Also by Henry Kissinger

A WORLD RESTORED: CASTLEREAGH, METTERNICH AND THE RESTORATION OF PEACE 1812–1822

NUCLEAR WEAPONS AND FOREIGN POLICY

THE NECESSITY FOR CHOICE: PROSPECTS OF AMERICAN FOREIGN POLICY

THE TROUBLED PARTNERSHIP: A RE-APPRAISAL OF THE ATLANTIC ALLIANCE

AMERICAN FOREIGN POLICY

as editor: PROBLEMS OF NATIONAL STRATEGY: A BOOK OF READINGS

The White House Years

HENRY KISSINGER

The White House Years

Weidenfeld and Nicolson
and
Michael Joseph

First published in Great Britain by
George Weidenfeld & Nicolson Ltd
91 Clapham High Street
London SW4 7TA
and
Michael Joseph Ltd
52 Bedford Square
London WC1B 3EF
1979

Copyright © 1979 by Henry A. Kissinger

ISBN 0 7181 1868 5

The author is grateful to the following publishers to quote from selected material:

The Brookings Institution for Henry A. Kissinger, "Central issues of American Foreign Policy"; Charles L. Schultze, "Budget Alternatives after Vietnam"; Carl Kaysen, "Military Strategy, Military Forces, and Arms Control"; in Kermit Gordon, ed., *Agenda for the Nation*, 1968. Reprinted by permission.

Encounter for Zbigniew Brzezinski, "Peace and Power," November 1968.

Foreign Affairs for Henry A. Kissinger, "The Viet Nam Negotiations," copyright 1968 by Council on Foreign Relations, Inc.; and Richard M. Nixon, "Asia after Vietnam," copyright 1967 by Council on Foreign Relations, Inc. Reprinted by permission.

The *New York Times* for excerpts © 1969, 1970, 1971, 1972 by The New York Times Company. Reprinted by permission.

Oxford University Press for Guenter Lewy, *America in Vietnam*, 1978.

Time Inc. for excerpts from *Time*, copyright 1969, 1970 Time Inc. All rights reserved.

The author is also grateful to the *Milwaukee Journal*, *St. Louis Post-Dispatch*, the *Washington Post* and the *Washington Star*.

The back cover photograph is by Tom Blau (Camera Press).

Printed in Great Britain by
Richard Clay (The Chaucer Press) Ltd,
Bungay, Suffolk

To the memory of
Nelson Aldrich Rockefeller

Contents

List of Illustrations

List of Maps

(Maps by Dick Sanderson)

Foreword

FOR better or worse I was called upon to play a prominent role in the making and execution of United States foreign policy, first as President Nixon's Assistant for National Security Affairs and later as Secretary of State under President Nixon and President Ford. This book is an account of our foreign policy during the first term of Richard Nixon's Presidency — from my appointment as national security adviser after the November 1968 election through the end of the Vietnam negotiations, roughly coincident with Nixon's second inauguration in January 1973. Inevitably, it is history seen through my eyes — a portrayal of what I saw and thought and did — and inevitably I have had to select and compress. A complete record in the historian's sense must await the publication of other documents, memoirs, and biographies — not all of American origin.

The period covered in this volume was marked by domestic division and international turmoil; it witnessed America's passage into a world in which we were no longer predominant though still vastly influential. It was a painful transition, not, I hope, without achievement, that began the process of a new and in the long run perhaps even more seminal American contribution to the prospects of free societies. For some, the treatment in this volume of controversial matters, especially the Vietnam war, will be the view from a side of the barricades unfamiliar to them. It is put forward here as honestly as possible, with the intention to reconcile, not to score retrospective debating points. As a nation we can transcend our divisions only by recognizing that serious people manned both sides of those barricades.

In a subsequent volume I intend to cover the period from January 1973 to January 1977, during most of which I was Secretary of State. That volume will discuss such matters as Watergate and the resignation of Richard Nixon; the October 1973 Middle East war and the "shuttle diplomacy" that followed; international economic problems such as the oil crisis and the North-South dialogue; Southern Africa; the fall of Salvador Allende and our Latin American policy; the Communist takeover of Indochina; negotiations on SALT II; the evolution of our relations with China; the Presidency of Gerald Ford and the 1976 election campaign; and others. On some topics I may hark back to events in the 1969–1972 period that were omitted here for reasons of space or continuity. Readers who hold this weighty volume in their hands may find it hard to believe that anything was left out, but will perhaps be grateful that some matters were indeed deferred to a second volume.

In writing this account I have tried to keep reliance on memory to a minimum; I have been able to refer to much documentary evidence and, for part of this period, to a diary I kept. I intend to leave an annotated copy of this volume with my papers for the use of scholars who may someday pursue the period in greater detail.

One of the paradoxes of the age of the memorandum and the Xerox machine, of proliferating bureaucracies and compulsive record-keeping, is that the writing of history may have become nearly impossible.

When an historian deals with previous centuries, the problem is to find sufficient contemporary material; when he writes of modern diplomacy, the problem is to avoid being inundated by it. If a scholar of impeccable credentials and unassailable objectivity were given free run of the millions of documents of any modern four-year period, he would have the greatest difficulty knowing where to begin. The written record would by its very volume obscure as much as it illuminated; it would provide no criteria for determining which documents were produced to provide an alibi and which genuinely guided decisions, which reflected actual participation and which were prepared in ignorance of crucial events. Before the era of instantaneous communication, instructions to a negotiator had to be conceptual and therefore they gave an insight into the thinking of statesmen; in the age of the teletype they are usually tactical or technical and therefore are silent about larger purposes and premises. Official files of our period would not necessarily disclose what decisions were taken by "backchannels" bypassing formal procedures or what was settled orally without ever becoming part of the formal record. A participant's account of conversations can easily be ex post facto self-justification. (Dean Acheson once said that he never read a report of a conversation in which the author came out second best in the argument.) By a selective presentation of documents one can prove almost anything. Contemporary practices of unauthorized or liberalized disclosure come close to ensuring that every document is written with an eye to self-protection. The journalist's gain is the historian's loss.

The participant in great events is of course not immune to these tendencies when he writes his account. Obviously, his perspective will be affected by his own involvement; the impulse to explain merges with the impulse to defend. But the participant has at least one vital contribution to make to the writing of history: He will *know* which of the myriad of possible considerations in fact influenced the decisions in which he was involved; he will be aware of which documents reflect the reality as he perceived it; he will be able to recall what views were taken seriously, which were rejected, and the reasoning behind the choices made. None of this proves that his judgment was right — only what it was based upon. If done with detachment, a participant's memoir may help future historians judge how things really appeared, even (and perhaps especially) when in the fullness of time more evidence becomes available about all dimensions of the events.

I owe a deep debt of gratitude to those who helped me in the preparation of this book. Peter W. Rodman, friend, confidant, and invaluable associate for a decade and a half, supervised the research, undertook major research himself, and helped with editing, checking, and many other chores. Without him this work could never have been completed. William G. Hyland, another trusted associate and longtime friend, contributed enormously to the research, especially on Europe, East-West relations, and SALT. Rosemary Neaher Niehuss and Mary E. Brownell, also colleagues of mine in government, were exceptionally skilled, dedicated, and helpful in their research and review of the manuscript.

Winston Lord and William D. Rogers permitted me to impose on their friendship to read the entire book. They made innumerable wise suggestions and an invaluable editorial contribution. Others who read portions of the manuscript were Brent Scowcroft, Lawrence S. Eagleburger, David Ginsburg, Richard Helms, John Freeman, Samuel Halpern, Jessica Catto, and John Kenneth Galbraith. I will not pretend that I took all the suggestions of such a diverse group. But I thank them warmly for their efforts.

Harold Evans, assisted by Oscar Turnill, read through the entire volume with a brilliant editorial eye; they taught me what skilled and intelligent editing can contribute to organization and to lightening prose. Betsy Pitha and the late Ned Bradford of Little, Brown were meticulous and helpful in going over the manuscript. The index was expertly prepared by Melissa Clemence. Catherine De Sibour, Kathleen Troia, and Jeffrey Yacker assisted with the research.

I owe appreciation to Daniel J. Boorstin, the Librarian of Congress, and the men and women of the Manuscript Division: John C. Broderick, Paul T. Heffron, John Knowlton, and their dedicated staff. They have my gratitude for their courtesy and assistance with my papers, of which they are now the custodians. The working arrangements they provided were a great boon to me and my staff. Treatment of classified materials in this book has been worked out with the office of the national security adviser, Dr. Zbigniew Brzezinski, to whom I express my appreciation. President Nixon has kindly given his permission to cite some materials from his Presidential files.

I am especially grateful to my personal assistant, M. Christine Vick, who took charge of organizing the handling of the manuscript, and typed it through several drafts, even while managing to keep my day-to-day business in order. Cheryl Womble and Mary Beth Baluta assisted in the typing with dedication. All worked many extra hours.

My wife Nancy encouraged me with her advice and love; as always she served as my conscience.

I have dedicated this volume to Nelson A. Rockefeller. He was my friend for twenty-five years until his untimely death in January of this year.

I alone am responsible for the contents of this book, as indeed I am for my actions as described herein.

Washington, D.C.
June 1979

PART ONE

Beginnings

I

An Invitation

THE Inauguration took place on a bright, cold, and windy day. I sat on the platform just behind the new Cabinet and watched Lyndon Johnson stride down the aisle for the last time to the tune of "Hail to the Chief." I wondered what this powerful and tragic figure thought as he ended a term of office that had begun with soaring aspiration and finished in painful division. How had this man of consensus ended up with a torn country? Johnson stood like a caged eagle, proud, dignified, never to be trifled with, his eyes fixed on distant heights that now he would never reach.

There was another fanfare and President-elect Richard Nixon appeared at the top of the Capitol stairs. He was dressed in a morning coat, his pant legs as always a trifle short. His jaw jutted defiantly and yet he seemed uncertain, as if unsure that he was really there. He exuded at once relief and disbelief. He had arrived at last after the most improbable of careers and one of the most extraordinary feats of self-discipline in American political history. He seemed exultant, as if he could hardly wait for the ceremony to be over so that he could begin to implement the dream of a lifetime. Yet he also appeared somehow spent, even fragile, like a marathon runner who has exhausted himself in a great race. As ever, it was difficult to tell whether it was the occasion or his previous image of it that Nixon actually enjoyed. He walked down the steps and took the oath of office in his firm deep voice.

Nelson Rockefeller

MY own feeling of surprise at being there was palpable. Only eight weeks earlier the suggestion that I might participate in the Inauguration as one of the new President's closest advisers would have seemed preposterous. Until then, all my political experience had been in the company of those who considered themselves in mortal opposition to Richard Nixon. I had taught for over ten years at Harvard University, where among the faculty disdain for Richard Nixon was established orthodoxy. And the single most influential person in my life had been a man whom Nixon had twice defeated in futile quests for the Presidential nomination, Nelson Rockefeller.

It was Nelson Rockefeller who had introduced me to high-level policymaking in 1955 when he was Special Assistant for National Security Affairs to President Eisenhower. He had called together a group of academics, among whom I was included, to draft a paper for the President on a fundamental diplomatic problem: how the United States could seize the initiative in international affairs and articulate its long-range objectives.

It was a revealing encounter. Rockefeller entered the room slapping the backs of the assembled academics, grinning and calling each by the closest approximation of his first name that he could remember. Yet this and his aura of all-American charm served at the same time to establish his remoteness: when everybody is called by his first name and with equal friendliness, relationships lose personal significance. Rockefeller sat down to listen as each of us, intoxicated by our proximity to power — and I daresay wealth — did his best to impress him with our practical acumen. One professor after another volunteered clever tactical advice on how to manipulate nations — or at least the bureaucracy; how to deal with a President we did not know; or (the perennial problem of national security advisers) how to prevail over an equally unfamiliar Secretary of State. As we finished, the smile left Rockefeller's face and his eyes assumed a hooded look which I later came to know so well and which signaled that the time for serious business had arrived. He said: "I did not bring you gentlemen down here to tell me how to maneuver in Washington — that is my job. *Your* job is to tell me what is right. If you can convince me I will take it to the President. And if I can't sell it to him I will resign."

Rockefeller proved to be true to his word. We wrote a report; one of its ideas, the "open skies" proposal, was accepted. The sections spelling out long-range objectives were stillborn, partly because of the prevailing mood of self-satisfaction in the country, but largely because of the opposition of a powerful Secretary of State pressing his own convictions. At the end of 1955 Rockefeller resigned.

I had been part of a typical Rockefeller venture. Of all the public figures I have known he retained the most absolute, almost touching, faith in the power of ideas. He spent enormous resources to try to learn what was "the right thing" to do. His national campaigns were based on the illusion that the way to win delegates at national political conventions was to present superior substantive programs. He spent an excruciating amount of time on his speeches. Untypical as he might seem to be, he was in a way quintessentially American in his boundless energy, his pragmatic genius, and his unquenchable optimism. Obstacles were there to be overcome; problems were opportunities. He could never imagine that a wrong could not be righted or that an honorable aspiration was beyond reach. For other nations utopia is a blessed past never to be recovered; for Americans it is no farther than the intensity of their commitment.

Nelson Rockefeller, I am certain, would have made a great President. He possessed in abundance the qualities of courage and vision that are the touchstones of leadership. But at the moments when his goal might have been realized, in 1960 and again in 1968, he uncharacteristically hesitated. In the service of his beliefs he could be cold-blooded and ruthless; he was incredibly persistent. Yet there was in him a profound ambivalence. A kind of aristocratic scruple restrained him from pursuing the prize with the single-mindedness required and led him to exhaust himself in efforts to make himself worthy of the office. His entire upbringing made him recoil from appearing before the people he wanted to serve as if he were pursuing a personal goal; being already so privileged, he felt he had no right to ask anything more for himself as an individual. So he sought the office by trying to present to the nation the most sweeping vision of its possibilities and the best blueprint on how to attain them.

In a deep sense Nelson Rockefeller suffered from the hereditary disability of very wealthy men in an egalitarian society. He wanted assurance that he had transcended what was inherently ambiguous: that his career was due to merit and not wealth, that he had earned it by achievement and not acquired it by inheritance. In countries with aristocratic traditions — in Great Britain, for example, until well after World War II — an upper class moved in and out of high office convinced that public responsibility was theirs by right. Merit was assumed. But in the United States, the scions of great families are extremely sensitive to the charge of acquiring power through the visible exercise of influence or wealth; they believe that they must earn their office in their own right. But no more than a beautiful woman can be sure of being desired "for her own sake" — indeed, her own sake is inseparable from her beauty — can a rich man in America be certain what brought him to his station in public life. If he is lucky he learns in time that it makes little difference. In high political office he will be measured by the challenges he met and the accomplishments he wrought, not by his money or the motives of those who helped him get there. History will judge not the head start but the achievement.

Nelson Rockeller never fully resolved this dilemma. After his untimely death it was said that he failed to win the Presidency despite the fact that he was a Rockefeller. The opposite was more nearly true. He failed largely *because* he was a Rockefeller. He was not above spending vast sums for his political campaigns, but at the same time he felt an inordinate obligation to justify his ambition by his programs and an extraordinary reluctance to realize his dreams by what he considered the demeaning wooing of delegates to national conventions. It is not quite the way our political process works, geared as it is more to personalities than to programs.

Through three conventions Rockefeller fought for what he considered respectable party platforms in defiance of one of the surest lessons of American political history: that party platforms serve the fleeting moment when delegates come together to choose a party's candidate and then quietly fade from public memory. In 1960, he advanced a major and comprehensive program a bare three weeks before the Republican National Convention, when his rejection was already foreordained and there was no practical hope of altering the outcome. By this device he forced Nixon into the famous "Compact of Fifth Avenue" — a document drafted in Rockefeller's apartment — tilting the Republican platform in a direction compatible with his views. But he paid a grievous price in terms of his standing in the party. In 1964, he opposed Barry Goldwater beyond all the dictates of prudence because he was genuinely convinced that Goldwater in those days was a stalking horse for a dangerous form of conservative extremism (though he came to admire him later). And Goldwater's less temperate adherents reciprocated by seeking to jeer Rockefeller off the stage at the Republican convention. In 1968, he withdrew from the race in March when he still had an outside chance and then, when Nixon had assured himself of a mathematical majority, reentered it by publishing a series of detailed and thoughtful policy positions.

The contrast with the style of Richard Nixon could not have been greater. In contemporary America, power increasingly gravitates to those with an almost obsessive desire to win it. Whoever does not devote himself monomaniacally to the nominating process, whoever is afraid of it or disdains it, will always be pursuing a mirage, however remarkable his other qualifications. With candidates for the highest office, as with athletes, everything depends upon timing, upon an intuitive ability to seize the opportunity. Convention delegates live the compressed existence of butterflies. For a brief period they are admired, wooed, pressured, flattered, cajoled, endlessly pursued. The day after they have chosen, they return to oblivion. They are therefore uniquely sensitive to any candidate's self-doubt.

The qualities required to grasp the nomination for the American Presidency from such a transient body may have little in common with the qualities needed to govern; indeed, as the demands of the nominating process become more intensive with each election the two may grow increasingly incompatible. The nominating procedure puts a premium on a candidate skilled at organization, who can match political expression to the need of the moment, a master of ambiguity and consensus, able to subordinate programs to the requirement of amassing a broad coalition. A man who understands the complex essence of the nominating process, as Nixon did so supremely, will inevitably defeat a candidate who seeks the goal by emphasizing substance.

As a personality, Nelson Rockefeller was as different from Adlai Stevenson as it was possible for two men to be. Rockefeller was made of sterner stuff; he was far more decisive. And yet their destinies were oddly parallel. In the face of opportunity they hesitated, or rather they disdained to fashion their opportunities by the means required by the new politics. If this was dangerous for a Democrat, it was fatal for a Republican, whose party, having been out of power for a generation, had turned inward to an orthodoxy and discipline that made it highly suspicious of bold new programs. All the frustrations of the two men flowed from this flaw. Just as Stevenson was defeated by the Kennedy organization in 1960, so Rockefeller was defeated by the Nixon machine in 1960 and again in 1968. Rockefeller's intense dislike of Nixon came from many factors, but crucial was the intuitive rebellion against the politics of manipulation that may yet be the essence of modern American Presidential politics.

In addition, the rivalry between Rockefeller and Nixon was not without an ingredient of personal antipathy that transcended even that automatically generated by competition for a unique prize. Nixon thought of Rockefeller as a selfish amateur who would wreck what he could not control, a representative of the Establishment that had treated him with condescension throughout his political life. Rockefeller considered Nixon an opportunist without the vision and idealism needed to shape the destiny of our nation.

In 1968 I shared many of these attitudes toward Nixon, although I had little direct evidence on which to base a judgment. I attended the gallant press conference in which Rockefeller conceded to Nixon and I was sick at heart. My feelings were very similar to those of a journalist who had covered the Rockefeller campaign and who broke down in the bar of the Americana Hotel when it came to an end. "This is the last politician to whom I will become emotionally attached," he said. "Politicians are like dogs. Their life expectancy is too short for a commitment to be bearable." A man who could have been one of our great Presidents would never achieve his goal. This knowledge was all the harder for his friends because we knew deep down that but for tactical errors and hesitations, it should have been otherwise.

The Phone Call

SOME months after that depressing day — with Richard Nixon now President-elect — I was having lunch with Governor Rockefeller and a group of his advisers in New York City in his small apartment on the fourth floor of the Museum of Primitive Art. It was Friday, November 22, 1968. The museum, which he had endowed, was connected with Rockefeller's gubernatorial office on West Fifty-fifth Street by a covered walkway traversing a back alley. The apartment had been designed by the architect Wallace Harrison, who had also built Rockefeller Center. Its dramatic curved walls done in red were covered with pictures by Toulouse-Lautrec; invaluable paintings which he had no room to hang were stored in closets. In this splendid setting we were discussing what attitude Rockefeller should take toward a possible offer to join the Nixon Cabinet and what Cabinet position he should seek if given a choice.

Views were divided. One group of advisers held that Rockefeller's influence would be greater as governor of a major state controlling a political party organization and patronage. Others considered indirect influence illusory. A governor could scarcely sway national policy consistently or across the board, and any attempt to do so was likely to reopen old wounds in especially unfavorable circumstances. Rockefeller leaned toward the first opinion, arguing that he would find it difficult to serve as a subordinate, especially to Nixon.

I was of the view that if given the opportunity Rockefeller should join the Cabinet; I further urged that he would be happiest as Secretary of Defense. I thought that the President-elect would almost surely carry out his announced intention to act as his own Secretary of State. The State Department, moreover, did not seem to me to offer the autonomy required by Rockefeller's personality. As Secretary of Defense he would be able to implement his decades-long interest in national security. From the example of Robert McNamara, I thought also that the Secretary of Defense could play a major role in the design of foreign policy.

We were debating these considerations in a desultory fashion when we were interrupted by a telephone call from the office of the President-elect. It was a poignant reminder of Rockefeller's frustrating career in national politics that the caller was Nixon's appointments secretary, Dwight Chapin, who was interrupting Rockefeller's strategy meeting to ask me — and not Rockefeller — to meet with his chief. In retrospect, it is clear that this phone call made our discussion pointless. But we returned to it as if nothing had happened. No one at the lunch could conceive that the purpose of the call could be to offer me a major position in the new Administration.

The call filled me with neither expectation nor enthusiasm. During my long association with Rockefeller, I had served as a consultant to the White House in the early days of John Kennedy's Administration, when professors for the first time moved from advisory to operational responsibilities. President Kennedy, who had read my newly published book,

The Necessity for Choice (or at least a long review of it in the *New Yorker*), asked me to join the White House staff. We had a long conversation in which I was charmed by Kennedy's vitality and his incisive mind, although at that early stage it did not seem to me that Kennedy's self-confidence was as yet equal to his energy and soaring imagination. Nor did I have the impression that his Special Asistant for National Security, my former Harvard colleague McGeorge Bundy, shared the President's sense of urgency to add to the White House staff another professor of comparable academic competence. In any event I was reluctant to sever my connection with Rockefeller, so we agreed that I would spend a day or two a week at the White House as a consultant.

The very nature of an outside consultancy, and my own academic self-centeredness, as yet untempered by exposure to the daily pressures of the Presidency, combined to make this a frustrating experience on all sides. A regular consultant is too remote to participate in fast-moving decisions, and yet too intimately involved to maintain the inward distance and mystery of the outside adviser. He becomes almost inevitably a burden alike upon those who must assist him and those whom he advises. With little understanding then of how the Presidency worked, I consumed my energies in offering unwanted advice and, in our infrequent contact, inflicting on President Kennedy learned disquisitions about which he could have done nothing even in the unlikely event that they aroused his interest. It was with a sense of mutual relief that we parted company in mid-1962.

Meeting Richard Nixon

WITH this unpromising background I had even less reason to expect to be invited to join the Nixon Administration. I did not know the President-elect. My friend William F. Buckley, Jr., the conservative columnist, had told me for years that Nixon was underestimated by his critics, that he was more intelligent and sensitive than his opponents assumed. But I had no opportunity to form my own judgment until after the 1968 election.

I had met Richard Nixon only once, when we both attended a Christmas party in Clare Luce's apartment in 1967. Nixon arrived just as I was about to leave. Mrs. Luce drew us into the library. Nixon said that he had read my first book, *Nuclear Weapons and Foreign Policy*. He had learned from it and had written me a note about it, which to my embarrassment I had forgotten. I replied stiffly, less out of the prejudice of two decades than from the awkwardness of our meeting. At that time I was still highly uncomfortable with small talk, and Richard Nixon has to this day not overcome his own social inhibitions. We exchanged a few strained pleasantries and went our separate ways.

My first encounter with the Nixon staff occurred at the Republican Convention in Miami in 1968. Before the balloting but after Nixon's nomination had become obvious, I met with Richard V. Allen, then Nixon's principal adviser on foreign policy, to try to reach agreement on a Vietnam platform that would avoid a convention fight. My major concern was to make sure that the Republican platform took account of the hopes for a negotiated settlement. With the nomination assured, the Nixon forces saw no point in the kind of bruising battle over substance that had marred the previous two conventions. A rather bland compromise emerged, which we in the Rockefeller camp — with little enough to celebrate — welcomed as a moral victory.

After the convention I returned to Harvard, my contribution to the American political process completed, I thought. During the national campaign in 1968 several Nixon emissaries — some self-appointed — telephoned me for counsel. I took the position that I would answer specific questions on foreign policy, but that I would not offer general advice or volunteer suggestions. This was the same response I made to inquiries from the Humphrey staff.

In any event, only one question was ever put to me by the Nixon organization. Early in October 1968, Bill Buckley introduced me to John Mitchell, then Nixon's campaign manager. Mitchell asked me if I thought the Johnson Administration would agree to a bombing halt in Vietnam in return for the opening of negotiations before the election. I replied that it seemed to me highly probable that the North Vietnamese wanted a bombing halt on these terms, and that they would seek to commit both candidates to it. Therefore I believed that Hanoi was likely to agree to it just before the election. I advised against making an issue of it. Mitchell checked that judgment with me once or twice more during the campaign. At one point he urged me to call a certain Mr. Haldeman if ever I received any hard information, and gave me a phone number. I never used it. My limited impression of the Nixon staff was of a group totally immersed in the mechanics of the election, deferring issues of substance until the campaign was over, a not uncharacteristic attitude for the staff of any Presidential contender.

Encounters at the Pierre Hotel

I N response to Chapin's phone call, I presented myself at ten o'clock on the morning of Monday, November 25, at the Nixon transition headquarters on the thirty-ninth floor of the Pierre Hotel, not knowing what to expect. I did not anticipate a conversation that would change my life; I thought it likely that the President-elect wanted my views on the policy problems before him. Clean-cut young men were monitoring security cameras in the reception area, where I was greeted by one of the cleanest-cut and youngest, who turned out to be Dwight Chapin. With firm politeness, he took me to a large living room at the end of the hall and told me that the President-elect would be with me soon. I did not know then that Nixon was painfully shy. Meeting new people filled him with vague dread, especially if they were in a position to rebuff or contradict him. As was his habit before such appointments, Nixon was probably in an adjoining room settling his nerves and reviewing his remarks, no doubt jotted down on a yellow tablet that he never displayed to his visitors.

When at last Nixon entered the room, it was with a show of jauntiness that failed to hide an extraordinary nervousness. He sat on a sofa with his back to the window overlooking Fifth Avenue, and motioned me to an easy chair facing him. His manner was almost diffident; his movements were slightly vague, and unrelated to what he was saying, as if two different impulses were behind speech and gesture. He spoke in a low, gentle voice. While he talked, he sipped, one after another, cups of coffee that were brought in without his asking for them.

His subject was the task of setting up his new government. He had a massive organizational problem, he said. He had very little confidence in the State Department. Its personnel had no loyalty to him; the Foreign Service had disdained him as Vice President and ignored him the moment he was out of office. He was determined to run foreign policy from the White House. He thought that the Johnson Administration had ignored the military and that its decision-making procedures gave the President no real options. He felt it imperative to exclude the CIA from the formulation of policy; it was staffed by Ivy League liberals who behind the facade of analytical objectivity were usually pushing their own preferences. They had always opposed him politically. Nixon invited my opinion on these subjects.

I replied that he should not judge the Foreign Service's attitude toward a President by its behavior toward a candidate or even a Vice President. In any event, a President who knew his own mind would always be able to dominate foreign policy. I knew too little about the CIA to have an opinion. I agreed that there was a need for a more formal decision-making process. The decisions of the Johnson Administration had been taken too frequently at informal sessions, often at meals — the famous ''Tuesday lunches'' — without staff work or follow-up. It was therefore difficult to know exactly what decisions had been made. Even with the best of goodwill, each interested agency was tempted to interpret the often ambiguous outcome of such meetings in the way most suited to its own preconceptions. And, of course, there was a high probability of outright error and misunderstanding. There was little opportunity for conceptual approaches, consecutive action, or a sense of nuance. A more systematic structure seemed to me necessary. It should avoid the rigorous formalism of the Eisenhower Administration, in which the policymaking process had too often taken on the character of ad hoc treaties among sovereign departments. But a new coherence and precision seemed to me essential.

Nixon outlined some of his foreign policy views. I was struck by his perceptiveness and knowledge so at variance with my previous image of him. He asked what in my view should be the goal of his diplomacy. I replied that the overriding problem was to free our foreign policy from its violent historical fluctuations between euphoria and panic, from the illusion that decisions depended largely on the idiosyncrasies of decision-makers. Policy had to be related to some basic principles of national interest that transcended any particular Administration and would therefore be maintained as Presidents changed.

At this point the conversation grew less precise. Nixon's fear of rebuffs caused him to make proposals in such elliptical ways that it was often difficult to tell what he was driving at, whether in fact he was suggesting anything specific at all. After frequent contact I came to understand his subtle circumlocutions better; I learned that to Nixon words were like billiard balls; what mattered was not the initial impact but the carom. At this first encounter I had no choice except to take the President-elect literally. What I understood was that I had been asked whether in principle I was prepared to join his Administration in some planning capacity. I replied that in the event that Governor Rockefeller was offered a Cabinet post, I would be happy to serve on his staff. The President-elect made no further comment about my future. He suggested that I put my views about the most effective structure of government into a memorandum.

In retrospect it is clear that my comment killed whatever minimal prospects existed for a Rockefeller appointment. Richard Nixon had no intention of having me join his Administration on the coattails of Nelson Rockefeller; even less was he prepared to create a situation in which I might have to choose between the two men. One of my attractions for Nixon, I understood later, was that my appointment would demonstrate his ability to co-opt a Harvard intellectual; that I came from Rockefeller's entourage made the prospect all the more interesting.

To indicate that the conversation was drawing to a close, Nixon pressed a buzzer; a trim, crew-cut, businesslike man appeared and was introduced as Bob Haldeman. Nixon told Haldeman to install a direct telephone line to my office at Harvard so that the President-elect could continue the conversation later. Haldeman jotted down this curious request, which presupposed the absence of normal telephone connections between New York and Cambridge, on a yellow pad. He never made any effort to implement it.

As I left the President-elect, I had no precise idea of what he expected of me. From the conversation it was unclear whether Nixon wanted advice or commitment and, if the latter, to what. On my way out Haldeman asked me to step into his office, which was next to Nixon's. He said nothing to enlighten me on my basic question and I did not ask. Instead, Haldeman seemed eager to describe his job to me. Matter-of-factly he explained that his principal function was to prevent end-runs. He would see to it that no memorandum reached the President without comment from the appropriate White House staffer, and that a member of that staff would be present at every conversation with the President, to guarantee implementation. He also pointed out that he was changing the title of senior White House personnel from "Special Assistant to the President" to "Assistant to the President," since no one knew what the "Special" meant. Having delivered himself of these pronouncements in a manner which did not invite comment, Haldeman cordially bade me goodbye.

I returned to Harvard that afternoon in time to teach my four o'clock seminar on National Security Policy. There was a general buzz of interest at my having seen the President-elect, but no serious speculation that I might be offered an appointment in the new Administration. No newspapers inquired about the meeting and few friends seemed interested.

The next day I received a phone call from Nelson Rockefeller. He had seen the President-elect and been informed that he could be of greater service to the country as Governor of New York than as a Cabinet member. Because of the crucial elections to be held in 1970, Nixon had said, it was essential that Rockefeller continue to head the state ticket. Nixon had asked him many questions about me, especially about my performance under pressure. Rockefeller told me that he had fully reassured the President-elect on that point. Rockefeller recounted his conversation blandly, without comment; he expressed no opinion as to whether I should serve under Nixon.

An hour later I received a second phone call. This was from John Mitchell's office, suggesting an appointment for the next day; the subject was to be my position in the new Administration. It was not explained what position he was talking about, whether he thought that I had already been offered one, or whether there would be simply another exploratory talk.

I went to New York that evening and called on McGeorge Bundy, who after leaving the White House had become head of the Ford Foundation. Bundy and I had had an ambivalent relationship over the years. I admired his brilliance even when he put it, too frequently, at the service of ideas that were more fashionable than substantial. I thought him more sensitive and gentle than his occasionally brusque manner suggested. He tended to treat me with the combination of politeness and subconscious condescension that upper-class Bostonians reserve for people of, by

New England standards, exotic backgrounds and excessively intense personal style.

On balance, I held Bundy in very high esteem. Had he lived in a less revolutionary period his career might well have rivaled that of his idol Henry Stimson, whose autobiography he had edited. Bundy would have moved through the high offices of government until his experience matched his brilliance and his judgment equaled his self-confidence. It was Bundy's misfortune to begin governmental service at a time of upheaval within the very institutions and groups that should have served as his fixed reference points. He was thus perpetually finding himself on the fashionable side, but at the very moment that fashion began to wane. A hawk on Vietnam, he was baffled by the demoralization of the Establishment whose maxims had produced the war; at heart he was a conservative whose previous associations had driven him into causes for which, ultimately, he had no passion. Torn between his convictions and his instincts, between his intelligence and his need for emotional support, Bundy gradually lost the constituencies that could have made him a kind of permanent public counselor like John McCloy or David Bruce; he surely possessed the brilliance, character, and upbringing to render the nation greater service than destiny has so far permitted him.

So high was my regard for Bundy that he was the only person I consulted before my meeting with Mitchell. I told him that I expected to be offered a position in the State Department. Bundy's estimate of the appropriate level for me was reflected in his remark that it would be unfortunate if the President-elect were to appoint Assistant Secretaries before designating the Secretary of State. The Kennedy experience showed, he said, that this procedure undermined the authority of the Secretary without increasing the influence of the President. Bundy urged that, if given a choice, I should seek the position of Director of the Policy Planning Staff, provided the Secretary of State was someone whom I knew and trusted. He expressed no strong objection in principle to my joining the Nixon Administration.

I found John Mitchell seated behind his desk puffing a pipe. Self-confident and taciturn, he exuded authority. He came straight to the point: "What have you decided about the National Security job?"

"I did not know I had been offered it."

"Oh, Jesus Christ," said Mitchell, "he has screwed it up again." Mitchell rose from his swivel chair and lumbered out of the room. He returned in five minutes with the information that the President-elect wished to see me, and he escorted me down the hall.

This time it was clear what Nixon had in mind; I was offered the job of security adviser. The President-elect repeated essentially the same arguments he had made two days earlier, emphasizing more strongly his view of the incompetence of the CIA and the untrustworthiness of the

State Department. The position of security adviser was therefore crucial to him and to his plan to run foreign policy from the White House. We talked briefly about the work. I emphasized that in all previous advisory roles I had refused to see the press. The President-elect readily agreed that I should continue my reticence. Neither of us proved especially far-sighted in this regard.

I did not have to remind myself that this was still the same Richard Nixon who for more than two decades had been politically anathema, and for that reason, if for no other, I felt unable to accept the position on the spot. I told the President-elect that I would be of no use to him without the moral support of my friends and associates — a judgment that proved to be false. I asked for a week to consult them.

This extraordinary request reflected to no small extent the insularity of the academic profession and the arrogance of the Harvard faculty. Here was the President-elect of the United States offering one of the most influential positions in the world to a foreign-born professor, and that professor was hesitating so that he might talk to colleagues who, to a man, had voted against Nixon and were certain to oppose him in the future. The President-elect was taking a perhaps enormous political risk; the prospective adviser was reluctant to hazard the esteem of his academic associates. Nixon would have been well justified had he told me to forget the whole thing. Instead, he accepted the delay with better grace than the request deserved. Rather touchingly, he suggested the names of some professors who had known him at Duke University and who would be able to give me a more balanced picture of his moral standards than I was likely to obtain at Harvard. He added that he would be delighted if I would regularly bring intellectuals to the White House to ensure that we had before us the widest range of ideas. He had a particularly high regard for men like Alastair Buchan from the United Kingdom and Raymond Aron from France.

Immediately after this meeting I began my canvass of friends and colleagues. Unanimously they urged me to accept. Their advice was, undoubtedly, tinged by the desire to know someone of influence in Washington who could provide the vicarious access to power that had become the addiction of so many academics in the aftermath of the Kennedy years. There and then were sown the seeds of future misunderstandings. Some friends and colleagues may have seen in our relationship not only a guarantee of access but also an assurance that their views would prevail. But this was impossible, for two reasons. The wary antagonism between Nixon and the intellectuals did have a profound basis in both philosophy and personality. Nixon did not really trust them any more than they accepted him; they could occasionally coexist, never cooperate. And although I respected my colleagues and liked many of them, as a Presidential Assistant my loyalty was bound to be to my chief whose policies I, after all, would have a major share in forming. As time went on, this difference in perspective was to cause much anguish to both sides.

The decisive conversation was with Nelson Rockefeller. I had no choice, he said. Such a request was a duty. To refuse would be an act of pure selfishness. If I rejected the offer I would blame myself for every failure of foreign policy and indeed I would deserve severe criticism. Late Friday afternoon, November 29, a week after receiving that first phone call in Rockefeller's dining room and two days after being offered the position, I called Nixon's adviser Bryce Harlow and asked him to convey to the President-elect that I would be honored to accept.

The announcement was set for Monday, December 2, at 10 A.M.

Thus it happened that the President-elect and I mounted the podium in the ballroom at the Pierre Hotel for what proved to be my first press conference. As usual Nixon was nervous, and in his eagerness to deflect any possible criticism he announced a program substantially at variance with what he had told me privately. His Assistant for National Security would have primarily planning functions, he said. He intended to name a strong Secretary of State; the security adviser would not come between the President and the Secretary of State. The security adviser would deal with long-range matters, not with tactical issues. I confirmed that this reflected my own thinking and added that I did not propose to speak out publicly on foreign policy issues.

But the pledges of each new Administration are like leaves on a turbulent sea. No President-elect or his advisers can possibly know upon what shore they may finally be washed by that storm of deadlines, ambiguous information, complex choices, and manifold pressures which descends upon all leaders of a great nation.

II

Period of Innocence: The Transition

Getting Acquainted

THE period immediately after an electoral victory is a moment of charmed innocence. The President-elect is liberated from the harrowing uncertainty, the physical and psychological battering, of his struggle for the great prize. For the first time in months and perhaps in years, he can turn to issues of substance. He and his entourage share the exhilaration of imminent authority but are not yet buffeted by its ambiguities and pressures. His advisers are suddenly catapulted from obscurity into the limelight. Their every word and action are now analyzed by journalists, diplomats, and foreign intelligence services as a clue to future policy. Usually such scrutiny is vain; the entourage of a candidate have no time to address the problem of governance; nor have they been selected for their mastery of issues. And after the election is over they are soon consumed by the practical problems of organizing a new administration.

So it was with me. One of the most delicate tasks of a new appointee is how to handle the transition with one's predecessors. I stayed out of Washington as much as possible. Walt Rostow, President Johnson's security adviser, gave me an office in the Executive Office Building next door to the White House and suggested generously that I begin following the daily cables. I thought this unwise since I had no staff to help me assess the information they contained.

My feelings toward Johnson and Rostow were warm and friendly; soon after my appointment I called on them to pay my respects. I had met President Johnson a few times but had never worked for him directly. In 1967, I had conducted a negotiation for him with the North Vietnamese through two French intermediaries. In that connection, I had attended a meeting he held in the Cabinet Room with his senior advisers. I was impressed and oddly touched by this hulking, powerful man, so domineering and yet so insecure, so overwhelming and yet so vulnerable. It was President Johnson's tragedy that he became identified with a national misadventure that was already long in the making by the time he took office and in the field of foreign policy for which his finely tuned political antennae proved worthless. President Johnson did not take naturally to international relations. One never had the impression that he would think about the topic spontaneously — while shaving, for example. He did not trust his own judgment; he therefore relied on advisers, most of whom he had not appointed and whose way of thinking was not really congenial to him. Many of these advisers were themselves without bearings amidst the upheavals of the 1960s. Some of them were growing restless with the consequences of their own recommendations and began to work against policies which they themselves had designed.

No President had striven so desperately for approbation, and none since Andrew Johnson had been more viciously attacked. LBJ had labored for a special place in history; his legislative accomplishments and authentic humanitarianism will in time earn it for him. But the very qualities of compromise and consultation on which his domestic political successes were based proved disastrous in foreign policy. Too tough for the liberal wing of his party, too hesitant for its more conservative elements, Lyndon Johnson could never mount an international enterprise that commanded the wholehearted support of either his party or the nation. He took advice that he thought better informed than his more elemental instincts, finally cutting himself off from all constituencies as well as from his emotional roots.

When I called on him in the Oval Office, President Johnson was in a melancholy mood. For the outgoing, the transition (as I later learned) is a somber time. The surface appurtenances of power still exist; the bureaucracy continues to produce the paperwork for executive decision. But authority is slipping away. Decisions of which officials disapprove will be delayed in implementation; foreign governments go through the motions of diplomacy but reserve their best efforts and their real attention for the new team. And yet so familiar has the exercise of power become that its loss is sensed only dimly and intermittently. Days go by in which one carries out one's duties as if one's actions still matter.

So it was with President Johnson. The walls of the Oval Office in his day were lined with television sets and news tickers noisily disgorging their copy. It was strange to see the most powerful leader in the world, with instant access to all the information of our intelligence services, jumping up periodically to see what the news ticker was revealing.

He launched into a long soliloquy about the war in Vietnam. He urged that we apply military pressure and at the same time pursue serious negotiations; he did not describe precisely what he had in mind for either course. He advised me to ensure that the bureaucracy was loyal; he had been destroyed, in part, he thought, by systematic leaking. "I have one piece of advice to give you, Professor," he said, and I leaned forward to profit from the distilled wisdom of decades of public service. "Read the columnists," he added, "and if they call a member of your staff thoughtful, dedicated, or any other friendly adjective, fire him immediately. He is your leaker." I left the Oval Office determined to do my utmost to spare the new Administration the heartache and isolation of Johnson's waning days.

The transition period leaves little time for such reflections, however. My immediate problem was more mundane: to establish my relationship with the advisers who had been with Nixon during the campaign and to recruit a staff.

It would have required superhuman qualities of tolerance for some in the Nixon team not to resent an outsider who seemed to have the best of all worlds: what they considered the glamorous aura of a Harvard professor and Rockefeller associate, and association with the President-elect after his victory. I had, after all, not been merely absent from the election struggle; I had been in the mainstream of those who had either been hostile to Nixon or disdained him. One of the most painful tasks of a new President is to cull from the entourage that helped him into office the men and women who can assist him in running it. This leads to almost unavoidable rivalry between those who have borne up the President-elect during his journey to election and the newcomers who appear to the old guard as interlopers reaping the fruits of their labors. Newcomers there must be because the qualities of a campaign aide are different from those of a policymaker. It takes a very special personality to join a Presidential aspirant early in a campaign when the odds against success are usually overwhelming. Campaign chores are highly technical and some are demeaning: the preparation of schedules, the "advancing" of rallies and meetings, the endless wooing of delegates or media representatives. A candidate's staffers are selected — or volunteer — on the basis of loyalty and endurance; they provide emotional support in an inherently anxious situation. With the firmest resolve or best intentions few can predict what they will do or stand for when the elusive goal of high office is finally reached; their performance in the campaign offers no clue to their capabilities in the Executive Branch.

This was a particular problem for the Nixon staff. The loyal few who had remained with Nixon after his defeat for the governorship of California in 1962 exemplified an almost perverse dedication and faith. According to all conventional wisdom, Nixon's political career was finished. His dogged pursuit of the Presidency was turning into a national joke (LBJ ridiculed him as a "chronic campaigner"). There were no early or obvious rewards — even the attention of those who bet on long odds — in sticking with so unlikely an aspirant. Only congenital outsiders would hazard everything on so improbable an enterprise. Such men and women were almost certain to feel beleaguered; they inherently lacked the ability to reach out.

Nor did this attitude lack a basis in fact; paranoia need not be unjustified to be real. When Nixon moved to New York in 1962, he was shunned by the people whose respect he might have expected as a former Vice President of the United States who had come within an eyelash of election as President. He was never invited by what he considered the "best" families. This rankled and compounded his already strong tendency to see himself beset by enemies. His associates shared his sense of isolation and resentment. The Nixon team drew the wagons around itself from the beginning; it was besieged in mind long before it was besieged in fact.

This fortress mentality, which was to have such a corrosive effect on the entire Administration, showed itself in many ways. The team was temperamentally unable, for instance, to exploit the opportunities of Washington's social life for oiling the wheels of national politics. Washington is a one-industry town where the work is a way of life. Everyone at the higher levels of government meets constantly in the interminable conferences by which government runs itself; they then encounter the same people in the evening together with a sprinkling of senior journalists, socially adept and powerful members of Congress, and the few members of the permanent Washington Establishment. To all practical purposes there is no other topic of conversation except government, and that generally in Washington means not the national purpose but the relationship to one another of the key personalities in the Administration of the day: who, at any given point, is "up" and who is "down."

The criteria of this social life are brutal. They are geared substantially to power, its exercise and its decline. A person is accepted as soon as he enters the charmed circles of the holders of power. With the rarest exceptions, he is dropped when his position ends, his column is discontinued, or he is retired from Congress. There is no need to expend effort to crash this charmed circle; membership — or at least its availability — is nearly automatic; but so is the ultimate exclusion. In Washington the appearance of power is therefore almost as important as the reality of it; in fact, the appearance is frequently its essential reality. Since the topic of who is "up" and who is "down" is all-consuming, struggles result sometimes about nothing more than abstract bureaucratic designations.

Precisely because the official life is so formal, social life provides a mechanism for measuring intangibles and understanding nuances. Moods can be gauged by newspapermen and ambassadors and senior civil servants that are not discernible at formal meetings. It is at their dinner parties and receptions that the relationships are created without which the machinery of government would soon stalemate itself. The disdain of the Nixon entourage for this side of Washington complicated its actions and deprived it of the sensitivity to respond to brewing domestic anxieties.

I, too, it must be said, was ignorant of the ways of Washington or government when I proclaimed at the press conference announcing my new position that I would have no dealings with the press. As soon as my appointment was announced senior members of the press began calling to look me over. I was no little awed by the famous men whom I had read or listened to for years and whom I now was meeting at first hand. I saw Walter Lippmann, James ("Scotty") Reston, and Joseph Alsop — of whom Reston and Alsop were to become personal friends. (Lippmann fell ill soon afterward.) Lippmann urged upon me the necessity of bringing American commitments into line with our resources, especially in Indochina and the Middle East. Reston talked to me with avuncular goodwill tinged with Calvinist skepticism, then and after, about the imperfectibility of man. Joe Alsop interviewed me with the attitude that his criteria for my suitability for high office would be more severe than Nixon's. He gave me to understand that his knowledge of the Indochina problem far exceeded that of any neophyte Presidential Assistant. I had the impression that he had suspended judgment about the wisdom of the President's choice and that I would remain on probation for some time to come.

The editors of *Newsweek* invited me to meet with them. Pedantically I explained once again the incompatibility between my position and any worthwhile briefing of the press. They greeted this information with the amused tolerance reserved for amateurs or victims.

I soon found how naive my attitude was. One of the most important functions of the Presidential Assistant is to explain the President's policies and purposes. I learned that I could not ignore the media and I began to see journalists, though at first almost always at their initiative. I experienced the symbiotic relationship in Washington between media and government. Much as the journalist may resent it, he performs a partly governmental function. He is the one person in town who can be reasonably sure that everyone who matters listens to him or hears him. Officials seek him out to bring their pet projects to general attention, to settle scores, or to reverse a decision that went against them. Whatever the official's motive, it cannot be disinterested. At a minimum he seeks to put himself in his best light. For the experienced Washington observer careful reading of the press or listening to the key commentators provides invaluable intelligence concerning the cross-currents of bureaucracy, or the subterranean gathering of pent-up political forces.

The journalist has comparably interested motives in his contacts with the official. He must woo and flatter the official because without his goodwill he will be deprived of information. But he cannot let himself be seduced — the secret dream of most officials — or he will lose his objectivity. A love-hate relationship is almost inevitable. Officials are tempted to believe that social relationships lay the groundwork for compassionate treatment; journalists often prove their "objectivity" by attacking precisely those who shower them with attention. If both sides are realistic and mature they will establish a mutual respect. The official will recognize that not seduction but the journalist's personal integrity is the ultimate guarantee of fairness. The journalist will accept that to the official duty is paramount, and that its requirements are not always identical with providing scoops. If both the makers of policy and its interpreters can respect each other's vital function, the resulting working relationship can be one of the strongest guarantees of a free society.

I soon discovered also that another of my original ideas could not survive. I had thought I could continue teaching at Harvard until just before Inauguration. It was impossible. I had to educate myself on my duties; I had to set up the machinery of analysis and planning promised by the President-elect during his campaign. Some of my education was supplied by consulting many men and women who had been prominent in the Eisenhower, Kennedy, and Johnson administrations. For the entire postwar period foreign policy had been ennobled by a group of distinguished men who, having established their eminence in other fields, devoted themselves to public service. Dean Acheson, David K. E. Bruce, Ellsworth Bunker, Averell Harriman, John McCloy, Robert Lovett, Douglas Dillon, among others, represented a unique pool of talent — an aristocracy dedicated to the service of this nation on behalf of principles beyond partisanship. Free peoples owe them gratitude for their achievements; Presidents and Secretaries of State have been sustained by their matter-of-fact patriotism and freely tendered wisdom. While I was in office they were always available for counsel without preconditions; nor was there ever fear that they would use governmental information for personal or political advantage. Unfortunately, when I came into office they were all in their seventies. My generation had men equal to them in intelligence; but none had yet been sufficiently tested to develop the selflessness and integrity that characterized their predecessors. As the older group leaves public office, they take with them one of the steadying and guiding factors in our foreign policy.

The member of this group whom I saw most frequently in the transition period was John McCloy; later, when I moved to Washington, Dean Acheson and David Bruce became close friends and advisers. With the body of a wrestler and a bullet head, John McCloy seemed more like a jovial gnome than a preeminent New York lawyer and perennial counselor of Presidents and Secretaries of State. On the surface, his influence was hard to account for. He had never served at the Cabinet level; the positions he had held were important but not decisive. He could be time-consuming with his penchant for anecdotes; his intelligence was balanced rather than penetrating. But high officials always face perplexing choices. Presidents and Secretaries of State found in John McCloy a reliable pilot through treacherous shoals. He rarely supplied solutions to difficult problems, but he never failed to provide the psychological and moral reassurance that made solutions possible. On my first day back in the office from an unsuccessful negotiation in the Middle East in 1975, I asked John McCloy to see me. He came, as requested, without a murmur. Only weeks later did I learn that it had been his eightieth birthday and that he had given up a family celebration, never dreaming of suggesting a twenty-four-hour postponement. He was always available. He was ever wise.

When I started choosing staff, frictions with the Nixon team developed immediately. By custom the responsibility for selecting the National Security Council staff fell to the President's national security adviser. As the first Presidential appointee in the foreign policy area I had the advantage of being able to begin recruiting early. As a White House assistant I was not limited by departmental or civil service practices. Thus, unrestrained by bureaucratic limitations and with the President-elect's charter to build a new organization from the ground up, I was determined to recruit the ablest and strongest individuals I could find.

While I hold strong opinions I have always felt it essential to test them against men and women of intelligence and character; those who stood up to me earned my respect and often became my closest associates. If my staff was to be of decisive influence in guiding interdepartmental planning, it had to substitute in quality for what it lacked in numbers. Indeed, its small size could be an advantage, since we could avoid the endless internal negotiations that stultify larger organizations. So I looked for younger men and women and promoted them rapidly, reasoning that someone well along in his career would have reached his level of performance and would be unlikely to do much better on my staff than in his present position. I recruited professional officers from the Foreign Service, the Defense Department, and the intelligence community, both to gain the benefit of their experience and to help guide me through the bureaucratic maze; I hired talented people from the academic world. For balance, I strove for representatives of as many different points of view as possible.

I took the position that I would abide by security objections but would accept no other criterion than quality. Peter Flanigan, a Nixon associate responsible for political appointments (who later became a good friend), sent me six names of people who had been promised political appointments. After interviewing some of them, I rejected all. In at least two cases Haldeman challenged my staff selections on grounds of security, which turned out to be more a matter of liberal convictions or a propensity to talk to journalists. In both cases I overruled Haldeman.

Nixon invariably supported me. He had his private doubts and later, as public pressures began to mount, he came to regard my staff with disquiet. He suspected some of my colleagues of disliking him, which was correct, and of fueling the debate with leaks, for which there was never any evidence. But during the transition period Nixon backed my choices. He did so because he treated foreign policy differently from the domestic area. In domestic politics, he had used — and would use again — rough tactics and relied on some odd associates. To be fair, Nixon remained convinced to the end that in the domestic area he was following traditional practice for which a hypocritical Establishment, following an incomprehensible double standard, condemned only him. But foreign policy he regarded as something apart. Where the basic national interest and the security and progress of the free world were concerned his touchstone was to do what was right, not expedient, whatever the conventional practice, and when necessary against the conventional wisdom. Only in the rarest cases did he permit partisan interests to infringe on foreign policy decisions.

Though some of my personnel choices proved in the end unwise, the dedication and ability of my staff contributed fundamentally to the foreign policy successes of the first Nixon Administration. The core members — Winston Lord, Lawrence Eagleburger, Helmut Sonnenfeldt, William Hyland, Harold Saunders, Peter Rodman, and Alexander Haig — remained with me through all vicissitudes and became close friends as well. The high quality of this team was an important reason for the growing influence of the office of the President's national security adviser, and the viability of my office became crucial since Richard Nixon appointed a Cabinet of able, astute, and willful men that were never able to operate effectively as a team.

The Uneasy Team

RICHARD NIXON was in a sense the first Republican President in thirty-six years. Dwight Eisenhower had been elected on the Republican ticket, but he owed little to the Republican Party and conducted himself accordingly. In almost two generations out of office the Republican Party had grown unused to the responsibilities of power. The consequences became clear soon after the Inauguration. The party's Congressional delegations often acted as if they were in opposition to a Republican President. The members of the new Administration — strangers to one another and whipsawed by the complex personality of the President — never really formed themselves into a cohesive team.

A French sociologist[1] has written that every executive below the very top of an organization faces a fundamental choice: he can see himself as the surrogate of the head of the organization, taking on his shoulders some of the onus of bureaucratically unpopular decisions. Or he can become the spokesman of his subordinates and thus face the chief executive with the necessity of assuming the sole responsibility for painful choices. If he takes the former course he is likely to be unpopular in the bureaucracy — at least in the short run — but he helps bring about cohesion, a sense of direction, and ultimately high morale. If he places the onus for every difficult decision on his superior — if he insists on playing the "good guy" — he may create goodwill among subordinates but he will sacrifice discipline and effectiveness; ultimately a price will be paid in institutional morale. Such a course, moreover, invites the very buffeting it seeks to avoid; it focuses attention on obstacles rather than on purposes.

This challenge to executives in any field is compounded in Washington by the close relationship between government and the media. Disgruntled officials use the press to make their case. The media have a high incentive to probe for disagreements within the Administration; some journalists do not mind contributing to the discord as a means of generating a story. The Congress increasingly seeks the raw material for many of its hearings in the conflicts of senior officials. A premium is placed, therefore, on divisive tendencies; Washington's crises are bureaucratic battles.

There can be little doubt that the so-called Nixon team never existed except in the White House, and even there it later disintegrated under stress. There were several reasons for this. Many in the media disliked Richard Nixon for his philosophy and his record. The temptation was thereby created to give credit for favorable developments to more admired associates and to leave him with the blame for everything that was unpopular. It would have required superhuman qualities of dedication and restraint by these associates to reject the proffered laurels. None, myself included, reached within himself for these qualities.

There developed, as a result, a reversal of the normal practice. In most administrations the good news is announced from the White House and unpopular news is left to the departments to disclose; in the Nixon Administration the bureaucracy developed great skill at both leaking good news prematurely to gain the credit and releasing bad news in a way that focused blame on the President. This in turn reinforced Nixon's already powerful tendency to see himself surrounded by a conspiracy reaching even among his Cabinet colleagues; it enhanced his already strong penchant toward withdrawal and isolation. The Administration turned into an array of baronies presided over by feudal lords protecting their turf as best they could against the inroads of a central authority that sallied forth periodically from its fortress manned by retainers zealous to assert their power.

In due course I became a beneficiary of this state of affairs and of this bias of the media. Ironically, one reason why the President entrusted me with so much responsibility and so many missions was because I was more under his control than his Cabinet. Since I was little known at the outset, it was also his way of ensuring that at least some credit would go to the White House.

Nixon compounded his problem by an administrative style so indirect and a choice of Cabinet colleagues with whom his personal relationship was so complex (to describe it most charitably) that a sense of real teamwork never developed. This was especially the case with respect to his Secretary of State.

I had not known William Pierce Rogers when he was selected. Shortly after my appointment, Nixon and I had a brief conversation about his choice for Secretary of State. He said he was looking for a good negotiator, rather than a policymaker — a role he reserved for himself and his Assistant for National Security Affairs. And because of his distrust of the Foreign Service, Nixon wanted a strong executive who would ensure State Department support of the President's policies. Nixon left me with the impression that his first choice was Ambassador Robert Murphy, an outstanding retired diplomat and at that time chairman of the board of Corning Glass. Murphy had served with distinction in many senior posts and I grew to value his judgment and wit. Years later, Nixon told me that Murphy had turned down the position.

A few days after my own appointment I met William Rogers for the first time in the dining room of Nixon's suite at the Pierre Hotel. The President-elect had asked me to chat with Rogers and to report my reactions. He told me only that Rogers was being considered for a senior foreign policy post. Since neither Rogers nor I knew exactly what the point of our meeting was, our conversation was desultory and a little strained. I formed no impression one way or the other except that I found Rogers affable.

The next day, without having talked to me about my meeting or asking for my views, Nixon informed me that William Rogers was to be his Secretary of State. He said that he and Rogers had been close friends in the Eisenhower Administration when Rogers was Attorney General, although their friendship had eroded when they were both out of office. As lawyers in private practice, the two had come to compete for clients. Despite this cloud over their relationship he regarded Rogers as the ideal man for the post. Nixon considered Rogers's unfamiliarity with the subject an asset because it guaranteed that policy direction would remain in the White House. At the same time, Nixon said, Rogers was one of the toughest, most cold-eyed, self-centered, and ambitious men he had ever met. As a negotiator he would give the Soviets fits. And "the little boys in the State Department" had better be careful because Rogers would brook no nonsense. Few Secretaries of State can have been selected because of their President's confidence in their ignorance of foreign policy.

It was probably unfair to appoint to the senior Cabinet position some-one whose entire training and experience had been in other fields. Rogers had been a distinguished Attorney General. But the old adage that men grow into office has not proved true in my experience. High office teaches decision-making, not substance. Cabinet members are soon overwhelmed by the insistent demands of running their depart-ments. On the whole, a period in high office consumes intellectual capi-tal; it does not create it. Most high officials leave office with the percep-tions and insights with which they entered; they learn how to make decisions but not what decisions to make. And the less they know at the outset, the more dependent they are on the only source of available knowledge: the permanent officials. Unsure of their own judgment, un-aware of alternatives, they have little choice except to follow the advice of the experts.

This is a particular problem for a Secretary of State. He is at the head of an organization staffed by probably the ablest and most professional group of men and women in public service. They are intelligent, compe-tent, loyal, and hardworking. But the reverse side of their dedication is the conviction that a lifetime of service and study has given them in-sights that transcend the untrained and shallow-rooted views of political appointees. When there is strong leadership their professionalism makes the Foreign Service an invaluable and indispensable tool of policymak-ing. In such circumstances the Foreign Service becomes a disciplined and finely honed instrument; their occasional acts of self-will generate an important, sometimes an exciting dialogue. But when there is not a strong hand at the helm, clannishness tends to overcome discipline. Desk officers become advocates for the countries they deal with and not spokesmen of national policy; Assistant Secretaries push almost exclu-sively the concerns of their areas. Officers will fight for parochial inter-ests with tenacity and a bureaucratic skill sharpened by decades of struggling for survival. They will carry out clear-cut instructions with great loyalty, but the typical Foreign Service officer is not easily per-suaded that an instruction with which he disagrees is really clear-cut.

The procedures of the State Department are well designed to put a premium on bureaucratic self-will. Despite lip service to planning, there is a strong bias in favor of making policy in response to cables and in the form of cables. The novice Secretary of State thus finds on his desk not policy analyses or options but stacks of dispatches which he is asked to initial and to do so urgently, if you please. He can scarcely know enough about all the subjects to which they refer, or perhaps about any of them, to form an opinion. In any event, he will not learn from these draft cables what alternatives he has. Even if he asserts himself and rejects a particular draft, it is likely to come back to him with a modifi-cation so minor that only a legal scholar could tell the difference. When

I later became Secretary I discovered that it was a herculean effort even for someone who had made foreign policy his life's work to dominate the State Department cable machine. Woe to the uninitiated at the mercy of that extraordinary and dedicated band of experts.

The irony of Nixon's decision to choose as Secretary of State someone with little substantive preparation was that he thereby enhanced the influence of the two institutions he most distrusted — the Foreign Service and the press. For the new Secretary of State had in effect only two choices. He could take his direction from the White House and become the advocate of Presidential policy to the Department, the Congress, and the country, or he could make himself the spokesman of his subordinates. In a quieter time Secretary Rogers might well have been able to balance the demands upon him. But in the turmoil of the domestic discord caused by Vietnam, to do so required more self-confidence and knowledge than he could reasonably have been expected to possess. As a result, he seemed quite naturally concerned to avoid the assaults inflicted upon his predecessor, Dean Rusk. Since he tended to identify the public and Congressional mood with the editorial position of leading Eastern newspapers, and since these also powerfully influenced his subordinates, Rogers at critical junctures found himself unwilling to do battle for the President and often sponsored positions at variance with Nixon's.

Paradoxically, he may have been reinforced in that tendency by the memory of his friendship with Nixon in the 1950s. Then Rogers had been much the psychologically dominant partner. In consequence he could not really grasp that in the new relationship his was the clearly subordinate position. Even less could he face the proposition that he might have been appointed, at least in part, because his old friend wanted to reverse roles and establish a relationship in which both hierarchically and substantively he, Nixon, called the tune for once.

This curious antiphonal relationship between the two men had the consequence of enhancing my position, but my own role was clearly a result of that relationship and not the cause of it. From the beginning Nixon was determined to dominate the most important negotiations. He excluded his Secretary of State, for example, from his first meeting with Soviet Ambassador Anatoly Dobrynin on February 17, 1969, four weeks after Inauguration, at a time when it would have been inconceivable for me to suggest such a procedure. The practice, established before my own position was settled, continued. Throughout his term, when a State visitor was received in the Oval Office by Nixon for a lengthy discussion, I was the only other American present.

The tug of war over responsibility for policy emerged early. For his part, Secretary Rogers took the position that he would carry out orders with which he disagreed only if they were transmitted personally by the

President. This was the one thing Nixon was psychologically incapable of doing. He would resort to any subterfuge to avoid a personal confrontation. He would send letters explaining what he meant; he would use emissaries. But since Rogers believed — quite correctly — that these letters were drafted by me or my staff, he did not give them full credence even though they were signed by the President. He frustrated the emissary, usually John Mitchell, by invoking his old friendship with the President and claiming that he understood Nixon better. This contest, which was partially obscured because both men blamed it on third parties, was unending. Nixon would repeatedly order that all outgoing policy cables were to be cleared in the White House. But this was frequently circumvented, and in any event, the means by which a Secretary of State can communicate with his subordinates are too manifold to be controlled by fiat.

As time went by, the President, or I on his behalf, in order to avoid these endless confrontations, came to deal increasingly with key foreign leaders through channels that directly linked the White House Situation Room to the field without going through the State Department — the so-called backchannels. This process started on the day after Inauguration. The new President wanted to change the negotiating instructions on Vietnam drafted at State that reflected the approach of the previous Administration. But he wished also to avoid a controversy. He therefore asked me to phone Ambassador Henry Cabot Lodge, our negotiator in Paris, to suggest that Lodge send in through regular channels, as his own recommendation, the course of action that the President preferred. Lodge readily agreed. Since such procedures were complicated and could not work in most cases, Nixon increasingly moved sensitive negotiations into the White House where he could supervise them directly, get the credit personally, and avoid the bureaucratic disputes or inertia that he found so distasteful.

Nor was the President above dissociating himself from State Department foreign policy ventures. Thus in March 1969 Nixon asked me to inform Ambassador Dobrynin privately that the Secretary of State in his first lengthy talk on Vietnam with the Soviet envoy had gone beyond the President's thinking. I did not do so at once, waiting rather for some concrete issue to come up. There can be no doubt, however, that the conduct of both the White House and the State Department made the Soviets aware of our own internal debate and that they did their best to exploit it. Nixon kept his private exchange with North Vietnam's President Ho Chi Minh in July–August 1969 from Rogers until forty-eight hours before he revealed it on television in November. In early 1970 Nixon sent word to the Jewish community through his aide Leonard Garment and Attorney General John Mitchell that the ''Rogers Plan'' on the Middle East was aptly named and did not originate in the

White House. In May 1971 the Secretary of State did not know of the negotiations in White House–Kremlin channels that led to the breakthrough in the SALT talks until seventy-two hours before there was a formal announcement. In July 1971 Rogers was told of my secret trip to China only after I was already on the way. In April 1972, the President gave Rogers such a convoluted explanation for my trip to Moscow — which had been arranged secretly and which Rogers opposed when he was told at the last minute — that it complicated the negotiations. Such examples could be endlessly multiplied.

I do not mean to suggest that I resisted Nixon's conduct toward his senior Cabinet officer. From the first my presence made it technically possible and after a time I undoubtedly encouraged it. Like the overwhelming majority of high officials I had strong views and did not reject opportunities to have them prevail. What makes the tension and exhaustion of high office bearable and indeed exhilarating is the conviction that one makes a contribution to a better world. To what extent less elevated motives of vanity and quest for power played a role is hard to determine at this remove; it is unlikely that they were entirely absent. But I am convinced that in a Nixon Administration foreign policy would have centered in the White House whatever the administrative practices and whoever the personalities.

Once Nixon had appointed a strong personality, expert in foreign policy, as the national security adviser, competition with the Secretary of State became inevitable, although I did not realize this at first. The two positions are inherently competitive if both incumbents seek to play a major policy role. All the incentives make for controversy; indeed, were they to agree there would be no need for both of them. Though I did not think so at the time, I have become convinced that a President should make the Secretary of State his principal adviser and use the national security adviser primarily as a senior administrator and coordinator to make certain that each significant point of view is heard. If the security adviser becomes active in the development and articulation of policy he must inevitably diminish the Secretary of State and reduce his effectiveness. Foreign governments are confused and, equally dangerous, given opportunity to play one part of our government off against the other; the State Department becomes demoralized and retreats into parochialism. If the President does not have confidence in his Secretary of State he should replace him, not supervise him with a personal aide. In the Nixon Administration this preeminent role for the Secretary of State was made impossible by Nixon's distrust of the State Department bureaucracy, by his relationship with Rogers, by Rogers's inexperience and by my own strong convictions. Rogers's understandable insistence on the prerogatives of his office compounded the problem and had the ironical consequence of weakening his position. In a bureaucratic dispute the side having no better argument than its hierarchical right is likely to lose. Presidents listen to advisers whose views they think they need, not to those who insist on a hearing because of the organization chart.

Beyond these reasons, tensions in the Nixon policy machinery were produced also by an honest difference in perspective between the Secretary and me. Rogers was in fact far abler than he was pictured; he had a shrewd analytical mind and outstanding common sense. But his perspective was tactical; as a lawyer he was trained to deal with issues as they arose "on their merits." My approach was strategic and geopolitical; I attempted to relate events to each other, to create incentives or pressures in one part of the world to influence events in another. Rogers was keenly attuned to the requirements of particular negotiations. I wanted to accumulate nuances for a long-range strategy. Rogers was concerned with immediate reaction in the Congress and media, which was to some extent his responsibility as principal spokesman in foreign affairs. I was more worried about results some years down the road. Inevitably, Rogers must have considered me an egotistical nitpicker who ruined his relations with the President; I tended to view him as an insensitive neophyte who threatened the careful design of our foreign policy. The relationship was bound to deteriorate. Had both of us been wiser we would have understood that we would serve the country best by composing our personal differences and reinforcing each other. This would have reduced Nixon's temptation to manipulate tensions that he both dreaded and fomented. But all our attempts to meet regularly foundered. Rogers was too proud, I intellectually too arrogant, and we were both too insecure to adopt a course which would have saved us much needless anguish and bureaucratic headaches.

But none of this would have made a decisive difference had Nixon and Rogers been, in fact, as close as they may have sincerely believed they were. The indispensable prerequisite of a Secretary of State is the complete confidence of the President. The successful Secretaries, such as Dean Acheson or John Foster Dulles, all established an intimate working relationship with their Presidents. Those who sought to compete with their President, like Robert Lansing or James Byrnes, soon lost either influence or position. Acheson frequently emphasized that while he felt free to disagree vigorously with President Truman he never put him into a position that seemed to test his authority nor would he ever join a cabal of other Cabinet members to bring pressure on the President. A President needs substantive advice, but he also requires emotional succor. He must know that his advisers are strong and self-confident, but he must also sense that they have compassion for the isolation and responsibilities of his position and will not willfully add to his psychological burdens. This intangible ingredient was precisely what was missing between President Nixon and his first Secretary of State, in part for reasons that antedated the Nixon Administration. The very closeness of their previous relationship prevented Rogers from acting on this truth and Nixon from admitting it.

Relations were different with the other senior Cabinet member in the foreign policy field, the Secretary of Defense, Melvin Laird. As with State, I had been under the impression for several days that someone else was in line for the job, believing that Senator Henry M. Jackson would accept the President-elect's offer. When he turned it down, I was informed of Mr. Nixon's decision in favor of Mel Laird; I was not consulted.

I had met Laird at the Republican Convention of 1964. He had been chairman of the platform committee and had skillfully outmaneuvered the Rockefeller forces. Later I had contributed to a collection of essays on conservatism that he compiled.[2] Mel Laird was a professional politician; he spoke a language that Nixon understood. Nixon had no psychological reservations or old scores to settle with his Secretary of Defense. Having served on the Defense Subcommittee of the House Appropriations Committee for most of his sixteen years in the Congress, Laird knew his subject thoroughly before he took office. And Laird had an important constituency. Remaining influential in the Congress, especially through his friendship with the powerful chairman of the House Appropriations Committee George Mahon, Laird could be ignored by the President only at serious risk. And while Laird's maneuvers were often as Byzantine in their complexity or indirection as those of Nixon, he accomplished with verve and surprising goodwill what Nixon performed with grim determination and inward resentment. Laird liked to win, but unlike Nixon, derived no great pleasure from seeing someone else lose. There was about him a buoyancy and a rascally good humor that made working with him as satisfying as it could on occasion be maddening.

Laird acted on the assumption that he had a Constitutional right to seek to outsmart and outmaneuver anyone with whom his office brought him into contact. This was partly a game and partly the effort of a seasoned politician to protect his options and garner whatever publicity might be available along the way. Laird was master of the inspired leak. After a while, I learned that when Laird called early in the morning to complain about a newspaper story, he was its probable source. Elliot Richardson used to say, not unkindly, that when Laird employed one of his favorite phrases, "See what I mean?" there was no possible way of penetrating his meaning.

Laird would think nothing of coming to a White House meeting with the Joint Chiefs of Staff, supporting their position, then indicating his reservations privately to the President and me, only to work out a third approach later with his friend Chairman Mahon. The maneuvers of Nixon and Laird to steal the credit for each announced troop withdrawal from Vietnam were conducted with all the artistry of a Kabuki play, with an admixture of the Florentine court politics of the fifteenth century. The thrusts and parries of these two hardy professionals, each seeking to divine the other's intentions and to confuse him at the same time, cannot be rendered biographically; only a novel or play could do them justice. But it was a game that Nixon, being less playful, more deadly, and holding the trump cards of the Presidency, rarely lost.

Provided he was allowed some reasonable range for saving face by maneuvering to a new position without embarrassment, Laird accepted bureaucratic setbacks without rancor. But he insisted on his day in court. In working with him, intellectual arguments were only marginally useful and direct orders were suicidal. I eventually learned that it was safest to begin a battle with Laird by closing off insofar as possible all his bureaucratic or Congressional escape routes, provided I could figure them out, which was not always easy. Only then would I broach substance. But even with such tactics I lost as often as I won.

John Ehrlichman, also an Assistant to the President, considered mine a cowardly procedure. In 1971, wanting some land owned by the Army in Hawaii for a national park, Ehrlichman decided he would teach me how to deal with Laird. Following the best administrative theory of White House predominance, Ehrlichman, without troubling to touch any bureaucratic or Congressional bases, transmitted a direct order to Laird to relinquish the land. Laird treated this clumsy procedure the way a matador handles the lunges of a bull. He accelerated his plan to use the land for two Army recreation hotels. Together with his friend Mahon, Laird put a bill through the Congress that neatly overrode the directive he had received, all the time protesting that he would carry out any White House orders permitted by the Congress. The hotels are still there under Army control; the national park is still a planner's dream. Ehrlichman learned the hard way that there are dimensions of political science not taught at universities and that being right on substance does not always guarantee success in Washington.

As a finely seasoned politician, Laird did not believe in fighting losing battles. He could solve daily problems with great skill; he was less concerned with those that might emerge tomorrow. In calm periods he could be maddening. In crises he was magnificent — strong, loyal, daring, and eloquent in defending Presidential decisions, including those he had opposed in the councils of government. Laird served as Secretary of Defense while our military strength was under unremitting assault by the Congressional majority, the media, academia, and antidefense lobbies. He preserved the sinews of our strength and laid the basis for expansion when the public mood changed later. Melvin Laird maintained our national power through a period of extraordinary turbulence. This was a major achievement.

Below the Cabinet level was another echelon of influential advisers: the Chairman of the Joint Chiefs of Staff, General Earle Wheeler, and the Director of the Central Intelligence Agency, Richard Helms.

When Nixon assumed the Presidency, "Bus" Wheeler was in his final year as Chairman of the Joint Chiefs. His term should have ended in July 1968, but Johnson generously extended it a year to give his successor the opportunity of selecting the next Chairman. Wheeler's integrity and experience proved so indispensable that Nixon extended his term by yet another year. Tall, elegant, calm, Wheeler by that time was deeply disillusioned. He looked like a wary beagle, his soft dark eyes watchful for the origin of the next blow. He had lived through the 1960s when young systems analysts had been brought into the Pentagon to shake up the military establishment by questioning long-held assumptions. Intellectually the systems analysts were more often right than not; but they soon learned that the way a question is put can often predetermine an answer, and their efforts in the hallowed name of objectivity frequently wound up pushing personal preconceptions.

Misuse of systems analysis apart, there was a truth which senior military officers had learned in a lifetime of service that did not lend itself to formal articulation: that power has a psychological and not only a technical component. Men can be led by statistics only up to a certain point and then more fundamental values predominate. In the final analysis the military profession is the art of prevailing, and while in our time this required more careful calculations than in the past, it also depends on elemental psychological factors that are difficult to quantify. The military found themselves designing weapons on the basis of abstract criteria, carrying out strategies in which they did not really believe, and ultimately conducting a war that they did not understand. To be sure, the military brought on some of their own troubles. They permitted themselves to be co-opted too readily. They accommodated to the new dispensation while inwardly resenting it. In Vietnam, they adopted their traditional strategy of attrition inherited from Grant, Pershing, and Marshall; they never fully grasped that attrition is next to impossible to apply in a guerrilla war against an enemy who does not *have* to fight because he can melt into the population. This played into the hands of a civilian leadership that imposed ever more restraints; military traditionalism and civilian supersophistication combined to waste whatever chances existed to bring about a rapid end to the war at a time when Johnson still enjoyed widespread public support. The longer the war lasted, the more the psychological balance would tilt against us and the more frustrating the military effort became.

Throughout the 1960s the military were torn between the commitment to civilian supremacy inculcated through generations of service and their premonition of disaster, between trying to make the new system work and rebelling against it. They were demoralized by the order to procure weapons in which they did not believe and by the necessity of fighting a war whose purpose proved increasingly elusive. A new breed of military officer emerged: men who had learned the new jargon, who could present the systems analysis arguments so much in vogue, more articulate than the older generation and more skillful in bureaucratic maneuvering. On some levels it eased civilian-military relationships; on a deeper level it deprived the policy process of the simpler, cruder, but perhaps more relevant assessments which in the final analysis are needed when issues are reduced to a test of arms.

Earle Wheeler had presided over this transition and was not at peace with it. He believed, rightly, that military advice had not been taken seriously enough in the Pentagon of the Sixties, but when the time came to present an alternative he offered no more than marginal adjustments of the status quo. He prized his direct access to the new President, but he rarely used it — partially because Laird discouraged meetings between the President and the Chairman in which he did not participate. Wheeler's demurrers more often took the form of expressing his concerns privately to me than in open confrontation with his superiors. At the June 1969 meeting in Hawaii where Nixon sought military approval for his Vietnam withdrawal plan, it was obvious to me that both Wheeler and General Creighton Abrams (our Vietnam commander) could not have been more unhappy. Every instinct told them that it was improbable that we could prevail by reducing our strength. The more forces were withdrawn, the less likely a tolerable outcome would be achieved. But they did not have the self-confidence to say this to their civilian chiefs who, including me, were arguing that withdrawals were essential to sustain the domestic basis for an honorable political solution. Wheeler and Abrams assuaged their premonitions by pressing for the smallest possible pullback. But soon they found they had acquiesced in a plan that gathered its own momentum. As withdrawal schedules became part of the military budget, they could be slowed down only at the price of giving up weapons modernization.

High military officers must always strike a balance between their convictions and their knowledge that to be effective they must survive to fight another day. Their innate awe of the Commander-in-Chief tempts them to find a military reason for what they consider barely tolerable. Contrary to some of the public mythology, they rarely challenge the Commander-in-Chief; they seek for excuses to support, not to oppose him. In this manner Wheeler had participated in a series of decisions any one of which he was able to defend, but the cumulative impact of which he could not really justify to himself. He was a gentleman to the core, a fine officer who helped his country through tragic times and was himself inwardly eaten up by them.

Wheeler's successor, Admiral Thomas Moorer, was a more elemental personality than Wheeler. He had spent the 1960s in command positions which, while not without their frustrations, did not produce the physical and psychological exhaustion of high-level Washington. A canny bureaucratic infighter, Moorer made no pretense of academic subtlety. If anything he exaggerated the attitude of an innocent country boy caught in a jungle of sharpies. What his views lacked in elegance they made up in explicitness. By the time he took office, Vietnam had become a rearguard action. He conducted its heartbreaking phaseout with dignity. No President could have had a more stalwart military adviser.

Another member of the National Security team was Richard Helms, whom Nixon inherited as Director of the Central Intelligence Agency. I had met Helms in the Kennedy period when, at the request of the White House in 1961, I had had several conversations with him about the Berlin crisis. His professionalism was impressive, then and later. We did not meet again until after I was appointed Assistant to the President when in the White House Situation Room he explained to me the structure and operation of his agency.

At the time Helms's situation was delicate. Even more than the State Department, Nixon considered the CIA a refuge of Ivy League intellectuals opposed to him. And he felt ill at ease with Helms personally, since he suspected that Helms was well liked by the liberal Georgetown social set to which Nixon ascribed many of his difficulties. I had no strong opinion about Helms, but I opposed his removal. I thought it was dangerous to turn the CIA into a political plum whose Director would change with each new President. Nixon compromised. He agreed to retain Helms as CIA Director but proposed to drop him from attendance at National Security Council meetings. This, in turn, was stopped by Laird, who correctly pointed out that for the Council to consider major decisions in the absence of the Director of Central Intelligence would leave the President dangerously vulnerable to Congressional and public criticism. Nixon relented once again. He agreed to let Helms attend NSC meetings but only to give factual briefings. Helms would not be permitted to offer recommendations and would have to leave the Cabinet Room as soon as he finished his briefing. Helms retained this anomalous status for six weeks. In time the situation became too embarrassing, too artificial, and too self-defeating to be sustained; intelligence information was usually highly relevant to the discussion even after the formal briefing; after all, a great deal depended on the assessment of the consequences of the various options being considered. Helms eventually became a regular participant in the National Security Council though never a confidant of the President.

My position of Assistant for National Security Affairs inevitably required close cooperation with the CIA Director. It is the Director on whom the President relies to supply early warning; it is to the Director that the Assistant first turns to learn the facts in a crisis and for analysis of events. And since decisions turn on the perception of the consequences of actions, the CIA assessment can almost amount to a policy recommendation.

Disciplined, meticulously fair and discreet, Helms performed his duties with the total objectivity essential to an effective intelligence service. For years, we had no direct social contact; we met very infrequently at dinners in other people's homes. I respected Helms not because he was congenial, though he was certainly that, but because of his professional insight and unflappability. He never volunteered policy advice beyond the questions that were asked him, though never hesitating to warn the White House of dangers even when his views ran counter to the preconceptions of the President or of his security adviser. He stood his ground where lesser men might have resorted to ambiguity. Early in the Administration a school of thought developed that the triple warhead on the Soviet SS-9 intercontinental missile was a multiple independently targeted reentry vehicle (MIRV) aimed at our Minuteman missile silos. The CIA maintained that the warheads could not be targeted independently. I leaned toward the more ominous interpretation. To clarify matters I adopted a procedure much resented by traditionalists who jealously guarded the independence of the estimating process. I assembled all the analysts in the White House Situation Room and played the devil's advocate, cross-examining the analysts closely and sharply. Helms stood his ground; he was later proved right.

No one is promoted through the ranks to Director of CIA who is not tempered in many battles; Helms was strong and he was wary. His urbanity was coupled with extraordinary tenacity; his smile did not always include his eyes. He had seen administrations come and go and he understood that in Washington knowledge was power. He was presumed to know a lot and never disabused people of that belief. At the same time I never knew him to misuse his knowledge or his power. He never forgot that his integrity guaranteed his effectiveness, that his best weapon with Presidents was a reputation for reliability.

CIA analyses were not, however, infallible. Far from being the hawkish band of international adventurers so facilely portrayed by its critics, the Agency usually erred on the side of the interpretation fashionable in the Washington Establishment. In my experience the CIA developed rationales for inaction much more frequently than for daring thrusts. Its analysts were only too aware that no one has ever been penalized for not having foreseen an opportunity, but that many careers have been blighted for not predicting a risk. Therefore the intelligence community has always been tempted to forecast dire consequences for any conceivable course of action, an attitude that encourages paralysis rather than adventurism. After every crisis there surfaces in the press some obscure intelligence report or analyst purporting to have predicted it, only to have been foolishly ignored by the policymakers. What these claims omit to mention is that when warnings become too routine they lose all significance; when reports are not called specifically to the attention of the top leadership they are lost in bureaucratic background noise, particularly since for every admonitory report one can probably find also its opposite in the files.

Despite these reservations, I found the CIA staffed by dedicated men and women and absolutely indispensable. Helms served his country and his President well. He deserved better than the accusations that marred the close of his public career after thirty years of such distinguished service.

These men were the team the new President brought together to fashion a global strategy, all the while seeking to extricate the country from a war left to it by its predecessors. The Cabinet members met for the first time on December 12, 1968, at a get-acquainted session in the Shoreham Hotel in Washington. It was a harbinger that briefings outlining the problems facing the new Administration were given not by the Cabinet officers (appointed only the day before) but by Presidential Assistants, including myself, who had been named in most cases more than a week earlier. Whether these able, astute, strong men could have formed a cohesive team under any leadership will never be known; their complex chief chose to manipulate them as disparate advisers while he undertook his solitary journey with a system of policymaking that centralized power in the White House.

Getting Organized

IN a radio speech of October 24, 1968, Presidential candidate Richard Nixon had promised to "restore the National Security Council to its preeminent role in national security planning." He went so far as to attribute "most of our serious reverses abroad to the inability or disinclination of President Eisenhower's successors to make use of this important council." When the President-elect announced my appointment on December 2, 1968, he revealed that "Dr. Kissinger has set up what I believe, or is setting up at the present time, a very exciting new procedure for seeing to it that the next President of the United States does not hear just what he wants to hear. . . ." Nixon did not explain how I could have accomplished all of this in the three days that had elapsed since I had accepted the appointment.

I agreed with the President-elect on the importance of restoring the National Security Council machinery. A statement issued by Governor Nelson Rockefeller on June 21, 1968, during his campaign for the nomination reflected my views:

There exists no regular staff procedure for arriving at decisions; instead, *ad hoc* groups are formed as the need arises. No staff agency to monitor the carry- ing out of decisions is available. There is no focal point for long-range planning on an inter-agency basis. Without a central administrative focus, foreign policy turns into a series of unrelated decisions — crisis-oriented, *ad hoc* and after- the-fact in nature. We become the prisoners of events.

When I was appointed, I did not have any organizational plan in mind. My major concern was that a large bureaucracy, however orga- nized, tends to stifle creativity. It confuses wise policy with smooth ad- ministration. In the modern state bureaucracies become so large that too often more time is spent in running them than in defining their purposes. A complex bureaucracy has an incentive to exaggerate technical com- plexity and minimize the scope of importance of political judgment; it favors the status quo, however arrived at, because short of an unam- biguous catastrophe the status quo has the advantage of familiarity and it is never possible to prove that another course would yield superior results. It seemed to me no accident that most great statesmen had been locked in permanent struggle with the experts in their foreign offices, for the scope of the statesman's conception challenges the inclination of the expert toward minimum risk.

The complexity of modern government makes large bureaucracies es- sential; but the need for innovation also creates the imperative to define purposes that go beyond administrative norms. Ultimately there is no purely organizational answer; it is above all a problem of leadership. Organizational remedies cannot by themselves remove the bias for wait- ing for crises and for the avoidance of long-range planning. We set our- selves the task of making a conscious effort to shape the international environment according to a conception of American purposes rather than to wait for events to impose the need for decision.

My unhappy experience as a regular but outside consultant to Presi- dent Kennedy proved invaluable. I had learned then the difference be- tween advice and authority. Statesmanship requires above all a sense of nuance and proportion, the ability to perceive the essential among a mass of apparent facts, and an intuition as to which of many equally plausible hypotheses about the future is likely to prove true. And author- ity is essential — the strength to take charge of a sequence of events and to impose some direction. Occasionally an outsider may provide perspective; almost never does he have enough knowledge to advise soundly on tactical moves. Before I served as a consultant to Kennedy, I had believed, like most academicians, that the process of decision-mak- ing was largely intellectual and that all one had to do was to walk into the President's office and convince him of the correctness of one's views. This perspective I soon realized is as dangerously immature as it is widely held. To be sure, in our system the President has the authority to make final decisions; he has larger scope for discretion than the chief executive of any other large country — including probably even the Soviet Union. But a President's schedule is so hectic that he has little time for abstract reflection. Almost all of his callers are supplicants or advocates, and most of their cases are extremely plausible — which is what got them into the Oval Office in the first place. As a result, one of the President's most difficult tasks is to choose among endless arguments that sound equally convincing. The easy decisions do not come to him; they are taken care of at lower levels. As his term in office progresses, therefore, except in extreme crisis a President comes to base his choices more and more on the confidence he has in his advisers. He grows increasingly conscious of bureaucratic and political pressures upon him; issues of substance tend to merge in his mind with the personalities embodying the conflicting considerations.

A Presidential decision is always an amalgam of judgment, confidence in his associates, and also concern about their morale. Any President soon discovers that his problem is not only to give an order but to get it implemented, and this requires willing cooperation. Bureaucratically unpopular orders can be evaded in a variety of ways. They can be interpreted by skilled exegesis to yield a result as close as possible to what the department most concerned wanted in the first place; there can be endless procrastination in implementation; leaks can sabotage a policy by sparking a controversy. And there is the intangible human quality; cut off from most normal contacts, Presidents are acutely uncomfortable with unhappy associates — and seek to avoid the problem if at all possible.

To be helpful to the President the machinery for making decisions must therefore meet several criteria. It must be compatible with his personality and style. It must lead to action; desultory talk without operational content produces paralysis. Above all, it must be sensitive to the psychological relationship between the President and his close advisers: it must enable the President's associates to strengthen his self-confidence and yet give him real choices, to supply perspective and yet not turn every issue into a test of wills. It must give scope for genuine Presidential discretion without promoting the megalomania that often develops in positions where one encounters few equals. At the same time, if every single decision is funneled into the President's office, he will lose the benefit of the technical competence and accumulated experience of the permanent officials.

If key decisions are made informally at unprepared meetings, the tendency to be obliging to the President and cooperative with one's colleagues may vitiate the articulation of real choices. This seemed to me a problem with decision-making in the Kennedy and Johnson administrations. On the other hand, if the procedures grow too formal, if the President is humble enough to subordinate his judgment to a bureaucratic consensus — as happened in the Eisenhower Administration — the danger is that he will in practice be given only the choice between approving or disapproving a single recommended course. Since he is not told of alternatives, or the consequences of disapproval, such a system develops a bias toward the lowest common denominator. It sacrifices purpose to administrative efficiency. This may be relieved by occasional spasms of Presidential self-will meant to convince others (and himself) of his authority, but such erratic outbursts are bound to prove temporary since his refusal to accept the agreed recommendation leaves him with no operational alternative.

Permitting the President to make a real choice seemed to me essential, not only to establish genuine Presidential authority but also to enhance his leadership by giving him the self-assurance that comes from knowing that he had considered all the valid alternatives. Putting before the President the fullest range of choices and their likely consequences was indeed the main job of the national security adviser. No President can avoid failures on some problems sometime in his term; I never wanted it said that they occurred because of events which were foreseeable but had never been considered. With the help of Morton Halperin, a young Harvard colleague, and General Andrew Goodpaster, a former adviser to President Eisenhower, I set to work.

General Goodpaster was assigned to Nixon's transition staff on a temporary leave of absence from his post as Deputy Commander in Saigon. He had helped run the NSC system during a part of the Eisenhower Presidency and had come to Nixon's attention in this capacity. A Princeton Ph.D., he belonged to the new breed of senior officers enlightened (if that is the word) by postgraduate studies at civilian universities. The combination of military training and scholarly pursuit can often produce a style so methodical that it borders on pedantry, but can also give a perspective far wider than that of other senior officers. It is possible that the military overestimated Goodpaster's academic suppleness and that the academicians were carried away by the phenomenon of an intellectual general. The fact remained that General Goodpaster was a man of vast experience, great honor, and considerable ability.

By the end of December 1968 I was ready to submit my recommendations to the President-elect. On December 27 I sent him a memorandum discussing the strengths and weaknesses of the previous systems as I saw them: the flexibility but occasional disarray of the informal Johnson procedure; the formality but also rigidity of the Eisenhower structure, which faced the President with a bureaucratic consensus but no real choices. Our task, I argued, was to combine the best features of the two systems: the regularity and efficiency of the National Security Council, coupled with procedures that ensured that the President and his top advisers considered all the realistic alternatives, the costs and benefits of each, and the separate views and recommendations of all interested agencies. The National Security Council was to be buttressed by a structure of subcommittees. Like the Council itself they would include representatives of all the relevant agencies; their task would be to draft analyses of policy that would present the facts, problems, and choices. Interdepartmental Groups covering different subjects would be chaired by an Assistant Secretary of State or (if appropriate) Defense. As in the Eisenhower period, the President's national security adviser would be chairman of a Review Group which would screen these interagency papers before presentation to the full NSC chaired by the President.

At the end of my memorandum appeared an innocuous sentence: "The elaborated NSC machinery makes the continued functioning of the existing Senior Interdepartmental Group unnecessary." This proposal to abolish the Senior Interdepartmental Group was to start a monumental bureaucratic row, the first in the new Administration. Esoteric as this dispute may seem, its conduct told much about the style of the President-elect and its outcome affected the perception of authority within the government for the entire Nixon Presidency.

The Senior Interdepartmental Group ("SIG" in bureaucratese) had been established in 1967. It was composed of the highest officials of the government just below Cabinet level — the Under Secretaries of State, Defense, and Treasury, the Deputy Director of the CIA, and the Chairman of the Joint Chiefs of Staff. It was chaired by the Under Secretary of State. Its role was to review the options to be presented to the National Security Council and to follow up on decisions reached. The SIG supervised a battery of interdepartmental groups covering different regions of the world; these were also chaired by the State Department representatives. Needless to say, the State Department considered this structure a major bureaucratic triumph because it formally enshrined the Department's preeminence in foreign policy. Equally predictable was the dissatisfaction of every other department. It made no difference that the National Security Council had rarely met in the Johnson Administration and therefore there had been little for the Senior Interdepartmental Group to do. Nor did it matter that the follow-up to the Tuesday lunches, where decisions *were* made, was outside the SIG structure. To the State Department, its preeminence, however hollow and formalistic, was a crucial symbol. And it was not wrong, given the Washington tendency to identify the reality of power with its appearance.

At first I was agnostic. Before an early meeting with the President-elect I had jotted down some notes setting out the requirements of my White House position as I saw it. These notes leave no doubt that my first instinct was to continue the existing structure since I was suggesting that I become ex officio a member of the SIG and that my staff participate in the various Interdepartmental Groups. The President-elect would have none of this. Firmly persuaded of the Foreign Service's ineradicable hostility to him, Nixon flatly refused to consider preserving the SIG. My notes after a meeting reflect this instruction: "Influence of State Department establishment must be reduced."

General Goodpaster and former President Eisenhower took an equally strong line, if for less personal reasons. Shortly after my appointment, General Goodpaster took me to call on the former President, who was bedridden at the Walter Reed Army Hospital. President Eisenhower was emaciated by his illness and largely immobilized by a heart pacemaker. I had never met him before, and held about him the conventional academic opinion that he was a genial but inarticulate war hero who had been a rather ineffective President. Two of my books and several articles deplored the vacuum of leadership of his Administration — a view I have since changed. Successive heart attacks had left little doubt that he had not long to live. Despite this, his forcefulness was surprising. His syntax, which seemed so awkward in print, became much more graphic when enlivened by his cold, deep blue, extraordinarily penetrating eyes and when given emphasis by his still commanding voice.

Eisenhower insisted that the SIG structure had to be ended because the Pentagon would never willingly accept State Department domination of the national security process. It would either attempt end-runs or counterattack by leaking. He had been fortunate to have a strong Secretary of State, but Dulles's influence had derived from the President's confidence in him and not from the State Department machinery. And for all his admiration for Dulles, he had always insisted on keeping control of the NSC machinery in the White House.

As time went on I came to see that President Eisenhower was right. Nixon's instructions may have been triggered by personal pique; they nevertheless reflected Presidential necessities. A President should not leave the presentation of his options to one of the Cabinet departments or agencies. Since the views of the departments are often in conflict, to place one in charge of presenting the options will be perceived by the others as giving it an unfair advantage. Moreover, the strong inclination of all departments is to narrow the scope for Presidential decision, not to expand it. They are organized to develop a preferred policy, not a range of choices. If forced to present options, the typical department will present two absurd alternatives as straw men bracketing its preferred option — which usually appears in the middle position. A totally ignorant decision-maker could easily satisfy his departments by blindly choosing Option 2 of any three choices which they submit to him. Every department, finally, dreads being overruled by the President; all have, therefore, a high incentive to obscure their differences. Options tend to disappear in an empty consensus that at the end of the day

permits each agency or department maximum latitude to pursue its original preference. It takes a strong, dedicated, and fair Presidential staff to
ensure that the President has before him genuine and not bogus choices.

The scheme I had submitted to the President-elect was not particularly
novel. It was, in effect, the Eisenhower NSC system, weighted somewhat in favor of the State Department by retaining the State Department
chairmanship of the various subcommittees. A similar system, but with
even greater formal White House control, had been completely dominated by Secretary of State Dulles in the Eisenhower Administration.

In the transition period, however, this was not the perception of the
departments. The President-elect assembled his senior appointees —
William Rogers, Melvin Laird, and myself — at Key Biscayne,
Florida, on December 28, 1968, to discuss my organizational proposals.
Characteristically, Nixon had approved my memorandum the day *before* — depriving the meeting of its subject, though the other participants did not know this. Like so many meetings in the Nixon Administration the Key Biscayne session had its script determined in advance.
After a desultory exchange Nixon informed his future Cabinet colleagues that he had approved the structure outlined in my memorandum.
There was no objection, which may have been because the Secretaries-
designate had failed to obtain staff advice or because the President-elect
presented his views so elliptically that their import did not sink in immediately. His only change was to remove the Director of the Central Intelligence Agency from the National Security Council.

Once they had left Key Biscayne, Rogers and Laird quickly reversed
themselves. Perhaps from long familiarity with the President-elect, they
in no way considered Nixon's approval of a memorandum to be a final
decision.

The first to be heard from was Laird, who in the process initiated me
to his patented technique of bureaucratic warfare: to throw up a smokescreen of major objections in which he was not really interested but
which reduced the item that really concerned him to such minor proportions that to refuse him would appear positively indecent. Applying this
tactic, Laird spoke with me and then submitted a memorandum that
identified some fundamental disagreements with the proposed new system. He objected to the intelligence community's lack of direct access
to the President; he feared an NSC staff monopoly of the right to initiate
studies; somewhat contradictorily, he asked for assurances against senior officials' ''going around the NSC and directly to the President as a
regular practice.'' (His chief worry here was to prevent the Chairman of
the Joint Chiefs of Staff from exercising too literally his legal prerogative as principal military adviser to the President.) But when I met with
Laird for dinner at the Sheraton-Carlton Hotel in Washington to discuss
his memorandum, it turned out that he sought no more than the partici-

pation of the CIA Director at NSC meetings and the right to propose the initiation of studies. These requests were easily accommodated.

Rogers's objections, however, went to the heart of the system. Rogers found that his new subordinates attached extreme importance to State Department chairmanship of the SIG and to this group's function as clearinghouse for all NSC business. U. Alexis Johnson, newly appointed Under Secretary of State for Political Affairs, was the principal champion of the State Department point of view. One of the most distinguished Foreign Service Officers, skilled, disciplined, prudent, and loyal, Alex Johnson represented with great ability an institution that I grew to admire — the corps of professional diplomats who serve our country with anonymity and dedication, regardless of Administration, and who thereby assure the continuity of our foreign policy. These same qualities caused Alex Johnson to encourage Bill Rogers to fight a rearguard action to defend the preeminence of the State Department — which even five minutes' conversation with Nixon could leave no doubt that the President-elect would never tolerate.

On January 7 I wrote the President-elect to explain the issues in dispute with the State Department. State proposed that it continue to be the "executive agent" for the President for the design and conduct of foreign policy. State wanted to control the staffing of the interdepartmental machinery; it also insisted on the authority to resolve disputes with other departments and the right to take disagreements to the NSC. I explained to the President-elect that the procedures he had already approved embodied his instructions. The State Department would be fully represented in the new NSC structure, chairing the Interdepartmental Groups and participating in the Review Group and the NSC. Only the final review was under White House chairmanship as it had been in the Eisenhower Administration. Though I had not started with a strong preference I did not think Nixon could afford to retreat on the issue. If he left it open he would begin his Administration with a bitter bureaucratic disagreement; if he reversed his own Key Biscayne decision he would encourage further challenges.

At this point I experienced for the first time two of Nixon's distinguishing attributes. Nixon could be very decisive. Almost invariably during his Presidency his decisions were courageous and strong and often taken in loneliness against all expert advice. But wherever possible Nixon made these decisions in solitude on the basis of memoranda or with a few very intimate aides. He abhorred confronting colleagues with whom he disagreed and he could not bring himself to face a disapproving friend. William Rogers was both. Suddenly Nixon was unavailable for days on end. When I did see him, he would assert vaguely that the organizational problem would resolve itself, without indicating how, and pass on to other matters. The public heard little of the new NSC system that had been announced so triumphantly three weeks earlier. In order to bring matters to a head, General Goodpaster and I drafted a directive and submitted it for Presidential signature. In bureaucratese it was entitled National Security Decision Memorandum 2 — abbreviated as NSDM 2.* NSDM 2 formally established the NSC system along the lines Nixon had approved in Key Biscayne.

Concurrently I sought to negotiate a settlement of the issue. Andy Goodpaster, I, and my assistant Larry Eagleburger visited the State Department to meet with Rogers and his Under Secretary–designate Elliot Richardson in the office set aside for Rogers during the transition. Goodpaster defended the directive forcefully. Rogers followed a brief which repeated the insistence that State chair the entire NSC machinery. Richardson started out on Rogers's side, but eventually switched and rather effectively defended NSDM 2. Richardson, I suspect, understood it was the President's preference and I believe his precise lawyer's mind also saw its sense and symmetry. Nixon, however, was prepared to accept neither NSDM 2 as drafted nor Rogers's objections. The reason had little to do with substance; his basic problem was tactical. Given Nixon's specific instructions, his strong views on the need for an NSC system, and his deep distrust of the State Department, the outcome was scarcely in doubt. But how to implement his preferences without giving a direct order was another matter. While everyone had offices at the Pierre Hotel in New York, Nixon found even a written order or action through an intermediary — normally his preferred method — difficult to implement. He therefore continued to envelop himself in silence and ambiguity on the threshold issue of our foreign policy machinery.

When Nixon secluded himself again to work on his Inaugural address, the situation changed. Geographic distance provided the mechanism for resolving the dispute. Quite unexpectedly, I received a phone call from Haldeman informing me that the President-elect had decided to sign NSDM 2 and that anyone opposing it should submit his resignation. It was all vintage Nixon: a definite instruction, followed by maddening ambiguity and procrastination, which masked the search for an indirect means of solution, capped by a sudden decision — transmitted to the loser by two consecutive intermediaries. It also explains why his White House Assistants came to play such a dominant role. They were the buffer that absorbed unwanted interlocutors, a category including anyone who wanted to express a disagreement face to face. They transmitted unpopular instructions. They bore the weight of departmental wrath.

NSDM 2 was signed on January 19 and issued shortly after Inauguration on January 20.

---

* NSDM 1 was a technical directive creating two series of Presidential directives: National Security Study Memoranda (NSSMs) and National Security Decision Memoranda (NSDMs).

In the light of Nixon's firm convictions, the outcome of this dispute was foreordained. Nor was it a crucial grant of power to me to the degree that was often alleged.[3] This incident was important less in terms of real power than in appearance and in what it foretold about the President's relations with his principal advisers. The fact that the contest ended in what was perceived to be a victory for me helped establish my authority early on. Further, it turned out to be the first of seemingly unending skirmishes between the President and his Secretary of State — all the more grating on both since each usually found someone else to blame for the disagreement. It was the futility of these battles that shaped in practice, much more than the organization chart, the relative influence of Nixon's key advisers. And the true origin of our policymaking procedures lay in Nixon's determination — antedating my appointment — to conduct foreign policy from the White House, his distrust of the existing bureaucracy, coupled with the congruence of his philosophy and mine and the relative inexperience of the new Secretary of State.

To be sure, the organization made White House control easier. It gave me a means to involve myself and my staff in early stages of policy formulation. Though this was not envisioned at the beginning, it also made possible the secret negotiations in which as time went on I was increasingly involved. Nixon and I could use the interdepartmental machinery to educate ourselves by ordering planning papers on negotiations that as far as the bureaucracy was concerned were hypothetical; these studies told us the range of options and what could find support within the government. We were then able to put departmental ideas into practice outside of formal channels. Strange as it may seem, I never negotiated without a major departmental contribution even when the departments did not know what I was doing.

But in the final analysis the influence of a Presidential Assistant derives almost exclusively from the confidence of the President, not from administrative arrangements. My role would almost surely have been roughly the same if the Johnson system had been continued. Propinquity counts for much; the opportunity to confer with the President several times a day is often of decisive importance, much more so than the chairmanship of committees or the right to present options. For reasons that must be left to students of psychology, every President since Kennedy seems to have trusted his White House aides more than his Cabinet. It may be because they are even more dependent on him; it may be that unencumbered by the pressures of managing a large bureaucracy the Presidential Assistants can cater more fully to Presidential whims; it may be as simple as the psychological reassurance conferred by proximity just down the hall. In Nixon's case the role of the Assistants was magnified by the work habits of the President. Nixon tended to work in spurts. During periods when he withdrew he counted on his assistants to carry on the day-to-day decisions; during spasms of extreme activity he relied on his Assistants to screen his more impetuous commands. They were needed to prevent the face-to-face confrontations he so disliked and dreaded. And they were to protect Nixon against impulsive orders or the tendency to agree with the visitors he did receive. Haldeman's staff system did not "isolate" the President as was often alleged; Nixon insisted on isolating himself; it was the only way in which he could marshal his psychological resources and his instructions could be given systematic review.

In this context the control of interdepartmental machinery and the right to present options at NSC meetings were useful but not decisive. The options were after all prepared by interdepartmental committees and usually debated at NSC meetings in the presence of all the principals, any one of whom — and even more devastatingly a combination of them — had the right to object if the presentation was one-sided. And there was an even more fundamental check: a President would not easily forget a failure resulting from inadequate presentation of the issues.

Eventually, though not for the first one and a half years, I became the principal adviser. Until the end of 1970 I was influential but not dominant. From then on, my role increased as Nixon sought to bypass the delays and sometimes opposition of the departments. The fact remains that the NSC machinery was used more fully before my authority was confirmed, while afterward tactical decisions were increasingly taken outside the system in personal conversations with the President.

Turning to Substance

IN the transition period, problems of substance usually appear as requests for meetings or pleas for continuity. Almost from the moment my job was announced, foreign diplomats sought appointments, driven by the necessity to write reports and in order to get a head start in dealing with the new Administration. The outgoing Administration sought to enlist the new appointees in support of its own preferences.

We had considerable respect for the leading members of the Administration, many of whom had served for five or eight years in Washington. We did our utmost to ease their transition into private life. No critical comment about any key official of the Johnson Administration came from the Nixon team either before or after the Inauguration. An effort was made to treat them with courtesy and to benefit from their experience; we regularly briefed former President Johnson and some of his advisers for years after they left office. Later on, almost every time a senior embassy opened up it was offered first to Dean Rusk; Cyrus Vance was asked to undertake a sensitive mission.

But we could not continue foreign policy by momentum; we were not prepared to submerge our doubts about some of the existing trends and procedures. In this respect the most painful problem was how to deal with the Johnson Administration's continuing effort to arrange a summit meeting between the outgoing President and Soviet Premier Alexei Kosygin. President Johnson had used the occasion of signing the Non-Proliferation Treaty on July 1, 1968, to announce that the two governments had agreed to begin talks on strategic arms limitation. A joint announcement was scheduled for August 21 to disclose that these negotiations would be launched on September 30 at a summit meeting between Kosygin and Johnson in Leningrad. This announcement was aborted by the Soviet invasion of Czechoslovakia.

Yet the Johnson Administration continued to press for a summit even after the invasion of Czechoslovakia and even after the American Presidential election. The Soviet Union, for its part, was eager for it. The Soviets wanted to commit the United States to the principle of strategic arms limitation before President Nixon took office (they could then blame Nixon for any later deadlock by contrasting him with his predecessor); they also sought to purge the diplomatic atmosphere of the stench of the Czechoslovak invasion. On November 14, 1968, a week after Nixon's election, Ambassador Dobrynin told Presidential Assistant Walt Rostow that his government felt it important not to lose momentum in the missile talks and that it was equally important that a good atmosphere be created for ratification of the Non-Proliferation Treaty. It would be a great contribution to the future of US–Soviet relations, Dobrynin added, if President Johnson would lay a basis for moving rapidly with the next Administration. Although Rostow replied that the continued presence of Soviet troops in Czechoslovakia was a problem, the conversation turned to discussion of a summit meeting. As late as December 15, Defense Secretary Clark Clifford on the television program "Face the Nation" was strongly urging an early US–Soviet summit meeting to launch the strategic arms negotiations.

It was impossible not to be moved by President Johnson's eagerness to go down in history for making a breakthrough toward peace and being thwarted by fate, personality, and events from realizing his dream. So brutally vilified for a Vietnam policy which he had partly inherited, President Johnson understandably wanted to leave office on a note of hope. Nevertheless, we thought a Soviet-American summit during the transition period inappropriate. Nor should a President of the United States have met with Soviet leaders within months of the invasion of Czechoslovakia. The impact of such a gesture would have been devastating, especially in Western Europe. It was particularly unwise for a lame-duck Administration. Whatever would be achieved would have to be carried out by officials with no hand in negotiating or shaping it. The Soviet Union with continuity in leadership might emerge as the authoritative interpreter of whatever agreement was reached. And any change of policy the new Administration might wish to make would be criticized as breaking solemn international commitments or would be contrasted unfavorably with its predecessor's.

One of the first decisions made after my appointment was announced on December 2, therefore, was to head off a summit before Inauguration. On December 8, Nixon's adviser Robert Ellsworth, with whom the Soviet Embassy had maintained contact during the campaign, was instructed to explain to Soviet chargé d'affaires Yuri N. Chernyakov that the President-elect would not look with favor on a summit meeting before January 20. I made the same point to Boris Sedov, a KGB operative who seemed to have had the Rockefeller assignment during the campaign and who had tagged along with me ever since. On December 18, Chernyakov handed Ellsworth a Soviet reply at the Plaza Hotel in New York. The Soviet note explained that the summit had been raised by the United States first in July, then again in the middle of September, and finally at the end of November. The Soviets had assumed that the President-elect had been kept informed. Now that "the situation in this respect" had been "clarified," the Soviets acknowledged that it was "difficult" for them to judge how successful a summit could be under present circumstances. Chernyakov added that he would be glad to convey any reply from the President-elect to Moscow. There was no reply. It was the end of the summit idea.

Sporadic contact continued with Sedov. His major preoccupation was that Nixon include something in his Inaugural address to the effect that he was keeping open the lines of communication to Moscow. This he said would be well received in the Kremlin. I was never clear whether this request reflected an attempt by Sedov to demonstrate his influence to Moscow or whether it was a serious policy approach by the Politburo. In any event I saw no harm in it. Nixon's Inaugural address proclaimed to all nations that "during this Administration our lines of communication will be open" and offered other now-standard expressions of our devotion to peace.[4]

Another problem of the transition period proved to be largely self-inflicted: the so-called Scranton mission.

I had met William Scranton briefly during his abortive try for the Presidency in 1964. Later I came to work closely with him when he became our Ambassador to the United Nations. I found him selfless and able. Reluctant to take on full-time duties, he was always available for advice and special missions. In early December 1968, Nixon sent him for nine days to six Middle East countries as his personal envoy. After crossing the Allenby Bridge from Jordan into the Israeli-held West Bank on December 9, Scranton spoke to reporters in Jericho and added a new catch-phrase to the vocabulary of Middle East diplomacy: "It is impor-

tant [that] U.S. policy become more even-handed" in the area, he proclaimed, adding that by "even-handed" he meant that the United States
should deal "with all countries in the area and not necessarily espouse
one." When Scranton arrived in Rome on December 11, he announced
that the Nixon Administration would draw up a new "peace plan" for
the Middle East. This set off an uproar in Israel, causing Nixon's press
spokesman, Ronald Ziegler, to state on the same day that the remarks
about an "even-handed" policy and a new "peace plan" were not necessarily those of the President-elect. But when Scranton returned to
report to Nixon on December 13, he held a press conference afterward
and, being a man of conviction, repeated his statement that the United
States should have "a more even-handed policy" in the Middle East.
Shock waves of alarm spread to Israel and among Israel's supporters in
the United States. We had a chance to calm the situation when Nixon
and I met on December 13 with Israeli Defense Minister Moshe Dayan.
Sharing Nixon's wish not to start off the new Administration with a US–
Israeli brawl, Dayan publicly denied news reports that Israel was dis-
pleased with the Scranton visit. His government felt, Dayan explained
ambiguously to the press, that Scranton left Israel with "a better appreciation of the issues." The Scranton flap was put behind us, but the
hard rock of the Middle East impasse remained.

This was not our only exposure to the complexities of the Middle
East. On December 17, the President-elect met with the Amir of Kuwait
at the insistent request of President Johnson, who, correctly, made it a
point of personal privilege that his last State visitor also be received by
Nixon. The occasion was notable mainly for giving me my first opportunity to prepare the President-elect for a high-level meeting — a test
which I flunked ingloriously. I assumed that the Arab-Israeli conflict
would be at the forefront of the Amir's concern and prepared an erudite
memorandum on the subject. Unfortunately, the Amir wanted, above
all, to learn what plans the new Administration had for the Persian Gulf
after the United Kingdom vacated the area, as it had announced it would
do in 1971. What were America's intentions if, for example, Iraq attacked Kuwait? Nixon gave me the glassy look he reserved for occasions when in his view the inadequacy of his associates had placed him
into a untenable position. Manfully he replied that he would have to
study the matter, but that, of course, we were interested in the territorial
integrity of all states in the area; what tactical measures we would adopt
would of course depend on circumstances. The Amir seemed content
with this Delphic utterance.

Later I learned to improve my forecasting — if necessary by asking
the visitor in advance what subjects he intended to raise with Nixon.

In the transition period a new Administration must be careful not to
intervene in the day-to-day operations of foreign policy. But it can make

gestures to establish a positive atmosphere. In early January the President-elect sent warm letters to President Charles de Gaulle, Prime Minister Harold Wilson, Chancellor Kurt Kiesinger, and NATO Secretary-General Manlio Brosio, affirming the priority he intended to give to strengthening Atlantic ties. Friendly messages were also sent to Japanese Prime Minister Eisaku Sato, President Josip Broz Tito, and Pope Paul VI.

The most important diplomatic initiative of the transition period was toward Hanoi. At my suggestion, the President-elect initiated two exchanges with the North Vietnamese in late December and early January, which stressed our readiness for serious negotiations. The intermediary was my friend Jean Sainteny, the former French Delegate General in Hanoi. These contacts proved stillborn because the North Vietnamese, having in effect achieved a unilateral bombing halt, immediately put forward the demand that the United States overthrow the government in Saigon.

Vietnam was in fact the subject of our principal mistake during the transition. It was as if Vietnam had a congenital capacity to becloud American judgment. A few days before Inauguration, we made it possible for the American negotiators in the Paris peace talks to settle the deadlock that had held up the start of formal negotiations ever since the bombing halt on November 1: the dispute over the shape of the negotiating table and the designation of the parties that were to sit around it. This was not a trivial issue; it was of great symbolic significance to our South Vietnamese allies, who, considering themselves the legitimate government, were not ready to accord equal status to Hanoi's arm in the South, the National Liberation Front. For three months, therefore, Saigon had resisted Hanoi's proposal for a four-sided table at which Hanoi, the NLF, Saigon, and the United States were each accorded equal status. By this proposal Hanoi sought to use the beginnings of the negotiations to establish the NLF as an alternative government.

In mid-January, the Soviet Union suddenly offered a compromise on behalf of the North Vietnamese. The agreement that quickly emerged was a circular table without nameplates, flags, or markings — an arrangement ambiguous enough for the Communists to speak of four sides and for the United States and South Vietnam to speak of two sides (the allies versus the Communists). The Communists' motive was transparent. If the deadlock continued into the new Administration, the new President, whose public pronouncements certainly sounded bellicose, might abrogate the bombing halt. If the deadlock were to be broken after the Inauguration, the new Administration would be able to use this sign of "progress" to strengthen its public support and therefore its endurance against the psychological warfare that Hanoi was about to unleash upon it. Settling with an outgoing Administration in its last days in office solved both problems for the North Vietnamese.

It would have been easy for us to encourage the South Vietnamese to continue to drag their feet and block the accord until after the Inauguration. Saigon would do this anyway even if we did nothing. But Bill Rogers authorized Secretary of State Rusk to inform Saigon that the President-elect urged it to accept the compromise *before* Inauguration. And Nixon, despite my urging, did not feel that he could go back on this commitment. Thus the outgoing Administration in its last days in office was given an opportunity to celebrate a success. The success was meaningless for it, yet as Hanoi had foreseen it weakened the new President by dooming him to an immediate deadlock that would soon rekindle the domestic debate. Not many weeks passed before Nixon was accused of inflexibility because of insufficient substantive progress in the negotiations.

The transition period proved much too brief; it always is. At noon on January 20 in the cold wind of the platform on the Capitol steps, I watched Richard Nixon take the oath of office. It now fell to us, who took up our new duties with hopes not untinged by trepidation, to make the decisions that could shape the future of our country and determine the prospects of peace and freedom in the world.

III

The Convictions of an
Apprentice Statesman

An Historian's Perspective

THE moment of responsibility is profoundly sobering, especially for one trained as an academic. Suddenly forced to make the transition from reflection to decision, I had to learn the difference between a conclusion and a policy. It was no longer enough to be plausible in argument; one had to be convincing in action. Problems were no longer theoretical; the interlocutors were not debaters but sovereign countries, some of which had the physical power to make their views prevail.

Any statesman is in part the prisoner of necessity. He is confronted with an environment he did not create, and is shaped by a personal history he can no longer change. It is an illusion to believe that leaders gain in profundity while they gain experience. As I have said, the convictions that leaders have formed before reaching high office are the intellectual capital they will consume as long as they continue in office. There is little time for leaders to reflect. They are locked in an endless battle in which the urgent constantly gains on the important. The public life of every political figure is a continual struggle to rescue an element of choice from the pressure of circumstance.

When I entered office, I brought with me a philosophy formed by two decades of the study of history. History is not, of course, a cookbook offering pretested recipes. It teaches by analogy, not by maxims. It can illuminate the consequences of actions in comparable situations, yet each generation must discover for itself what situations are in fact comparable. No academic discipline can take from our shoulders the burden of difficult choices.

I had written a book and several articles on the diplomacy of the nineteenth century. My motive was to understand the processes by which Europe after the Napoleonic wars established a peace that lasted a century; I also wanted to know why that peace collapsed in 1914. But I had never conceived that designs and strategies of previous periods could be applied literally to the present. As I entered office I was convinced that the past could teach us some important lessons. But I was also aware that we were entering a period for which there was no precedent: in the destructiveness of weapons, in the speed of the spread of ideas, in the global impact of foreign policies, in the technical possibility to fulfill the age-old dreams of bettering the condition of mankind.

If history teaches anything it is that there can be no peace without equilibrium and no justice without restraint. But I believed equally that no nation could face or even define its choices without a moral compass that set a course through the ambiguities of reality and thus made sacrifices meaningful. The willingness to walk this fine line marks the difference between the academic's — or any outsider's — perception of morality and that of the statesman. The outsider thinks in terms of absolutes; for him right and wrong are defined in their conception. The political leader does not have this luxury. He rarely can reach his goal except in stages; any partial step is inherently morally imperfect and yet morality cannot be approximated without it. The philosopher's test is the reasoning behind his maxims; the statesman's test is not only the exaltation of his goals but the catastrophe he averts. Mankind will never know what it was spared because of risks avoided or because of actions taken that averted awful consequences — if only because once thwarted the consequences can never be proved. The dialogue between the academic and the statesman is therefore always likely to be inconclusive. Without philosophy, policy will have no standards; but without the willingness to peer into darkness and risk some faltering steps without certainty, humanity would never know peace.

History knows no resting places and no plateaus. All societies of which history informs us went through periods of decline; most of them eventually collapsed. Yet there is a margin between necessity and accident, in which the statesman by perseverance and intuition must choose and thereby shape the destiny of his people. To ignore objective conditions is perilous; to hide behind historical inevitability is tantamount to moral abdication; it is to neglect the elements of strength and hope and inspiration which through the centuries have sustained mankind. The statesman's responsibility is to struggle against transitoriness and not to insist that he be paid in the coin of eternity. He may know that history is the foe of permanence; but no leader is entitled to resignation. He owes it to his people to strive, to create, and to resist the decay that besets all human institutions.

The American Experience

I REACHED high office unexpectedly at a particularly complex period of our national life. In the life of nations, as of human beings, a point is

often reached when the seemingly limitless possibilities of youth suddenly narrow and one must come to grips with the fact that not every
option is open any longer. This insight can inspire a new creative impetus, less innocent perhaps than the naive exuberance of earlier years, but
more complex and ultimately more permanent. The process of coming
to grips with one's limits is never easy. It can end in despair or in
rebellion; it can produce a self-hatred that turns inevitable compromises
into a sense of inadequacy.

America went through such a period of self-doubt and self-hatred in
the late 1960s. The trigger for it was the war in Vietnam. Entered into
gradually by two administrations, by 1969 it had resulted in over 31,000
American dead with no prospect of early resolution. It began with overwhelming public and Congressional approval, but this had evolved first
into skepticism and then into increasingly hostile rebellion. For too
many, a war to resist aggression had turned into a symbol of fundamental American evil. A decade that had begun with the bold declaration
that America would pay any price and bear any burden to ensure the
survival and success of liberty had ended in an agony of assassinations,
urban riots, and ugly demonstrations. The Sixties marked the end of our
innocence; this was certain. What remained to be determined was
whether we could learn from this knowledge or consume our substance in rebelling against the reality of our maturity.

The turmoil of the 1960s was all the more unsettling to Americans
because it came at the end of an extraordinary period of American accomplishment. We had built alliances that preserved the peace and fostered the growth of the industrial democracies of North America, Western Europe, and Japan. We had helped create international economic
institutions that had nourished global prosperity for a generation. We
had promoted decolonization and pioneered in development assistance
for the new nations. In a planet shrunk by communications and technology, in a world either devastated by war or struggling in the first steps
of nationhood, the United States had every reason to take pride in its
global contribution — its energy, idealism, and enduring accomplishment.

The fact remained that at the end of twenty years of exertion America
was not at peace with itself. The consensus that had sustained our
postwar foreign policy had evaporated. The men and women who had
sustained our international commitments and achievements were demoralized by what they considered their failure in Vietnam. Too many of
our young were in rebellion against the successes of their fathers, attacking what they claimed to be the overextension of our commitments
and mocking the values that had animated the achievements. A new
isolationism was growing. Whereas in the 1920s we had withdrawn
from the world because we thought we were too good for it, the insidi-

ous theme of the late 1960s was that we should withdraw from the world because we were too evil for it.

Not surprisingly, American self-doubt proved contagious; it is hard for foreign nations to have more faith in a country than it has in itself. European intellectuals began to argue that the Cold War was caused by American as well as by Soviet policies; they urged their governments to break out of the vicious circle by peace initiatives of their own. Many European leaders, catering to this mood, became fervent advocates of détente, playing the role of a "bridge" between East and West — visiting Moscow, exploring ties with Peking, urging disarmament and East-West trade.

These protestations were all very well until the United States, in the late Sixties, began to take them to heart and adopt the policy implicit in them. Suddenly European statesmen reversed course. Now they were fearful of a US–Soviet condominium, a "Super-Yalta" in which American and Soviet leaders would settle global issues over the heads of European governments. In the year that saw the Soviet invasion of Czechoslovakia, the United States was accused by many of its allies of being at one and the same time too bellicose in Southeast Asia and too accommodating in its dealings with the Soviet Union. This ambivalence gnawed at the unity of the Alliance. Unnerved by events in Czechoslovakia, pressed by public opinion toward conciliation, impelled by conviction to strengthen security, the Western Alliance was becalmed like a ship dead in the water.

Similar uncertainty marked our other policies. For two decades our contacts with China had been limited to the reciprocal recriminations of sporadic ambassadorial meetings in Warsaw. The Middle East was explosive, but in the aftermath of the 1967 war no diplomacy was in train. Our domestic divisions prevented decisive initiatives. America seemed reduced to passivity in a world in which, with all our self-doubt, only our power could offer security, only our dedication could sustain hope.

In my view, Vietnam was not the cause of our difficulties but a symptom. We were in a period of painful adjustment to a profound transformation of global politics; we were being forced to come to grips with the tension between our history and our new necessities. For two centuries America's participation in the world seemed to oscillate between overinvolvement and withdrawal, between expecting too much of our power and being ashamed of it, between optimistic exuberance and frustration with the ambiguities of an imperfect world. I was convinced that the deepest cause of our national unease was the realization — as yet dimly perceived — that we were becoming like other nations in the need to recognize that our power, while vast, had limits. Our resources were no longer infinite in relation to our problems; instead we had to set priorities, both intellectual and material. In the Fifties and Sixties we had attempted ultimate solutions to specific problems; now our challenge was to shape a world and an American role to which we were permanently committed, which could no longer be sustained by the illusion that our exertions had a terminal point.

Any Administration elected in 1968 would have faced this problem. It was a colossal task in the best of circumstances; the war in Vietnam turned it into a searing and anguishing enterprise.

Our history ill prepared us. Ironically, our Founding Fathers were sophisticated statesmen who understood the European balance of power and manipulated it brilliantly, first to bring about America's independence and then to preserve it. The shrewd diplomacy of Franklin and Jefferson engaged Britain's enemies (France, Spain, and Russia) on our side; our negotiating hand thus strengthened, John Jay secured recognition from the British Crown and liquidated the residual problems of our war with England. At that point, however, in the best traditions of the European balance of power, we cut loose from our temporary allies and went on our own way. For more than three decades after independence, we lived precariously, like other nations. We went to the brink of war with France and endured the capture of our capital by British forces. But we moved astutely to take advantage of new opportunities. The effective elimination of France and Spain from the Western Hemisphere, the new danger of Russian expansion in the Pacific Northwest, and Great Britain's growing estrangement from the European nations led us in 1823 to concert the Monroe Doctrine with Britain to exclude European power from our hemisphere.

Britain's perspective was that of the European equilibrium. Prime Minister Canning perceived that the Monroe Doctrine ''called the New World into existence to redress the balance of the Old.'' But in the New World it meant that we were free to turn our backs on Europe and to devote our energies to opening up the continent to the west of us. For the hundred years between Waterloo and 1914, we were shielded by our geographic remoteness and British sea power, which maintained global stability.

As the United States grew in strength and European rivalries focused on Europe, Africa, and Asia, Americans came to consider the isolation conferred by two great oceans as the normal pattern of foreign relations. Rather arrogantly we ascribed our security entirely to the superiority of our beliefs rather than to the weight of our power or the fortunate accidents of history and geography. After the Napoleonic upheaval, America stood apart from European conflicts throughout the nineteenth century — although in order to round out our national territory and maintain our national unity we fought as many wars as any European country and probably suffered more casualties. But these wars were not seen in terms of a concept of international relations; to Americans they reflected the imperatives of a manifest destiny.

Americans, whether Mayflower descendants or refugees from the failed revolutions of 1848, came to assume that we were immune from the necessities that impelled other nations. There was, of course, also a pragmatic and realistic strain. Admiral Mahan's perception of the role of sea power proved that Americans could think profoundly in geopolitical terms. The methods by which we acquired the Philippines and the Panama Canal proved that power politics was not totally neglected. Nevertheless, American political thought had come increasingly to regard diplomacy with suspicion. Arms and alliances were considered immoral and reactionary. Negotiations were treated less as a means of reconciling our ideals with our interests than as a trap to entangle us in the endless quarrels of a morally questionable world. Our native inclination for straightforwardness, our instinct for open, noisy politics, our distrust of European manners and continental elites all brought about an increasing impatience with the stylized methods of European diplomacy and with its tendency toward ambiguous compromise. In its day even the purchase of Alaska, which finally ejected Russia from our continent, was regarded as a towering folly explicable only by American gullibility in the face of Old World diplomatic machinations. Congress was prevailed upon only with the greatest difficulty to appropriate $7 million to complete the deal.

The mythology of foreigners' guileful superiority in the ways of diplomacy was carried into the twentieth century. Will Rogers was always assured of a laugh when he cracked: "America never lost a war and never won a conference."

Thus America entered the twentieth century largely unprepared for the part it would be called upon to play. Forgotten was the skilled statecraft by which the Founding Fathers had secured our independence; disdained were the techniques by which all nations must preserve their interests. As Lord Bryce observed in 1888 in *The American Commonwealth,* America had been sailing "on a summer sea," but now a cloud bank was "on the horizon and now no longer distant, a time of mists and shadows, wherein dangers may be concealed whose form and magnitude she can scarcely conjecture."

Though America was not to grasp its consequences for many decades, the Pax Britannica on which we had relied for so long was ending. We had developed into the world's major economic power; and we were fast becoming the only democratic nation with sufficient strength to maintain a precarious world balance.

Our entry into World War I was the inevitable result of our geopolitical interest in maintaining freedom of the seas and preventing Europe's domination by a hostile power. But true to our tradition, we chose to interpret our participation in legal and idealistic terms. We fought the war "to end all wars" and "to make the world safe for democracy." The inevitable disillusion with an imperfect outcome let loose the tide of isolationism. We fell back on our preference for law in repeated attempts to legislate an end to international conflict — automatic machinery for collective security, new disarmament schemes, the Kellogg-Briand Pact to ban war. Our refusal to accept that foreign policy must start with security led us in the interwar years to treat allies as rivals, whose armaments had to be limited because weapons by definition contributed to international tensions. We looked for scapegoats — the so-called munitions-makers — to explain why we had ever engaged in so sordid an undertaking as the First World War. Intelligence services were considered unworthy if not a threat to our liberties. Economic activity was seen as the only defensible form of American involvement abroad; its objectives were either humanitarian, exemplified by the relief efforts of Herbert Hoover, or essentially passive: free trade, as advocated by Cordell Hull.

Later, when totalitarianism was on the rise and the entire international order was being challenged, we clung to our isolation, which had been transformed from a policy preference into a moral conviction. We had virtually abandoned the basic precautions needed for our national security. Only with the greatest difficulty could President Roosevelt take the first tentative steps against the mounting threat, aiding Great Britain by subterfuge and rebuilding our military might. The Second World War was well under way before we were shocked out of isolation by a surprise attack against American soil. But then in our absorption with total victory, we spurned the notion that the security of the postwar world might depend on some sort of equilibrium of power. We were thus much surprised by the war's aftermath. The central fact of the postwar period was that the destruction of Germany and Italy and the exhaustion of Britain and France drew Soviet power into the heart of the European continent and for a while seemed to place Western Europe at Soviet mercy. Moscow's renewed ideological hostility increasingly challenged our comfortable wartime assumptions about postwar international harmony. And our scientists had unleashed the atom, ushering in a revolution in weaponry that set our age apart from all that had gone before.

When Dean Acheson said he was "present at the creation," he referred not only to the creation of our postwar foreign policy but to a new era in our own history. After two world wars in this century, the responsibilities and the burdens of world leadership proved inescapable. The United States had despite itself become the guardian of the new equilibrium. It is to the lasting credit of that generation of Americans that they assumed these responsibilities with energy, imagination, and skill. By helping Europe rebuild, encouraging European unity, shaping institutions of economic cooperation, and extending the protection of our alliances, they saved the possibilities of freedom. This burst of creativity is one of the glorious moments of American history.

Yet this period of exuberance was bound to wane, if only because we inevitably encountered the consequences of our success. The recovery of Europe and Japan required adjustments in our alliance relations; the developing world of new nations whose independence we had promoted was certain to claim a greater share of global prosperity. And nothing we could have done would have prevented the Soviet Union from recovering from the war and asserting its new power. Our early postwar successes did not equip us for a new era of more complex problems. Our early programs like the Marshall Plan and Point Four expressed our idealism, our technological know-how, and our ability to overwhelm problems with resources. In a sense we were applying the precepts of our own New Deal, expecting political conflict to dissolve in economic progress. It worked in Europe and parts of Asia where political structures existed; it would be less relevant in the scores of new nations. In the relatively simple bipolar world of the Cold War, we held fast against pressure or blackmail in Berlin, in Korea, in Berlin again, and finally during the Cuban missile crisis. These were successes. But in an important sense we had only begun to scratch the surface of the long-term problem of our relationship with the Soviet Union in the thermonuclear age, which would soon produce more ambiguous challenges.

Our deeper problem was conceptual. Because peace was believed to be "normal," many of our great international exertions were expected to bring about a final result, restoring normality by overcoming an intervening obstacle. The programs for European economic recovery were expected to bring lasting prosperity. Exertions to ensure security were aimed at a conclusive settlement with the Soviet Union. This was implicit in the concept of "containment" that expressed our postwar policy toward the Soviet Union.[1]

According to George Kennan's famous "X" article in *Foreign Affairs* in 1947, our task was to resist Soviet probes with counterforce, patiently awaiting the mellowing of the Soviet system. As applied in the diplomacy of Dean Acheson and to some extent John Foster Dulles, we were to mark time until we built the strength to contain Soviet aggression — especially the assault on Central Europe, which preoccupied our strategic thinking. After containment had been achieved, diplomacy would take over. "What we must do," said Secretary of State Acheson, "is to create situations of strength; we must build strength and if we create that strength then I think the whole situation in the world begins to change . . . with that change there comes a difference in the negotiating positions of the various parties, and out of that I should hope that there would be a willingness on the part of the Kremlin to recognize the facts. . . ."[2]

This definition of containment treated power and diplomacy as two distinct elements or phases of policy. It aimed at an ultimate negotiation but supplied no guide to the content of those negotiations. It implied that strength was self-evident and that once negotiations started their content would also be self-evident. It did not answer the question of how the situation of strength was to be demonstrated in the absence of a direct attack on us or on our allies. Nor did it make clear what would happen after we had achieved a position of strength if our adversary, instead of negotiating, concentrated on eroding it or turning our flank.

This policy of containment was flawed in three ways. First, our excessively military conception of the balance of power — and its corollary, the policy of deferring negotiations for a postwar settlement — paradoxically gave the Soviet Union time to consolidate ·its conquests and to redress the nuclear imbalance. To be sure, in the immediate postwar period the massive Soviet armies in Central Europe were much larger than the forces arrayed against them; Western Europe was prostrate and the United States was demobilized. But the real strength of the Soviet Union was but a fraction of our own. The Soviet Union had been exhausted by four years of war and 20 million casualties. We had an atomic monopoly and for twenty years a vast nuclear superiority. Our relative strength was never greater than at the beginning of what soon came to be called the Cold War.

Secondly, the nature of military technology was such that the balance of power could no longer be thought of as uniform. Nuclear weapons were so cataclysmic that as the arsenals grew they proved less and less useful to repel every conceivable aggression. For a while this reality was obscured by our nuclear monopoly and later by our numerical preponderance. But the point was inevitably reached when technology enabled the Kremlin to pose risks that reduced the credibility of the threat of nuclear retaliation. From then on, managing the military balance of power required vigilance on two levels: being strong enough not only strategically with nuclear power but also locally with conventional arms. Formal declarations of the unimpaired sincerity of our nuclear guarantee would not remove the fact of nuclear deadlock and the consequent requirement for alternative regional defenses. Yet every decade has had to relearn the essential duality of our burden.

Thirdly, our doctrine of containment could never be an adequate response to the modern impact of Communist ideology, which transforms relations between states into conflicts between philosophies and poses challenges to the balance of power through domestic upheavals.

In short, we never fully understood that while our absolute power was growing, our *relative* position was bound to decline as the USSR recovered from World War II. Our military and diplomatic position was never more favorable than at the *very beginning* of the containment policy in the late 1940s. That was the time to attempt a serious discussion on the future of Europe. We lost our opportunity.

In fact, I am inclined to doubt that Stalin originally expected to lock all of Eastern Europe into his satellite orbit; his first postwar steps — such as permitting free elections in Poland, Czechoslovakia, and Hungary, all of which the Communists lost — suggest that he might have been prepared to settle for their having a status similar to Finland's. Unexpectedly, we deferred serious negotiations until we had mobilized more of our potential strength. Thus we gave the Soviet Union time — the most precious commodity it needed to consolidate its conquests and to recover from the war.

As so often before, Winston Churchill understood this best. In a much neglected speech in October 1948, during his period out of office, he said:

> The question is asked: What will happen when they get the atomic bomb themselves and have accumulated a large store? You can judge yourselves what will happen then by what is happening now. If these things are done in the green wood, what will be done in the dry? If they can continue month after month disturbing and tormenting the world, trusting to our Christian and altruistic inhibitions against using this strange new power against them, what will they do when they themselves have large quantities of atomic bombs? . . . No one in his senses can believe that we have a limitless period of time before us. We ought to bring matters to a head and make a final settlement. We ought not to go jogging along improvident, incompetent, waiting for something to turn up, by which I mean waiting for something bad for us to turn up. The Western Nations will be far more likely to reach a lasting settlement, without bloodshed, if they formulate their just demands while they have the atomic power and before the Russian Communists have got it too.[3]

So it happened that the two wars in which America engaged after 1945 — in Korea and Vietnam — did not correspond to any of our political or strategic expectations. Korea was a war not initiated by an attack on the United States or our major allies. It was not aimed at the heartland of Europe. Nor did it directly involve the USSR. Little wonder that those responsible in Washington saw in it a strategic diversion to draw us into Asia while the Soviet Union prepared an onslaught in Europe. Our conduct of the war was, therefore, tentative. Our objectives fluctuated with the military situation. At various times our aim was declared to be repelling aggression, the unification of Korea, the security of our forces, or a guaranteed armistice to ratify the military stalemate.

Our perception of power and diplomacy as distinct and successive phases of foreign policy prevented us from negotiating to settle the Korean War after the landing at Inchon when we were in the strongest military position; it tempted us to escalate our aims. A year later it also caused us to stop military operations except of a purely defensive nature the moment negotiations got under way, thus removing the enemy's major incentive for a rapid diplomatic settlement. We acted as if the process of negotiations operated on its own inherent logic independent of the military balance — indeed, that military pressures might jeopardize the negotiations by antagonizing our adversary or demonstrating bad faith. Not surprisingly, a stalemate of nearly two years' duration followed, during which our casualties equaled those we had endured when hostilities were unconstrained. Treating force and diplomacy as discrete phenomena caused our power to lack purpose and our negotiations to lack force.

The result was domestic convulsion that represented the first breach in the new national consensus on foreign policy: the conflict between General Douglas MacArthur and the civilian and military leadership in Washington. MacArthur advocated victory in the Far East. His critics argued, among other things, that we had to conserve our strength for a possibly imminent all-out test with the Soviet Union, probably in Europe. MacArthur objected to his directives because they seemed to him too confining in terms of our traditional concept of war; to the political leadership, on the other hand, Korea was a strategic diversion: It was too big a war in terms of Washington's perception of Europe as the decisive arena.

Given the threat the growing Soviet nuclear arsenal would soon pose, it is possible to doubt the premises that time was on our side or that we had more to lose from an all-out war than the Soviet Union. The paradox we never solved was that we had entered the Korean War because we were afraid that to fail to do so would produce a much graver danger to Europe in the near future. But then the very reluctance to face an all-out onslaught on Europe severely circumscribed the risks we were prepared to run to prevail in Korea. The resulting deadlock sapped our domestic cohesion and contributed to the assault on our liberties in the form of McCarthyism.

Ten years later we encountered the same dilemmas in Vietnam. Once more we became involved because we considered the warfare in Indochina the manifestation of a coordinated global Communist strategy. Again we sought to limit our risks because the very global challenge of which Indochina seemed to be a part also made Vietnam appear as an unprofitable place for a showdown. At every stage we sought to keep our risks below the level which in our estimate would trigger Chinese or Soviet intervention. In short, our perception of the global challenge at the same time tempted us into distant enterprises and prevented us from meeting them conclusively. Once again, a war that we had entered with great public support turned into a frustrating stalemate that gradually forfeited public acceptance.

By 1969, the war in Vietnam had become a national nightmare that stimulated an attack on our entire postwar foreign policy. The hitherto almost unanimous conviction that the Cold War had been caused by Soviet intransigence was challenged by a vocal and at times violent minority which began to insist it was American bellicosity, American militarism, and American economic imperialism that were the root causes of international tensions. This home-grown radicalism never had many true adherents; it collapsed instantaneously once we left Vietnam. What is striking is not so much its temporary appeal as its shattering effect in demoralizing the very groups that might have been expected to defend the premises and accomplishments of our postwar policy. The internationalist Establishment, which had been responsible for the great achievements of our foreign policy, collapsed before the onslaught of its children who questioned all its values.

The new Nixon Administration was the first of the postwar generation that had to conduct foreign policy without the national consensus that had sustained its predecessors largely since 1947. And our task was if anything more complex. We faced not only the dislocations of a war but the need to articulate a new foreign policy for a new era. Sooner or later the Vietnam war would end. What were the global challenges we faced? What were our goals in the world? Could we shape a new consensus that could reconcile our idealism and our responsibilities, our security and our values, our dreams and our possibilities?

Problems of a New Equilibrium

EVEN as we entered office, it was clear that the agony of Vietnam threatened a new disillusionment with international affairs that could draw America inward to nurse its wounds and renounce its world leadership. This would be a profound tragedy, far more grievous than the tragedy of Vietnam itself. We would be back to our historical cycle of exuberant overextension and sulking isolationism. And this time we would be forsaking a world far more complex, more dangerous, more dependent upon America's leadership than the world of the 1930s. Therefore the Nixon Administration saw it as its task to lay the foundation for a long-range American foreign policy, even while liquidating our Indochina involvement. Crisis management, the academic focus of the Sixties, was no longer enough. Crises were symptoms of deeper problems which if allowed to fester would prove increasingly unmanageable. Moral exuberance had inspired both overinvolvement and isolationism. It was my conviction that a concept of our fundamental national interests would provide a ballast of restraint and an assurance of continuity. Our idealism had to be not an excuse for irresponsibility but a source of courage, stamina, self-confidence, and direction. Only in this manner would we be able to shape an emerging international system that was unprecedented in its perils, its promise, and its global nature.

Since we were beset by a malaise deeper than Vietnam, its solution was less a matter of expertise than of philosophy. In an essay published a few weeks before the 1968 election, when I had no inkling that I would be asked to put my ideas to the test, I wrote:

> The contemporary unrest is no doubt exploited by some whose purposes are all too clear. But that it is there to exploit is proof of a profound dissatisfaction with the merely managerial and consumer-oriented qualities of the modern state and with a world which seems to generate crises by inertia. The modern bureaucratic state, for all its panoply of strength, often finds itself shaken to its foundations by seemingly trivial causes. Its brittleness and the world-wide revolution of youth — especially in advanced countries and among the relatively affluent — suggest a spiritual void, an almost metaphysical boredom with a political environment that increasingly emphasizes bureaucratic challenges and is dedicated to no deeper purpose than material comfort. . . .
>
> In the best of circumstances, the next administration will be beset by crises. In almost every area of the world, we have been living off capital — warding off the immediate, rarely dealing with underlying problems. These difficulties are likely to multiply when it becomes apparent that one of the legacies of the war in Vietnam will be a strong American reluctance to risk overseas involvements.
>
> A new administration has the right to ask for compassion and understanding from the American people. But it must found its claim not on pat technical answers to difficult issues; it must above all ask the right questions. It must recognize that, in the field of foreign policy, we will never be able to contribute to building a stable and creative world order unless we first form some conception of it.[4]

The most ominous change that marked our period was the transformation in the nature of power. Until the beginning of the nuclear age it would have been inconceivable that a country could possess too much military strength for effective political use; every addition of power was — at least theoretically — politically useful. The nuclear age destroyed this traditional measure. A country might be strong enough to destroy an adversary and yet no longer be able to protect its own population against attack. By an irony of history a gargantuan increase in power had eroded the relationship of power to policy. Henceforth, the major nuclear powers would be able to devastate one another. But they would also have great difficulty in bringing their power to bear on the issues most likely to arise. They might be able to deter direct challenges to their own survival; they could not necessarily use this power to impose their will. The capacity to destroy proved difficult to translate into a plausible threat even against countries with no capacity for retaliation. The margin of the superpowers over non-nuclear states had been widening; yet the awesomeness of their power had increased their inhibitions. As power had grown more awesome, it had also turned abstract, intangible, elusive.

The military policy we adopted was deterrence. But deterrence is a psychological phenomenon. It depends above all on what a potential aggressor considers an unacceptable risk. In the nuclear age a bluff taken seriously is useful; a serious threat taken as a bluff may prove disastrous. The longer deterrence succeeds, the more difficult it is to demonstrate what made it work. Was peace maintained by the risk of war, or because the adversary never intended aggression in the first place? It is no accident that peace movements have multiplied the longer peace has been maintained. But if deterrence is effectual, then we dismantle the forces that sustain it only at our grave peril.

Nuclear weapons have compounded the political rigidity of a two-power world. The guardians of the equilibrium of the nineteenth century were prepared to adjust it to changes in the structure of power. The policymakers of the superpowers in the second half of the twentieth century have much less confidence in the ability of the equilibrium to right itself after disturbance. The "balance" between the superpowers has become both precarious and inflexible. As the world has grown bipolar, it has also lost the perspective for nuance; a gain for one side appears as an absolute loss for the other. Every issue seems to bear on the question of survival. Diplomacy turns rigid; relations are inherently wary.

At the same time, strangely enough, military bipolarity has encouraged, and not diminished, the global diffusion of political power. Smaller countries are torn between a desire for protection and a wish to escape big-power dominance. To the degree that smaller allies doubt that their senior partner would risk its own survival to preserve theirs, they are driven to seek some independent means for defending themselves. Even when they do count on the senior partner to defend them, they are all the more tempted to conduct independent foreign policies even in defiance of its wishes. It is probable that Charles de Gaulle's bold challenge to the United States in the 1960s reflected more his conviction that the United States would have no choice but to defend France in case of Soviet attack than his proclaimed fear that we would not. Similarly, the new nations have proved shrewdly adept at playing the superpowers against each other, even while the military predominance of the superpowers is enormous and growing.

Every new President soon learns that he faces two seemingly contradictory obligations. He must assemble adequate strength to protect the security of America and of its allies and friends. And he must face too the moral necessity of avoiding nuclear war. If he is perceived otherwise he will forfeit the domestic support he needs should a confrontation prove unavoidable. He must both assemble power and discipline its use; he must maintain America's readiness for both defense and peace. He can do neither without a public that has confidence in his purposes. Before he can act as a practical guide, the President must establish his moral leadership.

The elusive problem of peace would have been difficult enough in any circumstances; in our time it is compounded by ideological conflict. In periods heavily influenced by ideology, political loyalties no longer coincide with national boundaries. Communist parties everywhere adhere to a philosophy that asserts universal validity and historical inevitability and pay allegiance to a foreign nation often in conflict with their own; many new nations are swept by an ideology whose central tenet, if not Communism, is powerfully anti-Western in the name of anti-imperialism; a crucial new conflict is the struggle between moderates and radicals in the developing world. In such conditions a domestic upheaval in any country can cause a major shift in international alignments. Nations begin to feel threatened not only by foreign policies but also and perhaps especially by domestic transformations. A liberalized *Communist* regime in Prague, which in no way challenged Soviet preeminence in foreign policy, caused the Soviet Union in 1968 to invade rather than risk the contagion of ideas that it feared could spread elsewhere in its empire. Ten years later the upheaval in Iran shook stability throughout the Middle East.

And all these confrontations and uncertainties were being played out for the first time on a global scale. Throughout history the various continents had existed in relative isolation. As late as the outbreak of the Second World War, the crucial decisions of world politics were taken in a few European capitals. The postwar period was the first in which *all* the continents interacted. In 1945, the world community comprised fifty-one nations; by 1968 it had more than doubled, to nearly one hundred thirty. Modern communications transmitted news and ideas instantaneously. Events that used to be local — wars, rivalries, scandals, domestic upheavals, natural tragedies — suddenly began to assume global significance. When the Nixon Administration entered office all the elements of international relations were in flux simultaneously.

On the one hand the industrial democracies had gained in economic well-being and political vitality. Inevitably this produced a challenge to our previous predominance in our alliances. Most American leaders tended to lay the blame on the awesome, enigmatic Charles de Gaulle. I did not share the conventional view of de Gaulle. I saw him not as the cause of current difficulties and doubts but as the symptom of deepseated structural changes in the Atlantic relationship. It was not natural that the major decisions affecting the destiny of countries so rich in traditions, national pride, and economic strength as Western Europe and Japan should be made thousands of miles away. I had urged for years that it was in the American national interest to encourage a sharing of responsibilities. If the United States insisted on being the trustee of all the non-Communist areas we would exhaust ourselves psychologically long before we did so physically. A world of more centers of decision, I believed, was fully compatible with our interests as well as our ideals. This is why I opposed the efforts of the Kennedy and Johnson administrations to abort the French and if possible even the British nuclear programs, and Washington's tendency in the 1960s to turn consultation into the exegesis of American prescriptions.

At the same time, the so-called Third World of developing nations tested our intellectual and political understanding. Our experiences of the New Deal and the Marshall Plan were not entirely relevant to promoting economic progress and nation-building in countries with no political tradition and no middle class of managers and administrators. Instead, leaders were often overwhelmed by the task of establishing cohesion. We were dealing not with mature economies but with societies taking the wrenching first steps toward modernization. It became apparent that nation-building depended crucially on the ability to establish political authority. Economic aid, by accelerating the erosion of the traditional (frequently feudal) order, often made political stability even harder to achieve. By one of the ironies of history, Marxism has proved attractive to developing nations not because of the economic theory on which it prides itself but because it has supplied an answer to the problem of political legitimacy and authority — a formula for social mobilization, a justification for political power, a means of harnessing resentments against Western cultural and political dominance as a method of fostering unity. Democracy has less appeal, not because of the West's sins but because leaders in most developing countries did not undergo the risks of the anticolonial struggle in order to make themselves dispensable. By an historical joke, a materialist philosophy that has solved no country's economic problems has spread because of its moral claims, while the West, professing an idealistic philosophy, has bemused itself with economic and technical remedies largely irrelevant to the underlying political and spiritual problem.

Thus the new Administration confronted a world of turbulence and complexity, which would require of us qualities that had no precedent in American experience. Simultaneously we had to end a war, manage a global rivalry with the Soviet Union in the shadow of nuclear weapons, reinvigorate our alliance with the industrial democracies, and integrate the new nations into a new world equilibrium that would last only if it was compatible with the aspiration of all nations. We had to turn to new tasks of construction even while we had learned the limits of our capacities. We had to find within ourselves the moral stamina to persevere while our society was assailed by doubt.

In the late eighteenth century the philosopher Immanuel Kant, in his essay *Perpetual Peace,* had written that world peace was inevitable; it would come about either because all nations shared the same sense of justice or because of a cycle of wars of ever increasing violence that would teach men the futility of conflict. Our period was giving new meaning to Kant's prediction. When nations are able to inflict tens of millions of casualties in a matter of hours, peace has become a moral imperative. No one entering office could evade this fundamental responsibility. But the root dilemma of our time is that if the quest for peace turns into the *sole* objective of policy, the fear of war becomes a weapon in the hands of the most ruthless; it produces moral disarmament. How to strive for both peace and justice, for an end of war that does not lead to tyranny, for a commitment to justice that does not produce cataclysm — to find this balance is the perpetual task of the statesman in the nuclear age.

These, then, were the perceptions about which I had thought and written much as a professor. They would soon be tested by events. For once the oath of office has been taken by a new President, there is no longer time for calm reflection. The policymaker is then like a man on a tightrope; he can avoid a precipitous drop only by moving forward.

PART TWO

1969: The Start of the Journey

IV

European Journey

Nixon Visits Europe

RICHARD NIXON left on his first foreign trip as President on February 23, 1969, from Andrews Air Force Base near Washington. It was a rainy Sunday morning. A steady drizzle soaked the crowd that had traveled the half hour from downtown to bid him Godspeed. The Cabinet was in attendance, as was the Congressional leadership from both sides of the aisle. A gaggle of photographers jockeyed for position behind a steel barricade.

It was still the honeymoon period, the first time in Nixon's life that he enjoyed broad sympathy and popular support. He reveled in it like a man who has reached an oasis after traversing an inhospitable desert. He was too shrewd not to notice the irony of being praised for qualities of conciliation contrary to the record of his entire public life. He better than anyone knew that today's acclaim can turn into tomorrow's vilification. But for now he basked in an unaccustomed approbation.

Nixon bantered briefly and uneasily with the notables on the airport tarmac, then strode to the microphone to make his departure statement. It was a characteristic Nixon performance. What he said about foreign policy was sensitive and modest. He was going to Europe to consult with friends. This meant "real" consultation because "we seek not only their support but their advice" in many parts of the world — a slap at the deterioration of Alliance relations under his predecessors which he had criticized in his campaign. But the rest of his remarks had that curious downbeat quality with which he managed so often to chill enthusiasm and goodwill. He had been fretting for weeks that there might be demonstrations against him that, when shown on television, might weaken his domestic position. Nixon held the view that he could pull the sting of an unfavorable development by preempting it. If he made clear that he expected difficulty, somehow the damage would be eased. Occasionally, he was right. More often, the predictions of trouble or opposition only made him appear defensive if they proved false or to have courted disaster if they were borne out. This departure was one of those occasions. He chose to devote over half of his brief statement to the possibility of hostile demonstrators; he disparaged them by saying that they represented only a small fraction of the public. They would not deter him from his quest for peace. Partly provocative, oddly vulnerable, the statement was not well calculated to inspire, but it accurately reflected the complexities of the not inconsiderable man who was to shape the destiny of our country for a turbulent five and a half years.

I did not hear the end of his statement because before he had finished, advance men had bundled me and other members of the party aboard the Presidential aircraft, *Air Force One.* There were two reasons for this procedure, which was followed on every Presidential trip. The planners wanted the plane to leave the second the door had closed behind the President. More important, they were determined that when Nixon stood on the ramp to wave goodbye to the crowd for the benefit of the photographers, the picture would show no one else.

All this and much more was the work on this trip of John Ehrlichman and the advance men — so called because a small party of them descends on every Presidential stop days before his arrival to plan his every move. Ehrlichman had been Nixon's chief advance man during the 1968 campaign. He had joined Nixon's staff in 1962 when the prospects for success were minimal and only a consuming dedication could sustain their quixotic quest.

No one could prosper around Nixon without affecting an air of toughness; what started as an expedient pose could, if staged long enough, become a way of life. I did not think of Ehrlichman as a naturally tough man; he was, in fact, predisposed to be gentle. He had an attractive family whom he adored. He would have most liked to shape a forward-looking domestic program, a task that he was eventually given. But he was ambitious. He wanted, above all, to be recognized as a leading figure in the White House. Precisely because it did not come spontaneously, he could be extraordinarily aggressive and even unpleasant in the pursuit of that goal. He respected me; and he envied me because he thought — not wrongly from his point of view — that I skimmed the cream of the glories of power while he had to suffer the continuing social ostracism that resulted from the mutual distrust of the old Nixon acolytes and the Washington Establishment. He seized several opportunities to harass me, often by conducting investigations of leaks of information in a manner designed to demonstrate my staff's unreliability. But he also was often very helpful and encouraging. Most of the time our relations were cordial. In a different environment he might have performed a great service for his country. In the Nixon White House he was in time destroyed by the cult of the tough guy and the corrosive siege mentality that helped to bring on the very nightmares it feared most. Ehrlichman was a friend and competitor of H. R. (Bob)

Haldeman — their relationship improved as Ehrlichman rose to power on the substantive side of White House activity, in which Haldeman was aggressively uninterested. But on this trip there was considerable tension, for Haldeman was determined to get the advance men entirely under his control. He succeeded. It was the last trip Ehrlichman advanced. Thereafter, this responsibility was taken over by Dwight Chapin, a Haldeman lieutenant.

Ehrlichman had his hands full, for a Presidential trip is a major logistical undertaking. I understood so little of this for several years that when, during my secret trip to Peking in July 1971, Chou En-lai asked me how large Nixon's party would be, I guessed at about fifty. It was a demonstration of ignorance that evoked condescending pity from Haldeman. The Secret Service agents alone who accompany the President exceed that number. Then there are the immediate staff, and secretaries and baggage handlers, and the platoons of communicators, since wherever the President travels he and his staff must be able to reach any part of the world instantaneously by teletype or telephone. A President cannot travel, moreover, without the many assistants and departmental representatives for whom presence on a Presidential trip is a coveted status symbol, even when they participate in no meetings and scarcely if at all see the President. And the traveling press frequently numbers over three hundred. In total, a typical Presidential party is between six hundred and eight hundred people.

To move this whole entourage smoothly on a fast-paced trip is no small feat. The press by itself is a major challenge. They must cover both the President's arrivals and his departures. To solve this problem, the press planes usually take off after *Air Force One* (so they can attend the departure) but then overtake it in flight and land first (so they can cover the arrival). In addition, a small press pool of four to six flies on *Air Force One*. The journalists must be present at all important events yet still have opportunity to write and file their stories.

The slightly baffled official party is at the center of this wondrous undertaking. Each is given a little book outlining every event and every movement, timed literally to the minute, together with charts showing where everyone is to stand during ceremonies, sleeping accommodations, participation in meetings, and other vital information. Slavish obedience is the only safe course, though it taxes one's strength and sometimes sanity. When I was Assistant to the President, a position that despite its great power is low in protocol rank, I was seated far below the salt; I spent much time calculating the distance separating me from the Presidential person and the odds on my reaching my car before the Presidential limousine pulled out. At a splendid formal dinner in the enormous dining room of Madrid's Royal Palace, an elegant Spanish lady seated next to me said: "I would give anything to know what a brilliant man like you is thinking." She must have wondered about the emotional stability of senior American policymakers when I replied: "Frankly, I am close to panic that I will miss my motorcade."

The European journey was my first introduction to these rites of Presidential passage and the antics of the advance men: they were clean-cut, efficient, and disciplined individuals Haldeman had proudly picked from advertising agencies and junior executive positions. Some worked full-time as advance men; some were volunteers whose main employment was in the private sector. What they lacked in ideals and background they made up in assiduity. Later it would become clear how little was the commitment to the future of such people without a past. Those whose primary loyalty is to their own advancement have no ballast when their careers are in jeopardy. During the Watergate period this produced the unedifying spectacle of a rush for the lifeboats with each little caesar seeking safety by pushing his blood brothers over the side.

In 1969, however, Watergate was infinitely remote. The advance team was at the peak of their self-confidence, honed by political campaigns to a razor edge. They had had it drilled into them that their only obligation was to the President. Since during a campaign the hosts at each daily stop were left behind, consideration for the feelings of these dispensable strangers was not part of their charter. Their sole responsibility was to make certain that everything ran smoothly for Nixon, who must never face the unexpected contingencies he hated so much. And it was their job to arrange the extended rest periods — shown as "staff time" in the press releases — that he needed to maintain his concentration and prepare himself for important face-to-face encounters. Above all, the advance team held itself responsible for ensuring that Nixon was seen by others only in the most favorable light. This sometimes led to absurdities. On a State visit to Ottawa in 1972, an advance man decided that the tan furniture in Pierre Trudeau's office would not flatter Nixon on television and took it upon himself to redecorate the Prime Minister's private office with blue-covered sofas. He was stopped at the last minute by an incredulous associate of Trudeau almost incoherent with rage.

On the European trip, the advance men's first exposure to the world of diplomacy, they solved their problems by acting as if they were running a political stopover in Des Moines. They paid no attention whatsoever to our ambassadors, many of whom they distrusted as lame-duck Democratic holdovers, and only minimum heed to the sovereign governments that were our hosts. When Ehrlichman sought to prescribe a guest list for a dinner at 10 Downing Street, David Bruce, our Ambassador in London, who had seen too much in a distinguished diplomatic career to be intimidated by a new Administration, cabled: "Surely the absurdity of telling the British Prime Minister whom he can invite to his own home for dinner requires no explanation." Other advance men in

Paris, surveying the residence of our Ambassador there in preparation for the President's dinner for de Gaulle, gave rise to further palpitations. They noticed some photographs of John Kennedy. Special high-level dispensation was required before Ambassador Sargent Shriver — married to President Kennedy's sister Eunice — was permitted to keep the pictures of his brother-in-law on visible display. But these occasional inanities aside, the advance men did well with the logistics — seven stops in seven days without a hitch — and everything clicked into place in a remarkably well-planned exercise.

Once aboard *Air Force One*, Nixon turned assiduously to his briefing papers, which were extraordinary in range and detail. Speeches, of course, were already drafted. No matter what the pretense, no President has the time to draft his own speeches. Nixon's foreign policy speeches all had the same origin: a detailed outline prepared by the NSC staff under my supervision, which Nixon would review and perhaps alter a bit before assigning to a speechwriter. When he had a vital speech to make he might himself rewrite extensively, especially at the beginning and end, with particular attention to any political implications. If he thought I would approve the rhetorical changes, I might see the final text, but not otherwise. On a fast-moving foreign trip like the one we were launched upon, there would be no time for extensive editing, and the speechwriters would come into their own.

The choice of speechwriters always determined the tone and not infrequently the substance of a Presidential speech. The common conception is that speechwriters are passive instruments who docilely craft into elegant prose the policy thought of their principals. On the contrary, the vast majority of them are frustrated principals themselves who seek to use their privileged position to put over their own ideas. Well aware that a Presidential sentence can be used as a charter by the bureaucracy, they seek to monopolize the final process, rationalizing their efforts as a struggle for the soul of the President. Whatever it was we were struggling over, there were occasionally quite bitter exchanges between my staff and the writers when we saw the mutations they had wrought.

Nixon's speechwriting staff was unusually talented and varied; it carried specialization to the point that there was a writer for every chord Nixon wanted to strike. On this trip, where we worked well together, the principal speechwriter was Bill Safire, sporadically witty, flexible, with a brilliant sense of public relations and an ability to turn a phrase that sometimes obscured its meaning in clever alliterations. Safire was the speechwriter least likely to put his own substantive gloss on a speech, though his style was so individual that Nixon rarely used him for the occasions he wanted to mark with his rhetoric. Ray Price was the doyen of the speechwriters. Wise, balanced, leaning to the liberal side, he was used when the President wanted to convey lofty, somewhat philosophical nonpartisanship. Patrick Buchanan was the resident conservative, deeply wary of those whom he suspected of deflecting Nixon from his natural right-wing orientation, convinced that a cabal of intellectuals was confusing the pristine quality of the President's philosophy, unwilling to accept that it was in the nature of our many-faceted principal to show a different face to different people. He was rarely used in Nixon's foreign policy speeches — I can remember only the Cambodia speech.

In addition to a folder of speeches, Nixon had voluminous briefing books prepared for him by my staff and the State Department. They included an overall conceptual paper that explained our objectives, the strategy for achieving them, and their relationship to our general foreign policy. In addition there were talking points for each country, discussing the issues likely to be raised and biographical material about the leaders he would meet. In deference to the President's predilections, the talking points sought to turn each meeting to the greatest extent possible into a set piece. They were broken down into the issues the various leaders were likely to raise; they listed the suggested responses and warned about sensitive topics to avoid.

I already had some experience of the importance of this preparation for Nixon. The meeting of any new person filled Nixon with an undefined dread. He feared being confronted with some unexpected question, some unanticipated issue, or some line of argument for which he was not prepared and which might then make him appear less in control of events than his self-image required. He therefore insisted on briefing papers that set out the possible course of the conversation in meticulous detail. But since Nixon did not want to admit that he needed guidance, he would impose on himself the extraordinary discipline of committing these memoranda to memory. And to show how well he had done, as well as to play the little games which so delighted him, he would skate as close as he dared to the edge of what he had been advised to avoid. He sometimes cut it very fine, as his advisers inwardly squirmed, but he never went over the precipice.

As *Air Force One* headed for Europe the President, in addition to memorizing the point-by-point analyses, busied himself with a long essay on de Gaulle, adapted from a book I had written on the NATO alliance called *The Troubled Partnership.** I found myself anticipating our next days with eagerness. I was of course returning to the continent where I was born; but the real reasons for my interest were the geopolitical realities and historical ties between countries sharing similar histories, values, and institutions.

---

*This book sold modestly, as could be expected of a tome on NATO affairs, except in one city where it sold unusually well. Upon investigation, it was found that the main bookstore had placed it on the shelf under marriage manuals.

Later we became jaded with airport receptions, but it would be hard to exaggerate the thrill when *Air Force One* arrived in Brussels after dark. As soon as the door of the plane opened, we were bathed in the arc lights of television. A red carpet stretched past an honor guard. The gentle, sensitive King Baudouin of the Belgians stood at the foot of the ramp to greet the President, who proclaimed, in his brief arrival statement, that the trip would inaugurate a new search for peace. He quoted Woodrow Wilson, always one of his heroes. There were NATO as well as Belgian dignitaries — technically the visit to Brussels was to call at NATO headquarters — but the Belgians had claimed the evening for themselves and we were driven off to the imposing Royal Palace in the heart of the town. King Baudouin excused himself after some pleasantries, and the President was left with Belgian Prime Minister Gaston Eyskens, Foreign Minister Pierre Harmel, Secretary of State Rogers, and me. The Belgians were puzzled by my presence; their protocol had no provision for Presidential Assistants. My attendance also disturbed the precise numerical balance so dear to the heart of diplomats. Since they did not know how to get rid of me, they added a member of the Prime Minister's office on their side.

The Belgian ministers were no exception to the rule that all the leaders we were to visit saw their principal aim in establishing a close personal relationship with Nixon and, perhaps even more important, to be perceived to be doing so. Whatever animosities Nixon might arouse in the United States, then or later, in Europe friendship with the President of the United States was considered a political asset. Moreover, those who had met Nixon during his period out of office had favorable views of him, especially of his knowledge of world affairs. This respect for his competence in foreign policy increased progressively during his term in office.

Eyskens, a smallish, squarely built man, stressed Belgium's interest in a united Europe. Belgium hoped for an end to the Anglo-French quarrel that had blocked British entry into the European Economic Community. Obviously uneasy about a potential Franco-German condominium, Eyskens argued that British entry into the Common Market would bring a better balance and restrain excessive nationalism. He offered no suggestion of what Belgium might do to assist this process, other than offer goodwill. His hope seemed to be that somehow somebody — perhaps the United States — would bring about the desired result. The second preoccupation of the Belgian leaders was détente. Like most European leaders they were concerned about Nixon's reputation as a Cold Warrior. They clearly thought he needed prodding on the desirability of relaxing tensions. The Soviet Union, we were told, wanted détente because of its people's desire for consumer goods and its fear of China. The Belgians averred that a strong NATO defense was the prerequisite for a détente, but they also made clear that there was little prospect of an increase in European defense efforts. Essentially they pleaded for a continued substantial American troop presence in Europe. There was a tactful allusion to the domestic problems caused for European governments by the war in Vietnam.

Nixon was at his best in formal exchanges of this type. He calmly explained his commitment to a new era of peace; he agreed that it could only be founded on Western strength. He stressed his devotion to Atlantic unity and his determination to consult our allies before major initiatives.

The next morning, Nixon delivered a major speech to the North Atlantic Council, the assembly of the Alliance's permanent ambassadors. He raised a number of questions to which the Alliance had to address itself over the next twenty years:

NATO was brought into being by the threat from the Soviet Union. What is the nature of that threat today?

When NATO was founded, Europe's economies were still shattered by war. Now they are flourishing. How should this be reflected by changed relationships among the NATO partners?

We are all grappling with problems of a modern environment, which are the byproducts of our advanced technologies — problems such as the pollution of air and water, and the congestion in our cities. Together we can dramatically advance our mastery of these problems. By what means can we best cooperate to bring this about?

He affirmed America's determination, after proper preparations, to enter into negotiation with the Soviet Union on a wide range of issues. But his basic purpose was to reinvigorate the Alliance:

The tie that binds Europe and America is not the contemplation of danger, to be stretched or tightened by the fluctuations of fear.

The ties that bind our continents are the common tradition of freedom, the common desire for progress, and the common passion for peace.

In that more constructive spirit, let us look at new situations with new eyes, and in so doing, set an example for the world.

It would be an exaggeration to say that the representatives in council assembled responded electrically. They were ambassadors meeting a head of state; they were not used to engaging in searching debate on such occasions, nor were they authorized to do so. Moreover, the President was about to visit four other capitals; it is a reckless ambassador who would presume to preempt his chiefs. So the ambassadors to a man responded with expressions of gratification at the President's commitment to NATO. All avoided giving the impression that their countries might be willing to expand their defense efforts; they were unanimous, however, about the need for American forces in Europe. The French Ambassador was the only one to warn about the potential incompatibility of détente and defense; he cautioned the President against encouraging even the impression of a condominium with the Soviet Union.

The visit to Brussels was a cross-section of the problems of European-American relations in 1969. There was uncertainty about the future of Europe. The attitude to the common defense was a curious mixture of unwillingness to augment European efforts and fear of American withdrawal. European leaders were urging us toward détente with the East — but we had the uneasy sense that the principal motive was to lift the burden of difficult decisions from European shoulders. And Vietnam confronted European governments with a dilemma: they felt the need to respond to domestic pressures, but for their own security they feared an American humiliation or defeat and shrank from any step that would contribute to it. It was clear that all our perceptions and planning were about to be tested; and it is necessary to recall how we saw the Atlantic relationship, its disquiets and disunions, as philosophy gave way to politics.

Malaise of the Western Alliance

IN the late 1960s the Atlantic Alliance stood in a state of disarray that was the more painful for following a period of extraordinary success. American initiative had produced the Marshall Plan; American resources had sparked the economic recovery of Europe; American military forces had assured European security. Wise Europeans like Jean Monnet, Robert Schumann, Alcide de Gasperi, Konrad Adenauer, and Paul-Henri Spaak had fostered the concept of European integration within the framework of partnership with the United States. Sometimes inspiring these great Europeans, more often following their lead, American policy toward Europe during this period had been perceptive and consistent. Every postwar American administration had supported the idea of European political unity based on supranational federal institutions. Only a federal Europe, it was believed, could end Europe's wars, provide an effective counterweight to the USSR, bind Germany indissolubly to the West, constitute an equal partner for the United States, and share with us the burdens and obligations of world leadership.

In my essay written in 1968, I suggested that two decades of American military presence in Europe had reduced the fear of Soviet invasion and of American withdrawal and the new, stronger Europe was bound to act differently from the Europe of 1949: "The United States could not expect to perpetuate the accident of Europe's postwar exhaustion into a permanent pattern of international relations. Europe's economic recovery inevitably led to a return to more traditional political pressures."[1]

And again, in *The Troubled Partnership:* "A united Europe is likely to insist on a specifically European view of world affairs — which is another way of saying that it will challenge American hegemony in Atlantic policy. This may well be a price worth paying for European unity; but American policy has suffered from an unwillingness to recognize that there is a price to be paid." [2]

By 1968 the shift in the foundations of our Atlantic relationship had produced evident disappointment and anxiety. Walt Rostow, President Johnson's Special Assistant for National Security Affairs, listed European policy among his disappointments on leaving office,[3] and Francis Bator, a Harvard professor in the Johnson White House, declared frankly that early notions of Atlantic political integration had lost their hold: "None of the overarching visions designed to settle the Second World War and prevent a third is moving toward fulfillment." [4] In Europe, Alastair Buchan, for years the Director of the prestigious Institute for Strategic Studies in London, wrote in 1968 that it was a moment of slack water in the tide of European affairs:

The clarity that the Cold War imposed upon relations between the countries of the developed world, in particular the sense of solidarity within each of the two main alliances, has become blurred; the assumption of a natural community of interest between the nations of the Atlantic world has been weakened, and so has an equivalent sense of identity between Eastern Europe and the Soviet Union; the belief that economic association within Western Europe would lead naturally to political association has been called in question; and many traditional sources of division between the European powers, nationalism and diminishing confidence in governments, which were muted through much of the postwar era, have begun to reassert themselves.[5]

The structural changes in the Atlantic Alliance had their origin in the field of security, which had given the first impetus to the formation of the Alliance. The Atlantic Alliance had been formed to provide for the common defense; its military strategy was grounded in the American threat to wage all-out nuclear war in defense of Europe. American ground and air forces had been dispatched to Europe in the 1950s even when the official strategy was massive retaliation by forces based in the United States. As far as our European allies were concerned, the United States was to be deprived of any element of choice by involving US forces in a conflict from the outset. In the face of the risks of modern war, Europeans considered our constant reiteration of American steadfastness as insufficient, if not naive. Too many European countries had been let down by allies — or had let down allies themselves — to be totally comforted by rhetorical reassurances that became the staple of NATO meetings. Our troops, to put it bluntly, were wanted as hostages.

This being the case, our allies never had an incentive to contribute to a real capacity for regional defense. To be sure, our European allies made defense efforts of their own, to avoid Congressional complaints that we were carrying the whole burden. But the European effort was beset by ambivalence at its core. Too large to be a trip wire, too small to resist an all-out Soviet onslaught, the allied military establishment was an accidental array of forces in search of a mission. The best trained and equipped troops, those of the United States, were in the south, guarding the most beautiful scenery — primarily because they had happened to end up there in 1945. Unfortunately, the traditional invasion routes are located on the North German plain, which was the responsibility of some West German and British forces that had the least effective logistical support. The weapons of the various forces were — and are — a mix of the armories of various nationalities; neither the equipment nor the criteria for using it were standardized. NATO in the late 1960s — and, I fear, today — was strong enough to resist in the early phases of a conflict but would be incapable of concluding it. But that was perhaps exactly what our allies wanted; therein precisely lay the guarantee of an eventual American response with strategic nuclear weapons.

Periodic attempts to rationalize the defense structure in Europe were bound to run into resistance. Any American initiative to strengthen local defense raised questions whether it was a device to reduce our nuclear commitment. At least some of our allies felt concern that given an alternative we might not come to their defense at all, or at any rate quit if and when the tide of the ground battle turned against us. Europeans dreaded at one and the same time the devastation of a nuclear war on their densely populated continent and our apparently growing reluctance to resort to nuclear weapons. They wanted to make the Soviet Union believe that any attack would unleash America's nuclear arsenal. If the bluff failed, however, they were not eager to have us implement the threat on their soil. Their secret hope, which they never dared to articulate, was that the defense of Europe would be conducted as an intercontinental nuclear exchange over their heads; to defend their own countries, America was invited to run the very risk of nuclear devastation from which they were shying away.

The real concerns of each side remained masked. The Europeans dared not make their fears explicit lest they turn into self-fulfilling prophecies. The United States righteously proclaimed self-evident good faith but would not admit that the strategic equation had altered beyond the ability of words to repair. For most of the postwar period the Soviet Union had been virtually defenseless against an American first strike. Nor could it improve its position significantly by attacking, since our counterblow would have posed unacceptable risks. Hence, our strategic forces were an effective deterrent against any massive Soviet ground assault. In the early Sixties — despite our initial obsession with a nonexistent "missile gap" — our retaliatory forces were still so much larger that Soviet local military adventures remained foolhardy in the extreme. But starting in the middle Sixties, in the wake of the Cuban missile crisis, the Soviets began to augment their strategic arsenal at a rate that was bound to raise American casualties in a nuclear exchange — no matter how it started — into the tens of millions. When we came to office in 1969, the estimate of casualties in case of a Soviet *second* strike stood at over fifty million dead from *immediate* effects (not to mention later deaths from radiation).

To pretend that such a prospect would not affect American readiness to resort to nuclear weapons would have been an evasion of responsibility. The growth of Soviet nuclear power was bound to drain the threat of an automatic all-out nuclear response of credibility with every passing year.

It would have been equally irresponsible to ignore the profound concern that this new situation created in Europe. American efforts in the Sixties to remain the sole custodian of nuclear weapons in the Alliance, expressed in our opposition to the nuclear programs of Britain and France, were interpreted — by many more European leaders than avowed it — as an attempt by the United States to reserve to itself the definition of what constituted the vital interests of the entire Alliance. In its more extreme form, the American attempt to monopolize the central nuclear decisions could be portrayed as ensuring for us the option — whatever our immediate intention — of "de-coupling" our defense from that of our allies. This was the Europeans' nightmare — and remains so. After his retirement in 1969, de Gaulle expressed this concern in its most brutal form in a conversation with André Malraux: "Despite its power, I don't believe the United States has a long-term policy. Its desire, and it will satisfy it one day, is to desert Europe. You will see."[6]

In the Sixties, the United States was generally correct in purely military analyses; our allies on the whole acted like ostriches. They were as unwilling to confront the changed strategic relationship or make a greater defense effort as they were ready to attribute to complex, sometimes devious, American intentions what was in fact largely the result of an inexorable technological evolution. At the same time, the United States was slow in recognizing that the issue was political, and ultimately psychological. It was to be expected that under conditions of incipient parity the nuclear superpowers would attempt to make the nuclear environment more predictable and manageable. But this very attempt was bound to appear to others as a budding condominium: It clearly placed restraints on our decision to go to nuclear war — upon which Europe based its security. The allies grumbled about inadequate consultation, but their worries would have been scarcely muted by full consultation. Once the United States and the Soviet Union each possessed invulnerable retaliatory forces capable of inflicting unacceptable damage, allied cohesion would depend on the ability to make sure that American and European perceptions of vital interests were congruent, and perceived to be so by the Soviet Union.

The strategic debates were thus only the tip of the iceberg. The deepest challenge was that after centuries of Europe's preeminence, the center of gravity of world affairs was moving away from it. For nations to play a major international role, they must believe that their decisions matter. From the middle of the eighteenth century onward, the decisions of European powers determined war and peace, progress or stagnation. Conflicts in other continents were often encouraged by Europeans if not fought by them. Economic progress depended upon European capital and European technology. World War I — senseless in its origin, pointless in its outcome — produced a catastrophe out of all proportion to the issues at stake. Ninety percent of Britain's Oxford University graduates of 1914 perished as junior officers in the carnage of the Great War. Precisely because the suffering was so vast and so unexpected, after a century's smug belief in uninterrupted progress, European self-confidence was shaken and its economic foundation eroded. World War II and the period of decolonization completed the process, narrowing horizons further and compounding the sense of impotence. European governments suddenly realized that their security and prosperity depended on decisions made far away; from being principal actors they had become supporting players. Europe after 1945 thus faced a crisis of the spirit that went beyond its still considerable material resources. The real tension between the United States and Europe revolved about Europe's quest for a sense of identity and relevance in a world in which it no longer controlled the ultimate decisions.

The American answer in the 1960s was simple. American and European interests, we asserted, were identical; there was no possibility that the United States would knowingly jeopardize the vital concerns of its allies in either diplomacy or strategy. The real obstacle to allied cooperation, we argued, was the difference in power between Europe and the United States. Europe would assume global responsibilities as it gained in strength and this would come from integration on a supranational basis. American advocates of European unity sometimes embraced it more passionately than their colleagues in Europe. A few thoughtful Europeans, however, questioned whether it was all quite so simple. They doubted whether "burden-sharing" (the jargon phrase) would solve the problem of identity or of national purpose. Europe, they felt, needed a political purpose of its own and not simply a technical assignment in a joint enterprise.

Those who argued that Europe would be more willing to share global burdens if it were federally integrated seemed to me to follow too mechanical a concept of history. The reason Europe did not play a global role was not so much shrinking resources as shrinking horizons. I did not think that countries shared burdens merely because they were capable of doing so. Through the greatest part of its history the United States had the resources but not the inclination to play a global role; conversely, many European countries continued to maintain overseas commitments even after their resources began to dwindle. The largest colonial empire in the Sixties and part of the Seventies was maintained by Portugal, one of the weakest NATO members. Burden-sharing among the allies was likely only if two conditions were met: Europe had to develop its own perception of international relations, and Europe had to be convinced that we could not, or would not, carry the load alone. Neither condition obtained in the late Sixties. Europeans were absorbed with domestic problems. To the extent that they sought reinsurance against American withdrawal, they did so not by a division of labor with us but in duplicating our strengths, by building strategic weapons of their own. And Europe would need to articulate a policy of its own before it would assume greater burdens or responsibilities.

I favored European unity, but I was agnostic about the form it should take, whether it should be a confederation of nation-states or a supranational federation. I wanted Europe to play a larger international role, but we had to face the fact that this role would derive from an independent conception that would not always agree with ours. Shortly before the election, I had written about our relation to Europe:

No country can act wisely simultaneously in every part of the globe at every moment of time. A more pluralistic world — especially in relationships with friends — is profoundly in our long-term interest. Political multipolarity, while difficult to get used to, is the precondition for a new period of creativity. Painful as it may be to admit, we could benefit from a counterweight that would discipline our occasional impetuosity and, by supplying historical perspective, modify our penchant for abstract and "final" solutions.[7]

The vitality of free peoples would be tested by the answer they gave to the age-old dilemma of freedom: how to reconcile diversity and unity, independence and collaboration, liberty and security.

London and the "Special Relationship"

FROM Brussels, Nixon flew to London. The ease and warmth of his welcome concealed the fact that a major storm had just taken place: a nasty dispute between Britain and France over the future of Europe, symptomatic of what lay before us.

The flare-up had begun in private conversations which President de Gaulle had had with the British Ambassador in Paris, Christopher Soames, who as Winston Churchill's son-in-law was not wholly unfamiliar with greatness or overly awed by grandeur. The controversy told much about the debate within Europe and the Alliance as a whole. On February 4, 1969, President de Gaulle and Ambassador Soames chatted at the Elysée Palace (the Presidential residence and office) about the future of Europe; they had another meeting on the same subject on February 14. The British thereafter informed their other allies, including us, that General de Gaulle had described his concept of the future of Europe in rather provocative and somewhat novel terms.

To create a truly independent Europe, capable of making decisions on matters of global importance, de Gaulle had said that first of all it would be necessary for Europeans to free themselves from the encumbrance of NATO, with its "American domination and machinery." A successful European political organization would have to rely on a concert of the most significant European powers: France, England, Germany, and Italy. And in that relationship the central element would have to be Anglo-French understanding and cooperation. Secondly, in this process the structure of the Common Market had to change, and de Gaulle in any event had little confidence in its future. Instead, he could envisage its replacement by some sort of broad free-trade area, especially for agricultural products. Thirdly, since the Anglo-French relationship would be the keystone of this concept, the General was ready to hold *private* bilateral discussions with Britain on economic, monetary, political, and financial problems. He said he would welcome a British initiative for such talks.

The British told us that they had replied to de Gaulle that the United Kingdom still wished to join the Common Market and hoped that negotiations might soon be reopened. Though British views on NATO, relations with the United States, and the desirability of a four-power directorate in Europe differed materially from de Gaulle's, Britain considered the General's proposals to be very significant. It was willing to discuss them further, but only on the understanding that its NATO partners would be kept fully informed. In this connection, Soames had told de Gaulle at their second meeting that Prime Minister Wilson had felt it his duty to brief German Chancellor Kiesinger when the two met in Bonn on February 13–14. The British also conveyed the essence of the de Gaulle–Soames talks to us, the Belgians, and other allies; word spread like wildfire through NATO.

On February 17 and 18, French ambassadors to European capitals sought to ascertain how much of the de Gaulle–Soames conversations had become known and to offer assurances that the General had no intention of breaking up NATO. He had merely told Soames, they said, that the expansion of the Common Market would inevitably change its character and that its subsequent direction would have to be closely reviewed.

By February 21, the squabble over who said what to whom had reached such proportions that both the British and the French felt obligated to leak their rival versions to the press. A British backgrounder in the London *Times* matched very closely their earlier private account to us. An inspired story in the Paris newspaper *Figaro* replied that de Gaulle had simply sketched his views of an independent Europe, which could be realized "without having any effect on the conception of NATO." *Figaro,* for good measure, attacked Ambassador Soames personally for having spread around Europe a "sensational version" of the General's remarks, which "cast doubts on the credibility of Mr. Soames." French Foreign Minister Michel Debré soon afterward declared publicly that the General had wanted only to examine whether the British were interested in exploratory talks on "European political and economic perspectives."

Like old warriors of a battle whose memory sustained emotion and righteousness, all the American veterans of previous controversies with de Gaulle rushed into the fray. The new Administration was deluged with proposals from inside and outside our government to seize the opportunity to reaffirm our commitment to a federal Europe and to reject de Gaulle's proposal — which in any event had not been made to us — for a special directorate of the larger European powers. The new Administration was being asked to pick up the fallen lance of its predecessor and tilt once more against the windmills of European dogma, to resume the acrimonious debate with France exactly where it had been suspended by our election.

This we were determined not to do. We thought the organization of Europe was for Europeans to decide. The United States had wasted too much of its prestige over such doctrinal disputes. On February 22, the day before we flew to Europe, I sent Nixon a brief account of the affair, which I concluded as follows:

I believe that de Gaulle did expound his views on the future of Europe to Soames in much the terms originally reported by the British. In any case, the hope for a Europe independent of American "domination" and guided by the concert of the greatest European powers is completely in consonance with de Gaulle's recorded views. It is also characteristic that de Gaulle would have recognized that such a concert would have to be based on Anglo-French agreement, although on the supposition that England would emancipate itself from any "special relationship" with the United States. . . .

You will be under pressure to comment.

I recommend that you:

1. affirm our commitment to NATO;

2. affirm our traditional support of European unity, including British entry into the Common Market, *but*

3. make clear that we will not inject ourselves into intra-European debates on the forms, methods and timing of steps toward unity.

Nixon followed this approach carefully and subtly in his private talks; I repeated it often in background briefings before and after the European trip. Asked about the Soames–de Gaulle controversy, I told the press on February 21: "Our concern is the relationship of the United States to Europe, not the internal arrangements of Europe." We used the Soames–de Gaulle controversy to make clear that our emphasis would be on Atlantic relations; we would leave the elaboration of Europe's internal arrangements to the Europeans. In the long run this would be the stance most helpful to Britain's entry into the Common Market.

Nixon arrived in London from Brussels on a rainy Monday evening to be greeted at Heathrow Airport by Prime Minister Harold Wilson and the Foreign Secretary, Michael Stewart. Ceremony was subdued because Nixon was afraid of being accused of junketing while the war in Vietnam was raging and had asked to limit protocol to a minimum. This was a painful sacrifice since he dearly loved ceremony, especially in Britain, which has raised understated pomp to a major art form. More than that anywhere, British state protocol deftly reassures the insecure that they are entitled to their honors on merit.

Harold Wilson greeted Nixon with the avuncular goodwill of the head of an ancient family that has seen better times but is still able to evoke memories of the wisdom, dignity, and power that had established the family name in the first place. He took a jab at de Gaulle by announcing his rejection of "inward looking attitudes" toward foreign affairs and contrasted it unfavorably with the "wider world concept" put forward by Nixon, to which he pledged support. But Wilson's major theme was what had become ritual all over Western Europe — that the Alliance had to move from security to such positive ends as "cooperation and peace." The purpose of the Alliance in the late Sixties was no longer defense — at least in public rhetoric; its principal justification was becoming the relaxation of tension. Nixon was never to be outdone by others' high-sounding proclamations. He responded with a phrase he was to work to death in the 1972 campaign with a consequent inflation of expectations from détente: "I believe as I stand here today, that we can bring about a durable peace in our time." He was in a buoyant mood. He tackled head-on the so-called special relationship between Britain and the United States that was so contentious within our government — by referring to it explicitly twice and in most positive terms.

This gave no little pain to many of the European integrationists in the

Department of State and outside the government. The advocates — almost fanatics — of European unity were eager to terminate the "special relationship" with our oldest ally as an alleged favor to Britain to smooth its entry into the Common Market. They felt it essential to deprive Britain of any special status with us lest it impede Britain's role in the Europe they cherished. They urged a formal egalitarianism, unaffected by tradition or conceptions of the national interest, as the best guarantee of their Grand Design.

Even if desirable, which I doubted, this was impractical. For the special relationship with Britain was peculiarly impervious to abstract theories. It did not depend on formal arrangements; it derived in part from the memory of Britain's heroic wartime effort; it reflected the common language and culture of two sister peoples. It owed no little to the superb self-discipline by which Britain had succeeded in maintaining political influence after its physical power had waned. When Britain emerged from the Second World War too enfeebled to insist on its views, it wasted no time in mourning an irretrievable past. British leaders instead tenaciously elaborated the "special relationship" with us. This was, in effect, a pattern of consultation so matter-of-factly intimate that it became psychologically impossible to ignore British views. They evolved a habit of meetings so regular that autonomous American action somehow came to seem to violate club rules. Above all, they used effectively an abundance of wisdom and trustworthiness of conduct so exceptional that successive American leaders saw it in their self-interest to obtain British advice before taking major decisions. It was an extraordinary relationship because it rested on no legal claim; it was formalized by no document; it was carried forward by succeeding British governments as if no alternative were conceivable. Britain's influence was great precisely because it never insisted on it; the "special relationship" demonstrated the value of intangibles.

One feature of the Anglo-American relationship was the degree to which diplomatic subtlety overcame substantive disagreements. In reality, on European integration the views of Britain's leaders were closer to de Gaulle's than to ours; an integrated supranational Europe was as much anathema in Britain as in France. The major difference between the French and the British was that the British leaders generally conceded us the theory — of European integration or Atlantic unity — while seeking to shape its implementation through the closest contacts with us. Where de Gaulle tended to confront us with faits accomplis and doctrinal challenges, Britain turned conciliation into a weapon by making it morally inconceivable that its views could be ignored.

I considered the attacks from within our government on the special relationship as petty and formalistic. Severing our special ties — assuming it could be done — would undermine British self-confidence, and gain us nothing. In a background briefing on February 21 before our departure for Europe, I pointed out:

My own personal view on this issue is that we do not suffer in the world from such an excess of friends that we should discourage those who feel that they have a special friendship for us. I would think that the answer to the special relationship of Britain would be to raise other countries to the same status, rather than to discourage Britain into a less warm relationship with the United States.

Nixon had accepted my advice not to become involved in the Soames–de Gaulle controversy; he also had little interest in the dispute so long as it was confined to obtuse and theoretical bureaucratic backbiting. Believing in the "special relationship," he settled the issue by his arrival statement.

This fitted in well with the approach of our hosts. Everything was low-key, personal, and subtly flattering. The British had gone to extraordinary lengths to make us comfortable without being intrusive, to be available for an exchange of opinion without asking for any specific American action in return. We were taken from the airport to Chequers, the Prime Minister's country residence, which is comfortable but not ostentatious, full of just enough history to remind one of Britain's glorious past. But like its occupants, it is subtle and indirect in its lesson and its influence. The first conversations took place there over dinner, a small private gathering of Nixon and Wilson, Rogers and Stewart, Sir Burke Trend, the British Cabinet Secretary, and me.

When we first encountered him, Harold Wilson had the reputation of a wily politician whose penetrating intelligence was flawed by the absence of ultimate reliability. Some in the outgoing Administration had considered him too close to the left wing of the Labour Party; this and his vanity were supposed to make him unusually susceptible to Soviet blandishments. And he was accused of not being above using our discomfiture in Vietnam to shore up his own domestic position. In my experience with Wilson, none of these criticisms proved accurate. To be sure, any Labour Party leader has to take account of the views of the left wing of his party. Nor was he the first British Prime Minister to present himself as a special apostle of peace with the East — Harold Macmillan, after all, had gained himself the sobriquet of Super Mac by showing up in Moscow at the height of the Berlin crisis preaching conciliation and wearing an astrakhan hat. In my experience, Wilson was a sincere friend of the United States. His emotional ties, like those of most Britons, were across the oceans and not across the Channel in that region which in Britain is significantly called "Europe." He had spent much time in the United States; he sincerely believed in the Anglo-American partnership. It was not theatrics to invite Nixon, as he did, to attend a Cabinet meeting — an unprecedented honor for a foreigner. As for Wilson's reliability, I am in no position to judge his conduct on the British scene. With the United States I always found him a man of his word. He represented a curious phenomenon in British politics: his generation of Labour Party leaders was emotionally closer to the United States than were many leaders of the Conservative Party. The Tories seemed to find the loss of physical preeminence to the United States rankling, especially after what they considered our betrayal over Suez.

Though trained at Oxford, where he had taught economics for several years, Wilson had almost no interest in abstract ideas. He was fascinated by the manipulation of political power; he relished the enterprise of solving definable problems. Longer-range objectives elicited from him only the most cursory attention. He saw no sense in planning, because he had complete confidence that his many skills would see him through any tight spot. Wilson had an extraordinary memory that enabled him to recall the exact position on a page of a sentence he had read many years before. It was a skill he delighted in showing off; he exhibited almost equal skill in finding opportunities to do so. He was personally rather cold, though — not unlike Nixon — touchingly eager for approval, especially from those he respected. This category generally included men of power or academics; he prized especially his close relationships with American Presidents. Early on he suggested to Nixon that they call each other by their first names. A fish-eyed stare from Nixon squelched this idea. But the incident did not change Wilson's friendly attitude toward the United States. I personally liked him; he never let us down.

His colleague, Foreign Secretary Michael Stewart, was a different personality. Well-meaning, slightly pedantic, Stewart delighted in moral disquisitions that could drive Nixon to distraction. He had been a schoolmaster, and showed it, before becoming first Minister of Education and then Foreign Secretary. Like many who came late in life to international responsibility, he acted as if it consisted of the proclamation of theoretical maxims. Stewart, however, was dedicated by conviction to the close relationship between our countries. Despite his many doubts, he defended our position in Vietnam in a debate at the Oxford Union with more vigor and skill than was exhibited by many of the Americans who had made the decision to send our troops there; he never expressed his qualms to outsiders. He was a decent, solid man, not brilliant or farsighted, but of the sturdy quality to which Britain owes so much of its greatness.

The third senior Britisher at dinner was Sir Burke (later Lord) Trend, Secretary of the Cabinet. His office is as powerful as it is anonymous. A senior civil servant who remains in place through all changes of administration, he prepares the minutes of Cabinet meetings, supervises the permanent civil service machinery, and renders the disinterested advice of decades of accumulated experience. The influence inherent in this position was used with special effectiveness by its incumbent. Burke Trend was a slight and scholarly man, with a twinkle in his eye and a manner that proclaimed both wisdom and discretion. He unobtrusively steered discussion away from shoals which he knew had wrecked earlier impetuous adventures. He skillfully made the Cabinet ministers he served appear more competent than they could possibly be. He was a man of generous spirit. His erudition and advice were among the benefits to us of the "special relationship."

The dinner at Chequers seemed a family evening. The discussion was a *tour d'horizon* of world affairs, begun in the paneled dining room and continued over brandy in the famous Long Gallery. Men who would have to settle their countries' futures for the next years took one another's measure and were on the whole at ease with the results.

Nixon later called me to his suite at Claridge's to review the day's events. The day had started at the NATO Council in Brussels and had ended at the home of the British Prime Minister, to which Nixon ascribed a history dating back through the centuries. I did not have the heart to tell him that Chequers had performed its current function only since World War I. He was exuberant; he adored the vestigial ceremonies and was new enough to it to be thrilled at the succession of events. To land with *Air Force One* on foreign soil, to be greeted by a King and then a Prime Minister, to review honor guards, to visit Chequers — all this was the culmination of his youthful dreams, the conception of high office, seemingly unattainable for a poor, somewhat resentful young man from a little town in California. It all produced one of the few occasions of nearly spontaneous joy I witnessed in my acquaintance with this withdrawn and elusive man. Though the day's discussion had resolved no grand issues, Nixon loved philosophical conversations that involved neither confrontations nor haggling over details. Nixon desperately wanted to be told how well he had done. As he would do on so many other occasions, he asked me to recount his conspicuous role in the day's events over and over again. He had gone to bed, and as occasionally happened when under stress he began to slur his words or else struggle to form them very carefully. It was easy to reassure him. Although the day had presented no taxing challenge, he had conducted himself with dignity and ability.

The next day in the Cabinet room at 10 Downing Street (the residence as well as the office of the Prime Minister), a larger group on both sides touched on the themes of the night before. The main topics were Britain's decision to renew its application to the Common Market, the future of NATO, and the course of East-West relations. The British ministers claimed that they sought membership in Europe less for the economic than for the political benefits of the more outward-looking Europe they would help bring about. Nixon agreed with this concept, but stressed that it could not be furthered by American hostility to de Gaulle. He would try to improve America's relations with France; while this would not alter de Gaulle's basic views it might make him more amenable to practical accommodations. The British ministers averred that this was exactly their view as well — as if the Soames–de Gaulle controversy had never occurred.

The discussion of NATO revealed once again the ambivalences of the Atlantic Alliance. Everyone agreed with Nixon's assessment that the Soviet Union was closing the nuclear gap and that we would do well in the face of Congressional pressures to preserve the new defense programs we were starting. But there was no willingness to draw the obvious conclusion that European defenses had to be strengthened. Wilson argued that NATO required a new strategic doctrine; he doubted that any European country was prepared to undertake a major increase in its defense expenditures for fear that the United States would then reduce its commitment. Wilson left it to us to figure out what could be the significance of a new strategic doctrine not embodied in new forces.

Michael Stewart contributed what was becoming the standard European theme. Our negotiation with the Soviet Union, especially on strategic arms limitation, was essential. The young generation would no longer support the Atlantic Alliance solely as an instrument for defense; it was essential for the unity of the West that they see in it also a vehicle for détente. He was right, but he thereby revealed the profound ambivalence of our European allies. In times of rising tension, they feared American rigidity; in times of relaxing tension, they dreaded a US–Soviet condominium. They urged us to be firm, then offered their mediation to break the resulting deadlock. They insisted that we consult with them before we did anything, but they wanted the freedom and autonomy to pursue their own détente diplomacy without restraint. If we were perceived to block détente, we would lose the support of our West European allies, who would then speed up their own contacts with the East, with no coordinated strategy; they would be too weak to resist simultaneous domestic and Soviet pressures. We found ourselves in the paradoxical position that we would have to take a leadership role in East-West relations if we wanted to hold the Alliance together and establish some ground rules for East-West contacts. But if we moved too rapidly or raised unwarranted hopes, we would undermine our case for the military strength that was the only safe basis on which to deal with the Soviet Union. It was a problem that would remain long after the participants in the Downing Street discussion had all left office.

There was a luncheon at Buckingham Palace with Queen Elizabeth. I thought she had been wrongly stereotyped as rather stodgy. She has an impish wit and she impressed me with her knowledge of world affairs and her insight into the personalities involved. In the afternoon, the President spoke to the personnel of the United States Embassy and met with a group of British editors and intellectuals.

The evening was notable for showing a side of Nixon barely known to the public. During the spring of 1968, Harold Wilson had committed the extraordinary misjudgment of betting on a Democratic victory; he had therefore appointed John Freeman, an old friend of Hubert Humphrey's, as Ambassador to Washington. It threatened to be a nearly disastrous decision. Freeman had been a Labour minister on the left of the party. He had resigned in a row over government health charges and gone on to make a name for himself first as a television interviewer, then editor of the left weekly *New Statesman,* and Britain's High Commissioner to India. While editor of the *Statesman* Freeman had celebrated Nixon's defeat in California by congratulating Americans on removing "a man of no principle whatsoever except a willingness to sacrifice everything in the cause of Dick Nixon." When Nixon won the election seven months after Freeman's appointment, Wilson was stuck with his embarrassing choice. To his credit, Wilson refused to change ambassadors. Nixon was outraged. From the beginning of his Administration, he swore that he would have nothing to do with Freeman. He was reinforced by General Eisenhower, who told him in my presence in January that Freeman's appointment was an insult not only to Nixon as a person but to the Presidency. But since it was unthinkable that we would declare a British Ambassador *persona non grata,* it seemed there was nothing left for Nixon but to make Freeman's ambassadorial tenure as difficult and awkward as possible. There was no doubt that he was capable of doing so. Our advance men requested Wilson to remove Freeman from the guest list for the President's dinner at 10 Downing Street. Wilson courageously refused and we all approached the evening with trepidation.

But Nixon could astonish. At the end of the dinner, he rose to make a toast. Looking squarely at Freeman, who sat on the opposite side of the table, Nixon said: "Some say there's a new Nixon. And they wonder if there's a new Freeman. I would like to think that that's all behind us. After all, he's the new diplomat and I'm the new statesman, trying to do our best for peace in the world."

The impact was electric. Wilson called the toast the most gracious he had heard at 10 Downing Street. He wrote Nixon a note on his menu. "You can't guarantee being born a Lord. It is possible — you've shown it — to be born a gentleman." The usually imperturbable Freeman was close to tears. Thus was born a mission to Washington that proved a spectacular success. John Freeman was one of the most effective ambassadors I ever dealt with. The reason for this was not so simple. His style was unpropitious. Freeman eschewed all flattery; he met socially only those he respected; he made little effort to turn his Embassy into a fashionable salon. When he had a message to deliver, he prefaced it with a very formal statement that he was speaking under instructions. But Freeman was prepared to go beyond his instructions to express personal views. Since he was a man of superb intelligence and utter integrity, this soon proved invaluable. He had a shrewd geopolitical mind and, as it turned out, rather shared our philosophy of foreign relations. I thought so highly of Freeman's judgment that I frequently consulted him on matters outside his official purview; on one or two occasions, I let him read early drafts of Presidential speeches, tapping his talents as an editor. He had every right to report all his conversations to his Prime Minister; he almost certainly did so. But the intimacy and trust of the "special relationship" were meant precisely for such cordial collaboration.

For his part Nixon came first to trust, then to like Freeman. Freeman was the only Ambassador invited to the White House for a social occasion during Nixon's first term. He also became one of my closest friends; that friendship has survived both our terms of office. I consider it one of the greatest rewards of my public service.

So the London trip ended with a special bonus of goodwill. It had exposed more ambivalences than it solved. But as intended, it laid the basis for fruitful collaboration later.

Bonn and Berlin and the Enigma of Germany

OUR next stop was Bonn. The situation of the Federal Republic of Germany was more complex. German politics were in preelection flux and we arrived during an incipient Berlin crisis. The West German President, a largely ceremonial figure, is selected by a special assembly of the Bundestag or representatives of the states (*Länder*). On all prior occasions this session was held in the old Reichstag building in West Berlin. This was to emphasize Bonn's claim to represent the continuity of the legitimate German state. The Soviets and their East German associates had previously ignored this implied challenge; by 1969 they felt strong enough to make an issue of it. They protested the electoral meeting in Berlin on the ground that West Berlin was not legally part of the Federal Republic. They started harassing the access routes for the first time since 1962.

This was bound to cause profound anxiety in Bonn. Berlin's vulnerability had become proverbial. There was uncertainty about how the new Administration would react. There was a pervasive unease caused in part by Germany's exposed position, in part by policy disputes with the two administrations preceding us. Bonn had disagreed with the McNamara emphasis on non-nuclear regional defense, fearing that it might tempt Soviet aggression. Bonn saw in the Nuclear Non-Proliferation Treaty a clear example of discrimination against it in the nuclear field. Bonn resented American pressures to pay for the stationing of American forces on German soil. Two Chancellors — Konrad Adenauer and Ludwig Erhard — had seen their departure hastened by their controversies with the Kennedy and Johnson administrations.

All this reflected the shaky psychological position of the seemingly so powerful new German state. Defeated in two wars, bearing the stigma of the Nazi past, dismembered and divided, West Germany was an economy in search of political purpose. There was not in Bonn that British self-confidence born of centuries of uninterrupted political evolution and imperial glory. Bonn itself, chosen as the new capital for the personal convenience of the first postwar Chancellor (it was close to the small town where Adenauer lived), and embodying no previous tradition of government, symbolized the precariousness of Germany's postwar resurrection. The Federal Republic was like an imposing tree with shallow roots, vulnerable to sudden gusts of wind.

The tenuousness of its position was reflected in the sense of insecurity of its leaders. Adenauer, a truly great man, had considered it his primary duty to restore for Germany a reputation for reliability. He resolutely rejected many temptations to exploit Germany's opportunities for maneuver between East and West. He resisted the accusations of his domestic opposition that his pro-Western course threatened the prospects for German reunification. He disdained the occasional blandishments from the East. Instead, he sought to embed the Federal Republic in Europe, and Europe in the Atlantic Alliance, so fully that the nationalism which had produced Germany's disasters would never again have the opportunity to infect his people.

Adenauer succeeded dramatically. A dozen years after the creation of the Federal Republic, its pro-Western orientation was no longer a domestic German issue. The opposition, which only yesterday had urged a neutralist Germany equipoised between East and West, had dramatically changed its program and was now competing with the government in protesting its allegiance to Western ties even in the military field. By a twist of fate, the bright young men who ran the Kennedy Administration chose this moment to urge greater flexibility toward the East on the man who had placed so much value on steadiness and reliability and who had just accomplished the tour de force of bringing about a national consensus behind his policy of close Atlantic ties. This helped produce a domestic upheaval in Germany in the Sixties and a reversal of roles. The Social Democratic opposition, which a decade earlier had sought to tap the latent German nationalism and had opposed Adenauer's pro-Western orientation, now criticized the government for jeopardizing the American connection. The still-governing Christian Democrats clung rigidly to the maxims of the Fifties. Their near obsession with continuity provoked the impatience of an American Administration eager to turn over a new leaf, convinced of the validity of its Grand Designs, and on the whole more comfortable with leftist or at least reformist groups than with the Christian Democratic conservatives who had built postwar Europe.

Thus the inherent dilemmas of Germany's postwar policies were made explicit. Alone among the European powers the Federal Republic had unfulfilled national aims. This aspiration to reunification was expressed in a refusal to deal with the East German regime or even to maintain diplomatic relations with any government that did. (This was the so-called Hallstein Doctrine.) But no other European government shared this German aim. For all of them a united Germany evoked old nightmares of German hegemony; they shared Clemenceau's witticism that such was his affection for Germany that he wanted two of them. They knew, moreover, that German unity was achievable, if at all, only through a massive showdown with the Soviet Union. Thus an inevitable gulf existed between the Federal Republic's proclaimed goal of German unity and the actions it could take to implement it. And this gulf enabled the Soviet Union to press West Germany in periodic confrontations over Berlin, which were at least partially designed to bring about the Federal Republic's acquiescence in the status quo and to force its NATO allies to dissociate themselves from its national aspirations.

Exposed on the front line of a divided Europe, subject to repeated pressures from the East, conscious of the deep residue of distrust in the West, pained by its unfulfilled national aims, West Germany's leaders saw in the American connection their anchor to windward. They did not aspire to a role in global affairs. They lacked the self-assurance to seek to influence our policy on a wider scale. Their aim was more modest: to make certain that they could count on us for defense and that there would be no drastic shifts of policy toward the East that would leave Germany exposed either physically or psychologically.

Our boisterous political process therefore had a tendency to disquiet the West Germans. The periodic advent of new administrations loudly proclaiming new approaches or the obsolescence of previous policies raised the specter that at some future turn of the wheel would come the dreaded American disengagement from Europe.

Nixon's mission to restore confidence and stability in Bonn was especially opportune since, the Berlin crisis notwithstanding, German politics were in transition. Adenauer had resigned as Chancellor in October 1963 and had been succeeded by Erhard, then tremendously popular as the architect of the German "miracle" of economic recovery. But as Adenauer had predicted, Erhard's economic competence was not matched in politics. The governing coalition of Christian Democrats and

Free Democrats fell apart; in 1966, a new so-called Grand Coalition was formed between Christian Democrats and Social Democrats, with Kurt Georg Kiesinger as Chancellor and Willy Brandt as Vice Chancellor and Minister of Foreign Affairs.

It proved to be a fateful decision for the moderately conservative Christian Democrats, who had dominated the entire postwar period. The Social Democrats had languished in an opposition that threatened to become permanent. The principal reason was that enough voters felt that this party — despite its honorable democratic record — was the heir of too many radical traditions to be entrusted with the responsibilities of government. The Grand Coalition, engineered by the brilliant Social Democratic strategist Herbert Wehner, resolved the issue of whether in fact the Social Democrats were fit to govern; their mere participation in government finally gave them enough additional votes to win electoral victory toward the end of 1969. Painful though the miscalculation that produced the Grand Coalition proved for the Christian Democrats, it was a great boon to democracy in Germany. It demonstrated that the Social Democrats were in fact a responsible democratic party; this prevented in Germany the radicalization or polarization of political life that was endemic to so many other European countries.

But this outcome was still just around the corner. The government that welcomed us in Bonn, despite its exalted title of Grand Coalition, was deeply divided. Its leading figures would within months be contesting an election against each other; almost everything said during our visit reflected a careful jockeying for position. Chancellor Kiesinger,* courteous, grave, stolid, announcing the banal with an air of great profundity, was in a political trap because every day in office built up his principal opponent, who also happened to be Vice Chancellor — Willy Brandt. Brandt, hulking, solid, basically uncommunicative despite his hearty manner, suggested in no sense that he considered himself a subordinate of the Chancellor.

Where the British government had been ambivalent on the issues of deterrence, détente, Western unity, and East-West relations, the German leaders were individually clearer but divided among themselves. Both agreed on firmness over Berlin, but this was about as far as the harmony went. Kiesinger favored a strong line toward the East. Brandt formally emphasized nuances of accommodation. It required no great imagina-

---

* Kiesinger's fate shows how much political careers can turn on accidents. In the elections coming in September, Kiesinger received the second largest popular vote ever obtained by a Christian Democrat. But for the only time in the postwar period a tiny neo-Nazi party contested the election and deprived him, through a quirk of the German electoral law, of just enough seats for a majority. This enabled the Social Democrats and the Free Democrats to form a coalition and condemn Kiesinger's party, which had the largest number of seats, to opposition. He thereby crossed that thin dividing line between being hailed as the master politician and being scorned as the failed leader whose party lost its power during his term in office. At this writing the CDU has yet to regain it.

tion, however, to deduce that he was prepared to bite the bullet of East German recognition. Kiesinger prized the French connection; Brandt was prepared to emphasize Britain's entry into the Common Market. Kiesinger's views were closer to Nixon's; Brandt's were more compatible with the convictions of our State Department. The conversations in Bonn thus made clear that until the election in the fall, German policy would largely be a holding action.

The visit to West Germany concluded with a tour of Berlin. Huge crowds greeted the Presidential motorcade, but Nixon was ill at ease, worried that the turnout would be compared unfavorably with that for Kennedy in 1963. Only after he was assured repeatedly that no unfavorable comparisons could possibly be drawn did he relax. (I noted that the route of the motorcade was S-shaped so that "crowds" could shuttle easily from one street to another. I was told that this device had also been used during the Kennedy visit.)

Nixon sought to head off another Berlin crisis by staking the prestige of the Presidency early in his term unmistakably on Berlin. He did so in an eloquent speech at the Siemens factory: "Four Presidents before me have held to this principle, and I tell you at this time and in this place that I, too, hold fast to this principle: Berlin must remain free. I do not say this in any spirit of bravado or belligerence. I am simply stating an irrevocable fact of international life."

Rome Interlude

ITALY was our next stop. It was a dramatic change from the disciplined formality of Berlin to the exuberant chaos of the Rome airport. In the happy confusion, Secretary of State Rogers was taken off to review the honor guard until a petrified advance man recovered from his shock and replaced him with the President. After that everything ran smoothly, if always along a precipice.

This was the first of many visits I was to make to Italy during my term in office. I have always loved the stark beauty of the country and the extraordinary humanity of its people. But every visit confirmed that Italy followed different political laws and had a different concept of the role of the state from that of the rest of Western Europe. Perhaps Italians were too civilized, too imbued with the worth of the individual to make the total commitment to political goals that for over a century and a half had driven the rivalries and ambitions of the other countries of Europe. No doubt Italy's domestic problems claimed so much of the attention of the top leadership that foreign policy played a secondary role. Then there was the fact that Rome as a capital was less the focus of a national consciousness than of an historical tradition. It had been the governmental center of an ancient empire. For a millennium and a half afterward, it was the capital of the Papal states — indeed, the Quirinale Palace, now housing Italy's President, had been the summer residence of the Pope until 1871. In contrast to other European capitals, Rome was not the impetus for Italy's unification; rather, it was added to Italy a decade after the state had come into existence. The Italian government moved to the city of the Pope; the Papacy remained the central institution of Rome.

Whatever the reason, each visit left me with the feeling that its primary purpose was fulfilled by our arrival at the airport. This symbolized that the United States took Italy seriously; it produced photographic evidence that Italian leaders were being consulted. This achieved, Italian ministers acted as if they were too worldly-wise to pretend that their views on international affairs could decisively affect events.

During my period in office, the office of Prime Minister alternated between Mariano Rumor and Aldo Moro, with an occasional brief spell for Emilio Colombo. The leader who was not Prime Minister would then serve as Foreign Minister. Rumor exuded friendliness, goodwill, indeed eagerness to please. He was obviously a manager of party machinery who surfaced when temperatures needed lowering and dispensed goodwill among the various Christian Democratic factions. Colombo was an intellectual. Polite, thoughtful, more of an expert than a leader, he seemed to rise to the top when the factions were deadlocked and a caretaker Prime Minister was needed who would not tilt the balance in any direction until a new adjustment had been negotiated. Moro was clearly the most formidable. He was as intelligent as he was taciturn; he had a reputation of superb intelligence. My only evidence for this was the Byzantine complexity of his sentence structure. But then I had a soporific effect on him; more often than not he fell asleep in meetings with me; I considered it a success to keep him awake. International affairs clearly did not interest Moro. He was the party strategist par excellence, who would engineer new departures in domestic policy with extraordinary subtlety; foreign policy was a portfolio he assumed as a power base, never to pursue as a vocation. Obviously the leaders of Italy were chosen to reflect domestic necessities and above all the internal balance of the Christian Democratic Party.

The Presidents I served never fully understood this. Suffering from the illusion that the Italian Prime Minister possessed executive authority, they attempted discussions implying specific decisions. No Italian Prime Minister I met encouraged such an attitude, which in their view could only result from a crude attempt at flattery or from ignorance. They knew they headed unstable coalitions; they had the right to preside at Cabinet meetings but not to issue binding orders. Decisions were made by a consensus that included many people not in the government. In discussions with either Prime Ministers or Foreign Ministers, domestic politics remained the main preoccupation. The Italian Foreign Office included some of the most distinguished and thoughtful diplomats I have encountered. Still, one sometimes could not avoid the impression that to discuss international affairs with their Foreign Minister was to risk boring him.

There was, as it happened, every reason for concern about Italy's domestic predicament. The Christian Democratic Party had governed Italy since the war. It was fashionable to say that it had not solved Italy's fundamental problems and that inefficiency was widespread and corruption rampant. But this was only partly true. Italy had made remarkable economic progress; its economy had grown at an average rate of 5.5 percent over the previous decade. But, as everywhere, the process of development produced dislocations that strained political stability. South Italian farmers had always been very poor; they were morally buttressed by tradition and the Church. Economic development transplanted these men and women to the factories of the North. In this massive readjustment, their principal spiritual support turned out to be the Communist Party, which received them at the railroad station and sustained them in their rootlessness. If the Communist vote remained constant in Italy despite rapid economic growth — and against every fashionable theory — this was in large part because the Party was considered by many as the guarantor of their security and because the government in Rome failed to establish the human contact so decisive in Italy.

The endless American obsession with institutional solutions compounded the problem. For most of the postwar period, Italy had been governed by a coalition of Christian Democrats and moderate parties of the right and left. The Social Democrats represented the left wing of the governing group; their distinguishing feature was their refusal to work with the Communists. The opposition was the Communists supported by left-wing Socialists, and the Monarchists and Fascists on the right. In 1963, the United States decided to support the so-called opening to the left. Its aim was a coalition between left-wing Socialists and Christian Democrats, thereby, it was hoped, isolating the Communists. Under considerable American pressure, this coalition was in fact negotiated.

The results, though delayed for over a decade, were precisely the opposite of what was intended. With the new coalition, the Social Democratic Party lost its principal reason for existence — its role as non-Communist opposition on the left. It declined with every election into progressive insignificance. The free-enterprise Liberal Party was expelled from the government as an entrance price for the Socialists; it too declined with every election. The left-wing Socialists did not profit, because they remained in coalition with the Communists in the provinces while governing with the Christian Democrats in Rome. Such a party could only exhaust itself in ambivalence; unwilling to give up either of its alliances, it could neither function as a barrier against the Communists in the provinces, nor aspire to reform the Christian Democrats in Rome.

Thus, far from isolating the Communists, the opening to the left made them the sole significant opposition party. By destroying the smaller democratic parties, the experiment deprived the Italian political system of flexibility. Any crisis of government would henceforth benefit the Communists; Italy increasingly faced the choice between the Christian Democrats, frozen into immobility, and a radical antidemocratic change. In the late Sixties, this ominous historic process was just becoming apparent. The ministers still avowed their anti-Communism, but the electoral arithmetic increasingly belied these professions. Any fundamental change would threaten not only the rule of the governing party but the democratic system itself.

Rome was the only capital in which substantial riots greeted Nixon. The Communists had not yet made their ostensible public conversion to NATO (which would come when they were on the edge of power and it offered tactical benefit). They demonstrated under the slogan "NATO out of Italy and Italy out of NATO." Nixon repeated his basic themes of the other stops: his commitment to full consultation, his cautious approach to the Soviet Union, his desire for peace. All this was well enough received by the Italian leaders, but much as though it were news from a distant planet — interesting, but basically irrelevant to their main concerns.

Meetings occurred in a somewhat haphazard fashion. President Giuseppe Saragat insisted on receiving Nixon without his ministers, because in front of them he was afraid to express his forebodings about Communist gains. Saragat proved crisp and thoughtful in these private talks, but his impact was attenuated by the constitutional fact that the Italian President is not part of the political process. Saragat gave an enormous state dinner in the ornate Quirinale Palace. Since it permitted no serious conversation, and since no one had any idea who of the many Italian leaders would play a major role over the years, Nixon received a large number of them one by one in a smaller room of the Palace while brandy was being served to the rest of the guests. The impression created by this procedure was more kaleidoscopic than illuminating. None of the leaders of whatever party had any concrete program, since his action in office, should he reach it, would depend less on his personal convictions than on the balance of forces he would find there.

In a curious way Italy had not yet broken with its Renaissance tradition. Its parties acted like the congeries of city-states that had dominated much of Italy's history. The Christian Democrats were a combination of Naples and Florence, seductively smothering change in pliant forms and managing their rivals by the subtle strategems of Machiavelli; the Communists were Piedmont reinforced by Moscow as the traditional Piedmont had been encouraged by France; disciplined, rational, dour. The Republican Party was a modest city-state like Modena, getting by on the prestige of its intelligence. Only the Socialists were in trouble. They aspired to national and European foundations that had few roots in Italian history.

Many of these tendencies emerged at a large formal meeting with the government, in which almost all ministers were present, at the Villa Madonna, a beautiful Renaissance palace overlooking Rome. It was preceded by a private meeting between Nixon and Prime Minister Rumor that was doomed to inconclusiveness since Rumor could make no commitments without his ministers, and the assembled ministers were, in turn, too numerous to permit a focused discussion at the plenary session — which Nixon in any case abhorred because of its large size. The Italian concerns were to end the war in Vietnam in order to remove a Communist propaganda theme, to encourage British membership in the Common Market, to reduce Gaullist trends, and to conciliate the East to give the Alliance a purpose. These propositions were put forward as friendly exhortations to a trusted ally; they were not accompanied by any specific proposal. Italian ministers were silent on issues of defense.

The Colossus of de Gaulle

THE last stop of Nixon's odyssey was Paris, where we were greeted at the airport by the extraordinary figure of Charles de Gaulle, President of the Fifth French Republic. He exuded authority. Four weeks later, he was to visit Washington for the funeral of President Eisenhower. His presence at the reception tendered by Nixon was so overwhelming that he was the center of attention wherever he stood. Other heads of government and many Senators who usually proclaimed their antipathy to authoritarian generals crowded around him and treated him like some strange species. One had the sense that if he moved to a window the center of gravity might shift and the whole room might tilt everybody into the garden.

De Gaulle had become the spokesman of the nation-state and of European autonomy from the United States. Gallic logic often tempted him to carry his postulates to extremes unnecessarily wounding to Americans. When we took office mutual distrust had made calm discussion impossible; de Gaulle had become anathema to our policymakers. Their feelings were reciprocated. It was a pity because de Gaulle had raised an important issue about the nature of international cooperation. Washington dreamed of a structure that made separate action physically impossible by assigning each partner a portion of the overall task. De Gaulle insisted that cooperation would be effective only if each partner had a real choice; therefore, each ally must — at least theoretically — be able to act autonomously. Washington, postulating a web of common interests, relied on consultation to dissolve disagreements. And in the American view, influence in that consultative process was proportionate to a nation's contribution to a common effort, somewhat like owning shares in a stock company.

De Gaulle, as the son of a continent covered with ruins testifying to the fallibility of human foresight, did not accept so institutional an approach. European self-confidence, in his view, required not only the opportunity to consult; it also depended on the options available in case disagreement was beyond resolution. Therefore, where American spokesmen stressed partnership, de Gaulle emphasized equilibrium. To de Gaulle, sound relationships depended less on personal goodwill and willingness to cooperate than on a balance of pressures and the understanding of the relation of forces. "Man 'limited by his nature' is 'infinite in his desires,' " he argued. "The world is thus full of opposing forces. Of course, human wisdom has often succeeded in preventing these rivalries from degenerating into murderous conflicts. But the competition of efforts is the condition of life. Our country finds itself confronted today with this law of the species, as it has been for two thousand years."[8] The art of statesmanship, de Gaulle reasoned, was to understand the trend of history. A great leader may be clever, but he must be above all lucid and clear-sighted. To de Gaulle, grandeur was not simply physical power, but strength reinforced by moral purpose. Nor did competition, in his view, inevitably involve physical conflict. Paradoxically, de Gaulle could see true partnership emerge only from a contest of wills because only in this manner would each side maintain its self-respect: "Yes, international life, like life in general, is a battle. The battle which our country is waging tends to unite and not to divide, to honor and not to debase, to liberate and not to dominate. Thus it is faithful to its mission, which always was and which remains human and universal."[9]

With this philosophy, de Gaulle could not possibly accept the American conviction of the obsolescence of the nation-state. The problem was not that he wished to reactivate Europe's traditional national rivalries, as so many of his American critics alleged. On the contrary, he passionately affirmed the goal of unity for Europe. But where the American and European "integrationists" insisted that European unity required that the nation-state be subsumed in a federal supranational structure, de Gaulle argued that Europe's identity and ultimately its unity depended on the vitality and self-confidence of the traditional European national entities. To de Gaulle, states were the only legitimate source of power;

only they could act responsibly: ". . . it is true that the nation is a human and sentimental element, whereas Europe can be built on the basis of active, authoritative and responsible elements. What elements? The States, of course; for, in this respect, it is only the States that are valid, legitimate and capable of achievement. I have already said, and I repeat, that at the present time there cannot be any other Europe than a Europe of States, apart, of course, from myths, stories and parades."[10] And: "The States are, in truth, certainly very different from one another, each of which has its own spirit, its own history, its own language, its own misfortunes, glories and ambitions; but these States are the only entities that have the right to order and the authority to act."[11]

When de Gaulle excluded Britain from the Common Market in 1963, the outrage in Washington took an almost palpably personal form. When he withdrew from NATO's integrated command in 1966, that outrage turned into vindictiveness. Much of our European policy in the late Sixties was a futile effort to isolate France and punish it — futile because some Europeans agreed with him and others were too weak to oppose him.

As I have indicated, I never participated in the condemnation of General de Gaulle; in fact, I thought our European policy of the Sixties generally misconceived. We were, it seemed to me, extraordinarily insensitive to the psychological problems of a country like France, which had barely survived two world wars, which had been humiliated in 1940, and which in 1958, 1960, and 1962 had been at the brink of civil war. De Gaulle's overriding challenge was to restore France's faith in itself. How well he succeeded was shown by the fact that three years after the end of the Algerian war (which most observers had expected to enfeeble France with internal divisions for decades), the common complaint was that France was conducting a foreign policy more vigorous and assertive than its real capabilities should have allowed.

I was persuaded that a Europe seeking to play an international role, even if occasionally assertive, was more in our interest than a quiescent Europe abdicating responsibilities in the guise of following American leadership. Nor did de Gaulle's attitude toward supranational institutions seem to me extraordinary. Britain had exactly the same view; the chief difference was that British statesmen characteristically expressed their disagreements on more pragmatic grounds and in a less doctrinaire manner.* We did not need to insist on structures that enshrined our leader-

---

* Both parties in Britain rejected supranational institutions. When Harold Macmillan announced Britain's first application for entry into the Common Market in July 1961, he assured Parliament that he had no interest in a "federalist system" that was based on a "completely false analogy" with the American federal union. Labour Party leader Hugh Gaitskell opposed British membership because, despite Macmillan's assurances, he feared that Britain might lose the freedom to conduct its own socialist domestic policies if submerged in a Christian Democratic Europe.

ship position because, left to their own devices, Europeans were likely to come to conclusions about their vital interests parallel to ours on most matters affecting the security of the Atlantic area. Nixon's views coincided with mine, though he gave them a less theoretical cast.

Before and during our Paris visit, we took every opportunity to stress our determination to end the old disputes with France. On February 28 I told the press in a background briefing in Paris:

It is the conviction of the President that it serves no purpose, it serves nobody's purpose for the United States and France to have avoidable bad relations. The one clear message we got in every country that we visited was . . . that they do not want to be in the position of having to choose between the United States and France. . . . I think we are making it possible for every country to make their decision on the merits of the issues, if we are not in an organic permanent conflict with France. . . .

Nixon expressed his personal admiration for de Gaulle during the lavish state dinner at the Elysée Palace. He characterized de Gaulle's life as "an epic of courage, an epic also of leadership seldom equaled in the history of the world, leadership which now has brought this great nation to the rightful place that it should have in the family of nations." He described de Gaulle as "a leader who has become a giant among men because he had courage, because he had vision, and because he had the wisdom that the world now seeks to solve its difficult problems." De Gaulle reciprocated the respectful warmth, making the gesture (rare for him) of attending Nixon's return dinner at the American Embassy.

Nixon and de Gaulle had three long meetings. I attended only one of them but read the transcript of the others made by our masterful interpreter, General Vernon A. Walters. De Gaulle spoke with the graphic command of language on which so much of his authority rested. His historical sweep made necessity appear as the handmaiden of the statesman's perception. East-West relations were the topic of his first meeting, at the Elysée Palace. De Gaulle spoke of the Chinese people and the need to keep them from being "isolated in their own rage." He called for an end to the war in Vietnam, suggesting that we use a time limit on our withdrawal as a means of obtaining a political accommodation — though having sketched the objective, he supplied no clue as to how to achieve it. He urged an imposed solution in the Middle East; this should be achieved in a Four-Power forum, he thought. When Nixon suggested parallel US–Soviet talks he made a show of indifference that scarcely obscured his extreme reserve. De Gaulle had no interest in tempting a US–Soviet condominium. (This will be discussed further in Chapter X on the Middle East.)

As for the Soviet Union, de Gaulle coupled an insistence on the need for a strong defense with a broad historical argument for the necessity of détente. There was Russia and there was Communism, he said. The Communists were no longer advancing; the danger of Communism was not over, but it could no longer conquer the world. It was too late for that. The dynamic had gone. Russia was a vast country with a long history, great resources, pride, and ambitions that were not necessarily Communist. While the Soviet leaders would be delighted if the United States and Europe diminished their defense efforts, they were not likely to march west. That would lead to a general war, and Moscow knew it could not win. The United States could not allow it to conquer Europe, for that would also mean the conquest of Asia and the isolation of the United States on the American continent. In a war, Moscow might have initial success, but the United States would eventually use all of its power and destroy Russia.

The principal concern of the Soviet leaders, said de Gaulle, was China. The Russians viewed their relations with the West and the United States in light of the problems they expected to have with Peking. Thus, with prudence and some Western flexibility, they might well opt for a policy of rapprochement with the West in order to be sure that the West would not deal with China behind their back. They were thus sincere, he was convinced, in their desire for détente. And détente he thought might also serve other Western purposes. It meant contacts, trips, exchange of goods and of opinion. The trend toward freedom and dignity, which was not dead in Eastern Europe, would surely flourish in an atmosphere of détente. When people saw themselves at the edge of war, there was always a pretext for tight control, but this would not be maintained when tensions relaxed. Besides, what was the alternative? If one did not want to make war or break down the Berlin Wall, there was no alternative except to do nothing at all. And that was always the worst possible course.

De Gaulle therefore approved of American contacts with the Soviets, seeing in them an application of principles he was already implementing. But he cautioned against US–Soviet collusion. The United States should have "company" when it made agreements; it should avoid what "some people" called a "Yalta idea." He was not, in short, so much an advocate of détente as to wish to promote a US–Soviet bilateral arrangement.

Nixon and de Gaulle met a day later in the Grand Trianon Palace at Versailles. The General was eloquent about Atlantic relations. He sketched his perception of Europe: of Italy imprisoned in the Mediterranean and isolated by the Alps; of Germany, the source of all Europe's misfortunes, cut in two and watched by both sides; of France, a continental country with access to the sea; of Britain facing the oceans and made for overseas trade. These four countries, the only ones of real weight in Europe, were as different in their language, customs, history, and interests as they were in their geographic location. They, not some abstract conception of integration, were the political reality of a Europe that did not exist beyond them.

De Gaulle stressed that it was imperative for the Soviets to know that the United States would stand with its allies in Europe in case of attack. But NATO, the integrated command, was another matter. He did not object to other countries' willingness to accept an American protectorate. But to France, integration amounted to a renunciation of her own defense. If a war were fought by an integrated NATO, the French people would feel that it was an American, and not a French, war. This would mean the end of national effort, and therefore the end of French national policy. France, thus demoralized, would then quickly revert to a situation where she had thirty political parties. In de Gaulle's view, France, perhaps paradoxically, rendered the greatest service to the Alliance by being independent.

These views, so contrary to American postwar preconceptions, were those of an ancient country grown skeptical through many enthusiasms shattered and conscious that to be meaningful to others, France had first of all to mean something to herself. The General, while rejecting integration of military forces, favored coordination of foreign policies. Our approach in the past had tended to be the reverse. The Nixon Administration sought to bring about coordination in both fields.

There was a brief third meeting, at the Elysée, on Vietnam, China, and bilateral relations. On Vietnam de Gaulle summed up his views of the first meeting. I shall deal with the China discussion in the appropriate chapter. On bilateral issues Nixon maintained wisely that there was no way to bridge the theoretical disputes in the Alliance; therefore efforts should be made to work together on concrete projects of common concern. To this de Gaulle agreed.

Except on Europe and in the power of his presentation, de Gaulle's ideas were not drastically different from those of the other West European leaders. He favored a strong defense; it was the prerequisite of an era of negotiations. He made no greater effort than his colleagues to reconcile the potential incompatibility between détente and defense: the more successful détente, the less the incentive for defense. The major difference was that his colleagues justified their East-West policies by domestic pressures; de Gaulle placed his ideas in the service of an historical vision.

It would be pleasant to report that my own contact with de Gaulle was at a level equal to my sense of his historic importance. Unfortunately, this was not so. The General considered Presidential Assistants as functionaries whose views should be solicited only to enable the principals to establish some technical point; he did not treat them as autonomous entities. At the end of the dinner at the Elysée, while liqueur was being served, an aide told me that the General wished to see me. Without the slightest attempt at small talk, de Gaulle greeted me with the query: "Why don't you get out of Vietnam?"

"Because," I replied, "a sudden withdrawal might give us a credibility problem."

"Where?" the General wanted to know. I mentioned the Middle East.

"How very odd," said the General from a foot above me. "It is precisely in the Middle East that I thought your enemies had the credibility problem."

The next day I was asked to drinks before lunch with the two Presidents. Nixon had the amazing idea of asking me what I thought of de Gaulle's views on Europe. And I had the extraordinarily poor judgment to respond to Nixon's request. De Gaulle considered this invitation so astonishing that in preparing himself for the impertinence of my opinion he drew himself up to an even more imposing height. "I found it fascinating," I said. "But I do not know how the President will keep Germany from dominating the Europe he has just described." De Gaulle, seized by profound melancholy at so much obtuseness, seemed to grow another inch as he contemplated me with the natural haughtiness of a snowcapped Alpine peak toward a little foothill. *"Par la guerre,"* he said simply ("through war").

In order to give me a chance with a subject presumably within the grasp of a professor, de Gaulle turned to a discussion of history. Which nineteenth-century diplomat, he wanted to know, had impressed me most?

"Bismarck," I replied.

"Why?" asked the General.

"Because of his moderation after victory," I said. Had I stopped there, all might have been well. Unfortunately, I was on a losing streak and pressed on. "He failed only once, when in 1871, against his better judgment, he acquiesced in the General Staff's desire to annex both Alsace and Lorraine. He always said that he had achieved more than was good for Germany."

De Gaulle gave up at this point. "I am glad Bismarck did not get his way," he said. "It gave us a chance to reconquer everything in 1918."

I do not believe I made a lasting impression on the great French leader.

The Paris stop was the high point of Nixon's first European trip. He doubled back to Rome for a brief meeting with the Pope, discussing the philosophical attraction of Communism and the unrest of youth, before heading home.

When we arrived at Andrews, Nixon had every reason to be satisfied with his visit to Europe. His summary to Congressional leaders was a fair account. He had set out to establish a new relationship of confidence with the European leaders. He had succeeded within the limits of what was possible in one trip. He had sought to get the United States out of intra-European quarrels. Progress had been made in all these respects. He had to some extent calmed European fears of US–Soviet collusion at their expense; he had warned against détente for its own sake as raising the danger of complacency. He had emphasized the need for equitable burden-sharing in NATO and for adapting Alliance doctrine to new realities. A start had been made toward a new spirit of consultation.

Clearly no single visit or Presidential exchange of views could overcome the ambivalences in the Alliance: between the fear of a US–Soviet accommodation and the aspiration to détente; between its instinct for a strong defense and its temptation to sacrifice military to domestic programs; between its desire for an abiding American troop commitment and its concern that Europe be defended by American strategic forces that were not part of NATO. But the issues had been defined, and we would have the rest of the Presidency to shape the answers.

V

Opening Moves with Moscow

Introduction to Anatoly Dobrynin

THE Embassy of the Soviet Union in the United States was a stately private mansion when it was built at the turn of the century. But it has lost its garden. Tall modern office buildings peer down condescendingly at this squat, Victorian intruder which is now neither functional nor elegant. On its roof is a lush forest of radio antennae. These paraphernalia suggest either an extraordinary interest in watching American television on the part of Soviet Embassy employees, or else a more utilitarian purpose such as satisfying an unquenchable fascination with American telephone calls.

As one enters the Embassy one faces a long corridor at the end of which a Soviet security officer is monitoring closed-circuit television screens. On the second floor are several large, high-ceilinged rooms that were quite run down until they were given a new coat of paint and had their gilding restored in honor of Leonid Brezhnev's visit in 1973. These rooms were undoubtedly the drawing rooms when the capitalist owners still used the residence. Now they are used only for large receptions or dinners.

On February 14, 1969, I was invited to my first official reception at the Soviet Embassy. This one was in honor of Georgi Arbatov, head of a Soviet research institute specializing in studying the United States. Arbatov was a faithful expounder of the Kremlin line, whom I had met at various international conferences on arms control when I was still a professor. He knew much about America and was skillful in adjusting his arguments to the prevailing fashions. He was especially subtle in playing to the inexhaustible masochism of American intellectuals who took it as an article of faith that every difficulty in US–Soviet relations had to be caused by American stupidity or intransigence. He was endlessly ingenious in demonstrating how American rebuffs were frustrating the peaceful, sensitive leaders in the Kremlin, who were being driven reluctantly by our inflexibility into conflicts that offended their inherently gentle natures.

On this February evening the Embassy rooms were packed with the usual Washington cocktail crowd — middle-level officials, some lobbyists, an occasional Congressman. It was not a brilliant assembly by Washington standards. The Ambassador, Anatoly Dobrynin, was in his apartment upstairs, recuperating from a bout of flu, and the host was the Soviet chargé d'affaires, Yuri Chernyakov.

I said hello to Arbatov, mingled a bit, and was beginning to beat my retreat when a junior Soviet official tugged at my sleeve. He asked whether I could spare a few moments for his chief.

It was our first meeting. I found Dobrynin robed in a dressing gown in the second living room of his small apartment, which must have been the sleeping quarters in the original design. Two medium-sized living rooms open one onto the other, furnished almost identically in the overstuffed heavy Central European manner I remembered from my youth in Germany. Dobrynin greeted me with smiling, watchful eyes and the bluff confident manner of one who had taken the measure of his share of senior American officials in his day. He suggested that since we would work together closely we call each other by our first names. From then on, he was "Anatol" and I was "Henry" (or more often "Khenry," since the Russian language has no "h" sound).* He said that he had just returned from the Soviet Union from a medical checkup in the same sanitarium frequented by Brezhnev, Kosygin, and Podgorny. He left open whether they had been there with him or whether he had seen them in the Kremlin. He said he had an oral message from his leaders that he wanted to deliver personally to the new President. He told me that he had been in Washington since 1962 and had experienced many crises. Throughout, he had maintained a relationship of personal confidence with the senior officials; he hoped to do the same with the new Administration, whatever the fluctuations of official relations. He mused that great opportunities had been lost in Soviet–American affairs, especially between 1959 and 1963. He had been head of the American division of the Soviet Foreign Ministry during that period, and he knew that Khrushchev seriously wanted an accommodation with the United States. The chance had been lost then; we must not lose the opportunities at hand today.

I told Dobrynin that the Nixon Administration was prepared to relax tensions on the basis of reciprocity. But we did not believe that these tensions were due to misunderstandings. They arose from real causes, which had to be dealt with if real progress were to be made. Dobrynin's mention of the 1959–1963 period as a lost opportunity, I pointed out, was bound to sound strange to American ears. That was, after all, the time of two Berlin ultimatums, Khrushchev's brutal behavior toward

---

* We spoke in English. I did not make fun of him because he spoke with an accent.

Kennedy in Vienna, the Cuban missile crisis, and the Soviet Union's unilateral breach of the moratorium on nuclear testing. If the Soviet leaders sought an accommodation with the new Administration by these methods, crises would be unavoidable; more "opportunities" would be lost.

Dobrynin smiled and conceded that not all the mistakes had been on the American side. I promised to arrange an early meeting with Nixon.

The Enduring Philosophical Problem of US–Soviet Relations

FEW foreign policy issues have bedeviled the American domestic debate or challenged our traditional categories of thought more than relations with the Soviet Union. Little in our historical experience prepared us for dealing with an adversary of comparable strength on a permanent basis. We had never needed to confront nations sharply opposed to us for more than brief periods of great exertion. The shock of Russia's animosity after 1945 was all the greater because the wartime grand alliance had encouraged a confidence that peace would be maintained by a permanent coalition of the victors. Instead, we found ourselves in a world of political rivalry and ideological struggle, overshadowed by fearful weapons that at one and the same time compounded tensions and made them insoluble. No wonder the riddle of relations with the other nuclear superpower has been a persistent preoccupation for postwar American foreign policy.

It is remarkable that we ever thought we could retreat into our traditional isolation. Two world wars had destroyed the international system that had dominated world affairs for two hundred years. Germany and Japan temporarily disappeared as major factors; China was wracked by civil war. Every significant power abroad, with the exception of Great Britain, had been occupied either during the war or as a result of it. And Britain was so exhausted by its heroic struggle that it could no longer play its historical role as the guardian of the equilibrium. Somehow we cherished the idea that this vacuum could endure as, within months of victory, we demobilized our vast military establishment. Our diplomacy sought conciliation, disarmament, and global cooperation through the United Nations. Our secret dream in the first postwar years was to play the role that India's Prime Minister Nehru later arrogated to himself; we would have liked some other country, say Britain, to maintain the balance of power while we nobly mediated its conflicts with the Soviet Union. It was symptomatic of this attitude that President Truman refused to stop in Britain on the way to or from the Potsdam Conference because he did not wish to appear to collude against our Soviet ally. Our traditional revulsion against balance-of-power politics postponed our awareness that the very totality of our victory had created a gross imbalance of force and influence in the center of Europe. American demobilization became a Soviet opportunity; it accelerated the Communist domination of all of Eastern Europe, which may not even have been Stalin's original expectation; and it produced a pervasive alarm and insecurity in countries around the Soviet periphery.

Our age of innocence ended in 1947 when Britain informed us she could no longer assure the defense of Greece and Turkey. We were obliged to step in — but not merely as vocal guarantors of national integrity. Like it or not, we were assuming the historical responsibility for preserving the balance of power; and we were poorly prepared for the task. In both world wars we equated victory with peace, and even in the crises of 1947 we still thought that the problem of maintaining global equilibrium consisted in coping with a temporary dislocation of some natural order of things. We saw power in military terms and, just having dismantled the huge forces for a world war, we perceived a need for similar strength before we could have a serious negotiation with the Soviet Union. Once we had contained its expansionary drives, we reasoned, diplomacy could again come into its own as an exercise of goodwill and conciliation.

But the management of a balance of power is a permanent undertaking, not an exertion that has a foreseeable end. To a great extent it is a psychological phenomenon; if an equality of power is perceived it will not be tested. Calculations must include potential as well as actual power, not only the possession of power but the will to bring it to bear. Management of the balance requires perseverance, subtlety, not a little courage, and above all understanding of its requirements.

As I discussed in Chapter III, our first response was the policy of containment, according to which no serious negotiation with the Soviets could take place until we had first built up our strength; afterward, we hoped, the Soviet leadership would have learned the advantages of peace. Paradoxically, this approach exaggerated the Soviets' military advantage, underestimated our potential power and psychological advantages (not to mention our nuclear monopoly), and gave the Soviet Union the time it desperately needed to consolidate its conquests and to redress the nuclear imbalance.

I have also mentioned the transformation of the nature of power wrought by nuclear weapons. Because nuclear weapons are so cataclysmic, they are hardly relevant to a whole gamut of challenges: probes, guerrilla wars, local crises. The weakness of Dulles's "massive retaliation" strategy of the 1950s (the doctrine that we reserved the right to retaliate against local challenges by threatening to launch strategic war) was not that it brought us close to nuclear war, but that in a crisis it gave us only the choice between nuclear war and doing nothing. We ended up doing nothing (or using conventional forces, as in Lebanon in 1958, which contradicted our proclaimed strategy).

This was the context in which the United States attempted to grapple with the dynamics of the Soviet system.

The most singular feature of Soviet foreign policy is, of course, Communist ideology, which transforms relations among states into conflicts between philosophies. It is a doctrine of history and also a motivating force. From Lenin, to Stalin, to Khrushchev, to Brezhnev, and to whoever succeeds him, Soviet leaders have been partly motivated by a self-proclaimed insight into the forces of history and by a conviction that their cause is the cause of historical inevitability. Their ideology teaches that the class struggle and economic determinism make revolutionary upheaval inevitable. The conflict between the forces of revolution and counterrevolution is irreconcilable. To the industrial democracies peace appears as a naturally attainable condition; it is the composition of differences, the absence of struggle. To the Soviet leaders, by contrast, struggle is ended not by compromise but by the victory of one side. Permanent peace, according to Communist theory, can be achieved only by abolishing the class struggle and the class struggle can be ended only by a Communist victory. Hence, any Soviet move, no matter how belligerent, advances the cause of peace, while any capitalist policy, no matter how conciliatory, serves the ends of war. "Until the final issue [between capitalism and Communism] is decided," said Lenin, "the state of awful war will continue. . . . Sentimentality is no less a crime than cowardice in war."[1] Statements of Western leaders or analysts stressing the importance of goodwill can only appear to Soviet leaders either as hypocrisy or stupidity, propaganda or ignorance.

Soviet policy thus uses a vocabulary all its own. In 1939, it was the League of Nations that in Soviet propaganda threatened peace by condemning the Soviet attack on Finland. While Soviet tanks were shooting down civilians in Hungary in the fall of 1956, it was the United Nations that was accused by Moscow of threatening peace by debating Soviet armed intervention. When in 1968 the Soviet Union and its Warsaw Pact allies invaded Czechoslovakia, they did so amid a smokescreen of accusations against the United States, West Germany, and NATO for "interfering," even though the West had bent over backward *not* to involve itself in Czechoslovakia. In 1978, the USSR "warned" the United States against interfering in Iran, not because they feared it but because they knew it would not happen; it was a way to accelerate the demoralization of those who might resist the upheaval already taking place. The Soviet leadership is burdened by no self-doubt or liberal guilt. It has no effective domestic opposition questioning the morality of its actions. The result is a foreign policy free to fill every vacuum, to exploit every opportunity, to act out the implications of its doctrine. Policy is constrained principally by calculations of objective conditions. Soviet proclamations of peaceful intent must be judged by this vocabulary. They may well be "sincere" but for pragmatic reasons. Where there exists a danger of nuclear war they are unquestionably sincere because Soviet leaders have no intention of committing suicide. But fundamentally they reflect less of a principle and more of a judgment that the relation of forces is unfavorable for military pressure. And even during the most strenuous peace offensives Soviet leaders have never disguised their intention of waging a permanent war for men's minds.

In his report to the Party Congress outlining his new commitment to coexistence, Khrushchev explained his policy in purely tactical terms, as a device to enable capitalists to surrender peacefully: "There is no doubt that in a number of capitalist countries violent overthrow of the dictatorship of the bourgeoisie . . . [is] inevitable. But the forms of social revolution vary. . . . The greater or lesser intensity which the struggle may assume, the use or non-use of violence in the transition to socialism depend on the resistance of the exploiters. . . ."[2]

Historical trends are considered immune from tactical compromise. Marxist theory combines with Russian national advantage to place the Soviet Union on the side of all radical anti-Western movements in the Third World, regardless of what practical accommodations are made between East and West on nuclear matters. Leonid Brezhnev declared at the twenty-fourth Party Congress at the end of March 1971:

We declare that, while consistently pursuing its policy of peace and friendship among nations, the Soviet Union will continue to conduct a resolute struggle against imperialism, and firmly to rebuff the evil designs and subversions of aggressors. As in the past, we shall give undeviating support to the people's struggle for democracy, national liberation and socialism.

His colleague, Soviet President Nikolai Podgorny, declared in November 1973:

As the Soviet people see it, a just and democratic world cannot be achieved without the national and social liberation of peoples. The struggle by the Soviet Union for the relaxation of international tensions, for peaceful coexistence among states and different systems does not represent, and cannot represent, a departure from the class principles of our foreign policy.[3]

The arena of international struggle thereby expands to include the internal policies and social structures of countries, mocking the traditional standard of international law that condemns interference in a country's domestic affairs. In the centuries in which the European nations dominated the world, a country could increase its influence only by territorial acquisitions; these were visible and evoked after a time the united resistance of those threatened by the upset of the established order. But in the postwar period it is possible to change the balance of power through developments — upheavals, revolutions, subversion — within the sovereign territory of another country. Ideology thus challenges the stability of the international system — like the Napoleonic upheavals after the French Revolution, or the religious wars that convulsed Europe for centuries. Ideology transcends limits, eschews restraints, and disdains tolerance or conciliation.

Soviet policy is also, of course, the inheritor of an ancient tradition of Russian nationalism. Over centuries the strange Russian empire has seeped outward from the Duchy of Muscovy, spreading east and west across endless plains where no geographical obstacle except distance set a limit to human ambition, inundating what resisted, absorbing what yielded. This sea of land has, of course, been a temptation for invaders as well, but as it has eventually swallowed up all conquerors — aided no little by a hard climate — it has impelled the Russian people who have endured to identify security with pushing back all surrounding countries. Perhaps from this insecure history, perhaps from a sense of inferiority, Russia's rulers — Communists or tsars — have responded by identifying security not only with distance but also with domination. They have never believed that they could build a moral consensus among other peoples. Absolute security for Russia has meant infinite insecurity for all its neighbors. The distinction of Leninist Communism was that it, for the first time in Russian history, gave the expansionist instinct a theoretical formulation that applied universally around the globe. It salved Russian consciences; it compounded the problem for all other peoples.

These durable impulses of nationalism and ideology that lie behind Soviet policy emphasize the irrelevance of much Western debate whether this or that Soviet move is the prelude to a global showdown, or, alternatively, whether some new overture marks a thaw, a change of heart. The question is continually asked: What are the Soviet Union's ultimate aims? What are the Soviet leaders' real intentions? It may be the wrong question. It seems to imply that the answer lies in the secret recesses of the minds of Soviet leaders, as if Brezhnev might divulge it if awakened in the middle of night or caught in an unguarded moment. Focusing on the question of ultimate aims is bound to leave the democracies uncertain and hesitant at each new Soviet geopolitical move, as they try to analyze and debate among themselves whether the intrinsic value of the area at stake is of any "strategic importance," or whether it heralds a turn to a hard line. These are not the alternatives as the Soviet leaders see them. The Soviet practice, confident of the flow of history, is to promote the attrition of adversaries by gradual increments, not to stake everything on a single throw of the dice. "To accept battle at a time when it is obviously advantageous to the enemy and not to us is a crime," wrote Lenin.[4] By the same token, the failure to engage in the conflict when the relation of forces is favorable is equally a crime. The choice of Soviet tactics is, therefore, at each time and place determined by their assessment of the "objective correlation of forces," which as Marxists they pride themselves on discerning.

It seems to me more useful, therefore, to view Soviet strategy as essentially one of ruthless opportunism. No chance of incremental gain must be given up for Western concepts of goodwill. The immense reservoir of sympathy built up during World War II was sacrificed without hesitation to obtain a bastion in Eastern Europe. The Geneva summit conference of 1955 was used to perpetuate the Soviet position in East Germany and opened the way to the Soviet arms deal with Egypt, which helped to produce two decades of turmoil in the Middle East. In 1962 a new Administration that had eagerly — almost pleadingly — expressed its desire for a new era of US–Soviet relations was confronted with an ultimatum over Berlin and a Cuban missile crisis. In 1975–1976 a possible SALT agreement did not prevent the dispatch of Soviet-backed Cuban forces to Angola. In 1977 the hopeful prospect of a new Administration eager to revive détente did not tilt the balance in favor of restraint when an opportunity for proxy war presented itself in Ethiopia. In every policy choice the Soviet leaders have identified their interests not with the goodwill of countries that Soviet doctrine defines as organically hostile but with strategic opportunity as they saw it. To expect the Soviet leaders to restrain themselves from exploiting circumstances they conceive to be favorable is to misread history. To foreclose Soviet opportunities is thus the essence of the West's responsibility. It is up to *us* to define the limits of Soviet aims.

This is an attainable objective. The imposing monolith of totalitarian states often obscures their latent weaknesses. The Soviet system is unstable politically; it has no mechanism for succession. Of the four General Secretaries of the Soviet Communist Party two have died in office; the third has been removed by couplike procedures; the fate of the fourth is unsettled at this writing. Precisely because there is no "legitimate" means of replacing leaders they all grow old together in office. A ponderous bureaucratic machinery and the complexity of collective leadership make it rare that Soviet foreign policy shows great brilliance or even quick responses to fast-moving events.

Nor is their economic system impressive. Ironically, in a country that exalts economic determinism, the standard of living of the Soviet Union, a land rich in resources, still lags even behind that of its East European satellites over sixty years after the advent of Communism. Over time this inefficiency is bound to produce strains and competing claims on the resources now devoted so predominantly to military preparations. Nor is the Communist Party likely to remain forever mono-lithic and unchallenged. The system of total planning leads to top-heavy competing bureaucracies uneasily arbitrated by the aging leaders in the Politburo. It is one of the ironies of elaborated Communist states that the Communist Party has no real function even though it permeates every aspect of society. It is not needed for running the economy, for administration, or for government. Rather, it embodies a social structure of privilege; it justifies itself by vigilance against enemies, domestic and foreign — thus producing a vested interest in tension. Sooner or later this essentially parasitic function is bound to lead to internal pressures, especially in a state comprised of many nationalities.

Nothing could be more mistaken than to fall in with the myth of an inexorable Soviet advance carefully orchestrated by some superplanners. Coexistence on the basis of the balance of forces should therefore be within our grasp — provided the nature of the challenge is correctly understood. But this is precisely what the democracies have had difficulty doing. The themes dominant in the West's perceptions of the Soviet Union have been recurrent: first, that Soviet purposes have al-ready changed and the Soviet leaders are about to concentrate on economic development rather than foreign adventures; second, that im-provements in atmosphere and good personal relations with Soviet lead-ers will help mitigate hostility; and third, that the Kremlin is divided between hawks and doves and that it is the duty of the Western democ-racies to strengthen the doves by a policy of conciliation.

The eagerness of so many in the non-Communist world to declare an end to the tensions and perils of the Cold War does not lack poignancy. In the 1930s the prominent American historian Michael Florinsky argued: "The former crusaders of world revolution at any cost have exchanged their swords for machine tools, and now rely more on the results of their labor than on direct action to achieve the ultimate victory of the proletariat."[5] In the 1930s, the democratic freedoms described in the Soviet Constitution were admired in Europe and the United States even while the Gulag Archipelago was growing, the purge trials mocked any concept of justice, and the Soviet Union became the first major country to make an overture toward Hitler. After Stalin disbanded the Comintern in 1943, Senator Tom Connally of Texas, hardly known for his softness on Communism, was reported as saying: "Russians for years have been changing their economy and approaching the abandon-ment of communism and the whole Western world will be gratified at the happy climax of their efforts."[6] Wrote Under Secretary of State Sumner Welles, "Upon the conclusion of the present war, the Soviet government undoubtedly will have to dedicate its chief energies for a term of years to the rehabilitation and reconstruction of its devastated cities and territories, to the problem of industrialization, and to the achievement of a rise in the popular standard of living."[7]

This theme that the Soviet Union should prefer economic development has never died. The Western democracies, extrapolating from their own domestic experience, assume that popular frustrations are assuaged by economic advance and that economic progress is a more rational objective than foreign adventures. In 1959 Averell Harriman wrote: "I think Mr. Khrushchev is keenly anxious to improve Soviet living standards. I believe that he looks upon the current Seven Year Plan as the crowning success of the Communist revolution and a historic turning point in the lives of the Soviet people. He also considers it a monument to himself that will mark him in history as one of his country's great benefactors."[8] The bitter disappointments to follow did not inter this thought.

Thus in February 1964 Secretary of State Dean Rusk, hardly a dove, confidently asserted: "They [the Communists] appear to have begun to realize that there is an irresolvable contradiction between the demands to promote world Communism by force and the needs of the Soviet state and the people."[9] The suppression of the East German and Hungarian uprisings, the several confrontations over Berlin, the Cuban missile crisis, the invasion of Czechoslovakia, the massive supplies to North Vietnam, the exacerbation of tensions in the Middle East, the never-ending attempt to probe for weak spots in Africa — none of these affected the persistent conviction of many that a Soviet change of heart was imminent and that the Soviets would prefer economic development to foreign adventures. (Of course, one reason why it has been difficult to test this last proposition is that the industrial democracies have never insisted that the Soviet Union make this choice: credits and trade have continued even in periods of Soviet aggressiveness.)

Equally perennial has been the conviction that there rages in the Kremlin a continual struggle in which America can assist the more peace-loving element by a conciliatory policy. The West has been assiduous in finding alibis for a succession of Soviet leaders; the incumbent was always considered the leader of the "liberal" faction — even Josef Stalin. Perhaps the definitive example of this Western attitude was written in 1945; today we can appreciate the irony of it. After the Yalta Conference, White House adviser Harry Hopkins told the author Robert Sherwood:

The Russians had proved that they could be reasonable and farseeing and there wasn't any doubt in the minds of the President or any of us that we could live with them and get along with them peacefully for as far into the future as any of us could imagine. But I have to make one amendment to that — I think we all had in our minds the reservation that we could not foretell what the results would be if anything should happen to Stalin. We felt sure that we could count on him to be reasonable and sensible and understanding — but we never could be sure who or what might be in back of him there in the Kremlin.[10]

"The prospect that the survival of Nikita S. Khrushchev's liberal regime rests upon a meeting this year between the Soviet Premier and Western leaders is being discussed by Western diplomats," reported the *New York Times* on May 5, 1958, a view that led to Khrushchev's visit to Washington in 1959. After Khrushchev's effort to change the strategic balance was rebuffed in the Cuban missile crisis, Washington experts speculated that he was struggling against hard-liners in the Kremlin and needed understanding and support from the United States lest these hard-liners prevail — ignoring the fact that it was Khrushchev himself who had sent the missiles to Cuba and that he was being attacked mainly because he had failed.[11] A plausible argument can be made that we strengthen whatever moderate elements there are in the Kremlin more by firmness, which demonstrates the risks of Soviet adventures, than by creating the impression that seemingly marginal moves are free of cost.

The idea of the Kremlin struggle that America should seek to influence adds impetus to the other dominant idea that tensions are caused by personal misunderstandings which charm and sincerity can eradicate. A little more than two years after coming into office with the argument that it would roll back Communism, the Eisenhower Administration undertook a summit with the Soviets at which the personal magic of the President was widely hailed as ushering in a new era. "No one would want to underestimate the change in the Russian attitude," said the *New York Herald Tribune* on July 21, 1955. "Without that, nothing would have been possible. . . . But it remains President Eisenhower's achievement that he comprehended the change, that he seized the opening and turned it to the advantage of world peace." *Life* magazine averred on August 1, 1955: "The chief result of the Geneva conference is so simple and breath-taking that cynics and comma-chasers still question it and Americans, for other reasons, find it a little difficult to grasp. The championship of peace has changed hands. In the mind of Europe, which judges this unofficial title, it has passed from Moscow to Washington." It was open to question how a country that had in short order turned all of Eastern Europe into satellites, blockaded Berlin, and suppressed a revolt in East Germany should have qualified for the championship of peace in the first place. But the belief that peace depended on good personal relations was extraordinarily pervasive even in the 1950s. The most eloquent statement of this attitude was made by then British Foreign Secretary Harold Macmillan at the end of the Foreign Ministers' Conference in 1955. This meeting had deadlocked precisely because the preceding summit conference had achieved the Soviet aim of relaxing tensions entirely through atmospherics:

Why did this meeting [the summit] send a thrill of hope and expectation round the world? It wasn't that the discussions were specially remarkable.

. . . It wasn't that they reached any very sensational agreement. It wasn't really what they did or said. What struck the imagination of the world was the fact of the friendly meeting between the Heads of the two great groups into which the world is divided. These men, carrying their immense burdens, met and talked and joked together like ordinary mortals. . . . The Geneva spirit was really a return to normal human relations.[12]

A year later these same Soviet leaders suppressed the uprising in Hungary and threatened Britain and France with nuclear war over the crisis in the Middle East — after the United States had ostentatiously dissociated itself from its allies. A decade later, however, President Johnson in his 1965 State of the Union Address expressed the hope that Khrushchev's successors could also visit the United States, in order to reduce the risks of personal misunderstandings:

If we are to live together in peace, we must come to know each other better.

I am sure that the American people would welcome a chance to listen to the Soviet leaders on our television — as I would like the Soviet people to hear our leaders on theirs.

I hope the new Soviet leaders can visit America so they can learn about our country at firsthand.

In the face of the Soviet Union's ambiguous challenge, the West paralyzed itself, moreover, not only by excesses of conciliation but by excesses of truculence. In every decade the alternative to policies of sentimental conciliation was posed in terms of liturgical belligerence as if the emphatic trumpeting of anti-Communism would suffice to make the walls come tumbling down. Side by side with the idea that there had been a basic change in the Soviet system there existed the belief that Soviet purposes could never be modified, which would make the Soviet state the first in history to be immune to historical change. Those who denounced American intransigence were opposed by others who could not imagine that any agreement with the Soviet Union could possibly be in our interest; sometimes the very fact that the Soviets wanted an agreement was adduced as an argument against it. Both these attitudes sprang from the same fallacy that there was some terminal point to international tension, the reward either for goodwill or for toughness. They neglected the reality that we were dealing with a system too ideologically hostile for instant conciliation and militarily too powerful to destroy. We had to prevent its seizing of strategic opportunities; but we also had to have enough confidence in our own judgments to make arrangements with it that would gain time — time for the inherent stagnation of the Communist system to work its corrosion and to permit the necessity of coexistence based on restraint to be understood.

I had been a critic of both these schools — which had influenced all postwar administrations in the decade before I entered public service:

The obsession with Soviet intentions causes the West to be smug during periods of détente and panicky during crises. A benign Soviet tone is equated with the achievement of peace; Soviet hostility is considered to be the signal for a new period of tension and usually evokes purely military countermeasures. The West is thus never ready for a Soviet change of course; it has been equally unprepared for détente and intransigence.[13]

*   *   *

The heat of their argument sometimes obscured the fact that the advocates and the opponents of negotiation agreed in their fundamental assumptions. They were in accord that an effective settlement presupposed a change in the Soviet system. They were at one in thinking that Western diplomacy should seek to influence Soviet internal developments. Both groups gave the impression that the nature of a possible settlement with the Communist world was perfectly obvious. . . . They differed primarily about the issue of timing. The opponents of negotiation maintained that the Soviet change of heart was still in the future, while the advocates claimed that it had already taken place. . . .

In the process, more attention was paid to whether we should negotiate than to what we should negotiate about. The dispute over Soviet domestic developments diverted energies from elaborating our own purposes. It caused us to make an issue of what should have been taken for granted: our willingness to negotiate. And it deflected us from elaborating a concrete program which alone would have made negotiations meaningful.[14]

By the time the Nixon Administration took office, the political balance sheet was hardly in credit. The Soviet Union had just occupied Czechoslovakia. It was supplying massive arms to North Vietnam; without its assistance to Hanoi, a successful negotiation could have been assured. It had shown no willingness to help bring a settlement in the Middle East. And the Soviet Union at this point was nearing equality in strategic weapons. The decisive American superiority, which had characterized the entire postwar period, had ended by 1967, halting at self-imposed ceilings of 1,000 Minuteman ICBMs, 656 Polaris SLBMs, and 54 Titan ICBMs.* By 1969 it was clear that the number of Soviet missiles capable of reaching the United States would soon equal that of all American missiles available for retaliation against the Soviet Union, and, if Soviet building programs continued through the Seventies, would come to exceed them.

The new Administration had to attempt to resolve a series of contradictions. Whatever might be said about growing Soviet power, Communist ideology, Russian expansionism, and Soviet interventionism, anyone coming to office in the late Sixties could not fail to be awed by the unprecedented dimensions of the challenge of peace. No bellicose rheto-

---

* ICBM: intercontinental ballistic missile; SLBM: submarine-launched ballistic missile.

ric could obscure the fact that existing nuclear stockpiles were enough to destroy mankind; no amount of distrust of the Soviet Union could endorse adoption of the traditional balance-of-power politics of resolving crisis by confrontation. There could be no higher duty than to prevent the catastrophe of nuclear war. Yet mere sentimentality was treacherous. It would mislead our people and Communist leaders alike, exposing the first to shock and tempting the second to regard negotiation as a viable instrument of political warfare. We had to recognize that at home and among our allies we could gain support for firm action in crisis only if we could demonstrate it was not of our making. But in trying to construct a more peaceful world it would also be folly to lull people into ignoring the nature of an ideological and geopolitical challenge that would last for generations, or to shirk the unpopularity of spending for tactical and strategic defense. It was not going to be easy for a democracy, in the middle of a divisive war in Asia.

For those in positions of responsibility, devotion to peace and freedom is not tested by the emotion of their pronouncements. We had to express our commitment by the discipline with which we would defend our values and yet create conditions for long-term security. We had to teach our people to face their permanent responsibility, not to expect that either tension — or our adversary — would ever millennially disappear. Such a course might not be comfortable or easy, especially for a people as impatient as ours. But we would be judged by future generations by whether we had left a safer world than we found, a world that preserved the peace without abdication and strengthened the confidence and hopes of free peoples.

Reflections during the Transition Period

THE Kremlin tends to approach a new American Administration with acute wariness. Bureaucracies crave predictability, and the Soviet leaders operate in a Byzantine bureaucratic environment of uncompromising standards. They can adjust to steady firmness; they grow nervous in the face of rapid changes, which undermine the confidence of their colleagues in their judgment and their mastery of events. It was pointless, we concluded, to try to overcome this uneasiness at the start of a new Administration by appeals to a sense of moral community, for the Soviet leaders' entire training and ideology deny this possibility. Self-interest is a standard they understand better. It is no accident that in relations between the Soviet Union and other societies those Western leaders most bent on showing "understanding" for their Soviet counterparts have been least successful. A Soviet leadership proud of its superior understanding of the objective sources of political motivation cannot admit that it is swayed by transitory considerations. Thus the almost pleading efforts of the Kennedy Administration failed to make progress until a psychological balance was restored, first with the US military buildup after pressures on Berlin and then by the Cuban missile crisis. After these events some progress was made.

The Kremlin knew Nixon, by contrast, as a Communist-baiter; but it had never permitted personal antipathy to stand in the way of Soviet national interest. Stalin, after all, had made an overture to Hitler within weeks of the Nazis' advent to power. Despite the mutual distrust, relations between the Kremlin and the Nixon Administration were more businesslike than in most previous periods and generally free of the roller-coaster effect of first exalted and then disappointed hopes. That strange pair, Brezhnev and Nixon, ultimately developed a modus vivendi because each came to understand the other's perception of his self-interest. Nixon had visited the Soviet Union earlier in his career, when as Vice President he had had his famous "Kitchen Debate" with Khrushchev. Nixon had a far keener grasp of the characteristics of its leadership than any other recent Presidential contender. Moscow was concerned lest the new President begin a fresh round of weapons procurement, which would strain the Soviet economy. But it was prepared to inquire into the price for averting this prospect, even while it put up its time-tested pretense of imperviousness to threats and resorted to its traditional tactic of seeking to undermine American domestic support for the policy it feared.

It took some time for the relationship to prosper but when it did it was not by chance. No subject occupied more of the attention of the President-elect during the transition period; he and I spent hours together charting our course. Nixon had come to the problem by a more political route than I. Having made his reputation through a tough, occasionally strident anti-Communism, he was committed to maintaining his traditional conservative constituency. He considered his reputation as a hardliner a unique asset to the conduct of our policy. But he understood that as President he would need to stretch his political base toward the political center; indeed, he shrewdly saw in East-West relations a long-term opportunity to build his new majority. He tended to combine these keen instincts with extremely personal judgments. He had been afraid that the Glassboro summit might restore Johnson's fortunes — hence he considered that the Soviets had colluded with the Democrats to thwart him. But he had also seen how the inconclusive outcome caused Johnson's popularity to dissipate as rapidly as it had spurted — hence his determination not to have a summit unless success could be guaranteed.

My approach — as outlined above — was in essence quite similar, if, given my academic background, somewhat more theoretical. On December 12, 1968, the President-elect asked me to brief the new Cabinet on our approach to foreign policy. It seemed to me, I told my new colleagues, that Soviet foreign policy was being pulled in two directions. There were pressures for conciliation with the West, coming from a rising desire for consumer goods, from the fear of war, and perhaps from those who hoped for a relaxation in police-state controls. At the same time there were pressures for continued confrontation with the United States arising out of Communist ideology, the suspiciousness of the leaders, the Party apparatus, the military, and those who feared that any relaxation of tensions could only encourage the satellites to try once again to loosen Moscow's apron strings. Moscow's foreign policy since the August invasion of Czechoslovakia had focused on two problems: how to overcome the shock effect of the invasion on the rest of the Communist world, and how to cut its losses elsewhere, especially how to hold down damage to US–Soviet relations.

For the latter reason, the Soviets seemed particularly anxious to keep open the possibility of talks on strategic arms limitation. This had many motives: It could be a tactical device to regain respectability; it might be a maneuver to split the Alliance by playing up fears of a US–Soviet condominium; it could be that they believed a reasonably stable strategic balance was inevitable and had therefore decided to try to stablize the arms race at the present level. Our response depended on our conception of the problem. Our past policy had often been one of "confidence building" for its own sake, in the belief that as confidence grew tensions would lessen. But if one took the view that tensions arose as a result of differences over concrete issues, then the way to approach the problem was to begin working on those differences. A lasting peace depended on the settlement of the political issues that were dividing the two nuclear superpowers.

In fact, I spoke in almost the same vein to a key Soviet representative. When I saw Boris Sedov, the KGB operative masquerading as an Embassy counselor, on December 18 at the Pierre Hotel, I told him that the President-elect was serious when he spoke of an era of negotiation. The Soviet leadership would find the new Administration prepared to negotiate lasting settlements reflecting real interests. We believed that there had been too much concern with atmospherics and not enough with substance. In the view of the new Administration there were real differences between the United States and the Soviet Union and these differences must be narrowed if there was to be a genuine relaxation of tensions. We were, I said, prepared to talk about limiting strategic weapons. But we would not be stampeded into talks before we had analyzed the problem. We would also judge the Soviet Union's purposes by its willingness to move forward on a broad front, especially by its attitude on the Middle East and Vietnam. We expected Soviet restraint in trouble spots around the world. (This was the famous doctrine of "linkage.") I hoped he would convey these considerations to Moscow.

Moscow sent a soothing reply. Sedov brought me a message on

January 2, 1969, in which Soviet leaders dissociated themselves from the "pessimistic view" they claimed to have seen expressed "in many parts of the world" about the President-elect. The "key concern of Moscow" was not Nixon's past record but whether our leadership was animated by "a sense of reality." Disarmament was of preeminent importance. The Soviet leaders recognized that our relations would be favorably affected by a settlement of the Vietnam problem, a political solution in the Middle East, and "a realistic approach" in Europe as a whole and in Germany in particular. The Kremlin did not fail to note its own "special interests" in Eastern Europe.

Both sides had now stated their basic positions. The new Administration wanted to use the Soviet concern about its intentions to draw the Kremlin into discussions on Vietnam. We therefore insisted that negotiations on all issues proceed simultaneously. The Soviet leaders were especially worried about the impact of a new arms race on the Soviet economy; they therefore gave top priority to arms limitation. This had the additional advantage to them that the mere fact of talks, regardless of their results, would complicate new defense appropriations in the United States and — though we did not yet perceive this — would disquiet the Chinese.

Of course, nothing further could happen until the new Administration was in office. But in our deliberations at the Pierre Hotel the President-elect and I distilled a number of basic principles that were to characterize our approach to US–Soviet relations as long as we were in office:

The principle of concreteness. We would insist that any negotiations between the United States and the Soviet Union deal with specific causes of tensions rather than general atmospherics. Summit meetings, if they were to be meaningful, had to be well prepared and reflect negotiations that had already made major progress in diplomatic channels. We would take seriously the ideological commitment of Soviet leaders; we would not delude ourselves about the incompatible interests between our two countries in many areas. We would not pretend that good personal relations or sentimental rhetoric would end the tensions of the postwar period. But we were prepared to explore areas of common concern and to make precise agreements based on strict reciprocity.

The principle of restraint. Reasonable relations between the superpowers could not survive the constant attempt to pursue unilateral advantages and exploit areas of crisis. We were determined to resist Soviet adventures; at the same time we were prepared to negotiate about a genuine easing of tensions. We would not hold still for a détente designed to lull potential victims; we were prepared for a détente based on mutual restraint. We would pursue a carrot-and-stick approach, ready to impose penalties for adventurism, willing to expand relations in the context of responsible behavior.

The principle of linkage. We insisted that progress in superpower relations, to be real, had to be made on a broad front. Events in different parts of the world, in our view, were related to each other; even more so, Soviet conduct in different parts of the world. We proceeded from the premise that to separate issues into distinct compartments would encourage the Soviet leaders to believe that they could use cooperation in one area as a safety valve while striving for unilateral advantages elsewhere. This was unacceptable. Nixon expressed this view at his very first press conference on January 27, 1969. Strategic arms limitation talks with the Soviet Union would be more productive, he said, if they were conducted "in a way and at a time that will promote, if possible, progress on outstanding political problems at the same time." In a briefing for reporters on February 6, I used the term "linkage" explicitly: "To take the question of the linkage between the political and the strategic environment . . . [the President] . . . would like to deal with the problem of peace on the entire front in which peace is challenged and not only on the military one."

So strong is the pragmatic tradition of American political thought that this concept of linkage was widely challenged in 1969. It was thought to be an idiosyncrasy, a gratuitous device to delay arms control negotiations. It has since been repudiated as if it reflected the policy preference of a particular administration. In our view, linkage existed in two forms: first, when a diplomat deliberately links two separate objectives in a negotiation, using one as leverage on the other; or by virtue of reality, because in an interdependent world the actions of a major power are inevitably related and have consequences beyond the issue or region immediately concerned.

The new Administration sometimes resorted to linkage in the first sense; for example, when we made progress in settling the Vietnam war something of a condition for advance in areas of interest to the Soviets, such as the Middle East, trade, or arms limitation. But in the far more important sense, linkage was a reality, not a decision. Displays of American impotence in one part of the world, such as Asia or Africa, would inevitably erode our credibility in other parts of the world, such as the Middle East. (This was why we were so determined that our withdrawal from Vietnam occur not as a collapse but as an American strategy.) Our posture in arms control negotiations could not be separated from the resulting military balance, nor from our responsibilities as the major military power of a global system of alliances. By the same token, arms limitation could almost certainly not survive a period of growing international tensions. We saw linkage, in short, as synonymous with an overall strategic and geopolitical view. To ignore the interconnection of events was to undermine the coherence of *all* policy.

Linkage, however, is not a natural concept for Americans, who have traditionally perceived foreign policy as an episodic enterprise. Our bureaucratic organizations, divided into regional and functional bureaus, and indeed our academic tradition of specialization compound the tendency to compartmentalize. American pragmatism produces a penchant for examining issues separately: to solve problems on their merits, without a sense of time or context or of the seamless web of reality. And the American legal tradition encourages rigid attention to the "facts of the case," a distrust of abstractions.

Yet in foreign policy there is no escaping the need for an integrating conceptual framework. In domestic affairs new departures are defined by the legislative process; dramatic initiatives may be the only way to launch a new program. In foreign policy the most important initiatives require painstaking preparation; results take months or years to emerge. Success requires a sense of history, an understanding of manifold forces not within our control, and a broad view of the fabric of events. The test of domestic policy is the merit of a law; that of foreign policy, nuances and interrelations.

The most difficult challenge for a policymaker in foreign affairs is to establish priorities. A conceptual framework — which "links" events — is an essential tool. The absence of linkage produces exactly the opposite of freedom of action; policymakers are forced to respond to parochial interests, buffeted by pressures without a fixed compass. The Secretary of State becomes the captive of his geographic bureaus; the President is driven excessively by his agencies. Both run the risk of becoming prisoners of events.

Linkage, therefore, was another of the attempts of the new Administration to free our foreign policy from oscillations between overextension and isolation and to ground it in a firm conception of the national interest.

Public and Congressional Attitudes: A Spring Flurry

ONE of the bizarre elements of the election of Richard Nixon was that many of those who had fought him because of his strident opposition to Communism should interpret his election as a mandate for new overtures to the Soviet Union. The Nixon Administration was greeted with a barrage of advice to move forward rapidly to improve relations with the Soviet Union. Nixon was soon found wanting in this regard, too suspicious of Soviet intentions, too obsessed with military strength, too resistant to the necessities of détente.

A "get-acquainted" summit was one proposal; its purpose would be to initiate the strategic arms talks that the Johnson Administration had prepared, and to improve the climate of personal relations. This was widely espoused by, among others, Zbigniew Brzezinski, who wrote that a "useful device — both symbolically and practically — would be to initiate the practice of holding annually an informal two-day working discussion meeting between American and Soviet heads of governments. . . . The meeting need not always have a formal agenda. . . . Its purpose would be to provide the heads of the . . . two leading nuclear powers with a regular opportunity for personal exchange of views and for the maintenance of personal contact."[15]

A campaign began to urge the Administration to remove the barriers to East-West trade and use the promise of an expanded economic relationship as the wedge to open a political dialogue. The two superpowers had increasingly complementary economic interests and these, it was argued, could erode political distrust. Marshall Shulman, a prominent expert on the Soviet Union, wrote: "These common interests may not dissolve the differences that now drive the Soviet-American competition, but they may in time come to make these differences seem less important."[16] A panel of the United Nations Association chaired by Arthur Goldberg and consisting of several experts issued a report on February 1, 1969 — barely five months after Czechoslovakia — urging the easing of restrictions on East-West trade as "a matter of major priority." The Congress took up the call. Hearings had been held in the Senate during 1968 and a new series of hearings were held on the virtues of greater trade with the Soviet Union.

Arms control, of course, was seen almost universally as an area for a breakthrough: first because of the mutuality of interest in avoiding nuclear war, and second because the levels of strategic forces were thought to be roughly equal in 1969. A Council on Foreign Relations study group chaired by Carl Kaysen (deputy national security adviser in the Kennedy Administration) and joined by many of the foremost academic specialists on arms control sent the President-elect a report in January 1969 urging an early strategic arms limitation agreement as "imperative." It argued that a rare opportunity might slip away, and called for a unilateral moratorium on American deployment of antiballistic missiles (ABMs) and multiple independently targetable reentry vehicles (MIRVs) in order to make a strategic arms limitation agreement possible. The United Nations Association panel cited above urged "the necessary and urgent early initiation of bilateral strategic missile negotiations with the Soviet Union."

In Europe, a tendency emerged, intensified to some extent by our Vietnam involvement, to distance itself somewhat from American policy toward the Soviet Union. De Gaulle had pioneered in doing business bilaterally with the USSR; he visited Moscow in 1966. British Prime Ministers of both parties had posed at the Kremlin in astrakhan hats to show their commitment to peace. In West Germany, even before Willy Brandt's accession as Chancellor in 1969, the Grand Coalition of which

Brandt was Foreign Minister thawed Germany's earlier rigid stance toward Eastern Europe and engaged in direct talks with the Soviet Union. The more rigid the posture of the United States toward the Soviet Union, the greater the temptation of allied leaders to play the role of "bridge" between East and West. It was tempting to European leaders to assure their publics that they would not allow American recklessness to produce a world war. Allied countries found it prudent to show interest in mutual force reductions and the long-standing Soviet proposal of a European Security Conference. In these circumstances the prospect was real that a "differential détente" would develop; the Soviet Union could play to these attitudes in Europe while remaining intransigent on global issues of concern to us, thus driving a wedge between us and our allies.

The overwhelming impulse throughout the West, in the United States as well as in Europe, was to resume the active pursuit of détente and not to allow the Czech invasion to disrupt it. President Johnson declared in a speech to B'nai B'rith on September 10, 1968, barely three weeks after Czechoslovakia: "We hope — and we shall strive — to make this setback a very temporary one." It was strange that in the wake of Czechoslovakia it was America that was asked to demonstrate its good faith. Nor was it clear what concrete facts justified the undoubted sense of hope and urgency summed up by a *Washington Star* editorial which concluded on March 9 that "If there is to be a time for detente this is it." In this atmosphere the Soviet Union chose Inauguration Day to speak out for immediate commencement of strategic arms limitation talks (which came to be referred to as SALT).

The President was not willing to be stampeded. He was determined to impress on the Soviet leaders that we would not negotiate simply to create a better atmosphere, would not meet at the summit without preparation and the prospect of some genuine achievements, and would not accept a process in which the Soviet Union could determine the agenda of the conferences. I shared these views. We needed time to define our purposes, to develop our strategy, and to determine Soviet attitudes on the matters we considered vital. We did not think that the opportunity would prove as fleeting as the advocates of immediate talks implied or that Soviet leaders would react so petulantly. In fact, we believed the perfect way to wreck a negotiation was to enter it unprepared or to let the Soviet leaders believe that we could be pressured by propaganda.

In fact, we were quite willing to enter negotiations, perhaps of unprecedented scope, aiming for fundamental settlements. But we wanted these negotiations to reflect a deliberate strategy, not a reaction to Soviet maneuvers; we thought it essential to create the correct balance of incentives. In my February 6 background briefing to the press I stressed the importance of linkage: "What we have asked for . . . is that there should be some indication of a willingness to lower the level of political tensions, some demonstration of something other than words that together with reducing the competition on arms there will be an attempt to reduce the conflict in the political fields.'' In concrete terms this meant that we would not ignore, as our predecessors had done, the role of the Soviet Union in making the war in Vietnam possible. Nor would we refrain from seeking to exploit Soviet anxieties (for example, about China) to move it toward a more broadly accommodating policy.

But the public and Congressional temper was decidedly different. Unusual for the honeymoon period of a President's term was the barrage of criticism of the concept of linkage and the President's strategy toward the Soviet Union once these became apparent. ''The missile talks evidently can start at Mr. Nixon's convenience,'' the *Washington Post* editorialized one day after the Inauguration. ''They offer him an immediate opportunity, his first, to apply his expressed belief that the 'era of confrontation' in East-West relations has given way to an 'era of negotiations'. . . . His testing in the highest role he has staked out for himself, that of 'peacemaker,' is upon him.'' *Time* magazine in its post-inaugural issue (January 31) raised expectations of early progress: ''The Russians chose Nixon's inauguration day to prod the US — and to emphasize to the world that the next move is up to Washington. . . . Some diplomats and disarmament experts in Washington believe that Nixon and Rogers have already concluded that talks should be held — and that a conference may actually begin in two to four months.''

But, so the helpful advice ran, if this opportunity was to be seized, the opening for talks had to be freed of any preconditions or linkage. ''The President has indicated,'' editorialized the *New York Times* on February 18,

that he intends to reverse American policy of the past dozen years by linking projected Soviet-American negotiations on strategic arms control with those on political issues. But nothing is more likely to alarm the NATO allies. . . . [T]he kind of across-the-board negotiation with the Soviet Union that he seems to have in mind, covering a number of East-West issues, undoubtedly would arouse concern in most West European countries just when Mr. Nixon is seeking to gain their confidence. Moreover, East-West political issues, such as the Middle East, Vietnam and Germany, will be difficult to settle, while strategic arms issues are ripe for resolution.

(Within months our allies were to be alarmed precisely by the prospect of unlinking the issues.) The *Washington Post* weighed in with a similar theme on April 5:

President Nixon has got to stop dawdling and move quickly into missile talks with the Russians. The grace period allowed a new President to be briefed and to set his own tactics is over. Yet the Nixon Administration is still futzing around. . . . Well, when? The Russians have been ready almost a year.

And on linkage:

Reality is too complex and sticky to permit any President to believe he can line up so many different ducks in a row. Arms control has a value and urgency entirely apart from the status of political issues.
Moreover, the whole history of East-West relations warns against linkage.

It was "more urgent than ever" to start the talks, wrote *Business Week* on March 22. "The Nixon Administration is dragging its feet," R. H. Shackford of the Scripps-Howard newspapers had written on February 19. The *New York Post* demanded on March 27 that the Administration "cease stalling forthwith."

Leading Senators and other public figures struck the same themes; our predecessors gave us a period of grace lasting a few weeks at most. Senator Frank Church of Idaho on the Senate floor on February 4 warned that we had to come to the rescue of Kremlin "doves": "The position and credibility of those within the Soviet Government who argue for missile talks will be damaged, perhaps beyond repair, if President Nixon listens to those in the United States who argue against immediate talks on missile limitation." Senator Albert Gore of Tennessee opened hearings of his disarmament subcommittee in early March by declaring: "It may be that we have an unparalleled opportunity to arrest a developing escalation of another nuclear armaments race." Former Defense Secretary Clark Clifford, who two months earlier had submitted a defense budget containing funds for both ABM defense and MIRVs, made a speech in mid-March calling for a freeze in the programs he had himself proposed: "The hard fact is that we may never again expect to be in as favorable a position as we now enjoy for entry into talks about a freeze in strategic nuclear armaments. Technological developments may well make any arms limitation agreement more difficult to develop and enforce a year from now, or 6 months from now, than it is today."[17]

These views found resonance within the bureaucracy. Diplomats are always in favor of negotiations; they are the lifeblood of the profession. Soviet affairs in the State Department had attracted some of our most distinguished Foreign Service Officers, men like Llewellyn Thompson, Charles Bohlen, and George Kennan. Theirs had been a little appreciated specialty. They had sought to keep alive an interest in the Soviet relationship during a period when the bare recognition of the Soviet Union (not accomplished until 1933) seemed the ultimate limit for United States diplomacy. They were appalled when during the Second World War uncritical rejection of all things Soviet gave way to undiscriminating acceptance. They wrote prescient analyses on the dynamics of Soviet society during that period. George Kennan came as close to authoring the diplomatic doctrine of his era as any diplomat in our history. Perhaps it was inevitable that a lifetime of specialization would produce a commitment to US–Soviet relationships that was not without its emotional component. Having suffered through decades when communications were practically cut off, partly by the severity of our approach but above all by the paranoia of the Soviet leadership under Stalin, these diplomats saw in the periodic post-Stalin peace offensives the beginning at last of the realization of hopes of a lifetime.

When we came into office, Llewellyn Thompson, in particular, then senior State Department adviser on Soviet affairs, urged the rapid acceptance of Soviet overtures lest the balance of forces within the Kremlin shift again to a hard line. It did not stem the tide that Nixon at a National Security Council meeting on January 25 stressed his determination to control negotiations with the Soviet Union from the White House. It did not affect the bureaucratic momentum that the President used every opportunity to emphasize that he did not wish to commit himself to a specific date for talks on arms limitation until he had explored Soviet cooperativeness on political issues, especially Vietnam.

The NSC procedures that supposedly established my dictatorial control were not able in this instance to produce any coherent approach or settled policy. Late that month I asked for a study of alternative approaches and views "on the nature of U.S.–Soviet relations . . . in their broadest sense." It resulted in a synthetic options paper prepared by the State Department which, in a fashion soon to become standard, bracketed the only viable option, "Limited Adversary Relationship," between two obviously phony ones, hostility and all-out conciliation. Even the definition of "Limited Adversary Relationship" was worded in such a way as to permit each agency to pursue its preferences unimpeded. A principal problem was the flat refusal of the President to confront his advisers directly on the central question. There never took place a meeting at which the issue was formally thrashed out and settled because Nixon wanted to avoid a face-to-face confrontation with his Secretary of State. Instead, Nixon sent out a letter on February 4 to Rogers, Laird, and Helms — but really intended for Rogers — that reiterated linkage as official policy:

I believe that the tone of our public and private discourse about and with the Soviet Union should be calm, courteous and non-polemical. . . .

I believe that the basis for a viable settlement is a mutual recognition of our vital interests. We must recognize that the Soviet Union has interests; in the present circumstances we cannot but take account of them in defining our own. We should leave the Soviet leadership in no doubt that we expect them to adopt a similar approach toward us. . . . In the past, we have often attempted to settle things in a fit of enthusiasm, relying on personal diplomacy. But the "spirit" that permeated various meetings lacked a solid basis of mutual interest, and therefore, every summit meeting was followed by a crisis in less than a year.

I am convinced that the great issues are fundamentally interrelated. I do not mean this to establish artificial linkages between specific elements of one or another issue or between tactical steps that we may elect to take. But I do believe that crisis or confrontation in one place and real cooperation in another cannot long be sustained simultaneously. I recognize that the previous Administration took the view that when we perceive a mutual interest on an issue with the USSR, we should pursue agreement and attempt to insulate it as much as possible from the ups and downs of conflicts elsewhere. This may well be sound on numerous bilateral and practical matters such as cultural or scientific exchanges. But, on the crucial issues of our day, I believe we must seek to advance on a front at least broad enough to make clear that we see some relationship between political and military issues. I believe that the Soviet leaders should be brought to understand that they cannot expect to reap the benefits of cooperation in one area while seeking to take advantage of tension or confrontation elsewhere. Such a course involves the danger that the Soviets will use talks on arms as a safety valve on intransigence elsewhere. . . .

. . . I would like to illustrate what I have in mind in one case of immediate and widespread interest — the proposed talks on strategic weapons. I believe our decision on when and how to proceed does not depend exclusively on our review of the purely military and technical issues, although these are of key importance. This decision should also be taken in the light of the prevailing political context and, in particular, in light of progress toward stabilizing the explosive Middle East situation, and in light of the Paris talks [on Vietnam]. I believe I should retain the freedom to ensure, to the extent that we have control over it, that the timing of talks with the Soviet Union on strategic weapons is optimal. This may, in fact, mean delay beyond that required for our review of the technical issues. Indeed, it means that we should — at least in our public position — keep open the option that there may be no talks at all.

The letter stated what in fact Nixon carried out, if with many detours. But since the letter was assumed — quite correctly — to have been drafted by my staff and me, it was dismissed as reflecting the malign impact of the President's adviser. The State Department was most eager for liberalizing East-West trade unilaterally, for injecting us into the Middle East conflict in a way that magnified rather than reduced Soviet influence, and above all for beginning SALT as soon as possible. Any White House directive to the contrary was interpreted with the widest possible latitude if it was not ignored altogether. (In this case the letter, being a personal one to the Cabinet Secretaries, undoubtedly never reached the bureaucracy.)

In spite of the President's seemingly explicit and unambiguous statement that he believed in linkage and was not yet committed to the unqualified opening of SALT, on March 19 our disarmament negotiator Gerard C. Smith told his Soviet counterpart Alexei Roshchin in Geneva that the start of SALT "need not be tied, in some sort of package formula, to the settlement of specific international problems." On March 27 Secretary of State Rogers testified before the Senate Foreign Relations Committee that "we hope such talks can begin within the next few months. . . . We have already agreed with the Soviet Union that we will have these talks fairly soon." Asked at an April 7 press conference whether something stood in the way of SALT, Rogers replied: "No, there is nothing that stands in the way, and they can go forward soon. We are in the process of preparing for them now, and we expect they will begin in the late spring or early summer." A State Department draft for the President's address to the North Atlantic Council for April 10 had the President announcing: "I have instructed our Ambassador in Moscow today to advise the Soviet government that we shall be pleased to start these talks in Geneva on April . . . ," leaving it to the President to fill in a date for something he had explicitly rejected five weeks earlier. The stratagem was apparent: State, thinking the President had been unduly influenced by me, sought to bypass me via a speechwriter.

Day after day that spring the bureaucracy chipped away at the President's declared policy, feeding expectations of arms talks. In the *New York Times* of April 18, "officials" were reported contending that arms agreements with the Soviet Union "are an overriding goal of the Nixon foreign policy." On April 22 the *Times* cited "American diplomats" speculating about SALT talks in June. On May 4, Llewellyn Thompson told Dobrynin that Rogers hoped to discuss a date and place with Dobrynin before Rogers left May 12 on his trip to Asia. On May 8, Rogers told Dobrynin that he expected to be able to discuss a date, place, and modalities immediately after his return from Asia, citing the target of "early summer." The same day, our Ambassador in Moscow, Jacob Beam, saw Soviet Deputy Foreign Minister Vasily V. Kuznetsov and, on instructions from Rogers, repeated the target dates of June or July: Kuznetsov said the Soviets were ready. On May 13 Chalmers Roberts in the *Washington Post,* citing Administration sources, said Rogers would meet Dobrynin on May 29 and set a date; the Soviets had reportedly reiterated their readiness. On May 14, UPI reported from Geneva that the United States was ready to start SALT in early July. On May 14, the British government approached the State Department for guidance on how to comment publicly on SALT, which they were led to believe was imminent. Other NATO allies, under the same impression, followed suit. On May 16 in Washington, Gerard Smith gave West German Ambassador Rolf Pauls a briefing on SALT, speculating that negotiations would probably have to address both MIRV and ABM and could begin "during the summer."

These preemptive statements and cumulative pressures were not the result of an articulated conceptual difference between the Secretary of State and the President. They were a series of tactical day-to-day deviations from White House policy. They were intended to crystallize a decision. What they did was to expend, wholesale, assets we wanted to hoard in accordance with a careful strategy. The Soviets were eager for SALT; we intended to draw out the Soviets on other issues like Vietnam. For a brief period in the spring of that first year, the visible discrepancy between the White House and State Department gave the Soviet Union an opportunity to maneuver within our government, to egg on the State Department, media, and Congress as a deliberate form of pressure on the White House.

The cumulative impact of all the bureaucratic indiscipline, with media and Congressional pressures added, was that we had to abandon our attempt to use the opening of SALT talks as a lever for other negotiations. On June 11 we authorized Rogers to inform the Soviets that we were ready to start SALT — only to be met by four months of *Soviet* stonewalling.

But the bureaucracy's victory was Pyrrhic. After yielding on the opening date, Nixon, buttressed by me, moved the conduct of negotiations more and more into the White House. While his preference for secrecy would have inclined him in this direction anyway, the bureaucracy's indiscipline accelerated it. The Soviet leaders soon learned that while the President might be reluctant to confront his Secretary of State and while he might now and then withdraw tactically, Nixon had no intention to defer to others on the fundamental determination of our foreign policy. Once the Soviets understood that the decisions actually carried out were those made by the President, direct contact developed between Ambassador Dobrynin and the White House. There sprang into existence what came to be known in US–Soviet parlance as "the Channel."

The Channel

M Y encounter with the extraordinary Soviet Ambassador in his apartment on February 14 was the first of a series of intimate exchanges that continued over eight years. Increasingly, the most sensitive business in US–Soviet relations came to be handled between Dobrynin and me. We met almost invariably in the Map Room of the White House, a pleasant room off the Diplomatic Entrance whose view is obscured by the rhododendron bushes planted in the garden. Franklin Roosevelt had used it as his planning room during World War II — hence its name.

Dobrynin and I began to conduct preliminary negotiations on almost all major issues, he on behalf of the Politburo, I as confidant to Nixon. We would, informally, clarify the basic purposes of our governments and when our talks gave hope of specific agreements, the subject was moved to conventional diplomatic channels. If formal negotiations there reached a deadlock, the Channel would open up again. We developed some procedures to avoid the sort of deadlock that can only be resolved as a test of strength. With the President's permission I would sometimes sketch our view as my own idea, stating I was "thinking out loud." Dobrynin would then give me the Kremlin's reaction on the same non-committal basis. Sometimes the procedure was reversed. Neither side was precluded from raising the issue formally because of adverse reaction from the other. But at least inadvertent confrontations were prevented. It was a way to explore the terrain, to avoid major deadlocks.

Dobrynin was admirably suited to this delicate role. Ambassadors nowadays have little freedom as negotiators. The telephone and telex from home can give them a detailed brief; they can also change it within the hour. But if jet-age ambassadors have become diplomatic postmen they are crucial as political interpreters — and *before* there is an emergency. Officials at home spend so much time managing cumbersome bureaucracies that they have little feel for the complexities of other capitals and leaders — starkly less, certainly, than in the days when the world's significant diplomats all came from similar backgrounds and communicated within the same cultural framework. There is no substitute for the insight of a man on the spot who mixes enough to take the pulse of political life without becoming so absorbed as to lose perspective. His role is crucial in crises when judgments affecting matters of life and death depend on a subtle and rapid understanding of intangibles.

This is a particular challenge to Soviet ambassadors. They are the product of a bureaucracy that rewards discipline and discourages initiative; of a society historically distrustful of foreigners; of a people hiding its latent insecurity by heavy-handed self-assertiveness. With some Soviet diplomats one has the uneasy feeling that they report in a way to suit the preconceptions of their faraway but ever-watchful superiors, for in this manner they can most easily avoid the charge of flawed judgment. Most Soviet diplomats certainly cling rigidly to formal positions, for they can never be accused in Moscow of unnecessary compromise if they show no initiative. They repeat standard arguments because they cannot hazard a challenge to ideological orthodoxy. Only rarely do they explain the reasons for their positions in any but the most formal terms, for they do not want to risk being blamed at home for inadequate advocacy or suggest without authorization that Soviet purposes are subject to negotiation.

Dobrynin avoided these professional deformations. He was a classic product of the Communist society. Born into a family of twelve children, and the first member of his family to go to a university, he had benefited from the system that he represented so ably. He was trained as an electrical engineer and seconded to the Foreign Office during the war. Whether he owed his flexibility to his training in a subject relatively free of deadening ideology, or to a natural disposition, he was one of the few Soviet diplomats of my acquaintance who could understand the psychology of others. He was suave not just by Soviet standards — which leave ample room for clumsiness — but by any criteria. He knew how to talk to Americans in a way brilliantly attuned to their preconceptions. He too was especially skilled at evoking the inexhaustible American sense of guilt, by persistently but pleasantly hammering home the impression that every deadlock was our fault.

I never forgot that Dobrynin was a member of the Central Committee of the Soviet Communist Party; I never indulged in the conceit that his easy manner reflected any predisposition toward me or toward the West. I had no doubt that if the interests of his country required it he could be as ruthless or duplicitous as any other Communist leader. I took it for granted that his effectiveness depended on the skill with which he reflected his government's policies, not his personal preferences. But I considered his unquestioning support of the Soviet line an asset, not a liability; it enabled us to measure the policies of his masters with precision and buttressed his own influence at home. It would have been enough for our purposes that he should have an extraordinary understanding of the American scene. Occasionally he would give me his personal analysis of American politics; without exception it was acute and even wise. This gave us some confidence that the Kremlin would have at its disposal a sophisticated assessment of conditions here. An accurate understanding could not guarantee that Moscow would choose our preferred response, but it reduced the prospects of gross miscalculation.

Dobrynin was free of the tendency toward petty chiseling by which the run-of-the-mill Soviet diplomat demonstrates his vigilance to his superiors; he understood that a reputation for reliability is an important asset in foreign policy. Subtle and disciplined, warm in his demeanor while wary in his conduct, Dobrynin moved through the upper echelons of Washington with consummate skill. His personal role within the margin available to ambassadors was almost certainly beneficial to US–Soviet relations. If someday there should come about the genuine relaxation of tensions and dangers which our period demands, Anatoly Dobrynin will have made a central contribution to it.

In February 1969 we were at the very beginning. Each side was still trying to get a sense of the other. Dobrynin's request for an appointment with the President confronted Nixon with a procedural and a substantive problem. Procedurally, Nixon wished to establish his dominance over negotiations with the Soviet Union; in his mind, this required the exclusion of Rogers, who might be too anxious and who might claim credit for whatever progress might be made. Substantively, he wanted to begin the linkage approach at his own pace. Nixon sought to solve the Rogers problem in his customary fashion by letting Haldeman bear the onus (and no doubt Haldeman laid it off on me). Haldeman told the Secretary of State that the best guarantee for not raising expectations was for Rogers to be absent from the meeting. Attendance by Rogers would convey a sense of urgency contrary to our strategy; it might lead to an undue sense of optimism. Rogers, not used to such solicitude from his old friend, proved resistant to this thoughtfulness; a good part of the weekend was spent fighting off Rogers's pleas — basically not unjustified — that the Secretary of State participate in the first meeting between the new President and the Soviet Ambassador.

But this was the sort of issue on which Nixon never yielded as long as he could find someone else to do the dirty work. Rogers did not attend the meeting. As a sop to institutional prestige, Malcolm Toon, then director of Soviet affairs at the State Department (and later a first-class Ambassador to Moscow), was invited. Even that was deprived of significance, however, because Nixon dismissed Toon and me at the end of the session and then told Dobrynin privately that matters of special sensitivity should be taken up with me first.

The Channel was thus formally established.

Before his meeting with Dobrynin, Nixon asked me to write a memorandum outlining what Dobrynin was likely to raise, his objectives and the general attitude I would recommend. My response predicted that Dobrynin's line would probably be to assure us of Soviet readiness to begin negotiations, especially on SALT; to express concern that we were not sufficiently responsive to the conciliatory stance of the Soviet Union since January 20; to leave an implication that we should not pass up the favorable opportunity; and to establish a direct channel between the President and the Russian leaders. I recommended that if Dobrynin brought a message from the Soviet leadership, the President should be receptive to concrete propositions, but not let the Soviets force the pace by vague offers to talk without indications of substance. Progress, we must insist, depended on specific settlement, not personal diplomacy. Any summit meeting should come at the end of careful preparation. On specific areas the messages should be that continued harassment of Berlin access routes over the issue of Federal Presidential elections would end all hopes of negotiations; that in the Middle East, each side should use its influence for restraint and a flexible diplomacy; that we were determined to end the war in Vietnam and our overall relations with the Soviets depended on their help in settling that conflict. I also included an ambiguous formulation to the effect that if Soviet support failed to materialize "we do not exclude that others who have an interest would be enlisted to bring about progress. . . ." This was a cryptic reference to the Chinese — though it would not be opaque to the astute Dobrynin.

As was his habit, Nixon carefully underlined the sentences in my memorandum that seemed significant to him. He noted the passage emphasizing our commitment to the integrity and vitality of Berlin. He underlined almost every sentence in the sections on the Middle East and Vietnam; he noted the reference to China.

In meetings with foreign leaders Nixon was a superb expositor of carefully prepared positions; he also understood foreign psychologies better than those of most Americans — perhaps he considered them less of a threat. But the give-and-take of negotiations made him nervous; he hated any personal encounter that was not a set piece; he found it painful to insist on his point of view directly. He was impatient with small points and unwilling to confront the prolonged stalemates that are the mechanisms by which settlements are usually achieved. Though Nixon excelled at conceptual discussions, he was too proud to admit to visitors that he required the assistance of even a memorandum. As noted, he conducted his diplomatic encounters by learning by heart the talking points prepared for him — which, in fairness, were drafted to reflect his views if they had previously been discussed between us.

Nixon's antipathy to personal negotiation was not a weakness in a President but a strength. Some of the debacles of our diplomatic history have been perpetrated by Presidents who fancied themselves negotiators. As a general rule the requirements of the office preclude the follow-through and attention to detail negotiation requires. Moreover, when Presidents become negotiators no escape routes are left for diplomacy. Concessions are irrevocable without dishonor. A stalemate stakes the personal prestige of the office; a mistake requires an admission of error. And since heads of government would not have chosen this career without a healthy dose of ego, negotiations can rapidly deteriorate from intractability to confrontation. Negotiations at lower levels — and even the Secretary of State is a low level in relation to the President — permit the head of government to intervene at crucial moments; adjustments can be made at far less cost. By the time heads of government appear on the scene the texts of agreement should already have been settled — so it was most times with the Presidents I served — though a point or two may be left open to justify the claim that the intervention of the principals clinched the issue. Presidents, of course, are responsible for shaping the overall strategy. They must make the key decisions; for this they are accountable, and for it they deserve full credit no matter how much help they receive along the way. When they attempt the tactical implementation of their own strategy they court disaster. Nixon never made that mistake.

The first meeting between Dobrynin and Nixon took place on February 17, 1969. Dobrynin, now recovered from the flu, came into the Oval Office, was introduced to the President, and presented the views of his leadership much along the lines of his conversation with me a few days earlier. He hinted at the possibility of a summit meeting; he did not reject linkage. On the contrary, he asserted a Soviet willingness to negotiate on a number of subjects simultaneously. He said that the Soviet Union was prepared to use its influence to find a solution in the Middle East. And he inquired when we might be ready to engage in talks on the limitation of strategic arms.

Nixon, in the formal manner he adopted when he was keyed up, replied that summits required careful preparations. He stressed the importance of superpower restraint on a global basis; he insisted on the need to defuse the Middle East and Vietnam. Arms talks, too, he said, required careful preparation, and freezing arms would not assure peace unless there was also political restraint. He emphasized the importance we attached to the status of Berlin, to which Dobrynin replied that the Soviet Union would do its utmost to calm the situation.

It was characteristic of Nixon's insecurity with personal encounters that he called me into his office four times that day for reassurance that he had done well. He thought there had been a tough confrontation. My impression was rather the opposite — that the meeting had been on the conciliatory side. Or at least that it went as one would expect of the opening in a chess game between experts. Each side made moves to maintain the maximum number of options; each side sought to protect itself against some unexpected move by the opponent. I could tell Nixon in good conscience that he had done as well as possible.

The next morning, February 18, I sent Nixon a memorandum with my reflections on that first meeting. My conclusion was:

I believe the current Soviet line of conciliation and interest in negotiations, especially on arms control but also on the Middle East, stems in large measure from their uncertainty about the plans of this Administration. They are clearly concerned that you may elect to undertake new weapons programs which would require new and costly decisions in Moscow; they hope that early negotiations would at least counteract such tendencies in Washington. (I doubt that there is much division on this point in the Kremlin, though there may well be substantial ones over the actual terms of an agreement with us.) In a nutshell, I think that at this moment of uncertainty about our intentions (the Soviets see it as a moment of contention between ''reasonable'' and ''adventurous'' forces here), Moscow wants to engage us. Some would argue that regardless of motive, we should not let this moment of Soviet interest pass, lest Moscow swing back to total hostility. My own view is that we should seek to utilize this Soviet interest, stemming as I think it does from anxiety, to induce them to come to grips with the real sources of tension, notably in the Middle East, but also in Vietnam. This approach also would require continued firmness on our part in Berlin.

It was too soon to gauge what the Soviets were up to. Dobrynin had assented to linkage only in the sense that the Soviet leaders indicated their readiness to negotiate on a broad front; they did not agree to making the result of one negotiation conditional on progress in another. Dobrynin had agreed blandly that progress toward peace in Vietnam would help improve the overall relationship; but this formulation was also consistent with an attempt to blackmail us by "reverse linkage." The Soviet offer to be helpful on the Middle East in practice could have meant — and in fact proved to mean — no more than that they were prepared to support their Arab friends.

As it turned out, we were not to break out of our deadlock with the Soviets until 1971. Inconclusive exchanges in 1969 degenerated into a series of confrontations that lasted through 1970. On about ten occasions in 1969 in my monthly meetings with Dobrynin I tried to enlist Soviet cooperation to help end the war in Vietnam. Dobrynin was always evasive. He denied that the Soviet Union had any interest in continuing the war; he warned (extremely mildly in retrospect) against escalation; he never came up with a concrete proposal to end the war.

The President fared no better. On March 26 Nixon wrote to Soviet Premier Alexei Kosygin along the lines of his conversation with Dobrynin of February 17. (Leonid Brezhnev, the General Secretary of the Central Committee of the Communist Party, was to play no obvious public role in foreign policy until the middle of 1971.) Kosygin replied on May 27, adding little to the standard Soviet position. The major new feature of his letter was that, probably emboldened by American domestic criticism of our linkage concept, he now challenged the concept forcefully and openly. Kosygin argued that, "taking into account the complexity of each of these problems by itself, it is hardly worthwhile to attempt somehow to link one with another." We decided not to argue the point; we would simply continue our approach in practice.

On May 14 Dobrynin was given an advance copy of the President's Vietnam speech. By prearrangement, Nixon telephoned me while I was meeting with Dobrynin and invited both of us to the Lincoln Sitting Room to emphasize to Dobrynin his determination to end the war. There was no Soviet response. This was also the Soviet reaction to our proposal of a Vietnam peace mission by Cyrus Vance.* It was in part because of Soviet stonewalling that Nixon scheduled his trip to Romania in August. His purpose was to remind Moscow that we had options toward Eastern Europe and also toward the People's Republic of

---

* These US–Soviet discussions on Vietnam are described in Chapter VIII.

China, of which Romania was a sometime supporter. And in the autumn we refused to invite Andrei Gromyko to Washington for the by now almost traditional *tour d'horizon* with the President on the occasion of Gromyko's annual visit to New York for the UN General Assembly. We indicated that the President would receive the Soviet Foreign Minister should an appointment be requested; this, in turn, the Soviets refused to do.

There was a sameness to Soviet conduct in 1969 that left little doubt of their basic preference for form over substance. By April, as I recounted earlier, a series of lower-level public statements and leaks not authorized in the White House had precipitated a commitment to start SALT talks by "late spring or early summer." When the White House on June 11 authorized informing the Soviets that we were ready to begin talks, our bureaucracy confidently expected a reply in a matter of weeks or less. In fact, the Soviets did not reply for over four months. The reason almost certainly was that they wanted to await the end of the Senate's ABM debate and not spoil the argument of our critics that our ABM program was incompatible with arms control negotiations.

Whatever the reason, it was not until October 20 that Dobrynin called on the President to inform him of Soviet willingness to set a date for the opening of SALT talks. Dobrynin took the occasion to complain about the slow progress of US–Soviet relations in general. Nixon replied that the Soviet Union had every right to make its own decisions but general progress would depend on the Soviet attitude on Vietnam. To drive the point home, I gave Dobrynin the next day as an aide-mémoire the Vietnam portion of the transcript of his conversation with the President; I had deliberately sharpened some points for Moscow's consumption. Dobrynin, as was his practice, had taken no notes during the meeting with Nixon, but he spotted the discrepancies and asked which version he should transmit to Moscow as the official record. I told him to use the written version.

We made no progress on European security, especially Berlin, either. The East Germans started a mini-crisis by harassing access routes in protest of the Federal Presidential election in West Berlin, though three previous elections had passed without incident. On February 22, on the eve of his first visit to Europe, Nixon ordered a step-up of US military traffic to West Berlin. He did so over the anguished disagreement of the State Department. The incident passed because Dobrynin had promised Nixon on February 17 that the Soviet Union would keep the situation calm. On March 5 the Federal election took place in the Reichstag building without a crisis and harassment stopped. When I met Chinese Premier Chou En-lai on my secret trip in July 1971, he offered his own interpretation of these events. He argued that the Soviet Union had deliberately staged the March 1969 border clashes with China to provide a diversion while West German parliamentarians traveled unimpeded to

Berlin. In Chou's view the border clashes were manufactured to permit the Soviets "to escape their responsibilities over Berlin."*

In any case, President Nixon made a public proposal of a Berlin negotiation in his speech at the Siemens factory in West Berlin on his European trip on February 27. After reaffirming our resolve to defend the city, he expressed the hope that Berlin could become an object of "negotiation . . . and reconciliation" instead of threats and coercion. An offer to discuss Berlin was also included in the President's letter to Kosygin on March 26. At the NATO meeting in Washington in April, the three Western allies responsible for Berlin — France, Britain, and the United States — were urged by the Federal Republic to approach the Soviets about Berlin. Allied consultations to this end proceeded over the summer. On July 10 Gromyko publicly declared Soviet willingness "to exchange views as to how complications concerning West Berlin can be prevented now and in the future." West German Chancellor Kurt Kiesinger, not unaware of the benefits of an easing of tensions for the German elections scheduled for September, urged speedy acceptance. On August 7 the Western allies indicated a willingness to open talks. The Soviets waited until well into September — or just before the German elections — before giving an evasive reply; it did little but repeat Gromyko's general phrases and stress the sovereignty of the East German regime (not yet recognized by any of the Western powers). The Soviets evaded any commitment to talk about improving access and proposed instead a negotiation on curbing West German activities in Berlin.

This Soviet reply seemed to me "virtually no substantive advance," as I described it in a memorandum to the President. Once again the Soviets were seeking all the atmospheric advantages surrounding the opening of negotiations on another major issue without any indication that they were prepared for substantive progress. I concluded: "They are obviously in no hurry, and I see no reasons for us to be, especially since pushing the negotiation runs some danger of forcing the Soviets simply to repeat their rigid support for East German 'sovereignty.' "

What the Soviet leaders did try to arrange over Berlin were bilateral talks with the United States. Kosygin in his letter of May 27 had picked up the President's offer to discuss the subject and Dobrynin, in his conversation with Nixon on October 20, made the formal proposal. Given the Soviets' unwillingness to discuss the improvements in access to Berlin that we desired, I recommended that we discourage the notion of bilateral talks. The Soviets would only use them to stir up suspicions among our allies. We would do best to keep this issue in the regular Four-Power forum for the moment, I suggested.

---

* The March 1969 military flare-up along the Sino-Soviet border is described in Chapter VI.

The Soviets adopted a similar tactic on the Middle East. Once again they opened with urgent requests for talks. When these began, as Chapter X will describe, the Soviets embraced the standard radical Arab position, which they must have known was not negotiable. For months we were told that the Soviet Union could not ask its clients for concessions until the United States had clarified its positions on frontiers; we finally did so on October 28, substantially accepting the 1967 borders. No Soviet reply was received for two months; when it came it offered nothing. As far as the Soviets were concerned, 1969 was a flight from concreteness.

But if the Soviets procrastinated there was no shortage of Americans urging an acceleration of negotiations in almost all areas.

Preparing for SALT

A	MBASSADOR Gerard C. Smith was appointed our chief negotiator for SALT and head of the Arms Control and Disarmament Agency in early March 1969. Though he and I often disagreed, I considered it an excellent appointment. Dedicated, indefatigable, and shrewd, Smith was one of those talented executives who serve successive administrations and epitomize the ideal of public service. It was easy to underestimate him because of his occasionally ponderous manner. But he knew his way around Washington; he was no novice at the bureaucratic game. Considering that he had no power base of his own, he was able to generate astonishing pressures. He was agile in drafting instructions for himself that permitted his nominal superiors only a minimum influence over his discretionary powers; he was not unskillful either in interpreting directives he did not happen to agree with to make them conform to his preferences. Withal, he was always cheerful and honorable, a stolid warrior for a good cause. That cause was the control of arms; it was the assignment of his agency to keep that objective alive within our government; he did it with irrepressible persistence.

I have described earlier the pressures that moved the Administration toward offering a date for opening SALT talks and how, contrary to the campaigners, the Soviets did not respond for four months. This fortunately gave us the bonus of additional time for preparation and enabled us to impose coherence on the negotiations when they finally opened.

I had issued a directive on March 6 requesting options for the US negotiating position. This request was honored mostly in the breach. The officials at the second and third levels were mostly holdovers from the previous Administration. Naturally the option they preferred was the one that Johnson would have proposed to Kosygin had his cherished summit at Leningrad taken place. The bureaucracy had labored through the summer of 1968 and given birth to an elaborate consensus proposal.

A major advantage was that it had been accepted by the Joint Chiefs of Staff. This minor bureaucratic triumph lost some of its luster, however, when one examined its principal feature: a freeze on both land-based and sea-based strategic missiles. Though in 1969 the growing Soviet arsenal of land-based missiles was beginning to approach ours in number, the Russians remained far behind in submarine-launched missiles. When one added our large advantage in intercontinental bombers (omitted from the proposal), the probability that the Soviets would accept the freeze was not overwhelming.

My effort to broaden the President's choices involved unusual bureaucratic difficulties. Nixon took a keen interest in the strategy for SALT and in what channels it should be negotiated. But the details of the various plans bored him; in effect he left the selection of options to me. Yet if the bureaucracy had become aware of this, all vestige of discipline would have disappeared. I therefore scheduled over Nixon's impatient protests a series of NSC meetings where options were presented to a glassy-eyed and irritable President so that directives could be issued with some plausibility on his authority.

In order to bring some order into the NSC discussion I asked for a range of options, including both limited and comprehensive approaches. The conviction with which these were pursued was shown by the fact that when subjected to analysis all of the options except one left us strategically *worse off* than if there were no agreement at all. The unexpected delay in the opening of SALT provided us with the opportunity to get our house in order. I learned a great deal from an interagency panel Richardson and I set up charged with a systematic analysis of the strategic implications of limits on MIRVs, the verifiability of such limits, and the possibilities and risks of evasion. After some weeks I expanded this assignment to cover not only MIRVs but all strategic weapons potentially the subject of negotiations. The CIA was asked to assess the verifiability of each weapon limitation proposed — how we could check up on compliance, how much cheating could take place before discovery, and the strategic consequences of the possible violations. The Defense Department was requested to analyze what remedial measures were available and the time it would take to implement them. When the first interagency options papers came before the Review Group, I told my colleagues that the mind boggled at the possible combinations of negotiating positions and it was not fair to the President to ask him to sort them out. So we went back to the drawing board and tried a new approach. We analyzed the possible limitations weapon by weapon, singly and then in combination. The possible limitations were grouped into some seven packages, each of which we thought compatible with our security; these were to serve as building blocks from which to construct specific proposals or to modify them. We were thus in a position to respond flexibly to Soviet ideas without each time having to develop a new US position among ourselves. The result was the most comprehensive study of the strategic and verification implications of the control of weapons ever undertaken by our government and probably any government. Our negotiating position would reflect not bureaucratic compromise but careful analysis of consequences and objectives.

An unintended benefit of these studies was the education and bureaucratic backstopping they provided for my later negotiations on SALT with Dobrynin in the White House Channel. It enabled me to tell which options commanded a bureaucratic consensus and yet to maintain the secrecy of the talks. I would thus deal with Dobrynin knowing I was on relatively safe ground. (This did not totally protect me against Monday-morning quarterbacking, however.)

The first official session of SALT was to begin in Helsinki on November 17, 1969. As we examined the various building blocks and the absence of any governmental consensus it seemed to me wisest to treat the session as exploratory. We did not want to give the Soviet Union an opportunity to score a propaganda coup, or risk failure by putting forward clearly unacceptable proposals. Gerard Smith supported this view for his own reasons; he was afraid that he might not like the instructions which the President was most probably going to issue; he hoped to use the first session to elicit from the Soviets proposals that he favored for a ban on ABMs and a moratorium on MIRV testing. As often in big bureaucracies, different motives produced instructions to the effect that the opening talks were to develop a work program and to draw out Soviet views on procedures. We would make clear our willingness to discuss limitations on both offensive and defensive weapons systems. Verifiability would be stressed. To curb excessive enthusiasm, the delegation was instructed to refer any proposals for MIRV or other moratoriums to Washington.

The first round of the strategic arms limitation talks began as scheduled and lasted till December 22. An early impasse developed over what constituted a strategic weapon. The Soviets defined as "strategic" any weapon that could reach the territory of the other side, thereby sweeping in our forward-based aircraft in Western Europe as well as our carrier-based aircraft, but neatly excluding their own medium- and intermediate-range ballistic missiles and large fleet of medium bombers targeted at Western Europe. The scheme had the additional political advantage of elaborating a distinction between our security concerns and those of Western Europe, thus straining the Western Alliance. Needless to say, we rejected the Soviet definition. The Soviets similarly raised the issue of "non-dissemination" of nuclear weapons, which called into question our cooperation with our British ally on nuclear matters and indeed possibly with the whole NATO defense establishment.

The Soviets were most eager to talk about the weapons system that so many experts had opposed because they alleged that it would make all SALT negotiations impossible — the ABM. And much to the surprise of our SALT delegation, the Soviets showed no interest in a MIRV ban. They did not raise it, or respond when we brought it up. On the whole their tone was precise, nonpolemic, businesslike, and serious.

I evaluated the results in a Washington background briefing on December 18:

> We were told before we went to Helsinki by many people that if we didn't go there with a position, the Soviets would lose confidence in us, or we were told if we didn't go there with a detailed position the Soviets would preempt the field with a spectacular of their own.
>
> In fact the curious thing seems to have happened that the Soviet preparations have taken about the same form as ours; that is, they have made a detailed analysis of the problems and I consider that one of the more hopeful signs, regardless of what may come out in the next phase of the talks.

The SALT process with all its bureaucratic stresses had brought matters about where we wanted them. We had given up no strategic programs as an admission price. We had made no unilateral concessions. We had educated our government in both the importance and the complexity of the subject. We had made clear to the Soviets that they would have to be precise, that they would get nowhere with propaganda. But we were also committed to progress. We would not treat the nuclear weapon as simply another weapon; once started on the course we would proceed toward the limitation of strategic arms without illusion but also without respite, with dedication to security and also with the conviction that future generations should know that we seized all opportunities to push back the specter of nuclear war. We would not neglect our defenses; we would not risk falling behind; we never forgot that the future of freedom depended on our nuclear strength. But the nuclear buildup was unlike any other arms race in history. It staked the lives of all human beings. It imposed an obligation for arms control that we had no right to shirk.

East-West Trade

O NE of the curiosities of Communism is that an ideology founded on the inexorable influence of economics should do so poorly in delivering the goods. Whenever market economies and Communist economies have competed in roughly comparable circumstances, the Communist economies have been left far behind. By whatever standard one compares West and East Germany, Austria and Czechoslovakia, South and North Korea, or South and North Vietnam before the forcible unification, the market economies produce more and better goods and services, fulfill more human needs, and create far more pluralist societies than their Communist counterparts. Only in one category have Communist economies scored: the accumulation of military power. Unfortunately, history offers no guarantee that a more humane and beneficent style of life inevitably prevails. Those prepared to deprive themselves over decades may be able to achieve military dominance; sooner or later superior power almost inevitably produces political advantages for the stronger side. This is a challenge the industrial democracies dare not fail to meet.

There are many reasons for the inferior economic performance of Communist societies. Even with the development of modern computers — themselves a sophisticated central industry in which Communist economies are backward — planning cannot escape bottlenecks and bureaucracy. Communist planning creates incentives for managers not to produce more but to understate the productive potential so that they are not caught by failing to fulfill quotas. Communist executives tend to hoard scarce materials to make themselves independent of the vagaries of the planning process. Whatever the causes, it is little wonder that, with shortages and bureaucratic stumbling, the Soviet Union and the East European Communist states have since the late 1950s sought to expand trade with the West as a shortcut to modern technology and capital. We, for our part, have imposed restrictions since the onset of the Cold War in the late Forties, either unilaterally or in concert with our allies. American law prohibited the extension of Most Favored Nation treatment to imports from Communist countries except Poland and Yugoslavia.

As a result, big tariff cuts in later trade negotiations did not apply and imports had to pay the very high tariffs of the 1930 Hawley-Smoot Act. American exports of products or technical data that could enhance Communist military and economic potential needed licenses — rarely given — under the Export Control Act of 1949. United States Export–Import Bank credits or guarantees for any country trading with North Vietnam (effectively all Communist countries) were barred by the so-called Fino Amendment. Any financial or commercial transactions with North Korea, North Vietnam, or Cuba and (until 1971) China needed special license. A common list of prohibited strategic exports, not quite as severe as the American embargoes, was operated from 1950 by the Co-ordinating Committee on Export Controls (COCOM), representing the NATO countries and Japan. Travel to many Communist countries was restricted by US law.

The Nixon Administration came into office when nearly all these restrictions were under attack in the United States. Liberal opinion regarded them as archaisms of the Cold War, which, they argued, was in the process of liquidation. On October 7, 1966, President Johnson had announced a shift from "the narrow concept of co-existence to the broader vision of peaceful engagement." This was expressed in a series of minor liberalizing measures on trade and credits which he was able to take within his administrative discretion. The overture was rebuffed by Brezhnev on October 16: The United States labored under a "strange and persistent delusion" if it believed that relations could be improved while the Vietnam war continued — making Brezhnev the father of the linkage theory.

The issue was quiescent for two years. Then in the spring of 1968, former Presidential Counselor Theodore Sorensen and former Under Secretary of State George Ball led a campaign urging removal of restrictions on East-West trade. Senate hearings were held in June and July 1968. Senator Walter Mondale introduced a resolution urging that these trade barriers be lowered. The discussion of 1968 was only briefly submerged by the Soviet invasion of Czechoslovakia and the Presidential election; it quickly heated up again in early 1969, after Nixon's Inauguration, for the 1949 Export Control Act was due to expire on June 30 of that year.

Hearings were held from April through July of 1969. The only issue in disagreement was not whether but to what degree the existing law should be eased. The *New York Times* declared on June 3 that US trade restrictions were "self-defeating." They were "cold war policies" that were "inconsistent with the Nixon Administration's theory that it is time to move from an era of confrontation into one of negotiation and cooperation" — helpfully instructing the President on what his own policy was. The Administration's apparent reluctance to liberalize the Export Control Act was "inexplicable." The basic argument of Senators like J. William Fulbright, Walter Mondale, and Edmund Muskie was that the Cold War was over, that linking trade to foreign policy only caused suspicions and tensions. Mondale said the restrictions "hold back economic growth in the U.S., not in Eastern Europe." Muskie pointed out that some items could be bought from our European allies. Nicholas Katzenbach, former Under Secretary of State, built a political pyramid: Trade meant freer choices for Soviet consumers and managers, which was the beginning of a freer society, and a more sophisticated Soviet economy would undercut Soviet ideology and stimulate dissent. Maintaining the restrictions for political reasons was denounced as self-denying economically, as futile politically, and as playing into the hands of Stalinist hard-liners.

My own view was of a piece with my general attitude. Given Soviet needs, expanding trade without a political quid pro quo was a gift; there was very little the Soviet Union could do for us economically. It did not seem to me unreasonable to require Soviet restraint in such trouble spots as the Middle East, Berlin, and Southeast Asia in return. Nixon had similar views, with a political edge. He did offer Dobrynin increased trade for help on Vietnam but he was doubtful that the Soviets would take the bait. If not, he saw no sense in antagonizing his old constituency by accepting liberalizing legislation. On the contrary, given the "soft" position he was taking on Vietnam he used East-West trade to refurbish his conservative credentials.

Within the bureaucracy, East-West trade evoked the familiar opposition to linkage. Only the Defense Department generally supported the White House view. The State Department favored liberalization on the ground that it would improve the political atmosphere, which was of course exactly the opposite of the White House view that trade should follow political progress. The Commerce Department's view was the most interesting because it reflected the surprising attitude of much of the American business community. Business leaders are of course vocally anti-Communist. In the abstract they preach hard bargaining with the Communists and they are quick to blame their government for "giveaways." But when it comes to trade, their attitude changes. During my period in office the most fervent advocates of East-West trade without strings were in the group of capitalists so vilified by Leninist theory. They are dedicated to the free market, at least if it means more business for their companies. They resent as "government interference" the apparatus of regulations and restrictions that is the only way to subordinate economic relations to political goals. If the Soviet Union can enter our market for credit or goods on the basis of purely economic criteria, all political leverage disappears. Perhaps businessmen are in addition especially susceptible to the bonhomie with which Soviet officials flatter those whom they wish to influence — a style of slightly inebriated good fellowship not totally unknown in some of the reunions of capitalist trade associations.

East-West trade came up for discussion at an NSC meeting on May 21. The Administration had to take a position on the proposals in Congress to replace the expiring Export Control Act with a more forthcoming law. The government also had to decide on a number of specific licenses that had been requested: for materials for a foundry at a new Soviet truck plant, for an oil extraction plant, and for a small sale of $15 million of corn to the USSR at world market prices. Before the meeting I sent Nixon a briefing paper summing up the agencies' recommendations together with my own. My view was not to oppose but to acquiesce in a new law granting the President discretionary authority to expand trade, while exercising this authority only in return for a political quid pro quo. I also recommended bringing the United States export control list into line with the somewhat more liberal COCOM list, since otherwise we merely lost business to our allies without affecting Communist conduct. Finally, I favored issuing a license for the oil extraction plant because the long lead time for its construction would give us continuing leverage. I opposed licenses for the foundry and the corn sale.

Nixon went against my recommendations. Smarting from the Soviet refusal to help us on Vietnam, he told the NSC meeting: "I do not accept the philosophy that increased trade results in improved political relations. In fact just the converse is true. Better political relations lead to improved trade." This was my belief too, but Nixon took it one step farther. He decreed that the Administration would oppose all legislative efforts to liberalize trade; the specific projects, including the oil extraction plant, were to be "put on ice" for the time being. I pointed out the general consensus that we should bring our restricted list in line with the COCOM list, except for computers and other key items in which we still had in effect a monopoly. The President agreed. A directive was issued on May 28. I saw to it that the directive was phrased in a relatively positive way, keeping open the possibility of increased trade if the political context changed.

No sooner were these instructions issued than the departments began to nibble away at them. Departments accept decisions which go against them only if vigilantly supervised. Otherwise the lower-level exegesis can be breathtaking in its effrontery. It falls on the President's Assistant for National Security to do this policing in the field of national security. I soon had my hands full. Despite the President's explicit orders at the May 21 NSC meeting that trade was not to be liberalized, the Commerce Department in July was about to announce administrative decontrol of about thirty items for export to the USSR and Eastern Europe. This was based on the proposition that Nixon had ruled only against liberalized legislation, not against easing trade by administrative fiat; Commerce therefore considered itself free to undertake a major liberalization of East-West trade *within* existing law. I stopped this move, but had to fight off similar schemes at regular intervals. In October, for example, State and Commerce requested authority for a sale of computers to the USSR for its communications with Eastern Europe; Commerce Secretary Maurice Stans wanted to decontrol a long list of 135 items without any political reciprocity. I disapproved these requests, in accordance with Nixon's decision at the NSC.

We were somewhat more obliging with respect to Eastern Europe, however, but again in the service of a political strategy. Our trade was used as a carrot for those countries pursuing policies relatively independent of the Soviet Union. Thus when the President's trip to Romania was announced on June 28, I asked Elliot Richardson and the Under Secretaries Committee of the NSC to recommend trade concessions that could be offered to the Romanians. After the President's visit to Romania, the White House actively promoted trade with Romania by whatever administrative steps could be taken. Maury Stans was imaginative and the Science Advisor, Lee DuBridge, came up with excellent ideas on technical cooperation. No sooner had we moved toward Romania, however, than various departments pressed for the liberalization of trade with *all* of Eastern Europe. This would have undermined our deliberate strategy of using trade selectively to encourage political autonomy. It took many months before we made our point.

After prolonged debate, the Congress passed a bill in December, the Export Administration Act of 1969, that liberalized the old Export Control Act and declared it US policy to favor expansion of peaceful trade with the Soviet Union and Eastern Europe. But much of its implementation was left to Presidential discretion.* After a while Moscow began to understand that if it wanted liberalized trade it would have to show restraint in its international conduct and arrange for progress on key foreign policy issues. Eventually the time would come when, consistent with our strategy, we would seek to offer some concessions after the Soviet Union cooperated with us in the political field. Then we suddenly encountered a reversal of attitudes. Many of those who had castigated us for seeking to link trade to Soviet *foreign* policy began to criticize us for not linking it more aggressively to Soviet *domestic* policy. Then, too, we would have to come to grips in earnest with the fundamental issue of East-West trade: if well-designed it forges links whose cumulative effect can reinforce restraints against Soviet aggressiveness; but also it can add to the sinews of Soviet power. It is as wrong to overlook the possibilities as to ignore the dangers.

Eastern Europe: Nixon's Visit to Romania

THE division of Europe along the Elbe River in Central Germany corresponded neither to historical tradition nor to the aspirations of its peoples. In every country of Eastern Europe an essentially alien regime had been imposed by Soviet troops; in three of them popular revolts had been crushed by the Red Army. In no country of Eastern Europe could the Communists win a free election even after a generation of totalitarian rule. The Soviet Union had started on the route of selective détente by seeking to split our allies from us; it seemed to us that détente, to be genuine, had to apply in Eastern Europe as well as Western Europe.

But this raised a problem of extraordinary complexity and indeed tragedy. Clarion calls to liberation had been mocked in 1956 when we stood by as Hungary was brutally suppressed. And again we were para-

---

*Ironically, in light of later events, the President was not given the right to grant Most Favored Nation status to the Soviet Union and Eastern Europe although we could have gotten it had we asked for it. This came back to haunt us a few years later when we sought this authority, and the Congressional mood had meanwhile shifted 180 degrees.

lyzed in 1968 when the Prague uprising was crushed. Our sin was less
betrayal than the raising of expectations we could not possibly fulfill.
The Johnson Administration had announced a policy of "peaceful engagement" seeking to promote trade and cultural relations with Eastern
Europe but had not achieved much beyond enunciation of a clever
theory. We attempted a more differentiated policy to encourage the
countries of Eastern Europe to act more independently within their possibilities. We made no promises we could not back up nor used rhetoric
that might trigger actions doomed to disaster. We would reward those
with a more independent foreign policy and stay aloof where a nation,
by necessity or choice, slavishly followed the Soviet line. Differential
détente could work both ways.

Reacting to a report of the tumultuous greeting given astronaut Frank
Borman in Czechoslovakia, the President sent me a note in early June
1969: "Henry, I believe we could needle our Moscow friends by arranging more visits to the Eastern Europe countries. The people in those
countries, if given a chance, will welcome our Cabinet officers and
others with great enthusiasm."

A few weeks later, Nixon had a more concrete idea — that he should
visit Eastern Europe himself. He suggested including Romania on his
around-the-world trip, making him the first American President to pay a
State visit to a Communist country. He had done this for two reasons:
When he was out of office he had been treated with great respect by the
Romanian leadership on a visit in 1967, in contrast to his treatment in
other East European countries. Nixon never forgot courtesies of this
kind. But his principal reason was to needle the Soviets, or, as he told
me, "By the time we get through with this trip they are going to be out
of their minds that we are playing a Chinese game."

On June 21, on Nixon's instructions, I called in Ambassador Corneliu
Bogdan of Romania and noted that the President was thinking of taking
an around-the-world trip in the second half of July after watching the
Apollo 11 splashdown in the Pacific. Would it be convenient for the
President to stop in Bucharest on August 2 and 3? Within forty-eight
hours, on June 23, we were given the official reply that the Romanian
government welcomed the visit — despite the fact that it would force
postponement of a long-scheduled Romanian party conference to which
the Soviet leadership had been invited. There could be no greater proof
of the importance that Romania attached to a separate opening to Washington and to a Presidential visit.

The dramatic announcement was made on June 28. For the first time
an American President would visit a Communist nation in Eastern
Europe. I blandly told a press briefing that it was not "an anti-Soviet
gesture." The President had "very pleasant recollections" of his meetings with the Romanian leaders when they received him warmly as a

private citizen: "The United States is interested in dealing with the countries of Eastern Europe on the basis of mutual respect. . . . We feel under no obligation to check with the Soviet Union before making visits to sovereign countries."

So pervasive was the assumption that the Nixon Administration was hopelessly bellicose and anti-Soviet that the Romania visit was immediately denounced as reckless. Some in the State Department objected to the Romania visit (which had been arranged through White House channels) as dangerously provocative; they feared it would undermine SALT and other negotiations. The leading newspapers shared this view. The Romania visit was attacked as "disturbing," and as a possible threat to SALT; it was a "blunder" that would unnecessarily antagonize the Soviets, harden the Soviet attitude on all East-West questions — and also bestow American blessing on a "brutal Communist dictatorship."[18]

The Soviets also reacted — in a manner that made clear they understood the significance of the visit. The planned attendance of Brezhnev and Kosygin at the rescheduled Romanian party conference was canceled. I asked Bogdan on July 3 if his government had given the Soviets any advance word. He said he did not know; he thought they might have been informed shortly before the announcement. Romania made its own decisions, he said.

The President arrived in Bucharest on August 2 and received what the *New York Times* called "a warm reception from hundreds of thousands of flag-waving Romanians in the largest and most genuinely friendly welcome of his global tour." He toured a municipal market and a folk dancing school and joined in a dance with Romanian President Nicolae Ceauşescu. The *Times,* now convinced, exclaimed editorially on August 5 that the enthusiastic welcome demonstrated the enormous goodwill the United States enjoyed in Eastern Europe; that the President's themes of peace, national sovereignty, and peaceful coexistence were not clichés to Eastern Europeans, who vividly recalled the Czech invasion.

The overwhelming exuberance of the reception accorded Nixon was of course in part inspired and staged by the government. But even if the reception had been organized, it remained an extraordinary demonstration of Romania's independence from the Soviet Union. And it would have been difficult if not impossible for any government to create the emotional, joyful, human quality of the public outpouring. The streets of Bucharest were lined by hundreds of thousands of people at all times, waiting for a mere glimpse of the Presidential automobile. They did not merely line up along the boulevards coming in from the airport, or only around the guest house where the President stayed; they waited hour by hour in a continuous rain for the mere appearance of Nixon anywhere. It was profoundly moving, the emotional response of the people of a Communist state who so welcomed this first chance to greet the President of a nation that for many of them still stood, as it did in the nineteenth century, as the symbol of democracy and human freedom.

Nixon's public remarks in Bucharest reflected the recurring themes of United States policy: the importance of coexistence, repudiation of the Brezhnev Doctrine, our desire to settle problems by concrete negotiations:

> We see value neither in the exchange of polemics nor in a false euphoria. We seek the substance of détente, not its mere atmosphere.
>
> We seek, in sum, a peace not of hegemonies and not of artificial uniformity, but a peace in which the legitimate interests of each are respected and all are safeguarded.

It was also apparent that East European leaders, not unlike our own allies, feared a Soviet-American deal at their expense. This was not our policy; the President's visit — and his later unprecedented visits to Yugoslavia and Poland — were the best demonstration.

Conclusion

O NE of the innovations of the Nixon Presidency was the preparation of an annual report on foreign policy in the name of the President. I nad proposed this in a memorandum to Nixon in the transition period. It was to serve as a conceptual outline of the President's foreign policy, as a status report, and as an agenda for action. It could simultaneously guide our bureaucracy and inform foreign governments about our thinking.

This idea, patterned after the annual Defense Posture Statement initiated by Robert McNamara, created a whole host of problems. To begin with, the State Department asserted a proprietary interest, in spite of the fact that in the entire history of the Republic the State Department had never thought of issuing such a report. This led to the now customary tug-of-war between Rogers and me of which the most charitable description is that neither of us conducted ourselves better with respect to the annual report than with respect to other matters. Both the NSC staff and the State Department started preparing drafts while seeking to conceal this fact from each other. I and my staffers had the advantage of propinquity to the President and much greater knowledge of his views. The State Department draft further handicapped itself by seeking to please every bureaucratic fiefdom in that unwieldy structure; with every desk officer insisting on a mention of his country or countries of responsibility, the State Department draft was not distinguished by conceptual thrust or the ability to make any particular point.

Nixon resolved this dispute by methods that were becoming typical. He waited until Rogers was out of the country on an African trip and then ruled that both the NSC and the State Department could publish reports but that the Presidential one would appear at least a month before State's. This set off a frantic outburst of drafting on the Presidential report while my exhausted staff tried to deal with my revisions of their drafts and the objections of the bureaucracy. The high point of interagency wrangling was reached in 1971, when the State Department objected to a sentence about international protection of endangered species; our draft observed with some attempt at literary flair that such creatures were a fit topic for international cooperation since they moved without respect to national boundaries and could not totally be protected by national action. The State Department, ever careful, recommended changing the sentence to claim only that "some" of these creatures moved without respect to national boundaries. I did not accept the change, taking the risk of offending some patriotic bird.

Once the President's annual review became established, it produced some of the most thoughtful governmental statements of foreign policy. To our sorrow we never managed to get across its basic purpose of raising fundamental questions and expressing a philosophy. Try as we might, the media would cover only the section on Vietnam, probing for hot news or credibility gaps, ignoring the remainder as not newsworthy. In 1973 we ran into another problem. The report was issued in early May, after a year of Chinese and Soviet summits and climactic Vietnam negotiations; the date we had chosen weeks earlier for release of the report came four days after the resignation of Haldeman and Ehrlichman. Nevertheless, the reports performed a useful function. They served as rough guides to the bureaucracy. They were unusually candid. They were invaluable in conveying nuances of change to foreign governments. As I will show in various chapters, changes in attitude toward China, in defense policy, in the Middle East and elsewhere were often foreshadowed in the President's annual reports.

The President's first report, published on February 18, 1970, stated bluntly that "our overall relationship with the USSR remains far from satisfactory." In Vietnam, "to the detriment of the cause of peace," the Soviets had "failed to exert a helpful influence on the North Vietnamese in Paris" and bore a "heavy responsibility for the continuation of the war" because of its arms supply of North Vietnam. In the Middle East, the report charged that "we have not seen on the Soviet side that practical and constructive flexibility which is necessary for a successful outcome"; even more, the report noted "evidence . . . that the Soviet Union seeks a position in the area as a whole which would make great power rivalry more likely." (This would be proved true in two Middle East crises during 1970.)

These judgments reflected the reality that the Soviet Union was immobile in 1969. But, almost imperceptibly, there were the beginnings of a slow movement forward. The foreign policy decisions of any large state emerge from a complicated pattern of bureaucratic, domestic, and international pressures; the Soviet bureaucracy and policy process are especially tortuous. In 1969 the Soviets had to contend with a new US Administration, which is always a massive analytical problem for Soviet leaders, and we, in addition, were changing procedures. Operating on a broad front in simultaneous negotiations, for example, may not have been merely unfamiliar to the Soviet administrative process; it may have strained its capacity. Even though the apparatus is huge, it narrows to a very few decision-makers at the top. Their orders then filter back through an unwieldy line of command. Decisions tend to be made painstakingly, and since they put at stake the prestige of the top leadership they are changed only with the utmost reluctance. In 1969, furthermore, the conflict with China must have occupied much of the attention span of Soviet leaders. Serious military clashes along the Sino-Soviet border in March and in the summer prompted a major propaganda battle, probably serious policy debates, and later the opening of border talks.

The deepest reason for Soviet immobilism in 1969, however, was undoubtedly that conditions had not yet generated incentives and penalties of sufficient magnitude to impel decision. On Vietnam, the Soviets may have been moderately sincere in their avowed interest in helping us settle the war, knowing that it obstructed US–Soviet relations, but the difficult decision to exert pressure on their ally would never be made in the abstract. Indeed, as long as the risks to US–Soviet relations remained hypothetical, and the benefits of an Indochina settlement conjectural, the line of least resistance in Moscow was procrastination. Circumstances, in other words, failed to provide a spur to a Soviet decision. They faced no penalty for evading our requests for help. Their warnings against our escalation we took seriously at the time, though in retrospect I believe this was a mistake. In rereading the relevant documents for this volume, I am struck by the hedging and cautious tone of Soviet statements. They disparaged escalation as ''solving nothing,'' as ''aggravating the international situation,'' as being in a general way ''dangerous.'' At no time did the Soviets even approach the hint of a threat. On one occasion Dobrynin pointed out that if we resumed bombing of Hanoi and Haiphong, halted by President Johnson in 1968, Chinese engineer battalions withdrawn a few years earlier might reenter Vietnam, which would increase Chinese influence in Hanoi. I said, ''If you can live with it, we can''; Dobrynin was silent.

In retrospect it is clear that only if we posed specific tangible risks to important Soviet interests would the Soviets have an incentive to exert pressure on their monomaniacal clients in Hanoi. Offering positive inducements would help, but unless combined with risks posed by us, inducements would be rejected as too embarrassing to Soviet standing in the Communist world. When we finally did obtain Soviet help in 1972, it was through just such a combination of pressures and incentives. But before the North Vietnamese Easter offensive of 1972 we were never prepared to face the domestic and international consequences of such a course.

If the penalties were unclear to the Soviet leadership, so were the rewards. The President stated repeatedly that negotiations would accelerate in the Middle East once Vietnam was settled; I reinforced his comments. But we were not in a position to answer in precise terms Dobrynin's question to me on May 14: "Supposing the war were settled, how would you go about improving relations?" The best answer I could come up with was a summit and an unspecified promise to improve trade. In the Middle East our interest ran counter to Moscow's; it was the goal of our strategy, after all, to reduce Soviet influence in the Middle East, that of the Soviets to enhance or at least to preserve it. Nor were we prepared to trade that Middle East interest for a settlement in Vietnam.

No doubt domestic politics in America encouraged Soviet tendencies to procrastinate. The early fear that Nixon would embark on massive rearmament was soon superseded by awareness that in the face of mounting Congressional opposition the Administration would be lucky to maintain the existing defense budget. New military programs were fiercely attacked; some passed only by the thinnest of margins; once they were authorized their implementation was systematically whittled down and funds for them reduced annually. All pressures were in the direction of "reordering priorities" away from defense. Nor did it seem probable that America's allies would support a high-risk course in Vietnam. Thus again the Soviets had little reason to be forthcoming.

But while we may have been too optimistic about US–Soviet relations at the beginning of 1969, we began to lay the basis for ultimate progress by our moves in other areas — demonstrating the validity of linkage. We created the strategy that led to the reversal of alliances in the Middle East. We began to move decisively toward China. Our course in Vietnam made Soviet help dispensable for three years and then achievable in 1972. We strengthened Alliance relations. Through turmoil and tensions, we got across to the Soviets that if our style was sober, our policy would be serious and deliberate and at the right moment bold.

I sent the President an analysis of Soviet policy at the end of 1969, which I prepared with the help of Hal Sonnenfeldt and Bill Hyland of my staff. It began by rejecting the proposition that Soviet policy necessarily followed a master plan:

It is always tempting to arrange diverse Soviet moves into a grand design. The more esoteric brands of Kremlinology often purport to see each and every

move as part of the carefully orchestrated score in which events inexorably
move to the grand finale.

Experience has shown that this has rarely if ever been the case. From the
Cuban missile crisis, through the Arab-Israeli war, to the invasion of Czechoslovakia, there has been a large element of improvisation in Soviet policy.

I suspected that this was the case at present. The Kremlin had several
balls in the air. But Soviet actions seemed responses to particular situations. Some analysts saw a close tactical connection between the Sino-
Soviet talks and the Soviet conduct of SALT. By tying the United States
up in prolonged SALT negotiations, the Soviets could exploit the appearance of Soviet-American collusion against China. The main problem with this theory was that the Soviet position in SALT made good
sense without reference to the Chinese situation, and the deterioration of
the Chinese talks could easily be explained on the merits of the issues.
The Soviets had been noncommittal in SALT principally to explore the
terrain as we were doing, and also to determine to what degree we were
under domestic pressure to make concessions or unilateral cutbacks in
our military programs. The Chinese were responding to Soviet military
pressures by feelers toward us. Thus, if the Soviets designed their SALT
moves to impress the Chinese, they succeeded to some extent, but the
result might not have been to Soviet liking; it might, in fact, have
speeded up Chinese contacts with us. In Europe, instead of taking a
conciliatory line in order to free their energies to deal with China, the
Soviets were driving a hard bargain in initial talks with Willy Brandt's
new government — largely because the evident yearning in Western
Europe for détente seemed to provide an opportunity for cheap gains
through intransigence.

My analysis concluded: "In sum, there does not seem to be any
single unifying thread to Soviet policy."

Before this unifying thread could develop, the Soviet leaders had
probed in several directions at once. Only after we had resisted in some
bitter confrontations throughout 1970 and 1971 did our relations take a
turn for the better.

VI

First Steps toward China

WHEN we completed drafting the communiqué announcing my secret visit to China in July 1971, Chou En-lai remarked that the announcement would shake the world. He was right. Not only was it a sensation for the media; overnight it transformed the structure of international politics. After twenty bitter years of isolation an American emissary had stepped onto the mysterious soil of Peking; and his President would shortly follow. It was abrupt and astonishing, but behind the climax were thirty months of patient and deliberate preparation as each side felt its way, gingerly, always testing the ground so that a rebuff would not appear humiliating, graduating its steps so that exposure would not demoralize nervous allies or give a new strategic opportunity to those who did not wish them well.

We took even ourselves by surprise. Originally we had not thought reconciliation possible. We were convinced that the Chinese were fanatic and hostile. But even though we could not initially see a way to achieve it, both Nixon and I believed in the importance of an opening to the People's Republic of China.

Events came to our assistance, but I doubt whether the rapprochement could have occurred with the same decisiveness in any other Presidency. Nixon had an extraordinary instinct for the jugular. He was less interested in tactics or the meticulous accumulation of nuance; too much discussion of details of implementation, indeed, made him nervous. Once he had set a policy direction, he almost invariably left it to me to implement the strategy and manage the bureaucracy. But though I had independently come to the same judgment as Nixon, and though I designed many of the moves, I did not have the political strength or bureaucratic clout to pursue such a fundamental shift of policy on my own. Nixon viscerally understood the essence of the opportunity and pushed for it consistently. He had the political base on the right, which protected him from the charge of being "soft on Communism." And his administrative style lent itself to the secretive, solitary tactics the policy required. If the NSC system of elaborating options interested him for anything, it was for the intelligence it supplied him about the views of a bureaucracy he distrusted and for the opportunity it provided to camouflage his own aims.

There was a marginal difference in our perspectives. Nixon saw in the opening to China a somewhat greater opportunity than I to squeeze the Soviet Union into short-term help on Vietnam; I was more concerned with the policy's impact on the structure of international relations. Nixon tended to believe that ending the isolation of 800 million Chinese itself removed a great threat to peace. To me a China active in foreign policy would call for very skillful diplomacy to calibrate our policies in the more complicated context that would evolve and that would alter all international relationships. But these differences rested on the same fundamental judgment: that if relations could be developed with both the Soviet Union and China the triangular relationship would give us a great strategic opportunity for peace. We had both come to the same perception independently. In an important article in *Foreign Affairs* in October 1967 Nixon had written:

Taking the long view, we simply cannot afford to leave China forever outside the family of nations, there to nurture its fantasies, cherish its hates and threaten its neighbors. There is no place on this small planet for a billion of its potentially most able people to live in angry isolation. But we could go disastrously wrong if, in pursuing this long-range goal, we failed in the short range to read the lessons of history. . . .

For the short run, then, this means a policy of firm restraint, of no reward, of a creative counterpressure designed to persuade Peking that its interests can be served only by accepting the basic rules of international civility. For the long run, it means pulling China back into the world community — but as a great and progressing nation, not as the epicenter of world revolution.

In a magazine interview on August 9, 1968, immediately after his nomination for President, Nixon reiterated that "We must not forget China. We must always seek opportunities to talk with her, as with the USSR. . . . We must not only watch for changes. We must seek to make changes."[1]

China had not figured extensively in my own writings. In 1961, I had written about the possibility of a Sino-Soviet rift. Such a prospect, I argued, "must not be overlooked" and if it occurred "we should take advantage of it." But we could not promote this rift by our own efforts and we could not build our policy on the expectation of it.[2] (In fact, we know now that the rift had already occurred.) In my article on the Vietnam negotiations published in the January 1969 issue of *Foreign Affairs* but written three months earlier, I had argued that "the Soviet doctrine according to which Moscow has a right to intervene to protect socialist domestic structures made a Sino-Soviet war at least conceivable. For Moscow's accusations against Peking have been, if anything, even sharper than those against Prague.'' I saw this as a potentially serious problem for Hanoi and as a factor to press Hanoi toward a settlement. More fundamental, in July 1968, before the Soviet invasion of Czechoslovakia, I had worked with Nelson Rockefeller on a speech he gave on US–Soviet relations that contained a passage foreshadowing later policy: "We will have to learn to deal imaginatively with several competing centers of Communist power. . . . I would begin a dialogue with Communist China. In a subtle triangle of relations between Washington, Peking, and Moscow, we improve the possibilities of accommodations with each as we increase our options toward both.''

My perception owed something to my general approach to the conduct of foreign policy. Our relations to possible opponents should be such, I considered, that our options toward both of them were always greater than their options toward each other. If we could free our diplomacy from the dead weight of two decades, each Communist superpower would have greater inducement to deal with us constructively.

Though many scholars urged a rapprochement with China, such an approach to the question was not widely shared. A number of sinologists urged an improvement of relations as an end in itself, for which Americans should make concessions. A group of distinguished professors from Harvard and the Massachusetts Institute of Technology, for instance, sent a memorandum on China policy to Nixon during the transition period. They urged that we move toward China by such initiatives as relinquishing our ties to Taiway and inviting the People's Republic into the United Nations. Their memorandum did not mention — nor do I recall any other China experts who did so at the time — the geopolitical opportunities for us with respect to the Soviet Union or the possibility that the Chinese might have an incentive to move toward us *without* American concessions because of *their* need for an American counterweight to the Soviet Union.

But all ideas about rapprochement, whatever their rationale, it has to be said, were little more than nebulous theories when the new Administration came into office. For twenty years, there had been virtual isolation and ideological hostility, punctuated by the war in Korea in which American and Chinese soldiers fought ferociously against each other. Bilateral talks had been begun between consular officials of the United States and the People's Republic of China in 1954 in Geneva; these were raised to the ambassadorial level in 1955 and later moved to Warsaw. On September 10, 1955, an agreement was reached on repatriation of some nationals. And that was all. In the 134 meetings held from 1954 through 1968 the repatriation accord remained the only concrete achievement.

On May 28, 1968, Peking postponed the Warsaw talks, suggesting two dates in November, after the American Presidential election. Peking

Radio asserted that "there is nothing to discuss at present." The first faint glimmer of change followed the events of August 21, 1968, the Soviet invasion of Czechoslovakia. Whereas in the upheavals of 1956 in Poland and Hungary the Chinese had attempted to act as conciliators, this time their response was abusive condemnation of the Soviet Union. The Chinese Communist Party newspaper *People's Daily* on March 17, 1969, for example, called the Czech invasion "armed aggression and military occupation" by the "Soviet revisionist renegade clique." It denounced the Brezhnev Doctrine of limited sovereignty as an "out-and-out fascist theory." For in its literal meaning, the Brezhnev Doctrine applied as much to China as to any East European country; indeed, given China's unconcealed hostility to the Soviet leadership, perhaps even more so.

Thus, on November 26, 1968, three months after the Czech invasion and just after the US election, Peking proposed another Warsaw meeting with the United States to take place on February 20, 1969. True to the ancient Chinese tradition of never revealing any need for the cooperation of foreigners, Peking adopted a challenging tone, calling on the United States to join "an agreement on the Five Principles of Peaceful Coexistence" and "to withdraw all its armed forces from China's Taiwan Province and the Taiwan Straits and dismantle all its military installations in Taiwan Province."

There was no question that the Soviet Union was emerging as the principal Chinese foreign policy concern. Sino-Soviet hostility had many roots. What started as a close alliance soon showed increasing strains, which were at first papered over. There was an ideological disagreement over China's claims to have achieved Communism without passing through the stage of socialism — a doctrine of Mao Tse-tung's that implied that Peking was ideologically more pure than Moscow. There was also a national rivalry between two powerful states, and a growing mistrust. In the late 1950s Khrushchev refused nuclear cooperation; the Chinese retaliated by stepping up ideological attacks. In 1959 the Soviet Union pulled out its technical advisers and ended all economic aid. Personal antipathy developed between the two groups of Communist leaders, violating all Marxist-Leninist injunctions against "subjectivism." The Chinese resurrected ancient grievances, demanding the return of vast stretches of Siberian territory allegedly seized by the tsars in centuries of Russian expansion.

By 1969, the political conflict was beginning to take an ominous military form. Until about 1965–66, a rough military balance had existed along the Sino-Soviet border. Force levels on both sides were low. Opposite Sinkiang, Soviet forces were more numerous; the Chinese had numerical superiority near Manchuria. Soviet forces were, of course, consistently superior in quality and in logistical support. Border incidents began around 1959, and increased in frequency thereafter. Nevertheless, for several years there was no large-scale buildup by either side. Then in early 1966 the Soviets began transferring highly trained and well-equipped combat units from Eastern Europe to the Far East. Nuclear-tipped surface-to-surface rockets made their appearance. More worrying for Peking, in January 1966 the Soviet Union signed a twenty-year "Treaty of Friendship, Cooperation, and Mutual Aid" with Mongolia that allowed it to station troops and to maintain bases there. The number of Soviet divisions along the Chinese border increased from about twelve understrength divisions in 1964 to over forty modernized divisions by 1970.

On November 29, 1968, the Johnson Administration, with President-elect Nixon's blessing, accepted the Chinese offer to resume the Warsaw talks. (I had not yet been appointed as Nixon's Assistant.)

First Signals

IN retrospect all successful policies seem preordained. Leaders like to claim prescience for what has worked, ascribing to planning what usually starts as a series of improvisations. It was no different with the new China policy. The new Administration had the general intention of making a fresh start. But in all candor it had no precise idea how to do this and it had to take account of domestic realities, not the least of which was Nixon's traditional support among the conservative "China lobby" that had never forgiven Truman and Acheson for allegedly betraying Chiang Kai-shek.

The leaders in Peking probably had the same problem. It is likely that Mao Tse-tung decided to move toward the United States shortly after the Czech invasion. But he governed a country just emerging from the Cultural Revolution. Mao had sought by this extraordinary convulsion to head off the fatal tendency of Communist states toward bureaucratization and stagnation by imposing from the top a permanent revolutionary upheaval — surely one of the few times in history the head of a country deliberately overthrew his own institutions as an educational device. The impact of the upheaval on foreign policy is revealed by the fact that in 1969 China had only one ambassador serving abroad (he was Huang Hua, stationed in Cairo, later Ambassador to the United Nations and still later Foreign Minister).

One of the first and most important steps taken by the Nixon Administration was something we did *not* do. The Johnson Administration had used the specter of Asian Communism led by Peking as a principal justification for the Vietnam war. President Johnson in his speech at Johns Hopkins University on April 7, 1965, had argued that "the rulers in Hanoi are urged on by Peiping";* the contest in Vietnam was "part of a wider pattern of aggressive purposes." In the same vein Secretary of State Dean Rusk before the Senate Foreign Relations Committee on February 18, 1966, saw Peking as the instigator of aggression and Peking and Hanoi as in collusion. By contrast, the Nixon Administration, from the beginning, never cited, or even hinted at, an anti-Chinese motive for our Vietnam involvement; we did not agree with the analysis; we needed no additional enemies.

The first few months were full of contradictory tendencies. In his Inaugural address Nixon made a veiled reference to the new Administration's willingness to talk to China: "Let all nations know that during this administration our lines of communication will be open. We seek an open world — open to ideas, open to the exchange of goods and people — a world in which no people, great or small, will live in angry isolation." The phrase "angry isolation" harked back to his *Foreign Affairs* article of 1967. But there was no response. The Chinese were not to be impressed by a single conciliatory allusion.

The day after Inauguration the New China News Agency denounced Nixon as the new "puppet" chosen by the "monopoly bourgeois clique" to implement "the vicious ambitions of US imperialism to continue to carry out aggression and expansion in the world." Nixon's low-key rhetoric and the demonstrations against him at the Inaugural in Washington revealed, according to NCNA, that US imperialism was "beset with crises" and facing a "deathbed struggle." The *People's Daily* of January 27 gloated that US imperialism was "on its last legs." The article mocked: "Although at the end of his rope, Nixon had the cheek to speak about the future. . . . A man with one foot in the grave tries to console himself by dreaming of paradise. This is the delusion and writhing of a dying class."

Nixon's Inaugural address may have been more statesmanlike but the Chinese had more pungent writers.

Nixon was indeed somewhat schizophrenic in the early days. Five days after the Inauguration, Nixon sent me and Rogers a message complaining that our Ambassador in a European country had failed to prevent that country from announcing its recognition of Peking. The Ambassador, he said, was a "disaster"; we were told to "get rid of him" immediately. At his first news conference, on January 27, Nixon was asked whether he was planning to improve relations with Communist China. He gave a long account of Chinese hostility, concluding that at the forthcoming Warsaw meeting China would have an opportunity to prove whether it had altered its attitude. "Until some changes occur on their side, however, I see no immediate prospect of any change in our policy."

---

* Peiping was the Nationalist Chinese name for Peking; this usage was an additional insult.

The converse, of course, was that if China changed its attitude in some unspecified manner, we would be receptive. Formally this did not differ substantially from the pronouncements of previous administrations. And it was in sharp contrast also with more conciliatory references to the Soviet Union, SALT, and the Non-Proliferation Treaty in the same news conference. To the suspicious Chinese all this must have looked like the feared condominium. And they were already fretting over another incident. Three days before this news conference the Chinese chargé d'affaires in the Netherlands had defected and sought asylum in the United States. On February 6 the Chinese protested. On February 18 they canceled the Warsaw meeting scheduled for February 20, on the ground that the United States had "incited" the chargé "to betray his country and he was carried off by the CIA." Not to be outdone, Nixon, in his press conference of March 4, poured more cold water on the prospects of a Sino-American rapprochement: "Looking further down the road, we could think in terms of a better understanding with Red China. But being very realistic, in view of Red China's breaking off the rather limited Warsaw talks that were planned, I do not think that we should hold out any great optimism for any breakthroughs in that direction at this time."

Yet on February 1, in response to a report indicating some East European concern about possible Chinese-American contacts, Nixon had written me a memorandum:

I noted in your January 31 report the interesting comments from [the East European] source. I think we should give every encouragement to the attitude that this Administration is "exploring possibilities of raprochement [*sic*] with the Chinese." This, of course, should be done privately and should under no circumstances get into the public prints from this direction. However, in contacts with your friends, and particularly in any ways you might have to get to this . . . source, I would continue to plant that idea.

To be sure, the memorandum did not ask me to do anything toward the Chinese; it simply urged me to create the impression that we were *exploring* a move toward China. I was to plant the idea, moreover, not with friends of the Chinese but with East Europeans. The maneuver was intended to disquiet the Soviets, and almost certainly — given Nixon's preoccupations — to provide an incentive for them to help us end the war in Vietnam.

I used the Nixon memorandum to initiate a policy review, and on February 5 I called for an interagency study of China policy. The departments and agencies were asked to examine:

1. The current status of U.S. relations with Communist China and the Republic of China;
2. The nature of the Chinese Communist threat and intentions in Asia;

3. The interaction between U.S. policy and the policies of other major interested countries toward China;
4. Alternative U.S. approaches on China and their costs and risks.

China also featured in Nixon's conversations with President de Gaulle during the visit to Paris on March 1, 1969. Nixon did not actually ask de Gaulle for any particular assistance; indeed, it was de Gaulle who initiated the subject and Nixon who seemed to be skeptical. In characteristically sweeping terms, de Gaulle stressed the importance of China, a huge entity with great resources. As time passed, the Chinese would make their influence felt in all parts of the world; their ambitions matched their skills. It was unwise to isolate them ''in their own rage''; contacts could only be helpful. Nixon replied that in the short term there would be no change largely because of the unsettling impact of such a move on the rest of Asia; but over the long term — say ten years — we would have more communications with China, especially after it began to make progress in nuclear weapons. This indirect reply by Nixon was a sure sign that he meant to keep his options open. It was as compatible with an intention to wait ten years as with the objective of moving at the first opportunity. At best, it reflected the reality that the new Administration had no clear-cut plan.

Therefore on March 14, we talked again in a seemingly anti-Chinese direction. In announcing our ''Safeguard'' ABM program the President gave it in part the same anti-Chinese orientation that had also been the principal rationale of the Johnson Administration's ''Sentinel'' ABM program of 1967. The reason was the same in both Administrations: it seemed wise to obtain some protection against accidental launches or deliberate attacks by smaller nuclear powers, without attempting a massive population defense against the Soviet Union that raised arms control as well as budgetary problems. ''The Chinese threat against our population,'' Nixon's statement declared, ''as well as the danger of an accidental attack, cannot be ignored. By approving this system, it is possible to reduce U.S. fatalities to a minimal level in the event of a Chinese nuclear attack in the 1970's, or in an accidental attack from any source.'' To make matters worse from the Chinese point of view, Nixon went on to imply that the Soviet Union and the United States shared a common interest in containing China: ''I would imagine that the Soviet Union would be just as reluctant as we would be to leave their country naked against a potential Chinese Communist threat. So the abandoning of the entire system, particularly as long as the Chinese threat is there, I think neither country would look upon with much favor.'' Not surprisingly, the New China News Agency on March 16 denounced the ABM decision as American ''collusion with the Soviet revisionists to jointly maintain the nuclear threat and nuclear blackmail against the people of the world, particularly against the Chinese people.''

Thus by March 1969, Chinese-American relations seemed essentially frozen in the same hostility of mutual incomprehension and distrust that had characterized them for twenty years. The new Administration had a notion, but not yet a strategy, to move toward China. Policy emerges when concept encounters opportunity. Such an occasion arose when Soviet and Chinese troops clashed in the frozen Siberian tundra along a river of which none of us had ever heard. From then on ambiguity vanished, and we moved without further hesitation toward a momentous change in global diplomacy.

The Ussuri River Clashes

I N the remotest reaches of northeast Asia, a brief stretch of the 4,000-mile border between the Soviet Union and China is demarcated by the Ussuri River. If one drew a straight line from Vladivostok north-northeast to Khabarovsk, the Ussuri would run along most of its length. At a desolate point in the river about two hundred fifty miles from Vladivostok is a tiny island called Damansky by the Russians and by the Chinese Chenpao. (See the accompanying map.) The island is about a third of a square mile in area, wooded and uninhabited. It is somewhat closer to the Chinese bank of the river; the land opposite on both sides is marshy and barely populated. Apart from occasional fishermen and loggers from both sides, the only human presence in the region is the border outposts, Soviet and Chinese, guarding their respective river banks. The border with respect to the island has never been delimited. The Chinese had for some time asserted that the demarcation line ran down the middle of the river, which would have made the island Chinese. The Soviets maintained that the historical border put the entire Ussuri riverbed under Russian control. To this day no one has adequately explained why either side attached so much importance to an uninhabited island in a barren and largely empty territory.

On the morning of March 2, 1969, according to Soviet press accounts, 300 Chinese troops on the island ambushed a Russian patrol of frontier guards with machine-gun fire, killing twenty-three and wounding fourteen in the twenty-minute battle that resulted. Soviet reinforcements were sent, and they too were ambushed on arrival. Thereupon both sides withdrew from the island.[3]

The Soviets gave the clash enormous and immediate publicity. This was itself unprecedented. It seems to have been the first time either country had reported an armed incident or acknowledged casualties. The two sides traded protest notes and propaganda charges. The Chinese alleged that Soviet troops had made sixteen "intrusions" on Chenpao since 1967, eight of these in January and February of 1969; they recited a long list of Soviet incursions on other disputed islands in the Ussuri, and incidents of harassment and abuse of Chinese fishermen, frontier patrols, and local inhabitants. About ten thousand Chinese demonstrators mobbed the Soviet Embassy in Peking on March 3; a reported one hundred thousand Soviet demonstrators attacked the Chinese Embassy in Moscow on March 7, smashing windows and throwing ink bottles. Demonstrations spread to eighteen other Soviet cities over the next four days. *Red Star,* the Soviet Defense Ministry newspaper, reported on March 8 that Soviet troops in the Far East were on alert. A press conference at the Soviet Foreign Ministry displayed photographs of Soviet soldiers said to have been killed and mutilated by the Chinese, and Soviet television broadcast a special program on the border clashes. Chinese newspapers on March 4 proclaimed, "Down with the New Tsars!" Peking Radio reported that over four hundred million people (half the country's population) took part in various demonstrations across China.

In Washington we were still too preoccupied with Vietnam to respond to events whose origin we little understood and whose significance took some weeks to become apparent. And while I favored establishing a triangular relationship as a matter of theory, both Nixon and I still considered the People's Republic of China the more aggressive of the Communist powers. We thought it more than likely that Peking had started the fighting.

Ironically, it was heavy-handed Soviet diplomacy that made us think about our opportunities. On March 11, an emotional Ambassador Dobrynin raised the Ussuri incident with me. I had not even asked about it, but he insisted on giving me a gory account of the atrocities allegedly committed by the Chinese and an extended briefing. When I tried to change the subject by suggesting that it was a Sino-Soviet problem, Dobrynin insisted passionately that China was everybody's problem. I listened politely, thought a lot, but made no comment. Later that evening I described the encounter to the President. Nixon was intrigued, and remarked how sometimes unexpected events could have a major effect. I suggested that we stood to gain a great deal strategically. Nixon agreed that the incident must have shaken the Chinese.

On the morning of March 15 there was a second border clash on Damansky/Chenpao. In contrast with March 2, this time both sides were prepared. The battle lasted longer and casualties were higher. The Soviets had increased their patrolling, and a scouting party had camped on the island on the night of the fourteenth, probably to set a trap. Heavy fighting broke out and continued on and off for nine hours; tanks, armored cars, artillery, and antitank rockets were used. Both sides claimed victory (although the Chinese seem to have retained possession of the island).[4]

The origin of these incidents — who started what — will probably be forever unclear. But the Chinese argument that they were responding to a long series of Soviet intrusions has a certain plausibility. After all, inferior forces do not usually invite defeat by making unprovoked attacks. Over two years later, as I have mentioned, Chou En-lai claimed that the Soviets deliberately started the incidents to distract attention from their failure to block the West German election of the Federal President in West Berlin. Whatever the real cause, Communist diplomats saw to it that we could not ignore the clashes. In mid-March, in Budapest, the Soviets reportedly sought Warsaw Pact condemnation of China as the aggressor in the Ussuri incidents. They also appealed to each Warsaw Pact ally to send "symbolic military detachments" to the Sino-Soviet border area. The Romanians blocked both moves.

At the first private meeting of our new Paris negotiators with the North Vietnamese on March 22, Xuan Thuy volunteered the surprising outburst that the United States had nothing to gain by seeking to take advantage of the divisions between the Soviet Union and China. The Vietnamese would rely on themselves, he declared. The United States had raised no such issue either in Washington or Paris (although I had speculated about it in my *Foreign Affairs* article). But Xuan Thuy insisted that both Moscow and Peking had aided North Vietnam for years in spite of disputes lasting nearly a decade; he had no doubt that they would continue to do so.

On March 28, in a directive calling for a review of restrictions on trade with Communist countries, I specifically requested a reexamination of our embargo on trade with "Asian Communist countries."

On April 3, Dobrynin returned to the charge. He had read a press account that I was heading up a review of China policy (presumably the study directive of February 5). He wanted to learn more about it. Even though we had not had any communication with the Chinese, I gave an evasive reply which implied that the choice of rapprochement was up to us. Dobrynin suggested that there was still time for the two superpowers to order events, but they might not have this power much longer. He added that it seemed to many in the Soviet Union that Taiwan might well become an independent state. Summoning all my power to seem enigmatic, I did not respond.

On April 22 our Ambassador to Moscow, Jacob Beam, delivered a letter from President Nixon to Premier Kosygin covering a wide range of subjects in US–Soviet relations; China was deliberately *not* mentioned. However, we had instructed Beam to add orally that we did not intend to exploit Sino-Soviet difficulties — implying, of course, that we had the capacity to do so if we chose. The Soviets took the bait. On May 27, Foreign Minister Gromyko called in Beam to deliver Kosygin's reply. Gromyko added orally that the Soviet Union would not exploit *our* troubles with China either, and that in general US–Soviet relations should be based on "long-range considerations."

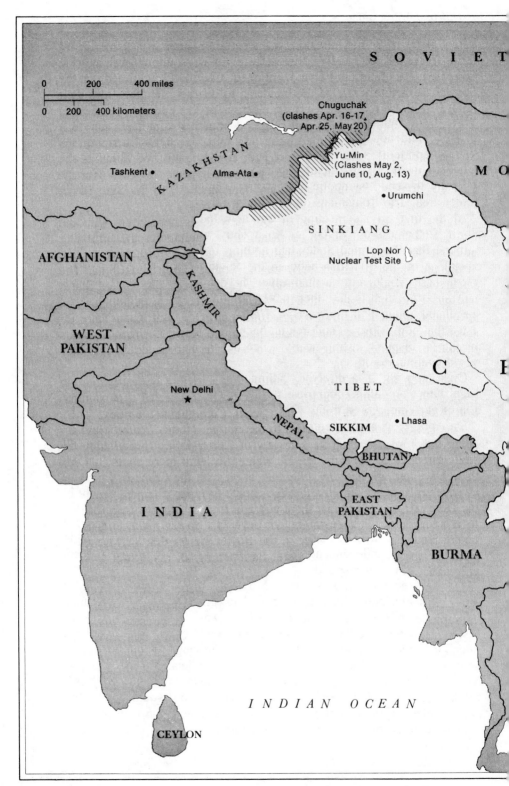

Sino-Soviet Border Clashes 1969

Hu-Ma
(clashes May 12-15)
Ai-Hui
(clash May 25)
Amur R.
Khabarovsk
Fu-Yuan (clash May 28)
Damansky/Chenpao
(clashes Mar. 2,
Mar. 14-15)
Ussuri R.

U N I O N

Ulan Bator

Harbin

Vladivostok

O L I A

Changchun

SEA OF
JAPAN

JAPAN

Mukden

NORTH
KOREA

Huhehot

INNER MONGOLIA

Peking

Pyongyang

Tientsin

Seoul

SOUTH
KOREA

Yellow River

I N A

Nanking

EAST CHINA
SEA

Shanghai
Hangchow

Yangtze River

Taiwan

STRAIT OF TAIWAN

PACIFIC

Canton

OCEAN

Hong Kong

NORTH
VIETNAM

Hainan

SOUTH CHINA
SEA

LAOS

PHILIPPINES

CAMBODIA

SOUTH
VIETNAM

SANDERSON

The triangular relationship, still highly tenuous, had shown its first tremor.

In the meantime, China had not been dormant. On April 1, Lin Piao, soon to be named Mao's heir, gave his political report to the Ninth National Congress of the Chinese Communist Party:

> We must on no account relax our revolutionary vigilance because of victory and on no account ignore the danger of U.S. imperialism and Soviet revisionism launching a large-scale war of aggression. . . . Chairman Mao said long ago we will not attack unless we are attacked; if we are attacked, we will certainly counter-attack. If they insist on fighting, we will keep them company and fight to the finish. The Chinese Revolution was won on the battlefield.

Despite its belligerent tone the speech had interesting, indeed tantalizing, innuendos. It emphasized that China would not attack unless attacked first, thus easing our fear of Chinese intervention in Indochina. It listed the Soviet Union and the United States as equal threats to the People's Republic, fulfilling one of the preconditions of triangular diplomacy, that the United States should not be the principal enemy.

On April 29, I sent the President a wrap-up of the Chinese Party Congress. The Congress seemed to reflect a continuing struggle in China over domestic, economic, and social policy and political control. Foreign policies seemed equally uncertain, but Chinese preoccupation with the Soviet, rather than the American, danger seemed to be growing. I informed Nixon:

> The direction of policy was not determined. . . . Support for class struggles in Southeast Asia, India and Israel was reaffirmed by Lin Piao, but given little emphasis.
>
> Denigration of the US was pro forma.
>
> Lin Piao mentioned that the Chinese had refused an urgent Soviet request to discuss the border issue, but he indicated that China was considering whether to engage in border discussions. . . .
>
> The public statements did not manifest any Chinese concern that war with the US or the USSR is imminent.
>
> Treatment of Vietnam was perfunctory, and the Chinese have not endorsed the North Korean position during the recent tension.*
>
> . . . The Congress had kind words for no governments and for only one Party, the Albanian. A combination of moralistic rigidity towards other Communists, together with a professed desire to see the overthrow of non-Communist neighbors, would appear likely to earn the hostility of both.

Whatever the long-term significance of my analysis, a reference in it to Mao's continuing battle to revamp educational policy caused Nixon to

---

*Referring to the North Korean shootdown of a US EC-121 reconnaissance aircraft. See Chapter IX.

discover a community of purpose with his erstwhile nemesis. He wrote in the margin: "HK: Note Mao [too] fights the educational establishment!"

While the Party Congress was going on in Peking, more fighting broke out along the Sino-Soviet border on April 16–17 — this time twenty-five hundred miles to the west on the frontier between Sinkiang and Kazakhstan. Another clash occurred there on April 25, and yet another on May 2. On April 26, the USSR publicly proposed to China the resumption of the meetings of the Joint Commission for Navigation on Boundary Rivers, which had been suspended since 1967. On May 8, the Soviet press disclosed military maneuvers by Soviet forces near the Chinese border. On May 9, Defense Minister Marshal Andrei Grechko's Order of the Day commemorating the twenty-fourth anniversary of V-E Day ranked China with the United States and West Germany among the USSR's major foes.

Apparently feeling the heat, the Chinese on May 11 accepted the Soviet proposal to resume discussions on river navigation. But there was more fighting all along the Amur River on May 12, 15, 25, and 28; and further clashes on May 20 and June 10 on the Sinkiang border (see the map on pp. 174–175). The hostilities in Sinkiang tipped the scales in my mind as to the probable aggressor. Originally I had accepted the fashionable view that the Chinese were the more militant country. But when I looked at a detailed map and saw that the Sinkiang incidents took place only a few miles from a Soviet railhead and several hundred miles from any Chinese railhead, it occurred to me that Chinese military leaders would not have picked such an unpropitious spot to attack. After that I looked at the problem differently. If the Soviet Union was the aggressor, however, we had a problem as well as an opportunity. The problem was that a full-scale Soviet invasion of China might tip not only the geopolitical but also the psychological equilibrium in the world; it would create a momentum of irresistible ruthlessness. But it was not an easy matter to resist such aggression on behalf of a country with which we had neither diplomatic relations nor effective communication at any level.

The opportunity was that China might be ready to reenter the diplomatic arena and that would require it to soften its previous hostility toward the United States. In such circumstances, the Chinese threat against many of our friends in Asia would decline; at the same time, by evoking the Soviet Union's concerns along its long Asian perimeter, it could also ease pressures on Europe. But for such possibilities to be clearer, we needed some communication with the Chinese leaders. If we moved too quickly or obviously — before the Cultural Revolution had fully run its course — the Chinese might rebuff the overture. If we moved too slowly, we might feed Chinese suspicions of Soviet-American collusion, which could drive them into making the best deal available with Moscow. As for the Soviets, we considered the Chinese option useful to induce restraint; but we had to take care not to pursue it so impetuously as to provoke a Soviet preemptive attack on China. And at home we had to overcome a habit of mind that had seen in the People's Republic either an irreconcilable enemy or a put-upon country concerned only with the issue of Taiwan.

My major concern at this stage was to make sure that the right questions were being asked in our government. My directive of February 5 had produced an interagency paper on China, which the NSC Review Group met to discuss on May 15. The paper paid heavy attention to the conventional Chinese-American bilateral problems: Taiwan, admission to the United Nations, trade and travel, and various disarmament schemes; it also discussed our opposing interests in Asia. All these concerns were treated as if they existed in a vacuum. No reference was made to the global implications of Sino-Soviet tensions and the opportunities for us in the triangular relationship. At the meeting I challenged what seemed to me excessive emphasis on China's ideology and alleged militancy; I thought the issue should be posed differently. The interagency paper assumed that American policy had the essentially psychological goal of changing the minds of the Chinese leadership, to turn Chinese minds from militancy toward conciliation. This ignored China's role in the power equation. A nation of 800 millions surrounded by weaker states was a geopolitical problem no matter who governed it. Which of our problems with China were caused by its size and situation and which by its leadership? What did we want from China and how could we reasonably influence its decisions? How did we view the evolution of Sino-Soviet relations; how much could we influence them and which side should we favor? I also questioned the view of most Kremlinologists that any attempt to better our relations with China would ruin relations with the Soviet Union. History suggested that it was usually more advantageous to align oneself with the weaker of two antagonistic partners, because this acted as a restraint on the stronger.

On June 8, the Soviets resumed their diplomatic offensive. Brezhnev, in a speech to the International Conference of Communist Parties in Moscow, denounced Mao and floated the concept of "a system of collective security in Asia." He did not elaborate, but such a "system" could only be directed against China. In late June, Soviet ambassadors made coordinated efforts to "expose" Chinese policy to their host governments and to discourage various West European nations from recognizing Peking. The Soviet Union sought to expand its contacts with non-Communist Asian nations; feelers were even extended to Taiwan. In a campaign to thwart any Chinese effort to break out of its isolation, Soviet diplomats hinted that in order better to isolate China the Soviet Union was prepared to avoid complicating relations with the United

States. I summed up these accumulating signs in a report to the President:

> I believe this is solid evidence of the growing obsession of the Soviet leaders with their China problem . . . at least it suggests that the Soviets may become more flexible in dealing with East-West issues. . . . Thus, Soviet concern may have finally reached the point that it can be turned to our advantage, if they are in fact attempting to ensure our neutrality in their Chinese containment policy, if not our active cooperation.

The President made enthusiastic comments in the margin, such as, "This is our goal." He suggested we "subtly encourage" all the countries being urged by the Soviets not to establish relations with Peking to proceed (a dramatic shift from his complaints about our Ambassador in Europe five days after his Inauguration).

We now redoubled our own efforts to establish contact with Peking. On June 26 the President sent me a message that we should encourage Senator Mike Mansfield, who had long been interested in China, to go through with his plan to seek a visa to visit China. I took the President's instructions a step further by urging Bryce Harlow, then in charge of Congressional relations at the White House, to encourage Mansfield to make his initiative public. But a more explicit gesture was necessary. The time had come to modify our trade embargo against China. The actual change was unimportant but the symbolism was vast. The worried deliberations necessary to bring about this relatively minor step are a measure of the distance we have traveled since. The decision grew out of an overall study of trade restrictions ordered on March 28. We decided to deal with Chinese trade as a special case. On June 26 I signed a directive to the agencies that: "The President has decided, on broad foreign policy grounds, to modify certain of our trade controls against China." The NSC Under Secretaries Committee, ably chaired by Elliot Richardson, was asked to prepare detailed recommendations to implement the Presidential decision.

It was at first assumed that any actual implementation had to await passage by the Congress of the revised Export Control Act expected in September. But Richardson and I soon realized that if we waited until then we might be overtaken by events in Asia, which seemed to be building to a climax. I pointed out to Nixon that the directive of June 26 was sure to leak and perhaps start a domestic debate that would dilute the favorable impact in Peking. Then there was the problem of US–Soviet relations. We expected at any time to announce the commencement of the SALT talks; if we coupled this with a relaxation of China trade restrictions, we would be open to charges by proponents of US–Soviet relations that it was a gratuitous slap at the Soviets and we would be held to blame for any deadlocks in SALT. Similarly, if the decision were announced after the President returned from his forthcoming trip to Romania (a friend of China), that trip would take on an "overly overt anti-Soviet significance."

Richardson and I finally settled on three recommendations: (1) permitting American tourists to purchase up to $100 of Chinese-made noncommercial goods; (2) eliminating the ban on travel to the People's Republic; and (3) allowing shipment of grain. The President agreed to the first two items, but on the advice of conservative Senators disapproved the third. Just as we were ready to make the announcement there occurred one of those trivial unforeseen events that can wreck the best-laid plans. On July 16, a yacht crewed by two Americans had capsized off Hong Kong; their lifeboat drifted into Chinese waters and they were captured by the Chinese. Richardson and I decided to postpone the announcement for a few days to see whether the Chinese would play the incident into an anti-American campaign. But Peking remained silent. On July 21, 1969, just before the President's departure for his around-the-world trip, the State Department made a low-key, matter-of-fact announcement that eased (but did not eliminate) restrictions on trade and travel to the People's Republic. The announcement asked for no reciprocity; the Chinese could consider it without reacting formally. On July 24 the Chinese released the American yachtsmen. Chou En-lai, too, knew how to make moves that required no reciprocity. Peking had understood.

By this time Nixon had set off on the trip round the world, during which he intended leaving visiting cards for the Chinese at every stop. Nixon began at once spreading the word of our readiness to open communication with Peking. In Indonesia and Thailand he told leaders that we would have nothing to do with the Soviet proposal for an Asian collective security scheme. This was an indirect reassurance to the Chinese, as well as a warning that we would resist the extension of Soviet influence to Southeast Asia. As he pointed out to the Thai Prime Minister: "A condominium is out of the question."

Nixon spoke more freely to Yahya Khan of Pakistan and Nicolae Ceauşescu of Romania, because he knew that both of them were friendly with the Chinese. On August 1, Nixon told President Yahya in Lahore that it was his personal view — not completely shared by the rest of his government or by many Americans — that Asia could not "move forward" if a nation as large as China remained isolated. (Nixon seemed to think that it enhanced his stature with foreign leaders if he indicated that he acted contrary to the advice of his subordinates — indeed, that if they knew what he was doing they would oppose him. What these leaders, used to more hierarchical arrangements, thought about such confessions will have to await their own memoirs.) He stressed that the United States would not be a party to any arrangements to isolate China. He asked Yahya to convey his feeling to the

Chinese at the highest level. Yahya later that day arranged a briefing for me at the State Guest House in Lahore by Air Marshal Sher Ali Khan, who had recently visited China. The Marshal believed that China's domestic upheaval was winding down, and that China would soon seek to end its self-imposed diplomatic isolation. He also described the Chinese leaders in terms quite contrary to our then widespread stereotypes of almost irrationally fanatic ideologues. He considered them disciplined, pragmatic, and reliable once they gave their word.

The next two days, August 2 and 3 in Bucharest, Nixon returned to his theme with President Ceauşescu. Once again he emphatically rejected the Asian security system on the ground that it was wrong for the Soviet Union to arrange a cabal in Asia against China. In twenty-five years China would have a billion people, Nixon argued. If isolated by others, it might turn into an explosive force. Our policy was to have good relations with the Soviet Union as well as with China. He hoped that Romania would agree to act as a channel of communication to the Chinese. Ceauşescu indicated that he was prepared to act as messenger; he promised to convey our views and report any Chinese response.

Contrary to our expectations, the Romanian channel turned out to be one-way. We had thought that the Chinese might prefer to deal with us through Communist intermediaries. In fact, they proved too wary for that, perhaps fearful of Soviet penetration of even a country as fiercely independent as Romania.

Back in Washington, I called in Pakistan's Ambassador, Agha Hilaly, to keep the Pakistanis in play and to establish a secure channel. Hilaly was an able professional, from an old Pakistani family, long active in public service. His brother at that time was Ambassador to China and later became permanent head of Pakistan's Foreign Ministry; in the 1950s, Hilaly's sister — an early advocate of women's rights in an inhospitable society — had been a student of mine at Harvard. Hilaly was meticulous and discreet. I asked him to reiterate to President Yahya that we thought Nixon's message should be delivered to the Chinese only at the highest level; in the meantime Pakistan could pass on our basic attitude in a low-key manner whenever a natural occasion presented itself. I told Hilaly of Nixon's preference that the Hilaly channel with me be the single confidential point of contact for any further discussion of this subject. Hilaly suggested that Yahya would reserve Nixon's detailed views for a conversation with Chou En-lai, who was expected to visit Pakistan in the near future.

On August 8, Secretary of State Rogers made a major speech in Canberra declaring our desire to improve relations with China:

We recognize, of course that the Republic of China on Taiwan and Communist China on the mainland are facts of life. We know, too, that mainland China will eventually play an important role in Asian and Pacific affairs — but

certainly not as long as its leaders continue to have such an introspective view
of the world. . . .

This is one reason why we have been seeking to open up channels of communication. Just a few days ago we liberalized our policies toward purchase of
their goods by American travelers and toward validating passports for travel to
China. Our purpose was to remove irritants in our relations and to help remind
people on mainland China of our historic friendship for them. . . .

Thus by the end of August we had communicated with the Chinese by
unilateral steps, intermediaries, and public declarations. All this had occurred through a series of ad hoc decisions. There had been no formal
consideration of China policy at the Cabinet level. The National Security Council did not meet on this topic until August. Before it met I gave
the President my analysis of the different views within the government
of how we should play our relations with China in light of our relations
with the Soviet Union. One view (which we might call the
"Slavophile" position) argued that the Soviets were so suspicious of
US–Chinese collusion that any effort to improve relations with China
would make Soviet-American cooperation impossible. Those who held
this view believed that we should give top priority to improving relations with the Soviet Union and, for this reason, should avoid efforts to
increase contact with Peking. An opposing view (a kind of "Realpolitik" approach) argued that the Soviets were more likely to be conciliatory if they feared that we would otherwise seek a rapprochement
with Peking. This school of thought urged that we expand our contacts
with China as a means of leverage against the Soviet Union. A third
"Sinophile" group argued that our relations with the Soviet Union
should not be a major factor in shaping our China policy. Marginal
actions to increase Soviet nervousness might be useful but fundamental
changes in the US–China relationship should be guided by other considerations.

Not surprisingly, I was on the side of the Realpolitikers.

When the NSC meeting discussed these issues on August 14, 1969,
little was decided, but the President startled his Cabinet colleagues by
his revolutionary thesis (which I strongly shared) that the Soviet Union
was the more aggressive party and that it was against our interests to let
China be "smashed" in a Sino-Soviet war. It was a major event in
American foreign policy when a President declared that we had a strategic interest in the survival of a major Communist country, long an
enemy, and with which we had no contact. The reason a Sino-Soviet
war was on his mind was that a new increase of tensions along the
border caused us grave concern. It also reinforced our conviction that
the need for contact was becoming urgent.

Rumors of War

ON August 8, the same day as Rogers's Canberra speech, the USSR and the People's Republic ended the talks that had proceeded since June in Khabarovsk and signed a protocol on the improvement of navigation on boundary rivers. Far from easing tensions, this seemed to spur them. A few days later, new and bloody fighting broke out along the frontier between Sinkiang and Kazakhstan. *Pravda* on August 14 reported on civil defense preparations in Kazakhstan; the New China News Agency on August 15 accused the USSR of preparing for war and exhorted the Chinese people to do the same.

Signals of tension multiplied. On August 18 a middle-level State Department specialist in Soviet affairs, William Stearman, was having lunch with a Soviet Embassy official when, out of the blue, the Russian asked what the US reaction would be to a Soviet attack on Chinese nuclear facilities. I took this sufficiently seriously to convene a meeting in San Clemente on August 25 of the Washington Special Actions Group (WSAG), the NSC subcommittee for contingency planning and crisis management. I asked them to prepare contingency plans for American policy in case of a Sino-Soviet war. When the WSAG papers proved inadequate, I had a group from my staff attempt a better analysis. As will be discussed in Chapter XVIII, an excellent paper was done in early 1970, cold-bloodedly analyzing our potential for either preventing a war or influencing its outcome. The President's conviction expressed at the August 14 NSC meeting that we could not allow China to be "smashed" was no longer a hypothetical issue. If the cataclysm occurred, Nixon and I would have to confront it with little support in the rest of the government — and perhaps the country — for what we saw as the strategic necessity of supporting China.

The Sino-Soviet propaganda war intensified markedly at the end of August. On August 28, *Pravda* warned China against further armed provocations and appealed to the rest of the world to recognize the danger of China before it was too late. *Pravda* added ominously that "no continent would be left out if a war flares up under the present conditions, with the existing present-day technology, with the availability of lethal weapons and the up-to-date means of their delivery." The same day, the Chinese Communist Party Central Committee issued a public order exhorting the population again to war preparations, including accelerated construction of underground shelters in the cities. In late August we detected a standdown of the Soviet air force in the Far East. Such a move, which permits all aircraft to be brought to a high state of readiness simultaneously, is often a sign of a possible attack; at a minimum it is a brutal warning in an intensified war of nerves. The standdown continued through September.

On the thirtieth anniversary of the beginning of World War II two prominent Soviet generals rattled sabers at Peking. Writing in *Izvestia,* the Soviet government newspaper, on September 1, Soviet Chief of Staff and First Deputy Defense Minister Marshal Matvey Zakharov pointedly recalled the Soviet onslaught that destroyed the seven-million-man Japanese army in twenty-five days. General S. P. Ivanov, commandant of the General Staff's Higher Military Academy, sounded the same theme in an article in the newspaper *Red Star* on September 2.

We therefore raised our profile somewhat to make clear that we were not indifferent to these Soviet threats. On August 27, CIA Director Richard Helms had spoken at a background luncheon for a group of diplomatic correspondents and disclosed that the Soviet Union seemed to be sounding out its European Communist brethren on the possibility of a Soviet preemptive attack on Chinese nuclear installations.[5] On September 5, Under Secretary Elliot Richardson told a New York convention of the American Political Science Association:

In the case of Communist China, longrun improvement in our relations is in our own national interest. We do not seek to exploit for our own advantage the hostility between the Soviet Union and the People's Republic. Ideological differences between the two Communist giants are not our affair. We could not fail to be deeply concerned, however, with an escalation of this quarrel into a massive breach of international peace and security.

It was another revolutionary step for the United States to take such public note of a threat against a country with which it had been in a posture of hostility for twenty years and with which it had had no kind of exchange since the advent of the new Administration.

There was no immediate impact. On September 10 a member of the Soviet mission at the United Nations remarked nonchalantly to a US delegate that the Soviets were militarily overwhelmingly superior to the Chinese and that if current Chinese hostility continued, a military engagement might become unavoidable. On the same day, the Soviet news agency TASS charged the Chinese with 488 premeditated violations of the Soviet border and with provoking armed clashes involving 2,500 Chinese in the period from June to mid-August 1969.

There was a brief interlude while a dramatic meeting took place on September 11 between the two Prime Ministers, Kosygin and Chou En-lai. Both Kosygin and Chou had visited Hanoi separately to pay their respects on the death of Ho Chi Minh. The strain between their countries was reflected in the fact that Kosygin flew to Hanoi via India instead of the much shorter route through China, and that he left Hanoi before Chou's arrival. TASS reported that he had departed for Moscow. He got as far as Dushanbe in Soviet Central Asia when his plane suddenly altered course and headed for Peking by what must surely be the longest route from Hanoi. His brief encounter with Chou at Peking airport was the first summit-level meeting between the two countries in four and a half years.

It is a common myth that high officials are informed immediately about significant events. Unfortunately, official information must almost invariably run the obstacle of bureaucratic review or the need for a cover memorandum to put the event into somebody's perspective. It happens not infrequently — much too frequently for the security adviser's emotional stability — that even the President learns of a significant occurrence from the newspapers. So it was with the Kosygin-Chou meeting. To my embarrassment the President read about it in the *Washington Star* before I could send him an analysis. He called me and asked for my reaction. I told him that at first blush the joint announcement of the meeting seemed rather cool. The absence of the standard adjective "fraternal" in describing the conversation implied a serious rift. The Chinese may have invited Kosygin to stop by, I speculated, because they thought it in the Chinese interest to "cool this off." The President wondered if this meant a "détente" between them. I thought not; it seemed to me an effort by both sides to position themselves for the next round of their conflict.

The origin of the meeting was capable of varied interpretations. The diversion of Kosygin's flight could suggest that the visit was a last-minute Chinese invitation. On the other hand, the minimal respect accorded to Kosygin, who was not permitted to leave the airport, and the fact that the Soviets announced the meeting first, could imply a Soviet move. Whether it was a Chinese approach toward accommodation or a last Soviet warning to Peking, it was clear that Sino-Soviet relations were approaching a crisis point.

On September 16, an ominous article appeared in the *London Evening News,* bearing out my analysis. Victor Louis, a Soviet "freelance journalist" whom we believed to be a spokesman for the Soviet government, often floated trial balloons. He now wrote that "Marxist theoreticians" were discussing the possibility of a Sino-Soviet war and suggesting that, if it took place, "the world would only learn about it afterwards." Louis mentioned the possibility of a Soviet air strike against the Chinese nuclear testing site at Lop Nor in Sinkiang. He claimed that a clandestine anti-Mao radio station was operating in China, which revealed the existence of anti-Mao forces who, it was "quite possible," might produce a leader who would ask other socialist countries for "fraternal help." "Events in the past year," Louis noted, "have confirmed that the Soviet Union is adhering to the doctrine that socialist countries have the right to interfere in each other's affairs in their own interest or those of others who are threatened."

A Soviet attack on China could not be ignored by us. It would upset the global balance of power; it would create around the world an impression of approaching Soviet dominance. But a direct American challenge would not be supported by our public opinion and might even accelerate what we sought to prevent.

On September 29, I brought the President up to date on the Soviet maneuvering over the previous month and urged that we do still more to respond:

I am concerned about our response to these probes. The Soviets may be quite uncertain over their China policy, and our reactions could figure in their calculations. Second, the Soviets may be using us to generate an impression in China and the world that we are being consulted in secret and would look with equanimity on their military actions. . . . I believe we should make clear that we are not playing along with these tactics. . . .

Before the President could act on this recommendation, on October 7 the New China News Agency suddenly announced that China had agreed to reopen the border negotiations with the USSR at the Deputy Foreign Minister level. In a conciliatory statement China affirmed its desire for a peaceful settlement; it denied that it was demanding the return of territories seized by tsarist Russia in the nineteenth century. The next day, China published a five-point proposal calling for a mutual troop pullback from disputed areas. On October 20, border negotiations resumed in Peking, conducted by Deputy Foreign Ministers Vasily V. Kuznetsov and Ch'iao Kuan-hua.

It seemed to me that in the war of nerves China had backed down. I wrote the President that in my view the shift in the Chinese position was due to two factors: a growing concern over a Soviet attack and the possible reassertion of control over foreign policy by the more pragmatic faction represented by Chou En-lai. But I did not believe that any fundamental change had occurred; the underlying tensions could not be reversed by procedural agreements. With his approval I proposed exploring some new administrative moves toward China with Elliot Richardson. Nixon agreed.

At this point — not surprisingly — the Pakistani channel suddenly began to show signs of life. On October 10, Air Marshal Sher Ali Khan, who had briefed me in Lahore, visited me in my office in the White House. He reported that Yahya had passed a general message to the Chinese about our willingness to improve relations but now felt he needed something more specific to convey when Chou En-lai came to Pakistan. I told Sher Ali of a step that Elliot Richardson and I had worked out a few days earlier. Since the outbreak of the Korean War in 1950, two American destroyers had been assigned to patrol the Strait of Taiwan to symbolize our commitment to the defense of the Republic of China. The destroyers were not, in fact, part of the defense of the island; their role was primarily symbolic. Richardson and I obtained the President's assent to withdraw a permanent patrol; we would show our continuing commitment to the defense of Taiwan by fifteen transits per month of other American warships. President Yahya was free to communicate this decision confidentially to the Communist Chinese Ambassador. He should ensure, however, that Peking did not misunderstand; our basic commitment to Taiwan's defense remained unchanged; this was simply a gesture to remove an irritant. I told Sher Ali that I would be in touch with Ambassador Hilaly when the President had decided upon something more precise to say to the Chinese. I reported all this to Nixon, who wrote at the end of my report: "K — also open trade possibilities." Since Sher Ali had already left Washington, and since I wanted to avoid the impression of overeagerness, I decided to hold this prospect for the next round.

On October 20, Ambassador Dobrynin, in the conversation with Nixon in which he conveyed the Soviet readiness to open SALT talks, also formally warned against any attempt to profit from Sino-Soviet tensions. Nixon told him that our China policy was not directed against the Soviet Union. At the same time, the United States did not intend to be a permanent enemy of the People's Republic of China any more than of the Soviet Union. We expected to accelerate trade, the exchange of persons, and eventually diplomacy. After this conversation I wrote Nixon my assessment:

> The Soviets again give vent to their underlying suspicion that we are trying to flirt with China in order to bring pressure on them. They warn us "in advance" that any such idea can lead to grave miscalculations and would interfere with the improvement of US–Soviet relations. You have already answered this point and I believe there is no advantage in giving the Soviets excessive reassurance. In any case we should not be diverted from our China policy.

Nor were we. To be certain that our meaning had been understood, on November 26 I authorized an additional signal, proposed by the State Department, by which the decision to end the destroyer patrol would be leaked to Chinese officials in Hong Kong.

Thus began an intricate minuet between us and the Chinese so delicately arranged that both sides could always maintain that they were not in contact, so stylized that neither side needed to bear the onus of an initiative, so elliptical that existing relationships on both sides were not jeopardized. Between November 1969 and June 1970 there were at least ten instances in which United States officials abroad exchanged words with Chinese officials at diplomatic functions. This was in sharp contrast to earlier practice in which the Chinese would invariably break off contact as soon as they realized they were encountering Americans. On at least four occasions Chinese officials initiated the contact. Then contacts started to go beyond social banter. In December 1969 our Deputy Consul General in Hong Kong heard through a reliable intermediary the "private" view of a Chinese Communist official that while all the differences between the United States and the People's Republic would take years to resolve, some form of relationship could be established before 1973.

We tried an initiative of our own. On September 9, at the height of the war scare, our Ambassador to Poland, Walter Stoessel, called on the President for a routine courtesy call. I had known Stoessel since 1959 when he was assigned as a postgraduate fellow to the Center for International Affairs at Harvard. I considered him one of the very best Foreign Service Officers — expert, thoughtful, disciplined. While we were waiting to see Nixon I urged Stoessel to walk up to the Ambassador of the People's Republic at the next social function they both attended and tell him that we were prepared for serious talks.*

Nothing happened for three months. Then on December 3, Stoessel spotted Lei Yang, the Chinese chargé d'affaires, at a Yugoslav fashion show held at the Warsaw Palace of Culture. When Stoessel approached, Lei Yang retreated down a flight of stairs. Stoessel pursued him and delivered his message through Lei's Polish-speaking interpreter. To convey to the Chinese that Stoessel's approach had not been a personal idiosyncrasy, we had the State Department spokesman announce at the next regular noon briefing that Stoessel and Lei had exchanged a few words. Chou En-lai told me many years later that we had nearly caused his worthy chargé a heart attack, and that Lei Yang, totally without instructions for such a contingency, had fled from Stoessel because he did not know how to respond.

But Chou En-lai knew. On December 6 the People's Republic released two other Americans who had been held since February 16 when their yacht had strayed into Chinese waters off Kwangtung province.†

On December 11, 1969, to our amazement, Ambassador Stoessel was invited to the Chinese Embassy — the first such invitation in *any* Sino-American contact since the Communists had taken power in China. Stoessel responded that he would be happy to arrive discreetly at the rear door; he was told that such delicacy was unnecessary; the main entrance was eminently suitable (presumably to avoid any chance that Soviet intelligence might miss the occasion). Stoessel indeed went through the front door and met his Chinese counterpart in a "cordial" atmosphere, as State Department spokesman Robert McCloskey announced the next day. Stoessel proposed the resumption of the Warsaw

---

* As it turned out, the Cultural Revolution had claimed this Ambassador; the highest-ranking official in Warsaw was the chargé d'affaires.

† This was a separate incident from the July episode described earlier, p. 180.

talks; no other subjects were covered. It was agreed that another meeting would take place within the month.

This contact by Stoessel was the first operational involvement of the regular State Department machinery in China diplomacy. Under Secretary Elliot Richardson, Assistant Secretary Marshall Green, their staffs, and high-level analysts had made a vital contribution to the various studies done in the NSC system; they had ably worked out the various schemes to ease trade restrictions. But the State Department as an institution had not been involved in the overall strategy and had had little diplomacy to conduct. Now its bureaucracy began to become active, for it thrives not on analysis but on negotiations. Having seen studies come and go, it is inclined not to argue over planning papers; it will fight to the death, however, over instructions to ambassadors. It is convinced that policy is made most efficiently by cable. Given the relatively short response time allowed by most negotiations, this has the added advantage of keeping to a minimum the intervention by outsiders (such as the President, or even the Secretary of State).

The Warsaw talks triggered all the latent reflexes of the State Department establishment. First to be heard from was the group that specialized in US–Soviet relations. Convinced that the nuclear superpowers held the key to peace and war, they wanted to run the minimum risks to this relationship; they saw little compensating advantage in a rapprochement with China. On the contrary, a triangular relationship would, they thought, upset all predictability in their sphere of policy. The argument that better relations with China might actually improve relations with the Soviet Union was considered by this group either absurd or reckless.* Their intellectual leader was the brilliant and dedicated former Ambassador to the Soviet Union Llewellyn Thompson, the State Department's foremost expert on Soviet affairs. As early as June he and his equally distinguished colleague Charles (Chip) Bohlen had, on their own initiative, called on Nixon when they had heard that we were planning to ease trade restrictions against China. Courageously, they warned the President against any attempt to "use" China against the Soviet Union. This could have nothing but dire consequences for US–Soviet relations and for world peace. Of course, we envisaged nothing so crude as "using" the People's Republic against the Soviet

---

*This was expressed as follows in a State Department paper submitted to the NSC Review Group in September:

> Soviet tolerance of U.S. overtures to Peking may be substantial — but these overtures will nevertheless introduce irritants into the U.S.–Soviet relationship. Moreover, if a significant improvement in the Sino-American relationship should come about, the Soviets might well adopt a harder line both at home and in international affairs. It is impossible to foresee the point at which the advantages in an improvement in Sino–U.S. relations might be counterbalanced by a hardening in U.S.–Soviet relationships. The fact that such a point almost certainly exists argues for caution in making moves toward better relations with China. . . .

Union; we wanted to create an incentive for both to improve their relations with us. Nixon performed in classic fashion — implying sympathy in their presence and then mocking what he considered the incorrigible softheadedness of the Foreign Service as soon as they left the room.

Learning of the imminent resumption of the Warsaw talks, Llewellyn Thompson now suggested that we keep Dobrynin informed of all our contacts. Rogers passed this proposal on to me, with the argument that he did not endorse it but wanted to "give the President the chance to think about it." I strongly disagreed. Since the Soviet Union did not brief us about its contacts with the Chinese or any other nation, I saw no reason to extend to it an unreciprocated courtesy or gratuitous reassurance. And I saw no point in giving the Russians the opportunity to gloat to Peking that they were being kept informed, thus heightening Chinese suspicions from the start. Nixon agreed with me. On December 12 I informed Rogers: "The President . . . has asked that under no circumstances should we inform Dobrynin of the talks or their content. If Dobrynin questions, we should respond with nonchalance that they concern matters of mutual interest but not go beyond that. The President is concerned that lower-level offices not go beyond this in informal conversations."

Unfortunately, another cog of the bureaucratic machinery was also working overtime. The State Department functions through a wondrous system of clearances by which the various offices of the Department as well as foreign governments are informed, more or less automatically, of important events. The motives are various: to make certain that key officials are aware of matters that may affect them in the discharge of their reponsibilities; to generate a sense of participation; to reassure nervous allies; and sometimes — in a profession where information is power — to create an obligation for the reciprocal sharing of information. The difficulty is that these worthy criteria are too often subordinated to very short-run considerations of vanity or bureaucratic prestige, and are implemented so routinely that senior officials find it hard to control them. Within days it became apparent that the State Department had sent accounts of the Warsaw meeting to our embassies in Tokyo, Taipei, and Moscow and to our Consulate General in Hong Kong. The governments of the United Kingdom, Australia, Canada, France, Italy, and New Zealand had been briefed either before or after Stoessel's meeting. While everybody was warned against public comment, such dissemination of a fairly juicy piece of news was bound to radiate through the diplomatic world. When I mentioned what had been done, the President sighed, "We'll kill this child before it is born." The difficulty of controlling the enormous bureaucratic communications machinery was a principal reason why control of China diplomacy was gradually moved into the White House.

On December 19 we took yet another initiative. A low-key announcement in the *Federal Register* announced a new easing of trade restrictions: lifting of the $100 ceiling on tourist purchases; permitting US–owned foreign subsidiaries to do business with the People's Republic of China; and shifting to the government the burden of proof with respect to what was Chinese-manufactured, thus easing imports of art objects.

Suddenly all channels seemed to spring to life. On December 17, Romania's First Deputy Foreign Minister Gheorghe Macovescu had called on me to report the Chinese reaction to Nixon's conversation with Ceauşescu. The Chinese had listened politely; they said they were interested in normal relations with the West; they had nothing specific to communicate. The People's Republic seemed to be saying two things: It was ready for contact, but not necessarily through the Romanian channel. Two days later, Ambassador Agha Hilaly conveyed the latest news of the Pakistani channel. He had much more to say. Reading from a handwritten letter — the way all Pakistani messages in the channel were transmitted, for security reasons — Hilaly reported that Yahya had told the Chinese Ambassador of both our general interest in improving relations and our decision to withdraw two destroyers from the Taiwan patrol. The Chinese Ambassador had first reacted very coolly, casting aspersions on American motives, but after a few days — obviously on receiving his instructions from Peking — had returned with a more conciliatory reply. He now expressed Peking's gratitude for Pakistan's role and efforts. The Chinese release of the two American yachtsmen on December 6 had been a tangible response to our overture, said Hilaly.

The President kept the ball in play with a long letter to Yahya on US–Pakistani relations. On China, Nixon wrote: "You know of my interest in trying to bring about a more meaningful dialogue with Chinese leaders. This is a slow process at best, but I have not abandoned it." When I handed this letter to Hilaly on December 23 he had already received another message. Yahya now informed us of his "impression" (in diplomatic vernacular, a nonattributable communication from a high Chinese official) that the Chinese were willing to resume the Warsaw talks without preconditions. It was clear that the Chinese attached special value to the Pakistani channel, Pakistan being in a less complicated position vis-à-vis Sino-Soviet relations than Romania.

Triangular Politics

THUS by the end of 1969, America's relationship with the Communist world was slowly becoming triangular. We did not consider our opening to China as inherently anti-Soviet. Our objective was to purge our foreign policy of all sentimentality. There was no reason for us to confine our contacts with major Communist countries to the Soviet

Union. We moved toward China not to expiate liberal guilt over our China policy of the late 1940s but to shape a global equilibrium. It was not to collude against the Soviet Union but to give us a balancing position to use for constructive ends — to give each Communist power a stake in better relations with us. Such an equilibrium could assure stability among the major powers, and even eventual cooperation, in the Seventies and Eighties.

On December 18 in a year-end press briefing in the East Room, I tried to sketch our general approach to *both* of the major Communist countries: "We have always made it clear that we have no permanent enemies and that we will judge other countries, including Communist countries, and specifically countries like Communist China, on the basis of their actions and not on the basis of their domestic ideology." I spoke favorably of the matter-of-fact style that had developed in our relations with the Soviet Union, of the absence of the tendentious propaganda that had characterized previous exchanges. We were ready for serious negotiations. We would prepare ourselves meticulously. But we would insist on reciprocity. We were prepared to have a summit meeting with the Soviet leaders, but we would prefer to have the summit register considerable progress, not be an end in itself. I spoke of China in a more philosophical vein, since we had so much farther to go to awaken that relationship:

The Chinese people are obviously a great people. They have the longest unbroken record of government in one area of any of the existing civilizations; and secondly, 800 million people representing 25 percent of the human race are a factor that cannot be ignored. They will influence international affairs whatever we intend to do and declaratory policy we adopt. They are a reality. And their policy, for good or ill, will determine the possibilities for peace and progress. And that is irrespective of what we do.

. . . if it is true that the big problem of the immediate post–World War II period was to avoid chaos, and if it is true that the big problem of the next 20 years is to build a more permanent peace, then it seems to us impossible to build a peace, which we would define as something other than just the avoidance of crisis, by simply ignoring these 800 million people. . . .

Nor do we over-estimate what we can do by unilateral actions towards them.

They will make their decisions on the basis of their conceptions of their needs, and of their ideology. But to the degree that their actions can be influenced by ours, we are prepared to engage in a dialogue with them.

On December 22 I had a private year-end review with Dobrynin. I was so certain that he would bring up China that I wrote out my response for the President's approval, which he gave. I wrote:

I will reiterate that
— we do not accept the proposition that permanent hostility is the iron law of US–Chinese relations;

— our policy is not aimed against the USSR;
— we take no sides in the Sino-Soviet dispute.

I was not to be disappointed. Dobrynin raised the subject of China yet again, asking what we were up to and what the Chinese had responded. I sidestepped the question, giving only the general assurances I had prepared.

By the end of 1969 it was apparent that China, too, had made a strategic decision to seek rapprochement with us, even while it fended off the Soviet Union by resuming an intermittent dialogue on the border dispute. As 1970 began, the Chinese agreed to another informal meeting at which Stoessel was to propose the formal resumption of the Warsaw ambassadorial talks. The meeting was to take place at the American Embassy on January 8. Preparing for it led to another minor dispute with the State Department. The President and I were anxious to use the occasion to tell the Chinese that we would not participate in a US–Soviet condominium in Asia or anywhere else. We wanted to have the Chinese hear directly what had until now been said to them only through third parties. There was also the danger that we would undermine the credibility of our private channels if American diplomats did not reiterate what the President and I had repeatedly said through intermediaries.

Assistant Secretary of State for East Asian and Pacific Affairs Marshall Green resisted, arguing that we should avoid substance at a meeting devoted to procedure. There were undoubtedly deeper reasons for this resistance: irritation at White House interference; a feeling among East Asian specialists that introducing a geopolitical consideration having to do with the Soviet Union was gratuitous; and perhaps still caution toward the China opening among experts accustomed to view China as a major threat, or else inhibited by painful memories of the penalties exacted for bold steps toward Communist China during the McCarthy era.

In the event, the Warsaw meeting of January 8 went extraordinarily well. The Chinese chargé arrived flamboyantly at the US Embassy in a limousine flying the Chinese flag. Procedural issues were amicably settled. It was agreed to resume the formal and regular Warsaw meetings between ambassadors. And the President's message about condominium was conveyed. Both sides avoided polemics (even though the Chinese press was still informing its public of the "iniquities" of the Nixon Administration). The Chinese accepted the principle of meeting alternately in the two embassies. The next meeting was set for January 20, in the Chinese Embassy. Lei Yang proposed that the meeting be announced.

Thus, one year to the day after the Inauguration of the President, the People's Republic of China and the United States were to engage in substantive talks again for the first time in over two years. But these were to be different from any of the 134 meetings that had preceded them. They had been painstakingly prepared over months by messages, first indirect but growing increasingly explicit, of a willingness to bring about a fundamental change in our relationship. We still had a long way to go. But we were at last in the foothills of a mountain range that it would take us another eighteen months to traverse.

It was a moment of extraordinary hope. Beyond the advantages of triangular diplomacy, there were other reasons. One was Vietnam. An opening to China might help us end the agony of that war. Xuan Thuy's outburst of March 22 had vividly shown Hanoi's sensitivity to the escalating feud between its two major allies. This Sino-Soviet conflict complicated North Vietnam's position, for (among others) the simple practical reason that much military aid from the Soviet Union came overland by rail through China and therefore required some minimal Sino-Soviet cooperation. Hanoi might have sensed the maneuvering room the feud would give us as it did in 1972. And any initiative that helped heal our domestic divisions also deprived Hanoi of one of its major assets.

The domestic impact in America of our China initiative had a far deeper significance. The agony of Vietnam seemed to bring on a despair about the possibility of creative policy, an abhorrence of foreign involvement, and in some quarters an insidious self-hatred. The drama of ending estrangement with this great people, in human terms and for what it meant to the global prospects of peace, would be a breath of fresh air, a reminder of what America could accomplish as a world leader. To do so in the midst of a divisive war would prove to ourselves and others that we remained a major factor in world affairs, able to act with boldness and skill to advance our goals and the well-being of all who relied upon us.

VII

Defense Policy and Strategy

Defense and the Strategic Balance

T HROUGHOUT history the political influence of nations has been roughly correlative to their military power. While states might differ in the moral worth and prestige of their institutions, diplomatic skill could augment but never substitute for military strength. In the final reckoning weakness has invariably tempted aggression and impotence brings abdication of policy in its train. Some lesser countries have played significant roles on the world scale for brief periods, but only when they were acting in the secure framework of an international equilibrium. The balance of power, a concept much maligned in American political writing — rarely used without being preceded by the pejorative ''outdated'' — has in fact been the precondition of peace. A calculus of power, of course, is only the beginning of policy; it cannot be its sole purpose. The fact remains that without strength even the most elevated purpose risks being overwhelmed by the dictates of others.

This has been a hard lesson for Americans to learn. Protected by two oceans, we were persuaded for over a century that it was unnecessary for us to address issues of strategy. Alone among the great powers, we imagined that we could prevail through the purity of our motives and that our impact on the world was somehow unrelated to our physical power. We tended to oscillate between isolation and spurts of involvement, each conceived in moralistic terms. Even our military efforts had an abstract quality about them, focused more on logistics than on geopolitics. In our wars, we generally wore down our adversary by the weight of resources rather than by boldness or strategic conceptions.

By the late 1960s we were once again tempted by withdrawal. The frustrations of an inconclusive war encouraged some to ascribe our problems to being too heavily engaged around the world. Criticism originally aimed at the war in Vietnam was soon extended to the entire spectrum of our military programs and commitments. The informed opinion that had sustained a generation of enlightened postwar international involvement seemed to be turning sharply against it.

This threatened to put our nation and other free peoples into a precarious position. The political stability of Europe and Japan and the future evolution of the developing countries of Latin America, Africa, and Asia would turn on whether the United States possessed power relevant to its objectives and was perceived as able to defend its interests and those of its friends. If the war in Vietnam eroded our willingness to back the security of free peoples with our military strength, untold millions would be in jeopardy.

Unfortunately, our domestic travail was most acute at a moment when technology, combined with earlier deliberate decisions, was altering the nature of the strategic balance. Throughout the postwar period the Soviet Union had enjoyed an enormous advantage in conventional land forces. Soviet military capabilities suffered from two handicaps, however: the Soviet reach was relatively short; it was confined in effect to areas adjoining the Soviet Union. And the American preponderance in nuclear strategic forces was overwhelming. The Soviet Union could not press its local advantage for fear of being confronted by the nuclear superiority of the United States. This was the primary reason why the Soviet Union, despite its occasional bluster, never used its vast conventional forces against countries allied with the United States. It is one of the ironies of our time that since 1945 the Red Army has been employed in force only against *allies* of the Soviet Union (in East Berlin in 1953, in Hungary in 1956, in Czechoslovakia in 1968, and on the border with China in 1969).

By the late Sixties, however, the strategic nuclear balance was tending toward parity. This should have changed all the assumptions of our postwar strategy. Unfortunately, at the precise moment that our national debate should have concentrated on the implications of this new situation, *all* our defense programs were coming under increasing attack. They were decried as excessive, blamed on reckless leaders, and criticized as contributing to crises and conflicts.

The administrations in office in the Sixties decided consciously to accept a parity in strategic weapons they considered inevitable; by accepting it, however, they also accelerated it. In the Sixties the United States voluntarily halted its construction of land-based ICBMs and sea-based SLBMs. We had no programs to build additional strategic bombers. It was decided to maintain a strategic force consisting of 1,054 land-based ICBMs, 656 SLBMs, and about 400 B-52 bombers. We adopted these ceilings at a time when we far outnumbered the strategic forces of the Soviet Union. But these ceilings were not changed even when it became clear that the Soviet Union, reacting in part to its humiliation in the Cuban missile crisis of 1962, had undertaken a massive effort to augment its military strength across the board.

In American folklore the Cuban crisis is remembered as a great

American victory. And indeed it was. But the American and Soviet governments drew diametrically opposite conclusions from it. In American policy it led to the pursuit of arms control and détente, exemplified by the Test Ban and Non-Proliferation treaties and indeed in the decision to cease our missile construction once we had reached a fixed number. In the Soviet Union, by contrast, Khrushchev's humiliation in Cuba was one cause of his overthrow two years later. The essence of the Soviet response to the Cuban experience is embodied in the pungent remark of Vasily V. Kuznetsov to John McCloy, when these two veteran Soviet and American diplomats negotiated the details of the removal of Soviet weapons from Cuba at the end of 1962: "You Americans will never be able to do this to us again!"[1] The Soviet Union thereupon launched itself on a determined, systematic, and long-term program of expanding *all* categories of its military power — its missiles and bombers, its tanks and submarines and fighter planes — in technological quality and global reach. The 1962 Cuban crisis was thus an historic turning point — but not for the reason some Americans complacently supposed.

Three years after the Cuban confrontation, in 1965, the Soviet strategic arsenal comprised about 220 ICBMs and over 100 SLBMs. By 1968 the numbers had grown to nearly 860 ICBMs and over 120 SLBMs. By 1971 the Soviets had caught up with us — and they continued to build. Our estimates of their plans invariably turned out to be low. The brilliant analyst Albert Wohlstetter has demonstrated convincingly that the belief fashionable in the 1960s — that the Pentagon exaggerated Soviet programs to win higher appropriations — was exactly the opposite of the truth. American planners in the Fifties and Sixties consistently *underestimated* the Soviet buildup.[2] The Soviet programs always were at the highest level of our estimates — not what was described as "most probable" but what was put forward as the "worst case." Instead of halting once they reached parity with us, as some expected, the Soviets continued to build — until stopped by the 1972 SALT accords, and then they switched to an energetic qualitative improvement.

The American response to the Soviet buildup in the Johnson Administration was twofold. There was a decision to build an antiballistic missile defense system (ABM), but it was forced on the Johnson Administration by an aroused Congress and it was left to Nixon to implement it. And on the offensive side, rather than match the numbers of Soviet missiles, our predecessors decided to develop MIRV warheads to multiply the offensive power of each of our existing missiles. The first US flight tests of MIRV'd missiles took place in 1968. Our predecessors had also decided to base our strategic force on light but highly accurate missiles, the Minuteman ICBM and Poseidon SLBM. (The Soviets had made the opposite decision, emphasizing missiles that were much larger than ours and therefore capable of delivering a far heavier payload. As Soviet technology improved, its advantage in numbers and payload would be enhanced by improved accuracy.) Thus decisions of the Johnson Administration determined the size as well as the numbers of our missiles throughout our period in office. This was because the lead time for most new weapons is at least six years between conception and production and because the Congress resisted new programs until the end of the Vietnam war. Hence no decision that we made could produce new weapons before the middle 1970s. And Congressional opposition threatened to delay this even further.

Thus, inexorably, the overwhelming preponderance that we had enjoyed in the Forties and Fifties was being eroded first into equality, eventually into vulnerability, of our land-based forces. The Soviets' heavier payload and imminent lead in numbers would be counterbalanced for a while by our technological lead. We were believed to be at least five years ahead in the development of MIRVs; the accuracy of our missiles was still superior, a crucial ingredient in any calculation about a hypothetical nuclear exchange. Our capacity to maintain a rough strategic balance was not yet endangered — provided our technological superiority was fully exploited. We could deploy an ABM to protect our cities or our missile sites. We could also speed up preliminary work on a more advanced bomber (later known as the B-1), a new submarine and submarine-launched missile (the Trident), and a new ICBM (the MX). After 1978 we would thus be in a strong position, provided all the programs started in the early 1970s were maintained. We took all these steps, but each was attacked both in the Congress and in the media. Our strategic dilemma was that without these future weapons systems our strategic forces would grow increasingly vulnerable; even with them our long-term security requirements were changing.

For *even with equality,* or a slight superiority, any new Administration would face an unprecedented challenge. Our defense strategies formed in the period of our superiority had to be reexamined in the harsh light of the new realities. Before too long an all-out nuclear exchange could inflict casualties on the United States amounting to tens of millions. A balance of destructiveness would then exist; and even if for a while our capacity to inflict casualties should exceed that of our adversaries, our reluctance to resort to nuclear war was certain to mount dramatically. The credibility of American pledges to risk Armageddon in defense of allies was bound to come into question. This raised critical issues: How could we maintain the independence and self-confidence of allied countries under the shadow of the Soviet Union's land armies (also growing) as well as its expanding nuclear arsenal? What should be our strategy for the use of our nuclear forces? If all-out thermonuclear war became too dangerous, would limited applications of nuclear forces still be feasible?

The Defense Debate

SUCH questions would have been difficult to answer in the best of circumstances. Unfortunately, the late 1960s and early 1970s were hardly a time for calm, rational analysis of strategic problems. The passionate critique of the war in Vietnam spread to an attack on the defense establishment as a whole; indeed, some saw in an assault on the defense budget a device for forcing an end to the war in Southeast Asia. "Reordering national priorities" from defense to domestic programs was the slogan of the period; it was a euphemism for severe cuts in the defense budget. Intellectuals who made fun of President Eisenhower's syntax and leadership when he was in office readily embraced as received truth his 1961 warning against permitting the so-called military-industrial complex to acquire a disproportionate influence on American life. Weapons — especially ours — were considered the cause rather than the symptoms of tension because it was alleged that our programs triggered Soviet responses rather than the other way around. The US government's assertions that the Soviet buildup faced us with a genuine defense problem were ridiculed as standard output of the "Pentagon propaganda machine,"[3] regurgitated every year to influence budgetary decisions in the Congress. The valid perception that the strategic arms race was different from any that preceded it was turned into the proposition that *any* new expenditure for strategic forces was absurd because there already existed enough weapons to destroy humanity several times over. The temper of the times was exemplified by a conference in March 1969 in Washington convened by a bipartisan group of ten Senators and nearly forty Representatives on the subject of "the Military Budget and National Priorities." It was attended by distinguished scholars, scientists, former government officials, and members of both houses of Congress. Their report, later published under the title *American Militarism 1970,* concluded that "our country is in danger of becoming a national security state."[4] The eighty-member bipartisan Members of Congress for Peace Through Law issued a report in July that attacked six major weapons programs, including the ABM, in what the *New York Times* described as an effort "to carry the momentum of the anti-ballistic missile debate into a much broader attack on military spending."[5] All things military came under assault — programs, budgets, strategic doctrines. A full-page advertisement opposing antiballistic missile defenses was entitled sarcastically: "From the same people who brought you Vietnam: the anti-ballistic missile system."[6]

The most frequently cited "lesson" of Vietnam was that the United States had to reduce its overseas commitments. The impression was created that our deployments abroad, rather than deterring aggression, actually encouraged it. By withdrawing US forces from overseas, it was said, the incidence of global conflict would go down, making lower defense expenditures possible. By the same token, reduced military budgets would force the government to curtail its foreign involvement. An additional benefit would be that funds would be freed for domestic welfare programs.

The novel theory that reduced defense budgets enhanced security was expressed by two former officials of the Kennedy-Johnson administrations writing at the end of 1968. They were Carl Kaysen, former Deputy Assistant for National Security Affairs under John Kennedy and then head of the prestigious Institute for Advanced Study in Princeton, and Charles L. Schultze, Director of the Bureau of the Budget for Johnson.[7] Kaysen argued:

The new political and technical realities point to the futility of a quest for security primarily through increased military strength and to the increasing importance of political factors and arms-control arrangements and agreements. Indeed, by giving weight to these factors in the next five years, we will have a better prospect of achieving higher levels of real security — that is, lower risks of harm to the United States and its vital interests, with armed forces and military budgets as much as a third lower than they are now — than we will have by continuing to follow the line of our past policy in a radically altered situation. In plain words, the course of arms limitation, restrictions in deployments, and arms control is not only cheaper than that of continuing competition in arms and military confrontation; it is safer.

Schultze concluded that the end of the Vietnam war would permit a reduction of the defense budget by $20 to $22 billion per year. But he was worried that this ''peace dividend'' was in danger of being eaten up by the procurement, already in process, of major new weapons. He therefore urged the greatest vigilance in approving new programs. Kaysen argued, and Schultze agreed, that an additional $15–16 billion savings per year could be realized beyond this so-called peace dividend if progress were made in SALT and if our conventional forces were reduced to a more modest size, reflecting a scaling-down in America's foreign commitments.

Thus critics drew from the approaching nuclear parity the amazing conclusion that we should cut our *conventional* forces in which we were already vastly inferior. They saw in the end of the Vietnam war not an opportunity to make up for long-neglected procurement but an occasion for cutting our defense budget. These cuts could of course be justified only if there was lessened foreign danger or if existing forces were redundant. These precise arguments were advanced by three Harvard professors in January 1970:

It is not clear that [conventional] forces contribute to deterring major nonnuclear conflicts or that such conflicts are sufficiently likely to justify their standing by in readiness. Only military planners, professionally committed to belief in the worst contingencies, today assign significant probability to a sudden Soviet march across the north German plain, a surprise attack by the Red Army on the Mediterranean flank of NATO, or even an unheralded descent by Communist China on Burma or Thailand. Equally, it is unclear what role American non-nuclear forces can play in the kinds of minor wars that do seem probable.[8]

The article did not address the question whether the probability of a Soviet conventional attack might be affected to some extent by the size of the opposing forces; it simply assumed that since there had been no aggression in the past there would be none in the future and therefore we were maintaining unnecessary forces.

It is, of course, inherent in deterrence that one can never prove what has prevented aggression. Is it our defense posture? Or is it that our adversary never intended to attack in the first place? Paradoxically, the more a given military posture deters aggression, the more arguments it supplies to those wishing to dismantle it. The three professors maintained that a smaller conventional force would permit budget reductions amounting to $30 billion, a defense budget $17 billion below the minimum post-Vietnam posture advocated by the Pentagon and $10 billion less than the force projected by President Nixon's first budget.

The same arguments were taken up, more significantly, in the Congress. Senator Mike Mansfield, the Majority Leader, declared in April 1969 that he would lead a fight to cut at least $5 billion from the $77.6 billion defense appropriation request in the Nixon Administration's first budget (which was already somewhat scaled down from the budget submitted by the outgoing Administration). Mansfield took aim at fifteen different defense programs. For example, he criticized a Navy proposal for a fleet of fast logistic deployment ships as "typical of those foot-in-the-door things about which we have to be careful."[9] In May, the *New York Times* reported that "a growing segment of Congress, propelled by the antimilitary climate generated by the war in Vietnam, is searching for some effective way to slash steadily rising military expenditures." This effort to "leash military spending" was bipartisan and included such Republicans as Senators Mark Hatfield of Oregon and John Sherman Cooper of Kentucky. The *Times* quoted freshman Republican Senator William A. Saxbe from Ohio: "We come to the Senate with the attitude that Nixon was elected because of the war — that the war wrecked Johnson and that it will wreck Nixon unless he responds. Those of us who come in with this group believe our election was largely responsive to this national attitude. I am really hopeful that we will beat the ABM and will go ahead with that foothold to attack the whole complex."[10]

On June 3, the Congress moved on two fronts. The Joint Economic Committee headed by Senator William Proxmire began eight days of hearings on how to reduce the defense budget. Charles Schultze, undeterred by the fact that the previous budgets had been prepared during his incumbency as budget director, opened the hearings by suggesting that the Congress create a new committee to review the Defense Department posture statement and bring about substantial reductions. One floor above in the New Senate Office Building, the Senate Armed Services Committee launched an inquiry into the $1.5 billion cost overrun on the C-5A supertransport aircraft (the plane that was later of vital importance in the 1973 Mideast war).

These pressures found their inevitable expression in the bureaucracy. On June 17 I reported to the President that a substantial body of opinion in the State Department, the Arms Control and Disarmament Agency, and even in the CIA believed strongly that

strategic initiatives or assertions of U.S. determination to remain strategically powerful would on balance disappoint and worry our Allies because of their fear of an accelerating arms race and would lead to a deterioration of East-West relations because of hardening Soviet attitudes. Also, it seems to be widely believed that Soviet strategic decisions are highly sensitive to our own decisions and that every U.S. action will provoke an offsetting Soviet reaction.

In commenting on these views I wrote to Nixon:

I do not believe the evidence justifies either the strength with which these views are held or the lack of strong dissenting views. It is equally plausible in my judgment that on balance Europeans would be relieved at clear demonstrations of U.S. strategic resolve and that the Soviet leadership, faced with very real economic problems, would be more rather than less interested in seeking some form of slow down in the competition.

From the beginning, Nixon was determined to resist these trends, believing that American power was not only morally defensible but crucial for the survival of free countries. But in the existing climate, strengthening our defenses proved no simple task. Not only the conduct of a war but the sinews of national security were under assault.

For me the debate brought much stress with old friends and former associates with whom I had served on arms control panels and study groups for over a decade. I agreed with them that nuclear weapons added a unique dimension to the arms race. To be sure, my reading of history did not support their view that all arms races caused tensions; arms buildups, historically, were more often a reflection rather than a cause of political conflicts and distrust. But I substantially agreed that what marked our time as a period of revolutionary change was the high state of readiness of strategic weapons and their destructiveness. Strategic forces, at once highly vulnerable and extremely powerful, could in a crisis tempt one side to strike first, especially if it feared that it might lose its means of retaliation to a first blow.

Like many in the academic community, I favored a conscious policy of stabilizing the arms race. I believed also that national leaders had a duty to disenthrall themselves of the simplistic notions that military power alone brought security, dating from a time when the penalties for misjudgment involved less catastrophic consequences. In my view it was in the interest of both sides to reduce the vulnerability of their retaliatory forces: by agreement on mutual restraint if possible, by unilateral actions if necessary. Even more important, I was convinced that a democratic society would never be able to brave the hazards of the nuclear age unless its people were convinced that its leaders responded rationally and soberly to the unprecedented existence of weapons of mass destruction. Given the dynamics of the Soviet system, I thought that military challenges were possible, perhaps even probable. I wanted the United States and its allies to be able to face them backed by a united public. One lesson of Vietnam was that firm counteractions, necessarily involving sacrifice, could always be undermined by domestic divisions if our people believed their governments needlessly sought or provoked confrontations.

Where I parted company with my friends and former colleagues was in my analysis of Soviet motivations. I did not accept the proposition that unilateral restraint in weapons procurement on our part would evoke a comparable response from the Kremlin. As believers in the predominance of "objective factors," the Soviet leaders were likely to interpret such steps less as gestures of conciliation than as weakness, caused by domestic or economic pressures. The Soviet Union after the Cuban missile crisis was going all out in its weapons procurement in every major category of arms. American abdication would tempt Soviet tendencies toward filling every vacuum; the USSR would accept a stabilization of the arms race only if convinced that it would not be allowed to achieve superiority. It was in our interest to demonstrate to the Soviet Union that given the inequality of resources it could not possibly win an arms race, that we would not stand by while the balance shifted against us, and that if sufficiently provoked we would simply outproduce them.

Nor did I agree with the military analysis so often advanced by critics of our defense programs. It was true that notions of military superiority had a different significance in the nuclear age; it did not follow that we could risk standing still while our adversaries built feverishly. Over the decades a growing imbalance against us was bound to deprive our pledges to defend our allies of *any* credibility; in extreme circumstances it might tempt an attack on the United States.

Even if the risks to the Soviet Union of an attempt to attack the

United States would always seem exorbitant, an eroding strategic equilibrium was bound to have geopolitical consequences. It would accentuate our known inferiority in forces capable of regional defense. The countries around the Soviet periphery would be more and more tempted to seek security in accommodation. Nor were our dangers exhausted by deliberate acts of Soviet military pressure. In a revolutionary period many crises were conceivable that were not sought by either side; Soviet willingness to run risks was bound to grow as the strategic balance shifted against us. This could not fail to demoralize countries looking to us for protection, whether they were allied or technically nonaligned.

I therefore favored new strategic programs and a strengthened conventional defense, even while urging a major effort in negotiations to control arms. In time my views were to provoke the wrath of both conservatives and liberals, the former because they opposed any arms control, the latter because they opposed any arms buildup. By the same token, the 1969 debate on the military balance came to affect national decisions on both weapons procurement and SALT negotiations for all the years of the Nixon Administration.

The debate focused on two new weapons systems: the ABM program and the deployment of MIRVs on our missiles. The new Administration inherited both of these programs from its predecessor. But Nixon's victory had altered the political equation; it liberated Democratic critics of defense programs who had muted their views while their own party was in office. They were soon reinforced by some of the very Johnson Administration officials who had originated these programs and were eager to rejoin the mainstream of their party. Though Nixon had cut the defense budget submitted by Johnson by $1.1 billion, he was nevertheless abused almost immediately by an insistent chorus of Democratic critics. Some Republicans, believing the antimilitary sentiment to be the dominant public mood, joined them.

Antiballistic Missiles (ABM)

THE ABM had become controversial in 1964 when it became apparent that the Soviet Union was deploying a missile defense system around Moscow in the apparent hope of protecting the Soviet capital against an attack. Under constant Congressional prodding, Secretary of Defense Robert McNamara, with considerable hesitation and reluctance, finally put forward the "Sentinel" ABM program in 1967. McNamara was torn between the doctrines of arms control and domestic pressures, between the imperatives of defense and the counsels of restraint. He opted for a compromise. He rejected the concept of full ABM defense of the United States against an all-out Soviet attack. Such a system would be prohibitively expensive; but there was also a theory that it might be perceived by the Soviets as a step toward a first-strike capability. (A country with a full ABM defense might imagine it could strike first and then use its ABMs to intercept the weakened retaliatory blow.) The Johnson Administration went even farther and actively discouraged the notion that the "Sentinel" ABM had *any* utility to limit damage from a Soviet attack on the United States. The principal justification put forward for the "Sentinel" program in 1967 was not the Soviet threat but the lesser danger from the small force of ICBMs that China might develop in the mid-1970s. In his last report to the Congress as Secretary of Defense, in January 1968, Clark Clifford stressed the point of view that in the strategic balance defense was secondary: "We remain convinced . . . we should continue to give primary priority in the allocation of available resources to the primary objective of our strategic forces, namely 'assured destruction.' "

By the time of Nixon's Inauguration the domestic mood had changed significantly from the period of the mid-1960s when Congress virtually forced ABM appropriations on McNamara. Opposition to ABM was growing in the Congress as well as in the academic and scientific community. All of Nixon's instincts were against unilaterally giving up a weapons program — especially one approved by his predecessor. I shared his view; I considered it highly dangerous to stop programs in the area of our traditional superiority — advanced technology — without any Soviet reciprocity.

But in order to pull the teeth of public criticism, Nixon on February 6 asked his Deputy Secretary of Defense, David Packard, to chair an interagency review of the ABM program. His purpose, as he told me, was to make us appear thoughtful. It proved a wrong calculation. As in the case of Vietnam, meeting critics halfway did not allay opposition; it whetted appetites. It encouraged the belief that the same political pressures which had produced the review could cause the Administration to abandon the ABM altogether. The *New York Times*, for example, gave the President no credit for ordering the review but ascribed it instead — not all that incorrectly — to Congressional pressure. The *Times* argued that the next step should be to question a whole range of military projects: "The Congressional pressure that spurred the Nixon Administration to halt deployment of the Sentinel antiballistic missile system signals a healthy new disposition on Capitol Hill to challenge the military-industrial complex, against which President Eisenhower warned eight years ago." And: "Now that the exercise of that right has prompted an Administration reassessment of the ABM system, there are encouraging signs that more such questions will be asked on Capitol Hill."[11]

On February 16 the influential Chairman of the Congressional Joint Committee on Atomic Energy, Representative Chet Holifield, said that he would oppose any missile defense against China or any antimissile site built close to his own home in California. This of course left no rationale whatever for the ABM program. On February 19 Senator Edward Kennedy took up the charge that the Pentagon review of the ABM had as its primary purpose to mollify critics. On February 26, in a speech at the University of Minnesota, Hubert Humphrey said that we should halt deployment of the ABM system and "begin as expeditiously as possible negotiation with the Soviet Union on the reduction of offensive and defensive strategic systems." On March 6, Senator Albert Gore's disarmament subcommittee opened hearings on the strategic and foreign policy implications of an ABM system. Almost without exception the witnesses were hostile to ABM defense.

The grounds for opposition were various, passionate, and not necessarily consistent. Six distinguished scientists — Hans Bethe, Herbert York, George Kistiakowsky, James R. Killian, Wolfgang Panofsky, and George Rathjens — testified in March that the ABM was not reliable; it was too technologically complex to function with adequate accuracy. A second argument was that even if ABM functioned as planned, it could be relatively easily defeated by various Soviet countermeasures. Carried away with enthusiasm for this line of reasoning, Professor Bethe in a public session outlined five scientific methods to defeat our ABM system.

On the other hand, the allegedly ineffective, unreliable, and easily defeated ABM system was considered a menace because it might spark an arms race and in the process might well weaken the deterrent effect of strategic weapons. Building an ABM, it was argued, implied that we might await a Soviet attack and seek to ride it out, while the better strategy was to let the Soviet Union believe we would launch our missiles immediately on warning of an attack: "If I were the Russians," said Senator Frank Church before Senator Gore's subcommittee, "and knew that an immediate counterlaunch of Minutemen would be the American response to any first strike against the United States, I would be far more reluctant to launch the attack than if I thought the United States might rely upon a defensive system in which I, as a Russian, had contempt. In other words, it seems to me that the very defensive system you are talking about . . . might even lead the Russians to conclude that they might hazard a first strike." The Senator did not explain why he would feel more secure when the United States could protect itself only by a hair-trigger response within the fifteen-minute maximum warning time available, a strategy that could not work unless the President delegated authority to field commanders to launch on the first warning of Soviet missiles — a warning that later might or might not prove correct.

Others argued that the need for our ABM was based on exaggerated estimates of the effectiveness of the Soviet ABM deployed around Moscow. However, the critics contended that it made no difference even if the Soviets had built an effective ABM. An American ABM program, whatever the provocation for it, would usher in a new round of the arms race threatening to the prospects for talks on strategic arms limitation. It was not explained why an American ABM still many years in the future would jeopardize the prospects for strategic arms limitation while an existing Soviet ABM system around Moscow would not.

Finally, the ABM — as indeed were many other military programs — was attacked as a wasteful diversion of resources from domestic priorities. In fact, strategic forces have always been a small fraction of our defense budget; most of our defense budget goes for conventional forces and manpower. In Fiscal Year 1970 *all* strategic forces accounted for about *one-ninth* of the total defense budget. Yet a highly visible new program like ABM was a natural target for attacks. In the Senate debate on the ABM, Senator Muskie argued:

The grim chain of urban sprawl and rural decline, of individual poverty and social disorganization, of wasted resources and hostile environments will not be broken by a government which is indifferent or a private sector which is inactive — or preoccupied with hunting the next arms contract.

Senator Mondale took a similar line:

This uneasy deterrence balance is threatened by the deployment of the . . . Safeguard . . . system. This threat comes from uncertainties — the uncertainties as to whether an anti-ballistic-missile system can work . . . the uncertainties which come with the inevitable introduction of offensive weapons to negate the effectiveness of an ABM defense . . . the uncertainties about our intentions when the deployment of more weapons indicates a decision to spend on military materials rather than on peaceful and domestic needs.

In early 1969 Senator Edward Kennedy sponsored publication of a book compiling a full battery of the political, diplomatic, economic, military, and technical arguments against an American ABM.[12]

This was the atmosphere in which the Nixon Administration's ABM review went forward. David Packard concluded his study in late February. He recommended that the Johnson Administration's 1967 "Sentinel" program be continued in a somewhat modified form. First, he proposed that the ABM radars face not only toward the north, whence an ICBM attack would come, but also toward the sea, from which submarines could launch missiles. Second, Packard recommended that more of the ABM interceptor missiles be used to protect our Minuteman ICBM fields. Third, he urged a slight thinning out of the number of missiles devoted to the defense of cities. The reasons for the first two recommendations were military: Defense of the circumference of the

United States was chosen to protect against accidental attack from any quarter or a small (a euphemism for Chinese) deliberate attack. It would also give us an option to expand the defense against the Soviet Union if SALT negotiations failed. And protecting Minuteman fields made a Soviet first strike more difficult. Thinning out the defense of the population was a purely political decision; it was designed to reassure arms control advocates fearful lest a heavy defense of our population would appear threatening to the Soviets. Our dilemma was that we could sell an ABM program to the Congress apparently only by depriving it of military effectiveness against our principal adversary.

I agreed with the conclusion that we should go forward with ABM. The decisive arguments in my view were both military and diplomatic. Soviet leaders and military theorists had never espoused the Western academic notions that vulnerability was desirable or that ABM was threatening and destabilizing. As Premier Kosygin declared at a London news conference in February 1967, an antiballistic missile system "is intended not for killing people but for saving human lives." And he had told President Johnson at Glassboro that giving up *defensive* weapons was the most absurd proposition he had ever heard. Moreover, being somewhat in awe of American technology, the Soviets could only assess an active *American* ABM program as a harbinger of future American superiority in a field that they considered important.

Thus, not only was it desirable to pursue an area of technology in which the Soviets were actively engaged; offering to limit our ABM could become the major Soviet incentive for a SALT agreement. Our own new offensive missiles were years away, and given the Congressional climate they might never be approved. In the immediate future we would not be able to counter the alarming buildup of Soviet offensive missiles except by deploying a defensive system and spurring the MIRV program. If these two programs were curtailed — as so many in the Congress urged — the United States would be without any strategic options at a time when the Soviets were building two to three hundred new missiles a year — an intolerable position in the long run. Our reasoning proved to be correct. The trade-off of Soviet willingness to limit offensive forces in exchange for our willingness to limit ABMs was the essential balance of incentives that produced the first SALT agreements three years later.

There were other reasons that caused me to support a limited ABM deployment. It seemed to me highly irresponsible simply to ignore the possibility of an accidental attack or the prospect of nuclear capabilities in the hands of yet more countries. China was only the first candidate; others would follow. Without any defense an accidental launch could do enormous damage. Even a small nuclear power would be able to blackmail the United States. I did not see the moral or political value of turning our people into hostages by deliberate choice.

Nixon faced what would clearly be a controversial decision; he paused briefly to canvass his associates. Laird was strongly in favor of proceeding. Rogers was mildly dubious; he called occasionally to tell me that some of his State Department colleagues suggested that we confine our ABM program to research and development, rather than production, but he stressed that he did not necessarily endorse their views. I asked Dave Packard if it was feasible to proceed in this manner. Packard replied that this was a way of killing the program. If we backed off now — which was the practical consequence of the proposal — the Congress was no more likely to support deployment the following year. The arguments for it would not be better then than now and the opponents would be strengthened by having imposed a one-year delay. Moreover, a pause of one year would result in an actual delay of two to three years in putting the system into operation: production facilities once closed down would take another year or two to start up again. Therefore a decision to postpone would mean a decision that the United States would be without any missile defense through the better part of the 1970s and with no assurance of Soviet restraint.

On March 14 Nixon announced his decision to go forward with an ABM program. Nixon's program called for twelve separate sites for area defense, of which four would also protect Minutemen, a total of nineteen radars, and several hundred interceptor missiles. It was to be completed by 1973. To show originality the Johnson "Sentinel" system was now renamed "Safeguard." It differed from "Sentinel" primarily in covering all of the United States with radars, providing a better base for rapid expansion against the Soviet Union, and concentrating somewhat more on defending ICBM bases. Nixon's statement added:

I have taken cognizance of the view that beginning construction of a U.S. ballistic missile defense would complicate an agreement on strategic arms with the Soviet Union.

I do not believe that the evidence of the recent past bears out this contention. The Soviet interest in strategic talks was not deterred by the decision of the previous administration to deploy the Sentinel ABM system — in fact, it was formally announced shortly afterwards. I believe that the modifications we have made in the previous program will give the Soviet Union even less reason to view our defense effort as an obstacle to talks. Moreover, I wish to emphasize that in any arms limitation talks with the Soviet Union, the United States will be fully prepared to discuss limitations on defensive as well as offensive weapons systems.

This announcement provoked a fierce and prolonged debate lasting from March until well into August. On August 6 the Senate, in a cliff-hanger, approved the authorization of funds for the ABM program by the barest margin of one vote.

But still the opponents did not give up. In succeeding years they managed to reduce appropriations until the original twelve-site "Safe-guard" program of 1969 had shrunk to three sites in 1972. The 1972 SALT treaty limited ABM to two sites for each country, including one for the defense of the national command authority and one for an ICBM field. In 1974 the United States and the Soviet Union amended the treaty to limit each side to one site (either an ICBM field or the national command authority). Congressional insistence and bureaucratic demoralization resulted in 1975 in a unilateral decision by the United States to scrap even the one site to which we were entitled under the treaty. But by then the ABM program had served its minimum purpose of making possible the 1972 SALT agreement, which stopped the numerical build-up of the Soviet offensive strategic forces. Nevertheless, I have always considered the 1975 decision to abandon our last site a mistake, even though I acquiesced in it.

Multiple Independently Targetable Reentry Vehicles (MIRV)

THE MIRV issue was the reverse side of the ABM problem. MIRVs had been developed in the Johnson Administration to counteract the Soviet deployment of an ABM defense by saturating it with incoming warheads and to do so without increasing our number of launchers, which was thought to be destabilizing. The theory was that if in reaction to the Soviet buildup we increased the numbers of our own missiles, we would spur the arms race; if, however, we increased the number of warheads carried on each individual missile we could guarantee our retaliatory capacity without running this risk. If the Soviets expanded their ABM system our missiles with multiple warheads could overwhelm it. And even if only a small number of our missiles survived a surprise attack, so the argument ran, those few would still be able to inflict unacceptable damage on an aggressor because they carried several warheads. The reasoning was a little cloudy because MIRV'd forces again gave a considerable advantage to the attacker. Even if both sides were equal, with, say, 1,000 missiles with three warheads on each, the side that struck first would be able to send 3,000 warheads against 1,000 targets, with a tempting chance for success. Why increasing warheads would be more stabilizing than multiplying launchers was neither self-evident nor was it explained. Nor was attention paid to our situation after the Soviets developed MIRVs of their own, when the number of launchers and their vulnerability would again become relevant.

MIRV did not arouse as intense a domestic debate as did ABM. One reason was that MIRV had already been funded by the Johnson Administration and testing had started in August 1968. The genie of MIRV was to all intents and purposes out of the bottle. But a new and final round of MIRV tests was scheduled to start in May. It was against this that opponents concentrated their fire, especially after Nixon's ABM decision of March 14. They followed what had become almost a ritual for opponents of new weapons systems. The new system is decried at one and the same time as unnecessary and destabilizing, as duplicating a perfectly adequate existing weapon, or as preempting a potentially much better one ten years down the road. Above all, it is alleged that our programs "lead" those of the Soviets; if we exercise restraint so will our adversary. (Of course, in the case of the ABM we were asked to exercise restraint even though our adversary had not.) This was the argument of the opponents of the hydrogen bomb; it was used again in the case of MIRV. In both instances the Soviets were well along in their own development programs while the debate raged in America.

In June, Senator Clifford Case offered an amendment to an appropriations bill to call for an end of MIRV testing; when this was rejected by the Appropriations Committee, Case threatened to reintroduce it on the floor. On June 17 Senator Edward Brooke introduced a resolution for a MIRV moratorium. It was cosponsored by forty other Senators, and Brooke told me there were at least ten more who would vote for it. On June 15 Senator Thomas Eagleton urged the President to halt MIRV development. In the House, Representative Jonathan Bingham submitted a resolution urging a moratorium; over one hundred of his colleagues joined him. On June 16 Representative John Anderson, Chairman of the House Republican Conference, recommended a halt to MIRV testing pending the arms control talks. On October 9, a House Foreign Affairs subcommittee issued a report calling on the President to give "high priority" to a freeze on MIRV testing in the SALT negotiations.

The thrust of the campaign was for the United States to halt MIRV tests unilaterally as a way to encourage the Soviets to do the same. The *New York Times* editorialized on June 12: "One way to entice Mr. Kosygin into a MIRV test suspension would be to offer to suspend American MIRV tests — or even actually suspend them with the announcement that they would not be resumed so long as the Soviet Union refrained from testing its multiple warheads." On June 20 it argued: "No decision Richard Nixon will face as President is likely to be more momentous than the decision he faces within the next few days on the proposals to suspend the flight testing of MIRV. . . . Continued testing for even a few more weeks threatens to take the world past a point of no return into an expensive and dangerous new round in the missile race."

A number of White House Congressional experts urged that we accede to a moratorium on MIRV testing in order to improve Congressional attitudes toward the ABM. I doubted this reasoning, writing to the President on May 23 that ending MIRV testing "might create pressures to halt the Minuteman III and Poseidon programs [the missiles designed to carry MIRVs] . . . thus further unravelling the U.S. strategic program.'' Since a major purpose of MIRVs was the penetration of ABM defenses, the logic that would lead Senators who favored a MIRV moratorium to become supporters of ''Safeguard'' was ''obscure.''

Senator Brooke continued to press his proposal. In an emotional conversation with me on May 23 Brooke stressed that if the tests were completed, then indeed the ''genie'' would be ''out of the bottle''; the whole issue was a matter of ''conscience.'' The academic community weighed in; many of my own friends in the universities wrote me to urge a unilateral halt to MIRV testing.

We were being pressed to take two momentous steps: first, to abandon our ABM without reciprocity; and second, to postpone our MIRV deployment as a unilateral gesture — in short, to forgo both our missile defense and the means to defeat that already deployed by the Soviet Union. All this was being advocated while the Soviet missile arsenal was growing at the rate of two to three hundred missiles a year. If the Soviets were building while we abandoned our programs, what would be their incentive to negotiate limitations in an agreement? Our unilateral restraint would be an incentive for the Soviets not to settle but to procrastinate, to tilt the balance as much in their favor as possible while we paralyzed ourselves. To abandon ABM and MIRV together would thus not only have undercut the prospects for any SALT agreement but probably guaranteed Soviet strategic superiority for a decade.

And so it happened that when the SALT talks started in November, contrary to the dire predictions of arms controllers the Soviets proved eager to negotiate on ABM; they showed, on the other hand, interest only in limits on the *deployment* of MIRVs, leaving them free to test and thereby catch up to us technologically. Neither our ABM program nor MIRV testing created difficulties for SALT. On the contrary, they spurred it.

The Attack on the Defense Budget

THE assault on ABM and MIRV in 1969, however, was soon enlarged into an attack on the defense budget as a whole. Nixon presented his first full budget on February 2, 1970. He tried to preempt the opposition by speaking eloquently of the need to reorder national priorities; in his State of the Union Address and Budget Message he proposed increased funding for family assistance, food subsidies, cleaner air and water, and transportation improvement. His defense budget of $73.5 billion cut over $5 billion in defense appropriations from the previous year. In fact, his spending proposals were the first by a President in twenty years in which defense was allotted less than "human needs": 37 percent went to the armed services, 41 percent to social and welfare programs. (In the year before — essentially Johnson's budget — 44 percent went for defense, 34 percent for social and welfare programs.) Richard Nixon had brought about the reordering of priorities that his critics had been passionately advocating for years.

I was not entirely happy with this trend since, despite all the talk of cutting only "fat," I was certain we would wind up reducing the combat effectiveness of our forces. Hence the military equation would move in the wrong direction with respect to both strategic and conventional forces. On January 14, 1970, I took the matter up with John Ehrlichman, who as Assistant in charge of domestic programs naturally defended domestic priorities. Ehrlichman said "everyone" knew Defense had been getting too much. I replied — with a prescience I did not realize — that they would not "know" this in 1973 when the Middle East blew up. Despite an injunction by Haldeman that Nixon was tired of all the budgetary pulling and tugging, later in the day I made the same point to the President: "The trouble is you could easily find yourself in a situation two or three years from now where you just don't have the forces for an emergency."

Nixon was sympathetic, but he calculated that if he did not offer some reductions the critics would take over the process and dismantle the military program altogether. He had reason to worry. His reductions did nothing to still the cries of critics who dismissed them as far too small. Our conventional forces were alleged to be excessive and incompatible with the reduced commitments implied in the President's Guam Doctrine (see page 222). The strategic forces budget, it was argued, could be cut further and still be a credible deterrent. The 1971 budget included long-term programs which it was said would only bloat future budgets, such as aircraft carriers and tactical air forces as well as expensive new strategic weapons. The *New York Times* complained on January 17, 1970, that Nixon's streamlined defense budget reflected only the reductions to be expected from the scaling down of Vietnam operations; they represented "no fundamental shifts in strategy, much less any reordering of priorities." James Reston wrote on January 18 that the defense budget could be safely reduced to the $58–63 billion range, citing former Defense Secretary McNamara and his deputy Roswell Gilpatric as authorities. Former Air Force analyst A. Ernest Fitzgerald, who had been fired for denouncing C-5A cost overruns and was now a spokesman for antidefense groups, said on January 27 that $20 billion should be cut from the defense budget, with $5 billion from procurement and development funds. A lengthy *New York Times* editorial two days later held that there was room for an $8 billion cut beyond the $5 billion anticipated: $2 billion from an ABM-MIRV moratorium; $1.5 billion from accelerated withdrawal from Vietnam; over $4 billion from a cutback of general purpose forces.

Congressional opinion reflected editorial views. At a meeting of the Democratic Policy Council Committee on National Priorities in February, Hubert Humphrey accused Nixon of devoting billions to military purposes at the expense of health and education needs. To the same group Senator Edward Kennedy suggested several areas where further cuts could be made, including the B-1 bomber program, the "Safeguard" ABM, and American conventional forces in Europe:

We should not repeat the mistakes of the fifties and sixties, when we overreacted to cold war fears and helped to stimulate the spiraling arms race. . . .

Since the federal budget is being sharply cut in so many areas, no aspect of military expenditures should be free from scrutiny. . . . I think I have demonstrated that the President's budget request for the Department of Defense is not rock bottom. Further major cuts can and will be made perfectly consistent with an enhanced national security.[13]

On May 2 a bipartisan group of twelve Senators announced plans for a rigorous review of the defense budget, with the intent to reorder "the relative priorities between military security and domestic needs." The Senators added: "We believe the result of such scrutiny can both substantially reduce the general level of expenditures and provide for as great if not greater real security for the United States." A group of liberal Representatives and Senators issued an unofficial report in late June recommending $4.65 billion in further cuts, taken from the programs for MIRV testing and deployment, and from procurement of the F-14 fighter, F-111 bomber, and "Safeguard" ABM.

In the event, by the time of its final vote on defense appropriations in December 1970, Congress had made up its mind to cut an additional $2.1 billion even though Nixon had already reduced it by $5 billion — or a total reduction from the previous year of over $7 billion. But even this does not measure the pervasive antimilitary atmosphere, the hostility to defense spending, the probability that any new military programs would lead to bitter fights, and the resulting cloud of uncertainty over defense planning and our long-term security as the decade of the 1960s came to a close.

To be sure, the most sweeping assaults were in the end turned back. ABM was passed; MIRV testing continued; we even succeeded in getting funds for the B-1 and the Trident, though at a slow rate; there were no drastic reductions in our vital overseas deployments. But at a time when the Soviet buildup required urgent reexamination of strategic doctrine and of forces, the energies of the Executive were consumed by a rearguard action to preserve a minimal arsenal. Pentagon planners were forced to concentrate on preserving the existing force structure rather than adapting it to changed circumstances.

The cuts would probably have been far worse had not Nixon attempted to respond to the national mood by trimming the defense budget himself, and had we not eased budgetary pressures by withdrawing troops gradually from Asia. We shall never know. I have wondered since whether it would have been wiser to meet the issue head-on. Perhaps there should have been an all-out national debate on our defense posture in 1969. Accommodation failed to placate the critics and may have demoralized supporters of a strong defense; as in the Vietnam controversy it tended to isolate the Administration because it seemed to· grant the precepts of the critics with which the Administration in fact disagreed and caused the debate to turn on the implementation of agreed assumptions. On the other hand, ringing Presidential speeches on the importance of defense, such as at the Air Force Academy in June 1969, were met with derision and indignation in the media and the Congress. The only issue in the Congress was not whether defense should be cut but by how much. Supporters of defense in Congress and the country did not rush to the barricades. In the antimilitary orgy spawned by Vietnam, to have challenged the overwhelming Congressional sentiment for ''domestic priorities'' was almost certainly an exercise in futility, pouring salt on the open wounds of the Vietnam debate.

Nixon and Laird in the end were able to preserve the essence of our military structure through years of turmoil, cuts, and conflict. The Nixon Administration began essential new programs — the B-1, the Trident, the cruise missile — and laid a foundation on which it was possible to build when the Congressional mood changed after the mid-1970s.

Strategic Doctrine

A MIDST this turmoil, my staff and I — with the President's strong support — undertook a reexamination of military doctrine. The purpose was to enable us in time to plan and defend our military programs according to reasoned criteria, to adjust our strategy to new realities, and to try to lead the public debate away from emotionalism.

The first problem was to redefine the strategy for general nuclear war. According to the doctrine of "assured destruction," which had guided the previous Administration, we deterred Soviet attack by maintaining offensive forces capable of achieving a particular level of civilian deaths and industrial damage.* The strategy did not aim at destroying the other side's missile or bomber forces; such an approach would have tied our force structure to the level of the other side's — which is precisely what the advocates of "assured destruction" sought to avoid. They preferred the apparent certainty of an absolute standard of destructiveness defined

---

* In 1965, "assured destruction" was defined in the Pentagon as the capacity to destroy one-fourth to one-third of the Soviet population and two-thirds of Soviet industry; by 1968 it was lowered to one-fifth to one-fourth of the Soviet population and one-half of Soviet industry.

in economic terms (systems analysis was, after all, an economists' technique), which freed us from the need to match the growing Soviet power. The number of nuclear weapons needed to achieve a huge level of destruction was fixed and not large.

Remarkably, the doctrine of "assured destruction," espoused by liberal advocates of arms control who were supposedly most moved by humanitarian concerns, implied the most inhuman strategy for conducting a war. The reasoning was that the more horrible the consequences of war the less likely we were to resort to it; the more controllable its consequences the greater the risk that a war would actually occur. Therefore, for the United States and Soviet Union to aim at each other's population, rather than at each other's missile bases, was desirable; if mutual extermination was the only course, neither side would resort to nuclear weapons. What would happen in case of miscalculation was left to the future. How we would defend allies in these circumstances was not analyzed.

The dilemma never resolved by this doctrine was psychological. It was all very well to threaten mutual suicide for purposes of deterrence, particularly in case of a direct threat to national survival. But no President could make such a threat credible except by conducting a diplomacy that suggested a high irrationality — and that in turn was precluded by our political system, which requires us to project an image of calculability and moderation. And if deterrence failed and the President was finally faced with the decision to retaliate, who would take the moral responsibility for recommending a strategy based on the mass extermination of civilians? How could the United States hold its allies together as the credibility of its strategy eroded? How would we deal with Soviet conventional forces once the Soviets believed that we meant what we said about basing strategy on the extermination of civilians?

Carried a step farther, the doctrine of "assured destruction" led to the extraordinary conclusion that the vulnerability of our civilian population was an *asset* reassuring the Soviet Union and guaranteeing its restraint in a crisis. For the first time a major country saw an advantage in enhancing its *own* vulnerability. "Assured destruction" was one of those theories that sound impressive in an academic seminar but are horribly unworkable for a decision-maker in the real world and lead to catastrophe if they are ever implemented.

I was also concerned that as strategic equivalence between the United States and the Soviet Union approached, strategic forces might be used in less than an all-out attack. I pointed out to the President in June of 1969 the dilemma he would face if there was a limited Soviet nuclear attack and urged him to request the Pentagon to devise strategies to meet contingencies other than all-out nuclear challenge. The President agreed. Orders to that effect were issued. But our military establishment resists intrusion into strategic doctrine even when it comes from a White House seeking to be helpful. When I entered office, former Defense Secretary Robert McNamara told me that he had tried for seven years to give the President more options. He had finally given up, he said, in the face of bureaucratic opposition and decided to improvise. I was determined to do better; I succeeded only partially. Civilian defense planners were reluctant because more options would require some new forces, complicating budgetary decisions. The service chiefs were reluctant because they prefer to negotiate their force levels by bargaining with each other, rather than submitting them to the tender mercies of civilian analysts who, experience has taught, are more likely to emasculate than to strengthen them. Since our military operations are planned by combined commands not subordinate to the military services, the various chiefs of staff are more heads of procurement enterprises than of organizations responsible for implementing strategy. They are deeply suspicious of any doctrinal formulation that later might interfere with their procurement decisions. So it happened that a specific Presidential directive of 1969 inquiring into the rationale of naval programs was never answered satisfactorily in the eight years I served in Washington. The response was always short of being insubordinate but also short of being useful. Despite semiannual reminders it was listed as incomplete on the books when we left office. The same attitude existed in other services.

Somewhat more progress was made in developing a more discriminating strategy for all-out war, partly as a result of considerable White House pressure. The Joint Chiefs cooperated because they understood that the doctrine of "assured destruction" would inevitably lead to political decisions halting or neglecting the improvement of our strategic forces and in time reducing them. We therefore developed in 1969 new criteria of "strategic sufficiency" that related our strategic planning to the destruction not only of civilians but of military targets as well. These criteria of "strategic sufficiency" that related our strategic planning to the destruction not only of civilians but of military targets as well. These backs with a rationale, rather than by reflex; they gave us at least the theoretical capability to use forces for objectives other than the mass extermination of populations.

Translating these doctrinal innovations into operational plans proved far more difficult. Planning started immediately, but it was not completed until the incumbency of James R. Schlesinger as Secretary of Defense (1973–1975). Some new targeting options were then produced. Unfortunately, by the time they were developed they had been overtaken by advances in technology. Expected casualties in a nuclear war had doubled even for minimum nuclear options. Defense Secretary Harold Brown has pursued this effort in the Carter Administration. Achieving a more discriminating nuclear strategy, preserving at least some hope of civilized life, remains to this day one of the most difficult tasks to implement, requiring a substantial recasting of our military establishment. If unsolved, the problem will sooner or later paralyze our strategy and our foreign policy.

Tactical Nuclear Weapons

A SIMILAR problem existed with respect to tactical nuclear weapons. One might have thought that if our strategic forces tended toward parity with the USSR and if at the same time we were inferior in conventional military strength, greater emphasis would be placed on tactical nuclear forces. This indeed was NATO's proclaimed strategy of "flexible response." But there was little enthusiasm for this concept within our government. Civilian officials in the State Department and the Pentagon, especially systems analysis experts, were eager to create a clear "firebreak" between conventional and nuclear weapons and to delay the decision to resort to *any* nuclear weapons as long as possible. They were reluctant, therefore, to rely on tactical nuclear weapons, which they thought would tend to erode all distinctions between nuclear and conventional strategy.

A passage from a study on NATO's military options reflected this state of mind. This particular study was unable to find *any* use for nuclear weapons in NATO even though our stockpile there numbered in the thousands: The primary role of our nuclear forces in Europe, the study argued, is to raise the Soviet estimate of the expected costs of aggression and add great uncertainty to their calculations. Nuclear forces do not necessarily have a decisive impact on the likelihood or form of aggression, the study concluded. This was an astonishing statement from a country that had preserved the peace in Europe for over twenty years by relying on its nuclear preponderance. Nor was it clear how forces thought not to have a decisive impact could affect the calculations of a potential aggressor. It was a counsel of defeat to abjure both strategic and tactical nuclear forces, for no NATO country — including ours — was prepared to undertake the massive buildup in conventional forces that was the sole alternative.

To confuse matters further, while American civilian analysts deprecated the use of nuclear weapons as ineffective and involving a dangerous risk of escalation, our allies pressed a course contradicting the prevailing theory in Washington. They urged both a guaranteed early resort to tactical nuclear weapons and immunity of their territories from their use. Inevitably, discussions that had been going on since 1968 in the NATO Nuclear Planning Group began to produce serious differences of opinion.

This Group had been set up by Secretary McNamara as a device by which our allies could participate in nuclear decisions without acquiring nuclear weapons themselves.* Denis Healey, then British Minister of Defense, had explained his government's view when Nixon visited London in February 1969. In Healey's judgment NATO's conventional forces would be able to resist for only a matter of days; hence early use of nuclear weapons was essential. Healey stressed the crucial importance of making the Soviets understand that the West would prefer to escalate to a strategic exchange rather than surrender. On the other hand, NATO should seek to reduce devastation to a minimum. The Nuclear Planning Group was working on solving this riddle; its "solution" was the use of a very small number of tactical weapons as a warning that matters were getting out of hand.

What Britain, supported by West Germany, was urging came to be called the "demonstrative use" of nuclear weapons. This meant setting off a nuclear weapon in some remote location, which did not involve many casualties — in the air over the Mediterranean, for example — as a signal of more drastic use if the warning failed. I never had much use for this concept. I believed that the Soviet Union would not attack Western Europe without anticipating a nuclear response. A reaction that was designed to be of no military relevance would show more hesitation than determination; it would thus be more likely to spur the attack than deter it. If nuclear weapons were to be used, we needed a concept by which they could stop an attack on the ground. A hesitant or ineffective response ran the risk of leaving us with no choices other than surrender or holocaust.

But what was an "effective" response? Given the political impossibility of raising adequate conventional forces, the Europeans saw nuclear weapons as the most effective deterrent. But they feared the use of them on their territories; what seemed "limited" to us could be catastrophic for them. The real goal of our allies — underlining the dilemma of tactical nuclear weapons — has been to commit the United States to the early use of *strategic* nuclear weapons, which meant a US–Soviet nuclear war fought over their heads. This was precisely what was unacceptable to American planners. Our strategy — then and now — must envisage the ultimate use of strategic nuclear weapons if Europe can be defended in no other way. But it must also seek to develop other options, both to increase the credibility of the deterrent and to permit a flexible application of our power should deterrence fail.

In 1969, a temporary compromise emerged that in effect papered over the dispute. The Nuclear Planning Group kept open the possibility of

---

*The NPG was composed of four permanent members and three members rotated at eighteen-month intervals. The permanent members were the United States, Britain, West Germany, and Italy. (France, to maintain its independence in nuclear matters, refused to participate.)

both "demonstrative" and "operational" uses of tactical nuclear weapons. In other words, a decision was avoided. Laird was correct when he reported to the President: "The longer term problem of divergence between American and European views on strategy remains."

One and a Half Wars

W HILE the nuclear issue was not resolved — and perhaps could not be — one major adaptation of our strategic doctrine did take place in 1969. It was destined to have profound consequences for our foreign policy. What started out as a highly esoteric discussion of military strategy turned into one of our most important signals to the People's Republic of China that we meant to improve our relations with it.

When the Nixon Administration came into office, the prevalent doctrine for conventional forces was the "two-and-one-half-war" strategy; according to it the United States needed forces sufficient to: (1) mount an initial (ninety-day) defense of Western Europe against a Soviet attack; (2) make a sustained defense against an all-out Chinese attack on either Southeast Asia or Korea; *and* (3) still meet a contingency elsewhere, for example, the Middle East. Our strategic planning assumed what was belied by the political facts: that we confronted a Communist monolith, that a general war would almost surely involve a simultaneous attack on our vital interests by both the Soviet Union and Communist China. To be sure, we never chose to build the conventional forces envisaged by this ambitious strategy. In military terms the two-and-one-half-war strategy was a paper exercise, in which certain divisions were earmarked for Europe and others for Asia. Its major result, however, was psychological. It connected the Soviet and Chinese threats in our thinking so inextricably that any analysis of possible use of nuclear weapons tended to presuppose that the Soviet Union and China were a single target area. Politically, it inhibited our understanding of the emerging split between the Communist giants and the opportunity this represented for the United States.

In one of my early initiatives as security adviser I launched a reexamination of the assumptions of the two-and-one-half-war concept. An Interdepartmental Group responded with five options, which my staff and I boiled down to three. Each alternative strategy was analyzed in terms of the contingencies it would enable us to meet and its budgetary implications. Strategies for NATO were matched in various combinations with strategies for Asia. These combinations were then related to projected domestic expenditures, so that the President could decide what level of risk he was running if he were to give up any particular strategic option for a specific domestic program. The three options were as follows:

• Strategy 1 would maintain conventional forces for an initial (ninety-day) defense of Western Europe against a major Soviet attack, and for simultaneous assistance (by logistical support and limited US combat forces) to an Asian ally against threats short of a full-scale Chinese invasion.

• Strategy 2 would maintain forces capable of either a NATO initial defense *or* a defense against a full-scale Chinese attack in Korea or Southeast Asia. That is, we would not maintain forces to fight on a large scale in Europe and Asia simultaneously.

• Strategy 3 (essentially our strategy before the Vietnam war) would maintain US forces for a NATO initial defense *and* a defense of Korea or Southeast Asia against a full-scale Chinese attack. The forces would be capable of meeting the major Warsaw Pact and Chinese threats *simultaneously*.

On October 2, 1969, I wrote to the President summing up the options and their military and budgetary implications. The agencies had varying views, which I reported fairly, but in case of a split view the President as always wanted my recommendation. I urged that he approve Strategy 2: "I believe that a simultaneous Warsaw Pact attack in Europe and Chinese conventional attack in Asia is unlikely. In any event, I do not believe such a simultaneous attack could or should be met with ground forces."

Nixon accepted my recommendation. It was one of the more important decisions of his Presidency. First of all, it harmonized doctrine and capability. We had never generated the forces our two-and-one-half-war doctrine required; the gap between our declaratory and our actual policy was bound to create confusion in the minds of potential aggressors and to raise grave risks if we attempted to apply it. There was no realistic prospect that the Chinese and the Soviets would move against us at the same time. But if there *were* a joint assault by China and the Soviet Union, we would be faced with a threat to the global equilibrium; to pretend that in these circumstances we would confine our response to a conventional war in two widely separated areas would multiply our dangers.

The political implications were even more decisive. We had to give up the obsession with a Communist monolith. By linking Soviet and Chinese purposes we created presumptions that circumscribed the flexibility of our diplomacy and ran counter to the demonstrable antagonism between the two major Communist powers. The reorientation of our strategy signaled to the People's Republic of China that we saw its purposes as separable from the Soviet Union's, that our military policy did not see China as a principal threat. Although our change of doctrine was never acknowledged by Peking, it is inconceivable that it was ignored by those careful students of geopolitics who so meticulously monitored all American public statements. For not only did we begin to reflect the new strategic design in our military planning for both nuclear and conventional war; to leave no doubt about our intentions, we took the extraordinary step of spelling out our rationale in the President's first Foreign Policy Report to the Congress on February 18, 1970, along the lines of the analysis I have just described. The key sentences read:

In the effort to harmonize doctrine and capability, we chose what is best described as the "1½-war" strategy. Under it we will maintain in peacetime general purpose forces adequate for simultaneously meeting a major Communist attack in *either* Europe or Asia, assisting allies against non-Chinese threats in Asia, and contending with a contingency elsewhere [emphasis added].

The choice of this strategy was based on the following considerations:

— the nuclear capability of our strategic and theater nuclear forces serves as a deterrent to full-scale Soviet attack on NATO Europe or Chinese attack on our Asian allies;

— the prospects for a coordinated two-front attack on our allies by Russia and China are low both because of the risks of nuclear war and the improbability of Sino-Soviet cooperation. . . .

And Western Europe — not Asia — was singled out as the theater in which the threat was most likely. We were, in short, concerned more with the danger of Soviet than of Chinese aggression.

We had sent an important signal to China. We would no longer treat a conflict with the USSR as automatically involving the People's Republic. We would treat our two adversaries on the basis of their actions toward us, not their ideology; we publicly acknowledged their differences and the unlikelihood of their cooperation. The Chinese had an option to move toward us.

The Nixon Doctrine

THE new strategy defined the forces we would generate. Contrary to the 1960s, the stated goals for our force levels were in fact met. But there remained the need to relate our intentions to the concerns of allies and friends, particularly in Asia. In contrast to some of our domestic critics, these threatened countries saw our withdrawal from Vietnam as irreversible. They feared that in the process the United States might shed *all* its responsibilities and turn its back on *all* its interests in the region. Countries not allied with us wondered whether we would begin to define our security concerns in the Pacific in strictly legal terms, confined to those countries with which we had written commitments. Where would this leave countries of great strategic importance, such as India or Indonesia? And those that had written commitments wondered about how we would interpret them.

Considering the domestic attacks on American overinvolvement and attempts to reduce even our commitments to NATO, these were not naive or trivial questions. But if the United States was perceived to be abdicating its role in Asia, dramatic changes in the foreign policies and perhaps even the domestic evolution of key countries would be probable. On the other hand there was no sense in indicating a doctrine for common defense that could not enlist a domestic consensus.

In preparing for Nixon's Asian trip in the summer of 1969 Nixon and I had discussed this problem often. We had concluded that it was important to make a distinction between three types of security dangers: internal subversion, external attack by a neighboring Asian country, and aggression by a nuclear power (in practical terms, the Soviet Union or the People's Republic of China). At the highest level of threat, we had to make explicit our unchanged opposition to the aggressive designs of any major power in Asia. At the low end of the spectrum, we had to avoid being involved in civil wars. For the gray area in between, no simple formula would suffice. The original intention had been to develop a Presidential speech along that line sometime during the summer. In a White House backgrounder on July 18 I had sketched the Administration's philosophy for post-Vietnam Asia:

The issue of the nature of commitments in the United States often takes the form of a discussion of legal obligations. But on a deeper level, and on the level that has to concern the President, the relationship of the United States to other countries depends in part, of course, on the legal relationships but more fundamentally on the conception the United States has of its role in the world and on the intrinsic significance of the countries in relationship to overall security and overall progress.

*   *   *

What we do want to discuss is, as I pointed out, how these countries visualize their own future because, as one looks ahead to the next decade, it is self-evident that the future of Asia, Southeast Asia, which we will be visiting, will have to depend not on prescriptions made in Washington, but on the dynamism and creativity and cooperation of the region.

We remain willing to participate, but we cannot supply all the conceptions and all the resources. The initiative has to move increasingly into that region. For that reason, it is important that we consider our views of their future.

Then, quite to my surprise, Nixon took up the theme in what I expected to be an informal background chat with the press on July 25 in an officers' club on Guam. We were on our way to the Philippines. It was at the end of a long day. We had been traveling for several hours across several time zones via Johnston Island to witness the splashdown of the first men to land on the moon. This moved Nixon to remark that we had witnessed the "greatest week in the history of the world since the

Creation'' — a statement that left the clergyman in the group somewhat nonplussed. To this day I do not think that Nixon intended a major policy pronouncement in Guam; his original purpose had been to make some news because of the empty period produced by the crossing of the international dateline. That a formal pronouncement was not at first on Nixon's mind is indicated by the fact that his remarks were made on background.[14] But, perhaps carried away by the occasion, Nixon, in an effective and often eloquent statement, spelled out his concerns and approach toward Asia.

Nixon saw potential military dangers in Asia from a major country, Communist China, and two relatively minor ones, North Korea and North Vietnam. But Nixon said that we ''must avoid that kind of policy that will make countries in Asia so dependent on us that we are dragged into conflicts such as the one that we have in Vietnam.'' Inevitably the correspondents pressed him for specifics. Nixon replied:

I believe that the time has come when the United States, in our relations with all of our Asian friends, [should] be quite emphatic on two points: One, that we will keep our treaty commitments, for example, with Thailand under SEATO; but, two, that as far as the problems of internal security are concerned, as far as the problems of military defense, except for the threat of a major power involving nuclear weapons, that the United States is going to encourage and has a right to expect that this problem will be increasingly handled by, and the responsibility for it taken by, the Asian nations themselves.

This still left open the question of what to do about aggression that came neither from a nuclear power nor from internal subversion. Nixon suggested that this might be dealt with by an Asian collective security system in five to ten years' time: ''Insofar as it deals with a threat other than that posed by a nuclear power . . . this is an objective which free Asian nations, independent Asian nations, can seek and which the United States should support.'' He avoided a follow-up question as to what we would do in the intervening period before such a security system came into being.

Nixon made more news than he bargained for. These comments from widely separated parts of an informal briefing were a sensation, dominating his conversations everywhere he went in Asia. Surprised at first by their impact, Nixon soon elevated them to a doctrine bearing his name — in fact, a considerable amount of his time was spent making sure that the initial label ''Guam Doctrine'' was rapidly supplanted in the journalistic lexicon by a more impressive phrase commemorating the person rather than the place. Nixon eventually elaborated his informal remarks into three key points in his Vietnam speech of November 3, 1969, and in his Foreign Policy Report of February 18, 1970:

— The United States will keep all its treaty commitments.
— We shall provide a shield if a nuclear power threatens the freedom of a

nation allied with us, or of a nation whose survival we consider vital to our security and the security of the region as a whole.

— In cases involving other types of aggression we shall furnish military and economic assistance when requested and as appropriate. But we shall look to the nation directly threatened to assume the primary responsibility of providing the manpower for its defense.

On one level there was less to the Nixon Doctrine than met the eye. If we were prepared to stand by our treaty commitments, this covered Japan, South Korea, the Philippines, Taiwan, Thailand, and South Vietnam. If we now pledged to protect even nonaligned countries against nuclear powers, this took care of the concern of countries like Indonesia, India, or Malaysia about hypothetical attacks from China. What the Nixon Doctrine excluded was automatic American participation in wars between other Asian powers, though we might offer military and economic assistance. That we should no longer involve ourselves in civil wars was — in 1969 — the conventional wisdom.

On the other hand, a formal statement of the American position provided for the first time clear-cut criteria for friend and foe. Domestically, it supplied a coherent answer to the charges of overextension; even those advocating a more far-reaching retrenchment had to take seriously the sweep and implications of Nixon's declaration. And nations in Asia dreading American withdrawal found in the Guam pronouncements considerable reassurance once they had understood them.

One ironic consequence was that those in our government and outside who wanted an even more significant retrenchment began to invoke the Nixon Doctrine against its author. It was amusing — and maddening — during the discussions on Cambodia, for example, to hear that American assistance was barred by a doctrine bearing the name of the man eager to assist a threatened country and who recognized no such incompatibility.

Thus, in the midst of an intense domestic debate over defense, we were able to preserve a base from which to build later as the Congressional and public mood changed. We developed a military strategy that fit our capacities for dealing with the more plausible dangers. And we advanced a doctrine for the security of the Pacific area that gave new assurance to our allies and friends. Of all the achievements of Nixon's first term, I consider the preservation of the sinews of our military strength among the most significant. Without it all efforts at relaxing tensions would have failed. For moderation is a virtue only in those who are thought to have a choice.

VIII

The Agony of Vietnam

I CANNOT yet write about Vietnam except with pain and sadness.
When we came into office over a half-million Americans were
fighting a war ten thousand miles away. Their numbers were still
increasing on a schedule established by our predecessors. We found no
plans for withdrawals. Thirty-one thousand had already died. Whatever
our original war aims, by 1969 our credibility abroad, the reliability of
our commitments, and our domestic cohesion were alike jeopardized by
a struggle in a country as far away from the North American continent
as our globe permits. Our involvement had begun openly, and with
nearly unanimous Congressional, public, and media approval.[1] But by
1969 our country had been riven by protest and anguish, sometimes taking on a violent and ugly character. The comity by which a democratic
society must live had broken down. No government can function without a minimum of trust. This was being dissipated under the harshness
of our alternatives and the increasing rage of our domestic controversy.

Psychologists or sociologists may explain some day what it is about
that distant monochromatic land, of green mountains and fields merging
with an azure sea, that for millennia has acted as a magnet for foreigners
who sought glory there and found frustration, who believed that in its
rice fields and jungles some principle was to be established and entered
them only to recede in disillusion. What has inspired its people to such
flights of heroism and monomania that a succession of outsiders have
looked there for a key to some riddle and then been expelled by a ferocious persistence that not only thwarted the foreigner's exertions but
hazarded his own internal balance?

Our predecessors had entered in innocence, convinced that the cruel
civil war represented the cutting edge of some global design. In four
years of struggle they had been unable to develop a strategy to achieve
victory — and for all one can know now such a strategy was not attainable. They had done enough to produce a major commitment of American power and credibility but not enough to bring it to a conclusion. In
the last year of the Johnson Administration the Communists had
launched a massive countrywide offensive. Few students of the subject

question today that it was massively defeated. But its scale and sacrifice turned it into a psychological victory. Under the impact of the Tet offensive we first curtailed and then ended our bombing of the North for no return except the opening of negotiations which our implacable adversary immediately stalemated. Public support was ebbing for a war we would not win but also seemed unable to end.

And in our country, opposition grew. It was composed of many strands: sincere pacifists who hated to see their country involved in killing thousands of miles away; pragmatists who could discern no plausible outcome; isolationists who wished to end American overseas involvement; idealists who saw no compatibility between our values and the horrors of a war literally brought home for the first time on television. And these groups were egged on by a small minority expressing the inchoate rage of the 1960s with shock tactics of obscenity and violence, expressing their hatred of America, its "system" and its "evil." All these groups had combined to produce the bitter chaos of the Democratic Convention of 1968, the campus violence, and the confusion and demoralization of the leadership groups that had sustained the great American postwar initiatives in foreign policy.

Richard Nixon inherited this cauldron. Of all choices he was probably the least suited for the act of grace that might have achieved reconciliation with the responsible members of the opposition. Seeing himself in any case the target of a liberal conspiracy to destroy him, he could never bring himself to regard the upheaval caused by the Vietnam war as anything other than a continuation of the long-lived assault on his political existence. Though he sympathized more with the anguish of the genuine protesters than they knew, he never mustered the self-confidence or the largeness of spirit to reach out to them. He accepted their premises that we faced a mortal domestic struggle; in the process he accelerated and compounded its bitterness.

Fairness compels the recognition that he had precious little help. After all, Hubert Humphrey, whose entire life was a reach for reconciliation, had been treated scarcely better during his campaign for the Presidency. And after Nixon took office those who had created our involvement in Vietnam moved first to neutrality and then to opposition, saddling Nixon with responsibility for a war he had inherited and attacking him in the name of solutions they themselves had neither advocated nor executed when they had the opportunity.

The Nixon Administration entered office determined to end our involvement in Vietnam. But it soon came up against the reality that had also bedeviled its predecessor. For nearly a generation the security and progress of free peoples had depended on confidence in America. We could not simply walk away from an enterprise involving two administrations, five allied countries, and thirty-one thousand dead as if we were switching a television channel. Many urged us to "emulate de Gaulle"; but they overlooked that it took even de Gaulle four years to extricate his country from Algeria because he, too, thought it important for France to emerge from its travails with its domestic cohesion and international stature intact. He extricated France from Algeria as an act of policy, not as a collapse, in a manner reflecting a national decision and not a rout.

Such an ending of the war was even more important for the United States. As the leader of democratic alliances we had to remember that scores of countries and millions of people relied for their security on our willingness to stand by allies, indeed on our confidence in ourselves. No serious policymaker could allow himself to succumb to the fashionable debunking of "prestige" or "honor" or "credibility." For a great power to abandon a small country to tyranny simply to obtain a respite from our own travail seemed to me — and still seems to me — profoundly immoral and destructive of our efforts to build a new and ultimately more peaceful pattern of international relations. We could not revitalize the Atlantic Alliance if its governments were assailed by doubt about American staying power. We would not be able to move the Soviet Union toward the imperative of mutual restraint against the background of capitulation in a major war. We might not achieve our opening to China if our value as a counterweight seemed nullified by a collapse that showed us irrelevant to Asian security. Our success in Middle East diplomacy would depend on convincing our ally of our reliability and its adversaries that we were impervious to threats of military pressure or blackmail. Clearly, the American people wanted to end the war, but every poll, and indeed Nixon's election (and the Wallace vote), made it equally evident that they saw their country's aims as honorable and did not relish America's humiliation. The new Administration had to respect the concerns of the opponents of the war but also the anguish of the families whose sons had suffered and died for their country and who did not want it determined — after the fact — that their sacrifice had been in vain.

The principles of America's honor and America's responsibility were not empty phrases to me. I felt them powerfully. I had been born in Germany in the Bavarian town of Fuerth, six months before Hitler's attempted beerhall putsch in Bavaria's capital, Munich. Hitler came to power when I was nine years old. Nuremberg, of which Fuerth was a neighbor with the same physical and psychological relationship as Brooklyn has to New York, was known for its Nazi support, massive Nazi Party rallies, and the notorious racial laws. Until I emigrated to America, my family and I endured progressive ostracism and discrimination. My father lost the teaching job for which he had worked all his life; the friends of my parents' youth shunned them. I was forced to attend a segregated school. Every walk in the street turned into an adventure, for my German contemporaries were free to beat up Jewish children without interference by the police.

Through this period America acquired a wondrous quality for me. When I was a boy it was a dream, an incredible place where tolerance was natural and personal freedom unchallenged. Even when I learned later that America, too, had massive problems, I could never forget what an inspiration it had been to the victims of persecution, to my family, and to me during cruel and degrading years. I always remembered the thrill when I first walked the streets of New York City. Seeing a group of boys, I began to cross to the other side to avoid being beaten up. And then I remembered where I was.

I therefore have always had a special feeling for what America means, which native-born citizens perhaps take for granted. I could not accept the self-hatred that took every imperfection as an excuse to denigrate a precious experiment whose significance for the rest of the world had been part of my life. I was enormously gratified to have an opportunity to repay my debt to a society whose blemishes I recognized but also saw in a different perspective; they could not obscure for me its greatness, its idealism, its humanity, and its embodiment of mankind's hopes.

The domestic turmoil of the Vietnam debate therefore pained me deeply. I did not agree with many of the decisions that had brought about the impasse in Indochina; I felt, however, that my appointment to high office entailed a responsibility to help end the war in a way compatible with American self-respect and the stake that all men and women of goodwill had in America's strength and purpose. It seemed to me important for America not to be humiliated, not to be shattered, but to leave Vietnam in a manner that even the protesters might later see as reflecting an American choice made with dignity and self-respect. Ironically, in view of the later charges of "historical pessimism" leveled against me, it was precisely the issue of our self-confidence and faith in our future that I considered at stake in the outcome in Vietnam.

I believed in the moral significance of my adopted country. America, alone of the free countries, was strong enough to assure global security against the forces of tyranny. Only America had both the power and the decency to inspire other peoples who struggled for identity, for progress and dignity. In the Thirties, when the democracies faced the gravest danger, America was waiting in the wings to come to Europe's rescue. There was no one now to come to America's rescue if we abandoned our international responsibilities or if we succumbed to self-hatred.

Unlike most of my contemporaries, I had experienced the fragility of the fabric of modern society. I had seen that the likely outcome of the dissolution of all social bonds and the undermining of all basic values is extremism, despair, and brutality. A people must not lose faith in itself; those who wallow in the imperfections of their society or turn them into an excuse for a nihilistic orgy usually end up by eroding all social and moral restraints; eventually in their pitiless assault on all beliefs they multiply suffering.

I could never bring myself to think of the war in Vietnam as a monstrous criminal conspiracy, as was fashionable in some circles. In my view our entry into the war had been the product not of a militarist psychosis but of a naive idealism that wanted to set right all the world's ills and believed American goodwill supplied its own efficacy. I had visited Vietnam as a professor. I saw there not ugly Americans — though, as in all wars, these existed too — but dedicated young men facing death daily despite the divisions at home; my recollection was of many idealistic Americans working under impossible conditions to bring government and health and development to a terrified and bewildered people. I thought the country owed something to *their* sacrifice and not only to the vocal protesters. Some of the critics viewed Vietnam as a morality play in which the wicked must be punished before the final curtain and where any attempt to salvage self-respect from the outcome compounded the wrong. I viewed it as a genuine tragedy. No one had a monopoly on anguish.

I saw my role as helping my adopted country heal its wounds, preserve its faith, and thus enable it to rededicate itself to the great tasks of construction that were awaiting it.

My Exposure to the Quagmire

M Y own exposure to Vietnam was imperceptibly gradual and progressively sobering; it paralleled the simplifications that led our government into an adventure whose ultimate cost proved out of proportion to any conceivable gain. I shared the gradual disillusionment.

In the early Sixties I did not pay much attention to Vietnam. Europe, strategy, and arms control were my academic specialties. Insofar as I held any views, I shared the conventional wisdom that the war was an effort by North Vietnam to take over South Vietnam by military force. This I continue to believe. In the early Sixties the possibility of sending American combat troops did not occur to me. As Chapter VI pointed out, the Johnson Administration saw Peking as masterminding the Vietnam aggression. The Kennedy Administration, which had sent the first 16,000 American military advisers to Vietnam, had also been fascinated by the phenomenon of guerrilla war, though it tended to see the inspiration in a January 1961 speech by Nikita Khrushchev endorsing "wars of national liberation."

When the Kennedy Administration sent those 16,000 advisers to

Vietnam, I remember asking Walt Rostow, then Director of the Policy Planning Staff of the State Department, what made him think we would succeed with that number when the French had failed with several hundred thousand. Rostow gave me the short shrift that harassed officials reserve for rank amateurs who should be minding their own business. The French, he explained, as if teaching the alphabet to an illiterate, did not understand guerrilla warfare; they lacked the mobility of the American forces. I did not pursue the matter, as my interest in Vietnam in those days was rather superficial.

It was not until November 1963 that I took strong exception to a government policy and then it was on a matter that enjoyed wide support. I was appalled by the direct role the United States had evidently played in the overthrow of South Vietnam's President Ngo Dinh Diem, which led to his assassination. This folly committed us to a course we could not foresee while undermining the political base for it; in the purge following, the country was bereft of almost its entire civil administration. For us to be seen to connive in the overthrow of a friendly government was bound to shake the confidence of other allies in Southeast Asia. I questioned the assumptions that had led us into such a gamble. Ngo Dinh Diem had to be overthrown, so argued his opponents, including much of the press corps in Saigon, because the war against the Communists would never be pursued with adequate energy or popular support while Diem was in office. His brother was accused of seeking a compromise with the Communists — precisely what seven years later became the orthodoxy of many of the same critics and for the refusal of which they now wanted to overthrow Diem's successor, Nguyen Van Thieu. But since the war concerned the legitimacy of the non-Communist government in South Vietnam, to overturn that government was a novel way to win it. The presumed military gains could not outweigh the loss of political authority. And we would be much more deeply committed morally to the government we had brought to office. We know today that Hanoi reached the same conclusion. While it had actively supported guerrilla warfare, it did not commit its regular forces until after the overthrow of Diem. I was in the process of writing an article along these lines, predicting a drastic deterioration in Vietnam, when President Kennedy was assassinated. I decided it would be in bad taste to proceed.

In 1964 I encouraged Governor Rockefeller to speak strongly on Vietnam in his primary campaign. Neither he nor I had a clear-cut view of an appropriate strategy and neither he nor I envisioned sending American combat troops. By 1965, however, I belonged to the silent majority that agreed with the Johnson Administration's commitment of combat forces to resist Hanoi's now clear direct involvement.

I ceased being a spectator in early August 1965 when Henry Cabot Lodge, an old friend then serving as Ambassador to Saigon, asked me to visit Vietnam as his consultant. I toured Vietnam first for two weeks in October and November 1965, again for about ten days in July 1966, and a third time for a few days in October 1966 — the last trip was made at the request of Averell Harriman. Lodge gave me a free hand to look into any subject of my choice; he put the facilities of the Embassy at my disposal.

I soon realized that we had involved ourselves in a war which we knew neither how to win nor how to conclude. The enemy's sanctuaries in Laos and Cambodia prevented the achievement of the classic military objective of war — the destruction of the military power of the enemy. In North Vietnam we were engaged in a bombing campaign powerful enough to mobilize world opinion against us but too halfhearted and gradual to be decisive. Thus our adversary was in a position to control the pace of military operations and the level of casualties, both his and ours. And the level of American casualties was to become a pivotal element in American public opinion.

I became convinced that in a civil war, military "victories" would be meaningless unless they brought about a political reality that could survive our ultimate withdrawal. Negotiations would occur only when Hanoi realized that it faced the progressive loss of its political influence over the local population the longer the war lasted. This was a monumental task. The North Vietnamese and Viet Cong, fighting on familiar terrain, needed only to hang on to keep in being forces sufficiently strong to dominate the population after the United States tired of the war. Our challenge was much more complex: We had to fight the war and simultaneously strengthen the South Vietnamese to survive without us — in other words, to make ourselves dispensable. It is a cardinal principle of guerrilla warfare that the guerrilla wins if he does not lose; the regular army loses unless it wins. We were fighting a military war against an elusive enemy; our adversary fought a political one against a stationary population. From the first I doubted that our planners had grasped this. On my way to Vietnam in October 1965, I stopped at our Pacific headquarters in Hawaii. After my first formal briefing on Vietnam, I wrote in my diary:

I was impressed by the fact that no one could really explain to me how even on the most favorable assumptions about the war in Vietnam the war was going to end. . . . I do not think we have even begun to solve the basic problem which is psychological. It seems to me that the Viet Cong and the North Vietnamese must be saying to themselves that even though their hopes for a victory this year were disappointed [because of American intervention], there is a possibility, even a probability, that if they can prolong the war sufficiently they will exhaust us. How does one convince a people that one is prepared to stay indefinitely 10,000 miles away against opponents who are fighting in their own country? . . . If we fail in our Pacific operations it will not be because of a failure in the technical realm, but because of a difficulty of synchronizing political and military objectives in a situation for which this enormously complex military establishment is not designed.

It seemed to me that regular North Vietnamese units, which were the chief target of our military operations, played the role of the matador's cape: they tempted our forces to lunge into politically insignificant areas while the Viet Cong infrastructure undermined the South Vietnamese government in the populated countryside. After a visit to a Vietnamese province on October 21, 1965, I wrote in my diary:

It is obvious that there are two separate wars going on here: (1) reflected in the army statistics about security of military units; and (2) that which affects the population. The two criteria do not match. For the army a road is open when it can travel in convoy along it. For the villager a road is open when he can travel it without paying taxes. For the army a village is secure when it can station its forces there. For the population a village is secure when it has protection not only from attacks by organized VC units but also from VC terrorism.

In the absence of criteria of success, self-delusion took the place of analysis. When I visited the province of Vinh Long in October 1965, I asked the province chief what percentage of his province was pacified; he proudly told me 80 percent. When I visited Vietnam for the second time in July 1966, I made a point of visiting the same provinces in order to assess the changes. In Vinh Long the same province chief told me that enormous progress had been made since my earlier visit. When I asked him how much of the province was now pacified, he proudly told me 70 percent!

I summed up my views of my first visit in a letter to Henry Cabot Lodge dated December 3, 1965:

Overshadowing everything is a social or maybe even philosophical problem: The Vietnamese have a strong sense of being a distinct people but little sense of nationhood. Our deepest challenge then is to discover how a nation can be built when the society is torn by internal schisms and in the middle of a civil war. All new countries have had the problem of achieving political cohesion; none have had to do so in the face of such overwhelming pressures as Vietnam.

On August 18, 1966, after my second visit to Vietnam, I wrote another letter to Lodge: "Candor compels me to say that I did not find any substantial change in the provinces. . . ." The attempt by American officials to judge security in the countryside was an attempt to quantify intangibles. Perhaps because of the inexperience of our province advisers (whose tour of duty was so short that by the time they learned their job they had to leave), our effort lacked political perspective. For

example, some areas listed as pacified might have been so because the
Viet Cong found it convenient to leave agriculture undisturbed as a
source of supply for themselves, because they were regularly collecting
the taxes. I added some recommendations: that the Embassy should attempt a more accurate assessment of the security situation, that local
government should be strengthened, and that priorities should be firmly
established. Also, we urgently needed a strategy for the negotiations for
which the Administration constantly proclaimed its eagerness. For a negotiation would be the beginning, not the end, of our difficulties.

And I had had some limited experience in dealing with the North
Vietnamese.

Between July and October 1967, at the request of the Johnson Administration, I served as an intermediary in an effort to get negotiations
started. I conveyed messages through two French intellectuals I knew,
one of whom had befriended Ho Chi Minh in the Forties, offering him
the hospitality of his house when Ho was in Paris to negotiate with the
French. I was authorized to encourage my friends to visit Hanoi to offer
compromise terms for a halt to American bombing as a prelude to a negotiation. They went and met with Ho Chi Minh. For several months I
traveled to Paris at intervals to convey or receive messages from the
North Vietnamese. Eventually the effort aborted, though it was a step in
the direction of the agreement that produced a bombing halt and the
opening of peace talks a year later.

After these negotiations had at last begun, at the end of 1968 I published my assessment in an article in *Foreign Affairs*.[2] It was written
before I was appointed security adviser but published afterward. I expressed my basic conclusions:

- that our military strategy was incapable of producing victory;
- that our military operations had to be geared to clearly defined
  negotiating objectives;
- that the South Vietnamese government could survive only if it
  developed a political program to which non-Communist South
  Vietnamese could rally;
- that the United States must cede increasing responsibility for the
  conduct of the war to the South Vietnamese; and
- that if in negotiations "Hanoi proves intransigent and the war
  goes on, we should seek to achieve as many of our objectives as
  possible unilaterally."
- that in our negotiations we should concentrate on military issues
  such as cease-fire while leaving the distribution of political
  power to the Vietnamese parties.

To some extent, I agreed with critics on both sides of the political
spectrum. The Johnson Administration, by its conduct of the war, had

abandoned whatever prospect of a conventional military victory existed; it had set a ceiling on our force levels and accepted a bombing halt. An honorable outcome depended on our ability to create political incentives for Hanoi to compromise — which would be impossible unless we could convert our military position on the ground into a durable political structure. Our negotiating position had to enlist enduring public support at home in order to make it clear to Hanoi that it would not gain by enmeshing us in protracted talks. To hold all these pieces in place while disengaging would be the task of any new Administration.

But while by January of 1969 I had become profoundly uneasy about the war, I differed with many of the critics in several respects. I did not favor an unconditional withdrawal. By 1969 the over half-million American forces, the 70,000 allied forces, and the 31,000 who had died there had settled the issue of whether the outcome was important for us and those who depended on us. Nor did I go along with the many critics of the war who acted as if peace depended above all on *our* goodwill. The hard men in Hanoi, having spent their lives in struggle, did not consider compromise a moral category. Driven by the epic saga of Vietnamese history — a history of wars against the Chinese, the French, the Japanese, and now us — they had sustained their undoubted heroism by the dream of victory; they would settle for compromise only on the basis of calculation and necessity. A negotiated peace would result from the reckoning of risks on both sides, not from a burst of sentiment. This judgment would forever separate me from many of the protesters — even when I agreed with their analysis that the war was draining our national strength and had to be liquidated.

What We Found

IT is a dubious achievement of many of our critics, including many from the administrations that brought about our Vietnam involvement, to have focused the Vietnam debate on the acts of the Nixon Administration, as if it were Nixon who had got us into Vietnam. It is well to remember that on January 20, 1969, when Nixon came into office, over half a million American troops were *in* Vietnam; indeed, the number was still rising toward the ceiling of 549,500 men that had been established by the previous Administration in April 1968. (The actual peak of troop strength was about 543,000 in April 1969.) The cost of our Vietnam effort had been $30 billion in Fiscal Year 1969.* American casualties had been averaging 200 men killed in action *per week* during the second half of 1968; a total of 14,592 Americans died in combat in

---

* Of this, $24 billion was the "additional cost" of the war, that is, excluding the costs that would have been incurred anyway in maintaining our forces had the war not been taking place.

1968. On January 20 the cumulative total of Americans killed in action in Vietnam since 1961 stood at over 31,000; South Vietnamese casualties were close to 90,000.

The fighting seemed to be stalemated. We had decisively defeated the Tet offensive in 1968; but its shock to American public support for the war led to the bombing halt and multiplied pressures for our withdrawal. The regular forces of our South Vietnamese ally numbered 826,000, greatly expanded from those of a year earlier (743,000). They were also much better equipped. But their task was daunting: to guard a trackless frontier of 600 miles and at the same time assure security for the population. And although the Viet Cong cadres had been decimated in the Tet offensive, North Vietnamese regular army forces took up the slack. Almost all of the fighting was now done by *North* Vietnamese main-force units — contrary to the mythology of "people's war."

South Vietnam seemed more stable politically than at any time in the previous four years. Nguyen Van Thieu, a northerner by birth, had been elected President in 1967 and included in his government more southerners and respected nationalists, such as Premier Tran Van Huong. Yet our Embassy in Saigon estimated that a Communist infrastructure still existed in 80 percent of the hamlets. Sixty-five percent of the total population and 81 percent of the rural population were estimated to be subject to some Communist influence, if only to Communist levies on their rice and production. In other words, the situation in the countryside had not changed significantly since my last visit in October 1966.

The enemy's strategy was to create a maximum sense of insecurity without seeking to hold any territory that could become a target for American attacks and thus lead to a pitched battle. Instead, the North Vietnamese launched sporadic attacks in all areas of South Vietnam. Main-force units attacked American forces to inflict casualties; guerrilla operations were designed to disrupt pacification; all the time efforts were made to strengthen the Communist political infrastructure for an eventual takeover.

In the second half of 1968, General Creighton ("Abe") Abrams had replaced General William Westmoreland as United States commander in Vietnam. Abrams had been a tank commander under George Patton and had led the battalion that liberated Bastogne in the Battle of the Bulge. Abrams had altered the American strategy. He abandoned large-scale offensive operations against the Communist main forces and concentrated on protecting the population. American troops were deployed for defense in depth around major cities. He had redeployed two American divisions from the northern part of the country to the more populated southern part. This was one military benefit of the bombing halt President Johnson had entered into on November 1, 1968, since the North Vietnamese had then agreed not to violate the Demilitarized Zone (DMZ) nor to launch indiscriminate attacks on major cities.

The bombing halt had come about for essentially two reasons. Opponents of the war had focused on the bombing partly because of its cost, partly because it was something the United States could halt unilaterally (unlike the rest of the fighting), partly because Hanoi had skillfully suggested that an end of the bombing would lead to rapid negotiation and negotiation would produce a quick settlement. On March 31, 1968, President Johnson announced his withdrawal from the Presidential race and a bombing halt above the twentieth parallel. A negotiation began in Paris between the United States and the Democratic Republic of Vietnam,* but it was confined to the procedural question of how to start talks. On November 1, President Johnson agreed to a complete bombing halt, though bombing of the North Vietnamese supply corridor through Laos (the so-called Ho Chi Minh Trail) and reconnaissance flights continued. There was an "understanding" that there would be "no indiscriminate attacks on the major cities" (such as Saigon, Danang, and Hué); no firing of artillery, rockets, or mortars from, across, and within the DMZ; no movement of troops from, across, or within the DMZ; and no massing or movement of troops near the DMZ "in a manner threatening to the other side." Hanoi never explicitly agreed to these provisions but rather "assented by silence," reinforced by an assurance from Soviet Premier Alexei Kosygin to President Johnson in a letter of October 28, 1968, that "doubts with regard to the position of the Vietnamese side are groundless." American chief negotiator Averell Harriman told the North Vietnamese in Paris on November 4 that indiscriminate attacks on the major cities "would create a situation which would not permit serious talks and thus the maintenance of a cessation [of the bombing]."

As matters turned out, serious talks did not begin as rapidly as Hanoi had led us to believe. As I have already described in Chapter II, there was a three-month haggle over the shape of the table, which was really a dispute over the status of Hanoi's front organization in the South, the National Liberation Front (NLF). The procedural haggle was ended on January 16, 1969, or four days before we came into office. On the day Nixon was inaugurated, not a single substantive negotiating session had occurred.

When the new team took over, our first necessity was a reliable assessment of the situation. Our desire to develop a coherent strategy immediately ran up against the paucity of facts, our attempt to modify established practice against the inertia of conventional wisdom. Vietnam was briefly discussed at the first NSC meeting, on January 21, and more extensively at an NSC meeting on January 25. But the team was too new and the career officials too demoralized. The briefings did not offer

---

*The Democratic Republic of Vietnam (abbreviated DRV or DRVN) was the official name of North Vietnam.

imaginative ideas to a new President eager for them, even from the military. For years, the military had been complaining about being held on a leash by the civilian leadership. But when Nixon pressed them for new strategies, all they could think of was resuming the bombing of the North. The only new instruction issued by Nixon at this point was to stop the constant controversies with Saigon; he had no intention of fulfilling Hanoi's desire by undermining the political structure of South Vietnam.

Our hunger for information was the origin of the first study directive issued by the new Administration. National Security Study Memorandum (NSSM) 1, entitled "Situation in Vietnam," requested the departments and agencies to respond to an enormous six-page, single-spaced list of twenty-eight major and fifty subsidiary questions. Each agency was asked to respond separately, to sharpen any disagreements so that we could pinpoint the controversial questions and the different points of view. NSSM 1 asked for explanations of events (for example, "Why is the DRV in Paris?" "Why did NVA [North Vietnamese army] units leave South Vietnam last summer and fall?"). It inquired into political factors affecting the negotiations, the enemy's military capabilities, South Vietnamese capabilities, the progress of security in the countryside, the political scene in Saigon, and United States military strategy and operations. In every case we asked, "What is the evidence?" or "How adequate is our information?"

Unfortunately, questions sometimes confirm the perplexities that have given rise to them rather than lead to their resolution. The responses to the NSSM 1 questionnaire arrived in February; my staff summarized and analyzed them in a forty-four-page paper that was circulated to the members of the NSC Review Group on March 14.[3] Perhaps not surprisingly, the summary found that the bureaucracy was divided along lines very similar to the rest of the country. There was a relatively optimistic school of thought that included Ellsworth Bunker (our Ambassador in Saigon), the Joint Chiefs of Staff, General Abrams, and Admiral John McCain (our Pacific commander). This group believed that the North Vietnamese had agreed to peace talks in Paris because of their military weakness, that pacification gains were real and "should hold up," and that "the tides are favorable." The opposite point of view reflected the civilian side of the Pentagon, the CIA, and to a lesser extent the State Department. It acknowledged the improvements in South Vietnamese capabilities but held that "these have produced essentially a stalemate." It argued that pacification gains were "inflated and fragile," that "inadequate political progress" was being made, that the enemy was not dealing from weakness either in Paris or on the ground, and that "a compromise settlement is the only feasible outcome for Vietnam."

There was agreement that the Viet Cong and North Vietnamese initiated the majority of military actions, and this determined the level of casualties on both sides; that the enemy had not changed its objectives; and that Hanoi was "charting a course basically independent of Moscow and Peking." There were, however, disturbingly large disagreements within the intelligence community over such elementary facts as the size and deployment of enemy forces, and the importance of Cambodia, particularly the port of Sihanoukville, as a supply route. The answers made clear that there was no consensus as to facts, much less as to policy.

Before we could resolve our internal debate — or even conduct it — on February 22, 1969, Hanoi preempted our analyses by launching a countrywide offensive in South Vietnam.

North Vietnamese Attacks and Cambodian Bombing

THE 1968 understanding with the North Vietnamese that led to the bombing halt included the "expectation" that there would be no attacks on major cities or across the DMZ. When we took office, however, enemy infiltration was mounting, which strongly indicated that a new offensive was in the offing.

The only plan we found for such a contingency was for renewal of bombing of the North. On November 24, 1968, Secretary of Defense Clark Clifford had declared on ABC-TV's "Issues and Answers": "If they, at some time, show us that they are not serious and that they are not proceeding with good faith, I have no doubt whatsoever that the President will have to return to our former concept and that is to keep the pressure on the enemy and that would include bombing if necessary." Averell Harriman made the same point in a White House briefing on December 4, 1968. General Earle Wheeler, Chairman of the Joint Chiefs, was only following inherited doctrine when he told Nixon at the NSC meeting of January 25, 1969, that everything possible was being done in Vietnam "except the bombing of the North."

No one in the new Administration, however, could anticipate a resumption of the bombing of the North with anything but distaste. We were savoring the honeymoon that follows the Inauguration of a new President; Nixon had never previously enjoyed the approval of the media. None of us had the stomach for the domestic outburst we knew renewed bombing would provoke — even if it were the direct result of North Vietnamese betrayal of the understandings that had led to the bombing halt. Above all, we had not yet given up hope, in the first month of the new Presidency, of uniting the nation on an honorable program for settlement of the war.

Unfortunately, alternatives to bombing the North were hard to come by. On January 30, I met in the Pentagon with Laird and Wheeler to explore how we might respond should there be an enemy offensive in

South Vietnam. Wheeler reiterated that American forces within South Vietnam were already fully committed; the only effective riposte would be operations in the DMZ or renewed bombing of the North. Laird demurred at the latter suggestion, emphasizing that the bombing halt had encouraged public expectations that the war was being wound down. Nor did I favor it, because I was eager to give negotiations a chance. On February 1, Nixon sent me a note: "I do not like the suggestions that I see in virtually every news report that 'we anticipate a Communist initiative in South Vietnam.' I believe that if any initiative occurs it should be on our part and not theirs." But my request to the Joint Chiefs for suggestions elicited the now familiar response outlining various levels of air or naval attacks on North Vietnamese targets and Mel Laird's (and my) equally standard reluctance to accept the recommendation.

Thought then turned to bombing of the North Vietnamese sanctuary areas in Cambodia, for reasons exactly the opposite of what has been assumed; it was not from a desire to expand the war, but to avoid bombing North Vietnam and yet to blunt an unprovoked offensive which was costing 400 American lives a week.

Revisionists have sometimes focused on the Nixon Administration's alleged assault on the "neutral" status of a "peaceful" country. These charges overlook that the issue concerned territory which was no longer Cambodian in any practical sense. For four years as many as four North Vietnamese divisions had been operating on Cambodian soil from a string of base areas along the South Vietnamese border. In 1978 the Communist victors in Cambodia put the uninvited North Vietnamese presence in northeastern Cambodia in 1969–1970 at 300,000, which far exceeded our estimates.[4] Cambodian officials had been excluded from their soil; they contained next to no Cambodian population.* They were entirely controlled by the North Vietnamese. From these territories North Vietnamese forces would launch attacks into South Vietnam, inflict casualties, disrupt government, and then withdraw to the protection of a formally neutral country. It requires calculated advocacy, not judgment, to argue that the United States was violating the neutrality of a peaceful country when with Cambodian encouragement we, in self-defense, sporadically bombed territories in which for years no Cambodian writ had run, which were either minimally populated or totally unpopulated by civilians, and which were occupied in violation of Cambodian neutrality by an enemy killing hundreds of Americans and South Vietnamese a week from these sanctuaries.

---

*The Communist deserter who helped pinpoint the location of the North Vietnamese headquarters reported that no Cambodians were permitted in the headquarters area. General Abrams reported this to the President in February along with an assurance that the target was at least a kilometer distant from any known Cambodian hamlets.

The first suggestion came from General Wheeler. When Laird on January 30 had expressed doubt that a renewed bombing of the North was politically supportable, Wheeler proposed, as an alternative, attacks on the complex of bases that the North Vietnamese had established illegally across the border in Cambodia. On February 9, General Abrams cabled General Wheeler from Saigon that recent intelligence from a deserter, as well as photo reconnaissance, showed that the Communist headquarters for all of South Vietnam was located just across the Cambodian border. (As a novice I was more impressed by such seemingly definitive evidence than I would be later on. As it turned out, the Communist leaders in Phnom Penh eight years later also confirmed that the deserter's information had been accurate on that score.) Abrams requested authority to attack the headquarters from the air with B-52s. Ambassador Bunker endorsed the idea in a separate cable through State Department channels.

These recommendations fell on fertile ground. In the transition period on January 8, 1969, the President-elect had sent me a note: "In making your study of Vietnam I want a precise report on what the enemy has in Cambodia and what, if anything, we are doing to destroy the buildup there. I think a very definite change of policy toward Cambodia probably should be one of the first orders of business when we get in." General Goodpaster had drafted a reply for my signature with detailed information about the North Vietnamese base areas along the Cambodian border. He reported that "our field command in South Vietnam is convinced that the vast bulk of supplies entering Cambodia come in through Sihanoukville. . . . What we are doing about this is very limited. . . . The command in the field has made several requests for authority to enter Cambodia to conduct pre-emptive operations and in pursuit of withdrawing forces that have attacked us. All such requests have been denied or are still pending without action."

The importance of Sihanoukville was one of the contested issues in the NSSM 1 study. The US military command in Saigon was convinced that between October 1967 and September 1968 some ten thousand tons of arms had come in through Sihanoukville. But CIA and State disputed this. According to them the flow of supplies down the Ho Chi Minh Trail through Laos was more than adequate to take care of the external requirements of *all* Communist forces in South Vietnam. At stake in this analysts' debate, of course, was whether the Cambodian sanctuaries were so crucial a target that they should be attacked; as happens all too frequently, intelligence estimates followed, rather than inspired, agency policy views. Those who favored attacks on the sanctuaries emphasized the importance of Sihanoukville; those who were opposed depreciated it. (When US and South Vietnamese forces moved into these sanctuaries in April 1970, documents in Communist storage dumps indicated that shipments through Cambodia far exceeded even the military's highest estimates.)

But whatever the dispute about whether the matériel traveled through Sihanoukville or down the Ho Chi Minh Trail, there was no dispute about the menace of the North Vietnamese bases in Cambodia to American and South Vietnamese forces. On February 18, I received a briefing by a two-man team from Saigon, together with Laird, Deputy Secretary Packard, General Wheeler, and Laird's military assistant, Colonel Robert E. Pursley. I reported to the President the conviction of General Abrams that no Cambodian civilians lived in the target area. Nevertheless, I advised against an unprovoked bombing of the sanctuaries. We should give negotiations a chance, I argued, and seek to maintain public support for our policy. We could review the situation again at the end of March — the classic bureaucratic stalling device to ease the pain of those being overruled. Nixon approved that recommendation on February 22, the day before he was to leave on his trip to Europe.

On the very day of Nixon's decision to defer action against the sanctuaries, the North Vietnamese transformed vague contingency planning into a need to deal with a crisis. After weeks of preparation antedating the new Administration, Hanoi launched a countrywide offensive. Americans killed in action during the first week of the offensive numbered 453, 336 in the second week, and 351 in the third; South Vietnamese casualties were far heavier, averaging over 500 a week. It was an act of extraordinary cynicism. No substantive negotiating sessions had been held in Paris with our new delegation, headed by Henry Cabot Lodge; the new Administration could hardly have formed its policy. Whether by accident or design, the offensive began the day before a scheduled Presidential trip overseas, thus both paralyzing our response and humiliating the new President. It occurred despite the fact that Nixon had communicated with the North Vietnamese in the transition period (as we shall see below), emphasizing his commitment to settle the war on the basis of the self-respect and honor of all parties involved. Without even testing these professions of intent, the first major move of Hanoi was to step up the killing of Americans. I noted in a report to the President that the North Vietnamese had been "able to achieve a relatively high casualty rate among US and South Vietnamese forces while not exposing their own main units."

Nixon received a military briefing on the enemy offensive in the Oval Office surrounded by piles of loose-leaf briefing books compiled by my staff and the State Department for each country he was to visit. (Nixon later came to use the Oval Office mostly for ceremonial occasions; he usually preferred to work in his informal office in the Executive Office Building.) Nixon was going through the books, committing them to memory, grumbling about the effort he had to make to do so. He was also seething. All his instincts were to respond violently to Hanoi's cynical maneuver. For years he had charged his predecessors with weakness in reacting to Communist moves. But he was eager also that his first foreign trip as President be a success. American retaliation might spark riots in Europe; passivity might embolden our adversary. He did not resolve this dilemma immediately. The only White House reaction on the day the offensive started was a phone call by me to Soviet Ambassador Dobrynin. The President wanted Moscow to understand, I said, that if the North Vietnamese offensive continued we would retaliate.

But the next day, on February 23, while in the air en route from Washington to Brussels, Nixon made up his mind; he suddenly ordered the bombing of the Cambodian sanctuaries. It seemed to me that a decision of this magnitude could not be simply communicated to Washington and to Saigon by cable from *Air Force One* without consulting relevant officials or in the absence of a detailed plan for dealing with the consequences. I therefore recommended to Nixon to postpone the final "execute" order for forty-eight hours and sent a flash message to Colonel Alexander Haig, then my military assistant in Washington, to meet me in Brussels, together with a Pentagon expert. I wanted to go over the military operations once again and to work out a diplomatic plan.

Haig, Haldeman (representing Nixon, who could not attend without attracting attention), the Pentagon planning officer, and I met on board *Air Force One* at the Brussels airport on the morning of February 24, just before the President spoke at NATO headquarters. The plane that Nixon used had been built to Johnson's specifications. Directly behind a stateroom for the President was a conference area with an oversized chair fitting into a kidney-shaped table; both the chair and the table were equipped with buttons that enabled them to develop a life of their own. The chair could assume various positions; the table could move hydraulically up and down. If one pressed the wrong button the table would slowly sink, pinning one helplessly in the chair; the situation could turn critical if the chair was rising at the same time. In this awesome setting we worked out guidelines for the bombing of the enemy's sanctuaries: The bombing would be limited to within five miles of the frontier; we would not announce the attacks but acknowledge them if Cambodia protested, and offer to pay compensation for any damage to civilians. In the short time available, we developed both a military and a diplomatic schedule as well as guidance for briefing the press. Haig and the Pentagon expert left immediately for Washington to brief Laird. Nixon later in London gave Rogers a cryptic account of his thinking but no details.

Before the day was out, Laird cabled his reservations from Washington. He thought that it would be impossible to keep the bombing secret, the press would be difficult to handle, and public support could not be guaranteed. He urged delay to a moment when the provocation would be clearer. It was symptomatic of the prevalent mood of hesitation, the fear to wake the dormant beast of public protest. In retrospect, it is astonishing to what extent all of us focused on the legal question of whether the understanding had been violated, and not on the four hundred American deaths a week by which Hanoi sought to break our will before we could develop any course of action. Even more astonishing now is that during this entire period no serious consideration was given to resuming the bombing of North Vietnam; the bombing halt, entered to speed a settlement, was turning into an end in itself.

I agreed with Laird's conclusions about the Cambodian bombing, if not with his reasoning. I thought that a failure to react to so cynical a move by Hanoi could doom our hopes for negotiations; it could only be read by Hanoi as a sign of Nixon's helplessness in the face of domestic pressures; it was likely to encourage further military challenges, as North Vietnam undertook to whipsaw Nixon as it had succeeded with Johnson. But the timing bothered me. I did not think it wise to launch a new military operation while the President was traveling in Europe, subject to possible hostile demonstrations and unable to meet with and rally his own government. I also did not relish the prospect of having Vietnam the subject of all our European press briefings or of privately trying to offer explanations to allied governments not always eager to reconcile their private support of our Vietnam efforts with their public stance of dissociation. I said as much to the President. The following day, while we were in Bonn, Nixon canceled the plan.

The so-called mini-Tet exposed the precariousness of our domestic position. The enemy offensive surely must have been planned over many months. It occurred when we were barely four weeks in office and before the enemy could possibly know what we intended — since we did not know ourselves. Yet the *New York Times* on March 9 blamed the new Administration for having provoked Hanoi by presuming to spend a month in studying the options in a war involving an expeditionary force of over 500,000 men: "The sad fact is that the Paris talks have been left on dead center while Ambassador Lodge awaits a White House go-ahead for making new peace proposals or for engaging in private talks out of which the only real progress is likely to come. Everything has been stalled while the Nixon Administration completes its military and diplomatic review." This theme soon was repeated in the Congress.

The President adopted a restrained posture in public while champing at the bit in private. At a news conference on March 4 he declared:

We have not moved in a precipitate fashion, but the fact that we have shown patience and forbearance should not be considered as a sign of weakness. We will not tolerate a continuation of a violation of an understanding. But more than that, we will not tolerate attacks which result in heavier casualties to our men at a time that we are honestly trying to seek peace at the conference table in Paris. An appropriate response to these attacks will be made if they continue.

On March 4 I passed on to the President without comment a Laird memo recommending against proposals by the Joint Chiefs to attack North Vietnam. Laird was far from a "dove"; in normal circumstances his instincts were rather on the bellicose side. He would have preferred to aim for victory. But he was also a careful student of the public and Congressional mood. He was a finely tuned politician and as such he had learned that those who mount the barricades may well forgo a future in politics; he was not about to make this sacrifice. He therefore navigated with great care between his convictions, which counseled some military reaction, and his political instinct, which called for restraint. He opposed bombing North Vietnam; he became a strong supporter of the attack on the Cambodian sanctuaries. (His only disagreement had to do with public relations policy; he did not think it possible to keep the bombing secret, on practical, not on moral, grounds.) The President, following a similar logic, ordered a strike against the Cambodian sanctuaries for March 9. On March 7 Rogers objected because of prospects for private talks in Paris.

Nixon retracted his order a second time. With each time he marched up the hill and down again, Nixon's resentments and impatience increased. Like Laird he kept saying that he did not want to hit the North, but he wanted to do "something." On March 14, Nixon was asked at a news conference whether his patience was wearing thin. He replied:

I took no comfort out of the stories that I saw in the papers this morning to the effect that our casualties for the immediate past week went from 400 down to 300. That is still much too high. What our response should be must be measured in terms of the effect on the negotiations in Paris. I will only respond as I did earlier. . . . We have issued a warning. I will not warn again. And if we conclude that the level of casualties is higher than we should tolerate, action will take place.

Next day the North Vietnamese fired five rockets into Saigon — a further escalation and violation of the understanding. There were thirty-two enemy attacks against major South Vietnamese cities in the first two weeks of March. At 3:35 P.M. the day the rockets hit Saigon I received a phone call from the President. He was ordering an immediate B-52 attack on the Cambodian sanctuaries. Capping a month of frustration, the President was emphatic: "State is to be notified only after the point of no return. . . . The order is not appealable." ("Not appealable" was a favorite Nixon phrase, which to those who knew him grew to mean considerable uncertainty; this of course tended to accelerate rather than slow down appeals.)

I told the President that such a decision should not be taken without giving his senior advisers an opportunity to express their views — if only to protect himself if it led to a public uproar. No time would be lost. A detailed scenario would have to be worked out in any event, and to prepare instructions would require at least twenty-four hours. A meeting was therefore scheduled for the following day in the Oval Office. I consulted Laird, who strongly supported the President's decision. To prepare for the meeting, I wrote a memo for the President listing the pros and cons. The risks ranged from a pro forma Cambodian protest to a strong Soviet reaction; from serious Cambodian opposition to explicit North Vietnamese retaliation — though it was hard to imagine what escalation Hanoi could undertake beyond what it was already doing. Finally, there was the risk of an upsurge of domestic criticism and new antiwar demonstrations. I recommended that our Paris delegation ask for a private meeting on the day of the bombing so as to emphasize our preference for a negotiated solution. I urged the President to stress to his associates that the proposed bombing was *not* to be a precedent. What my checklist did not foresee (what none of our deliberations foresaw) is what in fact happened: no reaction of any kind — from Hanoi, Phnom Penh, Moscow, or Peking.

The meeting on Sunday afternoon, March 16, in the Oval Office was attended by Rogers, Laird, Wheeler, and myself. It was the first time that Nixon confronted a concrete decision in an international crisis since becoming President; it was also the first time that he would face opposition from associates to a course of action to which he was already committed. He approached it with tactics that were to become vintage Nixon. On the one hand, he had made his decision and was not about to change it; indeed, he had instructed me to advise the Defense Department to that effect twenty-four hours before the meeting. On the other hand, he felt it necessary to pretend that the decision was still open. This led to hours of the very discussion that he found so distasteful and that reinforced his tendency to exclude the recalcitrants from further deliberations.

The Oval Office meeting followed predictable lines. Laird and Wheeler strongly advocated the attacks. Rogers objected not on foreign policy but on domestic grounds. He did not raise the neutral status of Cambodia; it was taken for granted (correctly) that we had the right to counter North Vietnam's blatant violation of Cambodia's neutrality, since Cambodia was unwilling or unable to defend its neutral status.[5] Rogers feared that we would run into a buzz saw in Congress just when things were calming down. There were several hours of discussion during which Nixon permitted himself to be persuaded by Laird and

Wheeler to do what he had already ordered. Having previously submitted my thoughts in a memorandum, I did not speak. Rogers finally agreed to a B-52 strike on the base area containing the presumed Communist headquarters. These deliberations are instructive: A month of an unprovoked North Vietnamese offensive, over a thousand American dead, elicited after weeks of anguished discussion exactly *one* American retaliatory raid within three miles of the Cambodian border in an area occupied by the North Vietnamese for over four years. And this would enter the folklore as an example of wanton "illegality."

After the meeting, the Joint Chiefs sought to include additional attacks on North Vietnamese troop concentrations violating the Demilitarized Zone. Laird and I agreed that it was more important to keep Rogers with us and the proposal was not approved.

The B-52 attack took place on March 18 against North Vietnamese Base Area 353, within three miles of the Cambodian border (see the map on page 248). For this strike the Pentagon dug into its bottomless bag of code names and came up with "Breakfast" — as meaningless as it was tasteless. When an air attack hits an ammunition or fuel depot, there are always secondary explosions that provide nearly conclusive evidence of a successful raid. The initial assessment by the crew of the March 18 Breakfast strike reported "a total of 73 secondary explosions in the target area ranging up to five times the normal intensity of a typical secondary."

Originally the attack on Base Area 353 was conceived as a single raid. Nixon ordered another strike in April 1969 partly because there had been no reaction from either Hanoi or Phnom Penh to the first, partly because the results exceeded our expectations, but above all because of an event far away in North Korea. Nixon had wanted to react to the shooting down of an unarmed American reconnaissance plane by bombing North Korea. (He had severely criticized Johnson for his failure to take forceful measures in response to the capture by North Korea of the electronic ship *Pueblo*.) Nixon had refrained, primarily because of the strong opposition of Rogers and Laird. But as always when suppressing his instinct for a jugular response, Nixon looked for some other place to demonstrate his mettle. There was nothing he feared more than to be thought weak; he had good foreign policy reasons as well for not letting Hanoi believe that he was paralyzed.

In May Nixon ordered attacks on a string of other Cambodian base areas, all unpopulated and within five miles of the border. The strike on Base Area 350 was given the code name of "Dessert"; Base Area 351 was "Snack," Base Area 740 was "Supper," Base Area 609 was "Lunch," and Base Area 352 was "Dinner." On the theory that anything worth doing is worth overdoing the whole series was given the code name of "Menu." From April through early August 1969 attacks

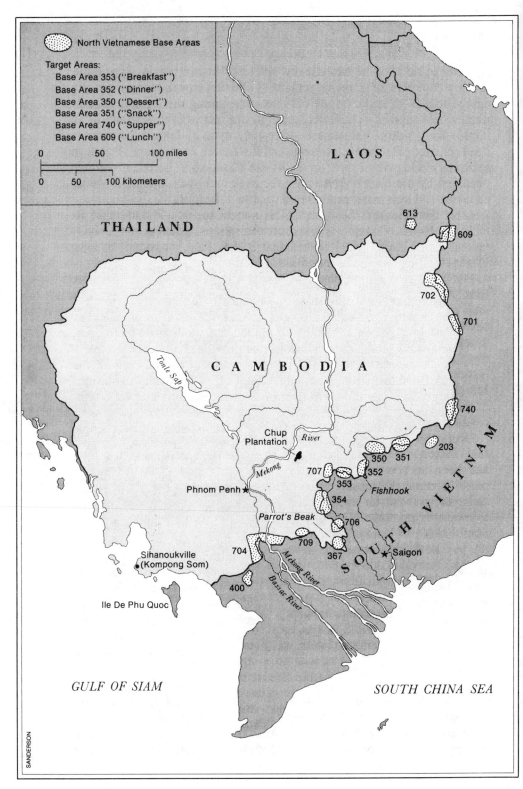

Cambodia: North Vietnamese Base Areas and
"Menu" Strikes 1969

were intermittent; each was approved specifically by the White House. Afterward, general authority was given; raids were conducted regularly. The map, defining the narrow strip of base areas within a few miles of the border, refutes the charges of "massive bombing of neutral Cambodia" that impelled twelve members of the House Judiciary Committee in 1974 to propose an article of impeachment on the theory that Nixon had concealed from Congress this "presidential conduct more shocking and more unbelievable than the conduct of any president in any war in all of American history," as Representative Robert Drinan imagined it.[6] Neither Cambodia nor North Vietnam ever claimed that there were Cambodian or civilian casualties. The statistics of tonnage dropped during these raids, so often invoked as an example of Administration barbarity, conveniently omit this salient fact or that it was confined to a strip only a few miles wide along the border. The series continued until May 1970, when strikes began openly in support of US and South Vietnamese ground operations against the North Vietnamese bases.

Periodic reports on the Menu strikes were sent to the President. In November 1969, he wrote on one, "continue them." In December 1969 and February 1970, he asked for an evaluation of their usefulness. Each time, Laird reported that General Abrams and Ambassador Bunker were convinced (as he reported on one occasion) that "Menu has been one of the most telling operations in the entire war." General Abrams credited the Menu operations with disrupting enemy logistics, aborting several enemy offensives, and reducing the enemy threat to the whole Saigon region. Laird endorsed the Joint Chiefs' and General Abrams's view that the Menu strikes "have been effective and can continue to be so with acceptable risks."

The original intention had been to acknowledge the Breakfast strike in response to a Cambodian or North Vietnamese reaction, which we firmly anticipated. For example, the CIA predicted in memoranda of February 20 and March 6 that Hanoi would "certainly" or "almost certainly" seek to derive propaganda advantages from charging an American expansion of the conflict. The Defense Department doubted that the attacks could be kept secret; my own view on that subject was agnostic. In a conversation with Nixon on March 8, I said: "Packard and I both think that if we do it, and if silence about it doesn't help, we have to step up and say what we did." The President agreed. A formal acknowledgment was prepared for the contingency of a Cambodian protest. It offered to pay damages and asked for international inspection.

Our initial reticence was to avoid *forcing* the North Vietnamese, Prince Sihanouk of Cambodia, and the Soviets and Chinese into public reactions they might not be eager to make. A volunteered American statement would have obliged Hanoi to make a public response, perhaps military retaliation or interruption of the peace talks. It would have required Sihanouk to take a public stand, tilting toward Hanoi as he tried to walk a tightrope of neutrality. It could have prompted reactions from the Soviet Union and China in the midst of our serious pursuit of triangular diplomacy.

But Hanoi did *not* protest. In fact, its delegation in Paris accepted Lodge's proposal for private talks on March 22 within seventy-two hours of our request. And Sihanouk not only did not object; he treated the bombing as something that did not concern him since it occurred in areas totally occupied by North Vietnamese troops and affected no Cambodians; hence it was outside his control and even knowledge.

In fact, our relations with Cambodia improved dramatically throughout the period of the bombing. Sihanouk's subtle and skillful balancing act between domestic and foreign pressures had been a cause of wonderment for a decade. An hereditary prince, Norodom Sihanouk had managed to obtain a mass support among the population that appeared to make him unassailable. He had established his country's independence and acquired the aura of indispensability. He had maneuvered to keep his country neutral. After the Laos settlement of 1962, he had concluded that the Communists, whom he hated, would probably prevail in Indochina. He adjusted to that reality by acquiescing in the North Vietnamese establishment of base areas in his country. In 1965 he found a pretext to break diplomatic relations with us. Yet his collaboration with the Communists was reluctant; Hanoi was encouraging the Khmer Rouge (Cambodian Communists), who began guerrilla activity long before there was any American action in Cambodia; Sihanouk sentenced the Communist leaders to death in absentia. For all these reasons I strongly supported a Rogers recommendation to the President in February 1969 that we approach Sihanouk with a view to improving relations.* These overtures were eagerly received. Our Embassy in Phnom Penh reopened, headed by a chargé d'affaires.

Sihanouk's acquiescence in the bombing should have come as no surprise. As early as January 10, 1968, during the previous Administration, he had told Presidential emissary Chester Bowles:

We don't want any Vietnamese in Cambodia. . . . We will be very glad if you solve our problem. We are not opposed to hot pursuit in uninhabited areas. You would be liberating us from the Viet Cong. For me only Cambodia counts. I want you to force the Viet Cong to leave Cambodia. In unpopulated areas, where there are not Cambodians, — such precise cases I would shut my eyes.

---

*Interestingly enough, these diplomatic overtures to Cambodia were opposed by the Department of Defense and the Joint Chiefs of Staff, who feared that they might interfere with possibilities of bombing the Cambodian sanctuaries. I received a memorandum from Defense warning against such "diplomatic action which implies a restraint or inhibition in any expansion of current operating authorities designed to protect our forces in South Vietnam." This was signed by Paul Warnke, then still Assistant Secretary of Defense for International Security Affairs.

On May 13, 1969, nearly two months after the bombing had begun, Sihanouk gave a press conference which all but confirmed the bombings, emphatically denied any loss of civilian life, and to all practical purposes invited us to continue:

I have not protested the bombings of Viet Cong camps because I have not heard of the bombings. I was not in the know, because in certain areas of Cambodia there are no Cambodians.

*   *   *

Cambodia only protests against the destruction of the property and lives of Cambodians. All I can say is that I cannot make a protest as long as I am not informed. But I will protest if there is any destruction of Khmer [Cambodian] life and property.

Here it is — the first report about several B-52 bombings. Yet I have not been informed about that at all, because I have not lost any houses, any countrymen, nothing, nothing. Nobody was caught in those barrages — nobody, no Cambodians.

*   *   *

That is what I want to tell you, gentlemen. If there is a buffalo or any Cambodian killed, I will be informed immediately. But this is an affair between the Americans and the Viet Cong–Viet Minh without any Khmer witnesses. There have been no Khmer witnesses, so how can I protest? But this does not mean — and I emphasize this — that I will permit the violation by either side. Please note that.

On August 22, 1969, Sihanouk said the same to Senator Mansfield* (according to the reporting cable):

there were no Cambodian protests of bombings in his country when these hit only VC's and not Cambodian villages or population. He declared that much of his information regarding US bombings of uninhabited regions of Cambodia came from US press and magazine statements. He strongly requested the avoidance of incidents involving Cambodian lives.

And on July 31, 1969, after four and a half months of bombing of North Vietnamese sanctuaries inside Cambodia, Sihanouk warmly invited President Nixon to visit Cambodia to mark the improvement of US–Cambodian relations. Relations continued to improve until Sihanouk was unexpectedly overthrown.

No one doubted the legality of attacking base areas being used to kill American and friendly forces, from which all Cambodian authority had been expelled and in which, according to Sihanouk himself, not even a Cambodian buffalo had been killed. We saw no sense in announcing

---

* Senator Mansfield did not know of the Menu program and undoubtedly assumed Sihanouk was speaking of accidental bombings.

what Cambodia encouraged and North Vietnam accepted. The reason for secrecy was to prevent the issue from becoming an international crisis, which would almost certainly have complicated our diplomacy or war effort. The war had been expanded into Cambodia four years earlier by the North Vietnamese, who occupied its territory. The war had been escalated within Vietnam from February 22 on, with North Vietnamese attacks on cities in violation of the 1968 understandings. To bomb base areas from which North Vietnamese soldiers had expelled all Cambodians so that they could more effectively kill Americans — at the rate of four hundred a week — was a minimum defensive reaction fully compatible with international law. It would surely have been supported by the American public. It was kept secret because a public announcement was a gratuitous blow to the Cambodian government, which might have forced it to demand that we stop; it might have encouraged a North Vietnamese retaliation (since how could they fail to react if we had announced we were doing it?). The North Vietnamese kept silent because they were not eager to advertise their illegal presence on Cambodian soil. Our bombing saved American and South Vietnamese lives.

This is why the press leaks that came from American sources struck Nixon and me as so outrageous. Accounts of B-52 or other air strikes against sanctuaries in Cambodia appeared in the *New York Times* (March 26, April 27) and *Washington Post* (April 27); a detailed story by William Beecher appeared in the *New York Times* on May 9; there was another in the *Wall Street Journal* on May 16; a widely disseminated UPI story appeared in the *Washington Post* on May 18; *Newsweek* reported it on June 2.

The conviction that press leaks of military operations were needlessly jeopardizing American lives, which I shared, caused the President to consult the Attorney General and the Director of the FBI about remedial measures. J. Edgar Hoover recommended wiretaps, which he pointed out had been widely used for these (and other much less justified) purposes by preceding administrations. The Attorney General affirmed their legality. Nixon ordered them carried out, in three categories of cases: officials who had adverse information in their security files; officials who had access to the classified information that had been leaked; and individuals whose names came up as possibilities in the course of the investigation according to the first two criteria. On the basis of these criteria, seventeen wiretaps were established by the FBI on thirteen officials and also four newsmen, lasting in some cases only a few weeks and in other cases several months. (My office was not aware of all of them.) Contrary to malicious lore, senior officials did not spend time pruriently reading over lengthy transcripts of personal conversations. What was received were brief summaries (usually about a page in length) of what the FBI considered discussions of sensitive military or foreign policy matters. The FBI's threshold of suspicion tended to be much lower than the White House's. In May 1971 Nixon cut off the reports sent to my office; thereafter, they went only to Haldeman, who had been receiving them all along.

I shall deal in another volume with the moral issues raised by national security wiretapping and the political style of the Nixon Administration in general. Here I simply wish to record that I went along with what I had no reason to doubt was legal and established practice in these circumstances, pursued, so we were told, with greater energy and fewer safeguards in previous administrations. The motive, which I strongly shared, was to prevent the jeopardizing of American and South Vietnamese lives by individuals (never discovered) who disclosed military information entrusted to them in order to undermine policies decided upon after prayerful consideration and in our view justified both in law and in the national interest. I believe now that the more stringent safeguards applied to national security wiretapping since that time reflect an even more fundamental national interest — but this in no way alters my view of the immorality of those who, in their contempt for their trust, attempted to sabotage national policies and risked American lives.

At the same time, we were wrong, I now believe, not to be more frank with Congressional leaders. To be sure, President Nixon and I gave a full briefing in the Oval Office on June 11, 1969, to Senators John Stennis and Richard Russell, Chairmen of the Senate Armed Services and Appropriations committees. Senate Minority Leader Everett Dirksen was also informed. In the House, Representatives Mendel Rivers and Leslie Arends, the Chairman and a ranking minority member of the House Armed Services Committee, as well as Minority Leader Gerald Ford, were briefed. Laird briefed key members of the Armed Services and Appropriations committees of both houses. Not one raised the issue that the full Congress should be consulted. This was at that time the accepted practice for briefing the Congress of classified military operations. Standards for Congressional consultation, too, have since changed, and this is undoubtedly for the better.*

Nor is it true that the bombing drove the North Vietnamese out of the sanctuaries and thus spread the war deep into Cambodia. To the extent

---

*The Pentagon's double-bookkeeping had a motivation much less sinister than that described in revisionist folklore. To preserve the secrecy of the initial (originally intended as the only) raid, Pentagon instructions were kept out of normal channels. The purpose was not to deceive Congress (where key leaders were informed) but to keep the attack from being routinely briefed to the Saigon press. The procedure was continued by rote when bombing became more frequent two months later. When Congressional committees asked for data four years later, new Pentagon officials, unaware of the two reporting channels, unwittingly furnished data from the regular files. This was a bureaucratic blunder, not deliberate design.

that North Vietnamese forces left the sanctuaries it was to move back into Vietnam, not deeper into Cambodia — until after Sihanouk was unexpectedly overthrown a year later. Then, North Vietnamese forces deliberately started to overrun Cambodian towns and military positions in order to isolate Phnom Penh and topple Sihanouk's successors, as I will describe in a later chapter.* And the widened war caused by that new act of North Vietnamese aggression, while searing and tragic, was not secret. It was fully known by our public, debated in the Congress, and widely reported in the press. Our air operations then were conducted under strict rules of engagement, supervised by our Ambassador in Phnom Penh and aided by aerial photography, designed to avoid areas populated by Cambodian civilians to the maximum extent possible. The "secret" bombing concerned small, largely uninhabited territories totally occupied by the North Vietnamese. The picture of a warlike, bloodthirsty government scheming to deceive is a caricature of the reality of harassed individuals, afraid alike of capitulation on the battlefield and more violent escalation, choosing what they considered a middle course between bombing North Vietnam and meekly accepting the outrage of a dishonorable and bloody offensive. The attacks on the enemy sanctuaries in Cambodia were undertaken reluctantly, as a last resort, as a minimum response, when we were faced with an unprovoked offensive killing four hundred Americans a week. We attacked military bases unpopulated by civilians and at most only five miles from the border. We would have been willing to acknowledge the bombing and defend it had there been a diplomatic protest. There was no protest; Cambodia did not object, nor did the North Vietnamese, nor the Soviets or the Chinese. Proceeding secretly became, therefore, a means of maintaining pressure on the enemy without complicating Cambodia's delicate position, without increasing international tensions in general, and without precipitating the abandonment of all limits.

Diplomacy for a Peace Settlement

ANOTHER of the many paradoxes of the Vietnam experience was how rapidly the public debate escalated. Negotiating terms were urged upon the government by the antiwar critics; specific concessions were advocated as essential for peace — until they were accepted by the government, at which point they were denounced as inadequate. The program of the "doves" was constantly in flux. (Hanoi was usually not interested in any of the doves' proposals for compromise; it exploited

---

*Sihanouk in a conversation with me on April 25, 1979, in front of witnesses denied that our bombing had had any effect in pushing the North Vietnamese to move westward. Our bombing "did not impress them," he said jovially. See Chapter XII.

them to undermine our domestic support but almost never negotiated on them; but that was a separate problem, to be discussed later.)

A good benchmark is the dove position during the 1968 Presidential campaign. The Nixon Administration (or at least I) had great hopes of bringing the country together because we were prepared in pursuit of negotiations to incorporate many of the ideas of the doves of 1968. This turned out to be a naive illusion.

Senator Robert Kennedy, for example, in early 1968 had offered a proposal for an "honorable negotiated settlement" compatible with our own conceptions:

- a halt to the bombing of North Vietnam;
- international supervision (by the United Nations, the International Control Commission, or another international organization) of "large" troop or supply buildups;
- reduction of American "search-and-destroy" missions and a shifting to defense of the densely populated areas;
- negotiations including all parties to the conflict, specifically the NLF;
- internationally guaranteed free elections to enable the South Vietnamese to choose their own government;
- an understanding with our adversaries that neither side would substantially increase the rate of infiltration or reinforcements during negotiations.[7]

After Robert Kennedy's assassination, the three leading antiwar Democrats — George McGovern, Eugene McCarthy, and Edward Kennedy — joined forces at the 1968 Democratic Convention behind the following platform:

- an unconditional halt to all bombing of North Vietnam;
- negotiation of a phased, *mutual* withdrawal of United States *and North Vietnamese* forces from South Vietnam;
- encouragement of South Vietnam "to negotiate a political reconciliation with the National Liberation Front looking toward a . . . broadly representative" government for South Vietnam; and
- reduction of US offensive operations in South Vietnam, "thus enabling an early withdrawal of a significant number of our troops."

This proposal was *defeated* at the Democratic Convention because it was considered too dovish.

The majority Democratic platform was more hawkish, calling for mutual withdrawal of all external forces, including those of North Vietnam, a bombing halt "when this action would not endanger the lives of our troops in the field,'' and internationally supervised free elections. The Republican platform, which I had a role in shaping,[8] explicitly rejected ''peace at any price'' or ''camouflaged surrender.'' But it pledged ''a positive program that will offer a fair and equitable settlement to all.'' It criticized the Democrats for having no peace plan, and pledged that a Republican Administration would ''sincerely and vigorously pursue peace negotiations.'' It pledged also a ''progressive de-Americanization of the war,'' full support for our servicemen, and a strategy that would concentrate on the security of the population and on strengthening the South Vietnamese.

By August of 1969 we had offered or undertaken unilaterally all of the terms of the 1968 *dove* plank of the Democrats (which had been defeated in Chicago). We had exceeded the promises of the Republican platform, expecting by our demonstration of flexibility to foster moderation in Hanoi and unity at home. We were naively wrong in both expectations. Hanoi wanted victory, not compromise. And its refusal to bargain was accepted as conclusive by many critics. At the same time several of the newly retired officials of the previous administrations did not feel inhibited, either by their role in getting us into the war or by the fact that their files were bare of any peace proposals, from adding to public pressures with proposals of their own. (Secretary of Defense Clark Clifford had declared on December 10, 1968: ''Let me reiterate that at the present time there is no plan for any net reduction in our troop level in Vietnam.'' This did not prevent him, within six months of leaving office, from calling on the new Administration to announce total withdrawal of American forces.) The only extant American negotiating proposal was the so-called Manila formula of October 24, 1966, which provided that ''allied forces . . . shall be withdrawn, after close consultation, as the other side withdraws its forces to the north, ceases infiltration, and the level of violence thus subsides. These forces will be withdrawn as soon as possible and not later than six months after the above conditions have been fulfilled.'' The South Vietnamese government offered, in ''a program of national reconciliation, to open its doors to those Vietnamese who have been misled or coerced into casting their lot with the Viet Cong.'' United States negotiators Averell Harriman and Cyrus Vance indicated to the North Vietnamese in private talks in Paris on September 15, 1968, that the Manila formula really meant *mutual* withdrawal, beginning simultaneously, but with the proviso that some US forces would remain until six months after all the North Vietnamese had left.

During the transition I solicited the private views of both Harriman and Vance on possible strategies for a negotiation. They did not differ much from the formal positions of the Johnson Administration.

Averell Harriman was completing the last regular diplomatic assignment of a distinguished career. I had first met him when he was serving as Assistant Secretary of State for East Asian Affairs in the early Kennedy Administration. The grizzled veteran carried out with extraordinary determination the duties of an office that lesser men would have spurned as a demotion. He was of a generation that considered public office an opportunity to serve the country and not an occasion for personal advancement. Once he had entered government service in his forties (before World War II) he never devoted himself full-time to any other activity. Harriman's patrician style was allied to a powerful determination to prevail in pursuit of strong beliefs. He affected a crotchety manner, and he used his relative deafness to great advantage. He would sit through meetings pretending to hear nothing unless some remark caught his interest, in which case he could be devastating or inspiring, depending on whether he liked what he heard. The drowsy manner that could give way to a sudden snap of the jaws earned Harriman, not for nothing, the nickname of "the crocodile."

No one could fail to be moved by his dedication, intensity, experience, and wisdom. Harriman was the last active statesman who had dealt personally with the great leaders of the Second World War, Churchill, Roosevelt, and Stalin. His endurance was in part due to his stamina, but in a deeper sense the stamina reflected a vital and youthful intellect. He undertook no assignment in which he did not deeply believe; he tended to transform every mission into a personal crusade. If he failed to achieve the highest offices to which his talents unquestionably entitled him, this was partially because of the insecurity his powerful personality evoked in lesser men and partially because of his tendency to become a passionate spokesman for his mandate of the moment, sometimes to the exclusion of larger considerations.

Early in the Vietnam conflict Harriman had become convinced that a military solution was impossible, partly because he thought that the actions necessary for victory might trigger Chinese intervention. Thereafter he turned into a tireless advocate of negotiations. He was an unrelenting bureaucratic infighter who did not shrink from using his charm and the prestige of his wealth to spin a web of social relationships to further his cause. And he was skillful in using the press.

When I saw him during the transition, he was the nation's veteran public servant, on the verge of leaving the Paris talks just as they were turning to substance and as I was about to enter office for the first time. As the years went by we had our share of disagreements. They did not affect my admiration and affection for him or his unfailing courtesy and helpfulness toward me. I have always regretted that President Nixon's profound distrust of the "Eastern Establishment" and Harriman's own partisanship prevented the administrations in which I served from using Harriman formally — though throughout my years in office I saw him regularly on a private basis, to my great benefit.

On January 7, 1969, Harriman submitted a memorandum, not

"cleared" by the Johnson Administration, which set out what he thought we should aim for. *All* North Vietnamese personnel should be asked to leave South Vietnam, not only regular army units and cadres, but even North Vietnamese replacements in Viet Cong guerrilla units. Provided the talks went well, he was prepared to recommend de-escalation of military operations. But he emphatically reaffirmed the Manila formula: "some [US] forces may have to remain in Vietnam for a considerable period until we are satisfied that all the North Vietnamese have been withdrawn." On the political side Harriman was equally firm, in this case with Saigon. He favored the "two-track" approach (which I had recommended in my *Foreign Affairs* article of January 1969), with the military issues discussed between the United States and Hanoi and the political issues left to the Vietnamese parties. He added acidly that the United States did not "have an obligation to retain the present government." Harriman's deputy, Cyrus Vance, endorsed the same approach in a memorandum he sent me on December 31, 1968.

Thus both our senior negotiators, who became active in the antiwar debate soon after, left office stressing the importance of *mutual* withdrawal, a six-month delay for the completion of the agreed American pullout to test North Vietnamese compliance, free elections, and leaving the political issues to be negotiated by the Vietnamese parties alone. Both were convinced that an American residual force would have to remain indefinitely. Neither urged or even hinted at the unilateral American withdrawal, coalition government, or unconditional cease-fire that within the year became the staple of the Vietnam debate and of their own contribution to it.

The other party to the dispute was Hanoi. In the innocence and exhilaration of newly acquired power I encouraged Nixon, even while President-elect, to lose no time to establish his good intentions. I encouraged him to open a private channel to Hanoi through my friend Jean Sainteny, a former French Delegate-General to Hanoi, then in private business. On December 20, 1968, we sent a message to the North Vietnamese stressing our readiness for serious negotiations:

1. The Nixon Administration is prepared to undertake serious talks.

2. These talks are to be based on the self respect and sense of honor of all parties.

3. The Nixon Administration is prepared for an honorable settlement but for nothing less.

4. If Hanoi wants, the Nixon Administration would be willing to discuss ultimate objectives first.

5. If Hanoi wishes to communicate some of their general ideas prior to January 20, they will be examined with a constructive attitude and in strictest confidence.

The North Vietnamese reply of December 31, 1968, was less concerned with honor or self-respect. It stated brutally two fundamental demands: the total withdrawal of *all* American forces and the replacement of what Hanoi called the ''Thieu–Ky–Huong clique,'' its pet phrase for the leadership in Saigon with which Hanoi was supposed to be negotiating. Hanoi simply repeated the formal position set forth by the Central Committee of the National Liberation Front (Viet Cong) on November 3, 1968, two days after the Johnson bombing halt. Far from evoking any sense of reciprocity as so many had expected, the bombing halt encouraged Hanoi to put forward maximum demands in the political field beginning with the overthrow of the government that we were supporting.

Thus was the Nixon Administration first exposed to the maddening diplomatic style of the North Vietnamese. It would have been impossible to find two societies less intended by fate to understand each other than the Vietnamese and the American. On the one side, Vietnamese history and Communist ideology combined to produce almost morbid suspicion and ferocious self-righteousness. This was compounded by a legacy of Cartesian logic from French colonialism that produced an infuriatingly doctrinaire technique of advocacy. Each North Vietnamese proposal was put forward as the sole logical truth and each demand was stated in the imperative (the United States ''must''). By 1971 we had been so conditioned that when the North Vietnamese substituted ''should'' for ''must'' we thought great progress had been made. On the other side, there was the American belief in the efficacy of goodwill and the importance of compromise — qualities likely to be despised by dedicated Leninists who saw themselves as the inexorable spokesmen of an inevitable future, absolute truth, and superior moral insight.

Throughout their history, survival for the North Vietnamese had depended on a subtle skill in manipulating physically stronger foreigners; the appearance of weakness was to be avoided at almost all costs, and admitting the possibility of compromise appeared to them as granting some validity to the point of view of the other side, in itself an unacceptable concession. Therefore the Vietnamese style of communication was indirect and, by American standards, devious or baffling. Because the United States had become great by assimilating men and women of different cultures and beliefs, we had developed an ethic of tolerance; having had little experience with unbridgeable schisms, our mode of settling conflicts was to seek a solution somewhere between the contending positions. But to the Vietnamese this meant that we were not serious about what we put forward and that we treated them as frivolous. They had not fought for forty years to achieve a compromise. The Vietnamese method of communication was opaque, designed to keep open as many options as possible and to undermine our domestic position. Ours

was matter-of-fact and geared to finding formulas to reconcile the irreconcilable, which Hanoi considered either a trick to be resisted or a
weakness to be exploited.

But the fundamental problem went deeper still. The North Vietnamese considered themselves in a life-and-death struggle; they did not treat
negotiations as an enterprise separate from the struggle; they were a
form of it. To them the Paris talks were not a device for settlement but
an instrument of political warfare. They were a weapon to exhaust us
psychologically, to split us from our South Vietnamese ally, and to
divide our public opinion through vague hints of solutions just out of
reach because of the foolishness or obduracy of our government. The
North Vietnamese were concerned lest we use the fact of the negotiations to rally public support; they would not compromise because any
appearance of "progress" might enhance our staying power. They preferred secret talks because this gave them an opportunity to reconnoiter
the terrain without paying the price of the appearance of progress. When
they settled an issue their motive was to have a maximum domestic impact in the United States. The bombing halt occurred just before the
1968 election in order to commit both Presidential candidates to it; the
shape of the table was settled just before Inauguration to prevent the
new Administration from enhancing its position by beginning with a
"success." Throughout the war we were taunted by the appearance of
great reasonableness by the North Vietnamese toward visitors, especially those opposed to the Administration. These guests were treated
with great civility and a catalogue of skillful and intriguing code words
that permitted a variety of interpretations, none of them so clear or firm
as to be reliable or so meaningful as the visitor imagined. All of them
evaporated as soon as we tested them in a serious forum.

The success of the North Vietnamese diplomatic campaign for the
bombing halt confirmed their faith in negotiations as a form of psychological warfare. They had invaded South Vietnam, Laos, and Cambodia
with substantial armies and without provocation; they had flagrantly
violated the Geneva agreement of 1962 on Laos, to which we were a
party. Yet when the United States sought to uphold international agreements and to maintain the freedom of allied peoples, Hanoi had demanded the end of bombing as the admission price to the conference
room and it had prevailed.

From the point of view of negotiations, the best strategy for us would
have been to formulate a very generous proposal and then to stand on it
without further concessions until there was reciprocity. But to the extent
that we maintained a firm position we were subject to domestic and bureaucratic pressures that gave Hanoi even more incentive to persevere in
its intransigence. Alternatively, we could have made one or two conciliatory gestures of de-escalation and withdrawal to demonstrate our

goodwill but then refused any more, pending some concession from Hanoi. This too was precluded by our domestic situation. Hanoi used every step toward de-escalation or withdrawal as proof of the validity of its cause and then condemned it as inadequate. The definition of "adequacy" was Hanoi's maximum position. We expended most of our energy in effect negotiating with ourselves.

The Paris talks quickly fell into a pattern. In the conference room the North Vietnamese acted like a stern tutor berating a wayward pupil; the student was being graded on answers to questions he had no right to participate in framing, by criteria determined exclusively by the professor. Outside the conference room the North Vietnamese created the impression that the negotiations were like a detective story. They threw out vague clues at whose answers we had to guess; if we missed the riddle the war would go on and we would be accused of having "missed an opportunity." Many of our critics fell in with this procedure. In our public debate it was rarely challenged; hardly anyone asked why Hanoi did not put forward an intelligible proposition and why they should proceed so allusively and indirectly. Of course when Hanoi was finally ready to settle (in October 1972) it proved as adept at real negotiating, as capable of framing concrete proposals as it had previously been skillful in obfuscation, and as impatient as it had previously been dilatory.

Between the hammer of antiwar pressure and the anvil of Hanoi, it was not surprising that there were important differences in the attitudes and expectations of the various leaders of the new Administration. It was the better part of a year before we had a settled strategy for negotiations. The President was the most skeptical. He did not believe that negotiations would amount to anything until the military situation changed fundamentally. He thought Hanoi would accept a compromise only if it had no other choice. On the whole, he favored a policy of maximum pressure; he was not too eager for negotiations until some military progress had been made.

Rogers was at the other extreme. His experience had been in the domestic arena; he had no settled views on foreign policy. His primary objectives were to avoid domestic controversy and the charge of rigidity. Many in the State Department shared the outlook advocated by the leading newspapers or the more dovish figures in the Congress partly out of conviction, partly out of fear. The practical result was that we were deluged by State Department proposals whose main feature was that they contained elements the other side had vaguely hinted it might accept. (As will be seen later, this almost invariably turned out to be a mirage.) Rogers often put these schemes forward with the argument that he was not endorsing them but that we would not be able to manage public pressures unless we were prepared at least to discuss them in Paris. Of course, once any of these propositions was on the agenda for discussion we had admitted their legitimacy and would soon be faced only with the choice of how much to concede.

Laird's view was more complicated. He was as skeptical about the utility of negotiations as about the possibility of military victory; and he was politically astute. His major concern was to get the United States out of Vietnam before we lost too much domestic support. But he wanted to do so without a collapse of the South Vietnamese. Hence his all-out advocacy of Vietnamization. He generally supported a hard line in negotiations and the most rapid possible pace of troop withdrawals. He had convinced himself that Vietnamization would work; it became his top priority.

I had great hope for negotiations — perhaps, as events turned out, more than was warranted. I even thought a tolerable outcome could be achieved within a year. Much of the impetus for negotiations came from me. As I will explain, I had my doubts about Vietnamization; nor did I think we had the time for victory — that opportunity, if it ever existed, had been lost by our predecessors. For diplomacy to succeed, however, we had to husband our negotiating assets. We needed a strategy that made continuation of the war seem less attractive to Hanoi than a settlement. I embraced the two-track negotiating strategy which Harriman and Vance had urged in their transition memoranda and which I had outlined in my *Foreign Affairs* article. Nixon on the whole supported this approach.

But the issue did not come up in quite this way. Rather, for several months we had a dispute over the inherited policy of mutual withdrawal embodied in the Manila formula. In those faraway days there was still a debate about whether our withdrawals should begin only *after* the North Vietnamese had completed their own withdrawal or simultaneously with it. The debate was absurd, first because Hanoi had no intention of withdrawing its own forces, and second because everyone knew that we intended to start a unilateral withdrawal in a few months. A second issue we wrestled with for several months was how large a residual force should be left after the *mutual* withdrawal. All agencies agreed that some substantial residual force had to remain, probably 100,000 support troops. (Harriman and Vance had embraced this view in their transition memoranda.) The Defense Department favored leaving combat personnel as well. This issue too was soon overtaken by events and public passions.

A third debate concerned de-escalation of the fighting on the battlefield. Our negotiating delegation in Paris anticipated (wrongly, as it turned out) that Hanoi would raise this issue and urged that we would be obliged to reply. The State Department and our Paris team argued that we offer to discuss the curtailment of B-52 strikes, of US offensive operations, and of the use of artillery for interdiction. Both our commander in Saigon and the Joint Chiefs of Staff disagreed strongly, insisting that such measures would cede the military initiative to the enemy and allow him to rebuild his strength in the populated areas. That too turned out to be a moot issue, since Hanoi never showed the slightest interest in de-escalation, even as we implemented it unilaterally. The North Vietnamese were less interested in stopping the fighting than in winning it.

Against Hanoi's obduracy we had the built-in momentum of imaginative bureaucracy, undisciplined at this stage by any strategy for negotiations. Whatever the Administration and regardless of the issue, American negotiators usually like to succeed. They deluge Washington with proposals to break deadlocks; they are tireless in thinking up initiatives. Imperceptibly at first, they tend to add their own pressures to the proposals of the other side. Animated by the high value they place on willingness to compromise or at least the appearance of it, they grow restive with deadlock. Since Washington's decisions as often as not are made by adversary proceedings, negotiators feel secure in urging far-reaching concessions, safe in the knowledge that other agencies holding opposite views will be equally one-sided in opposition. The President is left with seeking a compromise between contending pressures, not with developing a strategy. And if he is reluctant to dominate the process in detail he runs the risk that each bureaucratic contender pursues his favorite course unilaterally.

So it was with the negotiations in Paris. During February and early March, there was constant pressure from our Paris delegation to initiate private talks with the North Vietnamese based on all sorts of compromise schemes. When the first substantive private meeting finally took place on March 22, it produced not a negotiation but North Vietnamese demands for the unconditional withdrawal of all American forces and for dismantling the Thieu–Ky–Huong Administration.*

Instead of taking stock, the various departments reacted by pushing seemingly inexhaustible ideas for compromise.

Rogers was first off the mark. In a conversation with Soviet Ambassador Dobrynin on March 8, Rogers unilaterally abrogated the two-track approach of separating military and political issues. Rogers told Dobrynin that we were willing to talk about political and military issues simultaneously. Contrary to the President's decision not to hold private talks while Saigon was being shelled, Rogers proposed immediate private talks with Hanoi. Contrary to precedent, he implied that the private

---

* The only noteworthy occurrence at the first private meeting, already mentioned in Chapter VI, was the totally gratuitous and unexpected outburst by North Vietnamese negotiator Xuan Thuy to Lodge in Paris that the United States should not count on the Sino-Soviet split to help us settle the war in Vietnam, which, I must say, caused us to notice opportunities of which we had not been fully conscious.

talks include Saigon and the NLF. Rogers did not even require an end of attacks on major population centers as a condition. No wonder that Dobrynin replied that he believed what he had heard represented a major change in our position.

I was in despair. Rogers had in my view given away essential elements of our position without the slightest reciprocity and to no purpose; he was dissipating assets for one day's headlines — assuming the talks ever came off. Nixon was more philosophical. Nothing is more askew than the popular image of Nixon as an imperial President barking orders at cowed subordinates. Nixon hated to give direct orders — especially to those who might disagree with him. He rarely disciplined anybody; he would never face down a Cabinet member. When he met insubordination he sought to accomplish his objective without the offender's being aware of it. This might achieve the goal; it did little for discipline or cohesion. As often as not it revealed to outsiders a disunity that they might seek to exploit. Over time it led to a fragmented Administration in which under pressure almost every member looked out for himself. In the sense of isolation this produced in Nixon and the lack of cohesion among his team lay one of the root causes of Watergate. Thus it was in Nixon's reaction to Rogers's gaffe. He did not reiterate his strategy to his Secretary of State or call a meeting of advisers to insist on his approach. Instead he sent me to see Dobrynin on March 11 to tell him that the Soviet impression of a change in the US position was "premature." I explained delicately to Rogers on March 14 that the President's basic concern was that we start the private talks on a bilateral basis between us and Hanoi, before broadening them to include Saigon and the NLF. Rogers replied simply that he was "very anxious" to get the talks started.

Laird then followed with a unilateral step in the military field. On April 1, after several meetings on the subject, Nixon issued a directive prohibiting any proposals on de-escalation outside the context of mutual withdrawal. On that very day, the Pentagon announced publicly that we were reducing B-52 sorties by over 10 percent, effective June 30, because of budgetary considerations. When I complained, Laird explained blithely that he could not pay for the higher rate beyond June 30 and that he was actually continuing the higher rate three months longer than had been planned by his predecessor. Neither the President nor I had been aware of that plan or of the announcement.

I had no fixed view as to the right number of B-52 sorties, but I wanted to husband our relatively few negotiating assets. If we were going to de-escalate, it should be as part of a negotiation; the worst way to do it was unilaterally in response to budgetary pressures. In the absence of a Presidential willingness to confront his Secretary of Defense, I negotiated a rather ambiguous press statement with Laird: "It is the policy of the United States that reductions of military operations must be brought about by the phased mutual withdrawal of external forces. Budget planning figures will be brought in line with this policy on the basis of periodic review."

But the damage was done. A journalist told me that he took the B-52 reduction as a signal to both Hanoi and Saigon, because "you do not do a thing like this for budgetary reasons." He said it could not be read by Hanoi as anything except a move toward the withdrawal of our forces, or by Saigon as anything other than a warning that there were firm limits to the commitment of the United States. He was right in both judgments, though he gave us too much credit for thoughtful design. Ultimately, we made a virtue of necessity. Ambassador Lodge was instructed to cite the B-52 cutback in his public presentation at the Paris peace talks. The President referred to the reduction in sorties in his November 3 speech. Neither then nor later did the unsentimental leaders in Hanoi acknowledge these concessions. They did not pay for gifts they had already pocketed.

Our policy constantly ran the risk of falling between two stools. With Hanoi we risked throwing away our position in a series of unreciprocated concessions. At home, the more we sought to placate the critics, the more we discouraged those who were willing to support a strategy for victory but who could not understand continued sacrifice for something so elusive as honorable withdrawal. And we were not gaining the approval of those who wanted to turn the war into a moral lesson on the imperfections of America, even after we had gone beyond the program for which they had been demonstrating only nine months previously.

The Vance Mission

FOR all these reasons I concluded that time was working against us and that we should find some means of bringing matters to a head. I sought to involve the USSR in a complex maneuver and recommended Cyrus Vance as the ideal man for the mission.

I had met Cy Vance when he was Deputy Secretary of Defense in the Johnson Administration. Deliberate, soft-spoken, honorable, he struck me as the epitome of the New York corporation lawyer, meticulously executing his assignments, wisely advising his clients. Beneath his controlled manner, I thought I detected a passionate streak in harmony with progressive views now widely held in the circles in which he moved. On the Paris delegation he had come to share the ardent dedication of his chief, Harriman, to a negotiated settlement. After I was appointed Assistant for National Security Affairs, I recommended Vance for the position of Under Secretary of State, then the second position in the State Department. Rogers agreed, and the two of us met with Vance at

Rogers's home in Bethesda, Maryland. Vance was noncommittal but did not turn down the proposition out of hand. I saw Vance at length once again to make clear how interested the President-elect was in his services, and how important it was for the nation to have the benefit of his experience. Robert McNamara, his former chief, added his own urgings. Vance then declined, explaining that after nearly eight years of uninterrupted government service he needed to return to private life. When Vance left his position as Deputy Chief of the US delegation to the Paris peace talks on February 19, 1969, Nixon sent him a warm cable of thanks. I admired Vance's analytic ability and his judgment; I liked him enormously as a human being.

The mission which I had in mind was tailor-made for his qualities. It was nothing less than to enlist the Soviet Union in a rapid settlement of the Vietnam war.

In all my conversations with Dobrynin I had stressed that a fundamental improvement in US–Soviet relations presupposed Soviet cooperation in settling the war. Dobrynin had always evaded a reply by claiming that Soviet influence in Hanoi was extremely limited. In response, we procrastinated on all the negotiations in which the Soviet Union was interested — the strategic arms limitation talks, the Middle East, and expanded economic relations. But we had never made a comprehensive proposal to the Soviets on Vietnam.

I met with Vance on March 18 to explore his general willingness to undertake a mission to Moscow. The proposed mission involved linking the opening of SALT talks with an overall settlement in Vietnam. Vance would be sent to Moscow to begin SALT discussions and on the same trip meet secretly with a senior North Vietnamese representative. Vance would be empowered to make rapid progress in *both* areas, while seeking to keep them in tandem. (What I did not tell Vance was that I would recommend to Nixon a military showdown with Hanoi if Vance's mission failed.) The next day, Vance raised a number of sensible questions: How would the two negotiations in Moscow be related to each other; how could there be time to carry out both assignments adequately; how would his talks on Vietnam be kept secret from the team responsible for SALT?

On April 3, I formally proposed the Vance mission to the President. I pointed out the dilemmas inherent in the negotiations as they were proceeding in Paris. We had to convince the American public that we were eager to settle the war, and Hanoi that we were not so anxious that it could afford to outwait us. We had to continue military pressures sufficient to deter Hanoi from turning negotiations into another Panmunjom, but not act so provocatively as to tempt a fight to the finish. Our government had to be sufficiently disciplined to speak with the same voice. Relations with Saigon had to be close enough to deprive Hanoi of the expectation that the negotiations could be used to demoralize the

South Vietnamese government. I doubted our ability to fulfill these conditions. I thought that budgetary pressures and imminent withdrawals would reduce our military operations with no hope of reciprocity. The Paris delegation lacked discipline; our internal divisions made it unlikely that we could present a coherent policy or prevent oscillation between extremes. The temptation would grow to take out our frustrations on Saigon. An early settlement was in our interest because I suspected that all the trends I had described would bring about a situation in which our minimum program today would be much stronger than our maximum position a year from now. But Hanoi would not move without some pressure. Therefore Soviet participation could become crucial.

For all these reasons, I recommended that I approach Dobrynin with the warning that US–Soviet relations were at a crossroads. The President, I would say, was prepared to make progress in US–Soviet relations on a broad front. But the Vietnam war was a major obstacle. To resolve the impasse, Nixon was prepared to send a high-level delegation to Moscow, headed by Cyrus Vance, to agree immediately on principles of strategic arms limitation. While in Moscow, Vance would also be empowered to meet with a negotiator from North Vietnam and to agree with him on a military *and political* settlement for Indochina. (Since Rogers had already given away the two-track approach, I thought it best to develop a political program compatible with Saigon's survival.) On the military side, we would propose a cease-fire and mutual withdrawal. On the political side, we would offer guarantees that the NLF, if it renounced violence, could participate in the political life of the country without fear of reprisal. This would be coupled with agreement on a separate and independent South Vietnam for five years, after which there would be negotiations for unification. The President would give the effort six weeks to succeed. If the outcome of the Vance mission was positive, the President would also consider "other meetings at even higher levels" (that is, a possible summit).

I told the President, and proposed to hint to Dobrynin, that this course of action should not be approved unless the President was prepared to take "tough escalatory steps" if it failed.

The peace terms in my memorandum to Nixon went far beyond anything discussed in our government or for that matter argued by most doves. It exceeded, for example, the terms of the dove platform defeated at the Democratic Convention eight months before. It included a cease-fire — at that point violently opposed by the Pentagon. It accepted complete withdrawal (without residual forces) and it agreed to a role for the NLF in the political life of Saigon. We knew too little of Hanoi at that point to understand that its leaders were interested in victory, not a cease-fire, and in political control, not a role in free elections.

On the morning of April 5 when I spoke with the President at Key

Biscayne, he was dubious that the "Vance ploy," as he called it, would work. But he agreed we had to make a diplomatic move. On April 12, 1969, to bring matters to a head, I sent the President a memorandum reiterating the points I proposed to use with Dobrynin in a meeting scheduled for April 14. Nixon approved this with a few marginal notes in his handwriting, which extended the deadline to two months (rather than six weeks) and were more explicit than my draft in holding out the prospect of economic cooperation to the Soviets.

Using a technique I was to employ frequently later on, I let Dobrynin read these talking points together with the President's initials and handwritten amendments. This had the advantage of avoiding misunderstanding while authenticating that I was speaking for the President. Dobrynin took copious notes, stopping now and again to ask for an explanation. When he got through, Dobrynin asked whether we were making a Vietnam settlement a condition for progress on the Middle East, economic relations, and strategic arms. I replied that we were prepared to continue talking but that talks would move more rapidly if Vietnam were out of the way. Also, if there was no settlement we might take measures that would create "a complicated situation."

Dobrynin was voluble in emphasizing Moscow's desire to stay in negotiations with us whatever happened in Vietnam. He speculated that China was attempting to produce a clash between the Soviet Union and the United States. An escalation of the war in Vietnam, he added, could only serve the interests of China. I said that if this were so, the Soviet Union had a joint obligation with us to avoid complicating matters. Dobrynin's parting words were that this was a "very important" conversation.

Yet no reply was ever received from Moscow — no rejection, no invitation, not even a temporizing acknowledgment. In June Dobrynin mentioned in passing that our proposal had been transmitted to Hanoi but had not found favor there. The next time I heard from Dobrynin about the Vance mission proposal was eight months later, on December 22, when in the course of a global review he told me that Moscow had tried to be helpful with the Vance mission. Hanoi, however, had refused to talk unless the United States agreed ahead of time to a coalition government. Rather than return a negative reply, the Kremlin had preferred to say nothing. I answered coolly that some sort of acknowledgment, at least, might have been in order.

To this day, I do not know whether Moscow passed the proposal on to Hanoi and, receiving a negative reply, decided that it did not want to admit its impotence or run the risk of some American retaliation. It is also possible that Moscow never transmitted our proposal because the gains were too abstract and the risks of Soviet involvement in case of failure too great. I lean toward the former view. Given Hanoi's fanatical insistence on its independence and its skill at navigating between Moscow and Peking, Moscow as a site for a decisive negotiation was too risky. Peking might object; Moscow might use the occasion to go along with our maneuver and make concessions in Indochina to strengthen superpower relations. As for Moscow, it could not have been overly eager to host a negotiation for the results of which the respective sides might hold it accountable and which it could not influence decisively. We tried the same approach again in 1971, this time offering me as the negotiator. It was again rebuffed, probably for the same reasons. In the absence of either diplomatic or military pressures the Vietnam negotiations resumed their labored pace.

Return to the Treadmill

ON May 8, at the sixteenth plenary meeting in Paris, the Communists with great flourish put forward a ten-point peace program. Couched in the by now customary style of an ultimatum, the Ten Points listed what the United States "must" do to end the war. They demanded total, unconditional, and unilateral US withdrawal, abolition of the South Vietnamese government, and American reparations for war damage. They proposed that the South Vietnamese government be replaced by a coalition government to include all "social strata and political tendencies in South Vietnam that stand for peace, independence and neutrality."

The proposal for a coalition government did not sound unreasonable; many unwary Americans read it as simply a demand for Communist participation in the Saigon government. But once we started exploring its meaning we found that the Communists reserved for themselves the right to define who stood for "peace, independence and neutrality." The operational content of the Ten Points was that after we had decapitated the government of South Vietnam and demoralized the population by total and unconditional withdrawal, we would then collude with the Communists to force the remaining non-Communist elements into a structure containing the NLF and whatever groups the Communists alone would define as acceptable. And that new coalition government was to be only interim; the definitive political structure of South Vietnam was to be negotiated between it and the NLF, backed by Hanoi's army. Such was the Communist definition of a "just" political settlement.* Needless to say, when the Communists took over Saigon, no coalition government was established; in fact, even the NLF was excluded

---

*In July 1971, with Le Duc Tho I went over a list of Saigon politicians, including all known opposition leaders, who might prove acceptable as meeting the test of standing for "peace, independence and neutrality." Not *one* passed muster.

from any share in power. All key positions in the South today are held by North Vietnamese.

The proposal was one-sided in content and insolent in tone. But the mere existence of a Communist peace plan, however extraordinary in nature, generated Congressional, media, and public pressures not to pass up this "opportunity." If we were not going to be whipsawed we clearly needed to elaborate a clear-cut position of our own. In late April, I had proposed to the President that he give a speech presenting an American peace plan. On April 25, I called the President's attention to a remark made by Xuan Thuy: "If the Nixon Administration has a great peace program, as it makes believe, why doesn't it make that program public?"

But the President hesitated. He wanted to wait a little while longer for a reply from Moscow on the Vance mission. He was also inhibited by his uneasiness about the attitude of his Secretary of State. He was convinced that if the State Department saw the draft of a speech, it would either leak it or advance so many additions incompatible with his strategy that he would be made to appear as the hard-liner if he turned them down. As usual, Nixon found a solution as effective as it was devious. He waited until Rogers had departed on a trip to Southeast Asia on May 12, and then ordered me on the same day to supervise the preparation of a Presidential speech within the next forty-eight hours.

On May 14, Nixon went on national television and elaborated for the first time the premises of his Vietnam policy, the steps that had been taken, and a concrete new negotiating proposal. He reviewed the actions of his first four months in office: the blunting of the enemy offensive, the improvement of our relations with the Saigon government, the strengthening of the South Vietnamese forces, and, above all, the development of a coherent negotiating position.

He proposed an eight-point program that represented a quantum advance in the American negotiating position over that of the Johnson Administration. Specifically, he abandoned the Manila formula (Hanoi's withdrawal six months before ours) and advocated simultaneous withdrawal. Yet the North Vietnamese withdrawal could be de facto (by "informal understanding") rather than explicitly admitted by Hanoi.* The United States agreed to the participation of the NLF in the political life of South Vietnam; it committed itself to free elections under international supervision and to accept their outcome. The President offered to set a precise timetable for withdrawal, and he offered cease-fires under international supervision. In short, the May 14 speech provided every

---

* I explained in a White House background briefing before the speech, "We do not care whether they acknowledge that they have forces there, as long as they make sure the forces leave there and we will settle for supervisory arrangements which assure us that there are no longer any North Vietnamese forces in South Vietnam."

opportunity to explore the possibilities of a fair political contest. The only conditions it did not meet turned out to be the Communist *sine qua non:* unconditional withdrawal of United States forces and collusive installation of a Communist-controlled government.

North Vietnamese negotiator Xuan Thuy initially raised hopes by a relatively mild reaction, delicately noting that there were "points of agreement" between the Ten Points of the NLF and the Eight Points of the President's May 14 speech. But in the formal negotiations he adamantly refused to discuss them; soon the negotiating sessions reverted to the sterile reiteration of standard North Vietnamese positions. The stalemate continued.

And so did our efforts to break it.

The Beginning of Troop Withdrawals

AFTER the May 14 speech outlining our compromise terms for negotiation, we turned to the unilateral withdrawal of American troops. We had inherited, in one of the less felicitous phrases of foreign policy in this century, a general commitment to "de-Americanize" the war. The Johnson Administration had begun the effort to strengthen the South Vietnamese army, but there were no plans for American withdrawals. As Secretary of Defense Clark Clifford had said on September 29, 1968, "the level of combat is such that we are building up our troops, not cutting them down." In a news conference of December 10, 1968, Clifford reiterated that there were no plans for any reduction. In our innocence we thought that withdrawals of American troops might help us win public support so that the troops which remained and our enhanced staying power might give Hanoi an incentive to negotiate seriously. At the same time, if we strengthened the South Vietnamese sufficiently, our withdrawals might gradually even end our involvement *without* agreement with Hanoi.

Nixon favored withdrawal for both these reasons. In a news conference of March 14, he had laid down three criteria for our withdrawals: the ability of the South Vietnamese to defend themselves without American troops; negotiating progress in the Paris talks; and the level of enemy activity. Nixon's strategy in the early months, in fact, was to try to weaken the enemy to the maximum possible extent, speed up the modernization of Saigon's forces, and then begin withdrawals. He thought that would be a public relations coup.

General Wheeler at the January 25, 1969, NSC meeting had said he thought President Thieu would probably agree to a small reduction of US forces because it would help Nixon domestically and convey the image of a self-confident South Vietnam. Rogers thought we could buy an indefinite amount of time at home with a withdrawal of 50,000 troops. Laird and Nixon kept their counsel. Thieu expressed confidence publicly on February 6 that a sizable number of American forces could leave Vietnam in 1969. General Goodpaster, then serving as deputy to General Abrams, attended an NSC meeting on March 28 and reported that the South Vietnamese improvement had already been substantial; we were in fact close to "de-Americanizing" the war, he said, but were not at the "decision point" yet. Laird spoke up: "I agree, but not with your term 'de-Americanizing.' What we need is a term like 'Vietnamizing' to put the emphasis on the right issues." The President was impressed. "That's a good point, Mel," he said. Thus "Vietnamization" was born.

On April 10, I issued a directive requesting the departments and agencies to work out a schedule for Vietnamizing the war. Nixon decided the time was ripe soon after his May 14 speech. Whereas he had wanted to deliver his May 14 statement without interference from Rogers, he sought to proceed on troop withdrawals by preempting Laird.

A meeting was arranged for June 8 with South Vietnamese President Thieu to win his support. The site was to be Midway Island in the Pacific, chosen because of the fear that a visit by Thieu to the United States would provoke riots. Hawaii was rejected because Lyndon Johnson had held a meeting there with Vietnamese leaders. It was a symptom of the morass into which the Vietnam war had plunged our society that a meeting between the President and the leader for whose country over thirty thousand Americans had died had to take place on an uninhabited island in the middle of the Pacific.

On the way to Midway, Nixon convened a meeting in Honolulu on the afternoon of June 7 with Rogers, Laird, General Wheeler, Ambassador Lodge, and myself, in the conference room of the Kahala Hilton Hotel overlooking the Pacific. Ambassador Bunker, General Abrams, and Admiral McCain were also there. The meeting was to take the final decision on withdrawal strategy. It was clear that the military approached the subject with a heavy heart. Deep down they knew that it was a reversal of what they had fought for. However presented, it would make victory impossible and even an honorable outcome problematical. The process of withdrawal was likely to become irreversible. Henceforth, we would be in a race between the decline in our combat capability and the improvement of South Vietnamese forces — a race whose outcome was at best uncertain.

Contrary to mythology, the military rarely oppose their Commander-in-Chief, even privately. If they can conjure up a halfway plausible justification, they will overcome their misgivings and support a Presidential decision. It was painful to see General Abrams, epitome of the combat commander, obviously unhappy, yet nevertheless agreeing to a withdrawal of 25,000 combat troops. He knew then that he was doomed to a rearguard action, that the purpose of his command would increasingly become logistic redeployment and not success in battle. He could not possibly achieve the victory that had eluded us at full strength while our forces were constantly dwindling. It remained to sell this proposition to President Thieu.

The Midway meeting could not have had a more surrealistic setting. For the space of seven hours this atoll of no more than two square miles was invaded by the Presidential entourage of over five hundred officials, security men, communicators, journalists, and supernumeraries who considered themselves indispensable. The airport hangar was freshly painted; the Commander's house where the President was to meet Thieu received new furniture and a fresh coat of paint, making this Navy officer the one unambiguous beneficiary of the Midway meeting. Cars to transport the VIPs were flown in, as were supplies for a state luncheon. All this was observed with beady eyes by the gooney birds, who are native to this island and have grown insolent after being protected by the Interior Department for generations. No one has yet discovered the mystic bond between that dismal island and these strange birds, which soar majestically but take off like lumbering airplanes after an extended run. On Midway, the only island they deign to inhabit, they squat arrogantly in the middle of the roads, producing traffic jams to amuse themselves, happy in the knowledge that the Department of Interior will severely punish anyone who gives way to the all-too-human impulse to deliver a swift kick.

Thieu's position at Midway was less enviable than theirs. For days there had been reports (not discouraged by some in our government) that President Nixon would announce the beginning of the withdrawals of US forces and that this in turn would be intended as a warning to Thieu to put his house in order. By this his critics generally meant the early installation of Western-style democracy, if not a coalition government. Just how democratic freedoms might be ensured in a country overrun by 300,000 hostile troops and guerrillas those critics rarely made clear. Thieu was expected to accomplish within months and amidst a civil war what no other Southeast Asian leader had achieved in decades of peace. He was being asked simultaneously to win a war, adjust his own defense structure to the withdrawal of a large American military establishment, and build democratic institutions in a country that had not known peace in a generation or democracy in its history. His legitimacy as a nationalist leader was to be enhanced by reforms undertaken under pressure from the great power that had connived in the overthrow of his predecessor and thereby left the country bereft of its civil administration.

It was a poignant scene as Nguyen Van Thieu, for whose country 36,000 Americans had now died but who was not allowed to visit the soil of his powerful ally, stepped jauntily down the steps of his chartered Pan American plane. I felt sorry for him. It was not his fault that he was the focus of American domestic pressures; he was, after all, the representative of the millions of South Vietnamese who did not want to be overrun by the North Vietnamese army. He came from a culture different from ours, operating by different values. But all Vietnamese have an innate dignity, produced perhaps by the cruel and bloody history of their beautiful land. The Vietnamese have not "accepted their fate" as the Western myth about Asians would have it; they have fought for centuries, against outsiders and against each other, to determine their national destiny. And difficult, even obnoxious, as they can be, they have survived by a magnificent refusal to bow their necks to enemy or ally.

There were two sessions. The decisive one took place in the Commander's refurbished house. It included Nixon and me, Thieu and his personal assistant. In the Officers' Club there was also an experts' meeting dealing mostly with economic matters and chaired by the two foreign ministers. (It was a pattern that came to be followed in nearly all of Nixon's meetings with foreign leaders.) Thieu did not act as a supplicant. He conducted himself with assurance; he did not ask for favors. We had been concerned that the projected troop withdrawal would produce an awkward scene. Thieu anticipated us by proposing it himself. We suggested the initiation of private contacts with Hanoi at the Presidential level. Thieu agreed, provided he was informed about any political discussions. Because the five-hour time difference with the East Coast put the media under pressure to file, the two Presidents stepped outside the Commander's house after an hour-and-a-half discussion and President Nixon announced the first American troop withdrawal.

Nixon was jubilant. He considered the announcement a political triumph. He thought it would buy him the time necessary for developing our strategy. His advisers, including me, shared his view. We were wrong on both counts. We had crossed a fateful dividing line. The withdrawal increased the demoralization of those families whose sons remained at risk. And it brought no respite from the critics, the majority of whom believed that since their pressure had produced the initial decision to withdraw, more pressure could speed up the process, and who did not care — nay, some would have rejoiced — if accelerated withdrawals produced a collapse.

That June, former Secretary of Defense Clifford, who six months previously had stated that there was no United States plan for withdrawals, published an article in *Foreign Affairs* that grandly urged the unilateral withdrawal of 100,000 troops by the end of 1969, and of all other combat personnel by the end of 1970, leaving only logistics and air personnel.[9] President Nixon, never one to yield a debater's point, retorted impetuously at a press conference that he hoped to improve on Clifford's schedule. Though strenuous efforts were made to "interpret" the President's remark, the damage was done; our insistence on mutual withdrawal was by then drained of virtually any plausibility. Our commitment to unilateral withdrawal had come to be seen, at home, abroad, and particularly in Vietnam, as irreversible. The last elements of flexibility were lost when the Defense Department began to plan its budget on the basis of anticipated troop reductions; henceforth to interrupt withdrawals would produce a financial shortfall affecting the procurement of new weapons.

The North Vietnamese, on the other hand, were interested not in symbols but in reality. They coolly analyzed the withdrawal, weighing its psychological benefits to us in terms of enhanced staying power against the decline in military effectiveness represented by a shrinking number of American forces. Hanoi kept up incessant pressure for the largest possible withdrawal in the shortest possible time. The more automatic our withdrawal, the less useful it was as a bargaining weapon; the demand for mutual withdrawal grew hollow as our unilateral withdrawal accelerated. And the more rapid our withdrawal, the greater the possibility of a South Vietnamese collapse. Thus the North Vietnamese constantly complained that our unreciprocated withdrawals were just "driblets" or that we were not "sufficiently clear" about our ultimate intentions; they never deviated from their position that our unilateral steps created no obligation on their part. Within a year they were demanding an unconditional deadline.

These realities dominated our internal deliberations. Laird had prepared five alternative schemes for troop withdrawals in 1969. At the low end was a withdrawal of 50,000 troops, at the high end, 100,000. In between were various numbers and compositions of forces. Rogers supported a figure of 85,000; Laird, conscious of the views of the Joint Chiefs of Staff, officially supported the smallest figure (50,000) but indicated privately that he would not mind being overruled. As for the longer term, Laird offered timetables ranging from eighteen to forty-two months and ceilings for the residual American force — those troops remaining until Hanoi's forces withdrew — ranging from 260,000 to 306,000. In a memorandum Laird sent to the President on June 2, he offered a "feasible" timetable of forty-two months (stretching our withdrawal to the end of 1971) and a residual force of 260,000. He warned that in the absence of North Vietnamese reciprocity, a more rapid withdrawal would result in serious setbacks to the pacification program, a significant decline in allied military capacity, and the possibility of South Vietnamese collapse.

Within the bureaucracy two trends quickly developed. Since the credit (aside from Nixon's) for implementing the Vietnamization plan went to the Pentagon, the State Department could reach for a share in the glory of ending the war only by redoubling its political efforts. This unleashed a flood of cables on the hapless Thieu to speed up the process of political and economic reform. In fact, a sweeping change in the system of land tenure was put into effect. Our advocacy, however, may have weakened him by making his rather extensive reforms appear to result not from his strength and growing self-confidence but from American pressure. On July 11 Thieu offered free elections in which the Communists could participate, supervised by a mixed electoral commission of Vietnamese, including the Communists, and a body of international observers. Secretary Rogers leaked some of its details in a July 2 news conference, which led Thieu, out of pique, to delay sending us an advance draft of his new program.

These issues were to be discussed at a meeting of the President and his senior advisers on the Presidential yacht *Sequoia* on July 7. Rogers, Laird, Wheeler, Attorney General Mitchell, General Robert Cushman (Deputy CIA Director), and I were present. In the event, the principal topic of discussion was the meaning of an apparent lull in the fighting. Did it result from Hanoi's exhaustion, from a new negotiating strategy, or from an attempt by Hanoi to achieve de-escalation by tacit understandings? It was symptomatic of the intellectual confusion of the period that in the relief felt when a military lull eased both casualties and domestic pressures, no one asked the question whether the lull might not reflect the fact that our strategy was succeeding and should therefore be continued. Instead, there was unanimity that we should respond by a reciprocal slowdown. It was decided to make a basic change in the battlefield orders for General Abrams. The existing "mission statement" for US forces in Southeast Asia, inherited from the Johnson Administration, declared the ambitious intention to "defeat" the enemy and "force" its withdrawal to North Vietnam. The new mission statement (which went into effect on August 15) focused on providing "maximum assistance" to the South Vietnamese to strengthen their forces, supporting pacification efforts, and reducing the flow of supplies to the enemy. As it turned out, the President at the last moment changed his mind and countermanded the new instructions. But Laird had already issued them, and they stood. I do not know whether the changed orders — which were quickly leaked — made any practical difference. Given our commitment to withdrawal, they reflected our capabilities, whatever our intentions.

On July 30, Nixon made a surprise stop in Saigon on his around-the-world trip. He went there against the advice of the Secret Service, and for security reasons the Saigon stop was not announced until the last moment. Nixon was whisked from the airport to the Presidential Palace in a helicopter that seemed to go straight up out of range of possible sniper fire and then plummeted like a stone between the trees of Thieu's offices. I never learned how often the pilots had rehearsed this maneuver or how its risk compared with that of sniper fire. Nixon told Thieu that continued withdrawals were necessary to maintain American public support. He also argued that it was important that the reductions appear to be on a systematic timetable and at our initiative. We were clearly on the way out of Vietnam by negotiation if possible, by unilateral withdrawal if necessary.

A Secret Meeting with Xuan Thuy

IN June I initiated another attempt at negotiations, through my old friend Jean Sainteny, the former French Delegate-General in Hanoi. Sainteny's wife, Claude, had been a student of mine in the summer of 1953 in the International Seminar I conducted at Harvard for promising young foreign leaders. She was a writer and historian, as beautiful as she was intelligent. After she married Sainteny, I visited them occasionally at their apartment in the Rue de Rivoli overlooking the Tuileries Gardens. Sainteny was an elegant, highly intelligent man who during the years when there was no contact between the United States and Hanoi had given me my first insights into the Vietnamese mentality. He had spent much time with me recounting his experiences in Hanoi and giving me his assessment of our Vietnam involvement. Like many Frenchmen who had served in Indochina he considered our enterprise hopeless — an attitude not untinged with nationalism: How could America presume to succeed where France had failed? Unlike many of his compatriots, he understood the importance of an honorable exit for America and for other free peoples. I did not doubt that he would report our contacts to his government. This was of secondary importance, since this knowledge could confer on France no unilateral benefit; it would satisfy curiosity, not affect policy. I trusted Sainteny's honor and reliability in doing what he had undertaken. He was trusted by the North Vietnamese as well. No more can be asked of an intermediary.

So on June 24, I suggested to the President that we invite Sainteny to America to explore a new initiative: "My reading of the situation is that, in view of Hanoi's present state of mind, new overtures will probably not make much difference. However, I believe we should make another overture both for the record and because of the lack of real movement in the Paris negotiations." Sainteny saw the President in the Oval Office on July 15. Since no one knew of his presence in the United States, I had to act as interpreter. Given the shaky level of my spoken French, this surely did not help anybody's precision in understanding. Sainteny indicated that he would be prepared to visit Hanoi on our behalf and carry a message. Alternatively, he suggested a meeting between me and Le Duc Tho, a key member of the North Vietnamese

Politburo who visited Paris from time to time and had participated in private talks with Harriman.

We chose the first course. A private letter from Nixon to Ho Chi Minh was drafted. We asked Sainteny to deliver it personally to Hanoi. The letter stressed our commitment to peace; it offered to discuss Hanoi's plans together with our own. In concluded:

The time has come to move forward at the conference table toward an early resolution of this tragic war. You will find us forthcoming and open-minded in a common effort to bring the blessings of peace to the brave people of Vietnam. Let history record that at this critical juncture, both sides turned their face toward peace rather than toward conflict and war.[10]

But the North Vietnamese were not to be moved; they refused even to give Sainteny a visa. The letter was handed over to Hanoi's representative in Paris, Mai Van Bo. Determined to try for a breakthrough, we asked Sainteny to arrange for me to meet North Vietnamese negotiators.

At the end of July, I accompanied the President on his around-the-world trip, beginning with the *Apollo 11* splashdown and visiting Southeast Asia, India, Pakistan, and Romania. I split off from the President's party to visit Paris and Brussels while the President flew home. My secret meeting was scheduled for Sainteny's apartment on August 4. Le Duc Tho having left Paris, my interlocutor was to be Xuan Thuy, Hanoi's plenipotentiary at the plenary peace talks. This, as I learned later, guaranteed that little would be said other than the stock formulas that had come to dominate those plenary sessions. For Xuan Thuy was not a policymaker but a functionary. Representing the Foreign Ministry and not the Communist Party, he had been sent by Hanoi to read the official line at the public sessions. Tiny, with a Buddha face and a sharp mind, perpetually smiling even when saying the most outrageous things, he had no authority to negotiate. His job was psychological warfare. When Hanoi wanted serious talks, its "Special Adviser" to its Paris delegation, Le Duc Tho, would arrive from North Vietnam. He, too, could be described as flexible only by the wildest flight of fancy. But he, at least, had authority, and in the end it was he who concluded the negotiations.

The pretext for my visit to Paris was to brief President Georges Pompidou and Prime Minister Jacques Chaban-Delmas about President Nixon's world trip. Late in the afternoon of August 4, I left the American Embassy on the excuse of going sight-seeing, and together with my personal assistant, Anthony Lake, and our military attaché in Paris, General Vernon Walters, went to Sainteny's apartment not far away on the Rue de Rivoli. At that time I was not covered by journalists; reaching Sainteny's apartment unobserved was no great trick. General Walters was present because of his genius as an interpreter and because he was fully trusted by both President Nixon and me. (He was to set up all my early negotiating trips to Paris, as well as some contact there with the Chinese, with infallible precision, imagination, and discretion.) Walters spoke nine languages fluently. His skill at interpreting was phenomenal; he was also a great actor able to render not only the words but the intonation and attitude of the speaker. A fine flair for the dramatic ensured that the translation erred if at all on the side of improving on the original, but the speaker's composure was not eased by the fact that Walters's memory was so retentive that he refused to take notes. The meeting with Xuan Thuy lasted three and a half hours, partly because it required double translation. I spoke in English, translated into French by Walters, and then Xuan Thuy's interpreter rendered this into Vietnamese. When Xuan Thuy spoke, his interpreter went from Vietnamese into English.

I had anticipated the meeting with some nervousness. This would be the first negotiation in which I participated as a principal. It would be my first meeting with the elusive North Vietnamese, whom I had pursued without success for a whole summer on behalf of President Johnson. I still half believed that rapid progress would be made if we could convince them of our sincerity. My colleagues and I arrived at Sainteny's apartment a half hour before the scheduled time. Sainteny ushered us into his living room and showed us where the refreshments were located. His apartment contained some valuable artifacts from his days in Vietnam. "I hope if you disagree you will not throw the crockery at each other," said Sainteny dryly and excused himself.

Xuan Thuy and Mai Van Bo arrived exactly on time. We were seated on sofas facing one another, the American group with its back to the Rue de Rivoli, leaving the view of the Tuileries Gardens to the Vietnamese. As in all my later meetings, I was impressed by their dignity and quiet self-assurance. Here was a group of men who had made violence and guerrilla war their profession; their contact with the outside world had been sporadic and shaped by the requirements of their many struggles. But in meeting with the representative of the strongest power on earth, they were subtle, disciplined, and infinitely patient. Except for one occasion — when, carried away by the early success of the spring offensive of 1972, they turned insolent — they were always courteous; they never showed any undue eagerness; they never permitted themselves to appear rattled. They were specialists in political warfare, determined to move only at their own pace, not to be seduced by charm or goaded by impatience. They pocketed American concessions as their due, admitting no obligation to reciprocate moderation. They saw compromise as a confession of weakness. They were impressed only by their own assessment of Hanoi's self-interest. They admitted of no self-doubt; they could never grant — even to themselves — that they had been swayed, or even affected, by our arguments. Their goal was total power in South Vietnam, or at least a solution in which their opponents were so demoralized that they would be easy to destroy in the next round. They deviated from their quest for victory only after the collapse of their Easter offensive in 1972 left them totally exhausted.

After exchanging pleasantries, mostly about my abortive efforts to meet Mai Van Bo in 1967, I turned to the purpose of the meeting. I expressed my respect for the courage and the suffering of the Vietnamese people. The United States sincerely sought a settlement compatible with the self-respect of both sides. The fact remained that by November 1 the negotiations which had begun with the bombing halt would be a year old. In that period, the United States had made a series of significant unreciprocated gestures: We had stopped sending reinforcements, we had announced the unilateral withdrawal of 25,000 men, and we had promised further withdrawals. We had offered to accept the results of internationally supervised free elections in which the NLF could participate. There had been no response. I was in Paris, I said, to suggest from the highest possible level and in great earnestness that we make a major effort to settle the conflict by the time the negotiation was one year old — that is to say, by November 1. We were prepared to discuss the Ten Points of the NLF, but we could not accept the proposition that like the Ten Commandments they were graven in stone and not subject to negotiation. It was in the long term intolerable for us to be treated at every meeting like schoolboys taking an examination in the adequacy of our understanding of Hanoi's formal position.

I proposed intensified negotiations and an effort to find common ground between the NLF's Ten Points and Nixon's Eight Points of May 14. Specifically, the United States was prepared to withdraw all its forces, without exception, as part of a program of mutual withdrawal. We were ready to accept the outcome of any free political process. We understood that neither side could be expected to give up at the conference table what had not been conceded on the battlefield; we believed that a fair process must register an existing balance of political and military forces. As we were not asking for the disbanding of the Communist side, we should not be asked to disband the non-Communist political groupings. Successful negotiations required that each side recognize that its opponent could not be defeated without its noticing it. On behalf of the President, I proposed that we open a special channel of contact. If the negotiations proved serious, the President was prepared to adjust military operations to facilitate an agreement. At the same time, if by November 1 no progress had been made, the United States would have to consider steps of grave consequence.*

---

*Nixon made the same point to various host governments on his global trip, and to various leaders on State visits to Washington, in the expectation that these warnings would filter back to Hanoi. They did. But no plans yet existed to implement the threat if no progress resulted.

Xuan Thuy listened impassively without as much as hinting that he had heard a change in the American position. I had in fact presented the most comprehensive American peace plan yet. I had gone beyond the most dovish position then being advocated within the Washington bureaucracy by offering the total withdrawal of all American troops with no provision whatever for residual forces. I had proposed de-escalation of military operations. As was the North Vietnamese custom, he asked a few clarifying questions, especially about the procedures for intensified negotiations, and launched himself into a long monologue. He first recounted the epic of Vietnam's struggle for independence through the centuries. I was to hear this tale many more times over the next four years. It became a ritual, like saying grace — except that it took much longer. The heroic saga of how the Vietnamese defeated all foreigners was impressive, even moving, although after constant repetition over many years this litany came to test my self-control. Turning to substance after about forty-five minutes, Xuan Thuy denied that the Ten Points were, as I had said, the Ten Commandments; they were, however, the only "logical and realistic basis for settling the war" — a distinction my Occidental mind lacked the subtlety to grasp.

According to Xuan Thuy there were two problems, the military and the political. The military solution was the complete withdrawal of United States and what the North Vietnamese called "satellite" forces (troops contributed by allied countries). The United States had been very imprecise on that subject, he said — meaning that we had not given an unconditional schedule for their removal. The political solution required the removal of Thieu, Ky, and Huong (the President, the Vice President and the Prime Minister of our ally) and the establishment of a coalition government composed of the Communist Provisional Revolutionary Government* and the remnants of the Saigon administration as long as they stood for "peace, independence and neutrality." The two issues, military and political, were linked, said Xuan Thuy; one could not be solved without the other. In other words, not even a unilateral United States withdrawal would end the war or secure the release of our prisoners.

Hanoi thus continued to insist that the United States establish a new government under conditions in which the non-Communist side would be made impotent by the withdrawal of the American forces and demoralized by the removal of its leadership. If the United States had the effrontery to withdraw without bringing about such a political upheaval, the war would go on and our prisoners would remain. Over the years we moved from position to position, from mutual to unilateral withdrawal,

---

*The "Provisional Revolutionary Government," or PRG, was after June 1969 the designation of the National Liberation Front.

from residual forces to complete departure. But Hanoi never budged. We could have neither peace nor our prisoners until we achieved what Hanoi apparently no longer trusted itself to accomplish: the overthrow of our ally.

We were not prepared to do for the Communists what they could not do for themselves. This seemed to us an act of dishonor that would mortgage America's international position for a long time to come. Our refusal to overthrow an allied government remained the single and crucial issue that deadlocked all negotiation until October 8, 1972, when Hanoi withdrew the demand.

Though Xuan Thuy and I had achieved little except to restate established positions in a less contentious manner, we agreed that either party would be free to contact the other and that another meeting should take place. Xuan Thuy indicated that Hanoi did not like intermediaries from other countries and asked us to designate an American to receive or deliver messages in this channel. I designated General Walters. A summary was sent to Ambassador Bunker in Saigon to inform President Thieu, who had authorized such secret talks at the Midway meeting and who was kept thoroughly briefed on my secret negotiations from the beginning. In the absence of Ambassador Lodge in Paris, his deputy, Philip Habib, was briefed by me.

The newly established channel was not used again in 1969. Two days later, on August 6, there was a Communist attack on Cam Ranh Bay, which one could barely explain on the ground that it must have been planned well before the meeting with Xuan Thuy. On August 11, however, Communist forces attacked more than one hundred cities, towns, and bases across South Vietnam, ending the eight-week lull in the fighting. The most generous interpretation could not avoid the conclusion that Hanoi did not believe in gestures, negotiation, goodwill, or reciprocity.

Another Reassessment

NIXON reacted to the new Vietnam attacks by announcing on August 23 from the San Clemente White House that he was deferring consideration of the next troop withdrawal until his return to Washington. There was an unusually delayed and seemingly uncertain response from the North Vietnamese in Paris. The apparent delay in our unilateral withdrawal had given Hanoi pause — a hint of its respect for American forces and of what might have happened had our domestic situation permitted greater firmness. But it did not. Though Nixon's decision was exactly in accordance with two of the three criteria for troop withdrawal he had announced in March and frequently repeated (enemy activity, progress in Paris, and improvement of the South Vietnamese forces), the decision was greeted with outrage by the Congress and the media.

On August 25, Ho Chi Minh replied to President Nixon's letter of July 15. (Actually, the reply was received on August 30, three days before Ho's death.) Ho's letter, not reciprocating Nixon's salutation of "Dear Mr. President," reiterated North Vietnam's public position in a peremptory fashion:

Our Vietnamese people are deeply devoted to peace, a real peace with independence and real freedom. They are determined to fight to the end, without fearing the sacrifices and difficulties in order to defend their country and their sacred national rights. The overall solution in 10 points of the National Liberation Front of South Vietnam and of the Provisional Revolutionary Government of the Republic of South Vietnam is a logical and reasonable basis for the settlement of the Vietnamese problem. It has earned the sympathy and support of the peoples of the world.

In your letter you have expressed the desire to act for a just peace. For this the United States must cease the war of aggression and withdraw their troops from South Vietnam, respect the right of the population of the South and of the Vietnamese nation to dispose of themselves without foreign influence. This is the correct manner of solving the Vietnamese problem. . . .

Whatever the reason for Ho's reply — whether it was based on real or feigned outrage — it once again made clear that Hanoi would be satisfied only with victory. It counted on the nervous exhaustion of the United States; it would tolerate no appearance of "progress" in negotiations that might enable us to rally public opinion. A very natural response from us would have been to stop bringing soldiers home, but by now withdrawal had gained its own momentum. The reductions were always announced for a specific period; it was inevitable that pressures, partly public, partly bureaucratic, would build up as the end of each period approached. The August 23 riposte to Hanoi's belligerence was the last time Nixon tried to halt withdrawals.

On September 12, another NSC meeting was convened to discuss the next troop reduction. There was no longer any debate. On September 16, the President announced his decision to lower the troop ceiling by another 40,500 by December 15. The total reduction in the authorized ceiling now amounted to 65,500. This was 15,000 more than had been considered necessary by Rogers at the beginning of the year to convince the public that we were serious about ending the war. After the announcement on September 16 our withdrawals became inexorable; the President never again permitted the end of a withdrawal period to pass without announcing a new increment for the next. Hanoi was on the verge of achieving the second of its objectives without reciprocity: The bombing halt was now leading to unilateral withdrawal. We had come a long way: We had accepted total withdrawal, we had started out of Vietnam unilaterally, and we had de-escalated our military activities — all without the slightest response.

I was becoming uneasy about the course of our policy. At the NSC meeting on Vietnam of September 12, I took little part in the discussion but exclaimed toward the end: "We need a plan to end the war, not only to withdraw troops. This is what is on people's minds." Two days before the meeting I had sent the President a personal memorandum expressing my deep concern and questioning the assumptions of Vietnamization. Withdrawals would become like "salted peanuts" to the American public; the more troops we withdrew, the more would be expected, leading eventually to demands for total unilateral withdrawal, perhaps within a year (this in fact happened). I argued that our military strategy could not work rapidly enough against the erosion of public opinion and predicted, unhappily rightly, that Hanoi would probably wait until we had largely withdrawn before launching an all-out attack. In short, I did not think our policy would work. My memorandum of September 10 is reprinted in full in the notes at the back of this book.[11]

I followed this memorandum with another a day later that outlined the policy options as I saw them and warned once again that a strategy entirely dependent on Vietnamization would not work. A portion of this memorandum is also in the notes at the back.[12]

My preferred course was the one that had been at the heart of the proposed Vance mission: to make the most sweeping and generous proposal of which we were capable, short of overthrowing an allied government but ensuring a free political contest. If it were refused, we would halt troop withdrawals and quarantine North Vietnam by mining its ports and perhaps bombing its rail links to China. The goal would be a rapid negotiated compromise. Where the planning for the Vance mission had produced a detailed peace proposal, I assembled a trusted group of members of my staff in the White House Situation Room in September and October to explore the military side of the coin. Our present strategy was trying to walk a fine line, I told my staff, between withdrawing too fast to convince Hanoi of our determination and withdrawing too slowly to satisfy the American public. Assuming the President lost confidence in this policy and that he was not prepared to capitulate, how could he force a rapid conclusion? I asked for a military plan designed for maximum impact on the enemy's military capability; I requested also an assessment of the diplomatic consequences and a scenario for the final negotiation.

The planning was given the name "Duck Hook," for reasons that totally escape me today. Hal Sonnenfeldt and John Holdridge wrote analyses of the likely Soviet and Chinese responses to a major re-escalation.

Legal and diplomatic assessments were prepared. Roger Morris, Tony Lake,* and Peter Rodman worked on a draft Presidential speech (parts of which were later used on November 3). The Joint Chiefs of Staff devised a plan for mining North Vietnamese ports and harbors and destroying twenty-nine targets of military and economic importance in an air attack lasting four days. The plan also anticipated periodic attacks of forty-eight to seventy-two hours if Hanoi continued to avoid serious negotiation. The target date was to be November 1, 1969, the first anniversary of the bombing halt understanding that had promised us "prompt and productive" negotiations.

Our planning proceeded in a desultory fashion. As the scenario took shape, I concluded that no quick and "decisive" military action seemed attainable, and that there was not enough unanimity in our Administration to pursue so daring and risky a course. On October 17, I recommended to the President that he defer consideration of this option until he could assess the rate of North Vietnamese infiltration for the remainder of the year.† My doubts about Vietnamization persisted, reflecting the insoluble dilemmas of contesting both North Vietnam's army and domestic critics, of whom a significant percentage objected violently to the very concept of a coherent strategy. On October 30, I wrote another personal memorandum to the President, once again raising my doubts about the assumptions on which our policy was based:

We have seen so many Vietnam programs fail after being announced with great fanfare, that I thought I should put before you in summary form my questions about the assumptions underlying Vietnamization. To believe that this course is viable, we must make favorable assumptions about a number of factors, and must believe that Hanoi as well will come to accept them.

US calculations about the success of Vietnamization — and Hanoi's calculations, in turn, about the success of their strategy — rely on our respective judgments of:

— the pace of public opposition in the US to our continuing the fight in any form. (Past experience indicates that Vietnamization will not significantly slow it down.)

— the ability of the US Government to maintain its own discipline in carrying out this policy. (As public pressures grow, you may face increasing governmental disarray with a growing number of press leaks, etc.)

— the actual ability of the South Vietnamese Government and armed forces

---

* Morris and Lake later resigned, allegedly over the Cambodian operation of 1970; in the fall of 1969, however, they expressed no moral scruple over the much tougher option we were considering.

† This was, actually, an evasion. The strategy implied by the Duck Hook plan should have had nothing to do with the rate of infiltration — in fact, on the basis of my own prognosis infiltration would not pick up until we had reduced our forces much further. The plan should have been linked primarily to the progress of negotiations.

to replace American withdrawals — both physically and psychologically. (Conclusive evidence is lacking here; this fact in itself, and past experience, argue against optimism.)

— the degree to which Hanoi's current losses affect its ability to fight later — i.e., losses of military cadre, political infra-structure, etc. (Again, the evidence is not definitive. Most reports of progress have concerned security gains by US forces — not a lasting erosion of enemy political strength.)

— the ability of the GVN to gain solid political benefit from its current pacification progress. (Again, reports of progress have been largely about security gains behind the US shield.)

Our Vietnamization policy thus rests on a series of favorable assumptions which may not be accurate — although no one can be certain on the basis of current analyses.

By now my memoranda were growing quixotic. The only real alternatives to Vietnamization were immediate withdrawal or else the escalation that was part of the Vance gambit and Duck Hook planning. Not even the strongest critics in the mainstream of American life recommended immediate withdrawal in 1969. It would have been a blatant betrayal, precipitating the collapse of our ally, giving him no chance to survive on his own. It would have shaken confidence in the United States in Asia, particularly Japan; during the entire period not *one* European leader urged on us the unconditional abandonment of the war we had inherited. I doubt that our opening to China would have prospered after such a humiliation. China was inching toward us, after all, to find a counterweight to the growing Soviet threat on its borders. It was not even logistically possible to withdraw 500,000 men instantaneously; the Pentagon estimated that a minimum of twelve to eighteen months would be required to remove the numbers that had gone to Vietnam over a period of four years. They would have to be extricated amidst the disintegration and panic our collapse was certain to produce; the South Vietnamese army of close to a million might well turn on the ally that had so betrayed it. There was, moreover, next to no public support for such a course; every poll showed that unilateral withdrawal was rejected by crushing majorities. The public was as ambivalent as the government planners: It wanted us to get out of Vietnam and yet it did not want defeat. Above all, Hanoi had made clear repeatedly that the war could not be ended — or our prisoners released — even by our unilateral withdrawal. We were told throughout that as we exited we also had to remove our allies from power and install a Communist-dominated coalition government.

Starting in 1970, though not at first, our critics pressed us to announce a final deadline for our withdrawal. But that was either a variation of Vietnamization or the equivalent of capitulation. If the deadline was arbitrary — that is, too short — everything would disintegrate and it was a formula for collapse. If the deadline was feasible in terms of our own planning for Vietnamization, the only difference was that it was publicly announced. The issue was the tactical judgment whether an announcement would help or hinder our extrication from the war. For better or worse our judgment was that a public announcement would destroy the last incentives for Hanoi to negotiate; it would then simply outwait us. And how would we explain to American families why their sons' lives should be at risk when a fixed schedule for total withdrawal existed? It is important to remember that most responsible critics, including Clark Clifford, at first only asked for the withdrawal of *combat* troops by the end of 1970, leaving a large residual force behind. Our own schedule differed from this by exactly four months.

Another argument frequently pressed on us was that we should stop giving Saigon a "veto" over our negotiating position; more generally it was an attack on the alleged repressiveness of the South Vietnamese government. It would be absurd to deny that the government on whose territory our forces were located had some influence over our policies. Its self-confidence, legitimacy, and survivability were after all one of the key issues of the war; if we collapsed it by pressures beyond its capacity to bear, we would in effect have settled on Hanoi's terms. But our influence on Saigon was much greater than the reverse. There is no question that in response to our pressure the Saigon government made extraordinary efforts to broaden its base and to agree to a political contest with the Communists. A significant land reform program was instituted; an electoral commission on which the Communists would be represented was put forward. Saigon's politics were more pluralistic and turbulent than its American critics cared to admit — and vastly better in human terms than the icy totalitarianism of North Vietnam, which was in fact the alternative at stake.

The South Vietnamese government's internal security problem was not a flimsy excuse for autocracy but the reality of organized terrorism in the cities and almost daily assassinations and kidnappings in the countryside.* The independence and political weight of South Vietnam's military commanders and their tendency to warlordism were a challenge even to Thieu's personal authority, not to speak of constitutional government. But the United States shared some blame here, for it was the overthrow of Ngo Dinh Diem in 1963, with its resulting massive purge of the civil administration, that made successor regimes so dependent on the military. Obviously, the political practices of a prosperous country with a long libertarian tradition could not be

---

*The assassinations and kidnappings were usually aimed at the best, not the worst, of Saigon's officials, including schoolteachers, because they embodied Saigon's best claim to public support.

fully applied in an underdeveloped country wracked by civil war; they were not applied by President Lincoln during our own Civil War. Attacking Thieu too often was not an advocacy of concrete reform but an alibi for our abdication.

The fact was that the alternatives to simply getting out or dismantling Saigon were escalation or Vietnamization. We finally rejected the military option because we did not think we could sustain public support for the length of time required to prevail; because its outcome was problematical; and because had we succeeded Saigon might still not have been ready to take over. In truth I never examined it more than halfheartedly, largely because I and all members of the Administration not only wanted to end the war but yearned to do so in the least convulsive way. What separated the Administration from its moderate critics was not a philosophy but a nuance. Our course aimed at withdrawal; our desire to retain flexibility and therefore our rejection of a public deadline was due to our lingering hope that Hanoi might at some point negotiate, paying some price to accelerate our total withdrawal.

The Unpacifiable Doves

THE public atmosphere was hardly hospitable to nuance. For the war had set in motion forces transcending the issues and emotions that went beyond the substance of the debate.

A week before Inauguration, on January 12, 1969, the distinguished diplomatic correspondent of the *Washington Post,* Chalmers Roberts, had perceptively outlined Nixon's dilemma:

> At a guess, the country and Congress will give the new President six months to find the route to disengagement with honor from the Vietnam war. But very probably six months, or any limited extension that public attitudes may grant, will not be enough. . . .
>
> President Nixon is bound, not so much by his own words as the national mood, to continue on the Johnson course. . . .
>
> The election campaign made it very evident that the big majority of Americans want to get out of Vietnam, but in a way that does not make a mockery of the loss thus far of more than 31,000 American lives.
>
> This combination of attitudes restricts Mr. Nixon both as to time and substance. . . .

So it was. As the months went by in 1969, we were confronted by public protests and demonstrations and quickening demands in the media and the Congress for unilateral concessions in the negotiations. They had one common theme: The obstacle to peace was not Hanoi but their own government's inadequate dedication to peace.

Future generations may find it difficult to visualize the domestic convulsion that the Vietnam war induced. On July 2, 1969, antiwar women destroyed draft records in New York. On July 6, members of Women Strike for Peace flew to the University of Toronto to meet three women representing the Viet Cong. The mayors of two towns petitioned the President to stop sending their sons to Vietnam. Demonstrators launched a mock invasion of Fort Lewis on July 15. There were weekly demonstrations at the Pentagon, including such charming gestures as pouring blood on its steps. On August 14 twelve young soldiers from a base in Honolulu sought refuge in a church as an "act of deep involvement against all the injustice inherent in the American military system." A group called Business Executives for Vietnam Peace called on the White House on August 28 to inform the Administration that "the honeymoon is over." While Nixon was on the West Coast in August he was exposed to repeated demonstrations at his residence in San Clemente. On September 3, a group of over two hundred twenty-five psychologists demonstrated outside the White House, protesting the Vietnam war as "the insanity of our times." Protesters read lists of war dead at public rallies and had them inserted into the *Congressional Record*. (This turned into a favorite activity of some former members of the Johnson and Kennedy administrations who might have owed their successors something better than to imply that they were indifferent to sacrifices and deaths.) During August leaders of the protest movement announced a series of monthly demonstrations starting October 15 to bring pressure on the government — the so-called Moratorium. All of this was conspicuously and generally approvingly covered by the media. Very few, if any, of the protesters ever appealed to Hanoi for even a little flexibility or were ready to grant that just conceivably their own government might be sincere.

As the summer drew to a close and students returned to universities and the Congress ended its recess, the pace of protest quickened. The death of Ho Chi Minh on September 3 was alleged to present a new opportunity for ending the stalemate in Paris, though whatever evidence was at hand indicated the opposite. There was clamor that we propose a cease-fire in deference to the leader who had caused us so much discomfiture, and hope that such a cease-fire would then become permanent as if Hanoi might be made to slide without noticing it into an arrangement it had consistently rejected. In fact we observed a cease-fire on the day of Ho's funeral and of course it was not extended by our adversaries. As the summer drew to a close, Chalmers Roberts offered a thoughtful analysis in the *Washington Post* of September 5. He predicted that antiwar passions were just beginning to heat up:

[By staying in San Clemente] Mr. Nixon has been able to escape explaining what he is trying to do about the war. With Congress away and the college generation at the beaches . . . there has been no focus on the war's opponents.

But all this surely is about to change. Mr. Nixon will be back in the White

House next Tuesday and by then even the last congressional laggard will be in town. In a few days . . . the students will be back on campus. . . .

Ho's death is creating calls for new Nixon initiatives. And Ho's man in Paris, Xuan Thuy, on Tuesday seemed to hint that massive American withdrawals just might move the Paris talks off dead center.

Both events are likely to be grist for American doves. . . . The long summer is over and new forces are coming into motion in the area of American public opinion. The President will soon have to say more and probably do more if he wants public support. . . .

Roberts's prediction proved only too accurate. On September 3, Senator Edmund Muskie of Maine complained that President Nixon's plan for ending the war was "very ambiguous"; he also questioned whether Nixon was in fact seeking a negotiated settlement rather than a military victory. ("Victory" was turning into an epithet.) On September 5, Senators John Sherman Cooper and Gaylord Nelson suggested that the President use the "opportunity" created by Ho Chi Minh's death to propose new initiatives to end the war; they did not tell us how or what the opportunity consisted of. On September 6, Senate Majority Leader Mike Mansfield made the same suggestion. On September 18, two days after the President's announcement of withdrawal of 40,500 more troops, Senator Edward Kennedy attacked the President's Vietnam policy and branded the Saigon regime as the primary obstacle to a settlement. In an interview on September 21, Cyrus Vance called for a "standstill cease-fire," suggesting a "leopard-spot federal or confederal solution"[13] (though we had proposed a cease-fire to Dobrynin as part of the Vance gambit and Hanoi had shown no interest in it). On September 25, Congressman Allard Lowenstein of New York proclaimed plans to mobilize public support for another "dump Johnson"–style movement, this time with Nixon as the target. On the same day, Senator Charles Goodell of New York announced that he would introduce a resolution in the Senate requiring the withdrawal of all US forces from Vietnam by the end of 1970.

As the October 15 Moratorium drew nearer, Congressional critics from both parties grew more vocal. On October 2, Senator Mansfield called on the President to propose a standstill cease-fire. Senator Eugene McCarthy on the same day announced his support for the Goodell proposal. Senator Charles Percy on October 3 urged the Administration to halt allied offensive operations as long as the enemy did not take advantage of the situation — the same formula that had started the discussions of the bombing halt. Between September 24 and October 15, eleven antiwar resolutions were introduced in Congress. These included Senator Goodell's resolution to cut off funding for US combat forces by December 1970, Senators Mark Hatfield and Frank Church's bill calling for a schedule for immediate withdrawal of all US forces from Vietnam, and Senators Jacob Javits and Claiborne Pell's resolution for withdrawal of combat forces by the end of 1970 and for revocation of the 1964 Gulf of Tonkin Resolution under which President Johnson had first introduced American combat forces in Vietnam. Public statements by well-known personalities multiplied. On October 9, Kingman Brewster, president of Yale, called for unconditional withdrawal from Vietnam. On October 10, seventy-nine presidents of private colleges and universities wrote to President Nixon, urging a firm timetable for withdrawals. On October 13, Whitney Young of the National Urban League released a strongly worded statement calling the war "a moral and spiritual drain" and contending that it exacerbated racial tensions at home. On October 14, North Vietnamese Premier Pham Van Dong fed our public debate by an unprecedented open letter to American antiwar protesters in honor of the Moratorium, hailing their "struggle" as a "noble reflection of the legitimate and urgent demand of the American people . . . the Vietnamese people and the United States progressive people against United States aggression [which] will certainly be crowned with total victory."

The Moratorium demonstrations took place across the country on October 15. A crowd of 20,000 packed a noontime rally in New York's financial district and listened to Bill Moyers, President Johnson's former Assistant and press secretary, urge President Nixon to respond to the antiwar sentiment. Thirty thousand gathered on the New Haven Green. Fifty thousand massed on the Washington Monument grounds within sight of the White House. The demonstration at the Monument was preceded by a walk around the city of several thousand people carrying candles. At George Washington University, Dr. Benjamin Spock informed a large gathering that President Nixon was incapable of ending the war because of "limitations on his personality." The demonstration in Boston, where 100,000 people converged on the Common, appeared to be the largest of all. Thousands spilled over into neighboring streets. A number of speakers, including Senator George McGovern, addressed the huge crowd as a skywriting plane drew a peace symbol in the sky overhead. As each speaker finished, the crowd broke into a chant, "Peace Now, Peace Now." The common feature of all these demonstrations was the conviction that the American government was the obstacle to peace; that it needed not a program for an honorable peace — a concept evoking condescending ridicule — but instruction on the undesirability of war.

Both *Time* and *Newsweek* devoted several pages and vivid pictures to the demonstrations in major cities and on college campuses. *Time* interpreted the Moratorium's message to President Nixon as follows:

What in fact was M Day's message to Richard Nixon? Many participants demanded immediate and total withdrawal from Vietnam of all US forces. Yet the moratorium by no means constituted a call to the President for that solution — although it evidently gained new respectability and popularity. What M Day did raise was an unmistakable sign to Richard Nixon that he must do more to end the war and do it faster. Unless the pace of progress quickens, he will have great difficulty maintaining domestic support for the two or three years that he believes he needs to work the US out of Vietnam with honor and in a way that would safeguard US interests and influence in the world.

Even with the perspective of a decade, it is difficult to avoid a feeling of melancholy at this spectacle of a nation tearing at itself in the midst of a difficult war. By October the Administration had announced withdrawal of over fifty thousand troops, the reduction of B-52 sorties by 20 percent, of tactical air operations by 25 percent, and a change in battlefield orders to General Abrams that amounted to a decision to end offensive operations. The previous Administration had *sent* 550,000 Americans to Vietnam, had no negotiating proposal except that we would withdraw six months after the North Vietnamese left, and had strongly implied that it would insist on retaining a large residual force thereafter. Yet there was little compunction about harassing and vilifying a new President who had offered total withdrawal within twelve months of an agreement, free elections including the NLF, and mixed electoral commissions on which the NLF would be represented, and who had opened up the subject of a cease-fire.

The public malaise raised in a profound way the question of the responsibility of leaders to the public in a democracy. Lucky is the leader whose convictions of what is in the national interest coincide with the public mood. But what is his obligation when these perceptions differ? A shallow view of democracy would reduce the leader to passivity and have him simply register public opinion as he understands it. But such a course is a negation of the qualities that the public has a right to expect of those charged with conducting its affairs. Leaders are responsible not for running public opinion polls but for the consequences of their actions. They will be held to account for disasters even if the decision that produced the calamity enjoyed widespread public support when it was taken. In 1938 the Munich agreement made Chamberlain widely popular and cast Churchill in the role of an alarmist troublemaker; eighteen months later Chamberlain was finished because the Munich agreement was discredited. With the Vietnam war the problem was even more complex. Rightly or wrongly — I am still convinced rightly — we thought that capitulation or steps that amounted to it would usher in a period of disintegrating American credibility that would only accelerate the world's instability. The opposition was vocal, sometimes violent; it comprised a large minority of the college-educated; it certainly dominated the media and made full use of them. But in our view it was wrong. We could not give up our convictions, all the less so since the majority of the American people seemed to share our perception. At no time in 1969 did the Gallup Poll show support of the President's conduct of the war below 44 percent (and then opposition stood at 26 percent). At the height of the massive public demonstrations in October, 58 percent of the public supported the President and only 32 percent were opposed.

If we were to make progress in the negotiations, it was necessary to convince Hanoi that there were some irreducible conditions beyond which we would not retreat. We needed some program in the name of which to rally support. But as the years went by, every concession produced demands for further concessions. In the face of media and Congressional opposition, there never was any firm ground on which to stand.

Criticism of Hanoi was to all practical purposes nonexistent. Deadlocks tended to be ascribed to American shortsightedness if not to the malignity of our government; ending the war was presented as substantially within our control and as deliberately avoided because of psychological aberrations. The impression was created that some magical concession stood between us and a solution, prevented above all by United States rigidity, if not by more substantial moral defects. The issue came to be defined in terms both wounding and misleading: who was for and who was against the war, who liked bombing and who opposed it. A notable exception was the *Washington Post,* which, contrary to Nixon's view of its unalterable hostility, was in fact compassionate. It editorialized on October 12:

> The tragedy is that it is late — that there were no vigilantes in or out of government three or four years ago, organizing a Vietnam Moratorium. For what is going to be hard about Wednesday's manifestation is not the mobilizing of it; the problem is going to come in the interpreting of it and in the application of a great outpouring of protest in any practical, meaningful way. . . .
>
> Even the most anguished people in their prayers and protestations and teachings can give little useful or specific counsel to the President: a loud shout to stop the war, however heartfelt, is not a strategy. . . .
>
> It is almost impossible to believe both from what the President is doing and from any reasonable estimate of where his best interests lie, that he is not a charter member of this probable majority (of people desiring an end to the war).

But the general pattern can be demonstrated by a rereading of editorial columns of the *New York Times.* In October 1969 I had Peter Rodman, a member of my staff, trace the evolution of the *Times*'s editorial position. I did not mean to single out the *Times* for invidious comparison; it was among the more thoughtful of the critics and saw itself as making reasonable proposals for compromise, not mere demands for our capitulation. Yet the pattern of its proposals is instructive of what we faced.

The *New York Times* in 1969 regularly called for American concessions when the other side seemed conciliatory, in order, it was explained, to seize the opportunity for peace.[14] It also called for concessions, however, when the other side was intensifying the war, in that case because the Communist step-up had demonstrated that our military effort could never bring peace.[15] The recurring call for American concessions regardless of Hanoi's reactions led the *Times* into a series of constantly escalating proposals. In 1968 the *Times* advocated mutual withdrawal by both the US and North Vietnam, but this soon evolved into a recommendation that the United States initiate the process with a token withdrawal, then into a demand for withdrawals regardless of Hanoi's response, and then into pressures for a fixed and unconditional timetable for the complete evacuation of US forces.[16] As for the scale of American withdrawals, the *Times* first called for the United States simply to "initiate" or "begin" troop reductions; an editorial in May referred to anticipated US cutbacks of fifty to one hundred thousand men as "substantial." When Nixon began the withdrawal program at Midway in June, this was first welcomed as "a step toward disengagement"; by September, however, there was grumbling that the withdrawal of 60,000 was "timid" and "token," and not "significant" or "adequate."[17]

The same escalation of proposals occurred in the political dimension. In May 1969, the *Times* called for a "coalition electoral commission" to supervise free elections in South Vietnam. But less than four weeks later — a month before Saigon offered to establish just such a joint commission — the position had evolved to the negotiation of "an agreement . . . on the future government of South Vietnam," that is, an "interim coalition."[18] As for military tactics, the *Times* began calling for a cutback of search-and-destroy missions in April 1969. Its own news columns on July 25 reported that such a reduction was about to take place. Within two weeks, the *Times* was calling for a standstill cease-fire.[19] Even this proved insufficient. Nixon offered it on October 7, 1970; Hanoi promptly rejected it. The *Times* continued its criticism.

Each of these escalating concessions was advanced as the key to peace and as the only way to get negotiations started.[20] Once made, the concession was briefly applauded, and indeed Hanoi was called on to respond.[21] But when Hanoi ignored the proposals, the result was not a call for American steadfastness but for further US concessions[22] on the ground that the lack of progress was the fault of the United States[23] or of Saigon.[24] The importance of the earlier concession was now disparaged,[25] or else it was argued that Hanoi had in fact reciprocated[26] or that the United States had been hardening its position.[27] These calls for ever further American concessions were regularly explained by the argument that the United States had a special obligation to prove its good faith to the other side and to abandon the quest for military victory.[28] No such obligation was discovered for the other side. This evolution of editorial opinion was not unique. It was, instead, a vivid example of how our critics could rarely be satisfied for long, *even by the adoption of their proposals*.

The pattern was repeated in Congress. For example, Senator William Fulbright reacted to the President's May 14 speech by saying that although Nixon could have been more forthcoming, he did not "fault the President for not going further." Yet by June 22 — despite an intervening unilateral American troop withdrawal announcement of 25,000 — the Senator said that he was disillusioned and would reopen the Senate Foreign Relations Committee hearings on Vietnam.[29] In the same vein Senator Mike Mansfield reacted to the May 14 speech by saying that he was "impressed" and that "there appears to be a lot of room for . . . give and take." Two weeks later, he was attacking the Administration because its military strategy gave him no "indication of bringing the war to a conclusion."[30]

There was no civility or grace from the antiwar leaders; they mercilessly persecuted those they regarded as culpable. Walt Rostow was not reappointed to his professorship at the Massachusetts Institute of Technology; service at the highest level of his government for eight years had obviously reduced his qualifications for a professorship at that august institution. William Bundy's appointment as editor of *Foreign Affairs* was greeted by howls of protest. Dean Rusk, after eight years of unselfish, able, and dedicated service as Secretary of State, could find no position for months until his alma mater, the University of Georgia, appointed him to a professorship and gave him a part-time secretary. Hubert Humphrey, that gentle and conciliatory and lovable man, was subjected to harassment in a manner that still moved him to tears years later. Nor has the passage of a decade softened the implacability. In 1979 twenty-four professors of New York University protested McGeorge Bundy's appointment to the faculty on the ground of complicity in a "genocidal" war. A third of the faculty of the University of Chicago in the same month protested an award to Robert McNamara on the same grounds — ignoring the genuine genocide that has since occurred in Indochina after the Communist victory and that these men sought to prevent. It was never granted that serious men could have been pursuing perhaps misguided but honorable purposes over a decade ago. The doves have proved to be a specially vicious kind of bird.

To me the most poignant fate was that of Robert McNamara, who had been forced out by Johnson as Secretary of Defense in 1967 and then served as head of the World Bank. I had first met McNamara in 1961 shortly after President Kennedy had named him to head the Pentagon. He struck me as bright, dynamic, cocksure. I applauded his efforts to put our defense policy on a more analytical basis. But I thought that he overemphasized the quantitative aspects of defense planning; by neglecting intangible psychological and political components he aimed for a predictability that was illusory and caused needless strains to our alliances. His eager young associates hid their moral convictions behind a seemingly objective method of analysis which obscured that their questions too often predetermined the answers and that these answers led to a long-term stagnation in our military technology.

With all these drawbacks McNamara made substantial contributions as Secretary of Defense. His goal of a systematic approach to defense policy was long overdue; even when I did not agree with some of his answers I thought that he had asked the right questions. But though an outstanding Secretary of Defense, McNamara had proved an unfortunate choice for managing a war. The methods which on the whole had stood him in good stead in getting a grip on that most unwieldy of government departments were less appropriate to the conduct of a conflict whose outcome, too, depended on so many political and psychological intangibles. He managed at one and the same time to be too tough and too ambiguous, too narrowly focused on battlefield considerations and too ready to settle for atmospherics. But above all McNamara did not have his heart in the assignment. He had wanted to relate the awesome power of our nation to humane ends; he had no stomach for an endless war; he suffered from a deep feeling of guilt for having acquiesced in the decisions that made it both inevitable and inconclusive. When I returned from my first trip to Vietnam in 1965 he was the highest ranking member of the Johnson Administration to receive me. I found him tortured by the emerging inconclusiveness of the war; he was torn between his doubts and his sense of duty, between his analysis and loyalties. He knew that he would be able to restore many valued friendships by a dramatic gesture of protest, but he thought it wrong to speak out when he considered himself partially responsible and thought he could promote his convictions more effectively in office than outside.

In this, McNamara in the end had become an example of a larger reality. This same ambivalence had come to affect that Administration's conduct of the war, compelling its tentative character, its oscillation between periods of violence and escapism. McNamara from the beginning urged — nay, pleaded for — a negotiated and not an imposed peace. His door was open to those anguished by America's frustrations. In the councils of the government he supported the search for diplomatic initiatives more vigorously and consistently than the agencies conventionally charged with the mandate for solutions. In 1967 he had been the principal impetus behind the attempt to negotiate a bombing halt through two French intermediaries. He had been so anxious that he called me on the telephone after every contact with the North Vietnamese, using a cover name so transparent that it must have fooled the intelligence services listening in for all of ten seconds. Shortly after that effort failed, Johnson forced him out, reasoning — not entirely incorrectly — that McNamara's doubts had made the effective conduct of his office impossible, at the very moment when public denunciation of the Defense Secretary for being a warmonger was reaching fever pitch and he could make no public appearance without encountering the ugliest form of harassment.

After his resignation McNamara conducted himself with characteristic dignity. Beginning in 1969, he missed no opportunity to press on me courses of action that those who were vilifying him would have warmly embraced. Though he was physically assaulted on campuses and caricatured in print as a warmonger, he was always too much aware of the anguish of policymaking and of his own responsibility to choose the route taken by some of his previous associates of publicly damning the Administration for a conflict it had not started and thus easing his own personal position. He suffered cruelly but never showed it.

In such an atmosphere, communication broke down between an Administration that had inherited the war and which by every reasonable criterion demonstrably sought to liquidate it, and those elements that had formerly felt a stake in the Presidency and the international role of the United States. Part of the reason was the demoralization of the very leadership group that had sustained the great initiatives of the postwar period. The war in Indochina was the culmination of the disappointments of a decade that had opened with the clarion call of a resurgent idealism and ended with assassinations, racial and social discord, and radicalized politics. Our dilemmas were very much a product of liberal doctrines of reformist intervention and academic theories of graduated escalation. The collapse of these high aspirations shattered the self-confidence without which Establishments flounder. The leaders who had inspired our foreign policy were particularly upset by the rage of the students. The assault of these upper middle-class young men and women — who were, after all, their own children — was not simply on policies, but on life-styles and values heretofore considered sacrosanct. Stimulated by a sense of guilt encouraged by modern psychiatry and the radical chic rhetoric of upper middle-class suburbia, they symbolized the end of an era of simple faith in material progress. Ironically, the insecurity of their elders turned the normal grievances of maturing youth into an institutionalized rage and a national trauma.

There were other causes having to do with the structure of American politics. The Vietnam war toppled both Lyndon Johnson and Hubert Humphrey in 1968, not because the whole country shifted against the war (the Wallace vote and the Republicans, reflecting the majority view, were either pro-intervention or silent), but because the war split their base of power, the Democratic Party. Once out of the White House, the Democratic Party found it easy and tempting to unite in opposition to a Republican President on the issue of Vietnam. Those who opposed the war but reluctantly supported Johnson and Humphrey were now no longer constrained by party loyalty. On the Republican side, Richard Nixon as President was able to reconcile the Republican right to a withdrawal program and an inconclusive outcome for which conservatives might well have assaulted a Democratic President. Thus there was no conservative counterweight to the increasingly strident protests. By tranquilizing the right, Nixon liberated the protest movement from its constraints; the center of gravity of American politics thus shifted decisively to the antiwar side even though the public had not changed its basic view.

The basic challenge to the new Nixon Administration was similar to de Gaulle's in Algeria: to withdraw as an expression of policy and not as a collapse. This was even more important for the United States, on whose stability so many other countries depended. But de Gaulle was fortunate in his opposition; it came from those who wanted victory and who thought he was conceding too much. This gave him a margin for maneuver with the Algerian rebels; they were bound to consider the alternative to de Gaulle as worse. Our opposition came from those who wanted more rapid withdrawal, if not defeat, and this destroyed our bargaining position. Our enemies would only benefit from our domestic collapse. Thus — even though every opinion poll showed the majority of the American public eager for an honorable solution and firmly against capitulation, a sentiment Nixon was able to rally skillfully on many occasions — the momentum of American politics was in the direction of unilateral concessions. For the Nixon Administration to have kept these turbulent forces in harness as we designed a self-confident policy of orderly disengagement was no small feat. Indeed, to have maintained the initiative for four years and brought off a compromise settlement and a balance of forces on the ground in Vietnam, however precarious, was a political tour de force.

There is no gainsaying, however, that the ride was rougher than it need have been. The turbulent national mood touched Nixon on his rawest nerve. He had taken initiatives that reversed the course of his predecessor; he had withdrawn troops and de-escalated the war — all steps urged on him by the Establishment groups whom he simultaneously distrusted and envied. And instead of being acclaimed, he was being castigated for not moving more rapidly on the path on which they had not even dared to take the first step. It was not a big leap to the view that what he really faced was not a policy difference but the same liberal conspiracy that had sought to destroy him ever since the Alger Hiss case. Here were all the old enemies in the press and in the Establishment, uniting once again; they would even accept if not urge the military defeat of their country to carry out the vendetta of a generation. And Nixon possessed no instinct whatever for understanding the outburst of the young, and particularly the university students. Having worked his own way through college and law school, he thought they should be grateful for the opportunity of a higher education. He had an exalted view of Ivy League universities. When riots broke out at Harvard in the spring of 1969, he said to me that it might be a good thing, for the greatest university in the country would undoubtedly handle the challenge and thus set an example for all others. He seemed genuinely surprised when I gave him my opinion that under Harvard procedures nobody after three days would know who had done what to whom — which is exactly what happened. Recalling his own youth, he could see in the outrage of those he thought exceptionally privileged nothing but an indoctrination by sinister influences hostile to his person. He had no feeling for the metaphysical despair of those who saw before them a life of affluence in a spiritual desert. If what he was confronting was a political battle for survival, rather than a foreign policy debate, he believed himself justified in using the methods that had already brought him so far. On authentic international issues, Nixon was sensitive to nuance and comfortable with tactics of conciliation and compromise. In political battles he was a gut fighter; he turned without hesitation to uses of Presidential power that he never ceased believing — with much evidence — had been those of his predecessors as well.

Such tactics were inappropriate for our national anguish. Bridges needed building and the Chief Executive of the country, the only nationally elected official, should have taken the first step. Yet this is something Nixon just did not know how to do. He was too insecure and, in a strange way, too vulnerable. In fact he showed the protesters the respect in practice for which he never could find the words — by accepting their peace program. Perhaps it was precisely the irony that their program was being carried out by the man who had been anathema to them for two decades that so embittered some of his critics.

There is no question that generosity of spirit was not one of Nixon's virtues; he could never transcend his resentments and his complexes. But neither did he ever receive from his critics compassion for the task his predecessors had bequeathed to him. There was a self-fulfilling obtuseness in the bitterness with which the two sides regarded each other: Nixon's belief in the liberal conspiracy, the critics' view that the Nixon Administration was determined to pursue the war for its own sake. Both were wrong. In the process, each stalemated the other while demeaning itself.

I agreed with the President's Vietnam policy; I had designed much of it. If I had any criticism, it was that he procrastinated in facing the painful choices before him. But I thought that America's domestic problems went much deeper than a contest for political power waged in the name of a quarrel over peace terms for Vietnam. At one background briefing in 1970 I pointed out that

If you would look around the world, you will have to come to the conclusion that the turmoil is not caused primarily, or at least exclusively, by the causes that are ascribed to it. There are student riots in Berlin, where the students participate in [university] government, and there are student riots in Paris where they don't participate in it. There are student riots in Oxford, which has a tutorial system, and there are student riots in Rome, where there are huge lectures. There are riots in this country because of Vietnam, race and slums, allegedly, and there are riots in Holland which has no Vietnam, no race problem and no slums. In other words, we are dealing with a problem of contemporary society, of how to give meaning to life for a generation, for a younger generation in states that are becoming increasingly bureaucratic and technological.

For these reasons, my attitude toward the protesters diverged from Nixon's. He saw in them an enemy that had to be vanquished; I considered them students and colleagues with whom I differed but whose idealism was indispensable for our future; I sought to build bridges to them. I understood the anguish of the nonradical members of the protest movement; humanly I was close to many of them. While convinced that their policies were deeply wrong and their single-minded self-righteousness profoundly dangerous for our world position and domestic tranquillity, I attempted to maintain a serious dialogue between the Administration and its critics. In November 1969 Nixon asked me to comment on a memorandum sent to him by Pat Moynihan, then Counsellor to the President. It described a scene at a Harvard-Princeton football game in which the assembled graduates — worth, according to Pat, at least $10 billion — roared support when the Harvard University band was introduced, in a takeoff on Agnew's denigrating phrase, as the "effete Harvard Corps of Intellectual Snobs." Pat warned that while Nixon was right in resisting attempts to make policy in the streets, he should not needlessly challenge the young — because of their great influence on their parents. Nixon had made marginal comments that indicated his own skepticism about his ability to win over "Harvard types"; moreover, he was convinced that his political and financial support came from the South, the Midwest, and California, which were impervious to the shouts of a Harvard crowd. Nevertheless, a warning in Moynihan's memorandum about the "incredible powers of derision" of the young was significantly underlined by the President. I put some thought into my response of November 15, 1969. It appears here in major extracts:

Who are They?

They are a very mixed group — in social origin, in political outlook, in potential for help or harm. Of the young Moratorium marchers, some were certainly the offspring of the affluent, and therefore their politics are a sharp departure from their parents. Yet many have fathers who attended college under the GI Bill in the late '40s and who went on to vote for Stevenson. A lot of the marchers were undoubtedly the first generation to reach college from predominantly Democratic urban strata. And if Tom Wicker is speaking for himself and his colleagues in claiming that "those are our children" down there in the streets, these are also the offspring of some traditionally Democratic professional elements. . . .

Why Do They March?

Their motives are also quite varied. In the broader sense, most are casualties of our affluence. They have had the leisure for self-pity, and the education enabling them to focus it in a fashionable critique of the "system." But the psychological origins are probably irrelevant. Confusion, outrage, or evangelism have absorbed youthful energies in every generation. The group Pat talks about is special in the sheer breadth of its political consciousness and activism. It is drawn, after all, from the largest number of educated young people in history.

And to the degree that they are politically conscious, many are substantially anti-establishment simply because that is not only the natural bent of youthful alienation, but also because it is a major thrust of contemporary academic literature. Modern American sociology, psychology, political science, etc., have turned a glaring light (as they should have) on the faults in our society. So too is some of our best modern literature powerful social criticism. All this is bound to fall on fertile ground — and cover more of it than ever before — in a country that sends *8 million* kids to college.

The practical result is very mixed.

A small minority takes refuge (as it always has) in mindless radicalism.

But I believe that the overwhelming majority of these young people across the country remain remarkably open in terms of their future political affiliation. Many are bright and thoughtful. They are committed to right wrongs and find themselves. They are eager to participate, impatient for tangible results. They are wary of every answer — ready to suspect that arguments for gradual (*realistic*) progress (from peace in Vietnam to desegregation) mask some sinister conspiracy against the goal.

Their Political Impact

. . . They become formidable by adding to their own votes an enormous outburst of political activism, bound to have an influence on others as well as on their parents. We have ample proof of this in the McCarthy phenomenon.

Vietnam is only symptomatic. When that issue is gone, another will take its place. For they are fighting the establishment position as much as a given problem.

What Can You Do?

I agree with Moynihan that attacking this group head-on is counterproductive. This is not to say that you should be soft on the militants. There is a strong need here for firm leadership, both in psychological and political terms. . . .

There are strong arguments for simply neutralizing this potential force by avoiding a collision. This by no means requires appeasement. It does mean that the Administration be seen to take seriously the responsible majority of these young people. The posture would be that they may be wrong on the merits of the argument, but you do not doubt the authenticity and sincerity of their concerns.

Can you Gain Anything?

Beyond this neutralization, there just might be a chance, over time, to win some of these young people to your side. The old Democratic-Republican quarrels of the '40s and '50s do not encumber this generation of young Americans.

You have something basic in common with many of them — a conviction that the machinery of New Deal liberalism has to be fundamentally overhauled. You also share a concern that America play a more balanced and restrained role in the world. You are, in fact, turning over most of the rocks at home and abroad that these kids want to see turned over.

With a concerted and sensitive effort to get across the fresh approach of your Administration, you may well gain some converts among those who now seem irretrievable.

Whether Nixon in fact held all the views I ascribed to him or whether — like a good courtier — I sought to influence his behavior by giving him a reputation to uphold, I devoted a great deal of time and effort to meeting antiwar groups. Haldeman opposed my seeing such groups as at best a waste of my time and at worst appearing to give moral support to implacable opponents. I also gave background briefings to the press every time there was a Presidential speech on Vietnam and I traveled around the country with the President in 1970 talking to groups of editors, publishers, and broadcasters. My theme was constant, that the war had to be ended as an act of policy, not in response to demonstrations. At a meeting with a group of business leaders in October

1969 I argued that "capitulation would not terminate the demonstration phenomenon. If confrontation in the streets is to succeed on this issue, it could drastically alter the style of American politics. Some of the leaders are the same people who rioted in Chicago for demands which have long since been met. The true issue is the authority of the Presidency — not any particular President."

The paradox was that the Administration and its critics could frustrate each other but by doing so neither could achieve what both yearned for: an early negotiated end to the war in Vietnam. All this time Hanoi stood at the sidelines, coldly observing how America was negotiating not with its adversary but with itself.

Groping for a Strategy

WE were on a road out of Vietnam, attempting to pursue a middle course between capitulation and the seemingly endless stalemate that we had inherited. Whether we could succeed would depend on our ability to mesh a complicated series of diplomatic, military, and political moves while confronted by an implacable, impatient public protest.

Nixon sought to gain ascendancy over our domestic situation by various moves over and above our negotiating posture and de-escalation. On September 19, Nixon and Laird — who had already asked Congress for a draft lottery — announced at a White House briefing that the withdrawals of 60,000 men from Vietnam enabled us to cancel draft calls for November and December. Calls scheduled for October would be stretched out over the final quarter of the year. The Department of Defense began limiting induction to nineteen-year-olds; on November 26, the President signed into law the bill permittin'g a draft lottery.

A campaign on behalf of American prisoners of war in Vietnam was launched in August by demanding North Vietnamese compliance with the Geneva Convention and Red Cross inspection. This was followed by forceful American statements at the Paris peace talks and at the International Conference of the Red Cross in September 1969. Forty Senators signed a statement condemning North Vietnamese brutality against American POWs on August 13; two hundred Representatives signed a similar statement in September. The Johnson Administration, fearing reprisals, had been reluctant to press the issue. The Nixon Administration's approach proved to have a beneficial effect on the treatment of US prisoners of war. At the outset it rallied support at home, though in later years it was turned against us, as the prisoners became an added argument for unilateral withdrawal and dismantling of the South Vietnamese government.

But, as always, Nixon tried to play for all the marbles; and as was not infrequently the case, he began it with a maneuver that appeared portentous though it reflected no definitive plan. In short, he was bluffing. I have already mentioned that in a number of his talks with foreign leaders over a period of months in late 1969, Nixon had created the impression that the anniversary of the bombing halt on November 1 was a kind of deadline. On his world trip he dropped less than subtle hints that his patience was running out and that if no progress had been made in Paris by November 1, he would take strong action. So far as I could tell, Nixon had only the vaguest idea of what he had in mind. (There was certainly no prior staff planning; Duck Hook developed as an implementation of a threat that had already been made.) The first I heard of the deadline was when Nixon uttered it to Yahya Khan in August 1969. And because Nixon never permitted State Department personnel (and only rarely the Secretary of State) to sit in on his meetings with foreign leaders, no one else in our government even knew that a threat had been made.

Though Nixon kept referring to the deadline, at the same time he made moves that tended to vitiate his threats, such as announcing further troop withdrawals. In late September he confided to me that he contemplated making "the tough move" before October 15 so that it would not appear prompted by the Moratorium demonstrations. I advised against it, because to preempt his own deadline might confuse our adversaries. He never pursued the threat actively; it was perhaps a way to convince himself — and perhaps the historical record — that he was the tough leader thwarted by weaker colleagues.

On September 27, Dobrynin called on me to fish for an invitation for Foreign Minister Andrei Gromyko to meet with the President when visiting the US for the United Nations General Assembly. During our conversation, Nixon — by prearrangement — called my office and asked me to tell Dobrynin that Vietnam was the critical issue in US–Soviet relations, that "the train had left the station and was heading down the track" (a favorite Nixon phrase, used, for example, after the Oregon primary in 1968 to encourage wavering convention delegates). I repeated Nixon's observations and added that the next move was up to Hanoi.

On October 6, Nixon met with Rogers and prohibited any new diplomatic initiative on Vietnam until Hanoi responded in some way; for the first time he mentioned his deadline of November 1. Rogers took the threat seriously because, as he told me on October 8, he was convinced the President would in fact make some move on November 1, though he was evidently no clearer than I just what it was. On October 8, I suggested to Nixon that he announce a report to the people for around November 1. This would have the advantage of maintaining and perhaps heightening the sense of deadline in Hanoi and Moscow, for whatever benefit this might bring in unexpected North Vietnamese concessions. On October 13, the White House announced that the President would be giving a major speech to review Vietnam policy on November 3. (The date was chosen because November 2 would be the day of the New Jersey gubernatorial election, and Nixon did not wish to trigger a large turnout of protest votes against the Republican candidate — who, in the event, became the first Republican Governor of New Jersey in sixteen years.) To announce a Presidential speech so far ahead was a daring decision, because it compounded uncertainty and encouraged pressures to sway whatever decision he might be announcing.

In the interval, Nixon sought to elicit Soviet support. On October 20, he met with Dobrynin, who had just returned from one of his frequent consultations in Moscow. Nixon pointed out that the bombing halt was a year old; if no progress occurred soon, the United States would have to pursue its own methods for bringing the war to an end. On the other hand, if the Soviet Union cooperated in bringing the war to an honorable conclusion, we would "do something dramatic" to improve US–Soviet relations. Dobrynin was not prepared with any North Vietnamese offers but he did put forth a sort of Soviet concession. After months of sparring we had indicated to the Soviets in June that we were prepared to begin strategic arms talks immediately. Characteristically, even though the Soviets had professed their eagerness for talks for months, once we were committed they evaded a reply. On October 20 Dobrynin informed us that the Soviet Union would be prepared to start the talks by mid-November.

It was a shrewd move. Aware of the eagerness of much of our government to begin SALT negotiations, the Kremlin correctly judged that Nixon could not possibly refuse. In the resulting climate of hope, any escalation in Vietnam would appear as hazarding prospects for a major relaxation of tensions; this inhibition would thus be added to the domestic pressures dramatized by the Moratorium just a few days earlier. The Soviets, in short, applied reverse linkage to us. Their calculation proved to be correct. Despite White House efforts to hold up a reply on SALT until after the November 3 speech, Rogers insisted on announcing our acceptance on October 25. Nixon reluctantly agreed because he was afraid that otherwise he would face a week of leaks.

As was his habit Nixon sought to compensate for his unwillingness to face down his old friend by escalating the menace to the Soviets. He immediately told me that I should convey to Dobrynin that the President was "out of control" on Vietnam. In serving Nixon one owed it to him to discriminate among the orders he issued and to give him another chance at those that were unfulfillable or dangerous. This one was in the latter category. I knew that Nixon was planning to take no action on November 1. To utter a dire threat followed by no action whatever would depreciate our currency. So I waited to see whether Nixon would return to the theme. He did not.

Meanwhile Nixon isolated himself at Camp David to work on his November 3 speech. Its core was provided by my staff and me, but Nixon wrote the beginning and the end on one of his ubiquitous yellow pads and added rhetorical flourishes throughout. It proved one of Nixon's strongest public performances. Against the recommendations of all of his Cabinet he drew the line and made no concessions to the protesters. I agreed with his course. He took his case to the people, thereby to gain the maneuvering room he needed for what he considered "peace with honor." The speech had a shock effect since it defied the protesters, the North Vietnamese, and all expectations by announcing no spectacular shift in our negotiating position and no troop withdrawals. It appealed to the "great silent majority" of Americans to support their Commander-in-Chief. For the first time in a Presidential statement it spelled out clearly what the President meant when he said he had "a plan to end the war" — namely, the dual-track strategy of Vietnamization and negotiations. And it made the point that Vietnamization offered a prospect of honorable disengagement that was not hostage to the other side's cooperation.

I had advised the President not to defend the original commitment of troops to Vietnam, which he had inherited, but to present only his strategy for getting out. He disagreed, telling me — I now believe wisely — that the American public would not accept sacrifice for a war that had no valid purpose. The speech, despite its strong tone, did, moreover, mark some subtle changes in our negotiating position. Where the May 14 speech had proposed withdrawal of "the major portions" of our forces within one year, with residual forces left for policing the agreement, the November 3 speech accepted a *total* American pullout in a year in case of an agreed mutual withdrawal, thus bringing our public position into line with our private one with Xuan Thuy. The May 14 speech spoke of "supervised cease-fires," to include the possibility of local arrangements as well as general ones; the November 3 speech spoke of "cease-fire" in the singular. I explained in a backgrounder that we would be flexible; we would be willing to negotiate either local or general arrangements for cessation of hostilities. However, as Nixon declared, the issue was not a matter of detail but of basic principle: "Hanoi has refused even to discuss our proposals. They demand our unconditional acceptance of their terms, which are that we withdraw all American forces immediately and unconditionally and that we overthrow the Government of South Vietnam as we leave."

Nixon listed the steps taken to withdraw US troops, reduce air operations, and step up South Vietnamese training. He emphasized that Vietnamization envisaged "the complete withdrawal of all US combat ground forces and their replacement by South Vietnamese forces on an orderly scheduled timetable.'' As I had suggested, Nixon disclosed the secret correspondence with North Vietnam prior to Inauguration, the repeated discussions with the Soviet Union to promote negotiations, and the secret letters exchanged with Ho Chi Minh in July and August, the texts of which were released by the White House. He did not reveal my secret meeting with Xuan Thuy. But he explained candidly that ''no progress whatever had been made except agreement on the shape of the bargaining table.''

And he stated the fundamental issue:

In San Francisco a few weeks ago I saw demonstrators carrying signs reading: ''Lose in Vietnam, bring the boys home.''

Well, one of the strengths of our free society is that any American has a right to reach that conclusion and to advocate that point of view. But as President of the United States, I would be untrue to my oath of office if I allowed the policy of this Nation to be dictated by the minority who hold that point of view and who try to impose it on the Nation by mounting demonstrations in the street.

For almost 200 years, the policy of this nation has been made under our Constitution by those leaders in the Congress and in the White House elected by all of the people. If a vocal minority, however fervent its cause, prevails over reason and the will of the majority, this Nation has no future as a free society. . . .

The response to the speech was electric. From the minute it ended, the White House switchboard was clogged with congratulatory phone calls. Tens of thousands of supportive telegrams arrived which rapidly overwhelmed the general critical editorial and television comment. No doubt some of the enthusiasm was stimulated by Haldeman's indefatigable operatives who had called political supporters all over the country to send in telegrams. But the outpouring went far beyond the capacities of even the White House public relations geniuses. Nixon had undoubtedly touched a raw nerve. The polls showed a major boost in his support. The American people might be tiring of the war; they were not ready to be defeated.

Nixon was elated. Professing indifference to public adulation, he nevertheless relished those few moments of acclaim that came his way. He kept the congratulatory telegrams stacked on his desk in such numbers that the Oval Office could not be used for work, and for days he refused to relinquish them.

As soon as the public mood became clear, organized pressures began to slack off somewhat, so that for the first time since January the Administration had some maneuvering room.

We would need more than this, however, to outwait and outmaneuver the hard and single-minded leaders in Hanoi. In 1969 those leaders engaged in no effort that by even the most generous interpretation could be called negotiation. They refused to explore or even to discuss any compromise proposal — not the free elections or mixed electoral commissions or cease-fire. Unilateral withdrawals of men and planes did not improve the atmosphere; de-escalation did not speed up the negotiating process. Hanoi was determined to break our will at home and to achieve this it could permit not a flicker of hope or the appearance of progress. As the last convinced Leninists in the world, the North Vietnamese had no intention of sharing power.

In retrospect the reasoning behind my proposal of the Vance mission in April and my criticism of Vietnamization in September and October was almost certainly correct. Time was not on our side, and piecemeal concessions did more to encourage intransigence than compromise. Analytically, it would have been better to offer the most generous proposal imaginable — and then, if rejected, to seek to impose it militarily. Nothing short of this could have produced Soviet cooperation, for in the absence of crisis there was no incentive for a concrete Soviet step. (When a crisis finally developed in 1972, we induced some Soviet cooperation.) If we had offered at one dramatic moment all the concessions we eventually made in three years of war, and if the military actions we took with steadily declining forces over 1970, 1971, and 1972, in Cambodia, Laos, and North Vietnam (even without the last bombing assault), had been undertaken all together in early 1970, the war might well have been appreciably shortened — though it is hard to tell at this remove whether Saigon would have been ready to carry the burden of going it alone after a settlement. In the face of the domestic turmoil and the divisions within the Administration I did not fight for my theoretical analysis. I joined the general view that, all things considered, Vietnamization was the best amalgam of our international, military, and domestic imperatives.

Once embarked on it, there was no looking back. I knew that it would be painful and long — I had outlined its dangers repeatedly to the President — and that it might ultimately fail. I also believed that it was better than the alternatives that were being proposed to us by our domestic critics.

And so it happened that the year ended with two assessments; on the correctness of one, the outcome of the war would depend. The President's first Foreign Policy Report to the Congress, issued on February 18, 1970, summed up our Vietnam policy in strikingly sober terms. Rarely had a Presidential statement been as candid in admitting doubts and raising questions:

Claims of progress in Vietnam have been frequent during the course of our involvement there — and have often proved too optimistic. However careful our planning, and however hopeful we are for the progress of these plans, we are conscious of two basic facts:

— We cannot try to fool the enemy, who knows what is actually happening.
— Nor must we fool ourselves. The American people must have the full truth. We cannot afford a loss of confidence in our judgment and in our leadership.

The report admitted the existence of problems not yet solved and offered a benchmark by which progress could be judged in the future. We admitted that the Administration did not yet know the final answers to all the issues posed by the war — about enemy intentions, the prospects for Vietnamization, and the attitude of the Vietnamese people:

— What is the enemy's capability to mount sustained operations? Could they succeed in undoing our gains?
— What is the actual extent of improvement in allied capabilities? In particular, are the Vietnamese developing the leadership, logistics capabilities, tactical know-how, and sensitivity to the needs of their own people which are indispensable to continued success?
— What alternative strategies are open to the enemy in the face of continued allied success? If they choose to conduct a protracted, low-intensity war, could they simply wait out U.S. withdrawals and then, through reinvigorated efforts, seize the initiative again and defeat the South Vietnamese forces?
— Most important, what are the attitudes of the Vietnamese people, whose free choice we are fighting to preserve? Are they truly being disaffected from the Viet Cong, or are they indifferent to both sides? What do their attitudes imply about the likelihood that the pacification gains will stick?

This was not a clarion call for domestic confrontation or military victory; it was the sober reflection and analysis of leaders grown cautious by the disappointments of a decade, serious about basing their policy on reality, and willing to accept reasonable compromise.

As Hanoi's leaders were determined on victory, their perception of 1969 was the opposite of ours; they had no uncertainty about the outcome; nor did they talk of compromise. Hanoi's goal was a monopoly of political power. This was illuminated by a major policy document of the Communist military and political leadership captured in late 1969, Resolution No. 9 of the Central Office for South Vietnam (COSVN), the southern headquarters of the North Vietnamese Communist Party. It was a directive of guidance to the cadres in the field, which viewed American concessions not as efforts at compromise but as evidence of failure:

Their "limited war" strategy has met with bankruptcy. They are caught in a most serious crisis over strategy and *have been forced to deescalate the war step by step and adopt the policy of de-Americanizing the war,* beginning with the withdrawal of 25,000 U.S. troops, hoping to extricate themselves from their war of aggression in our country. . . .

After the great victory of the [1969] Spring Campaign, our army and people launched a new large-scale offensive in the military, political and diplomatic fields: we pushed our *summer offensive* while introducing the *10 point* peace solution at the Paris Conference and proceeding with the convening of the National Congress of People's Representatives which elected the *Provisional Revolutionary Government.* Thus the Nixon Administration, already beaten by our staggering attacks of the 1969 Spring Campaign, was dealt additional very heavy blows. Because of these new defeats on the battlefield and at the conference table, Nixon is under heavy attack by the people of the U.S. and of the world, demanding an end to the war of aggression in Viet-Nam. . . . The fact that Nixon was forced to issue the eight-point program, organize the meeting with Thieu at Midway, and begin to withdraw 25,000 troops, reflects the obduracy and guile of U.S. imperialism; on the other hand, it indicates that *the crisis and impasse in which the Nixon administration finds itself is developing to a new degree.* This is a *new opportunity* which demands that we make greater efforts in all fields of operations in order to win a great victory.

According to COSVN, the strategic objectives for 1969 were the killing of American troops to increase domestic strains in the United States, the weakening of the South Vietnamese Army and pacification efforts, and on this basis forcing the United States to accept a "coalition government working toward reunifying Vietnam":

a. *Fiercely attack American troops,* inflict very heavy losses on them, cause them increasing difficulties in all fields. . . .
b. *Strongly strike the puppet army, annihilate the most obdurate elements of the puppet army and administration, paralyze and disintegrate the remaining elements.* . . .
c. *Strive to build up our military and political forces and deploy them on an increasingly strong strategic offensive position.* . . .
d. Continue to destroy and weaken the puppet administration at various levels; *especially, defeat the enemy's pacification plan; wipe out the major part of the puppet administration . . . and promote the role of the Provisional Revolutionary Government.*
e. On this basis, *smash the Americans' will of aggression; force them to give up their intention of ending the war in a strong position, and to end the war quickly and withdraw troops* while the puppet army and administration are still too weak to take over the responsibility of the Americans; *force the Americans to accept a political solution,* and recognize an independent, democratic peaceful and neutral South Viet-Nam with a national, democratic coalition government working toward reunifying Viet-Nam. [Emphases in original.]

The North Vietnamese were cocksure; it was our duty to prove them wrong. I myself pursued the ambiguities of our complex policy with a heavy heart and not a little foreboding. But there was no acceptable alternative. We had the duty to see it through in a manner that best served its chances for success — because a defeat would not affect our destiny alone; the future of other peoples depended on their confidence in America. We would have to fight on — however reluctantly — until Hanoi's perception of its possibilities changed. And if we stuck to our course, in time Hanoi might sue for a respite, if not for peace. We would have to brave discord in the process, because we would be held responsible for disaster even if it resulted from overwhelming domestic pressures. We considered it our painful responsibility to continue the struggle against an implacable opponent until we had achieved a fair settlement compatible with our values, our international responsibilities, and the convictions of the majority of the American people.

IX

Early Tests in Asia

VIETNAM was tempting us into an obsession with a small corner of a vast continent while that continent on a larger scale was becoming ever more important in world affairs.

The security interests of all the great world powers intersect in Asia, particularly in Northeast Asia. China comprises the heartland of the continent. The Soviet Far East spreads across the top of Asia. The Japanese islands span two thousand miles of ocean off the mainland. America's Pacific presence encompasses the entire region. Western Europe has important economic links with Asia and feels indirectly the effects of any disturbance of the equilibrium in the area.

Asia contains more than half of the world's population and resources. In the last three decades, the Asian-Pacific economy has experienced more rapid growth than that of any other region. It is here that we have fought all our wars since 1945. It is here that the United States has its largest and fastest-growing overseas commerce. The influence of America and the West stimulated the transformation of much of Asia during the past hundred years. From the days of the New England transcendentalists to the modern period, Asian culture and ideas have significantly touched American intellectual life — reflecting the universality of human aspirations.

Early in 1969 we were tested in our first major crisis, which happened to be in Asia, and received praise that we did not deserve. In another test, in the same region of the world, an act of foresight and statesmanship went unheralded. These paradoxes of the early Administration were provided by the affair of the EC-121, where we acquiesced in the callous shooting down of an unarmed American plane, and Okinawa's reversion to Japanese sovereignty, where we laid the basis for a relationship of growing intimacy that weathered many shocks and turned into a key element of United States foreign policy. Our long alliance with the extraordinary Japanese — not without moments of farce and frustration, especially in economic matters — I will discuss later in this chapter. It must begin with the EC-121, where we learned so many lessons for even grimmer crises that lay ahead.

The EC-121 Shootdown

O N April 14, 1969, at 5:00 P.M. EST, a US Navy EC-121 of Fleet Air Reconnaissance Squadron One (an unarmed four-engine propeller-driven Constellation) took off from Atsugi Air Base in Japan on a routine reconnaissance mission over the Sea of Japan. These flights were important to give us information about hostile troop movements and dispositions. They were crucial to warn us of surprise attack — especially in Korea. The plane carried a crew of thirty Navy men and one Marine and some six tons of equipment. The aircraft was directed to fly from Atsugi to a point off the Musu peninsula on the North Korean coast (see the map on page 314), make a number of orbits on an ellipse about 120 miles long parallel to the coast of North Korea, and land at Osan Air Base in the Republic of Korea. Standing instructions for this kind of mission provided that the aircraft was not to approach closer to the coast of North Korea than forty nautical miles so that the plane would be at all times clearly over international waters.[1] North Korea claimed a twelve-mile territorial sea. On April 14 the aircraft commander was under orders from the Commander-in-Chief of the Pacific Fleet to fly even farther away from the North Korean coast, not approaching closer than fifty nautical miles.

As later determined, the aircraft — tracked at all times by our radar — deviated slightly from its approved track, presumably to investigate an electronic signal. But at no time did it approach closer to the coast than forty-eight miles. When it was alerted to the fact that an attack might be possible — three times within ten minutes — it acknowledged instructions to abort the mission and left its routine reconnaissance track to move farther out over international waters.

At a distance some ninety miles southeast of Chongjin, North Korea, at 11:50 P.M. EST, the aircraft disappeared from our radar screens. The EC-121 had been attacked and shot down by North Korean MiG aircraft over the Sea of Japan. It crashed about ninety nautical miles from the coast. No survivors were found. Thus was the Nixon Administration propelled into its first major crisis.

No new President can really know what kind of a "team" he has until faced with such a crunch. Its essence is the need to make high-risk decisions quickly and under pressure. In normal conditions it is never clear whether senior advisers are giving their own convictions or simply reflecting the consensus of their bureaucracies. It is easier to play safe. A reputation for moderation or wisdom can be picked up cheaply because success or failure is determined only after an interval when cause and effect have been obscured. But a crisis casts an immediate glare on men and policies. It illuminates above all those who husband their reputations and those willing to take the heat. A President is in a sense lucky

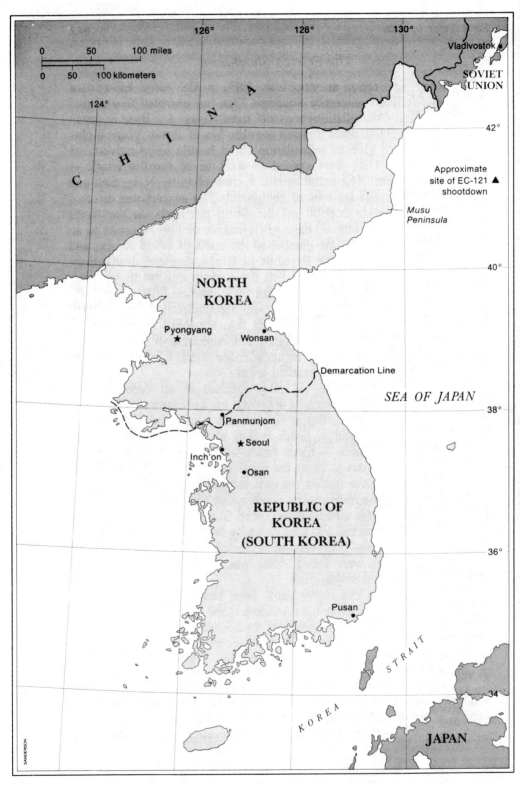

Korea and Area of EC-121 Shootdown 1969

if he is faced with a crisis early on; it enables him to shake down his team.

It cannot be said that the new Nixon Administration met the test with distinction. It was not so much that the wrong decision was made, though I believe it was. It was above all that our deliberations were banal or irrelevant; we rarely addressed the central issue. The NSC system became a device to accumulate options without supplying perspective or a sense of direction.

All the principals were so fascinated by the process of decision-making that they overlooked its purposes in ordering priorities for action. Like many new administrations, they were more concerned to avoid the charges they had made against their predecessors than to decide the issue on its merits. This reverence for campaign rhetoric is one of the most serious — and most tempting — mistakes of a new administration, so often leading it to believe it will be judged by its difference in style from its predecessors. In fact, within a year the choruses of the electoral campaign almost always fade into oblivion. The test of the new administration must inevitably become not its memory but its mastery of challenges. It will suffer no penalty for prevailing with the methods of its predecessor; it will reap no plaudits for failing with a style all of its own. Nixon was convinced that President Johnson had suffered from the "Situation Room syndrome," meaning that he had succumbed to the melodramatic idea that the world could be managed, in crisis, from this room in the basement of the White House. Ironically enough, though Nixon took up the cry of the "Situation Room syndrome," he fell victim to it himself the next time around.

The image of the Situation Room belied the reality. It is a tiny, uncomfortable, low-ceilinged, windowless room, which owes its chief utility to its location next door to a bank of teletypes and other communications equipment linking the White House to embassies around the world. Its name derived from the illusion of an earlier President that the international situation could be represented currently by maps on the wall. In my day, maps were neither current nor visible; in their place were drapes to add a human touch to the austere and cramped surroundings. Nixon's perception had some merit, in that Johnson liked to convey the impression he was spending a great deal of time planning individual bombing sorties, but ultimately Nixon became the victim of his own criticism. Because of his attack on the Situation Room syndrome he and his associates were reluctant to assemble advisers there (or anywhere) at the first sign of trouble. He did not want to be involved in tactics or planning battles. Everything had to be played cool.

And so it was when we learned that the EC-121 had gone down. We set the crisis machinery into motion with great deliberation, watching ourselves with rapt attention at each stop to make sure we were not shooting from the hip. Unfortunately, slow motion is no more likely than frenzy to guarantee correct judgment. The Situation Room was notified at 12:50 A.M. on April 15 that the EC-121 had been attacked by two North Korean aircraft. My military assistant, Colonel Alexander Haig, was notified at 1:07. Three minutes later Haig told me that there was an unconfirmed shootdown. I asked him to collect all information and to call back as soon as the incident was confirmed. I would not disturb the President until the shootdown was confirmed or there was a decision to be made by him. At 1:45 A.M. Haig called Colonel Robert Pursley, Laird's military assistant. Pursley decided as I had: Since the shootdown was unconfirmed he would not wake up Laird.

At 2:17 A.M. Radio Pyongyang announced that North Korea had shot down a United States reconnaissance plane when it intruded into Korean airspace. This was a blatant lie, for the plane, which was tracked at all times by our radar, was never closer to the Korean coast than forty-eight miles and was shot down at a distance of ninety miles. But for reasons unfathomable to me at this remove, everybody decided to ignore the broadcast. On the ground that we had no independent confirmation, the shootdown was still listed as "unconfirmed" as late as 7:20 A.M., when I briefed Nixon. Why North Korea would announce the shootdown of an American plane unless it had done so was never explained.

It was as if someone had pushed a button labeled "crisis management" and the answer that came up was "nonchalance." Nixon threw his vaunted NSC machinery into slow motion; it was a good way to collect options but also to waste time if one was reluctant to act. An NSC Review Group meeting was called for the afternoon following the shootdown, to prepare options for an NSC meeting that was scheduled for the following day, April 16, at 10:00 A.M. Nixon gave no indication of what action he proposed to take. He would await the presentation of the options. It was a mistaken procedure, in fact indicating that Nixon had no stomach for retaliation. It is all very well to make sure of alternatives. But when an unarmed American plane is shot down far from shore, a leisurely process of decision-making creates a presumption in favor of eventual inaction. What was needed was some analysis of the nature of the challenge and what it portended for American policy. Only in these terms could the options make any sense. There was a further source of inhibition. Nixon had scheduled a press conference for April 18 long before the crisis broke. It was an experience that usually filled him with such a combination of dread and exhilaration as to leave no energy for other reflection.

I thought that our reaction to North Korea's shootdown of an unarmed plane over international waters without provocation would be interpreted by many friendly nations — especially in Asia — as a test of the new Administration's decisiveness. I favored some retaliatory act, but was less clear about what it might be. My staff's advice that first day was amazingly hawkish. Even Morton Halperin — later to go into vocal opposition to the allegedly bellicose tendencies of the Administration — recommended an immediate air strike. But given the NSC schedule, no military forces could be moved for at least twenty-four hours, which turned out to be another error. An immediate mobilization of military strength would at least have put North Korea on notice that a grave offense had been committed. It might have elicited a gesture to indicate that it had backed down or admitted the need for some reparation. This is indeed what happened when the North Koreans beat two American officers to death along the DMZ in 1976.

In the absence of a clear-cut direction, each agency developed its own options geared to its own more or less parochial concerns. My staff developed alternatives ranging from stiff diplomatic protests at Panmunjom to seizure of North Korean ships at sea, and various kinds of military moves, from the mining of Wonsan harbor to shore bombardment or attacking of an airfield. What all of these plans lacked was the forces to implement them or a specific operational plan or a particular reparation we would demand from North Korea. In their absence we were engaged in academic exercises.

The State Department was preoccupied with a meeting of the Armistice Commission called by the North Koreans for April 18. The issue was whether to go, and if so, what to say; or whether instead to insist on an alternative date. The State Department sent us a memorandum expressing reservations about military retaliation. It did not address its objection to any particular form of military retaliation except the idea of seizing a Korean ship at sea, which it found legally unjustified.

The Defense Department took the most puzzling step of all. Apparently without consulting any other agency or the White House, it halted all reconnaissance flights near the Soviet Union, China, in the Mediterranean, and over Cuba. We found out about this only gradually when Nixon grandiloquently ordered military escorts for our Korean reconnaissance flights on April 17, only to discover that there were no planes to escort. Laird was undoubtedly right in his perception that these flights had multiplied over the years without a periodic analysis of their rationale. A review was long overdue. My concern was that halting all reconnaissance in response to a shootdown would convey an impression of insecurity; it hardly suggested that the Administration was determined to defend its rights against brutal challenge.

Much of the day of April 15 was, therefore, spent in inconclusive planning exercises. There seemed to be a growing consensus to pick up a North Korean ship at sea. Legal analyses were requested; they came to differing conclusions but were made irrelevant when it was realized that there were no Korean ships at sea nor had there been since the capture of the *Pueblo*. This disposed of another brilliant suggestion: that we use a submarine to torpedo some North Korean navy ship. There was a rumor to the effect that a Korean-owned ship under Dutch registry was somewhere in transit. Nixon wanted to seize it, keeping our lawyers in a dither for the better part of the day. As things turned out, we could never find the ship. For all I know it never existed.

In these circumstances the NSC meeting on April 16 was both unfocused and inconclusive. There was no discussion of the fundamental issue: whether our failure to respond to the shootdown of an unarmed reconnaissance plane over international waters might not create an impression of such irresolution that it would encourage our enemies in Hanoi and embolden opponents elsewhere. At the same time there was the usual reluctance of a new Administration to risk the honeymoon; at that time we were still basking in praise for moderation and restraint by comparison with our predecessors. And there was a natural fear of being involved in war in two theaters. Laird pointed out that our effort in Vietnam was certain to suffer if we became involved in a tit-for-tat with North Korea. Many of these considerations were implicit rather than formally stated at the meeting. Military options were reviewed in a haphazard way without ever being brought to the point of serious examination. They suffered from the disability that those that seemed safe were inadequate to the provocation, while those that seemed equal to the challenge appeared too risky in terms of the fear of a two-front war.

Later on, we were to learn that in crises boldness is the safest course. Hesitation encourages the adversary to persevere, maybe even to raise the ante. In retrospect it is clear that we vastly overestimated North Korea's readiness to engage in a tit-for-tat. This being still early in the Administration, I confined myself that first day to presenting the options; I made no recommendation. Nixon came to no conclusion at the NSC meeting. He spent much of the day inquiring about the Dutch/Korean ship, which seemed to offer a deus ex machina to navigate between risky military action and the sort of passivity Nixon had criticized so vociferously in connection with the *Pueblo*.

The next day, April 17, Nixon made two decisions. He accepted the second of the several options put before the NSC: the resumption of aerial reconnaissance accompanied by armed escorts. And he ordered two aircraft carriers into the Sea of Japan for possible retaliatory attacks. The reasoning behind the movement of the aircraft carriers was that to use tactical aircraft based in Japan would involve us in complicated consultations with the Japanese government that were certain to be leaked and produce public protests, possibly jeopardizing the Security Treaty talks with Japan. Using B-52s based in Guam seemed to be an overreaction. Everyone conveniently overlooked the aircraft stationed in South Korea. No doubt subconsciously, everyone drew comfort from the fact that it would take the aircraft carriers three days to get to where they could launch planes. Hawks could tell themselves that we were doing something; doves could console themselves that we still had a cushion of time. Every passing day would add to inhibitions against a retaliatory attack, all the more so as, erroneously, I now believe, we were demanding nothing of the North Koreans the acceptance of which could be considered compensation and the refusal of which would justify retaliation. Our protest at Panmunjom had been mild; State had pressed for a nonconfrontational tone; Rogers had opposed making any demands. Our political and military moves were substantially out of phase with each other. In this context the decision to move the carriers was essentially time-wasting; it looked tough but implied inaction.

On April 17 I assembled a special crisis management group composed of middle-level representatives of State, Defense, the CIA, and the Joint Chiefs of Staff, and me as Chairman. It was the nucleus of what later became the Washington Special Actions Group (WSAG), which handled all future crises. In the absence of clear-cut directives, planning was desultory in this first case. There was no real determination to use force: All discussions were theoretical and no concrete operational plan was ever put forward.

Nixon's press conference on April 18 announcing the resumption of armed reconnaissance was generally taken as our official response to the shootdown, even within our government. Alex Johnson thought there was no point continuing our contingency planning for a military response. I disagreed. I knew that Nixon, the press conference behind him, would now turn to a serious consideration of the issues.

In the late morning of April 18 — right after the press conference — Nixon and I reviewed the situation. I told him that failure to demand some redress or to engage in some retaliatory action would make it probable that he would have to act more boldly later on. However, there were three conditions about which Nixon had to satisfy himself: First, the action had to be significant; second, we had to be prepared to sustain it if North Korea responded (we could certainly not sustain a prolonged ground war); and third, he could not use force unless he had a united government behind him. My judgment was that North Korea would not escalate, although the President should act on the basis that it might. I suggested that I poll Rogers, Laird, and Helms individually about their views to avoid the danger that at an NSC meeting they would go along with what they might sense of the President's preference. Nixon agreed, partly because a press conference usually left him so drained that he sought to avoid stress for days afterward.

Rogers, Laird, and Helms were unanimous in their opposition to a military retaliation against North Korea: Rogers because of its impact on public opinion; Laird because he thought it would hurt the Vietnam effort and there was no Congressional support; Helms for a combination of these reasons. I reported the consensus of his advisers to Nixon late in the day of April 18; I added the recommendation that he could not run such risks over a close issue so early in his term with a divided team. Nixon and I met in the Treaty Room of the Residence. I never had had the impression that Nixon had his heart in a retaliatory attack. He had procrastinated too much; he had not really pressed for it in personal conversation; he had not engaged in the relentless maneuvering by which he bypassed opposition when his mind was made up. Now that he had in effect an alibi, he raged against his advisers. He would get rid of Rogers and Laird at the earliest opportunity; he would never consult them again in a crisis. He ordered new raids in our undisclosed Menu series against the sanctuaries in Cambodia so that Hanoi would not think us irresolute. But the bottom line was that we would make no military response against North Korea. I informed the Interdepartmental Group to that effect on the morning of April 19.

Nixon nevertheless ordered the carriers to proceed into the Sea of Japan as a show of strength. It was a threat unrelated to a comprehensible demand for action by the other side and therefore likely to be interpreted as empty posturing. In our inexperience we had not even asked for compensation from North Korea; there was no condition for them to satisfy; hence, no means of resolution. The carriers continued their majestic course for several more days, pursued by a flotilla of Japanese boats and blimps recording the event for television. What would have happened if matters had become serious can only be conjectured; in all probability several luminaries of Japanese television would have become casualties. However, once we had notified our bureaucracy, word leaked out rapidly that there would be no retaliation. Task Force 71 — as it was by then called — cruised peacefully in the Sea of Japan until April 26, eliciting a mild and private Soviet protest to which we responded sharply. By the end of the month the crisis had sputtered and died, leaving no results in terms of a North Korean penalty for the atrocity and little residue except Nixon's sense of not having quite measured up to his first full test. (That was surely my estimate of my own role.)

The residue of Laird's nearly incomprehensible decision to suspend all reconnaissance still had to be dealt with. (It was not until April 22 that the White House received a memorandum from the Pentagon detailing the extent of the standdown — not only around Korea, but also over China, the Soviet Union, and Cuba, and in the Mediterranean.) The President's order for armed reconnaissance was used to bring about another delay, on the basis that suitable fighter escort needed first to be assembled. Daily requests led to evasive answers. I was becoming increasingly worried, not because I considered every reconnaissance mission essential but because of the precedent that a shootdown of a single plane could put an end to our global reconnaissance system. The temptations this created for other incidents seemed to me overwhelming. It was not until May 8, after a standdown of nearly four weeks, that normal reconnaissance was ordered resumed.

The EC-121 incident was not primarily significant for the decision to do nothing — it was a close call, which probably should have gone the other way, but one on which reasonable men could differ. But it did show major flaws in our decision-making. We made no strategic assessment; instead, we bandied technical expedients about. There was no strong White House leadership. We made no significant political move; our military deployments took place in a vacuum. To manage crises effectively, the agencies and departments involved have to know what the President intends. They must be closely monitored to make certain that diplomatic and military moves dovetail. In this case we lacked both machinery and conception. We made no demands North Korea could either accept or reject. We assembled no force that could pose a credible threat until so long after the event that it became almost irrelevant. Coordination was poor; the President never really made up his mind. Still, the EC-121 incident was a blessing in disguise. It made us dramatically tighten our procedures. Future crises were handled crisply and with strong central direction. We established the Washington Special Actions Group for that precise purpose. We managed to project thereafter a much greater impression of purpose. Nixon's displeasure with Rogers and Laird was unjustified. They gave their best judgment, straightforwardly. The result nevertheless was to confirm Nixon in his isolated decision-making. In future crises he knew what he wanted and got it even if the maneuvers to reach that point were frequently convoluted.

Overall, I judge our conduct in the EC-121 crisis as weak, indecisive, and disorganized — though it was much praised then. I believe we paid for it in many intangible ways, in demoralized friends and emboldened adversaries. Luckily, it happened early and on a relatively peripheral issue. And the lessons we learned benefited our handling of later crises.

The US–Japanese Alliance

JAPAN and the United States have been allies for over twenty years; the keystone of our Pacific policy is without doubt our friendship, partnership, and interdependence with that extraordinary nation. Two peoples could hardly be more different than the pragmatic, matter-of-fact, legally oriented, literal Americans; and the complex, subtle Japanese, operating by allusion and conveying their meaning through an indirect, almost aesthetic sensitivity rather than words.

Japan and the United States have known each other for a century and a quarter. Our relationship has passed through an incredible range: from curiosity to competition, conflict, occupation, reconciliation, to alliance and mutual dependence. Americans are heterogeneous in our origins, constantly striving to redefine what we have in common. Japan, on the other hand, is a country of unusual cohesiveness and homogeneity. For Americans, contracts and laws are prime guarantors of social peace. The Japanese depend less on legal and formal rules to preserve social harmony than on the quality of human relationships and on unstated patterns of consensus and obligation.

The United States is blessed with vast land and ample resources; abundance is taken for granted. Japan is a great industrial power, but its prosperity is more recent and — because of the dependence of its industry on imported food, energy, raw materials, and external markets — more vulnerable.

The cliché that it is odd that two such different nations should have come together is, like most clichés, substantially true. But it would apply as well to Japan's relations with any other country. For Japan's achievements — and occasionally its setbacks — have grown out of a society whose structures, habits, and forms of decision-making are so unique as to insulate Japan from all other cultures. The further paradox is that the Japanese have used foreigners, acquiring their methods and technology the better to maintain their own vigor and identity.

A string of islands off the coast of China, with mist-shrouded mountain peaks growing out of a turbulent sea, its verdant valleys yielding bountifully to the discipline of its tillers but with few other natural resources, Japan flourishes as a triumph of discipline, faith, and dedication. Only the hardiest could wring a living out of so unpromising an environment. Influenced greatly by Chinese culture but then striking out independently, the Japanese developed over the centuries a style so much their own that it became at once a justification for their existence and a defense against outside encroachment; a national motivating force and even a weapon. Japan became more like a family than a nation, governed less by its laws (which regulated only the surface phenomena and the grossest violations) than by an intricate set of understandings which assigned each Japanese a specific role. The feudal values and obligations that in other countries were confined to a small upper class permeated the entire society. On these crowded islands men and women came to understand that survival depended on discipline and cooperation and thus on taking the edge off all confrontations. The exquisite Japanese form of communication depends on never putting forward a proposition that can be refused; on conveying the most delicate shades of meaning in a manner that permits retreat without loss of face, and that at the same time imposes consideration for the other point of view. Words in their subtle Japanese shadings are only a small part of that delicate process. Every gesture is invested with a symbolic significance — from the bow as a greeting whose fine gradations indicate a hierarchy, to the arrangements of flowers on a table.

Of course, there are dark edges to the intricate and close-knit Japanese social structure. It provides the individual Japanese with a defined sense of self and thus brings about restraint and mutual support in the Japanese context; but outside Japan these same people can become disoriented, even ferocious, when the criteria for conduct evaporate in confrontation with alien, seemingly barbarian, behavior.

The amazing thing is that the Japanese respect for the past and sense of cultural uniqueness have not produced stagnation. Other societies have paid for the commitment to tradition by growing irrelevance to the currents of modernity. Japan turned its feudal past into an asset by permeating its entire society with such a sense of shared respect that its internal differences could never mar the essential unity with which it faced foreigners. This spirit of uniqueness proved more serviceable than, for example, China's belief in its cultural superiority. Japan lost no face in adopting the methods of other societies; it could afford to adopt almost any system and still retain its Japanese character, which depended neither on forms of government nor on methods of economics but on a complicated, imbued, shared set of social relationships. Far from being an obstacle to progress, tradition in Japan provided the emotional security and indeed the impetus to try the novel.

After Japan was "opened" by Commodore Perry — a delicate euphemism for what everywhere else led to the beginning of colonization — the Japanese with iron determination adapted their feudal society to the imperatives of modernity. The institution of the Emperor ensured continuity while they developed an industrial nation which within fifty years grew strong enough to defeat a major European power — Russia — and within another generation to adopt itself the forms of colonialism that it had resisted, leading it into world conflict.

Defeat in the Second World War did not shake Japan's extraordinary cohesion and resilience. It seemed as if Japan had a finely calibrated radar that enabled it to gauge the global balance of power and to adapt its institutions to its necessities, confident that no adaptation could disturb the essence of Japanese society. Parliamentary democracy replaced authoritarianism, with the Emperor remaining as the symbol of Japanese distinctiveness. Japan changed its institutions, repaired the wartime devastation, and emerged within less than two decades more powerful than ever.

Faced by burgeoning competition from the other growing economies in free Asia, which began to enjoy the benefits of skilled, cheap labor that was once Japan's monopoly advantage, Japanese decision-makers brilliantly moved labor and resources from industries hit by competition

into others where their comparative advantage remained. The system
which gives workers lifetime job security was not allowed to become a
prescription for immobility. Of course, to some degree Japan benefited
at first from massive American aid and then from low spending on defense, made possible by its reliance on the Security Treaty with the
United States. But the success is above all a tribute to the cohesion of its
institutions and the talent of its people. The resilience Japan demonstrated in the 1973 energy crisis underlines the point. Within two years a
nation dependent upon imports for 90 percent of its oil had dug itself out
of its balance-of-payments deficit and restored its surplus by an awesome feat of national will. In my view Japanese decisions have been the
most farsighted and intelligent of any major nation of the postwar era
even while the Japanese leaders have acted with the understated,
anonymous style characteristic of their culture.

When the Nixon Administration entered office we had two concerns
with Japan: Our economic agencies were worried because of the increasingly unfavorable balance of our trade; our political departments were
pressing Japan to take on greater responsibilities for economic development and political stability and even security in Asia. These objectives
were straightforward enough, but the truth is that neither I nor my colleagues possessed a very subtle grasp of Japanese culture and psychology. We therefore made many mistakes; I like to think that we learned a
great deal and ultimately built an extraordinarily close relationship after
first inflicting some unnecessary shocks to Japanese sensibilities. The
hardest thing for us to grasp was that the extraordinary Japanese decisions were produced by leaders who prided themselves on their
anonymous style. To be sure, there were great prime ministers. But
they worked unobtrusively, conveying in their bearing that their policies
reflected the consensus of a society, not the idiosyncrasy of an individual. They might perform their duties with greater or lesser ability. In
the final analysis, however, they were the product of a continuous tradition, which would determine its necessities not through dominant personalities but by infusing its purposes throughout the society.

All of us brought up in Western-style decision-making, in which the
emphasis is on the act of deciding, had a maddeningly difficult time
grasping this point. Our style of negotiation is conversational; it is to
persuade the interlocutor to pursue our preferred course. But a Japanese
leader does not make a decision by imposing his will on subordinates;
his art consists of shaping their preference so that they will go in the
desired direction. A Japanese leader does not announce a decision;
he evokes it. Westerners decide quickly but our decisions require a long
time to implement, especially when they are controversial. In our
bureaucracy, each power center has to be persuaded or pressured; thus,
the spontaneity or discipline of execution is diluted. In Japan this pro-

cess *precedes* the setting of policy. Decision-making is therefore slow, but execution is rapid and single-minded; and it is given additional impetus because all those charged with carrying out the policy have participated in shaping it.

The Japanese do not like a confrontation, which produces a catalogue of identifiable winners and losers; they are uneasy with enterprises whose outcome is unpredictable. Meetings with them are preceded by the visits of innumerable emissaries who subtly probe the implications of one's position. After this exploratory stage there is an interval for the essential national consensus to coalesce before the formal stage of agreement. This is why at international meetings Japanese ministers rarely talk; they are there to collect raw material for their own decision-making process. Attempts to bypass this process and to pressure a Japanese interlocutor into agreement occasionally produce the appearance of success because the legendary Japanese politeness may override the judgment of what is possible. But they almost never result in action. This explains the success of the Okinawa negotiations and the failure of the textile negotiations in 1969–1970.

The Okinawa Negotiation

LONG after our postwar occupation of Japan had ended in 1952, Okinawa and the other Ryukyu Islands remained under American military administration. There was no serious dispute that the ultimate sovereignty of the islands belonged to Japan. We held onto the occupation status because Okinawa had become one of our most important military bases in Asia. We counted on its airfields for the defense of Korea and Taiwan; we used it as a staging area for Vietnam and as an emergency facility for B-52s. We stored nuclear weapons there. But important as Okinawa was strategically, our continuing occupation of it in the late Sixties mortgaged our long-range relations with Japan. In particular it cast a shadow on the US–Japanese Security Treaty, around which our entire Asian strategy was built. The treaty came into being in 1960 amid widespread anti-American riots in Japan that aborted President Eisenhower's planned visit.* It was due for possible termination after ten years, upon one year's notice by either party, which meant that 1970 would be a year of renewed agitation against the treaty by anti-American elements in Japan. We were doomed to that unhappy prospect if the repeated Japanese requests for revision of Okinawa's status went without a sympathetic American response. Japanese nationalists and rad-

---

*Nixon had hopes of completing Eisenhower's mission and becoming the first American President to visit Japan. The jinx worked against him, too. In November 1974, Gerald Ford paid the visit to Tokyo that was planned for Nixon.

icals were united on this issue, the latter as part of an antinuclear campaign of particular potency in the land of Hiroshima and Nagasaki, and the former to recover lost territories that had historically been Japanese.

When President Johnson and Prime Minister Eisaku Sato had met in November 1967, the Japanese had been told that because of our election the issue would have to wait until 1969. The issue of Okinawa thus was urgent when Nixon assumed office. It had only become hotter in the intervening period since the Sato-Johnson conversations. There had been public protests over our use of the bases for Vietnam operations. The visit of a nuclear carrier to Sasebo allegedly left traces of radioactivity in the water (which the United States denied had anything to do with the ship's visit). In February 1968 the Okinawa legislature adopted a resolution against basing B-52s on the island, and the Socialist opposition parties put forward a similar motion in the Japanese Diet (Parliament). In November 1968, in the first direct election there, a Socialist was elected Chief Executive of the Ryukyus. As one of his first acts, he announced that he would set up a commission to study the gradual closing of the bases and the return of the islands to Japan.

The day after Nixon's Inauguration I ordered an interagency study of our policy toward Japan, listing Okinawa among the priority issues to be examined. The urgency which the Japanese government attached to the reversion of Okinawa was discussed briefly at Nixon's first NSC meeting that same day and also in his first formal meeting with the Joint Chiefs of Staff on January 27. The Chiefs considered our Okinawa bases to be of inestimable value, not only because of their convenience for Indochina operations but also for our whole strategic position in the Pacific. The Chiefs were already coming to accept the judgment of the State Department, supported by me, that reversion to Japan was politically imperative. They wanted to make certain, however, that they would have the right to continue to use the bases with a minimum of interference (they hoped none at all). Also they wished to have the right to continue to store nuclear weapons on the island. If Okinawa reverted to Japan and our use were subject to the same restrictions as our bases on the Japanese home islands, the facilities could not be used for combat operations without prior consultation with Japan. Nuclear weapons would be excluded altogether, a restriction we had accepted on the main islands because of Japan's special sensitivity as the only nation to suffer nuclear attack; this would present a major problem of relocation for us since no convenient bases were close by. I was determined, however, in close cooperation with the State Department, to find a solution that would meet the needs of each side. While our interagency studies proceeded, Prime Minister Sato told the Diet in February 1969 of his "firm determination" to reunite Okinawa to Japan and to raise the matter with the new American President. As if to underscore his point, Okinawans staged massive demonstrations outside a US airfield, protesting the presence of B-52s used for our operations in Indochina.

A word is in order here about Eisaku Sato. Like all Japanese leaders, he operated anonymously; he never pretended that he had a power of decision beyond the national consensus. Yet his moral force was so great as to leave little doubt that it helped to shape that consensus. He was, it goes without saying, Japanese to the core; he was also a sincere friend of the United States, seeing in the partnership of the erstwhile foes the best guarantee for peace and progress in East Asia and the entire Pacific region. His fundamental commitment was to Japan; his foreign policy commitment was to the alliance with America; his passion was peace. He handled difficult negotiations with extraordinary delicacy and wisdom. He did not deserve the ill fortune that the Nixon shocks — the secret trip to Peking and the economic package of the summer of 1971 — inflicted in his term of office. (We thought we had no choice, as I shall explain in later chapters.) He was generous enough not to let it impair our close relations. I admired his character so much that I took a special trip to Japan in June 1972, during the last two weeks of his Prime Ministership, to consult with him ostentatiously and dine with him as a symbolic demonstration of our respect for this great leader. Even after he left office, I never visited Japan without requesting to see him. I am proud that he became a personal friend. When he won the Nobel Peace Prize in 1974, he regarded this as an additional bond between us. To me he embodied the serene inner strength, wisdom, and dignity that are the best of Japan. He died too soon for all who believe in peace and freedom.

As the interagency review moved forward, I gave Nixon frequent reports. On March 8 I sent him a paper by the Joint Chiefs of Staff, forwarded by Secretary Laird, reiterating the Chiefs' concern for both nuclear storage and unrestricted non-nuclear military use of the bases. Ten days later I sent Nixon a memorandum outlining the essential elements of the decision before him. The political reality was that the pressures in Japan for reversion were now unstoppable; agitation against our presence not only posed a physical danger to our use of the bases but also could jeopardize the political position of Sato and the governing Liberal Democratic Party, which had initiated and maintained Japan's alignment with the United States for two decades. In short, the military and political risks of seeking to maintain the status quo outweighed the military cost of having somewhat less flexibility in operating the Okinawa bases under Japanese sovereignty. Indeed, our refusal to negotiate an accommodation could well lead as a practical matter to our losing the bases altogether.

For once, the United States government was united on an issue. By April we were able to achieve a consensus on the major principles of our overall policy toward Japan. There was agreement that Japan was the cornerstone of our Asian policy and that it must be our basic objective to strengthen the relationship. We would seek to continue the Security Treaty without amendment after 1970, assuming Japan was not torn by domestic schisms over it. We would encourage Japan to play a larger political role in Asia and to make moderate increases in her defense capability, though we would not exert pressure on her to develop substantially larger forces. These principles were agreed upon at a Review Group meeting on April 25 and received Nixon's blessing at an NSC meeting on April 30.

Progress was made even on the technical issues of the reversion question. The Chiefs had reconciled themselves to reducing the number of bases on Okinawa; they agreed that if we could not obtain Japanese agreement to unrestricted use of the bases for combat operations throughout Asia we could settle for unrestricted rights for the defense of Korea, Taiwan, and Vietnam, reinforced by a Japanese endorsement of common defense concerns in Asia. Actually, this was a theoretical point without practical difference. It was difficult to imagine what areas we would want to defend from Okinawa other than those specified. The main point of contention was that the Joint Chiefs of Staff insisted on a continuing right to use our Okinawan facilities for nuclear storage. At the NSC meeting of April 30, Alex Johnson, the Under Secretary of State for Political Affairs and a former Ambassador to Japan, summed up the key issue: If properly handled, our reversion of Okinawa could serve as an incentive for Japan to assume greater responsibility for Asian stability and defense. But the nuclear issue was highly sensitive; we needed to show some understanding for Japanese sensibilities.

The Okinawa negotiations that followed the NSC meeting demonstrate how much nervous strain could have been avoided and how much more effectively our government would have functioned if the White House and the State Department had managed to achieve the same compatibility on other subjects. In the execution of Nixon's decision of April 30 Alex Johnson ran the day-to-day interdepartmental process in Washington; Ambassador Armin Meyer skillfully conducted the negotiations in Tokyo. My contribution was to provide a general climate of support and intervene with the Japanese at key moments. I saw it as my role to demonstrate the President's commitment to a successful outcome.

In that spirit I discussed Japan's view of its future role in Asia with Japanese Ambassador Takeso Shimoda on May 21. He emphasized that if the Okinawa issue were settled in 1969, Japan would be willing to assume Asian responsibilities to a far greater degree. I recognized that this was neither an enforceable commitment nor an excessively precise one, so I confined myself to an equally nebulous assurance that the

President would approach the forthcoming negotiations in a positive spirit.

Nixon's decision on the technical issues was disclosed to the agencies at the end of May. It followed the consensus of the NSC meeting: If we obtained a satisfactory understanding for the use of the bases for the defense of Korea, Taiwan, and Vietnam, Nixon would return Okinawa to Japanese sovereignty and take into account Japanese sensitivities on the nuclear issue — in other words, he implied that he might not insist on the right to store nuclear weapons in Okinawa. Within four days of this Presidential directive, its essence was helpfully leaked to the *New York Times*. Our fallback position was thus in print before our negotiations had even begun.

Formal negotiations between American and Japanese officials began in earnest in June 1969 in diplomatic channels. By then, another issue had arisen in the US–Japanese dialogue, unconnected with Okinawa but destined to be intimately linked to it: textiles. Where the Okinawa negotiations exemplified high policy, the textile problem proved a case of low comedy, frustration, and near fiasco.

For various reasons our balance of trade with Japan was chronically in deficit. Whether because of extraordinary Japanese productivity — as the Japanese claimed — or because of Japanese dumping in the American market and barriers to other countries' penetration of their own market — as some of our trade experts insisted — Japanese exports to America, particularly in manufactured products, far exceeded American exports to Japan. Japan had easy access to our market; we did not have an equal opportunity in Japan. The result was that Japanese competition became a fierce and sometimes overwhelming challenge for many American industries, evoking fears of unemployment caused by another nation's trade practices. American businessmen, legislators, and economic officials were vocal in insisting on some Japanese flexibility on economic matters to smooth the way for American action on Okinawa. Our economic agencies, each representing a different constituency, were bombarding the Japanese with a barrage of demands, including measures to restrict Japanese exports of wool and synthetic textiles or to reduce barriers to American capital investment. The plethora of proposals was actually self-defeating; the Japanese were choosing the least onerous ones. The Japanese had a coherent policy; we had only a set of separate demands. This enabled the Japanese to select from among our many schemes those least burdensome to them, often involving items out of which Japanese exporting had already shifted. They decided, for example, to liberalize conditions for American investment in Japan, well aware that there were many administrative, social, and cultural obstacles beyond formal legislation; they even announced a joint venture with Chrysler. I reported this to Nixon and recommended that we get our priorities straight. He agreed, writing on my memorandum: "This capital liberalization is not important to us politically. We have to get something on textiles."

Textiles were a sore point with Nixon. Textile manufacturers in the American South were among the industries hardest hit by Japanese competition; many mills had to be closed; they also represented a powerful and effective lobby. This had caused candidate Nixon to make a flat promise to Southern delegates and voters in the previous year, as part of the inscrutable American tribal ritual associated with years divisible by four, that he would do something about the textile problem.

The new Administration was determined to carry out Nixon's promise. Commerce Secretary Maurice Stans and White House aides Robert Ellsworth and Peter Flanigan wanted to confront the Japanese immediately to obtain a voluntary agreement to reduce Japanese textile exports. A political amateur, I did not think it appropriate to pick out one industry for special consideration until our overall political and economic studies had been completed. I therefore stalled, hiding behind the NSC decision-making process. I was soon educated: Nixon told me in no uncertain terms that he meant to have a textile agreement and that as a Presidential Assistant I was to contribute to the objective. This was easier said than done because my ignorance of the subject was encyclopedic. I had to learn an entire vocabulary of international trade, such as "export subsidy techniques" as well as the arcane complexity of "trigger points" (at which restraints would go into effect), and "categories" (which would be subject to restraint), all of which I have again mercifully succeeded in forgetting. The only enduring element in my memory is the awe of our economic experts in the face of Japanese ingenuity, causing them to insist on covering every conceivable category of textile in the negotiations; they were convinced that if any were left out the wily Japanese would use the loophole to evade the entire agreement.

So to my sorrow and later regret I was catapulted into these negotiations. My role was to lend Presidential clout to positions handed to me by Maury Stans and Peter Flanigan; I could only transmit them, not negotiate them, for once I abandoned the position I was given I had no intellectual foothold of any kind. As in a later negotiation with Pompidou on monetary issues this made me unshakable: Without a fallback position or the temptation to be imaginative on my side, it was up to the other side to yield if it wanted agreement.

My involvement started when Sato in good Japanese fashion sent out as a scout a personal friend of his and mine who had no official position in the Japanese government. The unofficial was now negotiating with the uninformed. Both the emissary and I could easily be disavowed; we soon constructed an intricate Kabuki play. On July 18 Sato's emissary came in to see me; we then established the secret channel bypassing the bureaucracies of both countries (except that in this case, because of my ignorance of subject, I kept the key players on our side meticulously informed). Sato wanted to come to an understanding with Nixon on the basic issues of principle on both the nuclear issue and textiles. Once the basic issues were settled, the bureaucracies of both sides would be told to work out the details. I called Nixon and told him of Sato's approach; he was enthusiastic: "Let's try to get it done and not fool around with the State Department."

Nixon had always been farsighted about relations with Japan. In his 1967 *Foreign Affairs* article, "Asia After Vietnam," he had written:

Not to trust Japan today with its own armed forces and with responsibility for its own defense would be to place its people and its government under a disability which, whatever its roots in painful recent history, ill accords with the role Japan *must* play in helping secure the common safety of non-communist Asia.

And in the same article Nixon's conception of Japan's important role in regional security related as well to his view of the evolution of the US role:

Weary with war, disheartened with allies, disillusioned with aid, dismayed at domestic crises, many Americans are heeding the call of the new isolationism. And they are not alone; there is a tendency in the whole Western world to turn inward, to become parochial and isolationist — dangerously so. But there can be neither peace nor security a generation hence unless we recognize now the massiveness of the forces at work in Asia, where more than half the world's people live and where the greatest explosive potential is lodged.

I spent a few days going over the issues with the emissary before my departure with the President on the trip to the *Apollo 11* splashdown and around the world. The emissary and I agreed on the general outlines of a textile settlement that would be negotiated through diplomatic channels. The nuclear issue was left for later consideration.

The harmonious atmosphere was marred by one of those mix-ups that no one can foresee and that once it happens never seems to end. Some US army nerve gas had been stored in canisters on Okinawa. A major whose aesthetic sense exceeded his judgment decided to have the canisters painted white. Blasting the surface smooth in preparation accidentally drilled holes in some of the canisters, and gas escaped. Media and Congressional pressures mounted rapidly. Japanese attention focused on Okinawa as never before. For a couple of weeks a great deal of the time of serious people was devoted to finding a place to which the gas could be moved in the United States when no state wanted to have it pass through on the way to its final destination. It was finally moved to Johnston Island in the middle of the Pacific and there destroyed.

Secretary of State Rogers visited Tokyo in late July (splitting off from the Presidential swing through Southeast Asia) to continue the formal talks with the Japanese over Okinawa. He was accompanied by Maury Stans and Agriculture Secretary Clifford Hardin, who joined him in Cabinet-level talks on trade and other economic subjects. The communiqué after their meetings disclosed only that Rogers and Foreign Minister Kiichi Aichi had "discussed the problem of reversion to Japan of administrative rights over Okinawa." But the Japanese quickly leaked to the press, and Rogers confirmed in a news conference on August 3, that the United States had agreed to the reversion of Okinawa in principle. This reinforced Nixon's and Sato's previous determination to confine the most sensitive discussions to the less porous private channel.

Negotiations proceeded smoothly enough for Sato to be invited to Washington in November for crucial meetings that were finally to settle the Okinawa issue. In effect two issues were left for the leaders: the nuclear storage in Okinawa, which was explicit; and textiles, where concessions would not be revealed lest they undermine Sato's domestic base. That the President insisted on a textile settlement was hammered home to me by the political side of the White House. I was far from enthusiastic about linking an issue of fundamental strategic importance with a transient domestic political problem, and in effect blackmailing the Japanese on a matter of this kind. But I was not in a strong enough position in 1969 to block the collective judgement.

Whereas for Nixon the avoidance of confrontation was a personal idiosyncrasy, for Sato it was a cultural imperative. The needs of the two leaders to have a well-rehearsed outcome totally coincided. Therefore, ten days in advance, Sato's emissary arrived to work out with me the main understandings to be reached and the language to be adopted in the published communiqué. Alex Johnson and Assistant Secretary Marshall Green, who were aware of my confidential talks with Sato's emissary, recommended holding the President's decision not to insist on nuclear storage in reserve until the last minute so as to obtain the maximum concessions on textiles. I coolly told the emissary that the final decision on the nuclear issue should be left for Sato's arrival, so that it would be "his achievement when he comes here."

The strategy worked in the short term; but it went beyond Sato's capacity to deliver. Sato was at a disadvantage. Once he had come, he could not let the negotiations fail on the nuclear issue, since that would have jeopardized the entire security relationship with the United States, the pillar of Japanese foreign policy. The emissary therefore told me that Sato would agree to a comprehensive arrangement by which the Japanese would limit their textile exports to the United States to specific levels. Maury Stans gave me a formula for these limitations that I handed over in pristine form; as far as I was concerned it might as well have been written in Japanese. The emissary flew back to Japan to brief Sato; after a few days he confirmed that the proposed limitations would be acceptable. The stage seemed set for a successful meeting between Nixon and Sato.

Then, two days before Sato's arrival, I received a frantic phone call from Tokyo. It was Sato's emissary. To disguise his identity and fool for two minutes any intelligence services listening in, he had adopted the nom de guerre of "Mr. Yoshida"; he spoke elliptically of "my friend" (Sato) and "your friend" (Nixon) in outlining the problem on the open line. (The "my friend"/"your friend" conversations were to become a feature of my life for an extended period and ultimately were to test my sanity.) In this conversation he informed me that Sato ("my friend") would not be able to settle textiles in a secret negotiation; he would simply not be able to deliver on his promises. For domestic reasons he preferred to have the agreed position emerge from ongoing formal trade talks in Geneva. "Yoshida" confirmed that the outcome would be the specific figures agreed to; but the somewhat more protracted process would permit the articulation of a Japanese consensus. I consulted all interested parties in our government; all agreed to this procedure. We should have realized what was going to happen. If Sato was not strong enough to deliver on his agreement when Okinawa hung in the balance, he would surely be unable to do so in a purely commercial negotiation wherein the concessions would have to be made largely by the Japanese side and no obvious pressures were available for us.

Sato arrived at the White House on November 19, 1969. He represented a country that had rested its entire security and foreign policy upon the United States. His Japan counted on American strength and resolve and leadership. Indeed, in his dinner toast that evening, Sato lavished praise on the American achievement in the *Apollo 12* moon landing, which had just taken place; to Sato this was "not only the victory of the superb power of organization of the United States, but also the victory of the imagination and courage of the American people."

This attitude animated his talk with Nixon. He met in Nixon a kindred spirit. As well as having given thought to US–Japanese relations, Nixon had visited Japan six times as a private citizen and had a high opinion of its potential and its leaders. He especially admired Sato's half brother Nobusuke Kishi, the former Premier who had resigned because of the embarrassment of having to cancel Eisenhower's planned visit in 1960. Sato, too, was favorably known to him.

Sato confirmed his government's strong commitment to continue the Security Treaty for a "considerably long period." An Okinawa agreement, Sato reaffirmed, would go a long way to defuse opposition to the

US–Japan relationship. With Okinawa out of the way, Sato indicated, Japan would be able to increase its defense capability. Nixon averred his personal commitment to Japan along the lines of his 1967 *Foreign Affairs* article. He encouraged Japan to assume a greater role in Pacific defense and expressed pleasure at recent Japanese efforts to increase air and naval forces. Nixon also hoped that Japan could contribute to the strength of free Asia by economic and technical assistance to the developing nations in the region. Sato agreed to these propositions, and indeed the joint communiqué went far in asserting Japan's stake in the security of South Korea, Taiwan, and South Vietnam. Japan also made a general pledge to "make further active contributions to the peace and prosperity of Asia." To give symbolic expression to these common concerns a hot line was set up between Tokyo and Washington. (These harbingers of Japanese activism were at first ill received in Peking. On my first visit to Peking Chou En-lai accused us of tempting Japan into traditional nationalist paths. It took me some time to convince him that the US–Japan alliance was not directed against China; indeed, that the surest way to tempt Japanese nationalism would be to set off a competition for Tokyo's favor between China and the United States.)

The effect of all this on the Okinawa issue was that the philosophical expressions of Japan's interest in the security of Korea, Taiwan, and Vietnam provided the formula for the principle of the essentially unrestricted right to use conventional weapons in the defense of these countries. This left the nuclear question. Nixon had agreed to give up the right to store nuclear weapons in Okinawa; we thought it important to retain the right to reintroduce them in an emergency. The result was a complicated exchange between "Yoshida" and me to find a formula to meet the domestic necessities of both sides. The Japanese wanted a statement that nuclear weapons would be dealt with in accordance with "the policy of the Japanese government as described by the Prime Minister." This could mean anything; in the Japanese context it was bound to be interpreted as prohibiting the introduction of nuclear weapons. Our Joint Chiefs, on the other hand, insisted on *some* formula on which they could base the reintroduction of nuclear weapons in an emergency. In a sense we were arguing about window dressing; a decision of the magnitude of introducing nuclear weapons would not depend on quoting clauses from long-ago communiqués but on the conditions prevailing at the time. Still, the reversion would need domestic approval in *both* countries and that was unattainable without some solution to the largely self-imposed dilemma.

Alex Johnson and I finally came up with a formula as ingenious as it was empty. The US–Japanese Security Treaty had a provision for prior consultation over emergencies. If we referred to it in the communiqué, both sides could satisfy their requirements: Sato could maintain the antinuclear stance of his government; Nixon could claim that the clause gave us the right to raise the issue of nuclear weapons on Okinawa even in advance of an actual emergency. I put this formula to "Yoshida," who in turn obtained Sato's approval.

This still left the problem of how the formula was to emerge and who would surface it. "Yoshida" and I worked out a careful script in which we rehearsed our principals several times so that the proper record would exist. "Yoshida" checked with Sato, who thought this might work.

Sato would open with the standard Japanese position opposing *any* introduction of nuclear weapons. Nixon would counter by tabling a very tough formulation of our maximum position. Sato upon a few minutes' reflection would then produce the previously agreed compromise. After pondering the matter for the benefit of officials (or at least of the record), Nixon would accept Sato's "compromise." That way the formula was a Japanese idea; it had not been imposed; the record would be pristine.

With that thorny issue out of the way the rest followed easily. Nixon and Sato agreed that administrative rights over Okinawa should revert to Japan and that technical discussions would begin with the aim of completing the turnover by 1972. (The deadline was met; Okinawa was officially turned over to Japan on May 15, 1972.) The use of the bases for conventional conflict was dealt with when both sides expressed agreement that reversion should take place "without detriment to the security of the Far East" and therefore "should not hinder the effective discharge of the international obligations assumed by the United States for the defense of countries in the Far East including Japan." The final communiqué of Sato's visit noted President Nixon's pledge to recognize with respect to Okinawa "the particular sentiment of the Japanese people against nuclear weapons." In other words, Okinawa would be as "nuclear-free" as the rest of Japan, but without prejudice to the possibilities of joint consultation in emergencies as provided in the Security Treaty.[2] Sato privately expressed "deep gratitude" to Nixon for this "magnanimous" decision to return Okinawa.

Thus ended a complex negotiation with an act of foresight and statesmanship. Crises avoided do not make for headlines. On the surface we yielded in Okinawa; in reality we preserved the US–Japanese relationship. We removed nuclear weapons from the island and accepted some limited restrictions on conventional use. By these measures we avoided losing everything. Our bases on Okinawa have continued to operate without any interference or significant public opposition since 1972. And the Okinawa negotiations laid the basis for a strengthened partnership with Japan. Nixon was buoyant and he was not far off the mark when he declared on Sato's departure: "It is customary on such occasions to say that a new era begins in the relations between the two countries involved. I believe today, however, that there is no question that this is a statement of the fact that a new era begins between the United States and Japan, in our relations not only bilaterally in the Pacific but in the world.'' And Sato replied in a similar vein in a letter: "I am convinced that our two countries have now entered an era of mutually cooperative relationship resting upon a far stronger foundation than ever before."

Happiness over our Japanese relationship was intensified by the results of Japan's general election on December 27, 1969, which returned Sato's Liberal Democrats to power with a Parliamentary majority even greater than expected (288 out of 486 in the House of Representatives). We considered it a vindication of the Okinawa negotiation. Japanese supporters of the American relationship were strengthened; Sato would be in a position to influence the choice of his successor when he retired. With some justification Nixon's Foreign Policy Report of February 1970 cited the Okinawa initiative as "among the most important decisions I have taken as President."

The Textile Fiasco

TEXTILES remained a far trickier problem. "Mr. Yoshida," who was present in Washington and resumed his covert intermediary role, called me the evening after Sato's arrival to tell me that Sato had second thoughts on the textile scenario by which our formula for comprehensive export limits would be arranged at Geneva and wanted to "think it over" overnight. I expressed dismay that our understanding should fall through so quickly. The next morning "Yoshida" called back to say that "his friend" would stick to the planned scenario. After the Japanese election Sato would move matters to the agreed outcome in the formal talks at Geneva. But this could work only if there was no reference to textiles in the communiqué. Since the solution had to emerge from a negotiation that had not yet started, Sato could hardly indicate its outcome in advance. And it would impair the new relationship if it appeared that we had traded Okinawa for concessions on textiles. The economic portions of the communiqué, therefore, waxed eloquent about other of Maury Stans's favorite themes, committing Sato's government to lowering the barriers to foreign imports and investment in Japan. But nothing on the textile problem.

Still, things seemed to be on track. In the second day's talks with Nixon, Sato explicitly promised that textiles would be resolved as the President desired. Sato declared that he took full responsibility, that it was his "personal credo" and "vow" to keep his word, that he committed his sincerity and all his efforts to that end. Nixon said that was good enough for him; the two leaders shook hands. Sato did not use the word "comprehensive," but "Yoshida" assured me in a conversation that evening that Sato would honor the understanding. After Sato returned home, "Yoshida" called me again in December to confirm Sato's assurance that there would be a bilateral accord on textiles that would be comprehensive in effect, although the word would not be used, to ease Sato's domestic problem. This was reasonable enough, since Sato had just called a general election for December 27.

In negotiations it is dangerous to aim for successes that go beyond the capacities of the domestic structure of one of the parties, let alone of both. The textile problem was never finally resolved as Nixon and Sato had agreed because practically no one in either government understood how to reach the objective or even precisely what the objective was. Lower-level Japanese officials immediately rejected our official proposals based on the Sato-Nixon agreement. I called "Yoshida," who told me again that Sato would honor the understanding but that Sato was keeping its existence secret in Japan in the hope that this would make it easier for him politically and bureaucratically to produce the desired result. I passed on all this to Alex Johnson, telling him, "It's a Kabuki play." It turned out to be more like a Kafka story.

Formal US–Japanese discussions over textiles continued at several levels; at none of them did the Japanese government offer or accept a position resembling what Sato had pledged. Sato was facing immovable opposition from the Japanese textile industry and from its advocates in the Ministry of International Trade and Industry (MITI), the Japanese counterpart to our Commerce Department. There was no legal way Sato could force a solution on his unwilling industry. At one point Sato effected a cabinet reshuffle that replaced the MITI Minister, but the new Minister ended up just as opposed to concessions.

Our side compounded the problem. To make the Sato-Nixon scenario work we were supposed to present a very tough position that would enable Sato to surface his agreement with Nixon as a compromise. However, our middle-level officials, whose knowledge of what was possible was based on the statements of their Japanese counterparts, never believed that we could achieve maximum demands. They insisted on putting forward what they considered realistic positions and would not long hold to the hard-line positions that the scenario required. Our negotiators put forward what we told them was the agreed outcome, rather than a hard-line position. That, of course, put Sato into the untenable position of being asked to accept the American position and evoked desperate phone calls from "Yoshida" accusing me of welshing on the promise of a tough American opening position — surely one of the very few occasions when a foreign government has complained about being given too conciliatory a proposal. All the time pressures grew in the US Congress to wheel out the heaviest artillery of economic warfare — legislation to impose severe quota restrictions on Japanese textile imports. Instead of being solved harmoniously, the textile issue threatened to turn into a confrontation.

In Feburary 1970 "Yoshida" invited me to Japan to settle the problem. Not at all eager to immerse myself so deeply in a negotiation I little understood and to whose solution I could make no substantive contribution, I urged Alex Johnson to come up with an alternative. Alex suggested Phil Trezise, a State Department trade expert. "Yoshida" rejected Trezise as being too low-level; he wanted a Cabinet member. The choice fell on Maury Stans. Having got his wish, "Yoshida" called five days later to tell me that we should delay. The Japanese could not get their house in order; there would be no point yet in Stans's coming.

Instead, a Japanese negotiator arrived in Washington in March with proposals that were unsatisfactory; "Yoshida" called me to say that the Japanese proposal only "looked" unacceptable; the actual Japanese position was more flexible. This was not apparent to Alex Johnson, Maury Stans, or me. I then got further phone calls from "Yoshida" promising better proposals and begging me not to break off the negotiation. I did my now customary round of checking with Johnson and Stans, and told "Yoshida" we would wait for his new proposals. We will never know what might have happened, but at that point a prominent US businessman favoring free trade and seeking to avert restrictive legislation put forward in Tokyo his own suggestions for a compromise. He was acting on his own; but the Japanese took refuge in his proposals. These were less than what the State Department had suggested, which in turn had been too "soft" to permit Sato to come up with a compromise, and less than what "Yoshida" had caused me to believe Sato might be ready to offer. No wonder then that the Japanese quickly accepted the businessman's ideas; on the advice of Stans and Johnson I had to call "Yoshida" to tell him that he was acting on his own, without authority. Nixon told me to "work out the deal" with Sato's emissary; there were "too many people in the act." I agreed; it was hardly wise to let the Japanese shop around for the offer they liked best.

The comedy went on for another two years, with almost the identical script. Japanese MITI Minister Kiichi Miyazawa visited Washington in June 1970 and met with Stans (with my and Johnson's approval). Miyazawa's proposals seemed to Stans to renege on everything to which the Japanese had ever agreed during the course of the negotiations, much less to embody the Sato plan (a "kamikaze attitude," suggested Stans grimly). This led the President to shift the Administration's position to one of "reluctantly" endorsing quota legislation. Several times I told Stans and Johnson of my eagerness to get out of the negotiation. They encouraged me to stay in; my "backchannel" seemed to offer the only hope of achieving any kind of coordination among the two sides' chaotic efforts. Peter Flanigan, Presidential Assistant for International Economic Policy, was brought into the act in the fall of 1970, and another abortive attempt was made to achieve an agreement with the Japanese.

Prime Minister Sato came to America for the United Nations anniversary celebration in the fall. The ubiquitous emissary preceded him — though this time it was not "Yoshida." The new man insisted that when Sato visited Nixon he wished to settle the textile issue as a matter of honor. I urged him strongly not to raise it unless Sato could deliver. Nixon understood that sometimes insuperable domestic obstacles could frustrate the best intentions of statesmen; he had had that experience himself. But another misfire might shake confidence.

Sato insisted on another go at the textile problem, however. The performance of the previous year was repeated. Sato purported to agree on fourteen of sixteen outstanding issues; he said he wanted to save the remaining two for his return, so that the final decision could be made in Tokyo rather than Washington. After saying goodbye to Nixon, Sato drove around the White House to West Executive Avenue and appeared unexpectedly in my office. He wanted to reaffirm his commitment in front of my associates, he said. He thereupon proceeded to repeat what he had told Nixon.

He did and returned to Tokyo. Still nothing happened; the talks remained stalemated. I have no doubt that Sato was sincere in his pledges. He was far too intelligent to attempt such clumsy evasions, far too honorable to resort to tricks with a country he genuinely liked and toward a President he respected. We had demanded too much of him; he promised more than he should have, and he was deeply embarrassed by his inability to deliver. The blame must be shared.

In early 1971, Congressman Wilbur Mills, Chairman of the House Ways and Means Committee, performed the extraordinary feat of negotiating an agreement directly with the Japanese textile industry. The US textile industry and the White House denounced it as unsatisfactory. Ambassador-at-large David Kennedy, former Treasury Secretary, was put in charge of textile negotiations in 1971. The dispute then merged with the New Economic Policy announced by Nixon on August 15, 1971; this was the second "Nixon shock" of 1971 (after the secret visit to China), and it was to a great extent a product of the failure of previous US–Japanese trade discussions. Finally, under this severe buffeting, combined with the obnoxious threat of quotas by Executive Order under the 1917 Trading with the Enemy Act, the Japanese reached agreement with Ambassador Kennedy on October 15, 1971.

The criticism has been made that the so-called Nixon-Kissinger diplomacy here showed its usual misunderstanding of the pluralistic political system of a democratic ally, in which national leaders could not dominate the decision-making as in a dictatorship.[3] While I did not then grasp all the subtleties of Japan's political culture, I came to understand the problem we were facing all too well. In reality, it was not a "back-channel negotiation" in the usual sense; I kept in contact with the key officials of the State and Commerce departments at every turn, by necessity, whatever Nixon's urgings to the contrary. The other agencies indeed hoped that the White House channel to Sato could make some sense out of the confusion on both sides. Nor did the dispute arise because Nixon misunderstood an elliptical pledge by Sato, as has been suggested.[4] Sato's explicit promise was reiterated over and over again by his designated emissary. It could be said that the basic mistake was Nixon's campaign pledge of 1968, which cost too high a price in terms of our foreign policy objectives.

But the real problem, of course, was deeper, and it is of fundamental importance to the future of all the industrial democracies. While Japan, the United States, Canada, and the nations of Western Europe are political and military allies, we are also inevitable economic competitors. As democracies, indeed, our systems disperse economic power as well as the political authority by which decisions are made on economic questions. No government has solved the problem of how autonomous national economic policies can be pursued without growing strains with political allies who are also trade rivals; even less have we solved the challenge of coordinating economic goals to reinforce the cohesion of free peoples. We proclaim interdependence but we have been reluctant to accept that this involves a measure of dependence.

Thus trade disputes among the industrial democracies are still with us; the competitive and protectionist pressures surged again after the 1973–1974 energy crisis threw the industrial world into a protracted recession. The textiles fiasco was one major lapse in Japan's otherwise impressive record of economic decision-making. Yet the vulnerability of American policy to protectionist pressures, which forced us to stake so much on the effort to get such an agreement from the Japanese (if only to head off more brutal legislative impositions), remains a serious weakness of the American system. Protectionism is the resort of the economically weak; a wiser national policy would seek to enhance the mobility of labor and resources so that we can shift out of declining industries and expand our more productive sectors. And protectionism is above all an untenable posture for a nation that seeks to be the leader of the alliance of industrial democracies. This has thrown us into conflict when the necessity of statesmanship is to reemphasize in the economic field the fundamental community of interest that would surely operate in the face of obvious external threats to our security. The danger, conversely, is that economic clashes of mounting bitterness could undermine that very unity of interest and aspiration that is the bulwark of our freedom. We have yet to rise to this challenge.

X

Words and Shadows: Evolution of Middle East Strategy

W HEN I entered office I knew little of the Middle East. I had never visited any Arab country; I was not familiar with the liturgy of Middle East negotiations. The first time I heard one of the staple formulas of the region's diplomacy was at a dinner at the British Embassy in February 1969. Someone invoked the sacramental language of United Nations Security Council Resolution 242, mumbling about the need for a just and lasting peace within secure and recognized borders. I thought the phrase so platitudinous that I accused the speaker of pulling my leg. It was a mistake I was not to repeat. By the end of my time in office I had become like all other old Middle East hands; word had become reality, form and substance had merged. I was immersed in the ambiguities, passions, and frustrations of that maddening, heroic, and exhilarating region. If the reader finds the diplomacy outlined in this chapter an agonizing swamp of endless maneuvering and confusion, he knows how I felt.

My personal acquaintance with the area before 1969 was limited to three brief private visits to Israel during the 1960s. I recall particularly vividly my visit to Kibbutz Ginossar, the home of Yigal Allon, a student in my International Seminar at Harvard in 1957 and later my colleague as Deputy Prime Minister and Foreign Minister of Israel. His kibbutz is on the shores of the Sea of Galilee. Every square inch of its intensively cultivated soil had been wrested by faith and suffering from the hostile circumstances of geography and conflict. Across the Sea of Galilee I remember seeing a solitary fishing boat at the edge of the escarpment of the Golan Heights, within easy range of Syrian rifles. I thought then how little the materialist philosophers understood of human motivation. Here were a people, sustained by faith through two millennia of persecution, come to reclaim dreams that for all this time had been more powerful than their tragic reality. But I thought too that the meaning of this faith must not be exhausted in the heroic defense of a country that threatened to turn into another beleaguered ghetto. Sooner or later there had to be a reconciliation with the men and women on top of the escarpment. Peace in the Middle East was not only a physical necessity but a spiritual fulfillment. It never occurred to me that some day I might join the struggle for it.

Nor did I then appreciate quite how the flood of words used to justify the various demands obscured rather than illuminated fundamental positions. In that barren region of deserts and stark mountains from which three of the world's great religions have emerged, there is a profound temptation toward exaltation, magnified by the fact that geography has set no bound to the human imagination. Only the dedicated can survive in such adversity of topography and climate; man's principal solace is not nature but faith and the human relationship. Nowhere else is there to be found such a collection of leaders of such sharply etched personality; nowhere else do the convictions of individual statesmen play so pivotal a role. Man is united with his fellows by faith, and the word plays here an often decisive role. Whether in the Israelis' Talmudic exegesis or the Arabs' tendency toward epic poetry, the line is easily crossed beyond what the pragmatic West would consider empirical reality into the sphere of passionate rhetoric and the realm of human inspiration. Woe to the unwary outsider who takes this linguistic exuberance literally and seeks to find a solution by asking adversaries what they really want.

What the parties to the Middle East conflict really want lies deep in an amalgam of convictions, resentments, and dreams. Formal positions are like the shadows in Plato's cave — reflections of a transcendent reality almost impossible to encompass in the dry legalisms of a negotiating process.

The conflict has not lasted for thousands of years, as is often said. It is very much a product of our twentieth century. The movements of Zionism and Arab nationalism, to be sure, were spawned in the late 1800s but they were not directed against each other. Only when the centuries of Ottoman rule had given way to the British Mandate, and the prospect of self-determination for Palestine emerged, did the Arab and the Jew, after having coexisted peacefully for generations, begin their mortal struggle over the political future of this land. The modern era, which gave birth to this communal conflict, then bestowed all its malevolent possibilities upon it. The Nazi holocaust added moral urgency to the quest for a Jewish state. But no sooner was it established and blessed by the international community in 1948 than it was forced to defend its independence against Arab neighbors who did not see why they should make sacrifices to atone for European iniquities in which they had had no part. Israel's victory in the 1948–1949 war in turn fueled the fires of Arab nationalism as traditional regimes, discredited by defeat, came under the sway of radical ideology — Pan-Arabism and socialism. Then the region became the focal point of Cold War rivalry, which both exacerbated local conflict and posed the danger that outside powers could be dragged into major confrontation.

By 1969, Israel had existed for twenty years unrecognized by its neighbors, harassed by guerrillas, assaulted in international forums, and squeezed by Arab economic boycott. Its very shape expressed the tenuous quality of its statehood; it was only *nine miles wide* at the narrowest point between the Mediterranean coast and the Jordan border; the main road between divided Jerusalem and Tel Aviv at some places was located less than a hundred yards from Arab outposts. With implacable adversaries on all its frontiers, Israel's foreign policy had become indistinguishable from its defense policy; its cardinal and ultimate objective was what for most other nations is the starting point of foreign policy — acceptance by its neighbors of its right to exist. It naturally saw in the territories occupied in 1967 an assurance of the security that it had vainly sought throughout its existence. It strove for both territory and recognition, reluctant to admit that these objectives might prove incompatible.

This gulf in perceptions — in which, as in all tragedies, both sides represented a truth — is what had given the Arab-Israeli conflict its bitter intractability. When truths collide, compromise becomes the first casualty. Agreements are achieved only through evasions. Progress evaporates as the parties approach specifics. This became increasingly apparent when we took office. The Middle East was still mired in the aftermath of the Six Day War. Positions had hardened, diplomacy was stalemated, and hostilities were increasing.

On June 5, 1967, Israel had exploded across its frontiers, climaxing a sequence of events in which Arab rhetoric had run away with Arab intentions. In May 1967 the Soviet Union had warned Egypt that an Israeli attack on Syria was imminent. This Soviet claim was false; whether it was a deliberate untruth designed to provoke tension and gain some cheap credit or whether it was an honest misunderstanding, it set in motion a fateful process. President Gamal Abdel Nasser impetuously ordered his army into the Sinai, which had been in practice demilitarized since 1956, and announced that he was closing the Strait of Tiran, which controlled access to the Israeli port of Eilat from the Red Sea. He asked United Nations Secretary-General U Thant to remove the United Nations Emergency Force, which separated Israeli and Egyptian forces along the international boundary. It is doubtful that Nasser sought a military showdown; it is even possible that he was astonished by the alacrity with which U Thant acceded to his request. Nasser may have intended to do no more than strike a heroic pose.

Sometimes events mocking the intentions of the actors race out of control. Once the Egyptian army replaced the UN force on its frontier, Israel had no choice but to mobilize, because Israel's territory was too small to absorb a first blow. And once Israel mobilized, its decision to fight had to be made in a matter of weeks, for its economy could not stand the indefinite loss of manpower absorbed by the mobilization, and it could not demobilize with the Egyptian army on its borders. But international diplomacy operated at its leisurely pace. Exploration followed consultation and reassurance; the world's statesmen discussed various formulas to overcome the announced blockade of the Strait of Tiran. Inconclusive exchanges drifted on until Israel wiped out the Egyptian air force in one blow by a surprise attack on the morning of June 5. The war ended in six days with Israel occupying territories in Egypt, Syria, and Jordan — the Sinai, the Golan Heights, and the West Bank of the Jordan River. The new territory seized was three times the size of Israel itself.

Arab radicalism grew exponentially in the wake of the 1967 war. The policy of Egypt, the pivotal Arab country, and indeed of much of the Arab world, was still driven by the volatile Nasser. The growing presence of Palestinian guerrillas in Jordan threatened the survival of the moderate, pro-Western Hashemite King Hussein; agitation by the same groups kept Lebanon effectively without a government through most of 1969. The Soviet Union implanted itself more firmly in the region by sending massive military supplies to Egypt, Iraq, and Syria; the Arab front-line states, having cut their ties to the United States in 1967, became dependent on Soviet support, diplomatic as well as material. Whatever the Soviets' formal diplomatic position, their arms supply reinforced the irredentist and intransigent streak of Arab policy, expressed by the Khartoum Arab Summit of late August 1967 in the unanimous proclamation of the "three no's" — "no peace with Israel, no negotiation with Israel, no recognition of Israel."

Gradually some quarters in the Arab world began to understand that intransigence would perpetuate continued Israeli occupation of captured territories. While Syria turned its back on negotiations, Egypt and Jordan undertook tentative and reluctant feelers toward some form of accommodation. They demanded Israeli withdrawal to the pre–June 5, 1967, boundaries, but indicated a willingness to consider declarations of nonbelligerency, the right of each state to a secure existence, and recognition of Israel. Though this marked a quantum advance from the hostility that had characterized Arab attitudes for two decades, it fell far short of Israel's stated requirements: face-to-face negotiations, secure and recognized boundaries (a euphemism for border changes), frontiers open to trade and travel, and a guarantee of free navigation through the international waterways. Even the moderate Arabs would settle for nothing less than total withdrawal and they rejected direct talks. (At least publicly. Jordan in fact maintained secret direct contacts with Israel during that period.) The radical Arabs refused a peace process on any basis.

The Palestinian commando organization Al Fatah in a policy statement of October 1968 rejected "all compromises aiming at halt of armed strife," warned Arab governments against pursuing such a course, and declared itself in favor of a "free, open, non-sectarian, non-racist society in Palestine"[1] — in other words, abolishing the state of Israel altogether.

Resolution 242, about which I was to hear so much more, merely papered over these differences when it was adopted by the UN Security Council on November 22, 1967, with the approval of the two sides. It spoke of a "just and lasting peace" within "secure and recognized boundaries"; it called for an end to "claims or states of belligerency," for Israeli withdrawal "from territories occupied in the recent conflict," and for acknowledgment of all states' "sovereignty, territorial integrity and political independence." But it soon became apparent that these ambiguous phrases were acceptable to each party only because it could interpret them in its own favor. Egypt and Jordan interpreted the clause "withdrawal from territories occupied" to require withdrawal from *all* captured soil; Israel took "secure and recognized boundaries" to *exclude* a return to the lines before the Six Day War. To Israel withdrawal meant giving up tangible safeguards and it demanded a quid pro quo; to the Arabs withdrawal meant getting back what in their view belonged to them — hence, they considered Israeli withdrawal their right and not an Israeli concession.

These clashing perspectives permeated the Middle East dispute and prevented any real bargaining; each side sought to achieve its primary goal as the entrance price into negotiations. Egypt insisted that Israeli withdrawal should *precede* fulfillment or even negotiation of any of the other conditions. Israel demanded face-to-face talks at the outset, which had the dual advantage of obtaining at least implied recognition and of minimizing the danger of great-power imposition. Jordan's acquiescence in Resolution 242 had been obtained in 1967 by the promise of our United Nations Ambassador Arthur Goldberg that under its terms we would work for the return of the West Bank to Jordan with minor boundary rectifications and that we were prepared to use our influence to obtain a role for Jordan in Jerusalem. Since there were no negotiations going on, the promise was meaningless.

Resolution 242 instructed Secretary-General U Thant to appoint a Special Representative to talk to the parties and try to get negotiations started. Thant selected the Swedish Ambassador to Moscow, Gunnar Jarring. To see whether the dissonant voices might yield some coherence, Jarring began his mission by sending questionnaires to the parties asking their positions. After months of evasion they finally told him, each in its own convoluted language, what they had already declared publicly in simplified and sometimes demagogic language. When Jarring visited the Middle East he found that the real positions of the parties were even more incompatible than their public statements.

There was no little pathos in the emotions underlying each side's arguments. Israel insisted on a "binding peace." Only a country that had never known peace could have attached so much importance to that phrase. For what is a binding peace among sovereign nations when one of the attributes of sovereignty is the right to change one's mind? For three centuries France and Germany had fought wars in almost every generation; each one was ended by a formal "binding" peace treaty that did nothing to prevent the next war. Nor did "open frontiers" in 1914 prevent the outbreak of a world war which shook Europe to its foundations. Most wars in history have been fought between countries that started out at peace; it was the special lunacy of the Middle East that its wars broke out between countries that were technically already at war.

Nasser insisted on unconditional withdrawal from all occupied territories — but he never explained what incentive Israel had for withdrawal in the face of his ambiguous offers of nonbelligerency. Nor did he cite a prior example of a peace settlement based solely on the unconditional withdrawal of the victor from the territory it had conquered. But for Nasser, the prospect of recognizing Israel was such a personal trauma that his mere mention of the phrase seemed to him to remove all necessity for giving it concrete meaning.

In other regions of the world these circumstances might have produced a stalemate broken from time to time by a series of wars until exhaustion produced the equilibrium that wisdom had been unable to define. But the Middle East, in the second half of the twentieth century, was at the vortex of global politics. Though in the late Sixties oil was not yet perceived as a scarce commodity, the importance of the Middle East — at the crossroads of continents and civilizations — was understood only too clearly. The Soviet Union, which in the late Forties had written off the Middle East as beyond its capacity to influence,[2] had leaped in ten years later by a sale of arms and twenty years later by the dispatch of thousands of military advisers to Egypt. The Soviet presence constituted a major geopolitical change since World War II. For fifteen years it helped exacerbate the conflict. As time went on the Soviets acted with increasing boldness. In 1956, they meddled marginally in Suez crisis diplomacy and made vague threats of military involvement *after* our pressure on Britain and France had made it safe to do so. After 1967 the number of Soviet military advisers in the Middle East increased fivefold. Through the Sixties Soviet influence grew dramatically in Egypt, Syria, Iraq, Algeria, Sudan, and in later years, Libya. The 1967 war, which they helped to provoke, enabled the Soviets for the first time in history to establish a permanent fleet of some fifty warships in the Mediterranean Sea.

The roles of outside powers were almost as complex as those of the principal actors. The Soviet Union acted as advocate of the Arab cause; it espoused Arab proposals and offered no hint of possible compromise. The West European countries were torn between their impotence and their premonition of the economic dangers of another conflict. The most active, de Gaulle's France, in effect embraced the Arab position after the Six Day War. As for the United States, President Johnson in a speech on June 19, 1967, sought to navigate the reefs of controversy by avoiding any precision; in his discussion of borders, recognition, and maritime rights he foreshadowed what later became the mystical ambiguities of Resolution 242. Egypt, together with other Arab states, had broken diplomatic relations with the United States in the aftermath of the 1967 war. We were thus without senior diplomats in the capitals of the key Arab countries, which nevertheless demanded our help in the negotiating process. Nasser insisted that we pressure Israel in his behalf, holding out in return the prospect of restoring diplomatic relations with us. Why we should pay a price for the restoration of relations which he had cut off under a totally false pretext was never made clear.* We had all the less incentive to do so as long as his policy continued to rely on Soviet support and catered to radical passions throughout the Arab world.

I had always believed it essential to reduce the scope of Soviet adventurist policies in the Middle East. For that reason the United States performance in the Suez crisis of 1956 had struck me as deplorable. We should have understood that our sudden withdrawal of financial support for Egypt's Aswan High Dam would be the beginning, not the end, of a crisis. And the crisis when it occurred was in my view mishandled. Whatever one's view of the wisdom of the British and French military action, I was convinced that we would pay heavily in the years ahead for our shortsighted playing to the gallery. I did not think that manhandling our closest allies would achieve the lasting gratitude of Nasser or those who admired him; on the contrary, he would probably be confirmed in a course fundamentally inimical to Western interests. The moderate regimes buttressed by British power and prestige, especially in Iraq, were likely to be weakened if not doomed by what they could only see as our siding with the radical elements exemplified by Nasser. Britain and France, their self-confidence and sense of global relevance shattered, would hasten to shed their remaining international responsibilities. The realities of power would then impel us to fill the resulting vacuum in the Middle East and east of Suez and so take on our own shoulders all the moral onus of difficult geopolitical decisions.

When I reached high office, however, my ability to implement my

---

* Nasser had accused the United States of direct military participation on Israel's side in the 1967 war. President Johnson insisted that Nasser recant this charge before diplomatic relations could be resumed. Nasser did so through the press, but Johnson insisted that Nasser make the gesture directly to the United States.

views on Middle East policy differed from my position on other issues. On other topics Nixon would listen to the agencies for a while and then act from the White House; thus my office assumed constantly growing responsibilities. But in the Middle East the President made a distinction between my planning and my operational functions. I was allowed to plan, to warn, to delay; I could force deliberations into the NSC framework — but until the end of 1971 I was not permitted to conduct diplomacy except in rare periods of acute crisis such as the Syrian invasion of Jordan in September 1970.

The two main reasons for this, in my view, were Nixon's ambivalent relationship with Secretary of State Rogers and his assessment of the domestic liabilities of an active Middle East policy. Because Nixon's distrust of the State Department thrust me forward and inevitably embarrassed and frustrated Rogers, Nixon constantly sought means to comfort his old friend. One was to reserve some area of foreign policy for Rogers's predominant influence. But what Nixon gave with one hand he tended to take away with the other. The areas he did not mind consigning were those where success seemed elusive, such as Africa, or those where the risks of domestic reaction were high. The Middle East met both of Nixon's criteria. He calculated that almost any active policy would fail; in addition, it would almost certainly incur the wrath of Israel's supporters. So he found it useful to get the White House as much out of the direct line of fire as possible.

He also suspected that my Jewish origin might cause me to lean too much toward Israel. And, like other Presidents, he was not above feeding the rivalry inherent (despite the ritualistic protestations to the contrary) between the offices of Secretary of State and security adviser in order to enhance his own control.

There was a further personality reason for the relatively more active role of the State Department in the Middle East, and it lay in the character of the Assistant Secretary who was appointed to head its bureau of Near Eastern and South Asian Affairs. Intense, gregarious, occasionally frenetic, Joseph Sisco was not a conventional Foreign Service Officer. He had never served overseas; only the insistence of Dean Rusk had earned him promotion to the highest rank of the service, which selection boards applying more conventional criteria consistently denied him. Once there, he turned out to be a living proof of what imaginative leadership could achieve in the State Department even under a President determined to conduct his own foreign policy. Enormously inventive, with a talent for the stratagems that are the lifeblood of Middle East diplomacy, sometimes offering more solutions than there were problems, Joe Sisco seized the bureaucratic initiative and never surrendered it. He was adroit in the ways of Washington and quickly established a personal relationship with me, perceiving that in the Nixon Administration Presidential authority would be the ultimate arbiter. In the end, he probably spent as much time mediating between Rogers and me as between the Arabs and Israelis. Much of the information that the White House was given about the day-to-day course of the State Department's Middle East initiatives came from Sisco to me or to Hal Saunders, my senior staff assistant on the Middle East. Joe managed to remain loyal to both his bosses, Rogers and the President, and served both well. After I became Secretary of State I made him Under Secretary of State for Political Affairs, the highest career policymaking position in the Department. In that capacity he became an indispensable collaborator and a close friend.

Initiatives Galore

WHEN a new Administration comes to office it is taken for granted that it will "tackle" the important world problems; new Presidents always chide their predecessors for leaving issues not yet conclusively "solved." It is difficult for any American leader to accept the fact that in some conflicts opposing positions are simply irreconcilable. Indeed, when readiness to compromise does not exist, forcing the issue prematurely will magnify insecurity and instability; events that should be slowed down may be accelerated; pressures are generated that cannot be controlled. Every new Administration must learn — often the hard way — that one of the most difficult responsibilities of policymaking is the patience to pick the right moment for decisive action.

Many temptations to "do something" awaited the new Administration when it took office. In early February 1969 Israeli sources reported that 1,288 incidents of sabotage and terrorism had taken place in the year and a half from the Six Day War to the end of 1968: 920 incidents on the Jordanian front, 166 on the Egyptian border, 37 on the cease-fire line with Syria, 35 on the Lebanese border, and 130 in Gaza. Israeli losses for the same period were reported as 234 dead and 765 wounded among military personnel and 47 dead and 330 wounded among civilians — a staggering total for a country with a population of 2.5 million, equivalent to over 20,000 dead and 100,000 wounded for a nation the size of America. Israel retaliated by air attacks on suspected guerrilla bases in Jordan; it staged a major attack against the Beirut international airport on December 28, 1968; and artillery duels across the Suez Canal were a regular occurrence.

There was no shortage of invitations for American diplomatic involvement. Two in particular were awaiting the new Administration: On December 30 the Soviets had suggested a peace plan to implement Resolution 242; it reflected the Arab demand for total Israeli withdrawal and a definition of peace so minimal as to be an obvious nonstarter. On

January 16, 1969, France proposed Four-Power consultations on the Middle East — among the United States, the Soviet Union, Britain, and France.

At our NSC meeting on February 1 we had to decide how to respond to these initiatives and basically whether to depart from the low-profile policy that had characterized the Johnson years. It rapidly became clear that the State Department was eager to launch an American initiative. What objective or strategy this involvement should serve would be left to emerge in negotiation. State believed that it was our responsibility to help bridge the gap between the parties and point them toward compromise under Jarring. Moreover, since the fighting was intensifying, so the argument ran, we could not afford to appear indifferent. All the parties in the area professed to believe that the United States held the key to a settlement; hence, the Department argued, we should indeed involve ourselves actively. It was hoped that common ground could probably be achieved among the parties as well as among the outside powers by the sheer momentum of the negotiating process. As for the Soviet problem, the Department contended that since Moscow seemed to gain by exploiting the tensions of the area, a peace settlement was bound to frustrate its strategy. At a minimum such a course would test Soviet intentions.

The new President was about to undergo his first experience of the bureaucratic steamroller. It is the nature of a bureaucracy to move by almost imperceptible stages toward a goal it may itself only dimly perceive. The first move is usually to ask the President or the Secretary of State for authority to "explore" a certain course "in principle," with solemn assurances that this decision creates neither precedent nor obligation for another step and that the policymakers will retain full control over the process. Invariably the first step implies a series of others; the exploration of a serious subject can only reveal its difficulties and spur pressures to overcome them. Soon the President is asked to act to remove an impasse his own policy has created. This is of course exactly what the advocates of an active policy desire; they are only too eager to put forward schemes to break the deadlock. Many Mideast experts in State had been unhappy with President Johnson's aloof posture toward the conflict, which they attributed to domestic politics. Their eagerness was further stimulated by the cast of mind of some American diplomats that a crisis is somehow not genuine unless we are a party to it. This was the origin of the thought that we must never be perceived (never specifying by whom) as indifferent to emerging confrontations.

I had serious doubts about rushing into negotiations whose objectives we had not defined and for whose outcome we would be held responsible. I also questioned the assumptions underlying the recommendation. It seemed to me unlikely that we would find common ground between the parties. I did not particularly like the negotiating forums offered to us. Given Soviet and French biases toward the Arab viewpoint (and the pressures this put on the British), a Four-Power forum as proposed by France was likely to produce a lineup against the United States. On the other hand, Two-Power talks — between the United States and the Soviet Union — might, if they made any progress, give the Soviet Union the credit for having pressed a Middle East settlement on us, and if they failed, saddle us with the blame.

More serious than the choice of forum was the constant and fundamental premise — stated explicitly by one of the State Department representatives at the February 1 NSC meeting — that the United States would have to deliver Israeli agreement. It meant that we were being asked to pressure an ally on behalf of countries which, with the exception of Jordan, had broken relations with us, pursued policies generally hostile to us, and were clients of Moscow. I therefore doubted the advisability of American pressure for a general settlement until we could see more clearly what concessions the Arabs would make and until those who would benefit from it would be America's friends, not Soviet clients. In the meantime I much preferred an Israeli-Jordanian negotiation, which would involve just such a friend, rather than an Israeli-Egyptian negotiation, in which we would be asked to bail out a Soviet protégé. In short, I thought the prerequisite of effective Middle East diplomacy was to reduce the Soviet influence so that progress could not be ascribed to its pressures and moderate governments gained some maneuvering room.

I expressed my concern to the President the day afterward. He had invited me to accompany him to Walter Reed Army Hospital to call on former President Eisenhower, then in an advanced stage of the illness that killed him seven weeks later. Propped up in an easy chair, Eisenhower appeared even more emaciated than the last time I had seen him. He spent much of the time warning Nixon against leaks of NSC proceedings. Nixon told him about our Middle East discussion. Eisenhower argued against major American involvement in the negotiations. Probably reflecting the agony he went through over Suez in 1956, he thought the best course was to let the parties work it out themselves. If we became active we would be forced in the end to become an arbiter and then offer the parties our own guarantee of whatever final arrangement emerged. This would keep us embroiled in Middle East difficulties forever.

The next day, I had not been in my office many minutes before an irate Eisenhower was on the phone. He had just read a *New York Times* story reporting that the NSC meeting had determined that the United States would now pursue a more active policy in the Middle East. With a vigor that belied my memory of his frailty — and a graphic vocabulary at variance with his sunny smile — he berated me for letting down the President by not restricting the number of NSC participants. It was my duty, he said, to prevent attempts by the bureaucracy to stampede the President with news leaks like this. What had happened underlined his strictures of the night before; we should keep hands off the Middle East.

The same day I sent Nixon my further reflections in a memorandum. I took it as given that he was about to decide on some form of active diplomacy, both in response to State's prodding and because of his campaign pledges of a new American initiative. I sought to explain the likely costs of such a course and my doubts about its chances of success. It was true, I argued, that the parties would never by themselves be able to achieve a settlement amid the mounting violence. But it did not follow that we would do better. I doubted whether Nasser would be able to commit himself to the minimum conditions of peace that Israel would accept. An all-out effort for a general settlement would probably fail; we would therefore be wasting our political capital, exacerbating the pressures toward conflict and crippling our ability to contain a conflict if it erupted. It seemed to me that we would be better off focusing on a partial settlement, such as one with Jordan,* which had a long and honorable record of friendship with the United States. I urged the President, if he proceeded, to obtain from State not only its procedural proposal but the outline of the substance of the peace terms it would be supporting — the articulation of which was, after all, the point of the exercise.

Nixon and I had a private talk on the afternoon of February 3. He felt himself "boxed in." He could not reject the French proposal outright since that would mortgage his effort to improve relations with de Gaulle; also, he saw in the Middle East a lever to pry loose some Soviet cooperation on Vietnam. And he did not want to overrule the State Department on an issue on which its views were unanimous and so strongly held. Unfortunately, these objectives were not compatible. In my opinion, as I told him, we were more likely to obtain Soviet cooperation in Vietnam by moving deliberately in the Middle East, where the Soviet clients were the weaker party, than by relieving its embarrassment through talks that would give the Soviets a dazzling opportunity to demonstrate their utility to their Arab friends. Nor would we placate the bureaucracy by going along with its opening gambit; it was certain to be back with requests for more specific instructions that would head us down the slippery slope. If we were not careful, we would be asked to break every deadlock by putting forward our own plan — which we would then be asked to impose on recalcitrant parties.

---

*This judgment turned out to be wrong because the West Bank and Jerusalem were the toughest issues for Israel to handle.

Foreign policy decisions rarely emerge from abstract analysis, however. For reasons already described Nixon did not wish to overrule the State Department, antagonize de Gaulle, or rebuff the Soviet Union. Sensing this, I suggested a way to move without committing ourselves irrevocably. Rather than choose between the Four-Power and the Two-Power forums, we could maintain some freedom of action by accepting *both*. We would make progress in the Four-Power forum depend on exploratory talks with the Soviets. In this manner we could attempt to tie the Middle East discussions to our broader concerns, including Soviet help on Vietnam. And in the Four-Power forum, our European allies would be more hesitant to side with the Soviets against us if they knew we had our own bilateral option. To prevent the process from gaining uncontrollable momentum, we could insist that the President review the results of the exploratory talks before proceeding to formal discussions.

The President agreed. On February 3 I let Rogers and Sisco know of the decision. On February 5 the State Department, as instructed, announced that the United States regarded the French proposal "favorably" and that we would begin consultations with the Soviet Union, Britain, and France, bilaterally to develop "the measure of understanding" that would make an early meeting of the Four "fruitful and constructive."

My scheme did not work; it was too clever by half. I could spark planning exercises and try to deflect bureaucratic energies but I could not control the pace of the negotiations. The Department treated the White House tactical gimmickry as a sop to domestic politics and rushed to complete the "exploratory" talks as rapidly as possible. Within less than two weeks, I discovered that the State Department was already planning for the next move: developing substantive, comprehensive principles for a Middle East peace settlement — exactly what I had hoped to string out over many months.

As the pace of diplomacy quickened so did domestic excitement. Within a week of the announcement of our "favorable" attitude to Four-Power talks, Israel's supporters reacted with the vigor I would come to know so well in the years to come. They reflected Israel's own concern that outsiders not seek to substitute for direct talks with the Arabs. A delegation of six Congressmen, headed by Emanuel Celler of New York and representing the House leadership of both parties, called first on me and then on the President on February 13. They viewed the start of Four-Power talks as a sign that the United States was heading toward an imposed settlement; they deeply distrusted the forum and feared it would move us closer to French and Soviet views.

If there was already concern in the Congress over the negotiating forum, I could imagine the outcry once we turned to substance. The dramatic gulf between the two sides' positions was demonstrated again by interviews granted by President Nasser of Egypt and Prime Minister

Levi Eshkol to an American news magazine.[3] The Egyptian demanded total Israeli withdrawal as the precondition for Arab fulfillment of the other provisions of Resolution 242. The Israeli made clear that Israel would not return to prewar lines under any terms, and that he had very specific ideas about the requirements for "peace." The situation was further complicated by the death of Prime Minister Eshkol at the end of February, which meant that Israel faced the prospect of complicated election-year politics until Golda Meir, named Eshkol's successor, received a fresh mandate in the elections scheduled for October.

This only reinforced my conviction that the time was not ripe for an active negotiation. And the resulting strategic disagreement was never really settled. The bureaucracy wanted to embark on substantive talks as rapidly as possible because it feared that a deteriorating situation would increase Soviet influence. I thought delay was on the whole in our interest because it enabled us to demonstrate even to radical Arabs that we were indispensable to *any* progress and that it could not be extorted from us by Soviet pressure. The State Department wanted to fuel the process of negotiations by accepting at least some of the Soviet ideas, to facilitate compromise. I wanted to frustrate the radicals — who were in any event hostile to us — by demonstrating that in the Middle East friendship with the United States was the precondition to diplomatic progress. When I told Sisco in mid-February that we did not *want* a quick success in the Four-Power consultations at the United Nations in New York, I was speaking a language that ran counter to all the convictions of his Department.

The Soviets, meanwhile, had quickly nibbled at our bait. At my very first meeting with Dobrynin on February 14, he told me that the Soviet leadership was prepared to talk bilaterally with us on the Middle East, preferably outside the UN framework. He repeated the same point during his first meeting with Nixon on February 17. Nixon evaded the offer of confidential bilateral talks on the Middle East at the White House level; he maintained his view that the Channel would be available only in return for cooperation on Vietnam.

The President's talks in Europe on his trip in late February and early March 1969 added to the pressures on the United States to become actively involved. The British and French naturally wanted the main talks to take place in the Four-Power forum; they did not flatly object to parallel US–Soviet discussions but their enthusiasm for this procedure was well contained. De Gaulle observed with Olympian detachment that the United States and the Soviet Union could talk about anything they chose so long as they avoided the impression of a condominium. Beyond these procedural concerns — and de Gaulle's general support for total Israeli withdrawal coupled with Four-Power guarantees — no European leader had a concrete idea of how to move the parties to a comprehensive agreement. They generously left such details to us.

By the beginning of March, then, foreign and bureaucratic pressures combined to generate irresistible momentum behind an active American role. Even in advance of the Presidential decision, Joe Sisco was already discussing with Dobrynin the virtues of Two-Power talks. Sisco's enthusiasm was not a little influenced by the fact that he would conduct the Two-Power talks, while the Four-Power talks were under the aegis of Charles Yost, our Ambassador to the United Nations.

Dobrynin, somewhat confused, over lunch with me on March 3 pressed for clarification about the relation between the Two-Power talks, which he was eager to start, and the Four-Power forum. He tried to tantalize me by revealing that the Soviet Union was prepared to discuss a package deal, that is to say, a scheme requiring the simultaneous execution of all its provisions, in contrast to the prior Arab-Soviet demand that the process *begin* with Israeli withdrawal. He wanted to know in what forum to surface his plan; he indicated a preference to discuss some of the more delicate subjects, such as frontiers, in the White House Channel. Applying our strategy of using the Middle East as leverage on Vietnam — and conscious of Nixon's reluctance to see me involved — I evaded the proposal; I encouraged Dobrynin to pursue his bilateral talks with Sisco.

The next day, March 4, it was the turn of the Israeli Ambassador to inquire into our purposes. Yitzhak Rabin had been a hero of Israel's war of independence and as Chief of Staff of Israel's defense forces he was an architect of the victory of the Six Day War. Except for his intelligence and tenacity, he was an unlikely ambassador. Taciturn, shy, reflective, almost resentful of small talk, Rabin possessed few of the attributes commonly associated with diplomacy. Repetitious people bored him and the commonplace offended him; unfortunately for Rabin both these qualities are not exactly in short supply in Washington. He hated ambiguity, which is the stuff of diplomacy. I grew extremely fond of him though he did little to encourage affection. His integrity and his analytical brilliance in cutting to the core of a problem were awesome. I valued his judgment, often even on matters unconnected with the Middle East, and trusted his motives even when his country's positions were not always identical with our own. We became good friends and remained so through all the vicissitudes and squabbles that our duties occasionally imposed on us.

In that first conversation I could not answer his question about our policy; we had not yet settled on it ourselves. But I was reasonably certain that the President would proceed with both the Four- and Two-Power forums. My private advice was that Israel should prepare a concrete program articulating a definition of "peace" that it could live with; only this could give us criteria by which to judge progress.

As I feared, the momentum of negotiations rather than considered strategy drove the decisions. By early March Sisco reported the success

I thought it wiser to postpone; he had now already fulfilled his first instructions and was asking for further guidance — which the Department had been working for two weeks to prepare, lest the President lose any time. In other words, less than a month after starting a "deliberate," "exploratory" process, Sisco and his colleagues were about to propose to Nixon that we put forward substantive comprehensive principles.

The argument of the State Department now was exactly the opposite of that by which the explorations had been sold to the President. Whereas a month earlier it had been argued that the decision to open Four-Power talks implied no commitment as to substance, now it was claimed that the informal explorations could not be sustained except with some specific scheme such as a set of principles. Unless we put forth our ideas, it was claimed, we would be stuck with less balanced positions presented by the other three powers. And we had to do so quickly. The State Department urged that the scheduled mid-March visit by Israeli Foreign Minister Abba Eban should be the deadline for Presidential decision. Eban was to be told that we planned to surface the document in the Four-Power forum and with the Soviets. The procedure I had devised in order to slow things down had been now fully exhausted in less than four weeks.

My views had not been changed by the events of the previous month. On March 5 I wrote to the President, summing up my concerns:

Everyone points out that we will be expected to deliver Israel in any negotiation. The Arabs assume — wrongly but irrevocably — that we can make Israel do what we wish. The French and British assume we could do more than we have. Perhaps only the Soviets — who know the limits of their own influence in Cairo and Damascus — realistically understand the limits of our influence in Jerusalem, but they find too much propaganda advantage in our support for Israel to admit the truth publicly.

Yet everyone also says that a settlement this year is unlikely, precisely because Israeli post-Eshkol and election-year politics will strictly limit Israel's ability to compromise.

The arguments commonly made for trying the unlikely are that (1) trying in itself would be a stabilizing factor in the Mid-East and (2) arranging a settlement this year is the only way to undercut the militant Palestinians. But a situation can be posed in which (1) trying too hard could make matters worse than not making an all-out effort now and (2) a settlement could actually strengthen the Palestinians and weaken the Arab governments that accepted it.

Our dilemma was that if we pressured Israel we would give encouragement to Arab radicals and Soviet clients, who would see it as a vindication of their intransigence and of their Soviet connection; for the same reason such pressure could also drive Israel to extreme actions, or at least to dig in and concede nothing. If on the other hand we failed to press Israel, the blame for the deadlock would fall on us. In the event that Israel agreed to compromise terms, the Palestinians would then probably block a settlement, with Syrian and Iraqi support; a moderate Arab government that agreed to the settlement would come under assault from the radicals. Hussein and even Nasser could become vulnerable. The result would be not merely a failed negotiation but increasing chaos and a new danger of war. In other words, given the influence and intransigence of the Soviets, the militance of Nasser, and the power of the fedayeen, I argued, the Middle East was not ready for a comprehensive American initiative.

The State Department came up with a paper of "general principles" which led precisely in that direction. It asserted that the object of negotiations was a binding contractual agreement, though not necessarily a peace treaty. Face-to-face talks were "not essential" in the early phase but would probably have to occur "at some point." The principles allowed minimal changes from preexisting borders, but such changes "should not reflect the weight of conquest." (The language about "the weight of conquest" was a State Department euphemism for insisting on near-total Israeli withdrawal; it had appeared earlier in a speech by President Johnson on September 10, 1968.) The clear assumption behind the principles was that, while the UN's Gunnar Jarring was to take the lead, with the Four-Power and Two-Power talks "backstopping" him, in the last analysis the effort could work only if the United States exercised its full leverage over Israel. An earlier version of State's general principles paper insisted on Israeli withdrawal to the prewar line with Egypt and Jordan, except for minor border rectifications only in the case of Jordan. On this provision, I did manage to soften State's principles in a session with Sisco, though an Israeli explosion was certain anyway.

On March 10, Nixon approved the State Department recommendation that the general principles paper be presented to Eban during his visit; then the paper would be discussed point by point between Sisco and Dobrynin and submitted to the Four-Power forum as the basis for consultations there. Nixon indicated to me that he shared my skepticism about what could come of it, but he said it would give State something to do, while we handled Vietnam, SALT, Europe, and China in the White House. (It is not to be excluded that he gave Rogers an opposite explanation.) Rogers proudly unveiled the new approach in public testimony to the Senate Foreign Relations Committee on March 27, telling the Senators that it was "a direct interest of the United States to exercise whatever influence it has, in whatever way would be useful and effective. . . ." Calling for "secure and recognized boundaries" and a "contractually binding," state of peace, Rogers added the crucial formula: "In our view rectifications from the preexisting lines should be confined to those required for mutual security and should not reflect the weight of conquest.''

Sisco's talks with Dobrynin stretched over nine sessions between March 18 and April 22 and followed predictable lines. The only topic discussed was the American general principles paper, with Dobrynin pressing Sisco to be more specific. Being more specific in this context meant spelling out a firmer position on issues such as final borders, which could only provoke an uproar in Israel by making it obvious that we had moved closer to the Soviet-Egyptian insistence on total withdrawal. We presented the general principles to the Four Powers on March 24 with the same result. Once again the American position was the focus of debate, with our allies seeking to nudge us into a greater effort. ''Greater effort'' had the same operational meaning as being ''more specific.'' We were being jockeyed from position to position, endlessly asked to modify our positions in order to rescue a negotiation that we ourselves had started presumably in order to ease pressures on us.

At the end of March, I sent an interim report about the Two-Power talks to the President:

> While we have so far avoided the worst dangers of an unprepared position, the whole burden of the talks could still fall on us — for producing all the substantive proposals and for bringing the Israelis around. . . . A good definition of an equitable settlement is one that will make both sides unhappy. If so, we must have Soviet help, and the Soviets must share the blame for pushing an unpalatable solution.

We had already separated ourselves from Israel's position; the Soviets had not reciprocated by differentiating their position in any way from the Arabs'. Before we took new steps, I reiterated, we needed to develop an agreed United States position on the terms of a final settlement, on the tactics of producing it, on how to relate the Two- and Four-Power talks, and on how to coordinate both of them with Jarring. Otherwise, the entire exercise would end in confusion.

All these procedural maneuverings would not spare us from the necessity to hear the view of the parties themselves — a process bound to bring us starkly into contact with reality once again.

Middle East Visitors

THE first to be heard from was the eloquent Abba Eban, who arrived in Washington in the middle of March for talks at the White House and State Department. I had met Eban socially in Israel when he was Minister of Education; this was my first professional contact with him. I have never encountered anyone who matched his command of the

English language. Sentences poured forth in mellifluous constructions complicated enough to test the listener's intelligence and simultaneously leave him transfixed by the speaker's virtuosity. The prose flowed evenly, without high points, rustling along inexorably like a clear mountain stream. To interrupt seemed almost unthinkable, for one knew that one would have to do so in an idiom that seemed barbaric by comparison. No American or British personality ever reminded me so acutely that English was for me, after all, an acquired language.

Eban's eloquence — unfortunately for those who had to negotiate with him — was allied to a first-class intelligence and fully professional grasp of diplomacy. He was always well prepared; he knew what he wanted. He practiced to the full his maxim that anything less than one hundred percent agreement with Israel's point of view demonstrated lack of objectivity. Even a most sympathetic position — say ninety percent — was deplored as "erosion," "weakening," or "loss of nerve." I was not always sure whether Eban's more matter-of-fact colleagues in Jerusalem appreciated his eloquence as much as I did; his Prime Minister seemed occasionally to bypass him in favor of more unorthodox channels. But I was hardly in a strong moral position to object to channels that bypassed a Foreign Minister.

Eban took vigorous exception to the very concept of Four-Power and Two-Power talks, on the ground that the deck would be stacked against Israel in either group. Eban stressed the one Israeli demand that he calculated was least likely to be met by the Arabs: the insistence on direct negotiations and Arab signatures on a joint peace treaty. A signed peace treaty was essential, he explained, because of the special reverence that the Arabs had always shown for written promises. I did not move him by suggesting that in my admittedly inadequate reading of Arab history I had found no greater or lesser adherence to signed treaties than in any other part of the world.

Eban was too shrewd to waste time debating history with me, however. He had a long meeting with Secretary Rogers on March 13 in the course of which he was shown the general principles paper, rejected it, and asked that it not be submitted. Eban objected strongly to our formulations regarding borders. It seemed to prejudge what Israel insisted could be negotiated only between the parties. Lest we grow too self-confident about any other portion of our principles paper, Eban rejected the notion of big-power guarantees as well. By "globalizing" every event in the Middle East, he said, we would turn the area into another Berlin. Egypt was not ready for the kind of peace Israel required; he was convinced the Soviet presence in Egypt made it increasingly unlikely that Nasser would be flexible. A negotiation with Jordan, less immoderate and free of Soviet influence, was more hopeful.

In the final analysis, Eban saw nothing intolerable in the status quo.

Israel much preferred that the United States avoid an active role and let
Jarring pursue his course. Israel was ostensibly willing to negotiate but
profoundly pessimistic about prospects for a comprehensive settlement.
This meant that there was no way of pursuing the course we had set for
ourselves without a massive clash with Israel.

The next visitors were Arab. They were no more tractable.

When former President Eisenhower died on March 28, Nasser designated Mahmoud Fawzi, his foreign affairs adviser, to attend the funeral
as Egypt's representative. Fawzi's presence to honor a leader of a
country with which Egypt had no diplomatic relations was a mark of
particular respect and courtesy. Fawzi was a fine gentleman, a professional with the ingratiating manner of the educated Egyptian and the
weary air of one who had seen much of man's foibles. Because I considered Egypt as a Soviet client state, I did not take advantage of establishing the closer human contact that the opportunity afforded. In the
light of my later experience I have regretted this.

Fawzi's visit came after nearly a decade and a half of eroding relations between Egypt and the United States. During the transition, Nasser
had sent a rambling letter to the President-elect listing his grievances
against the United States but hinting that in the right circumstances he
would be prepared to resume relations. This had also been Nasser's
theme when Governor Scranton visited Cairo in early December; Egypt
wanted to resume ties but would like to have a more favorable American
Middle East policy for a pretext. Throughout early 1969 Nasser repeated
the request for an American gesture to break the ice. Holding up the sale
of F-4 Phantom jets to Israel was one of his ideas; it was unlikely to
commend itself to Israel. Though it seemed to me that Nasser overrated
the boon he would confer on us by resuming diplomatic relations, I
wrote Nixon in March that we had already taken several of the steps
Nasser had suggested (if for different reasons). We had conducted an
active diplomacy; we had put forward general principles; Rogers had
stated a forthcoming position on frontiers before the Senate Foreign
Relations Committee. The basis for a possible rapprochement between
Washington and Cairo seemed to exist.

Against this backdrop I had two meetings with Fawzi preparatory to
his call on Nixon on April 11. But it soon transpired that Fawzi had no
authority to resume diplomatic relations. He would report our reaction
to Cairo; relations could be resumed only if there was some concrete advance; he did not spell out what he meant by that phrase. Egypt was
eager to make progress partly because the Soviets were pressing it in the
direction of peace, he said. They seemed to understand that they would
not be able to help their Arab friends any other way; in a stalemate Soviet standing in the Arab world was bound to deteriorate.

Fawzi's last point was, of course, precisely the strategic opportunity I

With President-elect Nixon at the press conference announcing my appointment as national security adviser, Pierre Hotel, December 2, 1968 (behind me, Nixon foreign policy aide Richard V. Allen).

At my desk in my White House basement office, May 1969.

With Colonel Alexander Haig, my military assistant, and Lawrence S. Eagleburger, my executive assistant, May 1969.

With my staff, as the President signs the Foreig

Policy Report to the Congress, February 25, 1971.

LEFT, ABOVE: *A pleasant moment with Secretary of State William Rogers in his State Department office, early 1969.*

LEFT, BELOW: *On the steps to Nixon's hideaway office in the Executive Office Building with Nixon, Secretary of Defense Melvin Laird, and (at right) Press Secretary Ronald Ziegler.*

ABOVE: *Before the first National Security Council meeting, January 21, 1969, looking for our seats. From left: General Earle G. Wheeler, Chairman, Joint Chiefs of Staff; Richard Helms, Director, CIA; HAK; Secretary of State Rogers; Vice President Spiro Agnew (back to camera); Defense Secretary Laird (partly hidden); Secretary of the Treasury David M. Kennedy.*

My parents, Louis and Paula Kissinger.

*My children, David and Elizabeth, meet former President and
Mrs. Lyndon Johnson.*

*Governor Nelson Rockefeller and his aide Jim Cannon visit Nixon at
San Clemente, September 3, 1969.*

*With Governor Rockefeller at a National Press Club luncheon, October 31, 1972.
From left: HAK, Happy Rockefeller, Jim Cannon, Governor Rockefeller.*

En route to the Midway meeting on Air Force One, *June 1969. Clockwise from left: the President, Rogers, Laird, General Earle Wheeler (Chairman, Joint Chiefs of Staff), General Creighton Abrams (Vietnam commander), Admiral John McCain (Pacific commander), HAK, Henry Cabot Lodge (Ambassador Paris talks), Ellsworth Bunker (Ambassador to Republic of Vietnam)*

Nixon and President Nguyen Van Thieu at Midway, June 8, 1969.

Meeting with Thieu in Saigon, July 30, 1969. Clockwise from left: Nixon, Thieu, aide Nguyen Phu Duc, HAK, Ellsworth Bunker.

ABOVE: *National Security Council meeting on Vietnam, September 12,
1969. Clockwise from left: HAK, Attorney General John Mitchell, Vice
President Spiro Agnew, Admiral McCain, General Abrams, CIA Director
Richard Helms, Ambassador Philip Habib, Ambassador Bunker, Rogers,
Nixon, Laird, General Wheeler*

RIGHT: *West German Chancellor Kurt Kiesinger visits the White House,
April 1, 1969, on the occasion of President Eisenhower's funeral*

LEFT: *With British Prime Minister Harold Wilson at Mildenhall RAF base, England, August 3, 1969.*

LEFT, BELOW: *Stopping off at Chequers to dine with British Prime Minister Edward Heath, October 3, 1970. (From left, on the ground: Rogers, Nixon, Heath, US Chief of Protocol Emil Mosbacher).*

RIGHT: *With West German Chancellor Willy Brandt and Brandt's aide Egon Bahr (center), taken at Munich, September 9, 1972.*

RIGHT, BELOW: *With former Japanese Prime Minister Eisaku Sato in Tokyo, after his retirement (February 1973).*

ABOVE: *King Hussein of Jordan visits the White House, April 8, 1969.*
BELOW: *Dean Brown, our new Ambassador to Jordan, in San Clemente before his departure for Amman (and the Jordan crisis), September 4, 1970.*

perceived for the United States. If the Soviet position in Egypt was bound to deteriorate the longer a settlement was delayed, we had no incentive whatever to accept the first Soviet or Egyptian offer, especially as long as the Soviet Union maintained large forces in Egypt and Egyptian diplomacy took its lead from Moscow. The terms offered by Fawzi were not likely to inspire optimism in any event. Egypt refused to sign a joint document with Israel; its obligations would run only to the Security Council (where the Soviet Union had a veto); it would not establish diplomatic relations with Israel; UN peacekeeping forces could be removed upon six months' notice. These positions would never suffice to bring about the full Israeli withdrawal Egypt demanded.

Fawzi urbanely assured Nixon on April 11 that Egypt was eager to reduce its military expenditures and devote its resources to domestic construction. He did not ask the United States to press Israel to do things against its interests; he did request even-handed treatment for Egypt. As for resuming relations, the time was not yet ripe, he said.

To this day I have not understood Nasser's motives. For months he had conveyed urgent signals pointing in the direction of resumption of relations. He sent Fawzi, known as a conciliator, to Washington. Fawzi conducted himself capably, but on that crucial issue his instructions, to his obvious discomfiture, did not permit him to budge. It was never clear how Nasser thought Nixon could brave domestic opposition, Israeli refusals, and Soviet aloofness to support the maximum goals of a country that refused diplomatic relations with us and whose foreign policy remained fundamentally unfriendly. Nasser, in effect, sought to deal with us by blackmail but had nothing to threaten us with. When later in the year the Administration put forward precise plans on both the Egyptian and Jordanian borders along lines previously declared acceptable by Nasser, he refused either to accept them or to resume relations. He gloried in his radicalism, which he thought essential to his Pan-Arab ambitions, and for this he must have felt compelled to remain in perpetual confrontation with us in the Middle East and the Third World, even at the cost of jeopardizing our willingness to move in his direction.

I have no doubt that the United States would have pursued the peace process more energetically early in the Nixon Administration had Nasser been more flexible. The principal obstacles to a more active American role were Nasser's anti-American foreign policy and the predominant role of the Soviet Union in Cairo. Fawzi was not in a position to reassure us that these did not represent fixed principles of Egyptian policy. Instead, with all his charm, Fawzi on Nasser's instructions calmly insisted on having everything for nothing: US support against Israel, Soviet support against the United States, and leadership of the radical movements throughout the Third World. Foreign policy does not work that way. Nasser could not make the choice between his rhetorical ambitions and his intuition of the limits of Egypt's ability to achieve those ambitions. He died without ever making the choice. Only his great successor, Anwar Sadat, would put the pieces together.

The failure of the Fawzi mission affected another Arab visitor, the doughty King Hussein of Jordan, who had never bargained about his friendship with the United States. Hussein was one of the most attractive political leaders I have met. The little King — as he was affectionately called by our officials — stoutly defended the Arab cause even when his Arab brethren failed to reciprocate his loyalty. Once I knew him reasonably well I could measure his irritation at what he considered insensitivity or bureaucratic pedantry by the heightening of his legendary courtesy; his use of the honorific "sir" would multiply while he assumed a glacial demeanor. (He, an hereditary monarch, called me "sir" even when I was a mere Presidential Assistant.)

He was as gallant as he was polite. Once he piloted my wife Nancy and me in his helicopter on a hair-raising ride at treetop level. To get him to fly higher, Nancy said innocently that she did not know helicopters could fly so low. The King assured her that they could fly lower still, making the rest of the trip almost on the deck. Had he exploited the opportunity he could have obtained my agreement to any political demand by promising to fly higher.

Hussein sought with dignity and courage to reconcile the roles of Arab nationalist and America's friend. A pro-Western monarch in the vortex of Arab radicalism, he maintained his independence as well as the respect of rulers in the region who were less than enchanted by the dynastic principle. Though substantially dependent on American aid he put up with our cumbersome and sometimes humiliating procedures, never losing his composure or patience but also never descending to the role of supplicant. He was the first Arab leader prepared to talk of making peace with Israel, maintaining an intermittent if fruitless contact with Jerusalem. It was a misfortune that the strength of Hussein's bargaining position did not match his moderation and that his available options were not equal to his goodwill. He thus had the capacity neither for independent action nor for blackmail, which are the stuff of Middle Eastern politics. In 1969, the fedayeen of the Palestine Liberation Organization formed a state within his state but did not deflect him from his moderate course; months later (as we shall see in Chapter XV) he courageously and decisively confronted their challenge to his authority.

In his meeting with Nixon on April 8, Hussein, speaking also on behalf of Nasser, stressed that both leaders were committed to Security Council Resolution 242 and were prepared to sign any document with Israel *except* a peace treaty. Hussein recognized the need for some minor border rectifications. If Israel would cede Gaza to Jordanian rule, the rectifications on the West Bank could be fairly substantial. (It seems unfortunate, in retrospect, that there was not more exploration of a separate Jordan-Israel arrangement involving a swap of Gaza for West Bank territories.) Hussein asserted that both Nasser and he were willing to consider demilitarized zones and free access through the Suez Canal as well as the Strait of Tiran. The pressure of Arab extremists was "eager" to resume ties with the United States. But the conciliatory impact of these remarks was largely vitiated by Fawzi's talks with me and his disappointing meeting with Nixon three days later, as already described.

Diplomacy: Ever-New Proposals

THE deadlock between the Middle East parties inevitably reflected itself in the Four- and the Two-Power talks. The solution that seemed obvious to our interlocutors in those talks was to throw us into the fray to impose a peace. On April 14 Dobrynin told me that the Two-Power exercise needed more concrete propositions, particularly on frontiers. What the Soviets and Arabs wanted was to get us to make specific the implication of our vague formulations about "minor rectifications" and the "weight of conquest," that is, an explicit insistence that Israeli withdrawal be *total*. Assuring me of Soviet eagerness to help promote a settlement, Dobrynin suggested we try a joint US–Soviet proposal; if the United States came up with more specific positions on each of the principles, the Soviets would then sell them to the Arabs. Since Dobrynin in effect was asking us to accept the Arab program, it was not clear what he proposed to "sell" to them. To me it seemed that he was looking to obtain credit in the Arab world for what would amount to a peace imposed by us on Israel. We were being pressed in the same direction in the Four-Power forum as well. De Gaulle, who had honored President Eisenhower by attending the memorial services himself, had told Nixon on March 31 that the Four should try to agree on common terms for a settlement. Yet we knew from our consultations in New York that each of the participants had his own idea of what those terms should be — and that none was acceptable to Israel. In each forum we were being asked to impose a peace, for which we needed no forum. This was precisely the outcome I had predicted.

At home, a majority of both Houses of Congress rallied to support Israel's position in a public declaration: direct negotiations, a contractual peace, and no pressure on Israel to withdraw prematurely. As in Vietnam, we would wind up negotiating with ourselves.

Not surprisingly, the more inconclusive the negotiations in March and April 1969, the more intense was the military confrontation on the ground. As violence spiraled, U Thant warned on April 22 that a "virtual state of active war" existed along the Suez Canal; a Cairo spokesman declared the 1967 cease-fire on that front void. Clashes mounted as Israel retaliated against fedayeen attacks from Jordan; Lebanon declared a state of emergency in the futile attempt to halt fedayeen raids into Israel from its territory. What came to be called the "war of attrition" was proceeding in earnest.

In other words, after two months of a new US initiative, we were more or less back at the starting point. We had proved again what we already knew: The parties had vastly different views about the meaning of secure and recognized frontiers, the timing and extent of withdrawals, the nature of recognition, and indeed the process of negotiation.

Another policy review was clearly necessary.

What had started in February as an exploration to determine the *feasibility* of negotiations had by May evolved into the proposition that the United States had an obligation to save the negotiations by producing new and increasingly specific proposals. But there was no getting around the fact that each side's propositions were totally unacceptable to the other. The parties could not be maneuvered by artful procedures into abandoning positions they had held and fought for in three wars over twenty years. The yawning gulf between them could be bridged only by formulations so ambiguous that they would simply repeat the evasions of Security Council Resolution 242.

In these circumstances, the vital question for us was not what general proposals we would make but whether we were prepared to insist — by pressure if necessary — that our proposals be carried out. Until we had answered this question — which meant, as the proposals were framed, pressure on Israel — the negotiation was bound to stalemate one way or another. If we stuck to our vague positions, the Four- and Two-Power talks would collapse, with the blame falling on the United States. If we were specific we would be in a major brawl with Israel without gaining the friendship of the Arabs. On the contrary, the Soviet Union and its clients would be the major beneficiaries. And if we shied away from pressing Israel, for either domestic or foreign policy reasons, the negotiation would again grind to a halt. To me, this was the inevitable consequence of attempting a comprehensive settlement when the parties' positions were so far apart, the Soviets supported the Arab position, and we had not yet maneuvered to a mediator's role.

Rogers argued that putting forth a detailed plan would improve our position even if it were rejected; there was, according to him, simply no way of knowing whether a settlement was possible without testing Egyptian, Soviet, and Israeli views. Therefore, the State Department now submitted for Presidential approval the draft of a detailed peace settlement between Egypt and Israel, based on the pre–June 5, 1967, lines. A draft of a Jordan-Israel peace agreement would follow shortly.

I expressed strong reservations to the President. I predicted that the scheme would probably lead to a blowup with both sides. The borders were certain to be unacceptable to Israel, and the Arabs, in Nasser's current frame of mind, were not ready to make the necessary commitment to peace. It would not improve our relations with the Arabs; it would strengthen the position of the Soviets; the Soviets and their clients would first get credit for having pushed us this far and then accuse us of not going far enough and not delivering Israel on what we had promised.

These issues were debated before the President at an NSC meeting on the morning of April 25. The President, torn between the warnings in my memoranda and the pressures of his bureaucracy, avoided a decision. Instead, he asked me afterward to work with Sisco on modifying the State proposal to mitigate the dangers I had foreseen. The paper, as revised, was approved by the President on May 5. The changes were mostly cosmetic. It was known that the President was not prepared flatly to overrule his Secretary of State on the Middle East; hence, my influence was weak. In the new version the United States would not present an overall plan for an Egyptian-Israeli settlement all at once; rather, its provisions would be put forward piecemeal in successive talks between Sisco and Dobrynin. Second, the United States would not commit itself initially to push for full Israeli withdrawal from the Sinai; rather, the formulation on boundaries would be left ambiguous, with withdrawal to the prewar line "not necessarily excluded." These changes could only delay — they could not arrest — the State Department steamroller; once the President had authorized the ultimate position it was certain to be put forward one way or the other.

This was all the more true because Joe Sisco did not believe in leisurely negotiations. As soon as the President had approved the revised strategy, he began his second round of talks with Dobrynin. He did not waste time; he started on May 6 and finished by June 9. Sisco briskly doled out the United States positions on the key issues. It soon became apparent that the Soviets were not about to accept them and would inevitably ask for more. For example, we insisted on direct Arab-Israeli negotiations at some stage. Dobrynin wanted to downplay this. On borders, we maintained that "the former international boundary between Egypt and the mandated territory of Palestine is not necessarily excluded." The Soviet Union demanded total withdrawal to the prewar lines without change. We favored demilitarization of the entire Sinai; the Soviets did not. We insisted on free navigation through international waterways such as the Strait of Tiran and the Suez Canal while the Soviets hedged their position by references to the Constantinople Convention of 1888 whose import was ambiguous when applied to current circumstances. There were also differences over the refugee issue. On June 11, Dobrynin complained to me about the new deadlock; he lamented

Sisco's lack of precision, particularly his "abstract" formulation on borders, as Dobrynin called it (which at least demonstrated to me that Joe was staying within instructions).

All this time, Israel made clear in its inimitable way that its unhappiness with the new American initiative was mounting, even as Dobrynin was attacking our formulas from the Arab side. On May 13 Ambassador Rabin inquired into the purpose of this new US–Soviet dialogue and expressed special concern that we might yield on the border issue. He criticized other provisions as well. Israel still preferred direct negotiations with the Arabs. Prime Minister Golda Meir sent an impassioned letter to President Nixon reiterating her concern that the United States was prejudicing the negotiations by predetermining the outcome on the main issues. To prevent the situation from getting out of hand, Rabin suggested that Mrs. Meir be invited to Washington at an early date. We were not ready for an immediate encounter. I secured an invitation from the President for Mrs. Meir to visit in the fall.

New fighting punctuated the diplomatic sparring. In May, June, and July, the Middle East exploded daily with fedayeen raids from Jordan and aerial combat over the Egyptian and Syrian fronts; Mrs. Meir promised that Israeli reprisals would be swift and severe, repaying "sevenfold" the Arab attacks on Israel. In May, Nasser told *Time* magazine that a settlement was possible if Israel agreed to total withdrawal and to giving Palestinians the choice of return — both of which Israel had already rejected. In the same interview he also said that he accepted the "reality" of Israel, but he demonstrated his ambivalence by ordering that sentence omitted from the Cairo media account of his interview. Then, in a major speech on July 23, Nasser seemed to reverse himself again; he now proclaimed that Egypt was passing into the "stage of liberation" in its war with Israel, and condemned the United States and Britain for supporting Israel. Meanwhile, on June 13 Soviet Foreign Minister Gromyko ended a Cairo visit with a communiqué that pledged full Soviet support for Egypt's struggle to "liquidate the consequences of aggression."

On June 17, the Soviet Union finally gave us a counterproposal. The Soviet reply had some positive elements: it talked of working for a binding agreement and of recognition of Israel. But it showed little flexibility on the major issues that concerned us most: Direct negotiations were not mentioned; final borders must rigidly follow the 1967 lines; freedom of navigation was left vague; the definition of final peace omitted any obligation to control the guerrillas; and it refused to embrace the proposition that Israel should have some control over which Palestinians returned to Israel.

Rogers, nevertheless, decided that the Soviet reply showed enough "forward movement" to warrant another American proposal. Since

Dobrynin had returned home for consultations, Rogers proposed on June 30 that Joe Sisco travel to Moscow to present some new ideas. Specifically, Rogers wanted Sisco to be authorized in Moscow, at his own discretion as a fallback position, to play our "trump card" — an explicit commitment to the prewar frontiers — if the Soviets were forthcoming on the issues of peace, security, and direct negotiations.

This I thought premature, to put it kindly. In my view, the Soviet reply reflected no significant concession. Basically, it sought to extract the total Arab program from us by subtly evasive and substantially unyielding formulas. It showed no willingness to match our leverage on Israel with similar pressure on the Arabs. It seemed designed for the overriding purpose of demonstrating the Soviet Union's indispensability to its Arab clients. If we went along, a blowup with Israel was inevitable. Nevertheless, I was not in a position to stop Rogers's initiative. I recommended to the President that he go along with the Sisco trip so long as we offered no new concession on borders. I advised the President: "I would not at this stage give him authority to commit us in any way to the fallback language. That puts us too far ahead of Israel and gives away our position without any return. I think the Russians — not we — should be setting the bait." My proposed strategy was to insist that the Soviet Union pay a price with its Arab friends commensurate to what we were expected to pay with Israel. This would both ensure a fairer negotiation and put some strains on the Soviet-Egyptian relationship. Nixon agreed; Sisco was authorized to go to Moscow but not to carry with him any new position on borders.

Sisco visited Moscow from July 14 to 17. His discussions were a replay of the exchanges of the previous two months. Even he returned skeptical about Soviet flexibility and intentions. He reported to the President that he found no evidence that the Soviets were prepared to press Nasser on the key issues of peace and direct negotiations. They viewed Nasser as their primary instrument in the Middle East; they were unwilling to risk either his political position or their influence with him by urging him to make peace on terms other than his own. Instead of pressing Nasser, their strategy seemed to be to sit tight and erode our position to a point where we were prepared to impose their terms on Israel. Sisco concluded, correctly in my view, that we, too, should sit tight.

The Sisco mission stilled the impulse for initiatives for exactly two months. Although for the moment the White House and State Department were in rare accord on doing nothing, diplomatic activity could be expected to resume in the fall. The arrival of foreign dignitaries, including the parties to the Middle East dispute, for the United Nations General Assembly would generate the incentive as well as the opportunity to try again.

Yet Another Initiative

THIS was particularly true since in August, fighting flared up again on all fronts, especially dangerously along the Suez Canal. It was not calmed by the burning of the Al Aqsa Mosque in Jerusalem by a deranged Australian. The Arabs predictably blamed Israel; both Nasser and King Faisal of Saudi Arabia called for a holy war to liberate Jerusalem. Terrorists hijacked a TWA jetliner to Damascus where Israeli passengers were held for several weeks. Israel's Labour Party, gearing up for the fall elections, proclaimed its intention of keeping parts of the occupied territories whatever the peace terms.

This grim scene called for another policy review. It took the usual form of State's pressing for an initiative and my urging the prior elaboration of a precise strategy. Gromyko was coming to the UN General Assembly; Rogers and our UN Ambassador Charles Yost asked Nixon for permission to present the American endorsement of the 1967 frontiers, conditional on satisfactory security arrangements. Sisco took a more cautious position.

These pressures illustrate what I take to be a basic maxim of US foreign policymaking. Once a fallback position exists — however hedged with qualifications — it will be put forward one way or the other, first by private comments and press leaks and ultimately as a formal position. A President who authorizes a fallback position in the expectation that he may never face its consequences is bound to be disappointed. The very existence of a fallback erodes the tenacity with which the approved position is maintained. And the process is accelerated if bureaucratic prerogatives and individual egos are committed to the fallback position and its expectations of success.

Therefore the by now familiar debate took place yet again, this time at an NSC meeting on September 11. The State Department representatives argued that without our putting forward the fallback position, progress was impossible (an argument which if pushed far enough would eventually lead us squarely to the Soviet position on every issue). I questioned the wisdom of a proposal that would certainly be rejected by Israel and that might not even be accepted by Egypt, hedged as it was by conditions of peace already rebuffed. In the next round, having committed ourselves to this course, we would be inevitably pressured to soften our position even further and then to impose it on Israel.

We were back to the strategic controversy with which we had started in February. The advocates of further concessions argued that time was working against us; the longer the deadlock lasted, the more our position in the Arab world would deteriorate. I stressed that the opposite was true. A continuing deadlock was in our interest; it would persuade Egypt to face the reality that Soviet tutelage and a radical foreign policy were obstacles to progress and that only the United States could bring about a settlement; it would demonstrate Soviet impotence and in time might impel a fundamental reconstruction of Arab, and especially of Egyptian, foreign policies. Rogers saw in the Two-Power talks a device by which the Soviet Union would help us out of our Middle East predicament. I thought it was the Soviets that faced a predicament, since they had no means of achieving their objectives except by our cooperation or through a war their clients stood to lose. If we stayed calm, they would sooner or later have to pay a price for our help, either in the Middle East or elsewhere. Rogers was concerned that the United States might be isolated in the Four-Power talks; my view was that this was inherent in the forum and could not be avoided by clever formulas.

Before the September 11 NSC meeting the President had brought John Mitchell into the discussions to advise him on the domestic politics of the choices before him. Mitchell, in spite of his gruff, pipe-smoking exterior and his later fate, was a man of discretion and shrewdness. Nixon valued his political judgment; he played the detached observer and protector of the President's interests, and he proved his insight on many occasions. Now Mitchell warned Nixon of the domestic buzz saw he was facing — the inevitable brawl with Israel, with no hope of achieving peace.

Nixon was thus well prepared for the NSC meeting and probed Rogers and Sisco sharply. "Do you fellows ever talk to the Israelis?" he asked. How did they think Israel was going to react to our accepting the 1967 borders? Rogers and Sisco assured him that the Israelis would be happy with the total package since it would include elements of their own definition of peace. I questioned this, pointing out that if I was right and we were not prepared to pressure Israel, we would lose with the Arabs by adding the charge of impotence to that of ill will. The President decided to keep our negotiations "exploratory" until Mrs. Meir's visit; in the meantime he ordered a study of the settlement terms for Jordan and Syria as well as Egypt. The NSC process might not be taken seriously as a device to produce options; it had a great advantage in providing an excuse for delaying decisions.

Mitchell told me afterward that the President had no preconceived notions on how to proceed. Nixon told me a few weeks later that he agreed with me that it would be best to delay specific proposals to see what tensions might develop between the Soviets and the Egyptians: "The summit and trade they [Moscow] can have but I'll be damned if they can get the Middle East." Rogers and Sisco were therefore instructed to say nothing new in their talks with Gromyko.

Golda Meir

GOLDA MEIR came to Washington on September 25 on her first trip to the United States as Israeli Prime Minister. She was an original. Her childhood in the Russia of pogroms and her youth as a pioneer in the harshness of Palestine had taught her that only the wary are given the opportunity to survive and only those who fight succeed in that effort. Her craggy face bore witness to the destiny of a people that had come to know too well the potentialities of man's inhumanity. Her watchful eyes made clear that she did not propose that those she led should suffer the same fate without a struggle. Yet she yearned to see her people realize their dream of peace; her occasionally sarcastic exterior never obscured a compassion that felt the death of every Israeli soldier as the loss of a member of her family. She was a founder of her country. Every inch of land for which Israel had fought was to her a token of her people's survival; it would be stubbornly defended against enemies; it would be given up only for a tangible guarantee of security. She had a penetrating mind, leavened by earthiness and a mischievous sense of humor. She was not taken in by elevated rhetoric, or particularly interested in the finer points of negotiating tactics. She cut to the heart of the matter. She answered pomposity with irony and dominated conversations by her personality and shrewd psychology. To me she acted as a benevolent aunt toward an especially favored nephew, so that even to admit the possibility of disagreement was a challenge to family hierarchy producing emotional outrage. It was usually calculated. My wife is fond of saying that some of the most dramatic theatrical performances she witnessed were between Golda Meir and me when we disagreed. Mrs. Meir treated Secretary Rogers as if the reports of his views could not possibly be true; she was certain that once he had a chance to explain himself the misunderstandings caused by the inevitable inadequacy of reporting telegrams would vanish; she then promised forgiveness. As for Nixon, Mrs. Meir hailed him as an old friend of the Jewish people, which was startling news to those of us more familiar with Nixon's ambivalences on that score. But it gave him a reputation to uphold. And in the event he did much for Israel if not out of affection then out of his characteristically unsentimental calculation of the national interest.

Her themes with Nixon were simple. The United States should not let Nasser avoid the responsibility for making peace by getting others to settle the terms; the Soviet Union had to know that the United States would not permit Israel to be destroyed; the Arabs had to understand that Israel was not weak. Only this would bring peace.

Nixon had not reached eminence, however, by being taken in by generalities. While he was restless with State Department steamroller tactics, he did not believe for a moment that peace would come automatically if we only held firm. He was not yet ready to press Israel, largely for domestic reasons, and he had no difficulty giving Golda Meir assurances of assistance against a Soviet attack. And he favored a strong Israel because he did not want the United States to have to fight Israel's battles — which was exactly Mrs. Meir's view as well. Nixon thought that Nasser would become more moderate only if faced by overwhelming power.

But he still had before him the policy recommendations of his Secretary of State; he could therefore scarcely promise that the United States would never advance new peace terms. He stalled, giving the impression that he was more sympathetic to Israeli concerns than his bureaucracy — which was true — and coming up with the formula that he would trade "hardware for software." This meant that he would be responsive to Israeli requests for armaments if Israel gave us some latitude in negotiations, which he strongly implied he would ensure would not amount to much.

It would be too much to claim that Mrs. Meir agreed; more accurate to say she acquiesced in a formulation whose meaning only the future would reveal. She reserved her right to do battle then, if necessary, and she would choose as her adversary someone lower in the hierarchy than the President. As it turned out she had occasion to do battle soon enough. The "hardware for software" formula the President had proposed was leaked to the press — in a way which implied that arms aid would thereafter be conditional on Israeli flexibility in negotiations. Mrs. Meir's outraged protests were targeted (probably correctly) on the State Department (which had been given a summary of the Presidential conversation with Mrs. Meir).

A serious bureaucratic battle was looming. On September 27 Dobrynin called on me with the perennial Soviet suggestion of a joint US–Soviet position, this time to provide guidelines for Jarring, the UN Special Representative. I rejected the overture with the argument that as long as the Soviets were so unhelpful on Vietnam, joint action elsewhere would be "difficult." I had no intention to act jointly with the Soviet Union when the Soviets clearly expected to get a free ride on our exertions. But my rebuff merely sent Dobrynin back into other channels. He continued intensive talks with Sisco in September and October. Picking up threads of the Moscow visit, Sisco and Dobrynin mulled over the various provisions of a possible Egyptian-Israeli settlement. By October 14, Sisco was reporting that there was enough progress on procedures (such as holding indirect talks, as Ralph Bunche had conducted twenty years earlier on the isle of Rhodes) to warrant moving ahead to the issue of boundaries the following week.

I had my doubts about this "progress." I thought the Soviets were using the Middle East, like SALT, to make Nixon think twice about his threatened November 1 "deadline" over Vietnam (see Chapter VIII). My concerns were not eased by the meeting between Dobrynin and the President on October 20. Dobrynin read from an aide-mémoire, putting all the blame for the Middle East impasse squarely on Washington. Nixon replied sharply, pointing out that the Soviets had been totally inflexible on Israeli withdrawal without indicating any sacrifice they would ask from Egypt; the Soviet client had lost the war, had lost the territory, and was in no position to be making demands.

While Nixon was facing down Dobrynin, Sisco was angling for authority to tell Dobrynin about our fallback position accepting the 1967 frontier linked to security guarantees. He wanted to move ahead at a meeting scheduled for October 28. I discussed this with the President, who agreed there should be no American initiatives of any kind before the November 1 Vietnam deadline. Nixon had, in fact, given a flat order that there be no further contacts at all with the Soviets until he had given his major November 3 speech on Vietnam. Sisco protested, because Rogers had already promised Gromyko that Sisco and Dobrynin would meet on October 28. (This was hardly a conclusive argument, since Sisco could always have stalled.) But Nixon was so absorbed with Vietnam, preparing his November 3 speech and dealing with the Moratorium, that he had even less stomach than usual for a fight with his Secretary of State. He yielded reluctantly. Characteristically, he sought to hedge his bets by asking John Mitchell and Leonard Garment — counselor to the President and adviser on Jewish affairs — to let Jewish community leaders know his doubts about State's diplomacy. Nixon implied strongly to them that he would see to it that nothing came of the very initiatives he was authorizing.

We were in the anomalous position of Nixon's leaning toward my strategy but going along with Rogers's tactics. The reasons for his relative deference to Rogers on Middle East policy are those I mentioned at the beginning of this chapter. Nixon understood well enough that the diplomacy would go nowhere; whenever it threatened a blowup he would usually follow my advice to abort it. And the final irony was that the resulting policy of fits and starts, of tantalizing initiatives later aborted, was the functional equivalent of what I wanted to achieve by design: to put us into the pivotal position in the negotiations and to demonstrate Soviet inability to produce progress.

Until this demonstration had been made, there was no gain for the United States in pursuing an active policy. Occasionally Nixon was tempted to impose a settlement. On one of my memoranda in late 1969, informing him of King Hussein's pessimism about peace prospects in the face of Israel's tough stand, Nixon wrote in longhand: "I am beginning to think we have to consider taking strong steps unilaterally to save Israel from her own destruction.'' But on further consideration he always stopped short, because in 1969 the beneficiaries of such a course would have been the Soviet Union and Soviet clients vociferously hostile to us.

On October 28 Sisco at last presented to Dobrynin the fallback position that State had been itching to put forward — committing the United States to the 1967 international boundary between Israel and Egypt. It included provisions on peace and security arrangements that State, without definite proof, gambled would be attractive enough to persuade Israel to withdraw and to convince the Soviets to press Egypt. Both hopes were to be disappointed.

Contrary to State's prediction, our offer evoked only a noncommittal Soviet response, and contrary to what Nasser had led us to believe earlier, accepting the prewar frontiers did not improve our relations with him. Instead, he made a fiery speech to his National Assembly on November 6 declaring that he would reclaim the occupied territories by ''fire and blood'' instead of political ''half-solutions,'' and accusing the United States of military involvement on Israel's behalf. So extreme was this Nasser outburst that, in a rare move, the State Department issued a rebuttal calling Nasser's position a ''setback'' to peace. Not long afterward Egyptian Foreign Minister Mahmoud Riad termed our peace plan (including its new line on borders) ''even worse'' than previous proposals. Even more predictable was the Israeli attitude. The concessions on the definition of peace, which were supposed to gain Israel's acquiescence, were brushed aside. Israel protested in the strongest diplomatic terms against our putting forward specific formulations on frontiers. American supporters of Israel expressed alarm. And the fighting escalated yet again, especially along the Suez Canal. A coup in Libya in September 1969, overthrowing the monarchy and establishing Qaddafi as ruler, aroused apprehension about the political future of the area (and cost us our basing privileges there). Lebanon was disintegrating; we held emergency meetings to review contingency plans should open civil war break out. Among our friends, moderate leaders in the Middle East — King Hussein, King Hassan of Morocco, Prince Fahd of Saudi Arabia, the Shah of Iran, and the Lebanese — told us either directly or through envoys of their despair at the growing radicalization of the region.

The Rogers Plan

BUT like a gambler on a losing streak, the advocates of an active American role wanted only to increase the stake. Ignoring the clearly stated positions of the two sides, they insisted that a compromise was still possible along our chosen route; they continued to believe that

Israeli flexibility on borders could be purchased by improving the content of the provisions on peace. In late November, therefore, the State Department formally recommended to the President that the Four-Power talks be resumed. It was proposed that we submit a Jordanian companion paper to our Egyptian plan embodying substantially the same principles. We could do no less for a friend than an adversary, it was said, and in any event President Johnson had in effect promised Jordan the 1967 borders with minor rectifications as a bait for Jordanian acceptance of Resolution 242. It was argued that this would give us a balanced position in the eyes of the world and might provide a starting point for later negotiations even if they failed now. What the "world" was to whose eyes we were appealing was not spelled out, nor the long-term benefit to be derived from a proposal almost certain to get nowhere. No one explained why this paper should achieve a happier fate than the Egyptian document or what was the purpose of accumulating rejections.

In transmitting this State proposal to the President I repeated yet again my by now tiresome refrain that all of these exercises were doomed to futility. No scheme was conceivable that could bridge the gap between the two sides: "It cannot produce a solution without massive pressure on Israel. It is more than likely going to wind up antagonizing both sides. It may produce a war." I feared that Israel in frustration might strike preemptively, or that the Arab countries would shift to hostility when we failed to impose our proposals. Every American initiative that failed played into the hands of the Soviets and strengthened the radicals.

Nixon scheduled an NSC meeting for December 10 to consider our course. In the meantime no further proposals were to be put forward. Secretary Rogers, however, had scheduled a comprehensive public statement of our Middle East policy for a speech on December 9. It was an odd choice of date, since the speech would be given the day *before* an NSC meeting that was supposed to decide on its subject matter. Rogers assured the President that he meant to break no new ground. Rogers and Sisco successfully argued that the speech would not prejudice any Presidential decisions that would come up at the December 10 NSC meeting. (It was a power play to circumvent the NSC system that would never have worked on another issue or at a later time.)

So Rogers spoke on the evening of December 9, 1969, to the Galaxy Conference on Adult Education, an undoubtedly distinguished group whose compelling requirement for a high-level pronouncement on the Middle East continues to escape me. The address became famous as the "Rogers Plan." Rogers stressed that our policy was balanced and that both sides had to make concessions. And he set forth the positions that Sisco and Yost had been presenting in the Two- and Four-Power forums. Rogers insisted that the conditions and obligations of peace had to be defined in specific terms on such issues as free navigation and sovereignty; reliable security arrangements had to be worked out by the parties with Ambassador Jarring's help. But his formulation of the territorial issue was what captured all the attention:

We believe that while recognized political boundaries must be established and agreed upon by the parties, any changes in the pre-existing lines should not reflect the weight of conquest and should be confined to insubstantial alterations required for mutual security. We do not support expansionism. We believe troops must be withdrawn as the resolution provides. We support Israel's security and the security of the Arab states as well.

Applying these principles to an Egyptian-Israeli agreement, Rogers went on to propose the withdrawal of Israeli armed forces to the international border between Israel and Egypt.

Within hours everyone was shooting at the speech. Precisely because the speech contained elements already rejected by both sides, it was bound to be attacked from all directions. The Arab press, mainly Egyptian, treated the speech as an American trick to pretend to Arabs that the United States was impartial, as well as to undermine Soviet-Egyptian relations. The Soviets first issued a fairly conciliatory statement saying the Rogers speech was long "overdue"; the real question was whether the United States would press Israel to withdraw. Later, *Pravda* fell into line with Egyptian reactions and denounced it as an American attempt to mask its partiality toward Israel. The day after the speech, the Israeli Cabinet rejected all outside efforts to prescribe boundaries; Prime Minister Meir said that Rogers was "moralizing" and that the major powers could not make peace on behalf of others. The Conference of Presidents of Major American Jewish Organizations expressed "grave concern"; members of the Congress weighed in. Eban was dispatched to Washington again to confer with American officials.

It was in this congenial atmosphere that the National Security Council on December 10 considered the State Department's proposal to put forward a plan on Jordan comparable to that on Egypt. What possessed the Department to persevere when all the evidence indicated certain failure must be left to students of administrative psychology. Perhaps when enough bureaucratic prestige has been invested in a policy it is easier to see it fail than to abandon it. I argued to Rogers — somewhat disingenuously — that in the light of his effective speech, there was no need for the United States to do more. This ploy, I should have known, would not long immobilize the steamroller. State sent a recommendation to the President that the detailed Israel-Jordan peace plan — originally claimed to be only for "guidance" — be formally presented in the Four-Power talks, to "round out" the US position.

By now the debate had become stylized. Those who wanted to advance specific proposals thought that this would improve our standing in the Arab world. My view was that if we were not ready to impose our proposals the mere presentation of them would gain us at most two to three weeks before we were again faced with the choice of offering more or letting the negotiation blow up. The proponents of specificity thought that the Soviet Union could be induced to be moderate. I believed that a steady stream of American concessions would increase Soviet temptations to act as the lawyer for Arab radicals. Proponents of an active policy wanted to win the radical regimes to our side by making increasingly generous offers. I argued that the radical regimes could not be won over; their moderation was more likely if we insisted on a change of course as a precondition of major American involvement.

At the NSC meeting itself, I challenged the fundamental premise of our diplomacy that the continuing stalemate strengthened the Soviet Union's position. In my view the opposite was the case; the longer the stalemate continued the more obvious would it become that the Soviet Union had failed to deliver what the Arabs wanted. As time went on, its Arab clients were bound to conclude that friendship with the Soviet Union was not the key to realizing their aims. Sooner or later, if we kept our nerve, this would force a reassessment of even radical Arab policy.

This was my strategy, which gradually became our policy from 1969 onward (over the corpses of various State Department peace plans, gunned down by the passions of the parties in the area rather than by me). In 1972 and 1973 the strategy began to succeed.

The outcome of the NSC meeting of December 10 was in a sense contrary to the thrust of its discussion. Unwilling to overrule his Secretary of State but also unprepared to face the consequences of a showdown with Israel, Nixon decided to let the Jordan proposal go forward while keeping the White House as far away from it as possible. Once again, he was hoping to deflect the expected criticism toward the State Department while gaining whatever diplomatic benefit there was from the presentation of the plan. On December 17, therefore, Nixon authorized the submission of the Jordan paper to the Four-Power talks. At the same time, Nixon ordered that private assurances be given to Mrs. Meir via Len Garment that we would go no further and that we would not press our proposal.

While the bureaucracy has been known to drag its feet in implementing directives with which it disagrees, its alacrity in carrying out instructions that it favors and that it fears may be changed is wonderful to behold. Ambassador Yost submitted the Jordan plan on December 18 within twenty-four hours of its approval.

Despite Nixon's assurances, the Israelis unleashed a public and private storm over the Rogers speech, the resumption of Four-Power talks, and the Jordan paper. Mrs. Meir called a special Cabinet meeting to consider US–Israeli relations. An Israeli official told Len Garment that Mrs. Meir was "bitterly disappointed" and "heartbroken" and thought the situation "a scandal" and "calamitous." Foreign Minister Eban publicly charged that the United States had withheld details of the Jordan paper from Israel before submitting it, even though he had met with Rogers on December 16. State Department officials retorted that Rogers described the plan to Eban in general terms. On December 22 a delegation of American Jewish leaders met with Rogers to express their concern. The Israeli Cabinet issued a statement flatly rejecting the US proposals; Mrs. Meir was said to consider them a dangerous "appeasement" of the Arabs.

To quell Israeli fears, Sisco suggested that we explain that the Nixon Administration positions differed little from those of the previous Administration — underscoring the home truth of our politics that a new administration is never so eager to demonstrate continuity as when it finds itself in trouble. He further recommended an early and positive decision on Israeli requests for economic and military aid. Nixon approved. This set in motion a cycle in which every negotiating step of which Israel disapproved was coupled with a step-up of Israeli assistance programs without achieving a real meeting of minds with Israel.

The Evolving Strategy

THOUGH we had moved in less than nine months from discussion of general principles to the presentation of specific plans, there was no diplomatic progress. Nor did relations with Egypt improve. A principal reason may well have been that we had little direct contact with Egypt, and Nasser could only conclude that the longer he waited the better our offers would become. He had no need to choose between his Soviet connection, his radical policies, and American support so long as every few months another unreciprocated American move occurred. Our position on frontiers had moved progressively in one direction — from the "weight of conquest" to "rectifications" to "insubstantial alterations." No corresponding shift had taken place on the radical Arab or Soviet side on the critical issue of peace. At the same time, the Soviet Union did not yet perceive that it had most to lose from a stalemate; all it did was to add its criticisms to Nasser's. On December 23, after two months of waiting, the Soviets finally replied to our proposal of October 28 which had supported essentially the 1967 borders. They *rejected* it. Dobrynin complained to me that the Middle East negotiations were stalled and going nowhere. Moscow, he said, now wanted the Middle East to be one of the subjects discussed in the Channel since it was clear that such questions could only really be settled "at the highest level.'' I told him that we had little to add to our existing formulations. As so often, the Soviets had saved us by overplaying their hand. The Four-Power as well as the Two-Power talks were dead. By now Nixon firmly shared my view that time was not ripe for a settlement; but he preferred to let our initiative run out of steam rather than give a clear-cut order.

Over the winter I tried to reflect his views in drafting the President's first Foreign Policy Report to the Congress. In order to lower public expectations the first draft had a sentence saying that the Arab-Israeli conflict was ''intractable.'' The State Department let out a howl of protest, arguing that this gloomy view undercut all their efforts. Rather than do battle, I softened the sentence to read in the final version (published February 18, 1970) that the Arab-Israeli problem ''has serious elements of intractability.'' This mollified the Middle East experts. The literary clumsiness of this phrase reflected the uneasy bureaucratic compromise. No better example could be found of the old maxim that a camel is a horse designed by a committee.

But through the diplomatic deadlock the underlying issues were becoming clear. The formal positions of the parties were but the tip of the iceberg. The Arab states, with the exception of Jordan, were clearly not prepared for a real peace expressed in normal relations with Israel or any concrete definition of security. Israel was not willing to return all the territories — probably not even in return for the definition of peace it was putting forward. The conflict between the positions of the parties then was in fact intractable.

Nasser counted on us to extricate him from the consequences of his recklessness in 1967. But he was unwilling to relinquish his role as champion of radical Arab nationalism, which forced him into a strident anti-American posture on almost all international issues. Nor was he ready to abandon the illusion that the best way to enlist the United States was through Soviet blackmail. This led him to conduct most negotiations through Moscow rather than deal with us directly. The Soviets, in turn, either through lack of imagination or in order to maintain their claim as defenders of radical nationalism, stuck to the rigid advocacy of maximum Arab demands. There was no reason why we should pull the chestnuts of this unlikely alliance out of the fire. And therefore all the various negotiating schemes of 1969 proved stillborn.

But through this turmoil the inherent strength of the American position in the Middle East also gradually emerged. Nobody could make peace without us. Only we, not the Soviet Union, could exert influence on Israel. Israel was too strong to succumb to Arab military pressure, and we could block all diplomatic activity until the Arabs showed *their* willingness to reciprocate Israeli concessions. If we remained steady and refused to be stampeded, the pivotal nature of our position would become more and more evident. Nixon equivocated, believing in my strategy but authorizing (and then aborting) State's tactics. In the process, partly by default, we began to follow my preferred course. The bureaucratic stalemate achieved what I favored as a matter of policy: an inconclusive course that over time was bound to induce at least some Arab leaders to reconsider the utility of relying on Soviet arms and radical posturing to achieve their ends. Once it became clear — for whatever reason — that a settlement could not be extorted from us, Arab leaders would gradually learn that Soviet pressures on us and their own intransigence only produced stagnation. They would, I thought, have to come to us in the end.

So in 1969, not without debate and much hesitation, the basis was laid for the later reversal of alliances in the Middle East. But it took a long time, further crises, and an anguishing war to complete it.

XI

The Uneasy Alliance:
Europe and the United States

Dilemmas of Europe's Success

EVERY new Administration since 1960 has come into office convinced
that its predecessor neglected Atlantic relations, proclaiming it
would give high priority to remedying this shortcoming, and
promising bold new programs. None brought about the dramatic improvement for which it aimed. Ironically, the greater the energy expended, the more the problems seemed to multiply.

This was no accident. There is a perpetual nostalgia about Atlantic
relations that harks back to the Marshall Plan. Then, a bold American
proposal elicited an enthusiastic and grateful European response; Atlantic and European institutions emerged in profusion to spell out a grand
design. It was the secret dream of US foreign policy come true: American moral leadership evoking a spontaneous and authentic consensus;
cooperation without a hint of coercion; the banishment of "outdated"
concepts of national interest and power politics.

In the heady exaltation of the postwar years, it was overlooked that
European attitudes were perhaps not as novel as they appeared; they
were quite compatible with a hard sense of national interests. The practical consequence of the new approach was to enable a prostrate and
ravaged continent to gain protection, economic assistance, and technology without any requirement of reciprocity. Yet for a whole generation
of American leaders, that experience represented the ideal pattern of international relations. They never reflected that while generosity makes
hegemony bearable it does not render it acceptable. The test would
come not in the formative years of the "new" Atlantic relationship, but
when its proclaimed goals were being reached. Then, when Europe had
regained its economic power and political self-confidence and the European countries were in a position to *insist* on their own views, when, in
other words, real options existed for them, we would know whether we
had participated in the birth of a new era or in the refurbishing of traditional patterns.

The 1960s ushered in the period of testing. Clearly, important new institutions of Atlantic cooperation and European integration had emerged. Consultation was more intense and more genuine than in any of our other foreign policy relationships. European economic integration was helping world trade and US exports rather than hurting them as some had feared. Europe was proceeding toward political unity — if not always along routes we favored. At the same time, the very achievement of the goals of the Forties was beginning to contribute to misunderstandings and tensions. As Europe grew more powerful it also became more assertive; not only did consultation register a consensus, more and more it became a means of articulating differences as well. American leaders who believed they had rendered nationalism obsolete in the Atlantic area reacted by endowing what came to be called the "great days of the Marshall Plan" with a nostalgia transcending even its undoubted success.

But new constructions in international relations by definition can be undertaken only at long intervals; their very success precludes early repetition. They may, in fact, be jeopardized by attempts to turn a singular tour de force into a stereotype. Inevitably, as postwar Europe took shape, Atlantic relations grew more mundane, the problems less dramatic. Paradoxically, Atlantic cooperation was most successful when it concentrated on housekeeping functions; it turned acrimonious when the goal became "architectural." It was no different with the Nixon Administration. Like its immediate predecessors it was most successful when its goals were most modest: to build confidence, to stress consultation, to maintain a domestic consensus behind our European troop deployments, to leave European integration to European initiatives. Yet during that period we were accused of "neglecting our allies." Later on when we decided to aim for the traditional "revitalization," we came up against the dilemma of both our predecessors and our successors: that one cannot base foreign policy on an abstract quest for psychological fulfillment.

In the early years of the Nixon Administration the Western Alliance was in ferment, much of it due to initiatives that were European in origin: Wilson's effort to secure British entry into the Common Market, Brandt's *Ostpolitik,* de Gaulle's and then Pompidou's interest in restoring the American connection. We aimed for no great breakthroughs, but we quietly encouraged Britain's admission to the Common Market. Our role was decisive for the ultimate success of *Ostpolitik* and the Berlin negotiations. We significantly improved cooperation with France. And we successfully defended the American troop deployment in Europe against fierce Congressional efforts to reduce it.

I summed up our approach in a memorandum to the President. It was written in March 1970 but it is appropriate here. Nixon had asked me whether American leadership in Atlantic affairs was still needed in the light of progress in European integration. Clearly, Nixon wanted reassurance. He had been raised on the convictions of the generation of Arthur Vandenberg that gave bipartisan support to our unprecedented alliance with Europe. Nixon's question was of the same category as his occasional musings about possibly not standing for a second term. When he asked about his political future he was really seeking confirmation of his indispensability. With respect to Europe he expected to hear me reaffirm the article of faith of his political apprenticeship: that American leadership remained central.

I had to stretch no conviction to render this verdict; it was the core of my own beliefs. American weight and leadership were still needed, I argued, because for all their economic progress the Europeans plainly had not developed the cohesion, the internal stability, or the will to match the power of the Soviet Union. Alliance unity, I wrote, required three things from the United States.

First, we had to remain sober in our own dealings with the Soviet Union. If we became too impetuous the European nations would grow fearful of a US–Soviet deal. This would cause them to multiply their own initiatives, perhaps beyond the point of prudence, to protect themselves by making their own arrangements with the USSR. But paradoxically, the same would happen if the United States stayed in the trenches of the Cold War. In that case European leaders would be tempted to appear before their publics as "mediators" between bellicose superpowers. The United States had to conduct a careful policy toward the Soviet Union: sufficiently strong to maintain the interest in the common defense; sufficiently flexible to prevent our allies from racing to Moscow.

Second, we had to be meticulous in consultation. Our allies had to be sure that their vital interests would be protected in negotiations such as SALT. Unless our own record was impeccable we could not hold the Europeans to a high standard of interallied consultation in return. Third, we had to avoid unilateral reductions of American forces in Europe, whether imposed by the Executive's financial stringencies or by the Congress's new mood of isolationism. This was a crucial test of our leadership, because significant reductions, whatever their cause, would seriously undermine NATO and foster tendencies of submission to the Soviet Union.

These were principles we sought to implement in our relations with our Atlantic allies. We did not always succeed. But the first few years of the Nixon Administration witnessed encouraging developments.

Consultations

TRUE to Nixon's promises during his first trip to Europe in early 1969, we pursued intensive consultation with allied nations in the following months. In March 1969 Nixon met in Washington with Canadian Prime Minister Pierre Trudeau. Canada's relations with NATO have always had a special character. Unlike the European countries, it was not directly threatened; unlike the United States, it could not be decisive in the common defense; the Canadian defense contribution would be marginal compared with that of the major European powers or the United States. Canada's ties, therefore, had above all a strong symbolic character. It was prepared to maintain the principle of collective security by supplying some military forces; at the same time it strongly favored measures for the relaxation of tensions.

Canada's somewhat aloof position combined with the high quality of its leadership gave it an influence out of proportion to its military contribution, however. It conducted a global foreign policy; it participated in international peacekeeping efforts; it made a constructive contribution to the dialogue between developed and developing nations. At the same time Canada had its own special relationship with the United States. Two-thirds of Canadian trade was with us; the dependence of its economy on ours was so great as to be a significant domestic issue within Canada. Canada, in fact, was beset by ambivalences which, while different from those of Europe, created their own complexities. It required both close economic relations with the United States and an occasional gesture of strident independence. Concretely, this meant that its need for American markets was in constant tension with its temptation to impose discriminatory economic measures; its instinct in favor of common defense conflicted with the temptation to stay above the battle as a kind of international arbiter. Convinced of the necessity of cooperation, impelled by domestic imperatives toward confrontation, Canadian leaders had a narrow margin for maneuver that they utilized with extraordinary skill.

It cannot be said that Nixon and Trudeau were ideally suited for each other. A scion of an old Quebec family, elegant, brilliant, enigmatic, intellectual, Trudeau was bound to evoke all of Nixon's resentments against ''swells'' who in his view had always looked down on him. He disdained Trudeau's clear enjoyment of social life; he tended to consider him soft on defense and in his general attitude toward the East. And yet, when they were together, Trudeau treated Nixon without any hint of condescension and Nixon accorded Trudeau both respect and attention. They worked together without visible strain. They settled the issues before them and did not revert to their less charitable personal comments until each was back in his own capital.

Their first encounter was no exception. Trudeau supported Nixon's position on the antiballistic missile defense. Reports that he would withdraw Canada from the NATO command proved unfounded. Economic matters were turned over to the experts. Frequent consultations were agreed to, and in fact carried out. United States–Canadian relations demonstrated that the national interest can be made to transcend personal sympathies.

At the end of March 1969, the death of President Eisenhower brought a galaxy of European leaders to Washington, among them Charles de Gaulle. He arrived wearing the uniform of a French brigadier general. Nixon sent me to the French Embassy to welcome him and tell him that the White House communications system was at his disposal. De Gaulle, who despite his residence of four years in London never used the English language, showed his appreciation by replying in English: "Tell your President that he is a very courteous man."

Nixon and de Gaulle met in the Oval Office for what turned out to be the last time. I warned Nixon beforehand to avoid "any suggestion that you share the General's currently bitter attitude toward the Wilson government" — the lingering aftermath of the Soames affair (see Chapter IV). De Gaulle, in fact, took Nixon on a *tour d'horizon* covering most of the points made a month earlier in Paris. He added one new note — a warning about carrying cooperation with Germany beyond the point of prudence. He opposed a recently concluded Anglo-German agreement for a centrifuge process to produce enriched uranium for nuclear reactors. He feared that this was the opening wedge for Germany's entry into the nuclear club; one should take care not to reawaken the driving ambition that had torn Europe twice in this century. Nixon replied blandly that he hoped a close and friendly relationship between France and Germany would be maintained.

There was about de Gaulle on this occasion a melancholy air of withdrawal, of already being a spectator at his own actions, of speaking in the abstract about a future he knew he would no longer shape — a harbinger of his retirement a few weeks later. He called to mind a poignant story told to me by Chancellor Kiesinger a few weeks earlier in Bonn, on the basis of which he predicted that de Gaulle would not serve much longer as Chief of State. According to Kiesinger, during one of their regular consultations, de Gaulle had characterized Franco-German relations as follows: "We and the Germans have gone through a lot together. We have traversed forests surrounded by wild animals. We have crossed deserts parched by the sun. We have climbed peaks covered by snow, always looking for a hidden treasure — usually competitively, very recently cooperatively. And now we have learned that there is no hidden treasure and only friendship is left to us."

The funeral was also the occasion for the discussion of a fundamental defense issue that was raised by an old friend, Denis Healey, then Minister of Defense of the United Kingdom. Healey and I had known each other since the mid-Fifties, when we had both written on strategic problems. He was brilliant and gregarious, extraordinarily well read and implacable in debate. His restless intellect sometimes caused him to shift his positions faster than his admirers could assimilate. But though like most politicians he was finely attuned to the moods of the moment, he was always constructive and stimulating.

Healey had written me a private letter asking what our attitude would be toward grouping the West European nations within NATO to concert their positions on defense matters. The prospect of a European caucus on defense raised an interesting question. The "integrationists" in our bureaucracy, as well as outside, passionately favored European economic unity; at the same time they strongly opposed a European identity in the defense field as likely to divide the Alliance. I thought the opposite was more likely to be true. In economic matters Europe and America were to some extent rivals; moreover, there was no risk or penalty for competition. In the military field there was no conceivable contingency in which Europe would be better off without American support. Our vital interests were complementary; the penalty for independent action was overwhelming. I was convinced that a European identity in the defense field would be less divisive than the European economic unity that all leading Americans, including myself, welcomed. Only by arriving at independent conclusions would Europe see the necessity of strengthening its defense effort.

I thought the issue sufficiently important to ask the President's guidance on how to respond to Healey:

> Some US officials . . . have noted that a European caucus could grow into a third force grouped around France, drawing its chief impulse to unity from anti-Americanism. . . .
>
> I believe that efforts to create a more coherent European voice in NATO are in our net interest, though not without some short term problems. Greater European coherence would be quite consistent with what you have said about the desirability over the longer run of our being able to deal with Europe as a true and more equal partner.

I therefore recommended that I inform Healey of our generally favorable reaction, provided such a grouping was not used as a device to isolate France. We would be prepared to tell other Europeans that "a stronger and more united European voice will make for a more equitable and hence a more productive Atlantic partnership." Nixon approved this approach. The "Eurogroup" gradually took shape, but no European consensus on defense emerged. The reason was lack of agreement on

Europe's political structure. France wanted a united European voice, but not within NATO; it was bound to consider the British initiative as a way of getting around the issue of British membership in the Common Market. The American bureaucracy, whatever the decision of the President, was lukewarm; it supported the scheme weakly and wherever possible surreptitiously opposed its implementation. The other Europeans were ambivalent. They favored unity in the abstract, but they feared that the attempt to articulate a European identity within NATO might give the United States an excuse for reducing its military establishment in Europe.

These attitudes came into focus again during the Washington meeting of foreign and defense ministers to celebrate the twentieth anniversary of the Alliance. In a memorandum of April 9 I had urged Nixon to emphasize our commitment to maintain strong American forces in Europe; but he should stress also that Congressional support in the United States required proportionate contributions from our allies. Second, he needed to counteract the notion that détente was just around the corner merely because the Soviet tone had softened. We should indicate a general readiness to explore concrete areas for agreement, rather than mere atmospherics, with the Soviet Union. Third, with respect to internal European arrangements I recommended that we encourage the European members of NATO to improve cooperation among themselves. But we should avoid support for a particular method; we should neither join in any effort to isolate France nor convey the idea that special rewards awaited those who contracted out of the Alliance.

Above all, I urged the President to underline the principle ''that the security of this alliance should be broadly construed to involve not only its physical safety against external attack but the ability of our countries to cope with the problems *within* our societies.'' To develop a sense of common interest above and beyond defense, I endorsed an idea, which Pat Moynihan had inspired, for a Committee on the Challenges of Modern Society. As modern industrial nations we all shared the problems of protecting the environment or improving transportation, and surely the resources and imagination of the Western nations could be brought to bear on the quality of life. In addition, to give tangible expression to his commitment to increased consultation, I recommended that the President propose that Deputy Foreign Ministers meet at least once between the semiannual Foreign Ministers' meetings. They could attempt longer-range planning, especially on East-West relations. Nixon accepted these recommendations and put them before the North Atlantic Council in an eloquent speech in April 1969.

One might have expected that, after years of complaining about inadequate American attention and insufficient consultation, our allies would have embraced our proposals with enthusiasm. But this ignored the psychological undercurrents. The Alliance's passion for "consultation" meant in practice the desire to limit America's freedom of action; not all of our allies were equally prepared to constrain their own. A political planning mechanism ran into France's quest for "independence" and received a lukewarm reception from the Federal Republic of Germany, advocating a more national policy. The Committee on the Challenges of Modern Society was greeted with the objection that NATO was never designed to address such questions — a far cry from the private expressions of *all* allied leaders during Nixon's trip to Europe that the common defense was no longer sufficient to inspire the younger generation.

The final communiqué of the April commemorative conference was therefore extremely reserved. It called for "consideration" of the President's proposal for periodic meetings of the Deputy Foreign Ministers and for "examination" of how the countries might "improve the exchange of views and experience . . . whether by action in the appropriate international organizations or otherwise, in the task of creating a better environment for their societies." It was clear that Europe was ambivalent about major American initiatives; it welcomed American commitments as long as they did not constrain its own freedom of action. At the same time, the new Administration was beginning to face a growing reluctance in this country to meet, let alone expand, our own commitments to Europe. We would have to navigate between these shoals for the remainder of Nixon's term.

De Gaulle's Departure and European Unity

IN 1969, actually, we succeeded in defusing much of the tension we had inherited within the Atlantic Alliance. Nixon's high regard for de Gaulle was reciprocated. De Gaulle, to be sure, did not change his basic principles, but he no longer pressed them so brutally. The reception given Nixon in France, de Gaulle's attendance at the return dinner at the American Embassy, his gracious gesture of coming to President Eisenhower's funeral — all helped ease the previous strains. The improvement in Franco-American relations, in turn, made the special Anglo-American relationship appear less of an obstacle to British membership in Europe. These trends were accelerated when President de Gaulle abruptly resigned on April 27, 1969. He had been defeated in two referenda on essentially secondary issues, one dealing with the structure of local government in France, the other with reform of the Senate. To resign over such matters raised the suspicion that the referenda had been arranged at least in part to provide de Gaulle with a pretext for leaving office. He had performed the dramatic feats required by the crises that had brought him to power. He had consolidated new political institutions. He had achieved the decolonization of French Africa while maintaining French self-confidence at home and its prestige in the former colonies. Barely overcoming incipient civil war, he had restored French pride by giving it a central role in the policies of Europe and the Western Alliance. His challenge to the United States had to a great degree the purpose of inspiring French self-assurance.

But the student upheavals of 1968 had shaken de Gaulle. And the challenges facing him thereafter were not of a magnitude he considered relevant to his vision of himself. To ensure a growing economy, to arbitrate contending claims on limited resources, to organize and manage a bureaucratic state — these were tasks for what he half-contemptuously called "quartermasters," not for heroic figures. The referenda of April 17 provided the occasion for a dramatic departure instead of the slow erosion of authority that he so feared. Afterward, all was solitude as de Gaulle retired to Colombey. He saw no political figures, made no pronouncements, worked on his memoirs, and awaited his death.

Upon de Gaulle's resignation I wrote to the President outlining what I saw to be the consequences. I expected Georges Pompidou to emerge as de Gaulle's successor in a more complicated political situation. De Gaulle had managed to stand above parties, appealing to the right with a moderate domestic program and to the left with his independent foreign policy. I thought it more likely that in the future French political life would be characterized by "a large, well-organized Communist Party on the far left, and a constantly shifting amalgam of left, center and right parties governing through a narrow consensus which permits little in the way of positive programs." I anticipated little change in the substance of French foreign policy, though the style might be more accommodating. Over the longer term, however, I thought that "French foreign policy may become more difficult for us to live with. With a less decisive Government, the left may well be able to move into a position — so common in other Western European democracies — of exercising a veto over foreign policy initiatives it does not like." These predictions proved, if not plain wrong, at best premature. Pompidou turned out to be a strong, decisive, and dominant President, at least until his last year in office when he was tormented by a cruel illness (he died in 1974).

At the time of de Gaulle's departure an interagency study under the chairmanship of the Department of State prepared a thoughtful analytical paper that predicted that Pompidou would move away slowly and unobtrusively from de Gaulle's opposition to Britain's membership in the Common Market; he would accelerate the improvement in relations with the United States that had already started under de Gaulle. I recommended that we not take any specific initiative during the French presidential election campaign. Rather, we should continue to expand "upon recent US efforts to give practical content to closer political rapport with France'' and encourage "discreetly any trend toward a more cooperative French attitude toward NATO.''

Shortly after the second round of the presidential elections, which gave Pompidou a victory over Alain Poher, I met with our Ambassador to Paris, Sargent Shriver, to discuss a possible visit by Pompidou to the United States. I proposed that the simplest solution would be to substitute Pompidou for de Gaulle, who had agreed to visit the United States in January or February 1970. Shriver was to sound out Pompidou and then a formal invitation would be sent. I told Shriver that the President was well disposed to explore the possibilities of military cooperation with France. The President would not let "NATO theology" stand in the way of an increase in French military cooperation with the United States. Not even the possibility of limited cooperation in the nuclear field was excluded.

Before his official visit, however, I had an opportunity to meet Pompidou on the way back from Nixon's visit to Asia and Romania in August 1969. The President stopped at an airfield in Britain to brief Prime Minister Wilson, and I left the party to brief Pompidou and the North Atlantic Council (and also to meet Xuan Thuy). Chancellor Kiesinger was coming to Washington in a few days and would receive his briefing there.

Pompidou expressed his appreciation for Nixon's gesture in sending me to Paris. As in all my later contacts I found him invariably polite and extremely penetrating, with the slightly sardonic manner of a graduate of one of the *grandes écoles* — the great educational institutions that have shaped so much of French leadership. He expressed support for Nixon's Guam Doctrine that Asians should assume a greater responsibility for their future; he thought this should apply to Europe as well. He accepted in principle the invitation to the United States for the early part of 1970. He was willing to be helpful on Vietnam if we asked, and made clear that he would not seek opportunities to harass us.

The precondition for de Gaulle's aloof policies toward the United States or Britain was in any event disappearing with the advent of the Brandt government in West Germany as a result of the elections of September 1969. Brandt was on record as favoring Britain's entry into the Common Market; his new policy toward the East (*Ostpolitik*) raised the specter of a more independent and more national course by Germany. All of this made Britain's participation in Europe seem more attractive to the French. Therefore, at a meeting of the heads of government of the European Economic Community on December 2, 1969, it was announced with French concurrence that the Community was prepared to negotiate with Britain and to consider political cooperation within "the context of enlargement.''

Thus at year's end the United States was face to face with the achievement of one of its long-held objectives — the expansion of European unity. For two decades it had been assumed that a united Europe would ease Atlantic relations, that it would inevitably pursue compatible policies while sharing a greater part of our burdens. I had never believed the results of European integration to be nearly so automatic. Divergences on monetary and trade policy were already increasingly apparent. A politically united Europe was more likely to articulate its own conceptions in other areas as well. At an interagency meeting on December 11 I noted that we would be faced with more assertive European positions on such questions as East-West negotiations and on the protectionist implications of the strengthening of the Common Market.

But it was a luxury to contemplate such problems, because they were the results of success. Our "low profile" on European unity had importantly improved Britain's prospects; our refusal to participate in intra-European quarrels had strengthened both European and Atlantic relations. To be sure, adherents of the previous policy of vocal American "leadership" were unhappy with our restraint.[1] In response to a query from Nixon I wrote the President on December 29:

There has been some criticism of our "low profile" in Europe from those who believe that we should continue the policy of the previous Administration of actively involving ourselves in intra-European affairs along conceptual lines which we have concluded are best for Europe. There remains a group of scholars, former officials and journalists on both sides of the Atlantic who believe that unless the US provides the momentum, the movement for European unity will die, particularly since the stimulus of fear of the Russians has largely disappeared.

Actually, our relations with Europe have improved immeasurably. The revised approach which you launched during your European trip and which is based on increased concern for what the Europeans want for themselves and a greatly improved consultative process on the major issues which affect Europe has been exceptionally successful. A case in point, of course, is your reversal of the formerly deteriorating relationship with France. I am personally convinced that you are on the right track and this has been confirmed by my numerous European contacts of varying political persuasions.

During 1969 the nations of the Atlantic area were increasingly absorbed with domestic problems; we with Vietnam, the Europeans with changing governments, their economies, or European integration. And looming before all members of the Alliance was an entirely new challenge: how to maintain security while seeking to improve — for the first time systematically — relations with the East; how to reconcile our solidarity with a policy of détente.

The Common Defense: The American Perception

THREE issues dominated discussions on NATO defense. First was the validity of the strategic doctrine of "flexible response," which had been officially adopted by NATO in 1967 under American pressure. Second was the allocation of the "burden" of the common defense between Europe and the United States; specifically, whether a greater European effort was possible. Third was the level of American forces to be stationed in Europe.

The official strategy of flexible response was pushed through NATO by Defense Secretary Robert McNamara after France had withdrawn from the integrated NATO command. In the 1950s Alliance military strategy had relied on the threat of massive retaliation — any attack on Europe would be answered by an immediate all-out American nuclear strike. With the growth of the Soviet nuclear stockpile the United States — inevitably — sought other options and a wider spectrum of choice. Under the doctrine of flexible response we would still resort to all-out war if necessary, but we would reach this point only by graduated escalation, starting with conventional weapons and moving up to nuclear weapons by discrete stages geared to the scale of the threat. The strategy had been accepted by our European allies with extreme uneasiness and only after a debate extending over five years. They saw it — correctly — as the symptom of growing reluctance by the United States to use its nuclear forces. They feared that a demonstrated reluctance to resort to nuclear war might cause the Soviets to seek to exploit the imbalance in conventional forces. They were concerned that a strategy which reduced the danger of nuclear war might make conventional aggression more likely.

The McNamara attitudes were still prevalent in our government. On June 17, 1969, I warned the President:

There seems to be a strongly held view in the Government that there is very little relationship between our strategic posture (and our tactical nuclear posture as well) and deterring or coping with conventional war. This view seems to be based on two conclusions: (a) our strategic forces can contribute to the deterrence of conventional war only if we have a credible first strike capability, which it is not possible to attain, and (b) tactical nuclear war in Europe would probably end in our defeat, so we have no incentive to rely on tactical nuclear weapons as a hedge against weaknesses in our conventional posture.

But if these judgments were true, we faced a nearly insoluble dilemma. If resort to our strategic forces was becoming too risky and if a tactical nuclear war would probably end in our defeat, we had in effect abdicated from the serious defense of Europe. To be sure, one could argue — and many did — that nations whose combined populations and

Gross National Products were at least three times the Soviet Union's should be able to mount a conventional defense against the Warsaw Pact. The difficulty was that no member of the Alliance, including the United States, was prepared to make the effort. (In preparation for an NSC meeting on September 10, my staff estimated that the additional cost of a conventional defense of Europe would be $12 billion a year for the United States alone, at the very time the Congress was insisting on drastic cuts in our defense budget.) Nor was there any prospect that the Europeans would increase their own efforts by anything like the amount necessary to provide a sustained conventional defense. They were under domestic pressure to show progress toward détente; a massive increase in defense spending was politically impossible. And they were convinced that any increase in their conventional forces would only encourage a further reduction of American forces. The result, in their perception, would be lowered nuclear protection at no increase in conventional defense capabilities.

This line of reasoning had led Prime Minister Wilson to affirm during Nixon's European visit that he was all in favor of a new strategic doctrine provided it did not lead to a major increase in defense expenditures. De Gaulle's doubts that the Soviets would march "west" reflected essentially the same view; he was convinced that even if the Soviets were to enjoy an initial success the United States would have no choice except to use *all* of its power — including strategic weapons — to prevent the loss of Western Europe. Hence, de Gaulle was more interested in a small strategic force of his own as a hedge against the off-chance of American failure to perceive US interests than in a conventional buildup. Put crudely, the predominant view in Europe was that a disparity in conventional strength on the ground was tolerable and even desirable since the defense of Europe rested ultimately on the American strategic nuclear deterrent.

The United States government undertook in 1969 to reexamine NATO strategy. In essence we saw four alternatives:

- A token American force in Europe to act as a "trip wire."
- A conventional defense posture capable of a short-term (ninety-day) non-nuclear defense of Europe. (This was current NATO strategy.)
- A sustained defense with conventional forces, adequate to defend Europe indefinitely without recourse to nuclear weapons against the standing Warsaw Pact forces.
- A total conventional defense that would allow us to counter an attack by the Warsaw Pact under full mobilization.

In analyzing these four strategies, our constraints became dramatically apparent. The trip-wire concept was rejected. It ran counter to our imperative to gain time for a deliberate decision on so fateful an issue as whether to initiate nuclear war, and the substantial troop withdrawals it implied would demoralize our European allies. A sustained conventional defense of Europe was also rejected. I pointed out to the President before the NSC meeting of September 10 that all our agencies except the Joint Chiefs of Staff believed that our NATO allies would resist this strategy because it contemplated prolonged ground conflict in Europe and thereby would erode the credibility of our intention to use nuclear forces in Europe's defense. This was even more true of the fourth option, total defense. An analysis of the budgetary costs of the four strategies further limited our choices. A sustained conventional defense would force us either to give up *all* new domestic programs or else to impose a surtax of 4 percent if the President limited himself to the domestic programs to which he was already committed (welfare reform, revenue sharing, and urban mass transit).

Allied sensitivities and budgetary constraints thus forced us to reaffirm the existing strategy of attempting a ninety-day conventional defense. But any close examination exposed its essential hollowness. Our studies showed that even the United States, with a declaratory policy of resisting for ninety days, did not have sufficient stockpiles in every significant category of supplies. And our ability to resist would be determined by the smallest critical stockpile, not some theoretical average number. An attempt to elicit from the Pentagon an estimate of which critical item was in short supply produced such an obfuscating runaround that it was clear that we would exhaust some essential items well before ninety days. Since weapons were not standardized, it was not possible to use the reserves of one ally to assist another. Moreover, no one could judge the supply levels of NATO as a whole because each ally computed the consumption rates differently. By whatever criteria were used, it was clear that NATO was far from meeting its own stated goals; the situation was a mess.

Like our predecessors we sought to deal with the problem by encouraging our allies to increase their defense expenditures. Mel Laird, in preparation for a NATO Defense Planning Committee meeting on May 28, had asked for authority to urge our allies to increase their contribution to NATO by an average of 4 percent annually from 1971 through 1975. I had supported Laird's recommendation, and the President had approved. The allies, however, would agree to no fixed percentage; they would go no further than to commit themselves to a "moderate" increase, defining no base from which this could be calculated. In the absence of a realistic strategy backed up by the ability to execute it, there was no practical solution to the problem. It remains without resolution to this day.

At first glance — indeed, at second glance as well — it would seem that in the new strategic circumstances there could be little debate over the importance of a continued American troop commitment to Europe. With nuclear parity on the way, the significance of ground forces on the continent — American and European — was increasing. But all the pressures on us came from the opposite direction. Our troop commitment to Europe was buffeted by the aftershocks of the Vietnam earthquake. Senators Mansfield and Fulbright and many others questioned it and saw it as another example of our global overextension that risked war. They were soon to introduce formal resolutions in the Senate to that effect. They reflected also a general resentment that twenty years after the end of World War II the Europeans, with a history of military autonomy, still would not raise forces adequate for their own defense. Our highly unfavorable balance of payments, moreover, was seen to require a reduction of foreign exchange costs, to be achieved in part by troop cuts in Europe. This set up a vicious circle: the greater the pressures for troop withdrawals in the United States, the greater the disinclination of our allies to augment their military establishments lest they justify further American withdrawals.

In fact, the United States had started a process of thinly disguised withdrawal during the Johnson Administration. In 1967–1968 part of one Army division and some Air Force units had been returned to the United States; altogether almost 60,000 troops had been brought home. Some of the equipment of these withdrawn units had been left behind in stockpiles, and periodic exercises were held to demonstrate our airlift capacity to return rapidly. But these steps missed the essential point: Europeans increasingly questioned not the capability but the willingness of the United States to carry out the commitment to their defense. They questioned not our airlift capability but our political will.

The unilateral reduction program of the Johnson Administration — with the acronym REDCOSTE ("Reduction of Costs in Europe") — had been justified on the ground that it was "cutting the fat" of administrative overhead; combat effectiveness would not be diminished. This followed hallowed convention. The cumulative impact of these cuts would tend to suggest that we possessed at one time the most bloated military establishment imaginable; or else that its combat effectiveness was so low that no amount of reductions could affect it. The problem of the Nixon Administration was how to deal with long-planned reductions which were taking place at the very time that we were urging our allies to do more.

At this point we witnessed the dazzling spectacle of Melvin Laird. Laird unilaterally decided to make his own cuts within NATO — barely three months after urging our allies to increase their expenditures by 4 percent annually. In early September 1969, Laird proposed reductions of naval forces committed to NATO by one attack carrier, six antisubmarine carriers, and forty-eight destroyers (now mothballed on the Pacific coast). He also recommended reducing the readiness of Army Strategic Reserve units assigned to NATO and — more important from the political point of view — of the elements of the 24th Infantry Division that were supposed to return to NATO in case of crisis. Laird included another pregnant sentence: "Further changes in our NATO committed force may be required as a result of reduction in defense expenditures already announced and under review." Basically, Laird was a staunch supporter of NATO. Why then did he seek to cut NATO forces so brusquely and so provocatively?

The principal reason, strangely enough, was Laird's concern to maintain the defense budget and with it NATO's defense capability. He was under pressure from the Bureau of the Budget (represented by its Assistant Director James R. Schlesinger) and the Congress to cut our defense budget by at least $5 billion on top of the reductions Nixon had judged expedient to make upon entering office. Laird calculated that NATO enjoyed a large constituency inside and outside the government. If he could demonstrate that overall cuts in the defense budget would immediately affect NATO, he might ease the pressures for reductions, or at least contain them. He decided that the best way to still ardor for budgetary cuts in the Executive or Legislative Branch was to make them as painful as possible. This proved to be a correct assessment.

But for this strategy to succeed it had to be carried out with nerve, of which Laird was never in short supply. And the more plausible Laird's maneuver — which was essential to its success — the more it was raising havoc with our position in NATO. When I conveyed Laird's recommendations to Nixon I wrote the following note:

These facts, as they become known, are going to be read in NATO against a background of other indicators that the US is actually cutting back on its commitments in Europe. The personnel reductions overseas and Secretary Laird's various comments all will be taken as part of a trend. . . . The fact that these reductions in effectiveness and readiness have already occurred, of course, raises the further question of consultation. . . .

To get some control over the situation I sent a directive to the departments on September 17 prohibiting further discussion of reductions publicly or within NATO, pending a "memo for the President describing what has already taken place," and providing recommendations for NATO consultation.

But Laird was too quick for me. Ten days after his first recommendations, he sent another memorandum to the President reminding us of the cryptic warning in his earlier communication that further cuts were possible: "This now proves to be the case. . . . There should be more changes required in our NATO-committed naval forces once our detailed analysis is completed. . . . The reductions are likely to be interpreted as inconsistent with your statements to the Europeans that we believe NATO forces should be maintained at current levels." Laird was in effect telling the President either to increase the defense budget or to break his word to European leaders.

Laird did not explain what could possibly have happened in ten days to bring about the need for another cut, or why he had not informed the White House of the scope of his intentions to begin with. It was clear that he was using European troop reductions to force the President's hand on increasing the defense budget. To add a bizarre touch, Laird admitted that the Joint Chiefs of Staff believed that these cuts would pose additional risks for the United States: "I agree with the Chiefs but believe that these cuts must be made, given our commitments in SEA [Southeast Asia] and the current tight fiscal situation." There was no doubt that the Commander-in-Chief was being blackmailed either to increase his defense budget (which he was reluctant to do because of Congressional opposition) or to take the money from Southeast Asia, thereby reducing his negotiating flexibility in Vietnam.

Once Laird had a winning position, it would only magnify one's losses to continue the battle. Laird proceeded to implement his plan. But I sought somehow to ensure that unilateral cuts would not happen again. On September 19 I wrote the President summarizing Laird's decisions and the Chiefs' objections. I recommended we set up a Defense Program Review Committee (DPRC) in the NSC system to enable the White House and the other agencies to have some voice in Laird's decisions. Nixon approved. The Committee was in fact established and did some useful work. Nevertheless, the White House never achieved the control over defense policy that it did over foreign policy. Laird was too nimble; the Joint Chiefs were too suspicious of outside determination of their priorities; and we had our hands full with the design and conduct of overall geopolitical strategy. But if the DPRC could not shape defense policy across the board, it could act as a brake on unilateral steps. This became apparent when Laird returned to the charge in October. He proposed cuts in reserve units and suggested that a passing reference to this prospect be made to our NATO allies. I urged the President to put an end to this piecemeal approach lest we create the impression of an endless process of withdrawal. Nixon agreed. From then on, we did manage to prevent unilateral cuts in our NATO forces.

Our allies, not used to the subtleties of our political process, did not immediately understand that all this was essentially for their own good. At the first meeting of the new DPRC on October 21, General Wheeler, Chairman of the Joint Chiefs, predicted that we would have a very hard time with our allies — correctly, he blamed the budget-cutters, not Laird. His guess was borne out. NATO Secretary-General Manlio Brosio visited Washington on November 14 and spoke pessimistically about the prospects for increasing European force levels while America was reducing its troops. He also reported a growing interest in the Alliance in negotiations with the Soviets on mutual troop reductions. Since the United States would be withdrawing anyhow, he argued, NATO might as well trade in our programmed reductions for some Soviet concessions.

In fairness it must be stated that Laird had achieved his principal aim. He had so scared various constituencies that his budget was cut by the absolute minimum. In the long run this was of great benefit to NATO and the defense posture of the United States. But in 1969 it certainly complicated the prospects for a coherent new NATO strategy and gave us an anxious time with our allies.

Basically, Laird had called attention to a fundamental issue. There was little doubt that the budget constraints were threatening to undermine our foreign policy. For the following year the same dilemmas surfaced again. By June 1970, budgetary planning for Fiscal Year 1972 was getting into gear. The Bureau of the Budget (now renamed the Office of Management and Budget, or OMB) foresaw a defense budget of $76 billion. Mel Laird, with my support, began to wield his formidable powers of maneuver. He considered $79 billion as the irreducible minimum; if he had to cut $3 billion, he wrote the President, the results would be ominous. Laird's genius for painting the most dire consequences if his budget requests were not met had not been impaired; if anything it had been sharpened by his successes during the past year. He submitted a staggering inventory of reductions, which included the loss of four aircraft carriers, deactivation of two Army divisions, retirement of 130 to 140 of our oldest B-52s, and cancellation of other major procurement programs. (If a $3 billion cut would have such an impact it was amazing that the full budget bought so few new weapons.)

To bring the choices and their consequences into focus I convened a meeting of the Defense Program Review Committee. Paul McCracken, Chairman of the Council of Economic Advisers, was worried that the projected federal budget of $237 billion would "scare hell out of the financial community" and demoralize the Federal Reserve Board to the point where it might put a damper on economic recovery. We would then wind up with the worst possible outcome — a sluggish economy and rekindled fears of inflation. McCracken wanted a $6 billion cut, twice that recommended by OMB. On the other side of the ledger, Deputy Defense Secretary David Packard argued that any cut in defense would be disastrous for our security.

Decisions were complicated by the inability of the military services to present an agreed rationale for their requests. In the years of relatively ample defense budgets each service had simply pushed its own pet projects, which were usually based on what was technically feasible. The "agreed" Joint Chiefs of Staff submissions were usually nonaggression treaties among the various services unrelated to a coherent strategy. I said to my colleagues: "I want a paper that will tell the President: 'If you do this, these are the consequences.' " If we could no longer destroy Soviet military power, what was the right level for our strategic forces? What would be the impact of that new situation on the defense of countries around the Soviet periphery, including Europe? Could one base the defense of peripheral areas indefinitely on a strategy of exterminating civilian populations? At a time that the American threat to launch general nuclear war was losing credibility we were under simultaneous pressure to cut all other forces. "We are cutting our general purpose forces and getting out of places like Korea.* How are we going to defend these areas? This question has to be put to the President. He must know what we are heading into."

It proved very difficult to get the issue submitted to the President in an agreed manner. No one had an interest in scrutinizing NATO doctrine and forces too closely. Such an investigation might well highlight the incongruity of a deployment that was a compromise between the European desire to guarantee an American nuclear response and our attempt to ensure that we would invoke it only as a last resort. A serious examination of NATO conventional strategy was further inhibited by the fear that such a study would discover shortfalls in essential supplies that could not be remedied in the existing mood of parliaments and media and thus might produce a pretext for unilateral reductions.

I kept raising at meeting after meeting the growing incongruity between our strategy and our force posture. No one denied this reality, yet no one was willing to do anything about it. At one session I found it impossible to obtain a definition of the term "marginally effective," which had been used to describe a category of weapons in our planning papers. To bring matters to a head I arranged a meeting of the Joint Chiefs of Staff with Nixon for August 18, 1970. It followed the time-honored pattern of such sessions. Each chief explained why his share of the recommended budget was the minimum required to carry out his "mission." Each treated the precise nature of that mission as self-evident and chose not to explain it. Baffled by these nurtured ambiguities, overwhelmed with technical detail, the President found it impossible to tell whether the arguments were self-serving or justified. They were usually both.

On the following day — August 19 — there was an NSC meeting to review the defense budget. The discussion rambled on inconclusively. Nixon made statements that were tough philosophically but that did not

---

* This referred to a plan to pull a division out of Korea, to compensate for which we would beef up South Korean forces.

change his budgetary ceiling; our capabilities would ultimately be determined by the ceiling, not by his exhortations. Nixon thought it imperative to present a "lean" budget in order to forestall even more severe cuts by the Congress. All that the discussion achieved was to reduce the proposed cut from $6 billion to $4.5 billion; the Congress then slashed another $3 billion. I expressed my premonitions to Nixon in a memorandum:

We are in danger of sliding into a period of relying on massive retaliation even though this is absurd. Our general purpose forces must be looked at. We have to have forces in which we can believe. We must be able to project a credible power abroad in a situation where general nuclear war is no longer a likely or reasonable alternative. The general purpose forces are the way we are seen by allies — they are the contact and the reality.

Mel Laird in a memorandum in November stressed that he too was concerned about the dangerous decline in conventional capabilities.

Laird, Packard, and I consoled each other with the determination that we would do our utmost to make up inadequacies in the "out" years — the years not covered by the current budget. Unfortunately, for the moment all pressures were in the opposite direction. The decision to move toward a volunteer army further reduced weapons procurement. It forced an increase in pay scales so that eventually nearly 60 percent of our military budget went to pay and allowances (as against a little over 30 percent in the Soviet Union), leaving a much smaller amount for new weapons. And despite those incentives it produced a manpower shortage. By November 1970, US forces in Europe were about 17,000 below authorized strength; almost two-thirds of that reduction had taken place since July.

And maintaining even the existing forces would face increasing political obstacles. Senator Mike Mansfield, Majority Leader of the Senate, now used Brandt's *Ostpolitik* to justify a substantial reduction of our troops in Europe.[2] Every easing of tensions led to pressures for cuts in the forces which had made that easing possible. Some favored a reduction of the American military presence in Europe because they thought it was no longer necessary; others considered our overseas deployment economically unbearable. Senator Stuart Symington made this point to Assistant Secretary of State Martin Hillenbrand:

The people of the United States want to see a reduction in the costs that we have in Europe, and they think and all the economists I have ever talked to before except you think this would significantly and favorably affect the US economy.[3]

In the Congress, *supporters* of NATO argued in the name of burden-sharing that if Europe did not do more, we should do less (because of our intractable balance of payments difficulties). "Burden-sharing" had, in fact, the same objective consequence as budgetary pressures: It was a way station in the direction of reducing our forces in Europe and our contribution to European security.

Our European allies, conscious of their military vulnerability, uneasy alike about their fears of American abdication and their political risks at home in expanding their own defenses, watched our debate with foreboding. They simultaneously feared our withdrawals and dreaded our pressures on them to build up their defenses. They were looking for ways out of their dilemma and they found two — at least intermediate — expedients.

Both were suggested in one sentence of the President's Foreign Policy Report of February 18, 1970:

> The forging of a common understanding on basic security issues will materially improve our ability to deal sensibly and realistically with the opportunities and pressures for change that we face, including suggestions in this country for substantial reductions of US troop levels in Europe and the possibility that balanced force reductions could become a subject of East-West discussions.

The energetic, able, and not a little wily NATO Secretary-General Manlio Brosio interpreted a phrase drafted by staff assistants as a Presidential signal for action. He proposed that NATO conduct a defense review as a means of slowing down American withdrawals. And he was a driving force behind NATO's growing interest in negotiations with the East for the mutual reduction of forces in Central Europe — what eventually came to be known as mutual and balanced force reductions, or MBFR. Both were designed — as Brosio frankly admitted to Nixon when they met privately in Naples in September 1970 — as devices to put a brake on unilateral American decisions. The presumption was that the US Congress would do nothing irrevocable until the two initiatives had been explored and completed. The revival of the idea of mutual reductions was not a passionate commitment to this ambiguous goal but an attempt — not at all discouraged by the Administration — to forestall unilateral American cuts.

The defense review proposed by Brosio occupied much of 1970. As part of it, the "Eurogroup" (the European caucus formed at Healey's initiative the year before) was to devise a program of new measures to beef up defense; this was to neutralize criticism in the US Congress that Europeans were not doing enough. Nixon gave the project an additional impetus when, in a meeting with NATO commanders in Naples on his Mediterranean trip in September 1970, he stressed that our approach to burden-sharing preferred additional European expenditures to be made for their own defense, rather than financial gimmicks to repay the United States for the stationing of American troops. His statement that we did not want Americans to act as mercenaries for Europeans was noble and theoretically correct; but it did not help Mel Laird's desperate attempt to get some budgetary relief in any form (such as the West German agreement to pay for our barracks and to buy American weapons, to offset some of our budgetary costs). Mel Laird was performing miracles in maintaining our NATO forces substantially at existing levels and laying the basis for modernization of our strategic arsenal. But modernization of NATO was out of the question when all our exertions were needed to keep the Congress from legislating a reduction of forces. The *Washington Post* correspondent in Bonn in a lengthy article on October 5 indicated that the strong statements made by the President had not allayed Europe's fears on this score: "After a long period of brushing the problem aside in hopes that it somehow would go away, the European members of NATO are beginning to realize that they have little time left to counter pressures in the US Congress for a wholesale reduction of the American commitment to NATO."

The projected military budget could leave no doubt about the direction in which Congressional and public pressures were inexorably pushing us. Though the dollar amount of the budget was slightly higher than the preceding one, inflation and the costs of the volunteer army produced a significant reduction in terms of constant dollars. Our allies were unwilling to step into the breach; they chose to implement the 1970 defense review by measures that avoided serious financial commitments. The NATO defense review was completed by December 1970 and submitted to the North Atlantic Council. It amounted to a collective contribution to the NATO infrastructure (aircraft shelters, barracks, other fixed facilities) of $420 million over five years, improvements of national forces amounting to about $450 to $500 million over the same period, and some other financial measures that would be interpreted to amount to $79 million. This was a total of about $1 billion, or $200 million a year for five years. There was no way of telling how much of this was genuinely new or how much represented simply bookkeeping changes. At best, it was an increase comparable to almost one-half percent of our defense budget. The amount was too trivial to go to the heart of the problem. The best that could be said for it was that it reversed the trend toward reductions.

On the whole our allies were clearly counting on the deus ex machina of mutual force reductions with the Warsaw Pact. They would urge us to keep American forces in Europe pending negotiations and would seek to avoid additional expenditures with the argument that they might be made irrelevant by new arms control agreements. This raised a whole new set of problems. I had no objection to using MBFR as a brake on unilateral Congressional cuts. But my doubts about its complexity and inherent disadvantages had not eased since the previous year. I wrote the President:

We have not been able to develop an approach to MBFR which would either maintain or improve NATO's military position although small mutual reductions could have a minimal adverse effect. We have not been able to identify negotiable "collateral constraints" which would inhibit Pact mobilization and reinforcement without harming NATO at the same time. We have just scratched the surface in thinking about verification problems.

In these circumstances an NSC meeting of November 19, 1970, to review NATO strategy could do little except to register our dilemma. I summed up the strategic problem again in a briefing memorandum to the President:

. . . we and our Allies must maintain strong enough conventional forces to be able to meet Soviet aggression or the threat of it implicit in their substantial forces. Unless we and our Allies rework our NATO strategy and forces so that they can provide this capability, we will soon experience the gradual "neutralization" of Western Europe. To avoid this situation, we must act vigorously to maintain NATO's conventional capability while developing a strategy for its use that makes sense in this fundamentally new strategic situation.

The assault on defense expenditures growing out of the Vietnam war prevented this effort until 1974.

The NSC meeting of November 19 was unusually serious and substantive. For once there was no bureaucratic maneuvering, because all the President's senior advisers were in agreement on the major issues. The meeting led to two significant decisions: another strong reaffirmation of our troop commitments in Europe, and a decision to reexamine the whole question of mutual force reductions. The European defense improvement program, however sparse and essentially irrelevant, thus achieved its immediate purpose. At the December meeting of Alliance Foreign Ministers, Secretary Rogers read a letter from Nixon that announced that in the light of Europe's increased defense efforts, the United States would maintain and improve its forces in Europe and would not reduce them except in the context of mutual reductions negotiated with the East.

In the nature of things these were stopgap measures sufficient to prevent immediate disaster, inadequate as a long-term remedy. An alliance whose only means of preserving its strength was to offer to negotiate force reductions (with an enemy aware of enormous pressures in the direction of unilateral reductions) was not in its most creative phase, especially when its basic force structure was inadequate. A fundamental reexamination would have to wait for a restoration of our national unity with the end of the Vietnam war.

East-West Relations in Europe

IN 1969, impatience with the rigors of the Cold War was pervasive in the West. All leaders were under pressure to demonstrate their commitment to peace; the Soviet Union played on these sensitivities cleverly. Within months after the brutal invasion of Czechoslovakia, *Western* governments had been maneuvered into the position of feeling obliged to prove their goodwill in East-West relations.

At each stop on his first European trip in early 1969, Nixon had found himself in discussions of how to respond to Soviet overtures. Each leader had urged him to start the SALT negotiations as rapidly as possible and to consult as they progressed; the axiom that the Soviets were ready for real détente because of domestic pressures for consumer goods and external pressures from China was unchallenged. Expanded exchanges and trade were also sought. De Gaulle strongly urged an approach to the Soviet Union. When Walter Scheel, leader of the West German Free Democratic Party and soon to be Foreign Minister, called on Nixon in June, he made the point that Europeans no longer feared a US–Soviet condominium; the majority of European public opinion not only endorsed détente but sought to become part of the process.

Though Nixon was skeptical, and I shared his view, these nearly unanimous appeals posed a serious challenge for us. In previous decades, American rigidity had become a target for leftist criticism in Europe, making NATO a controversial subject in every European country and forcing European leaders to shift to a détente line, purporting to act as a "bridge" between East and West. The stark fact was that if America was intransigent, we risked being isolated within the Alliance and pushing Europe toward neutralism. Similarly, within America we would be pummeled for our bellicosity, and the hysteria over Vietnam would spread to other areas of policy.

For all these reasons we came to the conclusion that we could best hold the Alliance together by accepting the principle of détente but establishing clear criteria to determine its course. On his trip through Europe Nixon never tired of preaching the gospel of his Administration: We were ready for an era of negotiations, but there would remain substantial elements of confrontation; negotiations had to be serious and concrete, not atmospheric. To that end, Atlantic unity and strength were vital. The Soviets must entertain no hope of dividing the Alliance by selective détente with some allies but not with others. We were determined to establish an agenda that did not permit the Soviets to pick their own issues, impose their own definition of détente, or lull the West into complacency.

The first tricky problem was SALT. When Nixon entered office one of the most insistent arguments of devotees of strategic arms limitation was that the Europeans desired it. And indeed when we delayed the talks in 1969 in order to review options and to link SALT to other issues, many European leaders stressed its urgency. This was easy for them since it involved no decisions on their part. As one of my associates wrote to me after a trip to Europe: "One can expect a growing appetite for detente, if only because it is so much more pleasant to think about than military problems." But the inevitable European ambivalence emerged when the negotiations that had been so insistently demanded were in fact approaching. As soon as we set a date for the opening of SALT and began briefing our allies, they began to grasp the strategic implications. An agreement between the Soviet Union and the United States to limit strategic weapons would inevitably ratify strategic equality. There could be no other basis for negotiation; and indeed our briefings pointed out to them that parity was approaching even *without* agreement as a result of the steady growth of Soviet forces. Josef Luns, then Dutch Foreign Minister, said to the President that the notion of parity was one of the most shocking propositions that he had ever heard. Similarly, Chancellor Kiesinger commented that he had not followed the strategic situation closely in recent years; it had come as something of a "thought-provoking" surprise to realize how close the two sides were to equality. Our allies had no reason to be surprised but every cause for concern: Strategic parity was bound to increase the dangers of the conventional superiority that the Soviet Union had long held on the European continent.

The British representative at the briefing of the NATO Council on June 30 questioned whether in view of the trend in the weapons development of both sides this was the moment for talks. West German Ambassador Rolf Pauls, in conversation with me on July 4, hit the nail on the head: SALT marked the end of American strategic superiority; the Soviet Union would erode our advantage either through its own buildup or through negotiations. I replied that I would hate to think that the world's greatest industrial power would be doomed to lose an arms race. But because of procurement decisions made in the 1960s, the trends of technology, the divisions caused by Vietnam, and the massive difficulty in obtaining Congressional approval for *any* new strategic programs, I knew that Pauls was right.

I summed up the European reaction for Nixon on July 10:

It is a fair estimate that some of the original enthusiasm for SALT is waning. One reason for this is the underlying concern over the effect of a SALT agreement. Some countries apparently fear that an agreement based on parity would leave the Soviet Union with a substantial margin of superiority in conventional forces in Europe, and the net result would be that the over-all deterrent against Soviet attacks might be weakened. There is also some concern, mainly German, that the connection between SALT and political matters is no longer to be maintained.

Fortunately for all concerned, the Soviet Union procrastinated in accepting the date proposed for opening the negotiations. This gave us an opportunity to complete our own internal studies and to achieve a satisfactory understanding with our European allies.

We could not fully overcome the disquiet of our allies, even though it was generated in large part by their urging us into détente and then shrinking before its consequences. On July 4 I had warned Ambassador Pauls — only half facetiously — that our allies henceforth had better be careful about what they proposed to us because we .might well accept their recommendations. The peril to Europe arose not from unilateral American concessions as a result of détente, however; it resulted from the fact that under conditions of strategic parity the inequality of forces on the continent of Europe would sooner or later make a difference. The governments of the Alliance for a variety of reasons, mostly domestic, were unwilling or unable to take the necessary remedial measures; in their absence they were bound to live increasingly dangerously. No amount of reassurance would be able to change this. But to synchronize allied cohesion and East-West negotiations on many subjects depended on some agreed view of the world we lived in, of the purposes we sought to achieve together, and of the requirements of the common defense.

Berlin and Brandt's Ostpolitik

THE relationship of the Communist world and the West can never have a uniform texture. SALT negotiations were confined to the United States and the Soviet Union, though our NATO allies had an obvious interest in them. Berlin involved all the wartime allies that had a legal responsibility for the city: Britain, France, the United States, and the Soviet Union. Because Berlin was technically under military occupation, West Germany had no legal status to negotiate. The almost perennial crises of two decades had made clear that the freedom of Berlin paradoxically depended on maintaining its status as a city still under occupation. This was the sole legal basis on which the United States and its Western allies could resist Soviet and East German pressures, anomalous though this was a generation after the end of the Second World War. In 1959 and again in 1961–1962, Western fortitude in maintaining occupation rights and Khrushchev's inability to stick to one strand of policy had preserved Berlin's freedom. But nothing could change the geographic realities of a city isolated a hundred miles deep in Communist territory, subject to harassment, susceptible at all times to new blackmail. Its vulnerability symbolized the tenuous nature of East-

West relations; it was the living proof of the importance of our concept of linkage. We could defend Berlin only by linking its freedom to other Soviet concerns. Any policy that dealt with Berlin as a separate issue was bound to find the Western allies at a significant negotiating disadvantage because of Berlin's military vulnerability.

The problem of Berlin reemerged almost accidentally early in the Nixon Presidency, largely as a result of the vagaries of the German constitutional cycle that made 1969 a presidential election year. As I have mentioned, Federal electors from the Bundestag and states intended, as before, to hold their special session to elect the President in West Berlin, in the old Reichstag building. In December 1968, the Soviet Foreign Ministry formally protested the coming session in Berlin to US Ambassador Llewellyn Thompson. The Johnson Administration decided to leave the response to its successor. On January 22, 1969, Secretary of State Rogers forwarded to President Nixon a draft rejecting the Soviet protest. I agreed with Rogers's proposed reply; however, I recommended — subject to German concurrence — that we not send it until much closer to the date of the German presidential election, which was March 5. It did not seem to me to be in our interest to invite what was bound to be an unproductive and potentially acrimonious exchange. The reply was held up.

The East Germans thereupon began some minor harassment of civilian traffic to Berlin. In memoranda of January 28 and February 11 I told the President that we should stay cool; this did not look to be the time for the Soviet Union to seek a confrontation with us. I also informed him of our contingency plans if harassment continued or increased. In my briefing paper for the President's first meeting with Soviet Ambassador Dobrynin on February 17, I recommended: "I think it especially important that you disabuse Dobrynin of the idea that Soviet–East German interference with access to Berlin in connection with the Federal Assembly meeting there on March 5 is a matter that does not directly concern the United States." Nixon made this point sharply to Dobrynin in his meeting of February 17. Dobrynin, showing that the Soviet Union was not prepared to test the new President so early in his term, hastened to reassure the President that Moscow sought no confrontation.

On February 22, the day before the President was to leave for Europe, Dobrynin passed a message to me urging us to intervene with the Kiesinger government to call off the election in Berlin. This would allow us to "avoid unnecessary tensions and cut short a tendency towards mounting of tension," said the Soviet note. I rejected the proposition; we would make no such request of Kiesinger. I warned Dobrynin sternly against unilateral acts; to underline my warning, the President, on my recommendation, ordered a step-up in US military traffic over the access routes to Berlin.

As I have already described, while visiting Berlin on February 27, Nixon in a speech at the Siemens factory strongly reaffirmed the American commitment to the freedom of the city: "Let there be no miscalculation: No unilateral move, no illegal act, no form of pressure from any source will shake the resolve of the Western nations to defend their rightful status as protectors of the people of free Berlin." After our return, and shortly before the election, Dobrynin complained mildly about the President's rhetoric. I replied that the President had simply reaffirmed existing commitments; we would consider any harassment of access to Berlin with the utmost gravity. Nothing would contribute more to the easing of tensions than to regularize access procedures to Berlin. Dobrynin for the first time suggested that there were "positive possibilities" to negotiate on that subject. The election of the new Federal President, Gustav Heinemann, took place on March 5 in Berlin without further incident. We had withstood our first, albeit minor, confrontation with the Soviets.

This mini-crisis set in motion a series of maneuvers that resulted in a formal negotiation over Berlin. None of the Western Powers and probably not even the Soviet Union had intended this early in 1969. (The process gathered momentum only slowly. But after many false starts it culminated in the late summer of 1971 in a new Four-Power agreement that put at least a temporary end to twenty-five years of tensions over Berlin.)

In the light of Dobrynin's hints, Nixon in his letter to Kosygin of March 26 repeated his offer to discuss Berlin. Kosygin replied on May 27 to the effect that the Soviet Union had no "objections" to a discussion of Berlin but that the Federal Republic was to blame for any tensions there. I recommended against pursuing the subject further in a bilateral channel: "I doubt that this is a good time to rush into any full-scale talks. Following the German election,* we might raise the issue with the new government in Bonn and then consider whether and how to follow up with Moscow."

Receiving no further reply from the United States, the Soviets turned to the public arena. On July 10, Soviet Foreign Minister Gromyko gave a speech affirming Soviet willingness to "exchange views as to how complications concerning West Berlin can be avoided now and in the future." Brandt, still Foreign Minister, had been urging his allies ever since the NATO ministerial meeting in April to seek to negotiate "improvements" in civilian access without telling us how to do this; he now urged rapid acceptance of Gromyko's offer. His sense of urgency was in my view not unconnected with the imminent German election. In any event, "rapid" in the cumbersome machinery of allied consultations translated into a four-week delay. On August 7, together with the

---

* The forthcoming parliamentary election scheduled for September 1969.

British and French, we informed the Soviet Union of our readiness to conduct exploratory talks.

The Soviets, however, waited well over a month to return what was a basically disappointing reply. They accepted Four-Power talks but resisted any discussion of improved access to Berlin; they wanted the discussions to focus on curbing the activities of the Federal Republic in West Berlin.

On October 20 when he met with Nixon, Dobrynin made another run at a bilateral US–Soviet negotiation, proposing a formal exchange of views. As I mentioned in Chapter V, I cautioned the President against it: "I think we should not encourage the notion of bilateral US–Soviet talks on Berlin at this stage. The Soviets would use them to stir up suspicions among the Allies and to play us off against each other. I believe we would do best to keep this issue in the quadripartite forum for the moment and not to press too much ourselves."

In fact, by then Soviet policy over Berlin was shifting its focus to Bonn after the advent of the new government of Willy Brandt.

As a result of the German general election of September 28, 1969, a new coalition of Social Democrats and Free Democrats came into office pledged to new openings toward the East.* The leader of the Free Democrats, Walter Scheel, had foreshadowed this approach in his conversation with Nixon on June 13. He had argued that the Hallstein Doctrine — which forbade diplomatic relations with non-Communist governments that recognized East Germany — would isolate the Federal Republic from the Third World. Closer relations between the two Germanies were essential either on the basis of a new treaty arrangement or some other legal formula.

But such a policy was not without its dangers. The State Department, in a thoughtful paper of October 6, pointed out that the new coalition could not pursue simultaneously active policies toward East Germany and integration of the Federal Republic into Western Europe. The State Department concluded — and I agreed — that "under an SPD-FDP coalition an active all-German and Eastern policy will have the first priority."

I shared these concerns in a memorandum to the President:

It should be stressed that men like Brandt, Wehner and Defense Minister [Helmut] Schmidt undoubtedly see themselves as conducting a responsible policy of reconciliation and normalization with the East and intend not to have this policy come into conflict with Germany's Western association. There can be no doubt about their basic Western orientation. But their problem is to control a

---

*Nixon, mistakenly assuming that the Christian Democratic plurality meant that Kurt Kiesinger would continue as Chancellor, had telephoned Kiesinger to congratulate him. When the Social Democrats (SPD) and the Free Democrats (FDP) formed a majority coalition instead, Brandt graciously forgave the gaffe by commenting: "To err is human, the more so at a distance."

process which, if it results in failure, could jeopardize their political lives and if it succeeds could create a momentum that may shake Germany's domestic stability and unhinge its international position.

It seemed to me that Brandt's new *Ostpolitik*, which looked to many like a progressive policy of quest for détente, could in less scrupulous hands turn into a new form of classic German nationalism. From Bismarck to Rapallo it was the essence of Germany's nationalist foreign policy to maneuver freely between East and West. By contrast, American (and German) policy since the 1940s had been to ground the Federal Republic firmly in the West, in the Atlantic Alliance and then the European Community.

Brandt's election, in fact, threw into sharp relief the central problem of German foreign policy. The German nation had been divided into two states for two decades. A brutal assertion of Soviet power had imposed a Communist regime on the eastern third of the country against the will of the population — the so-called German Democratic Republic. It was preposterous, of course, that in the center of Europe, where nationalism had originated, the world community should acquiesce in, if not positively endorse, the acceptance of a regime artificially imposed by foreign troops, a regime which could never have won a free election. Such "imperialism" in Asia or Africa would have produced outraged outcries and demonstrations; in Central Europe acceptance of the status quo became the test of reasonableness.

Any West German government was bound to avow the goal of reunification. But in prevailing circumstances this was unachievable without a massive collapse of Soviet power. The Western allies were willing to wait; they were not prepared to run significant risks on behalf of reunification — in part because a unified Germany raised in many West European and some American minds the specter of new German hegemony.

But the Federal Republic could not simply wait; it needed some plausible concept for dealing with a divided Germany. Throughout the Fifties and Sixties successive German governments had attempted to resolve this dilemma by ostracizing the East German regime. But by 1970 more and more countries were recognizing East Germany in defiance of Bonn's threat to cut off relations (the Hallstein Doctrine). The policy increasingly ran the risk of backfiring; it threatened to isolate Bonn rather than East Germany. By the middle Sixties the Federal Republic had felt obliged to make an "exception" for the countries of Eastern Europe on the weak excuse that they were not free in their decisions.

I had greatly admired Adenauer and his wise insistence on subordinating all other considerations to the need for gaining for his country a reputation for reliability and steadiness. But by the Seventies the Adenauer policies on reunification were bound to bring the Federal Republic into increasing conflict with both allies and the nonaligned. Bonn would have faced a possible crisis with the East practically alone had it held to its earlier course. It was to Brandt's historic credit that he assumed for Germany the burdens and the anguish imposed by necessity.

I cannot maintain that I came to this view immediately. But once I recognized the inevitable, I sought to channel it in a constructive direction by working closely with Brandt and his colleagues. Resurgent nationalism was a danger whichever course the Federal Republic pursued; it could be best avoided by a relationship of confidence that made a separate course appear too unrewarding and risky. We were determined to spare no effort to mute the latent incompatibility between Germany's national aims and its Atlantic and European ties.

For the deeper motivation of Soviet overtures both toward the Federal Republic and toward the other allies was to practice selective détente — to ease tensions with some allies while maintaining an intransigent position toward us. It would be achieved by elaborating presumed conflicts of interest between us and our allies; or by maneuvering us into appearing as the obstacle to an easing of tensions. Whatever the strategy, its purpose was to divide the Alliance and isolate us. But we were not without recourse. The Federal Republic did not have the bargaining tools to conduct its *Ostpolitik* on a purely national basis — and our other allies could not do without our security umbrella. On Berlin the negotiating strength of the two sides was too unequal; with the city isolated and East Germany occupied, the Federal Republic needed the support of its allies. Linkage was inherent. If *Ostpolitik* were to succeed, it had to be related to other issues involving the Alliance as a whole; only in this manner would the Soviet Union have incentives for compromise.

This was our attitude when Brandt asked that we receive his political confidant Egon Bahr on October 13, even before the new government was formally installed. I had known Egon Bahr from Brandt's days as Mayor of Berlin when Bahr was press spokesman. We had renewed our acquaintance when he headed the policy planning staff during Brandt's tenure as Foreign Minister. Bahr was a man of great intelligence and extraordinary confidence in his ability to devise formulas to overcome a diplomatic impasse. He was dedicated to improving West Germany's relations with the East; he believed that good personal relations with Soviet and East German personalities would assist this effort. His vanity caused him to flaunt these contacts and it was no doubt occasionally exploited by his counterparts. His enemies — and they were many — accused him of pro-Soviet sympathies; many distrusted what they interpreted as his deviousness. Though Bahr was a man of the left, I considered him above all a German nationalist who wanted to exploit Germany's central position to bargain with both sides. He was of the type that had always believed that Germany could realize its national destiny only by friendship with the East, or at least by avoiding its enmity. Bahr was obviously not as unquestioningly dedicated to Western unity as the people we had known in the previous government; he was also free of any sentimental attachment to the United States. To him, America was a weight to be added to West Germany's scale in the right way at the right time, but his priority was to restore relations between the two Germanies above all. As for his alleged deviousness, I tended to share Metternich's view that in a negotiation the perfectly straightforward person was the most difficult to deal with. I at any rate did not lack the self-confidence to confront Bahr's tactics.

So I met Bahr with the attitude of establishing a cooperative relationship. That I thought *Ostpolitik* was more likely to lead to a permanent division of Germany than to healing its breach was irrelevant. The Brandt government was asking not for our advice but for our cooperation in a course to which its principal figures had long since been committed. I thought we should receive Bahr so as to reduce the distrust produced by Nixon's unfortunate election-night telephone call to Kiesinger. It seemed to me important to work *with* Brandt rather than against him; opposing him would earn us the opprobrium of all the Germans of both parties who believed that Brandt deserved a chance. Moreover, Brandt's course was supported by all allies with the possible exception of France, which was, however, unwilling to make its opposition explicit. And in the long term Brandt's aim of conciliation in Central Europe was historically correct even if sometimes he pursued it with an enthusiasm and single-mindedness that weakened his bargaining position.

The first result of Egon Bahr's proposed visit was a procedural dispute with the Secretary of State. Rogers objected to the trip on the not unreasonable ground that negotiations should be conducted in the State Department. Rogers and I, dealing with each other like two sovereign entities, finally made a compact: I would receive Bahr but not negotiate with him, and Martin Hillenbrand, Assistant Secretary of State for European Affairs, would sit in on the meetings. There was a not insignificant deviation from my compact with Rogers in that Bahr, after leaving the White House by the front door, reentered it through the basement for a private talk with me, primarily to establish a channel by which we could stay in touch outside the formal procedures. As with my channels with Dobrynin to Moscow, with Pakistan to China, and on occasion with Israel and even Egypt, my contact with Egon Bahr became a White House backchannel by which Nixon could manage diplomacy bypassing the State Department.

Bahr informed us of the course Brandt intended to follow. He stressed that he wanted to pursue it in cooperation and friendship with the United States, but left little doubt that the policy itself was not subject to discussion. The major result was that Brandt would stay in close consultation with us and that we would cooperate with him. On November 11, Walter Scheel, the new Foreign Minister, announced that Bonn would shortly initiate talks with the Soviet Union on an agreement on the mutual renunciation of force. A formal proposal was made on November 16.* Meanwhile, the Western allies decided to reply to the Soviet proposal of September 24 on Berlin by offering their own detailed set of proposals. We wanted a guarantee for civilian surface traffic to and from West Berlin, regularized and simplified crossing procedures for West Berliners to travel to East Berlin, and the easing of postal, telephone, and other communications between the city's two halves. This note was dispatched on December 16.

By then a December NATO meeting of Foreign Ministers at US urging had set up a series of linkages to prevent "selective détente" and to strengthen Brandt's bargaining position. We made agreement to a European Security Conference conditional on progress in talks on Berlin and in Soviet-German negotiations. *Ostpolitik* was being embedded in a matrix of negotiations that enhanced the bargaining position of the Federal Republic but that also set limits beyond which it could not go without an allied consensus. Of these potential negotiations perhaps the most complicated was the European Security Conference.

European Security Conference

THE idea of a European Security Conference had been a staple of East-West discussions for a decade and a half. In the 1950s the Soviet Union had proposed it repeatedly. But it was equally repeatedly rejected out of hand as a transparent attempt to prevent German rearmament and the development of NATO, and indeed to prevent *any* American role in Europe, since the proposal usually excluded the United States as not "European." In the Fifties, also, several thoughtful observers — the most notable being George Kennan — advocated a disengagement of US and Soviet forces from Central Europe. In the prevailing climate this too was not seriously considered, if only because the distances to which the United States and the Soviet Union would withdraw were too unequal.

By the time Nixon entered office, political conditions had changed. In July 1966, the Warsaw Pact nations had issued a "Declaration on

---

* By approaching the USSR first, Brandt's government hoped to smooth the way for subsequent negotiations with East Germany and the other neighboring Soviet satellites. The Grand Coalition had attempted approaches to East European countries without first approaching the Soviet Union; the Soviets therefore blocked them.

Strengthening Peace and Security in Europe,'' urging a European Security Conference. In April 1967 a conference of European Communist parties followed suit. By December 1967 Western governments were facing domestic pressures to ease their earlier opposition. In the Harmel Report to NATO of December 1967, named after the Belgian Foreign Minister, therefore, the Alliance put the collective search for ''progress towards a more stable relationship'' with Eastern Europe high on its list of priorities, second only to deterrence of aggression. In June 1968 at the meeting of its Foreign Ministers in Reykjavik, NATO signaled its readiness to discuss mutual and balanced force reductions (MBFR) — the new technical term for disengagement — with the Warsaw Pact.

Communist policy is often described as diabolically clever, complicated, following well-thought-out routes toward world domination. This was not my impression. On the contrary, I found Soviet diplomacy generally rigid; nor is subtlety the quality for which Soviet diplomacy will go down in history. The Soviet Union has, in fact, had spectacularly little success in advancing its cause by diplomacy or moral consensus. Almost all of its advances have been due not to diplomatic skill but to the threat or reality of deploying massive military power.

But Soviet diplomacy has one great asset. It is extraordinarily persevering; it substitutes persistence for imagination. It has no domestic pressures impelling it constantly to put forward new ideas to break deadlocks. It is not accused of rigidity if it advances variations of the same proposals year after year. There are no rewards in the Politburo for the exploration of ever-new schemes, which turns so much of American diplomacy into a negotiation with ourselves. Like drops of water on a stone, Soviet repetitiveness has the tendency sooner or later to erode the resistance of the restless democracies. Pressures develop to accept the Soviet proposal ''in principle,'' or at least to talk about it. Once the subject is accepted as legitimate, the discussion immediately switches to the terms. The yearning for relaxation of tensions creates a presumption in favor of the Soviet agenda. The desire for agreement encourages constant pressures to find at least something in the Soviet position to accept.

So it was to some extent with the idea of the European Security Conference. Disparaged in the Fifties, rejected in the Sixties, it finally began to gain acceptance with the passing years by default, as it were. Soviet persistence was reinforced by domestic yearnings for an end to the Cold War, partly under the disillusionment caused by Vietnam. As American leadership of the Alliance began to be questioned, public opinion in allied countries looked for alternatives for their security. As the United States seemed to be withdrawing from Europe, the idea of mutual force reductions took on respectability. Some saw mutual force reductions as desirable in themselves; some advanced the idea as a means either to head off, or to gain some Soviet reciprocity for, the

American unilateral withdrawals from Europe that our domestic turmoil made appear inevitable.

The Soviet Union continued to press, partly to exploit the evident Western interest, partly to distract thoughts from Czechoslovakia. On March 17, 1969, a Warsaw Pact meeting in Budapest formally proposed an early conference on European security. It called for strengthening of political, economic, and cultural contacts; recognition of the inviolability of frontiers, including the Oder-Neisse boundary (between East Germany and Poland) and the frontier between West and East Germany; mutual recognition by West and East Germany of each other as sovereign states; renunciation by the Federal Republic of its claims to represent the entire German people; and recognition of West Berlin's separation from the Federal Republic. It was, in short, the maximum Soviet program for Europe, put forward in the name of enhancing European security.

On April 3 Dobrynin submitted the Warsaw Pact proposal to the White House through the Channel. He even accompanied it with a concession. He told me for the first time that the Soviet Union would not object to United States participation in what had previously been described as an "all-European conference." He also called to my particular attention the fact that the Budapest Declaration had dropped the requirement of previous declarations that alliance systems in Europe be dissolved; in other words, Moscow generously agreed to the continuation of NATO.

I was not prepared to treat the withdrawal of two absurd preconditions as a concession. Writing to the President on April 4, I pointed out that "anyone who is serious about making progress on European problems knows that we must be a party; we should not make the Soviets think that they are doing us a favor if they agree to such an obvious fact of life."

Nevertheless, the apparent conciliatory Soviet tone evoked enormous eagerness within the Alliance. While visiting Washington for Eisenhower's funeral, Mariano Rumor, then Italian Prime Minister, told Nixon that despite the propagandistic intent of the Soviet proposals the Italian political situation required a forthcoming response. Being forthcoming vis-à-vis a propagandistic maneuver is no mean feat; to keep it from turning into a slippery slope is more difficult still. Brandt favored a European Security Conference for the strange reason that it would legitimize the American presence in Europe. Pompidou embraced it as a means of avoiding separate German overtures toward the East and absorbing them in a multilateral framework. British leaders advocated it as a means to transcend the Cold War.

In these circumstances, I recommended to the President that to turn down the Soviet overture completely would leave us isolated within

NATO. But we should make our agreement in principle depend on progress on concrete European issues, especially Berlin. In a memorandum of April 8 I noted:

Without such progress, a conference would probably find the East European countries closely aligned with a rigid Soviet position, while the western participants would be competing with each other to find ways to "break the deadlock." The net result . . . would tend to set back prospects for an eventual resolution of European issues. Consequently, our emphasis should be on the need for talks on concrete issues and for consultations within NATO designed to develop coherent western positions on such issues.

This became the United States position; it was substantially adopted by the NATO ministerial meeting in April of 1969.

European security had thus been deliberately put on a slow track. No specific steps could be taken until the next NATO ministerial conference in December; it had been related to concrete issues; the imperative of American participation had been made clear; it had to be preceded by progress on the German question.

But once launched, a diplomatic process cannot be controlled simply by formal declarations — especially from the office of the security adviser in the White House basement. Good policy depends on the patient accumulation of nuances; care has to be taken that individual moves are orchestrated into a coherent strategy. Only rarely do policy issues appear in terms of black or white. More usually they depend on shades of interpretation; significant policy deviations begin as minor departures whose effect becomes apparent only as they are projected into the future. Inevitably, therefore, the European Security Conference raised the same issues about linkage and the philosophy of East-West relations that had divided our government all along. The White House approach was to make our participation in a European Security Conference conditional on Soviet concessions on Berlin and the intra-German negotiations. The State Department saw in a security conference a desirable forum that should be made to yield some results, perhaps on balanced force reductions, perhaps on principles of coexistence. It opposed linkage and as usual chipped away at White House resistance.

In the meantime Dobrynin weighed in with a proposal of the Warsaw Pact nations that a European Security Conference be assembled in the first half of 1970, with a two-point agenda: renunciation of the use or threat of force in relations between European states, and the widening of commercial, economic, technical, and scientific relations between European states. I opposed both the schedule and the agenda. We could not agree on a date until there had been progress in other negotiations, especially on Berlin; nor could we let the Soviets focus on recognition of the status quo in Europe until the results of Bonn's *Ostpolitik* were clearer; Bonn, not we, should assume the responsibility for accepting the division of Germany. And it made no sense expanding commercial and technical ties if tensions persisted. The President issued instructions along this line.

Rogers could report to the President with some satisfaction of the December NATO ministerial meeting:

> On the European Security Conference and East-West relations, we achieved a realistic and cautious NATO stand which stressed the need for further explorations and better prospects for significant results before we agreed to go to a Conference. We also obtained Alliance agreement on NATO initiatives vis-a-vis Eastern Europe including preparation of a negotiating position for mutual and balanced force reductions, support for initiatives on Germany and Berlin. . . . Euphoria for a conference for a conference's sake was contained. . . .

We had, in fact, blunted the Soviet strategy of selective détente by linking key issues to each other. The Soviets wanted a European Security Conference but they could not get one except by making progress in Berlin, where we had a veto as an occupying power. Brandt's *Ostpolitik* tended to confirm the European status quo no matter what we did, but Brandt would not be able to get his agreement with the Soviet Union or East Germany ratified by his Parliament in the absence of an agreement that improved access to Berlin. If we kept our head, therefore, we were in a position to encourage détente and to control its pace, to respond to our allies' pleas for an easing of tensions, and conduct a negotiation both precise and compatible with our security.

European Leaders Visit Washington: 1970

THERE was thus much to talk about when the West European leaders, reciprocating Nixon's visit of the year before, descended on Washington at monthly intervals starting late in January 1970. The first visitor was Harold Wilson; he was followed by Georges Pompidou in late February and by Willy Brandt in early April.

Wilson, as always with Nixon, affected his most avuncular manner, like a small-town banker who had decided that the best way to deal with his most improvident customer was to give him a reputation for parsimony to uphold. He urged on Nixon the benefits of Brandt's policy as if no other approach were conceivable. Nixon, whose suspicion of Brandt had not abated, went no further than to indicate that we would do nothing to oppose him. At the same time, Wilson was not above using *Ostpolitik* to further his goal of Britain's entry into the European Community, arguing that Britain's membership might serve to restrain German nationalist ambitions.

Much of the discussion was about Biafra, a province of Nigeria, populated by the Ibo tribe, that had sought to secede from the central government. The borders of Africa's nations were cruelly drawn by imperial powers on the basis of administrative convenience, cutting across tribal or linguistic ties. National unity within existing frontiers was both constantly at risk and passionately defended. Secession — especially on a tribal basis — threatened to disrupt all established order; once the precedent was established no state would be safe. The Organization of African Unity strongly supported the Nigerian federal government's war to preserve the unity of the country. So did Britain, convinced also that its colonial tradition conferred a special knowledge of African problems.

For some reason Biafra had become an issue in the American Presidential campaign of 1968. Nixon had claimed that the United States was not doing enough to ease civilian suffering in the besieged province. Our State Department shared the British view that to challenge Nigerian sovereignty would earn us the hostility of Africa's most populous nation and the suspicions of all others. I am inclined to believe that Nixon took the contrary view in part because he took no little pleasure in showing some of those who were wont to attack him for his alleged moral defects that they too were capable of expediency on the issue of human rights.

During Wilson's visit in January 1970 the Nigerian civil war was drawing to a bloody conclusion. The central government was about to overrun the seceding province. Independent studies had indicated that unless massive relief supplies reached Biafra immediately, a million and a half would starve to death. The Nigerian government insisted that all supplies be delivered through it. The White House — with Roger Morris of my staff playing an energetic and passionate role — was seeking to rush supplies directly. I supported Morris. So did Nixon, happy for once to be on the humane side of an issue. British obfuscation and State Department procrastination soon made the issue moot. We never succeeded in establishing an independent relief program. Federal troops took control of the province and snuffed out Biafran "independence." A curtain of silence descended. In the end, the Nigerian federal government successfully carried out a policy of reconciliation with the defeated Ibos. Wilson influenced Nixon's policy to a degree and curbed our interventionist impulses. From the point of view of our long-term interests he and the State Department were undoubtedly right.

Another noteworthy event of Wilson's visit was his attendance at a regular NSC meeting. It was Nixon's way of reciprocating for his equally historic attendance at a session of the British Cabinet when he visited London in February 1969. Both events were part charade, since obviously no serious debate would occur in the presence of foreign leaders — all the less so as Nixon was generally uncomfortable with any discussion whose outcome he could not foresee. The subject chosen, appropriately enough, was American policy toward Europe. The bureaucratic maneuvering preceding the meeting turned out to be far more interesting than the meeting itself. For a year my office had sought to extract an options paper on the subject from the European Bureau of the State Department. It had resisted bitterly. The State Department had considered European policy its special preserve and did not want to admit what was unfortunately inherent in the presentation of options: the possibility of a policy change.

After months of procrastination over subsidiary issues there emerged at last a governmental options paper. The choices being laid before the President hardly opened scintillating new vistas. They were: (1) maintaining the "present course"; (2) supporting an "enhanced Europe" (meaning British entry and closer integration); or (3) American disengagement. Here was the standard bureaucratic device of leaving the decision-maker with only one real option, which for easy identification is placed in the middle. The classic case, I joked, would be to confront the policymaker with the choices of nuclear war, present policy, or surrender. In this case, the bureaucracy took no chances. Options 1 and 2 were the same; our present course was an "enhanced Europe." "American disengagement" had pejorative connotations and no support in our government or in any allied government. Thus the preordained consensus quickly embraced the policy of encouraging an "enhanced Europe." Nixon laid down the gospel:

I have never been one who believes the US should have control of the actions of Europe. It is in the interests of the United States to have a strong economic, political and military European community, with the United Kingdom in that community. I have preferred that Europe move independently, going parallel with the United States. A strong, healthy and independent Europe is good for the balance of the world. For the US to play a heavy-handed role would be counter-productive. What we want is friendly competition with the United States.

Wilson generously told the NSC meeting that it was "fascinating as a form of governmental process." This was either a token of Wilson's personal affection for things American, or else classic British understatement. "Fascinating" was surely the least one could say for a procedure that brought forth alternatives no one would consider and that after months of study pointed to the course — British membership in an increasingly integrated Europe — which was already being carried out.

In a few months it began to appear that matters were not quite so simple. The "enhanced Europe" had its political promise, but it was also evidently capable of fierce economic competition with us, producing tensions not foreseen by the grand designs of the Sixties. But by then Harold Wilson was out of office. In June he called an election that he confidently expected to win — an opinion shared also by all our key officials save Nixon, whose prediction of a Heath victory never wavered and who never let his associates forget his prescient forecast.

The relationship with our next visitor, French President Georges Pompidou, proved more complex. He was the heir of the Gaullist tradition, having served as de Gaulle's Prime Minister for nearly a decade. De Gaulle had dismissed him after the student riots of 1968. Had de Gaulle not resigned in the spring of 1969, Pompidou would almost surely have slipped to the periphery of French politics. He rarely referred to de Gaulle, but when he did the deep injury showed through. I recall no occasion when he mentioned the positive qualities of his predecessor but several when he spoke of his aloofness and destructive suspiciousness. And yet Pompidou clearly was a President in de Gaulle's style; he practiced his own aloofness. His bearing was regal, in keeping with the elective monarchy with which the constitution of the Fifth French Republic had endowed its President, who is chosen for a term of seven years (renewable). He was acutely conscious of the prerogatives of his office, seeing in them, with some justice, the symbol of France's regained unity, self-confidence, and influence.

Pompidou was a man of extraordinary intelligence, dignity, and character. Wary eyes peering out behind bushy eyebrows betrayed the skepticism of a son of the Auvergne, that hardy region where French peasants have survived a stormy history by not trusting excessively in the unselfishness of their neighbors. He was supremely educated, one of the few statesmen with whom it was a pleasure to discuss subjects outside of politics. He had the skeptic's ability to get to the heart of the matter, and the French intellectual's tendency to endow issues with an intricacy more reflective of his own sophistication than of the cruder criteria employed by less complex personalities. And he had a sardonic sense of humor.

In regard to the United States, considerations of national interest were in ambivalent conflict with the prejudices of the French intellectual. He understood that to continue the confrontations of the de Gaulle period was bound to lead to the isolation of France; challenging the United States was a useful device for asserting French national identity only so long as the United States confined its displeasure to words. In an ultimate test France's relative weakness was bound to be demonstrated. Forced to choose between France and the United States, most European nations — and especially the Federal Republic of Germany — would have to abandon their French connection. Pompidou therefore was determined to follow the path, already initiated in the conversations between Nixon and de Gaulle, of ending the hostility between the two countries. Like de Gaulle he insisted on doing so on a bilateral basis; he distrusted multilateral organizations or decisions as dissolving French identity.

At the same time, Pompidou had the innate suspicion of many Frenchmen that in the end nothing good could come from the United States. Except for untypical representatives — like Nixon and, at the margin, myself — Pompidou really had little confidence that Americans understood international affairs, not to speak of more arcane subjects like political philosophy. He was not a little apprehensive that our characteristic combination of goodwill, great power, and energy might cause the United States to destroy more fragile structures such as the European Community or risk Europe's security by excesses of either hostility or conciliation with Moscow. Like most of his compatriots he did not doubt that we could benefit from French instruction in subtlety. He sought to build counterweights to our presumed impetuosity, even while cooperating to an unprecedented degree in common designs.

With all his doubts and innate suspicions, relations with France improved dramatically under Pompidou. He seemed to like Nixon for his grasp of international affairs and also for his many thoughtful gestures toward France. The latter included Nixon's attendance at the dinner in Pompidou's honor in New York after there had been hostile demonstrations in Chicago (which I will describe) and, later, his flying to Paris for the memorial service for de Gaulle in Notre Dame. (Nixon was, in fact, the first head of state to announce his attendance, thereby forcing a host of others to follow suit.) In return, as I will later describe, Pompidou was extraordinarily helpful in arranging my secret contacts with the North Vietnamese, going so far as to make his own jet available for my travel within France. I briefed him regularly on my talks with the North Vietnamese — more so than I did most of our own senior officials. He maintained complete discretion and never used these kindnesses to exact any kind of return.

Relations were no doubt eased because Pompidou's was the first "normal" Presidency of the Fifth Republic, in the sense that he had come to office by election and not through incipient civil war. He was the first President who could conduct a systematic foreign policy addressed to problems other than overcoming colonial wars or seeking to establish France's autonomy. In the process it became apparent that de Gaulle had built better than his American detractors had been willing to admit. His view that France could play an effective international role only if it pursued interests it perceived as its own proved to be correct. The proposition that an independent France would prove beneficial to the West was ridiculed when it was put forward; it turned out to be true. Under Pompidou and later his distinguished and able successor, Valéry Giscard d'Estaing, French foreign policy was often prickly, but it was serious and consistent. In its fundamentals it was compatible with our purposes, even when its tactics were occasionally grating. At times it was steadier and more perceptive than our own (such as in Africa in the late 1970s).

In its insistence on conducting a global policy by its own lights, France stood in growing contrast to other European allies, including even Great Britain. Britain still possessed the experience and intellectual resources of a great power and was governed by leaders of vast goodwill toward the United States. But with every passing year they acted less as if their decisions mattered. They offered advice, usually sage; they rarely sought to embody it in a policy of their own. British statesmen were content to act as honored consultants to our deliberations. And Brandt in his memoirs prided himself on the fact that his country had purged itself of any aspirations to a global role.[4] Of the NATO allies, therefore, only France aspired to a global policy and tried to assemble the means to carry it out. And, quite contrary to what had been predicted in the Sixties, as the years went on France's independent policy proved of significant help in far-flung areas. This was especially true in Africa, where it was never seduced by the sentimental illusion that the continent could be insulated from the physical and ideological realities of the contemporary world through the strenuous exercise of goodwill.

To be sure, French history and a Cartesian educational system occasionally produced convoluted theories of the motivations of others, especially Americans, that at times caused French policy to seek reassurance against mirages. But French leaders benefited from a tradition that saw no need to apologize for considerations of national interest. Their country had lost most when it engaged in ideological crusades or relied too much on others; it flourished when it understood the imperatives of the balance of power. The French President and Nixon were on the same wavelength when they reviewed international affairs.

Pompidou used the occasion of my first secret meeting with Le Duc Tho in February 1970 to invite me to lunch at his charming apartment in the Ile St. Louis, the ancient heart of Paris, within sight of Notre-Dame. He was clearly nervous about what would be his first visit to the United States as President of France. There had been reports of planned protests against the French sale of advanced airplanes to Libya. He was ill at ease about his coming encounters with our notorious press. I sought to reassure him on both counts. (In the event, I could have saved my breath about the media; he handled the press with natural aplomb. The protesters were another matter; they produced a fiasco.) We discussed the agenda of his imminent meeting with Nixon. I emphasized that we would not embarrass him. We would focus on practical cooperation rather than on the theory by which it might be justified. I told him that Nixon planned to attend a dinner at the French Embassy, the first such invitation he had accepted since entering the White House. Pompidou stressed that he was prepared to discuss all subjects of common interest so long as he was spared the liturgy of NATO integration. While he would not reverse de Gaulle's policy of national defense, he favored practical cooperation in the military field.

Nixon needed no urging to concentrate on the practicalities of cooperation; it reflected his own bent. At his first meeting with Pompidou he elaborated on his favorite theme of the balance of power: it was in the American interest to see an economically strong Europe, as well as Japan. Pompidou went straight to the heart of his concern, which turned out to be *Ostpolitik*. Like all his colleagues he claimed that he trusted Brandt but feared that Brandt's policies might unleash nationalistic tendencies that would prove impossible to contain. The streak of impatience in the German character made him uneasy. Defeats in two world wars had not been conclusive because the combined might of the rest of the world had been needed to accomplish them. German nationalism might break forth again and, if through calamity it had learned patience, it might prove even more dangerous. It was fear of a resurgent Germany, Pompidou averred, that had caused him to reverse de Gaulle's opposition to Britain's entry into Europe. Thus Pompidou's arguments were in fact not so different from Wilson's two weeks earlier; everybody wanted Britain in the Common Market to help restrain Germany. Pompidou even went so far as to ruminate on a London-Paris axis as a counterweight to uncontrolled German nationalism. Even Brandt favored Britain's entry, if obviously for a different reason. He sought to answer those critics who charged him with a one-sided leaning toward the East; it was the reason for his seminal speech in The Hague in early December, urging British entry into the Common Market. In short, Brandt's opening to the East had the unintended consequence of spurring West European integration. Of the three most important European leaders, two distrusted the tendencies unleashed by the third, and the third needed a gesture by which to assuage these suspicions. British entry into the Common Market provided the mechanism.

Pompidou followed the Gaullist approach to the Soviet Union. While profoundly distrusting Soviet purposes and fearful of growing Soviet strength, he advocated a policy of relaxation of tensions. The Soviets, according to Pompidou, were haunted by China and needed quiet in the West. Their desire for relaxation of tensions, therefore, was based not on sentiment but on economic, political, and military necessity. They also wanted economic support, especially for Eastern Europe. They would be tempted to obtain it from Germany. Germany as a Soviet partner was too dangerous, however, both for the Soviet Union and for the West. This is why France was determined not to let Germany get ahead of it in détente policy (thereby setting up unintentionally the preconditions of a race to Moscow). Closer contacts between the West and Russia were also desirable in their own right, according to Pompidou; ultimately they would weaken Moscow by encouraging the more liberal and reform-minded elements in Soviet society. Pompidou did not explain why the Kremlin would embrace a policy that by his analysis would lead to the transformation of its system. Perhaps he meant to imply that the policies of competing countries — especially superpowers — often involve competing assessments of the future, and he was betting on us. Probably, Pompidou was above all concerned with the legacy of Richelieu. Preventing a resurgent Germany on France's borders had a higher priority for him than fear of a more distant Russia, which in the final analysis had to be handled by us.

The visit of Pompidou achieved all that was possible, given the absence of concrete issues requiring solution. The talks were cordial and the two leaders had similar perceptions of European and Alliance questions if not of détente. Practical arrangements were made for intimate consultation by establishing a direct communications "hot line" and designating Pompidou's aide, Michel Jobert, and me as the contacts. The two leaders agreed to begin bilateral military discussions at the staff level. The only sour note occurred in Chicago, where Pompidou and his wife were pummeled by demonstrators protesting the sale of French planes to Libya. Pompidou nearly canceled the remainder of his trip. He was dissuaded only with difficulty and because Nixon announced that he would attend the dinner for Pompidou in New York.

History is sometimes made of small pieces. The incident reinforced Pompidou's inherent ambivalence toward the United States. He remained intellectually committed to close relations, but emotionally he never ceased considering the incident an insult to France and a grave discourtesy to his wife. In the agony of his last year (when he was dying of cancer) this emotional bias was to reinforce whatever substantive disagreements he had over the Year of Europe and lent passion to disputes that were then given added sharpness by Jobert, by then transformed from a staff assistant to Foreign Minister and from self-effacing aide to the oratorical terror of allied diplomacy.

Willy Brandt visited Washington in April 1970. As an unusual sign of respect Nixon had given Brandt the Presidential lodge ("Aspen") at Camp David for a few days of rest before the beginning of formal talks. As had become the custom before important Presidential conversations, I met with Brandt over lunch at Camp David to give him a preview of the President's approach and to sound him out about his own ideas.

Brandt greeted me wearing the Navy jacket with his name and the Presidential seal, which was given routinely to guests there. He had been very flattered by the invitation to Camp David (usually closed to foreign visitors) and the hospitality of the Presidential lodge. He sought to affect great confidence and bonhomie. But it was clear that he was worried about our reaction to his *Ostpolitik*.

I reassured him. There would be no attempt to change his basic course. We would not encourage any particular negotiating strategy. Nor would we comment on specific terms of his negotiation. For this he would have to take responsibility; we would not participate in the German domestic debate, on either side. We would support Brandt's objectives, stay silent on his methods, urge close consultation with his allies, warn against raising excessive expectations. And we would give him a sense of partnership, which was the best assurance against the latent dangers of a purely national policy. Brandt was greatly relieved.

The meeting between Brandt and Nixon was surprisingly cordial, given the fact that neither man would have sought out the other's company had not fate thrust the leadership of great nations upon them. Nixon had genuine doubts about those he saw as personalities of the left, and Brandt's habit of long silences made him nervous. Nixon made some amends for his gaffe of election night by a graceful dinner toast pledging to place all his telephone calls henceforth through the White House operators, since when he had dialed the call himself on the night of the German election it was to the wrong number. More important, Brandt left Washington with a public endorsement of his overall policy.

In his memoirs Brandt writes that Nixon and I missed the point of one of his more significant comments. It was to the effect that the Soviet proposal for a European Security Conference represented "a novel link with Europe which neither derived from legal rights acquired in the last war nor reposed solely on the North Atlantic Pact." [5] He was wrong. We got the point. We were simply not persuaded by the argument and we thought it more tactful not to pursue it. The "novel" feature of the European Security Conference was Soviet participation in its deliberations. We were willing enough to negotiate with the Soviets about outstanding issues; the implication that Soviet approval was needed to legitimize our role in Europe we considered dangerous. For us a European Security Conference had to be justified on quite different grounds.

Strangely, Vietnam played a minor role in the visits of European leaders. European public opinion, at least as represented by the media, opposed the war. But European leaders registered no objection. During the entire period of the war I recall no criticism by a European leader in even the most private conversation. They seemed paralyzed by the same dilemma that we faced. They wanted the war ended quickly because they traced some of the political unrest in their own countries to contagion from American universities and intellectual circles and because they feared that over time the conflict might sap our capacity to deal with threats to their own security. But they also wanted America's credibility unimpaired. Brandt and Wilson volunteered no comment and made sympathetic noises when Nixon outlined our Vietnam strategy. Pompidou stressed that as long as America demonstrated its desire to liquidate the war — which in his view we were doing — he would not second-guess our tactics. He knew how arduous and time-consuming the process of disengagement had been for France in Algeria. When Edward

Heath became British Prime Minister, he argued vigorously that an American withdrawal from Vietnam under conditions interpreted as a collapse of the American will might unleash a new round of Soviet aggression in Europe. It is impossible to determine whether these views were sincerely held or were the tactful responses of leaders unable to affect specific decisions and unwilling to jeopardize their relations with their principal ally. And it does not make much difference. Hidden motives may be the stuff of memoirs. The actual expression of views is what influences policy.

The visits to Washington of the three European leaders thus revealed that traditional patterns of European politics were beginning to reassert themselves. The British had told Nixon they might resume their historical role of balancing the continental powers. The French were speaking of the need to keep open the line to Moscow so as to watch German-Soviet relations. Both the Germans and the French, in the wake of their talks in Washington, were clearly moving toward Britain, each for their own essentially national reasons. The result was a consensus, however different the motives, on Britain's entry into the Common Market. But with Britain's entry into the Common Market imminent we were brought face to face for the first time with the full implications of what we had wrought.

Second Thoughts about the Common Market

As an enlarged European Community moved from theory to reality, it became clear that the more sentimental theories of earlier decades had painted too simple a picture. An economically strong Europe would be more self-reliant; but also a price would have to be paid for it. As the customs union, which was the Community's most tangible manifestation, began to affect American exports, and Europe came to compete with us in other areas of the world, our business community became restless and its rumblings soon affected governmental decisions. For the first time Atlantic relations became controversial. In the spring of 1970 I ordered a formal interagency consideration of Atlantic relations.

By the fall of 1970 fears about the effects of an expanded European Community, especially in our economic agencies, had become very vocal. The departments of the Treasury, Commerce, and Agriculture, following the tried and true pattern of the Pentagon, had constructed a "worst case" analysis of the consequences of the enlargement of the Common Market to include Britain and (it was then thought) Norway.* In effect they saw it as an economic monster dominating world trade

---

* The Norwegian voters turned down membership in the European Community by a referendum of September 26, 1972.

and monetary arrangements, excluding American agricultural products and manufactured goods, and gradually spreading its economic tentacles into the Third World. This last apprehension had been aroused by the preferential arrangements by which the Common Market nations granted and received special and exclusive trading relationships from their Mediterranean neighbors and former colonies. If all of Britain's former colonies now joined this network of exclusive trading arrangements, these dangers would be magnified. One study prepared for the NSC noted:

> In the long run we could be confronted by an "expanded Europe" comprising a Common Market of at least ten full members, associated memberships for the EFTA [European Free Trade Area] neutrals, and preferential trade arrangements with at least the Mediterranean and most of Africa. This bloc will account for about half of world trade, compared with our 15%; it will hold monetary reserves approaching twice our own; and it will even be able to outvote us constantly in the international economic organizations.

The ire of the economic agencies was inflamed by a passage in the President's Foreign Policy Report of February 1970, which, in the reading of those who had not participated in the drafting, amounted to a carte blanche for European economic nationalism:

> Our support for the strengthening and broadening of the European Community has not diminished. We recognize that our interests will necessarily be affected by Europe's evolution, and we may have to make sacrifices in the common interest. We consider that the possible economic price of a truly unified Europe is outweighed by the gain in the political vitality of the West as a whole.

Treasury and other agencies thought that this passage encouraged European economic pressure against us. It would have been a rash government that based policies so likely to stimulate American retaliation on an isolated and ambiguous sentence. But the passage provided a useful focus for an interagency debate. What the economic agencies wanted, and seriously proposed at an interagency meeting of May 13, was an official "reinterpretation" of the President's report — in effect, a declaration of war on the system of preferences and perhaps even on the concept of the European Community. The economic agencies insisted that we use the forthcoming negotiations for British entry into the Community to conduct the battle.

The State Department (not that it felt an overwhelming obligation to defend the report drafted by me and my staff) nevertheless was horrified by this assault on what had been one of the permanent features of American foreign policy. Expansion and further integration of the European Community had been pursued by us, especially in the Sixties, sometimes with more fervor than by the Europeans themselves. European policy had been the unchallenged preserve of the European Bureau of the State Department; it ruled out any alternative for Britain other than entry into Europe. Now that this project was so close to culmination, a challenge was being thrown down not by a domineering Frenchman but from the least expected quarter — within the United States government — threatening not only its substantive but its bureaucratic preeminence. The European Bureau resisted with time-honored tactics of procrastination and obfuscation. Hours were spent debating whether an interagency paper on British entry should say that European integration "would" or that it "could" pose problems. State fought valiantly against any comprehensive assessment of the negative economic consequences of the enlarged Community. It feared that American opposition would provide a handy scapegoat if for any reason the negotiations on British entry broke down.

But while the State Department was correct in the abstract, it overlooked the political realities, especially in a Congressional election year. It ran its congenital risk of being maneuvered into the position of seeming "soft" in defense of American interests. Congressional feeling soon found expression in a highly discriminatory trade bill aimed squarely at Europe and Japan. It was being pushed by the then extremely powerful House Ways and Means Committee Chairman, Wilbur Mills. This bill would have raised high protectionist barriers against certain imports, especially textiles and shoes. In the summer and fall of 1970 a trade war was clearly threatening; the Common Market countries would likely retaliate against our agricultural exports. Paul McCracken warned the President on July 2 of the danger and asked his intervention with Mills.

I agreed substantially with McCracken and the State Department. I had never shared the notion that a unified Europe would automatically rush to assume our burdens. In my view we had made too one-sided a strategic choice in the Fifties and Sixties. By stressing Europe's economic unification we had emphasized the dimension in which competition with us was most likely and our interests were most likely to diverge. By discouraging a European community in the defense field — at least after the failure of the initial project in 1954 — we downgraded the area in which Atlantic interests were most likely to overlap. But I preferred European unity in some form to a cacophony of conflicting nationalities whose impotence would sooner or later cause them to abdicate a serious concern with foreign policy and thus become functional, if not actual, neutralists. And we could not risk wrecking European unity without breaking the political influence of the very groups in Europe who had supported a strong Atlantic Alliance. The association of much of Africa, of Mediterranean countries such as Spain, Morocco, and Tunisia, to say nothing of Israel, with Western Europe, was in the geopolitical interest of the West. To thwart a relationship of these key countries with Europe would be the height of political folly.

On June 30, in a memorandum to the President, I came down

squarely on the side of our foreign policy objectives. Penalizing of textiles and shoes would hit countries with delicate domestic situations:
Spain, where it might blow up our base negotiations and risk our ties
with post-Franco Spain; Italy, where Communism was gaining; and
Japan. But to affect a Presidential decision it is not enough to oppose a
recommendation; one must offer an alternative. Internationally I proposed a negotiation to place our concerns before the European Community; domestically I put forward a mechanism to enable the economic
agencies to put their views before the President. The NSC Under Secretaries Committee would be augmented by the economic agencies and
be given a watching brief on the economic impact of the European
Community. This scheme was in reality a device to let the economic
agencies "win" on the reinterpretation of the Presidential report, but at
the same time to treat it as a foreign policy rather than economic issue
through the State Department chairmanship of the committee dealing
with the subject. And the requirement that disputed issues be referred to
the President — so dear to the heart of the economic agencies afraid of
State Department dominance — guaranteed that I would have an opportunity to weigh in (if not have the last word) if purely commercial
considerations threatened to overwhelm foreign policy imperatives.

The United States began negotiations with the European Community
on October 10. The European delegation was led by Ralf Dahrendorf, a
West German liberal (which in European terms meant a representative
of a party spanning the center of the spectrum and standing for free enterprise). In a meeting with me on October 15, Dahrendorf emphasized
his "deep concern" about trends in American trade policy. His analysis
of the Community's prospects was not too reassuring, however. Dahrendorf expected British entry, but he thought that the Community no
longer was thinking in terms of political unity; economic integration
would be pursued for its own sake. This is what I had described to the
interagency meeting on May 13 as the worst outcome for us. Without
compensating political progress, economic integration leading to brutal
competition and American retaliation was bound to undermine supporters of the Alliance on both sides of the Atlantic.

The precarious and increasingly strained relationship between the
United States and Europe was reflected in a note scribbled by the President. On a memorandum of November 13 in which I brought him up to
date on negotiations with the European Community, he wrote: "K — It
seems to me that we 'protest' and continue to get the short end of the
stick in our dealings with the Community. Agriculture is a prime example. The Congress is simply not going to tolerate this too passive attitude on the part of our representatives in such negotiations." Nixon was
too much of an Atlanticist to sit out the destructive battle. He appealed
to Wilbur Mills, to no avail. The protectionist trend was too strong;

Mills was not persuaded, and the restrictive trade legislation remained pending in the Congress throughout the summer and fall of 1970. To some extent the silent majority was taking out its frustration at America's being "kicked around" in the world. Our trade negotiations with Europe dragged on inconclusively for nearly a year, until Nixon in August 1971 made the subject at least temporarily irrelevant by his dramatic decision of August 15 to levy a 10 percent surcharge on all imports, to end the convertibility of the dollar into gold, and to establish wage and price controls.

The first contacts, then, had shown the Western Alliance ambivalent about the common defense, uncertain about relations with the East, and united only about the enlargement of the European Community, which in turn triggered an economic controversy with the United States. But the process of consultation led to an increasingly explicit articulation of common purposes. The Western leaders were beginning to come to grips with the fundamental issues. The right questions were beginning to be asked even if it would take some time longer to elaborate commonly accepted answers. Consensus among democracies is inherently more complex than negotiation with authoritarian states. The evolution from tutelage to partnership is never simple. And upon that evolution the Western Alliance was now embarked, to prove that the association of free peoples could flourish in a new generation.

PART THREE

1970-1971: From Turmoil to Hope

XII

The War Widens

W E still live with both the convulsions and the myths of 1970 in Indochina. The war engulfed both Laos and Cambodia. In early 1970 the still new Administration wanted nothing so much as to wind down the war. It was met with a deliberate escalation by the North Vietnamese, ingeniously orchestrating movements of armies and American public opinion while we were engaged in secret peace talks. In February there was a North Vietnamese offensive across the Plain of Jars in Laos. In March the North Vietnamese began to break out of the sanctuaries along Cambodia's frontier with South Vietnam, which they had been occupying without a shred of legality since 1965. They started cutting communications and harassing Phnom Penh with a view to overthrowing the Lon Nol government, which had replaced Sihanouk's without our knowledge or participation. (Lon Nol was recognized by both the UN and the Soviet Union.)

Yet the inflamed condemnation for the tragedies that ensued fell not on Hanoi but on the United States. In my talks in Paris with North Vietnamese emissary Le Duc Tho, he rejected neutrality for both Cambodia and Laos, and emphasized that it was his people's destiny not merely to take over South Vietnam but to dominate the whole of Indochina. The boasts were made in secret but the military moves that expressed these ambitions were plain to see. From an inexhaustible national masochism there sprang the folklore that American decisions triggered the Cambodian nightmare, and the myth survives even today when the Vietnamese, without the excuse of American provocation but with barely a whimper of world protest, have finally fulfilled the ambition of conquering the whole of Indochina. In Cambodia a rabble of murderous ideologues appear, it is true, to have been supplanted by an organized Communist state, but it has been done by the same force of alien arms that first attempted to do so in 1970. Hanoi's insatiable quest for hegemony — not America's hesitant and ambivalent response — is the root cause of Cambodia's ordeal.

The military responses we made were much agonized over, and in our view minimal if we were to conduct a retreat that did not become a rout.

There were certainly errors, but the persistence of the image of American officials plotting the overthrow of neutralist Prince Sihanouk in Cambodia and plunging deeper into war in Laos as well as Cambodia illustrates the prevalence of emotion over reality. The Richard Nixon who on April 30 announced our assault on the Cambodian sanctuaries was the same President who had announced on April 20 the withdrawal of 150,000 troops. The Administration which finally acted to prevent a complete Communist takeover of Cambodia was the same government that had offered the neutralization of Cambodia on April 4 — and been contemptuously rebuffed. The paradoxes of Indochina are many and painful. It was Hanoi that was implacable but it was America that reaped the whirlwind, nearly shattering the nerve of the Executive. Each of these interlocked major events requires a separate narrative in this chapter, but it has to begin with the reality of government at the time, which was that at the end of 1969 and the beginning of 1970 we engaged in a major attempt to understand what was happening on the ground in Vietnam — and to talk peace secretly once again with Hanoi.

The research work had begun in the fall of 1969 when Elliot Richardson and I set up an interagency committee, the Vietnam Special Studies Group, whose purpose was summed up in a memorandum by me to the President dated September 5, 1969:

> Looking back in our experience over the last few years, it is remarkable how frequently officials have let their preconceptions about Vietnam lead them astray even though a careful and objective analysis of readily available facts would have told them differently.

The group met for the first time on October 20. Elliot Richardson, Dave Packard, Richard Helms, and representatives of the Joint Chiefs of Staff and the Defense Intelligence Agency were in attendance. A Working Group, led by Larry Lynn and Bob Sansom of my staff, conducted an intensive study of twelve of the forty-four provinces in South Vietnam to solve the perennial problem of obtaining an accurate assessment of the situation in the countryside, that is, the contest over control of the rural population.

I read over the 100-page paper, covering it with handwritten questions. Why was it, for instance, that in 1965, 1966, and 1967 I was briefed that the South Vietnamese were making progress? What had changed? Did US advisers know what they were looking at? "I have found," I wrote, "that the most incompetent ones are those most easily satisfied. . . . If you have a lower level of incidents, does this mean you are doing well, or is it the enemy's deliberate intention? If it's the latter, is it a signal? How do we know what the infrastructure is that we've destroyed? . . . Everyone says land reform is important. It hasn't happened, yet we make progress in pacification. How can this be?'' After a new draft incorporated answers to these questions I summarized the paper's conclusions for the President on January 22. Thirty-eight percent of the population of South Vietnam lived in the cities, fairly securely under the authority and protection of the government (especially after the failure of the Tet offensive of 1968 decimated the Viet Cong cadre). But a primary objective of the enemy's strategy was to gain control of the 62 percent of the people that lived in the countryside, thereby to surround the cities so that they would ''fall like ripe fruit.'' The conclusion of the study was that since September 1968 the Saigon government's control of the countryside had risen from 20 to 55 percent; that of the Communists had fallen from 35 to 7 percent. Some four million rural South Vietnamese lived in contested areas, during the day controlled by Saigon, at night by the Viet Cong. We could not be sure that these percentages could be maintained, however, as we continued our troop withdrawals.

The statistics were moderately encouraging, but we also knew that North Vietnam's confidence was unbroken. Between December 14 and 20, 1969, Hanoi published a series of seven articles by its Defense Minister, General Vo Nguyen Giap, whose main thrust was that a protracted struggle could defeat America's superior technology. I predicted to the President, in a summary of these articles I sent him on January 7, 1970, that Hanoi would play for time until enough American forces had left to allow it to challenge Saigon's armed forces on a more equal basis. I summed up my doubts about optimistic reports in mid-January as follows:

(1) The North Vietnamese cannot have fought for 25 years only to call it quits without another major effort. This effort could come in many ways — through attacks on American forces, ARVN* forces or local forces. But if they had decided not to make the effort, they would presumably have been more forthcoming with regard to negotiations. [Here the President scribbled: ''makes sense.'']

(2) We have not seen proof that ARVN has really improved. It may be that the enemy forces have been hurt rather than that ARVN is significantly better than it was in the past. It could be that when the enemy drew back its main forces and cut down its activity in August and September, perhaps because of our threat in Paris at the beginning of August, they under-estimated the effect this would have on their guerrilla forces.

(3) There could be too much pressure from the top for optimistic reporting. . . .

For these reasons I recommended that the President send my military assistant Alexander Haig and a team of analysts to tour South Vietnam.

---

*ARVN, the Army of the Republic of Vietnam, that is, South Vietnamese forces.

Between January 19 and 29, 1970, they surveyed nine key provinces and confirmed the results of our Washington studies. They also warned, however, that the rate of improvement had definitely slowed in the last months of 1969: "There is no sign that the enemy has given up. . . . The pressures on the GVN* resulting from U.S. troop withdrawals may lead to . . . a deterioration of territorial security force performance and a loss of popular support for the GVN." Similar conclusions were reached by an independent CIA study that revealed a growing pessimism among South Vietnamese leaders deriving from fear of an overly hasty American withdrawal. When I sent this CIA report to Nixon, he wrote on it: "K — the psychology is enormously important. They must take responsibility if they are *ever* to gain confidence. We have to take risks on that score."

To be sure, there were contrary views. Sir Robert Thompson, the British expert on guerrilla warfare credited with devising the strategy that defeated the Communist guerrillas in Malaya, reported after a visit to Vietnam in November 1969 that Saigon held a "winning position" and would be able to maintain it unless the United States withdrew too rapidly and reduced its aid. This report was sent to all departments, and — somewhat in contradiction to their views expressed in the Vietnam Special Studies Group — they endorsed it.

But no amount of study, however objectively or prayerfully conducted, could solve our basic dilemma. An enemy determined on protracted struggle could only be brought to compromise by being confronted by insuperable obstacles on the ground. We could attempt this only by building up the South Vietnamese and blunting every effort Hanoi made to interrupt this buildup. Our strategy was certain to be bitterly contested by a dedicated, vocal, and growing minority of our people. The November 3 speech bought some time for Vietnamization. But time is fickle; we had to use the breathing spell to strengthen ourselves on the ground. Simultaneously, I was determined to probe the prospects for negotiations — the process by which the two sides tested their respective assessments of each other and we sought to shape a settlement from a seemingly intractable stalemate.

Return to Secret Negotiations

I HAVE always believed that the optimum moment for negotiations is when things appear to be going well. To yield to pressures is to invite them; to acquire the reputation for short staying power is to give the other side a powerful incentive for protracting negotiations. When a concession is made voluntarily it provides the greatest incentive for reci-

---

*GVN, or Government of Vietnam, that is, the South Vietnamese government.

procity. It also provides the best guarantee for staying power. In the negotiations that I conducted I always tried to determine the most reasonable outcome and then get there rapidly in one or two moves. This was derided as a strategy of ''preemptive concession'' by those who like to make their moves in driblets and at the last moment. But I consider that strategy useful primarily for placating bureaucracies and salving consciences. It impresses novices as a demonstration of toughness. Usually it proves to be self-defeating; shaving the salami encourages the other side to hold on to see what the next concession is likely to be, never sure that one has really reached the rock-bottom position. Thus, in the many negotiations I undertook — with the Vietnamese and others — I favored big steps taken when they were least expected, when there was a minimum of pressure, and creating the presumption that we would stick to that position. I almost always opposed modifications of our negotiating position under duress.

In November 1969 our position seemed the strongest since the beginning of the Nixon Administration. We had withstood a military offensive by Hanoi, as well as the Moratorium; the President had taken his case to the people and received substantial support. Henry Cabot Lodge had resigned as Ambassador to the Paris talks in November for personal reasons. Nixon, to show his displeasure with the slow progress of negotiations, refused to replace him. Hanoi construed this as a signal that we might end the bombing halt which had been tied to the opening of negotiations. Having stonewalled the Paris talks for a year, it now clamored insistently for the appointment of a new senior negotiator. I suggested to Nixon that we might use this period to make another attempt at secret talks. The North Vietnamese could not use the secret Paris channel for propaganda; if they refused to talk it could be used against them if we made it public; and if Hanoi was ready to settle — which I doubted — we would learn of it only in secret talks. In any event, if we were serious we could build a record by which we would be able to demonstrate that Hanoi was the obstacle to negotiations.

Nixon was skeptical of negotiations for a variety of complex reasons. On one level he did not believe that Hanoi would be prepared to settle for any terms we could live with without having suffered major military setbacks; in this he proved to be right. He was in general uneasy about any process of negotiation; he hated to put himself into a position where he might be rebuffed. And for that precise reason he always carefully constructed an excuse for failure. I never went into a negotiation without a written or oral injunction to hang tough and some expression that Nixon did not really expect success. But because Nixon, for all his bravado, genuinely wanted peace, he inevitably fell in with my argument that we owed it to our people to explore the possibility of an honorable settlement, however unlikely the chances, and to establish our record of having done so.

Accordingly, toward the end of November 1969 we asked General Vernon Walters, our defense attaché in Paris, to request a private appointment with Xuan Thuy; it was quickly granted. It was the first time in the Nixon Administration that we approached the North Vietnamese directly without a foreign intermediary. Walters proposed another secret meeting with me. But the North Vietnamese were not ready then. Meticulous planners, they had not yet made up their minds about the full implications of Nixon's November 3 speech. Or perhaps since Xuan Thuy was not a policymaker, they saw no point in another meeting at his level. Hanoi felt they had first to reestablish the psychological equilibrium by a show of nonconcern.

Whatever the reason, on December 12 General Walters was called to the North Vietnamese compound. Mai Van Bo, North Vietnamese Delegate-General in Paris, proclaimed Hanoi's unhappiness with the "warlike" speech of November 3 and the President's refusal to name a senior replacement for Henry Cabot Lodge. He called attention to Hanoi's proposal at the August meeting, which he described as "both logical and reasonable." Since we had already rejected that "logical and reasonable" offer before, there was no point, Hanoi said, in a new secret meeting unless we had something new to say.

Exactly one month after Hanoi's rebuff I persuaded Nixon — with much effort — to authorize another approach. Accordingly, General Walters saw Xuan Thuy on January 14 and suggested a meeting any weekend after February 8, "provided both sides were willing to go beyond the existing framework." Nixon was still skeptical. "I don't know what these clowns want to talk about," he said to me, "but the line we take is either they talk or we are going to sit it out. I don't feel this is any time for concession."

Hanoi did not respond for several weeks. But on January 26 we received the first indication that a negotiation might soon get under way. It was announced that Le Duc Tho, a member of the North Vietnamese Politburo (in fact, the fifth man in the hierarchy) and Hanoi's principal negotiator with Averell Harriman, would attend the forthcoming French Communist Party Congress. Then, on February 16 Walters was called to the North Vietnamese compound and informed that our insolent interlocutors accepted a meeting for February 20 or February 21 and after keeping us waiting for over a month they requested our answer within twelve hours. I have regretted ever since that we accepted the date of February 21, within the deadline. In retrospect, there is little question in my mind that to honor this unreasonable demand gave an unnecessary impression of eagerness; it enabled Hanoi to score one of the psychological points so dear to its heart. It did no lasting damage but it got us off on the wrong foot.

Thus began the secret negotiations between Le Duc Tho and me. Three meetings were held between February 20 and April 4, 1970.

The indefatigable Walters was in his element. If there was anything he enjoyed more than imitating the men for whom he was interpreting, it was arranging clandestine meetings. On a weekend or holiday, to provide better cover, I would leave Andrews Air Force Base near Washington on one of the Presidential fleet of Boeing 707s, accompanied by a secretary and two or three members of my staff. The plane's manifest indicated that it was one of the periodic training flights to check out itineraries for Presidential travel. It would land at Avord, a French Air Force base near Bourges in central France, where the French based both Mirage fighters and KC-135 tankers, roughly similar in appearance to the Presidential Boeing. My plane would touch down just long enough to let me off; its disappearance from radar tracking would not exceed twenty-five minutes; it would then proceed to Frankfurt's Rhein-Main Airport with my secretary. My associates and I would have meanwhile transferred to a Mystère-20 executive jet belonging to President Pompidou for the flight to Villacoublay Airport, a field for private airplanes near Paris.

There General Walters would come aboard to greet me, justifiably beaming with pride at his arrangements.[1] He would lead me and my colleagues to an unmarked rented Citroën, a sensitive subject for Walters since at first no official funds were available to reimburse him for the expense of a trip that could not be acknowledged to the Paris Embassy to which he was formally detailed. Walters would usually remind me of this as he drove us to his apartment building in the Neuilly section of Paris, where he smuggled us by elevator from the underground garage to his apartment. As far as his housekeeper was concerned I was a visiting American general named Harold A. Kirschman. We would spend the night there (he lent me his bedroom) and proceed the next day with Walters at the wheel to a house at 11 rue Darthé in Choisy-le-Roi, a lower middle-class neighborhood thirty minutes away on the outskirts of Paris where the secret meetings took place for a year and a half.

This routine went smoothly for two of the three trips, but the March 16 meeting was nearly aborted by a technical malfunction on my flight to Paris. The pilots suddenly noticed that the hydraulic system for the landing gear was not working; it would have to be lowered manually. This, however, would make it impossible to raise it again until the hydraulic fluid was replenished. A landing in Avord was out of the question because the pilots did not know whether a French military base had the equipment for this essential, if minor, repair; even were the equipment available, questions would be raised about the disappearance of a Presidential training flight for such an extended period from all radars tracking it.

The plane would have to go to Rhein-Main Airport in Germany, where, however, no one knew of our impending arrival, much less of our mission or predicament. Since the State Department bureaucracy had not been informed of my trip, there was no way to alert the German authorities that a French plane was coming to pick me up.

Fortunately, Presidential airplanes have superb communications. Tony Lake, then my special assistant, established contact from the airplane with General Walters in Paris — in a radio hookup through Washington. Walters went to the Elysée Palace — the residence of the French President — where Michel Jobert, then Director General of the French Presidency, and President Pompidou himself authorized the French Presidential jet to meet my plane, this time in Frankfurt.

I landed in a dark corner of the Rhein-Main airfield; Pompidou's jet was already waiting. I do not know to this day under what pretext Walters had obtained a ramp for a Boeing 707 in such an unlikely place. My staff and I transferred rapidly and were airborne again within ten minutes of landing. Walters claimed that West German cooperation was speeded up by their belief, encouraged by him, that the passenger was a secret girlfriend of Pompidou's.[2] Walters's flair for the dramatic made many extraordinary things possible, but I have often wondered why he thought the waiting ground personnel could have been fooled about the sex of the passenger.

In any event, Walters saved our March 16 trip with the imagination and tenacity that marked all his superb efforts and once again we were also in debt to Jobert and Pompidou. When Jobert was Foreign Minister later, he and I often crossed swords, but during the Vietnam negotiations he was unfailingly helpful and discreet. As for Pompidou, he never violated our confidence or sought to derive any special benefit from his knowledge; nor did he ask for any return for the many acts of friendship.

The house in Choisy-le-Roi where we met with the North Vietnamese might have belonged to a foreman in one of the factories in the district. On the ground floor there was a small living room connected to an even smaller dining room, which opened into a garden. In the living room two rows of easy chairs, heavily upholstered in red, faced each other. The American group — I, Richard Smyser (my Vietnam expert), Tony Lake, and General Walters — would sit alongside the wall to the left of the door; the North Vietnamese delegation, numbering six, sat along the other wall. There were four or five feet of floor space and eons of perception separating us.

At the first meeting on February 21, 1970, Xuan Thuy greeted me and led me into the living room to meet the man whose conceit it was to use the title of Special Adviser to Xuan Thuy, although as a member of the governing Politburo he outranked him by several levels.

Special Adviser Le Duc Tho and the First Round of Talks

L E DUC THO, gray-haired, dignified, invariably wore a black or brown
Mao suit. His large luminous eyes only rarely revealed the fanaticism that had induced him as a boy of sixteen to join the anti-French
Communist guerrillas. He was always composed; his manners, except
on one or two occasions, were impeccable. He always knew what he
was about and served his cause with dedication and skill.

It was our misfortune that his cause should be to break the will of the
United States and to establish Hanoi's rule over a country that we
sought to defend. Our private banter grew longer as our meetings progressed and some limited human contact developed; it revealed that Le
Duc Tho's profession was revolution, his vocation guerrilla warfare. He
could speak eloquently of peace but it was an abstraction alien to any
personal experience. He had spent ten years of his life in prisons under
the French. In 1973 he showed me around an historical museum in
Hanoi, which he admitted sheepishly he had never visited previously.
The artifacts of Vietnamese history — assembled, ironically enough, by
the French colonial administration — reminded Le Duc Tho not of the
glories of Vietnamese culture but of prisons in the cities or towns where
they had been excavated. As we walked through the halls I learned a
great deal about the relative merits of solitary confinement in various
prisons, the way disguises as a peasant can be discovered by the police,
and other tips that will prove invaluable should I ever decide to lead a
guerrilla struggle in Indochina.

Le Duc Tho had been sustained through his monumentally courageous exertions by a passionate belief in Leninist discipline and faith in
the Vietnamese nation. This transformed supreme personal self-assurance into a conviction that it was Vietnam's destiny to dominate not
only Indochina but all of Southeast Asia. His sense of national superiority made personal hatred of the United States irrelevant; we were simply
one of the hordes of foreigners whose congenital ignorance over the
centuries had tempted them into Indochina, whence it was Vietnam's
mission to expel them (not, I often thought, without driving them mad
first).

Le Duc Tho's Leninism convinced him that he understood my motivations better than I understood myself. His Vietnamese heritage expressed itself in an obsessive suspicion that he might somehow be
tricked; I sometimes suspected that the appearance of being outmaneuvered would bother him more than its reality. When the negotiation finally
grew serious after four years it would set him off looking for traps in the
most innocent of our proposals. At the outset it led him into lectures,
which in time grew tiresome, of his imperviousness to capitalist tricks.

I grew to understand that Le Duc Tho considered negotiations as another battle. Any settlement that deprived Hanoi of final victory was by definition in his eyes a ruse. He was there to wear me down. As the representative of the truth he had no category for compromise. Hanoi's proposals were put forward as the sole "logical and reasonable" framework for negotiations. The North Vietnamese were "an oppressed people"; in spite of much historical evidence to the contrary he considered them by definition incapable of oppressing others. America bore the entire responsibility for the war. Our proposals to reduce hostilities, by de-escalation or ceasefire — so fashionable among our critics — were seen by Le Duc Tho either as tricks or opportunities to sow confusion. In his view, the sole "reasonable" way to end the fighting was American acceptance of Hanoi's terms, which were unconditional withdrawal on a fixed deadline and the overthrow of the South Vietnamese government. As a spokesman for the "truth," Le Duc Tho had no category for our method of negotiating; trading concessions seemed to him immoral unless a superior necessity supervened, and until that happened he was prepared to wait us out indefinitely. He seemed concerned to rank favorably in the epic pantheon of Vietnamese struggles; he could not consider as an equal this barbarian from across the sea who thought that eloquent words were a means to deflect the inexorable march of history. Le Duc Tho undoubtedly was of the stuff of which heroes are made. What we grasped only with reluctance — and many at home never understood — is that heroes are such because of monomaniacal determination. They are rarely pleasant men; their rigidity approaches the fanatic; they do not specialize in the qualities required for a negotiated peace.

Luckily for my sanity the full implications of what I was up against did not hit me at that first meeting in the dingy living room in Rue Darthé, or I might have forgone the exercise. At the very least I would have curbed my sense of anticipation — almost of elation — at what I hoped would be the opening move in a dialogue of peace.

Le Duc Tho greeted me in the aloofly polite manner of someone whose superiority is so self-evident that he cannot derogate from it by a show of politeness approaching condescension. He laughed at my jokes, sometimes uproariously, sometimes with the impatience of one who had important business that was being delayed by trivia. He knew what he wanted; he had not suffered in prison for ten years and fought wars for twenty years to be seduced now by what a capitalist fancied to be charm. The meeting on February 21 took place in two sessions. We talked for three hours in the morning; we interrupted to permit General Walters and me to lunch with President Pompidou at his apartment in the Ile St. Louis to discuss, as I have mentioned, his imminent trip to the United States. We resumed in the late afternoon. Characteristically my interlocutors from Hanoi did not believe in giving away even the most minute procedural point; they did not agree to the afternoon meeting until just as I was leaving to see Pompidou.

Still half believing what was an article of faith among my former academic colleagues, that Hanoi's lack of trust in our intentions was the principal obstacle to a compromise peace, I opened the morning session with a prepared statement of our commitment to serious negotiations. I stressed that we sought to achieve a settlement which resolved the issues once and for all; we had no wish to repeat the experience of all previous agreements that had been armistices in an endless war. I pointed out that Hanoi's position had not improved since my meeting with Xuan Thuy in August. President Nixon had demonstrated his public support; the balance of forces on the ground did not warrant Hanoi's insistence on political predominance. Finally, it was our judgment "that the international situation has complications which may make Vietnam no longer the undivided concern of other countries and may mean that Vietnam will not enjoy the undivided support of countries which now support it" — an unsubtle reference to the Sino-Soviet dispute.

I then made two new points: that the United States was prepared to withdraw *all* its forces and retain no bases in Vietnam; and that in arranging for *mutual* withdrawal we did not insist that North Vietnamese troops be placed on the same legal basis as American forces. We sought a practical, not a theoretical, end to the war, I said. We did not insist that Hanoi formally announce its withdrawal so long as it in fact took place. On this basis I proposed that we set aside propaganda and work out some agreed principles. These could then be fleshed out in the plenary sessions at Avenue Kléber; we were prepared to send a new senior negotiator to Paris to complete an agreement.

Since Le Duc Tho was technically only "Special Adviser" to Hanoi's Paris delegation, Xuan Thuy as formal head of the delegation made the first response. He could not bring himself to forgo such an opportunity to impress his superior with his rhetorical skill (the content had obviously been worked out in advance). He insisted that before any negotiations the United States would have to set a deadline for unilateral withdrawal. The negotiations would then concern the modalities of our retreat; they could not affect its timing. North Vietnam's sole reciprocal obligation would be not to shoot at our men as they boarded their ships and aircraft to depart. The fighting against South Vietnam would continue until the Saigon government was overthrown; there was no mention of the release of our prisoners of war. Continuing its insistence on denying the significance of any American gesture, Xuan Thuy dismissed the announced departure of over 100,000 troops as "withdrawal by driblets." Our reduction of B-52 sorties by 25 percent and the change in military orders that severely curtailed offensive operations by American forces did not prevent an absurd allegation that we were escalating the war.

In the afternoon it was Le Duc Tho's turn. He began by challenging my assessment that events had moved in our favor since August. "Only when we have a correct assessment of the balance of forces," said Le Duc Tho in his role as Leninist schoolmaster, "can we have a correct solution." He revealed the importance Hanoi attached to our public opinion by giving it pride of place in his presentation. He denied that Nixon's public standing had improved, citing a Gallup Poll which showed that the number of Americans favoring immediate withdrawal had risen from 21 to 35 percent. This, however, was "only" public opinion. "In addition, I have seen many statements by the Senate Foreign Relations Committee, by the Democratic Party, by Mr. Clifford, which have demanded the total withdrawal of American forces, the change of Thieu–Ky–Khiem,* and the appointment of a successor to Ambassador Lodge." I replied sharply that I would listen to no further propositions from Hanoi regarding American public opinion; Le Duc Tho was there to negotiate the Vietnamese position. Painful as I found our domestic dissent, I did not think it compatible with our dignity to debate it with an adversary. It took several meetings to get that point across and I never succeeded totally.

Le Duc Tho next attacked our military assessment. He cut to the heart of the dilemma of Vietnamization. All too acutely, he pointed out that our strategy was to withdraw enough forces to make the war bearable for the American people while simultaneously strengthening the Saigon forces so that they could stand on their own. He then asked the question that was also tormenting me: "Before, there were over a million U.S. and puppet troops, and you failed. How can you succeed when you let the puppet troops do the fighting? Now, with only U.S. support, how can you win?"

From this analysis, Le Duc Tho's conclusions followed inexorably. He insisted that military and political problems be dealt with simultaneously — a position from which he never deviated until October 1972. According to Le Duc Tho, the only military subject for discussion was the unconditional liquidation of our involvement. The six-month deadline for withdrawal proposed by the NLF was fixed and would run regardless of other agreements. However, even if we withdrew, Hanoi would stop fighting only if there were a political settlement. This, in Le Duc Tho's view, presupposed the removal of the "warlike" President Thieu, Vice President Ky, and Prime Minister Khiem and the creation of a coalition government composed of three groups: those members of the "Saigon Administration" (without Thieu, Ky, and Khiem) who

---

*Tran Thien Khiem, who had replaced Tran Van Huong as Prime Minister of South Vietnam.

genuinely stood for "peace, independence and neutrality"; neutral forces who met the same criteria; and the Communist NLF. The NLF would determine who stood for "peace, independence and neutrality." This coalition government, loaded as it was in Hanoi's favor, was not, however, the final word. With one-third of it composed of Communists, with the remainder approved by the Communists, with all anti-Communist leaders barred, it was then to negotiate with the fully armed NLF for a definitive solution. Tho comforted me that this generous scheme would open hopeful prospects: "If you show goodwill and serious intent, a settlement will come quickly."

At the meeting on March 16 I tried another approach. I proposed to Le Duc Tho that neither side exert military pressure in Vietnam or in "related" countries during the negotiations — in other words a mutual de-escalation of military operations throughout Indochina. This was contemptuously rejected with a pedantic lecture that every war had its high points with which it was impossible to interfere. At the April 4 meeting I repeated the proposal. Once again the North Vietnamese spurned it without any exploration whatsoever. On March 16 I also put on the table a precise monthly schedule of total American withdrawal over a sixteen-month period. The North Vietnamese said it was unacceptable because it differed from the proposal of twelve months in the President's November 3 speech. (I had used sixteen months because it was the only precise schedule that existed in the Pentagon and reflected the technical assessment of how long it would take us to withdraw our 400,000 remaining men and their equipment.) When I explained that the schedule was illustrative only and that the deadline would of course be made to coincide with Presidential pronouncements, it was rejected because Hanoi supported the "correct and logical" deadline of six months put forward by the NLF. Our schedule was defective, in Le Duc Tho's view, because it would start to run only after the agreement was completed, while Hanoi wanted us to withdraw unconditionally on a schedule unrelated to any other issue. Furthermore, Le Duc Tho refused to discuss any political solution that preserved any leading member of the South Vietnamese government; he derided our proposal for mixed electoral commissions, including members of the Viet Cong, which we proposed as a fair means to supervise free elections. We were being offered terms for surrender, not a negotiation in any normal sense.

At the April 4 meeting Xuan Thuy summed up Hanoi's objections to our position. The deadline was "wrong" because it was longer than their demand of six months and depended on the settlement of other issues; mutual withdrawal was unacceptable; no settlement was possible as long as Thieu, Ky, and Khiem and other leaders "opposed to peace, independence and neutrality" remained in office; our delegation in Paris still lacked a senior replacement for Lodge. My suggestions that we explore ways to organize a fair political contest were answered with the unyielding response that only the overthrow of the Saigon government could solve the political question.

The most vitriolic comments were, however, reserved for Laos, where a North Vietnamese offensive had just been launched, and Cambodia. Le Duc Tho accused us of escalating the war in Laos. When I replied that one good test of who was doing what to whom was to see which side was advancing, Le Duc Tho argued that we had "provoked" the North Vietnamese offensive and that the fighting was being conducted by Laotian forces in any event. (This caused me to comment that it was remarkable how well the Pathet Lao spoke Vietnamese.) As for Cambodia, Le Duc Tho was aroused and implacable, ridiculing my offer for its neutralization. The war in Indochina had become one, he insisted, and would be fought to the finish on that basis. I will discuss Laos and Cambodia later in this chapter.

In short, Hanoi's position as it emerged in the three meetings with Le Duc Tho was peremptory and unyielding. The North Vietnamese rejected a schedule of mutual withdrawal, de-escalation, the neutralization of Cambodia, or a mixed electoral commission for South Vietnam. Le Duc Tho's idea of a negotiation was to put forward his unilateral demands. Their essence was for the United States to withdraw on a deadline so short that the collapse of Saigon would be inevitable. On the way out we were being asked to dismantle an allied government and establish an alternative whose composition would be prescribed by Hanoi and whose only role even then would be to negotiate final terms with Hanoi's front. When I asked Le Duc Tho whether his political program expressed a preference or a condition, he said flatly: "This is a condition." It was a condition to which Hanoi stuck resolutely until the fall of 1972.

The first series of secret negotiations with Le Duc Tho ended with his statement that unless we changed our position, there was nothing more to discuss.*

In going over the record with the perspective of time, I am astonished

---

*Typical of the never-never land of the public debate was an article that appeared the day after my first meeting with Le Duc Tho in the *Philadelphia Bulletin*. Its author, Roger Hilsman, had been Assistant Secretary of State for Far Eastern Affairs during the period of our initial involvement in Vietnam. He claimed that the President was "rebuffing a communist offer of a more-or-less immediate Vietnam peace on terms that many Americans might find perfectly acceptable." Hilsman claimed to be supported in his view by a number of experts, including Averell Harriman. On the basis of an exegesis of Hanoi's Delphic declarations, Hilsman and his associates professed to have discovered the following peace offer:

No election but an old-fashioned political deal setting up a coalition government including representatives of all political factions, Communist and non-Communist;

Although their propaganda still calls for immediate total withdrawal of American troops, privately they have indicated the withdrawal could be phased over two or three years;

by my own extraordinarily sanguine reporting. This was partly due to my desire to keep the channel alive. Aware of Nixon's skepticism, I fell into the trap of many negotiators of becoming an advocate of my own negotiation. No damage was done, because Hanoi never gave us the opportunity to make a concrete decision. Another reason for our optimism was that we were still relative innocents about the theological subtleties of Hanoi's unrelenting psychological warfare. For example, I reported to Nixon after the March 16 meeting that Hanoi had hinted at a willingness to discuss mutual withdrawal. In fact, as became evident at the next meeting, Le Duc Tho had actually insisted that Hanoi would discuss the role of its own forces only *after* our withdrawal and solely with the coalition government in Saigon whose composition it insisted on controlling.

The record leaves no doubt that we were looking for excuses to make the negotiations succeed, not to fail. Far from being determined on a military solution as our critics never tired of alleging, we went out of our way to give the benefit of every doubt to the pursuit of a negotiated settlement. Nixon shared this positive attitude despite his greater pessimism. And he was willing to run risks. In preparation for my March meeting I wrote to him on February 27:

> The positions we develop should be reasonable enough to be attractive, but strong enough so we would not have to back away from them in another more conventional negotiating channel if this one should break down. . . . The lack of an agreed position with the GVN will require you to make decisions on our position which could, if later revealed, embroil us in difficulties with Saigon. This is risky, but I see no other way to proceed if we are to maintain momentum and secrecy.

Nixon wrote into the margin next to the last sentence: ''OK — will do.''

Nor can Thieu be fairly charged with being an obstacle — except in the special sense that Hanoi objected to his existence. I cabled full reports after every session by backchannel to Ambassador Ellsworth Bunker in Saigon, to brief President Thieu. Thieu interposed no objections to either procedure or substance. Only slowly and toward the very end of the process did we come to understand that Thieu did not really agree with our positions. In the beginning he calculated that they would never be accepted and that acquiescence was his way of keeping our support for the conduct of the war.

One unhappy consequence of the secret talks was to sharpen the com-

---

Postponement of the reunification of North and South Vietnam for a period of between five and ten years;

International guarantees of the territorial integrity of Laos and Cambodia.

Hanoi, of course, had explicitly rejected each of these points.

partmentalization of knowledge, which was such a bane of the Nixon Administration. Rogers was not told of them until well into 1971. Since David Bruce was briefed after he became head of our Paris delegation in July 1970 and Bunker was always kept up to date, we had the curious result that these ambassadors knew more than their nominal chief. Laird was never formally told, though I am sure that he had adequate information about who was using the planes under his control and the likely reason. It was a poor system and even though I operated it I think it is one that ought never to be emulated. Nixon's distrust of his Cabinet members exaggerated their already strong self-will. Partly through ignorance, partly because they felt no commitment to policies they had not shaped, they consistently cut across our initiatives or challenged our strategies that had been clearly articulated.

The first round of negotiations with Le Duc Tho collapsed because diplomacy always reflects some balance of forces and Le Duc Tho's assessment was not so wrong. His sense of public opinion in America — and especially of the leadership groups he had identified — was quite accurate. The dilemmas of Vietnamization were real. The lack of discipline in the American bureaucracy meant that the philosophical disagreements within the Executive Branch were showing through. In these circumstances Le Duc Tho could see no reason to modify his demands for unconditional withdrawal and the overthrow of the Saigon government. He would see none until two and a half years later, when the military situation left him no other choice.

Laos Interlude

IN the northwest corner of Indochina, wedged between mountain ranges and the plain of the Mekong River, the tribes and peoples of Laos, ruled by a Buddhist king, led a peaceful existence for centuries, essentially unaffected by the wars and struggles of their more bellicose neighbors. In the nineteenth century Laos was conquered by the French without recorded resistance and then governed by them from Hanoi along with the rest of Indochina.

By one of history's little ironies, those struggling for independence sometimes inherit the imperial pretensions of their former colonial rulers. Thus the Leninist masters of Hanoi saw themselves as the natural heirs of all that had been ruled by France from the very headquarters they were now occupying. There had been previous efforts by Vietnam to dominate Laos and Cambodia in the eighteenth and early nineteenth centuries;[3] now there was added a proclivity to emulate the scale of French colonial rule. After the 1954 Geneva Agreement, which ended the French presence, the peace-loving peoples of Laos had the misfortune of being astride convenient routes by which North Vietnam could

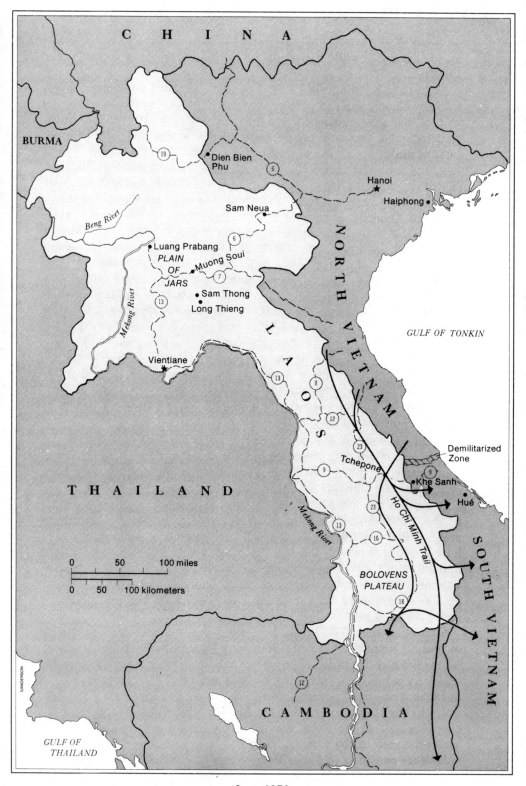

Laos 1970

invade the South while bypassing the Demilitarized Zone set up by that agreement.[4]

From the beginning the Pathet Lao (the Laotian Communists, dominated by Hanoi) retained control over two northeast provinces where the writ of the government in Vientiane never ran. By 1961 a three-cornered civil war was raging between the Pathet Lao in the northeast, neutralist forces in the center of the country on the fabled Plain of Jars, and a rightist group along the Mekong River bordering Thailand. (There is a map of Laos on page 449.) By 1961, over 6,000 North Vietnamese troops were involved. The conflict became sufficiently grave for President Kennedy to warn at a news conference on March 23, 1961: "Laos is far away from America, but the world is small. . . . The security of all Southeast Asia will be endangered if Laos loses its neutral independence." In May 1961 negotiations over the future of Laos opened in Geneva. Like all negotiations with Hanoi, they proved protracted; pursuing its normal tactic, Hanoi maintained military pressure until President Kennedy sent 5,000 US Marines to neighboring Thailand in May 1962. Within two months of that show of force, a new Geneva Agreement was signed by fourteen nations, including North Vietnam and the USSR, providing for neutralization of Laos. Accepting the Soviet and North Vietnamese proposal, the United States agreed to the withdrawal of all foreign military personnel and to a coalition government, headed by the neutralist Prince Souvanna Phouma, in which all three factions would be represented.

North Vietnam flouted the accords from the day they were signed. All 666 American military personnel in Laos departed through international checkpoints; of the 6,000 North Vietnamese in the country only *forty* (yes, forty) left through the checkpoints; the thousands remained.

In April 1963 the precarious coalition split apart. Fighting soon resumed. Southern Laos was in effect annexed by the North Vietnamese army, which constructed there an intricate system of infiltration routes into South Vietnam — the Ho Chi Minh Trail. By 1970 over half a million North Vietnamese troops had moved south along these paths. The number of North Vietnamese troops stationed in Laos had risen to 67,000 — ten times the number that in 1961–1962 had precipitated a major crisis under President Kennedy.

Starting in the mid-Sixties, the United States found itself extending increasing support to Premier Souvanna Phouma, the neutralist leader whom we had originally opposed but who had been recognized as the leader by all sides in the 1962 Geneva Accords. Our purpose was to maintain a neutralist government and also to secure Souvanna's acquiescence in our efforts to interdict the Ho Chi Minh Trail. We gave financial assistance to the Royal Laotian Army, to some irregular forces of Meo tribesmen led by General Vang Pao, and from time to time to Thai volunteers operating in Laos. Most of this was occasionally reported in the press; by 1970 all of it was known to the Senate Foreign Relations Committee because of a number of classified hearings conducted by Senator Stuart Symington. But the US government made no formal acknowledgment, so as to avoid giving Hanoi a pretext to compound its massive violations of the Geneva Accords by taking over all of Laos.

This history is of some importance because early in 1970 Laos briefly became the focal point of our Indochina concerns and domestic debate. A North Vietnamese offensive was threatening to overrun northern Laos. Domestic critics used the occasion to cry havoc about the danger that we might slide into another "open-ended" commitment in Indochina without noticing it.

Hanoi was fighting essentially two wars in Laos, though both for the same objective of hegemony in Indochina. In the south, the Ho Chi Minh Trail was Hanoi's link to the battlefield of South Vietnam. In northern Laos, Hanoi supported the Pathet Lao but it was restrained, we thought, by fear of American or Thai response. It had sought to maintain just enough pressure on the Laotian army to prevent it from consolidating itself as an instrument of authority; it would be dealt with after victory in South Vietnam. We did not, for our part, seek to disturb this uneasy equilibrium. No American administration could possibly desire a war in a country like Laos. It would not make sense to expand the conflict into Laos, except for the minimum required for our own protection, when we were busy withdrawing troops from South Vietnam. It was this position that the North Vietnamese disturbed in late January 1970 when they suddenly sent 13,000 reinforcements and a great deal of extra equipment to the Plain of Jars, where the neutralists were holding back the Pathet Lao. That threatened Souvanna, and our relations with him; if he abandoned his acquiescence in the bombing of the Ho Chi Minh Trail, Hanoi's logistic problem would be greatly eased, exposing us in South Vietnam to growing peril. Worse, if the North Vietnamese troops reached the Mekong, the war would lose its point for Thailand. Bangkok would then be under pressure along the hundreds of miles of the river dividing a plain without any other obstacles. We would almost certainly be denied use of the Thai airbases, essential for our B-52 and tactical air operations in Vietnam.

On January 23, an enemy offensive imminent, our Ambassador in Laos, G. McMurtrie Godley, requested B-52 strikes against a major North Vietnamese concentration containing, it was believed, 4,000 troops; it would have been the first use of B-52s in northern Laos. This inspired a stately bureaucratic minuet in Washington that told much about the state of mind of our government. We were caught between officials seeking to protect the American forces for which they felt a responsibility and a merciless Congressional onslaught that rattled these officials in their deliberations.

I scheduled a meeting of the Washington Special Actions Group

(WSAG) for January 26 to consider Godley's request. Two hours before the meeting Mel Laird told me that he favored using B-52s against that target; on the other hand he did not want it discussed in an interagency forum for fear of leaks. Laird urged approval in the same channels as the secret strikes in Cambodia. This was why, he told me, he had instructed his representatives on the WSAG to recommend *against* the use of B-52s in northern Laos even though he favored it. The record of the meeting thus would show Pentagon opposition whatever Laird's personal view; the President would take the heat for the decision. One hour before the meeting Bill Rogers called to tell me that he was against using B-52s in northern Laos and that he had Laird on his side. I mumbled some doubts about this claim but suggested a meeting of the three of us with the President. Unfortunately, the President chose this moment to go into seclusion at Camp David to prepare his first veto message, rejecting a welfare appropriations bill. As was his habit on such occasions he would not accept telephone calls, even from me. By the time he was again available all the principals were on record with some statement protecting themselves against all possible developments.

I therefore started around the track again — this time with General Earle Wheeler. I asked him whether the target of which Laird had spoken could be attacked with tactical aircraft rather than B-52s. (For some reason, tactical air strikes seemed to provoke less of an outcry than B-52s.) Wheeler informed me that it *was* being attacked by tactical aircraft but these could not compare in effectiveness with B-52s. When I went back to Laird he stressed that the concentration of 4,000 enemy troops would soon disperse; it was the best target for B-52s since he had become Secretary of Defense. On the other hand, he said, he would not be offended if it were turned down. I concluded that it was too late to obtain a consensus on this particular target but promised to get a clear-cut Presidential decision on the principle.

On February 12 the long-feared North Vietnamese offensive finally broke on the Plain of Jars. The next day, Premier Souvanna Phouma made a formal request for B-52 strikes — the first of several. By February 16 the North Vietnamese and Pathet Lao had driven government forces from most of the high ground that dominates the approaches to the Plain. The President called a meeting for the afternoon of February 16 with Laird, Acting Secretary of State Richardson, Helms, Admiral Moorer (Acting Chairman of the Joint Chiefs), and me. I recommended that the President authorize B-52 strikes if the enemy advanced beyond Muong Soui, the farthest point of Communist penetration before the government offensive of the previous summer. The President agreed. The Communists were beyond Muong Soui within twenty-four hours. An attack with three B-52s was launched on the evening of February

17–18. It had taken a month of discussion, a major North Vietnamese offensive, and the near collapse of the Laotian front to induce exactly one B-52 strike. I do not know to this day whether Laird favored or opposed the action; his stand was compatible with both positions. Wheeler was consistently in favor. Rogers moved from opposition to indifference.

But one B-52 strike was enough to trigger the domestic outcry. The very next day, February 19, the *New York Times* reported that B-52s had been diverted from South Vietnam to attack North Vietnamese and Pathet Lao forces in northern Laos. Senators Eugene McCarthy and Frank Church wasted no time in deploring the involvement of American planes and pilots in Laos; they made no reference to the North Vietnamese offensive. Senator Mike Mansfield, also without mentioning the continuing North Vietnamese onslaught, scored American "escalation" on February 21. Reports appeared of "armed Americans in civilian clothes" supporting the Laotian command.[5] On February 25, Senators Mathias, Mansfield, Gore, Symington, Cooper, and Percy attacked Administration "secrecy" over what they termed a "deepening U.S. involvement." Senators Gore and Mansfield on February 25 demanded publication of secret testimony taken by their subcommittee in October on US involvement. Senator Symington sent a letter to Secretary Rogers urging that Ambassador Godley be brought back from Laos to testify. On February 27 the *Wall Street Journal* halfheartedly supported the use of B-52s but warned against further escalation. The *Washington Post* on March 2 weighed in with a stinging editorial entitled "Laos: The Same Old Shell Game."

This was the culmination of a campaign extending over many months in the Senate and in the media to get at the "truth" in Laos. The issue was not to obtain the facts — they were widely known — but to induce the government to confirm them publicly, which was quite a different matter. The Senate Foreign Relations Committee had substantially full knowledge from its staff investigations as well as from its classified hearings. Similarly, the media had given the public a reasonably accurate picture. The issue for us was to what extent an official acknowledgment of our operations in Laos would wreck what was left of the 1962 Accords, give Hanoi a pretext for further stepping up its aggression in northern Laos, and fuel even more passionate controversy at home.

Our role in Laos had been "secret" in three administrations of two parties precisely because each President wanted to keep it limited. To spell out the limits publicly was as dangerous to this strategy as to spell out the extent of our involvement. We were being pressed to do both. From the critics' point of view the issue was useful for a challenge to the whole Vietnam enterprise. Some would even have considered it a bonus if a collapse in Laos had led to a collapse in Vietnam. They wanted not facts but ammunition.

Despite these hazards we came to the conclusion that some formal statement of our policy and intentions in Laos was required. The reasoning that led to this conclusion was somewhat Byzantine. Laird wanted a public statement to head off State Department leaks making him the fall guy; for this objective to be realized, the explanation had to come from anywhere but the Defense Department. Rogers opposed a State Department briefing for the same reason; he had no desire to mount the barricades over Laos. He suggested declassifying the secret State Department testimony that had already been given before the Symington subcommittee. Symington had behaved honorably. In those far-off years, secrets conveyed were still sacrosanct in many Congressional committees; Symington would not release classified information without the consent of the Administration. But if the Administration had given its consent it would have undercut the practice and principle of classified hearings. In the future, all that would be needed to force secret testimony into the public domain would be the generation of a public controversy; it would be a perpetual temptation to an unfriendly committee to structure the secret presentations so as to generate maximum adverse publicity and then compel disclosure.

I explained the issue in a memorandum for the President:

The real issue in Laos is entirely related to Vietnam:

— There is no question but that the North Vietnamese can overrun Laos at any point in time that they care to, providing they are willing to pay the political and psychological costs of upsetting the 1962 Accords.

— Should North Vietnam overrun Laos, our whole bargaining with respect to the Vietnam conflict would be undermined. In fact, if North Vietnamese military operations in Laos succeed to the point that Souvanna believes he must succumb to their influence in order to survive, we could then anticipate that he would refuse to permit us to continue our interdiction of the Ho Chi Minh Trail and thus our military operations in South Vietnam would be catastrophically damaged.

— These are the fundamental considerations with all the rest amounting to balderdash. . . .

— State regards the release of the Symington Subcommittee testimony as being the simplest way to do this. We might kill two birds with one stone: placate Symington, Fulbright, et al, and show the public what we are really doing.

— On the other hand, it is doubtful whether the release of the sensitive parts of the testimony will placate the Senators. They *know* what is going on in Laos, and why. The executive sessions have given them all this. . . .

— Releasing the testimony would help North Vietnam to document its case that we are violating the Geneva Accords, without admitting that it is violating them, and thus seriously undermine the real basis for our action.

It would also make it more difficult for the Soviets to preserve their present relatively friendly posture towards the RLG [Royal Laotian Government]. . . .

— Furthermore, by giving in on Laos, the Administration's stand on not releasing sensitive parts of the proceedings would be eroded with respect to other countries. We might be opening a real Pandora's box of problems for ourselves, not only domestically, but in our relations with other countries. Our good faith in preserving the sanctity of international agreements could no longer be trusted, and the usefulness of the diplomats who negotiated them would be compromised. I am particularly concerned over the reaction of the Thai, who already question our commitment to them.

An NSC meeting on February 27 dealt with our public position on Laos. The decision, to the enormous relief of the Cabinet members, was that a statement would be prepared by the NSC staff and issued by the White House. Why I agreed to a procedure that would put the White House in the direct line of fire on every factual dispute — whether it was bureaucratic inexperience or simply exhaustion with endless attempts to pass the buck — is impossible to determine at this late date. Whatever the reason, the NSC staff quickly began to draft a public statement explaining our involvement in Laos. To avoid its appearing excessively defensive, I cast it in the form of a new proposal to the two co-chairmen of the Geneva Conference, Britain and the Soviet Union, to convene a conference of signatories of the 1962 Accords to develop new guarantees for the neutrality of Laos. I had no illusion that this would happen. Neither London nor Moscow was eager to expose itself on this issue.

The statement, published on March 6, was a full and candid account of American involvement and the reasons for secrecy since the Kennedy Administration. But it generated a major controversy because of one inaccuracy, produced in part by the agencies' being less than meticulous about supplying my staff with all the details (since they would not be taking the heat), in part by an honest bureaucratic bungle. Nixon had felt that the best way to prove that no Americans were involved in ground combat in Laos was to emphasize that none had been killed in such activities. "No one cares about B-52 strikes in Laos. But people worry about our boys there," Nixon had told me after the NSC meeting. Winston Lord, my new special assistant — who was to become one of my closest friends — was in charge of drafting the statement. He and others scrupulously checked with the departments. They were given the impression that the only hesitation over an assertion that no US personnel had died in Laos related to some casualties among American reconnaissance teams that had sporadically entered southern Laos from Vietnam to observe and if possible harass infiltration on the Ho Chi Minh Trail (code-named "Operation Prairie Fire"). Since these activities were clearly related to the war in Vietnam and had nothing to do with the battles in northern Laos, we thought we could sustain a sentence to the effect that "no American stationed in Laos has ever been killed in ground combat operations."

Making a flat statement of fact on matters extending over nearly a decade is a certain sign of inexperience. One can never be sure what facts are stacked away in the recesses of the bureaucracy that will suddenly appear. I soon was to be given a lesson in the perils of being too categorical.

After the statement was issued on March 6, the bureaucracy suddenly began leaking to the press what it had not been able to bring itself to inform the President — that some very few Americans stationed in Laos, civilians and military personnel *not* in combat, had in fact been killed by random fire over the previous nine years. The White House was forced to acknowledge on March 8 that it now had information from the Defense Department that six civilians and one army captain who "was not engaged in combat operations" had been killed in Laos since the beginning of 1969. An average of about four American civilians had been killed in Laos in each of the preceding five years. On March 10, the Department of Defense helpfully announced that American military men serving in Laos had been entitled to "hostile fire pay" since January 1, 1966. Subsequent inquiry into who was responsible for the errors produced the unstartling conclusion that it was the result of a series of misunderstandings and a failure of communication. Lord did a postmortem, retracing the drafting process and the discussions between Defense and the NSC staff; it does not reflect the agony this brilliant and honorable man underwent in what were his first few weeks in the thankless job of being my special assistant.

Nixon was furious at what he considered a failure of my vaunted staff; for a week I could not get an appointment to see him. I took full responsibility. On March 9 I wrote to Laird, with a copy to the President:

Dear Mel:

In order to avoid any misunderstanding, I want you to know that your recollection is correct. Your staff lined out the phrase about no American combat deaths twice. I was under the misapprehension that this was a result of PRAIRIE FIRE and therefore adjusted the statement to take account of that. However, it is the duty of my office to prevent mistakes like this, and I wanted you to know that you bear no responsibility.

Warm regards,
Henry A. Kissinger

Naturally, the press and Congress were indignant at what was called — on the basis of four-to-five noncombat deaths a year — a confirmed American military involvement in Laos. Public debate focused on the new "credibility gap" rather than on the underlying reality — that American involvement in Laos was demonstrably minimal and that North Vietnam was engaged in an offensive.

The situation in Laos soon took another grave turn. The Communist advance reached the Long Thieng area, the last stronghold before the capital of Vientiane. It also threatened the headquarters of Vang Pao, the leader of the Meo tribesmen who were resisting Communist domination. With a Communist advance to the Mekong imminent, Thailand offered to send volunteers to Long Thieng if the Laotian government asked for them. This proposal was strenuously resisted by the State Department and received only lukewarm support from other agencies at two WSAG meetings. After we received a formal request from both the Laotian and Thai governments, the President overruled the agencies. He was convinced and I agreed that to refuse the offer would raise doubts in Thailand about our commitment to its defense and might panic Souvanna. On March 26 I told the WSAG of the President's decision.

The Laotian government launched a counteroffensive on March 27, aided by the Thai volunteers. Their intervention was decisive. On March 31 Laos government forces recaptured nearby Sam Thong; its airfield was soon back in use and our planes began ferrying supplies. North Vietnamese forces pulled back from the Long Thieng area the next day.

The Laos crisis thus subsided for the rest of the year; the political and military equilibrium in northern Laos was maintained. But the split within our government had been dramatized; and so corrosively untrusting was our opposition that we were accused of provoking what we sought to resist and were suspected of organizing the sequel — a coup in neighboring Cambodia. The facts were very different.

The Overthrow of Sihanouk

FOR nearly thirty years the political life of Cambodia had been synonymous with the tempestuous career and personality of Prince Norodom Sihanouk. Crowned King in 1941 at the age of eighteen, he abdicated the throne in 1955 to play an active political role as Prime Minister; in June 1960, by unanimous vote of the Cambodian National Assembly, he was elevated to chief of state. It was Sihanouk who had guided the kingdom of Cambodia to independence from France in 1953, shaped its political institutions, and dominated its policies.

In leading his country Sihanouk skillfully walked a tightrope between East and West in global politics, between the Soviet Union and China in the emerging Communist schism, between the opposing sides in the battle over Vietnam, and between right and left in his own country. Voluble, erratic, fun-loving — "mercurial" is the word usually used — he dexterously kept his country a haven of peace amid the bloody wars that ravaged the rest of Indochina. Finally — suddenly — in 1970, the nimble tightrope walker slipped and fell, and thus doomed his people to a hell far worse than even their neighbors had endured.

On January 7, 1970, Prince Sihanouk, with his wife Monique and a retinue of eleven, left their capital, Phnom Penh, for a two-month vacation at a clinic in Grasse on the French Riviera. It was his custom to "take the cure" there every two years to ease the discomfort of what he called his "obesity, blood disease, and albuminuria." In his absence his government was left in the hands of his own chosen leaders: Chairman of the National Assembly Cheng Heng (who became acting head of state); Prime Minister Lon Nol (whom Sihanouk had appointed in August 1969 and praised in September as "the only person I could trust because of his faithfulness to the Throne and Nation");* and Sirik Matak, First Deputy Prime Minister.

Relations between Sihanouk and his own government were not always smooth. Leftist elements had been discredited and expelled by Sihanouk in prior years (the leaders of the Communist Khmer Rouge had, in fact, been condemned to death in absentia). There were some differences with the Lon Nol–Sirik Matak Cabinet over Sihanouk's economic policies, his inability to rid the country of North Vietnamese and Viet Cong forces occupying Cambodia's eastern regions, the corruption of his entourage, and his unpopular decision to open a state casino in Phnom Penh. But none of these squabbles seemed critical enough in January 1970 to impede his departure for the south of France.

The United States had even less premonition of trouble. We had restored diplomatic relations in July 1969, as described earlier, and had a small mission headed by chargé d'affaires Lloyd Rives. There had been no US military or economic assistance program in Cambodia since Sihanouk canceled it in 1963. And, largely at Senator Mansfield's insistence, no CIA personnel were assigned to Phnom Penh after the restoration of diplomatic relations. In January, February, and into the first half of March 1970, the highest levels of the United States government were preoccupied with the burgeoning crisis in Laos and the related acrimony at home. On March 17 I lunched with Marshall Green and William Sullivan of the State Department's East Asian Bureau; our discussions focused on China, Vietnam, and Laos; the record suggests that Cambodia was not even touched upon.

---

* Lon Nol was also Sihanouk's representative to China's National Day celebrations in Peking on October 1, 1969, standing on Tien An Men with Mao Tse-tung.

From the American point of view the precarious political balance in neutral Cambodia under Sihanouk's skillful, if unpredictable, tutelage was the best attainable situation. To be sure, Hanoi's use of Cambodian territory for launching military operations against our forces, in flagrant disregard of international law, was a continuing danger. But here too a certain equilibrium had been established. Sihanouk had acquiesced in, if not encouraged, our air operations against these sanctuaries; we desisted from ground operations across the border; Hanoi continued to use the sanctuaries, if at a higher cost. And we had some idea of how precarious the internal balance in Cambodia was. When President Nixon met with President Thieu in Saigon on July 30, 1969, Thieu cautioned prophetically that if the balance in Cambodia were upset by the overthrow of Sihanouk, the Communists would win in the end:

The President [Nixon] asked for his views of Sihanouk. President Thieu replied that while Sihanouk is bad, we don't want to have something worse. He added that there are only two groups in Cambodia who can overthrow Sihanouk, the military or the Communists; the military are weak and ineffectual and it is more likely to be the Communists who would succeed. Even if the military moved against Sihanouk, he felt that the Communists would eventually take over. What Sihanouk does or can do depends very largely on what happens in Vietnam. Cambodia is a weak country and if Sihanouk were overthrown, or if we encouraged his overthrow, it is highly likely the Communists will take over.

We agreed with this assessment. Cambodia's tragedy was that its internal stresses finally upset the delicate equilibrium that Sihanouk had struggled to maintain, unleashing precisely the forces which Thieu had foreseen. The precipitating issue was the Communist sanctuaries from which the North Vietnamese had tormented our forces. These increasingly aroused the nationalist outrage of Cambodians, who over the centuries have seen successive Vietnamese rulers colonize their ancestral lands; indeed, the area around Saigon was taken by Vietnamese from Cambodians only in the early nineteenth century. Had French occupation not supervened, it is quite possible that all of Cambodia would have suffered that fate. The antipathy of Cambodians for all Vietnamese has ancient roots. Sihanouk's inability to dislodge the feared North Vietnamese from Cambodian soil undermined his position with every passing month.

Sihanouk's public statements of the period leave no doubt as to whom he considered the threat to his country's independence. Repeatedly and publicly he protested North Vietnamese "aggression" and infringement of Cambodia's sovereignty. In June 1969 — three months after the secret bombing started — he had complained at a press conference that Cambodia's Ratanakiri province was "practically North Vietnamese territory," and that "Viet Minh" (North Vietnamese) and Viet Cong forces had heavily infiltrated into Svay Rieng province. In the October 1969 issue of *Sangkum,* a journal of which Sihanouk was editor, an article entitled "The Implantation of Viet Cong and North Vietnamese along Our Borders" protested the North Vietnamese occupation at length; a map showed the location of 35,000 to 40,000 North Vietnamese and Viet Cong troops occupying Cambodian territory (not unhelpful to our intelligence). In a signed article in the December 1969 issue, Sihanouk went so far as to pay tribute to the American role in Vietnam. He argued that "in all honesty and objectivity," the presence of American forces in Southeast Asia established a regional balance of power that permitted small nations like Cambodia "to be respected, if not courted, by the European and even Asian Socialist camps." America's Asian allies could not compensate for a withdrawal of American power by turning toward the Communists because, wrote Sihanouk, like a bird before a serpent, "the bird, gentle or not, always ends up by being swallowed up." Sihanouk concluded his article with a ringing endorsement of the Nixon Doctrine:

It is possible and even probable that the new Nixon Doctrine which foresees not having American troops intervene . . . may enter into effect. . . . But, they [the Americans] will be obliged in their own interest to support the popular nationalists in their resistance against the new imperialism, that of Asiatic Communism. . . . If the US brings aid without conditions and without physical intervention . . . they will certainly have more hope of seeing the flood of Communism contained than if they assume this task with their own soldiers. In effect, they would thus contribute to cutting the wings from the subversive propaganda of Communism, which calls the nation to rebellion, and to the "liberation of the nation" when the region is "occupied" by foreign forces. . . .

I sent excerpts from this article to Nixon on February 12, 1970. On his instructions, I also sent the full text to Senator Mansfield on February 23.

Sihanouk had no doubt of which side had committed the fundamental aggression in Indochina. For example, in November 1969 the Viet Cong had fired on a US Special Forces camp in Vietnam from Cambodian territory; retaliatory — and publicized — American air attacks were said to have killed some twenty-five Cambodians. Sihanouk had protested this to the United States; our policy was to pay compensation. Nevertheless, in a speech on December 15, Sihanouk placed the responsibility for this incident on the North Vietnamese:

Who triggered the Dak Dam incident? It was the Viet Cong who fired at the Americans from our territory. When the Americans got hit, they became angry and bombed us. Then the Viet Cong and the Viet Minh fled, and only Khmer inhabitants were left to become victims. That is the whole story. . . .

The big Red powers who claim to be our friends, the European Reds at the United Nations, have forbidden us to complain to the United Nations. . . .

Sihanouk told his audience that he would not break diplomatic relations with the United States again, as some were urging, because if he did so, "we'll have to do the same thing with the Viet Minh and Viet Cong, because they still continue to commit aggression against our territory even after we established diplomatic relations with them."

On February 22, 1970, toward the end of his vacation in France, Sihanouk announced that on his way home in March he intended to visit the Soviet Union and China, "those great, friendly countries," to enlist their support to reduce or eliminate the North Vietnamese presence in his country.

But for the first time in his career Sihanouk lost his grip on events. On March 8, villagers in Cambodia's Svay Rieng province demonstrated against North Vietnamese occupation. On March 11, twenty thousand young Cambodians sacked the embassies of the North Vietnamese and the Viet Cong in Phnom Penh. (The Cambodian government clearly had a hand in organizing the demonstrations.) The two houses of the Cambodian Parliament held a special joint session and requested the government to reaffirm Cambodia's neutrality and to defend the national territory. The Parliament urged an expansion of the Cambodian army, which Sihanouk had kept deliberately weak because he feared that it might move against him.

From Paris, Sihanouk sent a public cablegram to his mother, the Dowager Queen, in Phnom Penh denouncing "certain personalities" in his government who were trying to "throw our country into the arms of an imperialist capitalist power." He announced his intention to return to Phnom Penh immediately "to address the nation and the army and ask them to make their choice." In an interview while still in Paris, Sihanouk warned the North Vietnamese and Viet Cong that they had a choice between respecting Cambodia's neutrality and seeing a pro-American faction take over his government.[6] For reasons never fully explained, he hesitated in Paris, however, and the kettle in Phnom Penh began to boil over. On March 12 Deputy Prime Minister Sirik Matak announced suspension of a trade agreement with the Viet Cong and the expansion of the Cambodian army by ten thousand men. New anti-Vietnamese riots took place in Phnom Penh with attacks on shops and churches of the Vietnamese community. On March 13, the Cambodian Foreign Ministry announced that it had notified the North Vietnamese and Viet Cong embassies that all Vietnamese Communist armed forces were to leave Cambodian territory by dawn on March 15, 1970 — two days later.

The same day, March 13, Sihanouk made his single most fateful decision. He left Paris, not to return to Phnom Penh as he had announced two days before, but to carry out his scheduled visit to Moscow. Attempting to regain the initiative on the issue of primary concern to his public, he announced in Paris: "I am going to Moscow and Peking to ask them to curb the activities of the Viet Cong and Viet Minh in my country." He reprinted a letter he had written in Agence Khmer Presse that he would fight "against the Communist Vietnamese who, taking advantage of the military situation, infiltrate and settle our territory." Despite his earlier intention to return quickly to Phnom Penh, despite Soviet President Podgorny's advice to fly home the next day, Siharouk spent five crucial days in Moscow haggling over military aid — in a last-ditch effort to placate his military, who were chafing at being cut off from all new equipment. Even then, he headed not for Phnom Penh but for Peking. In his own account Sihanouk asserts rather defensively that he "needed more time to watch developments in Phnom Penh";[7] at several points he claims that Lon Nol and Sirik Matak would have blocked any attempt to return. But it was not until March 18 that his own legislature dropped him and only then were the airports closed. Sihanouk learned that he had been deposed from Prime Minister Kosygin on the ride to Moscow's Vnukovo airport. He was stunned. For none of his aides had had the courage to tell him that earlier that day the ninety-two-strong Cambodian National Assembly and Council of the Kingdom, in another special joint session, had voted unanimously to remove him as chief of state.

Sihanouk arrived in Peking to be hugged by Premier Chou En-lai and feted by the Chinese as if nothing had changed; Chou assured him that China still regarded him as chief of state. In Phnom Penh, meanwhile, the Cambodian Parliament named Cheng Heng, whom Sihanouk had left behind in his place, as interim — instead of acting — chief of state. It was not a military "coup" in the classic sense; it was Sihanouk's own government without Sihanouk.

One account of Sihanouk's behavior came to me months later from Jean Sainteny. I met with Sainteny in his Paris apartment on September 27, 1970, before a meeting with the North Vietnamese. He revealed that he had lunched with Sihanouk in Paris on the very day that the North Vietnamese and Viet Cong embassies in Phnom Penh had been attacked (March 11). At that point Sihanouk planned to go back immediately — in which case Sainteny was convinced he would not have been deposed. Sainteny was convinced that Sihanouk changed his mind partly because of Princess Monique's desire to visit their children, who were students in Prague and Peking. Another reason, I believe, was that Sihanouk was overconfident; he could not believe his rule was in danger from the men who, after all, owed their office to him. He also hoped that Moscow would help him placate his military, by both military aid and pressure on Hanoi to leave Cambodia. Finally (as Sihanouk later told me), he had received a cable from his mother in Phnom Penh warning him that it was dangerous to return.

Any attempt to assess the blame for propelling Cambodia into the maelstrom of bloody conflict must begin here. For Lon Nol and Sirik Matak, the crucial step was their act of bravado to take up the popular battle against the hated — and far superior — forces of the North Vietnamese and Viet Cong. For Sihanouk, the crucial step was his week of hesitation, because what Lon Nol and Sirik Matak feared, and Podgorny advised, the United States also believed and preferred: that Sihanouk's bold reentry into Phnom Penh to face down his opponents would have turned the tide of events and was in everybody's best interest. Once returned to power, Sihanouk could have resumed his balancing role from his traditional position, which I described to Nixon on April 21 as one of "placing himself deliberately on the extreme left wing of the right wing." We would almost certainly have cooperated with this effort. By March 20 events were racing out of control.

The role of the United States through these events was hardly as purposeful as some imagine, or as effectual as others pretend. Preoccupied with Laos for the first three months of the year, and with no intelligence personnel in Phnom Penh, we found our perceptions lagging far behind events. We neither encouraged Sihanouk's overthrow nor knew about it in advance. We did not even grasp its significance for many weeks. My own ignorance of what was going on is reflected in two memoranda to Nixon. Though he received daily summaries of key events, I did not send forward a longer analysis of the first (March 11) demonstrations against Sihanouk until March 17, a week's delay that indicates that Cambodia was scarcely a high priority concern. Even more striking is my suggestion in that analysis that it all could have been an elaborate trick by Sihanouk:

Given the sharp competition between Sirik Matak and Sihanouk, it is possible that Sirik wanted to present Sihanouk with a fait accompli, or to challenge him to a test on grounds where Sirik Matak's position would be popular. On the other hand, nobody has challenged Sihanouk so directly in years, and it is quite possible that this is an elaborate maneuver, to permit Sihanouk to call for Soviet and Chinese cooperation in urging the VC/NVA* to leave, on the grounds that he will fall and be replaced by a "rightist" leader if the VC/NVA stay in Cambodia.

The recent behavior of Sihanouk and the RKG [Royal Khmer Government] would fit either thesis — i.e., that this is a collusive gambit; or that Sihanouk in fact faces a challenge from Sirik Matak and Lon Nol.

The motivations of the principal actors in Phnom Penh were quite obscure to me, not least because Lon Nol had been among those profiting from the smuggling trade with the very Communist forces that his government now challenged. On March 19 in another memorandum to

* Viet Cong/North Vietnamese Army.

the President, I still thought Sihanouk might attempt to return to Phnom Penh and put some of the pieces back together:

Lon Nol has heretofore been content to be Number Two, but this appears to be a straight power challenge. In popular anger against Vietnamese Communist incursions, he has found a good issue to challenge Sihanouk (and the Army fanned up that anger), but Lon Nol's dealings with the Communists do not suggest that he is a fervent anti-Communist or anti-Vietnamese patriot.

Future Choices. This situation will probably move in one of three ways:

— A Lon Nol/Sirik Matak–dominated new Government supported by the Army, with little popular support and forced to buy popularity with anti-Vietnamese slogans and economic progress.

— A shaky compromise akin to the barons' truce with King John in 1215, permitting Sihanouk to come back as Chief of State but with much limited powers. This would be an unstable situation, as Sihanouk maneuvered, probably successfully, to outflank and eliminate his challengers.

— A Sihanouk victory, by turning the Army against Lon Nol.

The Implications for Foreign Policy and for Us. Khmer nationalism has [been] aroused against the Vietnamese Communist occupation. Any future government will probably have to be more circumspect and covert about its cooperation with the Vietnamese. Lon Nol has chosen this issue, and he will need to be able to demonstrate publicly that he is taking action against the Vietnamese occupation. Similarly, Sihanouk will not for some time open himself to the charge of being "soft on the Vietnamese."

This will create serious problems for the VC/NVA, which will have considerable reason to take a more hostile line toward Cambodia.

None of my reports to the President discussed any US intelligence involvement or expressed any particular pleasure at the coup. Nor was CIA reporting more prescient, doubtless in part because the Agency had been banned from Phnom Penh. It was not until March 18 — the day of Sihanouk's ouster — that a CIA report was circulated in Washington. Its burden: that the Lon Nol–encouraged riots were a precursor to a coup against Sihanouk if Sihanouk refused to go along with an anti-Hanoi policy. The information had been acquired the week before from an Asian businessman not otherwise identified. The delay in distributing this report and the CIA's failure to predict the overthrow of Sihanouk were later the subject of an investigation by the President's Foreign Intelligence Advisory Board. I do not recall any document predicting the coup that came to my attention before the event, and I have not unearthed one in my papers. Of charges of intelligence failure, it should be remembered that the leader against whom it was directed had a far greater incentive to know the truth in his country, and he failed to anticipate the plot.

On March 20 Nixon and I discussed a forthcoming press conference by him. I recommended that he not comment on Cambodia beyond urging respect for Cambodian neutrality. Nixon agreed, adding that Sihanouk "may come back and take it over again." At the news conference, which took place on March 21, Nixon called the situation in Cambodia "unpredictable" and "fluid" and expressed hope that the North Vietnamese would respect Cambodia's neutrality. He repeated publicly what he had told me privately, that he still expected Sihanouk to return to Phnom Penh:

. . . we have, as you note, established relations on a temporary basis with the government which has been selected by the Parliament and will continue to deal with that government as long as it appears to be the government of the nation. I think any speculation with regard to which way this government is going to turn, *what will happen to Prince Sihanouk when he returns,* would both be premature and not helpful [emphasis added].

Our priorities were reflected in a meeting of the WSAG on March 19 called to discuss Laos and Cambodia; most of the discussion concerned Laos. My staff's briefing papers for me showed as much concern for the *Columbia Eagle,* an American ship impounded by the Cambodians after two sailors mutinied and diverted it to Sihanoukville, as for the long-range implications of the coup. On the political situation they regarded the outcome as uncertain and still left open the possibility of Sihanouk's return. My briefing paper asked a key question: "Does the presumably more pro-Western orientation of Lon Nol make up for the assumption that Sihanouk's departure may lead to increased instability?"

However, ignorance did not protect us against the necessity of decision. Not surprisingly, the Executive Branch was even more divided over Cambodia than it had been over Laos. Nixon from the first was in favor of a more active policy. Next to the passage in my memorandum of March 17 informing him of Lon Nol's plans to expand the Cambodian army by 10,000 men, Nixon wrote: "Let's get a plan to aid the new government on this goal." I had not yet acted on this note when Nixon returned my memorandum of March 19 informing him of Sihanouk's overthrow with the following note: "I want Helms to develop and implement a plan for maximum assistance to pro–US elements in Cambodia. Don't put this out to 303* or the bureaucracy. Handle like our [Menu] air strike." Haig conveyed the President's request directly to Helms on March 22 and I set up a meeting with Helms for March 23.

Helms's reply was largely procedural. He argued that the CIA could make few realistic recommendations unless permitted to open a station (the CIA term for a resident office) in Phnom Penh. He outlined possi-

---

* The 303 Committee, by then renamed the 40 Committee, was the interagency committee supervising covert intelligence activities.

ble actions ranging from clandestine airlifting to obtaining international support for Lon Nol, but implied that the Agency could not put forward a concrete proposal until it had better information. The President therefore decided to let CIA set up a station in Phnom Penh. This proved no simple matter, for the State Department fought it bitterly, partly out of fear of what Mansfield would do to it in Congress. On April 1, while I was away on vacation — another sure indication that I did not consider the situation critical — the President called Rogers and Helms into the Oval Office and conveyed his order that a CIA office be opened in Phnom Penh immediately.

Nevertheless, whether because Nixon was elliptical as he often was in his face-to-face meetings with Rogers, or because State felt strongly enough to ignore a direct order, the President's wishes were simply not carried out. On April 2, the next day, CIA nominated an officer and a communicator to move into Phnom Penh. But Rogers called Helms and said that he did not believe this was wise but agreed to look into the communications problem. There was further delay while the State Department decided whether to make a formal request to the Cambodian government. On April 7, chargé Lloyd Rives went to see a low-level Cambodian official; this maximized the likelihood of a refusal or at least of a delay. To the evident dismay of the East Asian Bureau, interim permission was granted on the spot, with the promise of an official notification in a short time. The Department insisted on waiting for the official reply, and in another delaying tactic recommended that the communications equipment be flown in by commercial rather than military aircraft.

By April 16, fifteen days after a direct Presidential order, neither CIA officer nor communicator nor equipment had yet moved. While Nixon hated giving direct orders, he could be brutal if sufficiently aroused. He called in Helms, his deputy General Cushman, Haig, and me (back from vacation) to register his outrage at the procrastination and defiance of his instruction. As a sign of his displeasure, no State Department representative was invited to the meeting. Nixon gave a twenty-four-hour deadline for introducing a CIA officer and communicator. He added a vindictive slap at State. Since State had protested that the small size of our Embassy was one of the obstacles, Nixon ordered one State Department official to leave Phnom Penh to make room.

Once again we beheld one of the wonders of the modern state, the relative inability of leaders to dominate their bureaucracy or to cut short its powers of endless exegesis. The twenty-four-hour period was consumed in further dithering. It was a full week before another Presidential explosion finally brought results. The reduction of Embassy personnel was never implemented because events overtook the Presidential directive.

Until the middle of April, therefore, our capability to monitor or influence the situation in Cambodia was severely limited. By then, however, the issue was no longer a quarrel between Cambodian factions, the success of either of which would have been compatible with our own interests. For in the last days of March Sihanouk made his second fateful decision. Ensconced in Peking (with which we had no contact of any kind at that stage), Sihanouk threw in his lot with Hanoi and turned violently against the United States. On March 20 — two days after he was deposed — he effectively declared war on the new government. He issued a statement calling for a national referendum and denouncing his removal as "absolutely illegal." He blamed the "turbulence" in Cambodia on CIA collusion with the "traitorous group" that had deposed him; he defended the North Vietnamese in Cambodia on the ground that they were "resisting American imperialism." The next day, Sihanouk vowed a struggle "until victory or death" against the new government, which he denounced as "stooges of American imperialists." Henceforth, Sihanouk's return would have meant not a restoration of neutralism but the victory of his new Communist patrons, whom he had lost all capacity to control.

In retaliation, the Cambodian National Assembly on March 21 voted to arrest Sihanouk and to charge him with treason if he returned. Newspapers and broadcasts in Phnom Penh were filled with lurid accounts of his corrupt personal life and attacks on his years of leadership. On March 22, after three days of avoiding direct comment on Cambodian events, North Vietnam labeled Cambodia's new leaders a "pro-American ultra-rightist group." The authoritative Hanoi party newspaper *Nhan Dan* claimed that Sihanouk's ouster had been engineered by the United States and affirmed that "our people fully support the struggle of the Cambodian people" against the new leadership. On March 23, Sihanouk in a five-point statement promised formation of a "liberation army" and "national united front," lauding the anti–US struggle of the Communist Vietnamese, Laotians, and Cambodians.

In early April the North Vietnamese and Viet Cong forces began making good their pledge of "support." Communist forces left their base areas and started penetrating deep into Cambodia to overthrow the new government. By April 3, the North Vietnamese began attacking Cambodian forces in Svay Rieng province. By April 10 Cambodian troops were forced to evacuate border positions in the Parrot's Beak area. Communists started to harass Mekong River traffic. By April 16, the North Vietnamese and Viet Cong troops launched raids on the capital of Takeo province south of Phnom Penh. Thus did the war begin in Cambodia, weeks before *any* American action.

At the same time, Sihanouk on April 2 denounced the United States as "the principal and sole culprit responsible for the war and political

instability in the three countries of Indochina.'' On April 3 he appealed
to his compatriots to take to the jungles and join the ''resistance zones
already there.'' On April 4 Premier Chou En-lai, while on a visit to
North Korea, formally endorsed Sihanouk's resistance movement. On
April 14 Radio Peking reported the formal establishment on April 6 of
the provisional committee of Sihanouk's ''national united front'' in
Cambodia's Svay Rieng province. In short, by the middle of April,
before we had undertaken *any* significant action, Sihanouk had irrevocably joined forces with the Communists, the Communists had dedicated
themselves to the overthrow of the Phnom Penh government, and North
Vietnamese units were attacking deep inside Cambodia.

Le Duc Tho's behavior in the secret talks removed any doubt that
Hanoi had formally linked Cambodia to its war in Vietnam. He emphasized Hanoi's intention to overthrow the Phnom Penh government, to
replace it with personnel acceptable to Hanoi, and to use Cambodia as a
base for operations in Vietnam. At the secret meeting of March
16 — two days before Sihanouk was deposed — Le Duc Tho accused
us of having organized the riots in Phnom Penh five days earlier, a
charge I vigorously denied. I considered Le Duc Tho's hot-tempered
assertions sufficiently worrying to report to the President: ''Their remarks on Cambodia were troublesome and may indicate increased pressure there.''

Fears about Hanoi's overall intentions could only be reinforced by the
sudden military ''high point'' in South Vietnam, which broke the lull
that had lasted since September. On March 31, while negotiations with
Le Duc Tho were still going on and in the face of our offer of de-escalation, the North Vietnamese launched scores of attacks throughout South
Vietnam. American dead for the week were 138, nearly double the
previous week's total.

This set the stage for our climactic Paris meeting of April 4. Le Duc
Tho blamed us once again for the upheaval in Cambodia and effectively
declared war on the new Cambodian government:

> You thought you could use a group of military reactionaries to overthrow
> Norodom Sihanouk and it would be all over. It is too simple thinking. It is pre-
> cisely your actions there which make the whole people of Cambodia fight
> against the agents of the U.S. They have responded to the appeal of Prince
> Sihanouk and the National Front of Cambodia. The Khmer people have stood
> up with all their strength to defend freedom and neutrality.

I rebutted his charges emphatically but futilely:

> I despair of convincing the Special Adviser that we had nothing to do with
> what happened in Phnom Penh, although I am flattered of the high opinion he
> has of our intelligence services. If they knew I was here, I would tell them of
> this high opinion.

Again, there is a simple test. Who has troops in Cambodia? Not the U S. I am impressed again with the linguistic ability of the people of the Indochinese peninsula. We discovered that the Pathet Lao speak Vietnamese, and now we find the same phenomenon in Cambodia.

We have shown great restraint vis-à-vis the bases you maintain in Cambodia and which you use in attacking our forces in Vietnam. . . .

I stressed to Le Duc Tho that the United States sought no expansion of the war. To achieve this goal I proposed to discuss *immediately* specific steps to assure the neutrality of Cambodia:

We are prepared to discuss immediately concrete and specific measures to guarantee the neutrality of Cambodia and to make absolutely certain it does not become a pawn in any international conflict. We are willing to do this bilaterally with you or in an international framework. . . . We shall be prepared to entertain reasonable propositions to guarantee that Laos and Cambodia — especially Cambodia, as it is a new problem — remain neutral.

But Le Duc Tho dismissed any suggestion of neutralization or of an international conference. The conflicts in Indochina had now become one, he asserted; he would not even discuss confining the war to Vietnam. Cambodia had become a theater of operations and Hanoi would brook no discussion about maintaining its neutrality. Over three weeks *before* our actions, Le Duc Tho said:

The three peoples of Indochina — the Vietnamese, Lao and Khmer people — have had traditional unity in the fight against colonialism. This cannot be broken by you. Now, faced with the extension of the war to Cambodia by the U S., the three peoples will continue to fight to have victory, no matter how great the sacrifices may be.

According to Le Duc Tho there could be no formal agreement on the neutralization of Cambodia. Instead, the regime that had seized power in Phnom Penh had to be overthrown: "We do not recognize the Lon Nol–Matak government. We support the Five Points of Norodom Sihanouk. We are convinced that so long as the Lon Nol–Matak government remains in Cambodia, then the Cambodian question cannot be settled."

In Cambodia, as in Vietnam, we were now faced with the proposition that the only key to peace was the overthrow of the established government (which most nations, including the Soviet Union, continued to recognize). A spokesman for United Nations Secretary-General U Thant declared on April 6 that the United Nations would "deal with the authorities which effectively have control of the situation in Cambodia," in effect recognizing the Lon Nol government.

In Cambodia, as in Vietnam, there was a refusal of negotiations and a deliberate expansion of the war by Hanoi. In Cambodia, as in Vietnam, Hanoi would discuss only the seizure of total power. Hence, the situation in Cambodia had been transformed fundamentally. Three weeks earlier, we would on the whole have preferred that Sihanouk remain in office. Now, if he returned through the military pressures of Hanoi and as its instrument, all of Cambodia would become an enemy sanctuary; the supply route through Sihanoukville would grow doubly menacing. Our nightmare, as a staff planning paper pointed out on April 1, was of "a communist-dominated Sihanouk government providing a secure sanctuary and logistics base for the VC/NVA."

The first official Cambodian request for US military assistance came as we gradually and reluctantly perceived the impossibility of Cambodia's neutrality, due to Hanoi's insistence on Communist domination of *all* of Cambodia. On the evening of April 9 Commandant Lon Non, Lon Nol's younger brother and commander of the Phnom Penh gendarmerie, requested a meeting with an Embassy official. Lon Non spoke of the expansion of the Cambodian army from 35,000 to more than 60,000 men; there was an immediate need for 100,000 to 150,000 weapons, and ultimately for 200,000 to 250,000, including ammunition.

Our chargé, Lloyd Rives, considered these quantities exaggerated and the need impossible to assess, since no breakdown was given as to types desired. To Washington Rives recommended "serious consideration of supplying weapons through a third party or parties, if such can be found." Lon Non's request was considered at first in intelligence channels because we still were eager to avoid direct intervention. Delivering arms clandestinely would avoid giving Hanoi a pretext for an all-out assault, and it also placed an inherent limit on the amount we could supply. The consensus was that American military forces and American arms should stay out of Cambodia. Our principal interest, it was agreed, was to prevent Cambodia's use as a supply base for Vietnam. We were even prepared to accept a degree of accommodation between Lon Nol and the Viet Cong if this proved essential to the survival of the Cambodian government. We sought to arrange military assistance through third parties as Rives had recommended. It was decided to instruct Rives to establish a private channel to the Cambodian government; to approach France to encourage more French assistance to Cambodia; to explore other possible intermediaries; and to have the Defense Department ascertain what captured *Communist* arms and ammunition were available in South Vietnam for transfer to the (hitherto Communist-equipped) Cambodian army. No American military assistance was authorized.

Rives carried out these instructions with selective exuberance, in harmony with the East Asian Bureau's passionate dedication to a version of Cambodian neutrality more stringent than that of Cambodia's government (and totally rejected by Hanoi). He turned the offer to be helpful through third parties into a disquisition on American reluctance to involve itself directly. He suggested to the Cambodian Foreign Minis-

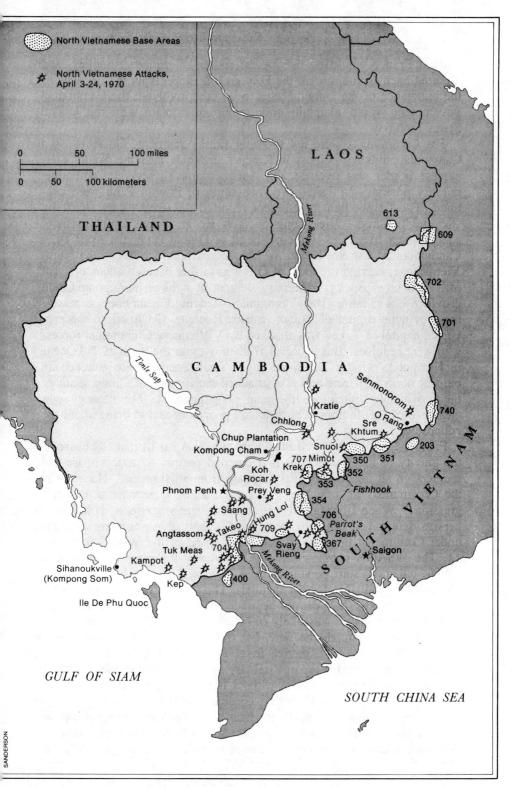

Cambodia: North Vietnamese Attacks
April 3–24, 1970

ter that France would be the logical source of military supplies, and reported back with approval the Foreign Minister's reply that in view of the reluctance of the United States to become involved, the Cambodian government would maintain only minimum contact with the United States Embassy.

The Communists were not showing similar restraint. On April 13 a Cambodian military outpost in Kampot province near the South Vietnamese border was overrun. On April 13 and 14 several Cambodian military positions in Takeo province south of Phnom Penh were captured. The Cambodian government reported on April 14 an attack by "several hundred" Viet Cong on Koh Rocar, Prey Veng province, about twenty-five miles to the northeast of Phnom Penh. On April 15, a Cambodian post at Sre Khtum in Mondolkiri province fell to the North Vietnamese, leaving the town of O Rang, farther east on Route 131, cut off. Also on April 15, a military outpost at Krek in Kompong Cham province was taken by the Communists, denying Cambodians access to the provincial capital of Mimot, astride Route 7. On April 16 the provincial capital of Takeo was attacked by Vietnamese Communist forces, who were repulsed. But on April 16 they overran the town of Tuk Meas in Kampot province. The same day a small enemy force attacked an outpost north of Kratie and also attacked the town of Chhlong south of the provincial capital (see the map on page 471). The strategy was clearly to cut off Phnom Penh from the provinces and to bring about the collapse of Lon Nol.

Premier Lon Nol declared in a broadcast on April 14 that "because of the gravity of the situation, it is deemed necessary to accept from this moment on all unconditional foreign aid from all sources." He accused the Communists of mounting "an escalation of systematic acts of aggression." When I brought this to the President's attention, Nixon said he was determined not to let the new Cambodian government collapse under Communist pressure. I called a meeting of the WSAG for April 14. The WSAG's composition was essentially the same as the earlier forum, but more staff personnel were permitted to attend and its documents were handled in formal channels. The shift reflected that the problem of Cambodia had grown beyond the intelligence framework. A major policy decision was likely to be required in the near future.

The committee might be new, but the participants had not changed their reluctance to see America involve itself. I asked the WSAG to recommend a level and type of military aid that would provide psychological reassurance to Lon Nol without furnishing a pretext for an even stronger offensive by Hanoi. The consensus was to send up to 3,000 captured Communist AK-47 rifles from South Vietnamese stocks and, to maintain our dissociation, to have them delivered through South Vietnamese channels. Everyone, including myself, agreed that it was "premature" to provide American M-1 rifles. For that very reason I reported to the WSAG that the President was not yet prepared to approve the delivery of 1,000-man packs of American equipment (CIA packages of hand weapons that were occasionally supplied to friendly forces on a covert basis). There was no discussion of heavier equipment. The State Department was reluctant to deliver even medical supplies overtly; it was finally agreed that the choice of their mode of delivery should be left to the Cambodians. In short, three weeks after the North Vietnamese had left their sanctuaries and were seeking to isolate Phnom Penh, the United States made available exactly 3,000 captured rifles delivered clandestinely. We gave no other aid.

The next day the Cambodian government submitted a request for military and economic assistance to expand their army to 200,000 men. This request clearly went beyond the framework of existing policy; it also far exceeded what in our judgment Cambodia could absorb. Anothe· WSAG meeting was held on April 15. It was decided that rather than start a formal US arms supply line we would channel $5 million to Cambodia through a friendly government (which we would then reimburse); Cambodia would thus have funds to buy its own arms on the open market. The sum was of course symbolic; it corresponded in no way to Cambodian needs, much less to Cambodian requests. It can hardly be called an heroic or urgent response to the pleas of a government on whose soil thousands of North Vietnamese were systematically undermining its authority, killing its citizens, and annexing its territory.

For by now the pattern of outside aggression was patent. North Vietnamese forces were attacking all over Cambodia, concentrating especially on provincial capitals and communications to and from Phnom Penh.

Against this backdrop of mounting North Vietnamese menace and his own growing frustration, the President took a personal hand in speeding aid to Cambodia. At a meeting with Helms and Cushman on April 16 called primarily to establish the CIA station in Phnom Penh, Nixon ordered delivery of the 1,000-man packs I had rejected at his instruction forty-eight hours earlier. A few days later he doubled the contingency fund approved by the WSAG to $10 million. In fact, none of these instructions could be implemented before they were overtaken by more escalation from Hanoi and Nixon's decision two weeks later to move against the sanctuaries.

There was a brief flurry of hope first. Yakov Malik, the Soviet Permanent Representative to the UN, suggested at a news conference on April 16 that "only a new Geneva Conference could bring a new solution and relax the tension on the Indochina peninsula." A Soviet call for a new Geneva Conference was a sensational event; it was bound to suggest parallels to the ending of the Korean War; it was analyzed solemnly by the US government and received massive media attention. We would have been most eager to explore it. I considered it practically impossible that Malik could have spoken without Hanoi's prior knowledge — especially as Le Duc Tho was at that moment in Moscow. I gave the President the following possible explanations:

— The North Vietnamese position is weaker than our intelligence reports have indicated, and Hanoi is particularly worried about yet another long war in Cambodia. It needs a breathing spell. It may then try to suspend the conference after it has gained some respite. (Both the 1954 and 1961–62 conferences were interrupted for periods of varying length).

— After the break-down of all valid contacts in Paris, Hanoi feels that it needs some forum to deal with us seriously. Also, it may want to deal seriously with the GVN, which it can do more easily in a larger framework.

— Any talk of a Geneva Conference (even if no conference is in the offing) would restrain our retaliation against any new military measures Hanoi might take. (But we doubt that the Soviets would let themselves be used this way when they have some serious business with us in Vienna [i.e., SALT].)

But before we could return a reply, Malik on April 18 retracted his "proposal." He did so with the cold-bloodedness of Soviet diplomats long practiced in sudden reversals that are then presented as the logical essence of orthodoxy. Malik suddenly and without explanation asserted that a Geneva Conference would be unrealistic and that "the Americans have to get out of Vietnam before anything much can happen." The negotiating route was slammed shut once again. There was to be no conference; the precondition for negotiations remained unilateral American withdrawal from Vietnam.

Nixon's irritation at the slow pace of our reaction continued to mount. Reading one report of a Viet Cong base in some mountain area deep inside Cambodia, he ordered a B-52 strike within two hours. This proved somewhat impractical because it would have taken more than two hours for the B-52s to get there and because the report was not confirmed; also because of the undesirable symbolism of a B-52 attack deep inside Cambodia before other fundamental decisions. Nixon urged a psychological warfare campaign to tie Sihanouk to the Communists and to dramatize US support for Lon Nol. He had an exalted view of the CIA's capacity for "black propaganda" and even more of its impact. This approach, too, was rapidly overtaken by events.

By the middle of April, then, over a month after the Cambodian coup, the United States had barely lifted a finger. We had as yet given no military aid, no intelligence support, and had only formalistic contacts with the new government. The coup itself had come without warning; its consequences threatened not only the freedom of Cambodia but our entire position in Vietnam. Instead of a strip of isolated sanctuaries close to the Vietnamese border we would, after the collapse of the Lon Nol government, confront *all* of Cambodia as a Communist base, stretching 600 miles along the border of South Vietnam and with short lines of supply from the sea. Vietnamization and American withdrawal would then come unstuck. So we were being driven toward support of Lon Nol hesitantly, reluctantly, in response to the evolving circumstances in Cambodia which we could neither forecast nor control, and with a series of half measures that always lagged behind the rapidly deteriorating situation. Of all the parties that made crucial decisions in that period — Hanoi, Lon Nol, Sihanouk, and the United States — we had the least freedom of choice. The record leaves no doubt that the North Vietnamese, also caught by surprise by the March coup, bear the heaviest responsibility for events in Cambodia. Their illegal and arrogant occupation of Cambodian territory had torn apart the fragile unity of Sihanouk's neutralist country; they created the Khmer Rouge as a force against Sihanouk well before his overthrow; they used him to give credence to that tiny band when he went into exile. On April 4 Le Duc Tho had rejected discussion not only of a cease-fire anywhere in Indochina, but of any scheme for the neutrality of Cambodia. It was they, not we, who had decided on a fight to the finish on the bleeding body of a small neutralist kingdom which wanted only to be left alone.

Cambodia's agony, then, unfolded with the inevitability of a Greek tragedy. The Communists were determined on total victory; Sihanouk's wounded pride caused him to make common cause with his erstwhile mortal enemies; and we were by then on the way out of Indochina and losing our power to control events.

But before the die was finally cast there was a brief interlude, during which to maintain our position in Vietnam we had to take another unilateral step toward weakening it; it was time for a new troop withdrawal decision.

The April 20 Troop Withdrawal Announcement

ON the surface, the issue was straightforward. The most recent withdrawal (announced December 15, 1969) had been 50,000 over a four-month period ending on April 15, 1970. With 115,000 troops already out, it was clear that the next increment would begin to cut sharply into our combat strength. The dilemma was plain to see. Troop cuts poulticed public sores at home, but they were evaporating Hanoi's need to bargain about our disengagement. And if Vietnamization was not making good the defensive gaps created by our withdrawals, we hazarded not only the negotiating lever but South Vietnam's independence and the entire basis of our sacrifices.

Though every agency paid lip service to Vietnamization, at least three schools of thought had developed by mid-1970. Secretary Rogers's experience had been in domestic policy. He was acutely sensitive to public and Congressional opinion. He had less of an instinct for the geopolitical consequences of an American defeat or for what decisions motivated by domestic considerations might do to our negotiating positions. He favored the largest possible withdrawal in the shortest possible time; the military effect he considered beyond the scope of his office. His Department deluged Saigon with a stream of proposals about political reform more attuned to our Congressional pressures than to the realities of a war-torn country with limited democratic traditions, overrun by several hundred thousand enemy troops and guerrillas.

Secretary Laird was the most politically subtle of the President's senior advisers. He understood the public's ambivalence, shown by every poll. It opposed unilateral withdrawal yet it wanted the war ended, and saw the reduction of our troop strength as a sign of progress. Laird aspired to stay in tune with this mood. He was prepared to give Vietnamization a real chance; for a long time he favored a residual US force of several hundred thousand. But he wanted to reduce to that residual force rapidly, and to maintain public confidence he thought it important to make our withdrawal look as inexorable as possible. He also saw Vietnam as an obstacle to his plans to modernize our armed forces; Congressional pressures to cut his defense budget could be reduced, he thought, if he was identified with troop pullouts. He sought to guarantee his preferred course by gearing the withdrawal rate to the defense budget in such a way that any slowdown of withdrawals was bound to reduce procurement — thus enlisting the support of the services for rapid withdrawal by threatening their cherished new projects.

Initially, I had been the most skeptical of the President's senior advisers, but once embarked on Vietnamization I did my utmost to give it a chance to succeed. Moreover, it was clear to me — if not to all my colleagues — that our commitment to Vietnamization was progressively reducing other options. Had we been prepared to accept Saigon's collapse we could have adopted any of the many proposals for setting a deadline that had become staples of the public and Congressional debate and that had some support among the middle levels of the Administration. But if we meant what we said about the global consequence of an American collapse, we had to give the South Vietnamese time to replace American forces without catastrophe. And if we wanted to husband negotiating assets, our withdrawal strategy had to provide the President some discretion to accelerate it or slow it down in response to enemy actions. This was also Nixon's view.

These differences of perspective, some of nuance, some of substance, were given added sharpness because each chief actor was acutely conscious of the public perception. Everybody wanted some of the credit for the withdrawal program; nobody desired the blame for failures or defeats it might produce. Memoranda proliferated to be available for later reference; the authors assumed that history would deal kindly with those advocating large withdrawals. The President, eager to garner whatever favorable publicity could be made to come his way, warily kept his own counsel. He feared that if he were more confiding his associates would leak higher withdrawal numbers than he was prepared to authorize and so place him at a disadvantage in the public eye.

This was a game in which Laird was not easily bested. He was a patriot whose every instinct was to win the war; he was also a realist who understood that the prospects for doing so were problematical at best. He was a politician to the core. He was perfectly prepared to support a strong policy so long as he was not identified as its principal author. In crises he was redoubtable. In the run-up to them he produced a blizzard of memoranda that would make it next to impossible to determine either his real intentions or — what was more important to him — his precise recommendation.

Every troop withdrawal decision set the stage for another of Laird's amazing tours de force. In 1970 Laird had started early. On February 27 he wrote the President explaining that his budgetary choices in allocating the "increasingly scarce resources" for the US military operations in Vietnam in Fiscal Years 1970–1971 would become more and more difficult. The budgetary situation was "tight by any reasonable standard"; changing combat requirements could also produce new "resource problems" for which reprogramming of funds would "not be an easy chore." Laird reminded the President that budgetary planning for Fiscal Year 1971 had been based on the assumption of reduced US combat and support efforts, and these constraints "restrict to a considerable degree our ability to impose added operations." In other words Laird opposed new or expanded military operations but sought to blame any military failures on budgetary constraints that prevented new operations.

On March 11 I sought General Wheeler's views on the relative merits of one four-month withdrawal increment (the largest period then being considered) or two withdrawals over two months each. Wheeler replied on March 20 in an unsigned memorandum, which he passed to the President through Haig, thus avoiding the inconvenience of Defense Department channels and the certainty of Laird's wrath. Wheeler recommended a "one bite approach," because the longer period provided greater flexibility by making it possible to retain key units until the end of the period. However, Wheeler added that he preferred "no further redeployment" at all because of the uncertain "overall situation." He strongly urged holding the next withdrawal decision in abeyance for ninety days.

Laird reentered the fray on April 4 with a long memorandum, the thrust of which was to remind everyone that our effort in Vietnam was "large and costly." He recommended a fixed monthly rate of withdrawal and a reduction in B-52 and tactical air operations in proportion to our withdrawals. Launching an incursion into the province of the State Department, Laird recommended that we seek a diplomatic solution to our dilemma. He urged that we offer a cease-fire in Vietnam and major new proposals for de-escalation in Laos and Cambodia, appoint a new senior ambassador to the peace talks in Paris, or explore a French proposal for an Indochina conference. Other than this, Laird pledged complete dedication to the President's policies and programs.

Laird cannot be blamed for not knowing that these schemes had all been rejected by Le Duc Tho; it was, in fact, a weakness of our method of government that the Secretary of Defense was operating in such a vacuum. But his memorandum raised issues that went beyond the scope of his tactical knowledge. And his military proposals, as I pointed out in a covering memorandum for the President, all assumed that the enemy threat would decline in parallel with our withdrawals. The opposite was more likely.

Throughout the war there were many exhortations, from within and outside the government, to eschew a military solution and to seek a diplomatic one. But the raw truth was that this distinction not only was unacceptable to our adversary; it was incomprehensible to him. Every time I met with Le Duc Tho, he spent most of our time depicting the hopelessness of our military position. This was the "objective" factor that he assumed would compel our eventual acceptance of North Vietnam's demands. There was no purely diplomatic alternative. Unless military and political efforts were kept in tandem, both would prove sterile. Until 1972 Hanoi never gave us a political option; its negotiating position was to demand our unilateral withdrawal on a short deadline and the overthrow of the Saigon government. It did so because it believed itself to be winning; it chose compromise only after a military stalemate had become apparent.

I was as committed to a political solution and even more prepared to come up with negotiating formulas than the other senior advisers, but it was precisely for this reason that I urged a military strategy that would persuade Hanoi to compromise and negotiate. Fixed deadlines and automatic withdrawals did not aid a political solution; they dissipated our negotiating assets. We were in danger, I thought, of having a withdrawal program too slow to satisfy our critics but too drastic for military or political effectiveness. This was not a policy but an abdication; it would make collapse inevitable through the very attempt to postpone it.

By April 8 General Abrams's assessment reached the White House. (It had actually been sent nearly three weeks earlier, but because its recommendations did not find favor, it had been held up in the Pentagon for "staffing.") It supported Wheeler's recommendation of a ninety-day moratorium on withdrawals. And it seriously challenged Laird's proposed reduction in tactical air operations and B-52 sorties. Abrams stressed that our withdrawals forced him to use the South Vietnamese forces in a static defense role. The B-52s thus became his sole strategic reserve. On April 15 I sent the President a memorandum arguing that since Vietnamization gains were "fragile" and allied forces were "stretched nearly to the limit of their capabilities," the sharp cutbacks in air operations implied by the defense budget had disturbing implications. I recommended that the President order a study of what air operations were required to support Vietnamization. Such an order was issued on April 17. It put an end to reductions during the immediate crisis, but the cutbacks in air operations were to resume — almost imperceptibly — in the fall, forcing us to send substantial reinforcements when the enemy offensive broke in 1972.

I took seriously Abrams's and Wheeler's pleas to maintain troop levels, especially in the light of North Vietnamese offensives in Laos and Cambodia. But I knew also that to stop withdrawals for ninety days would trigger the same public protests as had occurred in the previous summer and make the eventual, inevitable resumption of withdrawals appear as a defeat. I concluded that a primary flaw lay in the apparently immutable timetable. An announcement was expected every few months, always triggering a debate within the Executive Branch as well as in public. These self-inflicted deadlines were sapping our endurance and raising doubts about our purposes.

For all these reasons I proposed that Nixon announce a large withdrawal and stretch it over one year. After consultation with General Wheeler, I recommended a total reduction of 150,000 men. This represented a slight increase in the monthly rate of withdrawal; but to compensate for this I proposed that only a very small withdrawal take place over the next ninety days, with the bulk of withdrawals planned for 1971. Nixon understood the strategic discretion this gave him and the favorable public impact. But he was also convinced that if he revealed his intentions to his associates he would rapidly be embroiled in controversy on at least three fronts: They would seek to transform his plan into a fixed monthly rate; they would urge that the rate be increased; and there was in the end the near certainty of a leak arranged in such a way as to create the impression that others had recommended an even larger figure.

The result was a complicated bureaucratic chess game whereby Nixon, with my assistance, moved toward a foreordained decision while confusing his Cabinet as to his plans. We first needed Bunker's and Abrams's reactions. On April 6 I had sent a backchannel message to both:

. . . any announcement which is substantially less than the pattern set heretofore could be the source of major problems with domestic critics. He is therefore considering announcing a decision to withdraw at least 150,000 troops over the next year with just a token withdrawal, if any, over the next few months. I would be grateful for your views on the implications of this formulation.

Abrams and Bunker informed me on April 8 that they, and in their judgment President Thieu also, could accept a withdrawal of 150,000 extended over a year provided the bulk of the forces remained throughout 1970. In addition, Bunker and Abrams insisted that B-52 sorties be held at the highest possible level, particularly in the first half of 1971 when troop reductions would be rapid and large.

At this point bureaucratic games in Washington reached new degrees of intricacy. The President's writers began to draft a speech announcing new withdrawals but leaving the numbers and timing blank. On April 11 I notified Bunker and Abrams that the President now needed Thieu's concurrence. I stressed the need for ''absolute secrecy,'' since no one in Washington except Nixon and me knew of the President's intentions; Bunker was to stress to Thieu the importance of preventing any leaks. At the same time the agencies were sending instructions to Bunker based on their own studies and preferences, using figures substantially at variance with those being discussed in backchannels. Bunker and Abrams did an admirable job of keeping their two sets of instructions straight. Thieu concurred with the same provisos about timing and air sorties previously reported by Abrams and Bunker.

On April 17 Nixon went to Hawaii to greet the returning *Apollo 13* astronauts. In order to keep an eye on Cambodia as well as the maneuvering over withdrawals I did not accompany him. Admiral John McCain, our commander in the Pacific, briefed Nixon at length in Honolulu. This doughty, crusty officer could have passed in demeanor, appearance, pugnacity, and manner of speech for Popeye the Sailor Man. His son had been a prisoner of war in Hanoi for years; this tragedy left him undaunted. He fought for the victory that his instinct and upbringing demanded and that political reality forbade. McCain brought home to Nixon the danger in Laos and Cambodia; he reinforced Nixon's conviction that the withdrawal schedule had to be flexible.

Nixon and I rejoined forces in San Clemente on the evening of April 19. Separated from his Cabinet by three thousand miles, Nixon announced to the press that he would make a speech the next evening on redeployment from Vietnam but declined to give any indication of its content. We were besieged with calls from Washington, especially from Laird. Nixon refused to take them. He instructed me to tell Laird and Rogers the next morning that he was thinking of announcing only a monthly rate but no overall number — it was the exact opposite of the truth. His purpose was to avoid leakage of the total he had already decided upon or of any other figure.

Late that afternoon of the twentieth in San Clemente — too late for leaks to the evening newscasts — I called Laird and Rogers with the President's decision: a withdrawal of 150,000 by the end of spring of 1971, with 60,000 to be withdrawn in 1970 and the remaining 90,000 in 1971. Within 1970 the greater portion of the withdrawals would take place after August 1. Nixon made his surprise announcement on April 20. It was one of the tours de force by which we sustained our effort in Vietnam. It met the political need for a withdrawal schedule and the military necessity to retain the largest possible number of troops during the next three critical months while Hanoi's forces were assaulting Cambodia and pressing forward in Laos. Whatever the bureaucratic maneuvers or the monthly fluctuations in the withdrawal rate, the fact remained that we had within one year projected a total reduction of 265,500 below the troop ceiling of 549,500 we found when we came into office.

Rogers supported the President's decision, regretting only that by forgoing more frequent announcements, the President deprived himself of periodic respites from public pressures. Laird wanted the withdrawals spaced more evenly; he insisted on an appointment with Nixon. I arranged it for the next day in Washington. Nixon flew back to Washington immediately after his announcement. When they met on April 21, Nixon explained to Laird that "we must play a tough game" for the next two or three months and therefore had to postpone withdrawals. Laird demurred: "I want you to know you have a fiscal problem. You know that, don't you?" (a favorite Laird phrase, used whether or not one had any way of knowing what he had just communicated — especially when one had not). The President assured him he did know. Laird told the President that he had to take out 60,000 men by the time of the November Congressional election or "you might just as well forget about the election." Nixon replied that he would be judged not by how many men left Vietnam in a given period but by how we left Vietnam in the end. Nixon said he would "think about" Laird's warning.

When Nixon told a Cabinet member he would "think about" something, it almost invariably meant that he wished to avoid a face-to-face confrontation and that he would confirm his original decision either through Haldeman or by memorandum. So it was. The next day, April 21, the President initialed a short note to Laird:

Memorandum for the Secretary of Defense:

Following our discussion yesterday afternoon, I want to reiterate my decision that no more than 60,000 troops are to be redeployed this year. A plan to this effect should be submitted to me by May 1.

Until I have reviewed the plan, no further withdrawals should be scheduled.

Laird accepted the decision with apparent good grace. But he knew his chief well enough to return to the fray at a more propitious moment. In August he persuaded the President that he could dramatize the success of the Cambodian operation best by withdrawing 90,000 by the end of 1970 and 60,000 in 1971 — the exact opposite of the President's original intention. Laird got his way. Nixon acquiesced in part because he hated constant controversy, in part because Congressional elections were imminent.

I have discussed the troop withdrawal at such length because of the insight it gives on two related problems: the dilemmas of extricating ourselves from a war we inherited, whipsawed between an implacable domestic opposition and an implacable Hanoi; and the Nixon Administration's style of government.

The dilemmas of our Vietnam policy were reflected in the gulf between our perception of reality and the nature of the public debate. Our reality consisted of enemy offensives in Laos and Cambodia that threatened our military position in South Vietnam. Yet as the objective threats grew, we were required to continue a program of unilateral withdrawal. The public debate focused on the danger that we might slide into a new "commitment" in two other faraway countries. Our reality was that only by preventing a collapse of these countries could we strengthen the South Vietnamese and enable them to take up the slack of our withdrawal without turning it into a rout. The public debate challenged all military calculations on the assumption that military effort was futile and was either unrelated to or inconsistent with our diplomatic prospects. (This would have been news to General Giap.) We had seen enough of Le Duc Tho to know that without a plausible military strategy we could not have an effective diplomacy.

As for Nixon's style of government, he was prepared to make decisions without illusion. Once convinced, he went ruthlessly and courageously to the heart of the matter; but each controversial decision drove him deeper into his all-enveloping solitude. He was almost physically unable to confront people who disagreed with him; and he shunned persuading or inspiring his subordinates. He would decide from inside his self-imposed cocoon, but he was unwilling to communicate with those who disagreed. It was the paradox of a President strong in his decisions but inconclusive in his leadership. Making and enforcing decisions left so many scars on him and others that it sacrificed administrative cohesion on the altar of executive discretion; it perversely created the maximum incentive for strong-willed subordinates to evade his directives. Since Nixon disdained any effort to instill a team spirit and usually kept his designs to himself, his Cabinet was tempted to exaggerate its autonomy. This in turn reinforced his conviction that the bureaucracy did not support him; it surely rarely went out of its way to carry out the spirit of his orders. All this became a vicious circle in which the President withdrew ever more into his isolation and pulled the central decisions increasingly into the White House, in turn heightening the resentments and defiant mood of his appointees.

And soon these procedures would be tested by another crisis, with the White House once again in the vortex. The decision on what to do about Cambodia had become inescapable.

The Attack on North Vietnamese Sanctuaries

HISTORIANS rarely do justice to the psychological stress on a policy-maker. What they have available are documents written for a variety of purposes — under contemporary rules of disclosure, increasingly to dress up the record — and not always relevant to the moment of decision. What no document can reveal is the accumulated impact of accident, intangibles, fears, and hesitation.

March and April of 1970 were months of great tension. My talks with Le Duc Tho were maddeningly ambiguous. We faced what looked like a significant offensive in Laos; there was the coup in Cambodia soon to be followed by North Vietnamese attacks all over the country; Soviet combat personnel appeared in Egypt — the first time that the Soviet Union had risked combat outside the satellite orbit. Amid all these events, the President was getting testy. Nixon blamed his frustrations on the bureaucracy's slow and erratic response to his wishes, which he ascribed to the legacy of thirty years of Democratic rule. Haldeman joked that the President was in a "charming mood"; in the course of covering one subject on the telephone Nixon had hung up on him several times.

On April 13, just as Cambodia was approaching the decisive turn, an extraneous event occurred that took a heavy toll of Nixon's nervous energy: the mishap of *Apollo 13*. Soon after its launch on April 11 it became apparent that there was a severe malfunction and that the astronauts might have to circumnavigate the moon in the cramped and fragile vehicle designed for the brief lunar landing. I learned of the accident around 11:00 P.M. I sought to inform the President but ran into one of the mindless edicts by which Haldeman established his authority: The President could not be awakened without his specific authorization. This he refused to give for what he considered a technical problem involving no foreign policy considerations. I warned Haldeman that keeping the President ignorant would be hard to explain; he insisted that public relations was his province. The next morning Ron Ziegler had to go through verbal contortions to imply, without lying outright, that the President had been in command all night.

The rescue of the astronauts absorbed a great deal of Nixon's attention for the week that the pressures on Cambodia were multiplying. Fur-

thermore, *Apollo 13* caused him to travel to Hawaii on April 17 to welcome home the astronauts, who had almost miraculously survived their
brush with the infinite. The military briefing by Admiral McCain illuminated the perils we faced in Cambodia and its danger for Vietnamization. It magnified Nixon's restlessness and helped speed up his decisions. But there were above all pressing objective reasons for Nixon's
state of mind that no one who took Presidential responsibilities seriously
could ignore. Later on, during Watergate, Senator Howard Baker asked
the famous question: "What did he know and when did he know it?"
The question is apt in this case as well.

The first two weeks of April had seen a wave of Communist attacks
on Cambodian towns and communications. These now escalated further.
On April 17, several Cambodian government posts near the provincial
capital of Senmonorom were captured by the North Vietnamese. On the
same day, a Cambodian military spokesman announced that the enemy
had more than doubled its area of control in the preceding two weeks.
On April 18, a Cambodian army battalion was badly mauled on the west
bank of the Mekong twenty-five miles south of Phnom Penh. Farther
south on the Mekong, a Cambodian army headquarters at Hung Loi was
besieged for a week by a large enemy force. On April 20, enemy forces
unsuccessfully attacked Snuol in Kratie province. In Kandal province,
Communist forces temporarily captured the town of Saang, some twenty
miles south of Phnom Penh. On Tuesday, April 21, the day after the
President's troop withdrawal announcement, Communist forces struck
the town of Takeo and cut the road between it and Phnom Penh.

The pattern of Communist military actions was becoming clear (see
the map on page 471). General William Westmoreland, Acting Chairman of the Joint Chiefs in General Wheeler's absence, reported that the
Cambodian armed forces were only "marginally effective" against the
superior North Vietnamese and Viet Cong. He wrote: "The enemy objective may well be to isolate the city of Phnom Penh, bring military
pressure to bear on it from all sides, and perhaps, ultimately, to bring
Sihanouk back to regain political control at the appropriate time."

The Communists were escalating their political pressures as well. On
April 21 Sihanouk's "National United Front of Cambodia" broadcast
an appeal to overthrow Lon Nol over the Viet Cong's clandestine radio.
The same day, Sihanouk broadcast a message from Peking in which, according to Radio Hanoi, he urged Cambodians: "You should at once
abandon and isolate the clique of the Lon Nol–Sirik Matak reactionaries, you should point your guns at these traitors."

Revisionist history has painted a picture of a peaceful, neutral Cambodia wantonly assaulted by American forces and plunged into a civil
war that could have been avoided but for the American obsession with
military solutions. The facts are different. Sihanouk declared war on the

new Cambodian government as early as March 20, two days after his overthrow, throwing in his lot with the Communists he had held at bay and locating himself in Peking, then still considered the most revolutionary capital in the world and with which, moreover, we had no means of communication whatever. April saw a wave of Communist attacks to overthrow the existing governmental structure in Cambodia. Le Duc Tho on March 16 had rejected all suggestions of de-escalation of military activities and on April 4 had rejected all suggestions of neutralization. He had asserted that the Cambodian, Laotian, and Vietnamese peoples were one and would fight shoulder to shoulder to win the whole of Indochina. By the second half of April, the North Vietnamese were systematically expanding their sanctuaries and merging them into a "liberated zone." They were surrounding Phnom Penh and cutting it off from all access — using the very tactics that five years later led to its collapse.

If these steps were unopposed, the Communist sanctuaries, hitherto limited to narrow unpopulated areas close to the Vietnamese border, would be organized into a single large base area of a depth and with a logistics system which would enable rapid transfer of units and supplies. We would have preferred the old Sihanouk government, I told a group of Republican Senators on April 21. But Sihanouk's pronouncements left little doubt that this option was no longer open to us. If Lon Nol fell, the Sihanouk who returned would no longer balance contending forces in neutrality but lead a Communist government. His necessities (as well as his outraged vanity) would force him to purge the moderate groups on which his freedom of maneuver between contending factions had previously depended; he would be reduced to a figurehead. Sihanoukville would reopen to Communist supplies. Security throughout the southern half of South Vietnam would deteriorate drastically.

By April 21 the basic issue had been laid bare by Hanoi's aggressiveness; it was whether Vietnamization was to be merely an alibi for an American collapse or a serious strategy designed to achieve an honorable peace. If the former, neither the rate of withdrawal nor events in neighboring countries were important; in fact, anything that hastened the collapse of South Vietnam was a blessing in disguise. Some of the opposition, like Senator George McGovern, took this position. Though I considered it against the national interest, it was rational and honest. My intellectual difficulties arose with those who pretended that there was a middle course of action that would avoid collapse in Vietnam and yet ignore the impending Communist takeover in Cambodia.

There was no serious doubt that Hanoi's unopposed conquest of Cambodia would have been the last straw for South Vietnam. In the midst of a war, its chief ally was withdrawing forces at an accelerating rate and reducing its air support. Saigon was being asked to take the strain at the very moment Hanoi was increasing reinforcements greatly over the level of the preceding year. If Cambodia were to become a single armed camp at this point, catastrophe was inevitable. Saigon needed time to consolidate and improve its forces; the United States had to pose a credible threat for as long as possible; and Hanoi's offensive potential had to be weakened by slowing down its infiltration and destroying its supplies. It was a race between Vietnamization, American withdrawal, and Hanoi's offensives.

Strategically, Cambodia could not be considered a country separate from Vietnam. The indigenous Cambodian Communist forces — the murderous Khmer Rouge — were small in 1970 and entirely dependent on Hanoi for supplies. The forces threatening the South Vietnamese and Americans from Cambodia were *all* North Vietnamese; the base areas were part of the war in Vietnam. North Vietnamese forces that were busy cutting communications had already seized a quarter of the country. The danger of being ''bogged down in a new war in Cambodia'' was a mirage; the enemy in Cambodia and Vietnam was the same one. Whatever forces we fought in Cambodia we would not have to fight in Vietnam and vice versa. The war by then was a single war, as Le Duc Tho had proclaimed; there was turmoil in Cambodia precisely because Hanoi was determined to use it as a base for its invasion of South Vietnam and to establish its hegemony over Indochina.

By April 21 we had a stark choice. We could permit North Vietnam to overrun the whole of Cambodia so that it was an indisputable part of the battlefield and then attack it by air and sea — even Rogers told me on April 21 that if the Communists took over Cambodia, he believed all bombing restrictions should be ended. Or we could resist Cambodia's absorption, supporting the independence of a government recognized by the United Nations and most other nations, including the Soviet Union.*

---

*Curiously enough, one of the most implacable critics of our policy in Cambodia presents the same analysis of what our choices were:

> Back in March and April the administration had had freedom of choice in reacting to events in Cambodia. If it had decided not to encourage, let alone to arm Lon Nol, it could have compelled either the return of Sihanouk or, at least, an attempt, by Lon Nol, to preserve the country's flawed neutrality. This would not have been an ideal solution for Washington, it would probably have meant a government dominated by Hanoi and at the very least it would have allowed the Communists continued use of Sihanoukville (which Lon Nol renamed Kompong Som) and the sanctuaries. But as the suppressed National Intelligence Estimate had pointed out, short of permanent occupation the sanctuaries would always pose a military problem for a South Vietnamese government; that was a fact of both geography and revolutionary warfare.[8]

This passage is interesting, first of all, because it combines all the misconceptions about events in Cambodia in 1970. My narrative can leave no doubt that we did not encourage Lon Nol nor even begin to arm him for weeks after North Vietnamese troops were ravaging a neutral country. The option of Lon Nol's restoring Cambodia's neutrality did not exist; it had been explicitly rejected by Le Duc Tho. And by then Sihanouk was no longer in a position to be neutralist. He could return only by destroying the Lon Nol faction, which had previously constituted his own government and

There had been no consideration of attacking the sanctuaries before April 21. The final decision was taken on April 28. It is important therefore to review the decision-making process in some detail to know who knew what and when.

No doubt Admiral McCain's briefing of Nixon on April 18 gave focus to his inchoate anxieties about Cambodia. He was sufficiently concerned to ask McCain to come to San Clemente and give me the same briefing on April 20. Unquestionably, the accumulated nervous strain of the previous weeks caused Nixon to become somewhat overwrought; it does not alter the fact that his analysis was essentially right. On the trip to San Clemente to rendezvous with him I had come to the same conclusion. I did not see how we could stand by and watch Cambodia collapse without thereby producing at the same time the collapse of all we were doing in Vietnam. I would have raised the issue with Nixon had not McCain in a sense preempted me. Nixon's first step on returning to Washington was to schedule a meeting with Helms and me for 7:00 A.M. on April 21 to bring himself up to date. Helms's briefing showed that the North Vietnamese were attacking all over the country and that Phnom Penh could not long withstand this assault. In discussing the status of our (negligible) response, Nixon discovered that the $5 million for arms for Cambodia approved by the WSAG on April 15 and doubled by him shortly thereafter was still being held up by bureaucratic foot-dragging. Nor had the communications equipment for the CIA, which he had ordered on April 1 and insisted upon on April 16, been delivered. Nixon was beside himself. He ordered an immediate transfer of the money. He called an NSC meeting for the next day to determine overall strategy.

In preparation, I asked General Westmoreland about the feasibility of military operations by South Vietnamese forces into the sanctuaries. Westmoreland thought they could be effective, but not decisive without American support. I also sent a backchannel message to Ellsworth Bunker, asking for his and Abrams's "candid judgment" of the military, political, and psychological consequences of Sihanouk's return or

---

whose nucleus he would need to balance off against his newfound Khmer Rouge "friends." The real prospect before us, therefore, was exactly what the quoted paragraph describes as the most likely outcome: the reopening of Sihanoukville, a government in Phnom Penh dominated by Hanoi, and reopened sanctuaries now no longer an isolated strip but comprising all of eastern Cambodia. Where I differ sharply from the paragraph is in its assertion that we had "freedom of choice." This is precisely what we did *not* have, for the prospect it describes would have meant a massive shift in the military balance in Indochina: an overwhelming, insurmountable, and decisive menace to the survival of South Vietnam.

As for the allegedly "suppressed" National Intelligence Estimate, this is another fiction. No intelligence estimate was ever "suppressed" or inhibited by the NSC office. They were routinely distributed to all the principal agencies. The CIA input was an important element of every policy deliberation, including that before the Cambodian decision. Nixon received full briefings from Director Helms at at least three NSC meetings or Cabinet-level discussions in April, and indeed Nixon saw Helms privately on three additional occasions.

of a Communist victory in Cambodia. I also requested their suggestions of possible countermeasures.

Since February, the South Vietnamese had considered occasional shallow cross-border operations — to a distance of about three miles — into the sanctuaries with our logistical support. A company or less in size, these were designed to discover caches of weapons. General Haig had reported after his January tour of South Vietnam that there were enemy supply caches a few miles over the Cambodian border that could not be safely targeted by B-52s because they were too near populated areas. Laird had authorized General Abrams to give logistical support to South Vietnamese forces for shallow penetrations when he visited Vietnam in February. A cross-border operation by South Vietnamese forces had taken place on March 27. It was reported by the press. A second operation took place the next day and was also reported. White House Press Secretary Ron Ziegler had declared on March 28 that American field commanders were now authorized to cross the Cambodian border in response to threats to American forces.

Upon learning of the first cross-border operation, I requested a temporary halt to them until we could reach a considered and coordinated judgment in light of the new situation and to avoid giving Hanoi a pretext for expanding the war. I did not want policy determined by the tactical decisions of field commanders. After issuing these instructions I went on a (long-scheduled) vacation for a week. Haig therefore sent the implementing cable to Bunker on March 27:

If these operations continue we will be subject to accusation that South Vietnamese Government is drawing US into expanded war.

While recognizing that you are not a free agent in this respect, Mr. Kissinger hopes that you can encourage Thieu to refrain from these operations except in situations where current US rules of engagement would apply. Mr. Kissinger wants you to be aware that while President is understanding of South Vietnamese motives, he is concerned that short term military benefits of cross-border operations might be outweighed by the risks posed to our efforts to maintain our current levels of domestic support for our overall Vietnam policy.

On March 30, as instructed, Bunker met with Thieu and explained why cross-border operations should be held in abeyance. Our objective was to prevent the expansion of the war, Bunker told him. Thieu accepted our recommendation. On March 31, the *New York Times* warned that the Cambodian government's willingness to permit allied cross-border raids against Communist sanctuaries might draw the United States deeper into the war. The Cambodian government thereupon, on March 31, "faithful to its policy of strict neutrality," formally denied that the United States and South Vietnam were authorized to conduct such raids.

That same day, while I was still on vacation, Laird had called on the

President to protest the suspension of cross-border operations. I had instructed Haig by telephone to try to delay a response until after my return and in any case not to authorize further cross-border operations before my meeting with Le Duc Tho scheduled for April 4. The President overruled my recommendations. He ordered Haig to instruct Bunker by backchannel to reinstate cross-border operations, provided they were kept to the level of those carried out prior to the moratorium and were coordinated with the Cambodian armed forces. As far as I can determine now, four shallow cross-border operations took place during the first three weeks of April — all after my meeting on April 4 with Le Duc Tho, none lasting more than a day.

In the last two weeks of April, Communist forces stepped up assaults on Cambodian towns. On April 22 the border town of Snuol was attacked and the Cambodian government made a new appeal to the United Nations for help in fighting the invaders. It was ignored, as all others, though it would have been difficult to find a more flagrant case of aggression. In Washington, April 22 was the occasion of a major NSC meeting on Cambodia; it also saw a stream of typewritten messages from the President to me that reflected his increasingly agitated frame of mind.

In the first message, dictated at 5:00 A.M., Nixon stressed the need for a "bold move" in Cambodia, and expressed determination to "do something symbolic to help [Lon Nol] survive" even though he feared Lon Nol would not be able to do so. He thought we had "dropped the ball" by worrying that American help would destroy Lon Nol's neutrality and give the North Vietnamese an excuse to come in; the Communists never waited for an "excuse," as demonstrated in Hungary in 1956, Czechoslovakia in 1968, and in Laos and Cambodia. The President suggested sending Ambassador Robert Murphy to reassure Lon Nol. "In the event that I decide to go on this course," Nixon wanted me to stress with "some of the lily-livered Ambassadors from our so-called friends in the world" that their posture on this issue would show us "who our friends are." (The text of this message is in the back.)[9]

A second missive later in the day reiterated the same theme — that I should call in the Japanese, French, British, and other friendly ambassadors and stress that we counted on our allies to back us. A third memorandum commented on a recent letter from Sihanouk to Senator Mansfield. Sihanouk had compared the Lon Nol regime with Hitler and said that "the most severe ideology — as long as it is based on social justice — is infinitely preferable to a regime composed of greatly corrupted people and anti-popular reactionaries. . . ." Sihanouk said he was determined to liberate his country, even "at the price of an ideological change in Cambodia.' Nixon suggested that Sihanouk "parrots the Communist line in every respect," and asked me to pass the letter discreetly to Rogers and Helms. A fourth message asked me to call in the Soviet chargé and warn him that the President had made a "command decision" to react if the Communists moved on Phnom Penh.

The pace of events gave me no opportunity to carry out these instructions. In a meeting with the President later in the morning of April 22 I advised against sending Murphy (or Dean Acheson, his later suggestion) to Cambodia because it would just trigger an enormous debate and would probably be overtaken by the decisions at the NSC. The President said, "Well, whatever, I want to make sure that Cambodia does not go down the drain without doing something." He went on: "Everybody always comes into my office with suggestions on how to lose. No one ever comes in here with a suggestion on how to win." The President ordered a replacement for our chargé, Lloyd Rives, in Phnom Penh and US support for shallow cross-border operations. As with many Nixon orders to fire people, it was intended to show his displeasure; it was not meant to be carried out; it never was at lower levels.

Meanwhile, we had received a long backchannel reply from Bunker and Abrams, which sketched dire consequences if Sihanouk returned to power as a Communist figurehead: Viet Cong and North Vietnamese morale would be strengthened; Hanoi's capacity for protracted warfare would be enhanced; there would be shock waves in South Vietnam; Vietnamization would be jeopardized. Bunker and Abrams recommended both an immediate increase in shallow cross-border operations and combined US–South Vietnamese operations against the key Communist sanctuaries.

The NSC meeting was given in effect three tactical options: doing nothing (the preferred course of the State and Defense departments); attacking the sanctuaries with South Vietnamese forces only (my recommendation); and using whatever forces were necessary to neutralize all of the base areas, including American combat forces, recommended by Bunker, Abrams, and the Joint Chiefs of Staff.

Two base areas were of special concern. The so-called Parrot's Beak, Cambodia's Svay Rieng province, jutted into Vietnam to within only thirty-three miles of Saigon. It had sheltered North Vietnamese armies attacking the Saigon area and the rice-producing delta region during all the years of the Vietnam war. Farther north was a second area, code-named the Fishhook. Our intelligence analysts believed that COSVN, the Communist headquarters for all operations in the South, was located there; it also was the staging area for the Seventh North Vietnamese Division, which periodically threatened Saigon and always harassed the adjoining Tay Ninh province of South Vietnam. The Fishhook was well defended; we did not think the South Vietnamese army was strong enough to handle both operations simultaneously. Hence, to recommend that the actions be confined to South Vietnamese forces was tantamount to opting for operations against only one base area.

Momentous decisions are rarely produced by profound discussions. By the time an issue reaches the NSC it has been analyzed by so many lower-level committees that the Cabinet members perform like actors in a well-rehearsed play; they repeat essentially what their subordinates have already announced in other forums. In the Nixon NSC there was the additional factor that every participant suspected that there was almost certainly more going on than he knew. As usual, there was also an ambivalence between taking positions compatible with their complicated chief's designs and fear of the domestic consequences. There was a sinking feeling about anything that could be presented as escalation in Vietnam. No one around the table questioned the consequences of a Communist takeover of Cambodia. But we all knew that whatever the decision another round of domestic acrimony, protest, and perhaps even violence was probable. If Cambodia collapsed we would be even harder pressed to pull out unilaterally; if we accepted any of the other options we would be charged with "expanding the war." There was no middle ground.

The initial decision to attack the sanctuaries was thus taken at a subdued and rather random NSC meeting. Rogers opposed substantial cross-border operations even by South Vietnamese, but he took it for granted that unrestricted bombing of Cambodia would follow the overthrow of the government in Phnom Penh. Laird had been the strongest advocate of shallow cross-border operations, but he opposed General Abrams's recommendation of destroying the sanctuaries altogether. Helms was in favor of any action to neutralize the sanctuaries. Nixon normally announced his decisions after, not during, an NSC meeting; he would deliberate and then issue instructions in writing or through intermediaries. He did this to emphasize that the NSC was an advisory, not a decision-making, body and to avoid a challenge to his orders. On this occasion Nixon altered his usual procedure. He told his colleagues that he approved attacks on the base areas by South Vietnamese forces with US support. Since the South Vietnamese could handle only one offensive, Wheeler recommended that they go after Parrot's Beak. This led to a debate about American participation; Laird and Rogers sought to confine it to an absolute minimum, opposing even American advisers or tactical air support.

At this point Vice President Spiro Agnew spoke up. He thought the whole debate irrelevant. Either the sanctuaries were a danger or they were not. If it was worth cleaning them out, he did not understand all the pussyfooting about the American role or what we accomplished by attacking only one. Our task was to make Vietnamization succeed. He favored an attack on *both* Fishhook and Parrot's Beak, including American forces. Agnew was right. If Nixon hated anything more than being presented with a plan he had not considered, it was to be shown up in a group as being less tough than his advisers. Though chafing at the bit, he adroitly placed himself between the Vice President and the Cabinet. He authorized American air support for the Parrot's Beak operation but only ''on the basis of demonstrated necessity.'' He avoided committing himself to Fishhook. These decisions were later sent out in writing. After the meeting, Nixon complained bitterly to me that I had not forewarned him of Agnew's views, of which I had in fact been unaware. I have no doubt that Agnew's intervention accelerated Nixon's ultimate decision to order an attack on all the sanctuaries and use American forces.

The next day, April 23, began the effort of the various agencies to position themselves so as to deflect on to somebody else the public uproar certain to ensue. Rogers asked for permission to tell Congressional committees of the very large Cambodian aid requests; his reasoning was that this would make the planned operations appear restrained in comparison — indeed, look like a way of avoiding a full-scale military aid program. Laird wanted to make sure that no American ground personnel would enter Cambodia, not even air controllers for the tactical air support approved by Nixon only the day before. I held two WSAG meetings on April 23 to sort out the implementation of Nixon's decisions. Not surprisingly, the WSAG members echoed the views of their principals. The Defense Department wanted authority for each tactical air strike to come from Washington. It was hard to imagine what targets would hold still long enough for such cumbersome procedures. After two meetings the WSAG members agreed, somewhat reluctantly, to give General Abrams general authority to use US tactical aircraft when needed and authorized US air controllers to accompany the South Vietnamese. Nixon approved both WSAG recommendations on April 24.

The North Vietnamese, in any event, were free of such inhibitions. On Thursday, April 23, North Vietnamese and Viet Cong forces attacked the Cambodian towns of Mimot and Angtassom and captured an important bridge on Route 13 linking the town of Snuol and the capital of Kratie province. The Cambodian military headquarters at Hung Loi in Kandal province, under siege for several days, had to be abandoned on April 23 despite South Vietnamese air strikes. Two bridges west of Svay Rieng on Route 1 were captured by the enemy. Beginning on April 23 and continuing on April 24, Communist forces staged hit-and-run raids on the coastal city of Kep.

The Communists escalated politically as well. On April 24, a ''Summit Conference of the Indochinese Peoples'' was convened at an undisclosed location in the Laos–Vietnam–China frontier area, summoned at Sihanouk's initiative to coordinate strategy among the three insurgent groups. In attendance were Sihanouk, Prince Souvanouvong of the Pathet Lao, Nguyen Huu Tho of the Viet Cong, and Pham Van Dong, Premier of North Vietnam. A lengthy Joint Declaration published by

Sihanouk on April 27 in Peking pledged "reciprocal support" in the "struggle against the common enemy," that is, "US imperialism." Sihanouk in his closing speech to the conference hailed the birth of "People's Cambodia."

The period involved much tension. I did not believe that either Cambodia or South Vietnam could survive unless we reacted to the Communist offensive. But I was painfully conscious of the political upheaval that would certainly follow an attack on the sanctuaries as well as of the divisions on my staff. I had deliberately recruited the ablest young men and women I could find. I thought it important to tap their vitality and idealism; it seemed to me crucial that the concern so many of their contemporaries expressed in protest find an outlet also in the willingness to work on the more mundane matters by which a government gropes for peace. Three of those closest to me were Tony Lake, Roger Morris, and Winston Lord. They had no great use for Nixon; emotionally, each of them would probably have preferred a Democratic President. I worked hard to maintain their commitment because the problems before our country were not partisan and because I was convinced that they had to learn that in some circumstances morality can best be demonstrated not by a grand gesture but by the willingness to persevere through imperfect stages for a better world. Lake and Morris had already told me in February that they had decided to leave; in view of their ambivalences they were no longer willing to work the long hours required. I kept them on in less demanding planning functions until the fall when Lake returned to graduate school and Morris joined Senator Mondale's staff. Winston Lord stayed; he became an invaluable collaborator and cherished friend.

Just prior to the final decision I spent much time with Lake, Morris, and Lord. The best-reasoned and argued objections to the course we were planning came not from the departments but were expressed in a joint memorandum that they wrote me. Ironically, their reasoning accelerated the conclusion to which I was reluctantly moving: that our only realistic option was to destroy the sanctuaries. Their basic diagnosis was the same as mine. One of our major objectives, they argued, had to be to avoid the return of Sihanouk:

If he returned, it would be the result of a Communist decision to allow this, which implies meaningful assurances that he would do their bidding. . . . More importantly, Sihanouk's return as a Communist stooge would have a serious psychological effect in Vietnam and Laos, and would at least provide an issue for Thieu's opponents against him, especially and dangerously among hard-liners in the Army.

Nevertheless, their memorandum opposed American military operations against the sanctuaries. What they favored was a neutral Cambodian government under current or other non-Sihanouk leadership which has reached a private understanding with the Communists that they may use the border areas in the same fashion as earlier. This would mean that the Cambodian government would look the other way but not publicly acquiesce. This would imply the possibility of continuing Menu [the secret bombing] and defensive cross-border operations by the GVN — without active Cambodian opposition to military activity by either of the Vietnamese forces in the limited border area. Although not a good situation, this would be better than a Sihanouk government which actively opposed the GVN and would publicly oppose Menu, etc.

In other words, my three young friends and associates regarded continuation of the secret bombing of Cambodia and shallow cross-border penetration of a few miles as essential, but deep penetrations as indefensible — a distinction whose moral significance continues to escape me. Their preferred outcome, restoration of "the status quo ante without Sihanouk," was attractive but unattainable. To bring it about they urged that we encourage the Lon Nol government to reach an accommodation with Hanoi while warning Hanoi that we would resist by force the imposition of Sihanouk. There was no possibility of such a compromise in the face of Le Duc Tho's statements of April 4 that Hanoi would never deal with Lon Nol. More likely, the very attempt to arrange such a "solution" would have led to the collapse of Phnom Penh and a Communist victory. Nor could I conceive how the measures to convince Hanoi that we would oppose Sihanouk would have been compatible with a compromise. Cambodia unfortunately had already been polarized, as a result of forces over which we had no control and beyond our capacity to reconcile. The alternatives proposed were, in short, an evasion of our hard choices, a sop to consciences, not a guide to action.

I was becoming increasingly restless with the decision at the NSC meeting that was in effect my recommendation: to limit the attack on the sanctuaries to South Vietnamese forces. Agnew was right; we should either neutralize all of the sanctuaries or abandon the project. It was hard to imagine how a limited operation into just one sanctuary, in which South Vietnamese forces had at best strictly limited American air support, could make a decisive difference. We were in danger of combining the disadvantages of every course of action. We would be castigated for intervention in Cambodia without accomplishing any strategic purpose.

Before I could present these views to Nixon, there occurred another of those seemingly trivial events that accelerate the process of history. Journalist William Beecher in the *New York Times* reported the contents of a highly classified cable informing our chargé in Phnom Penh that we had decided to provide captured Communist rifles to the Cambodian government. Nixon exploded. Leaks infuriated him in the best of circumstances; this one seemed to him a clear attempt by the bureaucracy to generate Congressional and public pressures against any assistance to Cambodia. To make matters worse, at about the same moment Nixon found out that the signal equipment and CIA representative that he had ordered into Phnom Penh on April 1 and again on April 16 had still not been sent.

He flew into a monumental rage. On the night of April 23 he must have called me at least ten times — three times at the house of Senator Fulbright, where I was meeting informally with members of the Senate Foreign Relations Committee. As was his habit when extremely agitated he would bark an order and immediately hang up the phone. He wanted our chargé, Rives, relieved immediately; he ordered Marshall Green fired; on second thought his deputy Bill Sullivan was to be transferred as well; an Air Force plane with CIA personnel aboard should be dispatched to Phnom Penh immediately; everybody with access to the cable should be given a lie-detector test; a general was to be appointed immediately to take charge of Cambodia.

In these circumstances it was usually prudent not to argue and to wait twenty-four hours to see on which of these orders Nixon would insist after he calmed down. As it turned out, he came back to none of them. (I did get the CIA communications sent into Phnom Penh by military plane.) But his April 23 outburst did finally propel him to accept Agnew's advice: to proceed against Fishhook and Parrot's Beak simultaneously, using American forces against Fishhook. He called a meeting on the morning of April 24 with Admiral Moorer, Acting Chairman of the Joint Chiefs, and Helms and Cushman of the CIA. Nixon wanted to discuss the feasibility of a combined US–South Vietnamese operation against Fishhook, in parallel with the Parrot's Beak operation. It was a reflection of his extreme irritation at bureaucratic foot-dragging that he excluded both Rogers and Laird, on the pretext that he merely wanted a military and intelligence briefing. Helms and Moorer were both strongly in favor of an attack on the Fishhook sanctuary. They felt it would force the North Vietnamese to abandon their effort to encircle and terrorize Phnom Penh. The destruction of supplies would gain valuable time for Vietnamization. But Nixon was not prepared to announce a decision yet. Instead, he helicoptered to Camp David to reflect further and to figure out a way to bring along his Cabinet on a course toward which he was increasingly tending. In the meantime he left me to manage the bureaucracy.

The situation had its bizarre aspects. The departments were still dragging their feet on American air support of a South Vietnamese operation against *one* sanctuary when the President was beginning to lean more and more toward *combined* South Vietnamese–American operations against *all* sanctuaries. I did not think it right to keep the Secretary of Defense ignorant of a meeting between the Acting Chairman of the Joint Chiefs and the President; I therefore called Laird, describing it as a military briefing of options, including an American attack on Fishhook. Laird stressed that it would be highly desirable to avoid authorizing any American operation before Rogers's testimony to the Senate Foreign Relations Committee on April 27; this would enable Rogers to state truthfully that no Americans were involved in Cambodia. Laird reported that even the usually hawkish Armed Services Committees were restive about American involvement in Cambodia. Laird also argued — as he was to do on several occasions over the next few days — that Abrams and Wheeler were really opposed to the Fishhook operation. I checked with Admiral Moorer, who claimed (in a rough translation from his more colorful naval jargon) that his Secretary was under a misapprehension.

Once he was launched on a course, Nixon's determination was equal to his tactical resourcefulness. He decided to adopt Rogers's suggestion of scaring the Congress with the prospect of monumental aid requests from Cambodia but to use it to justify *American* operations in the sanctuaries, which Rogers never intended.

At Nixon's request I asked the Chairman of the Senate Armed Services Committee, Senator John Stennis from Mississippi, to meet with me. Stennis belonged to that generation of Senate leaders who, having achieved their position by seniority and being secure in their constituencies, embodied in their accumulated experience a sense of continuity. On domestic issues, especially the race problem, they sometimes lagged behind the moral currents of their time, but on national security and foreign policy they were towers of strength. Many were Southerners, sons of a region that had known its own tragedy. They understood, as most other regions of the country did not, that there can be irrevocable disasters, that mankind is fallible, that human perfection cannot be assumed, that virtue without power is impotent. Courtly, wise, and patriotic, Stennis, like his distinguished colleague Richard Russell, was one of the men who made the separation of powers function despite its formal intractability. Presidents could rely on his integrity; Cabinet members could count on his respect for their efforts.

I saw Stennis in the afternoon of April 24 and explained to him our reasoning that a US–supported incursion into Cambodia was a military necessity if Vietnamization were to proceed. I showed him a map with the base areas, which were an integral part of the war in Vietnam. In the middle of our conversation Nixon called my office, by prearrangement. In Stennis's hearing I summed up my briefing and reported Stennis's generally favorable reaction. Stennis then took the phone and expressed his support personally to the President.

Once again I reviewed the planning with Wheeler and Helms, asking Helms for a contingency study of what might go wrong. I stressed that if he had any hesitations he should tell me; if he developed second thoughts I would transmit them immediately to the President. Helms stood by his previous recommendation. He felt that we would pay the same domestic price for two operations as for one and the strategic payoff would be incomparably greater in the two-pronged attack.

I then spent an hour with members of my senior staff who opposed the proposed operation — Bill Watts and Larry Lynn, in addition to Lord, Lake, and Morris — to give them one final opportunity to express their objections. It was a painful session, for they felt deeply about what we were planning. Lake, Morris, and Watts resigned.

Since the NSC meeting two days earlier, the Secretaries of State and Defense had not been heard from. They knew of contingency plans involving US forces; indeed, Laird had originally transmitted the JCS plans for an attack on Fishhook. They could not have missed the President's increasing agitation; but they could not believe that Nixon might seriously decide to authorize a US incursion. They acted as if the problem would go away if they offered no alternative or even a systematic critique.

I urged Nixon to call an NSC meeting to give all parties an opportunity to express themselves. As I told Helms: "It is my judgment and strong recommendation that any decision must be discussed with the two Cabinet members — even if the decision has already been made and an order is in the desk drawer. You can't ram it down their throats without their having a chance to give their views." The meeting was set for Sunday afternoon, April 26.

By now Nixon was determined to proceed; his chief problem was to reduce the inevitable confrontation with Rogers and Laird to a minimum. When he was pressed to the wall, his romantic streak surfaced and he would see himself as a beleaguered military commander in the tradition of Patton. But personal idiosyncrasies aside, Nixon was putting the fundamental question: Could we in good conscience continue a gradual withdrawl from Vietnam with Sihanoukville reopened and all of Cambodia turned into one big contiguous base area? Those within the Administration who balked were mostly concerned about the domestic reaction. No one came up with an answer to the dilemma of how we could proceed with Vietnamization if the entire Cambodian frontier opened up to massive infiltration. Nor would inaction avoid our domestic dilemma. If we resisted, we would be charged with escalation; but if we acquiesced in the Communist takeover of Cambodia, our casualties started rising, and Vietnam began to disintegrate, we would be accused of pursuing a hopeless strategy.

On Saturday April 25 Nixon called me to Camp David to review the planning. I walked along at the edge of the swimming pool while he paddled in the water. We discussed the NSC meeting scheduled for the next afternoon. Nixon was determined to proceed with the Fishhook operation; indeed, he began to toy with the idea of going for broke: Perhaps we should combine an attack on the Cambodian sanctuaries with resumption of the bombing of North Vietnam as well as mining Haiphong. The opposition would be equally hysterical either way. I thought that this was one of the musings Nixon tended to put forward to demonstrate his toughness but which he really had no intention of carrying out, although he could use it later to demonstrate to trusted cronies that he had been let down by his staff. Nor did I conceive that the President could rise out a crisis of such magnitude with a divided team. For all these reasons I replied that we had enough on our plate; we could not abandon a strategy announced so recently and emphatically.

Nixon dropped the subject after ten minutes and never returned to it. I do not believe that he was seriously considering the option. But in retrospect I believe that we should have taken it more seriously. The bane of our military actions in Vietnam was their hesitancy; we were always trying to calculate with fine precision the absolute minimum of force or of time, leaving no margin for error or confusion, encouraging our adversary to hold on until our doubts overrode our efforts.

Perhaps the most difficult lesson for a national leader to learn is that with respect to the use of military force, his basic choice is to act or to refrain from acting. He will not be able to take away the moral curse of using force by employing it halfheartedly or incompetently. There are no rewards for exhibiting one's doubts in vacillation; statesmen get no prizes for failing with restraint. Once committed they must prevail. If they are not prepared to prevail, they should not commit their nation's power. Neither the successive administrations nor the critics ever fully understood this during the Vietnam war. And therein lay the seeds of many of its tragedies.

In all events, the poolside strategy session at Camp David was not the end of the deliberating for the day. We flew back to the capital and in the late afternoon Nixon invited John Mitchell to join Bebe Rebozo and me for a cruise on the Presidential yacht *Sequoia* down the Potomac. The tensions of the grim military planning were transformed into exaltation by the liquid refreshments, to the point of some patriotic awkwardness when it was decided that everyone should stand at attention while the *Sequoia* passed Mount Vernon — a feat not managed by everybody with equal success. On the return to the White House, Nixon invited his convivial colleagues to see the movie *Patton*. It was the second time he had so honored me. Inspiring as the film no doubt was, I managed to escape for an hour in the middle of it to prepare for the next day's NSC meeting.

On Sunday, April 26, North Vietnamese and Viet Cong troops gave urgency to our deliberations by attacking commercial shipping on the Mekong River route to Phnom Penh. Communist forces took the town of Angtassom (see map). The rail line leading south from Phnom Penh was cut at several points in Takeo province. Press statements from Hanoi and Peking rejected the proposal, advanced by Indonesia, of an Asian conference to restore the neutrality of Cambodia — a proposal we would have favored.

The President met that evening with his principal NSC advisers — Rogers, Laird, Wheeler, Helms, and me — in his working office in the Executive Office Building. Agnew was not included. Even though he was now taking his Vice President's advice, Nixon was still smarting from Agnew's unexpected sally and was determined to be the strong man of *this* meeting. From the outset, the meeting took an odd turn. Helms gave an intelligence assessment that Hanoi was expanding its base areas, linking them together and trying to create so much insecurity in Phnom Penh that the government would collapse. Wheeler described the proposed US operation against the Fishhook complex and a possibility of expanding it to include other base areas. Nixon tried to avoid a confrontation with his Secretaries of State and Defense by pretending that we were merely listening to a briefing. He would follow with a written directive later. To my astonishment, both Rogers and Laird — who after all were familiar with their elusive chief's methods by now — fell in with the charade that it was all a planning exercise and did not take a position. They avoided the question of why Nixon would call his senior advisers together on a Sunday night to hear a contingency briefing.

Nixon was immensely relieved. He construed silence as assent; at any rate, he had managed to avoid controversy. As soon as the meeting was over he called me over to the family quarters and instructed me to issue a directive authorizing an attack by American forces into the Fishhook area. I had it drafted, and he signed it. Just to be sure, the President first initialed the directive and then, beneath his initials, also signed his full name:

This double-barreled Presidential imprimatur by no means guaranteed compliance. I was chairing a meeting of the WSAG in the Situation Room the next morning to discuss implementation of the directive when I was called out to a phone call from Rogers. He wanted to know whether the directive which had just reached him meant that the President had ordered an American attack on one of the Cambodian sanctuaries. I allowed that there was hardly any other way to interpret it. Rogers said this would put him into a very difficult position with the Senate Foreign Relations Committee, since that very afternoon he was planning to testify that there was no American involvement in Cambodia. I suggested that he call the President.

I had no sooner returned to the Situation Room when the other senior Cabinet officer called. With his invariable tactic of raising the extraneous issue on which one was most vulnerable, Laird objected to a phrase in the directive that designated WSAG as the "implementing authority." Laird argued that this violated the chain of command which had to go through his office. I told him to substitute the word "coordinating" or any other suitable phrase he preferred. Laird then turned to what really bothered him. He claimed that the combined Parrot's Beak and Fishhook operations could cost 800 men killed in action in a week. He argued that Abrams and Wheeler did not think both operations feasible. When Wheeler had spoken on Sunday afternoon of two sanctuary operations, he was, Laird insisted, referring to Parrot's Beak plus Base Area 704, a sanctuary far to the south (which, as it turned out, served Laird's purposes very well by being completely waterlogged at this time of the year). I suggested that Laird, too, should call the President.

The WSAG meeting had barely resumed when I was called out again, this time by Haldeman, who told me that Rogers and Laird were both on their way to see the President. He invited me to attend, but reminded me to "let the President carry the ball."

The President's meeting with his senior Cabinet officers did not lack a surrealistic quality. Rogers was above all concerned with his appearance before the Senate Foreign Relations Committee that afternoon. He wanted to be able to testify that no Americans were involved in Cambodia; he therefore requested that the President withdraw his directive. Laird was more complicated. He repeated his fear of high casualties; he implied there had been a terrible misunderstanding about Abrams's recommendation, which really was for the waterlogged southern base area. Laird reiterated yet again his objections to the phrasing of the directive, a point which (as he well knew) I had already conceded.

Nixon said little, and what he said was ambiguous — a sure sign to anyone familiar with his methods that he meant to stick with his decision. He adjourned the meeting, telling his Cabinet officers that they would hear from him shortly. No sooner had Rogers and Laird left than

Nixon showered all his frustrations on me. He could not understand why his senior advisers never gave him a strategic argument and wasted his time on their personal political problems. He would not be deflected by this kind of behavior. I recommended that he delay execution of his directive for twenty-four hours; he might even withdraw it temporarily if this eased Rogers's problems. In the meantime, I would query Bunker and Abrams in his name to verify their views; we had to make sure that there was no misunderstanding about either their recommendations or the casualties they were expecting. I would also ask Laird to send over the cables on which he based his judgment that the field commanders did not favor the simultaneous operations against Fishhook and Parrot's Beak. Nixon accepted my suggestions. He withdrew the directive, and I informed his Cabinet members that a final decision would be forthcoming within twenty-four hours.

In the meantime I sent a backchannel cable to Ambassador Bunker asking his and General Abrams's views on a number of questions on a most urgent basis: the desirability of a combined US–South Vietnamese attack on Fishhook; whether this should coincide with the Parrot's Beak operation or follow it; whether comparable efforts within South Vietnam would bring better returns; whether other base areas — like Base Area 704 — would be more rewarding; what casualties would be expected. The cable concluded (in the President's name):

I am concerned whether General Abrams really wants to conduct this opera-tion on its merits or whether he favors it only because he assumes it represents my wishes. Therefore, please give me yours and General Abrams' unvarnished views on the foregoing questions and I will be heavily guided by them. Please show this message to General Abrams.

By early evening the memorandum from Laird and the reply from Bunker and Abrams had arrived. Laird restated his earlier position: He opposed the use of US combat troops in Cambodia; hence he favored the South Vietnamese operation against the Parrot's Beak, supple-mented if necessary by an attack on Base Area 704, also to be carried out by South Vietnamese forces. It is to Laird's enormous credit that once Nixon decided on the American operation he did not participate in the fashionable effort to dissociate himself; nor did this master-leaker of trivialities ever publicly reveal that he had, in writing, opposed the mas-sively important action in Cambodia.

As for Abrams and Bunker, they strongly recommended the com-bined allied attack on Fishhook as the "most desirable," preferably in parallel with the attack on Parrot's Beak, which was the second most important target. Base Area 704, Abrams confirmed, "does not rank in importance" with the other two. Bunker and Abrams did not believe that any operation within South Vietnam would produce comparable results.

Abrams cagily gave no estimate of probable casualties but pledged to do all he could to keep casualties to "an absolute minimum."

Nothing was heard from Rogers except news reports of his testimony to the Senate Foreign Relations Committee that no decision to use American forces in Cambodia had yet been made.

As in most decisions with major political consequences, Nixon decided to call in John Mitchell. The three of us spent until nearly midnight going over the memoranda and the pros and cons of the available options. In the end, Nixon decided to reaffirm his original decision and to tell Laird and Rogers in the morning, in Mitchell's presence. Nixon asked me to prepare a new directive changing the sentence to which Laird had objected so that WSAG would have "coordinating" instead of "implementing" authority. Otherwise the directive was to remain unchanged.

The next morning, Tuesday, April 28, Nixon met with Mitchell and me from 9:30 to 10:20 to review the operations once again. Nixon asked me to leave by a side door before his meeting with Rogers and Laird; he thought it desirable that I not become the butt of departmental criticism. In a twenty-minute meeting with Rogers, Laird, and Mitchell, the President then reaffirmed his decision to proceed with the combined US–South Vietnamese operation against the Fishhook. He noted that the Secretaries of State and Defense had opposed the use of American forces and that Dr. Kissinger was "leaning against" it. (This was no longer true; I had changed my view at least a week earlier. In my opinion Nixon lumped me with his two Cabinet members for his usual amalgam of complex reasons. He genuinely and generously wanted to shield me against departmental retaliation; no doubt he also wanted to live up to his image of himself as the lonely embattled leader propping up faltering associates.) Nixon assured them he would dictate a summary of events leading up to the decision that would make clear the contrary recommendations of his senior advisers; they would be on record in opposition; he would assume full responsibility. (Mitchell's record of the meeting is in the notes.) [10]

The final decision to proceed was thus not a maniacal eruption of irrationality as the uproar afterward sought to imply. It was taken carefully, with much hesitation, by a man who had to discipline his nerves almost daily to face his associates and to overcome the partially subconscious, partially deliberate procrastination of his executive departments. It was a demonstration of a certain nobility when he assumed full responsibility. The decision was not made behind the backs of his senior advisers, as has been alleged — though later on others were. Nixon overruled his Cabinet members; he did not keep them in the dark. This is the essence of the Presidency, the inescapable loneliness of the office, compounded in Nixon's case by the tendency of his senior Cabinet col-

leagues to leave him with the burden and to distance themselves publicly from him. His secretive and devious methods of decision-making
undoubtedly reinforced their proclivity toward selfwill. But his views
were well known; the agencies had had many opportunities to argue
their case. The fact remains that on the substance of Cambodia, Nixon
was right. And he was President. There is no doubt that the procrastination in carrying out direct Presidential directives, the exegesis of clear
Presidential wishes in order to thwart them, helped confirm Nixon's
already strong predilection for secretive and isolated decision-making
from then on.

A confrontation with people who disagreed with him took a lot out of
Nixon. After the meeting in the Oval Office he withdrew to his hideaway in the Executive Office Building, not to emerge until he delivered
his speech of April 30 announcing the Cambodian incursion. I spent
hours with him every day, bringing him up to date on the planning. Pat
Buchanan drafted the basic speech from a rough outline supplied by my
staff. But its major thrust was Nixon's. He supplied the rhetoric and the
tone; he worked for hours each day on successive drafts.

One morning he showed me a ruled paper from a yellow pad on
which he had jotted down the various pros and cons; I pulled a similar
yellow sheet from my pocket. We had reached practically the identical
conclusions, perhaps because we had rehearsed them so often orally to
each other. But in the days before announcing this most fateful decision
of his early Presidency Richard Nixon was virtually alone, sitting in a
darkened room in the Executive Office Building, the stereo softly playing neoclassical music — reflecting, resenting, collecting his thoughts
and his anger. The Churchillian rhetoric that emerged reflected less the
actual importance of the decision than his undoubted sense of defiance
at what he knew would be a colossal controversy over a decision he
deeply believed to be right, and in the making of which he received
little succor from his associates.

I was busy between helping the President and coordinating the implementation of the decision. Once a Cabinet department recognizes that a
decision is irrevocable and cannot be altered by artful exegesis or leaks,
it can become a splendid instrument, competent, efficient, thoughtful.
The WSAG meetings, which in previous weeks had been nightmares of
evasion and foot-dragging, now turned crisp and precise. U. Alexis
Johnson, the seasoned Under Secretary of State for Political Affairs,
produced one of those masterful overall plans (called "scenarios" in bureaucratese) that were his specialty, an hourly schedule of tasks for
every key individual and department down to and then after zero hour.

"Operation Rock Crusher," as it was labeled, or *Toan Thang* 42
("Total Victory") for the South Vietnamese, was launched against the
Parrot's Beak during the night of April 28. About fifty American ad-

visers accompanied the initial wave, joined by twenty-two more in the first four days.

On the fateful day of April 30 the President delivered his speech at 9:00 P.M., explaining to an anxious public that "the actions of the enemy in the last ten days clearly endanger the lives of Americans who are in Vietnam now and would constitute an unacceptable risk to those who will be there after withdrawal of another 150,000." He opened by explaining, with a map, that the North Vietnamese had begun to threaten Phnom Penh and expand their previously separated base areas into "a vast enemy staging area and a springboard for attacks on South Vietnam along 600 miles of frontier." We had three options: to do nothing; to "provide massive military assistance to Cambodia itself"; to clean out the sanctuaries. The decision he now announced was a combined US–South Vietnamese assault on "the headquarters for the entire Communist military operation in South Vietnam." The action was limited, temporary, not directed against any outside country, indispensable for Vietnamization and for keeping casualties to a minimum.

Adding rhetoric out of proportion to the subject though not to the stresses of the weeks preceding it, the President emphasized that America would not be "humiliated"; we would not succumb to "anarchy"; we would not act like a "pitiful, helpless giant." Nor would he take "the easy political path" of blaming it all on the previous administrations. It was vintage Nixon. He had "rejected all political considerations":

Whether my party gains in November is nothing compared to the lives of 400,000 brave Americans fighting for our country and for the cause of peace and freedom in Vietnam. Whether I may be a one-term President is insignificant compared to whether by our failure to act in this crisis the United States proves itself to be unworthy to lead the forces of freedom in this critical period in world history. I would rather be a one-term President and do what I believe is right than to be a two-term President at the cost of seeing America become a second-rate power and to see this Nation accept the first defeat in its proud 190-year history.

Afterward, the criticism was made that this was a divisive speech, apocalyptic in its claims, excessive in its pretensions. He would not have to face another election for over two years; no doubt he personalized the issue excessively. Certainly the speech was unsatisfactory to those for whom ending the war in Vietnam was the only aim and who identified this goal with ending all combat operations as rapidly as possible regardless of consequences. Without doubt Nixon should have been more compassionate toward the anguish of those genuinely torn by the ambiguities of an inconclusive war so foreign to our national experience. He played into the hands of his critics by presenting an essentially defensive operation, limited in both time and space, as an earthshaking, conscience-testing event, lending color to their claim that he had exceeded Presidential authority by "expanding" the war. And he added a sentence that was as irrelevant to his central thesis as it was untrue, that we had heretofore not moved against the sanctuaries — overlooking the secret bombing.

Yet in all fairness the critics made little effort to go beyond rhetoric to the realities of the decision. For behind the words, at once self-pitying and vainglorious, the merits of the case were overwhelming. We had not encouraged the coup in Cambodia or even known about it. We had done next to nothing to exploit it for four weeks. We were triggered into action when Le Duc Tho linked the wars in Vietnam and Cambodia; when Sihanouk threw in his lot with the Communists; when North Vietnamese forces broke out of the sanctuaries and began plunging deep into Cambodia with the obvious purpose of overthrowing the government and establishing a contiguous area from which the war in the southern half of South Vietnam could be pursued from a vastly improved logistics base. In these circumstances, either we would have to stop withdrawals or Vietnamization would become a subterfuge for the dismantling of an allied country. That Nixon's rhetoric was excessive did not change the reality that we had only the three choices he outlined. Doing nothing was the same as allowing the collapse of both Cambodia and South Vietnam. If we were serious about reducing our involvement in Vietnam and not leaving those who had relied on us to their fate, we had to thwart Hanoi's designs on Cambodia. The incursions into the sanctuaries, in short, were the only course compatible with a controlled retreat from Indochina and any prospect of preventing Hanoi's domination of the region.

The Elusive Communist Headquarters and Other Battles

AMERICAN and South Vietnamese forces pushed forward into the Fishhook area at 7:30 A.M. Saigon time on May 1. The same day Nixon visited the National Military Command Center at the Pentagon and — on the spur of the moment — ordered what he had long been considering, an incursion into all other base areas. As a result, twelve enemy base areas were attacked in the first three weeks. Some were combined allied operations; some were conducted by the South Vietnamese alone with US air and logistic support. Some were brief (a week to ten days); some were for the duration of the campaign.

Two US naval ships and naval patrol aircraft took up stations off the port of Sihanoukville (by then renamed Kompong Som) outside the twelve-mile limit. They were to watch the port and to effect a blockade if necessary. This terminated on June 13. On May 26, the secret Menu series was formally ended; B-52 strikes continued as open operations in support of the US ground forces in Cambodia. In addition, two days of air strikes were conducted in North Vietnam against three enemy supply bases just north of the Demilitarized Zone. General Abrams had called attention to this logistics complex in late April, considering it the hub of the enemy supply effort.

Nixon's speech had highlighted the presence of COSVN in the Fishhook area and had listed it as one of the targets of our assault. Laird had correctly cautioned against this specific reference in the speech but he did not see the draft until a couple of hours before it was delivered and Nixon was unwilling to change it. The result was one of the famous, self-inflicted credibility gaps irrelevant to the central issue but corrosive of public confidence. The Cambodian Communists confirmed eight years later what some Americans would not believe when Nixon stated it: that COSVN was indeed located in the Fishhook area.[11] In my briefings to the press in advance of the speech I admitted that COSVN was highly mobile and that we did not expect to capture it intact. And in fact, the assault into the Fishhook sanctuary severely disrupted COSVN's operations and captured or destroyed many of its personnel, supplies, and installations. On May 18, COSVN informed its subordinate units that it was being seriously threatened by allied attacks; it directed all its attendant radio stations to monitor closely since the headquarters would resume communications only briefly when needed. COSVN remained off the air for considerable periods while subordinates tried repeatedly to reestablish radio contact. But since we could not reveal intelligence information, we were naked before the media's merciless mocking of our pursuit of the elusive Communist headquarters.

COSVN aside, there was no doubt about the success. By the end of the first month, five and a half tons of enemy documents had been captured, including vital documentation of the enemy order of battle in Vietnam, its detailed plans for its campaign to overthrow the Phnom Penh government, and bills of lading for shipments through Sihanoukville that went beyond our highest estimates of Sihanoukville's importance. On May 22, the Defense Department estimated that 12,000 North Vietnamese troops were held up in the infiltration pipeline by our operations. Communist communications lamented these troops' consumption of stocks, scheduled for later use during the rainy season. The number of defectors from the Communist side increased substantially. In his final report to the nation at the end of June, Nixon listed the quantities of matériel captured:

— 22,892 individual weapons — enough to equip about 74 full-strength North Vietnamese infantry battalions and 2,509 big crew-served weapons —

enough to equip about 25 full-strength North Vietnamese infantry battalions;

— more than 15 million rounds of ammunition or about what the enemy has fired in South Vietnam during the past year;

— 14 million pounds of rice, enough to feed all the enemy combat battalions estimated to be in South Vietnam for about 4 months;

— 143,000 rockets, mortars, and recoilless rifle rounds, used against cities and bases. Based on recent experience, the number of mortars, large rockets, and recoilless rifle rounds is equivalent to what the enemy shoots in about 14 months in South Vietnam;

— over 199,552 antiaircraft rounds, 5,482 mines, 62,022 grenades, and 83,000 pounds of explosives, including 1,002 satchel charges;

— over 435 vehicles and destroyed over 11,688 bunkers and other military structures.

The military impact might have been even greater had we not withdrawn our forces arbitrarily in two months. The enormous uproar at home was profoundly unnerving.

Soon after his April 30 speech, Nixon started pressing for token, and then for substantial, withdrawals from the sanctuaries. The June 30 deadline began as an improvised and very approximate Nixon projection for Congressional leaders of how long the effort would last; it was soon made sacrosanct. At another Congressional briefing he suddenly introduced a limit of thirty kilometers for US penetrations (which was translated inexplicably by the Pentagon to mean twenty-one miles). The President was coming dangerously close to the perennial error of our military policy in Vietnam: acting sufficiently strongly to evoke storms of protest but then by hesitation depriving our actions of decisive impact. The limitations of time and geography placed on our forces' operations helped only marginally to calm the Congress and the media but certainly kept us from obtaining the operations' full benefit. The base areas by then extended over hundreds of square miles; hidden caches could not be discovered except by systematic searches; it then took some time to remove what was found. The time limit did not permit a thorough search. And the geographical restraints simplified the enemy's planning: He simply withdrew his forces and some of his caches to areas declared safe by us. I doubt if we would have attracted much more public hostility by extending our stay for the two or three additional months that a careful search needed. It might have prevented the Communists' maintaining some base areas from which they eventually prevailed in Cambodia itself. But the inhibitions, though regrettable for full success, did not prevent us from achieving our main goals. The attack on the sanctuaries made our withdrawal from Vietnam easier; it saved lives; even after the sanctuaries were partly reoccupied by the Communists they had been deprived of stockpiles for a sustained offensive.

Systems analysts on my own staff estimated that our operations destroyed or captured up to 40 percent of the total enemy stockpile in Cambodia. My own assessment was cautious. In press briefings at the beginning of the operation and in conversations with the President, I had predicted that the disruption of enemy supplies and operations would "buy us" between six and eight months. After a trip to Indochina on our behalf, Sir Robert Thompson thought the Communists would be unable to build up their supplies during the rainy season that year or to complete the restocking during the dry season. Only after the following rainy season could they rebuild their stocks to previous levels. In other words, he thought we had gained as much as two years.

Thompson proved to be correct. After 1969 the war in Vietnam had turned into a race between our withdrawals, the improvement of the South Vietnamese army, and the ability of Hanoi to interrupt the process by launching offensives. As the American combat role dwindled, anything that weakened Hanoi's combat capability was crucial for us. Because Hanoi had to fight far from its home base, interruption of its logistics line and depletion of its stockpiles threw off its calculations as well as its capabilities. Whatever the conclusions of systems analysts, there was no significant combat for nearly two years thereafter in the areas of South Vietnam that had been most exposed to attacks from the sanctuaries. The Mekong Delta and the heavily populated areas were effectively secured. And when Hanoi launched a nationwide offensive in the spring of 1972, its major thrust came across the DMZ, where its supply lines were shortest; its attacks from Cambodia were the weakest and the most easily contained.

For Americans, of course, the key criterion was our casualties. During the attack on the sanctuaries they rose briefly though they never reached more than a quarter of the 800 per week that Laird had feared. Afterward, the number of men killed in action dropped to below one hundred a week for the first time in four years. They continued to drop with every month thereafter. For each month beginning with June 1970, the casualty figure averaged less than half of that of the corresponding month of the previous year. By May 1971, a year later, it had fallen to thirty-five a week; in May 1972, ten a week. To be sure, the withdrawal of American forces was a factor; but we had several hundred thousand Americans in Vietnam through 1971, and had Hanoi possessed the capability it could have inflicted substantially higher casualties than it did. That it did not do so was importantly due to the breathing space provided by the Cambodian operation.

And in the international arena, the complications with other countries fiercely predicted by some critics did not materialize. The Soviet Union made ambiguous barbs, stopping well short of any specific threat. On May 4, Soviet Premier Kosygin held a tough press conference, asking what trust the Soviets could place in America's international undertakings given our "violation" of Cambodian neutrality. But he refused to apply this general complaint to the SALT talks. He did not pledge Soviet support to the "Indochinese Peoples' " Summit Declaration, or even disavow the Lon Nol government. On May 18, Soviet Deputy Foreign Minister Nikolai Firyubin told one of our European allies that the Soviets planned to keep their embassy in Phnom Penh since "there is nothing else to do." Firyubin described the situation in Cambodia as confused and Sihanouk as a prisoner of Peking.

The Chinese, though with more colorful language, were equally prudent. On May a government statement "sternly" warned the United States against its "flagrant provocation." Reminding everyone of Chairman Mao's dictum that the United States was a "paper tiger," China asserted that the "three Indochinese peoples" would "surely" win if they stayed united. A *People's Daily* editorial the next day reiterated the same themes, comforting the Indochinese revolutionaries with the thought that "the vast expanse of China's territory is their reliable rear area." In other words, as I told the President, "the Chinese have issued a statement, in effect saying that they wouldn't do anything." On May 20 an unusual statement was issued in the name of Chairman Mao with the calm title of "People of the World, Unite and Defeat the U.S. Aggressors and All Their Running Dogs!" Mao endorsed Sihanouk's new government in exile and the "Summit Declaration of the Indochinese Peoples," and pointed out again that "US imperialism, which looks like a huge monster, is in essence a paper tiger, now in the throes of its deathbed struggle." My analysis, forwarded to the President on May 23, was that this also offered little to Hanoi except verbal encouragement.

Far from hurting our relations with the two Communist giants, the Cambodia operations improved our position by adding another bone of contention between Moscow and Peking. With Moscow recognizing Lon Nol and Peking Sihanouk, the Sino-Soviet split was transplanted into Indochina. By June 10 Dobrynin and I were again exploring negotiations on SALT, the Middle East, and even a US–Soviet summit; tensions with Moscow that developed later in the summer resulted from conflicting interests in other parts of the world. And by the end of June we had received unmistakable signals from the Chinese that they were willing to reopen contacts with us.

The crisis was neither on the battlefield nor in our diplomacy but at home.

The Domestic Travail

NONE of these successes had any effect on the eruptions of the spring of 1970, thereby turning the period of the Cambodian incursion into a time of extraordinary stress. I had entered government with the hope that I could help heal the schisms in my adopted country by working to end the war. I sympathized with the anguish of the students eager to live the American dream of a world where ideas prevailed by their purity without the ambiguities of recourse to power. The war in Vietnam was the first conflict shown on television and reported by a largely hostile press. The squalor and suffering and confusion inseparable from any war became part of the living experience of Americans; too many ascribed its agony to the defects of their own leaders.

Repellent as I found the self-righteousness and brutality of some protesters, I had a special feeling for the students. They had been brought up by skeptics, relativists, and psychiatrists; now they were rudderless in a world from which they demanded certainty without sacrifice. My generation had failed them by encouraging self-indulgence and neglecting to provide roots. I spent a disproportionate amount of time in the next months with student groups — ten in May alone. I met with protesters at private homes. I listened, explained, argued. But my sympathy for their anguish could not obscure my obligation to my country as I saw it. They were, in my view, as wrong as they were passionate. Their pressures delayed the end of the war, not accelerated it; their simplifications did not bring closer the peace, of the yearning for which they had no monopoly. Emotion was not a policy. We had to end the war, but in conditions that did not undermine America's power to help build the new international order upon which the future of even the most enraged depended.

Nor is it fair to blame the upheaval primarily on Nixon's inflated rhetoric or even on the events at Kent State. The dialogue in our democracy had broken down previously. The antiwar movement had been dormant since November, awaiting a new opportunity. In mid-April there were protests in some two hundred cities and towns, and the temper was such that the April 28 news of the purely South Vietnamese operation in the Parrot's Beak evoked condemnation as a major escalation of the war. This was two days before the involvement of American soldiers or Nixon's speech. North Vietnamese forces had been romping through Cambodia for well over a month, without a word of criticism of Hanoi. Yet the South Vietnamese response was denounced in the *New York Times* (''a virtual renunciation of the President's promise of disengagement from South East Asia''), the *Wall Street Journal* (''Americans want an acceptable exit from Indochina, not a deeper entrapment'') and the *St. Louis Post-Dispatch* (''a shocking escalation''). The South Vietnamese thrust was intended to assist our orderly retreat. But in Congress barriers were being erected almost immediately against helping Cambodia, itself suffering a savage invasion by the same enemies and indeed the identical units that were fighting us in Vietnam. Senator

J. William Fulbright, Chairman of the Senate Foreign Relations Committee, told NBC news on April 27 after the briefing that had given Rogers so much anticipatory anguish that the Committee was virtually unanimous in the view that assisting Cambodia in its resistance to North Vietnamese conquest "would be an additional extension of the war."

All the critical themes of the later explosion were present before the President's speech: We were escalating the war. No military action could possibly succeed; hence, claims to the contrary by the government were false. We were alleged to be so little in control of our decisions that the smallest step was seen as leading to an open-ended commitment of hundreds of thousands of American troops. A credibility gap had been created over any effort to achieve an honorable exit from the war. Thus, the press greeted the arguments in Nixon's speech on April 30 with a simple counterassertion: They did not believe him. It was "Military Hallucination — Again" according to the *New York Times:* "Time and bitter experience have exhausted the credulity of the American people and Congress." To the *Washington Post* it was a "self-renewing war" supported by "suspect evidence, specious argument and excessive rhetoric." To the *Miami Herald* "the script in Cambodia shockingly is the same as the story in Vietnam in the days of Kennedy and Johnson. We have heard it all before — endless times." Debate was engulfed in mass passion.

Just as it was burgeoning before April 30, the new increase in tempo had begun with calls for strikes and marches by the student leaders, who had proved their skill in producing confrontation in previous seasons of protest. The President's statements, oscillating between the maudlin and the strident, did not help in a volatile situation where everything was capable of misinterpretation. His May 1 off-the-cuff reference to "bums . . . blowing up campuses," a gibe overheard by reporters during a visit to the Pentagon, was a needless challenge, although it was intended to refer only to a tiny group of students who had firebombed a building and burned the life's research of a Stanford professor. When on May 4, four students at Kent State University were killed by rifle fire from National Guardsmen dispatched by Ohio Governor James Rhodes to keep order during several days of violence, there was a shock wave that brought the nation and its leadership close to psychological exhaustion.

The Administration responded with a statement of extraordinary insensitivity. Ron Ziegler was told to say that the killings "should remind us all once again that when dissent turns to violence it invites tragedy."

The momentum of student strikes and protests accelerated immediately. Campus unrest and violence overtook the Cambodian operation itself as the major issue before the public. Washington took on the character of a besieged city. A pinnacle of mass public protest was reached by May 9 when a crowd estimated at between 75,000 and 100,000 demonstrated on a hot Saturday afternoon on the Ellipse, the park to the south of the White House. Police surrounded the White House; a ring of sixty buses was used to shield the grounds of the President's home.

After May 9 thousands more students, often led by their faculty, descended on the capital to denounce "escalation" and the "folly" of their government. A thousand lawyers lobbied Congress to end the war, followed by thirty-three heads of universities, architects, doctors, health officers, nurses, and one hundred corporate executives from New York. The press fed the mood. Editorials expressed doubts about the claims of success in Cambodia emanating from the Pentagon. Beyond these peaceful demonstrations antiwar students proved adept at imaginative tactics of disruption merging with outright violence. Some two thousand Columbia University students sat down in the road in the rush hour. Fires were set on several college campuses as bonfires for peace. At Syracuse University fire destroyed a new building as twenty-five hundred students demonstrated nearby. Students demonstrated in the financial district of New York City on May 7 and 8. In retaliation, construction workers building the World Trade Center descended on Wall Street and beat the protesters with clubs and other makeshift weapons. The incident shocked some into the realization that a breakdown of civil order could backfire dangerously against the demonstrators. But it did not slow down the pace of protest; it only encouraged Nixon in the belief that the masses of the American public were on his side.

Indeed, the Gallup Poll showed considerable support for the President's action. When people were asked, "Do you think the US should send arms and material to help Cambodia or not?" 48 percent of those questioned responded yes, 35 percent no, 11 percent expressed no opinion, while 6 percent gave a qualified answer. When they were asked, "Do you approve or disapprove of the way President Nixon is handling the Cambodian situation?" 50 percent expressed approval; 35 percent expressed disapproval; 15 percent expressed no opinion. And 53 percent of those questioned expressed approval of the way President Nixon was handling the situation in Vietnam; 37 percent expressed disapproval; 10 percent had no opinion.

The tidal wave of media and student criticism powerfully affected the Congress. From not unreasonable criticism of the President's inadequate consultation it escalated to attempts to legislate a withdrawal from Cambodia and to prohibit the reentry of American troops. On May 13 debate began in the Senate on the Foreign Military Sales Bill, to which Senators Frank Church and John Sherman Cooper proposed an amendment prohibiting the extension of US military aid to, and US military activities in, Cambodia after June 30. On the other hand, an amendment offered by Senator Robert Byrd would have granted the President authority to take whatever action he deemed necessary to protect US troops in South Vietnam. This amendment was narrowly defeated, 52–47, on June 11, in what was seen as a trial heat. Senate debate and parliamentary skirmishing lasted seven weeks, until on June 30 the Senate approved the Cooper-Church amendment in a 58–37 roll-call vote. The Senate had voted to give the Communists a free hand in Cambodia even though in the judgment of the Executive Branch this doomed South Vietnam. The bill then went to a House-Senate Conference. The entire Foreign Military Sales Bill remained in conference for the remainder of 1970, deadlocked over the House's refusal to agree to the Senate-passed amendment. By then the damage was substantially done; in the middle of a blatant North Vietnamese invasion, the enemy was being told by the Senate that Cambodia was on its own.

Whereas the Cooper-Church amendment focused on Cambodia, the McGovern-Hatfield amendment to the Defense Procurement Bill aimed at ending the Indochina war by the simple expedient of cutting off all funds by the end of 1970, later extended to December 31, 1971. The move was finally defeated by the Senate on September 1 by a 55–39 margin. But the pattern was clear. Senate opponents of the war would introduce one amendment after another, forcing the Administration into unending rearguard actions to preserve a minimum of flexibility for negotiations. Hanoi could only be encouraged to stall, waiting to harvest the results of our domestic dissent.

All this accelerated the processes of disenchantment. Conservatives were demoralized by a war that had turned into a retreat and liberals were paralyzed by what they themselves had wrought — for they could not completely repress the knowledge that it was a liberal Administration that had sent half a million Americans to Indochina. They were equally reluctant to face the implications of their past actions or to exert any serious effort to maintain calm. There was a headlong retreat from responsibility. Extraordinarily enough, all groups, dissenters and others, passed the buck to the Presidency. It was a great joke for undergraduates when one senior professor proclaimed "the way to get out of Vietnam is by ship." The practical consequence was that in the absence of any serious alternative the government was left with only its own policy or capitulation.

The very fabric of government was falling apart. The Executive Branch was shell-shocked. After all, their children and their friends' children took part in the demonstrations. Some two hundred and fifty State Department employees, including fifty Foreign Service Officers, signed a statement objecting to Administration policy. The ill-concealed disagreement of Cabinet members showed that the Executive Branch was nearly as divided as the country. Interior Secretary Walter Hickel protested in public. The *New York Times* on May 9 reported that the Secretary of State had prohibited any speculation on his own attitude — hardly a ringing endorsement of the President. A group of employees seized the Peace Corps building and flew a Viet Cong flag from it. Robert Finch, Secretary of Health, Education, and Welfare, refused to disagree publicly with his President and old friend — as indeed he did privately — and a large number of his officials occupied the department's auditorium in protest.[12] The President saw himself as the firm rock in this rushing stream, but the turmoil had its effect on him as well. Pretending indifference, he was deeply wounded by the hatred of the protesters. He would have given a great deal to gain a measure of the affection in which the students held the envied and admired Kennedys. In his ambivalence Nixon reached a point of exhaustion that caused his advisers deep concern. His awkward visit to the Lincoln Memorial to meet students at 5:00 A.M. on May 9 was only the tip of the psychological iceberg.

Exhaustion was the hallmark of us all. I had to move from my apartment ringed by protesters into the basement of the White House to get some sleep. Despite the need to coordinate the management of the crisis, much of my own time was spent with unhappy, nearly panicky, colleagues; even more with student and colleague demonstrators. I talked at some length to Brian McDonnell and Thomas Mahoney, two young pacifists who announced they would fast in Lafayette Park until all American troops had been withdrawn. I talked in the Situation Room with groups of students from various colleges and graduate schools about the root causes, as I saw them, of their despair, which I thought deeper than anxiety about the war.

I found these discussions with students rather more rewarding than those with their protesting teachers. When I had lunch in the Situation Room with a group of Harvard professors, most of whom had held high governmental posts, at their request, I offered to engage in a candid discussion of the reasoning behind the decision, but on an off-the-record basis. Most had been my close colleagues and friends. They would not accept this offer. They were there not as eminent academicians but as political figures representing a constituency at home, a campus inflamed by the Kent State tragedy as much as by the war. They had proclaimed to the newspapers beforehand — but not to me — that they were there to confront me; they announced that they would henceforth refuse any research or advisory relationship with the government.

Their objections to the Cambodian decision illustrated that hyperbole was not confined to the Administration. One distinguished professor gave it as his considered analysis that "somebody had forgotten to tell the President that Cambodia was a country; he acted as if he didn't know this. Had we undertaken a large commitment to Cambodia? If we had, this was rotten foreign policy. If we hadn't, this was rotten foreign policy." He was convinced that this action "clearly jeopardized American withdrawals" — though in fact it did the opposite. This professor was prepared to believe, on the basis of no evidence whatsoever, that Secretary of Defense Laird had been unaware of the military operations before the President announced them. He held the amazing view that "it was a gamble that shouldn't have been taken even if it succeeds on its own terms." Others said the decision was "incomprehensible," "more horrible than anything done by LBJ," "disastrous," "dreadful." One professor advanced the extraordinary hypothesis that an operation lasting eight weeks to a distance of twenty-one miles might lead our military commanders to believe that the use of nuclear weapons was now conceivable. Another declared that we had provoked all the actions of the other side.

The meeting completed my transition from the academic world to the world of affairs. These were the leaders of their fields; men who had been my friends, academicians whose lifetime of study should have encouraged a sense of perspective. That they disagreed with our decision was understandable; I had myself gone through a long process of hesitation before I became convinced that there was no alternative. But the lack of compassion, the overweening righteousness, the refusal to offer an alternative, reinforced two convictions: that for the internal peace of our country the war had to be ended, but also that in doing so on terms compatible with any international responsibility we would get no help from those with whom I had spent my professional life. The wounds would have to be healed after the war was over; in the event, these were not.

Cambodia was *not* a moral issue; neither Nixon nor his opponents should ever have presented it in those terms. What we faced was an essentially tactical choice: whether the use of American troops to neutralize the sanctuaries for a period of eight weeks was the best way to maintain the established pace and security of our exit from Vietnam and prevent Hanoi from overrunning Indochina. Reasonable men might differ; instead, rational discussion ended. The President's presentation that elevated his decision to the same level of crisis as some of the crucial choices of World War II was countered by the critics with the image of an out-of-control President acting totally irrationally, who had provoked the enemy and whose actions were immoral even if they *succeeded.*

But it was not the incursion into Cambodia that was the real subject of debate. It was the same issue that had torn the country during the Moratorium the previous year: whether there were any terms that the United States should insist on for its honor, its world position, and the sacrifices already made, or whether it should collapse its effort immediately and unconditionally. A political settlement as urged by Senator Fulbright — other than the quick imposition of a Communist government in Saigon — was precisely what Hanoi had always rejected, as Le Duc Tho had confirmed to me in the most unqualified terms not three weeks earlier. What none of the moderate critics was willing to admit was that if we followed their recommendations of refusing aid to Cambodia, we would soon have no choice but to accept Hanoi's terms, which none of them supported. Our opponents kept proclaiming an assumption for which there did not exist the slightest evidence — that there was some unspecified political alternative, some magic formula of neutrality, which was being willfully spurned. The panicky decision to set a June 30 deadline for the removal of our forces from Cambodia was one concrete result of public pressures.

The insecurity was even greater at the middle levels of government. Here the impact of the public protest was to shift discussion from how to make the operation succeed to an elaboration of various restraints: on the use of tactical air strikes; on South Vietnamese operations in Cambodia after we left on June 30; on the role of American advisers. The ambivalence of the government in Washington was bound to be transmitted to those in the field who soon sensed that Washington was not handing out prizes for imaginative and bold efforts to pursue the enemy in Cambodia. In this sense Cambodia was a microcosm of our whole effort in Indochina.

There are no winners when the dialogue in a democracy breaks down so completely. There can be no serious national policy when an attempt is made to coerce decisions by an outpouring of emotion and when those in high office are forced to take measures they do not really believe in simply to calm protests in the streets. Perhaps some of the critics might have been more understanding had they known of my conversations with Le Duc Tho, which were concealed by the Administration's conviction that secrecy was needed for successful negotiations. And yet it is impossible to avoid the impression that most of the critics did not need Presidential errors other than as a pretext. (They would probably have denounced the operation for jeopardizing all prospects for my negotiations had they known of them.) We were confronted by an undifferentiated emotion that dismissed every explanation as a repetition of excessive claims of previous administrations. The critics rarely addressed our root dilemma: how we could responsibly withdraw forces and reduce military operations — as we were doing — while permitting the enemy to open up a new front.

The effort to find a moderate alternative to our policy led to a renewal of pressures for a fixed deadline for our total withdrawal. On June 7, the *Los Angeles Times* called for an immediate and complete withdrawal from Southeast Asia: "The time has come for the U.S. to leave Vietnam and to leave it swiftly and without equivocation." An eighteen-month time period, said the *Times* without evidence, "would be much less hazardous than the policy the President is presently pursuing.'' In July, *Life* magazine followed suit.

Unfortunately, the arguments for a withdrawal deadline had not improved with age. Either the deadline was compatible with Vietnamization, in which case it coincided with our own policy but would deprive us of negotiating leverage. Or it was arbitrary, in which case it was a euphemism for a collapse; and it would have been nearly impossible to justify risking lives in the interval before the deadline expired. So we ended the Cambodia operation still on the long route out of Vietnam, confronting an implacable enemy and an equally implacable domestic opposition.

The Balance Sheet

THE ultimate victims of our domestic anguish were the gentle people of Cambodia. Years later, when the Cambodian government that we supported fell under Communist rule, those who had demanded for years that we abandon Cambodia acquired a vested interest in trying to evade by any contortion the responsibility for the horrendous consequences that their advocacy had a part in bringing about. There are assertions that the tensions within Cambodia that toppled Sihanouk resulted from the westward movement of Communist forces allegedly caused by our incursion of May 1970 [13] or our bombing since 1969. [14] In reality, as the map on page 471 makes obvious, the westward drive of the North Vietnamese began in early April, *before* our incursion, provoked only by a Cambodian government that had the effrontery to ask them to leave Cambodian soil.

Without our incursion, the Communists would have taken over Cambodia years earlier. That the rule of these fanatical ideologues would have been more benign under those conditions is not very likely; when tyrants are so remote from their people, so committed to frightful experiments of social transformation, so doctrinaire, no normal criteria apply. These were no misunderstood humanitarians who, in a fit of pique at our actions five years earlier, were driven to massacre their own population. The bizarre argument has indeed been made, with a glaring lack of substantiation, that the cruelty of the Khmer Rouge in victory was the product of five years of American and Cambodian efforts to resist them. [15] No one can accept this as an adequate explanation except apologists for the murderous Khmer Rouge. Sihanouk does not believe this; they were men he had kicked out of Cambodia in 1967 because they were a menace to his country. He told me in April 1979 that the Khmer Rouge leaders were ''always killers'' from the beginning. [16] The actions of the Khmer Rouge in power were a methodical application of economic theories nurtured in decades of ideological fanaticism. Leader

Khieu Samphan in his doctoral dissertation in Paris in the late 1950s had written that the Cambodian economy and social structure had to be transformed by mobilizing "the dormant energy in the peasant mass" against the corrupt cities — a theory applied two decades later with breathtaking thoroughness and brutality, to the point of genocide.[17]

That Hanoi would have respected the independence of a neutralist Sihanouk when it later squelched a fellow Communist regime precisely for the sin of independence defies plausibility; it is rebutted by every statement ever made to us by Le Duc Tho. We would have taken our chances on a neutralist Sihanouk. Unfortunately by late April 1970, events and his outrage had put him into a position where he could have come back only as the agent of the Communists. It was Hanoi — animated by an insatiable drive to dominate Indochina — that invaded Cambodia in the middle Sixties, that organized the Khmer Rouge long before *any* American bombs fell on Cambodian soil; it was North Vietnamese troops who were trying to strangle Cambodia in the month before our limited attack; and it is North Vietnamese troops who have overthrown the Khmer Rouge in 1978–1979. Had we not invaded the sanctuaries Cambodia would have been engulfed in 1970 instead of 1975. If anything doomed the free Cambodians, it was war weariness in the United States.

Poor Cambodia gradually turned into the butt of our national frustrations. Our domestic critics, thwarted in their various schemes to legislate an end of the war in Vietnam, were more successful in imposing abdication in Cambodia. Even though the same enemy was using Cambodia as a base, even though Hanoi had no means of reinforcing beyond what it was already doing so that any increase in Cambodian strength was bound to weaken it or put it on the defensive, American advisers were barred by law from Cambodia, and American aid was tightly constrained. The Cambodians tied down much of Hanoi's manpower in the South, but our aid funds were doled out grudgingly, amounting to about $200 million in 1970, and they were encumbered with the restriction that they could not be expended to "maintain the Lon Nol government" — an astounding policy of helping a country without assisting its government. This reflected both the fear that we might get "bogged down" in Cambodia, as in the other countries of Indochina, and the by now prevalent myth that we were being held hostage by Thieu rather than by Hanoi. It was never made clear how the deterioration of our allies' position in Cambodia and Laos would make it easier for us to disengage from Vietnam.

The Congressional ban on military advisers in Cambodia was taken so literally by our Ambassador that he prohibited our military attachés even from traveling to inform themselves of the conduct of Cambodian units. Cambodia became a backwater; South Vietnamese forces operated in its border area; American planes bombed enemy communications — and the weaker the Cambodian forces were, in large part as a result of the limits on our aid, the more they had to rely on our planes as their only strategic reserve. Not the least irony was that the critics produced what they professed to abhor: increasing reliance on air power. Nothing decisive was permitted; the North Vietnamese were given time to build up the Khmer Rouge forces when they might have been hard pressed early on. The Cambodian army had to live by the doves' version of the Nixon Doctrine, languishing until its merciless Communist enemy had gathered the strength for an all-out assault and while a doctrinaire America gradually throttled its capacity for resistance.

Cambodia's dilemma touched even two staffers of the Senate Foreign Relations Committee, Richard M. Moose and James G. Lowenstein, whose annual visits to Southeast Asia had been the terror of our officials because the two opposed the war and were adept at turning up bureaucratic bungling. Their reports were a semiannual salvo in the Congressional assault on our Vietnam policy. On a visit to Cambodia at the end of 1970, however, Moose and Lowenstein came to conclusions not very different from our own, and had the courage to state them. The thrust of their report was that the United States was really doing very little for Cambodia, that the Cambodian government had broad popular support, and that the United States was letting Cambodia down:

> It appeared to us that there is considerable support for the government of General Lon Nol among the youth and intellectuals, in marked contrast to the situation in South Vietnam, and among civil servants and members of the Senate and the Assembly. . . . There is an evident sense of national identity and purpose and a determination to defend the country without foreign troops. . . .
>
> Cambodians find it difficult to understand the complicated and involved elements of the American dilemma in Southeast Asia today. Looking back at the pattern of American behavior in Asia over the past two decades, they seem mystified by the signs of American hesitancy in arming them to defend against an invading force armed by China and the Soviet Union.

Whereas the earlier Moose-Lowenstein reports, supporting prevalent preconception, had been printed in fancy booklets and widely distributed, this report was bottled up for several days in committee. Then, apparently under pressure from some members, it was released — but in as inconspicuous a way as possible. Senator Fulbright simply inserted it into the *Congressional Record* on December 16, 1970, along with a few newspaper editorials, without calling attention to it and without a public reading.[18]

Whether to attack the sanctuaries was a close call, on which honest and serious individuals might well differ. But once the North Vietnamese forces had spread all over the country, once a "liberated zone" had been created under Communist control as a step toward overthrowing the non-Communist government in Phnom Penh (all antedating *any* American response), the die had been cast. Attacking the sanctuaries prevented an immediate collapse of Cambodia but could not remove the long-term threat. Those who had opposed the original decision now sought to undo it by blocking further assistance to the Cambodian government. But this neither undid the decision nor prevented an expansion of the war; all it accomplished was to give Hanoi and the Khmer Rouge a breathing spell to build up for the final assault. It doomed what was left of hope for an independent, free, and neutral Cambodia. Whatever the merits of the 1970 debate, a strong case can be made for the proposition that Cambodia was ultimately the victim of the breakdown of our democratic political process: Both government and critics could block each other's goals and frustrate each other's policies, preventing any coherent strategy. From this mélange of North Vietnamese determination, Cambodian rivalries, and American internal conflicts, everything followed with the inevitability of a Greek tragedy until there descended on that gentle land a horror that it did not deserve and that none of us have the right to forget.

In June 1970 we did not believe that matters were foreordained to end tragically. We still sought for the balance between firmness and conciliation which would provide the maximum incentive for a negotiation. This is why we asked General Walters to deliver a message on May 8, 1970, proposing another meeting with Le Duc Tho. I did not expect Hanoi to accept immediately. On May 6, Hanoi had "postponed" the scheduled public negotiating session at Avenue Kléber until May 14 and made another statement in support of the Khmer Rouge. But even this postponement was carried out, as my staff put it, "in a somewhat cautious manner" revealing an eagerness to keep the negotiating channel open — if only to give us no pretext to abrogate the bombing halt. Hanoi did not reply for many weeks to the offer to resume secret talks with Le Duc Tho. On June 5 it turned down our proposal for another meeting, calling it a "temporary suspension."

But it was clear that there would be a new round of diplomacy as the dust settled and a new balance of forces emerged on the ground. On May 25 I therefore requested from the departments and agencies a study of diplomatic initiatives the United States might take in Indochina. I also proposed to the President that we appoint a new senior negotiator in Paris. The North Vietnamese had insistently demanded this in both the public and the private talks. I had never thought that merely naming a negotiator would move the negotiations off dead center; Hanoi's main interest in the Paris forum was to keep us from resuming bombing the North on the ground that no serious talks were taking place. Nevertheless, I thought that a senior appointment would deprive Hanoi of a propaganda issue. I suggested David K. E. Bruce; Nixon enthusi-astically agreed; Bruce accepted with that sense of duty so characteristic of this extraordinary diplomat.

I have never met a more distinguished public servant or a finer man than David Bruce. Scion of an old Maryland family, he had deep roots in both Maryland and Virginia and had been at different times a member of both state legislatures. He had written about the early Presidents, and his admirers found in him many of the same sturdy qualities. He devoted his life to the public weal. He had proved his courage in the OSS in World War II. Handsome, wealthy, emotionally secure, he was free of that insistence on seeing their views prevail through which lesser men turn public service into an exercise of their egos. His bearing made clear that he served a cause that transcended the life span of an individual; he exuded the conviction that his country represented values that needed tending and that were worth defending. His dignity forswore the second-rate; his understated eloquence confirmed that in persons of quality substance and form cannot be separated. He saw man as uniquely capable of improvement through reason and tact in a world whose imperfections would yield — if only gradually — to patience and goodwill.

Bruce never turned down honorable requests by a President; nor did he evaluate them in terms of personal advantage. For thirty years he served Presidents of both parties as Ambassador to London, Paris, and Bonn. He was to work for Presidents Nixon and Ford in the Vietnam negotiations, in Peking, and in NATO — always with distinction. He spoke his mind, if necessary explicitly, but he did not use his own travail as a means of personal advancement. He had, in a word, character.

Few men have had a greater influence on me than David Bruce. On some of my most fateful decisions I instinctively turned to him. I did not always take his advice; I never failed to benefit from his judgment, his sense of humor, his unfailing tact. He kept me from taking myself too seriously; he never failed to inspire me with his conviction that our nation's future was a serious trust.

In July 1970, David Bruce, at the age of seventy-two and in fragile health, embarked on a mission in which he knew that his opposite numbers had as their primary objective to wear him down. He understood that debating skill could not substitute for the objective balance of forces on which his interlocutors placed so much stock. There would be little glory for him in Paris; nor did he seek it. But he knew that a nation's honor is not a trivial matter; we had not come through the centuries to betray those who had relied on our promises.

We were on a long road, certain to be painful. But with David Bruce as a companion its burdens would become more bearable. And any effort to which he was willing to commit himself had a strong presumption of being in the national interest.

The Soviet Riddle:
Europe, SALT, and a Summit

Hot and Cold

THE superpowers often behave like two heavily armed blind men feeling their way around a room, each believing himself in mortal peril from the other whom he assumes to have perfect vision. Each side should know that frequently uncertainty, compromise, and incoherence are the essence of policymaking. Yet each tends to ascribe to the other side a consistency, foresight, and coherence that its own experience belies. Of course, over time even two armed blind men in a room can do enormous damage to each other, not to speak of the room.

The problem with US–Soviet relations is not only that there are two competing bureaucracies with their assumptions and guesses; there are also conflicting conceptions of negotiation. Americans tend to believe that each negotiation has its own logic, that its outcome depends importantly on bargaining skill, goodwill, and facility for compromise. But if one side in a negotiation has only a vague mandate coupled with a general desire for agreement, negotiability — an elegant phrase meaning what one knows the other side will accept — becomes an end in itself and the outcome is foreordained: The negotiation will see the constant retreat of the party that is committed to it. Persistence in a negotiating position is disparaged domestically as "rigid," "stubborn," or "unimaginative." No position is ever final. Critics demand greater flexibility; soon the proposition is advanced that the United States has an obligation to overcome the stalemate by offering concessions. The other side, aware that we are in effect bidding against ourselves, has the maximum inducement to stand rigid to discover what else we may offer.

These attributes of American negotiators had complicated our efforts in 1969; they were compounded by our domestic debate. Within the Administration we had to fight a seemingly endless battle against those who wanted to fuel the momentum of negotiations with gestures of goodwill. Not a few argued, for example, that we should forgo our

ABM and MIRV programs lest we doom the prospects of strategic arms limitation — though in fact ABM and MIRV turned out to be among our few playable cards. Similarly, we were warned that an opening to China would cause relations with the Soviet Union to regress; in fact, the opening would break a logjam on several issues with the USSR.

Our internal divisions handed the Soviet leadership an irresistible opportunity to whipsaw us. The Kremlin would stress its eagerness to begin negotiations on SALT, for example. While the White House would try to gear our response to overall Soviet conduct, the rest of our government would find innumerable ways, from press leaks to informal hints, to let it be known that it was ready, nay eager, to start talking. The Soviet Embassy, under Dobrynin's sophisticated leadership, would spread the word among journalists and Congressional leaders that trade would make a major contribution to the easing of tensions. When the White House sought to insist that trade accompany and not precede an improvement of political relations, the various departments, as well as leading members of the Congress, pressed insistently for early relaxation of trade restrictions. Thus the better part of our first year was spent in convincing both the Soviets and our own bureaucracy that we intended to base our negotiations on a calculation of the national interest, not abstract slogans, and on strict reciprocity, not "gestures" or "signals." By the end of 1969 neither side had achieved any of its initial objectives, but it also seemed that the careful fencing was about to end. The Channel — my talks with Soviet Ambassador Anatoly Dobrynin — had become increasingly active at the end of 1969, usually on Soviet initiative. We had succeeded in making it clear to the Soviets, and with a little time lag to the bureaucracy, that the President's view was the decisive one. But what passed through the Channel early in 1970 was as inconclusive as an opening chess gambit. Each player was determined to avoid an irreparable mistake; the moves were careful; they revealed as little as possible of intentions and therefore inspired even greater caution on the part of the opponent.

When Dobrynin and I met for a general review on December 22, 1969, he remarked ingratiatingly that Moscow expected to have to deal with Nixon for seven more years. This was too long a time for Moscow to wait us out; indeed, it should be too long for Hanoi. Amazingly, he suggested that Moscow had no real interests in Southeast Asia; it had become involved on the basis of a "misunderstanding"; he did not explain what the misunderstanding consisted of. China, according to Dobrynin, was the sole beneficiary of a continuation of the war.

Dobrynin listed what he said were the Soviet Union's frustrations: the Administration's pressure for ABM, the stalled Middle East negotiations, the refusal to invite Gromyko to the White House while Nixon received the Deputy Foreign Minister of Romania, our attempt to make each negotiation conditional on some other one (linkage). All this culminated in his query whether we might begin fundamental discussions in the Channel even if we decided to delay implementing any understandings until the war in Vietnam was over. I told Dobrynin that I thought a positive answer probable.

We met again on January 20, 1970. The pretext was a Soviet note protesting meetings of committees of the West German Parliament in West Berlin. Significantly, the note was passed in the Presidential Channel where it would receive no publicity; Moscow, obviously, did not want a crisis in Central Europe.

Dobrynin took the occasion to ask about our recent round of Warsaw talks with the Chinese. He hoped I understood that this was a "neuralgic" point with Moscow. Would I brief him? This constant Soviet fretting about China is as inexplicable to me now as then; the same insecurity was in evidence nearly a decade later with respect to the Sino-Japanese treaty. The incessant inquiries could yield no positive benefit. If the Soviet Union had a real reason for concern, it was unlikely to receive a truthful reply; it was more likely to remind us of our strategic opportunity — this certainly was the result in 1969. Undoubtedly, Dobrynin's superiors in Moscow in their bureaucratic way thought that they could not be blamed for ignorance about the Warsaw talks if they could produce a record of having asked — with no sense of how insecure this made them appear.

I had always opposed briefing Moscow on our conversations with the Chinese because it gave the Soviets too easy an opportunity to play their version back to Peking to stimulate Chinese fears of a Soviet-American condominium. I therefore replied that if Moscow were so "neuralgic," his superiors would not believe anything I told him anyway. Even without a briefing it should be clear that we were in no position to "use" China as a military threat. At the same time Moscow had to understand that we too had our "neuralgic" point, which was Vietnam. I pointed out that recent broadcasts by American prisoners of war on Moscow Radio were an unfriendly act.

Dobrynin's real purpose for the meeting, however, was to continue the exchange of December 22 on using the Channel. He first made an uncharacteristically heavy-handed attempt to sound me out on a summit, asking about a supposed remark by the Japanese Ambassador that Nixon was aiming to meet with the Soviet leaders in late summer or early fall. I assured him that when we were ready for a summit we would not make our approach through another country.

At last, Dobrynin conveyed Moscow's reaction to our previous exchange. The Soviet leadership welcomed serious discussions in the Channel. He proposed that we take up one subject at a time. He would shortly present Soviet views on European security; perhaps before the

SALT talks resumed in April I could outline our basic approach. I agreed to this procedure.

Thus, by the end of January 1970 we seemed to be at the beginning of a serious dialogue. But, as so often, the Soviets veered unpredictably off course. The promised discussion on European security never took place; Dobrynin simply did not return to the subject. Nor were there substantive conversations on SALT. Instead, Dobrynin appeared in my office on January 31 with a warning from Premier Kosygin about Israeli military actions along the Suez Canal. If Israeli air raids deep into Egypt continued, said the note, the Soviet Union "will be forced to see to it that the Arab states have means at their disposal" to "rebuff" Israel. A cool but polite letter from Nixon rejected the allegations and left no doubt that the United States would resist any Soviet escalation in the Middle East.* On February 10 Dobrynin, somewhat chastened, returned to the charge, arguing that Kosygin's letter had been intended not to convey a threat but to define a dilemma.

A week later, Dobrynin came in with an extraordinary complaint that again demonstrated the congenital Soviet insecurity and at the same time skillfully put us on the defensive. He pointed out that in the recently published Presidential Foreign Policy Report, an epic of 40,000 words, the only foreign leaders mentioned by name were Presidents Thieu and Ceauşescu. His leaders were likely to conclude that we were not taking them seriously. I turned this amazing point aside politely, somewhat disingenuously telling him that the report was written primarily for an American audience. Dobrynin next asked about an innocuous phrase in the Europe chapter of the same report to the effect that "the only constant" in the world was "the inevitability of change." Did this mean we no longer recognized the existing dividing lines in Europe? I replied that it was odd for a Marxist to object to a philosophical reference to the inevitability of change. We did not challenge existing national frontiers, but we did not recognize the East German boundary as a national frontier. I knew that the Soviets were about to begin delicate negotiations with Chancellor Willy Brandt about internal German arrangements and I was not about to add to their leverage.

Dobrynin assured me again that his leadership was eager to continue his confidential exchanges with me, particularly on SALT. He was still without instructions on what specific subject to pursue, however. Then on March 10, shortly before the official SALT talks were scheduled to open, Dobrynin raised the question whether he and I should concentrate on a "comprehensive" or a "limited" SALT agreement. I told him the main problem was to get concrete about something. Within a week of this conversation we learned that the most advanced Soviet antiaircraft

---

*For details, see Chapter XIV.

missiles (the SA-3s) were arriving in Egypt together with Soviet personnel to man them. So, within ten days I met again with Dobrynin and told him firmly that this was reminiscent of their behavior during the Cuban missile crisis. We would surely see to it that the military balance was maintained. On April 7 Dobrynin again explored the possibility of an exchange on SALT: Moscow would consider it a sign of good faith if I outlined our position before it was tabled at Vienna. This would permit consideration at the highest levels in the Kremlin before the experts in the ministries maneuvered themselves into total inflexibility.

Before we could pursue these subjects, Dobrynin was recalled to Moscow for consultation, and the crisis in Cambodia intervened. But enough had taken place to make clear that the Kremlin had no clear line. It was trying pressure and accommodation simultaneously. It opened subjects it did not pursue and provoked a confrontation in the Middle East without definable purpose. What lay behind this confusing behavior?

The Riddle of Soviet Conduct

E VEN in the calmest periods, the picture of a Soviet leadership operating on the basis of profound long-range calculations is likely to be overdrawn. The Politburo, a committee of usually fifteen powerful leaders, makes the final decisions. To be sure, the Party General Secretary — Leonid Brezhnev since 1964 — has the most important voice. He can determine the agenda of Politburo meetings; he controls the Secretariat; he has decisive weight in selecting new members. Nevertheless, since Stalin no General Secretary has had unbridled discretion — even though Brezhnev clearly was increasingly preeminent since 1971. He must build a consensus; undoubtedly, there are competing schools of thought and centers of influence to be reconciled on every issue.

The ponderous nature of this machinery is magnified by the sharp separation between the policymaking body, the Politburo, and the executive organs of the government. The bureaucracy is entitled to a view only in its area of competence; it appears not to have the right to an opinion regarding some other department's specialization, even if it is related in substance. Thus the Ministry of Foreign Affairs can express its views on the political implications of arms control proposals, but not on military aspects. The Ministry of Defense is the sole authority on military questions; it enjoys little voice in diplomacy. All disputes between departments move for resolution to the Politburo. Until 1973, when Gromyko and Marshal Andrei Grechko joined the Politburo, neither the Foreign nor Defense Ministries, which they headed, had been represented on that body for a decade. Before he was elevated to the Politburo I occasionally had the impression that I was better informed about Soviet military deployments than Gromyko. Our SALT negotiators clearly made the military officers on the Soviet delegation uncomfortable when they discussed Soviet military dispositions in front of Soviet diplomats; early on, one of their officers suggested to our delegation privately that it would be better if technical military subjects were not raised in front of diplomats.

Soviet policymaking is thus cumbersome even when the General Secretary is preeminent and the Politburo unified. It tends to become muscle-bound during periods of change in the leadership. In such circumstances, the main lines of policy, once decided, are pursued with a single-minded rigidity reinforced by Russian stubbornness. During power struggles it is quite possible for incompatible courses to be pursued, until some crisis imposes the need for a clear-cut decision. The Soviet Union had slid into crises that were substantially unplanned and jeopardized goodwill because some event — such as a forthcoming Party Congress — monopolized the attention of the top leadership or gave greater weight to some part of its huge, complex bureaucratic machinery.

Such a period was early 1970. When Nixon became President, Alexei Kosygin, the Premier, seemed to be the dominant figure on foreign policy in the Politburo. Communications from the Soviet leadership were sent in his name; he had met President Johnson at Glassboro. When feelers were extended for a summit meeting his was the name invariably mentioned. But, equally obviously, throughout this period Brezhnev was gaining in influence. He seemed to extend his role from the management of party affairs and the domestic economy into international politics. A Party Congress, usually held every four years, was scheduled for 1970. (It did not, in fact, take place until the spring of 1971.) This would be the occasion for establishing Brezhnev's preeminence; after the spring of 1971 almost all high-level exchanges were with him.

This meant that 1970 was a year of transition in which the Soviet leadership, perhaps absorbed in its own internal maneuvering, reacted to events tactically. Moreover, the domestic turmoil in America over the war in Vietnam tempted it to exploit opportunities for making gains.

On February 2, I sent a memorandum to the President pointing out that this period of adjustment was exacerbated by serious and chronic Soviet domestic difficulties. The economic growth rate was declining, largely because of technological backwardness. After the fall of Khrushchev the new leaders had set out to increase the supply of consumer goods and at the same time to raise spending for defense, including a large buildup on the Chinese border. Though this stretched the economy, the Soviet leadership had hoped that industrial reform would provide a new stimulus to investment and growth. These hopes had been

disappointed: "The reason, of course, is that the Soviet leaders are reluctant to face up to the failure of their own industrial reforms. None of
the leaders can suggest a new program of reform which would spur
economic progress and at the same time preserve central political control. This is a central Soviet dilemma." (To this Nixon added his marginal comment: "The critical point.")

A tug-of-war at the top was therefore likely, I concluded:

> The Party Congress, which is expected this year, might bring problems to a
> head. All of the top leaders will want to ensure that their supporters retain key
> positions. The older group under Brezhnev may try to expand its mandate at the
> Congress, while the younger group would be inclined to block this prospect.

In the end, the internal tensions did not go to the breaking point. But
two of the individuals I identified as belonging to the "younger"
group — Dmitri Polyansky and Aleksandr Shelepin — were soon
purged from high office. Brezhnev apparently agreed with my analysis
of who was likely to grasp for power.

The uncertainties of Kremlin politics continued through the spring. In
a memorandum of May 5 to the President, I listed further signs of confused and contradictory Soviet policies, such as proposals rapidly retracted and references in speeches to decisions already changed:

> The consensus inside the government, and concurred in by some leading
> scholars, seems to be that there has, in fact, been trouble in the leadership, but
> that the resolution, if only temporary, has been in Brezhnev's favor.
>
> His image is sharper — as the result of intensive nation-wide television ex-
> posure; his confidence is apparently reflected in his wide-ranging speeches cov-
> ering all important internal and external topics. And several second level per-
> sonnel changes . . . suggest he is on top.

In June 1970 a Central Committee meeting and elections to the Parliament of the USSR (the Supreme Soviet) confirmed Brezhnev's predominance. In June I analyzed for the President the likely foreign policy
consequences:

> Brezhnev's predominance and growing strength does not immediately translate
> into policy terms. At the Congress he identified himself with the consumer at
> the expense of heavy and defense industry, and with his "peace program". He
> reiterated both themes in his closing speech. More important may be that if he
> is gaining more power and therefore probably some more freedom of action,
> he may thus be inclined to move on some of the international issues that we are
> engaged in — SALT, Berlin, etc.

But before the Soviets settled on a course of relaxing tensions they
sought to isolate us by "selective détente" — improving relations with
our European allies while increasing pressures on us. The Soviet leaders

saw an opening for this maneuver in the policies of the new Chancellor in West Germany, Willy Brandt; for some months *Ostpolitik* held the center of the stage.

Ostpolitik

As the months went by it became increasingly apparent why Dobrynin had never followed up his offer of January 20 to present Soviet views on European security. Moscow thought it could do better in dealing directly with Bonn than by involving us. In the winter of 1969 Willy Brandt had taken the initiative with offers to both the USSR and East Germany to renounce the use of force and accept the status quo in Central Europe. The Soviet leaders and their East German protégés were clearly intrigued by the prospect of dealing for the first time since the 1930s with a Social Democratic government in Germany. Moscow had opened negotiations simultaneously with Peking on the long-simmering border dispute. As the Soviets probably saw it, there was some chance of relieving pressure on both fronts at the same time; if they could secure Brandt's acceptance of the status quo in Europe, this would compound the isolation of the Chinese. And an accommodation directly between Bonn and Moscow would carry with it the additional dividend of excluding the United States from the solution of a major European problem, setting a precedent that might cause other Europeans to look increasingly to Moscow rather than Washington. Over time this was bound to weaken NATO ties.

While as I have indicated I had come to the view that Brandt's decision to modify the policies of his Christian Democratic predecessors was inevitable and potentially beneficial, this would be so only if it did not give the Soviets the whip hand over German and European policy. Unless we managed to get some control over the process Brandt would become more and more dependent on the Soviet Union and its goodwill for the fulfillment of German goals in the new policy. On February 16 I wrote to the President of the possible consequences:

The most worrisome aspects of *Ostpolitik,* however, are somewhat more long-range. As long as he is negotiating with the Eastern countries over the issues that are currently on the table — recognition of the GDR, the Oder-Neisse, various possible arrangements for Berlin — Brandt should not have any serious difficulty in maintaining his basic pro-Western policy. . . .

But assuming Brandt achieves a degree of normalization, he or his successor may discover before long that the hoped-for benefits fail to develop. . . . Having already invested heavily in their Eastern policy, the Germans may at this point see themselves as facing agonizing choices. It should be remembered that in the 1950s, many Germans not only in the SPD under Schumacher but in conservative quarters traditionally fascinated with the East or enthralled by the vision of Germany as a "bridge" between East and West, argued against Bonn's incorporation in Western institutions on the ground that it would forever seal Germany's division and preclude the restoration of an active German role in the East. This kind of debate about Germany's basic position could well recur in more divisive form, not only inflaming German domestic affairs but generating suspicions among Germany's Western associates as to its reliability as a partner.*

Yet there was no sense in seeking to derail Brandt's policy; the sole option available to us was to give the inevitable a constructive direction. Brandt's coalition had been elected on the program he was now implementing. We could abort his *Ostpolitik* only by massive intervention in German internal politics, the alienation of our allies, and (as President Pompidou feared) the refashioning of NATO into a German-American alliance for the liberation of Eastern Europe. And we had no alternative to offer. It was their fear of a German "liberation policy" that had caused Pompidou and Harold Wilson to endorse Brandt's approach publicly and to press us privately to follow suit. Nor would our public opinion understand a policy of insisting on German reunification *against* the wishes of the German government; we could not be more German than the Germans. On the contrary, we would become increasingly the butt of the charge that we had destroyed hopeful prospects for easing the harsh consequences of the division of Germany.

I therefore urged Nixon to go along with Brandt's policy and to use our influence to embed it in a wider framework than German nationalism. Brandt did his part in assuaging anxiety by keeping in close touch. To be sure, the new German government informed rather than consulted. They reported progress; they did not solicit advice. But this was also what we preferred. The last thing we wanted was to be held responsible for German negotiating positions that were turning into a bitter domestic issue in West Germany. I urged Nixon "that any endorsement we give Brandt should be no more than general support for the improvement of the FRG's [Federal Republic of Germany's] relations with the East — without approving specific FRG moves."

Nor were we without resources in preventing the Soviet Union from using *Ostpolitik* to divide us from our European allies. For one thing, no West German leader could afford to conduct a policy of which we strongly disapproved. His domestic position would not sustain it; his own convictions belied it; no rational calculation of benefits would encourage it. Moreover, the further Brandt went toward recognizing East Germany the more imperative a Berlin agreement became for him. Berlin became the key to the whole puzzle, for one simple reason. What-

---

*Something like this seems to be happening in Bonn as this book is being written.

ever treaties Brandt negotiated with the USSR and East Germany would have to be ratified by the West German Parliament, in which his coalition had the slimmest of majorities. An agreement improving the security of Berlin was the most tangible and convincing quid pro quo for Brandt's controversial treaties, which essentially embodied Germany's acceptance of its division. It became clear that only with a Berlin agreement would Brandt's Eastern treaties be ratified. A Berlin agreement required the concurrence of all four wartime powers (the United States, Britain, France, and the USSR). Thus our active cooperation was crucial; we alone had the strength to counterbalance the reality of Berlin's isolation; in time we would achieve thereby a major voice in the process, however it was started.

In this framework, without enthusiasm but not without confidence, we gave our support to Brandt's historic course. In a declaration of policy on January 14, 1970, he laid down six principles for negotiations with the East, including maintenance of Four-Power rights in Berlin and improvement of conditions in the city. Five days later, the East German Communist Party leader, Walter Ulbricht, agreed to negotiate without preconditions on inter-German relations. In another surprise move, on February 11 the East German Premier, Willi Stoph, proposed direct talks. After some haggling over location it was agreed that the two leaders would meet in Erfurt in East Germany on March 19. Parallel to the moves between the two Germanies, Bonn had also opened up discussions with the USSR on a treaty on the renunciation of force. Preliminary contacts by the West German Ambassador in Moscow had resulted in a predictable stalemate over Soviet insistence that the Federal Republic first recognize East Germany. Brandt then decided to escalate the level of talks by appointing Egon Bahr, his confidant, to lead the second round. Bahr informed me of this step by backchannel. On February 20, after his return from Moscow, Bahr used the backchannel again to convey his generally optimistic assessment of his talks there. He believed that the Soviets were "seriously interested" in the possibility of a treaty renouncing the use of force and were on the verge of submitting concrete proposals cleared by the Politburo.

But Bahr's talks had also brought home to him that the linkage to Berlin was our ace in the hole. Bahr assured me that he had pressed Gromyko to agree to undisturbed civilian traffic to Berlin, an essential quid pro quo for German public opinion. Gromyko had not reacted, but had taken note. Bahr wanted to make sure that Berlin negotiations did not lag behind the German talks. I had the opposite view; once the German talks were completed our bargaining position over Berlin would be vastly improved because the Soviets would be eager to see the Eastern treaties ratified.

After having stalled on Berlin talks for six months, the Soviets had begun to perceive the same realities. On February 10 the Soviets formally invited the United States, Britain, and France to begin negotiations about Berlin on February 18. The short deadline was totally unrealistic, given the glacial procedures of interallied consultation. But it bespoke Soviet eagerness; it highlighted our opportunity for improving our position in Berlin just so long as we did not let ourselves be stampeded. I recommended to the President that we accept the Soviet proposal but phase the talks so that the Soviets could not play off the allies against one another by two simultaneous sets of talks. This led to a careful minuet in which neither we nor our German ally could make our positions explicit. Brandt wanted to speed up the Berlin negotiations so that he could use them for leverage and, if necessary, shift the onus for any failure of his *Ostpolitik* to us. Conversely, we favored a more leisurely pace, lest we be asked to pay for progress in the inter-German negotiations in the coin of Four-Power rights in Berlin.

Brandt wrote to Nixon on February 25 reporting formally on Bahr's visit to Moscow and gently urging the early opening of Berlin negotiations. We waited until March 12 to reply; Nixon's letter agreed to work for a unified Western position; we suggested that the Four-Power Berlin talks might open on March 26. The intricacies of the Berlin question, the need to develop a common Western position, and the sharply conflicting views built up over the years all ensured that Berlin negotiations would be protracted. Brandt could set a much brisker pace in his bilateral initiatives; the style of Bahr, his chief negotiator, made it inescapable. All of this increased our leverage. To put it diplomatically, I did not consider the slow pace of the Berlin talks a tactical disadvantage.

Brandt's meeting with Willi Stoph in Erfurt was a major success. He was greeted with great enthusiasm by the East German crowds, who began chanting "Willy, Willy," and then, realizing that both participants had similar first names, changed their greeting to "Willy Brandt." No major agreement resulted; the significance was that for the first time the leaders of a divided Germany had met and talked. The classic Western position — that any European settlement presupposed the reunification of Germany — thereby passed into history.

This was the state of affairs when Brandt paid his first visit to Washington as Chancellor three weeks later. Before Brandt's arrival, I saw Egon Bahr privately on April 8 in my White House office. He briefed me in more detail on his talks in Moscow, though for some reason he omitted three "new papers" that he had handed to the Soviets but never discussed with us. (Dobrynin, never loath to widen any potential cracks in allied unity, had mentioned them to me!) Bahr was confident that the Soviets would urge the East Germans to normalize relations between Bonn and East Germany and that they would ease

Berlin access. What we wanted, of course, was not a Soviet administrative gesture revocable at will but a legal regimen to underpin West Berlin's viability. Brandt's meeting with Nixon went well, as I have described in Chapter XI. Brandt left Washington with a general endorsement of his policy. West German–Soviet talks resumed from May 12 to 22 and resulted in an agreement on "principles." At the semiannual meeting of Foreign Ministers of the Atlantic Alliance in Rome on May 26–27, Brandt received the solid support of all his allies.

All the time controversy was growing within West Germany. The opposition Christian Democrats launched a bitter attack on Brandt's policy. Former Chancellor Kiesinger warned that it was "five minutes to high noon"; Rainer Barzel, who was successfully challenging Kiesinger for the opposition leadership, declared ominously, "turn back before it is too late." Egon Bahr's negotiating paper was leaked in the German press, inflaming passions further. The furor made it starkly obvious that no treaty with the Soviet Union would be ratified by the West German Parliament unless there was a satisfactory agreement on Berlin.

Brandt, buttressed by a good showing in a local election in June, decided to proceed into the final phase of his negotiation with the USSR, appointing Foreign Minister Walter Scheel as chief negotiator. After twelve days in Moscow Scheel initialed a draft treaty on the renunciation of force with Foreign Minister Gromyko, and five days later Brandt followed to Moscow to sign the treaty and take the opportunity of an extended talk with Brezhnev. The Federal Republic had crossed its Rubicon: It had accepted the division of Germany; it had sealed the status quo in Central Europe.

Two days later Brandt wrote Nixon, saying that he had emphasized the crucial importance of solving the Berlin problem to both Kosygin and Brezhnev. The Soviets had been informed officially and repeatedly that the treaty would not come into force unless a satisfactory Berlin settlement was reached. On August 17 Bahr visited Washington again to brief me about Brandt's Moscow sojourn. His main concern was to emphasize Brandt's desire for rapid progress on Berlin. There was a danger, I pointed out to the President, that we were being set up as the fall guy should the intricate set of negotiations collapse. But I thought matters had gone too far for that. We had become the deciding element, though neither Moscow nor the Federal Republic was to understand this fully for five more months.

The Soviets had stalled the Berlin talks until the conclusion of their treaty with the Federal Republic. No doubt they calculated that the West Germans would then bring pressure on us to deliver a Berlin settlement — as they indeed halfheartedly did. But this was a grave miscalculation. Bonn's margin of maneuver was limited; it had exhausted its store of concessions; it was in no position to press us for more. To much of German public opinion the treaty with the Soviet Union seemed inequitable; Bonn forswore its national claims in return for an improvement of the atmosphere and easing of inter-German contacts, which should never have been interrupted to begin with. The treaty's fate in Parliament now depended on unambiguous Soviet concessions over Berlin. The linkage between the treaty and Berlin was clearly working against, not for, Moscow. To be sure, negotiations on Berlin would be complicated. The Western allies were seeking a Soviet, rather than East German, guarantee for free access across East German territory. This was bound to be resisted by East Germany. But the Soviets had another strong incentive to overcome East German hesitations: A European Security Conference could never take place without our agreement. We left no doubt that we would not even consider it before the Berlin talks were concluded. Thus we had harnessed the beast of détente, making both a European Security Conference and ratification of Brandt's Eastern treaties dependent upon a Berlin agreement that met our objectives.

We had to rein in our allies in the meantime. Brandt wanted the Alliance to agree on criteria for mutual and balanced force reductions (MBFR) in Europe, in order to prepare for negotiations and also to prevent unilateral American troop withdrawals. Britain urged the immediate creation of a Standing Commission for East-West relations. We deflected the German initiative by supporting a Canadian set of general MBFR principles of inspired vagueness. And we opposed the British proposal altogether. We wanted no institutions that would add their momentum to the already excessive pressures for a relaxation of tensions based on atmospherics.

Time was on our side; we were in a strong position, provided we kept our cool. This did not become apparent immediately to the Soviets, who still considered the agreement with the Federal Republic a major step in selective détente and continued to try to use it to weaken allied cohesion by a series of crises aimed at the United States. It took some months of firmness to bring home to the Kremlin the realities with which it would have to deal.

SALT and the Defense Debate

THERE was one negotiation with Moscow, however, that was developing a life of its own, the SALT negotiations, which alternated between Helsinki and Vienna. The first phase of these talks, held in Helsinki, had been exploratory; they were to be resumed in Vienna by the middle of April 1970. The principal Soviet concern had been to limit ABMs — a dramatic change from Kosygin's comment to President Johnson at Glassboro that the idea of limiting missile defenses was one of the most absurd he had ever heard. One might plausibly draw the conclusion that what changed Soviet perceptions was our decision to develop an ABM system of our own. Regrettably, this insight was not widespread. In fact, the bitter debate of 1969 over ABM was substantially repeated in 1970, this time over the size of the already approved program. The issue was whether to confine our ABM to the so-called Phase I, the two sites protecting Minuteman ICBM fields, which had been narrowly approved by the previous Congress; or whether to proceed with Phase II, building toward our announced objective of defending our population against accidental launches and attacks by third countries.

At an NSC meeting on January 23, 1970, I summed up the conflicting points of view. It was the perennial debate whether Soviet interest in compromise was best elicited by making unilateral American gestures or by presenting the Kremlin with risks and programs they were eager to stop. The issue has bedeviled our defense debate from the hydrogen bomb to the B-1 bomber. I know no instance where unilateral American restraint elicited a significant or lasting Soviet response.

The advocates of unilateral gestures urged a moratorium on further American ABM deployments and cited the Soviet interest in limiting defensive systems. They felt suspension of our program would signal our seriousness of purpose; Congressional critics of ABM would be mollified in the bargain. The moratorium could always be lifted if the Soviets dragged out the negotiations. This view was held by the State Department and the Arms Control and Disarmament Agency (ACDA). Those who wished to proceed with Phase II, however, including myself, argued that suspension of our ABM program would doom the prospects for agreement. The Soviets' attitudes toward missile defense had been reversed by the start of our program; they would have no incentive to negotiate seriously once we had ceased construction, all the less so since our Congressional opposition, having stopped Phase II, would surely seek to eliminate ABM altogether. The Soviets could achieve their objective of killing our ABM simply by dragging out the negotiations. It seemed to me improbable that our moratorium would be lifted, however much the Soviets stalled. Moratoria are always sold by fierce promises that the assumptions on which they are based will be vigilantly enforced; they almost never end unless there is a provocation so blatant that it simply cannot be ignored.

The NSC meeting of January 23 was unable to come to a decision; the issue had gone beyond SALT or ABM to the national debate over the nature of our country's security.

The dominant slogan of all attacks on our defense program was the need to "reorder national priorities" — a euphemism for cutting the defense budget. It was the counterpart of the Vietnam debate in the field of strategy. The plethora of amendments to restrict the use of funds for Vietnam was soon extended to specific weapons systems. Senator George McGovern proposed cutting off the B-1 bomber; Senators William Proxmire and Richard Schweiker urged postponing the C-5A transport plane until the end of an investigation of financially ailing Lockheed; Senator Birch Bayh wanted to limit the total size of our armed forces. Senator Edward Brooke was engaged in his annual campaign against ABM and MIRV. There were no resolutions or speeches indicating that the defense budget might be inadequate. The believers in strong defense were clearly fighting a rearguard action.

As with Vietnam, we were caught in a vicious circle. To preserve any support for national defense Nixon thought that he had to appear responsive to the pressures for trimming the defense budget and reducing the percentage of the Gross National Product devoted to military purposes. All senior members of the Administration except Laird and me agreed in this. They feared that otherwise the Congress would implement the drastic cuts proposed by antimilitary zealots in the Congress, the media, and academia. I had serious misgivings. I feared the long-term diplomatic impact of the persistent reduction of our forces at the very time that we were losing our relative strategic superiority, while we were visibly retrenching in Southeast Asia, and while the Soviet military expenditures were increasing steadily.

Nixon's defense budget, announced on February 2, 1970, called for a reduction of more than $5 billion under the previous year. (The figure, of course, does not tell the whole story, because even the previous year's budget had been inadequate, thanks to the same pressures operating in 1969.) The defense budget represented about 7 percent of the Gross National Product as compared with 8.7 percent the previous year, and 34.6 percent of the national budget as compared with 37.7 percent in 1969. (Indeed, the proposed defense budget in real terms was only 7 percent above the last peacetime budget of 1964, even though the war in Vietnam continued.) Within these constraints Mel Laird performed a miracle of management and planning by increasing, if only slightly, *all* strategic programs: the B-1 bomber, the Trident submarine and missile, the Minuteman III ICBM, and the "Safeguard" ABM.

But the effect of the reduction was nevertheless insidious. It prevented us from developing a coherent response to the growing imbalance in conventional forces. It froze our strategic planning into adaptations of the familiar. It caused the Pentagon to slight the ABM program, which cost us so heavily domestically and was at the heart of our SALT strategy, because the funds for it were bound to affect other priorities. We were thus negotiating disarmament on three fronts: at Vienna and Helsinki with the Soviets; at home *within* our government, and with the Congress. And even the sharply reduced defense budget was assaulted in the Congress. Senate Majority Leader Mike Mansfield objected to Phase II of the ABM program even before it was officially submitted. On January 31, forecasting a new Senate debate, he said: "Where the hell is it going to end? What is going to happen to people? . . . Where is the money coming from?" Senator J. William Fulbright called Phase II of ABM "a great mistake." When the new budget was announced on February 2, the criticism started in earnest. Senator Mansfield indicated that the new budget, while lower than that of the previous year, was still far too high. He warned that it contained "seed money" for many new projects. He was right, although after having voluntarily stopped our missile buildup in the Sixties, seed money was the least the new Administration could ask for in the face of the relentless growth of Soviet strategic forces.

In May a bipartisan group of Senators, including George McGovern, Philip Hart, William Fulbright, Walter Mondale, Clifford Case, and Mark Hatfield, announced plans to put forward an alternative budget demanding more severe cuts. On June 15 another group of liberal Senators and Congressmen recommended an additional reduction of $4.5 billion, specifically cutting money for the MIRV program, for Phase II of the "Safeguard" ABM, and for procurement of the Navy's F-14 fighter. A Brookings Institution report, prepared by high officials of the previous Administration, outlined a "low option" defense budget of $59 billion — $14 billion less than the President's.[1] The *Washington Post* of August 17, 1970, concisely summed up the situation:

> What was at one time an almost routine bit of legislation — passage of the annual military spending bill — has now been turned into a lengthy and frequently bitter battle over a score of military programs and policies. . . . [The long ABM debate] has obscured what is in fact the most widespread assault on all kinds of military activities ever made on Capitol Hill.

This call for defense retrenchment was all the more remarkable in light of the accelerating buildup of Soviet strategic and conventional forces. The Soviet Union had 250 operational ICBMs in mid-1966; 570 in mid-1967; 900 in September 1968; and overtook us with 1,060 in September 1969. By the end of 1970 they were expected to have close to 1,300 ICBMs. (They turned out to have 1,440.) No one knew what the upper limit might be; intelligence estimates over the previous five years had been consistently too low. Soviet submarine-launched missiles were expected to increase from 45 in September 1968 to over 900 by 1975. At the same time the expansion and modernization of Soviet conventional forces in both Europe and the Far East were proceeding rapidly.

Congress and the media dismissed these facts as typical Pentagon scare tactics to maintain an inflated defense budget. Even staunch advocates of a strong defense began to waver. Senator Henry Jackson, a key supporter of ABM who was up for reelection, opposed locating any ABM sites in his home state of Washington. Senator John Pastore, influential Chairman of the Joint Atomic Energy Committee, opposed any extension of ABM beyond the two sites already approved by the Congress: "People in my state wonder why more money for education is inflationary while more money for Safeguard is not." [2] Representative Mendel Rivers, the powerful Chairman of the House Armed Services Committee, favored cutting ABM to strengthen the Navy — showing how budgetary pressures were shaping Pentagon priorities. Even Speaker of the House Carl Albert, a long-time defense supporter, complained that domestic programs, especially for the environment, were being slighted to benefit defense, a criticism echoed by such key House members as Chet Holifield and Charles Vanik.

This was the atmosphere in which the Administration had to develop not only a viable defense program but also a coherent SALT strategy. Latter-day critics of SALT forget how difficult it was to maintain even embryonic strategic programs in the early 1970s and how some of them were even joining the attack. [3] The Administration had to marshal all its strength to keep the Congress from imposing unilaterally what we were seeking to negotiate reciprocally with the Soviets. We faced constant assaults on our overseas troop deployments, including the yearly struggle over attempts to reduce our forces in Europe. When we negotiated its mutual limitation in 1972, ABM was on the verge of being eliminated by the Congress or shrunk to a meaningless prototype. MIRV was attacked until the first SALT agreement, permitting modernization, put an end to the debate. If it wanted to maintain an adequate defense program, the Administration was increasingly pushed into the "bargaining chip" rationale for individual weapons programs — that is, arguing that it was building them not to fulfill strategic purposes but in order to give them up in arms control negotiations. This may have helped save minimum programs but was not likely to produce a profound strategic doctrine.

The domestic debate over ABM illustrated our dilemma. On one level it was highly technical, beyond the ken of most laymen. At the same time it involved serious issues of strategic doctrine and went to the heart of our arms control negotiations with the Soviet Union. Each of the conflicting approaches had its own spokesmen in the bureaucracy and in the Congress. Which of them prevailed depended on many factors, including the accidental one of whether the issue was posed as a defense problem or as a negotiating counter for SALT. This explains in part why the Administration wound up taking two incompatible positions on ABM. What was put forward in the defense budget, where the Pentagon predominated, was quite inconsistent with the position we put forward in SALT, which came out of a complex interagency process including State, Defense, the Joint Chiefs, ACDA, and the NSC staff. And the cacophony of public controversy gradually overwhelmed systematic consideration in any case.

The rationale for ABM put forward by two administrations was that it would provide protection for our population against attacks by third countries and some insurance against accidents; the defense of our Minuteman ICBMs had been a subsidiary objective. Yet our actual program was tending more and more in the latter direction. On February 7, I explained our dilemma to the President. If ABM were to fulfill its proclaimed purpose, we would have to begin Phase II, the defense of our population at least against attacks from third countries or accidental launches. The most logical next step would be to proceed with one more missile field (Whiteman Air Force Base in Missouri) and one site suitable for population defense in the Pacific Northwest. (Whiteman, being near St. Louis, had the additional advantage of providing some population defense as well.) However, the northwest site was ruled out by the campaigning Senator Jackson. The next best alternative was Whiteman plus a site that would protect Washington, D.C. (In the technical jargon this was the National Command Authority, or NCA.) But the already passionate opposition would become even shriller if we sought to protect "politicians and generals," not to mention the difficulty of finding the requisite real estate within fifteen miles of Washington. For all these reasons, Laird recommended Whiteman only. I had severe doubts about the logic of implementing a program presented a year earlier as population defense against third countries, by protecting missile sites from the Soviet Union.

Nixon, convinced that nothing else would pass the Congress and preferring an illogical ABM development to none at all, opted for Laird's recommendation of Whiteman. Thus within one year public and Congressional pressures had altered the character and objective of our ABM program by 180 degrees.

As almost always happens, retreat by the Administration spurred, rather than stilled, critics. Those within the government who had opposed the whole concept of ABM were encouraged to have another go. The Arms Control and Disarmament Agency had always been lukewarm at best in its support of ABM. (This, indeed, had caused Nixon to send me a note in April that Gerard Smith had better support ABM or resign as Director of ACDA. I transmitted the thought to Smith in somewhat attenuated form because, whatever his own opinions may have been, he had throughout loyally and honorably supported Administration policy. He could not always control the private expressions of passionate subordinates, however.) On March 10 even the President's General Advisory Committee on Arms Control and Disarmament, chaired by the stalwart

John McCloy, reflected the prevailing mood and recommended a complete ban on ABMs as well as suspension of MIRV testing. A week later, on March 18, during the first NSC Verification Panel meeting to examine the issues, Gerry Smith argued that the SALT delegation should be instructed to seek a total mutual ban on ABMs.

As the weeks went by, Smith, Rogers, Elliot Richardson, and Paul Nitze of the SALT delegation urged that in SALT we put forward an ABM system limited to Washington — primarily on the ground that this would make our program symmetrical with the Soviet ABM deployment around Moscow. Thus the bureaucratic and diplomatic requirements of SALT clashed with our defense program. Senior officials who had endorsed and indeed recommended three sites in the center of the country as part of our defense budget were suddenly, for purposes of SALT, urging a radically different deployment centering on Washington, which had never been put before the Congress. If the Soviets accepted our position we would have to tear down what we were building and start again from scratch.

All of this cried out for some coherence. In response to my request to that effect, a mind-boggling collection of nine different variations of ABM limitations was proudly put forward by an interagency committee of experts. In the Verification Panel meeting that I chaired on March 25, I complained that the process was becoming chaotic. For the President to make a decision we had to offer him some general concepts related to our national strategy, rather than make him arbitrate excruciatingly technical controversies.

The full National Security Council met on March 25. As I had feared, the discussion became a series of unrelated ventures by the principals into issues of high science. How did we limit the two sides' radar networks? And how did we guarantee that surface-to-air missiles (SAMs) against aircraft would not be covertly upgraded into antimissile ABMs?* Laird, Packard and General Wheeler, while lukewarm about ABM, were passionately in favor of MIRV. They demanded on-site inspection as the price for MIRV limitation though they were less clear about what was to be inspected and by whom. Rogers and Smith maintained their now well-established positions pressing for a ban on ABMs and a suspension of MIRVs. Since the issues were debated in the abstract and not reduced to discrete negotiating choices, a Presidential decision was not possible.

Someone leaked the Pentagon position to Chalmers Roberts of the *Washington Post* on March 27, to stir up a public reaction. Sure enough, within two weeks, proponents of the State Department and

---

*The jargon phrase for this problem was "SAM Upgrade," which one wag suggested was the name of a new analyst on my staff.

ACDA point of view had brought about a sense-of-the-Senate resolution on April 9, which by the overwhelming margin of 72–6 urged the President to propose that both sides "immediately suspend deployment of all offensive and defensive nuclear strategic weapons." The resolution was initiated by Ed Brooke and John Sherman Cooper — two Republicans; Henry Jackson supported it. Senator Edmund Muskie advocated an "interim strategic standstill," including an end to flight testing of MIRV. It would be a "negotiator's pause," for without it "all chances of banning MIRVs and ABMs are lost," he said. Even Senate Republican Leader Hugh Scott called the resolution "a useful and unrestrictive guideline" for the President.

On the eve of the opening of the next round of SALT talks in Vienna, scheduled for April 16, there was no consensus; there was a babble of discordant voices. Since the President had left the ordering of options on SALT to me (without telling the other principals), I decided that it was essential, first, to combine the various opinions into distinct packages so that the President could make a decision on general objectives rather than on abstruse technical problems. On March 27 I issued a directive asking the agencies to reduce the chaos to four options for Presidential decision.

Four options of increasing comprehensiveness — imaginatively labeled A, B, C, and D — were presented at the NSC meeting of April 8, 1970:

- Option A limited ICBMs and SLBMs to the US total of 1,710, and froze the numbers of bombers (527 for the US and 195 for the Soviets). It permitted a "Safeguard"-level ABM (twelve sites). In other words, it required a reduction of the Soviet missile force while leaving our bomber force and ABM program untouched. The agencies had no difficulty agreeing on this option; they left it to Gerry Smith to convince the Soviet Union.
- Option B offered the same offensive limitations as Option A. But ABM under this option was limited to National Command Authorities (NCA, that is, Washington and Moscow) or else banned altogether.
- Option C included the same offensive limitations as Options A and B. Like Option B it limited ABM to NCA or zero. But it added a ban on MIRVs (not covered in the first two options), provided the Soviets agreed to on-site inspection.
- Option D was somewhat different. It proposed major reductions going down from our existing total of 1,710 ICBMs and SLBMs by 100 per year until both sides reached a level of 1,000 by 1978. ABM was banned or limited to NCA; there was no ban on MIRVs.

These options illustrated the quandary in which the Executive Branch found itself. The agencies could agree on only two positions with respect to ABM: either the existing "Safeguard" program (which we already knew even pro-ABM Senators were no longer supporting) or a defense of Washington, D.C., which was contrary to what the President had already recommended to the Congress. Moreover, all Congressional experts agreed that Congress would never approve an ABM around Washington. And yet this doomed program was the only program on which *all* agencies could unite for SALT.

In retrospect I find it hard to explain how this option could ever be considered, much less adopted. The consensus demonstrates the extent to which parochial bureaucratic considerations can overwhelm substance. The Pentagon feared a complete ban on ABMs and therefore supported NCA because this would at least keep ABM technology alive and provide a base for future expansion. State and ACDA preferred no ABM at all, but they accepted NCA because it was symmetrical with the program of the Soviet Union and therefore "negotiable." Even more, they favored NCA because it would almost surely lead to their preferred option of a complete ABM ban on our side since Congress would kill it. I, in turn, acquiesced despite my better judgment for the not very elevated reason that over an issue so technical I knew the President would be reluctant to do battle with the agencies responsible for implementing it.

Nevertheless the proposal for NCA was a first-class blunder; it made no substantive sense whatever. We were proposing to the Soviets a program we knew the Congress would not approve and to the Congress a program contrary to what we were offering to the Soviets. Luckily no permanent damage resulted. Thanks to Soviet greediness, we managed to slide off our error before we were committed to a hopeless quandary.

The discussions of SALT at the NSC meeting of April 8 had all the elusiveness of a Kabuki play. Each department invoked complicated technical arguments in which the same facts were used to produce radically different conclusions. Each of the principals put forward two positions — one he believed in, and a tougher one as an opener that he calculated the Soviet Union would reject. Thus he could prove he was a "tough bargainer" and at the same time have his preferred proposal as the fallback. All of this feinting and posturing was performed before a President bored to distraction. His glazed expression showed that he considered most of the arguments esoteric rubbish; he was trying to calculate the political impact and salability of the various options, of which only the broad outlines interested him.

Gerry Smith argued for Option C — low ABMs and a MIRV ban — but he was willing to accept the reduction option, D. Dave Packard and Admiral Moorer, representing Defense and the Joint Chiefs respectively, preferred the smallest limitation (Option A, limiting offensive weapons but permitting "Safeguard") as a "good starting" point; as a fallback Packard surprisingly favored the reductions scheme of Option D (which would save Defense the yearly appropriations hassle). Paul Nitze argued that even with numbers frozen the Soviets would in time enjoy a superiority because of their edge in missile throwweight. He favored Option D, the deep reductions. He opposed a MIRV ban on the ground that it would enable the Soviets to catch up in one of the few areas where we were ahead. John McCloy commented that Nitze's approach was "crazy" but did not explain how he had reached this unfriendly conclusion. Rogers favored the reduction option but was willing to go along with Option A.

The happy task of distilling some recommendations out of this confusion fell on me. I regret to admit that in doing so I was swayed by bureaucratic and political considerations more than in any other set of decisions in my period in office. Basically, the security adviser ought not to play this game; he should submit to the President his own best judgment of the merits and leave political and bureaucratic considerations to the President. But in the case of SALT, I knew that my recommendation would carry an unusual weight. Nixon simply would not learn the technical details well enough to choose meaningfully. While I was quite prepared to overrule the departments on issues that the President followed closely, where I was in effect on my own I felt honor bound to exercise my mandate only within the broad limits set by the government consensus.

I considered Option B — a freeze on offensive weapons and an agreed level of ABM — the most realistic and most consistent with our interests. (I favored substituting the existing sites for NCA. This was in fact what eventually emerged, although it was at first recommended by no agency.) This would give us the greatest flexibility for modernization. It would arrest the Soviet offensive buildup, which was our most urgent concern. It would provide a ceiling from which later reductions could be negotiated. We would freeze our ABM — which Congress was in the process of killing — in exchange for a Soviet freeze on offensive weapons that they were still building.

But had Option B been put forward as our preferred position, all hell would have broken loose both in the Congress and in the bureaucracy. It would have been claimed that we had never even "explored" a ban on ABM and MIRV. It would have had a tepid reception in the Pentagon, which, while not eager to build "Safeguard," was not prepared to embody its convictions in an offer to limit it. The Defense Department preferred Option A, which constrained those offensive weapons that the Soviets were building but left weapons on which we were ahead (as well as defensive ones) unrestricted. Though Option A was a nonstarter, the failure to achieve it could always be blamed on the lack of vigilance of our negotiators. In any event, the domestic obstacles to Option A were even more serious than those to Option B.

As for the two more "comprehensive" options, I was convinced that the Soviets would never agree to a ban on MIRV technology before they had even tested their MIRVs, nor would they accept on-site inspection. And I did not believe that the Soviet Union would go along with the major reduction of offensive missiles called for in Option D; they were bound to consider this as aimed at reversing their buildup in midcourse while leaving our bomber force unconstrained. On the other hand, either of these options was compatible with our security and in many ways an improvement over what an arms race would produce.

My solution was to recommend to the President that we take Options C and D as our opening positions. This would respond to Congressional and bureaucratic supporters of MIRV and ABM bans; it would give us the positive public posture of having favored comprehensive limitations. If the Soviets accepted the proposals, we would have made a major step forward. If the Soviets rejected them, as I firmly expected, we could then put forward Option B from a much stronger domestic and bureaucratic position. If the Soviets surprised us by accepting our offer, the result would be compatible with our security. The President agreed. On April 10 I issued instructions accordingly.

During this time I had kept in loose touch with Dobrynin. On February 18 he had asked what position we intended to take on ABM and whether we preferred a limited or a comprehensive agreement. We arranged to meet again on March 10. I brought along Larry Lynn, my staff expert on systems analysis, to explain our general thinking on ABM. Dobrynin, however, put only a few perfunctory questions and then asked to see me alone. In a tone suggesting that I was being made privy to some important news, he indicated that the Kremlin was prepared for either a comprehensive or a limited agreement; a comprehensive approach might be better because it could lead to a solution of other political problems as well. It was all very titillating but without operational significance, for Dobrynin still did not define what the Soviets understood by either "comprehensive" or "limited." I replied that our main requirement now was to be concrete.

Dobrynin's skill at putting his American interlocutor on the defensive was infinite. On April 7 he complained that both sides were approaching the resumption of SALT talks with only the most minimal knowledge of each other's positions; he could recall no negotiation in which the two sides had been so ignorant of one another's purposes. There was some merit to his point. But he seemed to hold us wholly responsible for this state of affairs; he was not even slightly embarrassed by the idea that nothing prevented the Soviet Union from contributing to the general enlightenment. Throughout the SALT negotiations, without any exception that I can remember, the Soviet proposals either were totally self-serving and predictably unacceptable or else were reactions to our own.

On April 9 (thinking of Options C and D) I told Dobrynin, with the President's approval, that we would present several comprehensive proposals at Vienna. If, however, the Soviets decided they were interested in a more limited agreement in the interim, we were prepared to explore it as well. Dobrynin promised a reply after he returned from Moscow, where he was going again for consultation.

As it turned out the reply came not from him but in the course of the Vienna talks themselves, which reconvened on April 16. And what the Soviets had in mind, as we shall see, was neither a comprehensive nor a limited strategic arms agreement but a political alliance against China.

The Vienna negotiations fell into the pattern which I had anticipated. The United States delegation expectantly presented first Option C and then Option D. The offensive limitations in both schemes were quickly rejected by the Soviet negotiators. On the other hand, the Soviets accepted our proposal that ABMs be limited to national capitals with amazing and totally unprecedented speed — within a few days. The Soviets knew a good thing when they saw it. They did not mind keeping what they had while nailing us to what Congress would never approve.

But they were plagued by their temptation to overplay their hand. Instead of pulling the teeth of the American strategic program that concerned them most — the ABM — by putting forward a reasonable proposal on offensive limitations, the Soviets suggested a scheme so egregiously one-sided that even the most rabid proponents of limitations could not accept it. The Soviet position called for a ceiling on the aggregate number of ICBMs, SLBMs, and heavy bombers. They offered no numbers, but they insisted on counting all systems capable of reaching the USSR by virtue of their geographical deployment — in other words, all our bombers in Europe and on our aircraft carriers. MIRV deployment and production would be banned, but not flight testing. This, of course, was a neat device by which the Soviets would continue their own development and flight testing of MIRVs while freezing our deployments until they could catch up. And there was no reliable way to monitor a ban on production.

The Soviets proved flexible only with respect to the interests of their allies. The general fear of the SALT delegation that the Cambodian incursion would harm the negotiation proved groundless. Kosygin merely made an elliptical complaint in a news conference; the Soviet delegation in Vienna ignored Cambodia and did business as usual. And that meant endless esoteric debate, for it was becoming clear that the SALT talks had bogged down.

Our officials were growing restless, some because they wanted fresh instructions to break the deadlock, others because they feared them. Gerry Smith, leading our delegation in Vienna and in constant communication with Washington, was engaged with me in internal negotiations that were complex because we understood each other very well indeed. He wanted a freer rein and I was determined to prevent it. On May 20 Smith informed me that the delegation had exhausted its instructions and would need "search warrants" beyond the "holy writ" of the instructions. I was not prepared to agree to such a blank check. I had become aware of the tendency of some of the more passionate members of the delegation to put pet schemes of their own to the Soviets. When one's Russian counterpart did not respond, either out of bafflement or because he was without instructions, the delegation member would report eagerly to Washington that the Russian "did not disagree" or "showed great interest," implying that his own preference was clearly the preference also of the Russians. To curb such freewheeling I requested a specific proposal from Smith, as well as the views of the other agencies.

The result was that all the agencies, as I expected they would, were beginning to converge on Option B (the missile freeze and NCA level of ABMs), which they had ignored four weeks earlier. All agreed that we should accept an offensive ceiling of about 2,000 delivery vehicles, with MIRVs permitted. The Defense experts were committed to MIRV in order to counter the growing Soviet nuclear numerical superiority in launchers and to penetrate Soviet ABM defenses. (In any event, everyone agreed that the Soviet proposal banning MIRV production but permitting MIRV testing was totally unacceptable.) State and ACDA urged a total ban on ABM, while Defense wanted to stay with NCA (even though in practice this would have killed ABM). The most interesting single submission was from the Department of Defense. Deputy Secretary Dave Packard insisted that an early freeze on offensive weapons was imperative because the squeeze on our defense budget would make it nearly impossible to maintain existing strategic forces, much less to increase them.[4] He urged rapid conclusion of a SALT treaty on the basis of existing numbers.

In other words, Congressional and other pressures were threatening to deprive us of any bargaining leverage; we were being asked to stop the Soviet buildup by the threat of reducing our own forces. These circumstances were forgotten after we had achieved an agreement in 1972 and criticism became riskless. Then the numerical limits, which were almost exactly those put forward by the various departments in 1970 and urgently requested by the Pentagon, suddenly became controversial. Stopping the Soviet buildup in return for maintaining our existing program — which we had barely been able to do in the face of Congressional and media assaults — was represented by some as a "unilateral concession" by the United States.

What we were up against was shown by a vote of the Senate Armed Services Committee on ABM. It approved the two sites already authorized, but only two others for Minuteman defense. ABM as an area defense system was finished; indeed, there was a grave danger that the Senate would cut out the two sites when the authorization bill reached the Senate floor. We had now a program in search of a rationale, and a SALT position requiring us to dismantle what we had built and to build something we had not asked for.

Meanwhile in Vienna Smith was pressing for a new option, while Soviet negotiator Vladimir Semenov was suggesting a recess. I approached Dobrynin to determine Soviet intentions. Even more importantly, Nixon opened his three-year-long contest with Smith over who should get the credit for SALT by asking me to convey to Dobrynin that a SALT settlement should come at a summit and not in Vienna.

I met with Dobrynin in the Map Room of the White House on the evening of June 23. Semenov's suggestion of an early recess, I said, could be given three interpretations. First, the Soviet Union did not want an agreement on SALT this year at all; second, the Soviet Union wanted an agreement at Vienna and was using this device to elicit a different American proposal; or third, the Soviet Union wanted an agreement but not at Vienna and was stalemating the talks there to permit the top leaders to settle the issue. I would appreciate Dobrynin's guidance. Dobrynin replied that the first interpretation was clearly out of the question. The Soviet Union did want an agreement on SALT, even though our two positions were not yet close enough to predict a definite date. As for Vienna, it was the Soviet Union's judgment that an agreement including offensive and defensive weapons could not be negotiated in the time available. He was without instructions about a summit and he would have to inquire in Moscow. He made it clear, however, that Moscow preferred an agreement confined to limiting ABMs. At last we knew how the Soviets defined a limited agreement.

I left with the President for San Clemente on the morning of June 25. After our departure, Dobrynin replied with an aide-mémoire in effect proposing two immediate agreements: one on limiting ABM systems to Moscow and Washington, and a second on the problem of "reducing the danger of missile-nuclear war between the USSR and the US resulting from accidental or unsanctioned use of nuclear weapons." In other words, the Soviets wanted to stop the only strategic program we were actually building while they rejected all limitations on *offensive* missiles, which were our own principal concern. The Soviet delegation, Dobrynin said, had the necessary instructions to proceed in this fashion.

As for the "accidental war" agreement, it had the makings of a first-class booby trap. If it sought to safeguard the superpowers against a technical malfunction of their own weapons, it could be dealt with by establishing rapid communication links and agreed procedures for reacting. But if the "unsanctioned" use referred to the weapons of other nuclear powers, we faced a major political problem. We would be cooperating with the Soviet Union against two allies, the United Kingdom and France — and against the People's Republic of China, with which even then we were trying to establish contact. That this was what the Soviets had in mind became apparent when on June 30, out of the blue, Semenov at Vienna started expostulating on the dangers of accidental or unauthorized missile launches. And on July 2, Semenov said privately to one of our delegation that "what we need to do is jointly take a stand that the two governments intend to act together to prevent the outbreak of war by accidental, unauthorized or provocative action from any quarter. We need to let them [other countries] know that we would act together to deal with any attempted provocations." This was a violation of the rules of our Channel, which was supposed to be limited to explorations on the Nixon-Brezhnev level — perhaps explicable by the Soviets' difficulty in fathoming an Executive Branch that practiced the separation of powers within itself.

At any rate on July 4 I sent Dobrynin's proposal to Gerry Smith for his comment. Smith replied on July 5 that it seemed "too limited to be in the US interest. Any constraint on US ABM should be matched by constraints on USSR offensive weapons system. Desirability of positive Vienna outcome should not lead us to premature commitment of strongest bargaining counter."

I agreed with Smith, with one proviso. The proposal for an ABM agreement alone I agreed was much too limited; but the offer was much too sweeping in terms of the intended anti-China collusion reflected in the accidental-war ploy. I concluded that we had best return SALT rapidly to its subject matter: the control of strategic nuclear weapons. With Nixon's approval I informed Smith that we would insist on linking offensive and defensive limitations — because limiting Soviet offensive weapons was our main objective in SALT, and because we would not stop without reciprocity the only new weapons system we were in fact procuring. And we would not shatter our hopeful China policy and imply a US–Soviet condominium by making agreements directed against third countries. The best counter would be a proposal more realistic than Options C and D on which we could then take a stand for the long term.

I therefore submitted to the President a long memorandum suggesting a new proposal along the lines of Option B. However, I thought it essential to get off the NCA proposal, which, as far as we were concerned, amounted to an ABM ban. My preferred position was to maintain the deployment both sides were actually building. But an ABM ban was better than NCA because it would at least do away with the Soviet ABM, which I judged was the principal beneficiary of the NCA scheme.

Moreover, offering an ABM ban had the same practical bureaucratic consequence as putting forward Option C earlier in the year. It was certain to be rejected, especially when linked to an offensive freeze, and would enable us to move from there to insisting that the existing sites be continued. I therefore recommended that the President authorize our delegation to propose an ABM ban as an alternative to NCA (without as yet withdrawing the latter). The President approved my recommendation and a directive to that effect was issued on July 9. This proposal, subject to further refinement, was spelled out by the delegation for the remainder of the Vienna session, until adjournment on August 14.

This position was a major improvement; it introduced some of the elements that became the SALT agreements of 1972. It allowed us to proceed with a crucial technological development (MIRV), wherein lay our counterweight to the growing Soviet numbers (and which we knew the Soviets were proceeding to increase); it stopped no offensive program we were contemplating building. It committed us to a firm link between offensive and defensive limitations; we would not limit our ABM — Congress willing — except in exchange for an end to the Soviet offensive buildup. It made clear our refusal to allow SALT to limit our forward-based aircraft that defended Western Europe and Asia. And proposing a ban on ABM was the first step toward getting off the uncomfortable NCA position.

The Soviets — as so often — proved too greedy. They thought they could improve the terms still more by waiting out our domestic pressures for unilateral cutbacks. They wanted to stop our ABM program; they were as yet unwilling to face an offensive freeze, perhaps because their own buildup had not proceeded far enough. Nevertheless, in a meeting with the McCloy Advisory Committee in late July 1970, I predicted a SALT agreement along the lines of our proposal within two years. We beat this deadline by two months.

In the meantime, I had become concerned by the tendency of SALT to develop in the minds of many a momentum of its own; I feared — as it turned out, correctly — that SALT might have to bear the whole weight of East-West relations. This caused me on July 13 to send a memorandum to the President warning against treating a SALT agreement as the advent of the millennium. I pointed out that even under conditions of SALT the Soviet Union would be able in time to threaten our land-based missiles through a combination of throwweight, improvement in accuracy, and the development of MIRVs. "The Soviets could be fairly confident that they would never again be in a position of strategic inferiority. Indeed, they would expect to derive considerable political gain from the formal ratification of strategic 'equality.' " The Chinese would undoubtedly fear that a SALT agreement foreshadowed a US–Soviet condominium: "They would foresee a prospect for a general relaxation on the USSR's Western front, and might suspect a tacit deal in which the U.S. granted a free hand to the Soviets to deal with China.'' As for US–Soviet relations, they would continue to be marked by the ambiguous combination of threat and promise inherent in ideological conflict played out against the backdrop of awful weapons of mass destruction:

> None of the post war arms control agreements with the USSR have proved the turning point that their advocates hoped for. Yet a SALT agreement, even if limited, would probably have a much more deep-seated effect.
>
> The Soviets are currently drafting the next five year plan, and preparing for the 24th Party Congress. In addition, there is considerable evidence that the top leadership will probably be reshaped. An agreement in these circumstances could not help but influence the general course of Soviet policies. . . .
>
> At the same time — and we should be quite clear about this — this would not prevent Soviet leaders from moving drastically in Eastern Europe if they felt that the effects of "detente" undermined Soviet hegemony there; it would not stop the Soviets from seeking to advance their interests and to damage ours in Western Europe, the Middle East and Mediterranean and elsewhere. Moreover, the Soviet ruling elite would still remain highly sensitive to any contamination of their society through increased exchanges and the lowering of barriers to free movement of peoples and ideas. The Soviets would probably reason that our own stake in preserving the agreement is sufficiently great to oblige us to tolerate such a range of Soviet actions, especially if there were no plausible evidence that the USSR was violating the actual terms of the SALT agreement.

In my view SALT was not a cure-all. I saw in it an opportunity to redress the strategic balance but also to create the conditions for political restraint without which escalating crises were in my view inevitable, whatever happened to SALT. Militarily, SALT would delay the Soviet buildup and thus the ultimate threat to our land-based forces. It could help us preserve the sinews of our defense and to catch up numerically in the face of the stormy dissent produced by Vietnam. SALT could begin the process of mutual restraint without which mankind would sooner or later face Armageddon. It would have to lead to some change in political conduct. SALT, moreover, would have to be embedded in an overall strategy that preserved the coherence of the Western Alliance and left room for an opening to China. SALT was indeed important; but we must not make our entire foreign policy a hostage to it.

It remains only to deal with the final paradox of the SALT process: the Senate vote on ABM. We were in a weird position. The Senate was being asked to proceed with construction of one additional ABM site and preliminary work on five others at the very moment our Vienna delegation was proposing to the Soviets either a total ABM ban or a system limited to Washington for which we had not even requested funds. Indeed, we already had a tentative Soviet agreement on ABM defense of capitals. This confusion was emphatically not the proudest hour of the Nixon Administration.

The contradiction between the SALT position and the budget request became increasingly awkward as the SALT position began to leak out. On July 23, therefore, I met with ten key Senators and Congressmen to persuade them to stay with the Administration plan on ABM in order to strengthen our hand in SALT. The final vote in the Senate took place on August 12, 1970. An amendment offered by Senators John Sherman Cooper and Philip Hart to set aside all further construction was defeated 52–47. The vote was accompanied by a contretemps over a telegram to Senators from Gerard Smith in Vienna, where the talks were about to wind up. Smith had sent a cautious message affirming that "Safeguard" was an important element in his negotiations — which was about as far as he could stretch his convictions in deference to the Administration that he loyally served. According to the *New York Times,* Smith's telegram was decisive in switching the votes of Senators Thomas McIntyre and James Pearson. McIntyre told the press that a highly placed source in Vienna "made it very clear that the success of the negotiations rests almost exclusively on our not remaining 'static' in our ABM posture." Thus Gerry Smith, the passionate advocate of a complete ban on ABM and the butt of Nixon anger in April, saved the day for "Safeguard."

Pursuing a Moscow Summit

SOONER or later every President since Roosevelt has become convinced that he should take a personal hand in East-West relations through face-to-face meetings with the Soviet leaders. It is human to yearn to make a decisive breakthrough toward peace. And no one is more conscious of the cataclysmic possibilities of nuclear technology than the President who bears the burden of the ultimate decision. Presidents are strengthened in this temptation by an American public that finds it difficult to accept the existence of irreconcilable hostility and tends to see international relations in terms of the play of individual personalities. And a President rarely reaches his eminence without an abnormal ego; nor is his entourage likely to disabuse his estimate of himself. Almost by definition he has enormous confidence in his power of persuasion; after all, it got him where he is. Nor are Presidents unmindful of the political benefits of a well-publicized summit, especially in an election year. It is the ultimate "photo opportunity."

Nixon was less given to these tendencies than most. He was too skeptical to believe that one meeting could alter the course of events. He was

too experienced in international politics not to appreciate that decades-
long tensions between great powers are not the result of personal
animosities. Furthermore, he did not much like face-to-face negotiating;
it made him restless. And for him there was — as always — a strong
personal element. Having seen Johnson's popularity soar after the
Glassboro meeting with Kosygin and then collapse when the results
proved ephemeral, Nixon, who had been briefly panicked that Glassboro
threatened his own Presidential prospects, drew the conclusion that he
should avoid a similar trap. For all these reasons Nixon entered office
convinced that summits could succeed only if they were well prepared.
His original intention was to use the prospect of a summit only when it
could be a means to extract important Soviet concessions.

And yet in 1970, for one of the few times in his Presidency, Nixon
threw sober calculation to the winds and pressed for a summit. Tormented by antiwar agitators, he thought he could paralyze them by a
dramatic peace move. Meeting the Soviet leaders in the wake of Cambodia might show Hanoi that it could prove expendable in a larger
game; this indeed is what happened in 1972. He foresaw benefits for the
Congressional elections in the fall as well. Thus, as the year proceeded,
Nixon grew increasingly eager for a Moscow summit. What started as a
maneuver reached a point of near obsession until only the eternal Soviet
eagerness to squeeze one-sided gains from a negotiation saved us from
serious difficulties.

As I have said, the summit idea was launched innocuously enough
when Dobrynin on January 20, 1970, made one of his periodic feelers
for it. Following our established policy, I threw cold water on the idea.
But by April Nixon's attitude had changed. He foresaw no major
foreign policy achievements in 1970 and he turned longingly to the notion of a summit.

I maintained grave doubts. Though there were occasional tactical disagreements and strains caused by the interplay of our personalities, this
was to be one of the rare times in our association that I totally disagreed
with Nixon on a major foreign policy question. I believed that the
reasons that had caused us to be aloof toward a summit in 1969 were
even more valid in 1970. The Soviets had given us no help in Vietnam.
SALT was still substantially deadlocked. The Soviets had just introduced combat personnel into the Middle East — the first such Soviet
action in the postwar period. No negotiation with the Soviets had progressed to a point where success was guaranteed. Our China initiative
was still in the balance; it could easily be wrecked by the appearance of
collusion with the Soviets. A summit might thus easily fail; or else, in
order to rescue it, we would be induced to agreements and undertakings
we might later bitterly regret. Finally — though I could not make this
explicit — I did not think that face-to-face negotiation on the many unresolved issues was Nixon's forte.

But Nixon was adamant. Early in April he instructed me to explore the possibilities of a summit in 1970 in the Dobrynin Channel. I disagreed on tactical grounds; but it involved no issue of moral principle. So I plunged ahead, reservations and all. On April 7 Dobrynin invited me to the Soviet Embassy. He had some films about tiger hunting in Siberia that he erroneously believed would fascinate me. During dinner he gave me an opening by saying that every Administration in his experience had always moved too slowly on US–Soviet relations at the beginning of its term and too rapidly at the end, when it no longer made any sense. He cited the example of Lyndon Johnson's efforts to have a summit during his last six months in office. I replied warily that for us a summit was a practical matter; everything depended on its probable outcome. We were not opposed in principle if we had some assurance of concrete results.

Dobrynin was a thoroughgoing professional and grasped immediately what I was saying. Thus far, he and his leaders had operated on the assumption of no summit before 1971–1972, he said. Had they been wrong? I answered cautiously that a summit might be possible if a major breakthrough were imminent on some topic of mutual concern, such as Vietnam or SALT. I was prepared, however, to discuss the general principles now. Dobrynin, though clearly without instructions, decided to test our eagerness. He suggested that the easiest way would be for Premier Kosygin to head the Soviet delegation to the United Nations General Assembly in the fall and to meet with the President in that context. (The summit in 1970 was still perceived by both sides to involve Nixon and Kosygin, not Brezhnev.) I was confident that the President would not wish to repeat Johnson's experience of meeting in a UN context. But I told Dobrynin that I would obtain the President's views.

We met again two days later, after I had consulted the President. I told Dobrynin officially that we preferred that a summit be separate from the UN. Its purpose should be either to bless a completed SALT agreement or to break a deadlock in the SALT negotiations. Dobrynin now had the information he needed. He promised us a reply after he returned from consultations in Moscow. Cambodia did not interrupt this exchange. Dobrynin returned in early June while the Cambodian sanctuaries were still occupied by American forces. Nixon's yearning for a summit had increased in direct proportion to the public buffeting of the previous weeks. What would more discomfit his shrill opponents than emerging unexpectedly as a peacemaker and sitting down with the Soviets while beating up on their allies? He decided to make an all-out effort for a summit before the Congressional elections. Accordingly, I invited Dobrynin to have dinner with me on the Presidential yacht *Sequoia,* and to review the whole range of US–Soviet relations while we cruised on the Potomac.

Before we left, Nixon joined Dobrynin and me briefly in the White House Map Room. He told Dobrynin that he was prepared to let bygones be bygones; the time had come to put US–Soviet relations on a new basis. He was prepared to engage himself personally in this effort. Dobrynin agreed that there was no sense debating about the past. Neatly avoiding the hint about a summit, Dobrynin made a strong plea for US–Soviet cooperation in the Middle East, where the Soviets had just escalated tensions to unprecedented heights by sending advanced anti-aircraft missiles manned by Soviet crews. Obviously Moscow wanted to be paid for the summit in advance; the more eager we appeared the higher would be the price.

The cruise on the *Sequoia* did not change this impression. Dobrynin was keen to discuss in detail all outstanding issues — especially those of concern to the Soviet Union. He raised SALT, the Middle East, and Southeast Asia. But about the summit he was opaque. He claimed that the Kremlin's initial reaction had been favorable but then Cambodia had raised the thought that our proposal was a maneuver to obtain Soviet acquiescence in a tough Indochina policy. I denied this and indicated that our interest continued now that the Cambodian operation was drawing to a close. Dobrynin no more rose to this bait than he had risen to Nixon's. He returned to the question of how to deal with SALT and the Middle East, urging that we pursue them in our Channel. Obviously two could play at linkage.

We met again on June 23. This time the summit was not mentioned directly. Instead, after touching on the Middle East as set forth in the next chapter, I asked about Soviet intentions in SALT. Dobrynin claimed he had no instructions but promised an early reply. The Soviet response, in fact, was quick in coming. It was the June 25 aide-mémoire, which proposed the early conclusion of an agreement to limit ABM, coupled with the scheme to reduce the danger of "accidental war."

Collusion against China was to be the real Soviet price for a summit. It surfaced again in the best spy-novel tradition. Semenov encountered Smith at the Vienna Opera and handed him an unsigned paper outlining the Soviet notion of an accidental-war agreement. If a nuclear "provocation" were being "prepared" by a third country, each country was to inform the other. If a provocative act took place, each party would be obliged to take retaliatory action against the offending country. The two parties were to hold regular consultations on these subjects. We were in effect being asked to give the USSR a free hand against China; it was a blatant embodiment of condominium.

Nixon might have been willing to act against my tactical judgment on a summit. He needed no advice when our fundamental national interests or our overall global strategy was at stake. He and I were at one that the accidental-war proposal had to be rejected and promptly. On July 9 I saw Dobrynin to tell him that Semenov's overture was unacceptable. There were two aspects to the accidental-war problem, I said. One was the possibility of genuine accidents requiring technical safeguards and means of notification. This we were ready to address jointly with the Soviet Union. (Indeed, it eventually led to an agreement signed on September 30, 1971.) Political cooperation implying a major change in international alignments and clearly aimed against third countries was out of the question.

Dobrynin suavely pretended to be ignorant of Semenov's overture, an inconceivable idea. (It had probably, however, come through Semenov precisely to enable the Soviets to disavow it if we reacted unfavorably.) Dobrynin quickly shifted the conversation to an ABM agreement. At this point I reminded him that we had been talking about a meeting at the highest level since April. We had not had a reply; it was time to stop beating around the bush. Dobrynin mumbled something about Cambodia and the difficulties posed by the forthcoming Party Congress in Moscow. He then chose the route of pretending that he had not fully understood our overtures. Could he report to Moscow (1) that the President was proposing a summit meeting; (2) that it should discuss a fundamental reappraisal of US–Soviet relations?

When Dobrynin was instructed to stall he was masterly; he did not even mind pretending that he was a little dense. Of course, his queries had been answered several times in the past three months — most recently by the President himself four weeks earlier. Knowing the President's yearning for a summit I played the game; I solemnly assured Dobrynin that he could report in the sense he had indicated. But his perplexities on this occasion were so endless that one might have wondered how he had risen so high in the diplomatic service of his country. Were we thinking of 1971 or 1972?, he wished to know. No, I replied, we had 1970 in mind. He considered this gravely. Before or after the election?, asked this meticulous Soviet student of our democratic politics. This was one trap I did not yet need to fall into. I would let him know after hearing Moscow's reaction to the general project, I replied.

But no Soviet reaction was forthcoming. Instead, Dobrynin brought an aide-mémoire on July 20 asking for American help in convening a conference on European security. The Soviet leadership clearly had a long shopping list, and they were not about to satisfy Nixon's eagerness without going through the whole list to see how much of it they could get. But here too we had a well-settled strategy; I stonewalled.

Meanwhile, Dobrynin returned to Moscow once again for consultations on the same subjects he had said he had been consulting about in April and May. In early August an American businessman who claimed high Soviet connections reported that the Soviet leaders were expecting to see the President in the fall. I used this pretext on August 13 to inquire of Dobrynin's deputy, Yuli Vorontsov, what was going on. We had come full circle: This was the same ploy that Dobrynin had used in January when he had involved the Japanese Ambassador. And it received the same response. Vorontsov said predictably that he was without instructions but he knew that the subject was under "intense discussion" in Moscow.

On August 19 we received a formal reply. The Soviet leaders had a "positive approach" to the idea of a summit meeting, provided it was carefully prepared. It also invited our ideas for an agenda. They were playing our game of 1969. On August 24, on my behalf, my deputy Al Haig gave Vorontsov an agenda that listed SALT, European security, the Middle East, "principles of coexistence," and trade as possible items, without indicating our position on any of these topics. We invited Soviet counterproposals. None was forthcoming. We did not hear from the Kremlin again about the summit until Dobrynin finally returned to Washington in September, making further positive noises but accompanied by a procedural proposal for preliminary groundwork that would push the summit well into 1971. It was obvious that the Soviets were using the summit as another form of pressure on us in a summer filled with crises.

It was the best thing that could have happened. I shudder at how a summit would have unfolded in 1970. It was our low point domestically. We were still in the stage of laying foundations, of tentative probes. We had not yet achieved the breakthroughs and political surprises that established our grand strategy a year later. We would have been under tremendous pressures to bring back some success, and failing that, we would have been in an even worse position at home. The careful linkage of the German treaty and Berlin negotiations might have been destroyed, and European negotiations with Moscow, instead of being controlled, could have got out of hand. The pressure for an ABM-only agreement might have proved uncontainable; indeed, on July 11 Nixon specifically told me that he would pay this price to get to see the Soviet leaders. I waited for him to turn it into a formal instruction; he never did, partly because the Soviets never supplied the opportunity. But there is little doubt in my mind that in the context of a summit, Congress might well have killed ABM on its own. The Mideast crisis would have accelerated. The China initiative could have been nipped in the bud. Since agreements would not have been hammered out in advance, Nixon would have been under a handicap in being forced into protracted and detailed negotiations, with which he was always uncomfortable.

The Soviet leaders, luckily for us, had thrown away all this in order to score petty points. This is worth keeping in mind for those who perceive every Soviet action as part of a brilliantly calculated master plan. Moscow recognized well enough the obvious tactical advantage for them in Nixon's eagerness for a summit. But they had been so annoyed by Nixon's Romanian visit, his snub of Gromyko in 1969, and our aloof Middle East posture, and they were so tempted to squeeze the maximum concessions out of us, that they missed what could have been a great strategic opportunity. They wanted to be paid in advance for agreeing to the summit and then be paid again at the summit. They tried to obtain a de facto alliance against China, a European Security Conference, and a SALT agreement on their terms — all as an *entrance* price into the summit.

Nixon was not that eager. Nor was he incompetent. He agreed to none of these demands, and the Soviets achieved nothing.

The Soviet leaders acted so insensitively in part because they believed they had isolated us with their European initiatives, in part because they imagined us paralyzed by Vietnam. In the summer of 1970 they probably did not think they needed to deal with us urgently, calculating that the pressures which had made us press for a summit in 1970 would make us even more eager later. Moreover, they were in the process of fomenting tensions in the Middle East and attempting military deployments in the Caribbean that must have seemed to them to promise even greater opportunities the following year. And a summit would have made such actions extremely awkward.

But the first test of statesmanship is the accurate assessment of the bargaining relationship. This test the Soviets did not pass in the summer of 1970. Nixon sought a summit but he did not need it as desperately as Moscow reckoned. The German negotiations were bound finally to put us into the driver's seat in European diplomacy. Our weakest period with respect to SALT was behind us, and here too the Soviets had played into our hands by their inflexibility. The Soviets' rejection of our reasonable options put an end to our domestic debate on MIRV and, to some extent, on ABM. We could stand on our position without unbearable domestic pressure until the final breakthrough. The Middle East was moving in a direction where, with all its ups and downs, the Soviet inability to shape events was becoming more apparent as the months passed. And we had an ace in the hole in our China initiative.

The summer of crises in which these assessments would be severely tested was still before us. But crises temper administrations when they do not break them. They reveal who can be counted on. They establish the balance of strength internationally and within a government. And Nixon, with all his complex methods of government, was at his best when under pressures that cornered him and forced decisions. The summer and autumn of 1970 became such a period. And as so often before, its genesis was in the Middle East.

XIV

Middle East 1970

As 1970 began, the gods of war were inspecting their armaments, for it was clear they would soon be needed. There was daily combat along the Suez Canal. Then in January Israel began "deep penetration" air raids with bombing attacks around Cairo and the Nile Delta, designed to demonstrate Nasser's impotence and force an end to the so-called war of attrition. Israeli Prime Minister Golda Meir was quoted as telling visitors she could not say when peace would be possible so long as Nasser ruled Egypt. On the Jordan front the vicious cycle of fedayeen raid and Israeli reprisal accelerated. Israel and Syria clashed in the Golan. Finally, at the end of January, Nasser suddenly paid a secret visit to Moscow. Thereafter, the problems of the Middle East began increasingly to merge with the relations of the superpowers.

The United States was handicapped at this stage by a serious disagreement within our government on the nature of the problem. The perception of the State Department was that the root of our difficulties was the Arab-Israeli conflict over territory. Once that was resolved, the experts held, the influence of the radical Arabs would dwindle and with it the Soviet role in the Middle East. These views had guided our diplomacy throughout 1969 and had caused us to put forward increasingly specific proposals for comprehensive settlements.

I had grave doubts about these assumptions and the course they seemed to suggest. My assessment, as I explained to the President in a memorandum, was that Arab radicalism had five sources: Israel's conquests of territory; Israel's very existence; social and economic dissatisfactions; opposition to Western interests; and opposition to the Arab moderates. Only the first of these components would be affected by a settlement. The others would remain. Western capitalism would remain anathema to the radicals. Arab moderate regimes would continue to be unacceptable. The causes of social and economic unrest would persist. Israel would still be there for the Arab radicals to seek to erase. And the

Israelis understood this. It was precisely because the issue for them was the existence of Israel, and not its particular frontiers, that they were so reluctant to give up their conquests.

Nor was I convinced that Soviet influence would inevitably be diminished by a resolution of the Arab-Israeli conflict. Much would turn on the manner and detail of the settlement. A comprehensive approach involving all the parties would inherently favor the radicals by giving the most intransigent governments a veto over the entire process. If a settlement then appeared to result from Soviet pressure or blackmail, the radical regimes with their anti-Western and pro-Soviet orientation would be strengthened. Territories would be seen as returning to Soviet clients.

We needed to work not just for any solution but also to demonstrate that progress could be achieved best by our friends; that, in other words, the moderates held the key to peace in the Middle East. I was convinced that we were in a strong position to teach this lesson. "The advantage to us," I advised Nixon in early February, "is that the Arabs will come to realize that it is the U.S. and not the USSR that holds the key to what they want." And at a meeting of the Senior Review Group on February 25 I observed: "At some point it will become apparent that time is not working for the Soviets. If they cannot get Arab territory back, the Arabs may well come to us." Therefore, we should not yield to blackmail; we should not be panicked by radical rhetoric; patience could be our weapon. By the same token, once the breakthrough had occurred and the moderate Arabs had turned to us, we had to move decisively to produce diplomatic progress.

But I was in no position to carry out such a strategy. Nixon had assigned the Middle East to Rogers. The President was reluctant to intervene even when he had second thoughts. Nor was he — at this stage — convinced that my strategy was correct. He still believed that the Soviet Union had been the political victor of the 1967 war. He had not abandoned some vague notion of a trade-off with the Soviet Union between the Middle East and Vietnam. He considered himself less obligated to the Jewish constituency than any of his predecessors had been and was eager to demonstrate that he was impervious to its pressures. He also had his doubts as to whether my Jewish faith might warp my judgment. Normally I would have shaped his strategic options and given tactical guidance to the departments. But I was precluded from doing this in Middle East policy until late in 1971.

Thus, in the Middle East our policy lacked the single-minded sense of direction that Nixon usually demanded and I normally imposed. He let matters drift, confident that with my help he could always take over before matters got out of hand. He permitted a range of discretion to the State Department unthinkable in any other area. But because when all was said and done his convictions were closer to mine than to those of

Rogers, he applied the brakes just often enough to prevent a coherent application of the State Department approach.

In the process we had to learn the painful lesson that events can be dominated only by those with a clear set of goals. A nation gets no awards for confusion masquerading as moderation. For the adversary may mistake goodwill for acquiescence and confuse restraint with weakness. He may be genuinely surprised — indeed, feel tricked — when after much travail we finally and grudgingly turn to the defense of our interests. The result is a crisis.

From the perspective of a decade I do not doubt that our desire to avoid further showdowns in the year of Cambodia and domestic turmoil, and compulsive eagerness for solutions unrelated to the psychological necessities of the Mideast parties, tempted Soviet probes. I believe, too, that it was our ultimate decision to resist these probes that provided the basis for the eventual turn toward negotiations, both in the Middle East and with the Soviet Union generally.

The Kosygin Letter

O N January 31, 1970, Ambassador Dobrynin delivered a letter from Soviet Premier Alexei Kosygin to the President at my basement office in the White House. Normally, this would have made it part of the special Channel. On this occasion, however, we were informed that similar communications were being sent to Prime Minister Wilson and President Pompidou. Since the British and French were certain to consult with us, we thus had no choice but to put it into regular channels on our side. Obviously once the exchange had grown so formal it was bound to become public.

Kosygin's letter warned that Israel had in effect resumed military operations against the Arab states. The Soviet Union was studying to what extent Israel's operations had been coordinated with the diplomatic actions of "certain powers" — a not very subtle hint that our innocent 1969 peace proposals had been a cover for Israeli deep penetration air raids. If Israel's attacks continued, the letter said, "the Soviet Union will be forced to see to it that the Arab states have means at their disposal, with the help of which a due rebuff to the arrogant aggressor could be made." Kosygin called on the Four Powers to "compel" Israel to cease its attacks and to establish a lasting peace beginning with the "speediest withdrawal of Israeli forces from all the occupied Arab territories."

Forwarding this letter to Nixon, I pointed out that this was the first Soviet threat to the new Administration. While Kosygin stopped short of threatening any specific action, "the position that Israel must withdraw before other issues are settled is a return to the Soviet position of 1967, which seems to negate much of the progress made in the US–USSR talks last summer.'' At the same time I saw the Kosygin letter as part of the process through which our stronger position in the Middle East was being demonstrated:

Our policy of holding firm creates the following dilemma for them [the Soviets]: If they *do not* agree to our proposals, they get nothing, the onus for escalation falls on them and their client will lose if the escalation leads to a major clash. If they *do* agree, they would have to deliver their client on our terms. The strategy of our reply that I propose is to come down very hard on the Soviet threat; to relate Israeli observance of the cease-fire to corresponding observance by the other side, including irregular forces; to press the Soviets to spell out their views on what the Arabs would commit themselves to if Israel withdrew.

For once our government was at one on how to respond. Rogers and Sisco agreed that we needed a firm reply. A Presidential response was sent on February 4. It firmly rejected the Soviet allegations. It pointed out that the cease-fire was being violated by *both* sides; it had been Egypt that early in 1969 deliberately initiated the cycle of escalation by beginning the war of attrition. Nixon's reply warned that the Soviet threat to expand arms shipments, if carried out, could draw the major powers more deeply into the conflict: ''The United States is watching carefully the relative balance in the Middle East and we will not hesitate to provide arms to friendly states as the need arises.'' The message concluded by rejecting the Soviet position that Israel would have to withdraw *before* any other peace issues could be settled.

On the same day I sent the President further reflections on the Soviet note. I considered the note an odd maneuver and therefore disturbing:

It should not have taken much intelligence to expect at least the US (if not France and the UK) to reply that it favors restoration of the ceasefire on a reciprocal basis. . . . Thus the upshot of the Soviet move will be to place the onus for getting the ceasefire restored on Nasser and the Arabs, and through them on the Soviets themselves, rather than on us and the Israelis.

Two days later, in a long analysis for the President of basic issues of Middle East strategy, I reiterated my view: ''Now that he [Nasser] has turned to Moscow to lean on us to press Israel to stop the bombing, he is about to demonstrate Soviet inability to get him out of his box.''

Precisely because Kosygin's letter seemed so diffuse and asked for nothing that could in fact be done, I began to be convinced that it could not be an isolated move; it had to be part of a larger scheme, almost certainly the precursor of some concrete action in the military field. Its vagueness might be explained by the desire to discourage a response that might interfere with decisions already made. From the autobiographies of Anwar Sadat and Mohamed Heikal we now know in fact that while Nasser was in Moscow in late January a decision had been made to send Egypt the most advanced Soviet antiaircraft missiles. The Kosygin letter was not a warning but a smokescreen.

In the first week of February, indications appeared that the Soviets might send new arms to Egypt. I expressed to Nixon my doubts that military equipment alone would be of use. If the new arms simply augmented the existing arsenal, they would be destroyed by the Israelis; if they were more sophisticated, the Egyptians would not be able to operate them. This raised a more ominous possibility: If the Soviets sought to do something effective against Israeli attacks, "this would almost certainly seem to involve Soviet personnel." Reading my analysis, Nixon wrote in the margin: "I think it is time to talk directly with the Soviets on this. Acheson's idea — 'let the dust settle' — won't work.* State's 'negotiate in any forum' won't work. We must make a try at a bilateral talk to see if a deal in our interests is possible."

To carry out Nixon's wishes I moved on two fronts. Our Ambassador in Moscow, Jacob Beam, was instructed by the State Department to tell Foreign Minister Gromyko that the United States was prepared to work for restoration of the cease-fire and to discuss arms limitation on both sides. Not unexpectedly, Gromyko's response to Beam on February 11 was noncommittal. The USSR, he said, could not consider a cease-fire unless Israel first stopped its deep penetration raids. He was not against discussing arms limitations, but not so long as Israel occupied Arab lands; in other words, Israel would have to withdraw from all territories occupied in 1967. All this could be settled in the Two-Power talks, which the Soviet Union was prepared to resume.

One reason for Gromyko's evasiveness was undoubtedly that the Soviet Union was already examining a more authoritative statement of the American position. For the day before, on February 10, I met with Dobrynin on behalf of the President, and by the time Beam had his interview with Gromyko the Soviets could not have completed their analysis of my message. I told Dobrynin that "we want the Soviet leaders to know that the introduction of Soviet combat personnel in the Middle East would be viewed with the gravest concern." We chose this method of communication because we did not want to make a formal confrontation. At the same time, reflecting Nixon's instructions, I told Dobrynin of our willingness to begin bilateral discussions on the Middle East in the special Channel.

Dobrynin never wasted a meeting even when he was clearly without instructions — as was the case here. He fell back on his litany of com-

---

*This was a reference to a letter from Dean Acheson in January urging that we deal with the Middle East by "intelligent neglect." At that time Nixon had indicated his general agreement with Acheson's approach.

plaints about American actions; experience had taught him that in the Washington Establishment there was an inexhaustible reservoir of masochism eager to assume the blame for every impasse. Appealing to this trait, he objected to the publicity surrounding the Kosygin letter (which of course the Soviets had triggered by simultaneous démarches in Paris and London) and to the public position of the State Department, which, he argued, had erroneously interpreted Moscow's December reply to our proposals on borders (the "Rogers Plan") as a rejection. This latter revelation had clearly escaped everyone who had read Moscow's December note, including me. Nor had the Soviets previously contested the interpretation that they had rejected our formulations.

Nothing more was heard from the Soviet leaders for nearly a month. I sought to use the interval for contingency planning in anticipation of some significant Soviet move — almost certainly involving the introduction of military personnel in the Middle East. The various meetings of the WSAG once again exposed the divisions that had bedeviled the internal debate in 1969. My view was that if the Soviets introduced military personnel we had no choice but to resist, regardless of the merits of the issue that triggered the action. We could not accept a new Soviet military presence unless we were prepared to see the radical Arabs given a perhaps decisive momentum. I wanted a review of our plans in case the Soviets threatened Israel with retaliation. I also asked for measures to prevent the attrition of the Israeli air force should the Soviets introduce sophisticated equipment manned by their own personnel.

The departments were less than enthusiastic. Most in the government blamed the impasse on Israeli intransigence. All (except myself) were convinced that new large-scale aid to Israel would, at that juncture, "blow the place apart." As for contingency plans, no one could think of a plausible excuse to resist the effort to think ahead, but it was clear that implementation of any military counter to any major Soviet move would face massive bureaucratic opposition. The Defense Department submitted a formal memorandum stressing that it preferred political options — which meant, as in Vietnam, that some other department should carry the burden and risk. It did not explain just how we were going to bring about total Israeli withdrawal (which happened to be the only political option on the table) or how, if Soviet combat personnel showed up, the withdrawal would not appear to be the result of Soviet pressure.

Nixon's attitude was ambivalent, colored by both international and domestic considerations. He agreed with my geopolitical analysis. On one of my memoranda he instructed: " 'Even Handedness' is the right policy — But above all our interest is — what gives the Soviet the most trouble — Don't let Arab-Israeli conflict obscure that interest." At the same time he leaned toward the departmental views that Israel's policies were the basic cause of the difficulty, and he doubted whether demonstrations of Soviet impotence to produce progress would really disenchant the Arabs. He noted on a memorandum in which I had suggested this possibility: "I completely disagree with this conclusion — The Soviets know that Arabs are long on talk — We have been gloating over Soviet 'defeats' in the Mideast since '67 — & State et al said the June war was a 'defeat' for Soviet. It was *not*. They became the Arabs' friend and the U.S. their enemy. Long range this is what serves their interest."

The problem, of course, was how to reconcile Nixon's two notes; how we could give the Soviets trouble while letting them emerge as the dominant force in the region by acquiescing in the introduction of combat personnel. Nixon never settled such issues in the abstract, preferring to wait for a need for decision to arise. His usual ambivalence in the face of disagreements among his subordinates — at once fueling them and reacting only when they spilled over into his office — applied as well to the domestic implications of the Middle East crisis. The President was convinced that most leaders of the Jewish community had opposed him throughout his political career. The small percentage of Jews who voted for him, he would joke, had to be so crazy that they would probably stick with him even if he turned on Israel. He delighted in telling associates and visitors that the "Jewish lobby" had no effect on him.

Unfortunately for his image of himself, Nixon rarely had occasion to demonstrate this theory in practice. For on almost all practical issues his unsentimental geopolitical analysis finally led him to positions not so distant from ones others might take on the basis of ethnic politics. He would privately threaten dire reprisals to any constituency he thought was thwarting him. He would make gestures to demonstrate — in part to himself — that he was free of the traditional influences that had constrained other Presidents. But at the end of the day, when confronted with the realities of power in the Middle East — after much anguish and circuitous maneuvers — he would pursue, in the national interest, the same strategy: to reduce Soviet influence, weaken the position of the Arab radicals, encourage Arab moderates, and assure Israel's security. So Nixon and I often traveled different roads for part of the way, but at the points of decision in the Middle East we met, agreed, and acted in mutual support.

During February the annual Israeli shopping list of military assistance requests was being considered in our government. In 1970 it amounted to twenty-five F-4 Phantom jet fighter-bombers, one hundred A-4 Skyhawk attack bombers, and a substantial number of tanks and armored personnel carriers, all to be paid for by various forms of American credit. The consensus of the departments was that Israel could maintain its military superiority for the next three to five years without substantial new deliveries. This was buttressed by an interagency appraisal based on the arcane insights of systems analysis that remarkably paralleled the policy preferences of the heads of the agencies. (As events turned out, the 1973 Middle East war demonstrated that even after the fairly substantial military deliveries of 1970–1973 the military balance in the Middle East had become more precarious than any of our analysts had predicted.) The general reluctance in our bureaucracy to undertake new arms deliveries for Israel was reinforced by warning letters from our friends in the Arab world, such as the King of Morocco and the King of Jordan.

The government's deliberations were thus tending toward a minimum response when an event occurred that, while not directly relevant to the issue, triggered a resolution of it. At the end of February, President Pompidou was on his State visit to the United States, to which Nixon attached great importance. Insensitive to the likely domestic reaction in the United States, probably indifferent to it, Pompidou had in January completed an arms deal with the new revolutionary government of Colonel Muammar Qaddafi to sell Libya more than a hundred Mirage aircraft over four years. There was no rational Libyan need for such numbers of aircraft; indeed, at that time there were only a few pilots in all of Libya capable of flying high-performance aircraft. Clearly, these planes were intended for use by other Arab countries, probably Egypt. Predictably, supporters of Israel in the US Congress protested strongly. There were demonstrations in every city that Pompidou and his wife visited. A particularly egregious incident occurred in Chicago, where some demonstrators were especially offensive to Madame Pompidou. Pompidou abruptly cut short his Chicago visit and returned to New York. For a few hours it appeared that he might also cancel his New York sojourn and emplane for France. Pompidou never got over this inexcusable incident; it mortgaged his attitude toward the United States ever after.

Nixon was beside himself. He reacted in two ways, one generous, the other petty. The generous gesture was to fly unexpectedly to a dinner in New York on March 2 in honor of Pompidou where he delivered a speech that was as graceful as it was warm. The vindictive reaction was a Presidential order directly to State via Joe Sisco — apparently to avoid going through me — to defer consideration of the Israeli arms package indefinitely. Had I been consulted I would surely have emphasized the inadvisability of punishing a foreign country for the actions of an American minority and tempting the Soviet Union with the prospect of a free ride.

These were, in fact, the points I made when, characteristically, Nixon had second thoughts within hours of his order to Sisco. He had Haldeman tell me in effect that this was not a final decision and he would work things out on the plane to New York for the Pompidou dinner.

When Haldeman was assigned to such a task, one could be certain that the President meant business; Haldeman's studiedly cultivated disinterest in substance precluded debate. Still, Haldeman performed a therapeutic role; he provided a channel for protest but no means to implement it. Unable to reach Nixon, I warned Haldeman that the President's action had increased the chance of a Middle East explosion; to cut off Israel would head us into a simultaneous confrontation with the Soviets and the Israelis. Israel could scarcely avoid panic and might preempt; the Soviets were bound to be emboldened by our visible dissociation from our ally. We knew that the Soviets were planning some unspecified military move; this was not the time for the President to issue an order to cut off military aid to Israel, against which this imminent Soviet move was directed. Haldeman, with the long-suffering patience of a man caught between the outbursts first of his chief and then of those who — incomprehensibly to Haldeman — took substance seriously, assured me that the matter would be patched up. He did not say how. He proved to be wrong.

The State Department, when it receives an order of which its bureaucracy approves, is a wonderously efficient institution. When it wishes to exhaust recalcitrant superiors, drafts of memoranda wander through its labyrinthine channels for weeks and even months. But when it receives an instruction it considers wise, paperwork is suddenly completed in a matter of hours and the bureaucracy springs to marvelous action. Hence, within thirty-six hours of Nixon's order to Sisco, Rogers sent over a memorandum telling Nixon that he had already prepared and had in hand a scenario to "carry out your decision to postpone for now the question of additional aircraft for Israel."

I thought it unwise in the extreme to announce such a decision before we had any idea of the next Soviet move in the Middle East. By now I had had enough experience with Nixon's second thoughts to be certain that he would indeed, in Haldeman's words, seek to patch things up. Therefore, in transmitting Rogers's memorandum to the President, I pointed out that while the domestic implications were self-evident, "abroad, the appearance of bowing to Soviet pressure cannot be disposed of by simple denial." I therefore suggested that Rogers's recommendations be modified to soften the blow to Israel. Either we should agree to replace aircraft lost in the period 1969–1971 (up to a given number to avoid an incentive for costly raids), or else we should keep open the production line and earmark a specific number of Phantoms and Skyhawks that could be given to Israel immediately should a massive introduction of Soviet arms endanger the military balance. Even Sisco had told me (privately) that he agreed with my approach. To avert some of the backlash of the postponement I recommended that State, not the White House, announce it.

My proposal demonstrated that on the Middle East I was not in the dominant position. The best that could be said for it was that it provided a pause while the President reconsidered. Thus we might avoid tempting the Soviets at the very moment they were settling on their own next move.

We did not have to wait long for that move.

Soviet Soldiers and Missiles Appear in Egypt

O N March 10 Dobrynin appeared at the White House with the Kremlin's response to my démarche of February 10 warning against the introduction of Soviet combat personnel. We met in the office of the President's military aide, the Map Room being for some reason unavailable. The military aide's office in the East Wing of the White House is by its location far removed from policymaking. Offices of most substantive staff assistants are clustered around the Oval Office in the West Wing. There are worse yardsticks for measuring the importance of White House aides than their propinquity to the seat of power; many aides will gladly content themselves with a cubbyhole in the West Wing rather than risk losing status in more spacious and elegant quarters in the East Wing three hundred yards away or in the Executive Office Building across the street. But precisely because the offices in the East Wing deal largely with social or logistical matters it was a good place for an unobserved meeting.

Dobrynin exuded bonhomie. With respect to American exhortations for a cease-fire, he conveyed the conviction of his leaders that "if the Israelis stop their bombings of the UAR [Egypt], the UAR on its part will display restraint in its actions, without, of course, any official statements to that effect." In other words, Dobrynin was offering a de facto cease-fire along the Suez Canal. Moreover, Dobrynin was happy to announce that he had been authorized to resume bilateral talks with Rogers. He gave me a preview of two "concessions" that he would offer in these talks: First, a Mideast settlement would not simply end the state of war but would establish a state of peace; and second, Arab governments would undertake to control the operations of guerrilla forces from their territory.

There was less to these "concessions" than met the eye. It was a measure of the never-never land of Middle East policy that the suggestion that a peace settlement might establish peace was seriously put forward as a concession. To ask Israel to withdraw from all occupied territories without offering what is normal between most states, namely peace, would have been an absurdity. Nor could a commitment to end guerrilla attacks after peace had been made be described as a sacrifice; nobody could have maintained the opposite proposition. Still,

Dobrynin's offer of a cease-fire seemed sufficiently significant to prevent me from noticing that the Soviets had not responded to the chief thrust of the February 10 conversation — my warning against the introduction of their combat personnel. The reason for this omission was to become clear all too soon.

I reported to the President with what turned out to be premature elation: "Dobrynin made a number of significant concessions. . . . In the negotiations on Egypt our policy of relative firmness has paid off on all contested issues. The Soviet Union has made a first move and, while it may not be enough, at least it showed that holding firm and offering no concessions was the right course." The President reacted to this seeming softening of the Soviet attitude by modifying his original decision on Israeli military aid. Realizing that we could not approach Israel with the cease-fire proposal while rejecting its military requests, Nixon the same day approved my suggestion to replace Israeli aircraft losses with up to eight Phantoms and twenty Skyhawks in 1970. He endorsed with alacrity the suggestion that the bad news holding the overall package in abeyance come from State, but added a Nixonian wrinkle: I should inform Israeli Ambassador Rabin immediately of Nixon's decision to replace Israeli losses.

On March 12 I met with Rabin to inform him of Dobrynin's cease-fire proposal and also to convey the President's decision. At the same time I asked that Israel stop its deep penetration raids and agree to an undeclared cease-fire. An aide-mémoire from the President would formalize both the request and the assurance.

Yitzhak Rabin had many extraordinary qualities, but the gift of human relations was not one of them. If he had been handed the entire United States Strategic Air Command as a free gift he would have (a) affected the attitude that at last Israel was getting its due, and (b) found some technical shortcoming in the airplanes that made his accepting them a reluctant concession to us. Not surprisingly, he did not embrace the replacement formula. In fact, Rabin handed over two messages from Mrs. Meir to Nixon (one of them handwritten). These were generated by reports already in public circulation that we might postpone or turn down Israel's package of aircraft requests. Mrs. Meir wrote that such a decision would increase the military danger to Israel and encourage further Soviet and Arab aggression at the same time. The sense of "abandonment," she feared, would increase desperation and the capacity for irrational behavior in Israel: "One cannot overstate the seriousness of the situation that will result."

Rabin was also generally unenthusiastic about the cease-fire. It would save Nasser; it would settle nothing. Nevertheless, he considered the proposal important enough to take to Jerusalem personally. He flew to Israel and returned five days later with the Cabinet's reply: Israel would agree to an undeclared cease-fire provided all military activity ceased simultaneously, the replacement figure was doubled, and there was a public announcement of Nixon's assurance about maintaining Israeli air strength and the military balance in the Middle East. (I was now being directly exposed for the first time to Israeli negotiating tactics. In the combination of single-minded persistence and convoluted tactics the Israelis preserve in their interlocutor only those last vestiges of sanity and coherence needed to sign the final document.)

Before the issue with Israel could be resolved, however, we found out at last what military move the Soviets intended for Egypt. The very day — March 17 — that Israel accepted the cease-fire, Rabin informed me that a substantial shipment of Soviet arms had arrived in Egypt, including the most advanced Soviet antiaircraft system — the SA-3 surface-to-air-missile. This had never before been given to a foreign country, not even to North Vietnam. More disturbing still, the missiles were accompanied by 1,500 Soviet military personnel. Clearly, this was only the first installment of a major Soviet military move. It marked a unique turn in Soviet policy: Never before had they put their own military forces in jeopardy for a non-Communist country. It was apparent to me that as the Soviets increased their forces, they would develop a vested interest in protecting them and then in showing results for their commitment.

All experience teaches that Soviet military moves, which usually begin as tentative, must be resisted early, unequivocally, and in a fashion that gives Soviet leaders a justification for withdrawal. If this moment is permitted to pass, the commitment grows too large to be dismantled short of a major crisis. But a strong response when the challenge is still ambiguous is peculiarly difficult to organize. The evidence, by definition, is not likely to be conclusive. The early stages of a buildup are usually limited by the need to establish a logistic infrastructure. Intelligence agencies — contrary to the mythological perception of them as reckless adventurers — tend to play it safe; they generally flock to a cautious hypothesis. In my experience in almost every crisis there has been an initial dispute about whether we faced a challenge at all — a debate that quickly spreads from the Executive Branch to the Congress. Those opposed to a firm response claim that the Administration is "overreacting." And if the Administration acts in time and averts the danger, they will feel they were proved right. What they fail to consider is that the real choice is between seemingly overreacting (and containing the challenge) or letting events take over. By the time the true dimensions of the threat become unambiguous — when everyone agrees about its overwhelming nature — it is often too late to do anything. And somewhere along the line the question of what causes a Soviet move becomes irrelevant; American policy must deal with its consequences, not with its causes.

So it was with the Nixon Administration's reaction to the appearance of Soviet missiles and combat personnel in Egypt in the spring of 1970. Preoccupied with Vietnam, Cambodia, and Laos, shaken by domestic upheaval, more than half convinced that Israeli belligerence had provoked the Soviet move, the United States government vacillated and missed whatever opportunity there was to contain the challenge.

Our first reaction was in the right direction. On March 20 I called in Dobrynin for a tough dressing down. I said that we had taken the Soviet communication of March 10 extremely seriously. We had, in fact, recommended a cease-fire to Israel; Israel had accepted in principle. But at the precise moment that I was getting ready to approach him to settle on an agreed time for the cease-fire we had learned about the introduction of SA-3 missiles and Soviet combat personnel. The troops had been sent despite my explicit warning of the dangers of such a step. The tactic, I said, was reminiscent of the Cuban missile crisis. We had no choice except to terminate all our efforts for the cease-fire and to inform Israel accordingly.

Dobrynin did not return to the subject until April 7, when he asked whether we would have a different view of the Soviet weapon deployments if they were limited to Alexandria, Cairo, and Aswan; he was vague about the personnel. I asked him whether this was a formal proposal. He said he would let me know. He never did.

Once we laid down the challenge, our next move should have been to follow it up. The proper response to the introduction of advanced Soviet missiles and combat personnel would have been to increase military aid to Israel — not just to promise a few replacement aircraft. This would have shown that we would match any Soviet escalation and that Soviet military pressures were not the road to solving the political problems of the Middle East — an essential first condition to encouraging moderation and to fulfilling what I considered the optimum strategy. The rationale for my view was thoughtfully stated by Bill Hyland, a Soviet expert on my staff, on June 8:

> The Soviets respect power and strength. They understand military strength best of all. This does not mean, of course, that they are eager to fight, or that they believe in the indiscriminate use of force. But they do not understand restraint; it confuses them, and in the end leads them to conclude that there is room for their own forward movement.
>
> If the United States does not support Israel demonstratively with military assistance, the Soviets will ponder why we refuse to do so. Ultimately, they will conclude that we are deterred because of either domestic, political and economic concerns or because of the consequences of military escalation.

I did not succeed in getting such a strategy considered. Our agencies blamed Israel for the tension along the Suez Canal, arguing — not without evidence — that Israel had provoked the Soviet reaction by its deep penetration raids. Their "solution" to the Soviet military move was to press Israel to be more flexible. Precious time was wasted debating irrelevancies. Our intelligence community concentrated on trying to measure whether in precise hardware terms the military balance had in fact been upset. All this missed the essential point. Whatever one's view about greater Israeli flexibility, we now had first to face down the Soviets and the Arab radicals. Otherwise, Israeli concessions would be perceived as resulting from the introduction of Soviet military personnel. Our position would deteriorate as demands escalated. Once the Soviets established themselves with a combat role in the Middle East and we accepted that role, the political balance would be drastically changed, and the military balance could be overthrown at any moment of Soviet choosing. Israel was not free of responsibility for the present state of affairs, but we would be able to deal with the political problem only after mastering the military challenge.

This view did not prevail since I was still in the early years of my role as Presidential Assistant and the Middle East was substantially a State Department fiefdom. In any event, at that stage of my career in the White House, my influence was greatest when the agencies' views differed and the President had no strong views of his own; I was least likely to prevail when there was unanimity among the agencies, particularly on the Middle East. And in this case, Nixon's assessment was much closer to that of the departments than to mine. He spent much of his time on Cambodia; he was hankering after a Moscow summit; he hoped that the problem would go away, and, if it did not, that he and I could overpower it later.

In fact, at this very moment Nixon's earlier decision to hold the Israeli arms package in abeyance — taken in quite different circumstances — caught up with him. The State Department had gone ahead with the cumbersome process of drafting a public statement on the arms decision. And they had proceeded with their consultations with key Congressional leaders even after news of the latest Soviet move. The thinking was that our action would show our good faith to the Arabs; at a minimum it would prevent the explosion that our agencies considered inevitable if we proceeded with additional deliveries of hardware. Discouraged by previous rebuffs and convinced that the President's mind was made up, I let matters proceed. In retrospect I believe that I erred in not being more emphatic. So it happened that on March 23 — less than a week after we learned of the dispatch of Soviet combat personnel to Egypt — Rogers announced that "in our judgment, Israel's air capacity is sufficient to meet its needs for the time being. Consequently the President has decided·to hold in abeyance for now a decision with respect to Israel's request. . . ."

To be sure, the statement added that "if steps are taken which might upset the current balance or if in our judgment political developments warrant, the President will not hesitate to reconsider. . . .'' This qualification was understood for the soporific it was. No verbal reassurance could obscure the fact that less than a week after the introduction of Soviet combat personnel into the Middle East, and three days after canceling the cease-fire discussion with Dobrynin, the United States had publicly denied additional planes to Israel. The decision even seemed to imply that the most sophisticated Soviet weapons and Soviet combat personnel did not affect the military balance, an implication that almost invited their augmentation.

A trip long planned by Joe Sisco to the Middle East — ostensibly to consult ambassadors but in reality to sound out peace prospects — reinforced the impression of American indifference to the Soviet military presence. Sisco's mission so soon after a Soviet power play seemed to suggest that Soviet combat personnel in Egypt were no obstacle and might even be a spur to US peace efforts. The Israelis, in turn, rattled by the twin blows from the Soviet Union and the United States, suspended their deep penetration raids and adopted a more selective retaliatory policy. A gesture that a few weeks earlier might have contributed to improving the atmosphere became a concession to Soviet military blackmail. And to compound the errors, Nixon chose this moment to begin his overtures for a US–Soviet summit meeting — removing any remaining Soviet hesitations. April 1970 was not the proudest month of the Nixon Administration.

It was inevitable, given our weak response, that the Soviets should give the screw another turn. Soviet missiles multiplied; the number of combat personnel increased dramatically, to some ten thousand in the next six weeks. Rabin informed me on April 24 that Soviet pilots had been flying defense missions over Egypt's interior. Thus, the Egyptian air force was freed for attacking Israeli positions along the Canal and was becoming more aggressive. Air combat between Soviet and Israeli pilots was a virtual certainty.

At last the US government bestirred itself. The White House announced an "immediate and full" review of the situation. Nixon authorized me to tell Rabin on April 30 (the day he announced the Cambodian operation) that we would provide more planes despite his earlier decision. He was still sufficiently worried about the Arab reaction to request no publicity, thus depriving the decision of some of its deterrent effect. And since he gave no indication about the numbers he had in mind, he let himself in for weeks of additional interagency haggling from those who had opposed any plane sales to begin with. For even the appearance of Soviet pilots did not alter the cautious official analysis. The intelligence consensus was that the Soviet mission was purely defensive. But the intelligence community did not propose to trap itself by an unambiguous statement; an escape clause warned that "a shift in the situation, however, could radically alter their mission with little, if any, advance warning" — which was of course the heart of the problem.

On May 12, at the peak of the Cambodia hysteria, I was sufficiently concerned to sum up the developing impasse for Nixon: Nasser believed he could outwait the Israelis and Mrs. Meir thought that no peace was possible with Nasser. Mrs. Meir was prepared to stick it out until there was a change of heart on the Arab side. Israel wanted the United States to stand up more firmly to the Soviets and give Israel more planes. Even Sisco — as a result of his trip — now recommended a reevaluation of major assumptions about American strategy. Sisco was right, because those assumptions had been wrong across the board:

- We had assumed that major-power talks might break the impasse. In fact, they had not significantly changed the positions of any of the parties.
- We had assumed that the Soviets, in order to defuse the situation and limit Soviet involvement in Egypt, might feel an interest in pressing Nasser to compromise. On the contrary, Moscow had deepened its military commitment, thus encouraging Nasser's war of attrition against Israel.
- We had assumed Israel might in the end go along with a properly balanced American proposal. But the Israelis had flatly rejected our various plans while asking us to support them militarily and economically whether or not there was progress in negotiations.
- We had assumed that the Palestinians could be dealt with in a settlement purely as a refugee problem. Instead, they had become a quasi-independent force with a veto over policy in Jordan, and perhaps even in Lebanon.

My memorandum proposed a fundamental reexamination of our Middle East policy. The surrounding circumstances prevented the mustering of energies for such a battle. The physical and psychic toll of the Cambodia incursion was too great. Not until Watergate was Nixon so consumed and shaken; he was not prepared to add to his problems. When we turned again to the Middle East, it was in the context of a State Department peace initiative whose practical consequence was to ratify the Soviet buildup.

So the crisis in the Middle East deepened. Nasser in a speech on May I addressed an open message to Nixon, the peremptory tone of which emphasized the decline in our position. The United States "must *order* Israel to withdraw from the occupied Arab territories." If we were unable to do so, Nasser requested that we "refrain from giving any new support to Israel as long as it occupies our Arab territories — be it polit-

ical, military or economic support.'' Otherwise, ''the Arabs must come
to the inevitable conclusion that the United States wants Israel to continue to occupy our territories so as to dictate the terms of surrender.''
That the prospect of Soviet predominance in the Middle East was not
just the result of overwrought imaginations became apparent when Nasser told a distinguished American visitor, Eugene Black, a former head
of the World Bank, that he would prefer any American diplomatic initiative to be conducted through the Soviet Union; he did not trust us
enough to deal directly with us.

In this atmosphere the departments resisted Nixon's decision to keep
open the supply line to Israel (when current contracts for airplane deliveries ran out in July) by delays in implementation and by using the
loophole that he had not prescribed any overall numbers. The issue
eventually merged with the general debate over Middle East strategy.
Formally, the dispute resolved itself into the essentially phony question
of whether we should pursue a ''political strategy'' or a ''confrontation
with the USSR.'' Whenever issues are framed in this fashion, senior
policymakers should beware. No one in his right mind would *not* prefer
a political solution; confrontation cannot possibly be sought as a policy
objective. The question we faced in the Middle East in 1970 was, however, quite different; it was whether a political solution was achievable
without first making clear to the Soviet Union and its radical friends that
military pressure would not work. In such a situation, if confrontation is
rejected as a matter of principle, the term ''political solution'' becomes
a euphemism for settling on the opponents' terms. As I said in some
exasperation at a meeting of the Senior Review Group in late May:
''What will discourage the Soviets is fear of confrontation with us. We
have to have thought of how to convey that idea to them.''

But the time was not ripe for such an appraisal. Shaken by public protest, focused on Vietnam, half hoping for a negotiation with Moscow,
the Executive Branch was torn between its premonitions and its hopes,
between the reality of a Soviet challenge and the nightmare of concurrent crises. Reflecting this ambivalence, on June 2 Rogers called in
Dobrynin to read him the following extraordinary statement, without informing either me or (so far as I know) Nixon:

The USSR has indicated that Soviet military activities in the UAR will
remain defensive. We want to make clear that we would not view the introduction of Soviet personnel, by air or on the ground, in the Canal combat zone as
defensive since such action could only be in support of the announced UAR
policy of violating the ceasefire resolutions of the Security Council. We believe
that the introduction of Soviet military personnel into the delicate Suez Canal
combat zone [within thirty kilometers of the Canal] could lead to serious escalation with unpredictable consequences to which the U.S. could not remain
indifferent. . . .

On the surface this seems a strong warning. What it really did, however, was to give the Soviets a blank check; it acquiesced in the Soviet
combat presence in Egypt except in the immediate vicinity of the Suez
Canal. The Soviets were in effect told that they were free to build up
substantial forces in Egypt so long as they did not move them directly
into the combat zone. Build them up they did. And within two months
they were in a position to advance their units rapidly into the combat
zone whenever the opportunity presented itself. My associate Bill Hyland summed up the growing crisis:

Looking at our position and the Israeli standdown from deep raids, the Soviets must conclude that we have acquiesced in their direct intervention. Indeed, they could well read our latest statement (Rogers to Dobrynin) as confirmation that we accept the Soviet claim of "defensive" involvement, and are
only concerned that a movement toward the canal would not be "defensive." . . .

The conventional wisdom is that the Soviets will probably not move, mainly
because of the risk of combat with the Israelis. There is, however, some evidence that they are indeed already "inching" forward (the construction sites
along the canal). Moreover, it would seem a logical extension of Soviet strategy to do so. The near term Soviet objective in the Middle East is to destroy
Western influence. The main enemy is not Israel but the West in general and
the United States in particular. The road to the displacement of the West, however, now lies through Soviet demonstration that they cannot only protect their
clients, but reverse the losses they suffered in 1967. . . .

Warnings alone are not enough. Indeed, since we have presented several
serious warnings, the more we present the less credible. Breaking off contacts
serves no end, and moving military forces is at least premature. . . . Because
the dispatch of aircraft to Israel has become the symbol for measuring our policy, it has, perhaps unfortunately, become the only immediate issue.

Only *after* demonstrating our willingness to take up this option can we expect to convince Israel of the need to make some political concession and convince the Soviets and Arabs that we are not deterred by their recent actions.

But the United States government was not yet ready for such a course.
And the longer we delayed, the higher became the ultimate price. We
learned this painfully, albeit slowly. Events finally forced our hand.
They produced a series of confrontations over the autumn in the course
of which the Soviet advance was first arrested and finally reversed.

An American Diplomatic Initiative

OUR first move was the opposite of confrontation; it was another
peace initiative. I had tried to use an NSC meeting on June 10 to
bring about a fundamental review of our strategy. The State Department
preempted me by transforming it into a discussion of a tactical decision.

Rogers had prepared a complex scenario involving an American diplomatic initiative to get the parties to "stop shooting and start talking." Israel and Egypt would be asked to accept a ninety-day standstill cease-fire and indirect negotiations under UN Representative Gunnar Jarring. To encourage Israel the United States would offer — as the response to its arms needs — three Phantoms for July and August and four Phantoms and Skyhawks per month for replacement purposes thereafter. These supply arrangements were, however, subject to review "if negotiations . . . had started and showed signs of success."

Amazingly, the State Department proposal thus gave Israel an incentive to have the negotiations fail; the plane sales would be reviewed only if negotiations "showed signs of success." And the proposed scenario did not address at all the critical issue of the Soviet combat presence in Egypt. I had advised Nixon of my concerns in advance of the NSC meeting. I stressed that negotiations had to be seen in the context of the recent — and continuing — Soviet moves:

> The character of the Soviet move in the UAR should not be underrated. You may hear the argument made (by Defense) that this move was precipitated by Israeli action or that it is purely defensive and does not threaten Israel. These arguments do not meet the main point: This is a unique turn of Soviet policy — never before have the Soviets put their own forces in combat jeopardy for the sake of a non-Communist government.
>
> It is argued that now the Soviets have rescued Nasser both of them may suddenly change character and be prepared to negotiate seriously. This seems doubtful. Having scored a psychological gain with apparent impunity, it has generally been the Soviet tactic first to consolidate their gains and then to press forward, testing the ground as they move.

At the NSC meeting on June 10, CIA Director Helms summed up the deterioration. The Soviets had four to five regiments of SA-3s and three to five squadrons of Soviet-piloted MiG-21s in Egypt; there was no doubt about the numbers. The Soviet combat presence now amounted to ten thousand men introduced since March. Egypt's ability to destroy Israeli aircraft had been greatly augmented. Mounting losses would create new psychological pressures on Israel. With their preemptive option lost, Israel had an overwhelming incentive to control the area along the Suez Canal. The central questions therefore were whether the Soviets would move their SA-3 missiles toward the Canal and engage their airplanes there, and whether Israel would refrain from challenging them if they did. In any event, the situation could be altered to Israel's disadvantage very rapidly, by a sudden forward movement of the Soviet military complex.

Rogers then presented the State Department scenario for an immediate cease-fire and talks through Jarring as if Helms's briefing had not occurred. In effect, the proposal, like his June 2 conversation with Dobrynin, ratified the Soviet combat presence in Egypt.

Nixon confined himself to opaque philosophical statements that indicated he was not ready for a discussion of basic assumptions. He speculated about the impact of the 1956 Suez crisis on Britain's conception of herself as a world power. He considered the failure to deal with the problem of Arab refugees one of the major lapses of the postwar period. Even while we were considering a unilateral American initiative, he mused about the prospect for a joint US–Soviet enterprise, no doubt anticipating a meeting I would have with Dobrynin aboard the Presidential yacht *Sequoia* that evening to discuss his idea for a summit. All of this meandering was largely a smokescreen to enable Nixon to defer a formal decision. Nixon had no real belief that the State Department diplomatic plan would work, but also he had little stomach for overruling Rogers. He told me privately that he thought the current Middle East track would lead us into disaster. I agreed, adding that the worst course was to put in "a little arms and a little proposal." (This does not exclude that Nixon told Rogers the opposite.)

My meeting with Dobrynin on the *Sequoia* on the evening of June 10 was inconclusive. Dobrynin renewed his plea that we negotiate on the Middle East in the Channel. In order to have some carrot for Nixon's cherished summit I did not reject this possibility out of hand. But I insisted that it could work only if the Soviet Union would ask sacrifices from its Arab friends commensurate with the territorial concessions we would have to urge on Israel. Moreover, the presence of Soviet combat personnel in the Middle East was of the most profound concern to the United States. It was therefore crucial for us to know whether the Soviet Union would be prepared to withdraw its military forces as part of a negotiated peace. Dobrynin replied that he would ask for instructions.

The exchange with Dobrynin further strengthened my conviction that we were on the wrong track; the requisite balance of forces for effective negotiations simply did not exist. On June 16 I sent Nixon another assessment warning against the proposed initiative: The new proposal to "stop shooting and starting talking" had to be judged against the backdrop of our compulsive peace initiatives of the previous year: "They emboldened the Arabs, who stepped up their border pressures. Israel began making deep penetration raids which, in turn, caused Nasser to allow a massive influx of Soviet personnel and influence." The new proposal seemed to me to involve the same dangers; it would buy us at most two months:

The State approach would have us force the Israelis back to pre-war borders while they get no further planes after the summer. They would be asked to give up both elements of their security at the same time — their territorial buffers and the prospect of more aircraft. As peace with more vulnerable frontiers approached, their aircraft inventory would drop. If, on the other hand, Israel believes that she will get the larger aircraft package if negotiations are going badly, she will have no incentive to make negotiations go well. . . .

Nasser would interpret our action as a halfway move. He would seriously doubt that we could really press Israel to withdraw on the basis of six aircraft and perhaps others later on. . . .

To the Soviets, the State Department proposal would be a weak gesture in the face of their continued expansion of influence. Our formula would be of too little military consequence and too hesitant to convince them that we are prepared to match their escalation in the area. They considered our March announcement uncertain; they will read this one the same way.

Above all, I considered a major initiative inopportune unless it settled the issue of the Soviet combat presence, which seemed to me the heart of the problem. I therefore suggested an alternative approach: We would tell Nasser explicitly that only the United States could bring about Israeli withdrawal; all other routes would prove illusory, and we would see to it that this remained so. But we could urge Israeli withdrawal only in the context of an Israel made secure by substantial American military deliveries and an Egypt willing to negotiate detailed conditions of peace. Soviet combat personnel would have to be withdrawn as part of a settlement.

Such an approach, I argued, would give Israel an incentive to negotiate by offering detailed security arrangements, a contractual peace, and the withdrawal of Soviet troops. It would provide Egypt a greater prospect of regaining the Sinai. The Soviets would face the danger of escalation by a well-supplied Israel, and the escape hatch of an acceptable settlement. But I warned Nixon that to accept my plan would involve a bureaucratic nightmare: "Shortly after our Cambodian experience, you would have to override the recommendations of your top Cabinet advisers, and impose a wholly different policy upon a very reluctant bureaucracy, which would then be charged with implementing it."

Almost certainly for these reasons Nixon chose not to face the problem at that point. The policy implicit in my recommendations would require three more years to obtain his approval. On June 18, the President embraced State's proposal. He thought it would be rejected anyway; he would rather deal with a deadlock than another hassle with his bureaucracy. Thus, three months after we had turned down a cease-fire because of the first introduction of some one thousand Soviet combat troops into the Middle East, we accepted one even though Soviet personnel had since grown to ten thousand. That simple fact was to dog our footsteps in the Middle East until the Soviet Union finally overplayed its hand in September and gave us a new opportunity to restore the psychological as well as the physical balance.

The State Department responded to Nixon's decision with alacrity. The proposal for cease-fire and talks under Jarring was transmitted privately immediately to Israel, Egypt, the Soviet Union, and also Jordan. It was announced publicly on June 25.

The first rumbling response came from Israel. Already alarmed at the delays in military supplies and the weak American reaction to the influx of Soviet combat personnel, Israel now objected to a number of provisions in our scheme, but above all to the vagueness of the promise of airplanes. A letter from Nixon on June 20, drafted by State, did not allay Mrs. Meir's concerns because it stated, with less than dazzling clarity, that delivery of aircraft was conditional on the negotiations only with respect to timing — in other words, that we could postpone agreed deliveries if in our judgment this helped the negotiations. The Israelis, not unreasonably, considered that this exception deprived the commitment of much of its significance. Nixon, who from long campaigning considered promises to be the currency for dealing with tomorrow's problems, had a typical Nixonian solution. He told me privately that I could see Rabin and "tell them we've written the letter for the record. We're going to go forward on the planes unless there's an enormous change." (That too begged the question of what we would define as an enormous change.)

Then it was Moscow's turn. On June 23 Dobrynin reacted rather coolly to our Middle East overture. I asked if Moscow had given him any reply to my query about the withdrawal of Soviet combat troops; Dobrynin replied that I had put so many questions that he could not keep them all in mind. Dobrynin might well have thought he could evade the issue since the formal State Department initiative had made no reference to Soviet troops. He professed to be outraged by what he claimed was a "unilateral" American attempt to take over Middle East diplomacy. Negotiations were our problem now, he asserted, but he suspected we would have to come back to Moscow later. He did not know what "concessions" would be available then. In Moscow on June 29, Gromyko told Ambassador Beam that while the Soviets were studying our proposal they saw nothing new in it and that it had all the failings of previous efforts.

Egypt continued to envelop itself in silence.

In these conditions we decided to make clear that the President was not acting from weakness and that Soviet troops were a serious issue. On June 26 in San Clemente, in a background briefing, I took the initiative in challenging the Soviet military presence in Egypt. The Soviet Union's original intentions in sending combat personnel into the Middle East were irrelevant, I said. Even if they had been sent to shore up Nasser, their continued presence represented a strategic threat that had to be dealt with: "We are trying to get a settlement in such a way that the moderate regimes are strengthened, and not the radical regimes. We are trying to *expel the Soviet military presence,* not so much the advisors, but the combat pilots and the combat personnel, before they become so firmly established [emphasis added].''

The most accurate, if not elegant, way of describing the reaction is that all hell broke loose. I was accused by the State Department and pundits in the media of trying to scuttle the peace initiative, of making vainglorious threats beyond our capacity to carry out. The criticisms came from all quarters except the Soviets, who are usually provocative only when they can calculate a wide margin of safety and who had heard these views privately for three months. On June 30, in a backgrounder on the Cambodian operation, I was pressed on my alleged threat to "expel" the Russians. I stuck to my position; the Soviet military presence in Egypt created a dangerous new situation. Perhaps I should have used a more waffling expression than "expel," I said, but a Soviet combat presence was incompatible with peace. Moreover, "at some point of the Soviet presence in the Middle East there will be some indigenous Arab forces that will have their own reasons for not wanting to substitute one colonialism for another." Three years later we made this prediction come true.

By July 1 Nixon had substantially recovered from the trauma of Cambodia. And while he might not have been prepared yet to engage himself on the Arab-Israeli issue, he required no instruction on the geopolitical danger of Soviet combat troops in Egypt. With Rogers away on a trip, Nixon used a televised interview to express his essential agreement with my analysis. He warned that the two superpowers could be drawn into confrontation over the Middle East and that the United States would not tolerate the upsetting of the military balance there. "Once the balance of power shifts where Israel is weaker than its neighbors, there will be war. Therefore, it is in U.S. interests to maintain the balance. . . . As the Soviet Union moves in to support the UAR, it makes it necessary for the United States to evaluate what the Soviet Union does, and once that balance of power is upset, we will do what is necessary to maintain Israel's strength vis-a-vis its neighbors."

The Secretary of State would have none of this. From Europe he protested bitterly that "his" peace initiative was being torpedoed; he even reprimanded Sisco for supporting the President in a television appearance on July 12.

But Soviet sensitivities are not so tender; their calculations are based on an assessment of their interests, not on atmospherics. Now that Moscow suspected that we might mean business, Dobrynin's conduct in two meetings on July 7 and 9 could not have been more jovial. He exuded cooperativeness; he would have something to say on the Middle East soon. He made no reference to our warning. As it turned out, that had been none too soon. For in early July the Soviet missile complex, after securing the protection of Cairo, Alexandria, and Aswan, had begun inching toward the Suez Canal, despite Rogers's warning to Dobrynin of June 2. I summed up what we knew for Nixon on July 22: The Soviets and Egyptians were constructing a new defense barrier roughly parallel to the Suez Canal and at a distance of twenty to thirty nautical miles from it. That barrier included three SA-3 and eleven SA-2 sites, which could, of course, be augmented. It was close enough to the Canal to protect Egyptian artillery positions that were firing across it. At a minimum Egypt's capability for a war of attrition had been vastly enhanced; if the system grew in size and continued to move forward — as it gave every indication of doing — it might lay the basis for an Egyptian offensive into the Sinai.

In short, we were experiencing for the first time in the Nixon Administration the Soviet technique of using a military presence to enhance geopolitical influence. Within what it considers the Soviet orbit the Kremlin uses its military forces massively, rapidly, and ruthlessly. But when it operates beyond the dividing line between East and West, it moves with infinite care. The first commitment is usually moderate and justified by arguably defensive motives. At that point it is relatively simple to force a withdrawal by determined opposition. When no resistance is encountered, the Soviets tend to escalate rapidly. It is remarkable that a pattern so recurrent as to approach a stereotype should evoke — from Egypt to Angola to Ethiopia — the same doubts and hesitations that, far from encouraging moderation, serve only to guarantee that the Soviet involvement becomes massive.

So it was in the Middle East in July 1970. What had started as a protective move against deep penetration raids by Israel was on the verge of transforming the entire strategic equation. Some of our systems analysts already began to argue that Israel would be better served by having equipment suitable for resisting a cross-Canal invasion than by expending its aircraft in futile efforts to destroy the growing air defense system on the other side of the Canal. These arguments overlooked that a defensive strategy implies a war of attrition, a prospect fundamentally intolerable for a country outnumbered by around thirty to one. Israel was approaching the point of desperation, which might tempt it into preemptive action before the balance shifted irrevocably. Nasser might become reckless through euphoria. The Soviets were becoming indispensable to the radical Arabs. The United States seemed incapable of perceiving the essence of the danger, which was the growth of the Soviet military position in Egypt and the change in the regional balance of power. We had expended our prestige in starting talks based on incompatible premises and in paying each side for agreeing to negotiate about a peace that they needed more urgently than did we — the Israelis with airplanes and Nasser with hints of support on the territorial question. That we offered each side too little only compounded the tensions.

On July 1 Golda Meir wrote a bitter letter to the President. Noting that both SA-2 and SA-3 batteries were being installed to cover the Suez Canal, she pointed out: ''While these developments were going on, we were being told that the balance of power has remained intact.'' She warned that Israel would have no choice except to bomb these installations. But if Israel attacked a missile complex manned in part by Soviet personnel, there was a distinct possibility that the Soviets would defend it with their own aircraft. A direct clash between Israel and the Soviet Union was a danger that we could no longer ignore. I instituted urgent planning with unenthusiastic agencies who were still mumbling about forcing greater Israeli flexibility in negotiations — irrelevant to the problem we faced.

Then, on July 22 — just when a military clash seemed unavoidable — Nasser suddenly accepted our proposal for a cease-fire and negotiations.

Cease-fire and Standstill

WHY Nasser accepted our proposal at this point will not be known until Egyptian and Soviet archives become available. He may have feared an Israeli preemptive strike. He and his Soviet advisers may have interpreted the White House press statements by Nixon and me as raising a danger of American involvement. More likely, in the light of later events, he and the Soviets may have decided from the beginning to use the cease-fire offer much as they did the abortive initiative of March: as a cover for moving forward the missile complex with minimum risk.

The Administration was elated. Rogers claimed credit for having thought up the initiative — a claim privately disputed by Sisco, who insisted that he had fathered the idea. Nixon was convinced that his tough statement on July 1 had done the trick. Humility not being my strong suit, I was not loath to ascribe some of the ''success'' to my strong backgrounders of June 26 and 30 and my conversations with Dobrynin. Probably we were all somewhat right. In any event, it soon turned out that our elation was premature.

The early euphoria was deliberately encouraged by Dobrynin on July 23. He used a White House arrival ceremony for President Urho Kekkonen of Finland — Dobrynin was present as Acting Dean of the Diplomatic Corps — to give me a preview of what he would deliver at the State Department in the afternoon: The Soviet attitude to a temporary cease-fire was positive, and the Soviet Union also favored the resumption of the Jarring mission. However, Moscow believed that Jarring should have concrete guidance as to the meaning of the UN resolutions whose implementation he was supposed to promote. Dobrynin therefore urged that the Two- and Four-Power talks be speeded up to develop solutions on the outstanding issues. Showing that the Soviets had mastered our complex procedures, Dobrynin brought Rogers a special message as well. Delivering the note formally at the State Department, Dobrynin told Rogers what he neglected to convey to me — that the Soviets agreed to include a military standstill in the cease-fire. In compensation he subsequently gave me a note — of which Rogers was unaware — replying finally to my queries of June 10 and June 23 about the continued presence of Soviet troops in the Middle East. According to the note, the Soviets — *after* a comprehensive political settlement — would "probably" be prepared to consider withdrawal as long as it was a *mutual* obligation. When I pointed out that we had no troops in the Middle East, Dobrynin at first said that this was all the better for us and that the mutuality of obligation was put in as a matter of principle for cosmetic effect. Later he amended this to say that the United States would have to withdraw its military personnel from Iran.

Had we understood the situation better, we would have realized that we had cleared only the lowest hurdle. The negotiations we had arranged were certain to deadlock since Egypt still demanded restoration of the 1967 frontier and Israel still insisted on substantial territorial changes. Egypt expected American pressure on Israel; Israel, under the slogan of "no imposed settlement," wanted a free hand. Nixon had not yet decided on what he would do when the deadlock in the talks became apparent. Nor was the Soviet note all that reassuring. It defined neither "cease-fire" nor "standstill." It repeated the Soviet interpretation of the basis for Jarring's mission, which on all significant points was identical with the radical Arab program. Its willingness to discuss troop withdrawal was hedged by the word "probably" and linked to an absurd request for withdrawal of US military personnel from Iran. Above all, the Soviets might simply be repeating the maneuver of the previous March. The offer of a cease-fire now might mask, and then protect, the movement of the Soviet missile complex forward to the Canal.

At that time, such considerations were generally dismissed because our government was preoccupied with the Israeli reaction to our initiative, which was quite obstreperous, matching prickliness of behavior with shrillness of rhetoric. But this is scarcely extraordinary. Two thousand years of suffering have etched the premonition of tragedy deep into the soul of the Jewish people. And Israel's position as a tiny nation of 2.5 million surrounded by close to one hundred million potential enemies, in a region that has seen empires and states come and go, is a constant reminder to every Israeli of the transitoriness of historical existence. Israel's margin of survival is so narrow that its leaders distrust the great gesture or the stunning diplomatic departure; they identify survival with precise calculation, which can appear to outsiders (and sometimes is) pettifogging obstinacy. Even when Israeli leaders accept a peace proposal, they first resist fiercely, which serves the purpose of showing that they are not pushovers and thereby discourages further demands for Israeli concessions. And their acceptance is usually accompanied by endless requests for reassurances, memoranda of understanding, and secret explanations — all designed to limit the freedom of action of a rather volatile ally five thousand miles away that supplies its arms, sustains its economy, shelters its diplomacy, and has a seemingly limitless compulsion to offer peace plans.

This tendency is reinforced by a political system in which governments are usually turbulent coalitions of several parties and autonomous factions. Such a system does not make for rapid decisions or flexible diplomacy. Any leader who advocates a concession can be pounced upon by his colleagues and shrilly denounced in the Parliament as, if not a traitor, then at least a dupe of the wily (or foolish) Americans. An Israeli Cabinet meeting is well suited to nitpicking peace proposals to death, less adapted to developing a long-range policy. Israel sometimes finds it easier to shift the responsibility for difficult choices to its great ally than to make the decision itself; "American pressure" can be an excuse for what many Israeli leaders know in their hearts is necessary for Israel anyway.

For Israel to have responded enthusiastically to the cease-fire proposal and the prospect of negotiation would thus have been totally out of character. Nearly two more weeks of diplomatic exchanges and Presidential interventions were required to elicit a grudgingly favorable response. On July 23 Nixon sent Mrs. Meir another message urging the Israelis to take advantage of Arab acceptance of the US initiative. At the same time he assured her that we would not force Israel to accept the Arab interpretation of Security Council Resolution 242 in developing guidelines for the Jarring mission. It was just as well that this letter was not publicized until later, for the Arabs had been given precisely the opposite impression when the cease-fire initiative was presented to them.

Israel responded with requests for additional military assistance, especially weapons for the suppression of the Soviet surface-to-air missiles. We promised sympathetic consideration. Israel asked for further clarification of our position on such issues as withdrawals and refugees. Our answers clarified little because there was no unified Administration position and because those who had clear ideas were afraid to make them explicit lest they abort Israel's consent to the initiative. On July 30 Nixon bravely declared in a press conference that Israel could enter negotiations with confidence, "without fear that by her negotiations her position may be compromised or jeopardized in that period." Finally on July 31 we were told that the Israeli Cabinet had decided in principle to respond "affirmatively"; a formal response would be forthcoming soon. The President welcomed the decision in a statement from San Clemente.

Israeli concerns were far from groundless. Clearly, the Soviets and Egyptians were using the period before the cease-fire for a rapid buildup of missiles along the Canal, violating the spirit if not the letter of the projected standstill. The missiles would soon be able not only to protect the Egyptian artillery positions on the west bank of the Canal but to reach across it and protect an Egyptian landing. And in a cease-fire those missiles would be immune from retaliation.

On August 5 Rabin hurried in to paint a grim picture: Up to fourteen missile sites had been moved to within fifty kilometers of the Suez Canal; three missile ambush sites had been moved to within ten to twenty kilometers. On July 25; 27, and 30 Soviet-piloted aircraft had engaged Israeli aircraft; on July 30 four Russian-piloted aircraft had been shot down by the Israeli air force. Rabin reiterated Israel's determination not to permit the forward movement of the missile complex. He was so emphatic about it in a conversation on the evening of August 5 that I thought the Israelis might actually launch a ground attack against the SA-3 sites close to the Canal before a cease-fire, and so informed Nixon. At the last moment the Israeli Cabinet decided against such a move. I have never known whether Rabin exaggerated the likelihood of the attack or whether there was a last-minute change of heart in Jerusalem. At any rate, Israel informed us officially of its acceptance of the cease-fire on August 6. Rogers and Sisco rushed it to completion before anyone could change his mind, cutting some corners in the process with respect to the Jarring mission, which infuriated the Israelis.

On August 7 the cease-fire went into effect, born in fateful ambiguity. There was a cease-fire agreement between Egypt and Israel, which provided also for a military standstill in a zone fifty kilometers wide on either side of the Canal; unfortunately, the agreed text was vague as to what actions were prohibited by the standstill commitment. A separate "understanding" between Israel and the United States sought to fill this gap by outlining our joint view of what measures we felt would constitute violations of the Egyptian-Israeli agreement.*

Our chargé in Cairo was instructed to inform the Egyptians of the examples in the Israeli-American understanding but to say that they were only "illustrative" of activities which would be violations of the standstill. Aside from the fact that it was not self-evident how an understanding between Israel and the United States could bind Egypt and the USSR, there was also a serious problem of timing. The Egyptians formally accepted our proposal early on August 7 our time, and the

---

*These included prohibitions: "(a) not to introduce, move forward, construct or otherwise install missiles in this zone; (b) not to construct any concrete structures for the implacement of missiles; (c) not to carry out any work for the establishment of any new sites for missiles; (d) notwithstanding the consent to except maintenance of existing installations, no improvement should be made on the existing missile sites or implacements."

cease-fire went into effect at 1:00 A.M. August 8, Cairo time. But because of haggling with Israel over its terms, State's representative did
not communicate the "illustrative" catalogue of possible violations to
Cairo until 2:50 P.M. Cairo time on August 9, over thirty-six hours later.
This proved to be significant; the Israelis would later claim that Egypt
had violated the standstill agreement in the August 8–9 period even
before Egypt had any precise way of knowing what we understood by a
standstill.

The documents and "clarifications" were also passed on to the Soviets. But Moscow was not formally a party to either the cease-fire or
the standstill. And as the charges of violations mounted it increasingly
insisted that it was not bound despite its approving noises of July 23.

From this precarious base the first initiative for negotiations between the parties since 1967 was launched. The first day of the cease-
fire was quiet along the Canal though the Palestinian guerrillas based in
Jordan vowed not to observe it. While the Soviets used the occasion to
call once again for total Israeli withdrawal, they also publicly described
the cease-fire as an "important first step." The United States government began to prepare for the Jarring talks and to study Israeli military
aid requests. Sisco even told the NSC Senior Review Group on August
12 that, looking ahead to the Jarring talks, he was already beginning to
draft a "full agreement," to include definitive provisions on final borders. Our internal debate over Israel's aid requests rapidly bogged down
into abstract arguments about what kind of Israeli strategy to support.
This had the effect of delaying a decision, since the type of weapon
depended on a prior interagency agreement on military doctrine. These
somewhat esoteric discussions were soon overtaken by Israeli charges
that the military standstill was being violated.

Information on the early Egyptian-Soviet moves was confused and no
doubt was put in the most dramatic light by Israeli publicity. Verification was not eased by the amazing fact that the starting time of the
standstill was in the middle of the night, when reconnaissance aircraft or
satellites, assuming they were ready at such short notice, would have
been able to see little anyway. But there was no doubt that a substantial
forward movement of the Egyptian-Soviet air defense complex had
taken place in the nearly three weeks between Egypt's acceptance of the
American proposal and the beginning of the cease-fire and standstill. Almost certainly, whatever was under construction at the time the cease-
fire went into effect was completed afterward. This could be simple
cynicism; it could also be the case that the Soviets and Egyptians were
caught by surprise by the uncharacteristic speed with which our bureaucracy moved in launching the cease-fire.

By August 13 Israeli charges of Soviet-Egyptian violations had
reached our press. In Israel Menachem Begin withdrew his opposition

party from the emergency coalition in which it had participated since 1967 and violently attacked Golda Meir for having agreed to the United States plan in the first place. However, the State Department took the line that the United States had reached ''no conclusions'' about the Israeli reports of violations. Our Ambassador in Israel, Walworth Barbour, was instructed to urge the Israeli government to cease public discussion of the matter. Instead, Israel was asked speedily to appoint its representative to the Jarring talks.

On August 15 Ambassador Rabin came in to see me. He presented a démarche from Golda Meir reviewing the evidence that fourteen SA-2s backed up by SA-3s had been moved into the standstill zone. As a result Israel had lost five Phantoms (such are the wonders of a Middle East cease-fire). In other words, after our mild response to the first forward moves, made around the time the standstill went into effect, the Soviets and Egyptians had made *additional* deployments, this time clearly in violation of the agreement. Mrs. Meir asked to present her case to the President personally. This was judged inopportune by the State Department, which was eager to get the Jarring talks under way. Instead I arranged an opportunity for Rabin to show the Israeli intelligence to Nixon. Rabin used the occasion to complain bitterly about the reluctance of our intelligence community to accept Israeli evidence; the violations were genuine, he said. The upshot was that Nixon approved a rapid delivery of Shrike missiles for use against the SA-3 complex and later agreed to see Mrs. Meir in September when she would be in the United States for the twenty-fifth anniversary of the United Nations.

There was some merit in Rabin's complaint of the reluctance of the US intelligence community to find violations. As I explained to the President:

Israel, with her survival at stake, cannot afford to take chances. . . . The nature of the Israelis' situation is bound to influence their interpretation of ambiguous events. We, on the other hand, have an incentive to minimize such evidence, since the consequences of finding violations are so unpleasant. Violations force us to choose between doing something about them and thus risk the blowup of our initiative; or doing nothing and thus renege on our promises to Israel, posing the threat of her taking military action. Accordingly, we tend to lean over backwards to avoid the conclusion that the Arabs are violating the ceasefire unless the evidence is unambiguous.

Whatever the reason, it is probable that our hesitant first response encouraged Nasser to accelerate the forward deployment of missiles. We were witnessing, in fact, a replay of events of the spring: a seemingly marginal Soviet move, followed by a pause for consolidation and analysis of our reaction, succeeded by a rapid, dramatic buildup. Admittedly, the evidence in the first half of August was ambiguous as to whether the disputed activity had taken place just before or just after the cease-fire went into effect. There was no doubt, however, that whenever it occurred it was in defiance of the warning of June 2 by the Secretary of State to Dobrynin that Soviet missiles within thirty kilometers of the Canal could not be considered defensive.

By August 19 new evidence had been received confirming, as Israel alleged, clear-cut violations of the standstill agreement. This forced the State Department to formal action. But the public response, by way of a statement by the Department's press spokesman, was again so low-key as to suggest that we were looking for pretexts to avoid action rather than to seek remedies:

> We have concluded that there was forward deployment of surface-to-air missiles into and within the zone west of the Suez Canal around the time the ceasefire went into effect. There is some evidence that this was continued beyond the ceasefire deadline, although our evidence of this is not conclusive. . . . We are examining [additional information from Israel]. . . . We do not now anticipate making further public statements on this matter. . . .

In tandem with the public announcement, Egypt was informed of some of the evidence we had. But since the evidence was "not conclusive," we told the Egyptians that we would not make any public charges; we reminded them of what were considered violations and warned that further such activity would jeopardize peace talks. The Soviets were also informed of the approach in Cairo. Finally, a major effort was made to persuade the Israelis to react with restraint and not to cause future difficulties by publicity. A second American démarche was made in Cairo on August 22 when we presented "incontrovertible" evidence of violations.

If the United States protests an issue, it must do so forcefully and with a description of the remedial action it expects. A plaintive tone is the least likely to evoke a satisfactory response; it suggests that the protest may be for the record only. It deprives the offending country of a domestic pretext for changing course. This is especially important when the subject is politically sensitive and the policy not easy to reverse. On August 24, the day that Jarring announced the start of peace talks involving the chief UN delegates of Israel, Egypt, and Jordan, Egypt flatly rejected our charges of violations. Cairo took the position that its actions were consistent with its interpretation of the agreement; that it would not introduce additional missiles into the zone but reserved the right to "rotate" them in and out; that it would not construct any new sites but reserved the right to "maintain" and "repair" existing ones; that Israel was violating the cease-fire and that American arms supply to Israel ran counter to assurances given by Rogers as well as the cease-fire agreement.

At this juncture I advised the President that we were expending all our credit with the Israelis simply to establish a cease-fire before the talks had even begun. And these talks were certain to bring even more deep-seated disagreements to the surface. The Soviets and Nasser were likely to ''be tempted to believe that we are willing to acquiesce in their violations of the standstill cease-fire, despite our direct warnings to them and our promises to Israel. This has serious consequences for our current initiative in the Middle East, the longer term prospects for the area generally, and US–Soviet relations.'' It was crucial to take a harder line against violations of the cease-fire and to bring their responsibilities home to the Soviets.

A rational discussion of these issues was made next to impossible by the extraordinary diplomatic procedures that had developed in the previous eighteen months, and by the personal rivalry between Rogers and me. Nixon's penchant for operating through his Assistants rather than his Cabinet could be managed — if with great tension — so long as the White House was indeed in charge. But when operational control of sensitive negotiations left the White House, the weakness of the system became glaring. The State Department simply did not know enough about the President's thinking to pursue the nuances of his policy. Its tendency to nudge matters in its own preferred direction and to interpret Presidential instructions in a manner compatible with its preconceptions made matters worse. It was impossible to formulate Presidential instructions with any confidence that the intangibles underlying them would be understood or implemented.

I could have acted as an intermediary had my relations with Rogers been happier. But by the summer of 1970 it was clear to him that he was being excluded from key decisions on almost all issues except the Middle East, or else brought in so late that his role was that of a ratifier rather than of a policy formulator. Indeed, it must have occurred to him that it could not be happenstance that so many Presidential decisions were taken when he was on foreign trips. His pride did not let him admit that this could take place only at the instance of his old friend, the President. He therefore blamed me. Nor was he totally wrong. Nixon distrusted State and wanted sensitive matters handled by the White House alone, but my presence made the two-channel procedures possible and I was quite willing to step into the breach to conduct negotiations with my small staff and no interagency liaison. The procedures so painful to Rogers were clearly instigated by Nixon; it is equally evident that I nurtured them. Neither Rogers nor I mustered the grace to transcend an impasse that we should have recognized was not in the national interest. If we had been prepared to overcome our not inconsiderable egos, we could have complemented each other's efforts. Even then, of course, there would have remained large areas of disagreement on policy and tactics.

The Middle East was the one subject on which Rogers was given the responsibility and the authority. And the Middle East cease-fire had seemed like a great triumph, the first uncontroverted achievement of the Nixon Administration in foreign policy. Understandably, Rogers was reluctant to face the prospect that it might fail; he was acutely sensitive to any hint of White House interference. He tended to consider my concerns as an attempt to deprive him of his one field of glory. Sisco was caught in the middle. Heroically, he sought to navigate between conflicting, occasionally irreconcilable perspectives, and to remain loyal to both his Secretary and his President. He often steadied the ship, but he was in no position to give it a clear direction.

Only the President could do that, but having decided not to rely on the NSC staff for the Middle East, and distrusting the State Department machinery, he was left with no instrument for sustained governmental action. His usual response to controversy among his advisers was procrastination. In areas under White House control this did no ultimate damage because to some extent I could manage events until they forced a Presidential decision. But in the passionate circumstances of the Middle East the procedure risked being outstripped by events — a danger reinforced by Nixon's annual August sojourn in San Clemente, which slowed the administrative pace on all Presidential issues. Moreover, Nixon was still toying with the idea that he should weigh in personally with a Soviet summit.

A meeting in San Clemente on August 25 of the President, Rogers, Sisco, and me ended inconclusively and acrimoniously after Rogers accused me of seeking to foment a crisis by being so insistent on cease-fire violations. But crises cannot be avoided by denying the circumstances that produce them or blaming the bearer of bad tidings. By the end of August events began to assert their own logic; we were in danger of losing our margin for decision precisely because we pretended that we could extend it through the strenuous exercise of goodwill.

On August 28 the Soviets put themselves clearly on Nasser's side in this dispute, seizing the occasion of a US communication of August 8 that had informed them we would be monitoring the cease-fire with U-2 reconnaissance aircraft. (I thought that communication a mistake then because it would encourage the Soviets to take a position on an action which was needed to monitor the agreement. It is generally unwise in diplomacy to raise an issue when one is not prepared to accept the likely response.) Their reply, to Sisco in Washington and Beam in Moscow, took us to task on the U-2 flights, which were described as a "new complicating element"; in the Soviet view they contradicted the terms of the cease-fire, violated Egyptian sovereignty, involved "extremely serious complications," and also ran "the risk of special surprise." I informed the President, pointing out that the Soviets probably had every reason to be concerned about verification of the cease-fire in impartial hands. It would be easier for the Soviets and Nasser to reject charges of violations if they were based only on Israeli surveillance.

By August 29 the head of the State Department's Bureau of Intelligence and Research, Ray Cline, had concluded that instead of one SA-2 site within the thirty-kilometer zone, about which we had protested the previous week, there were now seven or eight, as well as three or four SA-3 sites. Most of these sites in his judgment were almost certainly built after the cease-fire went into effect. On August 31 a CIA assessment confirmed these conclusions.

A meeting of the President and his senior advisers — Rogers, Moorer, Laird, Helms, and me — was now unavoidable, and it took place on September 1 in San Clemente. The President directed that a very strong protest be made in both Cairo and Moscow, and that Israel be asked to send a representative to the Jarring talks in New York. On September 3 the State Department publicly confirmed the violations, this time less ambiguously but still with considerable restraint, and indicated that we would deal with the matter only in diplomatic channels; concurrently, State kept urging that the Jarring talks begin.

Both Egypt and the Soviet Union continued to reject our protests. Cairo denied the charges on September 4, in the process challenging our continued military supply to Israel as inconsistent with alleged assurances of restraint. On September 6, Deputy Foreign Minister Sergei Vinogradov told Beam that the Soviet Union had concluded no cease-fire agreement with the United States and was therefore not responsible for any violations. Vinogradov noted the "strange arrangement" whereby the United States was supervising the cease-fire without any request from Egypt and violating Egyptian territory by overflying the Sinai. About the same time, the Soviet chargé delivered a message in Washington expressing concern over an allegedly impending Israeli preemptive attack on the missile sites. The Soviets asked us to take steps to prevent this. We had no such evidence. I thought it was part of the perennial Soviet effort to put us on the defensive. I told Sisco to pass the warning to the Israelis without comment, but not to confirm to the Soviets that he had done so. There was no sense in letting them score easy points in Cairo as protector of the Arabs.

Israel Bows out of Negotiations

AFTER all the disputes and violations it was no surprise that on September 6, Israel announced that it could not participate in the settlement talks under Jarring. On September 6, moreover, Palestinian guerrillas hijacked three airplanes. What had started as a step toward peace a month earlier was precipitating a confrontation. I tended to share the view of the chief Soviet expert on my staff, Hal Sonnenfeldt, then and later an invaluable collaborator, who in September sent me an analysis drawing an analogy to the Cuban missile crisis:

> . . . my deep concern [is] that in the present Middle Eastern situation we may have (unwittingly) misled the Soviets to believe that cheating on the ceasefire was a matter of indifference to us and that we may have thereby contributed to a potentially much deeper crisis. . . . The nature, timing and speed of our cease-fire initiative, the relative looseness of its terms, the informality of its consummation, our reluctance to concede violations and our other statements and actions *after* violations began could have led the Soviets to conclude that all that really mattered to us was a ceasefire in a pre-election period in which we preferred not to confront the awkward choices of continued open warfare. . . . They could thus have been surprised by our subsequent apparently real indignation at what was happening (having meanwhile given the UAR and themselves the green light to proceed with violations and thus put their prestige on the line). Or they may even yet believe that we are merely play-acting.

At the same time, the Middle East expert on my staff, Hal Saunders, informed me that Soviet and Egyptian violations had actually *accelerated* after our protests of early September. Saunders, another superb analyst and fair-minded adviser, was not known for an anti-Arab bias. Yet he wrote me that, according to U-2 photography taken *after* our early September démarches in Moscow and Cairo:

> . . . it seems clear that the Egyptians are continuing SAM activity in violation of the military standstill provision of the ceasefire agreement. They have made no move to restore or rectify the situation on the 24 sites we have protested. . . . We have seen at least a 50 percent increase in the number of occupied SAM sites since August 10. . . . Activity is not levelling off. . . . The defensive missile complex along the Canal would seem to mean more to the Egyptians than the peace talks since the Israelis have made it very clear that they cannot go on with the talks until the pre-ceasefire situation is restored. . . .

Even then, some diehard analysts were determined to restore the peace initiative by making the facts fit their preferences. An inventive Defense Department expert came up with the extraordinary theory that perhaps Nasser had not violated the standstill after all. It could not be excluded, it was argued, that the missiles had been *hidden* in the fifty-kilometer zone before the cease-fire went into effect and had been surfaced only afterward. Hence, they had not been "introduced" into the zone; the standstill remained pristine. This sophisticated reasoning did not explain why the Egyptians would hide missiles when their deployment was permitted and surface them only when their deployment was proscribed. Nor was it possible to find through aerial photography sheds or warehouses large enough to house so much matériel, while to hide it in the sand would have required a hole the size of the pyramids.

There was simply no avoiding the fact that by the middle of September our initiatives had reached an impasse. In the bargain, we had fulfilled the Israeli arms request held in abeyance since March. We ended up increasing it, not so much to win Israel's flexibility in peace negotiations as to ward off an Israeli preemptive attack against the advance of the Egyptian missiles we had not been able to stop; we gained no credit for it in Israel and we magnified the displeasure of the Arabs. The Soviets had established a combat presence in Egypt that already threatened Israel and would be useful later in collusion with Nasser against any moderate Arab government. Our actions did not dominate events; they followed them, and often seemed to be overwhelmed by them. And the greatest danger resided in the apparent Soviet misperceptions of our firmness.

Almost inevitably, further crises descended on the Administration in September. We were faced simultaneously with a civil war in Jordan, a Soviet attempt to build a submarine base in Cuba, and the coming to power of Allende in Chile. It was at once the most dangerous and decisive period of the new Administration — far more perilous than the Cambodian incursion, for all the hysteria and media attention that received. Only after we had braved that storm would the various components of our global diplomacy, so laboriously assembled over a year and a half, begin to fall into place.

XV

The Autumn of Crises: Jordan

WITHIN a three-week period in September 1970 three major crises descended upon the Administration in corners of the world thousands of miles apart.

They could not have been more different. One was a civil war in a desert kingdom — Jordan — between the royal government and armed guerrillas seeking to secure a base to attack a neighboring country; the second was the sudden Soviet attempt to create a nuclear submarine base in Cienfuegos, Cuba, with prospects of direct superpower confrontation; the third was an election in a major country of South America — Chile — which risked a takeover by radicals allied with Communists. The causes of these events were fundamentally different, as were the concerns they raised for American policy. And yet they all represented — or seemed to us to represent — different facets of a global Communist challenge. None could have succeeded without Communist impetus or encouragement. The Soviet military thrust into Egypt and its incitement of radical Arabs spawned the crisis in Jordan; the naval base in Cuba was a direct Soviet challenge; and Chile's election, for all its ambiguity, presented the possibility that a nation would join the Communist family by democratic processes for the first time in history.

Crisis in Jordan

THROUGHOUT history boundaries in the Middle East have moved with the shifting sands. The Arab nation, glorious in its political constructions during the five hundred years after the birth of Islam in A.D. 622, found itself, for almost as long a period afterward, under the domination of various foreign rulers. Nationhood became at once a mystical concept and a nearly prophetic vision, a dream inspiring fervent believers and heroic actions but seldom realized. The last of these foreign empires, the Ottoman, was expelled from the region as a result of World War I. But it was not succeeded, as so many Arab nationalists had hoped, by one unified state. Rather, for another generation the Middle East was divided into semi-independent states under the tutelage of European powers. Each of these countries struggled for independence; they all achieved full sovereignty in the aftermath of World War II.

One of these states was the Hashemite Kingdom of Jordan. Called Transjordan before 1949, it had come about after World War I, when the League of Nations gave Britain a Mandate to govern Palestine, which then included all the territory from Iraq to the Mediterranean. In 1921, Britain split off from its Mandate what was then a trackless desert to create a kingdom for its Hashemite allies who had been disappointed in their hopes for other realms. In this unpromising setting talented rulers and an industrious people built the Jordanian state, which has been since its birth an element of restraint, progress, and stability in the Middle East. The partition of Palestine drew the Hashemite Kingdom onto the West Bank of the Jordan River. There it governed with its characteristic enlightenment until, from an excess of Arab solidarity, it involved itself in Nasser's reckless gamble of 1967. As a result, it lost the populous and fertile West Bank to Israeli occupation.

Fedayeen guerrillas — Palestinian refugees from the many Arab-Israeli wars — established themselves in Jordan, especially after 1967, in well-organized base camps from which to launch raids into Israel and Israeli-held territory. In addition, 17,000 Iraqi troops, representing the most radical of Arab regimes, remained encamped in eastern Jordan, left over from the 1967 war. King Hussein could not remove either group from his country without being challenged for his lack of "Arab solidarity." The presence of these radical armed forces both demonstrated the ascendancy of Arab radicalism in the age of Nasser and perpetuated the weakness of Hussein's authority. Nor were the fedayeen and Iraqis reluctant to wield their power heavy-handedly. The guerrillas raided Israel regardless of the risks this posed for Jordan; the Iraqis conducted military maneuvers on Jordanian territory.

The Jordanian army, descendant of the legendary Arab Legion trained by the British General Sir John Glubb (Glubb Pasha) in the 1940s, was composed largely of Bedouin fiercely loyal to King Hussein. But in 1970 it found itself engaged on two fronts; protecting the King against the fedayeen (and Iraqis) and safeguarding Jordanian territory against Israeli reprisals after fedayeen raids. Jordan learned (as did Lebanon six years later) that countries that harbor guerrillas run enormous risks. They are in constant danger of losing control over their destinies because others determine the question of war and peace for them. Indeed, if the guerrillas grow sufficiently powerful, they sooner or later seek to replace the authority of the host government.

By the summer of 1970 the young, able, and courageous King was in grave peril. The guerrillas, resentful of his efforts to promote a political settlement with Israel, increasingly challenged his army. On June 9 an attempt was made to assassinate him. Hussein dismissed some of his army leaders and assumed personal command. But he was reluctant to take on the Palestinians, whom he had ruled until 1967 and hoped to reunite with his kingdom. Conditions in Amman deteriorated. On June 11 I reported to Nixon that in the view of our chargé d'affaires (our new Ambassador, Dean Brown, not yet having arrived), "the situation has fallen apart." Our Embassy in Amman was given authority to evacuate dependents and nonessential personnel (about four hundred people, if all decided to leave).

That same day I called a meeting of the WSAG, our interagency mechanism for crisis management. We faced two major contingencies: first, evacuation of Americans, if necessary by military means; and second, our response if King Hussein appealed for assistance to maintain his authority against either the fedayeen or outside intervention from Iraq or Syria, both governed by leaders even more extreme and pro-Soviet than Nasser.

At the WSAG, opinions varied widely as to the wisdom, and indeed the feasibility, of American military action. If the Jordanian army should lose control over the airports, evacuation of Americans might require the landing of troops, a prospect that filled neither political nor military leaders with great enthusiasm. The problem, and the reluctance, would be even greater should the King ask for American intervention to ensure his continued rule. There was some hesitation even to *plan* for such contingencies. The Cambodian operation had not yet ended, our forces were stretched thin around the world, and the pickets surrounding the White House testified to our domestic disunity. Military action in Jordan was also technically difficult because in the more than ten years since our 1958 landing in Lebanon we had lost either the staging areas available then (in Libya, Greece, and Turkey) or the right to use them for Mideast conflicts. Reluctance to think of American military intervention was reinforced by the conviction of many that even if successful it would discredit Hussein in the rest of the Arab world and perhaps be his political death sentence.

I felt a bias toward supporting Hussein if at all possible. Just as I had sought to thwart Nasser as long as he relied so heavily on his Soviet connection and supported all radical movements, so it now seemed to me important to demonstrate that friendship with the United States had its benefits. Hussein had always advocated moderation, resisted the radical tide, and avoided fashionable anti-Western slogans. He was in difficulty because of his reluctance to permit the guerrillas free rein. His collapse would radicalize the entire Middle East. Israel would not acquiesce in the establishment of guerrilla bases all along its Jordanian frontier. Another Middle East war would be extremely likely. Thus, Jordan, in my view, was a test of our capacity to control events in the region. Nixon shared this perception. At a June 17 NSC meeting he said:

Let us suppose late in the summer we get a request from Lebanon or Jordan for assistance, or something happens in Lebanon. What can we do? . . . There comes a time when the US is going to be tested as to its credibility in the area. The real question will be, will we act? Our action has to be considered in that light. We must be ready. . . . Is the question really a military one or is it our credibility as a power in that area?

On June 22 I reassembled the WSAG to use the President's expressed wish to get some planning finally accomplished. By that time, the immediate danger having eased, the departments were ready to plan for contingencies that they did not think would arise. Even though the evacuation of the American citizens was proceeding, Hussein had emerged from the crisis gravely weakened. A report to the President drafted by Hal Saunders of my staff in early July abounded with ominous phrases: "The authority and prestige of the Hashemite regime will continue to decline. The international credibility of Jordan will be further compromised. . . . Greater fedayeen freedom of action will inevitably result in more serious breaches of the cease-fire in the Jordan Valley. . . . Hussein faces an uncertain political future. . . ."

The time of testing over Jordan therefore seemed imminent. Our contingency planning — however halfheartedly undertaken — stood us in good stead when early in September the tinder burst into flame and almost turned into a general Middle East conflagration.

Iraqi-Jordanian Showdown

I N any administration events occur that are not foreseen by intelligence; indeed, they are probably unforeseeable because they also surprise the victim who had the greatest interest in preventing them. The disturbance of the equilibrium may begin as a relatively minor event; its ever-widening ripples turn it into a crisis that either rages out of control or issues into that sudden calm indicating that a new equilibrium has been achieved. During the period of crisis the elements from which policy is shaped suddenly become fluid. In the resulting upheaval the statesman must act under constant pressure. Paradoxically, this confers an unusual capacity for creative action; everything suddenly depends on the ability to dominate and impose coherence on confused and seemingly random occurrences. Ideally this should occur without the use of force; however, sometimes one can avoid the use of force only by threatening it.

Some may visualize crisis management as a frenzied affair in which key policymakers converge on the White House in their limousines, when harassed officials are bombarded by nervous aides rushing in and out with the latest flash cables. Oddly enough, I have found this not to be accurate; periods of crisis, to be sure, involve great tension but they are also characterized by a strange tranquillity. All the petty day-to-day details are stripped away; they are either ignored, postponed, or handled by subordinates. Personality clashes are reduced; too much is usually at stake for normal jealousies to operate. In a crisis only the strongest strive for responsibility; the rest are intimidated by the knowledge that failure will demand a scapegoat. Many hide behind a consensus that they will be reluctant to shape; others concentrate on registering objections that will provide alibis after the event. The few prepared to grapple with circumstances are usually undisturbed in the eye of a hurricane. All around them there is commotion; they themselves operate in solitude and a great stillness that yields, as the resolution nears, to exhaustion, exhilaration, or despair.

The event in Jordan that triggered all forces occurred on September 1 when Palestinian guerrillas sought for a second time in three months to assassinate King Hussein, attacking his motorcade. Fighting immediately broke out between the loyal army and the fedayeen. The Iraqis threatened to use their troops stationed in Jordan to ''take all necessary measures to protect fedayeen action.'' The night before, the King had already informed our Embassy officials that he might be forced to take more drastic steps. The King expressed the hope that he could count on US support. He thought a strong public statement by the United States might discourage outside intervention; even better would be a joint statement with the Soviet Union.

The State Department's response to this message was hardly electric. Concerned with preserving its peace initiative, reluctant to add Jordan to a plate already overflowing with cease-fire violations in Egypt, the responsible officials did not (to my knowledge) immediately raise the matter to the White House or even the interagency level. Instead, an amazingly noncommittal reply was dispatched the next day, informing the King that public warnings by the United States had many implications which had to be carefully weighed — a truism that would not have conveyed excessive succor to the beleaguered Hussein. One reason for the initial aloofness was the conventional wisdom of the Middle East experts that Arabs were so excitable that any public warning was likely to drive them into frenzy. This judgment, in my view, confuses volubility with erratic behavior; in crises I found most Arab leaders to be circumspect and calculating.

Later in the day on September 1, Iraq issued another ultimatum warning that if Jordanian shelling of the fedayeen did not cease by 11:00 P.M. the Iraqi army would take steps to stop it. Zaid Rifai, close adviser to the King (and a former student of mine at Harvard), informed our Embassy and renewed the King's request for a big-power statement. He also inquired whether we knew what Israel would do if Iraq moved.

The latter was a question of grave import. It was improbable that Israel would permit Iraq, the most radical Arab state, to move its forces closer to her borders; nor indeed was it likely that Israel's army would be inactive while Palestinian guerrillas occupied the Jordan Valley. But to be joined by Israeli armed forces in his conflict was no trivial matter for the King. In defending his political independence he had no incentive to destroy his moral position in the Arab world. The question about Israeli intentions was not new. It had first been posed on behalf of Hussein on August 4 when the Iraqi troops stationed in eastern Jordan as a form of blackmail had refused to terminate their maneuvers on schedule. Our Ambassador in Israel had then reported to Washington the possibility that Israel would attack if Iraqi troops moved westward; he did not raise the issue with the Israeli government. The Near Eastern Bureau at State was so skittish about this subject that no reply was returned to the Jordanian query at that time. The need for it temporarily disappeared as the situation eased.

By September the problem had returned, as is the wont of unresolved issues, and with it the need to determine Israeli reaction. The State Department adopted its not uncommon practice of procrastination, probably because it did not want to complicate the efforts to deal with Egyptian-Israeli cease-fire violations even further. On September 2 our Ambassador Jacob Beam in Moscow called on Soviet Deputy Foreign Minister Sergei Vinogradov and in his low-key manner sought the Soviets' influence in restraining their Iraqi friends. Vinogradov affected avuncular concern. The Soviet Union was interested in preserving favorable conditions for peace talks but knew nothing, he said, about any Iraqi ultimatum; it was thus difficult for Moscow to take an official position. Vinogradov offered his personal opinion that Iraq would not intervene in Jordanian affairs — but, then again, he said, no one could predict what would happen in the Middle East. Moscow, in short, was keeping its options open. The fact that Anatoly Dobrynin was remaining in Moscow throughout the late summer left no doubt that the Soviets were not ready to spend any capital on calming the situation. The matter would thus have to be settled on the ground.

In Amman, on September 2, Zaid Rifai reported to our Embassy that the Iraqis had not implemented their threat. Three days later, he reaffirmed interest in a big-power statement urging restraint. Reflecting the State Department attitude, our chargé responded to renewed Jordanian queries about Israeli intentions with the extraordinary statement that he could not imagine Jordan's accepting help from its enemy Israel against a fellow Arab country. The King was, of course, much too subtle to put the issue this way and much too intelligent to require lectures by American officials on the implications of his own query.

Meanwhile, the situation in Amman continued to improve; talks began between the Jordanian government and moderate fedayeen leaders. On September 3, Beam in Moscow presented our protest of cease-fire violations along the Suez Canal. In the course of that conversation Vinogradov described things in Jordan as no worse and no better; he made no reference to any Soviet intercession with Iraq. To underscore the importance we attached to developments in Jordan, Nixon on September 4 received our new Ambassador to Amman, Dean Brown, in San Clemente.

By September 5 the crisis seemed to have abated. One more sign was the sudden Soviet warning to us against an Israeli crossing of the Canal, which they claimed was imminent. (As already described, this also had the function of deflecting attention from Egyptian and Soviet cease-fire violations.) It is a stereotyped Soviet tactic to fire off a threat as a crisis in which they have been reluctant to intervene winds down; evidently they hope to inspire the impression after the event of having been the principal factor in resolving the issue and thus establish a claim for compensation. (For example, in 1956 the Soviets had sent a stern warning to London and Paris to desist from the Suez invasion when the decision to withdraw was already apparent.) While the fedayeen had been prevented from taking over, the King's power was far from restored. Iraq's maneuvering remained an uneasy reminder of his waning authority in his own country. The American attitude — limited to nervous lecturing — had been ambiguous, falling far short of any action that could affect the situation concretely, much less dominate it. The calm was deceptive, however. Events in fact were now heading out of control.

Hijacking Crisis

THERE has never been a satisfactory explanation of why the fedayeen acted as they did during the period they themselves later described as "Black September." At the beginning of the month Nasser and the Soviets had successfully moved their missile system up to the Canal. The United States was getting ready to press Israel for negotiations in which Jordan was slated to participate, looking toward withdrawal from the West Bank. If left undisturbed, the process had many hopeful elements for the Arabs. Israel's military predominance along the Canal had been broken; pressures on Israel were certain to multiply once negotiations started. But the extremists among the fedayeen had their eyes elsewhere; their goal was not peace with Israel but its destruction. They were as yet unrecognized as a political entity — treated as refugees internationally, as objects of mixed fear and adulation in the Arab world, as terrorist criminals by Israel. They did not aspire to a political settlement in which their demands would be compromised; they sought a base under their control from which they could mount the decisive attack on

Israel and destroy it. In this sense their attempt to thwart diplomatic progress had a rational basis. On the other hand, the Palestinians were also gradually gaining ground in Jordan. They were approaching autonomy; by overplaying their hand, they destroyed their own prospects and ended up expelled to Lebanon. And the crisis they produced, ironically enough, handed the United States the opportunity to recoup much of what had been lost in the hesitations of the previous month, and so opened the road for the diplomacy of the years that followed.

The crisis erupted on September 6 when members of the Marxist Popular Front for the Liberation of Palestine (PFLP), the most extremist wing of the fedayeen movement, hijacked several aircraft. A Pan American 747 jumbo jet was flown to Cairo airport, its passengers released, and the plane blown up shortly after landing. An American TWA 707 and a Swissair DC-8 were flown by fedayeen to Dawson Field, a dirt strip some thirty miles from Amman. On September 9 a British VC-10 was also hijacked and joined the others at Dawson Field. The hijacking of an Israeli plane was aborted by its security personnel.

Altogether these hijackings involved several hundred passengers, including Swiss, German, British, French, Americans, and others. The most vulnerable group were the Israelis and dual-nationals — that is, those holding both Israeli and American passports. On September 7, the PFLP offered to release all passengers except Israelis and dual-nationals in return for the release of all fedayeen held in Swiss, German, and British jails. Israeli and dual-national passengers were to be held in return for guerrillas in Israeli jails. They gave a deadline of seventy-two hours.

Our immediate concern was to prevent the retention of American citizens, along with Israelis, after the other hostages had been released. Nor could we accept hierarchies established by foreigners among American citizens. We knew that Israel had a policy of never yielding to blackmail. It feared that if it ever yielded, no guerrillas could be held captive; terrorism would be encouraged. Our own view was roughly the same. The European countries involved did not believe that they could adopt such an uncompromising position. We urged them, at a minimum, to negotiate as a group.

On September 8, Rogers called a morning meeting in his office at State; Laird, Helms, Alexis Johnson, Joe Sisco, and I attended.

Allegations of a "Situation Room syndrome," discussed already in Chapter IX with respect to the EC-121 shootdown, sometimes include the accusation that officials manufacture crises in order to fulfill romantic notions of military prowess and machismo. This is nonsense. For one thing, the Situation Room is uncomfortable, unaesthetic, and essentially oppressive, as I have already described. For another, discussions there are usually highly technical. Because of the proximity of the most advanced communications equipment, those deliberating in the Situation Room have instant access to the latest information. Since they are usually sub-Cabinet officers, there is a good chance that decisions will be taken systematically through analysis and referred to higher levels for review.

The risk of rash decisions lies not there but in ad hoc meetings in the Oval Office, the Cabinet Room, or the personal offices of Cabinet members. There the danger is real that plausibility is confused with truth and verbal fluency overwhelms cool analysis. It is there that in the absence of staff work, decisions may be made which the facts do not support, where individuals talk to impress and not to elucidate at a time when precision is crucial. The temptation there is much greater than in the Situation Room to allow a fleeting and superficial consensus to ratify unexamined assumptions. There are the simultaneous risks of paralysis and recklessness. Principals cannot really know the consequences of their recommendations unless those recommendations have been translated into specific operational terms.

So it was at the meeting in Rogers's office. Wild ideas dominated desultory discussion. For example, considerable time was devoted to the possible use against the hijackers of some nerve gas that paralyzed victims without their knowledge. The lack of knowledge of whether a suitable gas existed in our arsenal impeded the discussion no more than the absence of a concept of how it was to be delivered, indeed, how any military action was to be organized or sustained. Rogers concluded with the conviction with which he had started the meeting — nothing could be done. The use of American troops was militarily impractical; Hussein would not move against the Palestinians; and Israeli intervention might be his death warrant.

The same arguments were repeated in the afternoon in a meeting with the President. Laird, Rogers, Johnson, Sisco, and I were present, along with J. Edgar Hoover and John Mitchell, who dealt with the domestic implications of hijacking. The President made no decision. He had earlier told me privately that the hijacking should be used as a pretext to crush the fedayeen; in the meeting he made no such comment. He did say that in an extremity he preferred American to Israeli military intervention. Rogers demurred, saying that we would pay an enormous price for an essentially useless act.

The President turned to me. I replied that we faced two problems, the safety of the hostages and the future of Jordan. If the fedayeen could use Jordan as their principal base and in the process destroy the authority of the King — one of the few rulers in the region distinguished by moderation and pro-Western sympathies — the entire Middle East would be revolutionized. Two months after our peace initiative the military balance along the Canal would have been altered by cheating at the very moment that the political balance along the Jordan front would have been destroyed by force. We could not acquiesce in this by dithering on the sidelines, wringing our hands, urging the resumption of peace talks, and then proclaiming our impotence.

Since no one was eager to face the implications of this analysis, the discussion turned to the prevention of hijacking. Mel Laird talked about electronic devices for airport security in the future. The President decided he favored both armed guards and electronic devices; he turned to me to "coordinate" this effort and asked Laird to take the "lead responsibility." He instructed Rogers to press diplomatic initiatives. My confusion as to what all this meant was not cleared up when the President wandered into my office ten minutes after the meeting and said he recognized we had a "terrible bureaucratic problem"; the Cabinet officers all wanted to "do something"; he had given them each something to do; I should sort it out. He did not say how, or even exactly what he intended.

Meanwhile, we were receiving disturbing accounts from Amman. The Jordanian army was reported to be in virtual mutiny because of what they considered insults and provocations by fedayeen. Loyal to the King but refusing any further compromise, they threatened to take matters into their own hands for the King's own good. Pressure was mounting on Hussein for forceful action.

With the President's approval, and to put an end to the bureaucratic confusion, I activated the NSC crisis machinery on September 9. For seventeen days thereafter, the WSAG would meet at least once a day virtually every day to discuss options, prepare contingency plans, and implement decisions on a coordinated basis. This was more than a procedural step; it was a warning to the bureaucracy that the vacillation over the standstill violations would not be repeated if Jordan deteriorated. My chairmanship of WSAG implied the threat that any unresolved issues would be passed on to Nixon.

The President is crucial in a crisis. He must be close enough to the process to give impetus to the ultimate decisions; yet he should not become so involved in the details that he precludes a thorough examination of alternatives. Kennedy wisely excluded himself from preliminary discussions during the Cuban missile crisis of 1962. Nixon followed the same procedure during the Jordan crisis of 1970 and almost all other crises of his Presidency. He was, in fact, at his best in such situations. He did not pretend that he was exercising his responsibilities as Commander-in-Chief by nervous meddling with tactical details or formative deliberations; he left the shaping of those to the governmental machinery under my supervision. He would hesitate before committing himself, sometimes in maddening ways. But he had a great sense of timing; he instinctively knew when the moment for decision had arrived; and he would then act resolutely, especially if he could insulate himself from too much personal controversy.

In the preliminary phase of the Jordan crisis I submitted daily at least two, and on occasion three, situation reports to the President. These informed him of WSAG recommendations, events in Amman, and the progress of negotiations for the release of hostages. Since all relevant agencies were represented on the WSAG, it could be assumed that full reports reached the appropriate Cabinet officers, who of course had the opportunity to appeal any disagreement to the President. During acute phases of the crisis — especially its last three days — Nixon called daily meetings of the principals to review WSAG recommendations.

On September 9, the primary problem was to set a course. In my view successful policy must have at least three components: a careful analysis to determine the realistic range of choice, meticulous preparation, and early seizing of the initiative. Passivity in a crisis leads to mounting impotence; one is forced to react on issues and in contexts contrived to one's maximum disadvantage. By contrast, the side that has the initiative can occupy its opponent's energies in analysis. And since the opponent will always assume the worst contingency, even relatively minor moves can have a major cautionary effect, unless they are so palpably bluffing as to encourage contempt. For maximum effectiveness one's actions must be sustained; they must appear relentless, inexorable; hesitation or gradualism invites an attempt to test one's resolution by matching the commitment.

On September 9, the WSAG met in the White House Situation Room for an hour, starting at 11:30 A.M. The intelligence briefing revealed that the deadline for the hostages had been extended; we did not know for how long. We agreed that American pressure had to be exerted to prevent the European countries from attempting separate deals that would leave them no choice except to yield to the hijackers. That would leave the United States isolated, with no recourse to free our citizens except by pressuring Israel, which believed — as did we — that surrender to terrorist blackmail was out of the question. Indeed, our view was shared by the able representative of the International Committee of the Red Cross, André Rochat, who was conducting the negotiations with the Palestinians. He sent a note to the governments concerned: "In case of a non-coordinated liberation of Palestinians, the Committee would be obliged to renounce the mandate which has been confided to it."

But if we wanted to prevent the negotiations from dragging on endlessly, we had, in my view, to begin conveying determination and start exerting pressure. An attitude of impotent scolding would only prolong our agony. American resolution was alike crucial for the fate of the hostages and for the survival of the King. Indeed, in a curious way the future of the King and of the hostages had begun to merge. If hundreds of hostages were killed on his soil, the collapse of royal authority in Jordan would be plain for all the world to see. Each successive inconclusive crisis had weakened Hussein a little further; matters were drifting toward showdown. Either Hussein in desperation would move against the fedayeen or the fedayeen would overthrow him.

Until that challenge was resolved no peace initiative had any chance; Israel would never discuss new borders with a government not in control of its own country. Since everyone agreed that a rescue operation was only a last resort, I listed three contingencies for which it was necessary to prepare: a fedayeen attack on the hostages, requiring emergency rescue; a breakdown of order in Amman, requiring the evacuation of Americans; a showdown between Hussein and the fedayeen, involving perhaps Syria and Iraq. An analysis of our capabilities indicated that we had only four brigades capable of reaching Jordan quickly, and such an operation would enlist our entire strategic reserve. It would take forty-eight hours to commit the brigade in Germany, seventy-two hours to commit the 82nd Airborne Division from the United States. Intervention of these forces would require overflight rights or ground access through neighboring countries. I requested the Joint Chiefs of Staff to submit within twenty-four hours proposals to heighten the alert status of forces in Europe; a study of the operational consequences of protracted American military engagement in Jordan; the forces required for each of the contingencies; and the related deployments needed to deter Soviet intervention.

In the meantime it was essential to convey to all parties that we were getting serious. The President ordered the Sixth Fleet aircraft carrier *Independence* be moved east to just off the coast of Lebanon, accompanied by four destroyers and joined within twenty-four hours by two more destroyers. Six C-130s were to be positioned at Incirlik airbase in Turkey for use in the evacuation of Americans. These steps were to be taken without announcement. I was certain that Soviet intelligence, probably aided by the normal process of Pentagon leaking, would cause them to become public. Our silence would give them an ominous quality.

The issue became more complicated when the WSAG considered under what circumstances these forces were to be used. Nobody relished another military involvement while several hundred thousand Americans were still fighting in Southeast Asia. We would have to commit our entire strategic reserve and supply it by air; we would become vulnerable to a Soviet thrust elsewhere. Operations would be difficult to sustain; our supply lines were tenuous and would have to cross several foreign countries. The longer the war continued, the more complicated our position would become. If Israel intervened in Jordan on its own, we would be conducting parallel military operations for different objectives. Even worse for our position in the Arab world and our prestige, if we got into difficulties we might have to ask Israel to bail us out.

For all these reasons I thought it desirable for our long-term interests to separate our military actions from those of Israel. My view was that American forces should be used for the evacuation of Americans because this could be done quickly and represented an immediate American interest; but in case of a major conflict provoked by an Iraqi or Syrian move, I favored letting the countries most immediately concerned take the principal responsibility. Since I considered an Israeli response to an Iraqi or Syrian move almost certain, I thought the best use of our power in that contingency was to deter Soviet intervention against Israel. A consensus developed around these propositions.

I informed Nixon. He still held to his earlier view that any military operations be American only; he wanted us to move alone against Iraqi or Syrian intervention or fedayeen upheavals and keep Israel out.

The position of the security adviser when he disagrees with the President is extremely delicate. The President must have the assurance that his adviser will act as his extension and will see to it that *his* wishes are carried out by the departments. On the other hand, the President must be able to count on being warned if his orders are dangerous. This was especially important for Nixon, given his tendency toward impetuous declarations that he never expected to see implemented. In the Jordan crisis I solved the problem by having two contingency plans prepared simultaneously: one embodying the President's preference for unilateral American action; the other reflecting the WSAG consensus for the United States to hold the ring against outside intervention. The President would then be able to choose when the moment for decision arrived.

On September 9, Soviet chargé Yuli M. Vorontsov informed us (via Sisco) that the Soviets had urged restraint in both Jordan and Iraq. However, the language of the Soviet admonition was hardly calculated to douse any fires. Moscow had told the Arabs that moderation was desirable because conflict among them would only help their enemies, specifically "the Israeli aggressors and the imperialist forces behind them" — a crude slap at us. In my view, the Kremlin was playing the Jordan crisis as it had the cease-fire. It made formally correct noises but did nothing constructive to reverse the drift toward crisis. By informing Jordan that it considered us an enemy of the Arabs, the Soviet Union was assaulting the very foundation of Jordan's traditional policy. Sending the text of this démarche to the State Department without attempting to soften its language was also provocative; Moscow obviously did not yet believe that it was running a serious risk.

The WSAG met again on the afternoon of September 10. By that time the Palestinians had changed their demands, partly as a result of the united front that we had managed to hold together. The British, Swiss, and Germans had agreed to hand over the fedayeen prisoners in their custody only after all hostages were released. The Palestinians then proposed the exchange of all women, children, and sick passengers for the fedayeen held in Europe; all the men would be ransomed for all the fedayeen held by Israel.

We accelerated our contingency planning. Once the departments understand that the White House is serious, they frequently discover possibilities for action unimagined when they believe the course is one of minimum risk. At the September 10 WSAG meeting Admiral Moorer reported that previously agreed alert measures had reduced the reaction time of our forces in Europe by nearly half. He had found two submarines to send to the Mediterranean to keep track of the Soviet fleet. An amphibious maneuver off Crete was due to end September 14; the forces in it, containing a Marine landing team, could be kept off the coast of Lebanon if the crisis continued. I asked the Joint Chiefs to study whether and how the United States could sustain military operations in Jordan if the President should follow his preference of unilateral American action. I knew that the group was opposed to such a course, but I did not want to be in a position where the President ordered something "without our knowing what we must do. . . ." Helms expressed the view that Hussein would probably seek to avoid a showdown with the fedayeen for fear of intervention by Syria or Iraq. I disagreed: "That means his end. There is no way for him to get back control without fighting." I considered a confrontation inevitable even though a new truce had been agreed to between the government and the fedayeen. It was a debate to which events would give a reply soon enough; it did not need to be resolved in the abstract. We had done what was possible to prepare for the coming storm.

On September 11 the alert measures of the previous two days began to pay off. Rumors of our fleet movements were translated by the gossip mill in Amman into reports of imminent American intervention. Red Cross representative Rochat reported that "fantastic tension" reigned at fedayeen headquarters, and he fully expected them to take some action to demonstrate that they would not be intimidated. All aircraft had been wired for bombing, but the passengers had been removed from them. That our threat was not without its effect became apparent at the end of the day when the fedayeen suddenly released a group of eighty-eight hostages, including some Americans (but not dual-nationalists).

The difference between Rogers and me in our approach to crisis management came into focus on that day. Rogers believed it desirable to reassure nervous adversaries that we intended them no harm. My view was the opposite, that once we were embarked on confrontation, implacability was the best as well as the safest course. Rogers thought calming the atmosphere would contribute to its resolution; I believed that it was the danger that the situation might get out of hand which provided the incentive for rapid settlement. Rogers now briefed the Congressional leaders with the same argument he had used three days earlier with the President: We had considered every possible military step for rescuing the hostages and concluded that nothing would work — thus vitiating the impact of the military movements that had been arranged to create exactly the opposite impression. It was fortunate that the Palestinians believed our actions and not our words; they probably considered the Congressional briefing as an attempt to trick them.

That morning the President, Laird, Rogers, and I met the Congressional leadership in the Oval Office. I was suddenly called out of the meeting by a frantic Sisco, who had brought with him a report that because of the menacing moves of the Sixth Fleet the Palestinians were threatening to kill the remaining hostages. We concluded the leadership meeting as rapidly as possible without creating a panic. The President asked Rogers and Laird to stay behind and invited Sisco to join us. Sisco and Rogers pressed for a public statement forswearing any American military action. I was opposed. Reassuring the fedayeen would simply reward outrageous threats, strengthen their bargaining position, and give us a harder problem later on if we had to act in an emergency. Instead, I favored a communication to Arab governments that the killing of hostages would have serious consequences. Nixon supported my recommendation.

As a result I drafted a carefully ambiguous statement for Ron Ziegler to read, which simply called attention to a Red Cross statement to the effect that no military action was "contemplated." This could mean anything. Sisco and I also drafted a warning note to Arab governments on the hostages. Even though the message had been ordered by the President, and its text approved by him, the Arab experts at State intervened at the last moment with the argument that threats were likely to trigger the excitable Arabs into exactly the opposite course from what was intended. I did not insist and urged the President to drop the matter. This was not the time for acrimonious debate over a telegram. Decisions would be determined by actions, not words.

With the President's approval I told Admiral Moorer that the Sixth Fleet should not be too meticulous about maintaining radio silence. In this way the Soviets would rapidly learn of our fleet movements; we would have conveyed a warning in a manner much more serious than a diplomatic note. On September 12 the Palestinians blew up the three empty planes with spectacular public effect, and continued to hold hostages in various unknown locations in Amman. Nixon and I discussed the increasing likelihood that our contingency plans would have to be activated. I reminded him of the interagency consensus in the WSAG that American ground forces would be preferable for the purpose of evacuation but that in case of a showdown between the King and the fedayeen backed by Iraqi forces we should let Israel take the brunt. The President still would not hear of Israeli intervention; he wanted to use American ground forces for both contingencies. It was not essential that we resolve the differences just then. But Nixon's preference had the practical consequence that I pressed in the WSAG to move more American forces into the area more rapidly than we might otherwise have done.

On September 13–14 our biggest concern was the growing evidence that at least the Germans, and probably the British, were on the verge of breaking the united negotiating front and dealing separately for their nationals. This fear was reinforced by a Palestinian statement that American hostages would be treated as Israelis. Soviet warships were beginning to shadow our Sixth Fleet off the coast of Lebanon; but the balance of naval strength in the Mediterranean was overwhelmingly in our favor and growing more so daily. There had been no diplomatic contact with the Soviet Union since September 9. The Kremlin seemed to have assumed its most advantageous course was observing from the sidelines the disintegration of the Kingdom of Jordan and the growing discomfiture of the United States.

It proved to be a mistaken calculation. In every crisis a point is reached where one side must decide whether to clinch its gains or to gamble for more. If the Soviet Union had around September 10 pressed for the release of hostages and a cease-fire, the gain for the fedayeen would have been massive; the authority of the King would have been gravely weakened. Instability in Jordan would have been added to insecurity along the Suez Canal; Soviet prestige would have been demonstrated and reinforced. But by getting too greedy — by not helping to rein in their clients — the Soviets gave us the opportunity to restore the equilibrium before the balance of forces had been fundamentally changed.

At the end of the second week in September the Palestinians had destroyed all four airplanes but had achieved no basic concessions either from the United States or from Israel. Our tone had become increasingly firm; above all, we were almost hourly augmenting our military forces in the area. At this point, whether because our readiness measures had given him a psychological lift or because he was reaching the point of desperation, the tough little King resolved on an all-out confrontation with the fedayeen. The showdown some of us had expected and others had dreaded was finally upon us.

Showdown with the Guerrillas

LATE on September 15, Dean Brown, our newly arrived Ambassador to Jordan, sent in an urgent cable from Amman that Hussein had decided to reestablish law and order in his capital. After surrounding the city with loyal army troops, the King would announce the formation of a military government early on September 16. He would not press the issue, but if the fedayeen resisted he was prepared to use whatever force was needed to affirm his authority. Hussein urgently requested that the United States use its influence to keep Israel from prejudicing or aggravating the situation. The King also noted that he might have to call for assistance if other Arab states intervened. Dean Brown added his own assessment: While matters were closer to a showdown than before, the King might be bluffing; he might also be making the opening move in a complex negotiation that could end in a compromise. Nor did Brown believe that intervention by Iraq or Syria was likely. I was convinced otherwise; in my view the showdown was now inevitable. The next day's events would tell the story.

Brown's cable arrived as I was en route by helicopter to Airlie House in Virginia, one of the many former private estates on the East Coast that have been given over to philanthropic and academic activities. Melvin Laird was being honored for his services to public health while in the House of Representatives. Laird had assembled all his associates and friends, which meant everybody of consequence in Washington. The WSAG was there in black tie: Packard, Moorer, Helms, Sisco, and I. Just as dinner was starting, I received a phone call from Al Haig informing me of Dean Brown's message. Shortly afterward, at about 9:00 P.M., I was called to the phone again. Haig informed me that Sir Denis Greenhill, the permanent head of the British Foreign Office, had tried to reach me. In my absence he had conveyed to Haig the judgment of Her Majesty's Government that a pitched battle between the Jordanian army and the fedayeen seemed inevitable. On behalf of Prime Minister Edward Heath he wanted to know what our intentions were, especially if the King should find himself in difficulty. And what was our attitude toward Israeli intervention? The Prime Minister might wish to talk to the President personally later during the night.

It was a good example of the "special relationship" between Britain and the United States, which enabled ideas to be exchanged at the highest levels outside of official channels without formality or protocol. It was, as well, a warning signal that could not be ignored. The Brown message had left some room for doubt, but Heath would not consider a call to Nixon unless Britain judged the situation to be grave. If the President was to talk to the Prime Minister, we needed to get our thinking in order. After consultation with Laird, Packard, and Sisco, I therefore collected the WSAG members and we returned to Washington by helicopter.

The WSAG convened from 10:30 P.M. to close to midnight in the White House Situation Room and continued afterward in my office upstairs. Still elegant in our dinner jackets, we reviewed the possible con-

tingencies: outbreak of war between the King and the fedayeen; Iraqi involvement (for some unknown reason no one in either Amman or
Washington expected Syrian intervention); or armed intervention by the
United States at least for purposes of evacuation. The meeting confirmed the judgments of the previous week. The King would probably
defeat the fedayeen. Israel would almost certainly intervene if the fedayeen seemed to gain the upper hand; it would surely do so if Iraq
moved. If Israel acted, everyone agreed that the United States should
stand aside but block Soviet retaliation against Israel. To show our support, material help should be offered to the King immediately. Whatever
happened, our readiness would have to be intensified.

Around midnight on September 15 I called Greenhill over a secure
phone* which is supposed to make intercepts impossible. It accom-
plishes this by making the conversation nearly unintelligible to the
speakers, tempting one to shout so loudly as to make it impossible for
others anywhere within reach of one's voice not to overhear, thus creating an additional security risk. I told Greenhill that we attached the
greatest importance to Hussein's survival. The President had not made a
final decision but American military involvement as a last resort could
not be excluded.

I was instrumental in shaping the WSAG consensus. I considered it
essential to preserve Hussein's rule; it was important to demonstrate that
friendship with the West and a moderate foreign policy would be rewarded with effective American support. It was necessary to arrest the
progressive radicalization of the Middle East, which had been accelerated by the dispatch of Soviet missiles and combat personnel to Egypt.
Nasser's technique of blackmailing the United States with Soviet threats
had to be shown as futile.

In my view our most effective role was to augment rapidly and threat-
eningly our military forces in the Mediterranean to deter the intervention
of radical Arab regimes in Jordan; to provide psychological support for
the King; and to match and overwhelm a Soviet response (including if
necessary military intervention). The massing of our military power in
the Mediterranean and the ambiguity of our pronouncements should be
used to stiffen Hussein, discourage his opponents, and deter the Soviets.

Accordingly, the next morning, September 16, after another brief
WSAG meeting to review the bidding, I sent a directive to the agencies
requesting detailed diplomatic and military plans for the following contingencies: material supply for Jordanian forces; armed US intervention
for the purpose of evacuation; US airstrikes or ground assault in support
of Hussein in the event of outside intervention (the President's prefer-

---

*The green secure phones throughout the US government normally had red circular plaques
reading "Secure Phone." Mine, thanks to the warped sense of humor of my staff, had the legend
in incorrect German: "Sichern Telefon."

ence); US acquiescence in Israeli air or ground strikes (the WSAG preference). I also requested that the existing plans for "deterring Soviet intervention" be adapted to the evolving situation. All plans and scenarios
were to be reviewed by noon on September 18.

That morning, too, I sent a report to the President outlining the
conclusions of the previous night's WSAG meeting. Unexpectedly, his
reaction was vehement. He had an election campaign on his mind and
was still hopeful of a Moscow summit. He questioned whether there had
been any need for an emergency WSAG meeting and covered my report
of the WSAG's views with angry scribbled comments. He wrote that he
preferred no confrontation at all; if it was unavoidable he wanted American forces used; he opposed any Israeli military moves unless he specifically approved them in advance, which he strongly implied he would
never do. I was not surprised by his preference for demonstrating American power directly and unilaterally; this had been his consistent view. I
was convinced that once he had studied its implications and our resources he would have second thoughts. There was no time for discussion because Nixon left immediately on a campaign trip to Kansas City,
Kansas State University, and Chicago.

September 16 was calm. Sisco and I flew briefly to Chicago for a
background session with Midwest editors and broadcasters. As planned,
the King announced the formation of a military government but took no
military action in Amman. However, he did raise with Dean Brown his
special concern that Syria, and not Iraq, might intervene. Brown's reporting cable shrugged this off; no one else in the government took it
seriously; our concerns were still focusing on Iraq because it already had
17,000 troops in Jordan. On the hijacking we struggled to maintain the
united front of the Western powers, resisting European importunings to
make separate deals for their own nationals.

On September 17 these discussions became largely theoretical because Hussein boldly ordered his army into Amman. Large-scale fighting broke out, spreading also to the north of Jordan around a Palestinian
concentration in the town of Irbid (see map facing). I convened
the WSAG twice that day. Ambassador Brown was instructed to
inform Hussein that the United States was sympathetic to his efforts and
that Brown would transmit rapidly any requests for material assistance.
Brown was told for his own information that American military support
against outside intervention was not precluded. Our chargé in Israel was
instructed to obtain Israel's assessment. (Nixon was in any event due to
see Golda Meir on the eighteenth.) We stayed in close touch with Britain
through frequent phone conversations with Greenhill, and we gave the
Shah, whose support in any Middle East crisis was crucial, our assessment.

But we decided not to communicate with the Soviet Union. I told the

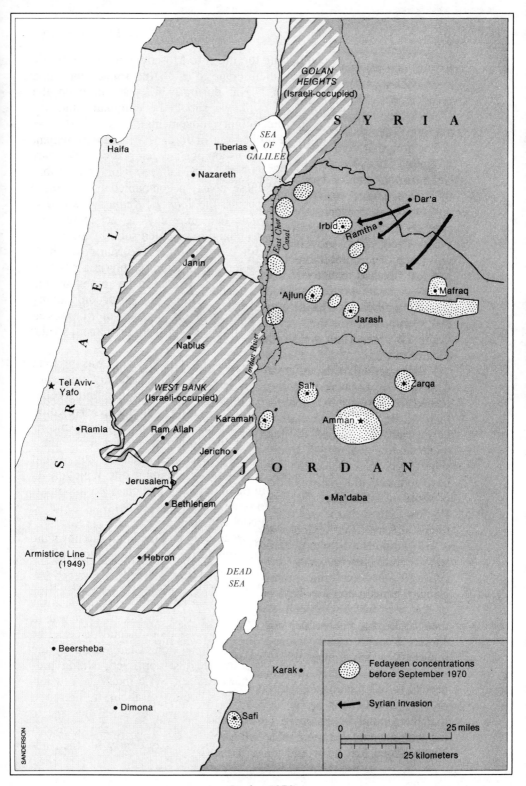

Jordan 1970

WSAG that we had been talking too much to Moscow without receiving a satisfactory response: "Let them come to us." And I made the same point in a conversation with Nixon during which he approved the WSAG recommendations: "I think we should be enigmatic and say nothing. They will pick up [our military movements]."

For now that civil war had broken out in Jordan, a rapid deployment of United States forces was vital to discourage any temptations. The carrier *Saratoga*, which had been stationed off Malta, was ordered to join the *Independence* near the Lebanese coast, accompanied by a cruiser and twelve destroyers. A third carrier, the *John F. Kennedy*, was dispatched to the Sixth Fleet; it would take nine days to get there from Puerto Rico, but its movement was bound to be noted soon by Soviet intelligence. The amphibious task force, including 1,200 Marines, which had just finished maneuvers off Crete, was ordered to stay in a position thirty-six hours off the coast of Lebanon. It was to be joined by the cruiser *Springfield*. The helicopter carrier *Guam* and an accompanying task group were on the way to pick up another group of Marines at Camp Lejeune. They were ordered to speed up their movement to the Mediterranean.

I discussed all this at great length with Nixon, who was now in Chicago. He approved all the deployments enthusiastically; they appealed to his romantic streak: "The main thing is there's nothing better than a little confrontation now and then, a little excitement." He could be dissuaded only with difficulty from having all our military movements announced, which would have created too much of a crisis atmosphere; the announcements would have backfired because they would have required too many public reassurances, draining our deployments of some of their effect. By late in the day Nixon had changed his mind. He now agreed that it was best to issue no warning, to continue to move forces and treat the Soviets with cool detachment.

He could afford to be generous because he had made all the news the traffic could bear at an off-the-record meeting with the editors of the *Chicago Sun-Times* that morning. I had urged Haldeman to keep the briefing general and low-key, but the traveling White House's definition of that term was unpredictable, especially in an election year. When his meeting began, Nixon had just learned of the outbreak of civil war in Jordan. Though usually his self-discipline was monumental, it could be breached by emotion at moments of high tension. Charged up by the news and the military movements he had just approved, Nixon proceeded to tell the amazed editors that if Iraq or Syria intervened in Jordan only the Israelis or the United States could stop them; he preferred that the United States do it. (It was also his way to get a message to me without confrontation.) Carried away by the spirit of the occasion, Nixon added that he would make the Russians pay dearly for their adventures with missiles along the Suez Canal. "We will intervene if the situation is such that our intervention will make a difference." It was too much to expect that such sensational news could be kept off the record. The *Sun-Times* ran the exact quote in an early edition. Though it was then withdrawn when Ziegler insisted on the off-the-record rule, this only heightened its foreign policy impact.*

Though Nixon was contrite after the event, I considered his statement on the whole helpful. When I was informed of it by the head of the US Information Agency, Frank Shakespeare, I told him that it gave me no pain. For one thing, it would prove to our bureaucracy that my pressures for a buildup in the Mediterranean reflected the President's approach, not my idiosyncrasy; indeed, it brought home to them that their real choice was between systematic interagency planning and ad hoc decisions in which they would not participate. Once I had convinced Rogers that I had not put Nixon up to it, the incident led to a brief period of improved relations between us.

As for the countries that concerned us most, the Soviet Union and the radical Arab states, the impact of Nixon's statement was likely to be beneficial because it proved that we meant business. In the afternoon I informed the President that Iraqi troops were standing by while the Jordanian army smashed fedayeen forces near them. And American actions during the day, including the President's statements, were bound to strengthen the resolve of our brave friend, the King of Jordan.

On Friday, September 18, the Moslem sabbath saw the Jordanian army systematically restoring its control of Amman, though more slowly. It met stiff fedayeen resistance in the north as well, where the Palestinians, in fact, proclaimed a "liberated zone." Syria, ten miles away, made threatening noises. The Iraqi army remained inactive; wherever necessary it moved itself out of harm's way. Nothing was heard from Nasser.

During the day Nixon received Golda Meir in the White House. Most of their talk concerned Israeli aid requests and Soviet-Egyptian violations of the cease-fire along the Suez Canal, reflecting the conviction of both leaders that the King was likely to prevail and that the crisis was almost over. Nixon said that he hoped Israel would do nothing precipitately. The Prime Minister assured Nixon that Israel would not move without informing the United States and that it saw no need to do so.

It was a day, too, of intensive newspaper speculation about the meaning of the President's Chicago comments. The adverse reaction was a storm warning of what we would face if we sought to implement the President's strategic preference for a unilateral American move. The

---

*That Nixon was not too upset is shown by the fact that he later congratulated the author of the piece, Peter Lisagor, for his skilled and careful handling of the story.[1]

highly respected Senator Richard Russell of Georgia, Chairman of the Appropriations Committee, senior member of the Armed Services Committee, and a consistent supporter of a hard line, phoned Rogers to tell him that he was unalterably opposed to the use of any American forces in the Middle East.

On September 18 it also became clear that Moscow had heard us. Soviet chargé Vorontsov called Deputy Assistant Secretary of State Rodger Davies to deliver a message from his government. Gone was the patronizing indifference with which Moscow had responded to the charge of violations of the standstill along the Canal; missing, too, was the incendiary invocation of the dangers of imperialism with which it had urged restraint on the parties a week earlier. Instead, the Soviets expressed their concern about the increasingly "complex" situation in the Middle East; there was no assessment of blame. Moscow expressed the "hope" that the United States shared its view that all states "including those not belonging to the region" exercise prudence. It "hoped" further that the United States would use its influence with Israel in that direction. For its part the Soviet Union had urged the governments of Jordan, Iraq, Syria, and Egypt to bring an end to the civil war in Jordan. "We are searching for ways of bringing our viewpoint also to the attention of the leadership of the Palestine movement" — thus conveying to us (probably truthfully) that Moscow had lost contact with the fedayeen and was dissociating itself from their actions, especially with respect to the hostages.

There was none of the "warning" of dire consequences that is a staple of Soviet diplomacy when the risk of having to implement it is low or when the balance of forces is favorable. Nor was there any accusation of American collusion with the King. The tone was rather plaintive, offering reassurance that the Soviet government "as before" stood for a settlement of the Middle East crisis on the basis of Security Council Resolution 242. Similar in tone was a TASS commentary warning us against intervention in terms whose ambiguity could not have escaped the notice of the Kremlin's clients in the Middle East.

All of this tended to support an analysis made earlier that day by Hal Sonnenfeldt of my staff in a forecast of probable Soviet reactions to our deployments and diplomacy:

The practical matter is that the Soviets will not be happy to see US military power used in the area in any way. They will have to denounce it, harass us (including by horse play and close UAR-based reconnaissance against the Sixth Fleet), and generally oppose us. The precedent is what will worry them most of all, and the demonstration that we could and will use our air power and naval presence will cast a shadow over their calculations about how far we might go in support of Israel at a later date in a new crisis, and our international posture generally. (This may be all to the good if our operations are, and are perceived to be, successful.)

The conviction that the Soviets were looking for a way out was reinforced by a conversation between Deputy Foreign Minister Vasily Kuznetsov and Ambassador Beam on September 19, a day when the Jordanian army continued its slow but undeniable progress against the fedayeen. Kuznetsov again expressed the "hope" that we had no intention of intervening in Jordan since this would create "difficulties" for all nations with interests in the area. He inquired into the purpose behind the buildup of the Sixth Fleet. Beam answered that he was uninformed about our military deployments, which was both the truth and also the response most likely to feed Soviet insecurities.

The best strategy, it seemed to me, was not to offer reassurance but to bring about a situation wherein the Soviet Union could ease its concerns only by urging its radical friends to refrain from intervening and by bringing the crisis to a decisive close. This is why I urged that no reply be returned for the time being. After all, the Soviets had kept us waiting for ten days before responding to our note on standstill violations. Silence was the best middle ground between reassurance, which would be self-defeating, and intransigence, which might turn out to be provocative.

On the whole, I thought that we were approaching the end of the crisis with much of our credibility reestablished. On the evening of September 19 I called Nixon, who was at Camp David, to inform him of the Soviet message. I suggested that it indicated an imminent retreat. Nixon, always wary of believing good news, expressed his doubts; whenever the Soviets volunteered reassurance, he said, something sinister was afoot. He proved to be right.

On the morning of Sunday, September 20, Syrian tanks invaded Jordan.

The Syrian Invasion

DURING fast-moving events those at the center of decisions are overwhelmed by floods of reports compounded of conjecture, knowledge, hope, and worry. These must then be sieved through their own preconceptions. Only rarely does a coherent picture emerge; in a sense coherence must be imposed on events by the decision-maker, who seizes the challenge and turns it into opportunity by assessing correctly both the circumstances and his margin for creative action. In crises this agility is akin to an athlete's. Decisions must be made very rapidly; physical endurance is tested as much as perception because an enormous amount of time must be spent making certain that each of the key figures at home and abroad acts on the basis of the same information and purpose. Whatever bureaucratic games might be played in normal times, during crises I made certain that each agency had the same information and that all principals and their key associates were willing collaborators in the overall design.

Sifting the facts from the welter of reports was peculiarly difficult during the Jordan crisis. After the King moved troops into Amman, our Embassy was cut off from the Palace. Occasionally the King and Rifai got through to our Ambassador by telephone. There was fitful use of radio between the Palace and our Embassy, but the transmission was in the open, likely to be intercepted and therefore unreliable. We were lucky in having on the spot Dean Brown, one of our ablest, bravest, and most knowledgeable diplomats. From time to time he went to look for the King and Rifai in an armored car; obviously this did not make for rapid communication. The British were more fortunate; their Embassy was closer to the Palace. Thus on occasion the King would send us messages via London. The practice inevitably produced a delay in transmissions since the British government understandably wanted to add its own comment — all the more so because London was somewhat concerned that we might act precipitately. The judgment was wrong but not the impression because at least the White House judged it a deterrent to rash action if London informed other capitals that things threatened to get out of hand. London delicately suppressed its misgivings with us, without however failing to suggest that it favored a more measured pace.

On Saturday, September 19, we had received the first reports that Syrian tanks had taken up positions some two hundred fifty yards inside Jordan. But since the report came from a British official in Cairo, and London had not seen fit to notify us directly, we did not believe that the British government attached too much importance to it. Nor did we. Despite all the communications difficulties, we believed that Hussein would have found a way to notify us had he been deeply concerned.

There was no doubt, however, about what was occurring on September 20, Sunday. At about 6:00 A.M. Washington time, both the King and Rifai in separate phone contacts with Brown reported two major incursions of Syrian tanks at Ramtha. The Jordanians had knocked out thirty tanks and pushed them back. Hussein requested American assistance, without being specific. At 12:30 P.M. Washington time Rifai became more concrete; on behalf of the King he asked for US reconnaissance to determine whether the Syrians were bringing up additional forces. At about the same time two more Syrian armored brigades crossed into Jordan and attacked on a broad front; we were not to confirm this until later in the afternoon.

I had no doubt that this challenge had to be met. If we failed to act, the Middle East crisis would deepen as radicals and their Soviet sponsors seized the initiative. If we succeeded, the Arab moderates would receive a new lease on life. On the whole, I was optimistic. The balance of forces was in our favor both locally and overall. I expressed the view to the President late that evening that the Soviets were ''either incompetent or forcing a showdown. If they are incompetent we will have an easy victory.'' I did not need to add that if they had decided on a showdown we had no choice in any case.

After consultation between Rogers, Sisco, and me a number of immediate steps were taken. Sisco and I jointly drafted a statement that was issued in Rogers's name, demanding in peremptory language the immediate withdrawal of Syrian forces and warning of the dangers of a broadened conflict. That afternoon Sisco called in Vorontsov and handed him a blistering message. In form a reply to the Soviet message of September 18, the operational part of our note read as follows:

At this moment, the situation is being further and dangerously aggravated by the intervention into Jordanian territory of armored forces from Syria and the concentration of further offensive forces in Syria along the Jordanian border. The US Government has condemned this intervention in Jordan and has called for the immediate withdrawal of the invading forces. This intolerable and irresponsible action from Syria, if not immediately halted and reversed, could lead to the broadening of the present conflict. The US Government calls upon the Soviet Government to impress upon the Government of Syria the grave dangers of its present course of action and the need both to withdraw these forces without delay from Jordanian territory and to desist from any further intervention in Jordan. The Soviet Government cannot be unaware of the serious consequences which could ensue from a broadening of the conflict. For its part, the US Government is urging restraint by all other parties in the area.

During the course of Sunday afternoon I recommended — and the President approved from Camp David — returning the airborne brigade in Germany to its base embarkation point from a maneuver area to which we had permitted it to move on September 18 when the crisis seemed to be cooling. The long-planned maneuver exercise extended the reaction time of the brigade to ten hours; at its home base its alert status would be reduced to four hours. One battalion was ordered to prepare for an airdrop. At 5:00 P.M. we requested our Embassy in Bonn to notify the German government of the movement of the airborne brigade. We explained that its heightened readiness was made necessary by the possibility of evacuating Americans from Jordan. The brigade was instructed to move rapidly and openly without any security precautions; we wanted Soviet intelligence to notice it quickly. The German government was likely to spread word of our moves to friendly European governments. Dean Brown was instructed to tell Hussein of our public statements and our note to the Soviets and not to close the door to possible United States intervention.

During the afternoon the scale of the new Syrian attack became clear. We had continued planning on the assumption of either an American or an Israeli military reaction; all in the government were agreed that the two must not take place simultaneously. On September 17 I had conveyed to the WSAG the President's preference for resisting Iraqi or Syrian intervention primarily with United States forces. I had requested that each course be examined in the light of three criteria: Who had the better reason for action? Who could sustain his actions better? Who had the greatest capacity to prevent escalation? I had asked for the best case that could be made for American action and the best case for standing aside and deterring the Soviets while the Israelis moved. These papers were available to the President over the weekend. I cannot tell whether he read them.

In order to make a final recommendation to the President I called a meeting of the WSAG for 7:00 P.M. Sunday evening, September 20. From then on until the NSC meeting next morning, the crisis for us in Washington took the form of almost uninterrupted meetings and telephone calls. The flavor can best be conveyed by tracing the events of the night hour by hour.

From 7:10 to 7:50 P.M. the WSAG principals met in the Situation Room in the White House basement, largely to bring one another up to date on events of the past hours and to look again at contingency plans. The intelligence and military briefings indicated that it was nip and tuck. Much of the discussion was a typical bureaucratic trauma over the trivial. Two portable military field hospitals were to be sent in response to the King's request for assistance; the debate was whether we should send them as an American contribution or under some multilateral aegis. A quick review of the pros and cons of American military intervention strengthened our conviction that our forces were best employed in holding the ring against Soviet interference with Israeli operations. To be effective unilaterally we would have to commit our entire strategic reserve; we would then be stretched to near the breaking point in two widely separated theaters and naked in the face of any new contingency. Our forces would have to go in without heavy equipment and with air support only from carriers. Our only overland supply route was across Israel, linking us with Israel when separation was the principal reason for an American action. If we got into difficulties, we would have to call on Israel for help. In short, if the situation in Jordan got out of control it could be remedied only by a massive blow against Syria, for which Israeli armed forces were best suited.

At 7:50 P.M. the President, having returned from Camp David, called me to his office. He and I had been in frequent touch during this Sunday afternoon. I had rehearsed my concerns about unilateral American military action on several occasions along the lines of the WSAG consensus;

late in the day he had changed his view; just before the WSAG meeting he had told me that if there were a military reaction it should *not* be by us. I'quickly brought Nixon up to date. I suggested that he call the senior members of the WSAG up to his office to give them some sense of his thinking and the psychological boost that can come only from Presidential leadership. Even though his view now coincided with that of the WSAG, I urged that he not reveal his change of mind so that the WSAG could go through the options again, free from the desire to fulfill Presidential preferences. He could then be sure to get the best judgment; he could make his formal decision after the WSAG meeting was concluded.

Once the point of decision was reached, Nixon acted with a kind of joyless, desperate courage — torn between his insights and understanding of the international reality and his fatalistic instinct that nothing he touched would ever be crowned with ultimate success. The biggest problem at that point was to keep the courage from turning into recklessness and the firmness into bravado. In these situations he would not be concerned with short-term political advantage; he would do what he thought was required by the national interest as he perceived it. No more can be asked of any President. Many have done much less.

From about 8:00 to 8:20 P.M., Nixon met with the WSAG principals — Alex Johnson, Tom Moorer, Dick Helms, David Packard, Joe Sisco. He gave them a pep talk expressing appreciation for their efforts. He said that their job was to save the King against outside intervention; he expected their judgment regardless of what they might previously have assumed to be his preferences. He stressed that I would be speaking for him.

At 8:20 P.M., the suitably inspired WSAG members left the President's office and resumed their deliberations downstairs in the Situation Room. I stayed behind for ten minutes to go over the options with the President. We both agreed that the odds favored our prevailing if we remained firm without being truculent and if we played our cards well.

At about 8:20 P.M., too, Denis Greenhill telephoned again on the secure phone. Since I was in the Oval Office, Haig in the Situation Room took the call. Greenhill passed on a message that Hussein had given to the British Ambassador in the morning and repeated again two hours before the phone call: In view of the deteriorating situation the King was requesting immediate air strikes.

At 8:35 P.M. I rejoined the WSAG meeting, which continued until about 9:15 P.M. The British message reinforced the predisposition in favor of standing aside for an Israeli move. We did not possess enough intelligence or target information to respond rapidly to the King's plea with American forces. At the same time, if the United States was to hold the ring against Soviet intervention we would have to accelerate our readiness; we would thereby also improve our capacity to conduct air operations should the Israelis prove more reluctant to act than we estimated. The WSAG approved the following recommendations to the President:

- improving the alert status of the airborne brigade in Germany even further;
- putting the 82nd Airborne Division on full alert (this would undoubtedly leak and thus force a rapid decision on both Moscow and Damascus);
- flying a reconnaissance plane from a carrier to Tel Aviv airport to pick up targeting information (this would undoubtedly be discovered by Soviet and Egyptian radar, and signal that American military action might be approaching).

In other words, we would heighten the perception that American or Israeli intervention was threatening.

In my view what seems "balanced" and "safe" in a crisis is often the most risky. Gradual escalation tempts the opponent to match every move; what is intended as a show of moderation may be interpreted as irresolution; reassurance may provide too predictable a checklist and hence an incentive for waiting, prolonging the conditions of inherent risk. A leader must choose carefully and thoughtfully the issues over which to face confrontation. He should do so only for major objectives. Once he is committed, however, his obligation is to end the confrontation rapidly. For this he must convey implacability. He must be prepared to escalate rapidly and brutally to a point where the opponent can no longer afford to experiment.

At about 9:27 P.M. I asked Sisco to join me conveying the WSAG's recommendations to the President; as the official who sat at the nexus of all the cable traffic it was crucial for Sisco to understand the nuances of White House thinking. It would also help keep Rogers informed; he had decided to stay near a phone at home to await developments. First we had to find the President because Nixon had decided to go bowling. With the aid of the Secret Service we finally tracked him to an obscure alley in the basement of the Executive Office Building. Nixon calmly listened to our report and approved the recommendations while incongruously holding a bowling ball in one hand. It was one of the few occasions that I saw Nixon without a coat and tie. He said that whatever was done must succeed; he was determined to stop the Syrian attack. He agreed that we needed urgently to establish contact with the Israeli Ambassador. I told him that I would call Rabin.

At about 10:00 P.M., I returned to my office in the White House and placed the call. It turned out that Rabin was attending a dinner in New York honoring Golda Meir. He had to be called from the dais and brought to a reasonably secure place, though throughout the conversation I could hear the distant babble of voices. Telling Rabin that Sisco was also on the line, I asked what information Israel had on Syrian moves. Rabin said Israel estimated some two hundred Syrian tanks to be in the area of Irbid. I told Rabin that we had been asked for assistance but had no intelligence. Could Israel fly some reconnaissance at daybreak (then only three hours away in the Middle East) and give us its judgment? Rabin, who was nobody's fool, asked whether we would look favorably on an Israeli air strike if the intelligence indicated significant Syrian advances. I replied that we would prefer to make this judgment *after* analyzing the results of the reconnaissance. We were in the process of discussing this when I was handed another urgent message from the King, this time directly to us. I told Rabin I would have to call him back shortly.

Hussein's message had come by telephone to our Ambassador two hours earlier. It spoke of a serious deterioration following a new massive Syrian invasion (the attack by the two brigades at noontime). Jordanian forces were no longer in contact with each other; Irbid was occupied. The troops in the capital were disquieted. In the King's view air strikes were imperative to save his country; he might soon request ground troops as well. Reversing his previous procedure, Hussein asked us to inform Britain of his plight.

At 10:10 P.M., Sisco and I jointly phoned Rogers from my office and told the Secretary of the conversation with Rabin and the new desperate message from the King. We were inclined to recommend to the President, we said, that we endorse an Israeli air strike. Rogers agreed we had no choice.

At 10:12 P.M., now familiar with the route, Sisco and I therefore went back to the bowling alley. (I never saw the bowling alley again after that fateful night.) We told the President of the King's request and the consensus of his own senior advisers. He accepted our recommendation and authorized us to approach Rabin. At 10:25 P.M. Sisco and I found our way back to my office.

At 10:35 P.M. I placed another call to Rabin with Sisco on the line. Just as the connection was being completed, Nixon, his bowling completed, walked into my office, conservatively dressed as usual. I told Rabin of the information we had received from Jordan, without specifying the source. After discussion with the President and the Secretary, I could inform him that if Israeli reconnaissance confirmed what he had told me, we would look favorably upon an Israeli air attack. We would make good the material losses, and we would do our utmost to prevent Soviet interference. Rabin carefully repeated what I had said to make sure that he understood; he would have to consult his Prime Minister.

At 10:45 P.M., in light of the possibility that Israel might act during our night, I called the WSAG back into session for a midnight meeting and asked my staff (principally Hal Saunders and Richard Kennedy) to gather all relevant information. I then called British Ambassador John Freeman to inform him of the King's message. I told him that we had been in touch with the Israeli Ambassador but did not go into details. Nixon, still in my office, chatted with me between phone calls.

At 11:15 P.M. I called Prime Minister Heath's private secretary on the secure line to read him the King's message, to inform him that we had been in touch with the Israeli Ambassador and that Israel would fly reconnaissance which would determine its next move. Nixon suggested I stop using the secure phone since more people on Pennsylvania Avenue could hear my shouting than would be likely to intercept a conversation on the open line.

At 11:30 P.M., Rabin called back with Mrs. Meir's answer. Israel would fly reconnaissance at first light. The situation around Irbid was "quite unpleasant"; Israeli military leaders were not convinced that air operations would be enough. Israel would pass its judgments on to Washington after studying the results of the reconnaissance, but would take no action without further consultation. Nixon heard my end of this conversation as well but made no comment. He then left my office.

At midnight, the WSAG convened again in the Situation Room. I briefed them about what had transpired since the last meeting. We discussed what to do if Israel struck during the next twenty-four hours. I requested urgent studies during the night on four topics: contingency plans against possible Soviet moves; assistance packages for Israel and Jordan to make up losses; a scenario for Congressional briefings; and a diplomatic plan to brief allies and urge the Soviets to stay out. With respect to the Soviets, I stressed: "We have two objectives: one, to get them to use their influence with the Syrians to get them to withdraw; two, to make sure they do not believe they can escape the dilemma of an Israeli move by putting the squeeze on Israel. . . . I think waffling now will give us more problems later."

At 12:45 A.M. I called Rogers at home to tell him of the Rabin conversation and the WSAG meeting. I inquired whether he had any problems. There were none. For once our senior people were united. At about 1:00 A.M. I called Nixon to give him a brief report on the WSAG. He listened to my summary of the various agency predictions about Soviet reactions. He snorted when I told him of a Defense Department fear that the Soviets might launch air strikes against Israel in retaliation: "I don't believe it."

I went home and to bed. It was 2:00 A.M., early Monday, September 21.

At 5:15 A.M. I was awakened by Al Haig, who had just received a call from Rabin. Though no report of reconnaissance was yet available,

Rabin said the Israelis did not consider air strikes alone adequate; *ground* action might also be necessary. Israel would appreciate the American view within two or three hours.

At 5:35 A.M., I phoned and awakened the President to tell him of Rabin's preliminary response. I urged him to defer a decision and to call a meeting of his senior advisers for 7:30 in the morning. But Nixon knew that a request for Israeli ground action would produce serious controversy, and he would have none of it. "We will make [the decision] now," he said. He reviewed the pros and cons of an Israeli ground attack with me for a few moments. He asked me to call Sisco for his view.

I began discussing with Haig the wisdom of calling Sisco without involving Rogers, and I had just concluded that I must talk to Rogers when Nixon called back. He had decided to approve Israeli ground action and dictated a thoughtful message to convey to Rabin. He said: "I have decided it. Don't ask anybody else. Tell him [Rabin] 'go.' "

I was not about to let the President run the risk of a major confrontation with the Soviet Union without consulting his senior advisers. An Israeli ground operation could produce a Mideast war. I owed it to Nixon to check with Rogers and Laird. Nor was there that much urgency. Israel would surely not move on land without mobilization. I called Sisco, who said he agreed with the President's decision. I next called Rogers, who had serious reservations, especially in the absence of a formal Jordanian request for ground support. Laird was ambiguous; he wanted to consider the intelligence. Between all these calls — which were all made from my home — the President called me frequently to add refinements to his decision. At 7:10 A.M. I urged him again to call a meeting of his senior advisers in view of the differences of opinion among them. He now reluctantly agreed. Haig informed Rabin that there would not be an American answer until midmorning.

From here on an hour-by-hour account is no longer necessary, the main issues having become defined during the night's events. Our government was united on approving Israeli air attacks; there was a difference of opinion as to Israeli ground operations. I did not think the issue required an immediate resolution because the Israeli reply, while adding the complicating threat of a ground war, also provided a political opportunity. If Israel considered a ground action essential, it would have to mobilize. Mobilization would take at least forty-eight hours. And Israel could not afford *not* to mobilize because it could not permit a Syrian victory, whatever our ultimate reaction. Thus we had a breathing space — if the King could hold on — during which pressures on Syria would mount and perhaps to the point where the crisis resolved itself without war. As Syria saw the increase in Israeli forces on the Golan Heights on the flank of its thrust into Jordan, it was bound to become extremely uneasy. Nasser was likely to press for an end to operations that might soon face him with the impossible dilemma that had led to the disaster of 1967: either breaking Arab solidarity by standing aside or risking another humiliating defeat by intervening. And the same considerations were certain to press on the Soviets. In short, Israeli mobilization, added to our own deployments, could "spook" all our adversaries and yet provide time for a solution short of war.

The National Security Council met at 8:45 A.M., Monday, September 21. Though the discussion concerned mainly the eminently practical issue of how to respond to the Israeli query of our attitude toward ground operations, it really came down again to a philosophical debate on how to handle crises. Rogers believed in very slow and measured escalation, if any. Nixon, as well as I, believed that this was the most likely way for a crisis to become unmanageable. Rogers was basically opposed to Israeli ground involvement for many reasons, including fear of a confrontation with the Soviets. Nixon and I held that if we wished to avoid confrontation with the Soviets we had to create rapidly a calculus of risks they would be unwilling to confront, rather than let them slide into the temptation to match our gradual moves. Rogers wanted to make the ultimate decision depend on whether the Syrians moved south from Irbid; in my view the crisis could be ended only by full Syrian withdrawal from its "liberated zone" in northern Jordan. Nixon finally decided that Sisco could inform Israel that the United States agreed to Israeli ground action in principle, subject to determining the King's view and consultation prior to a final decision.

I had my doubts about asking Hussein. Since in my view Israel should intervene only if the Jordanians were near collapse, we should not mortgage the King's already precarious position in the Arab world by asking him questions he could not afford to answer. Hussein might well acquiesce in what he could never request. But for the immediate management of the crisis it made no difference. Israeli mobilization had already quietly begun; when added to our own deployment, it would create its own menace and its own reality.

Had the Israeli government been eager to strike, our qualified response might have created doubts that could have transmitted themselves to our opponents. Fortunately, Israel had its own strategic assessment, which caused it to mobilize without asking for a final answer and thus to pursue precisely our preferred pace. Insatiable in its quest for reassurance, indeed showing remarkable caution, the Israeli government submitted a set of questions about American policy in the case of hostilities. The preparation of the answers took the better part of the day. No formal decision about ground action needed to be taken during that time. In the meantime, two Israeli brigades were moving onto the Golan Heights, threatening the flank of the Syrian forces in Jordan.

During the morning a message was received from French President Pompidou expressing his "great concern" about possible American intervention and urging Nixon to weigh his decisions with care. The message was not especially helpful, nor did we fail to notice France's attempt to dissociate from us in the midst of a crisis. It had the redeeming virtue, however, of showing that our deployments were being noted. What worried Paris could also disquiet Moscow and Damascus.

The rest of Monday, September 21, was devoted to WSAG meetings to improve our military readiness and to draft a reply to the Israeli questions in a manner that would not give Israel a veto over our relations with third countries.

The most significant event occurred late in the day. Soviet chargé Yuli Vorontsov called on Sisco with a reply to our message of the day before that had demanded immediate Syrian withdrawal. The speed of the reply — twenty-four hours compared to the week-long delays in responding to our complaints about cease-fire violations — showed that the Kremlin was worried indeed. The tone of the message was remarkably mild, considering the menacing, almost flaunting openness of our deployments. The Soviet government noted that we seemed to share its concern about the aggravation of the situation in Jordan and that we "also" (*sic*) considered intervention into the affairs of Jordan by other states to be unacceptable. Having thus obliquely arrayed themselves against Syrian intervention, the Soviets expressed the "hope" — a very gentle diplomatic term — that we too would urge such a course on Israel. To leave no ambiguity that it was pressing Syria to withdraw, the Soviet note added: "The Soviet government adheres to the same line in its contacts with the government of Syria."

Sisco skillfully compounded Soviet premonitions, following our strategy of creating maximum fear of a possible American move. When Vorontsov asked whether Jordan had asked for our assistance, Sisco replied that he was not authorized to discuss our exchanges with the King. When Vorontsov inquired into the purpose of the movements of the Sixth Fleet, Joe simply took note of the question. Altogether, I found Vorontsov's démarche encouraging. Unless the Soviets were tricking us, they were saying that they were pressing the radical government in Syria to halt its invasion. And tricking us while our strength in the Mediterranean was growing daily and Israel was mobilizing would have been extremely foolhardy.

This was the consensus, too, of another National Security Council meeting assembled at 6:00 P.M. It confined itself to factual briefings and concluded that no decision was needed until sometime the next day.

It had been a tense but potentially decisive twenty-four hours. What started out as an imminent Jordanian collapse was beginning to reverse itself. This was above all due to the courage of the King and his loyal army. But it was also because our deployments and assurance of material support were strengthening his determination while inspiring doubt and therefore hesitation among his adversaries. I was sufficiently confident to tell the President, in two phone conversations as he was retiring, not to cancel a trip to the Mediterranean scheduled to start the following Sunday, September 27: "If the Israelis don't move by Thursday the thing will settle down."

The WSAG meeting at 8:30 the next morning, Tuesday, September 22, received good news. The Jordanians, emboldened by our moves and by the fact that the Syrian air force (under a general named Hafez Asad) pointedly stayed out of combat, were beginning to attack Syrian tanks around Irbid from the air. The estimate was that Syria had lost 120 tanks, 60 to 90 to Jordanian arms, the rest to technical malfunctions. The Iraqi forces — which had been our original concern — still remained inactive. Egypt informed us that the Soviets had made a serious effort to get Syria to reconsider its course in Jordan. Israeli forces on the Golan Heights continued to increase. With the military situation stabilizing, Sisco and I agreed that we should ask Rabin once again that there be no Israeli military move without prior consultation. At the same time, to maintain the pressure, we increased our own readiness further. Additional aircraft, both fighters and transports, were flown to Europe. All unified commands were put on increased intelligence alert. Two battalions of the 82nd Airborne Division were placed on special six-hour alert.

My calendar shows repeated meetings with the President. An NSC meeting at noon lasted only a half hour and concluded with a Presidential decision to send a message of encouragement and support to Hussein. Basically, as I told the President, we had reached the point where we had done all that was possible; our contingency planning was essentially completed for whatever option he chose. The maximum pressures available had been assembled; the final decision would depend on how others assessed them and responded.

In the course of the afternoon we received two answers, one from Jordan, the other from Israel. The King was ambivalent about Israeli air strikes and negative about Israeli ground support. The Israelis informed us that their ground action, if it took place, would be confined to Jordan (that is, they would not attack Syria). Israel also wanted further clarification of our intentions — which reassured us that Israel was far from eager to jump in. The two messages tended to cancel each other out. But by then the final choices that Damascus and Moscow would make depended on developments that had already occurred — our augmentation and Israeli mobilization.

My optimism was reinforced by a conversation with the Soviet chargé. Contrary to my usual practice of never attending embassy receptions, I decided to stop by a party at the Egyptian mission on the evening of September 22 to show that our policy was not anti-Arab. Vorontsov excitedly stopped me in full view of many other guests and asked why we had not replied to the Soviet note of the previous day. I said that there was nothing we could add to what we had requested on Sunday; Syrian troops would have to withdraw. Vorontsov asked if we would consider it sufficient if the Syrians stopped where they were. I insisted on their return to Syria. Vorontsov then affected to be concerned about our well-being. Jordan, he averred, was not a vital Soviet interest, but American intervention would cause the United States terrible difficulties throughout the Arab world. "In that case," I cracked, "you should relax because you win either way."

All this occurred within the potential hearing of other guests, including reporters. Obviously, Vorontsov was eager for his view to become known. George Sherman of the *Washington Star* wrote the next day:

> Vorontsov was unusually candid about the Soviet desire to have Syrian intervention ended.
>
> He said that Soviet contacts with Syria are still not concluded. And under questioning he pointedly included Syria, as well as Israel and the United States, in a general statement that "we believe that there should be no outside intervention of any kind."

Soviet diplomats around the world were making similar comments. The unsettled question was whether these pressures would operate on Damascus before events in Jordan imposed their own pace.

In managing the conclusion of any crisis the problem is to calibrate pressures to produce the maximum incentive for settlement without giving the other side the impression that it has no way of avoiding a confrontation. Paradoxically, perhaps the most critical moment occurs when the opponent appears ready to settle; then it is the natural temptation to relax and perhaps to ease the process by a gesture of goodwill. This is almost always a mistake; the time for conciliation is *after* the crisis is surmounted and a settlement or modus vivendi has in fact been reached. Then moderation can be ascribed to generosity and goodwill; before, it may abort the hopeful prospects by raising last-minute doubts as to whether the cost of settlement need in fact be paid. Stopping our military actions in Korea in 1951 when cease-fire talks started almost surely prolonged the talks; in retrospect I would make the same argument about the Vietnam bombing halt in 1968, though I held a different view at the time.

That is why on Wednesday, September 23, even though a Syrian withdrawal was probable, I pressed for an augmentation of our forces in the Mediterranean. September 23 would be critical. If the Syrian forces did not withdraw — if, for example, they simply dug in — the point of maximum pressure would pass. Israel would either intervene with the attendant consequences or we would be seen to be bluffing. Then the war might start up again — or else the Syrians would maintain a "liberated zone" in Jordan, mortgaging the King's survival. I thought it wisest to strengthen the balance of incentives until we knew in fact that the Syrian forces had withdrawn. Letting up now would surely leak and could convey the wrong signal at a critical moment. Four more destroyers were therefore authorized to leave the United States for the Mediterranean; two attack submarines were slated to pass through the Strait of Gibraltar on September 25 and September 29. Contingency planning against Soviet intervention continued at the WSAG meeting in the morning.

This was the essence of a disagreement between Rogers and me at the National Security Council meeting later that morning. Rogers, with the crisis on the way to resolution, suddenly discovered that the pledges of support for Israeli action that the President had approved two days earlier in his presence were open-ended commitments and asked that they be formally revoked. It seemed to me that this was not the time to generate a dispute that would surely leak and inevitably raise questions about our resolution in Israeli, Soviet, and Syrian minds. There was time enough to clear the record *after* we were certain that the Syrian tanks had withdrawn. Moreover, we had indicated the previous day that we did not favor unilateral Israeli action, and Israel had shown no sign of anything except great caution. The President supported my view but asked Sisco to reiterate our request to Rabin not to act without consultation. Israel gave this assurance later in the day without any qualification.

My records show that the President and I met five times alone between the 9:30 A.M. NSC meeting and 2:50 P.M., the moment when we received conclusive word that Syrian tanks were withdrawing from Jordan.

There remained only the pleasant aftermath of success. I called each of the members of the Washington Special Actions Group to thank them for their superb support. I was especially appreciative of Joe Sisco's contribution. He had been an indispensable link between the State Department and the White House, in addition to handling the diplomatic moves with efficiency and dispatch. King Hussein wired his gratitude and admiration to the President. Congressional and press briefings were arranged.

Even Anatoly Dobrynin showed up again in Washington on Thursday, September 24, as if to underline that normality had returned. He called on me on September 25, expressing pain that we had never replied to the Soviet note of September 21. I pointed out that during the course of the year every Soviet note had been followed by an unfriendly action incompatible with it; hence, we simply awaited events. Dobrynin assured me that the Soviet Union had not known of the Syrian plan to invade Jordan. He weakened his case considerably by reassuring me that Soviet advisers had left their Syrian units before the latter crossed the frontier! He said pleasantly that the Kremlin was willing to let bygones be bygones and wanted to consult about Middle East issues. I evaded this by saying I would take it up with the President; in the meantime I could assure him that the United States would not undertake military action in Jordan unless other outside forces intervened.

On that day, too, we sent the following message to Israel:

> According to the latest available information, the forces which invaded Jordan have withdrawn to Syria. We believe that the steps Israel took have contributed measurably to that withdrawal. We appreciate the prompt and positive Israeli response to our approach. Because circumstances will be different if there is another attack, we consider that all aspects of the exchanges between us with regard to this Syrian invasion of Jordan are no longer applicable, and we understand that Israel agrees. If a new situation arises, there will have to be a fresh exchange.

The forces of moderation in the Middle East had been preserved. The King had prevailed by his own courage and decisiveness. Yet these would have been in vain but for his friendship with the United States. The Soviets had backed off, raising by another notch the growing Arab disenchantment with Moscow.

The Jordan crisis was over. But the repose was not to last long. Within forty-eight hours of the withdrawal of Syrian tanks we faced another crisis — this time over a Soviet naval base in Cuba.

XVI

The Autumn of Crises:
Soviet Submarine Base
at Cienfuegos

A Message from Moscow

THROUGHOUT most of that critical autumn of 1970 the Soviet Union was represented in Washington by a clever, amiable, and discreet but quite powerless chargé d'affaires, Yuli M. Vorontsov. Ambassador Anatoly Dobrynin had been recalled for consultations. I learned later that Dobrynin's absence often reflected the Kremlin's desire that no serious talks take place — in this case even, or perhaps especially, about the summit with which we were toying. Vorontsov's rank was quite high but such Soviet diplomats have little discretion; they usually deliver their messages woodenly and then carefully note the reply, limiting discussion to a few obvious questions and not venturing to pretend that they have any opinions of their own. Thus when Vorontsov was jovial, one could be certain it was on instructions; when he was stern, it was the Kremlin that was frowning.

At the end of July in San Clemente I received a call from Vorontsov, who said he had a message for me as soon as possible after my return to Washington; I assumed it concerned Soviet agreement to the summit. We met on August 4 in my White House office and Vorontsov was bubbling with joviality. He had no word from Moscow about a summit, which he knew was being actively and favorably considered; relations between our countries, he thought, had taken a "good turn." What he had come to convey was his government's desire to reaffirm the Kennedy-Khrushchev understanding of 1962 with respect to Cuba: "We would like to stress that in the Cuban question we proceed as before from the understanding on this question reached in the past and we expect that the American side will also strictly adhere to this understanding."

I was puzzled and said so. I was not aware of any special tension over Cuba; we were doing nothing unusual; there was no obvious reason why the Soviet Union should raise the question. Vorontsov was blandly reassuring. There had been news stories, he said, about American plans to strengthen the defense of Guantanamo Naval Base and alleged Soviet military activities in Cuba; he read me a note complaining about stepped-up subversive activities against Cuba by exiles operating from Florida. I asked in what way Moscow wished to confirm the 1962 understanding and what Vorontsov thought the understanding was. He said an oral statement from me would be enough, and he took the understanding to be that we would not invade Cuba by military force. I said I would have to discuss the matter with the President and let him know.

I at once asked the State Department for its records and interpretation of the 1962 understanding. Alex Johnson sent over excerpts from the Kennedy-Khrushchev correspondence and a summary of the subsequent negotiations between John McCloy and Vasily Kuznetsov on the arrangements under which the Soviet missiles and bombers were withdrawn. It emerged that there was no formal understanding in the sense of an agreement, either oral or in writing. The exchanges were, however, sufficiently lengthy and detailed to constitute mutual assurances, as I described to the President:

> The Khrushchev-Kennedy exchanges indicate clearly that there was an implicit understanding that we would agree to give assurances against an invasion of Cuba if the Soviet Union would remove its offensive missiles from Cuba under UN observation and would undertake, with suitable safeguards, to halt the re-introduction of such weapons systems into Cuba. However, the agreement was never explicitly completed because the Soviets did not agree to an acceptable verification system (because of Castro's opposition) and we never made a formal non-invasion pledge. The negotiations between McCloy and Kuznetsov, which were designed to work out a satisfactory means of formalizing the Kennedy-Khrushchev "understanding" eventually just fizzled out.
>
> The "understanding" we have with the Soviets, therefore, is an implicit one, which was never formally buttoned down. In fact, the Soviets removed their missiles and there is no evidence that they have re-introduced them; and we, of course, have not invaded Cuba.

The United States had also put its view on the record in public, and it had never been disputed. The question of a naval or submarine base had come up only briefly. John McCloy had raised the issue with Kuznetsov on November 5, 1962, stating that the United States objected to the establishment of *any* Soviet military base in Cuba. Kuznetsov said he understood.

Cuba was a neuralgic problem for Nixon. When he ran for the Presidency in 1960, it featured in the famous television debates with Kennedy. A few days before the debate of October 21, 1960, Kennedy had advocated intervention by American forces to topple Fidel Castro;

in those days a muscular stance was not considered incompatible with a liberal political philosophy. Nixon, who was aware of the planning for what turned out to be the abortive Bay of Pigs invasion, felt constrained to disavow the proposal. Whether his purpose was to protect the covert planning, as he claimed, or to assert his own statesmanship in contrast to Kennedy's "inexperience," he later convinced himself that his patriotic self-restraint had contributed to his defeat. In his memoirs, Nixon related with some bitterness: "In that debate, Kennedy conveyed the image — to 60 million people — that he was tougher on Castro and communism than I was."[1] Nixon was determined that no one would ever be able to make this charge again.

Nor was Nixon done with Cuba in 1960. In 1962, when he was running for the governorship of California, the Cuban missile crisis dominated the last three weeks of the campaign — the period Nixon always considered crucial to the outcome. Though he had already fallen behind by then, he was convinced that the crisis had deprived him of the opportunity to recover. He never ceased believing that Kennedy had timed the showdown to enhance Democratic prospects in the midterm elections. For Nixon the coincidence of Cuba with an electoral campaign set off waves of foreboding and resentment. In his view, nothing was more to be avoided than a Cuban crisis in a Congressional election year.

But in the middle of August of 1970 nothing was further from our minds. Nixon and I even speculated that the message delivered by Vorontsov might be a token of Soviet goodwill to improve the atmosphere for a summit in the fall. Our complacency was reflected in our reaction to an FBI report which, as chance would have it, reached us on August 5; it claimed that two boats hired by exiles in Miami would try to sink a Soviet tanker headed for Cuba. Nixon, who usually sympathized with the Cuban exiles, immediately agreed that we should assign two Coast Guard cutters to shadow the tanker and to protect it if necessary; an attack on a Soviet tanker by boats coming from Miami would have been difficult to explain to Moscow after its message. As it turned out, the attack never materialized. We had no other reason for special concern. The U-2 reconnaissance aircraft flying periodic photographic missions had noticed an increase in Soviet military activity in and around Cuba. But they had detected nothing that would indicate a violation of the "understanding."

On August 7 I gave Vorontsov our reply. It noted with satisfaction the assurance of the Soviet government that the understandings of 1962 were still in full force. We defined these as prohibiting the emplacement of any offensive weapon of any kind or any offensive delivery system on Cuban territory. We reaffirmed that in return we would not use military force to bring about a change in the governmental structure of Cuba. I added as a "personal" observation that there had been Soviet reconnaissance flights off our East Coast by converted bombers using Cuba as a final destination. In our view this was approaching the outer limits of the understanding. Reducing these flights to an absolute minimum would surely help our relationship; it would similarly be noticed if the greatest restraint were exercised with respect to Soviet naval operations in the Caribbean.

Vorontsov expressed his appreciation for the good spirit in which I had made these observations; he was certain that the Kremlin would be happy to receive our confirmation of the understandings of 1962. He repeated his earlier impression that our relations had taken a clear turn for the better.

In the light of events, it is hard to imagine what Vorontsov or his masters could have been thinking. In foreign policy crude tricks are almost always self-defeating. Even in a Machiavellian perception of international relations the resulting loss in confidence needs to be balanced by some decisive benefit. And decisive transformations are hard to come by; certainly what the Soviets were doing in Cuba in the late summer of 1970 involved risks that were out of proportion to the probable gains.

A Flotilla Heads for Cienfuegos

ON Cuba's southern coast there is a port named Cienfuegos. Its harbor can be reached only by a single channel leading to a bay dotted by a number of small islands and surrounded by steep hills. On one of these islands, called Cayo Alcatraz, a U-2 on August 26 photographed new construction activity that had not been evident during a flight eleven days earlier. It seemed to have been going on for several days; all that could be definitely identified was work on a wharf and on some new barracks. In itself this was not unusual. What made it of more than passing significance was another piece of intelligence: A flotilla of Soviet ships was on a course heading toward Cuba; it consisted of a submarine tender, a guided-missile cruiser, a guided-missile destroyer, an ocean-going salvage tug, a heavy salvage ship, a merchant tanker, and an amphibious landing ship carrying two eighty-foot barges. The submarine tender and the barges were of a type normally used for servicing nuclear submarines. The composition of this task force was so unprecedented that something more than a courtesy visit seemed to be involved. Suddenly, a succession of events over the better part of a year began to take on a new significance.

Castro had considered Khrushchev's conduct in the Cuban missile crisis an abject surrender. Relations between Moscow and Havana had deteriorated dramatically. In 1967 Castro even went so far as to attack the Soviets publicly for their failure to give effective assistance to their Arab friends during the Six Day War. He had resisted Soviet efforts to read the Chinese out of the Communist movement and had continued radical policies of "exporting revolution" in Latin America without Soviet help. Kosygin had met with Castro in 1967, but that November, at the time of the fiftieth anniversary of the Soviet revolution, the Cubans had virtually boycotted the Moscow festivities by sending a low-level delegation, which departed almost immediately without being received by any prominent Soviet leader. Relations began to improve, however, after the death of Ché Guevara in October 1967. In the spring of 1968 a new trade agreement was signed, including a Soviet credit of over $300 million. In August 1968 Cuba endorsed the invasion of Czechoslovakia, though belatedly and with qualifications. In early 1969 the Soviets resumed regular shipments of military aid for the first time in a year; they also refinanced the Cuban trade deficit with the USSR. By the time of the June 1969 Conference of Communist Parties the Cuban delegate said grandiloquently that Havana would support Moscow in case of a "provocation or aggression against the Soviet people come from where it may." It was the first time that Cuba had taken the Soviet side in the Sino-Soviet dispute.

The following month, July 1969, the Soviets undertook their first naval visit to Cuba. Seven ships, including two diesel-powered and one nuclear-powered attack submarine, paid a port call and then conducted some maneuvers in the Gulf of Mexico; the naval force left the area after visiting Martinique and Barbados. Simultaneously, a new Soviet Y-class ballistic missile submarine began its first patrol in the North Atlantic.

In November 1969 Soviet-Cuban relations in the military field advanced another step. The Soviet Minister of Defense, Marshal Andrei Grechko, paid a highly publicized visit to Cuba, accompanied by the Deputy Chief of the Soviet Naval Staff. After the event, it seems likely that it was this visit that led to the events I am about to describe. In the months that followed Grechko's visit, at any rate, Soviet military activity in and around Cuba gradually increased — almost certainly to get us accustomed to a Soviet naval presence in the Caribbean. In April 1970 the Cuban Defense Minister, Raul Castro, returned Grechko's visit with a five-week sojourn in the Soviet Union, where he met with Leonid Brezhnev. On April 22, in a Lenin Day speech, Fidel Castro proclaimed his readiness to establish closer military ties with the Soviet Union. Shortly afterward, long-range reconnaissance aircraft began to fly from the northern USSR to Cuba; these were Tu-95 jet bombers equipped with clearly visible electronic bubbles. Three separate flights preceded the second visit by a Soviet naval task force, which came in April on the heels of a major Soviet naval exercise ("Okean") in the North Atlantic. This time seven ships arrived for a two-week visit to Cienfuegos. They included a submarine tender and a nuclear-powered E-II-class submarine armed with short-range cruise missiles designed for use against shipping.

Neither the CIA nor the Defense Department raised any warning flags at the time, but the increasing pace of this Soviet air and naval activity concerned me sufficiently to summarize it for the President on June 1, 1970:

> While the Soviet naval visits may be part of the overall trend in recent years toward increased Soviet naval activity ever further from Soviet home ports, they may also be an effort to "accustom" Washington to greater Soviet use of Cuba by establishing gradually the precedent of visits and bunkering of active Soviet fleet and air units. The Soviets could conceivably wish to maintain Soviet naval units in the Caribbean–Southern Atlantic on a more or less permanent basis, refueling and resupplying out of Cuba. . . . It will be important to keep our eye on this situation.

Later in June my NSC staff expert in Latin American affairs, Viron P. (Pete) Vaky, called my attention to a CIA study which suggested that the Soviets, however cautiously, might intend to establish a new facility in Cuba, such as an installation for servicing either ships or reconnaissance aircraft.

This was the background against which we watched the Soviet flotilla reach Cienfuegos on September 9. On the following day the merchant tanker joined them. Daily U-2 flights were ordered to begin on the first clear day, which turned out to be September 14.

The Administration's concern at that point was the flotilla much more than the new shore installations. In an unusual gesture, Mel Laird had invited Pentagon reporters to his private dining room for coffee on September 2 for an impromptu press conference. Laird ranged over a number of issues, including the Middle East. It was his remarks on Cuba, however, that caught the headlines. He called attention to the Soviet ships moving toward the Caribbean, saying that news of them should be made public because there was evidence that the Soviet task force had weapons capable of reaching the United States. But, he added, "I do not see a crisis" because America had sufficient nuclear power to deter attack.[2] The story, however, received little sustained attention from the media. Cuba was vastly overshadowed by the cease-fire violations along the Suez Canal and the looming crisis in Jordan — which may have been one reason why the Soviets were so little eager to help calm the Middle East. It was a measure of the times that, while Jordan was blowing up and the Soviets were building a submarine base in Cuba, the Senate was debating ABM from the premise that defensive American strategic deployments were somehow provocative.

The Cuban reaction to our daily U-2 flights showed that something unusual was afoot. Our first flight on September 14 had to be aborted because MiG fighters scrambled after it. Another mission flying around the periphery of the island was also intercepted and forced to terminate its mission. On September 15 a US Navy antisubmarine aircraft was intercepted and shadowed for sixty miles while the MiG made several strafing passes. I was sufficiently concerned on September 16 to warn the Soviet Union that operating missile-carrying submarines or nuclear weapons from Cuba or servicing them from there would have grave consequences. I used the vehicle of a background briefing in Chicago. Since we did not yet have any concrete evidence or a settled policy, I stopped just short of making a direct charge that the Soviets were actually doing these things. It seemed best to leave open a line of retreat for them.

As it happened, conclusive evidence was being collected that very day by a U-2. What the photography showed was that in less than three weeks the Soviet Union had rushed to complete a fairly significant shore installation. Two new barracks and administrative buildings suddenly stood on Cayo Alcatraz, which had been barren only a month earlier. Recreation facilities had quickly risen on the island, including a basketball court and a soccer field. In my eyes this stamped it indelibly as a Russian base, since as an old soccer fan I knew Cubans played no soccer. More important, the submarine tender was moored in permanent fashion to four buoys in the bay. Alongside the tender were the two support barges, which had been unloaded from the amphibious ship. The tender was thus in a position to service submarines. Antisubmarine nets guarded the entrance to the harbor. On the mainland, a few miles from the town of Cienfuegos, there had arisen a new dock, a fuel storage depot, and the early stages of a major communications facility, undoubtedly the radio link to Moscow, guarded by antiaircraft missiles and surveillance radar. What we saw, in short, had all the earmarks of a permanent Soviet naval base.

I compiled the information for Nixon in a memorandum of September 18, along with a recapitulation of my exchanges with Vorontsov. I concluded:

Today's photography readout confirms that despite the exchange between Vorontsov and myself the Soviets have moved precipitously to establish an installation in Cienfuegos Bay which is probably designed to serve as a submarine staging base in the Caribbean. Because of the seriousness of this situation I have asked CIA to provide me with a briefing at 12:30 today at which time we will carefully evaluate the full range of photographic evidence now held in an effort to determine more precisely the full scope of Soviet activity in Cuba. I am also initiating, on an urgent basis, a detailed analysis of the strategic implications of this development.

The intelligence analysis that I received later in the day concluded that the Soviets were "establishing a support facility [in Cienfuegos] for naval operations in the Caribbean and the Atlantic.'' It added ominously that ''Soviet naval units, including nuclear powered submarines, may soon be operating regularly out of the Cuban port of Cienfuegos.'' Our naval experts pointed out that a permanent facility in Cuba would sharply reduce the time Soviet submarines lost in making long transits to operating areas in the Atlantic. The result would be to increase by approximately one-third the time that Soviet ballistic missile submarines could be on station in range of the United States, or to increase, also by approximately one-third, the number of submarines on station at any one time. This would be a quantum leap in the strategic capability of the Soviet Union against the United States.

The Showdown

EVIDENCE of the Soviet naval base in Cuba reached us while we were negotiating the release of the hostages held in Amman, while Hussein's troops were slowly advancing against the fedayeen, while American forces were either being rushed to the Mediterranean or mobilized, while the cease-fire violations along the Suez Canal continued, and while we were trying to design a response to Allende's plurality in Chile. We were facing that nightmare of policymakers: simultaneous crises in widely separated parts of the globe.

The reaction of senior officials reflected this. Secretary Rogers told me on September 18 — the day the intelligence about Cienfuegos was confirmed in Washington — that we had to guard against ''high-level tension.'' He wanted any paperwork restricted to a minimum so that we did not ''create a crisis in the public mind.'' The key issue, of course, was not whether there was a crisis in the public mind but whether there existed a crisis objectively, whether we could accept a permanent Soviet naval base in Cuba, whatever its immediate military significance, on top of the dispatch of Soviet military personnel to Egypt. I told Rogers that I would schedule a restricted meeting of the WSAG the next day, giving us an opportunity to collect our thoughts as well as any additional intelligence.

The Washington Special Actions Group met as scheduled on September 19, which coincided with the lull in the fighting in Jordan just before the Syrian invasion. Because the information about Cienfuegos had been restricted, there was no real staff preparation. Opinions therefore gyrated randomly in a conversational style. There was no dispute about the facts; all agreed that a base capable of servicing nuclear submarines was being built and that the Soviets were seeking to skirt the Kennedy-Khrushchev understanding by placing most of the facilities offshore. There was some dispute about whether Soviet activities violated the ''understanding''; I reminded the group that in 1962 President Kennedy had reacted not because the deployment of Soviet missiles to

Cuba had been "illegal" — it was, in fact, then technically "legal" — but because he considered it a threat to the security of the United States. The group then tried to gauge precisely the degree to which a fully operational base would affect the strategic balance (an issue that had also been debated during the 1962 missile crisis).

These reactions reflected the difficulty Americans have in dealing with the Soviet strategy of ambiguity. We were clearly facing a new naval facility. It had been built deceptively in less than three weeks. Even if no further facilities were added, it would increase the Soviet capacity to keep ballistic missile submarines at combat stations. If expanded, it might effectively double the Soviets' sea-based missile force against us. If the Soviets proceeded in their usual fashion, the first deployments, if not resisted, would be followed by a further rapid increase. The experience of the missile buildup along the Suez Canal would be repeated, this time against us. If we acquiesced in the original installation, we would have difficulty in resisting its expansion. But as yet our government could not be quite sure what the Soviets were up to, and thus we hesitated over our response. Since both the President and the Secretary of State wished to avoid a crisis atmosphere until we had set our course, I asked each agency represented at the WSAG to submit its assessment and recommendations on a very restricted basis by September 21. The State Department, in particular, was to solicit the views of Ambassador Llewellyn Thompson, then our leading Soviet expert.

Llewellyn Thompson responded that the Soviet move was largely symbolic; it was a symptom of their inferiority complex. Despite all ideological invective, we were the model of a great power that the Soviet Union sought to emulate, lagging some fifteen years behind us in its evolution. In other words, Thompson suggested, the Soviets were now developing overseas naval bases in imitation of our efforts of a decade and a half before. The remedy State proposed was a quiet talk between Rogers and Gromyko in New York, when they would meet normally at the United Nations General Assembly about a month hence. Rogers could then point out our concern. Thompson offered no suggestion as to what we should do if Gromyko stonewalled — which was almost certain.

The estimate of the Defense Department and Joint Chiefs of Staff was diametrically the opposite. They considered a submarine base at Cienfuegos a strategic threat to the United States; in their view it would enable Soviet submarines to extend their operational time at sea and enhance the ability of the Soviet undersea fleet to operate in the Gulf of Mexico, thus exposing additional areas of the United States to ballistic missile attack. The Defense Department and the JCS explained in technical terms how such a base would operate. Naturally, they recommended removal of the base but, as so many military planning papers did, left it to the political leadership to figure out how to accomplish such a sweeping objective. One step proposed was to delay the retirement of some of our older naval ships; how this would signal our resolution or remove the Soviets from Cuba was left to the imagination. Another perceptive suggestion in the fall of 1970 — six weeks after Cambodia — was the call-up of reserves.

I saw the Soviet move as going beyond its military implications; it was a part of a process of testing under way in different parts of the world. The Kremlin had perhaps been emboldened when we reacted to the dispatch of combat troops to the Middle East by pressing Israel for a cease-fire. I strongly favored facing the challenge immediately lest the Soviets misunderstand our permissiveness and escalate their involvement to a point where only a major crisis could remove the base. I opposed time-wasting moves such as waiting for a Gromyko-Rogers conversation in a month's time. The Soviets knew that we were photographing Cienfuegos almost daily; if we did nothing they had to assume that we were acquiescing. If we then suddenly confronted them, they might have run out of maneuvering room; the consequent crisis might well be sharpened by their belief that they had been set up for humiliation. Moreover, we were expecting an imminent reply to our suggestion of a summit. If the Soviets' answer was positive, we would face additional obstacles in confronting them, and if we did so, we would have to do it abruptly and at a level that would stake the prestige of the top leaders on both sides, making it even more difficult to contain the crisis.

The fact that so much of the equipment was seaborne indicated to me, however, that the Soviets had left themselves a way out. If challenged, they would bristle; they might bargain; but if permitted to so do, they would withdraw. It was not easy to convince the President of this strategy; indeed, I never really did; the final showdown was triggered by an accident.

A potential Cuban crisis during an election struck a raw nerve in Nixon. For anyone who knew him it was out of the question that he would tolerate the establishment of a Soviet naval base in Cuba for any length of time. Too much of his political life had been tied up with taking a tough stance on this issue; his friendship with Charles (Bebe) Rebozo, who hated Castro with a fierce Latin passion, guaranteed that he would be constantly exposed to arguments to take a hard line; he would never want to appear weak before his old friend. Sooner or later he would strike back, and he would then not rest until he had accomplished his objective. But we were now in the midst of the Jordan crisis; Syrian tanks had just crossed into Jordan; for all Nixon knew, that crisis might trigger a showdown with the Soviet Union. The President focused on the most immediate challenge. And Nixon had convinced himself that while Vietnam unleashed media and Congressional assaults on Presidential credibility, a new Cuban missile crisis in an election year would generate a massive *public* cynicism. Finally, Nixon was scheduled to leave on September 27 for the trip to the Mediterranean, on which he had set his heart, especially looking forward to a demonstration of firepower by the Sixth Fleet. He did not see how he could leave the country if we were in the middle of a Cuban crisis. For all these reasons, Nixon's preferred strategy was to confront the Soviets right after the election. He accepted my analysis, but for the interim he chose Rogers's policy of soothing delay.

To be sure, his initial reaction to my memorandum conveying the results of the U-2 mission of September 16 sounded tough. His handwritten note read:

> I want a report on a crash basis on: (1) What CIA can do to support *any* kind of action which will irritate Castro; (2) What actions we can take which we have not yet taken to boycott nations dealing with Castro; (3) Most important, what actions we can take, covert or overt, to put missiles in Turkey — or a sub base in the Black Sea — anything which will give us some trading stock.

But on close examination these were all time-wasting options. Harassment of Castro had been tried and failed in the Sixties; it would take months to organize; "irritating" Castro would have no effect on the Soviet base. Tightening the boycott on Cuba would be even slower; it would run counter to the prevalent trend of our allies' policies and it too would have no conceivable short-term impact. Putting missiles in Turkey whence they had been removed as a result of the Cuban missile crisis was hardly feasible rapidly. And if we did succeed, it would shake our relations with Turkey if it learned that we were using them only as "trading stock."

On September 19, when I reported to Nixon the results of the WSAG, he urged me to play it all down. He did not, he said, want some "clown Senator" asking for a Cuban blockade in the middle of an election (as Republican Senators had done in 1962). We were in an anomalous position. The President was heading for a confrontation, but his desire to delay the showdown for two months greatly increased its risks.

Whenever personal persuasion failed, I appealed to Haldeman, who would convey one's thoughts faithfully and literally without injecting his own views. It was risky to approach Haldeman, since he was likely to interpret any substantive concern as a sign of emotional instability; he had an invincible faith that there was no difficulty that could not be rectified by good public relations. But he was sure to communicate my uneasiness to Nixon even if he treated it as overwrought. I told Haldeman that the President was not focusing on the real issue. If there were a crisis in November or December we would have great difficulty explaining why we had done nothing in September; the Soviets might be misled by simultaneous summit preparations into steps that could cause the situation to get out of control.

The NSC meeting of September 23 helped concentrate the minds of senior officials. Some of the intelligence presented indicated that we had some time; some added to the sense of urgency. On the reassuring side was Helms's conviction that if the Soviets intended to base ballistic missile submarines in Cuba permanently, they would need additional heavy equipment, particularly large cranes. This equipment was not yet in Cienfuegos. Moreover, we knew of no missile-carrying submarine in the area. On the other hand, we had other intelligence suggesting that nuclear weapons might be on board one of the ships. In the event, the President decided to proceed along the lines he had already privately indicated to me. He asked for contingency plans for the mining of Cienfuegos, the blockade of Cuba, the tailing of Soviet ships, and the removal of all restraints on the Cuban exile community, to be implemented sometime in the future. In the interval, he ordered a very low-key public posture, confined simply to noting that we were aware of what was happening and were watching. Mel Laird pointed out that this would never work; too many people knew what was going on; the story would leak.

It must be remembered that at the time of the NSC meeting on September 23, we did not yet know that the Syrian tanks had turned around and that the invasion of Jordan was over. The President's procrastination was therefore understandable. Nevertheless, I was extremely uneasy. I thought the proposed policy was likely to tempt the Soviets to escalate their activity in the Caribbean; I did not see how we could move from a low-key posture in September to a confrontation in November if the installations remained the same, or how we would explain a showdown if the Soviets practiced a creeping expansion. If in the meantime the Soviets accepted our summit proposal, the problem would become nearly unmanageable. In short, the longer we waited the more difficult would be the decisions both for us and for the Soviets when we challenged them and the harder it would be to contain the looming crisis.

I convened a restricted meeting of the WSAG in the situation Room on September 24 — the day after the Syrian tanks had turned back — to implement the President's Cuban decisions, much as I disagreed with them. The discussion dealt entirely with press guidance should the construction in Cienfuegos become public while the President was in Europe. It was decided that if the issue came up, Defense would put out the bare-bones facts but offer no comment; State would express the view that the introduction of offensive weapons would be regarded with concern; and the White House would confine itself to stating that the President had been informed and was following events. The departmental press officers were given a detailed factual description; it was intended for their background guidance, not for use in briefings. We were on the way to implementing the President's decision when it was made irrelevant by a bureaucratic mix-up of monumental proportions.

First, Dobrynin returned to Washington after his absence of seven weeks. Exuding goodwill, joshing that I had broken my promise not to organize a crisis in his absence (referring to Jordan), he called on the evening of September 24 to say that he had a message concerning Jordan and the summit; he was instructed to deliver it personally to the President. I reported this to Nixon, who was unwilling to see Dobrynin. He was afraid the Soviets were turning down the summit and he did not wish to receive a rebuff personally. I told him that the Soviets would probably not rebuff him but seek to string him along and delay the summit until 1971. We both agreed, however, that to have kept the President waiting for six weeks for an answer to a summit proposed in August for October was an act of discourtesy that did not deserve a personal audience. Nor did Nixon want to see Dobrynin without mentioning Cuba, and he saw no way of discussing Cienfuegos without either stirring up the unwanted crisis or leaving an impression that we were acquiescing. It was finally decided that I would receive Dobrynin's message; it was the best signal of coolness we could give the Soviets. When I told him, Dobrynin pretended to have to check with Moscow.

Dobrynin and I finally met as usual in the Map Room of the White House at 10:00 A.M. on Friday, September 25. I cut off general discussion, pleading pressure of time caused by the President's imminent departure for Europe. Dobrynin's message was what I had expected: the Soviet Union agreed in principle to a summit; the agenda outlined in our communication of August 24 was acceptable. Dobrynin did not explain why it had taken so long to reach this profound conclusion. However, the Soviet government preferred that the summit take place in 1971 after the Party Congress in the spring, which in practice meant not before June. Dobrynin then wondered whether the President was thinking of Moscow as a venue. When I allowed for the umpteenth time that this thought had indeed crossed the President's mind, Dobrynin nevertheless stopped well short of an actual invitation. He left the site and date to further discussion. He also informed me that Premier Kosygin would not attend the twenty-fifth anniversary celebration of the United Nations in October 1970, thus closing off that opportunity for a high-level meeting before the Congressional election. Dobrynin also brought the Soviet leaders' reaction to the crisis in Jordan, which I have already described. I replied coolly that I would be in touch with him later.

By the time I returned to my office chaos had erupted. The morning had started with a column by C. L. Sulzberger in the *New York Times,* which, under the headline "Ugly Clouds in the South," warned of a possible Soviet submarine base in Cienfuegos. Contrary to our carefully planned press guidance, the spokesman of the Defense Department had filled in every detail when asked a question at his morning briefing. It was a Washington classic of misunderstood instructions. The Pentagon briefer had seen the contingency guidance but did not understand that he was to use it only in an extremity and was not to refer to the background material at all. He therefore volunteered everything he knew, giving a detailed account of Soviet construction and naval movements of the past few months.

The press reaction was predictable. The Associated Press led off with: "The Pentagon said today it has firm indications the Soviet Union may be establishing a permanent submarine base in Cuba." United Press International reported: "The Defense Department said today it has evidence that Russia has started construction of a submarine base in Cuba." Doubtless the evening television news and the next day's morning papers would dramatize it all further. It was inconceivable that the President could leave the country two days later without some White House statement on the new "crisis." Though Mel Laird and Dave Packard called to apologize for the inadvertent Pentagon briefing, the fat was in the fire. Laird offered to take a hard line so that the White House could appear conciliatory, but I would have none of it: "We can downplay it and say it is perfectly natural so we can go on the trip, but then how can we ever confront them on it, which is what the President wants to do?"

Yet when all was said and done the Pentagon bloopers were actually our salvation. The bare-bones press guidance originally planned was so reticent that it would surely have appeared to Moscow as acquiescence; the President's foreign journey would have provided an opportunity to complete the construction of the base; and the inevitable final confrontation would have been both bitter and far more risky. Now, however, we would be forced into my own preferred course. I told the President that we had no choice now except to face the Soviets down, but we should do so in a manner that gave them a way out. I proposed to use a briefing already scheduled that afternoon on Nixon's Mediterranean trip to issue a strong warning to the Soviets against building a submarine base in Cuba; I would leave open whether the base already existed, so that a clear line of retreat was available. I would then call in Dobrynin in the guise of giving him an answer to the summit proposal and confront him directly, telling him that we considered Cienfuegos an offensive base and would treat it accordingly. We would insist on its dismantlement. The President's trip would provide an interlude for that purpose.

When options were starkly defined, Nixon was always decisive. He understood immediately that waffling could only increase our dangers.

He approved my recommendation and suggested that I ask Admiral
Moorer to move a destroyer near Cienfuegos to emphasize our warning.
With the boldness that was his hallmark in foreign policy Nixon authorized a challenge to the Soviet Union on the eve of his departure on an
overseas trip. Accordingly, I went to the East Room of the White House
to brief the White House press — ostensibly on the President's trip.
When the predictable question on Cuba came up, I replied:

> With respect to Soviet naval activity in the Caribbean, we are, of course
> watching the development of Soviet naval activity and of possible construction
> there. We are watching it very closely. The Soviet Union can be under no
> doubt that we would view the establishment of a strategic base in the Caribbean
> with the utmost seriousness.
>
> I would like perhaps to call attention to a press conference statement that
> President Kennedy made on November 20, 1962, in which he said the follow-
> ing:
>
> "As for our part, if all offensive weapons are removed from Cuba and kept
> out of the Hemisphere in the future, under adequate verification and safeguards,
> and if Cuba is not used for the export of aggressive Communist purposes, there
> will be peace in the Caribbean."
>
> The operative part, of course, is here: "if all offensive weapons are removed
> from Cuba and kept out of the Hemisphere in the future."
>
> This, of course, remains the policy of this Government.

Later in the briefing I was asked whether this was not a bad time for the
President to take a trip. I replied:

> We are watching the events in Cuba. We are not at this moment in a position
> to say exactly what they mean. We will continue to observe them and at the
> right moment we will take the action that seems indicated. We are in excellent
> communication. Nothing very rapid and dramatic is likely to occur, and we are
> going to be in very close touch with the situation.

My briefing on the President's trip was subject to a press embargo —
it could not be used until Saturday, September 26, for the Sunday
papers, the day of the President's departure. The journalists pressed Ron
Ziegler to permit immediate use of my Cuba statement. We agreed.

Two hours after my briefing, at 5:30 P.M., I met Dobrynin again in
the Map Room. I had summoned him under the pretext of giving him an
answer to his summit queries; two could play the game of using summit
discussions to take some of the edge off confrontation. I told him that
we accepted the principle of a summit and suggested either June or September 1971, depending on the state of our preparations. Moscow was
acceptable as the site.

I then turned to the principal purpose of the meeting. Dobrynin had
no doubt seen the wire reports of my background briefing in the after-

noon. My words had been carefully chosen to suggest that the United States had not yet made up its mind about the precise nature of Soviet activities in Cienfuegos. I wanted him to understand that this was said only to give his government a graceful opportunity to withdraw without a public confrontation. We considered the construction at Cienfuegos unmistakably a submarine base. Moscow should be under no illusion; we would view continued construction with the "utmost gravity"; the base could not remain. We would not shrink from other measures including public steps if forced into it; if the ships — especially the tender — left Cienfuegos, we would consider it a training exercise.

Dobrynin was a thoroughgoing professional. He was usually genial, but he also knew when charm was wasted and when his usual recourse to cataloguing our sins was out of place. The issue now was a test between major powers involving important national interests. He was therefore all business as he sought to determine the extent and the limits of our challenge. Were we claiming that the 1962 understanding had been violated? I dismissed this as a legalistic quibble; in 1962 Kennedy had acted without claiming the violation of an understanding. Cuba, to us, was a place of extreme sensitivity. We considered the sequence of events, starting with Vorontsov's démarche of August 4, as acts of extremely bad faith. The installations had been completed with maximum deception; they could not remain. Dobrynin asked whether we were going to start a big press campaign on the issue, obviously calculating how much loss of face would be involved in a retreat. I replied that we had no such intention; the President was leaving for ten days in Europe and there would be no further briefings on the subject during that period. The Soviets thus had an opportunity to consider whether to go the route of conciliation or the route of confrontation; we were prepared for either. We were determined that there would be no Soviet submarine base in Cuba. Whatever the phraseology of the 1962 understanding, its intent could not have been to replace land-based with sea-based missiles. Dobrynin coolly said that he would report to Moscow and be in touch.

We kept our word; there was no government briefing. Rogers and Laird were with the President on his trip so that coherent press policy was easier to maintain than normally. The fact remained that less than forty-eight hours after the end of the Syrian invasion of Jordan, we were close to another confrontation, this time with a superpower.

Resolution of the Crisis

WE could not, of course, prevent newspaper or Congressional speculation sparked by the briefings that had already taken place. The *Washington Post* headlined the next day: "U.S. Warns Reds on Cuba

Sub Base.'' But the focus remained on the President's pending departure for the Mediterranean. The Cuban story was slow in building, and
there was no criticism that Nixon was departing in the midst of a crisis.
Senator Barry Goldwater was quoted in the *Washington Star* as considering the Pentagon disclosure of a possible Soviet nuclear submarine
base in Cuba evidence of a ''serious Russian bid for world domination.'' Senator Mike Mansfield was quoted also: ''I do view it with
alarm. It raises the most serious question in light of President John F.
Kennedy's statement after the 1962 Cuban missile crisis that offensive
weapons must be kept out of the Western Hemisphere to assure 'peace
in the Caribbean.' '' James Reston's column of September 27 was entitled ''Back to Cuba and the Cold War,'' and its lead paragraph ran:
''Something very serious and dangerous is now happening between the
leaders of the U.S. and the Soviet Union. They are clearly misjudging
one another in Southeast Asia, the Middle East and Cuba, and this could
be tragic for them and for the peace of the world.''

But this was the era of Vietnam. Almost immediately there was a second wave of reactions attacking the Administration. On Sunday, September 27, Senator J. William Fulbright voiced his skepticism on the
television show ''Issues and Answers,'' helpfully just as the Nixon
party departed from Washington: ''Nearly every year just before we
have an appropriations bill in the Senate, we get these stories; so it may
or may not be true.'' He said that it was a ''questionable proposition''
that the Soviets had no right to be in Cuba. He doubted that we could
''bluff'' the Soviets out of Cuba, because they now had a ''degree of
parity.'' Skeptical opinions in our bureaucracy made their way to the
front page of the *New York Times* in a September 30 story by Tad Szulc:

> American officials said today that the U.S. had only dubious and dated infor-
> mation to indicate that the Soviet Union might be planning to build a strategic
> submarine base in Cuba. For this reason, these officials, who include members
> of the intelligence community, said they were at a loss to explain why the
> White House chose last week to warn Moscow against the establishment of
> such a base.

The theme was picked up by Senator Frank Church, who, after an intelligence briefing, remarked on October 1 that the present evidence did
not suggest a reasonable conclusion one way or another. And on October 4, skeptical comments by a different part of our bureaucracy were
reported by Neil Sheehan of the *New York Times:* ''Military analysts say
they are not sure what the new construction ashore at Cienfuegos
signifies, but they say it could be a small facility for submarine-crew
housing and recreation. . . . In short the analysts think the Russians do
not need and may not want any large base at Cienfuegos for the
Yankee-class boats.'' This was not the view of the Joint Chiefs; it was

also clear that inaction was the best way to encourage the Soviet Union to build whatever it wanted and to expand whatever it was building.

And none of the critics noted that there was no word from the Soviet Union, neither denial nor outraged protest. In the whole period there was only a single, rather lame comment, complaining about hostile propaganda.

The Soviets had taken us seriously. As soon as we returned to Washington on October 5, Dobrynin requested an urgent appointment. He came in the next day with two messages, the first a face-saving one, to be shown to Arab clients, expressing satisfaction at my assurance of September 25 that we would not intervene in Jordan if other countries stayed out. The Kremlin chose to interpret this reaffirmation of the position from which we had never varied as a constructive contribution, and perhaps presented it to its Arab clients as having been exacted by Soviet diplomacy. I saw no point in disputing this; in diplomacy one collects claims on future restraint where one can.

The more important Soviet message concerned Cienfuegos. It began by noting the reaffirmation of the 1962 understanding in the previous exchanges and concluded with a precise commitment that no base was being built in Cuba:

> The Soviet side has not done and is not doing in Cuba now — that includes the area of the Cienfuegos port — anything of the kind that would contradict that mentioned understanding.

After rehashing the standard Soviet complaint about American overseas bases, and noting that the Soviet Union had proposed in the SALT talks to limit operational areas of ballistic missile submarines, the note concluded:

> In any case, we would like to reaffirm once more that the Soviet side strictly adheres to its part of the understanding on the Cuban question and will continue to adhere to it in the future on the assumption that the American side, as President Nixon has reaffirmed, will also strictly observe its part of the understanding.

Orally, Dobrynin added that while he could not make an agreement that Soviet submarines would never call at Cuban ports, he was prepared on behalf of his government to affirm that ballistic missile submarines would never call there in an operational capacity. I replied that we should make sure that the two governments understood the word "base" in the same manner. I would be back to him soon with some clarifying understandings.

The Soviets' reply was clearly positive in tone, committing them not to establish a naval base in Cuba — even if the definition was as yet vague — and Soviet actions were consistent with it: after my press statement, construction of port facilities had ceased, the tender had been moved to a pier rather than serving as a floating repair facility, and the next day two ships of the flotilla had departed.

On October 9 I handed Dobrynin a written definition of an operational "base" worked out with Captain Rembrandt C. Robinson, my staff liaison with the Joint Chiefs:

> The US Government understands that the USSR will not establish, utilize, or permit the establishment of any facility in Cuba that can be employed to support or repair Soviet naval ships capable of carrying offensive weapons; i.e. submarines or surface ships armed with nuclear-capable, surface-to-surface missiles.

The note then spelled out five activities, in particular, which according to the understanding would not be undertaken. In order to emphasize our determination, we headed it "President's Note."

Dobrynin accepted the document and said that he would have to await instructions from Moscow. However, he could tell me now that TASS would soon publish a formal statement. It appeared on October 13, and repeated the essence of the Soviet message of October 6. The spokesman of the Department of State described it as "positive." And so it was; submarines and offensive missiles on naval vessels were now for the first time incorporated into the 1962 understandings.

An interesting insight into the workings of the Soviet mind was given us two weeks later. Soviet Foreign Minister Gromyko, in the United States for the UN General Assembly, saw the President on October 22. On October 23 I spoke with Dobrynin at the Soviet mission in New York because Nixon had not yet given up the effort to extract some summit announcement before the election, an endeavor doomed — luckily for us — to disappointment. Dobrynin brought up Cuba. He said that Gromyko had been amazed because the President, after alluding to it briefly, had never returned to the subject. Naturally, Gromyko wondered about the reason. Could we be planning anything new? To the convoluted, ever-suspicious Soviet mind the President's omission had profoundly sinister connotations. In fact, Nixon had not pursued the subject because he did not wish to get into the sensitive Kissinger-Dobrynin exchanges in the presence of his Secretary of State. I asked Dobrynin what Gromyko would have replied had the President pursued the subject. Dobrynin said that Gromyko had been instructed to say the following: "We do not have a submarine base in Cuba nor are we building a military naval facility. We do not intend to have a military naval facility, and we will abide strictly by our understandings of 1962. We are also making the exchanges from August onward part of the understanding of 1962." Dobrynin added that our list of excluded activities could not be a formal agreement because it lacked reciprocity, but the

Soviet Union understood what we meant by a base. In other words, the "President's Note" became part of the understanding.

But nothing with the Soviets ever works this simply. The Soviet submarine tender and salvage tug, accompanied by four merchant ships and five Cuban patrol craft, indeed left Cienfuegos on October 10. On October 15, however, they turned in at the Cuban port of Mariel, on the northern coast of Cuba. They did not depart from Mariel until October 31; then, after heading in an easterly direction, they rounded the island again and arrived once again in Cienfuegos on November 7.

I protested angrily to Dobrynin on November 14. On November 24 the ubiquitous Vorontsov told a journalist that it was the task of a tender to tend submarines, and this was what it would do, though at sea. On December 22 I told Dobrynin that servicing submarines in or from Cuban ports would "lead to the most grave situation between the United States and the Soviet Union." On January 4, 1971, the President reinforced this by stating in a television interview: "In the event that nuclear submarines were serviced either in Cuba or from Cuba, that would be a violation of the understanding." On January 5 the White House elaborated on this statement, stressing that servicing of submarines "anywhere at sea" from tenders operating from Cuba was barred.[3]

The tender quit the Caribbean on January 3, 1971 — only to be replaced by a second tender that arrived in Cuba on February 14 with another Soviet naval task force, including a nuclear-powered attack submarine. I protested this to Dobrynin on three occasions and, after a WSAG meeting, handed him a note on February 22 saying that the presence of a tender in Cienfuegos for 125 of the last 166 days was inconsistent with the understanding. The tender and submarine left. But yet another Soviet flotilla returned in May, this time with a tender and a nuclear-powered cruise-missile submarine on a "training voyage," making a "brief rest" visit. Obviously the Soviets thought there was a loophole in port visits, and were exploiting it mercilessly. Every conceivable combination was being tried — except the most important one, the presence of a tender in conjunction with a nuclear-powered ballistic missile submarine.

We lodged another sharp protest. The tender left once more.

All this, it must be remembered, was handled almost entirely by private diplomacy. The process was essentially a series of messages in the Presidential Channel, backstopped by interagency coordination in the WSAG. Rather than a dramatic confrontation on the order of 1962, we considered that quiet diplomacy was best suited to giving the USSR an opportunity to withdraw without humiliation. By great firmness in the early stages of construction, we avoided a major crisis, yet we achieved our objective. Military construction was halted; the antiaircraft emplacements were dismantled; the communication facility never became operational. Admiral Thomas Moorer, Chairman of the Joint Chiefs of Staff, was able to tell the Economic Club of Detroit on November 9, 1970, that the Soviet Union did not have a submarine base in Cuba.

To be sure, the Soviets harassed us for a while longer through the loophole of port visits. But without shore facilities, port calls are strategically ineffective. And formally proscribing port calls would have widespread ramifications for the movement of the US Navy and our principle of freedom of the seas. What concerned us in Cuba in 1970 was an expansion of the Soviet Union's ballistic missile submarine capability against the United States by virtue of a base in the Caribbean. This was prevented.

We could not forget, of course, the deception that had been attempted. Nor would we be oblivious to the reality that Soviet restraint, when it was achieved, resulted only from our forcing of the issue and determined persistence. The Nixon Administration had told Moscow many times that we were prepared for a period of mutual restraint and conciliation. In the autumn of 1970 Moscow chose to test whether this willingness reflected indecision, domestic weakness due to Vietnam, or the strategy of a serious government. Having been given the answer, Moscow permitted Cienfuegos to recede once more into well-deserved obscurity.

XVII

The Autumn of Crises: Chile

ON September 4, 1970, Salvador Allende Gossens achieved a plurality in the Chilean presidential election, with a bare 36.2 percent of the popular vote, leading the next candidate in a three-man field by 39,000 votes. Ironically, this was a *decline* from the 38.9 percent he had received in the 1964 elections when he had lost to Eduardo Frei Montalva. But in 1970 the popular Frei was barred by law from succeeding himself, and the even higher anti-Allende vote (62.7 percent) was split between two candidates. The Chilean Congress would hold a runoff vote as required when no candidate received an electoral majority. Traditionally, it backed the candidate who received the plurality; it was expected to do so in this case and name Salvador Allende President of Chile.

Edward Korry, our Ambassador in Chile since 1967 and originally a Kennedy appointee, reported:

Chile voted calmly to have a Marxist-Leninist state, the first nation in the world to make this choice freely and knowingly. . . . *His margin is only about one percent but it is large enough in the Chilean constitutional framework to nail down his triumph as final.* There is no reason to believe that the Chilean armed forces will unleash a civil war or that any other intervening miracle will undo his victory. It is a sad fact that Chile has taken the path to communism with only a little more than a third (36 percent) of the nation approving this choice, but it is an immutable fact. *It will have the most profound effect on Latin America and beyond; we have suffered a grievous defeat; the consequences will be domestic and international;* the repercussions will have immediate impact in some lands and delayed effect in others.

The italicized sentences were underlined by Nixon when I sent him Korry's report. Korry was convinced that "Chile alone in the western and democratic world had the objective conditions to permit a unique constitutional transition to a communist state by an Allende government." He cited the strength and organization of the Marxist parties, the extensive powers of the presidency in Chile, the already advanced and growing trend toward state intervention in the economic sector, and the disarray among the democratic forces in Chile.

The Chilean election results came in just as Moscow and Cairo were rejecting our protests of Middle East cease-fire violations; Jordan feared an imminent move by Iraqi troops against the King; a Soviet naval force was steaming toward Cuba. By September 8, the day the Chilean developments were first discussed by an interagency committee, several airplanes had just been hijacked in the Middle East and the Soviet flotilla was nearing the port of Cienfuegos. Six days later, on September 14, when Chile was next considered, the Jordan situation had deteriorated, and Cuban MiGs intercepted a U-2 flight seeking to photograph Cienfuegos and the mission had to be aborted. In the weeks that followed, our government pondered Chilean events not in isolation but against the backdrop of the Syrian invasion of Jordan and our effort to force the Soviet Union to dismantle its installation for servicing nuclear submarines in the Caribbean. The reaction must be seen in that context.

In any circumstances, Allende's election was a challenge to our national interest. We did not find it easy to reconcile ourselves to a second Communist state in the Western Hemisphere. We were persuaded that it would soon be inciting anti-American policies, attacking hemisphere solidarity, making common cause with Cuba, and sooner or later establishing close relations with the Soviet Union. And this was all the more painful because Allende represented a break with Chile's long democratic history and would become President not through an authentic expression of majority will but through a fluke of the Chilean political system. Thirty-six percent of the popular vote was hardly a mandate for the irreversible transformation of Chile's political and economic institutions that Allende was determined to effect.

Two previous American administrations had come to the same conclusion. Two administrations had judged that an Allende government in Chile would be against fundamental American national interests. Our conclusion in 1970 was substantially the same.

Salvador Allende

ALLENDE's later martyrdom has obscured his politics. Socialist though he may have proclaimed himself, his goals and his philosophy bore no resemblance to European social democracy. Allende had founded the Socialist Party of Chile, which set itself apart from the Communist Party by being more radical in its program and no more democratic in its philosophy. He was willing enough to come to power by an election *before* undertaking the revolution; but the social and political transformation he promised afterward did not differ significantly from the Communist platform. It was a central tenet of the party's program that "bourgeois" democratic practices would be made irrelevant; by definition his would be the last democratic election.

In any case, Allende was the candidate of a coalition of the Communist Party and his own Socialist Party, called Popular Unity; it was joined by other radical splinter parties. The program of Popular Unity pledged to destroy the present system and bring about "revolutionary" and "profound" changes; it denounced "imperialist exploitation" and the "American monopolies." It called for wholesale expropriation of land, basic industries, and the commercial and banking system, and for a "radically transformed" educational system and a "national system to promote popular culture." Major portions of the Popular Unity program were drawn verbatim from the platform of the Chilean Communist Party,[1] whose subservience to the Moscow line was shown by the fact that it was one of the few Communist parties outside of Eastern Europe to welcome the Soviet invasion of Czechoslovakia. Among the planks borrowed from the Communists was one calling for a unicameral legislature and for subordination of the judiciary to this "Popular Assembly"; the purpose was to break down the traditional checks and balances and separation of powers provided by the Chilean constitution's bicameral legislature and independent judiciary. The Socialist Party's contribution to the program of the Popular Unity included the passages opposing "imperialism," condemning American "aggression" in Vietnam, calling for "active solidarity" with North Vietnam, and declaring "solidarity with the Cuban Revolution, which is the vanguard of revolution and construction of socialism in Latin America." Another notable passage denounced the Organization of American States as an "agent and tool of American imperialism."

In 1967 Allende had been one of the founders of the Organization of Latin American Solidarity, a Havana-based group whose political creed, in the words of Régis Debray, an idolatrous chronicler of revolutions, was "based on the conception of continental armed struggle against North American imperialism. Its basic functions are solidarity with, coordination of, and support for national liberation struggles throughout the continent. The declaration of the closing session of the conference made a frontal attack on the reformist positions of some of the left-wing parties in Latin America, pointing out that 'the revolutionary armed struggle constitutes the fundamental line for the Latin American revolution.' "[2] During the election campaign of 1970, Allende stated as his personal conviction: "Cuba in the Caribbean and a Socialist Chile in the southern cone will make the revolution in Latin America."

Indeed, there is no epithet that Allende would have rejected more indignantly than the notion that he was a democratic reformer. One should not needlessly insult the integrity of a man who spent his life dedicated to revolution by claiming him to be something he always emphatically denied. In his 1971 conversations with Régis Debray — at a time when he was, in fact, the constitutional President of Chile — he insisted that the democratic guarantees to which he had agreed in 1970 in order to persuade the Chilean Congress to ratify his election and the military to accept his accession to office were a "tactical necessity"[3] that did not affect his basic commitment to a revolutionary upheaval: "At the time the important thing was to take control of Government,"[4] Allende pointed out. He compared this tactic with Mao Tse-tung's decision to permit private enterprise for a few years after the Chinese Communists took power in 1949 or with Fidel Castro's restraint with respect to Guantanamo.[5]

The only inference one can draw is that the democratic guarantees Allende accepted reluctantly and, by his own account, for the sake of temporary expediency would be dismantled at the first opportunity. He explicitly distinguished his government from the earlier Popular Front government in Chile (like those in Europe in the 1930s), which had included democratic parties; these he disparaged as "bourgeois."[6] "In the Popular Front, Régis," he said to Debray in 1971, "there was a dominant Party, a majority party, the party of the bourgeoisie, the Radical Party. Today, there is no dominant party in the Popular Unity, but there are two parties of the working class, revolutionary parties, Marxist parties. Finally comrade, the President of the Republic is a socialist. Things are different, then, and I have reached this office in order to bring about the economic and social transformation of Chile, to open up the road to socialism. Our objective is total, scientific, Marxist socialism."[7]

Debray, still unconvinced, asked, "Who is using who? Who is taking who for a ride?" Allende replied: "The answer is the proletariat. If it wasn't so, I wouldn't be here."[8] At another point Allende expostulated: "As for the bourgeois State at the present moment, we are seeking to overcome it. To overthrow it!"[9]

What worried us about Allende was his proclaimed hostility to the United States and his patent intention to create in effect another Cuba. It was his explicit program and indeed long-standing goal to establish an irreversible dictatorship and a permanent challenge to our position in the Western Hemisphere. And in the month of Cienfuegos it was not absurd to take seriously the military implications of another Soviet ally in Latin America. Our concern with Allende was based on national security, not on economics.

Nationalization of American-owned property was not the issue. We never challenged the principle of international law that permits nationalization for public purposes, although we did emphasize our interest in prompt, adequate, and effective compensation (also required by international law). Every postwar administration in the United States had sought to discourage the expropriation of foreign companies by the developing nations and, where nationalization was unavoidable, to encourage its being done in a way that limited the adverse impact on the general investment climate. There existed a Congressional mandate, moreover, to terminate economic assistance under the Foreign Assistance Act of 1961 if American property was expropriated without compensation (the Hickenlooper Amendment).

But we had taken great pains not to let the expropriation issue interfere with the foreign policy objectives of the United States. Thus, in Chile in 1969, before Allende, Ambassador Korry had cooperated in what amounted to the negotiated nationalization of the Anaconda Company. And with Peru that same year, the Nixon Administration stretched our legislation almost to the breaking point to reach an equitable settlement of the nationalization of the International Petroleum Company's mining operations without having to invoke restrictive legislation. We repeatedly sought pretexts to postpone application of the Hickenlooper Amendment and made clear that we were prepared to accept a compensatory payment for IPC of less than full value, so as to maintain friendly relations with an important country — even though Peru was governed by a left-wing military junta that was aggressively nationalistic and leaning toward the more radical elements of the Third World. After patient and sustained efforts, we worked out a modus vivendi with the Peruvian government.

The challenge to our policy and interests posed by Allende was fundamentally different. He was not just nationalizing property; he avowed his dedication to totalitarian Marxism-Leninism. He was an admirer of the Cuban dictatorship and a resolute opponent of "American imperialism." His stated goal for over a decade before he became President had been to undermine our position in the entire Western Hemisphere by violence if necessary. Because it was a continental country, Chile's capacity for doing so was greater by far than Cuba's, and Cuba had already posed a substantial challenge; in fact, we were in the midst of the confrontation over Cienfuegos when Allende was elected. Chile bordered Argentina, Peru, and Bolivia, all plagued by radical movements. Allende's success would have had implications also for the future of Communist parties in Western Europe, whose policies would inevitably undermine the Western Alliance whatever their fluctuating claims of respectability. No responsible President could look at Allende's accession to power with anything but disquiet.

There was no dispute in our government about what Allende stood for. No one challenged Korry's first cable predicting the consequences of Allende's election. The only disagreement concerned Allende's capacity to achieve his aims in the face of indigenous resistance, and what the United States could do about it if Korry's prediction came true.

Influence and Intervention: The 40 Committee

W HETHER and to what extent the United States should seek to affect domestic developments in other countries is a complicated question, the answer to which depends on a variety of elements, including one's conception of the national interest. Presidents of both parties have felt the need for covert operations in the gray area between formal diplomacy and military intervention throughout the postwar period. I find it distasteful to discuss covert operations in print. But the material has already been published by the Senate Select Committee to Study Governmental Operations with Respect to Intelligence Activities (the so-called Church Committee) in a tendentious report in 1975 on Chile. There is no evidence that the authors of the report tried to weigh the concerns about an Allende victory that we felt so acutely at the time.

It is ironical that some of those who were vociferous in condemning what they called "intervention" in Chile have been most insistent on governmental pressure against Allende's successors. The restrictions on American aid to Chile have been far more severe against the post-Allende government than during Allende's term of office. The measures have admittedly been overt but overtness does not change the inconsistency with the principle against outside intervention on which at least part of the assault on covert operations was based. Paradoxically, American intervention in the domestic affairs of other countries has multiplied and become less discriminating since the covert operations of the CIA have come under attack. The earlier "Cold War" period of CIA activities observed certain limits: Its criteria were foreign policy and national security dangers to the United States, of which there were not that many. The new doctrine justifies unlimited intervention to promote internal change in countries that are both friend and foe; it has been directed against countries that do not threaten our national security and that may indeed be allies of the United States.

Of course, covert operations have their philosophical and practical difficulties and especially for America. Our national temperament and tradition are unsuited to them. Our system of government does not lend itself spontaneously to either the secrecy or subtlety that is required. We lack the elaborate conspiratorial apparatus of our adversaries. Those eager to dismantle our intelligence apparatus will have little difficulty finding examples of actions that were amateurish or transparent. But the men and women who have been prepared to carry out assignments in secret, with resources usually ridiculously inferior to those of our adversaries, under inhibiting restrictions, deserve better of their country than the merciless assault to which they have been exposed — assaults that threaten to leave us naked in a vital area of our national security. For we face an unprecedented problem. We live in an age of ideological confrontation; through every phase of coexistence the Soviet leaders have insisted that it did not imply any lessening of the ideological struggle. Soviet-line Communist parties around the world occasionally differ with their senior partner in Moscow on questions of internal Communist policy — as one would expect from strong-willed, power-oriented men who have reached eminence by a ruthless political competition. They almost never differ on international issues; even the most apparently "independent" Communist parties of Western Europe and Latin America follow the Soviet lead in foreign policy without significant exceptions, and those exceptions are as often as not on the side of greater radicalism than the Kremlin considers expedient.

Nor is the problem simply a matter of Communist parties. Radical politics in today's world encompasses a network of sympathetic organizations and groups that cover the globe, carrying out terrorist outrages or financing them, transferring weapons, infiltrating media, seeking to sway political processes. How funds are transferred from formal Communist channels to these front organizations is difficult to trace. Our Ambassador in Chile, for example, reported in September 1970 that one of the reasons why he was convinced Allende would succeed in establishing a totalitarian state was that "of the three TV channels in Santiago, in a still free society, one is totally controlled by the Marxist-Leninists of the University of Chile, another is controlled by a combination of Marxists and very left wing Christian Democrats of the Catholic University and the third is the State's." (The state's, of course, would also become dominated by radicals after Allende's accession to power.) And throughout 1970 we received credible reports that substantial covert funds and assistance from Cuba and other Communist sources were being funneled to Allende.

In these circumstances it was neither morally nor politically unjustified for the United States to support those internal political forces seeking to maintain a democratic counterweight to radical dominance. On the contrary, no responsible national leader could have done otherwise. There was nothing sinister about the desire of the United States to make it possible for democratic parties to maintain competing radio or television outlets or newspapers. These considerations had induced the Kennedy and Johnson administrations to make available over $3 million between 1962 and 1964 to the campaign of Allende's opponent, the reformist and able Eduardo Frei (though apparently without Frei's knowledge); and they became particularly acute in the light of Allende's relentless campaign of harassment, intimidation, and economic pressures to drive opposing media and democratic parties out of business once he came into office. This I will discuss at greater length in the next volume.

What the reader is entitled to know, however, is briefly how in a democratic society we maintained supervision over covert activities to ensure that they remained consonant with our national ethic and purposes.

When we came into office, covert operations were supervised by the so-called 303 Committee, named after a June 1964 Presidential Directive (National Security Action Memorandum 303) that affirmed its composition, functions, and responsibilities. Such an interagency coordinating mechanism has existed under various designations ever since the 1947 National Security Act, which created the CIA and the NSC. Early in the Nixon Administration the 303 Committee was identified in a news story. In those faraway days of innocence this was considered enough of a breach of security to require a change of name. National Security Decision Memorandum 40 reaffirmed the functions of the committee on February 17, 1970; it was given a new label, named after this directive.[10]

At that time, the 40 Committee was composed of the Attorney General, the Deputy Secretaries of State and Defense, the Director of Central Intelligence, the Chairman of the Joint Chiefs of Staff, and the Assistant to the President for National Security Affairs, who acted as chairman. The Assistant Secretary of State for the area in which the covert activity was proposed would almost invariably sit in. In other words, except for the Attorney General,* the composition of the 40 Committee was identical to that of the Senior Review Group and the WSAG; it comprised the senior officials responsible for the day-to-day conduct of our national security affairs. It was the group most likely to be sensitive to all the ramifications of our foreign policy. (The principal difference from the Senior Review Group was that staff members were excluded.)

The agenda was generally put forward by the Central Intelligence Agency in consultation with my office. The CIA usually cleared the agenda informally with the State Department and had a tendency to defer items until it had resolved State Department objections; this happened, for example, with Chile. (Since the Ambassador in the field was technically the supervisor of the CIA station chief, the CIA had learned that it needed State Department support to operate effectively.) A CIA officer familiar with the project under discussion would brief the Committee. Additional staff was not present except for the State Department expert on the area under discussion. Notes were kept by a CIA official assigned to the NSC for the purpose.

The overwhelming majority of covert activities were first suggested by the CIA or by our ambassadors abroad; while I was in office only in the rarest of cases did the White House propose agenda items. Chile was one of these, and even there the President only gave impetus to what the

---

* The Attorney General had participated in the committee supervising covert actions at least since the Kennedy Administration; he is today a formal member.

40 Committee was already doing on its own. The only change I made in the procedures I inherited was to require that each approved covert or reconnaissance operation be reviewed at least once a year by the 40 Committee; this was to prevent its continuation by bureaucratic inertia after the need had passed.

Subject to Presidential blessing, once the 40 Committee approved a covert activity — usually by authorizing the expenditure of a given amount of money — the CIA was responsible for its execution. The 40 Committee did not supervise the day-to-day conduct of what it had approved. It would ordinarily be briefed on a particular program only on completion or at the annual review or when more money was required, although in critical situations such as the first month after Allende's victory there were more regular briefings. In fact, the principal procedural weakness in our covert operations was that while they were initiated with full foreign policy review they were not thereafter controlled with the same attention to detail by the highest levels in our government; there was no subgroup to monitor operations. The 40 Committee authorized but did not supervise. Theoretically, the American ambassadors in whose countries covert activities were being conducted were supposed to supply the supervision. But they rarely had the time or the expertise.* With respect to Chile, the key question was whether the advent of an Allende government in Chile was of sufficient concern to our national security to justify the involvement of the 40 Committee.

The Chilean Election of 1970

As already noted, two previous administrations had concluded that Salvador Allende and the forces behind him posed a sufficient threat to our interests to warrant our opposing him in the 1964 election, to the extent of nearly $3 million; as late as 1968 several hundred thousand dollars were appropriated covertly by our predecessors to help defeat the Allende forces in the Chilean congressional elections scheduled for March 1969. Our official foreign assistance to Chile during the Frei Administration totaled well over $1 billion, the largest per capita program by far in Latin America — partly to strengthen the democratic forces against Allende. That an Allende government threatened our national interests was conventional wisdom when Nixon entered office.

Strangely enough, the Nixon Administration was initially less active

---

* In reading some of the internal communications of the Agency, which were published by the Church Committee — especially those after October 15, 1970 — I have come to believe that we should have insisted on the same clearance for those cables by the office of the President's national security adviser as that to which key State Department cables were subjected.

against Allende than its Democratic predecessors had been, partly because of its preoccupation with so many other crises; partly from a
wrong estimate of the likely outcome of the Chilean election. The mistaken estimate was readily accepted because it led to the most comfortable conclusion; it made it unnecessary to face up to the hard choices we
would be compelled to make in the conditions of 1970.

The United States government had for years actively supported
Frei because he was the most popular and able man in Chile. It
was a morally simple decision because it enabled us to be both anti-
Communist and on the side of reformist and progressive forces supported by the vast majority of Chileans. But in 1970 we were not to be
so fortunate; a choice would have to be made. President Frei was barred
by the Chilean constitution from succeeding himself. His Christian
Democratic Party had lost ground in the 1969 congressional election; its
vote had been reduced by 11 percent. The conservative National Party
had gained correspondingly. The Christian Democrats were splintering;
the most leftist members deserted when the party rejected their demand
for a "popular union" with the Marxist parties, and the party machine
fell into the hands of anti-Frei forces much more strident, less committed to the traditions of an open society and democracy, less truly reformist, more hostile to the United States.

The polarization of Chilean political life was evidenced when Frei, in
spite of the generous US aid program, felt obliged by leftist pressures in
early 1969 to take two significant steps. In the face of radical student
protests, he canceled a visit by Governor Nelson Rockefeller, whom
Nixon had sent on a tour of Latin America to help chart a new approach
to the Western Hemisphere. Almost simultaneously, Frei insisted on
renegotiating an agreement with the American copper companies concluded by his own government and put into effect only two years before, by which Chile had acquired a substantial, though not in every
case controlling, share of the ownership of the copper mines. He now
demanded an immediate majority interest and the progressive acquisi-
tion by Chile of the remaining American stock. Yet the desire to
strengthen what we and our predecessors considered the best hope for
moderate democracy in Chile was so strong that Ambassador Korry was
instructed to be helpful in arranging mutually satisfactory terms. "Satisfactory" in this context was a relative concept, given the companies'
knowledge that the alternative would be outright expropriation. (With a
lack of political foresight characteristic of many multinational companies, Anaconda had permitted its expropriation insurance to lapse in
reliance on the earlier agreement, in order to save insurance fees, which
undermined its bargaining position further.)

There were thus plenty of storm warnings in 1969. The increasing
leftward trend of the Chilean Christian Democrats and their shrinking

popular base made it unlikely that the nonrevolutionary parties could unite on a single candidate as they had done in 1964. The prospect was for a close three-way race among a conservative candidate, a weak Christian Democrat, and the radical leftist Allende — and a final decision by the Congress, in which Allende's grouping was not far from a majority. But the White House in 1969 was preoccupied with Vietnam and its domestic turmoil, Soviet relations, Western Europe, the Okinawa negotiations with Japan, and the beginnings of the China initiative. I knew too little about Chile to challenge the experts.

No agency called our attention to the gravity of the situation. Those that might have favored a more active American role were hesitant to challenge a State Department predisposition against an active covert role. Chile, indeed, is a classic example of how major events can unfold without the White House's knowing because the line agencies cannot agree on their significance: The "nonaggression treaty" by which agencies seek to avoid a contest in which a decision might go against them prevented Chile from being raised to the White House level throughout 1969. To be sure, the CIA on a number of occasions pointed out that if a serious effort were to be mounted in 1970, preparations for it had to begin in 1969. And in April 1969 the Agency had reckoned that the radical left stood an even chance of winning the presidency. But this was a practical judgment of what would have to be done if there were a decision to repeat our involvement of 1964; it was not a recommendation for action. Moreover, any such recommendation was certain to face the adamant opposition of the Latin American Bureau of the State Department, which could not bring itself to face Chilean political realities. In 1970 there was no viable reformist Christian Democrat to support; the party was divided; its candidate was weak and playing with the radical left. If Allende was to be stopped, it would have to be by the conservative Jorge Alessandri. Though he had impeccable democratic credentials — indeed, he had preceded Frei in the presidency — the Latin American Bureau disliked him, ostensibly for being too old, in reality because he was considered insufficiently progressive. Some in the Latin American Bureau, confusing social reform with geopolitics, did not consider an Allende presidency dangerous enough to overcome their ideological prejudices against Alessandri.

Ironically, the American tendency to identify politics with technical economic development had unintentionally contributed in the last years of the Johnson Administration to the weakening of the reformist political forces whom our officials really preferred and who were essential to resist the revolutionary parties. In 1968 — two years before the presidential election that brought Allende to power — the United States terminated grant economic aid to Chile on the ground that the Chilean economy had become largely self-sustaining. This may have been technically correct, but it is a clear example of the error of taking essentially political decisions on economic grounds. The cutoff of American aid was unpopular in Chile; it undercut the moderate element represented by Frei; it was exploited by the more radical anti-American wing of the governing party, which advocated an economic program substantially similar to that of the radical parties, thus further confusing the electoral situation.

The technical approach to development flourished side by side with a doctrinaire antimilitarism. In 1967 United States policy turned increasingly unfriendly to the Chilean military (and that of other friendly hemispheric nations). The theory was to encourage a shift of resources from military expenditures to social and economic development, on the premise that these countries had no need for a defense establishment. Ceilings were placed on our sale of arms; grant military aid programs were terminated; Frei was encouraged to sponsor various demilitarization and disarmament schemes for Latin America. By October 1969 discontent in the Chilean military about lagging professionalism and inadequate pay erupted into an abortive coup against the government. In response Frei instituted a state of emergency; rumors of military unrest continued. The Nixon Administration inherited in Chile both a radicalized Christian Democratic Party and profound resentment on the part of the Chilean military against the United States as well as against the Christian Democrats. This almost certainly enhanced Allende's ability to "buy off" or neutralize the military in the first years of his term.

Nothing illustrates more clearly — even tragically — the danger of applying the abstract theories of our better graduate schools to the domestic complexities of foreign societies than the policy toward Chile in the 1960s. The notion that social reform and economic development automatically produced political stability — drawn from the experience of our own New Deal — had only the most limited relevance in a country where two radical parties were determined not to reform but to overthrow the system. Our refusal to face the reality that what was going on was a deadly political struggle and not a debate between economics professors transformed us by 1970 from the dominant element of 1964 into a sort of mother hen clucking nervous irrelevancies from the sidelines.

To complete the process of self-stultification, the Latin American Bureau chose this moment to attack the very concept of covert support for foreign democratic parties, which had for so long been a central feature of our Chilean effort. The resources for any effort to block the Socialist-Communist climb to power, so the argument ran, could and should hereafter be found entirely *within* Chile. A great college term paper could have been written on that subject, but to raise it suddenly in 1970 was to run the kind of unacceptable risk that policymakers are hired to avoid. Such a policy was bound to demoralize the very forces we wanted to encourage; those who had benefited from American support would infer from it a new indifference. In a close election the resultant subtle change in the psychological balance could be decisive.

I was only dimly aware of these trends in 1969. In fact, the 40 Committee considered the subject only four times during the entire twenty-one months before Allende's victory on September 4. In April 1969 it decided to defer any decision on the possible need for action; in March 1970 it allocated a negligible sum for propaganda in support of democratic candidates five months before the election; in late June 1970 it allocated a somewhat larger sum for the same purposes — but in total a sum still only 15 percent of what the United States had spent covertly in 1964; and the funds reached Chile much too late, barely four weeks before the election. In August 1970 the 40 Committee decided that nothing further could now be done before the election. In other words, two of the four meetings took no action. The others approved a token effort.* At first the inaction was rationalized because there were not yet any candidates; hence, it was said, there was no basis on which to form a judgment or launch a strategy. By early December 1969, however, this excuse vanished. The conservatives nominated the venerable septuagenarian Alessandri, a former President of Chile. The Christian Democrats nominated Radomiro Tomic, a representative of their left wing whose program differed from Allende's largely on procedural points and in his sincere dedication to the democratic process. The Communists joined in a coalition with Allende's Socialists and chose Allende as the coalition candidate. I have already described the virulent anti-Americanism and radicalism of Allende's 1970 program. Now that there was a three-man race, the agencies comforted themselves with the fact that the polls showed Alessandri far in the lead; hence there was no need for an American role.

Until well into 1970 I did not focus on the dangers largely because the agencies with operational responsibility went through a complicated three-cornered minuet that kept the problem from high-level attention. Ambassador Korry took the position that an Allende victory was tantamount to a Communist takeover; it would be imprudent to act as if an Allende government would be anything but another Castro government; it might, in fact, be worse. But State's Latin American Bureau disagreed; it disparaged both the likelihood and the danger of an Allende victory. It wanted to do nothing to help the conservative Alessandri. The CIA tended to side with Korry but not to the point of asking the White House to resolve the difference; it knew it could not effectively

---

* On the basis of four meetings over eighteen months — only two of which made a decision — the Senate Select Committee charged darkly that Chile had been "for more than a year . . . on the 40 Committee's agenda."[11]

operate without strong State Department support. Thus the nonaggression treaty among the agencies caused me to be unaware for four months that in December 1969 the Embassy and the CIA station in Santiago had jointly submitted a proposal for a campaign to head off Allende; or that the upshot of the resulting interagency conference was agreement that a status report embodying the conflicting points of view was to be prepared for the 40 Committee. The Department and the Agency did not exactly expedite the process. It took them another two months to agree on a report; on March 25, 1970, they managed to submit to the 40 Committee a joint program for a ''spoiling'' action against Allende. It consisted of American assistance for the preparation of posters, leaflets, and advertisements opposing Allende without supporting Alessandri. The grand sum of $135,000 was recommended — and approved.* But the State Department circumscribed the expenditure of these funds even further by a strong caveat to the effect that if any of the covert activities tended to endorse Alessandri, State Department support would be withdrawn forthwith. The concept of defeating one candidate without helping his principal opponent was rather original; it was not obvious how Allende could be defeated without benefiting Alessandri. The appropriation and the caveat canceled each other out.

In retrospect it is clear that I should have been more vigilant. A security adviser serves his President best by never simply ratifying the bureaucratic consensus; he should always be the devil's advocate, the tireless asker of questions, the prober of what is presented as self-evident. But Latin America was an area in which I did not then have expertise of my own. I was lulled by the polls that predicted an Alessandri victory and by the consensus of the agencies — a consensus I would never have accepted so readily in an area where I had firsthand knowledge. And in the spring and summer Cambodia claimed most of my attention.

It was June 27 before Chile returned to the agenda of the 40 Committee, too late for an effective role in the remaining two months of the Chilean presidential campaign. Ambassador Korry's uneasiness about an Allende victory had multiplied because we now faced another danger: both CIA and State Department experts suddenly and unexpectedly concluded that Allende's supporters in the Chilean Congress might prevail even if Allende lost, unless Alessandri's margin of victory in the popular election — still confidently assumed — was more than 5 percent. Korry therefore recommended a two-phase program: an increase in expenditure for spoiling activities already approved, and funds to influence the congressional vote.

The State Department opposed both proposals; the only argument it

---

* All these figures have already been published by Congressional committees.

had found even partially persuasive was a query from Korry: "If he [Allende] were to gain power, what would be our response to those who asked what we did?" Expenditures were approved for the brief period remaining in the campaign and these were, as indicated, minor by the standards of 1964. For students of bureaucratic lore it should be noted that the vote was unanimous; the Latin American Bureau chose not to be recorded as holding the views it was advocating, thus preserving its flexibility whatever the outcome and protecting itself should Korry's question be raised again after an Allende victory. A decision on Phase II — seeking to influence the Congress — was deferred until after the election. The Latin American Bureau made sure that Ambassador Korry was not misled by the approval of funds. It informed him by backchannel that it opposed both pre-election (Phase I) and post-election (Phase II) programs on philosophical grounds, and it reiterated in the strongest terms its objection to using any of the approved funds to help Alessandri. There was no danger of our getting into trouble in Chile through an excess of enthusiasm or through a clear-cut strategic plan. Opposing Allende without helping Alessandri meant strengthening the weak Christian Democrat Tomic, thus reducing the vote of the only alternative to Allende who had a chance. A case can thus be made for the proposition that the anti-Alessandri bias of our bureaucracy ensured an Allende victory.

If the funds approved in March were much too little, those reluctantly voted at the end of June were far too late. (They were also too little.) The June 27 meeting took place barely two months before the election. Given the need for formal Presidential approval and the subsequent paperwork, it is unlikely that any of these funds reached Chile before the second half of July. And then the Embassy was constrained by instructions that made their effective use almost impossible.*

Despite the optimistic polls — which at the June 27 meeting still were said to show a comfortable margin for Alessandri — I was becoming increasingly uneasy. Accordingly, in late July I issued a directive to analyze our options in case Allende won in defiance of all predictions. I requested urgent answers to the following questions:

1. What policies and goals is an Allende administration likely to espouse? What probable alternative courses are developments in Chile likely to take under an Allende government?

2. What is the nature and degree of threat to U.S. interests of these alterna-

---

*I learned later that some representatives of the CIA had informally advised some American business interests in late July and August where to channel funds during the election. This was not known at the White House or in the State Department; at any rate, it also was too late. My own attitude was that any covert action in Chile should be carried out exclusively by our government; this was not a field for private enterprise. Accordingly, I turned down ITT's offer of $1 million to help influence the election. I may have agreed with the objective, but certainly not the vehicle.

tives, both in immediate terms and in terms of impact on our long-range goals and position?

3. What options are open to the U.S. to meet these problems?

Meanwhile, the 40 Committee met again on August 7 to review Chilean developments and reaffirmed its decision of June 27. It was now too close to the election for *any* decision to make a difference. The only issue was whether exploratory contacts with the Chilean Congress should be authorized in case Phase II was required. The risks of exposure seemed to outweigh the marginal benefits and the decision was held in abeyance.

Since my policy questions did not involve covert operations, they were considered by the Senior Review Group, which as I have already pointed out had the same membership as the 40 Committee except for the Attorney General. Staff members were permitted to attend and papers were much more widely circulated. The response to my request was a paper prepared by an interagency group chaired by the Department of State. Its conclusions reflected a strange ambivalence. On the one hand, it stated that the United States had no vital national interests "*within* Chile." The meaning of "*within* Chile," however, was not otherwise explained; nor was the conclusion supported by the subsequent analysis. For in answering my question of what threat Allende's accession might pose to American interests in the hemisphere, the interagency group came up with a conclusion which as summarized by my staff made it difficult to understand how our national interest was not affected:

An entrenched Allende Government would create considerable political and psychological losses to the U.S.:

(a) hemispheric cohesion would be threatened;

(b) a source of anti–U.S. policy would be consolidated in the hemisphere;

(c) U.S. prestige and influence would be set back with a corresponding boost for the USSR and Marxism.*

The Senior Review Group met on August 19, but no conclusions were reached or indeed could be reached until the election of Sep-

---

* Ambassador Korry had no illusions about the consequences of an Allende victory. Responding to a query whether a modus vivendi might prove possible, he replied: "A conscious effort to work out modus vivendi is a theoretical hypothesis without relation to reality. While Allende government would move internally with initial prudence to seek to maintain a framework of constitutionality and legality, it would be committed, as Allende has stated, to policies that treated US imperialism as 'public enemy number one' in the hemisphere. Aside from [specific actions including nationalization of US industries, recognition of Cuba, North Vietnam, etc.] which in themselves would make a modus vivendi a practical impossibility for the US, the profound changes in the structure of Chile would probably necessitate an external 'enemy' to justify an accelerating revolution. . . . The Allende forces cannot escape the conclusion that if he is inaugurated the United States has admitted its impotence."

tember 4. We could only wait with growing foreboding for the Chilean voters to go to the polls.

I have discussed our government's deliberations at such length because they have been substantially neglected in previous investigations of the subject — perhaps because they run so counter to preconceived conclusions. They leave no doubt that the United States acted in only the most minimal and ineffectual fashion prior to the Chilean election. Not only were the funds insufficient to have any significant impact, the insistence on not supporting the sole candidate with a chance of defeating Allende caused us to divide the resources in a way that probably increased the fragmentation of the anti-Allende vote. There was reluctance to become involved and even greater resistance to the possibility of being identified with a candidate of impeccable democratic antecedents whose principal liability in the eyes of our bureaucracy was that he was conservative. (That this opinion could be held at all — much less prevail — in a Nixon Administration shows once again how difficult it is even for a President to impose his views on the entrenched bureaucracy.)

By the time of the election, I had come to the view that I had been maneuvered into a position incompatible with my convictions — and, more important, those of Nixon. Had I believed in the spring and summer of 1970 that there was a significant likelihood of an Allende victory, I would have had an obligation to the President to give him an opportunity to consider a covert program of 1964 proportions, including the backing of a single candidate. I was resentful that this option had been foreclosed without even being discussed, first with the argument that a substantial program was unnecessary and later because it was then too late. If the unanimous analysis submitted to the Senior Review Group on August 19 spelling out the implications of an Allende victory was even partially córrect, the failure to examine other options earlier was inexcusable. The philosophical bias of our bureaucracy, the confusion between economic development and foreign policy objectives, had produced paralysis. The prevalent view in our government was apparently that it was acceptable for a radical candidate to receive substantial funds from Cuba and other Communist sources, but improper for the United States to assist the democratic candidate with the best chance of success, even if his program was less reformist than some might have wished. As I later summed up for the President:

The net effect of the State Department's position was that nothing could be done to stop Allende if it meant strengthening Alessandri. In view of the fact that the election came down to a very close race between Allende and Alessandri, with the Christian Democrat Tomic trailing far behind, the State position against strengthening Alessandri neutralized us. While it is not certain that a less circumscribed covert action program would have given the marginal victory to Alessandri. Helms feels the odds for success of an expanded program would have been reasonably favorable. An Alessandri victory might have presented some problems for us, but it clearly would not have been as threatening to our interests as Allende's victory; at a minimum, the serious problems we now face in dealing with a Marxist Government in Chile could have been postponed for perhaps six years.

Any fair assessment of our later conduct regarding Chile must start with this prologue.

The Coup That Never Was

IN the election of September 4, 1970, as already noted, Allende's percentage was a *decline* from the percentage he had received in 1964 when he lost to Frei, except that in 1970 the even higher anti-Allende vote was hopelessly split. According to Chile's constitution, since no candidate had received a majority, the Congress in joint session would decide between the top two candidates fifty days later, on October 24.

Maneuvering for the congressional runoff began immediately. On September 5, Allende at a press conference hailed his victory and pledged to enact the radical Popular Unity program on which he had campaigned. But to ease congressional fears he began to trim some of his pledges. He asserted that he would "never" favor a one-party system in Chile; he said he would retain Chilean membership in the OAS (despite the commitment in the Popular Unity program to "denounce" the organization); he also announced he would ask for a rescheduling of Chile's outstanding debt of $800 million to the United States. (He explained later to Régis Debray that he stayed in the OAS to neutralize American reactions while his real convictions lay with the revolutionary Havana-based Organization of Latin American Solidarity, which he had helped found.)[12] Next day Alessandri's supporters indicated that they would not accept the Allende victory; but their statement was not signed by Alessandri, who had declared during the campaign that he would recognize the candidate winning the most votes. On September 7, Allende met with President Frei, who agreed to set up a consultation arrangement with Allende (as he did also with Alessandri) on economic matters. While refusing Allende's request for a similar liaison on political matters, Frei did agree to take measures aimed at preventing economic panic in Chile.

The reaction in Washington, where during the summer everyone had taken refuge in consoling polls, was stunned surprise. Officials tend to react to unpleasant prospects by ignoring them in the hope that they will go away. And frequently they do; not all catastrophes predicted do in fact occur. But when conventional wisdom encourages inaction, it leaves no margin for the irrevocable. And it was the irrevocable that loomed before us so unexpectedly in September 1970.

Nixon was beside himself. For over a decade he had lambasted Democratic administrations for permitting the establishment of Communist power in Cuba. And now what he perceived — not wrongly — as another Cuba had come into being during his own Administration without his having been given the opportunity to make a decision. This explains the virulence of his reaction and his insistence on doing something, *anything*, that would reverse the previous neglect. Since he blamed the State Department and the Ambassador (incorrectly in the latter case) for the existing state of affairs, he sought as much as possible to circumvent the bureaucracy. That attitude was, in fact, quite unnecessary. For now that it was nearly too late, all agencies threw themselves into a frenzied reassessment. Some felt rather sheepish about their earlier sanguine evaluations or procrastinations; all felt frustrated; now at last there was unanimity that something should be done — spurred on by a likewise determined President. Unfortunately, it was now very late. A fraction of the effort behind one candidate before September 4 might well have prevented the new situation. Now we were forced to improvise while being confronted by a tight deadline and with no real preparations. With time running out our actions were inevitably frantic.*

When the 40 Committee met on September 8 to consider Chile, it was apparent that a congressional decision against Allende was unlikely — after all, we had been concerned only four weeks before that the Congress might vote for Allende even if Alessandri gained a plurality. It was not absurd to hope that the Chilean Congress *might* exercise its independent choice and deny the presidency to a minority candidate with a radical, almost certainly antidemocratic, program when there was still an overwhelming moderate majority in the country. But we knew this to be unlikely. Without real conviction we decided to instruct Ambassador Korry to prepare a ''cold-blooded assessment'' of the likelihood and feasibility of a military coup and of the pros and cons involved in ''organizing an effective future Chilean opposition to Allende.''

The possibility that Allende could be stopped received new life when on September 9 Alessandri announced that he would not withdraw from the congressional race after all. He announced that if elected by the Congress, he would resign and force new elections, which could then repeat the 1964 contest between Frei and Allende. Another presi-

---

*My interest here is in discussing White House knowledge, attitudes, decisions, and participations — not to give a complete account of all the CIA communications. I find publication of the 40 Committee deliberations against the public interest. Unfortunately, all the 40 Committee documents referred to here have already been published by the Church Committee.

dency having intervened, however briefly, Frei would be constitutionally eligible to run. He would almost certainly win. As for the military, on September 10 the army Commander-in-Chief, General Rene
Schneider, reportedly told a group of Chilean officers that the army
would not intervene in the electoral process. The army would, however,
demand ''guarantees'' from Allende that it would remain a fully professional institution and not be politicized. Ambassador Korry reported his
own conviction that such guarantees would be virtually worthless.

I had scheduled a 40 Committee meeting for September 14. On September 12, at the President's request, I solicited by backchannel Korry's
candid recommendations as to ''feasible courses of action available to
the US in the present circumstances.'' Nixon was increasingly restive about what he considered bureaucratic foot-dragging and a State
Department propensity to do business as usual, which reminded him of
what he always considered our early complacency toward Castro. (This
was in fact unjust. Whatever the State Department's procrastination
before the Chilean election, it strongly supported and actively implemented each subsequent 40 Committee decision.) Korry responded hopefully. Frei was reported to be alarmed by the prospect of an Allende
takeover and interested in possible ways to avert it.* Ambassador Korry
suggested to me a deep backgrounder by a high official in Washington
to bring the facts on Chile to the American public and to convey to hesitant Chileans the depth of our concern.

On September 14 the 40 Committee considered what we had by now
nicknamed the ''Rube Goldberg'' gambit: the election and subsequent
resignation of Alessandri, leaving Frei constitutionally free to run again
in an immediate special election. It was agreed to authorize Korry to
explore this possibility and to set aside $250,000 for projects in support
of it. On September 15 Korry was told of this decision by cable from
Under Secretary of State Alexis Johnson; he was also asked to intensify
contacts by all appropriate members of his Embassy with the Chilean
military ''for the purpose of assuring ourselves that we have the requisite intelligence to enable independent assessment of the military determination to back the Frei reelection gambit.''

On September 16 — the day on which we were informed that King
Hussein was about to initiate a showdown with the fedayeen and on
which it was becoming clear that Cienfuegos was being turned into a
submarine base — I gave a background briefing to a group of Midwest
editors and broadcasters in Chicago to put on record, among other subjects, our view of Allende's accession to power as Korry had requested:

---

* Frei has since emphatically denied that he would have lent himself to any circumvention of the
Chilean constitution. Korry's information came from Frei's lieutenants, who may well have acted
on their own authority. We at any rate had to act on the basis of what our Embassy considered to be
the facts.

The election in Chile brought about a result in which the man backed by the Communists, and probably a Communist himself, had the largest number of votes by 30,000 over the next man, who was a conservative. He had about 36.1 percent of the votes. So he had a plurality.

The two non-Communist parties between them had, of course, 64 percent of the votes, so there is a non-Communist majority, but a Communist plurality. I say that just to get the picture straight. . . .

Now, it is fairly easy for one to predict that if Allende wins, there is a good chance that he will establish over a period of years some sort of Communist government. In that case you would have one not on an island off the coast which has not a traditional relationship and impact on Latin America, but in a major Latin American country you would have a Communist government, [ad]joining, for example, Argentina, which is already deeply divided, along a long frontier, [ad]joining Peru, which has already been heading in directions that have been difficult to deal with, and [ad]joining Bolivia, which has also gone in a more leftist, anti–U.S. direction, even without any of these developments.

So I don't think we should delude ourselves that an Allende take-over in Chile would not present massive problems for us, and for democratic forces and for pro–U.S. forces in Latin America, and indeed to the whole Western Hemisphere.

By then Nixon had taken a personal role. He had been triggered into action on September 14 by Augustin Edwards, the publisher of *El Mercurio*, the most respected Chilean daily newspaper, who had come to Washington to warn of the consequences of an Allende takeover. Edwards was staying at the house of Don Kendall, the chief executive officer of Pepsi-Cola, who by chance was bringing his father to see Nixon that very day. (I met with Edwards and Mitchell for breakfast and had asked Helms to see Edwards for whatever insight he might have.)

After meeting Kendall, Nixon asked Helms, Mitchell, and me to his office in the early afternoon of September 15. In a conversation lasting less than fifteen minutes Nixon told Helms that he wanted a major effort to see what could be done to prevent Allende's accession to power: If there were one chance in ten of getting rid of Allende we should try it; if Helms needed $10 million he would approve it. Aid programs to Chile should be cut; its economy should be squeezed until it "screamed." Helms should bypass Korry and report directly to the White House, which would make the final decisions. The operational objective at the time was still the "Rube Goldberg" scheme. Nixon did not in fact put forward a concrete scheme, only a passionate desire, unfocused and born of frustration, to do "something."

This conversation is now treated as the inception of what was later called Track II — as opposed to the formal 40 Committee decisions, which in retrospect became Track I — so gleefully exposed by Congressional committees. But there was always less to Track II than met the eye. As I have shown many times in this book, Nixon was given to grandiloquent statements on which he did not insist once their implications became clear to him. The fear that unwary visitors would take the President literally was, indeed, one of the reasons why Haldeman controlled access to him so solicitously. In the case of Track II, for example, not only was there no expenditure of $10 million; no specific sum was ever set aside. The expenditures, if any, could not have amounted to more than a few thousand dollars. It was never more than a probe and an exploration of possibilities, even in Helms's perception.

Moreover, while the Presidential outburst undoubtedly gave impetus and urgency to approaches to the military as well as to the "Rube Goldberg" scheme, it only paralleled conclusions toward which the departments were coming on their own. Through the regular machinery of the 40 Committee (Track I), the Embassy received instructions closely paralleling the CIA activities growing out of Helms's conversation with Nixon. Track II was an expression of Nixon's profound distrust of State Department machinery, which he suspected would foil consideration of his wishes. In this case he was wrong, because after Allende's election there was no significant difference between the agencies.

Nixon was briefed at various times on Track II by Tom Karamessines, head of CIA's covert operations, always pessimistically. All the CIA reports to Haig and me were similarly negative. The effort was terminated by me on October 15, as I shall show, after one month; Nixon approved. Track I, with full State Department backing, sought to encourage a military move to produce a new election very much along the lines desired by the President. It was similarly unsuccessful and abandoned at the same point — this time by the 40 Committee.

Whatever the focus, whether Track I (the formal 40 Committee approach) or Track II (the unilateral CIA approach), deliberations were turning increasingly to the role of the Chilean military. By September 21 it was becoming clear that Frei was not pursuing any scheme that would result in his own reelection. Korry's fertile mind now turned to a maneuver — apparently cleared by associates of Frei — whereby key Cabinet members would resign and induce their colleagues to follow suit. This would give Frei, if he were willing, a pretext to replace them with military officers. In other words, Frei was to be given the means to trigger a constitutional crisis — designed, as in every other scheme, to lead to another election so that the country could choose between Frei and Allende, between democracy and potential dictatorship. There was doubt about Frei's willingness to do this. The principal obstacle, however, was perceived to be the Commander-in-Chief of the Army, General Schneider, who took the position that the politicians having put Chile into this mess, it behooved them to extricate her. Another stumbling block was reported to be the fear of the Chilean military that if they acted they would be treated like the Greek junta — that is to say, deprived of military aid by the United States and harassed by the left globally.

The 40 Committee therefore authorized Korry to approach selected military leaders. They would be given to understand that their involvement would not jeopardize American military assistance; I cannot determine from my records whether, when, or to whom these meassages were passed.

From September 26 to October 5 I was absent from Washington, going first to Paris to meet with South Vietnamese Vice President Nguyen Cao Ky and a secret meeting with the North Vietnamese, and then joining Nixon in Rome for his trip to Mediterranean countries on the evening of September 27. At every opportunity Nixon encouraged friendly governments to use their influence in Chile to prevent the accession of Allende or at least not to treat his victory as foreordained. He found he was not alone in his concern about Chile's future.

On September 29 the 40 Committee met, in my absence, under the chairmanship of Under Secretary of State Johnson and concluded that the Chilean military would move toward a new election only if they feared an economic crisis and the cutoff of United States military aid if they did not move. Steps to inform the Chilean military that these risks were real were approved in my absence; to lend emphasis, pipeline shipments of military aid were interrupted. After the President's return, a 40 Committee meeting on October 6 left us with exactly the perplexities that had existed before our departure. Frei not only did not move; he did nothing to prevent the Christian Democratic Party congress on October 5 from conditionally endorsing Allende's election by the Chilean Congress. The "Rube Goldberg" gambit was now definitely dead; the Congress would surely vote for Allende. Time was also running out on the Cabinet resignation route to a constitutional crisis. The sole remaining possibility for forestalling the accession of Allende was a military takeover as a prelude to new elections. Reflecting the consensus, Alex Johnson and I sent a joint backchannel to Korry — in Track I — asking him to reinforce with the military the serious consequences of an Allende presidency and authorizing him to reiterate the assurances of continued American military assistance if they moved.

Track I and Track II were, in fact, merging. On October 10 the Central Intelligence Agency reported to General Haig — as part of Track II — that the prospects for a military coup were even dimmer than before. On October 14 the CIA representative, Tom Karamessines, reported to the 40 Committee — as part of Track I — that "a coup climate does not presently exist.'' I observed to the group that there appeared to be little that we could do to influence the Chilean situation one way or another. On October 15 I received a similar briefing from Karamessines as part of Track II. The only remaining possibility was an amateurish plot organized by a General Roberto Viaux to kidnap General Schneider and take him to Argentina. I reported to Nixon: ''I saw Karamessines today. That looks hopeless. I turned it off. Nothing would be worse than an abortive coup.'' Nixon agreed. He was now resigned to an Allende presidency. His major concern was to keep State from pressuring him to resume aid relationships with an Allende government; if Allende expropriated American property, the Hickenlooper Amendment should be applied immediately, he ordered.

Karamessines carried from his October 15 meeting with me an instruction to turn off General Viaux's coup plot and a general mandate to ''preserve our assets'' in Chile on the (clearly remote) chance that some other opportunity might develop. The CIA passed this instruction to the Viaux group on October 17; our station in Santiago advised them that their scheme would fail, would thus backfire, and should not be carried out.

The Senate Select Committee, supposedly investigating assassination plots by the United States government, spent a great deal of space in its 1975 report mulling over whether Al Haig or I was misleading the Committee when we testified that coup planning had been ended on October 15 or whether the CIA proceeded without authority. The facts are these. The Senate Select Committee discovered a second group of plotters, in addition to the Viaux group, with whom the CIA was in contact and who also planned to kidnap General Schneider. Neither Haig nor I was ever aware of their existence for the very good reason that they never did anything. When I ordered coup plotting turned off on October 15, 1970, Nixon, Haig, and I considered it the end of both Track I and Track II. The CIA personnel in Chile apparently thought that the order applied only to Viaux; they felt they were free to continue with the second group of plotters, of whom the White House was unaware. They even provided them with three submachine guns on October 19 without informing anyone in the White House. Military plotters that needed foreign weapons should not have been regarded as serious. For they were not. In a comedy of errors worthy of the Keystone Kops, the plotters were set to kidnap Schneider in his car after a dinner party on October 19; they missed him because he left in a different car. The next day they tried again but lost sight of Schneider's car in Santiago traffic. The guns were returned unused to our CIA station. The plotters returned to a well-deserved obscurity which they mercifully enjoyed until their exploits were given great notoriety by the Senate Committee.

Then on October 22, the Viaux group, which had been explicitly told to desist by the CIA on October 17, proceeded on its own in defiance of

CIA instructions and without our knowledge. It attempted to abduct General Schneider, and bungled it. Schneider drew his pistol in self-defense and was mortally wounded by gunfire. The death of General Schneider, caused by the bungling of a *kidnapping* plot which we had ordered called off and to which we gave no support, no endorsement, no assistance, and no approval, is one of the featured events in the Senate Committee's investigation of *US government* plots to *assassinate* foreign leaders. Amid all its insinuation the Senate Committee did find that there was no US plot to assassinate General Schneider. Indeed, no one intended assassination, not even General Viaux. Assassination was never discussed or implied in any 40 Committee meeting on any subject during my tour of duty, nor was it ever considered as part of Track II. Viaux planned a kidnapping — and we told him not to do it; the second group of plotters did nothing. And all the schemes of either Track I or Track II, even the convoluted schemes involving the military, were designed to produce a new election that was to test in a two-man race whether the Chilean people wanted a democratic President or an avowedly Leninist one. It is a virtual certainty that in a two-man race the Chilean people would have chosen the reformist democrat, Eduardo Frei.

After October 15 our attention turned to the post-Allende period. I called a meeting of the Senior Review Group on October 17 to discuss our options after Allende's inauguration. On October 18 — before any of the various coup attempts were made — I sent a memorandum to the President that can leave no doubt that at the highest level all thoughts of coups had been abandoned: "It now appears certain that Allende will be elected President of Chile in the October 24 Congressional run-off elections."

I believe we were right in our assessment of the perils to our interests and to the Western Hemisphere of Allende's accession to the presidency. The solution we sought was to promote a clear-cut popular choice between the democratic and the totalitarian forces. To assist such efforts seemed right to me then and seems right to me today. I cannot accept the proposition that the United States is debarred from acting in the gray area between diplomacy and military intervention, a shadow world in which our adversaries have as instruments a political party, their own infinitely greater foreign resources, and innumerable front organizations to mask their role. The effort was amateurish, being improvised in panic and executed in confusion. The "covert operations" never got off the ground; in contrast to 1964 we did too little and acted too late. Allende was inaugurated; there was no coup; we had no further contacts aimed at organizing one after October of 1970 (despite some false and misleading innuendos in the Senate report). When Allende was finally overthrown, it was by his own incompetence and intransigence; military leaders without consulting us moved against him on their own initiative because they were convinced that he was intent on taking over total power and about to organize his own coup to that end. They had good reason to think so — but that is for my second volume.

Allende Inaugurated

AFTER OCTOBER 15 the impossibility of preventing Allende's accession to the presidency was acknowledged, and senior officials increasingly turned to the problem of relations with an Allende government. Ambassador Korry, who had urged earlier that a modus vivendi with Allende was an illusion, changed his mind and recommended the immediate opening of negotiations with the President-elect. Since Allende wanted international respectability and legitimacy, Korry now argued, and since this required our acquiescence, we should offer our nonhostility in return for Chilean restraint, especially on expropriation issues. I gave Korry an opportunity to present his views to Nixon on October 15. Nixon was reconciled to Allende's accession but not to cooperation with him. He replied evasively and thereafter unfairly classified Korry as a "softhead."

Korry's recommendation illustrated our policy dilemma. I outlined it to the Senior Review Group on October 17:

If we are publicly or prematurely hostile, our attitude may rally Chilean nationalists behind Allende. If, on the other hand, we are accommodating, we risk giving the appearance of weakness or of indifference to the establishment of a Marxist government in the Hemisphere.

What I got out of the meeting the other day is that no one believes a long-term accommodation is possible. We are faced only with a choice in tactics. The question is whether it would be better if a confrontation were seen to result from Allende's actions or whether the US should move immediately to a position of militant hostility.

Next day I outlined the state of play for the President. Allende's inauguration, I wrote him, as indicated above, now appeared certain.* The US government was unanimous that he was a tough, dedicated Marxist with a strongly anti-American bias who would seek close relations with Cuba and the Soviet Union, lead opposition to US influence in the hemisphere, and systematically promote policies hostile to ours. He would almost surely expropriate American investments and probably without adequate compensation. The very existence of such a government was bound to encourage elements hostile to us in other Latin American countries. To be sure, Allende started from a weak position. The coalition supporting him was fractious; the economy was deteriorating; Chile's democratic tradition would for a time inhibit moves to establish a totalitarian state; the military distrusted him. "To meet these weaknesses,"

---

* Leaving no doubt that we had no foreknowledge of Viaux's plot of October 22.

I wrote Nixon, "Allende's 'game plan' will almost certainly seek legitimacy and respectability; to reassure the apprehensive or concerned and to move carefully to avoid coalescing opposition to him prematurely; to keep his opposition fragmented and then slice their power bit by bit as he is able. Left to his own game plan and pace he probably has the capacity and skill to consolidate his power and neutralize his opposition in a year or two."

Thus we faced the dilemma that a policy of accommodation would not work: "Allende is not voluntarily going to modify his goals, nor is he likely to have any interest in negotiating such a modification just to get along with us. A U.S. policy of seeking accommodation with him, therefore, is unlikely to deter him from an anti–US course if he wants and is able to take it." In other words, our real choice was that defined by the Senior Review Group: whether we should adopt an openly hostile attitude or whether it would be better to pursue a "correct" but "cold" posture, leaving it to Allende to force the confrontation. I urged the President to have this issue deliberated at a National Security Council meeting. I made clear my preference for avoiding a confrontation and adopting the "cool but correct" stance.

A number of specific protocol questions had, however, to be decided immediately. They concerned our formal response to Allende's now imminent inauguration. I proposed that Ron Ziegler should declare that we had taken note of Allende's election and our future relationship was up to Chile to determine; that we send a small, low-key delegation headed by Assistant Secretary of State Charles Meyer to attend the ceremonies; that pipeline shipments to the Chilean military be resumed. I recommended that we close our Air Force atmosphere-testing station in Chile (since Allende was certain to request it), and that we consult with key Latin American governments to attempt to coordinate policies toward the new Chilean President throughout the hemisphere.

Nixon approved all my recommendations. They were conveyed to the agencies on October 21. The Chilean Congress voted Allende President on October 24. On October 30 I supported State's recommendation that Assistant Secretary Meyer be authorized to convey a message of congratulation, to the effect that President Nixon was cognizant of the great honor and responsibility accorded to Allende by the Chilean people. It was not an exuberant message, and I urged that it be conveyed orally rather than in writing, but it observed the appropriate courtesies and left the way open for a conciliatory response should Allende choose such a route.

On October 30 Allende announced the makeup of his new fifteen-strong Cabinet. All key economic and patronage posts were given to the Communist Party (Finance, Public Works, and Labor); the Ministry of Economy went to an independent very close to the Communists; four posts went to Allende's own Socialist Party (Interior, Foreign Relations,

Housing, and Secretary of the Presidency); seven others went to various other radical and splinter parties. The new Minister of Foreign Relations, Clodomiro Almeyda, was so far to the left that in the past he had opposed Soviet positions out of admiration for the more radical Chinese Communists and Cubans.

In his final address to the nation on October 31, outgoing President Frei stated his intention to remain politically active as a constructive opponent of the Allende Administration. He urged Chileans to defend democracy, warned against converting the universities into political battlegrounds, and appeared to reflect the widespread concern about the future of political liberties under Allende.

Allende was sworn in before a Joint Session of Congress on November 3. He pledged "to maintain the integrity and independence of the nation and keep and obey the constitution." He also called for "work and sacrifice" from Chileans as necessary for the construction of socialism. Attending the inaugural ceremonies were representatives from more than sixty foreign nations, including unofficial delegations from North Vietnam, the People's Republic of China, East Germany, and Cuba (the latter led by longtime Communist Party leader Carlos Rafael Rodriguez). As a foretaste of Allende's anti–US bias, the leaders of the Puerto Rican independence party were also invited to the inauguration. In public remarks related to the festivities, Allende was quoted as saying he planned to hold national plebiscites if the Congress (in which his Popular Unity controlled only 90 of the 200 seats) rejected the "new forms" of government he might propose.[13] On November 5, in a speech at a rally climaxing the three-day celebrations, Allende pledged a "republic of the working class" and blamed the capitalist system for social and economic inequities. He hinted at a major nationalization program.

Charles Meyer was received by Allende and delivered Nixon's message. Allende gave no evidence of a conciliatory approach. The tenor of his administration was set. A few days later, for example, a statue of Che Guevara was unveiled in a working-class district of San Miguel. Latin American revolutionary militants, including the Secretary General of the Cuban Workers Federation, were present for the dedication, which was marked by crowds singing the national anthems of Chile and Cuba.[14]

This was the atmosphere in which the National Security Council met on November 6 to review our policy toward Chile. And it was scarcely improved by a reliable report that day which described a clandestine meeting between Allende and members of the Chilean National Liberation Army, a radical group created to promote revolution in Bolivia. Allende was said to have pledged that once his administration was firmly in power, Chile would become a center of assistance and training for Latin American revolutionary organizations seeking to "liberate" their countries through armed struggle.

Nixon accepted, nevertheless, the consensus supporting a "cool but correct" posture. He expressed concern that Allende's successful consolidation of his power would encourage all our opponents throughout Latin America and might move many sitting on the fence into opposition to us. But he agreed that overt hostility might play into Allende's hands. He therefore decided on a policy that was embodied in a directive issued on November 9. It affirmed that the public posture of the United States would be "correct but cool, to avoid giving the Allende government a basis on which to rally domestic and international support for consolidation of the regime." But it also called for assembling pressures to prevent the consolidation of "a communist state in Chile hostile to the interests of the United States and other hemisphere nations." The President ordered that no guarantees of new private investment be issued, that old ones, if possible, be terminated, and that we use our influence in international financial institutions to limit credit or other financing assistance to Chile. No new bilateral economic aid commitments were to be undertaken for the time being. However, an exception was made for humanitarian programs. Existing commitments would be fulfilled.

The directive was stern but less drastic and decisive than it sounded. (It was, for example, much less so than the policy later pursued against Augusto Pinochet of Chile or Anastasio Somoza of Nicaragua.) With the Chilean government's new policy of expropriation without compensation designed to discourage any private investment, with government-fueled inflation reaching a level of some 350 percent (on the day of Allende's death) and destroying the middle class, and with default on its international debt repayments in 1971, the credit-worthiness of Chile would have dropped drastically between 1970 and 1973 whatever policy the United States pursued in international lending institutions. It would have been an imprudent financial institution, national or international, that extended substantial credit to someone who, in his 1970 campaign declaration ("The Popular Government's First Forty Measures") had pledged to "renege the commitments with the International Monetary Fund," or who in his 1970 Popular Unity program had proclaimed the intention of "expropriating imperialist capital and . . . increasing our capacity to self finance our activities" and who had regarded it "absolutely necessary to review, denounce or renounce, as befits each case, those treaties or agreements which involve commitments limiting our sovereignty, and, in particular, treaties of reciprocal assistance, pacts of mutual aid or other pacts which Chile signed with the U.S.A."

As for bilateral United States aid programs, grant aid, as has been mentioned, was terminated in 1968 while Frei was still President. The loan programs had dropped to some $40 million in 1969 and $70 million in 1970. Even under Allende the exception for humanitarian programs resulted in authorization of $16.8 million in Food for Peace programs, some $250,000 in special disaster relief, and favorable US action on Inter-American Development Bank loans of $11.5 million to two Chilean universities in January of 1971. And the Peace Corps remained. While Allende was in office, the United States also authorized over $42 million in military assistance, agreed to the rescheduling of around $250 million of Chile's debt, participated in $82.3 million IMF loans, and honored previous aid commitment amounting to some $25 million. Thus Chile under Allende remained one of the largest recipients of official American aid per capita in Latin America. Altogether, Allende received new credits of nearly $950 million from all sources, including well over $600 million from Communist sources.[15] Painful as it may be to admit for those who seek some extraneous reason for Marxist-managed economic disasters, it was not American economic pressure but Allende's own policies that brought him down.

Allende did not wait long to implement his program. On November 12 he announced reestablishment of diplomatic relations with Cuba, in contravention of the OAS resolution of 1964, which Allende denounced as lacking "juridical and moral basis"; the new agreement was negotiated by Carlos Rafael Rodriguez during Allende's inauguration. The State Department reacted the following day with a statement which "deplored" that Chile had acted without resort to the OAS consultative framework. The Allende government also moved rapidly to sign a pact with the North Korean delegation. While not mentioning diplomatic ties, it nonetheless constituted de facto recognition. Chile promptly withdrew from the UN Commission on Korea.

Allende's first move against American industry occurred on November 20, when he ordered an administrative takeover, under provisions of a 1945 labor law, of two Chilean companies controlled by Northern Indiana Brass and Ralston Purina. Allende charged that the companies had intentionally deprived Chileans of jobs. This was followed by a speech on November 26 — to the Communist Party plenum — in which he declared that his government would shortly propose legislation to nationalize US interests as well as Chilean and foreign banking, insurance, and unidentified industrial properties. It was reported that the legislation would probably be accompanied by a proposal to alter the guarantees of private property in the constitution to enable the government to take over working installations (such as industrial and mining plants), as well as privately owned land (already authorized). This speech was followed by disclosure of plans for large-scale nationalization of basic industry and central planning and direction of industry, banking, trade, and agriculture, as pledged in his 1970 program. Allende's Finance Minister, who outlined the economic program to a committee of the Chilean Congress, placed the blame for Chile's economic problems on the "capitalist system" and on foreign, especially United States, investors.

Within a month Allende had amnestied hundreds of revolutionary terrorists belonging to MIR — an organization to the left of the Communists dedicated to seizing power by violence. Within a year — in 1971 — dramatizing the breach in hemispheric unity, Fidel Castro paid a visit to Chile that lasted for nearly a month. The trip concluded with a joint communiqué affirming the "common struggle" and "common outlook of both governments and peoples in analyzing the world situation," condemning the "imperialist intervention" in Vietnam, hailing "the crisis of the capitalist monetary system" and "the gradual, substantial increase of the economic, political, social and technological power of the socialist camp."

In time Allende's Cuban son-in-law, Luis Fernandez de Ona, who had been actively involved in planning Ché Guevara's Bolivian expedition, was given an office in the presidential palace in Santiago. Allende organized his own private security force, made up largely of extremist members of the terrorist MIR group, outside the existing army and police structure. He clandestinely imported large quantities of Cuban weapons to arm supporters for street fighting — an interesting procedure for a "constitutional" President. Between ten and fifteen thousand visaless foreigners came in to help organize the guerrilla left within Chile and terrorist activities in neighboring countries. Attempts were made to overthrow the military structure; noncommissioned officers staged a coup to take over the navy with the tacit approval of the President in 1971.

The myth that Allende was a democrat has been as assiduously fostered as it is untrue. The fact is that various measures taken by Allende's government were declared to be unconstitutional and outside the law by the Chilean Supreme Court on May 26, 1973, by the Comptroller General on July 2, 1973, and by the Chamber of Deputies on August 22, 1973. It is the opposition he aroused *within* Chile that triggered the military coup of 1973, in the conception, planning, and execution of which we played no role whatever.

In November 1970 all this was still far in the future. We had been unable to prevent Allende's accession to power. We were open to accommodation should Allende, against all expectations, be prepared for one. But we were also prepared to defend our own interests in the more likely event that Allende was as good as his word.

So Chile took its own place in our autumn of crisis. We had prevailed in Jordan and Cienfuegos, but we were to face a continuing challenge in the Western Hemisphere. Our deliberations had honed our own capacity to deal with other, future crises. We had endured trials all the more complicated because they occurred practically simultaneously and followed so closely on the wrenching experience of Cambodia. Having grappled with challenges imposed upon us, we could now seek to shape events in the light of our own purposes.

XVIII

An Invitation to Peking

The End of the Warsaw Channel

THERE was, on the surface, nothing dramatic about the first official meeting in the Nixon Administration between the United States and the People's Republic of China. It took place in Warsaw at the Chinese Embassy, on January 20, 1970, with our Ambassador to Poland, Walter Stoessel, sitting across the table from Lei Yang, chargé d'affaires of the People's Republic. It was the first meeting in two years, but ambassadorial sessions of this kind had been going on sporadically for fifteen years and their major significance seemed to be that they represented the longest continual talks that could not point to a single important achievement. There had been 134 meetings and all of them had been sterile. The agenda for the 135th meeting was heavy with the same air of futility. The difference was that after bureaucratic bloodletting in Washington, Stoessel had been instructed to say something different — and so, it transpired, had Lei Yang.

The main point of the previous 134 meetings had been our relationship to Taiwan, a classic Catch-22 topic: no solution was conceivable so long as US–Chinese hostility persisted, and the hostility would not end so long as the Taiwan issue was unsettled. Other questions raised from time to time were the hoary standbys of bilateral perplexity: American claims to compensation for nationalized property and defaulted debts; Chinese efforts to recover assets in the United States, frozen after 1949 under the Trading with the Enemy Act; our efforts to secure the release of Americans imprisoned in China; and fitful attempts to gain access to China for American newsmen, or to explore the prospects for trade.

All the familiar themes were due for tedious rehearsal again at the 135th meeting. The instructions for our side were being prepared by the State Department's Bureau of East Asian and Pacific Affairs, which, unaware of the messages that had been passed to the Chinese during the previous year, saw no reason to change an approach that had seen it through 134 previous Warsaw meetings — without result, true, but also without debacle or controversy. Nixon, like me, while not indifferent to the hallowed agenda, saw an opportunity in Warsaw to convey a new and more significant message to China. None of the agenda subjects was capable of being defined, much less solved, so long as Peking considered the United States its principal foreign enemy and Washington viewed China as the fount of all aggression and revolutionary activity in Asia, including in Vietnam.

For twenty years US policymakers considered China as a brooding, chaotic, fanatical, and alien realm difficult to comprehend and impossible to sway. They had been convinced that the Vietnam war was a reflection of Chinese expansionism, and that the Cultural Revolution derived from an obsession with ideological purity alien, and not a little frightening, to the American temperament. The Chinese, for their part, saw the scale of our effort in Vietnam as disproportionate to any objective to be achieved, and hence believed its only rational purpose could be to turn Indochina into a springboard for an eventual assault on China. These twenty years of deadlock — reflecting sincerely held views — had blinded our experts, and no doubt their opposite numbers in the People's Republic, to a vital change: an emerging, still only dimly perceived community of interest between the United States and China. The leaders in two countries had begun, for the first time in a generation, to regard each other in geopolitical rather than ideological terms.

Impelled by the obvious menace of the Soviet buildup on the 4,000-mile common border, China wanted to reduce the number of its adversaries and to obtain another counterweight to Soviet pressure. Burdened by the traumas of Vietnam, yet determined to shape a new era of international relations, the Nixon Administration was convinced that contact with this one quarter of humanity could restore new perspective to our diplomacy. Both parties had to tread warily, feeling their way toward each other with significant but tenuous messages and gestures, which could be disavowed if rejected. It was perhaps not surprising that the subtle changes by which the Chinese signaled their willingness to alter course had been overlooked by our experts; and the issue had been confused by the well-meaning but woolly efforts of "Chinese friendship" groups in America.

Too many of them based their views on abstract notions of personal "goodwill," or even historical guilt, difficult for policymakers to reconcile with the realities of the American national interest — or of the new China. What the Chinese wanted was not vacuous benevolence, or even the practical steps that had been the essence of the previous dialogue, such as recognition, UN membership, claims, exchanges. They wanted strategic reassurance, some easing of their nightmare of hostile encirclement. This the new Administration was prepared to provide, and its much decried unsentimentality was a positive asset because it was in

tune with China's hardheaded needs. But we had to overcome the preconceptions of two decades, the paralyzing grip of experts brought up
on different precepts, and the bizarre rivalries within the Administration.
I thought we could do none of this unless we broke out of the stagnating
ritual of Warsaw and, specifically, until we arranged high-level talks
among special emissaries in one of the capitals, probably Peking.

American ambassadors to Warsaw were generally not selected for
their expertise on Chinese affairs. For each meeting, therefore, a
middle-level official had to be flown in with the text of a statement that
had been painfully cleared through the bureaucracy and among friendly
countries. Our Ambassador would then read his statement; he received a
reply no doubt produced by analogous procedures. The ambassadors'
permitted discretion did not go beyond a few clarifying questions. At
the next session they read out a response ponderously prepared anew in
the respective capitals. It all took time and got nowhere. In the prevailing atmosphere of distrust, neither side could be sure what use would be
made of a candid presentation of real aims or views. And the distrust
could not be dispelled without an unconstrained discussion. I considered
it essential to move the dialogue to a level where the negotiators could
engage in some give-and-take and were sufficiently familiar with the
thinking of their leaders to grasp the underlying strategy. I wanted to
use the January 20 meeting to indicate our willingness to send an emissary to Peking, and I suggested to the President that it did not matter
what else was said so long as it included our basic themes: that we
wanted to make a fresh start; that we would not participate in a Soviet-
American condominium; that we would proceed not on the basis of
ideology but on an assessment of mutual interest.

None of this was acceptable to those who had made China policy up
to that time. Each of these themes was fiercely resisted when it came to
drafting a statement for Ambassador Stoessel to read on January 20. The
Asian experts did not share our hopes for a new beginning (partly
because they did not know what was passing in secret channels); the Soviet experts were uneasy lest the Soviet Union be antagonized by the
mere fact of the talks, and still more by our including reassurances
about condominium. Progress was identified with a renunciation of
force in the Taiwan Strait, participation in arms control negotiations, or
assurances of peaceful conduct in Asia — none of which Peking would
even consider except in a wider context. As for sending an emissary to
Peking, the mere mention sent shivers down official spines, for the conduct of such talks was likely to be drawn into the White House and out
of the hands of the State Department.

The bureaucratic fight was settled by compromise in the traditional
bureaucratic way: I conceded all State's pet projects — references to
Taiwan, arms control, claims/assets, prisoners, and so on — in return

for the themes I considered essential. Stoessel's instructions as finally drafted were still more muted than I would have wished, but when I got to know the Chinese better I came to realize that understatement, from whatever motive, almost always impressed them. The Chinese, having manipulated foreigners for three thousand years — and not without success — tend to consider insistent reiteration a reflection on their subtlety.

As it happened, the Chinese had been thinking along parallel lines. At the January 20 meeting, Stoessel read a statement that repeated that the United States did not seek to "join in any condominium with the Soviet Union directed against China." He added a sentence whose matter-of-factness obscured the bureaucratic blood that had been spilled: The United States "would be prepared to consider sending a representative to Peking for direct discussions with your officials or receiving a representative from your government in Washington for more thorough exploration of any of the subjects I have mentioned in my remarks today or other matters on which we might agree."

Lei Yang, the Chinese chargé d'affaires, did not, of course, respond to this startling departure, but he read a statement notable for the conciliatory tone of its otherwise conventional rhetoric on Taiwan, and for two pregnant sentences hidden amidst familiar verbiage:

We are willing to consider and discuss whatever ideas and suggestions the U.S. Government might put forward in accordance with the five principles of peaceful coexistence, therefore really helping to reduce tensions between China and the U.S. and fundamentally improve relations between China and the U.S. These talks may either continue to be conducted at the ambassadorial level or may be conducted at a higher level or through other channels acceptable to both sides.

Two formal speeches drafted in capitals twelve thousand miles apart had made in effect the same proposal. But the nature of the Warsaw meetings meant we had to wait a month before seeing whether the idea could be moved forward at the next meeting.

I was encouraged in late January when I read a report of a conversation between Chinese Premier Chou En-lai and the Pakistani Ambassador in Peking. The Ambassador found Chou En-lai primarily concerned about the Soviet Union, secondarily about the revival of Japanese militarism. As for the United States, Chou clearly considered it a lesser threat; he seemed quite prepared for high-level talks with the United States, provided we took the initiative. In fact, according to this report, Chou En-lai had mused about our apparent unwillingness "to take a step like Kosygin" — in other words, to send a high official to Peking.

Throughout, the Soviets were characteristically heavy-handed. The day after the Warsaw meeting Dobrynin appeared at my office, seeking a briefing, undeterred by the fact that this was a favor Moscow never vouchsafed to us on any topic. When I evaded his request, he said that he hoped that we were not thinking of "using" China as a military threat, a proposition so grotesque when all that happened was one set-piece speech by each ambassador that I simply laughed it off. But other Soviet Embassy personnel made similar inquiries at other levels; clearly, Peking was a "neuralgic" point.

While we waited for Warsaw meeting 136, we redoubled our search for less constrained channels. One of the penalties of twenty years of isolation was that we had no idea how to approach the Chinese leaders. Henry Cabot Lodge introduced me to a friend of his, the chargé d'affaires of a West European country in Peking who claimed access to the Chinese leadership. With Nixon's approval I gave this diplomat a message pointing out the difficulty of conducting serious talks in Warsaw and suggesting another channel through our military attaché in Paris, General Vernon Walters (who had proved so adept at arranging my secret meetings with Le Duc Tho). Lodge's friend took the message and then reported faithfully every few weeks thereafter that he had not yet had an opportunity to deliver it. Finally, ten months later, on December 1, 1970, he informed us that he was about to do so — what gave him this confidence I cannot imagine — but by then we had already established an alternate channel.

Warsaw meeting 136, planned for February 20, 1970, produced another tug-of-war between the White House and the State Department. We were faced with the question of how to react if, as seemed likely, the Chinese accepted our proposal to send an emissary to Peking or receive theirs in Washington. I wanted Stoessel to indicate agreement in principle and refer the matter to Washington for a detailed reply. The State Department made the extraordinary recommendation that we pull back from our own initiative and simply note the Chinese reply without comment. Apart from the loss of control — and nothing makes the bureaucratic adrenalin flow like the defense of imperiled prerogatives — State was decidedly reluctant to have to explain a new venue to suspicious allies, insistent neutrals, and a querulous Soviet Union, not to speak of the media.

I prevailed. Nixon ordered me to instruct Stoessel to respond positively, without, of course, neglecting to recite the litany of bilateral issues (Taiwan, claims, assets, prisoners, and so on) that had sustained the previous 135 meetings. To make sure the Chinese understood our changed attitude, we spoke of China with unprecedented matter-of-factness in the President's Foreign Policy Report, which was published two days before the February Warsaw meeting: "The Chinese are a great and vital people who should not remain isolated from the international community. In the long run, no stable and enduring international order is conceivable without the contribution of this nation of more than 700 million people.'' We stressed that we were concerned not with rhetoric but with practical policy. The key to our relations would be the actions of each toward the other. The report explicitly rejected any desire to take sides in the Sino-Soviet conflict and hence any idea of condominium:

> Our desire for improved relations is not a tactical means of exploiting the clash between China and the Soviet Union. We see no benefit to us in the intensification of that conflict, and we have no intention of taking sides. Nor is the United States interested in joining any condominium or hostile coalition of great powers against either of the large Communist countries. Our attitude is clear-cut — a lasting peace will be impossible so long as some nations consider themselves the permanent enemies of others.

For good measure the part of the report dealing with defense policy, as I have mentioned, emphasized that we no longer considered the Soviet Union and the People's Republic a single adversary. Henceforth, our war planning would be based on the assumption that joint Sino-Soviet aggression against us had ceased to be an imminent contingency. We would deal with each country separately on the basis of its conduct toward us.

The messages were received and understood. At the 136th meeting Lei Yang made an extraordinarily conciliatory statement — and accepted our proposal to send an emissary to Peking. We seemed on the verge of a breakthrough. If we signaled our changed attitude before the Warsaw meeting, the Chinese did so immediately after. On February 22 we received a communication from Pakistani Ambassador Hilaly that his President, Yahya Khan, believed our initiatives had encouraged the Chinese. This circumlocution undoubtedly meant that Yahya had information from the Chinese, who preferred as yet to deal indirectly with us. According to Yahya, the Chinese were now much less worried about US–Soviet collusion. They would, however, be upset if the United States were to give the impression that Chinese overtures derived from weakness or from fear. Prospects for gradual progress were favorable, especially since "the possibility of expansion of the Vietnam war is seen as having lessened. A war between China and the US is seen now as a very remote possibility.'' In other words, Chou En-lai had understood us. He had even grasped by early 1970 what so many domestic critics had failed to acknowledge: that we were on the way out of Vietnam. And he coupled this with an unmistakable hint that China had no intention of entering the Vietnam war or, for that matter, of attacking any other vital American interest.

I replied immediately to Hilaly that we could not control press speculation, but the White House would scrupulously avoid any comments that might impugn China's motives or strength. I suggested again that we open a channel more suitable for confidential exchanges than the Warsaw talks. Nixon wrote "Good" on my memorandum reporting the conversation. The road to Peking was open if we were prepared to travel it with skill and delicacy.

But the encrusted suspicion of two decades is not easily overcome. Now that we were faced with a Chinese acceptance of our own proposal, all the latent uneasiness in our government surfaced again. At the next Warsaw meeting we could not evade the issue merely by filling the agenda with everybody's favorite project; even the most artful drafting of Stoessel's instructions could not obscure the reality that we now had to respond to a Chinese invitation to come to Peking.

The view in State's East Asian Bureau was that a trip to Peking, without prior progress on bilateral issues discussed for fifteen years, implied a concession to the Chinese and risked misunderstanding by allies, not to speak of hostility in Moscow. The Bureau wanted the Chinese to concede us our principal *Asian* concerns as an admission price to high-level talks. My view was that the bilateral issues were peripheral to the imperatives now driving the Chinese. Only extraordinary concern about Soviet purposes could explain the Chinese wish to sit down with the nation heretofore vilified as the archenemy. If I was correct, what the Chinese really wanted to discuss was the global balance of power. I was not concerned about State's fear that the Chinese might want to bog us down in protracted, humiliating negotiations in Peking; they could not possibly be wanting to humiliate us; the Peking invitation made sense only if the Chinese were seeking to *reduce* the number of their enemies. The mere opening of talks would revolutionize international relationships by demonstrating that we had options previously thought unavailable, and that we were capable of taking bold initiatives even under the pressure of the war in Vietnam.

The State Department view was summed up in a memorandum from Rogers to the President on March 10, proposing March 19 as the date for the next Warsaw ambassadorial meeting. If we allowed forty-eight hours for Presidential consideration, the memorandum was clearly timed with delay in mind. The Chinese could not prepare for a meeting on such short notice. And the suggested agenda made a fruitful meeting unlikely: agreement in principle to peaceful settlement of the Taiwan problem and expansion of trade and mutual contacts; some unilateral Chinese gesture of goodwill, such as the release of Americans or the expansion of travel. Only *after* the Chinese had yielded on these points, which Rogers optimistically expected would take "several" more Warsaw meetings, would it be safe to discuss even the modalities of a higher-level emissary to Peking.

On March 17 I had a long lunch in the Situation Room with Marshall Green, the Assistant Secretary of State for East Asian and Pacific Affairs, in which he pressed again for some prior indication of Chinese willingness to meet our concerns on bilateral matters. Afterward, he wrote me a personal note summarizing his anxieties:

To go to Peking without such clarification poses serious risk of our being used by Peking for its own purposes in its relations with the Soviets without any compensating gains either in terms of our bilateral relations with the Chinese or in progress toward a relaxation of tensions elsewhere, particularly in Southeast Asia. For the same reason, I think we should not offer to discuss with the Chinese modalities of a meeting such as communications, personnel, timing, security, etc., unless we have made a firm and final decision to go ahead with such a meeting. Our discussion of such modalities will be interpreted as a firm commitment to a higher-level meeting by Peking, and may reinforce the Chinese belief they need not discuss "substance" with us until such a meeting takes place. To make such a commitment at this point would thus weaken our ability to press the Chinese now to commit themselves further on their own intentions and negotiating position at a higher-level meeting.

I disagreed. The visit of an American emissary to Peking was bound to spark a geopolitical revolution; the effect on Hanoi alone would be traumatic. These were overwhelming "compensating gains." At the same time I could not conceive that in Warsaw the Chinese would publicly concede principles reversing their whole policy in Asia without having any idea of our overall approach. We would encounter, to be sure, serious complications in relations with our Asian friends, but we would face most of these anyway as China emerged, as it was bound eventually to do, from its self-imposed isolation. The United States should choose to be not an impotent bystander but rather the purposeful shaper of events.

Nixon shared my view. In several conversations he stressed his desire to move the venue to Peking and to send a special Presidential envoy rather than a conventional ambassador. This was, of course, exactly why State was so skittish about the enterprise. Nixon suggested that I circumvent the bureaucracy by letting Lodge's friend, the European chargé in Peking, inform the Chinese leaders of our agreement in principle to send a Presidential emissary. We did not yet know that this would-be matchmaker had wildly overstated his access to the Chinese leaders, but as he had not yet delivered his original message I saw no point in bothering him with something so startling.

This internal wrangling lasted a week beyond the date originally intended for the Warsaw meeting itself. To bring matters to a head I sent a memorandum to State on March 20 proposing an immediate Warsaw meeting and urging that Stoessel's instructions reflect a "positive" ap-

proach to the idea of higher-level talks; we should also take up Lei
Yang's hints that general Far Eastern problems could be discussed, and
not only the traditional Sino-American bilateral issues. State replied that
the earliest date at which it could prepare a "cleared" statement was
April 8 (raising some question in my mind whether it would have presented an uncleared statement had we approved March 19). This I accepted. Peking came back with April 15, though whether this was for
tactical or its own bureaucratic reasons was unrevealed.* The delay enabled State to think up yet another reason for postponement. Chiang
Ching-kuo, Vice Premier of the Republic of China (Taiwan) and son of
Chiang Kai-shek, was due to visit Washington on April 22. The East
Asian Bureau considered it unwise to schedule talks with Peking in
Warsaw within two weeks before or ten days after the trip (they never
shared with me how these figures were arrived at). On April 1, therefore, the United States proposed to the Chinese April 30 or any date
thereafter. The Chinese, clearly irritated by now, decided to play at
procrastination themselves. They waited for four weeks before replying.
On April 28 they suggested May 20 and we accepted.

It was extraordinary that we received any reply at all. By April 28
Sihanouk, in Peking, had established his Cambodian government in
exile and liberation army. Chou En-lai had passionately espoused his
cause. South Vietnamese forces were entering the Parrot's Beak. Our
troops were poised to move into the sanctuaries. In the face of all this,
China accepted further talks, the purpose of which was to arrange the
visit of a representative of the imperialist enemy to Peking. Not until
May 18, nearly three weeks after the start of our operations in Cambodia, did the Chinese put out through the New China News Agency a
terse statement that in view of the "brazen" invasion of Cambodia,
"the Chinese government deems it no longer suitable for the 137th
meeting of the Sino–US ambassadorial talks to be held on May 20 as
originally scheduled. As to when the meeting will be held in the future,
it will be decided upon later through consultation by the liaison personnel of the two sides."

It was just as well. China could hardly have attended such a meeting
without haranguing us harshly about Indochina. Acrimony would have
been unavoidable. Instead, the cancellation was accomplished in the
most restrained matter conceivable. Only the timing, not the fact, of a
meeting was deemed "unsuitable"; China made clear its willingness to
continue conversations and even suggested a procedure for accomplishing it. There were to be other interruptions due to events
beyond the control of either side, but thereafter China and the United
States never stayed long out of touch.

---

*Mao later explained to Nixon in February 1972 that there had been some bureaucratic re-
sistance or at least lassitude on the Chinese side.

The May 20 cancellation was providential for another reason. Our government was simply not ready to speak with a single voice. To be sure, after much effort I had succeeded in having the May 20 instructions modified to include a discussion of technical aspects of an emissary's visit, and to authorize Stoessel to talk about broader relationships, especially in the Far East. But the changes were accomplished so grudgingly and enveloped so ostentatiously in conventional rhetoric that Warsaw clearly would not do as the site of a serious discussion. The White House's interest in talking to Peking about common geopolitical concerns could not be dealt with — or perhaps even understood — there. The Warsaw talks never resumed. When we reestablished contact later in the year, it was in a different channel, with a sharper focus.

Triangular Relationships

THE disagreements within our government on the strategy for the Warsaw talks were serious, but there was none about the general desirability of continuing to signal our conciliatory attitude to Peking. The State Department skillfully dismantled various obstacles to trade and contacts established during the Korean war. On March 16 travel restrictions to North Vietnam, Cuba, North Korea, and what was then called Mainland China were formally extended for another six months. But in effect a partial exception was made for China. It was announced that henceforth American passports would be validated for travel there for any "legitimate" purpose. On April 29 American-made components and spare parts for nonstrategic goods manufactured in other countries were freed for export to China. The practical object was to reduce disputes with friendly nations over the extraterritorial reach of our controls; the fundamental purpose was a political gesture that Peking could hardly misunderstand.

I remained convinced that China's cautious overtures to us were caused by the rapid and relentless Soviet military buildup in the Far East. The prospect of military conflict along the Sino-Soviet border faced us with nightmarish choices. Any improvised response to such a dire event was bound to be erratic and probably inadequate. Throughout 1969 I had sought to elicit contingency plans from the interagency machinery. But the departments and agencies considered our choices too awful to contemplate, and so produced only careful evasions: their ingenious catalogue of eventualities seemed more insurance against accusations of lack of foresight than a set of practical choices for the President. Early in 1970 I decided to ask my own staff to draw up plans of our own, resulting in a lengthy and thoughtful study that for a few years served as our basic planning paper. In a book years later it was deprecated as another example of a step taken "in secret from the rest of the government''; with uncharacteristic modesty the author, who had left my staff, neglected to mention that he had written it! [1]

Meanwhile, we watched Sino-Soviet relations closely. In April 1970 there was a report of some progress in the Sino-Soviet border negotiations; Nixon read about it in his morning News Summary, an extremely thorough compilation of media reportage prepared overnight by an efficient team of White House aides. Nixon would jot comments in the margin; these would be passed on to the appropriate staff member in a pompous memorandum that a junior aide to Haldeman wrote in the passive voice, as if Nixon's jottings were thunderbolts from on high (''It has been requested that you note the report that appeared . . .''). This time I responded that while progress in the border talks (which was unconfirmed) might take some of the urgency out of the Chinese desire for higher-level meetings with us, it would not change underlying realities:

We know that the Soviets are extremely suspicious of the Chinese policies and intentions, and the Chinese have made it very evident that they have no use for the ''new Tsars'', as they now call the Soviets. . . . Thus no significant change in our strategy toward Communist China is likely to be required. The Chinese will probably still wish to continue to develop the contact with us as a counterweight to the Soviets. There also seems to be some interest on their part in opening up trade with us. They may, however, believe that there is less urgency in moving ahead with higher level talks in Peking, and we may find that the fairly rapid pace which developed in our contacts with the Chinese at Warsaw since December 1969 will slow down.

Nixon circled the reference to talks in Peking and wrote in longhand: ''Let us see that State does not drag its feet on this.''

All these efforts and speculations were temporarily hostage to events in Cambodia. When the incursions into the sanctuaries were announced, we were accused both within and without the government of torpedoing any hopes of improved relations with both Moscow and Peking. Indeed, it was even said that the two would now be driven together in opposition to us. But nothing remotely like it occurred. There were only the obligatory verbal fireworks; no action of any kind.

As we have already seen in Chapter XII, Chinese statements of May 4 and May 5 ''sternly'' warned the United States against its ''flagrant provocation.'' They consoled Hanoi not with promises of increased support but by the quotation of Chairman Mao's statement that the United States was a ''paper tiger,'' and that ''the vast expanse of China is their reliable rear area.'' I told the President: ''The Chinese have issued a statement, in effect saying they wouldn't do anything.''

Far from driving the two Communist giants together, events in Cambodia only created a new battleground for rivalry as Peking and Moscow jockeyed for influence over the various insurgent forces in Indochina.

Sihanouk remained ensconced in exile in Peking, to the discomfiture of both Moscow and Hanoi. And in a broader sense, the tempered Chinese and Soviet reactions to our military moves pointed once again to the possibilities of triangular diplomacy to help settle the war. It became unmistakably clear that neither Communist power could risk a sharp break with us over Vietnam for fear that we might then throw our full weight behind the other.

On May 18, *Pravda* published a bitter attack on China, charging the People's Republic with having rejected Soviet calls for joint action in Cambodia. The Chinese, acutely sensitive to such an accusation, responded by wheeling out their heaviest artillery, the declaration issued on May 20 in the name of Mao Tse-tung entitled "People of the World, Unite and Defeat the U.S. Aggressors and All Their Running Dogs!" Stripped of its exuberant rhetoric, this statement too revealed extraordinary caution. My analysis for the President pointed out:

In substance . . . it is remarkably bland. It offers only "warm support" to the three peoples of Indo-China, without even the usual phrases about China being a "rear area" for the struggle. It hammers home the thesis that a small nation can defeat a large one, which must seem cold comfort in Hanoi. It makes no threats, offers no commitments, is not personally abusive toward you, and avoids positions on contentious bilateral issues.

Tactically, Mao's statement serves several purposes:

— It makes propaganda capital of your action in Cambodia.

— It adds Mao's personal prestige to Chinese support for Sihanouk.

— It embarrasses the Soviets by noting pointedly that twenty (other) countries have recognized Sihanouk [which Moscow had not done nor was ever to do].

Next day Hanoi publicly thanked Mao, but in a statement exhibiting many subtle discrepancies between its views and Peking's. Whereas China had spoken of the need for a united front of the peoples of *Indochina* (a reference, among other things, to the perennial disagreements between Vietnamese and Cambodian Communists), Hanoi called attention to the imperative of a united *Communist world,* in effect asking Mao to compose his differences with Moscow.

Mao's statement reached Washington at a time when Nixon was in a particularly feisty mood. Without waiting for my analysis, he ordered every element of the Seventh Fleet not needed for Vietnam moved into the Taiwan Strait: "Stuff that will look belligerent. I want them to know we are not playing this chicken game. . . . I don't want any long paper prepared. No NSSM.* I want you to call Moorer that it's an order

---

* A National Security Study Memorandum — NSSM — was the usual Presidential directive asking for an interagency study.

from the Commander-in-Chief. You can tell Laird. There's no recourse. I want them there within 24 hours.'' It was one of those orders that close associates had come to recognize would better serve the public welfare if not implemented for twenty-four hours. And as I have indicated before, when Nixon used the phrase ''no recourse'' it dramatized his uncertainty. After we had a chance to discuss the real meaning of Mao's statement, Nixon thought better of new deployments in the Taiwan Strait. It could not be in our national interest to link Cambodia to the security of China; Mao had left a host of openings for renewing the long march of our two countries toward each other and nothing would be gained by closing them off in a fit of pique.

By the middle of June, when emotions over Cambodia were subsiding, we therefore sought again to reopen contacts. On June 15 General Walters was instructed to approach his Chinese counterpart in Paris, a defense attaché named Fang Wen, saying he had a message to deliver. Walters was given a text to read that contained our by now familiar theme: Since the Warsaw forum was too public and too formalistic, we would like to open another channel for confidential communications. But our backchannel system, which had so intrigued the Soviets, held as yet no attraction for the Chinese. Perhaps they did not understand how a serious government could be run in that way; if so, they were not alone. (Later they became masters at it.) The redoubtable Walters tried twice to pass his message, once during the summer and once in early September, each time without success. Both times Walters spotted Fang Wen and mentioned a message from Washington, Fang Wen mumbled that he would inform his government and sped off in his car. There was no response.

It may have been that China, too, was having internal difficulties with the new policy. There is every reason to suppose Communist countries share the human resistance to innovation; we had the impression that in Peking various, sometimes clashing, policy views were being pursued simultaneously, with the military, headed by Lin Piao, especially favoring a hard line. (This seemed confirmed when much of the top Chinese military leadership was replaced a short time after my secret trip to Peking.) On the one hand, Chou En-lai was reported to have told East European diplomats in early June that Peking looked forward to resuming contacts with the United States in Warsaw following the ''temporary'' interruption caused by the Cambodian crisis. Chou volunteered these comments to several visitors in the context of expressing China's desire to improve relations with countries everywhere.[2] This seemed to be confirmed by the mild manner in which the Chinese again postponed the Warsaw talks on June 20, stressing that their resumption would be ''discussed later at the proper time.'' On the other hand, there was also a bellicose strand in Chinese policy. On June 27, the Chinese ''commemorated'' the twentieth anniversary of President Truman's decision to interpose the Seventh Fleet in the Taiwan Strait, which they denounced as "US occupation of China's sacred territory Taiwan by armed forces.'' Peking accused the United States of repeated military "intrusions" against China's sovereign territory, including thirteen such incidents since Nixon came into office.

More worrying, on July 2 the Chinese sent up two MiG-19s in an apparently premeditated attempt to intercept and possibly shoot down a C-130 flying an intelligence mission one hundred miles off the Chinese coast. This was the first time since 1965 that China had sought to intercept a routine reconnaissance mission. I sent a memorandum to the President on "puzzling and even disturbing" aspects of this event. I emphasized that we could not abandon our intelligence missions far out at sea without playing into the hands of those in China advocating a tough line. But I was above all concerned about what the incident revealed of internal Chinese struggles:

Perhaps the most plausible hypothesis is that somebody in the power structure *did* want to wreck Sino–US relations. Discounting the usual stridency of their propaganda language, the Chinese for some two years have been cautiously and tentatively feeling us out to see what we might be willing to do to improve relations. This policy is usually associated with Chou En-lai and the moderate grouping which has dominated internal policy in the same period. In the past couple of weeks, there has been evidence of an upsurge of the zealots, and signs that they are fighting their relative exclusion from the reconstituted Party. The Air Force during the Cultural Revolution was the most radical of the armed services. The attempted shootdown may have been related to a policy/power struggle and been intended to stop the moderate drift of foreign policy. The perpetrators may also have hoped that by provoking us into reactions or angry statements they could discredit any proponents of limited accommodation with the U.S.

Suddenly, on July 10 it began to appear that the Chinese had resolved their internal controversy. Peking announced the release of Bishop James Walsh, who had been arrested in 1958 and sentenced in 1960 to twenty years' imprisonment as a spy. The simultaneous disclosure that Hugh Redmond, an American businessman sentenced in Shanghai in 1954 to life imprisonment for espionage, had committed suicide three months earlier tempered elation, but the timing of the release of Bishop Walsh was symbolic. It coincided with, and neatly counterbalanced, an announcement of the reopening of talks with the Soviet Union on the navigation of border rivers.

On our part, we continued with gestures that could not be rejected and did not need to be acknowledged. For example, in late June General Motors applied for permission to include US–made diesel engines and spare parts in a shipment to China of eighty large dump trucks produced by the Roberto Perlini company of Italy. The Defense Department raised objections to this first instance of the sale of spare parts for China. State and Commerce recommended approval. In a memorandum to the President (July 13) I supported State and Commerce. The Chinese had insisted on the US–made engines as part of the sale, in spite of their professed indifference to US trade and the fact that other engines were available; they might thus be testing our intentions. On July 24 Nixon approved the transaction and on July 28 the Commerce Department disclosed the decision. On August 26 the United States announced the lifting of restrictions that prohibited American oil companies abroad from refueling foreign ships carrying nonstrategic goods to or from China.

Though the Chinese continued to envelop themselves in silence, we did not keep secret the rationale of our actions. On September 16, 1970, I told a group of Midwestern editors and publishers in Chicago:

> The deepest rivalry which may exist in the world today is . . . that between the Soviet Union and Communist China. Along a frontier of 4,000 miles, there are territorial claims on one side and a military buildup on the other. This is made more severe by the dispute between the two great Communist states as to which of them represents the center of Communist orthodoxy, which gives a quasi-religious connotation to their conflict.

This is what gave urgency to the rapprochement with Peking. It was why, despite temporary interruptions, Washington and Peking were inexorably moving toward each other.

The Pakistani Channel

THESE signals were all very well, but both Nixon and I were convinced that the overriding necessity was to establish a confidential means of communication, unencumbered by vested bureaucratic interests and the traditional liturgy, which could be trusted by both sides. On September 27 while I was in Paris, my friend Jean Sainteny told me that he occasionally saw the Chinese Ambassador, Huang Chen, socially. I told him to mention our desire for a direct contact. This Sainteny did in December.

Chou En-lai and Mao Tse-tung quite independently decided that the time had come to send us a signal. Unfortunately, they overestimated our subtlety, for what they conveyed was so oblique that our crude Occidental minds completely missed the point. On October 1, China's National Day, Chou En-lai led the American writer Edgar Snow — an old friend of the Chinese Communists — and his wife to stand at Mao's side on Tien An Men (the Gate of Heavenly Peace) and to be photographed with Mao reviewing the annual anniversary parade. This was unprecedented; no American had ever been so honored. The inscrutable Chairman was trying to convey something. (As Snow himself later observed of the incident: "Nothing China's leaders do publicly is without purpose."[3] Eventually, I came to understand that Mao intended to symbolize that American relations now had his personal attention, but it was by then a purely academic insight: we had missed the point when it mattered. Excessive subtlety had produced a failure of communication.

Where Mao used a rapier, Nixon seized a sledgehammer to convey a signal of his own. Almost at the same moment that Snow was watching the National Day parade, Nixon granted an interview to *Time* magazine that focused on the recently concluded Jordan crisis. Buried in Nixon's exposition was a pregnant remark on the subject of China's assuming a world role and his own part in it:

> Maybe that role won't be possible for five years, maybe not even ten years. But in 20 years it had better be, or the world is in mortal danger. If there is anything I want to do before I die, it is to go to China. If I don't, I want my children to.[4]

Later in October Nixon gave another personal push to the effort. Several heads of government came to the United Nations for the celebration of its twenty-fifth anniversary. Nixon received many of them in Washington and took the opportunity to point out his interest in Sino-American rapprochement. Of crucial importance was his meeting in the Oval Office on October 25 with President Yahya Khan of Pakistan, who was about to visit Peking. The President briefed Yahya on all the points we had tried and failed to get into the Warsaw talks. He asked him to convey that we regarded a Sino-American rapproachement as "essential," that we would never join a condominium against China, and that we were willing to send a high-level secret emissary to Peking. Nixon mentioned Robert Murphy, Thomas E. Dewey, or myself as possible envoys.

Next day Nixon pursued the same themes with Romanian President Nicolae Ceauşescu, picking up on the conversations during his visit to Bucharest in 1969. Just in case this conversation should reach Soviet ears — not improbable — Nixon waxed eloquent about his desire for good relations with both China *and* the Soviet Union. Later in the day Nixon used Ceauşescu's visit for a public step forward. At the state dinner, Nixon toasted the many common interests of the United States and Romania, listing prominently that of good relations, such as Romania had, with the United States, the Soviet Union, and the "People's Republic of China." It was the first use of China's official name by an American President. And just to make sure that the Romanians got the message, I reiterated Nixon's themes and language in a private conversation with Ceauşescu at Blair House on October 27.

All we could do now was wait. November was not an auspicious month, for at the United Nations we once again succeeded in blocking Peking's admission, spurring the writers of the *People's Daily* to use a choice selection of their well-honed invective. On November 19, the day before the UN vote, I launched two interagency studies. One concerned our long-range policy toward the People's Republic of China; the other sought an exploration of the issues of Chinese representation in the United Nations in the light of the narrowing UN support for our position.*

A report in late November of a trade agreement between Moscow and Peking triggered another anxious query from Nixon. I did not consider the amounts involved significant. Nor did I believe that Sino–Soviet differences lent themselves to simple reconciliation. No commercial gesture could alter the fact that forty Soviet divisions were poised along a 4,000-mile border not recognized by China. Nor could commercial transactions still the uneasiness with which Soviet leaders were bound to view the 800 million irredentists to their south, eyeing covetously the vast and rich empty spaces of Siberia, so unattractive to Russians that they are pioneered by the outcasts of whatever regime governs in the Russian capital. As I wrote the President:

> For both the Soviets and the Chinese this appearance of more normal relations is an important counter to the widespread speculation in the West that the two countries are so preoccupied by their continuing disputes to be susceptible to pressure to reach some major accommodation with us and the West Europeans. Signs that relations are improving are thus useful for both Peking and Moscow.
>
> Nevertheless, most of this is in the realm of form rather than substance and there is no evidence that fundamental problems can be resolved. Indeed our intelligence shows a continuing improvement in military capabilities along the Sino-Soviet border, and this fact no doubt plays some role in Chinese willingness to go along with signs of normalization of state relations — a position which two years ago they rejected out of hand.

What we did not know at this time was that the Chinese had already sent us a message quite different in kind from anything we had received before. President Yahya Khan was in China from November 10 to 15 and we assumed nothing had happened. Then three weeks later, on December 8, Ambassador Hilaly contacted Hal Saunders of my staff and said that he had "a message" for me relating to Yahya's trip. We never received an adequate explanation why Yahya waited nearly three weeks after his return to Pakistan to transmit the message. Perhaps the Chinese for their own reasons established a date after which it could be communicated; perhaps the reason was Yahya's careful precautions. In

---

*As it happened, Nixon wrote me a note on November 22 urging me to begin a study of the UN problem.[5] By then the study was already under way.

any event, I invited Hilaly to the White House the next day, where in my office a few minutes after 6:00 P.M. he produced an envelope containing a handwritten missive on white, blue-lined paper which had been carried to him by hand, Yahya not trusting the security of cable communications. (This was to be the form for all messages through the Pakistani channel.) Hilaly said he was not authorized to leave the document with me. He therefore had to dictate it, speaking slowly as I copied it down. We were so preoccupied with this mechanical chore that we did not notice the incongruity of this elegant spokesman of the elite of a country based on an ancient religion dictating a communication from the leader of a militant Asiatic revolutionary nation to a representative of the leader of the Western capitalist world; or the phenomenon that in an age of instantaneous communication we had returned to the diplomatic methods of the previous century — the handwritten note delivered by messenger and read aloud. An event of fundamental importance took place in a pedantic, almost pedestrian, fashion.

I was, at any rate, too busy to give expression to the excitement I felt. Usually in diplomacy individual events are part of a series; they merge in a continuum whose ultimate significance can only be viewed through the prism of time. As a general rule, turning points are apparent only in retrospect. But the message brought by Hilaly was clearly an event of importance. This was not an indirect subtle signal to be disavowed at the first tremors of difficulty. It was an authoritative personal message to Richard Nixon from Chou En-lai, who emphasized that he spoke not only for himself but also for Chairman Mao and Vice Chairman Lin Piao. China, Chou declared, "has always been willing and has always tried to negotiate by peaceful means. . . . In order to discuss the subject of the vacation of Chinese territories called Taiwan, a special envoy of President Nixon's will be most welcome in Peking." Chou En-lai observed gracefully that many other messages had been received from the United States through various sources, "but this is the first time that the proposal has come from a Head, through a Head, to a Head. The United States knows that Pakistan is a great friend of China and therefore we attach importance to the message."

In short, a personal representative of the President was being invited to Peking. To be sure, the purpose of the meeting was said to be "the vacation of Chinese territories called Taiwan." But I considered this a standard formula, perhaps to ensure against leaks or bad faith in Washington; it was less of a breach of ideological purity to couch the invitation to the archenemy in such terms. Mao, Lin Piao, and Chou En-lai would not associate themselves with any invitation patently incapable of fulfillment. To be eager for the visit of an American emissary they had to be driven by some deeper imperative than the future of one of China's provinces; it had to involve the security of China itself.

The moment Hilaly left I walked down the hall to the Oval Office, where Nixon and I talked at length. We were as one in our readiness to accept the invitation. We could not, we agreed, confine an agenda to Taiwan, and were certain that this reflected Chinese preferences as well, however reluctant they might be to put this into a communication. I therefore drafted a reply that I handed to Hilaly on December 16. It established a procedure on our side as well. Where the Chinese notes in the Pakistani channel were handwritten, ours were thereafter typed on Xerox paper without a letterhead or a United States government watermark. They were not signed (and our bureaucracy was not informed).

Our reply made clear that the United States would be prepared for high-level talks in Peking for discussions

on the broad range of issues which lie between the People's Republic of China and the United States, including the issue of Taiwan. . . . the meeting in Peking would not be limited only to the Taiwan question but would encompass other steps designed to improve relations and reduce tensions. With respect to the U.S. military presence on Taiwan, however, the policy of the United States Government is to reduce its military presence in the region of East Asia and the Pacific as tensions in this region diminish.

(The last sentence was designed to encourage Chinese interest in a settlement of the war in Vietnam by tying troop withdrawals from Taiwan to an end of the conflict in Indochina. It was a formula which had been used in many interagency studies in our government; it found its way almost unchanged into the Shanghai Communiqué that ended Nixon's visit over fourteen months later.) Our message proposed a meeting of lower-level officials to work out arrangements for a visit by an emissary. The two sides had in effect agreed on a meeting in Peking.

Once launched on this course, the Chinese multiplied their signals. On December 18 Mao received Edgar Snow for a long interview, an action that, however, once again overestimated our subtlety and our intelligence capabilities. Whereas Nixon had first publicly expressed his wish to visit China in a *Time* interview in October, Mao first expressed willingness to welcome Nixon in what would later be a *Life* interview (undoubtedly driving the soul of Henry Luce into a state of torment). Mao observed dryly to Snow that "at present, the problems between China and the U.S.A. would have to be solved with Nixon." Therefore, Mao "would be happy to talk with him, either as a tourist or as President." In a subtle maneuver Snow was given interpreter Nancy T'ang's notes of the conversation but was not permitted to publish his article for several months. The Chinese surely calculated that we would learn of the interview and that the handing over of a verbatim transcript coupled with the refusal to permit its publication would heighten its authenticity. If so, they were disappointed. We did not learn of the interview until several months later and by that time we had had communications from Chou En-lai sufficiently explicit for our less supple minds to grasp.[6]

Nevertheless, Snow's interview with Mao is interesting for what it tells us about the state of mind of China's leaders in December 1970. It shows that they were considering a Presidential visit at that early date, an idea not yet broached officially in any of our communications. It reveals that the Chinese had taken note of all the unilateral American steps. Snow quoted a senior Chinese diplomat as saying: "Nixon is getting out of Vietnam." Understanding of the direction of our Vietnam policy seems to have been greater in Tien An Men Square than in Harvard Square. To be sure, Snow did suggest that it was our side that asked to send an emissary to Peking. The record is somewhat different. Both sides proposed higher-level meetings at the same Warsaw session of January 20. Until we received the formal Chinese invitation, we had kept open the possibility that Washington might be the venue. The Snow article also implied that the President had invited himself to Peking. In fact, while Nixon expressed an abstract desire to visit China in his October 1970 *Time* interview, the first reference to a Presidential visit in any of our exchanges came in a comment by Chou En-lai conveyed on January 11, 1971. Perhaps the Chinese retained their traditional self-image of being the Middle Kingdom to which barbarians came to pay tribute; China is not alone among major countries, in fact, in not liking to appear the supplicant.

On December 23, Jean Sainteny saw Chinese Ambassador Huang Chen in Paris, and the Ambassador said he had passed on to his leaders my message (which I had given Sainteny in September) indicating our desire to set up a secure channel. It was Peking's way of validating the other approaches.

As 1971 opened, the Chinese sent us another important message, this time through Romania. Obviously, the Chinese were no more certain how to communicate with us than we with them. Romanian Ambassador Corneliu Bogdan called on me at the White House on January 11 with a message given to Vice Premier Gheorghe Radulescu on a visit to Peking in late November. (Again, there was no explanation for the long delay in delivering it.) We were read a written message from Chou En-lai almost identical with the one passed through Yahya; this message, too, we were told had been "reviewed by Chairman Mao and Lin Piao." Taiwan was said to be the "one outstanding issue" between the United States and China; if the United States were prepared to settle this, an American special envoy would be welcome in Peking. There was, however, an entirely novel and startling comment by Chou En-lai. Chou disarmingly suggested that since President Nixon had already visited Bucharest and Belgrade, he would also be welcome in Peking.

Thus was a Presidential visit to China broached for the first time. And by bracketing Peking with Bucharest and Belgrade — two capitals we had visited precisely because of their independence from Moscow — Chou made clear that whatever was said formally about Taiwan, he was interested above all in the Soviet challenge. Neither Chinese note made any reference to Indochina. The war in Vietnam might impede domestic tranquillity in America; it was no obstacle to reconciliation with the People's Republic of China, the avowedly revolutionary state on the border of which the war was raging and which four years earlier had been considered the instigator of the conflict. I made these points in a memorandum to Nixon. He noted on it that we should not appear too eager to respond.

Accordingly, I waited until January 29 to reply to the Romanian Ambassador. He was returning to Bucharest for consultation, and would have considered it odd if I let the occasion pass without a reference to Chou En-lai's communication. In order to avoid any misunderstandings or an exegesis of the significance of different formulations, I gave Bogdan a message which was verbatim that given to Hilaly over a month earlier: We were prepared to talk about the whole range of international issues, including Taiwan. The only difference was that the message was oral and not typed, indicating our slight preference for the Pakistani channel; we reasoned that Pakistan's position vis-à-vis China and the Soviet Union was less complicated than Romania's. (It would be difficult for Bucharest to avoid briefing Moscow.) I made no reference to a Presidential visit. Until we had had a reply to our earlier message regarding the agenda, such an overture was premature and potentially embarrassing.

There was again nothing to do but wait. I used the interval to try to educate myself on China. Between the middle of December and early April I met three times with groups of academic experts on China from various eminent institutions of higher learning. It would be satisfying to report that my former colleagues conveyed to me flashes of illuminating insight. Outside advisers, as I should have remembered, labor under difficulties despite their learning. A policymaker's greatest need for outside advice is in an intermediate realm between tactics and goals. Tactics are usually so dependent on the immediate situation that outsiders without access to cables can rarely make a significant contribution. At the other extreme, ultimate goals reflect philosophical perceptions and political necessities; while an adviser can provide some insights here, to be effective he must be conversant with the perceptions of the policymaker — changes of course require self-confidence rather more than expert knowledge. The dimension for which outside advice is most useful is the medium term, to carry the policymaker beyond the urgent but short of the ultimate — the perspective of two to five years. Unfortunately, this is normally the routine preoccupation of academicians interested in political problems and they seem to feel themselves cheated, deprived of the excitement of proximity to power, if they are called to Washington to do no more than they can accomplish at home. So instead of focusing on the medium term they tend to flood the policymaker with minute tactical advice or elaborate recommendations as to grand strategy until, glassy-eyed, he begins to feel new and unaccustomed affection for his regular bureaucracy.

This is how it was with the sinologists early in 1971. The academic China experts were convinced that the issues of primary concern to China were Vietnam and Taiwan. This turned out to be quite wrong. Arms control was another priority urged on me; the Chinese never even raised this matter and rebuffed us when we did; they consistently took the Gaullist view that the whole subject was just another form of US–Soviet collusion. Another nearly universal expert opinion was that *before* US–Chinese relations could improve, we had to recognize Peking as the sole government of China or at least allow Peking into the United Nations. This too was wrong: The breakthrough occurred months before the latter event took place, and seven years before President Carter did the former. Bilateral trade and exchanges were another professorial priority (exchanges meant that professors could visit China); these turned out to be of marginal interest to the Chinese, doled out when necessary for symbolic purposes. It was widely held, again, that China would insist on reassurance that we were withdrawing from Asia. The opposite was true. China desperately wanted us *in* Asia as a counterweight to the Soviet Union. I listened politely to my colleagues' suggestions, chastening any impatience with the recognition that I could hardly have been more relevant when I had served as an academic consultant to two previous administrations.

The second opportunity for education while we were waiting for the Chinese reply was provided by the three interagency studies requested in 1969 and 1970 regarding China policy, the UN membership issue, and our military strategy in the Pacific.* One advantage of the NSC system for the secret diplomacy in which we were now involved was that it enabled the President and me to obtain agency views and ideas without revealing our tactical plan. Thus, as part of the study of our military posture in Asia, I requested a breakdown of which of our forces in Taiwan were needed for Indochina operations and which were required as part of the Mutual Security Treaty with Taipei. This gave me some idea of what it was possible to concede if we were to withdraw some forces as "tensions in the area diminished." As I told the Senior Review Group: "Something that we have never done well before is to extract concessions for changes in military deployments that we were

---

* The Senior Review Group met on March 12 and the NSC on March 25, 1971.

going to make anyway. It might not be a bad idea to have this sort of information available for Taiwan."

A great deal of bureaucratic and intellectual energy was expended on the issue of Chinese representation in the United Nations, with which I shall deal later.

Another preoccupation in February and early March of 1971 was the South Vietnamese military campaign to cut, with our logistic and air support, the Ho Chi Minh Trail in the Laos panhandle. Some of our critics in the Congress and the media professed to see in this limited operation — at the southernmost extremity of Laos, in an area in which the writ of the Laotian government had not run for nearly a decade — a provocation to Peking on the scale of MacArthur's advance to the Yalu in 1950. The hesitant efforts of the hitherto much-decried ARVN were denounced by many critics as the precursor of an attack on North Vietnam itself, which, it was said, Peking might intervene to prevent. (Had the South Vietnamese in fact possessed this capacity, the war in Vietnam would have ended much differently.) But we were convinced that China was playing a bigger game and would not volunteer to put itself into its worst nightmare — a US–Soviet collusion — by launching a war against us on Hanoi's behalf in the uninhabitable jungles of southern Laos.

Events bore out this judgment. To be sure, on February 4, 1971, the *People's Daily* ground out an eloquent denunciation of the operations in Laos. But just as in the preceding year over Cambodia, it carefully avoided personal attacks on Nixon; Mao was quoted directly only once and on the same theme as in the preceding year over Cambodia: "Strengthening their unity, supporting each other, and persevering in a protracted people's war, the three Indochinese peoples will certainly overcome all difficulties and win complete victory." In other words, Vietnam was perfectly capable of winning its own war; China would not involve itself militarily.

Lest we miss the point, Chinese leaders chose the day of the *People's Daily* tirade to send us another signal. Ch'iao Kuan-hua, Chinese Deputy Foreign Minister and an old friend and associate of Chou En-lai, told the Norwegian Ambassador in Peking, Ole Aalgard, that China was aware of a new trend in American policy. The Indochina war made it impossible to resume the Warsaw talks, Ch'iao said, but sooner or later the Chinese would want to sit down and talk to us. He expressed the special desire to meet with me, and requested that the conversation be brought to our attention. We noted the message and made doubly sure that China understood our limited purposes in Laos. Nixon declared at his press conference of February 17 that "this action is not directed against Communist China. It is directed against the North Vietnamese who are pointed toward South Vietnam and toward Cambodia.

Consequently, I do not believe that the Communist Chinese have any reason to interpret this as a threat against them or any reason therefore to react to it.'' Noteworthy also was the restraint shown by Chou En-lai during a visit to Hanoi from March 5 to 8. He offered the North Vietnamese moral and material support but stayed clear of any personal invective against Nixon or threat of Chinese intervention.

In the meantime, in the President's second Foreign Policy Report, issued on Feburary 25, 1971, we reiterated our desire to improve relations. For the first time an American official document referred to the People's Republic of China by its official name. And we continued the easing of restrictions on China trade. On March 15, the State Department disclosed the President's decision to terminate all restrictions on the use of US passports for travel to the People's Republic of China; thereafter, visits to China were permitted for any legitimate purpose. (The Chinese had been less liberal with entry visas, granting only three for Americans in eighteen months.) On my instructions Ron Ziegler called attention to the decision in a White House briefing: ''We hope for, but will not be deterred by a lack of, reciprocity.''

On March 17 the Chinese showed what pinnacles of invective they were capable of when they meant business: They launched a fire-breathing verbal assault *on the Soviet Union*. The three major Chinese newspapers published a joint editorial on the centenary of the Paris Commune of 1871, stressing that revolutionary victory required the ''power of the revolutionary masses.'' Brezhnev was denounced as a ''renegade.'' The United States was dealt with in a sharply contrasting, perfunctory manner. The Soviet Union had replaced us as the principal enemy of Peking.

Even though Moscow could only lose by exhibiting its sense of vulnerability, China was too raw a nerve for the Soviets to ignore even a verbal assault, as all were now enabled to see. On March 26 an article in the Soviet foreign affairs weekly *New Times* bitterly attacked the United States for conducting ''a diplomacy of smiles'' toward China in the hope of further aggravating Soviet-Chinese relations. Even ''ultra-reactionary'' groups in the United States were said to be in favor of establishing ties with Peking for this sinister purpose.

March drew to a close with the twenty-fourth Congress of the Soviet Communist Party in Moscow. General Secretary Brezhnev's official report on March 30 lamented the continuing stalemate in the USSR's relations with China, but ''resolutely'' rejected the ''slanderous inventions'' about the Soviet Union that were ''being spread from Peking and instilled into the minds of the Chinese people'':

It is the more absurd and harmful to sow dissent between China and the USSR considering that this is taking place in a situation in which the imperialists have been stepping up their aggressive action against the freedom-loving peoples. More than ever before the situation demands cohesion and joint action by all the anti-imperialist, revolutionary forces, instead of fanning hostility between such states as the USSR and China.

But Brezhnev's operational proposals proved that Moscow had little ability to prevent what it feared. He proposed a five-nation conference of nuclear powers — the United States, the Soviet Union, Britain, France, and China — "at which the problems of nuclear disarmament as a whole should be considered." Since Peking's rejection of all such schemes was a foregone conclusion, this was another transparent attempt to isolate China. And the United States, if it understood its own interests, could not have any motive for joining such an effort.

By the end of March the trend was clear. We were approaching the end of the first stage of our long and difficult journey. At this point Chou En-lai took another giant step forward.

Ping-Pong Diplomacy

THE dramatic events that were about to burst upon us were foreshadowed by China's systematic restoration of its global diplomacy after the self-inflicted paralysis of the Cultural Revolution. In May 1969 Peking had begun to replace the ambassadors of whom all except one had been recalled during that upheaval; in 1970 it sought new ties with countries with which it had not previously had diplomatic relations. By the beginning of April 1971, Secretary Rogers reported to the President that Peking had been recognized by seven more countries in the previous six months, more than in the preceding seven years. China was discussing renewal of diplomatic relations with such diverse countries as Austria, Lebanon, Peru, and Cameroon, Rogers reported. It had made overtures to restore ties and establish new economic aid missions in several African states; it was also seeking improved relations with Britain and Japan and was extending feelers even to Eastern European nations in the Soviet orbit. Much of Peking's effort, according to Rogers, seemed aimed at encouraging support of its admission to the United Nations. Chou En-lai made it clear to the British chargé in Peking on March 3 that the price of upgraded Anglo-Chinese relations would be a British switch on the issue of Chinese admission to the UN and withdrawal of the British consulate in Taipei.

On April 1, 1971, the State Department reported other significant developments. Chou En-lai, for example, had received former Japanese Foreign Minister Aiichiro Fujiyama in March and told him that "at some point a sudden dramatic improvement is possible" in relations with the United States. Chou said that he had "very carefully" read the

President's Foreign Policy Report and "took specific note of the fact that for the first time an American President called China by its official name." The same State memorandum included a report of Edgar Snow's impressions from his recent talks with Mao and Chou. State could not have had the full text of the interview, for it ignored the important element of the invitation to Nixon; it reported instead that Snow had come away from his meetings with the impression that "there was no immediate prospect of improving Sino–US relations because of the war in Indochina." Mao, said the memorandum, did not expect progress in US–Chinese relations before 1972. The depressing conclusion was belied, did we but know it, by another, apparently trivial sentence in the same report in a paragraph about China's ambiguous relations with Japan. The two countries had their difficulties, the Department pointed out, but among the positive signs was that "Peking has also sent its table tennis team to Japan to participate in an international tournament, the first such sports activity in several years." Five days later we all grasped the significance of this sentence.

The United States table tennis team was also competing in the tournament, the thirty-first World Table Tennis Championship, staged in Nagoya, Japan. The nine young Americans on our team did not know it, but they were about to be players also in a complicated chess game. On April 4, a day of rest in the competition, Glenn Cowan, a nineteen-year-old from Santa Monica City College near Los Angeles, approached the Chinese team captain, three-time world champion Chuang Tse-tung, and wangled a ride on the bus with the Chinese players to an outing at the pearl farms on Mie Peninsula. ("Wangled" is almost certainly the wrong word; the Chinese would not have agreed had they not come to Nagoya with firm instructions to befriend the Americans. One of the most remarkable gifts of the Chinese is to make the meticulously planned appear spontaneous.) The next day, Cowan waited for Chuang to finish a match and offered him a T-shirt as a gift. Cowan, a sophomore majoring in history and political science, later said he wanted to "promote friendship with everybody, including the Chinese." To his surprise, Chuang accepted, and in return gave Cowan a Chinese handkerchief showing printed Chinese scenes.[7]

On April 6, to everybody's stunned surprise, the Chinese invited the American team to visit China. Graham B. Steenhoven, President of the US Table Tennis Association and manager of the American team, phoned the American Embassy in Tokyo for advice. Without hesitation, the Embassy's China specialist, William Cunningham, who knew nothing of our overtures to Peking except our general desire to improve relations, recommended that Steenhoven accept.[8] Cunningham deserves much credit for his perception and initiative. The Washington bureaucracy was less daring. On April 7 the State Department made sure that it would not be accused of recklessness by reporting to the White House: "Though we have as yet no way of being sure, the invitation may be intended at least in part as a gesture in response to recent US initiatives." The visit was an international sensation; it captured the world's imagination, aided no little by Chou En-lai's careful stage management. Peking Radio broadcasts gave pride of place to the team's arrival in China even though several other national teams had also been invited.

The day after the Chinese invitation to the American Ping-Pong team, Nixon gave a speech on Vietnam. While announcing the withdrawal of 100,000 additional American troops between May 1 and December 1 of 1971, Nixon also made a ringing defense of his Indochina policy, including the Laos operation. This had no adverse effect whatsoever on Peking. The United States table tennis players were given a dazzling welcome in China. On April 14, in the Great Hall of the People, they were received by Chou En-lai himself, an achievement that was still an unfulfilled ambition of most of the Western diplomats stationed in Peking. "You have opened a new chapter in the relations of the American and Chinese people," said the extraordinary Chinese Premier. "I am confident that this beginning again of our friendship will certainly meet with majority support of our two peoples." When the stunned athletes did not respond, the Premier pursued the subject: "Don't you agree with me?" The Americans burst into applause. They quickly invited the Chinese team to tour the United States. The invitation was accepted immediately.

The whole enterprise was vintage Chou En-lai. Like all Chinese moves, it had so many layers of meaning that the brilliantly painted surface was the least significant part. At its most obvious the invitation to the young Americans symbolized China's commitment to improved relations with the United States; on a deeper level it reassured — more than any diplomatic communication through any channel — that the emissary who would now surely be invited would step on friendly soil. It was a signal to the White House that our initiatives had been noted. The fact that the players could not possibly represent a particular political tendency added to the attractiveness of the maneuver from the Chinese perspective. China would be able to make its point without any possibility of a jarring American commentary. Chou En-lai, too, knew how to make gestures that could not be rebuffed. Within China it helped condition the public and party cadres to an impending and revolutionary change of course. But it was also a subtle warning to us: If Chinese overtures were rebuffed, Peking could activate a people-to-people approach and seek to press its case in a public campaign much as Hanoi was doing.

What made the situation more intriguing was that we were expecting Dobrynin back from the Soviet Union any day with an invitation to a summit. An announcement of a Moscow summit might abort the Chinese overture and too active a Chinese diplomacy might frustrate our Soviet policy. In the event, the Soviets' undying quest for petty advantage brought Dobrynin back with another procrastinating answer. His masters had still not given up on using the summit as bait to obtain concessions on Berlin. Excessive cleverness usually backfires; in this case we held cards of which the Politburo was unaware. Moscow solved our problem for us; its pressure tactics allowed us to proceed without impediment to complete the construction of the triangle.

In many ways the weeks following the Ping-Pong diplomacy were the most maddening of the entire tortuous process. Only the President and I understood the full implications of Chou En-lai's move because we alone were aware of all the communications between Peking and Washington. We knew that something big was about to happen, but we were baffled as to which channel would surface it and precisely what form it would take. As often on the eve of great events, Nixon was assailed by conflicting premonitions and hopes, by his amalgam of high national purpose and political and personal calculation. He was afraid that China would pull back at the last moment; this I thought improbable. At the same time he had second thoughts about what had already been decided — that a subordinate emissary should visit Peking before any Presidential trip. Undeterred by the fact that we had never responded to the Chinese overture for a Presidential visit, he now wanted to skip the emissary stage lest it take the glow off his own journey. I reminded him that we had not heard directly from the Chinese for three months about either enterprise, and that an unprepared Presidential trip to China was much too dangerous. Nixon was excited to the point of euphoria about the prospect before us; but he also was assailed by his chronic anxiety that no enterprise of his would ever come to a totally satisfactory ending.

Naturally, I shared Nixon's sense of the occasion. I had fewer doubts than he did that the Chinese would pull back or follow Hanoi's path of psychological warfare. After all, its goals were quite different from Hanoi's. Hanoi wanted to break our will; Peking needed us as a counterweight to Moscow. Hanoi was engaged in a ceaseless assault on the authority of our government; China's stake had to be in a Washington with the authority and determination to maintain the global balance of power. What worried me more was whether Peking had understood our method of government well enough to know in what channel to approach us.

But we controlled our nerves, Nixon agreeing that we should pursue the overtures to Peking along the established lines and wait for a message from our enigmatic opposite numbers on the other side of the globe. We sent further signals to show our steady course. In 1970 the NSC Under Secretaries Committee had been instructed to develop a program to augment travel and trade with China. By the middle of March 1971, a lengthy list had been developed, cataloguing every conceivable step within the administrative discretion of the President and not in need of Chinese acceptance or reciprocity. Carried away by the spirit of the enterprise, the Under Secretaries Committee recommended immediate approval of the entire package. I was dubious. Though I had been one of the originators of the policy of "unrejectable steps," I did not favor a move of this magnitude without reciprocity and before we knew the nature of the Chinese response. In a memorandum to the President of March 25 — well before the invitation to the Ping-Pong team — I divided the list into three components. The first package would keep trade with China somewhat below that with the Soviet Union; Stage II would place China trade on a par with US–Soviet trade; Stage III would go beyond the level of trade with the Soviet Union. I recommended that the first package be carried out in the near future and unilaterally; implementation of the second and third should await the development of our relations with China and be based on reciprocity.

This memorandum was on Nixon's desk when the news of the table tennis invitation reached us. I told him that this was the optimum time for a Presidential decision. Nixon approved the basic strategy on April 12 and ordered that Stage I be implemented immediately. On April 13 I notified the various agencies. On April 14, the White House through Ron Ziegler announced the first major breach in the decades-old trade embargo against China. He placed the new measures in the context of the Administration's China policy as it had evolved since 1969, but acknowledged on a background basis that the Ping-Pong events had affected the timing of the announcement. On the same day I notified the agencies of a separate Presidential decision to approve the sale of French dump trucks containing American-made engines and transmissions to the People's Republic of China.

Triangular diplomacy, to be effective, must rely on the natural incentives and propensities of the players. It must avoid the impression that one is "using" either of the contenders against the other; otherwise one becomes vulnerable to retaliation or blackmail. The hostility between China and the Soviet Union served our purposes best if we maintained closer relations with each side than they did with each other. The rest could be left to the dynamic of events.

On April 13 I called in Yuli Vorontsov, once again Soviet chargé d'affaires, whose destiny it seemed to be to receive unpleasant news, to give him one day's advance word of our decision to open up China trade. I stressed that it reflected no anti-Soviet intent. This is the conventional pacifier of diplomacy by which the target of a maneuver is given a formal reassurance intended to unnerve as much as to calm, and which would defeat its purpose if it were actually believed. Soviet diplomats are not known for their gullibility, but I thought that the implications spoke for themselves. I also urged Ziegler likewise to deny anti-Soviet intent at a White House briefing. This he did, but as instructed he balanced it with a statement agreeing with Chou En-lai: "There is no question about the fact that the initiatives of President Nixon have turned a new page in our relations with China."

"Washington watchers" in Peking must have been amused by the signs of "factional feuding" in Washington. On the one hand the President rode the waves of euphoria. At a session at the convention of the American Society of Newspaper Editors, Nixon waxed eloquent on his long-range goals of normalizing relations between the United States and the People's Republic of China, "the ending of the isolation of Mainland China from the world community." He traced the various steps that had been taken and noted that his policy was beginning to bear fruit. True to his habit of walking so close to the edge of the precipice that his advisers would squirm with discomfiture, he mentioned that he had recommended to his daughter Tricia and her fiancé (who were to be married in June) that China was a nice place to spend a honeymoon. Nixon hoped they could see China some day. "As a matter of fact, I hope sometime I do."

On the other hand, Vice President Spiro Agnew told a group of reporters that he disagreed with the policy of normalizing relations with Peking and that he had argued against it at an NSC meeting before the Ping-Pong episode. The conversation was supposed to be off the record, but journalistic restraint has its limits. The relationship between the President and any Vice President is never easy; it is, after all, disconcerting to have at one's side a man whose life's ambition will be achieved by one's death. Nixon's sense of being surrounded by potential antagonists needed no such encouragement. He wrote off this gaffe as another example of Agnew's unsuitability to succeed him — a view he held about most potential candidates — and ordered Haldeman to ask Agnew to desist from further comments about China.

Anxieties multiplied as we waited; Nixon fretted that the whole enterprise might abort. Finally, on April 27 we decided to approach the Chinese directly. A courier was sent to Paris with a letter for Jean Sainteny, urgently requesting him to deliver to the Chinese Ambassador a formal proposal to open a channel with us in Paris. We chose Paris because of at least a possibility that the long Chinese silence in the Pakistani and Romanian channels might mean that neither was trusted. The letter, however, was never delivered. While it was still en route, the Pakistani channel became active at last and we stopped the messenger.

The first indication came at 3:45 P.M. on April 27 — word that Hilaly needed to see me urgently for five minutes. Told by Hal Saunders that I was leaving on vacation the next day, Hilaly insisted that his message could not wait. So I received him at 6:12 P.M. He handed me a handwritten two-page aide-mémoire conveying a message from Chou En-lai in response to President Nixon's message of December 16 (received, we now learned, by the Chinese on January 5). The message, in elegant handwriting, read exactly as follows:

Message from Premier Chou en Lai

Premier Chou en Lai thanked President Yahya for conveying the message of President Nixon on 5 Jan 71. Premier Chou en Lai is very grateful to President Yahya and he will be grateful if President Yahya conveys the following verbatim message to President Nixon:

"Owing to the situation at the time, it has not been possible to reply earlier to the message from the President of the USA to the Premier of People's Republic of China.

"At present, contacts between the People's Republic of China and the United States are being reviewed. However, if the relations between China and the USA are to be restored fundamentally, the US must withdraw all its Armed forces from China's Taiwan and Taiwan Straits area. A solution to this crucial question can be found only through direct discussions between high level responsible persons of the two countries. Therefore, the Chinese Govt reaffirms its willingness to receive publically in Peking a special envoy of the President of the US (for instance, Mr Kissinger) or the US Secy of State or even the President of the US himself for a direct meeting and discussions. Of course, if the US President considers that the time is not yet ripe, the matter may be deferred to a later date. As for the modalities, procedure and other details of the high level meeting and discussions in Peking, as they are of no substantive significance, it is believed that it is entirely possible for proper arrangements to be made through the good offices of President Yahya Khan. April 21, 1971"

I asked Hilaly when this message had been received in Pakistan. After returning to his office, he called me to say that it had arrived on April 23. The delay was due to its having been sent to Washington by courier.

One can only speculate why Chou had waited so long to contact us. The Laotian operation may have made it imprudent to do so earlier; the Chinese may have been as perplexed as we were about the best channel. We both had come to the same conclusion regarding Romania; it was simply too exposed, too tempted by its own necessities, and too unfortunately located geographically to handle the last phase of setting up the contacts, however helpful it had been at earlier stages. The Chinese had tried Norway; we had attempted Paris; it would be interesting to know why Peking eschewed the latter. Perhaps it had a high estimate of the efficiency of French intelligence; perhaps it was worried about Soviet penetration; perhaps its communications to Paris were not adequate.

Probably in the classic Chinese manner, Chou En-lai waited to see whether he could get the barbarians to solicit an invitation after the broad hint of the Ping-Pong diplomacy. He may well have been as mystified by our silence as we were by his. It was a close call, but our outward self-control triggered the Chinese into the uncharacteristic posture of having to make the first move.

So we were at last at the end of one road and at the beginning of another. Chou En-lai's warm tone indicated that we needed to fear no humiliation; the peremptory tone of previous communications had been dropped. The subject of the proposed meeting was still to be Taiwan, but the emphasis was on withdrawing our forces rather than abandoning our relationship. The Chinese sought a high-level meeting, the purpose of which was to be a fundamental restoration of the relationship with the United States. The President had been specifically invited, not simply in a disavowable oral aside but in a formal communication. Nor did Chou En-lai want to risk subordinates' thwarting of our common design by their haggling over "modalities." By keeping technical arrangements in the Pakistani channel, he ensured discretion, high-level consideration, and expeditious decisions.

Hilaly left my office after a bare twenty minutes. I immediately went to see the President. I found him in the Lincoln Sitting Room and read him the message. There was little need for conversation. The message spoke for itself.

Within an hour, Nixon called me back on the telephone. Even great events ultimately reduce themselves to operational questions; our first was whom to send to China. Originally, there was no thought of sending me. We agreed that David Bruce would be the ideal emissary; I indeed broached the subject with Bruce in late May for the contingency of a later mission. But we came to realize that Bruce's role as head of our delegation to the Paris peace talks on Vietnam could cause his choice to be regarded by the Chinese as a transparent ploy; we wanted no backfire at so formative a stage. (This judgment turned out to be correct. Peking rejected Bruce as part of my delegation for the second trip to China in October. Later, they would change their minds and welcome him as the first head of our Liaison Office in Peking.) We discussed a long list of other candidates, including George Bush and Elliot Richardson. There was an extended consideration of Nelson Rockefeller, perhaps accompanied by Al Haig. Each was found to present problems in arranging a secret trip, either because they were insufficiently familiar with the nuances of Nixon's thinking or because they might detract too much attention from Nixon's own trip. Nixon even raised the name of Tom Dewey several times and waxed eloquent about his abilities; unfortunately, Dewey was no longer available, having died a few months previously. Rogers's name did not come up; nor could it have, given Nixon's determination that he, not the State Department, should be seen — justly — as the originator of China policy.

Restraining our excitement, we talked of the significance of the occasion. Nixon thought that our firmness on Vietnam had paved the way strategically even if here and there it caused a brief delay. Only an America that was strong in Asia could be taken seriously by the Chinese. I told the President that the tide was turning; we were beginning to see the outline of a new international order. We had, in fact, linked the various strands of our policy as we had intended: "We have done it now, we have got it all hooked together." And so we had, in Europe, Berlin, SALT, and the Middle East. Nixon raised the question whether a forthcoming announcement on SALT (the May 20 agreement to consider offensive and defensive limitations simultaneously) would upset the Chinese. I doubted it; they were playing a bigger game. Nixon asked if the announcement of a Soviet summit for September — which we still considered possible — would hurt our China initiative. I did not believe the Soviet leaders could move this rapidly; they were still waiting for the Vietnam protests in this country to weaken us further; they had not yet done with trying to squeeze us into further concessions as an admission price to a summit. Chou En-lai, I felt, had made "a more sophisticated analysis." But if I were proved wrong, we would simply be faced with choosing the priority of two summits, an embarrassment of riches. These were good problems to have — a luxury we had missed for two years.

High office often involves harassments, frustrations, petty calculation. Rather than the dramatic peaks of the public imagination it usually means an accumulation of seemingly endless pressures and tensions in which every apparent solution proves to be only a ticket to a new set of problems. The character of leaders is tested by their willingness to persevere in the face of uncertainty and to build for a future they can neither demonstrate nor fully discern. But every once in a while a fortunate few can participate in an event that they *know* will make a difference. I went home a little later than usual that evening and sat alone reflectively in my study. For over two years my nightmare had been that Vietnam would sap our nation's self-confidence and drain it of its crucial capacity to preserve the free nations and to sustain all hopes for progress. While the postwar world was crumbling and our creative contribution was more than ever indispensable, we stood in danger of consuming our national substance in bitter domestic strife over a corner of Southeast Asia. Whatever happened in Indochina, we would have to begin a new era of international relations — a goal unachievable without national dedication and national consensus. The message from Peking told us above all that despite Indochina we had a chance to raise the sights of the American people to a future of opportunity. There was now, for once, the prospect that Americans could at last begin to unite behind a vision of a more constructive and peaceful world, and would be given hope by the demonstration that even in adversity America still had the inward strength for great enterprises. For the first time in two years I experienced, amid the excitement, a moment of elation and inner peace.

Nixon and I met again the next morning in the Oval Office. Nixon asked me to read out the Chinese note to Haldeman and to explain its significance. It was not that Nixon did not understand it; it was rather that he wanted to savor the moment of accomplishment by hearing it described to an old associate from the lonely days of exile. It was a kind of vindication, proof that the solitude and travail of those years had not been in vain.

There was another inconclusive discussion of possible emissaries, this time in Haldeman's presence. Nixon was still concerned that the Chinese might use the same tactics as Hanoi and bring pressure on us by inviting other American political figures in opposition to us (an apprehension he never conquered). I questioned that; Peking's strategic requirements did not coincide with Hanoi's. It would not want the opening to China to appear extorted; a reluctant Administration would not satisfy China's need for insurance in an emergency. Washington was being brought into play as a counterweight to Soviet pressures, and from the Chinese point of view it was desirable that this weight be heavy and spontaneous. Nixon nevertheless asked me to discourage any temptation for Peking to deal with his political opponents; it was easy to express my acquiescence, much more difficult to know what to do about it.

Later in the morning Nixon told me that he had decided on me as the emissary; I should start preparations at once. His motives were mixed, as is always the case with political leaders. Only romantic outsiders believe that men who have prevailed in a hard struggle for power make decisions exclusively on the basis of analytical ideas. Nixon's overriding motive was undoubtedly that I understood our policy best, and that being familiar with my complicated chief I would be able to arrange the sort of Peking visit for him with which Nixon would be most comfortable. He could ask me without embarrassment to raise the public relations requirements of his insistently eager advance men. Another factor was undoubtedly that of all the potential emissaries I was the most subject to his control. I was on the White House staff; I had no means of publicizing my activities except through the White House press office; my success would be a Presidential success. I was substantially unknown to the general public; in two and a half years in office I had never given an on-the-record press conference.

At that moment, I cannot say that I was vastly surprised. I felt, rather, an immense relief that after so long a preoccupation with its design I would be able to bring the enterprise to fruition. As for Nixon, whatever his complex motivations, he is owed the tribute for courage in revolutionizing our postwar foreign policy in spite of the profound shock that he knew many of his traditional supporters would feel. Assisted only by his security adviser, without the alibi provided by normal processes of bureaucratic clearance, he authorized a mission that, had it failed, would surely have produced a political catastrophe for him and an international catastrophe for his country. That the odds were in our favore is irrelevant to the loneliness of the choice when it was made; that Nixon was not normally confiding does not change the fact that it took a resolute man to walk along the edge of a precipice with only a single associate.

Plans and Aberrations

H AVING been kept waiting for four months, we did not wish to return a formal response immediately, lest we appear too eager. But the decision had to be translated rapidly into operational terms, especially since both Nixon and I were going on vacation, he to San Clemente, I to Palm Springs.

I called in Agha Hilaly on April 28 to give him an interim reply. Our messages to the Chinese were first drafted by me by hand after discussion with the President. They then went generally through several additional drafts to take account of comments by Al Haig and Winston Lord and my own second thoughts. They were then typed and shown again to Nixon; my records show that he approved them without change.

Our interim reply expressed our appreciation to President Yahya Khan for his delicacy and tact, and thanked Chou En-lai for his communication, which we evaluated as positive, constructive, and forthcoming. We would respond in the same spirit. Peking could expect a formal reply during the week of May 10. To take account of the President's concern that China might approach other American political figures, and to prevent Chinese nervousness, which might lead to the opening of new and complicating channels, I added some personal — and therefore disavowable — observations. I suggested that Yahya communicate to Chou En-lai as his own view the importance of confining US–Chinese exchanges to this channel until an official link was securely in place. We hoped that the Chinese would make no other initiatives until we had returned a formal reply and designated an emissary. This was without prejudice to the intensification of people-to-people exchanges — students, reporters, scholars — which we would greatly welcome. I stressed that this should be communicated not as an official American position but as Yahya's personal assessment of our attitude. I did not doubt that Chou En-lai would get the point. On May 5 the Pakistanis informed us that all messages had been passed to the Chinese on

May 1 — the very day that disruptive demonstrations sought to paralyze Washington in order, so the organizers claimed, to persuade the government of the necessity of working for peace.

But before the message could reach Peking, our curious system of government produced an aberration that complicated the entire enterprise; indeed, that it did not do more damage was a testimony to the determination with which the Chinese leadership was seeking a rapprochement with us. The State Department was, of course, unaware of the messages being passed — though it might well have sensed that something was afoot from the Ping-Pong diplomacy and the many study memoranda on China policy with which we burdened the NSC system. The one aspect of China policy unambiguously under its control was the issue of Chinese representation in the United Nations. And this topic was pursued with the intensity of injured prerogative.

The Department, correctly calculating that support in the UN for our traditional position was ebbing, was eager to engineer the admission of the People's Republic of China into the United Nations in some form without producing the expulsion of Taiwan. It sought to please the liberal wing of the Congress, which was tormenting us on Vietnam, without antagonizing the conservatives, not to speak of a President who had derived much early support from the "China lobby." It therefore came up with a number of schemes that had the common feature of being opposed by both Taiwan and the People's Republic; they were favored only by a small group of journalists and members of Congress. One was "universality": that both portions of all divided countries should be admitted separately to the UN. This was close to the two-China solution always vehemently rejected by both Taipei and Peking; it also would have provoked the opposition at that time of South Korea and West Germany. Another scheme was to admit the People's Republic by majority vote and give it the Security Council seat, while Taiwan remained in some undefined status in the General Assembly (under a procedural device that expulsion required a two-thirds vote). This, too, was unacceptable to both Taiwan and the People's Republic; it was acceptable, however, to many domestic critics of our China policy and it might get us through a year or two at the General Assembly. State had been pressing for months for a Presidential decision on what approach to pursue because it needed time to canvass for support for the preferred option. I had procrastinated, with the President's agreement, because I did not want to jeopardize the precarious beginnings of our new China policy with an issue that would be provocative without being capable of resolution, and would in any event be overtaken by the evolution of our relations with Peking.

It was a reflection on the theological nature of our China debate that many experts still regarded the "solution" of the UN issue, liturgically, as the absolute precondition of any improvement in our relations with Peking — a point that had not been made in any Chinese communication in any channel; indeed, no Chinese communication even raised the UN issue. Unable to obtain a Presidential ruling, the State Department simply put forward its theoretical position publicly to get a leg up in the bureaucratic debate. On April 28, the Department spokesman declared as our position that sovereignty over Taiwan and the Pescadores was "an unsettled question subject to future international resolution," something *both* parties of the China dispute rejected since both considered the territories as part of the sovereign state of China. The purpose of the statement was to enable us to lay the legal basis for admitting Peking to the UN while retaining a seat in the General Assembly for Taipei. To complicate matters further, on April 29 Secretary Rogers, in London for a SEATO ministerial meeting, appeared on television to proclaim that Mao's invitation to Nixon, as reported in *Life* magazine by Edgar Snow, was "fairly casually made"; he did not believe it was "a serious invitation." He went on to say that China's foreign policy was "expansionist" in many ways; China's policy had been "rather paranoiac" toward the rest of the world; and if our efforts to improve relations with the USSR and China stimulated their feud, that was a "dividend" — though, he added, not our objective. A Nixon trip to China, Rogers added, following the line his East Asian Bureau had been pressing for all along, might be possible "down the road a piece," but only provided that China decided to join the international community in some unspecified way and complied "with the rules of international law."

That Rogers did not know of our exchanges excused this confusion to some extent; it did not diminish the impact of his remarks. Nixon and I were thunderstruck. We were concerned that Peking might construe Rogers's statements as our reply to its message or conclude that we thought China was susceptible to pressure despite its warnings months earlier not to treat its opening toward us as a sign of weakness — a statement rarely made by countries that in fact feel themselves strong. The Chinese were clearly worried that we might escalate our demands; in that case, we feared, they might revert to brooding isolation or another spell of belligerent rhetoric, to demonstrate their imperviousness to pressure. We needed to send reassurance but it seemed unwise to overload the Pakistani channel, aside from the fact that it was not easy to formulate a disavowal of a statement of the Secretary of State that would not do more harm than good. Nixon did his best to restore some perspective at a press conference on April 29. He made it clear that no decision had been made on our UN approach; he listed the various proposals before him, ranging from a two-China solution to a single representation. This was the farthest he could go without publicly dissociating from his Secretary of State. He included a conciliatory reference to a possible visit to China, probably more meaningful in Peking than in Washington: "I hope, and, as a matter of fact, I expect to visit Mainland China sometime in some capacity — I don't know what capacity." It was a skillful performance.

A Chinese broadcast of May 4 defined the limits of Chinese acquiescence in our bureaucratic shenanigans. The State Department's assertion that Taiwan's status was "an unsettled question" was denounced as "brazen interference" in Chinese affairs and an act of "hostility to the Chinese people." Peking declared emphatically that "there is only one China in the world" and that "Taiwan is an inalienable part of China's sacred territory." It described the visit of the American table tennis team to China as a "new development" in the friendship between the American and Chinese peoples, but added that the Nixon Administration's moves to improve US–China relations were "fraudulent" and were attempts to "gain political capital and extricate itself from its isolated situation." The broadcast was a warning to us not to press too far; it did not in fact interrupt our exchanges.

For there were constraints, too, on China's freedom of action. We might be prone to official hiccups, but the divisions on China's borders were Soviet. The Soviets had moved new military units to the Mongolian border, bringing the total of these forces to forty-four divisions. The Chinese had substantially increased their own ground forces. The border talks between the USSR and China were stalemated. Brezhnev, in a meeting with the leaders of a Western Communist Party, had expressed considerable concern over the progress in US–Chinese relations. A Soviet TV commentator had declared on April 25, with respect to US–Chinese relations, that "pressure has no effect on the Soviet Union, and such a policy is doomed to failure." Countries that proclaim that they are unaffected by pressure are either bluffing or have had the good fortune never to be exposed to it.

I went ahead with planning my trip to China. I took with me on my vacation in Palm Springs a bagful of books on Chinese philosophy, history, and art. Winston Lord had the responsibility for preparing the briefing materials, a duty made excruciatingly painful by the necessity to keep it secret from his beautiful, charming, and intelligent Chinese-American wife, Betty, born in Shanghai, whose parents, originally from the Mainland, had close ties with Taiwan. Winston set about to produce voluminous notebooks on every subject that could conceivably come up.

To start the technical arrangements, I sent a backchannel message on May 3 to our Ambassador in Pakistan, Joseph Farland:

For the most sensitive reasons known only to the President and myself, the President wishes you to find some personal . . . pretext for undertaking an immediate trip to the United States in order that you may be able to confer with me. Our meeting will have to be completely covert, with its nature being divulged to no one with the exception of the President, you and myself. . . . I recognize the difficulties that this message will entail for you but I am sure you realize that the importance the President attaches to our meeting is the overriding consideration. The subject of our meeting will not require any preparation on your part.

The puzzled but loyal Farland flew to Los Angeles on what he described to his superiors as "private business"; I brought him from there to Palm Springs in a friend's private plane. On May 7 he met with me secretly at the private home where I was staying. We spent three hours together; Farland then returned to the Los Angeles airport; there was no record of Farland's having visited Palm Springs at all.

We were fortunate that our Ambassador in Pakistan at that moment was a man outside the regular Foreign Service Establishment. A traditionalist would never have responded without reinsuring himself by a "personal" communication to his departmental chiefs in Washington. Farland, moreover, was as matter-of-factly able as he was conscientious. He handled the complicated arrangement for my trip with unfailing skill and discretion. On May 7 in Palm Springs, I reviewed with him all the communications with Peking that had come through the Pakistani channel. I told him that technical arrangements for the trip should be made through him, to avoid the possibility of misunderstanding inherent in passing complex material through too many hands. And Farland could use his Embassy staff to look into the feasibility of some of the arrangements, so long as he did not tell them what their real purpose was. At that point my idea was to meet Chinese representatives either in Pakistan or at a convenient airport in southern China. I told Farland that I would also keep him informed of all messages I sent to Yahya through Hilaly. I would count on him to control the Embassy personnel while I was in Pakistan, and to back up my "cover" story.

Farland recommended that the meeting be held in China; it would be better to be taped by the Chinese, who would keep a record anyway, than by the Pakistanis. I told Farland that I would set up a Navy backchannel via our naval attaché in Karachi; Admiral Elmo R. Zumwalt, Jr., the Chief of Naval Operations, had set up a similar channel for me with satisfactory results during the Berlin negotiations. (Later we found the Navy channel too cumbersome. With Helms's cooperation we worked out an effective system through the CIA.)

Backchannels in those days were a curious phenomenon. For every bureaucracy they excluded, they made the user hostage to another — until eventually we were able to set up channels directly from the White House that went through no other agency. Essentially, a backchannel is a communication system that seeks to circumvent normal procedures; it requires, however, *somebody's* facilities. Usually the excluded party was the State Department, which had victimized itself by technology and habit: by technology because its computers automatically distribute even the most sensitive cables through the building by preestablished criteria; by habit because diplomats live on trading information and are infinitely ingenious in getting around formal restrictions. This is why even the State Department has set up its own system of internal backchannels and why almost every modern President has sought to evade State's formal communications machinery. Helms knew how to limit the flow of cables; he handled backchannels discreetly and competently.

I outlined to Farland the itinerary that I planned. I would leave Washington on an "information" trip taking me to Saigon, Bangkok, New Delhi, Islamabad, and Paris. At each stop I would schedule many orientation meetings but hold no press briefings. I would carry no newsmen on my plane. By the time I reached Islamabad a week later I hoped to have bored local journalists to such a point and have made so little news that there would be no great press interest left in covering me. Farland told me there was only one American stringer stationed in Islamabad.

Farland and I agreed that the most effective plan would be to have me arrive in Pakistan on a Friday morning. Farland would schedule a full day of activities both with the Embassy and with the Pakistani government. If President Yahya agreed, he might invite me to spend the weekend in some suitable retreat, say the Khyber Pass or some hill station. I would leave my plane at a conspicuous location at the airport. I would go to China in an American, Pakistani, or Chinese plane prepositioned in Pakistan; we would make the final decision after we knew the venue and had looked into the feasibility. I would conspicuously reappear after an absence of no more than thirty-six hours and proceed westward to Paris. Farland thought all this manageable; he promised to contact Yahya immediately upon his return. I told him that I would inform Hilaly of Farland's role.

May and June provided opportunities to move another step forward in our economic relations with China and also to send encouraging signals. On May 7 the Departments of State, Commerce, Treasury, and Transportation published regulations implementing the White House announcement of April 14 that liberalized economic relations with China. The Treasury Department removed all controls on the use of US dollars or dollar instruments (except those in blocked accounts) in transactions with Peking. As a result, Chinese-Americans were now permitted to send dollars to relatives on the Mainland. American-owned ships under foreign flags were also permitted to stop at Mainland China ports. United States flag vessels could henceforth transport goods destined for the Mainland from US to non-Chinese ports, or from one non-Communist port to another.

On May 9 I returned to Washington from my Palm Springs vacation, having drafted a reply to Chou En-lai's last message. Nixon approved it next morning and at noon I handed it to Hilaly, unsigned:

President Nixon has carefully studied the message of April 21, 1971, from Premier Chou En-Lai conveyed through the courtesy of President Yahya Khan. President Nixon agrees that direct high-level negotiations are necessary to resolve the issues dividing the United States of America and the People's Republic of China. Because of the importance he attaches to normalizing relations between our two countries, President Nixon is prepared to accept the suggestion of Premier Chou En-Lai that he visit Peking for direct conversations with the leaders of the People's Republic of China. At such a meeting each side would be free to raise the issue of principal concern to it.

In order to prepare the visit by President Nixon and to establish reliable contact with the leaders of the Chinese People's Republic, President Nixon proposes a preliminary *secret* meeting between his Assistant for National Security Affairs, Dr. Kissinger, and Premier Chou En-Lai or another appropriate high-level Chinese official. Dr. Kissinger would be prepared to attend such a meeting on Chinese soil preferably at some location within convenient flying distance from Pakistan to be suggested by the People's Republic of China. Dr. Kissinger would be authorized to discuss the circumstances which would make a visit by President Nixon most useful, the agenda of such a meeting, the time of such a visit and to begin a preliminary exchange of views on all subjects of mutual interest. If it should be thought desirable that a special emissary come to Peking publicly between the secret visit to the People's Republic of China of Dr. Kissinger and the arrival of President Nixon, Dr. Kissinger will be authorized to arrange it. It is anticipated that the visit of President Nixon to Peking could be announced within a short time of the secret meeting between Dr. Kissinger and Premier Chou En-Lai. Dr. Kissinger will be prepared to come from June 15 onward.

It is proposed that the precise details of Dr. Kissinger's trip including location, duration of stay, communication and similar matters be discussed through the good offices of President Yahya Khan. *For secrecy, it is essential that no other channel be used. It is also understood that this first meeting between Dr. Kissinger and high officials of the People's Republic of China be strictly secret* [emphasis in original].

We learned later that the Chinese were extremely suspicious of our desire for secrecy; perhaps they saw it as a device to allow us to reverse course quickly. Chinese wariness was compounded by doubts of our ability to maintain confidences.* It is difficult to recapture now the sense of mutual ignorance of the United States and China in those days.

---

* Edgar Snow later wrote: "Only one thing may have surprised the Chinese: Mr. Kissinger's success in keeping his visit secret. Experience with American diplomats during World War II had convinced Chinese leaders that Americans could not keep secrets."[9]

Except for the formalistic presentations at the Warsaw talks, we had had no contact of any sort with the Chinese leadership. The messages cited in this volume were quite literally our sole communication. Since Chinese leaders do not believe in idle chatter, most of the Western diplomats in Peking would go for months without seeing any important Chinese official; few of them ever encountered a senior Chinese leader except on purely ceremonial occasions. Thus we lacked even the tidbits that are occasionally exchanged between friendly governments; we had no idea what we would find in Peking.

In addition, we knew that if an announcement were made before a visit we would be caught between those who wanted a catalogue of concessions and others who wanted guarantees of our intransigence. Foreign countries would ask for briefings and reassurances about a meeting whose agenda consisted of nothing other than permitting each side to raise the issues of importance to it. All this would become public and be recited back to a capital with which we were able to communicate only via third parties. Some countries might have attempted to preempt our visit; others to thwart it. The tender shoot so painstakingly nurtured for more than two years might well have been killed. In time the Chinese came to understand our reasons; I have no doubt now that the secrecy of the first trip turned into a guarantee of a solid and well-managed improvement of relations.

The most significant part of the note was our formal acceptance of the invitation to the President to visit Peking. We stressed secrecy but sought to allay Chinese concerns by agreeing that the trip could be announced immediately afterward and that a second, *public* visit by an emissary could be arranged prior to the Nixon visit. We stressed that we could not agree to talk only about Taiwan; each side would be free to "raise the issue of principal concern to it." This message was received in Peking on May 17.

On May 20, after months of haggling, the United States and the Soviet Union announced a procedural breakthrough in the SALT negotiations. Heretofore, the Soviets had insisted that SALT deal only with limiting ABM; now Moscow and Washington agreed to deal simultaneously with offensive and defensive limitations as we desired. Nixon had worried that this might disturb the Chinese. I was less concerned — the demonstration of options is almost always an asset — but thought it an occasion to demonstrate to Peking the advantage of the American connection; we could assure the Chinese directly that the SALT announcement did not imply a US–Soviet condominium. With the President's approval I sent an advance copy of the official announcement to Farland to give to Yahya for the Chinese. An accompanying message assured them that we would "conclude no agreement which would be directed against the People's Republic of China," and that I would be prepared to discuss "this issue and related questions" on my forthcoming secret trip.

While we were waiting for Peking's reply, we found that we were not the only ones with an aberrant bureaucracy. On May 26 an old colleague from Harvard called up to say excitedly that he had been in Ottawa the day before and that members of the newly established Chinese mission there had complained that President Nixon had been invited to visit China but would not come. It was an odd signal — half on the mark; a Chinese official cognizant of the full story would have known that the United States *had* responded favorably to the invitation. It was also a warning — whether it was so intended or not — of what the Chinese could do to us publicly if the initiative faltered. We would soon find ourselves on the public defensive for having failed to seize the opportunity of improving Sino–US relations. I decided to make light of the possibility of a Presidential visit and to occupy the professor's energies by suggesting that he might try to arrange a meeting for me with the new Chinese Ambassador in Canada when he arrived.

On May 31 we received an excited but cryptic message from Hilaly: A long message from Peking was on its way by courier from Pakistan; Hilaly had been given only elliptical hints of its contents. Apparently it was encouraging; Hilaly was pretty sure that the Chinese accepted the essence of our proposal. We spent an impatient two days awaiting the Pakistani messenger. The State Department, unaware of our design and understandably anxious to begin canvassing for the UN vote on Chinese representation, chose that moment to press for a Presidential decision on a modified version of its two-China formula. The proposed vehicle was a speech by the Secretary of State toward the end of June. No worse timing could have been imagined, and it illustrated the pitfalls of our two-channel style of government. But Nixon was not about to confront his Secretary in a setting where he would have to give explanations. He therefore simply announced at a press conference on June 1 that he would not make a decision on the Chinese representation issue before July 15. The date was not chosen accidentally. Finally the messenger from Islamabad arrived. Hilaly hurried in to see me with Chou En-lai's reply at 8:10 P.M. on June 2:

Premier Chou En Lai has seriously studied President Nixon's messages of April 29, May 17th and May 22nd 1971, and has reported with much pleasure to Chairman Mao Tse Tung that President Nixon is prepared to accept his suggestion to visit Peking for direct conversations with the leaders of the Peoples Republic of China. Chairman Mao Tse Tung has indicated that he welcomes President Nixon's visit and looks forward to that occasion when he may have direct conversations with His Excellency the President, in which each side would be free to raise the principal issue of concern to it. It goes without saying that the first question to be settled is the crucial issue between China and the United States which is the question of the concrete way of the withdrawal of all the U.S. Armed Forces from Taiwan and Taiwan Straits area.

Premier Chou En Lai welcomes Dr. Kissinger to China as the U.S. representative who will come in advance for a preliminary secret meeting with high level Chinese officials to prepare and make necessary arrangements for President Nixon's visit to Peking.

Premier Chou En Lai suggests that it would be preferable for Dr. Kissinger to set a date between June 15 and 20th for his arrival in China, and that he may fly direct from Islamabad to a Chinese airport not open to the public. As for the flight, he may take a Pakistan Boeing aircraft or a Chinese special plane can be sent to fly him to and from China, if needed. . . . Premier Chou En Lai warmly looks forward to the meeting with Dr. Kissinger in China in the near future.

It would be difficult to exaggerate the relief I felt. Chou had accepted our proposal that each side should be free to raise the issues of most concern to it; this guaranteed a discussion of global issues that interested us most. Chou had again framed the Taiwan problem in a manner most susceptible to solution: the withdrawal of US forces. The Chinese leaders could not have gone so far were they not willing, even eager, for a fundamental reappraisal of the Sino-American relationship.

I walked from my office in the West Wing over to the mansion to inform the President. Nixon was hosting a dinner for President Anastasio Somoza of Nicaragua. I told the military aide standing outside the State Dining Room that it was imperative for the President to see me for a few minutes as soon as he could. I paced the hall for several minutes, waiting. Around 9:30 the President came out. I told him about the message; buoyantly he took me to the Lincoln Sitting Room, found some brandy and two glasses, and proposed a toast to what had been and what remained yet to be done. Nixon remembers the toast: "Henry, we are drinking a toast not to ourselves personally or to our success, or to our administration's policies which have made this message and made tonight possible. Let us drink to generations to come who may have a better chance to live in peace because of what we have done."[10] My recollection is not so precise; it was probably far too early to make such exalted claims. But the quotation reflects accurately the emotion and the rekindled hope that out of the bitterness and division of a frustrating war we could emerge with a new national confidence in our country's future.

I handed our reply to Peking — composed by Winston Lord and me after many drafts — to Hilaly two days later in the afternoon of June 4. In it President Nixon expressed appreciation for the warm welcome extended to my visit. "Because of the shortness of time available and the need to arrange a suitable pretext for his travel, Dr. Kissinger now finds it impossible to leave Washington before the first week of July. Accordingly, President Nixon proposes that Dr. Kissinger arrive in China on July 9 and leave on July 11, flying in a Pakistani Boeing aircraft from Islamabad to Peking." (This schedule was kept.) Our message appreciated Chinese willingness to observe secrecy and repeated that I would be empowered to settle on a communiqué to be issued shortly afterward "if this is mutually desired." We chose the weekend of July 9 because Rogers planned to be in London later in July and we could not make an announcement of a Presidential trip to Peking while the Secretary of State was traveling.

On June 11 Chou En-lai accepted the July 9 date in a brief note; we learned only later that this was at some considerable inconvenience and embarrassment, because a visit by North Korean Premier Kim Il-sung was scheduled for the same days. Yahya Khan, who had little to be cheerful about amid his travails in East Pakistan, was carried away by the spirit of the mission. Hilaly brought a handwritten note from Yahya on June 19: "The above message from Peking seems to clinch the issue finally. Please assure our friend that absolutely foolproof arrangements will be made by us and he need have no anxiety on this count."

We were now committed; all that remained was the act. The first problem was to convince the Secretary of State of the need for me to take a lengthy "information trip" through Asia — the first foreign trip I would take on my own as security adviser. He was understandably reluctant. It was painful enough to see me and the NSC staff dominate the policy process in Washington; it was harder still to accept the proposition that I might begin to intrude on the conduct of foreign policy overseas. The objection was, in fact, well taken. The State Department should be the visible focus of our foreign policy; if the President has no confidence in his Secretary of State he should replace him, not substitute the security adviser for him. If he does not trust the State Department, the President should enforce compliance with his directives, not circumvent it with the NSC machinery. Yet, while these postulates are beyond argument as a matter of theory, they are not easy to carry out. To achieve the essential coherence of policy there is need for a strong Secretary of State who is at the same time quite prepared to carry out Presidential wishes not only formally but in all nuances. The combination has been an historical rarity; in recent times, one or the other quality has, alas, often been missing.

In June 1971 I had a less detached perspective, and in any event this wisdom would have been irrelevant to the problems we faced. For after the Chinese accepted July 9, we had passed the point of no return. It made little difference when the State Department protested that my visit to the Indian subcontinent was badly timed or might be misunderstood in view of the tensions caused by the upheavals in East Pakistan. I briefly explored entering China from an American air base in Okinawa, but decided that it would be an unhappy symbol for Peking and needlessly humiliating to Japan to make the secret trip from what we recognized as Japanese territory without consulting the Japanese government. Nixon would not give a direct order; he assigned Haldeman the task of wearing Rogers down. At last the State Department grudgingly withdrew its objection to the trip. As for informing Rogers of my ultimate destination, the President conceived the idea of inviting Rogers to San Clemente for the major part of my Asian trip; he would thus be able to break the news under the best, or at least most controlled, circumstances.

Another complication was that the entire senior level of the United States government seemed to be seized by an irrepressible wanderlust for Taiwan at the very moment that I was slated to go to Peking. First we had to dissuade Vice President Agnew from making a long-awaited visit to Chiang Kai-shek; he was consoled with an around-the-world trip focusing heavily on the Middle East and Africa. Then Mel Laird conceived the idea of inspecting defense installations on Taiwan on just the days when I would be in Peking; he had already planned to go to Japan and Korea to meet with allied defense ministers. Laird was a good soldier; without inquiring into my reasons for asking, he rearranged his schedule.

One result of all this junketing, however, was that no Presidential plane was left for my trip. The President required two for his move to San Clemente; Agnew had another one, and Laird took the remaining VIP plane. We finally hunted up a command plane from the Tactical Air Command filled with electronic equipment, extraordinarily uncomfortable, and with engines so old-fashioned that it required long runways. On takeoff one had the feeling that the plane really preferred to reach its destination overland.

Just when all technical and bureaucratic problems seemed to be solved, there occurred an event that deflected our attention for much of the period remaining before I left on my mission: the publication of the so-called Pentagon Papers. After we had struggled for months to establish a secret channel to Peking, having overcome many obstacles and suspicions, the sudden release of over 7,000 pages of secret documents came as a profound shock to the Administration. The documents, of course, were in no way damaging to the Nixon Presidency. Indeed, there was some sentiment among White House political operatives to exploit them as an illustration of the machinations of our predecessors and the difficulties we inherited. But such an attitude seemed to me against the public interest: Our foreign policy could never achieve the continuity on which other nations must depend, and our system of government would surely lose all trust if each President used his control of the process of declassification to smear his predecessors or if his discretion in defending the classification system became a partisan matter. The publication of these documents was selective, one-sided, and clearly intended as a weapon of political warfare. It unfairly damaged personal reputations, such as that of John McNaughton; this distinguished public servant, whom I knew to have been essentially opposed to the war, was portrayed in the Pentagon Papers as an evil warmonger, but in 1971 he was no longer alive to defend himself, having perished with his family in an airplane crash.

Our nightmare at that moment was that Peking might conclude our government was too unsteady, too harassed, and too insecure to be a useful partner. The massive hemorrhage of state secrets was bound to raise doubts about our reliability in the minds of other governments, friend and foe, and indeed about the stability of our political system. We had secret talks going on at the same time with the North Vietnamese, which we believed — incorrectly, as it turned out — were close to a breakthrough. We were at an important point in the sensitive SALT talks. And we were in the final stages of delicate Berlin negotiations which also depended on secrecy.

I not only supported Nixon in his opposition to this wholesale theft and unauthorized disclosure; I encouraged him. An unsuccessful effort was made in court to block publication by civil injunction. (The idea to do so did not come from me, but I did not object to it.) I was not aware of other steps later taken, the sordidness, puerility, and ineffectuality of which eventually led to the downfall of the Nixon Administration. I consider those methods inexcusable, but I continue to believe that the theft and publication of official documents did a grave disservice to the nation. In the event, the release of the Pentagon Papers did not impede our overture to Peking. But this does not change the principle. We could not know so at the time; nor did those who stole the documents consider the consequences of their action, or even care — their purpose was, after all, to undermine confidence in their government. One can only speculate whether our vigorous defense of the principle of confidentiality reassured Peking or whether it was irrelevant.

After some weeks of excitement the secret trip was nearly upon us. I chose my associates: John Holdridge, a Foreign Service Officer and China specialist who handled East Asia on the NSC staff; Dick Smyser, another Foreign Service Officer and Vietnam expert on my staff; Winston Lord, formerly of State and Defense and now my special assistant on the most sensitive matters, a trusted confidant and close friend.

I have always believed that the secret of negotiations is meticulous preparation. The negotiator should know not only the technical side of the subject but its nuances. He must above all have a clear conception of his objectives and the routes to reach them. He must study the psychology and purposes of his opposite number and determine whether and how to reconcile them with his own. He must have all this at his finger-tips because the impression of indecisiveness invites hesitation or intran-sigence; the need for frequent consultation at the negotiating table un-dermines authority. This is why my associates and I repaired to Key Biscayne over the weekend of June 19–20 to review the briefing papers, which had already been rewritten many times — and were to be rewrit-ten again several times more before we set off. (I used to tell a story about a Harvard professor who demanded that a student write ten suc-cessive redrafts of a term paper, returning each one with the query: ''Can't you do better than that?'' After the tenth draft the student ex-claimed in exasperation: ''No, I can't do better than that.'' ''In that case,'' the professor said, ''now I will read it.'' Though the story is apocryphal, my staff came to believe that they lived through it.) The volumes of briefing papers included information on the topics I expected to discuss with Chou En-lai — Indochina, Soviet relations, India and Pakistan, trade and exchanges, Taiwan, and Americans imprisoned in China. The papers reviewed Peking's known attitudes on these issues and sketched the positions that I should take. (Much of this material was drawn from the interagency studies we had ordered within the NSC sys-tem.) There were a draft of an opening statement and a general paper on the purpose of the trip and the strategy to pursue. The exercise of com-posing these papers sharpened my own thinking; they could be reviewed by the President, giving him the opportunity to approve and shape the approach.

In that month of exhausting preparations we also had to look after the other side of the triangle. On June 8 I took Anatoly Dobrynin to Camp David for a leisurely discussion of US–Soviet relations. Dobrynin told me benignly that the Soviet Union had no objection to a gradual im-provement of our relations with China; he even gave me the Soviet assessment of individual Chinese leaders. He continued his cat-and-mouse game about a Moscow summit. The tentative schedule of Sep-tember 1971 was now slipping on various pretexts as the Soviets sought to extract additional concessions on other negotiations, especially Berlin and a European security conference. But it was comforting to hold cards of which the other side was unaware. When I told Dobrynin that after fourteen months of exploration the time for setting a date for the summit seemed to have arrived, he must have judged again that he was dealing with an exploitable impatience. In fact, I was in no great hurry; I simply wanted to determine the sequence of the looming summits. I slightly preferred the Peking summit first. Had he responded favorably, we would have had a tricky problem in deciding which summit should have precedence. The Soviets again inadvertently solved the problem for us. I tried to imagine Dobrynin's reaction if I had suddenly told him where I meant to be in a month's time.

On June 10 the White House published the list of items withdrawn from export controls for trade with China in accordance with the Presidential decisions of April 14. A press release and statement by Ron Ziegler announced that a broad range of nonstrategic goods was being made available for export to China; Chinese commercial imports were also being permitted for the first time in twenty years. The statement noted that we would "later consider the possibility of further steps" toward China. The greater part of the unilateral restrictions imposed on China since the Forties and Fifties had now been dismantled. The time of signaling was ending; negotiations were next.

On June 28 a gossip item in the *New York Times* listed me as a possible future ambassador to Peking. Bill Rogers thought it was funny; I joked that it was probably a State Department leak to get me as far away from Washington as possible. Rogers teased that it was not a bad trip if one wanted to get away from it all. I agreed. I loved the food, I said.

On June 30 the White House press secretary made a brief announcement at his regular briefing that President Nixon was sending me on a fact-finding mission to South Vietnam from July 2 to 5. I would then go to Paris to consult with Ambassador David Bruce; on my way to Paris I was to confer with officials in Thailand, India, and Pakistan. In addition, to distract the Soviets, who were always being kept informed by Hanoi, I had arranged for another secret meeting with Le Duc Tho in Paris for July 12. Thus there would be no gap in my schedule to arouse suspicion.

At last July 1 dawned, the day when my companions and I would set off in a cramped and uncomfortable plane for the most momentous journey of our lives.

XIX

The Journey to Peking

"Polo I": Prelude

I HAD one of the more painful meetings of my career on July 1, 1971. The Ambassador of the Republic of China, James Shen, came to see me about preserving Taiwan's seat at the next United Nations General Assembly vote on Chinese representation. Shen lodged an extensive objection to the State Department plan for "dual representation," which would have attempted to admit Peking to the UN without expelling Taiwan. I found it difficult to concentrate on the details, for that July 1 was the very day I was due to leave on my trip to Asia for the secret rendezvous in Peking. No government less deserved what was about to happen to it than that of Taiwan. It had been a loyal ally; its conduct toward us had been exemplary. Its representatives, most notably its Ambassador, had behaved with that matter-of-fact reliability and subtle intelligence characteristic of the Chinese people. I found my role with Shen particularly painful, since I knew that before long his esoteric discussion of UN procedural maneuvers would be overtaken by more elemental events; but I could say nothing to him, and indeed it was essential that I maintained as normal and nonchalant a schedule as possible.

My diary shows that as well as Shen I met the Counsellor to the President, Don Rumsfeld; the Mexican Foreign Minister, Emilio Rabasa; and the Indian Ambassador, L. K. Jha. I also had three meetings with the President for a total of over two hours to review my briefing books. Later accounts spoke of night meetings in the Lincoln Sitting Room with a thoughtful President and a reflective security adviser and Secretary of State, jointly planning strategy. These were mostly public relations hogwash. I was later asked by a journalist for an interview on these meetings and begged Haldeman to spare me. He agree. "You can only lie so far," he acknowledged, adding a new dimension to the moral imperative of truthfulness. In fact, though I had conversed there with Nixon when I relayed the Chinese message of June 2, we rarely met in the Lincoln Sitting Room and never with Rogers. Our talks on the China trip were almost always in the Oval Office or in Nixon's Executive Office Building hideaway. On July 1 we discussed primarily the impact the opening to China might have on Soviet attitudes and on the war in Vietnam. A great deal of time was spent on the order in which the prospective summits with China and the Soviet Union might be held; we still had not heard from Moscow about a September meeting. We decided that whatever the response, the China summit would now come first.

The trip heightened the nervous sensitivity of Nixon's public relations antennae. Having made the decisions without executive or Congressional consultation, Nixon had left himself quite naked should anything go wrong; in such lonely decisions he was extremely courageous. But in his complicated personality high motives constantly warred with less lofty considerations. He was eager to be known as the first American leader to visit Peking; he therefore requested me periodically to change the venue of my own visit to any other place in China. I did not know how to put this to either the Pakistanis or the Chinese. We had already raised suspicions by insisting on secrecy. Being unfamiliar with Chinese security or internal processes of consultation, we would probably feed these suspicions by seeking to prescribe the talks' location. So I procrastinated, as Nixon could tell from the messages to Peking — every one of which he saw before it went out and none of which suggested a different venue. I left Washington, however, still being urged to find another site.

Another desire of Nixon was that the communiqué announcing my visit not mention my name; he wanted his name and Chou En-lai's to be the first on an official Sino-American document. He did not explain how one could announce the visit of an American emissary to Peking without revealing the emissary's name unless one wanted to get a reputation in China for complete inscrutability. Reality took care of this problem. Nixon also wanted Chinese assurances that no other American political figure would be invited before his visit. I had raised this indirectly with Hilaly but decided to defer such requests until I arrived in Peking, all the more readily as none of us had the slightest idea of what we would find when we got there.

About a week before my departure I had shown the President the briefing book that my staff and I had put together. The big black tome had been given the code name "Polo," presumably after an earlier China visitor of European origin. Nixon studied the cover memorandum carefully and covered the front page with handwritten notes. The book began with a "scope paper" outlining China's probable purposes in inviting me, and our purposes in accepting.

No doubt, my paper argued, the Chinese expected to enhance their country's international standing and undercut that of Taiwan; some disarray among our allies and friends might result; the Soviet Union would be faced with new complexities. It might even turn out to be true, as many experts believed, that Peking's basic goal was that the United States get out of Asia; there was undoubtedly some advantage to be gained among militant revolutionaries by humiliating us. But on balance I did not think that such a course was likely or compatible with the circumstances that produced my visit and the invitation to the President. "We have assumed," my memorandum read, "that they are acting in part in response to the Soviet military threat along their borders, and it would not help them to humiliate us if they want to use us in some way as a counterweight to the Soviets." American withdrawal from Asia, which Chinese propaganda (and American domestic critics) had called for in years past, would not really suit Chinese purposes either, since it would leave a vacuum that the Soviets could attempt to fill. The Chinese were bound to realize that an attempt to pressure us might generate enough resentment to speed the much feared US–Soviet condominium. In time, my memorandum argued, the Chinese might even see value in the continuing close American relationship with Japan, which loomed increasingly large in Chinese eyes as a rival and potential threat.

In consequence, I proposed on my visit to concentrate on the fundamentals of the international situation that had brought about my visit, on the conjunction of purposes that each side seemed to wish to confirm. Within that framework I would discuss China's international role, some form of understanding not to resort to force in our bilateral relations, the reduction of our forces on Taiwan, and Chinese perceptions of the Soviet Union. I would seek some moderating influence on Indochina, keeping in mind that the mere fact of the meeting and the subsequent summit was bound massively to demoralize Hanoi. We would seek to set up some communication not dependent on third parties. We would no doubt encounter the Middle Kingdom syndrome that we were barbarians come to pay tribute to the center of culture and politics, but we could live with these pretensions "in full confidence of our own place in history and national strength."

In addition, the briefing book contained a lengthy draft opening statement, talking points on various issues, and extensive background papers. I cannot tell how thoroughly Nixon reviewed this material; his usual procedure was to concentrate on the cover memorandum and ignore the backup papers.

On July 1, Nixon and I spent most of our time together reviewing the comments he had scrawled on the cover page. They contained his invariable hard-line rhetoric with which he sent me off on every mission. He wanted me to stress that if pressed he would "turn hard on Vietnam." He thought I should keep in play a "possible move towards the Soviets," showing a subtle understanding of the triangular diplomacy.

He wanted me to emphasize that China's fear of Japan could best be assuaged by a continuing US–Japanese alliance. Not all of Nixon's concerns were on the plane of high policy. He also wanted me to repeat yet again what had already been conveyed through Hilaly — that he wanted "a severe limit on political visitors" prior to any Presidential visit. He asked me to arrange for grain shipments before his own trip, which would help placate his conservative critics. Giving vent to his dislike of Pierre Trudeau, he remarked that future contacts or channels with the Chinese could take place anywhere except Ottawa. Most of this was boilerplate on which I knew Nixon would not insist if I should succeed in arranging the cherished summit. Nixon was too experienced not to know that we could cover pages with words, but we would not be able to shape events until we had met the Chinese.

I set off from Andrews Air Force Base at about eight o'clock in the evening. I was to visit Saigon, Bangkok, and New Delhi before landing in Islamabad, capital of Pakistan and springboard to my real destination. At each stop, whatever the main subject of my conversations, I tried to soften in advance the impact of the announcement I knew would be forthcoming. Speaking of Ping-Pong diplomacy and our easing of trade restrictions, I explained the reasons why we had decided to try to move toward China, stressing principally the needs of the global equilibrium. I told Indira Gandhi that we would continue to oppose unprovoked military pressures by any nuclear power, as enunciated in the Nixon Doctrine. We must await the memoirs of my interlocutors to learn whether this was subsequently regarded as duplicity or understood as the only reassurance that circumstances permitted.

The unsung hero of this trip was Winston Lord. Not only had he supervised the substantive preparations, he also had to keep track of the distribution of documents within my party. This was a monumental task. For there were three levels of knowledge. Some knew where I was going and what I would say when I got there. Others knew of my destination but not of my agenda, being along to assist me on the other stops. Still others were aware of neither. Lord had to see to it that each group received papers and schedules appropriate to its knowledge, and no other. And he had to do this while making sure the briefing papers for each stop were up to date, urged on by my proverbially gentle and characteristically polite instructions. He managed to retain everybody's respect and his own sanity, not the meanest achievement of the journey.

Throughout the trip I received backchannel messages from Washington through which my deputy Al Haig kept me in touch with the feverish mood of the White House. Haldeman conveyed a Presidential injunction that my party refrain from commenting to State Department personnel about the Pentagon Papers. When I queried the meaning of this odd request, it transpired that Haldeman was merely expressing the President's long-standing disquiet about the loyalty of my staff; he feared that they might encourage what he took to be the sympathy of State Department officials for those who had leaked the documents. Within hours of my leaving town, Rogers showed that he had learned some bureaucratic lessons. He attempted to use my absence to obtain Presidential authority for a trip by Joe Sisco to the Middle East for another round of negotiations; indeed, two emissaries were already leaving for Cairo for preliminary contacts when Rogers's memorandum arrived. It was too transparent a maneuver. From Saigon I cabled that such a trip now would only accelerate tensions in the Middle East and should be deferred. I suggested the device of scheduling an NSC meeting on the Middle East for a date soon after my return. The President agreed.

Waiting was apparently more nerve-racking for those in Washington than for us who were all being kept busy. Repeatedly I received instructions saying yet again what I had already been told innumerable times before leaving: no names in the communiqué; no other politicians to China before Nixon. Another wave of panic hit when the White House learned that columnist James Reston would be visiting Peking just when I was. In the light of this "suspicious turn of events," I was advised to get an urgent message to my "hosts" (the cover name for the Chinese, subtly chosen to confuse communicators since Peking had been mentioned earlier in the paragraph) at my next stop (New Delhi), asking them to defer Reston's visit or to provide me "with the necessary assurances." I could not visualize marching into Peking's Embassy in New Delhi without attracting at least some Indian attention. I therefore cabled back: "As for Reston, host's decision will not be affected by my protestations. . . . I am sure they can maintain secrecy if they wish."

On July 5, while I was still in Bangkok, Haig informed me that Vorontsov had delivered the Soviets' long-awaited reply on a summit. They now proposed postponing it from September 1971, as had been scheduled, until later in the year; even then, it was made conditional upon progress in ongoing negotiations and upon the "assumption" that nothing happened in the interval to complicate the situation. Once again, the Soviets had unwittingly done us an enormous favor; they had outfoxed themselves. The Kremlin's reply freed us from the complexity of managing two parallel summits. Moscow could not blame us for opening first to Peking. We could now complete our design with a minimum of friction.

I cabled Haig that no reply should be returned to Vorontsov and that Ambassador Kenneth Rush in Bonn should find some pretext to avoid further Berlin negotiations until I was back. I commented that I considered the Soviet reply "not an unalloyed disadvantage" because a Soviet summit could now take place later and under much better psychological circumstances. Nixon was outraged by the Soviet reply and looked for ways to retaliate. I counseled against showing any irritation or indeed reacting at all. If we played a "cool, deliberate game" a favorable outcome was probable; we could not afford the luxury of "succumbing to pique." The next ten days, I was convinced, would supply a more effective riposte than any formal reply.

Against this backdrop of Washington apprehension and superpower maneuvering, I headed for Islamabad. My stay had been carefully planned by the indefatigable Farland through CIA backchannel cables. Code names that might have fooled a five-year-old for three minutes were used at every opportunity (mine was "the principal"). One problem was how to free myself from the ubiquitous protocol of a high-level visit. Our original thought was that Yahya should ostensibly invite me to a hill station for a quiet talk. This had the disadvantage that I would have had to schedule a stay of seventy-two hours. In the inflamed atmosphere of the civil war in East Pakistan and the flood of Bengali refugees into India, to stay a day longer in Pakistan than in India would have been interpreted as favoritism to Pakistan, with repercussions in New Delhi, our bureaucracy, the media, and above all the Congress. Yahya would have had to disappear for two days, raising the risk of a leak on the Pakistani side. And it was in any event inappropriate to use a head of state entirely for purposes of cover.

I had therefore suggested that we publish a schedule that would have me in Pakistan only forty-eight hours, from July 8 to 10, roughly equal to my stay in India. Upon arrival I would plead a stomachache. The Embassy dispensary would be asked for medication. My discomfort would get progressively worse until Yahya would invite me over dinner to use the Presidential rest house in Nathiagali in the mountains to recover. Under this pretext I could add an extra day to my Pakistan stay and disappear for two days to Peking. It was still not as easy as it looked. If I "fell ill," how could we prevent the Embassy doctor from rushing to take care of me? And how could one restrain Embassy personnel trained through years in the Foreign Service to be at the beck and call of Presidential emissaries twenty-four hours of every day? Our ingenious ambassador found a solution that can be best summarized in his own backchannel cable: "Embassy doctor no longer any problem. He departs 06 July. Embassy nurse is quite containable under these circumstances and would not seek to intrude herself. DCM [Deputy Chief of Mission] goes on leave 07 July; US AID director departs on home leave 02 July. Everyone else is manageable." It was almost surely the first time in the long and distinguished history of the Foreign Service that an ambassador prided himself on getting all his key people out of town for the visit of a representative of the President and that he was commended by Washington for his thoughtfulness. (The gods decided to punish me for human presumption; in New Delhi I developed a genuine stomachache through which I had to suffer in secret lest I ruin my credibility when we reached Pakistan.)

Our planning had even provided for the contingency of being found out. In that case a simple statement was to be released by the White House along these lines: "Dr. Kissinger is meeting with leaders of the People's Republic of China at their request. There will be a statement after Dr. Kissinger returns and reports to the President." I had no illusion that so bland a statement would have quieted the uproar.

My visit to Islamabad followed the script to the letter. There was a lunch at Ambassador Farland's residence with what was left of the Embassy staff, a meeting with President Yahya, a briefing at the Embassy, and then again a private dinner with Yahya and senior associates. I was probably responsible for the last pleasant day Yahya had before he was overthrown as a result of the India-Pakistan war in December of that year. For Yahya was enthralled by the cops-and-robbers atmosphere of the enterprise. He personally reviewed each detail of my clandestine departure; he put the full facilities of his government at our disposal and lent me his trusted personal pilot. He asked nothing in return — contrary to many media claims at the time. His courtesy was not matched by equally generous treatment from our government amid the upheaval in East Pakistan. Yahya was a bluff, direct soldier of limited imagination caught up after the convulsion in East Pakistan in events for which neither experience nor training prepared him. He made grievous mistakes. Yet he performed a great service for our country; and it must be recorded that he dealt with us honorably.

During the course of his dinner in my honor Yahya began implementing our plan. My stomachache became a topic of general conversation. He announced loudly that the heat of Islamabad would impede my recovery; he urged that I repair to Nathiagali, a private estate adjoining a presidential guest house in the hills above Murree. When I demurred, he insisted, against all the evidence of history, that in a Moslem country the host's and not the guest's wishes are decisive. He was so convincing that one of my Secret Service agents who overheard the conversation immediately arranged for a colleague to make an "advance" visit to the hill station. Around midnight the agent called in great distress; he had looked over the guest house and found it unsuitable. There was nothing left to do other than to ask the Pakistanis to detain the hapless agent in Nathiagali until my return from Peking.

One of my last communications from San Clemente before my departure informed me that the President had at last — on July 8 — informed his Secretary of State of my China trip, putting it that the visit was a last-minute decision in response to an invitation I had received while in Pakistan. I was also told by backchannel, hours before taking off for Peking, to keep in mind that the public relations experts considered

10:30 P.M. Washington time, July 15, the optimum time for any announcement. Finally, I was warned that Mel Laird, in Tokyo, had helpfully declared to a Japanese news conference that he was not opposed to an independent Japanese nuclear capability and that the SALT talks would confirm a strategic parity that might provide an incentive for a Japanese nuclear program.

None of this could still my sense of excitement and anticipation as I retired around 11:00 P.M. after my dinner with Yahya. For the only time in office I had difficulty sleeping. I tried to imagine what lay ahead. For the only time, too, I had a feeling of some insecurity about so momentous a mission in an unknown capital where I would be cut off from all communication.

At 3:30 on the morning of July 9 I arose in the state guest house in Islamabad and had an early breakfast. At 4:00 A.M. I and my party were driven in Pakistani military vehicles to Chaklala Airport, escorted by Foreign Secretary Sultan Khan. My assistants Winston Lord, John Holdridge, and Dick Smyser were with me, as well as Secret Service agents John D. Ready and Gary McLeod. At Farland's suggestion, I had with me a hat and sunglasses to ensure that no stray pedestrian spotted me — an unlikely contingency at that hour in Islamabad, where my name was scarcely a household word. A Boeing 707 of Pakistani International Airlines (PIA) was waiting at the military side of the airport. The plane had made a test run to Peking over July 6–7 and returned with Chinese navigators who would accompany the July 9 flight; they remained aboard and out of sight until my staff and I arrived. The aircraft was piloted by Yahya's personal pilot, who had been briefed on the dangers of intercepts of radio communications and would be accordingly circumspect. My own aircraft was parked on the civilian side of Chaklala, well out of sight of the PIA Boeing and well within view of any stray journalists or Embassy personnel.

Before departing, I wrote out by hand a brief cable to Haig confirming that I understood the preferred time for the announcement of Nixon's journey. I informed San Clemente that the Chinese had sent not merely three navigators but a senior four-man delegation to accompany me on the flight. President Yahya had told me that the Chinese were "very hurt" by the American insistence on secrecy and would probably wish a full announcement. "Got off in fine shape," my message concluded. At 4:30 A.M. we were airborne for Peking, a flight of twenty-five hundred miles and four and three-quarter hours.

A few hours later, at 8:00 A.M. on July 9, while I was already approaching Peking, the cover plan went into effect. A dummy motorcade proceeded without me on the three-hour, fifty-mile journey to Nathiagali; its passengers included Ambassador Farland, my aide David Halperin, two other Secret Service agents, and Pakistani aide M. M.

Ahmed. Hal Saunders (who was familiar with the plan) remained in Islamabad to discuss bilateral issues with Pakistani officials and to handle emergencies. At 9:00 A.M. the next day (when I had already been in Peking nearly twenty-four hours), David Halperin, from Nathiagali, phoned Hal Saunders in Islamabad to "inform" him that I needed an extra day's rest and to cancel my appointments. Halperin also phoned the pilot of my official aircraft and requested that he file the necessary changes in the flight plan. The Embassy was instructed to send out cables to the remaining stops — Tehran (a short refueling stop), Paris, San Clemente, and also Washington — notifying them of my "revised schedule."

Aboard the PIA Boeing at Chaklala Airport in the early morning of July 9, the first person I saw was Chang Wen-chin, head of the West European, American, and Oceania Department of the Chinese Foreign Ministry, whom Chou En-lai, as a token of the importance he attached to the visit, had sent to escort me to Peking. (Perhaps on the theory that all Westerners look alike, the Chinese Foreign Office grouped Western Europe, the Americas, Australia, and New Zealand into one department.) Looking like a Spanish cardinal in an El Greco painting — though of course in Mao uniform — Chang combined austere elegance and understated intelligence. His command of English was awe-inspiring. He rarely spoke it, but it stood him in good stead in drafting sessions. He greeted us as if it were the most natural thing in the world for a senior Chinese diplomat to travel twenty-five hundred miles to accompany a capitalist official to the seat of a government that proclaimed itself the fountainhead of world revolution.

With him was the interpreter T'ang Wen-sheng — the formidable Nancy T'ang — born in Brooklyn and therefore speaking perfect American English. I used to tease her that because she was born in the United States, she, unlike me, was not barred by the Constitution from becoming President. It was a prospect unlikely to tempt her; her intelligence and vivacity for a long time obscured her fanatical ideological dedication. She considered herself more than an interpreter; on several occasions she did not hesitate to argue with Chou En-lai in our presence. The third member of Chang's party was Wang Hai-jung, a Foreign Ministry official. She was reported to be Mao's niece or grandniece, a shy, gentle person with the look of an easily startled deer. (The two women would turn out to be at all my meetings with Mao as well as those with Chou.) The fourth member was T'ang Lung-pin from the protocol department.

I had never met any Chinese Communists; neither, I must add, had the members of my Secret Service detail, who had not been told of my destination and who nearly had heart attacks at what they were witnessing. Their charge was not merely flying in a foreign airplane — which was contrary to all the principles of their training — but was being whisked by a group of Communist Chinese to locations for which there had been no "advance" and in which they would have no way of telling who constituted a security risk. Jack Ready and Gary McLeod did their duty by sticking grimly by my side wherever we were taken; they insisted even on sitting in on the meetings with Chou En-lai. (Later on, the Chinese excluded security personnel.) They guarded our two heavy bags full of classified material, carrying them everywhere, including to meals and on the tour of the Forbidden City. They comported themselves as if they were a match for whatever 800 million Chinese might throw at them.

The Middle Kingdom: First Meeting with Chou En-lai

IT is not often that one can recapture as an adult the quality that in one's youth made time seem to stand still; that gave every event the mystery of novelty; that enabled each experience to be relished because of its singularity. As we grow older we comfort ourselves with the familiar for which we have developed rote responses. In the same measure, as the world becomes more routine time seems to speed up; life becomes a kaleidoscope of seemingly interchangeable experiences. Only some truly extraordinary event, both novel and moving, both unusual and overwhelming, restores the innocence of the years when each day was a precious adventure in defining the meaning of life. This is how it was for me as the aircraft crossed the snow-capped Himalayas, thrusting toward the heavens in the roseate glow of a rising sun. We flew very close to K-2, the second highest mountain in the world. I had always thought of China as a densely populated, highly cultivated country, but we flew for hours over barren deserts dotted by oases. Winston Lord is quite proud that he was standing farthest forward in the aircraft when it crossed the border and thus was technically the first official American into China.

The Chinese and we sat around a table in easy conversation, as if there had never been a day's interruption in contacts between our nations; there was nothing to remind one of the bitter invective that only yesterday had been routine in all our countries' public discourse about each other. They probed gently into the reason for our insistence on secrecy. Were we ashamed to acknowledge meeting Chinese leaders? The slight of John Foster Dulles's refusal to shake Chou En-lai's hand at the 1954 Geneva Conference on Indochina had not been forgotten; it was referred to on the flight and on many occasions in the days afterward and on subsequent visits. I told Chang that the purpose of my trip was to announce a new period in our relationship, but it was best that we agree first on the context. He said that Premier Chou En-lai would be prepared to explore all subjects.

We landed at a military airport at the outskirts of Peking at fifteen minutes after noon Peking time, Friday, July 9. We were greeted by Marshal Yeh Chien-ying, one of the most senior members of the Chinese Politburo and Vice Chairman of the Military Affairs Committee; Huang Hua, recently appointed Ambassador to Canada (later China's first UN Ambassador and later still Foreign Minister); Han Hsu, Acting Chief of Protocol (later Deputy Chief of the Chinese Liaison Office in Washington); and another interpreter, Chi Ch'ao-chu, who had studied chemistry at Harvard and since gone on to better things. He had been with Mao and Edgar Snow during the parade review.

Marshal Yeh Chien-ying took me into the city in a large limousine, with curtains drawn. Peeking from behind the curtain, I glimpsed wide, clean streets with little traffic except bicycles. We drove through the massive Tien An Men Square. Our destination was a guest house for state visitors, one of many in a large walled-off park in the western part of the city. The park, I was told, used to contain the imperial fishing lake. Each of the many guest houses is located on a small peninsula connected to its neighbor by a small elegant bridge. The whole complex conveys a sense of extraordinary spaciousness, jarred only by the shock of a sentry emerging from concealment behind a bush when one attempts to cross a bridge. (The sentries later became less obtrusive and the whole park was opened up to guests.)

The houses were legacies of the period of Soviet influence; they were built in the heavy, stately, Victorian style that in Communist countries confirms status. In the reception room, overstuffed heavy chairs and sofas formed a quadrangle, where Marshal Yeh made us feel at home and shared tea with us. On the drive to the guest house he had apologized for being unable to give me an appropriate public reception; this would be remedied when the President visited Peking (a prediction which was not, in fact, totally fulfilled). The Marshal invited us to one of the many meals of staggering variety and quantity that caused me to speculate to our hosts that somewhere thousands of years ago a Chinese had been accused of starving an important guest and they were determined not to allow this to occur again.

Chou En-lai arrived at 4:30. His gaunt, expressive face was dominated by piercing eyes, conveying a mixture of intensity and repose, of wariness and calm self-confidence. He wore an immaculately tailored gray Mao tunic, at once simple and elegant. He moved gracefully and with dignity, filling a room not by his physical dominance (as did Mao or de Gaulle) but by his air of controlled tension, steely discipline, and self-control, as if he were a coiled spring. He conveyed an easy casualness, which, however, did not deceive the careful observer. The quick smile, the comprehending expression that made clear he understood English even without translation, the palpable alertness, were clearly the features of a man who had had burned into him by a searing half-

century the vital importance of self-possession. I greeted him at the door
of the guest house and ostentatiously stuck out my hand. Chou gave me
a quick smile and took it. It was the first step in putting the legacy of the
past behind us.

Unlike Mao, Chou had lived abroad; born of a middle-class family in
1898, he had been a brilliant student and had studied and worked in
France and Germany in the 1920s. When I met him, he had been a
leader of the Chinese Communist movement for nearly fifty years. He
had been on the Long March. He had been the only Premier the People's Republic had had — nearly twenty-two years — and for nine of
those years he had also been Foreign Minister. Chou had negotiated
with General Marshall in the 1940s. He was a figure out of history. He
was equally at home in philosophy, reminiscence, historical analysis,
tactical probes, humorous repartee. His command of facts, in particular
his knowledge of American events and, for that matter, of my own
background, was stunning. There was little wasted motion either in his
words or in his movements. Both reflected the inner tensions of a man
concerned, as he stressed, with the endless daily problems of a people
of 800 million and the effort to preserve ideological faith for the next
generation. How to invite President Nixon in a manner that accommodated all these concerns was clearly a matter of some emotion and
difficulty for him.

For it was evident that to the Chinese our arrival had an even deeper
meaning than for the American party. To us it was the beginning of an
advantageous new turn in international relations. For the Chinese it had
to be a personal, intellectual, and emotional crisis. They had started as a
tiny splinter group, with no hope for victory, endured the Long March,
fought Japan and a civil war, opposed us in Korea and then took on the
Soviets, and imposed the Cultural Revolution on themselves. And yet
here they were — conferring with the archenemy of twenty-five years
while we intervened in what they considered a "war of liberation" on
their very border — acting out an encounter of philosophical contradictions. This moral ambivalence was reflected in a certain brooding
quality of Chou's, in the occasional schizophrenia of his presentation, in
the jagged rhythm in which the announcement of my visit was drafted,
interspersed with epic tales of the Long March and accounts of Mao's
inspirational leadership. Yet there was also about Chou an inner serenity
that enabled him, I would soon learn, to eschew the petty maneuvers
that characterized our negotiations with other Communists. All our
meetings on this and my subsequent visits lasted for many hours (sessions of five to seven hours were not uncommon); yet on no occasion
did he reveal any impatience or imply that he had anything else to do.
We were never interrupted by phone calls or the bureaucratic necessities
of running a huge state. I do not know how he managed it; I used to

*Strategy session over breakfast with Ambassadors David Bruce and
Ellsworth Bunker, July 22, 1970.*

Meeting in Ireland to discuss imminent Vietnam cease-fire initiative, October 3, 1970. From left: Bruce, Nixon, Rogers, HAK, Habib.

Planning the Laos operation, January 1971. From left: Helms, HAK, Rogers, Nixon, Laird, Admiral Thomas Moorer (Chairman, Joint Chiefs of Staff).

Conferring after the Laos operation has begun, February 10, 1971.

Greeted on my arrival in Pakistan, July 8, 1971, by three colleagues who know my real ultimate destination. From left: US Ambassador Joseph Farland, HAK, Foreign Secretary Sultan Khan, and Agha Hilaly, Pakistan's Ambassador to the US.

Secret arrival in Peking, July 9, 1971. From left: Wang Hai-jung, Chi Ch'ao-chu, Marshal Yeh Chien-ying, Huang Hua, HAK, Chang Wen-chin, Nancy T'ang.

Secret trip to Peking. ABOVE: *Meeting Chou En-lai, July 9, 1971.* RIGHT: *A banquet with Chou En-lai.*

A tour of the Forbidden City. Front, from left: Huang Hua, HAK, Chi Ch'ao-chu, the director of China's museums. Back row, from left: Winston Lord, Richard Smyser, Agent Jack Ready, unidentified, John Holdridge, Agent Gary McLeod.

Greeted by Nixon in San Clemente on my return from Peking, July 13, 1971 (in helicopter doorway, Al Haig).

After my China trip, September 1971.

At the Great Wall on my second trip to China, October 1971.

Nixon meets with the Old Guard, December 1970. From left: Lucius Clay, Thomas E. Dewey, Dean Acheson, Nixon, John McCloy, HAK.

A visit with Prime Minister Indira Gandhi in New Delhi as the India-Pakistan crisis builds, July 7, 1971 (center, US Ambassador Kenneth Keating).

Secretary of the Treasury John Connally (photo taken after he left office, July 1972).

In San Clemente, August 1971.

*With newsmen before my departure for my second trip
to China, October 16, 1971.*

In Nixon's hideaway office in the Executive Office Building, November 1971.

joke that senior officials in Washington would probably not be able to free so much time for the Second Coming.

Chou could also display an extraordinary personal graciousness. When junior members of our party took ill, he would visit them. Despite the gap in our protocol rank he insisted that our meetings alternate between my residence and the Great Hall of the People so that he would call on me as often as I called on him. After we had settled on Paris as our future point of contact, Chou nevertheless proposed that we continue to use the Pakistani channel occasionally because "we have a saying in China that one shouldn't break the bridge after crossing it."

On one occasion (in June 1972) I told him that the soldiers who stepped forward on the bridges connecting the various guest cottages made me feel like the plumber in Kafka's novel *The Castle,* who, having been summoned and then denied entrance, spent his life trying to get in, having quite forgotten why he was summoned in the first place. I did not know why I wanted to get across that bridge; but I knew I did. Chou laughed but did nothing during that trip. My next trip took place in February 1973; on my very last night, as I was packing my bags, a woman from protocol knocked at my door and told me that the Premier invited me to a private talk. We were driven to another guest house on the other side of the lake, where Chou En-lai and I talked until three in the morning. As I took my leave he suddenly said in English: "Let's take a walk." While continuing our chat, we crossed two bridges; he then entered his car, which had been following us, and drove off. It was an extraordinary gesture.

Even the Chinese seemed to regard him with special reverence, to see in him of all their leaders a special human quality. On a visit in late 1975 I asked a young interpreter about Chou's health; tears brimmed in her eyes as she told me he was gravely ill. It was no accident that he was so deeply mourned in China after his death, or that the extraordinary expressions of yearning for greater freedom that appeared in China in the late 1970s invoked and praised his name.

Chou En-lai, in short, was one of the two or three most impressive men I have ever met. Urbane, infinitely patient, extraordinarily intelligent, subtle, he moved through our discussions with an easy grace that penetrated to the essence of our new relationship as if there were no sensible alternative. The challenge of bringing together two societies so estranged by ideology and history was considerable. Conventional wisdom would have counseled the removal of specific causes of tension; but there was one cause of tension — Taiwan — that permitted no rapid solution, while the others were too trivial to provide the basis of an enduring relationship. The answer was to discuss fundamentals: our perceptions of global and especially Asian affairs, in a manner that clarified our purposes and perspectives and thereby bridged two decades of mutual ignorance. Precisely because there was little practical business to be done, the element of confidence had to emerge from conceptual discussions. Chou and I spent hours together essentially giving shape to intangibles of mutual understanding.

Chou set the tone within the first half hour of our encounter. I had prepared a long and slightly pendantic opening statement, reciting the history of US–Chinese relations that had led up to the present meeting. At the end of its introductory part I said with an attempt at eloquence: "Many visitors have come to this beautiful, and to us, mysterious land." Chou held up his hand: "You will find it not mysterious. When you have become familiar with it, it will not be as mysterious as before." I was taken aback, but Chou was certainly right. Our concern was not the bilateral issues between us — at least at first. We had to build confidence; to remove the mystery. This was his fundamental purpose with me, as was mine with him.

So it happened that the talks between Chou and me were longer and deeper than with any other leader I met during my public service, except possibly Anwar Sadat. Two ideological enemies presented their respective views of the world with a frankness rarely achieved among allies and with a depth that one experiences only in the presence of a great man. On my first visit, I spent seventeen hours in talks with Chou En-lai. On each succeeding visit during his premiership we spent between six to ten hours together each day with no interruption except for meals. And even then the conversation would be philosophical, humorous, and illuminating. The same pattern was repeated when Nixon visited China. Thus was built a structure that has withstood many stresses and has emerged as one of the foundations of contemporary international relations.

The impact of personalities on events is never easy to define. To be sure, China and the United States were brought together by necessity; it was not abstract goodwill but converging interests that brought me to Peking; it was not personal friendship with Chou but a commonly perceived danger that fostered the elaboration of our relationship. But that these interests were perceived clearly and acted upon decisively was due to leadership that — on both sides — skillfully used the margin of choice available. That China and the United States would seek rapprochement in the early 1970s was inherent in the world environment. That it should occur so rapidly and develop so naturally owed no little to the luminous personality and extraordinary perception of the Chinese Premier.

Of course, Chou and I used each other; that is on one level the purpose of diplomacy. But another of its purposes is to bring about a compatibility of aims; only the amateur or the insecure thinks he can permanently outmaneuver his opposite number. In foreign policy one must never forget that one deals in recurring cycles and on consecutive issues with the same people; trickery sacrifices structure to temporary benefit. Reliability is the cement of international order even among opponents; pettiness is the foe of permanence. This Chou En-lai grasped, and it enabled us to achieve not identical aims but comparable analyses of what was needed to use the international equilibrium to our mutual benefit at this particular moment in history.

Chou never bargained to score petty points. I soon found that the best way to deal with him was to present a reasonable position, explain it meticulously, and then stick to it. I sometimes went so far as to let him see the internal studies that supported our conclusions. Chou acted the same way; the suicidal method was sharp trading. On one occasion when negotiating the Shanghai Communiqué I objected to two sentences in the section of the communiqué explaining the Chinese point of view. Though we were not responsible for what the Chinese said, I thought that it would lead to controversy in a joint communiqué. I offered to give up two sentences in the section stating the American position in return. "Give your two sentences to your President if you wish," said Chou impatiently. "I do not want them. You do not have to trade; all you have to do is to convince me why our language is embarrassing." He was as good as his word; the most egregious passages disappeared from the Chinese text. (Nothing ever being wasted in China, two months later they showed up again in a Chinese UN speech, but since that was a unilateral document we could ignore them.)

I had no illusions about the system Chou represented nor did I doubt that in serving its purposes he could be as formidable a foe as he was fascinating as an interlocutor. The new society in China had been achieved at an enormous, by my values exorbitant, price. The sacrifices in freedom, spontaneity, culture, family life, seemed to me to go beyond what any group of leaders have a moral right to impose on their people. The Chinese were cold-blooded practitioners of power politics, a far cry from the romantic humanitarians imagined in Western intellectual circles. And yet when Chou died, I felt a great sadness. The world would be less vibrant, the prospects less clearly seen. Neither of us had ever forgotten that our relationship was essentially ambiguous or overlooked the possibility that as history is counted our two countries' paths might be parallel for only a fleeting moment. After that, they might well find themselves again on opposite sides. Should that day come, the Chinese would apply themselves to confrontation with the same determination and shrewdness with which they had practiced cooperation when it served their interests. But one of the rewards of my public life has been that in a moment, however brief in the pitiless measurement of history, I could work with a great man across the barriers of ideology in the endless struggle of statesmen to rescue some permanence from the tenuousness of human foresight.

Chou En-lai and I began our first talk on the afternoon of July 9 at my guest house about four hours after my arrival in Peking. We faced each other across a green-covered table, seated incongruously in large wicker chairs of the kind one finds in old-fashioned summer resorts. He was flanked by Marshal Yeh Chien-ying, Huang Hua, and Chang Wen-chin. Holdridge, Smyser, and Lord composed my team, all of us under the beady eye of Secret Service agents Ready and McLeod, who were not about to leave me to the mercy of unscreened foreigners. I had before me the voluminous briefing book, to which I did not refer again after Chou had interrupted my opening statement. Chou, as always, used only a single sheet of paper with a few words on it, presumably the general headings he wished to discuss.

Chou and I had both reached the conclusion that the most important result of this first encounter would be comprehension by each side of the fundamental purposes of the other. And if we had judged correctly, the necessities that had brought us together would set the direction for our future relationship, provided neither side asked the other to do what its values or interests prohibited. Thus ensued a conversation whose easy banter and stylized character, as if it were a dialogue between two professors of political philosophy, nearly obscured that the penalty of failure would be continued isolation for one side and sharpened international difficulties for the other. An aborted mission would heighten China's risks. It would unquestionably embolden the Soviets. It would discredit us at home; it could easily turn our retreat from Indochina into a rout. Although both Chou and I knew the stakes for each of us and despite an unbreakable deadline of forty-eight hours — I had to reappear in Pakistan within that period if suspicions were not to be aroused — neither of us at that first meeting tested the issue by which my trip would be judged: our ability to agree on a Presidential visit. We both acted as if this were a subsidiary matter that would be easily settled. By pushing each other against the deadline, we both sought to demonstrate that we had other options. With courtesy, philosophical digressions, and occasional humor we sought to convey that we could still turn back, that we had not crossed our Rubicon. And yet all the time we knew that the Rubicon was behind us; we had in fact nowhere to go but forward.

A Presidential visit to China was referred to briefly by us both at the beginning and then we did not return to it until the end of the second day, about eighteen hours before my departure. Instead, Chou spent some time in our first meeting, which lasted nearly seven hours (including dinner), expressing his general agreement with the concepts outlined by Nixon in a speech in Kansas City on July 6. This put me at some disadvantage since I was unaware of either the fact or the content of the speech, proving that even the most meticulous preparation is prey to the accidental. The next morning Chou characteristically had his own, marked-up copy of the English text delivered with my breakfast, with a request to return it since it was his only copy. It turned out to be extemporaneous remarks made by the President to a meeting of Midwestern news media executives gathered for a briefing on domestic policy by Cabinet members and White House aides. Nixon either startled or mystified the assembled executives by discussing the "broader context," "the relationship between these [domestic] programs and the problems that America has in the world." Impelled by his excitement at what he knew to be about to take place, Nixon praised the Chinese as "creative, they are productive, they are one of the most capable people in the world." This is why it was "essential that this Administration take the first steps toward ending the isolation of Mainland China from the world community." He foresaw a world of "five great economic superpowers" (the United States, Western Europe, Japan, the Soviet Union, and China) whose relationship would determine the structure of peace in our time. Chou rejected the appellation of "superpower"; China would not play that game. It was both true and prudent; China needed us precisely because it did not have the strength to balance the Soviet Union by itself.

Chou and I by tacit agreement did not press controversial issues to the hilt. Taiwan was mentioned only briefly during the first session. More time was spent on my explaining our policy in Indochina, with special emphasis on my secret talks with Le Duc Tho, which for a fleeting moment seemed to indicate the possibility of a breakthrough. (We were due for our next meeting with Le Duc Tho in a few days' time.) Whereas the Soviets often flaunted their knowledge of these secret talks, Chou professed to be unaware of them; he confined himself to asking probing questions. It was a good device to avoid being pressed to take a position. Our first day of talks ended at 11:20 P.M. and we had neither settled anything nor even discussed the issue that required a decision.

On Saturday morning, July 10, we were taken to the Forbidden City, the former Imperial Palace built in the fifteenth century. The enormous grounds, normally a popular tourist attraction, had been closed off to the public for a half day so we six Americans could be given a private tour. Accompanied by Huang Hua, we were guided through its beautifully proportioned courtyards, halls and gardens, awed as many foreign emissaries had been before us by the exquisite architecture of red and gold, the stone carvings and bronze lions, the yellow roofs seeming to tumble like waterfalls into the pools of sand that formed the many squares, the sweeping vistas that were once the residence of Chinese emperors who believed it to be the center of the universe and for long periods turned their pretensions into reality. The director of all Chinese archaeological museums took us to an exhibit of recently excavated treasures (many of which later toured the United States).

At noon my meetings with Chou resumed in the Great Hall of the People; that gigantic edifice — undecided between Mussolini neoclassicism and Communist baroque — faces the Forbidden City and was built within thirteen months in 1959 to celebrate the tenth anniversary of the Communist victory in the Chinese civil war. Each large room within it is named for a province of China; there are a banquet hall that can seat several thousand, at least one theater, and innumerable other meeting places. We met in the Fukien Room, named for the Chinese province opposite Taiwan, a subtlety which — like the Snow interview — unfortunately was lost on me since I did not then know the name of the room nor to my shame would have recognized its significance. There is some advantage in invincible obtuseness. (Chou was obliged to point all of this out on a subsequent visit when we met in another room.)

The mood on this occasion was different from that of the previous evening. With very few preliminaries Chou launched into a forceful presentation of the Chinese point of view. With little rhetorical flourish Chou put forward much of what I came later to know as Chinese Communist liturgy — that there was "much turmoil under the heavens"; that Taiwan was part of China; that China supported the "just struggle" of the North Vietnamese; that the big powers were colluding against China (not only the United States and the Soviet Union but also a militaristic Japan); that India was aggressive; that the Soviets were greedy and menacing to the world; that China was not and would never want to be a superpower like America and Russia; that America was in difficulty because we had "stretched out our hands too far." Chou recited this fierce litany and closed with a challenging question — whether, given our vast differences, there was any sense in a Presidential visit.

I responded equally firmly, pointing out that Peking had broached the Presidential visit and that we could not accept any conditions. I would not raise the question again; the Chinese leaders had to decide whether to issue an invitation. I then launched into a deliberately brusque point-by-point rebuttal of Chou's presentation. Chou stopped me after the first point, saying the duck would get cold if we did not eat first.

At lunch over Peking duck the mood changed and Chou's geniality returned. As the lunch ended, Chou turned to the subject of the Cultural Revolution. I demurred that this was China's internal affair, but Chou continued, insisting that if we were to deal with each other an understanding of this drama was critical. With grace masking undoubted anguish, Chou described China as torn between the fear of bureaucratization and the excesses of ideological zeal; he painted the dilemma of a society brought up on faith in a single truth when suddenly many factions representing different truths contended in the streets until the fruits of fifty years of struggle were in jeopardy. He recounted being confined in his office for a couple of days by the Red Guards. He had doubted the necessity of such drastic measures, but Mao had been wiser; he had the vision to look far into the future. In retrospect I doubt that Chou would have raised the point at all had he not wanted to dissociate himself from the Cultural Revolution at least to some extent and to indicate that it was over.

After lunch I resumed my rebuttal for another hour until Chou suddenly, matter-of-factly suggested the summer of 1972 for the President's visit as if all that was left was to decide the timing. He added that he thought it prudent if we met the Soviet leaders first. Aware of Soviet maneuvers regarding a summit, I replied that while a summit in Moscow was probable, the visits should take place in the order in which they had been arranged — first Peking, then Moscow. I did not have the impression that Chou was unhappy about this information. When I indicated that a summer summit close to our elections might be misunderstood, Chou proposed the spring of 1972. I agreed. We adjourned at six because Chou had to host a dinner for another unnamed visitor (we learned later that it was North Korean leader Kim Il-sung). Chou liked to work from about noon to early morning. He proposed that we meet again after dinner at 10:00 P.M. to draft a joint announcement of my visit.

I returned with my staff to the guest house for dinner. All Chinese officials had suddenly disappeared and we were left alone with the staff of the guest house. It was an agonizing evening of rescheduled and then postponed meetings, of nighttime strolls up to the sentries and barely concealed anxiety as to what would happen. (All our strategy talks were held on these walks for fear of eavesdropping.) For all we knew, the Chinese had had second thoughts. Finally, about 11:15 P.M. Chou came back, his state dinner having concluded late. But instead of turning to the communiqué, we ruminated for an hour on the future of India and Germany. His basic point was that India had been the aggressor against China in 1962; there was a great danger of the same policy's being applied to Pakistan in 1971. He designated Huang Hua as his representative for drafting the announcement, and then left.

But Huang Hua did not show up right away. The inexplicable waiting was all the more ominous because we were talking not about an elaborate communiqué but about a statement of a paragraph or two announcing a Presidential visit to Peking. We never found out whether it was a deliberate tactic to unsettle us, whether there was a Politburo meeting, whether Mao insisted on reviewing the talks, or whether, as was most likely, we faced a combination of all these. Finally, Huang Hua showed up without a word of explanation, urbane, affable, imperturbable.

Huang Hua had with him a draft communiqué that produced immediate controversy. In best Middle Kingdom tradition it suggested that Nixon had solicited the invitation. The purpose was stated to be a discussion of Taiwan as a prelude to the normalization of relations. I rejected both propositions.

We would not appear in Peking as supplicants. We would not come for the sole purpose of discussing Taiwan or even simply to seek ''normalization of relations.'' There had to be a reference to other issues of common concern. Huang Hua, in a gesture wise, practical, and characteristic, suggested that we put aside the drafting and each tell the other frankly what his needs were. Clearly, neither side wanted to appear the supplicant; both wanted a positive outcome; it was in nobody's interest to imply that the agenda would be one-sided. We spent two hours on this. I explained our concerns of principle and domestic requirements; we would not appear as having solicited the invitation; Taiwan could not be the sole agenda item. Huang Hua pointed out the shocking impact of the announcement on the Chinese masses. Rarely are negotiations this candid, almost never with potential adversaries. At about 1:40 A.M., Huang Hua proposed a thirty-minute recess in which they would try to work out language suitable to us, and left the room. We took another walk in the grounds and returned to await their arrival; at 3:00 A.M. we learned that they had left and would not return until 9:00 A.M.

We reconvened at 9:40 A.M. on Sunday, July 11, for three and a half hours before the unbreakable departure deadline. Huang Hua was still the Chinese spokesman, continuing my first exposure to the Chinese negotiating style. As I have mentioned before, other negotiators, eager to impress superiors or the public, sometimes use the ''salami'' approach; they try to slice their concessions as thinly as possible over as long a period of time as possible. This method confers an illusory impression of toughness. Since neither side can know which slice of the salami is the final one, each is tempted to wait out the process and thus protract it further. Inevitably, pressure grows for what has absorbed so much time, energy, and commitment to succeed; this can easily carry the negotiator beyond prudent limits. I preferred by far the style the Chinese employed with us, and to which Huang Hua introduced me that morning, which is to determine as well as possible the nature of a reasonable solution, get there in one jump, and then stick to that position. Wherever possible I sought to adapt it to the negotiations I later conducted — it was castigated as the tactic of the ''preemptive concession.'' In fact, while the initial concessions seem greater than in the salami approach, the overall concessions are almost certainly fewer. The strategy of getting in one jump to a defensible position defines the irreducible position unambiguously; it is easier to defend than the cumulative impact over a long period of a series of marginal moves in which process always threatens to dominate substance.

Be that as it may, Huang Hua presented a draft at 9:40 that morning so close to our needs that we could accept it with a change of only one word. Indeed, it was fortunate that I suggested the Chinese submit their version first; it was better for us than our own. (Each side had leaned over backward to consider the point of view of the other.) It was the joint announcement Nixon was to read on July 15.

As soon as the drafting was completed, Chou En-lai, who had been waiting nearby, reappeared. We discussed establishing a point of contact for the future and selected Paris — General Walters would deal with the Chinese Ambassador there, Huang Chen. We exchanged preliminary thoughts on the President's trip. When we had concluded our business, Chou in a characteristic gesture spent some time bringing me up to date on international news that had reached Peking while I was cut off from communications.

We bid farewell to Chou, and my staff and I and the other Chinese sat down to a final cheerful lunch. All tension was gone. Marshal Yeh's normally impassive face was creased in smiles. On the way to the airport he told me of his life. He had been an officer in the Nationalist army when he had heard of Mao's little band in the mountains; he had joined them because he saw Mao above all as a teacher. As we drove up toward the waiting Pakistani plane, he remarked that none of them on the Long March had ever dreamed of seeing victory in their lifetimes. They had thought their struggle was for future generations. With the Chinese artistry in making the carefully planned appear spontaneous, just as we reached the foot of the steps he said, "Yet here we are and here you are."

No account of the secret trip can be complete without the saga of my shirts. Knowing the vicissitudes of a hectic twelve-day trip through Asia, I had asked my aide Dave Halperin to be sure to set aside a couple of clean shirts throughout the long tour to be saved specifically for Peking. Undoubtedly I reminded Halperin of this necessity several times with my customary persistence. As the Pakistani plane took off from Chaklala and soared toward the Himalayas, Halperin, riding back to the hill station with the Secret Service, was stunned by the realization that he had set aside the shirts so carefully that I could not have packed them; at this thought he became physically sick. I was aghast when, in the plane, I wanted to change shirts before arriving in Peking. I invoked Halperin's name with somewhat less than the affection I actually felt for him. In desperation I borrowed some white shirts from John Holdridge — a six-foot-two trim former West Pointer whose build did not exactly coincide with my rather more compact physique. Souvenir photos taken by the Chinese of my party in shirt-sleeves on our tour of the Forbidden City show me smiling enigmatically, in garments that left me with the appearance of having no neck. Their size was the least of it; for these shirts, belonging to an old Asia hand, were prominently labeled "Made in Taiwan." I was telling the literal truth when I told our hosts that Taiwan was a matter close to me.

Then there was the James Reston drama. Scotty Reston, whose presence in Peking had caused such a worry in the White House, was naturally no problem for the Chinese. He and his wife arrived in South China on July 8, the day before I reached Peking. In Canton, their official guide informed them of a "change of plans"; they were to remain in the Canton area for two days and proceed by rail to Peking on the evening of the tenth, arriving in the capital on the morning of the twelfth. Reston protested and asked to fly to Peking at once. But the *New York Times* did not inspire the same terror in China as in Washington. He was told it was out of the question. Chou En-lai gleefully informed me on July 10 that Reston was on a slow train that would conveniently delay his arrival in Peking until well after my departure.

Reston was told on the morning of the fifteenth of the announcement that I had been in Peking. This was the source of acute pain. "At that precise moment," Reston later recounted,[1] "or so it now seems, the first stab of pain went through my groin. By evening I had a temperature of 103, and in my delirium I could see Mr. Kissinger floating across my bedroom ceiling grinning at me out of the corner of a hooded rickshaw." It turned out to be, in fact, not journalistic mortification but acute appendicitis. His appendix was removed on July 17 at Peking's Anti-Imperialist Hospital (the then current name of the facility built in 1916 by the Rockefeller Foundation, later renamed the Friendship Hospital in time for Nixon's visit). Acupuncture needles were stuck into Scotty's elbow and below his knees to help relieve postoperative discomfort. As he lay in bed with needles protruding, no medicine, not even Chinese, could relieve the agony he felt at being so near, yet missing a tremendous scoop.

My colleagues and I flew back to Pakistan on July 11 in a spirit of high excitement and loaded down by one last round of Chinese dishes delivered aboard the plane, the latest English version of Mao's works, and photo albums of our visit prepared during the night.

Lord and I drafted a report to the President; its conclusions summed up our perhaps excessively exalted and not overly humble frame of mind:

We have laid the groundwork for you and Mao to turn a page in history. But we should have no illusions about the future. Profound differences and years of isolation yawn between us and the Chinese. They will be tough before and during the summit on the question of Taiwan and other major issues. And they will prove implacable foes if our relations turn sour. My assessment of these people is that they are deeply ideological, close to fanatic in the intensity of their beliefs. At the same time they display an inward security that allows them, within the framework of their principles, to be meticulous and reliable in dealing with others.

Furthermore, the process we have now started will send enormous shock waves around the world. . . .

However, we were well aware of these risks when we embarked on this course. We were aware too that the alternative was unacceptable — continued isolation from one-quarter of the world's most talented people and a country rich in past achievements and future potential.

And even the risks can be managed and turned to our advantage if we maintain steady nerves and pursue our policies responsibly. With the Soviet Union we will have to make clear the continued priorities we attach to our concrete negotiations with them. Just as we will not collude with them against China, so we have no intention of colluding with China against them. If carefully managed, our new China policy could have a longer term beneficial impact on Moscow.

With Japan our task will be to make clear that we are not shifting our allegiance in Asia from her to China. On Taiwan we can hope for little more than damage limitation by reaffirming our diplomatic relations. . . .

For Asia and for the world we need to demonstrate that we are enlarging the scope of our diplomacy in a way that, far from harming the interest of other countries, should instead prove helpful to them.

Our dealings, both with the Chinese and others, will require reliability, precision, finesse. If we can master this process, we will have made a revolution.

The Announcement That Shook the World

THE return flight to Pakistan seemed much shorter than the journey to Peking. We were all elated; yet another group of barbarians had succumbed to subtle Chinese flattery and a hospitality all the more insinuating for appearing so matter-of-fact. We all agreed with Chou En-lai that the announcement now firmly scheduled for the following Thursday at 10:30 P.M. Washington time would "shake the world." How we managed to maintain security on landing in Pakistan, enveloped as we were by Mao's collected works and Chinese photo albums, I cannot now imagine. Perhaps security works best with undertakings no one thinks possible.

We arrived in Islamabad at the military side of Chaklala airport about 3:00 in the afternoon of July 11. Sultan Khan, helpful and unobtrusive as ever, was there to greet us. We drove a circuitous route to the Murree Road and thence back to Islamabad as though returning from the hill station. I paid a brief courtesy call on Yahya Khan, who was boyishly ecstatic about having pulled off this coup. I thanked him for his efforts and for the spirit with which he had carried them out. Five months later Yahya was ousted. I was not to see him again. Afterward, I made sure of meeting as many US Embassy officials as I could, including my escort officer, who in violation of all State Department procedures had lost touch with me and had not yet figured out just what had happened. By 6:00 P.M. we were back in our own plane heading west to Paris via

Tehran. I arrived at Le Bourget long after midnight, ending a day that had begun with a meeting with Chou En-lai eighteen hours earlier.

All attention in Paris focused on Vietnam. The Viet Cong had just published their annual peace program, again in effect calling for the overthrow of the South Vietnamese government. And the yearly ritual of Congressional and media pressure on us to show flexibility was gearing up. I was pursued by journalists all over Paris, not to determine the cause of my Pakistani stomachache but to see whether I might meet with Le Duc Tho, who was known to be in Paris. As it turned out, we did meet. David Bruce, head of our Paris delegation, came to the Embassy through the front door where the press was staked out; ostensibly he and I were to review Vietnam strategy. (Bruce was aware of both my China trip and my secret Vietnam negotiations.) I escaped through a rear gate by one of the procedures so exuberantly and efficiently worked out by General Walters (described in Chapter XII). My secret meeting with the North Vietnamese lasted three hours; it turned out to be the most hopeful I had had. For some intoxicating weeks we thought that we might have simultaneous breakthroughs toward peace in Vietnam and toward China; Winston Lord and I on the way back from seeing Le Duc Tho had sufficient hubris to speculate on which would be considered historically the more significant achievement. After sneaking back into the Embassy by the rear door, I met briefly with reporters as I bade Bruce farewell.

That evening I dined in a restaurant with my friend Margaret Osmer, an attractive and intelligent television journalist. A vacationing American woman caught up in the spirit of the time came up and chided me in a loud voice: It was a disgrace for me to be in a restaurant with a young lady when I should be working for peace. I was picked up at the restaurant by Ambassador Arthur Watson, who took me to my plane; the hour of departure had been set so that I would reach San Clemente early in the morning.

I arrived at El Toro Marine Corps Air Station, California, at 7:00 A.M. on Tuesday, July 13. My trip around the world had lasted twelve days. Al Haig, who had held the fort heroically and efficiently in my absence, greeted me and rode back in the helicopter with me to San Clemente. Richard Nixon was impatiently waiting at the helipad. He had learned of the success of my trip when I cabled the agreed code word on the way to Tehran. The word was "Eureka." This had sent him into such transports that contrary to our original understanding he had requested an immediate report by cable. I sent that from the plane and he responded, thanking me profusely and trying his hand at a joke by informing me I would get a day off upon my return. He also requested that I first give him a full private briefing after which a "sanitized" account should go to his "guest" — Haig's code name for the

Secretary of State, who was staying at San Clemente. We received a great deal of credit afterward for our skill in keeping the information secret; as I review the exchanges, I am bound to thank our pure good fortune and the extraordinary discretion of the CIA, which was handling the exchanges.

I spent from 7:20 to 9:30 A.M. with the President, giving him a detailed account of events and my long written report. We both recognized that we had opened up new opportunities for our diplomacy. Inevitably, there would be repercussions with the Soviet Union; we thought that over time they would be beneficial. The impact on the war in Vietnam could be profound. When I left, Chou had wished me well in our negotiations. Though I doubted that the Chinese leaders could or would do much to help directly, my trip would be a major defeat for Hanoi. It would take the Viet Cong's deceptive "Seven Points" off the front pages, for it undercut Hanoi's campaign to exhaust us psychologically and undermine our public support. The American people would see that their government was capable of bold moves for peace. This would encourage all those around the world whose security and progress depended on a confident and resolute America. We would face inevitable problems in Japan and Taiwan. Sooner or later they would have come upon us as Peking's diplomatic offensive developed. The trip enabled us to dominate events rather than await them passively.

We talked about these implications in Nixon's modest study in the aerie of his residence in San Clemente, looking out across the Pacific. It was tempting to imagine the far shore of China, thousands of miles distant.

Haldeman joined us around 9:30 A.M. and the discussion took a practical turn. He wanted to know about the size of the press contingent to accompany the President. He was disdainful when he learned that I had not settled this, incredulous when I informed him that I had estimated the total party to Chou En-lai to be around fifty; the Secret Service complement would be larger than that, not to speak of the press contingent. Haldeman saw no sense in making history if television was not there to broadcast it. This led to a lengthy back-and-forth between Nixon and Haldeman as to how to get maximum press, and above all television, coverage, while still retaining some control over who could go. It was one of Nixon's unshakable conceits that somehow he could blackmail the press into a more benign view of him by rewarding with special attention those who, as he saw it, treated him fairly. Needless to say, he never accomplished this; neither he nor Haldeman achieved a veto over whom the media chose to send with Nixon to Peking.

More serious was the question of how the President would present the joint announcement. All canons of public relations lore counseled one of those dramatic, emotional speeches that punctuated the Nixon Presidency. But I strongly opposed this. We were at the very beginning of a new relationship; the more we embellished it the more we would encumber the delicate diplomacy that would have to give it substance. We would have to placate troubled adversaries; we would be obliged to reassure uneasy friends. The time would come for all these enterprises, but at this early stage we should neither promise nor qualify. Nixon should let the announcement, however brief and stilted, speak for itself. Nixon agreed with some reluctance, Haldeman with grave doubt. Within a day Nixon entered into the spirit of the occasion and grew increasingly enthusiastic about the potential impact of a terse, enigmatic presentation. Lord and I prepared a short set of accompanying remarks (there went my promised day off). Two and a half years of planning, effort, and anticipation were boiled down into four hundred words.

There was some uneasiness about how to announce the President's appearance. If television time was requested there was certain to be speculation that the subject was Vietnam; the resulting disappointment, so Haldeman feared, might vitiate the impact of the announcement. He therefore favored explicitly stating that the President wished to address the nation on a subject not related to Vietnam. I argued against this. The speculation such an announcement would generate would defeat its purpose. I was convinced that the President would not have to apologize when he was finished.

Finally Rogers joined us. I gave him the "sanitized" version of my trip that Nixon had suggested. We discussed his role in the unfolding events. Notifying foreign governments would be the State Department's duty. Rogers ably took charge. A scenario was developed; he would begin with Japan about an hour before the Presidential speech.

The next forty-eight hours passed amidst anxiety as to whether we could keep the secret and in the decompression that follows great exertion. Throughout my public life my own emotions were somewhat out of phase with my surroundings. My moment of elation occurred when it was clear that success in some effort was probable; this was usually days, sometimes weeks, before the public and even some colleagues learned of it. By the time of full public impact I was preoccupied in dealing with the next phase. There are no plateaus in foreign policy; every achievement is purchased by new travail; every advance must be consolidated by additional effort. So it was in San Clemente in those tense, yet calm, two days before the President's speech. My colleagues were preoccupied with a performance in a television studio forty-eight hours away. I had the letdown of jet lag and growing concern over how to manage what we had brought into being.

On the afternoon of July 15 Nixon eased his own tension by one of those performances at the edge of a precipice with which he liked to demonstrate his virtuosity and, as a bonus, torment his associates.

Learning that I was having lunch with the (London) *Sunday Times* journalist Henry Brandon and his charming wife, Muffie, Nixon invited them both to his residence. Showing them the rooms and walking through the gardens, he kept dropping cryptic hints, while I was squirming about the risk of compromising our secret at the last minute. Nixon spoke musingly about China on the far shore of the Pacific before us, about the need for a new relationship and his desire to take a trip through Asia. Luckily, he spoke so elliptically that Brandon got the point only in retrospect; he surely strained my own emotional equilibrium.[2]

At 2:45 P.M. Pacific daylight time (5:45 P.M. Eastern daylight time) on July 15, the Western White House made a cryptic announcement that the President would make a "major statement" on all television and radio networks five hours later. The Associated Press carried a bulletin about twenty minutes afterward: "President Nixon is making a 'major statement' on all nationwide television and radio networks at 10:30 P.M. tonight [EDT] on a secret subject the Western White House refused to discuss in advance."

At 5:45 P.M. Pacific time I departed with the President by helicopter for Los Angeles. At NBC television studios in Burbank Nixon appeared before nationwide cameras and microphones and delivered a brief, seven-minute speech:

Good Evening: I have requested this television time tonight to announce a major development in our efforts to build a lasting peace in the world.

As I have pointed out on a number of occasions over the past three years, there can be no stable and enduring peace without the participation of the People's Republic of China and its 750 million people. That is why I have undertaken initiatives in several areas to open the door for more normal relations between our two countries.

In pursuance of that goal, I sent Dr. Kissinger, my Assistant for National Security Affairs, to Peking during his recent world tour for the purpose of having talks with Premier Chou En-lai.

The announcement I shall now read is being issued simultaneously in Peking and in the United States:

Premier Chou En-lai and Dr. Henry Kissinger, President Nixon's Assistant for National Security Affairs, held talks in Peking from July 9 to 11, 1971. Knowing of President Nixon's expressed desire to visit the People's Republic of China, Premier Chou En-lai, on behalf of the Government of the People's Republic of China, has extended an invitation to President Nixon to visit China at an appropriate date before May 1972. President Nixon has accepted the invitation with pleasure.

The meeting between the leaders of China and the United States is to seek

the normalization of relations between the two countries and also to exchange views on questions of concern to the two sides.

In anticipation of the inevitable speculation which will follow this announcement, I want to put our policy in the clearest possible context.

Our action in seeking a new relationship with the People's Republic of China
will not be at the expense of our old friends. It is not directed against any other
nation. We seek friendly relations with all nations. Any nation can be our
friend without being any other nation's enemy.

I have taken this action because of my profound conviction that all nations
will gain from a reduction of tensions and a better relationship between the
United States and the People's Republic of China.

It is in this spirit that I will undertake what I deeply hope will become a journey for peace, peace not just for our generation but for future generations on
this earth we share together. Thank you and good night.

As Nixon left the Burbank studios, a small but vocal group greeted
him with chants of "Get out of Vietnam."

About forty-five minutes earlier, Colonel Richard T. Kennedy, managing my office in Washington, had handed the unfortunate Vorontsov a
copy of Nixon's speech accompanied by a note reminding the Soviets of
"the sequence of events which has preceded the July 15 announcement" — a none too subtle reference to the way the Soviets had toyed
with us over the summit. It reaffirmed our willingness to place relations
with the Soviet Union on a new basis. It warned of "serious results" should our hopes be disappointed. All the assurances in the
speech and the note could not sugarcoat the fact that the bargaining
positions between Washington and Moscow had changed.

Nixon and his senior staff then went to Perino's Restaurant in Los
Angeles, where Nixon reveled in an unchallengeable triumph. He
moved slowly to our table in a booth in a corner, savoring the congratulations of some diners and inviting the good wishes of others who had
not yet heard the news. We celebrated with a dinner of crab legs and a
bottle of Château Lafite-Rothschild 1961. As we left he lingered once
again in the foyer, stopping other guests by introducing me as the man
who had traveled to Peking, to the puzzlement of several who had not
been glued to the television set. It was a touching occasion. Nixon was
not boastful; he acted almost as if he could not quite believe what he
had just announced. There was a mutual shyness; Nixon was always ill
at ease with strangers, and the other guests were not comfortable in
approaching a President. In his hour of achievement Richard Nixon was
oddly vulnerable, waiting expectantly for recognition without quite
being able to bridge the gulf by which he had isolated himself from his
fellow men. In this sense the scene at Perino's symbolized the triumph
and tragedy of Richard Nixon.

Several days of excitement — and absurdity — followed. Congratulations poured in from all over the globe. The media were nearly unanimous in their praise. There were some churlish comments, not only from conservatives but, interestingly, from a few American liberal critics who feared that we were needlessly antagonizing the Soviet Union. But these were submerged in an event that caught the world's imagination. We did not lack advice; some urged that the President visit Peking and Moscow on the same trip; every group had its own pet project for Nixon to carry out (ending the Vietnam war, expanding trade, and so on). But this was a good problem to have; we had not previously been overwhelmed by volunteers offering to support our policy.

Our Cabinet's Taiwan wanderlust was immediately replaced by a nearly unquenchable yearning of senior officials to visit Peking on suddenly essential business. Senators and Congressmen deluged us with suggestions that they travel to the Mainland and requests that I use my new contacts to arrange appointments with Chou En-lai. Even the agent of a nightclub singer managed to get through to offer his client's services for a tour of China's night spots. When told there were no nightclubs in China, he grumbled incredulously and wrote it off as an implausible excuse for White House uppityness.

Haldeman was pressured by his chief to treat the event as an unrivaled opportunity to "sell" Nixon, embellishing the drama into an epic poem. Thus was born the largely apocryphal saga of the Lincoln Sitting Room sessions among Nixon and me and Rogers. I was given detailed advice to brief the press on the resemblance between Chou En-lai and Nixon. Heroic efforts were required to convince the White House staff, browbeaten by Haldeman, that history happens, it is not invented, and that this time, anyway, Presidential restraint was the best public relations policy.

Nixon was at first uneasy that the praise came so lavishly from the liberal circles he despised and was more grudging from the conservatives who had his emotional allegiance. But after a few days and some efforts at explanation even conservatives began to recognize the potential. The principal sour note came from Japan, whose Prime Minister Eisaku Sato had been a staunch friend of the United States. It was particularly painful to embarrass a man who had done so much to cement the friendship between our two countries. The China announcement became known in Japan as the first "Nixon shock," to be followed a month later by the second shock of the emergency economic program that imposed wage-price controls at home and trade and currency restrictions abroad.

Armin Meyer, our able Ambassador in Japan at that time, was one of the most embarrassed. He heard the announcement over Armed Forces Radio while getting a haircut and first thought that Nixon's reference to

"China" was a slip of the tongue. According to his memoirs,[3] Meyer's initial reaction was bitterness at this insensitivity, a reaction that he says was shared by many other Americans and Japanese in Tokyo. However, "after days and weeks of reflection," Meyer reached the conclusion that "the President and his Assistant for National Security Affairs could not have handled it in an intrinsically different manner if its accomplishment was to be assured." Meyer advanced a number of reasons: that the Japanese were chronically unable to maintain confidentiality; that other allied countries (Taiwan, Korea, Southeast Asian allies, NATO) had a greater or equal claim to advance consultation (not to mention the Soviets); that Japanese policy was not undercut by ours but only deprived of its desired opportunity to stay *ahead* of us on a road it had started traveling long before we did — for as early as January 22, 1971, Sato had publicly offered to increase trade and press contacts with Peking and to initiate talks on the governmental level.

I believe in retrospect that we could have chosen a more sensitive method of informing the Japanese even though Meyer's considerations precluded earlier consultation. It would have surely been more courteous and thoughtful, for example, to send one of my associates from the Peking trip to Tokyo to brief Sato a few hours before the official announcement. This would have combined secrecy with a demonstration of special consideration for a good and decent friend. In the pressure of events the thought occurred to no one; it was a serious error in manners. The accusation of "mistreating our allies" was picked up by many critics whose devotion to our military alliances and conservative allies had previously been well hidden. But even with the perspective of nearly a decade I do not know how the fundamental secrecy could have been avoided. The delicacy of the event and the uniqueness of the opportunity made it essential that the United States be in control of the context of its presentation.

In his speech the President was able to stress that our policy was not directed against any other nation and would not be at the expense of our old friends. Clichés though these may be, one need only imagine the confusion if unfocused speculation had ruled the day. Had the trip been announced in advance, it would have triggered weeks of speculation to which we could not respond. Opponents would have had an opportunity to raise sinister implications that no reassurances would entirely dispel — especially since we did not really control the agenda of the talks. Even ostensible supporters could embarrass us by putting forward the traditional agenda we were determined to transcend. And some countries with the best claim to being consulted also had the highest incentive to sabotage the trip. To maintain our control over the presentation of the event was synonymous with maintaining control over our policy and its consequences. As the President's Foreign Policy Report of February 9, 1972, conceded, we paid a price for secrecy, but the price was "unavoidable" and the reasons for it "overriding."

The outcome of my trip was not foreseeable; we did not want to risk inflating expectations, generating pressures, and forcing the two sides to take public positions before the results were known. The shock effect of the reversal of positions would have been inevitable no matter how the trip had been handled (witness the Ping-Pong experience). In any event, the report argued, no substantive negotiations with the Chinese would take place until Nixon's trip, before which we would have months to consult with our allies — a promise faithfully carried out.

My colleague Bill Safire found a precedent for our position:

July 19, 1971.

MEMORANDUM FOR: HENRY KISSINGER
FROM: BILL SAFIRE

Here is a quotation about secrecy that you may find occasion to use:

> "The most dangerous of all moral dilemmas: When we are obliged to conceal truth in order to help the truth to be victorious."
>
>   — Dag Hammarskjold

"The China Card"

TRIANGULAR diplomacy, in which we were now engaged in public view, was not, understandably, appreciated at once by everyone. It could not be a crude attempt to play off China against the Soviet Union. "The China card" was not ours to play. Sino-Soviet hostility had followed its own dynamic. We had not generated it; we were, in fact, unaware of its intensity for the better part of a decade. Neither Peking nor Moscow was quarreling with the other to curry favor with us; they were currying favor with us because they were quarreling. We could not "exploit" that rivalry; it exploited itself. To the extent that we tried to aggravate rivalry we would lose in other ways. Paradoxically, we might even disquiet Peking by doing so: To speak of a China card implied that for a price we might not play it. The Chinese often expressed the fear that having achieved our objective with Moscow we might find Peking expendable; Mao warned us against "standing on China's shoulders to reach Moscow." Any attempt to manipulate Peking might drive China into detaching itself from us, perhaps to reexamine its options with the Soviet Union, to gain control of its own destiny. Equally, any move by us to play the Chinese card might tempt the Soviets to end their nightmare of hostile powers on two fronts by striking out in one direction before it was too late, probably against China, which was weaker and not protected by an American alliance system.

Equilibrium was the name of the game. We did not seek to join China in a provocative confrontation with the Soviet Union. But we agreed on the necessity to curb Moscow's geopolitical ambitions. The sending of combat troops to Egypt, the circumstances that led to the Syrian invasion of Jordan, the building of a naval base at Cienfuegos, and the clashes along the Sino-Soviet border were part of a uniform challenge to the global equilibrium that had to be resisted. Moreover, both China and the United States wanted to broaden their diplomatic options: Peking, to escape the self-imposed isolation of the Cultural Revolution; Washington, to strengthen security in an international system less dependent for stability on permanent American intervention.

But while China and the United States were brought together by a common concern, they did not automatically agree on how to deal with it; therein lay the seed of future difficulties. Peking confronted Moscow with the same dedicated, uncompromising zeal with which it had earlier prevailed in its own civil war. Peking's challenge was polemic and philosophical; it opposed not only Moscow's geopolitical aspirations but also its ideological preeminence. We agreed on the necessity of thwarting the geopolitical ambitions, but we had no reason to become involved in the ideological dispute. Also, the possession of vast arsenals of weapons of mass destruction imposed on us a fiduciary responsibility for hundreds of millions of lives. We had a moral and a political obligation to strive for coexistence if it was possible; we would not shrink from confrontation if challenged but the thermonuclear age evokes the imperative of mutual restraint. Critics — some in Peking — might sneer at this quest and proclaim its futility; but, paradoxically, only by pursuing it would we be able to rally our people when we needed to face up to military pressures.

From the beginning Nixon and I were convinced — alone among senior policymakers — that the United States could not accept a Soviet military assault on China. We had held this view before there was contact of any sort; we imposed contingency planning on a reluctant bureaucracy as early as the summer of 1969. Obviously, this reflected no agreement between Peking and Washington — not even the Warsaw talks were taking place at that time. It was based on a sober geopolitical assessment. If Moscow succeeded in humiliating Peking and reducing it to impotence, the whole weight of the Soviet military effort could be thrown against the West. Such a demonstration of Soviet ruthlessness and American impotence (or indifference — the result would be the same) would encourage accommodation to other Soviet demands from Japan to Western Europe, not to speak of the many smaller countries on the Soviet periphery. Clearly, triangular diplomacy required agility. We had somehow not to flex our own muscles but, as in judo, to use the weight of an adversary to propel him in a desired direction. If successful we would have a larger series of options toward either side than they had toward each other; there was always the risk also of antagonizing both sides. I summed up this strategy in a memorandum to Nixon (in October, before a second trip to China):

> We want our China policy to show Moscow that it cannot speak for all communist countries, that it is to their advantage to make agreements with us, that they must take account of possible US–PRC [China] cooperation — all this without overdoing the Soviet paranoia. The beneficial impact on the USSR is perhaps the single biggest plus that we get from the China initiative.
>
> We have already achieved this. There is nothing the Chinese need do. Our interests here are congruent and we need only to continue on the path we have set out upon. Pressure on the Russians is something we obviously never explicitly point to. The facts speak for themselves.

At the same time there was a natural congruence of interests on some matters between us and China. Contrary to academic and other expert opinion, China had not changed its policy toward us so markedly merely to regain Taiwan, in spite of its many prominent mentions. It wanted to take its place in international affairs and demonstrate to the world its prestige and importance. This would provide some security against Soviet pressures and reduce the danger of a US–Soviet condominium. I wrote to Nixon:

> The Chinese want to relieve themselves of the threat of a two-front war, introduce new calculations in Moscow about attacking or leaning on the PRC, and perhaps make the USSR more pliable in its dealing with Peking. Specifically from us they want assurances against US–USSR collusion.

These we were able to give. They were inherent in our initiative and in our own interest. We were on a tightrope; we had to be careful never to lean to one side or the other — regardless of buffeting — or we might drop into the abyss.

From my first visit I told Chou that we would continue to deal with Moscow, but we would inform Peking in detail of any understanding affecting Chinese interests that we might consider with the Soviets, and we would take Chinese views into account. These assurances were confirmed by Nixon in a message to Chou En-lai on July 16; we also enclosed the text of a background briefing on my Peking trip that I gave reporters on July 16 — a courtesy intended to establish our care in fostering the new relationship.

This message was the first contact in the new Paris channel agreed to in Peking, and was delivered on July 19 by General Walters to Chinese Ambassador Huang Chen. The messages in the Paris channel were drafted by my staff and me, approved by Nixon, carried by hand to Paris by a member of the Situation Room staff and delivered by the irrepressible Walters — who promptly gave us an incentive for additional messages by sending back graphic accounts of his meetings with the hospitable Chinese. Walters exceeded even his own high standards of hyperbole in detailing atmosphere, setting, personalities, and cuisine. A man of precise tastes, Walters regaled us with tales of exotic delicacies, some of which he said he ate only out of a sense of patriotic duty. He and Huang Chen, both military men, soon were swapping war stories with enthusiasm undampened by the fact that in some cases they had been in the same war on opposite sides.

We had many occasions to use the Paris channel, because we were soon deluged with communications from Moscow. Contrary to the fears of the Soviet experts, Moscow did not react with hostility — at least initially. Moscow Radio in its domestic service broke the news to Russian listeners, closely following the text of the communiqué but omitting the sentence "President Nixon has accepted the invitation with pleasure." The first authoritative Soviet comment came nine days later. With studied nonchalance *Pravda* declared on July 24: "Nobody here in the Soviet Union sees in the Chinese-American contacts any cause for sensation," and went on:

Of course, the further development of events will better reveal the true intentions of Peking and Washington. Our party and state will take into account all the possible consequences of the Chinese-American contacts. It goes without saying that any designs to use the contacts between Peking and Washington for some "pressure" on the Soviet Union, on the states of the Socialist community, are nothing but the result of a loss of touch with reality.

Of course, just as pressure is not achieved by proclaiming it, so it is not ended by denying it.

The authentic Soviet response was diplomatic, not propagandistic. The Soviet Union began to move energetically on two fronts to deal with the new international reality. First it sought rapidly to improve its relations with Washington: It was suddenly anxious to create the impression that more serious business could be accomplished in Moscow than in Peking.

On July 19 Dobrynin somewhat plaintively inquired whether the Soviet note of July 5, evading a summit, had affected our China policy. I avoided an answer; the truth, as I have noted, was that it had eased our road to Peking; we would have traveled it anyway but with more detours. Suddenly, the Moscow summit was not elusive. Would the President, inquired Dobrynin, consider visiting Moscow before Peking? My answer was identical to that given Chou En-lai: The summits would take place in the order in which they were announced. Other negotiations deadlocked for months began magically to unfreeze: Berlin, for example, and the talks to guard against accidental nuclear war. As I shall describe elsewhere, both these negotiations moved rapidly to completion within weeks of the Peking announcement.

But there was also an ominous side to Soviet policy. In the growing India-Pakistan conflict the Soviet Union discovered an opportunity to humiliate China and to punish Pakistan for having served as intermediary. Tensions in the subcontinent had multiplied after Pakistan's military government sought to repress East Pakistan's attempt to secede. India and the Soviet Union were brought into a natural de facto alliance. For its part, India had initially welcomed Nixon's July 15 announcement with a generous statement by Foreign Minister Swaran Singh that it was a "significant, positive development." But by July 20, India began to display second thoughts; it started to invoke fictitious Sino-American designs on the subcontinent as a pretext for its own arrangements with the Soviet Union. Answering questions in Parliament, Swaran Singh said: "We cannot look upon it [a Sino–US rapprochement] with equanimity if it means domination of the two countries over this region. . . . We cannot at present totally rule out such a possibility . . . [and] for some time we have been considering ways and means of preventing such a situation from arising." In a reference to the Soviet Union, Singh continued: "In this we are not alone. There are other countries both big and small who may be more perturbed than we are."

What Singh had in mind became public on August 9 when India and the Soviet Union signed a Friendship Treaty, which for all practical purposes gave India a Soviet guarantee against Chinese intervention if India went to war with Pakistan. By this action the Soviet Union deliberately opened the door to war on the subcontinent; it was the first of a series of moves throughout the Seventies whereby the Soviets fueled conflicts by giving arms and assurances to countries with high incentive to resort to force. I agreed with Hal Sonnenfeldt's and Bill Hyland's perceptive analysis:

> The escalatory aspects of this are obvious: if the Chinese come under pressure from Pakistan to counter the Soviet move, what will they do? If they do nothing the Soviets have made an important gain — certainly one of their objectives is to expose the Chinese as weak allies. If, on the other hand, the Chinese raise the ante, then the Soviets must also respond to maintain their credibility, a credibility which would have to be backed with at least more sophisticated Soviet weaponry, etc. . . .
>
> Thus, the India-Pakistan conflict becomes a sort of Sino-Soviet clash by proxy.

Sonnenfeldt and Hyland also predicted that the Soviets might seek to humiliate Romania, which had been a friend of China. In fact, the Soviets began to wage a war of nerves against that country in late summer.

We protested vigorously and may have helped bring an end to the harassment.

The only way to protect the tender shoot of our China policy from being crushed by this combination of Soviet embrace and menace was to make sure Peking understood our actions. We accordingly increased our contacts with the Chinese through Paris. Between August 1 and the end of September we exchanged more messages than we had in the previous twenty years. I used my visits to Paris for secret negotiations with Le Duc Tho to meet, also secretly, three times with Ambassador Huang Chen. An able, affable veteran of the Long March, Huang Chen later became the first Chief of the Chinese Liaison Office in Washington. I took great pains to keep the Chinese informed of all our moves with Moscow and of our assessment of Soviet intentions. We kept Peking posted about the sudden Soviet eagerness for a summit; we gave them a four-week advance warning of the contents of both the accidental-war and the Berlin agreements. Both sides exchanged views on the deteriorating situation on the Indian subcontinent. Knowing of China's unwillingness to join a conference of the five nuclear powers, we rejected Brezhnev's proposal for such a conference on the ground that it would make sense only if all parties attended.

Peking, of course, was offered no veto over our policy or our actions; nor was one sought. Our objective was to ensure that the Chinese leaders understood what we did and why, and how we saw the international situation. The Chinese leaders affected unconcern about the information they were given, a correct posture toward developments they could not alter. Though no doubt Peking would have preferred us to take an openly antagonistic stance toward Moscow, it learned that our approach to foreign policy was unsentimental and geopolitical. We were not prepared to pay for coexistence in the coin of the balance of power. We were ready for détente — in the face of domestic or foreign opposition — but only if the Soviets gave up military pressure and exercised political restraint.

Two other subjects occupied the new channel through Paris — one explicit, the other unspoken. The subject of formal exchanges was a second trip by me to China to prepare the Peking summit. It was soon overshadowed by a subject which was never discussed, but of which we were extremely conscious: the overthrow of Lin Piao in China. The upheaval was in all likelihood induced by the sharp new turn in China's policy toward us; so Mao told Nixon in February 1972. It clearly reflected deep-seated strains in Chinese politics. But we never raised the subject. A second journey to China by me had been discussed in our exchanges even before my July visit. In July, Chou En-lai was eager for this, perhaps to remove any possible stigma attached to the secrecy of the first visit, perhaps because he was experienced enough to understand that a Presidential trip was too risky unless the major issues had been settled in advance.

Nixon was still eager to make the next visit himself, but need soon overcame vanity. Nixon never left summit meetings to chance; all his were settled in their main parts before he arrived. He would not participate in one — until his desperate last months — without having a reasonable idea of its outcome. It is the only responsible course for a President. Heads of government have too much at stake to be principal negotiators. They usually are too busy to master all the manifold details on which successful negotiations depend. They are too self-centered to submit gracefully to the inevitable pressures of a protracted negotiation. If there is a deadlock, there is no recourse. Summits are, moreover, too brief to permit the meticulous analysis that assures the durability of an agreement. Nixon understood this and approved preparations for my second visit.

Exchanges with Peking leading to my second visit were not without their testy moments. For one thing, even in the millennia of their history the Chinese had never encountered a Presidential advance party, especially one whose skills had been honed by the hectic trips of a candidate in the heartland of America and disciplined by the monomaniacal obsession of the Nixon White House with public relations. When I warned Chou En-lai that China had survived barbarian invasions before but had never encountered advance men, it was only partly a joke. One message had to be devoted to explaining just what an advance party did and why its size needed to be almost equal to what in my naiveté I had told Chou En-lai would be the whole Presidential contingent. Also, we had never flown an American plane into China; this involved both political and technical complications. Finally, the Chinese rejected my suggestion that I be accompanied by David Bruce, despite Chou's having agreed to this in July. Peking now pleaded "understandable reasons," which was fair enough considering Hanoi's irritation and Moscow Radio's incessant accusations that Peking had made a deal on Indochina.

All these exchanges were taking place against the background of ominous if mystifying reports out of Peking. In September we suddenly became aware that all of China's leaders had disappeared from public view for five days; all Chinese planes had been grounded for the same time. As the month wore on, it became clear that several key leaders had been removed from office, including much of the top leadership of the armed forces. Foremost among the suddenly missing was Lin Piao: Minister of Defense, Vice Premier of the State Council, Vice Chairman of the Communist Party Politburo, Chairman of the Politburo Military Affairs Committee; and designated by the Ninth Party Congress in April 1969 as the heir and successor to Chairman Mao Tse-tung. On September 12 a Chinese military plane crashed mysteriously in Mongolia. On September 20 the annual parade to celebrate the Chinese Revolution on October 1 was canceled. Clearly, something massive was taking place in China.

We had no firsthand information. The Chinese communications to us on other subjects continued; they were unfailingly crisp. There was no interruption in planning my trip nor the slightest hint — except in our press — that the President's visit was in any jeopardy. There was an occasional tartness from the Peking end of the line, but there was usually an adequate explanation for it. For one thing, there were our suddenly blooming relations with the Soviet Union. Not only were the Berlin and accidental-war agreements concluded, but Gromyko visited Washington to bring a formal invitation to the President to visit Moscow. Whereas the year before the Soviets went to elaborate lengths to avoid any press speculation about the summit, they now could not rush a public announcement fast enough. We held them off long enough to give ourselves time to announce my second trip to Peking on October 5. Exactly a week later we announced the summit for Moscow, scheduled for sometime in May 1972. Whatever their private thoughts, the Chinese gritted their teeth and said nothing.

China at the United Nations

THE preparations for my October trip coincided with the annual debate on whether Taipei or Peking should represent China in the United Nations. Our opening to Peking effectively determined the outcome of the UN debate, although we did not realize this immediately. Even before 1971 we had been engaged in an essentially doomed rearguard action. Now all these processes accelerated.

The Republic of China was one of the founders of the United Nations; it was an original permanent member of the Security Council. After the Revolution of 1949, a vote was taken almost every year in the General Assembly on the question of which government — the Republic of China on Taiwan or the People's Republic of China in Peking — was the "real" representative of China. At first there was a majority against Peking's admission. But with the admission of dozens of new African and Asian nations, the number of countries favoring Peking increased with every year. The United States retreated to a procedural defense of Taiwan's position. From 1961 onward, we and a group of allies annually submitted a resolution making any proposal to change the representation of China an "Important Question," requiring a two-thirds majority of the General Assembly for approval. As long as we could muster a simple majority for the first vote, we could then block Peking by mustering one-third plus one votes on the second.

In 1969 the Important Question resolution had passed by a wide margin of 71 in favor, 48 against, and 4 abstentions. The Albanian resolution to seat Peking and expel Taiwan was then defeated by 48–56–21; in opposing it we had a plurality of only eight votes, compared with the fourteen-vote plurality of the year before. While the decision to admit the People's Republic would still be defeated by failing to obtain a two-thirds majority, the pro-Peking forces were clearly heading toward the psychological breakthrough of a simple majority. Not only were more new nations being admitted to the United Nations every year, but trendy Third Worldism was cutting into our usual Latin American bloc of support and even our NATO allies were growing restive.

On June 19, 1970, Secretary Rogers had sent the President a memorandum analyzing the lineup in the General Assembly as the 1970 vote approached. Rogers speculated (correctly) that the status quo could probably be maintained in 1970 but was eroding fast. He forewarned the President of the possible need to shift tactics, perhaps toward some formula for "dual representation." Rogers made no recommendation and implied that he favored maintaining the standard US opposition to Peking's admission for 1970; no Presidential decision was sought.

Eventual defeat was becoming increasingly likely, however. Canada recognized Peking on October 13, 1970. Ottawa informed us that Canada would continue to vote with us on the Important Question resolution but would probably vote for the Albanian resolution for seating Peking. As the General Assembly vote approached, pressures mounted. Senator Jacob Javits, a member of our delegation to the General Assembly, urged the Administration to "take a more positive line," to change our emphasis from keeping Peking out to maintaining Taiwan *in* the United Nations. The United States made a significant shift in that direction when on October 25 Ron Ziegler implied that we objected to the expulsion of Taiwan, not to the admission of Peking: "The US opposes the admission of the Peking regime into the UN at the expense of the Republic of China."

On November 19 I called for an interagency study of the long-term issue of Chinese representation. Next day came the vote. The Important Question resolution passed by 66–52–7 (the fourteen-vote margin contrasted with the twenty-three of the year before). The Albanian resolution received 51 votes for, 49 against, and 25 abstentions. It failed for want of two-thirds — but for the first time a majority had voted in favor of Peking.

As we had feared, the majority for the Albanian resolution proved the psychological watershed. The Japanese Foreign Ministry informed our Embassy in early January 1971 of its pessimistic assessment of the prospects for a dual-representation formula (toward which we were working) and for the Important Question resolution. On January 22 Prime Minister Sato at the opening of the new Diet session spoke of Japan's desire for better bilateral relations with Peking and offered to begin governmental contacts. Britain and Belgium indicated privately that they expected the US position to be defeated in 1971. Secretary-General of the United Nations U Thant said Peking would prevail in 1972; and signs appeared that the UN Secretariat was making contingency plans for Peking's admission. The British, hoping to upgrade their own ties to Peking, even hinted that they might oppose us on dual representation.

The State Department had indeed worked out a dual-representation formula, and it soon became apparent that this had its Catch-22 aspects. If we persisted with the Important Question tactic, dual representation, which probably could command simple majority support, would fail for lack of a two-thirds vote. On the other hand, if we dropped the Important Question, the Albanian resolution would probably pass by simple majority and Taiwan would be expelled. At a Senior Review Group discussion on March 9 I had indicated my own doubts about the dual-representation formula; if countries were looking for an elegant way out, our various dual-representation gimmicks would serve. But if they were determined to improve their relations with Peking, as we had been, they would vote to ensure Peking's admission even at the cost of expelling Taiwan. I guessed the latter was more likely. But China representation was the only piece of the action on China under State Department control; it therefore pursued it with unrelenting persistence. There were other incentives for maximum activity. The Department has never gotten over the charge of the Fifties that it had been ''soft on Communism'' with respect to China; Foreign Service careers had been destroyed by the issue. Many in the Department had what turned out to be an exaggerated estimate of the power of the ''China Lobby.'' Now, as I have already suggested, it was in the unusual position where, by advocating some form of dual representation, it could please both liberal and conservative constituencies — the liberals because they would see the move as a way to get the People's Republic into the United Nations, the conservatives because it was an effort to preserve Taiwan's seat in some form. The only thing wrong with dual representation was that both Peking and Taipei rejected it and a majority for it was getting harder and harder to assemble.

All this culminated in pressures to advance a dual-representation position publicly, preferably in a major speech by the Secretary of State — at the moment that we were taking the first tentative steps toward Peking. This is why the State Department on April 28 — the day after we received Chou's invitation to Nixon — had called the status of Taiwan ''unsettled''; it was the legal buttress of State's dual-representation position.

As the months went by I developed increasing doubt about the policy proposed by the State Department. It was bound to raise havoc with our relations with Peking and even to some extent with Taipei. There was no possibility that this position could be maintained for any length of time. Countries eager to get into the good graces of Peking would not embrace so transparent a maneuver. It was a position both awkward and self-defeating. Our new advocacy of Peking's admission increased Peking's support; but since Peking rejected our dual-representation formula, this new support went to the Albanian resolution expelling Taipei, not to our preference of keeping Taiwan in the General Assembly. We might delay Peking's entry for a year or two; the end result was foreordained.

Increasingly, I favored sticking with our existing position (blocking Peking), doomed as it was. It was at least principled; it avoided legalistic evasions. At the end of the day we would be defeated whatever position we adopted, unless we maintained a posture of uncompromising hostility against Peking and made it a test case in all our relations with other countries. This we were simply not willing to do. At an NSC meeting that had discussed the subject on March 25, after hearing the case for dual representation, both Vice President Agnew and Treasury Secretary Connally argued that we would be better off being defeated with a straightforward position than in effect engineering our own defeat by buying at most a one- or two-year delay. Nixon told me afterward that he agreed with that view.

But he, like me, was reluctant to go to the mat with Rogers on this issue. We could be accused of pigheadedness and of not trying a potentially fruitful way of saving Taipei's seat, all the more so since the State Department was telling us that there was some chance of Peking's acquiescence in the scheme. Nixon therefore chose delay. He would let the State Department have its way eventually — but not until we made a breakthrough with Peking or clearly failed. Not without anguish, he prevented a speech on dual representation by Rogers in January, then in April, and finally in June. Under constant pressure to announce our position, he told a press conference on June 1, as I have mentioned, that he would not make a decision until the middle of July.

On my secret trip I told Chou En-lai what position we were planning to take. Chou confirmed that dual representation in any form would not be accepted by Peking; on the other hand China had existed for a long time without membership in the UN and could wait awhile longer. I did not have the impression that he considered the issue central to Sino-American relations.

Convinced now that the price was manageable, the President, after my return, authorized Rogers to go ahead with proposing a dual-representation formula. This Rogers did on August 2 in a lengthy statement advocating Peking's entry into the United Nations but opposing the expulsion of Taipei. The General Assembly was to determine the disposition of China's Security Council seat. (By early September we were forced to retreat from this position and actually *recommend* that China's Security Council seat go to Peking, in the hope that the majority of nations would be attracted by the compromise.) In an interview with James Reston on August 5, Chou En-lai rather gently turned aside this proposal, calling it — not incorrectly — self-contradictory. On August 6 the Chinese Ambassador in Ottawa, my new friend Huang Hua, told the *New York Times* that China would not take its seat according to such a formula; this was just about the most circuitous and conciliatory way by which our proposal could be rejected. Both Chou and Huang Hua insisted, however, that the President's trip to China was not jeopardized by our position in the UN.

On September 22 we lost a crucial procedural vote, which was an augury of things to come. The UN General Committee placed the Albanian resolution on the agenda ahead of the US resolutions for dual representation. Since we had confined the Important Question to the issue of expulsion, it was all but certain that Peking would be admitted before our dual-representation formula could ever come to a vote. While we fought this procedural battle, Peking asked that we postpone the announcement of my October trip. (Interestingly, Peking seemed to feel that announcing my trip while this maneuvering was going on might imply Peking's blessing of our formula.) My trip was announced on October 5.

"Polo II"

WHEN I review the exchanges preceding what we code-named "Polo II," it is difficult to imagine how we had ever made it to Peking three months earlier with only the Pakistani channel. In the interval we had managed to enmesh the new relationship in bureaucratic complexity. The Chinese were astonished at the size of what we called an advance party for the Presidential trip, and the fact that it would need to be followed by a third visit by a yet larger technical team. They were about to learn methods of bureaucratic management unknown even in the country that had invented bureaucracy two millennia earlier. The compartmentalization of knowledge that Winston Lord had to keep track of on my first trip had grown in complexity as we brought with us a large group of technical personnel in October. My party would contain at least four levels of knowledge, which the indefatigable Lord had to keep straight; I, Lord, and Holdridge were familiar with both the policy and some of the technical side of the President's trip (though not with how he intended to exploit it domestically). Dwight Chapin, Deputy Assistant to the President and head of the advance team, was fully acquainted with all technical issues (and probably knew more than I did about the public relations plans). The security and communications technicians were familiar only with the necessities under their care. Finally, there was a State Department representative, the able, wise, and witty old China hand Alfred Jenkins. He was an expert in the bilateral issues that had been the staples of Sino-American discussions for two decades; my task was to give him a sense of participation without letting him in on key geopolitical discussions, especially the drafting of the communiqué.

I solved this problem as best I could by conveying to the Chinese through our Paris channel a logistical proposal about my trip of such complexity that a less talented people would never have straightened it out in time. It involved several levels of meetings, each tailored to the "need to know" of a particular group, preferably going on at the same time, so that Chou and I and a restricted group could settle the most sensitive issues undisturbed.

The Chinese, with long experience with the strange ways of barbarians, took all this with remarkable aplomb. They helped to solve our bureaucratic intricacies as if it were the most natural service to render to a country six months earlier still depicted as the capitalist archenemy. Indeed, the Chinese arranged the meetings so seemingly spontaneously as to give the impression that it was all their idea. First, of course, there had to be many meetings between the intrepid General Walters and the Chinese Embassy in Paris. He reported in characteristic style one session with Ambassador Huang Chen, lubricated by the powerful liqueur *mao-tai,* with which I was already painfully familiar:

Food was then brought in. First, stuffed pastries, stuffed round patties, fried shrimp and, finally, soup. Large quantities of all of these were heaped on my plate at regular intervals. All of this was washed down with a perfumed red wine and a colorless liquid that must have been related to 110 octane gas. Inasmuch as the smell of shrimp alone nauseates me, I had to drown it in soy sauce. He noted approvingly that I could eat with chopsticks. Each sip of the colorless liquid gave me the impression that the lining of my throat had been removed but then, unfortunately, the fishiness of the shrimp proved that this was not the case. I was very cautious with the strong beverage, raising it many times to my lips but drinking very little, both to avoid getting drunk and to save my alimentary tract. There was long chit chat about Chinese cooking at those times when I could speak.

Before I could set out on my journey there was the by now almost traditional dispute with the State Department. Rogers learned of my trip a few days before it was to be announced and objected strenuously, this time on the ground that it would interfere with our strategy on Chinese representation in the United Nations. He was right in principle: Presidents should not send emissaries who are independent of the Secretary of State. I did not think the UN vote would be decisively affected; nor did our UN Ambassador, George Bush. My October trip undoubtedly reinforced the conviction that China's emergence on the world scene was now a fact of life. On the other hand, it could also be seen to demonstrate that it was possible to have businesslike relations with Peking while opposing Taiwan's expulsion from the UN. (The Chinese, too, as noted, seemed to fear that this could cut both ways.) We tried to make this point to wavering allies. The problem was not any one trip but the basic trend: Now that Peking was emerging from its self-imposed isolation, countries would not base their vote on legal formulas but on the political importance they attached to their relations with Peking. The true watershed had been Nixon's July 15 announcement. The procedural vote of September 22 foreshadowed the outcome.

In any event, we could hardly change the date of a visit agreed to for two months without some cost to our new relations with Peking. If the President's trip was to take place in the early part of 1972 — as was necessary to avoid doubling up with the Moscow summit — we could not delay. (It was just as well that we did not postpone my trip, for had we delayed by a month I would have found myself in Peking in the midst of the India-Pakistan war.)

So I set out on October 16, this time much more comfortably in *Air Force One*, trying the route planned for the Nixon trip with stopovers in Hawaii and Guam; this was to permit the Presidential party to reach China without being too exhausted by time changes and jet lag. I arrived on October 20 in a China that only recently had seen a massive purge of its top leadership. The Chinese were undergoing a philosophical crisis, torn between the imperatives of Realpolitik and the dictates of ideology. This accounted in part for the chilly, or at least aloof, circumstances of our reception. When we landed in Shanghai the weather was partially overcast; only a handful of officials were on hand — the same four who had met us in Islamabad in July plus two representatives of the Shanghai Foreign Affairs Office. Their manner was correct but restrained. In Peking, too, the reception committee was similar to the one that had greeted us when we arrived secretly, although this time the visit was publicly announced. As before, Marshal Yeh Chien-ying headed the official welcoming party, joined this time by Acting Foreign Minister Chi P'eng-fei.

In our ride from the airport to the same guest house in which we had stayed before, the motorcade reached the city over roads that were again closed to traffic and heavily guarded. We discovered upon entering our rooms that each contained an English-language propaganda bulletin carrying an appeal on the cover for the people of the world to "overthrow the American imperialists and their running dogs." Similar signs were painted along the route of our motorcade, most in Chinese but one or two in English. I had no intention of accepting insults, no matter how much importance I attached to US–Chinese relations. I instructed a member of my staff to hand my pamphlet to a Chinese protocol officer with the remark that it must have been left there by the previous party. I had all the rest of the bulletins collected and presented to the Chinese without comment. They received them in silence.

The Chinese had not constructed the new and delicate mechanism of rapprochement with the United States to have it smashed now on the altar of ideology. A thaw began to set in as soon as Chou En-lai received our entire party in the Great Hall of the People later that day. After a group picture was taken at the entrance to the meeting room, Chou seated us behind the inevitable cups of green tea and proceeded to say a few words of personal greeting to everyone in the party. The Premier had done his biographical homework well and flattered my associates with references to their educational and professional history or, with Al Jenkins, to his residence in China twenty-five years before.

Our preliminary session was confined to generalities and the agenda. Chou En-lai then hosted a banquet in our honor at which he delivered a toast of extraordinary warmth, free of any ideological controversy, without any reference to the war in Indochina. He dedicated my visit to friendship between China and the United States. Nor did he omit subtle flattery, joking about my penchant for philosophy, picking up a remark of several months before — my opening statement calling China a land of mystery. The toast was not published, and since it was less formal, it gives a better picture of Chou's style than the official ones:

Dr. Kissinger and friends, I would like to take this opportunity to welcome President Nixon's special envoy Dr. Kissinger and the other American friends who have come to China for this interim visit. The purpose of Dr. Kissinger's present visit is to make preparations related to the political discussions and the technical arrangements of President Nixon's visit.

A new chapter will now be opened in the history of the relations between China and the United States after they have been cut off for twenty-two years, and we should say that the credit for this should go to Chairman Mao Tse-tung and President Nixon. Of course, there must be someone serving as a guide, and it was Dr. Kissinger who courageously made a secret visit to China, the so-called "land of mystery." That was quite a remarkable thing. This is now Dr. Kissinger's second visit to a land that should no longer be considered a "mystery." He has come as a friend, and has also brought with him some new friends.

As for me, although I have never been to the United States, I know quite a few American friends, and the United States is not unfamiliar to me. It is evident that the social systems of our two countries are different, and our respective world outlooks — Dr. Kissinger likes to use the word "Philosophy"

— are totally different, yet this should not prevent us from finding common ground. The Sino-American talks have gone on for sixteen years now, but no common ground has yet been found. Now President Nixon will personally come to Peking for discussions, and Dr. Kissinger is his advanceman. We hope these discussions will achieve positive results.

Our two peoples are great peoples. Although our two countries are separated by the vast Pacific Ocean, friendship links our two peoples together. After receiving the U.S. table tennis team this year, we received a number of other American friends. We hope that this new era will be approached in a new spirit.

I propose a toast to the friendship between the great American people and the great Chinese people and to the health of Dr. Kissinger and all our other friends!

Chou's reference to our earlier conversation, as if we were engaged in a continuous dialogue, was a characteristic touch, one of the most insinuating Chinese skills. Everything ever said to me by any Chinese of any station during any visit was part of an intricate design — even when with my slower Occidental mind it took me a while to catch on. And subjects were carried forward between meetings months apart as if there had never been an interruption.

At the end of the dinner Chou walked around the room, shaking hands and clinking glasses with every member of my party, including junior staff, secretaries, and the crew off the aircraft. This set the warm tone for the rest of the trip, which was partly designed by the Chinese stage managers to accustom the Chinese people to the new relationship.

First, however, the Chinese had to clear up the issue of the bulletins in our room and the posters that we had encountered on the way into the city. The Acting Foreign Minister called for me at the guest house the day after our arrival to escort me to a meeting with Chou En-lai. In the car on the way to the Great Hall of the People, he pointed out that each nation had its own means of communicating with its people; we used newspapers and television, the Chinese used wall posters. He pointed to a poster that we were just then passing as an example. Freshly installed where only yesterday a sign had castigated American imperialism, it now read in English: "Welcome Afro-Asian Ping-Pong Tournament." A few minutes later Chou En-lai mentioned in passing that we should observe Peking's actions, not its rhetoric; the anti-American propaganda was "firing an empty cannon."

I do not know whether the offending signs had been put up by Chou's opponents and Chou then used my protest to get Mao to overrule them; or whether they were erected with Chou's approval to test the limits of our tolerance; or whether they had been put up long before and left by bureaucratic inertia. Whatever the cause, there was no further untoward incident. We saw no other hostile posters and many examples of posters that had been blotted out. (When we left Peking five days later, similar signs at the airport had been replaced.)

The mood changed sharply after that. Indeed, the rest of my visit was marked by overwhelming courtesy and friendliness, and, even more important, by a major effort to establish in the Chinese public mind that Americans were there as honored guests. On the day of our arrival the official Party newspaper listed the welcoming committee; its high rank underlined the importance attached to the visit. On October 21, the *People's Daily* carried two photographs of Chou and me; it was the first time in twenty years that an American official had been pictured with a Chinese leader.

On the evening of October 22 we were taken to the Great Hall of the People to see a "revolutionary" Peking opera — an art form of truly stupefying boredom in which villains were the incarnation of evil and wore black, good guys wore red, and as far as I could make out the girl fell in love with a tractor. We were escorted by Marshal Yeh Chien-ying, Acting Foreign Minister Chi P'eng-fei, the Prime Minister's Secretary, and other leading Chinese personalities into an auditorium where, to our surprise, approximately five hundred middle-level Chinese officials had been assembled. It was a carefully selected group and this was the first time that our exposure was widened beyond the top leadership. We were about two hours late, a meeting with Chou having been unexpectedly protracted. Immediately upon entering, Marshal Yeh and the other top leaders began to clap loudly, inviting a response from the audience. I must in all candor admit that the American visitors did not exactly bring the house down, partly because we were unfamiliar with the Communist habit of clapping back. In any event, the point was surely driven home: these Americans were distinctly *personae gratae*.

The next day, October 23, my public exposure was advanced another step, with an ostentatious public appearance. In the morning I was taken to visit the Great Wall and the Ming Tombs, not at all shielded, as in July, from curious tourists. In the afternoon our hosts arranged a visit to the Summer Palace, about a half hour's drive west of Peking. My escort again was the eminent Marshal Yeh, who saw to it that he and I were properly displayed together before what the Chinese call "the masses." The Acting Foreign Minister and the Secretary to the Prime Minister were also present. The high point of this episode was our taking tea aboard a boat poled out onto the lake in plain view of literally hundreds of Chinese spectators — including, in addition, a North Vietnamese newsman who took pictures. Chou later mentioned his presence to me and apologized. I did not object; it did not bother me if Hanoi got the message; I suspected that Chou had the same purpose in mind. The fact that a strong, cold wind was blowing did not deter our hosts; they clearly wanted the boat ride to take place, and only a hurricane could have prevented this ''contact'' with the Chinese people.

Gradually escalating public exposure served Chinese domestic necessities, but the test of our visit would be our ability to arrange the President's trip, advance further our political rapprochement, and begin to agree on a communiqué. The details of the Nixon trip were settled very rapidly. We proposed two dates, February 21 and March 16; Chou chose the earlier. Since the size of our proposed party was so much larger than I had indicated in July, I had had my staff prepare a briefing book for Chou that showed the dimensions of past Presidential trips, a ''reduced optimum plan'' for Nixon's visit to China, and the ''bare minimum plan'' that we had finally made. My hope was that if we presented a reasonable proposition, Chou would not haggle. The Chinese studied the briefing book for two days and then accepted what we considered a bare-bones Presidential party, which still amounted to some several hundred. Chou for some reason used this occasion to tell me that he had seen the movie *Patton*, after hearing of Nixon's admiration for the film and its subject.

The remaining technical problems solved themselves as easily as was compatible with the obsessive single-mindedness of the advance men. The communications expert came up with an ambitious plan that would have preempted every telephone line in Peking. I told Chou that by the time we got through he would surely be able to call Washington; whether he could still reach Shanghai was another matter. The head of our security detail distinguished himself by requesting a list of subversives in each locality the President was likely to visit. This raised an interesting problem, because in China conservative Republicans would undoubtedly be classed as subversives and if we asked how many Communist sympathizers there were we would get the unsettling answer of 800 million. Our security expert also fiercely resisted the proposition that the President might travel in a Chinese plane or a Chinese limousine — in his manual there were no reliable foreigners and no reliable foreign machines. Eventually, Nixon had to overrule him.

Chou and I spent over twenty-five hours together reviewing the world situation, another fifteen working on a statement that later came to be known as the Shanghai Communiqué. The world review followed the pattern established in July but went into more depth. Chou and I understood that we were in no position to make formal agreements. We could strive to understand each other's purposes and tactics. To the extent that they were compatible they would lead to complementary policies.

I have already expressed my appreciation of Chou's outstanding qualities. I met no leader — with the exception of de Gaulle — with an equal grasp of world events. His knowledge of detail was astonishing, but where many leaders use detail to avoid complexity, Chou also had an extraordinary grasp of the relationship of events. He was a dedicated ideologue, but he used the faith that had sustained him through decades of struggle to discipline a passionate nature into one of the most acute and unsentimental assessments of reality that I have encountered. Chou did not identify leadership with the proclamation of personal idiosyncrasies. He understood that statesmen cannot invent reality, and was fond of quoting an old Chinese proverb: "The helmsman must guide the boat by using the waves; otherwise it will be submerged by the waves." Statesmanship required a knowledge of what could not be changed as well as an understanding of the scope available for creativity. In this extraordinary manner — without ever discussing common actions — did the United States and the People's Republic continue the process of coordinating their approaches to the issues of global peace and equilibrium.

The most dramatic encounter was over the communiqué for Nixon's visit. The outside observer tends to believe, and is encouraged to do so by heads of government, that these joint pronouncements grow spontaneously out of the discussions they purport to summarize. The opposite is usually true. The discussions of heads of government are framed by a communiqué usually drafted beforehand. To leave communiqué drafting for the actual visit is to court disaster. The protocol functions consume too much time; the danger of running up against a deadline is too great. Heads of government should use their time at summitry to gain an insight into the perceptions and thinking of their counterparts, not to quibble over language. This will help them make decisions in the future; it may make all the difference in crises.

Nixon had given me authority to negotiate the communiqué for his visit. I could communicate with Washington by the teletype on my airplane, but Nixon had no staff available to vet my recommendations — all the China experts were with me. Nor did he seek to; as in all negotiations after 1971 he had given me a wide area of discretion. Nixon had seen and approved a draft communiqué prepared by me and my staff. It followed the conventional style, highlighting fuzzy areas of agreement and obscuring differences with platitudinous generalizations; in this case it clearly implied more common ground than actually existed. I handed over this draft to Chou En-lai on the evening of October 22. The next evening Chou gave me his initial reaction — that our draft could serve as a basis for discussion. Naturally, the Chinese would want to add their views in some places; Acting Foreign Minister Chi P'eng-fei would begin the redrafting process with me the next morning.

To my surprise, at the appointed hour the Premier himself showed up. Quite uncharacteristically, he made a scorching one-hour speech — at the express direction of Mao, he said. He declared that our approach was unacceptable. The communiqué had to set forth fundamental differences; otherwise the wording would have an "untruthful appearance." Our draft implied that peace was an end in itself; the Chinese believed that struggle was more important than peace or at least that peace could grow only out of struggle. Ours pretended to illusory agreements; the Chinese were not afraid to face the reality of differences. In addition, we would have to renounce our Taiwan ties. Our present draft was the sort of banality the Soviets would sign but neither mean nor observe.

My normal approach to negotiations was to conduct them in a bantering tone to put my opposite number at ease, to avoid turning every issue into a test of will, and to emphasize the turn toward firmness when a line had to be drawn. I therefore replied in an unusually hard manner. I said that I respected Chou's convictions, but proclamations of infallible doctrine were out of place in a communiqué. The Chinese would not respect us if we started our new relationship by betraying our old friends; we would not renounce our Taiwan ties. Problems between us had to be solved by history, not force. We were here not simply to record philosophical disagreement but to chart a path. We could not just catalogue disagreements; there had to be some thrust into the future. I did not think we should risk drafting a communiqué from scratch during the President's visit; but the choice was up to Chou.

Following a break, Chou said that he would submit a proposed draft later in the day. After stuffing us with roast duck, Chou submitted his paper in the evening. It was unprecedented in design. It stated the Chinese position on a whole host of issues in extremely uncompromising terms. It left blank pages for our position, which was assumed to be contrary. It was intransigent on Taiwan. At first I was taken aback. To end a Presidential visit with a catalogue of disagreements was extraordinary; it was also, I thought, unacceptable internationally and domestically. But as I reflected further I began to see that the very novelty of the approach might resolve our perplexities. A statement of differences would reassure allies and friends that their interests had been defended; if we could develop some common positions, these would then stand out as the authentic convictions of principled leaders. We would avoid the exegesis of platitudes, which is the bane of the standard communiqué. And we would not run the risk of contradiction and ill will after the communiqué was issued and each side explained the meaning of vague language to its own advantage.

After a brief break I told Chou that I would accept his basic approach. The communiqué could contain an extended statement of differences; we would supply the American position for those areas later. However, the language of the disagreements had to be compatible with the occasion. Some of the Chinese formulations were stated in rigid and unacceptable fashion; the President could not put his name to a document repeating standard propaganda positions that were published every day in the newspapers. We would not accept language that tended to put us on trial or to humiliate an American President even if it was clearly labeled as the Chinese point of view. Also, there would have to be some common positions, or else the whole journey would be seen as an exercise in futility. I promised to submit a counterdraft the next morning.

It turned into a contest of physical endurance. Lord redrafted the communiqué while I got three hours of sleep. Then he went to bed and I reworked his draft for the remainder of the night. We concentrated on softening the language of the Chinese positions, writing the sections expressing the American position, and developing some common points of agreement. We deliberately chose moderate formulations for our point of view because this would be our first opportunity to present American values and purposes to the Chinese public. We sought a tone of firmness without belligerence.

Our counterdraft of October 25 ushered in a session that lasted the whole day, interrupted occasionally for several hours while the Chinese translated our text, studied it, and, no doubt, cleared their position with Mao. As I have already mentioned, Chou agreed to delete the most egregious sentences from the statement of the Chinese position. We outlined the key joint positions, especially the paragraph concerning both countries' opposition to hegemony. (Though this later became a hallowed Chinese word, it actually was introduced first by us.)

Taiwan, as expected, provided the most difficult issue. We needed a formula acknowledging the unity of China, which was the one point on which Taipei and Peking agreed, without supporting the claim of either. I finally put forward the American position on Taiwan as follows: "The United States acknowledges that all Chinese on either side of the Taiwan Straits maintain there is but one China. The United States Government does not challenge that position." I do not think anything I did or said impressed Chou as much as this ambiguous formula with which both sides were able to live for nearly a decade. (In fairness I must say that I adapted it from a State Department planning document for negotiations, which aborted in the Fifties.) The Chinese asked for a recess at 11:35 P.M. At 4:45 A.M. we were given a new Chinese draft and by 5:30 A.M. Chou returned. He and I refined the text for several more hours until at 8:10 A.M., concluding a nearly nonstop session of twenty-four hours, we had agreed on the main outline of what came to be known as the Shanghai Communiqué. It was an unusual document. Its explicit, sometimes brutal disagreements gave emphasis to the common positions — the concern with hegemony (a euphemism for Soviet expansionism), the commitment to normalize relations. The paragraph on the American defense relationship to Taiwan was left open, but the two sides' positions were within range of each other and the agreed portions needed beefing up. I was confident that we could find a solution when I returned with Nixon in February.

We had scheduled our departure for 9:00 A.M. Chou took me to the door of the guest house and spoke to me for the first time in English: "Come back soon for the joy of talking."

The United Nations

M Y plane was barely airborne for home when the teletype chattered out the news that in the United Nations we had lost the battle to preserve Taiwan's seat. Chou told me later that he had learned of the vote just before my departure but that he did not want to embarrass me by being the first to inform me. Ironically, on my visit I did not have the impression that the Chinese expected to prevail in that session. Chou had referred to the subject only once and briefly, pointing out that Taiwan's status was more important to Peking than membership in the United Nations; Peking would not take its seat under our dual-representation formula.

The vote had come a week earlier than expected mainly because fewer nations than expected chose to speak. Advocates of the Albanian resolution decided to force a vote on Monday night, October 25. Valiant efforts by our UN Ambassador, George Bush, failed to stall it. At 9:47 P.M. the tabulating lights above the podium in the General Assembly flashed the totals: The Important Question resolution, which we had still expected to win, *lost* by 59 votes against, 55 in favor, and 15 abstentions. Every NATO ally except Luxembourg, Portugal, and Greece voted "no" or abstained. The *New York Times* reported what followed:

> The Tanzanians, who were among the floor managers for Peking, jumped from their seats in the front row and did a little victory dance. The Algerians, fellow cosponsors, embraced one another. The Albanians sedately shook hands. Others stood up, applauded, cheered. Rhythmic clapping beat against the walls. The vote on the Albanian resolution 90 minutes later was anticlimactic. The result was 76–35, with 17 abstentions (and without a single NATO ally on the American side).[4]

Thus the Albanian resolution passed overwhelmingly. The US resolution for dual representation and the Security Council seat for Peking, which our government had labored so hard to shape and promote, never came to a vote. The essence of the matter was that friendly nations changed their position. Many of them had long been torn between their desire not to antagonize us and their self-interest in gaining the favor of powerful China. As long as the United States was in a posture of hostility to Peking, they feared that voting for the admission of the People's Republic would incur some penalty from us. Once we moved dramatically toward rapprochement with China, they no longer feared that we would impose such a penalty. Thus all of State's efforts to frame a "reasonable compromise" resolution were to no avail. By voting for Peking's admission, not only could other countries serve their geopolitical interest; supporting Peking was also a way to satisfy their domestic left, all the more useful if it seemed to be in defiance of the United States.

Reaction in Congress was bitter and surprisingly widespread. There was strong sentiment to retaliate against the UN and against countries that had voted to expel Taiwan. Secretary Rogers at a news conference on Tuesday, October 26, welcomed Peking into the UN but said that the United States "deeply regrets" the expulsion of Taiwan; it was a "most unfortunate" precedent "which will have many adverse effects in the future." He said the Administration would not support a reduction of funds for the UN in retaliation, but to preempt Congressional assaults he did suggest that "there has to be some hard thinking by member nations" about whether the UN was "living beyond its resources." The next day, Wednesday, October 27, Ron Ziegler issued a much sharper statement. Speaking from notes he had taken during an early-morning conversation with Nixon, Ziegler declared that the President was outraged by the "spectacle" of "cheering, handclapping and dancing" after the vote; Nixon found this a "shocking demonstration" of "undisguised glee" and "personal animosity." Careful not to condemn the vote itself, Ziegler warned that the offensive and undignified behavior "could very seriously impair support for the United Nations in the country and in the Congress" and "even affect foreign aid allocations," since some of the delegates that exhibited such jubilation were from countries to which the United States had been "quite generous." Ziegler's statement fanned the hysteria on Capitol Hill. The worst offenders, amazingly enough, were the liberals who had always advocated Peking's admission to the UN. Conservative amendments to cut back the US contribution to the UN were headed off in the Senate. But a group of liberal Senators, in a surprise late-evening vote on Friday, October 29, in a fit of Vietnam-era hysteria killed the Administration's *entire* $3.3 billion foreign aid authorization bill, after loading it with antiwar amendments and provisions to replace bilateral with multilateral aid. Nixon justifiably condemned this "highly irresponsible action which undoes twenty-five years of constructive bipartisan foreign policy and produces unacceptable risks to the national security of the United States."

Meanwhile, I returned late on October 26 to a White House already in a state of agitation. Some in the government saw an opportunity to weaken my position by leaking comments blaming the outcome of the China vote on my visit to Peking. And the President was becoming restive at the publicity I was receiving. He had selected me for the July secret mission in part because I had less visibility than any other candidate and was more easily controlled. But Nixon, like any other President, had no intention of being upstaged by his own Assistant. I could see a ripple of Washington's currents when I was asked to stop over in Alaska on the way back so that I would not arrive home on the day of the UN vote (this had been requested by Rogers) — a virtual acknowledgment that my trip was responsible for the outcome. And I was disembarked at a distant corner of Andrews Air Force Base, inaccessible to newsmen and photographers.

It was not a heroic homecoming, especially after the strenuous exertions of the preceding days. But it made no lasting difference. One cannot make it a political issue that a diplomatic setback which had been recognized as inevitable occurred a little earlier than expected. And while Nixon could be peevish and petty, he was not about to risk an imminent triumph or a key element of his foreign policy.

Planning for his trip to Peking accelerated and soon submerged other considerations. Peking took its seat in the United Nations, not without a private joke between Chou and me. For China's Deputy Foreign Minister Ch'iao Kuan-hua showed that the Chinese never waste anything; he included in his maiden speech in the United Nations almost all the polemics I had deleted from the draft of the communiqué. I, in turn, instructed George Bush to express regret that Peking had decided to begin participation in this world body by "firing these empty cannons of rhetoric." Chou understood, though some editorial writers found it harsh and others wondered at the strange metaphor.

On November 15 I proposed in our Paris channel that the new Chinese mission to the UN be authorized to deal with its American counterparts in an emergency. The Chinese agreed on November 20. This link was soon to be needed during the India-Pakistan war. In fact, I met secretly in New York about a dozen times over the next year and a half with Huang Hua, who was quickly moved from Ottawa to become China's UN Ambassador. These meetings, together with my annual trips to China, became the principal channel of communications until the creation of the Liaison Offices in Washington and Peking in mid-1973.

Over Thanksgiving, flying to San Clemente with me on *Air Force One*, my nine-year-old son David was teased by the White House press, who asked if he knew the still-secret date of Nixon's China trip. David had heard March mentioned on the radio, and said so. The press gleefully reported this as a scoop; for days afterward I was pursued by newsmen who wanted to know if I was going to "muzzle" my son for his leaking of state secrets. But the reports of David's "leaking" were as incorrect as the radio report that he had heard in the first place. On November 29 the White House announced the agreed date of Nixon's visit to Peking — luckily for my son, it turned out to be February 21, 1972.

The year that had started with elliptical and tentative messages to Peking through third parties had ended with face-to-face talks and several direct channels. After having had no communication with Chinese leaders for twenty years, we had conducted one of the most comprehensive reviews of international relations in my diplomatic experience. An American President was to visit the Chinese capital; a communiqué was already essentially agreed upon. In one giant step we had transformed our diplomacy. We had brought new flexibility to our foreign policy. We had captured the initiative and also the imagination of our own people. We had much farther to go, of course. But we had made a new departure and traveled some distance down the road.

XX

US–Soviet Relations: Breakthrough on Two Fronts

I T was in a brief interlude of calm that Andrei Gromyko came to Washington in October 1970, and Richard Nixon had his first meeting as President with a Soviet leader. The crises of Cienfuegos and Jordan were just behind us. The SALT talks were scheduled to resume on November 2, the Berlin talks were reconvening, and despite Soviet deceit in Cuba and the Middle East, Nixon's near obsession with a Moscow summit meeting had not abated. In Gromyko we were meeting a master craftsman, a Foreign Minister who had to design policy for a Politburo without significant experience of the outside world and who had to conduct the international affairs of a superpower from a bureaucratic jungle in which his only power base was his own competence. He was a survivor. He had lived through the Stalin period, the Molotov era at the Foreign Ministry, and Khrushchev's roller-coaster diplomacy. He was only thirty-four when he was made Ambassador to the United States in 1943. He had been Foreign Minister since 1957, when he replaced Dmitri Shepilov after a spell as Ambassador to the United Nations from 1946 to 1949. He had met in the Oval Office with Franklin Roosevelt and every American President since.

The price of survival included being the butt of the crude jokes of whoever was the top Soviet leader; Khrushchev and Brezhnev were alike in this respect. Khrushchev once boasted to a foreign visitor that if Gromyko were asked to sit on a block of ice with his pants down he would do so unquestioningly until ordered to leave it. Brezhnev's humor, though less brutal, made the same point. Neither left any doubt that in their view one of Gromyko's great assets was literal adherence to orders as a pliant instrument of arbitrary power.

Gromyko's face would crease in smiles when he was the butt of this heavy-handed joshing. Only his eyes remained wary and slightly melancholy, like those of the beagle who has endured the inexplicable foibles of his master yet bent them to his own will. Through all this Gromyko preserved an aloof kind of dignity; he was loyal and compliant but not obsequious. And inevitably a point would be reached where his competence would dominate the discussions. He became the indispensable drive-wheel of Soviet foreign policy, the consummate Soviet diplomat, well-briefed, confident, and tenacious. He never entered a negotiation without having mastered the subject. At first he knew little of strategic weapons, but he learned so well that he was eventually able to conduct dogged rearguard actions even on the most trivial issues. Indeed, for Gromyko there were no minor issues; every point was pressed with impartial tenacity, eroding all dividing lines and permitting him to trade what should never have been raised for something essential. He once drew me into a daylong discussion, on how to calculate the volume of Soviet missiles, that had no relationship to any known Soviet missile or program and was in fact technically absurd though logically impeccable. It was a maddeningly theoretical point, essentially irrelevant, but one which, once raised, had to be searched in case of booby traps. (This proved free of them; it disappeared from the negotiations at the next session.) On another occasion he claimed that each of the United States' new planned strategic bombers, the B-1, should count as three weapons in the SALT totals. When asked why, he paused and then argued that it was faster and would arrive over the USSR before the B-52. Introducing speed as a strategic criterion was a brand-new thought. He was nonplussed when it was pointed out that the B-1 was much slower than missiles that counted only as one. He finally abandoned this line of argument, in a grand gesture, but still contrived to claim this as a valuable concession for which he was due something.

Normally, Gromyko knew every shade of a subject; it was suicidal to negotiate with him without mastering the record or the issues. He was indefatigable and imperturbable. When he lost his temper, one knew it was carefully planned. Curiously enough, this removed much of the sting; it was obviously never personal. He had a prodigious memory that enabled him to bank every concession, however slight, he believed we had made — or perhaps even hinted at. It would then become the starting point for the next round. Gromyko did not believe in the brilliant stroke or the dramatic maneuver. His innate caution and Moscow's domestic politics were against them. Before he was elevated to the Politburo in 1973 he was an implementer, not a maker, of policy. Afterward, he became visibly more influential and self-confident; toward the end of my term in office, he would not hesitate to correct even Brezhnev if he thought his chief had strayed from the established line.

Gromyko's method of negotiation approached a stereotype. It seemed a reflection of the national character and of Russian history. Just as Russia had expanded over the centuries by gradually inundating the territories on the flat plain surrounding the original Grand Duchy of Muscovy, so Gromyko preferred steady pressure to the bold move. He patiently accumulated marginal gains until they amounted to a major difference. He relied on the restlessness of his opposite number to extract otherwise unachievable advantages. He would hold onto his own concessions until the last possible moment, almost invariably toward the very end of the last scheduled negotiating session. There was no sense wasting them, he seemed to reason, so long as there was the slightest possibility that the other side might yield first. Against inexperienced negotiators — and compared with Gromyko most negotiators were inexperienced — this technique was extremely effective. Once one had caught onto it, however, the tactic tended to be self-defeating. Eventually it dawned that if one could keep one's composure long enough, Gromyko would reveal he had more in his pocket than he had been prepared to admit.

Whenever possible, Gromyko tried to sell even the opening of a negotiation; that is to say, he would demand a concession as a price for sitting down at the bargaining table. After that he would seek to wear down his opposite number by endless haggling over "general principles." Once these were agreed, he would get a second crack at the issue by haggling over implementation; tentative agreements thus often tended to dissolve in the exegesis of their meaning. Whatever Gromyko might say disapprovingly about linkage in general, he was a great believer in linking every detail of a negotiation to every other. He offered every concession conditionally, dependent on some movement on some other subject. Only after this laborious process had demonstrated to him — and, perhaps even more important, to his superiors — that the lemon had been squeezed absolutely dry, would he move to a settlement, often very rapidly.

And then innate suspiciousness compounded by the congenital insecurity of the system and the bureaucratic structure within which he lived would take over. The only time this master negotiator would betray any emotion was in the last phase of a negotiation after the agreement was in essence complete. Then Gromyko seemed to be seized by an undefinable terror that his opposite number might pull some last-minute trick on him. He would seek to rush through the signature — showing that the stolid exertions of the preceding months and years had taken their toll on his composure after all. Or perhaps he feared the obloquy of his colleagues if their complicated decision-making should have proved in vain. The previous bullying then emerged as the ironic reflection of a profound absence of self-confidence, the fear of being tricked in the end despite one's most strenuous efforts.

No doubt the Soviet system shaped Gromyko's style. He was too experienced not to know that some propositions he advanced were unrealizable even when coupled with his dogged persistence. But most probably he could convince his chiefs, and later his colleagues on the Politburo, only by a succession of prolonged stalemates. Greater flexibility might have seemed suspiciously like ideological impurity, or mere softness.

Every negotiator must decide at what point marginal gains are no longer worth the loss of confidence caused by the kind of haggling that merges with sharp practice. Amateurs think of great diplomats as crafty; but the wise diplomat understands that he cannot afford to trick his opponent; in the long run a reputation for reliability and fairness is an important asset. The same negotiators meet over and over again; their ability to deal with one another is undermined if a diplomat acquires a reputation for evasion or duplicity. But there is no premium in the Soviet system for farsighted restraint. So Gromyko would proceed by splitting minuscule differences, selling every marginal change of position as dearly as possible. He was in the retail, not the wholesale, business. For Gromyko every negotiation was a *tabula rasa;* it started as if it had no history, and it established no claim or obligation for the future. Confidence, if it meant anything at all, depended on a balance of interests that had to be redefined from scratch in each negotiation.

If after 1973 I sought to keep Moscow out of Middle East negotiations, the reason was partly geopolitical, partly the Soviet negotiating style. I was convinced that progress in Middle East diplomacy depended on fluidity, on keeping the parties' positions relatively open until they had explored not only the legal but the psychological meanings of what was being said. But I knew that Gromyko, once involved, would advance some document with endless legalistic clauses and then work pedantically at going through them one by one. Even with Soviet goodwill (which I did not take for granted) this was the road to deadlock, to giving a veto to the most radical elements, and hence eventually to explosion.

Sometimes Gromyko's tactics left a bad taste. Occasionally he — or those who made the political decisions — overreached themselves. The absolute refusal to take any chance, the desire to squeeze every possible gain from a negotiation caused, as I have already shown, the Soviet leaders to miss the opportunity for a summit in 1970 when our bargaining position was weak, or in 1971 before our announcement of the Peking summit. Had the Soviets responded in 1970, they would at least have complicated our China initiative and inhibited our freedom of maneuver in the Middle East. Had the Kremlin ended its cat-and-mouse game about the summit in the spring of 1971 and announced a date, its bargaining position would have been greatly strengthened. Our perennial critics, and some Kremlinologists, would then have blamed every negotiating deadlock with Moscow on our move toward Peking. By continuing to squeeze us, the Kremlin inadvertently gave our diplomacy extraordinary scope toward *both* Peking and Moscow.

Withal, I grew to like and respect Gromyko. Within the framework imposed by the system he represented he was honorable. He was a man of his word. It might be difficult to get him to agree, but he stuck to his bargains — or if he was obliged to change course, he did so with visible embarrassment. Despite his dour countenance he had an excellent sense of humor, though the American style of wisecracking at first eluded him. We met for the first time at a reception given by the President for heads of delegations at the United Nations in September 1969. Gromyko walked up to me and said: "You look just like Henry Kissinger." I replied: "You look just like Richard Nixon." This took him a few seconds to hoist aboard, especially as his entourage was reluctant to laugh until he had given the signal. By the next year he had absorbed the style. When we discussed which entrance he should use for his White House meeting with Nixon, Gromyko said it did not make any difference; the guards would salute and let him through wherever he presented himself; who would stop the President? To make sure that everyone — especially his associates — understood that it was playtime, he gave a hearty laugh reminiscent of a street-corner Santa Claus.

During the Moscow summit of 1972 one of our Xerox machines broke down. Knowing the KGB's reputation for Orwellian ubiquity, I asked Gromyko during a meeting in the elegant St. Catherine's Hall in the Kremlin whether he could have some copies made for us if we held certain documents up to the chandelier. Gromyko replied without missing a beat that unfortunately the cameras were installed by the tsars; they were adequate for photographing people but not documents.

Gromyko's favorite verbal device was the double or even quadruple negative. "Not out of the question" was for him a resounding affirmative. When things were going badly, his face would take on an expression of such plaintive dejection that one was tempted into a compassionate obligation to yield. But above all he would persist in whatever course he was on, using whatever argument was at hand. Once we argued about two relatively minor paragraphs in a document. Gromyko insisted vociferously that paragraphs — *all* paragraphs — should be structured as a crescendo rising to a climactic last sentence. After letting him win his point, I confronted him with the identical argument for the next paragraph. Gromyko dryly responded that some paragraphs should be arranged as a diminuendo. I gave him his choice. He could not have both. He opted for crescendo in both paragraphs.

Without doubt, Gromyko was one of the ablest diplomats with whom I dealt. At one stage he was handling simultaneously negotiations on strategic arms limitations, prevention of accidental war, Berlin, trade, and a host of minor agreements; he conducted himself with great skill, patience, and discipline; he was on top of all these subjects. He did not embody a great vision or put forward a compelling model of a world order, but neither did the system he represented. It was not his assignment or his conception of his role to ask the ultimate questions. And he would not have survived so long if he had. Chou En-lai, possessing the sense of cultural superiority of an ancient civilization, softened the edges of ideological hostility by an insinuating ease of manner and a seemingly effortless skill to penetrate to the heart of the matter. Gromyko, as the spokesman of a country that had never prevailed except by raw power, lacked this confidence; he was obliged to test his mettle in every encounter. It was easy to underestimate him. His bulldozing persistence was a deliberate method of operation, not a gauge of his subtlety. He protected his country in times of turbulence and confusion; he masked its weakness; he advanced its purposes. Final greatness eluded him; but he achieved important objectives and he rarely made avoidable errors. There are few foreign ministers to whom one can pay such a tribute.

In October 1970, I was at the very beginning of my experience with Gromyko. He arrived in Washington during a brief period of hope. After the official termination of the Cienfuegos affair, it seemed Soviet-American relations would improve. Talks on Berlin and arms control were scheduled. The Middle East was cooling off. There seemed to be an agreement in principle on both the timing and agenda of a summit. While the Soviet reply of September 25 had pushed the date of a summit meeting into 1971, this, in Nixon's eager view, did not need to preclude the benefit of an early announcement before the November elections. Nixon also wanted to make sure that the planning of an eventual summit would stay in the White House Channel. He asked me to explore these possibilities with Dobrynin before he met Gromyko, especially to ensure that Gromyko did not let slip in front of Rogers, who would be present, that we had been exploring a summit since April — the Secretary of State had learned it only a few weeks earlier.

It rapidly became apparent that the suspicions and tensions of the summer and autumn had taken their toll on both sides. A preliminary meeting with Dobrynin on October 17 turned somewhat acrimonious. In addition to his customary litany of American errors he said that Gromyko had come to find out whether we had made a decision to adopt a hard line. I told him that he would find the President prepared to explore the prospects of a happier future. A speech that the President planned to deliver to the United Nations in a few days would be cast in conciliatory terms. Dobrynin indicated that Gromyko would be prepared to discuss the summit with the President.

Before his meeting with Gromyko, I wrote a memorandum to the President on the principal issues. The meeting was taking place, I pointed out, at a moment of unusual sensitivity in US–Soviet relations. We were bound to ask ourselves about the Soviets' performance in the Middle East, their military foray into Cuba, their continuing strategic buildup, the policy of selective détente seeking to divide us from the Europeans. We had no good evidence concerning the attitudes of Soviet leaders, the jockeying that must be going on among them in anticipation of the Party Congress, and the distribution of power within the Soviet leadership. I counseled against any attempt to play off factions in the Kremlin against each other; we did not know enough to pit doves against hawks. We did best in our relationship with the Soviet Union when we looked after our own interests and let the Soviets define theirs. It was still early enough in the President's term to achieve fundamental progress, but this, we should make clear, was incompatible with the unremitting pressure for unilateral advantage and constant efforts to exploit trouble spots that had characterized recent Soviet policy.

The meeting of October 22 between Gromyko and Nixon was attended by Rogers, me, and Dobrynin (and interpreters from both sides). Gromyko voiced the same complaints that Dobrynin had outlined on October 17. Nixon — partly because he wanted to keep open the summit option, partly because it was his style — rebutted in a more general way, stressing the importance of seeking areas for agreement, especially on SALT and trade. There was a review of the Middle East, Berlin, European security, and Vietnam. Gromyko introduced nothing new and Nixon restated the American position. The meeting provided a more cordial atmosphere, but no turning point of substance.

Toward the end, however, Gromyko raised the subject for which Nixon had been waiting eagerly: the idea of a summit. With his usual mastery of the double negative, Gromyko allowed that the President's thoughts on this subject were not inconsistent with those of the Soviet leadership. He suggested that the meeting be arranged for sometime after April 1971, in Moscow. Nixon, for the benefit of the State Department note-taker, pretended to weigh this as a new and momentous proposition. Nixon agreed that a summit in Moscow would be a dramatic event; indeed, it was so subject to misinterpretation that the decision to hold it should not be sprung on an unwary public and the Congress through a leak. He therefore recommended an early announcement. But Gromyko had not maintained himself for nearly fifteen years as Foreign Minister by giving away things for nothing. He intended to use the prospect of the summit to press us further on matters of concern to the Soviet Union, such as Berlin. He demurred. He had not meant to imply that a summit announcement should be made today or tomorrow. He would be returning to Moscow on October 29. Soon afterward the *timing* of the announcement could be agreed between them. Nixon, not wanting to pursue the subject in front of a large group, offered to show Gromyko his hideaway in the Executive Office Building. There, safely away from the group in the Oval Office, he explained to Gromyko that all preparations for the summit should take place between Dobrynin and me.

The next day Nixon delivered a major speech at the United Nations, focusing on US–Soviet relations. While not minimizing differences, Nixon took a conciliatory and hopeful line, as I had told Dobrynin he would. Nixon stressed our perennial themes: that in the nuclear age the classic pattern of exploiting tensions for unilateral gain was too dangerous, that the United States wished to move from a era of confrontation to an era of negotiation, that we were ready to settle outstanding issues on the basis of reciprocity. Moscow was given the choice between confrontation and negotiation; Nixon's strong preference was for the latter.

That day Nixon sent me to Dobrynin, who was in New York accompanying Gromyko to the United Nations, to make one more try at a summit announcement. We would like to announce the summit on October 29 or 30 from San Clemente, I told Dobrynin. One did not have to be too well versed in American politics to understand this rather transparent maneuver so close to our Congressional elections. Dobrynin immediately warned of poor communications (an amazing claim for a superpower) and slow decision-making. But he finally relented and promised to report to Gromyko and to Moscow with a view to speeding up a reply.

Nixon's conciliatory UN speech, in the meantime, was well received. The *Christian Science Monitor* of October 24 put the burden on the Soviets: "The President is stating the essential thinking of current American diplomacy. We applaud his responsible, high level appeal. We urge Moscow's leaders to respond in kind." The *New York Times* of October 25, noting that we were at a "crossroads," said Moscow's response to Nixon's new questioning "holds the answer not only to détente but to the future of world peace."

But relations were not destined to improve so dramatically. Minor issues seemed to arise almost spontaneously to sour things. First, two American generals in a small Beechcraft airplane wandered over the Turkish-Soviet border on October 21 and landed inside the Soviet Union. There was no dispute that the hapless officers had made an honest mistake. The Soviet leaders, however, not only looked gift horses in the mouth but would consider giving them up only for cash on the barrelhead. Dobrynin was instructed to raise the question of the release of a convicted Soviet espionage agent, Igor Ivanov. The idea of trading two generals who had nothing to do with intelligence for a convicted spy was galling, all the more so as Dobrynin knew that the United States was already considering releasing Ivanov. Then in November a Lithuanian seaman, Simas Kudirka, attempted to defect from his Soviet trawler onto a US Coast Guard ship during a fisheries negotiation off the coast of Massachusetts. The bemused Coast Guard commander permitted Soviet seamen to come on board and drag Kudirka back. This enraged Nixon and me, but it was all over long before any high officials were aware of the incident or could intervene. (It later turned out that Kudirka had a valid claim to US citizenship. He was permitted to emigrate to the United States after President Ford interceded privately on his behalf with Brezhnev.)

But the real cause of Soviet aloofness was elsewhere. Nixon's motive in seeking an early announcement was too obvious and political; the Soviets were not wrong in considering it ill-timed from a foreign policy point of view. The Politburo did not want a summit until the Berlin issue was settled, and it was afraid that once the summit was agreed we would not have an adequate incentive to proceed. Another and probably decisive cause of Soviet hesitation was the unsettled nature of the internal relations of the Soviet leadership. After Khrushchev's overthrow in 1964 the Soviet Union was governed by a troika of Brezhnev, Kosygin, and Podgorny. Until well into 1971 all our high-level communications with the Soviet Union were with Kosygin. As the Party Congress approached, Brezhnev was clearly becoming dominant, but we were still assuming that Prime Minister Kosygin would be Nixon's host. Gromyko did not demur when Nixon mentioned Kosygin's name in that context. Until Moscow had sorted out its internal priorities, the Politburo would be careful not to risk its cohesion at a summit.

Finally, the Soviet leadership had still not exhausted the opportunities for selective détente in Europe. By easing tensions with Western European allies while maintaining a hard line toward us, Moscow hoped to encourage divisions within the Western alliance. To the extent that we were blamed for tensions, NATO could be made to appear in Europe as an obstacle to peace that turned friendship with the United States into a source of danger rather than of security. Selective détente was a way of encouraging European neutralism.

Five days after the Gromyko-Nixon talk, Dobrynin gave me the reply to the proposition of an early announcement. It reaffirmed the Soviet desire for a summit. It agreed with the President that a summit had to be carefully prepared. Dobrynin and I should get to work on the subject immediately. As part of these preparations the timing of the visit and an appropriate announcement could, of course, be discussed. But October 30 was clearly premature for such an event. The Soviet leadership rejected Nixon's "fear" of a leak; it was convinced that with so few people aware of the summit discussions there could be no such danger. In this somewhat disdainful manner did the Soviets evade Nixon's overture.

But if the Soviet leaders believed that time was on their side, they had not calculated correctly. They could not complete their German policy without cooperation from us, because the German Parliament would drag its feet on ratification of the Eastern treaties without a Berlin settlement, and we had made *that* dependent upon an improvement in relations between Moscow and Washington. A few weeks later the Kremlin began to realize that its strategy of selective détente would not work either. In the middle of December 1970 it suddenly faced the danger of an upheaval in its own backyard.

The Polish Riots

THE folklore persists that revolutions occur when conditions are desperate. The reality, perceived since Tocqueville, is that most upheavals have taken place when conditions seem to be improving. The completely downtrodden are usually too demoralized to revolt. Violent change is more likely when governments become overconfident, when the population senses that it has some margin for maneuver, and when there is some progress that confirms this expectation.

So it was in Poland. On December 7, 1970, Brandt recognized the new borders of Poland and relinquished Germany's claim to recover the territories east of the Oder-Neisse line. He went to Warsaw for the signing of the treaty, knelt at the Warsaw Ghetto monument, and paid a moving and historic visit to Auschwitz. The Polish Party leader, Wladyslaw Gomulka, calculated — correctly — that the treaty with Bonn would ease the Polish people's perennial nightmare of an irredentist Germany. He thought — wrongly — that he could use his newfound popularity to solve Poland's chronic economic ills. Poland's massively inefficient industries had increased output but had been stockpiling unwanted goods until by 1970 their inventories reached the astonishing total of 50 percent of the Gross National Product. Two consecutive poor harvests compounded consumer goods shortages with a food crisis. Unemployment added to tensions; in early 1970, two hundred thousand "surplus" workers were laid off. These factors combined to give Poland, from 1966 to 1970, the slowest rate of increase in real wages in Eastern Europe.

On December 13, barely a week after the signing of the West German treaty, the Polish regime raised the price of meat products by amounts from 10 to 33 percent. The first sign of trouble came in Gdansk on the Baltic coast. Workers' protests led to rioting, which spread to two nearby cities, Sopot and Gdynia. By December 15 shipyard workers in Gdansk were marching on Communist Party headquarters. Two days later tanks had to be used to suppress riots in the port of Szczecin. On December 18 demonstrations spread to the mining city of Katowice. On December 20, Gomulka was replaced as Party Secretary by Edward Gierek, who told the people that the disturbances had been caused by "hasty concepts of economic policy" which "we will remove." On December 23 the Polish Parliament appointed Piotr Jaroszewicz to replace Premier Jozef Cyrankiewicz. He immediately ordered food prices frozen for two years.

These dramatic events presented us with two challenges. The most immediate one, and the focus of US governmental discussion, was how we might react if the Soviets suppressed the Polish disturbances militarily. Unfortunately, nearly thirty years of postwar history had left little doubt that we had a limited capacity for military intervention; contingency studies confirmed this. If we could not forestall Soviet repression, we would have few means to undo it.

Contrary to my views in the 1968 Czech crisis, I was convinced that the Soviets would be highly reluctant to undertake the military occupation of a country the size and importance of Poland. The most important aspect of the Polish riots was the lessons the Soviets might draw from them. Soviet policy had sought to encourage West European dissociation from the United States, but in encouraging a more national German policy the Soviet Union had evoked similar national trends in Eastern Europe. An agreement solving one of Poland's *national* foreign policy problems on a *bilateral* basis with Bonn had encouraged the Polish government to ease its domestic problems on a national basis and thus faced the Soviet Union with centrifugal tendencies in its empire in Eastern Europe. I thought that the Polish riots would drive Moscow toward the United States. On December 20 I wrote the President:

The Soviet leaders may also be inclined to believe that *Ostpolitik* has an unsettling effect on Eastern Europe. For example, they may believe that the treaty with Germany led Gomulka to conclude he could press unpopular price increases on the population. Thus, Moscow may also want a pause in its relations with Bonn. . . .

At the same time, with this detente with Bonn at least temporarily slowed down, the Soviet leaders, if they choose to maintain some prospect of detente, may be inclined to show some improvement in their relations with us.

Thus by the middle of December 1970 the bargaining position between us and Moscow had, in my view, changed; we were, in fact, in the strongest position since Nixon had come to office. We had Cienfuegos and Jordan behind us; we had demonstrated our determination to resist pressures; Moscow had experienced the brittleness of its East European dominion. And we had a safety valve of which the Kremlin was as yet unaware. About ten days earlier we had received the first direct communication from the Chinese leadership proposing high-level talks.

After submitting my memorandum, I had several extensive conversations with the President on the situation. I told him that the moment had come to test the Channel between Dobrynin and me. I conjectured that the Soviets might be ready to break the deadlock on a number of negotiations; of these SALT and Berlin were especially important, for SALT would influence our defense budget and Berlin would test allied cohesion.

I said that we were again about to face the now annual ritualistic assault by Congress on our defense budget, the symbol of which was the antiballistic missile (ABM) that was also our chief bargaining chip in SALT negotiations. For the identical forces of previous battles were mobilizing; the trenches were being manned by the same figures now so used to the confrontation that it had become an end in itself. The annual delegation of scientific and academic figures would appear at Congressional hearings, all opposing ABM as both ineffectual and menacing to strategic stability. Repetition had still not clarified how both of these criticisms could be simultaneously valid. Leading Senators would take up the call, submitting resolutions to dictate our deployments or our negotiating stance — it was the Vietnam syndrome extending into all other areas of policy. The *New York Times* and the *Washington Post* would supply the accompaniment with biweekly editorials. Our defense program would be cut first by the Administration to preempt Congressional assaults and then again by the Congress to assert its prerogative and to carry out the myth assiduously fostered by various peace groups: that only if the Congress emasculated our military establishment would our government behave responsibly and end the war in Vietnam. By agreement with the Soviets or by Congressional imposition, one way or another we were approaching the unilateral abandonment of ABM.

But once that happened the Soviets would lose any incentive to halt their offensive buildup. This is why the President and I insisted on tying limitations on our ABM program to a freeze on Soviet offensive deployments.* The Defense Department not only supported but pressed for this proposal. In December 1970 I urged the President to open negotiations to that end; if we failed, Congressional pressures might cause us to lose any leverage on the Soviet strategic buildup.

On Berlin I told the President I thought an agreement would be demanded by the German Parliament as the price of ratifying Chancellor Brandt's treaties with Moscow. That required our approval, as one of the four occupying powers (the United States, the Soviet Union, Great Britain, and France), and probably our active diplomacy. Our pivotal role constrained the nationalistic undercurrents of *Ostpolitik;* it also forced the Soviets to seek our support. I described the Soviets' problem in a memorandum to Nixon:

The Soviets may have some considerable concern that they cannot go into a Party Congress in March with their Western policy in a shambles — no Berlin progress, no move to ratify the German treaties, no prospect for economic assistance from the West Germans — but that we hold the key to this increasingly complicated tangle of issues.

---

*The formal proposal of freezing the construction of offensive weapons was, of course, to be applied to both sides. But since we had no new deployments we could undertake for a five-year period, we were in effect talking about a Soviet freeze.

At the same time we had a major interest in improving life in Berlin: to maintain the morale of its population and especially to eliminate this perennial pretext for Soviet blackmail. Unfortunately, the Berlin negotiations were bogged down in a maze of bureaucratic and legalistic complexity. Every proposal had to move through a cumbersome Four-Power machinery, which incidentally excluded the country with the biggest stake in the outcome, the Federal German Republic, whose officials attended only the meetings of an allied consultative group. Given the difficulty of negotiating every proposal within each government, then between the Western powers, and finally with the Soviets, progress was glacial. Every change involved weeks of controversy, comprehensible only to the few lawyers whose odd specialty was the arcane subject of the Potsdam Agreement of 1945 and its later legal history.

For us the negotiations presented special complexities. On the one hand, we could bring about an improvement of access to Berlin and move *Ostpolitik* into a multilateral framework only if we were prepared to sustain a prolonged deadlock; this would bring home to the Soviets that they needed a Berlin agreement more than we did. To some extent, we had already accomplished this. On the other hand, unless skillfully handled, a prolonged stalemate offering no hope of solution could damage US–German relations severely. We could become the whipping boy, accused by Brandt of blocking his policies, and charged by his opponents with having let him get too far out front. If there were another Berlin crisis, the onus could fall on us. We were constantly being told by Soviet diplomats that France and the Federal Republic blamed us for slow progress on Berlin. Though the Soviet intention was clearly to sow discord, the report had undoubtedly a kernel of truth; our allies were not above deflecting Soviet wrath to us, and France in particular seemed willing to be wooed.

Brandt's state of mind surfaced in a letter he wrote to Nixon on December 12, urging — not without implied criticism — an acceleration of Berlin negotiations. Brandt recommended that the talks go into "continuous conference." In these circumstances we could prevent the Berlin negotiations from getting out of control only if we played an active role; any other position might wind up with either dangerous concessions or a Berlin crisis. I had another reason, transcending the tactical handling of specific negotiations, to test the feasibility of a policy of mutual restraint. Through all turmoil and crises, despite my firm commitment to prevent Soviet geopolitical gains, I felt a moral and political obligation to explore the opportunities of coexistence, no matter how unpromising the prospects. Every political leader owes his people the reality as well as the appearance of exerting his best effort to spare mankind a nuclear holocaust. Skeptics were concerned lest such a policy, by blinding free peoples to their danger, undermined their readiness to defend themselves. The schisms of the Vietnam war moved me in the opposite direction. The "peace issue" had been exploited by some determined to undermine governmental credibility and perhaps the cohesion of our society. They could not be left a mischievous monopoly. If we were to resist Soviet expansionism, we had, paradoxically, to demonstrate that all peaceful initiatives had been exhausted. I had then retained, and still do, the confidence that free peoples can accomplish both, looking to their security through strong defenses while simultaneously exploring the ambiguous prospects for peace. Indeed, if they cannot pursue both objectives, they will fail in both.

In the long term I felt a period of international tranquillity was bound to present more problems to the Soviet Union than to us since its cohesion was in part maintained by the constant evocation of an external danger. A long period of peace, I was convinced, would unleash more centrifugal tendencies in the totalitarian states than in the industrial democracies. A stagnating economy, restless nationalities, and dissidents would absorb more and more of Soviet energies. The geopolitical prospects of the Soviet Union would become more problematical as China became stronger and Japan threw off the trauma of defeat. Time was not necessarily on the Soviet side.

I began testing the hunch that the Soviet leaders might be ready for serious talks in a long conversation with Dobrynin on December 22, two days after I wrote to Nixon on the Polish uprising. I reiterated our conviction that Moscow's recent policies were incompatible with improved relations: the deception at Cienfuegos and the subsequent attempt to test the limits of our understandings there; Soviet aggressiveness in the Middle East; the harassment of the Berlin corridors; the delay in releasing the two errant American generals. A fundamental decision was necessary. If the policy of petty advantage were continued, pinpricks could easily become wounds; suspicions could enlarge failure of communication into crisis. But there was the possibility of a more constructive relationship. I proposed that we use the Channel to solve some of the outstanding issues on a basis of strict reciprocity. Something should and could come out of our talks other than mutual recriminations.

Since Dobrynin was without instructions, he could only sum up the established Soviet position in a conciliatory fashion. But he agreed on the need to break the ice. He assured me that his government was committed to reach an understanding with the United States. He agreed that we should both review negotiating records to find areas of possible flexibility.

On January 6, Dobrynin left a note about Berlin at my White House office; I was in San Clemente with the President. In characteristic fashion it implied a concession by voicing a complaint; Gromyko specialized in double negatives in diplomatic correspondence as well as in personal conversation. On this occasion the complaint was that the United States had not lived up to a commitment allegedly made by Nixon in his talk with Gromyko. Nixon had said that the United States could not show greater flexibility on Berlin unless the Soviets accepted Berlin's organic cord to the Federal Republic. Moscow had in the meantime made a Delphic utterance that could be interpreted as recognizing an umbilical connection without, however, spelling out its nature or any Soviet obligation to see it respected. Gromyko's note pointed to that utterance as a dazzling concession opening up the possibility of negotiating simultaneously on "*all* questions . . . as a kind of package." The Soviets knew better than that; Nixon's remark had been one of those metaphorical flourishes by which heads of government avoid coming to grips with operational issues. But whatever Nixon's intention — and his basic motive had been to get through the Berlin part of his brief without making any commitment — Dobrynin's note in its convoluted way showed that they were getting ready to shift their position. They had hitherto insisted that the Berlin talks focus on reducing West German activities in the city in return for little other than the confirmation of the existing status. Now they were hinting at a readiness to move on Soviet guarantees of access and improvement in life in Berlin. On this basis a serious negotiation was possible.

I recommended to Nixon that we return a positive reply which would insist on Soviet guarantees of access and a clearly defined legal status for West Berlin. And I proposed linking the Berlin negotiations to progress in SALT; SALT, in turn, we would make depend on Soviet willingness to freeze its offensive buildup. Nixon approved. Dobrynin had been called back to Moscow for urgent consultation. This could mean that the Soviet leaders wanted to be out of touch because of a crisis they knew to be imminent, or that they wished to avoid an answer to a query, or that they were indeed engaged in a serious policy review. The latter hypothesis was the more plausible in this instance; Dobrynin had delayed his departure by twenty-four hours so that he could get our response to the feeler on Berlin.

On my return from San Clemente, Dobrynin and I met on the morning of January 9, 1971, at the Soviet Embassy. The two-hour meeting turned out to be a crucial one. I put forward new propositions on two subjects that I cleared in principle with Nixon. The first was our answer on Berlin. I told Dobrynin that it was senseless to engage in an abstract exegesis of the conversation between Gromyko and Nixon. We wanted two things from the Soviet Union: first, improved access for West Berlin and, second, a Soviet guarantee of the new access procedures. We did not want to have the freedom of Berlin depend on the goodwill of the East German regime, against which we had little leverage. If the Soviet leaders were precise on these two points, we would engage ourselves more directly in the Berlin negotiations. We would be prepared to conduct exploratory talks in the Channel and if they went well feed their results into the established Four-Power machinery. This would inevitably involve consultation with West German officials; we would reach no understandings with the Soviets not approved in advance by Bonn. I was proposing, as I made clear in a later conversation, an opportunity for greater speed, not for greater concessions.

With respect to SALT, I proposed to break the deadlock over the linkage between ABM and offensive limitations.* I told Dobrynin we would accept the Soviet proposal to negotiate an ABM treaty provided the Soviets undertook to begin negotiations immediately on offensive limitations; the two negotiations would conclude simultaneously. The offensive limitation would consist of an undertaking that neither side would start construction of new land-based ICBMs while the negotiations were going on. We would put forward later a new proposal on submarine-launched missiles. The results could be expressed in an exchange of letters between the President and Kosygin (still assumed by us to be Nixon's interlocutor).

What I was proposing on both SALT and Berlin was a mechanism to shortcut the cumbersome machinery that made stalemate probable and public acrimony certain. Any successful negotiation must be based on a balance of mutual concessions. But how to arrive at this balance is a complex process. The sequence in which concessions are made becomes crucial; it can be aborted if each move has to be defended individually rather than as part of a mosaic before the reciprocal move is clear. In the formative stages of a negotiation secrecy is therefore vital, as the Carter Administration learned when its efforts at open diplomacy exploded several promising initiatives. Speed also is often of the essence. Every negotiation reaches a critical point where it will move rapidly to a conclusion or lapse into stagnation. This is when the highest levels of government must engage themselves to overcome bureaucratic inertia. I had offered Dobrynin a mechanism and an assurance of secrecy and speed.

Dobrynin asked some penetrating questions. While he was at it, he tried for a breakthrough on the Middle East as well, but I put him off; I did not think conditions were ripe. Dobrynin by now knew me well enough not to have illusions about my intention to conduct the two negotiations — Berlin and SALT — in tandem. And I had learned enough about the Soviet system to be certain that the Soviet leadership could move with dispatch when it wanted to. Dobrynin promised an early reply; I was sure that this was one promise which would be kept.

---

*There was no Presidential letter to Brezhnev, or Presidential meeting with Dobrynin on January 9, as some accounts suggest,[1] but an initiative by me — approved by the President — in the Presidential Channel with Dobrynin. (The first communication between Nixon and Brezhnev took place in August 1971.)

Dobrynin was back in less than two weeks; on January 23 he came to the Map Room bubbling with enthusiasm. The Politburo, he said, had studied our propositions with great interest. He had seen all the top leaders and he could tell me that conditions for a summit were now excellent. (I had not, in fact, raised that point on January 9, but Dobrynin no doubt saw some mileage in playing on Nixon's presumed eagerness for a publicity coup.) The Soviet leaders would prefer July or August; September would, however, also be suitable. Of course, some progress had to be made first. But everybody was now quite optimistic. Having delivered himself of the Soviet conception of linkage, Dobrynin turned to ours. The Soviet leaders were delighted that I was willing to engage myself in the Berlin talks. They had been told by Brandt and Bahr that of all the American leaders I understood German conditions best. (This was probably true; at the same time Moscow must have decided that playing on my vanity could do no harm.) Though formal positions would not be put forward until the talks actually began, Dobrynin could tell me now that the suggestion that the Soviet Union provide some guarantee of access was being studied seriously in Moscow. As he spoke, it was becoming plain that the pressure for a rapid Berlin agreement was on Moscow. It now had begun to see that it would never get its cherished Eastern treaties unless there were a Berlin agreement. And it would pay a price for that.

As to SALT, Dobrynin was not yet in a position to be definitive. However, there was a good possibility that Moscow would accept the idea of combining a defensive treaty with an offensive freeze. He raised a number of practical questions. One was as difficult as it was embarrassing — which of the many versions of the ABM scheme that had been advanced either in the SALT talks or to the Congress were we really interested in. I could only say lamely that we had not yet decided; it was one of those cases where what is true is not necessarily plausible. It was not easy for the Soviets to find their way among our Congressional position (the three-site system protecting ICBMs), our formal SALT proposal (National Command Authorities, that is, Washington and Moscow), and the personal conviction of our SALT negotiator (which was for a total ban). I made clear that SALT would be kept in step with the Berlin negotiations.

Soviet diplomats never fail to go through an endless catalogue of Soviet proposals. The theory seems to be that one can never tell when an interlocutor might absentmindedly or inadvertently yield up a concession; at a minimum, the leadership in Moscow seems to require tangible proof that its representative has not failed for lack of persistence. After I disposed again of all of Dobrynin's old standbys — the European Security Conference and Middle East leading the list — we agreed to meet regularly and systematically once I had set up the appropriate procedures.

I was getting myself engaged in two negotiations of almost theological complexity. Berlin involved the vital interests of three other Western allies and the Soviet Union and two already established forums. SALT was addressed in a formal negotiation alternating between Helsinki and Vienna and backstopped by a bewildering maze of technical and substantive committees, some of which I chaired. Unless great care was taken, we could wind up blowing all the fuses.

The Channel Becomes Operational

B Y the end of 1970 I had worked with Nixon for nearly two years; we had talked at length almost every day; we had gone through all crises in closest cooperation. He tended more and more to delegate the tactical management of foreign policy to me. During the first year or so I would submit for Nixon's approval an outline of what I proposed to say to Dobrynin or the North Vietnamese, for instance, before every meeting. He rarely changed it, though he rarely failed also to add tough-sounding exhortations. By the end of 1970 Nixon no longer required these memoranda. He would approve the strategy, usually orally; he would almost never intervene in its day-to-day implementation. After each negotiating session I submitted a lengthy memorandum and analysis. Nixon thus had every opportunity to determine whether his wishes were being carried out. But I can recall no occasion after 1971 where he altered the course of a negotiation once it was in train. I knew what Nixon wanted to accomplish. We had jointly devised the strategy. He did not believe that the conductor need be seen to play every instrument in the orchestra.

But if I could be sure of Nixon's backing, I was on thin ice with the rest of the government. The risk of any negotiation in a large bureaucracy is that those who are excluded can always claim that they could have done better and the fewer engaged the more are tempted to do so. Uninvolved in the process of mutual adjustment, they can emphasize maximum objectives; unaware of obstacles, they can blame every concession on inadequate toughness or negotiating skill. The procedures I developed enhanced decisiveness in negotiations, but they made it more difficult to develop a consensus behind the results.

Then there was the problem of mastering the subject. My staff was too small to backstop two complex simultaneous negotiations. The control of interdepartmental machinery served as a substitute. It enabled me to use the bureaucracy without revealing our purposes. I would introduce as planning topics issues that were actually being secretly negotiated. In this manner I could learn the views of the agencies (as well as the necessary background) without formally "clearing" my position with them. What I proposed to Dobrynin would reflect a bureaucratic consensus and was probably tougher than a formal negotiating position would have been. For agencies usually take a harder line in in-teragency planning meetings, where it is possible to acquire a reputation for vigilance without risk, than in preparation for a conference where there are always some agencies with a vested interest in success.

These extraordinary procedures were essentially made necessary by a President who neither trusted his Cabinet nor was willing to give them direct orders. Nixon feared leaks and shrank from imposing discipline. But he was determined to achieve his purposes; he thus encouraged procedures unlikely to be recommended in textbooks on public adminis-tration that, crablike, worked privily around existing structures. It was demoralizing for the bureaucracy, which, cut out of the process, reacted by accentuating the independence and self-will that had caused Nixon to bypass it in the first place. But it worked; it achieved that elusive blend of laborious planning and crisp articulation on which successful policy depends. In 1971 and 1972 these methods produced the SALT breakthrough, the opening to China, a Berlin agreement, the Peking and the Moscow summits without any setback. The results should be judged on their merits, though I recognize a price was paid in the manner of their achievement and though I do not believe it should be repeated.

In the case of SALT, official negotiations were going on that required periodic formal Presidential instructions. Hence I knew the views of the agencies both in abstract planning and in relation to the actual negotia-tions. It was clear that pressures for an ABM-only agreement were growing within the government. Several members of the SALT delega-tion explicitly advocated it. The Defense Department representative would have settled for an ABM-only agreement if linked with a freeze on heavy missiles alone, leaving all other missiles to run free. Gerard Smith favored an ABM ban or NCA in return for some unspecified of-fensive limitations, but the bargaining-chip approach made it hard to sell any ABM program to the Congress, which was not eager to spend money for what we might have to dismantle. The State Department leaned toward an ABM-only agreement but was reluctant to press for it. In short, if I succeeded in linking an ABM treaty to a freeze on *all* stra-tegic missiles I would be on safe bureaucratic ground because I would have achieved more than any agency was advocating.

Berlin was more complicated to manage. The legal positions had grown up over the decades of Berlin crises; encrusted with tradition and a hard-won consensus, they could not simply be changed by Presidential decision. Our policy had to be worked out with three allies, any one of whom would not let previous charges of US foot-dragging stand in the way of blaming us for excessive flexibility.

It was impossible to proceed without Brandt's full backing, and for this I needed to see Brandt's close adviser, Egon Bahr. But at some point the talks with the Soviets would end up in a Four-Power forum.

So I also needed the cooperation of our Ambassador to Bonn, Kenneth Rush, who ex officio conducted the formal Berlin negotiations on our behalf.

Rush had come to the ambassadorship by way of private industry; his last major post had been President and Director of Union Carbide. Nixon knew of him because he had taught at Duke Law School, though he had not met Nixon then. He was a close friend of John Mitchell, then Attorney General. It turned out to be one of Nixon's best appointments. Calm, analytical, thoughtful, Rush performed his complex role in Bonn with subtlety and skill.

Bahr's problem was identical with mine. He would have to handle a negotiation without the knowledge of his Foreign Office. With Germany's long bureaucratic tradition this was more difficult to accomplish in Bonn than in Washington. No normal channel of communication appeared trustworthy enough. Nor could Bahr come to Washington under some pretext or other without reigniting the jurisdictional disputes of previous years. The State Department would insist on participation in any conversations and the German Foreign Office would require a report. To get around these problems, I sent a courier to Bonn on January 27 with personal letters to Bahr and Rush. I told Bahr that we were prepared to accept the Chancellor's suggestions to speed up the Berlin negotiations; hence it was urgent that he and I meet. I expected him to come with the full authority of the Chancellor. As to the overt purpose of his trip, I had instructed the messenger to convey an invitation of the Vice President (as head of the Space Council) to attend the launching of the *Apollo 14* moon shot on January 31, 1971. If Bahr accepted I would attend the event, and I would then arrange to fly him to New York and we could talk on the plane. Bahr accepted immediately, setting out for Washington within twenty-four hours. I avoided him there, meeting him on the flight to Cape Kennedy on January 30.

The letter to Ken Rush was delivered by the same messenger. To justify a visit by Rush to Washington I arranged a phone call from his friend John Mitchell. He used the pretext of wanting to discuss political appointments with the Ambassador. The State Department authorized Rush's visit for "consultations" and I met him on the evening of February 3 in Mitchell's Washington apartment in the Watergate, an as yet little-known apartment complex.

I informed Dobrynin that I was proceeding (his government was sure to learn through Bahr anyway); I added that Moscow might wish to put something forward to give all participants a sense of confidence. To my surprise Dobrynin appeared within twenty-four hours with an offer of something the Soviet Union had previously refused. The Soviets had insisted that access procedures concerned only the two Germanies; our recourse in case of trouble would be to the normal processes of international law with respect to East Germany, which we did not even recognize; hence, there was little we could do to enforce our claims. Heretofore the Soviets had sought to exploit Berlin's precarious geographic location to boost the international status of East Germany while disclaiming any responsibility for harassment of access. Now they proposed that in any new arrangement on Berlin each of the Four Powers would have the right to call violations to the attention of the others — a tenuous, as yet unsatisfactory, implication of Four-Power responsibility. It was only a tentative step toward the essential Soviet guarantee. But anyone familiar with Gromyko's tactics would know that he would never start with an excessively generous opening position.

The subterfuge with Bahr worked, and on January 30 he and I duly arrived at Cape Kennedy for the launch of the moon shot. I had always considered watching space shots as suitable primarily for children, but I was deeply moved that night when a small group of us visited the Saturn V rocket by moonlight. From the vantage of spectators miles away during lift-off, the rocket standing alone without any reference point did not look so overwhelming. But up close at night it dwarfed us by its size and it shamed us by its conception.

I knew that there was a debate about the utility of the space program. The early sense of adventure was beginning to be submerged in bickering about national priorities. But I reflected that we needed the space program, scientific arguments aside, because a society that does not stretch its horizons will soon shrink them. The argument that we must first solve all our problems on earth before venturing beyond our planet will confine us for eternity; the world will never be without problems; they will become an obsession rather than a challenge unless mankind constantly expands its vision. Columbus would never have discovered America if fifteenth-century Europe had applied the facile slogan that it needed first to solve its own problems; and, paradoxically, these problems would thereby have become insoluble and Europe would have suffocated in its own perplexities. Faith has provided the motive force for mankind's checkered odyssey. But how does one dream in a technocratic age? How do a people regain the faith that caused small peasant societies to build cathedrals with spires reaching toward the heavens, edifices that it would take centuries to complete, enshrining in stone a testimonial to the perseverance and sweep of their aspirations? No one could know what we would find in space: The moon was only the first small step. I remembered an astronaut telling me that his eeriest moment came when he finally entered the capsule for lift-off. For the first time there were no workmen. All was silence as he would soon be launched on a journey from which he knew he could not return by himself. And he nearly panicked.

It seemed to me that as I stood there at Cape Kennedy with my daughter Elizabeth, then aged ten, and my son David, aged eight, that we were all enveloped in our different ways in this special kind of loneliness. They would live in a world subjectively at variance with mine; their perception of reality was of a different order. I had known only national boundaries as a child. Space was beyond my imagination. Television was inconceivable. They would be both less constrained and more literal. The horizon was not their limit as it had been mine. Paradoxically, their physical reach was likely to be accompanied by an impoverishment of the imagination. My generation had been brought up on books, which force the reader into conjuring up his own reality; my children's reality was being presented to them daily on television screens; they could absorb it passively. And yet they lived in a world in which journeys of hundreds of millions of miles were determined by an impetus given in ten seconds, and were then in large part unchangeable — a concept beyond my imagination at their age.

For better or worse, I thought I was now one of those who had the power to provide an initial impetus, making future generations into passengers on journeys they had not selected. If our aim was wrong, even the most skilled navigator would not be able to correct it. Ours was the responsibility to find a trajectory toward a world where no one had ever been; but we also were in danger of hurtling toward a void. Our most important decisions would be whether to start a journey, and the crucial quality we needed was faith in a future created in part through the act of commitment.

As the astronauts who had stimulated reflection headed for the moon, Bahr and I headed back to New York and in the privacy of the Jetstar talked all the way about Berlin. Bahr favored speeding up the negotiations and was enthusiastic about my willingness to become involved. But how, on behalf of our heads of government, could we conduct major negotiations of which our own foreign ministers were unaware — and how could we stop the Soviets from playing off the four Western powers against each other? Since I knew that Bahr was in close contact with Soviet diplomats, I insisted we keep each other informed about every contact with the Soviets or East Germans over Berlin, and for the rest we agreed on an intricate process of consultation. Bahr and Rush together would formulate propositions in three areas — access procedures, guarantees, and activities of the Federal Republic in Berlin — and sound out allied reactions; I would then explore them with Dobrynin; and then Rush or Bahr would put them back into regular channels. Against all odds, this three-dimensional chess worked. We achieved within seven months an agreement that has stood the test of time.

Arrangements with Ken Rush were settled at our meeting on the evening of February 3 in John Mitchell's apartment. Rush agreed that probably no other plan would work in a practical time frame. If the stalemate proved too protracted, Brandt might seek to break out on his own, blaming us for Germany's unfulfilled national aspirations and perhaps charting a new and far more independent national course. Rush questioned whether we could handle a Berlin crisis and its accompanying German domestic uproar while the war in Vietnam was going on.

It remained to set up a communications channel. The CIA was, of course, available. Rush felt that the Station Chief could not avoid bringing in some of his subordinates; he was, in addition, very close to some of the Embassy personnel. Most important, the Station Chief could not call frequently on Bahr to receive or transmit messages without arousing suspicion. My deputy, Al Haig, found a solution. He worked out with our JCS liaison officer, Navy Captain Rembrandt Robinson, a complicated special communications link in Navy channels to a Navy officer in Frankfurt. It was established by Chief of Naval Operations Admiral Elmo Zumwalt — later a vocal opponent of such diplomacy. The officer in Frankfurt was described to me in a memorandum from Haig as "completely reliable" and free of any "responsibility to our embassy or any other intelligence or departmental interests." What he was doing in Frankfurt I cannot imagine and did not think to ask, which may have been just as well. In any event, the Navy officer, given special phone numbers from Bahr and Rush and one of his own, was the crucial link. State Department cables about Berlin frequently leaked; they had too wide a distribution. The Navy channel messages never did. And we were grateful to be spared that complication because by early February SALT as well as Berlin was ripe for secret negotiation.

The SALT Negotiations and the May 20 Agreement

W HEN I had begun exploring a breakthrough on SALT with Dobrynin, the formal talks, which had resumed in Helsinki in early November, were as stalemated as our domestic debate. There was formal agreement in our government that the United States should stand on its last proposal of August 4, 1970, which would limit both sides to an "agreed number" of missiles and bombers and limit the number of Soviet heavy missiles to 250 (a number that by the end of 1970 the Soviets had already exceeded). As I have pointed out, many members of the SALT delegation were privately weakening in their commitment to these proposals.

With respect to ABM, our negotiating position was in turmoil. The Soviets had accepted our proposal of a system limited to National Command Authorities (NCA), for which we had neither requested nor obtained funds from Congress. We had asked the Congress for funds for three sites, which, however, did not include the national capital. The gap between our negotiating position and our actual program was widening. Senator John Stennis told Gerard Smith in October that the ABM issue was "souring" the entire defense appropriation debate.

To clear the bureaucratic record I asked Smith by backchannel whether he still agreed that defensive and offensive limitations should remain linked. Smith's answer was not free of ambiguity; in fact, it left open all the possibilities for a ban on ABM in the negotiations and hence a cutoff of ABM by the Congress. His personal objection still stood to a separate ABM agreement, which the Soviets offered again in December. He nevertheless insisted that an "instant" rejection would be unnecessarily turbulent. The President might want to "review" his policy of opposing a separate ABM agreement. The upshot was that the entire ABM issue was reopened again within the Administration.

Indeed, the debate over the SALT position was beginning to merge with the almost religious annual opposition to ABM. Public pressures once more began to build. On January 17, 1971, the *New York Times* accepted the Soviet ABM offer for us, condemning the President's insistence on linking offensive and defensive weapons. On January 26 the front-runner for the Democratic Presidential nomination, Senator Edmund Muskie, announced his contribution to the encouragement of Soviet flexibility. On his recent visit to Moscow he had told Premier Kosygin, the Senator averred, that "there was a body of opinion in the United States that wanted to reduce US weapons spending." The Senator did not consider it harmful for our foreign policy for a Presidential candidate to tell the Soviet Premier that influential members of the Congress were seeking to reduce our defenses: "Since I can say it here on the Senate floor, I don't see any damn reason why I can't say it to Kosygin."[2]

The anti-ABM campaign was given inadvertent impetus when Secretary of Defense Laird disclosed that the Soviets seemed to have slowed down the construction of new ICBMs. This was taken by many as one of the ubiquitous Soviet "signals" by which those diffident fellows in the Kremlin hinted at their intentions. This was a puzzling concept, considering the repetitive abandon with which those same Soviet leaders were bludgeoning us on all issues of real concern to them. The alleged Soviet signal sparked a letter from Gerard Smith to the President suggesting that we declare a halt to further ABM deployments as a sign of our good faith. Should Soviet missile construction resume we would be in a strong position to go all out in our own missile defense program. This theme, with variations, was repeated in Congressional and media comment. On February 1, Senator Hubert Humphrey urged the Senate to freeze American ABM and MIRV programs. "At no cost to ourselves," Humphrey declared, "and with absolute guarantee of our own security — we can stop our part of the nuclear arms race in response to actions already taken by the Soviet Union."[3] By March the Soviet "signal" had evaporated. It turned out that the Soviets had merely halted SS-9 construction in order to begin construction of a new generation of ICBMs, the SS-18, while continuing to build silos for the SS-11s. Indeed, there were more Soviet missile starts in 1971 than in all but one year of the previous decade. This fact did not ease pressures for a cut in defense spending in the slightest. None of those who had asked us to respond to the Soviet "signal" of restraint suggested that we react to the Soviet buildup.

The drumbeat to stop ABM and to slow down other programs continued throughout the spring. On February 3, in a closed-door hearing of the Senate Foreign Relations Committee, Senator Frank Church called on the President to accept "an ABM-only agreement as a first step." On February 26 William Foster, head of the Arms Control and Disarmament Agency under President Johnson, called for "a complete ban on ABM deployment, production and testing."[4] By the end of March Senators Humphrey, Harold Hughes, and George McGovern had joined the call for an ABM-only agreement. Senator Stuart Symington proposed a mutual ABM freeze and claimed that this would render MIRV unnecessary. Senator Muskie promised to conduct closed-door hearings in April.

On April 5 the *New York Times* endorsed Senator Muskie's earlier suggestion that the United States abandon Poseidon and Minuteman III and agree to a mutual halt of ABM deployment — stripping us in one fell swoop of every strategic program. On April 6 Senator Muskie joined his colleagues in advocating an agreement limiting or banning ABM as a first step. By early May criticism from these quarters intensified, with accusations that the Administration was deliberately dragging its feet on SALT in order to continue the arms race. Senator Symington went so far as to accuse the Administration of "planning deliberately not to have any arms control agreement at all."[5]

The Administration's contention that ABM was a useful "bargaining chip" came under sharp attack. Senator Fulbright, Chairman of the Senate Foreign Relations Committee, claimed that "bargaining-chip reasoning" was fallacious and served only to escalate the arms race. The *Christian Science Monitor* of May 12 accused the Administration of tripling US nuclear striking power while the Soviets were deploying nothing — an extraordinary conclusion in the face of a Soviet buildup proceeding at the rate of 200 missiles a year over nearly a decade. The *Washington Star* reported on April 13 that a new coalition against military spending was being formed with the aim of cutting $6 to $8 billion from the defense budget. Senator William Proxmire launched this drive by opposing the B-1 strategic bombing, new aircraft carriers, and submarines, as well as the F-14 and F-15 aircraft and Cheyenne helicopter.

There was no new American weapons system, in short, that was not under fierce media and Congressional attack. At the same time Senator Mike Mansfield submitted his annual resolution to withdraw half of the American forces in Europe. It was narrowly defeated after a desperate battle (described in Chapter XXII).

The Congress eventually cut $3 billion from the Administration's request. On paper, we had asked for a slightly higher arms appropriation than that of the previous year, or $73.5 billion compared with $68.7 billion. But this meant considerably less to be spent on weapons, since $4.6 billion more was needed solely to meet pay increases made necessary by a shift toward a volunteer army and the rest was absorbed by inflation. In 1971, as in the year before, the Administration was fortunate to preserve the base for later expansion by maintaining a slow but steady program for the B-1 bomber, Trident submarine and missile, and modern tactical aircraft. Thus we barely maintained our negotiating position in SALT. But the danger was real that sooner or later one or the other of these programs would fall to the relentless Congressional assault.

In this atmosphere the internal debate of the previous year was repeated. At an NSC meeting on January 27, 1971, one school of thought, represented by the State Department and the Arms Control and Disarmament Agency, argued that SALT would be given impetus by a slowdown in our ABM program. Others (like me) maintained exactly the opposite, that an American ABM program was essential to any hopes for Soviet acceptance of offensive limitations. Mel Laird and the Joint Chiefs wanted to proceed with a "Safeguard" ABM program of four sites, though only two were actually being built and construction had not yet started on the third authorized site at Whiteman Air Force Base in Missouri. Discussion continued inconclusively for another month over whether we should bring our SALT position into line with our actual ABM program.

Nixon finally put a damper on the discussion in March. He was convinced, correctly, that the Congress would kill the NCA idea as a means to ban all ABMs. The upshot was a Presidential decision on March 11 to go forward with the four-site "Safeguard" system and to bring our SALT position into line with it. So powerful was the resistance of those favoring an ABM ban or NCA that this decision was not presented to the Soviets by our SALT delegation until after constant harassment from my office and a new formal instruction issued on April 22.

My negotiations with Dobrynin must be viewed against this background. The Soviets must have been sorely tempted to wait us out, to reap the results of our domestic debate which might relieve them of any need for reciprocity. On February 4 Dobrynin confirmed that the Politburo was agreeable in principle to discuss coupling an ABM agreement with a freeze on deployments of offensive missiles. But the seeming concession turned out to be only an admission ticket into a negotiation conducted with Moscow's characteristic roller-coaster tactics of alternating advances and retreats, of grudging concessions sold over and over again. And the negotiations were further complicated because Gromyko's strategy was the reverse of mine. Whereas I held out on Berlin to speed progress on SALT, Gromyko slowed up SALT to accelerate the discussions on Berlin.

On February 10, Dobrynin confirmed the understanding to link offensive and defensive limitations. If the two agreements could not be negotiated simultaneously, the Soviets would consider a freeze on offensive deployments pending the completion of negotiations. With respect to ABM, Dobrynin expressed a preference for the NCA option.

With normal negotiations this would have ended matters. One would go from an agreement in principle to drafting the relatively simple document expressing the decision to negotiate offensive and defensive limitations simultaneously. Technical teams would then take over until some deadlock required a resolution at the political level. But nothing works so simply with the Kremlin. We now were exposed to the Soviet tactic of first selling the principle and then seeking to sell the same merchandise again in the form of substance. Perhaps to flex their muscles — more likely, to fulfill some bureaucratic schedule established months earlier — the Soviets sent another submarine tender to Cienfuegos, with predictable reactions. On February 22 I called in Dobrynin and demanded its immediate removal. No negotiations would be conducted while the tender was in Cuba (it left shortly afterward). At the same time, I handed Dobrynin a draft exchange of letters between Nixon and Kosygin embodying the understanding that offensive and defensive limitations be negotiated simultaneously; these had been prepared by my staff, drawing on interagency preparations for SALT discussions. But here matters stalled. At meetings on February 26 and March 5, Dobrynin claimed genially that all his leaders were out of Moscow preparing for the forthcoming twenty-fourth Soviet Party Congress; it was therefore difficult for them to concentrate on so complex a topic as SALT. I could not resist the observation that they seemed to have no difficulty focusing on the even more complex and laborious subject of Berlin, as to which not a week passed without some detailed communication from Moscow.

Time was becoming crucial, complicated by our own procedures. The official SALT talks were resuming in Vienna on March 15. We had to formulate new instructions that were at a minimum not incompatible with what was going on in the special Channel. At the same time, Nixon was seized by the fear that Gerard Smith, rather than he, would get credit for the seemingly imminent breakthrough of linking offensive and defensive limitations. He had taken enough of a beating on Vietnam and Cambodia not to succumb to the human emotion of wanting the credit for the initiatives identified with peace. I reassured Nixon that such a breakthrough could occur in Vienna only if Moscow made a deliberate choice to bypass the Presidential Channel, not only on this issue but on all others. This would be a fateful decision and against the Soviet interest, at least as long as Brandt's Eastern treaties hung in the balance. Still, the guerrilla warfare continued, with Dobrynin on March 12 handing me a Soviet draft that went back on the principle of simultaneity of offensive and defensive limitations. It called for an ABM agreement "this year" confined to national capitals (NCA); offensive limitations would be discussed only *after* such an agreement had been reached and only "in principle." This restatement of the formal Soviet position at the SALT talks could not be serious; Dobrynin had to have something in reserve. The proposition was being put forward by the Soviet leadership as a final proof to itself that it would not get anywhere; there was no point in a special Channel if it merely repeated the lower-level deadlock. As soon as I rejected Dobrynin's proposal, Dobrynin immediately showed his hand: He did not ask for time to consult Moscow — which would have been normal had the first scheme been serious — but suggested that we try to merge Soviet and American drafts and attempt to bridge differences. Clearly, Dobrynin had been equipped with some latitude; he would never have offered redrafts on his own authority.

On March 15 we met to exchange the new drafts. Dobrynin gave me an abbreviated version of his March 12 draft. It did not change the Soviet insistence that an agreement on ABM *precede* offensive limitations; it did drop the principle that ABM be confined to the capitals. Our version continued to link offensive and defensive limitations, my main aim.

Dobrynin and I met the next day to attempt an amalgam. What emerged came close to meeting our principal requirements. Instructions would be issued to the two SALT delegations to reach an ABM agreement "immediately." This would be accomplished by a freeze on "strategic offensive weapons," both ICBMs and SLBMs. Modernization and replacement would be permitted, but only by weapons of the same category. In other words, the Soviet heavy missiles (SS-9s), which we considered such a threat to our Minuteman land-based missile force, would be frozen at the current level.

On March 25 I sent Dobrynin what in diplomatic parlance is called an "oral note" — a written but unsigned communication whose status is that of the spoken word and which can therefore be more easily disavowed. It laid out our view of the procedures to be adopted. The terms of an ABM agreement and the freeze on offensive weapons would have to be negotiated simultaneously and completed at the same time. (I left the nature of the ABM limitation to the negotiators.) The permitted levels would be the number of weapons operational or under construction on the date the freeze went into effect.

The next day, March 26, Dobrynin brought the Soviet reply to our March 16 draft, which it neither accepted nor rejected. The principle of a freeze on strategic offensive weapons was accepted, but the details were to be discussed *after* an agreement on defensive weapons had been reached. In the arcane world of Soviet diplomacy, where any concession must be made with a minimum of grace, this implied a compromise: that the agreements be discussed successively but signed simultaneously. This we could not accept. Once an ABM treaty was known to exist, we would be under irresistible pressure to sign; the minute we had signed, the offensive freeze would evaporate. (Even if we did not sign it, the Congress would never vote funds for the ABM program, so that the ideal outcome from the Soviet point of view would be an unconsummated ABM agreement in which the United States abandoned its program unilaterally.)

We were making progress, but at an excruciatingly slow pace. I left no doubt that we would insist on the principles of the note submitted the previous day. Dobrynin allowed that his leaders could not have had an opportunity to study it. Fortunately, he would soon be in Moscow to brief them personally, since he had just been recalled once again for consultation. In the style to which I had become accustomed, Moscow was slowing down negotiations further by the simple device of removing its negotiator.

All this time the formal SALT negotiations proceeded in Vienna, adding another complication because our negotiators were unaware of the special Channel. At the end of March Gerard Smith speculated in a backchannel to me that he had gone about as far as possible unless he was given the authority to include forward-based systems in the negotiations. Paul Nitze, representing the Defense Department, suggested that we accept an ABM ban in return for a freeze and eventual reduction of Soviet heavy ICBMs (the SS-9s). Domestically, pressures continued to build on us to accept the Soviet ABM-only proposal. *Time* magazine, the *Washington Post,* and Senator Muskie were among the advocates. Senator Symington compared the "Safeguard" ABM program to a company making parachutes that advertises "if it doesn't work send it back and we will give you another one."[6] In fairness, our secret style of negotiations left us vulnerable to these pressures; our critics did not know that we could do better. On the other hand, had they known they would have pressed us to accept the current Soviet proposals, which we were still seeking to improve.

Indeed, since public debate on offensive weapons focused on holding up the only new offensive program *we* had, deployment of the multiple warhead (MIRV), the United States was perennially on the verge of being forced to give up — *before* any SALT agreement — the two strategic weapons systems we were building.

Fortunately, on April 23 Dobrynin returned from Moscow and took us off the hook. He handed me a note that, in the glacially deliberate style of Soviet negotiators, accepted our proposal that the offensive limitations could be discussed *before* an ABM agreement was completed; it was a good definition of simultaneity, though phrased in one of Gromyko's double negatives. We had achieved our primary goal; typically, however, the Soviets took away a previous concession: The agreement was to be dependent on our accepting an ABM system limited to national capitals. Yet again the Politburo dissipated moral capital without any prospect of gain. Dobrynin must have known — even if Gromyko was reluctant to accept — that NCA was last year's windfall. On the other hand, the Soviets would not have gone this far if they were not willing to go the rest of the way. On April 26, in another oral note, I offered a way out by suggesting that the decision on the nature of sites to be permitted in the ABM agreement be deferred to subsequent negotiations. However, the note put the Soviets on notice that the American position would be based on the system we were actually building (that is, the defense of missile sites) and not on some hypothetical system centered on capitals. Dobrynin could not forgo scoring the debating point that, after all, the Soviets were only accepting our ABM proposal of the previous year. I acknowledged this slightly embarrassing truth but made clear that we would not budge.

As we were approaching agreement, a bizarre incident interrupted our efforts on May 2. Vladimir Semenov, the Soviet SALT negotiator in Vienna, suddenly broached to Smith over a private dinner the very proposal for an ABM agreement limited to capitals, followed by a freeze on ICBMs to be discussed *after* the ABM agreement was concluded, which had been rejected by me six weeks before. In other words, Semenov put forward the *old* Soviet position after Dobrynin had already conceded simultaneity. Since it went far beyond anything the Soviets had previously conceded at Vienna, and he could not know that he was being offered what we had already rejected and improved, Smith thought himself on the verge of a breakthrough. He urged acceptance — thus indicating what pressures we would have faced had the negotiation remained in formal channels. To this day I do not understand what Gromyko hoped to accomplish by this maneuver. Perhaps he could not resist the temptation of exploiting our double channel system and gave authority to explore how far our formal negotiators were willing to go. Perhaps he sought to test whether the President could make the program I had put forward stick. Conceivably, he wanted to give Semenov a part of the action, and Semenov in turn wanted to prove that he could do better than Dobrynin. (One should not assume that the Soviet system is more immune to bureaucratic infighting than ours; in all likelihood, it is more virulently prone to it.)

Whatever the reason, Semenov's move, as well as raising doubts about Soviet good faith, in effect circumvented the Presidential Channel. It also started a formal consideration within our agencies that soon escalated to media and Congressional pressure to accept this "compromise." I was in Palm Springs, ostensibly on vacation, in reality to set up the China trip. I therefore asked Al Haig to challenge Dobrynin. Dobrynin had no real explanation. He pointed out that Semenov had put forward the "old" position, as if this could somehow excuse the maneuver. Dobrynin promised to get matters under control.

A few days later, on May 9, Semenov returned to the attack, choosing as occasion this time a boat trip hosted by the Austrian government to demonstrate his addiction to bypassing the Channel. Semenov took Smith aside and proposed that they concentrate "this year" on reaching an ABM agreement, after which there would be an intensive negotiation for an offensive agreement. Deployment of ICBMs would be halted "for some period" while these negotiations proceeded. (He had now graduated from the position of six weeks before to the next-to-last one. He still insisted on consecutive negotiations and continued to exclude submarine-launched missiles.) Smith was jubilant about the new apparent "breakthrough." I was in a dilemma. I could hardly tell Smith that he had been handed shopworn goods, that Semenov's offer had been superseded by a better one in a channel of which he was ignorant. The best I could do was suggest that Smith return within a week to review the bidding.

In the meantime I decided to try to bring matters to a head with Dobrynin. In dealing with the Soviets a point is inevitably reached where it is important to make clear brutally that the limits of flexibility have been reached, that the time has come either to settle or to end the negotiation. This is a more complex matter than simply getting "tough." If the line is drawn too early, the Soviets will in fact break up the negotiation. If the line is drawn too late, they may no longer believe that the challenge is serious. Success in negotiations is a matter of timing, and nowhere more so than with Moscow.

What later developed into a deliberate device that we would use more than once was imposed by necessity — or Soviet clumsiness — in May 1971. Once Smith returned to Washington, Semenov's proposal would become the subject of formal interagency deliberation; it would be out of control of the Presidential Channel. On May 11 I had a rather blunt conversation with Dobrynin. The Soviets, I said, might think they could play off our two channels against each other; and indeed, we might have some difficulty convincing the agencies that what Dobrynin had already conceded was in fact achievable. But he could not doubt that sooner or later the President's tenacity and my control of the bureaucratic machinery would get matters to where we wanted them. The price, I told him, would be loss of confidence in the seriousness of a private, direct Channel. The President's anger at what he could only construe as a deliberate maneuver to deprive him of credit would be massive. I demanded an answer to our proposal of April 26 within forty-eight hours. Otherwise we would shift the whole subject into official channels. We would do the same with Berlin negotiations. On May 12 Dobrynin brought the answer. The Soviet Union dropped its insistence on the NCA system. It accepted simultaneity of negotiation in limiting of offensive and defensive systems. By May 15 we had agreed on an announcement to be made on May 20 and on the text of a private exchange of letters between Nixon and Kosygin.

This success gave Nixon considerable anguish, for he would now have to tell his Secretary of State that negotiations had been going on for months without his knowledge and were on the verge of being consummated by a formal announcement. His first instinct was to claim that a sudden Soviet communication had unexpectedly produced a breakthrough. (This was the explanation given seven weeks later for my trip to Peking.) I counseled against an account that the records would not sustain and that mischievous Soviet negotiators could exploit. Nixon's next idea was to suggest that he had written to Brezhnev in January and that he had just received a reply. This, too, I advised against on much the same grounds. Nixon finally handled the embarrassment by letting Haldeman break the news to his old friend. The obloquy later heaped on Haldeman must not obscure the fortitude with which he discharged many such thankless and essentially demeaning tasks. Rogers accepted the proffered explanation — the apocryphal Brezhnev letter — with a composure that did him credit.

The task of briefing Gerry Smith was left to me. It was not a pleasant assignment. Whatever my disagreement with Smith's views on policy, I respected his professionalism and loyalty. It was bound to be painful for him to be excluded from a culmination of years of work. It would have been too much to expect our chief negotiator to agree that negotiations in formal channels would have been far more protracted; I doubt if we could have sustained our ultimate position in the face of the public pressures to yield. I showed Smith all the exchanges with the Soviets and a summary of my conversations. Smith conducted himself with courtesy and restraint. Though he later privately expressed understandable bitterness, when such conduct could have detracted from the first major achievement of the Nixon Administration in East-West relations he put national unity before his own feelings.

At noon on May 20, 1971, Nixon stepped before the White House press corps and sprang what was to be the first of many surprises that year. He read the text of the announcement, whose sparse (and somewhat convoluted) words scarcely did justice to the labors of the previous six months and to its intrinsic significance:

The Governments of the United States and the Soviet Union, after reviewing the course of their talks on the limitation of strategic armaments, have agreed to concentrate this year on working out an agreement for the limitation of the deployment of anti-ballistic missile systems (ABMs). They have also agreed that, together with concluding an agreement to limit ABMs, they will agree on certain measures with respect to the limitation of offensive strategic weapons.

But nothing was destined to work smoothly in this negotiation with the Soviets. The agreed statement had barely been released when I was informed that the Soviet news agency TASS had published a different version implying that the discussion of offensive limitations would come "after" instead of "together with" an ABM accord. In other words, we were faced with an attempt to slip past us the earlier Soviet position in the form of a press release. When I brought this to Dobrynin's attention, he argued lamely that TASS must have done its own retranslation from a Russian text (an extraordinary explanation, considering that the original statement had been negotiated in English). Unfortunately, Dobrynin argued, it was now too late to reach Moscow because of the time difference. I told him that I would be conducting a briefing on the announcement in two hours. I would either discuss Soviet duplicity or present the agreed text as the first important step toward improved relations. It was up to him to choose. The Ambassador's ingenious solution was to have the correct English text typed on Soviet Embassy stationery. It was thus available, in time, for the specialists in credibility gaps who were already unlimbering their heavy artillery. It was probably the only time that a press release with a Soviet letterhead was distributed from the White House press office.

The breakthrough of May 20 was on the surface procedural. It settled that offensive and defensive limitations would be concluded simultaneously.* But there was more to the agreement than the words that announced it. For one thing, we had put before the Politburo the essence of our SALT position. The SALT agreement of 1972 confirmed what the May 1971 understanding implied: The Soviets had in effect accepted a freeze on new starts of strategic missiles; they had conceded a sublimit on heavy missiles; they had in effect dropped their claim that our aircraft based abroad be counted; and we had put them on notice that submarine-launched missiles would have to be limited or accounted for.

---

* Some academic arms control experts continued to believe that the President had accepted the Soviet proposal; they praised Nixon for agreeing to an ABM-only agreement when he had done exactly the opposite.[7]

In addition, we had managed to slide off our ill-advised NCA proposal of the previous year. In short, the final agreement negotiated a year later reflected in its basic aspects the exchanges leading up to the May 20 announcement.

Long after the SALT accords were signed in May 1972 it became fashionable to criticize their alleged "inequality." It is true that a freeze preserved for five years the numerical gap between the Soviet and US missile forces that had developed over the preceding decade. But as a result of decisions of our predecessors, no American programs existed that could possibly produce new missiles for at least five years. Mel Laird pointed out at an NSC meeting that the earliest date for the new submarines we were planning was 1977; he proved overoptimistic by at least two years. In the interval the Administration pressed forward with development of new programs — Trident, B-1, Minuteman III, ABM, and MIRV — in the face of active and vocal Congressional opposition. The freeze on numbers thus stopped no American program; it did arrest a continuing Soviet program that was deploying over 200 ICBMs and SLBMs a year. In exchange for this we accepted a limit on ABM, our bargaining chip, which our Congress was on the verge of killing anyway.

That we achieved it despite an obviously weak bargaining position — we were, after all, unable to argue plausibly that we could build up rapidly if the agreement failed — was due to several factors. The Soviet leadership chose not to exploit the domestic pressures unleashed by the Vietnam war; it came to this decision not out of charity but because it recognized that the special Channel might represent its only chance for a fundamental agreement in Nixon's first term. And the leaders were sufficiently wary of what was considered Nixon's "unpredictability" — which was really his way of forcing an issue — not to gamble on a seeming domestic discomfiture whose thin base in America Dobrynin, for one, understood better than many of our critics.

More important, the Soviets could not risk a crisis with us if they wanted the Berlin agreement concluded or the German treaties ratified. This linkage was never made explicit, but it was clearly reflected in the pace of our negotiations. (For example, during the week of Semenov's indiscretion I asked Rush to delay a meeting with the Soviet Ambassador in Bonn on some pretext for two weeks.) And there was no possibility that the German Parliament would ratify Brandt's Eastern treaties under Cold War conditions. We had our own reasons for not wishing to compound East-West tensions, but we were prepared to risk this prospect by holding out for a SALT agreement we considered compatible with our security.

Domestically, the May 20 agreement gave us breathing space. It briefly quieted the critics who were alleging the Administration's insufficient commitment to peace; it put to rest the defense debate for the remainder of Nixon's term. Once it became obvious that SALT would probably succeed, the pressures for various kinds of moratoria dwindled. The ABM remained in an embryonic stage, but this had been inevitable for a year. Indeed, we obtained a higher price for it than would have been thought probable after the Senate Armed Services Committee in May 1971 voted to confine deployment to two sites even in the absence of a SALT agreement.

Within the government, furthermore, the May 20 agreement was a milestone in confirming White House dominance of foreign affairs. For the first two years White House control had been confined to the formulation of policy; now it extended to its execution. Simultaneously, three major initiatives were being negotiated of which the regular bureaucracy was ignorant: the May 20 SALT agreement, the Berlin negotiations, and the opening to China. I have already indicated that I do not consider this a procedure that can stand institutionalization. But it has to be equally stressed that the departments did little to encourage Presidential confidence. Their tendency to take advantage of Nixon's reluctance to engage in face-to-face confrontations tempted him into an endless guerrilla war to circumvent his own subordinates whom he never considered as his own. Which came first — Nixon's suspicions of a lifetime or the distrust of him by a government staffed by the opposition for a decade — is a chicken and egg question. Nixon — assisted by me — found his own method of solving the problem. It was certainly disruptive of departmental morale. To individuals like Smith, it was unfair and demeaning. It was also tough on the nerves of the NSC staff, who had the sole responsibility of backstopping three major negotiations simultaneously in the midst of the Laos operation. And a lot of energy was consumed in servicing duplicative channels. But Nixon judged that, given his conviction and personality and subordinates, he could achieve results no other way.

With respect to the May 20 understanding he had every reason to worry that in regular channels it would have dragged on for months while our departments debated among the three ABM options and the various versions of the freeze, and leaked their favorite schemes to try to preempt his decisions. The Soviets would have been pressing constantly for an ABM-only agreement and successfully mobilizing strong media, academic, and Congressional pressure on us to accept it. The essential linkage of Berlin and SALT negotiations would have been almost certainly lost given the impossibility of fine-tuning of moves by two entirely different bureaucracies, each convinced that its responsibility was sufficiently difficult and worthwhile on its merits to justify proceeding independently.

The May 20 agreement also played a minor role in our China initiative. It showed Peking that we had an option toward Moscow, while giving us an opportunity to demonstrate that we understood fundamental Chinese concerns. We used the Pakistani channel to inform the Chinese leaders of our decision and the reasons for it, making clear that we rejected any ambitions to condominium. The May 20 agreement, finally, was the first sustained US–Soviet negotiation on the Presidential level — the forerunner of others in the years ahead. The two nuclear giants were beginning to feel their way — with many ups and downs — toward some ground rules of coexistence.

The Berlin Negotiation

THE negotiation with the Soviet Union over Berlin was also conducted on both a secret and an official level, but Berlin exceeded even SALT in its intricacy and esoteric jargon. Whereas in SALT we were in complete charge of our side, on Berlin we had not only to deal with the Soviet Union but also to keep in partnership with Britain and France as occupying powers, the Federal Republic of Germany as the ally most concerned, and the West Berlin government, which, after all, represented the people whose opportunity to live in freedom was at stake. Moreover, the negotiation was encrusted by years of haggling over legalisms. There was scarcely any topic, from the exact form of a stamp on a pass to the legal status of the entire city, that had not been squabbled over with the Soviets in the 1950s and 1960s. Any initiative had to contend with a long legacy of accumulated juridical formulas; and it had to bypass the stonewalling of the chief Soviet negotiator, Pyotr A. Abrasimov, Soviet Ambassador to East Germany, who was not a diplomat but a Communist Party functionary whose entire experience had been in dealing with East Europeans. He was thus peremptory and abrasive even by Soviet standards. He found it hard to accept that he could not simply issue directives to the Western negotiators.

The Western bargaining position was fundamentally unfavorable. The road, rail, and air links to West Berlin were easy prey to harassment by the Soviets and East Germans, to interruptions so seemingly trivial that they were difficult to challenge and yet in their cumulative impact profoundly threatening to the freedom of Berlin. West Berliners were forbidden to travel to East Berlin. There was no telephone service. Rail and road service for civilians was under the control of East Germany, which we did not even recognize at that time. Technically, military traffic passed through a Soviet-controlled checkpoint, but even this was a fiction, since actually an East German guard controlled the gates while a Soviet officer lounged in a nearby shack in case a dispute developed.

The "Western sectors" — the term always used by the allies to emphasize that Berlin still was a single city under Four-Power occupation — were supported economically by West Germany. Indeed, the Federal Republic had made a special effort under both the Christian Democratic and Social Democratic governments in Bonn to establish a political as well as economic presence in Berlin. These efforts had been supported and encouraged by the three Western powers. Nevertheless, in order to maintain the occupation status, which was the sole legal basis for holding the Soviets to account over Berlin, the three Western powers never acknowledged, and the Federal Republic never claimed, that West Berlin was part of the Federal Republic. It was therefore very much in the US interest to establish Soviet legal obligations to allow more normal access to West Berlin, and between West and East Berlin, which for a decade had been separated from each other by the Wall.

For a decade Berlin's vulnerability had been treated by the Soviets as an opportunity to exploit, not as an incentive to settle. What we had going for us in 1971 was Moscow's concern to achieve ratification of Brandt's Eastern treaties. Because it was inherent in *Ostpolitik* that its tangible advantages seemed to be one-sided — after all, Bonn was accepting the division of its country in return for nothing more than improvements in the political atmosphere — a favorable Berlin agreement had to supply the quid pro quo. Moscow was thus in the paradoxical position of being asked to make concessions not justified by the local balance of forces in order to achieve gains on other matters of importance to it. It was a classic case of linkage. The practical consequence of this linkage, however, was that in the process we became responsible for the ultimate success of Brandt's policy.

Two major issues had to be settled:

- the Western powers wanted a Soviet (not East German) guarantee that their access to Berlin would be preferential and unhindered;
- the Federal Republic wanted Soviet acceptance of significant political ties between the Federal Republic and Berlin, to remove the traditional pretexts of Communist pressures against West Berlin.

The Soviet Union had begun the Four-Power negotiations by attacking both issues with traditional subtlety; it put forth its maximum position with sledgehammer tactics. With respect to access, the Soviets denied any competence; they insisted that traffic crossing East Germany was not subject to their control or influence; it was a matter for the two German sides to discuss. If the Soviets as one of the occupying powers had no responsibility, then according to the Soviet approach neither did the Western allies. Civilian access to Berlin was thus a purely German matter; any crisis had to be resolved as an inter-German affair.

As for the "Federal presence" — the Soviet position was simplicity itself. The Soviets demanded nothing less than the complete elimination of any vestige of Bonn's "illegal" activities in the city, of which they put forward an encyclopedic list. And in characteristic fashion Abrasimov demanded that the issue of Federal presence be settled first; only then would access be discussed. The Soviets seemed to want to use the negotiations to turn West Berlin into a "free city," pressure for which had produced a major crisis in 1958–1959 and then again in 1961. It was a replay of their SALT tactics, in which the Soviets also wanted to settle the issue of greatest concern in Moscow — ABM — before turning to matters that we wanted. What point the Soviets thought was served by putting forward a proposition whose acceptance Brandt could not survive may remain forever mysterious.

Another tack the Soviets attempted just as I became personally involved in February 1971 was to try to bypass the Four Powers altogether. An East German official, Michael Kohl, appeared in Bonn to negotiate the normalization of relations between East Germany and the Federal Republic. I had set up the secret naval channel previously described to keep the Federal Republic's Bahr, our Ambassador Ken Rush, and myself in touch with one another, and I used it for the first time to warn Bahr that he should not be tempted to let the Soviets use him for an end-run in an all-German forum.

My next step was to discuss with Dobrynin, on February 10, the draft proposal the Western powers had submitted in the Four-Power talks on February 5. This insisted on unhindered access backed by a Soviet guarantee. As to the Federal presence, the draft offered that constitutional organs, such as the Parliament that elected the President, would no longer meet in Berlin, and that all West German ministries would be garnered under a single representative of the Federal Republic in Berlin. It was not much of a concession, since the offices would remain, but it gave the Soviets a face-saving institution with which they could deal. Everything that was not proscribed would be permitted.

Ken Rush was the linchpin. He kept me briefed for my negotiations with Dobrynin; he kept in close touch with the other Western allies to make sure that the allied positions remained compatible; he also had to curb Bahr's propensity for solitary efforts and for claiming credit with the Soviets for all concessions made. And Rush had to accomplish all this without the knowledge of his own State Department. It was an odd way to run a government. The miracle is that it worked, due in large measure to Rush's unflappable skill.

Dobrynin began by insisting that access procedures should be handled by the two Germanys, then suddenly dredged up a compromise: The Soviets would express their responsibility for access in the form of a unilateral declaration of what they understood the East German view to be. This statement would then be incorporated in a general guarantee of the whole agreement. I had to admit that this sounded like a distinct possibility, since it was in fact precisely the Western fallback position that was already being discussed in the formal channels. (It even occurred to me that rather than my acceptance of a Soviet compromise, what in fact was happening at the February 10 meeting was Soviet acceptance of our fallback position, which had been fed to Moscow from some other source.)

When I notified Bahr and Rush of my conversation with Dobrynin, they both affirmed that such a guarantee would be acceptable to the Western allies, provided that the access procedures which were being guaranteed were sufficiently detailed to improve Berlin's viability. Dobrynin reacted on February 22 by suggesting that I submit a detailed set of access procedures. This threw Bahr and Rush into a frenzy of drafting, complicated by frequent garbles in transmission of the long texts that were cabled to me in our backchannel. Their draft represented an amalgamation of the various allied positions and was therefore likely to be acceptable in the allied forums. On February 26 I submitted this document to Dobrynin.

On March 15 Dobrynin renewed his appeal for a further Western concession on Federal presence. I said that we could not go beyond the allied position as submitted in February. It was indicative of how eager the Soviets were for progress that Dobrynin immediately offered a compromise: some Soviet presence in West Berlin — for example, a consulate — in return for a Soviet guarantee of access. This seemed to concede the definition of Federal presence put forward by the allies on February 5.

Nothing, of course, works so simply in the Soviet system. By March 18 either Moscow had second thoughts or some other element of the Soviet bureaucracy demanded proof that more was not attainable. Dobrynin handed me a complete, detailed Soviet draft of a Berlin agreement that in effect withdrew most of the concessions made during the previous month. He invited my comments before Moscow offered the text in the Four-Power talks on March 26. It was impossible to deal with all the esoteric legal issues in a massive document in so short a time. On the other hand the formal submission to the Four was not of decisive importance; its main significance was to keep the Four-Power talks going.

After consultation with Rush and Bahr I replied to Dobrynin on March 22. I was in no position to offer a counterdraft and I did not want to be drawn into a detailed negotiation of a Soviet document that would ensure negotiations would be about *our* concessions. To force the Soviets to move toward our view — which I thought they would — I put forward, in consultation with Rush, a number of general principles: First, any agreement had to affirm Berlin's ties to the Federal Republic and Soviet acceptance of the authority of the Western powers in West

Berlin. Second, the undertaking on access must be a solid guarantee by the Soviet Union that surface access to Berlin, civilian as well as military, be unhindered. Third, there had to be a Soviet commitment to improvements in access between the city's two halves. Fourth, the agreement had to indicate that the form of West Berlin representation abroad was the responsibility of the three powers — this was a euphemism for permitting West Germany to represent Berlin, for the Western powers would delegate their authority to Bonn. And fifth, any understanding regarding a Soviet official presence in West Berlin had to be handled outside the Four-Power Berlin agreement. This was to prevent the Soviet Union from abrogating the provisions on access by using the pretext that the exercise of its consular functions in West Berlin was being interfered with. I handed Dobrynin an aide-mémoire spelling out in considerable detail the practical implications of these views.

Dobrynin and I came up with the idea of private talks between Abrasimov and Rush. It turned out to be one of those ideas easier to conceive than to implement. Abrasimov was in East Berlin, Rush in Bonn. They met only at Four-Power meetings. For either of them to contact the other meant becoming noticeable to the media by crossing checkpoints along the Wall. And for them to meet privately, even in the context of a Four-Power session, would be questioned by the other ambassadors — as well as reported in the frontchannels of the State Department, thus generating Washington demands for a full report.

We thought we had overcome the difficulties and arranged a meeting for March 25. Abrasimov, who either did not understand the mutual commitment to the two-channel system and its significance, or wanted to dam up the Dobrynin Channel (or both), thereupon did a Semenov: He put the request for a private meeting with Rush into frontchannels, creating a great deal of confused speculation in Washington. Then he equally mysteriously canceled the request. His meeting with Rush was rescheduled for the next Four-Power session on April 16. Abrasimov blamed the failure this time on Rush's having left the meeting early. It was a transparent subterfuge, for Rush had warned everyone that he would have to host a dinner for the Boston Pops Orchestra in Bonn that evening. Something deeper was obviously happening, perhaps a tug-of-war between the Soviet Ministry of Foreign Affairs (represented by Dobrynin) and the Party machinery (represented by Abrasimov). Or else Gromyko had decided that his March draft was a loser and would never serve as the basis for negotiation, and he chose this way to withdraw it. It is not impossible that the Soviets did not trust the Abrasimov-Rush channel alone and wanted to find a forum that would include Bahr, in whom they obviously had confidence. Whatever the reason, when I suggested to Dobrynin on April 23 that the Soviet Ambassador to Bonn, Valentin Falin, be substituted for Abrasimov, he accepted eagerly. In

Bonn, Falin, Rush, and Bahr could meet without attracting attention. From Gromyko's point of view it probably had the additional advantage of keeping everything in Foreign Office channels.

It was obviously necessary for me to meet with Egon Bahr again. Once more we needed a venue that could justify our getting together. We chose the Bilderberg Conference, an informal annual get-together of European and American political and business leaders scheduled for the weekend of April 24–25 in Vermont. There in sylvan setting — picketed by left-wing groups who saw the conference as a capitalist conspiracy and by right-wing groups who suspected such radical sponsors as David Rockefeller and Jack Heinz of selling out America to shady internationalism — Bahr and I reviewed the state of the negotiations. He had an ingenious suggestion: that both sides drop the legal justifications for their positions and work instead on describing their practical responsibilities and obligations. I agreed, subject to discussion with Rush, provided the access procedures were spelled out in a degree of detail that precluded later misunderstanding.

I explored Bahr's approach with Dobrynin on Monday, April 26. He accepted with an alacrity that suggested that he was not hearing it for the first time. I have known no Soviet diplomat — including Gromyko — who would accept a new major proposal without referring it to Moscow. It was not always absolutely clear how many channels were operating and who the principal negotiator was. I made sure of Bahr's authority by insisting that Rush request Brandt's personal endorsement of both procedure and substance. This he obtained on April 30.

On May 3, apparently under Soviet pressure, the dour Stalinist Walter Ulbricht was replaced as Party boss in East Germany by Erich Honecker, ostensibly for reasons of health. Honecker was said to be more flexible — recognizing that in Communist East Germany this is an extremely relative term.

Falin, Bahr, and Rush met for the first time on May 10. Thereafter, the central focus of the backchannel negotiations shifted into that forum, with Dobrynin and me breaking any deadlocks. Each of the three main negotiators reported all separate conversations to the other (at least in theory) as the only means of preventing chaos. An enormous amount of cable traffic frequently overloaded the special communication channel. The Navy took on more than it bargained for when it agreed to serve as communication link. It acquitted itself well.

On May 10 Falin, Rush, and Bahr met again. Following my instructions and his own beliefs, Rush resisted Bahr's pressures to submit detailed proposals on access procedures and Federal presence without clearance by the other allies. Rush insisted on a prior meeting with the Working Group of the Western occupying powers. We expected that they would approve the new approach in principle; we foresaw no difficulty in getting their agreement to detailed access procedures, especially if Bonn put them forward. Bahr objected to this procedure in Falin's presence, insisting on submitting tentative proposals immediately. Rush again wisely resisted. Eventually the Working Group went along with the new approach, which was presented as a planning, not a negotiating, paper.

There was another week's delay while Rush on my instructions postponed a meeting scheduled for May 19 as a response to Semenov's conduct in circumventing the Channel during the SALT talks. After the SALT breakthrough of May 20, I let things proceed. Falin followed the usual Soviet negotiating technique of retracting on June 4 what he had conceded on May 27 and 28, only to restore most of it on June 6. The rest of June was spent by Rush, Bahr, and Falin in drafting the incredibly complex, interlocking documents that constituted the final Berlin agreement. Each of these sessions produced agreements that I reviewed on behalf of the President and some contentious points that I sorted out with Dobrynin. At this stage, the Soviets' basic effort was to try to limit the significance of their guarantee of access by inserting qualifying phrases such as "within their area of competence" or vague references as to "canons of international law"; this would have enabled them later to argue about what their area of competence was or what provision of international law would apply to access procedures across sovereign territory.

The logjam suddenly broke because the Berlin negotiations turned into one of those occasions on which Gromyko seemed to be seized with a near panic that they might abort on the brink of success. He decided to blackmail us into a speedy conclusion by making final agreement to a summit conditional on the conclusion of a Berlin agreement. Whether this was because he was genuinely worried, or whether he wanted to acquire some additional kudos in the Kremlin for sharp marksmanship, the consequence was exactly the opposite of the intention. Once it became clear that there would be no summit in September, I sought to delay the conclusion of the Berlin agreement until after the announcement of my Peking visit. This would ease Soviet temptations to use our China opening as a pretext to launch a new round of crises. I succeeded, but only with some difficulty. Even Rush, like all negotiators, was getting carried away by the prospect of an agreement and procrastinated only with great reluctance (not knowing, of course, the reasons involved). And as the Western allies noticed an easing of the Soviet position in the formal Four-Power sessions, they too pressed for a rapid conclusion.

On July 7 Ambassador Falin returned from Moscow, where he had been for consultations, and told Bahr and Rush with a straight face that to his surprise Gromyko had approved all the concessions made in June.

This had spared him (Falin) the necessity of appealing to Kosygin and Brezhnev over Gromyko's head. Even skeptics like me, whose minds boggled at the vision of Gromyko's learning of a month's quota of major concessions for the first time from a subordinate who then threatened to go over his head if need be, could not doubt that the Soviets meant to press Berlin to a rapid conclusion.

Rush received another necessarily incomprehensible instruction from me: to stave off a final negotiating round until after July 15. When my visit to Peking was announced, Bahr informed me that the Russians in Bonn reacted emotionally but that they would nevertheless continue to proceed with the Berlin negotiation. This was not much of a favor, because they needed a Berlin agreement far more than we did. But it was a useful piece of intelligence, indicating that the fear of our Kremlinologists that an opening to Peking would wreck our relations with Moscow was false. Events bore out this early sign, for nine days after I gave Rush the go-ahead again, he and Bahr settled the last contentious issue.

The Soviets acquiesced in extending the consular protection of the Federal Republic to citizens of West Berlin and in West Berliners' right to travel on West German passports. In return we agreed to the essentially face-saving device of permitting a Soviet consulate to be established in West Berlin. It was of no help to the Soviet theory of separating West Berlin from the Federal Republic, since Soviet consulates exist in West German cities. (In the nearly ten years that the Berlin agreement has been in force the Soviet consulate has played no important role.)

At the end of the day Rush backchanneled with justifiable pride: "A draft of the tentative agreement is enclosed and it is still difficult for me to believe that it is as favorable as it is. It is still subject to the final approval of you, Gromyko and Brandt respectively. . . . We yesterday secured from Falin practically everything that we wanted." And he was right. Whereas before there had existed no legal basis for civilian access at all, procedures for it were now spelled out in meticulous detail, down to such technicalities as the use of sealed conveyances for manufactured goods. Whereas before the Soviet Union had washed its hands of Berlin access, claiming that it took place at the sovereign discretion of the East Germans, it now guaranteed it. The Federal presence in West Berlin was slightly reduced — especially with respect to activities that had never been recognized by the allies, such as the quadrennial election of the Federal President. But the Soviet Union had accepted the principle that ties between the Federal Republic and Berlin could be "maintained and developed" — thus providing a legal basis for strengthening economic and cultural ties between Bonn and Berlin. The accord empowered West Germany to represent Berlin in international agreements or bodies and enabled Berliners to travel on West German passports. In sum, the agreement implied and brought about a substantial improvement in the lives and safety of Berlin's population. The text substantially achieved the goal set forth by the Four-Power draft submitted on February 5, in fact paralleling it in major categories.

But the secret conclusion of the agreement among us, the Federal Republic, and the Soviets dramatized the bureaucratic problem generated by our system of two channels. Somehow we had to see to it that our own State Department did not complicate matters. Moreover, the agreement had to be ratified in a Four-Power forum staffed by diplomats exquisitely conscious of their prerogatives as representatives of occupying powers. In addition, the speed with which the "negotiation" had suddenly proceeded was mystifying to those who for a decade had been used to the rituals of stalemate. The problem was not insuperable, for many elements of the agreed draft had been drawn from the planning papers of the Working Group, but it was not trivial either. Rush and Abrasimov managed to introduce the noncontroversial items, while Bahr put forward the more difficult provisions with our support. So far so good, but once the formal Four-Power talks reopened on August 10, they were, of course, under the direction of the regular bureaucracy and it was determined to prove its mettle. Suddenly, Rush received instructions through State Department channels asking him to rephrase paragraphs already settled in private negotiations. The changes were not significant, yet they raised fears in Bahr's mind that we were opening ourselves to accusations of bad faith. I in turn complained to Dobrynin about Abrasimov's rough tactics, especially toward the British Ambassador, who had a low boiling point. On August 18–19 the problems seemed finally overcome. Full allied agreement was achieved. Rush sent a jubilant backchannel cable claiming that the bureaucrats "have been foiled."*

The truth was that they had just awakened. For the third time in three months a negotiation was being completed in which the regular bureaucracy had not participated, indeed, was unaware of its existence. There is no agreement that cannot be picked to death by professionals not involved in negotiating it. The German desk of the State Department did not go quite this far; after all, the British and French ambassadors had accepted the text of the agreement. Rogers simply called Rush back for

---

*I am aware that I am describing a complex multilateral negotiation from the perhaps inadequate perspective of a single participant. I do not know what bilateral contacts went on between the other participants whose contribution may have equaled or exceeded what I am here recounting. For example, when Jean Sauvagnargues, the French representative at these talks, became my colleague and friend as Foreign Minister, he referred several times to a central contribution he had made, and Sauvagnargues was not given to bragging; but his comments were enigmatic to me. I did not press for elucidation, for I was not eager to reciprocate. It is quite possible that there were other bilateral contacts with the Soviets. We shall have to wait for the memoirs of the other participants.

a two-week consultation so that the Department could conduct an "intensive review."

We were in a serious quandary. We had to convince the nearly paranoid Soviets that the delay was not significant, yet the State Department could scarcely be told that it had no right to review an agreement of such importance. We could not guarantee that some bureaucratic nitpicker might not force us to reopen issues settled already twice with the Soviets, first in the Rush-Bahr-Falin meetings and then again in the Four-Power ambassadorial talks with Abrasimov. Frenzied phone calls among the President, Rogers, Haldeman, and Mitchell (as Rush's old friend) followed. As usual Haldeman was assigned the task of fixing things. Brandt — at my suggestion — weighed in with a strong letter to Nixon endorsing the agreement as a "major achievement"; this would be useful with Rogers. Nixon had a genius for thinking up explanations for a fait accompli. He appealed for the support of his Secretary of State on the ground that the Europeans were so upset by Nixon's economic measures of August 15 imposing a 10 percent surtax on imports that we needed to let them have *their* way for a change (implying that he had had nothing to do with concluding the agreement). After a meeting with Rush on August 25, Rogers began to come around. The final act of the play was a Presidential invitation to Rush to San Clemente on August 27. This culminated in a press conference during which Rush announced that he had completed a final review with the President and that the agreement was a "major triumph for the foreign policy of President Nixon." That ended our internal bickering.

There was one more bizarre diversion, another little Communist game with translations: The East Germans produced a text that was at considerable variance not only with the English and Russian versions but also with the West German one. The French, however, refused to join in pressure on the Russians to get the East Germans to conform — the French Ambassador, Jean Sauvagnargues, stormed out of one meeting. The French position was based on their refusal to give German the status of an official language. While heartwarming to Frenchmen, it represented an interesting approach to an agreement dealing largely with German matters. But as often happens in diplomacy an essentially absurd formula ended the controversy. Only the French, Soviet, and English texts were considered "official." The negotiation ended with the anomaly that there is no authoritative German text of an agreement that defines the status of the former capital of Germany and whose implementation is to a great degree in the hands of Germans.

The Quadripartite Agreement on Berlin was officially signed on September 3, 1971. Kenneth Rush, whose skillful efforts had made it possible, paid the price of his exertions with a physical collapse from which it took him several weeks to recover. If the Berlin negotiation has a hero, it is Rush. He kept faith with our allies; he curbed Bahr's impatience; he conducted negotiations with two sets of Soviet ambassadors (in Berlin and in Bonn) with great ability and total discretion. Without him, our effort could never have achieved its dramatic success.

The unsentimental approach to Soviet relations was now clearly beginning to pay off. We were beginning to demonstrate that calculations of national interest were better solvents of East-West deadlocks than appeals to a change of heart. Linkage was working even if rejected by theorists; we had kept SALT and Berlin in tandem and substantially achieved our goals. And, of course, the Soviets were reasonably satisfied by Brandt's concessions; only amateurs believe in one-sided deals.

The Summit Finally

BOTH the SALT and Berlin negotiations had as their contrapuntal motif the attempt to arrange a summit meeting. We had raised the issue in 1970 but had been able to advance its prospects no further than a general suggestion first presented by Dobrynin on September 25, 1970, later reinforced by Gromyko to Nixon, that a suitable date would be sometime in the late summer of 1971. Gromyko had, however, stopped well short of issuing a formal invitation, and Dobrynin had continued to evade setting a date. Obviously, the Soviets considered the prospect of meeting their leaders an irresistible boon to us, worthy of being sold over and over again at a high price.

It was not until January 23, 1971, when I agreed to discuss Berlin in the Dobrynin Channel, that summit preparations speeded up. Dobrynin began to be more specific about the timing, while always avoiding ultimate concreteness. Clearly, if I linked Berlin to SALT, the Soviets linked Berlin to a summit. The problem with Moscow's strategy was that at the same time we were also quietly arranging another summit with Peking, and this made our bargaining position much stronger than it can have appeared.

Dobrynin came back to the summit a few more times in February 1971, reaffirming an autumn date, but he was not prepared to discuss any arrangements. Afterward, the summit disappeared from our agenda because the Soviet leadership was allegedly preoccupied by its twenty-fourth Party Congress. At the end of March Dobrynin left for one of his frequent consultations in Moscow, so that the autumn grew again elusive; a guardian angel must have been watching over us because we were far from prepared for a summit.

The Party Congress established Brezhnev's preeminent position. I wrote the President in mid-April that in my view Brezhnev had emerged as the dominant personality. I drew from that mixed prospects:

. . . in the major substantive issues between us, Brezhnev almost certainly sees himself as operating from considerable strength. His propensity for concessions is likely to be limited accordingly since he will expect to be able to wait us out and to let the "peace issue" do its work here as the election approaches.

Nevertheless, a reasonable net judgment would be (a) that Brezhnev has some room for genuine negotiation, and (b) has an incentive for some stabilization with us to help him accomplish his domestic goals and control divisive tendencies in his empire.

Nixon wrote in the margin: "We will have the answer in thirty days."

The answer, however, showed that the Soviets were no more prepared to make a clear-cut decision under the new leadership than under the old: They wanted a summit but they also wished to reinsure themselves by using it to put the heat on us during the Berlin negotiations. They wanted a new relationship but did not trust us enough to rely on our completing a negotiation which was in both our interests and on which both sides had invested a great deal of their effort, time, and prestige. Thus on April 23 Dobrynin suggested September but linked the summit explicitly to a Berlin agreement. I reacted sharply, insisting that we would accept no conditions (this was not a little disingenuous, from one of the chief exponents of the linkage theory). Dobrynin, using my own linkage arguments against me, insisted that Moscow was talking about reality, not conditions. I was less than grateful that Dobrynin should present himself as so apt a student. On April 26 — the day before the final confirmation of Peking's invitation — I warned Dobrynin not to play with the summit; the next time we discussed it he should be prepared to make an announcement.

The next time turned out to be June 8 at Camp David, to which I had invited Dobrynin for a general review of US–Soviet relations. Dobrynin asserted ingratiatingly that he counted on Nixon's reelection, and then used this argument to suggest that there was no hurry about a summit. It would come about naturally after the Berlin negotiations were completed. It was a petty and unnecessary maneuver because Gromyko must have known — despite Falin's epic fairy tales — that we were moving to an early conclusion.

By then, planning for my Peking trip was well advanced. At Camp David on June 8 I was more concerned that the Soviets would tie down the summit prematurely than I was with finding a mutually agreeable date. The last thing I wanted was the public announcement of a US–Soviet agreement to a summit while I was en route to Peking. I therefore asked Dobrynin to let me have a definitive answer by the end of June (I was to leave on July 1 for my twelve-day Asian trip); otherwise September would prove no longer feasible. Dobrynin no doubt thought the deadline revealed an impatience that it would be a pity not to exploit. It was, in fact, a reflection of prudent reinsurance in a game whose nature the Soviets had not yet grasped.

On July 5, while I was in Bangkok and four days from arriving in Peking, Moscow turned down the September date it had originally proposed. Dobrynin's deputy, Vorontsov, brought in a reply to Haig, who called Lord at 3:00 A.M., speaking in double-talk (which an illiterate child could have deciphered). The Soviet note not only put off the summit but introduced more conditions. It admitted that there had lately been movement in the discussion of some questions (meaning Berlin). "At the same time there is yet no full certainty whether agreements could be reached as soon as desired." The Soviets proposed a mutually acceptable time closer to the end of 1971. The date for an announcement was to be "pinpointed" in additional talks — in other words, another stall. At the end of the message there was a paragraph that suggested the Soviets were making the summit conditional not only on Berlin but also on American restraint in general (perhaps thinking of Vietnam): "It is necessary that both sides will allow in their activities nothing that would make the situation unfavorable for the preparation and holding of the meeting and would weaken the chances of getting positive results at such a meeting."

I cabled Haig that Vorontsov's note had its advantages. We could now complete the summits in our preferred order. The Soviet Union would find it more difficult to accuse us of bad faith in our opening to Peking (not a decisive factor, but helpful). And if the Soviets still wanted to go ahead with a Moscow summit — as I thought probable — it would take place in circumstances where the balance of interests was more visible. As already indicated, I also instructed Ken Rush in Bonn to slow down the Berlin talks for two weeks.

We could not completely ignore the advice of all leading governmental experts on the Soviet Union to the effect that an opening to China might cause Soviet policy to turn to a hard line. While I disagreed with this judgment, I thought it necessary to take out insurance in case I proved mistaken. On July 15, about forty-five minutes before the announcement of my trip to Peking, we sent a message to the Soviet leaders through Vorontsov, coyly reminding the Soviet government of "the sequence of events which preceded the announcement." We reaffirmed our willingness to continue improving relations. We stressed that the July 15 announcement was not aimed at any country; however, we were prepared for all consequences.

There was no need for concern, as our own previous analysis of Soviet motivations should have taught us. Soviet leaders do not challenge objective factors; they adjust to them. They were not about to drive us irrevocably to the Chinese side. They calculated instead that they had more to offer. In short, the Kremlin played its part in the triangular relationship grudgingly, no doubt waiting for an opportunity to get even, but given no choice by the logic of events.

When I saw Dobrynin on July 19, four days after the world had learned that Nixon was going to Peking, he was at his ingratiating best. He was now all for a Moscow summit. The question was, could it take place before the one in Peking? I put it as my personal opinion that the summits should be held in the order in which they were decided upon — exactly the same point I had made in Peking. Dobrynin — no doubt in deep trouble in Moscow for not having foreseen our move — regretted that we had not given him any advance warning. On reflection he admitted that this would have been asking too much. And he kept inquiring about the impact of Soviet rejection of the September date for a Nixon visit (probably to shift some of the blame to his superiors). His tone and demeanor had changed since the announcement of my China visit. Now that we clearly had other options, the annoying alternation of carrot and stick disappeared. We had totally misunderstood their July 5 message, he averred. It was produced only by scheduling difficulties; it reflected no lack of interest in high-level meetings. Since the Soviet leaders were visiting France in October, the suggestion of November or December had been largely a procedural preference. I chose not to remind him of the conditions or of the cat-and-mouse game that had extended over fourteen months.

The new Soviet tactic was obvious. It was to demonstrate, as I have said, that in a trilateral diplomacy Peking gave us a move but not a strategy; Moscow could offer concrete benefits. As Brezhnev was to put it later, Nixon went "to Peking for banquets but to Moscow to do business." By this approach Moscow attempted to bring home to Peking that it had no real options: Hostility to Moscow had led to a massive buildup on the border; an attempt to open channels to Washington would only lead Moscow to demonstrate once again that it was the side with the greater assets.

There was no reason to disabuse the Soviets of their belief. To have the two Communist powers competing for good relations with us could only benefit the cause of peace; it was the essence of triangular strategy. Our road through this maze was to play it straight with all the parties. Geopolitically, it was against our interest to have the Soviet Union dominate China or for China to be driven back toward Moscow. We would do nothing, therefore, to further Soviet designs to establish China's impotence. Indeed, if the worst were to happen, I was convinced that we could not stand idly by in case of a Soviet attack on China — a view few of my colleagues shared.

On the other hand, we could not wish to provoke that contingency. Sino-Soviet tensions followed their own logic; they were not created by us nor could they be manipulated by us directly. Each of the Communist antagonists was certain to be affected by our actions; each would seek to nudge us in the direction it favored; each would determine its relation to the other in part in terms of its assessment of our intentions and actions.

But to seek to manipulate them was to make us their prisoner. We had no capacity to fuel a conflict of whose origin we had been unaware, and the attempt to do so was likely to tempt the two sides to blackmail us seriatim.

We had to walk a narrow path. We would make those agreements with the Soviet Union which we considered in our national interest. But we would give no encouragement to visions of condominium, and we would resist any attempts by Moscow to achieve hegemony over China or elsewhere. We would keep China informed of our negotiations with the Soviet Union and in considerable detail; we would take account of Peking's views. We would conclude no agreement aimed at Chinese interests. But we would not give Peking a veto over our actions. We followed these principles toward both sides scrupulously from the beginning of the triangular relationship — although since Moscow was the stronger party we briefed it much less precisely or frequently.

In early August 1971 I recommended to the President to open direct communications with Brezhnev. Until then the rare exchanges between the top leaders had been with Kosygin. But the Party Congress had made clear — and Dobrynin had emphasized — that henceforth Brezhnev would take an increasing interest in foreign policy. On August 5, therefore, a letter was sent from Nixon to Brezhnev — drafted by my staff and me — outlining the basic elements of our policy toward the Soviet Union. It reiterated the theme we had stressed since Nixon's Inauguration: that progress in our relations required concrete solutions, of which SALT was one of the most important. It then sketched our views on other issues along well-established lines. It stressed that we would proceed with the normalization of relations with China not as a policy aimed at the Soviet Union but in pursuit of our conception of a stable world order.

After that the pace of relations accelerated. The tone of Soviet communications eased considerably. Gone were the conditions of the previous three months or the escape clauses geared to general American conduct. On August 10 the Soviets extended a formal invitation to President Nixon to visit Moscow in May or June 1972. The Soviet note indicated that the USSR "welcomed" the normalization of relations between Peking and Washington with the caveat that everything depended on how these relations would be developed. Whistling past the graveyard, the note asserted that the Soviets were not swayed "by transitory calculations no matter how important the latter may seem." But just as we could ruin the trilateral relationship by seeming to exploit it, so the Soviets could not escape its consequences by proclaiming its irrelevance.

That Moscow, whatever it professed, understood reality became apparent in all that followed. After the announcement of the President's trip to Peking the unsettled issues on Berlin were resolved in one week to our satisfaction. The accidental-war agreement, providing for rapid communication in case of technical malfunction but stripped of all anti-Chinese implications, was concluded by the end of August. It was signed on September 30 in Washington during Gromyko's annual visit to the United States for the UN General Assembly. The tone in all our other dealings changed dramatically. Coexistence — at least for a time — was coming about, not because of sudden moral insights but through the necessities of the international balance that we had helped to shape.

On August 17 I told Dobrynin that we accepted the summit invitation. The rest of the month was spent in drafting an announcement that, like the one in Peking, sought to avoid having either side appear as the supplicant. Dobrynin and I on September 7 finally settled on a neutral formulation that indicated enough progress had been made in US–Soviet relations for the leaders of the two countries to meet in the second half of May 1972 in Moscow. The announcement was to be made October 12 after Gromyko's visit to Washington.

Gromyko arrived at the Oval Office on September 29, 1971, exuding joviality, the double negatives all pointing in a positive direction. He announced that Moscow considered the US–Soviet relationship central to world peace; Brezhnev would have it under his personal care. He indicated a new approach to the Middle East; the Soviet Union would be prepared to withdraw its combat forces from Egypt in case of a final settlement (discussed more fully in Chapter XXX). He went so far as to offer to convey a message to Hanoi. He averred his interest in a rapid and successful conclusion of the SALT negotiations.

Just as the year before, it was arranged prior to the meeting that Nixon would take Gromyko to his hideaway in the Executive Office Building. It was vital that he do so because no one in our bureaucracy as yet knew that a summit had been agreed to, much less the text of an announcement. Nixon returned, beaming, from the private meeting to tell his Secretary of State that he and Gromyko had just settled plans for the Moscow summit, creating the impression that Gromyko had brought the invitation, that Nixon had accepted it on the spot, and that the two of them had jointly negotiated the announcement. (This had the added advantage of casting Nixon in the role of the principal negotiator and reducing thereby the tensions between Rogers and me.) Gromyko played his part in some bafflement but with the poker face and aplomb that had seen him through decades of the infinitely more lethal Kremlin politics.

I met with Gromyko the next day at the Soviet Embassy. The atmosphere could not have been more cordial. There was no longer any foot-dragging about the relationship between offensive and defensive limitations on SALT; on the contrary, Gromyko left little doubt that Moscow would do its utmost to complete both agreements in time for the summit. Gromyko volunteered that a forthcoming visit by Soviet President Podgorny to Hanoi had not been initiated by Moscow but had come about at the urgent request of the North Vietnamese. He wondered whether we might settle for a "neutral" government in Saigon, excluding Communists as well as Thieu. I replied that we would not overthrow Thieu as part of a settlement but that we were open to a political process in which all forces could participate after a settlement had been achieved. Gromyko pretended that this repetition of our formal position was news worthy of being transmitted to Hanoi. Given the fact that we had direct channels to the North Vietnamese, I saw no point in a Soviet mediation in which we could never be sure whether the mediator understood all the subtleties or had the same interest as we did in conveying accurate information. I did revive the idea behind the Vance mission of two years earlier; I offered to go to Moscow for high-level negotiations with a senior North Vietnamese if Hanoi saw some prospect of a rapid settlement.

This offer was caught up in a bureaucratic dilemma. Ever since my secret trip the Soviets were eager for me to visit Moscow to prepare the summit, wanting absolute parity of treatment with Peking. (Since I had made a secret trip to Peking, they wanted me to make a secret trip to Moscow!) Gromyko brought the first invitation; it was repeated in writing on December 1. It also reflected a real need. Summits are notoriously poor occasions for negotiation. They have a built-in deadline, protocol reigns, and if they are to succeed, any major agreement needs to be worked out in advance. And given the organization of our government, I was the interlocutor who could be most decisive.

Nixon agreed with the principle of my visit to Moscow, but saw no way to implement it and keep on terms with Rogers. In this judgment he was quite right. I shared it and never urged a visit until much later, when the North Vietnamese offensive broke upon us seven weeks before the projected summit and made immediate contact with Brezhnev imperative. Nixon had kept Rogers from visiting Moscow for nearly three years, partly because he wanted to be the first senior American to go there, partly because as time went on he and Rogers rarely explored each other's mind on the issues. But to send me — until events demanded — would have been unnecessarily wounding.

The proposal for high-level talks on Vietnam in Moscow was no more successful than the initiative of the Vance mission — except that this time we received an official reply. On October 16 we were officially told by Dobrynin that Hanoi preferred to deal with us directly rather than through Moscow.

During the course of 1971 we had fended off continual urgings from our economic agencies to ease restrictions on trade with the USSR. Our strategy was to use trade concessions as a political instrument, withholding them when Soviet conduct was adventurous and granting them in measured doses when the Soviets behaved cooperatively. In general, we favored projects that required enough time to complete for us to have continued leverage on Soviet conduct. We sat on a scheme for an American firm to sell gear-cutting machinery for a Soviet civilian truck plant on the Kama River for two years in the face of massive pressures from our economic agencies and the Congress; we received many threatening letters from individuals staunchly anti-Communist until they saw profits in jeopardy. After the Soviets agreed to the May 20 compromise on SALT, the plant was quickly approved. Some other projects related to the Kama River plant were held up until there was a breakthrough on Berlin after the announcement of my China trip. Part was held up again during the India-Pakistan crisis. Peter G. Peterson, then Assistant to the President for International Economic Affairs, worked out effective coordination that subjected all such economic decisions to our foreign policy strategy. He carried out the same role with ability and finesse after he became Secretary of Commerce in 1972.

This then was the manner in which we maintained our momentum, culminating in 1971 with President Nixon's announcement on October 12 of a May 1972 summit in Moscow. A year that had started in stagnation had seen the opening to China, the thawing of the relationship with Moscow, the conclusion of agreements on Berlin and accidental war, and the breakthrough on SALT. Vietnam could be included in the year's progress. It still dominated the passions of many, but it was now less a national obsession than a painful legacy on the way to resolution. Hanoi could not help but be affected by the knowledge that its two great Communist allies were each improving their relationship with Washington despite the war in Indochina. This was bound to improve our negotiating position. Beyond that, our various initiatives began to dispel the nightmare that Vietnam would sap the spirit and the confidence of our people. We had shown that America remained capable of great enterprise amidst travail. We could see ahead of us the prospects for a new international order reflecting the realities and yearnings of our period, and achieved by American vision and dedication.

All this was due in not inconsiderable degree to Nixon's insistence, with my help, on White House control of foreign policy. In 1971 we took over not simply the planning but also the execution of major initiatives. I have stated here that I do not consider the methods employed desirable in the abstract; certainly, they should not be regularly pursued. But it is difficult for a President to make new departures through the "system." The departments and agencies prefer to operate by consensus. They like to make policy through a pattern of clearances that obscures who has prevailed — and also any clear-cut direction. They tend to be attracted to the fashionable. They shun confrontation with one another, the media, or the Congress. When thwarted they do not shrink, however, from political warfare against the President by leaks, and, in extreme cases, by the encouragement of Congressional pressures. All Presidents have found necessary some way to avoid being stifled by bureaucratic inertia in the guise of clearance procedures, or by economic agencies pursuing objectives without political guidance. No doubt Nixon went to extremes in trying to achieve dominance. There were many dedicated members of the agencies who would have been willing to help. But as the accounts of the China initiative, the SALT negotiations, and the Middle East have shown, many of our conceptions would have run up against established wisdom.

That Nixon chose to circumvent the process rather than discipline it reflected his personality. It does not change the problem, which would be faced by any innovative President. And Nixon deserves great credit for tough decisions taken in the face of enormous public pressures; for his strategic grasp; for his solitary efforts; for his courage in running risks not only in war but also for peace. His administrative approach was weird and its human cost unattractive, yet history must also record the fundamental fact that major successes were achieved that had proved unattainable by conventional procedures.

We had no illusions about Soviet motivations. But I did not accept then, nor will I now, the proposition that we were bound to be outmaneuvered by the Soviets in a political contest. Indeed, the contest could be sustained domestically only if we were unafraid to explore the prospects of coexistence. Only then would we be able to face down challenges as a united people; no other course would enable us to hold our alliances together. Whether the Soviets were preparing for negotiation or confrontation, our task was the same: The United States had to champion peace but it had to make sure that the quest for peace reflected a sense of justice and did not turn into a stampede of unilateral concessions.

We were using an era of negotiation to achieve *our* purposes of securing peace and defending freedom. As I wrote to Nixon in reporting on my conversation with Gromyko on September 30:

We can expect the Soviets, even in this new "positive" line, to be pursuing their own interests, driving hard bargains for their friends, and doing their normal amount of tactical elbowing. But the prospects and interplay of your two summit meetings give us useful leverage. If we play our cards right, we can hope for some constructive results.

XXI

The Tilt:
The India-Pakistan Crisis of 1971

Origins of Tragedy

IN every administration some event occurs that dramatizes the limits of human foresight. In the year of uncertainty on Vietnam, the opening to China, and the evolving relationship with the Soviet Union, there was almost nothing the Administration was less eager to face than a crisis in South Asia. And as if to underscore the contingent quality of all our planning, it was triggered by, of all things, a cyclone.

Bordered on the south by the Indian Ocean, on the north by the Himalayas, and on the west by the Hindu Kush mountains that merge with the heavens as if determined to seal off the teeming masses, and petering out in the east in the marshes and rivers of Bengal, the Indian subcontinent has existed through the millennia as a world apart. Its northern plains simmer in enervating heat in summer and are assailed by incongruous frost in winter; its lush south invites a life of tranquillity and repose. Its polyglot peoples testify to the waves of conquerors who have descended upon it through the mountain passes, from the neighboring deserts, and occasionally from across the sea. Huns, Mongols, Greeks, Persians, Moguls, Afghans, Portuguese, and at last Britons have established empires and then vanished, leaving multitudes oblivious of either the coming or the going.

Unlike China, which imposed its own matrix of law and culture on invaders so successfully that they grew indistinguishable from the Chinese people, India transcended foreigners not by co-opting but by segregating them. Invaders might raise incredible monuments to their own importance as if to reassure themselves of their greatness in the face of so much indifference, but the Indian peoples endured by creating relationships all but impervious to alien influence. Like the Middle East, India is the home of great religions. Yet unlike those of the Middle East, these are religions not of exaltation but of endurance; they have inspired man not by prophetic visions of messianic fulfillment but by bearing witness to the fragility of human existence; they offer not personal salvation but the solace of an inevitable destiny. Where each man is classified from birth, his failure is never personal; his quality is tested by his ability to endure his fate, not to shape it. The caste system does not attract civilizations determined to seek fulfillment in a single lifetime. It provides extraordinary resilience and comfort in larger perspectives. The Hindu religion is proud and self-contained; it accepts no converts. One is either born into it or forever denied its comforts and the assured position it confers. Foreign conquest is an ultimate irrelevancy in the face of such impermeability; it gives the non-Indian no status in Indian society, enabling Indian civilization to survive, occasionally even to thrive, through centuries of foreign rule. Of course, so many invasions have had to leave a human, not only an architectural, residue. The Moslem conquerors, representing a proselytizing religion, offered mass conversion as a route for lower-caste Hindus to alleviate their condition. They succeeded only partially, for once converted the new Moslems lost the respect to which even their low-caste status had entitled them. Here were sown the seeds of the communal hatred that has rent the subcontinent for the past generations.

Britain was but one of the latest of the conquerors, replacing Moslem Mogul and some Hindu rulers in the north and propping up indigenous Hindu rulers in the south — carrying out the cycle, it seemed, of the ages. But in one important respect Britain's conquest was different. True, it was made possible precisely because the British replaced one set of rulers by another in a pattern that had become traditional; its psychological basis was that the concept of nationhood did not yet exist. But it was Britain that gave the subcontinent — heretofore a religious, cultural, and geographic expression — a political identity as well. The British provided for the first time a homogeneous structure of government, administration, and law. They then supplied the Western values of nationalism and liberalism. Paradoxically, it was their own implanting of values of nationalism and democracy that made the British "foreign," that transformed a cultural expression into a political movement. Indian leaders trained in British schools claimed for their peoples the very values of their rulers. And the halfheartedness of Britain's resistance demonstrated that it had lost the moral battle before the physical one was joined.

As the prospect of nationhood appeared, the polyglot nationalities that the flood of invasions had swept into India now were left alone with their swelling numbers, their grinding poverty, and above all with one another. Nearly a third of the total population was Moslem, concentrated in the West Punjab and East Bengal but with important pockets all over India. Many of these peoples, by now outcasts of Indian society, found it unacceptable to live in a secular state dominated by those who

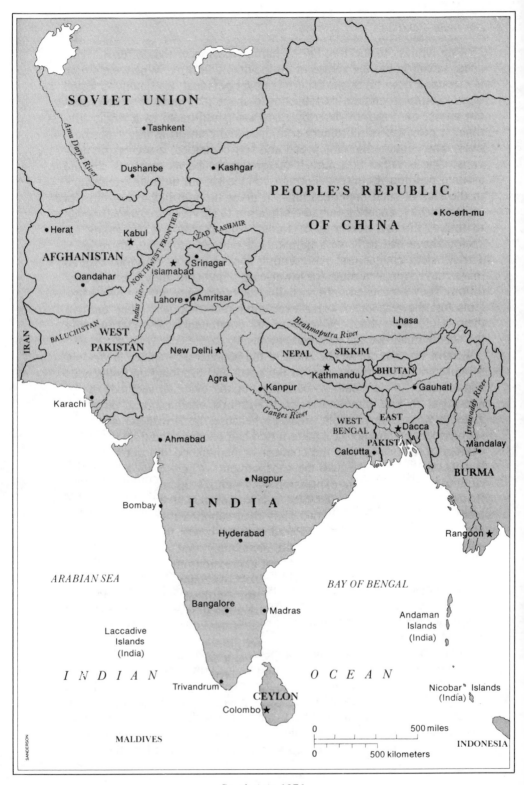

South Asia 1971

through the centuries had disdained them. The British solution in 1947 was partition along religious lines.

Thus were born, amidst unspeakable horrors and communal riots, the states of India and Pakistan. Pakistan was composed of two units: the West, dominated by the Punjab; and the East, Bengali,* separated by a thousand miles of Indian territory, with no common language, held together not by economics or history but by Islam and a common fear of Hindu domination. Pakistan's very existence was an affront to Indian nationalists who had, like other leaders of independence movements, dreamed of claiming all the territory ruled by the former colonial power. And India saw in the neighboring Moslem state a potential threat to its own national cohesion. Since more than fifty million Moslems remained under India's rule, either they would sooner or later claim their own national existence, or else the creation of Pakistan had been in fact the needless British imposition that some Indian nationalists never tired of proclaiming it was. For its part, Pakistan, conscious that even the lowest-class Hindus believed themselves part of a system superior to the Moslems, looked on its larger neighbor with fear, with resentment, and occasionally with hatred.

Few old neighbors have less in common, despite their centuries of living side by side, than the intricate, complex Hindus and the simpler, more direct Moslems. It is reflected in the contrasts of their architecture. The finely carved Hindu temples have nooks and corners whose seemingly endless detail conveys no single view or meaning. The mosques and forts with which the Moguls have covered the northern third of the subcontinent are vast, elegant, romantic, their resplendent opulence contrasting with the flatness of the simmering countryside, their innumerable fountains expressing a yearning for surcease from a harsh environment and a nostalgia for the less complicated regions that had extruded the invader.

In the 1950s and 1960s, America, oblivious to these new countries' absorption with themselves, sought to fit them into its own preconceptions. We took at face value Indian Prime Minister Jawaharlal Nehru's claim to be neutral moral arbiter of world affairs. We hardly noticed that this was precisely the policy by which a weak nation seeks influence out of proportion to its strength, or that India rarely matched its international pretensions with a willingness to assume risks, except on the subcontinent where it saw itself destined for preeminence. And we treated Pakistan simply as a potential military ally against Communist aggression. There was no recognition that most Pakistanis considered their real security threat to be India, the very country that we had enshrined in the

---

* Bengal was split by the 1947 partition. The eastern portion became East Pakistan; West Bengal remained part of India.

pantheon of abstract morality and that in turn viewed our arming of Pakistan as a challenge undermining our attempt to nurture its favor.

At one and the same time we overestimated the feasibility of obtaining India's political approbation and misjudged the target of Pakistan's military efforts. We were overly sensitive to the "world opinion" that India purported to represent. But we also sought to include Pakistan in a conception of containment that it did not share. The legal obligation to the common defense was thought to represent a deterrent to Communist aggression even when the members of the alliances in question could do little to reinforce each other's strength or had few shared objectives. Pakistan became our ally in the Southeast Asia Treaty Organization (SEATO) and in the Central Treaty Organization (CENTO).[1] Pakistan thus became eligible for US arms aid, which was intended for use against Communist aggression but was suspected by India of having other more likely uses.

The military alliances formed in the Eisenhower Administration became controversial in America when the Democratic opposition attacked them as examples of overemphasis on military considerations. India became the special favorite of American liberals, who saw in its commitment to democracy the foundation of a notional partnership and in its hoped-for economic success the best refutation of Communist claims to represent the wave of the future. No wonder that after the change of administrations in 1961, Washington's interest in Pakistan cooled noticeably; verbal assurances of American protection came increasingly to be substituted for military hardware. (The multiplication of these assurances came back to haunt us in 1971.) And all the while India worked tenaciously and skillfully to undermine the military relationship between Pakistan and the United States even after India had built up a significant weapons industry of its own and established a substantial military supply relationship with the Soviet Union.

The 1965 India-Pakistan war furnished us a pretext to disentangle ourselves to some degree. The United States stopped the supply of all military equipment to both sides (this policy was modified somewhat in 1966–1967, to permit the provision of nonlethal items and spares for all equipment). The seeming even-handedness was deceptive; the practical consequence was to injure Pakistan, since India received most of its arms either from Communist nations or from its own armories. President Johnson, aware of the one-sidedness of the action, promised to arrange a transfer to Pakistan of some obsolescent American tanks through a third party such as Turkey. But he never completed the transaction, in part because he did not want to spend his waning Congressional support on what must have appeared to him a marginally important decision, in part because the third parties developed second thoughts.

My own experience with the subcontinent should have forewarned me of its fevered passions. In January 1962, while I was still technically a consultant to President Kennedy, the United States Information Agency arranged a series of lectures for me on the subcontinent. Our Ambassador to India, John Kenneth Galbraith, a good friend of mine, was not a little disquieted about the impact on his presumptively sensitive and pacifist clients of a Harvard professor whose chief claim to fame at that time was a book called *Nuclear Weapons and Foreign Policy*. I promptly put his mind at ease by getting myself embroiled with Pakistan upon my arrival at the New Delhi airport. At the inevitable press conference I replied to a question about Kashmir with what I thought was a diplomatic answer — that I did not know enough about it to form a judgment. When queried about Pakistan's budding flirtation with China, I was loath to admit my ignorance of a development that, in the light of the prevalent view of China's congenital aggressiveness, seemed preposterous. I therefore opined that I could not imagine Pakistan doing such a foolish thing. Pakistan's leaders already felt discriminated against because a Harvard professor had been assigned as Ambassador to New Delhi while Islamabad rated "only" a career appointment. But they had been too circumspect to attack a personal friend of Kennedy. My airport interview was a godsend. It enabled the Pakistani press to vent its disappointment against another Harvard professor and lesser associate of Kennedy. My confession of ignorance about Kashmir was transmuted into a symbol of American indifference. Using the word "foolish" in the same sentence as "Pakistan" — even to deny that Pakistan was foolish — became a national insult. There was one compensation. The Pakistani press campaign turned me fleetingly into a figure of consequence in India. Thus in 1962, at least, the charge was that I was tilting toward India.

Matters eventually calmed down enough so that I could show my face in Pakistan on the same trip. I proved immediately that I had not lost my touch. Returning to Peshawar from sight-seeing at the Khyber Pass, I was waylaid by a Pakistani journalist who asked me whether I had seen any sign of Pushtoon agitation.* On the theory that the subcontinent had been deprived of my wisecracks long enough, I replied: "I would not recognize Pushtoon agitation if it hit me in the face." The resulting headline, "Kissinger Does Not Recognize Pushtoonistan," triggered an official Afghan protest in Washington, but at least it made me a momentary hero in Pakistan. There is no telling what else I might have achieved had I followed my wanderlust to visit Afghanistan. But the USIA judged that it had more than gotten its money's worth of cultural exchange and that home was a safer place for my talents.

---

*This referred to a movement to detach the border region from Pakistan and connect it with people speaking a similar language on the Afghan side of the Khyber Pass.

Thus perhaps I should have known better than to become involved in the frenzies of the subcontinent in 1971.

When the Nixon Administration took office, our policy objective on the subcontinent was, quite simply, to avoid adding another complication to our agenda. In their uneasy twenty-two-years' coexistence India and Pakistan had fought two wars. We sought to maintain good relations with both of them. Nixon, to put it mildly, was less susceptible to Indian claims of moral leadership than some of his predecessors; indeed, he viewed what he considered their alleged obsequiousness toward India as a prime example of liberal softheadedness. But this did not keep him from having a moderately successful visit to New Delhi in 1969 on his round-the-world trip. He quickly abandoned his vision of crowds comparable with Eisenhower's in 1956. The reception was restrained; crowds were merely adequate; the discussions were what in communiqué language would be called "constructive" and "businesslike." Nixon gave a very eloquent dinner toast, paying tribute to the wisdom of Mahatma Gandhi and ruminating thoughtfully on the nature of peace in the modern world.

But Nixon and Mrs. Indira Gandhi, Indian Prime Minister and daughter of Nehru, were not intended by fate to be personally congenial. Her assumption of almost hereditary moral superiority and her moody silences brought out all of Nixon's latent insecurities. Her bearing toward Nixon combined a disdain for a symbol of capitalism quite fashionable in developing countries with a hint that the obnoxious things she had heard about the President from her intellectual friends could not all be untrue. Nixon's comments after meetings with her were not always printable. On the other hand, Nixon had an understanding for leaders who operated on an unsentimental assessment of the national interest. Once one cut through the strident, self-righteous rhetoric, Mrs. Gandhi had few peers in the cold-blooded calculation of the elements of power. The political relationship in substance was thus far better than the personal one.

Whatever Nixon's personal qualms about its Prime Minister, India continued throughout his first Administration to enjoy a substantial constituency in the Congress and within the US government. Mrs. Gandhi had not yet disillusioned Americans by her nuclear test and assumption of authoritarian rule. Emotional ties with the world's most populous democracy remained. Large annual aid appropriations were proposed by the Administration and passed by Congress with little opposition. Between 1965 and 1971 India received $4.2 billion of American economic aid, about $1.5 billion of it during the Nixon years.

If India basked in Congressional warmth and was subject to Presidential indifference, Pakistan's situation was exactly the reverse. Pakistan was one of the countries where Nixon had been received with respect when he was out of office; he never forgot this. And the bluff, direct military chiefs of Pakistan were more congenial to him than the complex and apparently haughty Brahmin leaders of India. On the other hand, Pakistan had never found the sympathy in America that India enjoyed, at least among opinion-making groups. It did not represent principles with which Americans could identify as readily as with the "progressive" slogans and pacifist-sounding morality of the world's largest democracy. Moreover, India was much larger and had four or five times the population of Pakistan. There were thus hardheaded reasons for the priority attached to our relations with India.

Nixon made few changes in the policies he inherited on the subcontinent except to adopt a somewhat warmer tone toward Pakistan. He and I — as the only senior officials who knew the facts — were profoundly grateful for Pakistan's role as the channel to China. It was a service for which Pakistan's leaders, to their lasting honor, never sought any reciprocity or special consideration. The only concrete gesture Nixon made — and it was also to maintain the promise of his predecessor — was to approve in the summer of 1970 a small package of military equipment for Pakistan. This was to be a "one-time exception" to the US arms embargo. It included some twenty aircraft and 300 armored personnel carriers, but no tanks or artillery. The package amounted to $40 to $50 million (or somewhat more, depending on the type of aircraft chosen). India, which was increasing its military procurement at the average rate of $350 million a year — nearly ten times this amount — raised a storm of protest. At the same time India was accusing us of interfering in its domestic affairs because some of our Embassy personnel — in perhaps the most overstaffed Embassy of our diplomatic service — occasionally saw opposition leaders. This was not fulfilling a Washington-designed strategy but was a natural activity in a country with free institutions; it was an odd accusation for the leaders of a democracy to make. But the storm soon blew over.

By 1971 our relations with India had achieved a state of exasperatedly strained cordiality, like a couple that can neither separate nor get along. Our relations with Pakistan were marked by a superficial friendliness that had little concrete content. On the subcontinent, at least, alliance with the United States had not been shown to produce significant benefits over nonalignment.

At the beginning of 1971 none of our senior policymakers expected the subcontinent to jump to the top of our agenda. It seemed to require no immediate decisions except annual aid programs and relief efforts in response to tragic natural disasters in late 1970. It appeared to be the ideal subject for long-range studies. I ordered three of these in late 1970. Two addressed Soviet naval strength in the Indian Ocean and its implications; the third examined our long-term policy toward India and

Pakistan, including the objectives of the Soviet Union and Communist China and the interplay between them. Each of these studies was given a due date far ahead; no serious crisis was expected.

Two Cyclones

EVER since it had come into being, Pakistan had sought a sustained legitimacy. No government after the death of the founder of the state had served out its term. Every change had occurred through some sort of coup; military and civilian governments alternated, with the military dominant. The year 1970 was expected to see a constitutional government. Elections would finally take place in December. Pakistan's President Yahya Khan visited Nixon in October during the United Nations' twenty-fifth anniversary celebration, when Nixon gave him the message to Chou En-lai already described. I took the opportunity to ask Yahya what would happen to the powers of the President after the election. Yahya could not have been more confident. He expected a multiplicity of parties to emerge in both West and East Pakistan, which would continually fight each other in each wing of the country and between the two wings; the President would therefore remain the arbiter of Pakistan's politics.

Before his prediction could be tested a devastating cyclone struck East Pakistan over November 12–13. By most accounts, I wrote Nixon, this was the greatest disaster of the century in terms of destruction of property and human life; over 200,000 were thought to have died. The all-out relief program that Nixon ordered could only touch the surface of the suffering. Recovery efforts were chaotic and ineffective. The opposition charged the Yahya government with gross incompetence and worse. The political storm turned out in the end to be even more destructive than the natural one.

Whether the cyclone crystallized opposition to the central government and enhanced East Pakistan's sense of grievance and identity, or whether Yahya had misjudged the mood all along, the elections held on December 7, 1970, turned into a plebiscite on Yahya's handling of the crisis and produced a catastrophe for the military rulers. The Awami League, dedicated to East Pakistani autonomy, won 167 out of 169 seats contested in the East, giving it a majority of the 313 seats in the National Assembly. Its leader, Sheikh Mujibur Rahman (known as Mujib), was thus bound to be an unchallengeable figure in East Pakistan and a powerful influence in the entire country. To heighten the political drama, Zulfikar Ali Bhutto, leader of the Pakistan People's Party, emerged in a comparably dominant position in West Pakistan. While opposed to military rule, Bhutto was an advocate of a strong central government and of a united Pakistan; he fiercely resisted Mujib's insistence on East Pakistani autonomy and in this he was certain to be supported by the military. (Indeed, he may well have adopted this position in order to become more acceptable to the military.) The Awami League had put forward a six-point program for full provincial autonomy for East Pakistan that left the central government some vague responsibility only in the fields of foreign policy and defense. Each of the two constituent units of Pakistan, it proposed, would have its own currency, keep its own separate account for foreign exchange, raise its own taxes, set its own fiscal policy, and maintain its own militia and paramilitary units. Yahya and Bhutto rejected this as tantamount to secession. A stalemate — or crisis — was imminent.

On February 16, 1971, I requested an interagency study of the alternatives should East Pakistan try to make a break; on February 22, I sent my own analysis to the President:

[Mujib and Bhutto] have failed so far to forge even the beginning of an informal consensus on the new constitution. President Yahya remains committed to turning his military government over to the civilian politicians, but maintains that he will not preside over the splitting of Pakistan. . . . [Mujib] is now planning to stick with his demands for the virtual autonomy of East Pakistan and if he does not get his way — which is very likely — to declare East Pakistan independence.

Yahya was caught between his reluctance to make common cause with Bhutto and his resistance to the quasi-independence of East Pakistan demanded by Mujib. He postponed the convening of the National Assembly set for early March to give the political leaders more time to sort out their differences, but this move further antagonized the East. Yahya ultimately rescheduled the Assembly for March 25, gambling that the two civilian antagonists, faced with a deadlock that might break up the country, would choose to compromise. In this judgment, too, Yahya proved to be mistaken. Bhutto was undoubtedly the most brilliant man in Pakistani politics; he was also arrogant and strong-willed. Later on he would preside over the recovery of his dismembered country with statesmanship and courage. In early 1971 he feared that compromise would bring down on him the wrath of the very masses in West Pakistan whose support had swept him to the threshold of power. Mujib, for his part, could not arrest the forces he had unleashed. He was far less inclined to do so than Bhutto, and more prone to believe in his own rhetoric. Like figures in a Greek tragedy, each of these two popular Pakistani leaders refused to let the other cross the threshold beyond which lay power for both of them; they would yield to necessity but not to each other.

As the tension increased, our government reviewed its options. The Senior Review Group met on March 6 to consider the interagency study I had requested on February 16. Our consensus was that Pakistan would not be able to hold the East by force. I made it clear to the agencies that the President would be reluctant to confront Yahya, but that the White House would not object to other countries' efforts to dissuade him from using force. If Pakistan broke up, it should be the result of its internal dynamics, not of American pressures. All agencies agreed that the United States should not get involved. This was also the policy of Great Britain, which had a much longer historical relationship.

During March we experienced the confusions that mark the onset of most crises. In a major speech on March 7, Mujib stopped short of a total break with West Pakistan, but he demanded an end to martial law and a return to popular rule, making clear his goal remained the ''emancipation'' of the East. Yahya announced that he was flying to Dacca, capital of East Pakistan, to negotiate with Mujib on March 15. Meanwhile, in India in early March, Prime Minister Gandhi scored an enormous victory in the Indian general elections. Until then events in Pakistan had been the internal problems of a friendly country; we might have our view but they were not a foreign policy issue. Busy with the election campaign and its immediate aftermath, Mrs. Gandhi adopted a hands-off policy. As late as the middle of March, the permanent head of the Indian Foreign Office, T. N. Kaul, told our Ambassador in New Delhi, Kenneth Keating, that India wanted Pakistan to remain united. On March 17 the Indian Ambassador in Washington, the skillful L. K. Jha, spoke in the same sense to me. Neither gave the slightest indication that India would consider the troubles in neighboring East Pakistan as affecting its own vital interests.

But sometimes the nerves of public figures snap. Incapable of abiding events, they seek to force the pace and lose their balance. So it was that Yahya Khan, with less than 40,000 troops, decided to establish military rule over the 75 million people of East Pakistan, to suppress the Awami League, and to arrest Sheikh Mujibur Rahman.

The crisis in Pakistan then became international.

Military Crackdown

WHAT prompted Yahya to his reckless step on March 25 is not fully known. No doubt the Bengali population taunted the Pakistani soldiers drawn almost exclusively from the West. Mujib's version of autonomy seemed indistinguishable from independence. Almost all nations will fight for their unity, even if sentiment in the disaffected area is overwhelmingly for secession. So it was during our Civil War, with Nigeria toward Biafra, and with the Congo toward Katanga. Pakistan was unique, however, in that the seceding province was separated from West Pakistan by a thousand miles of Indian territory. There was no likelihood that a small military force owing loyalty to the one wing of the country could indefinitely hold down a population of 75 million of the other. Once indigenous Bengali support for a united Pakistan evaporated, the integrity of Pakistan was finished. An independent Bengali state was certain to emerge, even without Indian intervention. The only question was *how* the change would come about.

We wanted to stay aloof from this if we could, as did Britain. We even received reports of West Pakistani suspicions that we might favor an independent East Pakistan, but neither the British nor we wished to be made scapegoats for the country's breakup. We had few means to affect the situation. We had, moreover, every incentive to maintain Pakistan's goodwill. It was our crucial link to Peking; and Pakistan was one of China's closest allies. We had sent a message in December through Pakistan accepting the principle of an American emissary in Peking. In March and April the signs were multiplying that a Chinese response was imminent. April was the month of Ping-Pong diplomacy.

In this first stage of the crisis the consensus of the US government was to avoid precipitate action even among those who knew nothing of our China initiative. At a WSAG meeting on March 26 I repeated my own view that the prognosis was for civil war leading to independence fairly quickly. A State Department representative noted that Britain was unwilling to engage itself in pressing Pakistan. I told my colleagues: "I talked to the President briefly before lunch. His inclination is the same as everybody else's. He doesn't want to do anything. He doesn't want to be in the position where he can be accused of having encouraged the split-up of Pakistan. He does not favor a very active policy."

Yet pressures for an active policy began to mount. There was general and justified outrage as during April reports began to come in of Pakistani atrocities in Bengal. Our Consul General in Dacca was sending cables to Washington urging a public American stand against Pakistani repression; other members of the consulate staff signed a similar message in early April. Secretary Rogers told me he found it "outrageous" that his diplomats were writing petitions rather than reports. But in a favorite device of subordinates seeking to foreclose their superiors' options, the cables were deliberately given a low classification and hence wide circulation. Leaks to the Congress and press were inevitable. A Pakistani editor who visited East Pakistan wrote a firsthand account of army killings for the London *Sunday Times*. Our Ambassador in New Delhi, Kenneth Keating, reported to Washington that he was "deeply shocked at the massacre" and was "greatly concerned at the United States' vulnerability to damaging association with a reign of military terror." He urged that the United States promptly, publicly, and prominently deplore "this brutality," privately intervene with Yahya Khan, abrogate our "one-time exception," and immediately suspend all military deliveries to Pakistan.

We faced a dilemma. The United States could not condone a brutal military repression in which thousands of civilians were killed and from which millions fled to India for safety. There was no doubt about the strong-arm tactics of the Pakistani military. But Pakistan was our sole channel to China; once it was closed off it would take months to make alternative arrangements. The issue hit Washington, moreover, in the midst of another of the cyclic upheavals over Vietnam. A massive campaign of disobedience was planned for May 1. To some of our critics our silence over Pakistan — the reason for which we could not explain — became another symptom of the general moral insensitivity of their government. They could not accept that it might be torn between conflicting imperatives; some had a vested interest in undermining their government's standing on whatever issue came to hand in the belief that this would collapse our effort in Vietnam. The Administration reacted in the same ungenerous spirit; there was some merit to the charge of moral insensitivity. Nixon ordered our Consul General transferred from Dacca; he ridiculed Keating for having been "taken over by the Indians." A tragic victim of the war in Vietnam was the possibility of rational debate on foreign policy.

The State Department moved on its own to preempt the decisions. Ignorant of the China initiative, heavily influenced by its traditional Indian bias, in early April — without clearance with the White House — the Department moved toward a new arms embargo on Pakistan: It suspended issuance of new licenses for the sale of munitions and renewal of expired licenses; it put a hold on the delivery of items from Defense Department stocks and held in abeyance the "one-time exception" package of 1970. Some $35 million in arms to Pakistan was cut off, leaving some $5 million trickling through the pipeline. (This $5 million became a contentious issue with the Congress in early July.) The State Department also began to throttle economic aid to Pakistan, again without White House clearance, by the ingenious device of claiming that our existing programs could no longer be made effective throughout the entire country because of the civil war. My NSC staff expert Hal Saunders wrote me that the State Department was moving from a posture of detachment to one of dissociation from the Pakistani government, but "they are not acknowledging to themselves that this is what they are doing. They are justifying their move on technical grounds."

Anyone familiar with Nixon's attitudes could not doubt that this was contrary to his wishes; those unfamiliar should have checked with the White House. The preemption of Presidential prerogatives goes far to explain Nixon's (and my) attitude later that year. Throughout April my major task was to get control of the governmental process, with two objectives: to preserve the channel to Peking and to preserve the possibility of a political solution in Pakistan. By then, Islamabad was not only a point of contact but also my likely place of departure for China. And signs began to appear that India's proposed solution to the undoubted burden of millions of Bengali refugees was not so much to enable them to return as to *accelerate* the disintegration of Pakistan (or at any rate to identify one objective with the other). On March 31 the Indian Parliament unanimously expressed its wholehearted "sympathy and support" for the Bengalis. As early as April 1, I reported to the President that "the Indians seems to be embarking on a course of public diplomatic and covert actions that will increase the already high level of tension in the subcontinent and run the risk of touching off a broader and more serious international crisis." On April 14 a Bangladesh government in exile was established in Calcutta. By the middle of April we received reports that India was training Bengali refugees to become guerrilla fighters in East Pakistan (the so-called Mukti Bahini). By the end of April we learned that India was about to infiltrate the first 2,000 of these guerrillas into East Pakistan.

I considered a policy of restraint correct on the merits, above and beyond the China connection. For better or worse, the strategy of the Nixon Administration on humanitarian questions was not to lay down a challenge to sovereignty that would surely be rejected, but to exert our influence without public confrontation. In retrospect I believe that we sometimes carried this basically correct approach to pedantic lengths which antagonized potential supporters. In the case of Pakistan it seemed appropriate because its government was an ally that, we were convinced, was bound soon to learn the futility of its course. We undertook to persuade Yahya Khan to move toward autonomy, advising him as a friend to take steps that he would almost surely have rejected had we demanded them publicly. As I wrote the President on April 29, the central government "may recognize the need to move toward greater East Pakistani autonomy in order to draw the necessary Bengali cooperation. What we seem to face, therefore, is a period of transition to greater East Pakistani autonomy and, perhaps, eventual independence." Yet, I noted, India's policy was bound to work against such a settlement: "By training and equipping a relatively small Bengali resistance force, India can help keep active resistance alive and increase the chances of a prolonged guerrilla war. From all indications, the Indians intend to follow such a course."

Following our customary procedure, I asked the State Department in April to suggest options in preparation for a decision by the President as to what our policy should be in light of the unfolding crisis. A broad policy decision would provide the framework for handling the specific economic and military aid issues with Pakistan; it was especially needed in view of the fact that State had already begun moving in its own desired direction. As usual, the Department placed its preferred option between alternatives so absurd that they could not possibly serve as a basis of policy. (One proposal, for example, was all-out support for Yahya. This was neither the White House conviction nor a feasible course of action.) I distilled a recommendation from the range of options that State proposed. To respond to Congressional and public desires I proposed that the President ratify the State Department's unauthorized action of early April shutting down the military supply pipeline, allowing only some spare parts and nonlethal equipment to move. I also urged that economic aid be used as a carrot to induce political concessions, "to make a serious effort to help Yahya end the war and establish an arrangement that could be transitional to East Pakistani autonomy." Nixon approved my recommendation on May 2, and added a handwritten note: "To all hands. Don't squeeze Yahya at this time. RN."

But we ran up against three obstacles: the policy of India, our own public debate, and the indiscipline of our bureaucracy.

On May 18 — when we were already in the advanced stage of preparing the secret trip to Peking with Islamabad — Mrs. Gandhi warned Pakistan in a public speech that India was "fully prepared to fight if the situation is forced on us." Indian ambassadors alerted Britain and France that India "may be forced to act in its national interest" in view of the flood of refugees, by then an estimated 2.8 million.[2] The burden of refugees was indeed monumental; the danger of communal riots could not be dismissed. But as the weeks passed, we began increasingly to suspect that Mrs. Gandhi perceived a larger opportunity. As Pakistan grew more and more isolated internationally, she appeared to seek above all Pakistan's humiliation, perhaps trying to spread the centrifugal tendencies from East to West Pakistan. When the United States agreed to assume the major cost of refugee relief, India switched to insisting that the refugee problem was insoluble without a political settlement. But India's terms for a settlement escalated by the week. When the United States offered to alleviate famine in East Pakistan, India — together with many in the United States — demanded that the relief program be run by an international agency. The reason was ostensibly to ensure its fair distribution, but it would also prevent the Pakistani government from gaining credit with its own population.

In May 1971 we learned from sources heretofore reliable that Mrs. Gandhi had ordered plans for a lightning "Israeli-type" attack to take over East Pakistan. And we had hard evidence that India was dispersing aircraft and moving combat troops and armor to the border. Nixon took the reports seriously enough to order on May 23 that if India launched such an attack, US economic aid to India was to be cut off. I assembled the WSAG on May 26 to review our policy in the event of a war. Around this time we learned that Indian military leaders thought Mrs.

Gandhi's proposal of an attack on East Pakistan was too risky. They feared Chinese intervention, the possibility of other countries' military aid to Pakistan (especially Iran's), the uncertainty of resupply of Soviet weapons, and the likelihood that *all* of Pakistan might have to be occupied to bring the war to a conclusion. The Indian commanders insisted, at a minimum, on waiting until November when weather in the Himalayas would make Chinese intervention more difficult.

While Mrs. Gandhi set about systematically to remove these objections and waited for the snows to fall in the mountains, we had a breathing space. (I must stress that most in the United States government did not credit these reports as I did; most senior officials considered an Indian attack improbable.) We used the interval first of all to step up our assistance to the refugees; the original authorization of $2.5 million in the spring was eventually multiplied a hundredfold to $250 million. At the same time we pressed Pakistan to take steps of political accommodation, urging Yahya first to internationalize the relief effort in East Pakistan and then to come up with a political proposal. And we recommended the replacement of the military governor in the East by a civilian; we succeeded in securing a general amnesty covering all persons not already charged with specific criminal acts.

On May 28 Nixon sent letters to both Mrs. Gandhi and Yahya Khan outlining our policy. The letter to Yahya was not exactly strong; it reflected our need for Yahya as a channel to Peking. But it left no doubt that we favored a political and not a military solution to the problem of East Pakistan. Nixon acknowledged Yahya's readiness to accept the internationalization of relief. He encouraged Yahya to continue on the course of "political accommodation": "I have also noticed with satisfaction your public declaration of amnesty for the refugees and commitment to transfer power to elected representatives. I am confident that you will turn these statements into reality." Nixon urged restraint in Pakistan's relations with India; he deemed it "absolutely vital" to restore conditions in East Pakistan "conducive to the return of refugees from Indian territory as quickly as possible."

The President's parallel letter to Mrs. Gandhi on May 28 stressed our desire to reduce the refugee flow into India and to help ease the burden on India by financial and technical aid. Nixon informed her of our efforts to move Yahya:

We have chosen to work primarily through quiet diplomacy, as we have informed your Ambassador and Foreign Minister. We have been discussing with the Government of Pakistan the importance of achieving a peaceful political accommodation and of restoring conditions under which the refugee flow would stop and the refugees would be able to return to their homes. I feel that these approaches were at least in part behind President Yahya's press conference on

May 24 and especially his public acceptance of international assistance, offer of amnesty to the refugees and commitment to transfer power to elected representatives.

Nixon complimented India on the vitality of its democracy and its economic and social progress, and added a veiled warning against a military solution: "India's friends would be dismayed were this progress to be interrupted by war." On June 3 I explained our strategy to Kenneth Keating. I was convinced that East Pakistan would eventually become independent. Our policy was to "give the facts time to assert themselves."

During June Indian Foreign Minister Swaran Singh arrived in Washington to urge termination of both military and economic aid to Pakistan. India was increasingly presenting us with a Catch-22 dilemma. It claimed that the enormous flow of refugees would sooner or later force India into drastic measures. But at the same time India would do nothing to curb — indeed, it trained, equipped, and encouraged — the guerrillas whose infiltration from Indian territory guaranteed unsettled conditions that would generate more refugees. Despite Yahya's proclamation of an amnesty, India made the return of refugees to East Pakistan depend on a political settlement there. But India reserved the right to define what constituted an acceptable political settlement on the sovereign territory of its neighbor. In mid-June Mrs. Gandhi declared that India would not agree to any solution that meant "the death of Bangladesh"; in other words, India's condition for staying its hand was the breakup of Pakistan. With evolution to autonomy rejected, refugees encouraged, and their return precluded, India had made a mounting crisis inevitable.

Many in our country saw it differently. Unfortunately, the debate began to take on some of the bitterness and impugning of motives characteristic of the Vietnam debate. And the Administration, which had a case, did not help matters by enveloping itself in silence. Congressman Cornelius Gallagher of New Jersey, Chairman of the House subcommittee concerned with the problem, declared on the floor of the House on June 10 after a visit to Indian refugee camps that India had shown "almost unbelievable restraint" in the face of the refugee burden. (This was three weeks after Mrs. Gandhi's public threat to go to war.) On June 17, the *New York Times* took the Administration to task, calling our public statement urging restraint on both sides "belated"; our appeal would be fruitless, said the *Times,* unless we matched word with deed, that is, cut off all American aid to Pakistan until there was a genuine political accommodation in East Pakistan. The *Times,* too, praised Mrs. Gandhi for having shown "remarkable restraint" in the face of the staggering refugee problem.

Then there occurred one of those media events by which small facts become surrogates for larger debates, focusing and in the process distorting the issues. On June 22, the *New York Times* carried a story that a Pakistani freighter was preparing to sail from New York City with a cargo of military equipment for Pakistan, seemingly in violation of the Administration's officially proclaimed ban. Soon a second ship carrying military items was reported on its way to Pakistan. There was outrage from the press and Congress, and from India. The next day the *New York Times* charged that the shipments were a "breach of faith" with the American people and Congress and with India and "further" undermined American credibility. Senator Stuart Symington said it was either ignorance or deliberate deception. State's announcement of June 24 that Washington was providing an additional $70 million to India for refugees was drowned out by reports that a third Pakistani freighter had sailed from New York to Karachi with military equipment.

It did not still the charges of governmental duplicity that all the equipment in question had been purchased under licenses issued *before* the ban and was thus legally out of our control; and that the third freighter had sailed four days *before* the State Department suspension of licenses went into effect.[3] Here was another of the credibility gaps so cherished during the Vietnam period. We could convince no one that we simply had no mechanism to track down licenses already issued, nor that the amount of "seepage" was minuscule and could affect the military balance neither on the subcontinent nor in Bengal. The *Washington Post* on July 5 could barely contain its outrage: It was

an astonishing and shameful record . . . [which] must be read in the context of the current controversy over the Pentagon Papers, which turns on the public right to know and the government's right to conceal. Here we have a classic example of how the System really works; hidden from public scrutiny, administration officials have been supplying arms to Pakistan while plainly and persistently telling the public that such supplies were cut off.

The irony was that the "credibility gap" was caused by the State Department, whose precipitate action in the embargo had so angered the White House. The department most in accord with media and Congressional criticism became, unintentionally, its focus.

The Crisis Accelerates

JUST before my departure for Asia, Yahya on June 28 announced a plan to transfer political power to civilians. A new constitution drawn up by experts would be proclaimed within four months; Awami League members not associated with secession would be eligible to participate in the government. Yahya did not explain to what category of leaders this might apply.

While I was en route, I received disturbing information that the Soviet Union had at last perceived its strategic opportunity. Abandoning its previous caution, it had informed India of its approval of guerrilla operations into East Pakistan and had promised India protection against Chinese reprisals. A new and ominous dimension had been added to the conflict. (This occurred well *before* our China initiative.)

In visiting New Delhi I had two partially contradictory missions. One was to prepare India circumspectly for the news of my visit to China. Noting the Ping-Pong diplomacy and our two-year record of overtures in trade and travel, I stressed that we were bound to continue to improve our relations with Peking. On the other hand, we would take a grave view of an unprovoked Chinese attack on India. If this unsolicited comment did not utterly mystify my interlocutors, it may have given them a brief moment of encouragement — though that moment of euphoria surely ended with the July 15 announcement of my trip to China.

We must await the memoirs of my interlocutors to see whether the Indian ministers considered my reassurances the best we could do given our constraints, or an effort at deception. The major topic of my talks in New Delhi was the crisis in East Pakistan. I reported to the President:

> There seems to be a growing sense of the inevitability of war or at least widespread Hindu-Muslim violence, not necessarily because anyone wants it but because in the end they fear they will not know how to avoid it. . . .
>
> I assured [Mrs. Gandhi] the whole point of our policy has been to retain enough influence to urge creation of conditions that would permit the refugees to go back, although we would not promise results. I asked how much more time she thought there was before the situation became unmanageable, and she replied that it is unmanageable now and that they are "just holding it together by sheer willpower."

The conversations with Indian leaders, in fact, followed the ritual of the previous weeks. As I had done on many occasions with Indian Ambassador Jha in Washington, I tried to assure them that the United States was eager to maintain good relations with India. We did not oppose Bengali autonomy, and we were confident we could encourage a favorable evolution if we dealt with Yahya as a friend instead of as another tormentor. I invited Mrs. Gandhi to visit the United States for a fundamental review of Indian-American relations with President Nixon.

But Mrs. Gandhi and her ministers were in no mood for conciliation. The invitation to Washington was evaded. They avowed their desire to improve relations with the United States but passionately accused us of deception over arms sales to Pakistan. The stridency of these complaints was in no way diminished by the facts: that almost all arms shipments to Pakistan had been stopped, including the "one-time exception"; that no new licenses were being issued; and that the only items still in transit were the trickle licensed *before* the ban went into effect. India could have no serious concern about this minuscule flow; it would end automatically as licenses expired; our estimate, indeed, was that nothing would be left in the pipeline after October. Mrs. Gandhi even admitted to me that the amounts were not the issue, but the symbolism. In other words, India wanted the demoralization of Pakistan through the conspicuous dissociation of the United States. I was pressed to cut off not only arms but all *economic* aid as well. Indian leaders evidently did not think it strange that a country which had distanced itself from most of our foreign policy objectives in the name of nonalignment was asking us to break all ties with an ally over what was in international law a domestic conflict. The American contribution to refugee relief by July had reached nearly $100 million; this did not keep Mrs. Gandhi from broadening her criticisms to encompass the entire twenty-four-year record of our policies toward Pakistan. I left New Delhi with the conviction that India was bent on a showdown with Pakistan. It was only waiting for the right moment. The opportunity to settle scores with a rival that had isolated itself by its own shortsightedness was simply too tempting.

On my visit to Islamabad I was preoccupied with my impending journey to Peking. But I had several conversations with President Yahya and Foreign Secretary Sultan Khan. I urged them to put forward a comprehensive proposal to encourage refugees to return home and to deny India a pretext for going to war. I urged Yahya and his associates to go a step farther in the internationalization of relief by admitting the United Nations to supervise its distribution. And I recommended the early appointment of a civilian governor for East Pakistan. Yahya promised to consider these suggestions. But fundamentally he was oblivious to his perils and unprepared to face necessities. He and his colleagues did not believe that India might be planning war; if so, they were convinced that they would win. When I asked as tactfully as I could about the Indian advantage in numbers and equipment, Yahya and his colleagues answered with bravado about the historic superiority of Moslem fighters.

There simply was no blinking the fact that Pakistan's military leaders were caught up in a process beyond their comprehension. They could not conceive of the dismemberment of their country; and those who could saw no way of surviving such a catastrophe politically if they cooperated with it. They had no understanding of the psychological and political isolation into which they had maneuvered their country by their brutal suppression. They agreed theoretically that they needed a comprehensive program if they were to escape their dilemmas. But their definition of "comprehensive" was too grudging, legalistic, technical, and piecemeal. The result was that never throughout the crisis did Pakistan manage to put forward a position on which it could take its international

stand. In fact, its piecemeal concessions, though cumulatively not inconsiderable, played into India's hands; they proved its case that something was wrong without providing a convincing remedy. Yahya found
himself at a tragic impasse. Accused by conservative colleagues of
hazarding his country's unity and by foreign opinion of brutally
suppressing freedom, he vacillated, going too far for his conservatives,
not far enough for world, and especially American, public opinion.

At a dinner given for me the night before I left for Peking, I had an
opportunity to chide Yahya for the mess that had been created. "Everyone calls me a dictator," bellowed Yahya in his bluff imitation of the
Sandhurst manner. "Am I a dictator?" he asked every guest, American
as well as Pakistani, in turn. Everyone protested with varying degrees of
sincerity that of course Yahya was not a dictator. When he came to me,
I said: "I don't know, Mr. President, except that for a dictator you run a
lousy election."

The festering crisis naturally came up in my conversations in Peking.
Chou En-lai's perspective could not have been more different from the
conventional wisdom in Washington. He quite simply considered India
the aggressor; he spent an hour of our scarce time recounting his version
of the Sino-Indian clashes of 1962, which he claimed had been provoked by Indian encroachments. Chou insisted that China would not be
indifferent if India attacked Pakistan. He even asked me to convey this
expression of Chinese support to Yahya — a gesture intended for Washington, since Peking had an Ambassador in Islamabad quite capable of
delivering messages. I replied that the United States had traditional ties
with Pakistan, and we were grateful for its arranging the opening to
China. We would continue to maintain friendly relations with India, but
we would strongly oppose any Indian military action. Our disapproval
could not, however, take the form of military aid or military measures
on behalf of Pakistan.

I returned to Washington with a premonition of disaster. India, in my
view, would almost certainly attack Pakistan shortly after the monsoon
ended. Though I was confident that we could succeed in nudging Islamabad toward autonomy for East Pakistan, I doubted that India would
give us the time and thus miss an opportunity, which might not soon
come again, of settling accounts with a country whose very existence
many of its leaders found so offensive. China might then act. The Soviet Union might use the opportunity to teach Peking a lesson. For us to
gang up on Pakistan — as our media and Congress were so insistently
demanding — would accelerate the danger; it would give India an even
stronger justification to attack. It would jeopardize the China initiative.
At that time, prior to Nixon's visit to Peking, we had no way of knowing how firm China's commitment to the opening to Washington really
was.

Nixon called the National Security Council together on July 16, the day after he announced his trip to China. It was a sign of how seriously he took the crisis. He asked me to sum up the issues. I said India seemed bent on war. I did not think that Yahya had the imagination to solve the political problems in time to prevent an Indian assault. On the other hand, 70,000 West Pakistani soldiers (they had been augmented since March) could not hold down 75 million East Pakistanis for long. Our objective had to be an evolution that would lead to independence for East Pakistan. Unfortunately, this was not likely to happen in time to head off an Indian attack. Therefore, immediate efforts were needed to arrest and reverse the flow of refugees and thereby remove the pretext for war.

There was no disagreement with my analysis. Rogers added his judgment that India was doing everything in its power to prevent the refugees from returning. Nixon concluded that we would ask the Pakistanis to do their maximum on refugees. We would not countenance an Indian attack; if India used force, all American aid would be cut off. Every effort should be made to avoid a war.

On July 23, Pakistani Ambassador Agha Hilaly informed us that his government accepted our suggestion of UN supervision of the resettlement of refugees to guarantee them against reprisals. Yahya also went along with our recommendation to appoint a civilian administrator to oversee refugee relief and resettlement. I strongly urged Hilaly to accelerate their efforts.

Unfortunately, India would have none of it. The very reasons that made the strategy of concentrating on refugees attractive to us caused India to obstruct it. As early as July 15, Indian Ambassador Jha told us that India could not accept proposals to curb guerrilla activity from its territory. On July 16, Indian Foreign Secretary Kaul told us that India would not accept UN personnel on its side of the border even to handle refugees. This was Catch-22 again. Everyone agreed that a condition for political progress in the East was the return of the Pakistani army to its barracks, which was one reason we were pressing for the appointment of a civilian administrator. But there was no way to induce the Pakistani army to do so as long as its neighbor conducted a guerrilla war against it — and proclaimed its determination to escalate that war. Pakistan had agreed to place the resettlement of refugees under UN supervision. But this could not be implemented if the refugees could not even learn of Pakistan's offers because UN personnel were barred from any contact with them in India to explain their prospects if they returned. In the absence of any outside observers in these camps we could not even be sure of the actual number of refugees.

Two Senior Review Group meetings, on July 23 and July 30, discussed these dilemmas. On no issue — except perhaps Cambodia —

was the split between the White House and the departments so profound as on the India-Pakistan crisis in the summer of 1971. On no other problem was there such flagrant disregard of unambiguous Presidential directives. The State Department controlled the machinery of execution. Nixon left it to me to ensure that his policy was carried out and to bring major disagreements to him. But what we faced was a constant infighting over seemingly trivial issues, any one of which seemed too lightweight or technical to raise to the President but whose accumulation would define the course of national policy. Nixon was not prepared to overrule his Secretary of State on what appeared to him minor operational matters; this freed the State Department to interpret Nixon's directives in accordance with its own preferences, thereby vitiating the course Nixon had set.

No one could speak for five minutes with Nixon without hearing of his profound distrust of Indian motives, his concern over Soviet meddling, and above all his desire not to risk the opening to China by ill-considered posturing. Nixon had ordered repeatedly that we should move Pakistan toward political accommodation through understanding rather than pressure. The State Department had every right to a contrary view: that massive public pressure would make Pakistan more pliable. What strained White House–State relations was the effort by State to implement its views when the President had chosen a different course. For example, in early September we found out through the Pakistanis that the State Department had privately opened negotiations with them to cut off even the trivial amount of military equipment licensed before March 25. The White House thought that Pakistan was moving through the painful process of disintegration and wanted to take account of the anguish of an old ally, the limited horizons of its leaders, and its internal stresses; therefore we wanted to avoid announcing a formal embargo, although our actions amounted to as much. The State Department was more conscious of our critics at home and was loath to antagonize India. My nightmare was that the effort to placate India would generate a war. As I told the Senior Review Group on July 30, "We should urge Yahya to restore an increasing degree of participation by the people of East Pakistan. But the clock of war is running in India faster than the clock on political accommodation. We are determined to avoid war." I had told the President on July 27 that State was beginning to throttle even our economic aid to Pakistan: "If anything will tempt the Indians to attack, it will be the complete helplessness of Pakistan." Whatever the merits of this debate, the fact was that Nixon was President and that departments, after having stated their case, should carry out not only the letter but also the spirit of Presidential decisions even if they disagree and even if they have to face outside or Congressional criticisms in doing so.

The problem was accentuated by the anomaly that some long-forgotten State Department reorganization had placed the subcontinent in the Near East Bureau, whose jurisdiction ended at the subcontinent's eastern boundary; it excluded East Asia and any consideration of China. Senior officials who might have been conscious of China's concerns had been excluded from the opening to Peking. Hence, there was no one at State who felt fully responsible for the "China account" or even fully understood its rationale — this was one of the prices paid for our unorthodox method of administration. In interagency debates my office was not infrequently accused of an obsession with "protecting the trip to China," as if preserving that option were somehow an unworthy enterprise. Not a single bureaucratic analysis of India-Pakistan during the period seriously addressed the impact of our conduct on China. Peking was not rejected by our bureaucracy. It was simply ignored. The gulf in perception between the White House and the rest of the government became apparent in an options paper prepared for the July 23 Senior Review Group meeting. It recommended that if China intervened in an India-Pakistan war, the United States should extend military assistance to *India* and coordinate its actions with the *Soviet Union* and Great Britain. Nothing more contrary to the President's foreign policy could have been imagined.

Nixon stated succinctly at his August 4 press conference that we were not going to engage in public pressure on Pakistan: "That would be totally counterproductive. These are matters that we will discuss only in private channels." Despite this, nearly all operational proposals by the bureaucracy were aimed at increasing the pressure on Pakistan. I asked at the July 30 Senior Review Group meeting: "What would an enemy do to Pakistan? We are already cutting off military and economic aid to them. The President has said repeatedly that we should lean toward Pakistan, but every proposal that is made goes directly counter to these instructions."

As I have mentioned, State had come up with the proposal that the remaining $3-to-4 million in the military pipeline be canceled by agreement with Pakistan. The justification was that this would make it easier for us to maintain economic assistance. I reluctantly went along, though I thought it an unworthy response to Pakistan's assistance on China. The negotiation for drying up the pipeline took two months. It was finally accomplished in early November, woundingly for Pakistan, just in time to create a "good atmosphere" for Mrs. Gandhi's visit. But no sooner did Pakistan agree to negotiate a total arms cutoff than foot-dragging began on economic assistance. No new development loans were made throughout 1971. As I said acidly on September 8 at a Senior Review Group meeting, the State Department sold us a dried-up arms pipeline in return for a dried-up economic aid policy.

And none of these maneuvers addressed the central issue. I was convinced that East Pakistan would become independent Bangladesh relatively soon. But Yahya could not possibly accomplish this before October or November, when the Indians were most likely to attack. Hence I thought it imperative to make a massive effort to alleviate the refugee problem immediately and to bring our influence to bear in the direction of constitutional rule at as fast a pace as the Pakistani political structure could stand. Constitutional government, in turn, was almost certain to produce at least Bangladesh autonomy and eventually independence. So we multiplied our aid contribution, providing some $90 million to India and over $150 million for internationally supervised famine relief in East Pakistan to reverse the tide of refugees. We appointed an able senior official of our Agency for International Development, Maurice Williams, to coordinate all US refugee relief.

But it was to no avail. Our actions were outstripped by India's deliberate acceleration of tensions. On July 24 Kaul again rejected the idea of UN personnel on the Indian side of the border. On August 4, Ambassador Jha rejected suggestions of Under Secretary of State John Irwin that India control the guerrillas operating from its territory. Jha made a new suggestion — that the United States take up an offer of contact with the Bangladesh exiles in Calcutta. When we did so, as will be seen, it was aborted in part because of Indian obstruction.

The Soviet-Indian Friendship Treaty

ON August 9 came the bombshell of the Soviet-Indian Friendship Treaty.

We learned first from the newspapers that Soviet Foreign Minister Gromyko had concluded a visit to New Delhi by signing a twenty-year Treaty of Peace, Friendship, and Cooperation. Its bland provisions could not obscure its strategic significance. It contained the usual clauses on lasting friendship, noninterference in each other's affairs, and cooperation in economic, scientific, technical, and cultural matters. More important, the two parties pledged to consult regularly "on major international problems" affecting both sides. The decisive provision was Article IX, which called on the signatories to refrain from giving assistance to any third country taking part in an armed conflict with the other, and committed each side to consult immediately with a view toward taking "appropriate effective measures" in case either party was attacked or threatened with attack.

The initial reaction of our government was astonishingly sanguine. The intelligence assessment may have been subconsciously colored by the long-standing perception of India as a pacifist country, above power politics. Nor was it easy to accept the proposition that Nehru's daughter was deliberately steering nonaligned India toward a de facto alliance with the Soviet Union. Hence as of August 11 the assessment was that Mrs. Gandhi was resisting a tide of public opinion in favor of a show-down. The Soviets were allegedly fearful that she might be forced against her inclinations to recognize Bangladesh and thus trigger a Pakistani declaration of war. By signing the treaty, so the analysis went, the USSR gave Mrs. Gandhi a diplomatic success that would help her maintain her policy of moderation and restraint; in return, the Soviet Union could rest assured that Indian territory would not be used for hostile bases.

In retrospect, it would have been nearly impossible to concoct a more fatuous estimate. It was a classic example of how preconceptions shape intelligence assessments. There was no realistic prospect of any foreign base's being established on Indian soil; not enough of one, surely, to warrant such an extraordinary departure from previous Indian conduct and Soviet caution. We knew that the principal deterrent to a military conflict was the fear of India's military planners that a war of which the Soviets disapproved might dry up the Soviet supply line and encourage China to intervene. The Soviet-Indian Friendship Treaty was bound to eliminate these fears; it therefore objectively increased the danger of war. The Soviet Union had seized a strategic opportunity. To demon-strate Chinese impotence and to humiliate a friend of both China and the United States proved too tempting. If China did nothing, it stood re-vealed as impotent; if China raised the ante, it risked Soviet reprisal. With the treaty, Moscow threw a lighted match into a powder keg.

On the day of the announcement of the treaty, I lunched with the In-dian Ambassador at his request. L. K. Jha served in Washington at a difficult period. He was a superb analyst of the American scene; he un-derstood international politics without sentimentality. At least toward me he never used the hectoring tone of moral superiority with which In-dian diplomats sometimes exhaust if not the goodwill, at least the pa-tience of their interlocutors. He was skillful in getting the Indian version of the issues to the press; I could always trace his footprints through the columns, and it was a painful experience when we found ourselves on opposite sides. (I was supposed to be skillful in dealing with the press. On the India-Pakistan issue Jha clearly outclassed me.) Yet I had high regard and even affection for Jha. I saw him frequently, socially or to exchange ideas — partly because I considered India important in world affairs whether or not we agreed with all its policies, partly because I always learned from his tough-minded analyses.

On this occasion Jha brought a letter from Mrs. Gandhi to the Presi-dent. She blamed tensions entirely on Pakistan. Her letter took no notice of our substantial economic assistance for the refugees or of the steps of conciliation into which we had nudged the government in Islamabad.

Instead, she devoted much space to the implication that we had deceived India with respect to our arms policy and, indeed, had fueled *all* tensions on the subcontinent by selling arms to Pakistan between 1954 and 1965. She rejected once again the stationing of UN personnel on Indian territory. She made no mention of the treaty with the Soviet Union, but hinted at an acceptance of the invitation to Washington I had conveyed on behalf of Nixon when I visited New Delhi in July. This conciliatory gesture was coupled with a catalogue of charges that left little doubt as to who was slated for the dock when the two leaders met.

It was left to Jha to supply the formal explanation of the treaty. Interestingly, his account totally contradicted the editorial criticism according to which we had driven India to the Soviets as a desperate last resort. He confirmed what I suspected — that the Soviet treaty was not a reaction to American policy in the India-Pakistan crisis but a carefully considered Indian strategy that had been in preparation for over a year. I have never understood why Jha would consider this reassuring. (Dobrynin made the same point to me.)[4] I replied that, read literally, the treaty was a matter of secondary concern, though it was hard to reconcile with India's nonalignment. What did concern us was the possibility that India might draw the conclusion that it now enjoyed freedom of action toward Pakistan. I could not be more unequivocal in warning that a war between India and Pakistan would set back Indian-American relations for half a decade. No matter what the Ambassador was told by others in the Administration, I wanted him to understand that military intervention in East Pakistan would involve the high probability of a cutoff of aid to India. There was no reason for the United States and India to quarrel over a problem whose solution seemed foreordained. We took India seriously as a world power; we sought good relations. East Bengal was certain to gain autonomy, if we only gave the inevitable a chance; we wanted it to come about peacefully. Jha denied that the Soviet treaty was incompatible with nonalignment. He evaded any discussion of Indian-Pakistani issues, arguing that Mrs. Gandhi's visit would give us this opportunity. I warned once more against trying to settle the issue by war; an evolutionary process would with our support lead to self-determination for East Bengal.

India was not interested in evolution, however. And Yahya did not grasp his peril. Swept up in events beyond his capacity, he complicated our task with one of those truculent moves with which desperate men reassure themselves that they still have a margin for decision. On August 9 Yahya's regime announced that Mujib would be tried in secret for treason. I have never understood what Yahya hoped to accomplish by this stroke. He was certain to mobilize even greater world pressures against him and fuel Indian intransigence. Mrs. Gandhi promptly sent messages of protest to world leaders. Eleven Senators and fifty-eight

Representatives demanded that the United States press Pakistan to show compassion. On August 11 Secretary Rogers conveyed the American concern to Ambassador Hilaly.

On August 11 I arranged for the President to meet with the Senior Review Group to overcome the bureaucratic foot-dragging fostered by the suspicion that I was transmitting my own preferences as the President's orders. Nixon made a strong statement along the lines of what he had told the NSC on July 16. He wanted a massive refugee relief program; we would do everything in our power to alleviate suffering. He thought that most of the media attacks were politically motivated; for his critics, Pakistan was turning into a surrogate for Vietnam, which was being made irrelevant by the opening to China. He held no brief for Yahya's actions; they did not, however, justify war. No one should doubt his determination to cut off aid to India if it attacked. The Soviets' conduct reminded him of their behavior in the Middle East in 1967 when they started a sequence of events that got out of control. There would be no public assault on the Pakistani government about political evolution, the President said; "we will deal with the political problem in private."

And this was our course. On August 14 Nixon sent a letter to Yahya urging him to speed the process of national reconciliation by pressing the relief program and enlisting the support of the elected representatives of East Pakistan. Such measures, Nixon wrote,

will be important in countering the corrosive threat of insurgency and restoring peace to your part of the world. They will also hasten the day when the United States and other countries can resume, within a revised national development plan, the task of assisting your country's economic development which has been so tragically complicated and slowed by recent events.

However diplomatically worded, the letter's import was clear: Sustained economic assistance was linked to turning over power to elected representatives. We were, in fact, asking in the name of friendship for self-determination for East Pakistan. Our main difference with New Delhi lay in its demand for a pace of change that might undermine the cohesion of even West Pakistan.

Contacts with the Bangladesh Exiles

WE also took up Jha's suggestion of direct contacts between the United States and the Bangladesh exiles in Calcutta. This led to a futile three-month pursuit of political accommodation that could have amounted to something if India and the Bengalis had wanted. On July 30, a Mr. Qaiyum, an elected member of the Awami League closely associated with the Bangladesh government in exile, approached our Consulate in Calcutta to say he had been designated to establish contact with the United States. He would return in two weeks for an answer. The Consulate reported this approach in State channels.

We recognized that this contact would be explosive if it surfaced in Islamabad — and we had to assume that India would have every incentive to publicize it. Nevertheless, after checking with the President, I approved a State suggestion that our Consulate receive Qaiyum and probe for the readiness of the Awami League to negotiate with the Pakistani government. (The instructions for this initiative were prepared in State's Near East Bureau and cleared in the White House.) Qaiyum appeared on schedule on August 14. He affirmed that if Mujib were allowed to participate in these negotiations, his group might settle for less than total independence so long as Islamabad accepted the Awami League's six points. He hoped the United States would encourage such an evolution. In a second meeting a few days later, Qaiyum observed that once India formally recognized Bangladesh, even this essentially face-saving proposal would no longer be possible.

We did not think we could proceed further without informing Yahya; at the same time the Calcutta contacts might be an opportunity to nudge Islamabad toward a political solution. State instructed Ambassador Joseph Farland to tell Yahya of our contacts in Calcutta and of the possibility of a settlement based on the six points. Farland was asked to avoid any recommendations but the import of the démarche could hardly be lost on Yahya. Governments do not normally transmit proposals on behalf of exiles outlawed in their own country.

Yahya's reaction was surprisingly favorable. Recognizing that he had trapped himself, he was groping for a way out. He welcomed our contacts in Calcutta, asking only to be kept informed. He even accepted Farland's suggestion that we use our good offices to arrange secret contacts between his government and the Bengali exiles.

When on August 27 Qaiyum showed interest in expediting contacts, we went one step farther. On September 4 Farland suggested to Yahya that we contact the Bangladesh "foreign minister," ostensibly to check out Qaiyum's bona fides; we would tell him of Yahya's willingness to engage in secret talks. It was an extraordinary proposal to make to the President of a friendly country that we would approach the "foreign minister" of a movement he had banned as seditious, an official whose very title implied at a minimum a constitutional change if not treason. Such was Yahya's quandary that he agreed.

Yahya accepted our suggestions in other fields as well. On September 1 he appointed a civilian governor for East Pakistan, replacing the hated martial-law administrator. On September 5 Yahya extended the amnesty previously offered to refugees to cover all citizens except those against whom criminal proceedings had already been instituted. (This excluded

Mujib, however.) Around the same time, Yahya assured Maury Williams, our aid coordinator, that a death sentence against Mujib would not be carried out. On October 1 Nixon announced that he would ask for $250 million in additional funds for refugee relief, bringing our contribution to nearly twice that of the rest of the world combined.

The surest way to intensify a crisis is to reject all the other side's initiatives without offering an alternative. This was India's course. No government offers its ultimate concessions at the outset, and it may not even know how far it is prepared to go until there is some process of negotiation. This was particularly true of the harassed military leaders of Pakistan in 1971. They knew by now that their brutal suppression of East Pakistan beginning on March 25 had been, in Talleyrand's phrase, worse than a crime; it was a blunder. Yet they had stood for a united Pakistan all their lives; it was impossible for them to accept the secession of half their country. Yahya feared both a war caused by his inflexibility and an overthrow based on the accusation that he made too many concessions. Faced with this dilemma, he sought to turn over authority to a civilian government as rapidly as possible, shifting to it the responsibility for the ultimate debacle. In the meantime he hoped to stave off a conflict by making some concessions while avoiding West Pakistani unrest.

Mrs. Gandhi, however, had no intention of permitting Pakistan's leaders to escape their dilemma so easily. She knew that once discussions between Pakistan and the Awami League started, some sort of compromise might emerge; India might then lose control of events. Mrs. Gandhi was not willing to risk this. She would not soon again have Pakistan at such a disadvantage, China in the throes of domestic upheaval (the Lin Piao affair), the United States divided by Vietnam, and the Soviet Union almost unconditionally on India's side. On September 1 we learned that Indian armed forces had been put on general alert. Predictably Pakistan reacted on September 4 by moving additional forces into forward positions near the West Pakistan–India border. On September 9 units of India's only armored division and an independent armored brigade moved toward the West Pakistan frontier. On September 16 there was a report that India planned to infiltrate some 9,000 more Mukti Bahini guerrillas into East Pakistan starting in early October.

At the same time, our contacts with the Bangladesh representatives in Calcutta began to dry up. On September 9 our Consul met with Qaiyum to arrange the meeting with the Bangladesh "foreign minister." But Qaiyum now demanded not only the immediate release of Mujib, but the immediate departure of the Pakistani army from East Pakistan and a guarantee for Bangladesh's security by the United Nations — in short, immediate independence. On September 14 Qaiyum told us that his "foreign minister" saw little point in a meeting. He ascribed this reluctance to surveillance by the Indian government, which he said was skittish about any contacts with the United States. On September 21 Yahya revealed his anxiety by asking Farland about our contacts in Calcutta. He hoped Farland would keep him informed of any new developments. Farland was sufficiently encouraged to recommend that our Consul be permitted to meet with the "acting president" of the Bangladesh government in exile if the foreign minister remained unavailable.

But in Calcutta all signals were now pointing in the opposite direction. On September 23 Qaiyum sent a messenger to tell our Consul that the Indian government had become aware of his contacts with us and had formally warned against them. We responded by proposing a meeting with the "acting president." Qaiyum presented himself shortly afterward and confirmed what his messenger had said: India wanted all contacts handled through New Delhi.

At the same time, the Indians were telling us exactly the opposite — at least about refugees. Whenever we proposed joint US–Indian relief programs we were given the stock reply that this should be taken up with Bangladesh representatives in Calcutta. We could be excused for suspecting that we were being given the runaround: The Indians urged us to talk to the Bengali exiles, who then avoided high-level contact under the pretext of Indian displeasure.

On September 27 Joe Sisco sought to straighten out the mess by proposing to Jha direct negotiations between representatives of Pakistan and Bangladesh without conditions. Jha was negative. He professed not to see any advance in this offer (even though such talks implied a recognition of Bangladesh and could hardly lead to any result other than autonomy and eventually independence). He fell back on the stock demand, which he knew could not be immediately fulfilled: that any talks with Bangladesh representatives include Mujib at the outset and be aimed at immediate independence. (At this point the release of Mujib was essentially a problem of face. The military government could not bring itself to commence negotiations with so humiliating a reversal. On the other hand, it must have been clear to it that any negotiations it initiated with the Awami League could not go far unless its leader was eventually released from jail.)

The next day the Bangladesh "foreign minister" finally met with our Consul in Calcutta; he said talks were useless unless the United States used its influence to bring about Bengali "desires," which included full independence, freedom for Mujib, US aid, and normal relations. Lest there be any temptation to yield, Qaiyum returned on October 3 with an escalation of Bangladesh's "desires." He wanted the Soviet Union to participate in the talks. He saw no need for concessions since the Indian army would keep Pakistani forces busy at the border, freeing the guerrillas for eventual control of the country. On October 16 Qaiyum ruled out a meeting between our Consul and the "acting president" of Bangladesh, citing Indian objections. On October 20 another senior Bangladesh official, Hossain Ali, told our Consul that his organization was not interested in passing messages to Yahya; the "obvious solution" was Mujib's release and immediate independence for Bangladesh. By the end of October, the Indian press was publicly warning against Bengali negotiations with "foreign representatives." In short, the effort to encourage negotiations between the government of Pakistan and the Bangladesh government in exile was finished.

Mrs. Gandhi Comes to Washington

CONCURRENTLY, we made every effort to come to an understanding with India. In my conversations with Ambassador Jha I reiterated my constant theme. We considered Indian and American long-term interests as congruent. We would do our utmost to turn Mrs. Gandhi's visit into a watershed in our relations. On August 25, September 11, and October 8 I emphasized that the United States did not insist that East Bengal remain part of Pakistan. On the contrary, we accepted autonomy as inevitable and independence as probable. A war was senseless; Bangladesh would come into being by the spring of 1972 if present procedures were given a chance. We differed over method, not aim. If Mrs. Gandhi was prepared for a fundamental improvement of our relations, she would find us an eager partner. If she was using her visit as a cover for an Indian military attack, our relations would not soon recover. The State Department was instructed to follow a similar line. On October 7 I told a WSAG meeting that if India would accept an evolutionary process, it would achieve most of its objectives with our assistance. "If they would cooperate with us we could work with them on 90 percent of their problems, like releasing Mujib or attaining some degree of autonomy for Bangladesh, and these steps would lead eventually to their getting it all."

Unlike our domestic critics, Jha understood only too well that we were not anti-Indian; he counted on it to limit our reaction to what India was clearly planning. India continued to invoke the intolerable burden of refugees, now reportedly on a scale of seven or eight million. Yet India would not encourage their return after Yahya's amnesty or cooperate in stemming that flow, or permit the posting of UN personnel in the camps to inform the refugees of the amnesty. It took no responsibility for the Bengali guerrillas' contribution to the chaos. Though they were recruited on Indian soil, trained by Indian officers, equipped with Indian arms, and supported by Indian artillery from the Indian side of the frontier, India claimed that they were not under its control. New Delhi even refused to promise that the guerrillas would refrain from interfering with relief supplies. The threats of war were becoming ever

more explicit. Jha told me on October 8 that India would act by the end
of the year if its terms were not met; similar statements were made to
American diplomats in New Delhi by the Foreign Minister and the
Foreign Secretary. India deliberately set a deadline so short that it was
bound to shake the constitutional structure of Pakistan.

The Soviet Union played a highly inflammatory role. Though protesting
repeatedly its dedication to peace, it defined terms that were indistinguishable from New Delhi's and therefore represented the backing for
India that would guarantee a showdown. Though repeatedly affirming
its newfound devotion to détente, it used the budding improvement of
relations with us not to prevent an explosion but to deflect the consequences from itself. Moscow was acting throughout like a pyromaniac
who wants credit for having called the fire department to the fire he
has set.

My first discussion of the India-Pakistan crisis with Dobrynin took
place on July 19 shortly after my secret trip to Peking. Dobrynin, oozing conciliation, asked for my views. I replied that we favored a peaceful political evolution because a war could not be localized. Dobrynin
said this was also the Soviet view; Moscow supported India's political
goals but was strongly discouraging military adventures. We met again
on August 17 after the signing of the Soviet-Indian Friendship Treaty.
Dobrynin gave me the same interpretation as Jha had previously, insisting that the treaty had been in preparation for a long time. No more than
Jha did he explain why premeditation should assuage our concern. The
treaty was not directed against anybody, he said. (This, as I have noted,
is the conventional pacifier of diplomacy by which diplomats give a formal reassurance to those they wish to keep in suspense; it is an elegant
way of suggesting that one has the capacity to do worse.) I warned that
we would react sharply to a military challenge. Dobrynin's response
was that the Soviet Union was urging a peaceful solution.

Unfortunately, Soviet actions increasingly contradicted these assurances. Toward the end of August we received incontrovertible evidence
that, far from restraining the Indians, Moscow had promised to use its
veto in the United Nations if India were brought before the Security
Council as an aggressor; further, if Pakistan or China attacked India, the
Soviet Union would respond with an airlift of military equipment. The
Soviet Union, in other words, came close to giving Mrs. Gandhi a blank
check. Published accounts of Mrs. Gandhi's visit to Moscow in late
September supported this interpretation. Premier Kosygin jointly with
Mrs. Gandhi called on Yahya to liquidate tensions — placing the entire
blame on Pakistan. Kosygin declared an early political settlement essen-
tial to avoid war — the strongest endorsement yet by the Kremlin of the
Indian strategy. A visit by Soviet President Podgorny to India in early
October further dramatized Soviet support.

On September 29, Nixon met with Gromyko in Washington and told him that our two countries had a mutual interest in discouraging India from war. Gromyko was noncommittal. Avoiding war was indeed desirable; unfortunately, it was his considered judgment that the risk of war resided, above all, in Pakistani provocation. He gave no evidence for his interesting judgment that the demonstrably weaker country, cut off from all supplies of arms, was likely to attack the stronger. Nor did he explain why we could not be given the period till March to see what could be done after the transfer of power to civilian hands in Pakistan.

On October 9 I urgently sought Soviet help in discouraging the infiltration of 40,000 guerrillas into East Pakistan, after we had received disturbing reports that this was about to occur. The President, I said to Dobrynin, attached the utmost importance to the avoidance of war. Dobrynin could not have been friendlier — or less helpful. The Soviets were appealing to both sides, he said, but the Indians were becoming extremely difficult. I said we were prepared to consider acting jointly with the USSR to defuse the crisis. The offer was never taken up. India's opportunity to humiliate Pakistan was also the Soviet Union's opportunity to humiliate China. Moscow had every incentive to raise the stakes. Pakistan was the weaker country. The United States, which might have equalized the scales, was barred from helping Pakistan by a self-imposed arms embargo, a Vietnam-induced fear of any foreign involvement, and a nearly unanimous Congressional and media sentiment that India was justified in any action she might take. And China was temporarily paralyzed by its own internal travails.

Throughout October the Nixon Administration was subjected to a drumfire of criticism. On October 5, the Senate Foreign Relations Committee voted to suspend all US economic and military aid to Pakistan. Many Senators were clamoring for tougher measures still. This attitude was summed up in an editorial of October 22 in the *Washington Post:*

> The American position remains disgraceful. The other day the State Department mustered a feeble call for restraint on both sides. It was an appeal rendered grotesque by the twin facts that one side, Pakistan, is almost entirely responsible for the threat to the peace, and the United States is a partisan — arms, supplies, political support, relief and so on — of that side. In fact, the danger to peace on the subcontinent does not lie in the traditional differences between India and Pakistan but in Pakistan's policy of exporting an internal political problem — in the form of refugees — into India. American leadership in the provision of relief is simply not enough. It must be accompanied by stern political efforts to induce Pakistan to halt the persecution of its own people.

That Pakistan was to blame for the origin of the crisis was incontestable. But by October the central issue was how to remedy the original error and avoid a war with consequences far transcending the subcontinent. The Soviet aim in the wake of our China initiative was to humiliate Peking and to demonstrate the futility of reliance on either China or the United States as an ally. Furthermore, if India got away with such tactics, these might well spread to the Middle East, where Egypt, which also had a friendship treaty with Moscow, was threatening in a so-called year of decision to settle its grievances by war. For the Soviets to be able to point to South Asia as evidence of the efficacy of war and the impotence of the United States opened, I thought, ominous prospects for the Middle East.

I convened the WSAG in the Situation Room on October 7 to consider what could be done to arrest the drift to war. There was the reflex concern about Chinese intervention; some proposed a formal warning to Peking, which would have had the practical result of removing yet another of India's inhibitions. However, the meeting concluded harmoniously enough. State proposed that we ask both India and Pakistan to pull back their military forces from the borders; Moscow and Tehran would be approached to support this idea; it would again be made clear to both sides that war would lead to a cutoff of American aid; Pakistan would be encouraged to open a dialogue with the elected Bengali leaders — a not-too-subtle hint to reconsider its attitude toward Mujib. State's plan was approved.

It is clear in retrospect that we vastly overestimated the impact on India of the threat to cut off aid. Because of the complexity of determining and affecting what is already sold and on the way, an aid cutoff is never all that surgical. India could calculate — as it turned out, correctly — that it could rely on the pipeline to tide it over until another change in the climate of opinion would permit the renewal of aid.

Our first overture was to Yahya, with encouraging results. On October 11, he accepted our proposal of a mutual pullback of troops from the borders. He now gave us a timetable for a political solution. He would convene a new National Assembly before the end of the year and submit a constitution to it. Shortly after the National Assembly met he would turn over power to a civilian government. Provincial assemblies would meet in both West and East Pakistan. East Pakistan would have a majority in the civilian national government (in effect guaranteeing an outcome compatible with Bengali aspirations). He promised again that Mujib's death sentence would not be carried out; the civilian government could deal with his future within three months. On October 16 our chargé in Islamabad met with Bhutto, who agreed that the leading positions in a new government should go to East Pakistan; Mujib could play an active role. There was now little doubt left that East Pakistan would be able to decide its future once Yahya had stepped down.

The results in India were less auspicious. On October 12 Ambassador Keating saw Swaran Singh and was given the familiar catalogue of Indian grievances: The United States was not using its influence with Islamabad adequately; the efforts to start a dialogue with the Bangladesh exiles were a subterfuge to bypass Mujib. A mutual troop withdrawal, the Foreign Minister indicated, was unacceptable, but a unilateral Pakistani withdrawal from the frontier would be useful and India might reconsider if the Pakistanis in fact withdrew. Singh did not explain how Pakistan could withdraw troops while the Indian army was massed at its frontier and infiltrating thousands of guerrillas.

Learning of these rebuffs, Nixon ordered Haig on October 19 to "hit the Indians again on this." (I was en route to Peking and Haig was standing in for me.) Before the instruction could be carried out, the Indian Defense Secretary once more rejected a mutual troop pullback, this time on October 20 to Maury Williams. There was no danger, the Indian added ominously, of *accidental* confrontation.

On October 18 Ambassador Beam in Moscow presented our proposal for mutual troop withdrawal to Gromyko. This was buttressed by a Haig warning to Dobrynin to reinforce Nixon's concern. On October 23 we received the Soviet answer. It was identical with New Delhi's. The only effective way of avoiding war was the immediate release of Mujib and the "speediest political settlement in East Pakistan." Mutual troop withdrawals were deemed useful only in the context of a "complex of [other] measures." Clearly, Moscow was not going to cooperate in bringing about restraint.

The war danger meanwhile was developing its own momentum. On October 18 the Indian army and navy were placed in the highest state of alert. Clashes in the East were increasing. On November 1 the Indian army took major action to silence Pakistani artillery batteries, which they claimed had fired on Indian territory. (Considering that Pakistani forces in the East were outnumbered by some five to one and had to fight a guerrilla war, their incentive to initiate hostilities could not have been high.) On November 6, *after* the Nixon-Gandhi talks, we learned that small Indian regular army units had begun crossing the East Pakistan border on October 30. On November 1 a Soviet airlift of military equipment to India started. Soviet Deputy Foreign Minister Nikolai Firyubin visited New Delhi in late October; the press in India reported that he was urging restraint. Presumably he was aided in this by a follow-on visit by Marshal Pavel S. Kutakhov, Deputy Defense Minister and Chief of Staff of the Soviet Air Force.

We made one more effort to lower tensions before Mrs. Gandhi's arrival in Washington. Ambassador Farland was instructed to suggest that Pakistan consider *unilateral* troop withdrawal from the borders after all, and to urge Yahya to go to the outer limits of his flexibility in making political changes. On November 2 Farland brought Yahya a letter from Nixon that was none too subtle:

I know the importance you attach to enlisting the maximum degree of participation by the elected representatives of the people of East Pakistan. I also
believe you agree that this process is essential to restoring those conditions in
the Eastern wing of your country which will end the flow of refugees into India
and achieve a viable political accommodation among all the people of Pakistan.

To our surprise Yahya agreed to the unilateral withdrawal. The next day
his Ambassador in Washington reiterated the offer in a meeting with
me, on condition that Mrs. Gandhi agree to withdraw Indian forces
"shortly afterwards." Yahya accepted further that the total drying up of
the arms pipeline to Pakistan could be announced in connection with her
visit — a galling concession that he made with good grace. Yahya was
prepared, finally, to hold discussions with some Awami League leaders,
or some Bangladesh leaders in India not charged with a major crime,
and he said he would consider the idea of meeting with someone designated by Mujib. If we wanted to go further, we would have to wait for
the advent of the civilian government — then less than two months
away by Yahya's timetable. On November 3 Bhutto told Farland that
talks with Bangladesh representatives — including Mujib — were essential; in two months' time Bhutto would probably be a leader, if not
the head, of the new civilian government in Pakistan.

   This was the context of what were without a doubt the two most unfortunate meetings Nixon had with any foreign leader — his conversations on November 4 and 5 with Prime Minister Indira Gandhi. It was
not that the participants were belligerent or the tone impolite. In fact, they
studiously followed the convention for such encounters. Heads of government rarely make disagreements explicit; they do not want to solidify
a deadlock that they have no means of breaking — this would be a confession of either lack of negotiating skill or failing resolution. The inability of heads of government to arrive at a meeting of the minds tends
to be reflected in monologues that bear no relationship to what the opposite number has said, and in pregnant silences during which both no
doubt ponder the political consequences of the impasse. Or else — as
happened in the Nixon-Gandhi talks — the key subject is suddenly
dropped altogether.

   The President and the Prime Minister sat in two wing chairs on either
side of the fireplace in the Oval Office with her Cabinet Secretary, P. N.
Haksar, and me on the sofas adjoining each chair. After the news photographers had taken their hurried pictures and been hustled out, Mrs.
Gandhi began by expressing admiration for Nixon's handling of Vietnam and the China initiative, in the manner of a professor praising a
slightly backward student. Her praise lost some of its luster when she
smugly expressed satisfaction that with China Nixon had consummated
what India had recommended for the past decade. Nixon reacted with

the glassy-eyed politeness which told those who knew him that his resentments were being kept in check only by his reluctance to engage in face-to-face disagreement.

Nixon had no time for Mrs. Gandhi's condescending manner. Privately, he scoffed at her moral pretensions, which he found all the more irritating because he suspected that in pursuit of her purposes she had in fact fewer scruples than he. He considered her, indeed, a cold-blooded practitioner of power politics. On August 11 Nixon had admitted to the Senior Review Group that in Mrs. Gandhi's position he might pursue a similar course. But he was not in her position — and therefore he was playing for time. He, as did I, wanted to avoid a showdown, because he knew that a war would threaten our geopolitical design, and we both judged that East Pakistani autonomy was inevitable, if over a slightly longer period than India suggested. (In fact, India never put forward a specific timetable, implying throughout that yesterday had already been too late.)

Mrs. Gandhi, who was as formidable as she was condescending, had no illusions about what Nixon was up to. She faced her own conflicting pressures. Her Parliament would be meeting in two weeks, thirsting for blood. Though she had contributed no little to the crisis atmosphere, by now it had its own momentum, which, if she did not master it, might overwhelm her. Her dislike of Nixon, expressed in the icy formality of her manner, was perhaps compounded by the uneasy recognition that this man whom her whole upbringing caused her to disdain perceived international relations in a manner uncomfortably close to her own. It was not that she was a hypocrite, as Nixon thought; this assumed that she was aware of a gap between her actions and her values. It was rather that for her, her interest and her values were inseparable.

My own views of Mrs. Gandhi were similar to Nixon's, the chief difference being that I did not take her condescension personally. Later on, Nixon and I were accused of bias against India. This was a total misunderstanding; a serious policy must rest on analysis, not sentiment. To be sure, as I have suggested, I did not find in Indian history or in Indian conduct toward its own people or its neighbors a unique moral sensitivity. In my view, India had survived its turbulent history through an unusual subtlety in grasping and then manipulating the psychology of foreigners. The moral pretensions of Indian leaders seemed to me perfectly attuned to exploit the guilt complexes of a liberal, slightly socialist West; they were indispensable weapons for an independence movement that was physically weak and that used the ethical categories of the colonial power to paralyze it. They were invaluable for a new country seeking to vindicate an international role that it could never establish through power alone.

Mrs. Gandhi was a strong personality relentlessly pursuing India's na-

tional interest with single-mindedness and finesse. I respected her
strength even when her policies were hurtful to our national interest; but
I could not agree with Indian pretensions that we might "lose" India's
friendship forever unless we supported its hegemonic ambitions on the
subcontinent. I was confident that whatever the momentary passions we
could no more permanently "lose" India than we could permanently
"win" it. Less than most, in my mind, would Mrs. Gandhi hold the
pursuit of our interests against us. She would not lightly give up the
nonalignment on which her bargaining position depended, including at
least the appearance of an option toward the United States. When she
thought India's needs required it, Mrs. Gandhi would cooperate with us
with the same unsentimentality with which she now pursued the dismemberment of Pakistan. She would repair our strained relations rapidly
after the immediate blowup was over; paradoxically, the greater the
strains, the higher her incentive to restore at least the appearance of
normality. And so it turned out to be.

But in November 1971 relations were still deteriorating. All the reasons that led Nixon to play for time led Mrs. Gandhi to force the issue.
The inevitable emergence of Bangladesh — which we postulated —
presented India with fierce long-term problems. For Bangladesh was in
effect East Bengal, separated only by religion from India's most fractious and most separatist state, West Bengal. They shared language,
tradition, culture, and, above all, a volatile national character. Whether
it turned nationalist or radical, Bangladesh would over time accentuate
India's centrifugal tendencies. It might set a precedent for the creation
of other Moslem states, carved this time out of India. Once it was independent, its Moslem heritage might eventually lead to a rapprochement with Pakistan. All of this dictated to the unsentimental
planners in New Delhi that its birth had to be accompanied by a dramatic demonstration of Indian predominance on the subcontinent.

Yahya's mounting concessions aggravated Mrs. Gandhi's problem. If
she could have been sure that Yahya was insincere, that there would be
no civilian government, that Mujib would not be released, that East
Pakistan would not become first autonomous and then independent in a
matter of months, she could have played out the string and used the failure of our program as a pretext for a showdown. It was precisely the
near certainty of a favorable outcome that gave urgency to her actions.
A civilian government could have led Pakistan out of its isolation. A negotiation between Bangladesh representatives and Pakistan would have
circumscribed, if not ended, India's ability to force the pace. India had
to act before this sequence came to pass. Mrs. Gandhi was going to war
not because she was convinced of our failure but because she feared our
success.

The Nixon-Gandhi conversation thus turned into a classic dialogue of the deaf. The two leaders failed to hear each other not because they did not understand each other but because they understood each other only too well. Nixon stressed his conviction that the outcome was bound to be autonomy for East Pakistan leading to independence; all we asked for was a timetable that would not shatter the cohesion of West Pakistan, whose government was already in process of being handed over to civilians. He listed what the United States had accomplished through persuasion: aversion of a famine in East Pakistan; internationalization of relief; appointment of a civilian governor for East Pakistan; proclamation of an amnesty; the promise not to execute Mujib; agreement to unilateral withdrawal of Pakistani forces from the border; and, very important, Yahya's willingness to talk to some Bengali leaders. A war in such circumstances would simply not be understood by the United States and would not be accepted as a solution to problems whose seriousness we did not deny.

Mrs. Gandhi listened to what was in fact one of Nixon's better presentations with aloof indifference. She took up none of the points he made, although some of them — such as Pakistan's offer of unilateral withdrawal and Yahya's willingness to talk to Bangladesh leaders — she was hearing personally for the first time. Pakistan's concessions were of no fundamental interest to her. Her real obsession was the nature of Pakistan, not the injustices being committed in a portion of that tormented country. Ignoring the issues that had produced the crisis, she gave a little lecture on the history of Pakistan. She denied that she was opposed to its existence, but her analysis did little to sustain her disclaimer. Her father, she averred, had been blamed for accepting partition. And there was an element of truth, she said, in the often-heard charge that India had been brought into being by leaders of an indigenous independence movement while Pakistan had been formed by British collaborators who, as soon as they became "independent," proceeded to imprison the authentic fighters for independence. Pakistan was a jerry-built structure held together by its hatred for India, which was being stoked by each new generation of Pakistani leaders. Conditions in East Pakistan reflected tendencies applicable to *all* of Pakistan. Neither Baluchistan nor the Northwest Frontier properly belonged to Pakistan; they too wanted and deserved greater autonomy; they should never have been part of the original settlement.

This history lesson was hardly calculated to calm anxiety about Indian intentions. It was at best irrelevant to the issues and at worst a threat to the cohesion of even West Pakistan. Mrs. Gandhi stressed the congenital defects of Pakistan so insistently that she implied that confining her demands to the secession of East Pakistan amounted to Indian restraint; the continued existence of West Pakistan reflected Indian forbearance. She treated Yahya's concessions of November 2 as of no account. She was not opposed to unilateral withdrawal by Pakistan, but she refused to say whether India would follow suit, promising a formal answer the next day. Nixon assured the Prime Minister that she could count on us to use all our efforts to ease the crisis, including the encouragement of a speedy political solution. But the steely lady deferred all such discussion to another meeting.

In the afternoon I went over Yahya's concessions once again with her aide Haksar. I assured him that we would press the soon-to-be-formed civilian government insistently in the direction of Bengali self-determination. I foresaw autonomy for East Pakistan by March and independence shortly thereafter. I proposed that we work on a joint timetable. Haksar showed no interest.

The conversation between Nixon and Mrs. Gandhi the next day confirmed the never-neverland of US–Indian relations. Mrs. Gandhi made no reference to Pakistan at all. The entire meeting was confined to a world review in which Mrs. Gandhi asked penetrating questions about *our* foreign policy elsewhere, as if the subcontinent were the one corner of peace and stability on the globe. She gave us honor grades everywhere except there. Nixon on his part was willing enough to ignore the subject of the previous day, partly because he dreaded unpleasant scenes, partly because he correctly judged that this was Mrs. Gandhi's way of rejecting the various schemes we had put forward. It was a classic demonstration why heads of government should not negotiate contentious matters. Because their deadlocks seem unbreakable, their tendency to avoid precision is compounded. Thus Mrs. Gandhi's visit ended without progress on any outstanding issue or even on a procedure by which progress could be sought.

By November 10, news of penetration by Indian troops into East Pakistan — in one confirmed report, two battalions — could no longer be ignored, and there was the risk of Pakistani retaliation. Sisco called in both the Pakistani and Indian ambassadors to urge maximum restraint. The new Pakistani Ambassador, N. A. M. Raza, promised that his government would avoid all provocative action. Jha denied any Indian involvement; we could not challenge this untruth without revealing our intelligence sources. In the first half of November we received reports that some Indian officials were speaking of the probability of war before the end of the month. They proved to be off by only a week.

I called a WSAG meeting on November 12. The State Department proposed to press Yahya for another maximum political program as a way of "helping [him] out of a box short of war," as one State representative noted. Unfortunately, the only concessions he had not yet made were the immediate release of Mujib and the proclamation of the independence of half his country — concessions he considered humiliating and therefore deferred to the soon to be installed civilian government. There was nothing to suggest that this could be achieved in time to avert India's headlong rush into conflict. The single approach that had a slight chance of working would have been a threatening démarche to New Delhi; no one was willing to put this forward. I told my colleagues again that we would encourage political evolution, but we would not support the Indian strategy of so forcing the pace that West Pakistan could not survive:

If Mrs. Gandhi wants a way out, we should try to give it to her. But we have broken our backs to help her and what has she done? She hasn't accepted one thing we've offered. She has said friendly things about the President, but they were not related to what he said. She's merely trying to jockey us into position as the villain of the piece. The question is how are we restraining her by giving her two-thirds of what she wants and letting her use that as a basis for the next move?

The time for recrimination, however, had passed. We faced a crisis with few tools save remonstrance. So we went back to the cable machine. We would further test Yahya's flexibility with respect to Mujib. State also sent its dispatches counseling restraint. India hardly bothered to respond; it complained that our démarches put it on the same level as Pakistan. Indian diplomacy, having obtained most of the concessions it had asked for, was now confined to having its Ambassador inquire into the status of the one condition it knew to be unfulfillable in the short run: the release of Mujib and his recognition as sole negotiator with Pakistan.

I did my part in a meeting with Pakistani Foreign Secretary Sultan Khan, who was visiting Washington, on November 15. This decent and able man had seen me off at Islamabad for Peking only four months previously. I now had to urge him as tactfully as I could to show the utmost flexibility over Mujib. He replied that in his view the present military government had reached the limits of concession. Once a civilian government were formed, however, some six weeks hence, the issue would be reconsidered. Yahya himself made the same point to Ambassador Farland on November 18, emphasizing that his main objective was to implement his timetable for a civilian government: "If the civilian government then wants to deal with Bangladesh through Mujib or otherwise, that will be the business of the civilian government and of no concern to me. I will have accomplished my objective of turning the power back to the people."

I talked to Dobrynin twice, on November 15 and 18. On both occasions I warned that the continuing Soviet airlift of arms was adding to the tensions. Dobrynin suavely replied that in fact the Soviet Union was counseling restraint. On November 19 I discussed with Jha a timetable according to which full autonomy would be achieved in East Bengal by March. He shrugged it off.

The prospects for peace diminish when a potential aggressor sees a

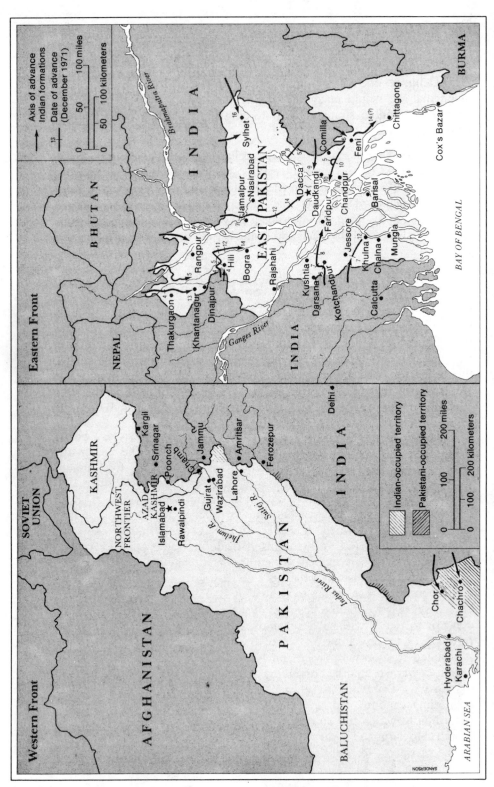

India-Pakistan War 1971

prize close at hand, enjoys overwhelming superiority on the ground, and perceives the intended victim to be isolated, demoralized, and disarmed. On November 22, the first stage of full-scale war broke out on the subcontinent, though nearly a week passed before India admitted it and before all of our agencies were prepared to face its implications.

War between India and Pakistan

O N November 22 I reported to Nixon:

The Pakistanis today claim in radio broadcasts that India "without a formal declaration of war, has launched an all-out offensive against East Pakistan." . . . The Indians claim that these reports are "absolutely false." . . . At this point, we have no independent evidence but it seems apparent that there had been a major incident.

Crises always start as confusion, this one more than most. The Pakistani Ambassador had no information; Secretary Rogers, who had no better sources than I, could only note the conflicting reports. Nixon was raring to carry out his threat, reiterated since May, that he would terminate aid to India. To head off domestic criticism he wanted to announce this as a cutoff of aid to both belligerents, knowing that aid to Pakistan was already being dried up. I recommended that he delay a decision until after a WSAG meeting called for the afternoon. I was skeptical even of announcing a cutoff for Pakistan if it turned out that India was the aggressor. It was just too cynical; it might be misunderstood in Peking. Nixon was for whatever course would hurt India more.

I had no doubt that we were now witnessing the beginning of an India-Pakistan war and that India had started it. Despite popular myths, large military units do not fight by accident; some command sets them into motion. No amount of obfuscation could offset the improbability that 70,000 Pakistani soldiers engaged in a guerrilla war would attack 200,000 Indian troops, or that the Pakistani air force of twelve planes in East Pakistan would have taken on the 200 Indian planes ranged against it. There was no pretense of legality. There was no doubt in my mind — a view held even more strongly by Nixon — that India had escalated its demands continually and deliberately to prevent a settlement. To be sure, Pakistani repression in East Bengal had been brutal and shortsighted; and millions of refugees had imposed enormous strain on the Indian economy. But what had caused the war, in Nixon's view and mine, went beyond the refugee problem; it was India's determination to use the crisis to establish its preeminence on the subcontinent.

But our paramount concern transcended the subcontinent. The Soviet Union could have restrained India; it chose not to. It had, in fact, actively encouraged war by signing the Friendship Treaty, giving diplomatic support to India's maximum demands, airlifting military supplies, and pledging to veto inconvenient resolutions in the UN Security Council. The Soviets encouraged India to exploit Pakistan's travail in part to deliver a blow to our system of alliances, in even greater measure to demonstrate Chinese impotence. Since it was a common concern about Soviet power that had driven Peking and Washington together, a demonstration of American irrelevance would severely strain our precarious new relationship with China. Had we followed the advice of our critics — massive public dissociation from Pakistan and confrontation with it in its moment of desperation — we would have been operating precisely as the US–Soviet condominium so dreaded by Peking; this almost surely would have undone our China initiative. I heard occasional comments in the interagency meetings implying that we were obsessed with preserving the trip to China. But as I said to Nixon, "These people don't recognize that without a China trip we wouldn't have had a Moscow trip."

Nor were we defending only abstract principles of international conduct. The victim of the attack was an ally — however reluctant many were to admit it — to which we had made several explicit promises concerning precisely this contingency. Clear treaty commitments reinforced by other undertakings dated back to 1959. One could debate the wisdom of these undertakings (and much of our bureaucracy was so eager to forget about them that for a time it proved next to impossible even for the White House to extract copies of the 1962 communications), but we could not ignore them. To do so would have disheartened allies like Iran and Turkey, which sympathized with Pakistan, had the same commitment from us, and looked to our reaction as a token of American steadiness in potential crises affecting them. High stakes were therefore involved. On December 5 I told Nixon that the India-Pakistan conflict would turn into a dress rehearsal for the Middle East in the spring. I made the same point to John Connally before and after the December 6 NSC meeting.

There was no question of "saving" East Pakistan. Both Nixon and I had recognized for months that its independence was inevitable; war was not necessary to accomplish it. We strove to preserve *West* Pakistan as an independent state, since we judged India's real aim was to encompass its disintegration. We sought to prevent a demonstration that Soviet arms and diplomatic support were inevitably decisive in crises. On December 4 I told Nixon that precisely because we were retreating from Vietnam we could not permit the impression to be created that all issues could be settled by naked force. Though it was now too late to prevent war, we still had an opportunity — through the intensity of our reaction — to make the Soviets pause before they undertook another adventure somewhere else. As I told Nixon on December 5, we had to become sufficiently threatening to discourage similar moves by Soviet friends in other areas, especially the Middle East. And if we acted with enough daring, we might stop the Indian onslaught before it engulfed and shattered West Pakistan.

It was nearly impossible to implement this strategy because our departments operated on different premises. They were afraid of antagonizing India; they saw that Pakistan was bound to lose the war whatever we did; they knew our course was unpopular in the Congress and the media. And Nixon, while he understood the strategic stakes, could not bring himself to impose the discipline required to implement the operational details.

The Foreign Service is a splendid instrument, highly trained, dedicated, and able. When I was Secretary of State I grew to admire it as an institution, to respect its members, and to develop a close friendship with many of them. But it requires strong leadership to impose coherence on the parochial concerns of the various bureaus which are most conscious of the daily pressures; this is especially true if the policy to be pursued is unpopular or at variance with long-held predilections. That sense of direction must be supplied by the Seventh Floor — the office of the Secretary of State and of his immediate entourage. Unfortunately — to the credit of neither of us — my relations with Rogers had deteriorated to the point that they exacerbated our policy differences and endangered coherent policy. He was likely to oppose any recommendation of mine simply as an assertion of prerogative; I tried to bypass him as much as possible. (Which came first must be determined by more neutral historians.) Rogers was convinced that our course was mistaken and that Nixon took it only because of my baneful influence. I believed that Rogers had no grasp of the geopolitical stakes. The result was a bureaucratic stalemate in which White House and State Department representatives dealt with each other as competing sovereign entities, not members of the same team, and the President sought to have his way by an indirection that compounded the internal stresses of our government.

At the first WSAG meeting after the war began, on November 22, the State Department argued that we did not have enough facts to make any decision. It recommended that we press *Pakistan* for further political concessions. Though the war was a clear violation of the UN Charter, the Department was ambivalent about going to the UN; determined not to clash with India, it saw merit in going to the UN not in order to invoke Charter provisions against armed attack but only to wash our hands of the entire affair. I asked — I fear none too patiently — what sense there was in rewarding India for its aggression by pressing for new concessions from Pakistan. Was it unreasonable to ask India to wait for four weeks to see how the transfer to civilian authority would come out? As for going to the UN, I asked State to prepare a scenario by the opening of business the next day. That same evening the President sent me an instruction that strong cables cautioning against war be sent to New Delhi, Moscow, and Islamabad. Nixon wanted Moscow, in particular, to be warned about its supply of arms to India.

The military outcome was becoming obvious. Pakistan told us that two Indian brigades were operating inside East Pakistan. On November 23 Nixon received a letter from Yahya describing Indian military dispositions as in effect a noose around the government forces in East Pakistan that was being tightened through large and unprovoked attacks. Assuring Nixon of his desire to avoid war even at this late stage, Yahya appealed for Nixon's "personal initiative at the present juncture" which "could still prove decisive in averting a catastrophe."

On the same day — November 23 — we received a letter from Mrs. Gandhi, inexplicably dated November 18. Speaking as if addressing a partner in a joint enterprise, Mrs. Gandhi gave herself high marks for restraint, which she ascribed to faith that justice would prevail and which had been "sustained by the discussion I had with you." While Indian units were roaming over a neighboring country, Mrs. Gandhi advised against convening the Security Council, arguing that "such a move would obstruct the path of the solutions which we jointly seek." It was an interesting doctrine of international law that recourse to the United Nations might obstruct the solution of a military conflict. And the implication that, now that India had attacked its neighbor, we were seeking "joint solutions" did little to calm the Presidential temper. Mrs. Gandhi appealed to Nixon to use his "great courage" to inspire a solution and expressed the hope for better relations between the United States and India. She did not vouchsafe what solution she was aiming for or what better relations between India and the United States would consist of. But it was clear she did not want to be called to defend and justify India's policy before the world community at the UN.

The WSAG meeting of November 23 shed no light on the direction in which American influence — now requested by both sides — could be brought to bear. The State Department had no objection to the cables to Moscow and Islamabad urging restraint (in the latter case, no one considered it odd to ask the victim of a military attack to show restraint). It was the cable to New Delhi that was giving trouble. Under Secretary of State Irwin recommended delaying until we had "independent" confirmation of an Indian attack. "We can play this charade only so long," I replied.

Nor was State ready to cut off military aid to India, as Nixon demanded. Its representatives questioned whether a cutoff was consistent with our efforts to restrain Mrs. Gandhi and doubted its effectiveness. This was exactly the opposite of what had been alleged for months with respect to Pakistan! And after months of demonstrating enormous ingenuity in drying up the Pakistani pipeline, they seemed totally at a loss on how to accomplish it with India, pleading the difficulty of tracing equipment already licensed. It also turned out that ending economic aid to both sides would hurt Pakistan more than India. I pointed out what should have been axiomatic: that it made no sense to refrain from cutting off military equipment to the attacking country when we had already done so to the victim.

November 23 was also the day of my first secret meeting with the Chinese in New York. Huang Hua was now Permanent Representative of the People's Republic of China to the United Nations. Peking had agreed that we could use Huang Hua in New York as a contact on UN matters or for emergency messages; the rest of our business was to be conducted through Paris as heretofore. I thought it important to keep Peking meticulously informed of our moves; at a minimum, the Chinese leaders had to understand that we were not in collusion with the Soviet Union. Peking needed to appreciate our determination to resist expansionism as well as the limits on our practical possibilities in this case.

Huang Hua and I met at a secret location in New York City in the East Thirties, a seedy little apartment in an old brownstone that the CIA had used as a safehouse. One requirement was that it have no doorman and few other occupants. Otherwise we would be tempting fate if too many sharp-eyed New Yorkers could see three Chinese diplomats wearing Mao suits walk into a building, to be followed by Henry Kissinger. (Later we moved our meeting place to an equally seedy if slightly more pretentious establishment in the East Seventies.) At this point I could do little more than brief Huang Hua on the military situation. I showed him the draft resolution we would submit to the Security Council if the issue were taken up there, indicating we had not made a final decision. Huang Hua emphasized that China would support Pakistan in the Security Council, but would follow Pakistan's lead as to whether to take the issue there.

On November 24, Mrs. Gandhi acknowledged for the first time that Indian troops had crossed the Pakistani border. They had done so only once, she said, on November 21. And, she informed the Indian Parliament, Indian troops had acted in their right of self-defense. Future decisions to cross the border would be left to the "man on the spot" — a group of commanders eager to demonstrate their prowess.

In the face of all this evidence, the WSAG meeting on November 24 marked time as we awaited the responses to our démarches in New Delhi, Islamabad, and Moscow. I asked the departments whether there was any doubt that Indian regular forces had invaded East Pakistan. Most agreed, but — in spite of Mrs. Gandhi's admission — the State Department representative still regarded the evidence as inconclusive.

The operational advice offered was, again, to press Pakistan for further political concessions. If there was a "tilt" in the US government at this stage, objectively it was on the side of India. Bureaucratic paralysis had the practical effect of cooperating with the delaying action that India was conducting on the diplomatic front.

At noon on November 24 Nixon met with Rogers and me in the Oval Office. The positions followed those of the WSAG, with Rogers arguing that we did not have enough evidence for a Security Council move. Unfortunately, the immediate issues were all extremely technical — phraseology for possible UN resolutions and methods to achieve various degrees of aid cutoff. Nixon hated this sort of detail; discussing it made him visibly nervous. Overruling his old friend went against his grain in any event. So the meeting ended inconclusively, with Nixon afterward fretting to me about how to deal with his Secretary of State; he played with the idea of getting John Mitchell to rein in Rogers but in the end did nothing.

The outcome was that everyone went his own merry way. The State Department had publicized its view by having its spokesman declare at a press briefing that the United States had no evidence to charge India with aggression. When the Pakistani Ambassador protested to the Secretary, Rogers reiterated that we had "no independent information to confirm or deny" Indian complicity in armed attack. Rogers explained that Washington did not want to be in a position to take sides as to the truth of conflicting reports. Of course, the location of the battle line deep inside Pakistani territory would have given us a pretty good clue as to who was probably doing the attacking.

Bureaucratic infighting caused a third day to pass without any serious US reaction. I have pointed out in previous chapters that crises can be managed only if they are overpowered early. Once they gain momentum the commitments of the parties tend to drive them out of control. A stern warning to India on the *first* day, coupled with a plausible threat of an aid cutoff brutally implemented, might possibly have given Mrs. Gandhi pause before she escalated. (It would, of course, have been even better to do so *before* the attack.) Doubts about who had attacked were largely spurious. Guerrilla forces do not operate tanks and airplanes across hundreds of miles of territory. Plaintive appeals for restraint only revealed our hesitation; they may have spurred Indian military action instead of restraining it.

Ambassador Keating's experience with Swaran Singh on Thanksgiving Day, November 25, revealed that India was implacable. In a stormy reply to our plea for restraint, Singh complained that there had been no political progress since Mrs. Gandhi's visit. He did not tell us how it could have been made, since his Prime Minister had never deigned to react to our proposals and did not communicate with us until November 23, forty-eight hours earlier. He said that if Pakistan unilaterally withdrew its troops, this would create a new situation, but he refused to tell us whether India would follow suit. It was Pakistan that threatened India, said Singh, not the other way around. When Keating referred to Indian troops on Pakistani territory, Singh blithely replied this did not tally with the facts as he knew them. Even Keating, who strongly supported the Indian point of view, lobbied for it in Congress, and frequently castigated both Nixon and me privately, found himself obliged to admit in an understatement that Singh was "less than completely frank with me with regard to Indian military personnel inside East Pakistan."

On November 25, too, we learned reliably that Mrs. Gandhi had told colleagues that India would continue its attacks and escalate them. Her commanders were as good as her word. On November 26 new Indian attacks were launched in the Jessore area. The Soviet Union blocked a Japanese feeler to call a Security Council meeting. Ambassador Beam was told that the Soviet Union would support an end to military operations only if there were a political solution satisfactory to India. Nixon phoned British Prime Minister Heath to tell him of his fear that Indian objectives might well go beyond East Pakistan. He received general expressions of agreement but a clear indication that Britain would stay aloof.

On November 26 Farland managed to see Yahya, who accepted Farland's suggestion that he request the UN to send observers to the Pakistani side of the line. He would also ask the UN to take over the refugee facilities in East Pakistan and would consider allowing Bengali oppositionists to meet with the still imprisoned Mujib. In New Delhi Keating saw Mrs. Gandhi in the context of a visit by Senators Frank Church and William Saxbe. Her line had hardened even further. She repeated the complaint that there had been no political progress since her talks with Nixon. The issue in any event was no longer East Pakistan but India's national security in the face of unstable neighbors, she said. Playing to the end the role of a peace-loving moderate overwhelmed by events, Mrs. Gandhi said that she was barely able to resist tremendous domestic pressure for even more drastic action — though it was not obvious what more India might do to harass, injure, and invade her neighbor.

Nixon's instinct, again, was to reply to Mrs. Gandhi with a cutoff of aid. I urged him to wait for the next Indian move. We would be better off reacting when the provocation was unambiguous and the facts unconstestable. The State Department came forward with the idea of Presidential letters to Yahya, Mrs. Gandhi, and Kosygin, again urging troop withdrawals, though without any indication that there was a penalty for refusing us. Though Presidential letters had grown so frequent as to debase the currency, I went along because they could do no damage and could provide a platform later for stronger action.

The President's letter to Mrs. Gandhi informed her of Yahya's willingness to permit UN observers on the Pakistani side of the border and reminded her of Pakistan's standing offer of unilateral withdrawal. Noting her admission that Indian forces were engaged on Pakistani territory, the letter stressed that "the American people would not understand if Indian actions led to broad scale hostilities."

The message to Kosygin called once again for Soviet cooperation in promoting a peaceful resolution to the crisis and urged the Soviet Union to press New Delhi on troop withdrawals. It was a futile gesture. The Soviet definition of an acceptable solution was identical with India's.

The letter to Yahya sought to discourage him from seeking to relieve the pressure on beleaguered East Pakistan by attacking India from the West, where the bulk of the Pakistani army was located. Even though such a move was also doomed to failure, desperate leaders might feel it required by their honor. We were concerned that a Pakistani attack in the West would merely supply the final pretext for India to complete the disintegration of *all* of Pakistan. The Nixon letter listed our various futile efforts to urge restraint on India; nevertheless, it warned against expansion of the war. Yahya received Farland on November 27. He was desperate and cooperative. He offered to ask the United Nations immediately to furnish observers for the Pakistani side of the border to guarantee Pakistan's defensive intent. He offered to permit Farland to meet with Mujib's lawyer. (As the war escalated Yahya later withdrew his offer.) And he reaffirmed his willingness for contacts with members of the provisional Bangladesh government in Calcutta and "they will not find me unresponsive."

The winning side in a war is rarely eager for negotiations; the longer the battle lasts, the better will be its bargaining position. The only restraint is the fear that if it overplays its hand it will trigger outside forces that might deprive it of the fruits of its victory. Mrs. Gandhi at the end of November was riding the waves of success, and the actions of neither the United States nor China gave her much reason for caution. The Nixon Administration was being pressed to turn on Pakistan; China at the end of its Cultural Revolution proved to be militarily unprepared and had just surmounted a domestic crisis involving the loyalty of its military.

Meanwhile, the State Department spokesman surfaced with a comment that showed how hard his colleagues found it to follow the White House strategy or to break with three decades of sentimental attachment to India. A former US Ambassador to Pakistan, Benjamin H. Oehlert, Jr., had written a letter to the *New York Times,* published on November 3, to the effect that the United States had commitments to come to Pakistan's aid "even with our arms and men, if she should be attacked by any other country." The State Department spokesman replied to a question on November 26 that there were no such secret commitments binding the United States to come to Pakistan's aid. If enough emphasis were placed on the phrase "arms and men" and if a sharp lawyer were permitted to define the meaning of "binding," this statement was at the very edge of truth. It also happened to be exactly the wrong signal if we sought to restrain an Indian assault on an allied country.

Mrs. Gandhi was unavailable to receive the President's letter. She had decided to visit her troops near the border. She blasted the superpowers (meaning the United States) for having the nerve to complain "because we have taken action to defend our borders." This speech was little likely to turn the thoughts of the military commanders, who now had discretion to cross the frontier, toward peace. That same day Indian Defense Minister Jagjivan Ram disclosed to a cheering crowd at a political rally in Calcutta that Indian forces had been authorized to advance into Pakistan to "silence" Pakistani artillery. At the same rally a speaker declared, "India will break Pakistan to pieces." And an Indian colonel told a reporter on November 28 what part of the US government was still unwilling to acknowledge — that "our troops went in because the Mukti Bahini called for help."[5]

Keating finally caught up with Mrs. Gandhi on November 29 and was received with another frosty recital of India's complaints. Yahya's problems, she pointed out not inaccurately, were self-created and "we are not in a position to make this easier for him." She could not continue to tell her people to wait and added ominously, "I can't hold it." When Keating tried to raise the issue of border incursions into Pakistan, Mrs. Gandhi cut him off: "We can't afford to listen to advice which weakens us."

This moved matters back to the WSAG, which on November 29 debated inconclusively whether India had made a decision to attack before or after the Nixon-Gandhi talks. The issue was as irrelevant as the answer was self-evident. Clearly, Mrs. Gandhi had planned it well in advance and used her trip not as a means to seek a solution but as a smokescreen for her actions. There was no way by which the Indian deployment could have been completed in the ten-day period between Mrs. Gandhi's return and the first cross-border operations. The WSAG had at last reconciled itself to the fact that the President meant to cut off some aid to India, but the State Department fought a dogged rearguard action to keep the reduction to a minimum and the directive sufficiently vague to permit the maximum administrative discretion. Matters reached such a point of confusion concerning what categories of arms we might cut off that I said, "We have contracts without licenses and licenses without contracts," asking which we were to terminate. It transpired that what was favored was a refusal to grant new licenses — undoubtedly on the theory that this decision could always be reversed after the war when passions had cooled. I should have known from the ease

with which interagency agreement was obtained that the amounts involved were small (around $17 million). The first step, a ban on new
licenses for military equipment for India, was announced by State on
December 1.

On November 29 I informed Peking via the Paris channel of all our
overtures to other countries and their responses.

By November 30 Mrs. Gandhi raised pressures another notch. Speaking to her Parliament, she sarcastically welcomed the call for troop
withdrawals but "the troops that should be withdrawn straight away are
the Pakistani troops in Bangladesh." She threw cold water on any negotiations with Pakistan on the ground that only the elected representatives
of Bangladesh could decide its future and that in her view they would
not settle for anything less than "liberation." Thus, there was nothing
to negotiate with Pakistan other than its dismemberment.

So the WSAG met again on December 1 to discuss whether, over a
week after the start of hostilities, the time had come for a UN Security
Council meeting and what additional steps could be taken to implement
an arms cutoff to India. There was surprising international unanimity
not to go to the Security Council. India did not want a Security Council
meeting because hypocrisy could not be stretched even in that body to
avoid the admission that an invasion of a sovereign member of the UN
had taken place. It would be able to escape condemnation only by the
promised Soviet veto. Pakistan did not want a Security Council discussion because it feared that it might broaden into a general criticism of
the repression in East Bengal; also, it wanted to keep the spotlight on its
invitation that UN observers be stationed on the Pakistani side of the
border — a proposal that had already been formally submitted to the
UN Secretary-General. The Soviet Union was not eager to be forced to
invoke its veto; Huang Hua had told me that China would back whatever Pakistan wanted. Within our government the State Department was
not eager to go to the Security Council because it feared the "tilt" of
White House instructions. I was reluctant because I was loath to take on
the domestic brawl that our instructions would evoke. It was a sad commentary on the state of the United Nations when a full-scale invasion of
a major country was treated by victim, ally, aggressor, and other great
powers as too dangerous to bring to the formal attention of the world
body pledged by its Charter to help preserve the peace.

The War Spreads

ON December 2 Pakistani Ambassador Raza delivered a letter from
Yahya to President Nixon invoking Article I of the 1959 bilateral
agreement between the United States and Pakistan as the basis for US
aid to Pakistan.[6] The American obligation to Pakistan was thus formally
raised. The State Department was eloquent in arguing that no binding

obligation existed; it regularly put out its view at public briefings. It pointed out that Article I spoke only of "appropriate action" subject to our constitutional processes; it did not specify what action should be taken. The Department also claimed that the obligation was qualified by its context, the 1958 Middle East "Eisenhower Doctrine" resolution, which, it was argued, intended to exclude an India-Pakistan war. State simply ignored all other communications between our government and Pakistan.

The image of a great nation conducting itself like a shyster looking for legalistic loopholes was not likely to inspire other allies who had signed treaties with us or relied on our expressions in the belief that the words meant approximately what they said. The treaty with Pakistan was identical to several other bilateral and multilateral agreements — all of which our pronouncements seemed to cast into doubt. And it had been buttressed in the case of Pakistan by many additional assurances of support. The fact was that over the decades of our relationship with Pakistan, there had grown up a complex body of communications by the Kennedy and Johnson administrations, going beyond the 1959 pact, some verbal, some in writing, whose plain import was that the United States would come to Pakistan's assistance if she was attacked by India.[7] To be sure, their purpose had been to evade Pakistani requests for arms after the Indian attack on Goa of December 1961 and the India-Pakistan war of 1965. Assurances of future US support were the substitute for immediate material aid. But if anything, this made matters worse. It made it appear as if the United States avoided supplying weapons to an ally first by promising later support if the threat materialized and then by welshing on its promises by superclever legal exegesis.

I am not suggesting that we should have blindly set our policy solely because of what our predecessors had said. The decisions of a great power will be shaped by the requirements of the national interest as perceived at the moment of decision, not only by abstract legal obligations whether vague or precise. No country can be expected to run grave risks if its interests and obligations have come to be at total variance with each other. But equally a nation that systematically ignores its pledges assumes a heavy burden; its diplomacy will lose the flexibility that comes from a reputation for reliability; it can no longer satisfy immediate pleas from allies by promises of future action. Pakistan, moreover, was an ally of other allies — Iran, Turkey — and a friend of Saudi Arabia and Jordan, then isolated in a still largely radical Middle East. And it was a friend of China and in close touch with a Peking that was gingerly feeling its way toward a new relationship with us based on the hope that we could maintain the global equilibrium. A reputation for unreliability was not something we could afford.

Nixon was ensconced in Key Biscayne; we talked frequently. He had no intention of becoming militarily involved, but he was determined that *something* be done. He ordered that the remaining licenses for Indian arms be terminated. He wanted a complete cutoff of economic aid (this I knew would never happen, given the biases of our bureaucracy). He wanted a State Department statement castigating Indian intransigence. "If they don't want to, Ziegler will do it from Florida, and it will be a blast." I transmitted these instructions to an unenthusiastic Rogers, who began trying to figure out ways to make the announcement so late in the day that the scope of press coverage would be reduced.

Once more events in the subcontinent overtook us. Yahya had at last been cornered by his subtly implacable opponent in New Delhi. Throughout the crisis, long periods of paralyzing inactivity by Yahya had been succeeded by sudden spasms as he sought to adjust to his predicament — usually too late. For eleven days he had stood by while Indian forces pressed deeper and deeper into East Pakistan, in effect dismembering his country. For his main forces to remain inactive on the borders of West Pakistan would amount to abdication; yet to respond would be to fall into the Indian trap and provide a pretext for an all-out onslaught on East *and* eventually West Pakistan. Yahya chose what he considered the path of honor. On December 3 he launched his army into an attack in the West that he must have known was suicidal. In simple-minded soldierly fashion he decided, as I told Nixon, that if Pakistan would be destroyed or dismembered it should go down fighting.

The reaction in our government was to use the Pakistani attack as a perfect excuse to defer the statement attacking Indian transgressions, which Nixon had ordered the day before, on the pretext that once again we did not have all the facts. This led to repeated arguments between me and Rogers, who took the view that the war having spread, a move to the Security Council was now inevitable. Criticizing India in these conditions would be assuming for ourselves a judicial role better left to the world organization; in other words, we would act as judges, not as an ally or even as a superpower with interests and commitments. Having opposed recourse to the Security Council earlier, State now favored it as a pretext to avoid a unilateral United States response and to delay our having to take any position at all. I finally acquiesced and let the Department slide off the condemnation of India that Nixon had ordered. Now that the Security Council would address the issue of the expanded war we could make our case there. And I knew that George Bush, our able UN Ambassador, would carry out the President's policy. After much pulling and hauling, State finally announced on December 3 the cutoff of remaining licenses on arms to India — hardly an overwhelming response to the outbreak of full-scale hostilities on the subcontinent.

By now Nixon was in high gear. As always, his attitude was woven of many strands. He wanted to preserve his China initiative, and he understood that "even-handedness" would play into India's hands. He wanted to deflect blame for what was happening from himself. He dreaded conflict with Rogers. But he was insistent on taking a strong line at the Security Council. His initiatives came cascading into my office, specific in indicating directions, less so in defining the methods.

In this atmosphere the WSAG assembled on December 3 to chart a course. It was a meeting memorialized in transcripts that were leaked to the columnist Jack Anderson. Out of context these sounded as if the White House were hell-bent on pursuing its own biases, but they can only be understood against the background of the several preceding months of frustrating and furious resistance by the bureaucracy to the President's explicit decisions. "I've been catching unshirted hell every half-hour from the President who says we're not tough enough," I commented in what I thought was the privacy of the Situation Room. "He really doesn't believe we're carrying out his wishes. He wants to tilt toward Pakistan and he believes that every briefing or statement is going the other way." That was of course a plain statement of the facts.

My sarcasm did nothing to affect departmental proclivities. When I transmitted the President's instruction to cut off economic aid to India, State suggested a similar step toward Pakistan — in spite of the President's view that India was the guilty party for its bellicosity. This provoked me in exasperation into another "tilt" statement: "It's hard to tilt toward Pakistan, as the President wishes, if every time we take some action in relation to India we have to do the same thing for Pakistan. Just hold this informally until I get to the President."

The State Department representatives at interagency meetings were in an extremely uncomfortable position. Castigated sarcastically by me for foot-dragging, pressed by their own chief to be more assertive in opposing the White House, they had to navigate in treacherous shoals. Joe Sisco, for example, was ordered by the White House on December 4 to brief the press informally to explain our criticism of Indian policy. This he did loyally and ably, to the intense displeasure of his Secretary of State, who subsequently prohibited him from appearing on television to repeat the same points on the record. The responsibility for the conditions I describe must fall on the personalities at the top, including myself. I have recounted the bureaucratic battles not to assess blame but to illuminate the public record, which is incomprehensible without them.

The issue hinged on the geopolitical perspective of the White House as against the regional perspective of the State Department, and on the relative weight to be given to China and India in the conduct of our foreign policy. The White House viewed the conflict as a ruthless power play by which India, encouraged by the Soviets, used the ineptitude of the Pakistani government and the fragility of the Pakistani political structure to force a solution of the East Pakistan crisis by military means when a political alternative seemed clearly available. Whether our officials liked it or not, Pakistan was an ally to which we had treaty commitments backed up by private assurances; its fate would thus affect the attitudes of several key countries that had rested their security on American promises. It would be watched carefully by China. And those countries in the Middle East eager to settle the issue by force could easily be tempted to adopt military means. And if its policy in the subcontinent succeeded too easily, the Soviet Union might resort to comparable tactics in other volatile areas — as indeed it later did when Watergate had sapped Executive authority. The dismemberment of Pakistan by military force and its eventual destruction without any American reaction thus would have profound international repercussions.

The opposing view was that we were needlessly sacrificing the friendship of India, that nothing could be done to save East Pakistan, and that it would, in any event, be undesirable to do so. We were taking the "Chinese position," Rogers complained. We were acting impetuously. We ran a needless risk of involving ourselves militarily. India was a country of huge potential that we needed as a friend. But Nixon and I were not being impetuous. We were convinced that India's nonalignment derived not from affection for the United States but from its perception of its national interest; these calculations were likely to reassert themselves as soon as the immediate crisis was over. The issue, to us, was the assault on international order implicit in Soviet-Indian collusion. I told the WSAG on December 4 that "everyone knows we will end up with Indian occupation of East Pakistan." But we had to act with determination to save larger interests and relationships. We were playing a weak hand, but one must never compound weakness by timidity. "I admit it's not a brilliant position," I said to Nixon on December 5, "but if we collapse now the Soviets won't respect us for it; the Chinese will despise us and the other countries will draw their own conclusions."

Once the war had spread to the West, moreover, at issue was not the method for establishing Bangladesh but the survival of Pakistan itself. India's military power was vastly superior to Pakistan's, partly the result of the six-year American embargo on arms sales to both sides, which hurt mainly Pakistan. Because of India's access to Soviet arms and a large arms industry of its own, India was bound to crush Pakistan's armed forces. The State Department's legal advisers might find a way to demonstrate that we had no binding obligation to Pakistan, but the geopolitical impact would be no less serious for it. Our minimum aim had to be to demonstrate that we would not compound our weakness by fatuousness. We had to act in a manner that would give pause to potential Soviet adventures elsewhere, especially in the Middle East, where Egypt's President had now proclaimed 1972 as another year of decision.

Our weakness on the ground forced us to play a bold game; when the weak act with restraint it encourages further pressures and brings home to their opponents the strength of their position. I had no illusion about our assets; but sometimes in situations of great peril leaders must make boldness substitute for assets. "We are running a tremendous bluff in a situation in which we are holding no cards," I told Haldeman on December 11, pleading with him to get the President for once to insist on some discipline in our government. "Unless we can settle on a strategy," I said in an appeal to my fractious colleagues on the WSAG on December 9, "speak with the same voice, and stop putting out all these conflicting stories from the various agencies and all this leaking, we don't deserve to succeed."

It was impossible to keep the government united and not easy to get it to act with any coherence. Most of December 4 was expended in getting the State Department to agree to a speech by George Bush challenging India's resort to arms and supporting a Security Council resolution calling for both a cease-fire and withdrawal of forces (that is, Indian).

Bush introduced a resolution along these lines on December 4. The Security Council supported our position, with eleven members favoring our resolution. But it failed of adoption because it was vetoed by the Soviet Union. (Britain and France abstained — another example of the tendency of our West European allies to let us carry the burden of global security alone.) With the Security Council stalemated by the Soviet veto we took the case to the General Assembly under the Uniting for Peace resolution. We prevailed in that body by a vote of 104 to 11 on December 7. Our position was opposed only by the Soviet bloc and India.

It was a weird situation. For years the Administration had been accused by its domestic critics of paying insufficient attention to world opinion. But here was an issue on which we enjoyed more support in the world community than on any other in a decade. Almost all the nonaligned were on our side for once. Many of them had border conflicts or ethnic divisions; none of them had an interest in letting outside force become the ultimate arbiter of such disputes. The Soviet bloc was isolated as it had not been since the early days of the United Nations. The numbers in our favor were overwhelming. Yet the usual votaries of world opinion in our country were busy castigating the White House as if it stood irrationally against the decent opinion of mankind. Little consideration was given to the global impact of a demonstration of American impotence combined with UN paralysis. For two years we had been talking about Security Council guarantees as a key to peace in the Middle East. What would be the implications for Middle East diplomacy of a blatant military attack in continuing defiance of UN resolutions and without any US action on behalf of a country with which it was allied?

All the while, the Soviet Union was buying time for India to complete its military operations. TASS issued a blistering statement on December 5 supporting India without reservation and opposing any cease-fire unless accompanied by a political settlement based on the "lawful rights" of the people of East Pakistan. When Nixon learned of this he decided to bring pressure on Moscow. Dobrynin, as in most crises, was out of town. His chargé, Vorontsov, had authority only to receive and transmit messages, not to negotiate.

On December 5 I told Vorontsov that we were at a watershed. Moscow's encouragement of Indian aggression was inconsistent with improvement in US–Soviet relations. Vorontsov was soothing. The crisis would be over in a week; it need have no impact on US–Soviet relations. If the Soviet Union continued on its present course, I snapped, it would not be over in a week, whatever happened on the subcontinent.

On December 6, Mrs. Gandhi officially recognized the independence of Bangladesh. While this had been implicit in her policy all along, her declaration had the effect of closing off all remaining possibility of political accommodation. The State Department at last announced the cutoff of economic aid to India that Nixon had ordered four days earlier (but it was carried out so halfheartedly that it had little impact).

Nixon convened an NSC meeting on December 6 because he had become convinced at last that some discipline was essential. But as usual his efforts to impose it were so ambiguous that they made things worse. Since Nixon took an essentially passive role, the meeting served only to make explicit the philosophical differences between Rogers and me, exacerbated by personality clashes that did neither of us any credit. Nixon made plain his displeasure with Mrs. Gandhi; but to avoid unpleasantness he gave no operational orders. His advisers had barely left, however, when he characteristically ordered me to get John Connally and Mel Laird to get Rogers to follow the White House line. But since Rogers had heard no such words from Nixon, he was confirmed in his view that he was carrying out Presidential wishes and that I was pursuing my own course. Ziegler was instructed by Nixon to say that India's actions went "against the international trend" of trying to settle international differences peacefully. But the departments — unaware that everything Ziegler said needed the approval of Haldeman or Nixon — took this as another maneuver by me.

In these circumstances, more and more of our policy was pulled into the White House, where Nixon and I could control it. And by now the departments were only too happy to let us bear the responsibility and the almost certain blame whatever happened. We decided that the best hope to keep India from smashing West Pakistan was to increase the risk for Moscow that events on the subcontinent might jeopardize its summit plans with the United States; in that case the Kremlin might urge restraint on India. Therefore, a letter from Nixon to Brezhnev was delivered to Vorontsov on December 6. It stressed that the "spirit in which we agreed'' to a summit required "utmost restraint and most urgent action to end conflict and restore territorial integrity in the subcontinent"; an Indian "accomplished fact" would "long complicate the international situation," "undermine confidence" and have an "adverse effect on the whole range of other issues."

Late that evening, at eleven, we received a Soviet reply to my conversation with Vorontsov of the day before. Conciliatory in tone, it took the traditional stance of the side whose military operations are going favorably — it stalled. The Soviets denied that what happened on the subcontinent represented a watershed. In more elegant form it followed TASS's line of calling for a political solution in East Pakistan as a precondition for a cease-fire. And the Soviet definition of a political solution was identical with India's: immediate independence. Clearly, Moscow wanted the war to continue.

Nixon responded by ordering, on my recommendation, a slowdown in economic negotiations with Moscow. This was easier said than done. By now enough departments had developed a vested interest in East-West trade to seek to protect their turf if only by inertia in carrying out orders. The resistance was led by Secretary of Commerce Stans, who reflected the passionate view of many businessmen that profits should not be sacrificed to politics. On top of it, Stans — surely an ardent anti-Communist — fancied that he had established a good personal relationship with Soviet leaders which he was most reluctant to jeopardize for arcane diplomatic maneuvers thousands of miles away.

On December 7 Yahya informed us that East Pakistan was disintegrating. For us the day began with a *Washington Post* editorial sharply attacking Administration policy on the subcontinent, calling the aid cutoff of India "puzzling," "purely punitive," and its reasons "laughable." The *Post* came to this conclusion on the very day on which all further doubt was dispelled that the issue had gone far beyond self-determination for East Pakistan. A report reached us from a source whose reliability we had never had any reason to doubt and which I do not question today, to the effect that Prime Minister Gandhi was determined to reduce even West Pakistan to impotence: She had indicated that India would not accept any General Assembly call for a cease-fire until Bangladesh was "liberated"; after that, Indian forces would proceed with the "liberation" of the southern part of Azad Kashmir — the Pakistani part of Kashmir — and continue fighting until the Pakistani army and air force were wiped out. In other words, *West* Pakistan was to be dismembered and rendered defenseless. Mrs. Gandhi also told colleagues that if the Chinese "rattled the sword," the Soviets had promised to take appropriate counteraction.* Other intelligence indi-

---

* These reports of Indian deliberations — among the most important reasons for our policy — were published by Jack Anderson, but without apparent understanding of their significance.[8]

cated that this meant diversionary military action against China in Sinkiang. Pakistan — West Pakistan — could not possibly survive such a combination of pressures, and a Sino-Soviet war was not excluded.

Against this background I gave a press briefing that became highly controversial later. I did so because Rogers had prohibited State Department personnel from undertaking public briefings, because massive leaks sought to undermine what the President had repeatedly ordered, and because we needed to state a coherent case for our position. I sought to set out our reasoning, warn India while giving it assurances of basic goodwill, and try to convey to the Soviets that matters were getting serious. I denied that the Administration was "anti-Indian." I emphasized that we had not condoned the Pakistani repression in East Bengal in March 1971; military aid had been cut off and major efforts had been made to promote political accommodation between the Pakistani government and Bangladesh officials in Calcutta. Nevertheless, in our view India was responsible for the war. India, I pointed out, "either . . . could have given us a timetable or one could have waited for the return to civilian rule which was only three weeks away, to see whether that would bring about a change in the situation. . . ." We had concluded that "military action was taken, in our view, without adequate cause." India had spurned or ignored our overtures. I warned the Soviet Union that it had an obligation to act as a force for restraint, for "the attempt to achieve unilateral advantage sooner or later will lead to an escalation of tensions which must jeopardize the prospects of relaxation." [9] I believed then, and still do, that this represented an accurate statement of the record.

George Bush, on instructions, went a step farther at the UN, labeling India the aggressor. The resolution we supported in the General Assembly, calling for cease-fire and withdrawal of forces, won overwhelming support, passing, as I have pointed out, by 104 to 11. But neither our briefings nor the overwhelming expression of world opinion softened media or Congressional criticism. The *New York Times* ridiculed my argument that a political accommodation with Yahya had been attainable. The *Washington Post* continued to express its "serious reservations about Mr. Nixon's pro-Pakistan policy."

To us the issue was now to prevent the dismemberment of *West* Pakistan. I told the WSAG on December 8:

Let's now turn to the key issue. If India turns on West Pakistan, takes Azad Kashmir and smashes the Pak air and tank forces, a number of things seem inevitable. Should we, in full conscience, allow the liberation of the same disintegrating forces in West Pakistan as in the East? Baluchistan and other comparable issues are bound to come to the fore, as Mrs. Gandhi indicated to the President and as she told a Columbia University seminar in New York, I understand. Pakistan would be left defenseless and West Pakistan would be turned into a vassal state.

Climax: A Fateful Decision

FUNDAMENTALLY, our only card left was to raise the risks for the Soviets to a level where Moscow would see larger interests jeopardized. Recognizing this, Nixon suggested to me on the evening of December 8 that perhaps we should cancel the Moscow summit. This showed the degree of the President's displeasure; it did not necessarily mean that he wanted me to carry out his suggestion. The statement had the additional advantage of establishing an historical record of toughness. It might be used later to demonstrate that one's associates had wavered while one stood like a rock in a churning sea. I was to learn before the week was up that to take it literally ran a major risk of Presidential displeasure. But at this point I told Nixon that such a move was premature. We had not yet received Brezhnev's formal answer to the Presidential message of December 6. And once pushed into a corner publicly, the Soviets would have no further incentive to call a halt to the Indian assault on Pakistan. But I did favor stepping up the pressure, keeping the threat of canceling the summit in reserve: "The major problem now is that the Russians retain their respect for us," I said. "We have to prevent India from attacking West Pakistan; that's the major thing." If we did absolutely nothing, "we will trigger the Soviets into really tough actions." I made the same point to Helms: "If we do nothing we will surely lose. If we do something and do it daringly enough and do other simultaneous steps, we might get the Russians to call a halt to their games."

On December 9 we received Brezhnev's reply. It had its hopeful side, proposing a cease-fire and the resumption of negotiations between the parties in Pakistan at the point, the message said, where they had been interrupted. If the Soviets intended by this to urge that the parties return to the situation as of March 25, there was promise in it; this would provide a fig leaf in that negotiations could be said to *begin* within the framework of a united Pakistan even though the outcome of an independent Bangladesh was foreordained. Brezhnev also demanded negotiations with Mujib, which would take time to accomplish; this might be a device to play for time while we were exploring the meaning of the proposal with Moscow. And we had to make sure that India would not use the interval to carry out its intention to destroy West Pakistan.

That ominous possibility became more evident in a conversation between the Indian Ambassador and the Under Secretary of State. John Irwin called in Jha to seek assurances from India that it would not seize any territory in West Pakistan, including any part of Azad Kashmir. Jha responded that there was no intention of territorial annexation in the West; however, with respect to Azad Kashmir, he would have to ask New Delhi. (India had never recognized Kashmir as part of Pakistan, hence claiming it was not, in its view, dismembering West Pakistan.) The meeting concluded with Irwin's stressing that we were approaching a climactic moment in Indian-American relations.

There was no way Pakistan could survive the simultaneous loss of Bengal and Kashmir; all centrifugal forces would be unleashed. We used the December 9 visit of Soviet Minister of Agriculture Vladimir Matskevich with Agriculture Secretary Earl Butz as a pretext to underscore our grave view. To his surprise Matskevich was invited to meet with the President in the Oval Office. Bullet-headed, hearty, bubbling with innocent goodwill, Matskevich conveyed a personal greeting from Brezhnev, who was looking forward with anticipation to the Moscow summit. Nixon replied that all progress in US–Soviet relations was being threatened by the war on the subcontinent. We insisted on a cease-fire. If India moved forces against West Pakistan, the United States would not stand by. Nixon added: "The Soviet Union has a treaty with India; we have one with Pakistan. You must recognize the urgency of a cease-fire and political settlement of the crisis." Matskevich was in a splendid position to claim that such matters of high policy were outside his province; nor was Vorontsov, who accompanied him, able to enlighten us. Time was thus gained for a further Indian advance.

The tensions in our government surfaced on December 9 when Nixon, beside himself over press stories that senior US diplomats were opposing the President's "anti-Indian bias," called in the principal officials of the WSAG. He told them that while he did not insist on the State Department's being loyal to the President, it should be loyal to the United States. It was one of the emotional comments Nixon later regretted and that cost him so much support. The Department was being loyal to the United States by its lights; it happened to disagree with the President's policy and it was following the guidelines of its Secretary. As I told Alex Johnson, cables with instructions to Keating to criticize New Delhi took days to be drafted and cleared; cables to Islamabad criticizing Pakistan were miraculously dispatched in two hours.

The root fact, which few were willing to face, was that the Soviet Union and India could have ended the crisis (and our own domestic disputes) by one simple gesture. All we required to let matters take their course was an assurance that there would be no attack on West Pakistan and no amputation of Kashmir. The war in East Pakistan would have then wound down on its own momentum. The Indian forces, with a six-to-one margin of superiority, were clearly prevailing. But this assurance was precisely what India refused to give or the Soviet Union to encourage. Jha remained without instructions from New Delhi. Vorontsov brought no such word even after Nixon had personally intervened.

On December 10 we worked out with Yahya a new proposal to the United Nations, drawing upon Brezhnev's suggestion that negotiations be resumed where they had been broken off. Our proposal abandoned the demand for an Indian withdrawal; it called for a cease-fire and stand-still to be monitored by UN representatives both in the East and the West; as soon as the cease-fire took effect there would be negotiations directed at troop withdrawals and the satisfaction of Bengali aspirations. In short, Pakistan, in return for an end to Indian military operations in the West, was prepared to settle for the military status quo in the East (largely occupied by India by now) and to enter negotiations whose only possible outcome could be the emergence of an independent Bangladesh.

I submitted this proposal to Vorontsov during the morning of December 10. It was accompanied by a letter from Nixon to Brezhnev which stated that Brezhnev's proposals for the political solution in East Pakistan were in the process of being met. "This must now be followed by an immediate cease-fire in the West." Following the procedure in the Cienfuegos crisis, I read Vorontsov the aide-mémoire of November 5, 1962, in which the United States promised assistance to Pakistan in case of *Indian* aggression. I warned him that we would honor this pledge. Vorontsov was, of course, without instructions. Nor would we hear from him for forty-eight hours.

"In foreign policy," Bismarck once said, "courage and success do not stand in a causal relationship; they are identical." Nixon had many faults, but in crises he was conspicuously courageous. An aircraft-carrier task force that we had alerted previously was now ordered to move toward the Bay of Bengal, ostensibly for the evacuation of Americans but in reality to give emphasis to our warnings against an attack on West Pakistan. We held it east of the Strait of Malacca, about twenty-four hours' steaming distance from the Bay of Bengal, because I wanted to consult the Chinese before we made our next move. In explaining the purpose of the fleet movement to Mel Laird, I pointed out that we recognized the Indian occupation of East Pakistan as an accomplished fact; our objective was to scare off an attack on West Pakistan. (I did not add that we also wanted to have forces in place in case the Soviet Union pressured China.) As always in crises, Laird was staunch and supportive.

Before I could leave for New York and a secret meeting with Huang Hua, we received word that the Pakistani commander in East Pakistan was offering a cease-fire. The State Department was jubilant. At the daily WSAG, Alex Johnson discussed how to carry it out. I was disconcerted. A separate cease-fire in the East would run counter to what had just been proposed to the Soviets. It would settle the already declining war in the East, but it would magnify our principal worry by freeing the Indian army and air force for an all-out attack on West Pakistan. We knew that Mrs. Gandhi had ordered a rapid transfer of the Indian army to the West and all-out attack as soon as operations against East Pakistan were concluded. I called in Pakistani Ambassador Raza and urged him to make the cease-fire proposal consistent with what had been agreed to with Yahya. The WSAG agreed to do the same in formal channels. A cease-fire must include *both* East and West Pakistan; otherwise the danger to the West would mount as operations in Bengal concluded. Islamabad therefore pulled back its proposal for a cease-fire in the East temporarily. But it was clear that this gave us only a brief breathing space. Within a short time the Pakistan army in the East would be destroyed. Indian troops would be freed for their planned assault on West Pakistan. We absolutely had to bring matters to a head.

Huang Hua and I met around six o'clock in the CIA's walk-up apartment in the East Seventies. Its heavily mirrored walls and gaudy paintings suggested purposes other than a meeting between the representative of a puritanical Communist regime and the Assistant to the President trying to save the faraway country that had brought them together.

I briefed Huang Hua in great detail on our exchanges with all the parties, including the Soviets. I told him of our reliable information of Indian plans to destroy West Pakistan's armed forces. We had come to the reluctant conclusion that if Pakistan was to be saved from complete destruction we had to exert maximum political pressure for a standstill cease-fire along the lines of the scheme worked out with Yahya. No other course would prevent the planned Indian offensive against West Pakistan, the success of which was foreordained. We were doing our part by moving a carrier task force near the Strait of Malacca.

Huang Hua, obviously without instructions, took a hard line. He insisted that a cease-fire in place amounted to an objective collusion with the Soviets. Aggression was being rewarded. East Pakistan would have been sacrificed to superior force. We should not give up the principle of Indian withdrawal *prior* to negotiations. I replied sharply that if Pakistan and China insisted on such a position we would go along with it in our vote in the UN. It would, however, prove futile; it would play right into the hands of Indian and Soviet strategy to dismember *all* of Pakistan. Huang Hua now came to the real Chinese concern — that a precedent was being set by which other countries might be dismembered by Indian-Soviet collusion. I told him that the United States would not be indifferent to further Soviet moves. An attack on China especially would have grave consequences; indeed, this was why we had maintained so strong a stand in defiance of public opinion, Congress, and the bulk of our bureaucracy. We had even moved our fleet toward the threatened area. It was an extraordinary state of affairs; an active if tacit collaboration was developing with a country that we did not recognize. Huang Hua said he would inform Premier Chou En-lai of our views; he could tell me now, he added, that China would never stop fighting as long as it had a rifle in its armory; it would surely increase its assistance to Pakistan. I took this — as it turned out, wrongly — to be an indication that China might intervene militarily even at this late stage.

To increase the pressures on the Soviets for a cease-fire I had Haig call Vorontsov late on December 10 to tell him that the United States would taking strong measures, including fleet movements, if we did not soon receive a satisfactory reply to our proposal.

The next morning, still in New York City, I met for breakfast with Zulfikar Ali Bhutto, who had been appointed Deputy Prime Minister a few days before, in the elegant apartment of our UN Ambassador at the Waldorf Towers. Chinese wallpaper and discreet waiters made one nearly forget that eight thousand miles away the future of my guest's country hung by a thread. Elegant, eloquent, subtle, Bhutto was at last a representative who would be able to compete with the Indian leaders for public attention. He had had a checkered past. Architect of Pakistan's friendship with China at a time when American leaders regarded the People's Republic as a menace to world peace, he was not above playing a demagogic anti-American tune when it served his domestic purposes. The legacy of distrust engendered by his flamboyant demeanor and occasionally cynical conduct haunted Bhutto within our government throughout his political life. I found him brilliant, charming, of global stature in his perceptions. He could distinguish posturing from policy. He did not suffer fools gladly. Since he had many to contend with, this provided him with more than the ordinary share of enemies. He was not really comfortable with the plodding pace of Pakistan's military leaders. No doubt he was later carried away by excessive self-confidence in his manipulative skills. But in the days of his country's tragedy he held the remnant of his nation together and restored its self-confidence. In its hour of greatest need, he saved his country from complete destruction. He later brought himself down by excessive pride. But his courage and vision in 1971 should have earned him a better fate than the tragic end his passionate countrymen meted out to him and that blighted their reputation for mercy.

When we met on December 11 I told Bhutto that Pakistan would not be saved by mock-tough rhetoric; we had to develop a course of action that could be sustained. We had gone to the limit of what was possible: "It is not that we do not want to help you; it is that we want to preserve you. It is all very well to proclaim principles but finally we have to assure your survival." I urged him to work out a common position with the Chinese; we would not accept being buffeted by those we were trying to help. If it kept up, we would help pass formalistic UN resolutions but we would lose the ability to be effective. The next forty-eight hours would be decisive. We should not waste them in posturing for the history books, I said.

Bhutto was composed and understanding. He knew the facts as well as I; he was a man without illusions, prepared to do what was necessary, however painful, to save what was left of his country. The Chinese were confused, he said, by the evident schism in our government. They had heard too many conflicting statements during the week, ranging from the speech by George Bush charging Indian aggression to a State Department statement avowing strict neutrality. What should they believe? I told him that it was no secret that there were disagreements; there was equally no secret where Nixon and I stood, and the White House made the final decisions. It was his obligation to cooperate with those of us who wanted to save West Pakistan; we could not let our domestic opponents achieve their goals by confusing our friends. Bhutto and I finally agreed that if we did not hear from Moscow by noon the next day we would return the issue to the Security Council, taking as a pretext the imminent end of hostilities in East Pakistan. We would begin by demanding a cease-fire and Indian withdrawal, but we would settle for a simple cease-fire in place, in effect accepting the Indian fait accompli in Bengal. I had to count on Bhutto to make sure the Chinese understood our position.

Returning to Washington, I called Vorontsov to say that he had until noon on December 12 or we would proceed unilaterally. Vorontsov told me that Deputy Foreign Minister Vasily Kuznetsov had been dispatched to New Delhi to arrange for a satisfactory outcome and to urge Indian restraint. I told Nixon that this was probably true; the Indians needed no Soviet visitor to strengthen their determination to destroy Pakistan and Kuznetsov was known to us as a moderate professional. But whether the Soviets were pressing for a cease-fire or egging on the Indians, our course had to be the same: We had to increase the pressure until we were assured by India that there would be a cease-fire and no annexation in the West.

India was not yet prepared for either contingency. Foreign Minister Singh, now in New York, objected to returning the issue to the United Nations; and in the absence of a UN decision there could be no relevant cease-fire resolution. He forswore any territorial ambitions in West Pakistan but then conspicuously excepted Azad Kashmir as not recognized by India as part of Pakistan. Ambassador Jha at last returned a reply to Under Secretary Irwin's query of two days earlier as to Indian intentions. He, too, denied territorial ambitions, but he also left open India's options over Kashmir. Kashmir, he argued, belonged to India and the Pakistani part of it was illegally held. When all the soothing phrases were assembled, they amounted to careful evasions. India and the Soviet Union still refused to recognize the territorial status quo in the West; they deliberately kept open the possibility of the kind of annexation achievable only by the total destruction of the Pakistani army and the consequent disintegration of Pakistan.

Such was the situation when Nixon, Haig, and I met in the Oval Office on Sunday morning, December 12, just before Nixon and I were to depart for the Azores to meet with French President Pompidou. There was a sense of urgency. We expected some Chinese reaction to my conversation with Huang Hua. It was symptomatic of the internal relationships of the Nixon Administration that neither the Secretary of State nor of Defense nor any other representative of their departments attended this crucial meeting, where, as it turned out, the first decision to risk war in the triangular Soviet-Chinese-American relationship was taken.

Rogers had been at a NATO meeting when the war had spread to West Pakistan. Upon his return he had made plain his displeasure with the President's policy by prohibiting Joe Sisco from appearing on television to defend it. As usual, Nixon was prepared neither to confront his old friend nor to overrule him. And Rogers was not eager to get involved: The outcome of the crisis was not likely to be glorious; success would be the avoidance of catastrophe, hardly an achievement that invites acclaim.

So Nixon and I and Haig met in the Oval Office in the solitude that envelops all crises, amidst the conflicting pressures and conjectures and gradually building tensions that one knows will soon break, though not yet in what direction. Vorontsov interrupted with a phone call at 10:05 A.M. to tell us that the Soviet reply was on the way. It assured us that India had no aggressive designs in the West — but again was silent on the key point: its territorial aims in Kashmir. It was as compatible with a maneuver to gain time for a further fait accompli as with a genuine desire to settle. We decided that the best way to stress how gravely we took the crisis was for us to take it to the United Nations. This would give us an opportunity to stress the urgency of the situation as well as put forward our proposal of a standstill cease-fire.

Therefore at 11:30 A.M. we sent a message, drafted by Haig and me, on the Hot Line to Moscow to keep up the pressure. This was the first use of the Hot Line by the Nixon Administration.* Actually, we knew that this Moscow-Washington telegraphic link worked more slowly than did the communications of the Soviet Embassy. But it conferred a sense of urgency and might speed up Soviet decisions. The one-page Hot Line message declared that after waiting seventy-two hours for a Soviet response to the conversations with Vorontsov and Matskevich, the President had "set in train certain moves" in the UN Security Council that could not be reversed. "I must also note that the Indian assurances still lack any concreteness. I am still prepared to proceed along the lines set forth in my letter of December 10" — in other words, a standstill

---

* Brezhnev later made use of the Hot Line during the alert in the October 1973 Middle East War.

cease-fire and immediate negotiations. Nixon's message concluded: "I cannot emphasize too strongly that time is of the essence to avoid consequences neither of us want."

Just when we had finished dispatching the Hot Line message to Moscow, we received word that Huang Hua needed to see me with an urgent response from Peking. It was unprecedented, the Chinese having previously always saved their messages until *we* asked for a meeting — this was one of the charming Middle Kingdom legacies. We assumed that only a matter of gravity could induce them into such a departure. We guessed that they were coming to the military assistance of Pakistan, as I thought Huang Hua, forty-eight hours earlier, had hinted they might. If so, we were on the verge of a possible showdown. For if China moved militarily, the Soviet Union — according to all our information — was committed to use force against China. We would then have to decide whether to assist a country that until a year earlier had been considered our most implacable enemy.

Nixon understood immediately that if the Soviet Union succeeded in humiliating China, all prospects for world equilibrium would disappear. He decided — and I fully agreed — that if the Soviet Union threatened China we would not stand idly by. A country which we did not recognize and with which we had had next to no contact for two decades would, at least in this circumstance, obtain some significant assistance — the precise nature to be worked out when the circumstances arose. Nixon made this decision without informing either his Secretary of State or Secretary of Defense; it was not an ideal way to manage crises. Since Nixon and I were both leaving for the Azores, Al Haig and Win Lord would have to go to New York to receive the Chinese message. If the message contained what we both suspected and feared, Haig was instructed to reply to the Chinese that we would not ignore Soviet intervention. To provide some military means to give effect to our strategy and to reinforce the message to Moscow, Nixon now ordered the carrier task force to proceed through the Strait of Malacca and into the Bay of Bengal.

It now became urgent to determine Soviet intentions and at the same time convince them that we meant business. At 11:45 A.M. I phoned Vorontsov to tell him of the Hot Line message and of the projected fleet movements, but also of our continued willingness to cooperate along the lines of the President's letter to Brezhnev — that is to say, accept a standstill cease-fire. We were returning the issue to the Security Council but were prepared to conduct the UN debate in a conciliatory manner. The choice was up to the Soviet Union. Vorontsov suggested that, based on his reports from Kuznetsov, we were working for the same objectives. He hoped that by the time the Security Council met the Soviet efforts in New Delhi would have borne fruit. I told him that time was running out.

At noon, Ron Ziegler announced that in view of India's continuing defiance of the overwhelming General Assembly call for a cease-fire, the United States was now returning the issue to the Security Council. He warned: "With East Pakistan virtually occupied by Indian troops a continuation of the war would take on increasingly the character of armed attack on the very existence of a member state of the United Nations."

In the event, the Chinese message was not what we expected. On the contrary, it accepted the UN procedure and the political solution I had outlined to Huang Hua forty-eight hours earlier — asking for a cease-fire and withdrawal, but settling for a standstill cease-fire. Chou En-lai's analysis was the same as ours. Amazingly, Pakistan, China, and — if Vorontsov could be believed — the Soviet Union, were now working in the same direction under our aegis. But Nixon did not know this when he made his lonely and brave decision. Had things developed as we anticipated, we would have had no choice but to assist China in some manner against the probable opposition of much of the government, the media, and the Congress. And we were still in the middle of the Vietnam war. History's assessment of Nixon, whatever its conclusions, must not overlook his courage and patriotism in making such a decision, at risk to his immediate political interest, to preserve the world balance of power for the ultimate safety of all free peoples.

When we received the Chinese message we held up the fleet's movement for twenty-four hours to give Moscow an opportunity to reply to our Hot Line message. It came in, also over the Hot Line, at 5 A.M. on December 13 while the President and I were in the Azores. It repeated what Vorontsov had already told us: The Soviets were "conducting a clarification of all the circumstances in India." They would inform us of the results without delay. Thus, the issue was left exactly as George Bush had defined it, on our instructions, in the Security Council the night before:

The question now arises as to India's further intentions. For example, does India intend to use the present situation to destroy the Pakistan army in the West? Does India intend to use as a pretext the Pakistan counterattacks in the West to annex territory in West Pakistan? Is its aim to take parts of Pakistan-controlled Kashmir contrary to the Security Council resolutions of 1948, 1949, and 1950? If this is not India's intention, then a prompt disavowal is required. The world has a right to know: What are India's intentions? Pakistan's aims have become clear: It has accepted the General Assembly's resolution passed by a vote of 104 to 11. My government has asked this question of the Indian Government several times in the last week. I regret to inform the Council that India's replies have been unsatisfactory and not reassuring.

Our fleet passed through the Strait of Malacca into the Bay of Bengal and attracted much media attention. Were we threatening India? Were we seeking to defend East Pakistan? Had we lost our minds? It was in fact sober calculation. We had some seventy-two hours to bring the war to a conclusion before West Pakistan would be swept into the mael- strom. It would take India that long to shift its forces and mount an as- sault. Once Pakistan's army and air force were destroyed, its impotence would guarantee the country's eventual disintegration. We had to give the Soviets a warning that matters might get out of control on our side too. We had to be ready to back up the Chinese if at the last moment they came in after all, our UN initiative having failed. The Kremlin needed an excuse to accelerate the pressures it claimed it was exerting on India. However unlikely an American military move against India, the other side could not be sure; it might not be willing to accept even the minor risk that we might act irrationally. It was also the best means to split the Soviet Union and India. Moscow was prepared to harass us; it was in our judgment not prepared to run military risks. Moving the carrier task force into the Bay of Bengal committed us to no final act, but it created precisely the margin of uncertainty needed to force a decision by New Delhi and Moscow.

On December 14 at 3:00 A.M., Vorontsov came in to hand Al Haig a formal Soviet note. A nine-page handwritten memorandum professed to see a "considerable rapprochement of our positions." It reported "firm assurances by the Indian leadership that India has no plans of seizing West Pakistani territory." This was some small progress but it still begged the principal question of whether India considered Pakistani-held Kashmir as Pakistani territory. And it was silent on the subject of a cease-fire. Nor was anything heard from India. And if there was not a cease-fire soon, the Indian army would be in a position to turn on West Pakistan and thus make all our discussions academic.

This is why on the return flight from the Azores I said on background to the press pool on *Air Force One* that Soviet conduct on the subconti- nent was not compatible with the mutual restraint required by genuine coexistence. If it continued, we would have to reevaluate our entire rela- tionship, including the summit. I had not cleared that last point specifi- cally with Nixon. I had assumed it reflected his thinking since he had himself mentioned this to me on December 8. The threat to cancel the summit caused the *Washington Post* to break the background rules and identify me as the speaker, in the name of the "people's right to know." This was a temporary fit of doctrinal puritanism from which the *Post* afterward recovered in order to be invited to later backgrounders.

The resulting hullabaloo occupied much of December 15. Though there were frantic disavowals at State and even some public backtrack- ing by Ron Ziegler, the message got through to Moscow, which had by then learned that my voice reflected the probable course of the Presi- dent's thinking. (Indeed, if my critics in the bureaucracy had analyzed the situation, they would have known that I could not have survived, much less prevailed, on any other condition.) Vorontsov appeared several times with increasingly urgent, soothing comments and requests for reassurances. By the next morning, December 16, we were receiving reliable reports that Kuznetsov was in fact pressing New Delhi to accept the territorial status quo in the West, including in Kashmir.

Late in the day on December 15, the commander of the outnumbered Pakistani forces in the East again offered a cease-fire. He had held out five days longer than we thought possible when the first cease-fire offer was put forward on December 10. The resistance of his forces had given us the time to mount the pressures that prevented the onslaught on West Pakistan.

Next day Mrs. Gandhi offered an unconditional cease-fire in the West. There is no doubt in my mind that it was a reluctant decision resulting from Soviet pressure, which in turn grew out of American insistence, including the fleet movement and the willingness to risk the summit. This knowledge stood us in good stead when Vietnam exploded four months later. It was also Chou En-lai's judgment, as he later told Bhutto, that we had saved West Pakistan. The crisis was over. We had avoided the worst — which is sometimes the maximum statesmen can achieve.

The Aftermath

THE India-Pakistan war of 1971 was perhaps the most complex issue of Nixon's first term. Not that emotions ran as high as on Vietnam, or that its effects were very long-lasting, though the "tilt toward Pakistan" entered the polemic folklore as a case history of political misjudgment. What made the crisis so difficult was that the stakes were so much greater than the common perception of them. The issue burst upon us while Pakistan was our only channel to China; we had no other means of communication with Peking. A major American initiative of fundamental importance to the global balance of power could not have survived if we colluded with the Soviet Union in the public humiliation of China's friend — and our ally. The naked recourse to force by a partner of the Soviet Union backed by Soviet arms and buttressed by Soviet assurances threatened the very structure of international order just when our whole Middle East strategy depended on proving the inefficacy of such tactics and when America's weight as a factor in the world was already being undercut by our divisions over Indochina. The assault on Pakistan was in our view a most dangerous precedent for Soviet behavior, which had to be resisted if we were not to tempt escalating upheavals. Had we acquiesced in such a power play, we would have sent a wrong signal to Moscow and unnerved all our allies, China, and the forces for restraint in other volatile areas of the world. This was, indeed, why the Soviets had made the Indian assault on Pakistan possible in the first place.

But an essentially geopolitical point of view found no understanding among those who conducted the public discourse on foreign policy in our country. (By "geopolitical" I mean an approach that pays attention to the requirements of equilibrium.) This dramatized one of the root dilemmas of the foreign policy of the Nixon Administration. Nixon and I wanted to found American foreign policy on a sober perception of permanent national interest, rather than on fluctuating emotions that in the past had led us to excesses of both intervention and abdication. We judged India by the impact of its actions, not by its pretensions or by the legacy of twenty years of sentiment. But our assessments depended on conjecture about the wider consequences of India's assault. To shape events one must act on the basis of assessments that cannot be proved correct when they are made. All the judgments we reached about the implications of an assault on Pakistan were undemonstrable. By the time the implications were clear it would be too late; indeed, there might then be another dispute as to what had actually produced them.

The majority of informed opinion sought to judge the confrontation on the subcontinent on the merits of the issues that had produced the crisis. Pakistan had unquestionably acted unwisely, brutally, and even immorally, though on a matter which under international law was clearly under its domestic jurisdiction. But even here, I would have to say we had an assessment of the facts different from that of our critics. I remain convinced to this day that Mrs. Gandhi was not motivated primarily by conditions in East Pakistan; many solutions to its inevitable autonomy existed, several suggested by us. Rather, encouraged by the isolation of Pakistan, the diplomatic and military support of the Soviet Union, the domestic strains in China, and the divisions in the United States, the Indian Prime Minister decided in the spring or summer of 1971 to use the opportunity to settle accounts with Pakistan once and for all and assert India's preeminence on the subcontinent. Her delay until November was to allow military training and preparations to be completed and to wait until winter snows in the Himalayas complicated Chinese access. After that decision, every concession by Pakistan was used as a starting point for a new demand escalating the requirements and shortening the time span for a response to the point that showdown was inevitable. We had no national interest to prevent self-determination for East Pakistan — indeed, we put forward several schemes to bring it about — but we had a stake in the process by which it occurred. We wanted it to be achieved by evolution, not by a traumatic shock to a country in whose survival the United States, China, and the world community (as shown in repeated UN votes) *did* feel a stake, or by a plain violation of the rules by which the world must conduct itself if it is to survive. India struck in late November; by the timetable that we induced Yahya to accept, martial law would have ended and a civilian government would have taken power at the end of December. This would almost surely have led to the autonomy and independence of East Pakistan — probably without the excesses of brutality, including public bayoneting, in which the Indian-trained guerrillas, the Mukti Bahini, engaged when they in turn terrorized Dacca.

If shortsighted and repressive domestic policies are used to justify foreign military intervention, the international order will soon be deprived of all restraints. In the name of morality we were lambasted for having supported the losing side and offended the winner — an interesting "moral" argument, not to mention that, historically, prudence and equilibrium usually suggest siding with the weaker to deter the stronger. After three years of harassment for insufficient dedication to peace, we were now challenged by one liberal columnist with the mind-boggling argument that war could not always be considered an evil because sometimes it was the instrument for change.[10] The principle seemed to be that if Richard Nixon was for peace, war could not be all bad.

There is in America an idealistic tradition that sees foreign policy as a contest between evil and good. There is a pragmatic tradition that seeks to solve "problems" as they arise. There is a legalistic tradition that treats international issues as juridical cases. There is no geopolitical tradition. All the strands of our international experience ran counter to what we were trying to accomplish on the subcontinent in the autumn of 1971. India had much sympathy as the world's most populous democracy; the problem to be "solved" was self-determination for East Pakistan; the "case" should be turned over to the United Nations, as Rogers never tired of pointing out. Our geopolitical concerns were given no credence and were attributed to personal pique, anti-Indian bias, callousness toward suffering, or inexplicable immorality.

Had we followed these recommendations, Pakistan, after losing its eastern wing, would have lost Kashmir and possibly Baluchistan and other portions of its western wing — in other words, it would have totally disintegrated. We maneuvered with some skill — and considering the few cards we held, considerable daring — to avert disasters. We succeeded in confining the impact of the conflict to the subcontinent. The Indian power play did not shake the foundations of our foreign policy and wreck our China initiative as it well might have, and as the Soviets undoubtedly hoped it would. But since there was no general recognition of these dangers, we could expect little understanding of our motivation.

Instead, attention focused on costs. We believed they would prove as temporary as they were unavoidable. We did not think that we had per-

manently jeopardized our relations with India or driven India irrevocably to the Soviet side, as was so often and passionately claimed. Nor
could we ever have competed with what the Soviet Union offered India
for this crisis: six years of weaponry while we embargoed arms to both
sides, military threats against Peking to deter Chinese interference, and
two vetoes in the Security Council blocking a cease-fire and UN peacekeeping efforts. We could not have outbid the USSR in this dimension — nor do I recall any of our domestic critics recommending that
we attempt to do so. Just as our wooing for two decades had not managed to tempt India out of its nonalignment, so India was unlikely to
move irrevocably to one side as a result of our defending our own interests. Nonalignment enabled India to navigate the international passage
with a maximum number of options. For that reason we were convinced
that India would sooner or later seek a rapprochement with us again if
only to keep Moscow from taking it for granted. When the immediate
crisis was over I reminded Dobrynin of a comment by the Austrian minister Schwarzenberg after Russian troops had helped put down the Hungarian revolt of 1848: "Some day we will amaze the world by the depth
of our ingratitude."

And this is exactly what happened. After the crisis, US–Indian relations returned quite rapidly to their previous state of frustrated incomprehension within a framework of compatible objectives. We were
not so fortunate as to be spared the usual hectoring, but within three
years US–Indian joint commissions were working on cooperative projects in a variety of economic and cultural fields. T. N. Kaul, the
Foreign Secretary who venomously pushed the policy of confrontation
in 1971, was sent to Washington as Ambassador with the assignment to
repair relations — a task to which he devoted himself with the same
single-mindedness that had characterized India's implacable dismemberment of Pakistan in 1971.

Nixon put it well when he told Prime Minister Heath in Bermuda on
December 20, after the crisis was over, what we had tried to accomplish:

I felt that if it was true that her [Mrs. Gandhi's] goal was to force Pakistan to
surrender in the West, there would be serious repercussions on the world scene.
It could be a lesson for other parts of the world. . . . The Soviets have tested us
to see if they could control events. Of course you have to consider the much
bigger stakes in the Middle East and Europe. Part of the reason for conducting
our Vietnam withdrawal so slowly is to give some message that we are not
prepared to pay *any* price for ending a war; we must now ask ourselves what
we are willing to pay to avert war. If we are not, we have tough days ahead.

Nixon's view, with which I agreed, was not shared by the media, our
bureaucracy, or the Congress. I still believe it was correct. The crisis

also demonstrated the error of the myth that Nixon, aided by me, exercised an octopuslike grip over a government that was kept in ignorance of our activities. On some initiatives — especially in the realm of bilateral negotiations — this was true. But in other areas Nixon's methods in part resulted from the fractiousness of the bureaucracy and in part from his own reluctance to discipline the bureaucracy. As so often, the handling of the India-Pakistan crisis reflected deep divisions within our government that were compounded by Nixon's indirection in conveying his views. The upshot was the opposite of the folklore: not widening White House dominance but bitter departmental rearguard resistance; not clear-cut directives but elliptical maneuvers to keep open options; not the inability of the agencies to present their views but the difficulty faced by the Chief Executive in making his views prevail. That these conditions reflected some of Nixon's psychological peculiarities does not change the fundamental conclusion. The history of the "tilt" is less a tale of Presidential self-will than of the complexity of managing a modern government — especially by a President unwilling to lay down the law directly. Who was right in this dispute is irrelevant; Presidents must be able to count on having their views accepted even if these run counter to bureaucratic preconceptions. I have repeatedly stated that the administrative practices of the Nixon Administration were unwise and not sustainable in the long run; fairness requires an admission that they did not take place in a vacuum.

The crisis was no sooner over than the White House found itself in the vortex of a storm of leaks and denunciations. As early as December 13, the columnist Jack Anderson began to publish excerpts from Defense Department notes of WSAG meetings. Our opposition to India's military action — our *public* position, for which we were indeed attacked — was held to be a startling revelation that proved us liars when we denied an anti-Indian bias. Reams of other classified information sprouted in the newspapers — cables from Kenneth Keating in India, for example, which urged pressure on Yahya or disputed my December 7 backgrounder.[11] The movements of our fleet, which are as a rule secret, found their way instantly into print. Rogers gave vent to years of frustration by contradicting my remarks on *Air Force One* and announcing at a press conference on December 23 that the Moscow summit was by no means impaired by events on the subcontinent. He also denied that we had any kind of military commitment to Pakistan if threatened by India — which was a fine lawyer's point. And the investigation of the leaks revealed that a Navy yeoman who had served as a clerk on my staff had systematically copied NSC documents entrusted to him and passed them on to his superiors at the Pentagon.

Nixon could be as petty in calm periods as he was bold in crises, as small-minded in dealing with his associates as he could be farsighted in defense of the national interest. After the first flush of elation over Mrs. Gandhi's cease-fire, Nixon gave strict orders that all briefings emphasize his central role. But as the criticism mounted, he began to look for ways to get out of the line of fire. No doubt he was influenced in part by an understandable resentment that I had received what he considered exorbitant credit for the foreign policy successes of the Administration, while all the blame for its harsher measures had fallen on him. But the proximate cause was the summit. Though Nixon had talked of canceling the summit on December 8 and was to do so again on December 16, my actually mentioning it to the press on December 14 triggered all his ambivalences. He had his heart set on completing the journey that Eisenhower had planned in 1960 but never accomplished. It meant a great deal to him to be the first American President in Moscow. Though he formally backed me, he was not in fact willing to jeopardize that coup. The result was an effort by the White House public relations experts to deflect onto me the attack on our conduct during the India-Pakistan crisis. The policy became *my* policy. For several weeks Nixon was unavailable to me. Ziegler made no statement of support, nor did he deny press accounts that I was out of favor. The departments were not admonished to cease their leaking against me. Nixon could not resist the temptation of letting me twist slowly, slowly in the wind, to use the literary contribution of a later period. It was a stern lesson in the dependence of Presidential Assistants on their chief. I did not take kindly — or even maturely — to my first experience of sustained public criticism and Presidential pressures.

And then suddenly it was all over. The crisis on the subcontinent did not linger and so there was no focal point for festering criticism. I was soon enough returned to favor with the President and we resumed our previous wary relationship — close on substance, aloof personally. There was other business to turn to. The basic structure of our foreign policy was intact. Planning for both summits was soon resumed. A string of spectacular foreign policy successes soon wiped out the episode and gained popular support. Peking had learned that we took seriously the requirements of the balance of power; Moscow had seen a sufficiently strong reaction not to be tempted to test us in areas of more central concern. We had survived the storm with the rudder intact. We could resume our course.

XXII

Crisis in the Alliance:
The Mansfield Amendment and the
Economic Confrontation

Mediterranean Journey

ALL Presidential trips are inevitably presented as grand exercises in diplomacy. Nobody who has traveled with Presidents can take the description seriously for most such journeys. Diplomacy operates through deadlock, which is one way by which two sides can test each other's determination. Even if they have the egos for it, few heads of government have the time to resolve stalemates; their meetings are too short and the demands of protocol too heavy. Hence, trips by heads of government usually find their principal justification in creating a symbolism, in setting deadlines for lower-level negotiations, and in permitting leaders to take each other's measure. They are also a way to demonstrate intentions and to emphasize a commitment.

There is, of course, a narrower political bonus. To say that Nixon in deciding on his second European trip was unaware of the glow it might cast on the forthcoming Congressional elections would be to deny him the qualities that led him to the Presidency. He had, after all, strenuously sought a Soviet summit for this period, and he was briefly tempted by a meeting with the heads of government of Britain, France, and the Federal Republic that had been proposed by Willy Brandt to give impetus and sanction to *Ostpolitik*. Pompidou had balked because he wanted to avoid the implication that Brandt was negotiating on behalf of the West as a whole. And Nixon's views on *Ostpolitik,* described earlier, did not make him eager to endorse it so dramatically. The trip, therefore, was built around visits to Italy, Yugoslavia, Spain, and Ireland, plus an overnight stop with the Sixth Fleet and a luncheon meeting with the new British Prime Minister, Edward Heath, at Chequers. The Mediterranean focus, and the stay with the Sixth Fleet, emphasized our continuing determination to play a role in the security and evolution of the area. Soviet influence in the Middle East had been growing since

1967. We had just gone through the autumn of crises along the Suez Canal and in Jordan. Libya had been taken over by a radical regime.

Nixon's journey began in Rome on September 27, 1970, where I joined him after my meeting with Xuan Thuy in Paris. By that fall Italian politics were in the throes of one of those convoluted maneuvers which to an outsider seemed a routine change of government but which in fact amounted to an acceleration of the leftward trend characteristic of Italian politics since the "opening to the left" in 1963. When Nixon had visited Italy in 1969 Mariano Rumor had been Prime Minister in a government composed entirely of Christian Democrats but governing with the tactical support of the Socialists. During the "hot autumn" of 1969 the Communist-dominated trade unions made their strength felt in a series of violent strikes often winding up as riots. The unions succeeded in getting passed the so-called Workers' Statute, which in addition to relieving many injustices also shifted the balance of power in labor negotiations decisively toward the unions. West European Communists had not yet discovered the virtues of NATO; both of Nixon's visits to Italy were greeted by Communist-sponsored riots directed against NATO, Vietnam, and, for good measure, the President.

The Italian regional elections in June had temporarily halted the Communist progress but had produced new frictions within the governing coalition. The Socialists, having gained slightly, interpreted their success as an endorsement of a move farther to the left, all the more so as the parties on the right were routed. The Christian Democrats were in disarray, torn between a left wing separated from the Communists largely by religious faith and a right wing split from the neo-Fascists primarily by democratic convictions. The Communists with their disciplined organization were tilting the entire spectrum to the left. They were following the strategy of their theorist Antonio Gramsci, which was systematically to infiltrate the key institutions of the society — trade unions, the judiciary, schools — before a final push to obtain participation in government.

On July 7 Rumor resigned and Emilio Colombo became Prime Minister of a four-party coalition (Christian Democrats, Republicans, Social Democrats, and Socialists). Aldo Moro was Foreign Minister. The government itself was short-lived; the coalition was not. The "opening to the left" had prospered to a point where it was no longer possible to govern without the Socialists. And the Socialists in turn were loath to open too wide a gulf between themselves and the Communists, with whom they were in coalition in many provincial governments. The Communists thus had a growing, if indirect, influence on the Italian government — a result exactly opposite to what the fathers of the "opening to the left" intended. So much influence, in fact, that in time the wily Moro decided that he could use the Communists to emasculate the Socialists. If tacit Communist acquiescence was needed in any event, it might as well be formalized. The Communist influence therefore graduated from a tacit to a formal veto under Moro's sponsorship.

These trends seemed obvious to me then, but they were hotly contested inside and outside the United States government. It was felt either that Communist influence was not in fact growing or that it might not be a bad thing if it were because it might shock the Christian Democrats into reform. At any rate, there was nothing concrete to be done about it. Christian Democratic political leaders seemed convinced that periodic visits by leading Americans confirmed Italy's international importance and thus strengthened their own prospects. We were happy enough to oblige: Nixon's visit had that point and so did some of my own later on when I was Secretary of State. I never saw any evidence that Presidential or high-level visits affected Italian politics one way or the other. But then it is difficult to prove the negative — no one knows by how much the leftward trend would have accelerated if the absence of such visits had been construed as American neglect.

The general sense of impotence was reflected in a State Department memorandum to the President of January 22, 1970, which I later saved in a file of vacuous recommendations: It urged that we "keep the problem under close scrutiny and continually assess the means of using our resources to make our view known in a discreet, but effective fashion." On how to be both discreet and effective the author was prudently silent. In fairness to him I had no better idea. There are problems that are out of the control of American policymakers. The best they can do in some situations is not to accelerate unfavorable trends by proclaiming the probable outcome as the desirable one. (This was, in my view, the error of the "opening to the left" in 1963 and the flirtation with Eurocommunism in 1977.)

We arrived in Rome at night to a reception ceremony held for security reasons in the courtyard of the Quirinale Palace. Colorful lancers on horseback were lined up in neat rows as the national anthems were played. The charming Italian anthem is probably the least martial-sounding one in the world; it is not easy to go forth to battle to the strains of what sounds almost like a waltz. After the ceremony chaos descended. The Quirinale, the former summer residence of the Pope, is one of the largest structures of its kind in Europe. Throngs of reporters and officials pushed us every which way, inspiring panic with the realization that if one headed down the wrong corridor one might not be found again for weeks. Finally, the mob converged on the central point of a large reception hall. Nixon and I were culled out to be reunited with President Saragat for a first, private review of the world situation.

Giuseppe Saragat was the most impressive by far of the Italian leaders — thoughtful, decisive, and a good friend of the United States.

Unfortunately, he suffered from two handicaps. His party, the Social Democrats, was atrophying under the impact of the "opening to the left" and its declining control of the levers of power. And his constitutional position as head of state prevented him from active participation in the policy process despite his considerable moral influence. But his opinions were always worth hearing. Saragat was concerned about the growth of Communist influence. He thought it an illusion to believe that Communist gains would be confined to his country; if not arrested they would surely spread elsewhere in Europe. But he offered no remedies. He implied there must be some deus ex machina that the United States could conjure up.

He was eloquent about the psychological impact of American actions on Europe. Our domestic debates on Vietnam were undermining European confidence in our stability and steadiness; this would affect politics in many European countries. *Ostpolitik* made Saragat uneasy; it was a way for the Federal Republic to seek a separate deal with Moscow; it had been triggered in part by diminished American credibility. The United States should be careful that détente with the Soviet Union appear to result from strength, or else all of Europe would follow the German example.

This gave Nixon an opportunity to proclaim his commitment to NATO; he did not spare hyperbole. He was prepared to risk his political life on that issue and he did not intend to "die easily." It was an eloquent phrase, though perhaps some dramatic license had been taken with the choices before us. Nixon faced nothing like the stark alternatives he painted. NATO was the one pillar of our foreign policy that still had some domestic constituency; most neo-isolationists proclaimed their devotion to it while attacking our involvement everywhere else. There was no possibility of Nixon's dying over that issue. When the meeting was expanded to include foreign ministers, Nixon eloquently reiterated his beliefs: "If we allow this great Alliance to fail, if we allow it to become fragmented, not because of the lack of economic capacity to defend our interests but because of the lack of will, determination, intelligence and leadership to maintain it and strength it, this would be a tragedy for mankind." Nixon had posed the right issue. It was the will to renew faith in democracy that was being challenged in too many countries, in the riots, bitterness, and divisions of the early 1970s.

The precision of the discussions did not improve at the state guest house, the Villa Madama, on another of Rome's hills. The meeting here illustrated the fundamental obstacles to a genuine dialogue. Italian politics — which concerned us most — were outside the purview of formal discussions. In turn, foreign policy issues seemed to the Italian leaders subsidiary to their internal dilemma and irrelevant because they were outside Italy's capacity to affect. It was no accident that the discussions grew more banal as the circle of participants expanded.

The procedure followed that of the Quirinale. There was first a private meeting between Prime Minister Colombo and Nixon, attended only by interpreters (part of the time I sat in as note-taker). It was followed by a very large meeting of practically the entire official party on each side. The private meeting was needed to pretend that the Italian Prime Minister has executive authority comparable to the United States President or even the British Prime Minister. But he has not, except in the rarest of circumstances. Italian Prime Ministers are chairmen of a coalition of many autonomous forces; they reflect a political equilibrium, not an executive authority. They proceed not by decision but by compromise. In this respect the Italian government is rather similar to the Japanese, though it is more likely to split its differences than to resolve them by consensus. And Colombo, in any event, was clearly an interim figure. He was a facade behind which the much more powerful Moro was preparing in his indirect, almost imperceptible manner the fundamental changes that were to bring the Communist Party close to the seats of power while the Christian Democrats were seeking to pull its revolutionary sting. The session was rescued from total irrelevance when the President was told that some of the hostages of the hijacking that had triggered the Jordan crisis (see Chapter XV) were passing through Rome. On the spur of the moment it was decided that Nixon and Colombo should helicopter to the airport to express their satisfaction at the rescue — leaving their associates to continue in amicable social banter.

All these meetings were squeezed into one morning because the schedulers had arranged for a visit to the Vatican in the afternoon, whence the President proposed to depart for the Sixth Fleet. This led to a series of incidents that unintentionally let loose one of Nixon's obsessions and caused unending discomfiture to the White House staff.

The President of Italy gave a luncheon in the tower room of the Quirinale Palace, overlooking the lush roofs and beautifully proportioned squares of the Eternal City. In this glorious setting, because of the President's tight schedule, an exquisite meal was served in about fifty-five minutes — proving to Nixon that one of his obsessions was clearly capable of fulfillment. For nearly two years his associates had heard him complain about the ineffable boredom of state dinners. He had cajoled and threatened to speed up the serving of White House meals in order to reduce the time he had to spend in small talk with his visitors. He had given personal attention to those courses that expedited service, and those that might be eliminated altogether. On some occasions he had even arranged for the interpreter to arrive late, as a means of cutting down the time for conversation. But the fastest service he had ever attained, even under the merciless prodding of Haldeman — the world record for White House dinners, so to speak — was an hour and twenty minutes. The Quirinale luncheon set a new standard that he never per-

mitted the White House staff to forget. Alas, like many Roman achievements, it proved impossible to emulate. Even Haldeman could not succeed in reducing the White House service by more than another ten
minutes. The Quirinale retained the speed-in-serving championship by a
good fifteen minutes, to the perpetual and vocal annoyance of the President.

The visit to the Vatican provided an opportunity for a review of the
international situation with one of the most sensitive and thoughtful men
I encountered in my public service: Pope Paul VI. The Holy Father
headed a Church thrust into ferment by the tremendous reforms of his
predecessor. But John XXIII had died after shaking up the existing
framework; he had not yet settled on the ultimate direction his changes
would take. This was left to Paul VI. He had served in the Vatican
diplomatic service for many years; he understood very well that change
can gain its own momentum and transmute the intentions of reformers.
Saints prevail by the purity of their motives; institutions are sustained by
durable standards. Pope Paul VI in many ways symbolized the travail of
his era. Better than almost any leading figure I encountered, he understood the moral dilemmas of a period in which tyranny marched under
the banners of freedom, and how "reform" ran the risk of creating
soulless bureaucracies. He struggled to retain a margin for conscience
and human dignity. He felt deeply the anguish of a time in need of both
rapid transformation and enduring moral verities. Although he yearned
for peace, it was never at the price of justice. Pope Paul was not free of
foreboding, but he was too sustained by faith to give in to his premonitions. He struggled to ease suffering in a world in some ways too gross
for his subtle intelligence and sensitivity, making him reluctant to tackle
frontally some of the trends he understood only too well. I never was in
his presence without being moved and humbled by the incommensura-
bility between the time frames of political leaders concerned with the
attainable and that of an institution committed to the eternal.

Pope Paul had wide and informed knowledge of international affairs.
He and Nixon reviewed the world with general agreement. At one point
Nixon was waxing eloquent about the leftward trend of priests in Latin
America. The Holy Father interrupted him gently, with a smile: "As a
matter of fact, Mr. President, this is even more of a problem for us than
it is for you."

The visit to the Vatican led to one of those scenes that are comic in
retrospect but mortifying when experienced. Our advance men had conceived the extraordinary idea that the President should leave for the
Sixth Fleet directly from St. Peter's Square in a US military helicopter.
The Curia, feeling that this represented enough martial trappings for one
day, tactfully suggested that the Secretary of Defense not be included in
the general audience that the Holy Father would offer to the members of

the President's party after his private audience with Nixon. The schedule was made accordingly, and Mel Laird was not with the group that engaged in separate talks while the Pope and Nixon were secluded. However, to exclude a practicing politician of Laird's ingenuity from a papal audience required more than the distribution of a printed schedule. As the official party was moving into the papal chamber for the general audience, Laird suddenly appeared, chewing on his ubiquitous cigar. Asked what he was doing there, he mumbled something about looking for the helicopters, though it was not clear what he thought these might be doing *inside* the Vatican when they were so conspicuously parked on either side of the obelisk in St. Peter's Square at the entrance to the Vatican. I urged Laird at least to do away with the cigar while we were in the papal presence.

The American group was placed into two rows at right angles to Nixon and the Holy Father, who were seated side by side. The Pope was making a graceful little speech when suddenly smoke came pouring out of the pocket of Laird's suit. Laird attempted to quell the fire caused by his cigar, at first inconspicuously, but he finally gave up and started slapping his side. Some of the others whose angle of vision prevented them from grasping the full drama of the Secretary of Defense immolating himself in front of the Pope took Laird's efforts at fire-extinguishing as applause, into which they joined. Only wisdom accumulated over two millennia enabled the Vatican officials to pretend that nothing unusual was going on and thus permit events to reach their planned conclusion.

One bizarre interlude succeeded another. As on all of Nixon's foreign trips, what the advance man's manual described as "photo opportunities" had to be created and scheduled so that pictures could make the evening television shows. And there was an implacable demand for color and crowd scenes. Lashed on by Haldeman, whose comprehension of the concept of sovereignty was not his most highly developed attribute, the advance men descended on governments baffled by modern public relations as practiced in America but unwilling to offend a Presidential party. Thus the Vatican, which had its doubts that a picture of military equipment in front of St. Peter's gave a true impression of its spiritual mission, had finally yielded to the argument that the President's tight schedule left no other choice.

Unfortunately, at the precise moment set for leaving, the advance men were struck with the realization that there had been no crowd scenes of Nixon in Rome. This was not unusual. Foreign dignitaries have been visiting Rome since records were kept. Romans, residing where heroes have paraded for hundreds of years, are rather jaded by political leaders. Basically, Rome is the city of the Popes; only their movements attract attention. Not even John Kennedy drew a crowd in

Rome. But Haldeman was not interested in historical comparisons. He applied the wisdom acquired in many years of barnstorming in America: Nothing produces an emotional crowd like a traffic jam. Since Mrs. Nixon was prevented by then existing Navy regulations from visiting the fleet, it was decided on the spot that the President would take her to her hotel by limousine. A motorcade was improvised and set off for the center of Rome at the height of the rush hour while the rest of us waited in the helicopters in front of the Vatican. The operation could not have been more successful. Those of us not part of the motorcade did not see our leader again for two hours. When the helicopters finally lifted off, a beaming Haldeman told us that the traffic jam had indeed been monumental; the crowds enormous; their passions nearly uncontainable. All of this made great television film. What the Curia thought of the helicopters waiting in St. Peter's Square for two hours will never be known. This is probably for the best.

We reached the aircraft carrier *Saratoga* at night to begin our visit to the Sixth Fleet. There is something abstract and esoteric, at least for laymen, about a fleet at sea. It follows unheard commands in response to dangers rarely seen. It affects people who almost never get a glimpse of what protects or threatens them. Throughout recent crises the Sixth Fleet had been the principal extension of our military power in the Middle East. It had helped mold events without ever approaching closer to them than two hundred miles. Highly vulnerable to Soviet land-based planes, the Sixth Fleet nevertheless had a decisive impact because an attack on it would bring into play the full force of the United States. The dramatic reinforcement of our naval power had been a crucial signal of our determination to prevent the Jordan crisis from getting out of hand. The fleet's importance had been enhanced by the progressive loss of our land bases and by political restrictions on those remaining.

The original plan was to spend the night aboard the carrier and watch a demonstration of firepower the next day. But this was to be one of those trips where nothing worked according to plan. Rogers, Laird, and I were watching a movie — *A Man Called Horse* — in the officers' wardroom when a Reuters dispatch was brought in containing an unconfirmed report of Nasser's death. I handed the dispatch to Rogers, who said that if it were true we would surely have heard in official channels. I tended to agree, and we all resumed watching the movie. After about ten minutes I grew uneasy; the dispatch was an unlikely story to have no foundation in fact. I sneaked out and contacted Washington. I received a classic reply: Little was known except that Cairo Radio had stopped its regular programming several hours earlier and started playing funeral music. "We consider this highly unusual," said the report cautiously. The conclusion that there had been a high-level death would not have been excessively daring.

Nixon had retired and Haldeman would not authorize awakening him until we had a confirmed report. I worked frantically with my associates on alternative plans for the trip. We guessed that Tito would go to Nasser's funeral, aborting our Belgrade visit. Cables started flying; phone calls were made all over, thanks to the ever-efficient White House Communications Agency. We played with the idea of reversing the Madrid and Belgrade stops, but our Embassy in Madrid though that the logistical obstacles to moving all preparations up by forty-eight hours would prove insurmountable; our advance men were approaching a nervous breakdown at the very thought. On the other hand, what to do with a President for forty-eight hours was not easy to resolve. The huge apparatus of a Presidential party cannot simply be imposed on a country without extensive preparations. We were in the process of developing several alternative plans when Tito took us off the hook the next morning. He attached more importance to the symbolism of the first Presidential visit to Belgrade than to the funeral of his fallen friend. Meanwhile, when Nasser's death was confirmed, I had awakened Nixon, told him the news, obtained his agreement to send a high-level delegation to the funeral, and informed him of the as yet unsettled status of his Belgrade stop.

Several hours later, about 2:00 A.M., I awoke with a start and remembered that we had scheduled a firepower demonstration for the next day. It seemed to me that to commemorate Nasser's death by setting off high explosives in the Mediterranean would be an act of supreme insensitivity. After checking my judgment with Rogers and Laird, I canceled the firepower display without rousing the President again.

It proved to be a grievous error. Presidential Assistants should not overwhelm their chief with trivia; after a while they should be sufficiently aware of Presidential preferences to make some decisions in his name. But they had better be sure, for they have no authority except the President's confidence. It turned out that Nixon had his heart set on the firepower demonstration. I could almost certainly have talked him out of it. But presenting him with a fait accompli the next morning produced a rare display of Nixonian temper. For twenty-four hours I was subjected to the little gestures by which others can read Presidential disfavor. For example, I was consigned to the backup helicopter for one of the Presidential movements on that day. I was seated at the periphery of meetings on the Sixth Fleet flagship. Soon the storm blew over. It was a small foretaste of what I would later undergo after the India-Pakistan crisis. I was correct on the issue. But I had also been given a lesson in the limits of my authority.

We were greeted at the airport in Belgrade by Marshal Tito in gray-blue uniform with golden epaulets — an incongruous dress for a Communist chief of state were it not for the fact that nowhere in Europe are

the middle-class values of the 1930s preserved in more pristine form
than in the "classless" societies of Eastern Europe. There, where life is
colossally dull, bureaucracy suffocating, planning all-pervasive, it is not·
the notion of the proletariat or Marxist ideology that moves people. Internal cohesion is achieved, even after a generation of Communist rule,
by nationalism of a kind nearly extinct in the more cosmopolitan Western Europe.

Josip Broz Tito was by now the last survivor in office of the legendary figures of the Second World War — a storied guerrilla chieftain,
the first Communist leader who dared to challenge Stalin, the inventor
of nationalistic Communism, and now one of the champions of
nonalignment. By September 1970 he had been in power for twenty-five
years. He exuded the authority of a man who has disposed of all possible rivals. His manners were those of a middle-class Central
European — courteous, clearly enjoying life, a rather self-satisfied
sense of humor. But he was also wary and careful. His eyes did not
always smile with his face. He had learned to deal with capitalists but
not necessarily to accept them. In the immediate postwar era he had
been one of the most intransigent of Communist leaders. There had even
been a brief confrontation with the United States in 1946, when Yugoslavia shot down an unarmed American transport plane and detained its
crew.

After his break with Stalin the Western perception of Tito changed.
His concern to preserve his regime was seen — in no small part thanks
to his own skill — as an abjuration of the values that had helped to establish it. All but forgotten was the fact that Tito had broken with Stalin
over the issue of national autonomy, not over the validity of Communist
theory. Through all vicissitudes Tito remained a member of the Leninist
faith. The requirements of survival forced him to reinsure himself
against Soviet aggression; they did not significantly alter the convictions
shaped by a lifetime of revolutionary dedication — nor should they
have been expected to. Only strong beliefs could have sustained a man
through the perils and ordeals of conspiracy and guerrilla warfare. Why
should he give these up in his hour of victory?

The reluctance to face this fact caused endless misunderstandings.
Yugoslavia was an asset to us in the Balkans and to a lesser extent in
Eastern Europe. It symbolized the possibility of independence. It relieved to some extent the threat to NATO. But outside of Europe Tito
pursued his convictions, which on the whole were not hospitable to
Western interests or ideals. His sympathy for revolution in developing
countries did not differ significantly from Moscow's. Indeed, Tito was
even more aggressive in catering to the radical developing nations; he
saw in their support a buttress for his own independence and an additional political inhibition to Soviet pressures. In turn, his autonomy

from the Soviets gave him a greater influence in the developing world than would have been possible for any of the satellite regimes of Eastern Europe. Therefore Yugoslavia rarely supported our position in international forums. It was, for example, a sponsor of the annual UN resolution for Puerto Rican independence. In the Middle East it generally encouraged the radical Arabs.

I faced this with equanimity. Yugoslavia had not broke with Stalin to do us a favor; it did not pursue its course to further our interests. Yet whatever Tito's motives, Yugoslavia's autonomy improved our global position. Stalin was quite right in worrying about the disruptive example it established for other countries of Eastern Europe. In addition, the security of Europe was enhanced by Tito's refusal to join the Warsaw Pact. Finally, there was a limit beyond which he would not go: He could not afford to antagonize us to a point that made his security depend on the goodwill of the Soviet Union. He needed us to maintain his sense of equilibrium. We therefore were under no pressure to curry his favor. We had no reason to be obsequious or reluctant to stand up for our interests with the same intensity as he pursued his own.

There were several areas of potentially fruitful cooperation between Yugoslavia and us. Belgrade was a useful source of information about trends in both the Communist and developing worlds. It could convey our attitudes to its friends, though it had too many separate purposes to be a reliable intermediary on detail. Periodic high-level exchanges were important in order to synchronize policies as much as possible and to underline our interest in Yugoslavia's independence.

We did not seek to win Yugoslavia over to our point of view. We recognized that its policy of nonalignment, like India's, reflected a cold analysis of its self-interest. The serious nonaligned countries — not those which, removed from all danger, traffic in slogans — seek to calculate the margin within which they can manipulate the international equilibrium. They will not hazard their security or well-being in quixotic gestures against us (unless tempted to do so by American supineness or sentimentality). Nor will they run the risk of becoming too closely associated with us no matter how "understanding" of their proclamations our policy may be. Paradoxically, if we approach too closely, they will have to move away; as we distance ourselves, they will have to move toward us; that is the almost physical law of nonalignment. In short, we did not succumb to the sentimental illusion that nonalignment resulted from specific grievances or misunderstandings. But we paid the nonaligned, and most particularly Yugoslavia, the compliment of recognizing that they were conducting a serious policy. Yugoslavia could not be won over by accepting its rhetoric nor could it be permanently antagonized when we defended our own interests.

Tito's assessment of the international situation was unsentimental, slightly doctrinaire, and always interesting. As it turned out, on this visit his principal concern was the Middle East. He warned us against putting all our chips on Israel. He considered Nasser the outstanding leader in the area; his death had dealt hopes for peace an extremely serious blow. He told us that during the September of crises the Soviet Union had urged Syria and Iraq to withdraw from Jordanian territory, which accorded with our own information. Some of his associates sought to explore how America would react to a Soviet attack on Yugoslavia. Tito never raised the subject, perhaps because he was too proud, perhaps because he knew that it would not come up in his lifetime. Nixon had now visited two capitals in Eastern Europe, Bucharest and Belgrade. The symbolism was inescapable. The United States would pay special attention to those Eastern European countries pursuing an autonomous foreign policy. The Chinese were to notice this, as I have mentioned.

The only other noteworthy feature of our visit to Belgrade was to expose our Communist hosts to the wonders of American public relations. The sorely beset Haldeman faced the same problem in Belgrade that he had overcome in Rome: the absence of a "photo opportunity" involving crowds. His dilemma stemmed from an inexplicable lapse of the advance team. One of the fixed Presidential acts in any country is to lay a wreath on the Tomb of the Unknown Soldier. It is a thoughtful gesture; it cannot fail to draw a crowd. Such a wreath-laying had been arranged in Belgrade as the first item on the President's schedule. Unfortunately, the Yugoslav tomb is located some twenty miles outside of Belgrade. The advance team had apparently neglected to report this fact — or perhaps the distance had simply not registered. As the motorcade wound its way deeper and deeper into a sylvan setting where no crowds disturbed the opportunity for reflection, the radios carried by all advance men crackled ever more insistently with the incredulous exchanges between Ziegler and Haldeman, whose joint outrage knew no bounds. But Haldeman was equal to the challenge. On the way back the Presidential limousine suddenly left the motorcade and, drawing all other cars with it, headed for the center of Belgrade, where its bewildered police escort ultimately caught up with it. Once more a monumental traffic jam developed; again the emotion of the captive audience reached extraordinary heights. And Nixon, jumping onto the hood of his car and waving to the crowd, in fact evoked genuine enthusiasm.

Whatever his satisfaction with a Presidential visit, Tito could not have been overjoyed that Madrid was our next port of call, that we were going from the capital of one aged autocrat to the lair of another, who antedated even Tito. Franco had come to power during the Fascist ascendancy in Europe. He had not permitted the debt he owed his fellow dictators to stand in the way of keeping his country neutral in the Second World War. But when the Fascist empires collapsed, Franco found himself in an inhospitable international environment. By the time of Nixon's visit he had, however, survived all pressures with the aid of the historic insularity and proud nationalism of his people. He had fostered the industrial modernization of Spain, gradually easing his rule and laying the foundation for the development, after his death, of more liberal institutions. In the Seventies, many reacting by rote found it hard to admit that Spain was far less repressive than *any* Communist state and than most of the new nations.

Now in his dotage, Franco had presided over his country's destinies for over a generation. Spain was as if suspended, waiting for a life to end so that it could rejoin European history. Its location makes Spain's strategic importance to the West self-evident. For this reason alone we were concerned that its politics after Franco's departure should evolve with moderation — in defiance of Spain's history. Our choice was whether to ostracize and oppose the existing regime or, while working with it, to extend our contacts and therefore our influence for the post-Franco period. We chose the latter course.

The immediate issue was our military relationship with Spain. Since the 1950s, successive administrations of both parties had concluded agreements with Franco's government on bases for our strategic bombers and Polaris submarines. As his end approached, the lease agreements came up again and, like most military measures in that era of the Vietnam war, were denounced by opponents as an unnecessary and morally indefensible arrangement with a Fascist country. The Administration did not believe that with the Middle East in turmoil and our other bases in the Mediterranean in jeopardy we could afford to abandon the Spanish bases and compound the impression of a global American retreat. And we saw no sense in a confrontation with an aged autocrat whose term of power was clearly ending, a confrontation that would stimulate the proverbial Spanish nationalism and pride.

Encouraging a democratic Spain after Franco would be a complex challenge in the best of circumstances. Spain's history had been marked by an obsession with the ultimate, with death and sacrifice, the tragic and the heroic. This had produced grandiose alternations between anarchy and authority, between chaos and a total discipline. Spaniards seemed able to submit only to exaltation, not to each other. There was no precedent in Spanish history for change that was moderate and evolutionary, not to say democratic rather than radical and violent. International ostracism ran the risk of making Spain a prisoner of its own passions. Throughout this crucial period of transition we maintained our friendship with the future King Juan Carlos, and with moderate elements in Spanish government and society. Indeed, America's contribution to Spain's evolution during the 1970s has been one of the major achievements of our foreign policy.

Nixon was not the first American President to stop in Madrid. Eisenhower had paid a triumphal call in December 1959. One of Nixon's obsessions, in fact, was to ensure that the crowds for him at least equaled, and, he hoped, exceeded, those of the predecessor whom he both respected and envied. There was no reason for concern. Madrid gave Nixon a magnificent reception, marred only by the unfortunate fact that the control tower neglected to close the runways after the arrival, and the whine of jet engines drowned the welcoming speeches. Since on both sides these had been honed to a fine edge of platitude, history is unlikely to feel their loss. On the ceremonial route into town not even Haldeman could complain about the splendid and photogenic scene, as mounted lancers flanked his chief and Franco, erect in an open limousine, amidst scenes of wild enthusiasm. He was able to assuage Nixon's unease over unfavorable comparisons with Eisenhower's reception by commenting sagely that once crowds exceeded several hundred thousand the only problem was to announce some plausible figure.

Of all the visits this was the one in which the symbolism of continued American interest was most clearly the message. The negotiations on bases had been concluded; the post-Franco transition was a subject too delicate for even the most oblique allusion. And the conversations with Franco were not memorable — at least to me — for yet another reason. When Nixon, accompanied by me, called on Franco for what were billed as substantive talks, we found the aged dictator exhausted by the long motorcade and tending to doze off while the President was talking. This had a weirdly mesmeric effect on me. Despite my most desperate efforts to contribute to the Spanish-American dialogue, at least to the extent of staying awake, I found myself also dozing off. Nixon was left exchanging ideas with Gregorio Lopez Bravo, the Spanish Foreign Minister, while Franco and I recuperated peacefully from our exertions. I was admitted to the meeting as note-taker. We owe whatever historical record of the event as now may exist to the wakeful General Walters, acting as interpreter.

We flew off and stopped for lunch at Chequers, the country home of British Prime Ministers, for Nixon's first talks with Edward Heath. The relationship with Heath was one of the most complex of Nixon's Presidency. There was no foreign leader for whom Nixon had a higher regard, especially in combination with Sir Alec Douglas-Home, Heath's Foreign Secretary, whom Nixon positively revered. During the British election campaign, Nixon had been an unabashed partisan of the Tories. Despite the evidence of the polls and contrary to the opinion of all of his advisers, including our Embassy in London, Nixon had been convinced that Heath would win. When his prediction came true, he was so elated that he called me four times in one night in Mexico City, where I was attending the soccer World Cup, to express his joy and receive my confirmation of his prescience. He wanted nothing so much as intimate collaboration of a kind he would grant to no other foreign leader. At last, he said, there would be a kindred spirit in one major country, a group of leaders who did not lean on us, whom we did not need constantly to buttress, and from whom we might learn a great deal.

The relationship never flourished. Like a couple who have been told by everyone that they should be in love and who try mightily but futilely to justify these expectations, Heath and Nixon never managed to establish the personal rapport for which Nixon, at least, longed in the beginning. Both were rather austere personalities, vulnerable and eager for acceptance but incapable of the act of grace that could have bridged their loneliness. Of all British political leaders, Heath was the one I knew best and liked most when I came to office. We have remained good friends, despite some differences of opinion when we were both in government. He was one of the ablest world leaders I met. He was not free of the complexes imposed by Britain's class history; he rose from modest beginnings to lead a party imbued with Britain's aristocratic tradition. The ruthlessness necessary to achieve his ambition did not come naturally and was all the more noticeable for that reason. His renowned aloofness was more apparent than real. He was a warm and gentle person who anticipated rejection and fended it off with a formal politeness (punctuated often with a laugh distinguished by its lack of mirth). He was in many respects the most untypical of British postwar political leaders. He had a theoretical bent closer than the rest to that of the continental Europeans, which gave his ideas an abstract cast sometimes verging on the doctrinaire.

And of all the British leaders Heath was probably also the least committed emotionally to the United States. It is not that he was anti-American. Rather, he was immune to the sentimental elements of that attachment forged in two wars. For most British leaders, whatever the facts of geography, America is closer than "Europe." This is a vestige of a time when Britain sought its fulfillment across the oceans and the continent was a source of danger, never of self-realization. Heath, however, was persuaded that Britain's future was in Europe and that Britain should join Europe not reluctantly and calculatingly but with real conviction. He had been the principal British negotiator in Macmillan's effort to enter the Common Market, aborted by de Gaulle's veto in 1963. More than half convinced by the Gaullist argument that the principal obstacle had been Britain's "special relationship" with the United States, Heath as Prime Minister was determined not to repeat Macmillan's mistake. His commitment to Europe was profound: The United States was a friendly foreign country, entitled to the consideration that reflected its power and importance, but the "special relationship" was an obstacle to the British vocation in Europe. Heath was content to enjoy no higher status in Washington than any other European leader. Indeed, he came close to *insisting* on receiving no preferential treatment.

A paradox was in the making. Wilson, whom Nixon distrusted, had reached for an easier and more personal relationship than did Heath, whom Nixon greatly admired. The Labour Party, whose domestic philosophy was far less congenial to a Republican Administration, established a closer rapport than the Conservatives, who in one sense were a kind of sister party. Some of this was due to Heath's personality and convictions; some of it brought to the surface deeper currents in Tory thinking. The Conservative Party felt acutely the decline in Britain's global role, with which it had historically been so identified. Some of its elements were not free of resentment about America's part in the process of decolonization, from Franklin Roosevelt's strictures during World War II to the Suez crisis of 1956.

Whatever the reason, Heath kept Washington at arm's length. He was being offered for nothing the preferred status in consultation for which his predecessors had struggled with patience and persistence and not a little straight flattery. He chose not to avail himself of the opportunity, and by making this rejection explicit he both smoothed Britain's entry into Europe and complicated his relationship with Washington. There was no meeting between the President and the Prime Minister immediately after Heath's election, as Nixon had hoped and as every previous postwar British leader had sought. There were very few personal calls on the telephone, though Nixon had made clear to those charged with handling all his phone calls that his refusal to accept "unscreened" calls did not apply to the British Prime Minister, and even though I repeatedly urged the British Ambassador, John Freeman, to encourage this sort of contact. The new British Prime Minister thus implemented what the American apostles of European integration had urged when Nixon had entered office and what had then been explicitly rejected. Indeed, inviting Nixon to stop briefly at Chequers — even in a most cordial atmosphere — served Heath's purpose of delaying a formal consultative meeting for several months more. It gave Heath an opportunity to present the meeting to his European colleagues as an informal courtesy call in which nothing of substance could possibly have been concluded because of the pressures of time, and to consult his European colleagues *before* launching himself on a trans-Atlantic dialogue.

Future historians will have to decide whether Heath's judgment of the European mood was correct. Did he really need to pay the price in intimacy with Washington to establish his European credentials, especially at a time when Brandt and Pompidou were heading in the opposite direction of strengthening their countries' ties with us? Did he, in fact, pay a price except for a slight change in atmospherics? Heath pursued a long-term policy with vision and tenacity. It may be argued that by making the Anglo-American relationship more formal, he adapted it to an inevitable reality. It was nevertheless a pity that so formidable and attractive a man could have such a blind spot for the importance of intangibles.

Outwardly, the meeting at Chequers could not have gone better. Nixon still ascribed the relative aloofness of the new British government to the need to get its feet on the ground — confusing British with American practice. (British administrations, inheriting the permanent civil service, and consisting of a handful of party leaders with long Parliamentary exposure to the issues, usually do not require an extended shakedown period.) The talks were conducted in two sessions. Before lunch Heath met with Nixon; only Cabinet Secretary Sir Burke Trend and I were also present. During lunch Rogers and Sir Alec joined the group. Altogether, there was less than two hours' time for conversation. Significantly, Europe was not discussed at all, except for Nixon's general comment that we were prepared to be discreetly helpful in the British negotiations with the European Community, an offer that was not pursued. All the conversations concerned international issues: Vietnam and Africa before lunch; the Middle East afterward. Heath was at his best in this sort of dialogue — incisive, decisive, and astute. He also substantially shared our perception of international affairs. He called our attention to the strategic significance of Africa and the Indian Ocean at a time when these were not yet high priorities on our agenda. He agreed with us that how we disengaged from Vietnam would affect the world beyond Southeast Asia: "If the Soviets feel you are in retreat and humiliated, they will reactivate their policy in Europe." Under the guise of briefing us on his attendance at Nasser's funeral, Sir Alec sought to nudge us gently toward greater activism in the Middle East, especially in the Four-Power talks. Nixon disagreed, believing, as I did, that the radical forces had not yet run out their string. He thought more crises inevitable, no matter what we did. There was no time to resolve the issue since our schedule forced us to leave for Ireland if we were not to arrive too late for the cherished "photo opportunity." The meeting had been useful, friendly, even warm, but strangely inconclusive, a harbinger of a more complex future.

The last stop of the Presidential trip was Ireland. My briefing book for Nixon said the maximum that was possible: "The Irish stop has no great international significance, except that Ireland has not been totally passive in world affairs. It has served, and can in the future, as a constructive and reliable neutral." This worthy objective would not normally require personal Presidential attention for a full forty-eight hours. The stop was frankly a domestic political one. It enabled Nixon to bring his claim to Irish ancestry to the attention of Irish-American voters and to pay off an obligation to a wealthy American contributor at whose extravagant castle we stayed. The contributor decided to put on a pageant of Irish history that started at one in the morning and, given the passion and drama of the subject, did not conclude until around four-thirty. By accident of propinquity my staff and I became the target of Presidential wrath, though we had had nothing to do with the scheduling.

Nixon's visit to Ireland followed distinguished precedents. In fact, the schedule let us off easy. An earlier scheme put forward by an advance man carried away by his imagination had proposed having Nixon lead a St. Patrick's Day parade in Dublin. Luckily for everyone's sanity, the date was inappropriate and no pretext ever developed for a Presidential trip to Europe in March.

The Irish stop, an otherwise conventional visit, unexpectedly provided one of the biggest news stories of the trip, occasioned by a review of the negotiations on Vietnam with David Bruce and Philip Habib, who had flown in from Paris. (As related in the next chapter, a major Presidential speech was being prepared, offering a standstill cease-fire.) This meeting gave the press an opportunity for another spate of speculative stories on Vietnam and its peace prospects. Nixon could not escape the subject even while searching for his roots in Ireland.

De Gaulle's Funeral and Heath's Visit

W ITHIN little more than a month of our return, Nixon was back in Europe, this time for the memorial Mass for Charles de Gaulle. In part because of Nixon's immediate decision to attend, which set the protocol level and guaranteed the attendance of many other heads of state, Pompidou and Nixon had an unusually warm meeting. Pompidou repeated his readiness to see Britain enter the European Community, supported our general approach to settling Vietnam, and expressed again his wariness about long-term German trends.

The visit, having been quickly improvised, could not pass without its bizarre aspects. At first Nixon had indicated that he wanted to leave immediately after the memorial Mass. To Haldeman's irritation, I persuaded Nixon that he would lose much goodwill if he did not stay for Pompidou's reception for visiting delegations in the late afternoon. Haldeman's opposition was partly a question of prerogative; he did not like interference in his area of jurisdiction, which was the President's schedule. More important, he knew better than anyone Nixon's crucial need for regular rest periods; it was the essential guarantee for consistent decisions. In fiercely protecting the President's schedule — especially the rest periods, for which the euphemism in the press release was "staff time" — Haldeman served the country and contributed to the strong decisions that were the hall-mark of the Nixon Presidency in foreign policy.

Once I had succeeded in interfering with his precious schedule, however, Haldeman's problem became the practical one of how to fill the gap. Like many of Nixon's associates, he had been made repeatedly aware of his chief's fondness for Maxim's restaurant. He therefore suggested that Nixon might care to lunch there with his official party. The idea of the President of the United States repairing from a memorial service at Notre-Dame to Maxim's was, of course, mind-boggling. But it did not seem so to an ebullient Nixon when he thought about it after a good dinner at the residence of our Ambassador, Arthur (Dick) Watson. Plans were therefore being laid to proceed. In good bureaucratic fashion I clothed my objection to principle in the technical argument that the President could not possibly be photographed drinking wine after a memorial service. I was overruled. An edict was issued reaffirming Maxim's but banning wine from the meal. Luckily, our Ambassador was a sensible man. By a stroke of destiny, he rather than an advance man had been assigned to contact the restaurant. I took Watson aside and warned him that his position would become intolerable when the French public outrage at our insensitivity spilled over into official relations. He should not do anything that night. If there were any complaint I would take the responsibility. As it turned out Nixon, after a good night's sleep, himself had had second thoughts. When I told him the next morning that he would undo all the good his trip had accomplished by such an action, he instructed me to cancel the preparations. I had no difficulty promising a speedy execution of that order.

Edward Heath visited Washington a month later, in December 1970, for his first formal consultation with Nixon. Britain's prospective entry into the European Common Market had brought to a head increasing tensions between Europe and America, though it did not cause them. The underlying reason was a clash of perception due essentially to economic rivalry between the United States and a resurgent Europe. Some of the dispute had a slightly unreal quality. We spoke of nondiscriminatory trade, ignoring that a common market is inherently discriminatory; after all, it is formed by raising tariffs and other obstacles against imports from the outside world that do not apply to the trade of the states within it. The imminence of Britain's membership forced us to face the long-ignored problem inherent in the very concept of European integration. Heath's visit defined the issue; Heath was in no position to resolve it. He left no doubt about the new priorities in British policy. He stressed that his overriding goal was Britain's entry into the Common Market. Once in, Britain would play a constructive role with respect to our concerns. But he could not risk making any concessions to us in advance; he wished neither to negotiate Common Market issues bilaterally with us nor to appear as — or, for that matter, to be — America's Trojan Horse in Europe. No previous British Prime Minister would have considered making such a statement to an American President. Neither the amiable context nor Nixon's understanding reply could obscure the fact that we were witnessing a revolution in Britain's postwar foreign policy.

However painful the transformation, this revolution had its positive

aspects. Britain's global experience and pragmatic style were bound to
be helpful in European councils whether its views were coordinated beforehand with the United States or not. Heath was surely right in stressing that the major benefit to us of Britain's entering into Europe would
be political, not economic. (This, of course, begged the question of how
big an economic price we were prepared to pay for political benefits.)
And his conversations with Nixon on world affairs demonstrated — as
at Chequers — a substantial harmony of views.

As did all the other European leaders, Heath expressed misgivings
about the long-term trends in Germany; though like all his colleagues he
almost surely did not convey them in Bonn, leaving it to us — if anybody — to bear the onus of expressing what everyone seemed to fear.
He opposed Brandt's idea of a permanent conference on Berlin. He
thought the allies had to bring home to the Soviets the need for reciprocity, especially on Berlin, if Brandt's policy was not to become a series
of unilateral concessions. Nixon agreed, explaining our concept of linkage. He reassured Heath that he would not permit SALT to give the Soviets strategic superiority. There was a review of Indochina, again with
substantial agreement. Heath was a new experience for American
leaders: a British Prime Minister who based his policy toward the
United States not on sentimental attachments but on a cool calculation
of interest. At the same time his convictions so nearly coincided with
ours that close collaboration would result from that self-interest.

The Heath visit concluded another year of intensive allied consultations. We had after some hesitation supported the breakthrough of
Brandt's policy. Britain's entry into Europe would in time have significant consequences. But on the whole we were engaged in a holding action. In the early part of 1971 we were preoccupied with the effort to
sever the North Vietnamese communications in Laos, the opening to
China, and the May 20 breakthrough linking offensive and defensive
weapons in the SALT negotiations with the Soviet Union.

In high office competing pressures tempt one to believe that an issue
deferred is a problem avoided; more often it is a crisis invited. Both the
military and the economic dimensions of our European relationship
came back to haunt us in 1971.

The Mansfield Amendment: The Old Guard Steps into the Breach

THE first crisis was military. On May 11, 1971, we learned without
any warning that the gentle Senate Majority Leader, Mike Mansfield, would revive his perennial proposal to cut our forces in Europe by
half, or 150,000 men. The vehicle would be an amendment to the Draft
Extension Act having the force of law. Mansfield was not just any

Senator. He was the Majority Leader, widely respected for his fairness, universally liked for his decency. Mansfield was not a member of a radical fringe but a charter member of the Senate Establishment, one of that small band of patriots who have made our maddeningly delicate system of checks and balances actually work. He was a passionate opponent of the war in Southeast Asia. But his opposition, while fierce, never passed the bounds of the civility and comity that are so vital to a democracy. At heart Mansfield was an isolationist, eager to reduce all American overseas commitments, reflecting the historical nostalgia that sought to maintain America's moral values uncontaminated by exposure to calculations of power and the petty quarrels of shortsighted foreigners.

Mansfield's amendment was thus a formidable challenge. All our studies indicated that our conventional forces in Europe needed to be enhanced, not reduced; the Mansfield amendment would dismantle them. If the Senate of the United States went on record as legislating a massive troop cut, NATO would have joined the other elements of our foreign policy as a victim of unrelenting domestic political controversy. Soon we would see the Vietnamization process repeated in Europe, whereby in order to salvage a bare minimum we would have to emasculate the essential. The long-term goal to adapt Alliance defense to new strategic realities would be destroyed.

The issue had come up as part of the annual debate over the defense budget, which critics of the Vietnam policy increasingly turned into an assault on all elements of our military strategy. The Administration, already publicly committed to a volunteer army, had asked for a two-year extension of the draft. When the bill reached the Senate floor, Senator Mansfield revived his annual proposal to cut American forces in Europe — this time not in the form of a "sense of the Senate resolution," as he usually did, but as binding law. He asked for a vote the next day, May 12. Leading Senators of both parties warned the White House that Mansfield probably would prevail.

It was symptomatic of the bitter and destructive mood of the period and of the substantial breakdown of national consensus that a bill of such magnitude could reach the floor of the Senate without committee hearing and that it stood a serious chance of passage. Our massive balance-of-payments deficit lent weight to any call to cut overseas expenditures; respect for Mansfield made his colleagues reluctant to vote against him. But the real problem went deeper. It was the national malaise that made the United States Senate willing to hazard institutions built up on a bipartisan basis over more than twenty years and five administrations. The Administration was determined to resist. The White House immediately (on May 12) issued a statement warning that the amendment would have "a serious detrimental effect on the structure of the alliance.'' Our next move was to delay the vote to give us time to rally support. We obtained an extension of five days which, while niggardly and almost preposterous in the light of the issues involved, probably made the difference.

Our determination to defeat the Mansfield amendment confronted severe obstacles. For one thing there was the passion of its supporters. Many of these were more concerned with Southeast Asia than with Western Europe, and some of them considered it a bonus to dismantle the structure of a foreign policy that they considered misconceived and Cold War–oriented, and a major contributor to international tensions. But the decisive element was that the liberal Establishment, which throughout the century had extolled the importance of a strong Executive, had reversed itself and had pressed on the Congress its obligation to control tightly an allegedly power-mad and war-obsessed Administration.

That the Congress should play a major role in the conduct of foreign policy was beyond argument. But in the Seventies passion overwhelmed analysis. Our system cannot function when Congress and the President have sharply conflicting goals or when the Congress attempts to prescribe day-to-day tactical decisions. The Congress can and ought to scrutinize the consequences of diplomacy. It cannot carry it out. When it has tried, the results have been unfortunate, as I will discuss at greater length in my second volume. The prime function of Congress is to pass laws with a claim to permanence: It deals in the predictable. Diplomacy requires constant adjustment to changing circumstance; it must leave a margin for the unexpected; the unpredictable is what always happens in foreign affairs. Nuance, flexibility, and sometimes ambiguity are the tools of diplomacy. In law they are vices; certainty and clarity are the requirements there. Lawmaking and diplomacy are not only starkly contrasted in their methods and consequences; they are done differently. Legislation often emerges from the compromise of conflicting interests; random coalitions form and fade. The coalitions and power centers of Congress shift in response to the stimuli of various pressure groups. Foreign policy requires a consistent view of the national interest. The legislator practices the art of reconciling pressure groups on a single issue; the foreign-policymaker deals with the same international actors over and over again, rarely concluding an issue or terminating a relationship.

The Mansfield amendment resulted from a coalition of frustrations. But it could have had grave consequences long after the coalition that produced it had disintegrated. It illustrates also that Congress is in no position to make coherent tactical decisions because its knowledge of the mosaic of foreign policy is so fragmentary. The amendment came forward in a week in which we concluded the negotiations for a breakthrough on SALT, set up the secret trip to Peking, were engaged in delicate talks on Berlin, and arranged for another round of private talks with the North Vietnamese. Even granting that the Nixon Administration sometimes carried secrecy to excessive lengths, sensitive negotiations will always be taking place or be in formative stages of which the Congress is bound to be unaware. In fact, the Congress's capacity to do damage is considerable even when the policies affected are fully in the public domain. In May 1971 the Congress knew that major negotiations were taking place on SALT and on Berlin, and that we were urging our allies with some success to improve their NATO forces. The Mansfield amendment jeopardized every one of these policies.

The habits of the Senate provided another complication. Even Senators who had always championed the Atlantic Alliance were torn between their convictions and their membership in an exclusive club, between their knowledge that the Mansfield amendment jeopardized fundamental American foreign policy interests and their reluctance to inflict a clear-cut defeat on a revered colleague. Our supporters in the Senate were therefore urging a compromise that would avoid a specific mandatory cut by calling upon the Administration to negotiate reductions with both the Soviet Union and our European allies. The President was to report to the Congress on September 15, 1971, and every six months thereafter on the progress of these negotiations.

Views in the Administration differed. Rogers, as well as the Congressional liaison staffs of the White House and the State Department, favored the compromise. In their view the Mathias amendment committed us to nothing more than consultations; it was a neat way of avoiding an obligatory reduction. Laird disagreed, largely for tactics. He wanted a straight vote on the Mansfield amendment without modifications; he thought that the "worse" the amendment, the better our chances of prevailing in the end. Nixon tended to support Laird. He was deeply committed to the Atlantic Alliance. He was experienced enough to understand that once the principle of reduction was accepted the floodgates would be opened. He was, as it happens, principally concerned at the time with concluding the preliminary understanding on SALT (linking offensive and defensive limitations), scheduled for a week hence, but he was willing to do what was necessary to defeat the Mansfield amendment. He assigned the brunt of the effort to me.

I was only too eager to accept it. I considered the Mansfield amendment a serious threat to our entire foreign policy. The national anguish over Vietnam could be ascribed, by countries that depended on our steadiness, to rash decisions and an inconclusive war. An assault on our deployments in Europe, on the other hand, would shake the very foundations of our postwar policy. I was adamantly against the proposed compromise. Even if it avoided immediate reductions, it established the principle and the semiannual reports would revive the pressure for unilateral withdrawals. The compromise amendment was already being spoken of — by Senator Humphrey, for example — as a Congressional instruction to the Administration to undertake speedy reductions. And a whole host of other amendments elaborating the same theme was waiting for Senate action. If any of the many compromise variations were on the books, the NATO force improvement program, however modest, would be out the window; our allies would lose heart; and the negotiations with the Soviet Union on mutual reductions were likely to atrophy. We would be on the road to Vietnamizing Europe.

I spent most of May 12 on the telephone, heatedly arguing along these lines to our supporters in the Senate. Experienced leaders such as John Stennis were convinced that Mansfield had the votes and that only a compromise could head him off. I preferred the Mansfield amendment. All the proposed compromises had the disadvantage of making the Administration a party to the decision to reduce troops in Europe; once we had given that much ground we would soon be driven from one position of disadvantage to another. At the same time, a straight vote would provide an opportunity to demonstrate that the essence of our postwar foreign policy could survive our divisions over Vietnam. For the first time in the Nixon Administration we might succeed in mobilizing the Establishment figures who had been responsible for so many of America's great postwar achievements.

One of the first was Dean Acheson. The capacity to admire others is not my most fully developed trait. That frailty did not apply to the figure of Acheson, so out of scale in his achievements and in his passion, in his moral convictions and in his prejudices. I had met him when he had just stepped down from the office he loved into that emptiness which marks the aftermath of a great mission, and into that loneliness known only to those who have lived with exertions for an important cause. Acheson once described his leaving office as akin to the end of a love affair. I had interviewed him in 1953 at his law firm; mustache bristling, he was impeccably tailored, sufficiently bored with the practice of law to be willing to help a graduate student with a research paper on some arcane aspect of the Korean War. I asked scholarly questions that later acquaintance taught me he must have considered recherché and irrelevant. He answered patiently, sometimes acerbically, always precisely. All went tolerably well until I inquired into his reaction to one of MacArthur's particularly muscular dispatches. "You mean before or after I peed in my pants?" asked this paragon of old-world diplomacy. Our paths did not cross again until he took me to lunch some years later, and gave me this description of a leading figure in a then new administration: "He reminds me of an amateur boomerang thrower practicing his art in a crowded room."

Acheson was a man of dignity — in his person and in his view of the public process. His exertions were always in the service of ideals that transcended the individual. For the better part of the three decades he made a seminal contribution to the shape and design of American foreign policy. He and the President he so loyally served ushered in the transformation from isolationism to the understanding that without America's strength the world would have no peace, and without our commitment it would know no hope. This unlikely pair fashioned the North Atlantic Alliance, the building of cooperative relations with former enemies, the economic institutions that helped Europe rebuild and launched a wartorn world toward peace, security, and unprecedented prosperity.

On a personal level I can never forget the graceful — I might almost say gentle — way in which Dean Acheson welcomed me to Washington when I arrived as national security adviser, and the wisdom and patience with which he sought thereafter to bridge the gap between the perceptions of a Harvard professor and the minimum requirements of reality. "Can I put it this way?" I once asked him about a particularly ponderous proposal. "Certainly you can put it that way," said Dean, "but not if you want to get anywhere."

Dean Acheson prized moral integrity, but he despised those who used the ideal as a device for avoiding the attainable. He would often mock the foibles of man, but he never denigrated the values of his nation. He strove mightily for peace and liberty, but he was too wise to believe that any one man's efforts could mark more than a stage of an endless journey. Justice Holmes once said in a speech that Acheson was fond of quoting: "Alas, gentlemen, we cannot live our dreams. We are lucky enough if we can give a sample of our best and if we can know in our hearts that it was nobly done." Dean Acheson surely lived his dreams; and it was, indeed, nobly done.

In his time he had been the object of much abuse, some of it directed at him by the President who was now in office. The creativity, excitement, and achievement that so marked his time as Secretary of State were overshadowed by a pervasive distrust and suspicion of which he became a conspicuous symbol. But he faced adversity jauntily, with determination and without compromise of principle. And history gave Dean Acheson its highest accolade — it proved him right.

Nixon's shabby treatment of him in the 1952 campaign did not keep Acheson from assisting his President when he was needed almost two decades later. His loyalty ran to the office, not the man. He had responded to several of Nixon's requests for his counsel, always without publicity. Now he offered to assist publicly. He told me that he would call any Senators where he could help, or any newspaper — though he felt that he might have outworn his welcome with the *New York Times* and the *Washington Post*. He gave me a list of "worthies" — John McCloy, George Ball, McGeorge Bundy, Cyrus Vance, and others — whose support I should try to enlist. I told him I would report to him after having taken soundings.

The response was divided. Contemporaries of Acheson — like Mc-Cloy — came to our assistance unconditionally. My own contemporaries still had futures to protect; they were willing to lend their names though not their muscle; basically, they preferred compromise. George Ball was in between in age — and in response. He gave us his judgment that a compromise was necessary. But he loved a fight in a good cause, and he went to work with effectiveness and characteristic passion for the outright defeat of the Mansfield amendment.

When I reported to Acheson the various reactions, he had another idea: "It seems to me what we want is a little volley firing and not just a splattering of musketry." He urged that President Nixon immediately gather together an array of former Secretaries of State, Secretaries of Defense, High Commissioners for Germany, NATO commanders, and Chairmen of the Joint Chiefs of Staff. This embodiment of a bipartisan postwar foreign policy should issue a statement supporting the President's determination to maintain our present military strength in Europe. Nixon shared my enthusiasm for Acheson's proposal. He reveled in the prospect that for the first, and in the event the only, time in his public life he would have the Establishment on his side — the men he revered and despised, whose approbation he both cherished and scorned. What tragedies might have been avoided if a permanent bridge could have been built to this group to give inward security to this lonely, complex President? What if the men who had sustained our nation's policy in their own time had helped Nixon to leave the dark land of his fears and premonitions and transcend that strange sense of his inadequacy? It is a pity it never happened; both sides must share the blame.

The meeting in the late afternoon of May 13 was a splendid occasion. Present in the Cabinet Room were such luminaries as Acheson, McCloy, Ball, Henry Cabot Lodge, Vance, Lucius Clay, Alfred Gruenther, Lauris Norstad, and Lyman Lemnitzer. It was the final meeting of the Old Guard, a group united in the national interest, still dedicated to the self-confident perception of world order by which American idealism had restored war-ravaged societies and turned enemies into allies. Nixon was at his best. He made an eloquent speech: He had never asked those present for their support on Vietnam. But they had never disagreed on NATO. The President recalled that since the Eightieth Congress, when President Truman proposed the North Atlantic Treaty and related programs and a Republican Congress supported them, we had always been at one on this subject. In opposing the Mansfield amendment, he represented the continuity of American policy. Alluding to the title of Acheson's autobiography, he said that he too had been "present at the creation." Perhaps we were on the verge of a breakthrough with the Communist world (he was thinking of SALT and the preparations for my trip to Peking). But we could achieve these goals only if the Atlantic Alliance stayed strong.

All present responded in the same spirit. There was some discussion about the desirability of compromise. But Acheson, who shared none of Nixon's reluctance to engage in face-to-face confrontations, effectively squelched it. At a strategic moment Acheson surfaced a brief statement of support for the others to sign. Rogers — unaware that Nixon himself had originated the notion of an Acheson draft, perhaps put off by the elegant self-assurance of his predecessor, perhaps worried about Mansfield, with whom he would have to continue to work — urged that it be kept in abeyance. Acheson, who knew that the existing consensus might evaporate once everyone returned to his normal pressures, urged agreement in principle on the spot and release of the statement as soon as possible, but no later than Saturday, May 15, or forty-eight hours later. Nixon managed to convey to his Secretary of State that he was in accord, and Rogers joined the consensus.

Acheson was selected to report to the press. Reticence was not his style. He gave as his impression that the President was adamant against the Mansfield proposal and any variation of it. It would be "asinine," he said, and "sheer nonsense," to cut forces without a cut in Soviet forces. He said he thought that we could win the vote. He reported that the President had called on the people who created NATO and saw it through for twenty years. "All of us had our fighting gloves on." Asked why the meeting took so long, he replied, "We are all old and we are all eloquent." George Ball added that it was a relief to be told by the President that he did not want to compromise.

Having thus laid the basis for public support, Nixon departed for Key Biscayne and left the management of the battle to me. In Bonn, McCloy had been busy with Brandt, who issued an effective statement warning that a unilateral American withdrawal would leave "the irradicable impression that the United States is on its way out of Europe," transforming détente into appeasement. Brosio, at the NATO Secretariat, released a letter to the President warning that a major reduction of US forces would "withdraw all credibility from NATO's ability to keep its commitments."

On the Saturday, as agreed, a brief Presidential statement opposing the Mansfield amendment was released from Key Biscayne, and was immediately endorsed by the luminous list of supporters who had been marshaled. In addition, former President Lyndon Johnson issued a statement in support; endorsements came from former Secretary of State Dean Rusk; former Secretaries of Defense Robert Lovett, Neil McElroy, and Tom Gates; former senior Defense Department figures like Roswell Gilpatric; diplomats Robert Murphy, Livingston Merchant, and Douglas Dillon; former NATO commanders such as General Matthew Ridgway and all former High Commissioners for Germany. Only Robert Mc-Namara and Clark Clifford opted out of the joint statement, the former because he was head of the World Bank and thus an international civil servant; the latter for reasons he chose not to reveal.

The media reaction showed that the old foreign policy Establishment still carried quite a wallop. The *New York Times* published an editorial on May 16 entitled "Senator Mansfield's Folly," criticizing the amendment as coming at an "inopportune time" and predicting certain rejection unless the Senate "has lost all sense of responsibility." Its "mere introduction could harm nearly every ongoing negotiating effort by the United States and its allies." And it further argued that "even a narrow defeat for the amendment will shake the confidence of the European allies."

On the very day of the Nixon statement, May 15, support came from a most unexpected quarter. In a major speech in Soviet Georgia, Leonid Brezhnev went out of his way explicitly to declare Soviet readiness to begin negotiations over *mutual* troop reductions in Europe. Brezhnev said that Western spokesmen were asking "whose armed forces — foreign or national — what armaments, nuclear or conventional, are to be reduced?" He compared such speculation to a man who tried to judge the flavor of wine by its appearance and not its taste; "translated into diplomatic language this means — to start negotiations."

The Administration, Congress, and the media alike seized upon Brezhnev's statement like manna from heaven. Here was a way out for uneasy supporters of Mansfield as well as for his Administration opponents. Both could unite behind the proposition that the imminence of negotiations made unilateral reductions of American forces untimely. On May 16 the *Washington Post* printed an editorial entitled "Brezhnev's Bid; Nixon's Opportunity," urging early negotiations on mutual force reductions. The *New York Times* and other leading journals followed a similar theme. On May 16 Secretary Rogers announced that Ambassador Jacob Beam had been instructed to ask Soviet officials to elaborate on Brezhnev's offer. We were well on the way to defeating the Mansfield amendment by committing ourselves to negotiations whose content we were as yet unable to define.

What possessed Brezhnev to make his mutual force reductions offer on that particular day is not clear. It was long-standing Soviet policy; he had said exactly the same thing in a speech in March. The Mansfield amendment must have caught the Kremlin even more than the Administration by surprise. Nor could Moscow have expected it to pick up such a head of steam. The Brezhnev proposal was undoubtedly planned to give impetus to the Berlin negotiations by suggesting that they would unlock the doors to a hopeful future. Nothing illustrates better the inflexibility of the Soviets' cumbersome policymaking machinery than their decision to stick to their game plan even when confronted with the Mansfield windfall. It should be pondered by those who see every Soviet maneuver as part of a well-considered design; Soviet momentum results generally from persistence and brute power, not from strategic vision or even tactical flexibility.

As often before, our biggest problem remained the institutional desire for a compromise in the Senate, and among several members of the Administration — a desire that even the combined impact of the "worthies" and Brezhnev could not quench totally. I explained to Senator Robert Griffin, the Republican whip, that none of the compromise proposals was as "innocuous" as he thought. All committed the Administration to the principle of unilateral withdrawal and to periodic reports to Congress about "progress." I also reminded George Ball, who was loyally lining up votes on the Hill despite his belief in the necessity of a compromise, that the White House would hold firm. Any hints otherwise from elsewhere in the Administration did not reflect the President's thinking.

The final vote came none too soon for our sanity, on May 19. The compromise amendment adamantly opposed by the Administration was beaten 73–24. A similar amendment put forward by Senator Peter Dominick was rejected 68–29. Senator Frank Church then proposed a modification of the Mansfield position, a cut of only 50,000 instead of Mansfield's proposal of 150,000. That was defeated 81–15. The mood in the Senate was revealed by one of our supporters who balked when I tried to brace him on the vote against another of the cascade of amendments: "How many times a day can a man vote no?" Finally, Mansfield's amendment came to a vote after an impassioned speech by the Majority Leader. It went down 61–36.

The next morning, May 20, Nixon announced the breakthrough on the SALT negotiations. It had been a close call. We had barely avoided the dismantling of twenty-five years of foreign policy on the eve of entering the conclusive phase of the Strategic Arms Limitation Talks.

The debate had one by-product: It gave impetus to the mutual force reduction negotiations. Our strategy previously had been to stall, partly to link these negotiations to other issues, but above all because we really had not thought through what would be desirable. Every scheme we had examined increased the imbalance of forces in Central Europe. The Warsaw Pact had far more troops than we had along the central front; its initial advantage would grow rapidly once mobilization began, particularly because of the proximity of Soviet divisions in European Russia. In such circumstances, agreed mutual reductions, if both sides reduced by an equal percentage, would compound NATO's problem; they would weaken the already thinly held NATO front without degrading the Soviet capacity to reinforce. One of our studies showed that while a 10 percent mutual reduction would not have any substantial effect, a 30 percent reduction would significantly improve the Warsaw Pact's position. Inevitably, this led to the view that the only safe agreement was "asymmetrical" reductions, in other words, that the Warsaw Pact would cut its forces by a larger amount than NATO. This concept first faced tough sledding in a bureaucracy dedicated to the proposition that we needed to put forward "negotiable" proposals; nobody believed that such an "unequal" approach would be accepted by the Soviets. The debate over the Mansfield amendment guaranteed that we would have to sort out our thinking *during* negotiations on mutual reductions, and not before them as we would have preferred.

The move toward negotiations was given a major push in the Lisbon meeting of NATO foreign ministers that adopted a plan by Rogers of early explorations to be conducted by Secretary General Brosio. And Nixon as usual was his own worst enemy after he had won the battle. Euphoric over the SALT breakthrough and the Senate vote, he used a press conference on June 1 to score a point off his liberal tormentors. He announced that after consultations which were already in progress the United States would be prepared to "move forward" toward early negotiations. He thus would have made negotiations for which we were quite unprepared nearly inevitable had the Soviets seized their opportunity. Luckily, they were looking for loose change; this gave us time to get our house in order.

For after having raised the issue of troop reductions in Europe at a fortuitous moment in the Mansfield debate, the Soviets as quickly dropped it. Perhaps they regretted the favor they had done us in helping to defeat the Mansfield amendment. Perhaps they had the same difficulty in developing unified positions that we did. Perhaps they feared the impact on their control of Eastern Europe if *any* Soviet withdrawal took place. Perhaps they wanted to wait until after the Berlin negotiations. Perhaps Brezhnev had just made a mistake.

Whatever the reason, no sooner had NATO shown an interest in mutual force reductions than the Soviets stalled, linking it to their pet project of the European Security Conference. And they refused to receive Brosio for exploratory talks on the ground that they did not wish to participate in bloc-to-bloc negotiations. This suited France very well, since Paris saw in the Brosio mission a diminution of its cherished independence. And France preferred the European Security Conference to mutual force reductions as a counterweight to Brandt's unilateral diplomacy. The Soviets insisted the European Security Conference be convened first. We, backed by all allies save France, took the position that both negotiations should proceed simultaneously. We succeeded in keeping the issue of mutual force reductions alive to block unilateral American withdrawals by the Congress; at the same time we succeeded in prolonging the negotiation without disadvantageous result.

As it turned out, the debate over the Mansfield amendment was a benchmark in the American domestic debate over foreign policy, though none of the participants understood this at the time. Until then the Administration had been on the defensive on the whole range of its policies. It had fought desperate, seemingly hopeless rearguard actions to prevent emasculation of our defense budget and unilateral reduction of our forces. With the SALT announcement on May 20 we seized the initiative. It was followed by my secret trip to Peking, the announcement of the Moscow summit, and a nearly uninterrupted series of unexpected moves that captured the "peace issues" and kept our opponents off balance. In later years — when it was safe to do so — some who had harassed us most shifted their views with the prevailing public mood and came to criticize us for insufficient attention to our allies; détente was attacked for being "oversold." As I have explained earlier, we considered a détente based on strict reciprocity in the national interest. But whatever one's views about détente in the abstract, in the context of 1971 and 1972 the .carefully calibrated measures of the Administration toward the Soviet Union were imperative to prevent a headlong rush toward abdication of responsibility in America and among the allies. Our willingness to discuss détente had lured Brezhnev into an initiative about mutual force reductions that saved our whole European defense structure from Congressional savaging. It was a classic example of why such a policy was needed to maintain the essential elements of national security if we were to avoid the destruction of our national defense and Alliance solidarity in the era of Vietnam.

The Economic Crisis: The Second "Nixon Shock"

THE Mansfield amendment and the flurry over negotiating with the Soviets temporarily overshadowed the economic conflict that had been steadily building for over a year. It came to a head in 1971 as a result of three developments: the imminent entry of Britain into the Common Market, the appointment of John Connally as Secretary of the Treasury, and the growing strain on the dollar.

By May 1971 the last obstacles to Britain's entry had been overcome. As I have already explained, Willy Brandt supported Britain's membership in the Common Market at least in part to give balance to his *Ostpolitik*. Pompidou abandoned de Gaulle's reservations lest France be left alone with a potentially nationalist Germany. Heath and Pompidou met on May 20–21 to resolve the remaining issues, all highly technical.

Afterward Pompidou, taking care to avoid inflaming hard-line Gaullists, announced the essentially positive results in a double negative which would have done Gromyko proud: "It would be unreasonable to think that we will not reach an agreement." He was as good as his word. By July Heath was in a position to announce that he would submit an agreement to Parliament before the end of the year.

This culmination of two decades of effort and American encouragement should have come as a gratification to the United States. Unhappily, it coincided with a period when the frustrations of the Vietnam war were encouraging xenophobia. Those who wanted to shake the edifice of American foreign policy now made common cause with those who saw in the enlarged Common Market a challenge to our economic preeminence. Both sought to reduce our international commitments. The criticism of the European system of preferences and Japan's surplus in its trade with us began to mount. Urgency was added by the increasingly apparent plight of the dollar, the world's reserve currency. A number of factors — inflation, high wage settlements, and a worsening balance-of-payments deficit — combined to cause a wave of dollar selling as the spring began. It began to appear that a major change in exchange rates could be stemmed only by the massive and escalating intervention of the European central banks. On May 10 the German Federal Republic finally stopped buying dollars; the mark began to float upward and the dollar's value fell. The appreciation of the deutsche mark in relation to the dollar would — theoretically and over time —aid our exports by making them cheaper and reduce our imports by increasing their cost. It was a "victory" of sorts, since our monetary authorities had been pressing for a realignment of rates for some time. But since it was achieved by what the Europeans considered our "benign neglect" of the dollar, it was treated as a pressure tactic that further increased tensions.

My own participation in the economic deliberations during this period was peripheral. From the start I had not expected to play a major role in international economics, which — to put it mildly — had not been a central field of study for me. Only later did I learn that the key economic policy decisions are not technical but political. At first I thought that I had enough on my hands keeping watch on the State and Defense Departments and the Central Intelligence Agency without also taking on Treasury, Commerce, and Agriculture. I took a crash "tutorial" from Professor Richard N. Cooper of Yale University to learn the rudiments of the subject. I appointed the brilliant economists Fred Bergsten and Robert Hormats to my staff. But on the whole I confined myself to a watching brief. Thus I attended meetings on the subject and I sent information memoranda to the President. But I did not seek to manage, much less dominate, the process of policy formulation as I did in other areas of national security. (This did not prevent those who criticized me for "dominating" State and Defense from also criticizing me for *not* dominating international economic policy.)

I agreed enthusiastically when, at OMB Director George Shultz's urging, the new post of Assistant to the President for International Economic Affairs was created at the White House — though it technically represented a diminution of my power. Peter Peterson, its first incumbent, and I established a close working relationship reinforced by personal friendship. Peterson, equipped with a subtle and wide-ranging mind, taught me a greal deal about international economics; I respected him enormously, and this was another reason why I intervened rarely and only when an overwhelming foreign policy interest seemed involved. The arrangement worked well until the frontal assault on the White House staff system by the new Secretary of Treasury, John Connally.

Connally had been appointed to the post in December 1970. Nixon considered his choice of one of the most formidable Democrats an extraordinary coup that sent him into transports of self-congratulatory pride for weeks afterward. For toward Connally there was none of that ambivalent sense of competition and insecurity that marked Nixon's relations with the other Cabinet members. Unlike Rogers and Laird, Connally had not had any contact with Nixon during previous crises in Nixon's life. Nixon therefore did not have with Connally the same fear of not being taken sufficiently seriously; from Connally he did not need the constant reassurance that he was indeed the President. Connally's swaggering self-assurance was Nixon's Walter Mitty image of himself. He was one person whom Nixon never denigrated behind his back.

And Connally was indeed the most formidable personality in the Cabinet. Highly intelligent, superbly endowed physically, he looked and acted as if he were born to lead. His build was matched by his ego — but those who aspire to the apex must not be criticized for that; they could never lead effectively without extraordinary self-confidence. His amiable manner never obscured the reality that he would not hesitate to overcome any obstacle to his purposes. He had a great sense of humor; but even when laughing he never gave the impression that the moment dominated him. He was not timid nor did he lack courage. "You will be measured in this town," he said to me once, "by the enemies you destroy. The bigger they are, the bigger you will be." John Connally was never afraid of his opponents; he relished combat in defense of his convictions. Whatever one might think of his views, he was a leader.

Like many self-made Texans he preferred the frontal assault to the indirect maneuver. He was convinced that the best way to transcend the malaise of Vietnam was for our leaders to be visibly engaged in a tough defense of the American interest. He demonstrated immediately that the notorious Nixon "Palace Guard," which forced Cabinet members to deal with the President through White House Assistants, could not survive the challenge of a determined Cabinet member. He simply ran over Pete Peterson on international economic policy. He refused to send memoranda through or receive instructions from him; if he needed White House guidance he simply crossed the street from the Treasury and went to the Oval Office. He showed that the White House dominance of which so much was written reflected the passive acquiescence of the Cabinet as much as the formal organization chart. He had reduced Peterson to the role of a spectator even before Nixon ended Peterson's agony by appointing him Secretary of Commerce, a position he filled with great distinction.

Connally saw no reason to treat foreigners with any greater tenderness. He believed that in the final analysis countries yield only to pressure; he had no faith in consultations except from a position of superior strength. His presence as Secretary of Treasury guaranteed that the economic dialogue with Europe would not be dull; it also ensured that the European contribution would have to be something more solid than ritual incantations of goodwill.

Such was the state of bureaucratic affairs when in the spring of 1971 Britain's imminent entry into the Common Market and the pressures on the dollar suddenly revived the issues and arguments that had become staples in the political and security field. Just as the need for "defense burden-sharing" had become a euphemism for the reduction of American forces and a policy of retrenchment, so the newfound strength of the industrial democracies was invoked as an argument for structural changes in the international monetary system. Usually the push was in the direction of greater flexibility of exchange rates, which, since it was increasingly clear that the dollar was still overvalued, would in fact mean a further decline for the dollar. All this was accompanied by a new tone of economic nationalism, even more strident after the German revaluation of the mark.

In Munich on May 28 Connally spoke of the responsibility of the Europeans and Japan in a manner that was unmistakably a challenge:

We today spend nearly 9 percent of our Gross National Product on defense — nearly $5 billion of that overseas, much of it in western Europe and Japan. Financing a military shield is a part of the burden of leadership; the responsibilities cannot and should not be cast off. But 25 years after World War II, legitimate questions arise over how the cost of these responsibilities should be allocated among the free world allies who benefit from that shield. . . .

No longer does the U.S. economy dominate the free world. No longer can considerations of friendship, or need, or capacity justify the United States carrying so heavy a share of the common burdens.

And, to be perfectly frank, no longer will the American people permit their government to engage in international actions in which the true long-run interests of the U.S. are not just as clearly recognized as those of the nations with which we deal.

And on June 7, at a meeting of the Organization for Economic Cooperation and Development, Secretary Rogers and Under Secretary of State Nathaniel Samuels followed with a comparably assertive, if more delicately phrased, approach.

Such language had not been heard since the formation of our alliances. It shook the crockery of our bureaucracy almost as much as it did the comfortable assumption of our allies that the doctrine of consultation gave them a veto over unilateral American actions. First of all, Connally's explosion ignited a contest in Washington. Paul McCracken wanted to move the discussion of our response to the emerging monetary crisis into the White House Council for International Economic Policy, where all the economic agencies (as well as my staff) were represented. Connally did not relish allowing his authority to be diluted in this way. Connally's preeminence was made unambiguous when Nixon decided to bypass his own system and asked Connally to submit recommendations based only on "consultation" with Paul McCracken, Arthur Burns (head of the Federal Reserve Board), George Shultz, and Peter Peterson. None of them had the bureaucratic clout to stand up to Connally. State and Defense were excluded from the process altogether.

The economic agencies agreed that the dollar was overvalued and that this worsened our balance of payments. They disagreed on the remedy. Shultz favored continued "benign neglect" of the dollar — in effect letting the dollar float. Burns leaned to increasing the price of gold. McCracken urged the orthodox approach of multilateral consultations for greater exchange-rate flexibility. Each of the proposals had major foreign policy consequences. "Benign neglect" of the dollar would be construed as a deliberate pressure tactic by the other industrial democracies. Increasing the price of gold would penalize those countries, like the Federal Republic, that had been trying to help at our urging by holding their reserves in dollars rather than gold. Multilateral consultations would be a signal of business as usual; they gave a veto to any significant participant. At the time Connally favored maintaining the existing system of fixed exchange rates: an unorthodoxy then that does not now look so odd in the light of experience with floating rates.

By early August protectionist sentiment and talk about retaliation against discriminatory trade practices were increasing. Peterson urged import restrictions against Japan unless it revalued the yen. Connally suggested an import surcharge. With foreign policy consequences clearly imminent by now, I assembled the Senior Review Group. This, for the first time, brought the State Department formally into the policy-making process. The discussion was inconclusive because everyone recognized that I had neither the power nor indeed the knowledge to insist on any particular policy line. Each agency therefore preferred to reserve its position for the meeting of principals under Connally's aegis where the final decisions would have to be made. Nevertheless, I asked the Review Group for options by August 17.

Within a few days events had overtaken the leisurely pace of interagency deliberations. The crisis Connally had foreseen, and perhaps sought, was upon us. On Monday, August 9, the dollar fell to its lowest point vis-à-vis the mark since World War II. On Wednesday speculation against the dollar abated somewhat. However, on Thursday European central banks were again forced to buy over $1 billion. An NSC staff memorandum pointed out:

> There is little likelihood that the situation will work itself out without either a revaluation of European currencies (which is the most probable course of action for the Europeans, given the present crisis); a devaluation of the dollar; or U.S. measures to restrict the imports of foreign goods to this country and encourage U.S. exports (which will take legislation). There will also probably be strong efforts on the part of the Europeans to restrict the amounts of dollars held by their central banks and to apply other stringent measures against the dollar.

Connally now urged Nixon to adopt a whole series of sweeping measures; it turned out that he favored *all* of the measures that my staff was putting forward as alternatives. That Saturday, August 14, just before leaving for a secret meeting in Paris with Le Duc Tho, I had a conversation with Nixon. In a favorite technique for breaking news his interlocutor might not like, Nixon was elliptical. He mentioned in passing that he would make a major speech on economic policy the following night. With his finely honed skill in avoiding unpleasant subjects he ran his planned surcharge on imports by me so lightly that its impact did not hit me until afterward. I should not have been surprised. I had seen him use the same technique on Rogers twice within recent months when his Secretary of State had been excluded from major policy deliberations — and he was going to use it on Rogers again within a week over the Berlin agreement, this time advancing the ingenious argument that it would take some of the sting out of our allies' reactions to his new economic policy. The fact was that a decision of major foreign policy importance had been taken about which neither the Secretary of State nor the national security adviser had been consulted. I asked some perfunctory questions about the attitude of Congress but made no other comment. There was no point to it. Since Nixon had already made his decision, there was no sense in debating it. The time for me to express my views would come if foreign policy consequences were obviously overwhelming.

The next day, August 15, the President made a television address outlining his new economic policy. On the domestic side he announced various measures to reduce both unemployment and inflation, such as investment credits, repeal of the excise tax on automobiles, acceleration of income tax exemptions, a $4.7 billion cut in government spending, postponement of government pay raises, and a ninety-day freeze on wages and prices. The real thrust of the new program, however, was in the measures to defend the dollar abroad and to rectify our balance-of-payments deficit. Nixon announced a 10 percent reduction in foreign economic assistance, a 10 percent surcharge on all imports, and suspension of the convertibility of the dollar into gold or other reserve assets.

With one dramatic gesture Nixon had broken the link between the dollar and gold, thereby opening the way for effective devaluation; he matched the international move with a program to cope with inflation and protectionism at home — and began the tortured process of systematic international adjustment. It was an extension of his bold strokes in foreign policy to the field of economics. The Bretton Woods agreement, which had regulated international monetary arrangements since 1944, was being made irrelevant. This was to have many, largely unforeseen, consequences as the years went on. The immediate significance of the new program was its effect abroad; it was seen by many as a declaration of economic war on the other industrial democracies, and a retreat by the United States from its previous commitment to an open international economic system. The industrial democracies, especially Japan, were in a state of shock because of the suddenness of the announcement, the unilateral nature of some of the measures, and the necessity they imposed to consider a formal restructuring of the entire international economic system. Clearly, we were heading into a period of intense negotiations, conflict, and confrontation.

When during the evening of August 16 I returned from Paris to a fait accompli, I found Nixon elated. For the second time in a month he had taken the world by stunning surprise; he saw himself as revolutionizing international economics as he had already transformed international diplomacy. He reveled in the publicity coup he had achieved. As he often did he asked me innumerable times to recite foreign reactions, which were mixed at best; he was delighted by the domestic approval. In this mood of euphoria, Nixon on August 19 stopped in Dallas and (proving that Presidential minds run in tandem) uttered the following memorable words: "The great challenge of peace is for each of us individually and for all us, as 'one nation under God,' to rededicate ourselves to this magnificent American dream. With this as our moral equivalent of war we can move into a generation of peace." It was hard to go wrong with a platform that offered peace as the moral equivalent of war.

My own views about the August 15 measures were agnostic. Later I grew concerned about the unsettling impact of a prolonged confrontation on allied relationships. At that time, however, I did not trust my judgment enough to take a position on the merits of the new measures. After the event I came to the view that some shock had probably been needed to bring about serious negotiations. My major concern was to end confrontation when it had served its purpose and to prevent economic issues from overwhelming all considerations of foreign policy.

Formally, the measures represented an effort to force new parities, that is to say, to establish values for the various currencies more in line with their real purchasing power and thus to deprive some allied countries of the unfair advantage of pegging their currencies at levels most helpful to their exports. In time, in fact, it led to the abandonment of a fixed system of exchange in favor of our present "floating" system in which each currency finds its own level on the basis of short-term supply and demand.

It took us nearly two years to get a fully floating exchange-rate system accepted by our allies. Its advocates thought it would avoid the periodic crises in which fixed rates were devalued when currency reserves ran out or revalued in the face of surpluses. There would be "painless" daily adjustments; speculators would disappear; exchange rates would more faithfully reflect underlying economic strengths; countries would not be bankrupted of their gold and currency reserves supporting "artificial rates." It has not quite worked out that way. The new system has been subject to crises and panics even more dramatic than the old system of fixed rates. It has given speculators new opportunities. Far from being immutably tied to economic performance, rates have been vulnerable to uncertainty and speculation and especially to transfers of capital balances. Reserves have still been spent to preserve some semblance of stability in a variation of the old system of fixed parities. Nobody in 1971, of course, predicted that the Organization of Petroleum Exporting Countries would raise the price of oil fivefold and create new billions of dollars of volatile money. But this is to anticipate a sequel to the Nixon-Connally spectacular that is still working itself out and that was then unforeseeable; problems of the dollar, the OPEC balances, and the whole system of international payments will, I suspect, remain on the international agenda for the indefinite future. The immediate confrontation in 1971 was the urgent concern to bring about a realignment of currencies within the fixed system (which had something like two more years of life). It was not just the rate for the dollar that was affected; the rates among other currencies were inevitably interlinked.

Connally's strategy was to put forward no specific American proposal to resolve the crisis. He reasoned that the longer the import surcharge remained, the stronger our bargaining position would be. He feared that *any* American proposal would enable all other nations to combine against it even though they would never be able to agree on a positive program of their own. Hence, a series of meetings of deputy finance ministers on September 3 in Paris and of finance ministers in London on September 15–16 ended inconclusively. Deputy Secretary of the Treasury Paul Volcker announced that the United States did not have a particular plan for solving the crisis. Talks were in a phase of "consultations, not negotiations."

Mounting tensions were therefore inevitable. The other industrial nations resented being pressured into adaptations of their economic policies even though they knew very well that without pressure they would almost surely not have acted at all. Many were shocked by the new American assertiveness. We would have to tread a narrow path between maintaining enough pressure to provide an incentive for the adjustments we were seeking, and evoking a trade war as well as jeopardizing political relationships built up over decades. I sought to make my contribution in finding that balance.

At first, I had sympathized with Connally's view that without a measure of confrontation our trading partners would avoid the hard choices implicit in a major realignment of the grid of exchange rates. But as time went on I began to suspect that Connally was sufficiently Texan to relish a good scrap for its own sake. At least he judged it would strengthen the Administration at home if it was perceived as a rugged defender of American national interests. But in my view the optimum time to settle is when the other side is still suspended between conciliation and confrontation. Once it has decided on confrontation, it cannot yield until the test of strength is far advanced. My preference was, therefore, to go along with hard-nosed negotiating for a time but to stop short of all-out confrontation that would threaten our Alliance relationships. I was reinforced in this view when Arthur Burns showed me a list of retaliatory measures planned by our major trading partners which would produce an outcome on balance highly disadvantageous to us.

While waiting for the moment to enter the fray, I moved on two fronts. I used the regular NSC machinery to work out political and economic approaches, especially to Japan, in order to soften the effect of the August 15 shock and to give us a running start for a new period of cooperation once we had surmounted the present crisis. Under Secretary of State and former Ambassador to Japan Alexis Johnson performed yeoman service here. At the same time I sought to move toward articulating some definable objectives that would permit negotiations to start. I proposed to Nixon that he form a small group to establish a negotiating position. It was composed of Connally, Paul McCracken, George Shultz, and me. Arthur Burns was kept advised. Nixon excluded Peterson because of Connally's objections, but I kept in close contact with Pete informally and he made a major contribution. The group met about once a week during October. It developed the basic scheme on which the settlement was ultimately achieved. The final plan was largely the work of Connally, Shultz, and Burns; my effort was to encourage a resolution, to explain the political implications, and in the end to move matters to a conclusion.

For a while matters got worse. In a press conference on September 16 Nixon had related the lifting of the surcharge not only to reform of the monetary system but also to burden-sharing, trade restraints, and non-tariff trade barriers — an agenda so incapable of rapid fulfillment as to threaten to make the surcharge permanent. He repeated the same theme on September 23. By the end of September, however, the meetings of the small group were beginning to bear fruit. At the annual meeting of the International Monetary Fund Connally linked the end of the sur-charge exclusively to an agreed monetary reform. Tensions mounted again when, in October, Connally still refused to put forward a specific scheme for monetary reform; he had not yet in his view squeezed the maximum out of the situation. Since the Europeans and Japanese could not agree among themselves, the practical result was that the import surcharge continued in force, thus raising the danger that sooner or later the other countries would retaliate in a bout of economic nationalism. Moreover, I feared that if the European countries and Japan suffered a recession which could be ascribed to our actions, there would be no want of voices blaming it on us, and permanent damage would result not only to our foreign policy but to the domestic structures of our allies. No new economic arrangement, however beneficial, could com-pensate for such a change.

To bring matters to a head, I recommended to Nixon that he inter-vene personally with the European heads of state. My original idea was a summit of the Western leaders. However, Pompidou made it clear that he was not interested; he knew he would not be able to create a common European front; in case of a stalemate Brandt would be under great pressure to side with the United States. Therefore we decided to initiate a series of bilateral talks. The key was Pompidou. Heath would avoid choosing sides between France and the United States. If we lined up with Brandt, we would evoke French resentment; we could always do that if the approach to Pompidou failed. Our preferred strategy was to permit Pompidou to establish a position of leadership in Europe by negotiating the terms of a settlement with us. We always had in reserve the threat to isolate him if he were totally intransigent. I did not think this likely. I judged that everyone would be eager to settle if an Ameri-can proposal gave the opportunity. And I was confident that Nixon would not want a public impression of deadlock to emerge from meet-ings in which he was involved.

On November 9 our Ambassador to France, Dick Watson, called on me at the White House, and I asked him on his return to Paris to arrange a meeting between Nixon and Pompidou. Pompidou agreed in principle. The project nearly ran aground in a dispute over the venue, essentially an issue of prestige. The French were at their prickliest. It was Nixon's turn to visit France, but he could not visit one capital alone. A tour of Europe, however, would destroy the idea of separate negotiations. On the other hand, Pompidou would not accept our proposal of a French island in the West Indies because it would force him to travel a disproportionate distance and because, though French soil, it would not be considered as comparable to his own visit to America. We finally settled on the neutral site of the Portuguese islands of the Azores. The meeting was scheduled for December 13. Pompidou, as I had suspected, insisted that we should not discuss economic issues with any other European leader before; this suggested that he was in a mood to settle. He urged that the Group of Ten, the finance ministers of the major economic countries, move up and dispose of a meeting scheduled for December 15, thus assuring that any settlement would be in the first instance bilateral between France and the United States. Nixon agreed. The Group of Ten met on December 1 in Rome without major results, as planned. The stage was thus set for the decisive meeting in the Azores. (Meetings had also been scheduled with Heath for December 20–21 in Bermuda and with Brandt for December 28–29 in Key Biscayne.)

We left for the Azores on the day that the India-Parkistan crisis was reaching its climax. On the journey Nixon and I knew that Al Haig was meeting with the Chinese, and we expected that they would inform us if they had decided to help Pakistan and thus move matters to the brink of general war. Even after the Chinese note removed the need for a military decision, we were preoccupied throughout our stay in the Azores with preventing a final assault by India on West Pakistan.

Most of my time in the Azores was spent in negotiating the monetary issue — not my strong suit. I had arrived at this extraordinary situation because of the vagaries of both American and French domestic politics. On our side I was the senior official most convinced that the political costs of the economic crisis were growing prohibitive, and that the Europeans were prepared to settle on reasonable terms. Once the President was involved he wanted a success. And true to his usual pattern, he identified this with his being seen to be the chief actor — at that time he still saw me as a surrogate, not as a competitor for public attention. Connally, in turn, was not eager to be perceived as having moved to compromise. He was willing enough to *have* a negotiation, but he preferred to keep himself in reserve for a deadlock (and as a brooding threat).

As for the French, Pompidou was eager to be perceived as the chief architect of a settlement. Relations with his Finance Minister, Valéry Giscard d'Estaing — destined to be his successor — did not seem close; Pompidou seemed determined to exclude him from the negotiations. (This in turn made it impossible, in any event, for Connally to participate directly.) Looked at practically, however, it gave us an important clue. For if Pompidou insisted on handling the negotiations, he was expecting them to succeed.

So it happened that a solution to the monetary crisis was being negotiated between Pompidou, a leading financial expert and a professional banker, and a neophyte; even in my most megalomaniac moments I did not believe that I would be remembered for my contributions to the reform of the international monetary system. From the American military base where our party was ensconced in barracks (except for the President, who was given the base commander's modest house), I helicoptered to Pompidou's elegant villa at a far end of the island. I was accompanied only by General Walters, who was to act as interpreter. Pompidou greeted me with his unfailing courtesy, attended by his interpreter, Prince Constantin Andronikof. We breakfasted overlooking the lush meadows and gentle hills of Portugal's outpost in the Atlantic, one of the relics of the period when that small country sent its sons on stupendous explorations of unknown seas, inspired by faith and sustained by greed.

As things turned out, my negotiations with Pompidou were less one-sided than our relative competence in economics might have implied. Connally had given me a range of positions that he was prepared to accept. I decided that it would be suicidal to engage in a technical negotiation. Once I started retreating from our maximum position, I would have no logical stopping point until we had reached our final fallback. My best tactic was to turn ignorance into an asset, and technical incompetence into a weapon. If I advanced one position only and refused to bargain, it could be presented — without belligerence — as the inability of an amateur to compete with a professional. I therefore chose to use the first session to reconnoiter the terrain. Afterward I would develop a position with Connally and submit it the next day.

To determine France's real position I presented the issue to Pompidou in philosophical and political terms. A settlement was necessary and inevitable. It was bound to be reached with *some* of the European countries, given their inability to arrive at a common position. We would like it best if France would take the lead. My presence as a negotiator guaranteed that we wanted an outcome compatible with the self-respect and needs of each side; it was the only politically viable result. In the establishment of a new international monetary system nobody could afford a "victory," since the new arrangement could be maintained only by the willing cooperation of all its members. I had come to negotiate, not to impose. It would help me if Pompidou would state his minimum requirements. I would do my best to bring about an understanding response when Nixon discussed them with Pompidou in the afternoon. If they agreed, I would submit a concrete proposal the next morning if he were disposed to invite me to breakfast again.

It turned out to be the right approach. Pompidou could not forgo some biting and not entirely unjustified comments to the effect that our economic policies seemed to him more geared to our electoral processes than to global concerns. And he asked how we would react if he were to ask us to accept some economic restraints because it would help him with some constituencies. But having made his point, he gave me a brilliant analysis of the monetary situation from which I distilled that Pompidou would not accept a freely floating system. He would in the end go along with some upward revaluation of the franc — if only for reasons of national pride — but to maintain France's competitive position it had to be less than the revaluation of the mark. He would not resist devaluation by the United States. The total package of American devaluation and European revaluation would be around 9 percent, with the franc at some distance from the mark along that scale. And Pompidou insisted that we defend the new parities. For this, he was willing to acquiesce in our going off the limited gold standard. It was agreed that the morning session with Nixon would deal with a review of the international situation. The afternoon session would cover monetary matters.

Nixon, Connally, and I reviewed Pompidou's presentation during the lunch break. Connally agreed to give me a proposal for establishing new parities in time for my breakfast meeting with Pompidou. He was extraordinarily helpful.

It was not easy to judge how well the afternoon session went, because Nixon did not plan to leave his mark on history in the field of economics. Pompidou repeated his presentation of the morning. Presciently, he stressed that a floating system would lead to chaos. He was prepared to help establish new parities provided they reflected relative economic strengths. It cannot be said that Nixon was clearly on top of the subject. He wanted a solution, not a discussion of exchange rates. If given truth serum, he would no doubt have revealed that he could not care less where in the new scale the various currencies were to be pegged. And as always when involved in negotiations rather than general exchanges of views, he was nervous to the point of anxiety. He wrapped himself in general observations, not all of them equally germane. But they were enough for Pompidou to sense general agreement to what had been discussed in the morning. The final details were to be worked out at breakfast between Pompidou and me.

In the evening Connally and I put the proposal to Pompidou into final shape. I told Connally that it was senseless for me to bargain, since I would be on my weakest ground. I would prefer to present a position somewhere between our minimum and maximum positions and stick to it. It should be reasonable enough for Pompidou to be able to accept it in principle, and adequate to our needs. Connally was not by temperament inclined to this negotiating method, but he finally agreed that it was the best he could do with an unworldly professor.

I submitted the numbers worked out between Connally and me to Pompidou over breakfast. The extraordinary aspect of the encounter was that France and the United States should have taken it upon themselves to work out the exchange rates for every one of the world's important currencies. Agreement, in fact, was reached rather quickly, for our proposal had taken Pompidou's reasonable requirements seriously. We drafted a document that was ratified by the principals in the afternoon, at a session in which for the first time the finance ministers participated. The agreement led to a conference of the Group of Ten a week later in Washington. All the other nations fell into line; the Smithsonian Agreement ratified the new monetary arrangements.

The economic crisis was over, at least until 1974 when the fivefold increase in the price of oil placed before the industrial nations the necessity of reassessing the entire world economic stystem. It had been accomplished with the inevitable apprehension, confusion, and anxiety that come when any well-established structure for conducting affairs is scrapped. The United States abandoned gold convertibility in order to secure a more realistic and defensible set of exchange-rate relationships. But the system could not last. Despite the Smithsonian Agreement, a floating dollar was inevitable. As Raymond Aron correctly pointed out, nonconvertibility into gold presented our partners with the choice of either accumulating dollars indefinitely or consenting to a devaluation with all its commercial disadvantages to them.[1] We were strong in monetary affairs; our partners were increasingly powerful commercially. The new system was bound to generate increasing pressures on the dollar, requiring sooner or later an even more basic structural reform of the world economic system.

Nixon's unilateral decisions of August 15, 1971, had their desired effect. Allied cohesion had been strained but not broken. At this remove it is difficult for me to assess whether the brutal unilateralism coming so soon after the shock of the secret trip to Peking mortgaged relations unnecessarily for many years to come, or whether our allies by their immobilism left us no other option.

High-Level Consultations: The Final Round

NINETEEN seventy-one ended with another series of meetings between Nixon and the leaders of our closest allies: France, Britain, and the Federal Republic of Germany. Except for the monetary issue, no great decisions emerged. Most of the fundamental issues remained in abeyance; but foundations were laid for new approaches after we had extricated ourselves from Indochina. Only then would we be able to overcome the European ambivalences: doubt about American constancy coupled with the unwillingness to assume a larger burden of the common defense; pressures for détente side by side with fears of a US–Soviet condominium; insistence on consultation over any American global move while catering to domestic popularity through the appearance of independence from and sometimes opposition to American preferences.

Given Nixon's lack of interest in economic issues, the political conversations were by far the most significant part of his meeting with Pompidou at the Azores. They had remarkably compatible views of international affairs. Both were profoundly suspicious of the Soviet Union, yet convinced of the need to demonstrate a desire for coexistence as the precondition of domestic support for a strong foreign policy. Both sought security not in abstract proclamations of goodwill but in strong defenses and an international equilibrium in which China played a prominent part.

They diverged because Pompidou shared de Gaulle's premonitions that, however able Nixon's conduct of foreign policy, the United States' internal dynamics would induce it sooner or later to withdraw from Europe. He therefore favored creation of a European political union backed up ultimately by a common European defense — an idea to which America had been inhospitable at least since the 1950s. Pompidou saw a potential incompatibility between our strategy of nuclear deterrence and the requirements of European security. "We want to be protected, not avenged," he said. "Revenge would be small consolation to us in a cemetery." Pompidou had urged Nixon toward conciliation with the Soviet Union when they first met in February 1970. Now that his advice was being adopted and the Moscow summit was scheduled, Pompidou shared also de Gaulle's long-standing distaste for a US–Soviet condominium; and he remained profoundly suspicious that in the long run German nationalism would respond to the siren calls from the East. He offered no better solution to his dilemmas than a European Security Conference, which he thought would curb everyone's appetite for going it alone. But on the whole, Pompidou's ruminations were intellectual exercises justifying that combination (so strange to Americans) of Alliance commitment and French independence that in fact has enabled France to conduct a serious and responsible foreign policy throughout the Fifth Republic.

In these general surveys Nixon was at his best. He had an excellent grasp of overall relationships and he could articulate our position concisely, often eloquently. Nixon did not differ with Pompidou's analysis of European conditions. After some initial hesitation he now favored the fostering of European unity; he objected, however, to basing it on the prospect of American withdrawal, which he feared would turn into a self-fulfilling prophecy. He concentrated on Soviet relations and the opening to China. He expressed his own fears about the long-range implications of *Ostpolitik*. He promised that his trips to Moscow and Peking would not encourage sentimental illusions. He explained our policy in the India-Pakistan crisis; Pompidou professed to agree with our analysis. But he left little doubt that since we were making the difficult decisions, France had some scope for cynical opportunism. Since we would protect the equilibrium, France would lean toward India as the stronger and more populous country.

Pompidou's reactions reflected the basic European ambivalence. In times of tension Europeans advocated détente; in periods of relaxation they dreaded condominium. In crisis they looked to us to maintain the equilibrium outside of Europe, and under the umbrella of the risks we were running they did not hesitate to seek special advantages for themselves. These attitudes acted at once as a spur and a brake to our European policy. It impelled us to a degree of sharing of views unprecedented among allies, but it left us finally face to face with the necessity of making the ultimate decisions on the most critical issues, especially outside of Europe. And it provided an additional incentive for us to develop our own strategy for détente. In its absence European leaders would make their own forays to Moscow and be tempted to gain the support of their left by pretending to act as a brake on an alleged American bellicosity, which they secretly welcomed. If we had our own option toward the East, these tendencies would be restrained by the fear that if pushed too far we could outstrip our allies in a race to Moscow.

The meeting with Heath on December 20–21 followed a similar pattern, except that Heath, being more familiar with American thought processes, was less explicit about long-term trends than Pompidou. He was more prepared to take Nixon at his word when he explained our priority of Atlantic over East-West relations. Heath pursued his favorite theme of European unity and reassured the President that it would be "competitive," not confrontational. It was an interesting and not entirely reassuring formulation, a considerable step away from the automatic cooperation taken for granted by our own "twin pillar" Atlanticists in the 1960s and by all of Heath's predecessors. Heath explained his ideas for the best procedure for Atlantic cooperation. First Europe should develop a common policy at a European summit or foreign ministers' conference. After that an effort would be made to coordinate with us — another important modification of the old "special relationship" based on prior consultations between London and Washington. Heath spoke more passionately than Pompidou about European defense. We faced in Heath the curiosity of a more benign British version of de Gaulle.

Except on these issues Heath's views paralleled ours. He shared our skepticism about the European Security Conference. He gave some credence to Pompidou's belief that it might buttress the independence of East European countries but sympathized with my view that it was hard to explain why then the Soviets would push it so energetically. Heath's major concern was not to be caught in a dispute between France and the United States on the subject. He suggested we put the issue off until 1973, using as a pretext the need to ratify Germany's Eastern treaties first.

The review of the world situation was warm and harmonious. On the Indian subcontinent Britain's historic relationship was too emotional to countenance our colder geopolitical assessment. The two leaders discussed what was perhaps the most profound philosophical question faced by all the nations of the West in common. It was posed by Heath: "We are moving more and more into a state of world affairs in which effective action is no longer possible. How much can you do?" It led to one of Nixon's more effective presentations, part of which has already been quoted in the previous chapter:

Part of the reason for conducting our Vietnam withdrawal so slowly is to give some message that we are not prepared to pay *any* price for ending a war; we must now ask ourselves what we are willing to pay to avert war. If we are not, we have tough days ahead. . . . The Establishment has a guilt complex. They can't stand the fact that I, their political opponent, am rectifying their mistakes. In addition, the Establishment has this growing obsession with domestic problems. The intellectual establishment is confused and frustrated by their own role, and by the United States' role. They have never believed that there was any real danger from the Left. They are turning inward. They have made it a problem whether we are going to continue our involvement in the world. The point of this too-long discourse is this: I know the issue; I'll see it through; we will have a world role. You'll wake up day after day wondering what's happening to us. Our initiatives are necessary to give our people hope. A political leader must constantly feed hope — but he must constantly know what he is doing, without illusion.

Nixon's later fate must not obscure the importance of this passage. He was right; he had diagnosed both the American and the Atlantic problem correctly.

The last visitor was Willy Brandt. As with the other European leaders there were few outstanding issues. But unlike the other leaders Brandt made no claims to a global role; he prided himself on avoiding it. As a result there was relatively little to discuss. The purely German problems had been negotiated. Both the Eastern treaties and the Berlin Agreement were awaiting ratification by the German Parliament. When Brandt visited Nixon at Key Biscayne on December 28 and 29, 1971, I did not attend the discussions, being laid up with influenza. This did not inhibit Nixon from following his usual procedure of meeting his visitor accompanied only by one White House aide (in this case Haig sat in for me). Rogers and German Foreign Minister Walter Scheel held separate discussions.

The major topic of conversation was East-West relations. In those far-away days Brandt was the leading expert on the Soviet leaders; he had met them more frequently than anyone; none of our senior officials had dealt with Brezhnev, Kosygin, or Podgorny — except for a brief encounter between Nixon and Podgorny at the reception in the Elysée Palace after the memorial service for de Gaulle. Brezhnev especially was an enigma to us. Brandt's assessment of him was on the whole positive. Brezhnev, according to Brandt, initially had been unfamiliar with foreign policy but in the past year had gained a great deal of confidence. He no longer simply read carefully prepared notes. Brandt thought that the Soviets genuinely wished détente partly because of their fear of China. He expressed his gratification at NATO's support for his *Ostpolitik*. Nixon frostily corrected him, saying that the Alliance did not *object* to the policy. But the Federal Republic had to make the decision and accept the responsibility. Brandt suggested that the Soviets resented the linkage between the German treaties and the Berlin Agreement. Haig had the impression that Brandt was not all that enthusiastic about linkage himself, fearing "reverse linkage" — Soviet pressure on the access routes to Berlin to accelerate the ratification process. However, given German politics, Brandt saw no way to avoid it. The Bonn Parliament would surely refuse to ratify the treaties without a satisfactory implementation of the Berlin Agreement. As for us, the state of affairs described by Brandt was not without its compensations. It gave us a lever to exact restrained Soviet behavior, especially if we had to react to a Vietnam offensive. The Soviets would not want a global crisis before the German Parliament had voted.

Nixon gave a preview of his approach to the Peking and Moscow summits, also following familiar lines. Brandt argued that East-West trade should not be linked to political negotiations; he considered commerce a way to leaven the Soviet system. He also urged a European Security Conference, invoking the standard European argument that it was desired precisely by the most independent countries of Eastern Europe as a means of buttressing their autonomy. No more than Pompidou before him could he explain why the Soviets were pressing for a conference that would loosen their hold on the satellite orbit.

Nixon, like me, was more skeptical. He warned that a European Security Conference might furnish an excuse to Congressional critics for troop reductions. He urged that all of the allies move in a deliberate fashion. Nixon and Brandt both noted that after the brief flurry of May the Soviets had cooled to the idea of mutual and balanced force reductions. Brandt stressed his interest in fostering the ties between Europe and the United States. It was a friendly meeting, successful even though it did not aim for results.

These general, largely philosophical discussions between the leaders of Europe and the United States that marked the beginning and the end of the 1970–71 period reflected the fact that these years of the Nixon Administration were an eventful period in our relations with the other industrial democracies. The Federal Republic was on the verge of completing its *Ostpolitik*. Our support of it had helped channel it in a direction compatible with Atlantic unity and Western cohesion. The economic adjustment entailed by Britain's imminent entry into the Common Market had produced a period of tension. But in the end, a new monetary system had emerged, reached — at least in its final stages — in a cooperative manner that gave the principal nations a stake in maintaining it. The military strength of the Western Alliance had been maintained in the face of bitter assault in the Congress.

Much remained to be done. A period of détente was clearly approaching. It remained to be seen whether the Alliance would succeed in distinguishing between form and substance, whether a period of relaxation of tensions would slacken the efforts to maintain the equilibrium or provide a spur to cohesion and new creativity. We hoped to infuse the Atlantic relationship with a new spurt of leadership after the Vietnam war was behind us, for it would — and must — remain the cornerstone of our foreign policy.

XXIII

Vietnam 1970-71:
Forcing Hanoi's Hand

ONTH by month the design of our foreign policy was piecing
together: Atlantic relationships, the opening to China, the
consequent improvement in Moscow's attitude to serious
negotiations. But we had one nightmare that might shatter all we were
trying to achieve: the war in Vietnam. We could not end it on terms acceptable to Hanoi without jeopardizing everything else we were doing
abroad; we could not pursue it to a decisive military result without risking all cohesion at home. So we navigated between conflicting necessities: holding out hope to our citizens that there would be an end, but
posing sufficient risk to Hanoi to induce a settlement compatible with
our international responsibilities and our national honor.

By the summer of 1970 the participants in our Vietnam debate were
for the moment spent from the trauma of Cambodia. The Administration
had achieved its objective of reducing Hanoi's capacity for offensive
operations. But it had done so at the cost of psychological exhaustion;
the fear of another round of demonstrations permeated all the thinking
about Vietnam in the Executive Branch that summer — even that of
Nixon, who pretended to be impervious. So weariness provided the
respite that a consensus could not furnish. And the crises along the Suez
Canal, in Cienfuegos, Jordan, and Chile absorbed some of the government's attention and focused public concern on other parts of the world.

We had one piece of good fortune. I had suggested, and Nixon had
enthusiastically agreed to, David Bruce's appointment as Ambassador to
the negotiations in Paris. Bruce had accepted at once. In the summer of
1970, as the national obsession with Vietnam seized hold of us again,
Bruce was a steadying influence. He asked to study the issue for two
months before making proposals; he did not wish the impression to be
created that he had received fresh instructions. Hanoi would settle only
if it believed that it could not extract fresh concessions simply by dig-
ging in.

It had a calming effect, for in the wake of the turmoil over Cambodia

Nixon's mood oscillated wildly. Nixon was talking in resolute terms on July 4 when he met Bruce and Phil Habib, his Paris negotiating team, at San Clemente. He would stay the course regardless of the political risk. He did not think de-escalation or unilateral withdrawal would budge the North Vietnamese; every time we withdrew troops Hanoi became more difficult. If negotiations failed, he would throw restraint to the winds and return to massive bombing. But a week later, on July 11, he fretted to me privately that the war was sapping his domestic support and therefore had to be ended before 1972; if any of his likely opponents were elected President, America's world position would be undermined. His solution was to combine all-out bombing with a total withdrawal. But by July 22 at breakfast in the White House with Bruce and Ellsworth Bunker and me, he had a more optimistic estimate of our endurance:

I am utterly convinced that how we end this war will determine the future of the U.S. in the world. We can maintain the American position in Europe and Asia if we come out well. The American people are evenly divided. The establishment is against me, but I'll see it through if I'm the only person in the country to do it. We'll see the end of our participation one way or another. . . . I came into office without the support of all the people who oppose me today and I can get reelected without their support.

Yet by August 10 Nixon was shaken by a conversation with Senators Harry Byrd and Gordon Allott, who had urged him to end the war quickly. "We've got the Left where we want it now," he told me. "All they've got left to argue for is a bug-out, and that's their problem. But when the Right starts wanting to get out, for whatever reason, that's *our* problem." Therefore he wanted to bring matters to a head by blockading the North, resuming bombing, and simultaneously withdrawing all our forces. I warned that in view of the trouble we had had in sustaining a campaign of eight weeks' duration to a distance of twenty miles in Cambodia, we would not be able to stick to such a course unless there had been overwhelming provocation. And withdrawal would convey a signal exactly the opposite of our military actions. Nixon's scheme might well produce a collapse in Saigon amidst carnage in the North. Nixon did not pursue the subject.

During the summer our studies confirmed that the North Vietnamese supply system through Cambodia had been disrupted and enemy forces based there severely weakened. More important, the North Vietnamese troops in the southern half of Vietnam — the so-called Military Regions 3 and 4 — would now have to be used not for offensive operations in South Vietnam but to protect new base areas and to train Cambodian guerrillas; their capacity for offensive operations had been gravely undermined for at least a year. Allied casualties dropped correspondingly.

In the twelve months before Cambodia over 7,000 Americans were killed in action. In the year after, the figure was less than 2,500. The next year it fell to less than 500.

But the political problem remained. Hanoi was not weakened to the point of abandoning hope and continued to demand the unilateral withdrawal of *all* American forces and the overthrow of the Saigon government. There was no hint of compromise. We were offered no terms other than unconditional surrender and betrayal of the millions who had relied on us to the tender mercies of Communist rule. Our opponents at home derided our definition of honor, but their alternative, fixing an unconditional withdrawal date, was an act of futility as well as dishonor. By the end of August the Senate was debating the McGovern-Hatfield amendment, which set a deadline for American withdrawal on December 31, 1971, allowing the President to extend the deadline by sixty days in an emergency. This scheme received wide editorial support. For the *Washington Post*[1] it would "end the shell game"; to the *St. Louis Post-Dispatch* we were "dropping the mask" by opposing McGovern-Hatfield, and revealed that our purpose was military victory (which had become a term of opprobrium). But once a final withdrawal date had been established by law, the already narrowing margin for negotiations would evaporate. We would lose the capacity to bargain even for our prisoners, for we would have literally nothing left to offer except the overthrow of a friendly government and the abandonment of millions to a brutal dictatorship. To end the war honorably we needed to present our enemy with the very margin of uncertainty about our intentions that our domestic opponents bent every effort to remove.

The ideal bargaining position would have existed if our public had trusted our goals and our enemy had been uncertain about our tactics. Our domestic discord produced exactly the opposite state of affairs. We faced a constant credibility gap at home while our opponents understood only too well the direction in which we were being pushed. Nor, once we were committed to a fixed withdrawal date, would it be so simple as was claimed to return to Congress to ask for the extension the McGovern-Hatfield amendment purported to offer. The very forces that had established the deadline would surely strive to preserve it. And the issue was unlikely to arise in a clear-cut way. The mere passage of the amendment might well lead to the collapse of the South Vietnamese morale and with it their armed forces. Thailand would probably close the bases so essential for air operations in Vietnam, and Souvanna Phouma of Laos would almost certainly request us to end the bombing of the Ho Chi Minh Trail, as these two threatened countries sought to adjust to new realities. No responsible administration could accept these risks merely in the hope of reassuring critics, most of whom, as events showed, were not to be placated. As things turned out, we managed to remove the overwhelming majority of American armed forces within the time period of the McGovern-Hatfield amendment and the remainder fifteen months later. Enough remained to help blunt the North Vietnamese offensive of 1972. But we withdrew without overthrowing our allies, and to have bound ourselves in September 1970 to a known date that we had no way of meeting would have had a vastly different result.

The McGovern-Hatfield amendment was defeated on September 1, 1970, 55–39. It was technically an Administration victory. But that thirty-nine Senators sought to prescribe the conduct of peace negotiations, in the face of Administration warnings that they were legislating a debacle, dealt a serious blow to the psychological basis for a coherent strategy. Nor was that vote the end of the amendment. It would come back month after month with constantly increasing support, dramatizing to Hanoi the erosion of our position and thus reducing the North's incentive for serious negotiation. And North Vietnam had another disincentive to negotiate. We were pulling out American troops so fast as to place a burden of credulity on Vietnamization; in the process we lost the bargaining leverage inherent in offering a speedup in our withdrawals in return for a genuinely free political choice by the people.

The concept of a free choice would have been hard to sell to the North Vietnamese in the best of circumstances, for they had no category of experience to which to refer it. They had seized power by the gun; they had expanded it by struggle. They were dedicated Marxist-Leninists. To them political legitimacy resided in the militant elite that embodied the "real wishes" of the people; dissenters had to be reeducated or eliminated. Nor did Vietnamese history offer succor: Past rulers had governed by the mandate of heaven and endured by success. Our schemes for impartial electoral commissions and free ballots were rejected disdainfully by Hanoi; they were accepted reluctantly by Saigon to indulge a rich benefactor whose support was essential for survival, though his naiveté constantly courted disaster. How in the light of Communist ideology and Vietnamese history it could ever have been supposed that all the Communists were fighting for was a coalition government — or that indeed any Vietnamese would accept it — must be left to studies of mass psychology.

I wrote to Nixon on July 20, warning him once again that a strategy relying on Vietnamization would not be compatible indefinitely with a strategy of negotiations. Each unilateral withdrawal tended to weaken our bargaining position. If troop withdrawals were already at the fastest rate consistent with Saigon's survival, our margin for speeding them up was limited; hence we had little to offer Hanoi. Somewhere down the road, probably by the middle of 1971, we might have to choose between Vietnamization and negotiation. It was mainly to try to explore hidden possibilities for breaking the deadlock that during July and August 1970 the Administration's thinking crystallized around the idea of a standstill cease-fire (or cease-fire in place), a proposal previously broached by Cyrus Vance after he retired as negotiator in Paris,[2] Averell Harriman, the *New York Times*,[3] and Senator Mike Mansfield. Its appeal as a "compromise" proposal was that both sides would thereby be renouncing military victory. In 1969 a standstill cease-fire had become a favorite formula for moderate opponents of the war who did not yet wish to advocate American capitulation or a fixed deadline for withdrawal. Their views were shared by many senior officials, from various motives. Some in the Defense Department favored a cease-fire to ease budgetary pressures and free funds for weapons procurement. The State Department urged it partly to please the Congress and the media, and partly from its own congenital wish to fuel negotiations with ever-new proposals. Nixon was generally disdainful of all these schemes. The day after his November 3, 1969, speech, the President had written to his Secretaries of State and Defense, specifically rejecting any initiative for a cease-fire. Nevertheless, on November 8 Rogers urged that we support the Mansfield Resolution for a Vietnam cease-fire as a means of winning over the doves. On November 10 a formal State Department memorandum arrived at the White House proposing a cease-fire initiative.

Unfortunately, there were two considerable obstacles: the North Vietnamese had shown no interest in cease-fires of any kind; and in 1969 the South Vietnamese government, our military commanders, and the Saigon Embassy had all been convinced that a standstill cease-fire would precipitate the military collapse of South Vietnam. The Vietnam Special Studies Group studied the impact of a cease-fire province by province. Its conclusions tended to confirm the Saigon judgment.

We had nevertheless kept the idea in play, on the theory that if it were accepted in principle we would insist on terms that gave the South Vietnamese a reasonable chance to survive. In February and March 1970, I had proposed to Le Duc Tho a cease-fire for Laos and Cambodia; I listed it among the subjects we were prepared to discuss for Vietnam.

But Le Duc Tho refused any such discussion. At every turn — until October 1972 — he contemptuously lectured me about the impossibility of a cease-fire without a prior political settlement; and his terms for that were a thinly disguised Communist takeover. I do not know whether Hanoi was so disdainful because it thought its prospects in the countryside better than we did, or because it feared that we would keep our troops in Vietnam after a cease-fire, or because of a doctrinaire Marxist-Leninist mistrust of any concept of equilibrium. For whatever reason, Hanoi ignored the suggestion in Nixon's May 14, 1969, speech and paid no attention to its reiteration on November 3 (both of these were in the form of offering local cease-fires, but the hint could have been easily picked up).

In late May of 1970 I ordered a special study that produced a variety of options to be discussed at interagency meetings in June and July, including an NSC meeting on July 21. Everyone agreed that Hanoi would reject a cease-fire involving regroupment or withdrawal; the only kind with any chance of being accepted by the other side was a cease-fire in place. The success of the Cambodian operation now made the risks tolerable; the North Vietnamese had regrouped their forces, withdrawing them closer to the border and using them to protect training bases for the Cambodian Communists. Nevertheless, our studies predicted that in a cease-fire in place, Saigon's control over the population would erode by at least 6 percent.

Yet it was a measure of the tightrope we were walking domestically that during the summer a consensus developed around putting forward a standstill cease-fire proposal. Inside the government opinions had not changed, except that Nixon was coming around to the need for putting forward some peace proposal after the Cambodian trauma. Outside government, too, the concept gained momentum. On the day the McGovern-Hatfield amendment was defeated a bipartisan group of fourteen Senators whom the *Washington Post* called "an unusual cross-section of hawks and doves"[4] sent Nixon a letter urging him to devote his efforts at the Paris peace talks toward "an internationally supervised standstill cease-fire throughout Vietnam." Sixteen more Senators joined by September 18. At the same time Clark Kerr's National Committee for a Political Settlement in Vietnam was in the forefront of those pushing the proposal. The concept temporarily united all points of view in the government: those who thought it should be offered in order to preempt our critics even though it was almost certain to be rejected; those who saw it as an opening wedge for more sweeping proposals that they were as yet reluctant to articulate; and those who sincerely believed that a cease-fire proposal would break the negotiating stalemate.

Even Nguyen Van Thieu went along; as was his tactic when facing the inevitable, he even recommended it. Only too aware of the growing war-weariness in America, Thieu was in the near impossible position of being asked to replace ever-decreasing American forces, to offer to share power with an adversary that daily proclaimed its determination to destroy him, and to carry out political reforms. Any one of these tasks would have tested the fabric of a stable society; to succeed in them all in the midst of a civil war with hundreds of thousands of foreign troops on his soil was impossible. That he accomplished as much as he did is a tribute to his considerable abilities. Thieu knew that he was a convenient target for war critics, who vilified him as the true obstacle to peace; and that he could end their attacks only by arranging for his own and his country's demise. Like all Vietnamese he could not see how power might be shared. He knew he needed time and that it would be a close race under the best of circumstances. Thieu sought to purchase it by making what he considered the least damaging concessions to this strange ally who sought to induce flexibility on the part of an implacable opponent by unilaterally weakening his own position. So he went along with our proposal partly because he thought it a tolerable gamble, partly because he suspected that Hanoi would reject it, partly because it might avail him some relief from the incessant pressures for coalition government.

During August, therefore, Nixon decided to offer a cease-fire after Bruce was well established. His target date was the end of the summer. It proved to be a decision of profound long-term consequence. The standstill cease-fire was put forward as being provisional. If achieved, it was to be followed by a diplomatic conference to settle the war, at which we would presumably continue to put forward the demand for the withdrawal of North Vietnamese forces. If rebuffed, we could then maintain a residual force in South Vietnam. But nobody could take such a prospect seriously. Even with a war going on, Congressional pressures for the unilateral withdrawal of our forces were mounting; not a month passed without some sort of legislated deadline being before one of the Houses of Congress. In such an atmosphere, it was inconceivable that Congress would permit us to keep troops in Indochina when a cease-fire had already been achieved, no matter what Hanoi did about its forces. The decision to propose a standstill cease-fire in 1970 thus implied the solution of 1972. That North Vietnamese forces would remain in the South was implicit in the standstill proposal; no negotiation would be able to remove them if we had not been able to expel them by force of arms. But before we could make our formal proposal the North Vietnamese were heard from again.

Madame Binh's Eight Points

As the Cambodian operation came to an end, I had sent a message to the North Vietnamese on July 5 through General Walters, suggesting a meeting with Le Duc Tho for any weekend after July 25. Characteristically, Hanoi did not reply until August 18, six weeks later, when it proposed a meeting with Xuan Thuy for August 29. This time we did not repeat the demonstration of eagerness of the previous February. The meeting finally took place on September 7, a week after we had survived the McGovern-Hatfield amendment.

I went to Paris secretly by the now familiar route. I flew from Andrews Air Force Base to the military base in Avord near Bourges in central France. My chief aides now were Winston Lord, who never missed a meeting after that and who took charge of my preparations, and Dick Smyser, the Vietnam expert on my staff. A French presidential jet took my party to Villacoublay Airport, where General Walters took us in hand. After a night in his apartment, where I was introduced to his maid as General Kirschman (my colleagues had their own code names), we went to see our Vietnamese interlocutors in the familiar simple house at 11 rue Darthé in Choisy-le-Roi at the outskirts of Paris.

Xuan Thuy greeted us, his Buddha face suffused by smiles, along with the familiar cast of characters: Mai Van Bo, the North Vietnamese Delegate-General in Paris; two other assistants; and the interpreter, who had become extremely skilled at delivering the same standard speech with the same intonation and emphasis on exactly the same phrases for three years — which had the effect of nearly undermining my sanity.

I had told Nixon that as a result of Cambodia I expected little but vituperation at this first meeting; progress was even less likely because Xuan Thuy was my opposite number. If Hanoi wanted serious talks they would be conducted by Le Duc Tho, who was a member of the Politburo. But there was no vituperation; Cambodia was barely mentioned; I was able to report to Nixon later that "the atmosphere was the friendliest of any of these sessions — indeed of any session with the Vietnamese." They seemed to drop their demand for a six months' withdrawal timetable (this turned out to be an illusion). They repeatedly indicated their desire for additional meetings. Xuan Thuy even permitted me to explain our proposal of mixed electoral commissions to supervise elections. In the never-never land of Vietnam negotiations, having negotiators from Hanoi listen to a proposal from us was considered progress; I drew from it the naive conclusion that Xuan Thuy might go so far as to consider it.

But nothing had really changed; not the speech, nor Xuan Thuy's instructions. In this phase when the negotiations were sporadic, the first session in a series was always the friendliest. (Later on, when Hanoi got down to serious bargaining, the opposite applied; the opening position was invariably tough.) The North Vietnamese negotiators used it as a come-on to encourage us to put the largest possible number of concessions on the table. These would then become the starting point for the next round of talks.

I made a carefully prepared opening statement that suffered from the professional deformation of all negotiators who are tempted to believe that impasses yield to eloquence. I explained to Xuan Thuy, as I had previously to Nixon and in much the same language, that we were approaching a fork in the road:

I ask you once again to take the path of negotiation with us. It is consistent with the self-respect and the objectives of both sides. We recognize the depth of your suspicions but they will not fade as time goes on and the struggle persists. This is the nature of war.

We are nearing the time when the chances for a negotiated settlement will pass. After a certain point you will have in effect committed yourselves to a test of arms. I do not want to predict how this test against a strengthened South Vietnam, supported by us, will end nor how long it will last. But you must recognize that it will make any settlement with the United States increasingly difficult.

Let us therefore move toward a negotiated settlement while there is still time.

I then introduced two changes in our position, one important, the other cosmetic. The significant concession was to make clear that the American withdrawal after the war would be complete; no residual forces, bases, or advisers would be left behind. Cosmetically, I brought our private position into line with our public one. In April I had given Le Duc Tho a sixteen-month withdrawal schedule; since we had already publicly offered to withdraw within a year I now gave Xuan Thuy a schedule of twelve months. (We were still talking in the context of mutual withdrawal.) I proposed free elections supervised by a mixed electoral commission composed of representatives of Saigon, the Communists, and neutrals. We did not seek to determine their outcome in advance: "We have no intention of interfering with the political evolution produced by the process agreed upon here." International observers would offer additional guarantees.

These proposals were not without their weird quality. Given the domestic pressures for unilateral withdrawal, which were accelerating by the month, we were telling the North Vietnamese that they had better agree to mutual withdrawal now lest we punish them by withdrawing unilaterally later. And we were seeking to persuade the most doctrinaire of Leninist regimes to rest the outcome of a lifetime's struggle on free elections such as they had never risked in their own country.

Xuan Thuy, in any event, had no authority to modify even slightly the standing Hanoi position. Nor was he impressed by my rhetoric. He was a little opaque about their six months' deadline for unconditional American withdrawal but only because, as we found out within ten days, Hanoi was about to unveil a new proposal; this new formula, however, was no different in essence. Xuan Thuy did not spend much time on the withdrawal question; no one who followed our Congressional debates or our media could doubt that the pressures for unilateral withdrawal had their own momentum. He dismissed our appointment of David Bruce as senior negotiator, despite the fact that at every meeting in February and March Le Duc Tho had castigated us for failing to replace Henry Cabot Lodge with a man of comparable distinction. Now Xuan Thuy claimed that Bruce's appointment simply put an end to what we should never have done in the first place; it implied no reciprocity.

What interested Xuan Thuy above all else was the political structure that Hanoi wanted to see in South Vietnam. Much as Hanoi wanted us out of Vietnam, it had assigned us a final role of honor: We were not to leave until we had overthrown all the leaders who had been our allies — President Thieu, Vice President Ky, and Premier Khiem, and, it soon appeared, almost any other South Vietnamese leader of prominence. If we did not overthrow this government, Xuan Thuy said, "no settlement can be reached." In defiance of past and current experience Xuan Thuy informed me that "the Vietnamese love one another. It is always easy to find solutions among the Vietnamese themselves." Xuan Thuy strenuously denied that the presence of nearly 200,000 North Vietnamese troops in the South (and substantial additional forces in Laos and Cambodia) was designed to exercise pressure; they were there through the free choice of the local population. When I jokingly invited him to Harvard to teach a seminar on Marxism and Leninism after the war, he declined, saying that Marxism-Leninism was not for export — which will come as remarkable news to all the inhabitants of Indochina today. All of this was highlighted by the perennial claim to epic stature: "We are afraid of nothing. We are not afraid of threats. Prolongation of fighting doesn't frighten us. Prolongation of negotiations doesn't frighten us. We are afraid of nothing." At the end of the meeting we agreed to study each other's presentations and to meet again on September 27.

Before the next meeting could take place, however, the Communists published a new peace program. Ten days after the secret meeting, on September 17 Madame Nguyen Thi Binh unveiled a new eight-point "peace program" in Paris. It was hardly a sign of the "serious intent" always professed by Hanoi's negotiators that Xuan Thuy had given me no advance word of this; clearly, Hanoi was more interested in propaganda than in negotiation. (Formally, all proposals were put forward by Madame Binh, the so-called foreign minister of the Provisional Revolutionary Government. Her actual stature is shown by the fact that after Hanoi overran the South she was relegated to the Ministry of Education and never heard of again.) Her eight points asked for total and unconditional US withdrawal in nine months, specifically by June 30, 1971. This looked like a generous extension of Hanoi's previous demand for withdrawal in six months. In fact, it was a retrogression. The previous proposal was for six months *after* an agreement had been concluded. Madame Binh's new scheme had the nine months starting immediately, and the American withdrawal would have to be completed whatever happened in the rest of the negotiations. Once we had agreed to it, we would have to go through with it even if Hanoi stalemated all other issues. And that unconditional withdrawal was only the first installment; it had to be coupled with our installation of a provisional coalition government in Saigon. This government would be composed of three segments: the Communist PRG; neutralists "standing for peace, independence, neutrality and democracy"; and members of the Saigon government other than Thieu, Ky, and Khiem who also "really stand for peace, independence, neutrality and democracy." Hanoi, of course, would decide who "really" incarnated these worthy goals. In other words, Hanoi's coalition government would consist of its own people, handpicked neutralists, plus handpicked remnants of the non-Communist element decapitated of its leadership and cut off from American military support. But the professional revolutionaries in Hanoi were not prepared to take any chances. This totally stacked coalition, according to Madame Binh, was to be considered only "provisional"; its job was then to negotiate a final settlement *with the Communist PRG.* After we had overthrown our own allies, a Communist-dominated government was to negotiate with the Communists to decide South Vietnam's future.

This was Hanoi's version of a fair negotiated outcome. Our unwillingness to accept it was decried by critics in America as pigheaded intransigence, explicable only by the bloodthirsty pursuit of military victory. In return Hanoi was prepared not to release our prisoners but only to "engage at once in discussions on" that subject, during which they would no doubt think up additional demands. A cease-fire would take effect only after we had agreed to all the other conditions, including the betrayal of our friends.

In this atmosphere I met with Xuan Thuy on September 27, 1970. Since the President was leaving for Rome that day, I had come to Paris openly the day before to consult with David Bruce and to have a talk with South Vietnamese Vice President Nguyen Cao Ky, who happened to be in the city. Ky had thrown Washington into a dither by indicating that he might visit us in October. It was symptomatic of the mood of the times that the visit of the Vice President of a country where over 40,000 Americans had already died should be considered disastrous by many Republican Congressional candidates, including those who had generally voted with the Administration. It took some delicate footwork to dissuade Ky; our meeting in Paris was offered as a substitute. Rogers even argued against this as risking the wrath of the protesters.

Going to Paris openly presented a novel logistics problem, as I had now to find a way of disappearing temporarily although my presence was already known. Our genial Ambassador, Dick Watson, stepped into the breach by ostensibly taking me for a drive into the country; at the edge of town we switched cars and General Walters took me, Lord, and Smyser to our meeting place.

Since I had made the opening presentation previously, it was Xuan Thuy's turn this time. He proved that he had indeed studied our twelve-month withdrawal schedule, and now put forward his own — it was Madame Binh's nine-month deadline, with withdrawals so arranged that all but about 20,000 Americans of the some 350,000 remaining would depart within the first six months. His terminal date remained inflexibly June 30, 1971, even if the negotiations on the remaining issues reached a complete deadlock. He elaborated slightly on the eight points. There would be a "cease-fire" between United States and Communist forces while we withdrew; Xuan Thuy was negative about whether fighting with the South Vietnamese forces would stop. We were being asked to withdraw even while our allies were being attacked. The government would not apply to Laos or Cambodia. As for the political side, Xuan Thuy rejected any discussion of the mixed electoral commission. He insisted on the removal of Thieu, Ky, and Khiem. He threw in Huong, who had previously served as Prime Minister, for good measure. The next year I was to find that no political figure known to me would prove acceptable to our implacable adversaries.

The only novelty introduced by Xuan Thuy was the rather ominous assertion that peace, to be effective, required a wider framework than South Vietnam; all neighboring states had to become "independent and neutral" as well. Under my questioning, he listed Laos, Cambodia, Burma, Indonesia, Australia, and Thailand: "In our view such countries should follow the path of peace and neutrality, so that this area will be peaceful." (New Zealand was for some reason excluded.) Incredulous, I asked him whether the Vietnam war had to continue until all these countries became neutral. He backed off. It was just Hanoi's "desire," he said. (The fact is that as of this writing it has realized its "desire" with respect to Laos and Cambodia and is threatening Thailand. Xuan Thuy might yet turn out to be prophetic.)

Whatever Hanoi's grandiose ambitions outside Indochina, within Indochina it demanded unconditional surrender and political desertion. With an immutable deadline set for our withdrawal, with all known non-Communist leaders excluded from political participation, and with the existing government overthrown, there was no possible outcome except a Communist takeover in which we were asked to collude. It was not just a matter of our pulling out and letting the chips fall where they may, nor of pulling out abruptly without any quid pro quo whatever. *Our unilateral exit was not enough;* we had to engineer a political turnover before we left, or else the war could not end, we would have no assurance of a safe withdrawal of our remaining forces, and we would not regain our prisoners. Our dilemma was that Hanoi maintained this position until October 1972. As long as it did so, no negotiated settlement was available. We were caught between an enemy unwilling to compromise and an antiwar movement in the Congress refusing either to admit that Hanoi might be implacable or to countenance military action that might have induced Hanoi to alter its terms. Madame Binh's public proposal summarized what we were also being told in secret. Hanoi's "private" view was identical with its public one.

After the September 27 meeting with Xuan Thuy I was convinced that our embryonic idea of a standstill cease-fire would be rejected out of hand. But so many in our government had invested so many hopes in it (and so few knew of the secret talks) that the Administration was governed by a rare unanimity as planning proceeded. All senior officials came to favor anything that might get the negotiations off dead center and our critics off the front pages, if only for a few days. Nixon met to consider his cease-fire speech with Rogers, Bruce, Habib, and me on Sunday, October 4, at Dromoland Castle, County Clare, Ireland, on the way home from his European trip. The meeting could not have been more optimistic. Habib was certain that the North Vietnamese would take the bait. From my conversations with Xuan Thuy (of which Bruce was fully informed) I had my doubts but did not express them. At a minimum, I thought, the President's proposal would give us some temporary relief from public pressures.

At the end of the meeting David Bruce made a statement unique in my experience with American negotiators. He said that he was aware of the many pressures on the President to make concessions; he would not add to these, since he thought the proposed speech by the President went to the limit of what we could offer. He had seen too much lost through the impatience of negotiators, even more through their vanity. He was by nature not impatient, and now too old for vanity. He was content to stand on the proposal.

We went immediately into the preparation of the speech for delivery October 7. The day before he was due to give it Nixon put on one of his classic performances. He stepped unexpectedly into the White House press briefing room to tell the startled journalists that he would deliver the next evening "the most comprehensive statement ever made on this subject since the beginning of this very difficult war." His penchant for hyperbole ensured that almost nothing he could say would live up to the advance billing. Nixon cautioned the assembled press against speculation. Speculation now being guaranteed, he returned to the Oval Office simultaneously to enjoy the discomfiture and confusion of his enemies in the media and to worry about the leaks his enthusiasm had encouraged.

Nixon's speech on October 7, 1970, in fact presented a comprehensive program that could well have served as a basis for negotiation except with an opponent bent on total victory. Nixon offered a standstill cease-fire, including a halt to our bombing *throughout* Indochina. He proposed a peace conference to bring an end to the wars in all the countries of Indochina. He expressed a readiness to negotiate an agreed timetable for the total withdrawal of American forces. He put it in the context of mutual withdrawal, but in a language so deliberately fuzzy as to invite exploration. He invited Hanoi to join us in a political settlement based on the will of the South Vietnamese people. He offered to abide by the outcome of the agreed political process but rejected the "patently unreasonable" demand that we dismantle the organized non-Communist forces and guarantee in advance the victory of the Communists. Finally, he called for the release by both sides of all prisoners of war.

For once a speech on Vietnam received almost unanimous praise. The Senate adopted a resolution, sponsored by Senator Charles Percy and a number of other Senators, calling the President's new peace initiative "fair and equitable." Senator Fulbright expressed his hope that the President's initiative might lead to a breakthrough. Senator Mike Mansfield said the speech was excellent; he would do his "very best to support it." Former Vice President Hubert Humphrey, running for the Senate in Minnesota, described the offer as "sound, welcome and heartening." Averell Harriman coupled one of his few favorable comments about a Nixon initiative with one of his obsessive warnings that the Thieu government was largely responsible for the negotiating impasse and should be prevented from blocking the cease-fire. House Speaker John McCormack described the initiative as "timely and strategically and psychologically sound." [5]

The newspapers joined the chorus of praise. The *New York Times* of October 9 called Nixon's approach a "major new peace initiative." The *Wall Street Journal* said: "However Hanoi finally responds, in fact, the President has put forth an American position so appealing and so sane that only the most unreasonable critics could object to it." The *Chicago Daily News,* usually opposed to the President's Vietnam policies, said that "Americans of almost every political persuasion must surely back the President to the utmost in his urgent attempt to write an end to the longest, most dismal war this nation has ever known." [6] The usually antiwar *St. Louis Post-Dispatch* on October 8 hailed the "significant and welcome changes" in Nixon's speech, his "statesmanlike proposals," his "constructive" and "responsible" statement; "we commend him on it."

But it was a short-lived honeymoon. Xuan Thuy made a statement in Paris the next day rejecting Nixon's proposal out of hand; he refused even to talk about it at plenary sessions. The classic pattern of the Vietnam debate reappeared. Some proposal would emerge and become the subject of passionate advocacy; it would be urged as the key to a breakthrough. At last the Administration would accept it, sometimes against its better judgment. Hanoi would refuse. The proposal would then immediately disappear from the public debate and some other pet scheme would become the national obsession. Within weeks our critics were back with demands for additional concessions. The new gimmick was to urge setting a withdrawal deadline unilaterally, in the belief — against all evidence — that this was acceptable to Hanoi. [7] Another was coalition government. The *St. Louis Post-Dispatch* on November 5 — less than a month after it had hailed the President's cease-fire offer — argued:

The Communists demand some sort of coalition government, and since they have fought for so many years there is no reason to think they will settle for anything less. Why should they? It seems to us a coalition, which would give each side a certain responsibility and authority, is the logical way to avert the bloody post-hostilities revenge Mr. Nixon so often envisions.

Unhappily, Hanoi had no concept of sharing political power; the coalition it demanded included none of our friends. Also on November 5, Averell Harriman now asserted, on the NBC television show "Today," that the Nixon Administration had "made no attempt to come to an agreement."

Our critics were stirred up even more when, with simultaneous air strikes, a brave band of American commandos conducted a raid on an installation twenty miles from Hanoi — the Son Tay prison — thought to house sixty American prisoners of war. The incident illustrated a basic axiom of policymaking: A President, and even more his security adviser, must take nothing on faith; they must question every assumption and probe every alleged fact. Not everything that is plausible is true, for those who put forward plans for action have a psychological disposition to marshal the facts that support their position. The Son Tay raid, carried out on November 20, was meticulously planned and heroically executed but was based on an egregious failure of intelligence: The prison had been closed at least three months earlier. We knew the risk of casualties, but none of the briefings that led to the decision to proceed had ever mentioned the possibility that the camp might be empty. *After the failure of the raid I was informed of a message sent in code by a prisoner of war that the camp was "closed" on July 14. This was interpreted by military analysts to mean that the gates were locked; it had not been considered of sufficient importance to bring to the attention of the White House.*

The raid produced a rather bizarre footnote generated by my warped sense of humor. An officer briefing me on the raid apologized for its failure. I told him not to apologize, joking that no doubt they had brought back a baby water buffalo, and the North Vietnamese were going crazy trying to figure out why we had mounted a big operation for that purpose. The officer, patriotically presuming that the President's security adviser could not be totally mad, reported this to his superiors. His superiors started a hunt for the animal. The troops in the field, convinced by now that Washington had lost its mind, reported they knew nothing about any kidnapped baby water buffalo. The Pentagon refused to believe I had made my comment lightly. Back went a cable asking to make sure by checking the helicopter for buffalo dung. The whole incident has been memorialized in a book.[8]

The Son Tay raid was accompanied by a two-day strike by 200 airplanes against North Vietnamese supply installations. There were three reasons for these attacks: to divert Hanoi's defenses from Son Tay; to retaliate for the abrupt rejection of our peace proposal; and to slow down the North Vietnamese dry-season supply effort into the South, now running at twice the rate of the previous year. Outrage in the Congress and the media, as usual, focused on American actions and not Hanoi's provocations. Two themes predominated: that bombing "demonstrably" never worked, and that the Administration once again was misleading the public. The self-evidence of the ineffectiveness of air interdiction is much less clear today than it seemed to many in the passion of the Vietnam debate. There is much evidence that at the time of the 1968 Tet offensive Hanoi was on the point of exhaustion when saved by our unilateral bombing halt. There is no doubt in my mind that the resumption of bombing in May 1972 hastened the end of the war. Whether a two-day bombing effort in 1970 bought us more time in the destruction of supplies than it lost in stirring up opposition is a close question, but not a trivial one. The military steps that were making it possible for us to withdraw from Vietnam were denounced as if they were escalating our involvement.

Neither government nor opposition dealt well with the raids. Officials desperately eager to avoid Congressional and media wrath belittled our offensive efforts or explained them by what was a patent subterfuge ("protective reaction"). Media and legislators smelling blood used every sign of panic and insecurity to build their case against a government they demagogically described as eager for war. Though much of the credibility gap was caused by the Administration, a not inconsiderable part was brought about by those relentless opponents who started from the presumption that nothing their government did in the war could have any moral foundation or serve any national purpose and who were committed to discrediting an Administration desperately trying to extricate our country from a war it had inherited. Such was the paranoia of the period that a distinguished senior professor told me in all seriousness that the Son Tay raid had been engineered so that some POWs would be killed in order to have a pretext for escalation of the war.

By January 19, 1971, Clark Kerr's National Committee for a Political Settlement in Vietnam was right back to where it had been before Nixon's October 7 speech. The group that had pressed so passionately for a US cease-fire proposal as the key to peace, now, after we had made one and been flatly turned down, did not draw the conclusion that we should maintain our position because the other side was unreasonable. Instead, it now urged a *unilateral* American cease-fire in Vietnam.

Hanoi's rejection was attributed not to intransigence but to our own actions in the Son Tay raid, protective reaction strikes, and failure to extend the Christmas cease-fire. All this despite the fact that Xuan Thuy had already rejected our offer *before* these events. Hanoi's rigidity was to be overcome by further American concessions. "A diplomatic effort is essential in the coming months," Kerr's Committee wrote the President, "if we are to break down the resistance of the other side to a cease-fire, and build pressures on them eventually to negotiate an agreement. . . . We remain convinced that such an agreement can be achieved eventually through vigorous diplomatic and political efforts and initiatives." The Committee gave no evidence on which to base such a conviction; we had considerable proof of the contrary.

The Setting of a Strategy

B Y the end of 1970 we ran the risk that our Vietnam strategy would turn into a debate about the rate of our unilateral withdrawal. Even within the Administration there was tremendous weariness. The constant pressures that transformed even the most minor military action into a test of credibility, the endless testimony before Congressional committees, the incessant probing by the media — which ranged from skeptical to hostile — all tended to work against a coherent strategy. There was simply no negotiating scheme that could possibly work with the cold-eyed planners in Hanoi unless it was related to some calculus of the balance of forces. Critics took it for granted that it was up to us to supply all the concessions and demonstrations of goodwill and flexibility; demands for ingenuity were rarely addressed to the other side, and never persistently. But the more the negotiating process degenerated into an accumulation of unreciprocated concessions, the greater was Hanoi's incentive to hold on in order to see what further movement toward its position our growing psychological exhaustion would produce.

One unilateral concession occasioned by domestic pressure was an acceleration of our withdrawal schedule in the fall of 1970. When on April 20, 1970, Nixon had announced a withdrawal of 150,000 men over twelve months, one of his reasons was to retain maximum flexibility in the timing of actual pullouts. The intention, confirmed in a written Presidential directive of April 22, was to withdraw no more than 60,000 during the remainder of 1970; this was to give us a cushion during the dry season, which ran from October to May (depending on the part of the country). It was during the dry season that Hanoi pushed its supplies down the Ho Chi Minh Trail; it was from February onward that Communist offensives took place. The President, on the advice of General Abrams, had wanted to defer the bulk of the reduction until 1971 to deter a new Tet offensive and to husband the last substantial combat forces for any emergency. But Congressional pressures on the Pentagon budget and the political need to reduce draft calls had made it impossible to fulfill Nixon's directive. On August 20 Laird wrote me, pointing out that "we continue to be tightly constrained" by the budget. Therefore, he said, General Abrams, our Pacific Command, and the Joint Chiefs of Staff "have recommended to me" a withdrawal schedule calling for withdrawal of 90,000 in calendar year 1970 and the remaining 60,000 by May 1, 1971.

I sent this memorandum to the President on August 27, pointing out its "serious implications." The figures represented the exact opposite of what the President had ordered and had promised to Thieu. The JCS "recommendations" were the product of fiscal guidance, not of a strategic preference: "The proposed accelerated redeployments would in effect spend all the benefits of the Cambodian operation on our withdrawal schedule rather than using these benefits as possible leverage in achieving a negotiated peace."

In the first round Nixon held firm. On September 4 I sent Laird a note that the President insisted on the original schedule. But it was a losing battle. By October it was clear that Laird was proceeding according to his own fiscal guidance. Never lacking daring, he proposed to announce the accelerated withdrawal at the regular Pentagon briefing on Monday, October 12. At this point I threw in the towel. Thieu took our volte-face with good grace, having long since decided that there was no point in debating our inexplicable domestic maneuvers. He pointed out that to replace the departing American forces he would have to withdraw into Vietnam a task force that had sought to keep roads open in Cambodia and complicate the reestablishment of Communist sanctuaries there. We were thus sloughing off our domestic problems onto Saigon, and Saigon was passing its difficulties on to Phnom Penh, which became the ultimate victim of everyone's frustrations.

In this autumn of seeming lull it became imperative to develop a strategy for ending the war. In November, under the impact of the unexpected setback in the Congressional elections, Nixon came back again to his project of announcing in 1971 an almost total withdrawal, coupled with a quarantine of North Vietnam and the resumption of heavy bombing. I still did not believe that such an attempt to force a rapid conclusion could work. The sudden withdrawal, even if it did not wreck the South Vietnamese government and the prospects of Vietnamization, would convey such a sense of impatience to Hanoi that the quarantine and the bombing would serve little purpose. Hanoi would simply buckle down and endure, counting on the domestic uproar here to stop our military pressure. I told the President that even from the political point of view his problem was less one of withdrawing in 1971 than of preventing a collapse in Vietnam in 1972.

Nixon and I spent a great deal of time in November 1970 working out a more practical strategy. We had to put a stop to the endless maneuvering over withdrawal rates. I recommended that when the current withdrawal increment was completed in May 1971 we should announce another substantial reduction, perhaps on the order of 100,000 over six months. This would still maintain security in South Vietnam through its Presidential election scheduled for October. After that, when our forces would be down to about 180,000, we would announce fairly frequent smaller reductions until we had reached a residual force of about 50,000 volunteers by the summer of 1972. These would remain until there was a settlement. Sometime in 1971, depending on the situation, we would announce the end of American participation in ground combat operations. Sometime in 1971, too, we would offer the North Vietnamese a more rapid withdrawal in return for a cease-fire. If it were rejected, we would know that we would face an offensive in 1972. The outcome of the war would then depend on whether the South Vietnamese, aided only by American air power, would be able to blunt the assault. Peace would thus come either at the end of 1971 or at the end of 1972 — either by negotiation or by a South Vietnamese collapse.

For this strategy to succeed, however, it was imperative to weaken the North Vietnamese as much as possible in the interval. The Cambodian operation had delayed Hanoi's logistics buildup for at least fifteen months; every month gained, we hoped, strengthened the South Vietnamese. We looked for ways to consume Hanoi's supplies, to postpone further its readiness for offensive operations, and to blunt the assault should it come. If we were serious about Vietnamization, we had to manage, in spite of our domestic dissent, three concurrent efforts until Saigon could stand on its own feet: American troop withdrawals; the rapid strengthening of South Vietnamese forces; and the progressive weakening of the enemy.*

The strategy Nixon and I devised in November 1970 was carried out in essence in 1971 and 1972. And it worked. We managed to withdraw all our forces within little more than a year of the chosen date of the McGovern-Hatfield amendment. And we accomplished this without overthrowing an allied government.**

It was the pursuit of this strategy that led us to the Laos operation of 1971.

---

* The demand for total withdrawal, incidentally, was never imposed on South Korea under much more favorable circumstances even twenty-five years after the end of hostilities.

** The one circumstance we could not foresee was the debacle of Watergate. It was that which finally sealed the fate of South Vietnam by the erosion of Executive authority, strangulation of South Vietnam by wholesale reductions of aid, and legislated prohibitions against enforcing the peace agreement in the face of unprovoked North Vietnamese violations.

The Laos Operation

THAT there was bound to be another test of strength was evident in the stridency of North Vietnam's public statements. For example, at the 100th plenary session of January 21, 1971, Xuan Thuy ridiculed our October 7 cease-fire proposal. Quoting liberally from American war critics (a common practice), he demanded that we respond positively to Madame Binh's eight points. Reporting on a plenary session of the Central Committee, the North Vietnamese Party newspaper *Nhan Dan* called for a relentless war effort no matter how "fierce" and "protracted" the war might be.

During the last months of 1970 I asked the experts in the government and on my staff to submit their assessments of the military and political prospects for the next two years.

It was clear at the end of 1970 that Hanoi would need most of 1971 to protect, enlarge, and rebuild its supply system. Hanoi's big push was expected for 1972, in order to have a maximum impact on our Presidential election. A meeting of the Senior Review Group on January 15, 1971, tried to forecast more precisely the situation the South Vietnamese would face in 1972. Our studies concluded that if US troop withdrawals and the enemy's supply buildup continued at their current rates, the South Vietnamese might be short by eight battalions of what they needed to resist, even if we continued to stalemate the enemy in Cambodia and Laos. (This was called the "battalion deficit" in systems analysis jargon.) The deficit would be thirty-five battalions if Hanoi were to achieve a decisive victory in Laos and Cambodia before its offensive of 1972.

The Communist strategy would depend on a combination of guerrilla and regular (called main-force) units that whipsawed the defenders. If we concentrated on guerrillas, the enemy's main-force units would occupy large parts of South Vietnam. If we dealt with the main-force units, the guerrillas would make gains in the countryside. Wherever the nexus between guerrilla and main-force units could be broken, enabling Saigon to concentrate on one or the other, Saigon gained the upper hand fairly rapidly. After the Cambodian operation the war virtually ended in the southern half of South Vietnam until well into 1972, and even then never regained full force. The North Vietnamese divisions in Cambodia were absorbed with rebuilding and protecting the Cambodian sanctuaries; they were confined to shallow hit-and-run raids across the frontier. In the northern regions the nexus between main-force units and guerrillas continued; North Vietnamese supply lines were short. Pacification progress was correspondingly slow.

It was here that the deficit in troops showed up in our statistics. But the figures did not truly reflect the nature of the problem. It was not just

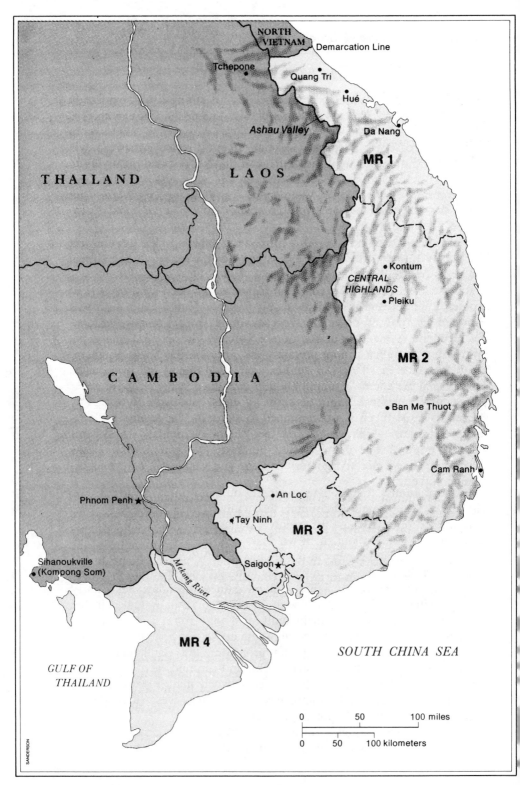

South Vietnam: Military Regions

a question of numbers but where the units were located. The South Vietnamese army was organized on the basis of two divisions for each of four Military Regions, with an airborne division, a marine division, and various Ranger and Special Forces units representing a strategic reserve. Thanks to the success of the Cambodian operation, there were excess troops (in the jargon, a battalion surplus) for every foreseeable contingency in Military Regions 3 and 4, southern South Vietnam. In the northern regions we expected a substantial deficit despite the military stalemate in Cambodia and Laos.

But we could not meet our problem by moving "surplus" southern troops into the "deficit" northern areas. Except for the strategic reserve, each division was tied to the Military Region in which it was stationed; and southern divisions were judged not to be useful for fighting in the northern Central Highlands and along the Demilitarized Zone (DMZ). There were several reasons. Divisions were stationed where they were recruited. The dependents of the troops lived near their bivouac areas; and experience had shown that a division which was moved out of its home region would rapidly suffer desertions and loss of morale. (During the North Vietnamese offensive in 1972 the 21st Division, which had been outstanding in the Mekong Delta, was moved into the Saigon area not seventy-five miles distant; its performance was pathetic.) Moreover, any such redeployment would be resisted by the generals commanding the affected Military Region; these were indispensable props of the Saigon government; they judged — correctly — that their political influence at the capital bore some relationship to the number of troops they commanded. South Vietnamese commanders were also constrained in the number of casualties they could tolerate — especially in offensive operations that the nearby dependents might consider unnecessary. For all those reasons statistical analysis understated the strategic problem. In practice we had only the strategic reserve available to fill the gap in the north.

If this analysis were correct, two conclusions followed. The enemy had to be prevented from taking over Cambodia and Laos if Vietnamization was to have any chance of success. And the enemy's dry-season logistics buildup would have to be slowed down, or if possible interrupted. One obvious solution would have been to keep an additional American combat division in the country through the 1972 dry season as a strategic reserve. Behind its shield, pacification could have been accelerated in Military Regions 1 and 2, freeing the South Vietnamese divisions to resist an enemy main-force attack in 1973. This could never be considered, however, in the face of our domestic situation. Our problem thus became how to make up the eight-battalion deficit either by strengthening the South Vietnamese or by weakening the North Vietnamese, especially by disrupting their logistics buildup.

This is why thought turned to an *allied* dry-season offensive, which would disrupt the Communist logistics effort, reduce the battalion deficit expected for 1972, and enhance Hanoi's incentive to negotiate. The winter of 1971 would also be the last year that American combat troops would be available. While our redeployments and domestic situation precluded the use of American troops in offensive operations, our forces could assume static security functions and so free South Vietnamese troops for spoiling attacks.

I strongly encouraged the concept of a dry-season offensive in 1971, in the face of the essential indifference of the departments, who were battening down against domestic storms. There were never any complaints about bureaucratic prerogatives when the White House assumed responsibility for Vietnam planning; the departments were only too eager to saddle the White House with the onus for the inevitable domestic uproar. I thought it my duty as security adviser not to await disasters passively or simply to gamble on the most favorable hypothesis. Hanoi's resupply effort was running at twice the rate of the previous year. A campaign to weaken Hanoi's capacity to launch attacks for as long as possible would give us a margin of safety. Faced with the prospect of yearly spoiling offensives, Hanoi might prefer to negotiate.

Originally, I thought that the best place for a dry-season offensive was Cambodia. My idea was to commit Saigon's strategic reserve and one of the divisions guarding the border to wipe out North Vietnamese supplies and forces in Cambodia and to destroy the growing Cambodian Communist infrastructure. This would eliminate any residual threat to the southern half of South Vietnam; it would squelch the still-developing Khmer Rouge and perhaps enable the Lon Nol government to control most of the country. Thieu would be able to shift his strategic reserve to the north to repel a Communist attack in 1972, or perhaps to mount another spoiling offensive before North Vietnam's logistics preparations had run their course in the following year. It might even have been possible to move one of the regular divisions north for pacification purposes.

The advantage of the Cambodian operation was that it was almost certain to succeed. North Vietnamese forces in Cambodia were still substantially occupied with containing Lon Nol's forces; the Cambodian Communists were not yet strong enough to stand on their own. There were practically no North Vietnamese reserves available; in Cambodia North Vietnamese units could not, as in Vietnam, hide in the population. Cambodia was at the end of the North Vietnamese supply lines; it could not be significantly reinforced. And a demonstrable success would strengthen the self-confidence of the South Vietnamese and lend a psychological boost for the almost inevitable showdown in 1972. The drawback of my concept was that it dealt only indirectly with our biggest strategic concern for 1972: a possible North Vietnamese attack in the Central Highlands and across the Demilitarized Zone.

The President agreed with my recommendation. With his approval I sent Al Haig and a team of NSC staff members to Vietnam to study the prospects. Haig returned with the report that Bunker, Abrams, and Thieu thought a dry-season offensive imperative. However, they recommended a much more daring concept than mine. They proposed to deal with the enemy's logistics buildup in one fell swoop by cutting the Ho Chi Minh Trail in Laos near the Demilitarized Zone.

In the dense jungles of southern Laos — on the sovereign territory of a state whose neutrality Hanoi had formally recognized in the Geneva Accords of 1962 — the North Vietnamese over nearly a decade had built a complex system of routes through which they funneled their soldiers and supplies into South Vietnam. The Ho Chi Minh Trail in fact consisted of more than fifteen hundred miles of roads and an elaborate trail network (see the map on page 449). At its hub was the small provincial town of Tchepone, on which all trails converged and from which supplies and men were then infiltrated into South Vietnam. The Ho Chi Minh Trail was manned by some 40,000 to 50,000 North Vietnamese logistics troops, together with supporting security forces. It operated each year from about October to May, when the onset of the rainy season mired it and made it impassable. At that point North Vietnamese troops generally withdrew until the next dry season.

Between 1966 and 1971 the Communists had used the Ho Chi Minh Trail to infiltrate at least 630,000 North Vietnamese troops, 100,000 tons of foodstuffs, 400,000 weapons and 50,000 tons of ammunition, or the equivalent of 600 million rounds into South Vietnam. Since the overthrow of Prince Sihanouk and the closing of the port of Sihanoukville, Hanoi had become almost completely dependent on the Ho Chi Minh Trail for its logistics effort into South Vietnam.

It was General Abrams's view, as conveyed by Haig, that if the Ho Chi Minh Trail could be denied to the Communists, or effectively disrupted for even *one* dry season, Hanoi's ability to launch major offensive operations in the South (and Cambodia) would be significantly curtailed, if not eliminated, for an indefinite future. Abrams therefore proposed a bold plan. American forces would set up blocking positions along the DMZ in South Vietnam westward to the Laotian border. In the process the important road junction and airstrip of Khe Sanh — scene of a bitter seige by the North Vietnamese during the 1968 Tet offensive and since abandoned — would be reoccupied. American artillery would move up to the Laotian frontier. The crack South Vietnamese First Division would then cross into Laos along Route 9 and head for Tchepone, building defensive fire bases along its exposed northern flank. When it was about halfway to the objective, the airborne division would seize the Tchepone airfield and link up with a tank column coming overland. (See the map facing.) The entire assault would take four or five days. The rest of the dry season would be spent in interdicting the trail and destroying the logistics complex assumed to lie along it, and especially around Tchepone. A successful campaign was expected to gain us at least two years, since the enemy would need one year to rebuild the logistics structure, perhaps longer if there were later South Vietnamese spoiling offensives.

As for Cambodia, Abrams proposed a more modest operation than I had envisaged originally. He would use one of the Vietnamese divisions from Military Region 3 to cross the border into the Chup rubber plantation where the North Vietnamese were establishing a new base area. Since Military Region 3 was commanded by General Do Cao Tri, considered South Vietnam's ablest, most daring (and incidentally most corrupt) commander, Abrams promised himself a maximum disruption of Hanoi's logistics structure in Cambodia. Both of these plans were strongly endorsed by the Joint Chiefs of Staff.

It was a splendid project on paper. Its chief drawback, as events showed, was that it in no way accorded with Vietnamese realities. South Vietnamese divisions had never conducted major offensive operations against a determined enemy outside Vietnam and only rarely inside. They would be doing it this time without American advisers because these were barred by the Cooper-Church amendment. The same amendment proscribed even the American officers who guided our tactical airstrikes, thus sharply reducing the effectiveness of our air support. Washington did not understand that Vietnamese units had practically no trained ground controllers who could speak English; excessive amounts of time would be lost as requests for air support went up and down the entire chain of command of the two sides. The South Vietnamese divisions were simply not yet good enough for such a complex operation as the one in Laos. Nor was the South Vietnamese high command sufficiently experienced to handle two major operations at the same time. Finally Tchepone was located at the precise point that Hanoi could most easily reinforce. Its strategic location made it possible to bring up troops from both North and South Vietnam.

In 1962 I had been asked by President Kennedy to brief the crusty West German Chancellor Adenauer on some of the military ideas of the young Administration. Adenauer had his doubts about statesmen of Kennedy's generation; he was even more skeptical about the strategic doctrines McNamara was developing. At one point he interrupted me in the full flight of my oratory to ask how I knew what I was presenting was true. I had been briefed by a general, I responded. Had the general worn a uniform, the Chancellor wanted to know. When I allowed that I did not remember, he suggested that I ask the general to repeat his briefing in civilian clothes; if I was still impressed I should let him know.

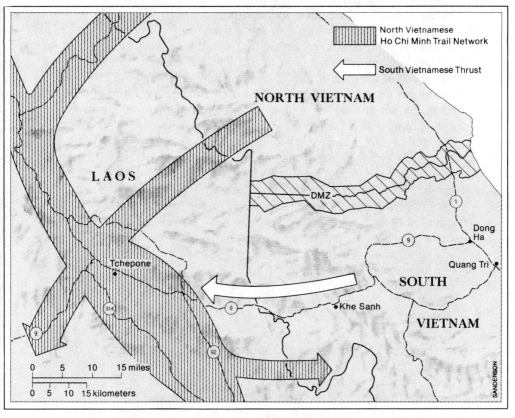

Laos Operation 1971

This sardonic advice would have stood us in good stead in 1971. Instead, we allowed ourselves to be carried away by the daring conception, by the unanimity of the responsible planners in both Saigon and Washington, by the memory of the success in Cambodia, and by the prospect of a decisive turn. Energies were soon absorbed not in careful analysis but in the interdepartmental maneuvering through which the Nixon Administration made its decisions.

Nixon was determined not to stand naked in front of his critics as he had the year before over Cambodia. This time he would involve his key Cabinet officers in every facet of the decision-making, to force them to take some of the heat of the inevitable public criticism. But this determination did not extend to confronting both Rogers and Laird at the same time. To get around his reluctance to give orders to his subordinates, and judging Rogers to be the most likely recalcitrant, Nixon conceived the idea of first maneuvering Laird into the position of proposing what Nixon preferred, and then letting his Secretary of Defense become the advocate of the plan within the National Security Council. He therefore considered it time well spent to preside over a succession of meetings, each covering exactly the same topic. For each meeting one more participant was added — someone whose view Nixon did not know in advance or whom he judged to be potentially hostile. The theory was that any recalcitrant was more likely to go along with a consensus backed by the President than with a free-for-all. By late January I had heard the same briefing at least three times and was approaching battle fatigue. Nixon was earning himself high marks for acting ability. He listened each time with wide-eyed interest as if he were hearing the plan for the first time. His questions — always the same — were a proper mixture of skepticism, fascination, and approval designed to convey to the new recruit that his chief was interested and well disposed. And since everybody else had already agreed, it took a strong individual to stand his ground in opposition. No one tried.

Thus Haig first reported to the President about his trip to Indochina in my presence. Nixon next added Tom Moorer, Chairman of the Joint Chiefs of Staff, to confirm that he was aboard. On December 23, Haig presented the same report to Nixon in the presence of Mel Laird; Moorer, not indicating that he had been in touch previously, supported the Laos plan. Nixon indicated that he favored the operation in the Chup plantation in Cambodia and that he was well disposed toward cutting the Ho Chi Minh Trail. He asked Laird to look into the concept during a trip he planned to take to Southeast Asia in early January.

Laird, as always, was complex. He was aware of the domestic pressures against the war; but he also favored moves that would reduce the risks of withdrawal. He probably had also already heard something from Moorer and Abrams through his own backchannels about a possible

Laos-Cambodia operation. Whatever the reason, Laird backed the concept of cutting the Ho Chi Minh Trail, arguing that it would buy us at least a year. He thought that the first major offensive operation by the South Vietnamese army without *any* US ground support would be clear-cut evidence of the success of Vietnamization. Vastly relieved, Nixon approved both plans in principle, subject to review after Laird's forthcoming trip.

No other senior officials were informed of the planning, which continued in the Pentagon and in Saigon while Laird took his trip, starting on January 5, 1971. On his return Nixon called another meeting in the Oval Office for January 18. Its participants were those of the December 23 meeting plus Rogers and Helms. As before, the one significant unknown quantity, Rogers, was to be presented with a united front of all of his colleagues. Helms did not count, because as CIA Director he was not supposed to put forward policy recommendations. Nixon could also assume from experience that Helms, having stated his views, would not pursue them in public. The pretext for the meeting was Laird's report on his trip.

Laird played his role to perfection. He spent a great deal of time on technical aspects of Vietnamization, the forthcoming presidential election in Vietnam, the performance of Thai forces in Laos, the need to monitor equipment deliveries in Cambodia. He covered, in fact, every conceivable subject except a dry-season offensive. After his audience was thoroughly anesthetized, Laird turned to the subject of dry-season operations by way of their effect on speeding up our rate of withdrawal, a subject presumed to be close to Rogers's heart. Throughout, Nixon made encouraging noises, asking questions with feigned amazement while steering the conversation to its ordained conclusion.

But Laird did not drop the other shoe immediately. He introduced Rogers to the concept of a dry-season campaign by describing a small South Vietnamese operation in Cambodia, involving some 4,000 ARVN marines, to open Route 4 from Phnom Penh to the sea. He went on from there to describe the South Vietnamese plan to seek to destroy the bases in the Chup plantation, which he characterized accurately as similar in concept to the Cambodian incursion of the previous year. No objections were raised by anyone once Laird had made clear that no American forces would be involved. Nearly two hours had by now elapsed without our having reached the heart of the matter. At this point Nixon called a fifteen-minute recess, perhaps to savor the unusual harmony among his advisers.

When the meeting resumed, Laird at last presented the concept of the Tchepone thrust, with the aid of maps. He indicated that the first phase, the movement by US forces to take up blocking positions along Route 9 inside South Vietnam and to reoccupy Khe Sanh as a forward base, should start around January 29. Phase II — the leapfrogging of Vietnamese units along Route 9 into Laos — would follow around February 8.

It was now time for the one remaining major official who had not been part of the previous planning to take a position. Rogers's reaction was almost a carbon copy of Laird's four weeks earlier. After reassuring himself that there would be no significant increase in casualties, he supported the plan as presented by Laird. He insisted that it was crucial that the operation succeed; Laird and Moorer vehemently affirmed their complete confidence. Helms, who also had not participated before but whose opinion was not decisive for Nixon, turned out to be the only adviser to raise serious questions. He pointed out that the proposed operation had been frequently considered in the past and had always been rejected as too difficult. Later I learned that four years earlier our then Vietnam commander, General William Westmoreland, had thought that such an operation would require two corps of *American* troops. Though he was now a member of the Joint Chiefs of Staff, no such view was submitted to the White House in 1971.

The die was cast. Nixon gave his tentative approval to proceed. I scheduled WSAG meetings starting January 19 to carry out detailed planning for the first time on a full interagency basis.

The strength of this elaborate procedure was that Nixon, when confronted with a sober analysis of his strategic options, had the courage to face the reality that unless some steps were taken to interrupt the North Vietnamese buildup, the situation of South Vietnam in the next year would become precarious indeed. The concept of a dry-season offensive was correct; Nixon acted boldly in ordering it. The flaw in Nixon's method of administration soon became evident, however. So much time, effort, and ingenuity were spent in trying to organize a consensus of the senior advisers that there was too little left to consider the weaknesses in the plan or to impose discipline on the rest of the government. There was no role for a devil's advocate. At every meeting, to gain the acquiescence of the potential recalcitrant, Nixon would offer so many modifications that the complex plan he was seeking to promote was eventually consumed. Since each Cabinet member was concerned about the domestic reaction to American involvement, Nixon at every Laos planning session agreed to reduce the American participation and to put new restraints on our actions. Each of these steps may have been minor; the cumulative impact was considerable, practically and above all psychologically. Filtering down through layers of command, it was bound to convey a sense of hesitation to the field commanders; they in turn had to focus as much on the restraints as on their main job: prevailing on the battlefield.

A President cannot take away the curse of a controversial decision by hesitation in its execution. The use of military force is a difficult decision that must always be made with a prayerful concern for Bismarck's profound dictum: "Woe to the statesman whose reasons for entering a war do not appear so plausible at its end as at its beginning." A leader's fundamental choice is whether to approve the use of force. If he decides to do so, his only vindication is to succeed. His doubts provide no justification for failure; restraint in execution is a boon to the other side; there are no awards for those who lose with moderation. Once the decision to use force has been made, the President has no choice but to pursue it with total determination — and to convey the same spirit to all those implementing it. Nations must not undertake military enterprises or major diplomatic initiatives that they are not willing to see through.

The Nixon method of government worked well when the military problem was relatively straightforward and could be carried out in one daring move as in Cambodia. It was effective also for purposeful solitary diplomacy conducted by a trusted associate working with a small staff, such as in the opening to China, the Vietnam negotiations, and the various diplomatic moves toward the Soviet Union. Difficulties arose when a sustained military effort was needed, as in Laos, or when the diplomacy was too complex to be handled by the security adviser's office, as in the India-Pakistan crisis. Then the absence of consensus or even understanding inhibited coherence and commitment. Departments excluded from key decisions were tempted into assertions of bureaucratic self-will. When only a very small group knew what the President intended and only part of that group agreed with the purposes, an inordinate amount of time would be consumed later by wrangling, dissociation, or attempts (usually in vain) to impose discipline. Though the President's complex personality provided the impetus, I, as the organizer of these procedures and as their driving force, must, of course, share the responsibility for the shortcomings, just as I have been given perhaps undue credit for the successes.

What happened in 1971 was that the governmental consensus of the December 23 and January 18 meetings began to evaporate as soon as Rogers was exposed to the passionate opposition of his experts. By January 21 it became apparent that State was dragging its feet. At WSAG meetings Under Secretary Alex Johnson began to surface objections that did not challenge the decision but would have delayed its implementation indefinitely — a bureaucratic maneuver in which Johnson was superbly skilled. The device to procrastinate was insistence on the prior approval of the Laotian Prime Minister, Souvanna Phouma.

It was a strange argument. The North Vietnamese had been occupying part of Laos for a decade, in flagrant violation of two Geneva Accords. They had in effect seized all the territory adjoining their border and most of southern Laos as the logistics base for operations in Vietnam. No Laotian writ had run in southern Laos for years; whatever sparse Laotian population had lived there had been expelled by the North Vietnamese. We had been bombing the Ho Chi Minh Trail for at least five years with Souvanna's acquiescence but without his formal approval. Anyone familiar with Souvanna had to know that he welcomed our actions but feared to endorse them lest he supply to his pitiless neighbor a pretext for further escalation. It was an extraordinary concept that our legal position to interrupt the logistics base aimed at South Vietnam would require the concurrence of the leader whose own officials were not permitted in the southern part of his country and who was barely holding on in the face of the North Vietnamese onslaught in the north. Anyone even vaguely familiar with Souvanna had to know that he would welcome the operation but would not want to be consulted beforehand. What he would have preferred was to adopt the position of Sihanouk with respect to the bombing of the sanctuary areas: Since no Laotian officials were present, he did not know what was going on and could not take the responsibility for the actions of either side.

In the event, days were consumed in exchanges with our Embassy in Vientiane about how to approach Souvanna — which was, of course, why the idea was put forward to begin with. To the acute disappointment of at least some of our officials, our Ambassador in Laos, Mac Godley, reported that Souvanna's tacit concurrence was probable, provided we kept him informed. Godley was instructed to obtain a more specific endorsement. Once again, Souvanna, who knew very well that his country's survival depended on a North Vietnamese defeat, failed to live up to the hopes of the opponents of the operation. He gave qualified approval so long as it did not last more than three weeks. Godley was sent back in with a yet more formal approach. But Souvanna, who understood his country's needs, refused to play: No matter how many opportunities he was given, he would not oppose the operation, which meant that he in fact welcomed it.

It was becoming clear that the State Department objections went beyond the procedural. Rogers was quite explicit in several conversations with me. I therefore recommended to the President that he overcome his reluctance to debate with his friend and hold another meeting of the senior members of the NSC. It was scheduled for January 27.

Before that meeting, on January 25 I reviewed the military planning with Admiral Moorer. I raised — perhaps too late — a number of concerns. If cutting the Ho Chi Minh Trail was potentially as decisive as Abrams thought, it was certain that the North Vietnamese would fight. They might even welcome an opportunity to inflict a setback on the South Vietnamese. And Tchepone at the hub of communications could be reinforced with North Vietnamese divisions redeployed quickly from both North and South Vietnam. How many casualties could we risk having inflicted on the South Vietnamese? How long could they sustain operations? Given the immobility of the South Vietnamese divisions, where were replacements going to come from? How would these divisions react when deprived for the first time of American advisers and air controllers during the most bitter fighting of their experience? And were we sure that our air support would be adequate and timely under these novel command arrangements? If the objective was so important, should we reinforce our air power? I submitted a memorandum to Nixon with questions along this line for use with Moorer and arranged for a meeting of the two for January 26.

Nixon did not, in fact, ask the questions with the explicitness that I had suggested, but in his indirect way he managed to touch on all the points. Moorer was emphatic in his reassurances. If the enemy fought — and probably it would — American air power would isolate the battlefield and inflict heavy losses that would be difficult to replace. If it did not, its supply system would be destroyed. The operation would ensure the success of Vietnamization, increasing our ability to withdraw forces more rapidly. It would help the Cambodian government in its struggle for survival by cutting off enemy supplies. In short, "decisive" results were probable.

Thus armed, Nixon met all his senior advisers — Rogers, Laird, Helms, Moorer, Haig, and me — on January 27. As usual, over half of the meeting concerned irrelevancies: how to testify with respect to American air activities in Cambodia; the public relations handling of the small South Vietnamese operation to open Route 4 in Cambodia; the precise meaning of Presidential statements of the previous June forswearing American combat activity in Cambodia except for interdiction; the planned operation in the Chup plantation in Cambodia.

After about an hour of this the President asked Admiral Moorer to review the attack on Tchepone. Moorer's presentation followed substantially his briefing of the President. When Moorer finished, Nixon had run out of stalling time; Rogers had to be given his day in court. In an extraordinarily effective presentation Rogers argued that the risks were excessive. The enemy had intelligence of our plans. A battle was certain. We were asking the South Vietnamese to conduct an operation that we had refused to undertake when we had 500,000 troops in Vietnam because we thought we were not strong enough. If Saigon were set back, we would risk all the gains of the previous year and might shake Thieu's position in the process. Less convincingly, he raised the issue of Souvanna's concurrence; the Laotian Prime Minister might well be overthrown as a result of the operation, he thought.

Except for the last point, Rogers was right on target. Unfortunately, Nixon simply did not believe that his Secretary of State knew what he was talking about. He had heard similar objections the year before over Cambodia and none of the predicted horrible contingencies had materialized. He accepted Abrams's and Moorer's word as to military feasibility; he knew from Godley that Souvanna was sympathetic regardless of what public position he might take. He therefore ordered the Chup operation and Phase I of the Tchepone operation to proceed immediately. (Phase I was the securing of Route 9 to the Laotian border by American forces.) But he also ordered Admiral Moorer to study whether the airborne assault on Tchepone could either be eliminated or conducted without American airlift. (The issue here was whether helicopters touching down to deliver South Vietnamese troops constituted "ground combat in Laos," proscribed by the Cooper-Church amendment.) Anyone familiar with Nixon should have known that once he had gone this far, he would not be deflected. The order to proceed with Phase I made certain that he would order Phase II, however tortuous the maneuvers before he gave the final word. But not all the participants understood Nixon. Even regular associates like Moorer could not be certain that he had in fact made up his mind that day. The uncertainty and hesitation suggested by his request for further study of the airborne operation was bound to be magnified as it moved down in the military hierarchy.

The onset of another military operation automatically excited Congressional and media pressures. On January 21, having read reports of American air strikes in support of South Vietnamese operations in Cambodia, sixty-four members of the House of Representatives introduced legislation to ban the use of funds "to provide U.S. air or sea-combat support" for *any* military operations in Cambodia, apparently on the theory that Hanoi was entitled to undisturbed sanctuaries from which to attack our allies and to install a Communist government in Phnom Penh. On January 27 Senators George McGovern and Mark Hatfield, along with nineteen Senate colleagues, reintroduced the proposed Vietnam Disengagement Act, which, to allow for the passage of time, now required the withdrawal of all American troops by December 31, 1971 (instead of June 30).

As Phase I of the Laos operation began, the Defense Department urged, and the WSAG agreed, that the press in Saigon be briefed on the military movements, but under an embargo; this would both protect security and prevent inaccurate and misleading reports. This proved to be a naive mistake. The official briefings accelerated a growing spray of leaks. The Saigon press corps might observe the embargo, but they were free to inform their colleagues in Washington of the basic facts and these were under no restraint. In an extraordinary performance the Washington press corps and the TV networks not only dropped the broadest possible hints of an imminent allied operation in Laos; they also treated the embargo as a major story in itself, a sinister plot of deception and coverup.

Editorial comment was not long delayed. On February 3 the *New York Times* and the *Los Angeles Times* expressed disquiet about the planned operation. On February 5 the *Wall Street Journal* joined in, and lest it be ignored the *New York Times* added another editorial emphasizing that any attempt to choke off supplies through Laos was bound to fail because there was so little to choke off. Obviously the *Times* had different statisticians from the CIA's, who estimated that 18,000 tons had already passed through Tchepone in the current dry season. Many other journals joined the chorus. On February 1 the State Department briefed Republican Senator George Aiken on the same basis as the press corps in Saigon had been briefed by Abrams and with identical results; the story was out within twenty-four hours.

To Nixon, all this was only too reminiscent of his 1970 experience over Cambodia. And as in 1970 he withdrew into his shell and sought the support of those advisers who he thought backed his policy. On February 1, I briefed Agnew, Connally, and Mitchell about the Laos operation. I gave them a detailed account of the pros and cons — allowing for my own bias in favor of the operation — including detailed notes of Rogers's presentation of January 27. Not surprisingly — this was, after all, why they were being brought in — they favored going ahead. The next morning, February 2, I circulated to Rogers, Laird, and Helms a five-page memorandum that set out the pros and cons and included Rogers's points of January 27 opposing the project; I invited comments. None was forthcoming. Nixon met with Rogers, Laird, Helms, Moorer, Haig, and me at 5:00 P.M. that day. No new arguments emerged.

Late that evening, after a performance by the singer Beverly Sills at the White House, I saw Nixon again. My diary indicates — it was an incident I had forgotten until I consulted my notes — that I suggested he take another look at the proposed operation, whatever its undoubted military advantages. Surprise had been lost; our government was clearly divided. Nixon appeared relieved; he seemed more interested in a Soviet summit.

Once launched on what he considered the strong course, however, Nixon was generally not to be deflected. The next morning, February 3, he told me that he had decided to go ahead and to pay the price both domestically and with the Soviets. He then called in Mitchell and Connally, who urged him to proceed. From about 12:30 to 2:00 P.M., Admiral Moorer and I briefed Senator John Stennis in my office; Nixon wandered in and took the three of us back to his own office to continue the discussion. When Stennis agreed that the operation made sense, Nixon gave the "execute" order. I held it up a few hours to have a chance for one more review with the WSAG and one more discussion with the President. At 6:00 P.M. I informed the principals of the President's decision.

On February 8 South Vietnamese troops began Phase II by crossing the Laotian border. On February 9 Representative Thomas P. O'Neill and thirty-seven cosponsors introduced legislation not only forbidding direct US intervention in Laos but also American support of any kind for any military operation in Laos. We were embarked on another act in the Greek tragedy by which each participant in our national debate, following the logic of his own nature, brought about national paralysis. The Laos operation sought to speed our extrication from Vietnam while preserving South Vietnam's chances for survival and our international credibility. The debate was over motives: whether an Administration that was withdrawing over 150,000 troops a year might be bent on victory (a term long since turned into an epithet), whether the effort to end a war while fulfilling an obligation to an allied people was really a subterfuge for its indefinite continuation. All the time, a flood of Congressional resolutions sought to cut off any flexibility or freedom of maneuver.

Lam Son 719: The Military Operation

THE operation, conceived in doubt and assailed by skepticism, proceeded in confusion. It soon became apparent that the plans on which we had been so eloquently and frequently briefed reflected staff exercises, not military reality. As a visitor to Vietnam, I had been impressed that one of the most unambiguous successes of Vietnamization was in exporting to the South Vietnamese our techniques of military briefing. The essence of what I came to dub the "idiot briefing" is to overwhelm the victim with so many facts presented with such invincible self-assurance that he is fortunate if he can keep up with the words. His chance of questioning the substance disappears in the insinuating sequence of charts, arrows, and statistics. He is so proud to be able to distill a question out of the welter of material that he loses the faculty of insisting that the answer make sense.

The Vietnamese staff plan, approved and no doubt reviewed by our military commanders, had impressively predicted a rapid interruption of the trail system to be followed by a systematic destruction of the logistics structure. But from the beginning it became clear that the South Vietnamese divisions had not been trained for the daring thrust envisaged by "Lam Son 719" — the Vietnamese name for the operation.* Their experience had been with static defense in South Vietnam; their offensive operations had been usually unopposed sweeps of the countryside in support of pacification. Here they were propelled into an alien landscape, deprived for the first time of American advisers and air

---

*Lam Son was the place of a battle in northern Vietnam where the Vietnamese won an ancient victory against the Chinese.

controllers, and asked to take on the formidable North Vietnamese divisions close to their vital supply bases. They proceeded in so cautious a fashion as to invite the sort of set-piece battle in which, as I pointed out to Admiral Moorer on February 22, the North Vietnamese excelled. If the South Vietnamese continued their defensive tactics, I warned, they might well be run out of Laos.

As for us, by 1971 our command in Saigon had concentrated for nearly two years on preventing disaster while redeploying forces. Indeed, it was being asked to reduce its forces by 60,000 while the Laos operation was going on. It simply could not adjust to performing both of its missions: withdrawal and offensive operations. It remained silent while the Vietnamese headquarters for the battle remained in a comfortable permanent base over fifty miles from Tchepone. It did not set up a special command structure for what was described to Washington as a "decisive" operation. It never tested whether Vietnamese air controllers could replace American ones; too late we found out that many of the Vietnamese spoke no English. The untested Vietnamese divisions were thus deprived of much of the air support on which the original plan had counted to control the battle. With business as usual, the Laos operation had to compete for resources with all the other requirements for Indochina. Inevitably, the effort became stalled, and the hopes for a decisive turn were thwarted.

With every passing day after Phase II started on February 8, it became more obvious that what was taking place resembled the original plan only in the briefings a hapless JCS Colonel was inflicting on me every morning. The usual procedure when things go wrong is to try to avoid informing the highest levels of government in the hope that the problem will go away and on the theory that too many raw facts might panic Washington. But the problem did not go away. Nothing could obscure the reality that the South Vietnamese units, after penetrating only eight to twelve miles, simply stopped and dug in. We found it impossible to tell what they were doing, whether they were cutting supply routes, searching for caches, or simply awaiting a North Vietnamese assault.

Military commanders, like most officials, tend to develop a heavy investment in their own plans. In the face of a clearly stalled operation I was given a new date for the promised movement into Tchepone on six different occasions between February 8 and 22. None materialized. On February 13, I began to press Admiral Moorer for an assessment by General Abrams comparing "actual ARVN troop movements and time phasing with those originally planned, and reasons for any deviations therefrom." It was not until February 16 that General Abrams replied, giving some technical reasons primarily having to do with enemy antiaircraft fire, considerations that to a layman appeared foreseeable in the original planning. Abrams concluded optimistically: "I am confident that the task that was initially laid out will be done."

But not much changed over the next four days. Optimistic reports from the field did not square with the obvious stalemate on the ground. Not until March 18 — after the operation was over — did Washington find out that on February 12 President Thieu had ordered his commanders to be careful in moving west and to stop the operation altogether as soon as they had suffered 3,000 casualties. Given Hanoi's probable penetration of the South Vietnamese high command (far better placed than we were to understand its workings), this had to be known to the enemy, who therefore could organize a response designed to maximize casualties rather than contest territory. We would never have approved the Tchepone plan in the White House had such a restriction been communicated to us.

On February 20 I asked Bunker again for his and Abrams's appraisal, adding: "In my view it is essential that there be a clear understanding that the objective of this operation is not to seize real estate or supplies but to disrupt and interdict to the extent possible the trail itself." This led Abrams and Bunker to call on Thieu and his military chief of staff, General Cao Van Vien. On the basis of this conversation Ambassador Bunker reported: "We both came away feeling that there is no question about the GVN's steadiness and their determination to see the operation through." On the same day I was sufficiently worried to ask Haig to visit Vietnam for his on-the-spot assessment. The idea was squelched by Laird and Moorer, who considered the sending of a White House emissary as a demonstration of lack of confidence in General Abrams, which they would not countenance.

On February 23, Moorer was absent from Washington, which made General Westmoreland Acting Chairman of the JCS on the basis of seniority. I used the occasion to ask for a briefing; in reality I wanted Westmoreland's assessment. According to the protocol of the Joint Chiefs, the White House was supposed to deal with the Chairman, not individual chiefs; hence, we could not have earlier approached Westmoreland directly.

Westy looked like our beau ideal of an American officer: straight as an arrow, handsome, serious. Like so many of his colleagues he had launched himself into Vietnam with self-confident optimism only to withdraw in bewilderment and frustration. Saddled with restrictions for which there was no precedent in manuals, confronted with an enemy following a strategy not taught in our command colleges, he soon fell into a trap that has been the bane of American commanders since the Civil War: substitution of logistics for strategy.

With rare and conspicuous exceptions like Douglas MacArthur, our modern generals have preferred to wear down the enemy through the weight of matériel rather than the bold stroke, through superior resources rather than superior maneuvers. In this they reflected the biases of a nonmilitary, technologically oriented society. But wars of attrition cannot be won against an enemy who refuses to fight except on his own terms. The Vietnam terrain, the nature of guerrilla warfare, the existence of sanctuaries, all combined to make it impossible for Westmoreland to wear down his adversary as he sought. Instead, the North Vietnamese hiding in the population and able to choose their moment for attack wore us down. And then the 1968 Tet offensive, though a massive North Vietnamese military defeat, turned into a psychological triumph by starting us on the road to withdrawal. (In fairness it must be stressed that Westmoreland labored under political restrictions that barred any of the major maneuvers that might have proved decisive — sealing off the Ho Chi Minh Trail in 1967, for example.)

Whatever the reason for his failure, Westmoreland lived through the neglect suffered by those who have teetered on the edge of popular acclaim and whom the public then punishes for not living up to their assigned roles. Whoever is at fault, they are consigned to an oblivion all the more bitter for having been just one step away from being cast as hero. Westmoreland sat in the sumptuous office of the Army Chief of Staff, deliberating over weapons procurement, enjoying the deference of the uniformed service due to his position, but ignored by the policymakers. He was almost never consulted about the war he had conducted with gallantry, if not always ultimate success. His advice had not been sought individually about the proposed assault on Tchepone, though we were told that he had endorsed it together with the other Joint Chiefs of Staff.

When I saw Westmoreland on February 23, his assessment was bleak. He did not think that the forces assigned to the Laos operation were adequate; he himself had considered that four American divisions would be needed to seize and hold Tchepone; the South Vietnamese had allotted less than two to the operation. Nor did he consider a frontal assault the best way to interrupt the trail system. He recommended hit-and-run raids by air-mobile units out of Khe Sanh to cut the trails at various points. This would throw the Communist supply system into a maximum of turmoil and achieve our objectives at much less risk. Even allowing for a natural bias against his successors, Westmoreland's comments made a great deal of sense to me.

They did not make sense to Laird and Moorer, who argued that Westmoreland had failed to object while the plan was under consideration. They were convinced Abrams would resent being second-guessed by his predecessor. They insisted on the hallowed principle of the autonomy of the field commander. But theories of command did not solve our basic problem: to find out whether we were achieving the objective of interrupting the Communist supply system. No doubt we were having *some* effect. The supplies being consumed in the battle would not be available farther south. Not all of the reports of caches found could be wrong — though one could not help noticing that the claims were much less exuberant than in the Cambodia operation of the previous year.

Beyond that, it was hard to know. We were being told daily that the trails were being cut. Yet reports from automatic sensors along them indicated considerable traffic on some stretches. The JCS Colonel briefing me every morning argued that this was because of the enemy's desperate shuttling of supplies between way stations in the stress of combat. It made no sense to me. The truth probably was that the supplies were being slowed down and used up; they were not interrupted.

An interesting study of the pathology of military campaigns would be to determine at what point an objective becomes an obsession. Moscow for Napoleon, Verdun and Stalingrad for the Germans, Gallipoli for the British, became magnets that attracted ever-mounting resources long after the original reason for the campaign had disappeared. So it was on a much smaller scale with Tchepone. On February 24 I put three questions to my briefing officer: (1) Why were we heading for Tchepone, where the enemy was waiting, when the roads could be cut just as well farther south? (2) Why were we not bypassing Tchepone to the west and cutting Route 23 (paralleling the Thai frontier) with a helicopter assault? (3) If we were determined to take Tchepone, why were not more reserves being committed? The replies simply reiterated the plan for the original operation; they told me what we were doing but not why.

By late February North Vietnam had shifted more than 40,000 troops toward the battle, a much larger number than we had been told was possible.* Saigon's forces, because of the territorial base of its divisions, remained constant. At the WSAG meeting on February 23 I pointed out the risks and asked Air Force General John Vogt, representing the JCS, for the rationale of the continued frontal attack on Tchepone. He replied: "A rationale is lacking in the report." It became embarrassingly difficult to explain our policy when the facts were so elusive and I began to suspect that even the Pentagon had no idea what was going on.

On March 1, I cabled my concerns directly to Bunker via backchannel:

Since the operation has been launched, the President has received reports on a wide range of modifications to the plan brought on by the host of very real difficulties with which the ARVN have been confronted, only to discover that events on the ground and subsequent operational reporting have not been con-

---

* At one point I discussed the Laos operation with Yitzhak Rabin, Israel's brilliant Chief of Staff in the Six Day War and then Ambassador to Washington. He predicted that the North Vietnamese reaction would come from divisions temporarily withdrawn from South Vietnam and attacking from the South, not from the North as we had expected. He was proved right.

sistent with the forecasts. Specifically, we have found ourselves in the following position:

(1) The President was initially briefed to the effect that ARVN forces would seize Tchepone four to five days after H-Hour;

(2) On February 15, he was told that weather, supply problems, conditions on Route 9, and enemy resistance would delay achieving this objective for a period of 8 to 10 days.

(3) Subsequently, the President was informed that Tchepone was less important because all routes going through Tchepone were being cut southeast of Tchepone.

(4) Subsequently, the President was informed that a modified scheme of maneuver would be adopted which would place two regiments attacking on a northwest axis along Route 914 and the high ground to the north with the objective of seizing Tchepone.

Since receiving information on these various conceptual approaches, events on the ground have not confirmed our ability to accomplish them. This has quite naturally resulted in concerns here as to the overall future outlook of the operation. An additional factor which concerns me greatly is the limited ARVN strength which has been involved in this operation at a time when the enemy has obviously committed his full resources. . . .

We will do our best to hold the fort. But we must know what we are up against. There is no chance to keep panic from setting in if we are constantly outstripped by events.

But our Saigon command had seen too many hortatory cables from anxious civilians over six years of war. The temptation was to ignore the fevered Washington policymakers and to persevere; too many crises had been weathered in this manner to change the mode of operation now. Bunker sent back a soothing telegram on March 3 describing the dedication of Thieu and Vien to success (which was not the issue): "In operations of this kind, one cannot be tied to preconceived ideas of what might be thought of as ideal procedures. A posture has to be maintained flexible enough to adapt to fluid conditions which may be governed by weather, terrain or changes in enemy tactics." This was unexceptionable, but it did not answer our fundamental concern, which was not procedural: To what extent, if any, were we interrupting the enemy buildup by whatever plan? The conclusion seemed to put our fears to rest: "General Abrams and I are both confident that if we hold steady on our course, the Cambodia and Laos operations will have the impact on the enemy's activities in South Vietnam and our troop withdrawals which we originally contemplated."

And for a few days things seemed to improve. In major battles between South Vietnamese and North Vietnamese units the North Vietnamese grudgingly gave ground (at least if our reports were to be believed). A new assault was launched in the direction of Tchepone on March 3, and by March 6 the South Vietnamese were close enough to that objective to sustain the claim of having captured it. But soon the suspicion grew that they wanted Tchepone only so that they could withdraw from Laos altogether without loss of face. As early as March 8 Abrams informed us that South Vietnamese commanders, having occupied the Tchepone area, considered their mission accomplished and were eager to retreat.

This ran counter to any concept of the operation as I had understood it; there was no point in risking so much to occupy an abandoned Laotian town for three days. The whole point of the exercise was to disrupt the North Vietnamese trail system for the better part of the dry season and to destroy as many caches as could be found. When I called this to Bunker's attention on March 9, he and Abrams paid another of their visits to Thieu, from which they emerged with a mystifying clarification: Thieu was not withdrawing from Laos but rotating his units. He would pull back elements of his strategic reserve but replace them with fresh units. After some weeks of exploring for caches in the Tchepone area, these new units would then withdraw to the southeast along Route 914 through Communist Base Area 611, destroying the Communist supply system along the way. (See the map on page 993.)

Two factors prompted my doubts. Thieu did not vouchsafe to us what fresh units he was talking about, and we could not imagine what they might be; we certainly did not know of any. For over ten days we had been urging him to commit the other division from Military Region 1 — the Third Division. Thieu had refused, judging — correctly, as events the following year proved — that the Third Division was no match for battle-hardened North Vietnamese. Where, then, were the replacements coming from? The poor Colonel from the JCS who briefed me every morning found himself the victim of my sarcasm when he recited the official version in the face of overwhelming evidence that the South Vietnamese were, in fact, retreating from Laos. There was not even a pretense of an attempt to exit via Base Area 611. We did not know it, but the South Vietnamese had reached Thieu's quota of casualties: The operation was over, though they did not tell us.

Now I insisted on sending Haig to take a firsthand look. By this time Laird knew something was wrong; he was eager to spread responsibility, and acceded readily. In the meantime I sent off another backchannel to Bunker on March 18:

I hope Thieu understands that the President's confidence is an asset he should not lightly dissipate and that this may be his last crack at massive U.S. support.

By March 19 Haig's arrival in Vietnam put an end to all illusions. He reported that after three weeks of uninterrupted combat the commanders of the two South Vietnamese divisions were no longer willing to continue the operation: "My visit to I Corps has convinced me that the issue now is not feasibility of reinforcing and remaining in Laos, but urgent need to impress upon ARVN the necessity of moving out only with full concentration of US firepower in an orderly and tactically sound fashion."

Within a few days the retreat from Laos was in full swing. On the whole the South Vietnamese extricated themselves in tolerable fashion, except for the unedifying and untypical television pictures of a few panicky soldiers clinging to the landing gear of the helicopters. It would have been difficult in the best of circumstances for the White House to give a balanced assessment; those pictures destroyed any such prospect, and Washington was so badly informed and the operation deviated so much from the original plan that an alternative set of facts was not available in time.

The attack on the Chup plantation in Cambodia was similarly inconclusive. It achieved good results so long as it was commanded by General Do Cao Tri, one of the few offensive-minded commanders in the South Vietnamese army. But after Tri's death in a helicopter crash on February 23 it bogged down in the kind of South Vietnamese caution that invited what it sought to avoid. Gradually, the operation simply petered out, though not without a sharp local setback near the Cambodian town of Snuol.

The dry-season offensive of 1971 was a watershed. It marked the last offensive operation in which American troops participated, even in a supporting role, in Indochina. It clearly did not realize all our hopes; nor did it fail completely. As always in Vietnam the truth lay somewhere between the claims of the Administration and the abuse of the critics. The assault on Tchepone did not interrupt the North Vietnamese logistics buildup sufficiently to prevent an offensive by Hanoi in 1972. It slowed it down, however, enough to delay the start of the 1972 offensive for several months until toward the end of the dry season and to confine its maximum impact to the areas closest to North Vietnam. The major enemy thrust in 1972 came across the Demilitarized Zone, where Hanoi's supply lines were shortest and least affected by the operations in Cambodia and Laos. The farther south the North Vietnamese attempted to attack in 1972, the weaker was their impact, because their sanctuaries and supply system had been disrupted by our operations in the previous two years. As it was, the combination of South Vietnamese ground forces and American air power enabled us just barely to blunt the North Vietnamese offensive in 1972. Without the attrition caused by the incursions into Laos and Cambodia, this would have been impossible. The campaigns of 1970 and 1971, in my view, saved us in 1972.

At the same time, the Laos incursion fell far short of our expectations. There were several reasons for this. Our planners proved less meticulous in assessing Vietnamese operations than in studying our own. Had the forces been American, they would never have undertaken so major a challenge to North Vietnam's capacity to sustain the war in the South with so little margin for error. Our command in Saigon had been transformed by Washington pressures into a redeployment headquarters. Suddenly it was being asked to oversee complex offensive operations in two widely separated theaters while adhering to a withdrawal schedule in which it did not believe. It was barred by law from having its own men on the ground with the advancing troops even to control our air operations; and it was in the straitjacket of limitations on air sorties mechanically imposed by budgetary cuts. Our command in Saigon operated by rote; it did not change established procedures to ensure the success of a potentially decisive operation. And Washington acted by reflex; it was more absorbed in fending off the assaults of its critics at home than the assaults of the enemy in the field.

As for the South Vietnamese, Laos exposed many of their lingering deficiencies. Their planning turned out to be largely abstract. It formalistically imitated what was taught at our command and general staff schools without adaptation to local conditions. In retrospect I have even come to doubt whether the South Vietnamese ever really understood what we were trying to accomplish. Our objective surely was not Tchepone or any other geographic trophy. It was to slow up North Vietnamese resources and logistics throughout the dry season so as to pull the teeth of the 1972 offensive, when only residual American forces would be left. What Thieu seemed to want — it later emerged — was a quick spectacular, not a long-range strategy. Above all, the South Vietnamese suffered from the flaws inherent in their military organization. They had few reserves; their tolerance for casualties was small, except in defensive battles. Each commander, aware that his political influence depended in part on the strength and morale of the units he commanded, was eager to husband his assets and reluctant to incur losses for what seemed a distant objective. The South Vietnamese had fought better than before; but there was no blinking the fact that the result had been inconclusive. The dry-season offensive of 1971 did not foreclose an assault by Hanoi in 1972 as we had hoped though it almost surely lessened its impact. It was probable now that we would face another major military challenge the next year.

The Marches on Washington

At this moment that uneasily dormant beast of public protest — our nightmare, our challenge, and, in a weird way, our spur — burst forth again. When objectives are shared, the domestic debate can address tactics; even when objectives differ, there is occasionally room for some synthesis between opposing points of view in pursuit of some larger goal. But when there is no agreement on fundamental premises, when the challenge is not only to perception but to motive, then differences take on the character of a civil war.

With Laos, the "credibility gap" became not so much an Administration failure as a weapon of the opposition. Opponents deliberately chivied the Administration until harassed officials either made some prediction that turned out to be wrong (the famous "light at the end of the tunnel" had been an error of perception and judgment, but not a lie) or tried to embellish facts with evasions. This was then mercilessly exploited to undermine confidence in all governmental purposes. The cry for full disclosure was unending but unfulfillable — partly, as in the Laos operation, because Washington had difficulty learning the facts; partly because some elements of military or diplomatic plans can be revealed only at the risk of destroying the possibilities of success. And, of course, many critics wanted not facts but ammunition. They often demanded public disclosure of what they had already learned in classified briefings.

The days were long since gone when the antiwar platform asked for *mutual* withdrawal. Two years before, we had been urged to show our good faith by some token unilateral withdrawal. Several hundred thousand American troops had been withdrawn since; the end of American participation in ground combat was imminent. But the critics now demanded that we set an unconditional date for final withdrawal, and they were soon to urge the overthrow of Thieu — in other words, adoption of Hanoi's terms.

On February 26 the *Washington Post* — which had been among the more compassionate of the war critics — objected even to a statement by Nixon that "as long as North Vietnam continues to hold a single American prisoner, we shall have forces in South Vietnam." This was not treated as a backhand way of announcing that there was to be no American residual force (a point already conceded in the secret negotiations months earlier). Rather, it was seen as a token of an open-ended commitment: "It is also an admission that the Nixon Administration has no unilateral, irreversible plan which promises to end this country's involvement in this war. . . ." But the only way to end a war unilaterally and irreversibly is to accept the enemy's terms unconditionally; unilateral withdrawal, as Hanoi had made clear, would not do the trick; it would leave our prisoners in Hanoi's hands. On March 3 the usually supportive *Wall Street Journal* joined the chorus. Explaining that the Administration had two objectives in the war — to withdraw American forces and to ensure a non-Communist government in Saigon — it warned that the latter objective, while desirable, must not obscure the imperative of withdrawal. And the *Milwaukee Journal* put the same point more brutally on March 4: "The South Vietnamese will rely on us as long as we are there. They have one of the world's biggest armies. If they can't stand on their own feet now it is too late. The United States can no longer stand the internal frustrations and disruptions that the bloody, tragic and immoral war is costing."

These attitudes did not take long to make themselves felt in the Congress. Between the beginning and the end of the Laotian operation no fewer than five Congressional resolutions were introduced, aimed at limiting Presidential discretion in the conduct of military operations, prohibiting expenditures for combat in Cambodia and Laos (which all our studies had shown were pivotal to the war in Vietnam), or fixing a date for unconditional withdrawal. On February 22 the Senate Democratic Policy Committee unanimously demanded the withdrawal of *all* American forces, including air and support troops, from Indochina by December 31, 1972. On February 25 Senator Walter Mondale, along with Senator William Saxbe and sixteen cosponsors, introduced legislation to prohibit American forces from supporting an invasion of North Vietnam without "prior and explicit" Congressional authorization. The significance of the amendment was not that it constrained any Administration plan, but that it sought to legislate immunity for the country whose armies were marching at the very moment through every neighboring country and thus to remove any need for it to keep defensive forces at home.

After the withdrawal from Laos, both media and Congressional pressures escalated. Between April 1 and July 1 there were seventeen House or Senate votes seeking to restrict the President's authority to conduct the war or to fix a date for unilateral withdrawal (making a total of twenty-two for the year). On June 22 the Senate adopted, 57-42, Senator Mansfield's Sense of the Senate resolution that declared that "it is the policy of the U.S. to terminate at the earliest practicable date all military operations in Indochina and to provide for the prompt and early withdrawal of all U.S. forces not more than nine months after the bill's enactment subject to the release of American POW's." Though Sense of the Senate resolutions are not legally binding, the Mansfield resolution illustrated the Vietnam tragedy: The opposition was unwilling to accept ultimate responsibility for its views, but it would move heaven and earth to keep the Administration from pursuing a coherent strategy.

The pervasive exhaustion reflected itself in ever more explicit assertions that no conceivable objective in Vietnam could outweigh the domestic revulsion against the war. Vietnamization, urged two years previously as a means of ending our involvement, now was attacked as prolonging the war. On April 16, *Life* magazine criticized the refusal to set a withdrawal date: "Prolonged and open-ended withdrawal is too much like prolonged an open-ended warfare. . . . A country that finds the war intolerable will find such a prospect unacceptable.'' The *New York Times* proclaimed on April 25: "Mr. Nixon can be assured of broad public support if he will abandon the cruel delusion of Vietnamization and declare unequivocally his intention to withdraw all American forces from Vietnam by an early fixed date, contingent on agreement by the other side to release all United States prisoners and to guarantee the safe exit of American troops.'' In the more moderate formulations, unilateral withdrawal was coupled with injunctions to President Thieu to broaden the base of his government, to "compromise" with the Communists — as if he were the principal obstacle to accommodation and as if any such negotiating possibilities in fact existed. "Saigon's choice," editoralized the *New York Times* on April 6, "is between going on indefinitely with the war or negotiating a compromise settlement. Moves to broaden the Saigon Government and open this year's elections to the Communists, if they agree to a cease-fire, would be useful steps toward a political solution.''

Former officials of the Johnson Administration, having had no plan for even a limited withdrawal when they were in office, continued to be convinced that the promise of a total, unilateral withdrawal would guarantee an early peace. Clark Clifford and Averell Harriman never missed an opportunity to press this view; other ex-officials led delegations to lobby the Congress for a fixed deadline. Praise for the cease-fire initiative of the year before had completely disappeared amid unrelenting castigation of the Administration for not making another proposal, which all evidence showed had no attraction for Hanoi whatever. Both publicly and secretly Hanoi never deviated from its demand that the war would not end until we had overthrown the Saigon government. Nor was it ever explained what the point was in continuing the war once a fixed deadline had been established and how we could justify additional casualties when we had already announced the abandonment of the enterprise. In April and May of 1971 there were six weeks of demonstrations in Washington: rallies by the Vietnam Veterans Against the War (including candlelight marches, "guerrilla theater," Congressional testimony, and symbolic throwing away of medals); distribution of antiwar leaflets in government buildings; and a massive May Day campaign of civil disobedience, disruption, and vandalism designed to "bring the government to a halt.''[9]

Weariness was not confined to the critics. Nixon persisted in his course and I in my defense of it, not because we wanted to continue the war but because we could not agree that we should overthrow a friendly government (put into office by a coup organized by our predecessors) and mock the sacrifice of millions who had relied on us, as the price for getting out. And we did not know how to explain to American mothers why their sons should be at risk when a deadline for unilateral withdrawal had already been established. Nixon found it difficult to articulate this issue in a generous manner. But he made valiant efforts in press conferences and speeches: "The issue very simply is this: Shall we leave Vietnam in a way that — by our own actions — consciously turns the country over to the Communists? Or shall we leave in a way that gives the South Vietnamese a reasonable chance to survive as a free people?" [10]

The fact that most critics were bored with the question — or ridiculed it as an "open-ended" commitment — did not make it any the less valid and central. The America that was the bulwark of free peoples everywhere could not, because it was weary, simply walk away from a small ally, the commitments of a decade, 45,000 casualties, and the anguish of their families whose sacrifices would be retroactively rendered meaningless. And the end result might well be an increased risk of war. I told a press briefing in February:

> In September, the situation in the Middle East hung by a razor's edge. If any of the chief adversaries had acted more precipitously there would have been an explosion. . . . We avoided a Middle East war also by being both firm and restrained. Neither our firmness nor our restraint would have meant a thing in September if we had not established the degree of credibility by our actions [in Southeast Asia] earlier.

We could not convince our opposition at home that it was so. Nothing Hanoi did was perceived as cynical or bellicose. When the Administration put forward a proposition, there seemed almost a vested interest in belittling it or a presumption that it was either duplicitous or insignificant. Each ploy of the North Vietnamese, no matter how transparent, was treated as an opening that an Administration bent on war was obtusely ignoring. Nixon certainly did not help matters by inflated claims and ungenerous comments. But it is not possible to understand the tragedy of Vietnam without a willingness to admit that some of the best people in our country thought they could serve peace best by discrediting their own government. I summarized this, our deepest problem, at a background briefing on April 8:

> I remember three years ago it used to be considered the height of enlightenment to believe that negotiations were a useful way of ending the war.
>
> Today, it is considered by many the height of obtuseness to believe that negotiations can still be a means of ending the war.
>
> There used to be a time when it was said that we should substitute Vietnamese for Americans. Now that is under attack. . . .
>
> We believe that we have to give the South Vietnamese a reasonable chance to stand on their own feet, and that what would happen to the American body politic if an American President, after seven years of war and 40,000 casual-

ties, consciously turned the country over to the Communists, would be something from which we would suffer for many years, even if there is a temporary feeling of relief in the immediate aftermath of such a settlement.

I had not given up hope that I could bridge somewhat the chasm between the Administration and its critics. Between April 1, 1970, and April 1, 1971, without publicity I met with groups of students and young protestors nineteen times, with academic critics of the war twenty-nine times, and Senators and other prominent critics thirty times — a total of seventy-eight occasions, or more than one a week. Many of them were former academic colleagues; some became new friends.

During the 1970 Cambodian operation I had become acquainted with a young pacifist who had pledged to fast until the operation was called off or he had been able to put his case to the President. Brian McDonnell and a friend sat in Lafayette Park, across Pennsylvania Avenue from the White House, for an hour each day to dramatize their willingness to sacrifice to end the war. Early in June 1970, on a mutual friend's suggestion, I called on McDonnell, without White House permission, at the simple residence in Georgetown where he was staying. I was moved by his sincerity even while I disagreed with his conclusions. I told him that he was sacrificing himself for a purpose that was already accomplished. The decision to leave Cambodia had already been made; I assured him we would carry it out. Furthermore, he could hardly expect to see the President through moral blackmail; if he ended his fast I would do my best to arrange a meeting with the President. He ended his fast. We kept to the deadline for withdrawal, but I could never succeed in persuading Nixon to receive him.

Brian and I met frequently afterward, usually in my office, always without publicity. Often he brought his extraordinary wife, Alice, a young black woman who did social work in the ghetto of Philadelphia. Months later she was brutally murdered in a random killing in the ghetto. How cruel was destiny to inflict such horror on two gentle people whose passion was the abhorrence of violence! I went privately to her funeral.

In early 1971 Brian conceived one of the wildly romantic ideas that proved his Irish ancestry. He suggested that I meet with a group of his friends who, he said, would welcome a discussion with me on the war and the problems of our society. I invited them to the White House. In fact, the three friends were a nun and two Catholic laymen who had been named as unindicted coconspirators in an alleged plot to kidnap me. When the press later learned of the meeting through one of McDonnell's friends, I was admonished by the Secret Service and the Attorney General, who demanded an explanation.

I met with Brian and his friends on a Saturday morning in March

1971 in the Situation Room of the White House, and we struggled to fashion at least a temporary bridge across the mutual incomprehension that was rending our society. Gently, they expressed their deep and passionate opposition to the war; but they had no idea how to end it. The problem for me, on the other hand, was to translate inchoate ideas — however deeply held — into concrete policy. Ours was the perpetually inconclusive dialogue between statesmen and prophets, between those who operate in time and through attainable stages and those who are concerned with truth and the eternal.

I found it easier to respect these committed and consistent pacifists, who hated all killing, than those whose morality was selective, who condemned American military actions but not North Vietnamese or Indian or Soviet. McDonnell argued that by continuing the war in Vietnam we were disintegrating morally; we were destroying the chance of any healing within our society. We were contributing to the idea that human life was cheap and irrelevant, that power alone was decisive. I thought the opposite was true. We could not establish our moral position by sacrificing our friends, thereby shaking the confidence of all who depended on us. In my view our society was suffering a malaise that went far beyond Vietnam. A feeling of self-pity was rampant, and a private grief that had become almost liturgical in nature. At the end of the meeting I tried to express the inconclusiveness, frustration, and anguish of the dialogue: "Somebody, and I don't know who, has got to build a bridge between those who *care* and those who *do*. I admit that four-fifths of the bridge has to be built by the government, by those in power and those who can do. But the other fifth must come from you and I don't even know how to tell you to try to do it."

With deep foreboding, but also a prayerful sense of the long-term national interest, the United States government had concluded that the security of free peoples everywhere would be jeopardized by an essentially narcissistic act of abdication. We could not simply turn tens of millions in Southeast Asia over to a Communist rule we knew would be repressive and brutal. We would settle for minimum terms. But we would not dishonor our country by joining our adversary against our friends. And if we would not accept Hanoi's terms, only two possibilities existed: Either we would negotiate a compromise compatible with our values, or else there would be another military test in 1972.

The Negotiations Are Resumed

THERE was no goal to which I was more passionately committed than to restore the unity and cohesion of my adopted country by ending its agony in Vietnam through negotiation. Nixon acquiesced somewhat grudgingly; as I have explained, he was always more skeptical than I that any negotiation would succeed until there had been a military showdown. He turned out to be right. After Laos, we first assessed the military prospects for 1972, and, second, considered how we could vary our negotiating terms to encourage flexibility from Hanoi.

The military conclusions of my systems analysis staff under Wayne Smith proved remarkably prescient. They considered that the Laotian incursion had gained us a year. They predicted that as a result of the Cambodian and Laotian operations the North Vietnamese would retain the capacity for a major offensive only in the northern part of South Vietnam across the DMZ in Military Region 1 and, to a lesser extent, the Central Highlands of Military Region 2. Because of the Cambodian incursion Hanoi's offensive operations in Military Region 3 would be deprived of guerrilla support; conventional attacks could not be sustained there for a long period. There was no main-force offensive threat to Military Region 4 at all. Because the Laos operation had disrupted Hanoi's logistics system, an offensive was unlikely before the second half of the dry season, probably not before early March 1972. (The estimate was off by only three weeks; the offensive, in fact, started at the end of March.) The question was whether Hanoi had made the same calculations and, if so, whether it would gamble on the outcome of an offensive in 1972 or attempt a serious negotiation in 1971.

With these questions in mind, I went back to Paris for another round of secret talks. While the Laos operations were taking place, negotiations inevitably had languished. In mid-April 1971 Xuan Thuy at a plenary session challenged the United States to set a withdrawal date; in return Hanoi would guarantee the security of our retreat and "discuss" prisoners of war. We did not take up these schemes at the plenary meetings because we had heard them the year before and because a separate US–Hanoi cease-fire was unthinkable. Hanoi's conception of a deadline was unchanged; once a fixed date was accepted the clock would then begin to run regardless of what else happened. We also knew that if Hanoi had anything new and significant to say, it would save it for my next secret meeting. On April 24 General Walters contacted the North Vietnamese in Paris, proposing May 16 as the date for a renewal of discussions "on the basis of new approaches." With its characteristic generosity of spirit Hanoi waited until May 14 to reply. It was not hard to imagine what our critics would have said if the roles had been reversed and we had let Hanoi wait for three weeks before replying, and then had done so only forty-eight hours before the suggested date. Hanoi accepted, but offered May 30 instead. We countered with May 31, partly so as not to accept Hanoi's date, but also for logistic and security reasons. (It was the last day of a long weekend; my absence would therefore not be noted.)

Before the meeting I submitted to Nixon a new seven-point peace program I proposed to table. Though basically skeptical, and afraid that Hanoi would try to string us along, Nixon authorized our proposal to be put forward as a "final offer." It was, in fact, the most sweeping plan we had yet offered, worked out by me, Lord and Smyser of my staff, cleared by Bunker, and approved by Thieu. It sought to bring our negotiating proposals into line with our actions.

The seven-point plan recognized that since we were withdrawing most of our forces unilaterally we could not use them to bargain for total Hanoi withdrawal. We would try to use our residual force as a bargaining counter while recognizing that the mounting Congressional pressures for deadlines — reflected in the ever-increasing votes for the McGovern-Hatfield type of amendment — would sooner or later make irrelevant even this potential concession. We offered, as our first point, to set a date for total withdrawal. We gave up the demand for mutual withdrawal, provided Hanoi agreed to end all additional infiltration into the countries of Indochina. The proposal sought to get us off the treadmill of demanding mutual withdrawal while we in fact carried ours out unilaterally; we would, in effect, trade our residual force for an end of infiltration. Theoretically, North Vietnamese forces would wither away if they could not be reinforced. To be sure, they might violate the prohibition against reinforcement (our point 4); but in that case they would ignore a provision for withdrawal as well, as in fact they had done in Laos a decade earlier and were to do in Laos and Cambodia a few years later. Whatever the agreement, it would depend on our willingness to enforce it. We proposed, as our third point, a cease-fire in place throughout Indochina to become effective at the time when US withdrawals began, based on a final agreed timetable under international supervision (point 5). Our sixth point called for guarantees for the independence, neutrality, and territorial integrity of Laos and Cambodia, with both sides renewing their pledge to respect the 1954 and 1962 Geneva Accords. We repeated our proposal for the immediate release by both sides of all prisoners of war and innocent civilians on humanitarian grounds and as an integral part of the US withdrawal timetable (point 7). The political future of South Vietnam was to be left to the South Vietnamese to settle (point 2). Our unilateral withdrawal, needless to say, was contingent on agreement on all other issues. The deadline would start running only *after* an agreement was reached. The text of the proposal is given in the notes.[11]

The proposal marked a turning point in our diplomacy in Vietnam. Indeed, in its essence it was accepted sixteen months later by Hanoi. It isolated the military issues for a separate solution: US withdrawal, cease-fire, return of POWs. This was the approach I had recommended in my *Foreign Affairs* article written in 1968, before my appointment as security adviser. Its acceptance by Thieu in 1971, when he was hard-pressed, misled us into believing that he would still welcome it in 1972 when he thought he was winning.

The May 11 meeting took place in the dingy living room on Rue Darthé. Once again the American and Vietnamese delegations faced each other across a narrow strip of carpet and a chasm of misperception. It was to turn into the first real negotiation with the North Vietnamese. It lasted three months and failed because in the end Hanoi continued to insist that we dismantle our ally and establish a Communist-controlled government before it would agree to a cease-fire and the return of our prisoners.

Xuan Thuy was too subtle not to recognize immediately that we had made a major change on the military issues, though he pretended to have difficulty understanding it. He still argued that the "correct and logical" solution was for us to set a deadline for unilateral withdrawal unrelated to any other aspect of the negotiation. He refused to move from the position that Hanoi would only "discuss," not guarantee, the release of our prisoners even if we set a withdrawal date; clearly, the prisoners were to be used as a lever to get us to overthrow the Saigon government. Nor could he refrain from lecturing me on our precarious domestic situation, leading to a sharp exchange:

KISSINGER: We'll take care of our public opinion and you of yours.

XUAN THUY: Since your public opinion speaks on the situation, therefore we must give an interpretation.

KISSINGER: I won't listen to it at these meetings.

Xuan Thuy maintained Hanoi's political terms: the replacement of Thieu, Ky, Khiem, and other "warlike leaders." He even tried to be helpful in this effort; drawing on a lifetime of experience in rigged elections, he pointed out that the imminent South Vietnamese presidential election gave us a great opportunity to get rid of our allies in a "natural" way.

Even though I adamantly refused to embrace his loaded political proposals, he was clearly eager to keep the discussion of our new military proposal alive, which suggested to me that Hanoi might be in the process of reconsidering its political demands. On the whole Xuan Thuy treated our propositions with more care than usual. He did not, for once, denounce them as "nothing new." He said again and again that Hanoi would study our offer seriously. In our shell-shocked state we considered that this minimum prerequisite of negotiations showed a new flexibility. At one point he even said that "in case your proposal is accepted in general, then next time we should be prepared to discuss all concrete questions." He stressed Hanoi's desire to negotiate. He did not repeat the usual insistence that a cease-fire was impossible in the absence of a full political settlement. He repeatedly asked for another meeting. For the first time he showed impatience, suggesting a date well before July 1. We settled on June 26. Soon we received word that Le Duc Tho had left Hanoi, stopping in Peking and Moscow on the way to Paris. A serious negotiation seemed in the offing for the first time, and there were other hints of breakthrough. We were also engaged in putting the finishing touches on my secret trip to Peking (the definitive invitation reached Washington on June 2), and we were still exploring a summit with the Soviet Union. It was a moment of extraordinary hope.

All the while, of course, Xuan Thuy in Paris threw out tantalizing public hints to egg on Congressional pressures to fix a deadline. At the June 3 plenary, while he repeated that the political and military issues were "the two crucial and inseparable questions," he added ambiguously that the withdrawal deadline was "the immediate crucial point." Clark Clifford, addressing a June 8 dinner meeting of lawyers lobbying against the war, declared that he had "reason to believe" that a withdrawal deadline of December 31, 1971, would secure the release of our prisoners. But under sharp probing by a journalist, Xuan Thuy himself refuted this. Chalmers Roberts concluded, after an interview published in the *Washington Post* of June 10: "The central issue between the United States and North Vietnam at the Paris peace talks has always been the political future of the South, despite the recent concentration in Congress and elsewhere on American troop withdrawal and the release of prisoners of war."

June, too, was the month in which for the first time a House of the Congress voted to override the Administration's Vietnam policy by legislation. On June 22, to the editorial acclaim of the leading journals, the Senate passed by a vote of 57 to 42 the Mansfield amendment calling on the President to withdraw all American forces from Vietnam within nine months if Hanoi agreed to release all our prisoners. The practical effect was to make irrelevant five of our seven points in the secret negotiations. Hanoi now knew that there was a floor under its risks; if these pressures mounted, it would not need to negotiate about a cease-fire anywhere in Indochina, or pledge to cease infiltration, or promise to respect the neutrality and independence of Laos and Cambodia. If it agreed to release our prisoners, there was a good chance that the Congress would impose an unconditional total withdrawal of American forces.

In retrospect, I wonder whether we paid too high a price for secrecy. Hanoi wanted secrecy because it sought to deprive the Administration of the possibility of using the negotiations to rally public opinion. We went along because we thought success was more important than publicity but also because experience had shown that no matter what we proposed, our critics would push us further, undermining our position. There is no doubt that in 1971 secrecy enabled Hanoi to whipsaw us; the question whether more openness would have stopped this or produced an even earlier stalemate must remain in the realm of conjecture.

June, finally, was the month the Pentagon Papers were published. The intensity of the Administration's reaction cannot be understood except in the context of our China initiative and Vietnam negotiations. For the first time in the war Hanoi had deigned to say that it would study an American proposal. We believed, rightly or wrongly, that Hanoi was approaching a fundamental decision on whether to end the war before the Vietnamese presidential election in October. And yet, at the very moment these decisions were being made in Hanoi, thousands of documents suddenly appeared in the press, leaked by those whose motive was to discredit all US efforts in Vietnam. That the villain of the papers was a previous Administration did not change our problem. If Hanoi concluded that our domestic support was eroding, for whatever reason, it was bound to hold fast to its position. The war would continue; there would be no chance for peace in 1971 except through capitulation. I do not believe now that publication of the Pentagon Papers made the final difference in Hanoi's decision not to conclude a settlement in 1971. But neither those who stole the papers nor the government could know this at the time.

When Le Duc Tho and I met on June 26, it was not under ideal conditions. To minimize the risk of discovery I had chosen a new route to Paris. I arranged for a two-day visit to London for which my good friend Sir Burke Trend, the Cabinet Secretary, supplied the invitation. He had devised the pretext of wishing to learn about the operation of the NSC system; it was a subterfuge more likely to fool Americans than the British, who knew very well that such procedures were next to impossible to graft onto the British Cabinet system. But it took a courageous British civil servant to pretend that Britain had anything to learn from the United States in bureaucratic management. On the second of two days set aside for consultations Burke suggested a trip to the countryside. The "countryside" in question was a British military airport whence a British plane took me to Paris. There was an unexpected hitch when Villacoublay Airport was closed for an hour because the French President was departing from it. At last we reached Rue Darthé, where for the first time in fourteen months Le Duc Tho was waiting for me.

"Ducky," as we had come to think of him, could not have been more cordial. Instead of our sitting in the living room as usual, he took us into the tiny dining room, which had been equipped with a green-covered conference table. For the first time in our private encounters the setting would be like that for a formal bargaining. He meant to symbolize that he was there for serious business, not vilification or psychological warfare. Le Duc Tho was so determined to create a friendly atmosphere that he even permitted me to interrupt his epic poem on American perfidy in

Cambodia. When I again emphasized that we had nothing to do with Sihanouk's overthrow, Ducky's reply added a new dimension to epistemology (the philosophy of knowledge). With a maximum effort at generosity he said: "I *temporarily* believe that you had nothing to do with the coup in Phnom Penh." Lest I be carried away by this unprecedented — if limited — declaration of faith in me, Le Duc Tho immediately added that it was an assertion based on politeness rather than on conviction.

While he was at it, Le Duc Tho enlightened me on relations with his Communist allies. On January 9 I had told Dobrynin that I was ready to resume private talks with the North Vietnamese, and Dobrynin had brought me the reply that Hanoi preferred to deal through existing channels in Paris. Le Duc Tho now complained bitterly about our use of intermediaries. He also implied strongly that Hanoi had invited a direct approach well *before* the Laotian operation. It led to melancholy reflections. If Le Duc Tho were telling the truth, Moscow had delayed transmitting a reply that we would surely have taken into account in planning the Laotian enterprise. If Dobrynin were telling the truth, Hanoi was trying to sow distrust between us and the Kremlin, perhaps to discourage any temptation in Moscow to impose a settlement. I considered it more likely that Dobrynin had told the truth. Thenceforward, we never used Moscow as an intermediary to Hanoi; whatever we told Moscow we also passed to Hanoi directly via Paris, and usually well ahead of time.

When we finally got around to the subject of our meeting, Xuan Thuy, being technically the chief negotiator, opened with some pointed questions about our May 31 proposal. Le Duc Tho, playing the role of Special Adviser to Xuan Thuy, followed with a lengthy, generalized statement about the history of negotiations, and alleged that allied military moves had interfered with a negotiated settlement. Both were very careful to avoid saying anything that suggested rejection. And their tone quickly became more conciliatory whenever I made a sharp reply.

After two hours of sparring there was a tea break. Xuan Thuy went upstairs, presumably to work on his next statement, but Le Duc Tho for the first time joined me for a sociable chat in the small garden behind the house. I invited him, too, to Harvard after the war to give a seminar on Marxism-Leninism. Le Duc Tho delicately suggested that his views might be strong medicine for a capitalist country. I assured him that he was more likely to be received cordially by my Harvard colleagues than I.

After the break the probing resumed, until I said: "We have made our proposal. If you have no other proposals of your own, I have nothing more to say." This triggered Xuan Thuy into a long recital of the saga of Vietnemese history that turned out to be preliminary to a new North Vietnamese nine-point proposal. Since Hanoi felt obligated to demonstrate its moral superiority at every turn, Xuan Thuy presented Hanoi's program by stating, only half in jest: "This proves our desire is more earnest than yours to end the war because we have more points [than you]!"

The program proposed a deadline for our withdrawal of December 31, 1971 — or six months away, a retrogression from Madame Binh's eight points of the previous September, but matching the most recent versions of the McGovern-Hatfield amendment. It explicitly agreed, for the first time, that American prisoners of the Vietnamese would be released — instead of merely "discussed" — simultaneously with our withdrawals, thus also fulfilling the Mansfield amendment. A standstill cease-fire would be instituted on completion of the agreement, and would be subject to international supervision and guarantees. The political proposals were a little more ambiguous. Hanoi had understood that we would never agree to its version of a coalition government. Therefore, we were now being asked to "stop supporting" Thieu, Ky, and Khiem so that "a new administration standing for peace, independence, neutrality and democracy" would be set up. To "stop supporting" our allies could mean anything from withdrawing our forces to ending all economic and military aid, or even conniving in their overthrow.

The obligation to respect the neutrality and independence of Laos and Cambodia (our sixth point) was referred to in one paragraph saying that the problems between Indochinese countries should be settled by them on the basis of mutual respect for their sovereignty, which was fine, but it added that Hanoi was "prepared to join in resolving such problems"; the Geneva Accords were invoked as if they were addressed only to the United States. The implication was that restrictions did not apply to North Vietnam and that Hanoi had a special status in determining the future of the countries of Indochina. And there was a demand — which I rejected out of hand — that the United States pay reparations "for the damage caused by the US in the war zones of Vietnam." The proposals were put forward as an "integrated whole"; in other words, Hanoi would not countenance the withdrawal-for-prisoners exchange that was the staple of our domestic debate.

In the fairy-tale atmosphere of Vietnam negotiations, after two years of Communist stonewalling and domestic flagellation, my colleagues and I were elated that Hanoi had for the first time responded to a proposition by us, even though the response could hardly be called generous. It was a major step forward only by the standards of previous exchanges. For the first time Hanoi presented its ideas as a negotiating document and not as a set of peremptory demands. Le Duc Tho repeatedly stressed that these were subjects for negotiation; we were invited to make counterproposals. In dealings with Ducky one was grateful for small favors. The fact that the North Vietnamese used the phrase "the United States should" rather than the traditional peremptory "the United States must" was considered by the Hanoi demonologists on my staff as a huge advance. Le Duc Tho offered to stay in Paris until the negotiations were completed.

In fact, I judged that for us every one of Hanoi's proposals, however unacceptably phrased, was negotiable, except the demand for reparations and the ambiguity with respect to the political solution. If the latter masked the old demand that we overthrow the Saigon government, we were once again at a dead end. But if it marked a stage in the retreat from that position, a settlement would be possible. I reported to Nixon:

> The real meaning of their counter-proposal and their discussion is as of now unclear. There remains the strong possibility that there can be no negotiated solution except on terms which we cannot accept. Their position and approach were consistent with an attempt on their part to gain time. It was also consistent, however, with moving toward our approach, for if they are to do that they must first go through the exercise of fighting for their political demands and showing that we were unyielding. Also, they do not need to send Le Duc Tho to Paris to string us along, and in any event, it is not clear what that tactic really buys them; there is nothing we lose by waiting right now; their proposal had some positive as well as tough elements, and they were clearly eager to negotiate further and concretely.

My colleagues and I had never had experience with Hanoi's offering to reconcile parallel points in comparable documents. I proposed to Nixon — and he agreed — that on July 12, at the end of my trip around the world (including Peking), I would submit a counterproposal seeking to merge Hanoi's document and ours. But before that meeting could take place, the North Vietnamese pulled another of their characteristic duplicitous stunts that so heightened our sense of outrage when in our domestic debate it was we who were accused of bad faith. The agent for their maneuver was Madame Binh. On July 1, just as I was leaving on my trip around the world, she published a new seven-point plan that partly duplicated Le Duc Tho's nine points, spelled some of them out in greater detail, omitted others altogether, and added some new ones.

Madame Binh's plan was cleverly geared to the American public debate, dangling the prospect of a simple withdrawal-for-prisoners deal by grouping together the provisions on withdrawal and prisoners and creating the impression that the two were linked and perhaps could be separated from the rest of the package. The other points omitted any reference to Cambodia and Laos and were more vaguely expressed on some issues and more intransigent on others. For example, Madame Binh's proposals were sharper in spelling out a coalition government along familiar lines; they also deferred a cease-fire until such a government was formed, rather than its going into effect when our agreements were signed, as Le Duc Tho had had it.

Almost concurrently, Le Duc Tho strongly implied to Anthony Lewis of the *New York Times* on July 6 that Madame Binh's point 1 — withdrawal for prisoners — could indeed be settled separately from the other provisions. This was a flat untruth; it was contradicted by the secret nine points, which explicitly linked all the provisions, calling them ''an integrated whole.'' (Le Duc Tho at our meeting on May 2, 1972, confirmed that journalists holding Lewis's view had just been ''speculating.'') Similarly deceptive interviews were given to prominent antiwar Americans, including Senator George McGovern. Neither journalists nor legislators hesitated to take for granted the truth of Hanoi's claims and the deceit of ours. Ducky, in great form, reached new heights of cynical implication when he suggested to journalists that he would be ready to meet if I asked him to do so.

Madame Binh's plan had its intended effect. The Congress and media were at one that the Administration was passing up yet another unparalleled opportunity for peace. A *Baltimore Sun* editorial of July 3 spoke of an ''opening in Paris.'' The *Washington Post* on July 8 saw ''New Possibilities in Vietnam.'' The *Chicago Daily News* on July 9 detected a ''faint scent of peace.'' *Newsweek* on July 12 headlined: ''A Way to End the War?'' Averell Harriman weighed in on July 15 with an article in the *New York Times* to the effect that Madame Binh had given us a ''reasonable chance'' to end it. *Life* on July 23 had few doubts: ''We hope President Nixon seizes the chance.''

We were constrained from demonstrating that the ''chance'' was bogus and at variance with the entire record of the secret — and the public — negotiations, for precisely the opposite of the reason alleged by our critics. It was our eagerness to score a breakthrough that made us preserve a secrecy which enabled our cynical adversaries to whipsaw us between a public position we dared not rebut and a private record we could not publish.

No wonder that Nixon, always skeptical of negotiations, bombarded me with missives on my round-the-world trip to toughen up our stance in Paris and bring matters to a head. On almost all the negotiations I conducted I was faced by this ambivalence on his part. He usually had to be persuaded to enter them at all; each new visit to Paris was preceded by a more or less protracted internal debate. Once that hurdle was passed, Nixon invariably approved the negotiating plan that I submitted to him. Then, when I was under way, he would deluge me with tough-sounding directives not always compatible with the plan, and some incapable of being carried out at all. The reason may have been his unease with the process of compromise or the fear of being rejected even in a diplomatic forum. A contributing cause was undoubtedly his highly developed sense of the historical record, which tempted him to ensure that he appear tougher than his associates; he was thus protected, whatever happened. And yet he never insisted on these second thoughts; he invariably returned to and backed up the original plan.

Ambivalence was compounded in this instance by the wish to be out of Vietnam before the Presidential election of 1972, yet without having Saigon collapse. When the secret visit to Peking succeeded, the first flush of euphoria caused Nixon to harden his Vietnam stand. Even the idea of suddenly announcing a total withdrawal coupled with an all-out air assault resurfaced in a Haig cable on July 10:

> You should be aware that he is seriously considering the alternative plan which he has mentioned previously of moving out precipitously and concurrently undertaking major air effort against North. Obviously this message is characterized by overkill and instructions must be interpreted in the light of your discussions at previous stop [Peking]. I did feel you should have the benefit of atmosphere here.

Nothing could stop Nixon from calling me in Paris on an open phone line the morning of July 12 to give me graphic and bloodcurdling instructions even while repeating his approval of the counterproposal I was about to submit. He reasoned that the conversation would be overheard by the French — which was probable — who would warn Hanoi — which was more doubtful and technically impossible in time for the afternoon meeting with Le Duc Tho.

Though my getting to Paris was easy this time — I arrived openly from Pakistan — Le Duc Tho's public invitation to a meeting had alerted the press. It was staked out in force at the Ambassador's Residence on Avenue d'Iéna where I was staying. I solved the problem by having David Bruce arrive conspicuously for what was announced as a review of the Paris negotiations. I greeted him at the front door and took him into the Residence. Once he was settled, I sneaked out the back into the courtyard where General Walters was waiting in his personal car; he had even thought of equipping me with a hat. Sliding down low in the seat in case the press was covering the rear exit — which it was not — we followed instructions previously cabled to me by Walters, who was having so much fun that he probably would have paid us for the privilege of participating. Written in the most portentous Pentágonese and labeled "Plan for Movement to and from Location," his scenario read:

> 1. My [Walters's] personal Chevrolet convertible, 6CD408, is prepositioned in rear countyard of Embassy Residence one day before action.
>
> 2. I arrive at Embassy on foot at 1245. Gen. Kirschman [my code name]

and I go down Embassy back stairs, get in my car and leave rear of building. We proceed by circuitous route to my home at 49 Blvd Charcot, Neuilly.

3. On arrival here two courses are possible.

a. Gen. Kirschman gets out, goes through electronic door which locks behind him, takes elevator and goes down to basement. Meantime I have driven into basement. My Warrant Officer locks garage door behind me and we emerge from rear exit on rue St. James.

b. Gen. Kirschman goes into garage with me and remainder of alternative *A.* is carried out.

4. My Warrant Officer remains at my home to make sure phone is not answered and no one is let into apartment.

5. Gen. Kirschman and I proceed to predetermined point 10 blocks from location. Here we meet my secretary in rental car who has just "cased" location. If all is clear we proceed to location.

6. We return to my basement via rue St. James, switch to my personal Chevrolet, emerge from Blvd. Charcot exit and return to Residence.

We eventually carried out Option 3b since Walters did not trust me to find my way to the basement unaided. The plan worked perfectly, mostly because no one was following us.

At last I was again face to face with Le Duc Tho and Xuan Thuy across a rectangular table covered with a green cloth. But the negotiating framework would never be the same again; it had been fundamentally changed by my trip to Peking, though Le Duc Tho did not yet know this. Xuan Thuy again spoke first for Hanoi. His role was that of the picador in a bullfight. He was to bloody us and perhaps let Le Duc Tho study our reactions. When serious exchanges began, Le Duc Tho would take over with his set monologue of Hanoi's view.

Not unexpectedly, the July 12 meeting began testily; I accused the North Vietnamese of bad faith in publishing Madame Binh's seven points. Xuan Thuy answered with a grab bag of accusations, mostly about military actions within South Vietnam, which were as misleading as they were irrelevant. He knew and I knew that no major military actions by either side were going ahead in South Vietnam. However, the North Vietnamese were eager not to push these matters too far. They seemed anxious to engage in negotiations. Not yet knowing of my trip to Peking, they thought they had us on the run; they probably wanted to see whether we would buckle.

"Negotiations," however, is a relative term in Hanoi. Le Duc Tho and Xuan Thuy would characterize their proposals as "concrete" and "factual"; ours by contrast were "unrealistic" and "vague" and "abstract," no matter how specific they might be. "Realism" was measured by correspondence with Hanoi's point of view. Ducky would treat his presence as a concession, his willingness to discuss our points — if only to reject them — as a sign of goodwill. He would introduce each new demand with the proposition that it was based on reason, fact, and history, which he would then explain at excruciating length — causing me on one occasion to remark that if he would emphasize reason and go easier on history we would all gain.

Even formal agreements tended to have a special meaning. For example, on the face of it, our seven points of May 31 and their nine points of June 26 were very close in their affirmation of the independence, neutrality, and territorial integrity of Cambodia and Laos on the basis of the Geneva agreements of 1954 and 1962. But whenever we approached the point of putting these issues aside as settled, Le Duc Tho would unnervingly point out that Hanoi was *already* living up to the Geneva Accords (at a time when several hundred thousand North Vietnamese troops were roaming around these countries). When I questioned this, Le Duc Tho would explain coolly that there were Vietnamese in many countries of the world; or if he wanted to be more formalistic, he would argue that the North Vietnamese were there to protect the neutrality of Laos and Cambodia. And the North Vietnamese were vague about the deadline for withdrawal, whether it followed an agreement or was to run independently of the rest of the negotiation, as Madame Binh had it.

But with all these qualifications the July 12 meeting did turn into a real negotiating session. We took the individual points of both documents, laying them side by side. It was apparent that agreement *was* within reach on most of the points (the principle of total US withdrawal, release of POWs, reaffirmation of the Geneva agreements of 1954 and 1962, internationally supervised cease-fire at the end). There were two basic disputes: the demand for reparations, and Hanoi's insistence that we overthrow the Saigon government. In spite of my previous rejection of it, the reparations question was not beyond compromise: It was primarily a matter of form, not substance. We had said repeatedly in the private talks, and Nixon had stated publicly (as had President Johnson before him), that we would contribute generously to the economic rehabilitation of all of Indochina, including North Vietnam, after the war. But we would do it of our own accord, not as an act of penance.

Inevitably, it was the political issue that turned into the bone of contention. Le Duc Tho repeated: "I tell you in a serious way that you have to replace Thieu. . . . You have many means [to do this]." For one, he repeated, the forthcoming presidential election presented us with a perfect opportunity. Though phrased in terms of a single individual, it soon transpired that the demand included everyone not considered "peaceful" by Hanoi. And since Hanoi proposed to fight until it achieved what it wanted, anyone opposing it was causing war, hence was not peaceful, therefore had to be replaced. With every major non-Communist political figure thus disposed of, Le Duc Tho and Xuan Thuy took turns in seeking to cajole me into accepting their proposal. If this were done, we would have made a "big step forward" and "favorable conditions will be created for a settlement." (Hanoi carried caution to the point of paranoia. It did not believe in making unconditional promises. Even if we accepted its demand to overthrow Thieu, that would merely create "favorable conditions"; Hanoi left itself running room to put forward additional demands.)

Le Duc Tho disposed definitively of the argument of our critics that we could settle only the military issues and get out. The dour and heroic men from Hanoi had not spent their lives fighting just for the chance to stop fighting. As Le Duc Tho told me on June 26: "There is no war without political goals. Military operations aim to achieve political goals. Military means are only the instruments to reach political ends." Clausewitz was alive and well and living in North Vietnam.

For some weeks, my colleagues and I were intoxicated by having settled in effect seven of the nine points; one hoped that Le Duc Tho's impassioned pleas to dismantle the Saigon government were a last-ditch effort to prove to his colleagues in Hanoi that we had reached the limit of our concessions and that they had better settle now for what was attainable. No doubt he assessed our conduct the same way. He must have thought it worth his while to persist in the negotiations with uncharacteristic flexibility to see whether with all other issues "solved" we would then throw the non-Communist South Vietnamese to the wolves.

The talks had lasted four and a half hours. We set a new date for a meeting two weeks later, on July 26, indicating that we would in the meantime review each other's positions. I returned to the Ambassador's Residence by reversing the Walters procedures. Around 7:00 P.M. David Bruce and I emerged at the front door of the Residence to announce to the waiting media that we had completed our review of the negotiations.

Before the July 26 meeting I submitted a memorandum to Nixon indicating that we had narrowed differences to one issue — the political arrangements in Saigon:

It is obvious that we cannot do their political work for them. For all his faults, Thieu has been a loyal ally. Moreover, the recent publication of the Pentagon papers with their revelations about American complicity in the coup against Diem would make our involvement in Thieu's removal even more unpalatable. Last but not least, I am not even sure we could remove Thieu if we wanted to, unless we were prepared to engage in a major confrontation whose only certain result would be the destruction of South Vietnam's political fabric and everybody's self-respect.

I reaffirmed, and Nixon agreed, that we could not make peace at the price of overturning the South Vietnamese government. If, however, Hanoi wanted to negotiate a genuinely open political process, we could make the following proposals: a complete withdrawal of our forces; the closing of our bases; and guaranteed neutrality for South Vietnam. I continued to think that there was a good chance that Le Duc Tho would drop his political demands.

I was wrong. At the meeting on July 26 we made further progress in meshing the formulations on all points save the political one. But it was becoming increasingly clear that these concessions were only come-ons to induce us to overthrow Thieu. Even in the issues on which we seemed to be making progress the wily Vietnamese had left themselves innumerable loopholes. No Martian observing the negotiation could have concluded that the men from Hanoi were representing an underdeveloped country. They were sinuous, disciplined, superbly skillful in nuances of formulation, endlessly patient. They had earned their place at the conference table by ruthless struggle; they would not give up its fruits for bourgeois notions of compromise, sentimental invocations of goodwill, or liberal ideas of free elections. Unfortunately, only in epic poems are heroes humanly attractive. In real life their dedication makes them unrelenting; their courage makes them overbearing; they are out of scale and therefore not amenable to ordinary mortal intercourse. It was our misfortune to stand in the way of Hanoi's obsessive drive for hegemony in Indochina. They fought us as strenuously and ably as they contemptuously used the sentimental misconceptions of so many of their supporters, our critics.

I put forward the various proposals I had gone over with Nixon. Le Duc Tho and Xuan Thuy had no interest in an American pledge of neutrality or in a free political process that they disdained. They would not hear of agreed limits on military aid by the United States; they wanted to cut off Saigon from *any* military supplies. For the third straight meeting they zeroed in on the theme that having put him in office we had "the capability" to replace the "warlike and fascist" Nguyen Van Thieu. This time Xuan Thuy offered us a secret understanding on the removal of Thieu: "We do not ask you to make a public statement. You should do that secretly." When I suggested that it would become obvious, Thuy persisted: "This understanding is between us only. It is not divulged." At an earlier point in the meeting, he made clear that a mere change of personalities would be insufficient: "If you change the person," he said, "and not change the policy . . . there is no change at all." Hanoi wanted domination of Saigon, not compromise. Le Duc Tho was eager to be helpful. He even offered me the benefit of his professional advice as a revolutionary. During a break he took me aside and suggested that if we did not know how to replace Thieu by means of the presidential election, assassination would do admirably. The vehemence of my refusal produced one of the few occasions when I saw Le Duc Tho temporarily flustered. He obviously had trouble understanding what

I was getting so excited about. But he soon regained his aplomb. As we returned to the table I summed up, almost plaintively, my problem with Hanoi's political "solution":

We have offered to do a number of things which would make it easier for the forces you support to participate in a political process and to affect the political future. We have expressed our willingness to accept neutrality for South Vietnam, to announce our withdrawals from South Vietnam, to accept limitations on military aid for South Vietnam, to declare publicly we are not supporting any particular force in South Vietnam, and to carry this out strictly. We are willing to listen to other proposals along this line.

What we cannot do is what you ask, to make a secret agreement to replace the leader of a country which is still an ally; which would then lead to endless debate, moreover, as to what exactly a peaceful administration is, in which you have a veto because you are the only one who knows what is meant by peaceful. . . .

We want to end the war. We do not want to stand in the way of the people of South Vietnam. We are not permanent enemies of Vietnam. But you must not expect us to do impossible things.

So the issue was left at the meeting of July 26. The prize of peace was as far away as ever.

The South Vietnamese Presidential Election

I N the meantime attention was increasingly focused on the presidential election scheduled for October 3 in South Vietnam. Hanoi had already shown that it was alive to the pretext the voting offered for removing Thieu. In the United States, there were many sincere and concerned individuals who thought that a fair democratic process in South Vietnam would unlock the door to negotiations. Why this should be so was never explained. The so-called Democratic Republic of Vietnam permitted no alternative political parties, had never held an election, and ridiculed the notion of free choice. With the self-assurance of experts who knew whereof they spoke, Xuan Thuy and Le Duc Tho never ceased explaining to me that the concept of a free election was meaningless: Whoever controlled the government would win. In terms of Vietnamese history they were substantially right. Liberal democracy has flourished in essentially homogeneous societies where minorities accept the electoral verdict in the hope of one day becoming the majority. But this development has been the product of centuries. Even in the United States democratic liberties took over a century to reach the stage of universal adult suffrage. In Vietnam we were seeking to force the developing of a democratic tradition to its culmination in a matter of months, among a people who had been killing each other in a civil war for two decades, in circumstances where loss of political power meant not only giving up office but risking one's life.

Yet with all these handicaps great progress had been made. Whereas Britain, in much less complex circumstances, had postponed elections for the duration of World War II, several elections had been held in South Vietnam with several hundred thousand North Vietnamese troops in the country. In August 1970, in elections for the upper house of the National Assembly, sixteen slates competed and opposition Buddhists won the most votes. In August 1971, in elections for the lower house, 1,200 candidates representing twelve major political parties and groups contended for the 159 seats and, again, opposition Buddhists won the most seats. Elections for local chiefs and councils had been held in over 95 percent of the country's villages; province chiefs and mayors were to be chosen by vote in November 1971.*

The constitution of the Republic of Vietnam, promulgated in April 1967 and drafted with American advice and assistance, bestowed upon South Vietnam the blessing of a four-year presidential term. In the first presidential election, on September 3, 1967, Nguyen Van Thieu won with 35 percent of the vote. The second presidential election was scheduled for Sunday, October 3, 1971. Thus, at a crucial point in the history of America's involvement in Vietnam, an event imposed on Vietnam essentially by American choice turned into a new source of turmoil and uncertainty.

The State Department had been indefatigable in urging Thieu to make new political offers to the Communists; many of its experts favored a coalition government. (I have never understood the dedication to this device, which our bureaucracy tends to surface as its patent remedy for civil strife. In the United States, a homogeneous society, the appointment of any member of the opposition party to a Cabinet is considered as newsworthy as it is extremely rare. The idea that a civil war can be ended by joining the people who have been killing each other in one government is an absurdity. Generally, a coalition government is a gimmick or an excuse, not a solution. It works best where it is least needed.) Now the Department threw all its enthusiasm behind free elections for the presidency. On May 19 the State Department issued elaborate instructions to American personnel in Vietnam to be neutral "in word, deed or acts." American aid would continue during the election, but it should be "carefully administered so it will not be misconstrued as U.S. Government support for, or opposition to, any individual bid for election to office." Many in the bureaucracy were hoping that Thieu would be defeated by a candidate prepared to accept a coali-

---

* In nationwide "elections" for North Vietnam's National Assembly in April 1971, 99.88 percent of eligible voters cast their ballots and the Politburo leaders averaged over 99 percent approval. There was no opposition slate. South Vietnam was much less efficient and ruthless.

tion government. I hoped that a democratic election would increase support for an ally.

The premise of neutrality made sense only if there was a real political contest with at least two authentic candidates. We thus wound up in the curious position of searching for opponents to a President who was conducting a war as our ally. The two most likely prospects were Vice President Nguyen Cao Ky and General Duong Van Minh. Less than a year before, Ky had been considered so unpalatable to American critics that we had discouraged a visit to Washington. But now there was a great effort to keep him in play as a candidate. When Minh headed the junta that overthrew President Diem, one of the grievances had been that Diem and his brother Nhu were plotting a coalition government. Minh now became the hope of many critics because his opaque comments lent themselves to the interpretation that he would accept Communists into his administration. He was clearly the preference of Hanoi; Xuan Thuy implied on one occasion that he might be acceptable as a replacement for Thieu. (As usual, Xuan Thuy was vague. He made no unambiguous commitment if we were to go along with his proposal.) But if Xuan Thuy's Delphic utterances meant what they implied, the reason was surely that all Vietnamese who knew Minh were agreed on one point: Minh was the most incompetent and lackadaisical of the principal figures.* If Hanoi accepted him — which was unclear — it would be because he was the easiest of all candidates to overthrow should he become President. (Minh finally became President two days before the Communist takeover of Saigon in 1975. He was led out of the Presidential Palace by two North Vietnamese soldiers and has not been seen since. So much for coalition government.)

And then, of course, there was Nguyen Van Thieu. He had not become President by accident. He was unquestionably the most formidable of the military leaders of South Vietnam, probably the ablest of all political personalities. Like most men who reach high office, he represented an amalgam of personal ambition and high motive. Those who do not find the exercise of power a tonic rarely aspire to exercise it and almost never gain it. Equally, those without strong values cannot withstand the ambiguities, pressures, and anguish that are inseparable from great responsibility. Thieu clearly enjoyed his office; in this attribute he was hardly alone among chief executives I have known. But he was also a man of principle; strongly anti-Communist, deeply religious and patriotic, highly intelligent, defending his compatriots with great courage against an onslaught from within and without South Vietnam.

---

* John Negroponte of my staff pointed out perceptively that Minh as President would have great difficulty in making moves of accommodation to the enemy because he was not trusted by the northern Catholics and senior military officers; the ''hard-line'' Thieu, on the other hand, would probably be able to make such moves without losing the confidence of those conservative elements.

He did not deserve the obloquy that those who sought excuses for our abdication insisted on visiting on him. He inherited a civil administration torn apart by the reckless coup against Diem, a guerrilla army threatening to overwhelm his country through systematic terror, and an invasion along a trackless border of 600 miles. He was saddled with an ally who first flooded his country with hundreds of thousands of troops and trained his army for a war not relevant to Southeast Asia; and then, while withdrawing at an accelerating rate, urged on him escalating concessions to an implacable enemy. He knew he could not possibly handle all these things simultaneously without his government's collapsing. But he did as many as he thought feasible, and more than many would have thought possible, including a major land reform. It was not his fault that our domestic critics proved insatiable and that to many he became a convenient scapegoat. He was not an obstacle to negotiations until the end, and — as I shall explain — he was in a terrible predicament even then. He was kept fully informed of my talks with Le Duc Tho, approving every proposal and being given a summary of each session through Bunker, with whom we communicated by an infantile code. Periodically, Haig would visit Saigon to make a survey and to bring Thieu up to date. Though he must have had serious misgivings, Thieu conducted himself toward us — that eviscerating ally — without whining, with aloof dignity not untinged with contempt. (I pay Thieu this tribute, which is his due, notwithstanding his venomous hatred for the manner in which I negotiated the final settlement.)

Thieu was convinced that South Vietnam could not afford a protracted period of ambiguous authority in the middle of a bitter war. His army had just suffered severe casualties in Laos. His ally had accelerated its withdrawals. He knew I was negotiating with Hanoi. And while he was familiar with the main outlines of our proposal, and had indeed approved them, he understood that Hanoi would be insisting in all our meetings in Paris on his overthrow. His morbid suspiciousness — a quintessential Vietnamese trait — no doubt led him to fear that the offer might prove tempting. Nor was he ready to step down. Reminded repeatedly after 1967 that he had won with only a 35 percent margin, he was determined this time to secure a bigger mandate. He therefore used the perquisites of incumbency without excessive delicacy.

His opponents, in turn, had no interest in participating in an election they were certain to lose even if it were conducted fairly. Minh easily collected the signatures required to qualify for the race but was uncertain about running. Ky, who wanted to run, had difficulty accumulating signatures because of Thieu's heavy-handed tactics. The Supreme Court of South Vietnam reinstated Ky in the race, but by then both he and Minh had chosen to withdraw. Ambassador Bunker tried in vain to persuade both to run. But they wanted in effect the same as Le Duc Tho: an

American guarantee of their success. With Ky and Minh unwilling to run, the election was then turned into a referendum: voters were given the options of voting for Thieu, defacing their ballots, or boycotting the election. Eighty-seven percent of eligible voters participated in the election, and Thieu received 94 percent of the ballots cast.

As the campaign progressed, I thought that Thieu was acting unwisely in using his incumbency to discourage rival candidacies. On my visit to Saigon in July I ostentatiously called on Ky, Minh, and the leader of the Buddhist opposition to emphasize our interest in a contested election. In August I sent several backchannel messages to Ellsworth Bunker, reinforcing the formal instructions of the State Department, to explore the possibility of finding other opposition candidates or fixing a new date for an election for which they could qualify. I cabled Bunker that Thieu should not doubt the depth of the public reaction in America to his high-handed methods. But neither Nixon nor I was prepared to toss Thieu to the wolves; indeed, short of cutting off all military and economic aid and thus doing Hanoi's work for it there was no practical way to do so. We considered support for the political structure in Saigon not a favor done to Thieu but an imperative of our national interest. We weathered the storm. It would be preposterous to maintain that Hanoi lamented the absence of a fair election in Saigon. What bothered it was our refusal to use the election as a pretext to decapitate the leadership of the non-Communist political structure in South Vietnam.

I met again with the North Vietnamese on August 16. Le Duc Tho was in Hanoi, which guaranteed that no breakthrough was possible. I opened the meeting by giving Xuan Thuy some unclassified technical material about the *Apollo* moonshots since Le Duc Tho had asked about them at the previous session. Xuan Thuy could not resist a wisecrack that although we had sent men to the moon, I had been a half hour late to the meeting. (This was due to a private session I had had with the Chinese Ambassador to Paris, Huang Chen.) But when we got down to business, it became evident that this series of talks had deadlocked. Both sides knew that the military issues were capable of fairly rapid resolution. Each regularly made minor adjustments in its position to bring the formulations on those issues even closer together, and to tantalize the other side into concessions on the intractable political problem. We modified our original proposal that all our prisoners be released two months *before* our final withdrawal; we agreed that it could be simultaneous. We gave Xuan Thuy a rough estimate of economic assistance to all of Indochina after the war, though not as part of the agreement or as reparations. Hanoi agreed that all our prisoners throughout Indochina would be released and not only those held by the Vietnamese, as had been their original position.

But nothing could obscure our mutual incapacity to settle the political issue. We would not make peace on Hanoi's terms of overthrowing an allied government. And for our principles we were willing to brave domestic turmoil — focused irrelevantly on the essentially settled schedule for our unilateral withdrawal. At the end of one particularly bitter exchange I summed up the impasse, not without some barbs at Xuan Thuy's subordinate status, and with a bravado that time (contrary to much of the evidence) was on our side:

Now Mr. Minister, I know you have your instructions. And I know you are not authorized to be convinced by me. And you will make a reply that everything that happens is our fault. It is a pity. . . . The tragedy is that if we continue the war, then a year from now we will be at about the same point, and one day we will arrive at an agreement more or less on the terms we are discussing now. We have told you that we will not stand in your way if you can win the political contest. Sooner or later this is what you have to do anyway. But it is obvious from what you have said that you are not now disposed to do this. I have enough experience to know that nothing I can say can change your conviction, and even more, your instructions. . . . The only thing that remains for me to say is to express the hope that someday Hanoi will approach us with an attitude that we will make peace. If there is that attitude I know the Minister and I can find formulas to make peace. Until then, until we can find that attitude, we will stay as we are.

And this is what happened. Fourteen months later we were to meet and settle essentially on the terms I had presented in the 1971 talks.

For some reason Xuan Thuy insisted on another session about a month later. His eagerness gave us another flicker of hope that maybe the Hanoi Politburo was using the time to review its position. Though Nixon was eager to break off the increasingly sterile contacts, I just managed to persuade him that to meet would improve our negotiating record, that it gave Hanoi one more opportunity to modify its position, and that we had "nothing to lose, except my 36 hours of inconvenience." We would achieve nothing by breaking off now, and Hanoi was not keeping us from anything we wanted to do. So we met again in Paris on September 13. The absence of Le Duc Tho could leave no further doubt that we had run out the string on this series of meetings. Xuan Thuy made no effort to say anything new, in effect reading a propaganda speech of the kind put forth repetitively in the plenary sessions of Avenue Kléber. The meeting adjourned after two hours, the shortest secret session ever. We parted with the understanding that either side could reopen the channel if it had something new to say.

All that was left of the debates and negotiations of the summer was to permit our domestic critics to catch up with reality. Senator George McGovern had the opportunity of meeting with Xuan Thuy for four hours on September 11. He left with the firm impression that the Communists were offering peace on the basis of a fixed date for US withdrawal in exchange for the release of prisoners. Though I thought such a deal was clearly inconsistent with Hanoi's nine points, Ambassador William Porter was instructed to explore it at the 129th session of the formal Paris peace talks, in order to put an end to the speculation once and for all. Porter told reporters after the meeting: "We spent the day trying to get them to confirm or deny officially things they have said in interviews. They refused." In fact, the North Vietnamese shortly eliminated the previous ambiguity of their public position and announced yet again that the release of our prisoners was conditional on a political settlement. In the process they left McGovern and several journalists high and dry. The *Washington Post* reported the next day:

North Vietnam toughened its peace terms today, thereby scuttling its carefully nurtured efforts over the past two months to appear more accommodating.

Hanoi delegate Xuan Thuy made clear that the United States must "simultaneously" announce the end of its support for South Vietnamese President Thieu and total United States troop withdrawal before American prisoners could be released. . . . More optimistic impressions voiced by antiwar Sen. George McGovern (D-S.D.) and a hitherto unquestioned statement by Le Duc Tho, a Hanoi politburo member, were left in shreds.

The hapless *Post* correspondent, Jonathan Randal, had for months been reporting the opposite on the basis of innuendoes assiduously fostered by the North Vietnamese. Randal pleaded with the North Vietnamese press spokesman after the September 16 plenary meeting:

You have known me for almost three years. Don't you understand why we no longer understand anything, and do you not understand the confusion in our minds? Either things are not clear or I am a fool. . . . What you have said today contradicts not only the significance but maybe even the literal meaning of what we understood and filed. I feel like a fool.

I knew how Randal felt. We had ridden the same roller coaster.

Revealing the Secret Talks

XUAN THUY's reaffirmation of Hanoi's rigid negotiating program had amazingly little effect on our domestic debate. Even so staunch a figure as Senator Henry M. Jackson on September 10 urged a cutoff of aid to Vietnam unless Thieu arranged for a contested election. The *New York Times* of September 18 castigated Nixon for stating that we would stay until Saigon was able to defend itself against a Communist takeover. Even the *Chicago Tribune* printed on September 20 a column by Frank Starr urging us to leave Vietnam immediately. American bombing raids on North Vietnam — undertaken partly in reaction to attacks on reconnaissance aircraft, largely to demonstrate to Hanoi that breaking off negotiations was not costless — evoked editorial outrage. On September 30 the Senate voted a new version of the Mansfield amendment, making it national policy to pull all US forces out in six months, dependent only upon return of our prisoners. It received widespread approval. Hanoi, ironically, showed more faith in Vietnamization and the strength of the South Vietnamese resistance than our own Senators or editorial writers. Its insistence that *we* overthrow the South Vietnamese government betrayed Hanoi's uncertainty whether it could accomplish the objective by itself even after our withdrawal.

In this atmosphere I submitted a long analysis to Nixon on September 18, summing up where we stood on Vietnam diplomacy. I reiterated that if we overthrew the political structure of South Vietnam either by precipitate withdrawal or by excessive political concessions, friends and adversaries would conclude — after a brief moment of relief — that America's post–World War II leadership was giving way to a post-Vietnam abdication. An ignominious end in Vietnam would also leave deep scars on our society, fueling impulses for recrimination and deepening the existing crisis of authority. I continued to believe that we needed to leave Vietnam as an act of governmental policy and with dignity, not as a response to pressures and a collapse of will.

Vietnamization, I agreed, might achieve that goal but it was inherently precarious. If it were played out to the end, a delicate point would inevitably be reached where our withdrawals would create uncertainty about South Vietnam's political future, jeopardizing the whole enterprise at the final hour. A negotiated settlement that would give South Vietnam a fair chance to survive had always been far preferable; it would end the war with an act of policy and leave the future of South Vietnam to an historical process.

But, my analysis continued, we now found ourselves with our negotiating assets wasting. Vietnamization, for all the anguish caused by protests, had bought time at home with the steady reduction of American forces, casualties, and expenses. And it had generated two pressures on Hanoi. First, the measured pace of our withdrawal conveyed to the North Vietnamese that if they wanted us to leave quickly or totally they would have to pay a price. Second, it evoked the prospect that eventually a strengthened South Vietnamese government would be able to stand on its own. Unfortunately, I reasoned, our first asset had all but withered away. Domestic pressures and the indiscipline of the bureaucracy combined to assure the North Vietnamese in an almost daily and compulsive manner that we would be completely out of Vietnam soon. Why should they pay for what would fall into their laps? Until the autumn of 1971 it seemed that our second asset — the growing strength of

Saigon — was still giving Hanoi serious pause. The South Vietnamese government had maintained a remarkable degree of stability. The irony was that this stability was now threatened because of the accident of the four-year presidential term that Americans helped to write into the constitution. In South Vietnam, the combination of presidential election, major US withdrawals, and domestic dissidence was causing the currents of unrest to flow again. Some within the Thieu administration and the army were beginning to hedge their bets and burnish their credentials for the Viet Cong.

In the United States, my memorandum continued, the momentum for rapid disengagement was rising. We now faced the real danger that Congressional legislation would set an obligatory date for our withdrawals and perhaps limit our assistance to South Vietnam. The politically and morally wrenching fact was that much of the opposition had given up on the merit of the issues. The more they were convinced we were getting out, the more they were trying to impose restrictive conditions on our exit so as to claim credit for what they knew we would do anyway. It was impossible to stay ahead of the momentum of this emotion.

For all these reasons I concluded, first, that we needed to stop weakening the political structure in Vietnam by well-meaning panaceas, since it was just about the only card we had left. Secondly, we should make one more effort at negotiation before our assets were dissipated completely. A withdrawal-for-prisoners swap had already been rejected by Xuan Thuy, who had insisted on Thieu's removal and a clean sweep of Saigon's political scene. Vietnamization pursued to the end would not return our prisoners. In any case we were approaching restrictive legislation on both troop and aid levels. Finally, escalation was not sustainable domestically in the absence of overwhelming provocation.

Therefore I urged Nixon that he authorize a new negotiating proposal on the political issue, which would go to the limit of what was compatible with our obligations, our sacrifices, and our honor. I proposed that we modify the eight points I had submitted on August 16 — which dealt mostly with military issues — by putting forward a provision for a new presidential election in South Vietnam within six months of signing the final agreement. The election would be run by an electoral commission representing all the political forces, including the Communists, under international supervision. One month before this election, President Thieu would resign and his function would be assumed by the President of the Senate. At that point the small residual American force would be withdrawn. We would also shorten our withdrawal deadline from nine months to seven.

Nixon approved this offer on September 20. Haig left for Saigon on September 21. Thieu accepted it on September 23, telling Haig that he was prepared to announce also that he would not even be a candidate in a new election once peace was achieved. This we thought would go too far; we recommended he keep his options open. But Thieu announced in a public speech three days before his election that if peace were achieved he would return to civilian life.

In the past we had always handed Hanoi any new proposals at a meeting. Now I thought we might save time if we submitted it in writing along with our request for a meeting. And I wanted to have our proposal on record in case Hanoi refused to meet and instead launched the now all but certain offensive. On October 11, General Walters called on the North Vietnamese Delegate-General in Paris to request a meeting with Le Duc Tho for November 1. Walters read a message saying we were responding to Minister Xuan Thuy's statement on September 13 that the North Vietnamese side would be forthcoming if a general proposal were made by the US side. Our proposal was "one last attempt" to reach a just settlement before the end of 1971. (The US proposal of October 11 is in the notes.) [12]

But Hanoi's grim and implacable leaders would compromise only as a last resort; protracted warfare was their profession. If they were to compromise, they had to prove to themselves that they had no other choice and they were not yet at that point. They were determined on another military throw of the dice. Hanoi replied on October 25 — with customary insolence, only six days before the date suggested for the meeting. There was no expression of goodwill, no comment on our proposal, no reference to an eagerness to settle in any particular time frame. It coldly proposed November 20, giving as a reason that "Special Advisor Le Duc Tho has at the present time activities under way in Hanoi and furthermore Minister Xuan Thuy is still under medical treatment." Hanoi did not even deign to characterize the activities in Hanoi as "important." Walters reported that the note was handed over in the briefest meeting ever. "No small talk and no tea," he lamented, simply the reading of a prepared text.

We accepted the date in a curt note of November 3, and afterward expected the usual report that Le Duc Tho had left Hanoi. It never came. On November 17, or less than forty-eight hours before I was supposed to leave for Paris, Hanoi informed us that Le Duc Tho would not be present because he had "suddenly become ill." No alternative date was offered; no expression of readiness to settle accompanied the message; there was still no comment on our major new proposal — offering the resignation of an allied leader — over a month after we had transmitted it. The only grace note — which was also a sign of disdain — was that Xuan Thuy was "still agreeable" to meeting me. But it was clear from the whole record of previous meetings that Xuan Thuy had no authority to negotiate.

On November 19 we returned a long reply summing up the status of the negotiations and concluding:

On November 17, 1971, the North Vietnamese side informed the U.S. side that Special Adviser Le Duc Tho was now ill and unable to attend the November 20 meeting. The U.S. side regrets this illness. Under these circumstances, no point would be served by a meeting.

The U.S. side stands ready to meet with Special Adviser Le Duc Tho, or any other representative of the North Vietnamese political leadership, together with Minister Xuan Thuy, in order to bring a rapid end to the war on a basis just for all parties. It will wait to hear recommendations from the North Vietnamese side as to a suitable date.

We never received a reply. The North Vietnamese, in the late stages of planning their major military offensive of 1972, were bending all their energies toward one last test of strength.

Many factors contributed to Hanoi's decision, including the monomania of a lifetime. But in my view the biggest single factor was the divisions within America. The North Vietnamese could only conclude that one more military push might propel us into essentially unconditional capitulation. The Politburo knew that Congress would impose withdrawal if they offered to release prisoners; they had little to lose by trying to force us to complete their victory by dismantling Saigon. No meeting with the North Vietnamese was complete without a recitation of the statements of our domestic opposition. On one occasion, when Le Duc Tho asserted that we would be forced to give in by our opposition, I lost my temper: "Mr. Special Adviser, you are a spokesman for one of the most totalitarian states. You have brutally destroyed any sign of opposition in your country. Kindly leave the interpretation of opposition to those who tolerate one and do not interpret matters about which you know nothing." After that, Ducky made fewer references to our public discomfiture, but there was no way to eliminate it from their calculations.

To be sure, our critics were not aware of all the proposals we had made. This was the perhaps unnecessary price we paid for a secrecy we thought essential for a serious negotiation. But Hanoi's conception of a "political settlement" was on the record; it required no great analytical skill to determine that it amounted to a Communist takeover. The fact was that most opponents of the war were at this point beyond caring about the particular issues in dispute; they simply yearned for the war to end. In spite of many public hints by Nixon that we were seeking a settlement, it seemed to be taken for granted that the Administration which had arranged summits with Peking and Moscow within a three-month period was lax in negotiating with Hanoi. On November 17 the *New York Times* editorialized:

The President made repeated references to his continuing desire for a negotiated settlement. . . . But he made no new move to reactivate the direct channel he already has to Hanoi in Paris. Nor did he make any effort to respond to
the openings offered in July by the Viet Cong's seven-point proposal, which
has remained largely unanswered for more than four months.

And on January 3, 1972, Senator McGovern pressed the same theme:

It is simply not true — and the President knows it is not true — that our negotiators in Paris have ever discussed with the North Vietnamese the question
of total American withdrawal from Indochina in conjunction with the release of
our prisoners.[13]

All the time Congressional resolutions to force a withdrawal simply in
return for prisoners multiplied. The Senate was passing them regularly;
the House of Representatives had repeatedly rejected them but with
steadily diminishing margins. On April 1, one was rejected by 122 to
260; on June 17, by 158 to 254; on June 28, by 176 to 219; on October
19, by 192 to 215. The day when the Congress would legislate a deadline was clearly approaching. On October 13 the Senate Foreign Relations Committee voted to limit American assistance to Cambodia to
$250 million and the number of Americans permitted to serve in Cam-
bodia to 200. Finally, on November 5, House and Senate conferees
agreed to a compromise on the Mansfield amendment. The new language stated it as "the policy of the United States" to require a termination of military operations and a "prompt withdrawal from Indochina," subject to the release of all American POWs and an
accounting for those missing in action. While Mansfield's original six-
month deadline was deleted, the resolution urged and requested the
President to set a date and negotiate an agreement for phased withdrawals parallel with the phased release of our prisoners. Hanoi now
knew that it could do no worse than a withdrawal-for-prisoners deal.
    What prevented total collapse was that the North Vietnamese, too,
were at the end of their tether. They might have had enough left for one
big push but their military resources were strained to the utmost. Their
logistics buildup had been disrupted; our diplomacy with Moscow and
Peking had prevented them from mobilizing the full fury of public dissent. The worldwide propaganda campaign scheduled to promote Madame Binh's seven points of July 1, 1971, had been blown off the front
pages by our China announcement two weeks later. The Russians did
not endear themselves to Hanoi by the announcement on October 12 of
Nixon's summit in Moscow. Nixon's public approval remained well
above 50 percent in the second half of 1971. We had made the two great
Communist powers collaborators in holding our home front together.
    As the dry season began, the large North Vietnamese logistics

buildup left little doubt that a Communist military offensive was approaching. It was essential that we seize the initiative. In December we bombed supply complexes south of the twentieth parallel for two days, to editorial and Congressional outrage. We sent strong notes to both Moscow and Peking summarizing our exchanges with the North Vietnamese and warning that an offensive would evoke the most serious retaliation. We did not think that either capital would prove helpful in the negotiation, but we considered it probable that they had their own objectives to protect at the forthcoming summits and that they would therefore probably pass on our warning. No reply was received from China — in itself a significant sign of dissociation by what had been considered until then the capital of world revolution. Dobrynin had a novel twist. As part of one of our periodic global reviews, he tried to blame Hanoi's intransigence on China. My invitation to Peking became known in Hanoi only thirty-six hours before it was announced, he said. This had so infuriated Hanoi it had put the negotiations on ice to show that peace had to be made with it and not imposed by the great powers.

As the euphoria of the China announcement wore off, as a US election year approached, and as a North Vietnamese offensive grew imminent, our domestic position was sure to be under assault again. We could not weather the storm unless we were clearly perceived as having made every effort to negotiate an end to the war, as having gone the extra mile. Presidential candidates and other critics were taking up Hanoi's duplicitous theme that we had not responded to Binh's seven points when we had indeed responded to — and in part accepted — Le Duc Tho's parallel nine points in the secret talks. We were being pressed continually to set a terminal date for our withdrawal when we had already offered one in the secret meeting and had been rejected. Nixon therefore decided to lay our negotiating record before the American people on January 25, 1972.

This decision had been preceded by some touchy encounters in Saigon, because while Thieu had approved our offer, he had not known that we had in fact transmitted it to Hanoi before the projected meeting with Le Duc Tho on November 20.* There was also some prickliness when Thieu realized that mutual withdrawal was being dropped from our public position. He knew of — and had approved — our May 31 proposal, which had abandoned it; he now claimed that any public formal change would weaken his domestic situation. (It was a harbinger of disputes later in 1972.) Finally Thieu went along with the speech and its reaffirmation of the US negotiating position because he knew we were withdrawing anyway, and because he probably judged that Hanoi, hav-

---

* This was only a pretext; a year later, during our showdown over the final terms, Thieu was to tell us that he had been deeply offended by the basic proposal; he gave us no hint of it at the time.

ing not even replied to a private offer, was unlikely to accept a public one.

Nixon's speech was one of his most dramatic and impressive. He laid out the negotiating record of my twelve secret meetings with the North Vietnamese. He revealed that we had offered on May 31, 1971, to set a deadline for withdrawal but had been turned down. He reaffirmed our proposal of October 11, 1971, which spelled out a political settlement — internationally supervised free elections, with Communist involvement, and Thieu's willingness to step down a month before the election. He even improved on our last secret offer by reducing the withdrawal deadline from seven months to six months. Nixon reiterated that the "only thing this plan does not do is to join our enemy to overthrow our ally, which the United States of America will never do. If the enemy wants peace it will have to recognize the important difference between settlement and surrender."

The reaction was stunned surprise both at our long record of efforts and at the sweep of our new proposal. The various Presidential contenders responded with cautious support. The front runner, Senator Edmund Muskie, called the plan "a welcome initiative." Hubert Humphrey responded with characteristic ebullience: "So what, there are plenty of other issues" — implying that the speech had removed Vietnam as a political issue.[14] The *Washington Post* on January 27 churlishly called the plan "The Same Old Shell Game," but the *New York Times* the same day briefly abandoned its months-long carping and indicated cautious support, if not for every provision, at least for the overall approach. Most editorial comment followed this line.

Within a week, many of the critics were back in chorus. Once again the deadlock — Hanoi's rejection of our proposals — was treated as entirely the Administration's fault. But this time the criticisms demonstrated that we had won the psychological battle. The only alternatives left for critics to offer were unilateral withdrawal tied only to release of prisoners (already rejected by Hanoi) and the overthrow of the South Vietnamese government. Senator Muskie responded in a speech on February 2 with a new turn of the screw: The United States should cut off all aid to Thieu, even after our unilateral withdrawal, unless he reached a settlement with the Communists. (It was a "heads-I-win, tails-you-lose" proposition: Since the only terms available from Hanoi called for his overthrow, Thieu was being given the choice between execution and suicide.) This program became the new platform of antiwar protests and editorials. But the base of opposition support was narrowing. The war was deeply unpopular. Yet it seemed plain that however weary the public might be, it was not prepared to join an enemy in defeating an ally. To most Americans, our long and vigorous negotiating record was now clear, as was the fact that it was Hanoi which had been steadily blocking a settlement by its exorbitant and insolent demands.

After Nixon's speech, I could never escape Washington for long without press scrutiny and queries. Therefore, all subsequent meetings were announced by the White House when I was in Paris and already in session. This had its advantages. It continually reminded the public that negotiations were taking place and the opposition that a dramatic development was possible at any moment.

We sent the text of the President's speech to Moscow and Peking with another emphatic warning that we would react strongly to a new offensive. Brezhnev replied in soothing fashion that he thought peace was still possible. Peking, no doubt stung by Hanoi's charges as reported to me by Dobrynin, returned a tart reply on January 30 accusing us — not unjustly — of seeking to enmesh China. We responded sharply. The exchange had no effect on the Peking summit three weeks later.

As for the North Vietnamese, we found them off stride. This was new in our experience. For a second time in six months we had outmaneuvered them (the first time being my trip to Peking). On January 31, they responded in Paris by publishing their side of the correspondence, including the nine-point peace plan that Le Duc Tho had presented to me on June 26, 1971.* Hanoi's spokesman, Nguyen Thanh Le, contrasted the two sides' peace plans, whose differences, he said, were "fundamental — like night and day." Le alleged that Hanoi had always wanted the substance of the negotiations to be public, but it had refrained "as wished by the US party." Yet, in an effort "to shift onto the DRV side the responsibility for the deadlock of the negotiations," he said, the United States "has broken its engagements and created serious obstacles to the negotiations." He did not explain how the publication of positions that Hanoi had always wanted to publish could create obstacles to negotiations.

It was obvious that Hanoi sensed that it had offered thin gruel and was on the defensive, because soon afterward, on February 2, it published a two-point "elaboration" of its nine points. It was a slightly reworked version of the old plan. Hanoi now explicitly agreed that our prisoners would be released on the date that our last troops withdrew. But this was linked to a political program that called for Thieu's immediate resignation, coupled with the dismantling of the "machine of oppression," meaning the police, the army, and the pacification program. So emasculated, the remaining South Vietnamese government was to negotiate with the fully armed Communists for setting up a coalition govern-

---

* I had indicated in a January 26 briefing that we would not publish Hanoi's documents but would "have no objection" if Hanoi did.

ment containing the familiar tripartite structure. Not even the most ardent peace groups could find much sustenance in these propositions. It was no accident. After we had concluded the negotiations a year later, Le Duc Tho, in a candid access of cynicism, explained that the two-point "elaboration" elaborated nothing; it was put forward simply to have some "new" North Vietnamese position available to answer ours.

By any normal standards our Vietnam policy in early 1972 was a considerable success. We had withdrawn over 410,000 troops while improving the military position of our ally. We had isolated Hanoi diplomatically from its main sources of support. At home we had withstood the most bitter assault on a government's policy in this century. We had done all this while fulfilling our global responsibilities by standing on the principle that we did not abandon allies and turn over friendly peoples to repression. I continue to believe that those initiatives with Peking and Moscow would have been impossible had we simply collapsed in Vietnam. Both took us seriously only so long as we were a weight in the scale. And we had shown to our people that even in the midst of a divisive war America could undertake major creative initiatives.

None of this would matter if the all but inevitable Communist military offensive in 1972 overwhelmed the South Vietnamese. But domestically we were in a solid position to take strong action in South Vietnam's defense. If we could weather the Communist offensive, the President could go to Peking and Moscow with hope that we could begin the construction of a new international order.

PART FOUR

1972: From War to Peace

XXIV

Nixon's Trip to China

The Haig Mission

ON the third anniversary of Nixon's Inauguration Day we were in the thick of planning an event nobody imagined possible in 1969: the visit of a United States President to Peking. We had hopes for other progress at the beginning of 1972 — in relations with the Soviet Union, for example, and in negotiating an end to the war in Vietnam — but the China summit was our immediate focus.

China was not important to us because it was physically powerful; Chou En-lai was surely right in his repeated protestations that his nation was not a superpower. In fact, had China been stronger it would not have pursued the improvement of relations with us with the same single-mindedness. Peking needed us to help break out of its isolation and as a counterweight to the potentially mortal threat along its northern border. We needed China to enhance the flexibility of our diplomacy. Gone were the days when we enjoyed the luxury of choosing the moment to involve ourselves in world affairs. We were permanently involved — but not so physically or morally predominant as before. We had to take account of other power centers and strive for an equilibrium among them. The China initiative also restored perspective to our national policy. It reduced Indochina to its proper scale — a small peninsula on a major continent. Its drama eased for the American people the pain that would inevitably accompany our withdrawal from Southeast Asia. And it brought balance into the perceptions of our friends around the world.

Early in the New Year an American technical team descended on Peking. It was headed by Brigadier General Alexander Haig, my deputy, whose assignment was to try to maintain some limits on the flights of imagination of our advance men. Haldeman and Nixon had decided to apply in China their maxims of public relations. They never tired of explaining to the uninitiated that print journalism, that is to say, newspapers, had only a negligible public impact, but that television could change perceptions in a matter of minutes. Moreover, they felt they had been tormented more by the writing journalists than by the broadcasters;

the trip to Peking would be a great opportunity to get even, by weighting the press contingent heavily toward television people. The decision turned out to be a great boon to network executives. Since there were only so many hours the networks could broadcast, the number of TV correspondents and technicians required, even for saturation coverage, was limited. And since the White House public relations experts had assigned a larger number of media places to the networks than they could use, a fair number of top echelon personnel who had not been near reporting for a decade received a free trip to China, while some newspapers were excluded altogether.

From the point of view of television China offered the added convenience of a country thirteen hours ahead of us: morning events could reach America at prime time in the evenings, and evening events could be broadcast live on morning television — provided only that our hosts cooperated. So it became the advance party's task to bring home the wonders of American public relations to a Chinese officialdom that had just barely survived the Cultural Revolution. Fortunately for us, the Chinese had time-honored ways of withstanding barbarian invaders. Once they understood what our advance men had in mind, the veterans of the Long March immediately grasped the benefit of being introduced on American television by an American President and thus becoming instantly acceptable. They agreed eagerly to the Haldeman conception. The fact that there was no means of televising directly from Peking to the United States proved only a temporary problem, solved by a ground station to transmit pictures by satellite. True to Mao's dictum of self-reliance, the Chinese purchased the ground station, rejecting our networks' offer to construct it at their own expense.

Haig's advance trip in early January helped resolve most of the conflicts between the obsessions of our advance men and the inconvenient reality that China was a sovereign state. The Secret Service did not want the President to ride in Chinese cars, but the Chinese leaders thought it would strain the comprehension of the "masses" if they suddenly started moving about in huge American limousines. The compromise was that Nixon could use his own armor-plated limousine when moving about on his own, but that he would ride in the Premier's car when traveling with Chou En-lai. A similar problem arose over the Chinese offer to fly the President in a Chinese airplane within China. After some internal struggle, the Secret Service reluctantly accepted that it simply would not do to tell a host country that its airplanes were unsafe. The realization that if the Secret Service persisted we might not get to travel within China at all helped a great deal. Altogether, the Chinese handled our advance party with extraordinary skill. Those requests with which our hosts agreed were carried out with magical efficiency. Other projects simply disappeared into an impermeable cloud of bland politeness which never provided an occasion for confrontation.

Haig had two private meetings with Chou En-lai to discuss political matters. He gave Chou our assessment of the recently concluded India-Pakistan crisis. Chou agreed with our handling of the conflict. He saw in Soviet policy on the subcontinent not a change provoked by the Sino-American rapprochement but the historic expression of Russia's expansionist tendencies. On Vietnam, Chou reiterated his moral support for Hanoi and urged a rapid settlement of the war in order to reduce Soviet influence in Indochina. Haig also submitted to Chou a new American counterdraft for the sensitive Taiwan passage in the proposed final communiqué — the major issue left over from my October 1971 trip. Chou En-lai promised only to consider it before the President arrived. The negotiation of a few sentences on Taiwan was to take a great deal of time during the President's visit.

I know of no Presidential trip that was as carefully planned nor of any President who ever prepared himself so conscientiously. The voluminous briefing books (produced under my supervision by Winston Lord and John Holdridge of my staff) contained essays on the trip's primary objectives and on all subjects of the agenda previously established with the Chinese. They suggested what the Chinese position would be on each topic, and the talking points the President might follow. All of my conversations with Chou in July and October were excerpted and arranged by subject matter. As background material, there were lengthy analyses of the personalities of Mao and Chou, prepared by the CIA and by Richard H. Solomon, a China expert on my staff. There were copious excerpts from articles and books by Western students of China, including Edgar Snow, Ross Terrill, Dennis Bloodworth, John Fairbank, C. P. Fitzgerald, Stuart Schram, and André Malraux. Nixon read all the briefing books with exquisite care, as we could tell by his underlining of key passages throughout. As was his habit, he committed the talking points to memory and followed them meticulously in his meetings with Chou En-lai while seeking to cultivate the impression that he was speaking extemporaneously.

Our excerpts from Malraux's *Anti-Memoirs* triggered Nixon into inviting that great Frenchman to the White House at the last minute. Nixon was not a little influenced by the gala occasion John and Jacqueline Kennedy had arranged for Malraux when France had lent us the *Mona Lisa*, and wanted to go one better than his envied predecessor. Whereas the Kennedy evening had been essentially artistic, and therefore "frilly" in Nixon's eyes, his meeting with Malraux was to be all business. He and the French writer were to collaborate not in staging a social event but in preparing an historic mission.

Unfortunately, Malraux was grossly out of date about China. And his predictions of China's immediate purposes were outrageously wrong. He believed, for example, that the invitation to Nixon reflected China's need for economic aid; the President would be judged by his ability to come up with a new Marshall Plan for China. Given Mao's philosophy of self-reliance, there was no chance of this happening; at best Malraux was several years premature.

And yet Malraux's intuitions proved that an artist's insight can often grasp the essence of problems better than experts or intelligence analysts can. Many of Malraux's judgments proved remarkably incisive. The rapprochement between China and the United States was inevitable, he argued; it was inherent in the Sino-Soviet split. The war in Vietnam would not prove an obstacle, for China's actions were reflections of its domestic necessities. China's role in Vietnam was an "imposture"; China would never help Vietnam effectively; the historical animosity toward Vietnam was too deep. The Chinese did not believe in any ideology; they believed primarily in China.

In essence America's role in Vietnam was now irrelevant, Malraux argued. What mattered was our Pacific policy. If Japan ceased believing in our nuclear protection, it would move toward the Soviet Union. If we could keep Japan tied to us, this might accelerate the need of the Soviet Union and even of China to attend to the satisfaction of their populations. Somewhere down the road, Malraux warned, maybe as early as within two years, our Chinese and Japanese policies would begin to conflict and require careful management. In the process the United States must never be perceived to hesitate; all of Asia expected firmness from the United States. Above all, said Malraux, China was looking for unity, for glory, and for dignity. Eventually it would look for economic salvation, too.

It was a stunning performance, not fully appreciated by an audience still imprisoned in the stereotypes of a decade. Words cascaded in torrents from Malraux as he fixed his hearers with his visionary gaze. He developed less a coherent analysis than a series of brilliant tableaux. Malraux had not visited China for nearly a decade; he had clearly not kept up with current developments; he had no inside information. All he had was sensitivity, brilliant perception, and shrewd understanding. Our task was to marry his intuition to the operational knowledge we were gradually acquiring.

February was spent in anticipation. We had a testy exchange with Peking at the end of January when, in the context of the President's January 25 speech, we informed the Chinese in detail of our repeated rebuffs from Hanoi. Chou sent back an acerbic note accusing us of seeking to enmesh the People's Republic in the Vietnam problem. It was partly true and partly instructive. We would have preferred Chinese pressure on Hanoi. But we would be quite content with Peking's posture of noninvolvement.

On February 9 we published the President's annual Foreign Policy Report, drafted, in each of Nixon's first four years, by my staff and me.

To our sorrow, no matter how thoughtful we sought to be, we always failed in our basic aim of getting the media to treat it as a statement of the basic philosophy of American foreign policy. Almost all that the press would cover each year was the section on Indochina; instead of a debate over America's purposes in the world, we invariably generated a discussion of tactics in Vietnam. Still, the 1972 report presented a long essay on China that addressed questions which had been raised since the dramatic July 15 announcement: what was the status of our existing commitments to Taiwan; whether we were "shifting our priorities" from Tokyo to Peking; what were the implications for our policy toward the Soviet Union. The President's report affirmed all existing alliance commitments; we would not give up a close relationship of twenty years' standing with Japan for a new opening to China. Less than two weeks before our arrival in Peking, the report affirmed our "friendship, our diplomatic ties, and our defense commitment" to Taiwan; it stressed that "a peaceful resolution of this problem by the parties would do much to reduce tension in the Far East."

As for the Soviet Union, we made the conventional disclaimer: Our policy was not "aimed against Moscow." But the fact was that it had been the Soviet Union whose menace had brought China and us together; our cooperation reflected a geopolitical reality produced by concern at the growth of Soviet military power. We could avoid provocative actions; we would not be able to eliminate the plain impact of the new relationship. If skillfully handled, it could provide an incentive for Soviet restraint and cooperation; if clumsily administered, it might tempt the very crisis it sought to avoid.

On February 11 the President made another gesture to China. He approved a new set of recommendations of the NSC Under Secretaries Committee for easing trade relations. This was announced on February 14. Henceforth, all commodities available for sale to the Soviet Union and Eastern Europe would also be available to the People's Republic. It was the last unilateral economic gesture toward Peking.

On February 17 the President stood by his helicopter on the White House lawn after a brief farewell meeting with Congressional leaders. For once, Nixon avoided the downbeat. He spoke simply of the many messages that had wished him well. He hoped that the future would record of his trip what was written on the plaque the *Apollo 11* astronauts had left on the moon: "We came in peace for all mankind."

Arrival: The Handshake

N IXON's first stop was in Hawaii, where he stayed at an Army base in order to avoid criticism of ostentatious living, and regretted it as soon as he saw his spartan surroundings. Putting up with a commandant's quarters in the Azores and now in Hawaii seemed a great deal of patriotic sacrifice. On the journey I benefited from Haldeman's instructions on how to make sure Nixon would get the most flattering television shots. Ziegler was in a state of advanced agitation because he had been told that he could give no briefings on matters of substance in Peking, and he was already dreading the prospect of facing his journalistic tormentors, who would be driven by the goad of daily deadlines. Throughout the journey, Nixon oscillated between anxiety that his otherwise competent staff was oblivious to the finer points of public relations and serious, indeed dedicated, preparation for his sojourn in China. Having read every briefing book, he plied me with questions on the long hours of the plane ride.

At 9:00 A.M. on Monday, February 21, we arrived in Shanghai for a brief stop to take on Chinese navigators. The only difference from my previous trips was a lonely American flag now fluttering on one of the poles in front of a modern terminal; on repeated visits to this airport I never saw a sign of any other passenger or an arriving or departing plane. Nixon was greeeted by Ch'iao Kuan-hua, technically Deputy Minister of Foreign Affairs but in fact the key figure in the Foreign Ministry. He was reputed to be one of Chou's closest associates, a plausible hypothesis since this impressive man was a lesser copy of Chou's charm, erudition, and intelligence. Present also were two familiar faces from my previous visits: Chang Wen-chin (head of the American Division) and Wang Hai-jung (Deputy Chief of Protocol and allegedly related to Mao), who had accompanied me from Pakistan in July 1971. True to the Chinese tradition that barbarian guests must be assumed to be starving, we were served an elaborate breakfast in record time — discomfiting the White House staff, who knew that it would generate new Nixon pressures for speeding up service on Pennsylvania Avenue. We arrived in Peking at 11:30 A.M., which conveniently was 10:30 P.M. Sunday night Eastern standard time — a prime television period.

This historic moment of arrival did not go unplanned. Nixon and Haldeman had decided that the President should be alone when the television cameras filmed his first encounter with Chou En-lai. Nixon had read my account of the July visit and Chou's sensitivity that Dulles had snubbed him by refusing to shake his hand in 1954. The President was determined to have no other American distract the viewer's attention while he rectified this slight. Rogers and I were to stay on the plane until the handshake had been accomplished. We had been instructed on this point at least a dozen times before our arrival in Peking; there was no way we could have missed the message. But Haldeman left nothing to chance. When the time came, a burly aide blocked the aisle of *Air Force One*. Our puzzled Chinese hosts must have wondered what had happened to the rest of the official party that usually files down the steps right behind the President. We all appeared magically — moments after the historic Nixon-Chou handshake had been consummated in splendid solitude.

We stood on a windswept tarmac, greeted by an honor guard, the frail and elegant figure of Chou En-lai, and a collection of Chinese notables exhibiting in their identical Mao jackets no discernible hierarchy, though of course they were lined up in precise order of political standing. The reception was understated in the extreme. Except for the 350-man honor guard — perhaps in its rigid discipline the most impressive of any I saw on Presidential trips — it was stark to the point of austerity. This very severity reflected the truth that only the most dire necessity could bring together countries whose other relations warranted none of the joyful ceremony usually associated with state visits.

We had been given no indication whether any kind of public welcome was being planned. As our motorcade sped into the center of town there was still some errant hope crackling over Haldeman's radio to Ziegler that perhaps the real welcoming ceremony involving photogenic Chinese multitudes might be awaiting us at Tien An Men Square. The hope was vain. The ever-present Chinese crowds were held back in the side streets as our motorcade swept through the square, vast in its emptiness; past the red walls of the Forbidden City on one side, the massive, squat Great Hall of the People on the other; by huge portraits of Marx, Engels, Lenin, and Stalin (surely one of the last of Stalin to be on display anywhere in the world); and on to the state guest houses located around the old Imperial Fishing Lake.

We were housed in two of the residences, the President and most of his staff (including me) in the larger one; the Secretary of State and his entourage in the small residence (a few hundred yards away) that I had used on my previous trips. Each had its own dining facilities, thus keeping spontaneous contact between the two American bureaucracies to a minimum. The Chinese had well understood the strange checks and balances within the Executive Branch and had re-created the physical gulf between the White House and Foggy Bottom in the heart of Peking.

On arrival at the Presidential guest house, the entire party was seated in easy chairs arranged in a circle in the very large living room, with a large open area in the center. Chou En-lai's wife was there to greet us, as were Marshal Yeh Chien-ying, Acting Foreign Minister Chi P'eng-fei, Deputy Foreign Minister Ch'iao Kuan-hua, and other officials. Tea was brought. Chou led a friendly, bantering conversation in which, as always, he managed to pay attention to every member of the American party.

In this manner Nixon was exposed for the first time to the Chinese style of diplomacy. The Soviets tend to be blunt, the Chinese insinuating. The Soviets insist on their prerogatives as a great power. The Chinese establish a claim on the basis of universal principles and a demonstration of self-confidence that attempts to make the issue of power seem irrelevant. The Soviets offer their goodwill as a prize for success in negotiations. The Chinese use friendship as a halter in advance of negotiation; by admitting the interlocutor to at least the appearance of personal intimacy, a subtle restraint is placed on the claims he can put forward. The Soviets, inhabiting a country frequently invaded and more recently expanding its influence largely by force of arms, are too unsure of their moral claims to admit the possibility of error. They move from infallible dogma to unchangeable positions (however often they may modify them). The Chinese, having been culturally preeminent in their part of the world for millennia, can even use self-criticism as a tool. The visitor is asked for advice — a gesture of humility eliciting sympathy and support. This pattern also serves to bring out the visitor's values and aims; he is thereby committed, for the Chinese later can (and often do) refer to his own recommendations. The Soviets, with all their stormy and occasionally duplicitous behavior, leave an impression of extraordinary psychological insecurity. The Chinese stress, because they believe in it, the uniqueness of Chinese values. Hence they convey an aura of imperviousness to pressure; indeed, they preempt pressure by implying that issues of principle are beyond discussion.

In creating this relationship Chinese diplomats, at least in their encounters with us, proved meticulously reliable. They never stooped to petty maneuvers; they did not haggle; they reached their bottom line quickly, explained it reasonably, and defended it tenaciously. They stuck to the meaning as well as the spirit of their undertakings. As Chou was fond of saying: *"Our* word counts."

Every visit to China was like a carefully rehearsed play in which nothing was accidental and yet everything appeared spontaneous. The Chinese remembered every conversation, from those with the lowliest officials to those with the most senior statesmen. Each remark by a Chinese was part of a jigsaw puzzle, even if at first our more literal intelligence did not pick up the design. (Later on Winston Lord and I actually got quite good at it.) On my ten visits to China, it was as if we were engaged in one endless conversation with an organism that recalled everything, seemingly motivated by a single intelligence. This gave the encounters both an exhilarating and occasionally a slightly ominous quality. It engendered a combination of awe and sense of impotence at so much discipline and dedication — not unusual in the encounter of foreigners with Chinese culture.

And so it was on Nixon's visit. By the time we had taken tea, all present felt convinced — just as I had seven months earlier during my secret visit — that they had been admitted into a very exclusive club, though there had yet to take place a single substantive conversation.

Mao Tse-tung

THAT conversation was not long delayed. We had just finished an opulent lunch when at 2:30 I was told that Chou En-lai needed to see me urgently in the reception room. Without the usual banter he said: "Chairman Mao would like to see the President." I asked whether I could bring Winston Lord. Chou agreed and was uncharacteristically persistent: "Since the Chairman is inviting him he wants to see him fairly soon." I decided to play it somewhat cool by asking Chou whether he would read his toast at the evening's banquet or speak extemporaneously; he indicated that he would read it. I inquired whether ours should be muted or tough, to respond to his mood. Slightly impatiently, Chou suggested that he would send me his text in advance. Finally I said that I would fetch Nixon.

So the President and I set off in Chinese cars to the Imperial City for the first encounter with one of the colossal figures of modern history. Lord came along as note-taker. His presence was not revealed, lest salt be rubbed in the wounds of the Department of State, which went unrepresented at any of the talks with Mao. Nixon had told me five days before that he wanted Rogers and Assistant Secretary of State Marshall Green to be occupied elsewhere so he could discuss sensitive matters with Mao and Chou. Nor was Rogers invited to the meeting by the Chinese, perhaps because of comments that State had made about Taiwan's "unsettled" juridical status during the previous year. Yet I could have insisted that Rogers come, and had I done so neither Nixon nor the Chinese would have refused; it is one of the prerogatives, indeed obligations, of the security adviser to appeal Presidential decisions he considers unwise. I did not. The neglect was technically unassailable but fundamentally unworthy. The Secretary of State should not have been excluded from this historic encounter.

Mao Tse-tung, the ruler whose life had been dedicated to overturning the values, the structure, and the appearance of traditional China, lived in fact in the Imperial City, as withdrawn and mysterious even as the emperors he disdained. Nobody ever had a scheduled appointment; one was admitted to a presence, not invited to a governmental authority. I saw Mao five times. On each occasion I was summoned suddenly, just as Nixon was. On one of my visits Mao expressed an interest in meeting my wife, Nancy. The fact that she was shopping presented no obstacle to our hosts. She was hustled out of a shop by a protocol officer who seemed to know exactly where she was and brought to Mao's presence while her accompanying State Department security officer, now bereft of his charge, was left to vent his dismay about a kidnapping in central Peking to a storekeeper who spoke no English.

We approached Mao's residence through a red gate where two soldiers of the People's Liberation Army impassively observed the traffic on the broad east-west axis road that has been carved from the former city wall. After passing the vermilion wall we traversed a thoroughfare, at first lined on each side with undistinguished-looking facades; one could not tell what kind of houses stood in the courtyards behind the nondescript exteriors. A mile farther on, the dwellings ended and the road followed a lake on one side and woods on the other. Mao's house stood alone; it was simple and unimposing; it could have belonged to a minor functionary. No special security measures were apparent. The car drove right up to the front door, which was sheltered by a portico. We entered through a small sitting room that opened into a wide hallway; on at least two of my visits it contained a Ping-Pong table.

Mao's study, a medium-sized room, was across the hallway. Manuscripts lined bookshelves along every wall; books covered the table and the floor; it looked more the retreat of a scholar than the audience room of the all-powerful leader of the world's most populous nation. On my first few visits a simple wood-frame bed stood in one corner; later it disappeared. Our first sight was of a semicircle of easy chairs, all with brownish slipcovers as if a thrifty middle-class family wanted to protect upholstery too expensive to replace. Between each pair of chairs stood a V-shaped coffee table, covered with a white napkin, fitting into the angle made by adjoining arm rests. The tables next to Mao, being generally piled with books, had just enough room for the ever-present cup of jasmine tea. Two standing lamps with unusually large circular shades stood behind the chairs; in front of Mao, to his right, was a spittoon. When one entered the room, Mao rose from one of the easy chairs; on the last couple of visits he required two assistants' help, but he never failed so to greet his visitors.

One usually cannot tell when meeting a famous and powerful leader to what extent one is impressed by his personality or awed by his status and repute. In Mao's case there could be no doubt. Except for the suddenness of the summons there was no ceremony. The interior appointments were as modest as the exterior. Mao just stood there, surrounded by books, tall and powerfully built for a Chinese. He fixed the visitor with a smile both penetrating and slightly mocking, warning by his bearing that there was no point in seeking to deceive this specialist in the foibles and duplicity of man. I have met no one, with the possible exception of Charles de Gaulle, who so distilled raw, concentrated willpower. He was planted there with a female attendant close by to help steady him (and on my last visits to hold him up); he dominated the room — not by the pomp that in most states confers a degree of majesty on the leaders, but by exuding in almost tangible form the overwhelming drive to prevail.

Mao's very presence testified to an act of will. His was the extraordinary saga of a peasant's son from southern China who conceived the goal of taking over the Kingdom of Heaven, attracted followers, led them on the Long March of six thousand miles, which less than a third survived, and from a totally unfamiliar territory fought first the Japanese and then the Nationalist government, until finally he was ensconced in the Imperial City, bearing witness that the mystery and majesty of the eternal China endured even amidst a revolution that professed to destroy all established forms. There were no trappings that could account for the sense of power Mao conveyed. My children speak of the "vibes" of popular recording artists to which, I must confess, I am totally immune. But Mao emanated vibrations of strength and power and will. In his presence even Chou seemed a secondary figure, though some of this effect was undoubtedly by design. Chou was too intelligent not to understand that the Number Two position in China was precarious to the point of being suicidal. None of his predecessors had survived.*

Mao's impact was all the more impressive because it was so incongruous in relation to his physical condition. Before our first meeting he had already suffered a series of debilitating strokes. He could move only with difficulty and speak but with considerable effort. Words seemed to leave his bulk as if with great reluctance; they were ejected from his vocal cords in gusts, each of which seemed to require a new rallying of physical force until enough strength had been assembled to tear forth another round of pungent declarations. Later on, as Mao's health deteriorated even further, the effort became so evident as to be painful to observe. In my last private meeting with him in October 1975, as well as during President Ford's visit of December 1975, Mao could barely speak; he croaked general sounds that Nancy T'ang, Wang Hai-jung, and another aide wrote down after consulting with each other and then showed him to make sure they had understood before translating. And yet even then, in the shadow of death, Mao's thoughts were lucid and sardonic.

Mao, in contrast to all other political leaders I have known, almost never engaged in soliloquies. Not for him were the prepared points most statesman use, either seemingly extemporaneously or learned from notes. His meaning emerged from a Socratic dialogue that he guided effortlessly and with deceptive casualness. He embedded his main observations in easy banter and seeming jokes, maneuvering his interlocutor for opportunities to inject comments that were sometimes philosophical and sometimes sarcastic. The cumulative effect was that his key points were enveloped in so many tangential phrases that they communicated a meaning while evading a commitment. Mao's elliptical phrases were

---

*Neither, in fact, did he. I am convinced — though I cannot prove it — that only illness and death saved him from an assault by what was later called the Gang of Four, tolerated if not backed by Mao. During the last year or so of his life he was rarely mentioned in the Chinese press or by other Chinese leaders to me.

passing shadows on a wall; they reflected a reality but they did not encompass it. They indicated a direction without defining the route of march. Mao would deliver dicta. They would catch the listener by surprise, creating an atmosphere at once confused and slightly menacing. It was as if one were dealing with a figure from another world who occasionally lifted a corner of the shroud that veils the future, permitting a glimpse but never the entire vision that he alone has seen.

Yet Mao could be brutal in cutting to the heart of a problem. On one of my later trips I commented to Teng Hsiao-p'ing that the relations of our two countries were on a sound basis because neither asked anything of the other. The next day Mao referred to my comment and at one and the same time showed his attention to detail. He firmly rebutted my banality: "If neither side had anything to ask from the other, why would you be coming to Peking? If neither side had anything to ask, then why . . . would we want to receive you and the President?" At another point he indicated his displeasure with what he took to be American ineffectuality in resisting Soviet expansionism; he compared us to swallows in the face of a storm: "This world is not tranquil," said the gusts painfully emitted from the shattered hulk, "and a storm — the wind and rain — are coming. And at the approach of the wind and rain the swallows are busy. . . . It is possible to postpone the arrival of the wind and rain, but it is difficulty to obstruct the coming."

This was the colossus into whose presence we were now being ushered. He greeted Nixon with his characteristic sidewise glance. "Our common old friend, Generalissimo Chiang Kai-shek, doesn't approve of this," he joked, taking Nixon's hand in both his own and welcoming him in front of the photographers with great cordiality — in itself an event of considerable symbolic significance, at least for the Chinese who were present or who would see the photograph in the *People's Daily*. Mao remarked about a statement Nixon had made on the plane ride to Ch'iao Kuan-hua, that he considered Mao a man with whom philosophical discourse was possible. (This was yet another example of the extraordinarily rapid Chinese internal communication, as well as of Mao's careful briefing.) Mao joked that philosophy was a "difficult problem"; he had nothing instructive to say on the subject; maybe Dr. Kissinger should take over the conversation. But he repeated the formula several times to avoid specifics on the international problems Nixon was raising. When Nixon put forward a list of countries requiring common attention, Mao's response was courteous but firm: "Those questions are not questions to be discussed in my place. They should be discussed with the Premier. I discuss the philosophical questions."

Nixon's memoirs give a graphic and accurate account of the meeting.[1] There were the jokes about my girlfriends and how I used them to set up a cover for my secret journeys. There was a mocking exchange about the epithets the leaders of Taipei and Peking were hurling at each other. There was an extraordinary indication of Mao's preference for the greater calculability of conservative leaders over the sentimental oscillations of liberals: "I voted for you during your election," he told the startled Nixon. "People say you are rightists, that the Republican Party is to the right, that Prime Minister Heath is also to the right. . . . I am comparatively happy when these people on the right come into power."

Mao used the context of a generally teasing conversation about Nixon's political prospects to mention his own political opposition. There was a "reactionary group which is opposed to our contact with you," he said. "The result was that they got on an airplane and fled abroad." The plane crashed in Outer Mongolia, Mao and Chou explained, in case we had missed the reference to Lin Piao. Nixon made an eloquent statement (reproduced in his memoirs) of his long journey from anti-Communism to Peking, based on the proposition that the foreign policy interests of the two countries were compatible and neither threatened the other. Mao used the occasion to give us an important assurance with regard to our allies as if the thought had occurred to him only while Nixon was speaking: "Neither do we threaten Japan or South Korea."

Later on, as I comprehended better the many-layered design of Mao's conversation, I understood that it was like the courtyards in the Forbidden City, each leading to a deeper recess distinguished from the others only by slight changes of proportion, with ultimate meaning residing in a totality that only long reflection could grasp. In the pleasantries recorded by Nixon there were hints and themes that, like the overture to a Wagner opera, needed elaboration before their meaning became evident.

Mao was elliptical, for instance, in conveying his decision to expand trade and exchanges with us. He couched this in the form of an explanation of China's slowness in responding to American initiatives over two years. China had been "bureaucratic" in its approach, he said, in insisting all along that the major issues had to be settled before smaller issues like trade and people-to-people exchanges could be addressed. "Later on I saw you were right, and we played table tennis." This was more than a recitation of history and a disarming apology; it meant that there would be progress with respect to trade and exchanges at the summit, as I had urged on Chou during my trip in October. Mao, in short, had willed the visit to be a success. After our presence received Mao's imprimatur, all Chinese officials seemed to have little difficulty discerning the instructions of the Chairman. Phrases originally obscure to me were quoted as indicating a direction. During the week that followed, all the Chinese — and especially Chou — kept coming back time and again to Mao's themes, which grew out of a conversation lasting only sixty-five minutes, half of it consumed in translation.

Amidst the teasing, the jokes, the light repartee, one had to pay attention, for Mao was putting forward major points in a manner deliberately offhand so that failure of the Nixon visit would not involve a loss of face. He delicately placed the issue of Taiwan on a subsidiary level, choosing to treat it as a relatively minor internal Chinese dispute; he did not even mention our military presence there. The only specific political reference to it was in the banter about the names the two groups were calling each other. And even this was a way of telling us that ultimately the Chinese would find their own solutions. Referring to their alliance in the Twenties, Mao reminded Nixon that "actually, the history of our friendship with him [Chiang Kai-shek] is much longer than the history of *your* friendship with him." Neither then, nor in any subsequent meeting, did Mao indicate any impatience over Taiwan, set any time limits, make any threats, or treat it as the touchstone of our relationship. "We can do without them for the time being, and let it come after 100 years." "Why such great haste?" "This issue [Taiwan] is not an important one. The issue of the international situation is an important one." "The small issue is Taiwan, the big issue is the world." These were Mao's thoughts on Taiwan as expressed to us on many visits. (These were also the views of Chou En-lai and Teng Hsiao-p'ing.) But Mao, like Chou and Teng, spent very little time in our talks on this issue.

What concerned Mao then, and even more fully when I saw him later alone at greater length, was the international context — that is, the Soviet Union. To a long disquisition by Nixon on the question of which of the nuclear superpowers, the United States or the Soviet Union, presented a greater threat, Mao replied: "At the present time, the question of aggression from the United States or aggression from China is relatively small. . . . You want to withdraw some of your troops back on your soil; ours do not go abroad." In other words, by a process of elimination, the Soviet Union was clearly Mao's principal security concern. Equally important was the elliptical assurance, later repeated by Chou, which removed the nightmare of two administrations that China might intervene in Indochina militarily. In foreclosing Chinese military intervention abroad and in the comments on Japan and South Korea, Mao was telling us that Peking would not challenge vital American interests. And since Westerners were notoriously slow-witted, Mao reverted to a recurrent theme of my meetings with Chou: "I think that, generally speaking, people like me sound a lot of big cannons. That is, things like 'the whole world should unite and defeat imperialism, revisionism, and all reactionaries, and establish socialism.' " Mao, seconded by Chou, laughed uproariously at the proposition that anyone might take seriously a decades-old slogan scrawled on every public poster in China.

The leaders of China were beyond ideology in their dealings with us. Their peril had established the absolute primacy of geopolitics. They were in effect freeing one front by a tacit nonaggression treaty with us.

Not all was strategy, however, in the encounter with Mao. Even in our brief meeting he could not escape the nightmare that shadowed his accomplishments and tormented his last years: that it might all prove ephemeral, that the exertions, the suffering, the Long March, the brutal leadership struggles would be but a brief incident in the triumphant, passive persistence of a millennial culture which had tamed all previous upheavals, leaving little more in their wake than the ripples of a stone falling into a pond. "The Chairman's writings moved a nation and have changed the world," said Nixon. "I have not been able to change it," replied Mao, not without pathos. "I have only been able to change a few places in the vicinity of Peking."

It was a modest claim after a lifetime of titanic struggle to uproot the very essence of his society. In its matter-of-fact resignation it underlined the revolutionary dilemma. The qualities needed to destroy are usually not those needed to sustain: The greater the upheaval, the more it may lead to a new apparatus even more pervasive and usually much more efficient than the one replaced. Revolutions conducted in the name of liberty more often than not refine new tools of authority. This is no accident. Academicians may define human freedom by concepts of human rights; historians understand that freedom resides not only in legal structures but in the general acceptance of institutions and the ease of human relationships. A society not scourged by irreconcilable schisms can practice tolerance and respect human dignity even in the absence of legally defined rights. Tolerance is inherent in its structure. Britain has never had a written constitution; civil rights are guaranteed by tradition. But a nation riven by factions, in which the minority has no hope of ever becoming a majority, or in which some group knows it is perpetually outcast, will seem oppressive to its members, whatever the legal pretensions.

The essence of modern totalitarianism is the insistence on a single standard of virtue and the corresponding destruction of all traditional restraints. The effort to make uniform the new morality has given rise to passions unknown since the periods of religious conflict and it has caused governments to arrogate powers to themselves unprecedented in history. (The American Revolution was not a revolution in this sense. It did not seek to uproot existing institutions but to return them to their original purpose.) To be a true revolutionary one requires a monstrous self-confidence. Who else would presume to impose on his followers the inevitable deprivations of revolutionary struggle, except one monomaniacally dedicated to the victory of his convictions and free of doubt about whether they justified the inevitable suffering? It is the pursuit of this charismatic truth — sometimes transcendental, as often diabolical — that has produced the gross misery as well as the profound upheavals that mark modern history. For "truth" knows no restraint and "virtue" can accept no limits; they are their own justification. Opponents are either ignorant or wicked, and must be either reeducated or eliminated. The more violent the uprooting, the more the need to impose new order by discipline. When spontaneity disappears, regimentation must replace it.

So it was with the China that Mao Tse-tung had wrought. No doubt many of the institutions he overthrew were corrupt. Unquestionably, there was something grandiose about Mao's commitment to egalitarianism in a population of 800 million and to the eradication of institutions grown up in the longest uninterrupted period of self-government on the globe. But the suffering inseparable from an enterprise so far beyond the human scale was vast. And the primeval resistance of a society grown great by the smothering of shocks evoked ever-greater spasms from that colossal figure, who challenged the gods in the scope of his aspirations.

To Mao, Communism was the truth. But as he achieved the dreams of his youth he — alone among all the fathers of twentieth-century Communism — espied a deeper truth. He discovered that the evolution of Communism could wind up mocking its pretensions, and that the essence of China might transmute his upheavals into a mere episode in its seemingly eternal continuity. Millions had died for a classless society, but in the hour of its realization it dawned on Mao that the enthusiasm of revolutionary fervor and the stifling controls necessary to transform a society would both in time run up against the traditions of his people whom he both loved and hated. The country that had invented the civil service would turn the Communist bureaucracy into a new mandarin class more confirmed in its prerogatives than ever by the maxims of a true dogma. The nation whose institutions had been shaped by Confucius into instruments for instilling universal ethics would before long absorb and transform the materialist Western philosophy imposed on it by its latest dynasty.

The aging Chairman railed against a fate that so cruelly mocked the suffering and meaning of a lifetime of struggle. Unable to bear the thought that the new was turning into a confirmation of what he had sought to destroy, he launched himself into ever more frenzied campaigns to save his people from themselves while he still had the strength. Many revolutions have been made to seize power and to destroy existing structures. Never has their maker undertaken a task so tremendous and possessed as to continue the revolution by deliberate systematic upheavals directed against the very system he has created. No institution was immune. Each decade an assault was launched against the huge, bloated bureaucracies — the government, the Party, the economy, the military. For several years all universities were closed. At one point China had only a single ambassador abroad. Mao destroyed or sought to destroy every Number Two man — Liu Shao-chi, Lin Piao, Teng Hsiao-p'ing, and possibly even Chou En-lai. In the nature of their position these men were forced to deal with the practical, hence the continuing, issues of Chinese life — the very problems that evoked Mao's premonition of ephemerality and his all-too-Chinese fear that they would erode the moral distinctiveness of the Middle Kingdom.

And so each decade the fading Chairman would smash what he had created, forgoing modernization, shaking up the bureaucracy, purging its leadership, resisting progress in order to maintain undefiled values that could be implemented, if at all, by a simple peasant society, encapsulating his people in its superior virtue while sacrificing all the means to defend it. And in the process he acted like the emperors whom he replaced and in whose compound he now lived, becoming like them in his practices in the struggle to prevent the return to their values.

One of history's monumental ironies is that probably no one better understood the built-in tensions of Communism than the titanic figure who made the Chinese Revolution. He had the courage to grapple with the implications of that insight. Pragmatic Communism leads to mandarinism, nationalism, and institutionalized privilege. His critique of Soviet Russia was so wounding to the Russians because it was essentially true. But truly revolutionary Communism leads to stagnation, insecurity, international irrelevance, and the continuing destruction of disciples by new votaries who prefer purity to permanence. Mao in his last decades oscillated between these two choices. Having understood the inherent dilemma of Communism, he would periodically permit a small dose of modernization, only to destroy those who had defiled his vision by carrying out his orders. And these series of planned upheavals still did not preoccupy him so much that he neglected the traditional Chinese statecraft of using one set of barbarians to balance another.

Until his death he was quintessentially Chinese in never doubting the cultural superiority of what he had wrought. He resisted modernization because it would destroy China's uniqueness, and he fought institutionalization because it banked China's ideological zeal. It has been said that revolutions destroy their makers. The opposite was true of Mao; he was the maker who destroyed one revolutionary wave after another. He fought the implications of his own revolution as fiercely as he did the institutions he had originally overthrown. But he had set a goal beyond human capacity. In his last months, bereft of speech, able to act only a few hours a day, he had passion strong enough for one last outburst against the pragmatists, again represented by Teng Hsiao-p'ing. And then that great, demonic, prescient, overwhelming personality disap-

peared like the great Emperor Ch'in Shih Huang-ti with whom he often
compared himself while dreading the oblivion which was his fate. And
his words to Nixon, like so much of what he said and attempted, had the
ring of prophecy: "I have only been able to change a few places in the
vicinity of Peking."

Walks, Talks, and Toasts

AFTER our encounter with history we turned to the practical issue of
how to distill from it a direction for policy. While I had outlined
the American approach to world affairs in considerable detail to Chou
En-lai on two previous visits, only the President could confer final authority and conviction. Much would depend on the Chinese leaders' assessment of Nixon's ability to execute, parallel with them, a global policy designed to maintain the balance of power which was the real
purpose of their opening to us.

And there was need, too, for a formal expression of the new relationship between two countries that had had no communication for over
two decades, no diplomatic ties, and no framework for dealing with
each other. So the final communiqué was crucial. What was required
was a document equally symbolic for Communist cadres and capitalist
observers, capable of squelching criticism from the ideological left in
China and the conservative right in America. It had to encompass Taiwan but remove it as a bone of contention. It had to suggest our real
mutual security concerns without spelling them out in provocative fashion. What was required was easier to state than to achieve. We had
made major progress during my October trip. Three paragraphs remained to be settled, one dealing with India-Pakistan, a second with
trade and exchanges, and the third with Taiwan. They took four late-
night sessions to complete.

Meanwhile, the Peking summit unfolded on other levels as well, all
intricately interwoven by our subtle hosts and our not so subtle advance
men. The Chinese wanted to use the majesty of their civilization and the
elegance of their manners to leave an impression that nothing was more
natural than an increasingly intimate relationship between the world's
most avowedly revolutionary Marxist state and the embodiment of capitalism. Our advance men had simpler objectives. They sought exposure
in prime television time. The purposes intersected to produce a spectacular show, a string of Presidential visits to the architectural and artistic
monuments of China's past: the Great Wall, the Forbidden City, the
Ming Tombs, the Summer Palace, and the Temple of Heaven, where
the emperors had carried their self-absorption and presumption to the
point of locating the precise geometric center of the universe within a
series of concentric circles in what is now downtown Peking.

I participated in none of the sight-seeing. I had seen the landmarks on my two previous visits, having indeed been used by the meticulous Chinese as a guinea pig for their study of timings and required security precautions, as well as of how these strange Americans behaved in the presence of the wonders of Chinese history. I therefore used the time to negotiate the communiqué with Ch'iao Kuan-hua and to attend to the Washington business of the Presidential security adviser.

From all accounts Nixon's sight-seeing proceeded according to scenario. No matter how many stops had been planned, one could set one's watch by initial departure and final return time. Yet regardless of how many digressions the Americans made, they were never under pressure from their Chinese hosts to meet a schedule. They were free to wander and explore, or to fail to do so; the schedule always came out to the minute. When I had experienced this marvel of planning some months earlier, I had asked a Chinese protocol officer how they managed to combine so much precision and latitude without any of the frenzied huffing by which protocol departments of other countries, including our own, demonstrate their virtuosity. It was all very simple, said the Chinese diplomat. Visitors were given only the time of the departure and of return and the places to be visited. They were under no psychological pressure from the detailed minute-by-minute schedule with which protocol officers usually discipline their charges (and demonstrate the intricacy of their preparations). For their own planning the Chinese broke down the allotted time into segments of eight minutes (though why eight remains suitably enigmatic). If guests spent more time in one place than was allowed for, equivalent eight-minute segments were removed from later parts of the tour; if less, eight-minute segments could be added.

In other words, the Chinese had hit on a characteristically simple idea: Instead of the guests' complying with the host's schedule, the host would gear himself to the wishes of the visitor. Chinese protocol thus inspires a strange sense of repose; it conveys both respect and a flattery all the more effective for appearing totally matter-of-fact.

With this preparation, the various sight-seeing trips went off as magnificent spectacles. Hordes of famous television commentators and senior journalists converged on each set piece, eager to record the profound thoughts of the leading actors. "This is a great wall," said Nixon to the assembled press at the Great Wall, placing his seal of approval on one of mankind's most impressive creations. The fact that the excursions were geared to television only reinforced that here, if ever, the medium was the message. In the mind of the American public, television established the reality of the People's Republic and the grandeur of China as no series of diplomatic notes possibly could have. The advance men had, after all, made their own contribution to history in a way that I had not comprehended or appreciated beforehand.

The symbolic events were continued each evening — in banquets, an exhibition of gymnastics and table tennis in the Sports Palace, and a performance of the stupefying revolutionary ballet entitled *The Red De-tachment of Women*. After my ten trips to China, the banquets now seem very stylized. In February 1972 they were still marvelously novel and imbued with the deft little touches with which the Chinese demonstrate that they consider their visitor special. They had acquired a list of Nixon's favorite tunes, and their splendid army band played a selection of them at each dinner. There were formal banquets on four of the seven nights we were in Peking: a welcoming banquet by Chou En-lai; a return one hosted by Nixon; and feasts in our honor by the municipalities of Hangchow and Shanghai. In addition, Chou En-lai gave a private dinner for the American delegation in Peking.

The banquets in the capital took place in the gigantic Great Hall of the People that commemorates the Communist takeover. Its combination of neoclassicism and Communist baroque, so explicit and sullen in contrast to the subtle and suggestive designs of China's past, faces the vermilion walls of the Forbidden City across Tien An Men Square. In that vast expanse, which is still enormous even with the huge bulk of the building filling one corner, the Hall is stranded like a beached whale, inspiring awe by its scale, and obliterating conventional reflections about its design by the defiance of mortality that it expresses.

The banquet protocol throughout my visits was unvarying. One reached the banquet hall by a grand staircase that rose steeply through various levels to seemingly distant heights. No visitor with a heart condition could possibly make it to the top alive. (There were elevators, but on Presidential visits the party was so large that we had to use the stairs.) The Chinese leadership waited at the head of the staircase. Several wooden stands had been arranged in ascending rows so that unobtrusive officials could assemble us in precise protocol rank for the obligatory group picture. No matter how large the group, it was rapidly arranged and the whole picture-taking process completed in no more than three to five minutes. The honored guests were then escorted into the banquet hall to the strains of a march and shook hands with a long line of dignitaries. The hall can seat as many as three thousand guests. During Nixon's visit the number was about nine hundred, but the large round tables were so arranged that no sense of empty spaces was created. The head tables were located at the foot of a stage on which were placed two sets of microphones, one for the leader proposing a toast, the other for the interpreter. I sat at a table with the Nixons and Chou En-lai, although too far away to participate in their conversation. The atmosphere was convivial. Not only did the courses of the meal seem to go on forever, but each Chinese at the table, in keeping with Chinese custom, concentrated on making sure every American plate was filled with heaps of food.

And then, of course, came the endless rounds of toasts. We drank *mao-tai*, that deadly brew which in my view is not used for airplane fuel only because it is too readily combustible. I received graphic proof of this when Nixon on his return to Washington sought to illustrate the liquid's potency to his daughter Tricia. He poured a bottle of it into a bowl and set it afire. To his horror the fire would not go out; the bowl burst and sent flaming *mao-tai* across the table top. The frantic combined efforts of the First Family managed to extinguish the fire just before a national tragedy occurred. Otherwise the Nixon Administration would have come to a self-inflicted premature end even earlier than it did.

Each Chinese around the table would drink only by toasting an American. This was done with a cheery *"gam bei"* — which means "bottoms up" and is taken literally. The glass must be emptied each time; the individual proposing the toast makes sure there is no cheating by showing his empty glass to shame his opposite number into following suit. Since the Chinese outnumbered us two to one and were more used to their national drink, exuberance mounted as such evenings progressed. Fortunately, the banquet toasts were prepared ahead of time, and were read. Only in Shanghai did euphoria carry one away when Nixon proposed what sounded like a defensive military alliance in his only extemporaneous toast of the trip.* Luckily, by that hour the press was too far gone itself. Nor were the correspondents looking to top the big story of the Shanghai Communiqué. My own problem at these banquets was that I generally had to meet Ch'iao Kuan-hua *after* each one for several hours to work on the drafting. I told him on one occasion that given everybody's happy mood we might as well negotiate it in Chinese.

But the banquets, televised live on the morning shows in America, performed a deadly serious purpose. They communicated rapidly and dramatically to the peoples of both countries that a new relationship was being forged. In his exceptionally warm welcoming toast at the first state dinner, Chou En-lai proclaimed that despite ideological differences, normal state-to-state relations could be established on the basis of the five principles of coexistence. He made no reference to Taiwan; he specifically abjured recourse to war to solve outstanding disputes. This only made explicit what we had learned privately. It was another, if implicit, assurance that we need no longer fear Chinese military intervention in Indochina. It was knowledge that stood us in good stead five weeks later when the Vietnamese offensive broke over us, especially when accompanied by similar (if less eloquent) assurances from Moscow.

Nixon replied in a more emotional vein. He had worked over the draft

---

* "... this great city, over the past, has on many occasions been the victim of foreign aggression and foreign occupation. And we join the Chinese people, we the American people, in our dedication to this principle: That never again shall foreign domination, foreign occupation, be visited upon this city or any part of China or any independent country in this world.

"Mr. Prime Minister, our two peoples tonight hold the future of the world in our hands."

I had submitted to him, casting it into his personal idiom and adding quotations from Mao. He stressed that we shared common interests that transcended the ideological gulf (without, however, specifying what they were):

What legacy shall we leave our children? Are they destined to die for the hatreds which have plagued the old world, or are they destined to live because we had the vision to build a new world?

There is no reason for us to be enemies. Neither of us seeks the territory of the other; neither of us seeks domination over the other; neither of us seeks to stretch out our hands and rule the world.

Chairman Mao has written, "So many deeds cry out to be done, and always urgently. The world rolls on. Time passes. Ten thousand years are too long. Seize the day, seize the hour."

This is the hour. This is the day for our two peoples to rise to the heights of greatness which can build a new and a better world.

After my many trips the banquets, the toasts, the music, have become commonplace, but I confess that when on this first occasion the Chinese Premier began circling the tables to toast each American member of the official party individually, to the strains of "America the Beautiful" played by musicians of an army with which two decades before we had been at war, I was deeply moved. In any event, when Richard Nixon could quote Mao Tse-tung to support American foreign policy on Washington's birthday, a diplomatic revolution had clearly taken place.

The symbolism was meaningful only if it could be matched by substance. This was approached on three levels. There were meetings between the Secretary of State and the Chinese Foreign Minister and their staffs that were devoted to the obsessions of our East Asian Bureau: the promotion of more trade and exchanges of persons — in other words, the subject matter of the Warsaw talks these many years. These meetings also served the purpose of keeping the State Department delegation occupied while Nixon was in meetings with Mao and Chou. (Nixon was convinced — and so told Chou — that "our State Department leaks like a sieve.") This group met in the guest house set aside for the Secretary of State. The major problem was to prevent the Chinese, whose internal communications were less constrained than ours, from revealing in the foreign ministers' meetings matters that had already been essentially settled in other forums, such as the structure and content of the communiqué. I attended none of these sessions.

The second level of meetings was the daily sessions between President Nixon and Premier Chou En-lai in the afternoons, following the morning sight-seeing. Four of these took place, extending over some twelve hours, alternating between the Great Hall of the People and the guest house where Nixon was staying. Nixon and Chou reviewed the international situation and made explicit the parallelism of views and de facto cooperation between the two countries that had grown up since my secret trip to Peking. On our side the participants were Nixon, I, and Winston Lord and John Holdridge of my staff.

The third level was the drafting of the communiqué, which involved primarily Deputy Foreign Minister Ch'iao Kuan-hua and me, with occasional recourse to the principals. These drafting meetings took up a total of about twenty hours, with an additional two hours between me and Chou En-lai, who stopped by our meetings on two occasions to let me explain a point to him personally. We met in a separate guest house set aside by the Chinese for their deliberations.

But before these meetings could take place, Chou and I had to sort out the scenario to make sure who would participate in which meeting and who knew what. About twenty minutes after the meeting with Mao ended, Chou and I conferred for about an hour in the guest house that had been reserved for communiqué drafting. My major task was to convey to Chou which topics should be raised in what group. ''The American folklore has it,'' I told him, ''that the Chinese are complicated and we are simple, but when I hear myself talk I think we are complicated and you are easier.'' Chou handled the exotic Americans with aplomb. In contrast to the Soviets, with whom no secret negotiation was complete without some attempt to play our various channels off against each other, the Chinese never dropped a stitch. They scheduled the meetings and kept the information compartmentalized as if they had dealt with our strange practices all their lives. It turned out that Chou did not mind keeping his own Acting Foreign Minister Chi P'eng-fei otherwise occupied. ''He has his limitations,'' Chou explained dryly to Nixon.

Before Chou and I could discuss substance, another bizarre bit of Americana required attention. Because of modern communications the President, wherever he may be located, is always in charge of the government. But every President believes he needs some symbolic event to demonstrate this. For this trip it had been decided that the President would sign before the assembled press a bill providing for arbitration to settle a West Coast dock strike; in conjunction with that event he would issue a statement calling for action on labor legislation in Congress. The public relations geniuses undoubtedly calculated that these were ideal subjects to have emanate from the capital of a country calling itself a workers' state. All would have been well had not one of the advance men conceived the idea that Nixon might present the pen with which the legislation was signed to Chou En-lai. For once, our usually imperturbable host was nonplussed. He had not heard of the custom of bestowing Presidential pens that had signed public documents. He did not like his role in it when I explained it to him. He tactfully pointed out that to accept the pen might look like interference in our internal affairs. Perhaps, he helpfully suggested, if we insisted on giving him a pen we could send another one after we returned to America. I finally told Chou that we would all be better off if the subject were dropped.

At last Chou and I got around to reviewing the communiqué. Three matters required further discussion. The two sides' statements on India and Pakistan, drafted on my October trip, had been overtaken by the crisis in November and December; we foresaw no problems in revision. The slim section on trade and exchanges, in our view, required expansion; it was one criterion by which the American public would measure progress. The section on Taiwan, finally, was incomplete. On this, neither side's current draft was acceptable to the other. Chou and I agreed that much negotiation lay ahead.

The first official meeting of the full delegation of each side occurred at a brief plenary session on Monday afternoon, February 21. Tacit cooperation was well advanced when each of the leaders could, seemingly spontaneously, propose a scheme thought up by the other. Chou put forward as his own idea the very work program I had outlined to him not half an hour earlier, thus taking the responsibility for setting up a separate group for the Foreign Ministers and sparing us much internal anguish. Not to be outdone, Nixon proclaimed his opposition to "weasel-worded" communiqués. In meetings of such importance, he declared, leaders showed their strength by being unafraid to avow their differences. Chou happily agreed that the communiqué should follow a format he had originally proposed in October. The bureaucratic books thus having been cleared, the meeting concluded on the high note of Nixon's declaration that he grouped countries not by ideology but by the foreign policy they conducted.

The next meeting took place with more restricted attendance and got down to serious business. On Tuesday afternoon, Nixon skillfully and succinctly described to Chou En-lai the outlines of American policy. He repeated that his diplomacy was based on other nations' foreign policies, not their domestic structures. His Kansas City remarks of July 1971, while extemporaneous, had reflected his well-considered conviction that a new world order was emerging, based on the five power centers of the United States, Soviet Union, China, Japan, and Western Europe. America had no territorial designs in Asia, and he was convinced that China had none on us. The basis of a cooperative relationship thus existed. Our friendship and alliance with Japan were in China's interest, Nixon pointed out, for they guaranteed that we would be a major factor in the Western Pacific to balance the designs of others, and would keep Japan from pursuing the path of militaristic nationalism. That was why our presence in the Philippines and even South Korea contributed to China's security, by maintaining a balance of power in areas close to China. Nixon summed up our efforts to negotiate a settlement in Vietnam. We would not impose a political solution on Vietnam, as Hanoi wanted. If we did, no country would ever trust us again — implying that our reliability was relevant also to Chinese security concerns. He warned that we would react violently if Hanoi launched another major offensive in 1972.

With respect to Taiwan, Nixon elaborated some fundamental principles that I had already foreshadowed to Chou: that we would not encourage a "two-Chinas" solution, or a "one-China, one-Taiwan" solution, or encourage other countries to replace our military position on the island. Nixon expressed his hope of completing the "normalization" process during his second term. He did not state our conditions for this, but he left no doubt that he would insist on a peaceful resolution. And he made clear that the withdrawal of our forces depended on the state of tensions in the area. Nixon repeatedly affirmed that he could make no "secret deals" on Taiwan; he made none.

Chou, as always, was impassive during Nixon's presentations and incisive in his own. He left no doubt that he feared Soviet expansionism above all. South Asia was but the most recent example, though Indian imperialist designs were well developed even before the Soviet Union stoked the fire of conflict. The primary problem, as China saw it, was to maintain the world balance of power. He regarded the estrangement between the United States and the new China as ended. The task now was joint opposition to hegemonic aspirations.

Chou's treatment of Vietnam was a masterpiece of indirection. He rebutted Nixon more in sorrow than in anger. He indicated "sympathy" for the North Vietnamese but did not allege a community of interest. He derived the obligation to support Hanoi not from ideological solidarity, much less from congruent national interests, but from an historical debt owed to Vietnam from China's imperial past. China would express no view on the continuing negotiations. He reiterated that differences between China and the United States would be settled peacefully. We interpreted this to mean that China would not intervene militarily in Vietnam; that North Vietnam was not an extension of Chinese policy; and that Chou treated Vietnam largely in the context of long-term Soviet aspirations in Southeast Asia. His principal argument for ending the war quickly was that it bogged down the United States and deflected our energies from more important parts of the globe. Chou criticized our negotiating position in only the most perfunctory manner. He urged our military withdrawal from Vietnam; he never really pushed for Hanoi's — and our critics' — political program of coalition government and the overthrow of Thieu.

With respect to Taiwan, Chou repeatedly emphasized the Chinese intention to "liberate" Taiwan peacefully, though he continued to insist that the process was China's internal affair. The overwhelming impression left by Chou, as by Mao, was that continuing differences over Taiwan were secondary to our primary mutual concern over the international equilibrium. The divergence of views on Taiwan would not be allowed to disturb the new relationship that had evolved so dramatically and that was grounded in geopolitical interests. The basic theme of the Nixon trip — and the Shanghai Communiqué — was to put off the issue of Taiwan for the future, to enable the two nations to close the gulf of twenty years and to pursue parallel policies where their interests coincided.

Such was the distilled essence of many conversations conducted, especially on the Chinese side, with extraordinary indirection and subtlety. There were no reciprocal commitments, not even an attempt to define coordinated action. A strange sort of partnership developed, all the more effectual for never being formalized. It had begun on my secret trip in July and continued on my interim visit in October. It culminated in and was legitimized by Nixon's skillful and lucid presentations in China. And it was then elaborated in my subsequent six visits. Two great nations sought cooperation not through formal compacts but by harmonizing their respective understanding of international issues and their interests in relation to them. Cooperation thus became a psychological, not merely a legal, necessity.

This is why Chou spent almost all of his time with Nixon discussing neither the communiqué (which came up only briefly and tangentially) nor operational decisions. The focus of the discussion — during Nixon's visit as in my own separate encounters with Mao or Chou or Teng Hsiao-p'ing or Chinese ambassadors — was on the requirements of the balance of power, the international order, and long-term trends of world politics. Both sides understood that if they agreed on these elements, a strategy of parallel action would follow naturally; if not, tactical decisions taken individually would prove ephemeral and fruitless.

The Shanghai Communiqué

I N fact, our perceptions grew coldly congruent. Yet the parallel strategies did require some tangible expression. The communiqué concluding the visit would be a symbol to the world and our two peoples. It would also guide the two bureaucracies (who would not have access to all the exchanges) in the new direction of policy. It would thus become a touchstone of the relationship between two countries whose diplomatic ties would remain unconventional as long as Washington continued officially to recognize Taipei as the seat of the government of all of China.

On many controversial topics most of the text, as I have said, had been settled during my visit in October, including the unprecedented format of stating conflicting points of view. These opposing presentations gave added emphasis and credibility to those matters on which we were able to endorse a common position, especially with respect to opposing "hegemony" (the new code word for Soviet expansionism). The communiqué was thus less subject to misinterpretation or inconsistent elaboration by the two sides than is the case with the normal document that tends to fudge disagreements as well as agreements; the former to convey an impression of harmony, the latter to avoid the charge of collusion. It was more reassuring to our respective allies and friends.

Taiwan, however, was a thorny problem. During my October visit we had agreed that each side, as on other issues, would state its own position. Peking had set out its claim to be the sole legal government of China and its insistence that Taiwan was a province of China. It had said that the future of Taiwan was an internal affair. For our own statement I had agreed not to challenge the view held by Chinese on both sides of the Taiwan Strait: "The United States acknowledges that all Chinese on either side of the Taiwan Strait maintain there is but one China and that Taiwan is a province of China. The United States does not challenge that position." Peking, for its part, had agreed not to attack — or even to mention — our defense treaty with Taiwan in the statement of its own position while calling for the evacuation of American forces. But when Nixon arrived in Peking, we still differed over the consequences to be drawn from the agreed statement on China's unity. The Chinese wanted us to state that a peaceful solution was our "hope." We insisted on affirming it as an American interest, indeed, on "reaffirming" it, implying that it was a continuing commitment. The Chinese wanted us to commit ourselves unconditionally to the total withdrawal of American forces from Taiwan. We were willing to go no further than to describe our withdrawal as an objective, and even then we insisted on linking it both to a peaceful solution of the Taiwan problem and to the easing of tensions in Asia in general.

In the twenty hours Ch'iao Kuan-hua and I needed to resolve these conflicting approaches, just as on my secret trip, each side pushed the other against the time limit to test whose resiliency was greater. Determination was masked by extreme affability. The best means of pressure available to each side was to pretend that there was no deadline. Conciliatory conduct would heighten the sense of urgency without producing personal strain. Yet while pressure is inescapable in any negotiation, the talks were also conducted with unusual delicacy. Each side took care not to make irrevocable demands or to bargain as if a move by one required a concession by the other. For different reasons Taiwan involved issues of principle for both countries. And to suggest that principles have a price can be offensive. This is why the two sides conducted themselves as if we had to solve a common problem not by a sharp bargain but by a joint understanding. We took pains to explain our domestic necessities to each other with great frankness, because we knew that the communiqué would not survive if negotiated through trickery or found unacceptable at home. We recognized that on some issues the only thing negotiators can achieve is to gain time with dignity. On Taiwan it was to leave the ultimate outcome to a future that in turn would be shaped by the relationship which would evolve from the rest of the communiqué and by the manner in which it was negotiated.

While Nixon attended to White House business, Ch'iao and I spent the first day of negotiation going through the existing draft line by line to confirm what was already agreed. I explained our requirements on Taiwan; Ch'iao indicated that he had no authority to change the existing Chinese proposal. I decided to let matters lie for a day and used the second day's "negotiating session" — on February 23 — to brief the Chinese on the agreements we planned to reach at the Moscow summit.

The Chinese were clearly not happy with our policy toward Moscow, but they would have to adjust to this reality of triangular diplomacy. We and they had a common interest in preventing the Soviet Union from upsetting the global balance of power by any means, including an attack on China. But we had no vested interest in permanent hostility with Moscow unless Moscow challenged the international equilibrium. As nuclear superpowers, we had indeed an obligation to reduce the threat of nuclear confrontation. Peking would no doubt have preferred a simpler pattern of overt hostility between Washington and Moscow. This would have eased its calculations and improved its bargaining position. Our necessities were more complicated. Peking's domestic imperatives pushed it toward confrontation; our imperative was to demonstrate to our public and to our allies that we were not the cause of conflict, or else the Congress would dismantle our defenses and our allies would dissociate from us. Only from a conciliatory platform could we rally support for firm action in a crisis. We were prepared to confront Soviet expansion. But we were not willing to foreclose the option of a genuine easing of tensions with Moscow if that could in time be achieved. Thus we had to make sure that China understood our purposes and would not be surprised by our actions. We kept Peking assiduously informed of our moves. We sought to avoid any implication of condominium. What we could not do was to give Peking a veto over our relationship with Moscow any more than we would give a veto to the Soviets over our relations with China. It was a three-dimensional game, but any simplification had the makings of catastrophe. If we appeared irresolute or leaning toward Moscow, Peking would be driven to accommodation with the Soviet Union. If we adopted the Chinese attitude, however, we might not even help Peking; we might, in fact, tempt a Soviet preemptive attack on China and thus be faced with decisions of enormous danger.

The deadline Ch'iao and I faced was Nixon's departure from Peking for Hangchow on the morning of February 26. There would be little opportunity to negotiate while traveling, and it would be difficult for the Chinese leaders to assemble their Politburo to ratify the outcome. On the third day of our negotiation, February 24, Nixon and his party were sight-seeing at the Great Wall. With only some thirty-six hours left the real negotiation between Ch'iao and me now began. In a two-and-a-half-hour session that morning Ch'iao put forward once again the formula that the United States "hoped" for a peaceful Taiwan solution. He asked us to assert — unrelated to any other conditions — that the United States "will progressively reduce and finally withdraw all the US troops and military installations from Taiwan." I rejected the formulation, saying that it jeopardized the entire relationship because American public opinion would never stand for it. Ch'iao and I met briefly in the afternoon to permit me to offer a compromise, which was in fact a slightly modified version of our original proposal. We tied withdrawals to the "premise" of a peaceful resolution of the Taiwan question and reduction of tensions in the Far East (thereby creating a linkage to Vietnam). Ch'iao promised to study the proposal. After midnight, following another banquet, Ch'iao rejected it. With only about eighteen hours of negotiating time left, we were stuck. On Friday, February 25, Ch'iao and I met again for ninety minutes in the morning while Nixon toured the Forbidden City. Neither of us showed much sense of urgency. We tossed ideas around, "thinking out loud," enabling both sides to pretend that they were not committed. I insisted on some form of conditionality for American withdrawals, especially the premise of a peaceful solution. That afternoon, Ch'iao and I met twice more, while Nixon was resting. At 2:35 P.M. Ch'iao came forward with a formulation which for the first time met our basic principle. China would no longer object if we affirmed an interest in the peaceful solution of the Taiwan issue so long as it also included a reference to total withdrawal of United States forces. I promised him a quick reply.

After I conferred with my associates and then with the President, we met again at about 3:30 P.M. I had hit upon the idea of separating the two problems — the final objective of total withdrawal and our willingness to withdraw troops gradually in the interval, which up to now had been in the same sentence. My proposal was to tie the final withdrawal to the premise of peaceful settlement, and to link the progressive reduction of forces to the gradual diminution of "tension in the area." Ch'iao showed some interest. He came up with a variation. He preferred to speak of the "prospect" of a peaceful settlement, rather than "premise," claiming that it had a more active and more bilateral connotation; "premise" sounded like a unilateral imposition by Washington. I thought this, if anything, better from our point of view; it implied some degree of Chinese commitment. In any event, I did not believe that the fate of Taiwan would be determined by such supersubtle shades of meaning. Ch'iao was not yet prepared to accept linking our withdrawal to our other requirement, the diminution of "tension in the area."

I was convinced that we had made our breakthrough. In every negotiation a point is reached where both sides have gone too far to pull back. Accumulated mutual concessions create their own momentum; at some stage retreat puts into question the judgment of the negotiators. Mao had put this same principle in his usual indirect fashion while pretending to Nixon that agreement was not essential: ". . . if we fail the first time, then people will ask why we are not able to succeed the first time? The only reason would be that we have taken the wrong road. What will they say if we succeed the second time?" Mao was quite right. An initial failure was bound to blight a later success: "What use is there if we stand in deadlock?"

Chou joined the negotiation for half an hour that afternoon, a clear indication of his confidence that we would not fail the first time. Chou was not needed to confirm an impasse; his presence showed that he would take the responsibility for the requisite compromise. I explained once again that we could make no unconditional commitment to withdraw and that the conditions of even a partial withdrawal had to be realistic and explicable to our public. We did have an interest in a peaceful solution of the Taiwan issue, and the war in Southeast Asia would in fact influence our deployments on Taiwan. By stating these concerns honestly we would be able to defend the communiqué in America. If not, we would be forced into stating the same conditions unilaterally, undermining the mutual confidence that was the most crucial purpose of the negotiations and the visit. Chou said that he would think my arguments over.

There was, in fact, an incongruity between the intensity of the discussion and its intrinsic importance. Chou knew well enough that the Taiwan issue could not be resolved during the President's visit. Indeed, any attempt to do so would run counter to China's objective of establishing a cooperative relationship. It would either raise a domestic storm in America or produce a deadlock in Peking; either contingency would stifle the new ties in their infancy. The fundamental objective of both sides was not territorial but geopolitical. Each had concluded that it needed the other for maintaining the balance of power. China's need was somewhat greater from the point of view of security, ours from the point of view of psychology. We required maneuvering room for our diplomacy and to give hope to our people after a tormented decade at home and abroad.

Matters would no doubt have been concluded then and there had we not been obliged to adjourn for a brief Nixon-Chou meeting, which was followed by another banquet. Chou En-lai's toast was rather brief, and noted the "great differences of principle between our two sides." Though Nixon's and Chou's standard rhetoric had repeated this same point all week, and though Chou En-lai at the end of his toast hailed the Chinese commitment to friendship with the United States, some restless newsmen thought they had detected a sudden "tension" in the negotiations because of the nuances of the toast and because the general mood at the banquet seemed deflated compared with the euphoria of the first night. Of course, since both sides had agreed to keep the substance of the conversations secret, the press, having had little guidance, must be forgiven for emphasizing the most dramatic possibilities. The fact was that by the time of the banquet the back of the communiqué was broken — except for some bickering within our delegation. Nixon and Chou in their one-hour meeting on Friday afternoon did not even discuss the communiqué. If conversation seemed to flag at the head table, it was partly because of the general exhaustion produced by successive late-night sessions, especially among the negotiators, and partly because we were all seated in protocol order, which meant that we found ourselves next to the same people at banquet after banquet. Inevitably we had by then explored every conceivable avenue of small talk. The American press self-centeredly assumed that its presence, indeed the intensive media coverage, made Nixon vulnerable to Chinese "pressure" because he needed a successful outcome — as if the Chinese did not have an equal if not greater stake. Whatever the cause, there were sensational headlines that "Banquet Toasts Hint Trouble" (in the *Washington Star*) or "Nixon-Chou Talks Appear Deadlocked" (in the *Washington Post*) and elaborate accounts of impasse based on no particular information.

Ch'iao and I met again at 10:30 P.M. after this Friday banquet and settled the key issue in fifteen minutes. He immediately accepted all the American formulations as I had explained them to Chou. In the process, we secured Ch'iao's agreement to stating that we acknowledged Taiwan as a "part" rather than a "province" of China, thus eliminating a suggestion of subordination. The relevant paragraph now read as follows:

> The U.S. side declared: The United States acknowledges that all Chinese on either side of the Taiwan Strait maintain there is but one China and that Taiwan is a part of China. The United States Government does not challenge that position. It reaffirms its interest in a peaceful settlement of the Taiwan question by the Chinese themselves. With this prospect in mind, it affirms the ultimate objective of the withdrawal of all U.S. forces and military installations from Taiwan. In the meantime, it will progressively reduce its forces and military installations on Taiwan as the tension in the area diminishes.

I had the Taiwan paragraph typed and took it to Nixon in the adjoining guest house. As in all negotiations, once we had agreed on our general objectives, Nixon had left the conduct of the talks to me. He took no special interest in the various formulations until there existed a version requiring his final approval. At one point I asked him to write a marginal comment on one of the Taiwan drafts which I then showed Ch'iao to lend emphasis to my insistence on conditionality for our withdrawals. Now the point of decision had been reached. We had a draft that I considered acceptable. At 10:50 P.M. Friday night Nixon and I reviewed it in detail. A comparison with earlier drafts indicated that we had achieved our basic objective. We would *reaffirm* our interest in a peaceful solution of the Taiwan question. Our agreement to the principle of total withdrawal of our military forces from Taiwan was stated as an *ultimate* objective linked to the *prospect* of a peaceful settlement of the Taiwan issue (implying that there was some ground for expecting it); withdrawals until then would depend on a reduction of tensions in the area. Both sides understood that the American role in the defense of Taiwan did not depend on the few forces on Taiwan, which were mostly communications personnel for our operations in Southeast Asia. The real American security role on Taiwan was defined by the 1955 mutual defense treaty. Neither side mentioned this in the Shanghai Communiqué, and its continued validity had been reaffirmed in the President's Foreign Policy Report published a week before his departure for Peking. Furthermore, not the least anomalous aspect of the China trip was that our defense commitment to Taiwan was reaffirmed yet again, this time on Chinese soil when I later briefed the press in Shanghai on February 27.

The Taiwan paragraph of the communiqué was not a "victory" by one side over the other; no constructive relationship can be built on that basis. In a joint enterprise of sovereign states only those agreements endure which both sides have an interest in maintaining. Rather, it put the Taiwan issue in abeyance, with each side maintaining its basic principles. Despite the continuing difference over Taiwan our rapprochement with China accelerated because we shared a central concern about threats to the global balance of power.

After Nixon approved the Taiwan paragraph, negotiations with Ch'iao on the other unsettled issues, mostly trade and exchanges, were concluded rapidly. The original Chinese draft had contained only a brief, noncommittal sentence, but we stressed that to many Americans progress here would be a measure of the new relationship. Ch'iao now accepted our proposals to expand the section on trade and exchanges. We went over the communiqué once again line by line. By 2:00 A.M. we had completed our labors. The text was subject only to confirmation by our principals, which from previous exchanges we knew would be a formality.

On Saturday, a brief plenary session was improvised in the waiting room at Peking airport before our departure for Hangchow in a Chinese aircraft (with the Secret Service oozing displeasure). The purpose was to give the Foreign Ministers their moment in the limelight by joining a session with the principals covered by the press, as well as to bless the work of the previous night. Unfortunately, someone had neglected to inform the honor guard that departure was not imminent. They were called to attention as soon as the limousine carrying Chou and Nixon arrived at the airport and remained in this posture in biting cold for the fifty minutes that the plenary session lasted. It was an astonishing display of discipline and endurance.

The session went off agreeably enough. Discussion of the communiqué was dampened by the inconvenient fact that most members of our party had not yet seen it, typing having been completed only just before we left the guest house. The two Foreign Ministers were invited to report on their deliberations during the week. This did not take long. Chou filled the void by speaking of an incident on Nixon's visit to the Ming Tombs. A keen-eyed American journalist had noticed that some of the children playing in colorful dresses seemed extremely well-rehearsed, raising some questions about their spontaneity. Chou gracefully apologized:

Some people got some young children there to prettify the Tombs, and it was putting up a false appearance. Your press correspondents have pointed this out to us, and we admit that this was wrong. We do not want to cover up the mistake on this, of course, and we have criticized those who have done this.

I did not go myself to the Ming Tombs, and I admit that I did not know about it previously that they would do that. I came to know that only through your press last night, and when I investigated the matter I found out that that had truly been the case, and I must thank that correspondent. I may have a chance to do that when we arrive in Hangchow and Shanghai.

Chou's comment on the danger of cover-ups evidently made no lasting impression on his principal guest. Nixon replied gracefully that he had enjoyed seeing the little girls, however they had gotten there — and then knocked the press as untrustworthy. It took great self-confidence and no little shrewdness for Chou to admit this mistake. Aside from displaying an admirable candor, it had the added advantage of reinforcing the seriousness of Chinese purposes on issues of principle where not even the possibility of error was admitted. Unfortunately, Chou's words did not seem to percolate through the Chinese bureaucracy with customary efficiency. In Hangchow we encountered once again groups of youngsters in colorful national dresses playing games — a sight never to be seen under other circumstances at that period on the somber streets of Chinese cities. And two years later when Chou had withdrawn from government because of illness, I encountered the same tableau in

Soochow. It seemed to be a standard operating procedure for distinguished visitors that not even the great Chou had authority to erase.

It would be pleasant to report that after our departure from Peking the business portion of the trip was completed. And indeed Hangchow, at the mouth of the lower Yangtze River, is one of the most beautiful cities in China. Built along romantic lakes, filled with exquisite gardens, temples, and palaces, blessed with a mild climate and an early spring, it is an ancient center of culture, scholarship, and poetry. Marco Polo, visiting in the thirteenth century, extolled Hangchow as ''the greatest city which may be found in the world'' and so beautiful that ''one fancies onself to be in Paradise.''[2] Ambassador Huang Chen in Paris had told General Walters of a Chinese saying that there were two places worth seeing, Heaven above and Hangchow below. The setting was reduced to Nixonian prose when the President pointed out to Chou En-lai on visiting the West Lake that the scene ''looks like a postcard.''

The only sight-seeing excursion that I personally made was in Hangchow. One of its most beautiful spots is an island in the middle of a lake that is itself on an island inside a larger lake. On that inner island the Chinese have placed a series of simple structures which are essentially frames through which to view the vistas as if they were paintings. During this particular side trip I was looking at the gentle hills rising like some large plant out of the water. A solitary birch was bending gracefully at the edge of the frame. All was tranquillity and repose. Suddenly into the picture staggered Walter Cronkite. He was a little the worse for wear, dressed in heavy furs more appropriate for a polar expedition and weighted down by a spectacular assortment of photographic gear around his neck. Fond as I am of Walter, the scene lost some of its serenity.

In any event the mood of the American party did not match the tranquillity of the scenery. On the plane to Hangchow the State Department experts were given the communiqué, in the preparation of which they had had no part. Predictably, they found it wanting. It is the price that must be paid for excluding the professionals from a negotiation. Unfamiliar with the obstacles overcome, those not participating can indulge in setting up utopian goals (which they would have urged be abandoned during the first day of the negotiation had they conducted it) and can contrast them with the document before them. Or they can nitpick at the result on stylistic grounds, pointing out telling nuances, brilliantly conceived, which the world was denied by their absence. I had recommended that Assistant Secretary Green join our negotiating team. Nixon had vetoed this for fear of leaks and because he preferred to have his inevitable confrontation over drafting with Rogers all at once rather than day by day. As over Rogers's absence from the meeting with Mao, I should have insisted; we now paid the price.

No sooner had we arrived in Hangchow than Secretary Rogers — just as after the Berlin negotiations — informed the President that the communiqué was unsatisfactory. He submitted a list of amendments prepared by his staff, as numerous as they were trivial. For example, his experts objected to the phrase that *all* Chinese on either side of the Taiwan Strait maintained that there was but one China. It seemed to them too inclusive; there might be some Chinese who disagreed. They proposed that we replace "all Chinese" with "the Chinese" — a distinction beyond the grasp of my untrained mind. Another recommendation was to drop the word "position" in the phrase "does not challenge that position." There were about fifteen changes of the same order of magnitude, including the reasonable proposal that the English text put the American statement of position first while the Chinese text would reverse the procedure. (This is conventional diplomatic practice.)

Nixon was beside himself. He recognized his political dilemma. He was already edgy about the reaction of his conservative supporters to the trip; he dreaded a right-wing assault on the communiqué. And he could see that leaks that the State Department was unhappy about American concessions might well be the trigger. He also knew that reopening the communiqué after the Chinese had been told he agreed to it might well sour his trip — especially since the importance of the proposed changes was next to impossible to explain. He was so exercised that he started storming about the beautiful guest house in Hangchow in his underwear. He would "do something" about the State Department at the first opportunity — a threat he had made at regular intervals since my first interview with him those many years ago at the Pierre Hotel, and never specified or implemented. One minute he insisted that he would stick to his word, the next that he could not go home with a divided delegation. I recommended that I have a go at Ch'iao Kuan-hua after dinner, however painful the occasion. If the Chinese insisted on the existing draft, we would have no choice but to stick with our commitment.

I did not enjoy this particular banquet, of southern cuisine, despite its extraordinary quality, from apprehension of what was to follow. Ch'iao Kuan-hua and I met at 10:20 P.M. I decided our only hope lay in perfect frankness. I explained that normally a Presidential decision settled a communiqué. But in this case we had not achieved our full objective if we merely announced some formal propositions; we needed to mobilize public opinion behind our course. It was therefore in our common interest that Ch'iao cooperate in giving the State Department a sense of having contributed. I then presented the proposed changes.

My arguments did not exactly overwhelm Ch'iao. He replied sharply that both sides had come very far and China had made many concessions in response to American wishes. The Politburo had approved the text the previous night on the basis of our assurance that the President had accepted it. How could we reopen it less than twenty-four hours before the communiqué was to be published? But the Chinese are pragmatic, and their leadership wise. Creating a psychological basis for a new relationship with the United States was more important than these valid objections of Ch'iao's. After a brief interruption — no doubt to consult the Premier — Ch'iao returned with a compromise. The Chinese would consider no changes in the Taiwan section; they had made major accommodations to our view; their leadership had approved the text after much debate. Any attempt to change it would preclude issuing a communiqué the next day. But Ch'iao would be prepared to discuss our other proposals on their merits.

We were thus launched into another late-night session. After firing many "empty cannons," the Chinese agreed to much of what was proposed on the parts of the communiqué not dealing with Taiwan. By 2:00 A.M. another "final" draft was at last completed, subject once again to the formal approval of our principals. This was obtained early the next morning. Ch'iao and I met once again for two and a half hours at midday on Sunday in Shanghai to review the new completed text. We read through it line by line, checking even punctuation, and agreeing on a few stylistic changes. (The full text of the communiqué is given in the notes.) [3]

I then outlined to Ch'iao Kuan-hua the briefing I would give to the press on the communiqué that afternoon. It was essential that neither side claim a victory. It was important not to exhibit our brilliance in interpretation. This was a not so subtle dig at the able (and often helpful) Assistant Minister Chang Wen-chin, whose capacity to develop fine shades of meaning had an heroic cast. My main purpose at the session was to make Ch'iao aware that I would reiterate the defense commitment to Taiwan in my briefing. I hoped that there would be no Chinese reaction. Ch'iao replied that he would rely on my tact.

My news conference in the Industrial Exhibition Center Banquet Hall in Shanghai was surely one of the most paradoxical events to take place on Chinese soil since the revolution. A foreign official explained that his country would continue to recognize a government which was the rival to that with which he had been negotiating, and would defend it with military force against his hosts. I reiterated the continued validity of the defense treaty by reaffirming the appropriate sections in the President's Foreign Policy Report published just weeks previously. And it is a measure of their wisdom that there was no Chinese reaction. Our hosts understood their priorities.

The Chinese grasp of essentials was also shown by their handling of the communiqué's translation. We had used Peking's interpreters in all the meetings, largely because of Nixon's belief that State Department interpreters would leak; theirs were also much better than ours. This was not a handicap, as sometimes alleged, because the Chinese would be bound by the English text. (Also, many on the Chinese side understood

English, and Holdridge understood Chinese. In cases of dispute the English text would be controlling.) Because of the pressure of time we had
no opportunity even to check the Chinese translation — a suicidal omission when dealing with the Russians, as we had learned when we announced our first SALT breakthrough. But Chou En-lai played no petty
games; he understood that mutual confidence was more important than
scoring debating points. The Chinese translation, amazingly enough,
turned out to be *more* favorable to our position than the English one. I
later forwarded to the President an analysis done by Richard Solomon of
my staff, which concluded:

Significant variations between the Chinese and English texts were found
regarding the three issues of Taiwan, the Indochina war, and cultural
exchanges. In virtually every case, however, the Chinese version clarifies a bit
of ambiguity in the English text, or states our position in a way that is more
rather than less favorable to our objectives.

Regarding the future of Taiwan, the Chinese version conveys even less of a
sense of U.S. acceptance of the PRC [Peking] view that the island is Chinese
territory than does the English. It more strongly conveys the idea that we do not
wish to get involved in a debate regarding the Chinese position on Taiwan, and
strengthens the sense of our concern that there be a peaceful resolution of the
Taiwan question.

The Shanghai Communiqué was as unusual as the new relationship it
confirmed. Its opening section expressed the conflicting views on a
whole host of issues including Korea, Vietnam, and Japan. The American position was phrased in conciliatory fashion, stressing our commitment to peaceful solutions and the principles of individual freedom and
social progress for all the peoples of the world. In this first statement of
our values to the Chinese people, we sought to emphasize that America
stood for humaneness and hope. The Chinese rhetoric was more militant, though toned down considerably from the conventional style. It
was difficult enough to habituate cadres brought up during the Cultural
Revolution to the sight of Americans meeting with Chinese leaders; it
was not possible to dispense totally with revolutionary rhetoric. It was
clear, as Mao and Chou frequently admitted, that the occasional firing
of "empty cannons" was for the record.

These contrasting statements merely served to highlight the revolutionary change in the Chinese-American relationship embodied in the
views that the two sides expressed in common. China and the United
States in effect renounced the use of force in settling disputes with each
other. They announced their common opposition to the hegemonic aspirations of others. They agreed not to enter into any agreements aimed at
the other. They undertook to promote exchanges and trade. And Taiwan
was handled in a manner preserving the dignity, self-respect, and commitments of each side.

The Shanghai Communiqué was probably unique in its success in guiding relations between two great nations for seven years without ever a dispute over its meaning until it was superseded by diplomatic relations in 1979. It had no secret clauses or codicils. Its significance lay not only in its words but in the assumptions underlying it. Despite the media's emphasis, the communiqué was not about Taiwan or bilateral exchanges, but about international order. It brought together two previously hostile nations not because they desired to settle bilateral problems — these could have been postponed for a substantial time — but to deal across the gulf of ideology with common security concerns.

Our sojourn in China was nearing conclusion. There was a final banquet in Shanghai where, with all tension gone, *mao-tai* flowed like water and Nixon, carried away with it all, delivered his extemporaneous toast (already noted) which edged up to an American military guarantee of China. Ch'iao and I had seemingly become so habituated to our late-night sessions that we could not do without another one. We met on February 27–28 from 11:05 P.M. to 12:30 P.M. in a session devoted to Vietnam. I explained our negotiating position in greater detail than Nixon had to Chou, and our determination to defeat an offensive by all available means should Hanoi seek a military resolution. Ch'iao repeated China's moral and material support for North Vietnam but, following Chou, dissociated China from Hanoi's negotiating position. These were a matter between us and the North Vietnamese on which China would express no views. He issued no warnings. He indicated no penalty if we carried out our threat.

There was one more conversation before my day was done. At three o'clock in the morning I was called to Nixon's room on an upper floor of the high-rise hotel that served as our domicile. Before us lay the immense city of Shanghai, with just a few flickering lights barely suggesting the presence of close to eleven million people. All else was blackness. The mass of China lay before us, all-pervasive but invisible. Nixon had also awakened Haldeman to share with him the tensions, the exhilaration, and the inchoate fears that always marked the end of his great exertions. Nixon talked about his accomplishments, asking for confirmation and reassurance. And we gave him both, moved in part by an odd tenderness for this lonely, tortured, and insecure man, in part also by an all-consuming desire to get to bed after an exhausting week. Yet it was easy to give Nixon the reassurance he wanted. The embellishments generated by the Walter Mitty side of his nature were trivial, in some ways touching. He had indeed wrought a genuine historic achievement. He had thought up the China initiative (even though I had reached the same conclusion independently); he had fostered it, had run the domestic political risks of going it alone, and had conducted himself admirably during the journey.

Chou En-lai paid a farewell call on Nixon just before escorting him to the airport early in the morning of February 28. It was a gentle and pensive conversation between two men who had taken each other's measure and were comfortable with each other's purposes. Since one could never be sure whether Occidentals had gotten the point, Chou reviewed once again the Chinese position on the two issues most likely to be immediately troublesome: Taiwan and Vietnam. With respect to Taiwan he again counseled patience: "We, being so big, have already let the Taiwan issue remain for twenty-two years, and can still afford to let it wait there for a time." About Vietnam Chou was at his best. He averred support for Hanoi but he again based it not on national interest or ideological solidarity but on an historical debt incurred by the Chinese Empire several centuries before. Clearly China might make some material sacrifices; it would not run the risk of war to discharge such a debt. China, insisted the subtle Premier, had refrained from avowing any special link to Vietnam in the communiqué because it did not want to leave the wrong impression. Chou told Nixon:

We have extreme sympathy for the people of that area. We believe they are closely linked with us. We thought of using wording in the communiqué but then we thought maybe there would be other implications and so we did not do so. . . . As Chairman Mao has pointed out, we who have been victorious have only an obligation to assist them, but not the right to interfere in their sovereignty. The debt we owe them was incurred by our ancestors. We have since liberation no responsibility because we overthrew the old system. . . . Dr. Kissinger can bear witness that we have exerted extreme restraint since July of last year. Yet the key to easing tensions in the world does not lie there and Mr. President and I and Chairman Mao all understand that.

We indeed understood each other; the war in Vietnam would not affect the improvement of our relations. The avowal of restraint and of the fact that the key to easing tensions did not lie in Indochina left no doubt that Peking's priority was not the war on its southern border but its relationship with us. Three months later Moscow revealed the same priorities, more crudely. Moscow and Peking, for all their hatred of each other, and perhaps because of it, were agreed on this point: North Vietnam would not be permitted to override their greater geopolitical preoccupations. Against all odds, our diplomacy was on the verge of isolating Hanoi.

Assessments

NIXON's trip ended on a high note of sentiment, but it was not from that impetus that Sino-American relations subsequently prospered. For all their charm and ideological fervor, the Chinese leaders were the most unsentimental practitioners of balance-of-power politics I have encountered. From ancient times Chinese rulers have had to contend with powerful non-Chinese neighbors and potential conquerors. They have prevailed, often from weakness, by understanding profoundly — and exploiting for their own ends — the psychology and preconceptions of foreigners. In the nineteenth century China was the only great prize to escape complete capture and subjugation by European nations. Though humiliated and mistreated it managed to maintain self-government through the skillful use of Western legal concepts of sovereignty (which have no exact Chinese equivalent) and the proposition that domestic matters are beyond foreign challenge. Throughout its history, whenever threatened, China has sought to pit potential adversaries against one another, and as a last extreme — as in the nineteenth century — it embroiled them over the division of Chinese spoils. Explaining how China avoided the fate of Africa and India in the colonial era, Chou said to me on one occasion: "On the one hand it was because of the strong desire for unity. On the other, so many countries were trying to get something out of China that other countries could not control it."

When the Nixon Administration came into office, two Chinese governments claiming legitimacy were dealing with their foreign problems by startlingly similar methods. Chiang Kai-shek dealt with us from a position of weakness; Mao maneuvered the Soviets also from a position of weakness. Both were doing well.

Mao and Chou, practicing high Chinese statesmanship in which ideology reinforced history and culture to confer psychological assurance, found a natural partner in Nixon. He was President during a period when the conventional wisdom decried the exercise of power; his critics asserted that America would prevail if at all because of the purity of its motives. But it was precisely the unpredictable, idiosyncratic nature of a policy founded on this illusion that needed to be overcome. Emotional slogans, unleavened by a concept of the national interest, had caused us historically to oscillate between excesses of isolation and overextension. The new "morality" was supposed to extricate us from excessive commitments. But moral claims lent themselves as easily to crusades as to abstinence; they had involved us in the distant enterprises to begin with. This American volatility unsettled the international equilibrium and those who relied on us. It was ultimately dangerous to the maintenance of peace. What the intellectual community's loathing of Nixon kept them from understanding was that we agreed with their professed desire to relate ends to means and our commitments to our capacities. We parted company with many of them because we did not believe it sensible to substitute one emotional excess for another. Indeed, one reason why the Vietnam debate grew so bitter was that both supporters and critics of the original involvement shared the same traditional sense of universal moral mission.

What made the Nixon Administration so "un-American" was its attempt to establish a sense of proportion out of the welter of conflicting emotions and to adjust to a world fundamentally different from our historical perception. The impulses to lurch toward either isolationism or global intervention had to be cured by making judgments according to some more permanent conception of national interest. Values and principles would inspire our efforts and set our direction. But it was no use rushing forth impetuously when excited or sulking in our tent when disappointed. We would have to learn to reconcile ourselves to imperfect choices, partial fulfillment, the unsatisfying tasks of balance and maneuver, given confidence by our moral values but recognizing that they could be achieved only in stages and over a long period of time.

It was a hard lesson to convey to a people who rarely read about the balance of power without seeing the adjective "outdated" precede it. It was not one of the least ironies of the period that it was a flawed man, so ungenerous in some of his human impulses, who took the initiative to lead America toward a concept of peace compatible with its new realities and the awful perils of a nuclear age, and that the foreign leaders who best understood this were the two grizzled veterans of the Long March, Mao and Chou, who openly expressed their preference for Richard Nixon over the wayward representatives of American liberalism. Their praise of Nixon was more than subtle Chinese flattery. "A sentimental policy knows no reciprocity," wrote Bismarck over a century earlier. For sovereign nations, predictability is more crucial than spasmodic brilliance or idiosyncratic moralistic rhetoric. They must gear their actions to the performance of others over extended periods of time; their domestic survival and international security alike may depend upon it. And it was on this level of shared geopolitical interest transcending philosophies and history that the former Red-baiter and the crusaders for world revolution found each other.

Out of these contacts, meticulously nurtured in the years to come, grew a relationship in which America and China reinforced each other while almost never coordinating tactics explicitly. From an early hostility to the American alliance with Japan (still to be found in the Shanghai Communiqué), the Chinese leaders soon came, in part under our persistent persuasion, to view it as a guarantee of America's continued interest in the Western Pacific and a rein on Japanese unilateralism. Soon they strongly supported close relations between Japan and America. On one occasion Mao went so far as to advise me to make sure that when I visited Asia I spend as much time in Tokyo as in Peking; Japan's pride should be respected. I accepted the recommendation. The Chinese, indeed, came to stress that US–Japanese relations were more important than US–Chinese relations. One of the advantages of our relationship with Peking has been that neither we nor the Japanese have been pressured by China to make a choice of priorities or induced to jockey for Peking's favor.

Over the years China's interest in an economically and militarily strong Western Europe grew to the point that I only half-jokingly called the People's Republic one of our stronger NATO allies. Surely the lectures that West European leaders heard in Peking about the importance of Atlantic defense were if anything more stern than the ones they received in Washington. And, as with Japan, the Chinese urged close relations between America and Europe. China tacitly encouraged our presence in the Philippines and Thailand and, while it followed Pyongyang's basic line, it never really pressed us to remove our forces from Korea. It correctly judged that the visible presence of American power was crucial for maintaining a balance of power in Asia and Europe. On my every visit the Chinese leaders urged us to pay close attention to the crucial southern rim of Eurasia — Turkey, Iran, and Pakistan — three close friends of the United States (and China), whose security was a barrier to a Soviet breakthrough to the Indian Ocean and a check on pro-Soviet radicalism in the Middle East. In the Middle East itself they continually encouraged our negotiating efforts, knowing that this was the best means of eroding Soviet influence. While they had little interest in Latin America, their contempt for Cuba as a Soviet agent was evident. The Chinese have shown a greater concern with and understanding of the spread of Soviet-sponsored radicalism in Africa than any Western country with the exception of France.

In most critical areas China has been a stabilizing force. Its motives, to be sure, are not to foster American designs but to contain Soviet expansion. But this approach is anti-Soviet only if Moscow's compulsion to spread its influence is so inherent in the Soviet system that it cannot survive without it. There is nothing incompatible in close relations with both Peking and Moscow so long as Moscow pursues a restrained foreign policy.

It would be dangerous in the extreme to assume that Chinese objectives and ours are in all respects identical. Peking would prefer to see us so embroiled with the Soviets that it need pay no price at all for a collaborative relationship with Washington. In such conditions, the protection afforded by the American option would be "free." Chinese leaders unquestionably would aspire to a clear-cut alignment rather than an American policy of equidistance between Moscow and Peking that tilted toward Peking only because it was the weaker and more threatened of the Communist giants. For our part, we did not have any illusions about the permanence of the new relationship. Peking and Washington were entering a marriage of convenience transformed into an emotional tie primarily by Chinese psychological skill and American sentimental recollection of a China that no longer existed, if ever it had. Once China becomes strong enough to stand alone, it might discard us. A little later it might even turn against us, if its perception of its interests requires it. Before then, the Soviet Union might be driven into a genuine relaxation of tensions with us — if it has not first sought to break out of its isolation by a military assault on China. But whatever China's long-term policy, our medium-term interest was to cooperate, and to support its security against foreign pressures.

To understand the contribution of the China initiative to international stability, we merely need to ask ourselves what the world would have been like if Chinese pressures in Asia had been added to Soviet global adventurism during the Vietnam war and afterward. By restoring hope to the American people, it also gave us a chance to shape a new concept of international order even while emerging from a debilitating war and a wrenching decade at home. The ultimate significance of the opening to China thus resided less in the formal exchanges than in the tacit understandings that grew out of Nixon's visit. They provided the foundation for a common if informal strategy, by which different — even clashing — purposes produced an extraordinary parallelism in action. It was a triumph of the intangible in the conduct of foreign policy.

The press corps accompanying Nixon did not concern themselves with the long-range implications of the journey. Maddened by a week without briefings, driven around the bend by endless banquets and deadly toasts, perhaps convinced in their hearts that nothing good could possibly come of a Nixon initiative, satiated but unstimulated, they fell on the Shanghai Communiqué like tigers on raw meat thrown into their cage. The *Washington Post* of February 28 began its story:

> President Nixon has acceded to Chinese Communist demands by publicly pledging, for the first time, to withdraw all American forces and military installations from Taiwan. . . . The considerable concessions by the President appeared to have been made in return for a relatively minor Chinese agreement to "facilitate" bilateral scientific, technological, cultural, sports, journalistic and trade exchanges between the United States and China.

> Weighing the concessions made by the President, many observers here feel that the Chinese got the better of the bargain. . . . Chinese officials appeared pleased by the outcome of the discussion.

The section on hegemony and renunciation of force totally escaped the writer, as did the conditionality of our undertaking to withdraw from Taiwan.

One television commentator, noting that there was no written mention or affirmation of the American defense commitment to Taiwan, concluded that in the communiqué China had won "a giant step" and given away little. China's omission of its customary condemnation of our defense treaty with Taiwan could equally be cited as a *Chinese* concession, as indeed Ch'iao Kuan-hua argued to me, since it seemed to abandon a long-held Chinese position. In any case, the same commentator ignored that on Chinese soil I reiterated our defense commitment to Taiwan.

On February 28 in the *Detroit Free Press,* an equally profound observer was quoted: "They got Taiwan; we got egg rolls." *Newsday* headlined its stories: "Goodbye Waves; Waves of Shock" and "Consensus — US Paid High Toll for Diplomatic Bridge to China." The *Boston Globe* headlined: "Nixon Makes Concessions on Taiwan, Pledges Pullout." It quoted an Australian reporter as giving this expert assessment: "Chou battled all week" for the Taiwan section "and he got what he wanted." Likewise the *Philadelphia Bulletin:* "Nixon Flying Home; Yielded on Taiwan." That the deal was struck when the Chinese accepted *our* formulations would have seemed as implausible in the era of the credibility gap as it was true.

Eventually, the lurid headlines calmed down, particularly after Nixon's arrival statement in Washington reiterating that our commitments were unaffected. The *Christian Science Monitor* wrote wisely that "what President Nixon agreed to was what he was doing anyway." So long as the defense treaty remained in force, "nothing is changed." The *Washington Post* in an editorial of February 29 analyzed the Shanghai Communiqué intelligently and defended Nixon against accusations of "selling out" Taiwan — accusations fostered among others by its own correspondent. Negative stories were in any event overwhelmed by the visual impact of Nixon's visit to Peking, which nearly every American family had been able to witness on its television screen. For once a White House public relations strategy succeeded, and performed a diplomatic function as well. Pictures overrode the printed word; the public simply was not interested in the complex analyses of the document after having watched the spectacle of an American President welcomed in the capital of an erstwhile enemy.

And what followed left no doubt about the real priorities of both sides. For years the United States was the only country enjoying political relations with Peking that did not have to sever its diplomatic ties with Taipei. Again and again in the years following the Nixon visit, the Chinese leaders stressed to us Mao's precept that Taiwan was a subordinate problem; the major common issue was the maintenance of the international equilibrium. We enjoyed diplomatic ties in all but name; we had throughout a regular channel of intimate communication at the highest level and more frequent exchanges than had most of the Western governments which had recognized Peking many years earlier. After the formation of Liaison Offices in each other's capitals in 1973 (following the Vietnam settlement), the two countries even had de facto embassies to promote the broader economic, cultural, and people-to-people exchanges that characterize relations between friendly states. The only element lacking was the willingness of Chinese leaders actually to set foot in Washington while a rival embassy was present.

Major expansion of trade and exchanges, which some saw as goals we were disappointed in not obtaining, were of secondary importance to both sides. On the Chinese side, the reluctance mostly came from Mao's ideological and Middle-Kingdom faith in self-reliance, not from the absence of diplomatic relations; no other country did much better than we did in this regard as long as Mao was alive. In 1977 and especially 1978, a new Chinese leadership moved out aggressively to expand economic and educational exchange with the West; the United States was a major participant and suffered little penalty because of the absence of formal diplomatic relations before January 1, 1979.

But this evolution being then unknown, there was an odd sense of ambivalence on the plane back from Peking. Nixon understood international affairs too well not to grasp that he had sealed a genuine diplomatic triumph. But he was also sufficiently political to recognize the danger he might face from his old conservative supporters if the first press accounts determined the national mood. Pat Buchanan, a speechwriter who considered himself Nixon's conservative conscience, was morose. In the best tradition of Presidential entourages he blamed pernicious advisers (meaning me) for the President's departure from grace. (Ray Price, the liberal conscience, often had the same tendency and the same target.) Nixon stewed in his cabin, not knowing what he would find on his return. It was unnecessary. The pictures of a President working for peace moved a country that was exhausted by years of turmoil over an inconclusive war. Nixon received a triumphal welcome at Andrews Air Force Base from a bipartisan group of Senators and Congressmen headed by the Vice President. Nixon used the occasion to remind listeners of his achievements but also to make clear that we had not given up "any United States commitment to any other country."

Within five minutes of reaching my office at ten o'clock in the evening I called two leading conservatives, Governor Ronald Reagan and Senator Barry Goldwater. Both promised their support if the President did not deviate from the commitment to Taiwan expressed by me in Shanghai and by the President at Andrews Air Force Base. Reagan joked that the China visit had been a great television "pilot" and ought to be made into a series.

The next day Nixon met with the bipartisan leadership of both Houses of Congress and received strong support. Euphoric, he even thought he might settle all his problems in one fell swoop. As the meeting broke up he stopped Senator Fulbright and urged him to end his public criticism of Vietnam because it was a very delicate issue and the "string could break" if there were a continuing hassle over it. Nixon pointed his finger at the startled Fulbright and said, "OK, Bill, agreed?" The distinguished Senator stood there in some disbelief, nodding (or maybe shaking) his head — the chronicler, Tom Korologos of the Congressional Liaison staff, is not precise on this point.

I briefed the press in greater detail than was possible in Shanghai and also met informally with the Senate Foreign Relations Committee. The machinery that accompanies great events moved into action. Ambassadors had to be informed. The most painful was my meeting with Ambassador James Shen from Taiwan; we had not in fact made any commitments undercutting Taiwan's security, but the entire process was bound to be inimical to its status. The most thorough, inquisitive caller proved to be the Ambassador from Japan, who having earlier missed my secret trip to Peking was not about to fail to unearth some new great secret if it could be accomplished through persistence.

The trip was increasingly perceived as a great success. As the American public gained hope from the China visit, Vietnam became less an obsession and more a challenge to be mastered. The Administration that had revolutionized international relations could not so easily be accused of neglecting the deepest concern of the American people.

Once more, though, we encountered the curious phenomenon that success seemed to unsettle Nixon more than failure. He seemed obsessed by the fear that he was not receiving adequate credit. He constantly badgered his associates to press a public relations campaign that would call more attention to the China visit. He followed the press carefully, so that any criticism could be immediately countered. He read some commentator's criticism that the Chinese statements of their position in the Shanghai Communiqué were more aggressive than the statements of our position. On March 9, therefore, he sent me a memorandum asking me to make clear to the press the deep thought and analysis that lay behind this "decision" to state our position moderately. His preference for this approach dated back, he said, to a speech he gave in the Soviet Union in 1959, which he urged me to read in his book *Six Crises*. Though Chou En-lai had originally proposed the idea of separate and conflictinging statements, though Chou and I had drafted almost all of that part of the text in October 1971 without reference to Washington, and though Nixon had learned of both the approach and the content only after I returned, he wanted me to explain to the press — and I believe had convinced himself — that he had conceived it:

You could begin by pointing out that I made the decision with regard to the tone of the statement of our position for two basic reasons. First, the more aggressive we stated our position the more aggressive the Chinese would have to be in stating their position. As a result of our presenting our position in a very firm, but non-belligerent manner, their position, while it was also uncompromising on principle, was not nearly as rough in its rhetoric as has been the case in previous statements they have issued over the years. . . .

I was determined that in this document, which would be the first time Chinese leaders, and cadres, and to a certain extent even Chinese masses, would ever hear the American position expressed, I had to make the strongest possible effort to set it in a tone which would not make it totally incredible when they heard it. It would not have been credible, of course, had we set forth our position in more aggressive terms because 22 years of propaganda at the other extreme would have made it impossible for the reader of the communiqué, or those who heard it read on radio, to believe it at all if the tone was too harsh.

Nixon, of course, deserves full credit for the Shanghai Communiqué. A President is always responsible for the policy, no matter who does the technical labors. A less courageous President could have pulled back from the separate statements, when I presented them to him upon my return in October, in favor of a more orthodox presentation. This trivial incident does not derogate from Nixon's boldness in his historic opening to China. What it illustrates, however, is the tendency for illusion to become reality, a brooding and involuted streak that, together with starker character traits, at first flawed, and later destroyed, a Presidency so rich in foreign policy achievements.

What Nixon hinted, Haldeman made explicit. On March 14 Haldeman sent me a memorandum whose thrust was that my briefings devoted too much time to substance; I would serve the President better by stressing to the press and above all on television the great personal qualities that made the achievements possible. Helpfully, Haldeman recited a catalogue of some ten of them. Since Haldeman never sat in on the negotiations, he could only have gotten all this information from one source. For anyone familiar with Oval Office procedure, the memorandum evoked a familiar scene: Haldeman, equipped with the yellow pad that every White House staffer (including me) carried with him as if part of our uniform, jotting down the musings of the chief. Some of Haldeman's descriptions were on the mark; others were bizarre; the whole concept was irrelevant. Leaders do best by emphasizing performance; surely this is all that history cares about. The conviction that Nixon's standing depended less on his actions than on their presentation was a bane of his Administration. It conveyed a lack of assurance even during his greatest accomplishments. It imparted a frenetic quality to the search for support, an endless quest that proved to be unfulfillable. It made it impossible for him ever to trust the momentum of events. It caused him to seek to embellish his most incontestable achievements, or to look for insurance in the face of even the most overwhelming probability of success. It was the psychological essence of the Watergate debacle.

In 1972 I read these memoranda with amusement tinged with exasperation, for I was still too close to events. Today I find them not without pathos — of a lonely man in his hour of high achievement reassuring himself with a catalogue of accomplishments and laudatory adjectives when the deed spoke for itself. Nixon had triumphed in the most important purpose of the visit. Leaders of two powerful nations had taken the measure of each other and judged that they could conduct compatible foreign policies, revolutionizing world diplomacy.

The bipolarity of the postwar period was over. There would be greater demands on America's creativity, endurance, and sophistication — but also new opportunities. At the end of the process stood what we had longed and suffered for during four tumultuous years: an honorable negotiated peace in Vietnam.

XXV

Hanoi Throws the Dice:
The Vietnam Spring Offensive

Invasion

FOUR weeks after our return from China, the long-awaited offensive in Vietnam finally broke over us. On March 30 North Vietnamese artillery and infantry units launched coordinated attacks against South Vietnamese bases in northeast Quang Tri province. In total disregard of the understandings associated with the bombing halt four years earlier, three North Vietnamese divisions poured across the Demilitarized Zone (DMZ), supported by more than two hundred tanks and large numbers of new 130mm recoilless artillery, all furnished by the Soviet Union. Fresh units were poised to invade the northern part of South Vietnam from Laos along Route 9, reversing the direction of the South Vietnamese thrust into Laos the previous year, and to attack through the Ashau Valley toward Hué. There were ominous troop concentrations in the Central Highlands threatening the cities of Kontum and Pleiku. Three North Vietnamese divisions from Cambodia were moving into Military Region 3, which included Saigon. An enemy offensive was expected there at any moment. The pretense that the Vietnam conflict was a "people's war," a guerrilla uprising in the South, was over; this was an invasion by the North Vietnamese regular army in division strength.

In Washington, as is usual at the onset of great events, it was hard to find out exactly what was taking place. As early as March 31 (Good Friday) Secretary Laird reported that the enemy offensive was a major one. But accounts from the Pentagon were initially soothing. General Abrams, we were told, did not consider that the attack had yet reached a critical stage; South Vietnamese fire-support bases seemed to be holding. There was no need for decisions at the highest level. For two days the attacks were treated as only a major enemy probe, partly because the battle seemed to be going well; perhaps also because civilian officials were afraid that Nixon might be tempted to implement his oft-repeated threat of an all-out response if this was *the* long-awaited Communist offensive.

On April 1, Nixon authorized American air attacks against military concentrations in North Vietnam, limited to within twenty-five miles north of the DMZ. But we encountered one of the perennial frustrations of the Vietnam war: bad weather preventing air operations. Since the ceiling was constantly below 2,500 feet, very few missions could be flown into the North. I called Admiral Moorer several times a day to ask if we were yet in the air; his answer for the first forty-eight hours was negative. Poor Moorer, who was not to blame, endured my badgering and sarcasm. It seemed to me that our entire Air Force consisted of delicate machines capable of flying only in a war in the desert in July. I suggested that if they could not fly maybe they could taxi north for twenty-five miles.*

On April 2 the South Vietnamese were forced to evacuate fourteen bases just south of the DMZ. There was no longer any doubt that the enemy offensive was under way. The next two months would be a decisive test of Vietnamization. We would now see whether the effort and agony of the past three years had been productive or would vanish like a wisp of smoke in a breeze.

I was convinced that, whatever the outcome of the offensive, it would end the war. This was Hanoi's last throw of the dice. One way or another, there would now be serious negotiations; their substance would depend upon which side prevailed on the battlefield. If South Vietnam collapsed, the war would have ended in a debacle. If Saigon, with our help, held back the entire North Vietnamese army, Hanoi would have no choice but to come to terms.

There were larger stakes. If we collapsed in Vietnam, the patient design of our foreign policy would be in jeopardy. The Moscow summit would take place — if at all — against the background of two successful assaults on American interests made possible by Soviet weaponry (first India-Pakistan, and now Indochina). Our negotiating position in the eyes of the cold calculators of power in the Kremlin would be pathetically weak. China might reconsider the value of American ties. Allies, whatever they thought of the merits of our Vietnam policy, would question our judgment and our mastery of events. In other parts of the world, those who believed in the arbitrament of arms would be emboldened; this might unhinge the Middle East. The grave consequences that we thought would flow from a political surrender would be aggravated by a military collapse. We were determined to prevent this

---

*The high rate of cancellation of air sorties became nearly an obsession of mine. A memorandum by Laird on August 19, submitted at my request, gave the glum statistics. Between May 8 and August 12, 1972, 53 percent of all scheduled strikes against primary targets in North Vietnam were canceled, 42 percent because of weather.

disaster; we would blunt the offensive and conclude the war on honorable terms. The last, but perhaps most painful, ordeal of the Vietnam war was upon us.

The Buildup

THE enemy offensive of 1972 had long been anticipated. The North Vietnamese had demonstrated in 1968 that they understood the impact of a major blow in a Presidential election year. Now its onslaught coincided with the critical moment in the process of Vietnamization when our own forces had been reduced to a residual level, tempting Hanoi to determine whether in fact the South Vietnamese could take over their own defense. The principal purpose of our Cambodian incursion of 1970 and Laotian dry-season offensive of 1971 had been to disrupt Hanoi's timetable for the contingency we were now facing. Since offensives were technically feasible only in the dry season from December to July, our blows had forced Hanoi to spend precious time each year rebuilding supply lines and replenishing stocks. Every month gained would, we hoped, bring a strengthening of South Vietnam's capacity to resist; every weakening of Hanoi's power would reduce the effectiveness of the attack when it came. And indeed the North Vietnamese offensive came two months after we expected it and never gained a coordinated momentum.

Throughout the second half of 1971 Hanoi's public statements had turned ominous. On September 20, 1971, Dick Helms, briefing an NSC meeting, reported considerable enemy reinforcements and great potential for offensive action just across the DMZ. At about that time it was becoming apparent that Hanoi's interest in secret negotiations with us had obviously flagged; the conversations about the seven points and the nine points were broken off by Le Duc Tho. Our new proposal presented to Hanoi by General Walters in October 1971 had received no reply; a meeting with Le Duc Tho scheduled for November 20 was canceled on three days' notice, allegedly because of illness; our offer to meet on another mutually convenient date was ignored.

Starting on January 4, 1972, General Abrams warned of an imminent offensive. In a dispatch of January 20, he predicted that the enemy would attempt "to face us with the most difficult situation of which he is capable." Abrams predicted an offensive for as early as the first part of February, just before Nixon's trip to Peking. He requested authority to disrupt the enemy's preparations by air attacks north of the DMZ. He concluded with a reminder that this would be the decisive battle and that he as field commander needed the maximum flexibility in advance. "In the final analysis," Abrams added perceptively, "when this is all over, [the] specific targets hit in the southern part of North Vietnam will not be a major issue. The issue will be whether Vietnamization has been a success or a failure."

I convened a meeting of the Senior Review Group on January 24 to consider General Abrams's requests. No one was eager to renew attacks on the North. The White House thought it would interfere with the trip to Peking; the State Department feared it would ruin the prospects of negotiation; Defense was loath to assume new budgetary burdens. Everybody dreaded the public outcry sure to be unleashed by our resuming the bombing of the North, even in a limited area. Some took refuge in minimizing the threat we faced, a not infrequent device to evade the need for decision. The consensus of the group was that the assault would come in the Central Highlands; there was disagreement over General Abrams's concern with the enemy's concentrations just above the DMZ. On January 26 Mel Laird found a classic compromise. He recommended that the President let Abrams have part of his cake but not the bombing of the North. He approved instead stepped-up air activity in the South and the placing of more sensors in the DMZ. Of course, the sensors would tell us whether an attack was taking place; they did not prevent it or increase our capability to resist it. I went along with Laird's refusal to authorize new attacks on the North for two reasons: It seemed unwise in the two weeks before Nixon's visit to China; and I thought that bombing made sense only if it were sustained, which it could not be except in reaction to an overwhelming provocation. We had to lean over backward to neutralize those ready to blame their own government for every crisis. I therefore favored delaying giving authority for resumed bombing until we could judge any offensive's dimensions.

I favored using the period of waiting, however, to strengthen ourselves to the maximum extent possible. I pressed Laird to change the composition of our withdrawals so that we retained as many helicopters as possible for mobility. I also recommended beefing up our B-52s, our all-weather aircraft, and our aircraft carriers. To accomplish these objectives Nixon called an NSC meeting on February 2 to which he invited Treasury Secretary John Connally, as he did in all cases where opposition to a strong course was likely and support was needed. The President's line reflected the talking points I had prepared (I cannot find a record of the meeting):

I will not accept any failure which can be attributed to a lack of available US support or shortcomings in our own leadership or decisiveness. We must do all we can to assist the South Vietnamese and to ensure that they have both the means and the will to meet Hanoi's challenge this year.

In the final analysis we cannot expect the enemy to negotiate seriously with us until he is convinced nothing can be gained by continuing the war. This will require an all out effort on our part during the coming dry season. I can think of no more crucial period in this painful conflict and I expect each of you to bring promptly to my attention any proposal you might have for additional steps which might be taken to guarantee success.

Nixon made decisions at NSC meetings only in the rarest of cases. He wanted to avoid pressure while he was in the room. He did not like the implication that the NSC had any role other than advisory. Therefore he waited until the afternoon to order the reinforcements: another carrier, more B-52s, and additional all-weather planes.

Meanwhile, we were confronted with the contradictory necessities of our domestic situation. These undercut at least part of our readiness measures. On January 13, even while North Vietnamese forces were massing, we thought it necessary to announce a withdrawal of another 70,000 American troops by May 1. In less than three years we had withdrawn 480,500 of the 545,000 troops that we had found in Vietnam when we entered office. We had done so while improving the military situation and extending the area controlled by the government in South Vietnam. But the appetite for withdrawals was insatiable; retreat had become an end in itself. And so by early March, with a decisive offensive clearly approaching, we found ourselves in the anomalous position of augmenting with forces that did not count against the troop ceiling — B-52s, aircraft carriers — while continuing the promised withdrawals of ground troops and planning the announcement of the next round of withdrawals, which would be expected about May 1. Neither Nixon nor I thought we could risk the most sensible decision, which would have been to halt withdrawals when a major offensive was imminent.

March thus turned into a period of waiting and of decisions that reflected the national schizophrenia: Withdrawals were combined with reinforcements; threats of retaliation alternated with fleeting moments of hope that maybe for once Hanoi was bluffing. We were neither anxious nor confident, but rather resigned to events. General Abrams, expecting simultaneous attacks across the DMZ and in the Central Highlands, now began to contemplate the further possibility of a third concurrent enemy thrust from across the Cambodian border facing Military Region 3. On March 10 I told Nixon to expect an attack within ten days on three fronts in South Vietnam. I urged him to stay his hand against the North itself until any fair-minded person could see that it was not we who had sought a test of arms; then we should hit in great force. In the meantime the recently arrived air reinforcements should be used to interrupt the enemy buildup in South Vietnam, Laos, and Cambodia and inhibit the launching of the offensive for as long as possible. Nixon suggested what he considered a "Churchillian strategy": to stand down all our aircraft in Southeast Asia for a few days and then use them all at once in one massive blow. I saw neither harm nor great sense in it. Laird agreed to do it. For two days all planes stood down and on the third they all flew. I do not know whether it made any difference; it surely must have driven Hanoi's intelligence analysts crazy trying to figure out what we were up to. Whatever the reason, whether because of the air attacks or our offensives of the previous two dry seasons, the date for the offensive was constantly slipping. Our intelligence was growing daily, however, that it would be upon us in full force before too many weeks had passed.

Diplomatic Maneuvers

As the North Vietnamese military preparations threatened three fronts in Vietnam, so we were active on three diplomatic fronts — with Hanoi, Moscow, and Peking. We continued the strategy surfaced by Nixon in his January 25 speech, when he revealed our secret negotiations with Hanoi, to bring home to the American people that their government had explored every avenue toward peace and to make clear to Hanoi that the negotiating option was still open. As I told a White House press conference on January 26, the day after the President's speech:

> Now the question is: Is there to be another round of warfare? We believe that we can contain the offensive, and it is even possible, maybe even probable, that the reason they make the offensive is as a prelude to a subsequent negotiation. This at least has been their pattern in 1954 and was their pattern in 1968. So this is an attempt to say to them once again, "It is not necessary. Let's get the war over with now."

Later that day I made the same point privately to another journalist. I told him that the North Vietnamese would probably "shoot their wad" militarily later in the year and, if the effort failed, would negotiate on the basis of something like our current proposal.

Nixon and I both sought to end the war as rapidly as possible. But there was a nuance of difference between us over the strategy for doing so. My aim was to weave a complex web that would give us the greatest number of options. Though favoring a strong military reaction, I never wanted to rely on power alone or, for that matter, on negotiation by itself. In my view diplomacy and strategy should support each other. I always favored preceding or at least accompanying a military move with a diplomatic one, even when I rated the chances of success as low. If it were accepted, we would achieve the goal of our diplomacy. If rejected, a conciliatory offer would help sustain our military effort with our public. By preempting critics' charges that we had somehow missed opportunities, we would enhance our endurance in holding out for honorable terms — which was the name of the game in Vietnam. To be sure, our exchanges with the North Vietnamese were secret. But I always conducted them with their ultimate public impact in mind. If pressed too far, we had the option to disclose them as we had done in Nixon's speeches of November 3, 1969, and January 25, 1972.

Nixon was in general wary of negotiations. He was less interested in increasing our options than he was in the public impact of failure. He was afraid that Hanoi — as well as his conservative constituency — might confuse negotiations with weakness. I agreed with him that Hanoi was seeking to use negotiations to undermine our domestic support. I did not think we could counteract this strategy by refusing to negotiate. This would only put us in the position of being the intransigent party and mobilize against us the same pressures that had brought down Lyndon Johnson and split our country. I was confident that if we accepted Hanoi's diplomatic challenge we could turn it to our advantage by elaborating our definition of an honorable peace; at the very least we would defuse the argument that we were not doing enough to end the war.

Therefore I always advised Nixon to keep some offer before Hanoi — even if only an offer to meet. This would enable us to deal with the periodic new Communist proposals (the eight points, the seven points, the two-point elaboration, and so on) from a stance of having an alternative program. It gave us an opportunity to test whether Hanoi was willing to settle and a program in the name of which to resist if honorable terms remained unavailable. On the few occasions when we gave up this posture — by canceling plenary meetings or refusing to send an ambassador to the peace talks, for example — we soon found ourselves buffeted by the North Vietnamese and our media and Congressional critics in a public debate over procedural issues. I therefore urged that we couple Nixon's January 25 speech with a private message to Hanoi suggesting the resumption of private meetings. Nixon reluctantly went along. The message was sent on January 26.

At the same time, we communicated with Moscow and Peking. Nixon sent a letter to Brezhnev; a note was delivered by General Walters to Huang Chen, the Chinese Ambassador in Paris, who was still functioning as our principal contact. Both communications made essentially the same point: We had gone to the limit of what we could honorably offer. We would react strongly if Hanoi responded with a military offensive.

Both Peking and Moscow were becoming restless. Neither wanted to be perceived as derelict in its duty to its North Vietnamese ally, lest it lose support in the rivalry within the Communist world. Neither was eager to pull our chestnuts out of the fire. Yet both feared that Hanoi in its intractability might thwart major designs with us that had matured over a period of years. And they feared that our military reaction would sharpen their dilemma. By threatening serious reprisals if Hanoi challenged us, we did our best to feed the nervousness of Moscow and Peking.

Peking's reply — in the private channel used whenever China (or Moscow, for that matter) sought to avoid a public row — disclaimed all knowledge of the Vietnam negotiations; it asserted no national or ideological interest, only its moral obligation toward a beleaguered people to which it owed an historical debt. China had never asked the United States to make any commitments over Vietnam, the note stated significantly; nor had China made any, which was true. China rejected any effort to "enmesh" it in Indochina. It seemed to us that Peking was in effect washing its hands of the whole affair. Since its material support for Hanoi was marginal because of its limited resources, a posture of indifference did not conflict with our purposes. And we did not press China further.

Moscow was more assertive, though its basic thrust was the same. It was not secure enough to admit ignorance of the negotiations; on the contrary, the Soviets flaunted their familiarity with the negotiating record. In general, Moscow supported Hanoi's position but without fervor. On February 7 Dobrynin, in conveying Brezhnev's reply to Nixon's message, took care to point out that the arguments made against our latest proposal were not put forward in Moscow's name; they were all ascribed to the North Vietnamese. Moscow could not stick to this complex position forever. But the Soviet Union procrastinated for an uncommonly long period — well over a week — before finally endorsing Hanoi's negotiating position. Even that endorsement was elicited only after the North Vietnamese Ambassador had called on Premier Kosygin. That meeting was described by *Pravda* as having taken place at the Ambassador's request — which indicated a Soviet effort to dissociate from its client. And their talk took place in a spirit of "friendship and comradely frankness," which in Communist parlance generally means some disagreement. The TASS commentary was noticeably cool.

But we could not let Moscow disengage as easily as the Chinese. Almost all of the weapons being assembled for Hanoi's assault were Soviet. If Moscow did not encourage Hanoi's military effort (as it constantly claimed), it surely made it possible. We had long since decided, therefore, to turn on Moscow if an offensive developed. I warned Dobrynin repeatedly that the Moscow summit would be jeopardized if Hanoi sought to force a military decision. To give Moscow an additional incentive to press its ally I accepted early in the year the Kremlin's repeated invitation to go to Moscow to help prepare the summit with the Soviet leadership. However, I made my visit conditional on some move by Moscow to end the war, preferably a North Vietnamese negotiator in Moscow empowered to settle.

There matters rested with the Soviet Union while Nixon visited China. After returning, we received low-key protests from Peking and Moscow about alleged American bombing attacks against North Vietnamese. Apparently Hanoi was giving its allies the same misinformation it used to influence our public opinion and as a pretext to delay negotiations. There was in fact no basis for the charge, because we had deliberately held our fire against North Vietnam during the President's visit to Peking, despite the increasingly ominous North Vietnamese buildup in January and February. And we restrained our air operations in March to avoid the perennial debate as to whether we had "provoked" the Communist assault. Hanoi had obviously put up its "fraternal" Communist allies to their démarches; they could not refuse to make them, but they showed their discomfort by simply going through the motions.

While all the major powers — the United States, China, and the Soviet Union — were painting on a canvas larger than Indochina, there was one group of men with only one concern and a monomaniacal passion: the Politburo in Hanoi. Not used to being on the defensive, they responded to the President's January 25 speech by announcing on February 2 their "two-point elaboration" of the seven points they had put forward the previous July. But these points were so obscure and empty that they were not embraced even by the most ardent of Hanoi's supporters in the West. On February 14 we received a reply to our note of January 26, which had proposed another meeting with Le Duc Tho. To our astonishment Hanoi accepted. It broke with precedent by proposing a date for any time convenient to us after March 15.

We should have been alerted by the excessively conciliatory tone, so out of keeping with past North Vietnamese practice and so inconsistent with the frantic military preparations going on above the Demilitarized Zone. Never before had Hanoi proposed a date so far ahead. (Thieu, being Vietnamese, spotted this last feature immediately when we informed him, as we always did.) Never had it left the date to our convenience. Had we reflected, we might have concluded that Hanoi was gearing the resumption of negotiations to the timing of its forthcoming offensive. It wanted to have talks take place under conditions of maximum pressure and discomfiture for us. But even if we had come to that conclusion, we would not have changed course. Delaying a counterblow against North Vietnam until *after* the offensive had started would still put us into the best political and psychological position to overcome the approaching onslaught and to sustain our retaliation publicly.

On February 16, the eve of our departure for China, we responded to Hanoi by proposing March 20 for the meeting with Le Duc Tho. We warned that "the attempt to place one side under military duress by escalating the level of military activity is inconsistent with the purpose of these meetings." On February 29 (after we had left China), Vo Van Sung, Hanoi's delegate in Paris, summoned General Walters to inform him that Hanoi was "of course agreeable to a meeting on the 20th of March at 11:30," as the United States had proposed. That genteel formulation, too, was unusual. It was far from a matter of course that Hanoi would accept a date we proposed this far ahead; it was downright unprecedented. Again, we paid the nuance no special heed.

A few days later Hanoi made an about-face. On March 6 it informed us that March 20 was no longer suitable; it wanted to postpone the meeting to April 15. The pretext was weak, even fishy: that the United States had engaged in extensive aerial attacks just before and just after the President's trip to Peking. Not only was the charge untrue, it was absurd, for Hanoi had accepted the March 20 date two weeks *after* some of the fictitious air attacks were alleged to have taken place. As for attacks *after* Hanoi had replied, they would have been totally inconsistent with our strategy. We were staying well clear of the North precisely to avoid this sort of accusation.

By now it had become evident to us that it was the forthcoming offensive which controlled the timing of North Vietnamese diplomacy. They would launch the assault that they were so frenetically preparing and then use my meeting with Le Duc Tho to inhibit our military response; they thought we would hesitate to attack while a "negotiation" was going on. But this time the maneuver was too crude; Hanoi had overplayed its hand. The better our public record for having sought a negotiated alternative, the better our position to respond violently to an offensive — as we were determined to do. Our record of having sought negotiations would now be impeccable when we made it public. No fair-minded person could be under any illusion about Hanoi's cynicism.

So we reacted only verbally. On March 13 we returned a very sharp note going over the record of our exchanges. We "utterly rejected" Hanoi's charges: "A careful rechecking of the facts makes clear that the allegations of U.S. aerial attacks in the period March 1 to March 6 is totally unfounded." In diplomatic language we were calling the leaders in Hanoi liars. We declined the offer to meet on April 15 (I had tentatively planned a visit to Japan for that date) and suggested April 24. We used the occasion to repeat our warning against escalation of military activity.

All this time the plenary sessions in Paris were proceeding across the round table at Avenue Kléber. Starting them had rent our country in 1968. But they already had achieved a great distinction in the annals of diplomacy. In four years of negotiation and more than 140 meetings not even the most minor issue had been settled; it was the only regular conference of such length that could not point to a single accomplishment, however trivial. (Nor was this record ever to be broken; the settlement was achieved in a different forum; the conference's only role in the peacemaking process was the final signing ceremony on the accords after 174 fruitless meetings.) Each week the plenipotentiaries assembled in the Hotel Majestic. Each ambassador read a set speech and made one rebuttal; then they adjourned. Afterward each briefed the press separately about his (or her) eloquent presentation. For Xuan Thuy and Madame Nguyen Thi Binh, the press conferences were clearly more important than the meetings themselves.

Three distinguished ambassadors had represented the American side during this charade: Henry Cabot Lodge, David Bruce, and now William Porter. Not enough can be said for the dedication and ability with which they acquitted themselves. Each was backed up by one of the most extraordinary Foreign Service Officers I know: Phil Habib, an energetic and indomitable deputy, who held our delegation together and buttressed his superiors until he was appointed Ambassador to Korea in 1971. To endure weekly harangues without any hope for a breakthrough, which they knew must come in the private channel, required unusual reserves of patience, devotion, and self-discipline. They were all now briefed fully about my meetings with Le Duc Tho, and I often sought their advice. (I had even invited David Bruce to sit in, but since his South Vietnamese colleague would not be attending, Bruce thought it best to be informed rather than to participate. William Porter finally sat in on the last stage of the negotiations in 1972.)

Nixon had never liked the plenary sessions at Avenue Kléber. He associated them with the bombing halt, which he thought had nearly cost him the election in 1968. He considered that they gave the North Vietnamese a weekly forum on television to undermine our domestic support. And he constantly sought ways to diminish their importance. In 1969 he had refused to name a replacement for the retired Lodge for seven months. Now he seized the occasion again.

When Hanoi did not respond to our March 31 note for a week, Nixon suspended the Paris sessions. In his March 24 news conference he said that we were trying to "break a filibuster"; the enemy was using the Paris forum for propaganda and on this basis "there was no hope whatever."

I was not much in favor of this move. In my view, it would have been better to reserve a break-off in Paris as retaliation for the offensive. The North Vietnamese were bound to attack it as further evidence of our intransigence. They would start a propaganda campaign to get us back to the conference table. American critics would pick up the theme. Sooner or later we would yield; what had started as a pressure tactic would thus be seen in the end as a diplomatic retreat. And this is exactly what happened. Hanoi was not about to give up its propaganda forum; it saw in the Paris conference the legal underpinning of the bombing halt. Just as in 1969 they had reacted to our refusal to replace Lodge by making progress conditional on our appointing a senior representative, so now they did their utmost to resurrect the Paris conference. On March 27, with its offensive preparations nearly complete, Hanoi accepted our date of April 24 for a private meeting — on condition that the public talks were resumed before then.

I suggested to Nixon that we go along. We would be at a propaganda disadvantage if the secret meetings failed simply because we refused to attend plenary sessions whose subject matter was after all largely in our control. Since plenary sessions were always scheduled a week in advance, I suggested that Ambassador Porter propose a new plenary session for April 13. If the secret meeting on April 24 proved sterile, we could then interrupt the plenary sessions again. By then we would know more about how the offensive was going. Nixon agreed.

On April 1, when we were as yet uncertain whether the attack across the DMZ was a major offensive or a probe, we returned our reply to the North Vietnamese proposals. Our purpose, as I informed Bunker, was to "write an impeccable record of reasonableness" and to give Hanoi a last warning that we were reaching the limits of our restraint. We told Hanoi that Porter would propose a plenary session for April 13 and on this basis we were planning for a secret meeting on April 24. The message concluded with another grave warning:

> The U.S. side points out that the military operations launched by the North Vietnamese in recent days near the Demilitarized Zone and elsewhere and the firing of missiles from North Vietnamese territory into South Vietnamese airspace are inconsistent with the purpose of these meetings. The U.S. side has been showing great restraint in its response in order to give negotiations every chance to succeed but it cannot remain indifferent if the step-up of military operations continues.

The diplomatic minuet was about to be overwhelmed by the fury of the battle. On April 2, the day our message was delivered to the North Vietnamese, the full extent of the offensive became clear, including its blatant violation of the 1968 understandings to respect the Demilitarized Zone. But this time we had prepared our ground with good effect. Having tried our utmost to head off a test of arms, we were in a strong psychological position to resist; and militarily we were determined to prevail.

What Strategy?

ONCE the scale of the offensive became apparent, several schools of thought developed within our government. An important group of officials thought that we should let events take their course, continuing our present level of assistance but not augmenting it for the crisis. This view — held by the civilian officials in Defense, much of the State

Department, and the systems analysis experts on my staff — rested on the proposition that the conclusive test of Vietnamization was at hand. Therefore, we should strengthen South Vietnam's capacity to defend itself; we should not increase our own effort. "We all recognize," said a summary memorandum submitted to me by my staff, "that the key is not what we do but what the South Vietnamese do."

But neither Nixon nor I recognized any such thing. North Vietnam had brutally and cynically chosen a test of arms. It had played with us for months, using negotiations as a smokescreen for a massive invasion. For three years it had rejected all efforts to negotiate seriously. On March 20, ten days before the offensive, North Vietnamese Premier Pham Van Dong made an egregious public speech rejecting the very concept of compromise: "Now, as in the past, the U.S. aggressors are indulging in this contention: 'Each side must go half way in negotiation, the Seven Points must be conciliated with the Eight Points, and so on.' This is the logic of a gangster." Peace could come only if the United States ceased "all its support and commitments to the Nguyen Van Thieu puppet régime." Now, as before, we were given only one way out of the war — to dismantle our ally and withdraw unconditionally. We had rejected surrender at the conference table; we would refuse it on the battlefield.

Starting on April 2, Nixon and I reviewed the situation several times a day. The Washington Special Actions Group met virtually every day. On April 3 I told the President that the attack would now precipitate matters; we would get no awards for losing with moderation. If we defeated the offensive, we would get a settlement out of it. The North Vietnamese had thrown everything into their effort; if it failed, they would have no choice except to negotiate. If they waited until after the election, they might have to face a President whose unpredictable reactions they had come to fear and who was freed from any electoral pressures during his final term.

Nixon needed no reminders. He had warned for years that he would react strongly to a North Vietnamese offensive. And he was as good as his word. Against intense bureaucratic opposition, he ordered repeated augmentations of our air and naval forces in Southeast Asia. He took off all budgetary restraints on air sorties. He directed naval attacks extended twenty-five miles up the coast of North Vietnam. On April 4 he authorized tactical air strikes up to the eighteenth parallel in North Vietnam (see the map on page 1110). Twenty additional B-52s, four more squadrons of F-4 fighter-bombers, and eight more destroyers were sent to Southeast Asia. On April 4 I told the WSAG that the President was determined to defeat the offensive. If we were run out of Vietnam under these conditions, our entire foreign policy would be in jeopardy. Hanoi had committed so many resources to the effort that once stopped, it

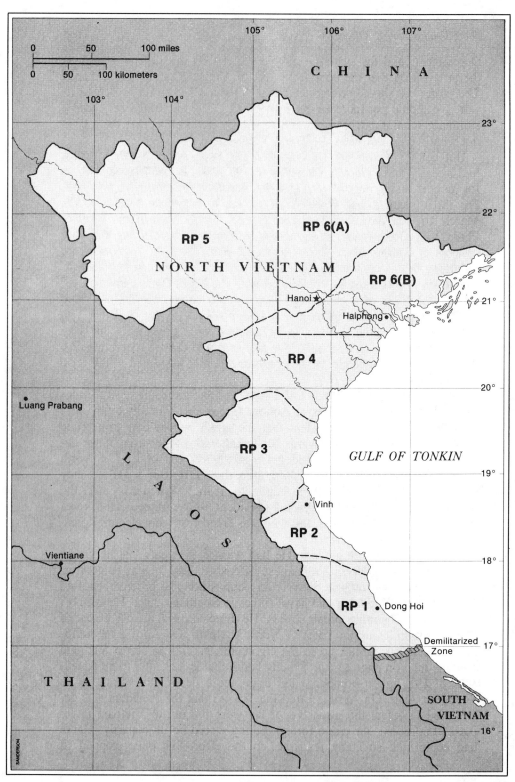

North Vietnam: Route Packages 1972

would almost certainly be obliged to settle. I asked every agency to give absolute priority to defeating the offensive.

But it proved difficult to translate this determination to the battlefield. One reason was the foul weather, which, to our frustration, grounded most of our planes during the first week. More fundamental was the frame of mind that had developed among our military leaders during a decade of restraints and three years of withdrawal. ''Our impression,'' I told the WSAG on April 5, ''is that our commanders have had it drilled into their heads that we want a minimum of activity and that they will receive rewards for getting out fast. They are not aggressive enough.''

Even after the message had gotten across, serious differences developed between the field commander (backed by Laird) and the White House. For four years General Abrams had performed, with dignity, one of the most thankless jobs ever assigned to an American general. He took over a force of 540,000 men in 1968 but was immediately shackled by mounting restrictions. He was continually given assignments that made no military sense. Starting in the middle of 1969, he was asked to dismantle his command at an ever-accelerating rate while maintaining the security of South Vietnam and putting the South Vietnamese forces into a position from which they could undertake their own defense. He succeeded to a remarkable degree. By the time Hanoi struck in 1972, more of the countryside than ever before was under Saigon's control; most of the South Vietnamese units had vastly improved. Still, deep down, General Abrams knew that he was engaged in a holding action in a battle for which even a small strategic reserve of American ground forces would almost surely have been decisive. For three years his command had been turned into a withdrawal headquarters. Now he was urged to win the crucial final battle.

It is intended as no derogation of a superb military leader to say that General Abrams could not adjust rapidly to this new situation. I had met him for the first time in 1961 during my short tenure as White House consultant when, as the commander of the armored division responsible for Berlin contingency planning, he had given me a brilliant briefing. He had then exuded daring and imagination. But four years of frustration in Saigon had taken their toll. Torn between his convictions and his obedience to civilian authority, he increasingly took refuge in routine. His refusal to change normal operating procedures even for the Laos operation contributed to its failure to achieve decisive results. (The basic fault, however, was to attempt decisive results with insufficient forces, for which all senior officials, including myself, must bear the responsibility.) And in 1972 he saw the North Vietnamese offensive in strictly local terms. For three years Washington had been hurrying him out of Vietnam; now it suddenly urged him to prevail with his shrunken assets. His responses were testy, occasionally pedantic, disquisitions on the prerogatives of the field commander. This finally drove me at one point to tell Moorer in exasperation that the Commander-in-Chief had some prerogatives as well.

One of the obstacles that prevented Abrams from raising his sights was the bizarre way the air campaign had been organized throughout the war. It told more about the Pentagon bureaucracy than about military realities; indeed, it showed that Washington's organizational requirements overrode strategy. For purposes of air operations North Vietnam was sliced into many segments — called Route Packages — with different military commanders having jurisdiction over particular target areas. (See the map on page 1110.) Only the Pacific Command in Hawaii, CINCPAC, four thousand miles away, was responsible for the whole campaign. How and by what reasoning these Route Packages were established in 1965 must be left for a student of bureaucratic psychology.

The Seventh Air Force had responsibility for targets in the Hanoi area, the northwest rail lines, and above the DMZ (Route Packages 1, 5, and 6A). The Seventh Fleet controlled the planes targeted against Haiphong and northeastern North Vietnam (Route Packages 2, 3, 4, and 6B). All these units except one reported to commanders of the Pacific Air Force and Pacific Fleet, respectively, who in turn reported to CINCPAC in Honolulu. General Abrams had authority only over targets in southernmost North Vietnam (Route Package 1); in that area the Seventh Air Force reported to him. Allocation of B-52s was separate and equally complex. These were controlled by our Strategic Air Command (SAC) and allocated in coordination with Abrams for South Vietnam and southernmost North Vietnam; for the other Route Packages, SAC coordinated with the appropriate command.

In short, there was institutionalized schizophrenia. As soon as aircraft left targets in Route Package 1, Abrams had no further control over them; he therefore could not tell whether the air campaign in the North was easing the immediate pressures on him or diverting resources. He tended to the latter view. The air war in the North was conceptually and organizationally separated from the war in the South. This, at least as much as political restrictions from Washington, produced the random quality of the air campaign and the constant disputes over priorities. Nixon at my urging made several attempts to change these command arrangements; indeed, he ordered a change just before the resumption of unrestricted bombing of North Vietnam. But Laird and Moorer resisted furiously. The same vested interests that had produced the original pattern opposed any change; Laird and Moorer felt that they had enough on their hands without taking on an internal row this late in the game. Like almost all of Nixon's attempts at reorganization, it aborted. Nixon decided that he could not risk an internal split just as he was entering the biggest foreign policy crisis of his Presidency.

A dispute was therefore inevitable between the command in Saigon and other decision-makers over whether our air assets should be confined to the battle in the South or whether we should start bombing North Vietnam as Nixon was eager to do. Now that there were more airplanes available than Abrams — or the Pentagon, for that matter — had ever requested, the command in Saigon nevertheless wanted *all* of them targeted on South Vietnam. Laird supported Abrams because he thought this would best prove the validity of Vietnamization. Nixon (as did I) saw it producing a stalemate. It would not generate enough pressure on Hanoi or its Soviet and Chinese patrons; Hanoi could simply halt its advance and sit on its newly conquered territory; Moscow and Peking would have no decisions to make. North Vietnam would get a free ride despite its cynical disregard of the 1968 bombing halt understandings. Now that the gauntlet had been thrown down, Nixon was determined on a showdown. He saw no point in further diplomacy until a military decision had been reached.

I agreed with Nixon that we had to carry the war to North Vietnam; only this could now force a conclusion of the war. At the same time, I thought that the North Vietnamese had acted partly out of weakness. The repeated postponements of the private meetings indicated that Hanoi must have been having great difficulty in assembling the necessary forces for the offensive. It occurred two months after the date General Abrams had considered the optimum time for Hanoi, and even then the North Vietnamese never managed to coordinate their three-pronged offensive. The attacks in the Central Highlands and on An Loc were spaced sufficiently far apart to let us throw the whole weight of our air power against each of them separately; and even Saigon's strategic reserve could be moved against the uncoordinated attacks in a limited way. These North Vietnamese difficulties reflected the combined impact of the Cambodian and Laotian operations and of our air interdiction. Moreover, Hanoi was undoubtedly feeling the psychological pressure of our overtures toward Peking and Moscow. We had seen reports of disagreements between Hanoi and its two powerful allies for months. Hanoi's displeasure with Peking, in particular, found its way into some of Le Duc Tho's comments to me.

While Nixon and I agreed on the importance of an all-out military response, we differed on how to treat Hanoi in relation to its patrons in Moscow and Peking. We were in complete agreement that there could be no Soviet summit if the North Vietnamese offensive succeeded. He could not go to Moscow after a humiliation imposed by Soviet arms. But whereas Nixon wanted to confront Hanoi and its patrons as a group, I preferred differentiating our pressures against Moscow, Peking, and Hanoi so as to isolate North Vietnam and demoralize it. Nixon saw in diplomacy a sign of potential weakness; I considered it a weapon. Nixon wanted to lump the purposes of Peking and especially of Moscow with

Hanoi's. I favored sharpening the distinction between the interests of the patrons on the one hand and the client on the other. Ultimately, Nixon gave his approval for my proposed strategy of seeking to split Hanoi from the Communist giants, so long as this did not interfere with stepped-up air action against the North. But he was never really comfortable with it, as he was to show at several crucial junctures during the next few weeks.

I began by moving in the direction Nixon favored, to the extent of holding Moscow responsible for Hanoi's offensive. At the same time, to give Moscow an incentive to dissociate from North Vietnam, I emphasized the larger interests it was jeopardizing. On April 3 I saw Dobrynin in the Map Room of the White House and accused the Soviet Union of complicity in Hanoi's attack. If the offensive continued, we would be forced into measures certain to present Moscow with difficult choices before the summit. In the meantime we would have to call off some steps of special concern to Moscow. For example, Moscow had asked us to send a message to West German leaders to urge the ratification of the Eastern treaties, scheduled for a vote in about a month's time. We had been reluctant to intervene to such an extent in Germany's internal politics. We used the North Vietnamese offensive as a pretext to avoid what we were reluctant to do in any event. Under current conditions, I told Dobrynin, we could not be active in Bonn. Moscow could not ask for our assistance in Europe while undermining our position in Southeast Asia. The Kremlin was put on notice that North Vietnamese actions might jeopardize some fundamental Soviet goals.

That same day I sent Winston Lord secretly to New York to see Huang Hua, the Chinese UN Ambassador. The formal reason was to reply to a Chinese protest (conveyed, it should be noted, privately) at the intrusion of American vessels into what China claimed as territorial waters around the Paracel Islands (a chain of islands lying off the coast of Vietnam). It was partly a dispute over the definition of territorial waters. Peking claimed twelve miles; our historical position had been three miles. Lord, known to the Chinese because he had been on every trip to China and attended every meeting with Chinese leaders, handed over an "oral note" informing Huang Hua that without prejudice to our legal position on territorial waters our Navy would be instructed to stay at a distance of twelve miles from the islands. But the main portion of our note was a reminder to Peking of our stake in Vietnam. In the sharpest language ever used in any of our messages to the Chinese, we protested China's public backing of the North Vietnamese invasion. We pointed out that Peking could be under no misapprehension about the profound importance of the issue for the United States. Indeed, we emphasized — presciently — that it could not be in the long-term interest of China for the United States to be humiliated in Indochina. The note warned that "major countries have a responsibility to use a moderating influence on this issue and not to exacerbate the situation." Attempts to "impose a military solution upon the US can only lead to unfortunate consequences." We repeated that we attached "extreme importance" to the improvement of our relations with China — implicitly warning that Vietnam was an obstacle.

On the following day, April 4, we began to hold the Soviet Union *publicly* accountable for the offensive. On my instructions Haig asked Robert McCloskey, the State Department press spokesman, to point out at his regular briefing that the North Vietnamese invasion of the South was made possible by Soviet arms. McCloskey, perhaps the ablest press officer I have known, carried off the assignment so well that he triggered a series of confirming comments from other agencies, raising speculation that the entire US–Soviet relationship, including the summit, was in jeopardy. This was a little more than we wanted, but it erred in the right direction.

On the same day, we also decided to bring home to Hanoi that we meant business. We had informed it that we would resume plenary sessions of the Paris conference on April 13. Following the elaborate procedures that were in inverse proportion to the significance of the agenda, this would normally have required a formal proposal to be submitted a week before, or by April 6. With the offensive mounting in fury by the day, it had become absurd to request a plenary session. Therefore, we forwarded a message to Paris to be delivered on April 6, informing Hanoi that we had changed our minds:

> The Government of North Vietnam has intensified military operations against the territory of the Government of South Vietnam to include the most flagrant violations of the understandings of 1968. Because of this grave escalation of military activity, and the flagrant violation of the Geneva Accords and the understandings of 1968, Ambassador Porter will not now propose a Plenary Session for April 13, 1972. A decision about the Plenary Session for April 20 will depend on the circumstances existing at that time.

We said nothing about the secret meeting of April 24; we put the onus on Hanoi to cancel that if it chose.

As it happened, our note of April 6 crossed a North Vietnamese message (in reply to our preliminary proposal of April 1) that illustrated what Hanoi promised itself from the secret meeting. In the midst of an offensive that violated every previous understanding, our insolent interlocutors made their agreement to a private meeting conditional on our keeping our "engagement" to halt the bombing of the North. In fact, we had not yet really resumed bombing because of the weather. Nevertheless, it took extraordinary gall to try to hold the United States to an "engagement," every provision of which North Vietnam had already broken.

On April 6, too, I had another meeting with Dobrynin. I told him the present situation was intolerable. As I had warned him in January, a North Vietnamese offensive would force us to bring the war to a decisive military conclusion. As for the Soviets, either they had had a hand in planning it or their negligence had made it possible. Either interpretation raised unpleasant prospects. I briefly reviewed our preparations for the summit, to give Moscow a sense of what it stood to lose in terms of the various agreements shaping up. We would now insist, I stressed, on ending the war by negotiation if possible, by force if necessary.

While putting on the diplomatic pressure, we continued the buildup of our forces. On April 9 twenty-eight more B-52s were sent to Guam. On April 10 a fifth aircraft carrier was ordered to Vietnam. The cruiser *Newport* and another carrier were moved from the Atlantic to Southeast Asia. By the end of the first week of April the weather had lifted enough to begin bombing of tactical targets in North Vietnam. Authority was given to attack as far north as the nineteenth parallel.

Antiwar critics who depicted the military establishment as champing at the bit to sow death and destruction would have been amazed that almost all reinforcements occurred over the opposition of at least the civilian leadership of the Pentagon. Concerned by the budgetary costs, eager to use the offensive to settle the fate of Vietnamization, the Pentagon civilians on the whole maintained that the forces in the field were already sufficient. This might have been accurate enough by the sophisticated calculations of systems analysis; it was not adequate for the political goal of bringing matters to a head and overawing outside intervention. If we wanted to force a diplomatic solution, we had to create an impression of implacable determination to prevail; only this would bring about either active Soviet assistance in settling the war or else Soviet acquiescence in our mounting military pressures, on which we were determined should diplomacy fail. Nixon's driving leadership shook the Pentagon out of the torpor induced by years of frustration; and I backed him up in the day-to-day monitoring of the implementation of his decisions and by the design of the diplomatic strategy.

As the new forces were being assembled in Southeast Asia, my staff prepared contingency plans for their use. A planning paper by Al Haig dated April 6, based on my instructions, outlined our course of action should South Vietnamese forces fail to halt the offensive. It provided for the bombing of all military targets throughout North Vietnam (except in a buffer zone along the Chinese border) and for the mining of all North Vietnamese ports. It was in effect the plan that would be implemented on May 8.

Nixon briefly played with the idea of going on television to report on the offensive to the American people. Safire was assigned to write the speech.[1] The project was abandoned as premature after a few days, around April 10. If the South Vietnamese held, there was no need to create a crisis atmosphere. If the North Vietnamese assault gained momentum, we would have to take drastic measures; that would be the right moment for a Presidential speech. But as I told the President, if we failed, not even ten speeches would do us any good. We had a somber, philosophical conversation. Nixon mused that if we failed, it was because the great forces of history had moved in another direction. Not only South Vietnam but the whole free world would be lost. "No," I replied, "if it fails, we'll have to tighten our belts and turn the forces around."

We kept up the diplomatic pressure. On April 8 I sent a note to Egon Bahr, Willy Brandt's adviser, warning him that we were reassessing our entire Soviet policy. Two military offensives against American interests made possible by Soviet arms within the space of six months was too much. We doubted the value of a policy of détente in these circumstances. Bahr, with the ratification of Brandt's Eastern treaties hanging in the balance, was certain to convey these sentiments to the Soviet Ambassador in Bonn. And Moscow would be reminded that we were not without means of pressure.

On April 9, in what surely was a unique exercise of triangular politics, I invited Anatoly Dobrynin to the White House to watch Chinese-made films of my Peking visits, which he had expressed an interest in seeing. At the end Dobrynin complained that our buildup in Southeast Asia was growing ominous. "Anatol," I replied, "we have been warning you for months that if there were an offensive we would take drastic measures to end the war once and for all. That situation has now arisen." Dobrynin volunteered that Moscow was extremely interested in a successful outcome of my projected private meeting of April 24 with Le Duc Tho and had informed Hanoi accordingly.

Clearly, Moscow was getting nervous. I warned Dobrynin that we would no longer agree to talk while the fighting was going on. We would insist on an end to the offensive or we would take even more serious measures. He did not bristle at this threat. The Soviets rarely bully when they believe the opponent to be strong and serious. Dobrynin replied that he would transmit this warning to Moscow; he was certain there would be an early response.

As I have pointed out in other chapters describing crises, once embarked on confrontation it is more dangerous to stop than to proceed. A pause in one's moves causes the other side to wonder whether it has seen the limit of the response and to test whether the status quo can be sustained. Confrontations end when the opponent decides that the risks are not worth the objective, and for this the risks must be kept high and incalculable. We therefore continued to raise both the diplomatic and military stakes. On April 10 the President attended a State Department ceremony at which he signed a multilateral convention banning biological weapons. Dobrynin was present. Nixon took the occasion to remind the Soviet Union that a "great responsibility particularly rests upon the great powers" not to "encourage directly or indirectly any other nation to use force or armed aggression against one of its neighbors." It was another not too subtle warning that we held Moscow accountable for Hanoi's offensive.

I spoke to Dobrynin an hour later to elaborate on the President's remarks. We would not stand still for the tactic by which Hanoi had whipsawed us in the last two series of secret talks. If Hanoi once again published new proposals in the middle of negotiations, the secret channel would be at an end. Dobrynin used this occasion to mention that we could take a hundred reporters to the summit in Moscow. Clearly, nothing had yet happened to change the Kremlin's priorities.

To keep up the pressure, I asked Hal Sonnenfeldt, my principal adviser on Soviet affairs, what negotiations with the USSR we could slow down that were of substantial interest to the Kremlin leaders. Sonnenfeldt proposed: ensuring that the US–Soviet talks in Moscow on grain sales yielded no results for now; avoiding unnecessarily friendly contacts during other negotiations; maintaining our tough demands in the talks on a Lend-Lease settlement; freezing other bilateral negotiations; using the Washington visit of Soviet Minister of Commerce Nikolai Patolichev, scheduled in early May, to get across our tough line; canceling the Patolichev visit if the situation deteriorated. I approved all these steps. The one recommendation I disapproved was to harass Soviet ships on the way to Cuba — this seemed unduly provocative.

Where we stepped up our military pressure was in Vietnam. Even before the President put the Soviets on notice at the State Department ceremony, twelve B-52s had struck supply dumps near the North Vietnamese port of Vinh, about 150 miles north of the Demilitarized Zone. It was the first use of B-52s in North Vietnam by the Nixon Administration.* It was a warning that things might get out of hand if the offensive did not stop.

April 10 was a busy day. The Chinese Foreign Ministry issued a rare public criticism of our air attacks on North Vietnam and hailed Communist victories in the South. Despite its polemic tone, we considered the statement to be minimal for the occasion. Its condemnation of our bombing demonstrated ideological solidarity; the catalogue of Communist victories forestalled any claim on additional Chinese resources. We noted that the Chinese statement failed to pledge the conventional "res-

---

* B-52s had been used against North Vietnam by the Johnson Administration in 1967.

olute'' support nor did it demand — as previous statements had — that the United States accept Hanoi's terms. Throughout the spring and summer, China confined most of its protests to the private channel, and even there, in almost every case, protested only instances of American aircraft or vessels impinging on *China's* sovereign airspace or territorial waters.

By now the offensive was in full swing on all three fronts. Several Communist divisions were knifing across the DMZ deep into Quang Tri province in Military Region 1. An attack was developing in the Central Highlands, and further south against the provincial capital of An Loc. We responded on April 11 by canceling the plenary session scheduled for April 20. We told Hanoi: "In light of the continued flagrant violation of the Demilitarized Zone by the North Vietnamese and the extension of military operations into Military Regions 3 and 4 of South Vietnam, no useful purpose would be served by the holding of a plenary session of the Paris Conference on April 20." Our note offered to proceed with the secret meeting of April 24 and to resume plenaries should that meeting prove successful.

But the pressure was beginning to tell on Hanoi as well. Though its offensive was now in high gear it faced an American buildup that was as menacing as our bombing was unexpected. The South Vietnamese, though gradually being driven back, were still holding. Too cautious in attack, they were fighting adequately when on the defensive. On April 15 Hanoi turned down the proposed private meeting with Le Duc Tho for April 24 until we agreed to resume the public sessions. But it did so in an uncharacteristically halfhearted way that showed profound confusion. It suggested April 27 for resuming the plenaries and May 6 for the secret meeting; May 6 was chosen, the note said, to give Le Duc Tho time to travel. Rarely before had Hanoi answered so rapidly or offered an explanation for any of its decisions.

We decided to stick to our strategy. On April 16 we proposed that the secret meeting take place as scheduled on April 24, *after* which we would attend the plenary meeting on April 27. The North Vietnamese replied on April 19 — again with unprecedented speed. After condemning the "atrocious" intensification of the air and naval war against North Vietnam, including the B-52 raids against Hanoi and Haiphong (see below), Hanoi added a slight sweetener to its previous proposal. It stuck to April 27 for a plenary and May 6 for a secret meeting, but said that if the United States announced its willingness to return to the plenaries, Le Duc Tho would leave immediately for Paris.

Both sides were clearly shadowboxing, half-wanting a secret meeting, half not, careful above all to avoid the onus of canceling. In effect, both sought to keep the possibility open until the opportune moment. The North Vietnamese wanted to time a meeting for the moment of our maximum humiliation after a massive defeat. We wanted to hold it only after the Soviets had been brought fully into the game. It would have been a simple matter for us to fix some formula for simultaneous agreement on secret and plenary meetings; this would quickly have resolved the matter. But I wanted to play *that* card with Moscow.

A great deal now depended on our exchanges with the Soviet Union. The Soviets had begun to engage themselves in earnest on April 12. During a luncheon to review summit preparations, Dobrynin let it be known that my planned (but shortly to be canceled) meeting with Le Duc Tho was crucial. He assured me that his leadership was not interested in a showdown. I replied that the Soviets had put themselves into the position where a miserable little country could jeopardize everything that had been negotiated for years. The Soviet Union must have known when it signed two supplementary aid agreements during the year that it was giving the North Vietnamese the wherewithal to launch an offensive. What did the Soviet leaders expect? Did they think the President would run the risk of being defeated and having 69,000 Americans taken prisoner? Dobrynin objected that the North Vietnamese had often offered to repatriate all Americans immediately. I said "Anatol, this is not worthy of comment, and that situation will not arise. There must be a meeting this month. It must lead to concrete results, and if it does not there will be incalculable consequences."

Dobrynin replied that it seemed to him that a visit by me to Moscow, which had been discussed since early in the year, was now urgent. The agenda could be Vietnam, as well as accelerated preparations for the summit. I told Dobrynin I would put this idea to the President.

The proposition evoked the most diverse emotions in Nixon. He longed for the summit. To be the first American President in Moscow stimulated his sense of history; to go where Eisenhower had been rebuffed would fulfill his ambition to outstrip his old mentor. To be sure, he often spoke of canceling the summit. But anyone familiar with his style knew that such queries, like occasional musings about his dispensability,[2] were really a call for reassurance. As I had learned painfully during the India-Pakistan war, one acted on these musings at one's peril. On the other hand, Nixon did not want to go to Moscow in a position of weakness, and he was suspicious of a Soviet ploy to delay or complicate our planned military campaign against North Vietnam by dragging me into prolonged negotiations in Moscow. Not the least of Nixon's concerns was how he would explain to Rogers yet another secret mission by his security adviser, this time to Moscow, which he had prevented his Secretary of State from visiting for nearly four years. (Rogers had wanted to make an advance trip to Moscow to match my advance trips to Peking; Nixon had turned him down.)

Vanity can never be completely dissociated in high office from the perception of national interest. My eagerness to go was no doubt affected by my sense of the dramatic. But its serious basis was that we had little to lose and much to gain. For the first time Moscow had offered to engage directly in discussions on Vietnam at a high level and without conditions. That mere fact was bound to disquiet Hanoi. The Kremlin could not string us along; it could gain no more time than the days I spent in Moscow. As for the summit preparations, they provided the vehicle by which to separate Moscow's interests from Hanoi's; the summit was Moscow's incentive either to press Hanoi toward compromise or to acquiesce if we forced the issue by military means. If my trip advanced the prospects for the summit — as was likely — it would help neutralize a Soviet response to our retaliation in Southeast Asia; Moscow would then know clearly what price it would pay by reacting against us. It was, of course, possible that Moscow was playing the same game. But we had more to lose in Vietnam than Moscow stood to gain by our humiliation. Thus in an odd way our bargaining position was stronger; our threats were more plausible.

Nixon at first agreed with my arguments. On April 12 he authorized me to inform· Dobrynin that I would arrive in Moscow on April 20. I even resurrected the proposal to meet a senior North Vietnamese official in Moscow, an offer unlikely to be accepted but useful in keeping the Kremlin on the defensive and us in the position of being ready to negotiate. But Nixon's mood fluctuated. On April 12 he urged me to discuss not only Vietnam in Moscow but also the summit. However, by April 15 he was worried that Brezhnev would "filibuster" me and our hands would be tied militarily for a week. The summit was sure to go down the drain if we played our "hole card" of blockade against the North. Perhaps we should preempt by canceling the summit ourselves, he told me. I assured him that even while I was in Moscow we could bomb all over North Vietnam except in the sensitive area of Hanoi and Haiphong. Moreover, my trip to Moscow would itself be a "hole card" to neutralize domestic critics and Soviet responses. Nor did I believe that cancellation of the summit was a certainty. Nixon then agreed that my trip was "a good thing to do. . . . I think it's right; you've just got to go," he said. He now was sure that "the strategy, which you and I both agree on, is the right one" — but he clearly wanted reassurance. At any rate, Nixon's memoirs leave no doubt that by the end of the day on April 15 he came back to the conclusion that I should proceed.[3]

To make sure that both Hanoi and Moscow understood our determination, I had recommended, and Nixon had approved, a dramatic two-day B-52 attack on fuel storage depots in the Hanoi-Haiphong area together with a shore bombardment by naval gunfire. It took place on the weekend of April 15–16 — over the opposition of Abrams but with the support of Laird. By chance April 15 was the day that Hanoi turned down our proposal for a meeting on April 24, a decision which — allowing for transmission time for its messages — it clearly had made before the attack. This postponement gave us the opportunity to assume the offensive. When one is running risks, it is almost always preferable to be bold. We sent a strong message to the Soviets on April 15 questioning whether any progress could be made on Vietnam during my visit to Moscow if the Soviet Union could not bring about even one meeting on an agreed date.

That evening Dobrynin came to my home to discuss the message and to urge me to go ahead with the plan to visit Moscow. Dobrynin, who must have known from the news tickers of the B-52 attacks, did not mention them. In an extremely friendly manner he suggested that great powers must be able to put local differences aside to settle fundamental issues. I said, "Anatol, for us it isn't just an international problem; it has now become a major domestic problem. We cannot permit our domestic structure to be constantly tormented by this country ten thousand miles away. The war must now be brought to a conclusion, and we will do it either together with the other great powers or alone."

The next morning, April 16, Dobrynin read me a message from the Soviet leadership stating that they had brought my complaint about the aborted secret meeting to the attention of Hanoi. Hanoi "could agree" to a secret meeting on April 24 if the plenary meetings were also resumed; this was puzzling since Hanoi the day before had rejected a meeting on April 24. There was also an implication that its agreement was dependent on a halt to the "expanded" bombing of North Vietnam. Hanoi had not yet responded to my suggestion to meet with North Vietnamese representatives in Moscow. Hanoi was clearly thrashing around. Its reply lacked the insolent self-assurance of previous years.

Finally, at the end of the day, a formal Soviet protest arrived. Our bombing had accidentally hit four Soviet merchant ships in Haiphong harbor, with loss of life. Like the Chinese, the Soviet protests about the bombing of North Vietnam took on a grave tone only when Soviet lives or property were in jeopardy. About the B-52 attacks Moscow confined itself to an expression of regret because it "seriously complicates the situation." Nevertheless, the Kremlin assured us that our views were being conveyed to Hanoi. Considering that we were bombing Hanoi and Haiphong four days before my visit to Moscow, this was restraint of a high order. What was significant was not that the criticism stopped well short of a protest but that Moscow maintained its invitation even in the face of an unprecedented assault on its client. Moscow obviously would not lightly hazard the forthcoming summit after Nixon had already visited Peking.

In the next few days Nixon reverted to his worry that my trip might prove "indecisive" — an augury of his later unease. I answered that my trip to Moscow was a stage in a process to put ourselves into the best possible position for a showdown with Hanoi; it could not possibly be decisive in itself. But even an indecisive trip could contribute to a decisive outcome.

That left only one more worry: how to tell the Secretary of State. Nixon decided to resort to the tested method used so many times during the previous year. He would go to Camp David while I was in Moscow; he would, in fact, be my "cover," since it would be announced that he and I were reviewing the situation together. From there, after I had left, he would break the news to his old friend that we had received a sudden invitation from Brezhnev to discuss Vietnam and that in view of its urgency he had accepted it on the spur of the moment.

As for Peking, on April 12 we had received a stiff reply to our note of April 3 in the private channel. China expressed solidarity with North Vietnam and warned us that we were getting bogged down further. But the note made no threats and concluded with a reaffirmation of Chinese interest in the normalization of relations with the United States.

As I departed on my secret trip to Moscow, I reflected that we had not been panicked by the offensive; we had assembled massive power to blunt it should Hanoi refuse negotiations. We were in the process of separating Hanoi from its allies. The next weeks would tell whether there would be a negotiation or another brutal test of arms.

XXVI

The Secret Trip to Moscow

I DEPARTED for Moscow on a Presidential aircraft shortly after one o'clock in the morning of Thursday, April 20. With me were my aides Hal Sonnenfeldt, Winston Lord, John Negroponte, Peter Rodman, two Secret Service agents, two secretaries — and also Anatoly Dobrynin, since it was the quickest way for him to get to Moscow. A Soviet navigator was aboard to guide us over Soviet territory.

The departure time had been chosen, as on almost all of my trips, to permit me to arrive in Moscow too late in the evening for serious talks. This reduced the effects of jet lag by guaranteeing a night's rest before important conversations. Twice when I violated this principle and went straight from an overnight flight to negotiations with Le Duc Tho, I paid a psychological price. The North Vietnamese method in those days was to wear us out by moving at a glacial pace, repeating the same basic speech at each session, and refusing to acknowledge the slightest merit in any idea we put forward. To show that we were equally patient, I normally responded by banter or by raising the same issues again and again, or by making the same concession in my turn over and over as if it were new. But when I went directly from a transatlantic flight into talks, I found I was on the verge of losing my temper at North Vietnamese insolence — nearly falling into their trap by playing the role they had assigned to me. From then on I never began a negotiation immediately after a long flight.

My Moscow trip was secret; it was to be announced only after I had returned. The Soviets had pressed for months for a clandestine visit, almost certainly for the simple reason that Peking had had a secret trip and they were entitled to equality! Nixon also welcomed the secrecy because, among other reasons, it postponed an argument with his Secretary of State. I favored secrecy because it freed me from the necessity of living up to criteria set beforehand by the media and critics. When we gave briefings after the event, we would be able to do so in the context of whatever had been achieved, not what other people expected or desired or invented.

I arrived in Moscow at about eight in the evening, local time, of the same day. Our airplane taxied to a dark secluded corner of a military airfield. Greeting me at the foot of the ramp was First Deputy Foreign Minister Vasily V. Kuznetsov, a grizzled veteran of the Soviet Foreign Office in the Gromyko mold: professional, disciplined, more concerned with the tactics than with the strategy. He was accompanied by KGB General Sergei Antonov, who would be responsible for Nixon's security. Where Chinese protocol had used me as a guinea pig for Presidential scheduling, Antonov used me as a test of his security procedures.

A terrifying motorcade whisked us at a seemingly hundred-mile-an-hour clip to the complex of guest houses in the Lenin Hills overlooking the Moscow River, near the Stalinist Gothic skyscraper of Moscow University. The architecture of the guest houses was almost identical with that of Peking; it was one Soviet export to China that had stood the test of time. They looked like the villas of upper middle-class, self-made industrialists trying to convey their new solidity by the solemnity of their appearance and the scale of the furniture. The chief difference was the location. The Chinese guest houses are situated around a lake in a large park from which the other residences are visible, though soldiers block access from one to the other. The Soviets take no chances on human frailty. Each house is self-contained behind walls and closed gates. No other dwelling is visible, only Moscow stretching before one's gaze across the river on the endless Russian plain.

The guest house was extremely comfortable. Traditional Russian hospitality was in this case blended with legendary Soviet subtlety. In the room set aside for a staff office was a safe, which the manager of the guest house graciously invited us to use for storage of our classified papers. It was a rickety old contraption whose construction suggested that its inner chambers might even be moving parts; one could easily imagine that its shelves, like dumbwaiters, would transport the contents downstairs for our hosts' leisurely overnight review. We politely declined the kind offer. Our classified materials were kept in a big tin box that was guarded during all waking hours by Secret Service Agent Gary McLeod. At night it sat in the room he shared with Agent Jack Ready, between their beds.

The trip also marked my introduction to the use of the "babbler." This was a cassette tape I had brought with me, which played a bizarre recording of what seemed like several dozen voices talking gibberish simultaneously. If I wanted to confer with my colleagues without being overheard by listening devices, we would gather around the babbler, speaking softly among ourselves. We could understand each other, but theoretically anyone listening in would be unable to distinguish the real conversation from the cacophony of recorded voices. Whether it worked or not we could never be sure. The only certainty was that anyone trying to talk through the mind-numbing babble for any length of time would lose his own sanity. Thus we used it sparingly. Usually we spoke elliptically or wrote notes to one another. A colleague and I sometimes took a walk in the garden, even there whispering to each other because Willy Brandt's security people had warned us that the trees contained listening devices. I once joked to Gromyko that there was a strange tree in the garden whose branches followed my every movement. Our respect for the KGB was such that our secretaries used manual typewriters brought from home lest the "telemetry" of electric machines be read by our solicitous hosts.

Gromyko and Dobrynin called on me at the guest house at 11:00 P.M. to settle the next day's program. I had my secretary, Julie Pineau, sit in to take notes. It clearly made Gromyko uncomfortable. Apparently not wanting a stenographic record kept, he spoke quietly in English, as if trying to make it difficult for her to hear. Gromyko did not mind notes taken by staff members; it was the secretary who was bothering him. Female stenographers offended either Russian male chauvinism or Soviet secretiveness (until Brezhnev a few years later had two Soviet girls sit in on a meeting, perhaps to impress me.)

Gromyko told me that Brezhnev would conduct all the discussions on the Soviet side except on Sunday, when he would attend his granddaughter's wedding. I stressed to him that my primary mission was to remove Vietnam as an obstacle to the summit. Our two countries' ability to destroy humanity imposed an obligation to improve our relationship. An opportunity now existed, but it was being thwarted by Hanoi. I was authorized to discuss a broad range of issues, but I was instructed above all to explore means to end the war in Vietnam. Gromyko affirmed Brezhnev's readiness to discuss the war in detail — in itself an unprecedented step. He spent most of his time stressing the importance that the Soviet leadership attached to the summit and the earnestness with which they were preparing themselves to meet the President. Gromyko's eagerness, within four days after a massive B-52 attack in the Haiphong area, dramatized to me that the summit could be used as a restraint on Soviet conduct while we pursued our strategy for ending the war.

Preparing the Summit

SUMMIT preparations had begun in earnest when Dobrynin had returned from Moscow by January 21, filled with good cheer. He claimed that he had had important sessions with the Soviet leaders who were eager for the summit to be successful. He brought with him a letter from Brezhnev to Nixon urging that the two sides get down to "practical work" on the summit by "periodically comparing our viewpoints on the key aspects of the most important issues." These were defined as

SALT; the Middle East; European security; removal of obstacles to trade and economic cooperation; and expanding exchanges in science and technology, including outer space, protection of the environment, and public health. With the summit as a deadline it was hoped that agreements would be signed in Moscow in several of these fields. Brezhnev's letter ended by assuring Nixon of the "great significance that we attach to the forthcoming meeting with you as well as to the kind of situation it will be taking place in." This clumsy phrase indicated Soviet nervousness over Nixon's China trip, or perhaps revealed his premonition of what was ahead in Vietnam.

Dobrynin bubbled over, I told Nixon, with "effusive cordiality." Dobrynin blamed the Vietnam deadlock on the Chinese — never unintentionally failing to remind us of the opportunities opened to us by Soviet sensitivities. I warned him that we would respond to an offensive with the strongest possible action, whatever its effect on US–Soviet relations. After discussion with Nixon, it was agreed I should accept the invitation to Moscow on condition Moscow made some move to end the war, preferably by producing an interlocutor from Hanoi empowered to settle.

Summit preparations now speeded up, and, as usual, they started with an internal row over who would supervise them, Secretary of State Rogers or I. By this time our relations had so deteriorated that there was no longer any pretense that it could be done jointly. Symptomatic of the state of affairs was the annual battle over drafting and publication of our lengthy foreign policy reports to the Congress and public. Three times the State Department put out a voluminous report on its own, side by side with the President's on the same subject. It had never done so before there was a Presidential report; it has never done so since. Theoretically, the two reports were complementary. The White House document, drafted by a few associates and me, was analytical, relatively short, and confined to general principles. The State document reflected the bureaucratic imperatives of the Department. It was drafted by committee and was therefore vaguer. At the same time, it was exhaustively comprehensive; every bureau and country director made sure his area of concern was included. Inevitably, this produced a stupefying catalogue of countries and technical issues. Each year there were bitter disputes between the White House and the State Department over, among other things, whose report would appear first. Predictably, the President's always did. This rivalry was not always on the plane of high policy. I saw to it that the President's report always gave some credit to Secretary Rogers, though of course stressing the central role of the President and by implication my own. The State Department entered readily into the spirit of the competition. In 1972 the State Department's report referred to the President 172 times, to Rogers 96 times, and to me once — in reprinting the text of the announcement of the President's trip to China, from which I simply could not be deleted. It included four photographs of the President, eight of Rogers, none of me. This was not much to show for a year in which it was revealed that I had made a secret trip to China and engaged in seven secret sessions with the North Vietnamese, not to mention the SALT breakthrough and the Berlin agreement. Someone on my staff counted the references; I do not know which was more petty, State's snub or my noticing it.

It was in this atmosphere that Rogers sent a memo to the President on March 14 saying that he planned to "take personal charge" of Moscow summit preparations. Anyone familiar with Nixon knew that this was never going to happen. On Nixon's order Haldeman sent a careful reply asking that every State Department contact with Dobrynin be cleared in *advance* by the White House. When this did not do the trick, on March 17 Nixon dropped in on one of my meetings with Dobrynin and told him that I was to supervise all major summit preparations. Technical negotiations on economic relations or scientific or cultural exchanges were turned over to the Cabinet departments, with the State Department playing the lead role, but the key policy issues were to be handled in the Channel.

Our interest in the subjects listed in Brezhnev's January letter was not uniform. We were prepared to finish SALT. We thought a European Security Conference should wait on the Bundestag's ratification of the German-Soviet treaties, which in turn we considered as an inducement to restrained Soviet conduct overall and on Vietnam in particular. As to the Middle East, we saw no possibility of a settlement on the terms the Soviets had heretofore proposed. Our strategy in that area, as I have described, was more designed to demonstrate the limitations of Soviet influence than to achieve a cooperative solution — at least so long as Moscow supported extreme Arab demands. With respect to the economic and technical agreements, Dobrynin knew our approach to linkage well enough to recognize that nothing would be concluded until the fundamental issues were out of the way. And of course we would have to work out a communiqué as the preparations advanced.

On SALT, major issues had been narrowed down to three. The Soviets, after first insisting that an agreement limiting ABMs be concluded *before* we turned to limitation of offensive systems, had agreed in the May 1971 announcement to deal with both issues simultaneously. But the nature of the ABM limitation was still in dispute. We insisted that we be permitted two ABM sites (either the two we were building at Malmstrom and Grand Forks, or one of those plus Washington), while the Soviet system be confined to the existing one around Moscow. The Soviets proposed equality; each side should be free to protect its capital and an equivalent number of missiles. Since Soviet missile fields were smaller than ours, this meant that under this proposal the Soviets would

*The Channel. In the Map Room
with Soviet Ambassador Anatoly
Dobrynin (taken in March 1972).*

*Soviet Trade Minister Nikolai Patolichev visits Nixon three days after the mining
of North Vietnam, May 11, 1972. Seated, clockwise from left: Peter Flanigan,
Dobrynin, Patolichev, Nixon, Peter Peterson, HAK.*

At the summit. RIGHT: *A walk with Nixon in the Kremlin, May 1972.* BELOW: *With Mrs. Nixon in the Kremlin, watching the President's address to the Soviet people, May 29, 1972.*

Dobrynin and I take a ride in a Soviet hydrofoil on the Potomac, August 1972.

With Brezhnev in the Kremlin, September 1972. From left: Gromyko, Dobrynin, Brezhnev, Sukhodrev, HAK.

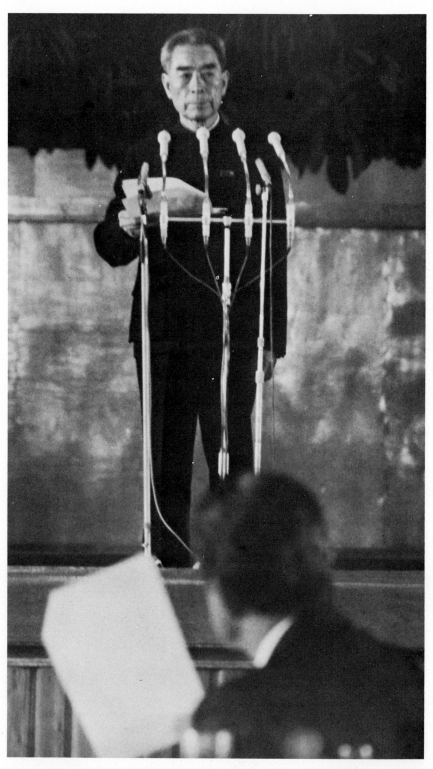

Premier Chou En-lai reads his banquet toast, February 1972.

The Presidential Guest House in Hangchow, February 1972.

Strategy conference in China. From left: Haldeman, HAK, Nixon, Ziegler.

ABOVE: *President Thieu greets me in Saigon, August 17, 1972 (at left, Ambassador Ellsworth Bunker).*

RIGHT, ABOVE: *Conferring after my Moscow trip and session with Le Duc Tho, September 16, 1972.*

RIGHT, BELOW: *Breakfast meeting after the Vietnam breakthrough, October 13, 1972. From left: Rogers, Nixon, HAK, Haig.*

With Lon Nol of beleaguered Cambodia, October 22, 1972.

On Air Force One *returning to Washington from San Clemente, November 7, 1972.*

Le Duc Tho confers with his aide Nguyen Co Thach in the garden at Gif-sur-Yvette, France, as the talks resume, November 20, 1972.

With my staff in Paris during the abortive December negotiations. From left: Peter Rodman, HAK, Winston Lord, Al Haig, William Sullivan, David Engel, John Negroponte (seated).

Announcing the breakdown of the talks, in the White House press briefing room, December 16, 1972.

At the Ambassador's residence in Paris during the December negotiations.

LEFT: *The two delegations meet toward the conclusion of the negotiation, Gif-sur-Yvette, January 12, 1973.*

LEFT, BELOW: *En route to Paris for initialing of Vietnam agreement, January 23, 1973.*

RIGHT, BELOW: *En route to Paris, January 23, 1973. From left: HAK, Lord, Negroponte (leaning back), Rodman.*

Initialing of the Vietnam agreement, January 23, 1973. From left: Heyward Isham, Sullivan, HAK, George Aldrich (standing), Winston Lord. BELOW: *Le Duc Tho initials the Vietnam agreement, January 23, 1973. Seated to his right, Xuan Thuy; to his left, Nguyen Co Thach. To my left, Aldrich; to my right, Sullivan.*

After the initialing, January 23, 1973. From left: Thach, Thuy, interpreter Nguyen Dinh Phuong, Le Duc Tho, HAK.

Outside after the initialing, shaking hands, January 23, 1973, Avenue Kléber, Paris (to Le Duc Tho's right, Xuan Thuy).

have three sites to our two. Second, we had agreed to freeze the deployment of ICBMs, but the duration of the freeze was unsettled. The Soviets had characteristically begun by suggesting a moratorium of from one and a half to two years. We wanted five years. By the time of my Moscow trip the Soviets had hinted that they might settle for a freeze of three years. The third problem was the Soviets' unwillingness to limit submarine-launched ballistic missiles (SLBMs) at all.

As always, our negotiating stance was heavily influenced by our unilateral decisions in the defense budget. I had been concerned at the growing divergence between our SALT positions and our defense decisions. On December 2, 1971, I had written to Laird to convey the President's decisions on the forthcoming defense budget for Fiscal Year 1973. A strong defense posture was vital for our foreign policy, I wrote, especially in the coming year "as we undertake diplomatic initiatives that require bargaining from strength, not weakness." For leverage on the negotiations the new budget should plan for four ABM sites even though we might wind up with only two if a SALT agreement were concluded. Similarly, I requested Laird to give favorable consideration to "an expanded strategic submarine program" in a way that was highly visible to the Soviets. I told Laird that the President had directed a substantial increase in the defense budget to accomplish these objectives.

The ABM directive went the way of many other Presidential instructions to the Defense Department. Opposition was simply too powerful. Since the Congress had repeatedly deprived the program of military significance, the services were reluctant to spend scarce procurement funds for it; the Pentagon gave it at best halfhearted support. The Senate Armed Services Committee had already in 1971 declined to authorize more than two sites. The State Department leaned toward a total ban on ABM and supported Gerard Smith's preference for a single site. Smith testified before the Armed Services Committee on March 16 in support of the conclusions which it had already reached. For his purposes, he argued, authorization for two sites would be enough; funds for additional sites could be put into escrow pending the outcome of the negotiations. With the negotiation nearing its climax and the summit only two months away, the President's decision to expand ABM was in effect being ignored.

The question of SLBMs was more complex. We were building none; our predecessors had halted construction after reaching a ceiling of forty-one Polaris- and Poseidon-carrying nuclear submarines. The Soviets were starting about eight new submarines a year, carrying a total of ninety-six to 128 missiles, depending on the type of submarine.* By

---

*The Y-class, with sixteen missiles each, was comparable to our Polaris; the D-class, with twelve missiles each, was comparable to our Poseidon — although our submarines were better and quieter.

1972 the Soviets had already launched or laid the keels for forty-three submarines. Our estimate was that their number could exceed eighty by 1978.

We faced a major procurement decision that in turn would determine our SALT posture. We had two choices: to proceed rapidly with the production of an improved version of the Poseidon vessels; or to wait for the entirely new Trident submarine, which could not be produced before 1978 at the earliest. If we chose to build improved Poseidons, we would prefer to leave submarine-launched missiles out of the SALT freeze; we would have an opportunity to match the Soviet Union by building new submarines rapidly. If on the other hand we chose to invest in the new Trident program, we would have to insist on the inclusion of SLBMs in SALT so as to freeze Soviet numbers while we used the five-year period to develop our new system.

The Pentagon opted for the Trident program, for many good reasons. Resources were better spent on a new generation of submarines and missiles than on a modified version of the existing Poseidon system. A crash program to build new Poseidons would, by tying up shipyards, compete with other building programs. Secretary Laird in a memorandum of January 4, Admiral Moorer at a Verification Panel meeting of March 8, and both Laird and Moorer at a National Security Council meeting of March 17 argued passionately that it was better to have a new submarine in 1978, even at the cost of having fewer strategic submarines in the interval. Admiral Elmo Zumwalt, Chief of Naval Operations, took the same position.[1] Mel Laird summed up the arguments against various options to build more of existing types: "Each of these options . . . reflects more of an emergency reaction than a deliberate, constructive, long-range program; these may therefore be counterproductive, politically and diplomatically."

If we chose the Trident, however, we had to move rapidly to reach agreement on an SLBM freeze. It had to be negotiated before the Soviets understood that we had decided to build no additional missile-carrying submarines during the moratorium period. Otherwise they would have no incentive to agree to a freeze, and we might wind up with the worst of all solutions: an unrestricted Soviet program not countered by any new American sea-based missiles for several years. Unless there was a freeze on offensive weapons, including SLBMs, the numerical gap against us would widen with every passing month. But how could we induce the Soviets to stop a program when we had none and could not have one for five years? Laird on January 18 came up with an ingenious solution. In a memorandum to the President he urged a rapid negotiation of an offensive freeze; in order to get some handle on the submarine question he would favor permitting the Soviets to continue building SLBMs — if at a slower rate — provided that they dismantled older ICBMs and SLBMs on a one-to-one basis as a trade-in. We estimated that the Soviets had some 209 older ICBMs and about thirty older SLBMs on nuclear-powered boats, making a total of about 240. If the Soviets exercised their full option, we would have eliminated several hundred of their older heavy-throwweight missiles, which because of their vulnerability were useful only for a Soviet first strike. At the same time we would keep the total number of Soviet submarine-launched missiles at nearly 200 below what Admiral Moorer estimated their potential program was.

Laird's scheme was discussed by the Verification Panel on March 8 and by the full NSC on March 17 with general approval (though, as was his custom, the President deferred a final decision). At the March 8 Verification Panel meeting, both Gerard Smith and Under Secretary of State John Irwin urged that the SLBM issue be left for the President to negotiate in Moscow. I demurred on the ground that I had a horror of the President's having to negotiate at the last minute on an issue involving so many technical judgments. I feared that the pressures to settle might prove too great for a reasonable outcome. (This exchange is ironic in the light of later claims that too many issues were negotiated in Moscow during the summit under too great a pressure of time. In fact, all except one of the key issues were settled before the summit and that one was much less complex than the SLBM question.)

The President agreed with me, but rather than fight his arms control negotiator and State, he asked me to put Laird's scheme to Dobrynin in the special Channel. If the Soviets accepted it, we could argue with the bureaucracy then; if they rejected it, no harm would have been done and much controversy avoided. I did this on March 9, "thinking out loud" as if it were my own idea for breaking the deadlock; Dobrynin showed no interest. I threatened that we would undertake a crash program to build submarines. (The impact of my threat could not have been helped by the budding press campaign attacking Laird for his Trident program and urging that we exchange the concept of a new generation of submarines for a moratorium on all submarine construction.)[2] Dobrynin urged the same line as our critics: He thought it best to complete only the ABM agreement and ICBM freeze; SLBMs should be left for later. I insisted that we would not let Soviet SLBMs run free; Dobrynin indicated that in that case a deadlock was probable. By early April, Dobrynin hinted that the Soviet leadership was studying the SLBM issue, but he gave no indication of their conclusions. And there matters rested when I left for Moscow.

The other important summit problem on which significant exchanges had taken place in the Channel was the final communiqué. Dobrynin had broached the subject in a gingerly fashion on January 21, asking me whether we were thinking of a single document that listed the issues discussed or whether we were open to a separate "Declaration of Principles." The Soviets are much addicted to declarations of principles. Probably they see in them an acknowledgment of equality and a device to create the impression that major progress is taking place in bilateral relations. Perhaps there is something in Russian history that leads them to value ritual, solemn declarations, and visible symbols. Whatever the reason, by the time our summit preparations were well launched, the Soviet Union had signed a long and effusive Declaration of Principles with President Pompidou, and one with Turkey; and a protocol on consultation with Canada, not to mention the German-Soviet nonaggression treaty. I responded to Dobrynin noncommittally, although I knew we were planning to include a statement of principles in our communiqué from China. I thought it important to avoid any impression of US–Soviet condominium, and I delayed until the Chinese trip was behind us lest preliminary drafts be played back misleadingly to Peking.

Nixon and I agreed that, given the precedents, a declaration of principles would be hard to avoid. Therefore we sought to use it to achieve some positive ends. We could elaborate *our* principles of international restraint — such as those Nixon had enunciated in his address to the United Nations in October 1970 — which if implemented would ease tensions, and if flouted could provide a rallying point for opposition to Soviet aggressiveness. So when Dobrynin raised the matter again on February 7 (still before the Peking summit), I told him we would be glad to look at a Soviet proposal. Dobrynin was too nimble for that; he was afraid that his own government's submission was likely to be rejected. At a minimum, the final draft would show that the Soviets had made major concessions. On March 9, after Nixon's China trip, Dobrynin suggested we use the French declaration as a model. I again asked for a Soviet draft. Dobrynin demurred on the ground that once a Soviet draft existed any modification would require government approval; long-distance negotiations would prove extremely complicated.

By the middle of March I thought that enough time had passed since the Peking summit. With the President's approval I handed Dobrynin on March 17 a draft communiqué spelling out, as did the Shanghai Communiqué, the principles we thought should govern US–Soviet relations. We emphasized mutual restraint, noninterference in the affairs of other states, and the renunciation of pressures for unilateral advantage. There was no reply. Nothing further was heard of this project until I arrived in Moscow a month later.

On the Middle East, Dobrynin sought to engage me in a dialogue designed, in effect, to impose the extreme Arab program. This did not fit into our strategy as long as Soviet troops and advisers were so prominent in Egypt and as long as the Soviet Union was supporting the radical Arabs. When I countered with proposals related to Israel's security concerns, he rapidly lost interest.

For the rest, the prospect of the May summit was used to prod our two bureaucracies to work out detailed agreements on various technical subjects suitable for bilateral cooperation. These accords were not politically significant, but they would demonstrate that the United States and the Soviet Union as major industrial powers had common interests in a variety of fields. Once unleashed, the bureaucracies dug up every project that had lain dormant for years and pushed them to a conclusion with the summit as the deadline. The biggest problem was still the unending rivalry between the White House and the various departments as to who would get credit. For example, in February an agreement was reached to expand commercial air services between the United States and the Soviet Union. It was signed routinely at the State Department on March 17. When I informed the President by memorandum on March 22, Nixon wrote on it: "K, get some credit for us."

A compromise was finally reached between the departments' desire for recognition for having done the negotiating and Nixon's insistence on a share of the glory. The signing of most of the bilateral agreements was postponed until the summit. There they would be signed by the Cabinet members whose staffs had negotiated them, in the presence of a beaming Nixon and Brezhnev. Rogers signed the agreements on health and science and technology; John Warner, Secretary of the Navy, signed an agreement on procedures to avoid incidents at sea. For some reason lost in the murk of time, Nixon decided that he would sign the agreement on environmental protection. One effect of holding up the signing of the agreements was an incidental linkage: If the summit did not take place, these agreements, which the Soviets so desired, would not be consummated.

On the economic front we were facing two pressures, Soviet and domestic. The Soviets had indicated an interest in trade since early in the Administration, as I discussed in Chapter V. In the fall of 1971, with a summit finally scheduled, Gromyko formally raised the issue with Nixon. Dobrynin followed up by proposing an exchange of visits of Cabinet officers responsible for trade. Secretary of Commerce Maurice Stans went to Moscow late in November and returned enchanted by Soviet hospitality and with great expectations of a boom in Soviet trade. There were three obstacles — Most Favored Nation (MFN) status for the Soviet Union, Soviet Lend-Lease debts, and linkage. The United States had withdrawn MFN status from the Soviet Union during the Korean War; even though restoring it would have marginal impact on our trade, it was of considerable symbolic importance. But MFN status could not be granted without Congressional support, for which it was necessary to clear away one old wartime issue, the repayment of Russia's Lend-Lease debt. The Soviets passionately resented the proposition that they should be asked to pay for assistance in a war against a common mortal enemy in which they had suffered the

heaviest in terms of human lives. The Congress felt otherwise; it believed that we should be repaid at least for the consumer goods, all the
more so as Britain had made a settlement on that basis. MFN status and
the Lend-Lease debt became linked, though the discussions remained inconclusive in early 1972. The United States asked for $800 million to
settle the matter; the Soviets offered $300 million. They indicated also
an interest in purchasing grain — though they played their cards so
skillfully and close to the chest that we did not become aware of the
critical nature of their needs until much too late.

The third and final obstacle faced by Maury Stans was linkage: the
White House's determination to have trade follow political progress and
not precede it. Nixon and I agreed that it was best to proceed deliberately on grain sales (by delaying a trip to Moscow by Secretary of Agriculture Earl Butz until April). We would make a Lend-Lease settlement
a prerequisite for MFN. We would hold off on the joint exploitation of
natural resources, such as Siberian natural gas, until after the Vietnam
war ended. We would, in short, make economic relations depend on
some demonstrated progress on matters of foreign policy importance to
the United States.

It proved difficult to convince Stans of the wisdom of this course. The
basic issue was, as I told him, "whether we will use them or they will
use us." He resisted this; to him trade was a good in itself; by definition
it involved mutual benefit. A conservative Republican, he joined the
chorus of liberal critics who continued to disparage all barriers to US–
Soviet trade as outdated relics of the Cold War and who denounced
linkage as a perverse obstacle to the relaxation of tensions. At regular
intervals Maury would implore me to lengthen the short leash on which
he was operating. When we stuck to our policy, his associates would
complain to the press or else Stans would tell Dobrynin that the White
House was the real obstacle to expanded trade. This unintentionally conferred credibility on our strategy. Dobrynin was sophisticated enough in
American ways to take in his stride the phenomenon of a Cabinet officer
complaining to a Communist ambassador about the political restrictions
under which he was laboring. But, as Dobrynin explained it to me,
Moscow saw Stans's fervor as part of a deliberate, clever design. What
Stans intended as evidence of his personal goodwill was interpreted in
Moscow — where it was assumed to be orchestrated from my
office — as a particularly subtle form of political pressure.

All these strands of policy, many of them interwoven, would be
tested on my trip to Moscow. But overshadowing them all, when the
time came for departure, was the offensive launched on March 30 by the
North Vietnamese army. Could the Soviet Union be induced to pressure
its client, for the sake of the summit? Or were we ourselves in danger of
being manipulated by the Soviet Union so that we would hesitate in

responding militarily to North Vietnam's challenges? Nixon, as I have described, had become visibly anxious in the week's interval between the April 12 decision that I should go and my departure. He worried that the Soviets would stall on Vietnam and thereby inhibit our reaction. I thought the opposite more likely: that the imminence of a summit could be used as a brake on Soviet responses and thus separate Hanoi and Moscow.

Before I left, Nixon gave me his familiar instructions to take a hard line. This was not unusual; it accompanied my departure for every negotiation. Nor in this case did it conflict with my own views. Now that Hanoi had committed its entire army to the offensive, I strongly favored bringing matters to a head. I was convinced that negotiations were inevitable once Hanoi's offensive was blunted. On the other hand, I did not think Moscow could halt the war by ukase, or be expected to turn openly against its ally. The dedicated revolutionaries in Hanoi had fought all their lives; by now they had accumulated enough supplies to see the offensive through regardless of pressures from Moscow. They had staked the war's outcome on its success; it was now too late for Moscow to order them to stop. It was up to the South Vietnamese — and the United States — to take the steps necessary to defeat it. Moscow could not act as our surrogate, though its acquiescence in our reaction would ease our job.

I presented my proposed strategy to Nixon in a memorandum. I would make clear to Moscow, I wrote, that "you intend to do what is necessary militarily to stop the Communist offensive and in that sense are prepared to subordinate your relationship with the USSR to the immediate requirements of the Vietnam situation." I said that I would insist on discussing Vietnam "before we turn to the summit-related substantive issues of US–Soviet relations." I would ask the North Vietnamese to

desist from their invasion across the DMZ; to pull back to North Vietnam the three NVA divisions, accompanying armor, artillery and anti-aircraft equipment involved in that invasion; and to fully restore the 1968 understandings, including complete respect for the DMZ and no shelling attacks on major South Vietnamese cities.

If this is agreed and, as it is being implemented, we will correspondingly reduce our air and naval bombardments against the DRV and cease them completely when the foregoing has been accomplished.

The Soviets' incentive, according to my memorandum, lay in their overall relationship with us:

The Soviets must bear considerable responsibility for the Communist offensive in Vietnam and we should therefore not be expected to "reward" them for using their influence to bring about deescalation. Nevertheless, the most promising *tactic* for implementing the general strategy will probably be to hold out to Brezhnev the *prospect* of a broad improvement in relations with us.

In other words, a carrot and a stick. We would not shy away from the military measures necessary to defeat Hanoi's offensive, whatever the embarrassment this would cause the Soviet Union, whatever the risk to our relationship with Moscow, and in the face of the predictable domestic outcry. At the same time, we would put before the Soviet leaders the carrot of substantial progress in US–Soviet relations. I explained to Nixon the positions I would take on such issues as SALT, European security, and the communiqué concluding his visit. I would link economic relations to political progress, including Soviet help on Vietnam.

Nixon initialed his approval of my memorandum, adding "OK — as modified by RN oral instructions." A fuller account of these oral instructions will have to await release of the relevant Nixon tape recordings. My only source is the handwritten notes I jotted down on the yellow pad that was standard equipment in the Oval Office. According to these notes, my instructions were not free of Nixon's customary hyperbole. I was to stress that the Soviet Union and the United States were the two nations with the greatest responsibility for international peace. The summit had the potential of being the most important diplomatic encounter "of this century." It was indispensable to have "progress" on Vietnam *by the time of the summit*. My notes also contained the detailed characterization of Nixon that I should give to Brezhnev: "direct, honest, strong . . . fatalistic — to him election [is] not key. Will not be affected one iota by public opinion. No other President could make SALT agreement while war is still going on." On the other hand, there would be Congressional opposition to economic deals unless progress was made on Vietnam. I should express the President's personal respect for Brezhnev. In the communiqué I was to emphasize the need for a single standard; we could not accept the proposition that the Soviet Union had the right to support liberation movements all over the world while insisting on the Brezhnev Doctrine inside the satellite orbit.

Nixon's oral comments were for the most part elaborations of the basic strategy in my paper. Whatever differences existed were not explicit in, and did not arise from, the conversations with me — these were essentially identical with the words that had sent me off on other journeys. But an important difference in emphasis was soon to become evident.

It began to emerge, in fact, when I was on the plane heading for Moscow. For the first time, there had obviously been no complete meeting of minds between us on the strategy for an important negotiation. Nixon cabled the aircraft that on reflection he had become convinced that I should go immediately to the subject of Vietnam and not permit Brezhnev to filibuster. I should stick to that subject until Brezhnev and I had reached "some sort of understanding." Nixon said he felt that my trip would be considered a failure by our critics if Moscow kept up its posture of all-out public support for Hanoi. "This will be much more the case with the Soviets, incidentally, than with the Chinese. With the Chinese, we made no pretense about having made progress on Vietnam. On the other hand, with the Soviets we are going to try to leave the impression that we have made some progress." To avoid the danger he urged me to include a phrase in the announcement of my trip stating or implying that Vietnam would be one of the priority items on the summit agenda. For the rest, Nixon told me to stick to the agreed program of demanding withdrawal across the DMZ of the additional North Vietnamese units taking part in the offensive, as a precondition of our ending the bombing of North Vietnam.

It was a strange instruction, at once too soft and too tough. As I read the cable, I jotted notes to myself in the margin for a reply. It was not the "pretense" of progress that we needed, but the reality. Nixon's instruction to put Vietnam publicly on the summit agenda seemed to me "too dilatory." Such an announcement would make it difficult for us to retaliate against Hanoi until the summit was concluded. I cabled back to him via Haig: "I do not think it is a good idea to have a statement which defers Vietnam to the summit agenda. We now have maximum momentum and Hanoi for the first time in the war is backing off. Also, the summit is one of our best bargaining counters. We therefore must get some concrete results now."

Nixon quickly cabled back his concurrence and the difficulty seemed to recede. But not for long.

Leonid Brezhnev

M Y first meeting with Brezhnev was scheduled for eleven o'clock in the morning of April 21. Dobrynin paid me a preliminary visit to make sure that everything was on track. Dobrynin was, I am convinced, sincerely dedicated to the improvement of US–Soviet relations; he was eager that nothing unforeseen should derail the product of his devoted labors. He was clearly unsure of how his General Secretary, with limited experience in foreign policy and regular contact with foreign leaders only in the last two years, would conduct himself.

Dobrynin's nervousness proved unjustified. Leonid Brezhnev was awaiting us in the largest guest house of the complex of villas where we were staying. Flanked by Gromyko and Dobrynin, with his aide Andrei Aleksandrov hovering unobtrusively a step behind, the successor to Lenin, Stalin, and Khrushchev welcomed me ebulliently. Obviously torn between the advice he must have received to behave discreetly and his own gregarious impulse, he alternated between pummeling me and wearing a grave mien. He took me into a dining room where the table had been covered with green baize to connote that negotiations would be taking place. I thanked him for the warmth of the welcome. Brezhnev joked that they hoped to make me feel warmer still. I asked whether this was a threat or a pleasant prospect. Brezhnev replied that the Soviet Union did not believe in threats — a welcome piece of information that struck me as new.

Within the space of two months, then, I had come face to face with the powerful heads of both Communist giants. Brezhnev could not have been more different from the Chinese. Both sets of leaders guided vast countries that had often been the subject of foreign invasions. But culture, history, and personal experience combined to produce vividly contrasting personalities and styles. Mao Tse-tung and Chou En-lai represented a society with the longest uninterrupted experience in the art of government, a nation that had always been culturally preeminent in its region. China had absorbed conquerors and had proved its inward strength by imposing its social and intellectual style on them. Its leaders were aloof, self-assured, composed. Brezhnev represented a nation that had survived not by civilizing its conquerors but by outlasting them, a people suspended between Europe and Asia and not wholly of either, with a culture that had destroyed its traditions without yet entirely replacing them. He sought to obscure his lack of assurance by boisterousness, and his sense of latent inadequacy by occasional bullying.

Appearances meant a lot to Brezhnev. On my secret visit, he arranged with great pride a tour of the spacious and elegant Tsars' Apartments in the Kremlin where Nixon would live, obviously expecting approval; such an action could not conceivably have come from a Chinese leader. Along the corridor marble pedestals bearing huge vases stood between every two windows. All the vases were draped except one, which was shown to me as an example of the high polish that patient labors had achieved; the shrouds would stay on to preserve the sheen, it was explained, until an hour before Nixon's arrival. All this suggested an uneasy, quite touching, meld of defensiveness and vulnerability somewhat out of keeping with the assertive personal style. At this point the personalities of Nixon and Brezhnev intersected.

To be sure, no one reached the top of a Communist hierarchy except by ruthlessness. Yet the charm of the Chinese leaders obscured that quality, while Brezhnev's gruff heavy-handedness tended to emphasize it. The Chinese even amid the greatest cordiality kept their distance. Brezhnev, who had physical magnetism, crowded his interlocutor. He changed moods rapidly and wore his emotions openly. These contrasting styles seemed also to be reflected in Chinese and Russian food.

Chinese cuisine is delicate, meticulous, and infinitely varied. Russian meals are heavy, straightforward, predictable. One eats Chinese food gracefully with chopsticks; one could eat most Russian food with one's hands. One walks away from a Chinese meal satisfied but not satiated, and looking forward to the next experience. After a Russian meal one is stuffed; one can barely face the prospect of the next round.

The Chinese leaders whom we first met had made their own revolution. Mao and Chou had themselves launched what they saw as a new epoch in history. Brezhnev was already the fourth in the revolutionary succession — a small number compared with Western countries, but still enough to place him in a long tradition. The Chinese drew inspiration from their heroic personal experiences, especially the legendary Long March. Brezhnev and his colleagues' long marches had been through savage infighting and bureaucratic jockeying within a Communist system. Their lifetimes had been spent clawing their way to the top and pushing aside (or putting away) formidable fellow Marxists. In the various successions strategic vision may have become impaired, but tactical skill had been sharpened.

The fact that in sixty years there had been only four Soviet leaders tells much about the Soviet system — or maybe any Communist one (although the Soviets have lived with the problem longest). No Communist state has solved the problem of regular succession. Every leader dies in office, or is replaced by couplike procedures. Honorific retirement is rare and nonexistent for the supreme leader. No Soviet leader's reputation, except Lenin's, has survived his death. In every Communist state a leadership group seize power, grow old together, and are eventually replaced by successors whose ability to reach the pinnacle depends on their skill in masking their ambitions. They live uncertainly on the way to the top, and they are aware of impermanence when they have supreme power — for they know that they will probably be denied by their successors the accolade of history, which is the incentive of most statesmen. In an ultimate paradox the political system based on historical truth denies historical significance to its votaries. They gain a long tenure in office at the price of final oblivion.

Leonid Brezhnev, when I met him, was clearly the leading Soviet figure. But equally he was obviously not yet in complete charge and already was on the verge of waning physical power. During the summit he went to great lengths to involve Premier Kosygin and President Podgorny in the meetings. Even in his first encounter with me he left the impression that he was expounding the agreed position of a collective to which he was under some obligation to report back. (Of course, visibly depriving oneself of flexibility is also an effective bargaining device that I occasionally used myself.) Brezhnev, it seemed, had authority to add nuances to an agreed position, but could not make radical shifts on his own — as an American President's authority and independence allow. At the same time, Brezhnev left the impression that if convinced that a change was necessary he would be able to carry the Politburo with him. As time went on, Brezhnev gained visibly in authority. After 1975, however, his declining health and limited attention span forced him to give Gromyko an increasing role in foreign affairs.

During our first encounter Brezhnev seemed nervous, probably because he felt insecure dealing with senior Americans for the first time, and partly because of his copious consumption of tobacco and alcohol, his history of heart disease, and the pressures of his job. His hands were perpetually in motion: twisting his watch; flicking ashes from his ever-present cigarette (until he was put on the regimen of a locked cigarette case that would open only at preset intervals, which he found ingenious ways to get around); clanging his cigarette holder against an ashtray. He could not keep still. While his remarks were being translated he would restlessly bound up from his chair, walk around the room, engage in loud conversations with his colleagues, or even leave the room without explanation and then return. Negotiations with Brezhnev thus included the bizarre feature that he might disappear at any moment; or while you were being most persuasive he could be concentrating not on your remarks but on forcing food on you. On one occasion he brought along a toy cannon to the conference room, normally used for meetings of the Politburo. It refused to fire. Making it work preoccupied him far more than whatever profundities I might be uttering at the moment. Finally the contraption went off with a roar. Brezhnev strutted around the room like a prizefighter who has knocked out his opponent. Negotiations then resumed as an uneasy tranquillity descended, which those of us by now familiar with Brezhnev knew would be temporary.

Before his health declined he liked to interrupt talks with anecdotes of varying quality, occasionally but not inevitably germane. At our first meeting, trying to stress the importance of making major progress, he told this tale:

There is a story of a traveler who wants to go from one place to another village. He does not know the distance; he knows only the road and his goal. He sees a man along the road chopping wood, and asks him, how much time does it take to get to that village? The woodsman says he doesn't know. The traveler is somewhat offended at the woodsman, because he is from there and surely must know. So the traveler heads off down the road. After he had taken a few strides, the woodsman calls out, "Stop. It will take you 15 minutes." "Why didn't you tell me the first time I asked?" the traveler asked. "Because then I didn't know the length of your stride."

Brezhnev cited this banal parable to urge me to "take long strides" in the negotiation.

Another Brezhnev anecdote gives some of the flavor of the conversation at our first encounter:

BREZHNEV: There is an anecdote about the Tsar who had before him a case of an arrested man. The question was, would he be executed or pardoned? The Tsar wrote out a piece of paper with only three words on it: "Execution impossible pardon," but the commas were misplaced. It should have read: "Execution impossible, pardon." But the official receiving it read it as "execution, impossible (to) pardon." No, that wasn't quite it; actually the Tsar wrote it without commas and then the lawyers had to decide which he meant.

KISSINGER: What happened to the man?

BREZHNEV: I will tell you that at the end of our discussions, before you go. My answer will depend on how our talks go.

GROMYKO: Maybe the answer should be given only at the Summit.

BREZHNEV: No, Dr. Kissinger has to leave Moscow with clear answers to all his questions. Because you might want to tell the President this story. He will want to know the ending. If you don't know it, he will wonder what you were talking about here.

KISSINGER: From my experience with bureaucracies, they probably did both.

I never did receive the answer.

Brezhnev was, in short, not only head of the Central Committee of the Communist Party of the Soviet Union but quintessentially Russian. He was a mixture of crudeness and warmth; at the same time brutal and engaging, cunning and disarming. While he boasted of Soviet strength, one had the sense that he was not really all that sure of it. Having grown up in a backward society nearly overrun by Nazi invasion, he might know the statistics of relative power but seemed to feel in his bones the vulnerability of his system. It is my nightmare that his successors, bred in more tranquil times and accustomed to modern technology and military strength, might be freer of self-doubt; with no such inferiority complex, they may believe their own boasts and, with a military establishment now covering the globe, may prove far more dangerous.

Equality seemed to mean a great deal to Brezhnev. It would be inconceivable that Chinese leaders would ask for it — if only because in the Middle Kingdom tradition it was a great concession granted *to* the foreigner. To Brezhnev it was central. In the first fifteen minutes of our meeting he complained about Nixon's impromptu toast in Shanghai to the effect that the United States and China held the future of the world in their hands. Brezhnev thought this downgraded the Soviet Union, to say the least. He expressed his pleasure when in my brief opening remarks I stated the obvious: that we were approaching the summit in a spirit of equality and reciprocity. What a more secure leader might have regarded as cliché or condescension, he treated as a welcome sign of our seriousness. (Even if his motive was flattery, it was an odd choice of object; flattery can be effective only if it is graced with some plausibility.)

Brezhnev led a nation that after nearly sixty years of horrible exertions still lagged behind Western Europe in technology and standard of living. He seemed in awe of American technology; he backed off in a crisis whenever we confronted him unambiguously with American power. The Soviet Union had acquired a tremendous military potential; it was a superpower; it had to be taken seriously. But it could not avoid the reality — perhaps even the premonition — that the Communist system is incompatible with the human spirit, that a modern economy cannot be run efficiently by total planning, that man cannot flourish without freedom. The state that sought to abolish the contradictions of the capitalist system emerged with a contradiction at once consoling to us and menacing: It could not possibly flourish with its existing structure because it stifled all creativity in a soulless bureaucracy. But its single-minded concentration on the one thing it did well, the accumulation of raw military power, gave it the means to disturb every equilibrium and the incentive to seek foreign success, even as its core grew more and more hollow. It thus faced us with the grave danger that its leaders at some point might seek to escape their historical perplexities by using the weapons they had so implacably accumulated over the decades.

Brezhnev was the incarnation of this ambivalence. Under his stewardship the Soviet Union had undertaken a colossal military buildup. Its origin may well have been Brezhnev's need to keep the military establishment on his side in the struggle to overthrow Khrushchev, as much as a well-thought-out design for world domination. In time the original motive would grow irrelevant. The accumulating military means would create their own opportunities and an inherent threat to the global balance of power. On the other hand, the massive devotion of scarce resources to military hardware would also inhibit the modernization of Soviet society. Brezhnev sought to escape the dilemma by relaxing tensions so that he could acquire Western technology without changing his domestic structure or impairing his military buildup or reducing Soviet global pressures. He was all the more tempted to do this because geopolitically the Soviet Union, despite its seeming power, was in an uncomfortable position. With our opening to Peking the time would be not far off when all the major power centers — the United States, Western Europe, China, and Japan — would be on one side and the Soviet Union on the other. Brezhnev was a man in a hurry caught between two challenges: He wanted to calm the threat from Russia's Western past so that he could deal with its Chinese future. Détente was his way of seeking this. The Chinese were not wrong when they saw it as a potential peril to themselves. Our challenge was whether by bringing our power to bear wisely we could induce a genuine reduction of tensions, genuine in the sense that it reduced the dangers to Europe without magnifying the menace to Asia.

We will never know whether a real relaxation was possible in the period immediately after 1972. No doubt Brezhnev justified détente to his colleagues as a way to beguile the West. And that was surely one of its dangers. But I also believe that part of Brezhnev sincerely sought, if not peace in the Western sense, then surcease from the danger and risks and struggles of a lifetime. I read a novel once, based on the proposition that each human being has a finite amount of qualities like courage and endurance and wisdom, and that life consists of expending these ever-dwindling resources. Something like that seemed to have happened to Brezhnev. When I met him he had gone through the Stalin purges of the Thirties (indeed, his first big jump up the ladder took place then), the Second World War, a new wave of purges, the power struggle following the death of Stalin, and the intrigue that led to the overthrow of Khrushchev and catapulted Brezhnev to the top. He seemed at once exuberant and spent, eager to prevail but at minimum risk. He had had enough excitement for one lifetime. He spoke often, and on occasion movingly, about the suffering and trauma of the Second World War.

None of this, of course, changed the realities of Soviet power, which he was augmenting energetically. And this would have to be balanced by our strength, whatever Brezhnev's intentions or professions. Détente could never replace a balance of power; it would be the result of equilibrium, not a substitute for it. And I therefore consistently spurred the strengthening of our own defenses. Maybe Brezhnev's performance was all theater, though I believe outsiders exaggerate busy leaders' capacity for sustained dissimulation. I thought he was genuine in his desire for a respite for his country. What I was unsure of was the price he would be willing to pay for it. Was he prepared for an end to the constant probing for openings and the testing of every equilibrium? Was he ready to begin a true period of coexistence? Or was it all a tactical maneuver to weaken our vigilance before the next round of pressures would be exerted with growing power?

Our strategy of détente always depended on a firm application of psychological and physical restraints and determined resistance to challenges. We had shown this in Jordan, Cienfuegos, India-Pakistan, and shortly would show it in Vietnam; we sought to show it later in Angola. In later years, the collapse of our executive authority as a result of Watergate, the erosion of the leadership structure even in the Congress, the isolationism born of the frustrations of Vietnam, and an emerging pattern of geopolitical abdication conspired to prevent the establishment of the balance of incentives and penalties that might have preempted several crises and in the long run given us a genuine period of restraint. Instead, we ended up achieving the worst of all results: constant pinpricks of the Soviet bear (denial of MFN status, for example), but not coupled with a readiness on our part to run the risks that alone could produce Soviet caution (in Angola, for example). In the absence of an equilibrium, without the provision of incentives and penalties, the inherent dynamics of the Soviet system again tempted it into expansion a few years after the 1972 summit. And Brezhnev's failing health may have enabled more energetic hands to design a conscious challenge to the West in the latter part of the 1970s. Now, not even Brezhnev will ever know how much he might have been prepared to pay in restraint for a genuine peace immediately after 1972, had we maintained the right balance between firmness and conciliation.

Conversations with Brezhnev and Gromyko

W HEN he opened our meeting on April 21, Brezhnev spoke from notes — a departure from what we had learned of his practice in early encounters with foreign leaders when he was dependent upon reading prepared statements. Brezhnev effusively expressed his commitment to the success of the forthcoming summit. There would be agreements, he insisted. "We have no wish to bring about a quarrel in the [summit] meeting. That is something we could easily do by staying in Washington and Moscow." He referred only tangentially to Vietnam. In uncharacteristically delicate reference to the B-52 bombing of Hanoi and Haiphong four days before my arrival, he observed: "Unfortunately it so happens that events in the recent period — shortly before this private meeting between us — dampened the atmosphere somewhat." It was not much of a statement of support for an ally even now being bombed on a daily basis. And even this was immediately qualified by a reassurance: "I am not saying this will reduce the prospects for our meeting." The next day Brezhnev said that he controlled neither our peace proposals nor our bombers, offering no suggestions for the former and uttering no threat with respect to the latter. His priority was clearly the summit and US–Soviet relations, not Vietnam.

All of the first day, however, was to be devoted to the war. Rather than begin with ultimatums, I expressed on behalf of the President our commitment to a successful summit. We wanted to improve not only the atmosphere but also the substance of East-West relationships. This was to set the stage for an exposition of North Vietnamese duplicity and of our determination to bring matters to a head in Vietnam. I said bluntly that Hanoi's offensive threatened the summit. I went so far as to advance the startling thesis that the Soviets had an interest in preventing a North Vietnamese victory; I doubted that the President could come to Moscow if we suffered a defeat. Even if the outcome were still in doubt by then, the American people would be aware that it was Soviet equipment which had made Hanoi's offensive possible; hence the President's freedom of action would be serverely limited: "I must in all honesty tell the General Secretary that if developments continue unchecked, either we will take actions which will threaten the summit or, if the summit should take place, we will lose the freedom of action to achieve the objective which we described.'' I insisted that there had to be a private meeting with Le Duc Tho before May 6 and that it would have to be conclusive: ''We are not interested in talks. We are interested in results. I like Mr. Le Duc Tho. He is a most impressive man, but the reason I want to see him is not for the pleasure of his company, but to have some concrete results.''

Brezhnev's response was mild in the extreme. He did not dispute my characterization of the North Vietnamese. He did not answer my thinly veiled threats. He read instead a note from Hanoi refusing to send an emissary to meet me in Moscow. He proudly showed me the cable, which I was of course unable to read, to demonstrate that he alone was listed on the distribution. (If this was genuine, he clearly expanded its circulation on the spot.) The North Vietnamese were now insisting on resumption of the plenary sessions on April 27 to be followed by a secret meeting on May 6. They added two minor concessions, however: Le Duc Tho would leave Hanoi as soon as we had accepted a plenary session, and we could propose an earlier date provided we gave Le Duc Tho a week to reach Paris. (He usually traveled via Peking and Moscow, stopping for consultations in each ''fraternal'' capital.) The North Vietnamese, who trusted no one, not even their principal supporter, forty-eight hours earlier had sent us directly the very proposal Brezhnev read to me. They felt no need to remind us, however, of their long-standing refusal to meet me in Moscow.

As was already clear before I went to Moscow, what was needed to have a private meeting was some formula to preserve everyone's face. For this we did not need Soviet assistance. What we had to accomplish in Moscow was to convey our determination to bring matters to a head; to estimate our host's likely response if we proceeded unilaterally; and to engage the Kremlin in a manner most likely to bring home to Hanoi its increasing isolation. I told Brezhnev ominously: ''So we have two requirements. The first is that the meeting cannot take place on May 6; first, because I am occupied on that day, and secondly, because that is too late, as I told your Ambassador. May 2 is the latest date I can attend and on which private talks still make sense.'' I warned that at the next meeting Le Duc Tho had to change his negotiating habits. We would no longer hold still for a recital of ultimatums in which Hanoi's demands were treated as the sole revealed truth: ''If this process is maintained we will act unilaterally at whatever risk to whatever relationship.''

It was a measure of Brezhnev's commitment to the summit that he listened to these provocative remarks without demur. Only the Chinese, he said, opposed the summit: ''You should bear in mind that powerful forces in the world are out to block the summit meeting. It certainly would be quite a big gift to the Chinese if the meeting did not come off. It would only help China.'' This statement convinced me that Brezhnev would go to great lengths to avoid canceling the summit. And nothing could reveal better the Soviet fixation with China than Brezhnev's apparent assumption that something that helped China would by definition be anathema to us. The "Chinese menace" had become second nature; it supplied its own justification even when cited to an American who, not two months previously, had drafted a communiqué in Peking whose condemnation of hegemony was clearly aimed at Soviet expansionism. This obsession also accounted for the compulsive manner in which the Soviet leaders kept raising China, oscillating between seeming uneasiness and the unshakable conviction that sooner or later — if they only kept at it long enough — we would join them in a condominium to stifle what they considered the overwhelming threat from the East.

I did not immediately put forward a formula for breaking the procedural deadlock with Hanoi. Nor did I submit our substantive proposal for the negotiations because I thought I had reached the limit of what the traffic would bear in that meeting. And since the hour was getting late I did not want to end the session by putting forth terms that might be rejected and thus give Brezhnev a night to think up reasons for doing so.

Brezhnev ended the five-hour meeting by suggesting we both reflect on our exchanges and "reach results" so that he would not be criticized by the Central Committee or I by the President. I replied that I ran a greater risk of being scolded by the President than he by the Central Committee. He did not know how truthful I was.

The next day, April 22, involved another five-hour session. I began by presenting a compromise proposal to break the deadlock over the sequence of plenary and private meetings with the North Vietnamese: We would attend a plenary session on April 27, provided Hanoi agreed in advance of it to a private meeting on May 2. I pointed out ominously that this was the last practicable date before we had to make "other decisions''; results therefore had to be achieved at that meeting. To give emphasis to the not very subtle warning, I said that we would not bomb in the Hanoi or Haiphong area pending the meeting. Brezhnev hailed my proposal as "constructive." As far as I was concerned, its major utility was to make the Soviets share responsibility for the meeting's outcome and to put the onus on Hanoi for its failure.

I therefore also described the substantive proposal that I would make to Le Duc Tho on May 2. It was the proposal I had outlined in my strategy memorandum for the President, who had approved it on April 19: withdrawal of those North Vietnamese units that had entered South Vietnam since March 29, respect for the DMZ, immediate exchange of prisoners who had been held for more than four years, and a serious effort to negotiate a settlement within an agreed time period. In return the

United States would halt the bombing of North Vietnam and withdraw the air and naval forces we had introduced since March 29.

This proposal has been the subject of some fiction. One account claims that it was a "concession of enormous magnitude" which left Brezhnev "astonished," a "veritable diplomatic bomb," "the first major turning point in the Vietnam negotiations."[3] Even apart from my impression that Brezhnev was not all that familiar with the details of the Vietnam negotiations, the account is pure nonsense. There was less to my proposal than met the eye. It was *tougher* than the standard US position in that it added the rather ambitious demand that the North Vietnamese units which had invaded in the March offensive should withdraw unilaterally. This demand was a throwaway; no one has devised a way to accomplish at the bargaining table what has not been achieved on the battlefield. The demand could be discarded when Hanoi was ready for serious negotiation; it was to be quietly dropped in Nixon's May 8 speech. The importance of my April trip was not the substantive proposal but the fact that the USSR engaged itself in the process in a manner that worked to our advantage.

Brezhnev responded to my somewhat insolent proposal in an extraordinarily conciliatory manner. He mumbled something about the difficulty of withdrawing North Vietnamese divisions in the midst of an offensive. "Just by listening by ear" — assuring me he did not want to "raise any conditions" — he wondered if we could "perhaps" exclude that provision. What would I think of a cease-fire along existing lines with all units staying in place? I said that three weeks earlier we would have jumped at such an opportunity. Now that Hanoi had put its entire army into the South, it would no longer do:

But now we have a situation where North Vietnam has violated the understanding we had with them in 1968. You know very well in this room that there was an understanding to respect the Demilitarized Zone. Therefore, it is imperative, if we are to stop the bombing, that they withdraw the divisions that crossed the DMZ, and that henceforth the DMZ be respected.

I had my doubts whether Hanoi would yet accept a cease-fire in place — a proposal that had been on the table since May 31, 1971. If Hanoi were interested, we would surely hear about it on May 2. That would be the time to make the decision; it was not an issue to be settled in Moscow. And my Soviet hosts were in no mood to debate Vietnam proposals. Brezhnev was obviously eager to get on to other business. He therefore agreed to submit our proposals to Hanoi. And, in fact, the head of the Soviet Central Committee section dealing with foreign Communist parties, Konstantin Katushev, left on a special plane for Hanoi shortly afterward. Moscow was now engaged. Nations do not generally transmit offers with whose rejection they intend to associate themselves.

Brezhnev's low-key treatment of Vietnam, his refusal to seek to soften our threats or contest our tough demands, was further indication that we could go quite some distance before the Soviets would jeopardize the summit. This was crucial intelligence for the crisis that would be ahead, either if the North Vietnamese refused the May 2 meeting or if it failed.

At this point, I made a crucial decision. I agreed to put Vietnam to the side and proceed with summit preparations. Thanks to a communications snarl to be discussed below, I had not received contrary instructions. I had little doubt from the ambiguous cable exchange with Nixon while I was on the plane that he was nervous about my discussing any subject but Vietnam. The night before, I had received an instruction — which I immediately appealed — to cut short the talks and return home pending a Soviet decision to bring the Indochina war to a conclusion. I judged this to be dangerous and unwise and I therefore went to the limits of my discretionary authority and proceeded to the rest of the agenda. Brezhnev had held still for a day and a half of menacing statements directed against a Soviet ally obviously because he wanted to make progress toward a summit. If I now left Moscow without even giving him a chance to make whatever proposals he had clearly prepared, he was bound to consider it an affront, a putdown in front of his associates, a fundamental reversal of course, and a deliberate effort to force a showdown not over Vietnam but over US–Soviet relations in general. I thought the logical opponent for a confrontation was Hanoi. Moscow should be maneuvered into the position where *it* would have to make the choice about proceeding with the summit; we should not preempt it by forcing the decision upon it. For these and other reasons which I will discuss more fully below, I decided to let Brezhnev present his proposals on the major issues for the summit. If we wanted a showdown, the President could always reject them; it was a much better course than to refuse even to listen to Soviet offers in Moscow and to seek to face down Brezhnev demonstratively in full view of his Politburo.

One of Brezhnev's most striking characteristics, as of almost all Soviet negotiators, was his anxiety to get matters wrapped up once he had decided on a breakthrough. He could haggle and stall for months, even years. But once his own cumbersome machinery had disgorged a design, his domestic standing seemed to depend on his ability to get it implemented rapidly.

Brezhnev had come prepared with major proposals. They went most of the way toward our positions on the two principal outstanding issues, SALT and the communiqué. He began with a new proposal on ABMs. Arguing that he wanted to show "how the Soviet side solves problems in a constructive spirit," he abandoned the complicated formulas of the previous Soviet position, which amounted to three ABM sites for the

Soviets to two for us. His new plan permitted each side to protect its capital and one ICBM site. Brezhnev noted that given the Soviet pattern of deployment, this would mean that the Soviets were protecting only half the number of missiles that we were. Except for the last wrinkle, this happened to be exactly the position of Mel Laird. I had my doubts that we would ever get the funds for a missile defense of Washington. I therefore preferred each side to have the right to select whatever two locations it chose. In our case the second site would have been the missile field at Malmstrom where construction had already started (the first being at Grand Forks). But having come this far, the negotiation would surely not deadlock on the relatively minor difference now remaining between the two sides' ABM formulas — especially since the Pentagon seemed to prefer Brezhnev's formula.

I did not respond to the proposal, however, because I could see that Brezhnev had another paper that he was eager to put forward. First there was some byplay, which I reprint here to convey some of the atmosphere:

KISSINGER: Mr. General Secretary, let me say this is a constructive approach. I will reserve comment until I hear what you say about submarines.
BREZHNEV: Nothing.
KISSINGER: Nothing?
BREZHNEV: Be patient. What can I say about them? They travel under water, we can't see them. They're silent —
GROMYKO: [in English] Puzzle, puzzle!
KISSINGER: You do have something on submarines?
GROMYKO: You can't read it before Sukhodrev!*

It turned out that Brezhnev's new paper in effect accepted Laird's formula of January 18, which I had put forward while "thinking out loud" with Dobrynin in March. The Soviet Union agreed to a ceiling of 950 submarine-launched ballistic missiles (at least 200 less than our estimate of their capacity to reach over that period) and would "trade in" older SLBMs and older ICBMs to stay under that figure. (The number to be traded in still needed to be negotiated.) Brezhnev also agreed that the agreement limiting offensive forces could last for five years, as we had sought, rather than three years, which the Soviet delegation in Helsinki was still maintaining. I spent the rest of the meeting probing the

---

* Viktor Sukhodrev was the brilliant Soviet interpreter. I was frequently criticized for relying on Soviet interpreters. This was as nonsensical a charge as in the Chinese case. In fact, three members of my staff knew Russian (Sonnenfeldt, Hyland, and Rodman); several on Brezhnev's side of the table knew English (Gromyko, Dobrynin, and Aleksandrov). If Sukhodrev ever had difficulty with a word or phrase, a chorus of voices chimed in to help him. Aside from this, it was never clear to me how the Soviets could gain by deliberately mistranslating what I said to Brezhnev or what Brezhnev said to me. For all documents to be signed, we were able to examine the Russian-language text.

exact meaning of the "trade-in" provisions and discussing how to conduct the official SALT negotiations so as to conclude before the summit. I told Brezhnev that he had made a major step forward. We would convey our reply within ten days of my return.

Brezhnev's offer on SLBMs and of a five-year moratorium represented major Soviet concessions. Considering that our Trident program would produce no new submarine-launched missiles for five years, putting a ceiling on the Soviets' program below their potential was a limitation that affected only them. And the dismantling of several hundred older missiles was another boon. A five-year moratorium covered exactly the period we needed to develop the new weapons to fill the gap caused by the decisions of the Sixties, which had in effect stopped our development of new strategic missiles.

At the end of the session, with further joking and banter, Brezhnev came up with yet another document, a new draft of the Declaration of Principles. The Soviets had taken the six principles I had submitted on March 17, split them into twelve, and flavored them with *Pravda*-like rhetoric. Brezhnev must have been warned by Gromyko or Dobrynin that I would never accept this version, even though it included many of our ideas on restrained international conduct, for he urged me to "strengthen" his document, promising me the accolades of history if I took his advice. Even with my proverbial vanity I did not believe that history would remember a set of principles so watered down as to be equally acceptable to the principal capitalist and the strongest Communist state. But I recognized that having come this far, the Soviet leaders would not let the document fail over their own rhetoric. His invitation to "improve" the document clearly implied that there was room for bargaining to produce a version acceptable to us. It was left that I would try my hand at a new draft and that Gromyko and I would review it the next day (Sunday) while Brezhnev would be at his granddaughter's wedding.

The only other event of note was that Brezhnev and Gromyko asked for our assistance with the ratification of the Eastern treaties soon to come to a vote before the Bonn Parliament. (They wanted us to help Brandt win two crucial by-elections, as if we had any means of doing so.) I replied in a friendly but noncommittal way; I pointed out that Hanoi's offensive made it difficult to be of real use. Indeed, the Soviets' eagerness to complete these treaties would be one of our assets if Vietnam should reach crisis proportions in the weeks ahead. From our point of view, having the Eastern treaties in abeyance was exactly the ideal posture.

On Sunday Gromyko and I completed the "Basic Principles of US–Soviet Relations" on the basis of a counterdraft that Sonnenfeldt and I prepared overnight. It emphasized the necessity of restraint and of calming conflicts in the world's trouble spots. Both sides renounced any claim for special privileges in any part of the world (which we, at least, interpreted as a repudiation of the Brezhnev Doctrine for Eastern Europe).

There was an inconclusive discussion of the Middle East. Gromyko sought to commit me to some general principles that the United States and Soviet Union could jointly endorse. Rather than turn him down flatly, I replied soothingly with comments long on goodwill, sparse on specifics. I suggested that a detailed discussion be deferred to the summit. In fact, a Middle East condominium was a card that we had no interest in playing at all. My objectives here were modest: to gain time and to use the prospect of future US–Soviet consultations for whatever effect it might have as an incentive for Soviet restraint.

Finally, Gromyko and I finished the text of a brief announcement of my visit. The Soviets wanted to leave the impression that we had asked for the meeting and that its agenda was confined to summit preparations. Nixon's instruction was exactly the opposite: to state or imply that I had discussed Vietnam in Moscow — in order to unnerve the North Vietnamese and encourage our public. I was prepared to leave open the question of who had originated the invitation so long as it was not implied that we were the supplicant. We finally agreed on the following text:

Between April 20, and April 24, Dr. Henry A. Kissinger, Assistant to the President for National Security Affairs, was in Moscow to confer with the General Secretary of the Central Committee of the CPSU Brezhnev, and Foreign Minister Gromyko. The discussions dealt with important international problems, as well as with bilateral matters, preparatory to the talks between President Nixon and Soviet leaders in May. The discussions were frank and useful.

"Important international problems" was at that point in history (three weeks after Hanoi's offensive) an obvious reference to Vietnam.

I had another session with Brezhnev the following morning. He began with a long emotional discourse on Vietnam, stopping well short of endorsing Hanoi's objectives. Brezhnev stressed that Moscow was not behind the offensive; Hanoi had been hoarding Soviet weapons for two years; America was being challenged not by Moscow but by those opposed to the summit, principally the Chinese, and also Hanoi. Brezhnev insisted that he was committed to an improvement of US–Soviet relations. He was proceeding with the summit in the teeth of a formal request by Hanoi to cancel it, he said. And he was transmitting our proposals to Hanoi.

Talk then turned to economic relations. Brezhnev hailed the potential benefits of joint ventures in Siberia. He argued for such projects on the grounds of altruism; they would be of great benefit to the United States because of our impending shortage of natural gas. Brezhnev's solicitude about easing American economic difficulties was as heartwarming as it was preposterous. Brezhnev spoke of MFN status and credits. Shrewdly, he did not mention his real need, which was grain. My approach was to defer economic programs until there had been political progress. If relations went as hoped for at the summit, I told him, then "during the summit we can work out a complete project and make it concrete in the summer." But I did not fail to note that Congressional reaction would be affected by Vietnam: "It is a little tough when the trucks carrying weapons in Vietnam are Russian."

Brezhnev nonetheless was in an expansive mood. He asked to see me alone and suddenly introduced the idea of an "understanding" not to use nuclear weapons against each other. He called it a step of "immense significance," a "peaceful bomb." That it was. It would have produced an explosion in the NATO Alliance, in China, and throughout the world. It would have been considered either a US–Soviet condominium or an American abdication. I politely turned it aside. (The Soviets did not stop pursuing the idea. We eventually agreed in June 1973 on a bland set of principles that had been systematically stripped of all implications harmful to our interests.)

Then Brezhnev departed for what he claimed was a Politburo meeting, saying that he thought the announcement of my visit which Gromyko and I had worked on the day before was generally acceptable except for "some minor alterations," which he had marked on his copy. He threw it across the table and marched out. The document turned out to be the original Soviet draft that I had rejected the previous day. The purpose of my visit was stated to be summit preparations exclusively and the impression was created that we had sought the invitation.

Predictably, I exploded. Gromyko claimed that my choice was between Brezhnev's draft or none, since he could not interrupt a Politburo meeting. I warned him that it would make a devastating impression to conclude the visit without an announcement. It could only be read as an admission of total failure by the public and the press. But I would rather face this than deviate from the requirement that a discussion of "international problems" had to be mentioned (as code words for Vietnam). Gromyko continued to plead his inability to change the text. I was adamant. Finally, Gromyko decided that Brezhnev might be reachable after all. He excused himself for a few minutes, and when he returned, he quickly accepted a slightly modified version of the draft he and I had agreed upon the day before. The principal change was to drop the final phrase that the talks had been "frank and useful"; however, Gromyko agreed that I could use this phrase in briefings and that the Soviets would confirm it. In other words there would be a version for America and another for Hanoi.

The episode is significant precisely because it was so petty. Anything that could conceivably be gained by such a crude maneuver must surely be outweighed by its powerful reminder that in dealing with Soviet leaders one must be constantly on one's guard. It is illustrative of the Soviet tendency to squander goodwill for marginal gains and of a nearly compulsive tendency to score points meaningful only, if at all, in terms of the Politburo's internal rivalries.

After that stormy session, all was again serene and jovial, as is the way of Soviet negotiators when they have at last discovered what the negotiating limits are. Gromyko brought up Vietnam again. He said he was authorized to tell me that Moscow had not been fully aware of the seriousness of the situation until ten days previously. The Soviets now needed some time to make their influence felt. They were going to try to help bring about a rapid solution of the war. There was no reference to an end of bombing.

Before leaving Moscow I had one last painful duty to perform: to brief our Ambassador about my visit. Jacob Beam was a true professional who had earned Nixon's gratitude by treating him respectfully while Nixon was out of office. He conducted himself with gentle, unassuming skill during his tour of duty in Moscow. He deserved better than this apparent vote of no confidence that our strange system of government imposed on him. He conducted himself at our meeting with dignity and the attitude that stressed the word *Service* in his title of Foreign Service Officer. After that, I never visited Moscow again without having our Ambassador participate in the meetings.

Thus my secret Moscow visit ended. My last reporting cable to Nixon summed up what I believed we had accomplished:

(a) Moscow's readiness to receive me three days after we bombed Hanoi and Haiphong and while we were bombing and shelling [North Vietnam].

(b) An announcement that when properly briefed makes plain Vietnam was discussed. The distinction between important international problems and bilateral matters related to the summit is a euphemism for Vietnam.

(c) Soviet willingness to transmit our procedural proposals to Hanoi and to urge private talks even while we continue bombing.

(d) Soviet willingness to transmit a very tough substantive proposal to Hanoi.

(e) Soviet recognition that we are deadly serious about Vietnam and that everything else is dependent on it.

(f) A SALT offer which culminates the private channel and accepts most of our proposals.

(g) Agreement on a declaration of principles to be published at the summit which includes most of our proposals and indeed involves a specific renunciation of the Brezhnev doctrine.

(h) Agreement to begin exploring MBFR.

(i) Agreement not to go beyond the FRG [West Germany] in pushing the GDR [East Germany] admission to UN.

(j) Enough holding actions in bilateral matters to give us a control over the implementation of the above.

For all this we give up the bombing of Haiphong for one week.

A Disagreement with the President

UNFORTUNATELY for my peace of mind, Washington did not share my perception of success. Throughout my stay in Moscow I was, in fact, embroiled on two fronts: with Brezhnev across the conference table, and with Nixon brooding in Camp David.

At bottom, though he never categorically insisted on this at the time, it is now obvious that Nixon at heart objected to my discussing any other subject in Moscow except Vietnam, and that I stretched whatever authority I had to include other subjects to the limit.[4] He wanted me to force a massive shift in Soviet Vietnam policy by the threat of bringing summit preparations to an end. This I judged to be dangerous — and certainly impossible if I cut my stay short as he suggested. There was no disagreement between Nixon and me about the measures that would have to be taken against North Vietnam if it did not stop its offensive. I had advocated the B-52 attack on the Haiphong fuel storage depots four days before my departure for Moscow. I urged a B-52 strike on the Thanh Hoa airfield south of the twentieth parallel while I was in Moscow, to give emphasis to my warnings. I was at one with Nixon on the need to expand our bombing regularly north of the twentieth parallel and to resort to a blockade either if the North Vietnamese refused another private meeting or if the meeting failed.

As the issue developed in the cable exchange between Moscow and Washington, where Nixon and I apparently differed was on the relationship of these decisions to the impending Moscow summit. Nixon wanted to use the threat of canceling the summit to obtain Soviet cooperation in Vietnam; I judged it wiser to shift the risks and the onus for cancellation to the Soviets and to use Moscow's eagerness for the summit as a device for separating Moscow from Hanoi. It was maddeningly frustrating to watch this divergence develop because we were locked into a communications cycle and a time-zone difference that left Washington hours behind events. Thus Nixon's comments on my reports arrived long after the day's meetings had taken place and often while I was already in the next session. This would have made it hard for me to carry out his instructions even in the best of circumstances. Because the trip was secret we could not use the Embassy communications system; the President would not have been comfortable with this anyway because of his determination to keep summit preparations in White House channels to prevent leaks. We therefore used our aircraft for communications. It had excellent facilities, and we had taken two members of the White House Communications Agency with us. However, when we had a message, they had to drive to the airport nearly an hour away and transmit it. When a message arrived from Washington, the procedure was reversed. Since we generally did not finish our reports until late at night, they arrived in Washington — allowing time for them to get to the airport and be transmitted — after the close of business. There was an additional delay caused by interference with the communications.* Whatever the cause, on this Moscow trip my first report arrived garbled in Washington and had to be retransmitted — adding to Nixon's frustrations. His anxiety mounted that I might be proceeding on a course he did not wish (or at least no longer wished) me to follow.

Even had communications worked better, I do not know what I could have done with the feverish messages I received. Al Haig in my office was my point of contact with Nixon, who was ensconced in Camp David with his friend Bebe Rebozo — a conjunction that did not usually make for the calmest reflection. And the Soviets needlessly added other complications. Our SALT negotiator Gerard Smith cabled from Helsinki on April 21 that his opposite number Vladimir Semenov had indicated that the SLBM issue was under intense reconsideration in Moscow. He did not tell Smith more, but the mere hint was enough to trigger an excited Smith backchannel to the White House, a Rogers phone call to the President, and a conclusion by Nixon that the wily Soviets were trying to deprive him of personal credit for a potential SALT agreement. What possessed Semenov again to play our two channels against each other just as he had done the year before can only be answered from Soviet sources. It seemed either Soviet bureaucratic disarray or a calculated effort to exert pressure. It is not impossible that the Soviets were trying to reinsure against the very instructions I was receiving. If I broke off the talks in Moscow over Vietnam, it would be on record that *before* the event they had hinted of a new position on submarine-launched missiles. Not only the summit but a virtually settled SALT agreement would have appeared to be hostage to Vietnam. If we had abandoned both, the domestic uproar from the press, academia, and Congress might have been uncontainable.

Smith's cable and Rogers's phone call compounded Nixon's nervousness about my Moscow talks and reinforced his suspicions about Soviet motives. He was now convinced that it was all an elaborate collusion by Moscow and Hanoi to make it more difficult for us to take strong action on Vietnam, as well as to deprive him of the credit for whatever might be achieved at the summit. On this theory Moscow was using the summit prospects as leverage against *us* to prevent our bomb-

---

*I paid no attention to this at the time, ascribing it to atmospheric conditions. When I was in Moscow in 1973 to arrange a cease-fire for the Middle East war and time was of the essence, it happened again — and it occurred to me that it might more than coincidence.

ing of the North — a not unreasonable conjecture. The hints of flexibility in SALT were designed, Nixon wrote me, as a "sweetener for concessions by us on South Vietnam" — though none had been asked for or made. Nixon was afraid that I would agree in Moscow to end the bombing of the North — which was never on the agenda and, interestingly enough, was never even suggested by Brezhnev.

Nixon's cabled instructions throughout my Moscow trip were, in fact, highly ambivalent. He was hopping mad that Semenov's hints to Smith would deprive the Presidential Channel of the credit for a SALT agreement. At the same time, if I followed his suggestions to stonewall Brezhnev on all topics except Vietnam, this would make it highly *likely* that whatever SALT offers Moscow had would surface in the regular channels in Helsinki, and then these offers would be used to show what opportunities we had missed by our intransigence on Vietnam. In one and the same cable I was told that I should stall all summit preparations — and also that I should give strong support to the technical advance team even then visiting Moscow to arrange the President's summit schedule.* For forty-eight hours I was castigated by the President for discussing summit substance. But then Nixon read a news report that the Kremlin had downgraded his trip in protocol rank from a State visit to an official working visit, and I was forthwith instructed to inform Gromyko that this was inadmissible. (I did so. The news report turned out to be false.)

Leaving aside the internal contradictions in the messages, there emerged from all these heated long-distance exchanges a difference that was fundamental. In my view one of the worst mistakes in a negotiation is to ask for something that is clearly unfulfillable. However tough such a demand sounds, it changes the psychological balance in a perverse way. Since the other side may not wish to admit the limitations of its power or influence, it may invent reasons for the refusal that sour the entire relationship. And the party that has put forward the proposal will be faced with either breaking off the negotiation or, if it proceeds, suggesting that its demands need not be taken seriously. In my view the course pressed on me from Washington would soon face us with precisely this dilemma. It was inconceivable that the North Vietnamese would agree to give up a lifetime's struggle in the less than ninety-six hours scheduled for my visit to Moscow. Even if pressed by Moscow, Hanoi would want to play to the end its current offensive, to which it was already

---

* The advance team was headed by the President's Military Assistant, Brigadier General Brent Scowcroft, a brilliant officer who later became my deputy. Scowcroft knew of my visit, having arranged the aircraft for me. Bill Hyland of my staff, who accompanied him, had to fend off eager KGB men who kept asking if he had a secret message from Kissinger for Brezhnev. Hyland politely said no, knowing that I was on the other side of town and needed no such circuitous procedures.

fully committed, to improve its bargaining position. Whatever Moscow decided, stopping the offensive and turning it back was *our* responsibility. If we slackened our military effort, we would be in a hopeless position in the negotiations that would inevitably follow. If we stepped up our response, the best form of Soviet pressure on Hanoi would be acquiescence in our actions.

If Nixon had wanted to adopt a stonewalling strategy on the summit, he should not have let me go to Moscow. That was best accomplished from Washington. He sent me because he knew that if I did not go he would then face the same dilemma on his own trip. Logically that, too, would have had to be canceled unless Vietnam were settled. If Nixon went anyway, *he* would have appeared to back down — and would have been in Moscow with most of the key SALT issues unresolved and under much greater pressure when resolving them than proved to be the case. On the other hand, had Nixon canceled his own trip, the major motive for Soviet restraint on Indochina would have disappeared. We would then have had to pursue our Vietnam policy in the face of an all-out Soviet propaganda and political assault, accused at home and abroad of risking global peace in the illusory pursuit of a military solution in Southeast Asia. The precedent of the abortive Eisenhower summit of 1960, which so haunted Nixon, would have been repeated after all.

Paradoxically, therefore, the condition for a tough policy in Vietnam was to leave the onus of any summit cancellation on Moscow and to complicate Soviet decisions to the maximum by holding out prospects of major progress in US–Soviet relations. We were in a good position to do so. Brezhnev had engaged his prestige by offering to conduct the talks with me personally. He was now committed to the success of the summit; Soviet stonewalling could have been equally accomplished by Gromyko or by Dobrynin in Washington.

As Nixon instructed, I devoted my first day and a half in Moscow to bearding the Russians on Vietnam. He then wanted me to cut off the talks, discuss nothing else, and come home early. I cabled my disagreement and Nixon relented, but by then I was already launched on the talks on my own. Because of the lengthy communications lag, I had no choice.

To follow my instructions literally, if Nixon had insisted on them, would have been to throw down the gauntlet to the Soviet leadership in Moscow with a series of unfulfillable demands — all the more pointlessly when Brezhnev in his eagerness to get Nixon to Moscow was accepting *our* positions on SALT and the communiqué that I had previously communicated through Dobrynin. We would have had a simultaneous crisis in Vietnam and in relations with the Soviet Union. Down the drain would have gone our strategy of creating a triangular relationship to stabilize the global equilibrium and to foster a Vietnam settlement, isolating Hanoi and giving hope to our public that we could, amid the passions of the war, conduct a creative foreign policy. Vietnam would have consumed our substance after all — the nightmare that we, and not only our critics, feared. To abandon the entire design of our foreign policy now would inevitably be interpreted in Moscow as a fundamental change of course for which Hanoi was only a pretext. It would be viewed by the Soviets as a shift to the Chinese option, with unpredictable consequences both for East-West relations and even for the security of China.

An abrupt reversal of our strategy, implicit in making a peremptory demand the Soviet leaders could not possibly fulfill, cut directly across our long-term strategy for dealing with the Soviet Union. The conceptual problem that America faces in the era of Soviet power, in my view, is that our liberal pragmatic tradition can make us unwilling to confront challenges in their incipient stage when they are ambiguous, while our moralistic bent, in its anti-Communist incarnation, can hold us back from exploring realistic opportunities for a more constructive long-term relationship. It was essential to react strongly, if necessary violently, in the early stages of Soviet expansion — I advocated this over Cienfuegos, Jordan, India-Pakistan, and was to do so over Angola. In May I was prepared to risk the Moscow summit for whatever was necessary to break Hanoi's offensive. It was mandatory to prevent the Soviet Union from gaining so much momentum that we were faced with either the collapse of the balance of power or a colossal confrontation.

But also we had never to lose sight of the duty imposed by the nuclear age. Peace is a goal that the horror of their technology compels the two superpowers to pursue in defiance of ideology, greed, and the momentum of the past. The option for peace should never be closed off. As the President's 1972 Foreign Policy Report suggested:

The USSR has the choice: whether the current period of relaxation is to be merely another offensive tactic or truly an opportunity to develop an international system resting on the stability of relations between the superpowers. Its choice will be demonstrated in actions prior to and after our meetings.

These were the considerations that impelled me to discuss the summit agenda with Brezhnev — not in defiance of Presidential instructions, which were too late and too vague, but in the execution of our consistent policy of two years and our tactics agreed only a few days earlier.

I reported fully to Washington at the end of each day. The reaction to my first day's report was a complaint from Haig about poor communications and Nixon's warning against a precipitate "deal" on Vietnam. (I received this at the end of the day on April 21.) This was irrelevant since no such deal was in the making. He asked me to return to Washington by the evening of Sunday the twenty-third. I had planned to stay through noon of Monday the twenty-fourth (having arrived Thursday night) because of Brezhnev's being unavailable on the Sunday of his granddaughter's wedding. I had consumed Friday and part of Saturday over Vietnam. The Soviet leaders knew I was free because they knew of my original offer to meet with Le Duc Tho on that date. The practical result of going back to Washington would have been to end all serious discussions with Brezhnev on Saturday. I sent back a somewhat ill-tempered reply to Haig early on April 22:

The situation seems to me as follows: Brezhnev wants a summit at almost any cost. He has told me in effect that he would not cancel it under any circumstances. He swears that he knew nothing of the offensive. He told me they did not step up aid deliveries. Even though untrue, this gives us three opportunities:

(a) We may get help in deescalating or ending the war.

(b) If not, we can almost surely get his acquiescence in pushing [North Vietnam] to the limit.

(c) We can use the summit to control the uproar in the U.S.

We have got to this point by a judicious mixture of pressure and flexibility. But here we have shown no flexibility whatever. Why blow it now? And for what? . . .

I have demanded concrete progress at the May 2 meeting [with Le Duc Tho] in the toughest possible terms. Today I shall give Brezhnev our program demanding the withdrawal across the DMZ., release of some prisoners, etc. They have all but promised to try to help. It seems to me better to step up actions south of the 20th parallel this week, go to the private meeting [on May 2] and then go all-out if it fails. The very people who are now screaming for blood will collapse when the going gets really tough. But you may assure the President that under no repeat no circumstances will I agree to an end of bombing here; nor have Soviets even asked for it. It is however essential that I play out the string and not be provocative. And above all he must trust me. I have not exactly let him down on other missions.

I am counting on you to help keep things in perspective. We are within sight of all our objectives. Let us keep steady on the homestretch. You may also show this to the President.

Haig's reply made clear what I had suspected. Nixon was tempted to cancel the summit mainly because he feared that the Soviets would do so if he stepped up the pressure on North Vietnam, as both he and I were determined to do if my projected May 2 meeting with Le Duc Tho failed. Even before I left for Moscow he had been considering cancellation. I came to suspect that it was another gnawing fear derived from his political past, like his neuralgia about Cuba which I have explained in Chapter XVI. He was convinced that he had been defeated in 1960 by two foreign policy events above all: his restraint on Cuba in the debate with Kennedy, and Khrushchev's cancellation of Eisenhower's projected Moscow summit. Nixon wanted to be the one to cancel, if it came to that; this would be less humiliating than having the Soviets knock the summit out from under him in an election year. Yet another factor influenced the tough-sounding messages that I was receiving from Haig: "You should be aware that President has received results of Sindlinger Poll which indicates his popularity has risen sharply since escalation of fighting in Vietnam. . . . As you can see, President's starchy mood has since this afternoon increased immeasurably," Haig told me.

Whatever his doubts, Nixon in the end authorized me to stay through Monday — provided it was warranted by "progress on the Vietnam question." This again cast doubt on whether Nixon was really in accord on the strategy or was merely needling; in seventy-two hours it was simply impossible technically to get concrete results on Vietnam from Moscow. Haig described the President's increasing nervousness:

President is also increasingly restless in Camp David and has asked me to advise you that you must be at Camp David not later than 6:00 p.m. Washington time Monday evening. This means your departure from Moscow must have occurred by 1:00 p.m. Moscow time. As I completed this message, the President just called again and added that he views Soviet positions on South Vietnam as frenzied and frivolous and, therefore, is determined to go forward with additional strikes on Hanoi and Haiphong unless some major breakthrough occurs. I have insisted with him that twenty degree restriction must be maintained until completion of May 2 meeting but President terminated conversation with the following: "It may or may not hold."

To say that my response to Haig was charitable would be stretching the truth:

I am reading your messages with mounting astonishment. I cannot share the theory on which Washington operates. I do not believe that Moscow is in direct collusion with Hanoi. At this time the leaders here seem extremely embarrassed and confused. Their summit objectives go far beyond Vietnam and would be much more easily achievable without it. They may want to disintegrate NATO, ruin our other alliances, and soften us up by an era of seeming good will. But they do not need Vietnam for that. Indeed right now Vietnam is an obstacle to it.

Moreover what in God's name are they getting out of all this? They see me three days after we bomb Hanoi. Their agreeing to a public announcement must infuriate and discourage Hanoi. They are willing to see the President while he is bombing North Vietnam. . . . we can get the best of all worlds: (1) inflicting maximum punishment on Hanoi, (2) appealing to hawks, (3) appealing to doves, (4) making historic progress on SALT, (5) getting a highly acceptable communiqué. I do not see how we can even consider blowing it all by the kind of attitudes which you describe. . . . Please keep everybody calm. We are approaching the successful culmination of our policies. Must we blow it in our eagerness to bomb targets which will not move and when the delay is only one week?

It was left to Al Haig to convey my thoughts more tactfully to the President of the United States. There was more back and forth along the same lines, but the basic issue was clear. The President was eager to go all out against North Vietnam immediately and preferred to cancel the summit rather than forgo this option. I favored the same measures to defeat the North Vietnamese offensive, but I sought to use the imminence of the summit and another meeting with Le Duc Tho to gain maneuvering room at home, leverage with the Soviets, and the isolation of Hanoi. Nixon in April 1972 was focused almost exclusively on the impact of the immediate crisis in Vietnam on American public opinion; I believed that we should relate it to a wider strategy; we demoralized Hanoi more — and ultimately gained more public support — by sharpening differences between it and its patrons than by forcing Moscow and Hanoi together. No one could spare us the necessity of confronting the North Vietnamese if they pursued their offensive and refused to negotiate. But to sustain a strong line at home, we had to have a clear demonstration of North Vietnamese intransigence. Thus, paradoxically, we needed another meeting with Le Duc Tho. And to isolate Hanoi, we had to continue the preparations for the Moscow summit.

A few weeks earlier Nixon would have been elated at the accomplishments of my trip to Moscow: A successful summit was guaranteed; SALT would be concluded essentially on the basis of our own proposals; we had a summit communiqué compatible with our principles. But alone in Camp David, with only Rebozo for company, Nixon was in a feisty mood. While my associates and I were aware of major breakthroughs, we were being bombarded with missives from Washington that we had been "taken in" by the wily Soviets. Nixon was obsessed with the fear that we might be tricked into the very kind of bombing halt for which he had attacked Johnson in 1968 and which he believed had nearly lost him the election. That there was not the slightest evidence for this, that neither Brezhnev nor any Soviet leader had even asked for it, did not in any way calm his suspicions. Nor did I succeed in convincing Nixon that Brezhnev was not maneuvering to deprive him of credit for the results of the summit, that all the evidence pointed in the opposite direction; after all, Brezhnev had as big a stake as Nixon had in being associated with a SALT agreement.

The full range of Presidential apprehensions was finally catalogued in a long memorandum he dictated at Camp David. (Because of the time difference it did not in fact reach me until all the Moscow meetings were concluded and the communiqué announcing my visit was agreed.) Nixon began with compliments about my "skill, resource-fulness, and determination," which he then in effect retracted in the subsequent paragraphs that suggested I had been doing it all wrong: "It seems to me that their primary purpose of getting you to Moscow to discuss the summit has now been served while our purpose of getting some progress on Vietnam has not been served, except, of course in the very important, intangible ways you have pointed out. . . ." Nixon continued to fear that our returning to the Paris plenaries in the wake of my Moscow trip would appear as a retreat. We would be attacked from both the right and the left for going to Moscow and failing to settle Vietnam. If Hanoi proved intransigent at the May 2 meeting, "then we will have to go all-out on the bombing front." He could not go to Moscow himself from a position of weakness. Nixon continued to see a problem on SALT in that Semenov had given Smith "exactly the same offer that you set forth in your message of April 22." Since the details of the SALT negotiations did not interest him, I could not convince him that this quite simply was not so. Semenov had indicated only that Mos-cow was studying the issue; he had given no details of any kind. SALT, in any case, argued Nixon, was of concern only to "a few sophisti-cates"; the main issue was Vietnam and there we had failed. But lest I be discouraged, Nixon ended on a friendly note of reassurance: "How-ever it all comes out, just remember we all know we couldn't have a better man in Moscow at this time than Kissinger. Rebozo joins us in sending our regards." In the light of the previous catalogue of errors one could only conclude that the Administration was in parlous shape indeed if its best man could not do better than that.

I replied ambiguously from the plane that Nixon's cable had meant a great deal to me. I disagreed with him about the Paris plenaries:

I do not share your fear. First, after the Moscow trip announcement everybody will figure that more is going on than meets the eye. Second, we can strongly hint that this is tied to private meetings. Third, we can confine the plenary to a discussion of how to end the North Vietnamese invasion and make clear that we shall discuss no other subject till that is done.

And I made one more effort to explain my proposed strategy in a long memorandum to the President drafted on the airplane:

Brezhnev's performance suggests that he has much riding on the summit. . . . We may have an election in November; he acts as if he has one next week and every week thereafter. . . . Soviet options in the present situation are beset with dilemmas. If they stay passive vis-a-vis Hanoi while the offensive con-tinues, they must now assume you will go all out against the North. To go forward with the summit in those circumstances is for them psychologically and politically an agonizing prospect. To cancel the Summit may, in their view, lead to your defeat in November, but not without our having meanwhile pulverized the DRV and Brezhnev's Western policy having collapsed. Much the same would happen if you cancelled the Summit or if you came but were hobbled by right-wing pressures. But the [Soviets'] alternative to all this — pressure on Hanoi to desist — means the betrayal of a socialist ally, the loss of influence in Hanoi and no assurance that Hanoi will stop the offensive, and we our retaliation.

In sum, I would have to conclude that Brezhnev personally, and the Soviets collectively, are in one of their toughest political corners in years. They must want the Vietnamese situation to subside and I would judge that there is just a chance that of all the distasteful courses open to them they will pick that of pressure on Hanoi — not to help us but themselves. The dispatch of Brezhnev's confidant, Katushev, to Hanoi tends to bear this out.

The stick of your determination and the carrot of the productive summit with which I went to Moscow, which I used there and which we must now maintain, give us our best leverage in Kremlin politics as well as the best position in our own.

By the time Nixon read my memorandum he had calmed down sufficiently to write "Superb job" on it. This might have reflected his real judgment, or his acceptance of a fait accompli. For the results of the Moscow meetings were gaining their own momentum. Events proved that no options had been given up and that in fact our freedom of maneuver had greatly increased. On April 23, from Moscow, we sent the procedural proposal to the North Vietnamese through our Paris channel. (General Walters having been appointed Deputy Director of the CIA, that channel was now operated efficiently, if less flamboyantly, by our air attaché, Colonel Georges R. Guay.) If we immediately received Hanoi's agreement to a secret meeting on May 2, we would be prepared to announce on April 25 our return to the plenary session of April 27. In other words, we gave Hanoi twenty-four hours to reply. And Hanoi, which had kept us waiting for weeks and even months on previous exchanges, accepted our proposal the next day.

On April 25 we announced at the White House that I had been in Moscow. My estimate of the impact proved correct. Later that day and long enough afterward in the news cycle to have a separate effect, we announced our willingness to resume the plenary sessions of the Paris peace talks. Without any hints on our part, the media tended to link this to my talks in Moscow as I predicted. And when Le Duc Tho's departure for Paris became known, hopeful speculation about diplomatic initiatives received additional impetus.

The importance of having separated Soviet and North Vietnamese policies became ever clearer. On April 19 the *New York Times,* in a stinging editorial called "Strategy of Failure," had castigated the Administration for risking a SALT agreement by its bombing of North Vietnam. But on April 26, after my Moscow trip was disclosed, a much more sanguine editorial expressed the conviction that it would be surprising if my visit to Moscow "had not added another chapter to the history of secret diplomacy about Vietnam." Other journals, including the *Washington Post* and the *Wall Street Journal,* reflected the consensus.

My trip to Moscow had conveyed the impression that we might not have to choose between our Soviet and our Vietnam policies; it thus had gained us some time. But it had not answered our basic question: How far we could push Moscow without risking the summit and the resulting domestic turmoil? My visit to Moscow had given the Kremlin an increased stake in the summit because it had whetted the Soviet appetite and practically guaranteed a successful outcome. It had removed the congenital suspicion that we might reverse course. But it had not enabled us to solve the riddle of the precise limits of Soviet tolerance. The answer to this would depend on two factors: the success of the North Vietnamese offensive, and the outcome of my private talk with Le Duc Tho on May 2.

XXVII

The Showdown: Mining of North Vietnamese Harbors

Preparing for Decision

As the showdown in Vietnam neared, we were in a strong position, both militarily and politically. The South Vietnamese had held; we had not panicked. Our air and sea power had been massively reinforced; bombing of the North had resumed. My trip to Moscow and the President's dramatic visit earlier to China had eased domestic pressures at least temporarily. It was clear that our diplomacy was not paralyzed by the war, and that the Administration was making major and successful efforts to construct a new international order. Moscow and Peking, wary of each other and aware of their stakes in relations with us, distanced themselves carefully from their North Vietnamese ally.

But Hanoi still had an offensive punch left; it would not quit without at least one more all-out effort. On April 24, the very day that it accepted our proposal for a private talk on May 2, Hanoi launched a military offensive in the Central Highlands. A powerful assault threatened the provincial capitals of Kontum and Pleiku, in the process destroying about half of the South Vietnamese 22nd Division. Attacks also multiplied against An Loc, another provincial capital sixty miles north of Saigon. Clearly, the North Vietnamese did not believe in the utility of those gestures of goodwill so incessantly urged on us by our critics. They wanted us in a position of maximum military disadvantage when the talks resumed; they hoped to bring about a South Vietnamese collapse before our pressures, political or military, could work.

Nevertheless, we had to go through with the meeting of May 2 with Le Duc Tho, however painful it was to wait before retaliating to the new offensive. Our challenge was as much psychological and political as military. We needed to keep our domestic, diplomatic, and military moves in tandem. When we retaliated, it had to be clear that it was Hanoi that had chosen a test of strength rather than a negotiated settlement. Domestic support was for us an essential part of the effectiveness of any military measure. And the closer to the summit we could act, the more the Soviet leadership would be committed to its success and the more likely would it respond minimally to any military move we made.

At first, everything seemed to fall into place. On the morning of April 25 we revealed my secret trip to Moscow; in the evening we announced resumption of the Paris plenaries. The next morning, April 26, Nixon announced the next slice of troop withdrawals. This was imposed upon us once again by the completion of the 70,000-man withdrawal announced three months earlier, and with it came the dilemma that intensified with every increment of our retreat. The fewer troops we had left, the deeper would be the impact if we kept withdrawals constant. At the current rate we would soon have no residual forces left as negotiating counters. But if we slowed them down, our critics would proclaim Vietnamization a failure and add another domestic complication to the growing uneasiness about the outcome of the North Vietnamese offensive.

Caught between the Scylla of our inability to stop withdrawals and the Charybdis of not wanting to compound the burden already borne by Saigon, we went through our usual interagency maneuvering. Laird, as always, favored the maximum withdrawal as the best means of tranquilizing public opinion. He wanted to pull out 54,000 troops between May 1 and December 31, 1972. This would bring us down to a residual force of 15,000 which, he argued, would demonstrate our confidence in our ability to withstand the offensive while convincing our public that withdrawals would continue. I disagreed. The reduction seemed to me excessive in the face of the immediate threat and much too inflexible from a negotiating point of view. It could demoralize Saigon and give up our remaining leverage on Hanoi. Nixon finally settled on a figure of 20,000 over two months, having reached another understanding with General Abrams that most of the withdrawals would occur at the end of the period; by then, we expected the North Vietnamese offensive to have run its course. The major advantage of announcing the withdrawals was that Nixon could report about the military situation on television in a context that offered hope, rather than in the crisis atmosphere that would have surrounded a Presidential speech addressed solely to the North Vietnamese offensive. Nixon, speaking from the Oval Office, mixed determination with conciliation. He contrasted our record of peace proposals with the enemy's steady buildup for a new offensive. This "invasion" was "a clear case of naked and unprovoked aggression across an international border." Twelve of North Vietnam's thirteen regular combat divisions were in South Vietnam, Laos, or Cambodia. The South Vietnamese forces were doing the ground fighting, with United States air and naval forces engaged in support. Nixon announced the 20,000-man withdrawal. His instruction to Ambassador William Porter to attend the plenary session the next day (announced by Ziegler the day before) was a sign of our readiness to negotiate. Nixon could take justifiable pride in the record:

By July 1 we will have withdrawn over 90 per cent of our forces that were in Vietnam in 1969. Before the enemy's invasion began, we had cut our air sorties in half. We have offered exceedingly generous terms for peace. The only thing we have refused to do is to accede to the enemy's demand to overthrow the lawfully constituted Government of South Vietnam and to impose a Communist dictatorship in its place.

No amount of righteous indignation about our bombing could obscure the fact that this was the *sole* remaining issue. And Nixon, regarded by his opponents as an immoral man, increased their hostility by reiterating what he believed — and I agreed — was the fundamental moral issue:

I do not know who will be in this office in the years ahead. But I do know that future Presidents will travel to nations abroad as I have on journeys for peace. If the United States betrays the millions of people who have relied on us in Vietnam, the President of the United States, whoever he is, will not deserve nor receive the respect which is essential if the United States is to continue to play the great role we are destined to play of helping to build a new structure of peace in the world. It would amount to a renunciation of our morality, an abdication of our leadership among nations, and an invitation for the mighty to prey upon the weak all around the world. It would be to deny peace the chance peace deserves to have. This we shall never do.

The course of events since had underscored that Nixon was right; the fate of the peoples of Indochina has been precisely what he predicted. His opponents were entitled to their distress at the war — it was shared by the President and his Administration. But they owed him the recognition that they had no monopoly of anguish or virtue, and that their government was trying to deal decently with a complex problem which would affect our future and the lives of tens of millions.

Hanoi answered our withdrawal announcement by launching another offensive, this time in the far north, against Quang Tri. (Preparations must have been well under way long before the speech.) On April 27, five days before I was to meet with Le Duc Tho, the North Vietnamese attacked with the heaviest artillery barrage of the war and large numbers of tanks. In the next few days the South Vietnamese Third Division was destroyed. The North Vietnamese captured their first provincial capital when Quang Tri city fell on May 1, and most of the province was doomed. Many South Vietnamese units panicked. Without plans for orderly retreat, deserted by their officers, South Vietnamese soldiers and thousands of civilians headed for Hué. North Vietnamese artillery pounded the refugee column mercilessly. We estimated 20,000 casualties, a large percentage of them civilians. Over a thousand civilians were killed when North Vietnamese troops deliberately shelled the refugees fleeing south. Indeed, the number of refugees thus ambushed and killed in the retreat from Quang Tri was almost certainly more than the total casualties claimed by North Vietnam from the B-52 bombing of Hanoi eight months later, in December.* No public protests are recorded about North Vietnamese brutality.

Nixon grew increasingly restive. We were bombing up to the twentieth parallel, but refrained from attacking Hanoi and Haiphong pending my May 2 meeting with Le Duc Tho. In the face of Hanoi's renewed offensive Nixon was eager to do something. On April 30 he told me that he had "decided" to cancel the summit "unless we get a settlement." As usual, it was part of the Assistant's task — expected by Nixon — to winnow out those "decisions" that he really did not mean to have implemented. A good rule of thumb was that the President's seriousness was in inverse proportion to the frequency of his commands and the emphasis with which they were put forward. Haldeman's indispensability derived from his extraordinary instinct for fathoming what his mercurial boss really had in mind. Haldeman was later disgraced for orders he carried out; he must be given his due for those he ignored or mitigated. In foreign policy I had this responsibility. I urged Nixon to stick to our course of deferring any escalation until after the May 2 meeting. We would know within forty-eight hours whether Hanoi was seeking a showdown or a negotiation.

On April 30 Nixon sent me a long memorandum ordering a three-day B-52 strike against Hanoi and Haiphong for the following weekend (May 5–7), apparently regardless of the outcome of my meeting with Le Duc Tho. The memorandum showed that Nixon again was seized by the same fear as during my Moscow trip, that somehow, because of the scheduled secret meeting, the North Vietnamese were getting the better of us. He was determined, he said again, to cancel the summit unless the situation improved.[2] Speaking to the press at John Connally's ranch in Texas that evening, Nixon warned that Hanoi was "taking a very great risk" if it continued its offensive in the South.

On May 1, Brezhnev wrote to Nixon suggesting that prospects for negotiations would improve if we exercised restraint. This was damaged merchandise; it was exactly the same argument used to obtain the bombing halt in 1968, but a bit shopworn after 147 fruitless plenary sessions. Brezhnev, trying a little linkage in reverse, suggested that such a course would also enhance the prospects for the summit.

Nixon saw in the letter a confirmation of all his suspicions that Hanoi

---

* Hanoi Radio on January 4, 1973, cited a preliminary figure of about thirteen hundred persons killed after twelve days of bombing.[1]

and Moscow were in collusion.[3] To me, however, Brezhnev's intervention seemed no more than standard rhetoric. His letter made no threat; it spoke of the impact of bombing on the "atmosphere" of the summit; it made no hint at cancellation. Since I was leaving that evening for Paris, it was idle to speculate. Our course would have to turn on Le Duc Tho's attitude, not on what the Soviets said. There was no doubt that if the meeting failed, some new, fundamental decisions were in order. Whatever happened, we had prepared the terrain.

The May 2 Secret Meeting

M Y meeting with Le Duc Tho was brutal. Contrary to the mythology of the time, the North Vietnamese were not poor misunderstood reformers. They were implacable revolutionaries, the terror of their neighbors, coming to claim the whole of the French colonial inheritance in Indochina by whatever force was necessary. Furthermore, in my experience the North Vietnamese were never more difficult than when they thought they had a strong military position — and never more conciliatory than when in trouble on the battlefield. Unfortunately for our emotional balance, Tuesday, May 2, was a day on which Le Duc Tho was confident he had the upper hand. Quang Tri had fallen the day before. Pleiku was in peril. An Loc was now surrounded. (Surrounding An Loc turned out to be a North Vietnamese misjudgment; had they left open a route of retreat the defenders would probably have fled as at Quang Tri, and An Loc would have fallen.) For all Le Duc Tho knew, a complete South Vietnamese collapse was imminent. Hanoi was prone to insist that it was impervious to military pressure; it clearly did not believe that we were.

Le Duc Tho immediately went on the offensive. He opened by accusing the United States of having interrupted the private meetings — an extraordinary effrontery given the record of Hanoi's canceling the November 20 meeting on three days' notice, not responding for two months to our offer to meet on an alternative date, and then postponing several scheduled sessions to fit in with the North Vietnamese offensive. Our decision to force a showdown, combined with my tenseness after coming directly to the meeting from an overnight transatlantic flight, made me lose my temper: "I don't know what world you live in, but I'm under the illusion that you postponed the private meetings. In fact, a man who says he is your representative was giving us notes, so we have it in writing."

Le Duc Tho was not to be put off. He resumed his attack with the argument that Hanoi's offensive was not in fact an offensive since it had been provoked by the United States, which was the real aggressor. He proceeded to quote statements from our American critics to support his argument, which led to a testy exchange:

KISSINGER: I won't listen to statements by American domestic figures. I have told this to the Special Adviser.

LE DUC THO: I would like to quote a sentence from Senator Fulbright to show you what Americans themselves are saying.

KISSINGER: Our domestic discussions are of no concern of yours, and I understand what the Senator said.

LE DUC THO: I would like to give you the evidence. It is an American source, not our source. Senator Fulbright said on April 8 that the acts of the liberation forces in South Vietnam are in direct response to your sabotage of the Paris Conference —

KISSINGER: I have heard it before. There is no need to translate. Let's get on to the discussion.

LE DUC THO: I would like to quote —

KISSINGER: I have heard it before. Please go ahead.

When we finally got down to business, I stated our position, hinting that we had discussed it with the Soviets:

We are meeting with you today in the expectation that you have something constructive to say. There are three requirements for effective negotiations. First, your offensive must stop. Second, the 1968 Understandings must be restored. Third, there must be serious, concrete and constructive negotiations leading to a rapid conclusion of the conflict.

We are prepared to make our contribution to this last point. We are willing to work with you to bring about a hopeful opening towards a peaceful settlement. But I don't want to underrate the seriousness of the point at which we meet and your side, which has chosen to launch a major offensive while pretending to prepare for private meetings with us, now has the responsibility to put forward concrete suggestions.

That is all I have to say at this moment. Besides, I understand your allies have already told you some of the ideas we have.

But Le Duc Tho had no suggestions, concrete or otherwise. He simply went through the motions. Hanoi had never responded to our proposal of October 11, 1971, or its modification in Nixon's speech of January 25, 1972. Le Duc Tho took the occasion to drop it without further discussion. Quoting a statement by Secretary Rogers that our eight points were "not an ultimatum," he suggested that we should begin the negotiations with our fallback position: "Now show us what flexibility you have and I am prepared to discuss your new flexibility, the new position you will express. We know that time is not on your side."

We had never been given the courtesy of an explanation of what Hanoi found inadequate in an American proposal that offered a cease-fire, total withdrawal, and the resignation of an allied head of government a month before an internationally supervised free election in which the Communists could participate. We were given no explanation now. All Xuan Thuy would do was to read me the published text of their "two-point elaboration," issued three months before. Since major decisions flowed from this meeting it is important to catch its flavor:

KISSINGER: What's new about that? I have read it. I know what it says. What do we have to answer? We went through the seven and nine points. Is there anything there that we did not discuss last summer?

XUAN THUY: It says that . . . [continues to read from Point One of the two-point elaboration].

KISSINGER: I have read it. There is no need to read it again. That's not my question. This is what we discussed last summer. We gave an exhaustive answer last summer. What additional answer is needed?

XUAN THUY: You don't set a specific date for withdrawal of your forces. You put only a six-month period.

KISSINGER: I know you are asking for the same thing we refused to do last summer [a deadline that would run independent of any agreement]. I'm asking whether you said anything new that requires an additional answer.

XUAN THUY: But since you refused, we have to continue our demand. The more you refuse, the more we have to continue our demand.

The second point of the two-point elaboration deals with the political problem in South Vietnam. [He reads Point Two.] "The U.S. Government should really respect the South Vietnamese peoples' right to self determination . . ."

KISSINGER: I have read it. I know the words very well.

XUAN THUY: You don't respond.

KISSINGER: We rejected it not because we don't understand it but because we understand it only too well.

XUAN THUY: Since you still refuse to answer, it shows you have not understood. So if you want us to present it again, I will.

KISSINGER: You don't have to present it again.

My first secret meeting with the North Vietnamese in nearly eight months, the object of so many weeks of effort, thus consisted of nothing more than Hanoi's reading its public position to me without explanation, modification, or attempt at negotiation. I suggested that there was really nothing left to discuss. Le Duc Tho thought otherwise. In his view I had been deprived for too long of his epic poem of American treachery and Vietnamese heroism and he now made up for this neglect. I suggested that perhaps one way to start the discussions would be to return to the situation of March 29, before the North Vietnamese offensive, in which case we would end our bombing and also withdraw our reinforcements. Le Duc Tho contemptuously dismissed this as to our unilateral advantage. I summed up where we now stood:

Mr. Special Adviser and Mr. Minister, much as I enjoy this conversation about the history of war, I don't see that you are ready to talk seriously about bringing about a rapid solution to the war. Since that is not the case, much as I regret coming a long distance for a very brief meeting, I propose that we adjourn the meeting and meet again when either side has something new to say. . . .

I want to make it perfectly clear that we notified you in February that we were prepared to discuss our eight points and include discussion of your points. You have refused to discuss our eight points at all. Since you are prepared to discuss only your points, points which we already explored last summer, there is no basis for discussion. We have invited you to make counter-proposals to our suggestions. But they have not been made. We have asked you whether there was anything new in your proposals and you simply read me your proposal. We told your Soviet allies last week what we wanted to discuss and they said they would transmit them to you. I find it difficult to understand why you meet with us at all since you knew what we wanted to discuss.

I want to make it absolutely clear, so that there is no misunderstanding, we are prepared to discuss any political process which genuinely leaves the political future of South Vietnam open. We are not prepared to discuss proposals which have the practical consequence of simply installing your version of a government in Saigon. We told you this last summer. We tell you this again.

At this point, Xuan Thuy, evidently thinking the record was not yet complete, responded by reiterating the demand for the immediate resignation of Thieu — "the sooner the better. If . . . tomorrow, it would be better. . . ." After that, the remaining "Saigon Administration" should change its policy, abolish the system of repression, abandon Vietnamization. When I asked him to explain why a Vietnamese government should abandon a policy of Vietnamization, he reverted again to Hanoi's unchanging demand for a tripartite coalition government in which the anti-Communist government, decapitated and deprived of its police and army, was supposed to join a coalition with "neutralists" (approved by Hanoi) and the fully armed Communists backed by the North Vietnamese army, which coalition would then negotiate with the fully armed Viet Cong, backed by Hanoi's entire field army. That is what Xuan Thuy called "the real situation in South Vietnam."

Xuan Thuy was so carried away by the spirit of the occasion that he complained about restrictions on freedom of the press in Saigon. This led to another exchange:

KISSINGER: Can anybody publish a paper in North Vietnam? I ask just for my own education.

XUAN THUY: The Democratic Republic of Vietnam has a completely different system and we do not impose this system on South Vietnam. If now they require us to apply a system like South Vietnam, we refuse that.

LE DUC THO: In our view the social democratic system is, however, the most democratic form of government.

Since my interlocutors were in such a feisty mood, I decided to use the occasion to nail down once and for all an issue that had rent our public debate for over a year. All that time Hanoi had given in public the impression that the military and political issues could be separated, that if we withdrew our forces, our prisoners would be released, while in all meetings with me, it consistently and totally rejected the notion. As I have already pointed out, media and Congressional urgings in that direction were unending. The following exchange settles the issue:

KISSINGER All last summer — you know well — there was a whole succession of journalists and senators who came to see you. They came away with the impression that you were prepared to discuss a military solution only. It is true that you never said so explicitly, but with great skill you left that impression. . . .
Let me sum up where we go from here. We are prepared to reopen these talks either on the military issues alone, that is the complex of issues on withdrawal and prisoners of war. But my impression is that at this moment you are not prepared to discuss this. I want to make sure I learned my lessons properly.
LE DUC THO: So you have correctly learned this lesson because I never separated these two questions. And when I talked to newspapermen I did not tell them this. The newspapers were just speculating.
KISSINGER: But you didn't do much to discourage them.
LE DUC THO: They speculate too much.

Enough has been said to make clear that there was no point in continuing the meeting. Contrary to Nixon's fears, Le Duc Tho was not even stalling. Our views had become irrelevant; he was laying down terms. He acted as if every passing day would make our position more untenable. Hanoi would not use the talks to try to forestall American retaliation because it wanted no inhibition on its own freedom of action. Le Duc Tho insisted that both the fact and the substance of the meeting be kept secret — presumably to deprive our public of any hope of progress. He compounded his insolence by handing over "some documents for your information." They turned out to be propaganda material of the kind routinely distributed by North Vietnamese press officers at the briefings following the plenary sessions. As I got up to leave after one of the briefest meetings ever — three hours — Le Duc Tho took me aside and said in the tone of a fellow-conspirator that his side's prospects were "good."

The die was cast. I had advocated delaying an all-out response until we had explored every diplomatic avenue. I had thought it desirable to make sure that we had assembled enough power for a massive blow. I wanted to bring about the greatest possible diplomatic isolation of Hanoi. And it was crucial that our negotiating record be above reproach to withstand the domestic fury ahead. Now there was no question that we would have to have a showdown. The back of the North Vietnamese offensive had to be broken militarily. We might obtain Soviet acquiescence in what was necessary, but Moscow clearly either could not or would not affect Hanoi's decisions until the outcome of the offensive was clear. We had no choice. Perhaps Moscow would cancel the summit, but the summit was not worth having if Saigon collapsed under the weight of Soviet arms. The point of decision had arrived.

The Mining of North Vietnam

O N my way home from Paris on May 2, I cabled the White House and Saigon to begin preparing for the crucial choices. Haig informed me that the President had received my preliminary report calmly and with resignation. Haig had passed on to him my recommendation that he withhold any decision until we had analyzed the implications of the meeting. It seemed to me that we needed not a spasm produced by disappointment but a precise plan of action. Haig's cable also carried the distressing news that a South Vietnamese base on the perimeter of Hué had been evacuated under heavy enemy assault. If the old imperial capital fell, the rout might well be on; South Vietnam could be on the verge of disintegration.

A little later another report arrived from Haig. Nixon was adamant about ordering a two-day B-52 strike on Hanoi, starting Friday, May 5. (Earlier, it had been a three-day strike on the weekend.) He thought this essential for public opinion, for South Vietnamese morale, and as a signal to the Soviets and North Vietnamese. Again Nixon had mused about canceling the summit, referring to it as a "political" question — meaning that it was outside my sphere of competence. Haig knew my views; he repeated that he had told Nixon to be careful not to pursue a course "which will cost us both the summit and not achieve what we are seeking with respect to Southeast Asia." Haig urged me to reflect on our options on the way back. He and a helicopter would meet me at Andrews Air Force Base and take me to the Washington Navy Yard and the Presidential yacht, *Sequoia*, where Nixon would discuss our strategy.

The *Sequoia* had clearly seen better days. Its lower level had a covered deck that adjoined a heavily paneled dining room; upstairs was a sun deck where Nixon liked to lounge with a drink before dinner. Its engine made an infernal noise, inhibiting conversation in the dining room. The furniture was squat and heavy and undistinguished; banal pictures of nautical scenes covered the walls. The *Sequoia* could make it to Mount Vernon and back; one shuddered at what might happen to it on the open sea. But it served a useful purpose in enabling Presidents to escape the claustrophobic tension of the White House. For the White House imprisons as well as exalts. The combination of living quarters and office in the same building may produce a sense of isolation as if the President and his aides were alone in the midst of a hurricane. The White House has a tendency to evoke simultaneous overconfidence and paranoia in its occupants; periodic release from its pressures is a necessity. The *Sequoia* provided a quick sanctuary; it was handier than Camp David, easier for casual, informal discussions. It is a shame that it was later dispensed with. It was made to order for the fateful discussions now to take place.

Nixon's journey to a decision was often tortuous. In general, he would put forward propositions disguised as orders that he expected to be challenged. Until the last possible moment he would put forward several often contradictory options. But when the final moment of decision was reached, the nervous agitation would give way to a calm decisiveness. At moments of real crisis Nixon would be coldly analytical. He might shrink his circle of advisers to a very few who agreed with him; he would surely withdraw to his hideaway in the Executive Office Building. He would sit there with his yellow pad, working out his choices. He would call in his close associates for endless meetings, going over the same questions again and again until one almost began to hope that some catastrophe would provide a pretext for going back to one's own office to get to work. But once launched on the process he would — in foreign policy matters — invariably get to the essence of the problem and take the courageous course, even if it seemed to risk his immediate political interest.

So it was on this occasion. I described my meeting with Le Duc Tho to the President and Haig, gathered around the *Sequoia* wardroom table. Its significance was not that the North Vietnamese had been unyielding, even bloodyminded. That had been true of many previous meetings. What the May 2 meeting revealed was Hanoi's conviction that it was so close to victory that it no longer needed even the pretense of a negotiation. It would have been easy for Le Duc Tho to sound conciliatory, to advance some ambiguous formulation that would have put us in the dilemma of whether to escalate the conflict in the face of a possible diplomatic breakthrough. An offer of a cease-fire in place, for example — with Communist forces at the outskirts of Hué, encircling An Loc, and threatening Kontum and Pleiku — would have demoralized Saigon had we accepted it, and shaken our domestic support if we refused. Le Duc Tho's disdain of any stratagem indicated that in Hanoi's judgment the rout had begun, beyond out capacity to reverse by retaliation. Our action had to provide a shock that would give the North pause and rally the South.

Nixon was still eager for B-52 strikes against Hanoi and Haiphong starting Friday, May 5. I did not believe a one-shot operation would meet our needs; I urged Nixon to wait until Monday and to give me forty-eight hours to develop some plan for sustained operations. In addition I knew that General Abrams was opposed: As usual he wanted to throw all B-52s into the ground battle in the South. How specifically to react was primarily a tactical question. But Nixon, Haig, and I were all agreed that a major military move was called for and that we would decide on its nature within forty-eight hours.

What concerned Nixon most was the imminent Moscow summit. Haunted by the memory of Eisenhower's experience in 1960, he was determined that any cancellation or postponement should come at his initiative. My view was that we had no choice; we would have to run whatever risk was necessary. If Le Duc Tho was right and the collapse was at hand, we would not be able to go to Moscow anyway. We could not fraternize with Soviet leaders while Soviet-made tanks were rolling through the streets of South Vietnamese cities and when Soviet arms had been used decisively against our interests for the second time in six months. I had sought to give Hanoi every opportunity for compromise and the Soviets the maximum incentive to dissociate from Hanoi. That strategy would now have to be put to the test. We would have to break the back of Hanoi's offensive, to reestablish the psychological equilibrium in Indochina. Whether to preempt the expected cancellation or leave the decision to the Soviets seemed to me a matter for Nixon's political judgment.

He was adamant that a cancellation by Moscow would be humiliating for him and politically disastrous; if it had to be, we must cancel the summit ourselves. He ordered preparation of a set of severe retaliatory military measures against the North Vietnamese; since I told him that these could well cause the Soviets to cancel, he instructed me to plan on the assumption that he would preempt Moscow. He would address the nation early the following week to explain whatever military moves he finally decided on, and announce his cancellation of the summit. SALT would go forward, however; it could be signed in a low-key way at a lower level. And so the fateful *Sequoia* meeting ended.

Our first move was to warn the Soviet leaders that grave decisions were impending. On May 3 a Presidential letter, drafted by Sonnenfeldt, Lord, and me, was sent to Brezhnev informing him of my fruitless meeting with Le Duc Tho. It seemed to us, the letter told Brezhnev, that Hanoi was attempting to force us to accept terms tantamount to surrender. We would not permit this. After our experience at the Paris meeting, we would communicate no further proposals; in the light of Hanoi's conduct there was no reason to believe they would have any positive effect. The letter spoke of "decisions" about to be made. It implied that the Soviet Union was at least partly responsible. It asked coldly for Brezhnev's "assessment of the situation" on an urgent basis.

The rest of May 3 was spent in preparing the military plans. They included various levels of air attacks north of the twentieth parallel. Nixon went over the options with me late at night in the Lincoln Sitting Room without, however, making any decisions. Haldeman sat in on some of these meetings. He had no views on the military operations, but he strongly opposed our cancellation of the summit, and said so. He saw no benefit in taking the initiative; it would, on the contrary, damage the President by making him appear impulsive. Nixon suggested that Haldeman and I solicit John Connally's views.

We called on Connally at the Treasury Department around noon on Thursday, May 4. The office of the Secretary of the Treasury is free of the Mussolini-style vastness of the Cabinet offices built in the Thirties, like Interior or Commerce or Justice. Nor does it have that atmosphere of an oversized boardroom of a provincial corporation which has been the Secretary of State's lot since 1947. It is elegant and yet of human proportions, situated where Andrew Jackson settled the controversy about its location by pointing with his walking stick, thereby forever cutting off the view to Capitol Hill from the White House and undoing L'Enfant's meticulous artistry in laying out Washington's streets.

Haldeman and I sat on a sofa, Connally on an easy chair facing us. His eyes were narrowed, squinting, as was his habit when he was gauging his challenge. We explained that the President was determined to resume bombing in the Hanoi-Haiphong area, beginning with a three-day B-52 strike, and had decided to preempt Moscow's probable reaction by canceling the summit. Haldeman said that he disagreed with the latter. Connally resoundingly seconded Haldeman. He would hear nothing of cancellation; it would gain us nothing domestically. Either way we would be charged with jeopardizing East-West relations; if we took the initiative the accusation of rashness would be added to the usual barrage of criticisms. We should do what we thought was necessary and leave the dilemma to the Soviets, whose arms had made it all possible. Anyway, Connally did not think it a foregone conclusion that the Soviets would cancel.

As soon as Connally had spoken I knew he was right. For a month I had been pursuing a strategy of seeking Soviet acquiescence in our military moves by enhancing the prospect of a successful summit; after nursing matters to this point it made no sense to refuse even to test the efficacy of what we had labored so hard over. I had gone along with Nixon's preliminary decision in deference to his superior knowledge of the domestic political consequences. But when the Cabinet officer generally believed to have the best political brain in the Administration considered cancellation a domestic liability, I guiltily realized that on the

Sequoia I had fallen into that cardinal sin of Presidential Assistants: permitting oneself to be seduced by arguments because they comported with Presidential preference. My duty was to speak unambiguously to those subjects for which I had responsibility. Clearly, I had not made the foreign policy case against cancellation on the *Sequoia*. In fact, the principal purpose of my Moscow trip had been to shift the onus of cancellation to the Soviets and to make it as difficult for them to do it as possible. Connally's strong stand gave me an opportunity to rectify my mistake.

Connally's second contribution was to stress that while *we* should not cancel the summit, we also should not refrain from doing what we thought necessary out of fear of the Soviets' doing so. Whatever measures we took had to be decisive. Challenging the Soviet Union was, in fact, safer if we showed no hesitation. The principal issue, he said, was simply what would be the most effective military response. That too cleared the air. Too much governmental discussion focuses on marginal issues. But the answers cannot be better than the questions asked. The most vital contribution that advisers can make is to define the central issue. Connally had done that.

I told Connally that we needed a military step that would at once shock Hanoi sufficiently to change the course of events in Vietnam and be sustainable in terms of American public opinion. A three-day B-52 attack on Hanoi and Haiphong would give the shock but would be too brief. In the longer term it might be negated by the public outrage that it would probably generate at home; it would be a godsend for our critics. (It also had to contend with the reluctance of General Abrams, who, even though his air forces had been augmented far above his recommendations, still insisted that he needed all his assets for the crucial battle in South Vietnam.) My preferred strategy was the plan first developed by my staff in 1969 and resubmitted by Haig on April 6: the blockade of North Vietnam, to be accomplished by mining.

I favored a blockade because it would force Hanoi to conserve its supplies and thus slow down its offensive at least until reliable new overland routes had been established through China. Since most of the supplies would be Soviet, this would not be an easy assignment. I preferred mining because after the initial decision it was automatic; it did not require the repeated confrontations of a blockade enforced by intercepting ships. Even though the brunt of stopping the offensive would still have to be borne by the forces in South Vietnam, once enemy supplies in the South were exhausted, the mining would create strong pressures for negotiations. I agreed with the necessity of bombing north of the twentieth parallel, including Hanoi and Haiphong, especially concentrating on road and rail links to China by which Hanoi would try to circumvent the blockade. But it should be carried out steadily by fighter-bombers and not dramatically by B-52s.

As soon as I finished with Connally, I placed these arguments before Nixon in the Oval Office. Nixon's ready acceptance demonstrated how reluctant, despite all the bravado, had been his "decision" to cancel the summit. He scheduled a meeting for 3:00 P.M.; he, Haig, Haldeman, and I were to be the sole participants. In the meantime I asked Admiral Moorer about the Joint Chiefs' view of the mining option and when it could be implemented. Moorer was enthusiastic, having repeatedly recommended it in the Sixties; he had also participated in the Duck Hook planning in 1969 and had been consulted by Haig on the subject in early April. He thought that the mining could be carried out as early as May 9, Indochina time, or the evening of May 8 in Washington.

When we met in Nixon's hideaway in the Executive Office Building at the appointed hour, the President was in good form, calm and analytical. The only symptom of his excitement was that instead of slouching in an easy chair with his feet on a settee as usual, he was pacing up and down, gesticulating with a pipe on which he was occasionally puffing, something I had never previously seen him do — yet one more from my chief's inexhaustible store of surprises. On one level he was playing MacArthur. On another he was steeling himself for a decision on which his political future would depend. Playacting aside, he was crisp and decisive, his questions thoughtful and to the point. Why was mining preferable to a blockade, he wanted to know. I replied that its chief advantage was that it required only one decision; after the mines had been seeded, that was that, until they turned themselves off, usually after four months. A blockade, in contrast, would produce daily confrontations with the Soviets. Every time a ship was stopped we would see a repetition of the drama of the Cuban missile crisis; our challenge and the Soviet reaction to it would have to be acted out over and over again, probably on television. The danger of some slip or of a pretext for serious incident would be too great.

Interestingly enough, Nixon did not again mention canceling the summit. Whether persuaded by Connally's argument or by his own longstanding yearning to complete Eisenhower's plan to visit Moscow, he proceeded with a much stronger military response than any previously considered and yet was willing to put the burden of abandoning the summit on the Soviets. Nixon then and there decided upon the mining of North Vietnamese ports. He would speak to the nation on Monday evening, May 8, or as soon thereafter as the mining could be implemented. He would convene the National Security Council on Monday morning to give his advisers an opportunity to express their opinions. The summit would then be up to the Soviets.

It was one of the finest hours of Nixon's Presidency. He could have taken the advice of his commander in the field, supported by his Secretary of Defense, and concentrated on the battle in South Vietnam. That would have probably seen him through the election without a debacle but would have faced him at the end of the year with substantially the same problem and no prospect of a negotiated end. He could have temporized, which is what most leaders do, and then blamed the collapse of South Vietnam on events running out of control. He could have concentrated on the summit and used it to obscure the failure of his Vietnam policy. Nixon did none of these. In an election year, he risked his political future on a course most of his Cabinet colleagues questioned. He was willing to abandon the summit because he would not go to Moscow in the midst of a defeat imposed by Soviet arms. And he had insisted on an honorable withdrawal from Vietnam because he was convinced that the stability of the post-Vietnam world would depend on it. He was right on all counts.

We no longer sought to hide that major decisions were imminent; the less surprising they were, the less likely that Moscow would react by a spasm. On May 4, one of the regular plenary sessions took place in Paris; they had been resumed only the week before. At its end, Ambassador Porter, as instructed, refused to schedule another meeting, by reason of "lack of progress in every available channel." On May 5 Hanoi violated the secrecy pledge on which it had itself insisted and disclosed that Le Duc Tho and I had met on May 2. It did not characterize the meeting or reveal that I had refused another date. Instead, it floated rumors that I had agreed to a coalition government. Such crude duplicity could be explained, if at all, only as an attempt at psychological warfare, to create an impression that would compound the demoralization of Saigon. The ploy was too transparent and cynical. It actually played into our hands by enabling us to use Hanoi's intransigence at the May 2 meeting to explain the actions that would now be inevitable. We advised Thieu to ignore Hanoi; we were on course and would not be deflected. He was free to deny the rumors of a coalition government in any manner he saw fit.

My staff and I bore the burden of the planning normally conducted by the Washington Special Actions Group. We informed the relevant Cabinet officers, but to avoid leaks the President wanted no interagency activity before the NSC meeting scheduled for May 8. I obtained the views of the principals separately. Moorer was enthusiastic. He was planning at full speed. The mining could begin the evening of May 8, Washington time. Laird was opposed. He thought the battle would be decided in South Vietnam; the battlefield impact of mining would come too late to affect the offensive. (I agreed, but I was concerned with Hanoi's actions *after* the offensive.) He also thought the North Vietnamese would be able to replace seaborne supplies with overland routes. Rogers was in Europe; he was asked to return for the NSC meeting on May 8. I expected that his associates would not favor the President's decision. Helms was unambiguously opposed. The analytical side of the

CIA, never the group of wild-eyed Cold Warriors that media and Congressional investigators later suggested, generally reflected the most liberal school of thought in the government. They had long since given up on Vietnam; they tended to believe that nothing could work. At a minimum they knew that they could suffer great damage by making hopeful predictions that turned out to be wrong; they ran few risks in making pessimistic forecasts. They now provided the analytical rationale for what Laird had suggested. Hanoi, they said, would be able to replace its sea imports by overland routes, using a port in South China tied into the North Vietnamese rail system or transporting all the way overland through China.

For all my respect and affection for Helms, I thought this nonsense. Our estimate was that Hanoi received 2.1 million tons of supplies through Haiphong harbor, including *all* its oil. Railways now carried only 300,000 tons, or one-seventh of the Haiphong total. To shift the remaining six-sevenths, even if feasible, would require time, and, above all, political decisions by the Soviet Union and China. Having seen the Chinese distrust of the Soviets, I did not think that either the Chinese seaports or rail system would be automatically available to Moscow. Nor did it seem to me quite so simple to shift an elaborate seaborne logistical system based on Odessa, Murmansk, and Vladivostok to rail transport across an unfriendly country. To ship oil thousands of miles overland without pipelines would be a formidable undertaking. At best it would take months, while Hanoi's supplies would dwindle with every passing day. We went on with our planning.

On May 5 I stressed again to Dobrynin that grave decisions were in train. I told Dobrynin that the President was not angry; he was preparing our actions coldly and deliberately. We were no longer asking Moscow to do anything. We would look after our own needs. We asked of Moscow only understanding of what had brought us to this point.

On May 6 I did my best to avoid the mistake of the Laos operation, of attempting a major blow with insufficient forces. To make sure that our command in Saigon was under no misapprehension about the President's determination, I sent a backchannel to Ambassador Bunker:

> To put it in the bluntest terms, we are not interested in half-measures; we want to demonstrate to Hanoi that we really mean business and we want to strike in a fashion that maximizes their difficulties in sorting out what their priorities should be in responding to these retaliatory actions.
>
> There should be no question in either your or General Abrams' mind that we want to devote the necessary assets to this action. If in your judgment the assets required for operations in the North lead you to conclude that more air is needed to meet tactical exigencies in the South, then that air should be promptly requested and we will get it to you.

Abrams responded through Bunker that his forces were sufficient — making him unique among American military leaders, whose readiness to request additional forces, if only as an alibi should failure follow their refusal, is usually insatiable. Of course Abrams had recently been the recipient of massive and unexpected Presidential largesse. He had received without any request, and against considerable opposition from the civilian side of the Pentagon, fifty-six more B-52s, three more aircraft carriers, and 129 more F-4 Phantom jets. Seventy-two additional Phantoms were on the way. Bunker added his own personal appreciation for the President's courage.

My conversation with Dobrynin triggered a rapid reply from Brezhnev to the President's letter of May 3. On the afternoon of Saturday, May 6, Dobrynin delivered a letter distinguished by its near irrelevance to the real situation. In defiance of all evidence, Brezhnev insisted that our "pessimism" about my meeting with Le Duc Tho was "unjustified." On the basis of Katushev's visit to Hanoi he could assure us that North Vietnam was ready to seek a political settlement; of course, he added offhandedly, this required a coalition government. In other words we could have peace by accepting Hanoi's terms; for this insight Brezhnev was not needed. Brezhnev tactlessly mentioned the Pentagon Papers among the reasons that Hanoi allegedly had to mistrust the actions and intentions of the United States — a gaffe hardly likely to elicit a calm reaction from Nixon. Brezhnev cautioned us against attempting to exert military pressure on Hanoi, hinting darkly that this could "entail serious consequences" for peace and for Soviet-American relations. Brezhnev urged that we show "restraint" and not miss the "opportunities" for settling the war by negotiation. But he made clear that Moscow would not involve itself in the diplomacy. The issue would have to be settled between Washington and Hanoi.

Brezhnev's letter served only to reinforce our determination. He threatened no specific responses; the danger to peace he foresaw was stated hypothetically and as arising "even irrespective of our wishes." In any event, the United States could not delay because of vague Soviet predictions and elliptical threats. We did not answer the letter until we had already acted.

To make sure that we had considered all the possibilities, I met with my staff experts that same Saturday afternoon of May 6: Al Haig, my deputy; Hal Sonnenfeldt, my Soviet expert; John Holdridge and John Negroponte, specialists on Asia and Vietnam; Richard T. Kennedy; Winston Lord; and Commander Jonathan Howe. In addition I invited George C. Carver, the principal CIA expert on Vietnam. It was a varied assembly: Foreign Service Officers, military officers, a CIA representative, and several civilian experts. But they held varying views on the Vietnam war and were an outspoken group. We debated the implications of the President's decision. Sonnenfeldt, the Soviet expert, thought the Soviets would cancel the summit. Holdridge, the China expert, expected that Peking would freeze all its relations with us except the less significant people-to-people contacts. Negroponte argued that the favorable impact on morale in South Vietnam would be dramatic. Carver repeated the CIA analysis that overland supply lines would be able to substitute for sea imports.

I summed up the arguments for and against the operation. The arguments in favor were that the North Vietnamese already faced severe constraints and now would have to confront new pressures on their limited manpower and resources. The mining would shake Hanoi's faith that time was on its side. It would strengthen morale in South Vietnam. It would give us an additional bargaining counter for the return of our prisoners. It might accelerate negotiations. It would restore the psychological balance with the Soviets and thus might make a summit possible. The negative arguments were that the further investment of American prestige would exacerbate the gravity of our defeat if the South Vietnamese collapsed despite our best efforts. Cancellation of the summit and of all the ripening agreements, including SALT, was conceivable. Relations with Peking would cool. There would be another domestic upheaval, which in turn could encourage Hanoi's intransigence.

After my summary I asked each participant for his recommendation. Winston Lord opposed our action; he thought the potential gains not commensurate with the costs. The consensus of the rest was to proceed. There was agreement also that if it were done it should be done "thoroughly"; we were going to pay the domestic price anyway and therefore we might as well succeed.

In Vietnam, meantime, a lull had settled over the battlefronts. An Loc remained surrounded; the North Vietnamese were still moving up supplies for the attack on Hué and Kontum. This reinforced our determination to act to strengthen Saigon's morale before the storm broke again.

Sunday was spent in preparing for the NSC meeting. In contrast with the Cambodian operation two years earlier, the mood was one not of incipient hysteria but of resigned determination. I acknowledged to Winston Lord that all we had patiently put together over three years might go down the drain in a twenty-minute speech. But we had no choice. Seeing the President toasting Brezhnev while we were being defeated by Soviet arms in Vietnam would not be understood by Americans whose sons had risked or given their lives there. It would be better to stand firm, gain respect, and pick up the pieces later. Lord and I spent the beautiful spring day at Camp David working with the President on the speech he proposed to deliver the next evening. The imminence of a television appearance had its usual electric effect on Nixon. While every public appearance made him nervous, once he had leaped the psychological hurdle toward decision the momentum of preparation took over. Though technically the decision to proceed was not to be made until the NSC meeting the next morning, every succeeding speech draft made its outcome more certain.

The NSC met next day, Monday, May 8, in the unreal atmosphere that Nixon's procedures generated. All present knew that he had almost certainly arrived at his final decision. They therefore had much less interest in considering the issues than in positioning themselves for the certain public uproar. Nixon, with his back to the wall, was at his best: direct, to the point, with none of the evasions that often characterized his style when facing opposition. He led off the meeting with a long monologue emphasizing his determination not to let South Vietnam fall. He was convinced that "there will be no summit" — whichever course we took. If we took strong action, this would "jeopardize" the summit; if we did nothing and Vietnam was collapsing, he could not go anyway.

Admiral Moorer presented the mining plan and the campaign to interdict railroads. Helms presented an intelligence appraisal. The CIA's considered assessment was that Moscow "would almost certainly move to cancel the summit" and perhaps bring pressure to bear on Berlin; China would "probably" provide direct support to Hanoi analogous to the 90,000 support troops it had sent during the pre-1968 American bombing; the overland routes would effectively replace the sea route. Helms concluded with the noncommittal prediction that Hanoi would wait for the outcome of the military test before deciding its course. (While not very illuminating, it turned out to be the single correct prediction in the assessment.) Laird argued that the most critical supplies came in by rail and in any case the North Vietnamese had four to five months of stocks in reserve. He expressed confidence that the South Vietnamese "can make it. Hué may go but it will not be as bad as 1968." His conclusion was that the mining and interdiction campaigns were unnecessary. The cheaper solution from the budgetary point of view was to send more equipment to South Vietnam. Nixon interjected: "Suppose we are wrong? Suppose Vietnam falls? How do we handle it? You don't assess the risks for our policy."

John Connally and Vice President Agnew rejected Laird's analysis altogether. Agnew was unequivocal that we simply could not afford to let South Vietnam collapse; it would have disastrous international consequences, especially in the Middle East and around the Indian Ocean. We were "handcuffing ourselves" by being "compulsive talkers"; the President really didn't have an option. Connally agreed: "If Vietnam is defeated, Mr. President, you won't have anything."

Rogers was ambiguous, agreeing that a failure in South Vietnam would be "disastrous for our policies" but pointing out the risks that the proposed actions might not be effective and would only compound our problem. We had to rely on the military's judgment of how effective it would be. On the other hand, couldn't we wait a few weeks, rather than torpedo the summit? In other words, he was for the operation if it succeeded and against it if it failed. He consoled the President that even if we did nothing and lost, the American people would support the President, knowing he had done all that was possible. Connally emphatically rejected that proposition. A collapse of Vietnam discredited the President's whole foreign policy; no excuse would be accepted.

This led to a discussion of what would happen to the summit if we proceeded. I expressed my judgment that there was a "better than even chance that the Soviets will cancel the summit." Connally did not think this certain; in any case he thought it better if the Soviets canceled than if we did.

I then answered the analyses that disparaged the effect of mining. The North Vietnamese would have to find alternative routes for more than 2.1 million tons of seaborne imports. Silhanoukville was closed. They could use railroads only by night for fear of our air interdiction: "You can't throw these figures around without a better analysis. It is easy to say that they have a four months' [reserve] capacity and could go all out and end the war, but they would end with zero capacity. . . . One thing is certain, they will not draw their supplies down to zero."

Nixon summed up:

The real question is whether the Americans give a damn anymore. . . . If you follow *Time, The Washington Post, The New York Times* and the three networks, you could say that the U.S. has done enough. "Let's get out; let's make a deal with the Russians and pull in our horns." The U.S. would cease to be a military and diplomatic power. If that happened, then the U.S. would look inward towards itself and would remove itself from the world. Every non-Communist nation in the world would live in terror. If the U.S. is strong enough and willing to use its strength, then the world will remain half-Communist rather than becoming entirely Communist.

The meeting ended at 12:20 after three hours and twenty minutes. Nixon announced that he would make a decision at two o'clock — the last moment, according to Moorer, to issue the "execute" order if the mining was to coincide with the President's speech. Nixon asked Connally and me to join him in the Oval Office immediately. He asked us whether anything had happened at the NSC meeting to change our minds. We both told him that the discussion had reinforced our conviction to proceed. Nixon calmly said that he would. I should bring the necessary papers to his Executive Office Building hideaway at two o'clock.

When I arrived, Haldeman was there. Before I could hand Nixon the order, he told me that Haldeman had raised new questions, which I should hear. To my amazement Haldeman described the dire impact that the proposed action would have on public opinion and the President's standing in the polls. If the President were defeated as a result of it, we would have lost everything. I passionately defended the decision; all the arguments we had so endlessly rehearsed for days were still valid. They were reinforced by the consideration that if the President pulled back now at the last moment — when all the key allies had already been briefed — he would risk his leadership and produce panic in Saigon. When Nixon excused himself to go to the bathroom, I whirled on Haldeman, who had never meddled in substance, and castigated him for interfering at a moment of such crisis. His job when no choices were left was to give the President confidence, not to agitate him on subjects about which he knew nothing. Haldeman grinned shamefacedly, making clear by his bearing that Nixon had put him up to his little speech. I was used to many games from my complex leader; this one was beyond my comprehension — until the revelation of the tapes suggested a possible motive: Nixon wanted me unambiguously on record as supporting the operation lest the hated "Georgetown social set" seek to draw a distinction between him and me as they had on Cambodia. Be that as it may, Nixon returned from the bathroom, and without another word signed the execute order.

The Summit in the Balance

I IMMEDIATELY passed the order to a jubilant Moorer. It was what he had been recommending for five years. He guaranteed that there would be no repetition of Laos; the effort would not fail because the military devoted inadequate resources or attention to it. I called all the other principals. As always in the face of great events, they seemed relieved that the uncertainty was over. (And of course several had positioned themselves to avoid the blame for any failure.) I knew from past experience that whatever Laird's attitude at the meeting, he would be staunch and imaginative in defending and carrying out the decision. Rogers would keep a low profile. Helms would act like the superb professional he was. And so it proved.

On Sunday I had spent nearly an hour with Alex Johnson working on the obligatory scenario: which country was to be notified by whom at what time. My office would take care of the Soviets and the Chinese; the State Department would handle all the others. Contrary to past practice, I would give no press briefing *before* the speech; it would carry its own message. I would hold an on-the-record news conference the next day explaining the decision. There was never any contest over White House preeminence where taking the heat over Vietnam was concerned; the other departments were only too eager to leave us to the inevitable public buffeting. The President would brief the Congressional leaders at eight o'clock in the evening. I would see Dobrynin at the same time. Peter Rodman would go to New York to tell the Chinese at their UN Mission.

With these preparations on track, all was quiet. I sat in my office, knowing that the next few days would determine the fate of our foreign policy and perhaps of the Nixon Administration. I felt like a boxer in the hours before a championship fight, unable to do anything further to improve his chances for success. To ease the tension I spent most of the interval making personal phone calls to friends who must have been astonished by my uncharacteristic solicitude. Some of them complimented me afterward on my "cool." They gave me too much credit. I was fatalistic; unknowingly they did me a great kindness by helping me pass the time, providing me with a personal warmth that would not be in plentiful supply when the storm broke and that would help sustain me in the trials ahead. And in one or two cases they gave me a last glimpse of a relationship that would shortly be sundered forever.

At 8:30 P.M. the lull was over. While the President briefed the Congressional leadership,[4] I saw Dobrynin, whom I had called away from a dinner. Dobrynin, a thoroughgoing professional, exhibited in crises none of the camaraderie with which he normally eased the processes of diplomacy. He began by telling me that whenever I saw him before a speech he knew it would not be good news. I joked that normally he was out of town in a crisis and let Vorontsov bear the brunt; we had obviously caught him unaware. I handed him a letter from Nixon to Brezhnev. At once firm and conciliatory, it pointed out that Brezhnev's message of May 6 did not change the situation; indeed, it confirmed it. There had been no indication, however minimal, that Hanoi would halt its offensive and resume negotiations on any acceptable basis. The letter then outlined the measures that would be announced in his speech. It also set out the terms on which he would end the blockade and bombing: an end to the offensive; an internationally supervised cease-fire in place (thus dropping my April demand for withdrawal of North Vietnamese units that had entered South Vietnam after March 29); and withdrawal of all United States forces from Vietnam within four months. (This was an improvement of our previous position of withdrawal in six months.)

Nixon's letter followed the same strategy as my trip to Moscow in April: painting the prospect of a successful summit as an incentive for Soviet restraint. It tantalizingly summarized what had already been agreed on SALT, the Declaration of Principles, and expanded trade, and waxed eloquent about the possible accomplishments of "our forthcoming meeting." Nixon concluded with an appeal to the elevated sentiments that he flatteringly implied might animate the Soviet leaders:

In conclusion, Mr. General Secretary, let me say to you that this is a moment for statesmanship. It is a moment when, by joint efforts, we can end the malignant effects on our relations and on the peace of the world which the conflict in Vietnam has so long produced. I am ready to join with you at once to bring about a peace that humiliates neither side and serves the interests of all the people involved. I know that together we have the capacity to do this.

After all our weeks of toing and froing, Nixon's letter thus made clear *our* willingness to proceed with the summit. The onus was now squarely on Brezhnev's shoulders if he chose to cancel it.

Dobrynin was all business. He asked what precise measures were implied in the blockade. He lost his cool only once when I asked him how the Soviet Union would react if the 15,000 Soviet soldiers in Egypt were in imminent danger of being captured by Israelis. Dobrynin became uncharacteristically vehement and revealed more than he could have intended: "First of all, we never put forces somewhere who can't defend themselves. Second, if the Israelis threaten us, we will wipe them out within two days. I can assure you our plans are made for this eventuality." His temper quickly subsided. It was explicable by the disappointment of a man who I believe was always sincerely dedicated to the improvement of Soviet-American relations (within the essential framework of Soviet world interests) and now saw the work of years in jeopardy. Dobrynin asked for a copy of the President's speech. It was quite literally still being typed a half hour before it was to be delivered because Nixon was making revisions until the last moment. Dobrynin did not believe this for one second. He said it was sad that I did not trust him to keep a secret for even fifteen minutes. At last a copy arrived. Dobrynin noted a sentence to the effect that my meeting with Le Duc Tho on May 2 had been based on Soviet assurances; this would be taken very ill in Moscow. I excused myself for a few minutes and went to the Oval Office, already crowded with cameras and technicians. I met with Nixon in a small office off the formal room. He agreed to delete the offending phrase; by some miracle, Ron Ziegler managed to correct the press copy in time. When I told Dobrynin, he said resignedly that at least he had achieved something in his dealings with our Administration.

Speaking privately, he was gloomy about the reaction in Moscow. Knowing Nixon, he averred, he was not surprised about our reaction to the May 2 meeting, though this particular course had not occurred to him. A drastic Soviet response was likely; the pity was that we had been so close to success. Because of the way decisions were made in the Soviet Union, once the Politburo had adopted a new and more hostile policy it would be hard to reverse it; US–Soviet relations were likely to be in for a long chilly period. I replied that the Politburo could have been under no misapprehension after my April trip to Moscow that a failure of the May 2 meeting would lead to a drastic American response. Dobrynin, with some melancholy, agreed. Still, it was a pity; we had come closer to an understanding than in any previous period of his tenure in Washington.

At 9:00 P.M. Nixon addressed the nation. Early drafts of the speech had contained the same strident, apocalyptic tone as his address announcing the incursion into Cambodia. By the end of Sunday, Lord and I — together with the very thoughtful White House speechwriter John Andrews — had managed to rework it. The speech now was more in sorrow than in anger. It left a way out to both Hanoi and Moscow. In a restrained and powerful address Nixon stressed that we would not accept Hanoi's terms but that a negotiated outcome was still our preference. He explained the sequence of our most recent negotiating effort: my April trip to Moscow, the disappointing May 2 meeting with Le Duc Tho. He repeated his willingness to settle the war. But the North Vietnamese "arrogantly refuse to negotiate anything but an imposition." The only way to stop the killing, therefore, was "to keep the weapons of war out of the hands of the international outlaws of North Vietnam." He recited the military actions he was taking; he stated our negotiating position in the terms he had outlined in the letter to Brezhnev.

The terms were, in fact, the most forthcoming we had put forward: a standstill cease-fire, release of prisoners, and total American withdrawal within four months. The deadline for withdrawal was the shortest ever. The offer of a standstill cease-fire implied that American bombing would stop and that Hanoi could keep all the gains made in its offensive. We were pledged to withdraw totally in return for a cease-fire and return of our prisoners. Nixon's speech publicly addressed Brezhnev in terms similar to the letter:

> Our two nations have made significant progress in our negotiations in recent months. We are near major agreements on nuclear arms limitation, on trade, on a host of other issues.
>
> Let us not slide back toward the dark shadows of a previous age. We do not ask you to sacrifice your principles, or your friends, but neither should you permit Hanoi's intransigence to blot out the prospects we together have so patiently prepared.
>
> We, the United States and the Soviet Union, are on the threshold of a new relationship that can serve not only the interests of our two countries, but the cause of world peace. We are prepared to continue to build this relationship. The responsibility is yours if we fail to do so.

That same evening Peter Rodman delivered a letter from Nixon for Chou En-lai to the Chinese UN Mission in New York. Ambassador Huang Hua read the letter somberly but made no comment; its content did not prevent him from making pleasant small talk and from offering Rodman several cups of jasmine tea. Nixon's letter to Chou En-lai characterized our negotiating proposals as fair and reminded him of our repeated warnings that we would react strongly to an enemy offensive. It reminded Chou in a pointed and prescient reference to the Soviet Union that "it is not the United States which seeks a long-term presence in Indochina." The letter expressed hope that this crisis would not interfere with progress in US–Chinese relations:

During the past three years the People's Republic of China and the United States have been patiently opening a new relationship based on the profound interests of both countries. We now face an important decision. We must consider whether the short-term perspectives of a smaller nation — all of whose own reasonable objectives could so clearly be achieved — can be allowed to threaten all the progress that we have made. I would hope that after the immediate passions have cooled, we will concentrate on longer-term interests.

I briefed the press next morning in the East Room of the White House. Important though explanations to our public were, they also served a vital diplomatic function. Every statement was part of an effort to persuade Moscow and Peking to acquiesce in our course and thus to move Hanoi, by isolating it, to meaningful negotiations. Our most important concern, of course, was the summit, now less than two weeks away. I adopted a posture of "business as usual." I explained that we had not heard from Moscow — nor could we have — but that we were "proceeding with the summit preparations, and we see at this moment no reason from our side to postpone the summit meeting." We recognized that the Soviet leaders would face "some short-term difficulties" in making their decision, but we, for our part, still believed that a new era in East-West relations was possible. Because I did not want to embarrass the Soviets I sidestepped a question about whether on my visit I had forewarned Brezhnev of our intended actions. I simply stated that after my visit the Soviet leaders could not have been "under any misapprehension of how seriously it would be viewed if this offensive continued." I concluded with an appeal to Hanoi:

Leaving aside how possible it is to have really complete private meetings under present circumstances, we believe that the most effective way of ending the war, the most certain way, is by negotiations. We respect Le Duc Tho as a serious, dedicated spokesman for his side, and we are prepared on our side to resume negotiations with him at any time that he is prepared to discuss propositions that are consistent with our principles. And we would make every effort to understand his point of view.

For the moment, the explanations and the signals were overwhelmed by Congressional and media outrage. Senator William Proxmire denounced the President's action as "reckless and wrong." Senator Mike

Mansfield was convinced that our decision would protract the war. Senator George McGovern called for Congressional action: "The President must not have a free hand in Indochina any longer. . . . The nation cannot stand it. The Congress must not allow it. . . . The political regime in Saigon is not worth the loss of one more American life." Senator Edmund Muskie thought the President was "jeopardizing the major security interests of the United States." Senator Frank Church, in condemning the action, was one of the few to recognize that we had made a major negotiating offer: "The one thing that has been overlooked is that in the same speech he [Nixon] made a proposition for peace that needs to be given closer attention, not only by this body, but also by Hanoi and by Moscow. . . ."[5]

The media's outrage was nearly uniform. The *New York Times*'s first reaction was predictable: "The many dangers that lie ahead in Vietnam are exceeded only by the threat to the peace of the world if a new Soviet-American crisis blocks the strategic arms limitation accord that is virtually assured in Helsinki."[6] After further reflection the *Times* decided to raise the decibel count, denouncing the President's "desperate gamble." The *Times* called upon the Congress to cut off all funds for the war to "save the President from himself and the nation from disaster." The *Washington Post* declared that Nixon "has lost touch with the real world. . . . The Moscow summit is in the balance, if it has not yet toppled over. . . . The only relief in this grim scene is that Mr. Nixon is coming to the end of a term and the American people will shortly have the opportunity to render a direct judgment on his policy." Even the *Christian Science Monitor* found that "the wisdom of that decision and the rightness of it are clearly open to question." The *Boston Globe* admitted that Nixon's peace terms added up to "the most reasonable offer this country has so far made." But of the risky challenge to Moscow, the *Globe* wrote: "Somehow it all seems even more immoral than our involvement in the war itself."[7]

On May 10 nine former members of my staff signed a letter of protest to me. Though in almost all cases their association with me had been only for a few months, two or three years earlier, they did not mind trading on the relationship to gain attention. In a letter that received much publicity, they assailed the mining and bombing on various grounds — that the "councils [*sic*] of common sense" had failed to be heeded; that the President's action "so jeopardized" détente and arms control; that it was clearly "dangerous and probably ineffective." It was "fruitless," "ill-conceived," "doubly shocking," "perilous and false."

If the critics had paid closer attention to reality and less to personal outrage, they would have noted that the Communist reaction was much more restrained than their own. They could not have known, of course, that Dobrynin and I spoke early on May 9, when I told Dobrynin of an accord worked out between West German Chancellor Brandt and opposition leader Rainer Barzel that would lead to ratification of the Eastern treaties now before the Bundestag. We had not planned it this way — we had no influence over the procedures of the German Parliament — but the linkage so disparaged by commentators was obvious. I told Dobrynin soothingly that at least outside of Southeast Asia we would continue to do business (implying, of course, that if the Soviets got tough so could we). Dobrynin then said that since this was a holiday in the Soviet Union (V-E Day), the official reaction to the President's speech might be somewhat delayed — a truly extraordinary explanation in the midst of an international crisis. If Soviet leaders were not prepared to interrupt a holiday, they could not be viewing the crisis as all that serious. He assumed that a statement or message could be expected sooner or later, however. I told him I would send a copy of my press conference remarks, which spoke positively about US–Soviet relations.

Our critics, as I said, were unaware of these exchanges. But there were many public Soviet signals that the response might be low-key. Hanoi fulminated against the "insolent challenge" and asked for increased support from its Communist backers. But there was no rush to the barricades in either Moscow or Peking. The Soviet SALT negotiators in Geneva continued their work. (We had instructed our delegation to proceed as if nothing had happened — but to refuse to discuss Vietnam.) A Soviet commercial delegation headed by Trade Minister Nikolai Patolichev was in Washington on a visit reciprocating that of Commerce Secretary Maurice Stans the preceding November. It missed sessions for one day but stayed in Washington. The only Soviet public comment was a TASS article on May 9 summarizing the President's speech and, interestingly, calling attention to Nixon's assurance that our efforts were not directed against any other country. Rather plaintively, TASS asserted that our actions were not compatible with our professed desire to end the war.

The Chinese response was more subtle still. A public statement on May 9 protested attacks on Chinese ships on May 6, 7, and 8 (before the President's speech), thus maintaining the distinction of recent months: Peking might complain of American actions against North Vietnam, but it would ''protest'' (implying some governmental sanction) only when Chinese lives or property were involved. We immediately notified the Chinese UN Mission in New York that special care would be taken to avoid Chinese ships; the point was in any case moot, since the North Vietnamese ports were now closed. That evening the Chinese gave us another lesson in indirection. Their Embassy in Paris — the point of contact for routine business — matter-of-factly inquired about technical arrangements for the trip to China of House leaders Hale Boggs and Gerald Ford, which was to take place at the end of June, nearly two months away. We knew well enough by now that nothing the Chinese do is accidental. Peking was telling us that the trips were still on; the steady improvement of our relations was not affected by the President's action.

On the afternoon of May 10, Dobrynin came to the Map Room of the White House to hand me a brief Soviet note of protest. Significantly, it was confined to damage caused to Soviet ships by our bombing, including the loss of life. The note asked for assurances against a recurrence. It said nothing about the mining. The fact that it came through our private Channel indicated the Soviet desire to keep their response out of the public realm. Dobrynin even gave us his ''personal view'' — an unlikely possibility — that Moscow's decision to move this way was ''encouraging,'' but it was perhaps ''premature'' to draw final conclusions. Playfully, he asked me what I thought the Politburo would decide. I replied that I would place my answer in a sealed envelope for both of us to look at when the crisis was over. (I never did, but if I had, the note would have predicted that Moscow would postpone the summit to a fixed early date.) I reminded him of the President's interest in a new era in our relations. Dobrynin asked detailed questions about our cease-fire proposal. We both spoke delicately about the discussions that would take place ''if'' the two leaders met.

Dobrynin was a good chess player. At the end of the meeting, out of the blue, he asked whether the President had as yet decided on receiving Trade Minister Patolichev. I was not a little startled by the request; it could only mean that the Soviet leaders had decided to fall in with our approach of business as usual. Trying to match the Ambassador's studied casualness, I allowed that I probably would be able to arrange a meeting in the Oval Office. Playing a little chess myself, I mentioned that it was customary on these occasions to invite press photographers. Dobrynin thought this highly appropriate.

In every crisis tension builds steadily, sometimes nearly unbearably, until some decisive turning point. The conversation with Dobrynin, if not yet the turning point, deflated the pressure. We knew that the summit was still on. Every day that passed without cancellation made it more likely that it would take place. In that case Hanoi would be isolated; we would have won our gamble. I quickly scheduled a meeting between the President and Patolichev for the next morning.

We awoke on May 11 to the first official statement released by TASS. It was both belated and mild. The Soviet Union considered our action ''inadmissible'' and ''will draw from this appropriate conclusions.'' The United States was advised to return to the conference table in Paris. The Soviet government ''resolutely'' insisted that the American military measures be ''cancelled without delay,'' which Moscow knew was technically impossible; and that freedom of navigation be respected, which was irrelevant since we were not interrupting ships at sea. As for the aid for the North Vietnamese, TASS employed some strange language. It noted that the Soviet "people" (that is, not the government) "associates itself" with the struggle. The Soviet "people" would continue to give the Vietnamese people "the *necessary* support" (not "increased" support, as Hanoi asked). The statement reeked of procrastination and hesitation.

That was not the attitude of Nikolai Patolichev when he appeared for his thirty-minute courtesy call in the Oval Office. Press and photographers were ushered in to witness what has been called "the usual contrived cordiality."[8] But in this case, contrived or not, the smiling pictures conveyed the Soviet message and it unambiguously spelled summit. Even the banter for the press was symbolic and by Soviet standards extremely subtle; the subject (I have no idea why) was the differing pronunciation in Polish and Russian of the word "friendship." Lest anyone miss the point, Patolichev was all smiles when he left the White House. A television reporter asked him if the summit was still on. "We never had any doubts," replied the Soviet Minister, wide-eyed at the seemingly inexhaustible obtuseness of Americans. "I don't know why you asked this question. Have you any doubts?"

The last remaining uncertainty was removed when Dobrynin and I met over lunch the same day to continue our regular discussion of summit preparations. Dobrynin claimed that the United States was "making too much" of the Soviet role in Vietnam; I stressed that the important thing was to settle the war. For our part, we were prepared to resolve the military issues alone or to agree on general principles of a political settlement. In the middle of the luncheon, one of Dobrynin's aides brought in a message from Brezhnev in Russian replying to Nixon's letter of May 8. Usually the Soviet Embassy supplied a written translation. In this case Dobrynin's assistant did the honors in a way which, had the meaning of the letter depended on precision, might well have defeated its purpose. But even a rough oral translation left no doubt that Brezhnev was avoiding any hint of confrontation, despite the letter's conventional bluster warning against the consequences of our actions. I asked innocently whether Brezhnev's warning referred to new actions or to steps that had already been taken. Obviously, replied Dobrynin, his patience seemingly tried by my denseness, the General Secretary could only have meant *additional* measures to those announced on May 8. Since it clearly pleased Dobrynin to play the professor, I asked why the letter had not referred to the summit. Dobrynin answered that since we had not asked about it in our communication of May 8, the Politburo had seen no need for a response. (For anyone familiar with Soviet diplomatic tactics such delicacy was a novel experience.) I asked whether we should have asked a question about the summit. "No," said Dobrynin, "you have handled a difficult situation uncommonly well."

The summit was on. That crisis was over.

On May 11 Peking, too, was heard from. A *People's Daily* commentator expressed resolute support for the people of Vietnam and "extreme indignation and strong condemnation" of the mining of North Vietnam. But the author neither denounced Nixon nor indicated any Chinese response to the interdiction campaign. China was Vietnam's "reliable rear area," which is to say it would take no action. Even more astonishing, the *People's Daily* printed the entire text of the President's speech. Probably the Chinese leaders wanted their people to learn of our challenge to the Soviet Union. Whatever the motive, it was the first time the Chinese "masses" had seen an account of Hanoi's intransigence and of our peace program. The dour fanatics of the North Vietnamese Politburo could only interpret it as cool dissociation by their two major allies.

The Soviet Union's Eastern European allies quickly fell into step. A Polish Vice Foreign Minister indicated publicly that Nixon's projected visit to Poland was still on. Since face-to-face talks were imminent, Poland had no need to say any more about the mining of North Vietnam; in other words, we were spared even a pro forma protest.

By then, too, New Zealand, Australia, Thailand, South Korea, and Britain had publicly indicated full support; the rest of our NATO allies and Japan had privately expressed understanding. None had expressed opposition. A Sindlinger telephone poll showed that 86 percent of the American public supported the President's speech; Opinion Research put the approval at 74 percent. And the Soviet response neutralized almost all vocal opposition.

From then on, summit preparations continued amicably with Dobrynin. On May 12, he and I were already discussing protocol points, such as the gifts to be exchanged. After that the emphasis was on SALT and other summit topics.

On May 11 I judged Hanoi sufficiently isolated to resume contact. I sent Le Duc Tho, who was still in Paris, an extract from my press conference of May 9, which stressed our readiness to resume negotiations. Le Duc Tho cutely replied by sending me an extract from *his* press conference of May 12; he had repeated the insistence on a coalition government, though in a language much more moderate than he had used to me on May 2. Once more this demonstrated the fallacy of the popular myth that Hanoi would be conciliatory only when we showed "goodwill." The opposite was in fact true. On May 12 Ducky had affirmed an unconditional readiness to resume talks:

If Mr. Nixon really desires serious negotiations, as far as we are concerned, faithful to our serious attitude and good will, we are disposed to seek together with the American side, a logical and reasonable solution to the Vietnamese problem. During the course of the last two decades, in its fight for independence and liberty, the Vietnamese people negotiated for a peaceful solution to the Vietnamese problem with the French Government in 1954, and participated in the peaceful solution of the Laotian problem with the United States in 1962. Consequently at present, there is no reason not to arrive at a negotiated solution to the Vietnamese problem. This question, of course, depends on Mr. Nixon's attitude.

I was certain now that serious negotiations would resume once Hanoi's offensive had run its course.

And the offensive stalled. The North Vietnamese attack on Hué never developed full steam. Kontum did not fall; neither did besieged An Loc. The South Vietnamese counteroffensive to relieve An Loc developed with excruciating slowness. But the tactical use of B-52s in the South was clearly disrupting the North Vietnamese buildup, and after some months the mining would make it increasingly difficult for the North Vietnamese to accumulate supplies for another big push.

Unbelievably by the standards of our fevered domestic debate, Vietnam disappeared entirely as a point of contention in our dialogue with the Soviet Union. On May 12 Dobrynin handed me a note — in the private Channel — that grudgingly accepted the President's expression of regret at the harm to Soviet ships and seamen and his assurance that care would be taken to avoid such incidents in the future. Nothing was said about the blockade of North Vietnam. On May 14 we returned a conciliatory reply repeating our assurances with respect to Soviet shipping. We also informed Moscow that while the President was out of the country Hanoi would not be attacked. By implication bombing would continue against all the rest of North Vietnam, including Haiphong. This was done.

Later in the day of May 14, Dobrynin delivered a note that urged a resumption of the Paris negotiations. If it were possible to announce this in advance of the summit, "that would in many ways be favorable to the Soviet-American meeting." The Soviets proposed that neither side set preconditions and that the plenary and secret meetings proceed in tandem. These were presented as Soviet suggestions "on our own behalf" and not from Hanoi. However, the Kremlin was prepared to pass our response on to the North Vietnamese.

Clearly, someone had blinked. Less than a week after the resumption of full-scale bombing and the blockade of North Vietnam, efforts were being made to resume negotiations "without preconditions" — a far cry from Hanoi's previous smug insistence on the "correctness" of its terms. If Moscow presented these propositions on its own — which it claimed but I doubted — the isolation of Hanoi had proceeded more rapidly than any of us had dared to hope. If Hanoi was using Moscow as an intermediary, it had at last begun its retreat toward a more negotiable position.

We thought it premature to announce a return to the plenaries. It would confuse our public; it might generate demands for military restraint when the best chance for a rapid solution was to convey our implacability. On May 15 I handed an unsigned note to Dobrynin that agreed in principle to the reopening of the plenary sessions. However, to avoid raising false expectations it should be preceded by a private meeting with Le Duc Tho. If we made progress, plenaries could resume. Originally, our note had included a tough paragraph warning of "the most serious consequences" if there was further military escalation by the North Vietnamese. When Dobrynin balked at being asked to pass on a threat, I had the offending paragraph typed on a separate sheet of paper and called it an "oral note." Dobrynin withdrew his objections and accepted it in this form. Such are the little victories of diplomats over one another.

On May 17 Dobrynin told me that Moscow had urged our procedural proposal on North Vietnam in the strongest language. No reply was ever received from Hanoi — perhaps because its planners lacked a strategy for the new challenge, perhaps because they feared that failure of a new meeting would lead to another round of escalation.

Meanwhile, I met almost daily with Dobrynin to work out the summit agenda and schedule. The SALT negotiators were putting their text into final shape. The various subsidiary negotiations were making rapid progress. On May 17 Dobrynin was invited to spend the night at Camp David. After breakfast with the President he told me that Moscow would spare no effort to make the summit a success. However, because of Vietnam the public welcome in Moscow could not be as warm as had originally been planned, Dobrynin suggested. This clever jab hit Nixon where it hurt — in the public relations field. (It also gave an insight into the "spontaneity" of the Soviet masses.)

Peking, too, demonstrated that it had its priorities straight. In a conversation with me in New York on May 16, UN Ambassador Huang Hua repeated the official line that China stood behind its friends. But he did not demur when I pointed out that we had warned Peking at least half a dozen times of our determination to react strongly if Hanoi sought to impose a military solution. Nor did our actions in Vietnam prevent Huang Hua from encouraging a visit by me to Peking in June. We had not only achieved a free hand in Vietnam; we would be able to continue at the same time the construction of the larger design of our foreign policy.

Postlude

THE media and Congress soon shifted their position, retreating to the familiar attacks on "indiscriminate" bombing and demands for a legislated deadline to end the war. Some praised the Soviets for their restraint; praise for Nixon's courage was sparse.

It was my fate throughout the Vietnamese war to be in the middle of the crossfire between my former associates and my new chief. Perhaps my most poignant and frustrating encounter of that period was with seven presidents of Ivy League universities who came to the Roosevelt Room of the White House on May 17, three days before we left for Moscow. These men, heads of the most prestigious American universities, had come to tell me, in effect, that rational judgment was no longer relevant to the war in Vietnam. One of them complained of destruction being inflicted "for reasons that are not clear and for a cause that no one seems willing to defend." When I tried to explain the issues posed by the North Vietnamese invasion and above all by Hanoi's insistence that we collude with them to impose Communist rule, he took refuge in the passions of the students: "Be that as it may, it is turning large numbers of young people away from their country." I replied that I was aware of the students' despair, but "we in government have an obligation not only to register what the students say but also to put it into the framework of the longer term." We were willing to take "any reasonable step," but turning Vietnam over to an enemy relying on brute force was not a reasonable step. Another of the group asked how he should explain the cost of the war to the students. I could only respond by asking how he would explain it if after eight years of war we did for Hanoi what it could not do for itself.

But it was a dialogue of the deaf. The distinguished Ivy League presidents were not interested in the merits of the issues in dispute between us and North Vietnam. They were there as spokesmen of an emotion. One of them stated that none of the students would really care if Saigon fell. Another allowed that our principles might be "persuasive," including the principle of "not letting one group dominate another," but since we did not help people in similar circumstances elsewhere, why did we have to do it in Vietnam? In other words, unless we defended every moral purpose everywhere we had no right to defend any principle anywhere. But the real problem boiled down to a more practical concern. One of them admitted: "I don't see how we can continue to run our universities if the war escalates. . . . What will we face in September?" Against this line of reasoning no persuasion was possible, as illustrated by the following exchange:

KISSINGER: If we are to do anything for your concerns we have to face them operationally. . . . The question of ending aid to people to defend themselves — against a people who are heroic and also brutal — is not obvious to me even as a moral issue. . . . This offensive will establish a new balance of forces one way or another. If Saigon collapses, the new balance is a fact. If not, that is also a new fact. The reaction of Peking and Moscow is also a new fact. If it fails, they can't go on.

But if we can just introduce some compassion in our debate, if instead of assuming that some of us want to kill and some have a monopoly on anguish over this war, if we could raise the level of the debate to try to find things we can do together. We never will agree on Vietnam. The debates pass each other like trains, without thinking that there are serious people on the other side.

We think — odd as this may seem to you — that it is important for the health of the society and the stability of the international system that we get out with some dignity.

UNIVERSITY PRESIDENT: We try to introduce fairness and reason to the debate — but only at risk to our own lives. That is a fact.

In other words, the heads of the nation's greatest universities had lost control of their campuses and expected the President of the United States to ease their difficulty by reversing a considered national policy then involving nearly 70,000 American troops and several of the world's major powers. This was to be done in the name of morality even though its admitted consequence was to consign millions of South Vietnamese who had relied upon us to a Communist dictatorship that the overwhelming majority of them rejected and feared. Consideration of the issues was dismissed; the profound emotion that now dominated the campuses was beyond rational analysis. The idea that the President of the United States was responsible for keeping order in our universities was novel, especially coming from liberal academicians. It was the ultimate expression of the abdication of institutional leaders in our society, of the abasement of the middle-aged before the young, of the dismissal of rational discourse by those with the greatest stake in reason.

From the other side of the barricades I was the recipient of frequent missives from Nixon, berating me for the insufficient audacity and toughness of the military's prosecution of the war. On May 9 a memorandum descended on me, urging me to look for new ways of hurting the enemy with air power:

We have the power to destroy his war-making capacity. The only question is whether we have the *will* to use that power. What distinguishes me from Johnson is that I have the *will* in spades. If we now fail it will be because the bureaucrats and the bureaucracy and particularly those in the Defense Department, who will of course be vigorously assisted by their allies in State, will find ways to erode the strong, decisive action that I have indicated we are going to take. For once, I want the military and I want the NSC staff to come up with some ideas on their own which will recommend *action* which is very *strong, threatening* and *effective*. [9]

On May 10 came a Presidential ukase, one of a long series, expressing his faith in the efficacy of psychological warfare; as usual, he wildly overestimated the CIA's capability in this area. He wanted the word to be put out that entire North Vietnamese regiments had ceased to exist and that North Vietnamese morale was collapsing. Nixon thought the CIA had a "total lack of imagination" in these matters. On May 13 came a memo undercutting the previous toughness somewhat by saying that the three new Air Force squadrons sent to Vietnam should make it possible for us to *accelerate* our withdrawal program by allowing us to remove additional support forces. By May 15 Nixon was proposing that we amass all tanks in South Vietnam for "at least one surprise offensive against the enemy" in some area where they could effectively be used. He surmised — not without reason — that these ideas might not all be appreciated by Moorer, Abrams, Haig, and me, but he reminded Haig and me of the unconventional brilliance of Patton and MacArthur and urged that we read an inspiring passage from Churchill. Correctly he lamented that the military, abused for years by civilian leadership, proved unable to respond imaginatively when given a freer hand. (Al Haig, he granted, "certainly is an exception.") On May 18, Haig was appropriately honored by a Presidential memo ordering that our bombing continue while the Presidential party was in Moscow. (Haig was to remain behind in Washington.) Nixon wrote that he would not make the same mistake as when he limited the bombing in connection with the China trip. After the Moscow summit he wanted more B-52 strikes in the Hanoi-Haiphong area. On Saturday, May 20, the day we were leaving for Moscow, the blizzard of paper ended with a long memorandum for Haig with further guidance for the military campaign against North Vietnam while Nixon was away. He wanted no basis for press stories that we were "letting up" during this period. He wanted a "relentless air attack" and yet more done on the propaganda front.

Nixon was entitled to some release for his nervous tension. For all his vulnerability and bravado, the fact remains that he had acted boldly and won a brilliant gamble. He challenged the Soviet Union and to a lesser extent China and in the end improved relations with both. He prevented the military collapse of South Vietnam, which (in 1972) would have undercut these relationships and the entire design of our foreign policy. After weeks of impatient musings about canceling the Moscow summit, he settled on the wiser strategy of using the Soviet stake in a successful summit to restrain a Soviet response, to gain a free hand in Vietnam, and eventually to bring to fruition our patient efforts to build a more constructive US–Soviet relationship.

In retrospect all events seem inevitable. The fact remains that I, the Soviet expert on my staff, as well as the CIA and the State Department, all expected the Soviets to cancel the summit and that was the background against which the President made his decision. (I nevertheless urged the military action, because a summit held under conditions of demonstrated weakness would not be worth holding.) That the risk did not materialize does not detract from Nixon's courage in running it.

With hindsight it is possible to see why the Soviets chose not to confront us. With all the ups and downs the Kremlin had learned the central importance of the US–Soviet relationship. No matter what our Congressional embarrassments, we were likely to prevail in a real arms race — if not immediately, then certainly as the American public mood changed under the impact of mounting tensions. Linkage was no rhetorical idiosyncrasy in Soviet eyes. Cancellation of the summit would bring about the Soviets' worst nightmare: an American relationship with Peking not balanced by equal ties with Moscow. And it would have undermined the Soviet Union's entire European policy. For thirty years and for understandable reasons, Moscow had been preoccupied by the German question; Brandt's Eastern treaties were moving toward a resolution before the German Parliament, but their fate was hanging by a thread. Our action would be pivotal. A new Cold War would almost certainly have upset the apple cart of Brandt's policy; the Soviet Union's carefully nurtured strategy for Europe would have collapsed. A cancellation would also have jeopardized the Soviet Union's economic prospects: Brezhnev had made a strategic decision to seek Western, and particularly American, trade and technology; that hope would vanish without a summit. And in many other crucial areas such as the Middle East, an era of confrontation opened unpleasant prospects before the Soviet leaders.

Conscious of its own vulnerabilities, the Kremlin therefore cut loose from its obstreperous small ally on the other side of the globe. By proceeding with the summit, Moscow helped neutralize our domestic opposition, which gave us freedom of action to break the back of North Vietnam's offensive. Our strategy of détente — posing risks and dangling benefits before the Soviets — made possible an unfettered attempt to bring our involvement in the Vietnam war to an honorable close. Nixon could leave for Moscow with dignity, for we had not sacrificed those who had put their trust in us; with confidence, since the interlocking design of our foreign policy had withstood extraordinary stress; and with hope that we were laying the foundations of a global equilibrium which could bring safety and progress to an anxious thermonuclear world.

XXVIII

The Moscow Summit

Richard Nixon in the Kremlin

WHEN against all expectations we took off for Moscow in *Air Force One* on Saturday morning, May 20, the mood was one of optimism, even elation, untinged by excessive humility. Despite the assaults by both Hanoi and our critics we had stood our ground; we were going to Moscow with dignity. We had behind us a rare public consensus produced by the stunning events of the preceding month. Conservatives reveled in the mining of North Vietnam; they interpreted the summit as a Soviet retreat. Liberals were relieved that the summit was taking place at all. Some editorialists, it is true, were concerned that we might be walking into a trap similar to that which had snapped shut on the Khrushchev-Eisenhower summit in Paris in 1960;[1] but none of us on the plane believed this.

The two negotiating teams on SALT were almost daily settling issues at Helsinki, and during my April trip we had in effect agreed with Brezhnev on a statement of principles of international conduct. The holding of the summit was the culmination of our four years of insistence on linkage — that arms control could not stand by itself, that Soviet help on Vietnam and restraint in the Middle East were essential preconditions of progress in other fields. In addition to the major agreements on SALT and the principles of conduct, a whole host of other accords had been negotiated under the impact of the summit deadline. The two leaders were rarely involved in the actual negotiations on these topics; on a few occasions a deadlock was referred to Dobrynin and me in the Channel and rapidly settled. Usually the knowledge that Brezhnev and Nixon wanted a document ready for signature at the summit encouraged a spirit of compromise on both sides. As a result, six subsidiary agreements awaited the principals: on cooperation in environmental protection; on medical science and public health; on the exploration and use of outer space for peaceful purposes; on science and technology; on avoiding incidents at sea by establishing "rules of the road"; and on establishing a joint US–Soviet economic commission.

Of course none of these agreements, even when the ink was dry, would obliterate the fundamental causes of conflict over which there was a sharp division in our country. Liberals in those days (before Solzhenitsyn's *Gulag* volumes) tended to believe either that the Soviets had already mellowed and it was left to diplomacy only to sweep up the cobwebs left over from an already transcended Cold War, or at worst that the few remaining authentic causes of tension could be ended by the strenuous exercise of goodwill on our part. Conservatives, uneasy at summitry, on the whole preferred to sound the trumpets of anti-Communism, as if rhetoric would crumble the walls of the Soviet empire. They did not explain how we could sustain such a course domestically amid the Vietnam hysteria. We had a somewhat different perspective from either liberals or conservatives. On Soviet motives I leaned toward the conservative analysis; in tactics I sought to incorporate some of the liberal views. In a memorandum for the President before leaving, I summarized Soviet policies in various parts of the world and described the outlook starkly:

The prospect for a fundamental change in Soviet-American relations is not bright. A SALT agreement, of course, would mark some forward progress and might be a precursor to more normal relations, particularly if there were also some improvement in economic ties. On both counts the Soviets would begin to have a stake in a less erratic and more stable relationship. The ratification of the German treaties and the implementation of the Berlin agreements would also add to elements creating a more permanent Soviet interest in stable relationships.

At the same time, in Europe the Soviets have interests in arrangements and agreements which contribute to the security of their own sphere but not in a genuine European settlement. And the conflict of interest in the Middle East and in Asia is likely to be prolonged.

For reasons deeply rooted in the ideology of the regime and the structure of internal Soviet politics, Soviet foreign policy will remain antagonistic to the West and especially the US. The world power ambitions of the Soviet leaders, and any likely successors, plus their confidence in their capability to support their ambitions with material resources, suggest that the USSR will press their challenge to Western interests with increasing vigor and in certain situations assume risks which heretofore would have seemed excessively dangerous.

But skepticism was not a viable policy by itself. We had to conduct a complex policy — and suffer attacks from both liberals and conservatives for it — ready to confront Soviet expansionism and yet receptive to more hopeful possibilities. We could not permit the Soviets to monopolize the world's yearning for peace; we could not maintain the moral leadership of free peoples if we were perceived as the cause of world tensions, for the ineluctable fact was that nuclear weapons required us to explore all opportunities, however tenuous, to achieve mutual restraint. If we denied the Soviets all opportunities for expansion and kept the door open for genuine cooperation, we might inculcate habits of moderation and bring about a more constructive future.

This was the emphasis I gave in my press briefing on May 21, when we stopped for a day in Salzburg to adjust to the time change: The two major nations that alone possessed the panoply of weapons had to conduct themselves, I said, "with a degree of foresight commensurate with their power."

The residence where we stayed in Salzburg was a fittingly spectacular prelude to our entry to Moscow. It was the castle of Klessheim, about ten miles out of town, with huge baroque staterooms and elegant formal gardens. A fence kept the press at a distance. Cameramen were permitted only one photo opportunity, which consisted of Nixon and me, looking our most reflective, pacing along the gravel paths between stately hedges. I do not now remember what we were discussing, but most often on such occasions it was more likely baseball than some profound matter of high policy.

Nixon had a meeting with Austria's shrewd and perceptive Chancellor Bruno Kreisky, who had parlayed his country's formal neutrality into a position of influence beyond its strength, often by interpreting the motives of competing countries to each other. That he could bring off this balancing act was a tribute to his tact, his intelligence, and his instinct for the scope — and the limits — of indiscretion. He was much traveled; his comments on trends and personalities were invariably illuminating. He had a great sense of humor and far more geopolitical insight than many leaders from more powerful countries. One of the asymmetries of history is the lack of correspondence between the abilities of some leaders and the power of their countries (Prime Minister Lee Kuan Yew of Singapore is another good contemporary example). Kreisky and Nixon exchanged good-humored reflections on the international situation. As a practicing politician Kreisky could not help admiring a man who stakes his election on a bold move and brings it off. Nixon remarked later that he wished Kreisky could change places with some of the Socialist leaders in larger European countries whose insight and sturdiness Nixon rated less highly.

While in Salzburg we received news suggesting that Brezhnev had newly strengthened his domestic position. The Soviet Party Central Committee had met to give formal approval to his decision to proceed with the summit. That ritualistic act acquired significance by the simultaneous removal of the Ukrainian Party chief Pyotr Shelest from the Politburo and his demotion to Deputy Prime Minister (in Communist states the Party functions are much more important than governmental office). Shelest had been regarded as an influential hard-liner; in dismissing him

Brezhnev was demonstrating to the Soviet ruling group that he was in charge. The move improved our bargaining position, for Brezhnev would now be under additional pressure to produce significant results at the summit.

As we set off for Moscow on Monday morning, May 22, Nixon was in high spirits, even though he was still concerned about how to surface the declaration of "Basic Principles of US–Soviet Relations," of which Secretary Rogers did not yet know. I told Nixon that I would try to get Brezhnev to bring it up in a manner that made it appear to emerge from the summit. In candor I did not rate Soviet subtlety sufficiently high to be sure that we would bring it off. Nixon agreed, however, and temporarily morose, reconciled himself to an explosion as in Hangchow when the Shanghai Communiqué had been surfaced suddenly.

For the rest Nixon prepared himself assiduously for the summit encounters by studying the voluminous briefing books prepared by my staff in collaboration with the State Department. One briefing memorandum analyzed Brezhnev's political position and recommended that Nixon avoid the impression that we were under pressure "to settle everything at these meetings this week." A second described in detail the maneuvering within the Politburo. A third dealt with Brezhnev's personality and objectives, comparing them with the Chinese leaders':

> Brezhnev and company lead a superpower, one equal in many respects to our own nation. They speak with the weight of current strategic equality, while the Chinese strength derives from a combination of their long past and their inevitable future. . . .
>
> Given the stage of our bilateral relations and personal inclination, Chou could spend time with us on history and philosophy. Brezhnev will want to talk about concrete issues — the format of a European Security Conference, the major elements of a SALT agreement, the mines in Haiphong Harbor, the drawing of lines in the Middle East. Although he obviously won't know all the details like Gromyko, he will be well briefed and in command of his material, prepared to press you on specific questions. He will want results and agreements, and he will not hestiate to do some tactical elbowing in the process.

Nixon marked up his briefing papers; he asked me searching questions. He also read excerpts from my April talks with Brezhnev. But there was not the same sense of tension, uncertainty, and insecurity as on the trip to Peking. He knew Moscow and was therefore more confident. He also knew — even if it was not yet public — that the basic issues had been essentially settled during my trip in April or in the negotiations by the various departments. Nixon's major task would be to conduct a *tour d'horizon* with the Soviet leaders. This was his strong suit, and he was rightly confident that he would carry it off.

We landed in Moscow at 4:00 P.M. on Monday, May 22. All day the sun had been unable to decide whether to join the arrival ceremony; its final judgment about the summit turned out to be as ambiguous as US–Soviet relations. Just before we arrived, it hid behind clouds so that the arrival ceremony took place in a light rain. As soon as the ceremony was over the rain stopped. For our arrival at the Kremlin the pale northern light of the Moscow spring shone on the American flag that only minutes before had been raised over the towers to denote the extraordinary fact that an American President was in residence.

President Nikolai Podgorny and Premier Alexei Kosygin greeted Nixon at the airport. Leonid Brezhnev stuck to protocol; as Party General Secretary he had no need to be present. He almost never attended the arrival of non-Communist dignitaries. Some learned press commentaries nevertheless found great significance in his absence. The ceremony was a shade less austere than that in Peking. The word was obviously out to improve on the Chinese reception but not to the point of offending Hanoi. A small crowd waved paper flags at one side of the terminal building; dignitaries were lined up on the other. Psychologists can determine which conveys a cooler impression — an empty tarmac as in Peking, or a crowd so conspicuously small as to symbolize minimum formality. There was about the arrival ceremony the quintessential Soviet mixture of brute strength and surface efficiency, coupled with the latent sense that some minor problem could make the whole splendid machinery grind to a halt. An impressive honor guard passed in review before we were moved pell-mell toward a huge fleet of waiting Soviet ZIL limousines — cars that have the look of a 1958 Packard and feel as if they have the same basic chassis as the Soviet light tank.

The wide avenues of Moscow had been cleared of traffic as our motorcade, some fifty vehicles, raced toward the Kremlin. It seemed bent on breaking the speed record set during my secret trip; it probably succeeded. Buses were blocking all side streets, thus preventing any member of the "masses" from paying tribute to the President. Here and there one could see crowds of curious onlookers behind the barricades. They were too far away for us to be able to judge their mood.

The Kremlin has sinister connotations; one expects buildings where menacing parapets reflect the violent history to which they have borne witness. The aesthetic reality is otherwise. What started as the fortress of Moscow had been transformed by Italian architects in the fifteenth century into an ornate conceit whose bright colors and classic proportions give the inhabitants of wintry Russia a brief vision of a less harsh and solemn environment. The Kremlin rises over Moscow like a beautiful mirage sustaining a weary traveler. Yellow-ochred facades with white trim peek over the red brick walls. Once inside its vast enclosed expanse, one might almost enjoy the illusion of being in an Italian Renaissance city, were it not for the various medieval churches with their characteristic multiple golden towers and the hideous semimodernistic Palace of Congresses, which neo-Stalinist architecture has inflicted on one of the beautifully proportioned squares. It is a tribute to the original design that even this incongruous structure of marble and glass is unable to disrupt the underlying harmony.

Nixon's apartment was in the palace of the Tsars' Apartments, which also houses the Armory Museum, a striking collection of jewelry, robes, and carriages, and other treasures from Tsarist days — Ivan the Terrible's throne, Boris Godunov's suit of armor, Catherine the Great's gowns, Fabergé eggs, and so on. This museum is sustained by the current regime, one supposes, to maintain the national pride, while reminding the public, in accompanying descriptions, of the exploitation on which the wealth was based. The Presidential quarters were located at the side of a long corridor lined with the urns that Brezhnev had proudly shown me and that were now resplendent in their carefully preserved sheen. Whoever had polished them no doubt strongly supported the decision to receive us despite our actions in Indochina. The suite was on the grandiose side, with beautiful rococo furniture. Several sitting rooms led to the President's bedroom. Across a courtyard along a parallel corridor were the suites of the senior White House staff. They had the better view, facing the outside, but the rooms were of more modest proportions. The furniture was from the Communist period, which is to say it was heavy and not very comfortable. Rogers was housed in the new Rossiya Hotel near Red Square, about five minutes' drive from the President's quarters. To the uninitiated this seems close enough; but even more than the adjacent guest houses in Peking it perpetuated the psychological gulf between the two bureaucracies, as if he were in Siberia.

Alas, the splendid Presidential apartment proved unsuited to the conduct of business. Our security experts were certain it was bugged by sophisticated equipment. Nixon refused to use the babbler; its noise drove him crazy. Thus the President and I were reduced to using his American limousine parked outside for really private conversations, hoping that its bulletproof windows would inhibit any electronic equipment aimed at it.

But this was not our concern upon arrival. Nixon's romantic streak was touched by the history of the Kremlin and by being the first American President to visit there. Kosygin and Podgorny made some small talk and then excused themselves. The summit was at last under way.

Greetings and Meetings

NIXON's first meeting with Brezhnev was sprung about an hour later — probably in imitation of the Mao procedure — just before the welcoming dinner. Brezhnev insisted on seeing Nixon alone. Nixon

followed his usual practice of not taking a State Department interpreter — which, now that I too was excluded, I found irksome. As
was his custom, he also did not dictate an official record, though he
briefed me orally. I was reduced to asking the splendid Soviet interpreter Viktor Sukhodrev to dictate his account to Julie Pineau, my
secretary. He obviously did not give his chief the worst of the exchanges — recalling Dean Acheson's famous dictum that no one ever
lost a debate in a memorandum of conversation dictated by oneself.
Sukhodrev's account shows much of the meeting taken up by a long
monologue by Brezhnev. He began by saying that it had not been
"easy" for the Soviet Union to agree to the meeting in the light of what
we were doing in Vietnam; it sounded plausible, though it grew tiresome as the week wore on and it became a refrain. No meeting seemed
official until the senior Soviet leader present had pronounced this liturgy
and implied that Soviet restraint required some American reciprocity.

Brezhnev avowed his dedication to a fundamental improvement in
US–Soviet relations; hence, he averred, he considered the "Basic Principles of US–Soviet Relations" even more important than the projected
SALT agreement. Brezhnev complained that the technical preoccupation
of the SALT delegates needed "looking into." In part, this complaint
may have been genuine; in part, it enabled the two leaders to act out the
seeming psychological necessity, at any summit, of pretending that they
have personally broken a deadlock produced by their less inspired subordinates. Brezhnev stressed his interest in a European Security Conference. And he managed to try out on Nixon the project that he had
sprung on me weeks earlier, an agreement that neither side would use
nuclear weapons against the other.

Nixon was not anxious for detailed negotiations at this point. He was
more eager to demonstrate how well he had prepared himself by quoting
back to Brezhnev excerpts from the latter's conversations with me in
April. He avoided Vietnam. He agreed to a European Security Conference "in principle," saying that only procedural obstacles remained.
This could mean anything. He shunted the accord to refrain from the use
of nuclear weapons back to me, thereby exposing me to another year of
heavy-handed Soviet cajolery. He implied that he might be prepared to
discuss Middle East issues. Neither of the leaders having achieved high
office through their mastery of detail, the only agreement they could
reach at this point was on the untrustworthiness and inadequacy of their
bureaucracies. Nixon suggested that Brezhnev and he should return to
the wartime atmosphere when fundamental issues were settled by heads
of government, with subordinates confined to technical implementation.
"If we leave all decisions to the bureaucrats we will never achieve any
progress," said Nixon. "They would simply bury us in paper," Brezhnev assented happily.

Having established this community of interest, the two leaders proceeded to swap accounts of their domestic difficulties. Brezhnev allowed that he would have to bring Kosygin and Podgorny to most meetings; Nixon reciprocated by pointing out that Rogers did not yet know about the "Basic Principles." He asked Brezhnev's help to introduce the document in a manner compatible with our bureaucratic necessities. This was a game Brezhnev could recognize; he readily agreed.

The two leaders kept the other guests waiting at the state dinner, scheduled to start at 8:00 P.M. This had the additional benefit of creating the impression that matters of the gravest import were being discussed. The dinner took place in the splendid Granovit Hall of the Grand Kremlin Palace, an exquisite fifteenth-century room with vaulted ceilings and walls covered with religious paintings. Because the room was relatively small, the guests were fewer than on similar occasions in China — about two hundred. They included the top leadership of the Soviet Union and the official parties of both sides. The dinner lacked the precise planning of the Peking banquets; it was more like the gathering of a slightly disorganized family. While we waited for the principals to arrive, there was aimless milling about with each delegation keeping generally to itself. The Soviet leaders entered at irregular intervals; there was no receiving line. Finally Brezhnev and Nixon appeared and made some jocular remarks to a few of the people they knew. Whereupon without any further ceremony, everyone went in to dinner about an hour late.

Both Nixon and Podgorny (Nixon's equivalent in protocol rank) made long but unsensational toasts. Podgorny reaffirmed the Soviet commitment to peaceful coexistence, which he said had been a principle of Soviet behavior since Lenin's time; we would have preferred intimation of some change in Soviet conduct; continuity was not without menace. Podgorny left unanswered the fundamental questions: Was relaxation of tensions only a tactic in an unending struggle to overturn the world equilibrium? Or were we at the beginning of a new phase of Soviet policy?

Nixon's response took the themes that we would seek to usher in a period of genuine great-power restraint. In contrast to his speech in Peking, he eschewed hyperbole. He wished the summit to be remembered, he said, for substance rather than atmosphere:

We should recognize that great nuclear powers have a solemn responsibility to exercise restraint in any crisis, and to take positive action to avert direct confrontation.

With great power goes great responsibility. It is precisely when power is not accompanied by responsibility that the peace is threatened. Let our power always be used to keep the peace, never to break it.

We should recognize further that it is the responsibility of great powers to influence other nations in conflict or crisis to moderate their behavior.

The Soviet summit thus began auspiciously enough. However, it never developed the uniform texture of the one in Peking; it was more random and jagged. We had had little practical business with the Chinese. The Peking summit had therefore focused on creating the philosophical and psychological ties that would cause coordinated policies to emerge from a common appreciation of the international situation. But we were geopolitically too competitive with the Soviet Union for such an approach to be possible in Moscow. And the Soviets leaders were psychologically too insecure and insensitive to intangibles to trust themselves in theoretical discussions. They had reached eminence by the cold elimination of rivals who were also colleagues. They could hardly trust a capitalist statesman more than they trusted one another. Collective leadership aggravated the unease. A mistake made collectively could be survived; a setback caused by an individual's excessive trust seemed unforgivable. Soviet leaders therefore reinsured themselves over and over again by documents and written interpretations. Philosophical discussions made them visibly nervous; they considered them either a trick or a smokescreen; they maneuvered them as rapidly as possible in the direction of some concrete result that could be signed. The result was that even written agreements were achieved by so much haggling along the way that they stood alone and on their own terms; they left little residue of goodwill. One had the sense that only the literal meaning of documents would be observed (if at all) and that what was not written down had no significance whatever. The "spirit" of a document was a meaningless phrase to the Soviet leadership.

This meant in practice that the discussions between Nixon and the Soviet leaders lacked a central theme. There was one dramatic meeting on Vietnam. For the rest the Soviet leaders met with Nixon at irregular intervals, discussing a grab bag of subjects, including Europe, the Middle East, and economic relations, without achieving either precise conclusions or profound political insight. On the whole what emerged were formal expressions of standard positions not significantly different from the written exchanges that had gone back and forth through the Channel, either summaries of concluded negotiations or precursors of later ones. What was left to negotiate was turned over to Gromyko and me for late-night sessions during the week and meetings most of the day on Saturday, May 27, while the President was sight-seeing in Leningrad, and on May 28, while he was preparing his television address to the Soviet people.

The summit's jagged rhythm was compounded by the fact that schedules in the Soviet Union seem to have at best an approximate quality. The meeting times printed on our programs were largely theoretical. We would sometimes be kept waiting for hours while the Soviet leaders caucused, attended Politburo sessions, or simply disappeared. One could never be sure of the time, place, or subject of a meeting, regardless of what had been agreed in advance. (This was true only of the top leaders. Gromyko as Foreign Minister was meticulously punctual.) It was never clear whether the numerous delays and the constant switching of topics were a form of psychological warfare or simply reflected the Soviet working style. In any case, the procedure never varied throughout my dealings with top Soviet leaders. When Brezhnev visited the United States in 1973, he sat on his veranda at Camp David in full view of Nixon's cabin, talking with his advisers right through a scheduled meeting with the President, whom he kept waiting for two hours without explanation or apology. That same year, after being kept waiting for four hours during a visit to Moscow, I finally got results by telling a Soviet protocol official that I had always wanted to spend my winter vacation in Moscow. This produced Brezhnev within half an hour (or maybe he was ready anyway). Whenever possible Dobrynin would show up during these unscheduled intervals, suavely conciliatory but obviously not able or willing to explain what was happening.

The one fixed item in the daily schedule was the signing ceremony, generally at 5:00 P.M. each day, for the subsidiary agreements negotiated beforehand. The entire Soviet and American delegations would meet in the Kremlin in a large room behind the impressive St. Vladimir Hall where the signings were to take place in front of a crowd of journalists, photographers, officials, and onlookers. The waiting room looked like the recreation hall of a self-made industrial tycoon: potted plants arranged in no discernible pattern and punctuated by massive furniture that was more expensive than elegant. The American and Soviet delegations awkwardly segregated themselves in opposite corners, perhaps because the Soviet officials responsible for the technical subjects had had little previous contact with non-Communist foreigners and simply did not know how to behave on an informal or personal level. What they lacked in parlor graces they made up for in determination. When the signal was given that the time for signing had arrived, they showed Russian resilience and toughness in elbowing their way through the doors ahead of their startled guests. They acted as if Soviet prestige was at stake in getting to the signing ceremony ahead of the American delegation. Such dedication deserves not to go unrecognized. History must record that in a week of signing ceremonies the Soviet delegations, however different their composition, never let their side down. They won every race to every signing ceremony.

The random nature of the planning emerged with the first plenary session on Tuesday, May 23. The meeting took place in St. Catherine's Hall, a large, ornately gilded room, furnished sparsely with elegant candelabra and carved chairs around a long rectangular table covered in beige felt. The Americans entered at one end of the long room and the Soviets from the opposite one; the two delegations met and milled about until they finally sorted themselves out and took their places opposite each other. On the American side Nixon was in the middle, flanked by Rogers and me; the full complement of White House and State Department aides was present, guaranteeing that Nixon would say nothing significant. The top Soviet leadership was seated with Brezhnev in the middle, flanked by Podgorny and Kosygin; the Soviet group included, among others, Gromyko and Dobrynin plus the interpreter Sukhodrev. The table was divided in the middle — as if it were a frontier — by a row of bottles of fizzy Georgian mineral water and crystal glasses. After a few minutes of the obligatory press and television photographs, the official conversations of the summit conference began.

They immediately ran squarely into the unpredictable. We had been led to expect that Europe would be the main topic, and the NSC staff had prepared the President's briefing with that in mind. That subject never really came up. This turned those staff aides who had worked on the papers rabidly anti-Soviet, there being no fury like that of a Presidential adviser who has been shown to be less than prescient before his chief.

Brezhnev's welcoming speech repeated the soon to be familiar point that it had not been "easy" for the Soviets to agree to the meeting. The next half hour was devoted to familiarizing the other participants with decisions long since reached in the Channel. Brezhnev proposed that there be a signing ceremony each afternoon. Nixon fell in step, observing that the Moscow morning papers would thus have something to report while in the United States the signings would make the evening television shows. What Brezhnev thought of the proposition that the Moscow journals needed Nixon's help in finding news must be left to his autobiography. Nixon then held forth at some length about the importance he attached to the meetings. He was careful to include caveats about continuing differences, noting that he had the reputation of a Cold Warrior. Kosygin intervened dryly that he seemed to have heard some rumors to that effect sometime in the past.

Banter continued even after the conversations turned to economic relations and SALT. Brezhnev said, half seriously, that US–Soviet relations would make great progress if we could grant credits of three to four billion dollars for twenty-five years at 2 percent interest. Kosygin interjected that it would then be possible to supply the United States with large quantities of genuine Soviet vodka, which was far better than the émigré vodka we were used to; Brezhnev suggested that he and Kissinger could set up a company. Nixon responded that I already made enough money — where he got this erroneous idea I do not know.

Nixon did not much like small talk. He therefore quickly moved to spell out the linkage between trade and credits and progress on SALT. He said that a SALT agreement would help him get the support in the Congress for expanded trade relations. Kosygin and Brezhnev insisted that trade was important in its own right. To our astonishment Podgorny suddenly intervened to say that SALT was more important than commercial ties because it dealt with national security. Brezhnev acknowledged this but added that the trade matters were "close to the heart of the people." Podgorny was not to be put off, however, and reiterated that SALT was more difficult and more important. Rogers spoke up to repeat what Nixon had said about the difficulty of getting support in the Congress for Most Favored Nation treatment unless there were other agreements. Podgorny hung in: While trade was important, SALT was more important still. Finally, Kosygin switched sides, stressing the importance of reaching a SALT agreement while the United States and the Soviet Union still enjoyed a practical duopoly of nuclear weapons; there was really "no other alternative." Nixon, looking for a way to avoid the blowup of Hangchow, suggested that Gromyko and Rogers concentrate on European security issues, and thus implied that I should handle all other topics. Brezhnev took his cue and proposed that Gromyko and I work on SALT; while we were at it, he added rather skillfully, we might also give some thought to general principles that should govern relations between our two countries. Brezhnev also noted that the SALT negotiators in Helsinki had so far failed to reach agreement on one or two points, and suggested that he and the President take them up at 4:00 P.M. between themselves. The bureaucratic books being finally cleared, the first plenary session had achieved its principal purpose and adjourned. Gromyko was the one clear victim, since he had been designated to negotiate with each American bureaucracy and to attend all plenary sessions as well.

This set the tone for all other formal sessions. Except for the discussion on SALT and a brief final discussion on Vietnam, the Soviet team operated as the troika of Kosygin, Podgorny, and Brezhnev. Brezhnev usually made the opening statement for the Soviet side, but with a great show of eliciting the agreement of his colleagues and giving them ample opportunity for comments of their own. Podgorny used the platform erratically and, at least as far as the American side was concerned, unpredictably. Kosygin, always disciplined and incisive, bore the burden of discussion on economic matters after introductory remarks by Brezhnev, and he chaired one plenary session from which Brezhnev was absent.

On the American side the composition depended on the subject matter, and since the Soviets changed topics continually there was an occasional scramble to field the correct line-up. I attended all high-level meetings, and was the sole senior adviser in the ones dealing with SALT and Vietnam. When economic subjects were discussed — as in the first plenary session on May 23 and the afternoon of May 25 —

Rogers, Peter Flanigan (Assistant to the President dealing with international economic affairs), and even Ron Ziegler were present. The discussions on Europe on May 24 included Rogers as well as his State Department advisers. The exchange on the Middle East on the afternoon of May 26 included the entire Soviet leadership but only three Americans — the President, me, and Peter Rodman as note-taker. But since State Department participation in the summit was more frequent and more visible than it had been in China, we avoided the internal bickering that so marred the end of the Peking summit.

The Soviet Power Structure: Kosygin and Podgorny

THESE meetings with the top Soviet leadership, though inconclusive, provided interesting insights into the Soviet power structure. Brezhnev held no governmental position but was clearly the top man; yet he appeared to need the support of Kosygin and Podgorny to carry the Politburo with him. At any rate, he made a great show of involving them in all decisions, going so far as to insist that the invitation for a Soviet return visit to the United States — which was included in the communiqué — mention the names of his associates. On military matters Brezhnev as Chairman of the Council of National Defense seemed to have exclusive authority; hence he met Nixon alone to discuss SALT. On Vietnam, too, he seemed to have a dominant voice, suggesting that relations with Hanoi were probably handled primarily as a Party matter — except for one collective attempt to browbeat Nixon, during which Kosygin showed the greatest passion.

Of Brezhnev's colleagues Kosygin was by far the most impressive. Though subordinate to Brezhnev in power and authority and not charged with conducting definitive talks on sensitive issues, he spoke on them with assurance and always with great precision. He seemed to master details more completely than Brezhnev. Among our own experts Kosygin had the reputation of being more liberal than Brezhnev. On the basis of my contact with him I considered that a superficial judgment. As Prime Minister, he was in operational control of day-to-day activities of the Soviet government — outside of the security and foreign policy fields. Inevitably, this produced a certain pragmatism. He was clearly fascinated by Western technology, and could speak eloquently about the advantages of increased commerce with the United States, though he never failed to claim that he was doing us the greater favor by opening up the Soviet market to our exports. But outside the economic area, on foreign policy questions, for example, Kosygin struck me as orthodox if not rigid. It seemed almost as if he compensated for managerial pragmatism by the strictest piety on ideological matters.

Kosygin was clearly more polished and better educated than his colleagues. Perhaps this was because he had been accustomed to function at the upper reaches of Soviet power for more than thirty years. Brezhnev, for example, was still a middle-level party official when Kosygin had joined the top group of twenty or so Soviet leaders. On the other hand, Kosygin's capacity for survival may well have derived from the fact that he never aspired to the very summit of power. Successive leaders beginning with Stalin had valued his competence; none had seen him as a potential rival. His main career having been on the governmental side, he lacked, in any event, the power base within the Party machinery from which to aim for the pinnacle. At the same time, Kosygin could neither have reached so near to the top nor maintained himself there for so long if he were entirely unskilled in Kremlin politics. He must have played one of the key roles in the palace revolt that overthrew Khrushchev, for example. But his longevity was due to the fact that his actions were not in service to personal ambition. His commitment to duty was vividly illustrated when his wife was fatally ill; Kosygin went ahead with his day's chores, even continuing to stand on Lenin's tomb to review a Red Square parade after the message of her death reached him.

Kosygin was shrewd in assessing character — obviously a requirement for survival in the Soviet system. Brezhnev seemed to play on the aspirations, ambitions, and weaknesses of his interlocutors by instinct; Kosygin gave the impression of doing so on the basis of skillful calculation. He even inspired Commerce Secretary Maurice Stans to dream that the two of them might join as hard-headed businessmen to settle the world's ills by economic exchange; innumerable other American business leaders came away from meeting with him salivating at the prospect of huge contracts and prepared on their return to do battle with an obdurate Administration for credits and export licenses. At the same time, Kosygin was equally skillful during the Vietnam war in holding out prospects for arms control to visitors like Averell Harriman, provided only that we would end the conflict in Indochina on Hanoi's terms.

Kosygin had the reputation of being dour. And I saw little evidence of the sense of humor some of our experts had detected beneath the glacial exterior. Either my only attempt to strike a light tone backfired, or else Kosygin's humor was too subtle for me. The Soviets, like the Chinese, had insisted that Nixon use one of their planes for internal travel, from Moscow to Kiev. As always, the Secret Service resisted; as in China, its objections were finally overcome. At the end of the summit, after the departure ceremony at Vnukovo Airport, we boarded the Soviet VIP plane, which was somewhat larger and considerably more ostentatious than *Air Force One*. In full view of the world press, and to the considerable chagrin of our Soviet hosts, its engines refused to start. While a backup plane was being readied Kosygin stormed on the plane and said: "Tell us what you want to do with our Minister of Aviation. If you want him shot on the tarmac we will do so." He looked as if he might be serious. I attempted to ease his embarrassment by speaking of the wickedness of objects. If one dropped a piece of toast it would fall on the buttered side in direct proportion to the value of the rug, I said; when one dropped a coin it always rolled away, never toward one. Kosygin was not to be consoled by such transparent attempts to shift responsibility. "This is not my experience," he said, fixing me with a baleful glance. "I have dropped coins which rolled toward me."

As for Podgorny, he was the hardest to fathom, perhaps because there was no depth there to penetrate. He clearly was third in influence among our hosts, though by protocol rank — the equivalent of head of state — he came before Kosygin. He had a grandfatherly air about him and seemed more relaxed than his colleagues, though his chain-smoking reflected the reality that the climb to even near the top of the Soviet pyramid generates enormous inner tensions. He had neither the elemental force of Brezhnev nor the sharp intellect of Kosygin. He spoke his piece; he sometimes intervened in eccentric ways; but he never gave the impression of someone who was expected to prevail, dominate, or exercise a decisive influence.

This was the trio that confronted Nixon at most sessions — especially at the dramatic one concerning Vietnam, on the evening of May 24.

Round One on SALT: Brezhnev and Nixon

By the time of the summit, discussions on strategic arms limitation had been in progress for nearly three years. The detailed talks were conducted by our SALT delegation, led by Gerry Smith with great persistence and skill both in diplomacy and in the bureaucratic maneuvering of Washington. The meetings alternated between Helsinki (the preferred Soviet site) and Vienna (which for some reason Nixon preferred). For the final phase of the negotiations the two delegations were meeting in Helsinki.

Whenever a deadlock persisted in these formal talks, the White House tended to interject itself through the Channel. Generally Dobrynin and I would work out an agreement in principle on the stalemated issue; the delegations would then develop elaborate technical implementation and the textual language. The first time was in May 1971, when Dobrynin and I negotiated the breakthrough to include offensive as well as defensive limitations in SALT. The second occurred during my April 1972 Moscow talks, when Brezhnev agreed to include submarine-launched ballistic missiles (SLBMs) in the offensive freeze.

There had been several reasons for these high-level interventions. One was the perennial problem of leaks. Instructions to the delegation went through a machinery that spewed forth hundreds of copies of each document; however discreet individual delegation members were, it was impossible to maintain secrecy, especially on issues politically most sensitive to both sides. Second, the complex machinery set up in our government to review SALT issues was extremely time-consuming. Rapid decisions were impossible; every element of the bureaucracy had at least an initial veto. Third, Nixon was determined that the credit for SALT go to him and not to Smith. Innumerable instructions to that effect were issued either directly from the Oval Office or through Haldeman. And the feeling was understandable enough. Nixon had been harassed for years for his alleged bellicosity; antiwar demonstrators had marched against him continually since he became President. It is no discredit to Nixon that he wanted to be remembered as a peacemaker; nor was it a distortion of the facts, however this might discomfit his perennial critics. He had seen the SALT process through to near culmination. Nixon's penchant for hyperbole — such as "a generation of peace" — could not obscure the reality that after years of domestic turmoil and divisive war a new international order was gradually emerging in which SALT was playing an important part.

Needless to say, the official SALT delegation was not enamored of this periodic White House involvement. They had gone through years of painstaking effort, largely unrecognized by the public. It was only human that they wanted to play a central role at the turning points which their dedication and ability had made possible. It was not their fault that the key decisions were political, involving domestic as well as foreign policy considerations for both sides. At the same time, we could not slow our efforts to resolve deadlocked issues simply to maintain the morale of our delegation. Painful as it was for our negotiating team, occasionally high-level intervention was essential. (The practice has been continued by our successors as well.)

By the time of the summit only three issues stood in the way of completing a SALT agreement. They had not been left by design, though no doubt Brezhnev and Nixon would have reserved one issue for themselves for a ceremonial concluding negotiation if the Helsinki talks had progressed with unexpected speed. While we were in Moscow, in fact, the Helsinki delegations made some progress each day. Brezhnev and Nixon (and ultimately Gromyko and I) picked up the remaining deadlocks. All the time the delegations continued their work. This arrangement created, as we shall see, some considerable tension.

The three remaining issues were (1) the distance between the two ABM sites permitted by the treaty; (2) what increases in size or volume, if any, of existing ICBMs and ICBM silos should be permitted; and (3) what SLBMs were to be counted. Each of these issues was, regrettably, highly technical. I shall try to render them in lay language; some understanding of them is essential for an evaluation of the SALT debate.

(The reader can skip to the next section if his or her interest in these details is not overwhelming.)

The spacing between the ABM sites was one of those trivial problems that emerge as a residue in the last stages of any negotiation; they are generally as complex as they are unimportant because by then both sides have exhausted their store of concessions. The problem was to prevent the two ABM sites from being so situated that they could support each other and thereby merge into a nucleus from which it would be possible to expand rapidly into a defense of a large part of the country. For this reason we advocated the widest possible spacing. We proposed 1,500 kilometers (937 miles); the Soviets put forward 1,300 kilometers (812 miles). The difference was insubstantial; political leaders, it soon turned out, could make no contribution to resolving it; it quite literally solved itself.

The other two issues were potentially more serious; they were still open precisely because they were politically intractable.

First, how to define and limit "heavy" missiles; that is, what should be the size of ICBMs permitted by the agreement? The offensive freeze banned the construction of new ICBM silos but permitted "modernization" of ICBMs. Only those silos that were actually being built at the time the agreement was signed could be completed. These provisions presented no special problem for us, because we had only one important type of ICBM, the Minuteman, nor were we building any new silos. The Soviets, however, had two main types of missiles: a "light" ICBM — the SS-11, which was in fact larger than the Minuteman — and a "heavy" monster — the SS-9, of great throwweight, which had no equivalent in the American arsenal. If the ICBM freeze left the Soviets free to place "heavy" missiles into the silos now housing SS-11s, the agreement would be meaningless and the Soviets would be able to build up a huge edge in throwweight despite the agreement.

Accordingly, conversion of silos from "light" to "heavy" was prohibited — but the Soviets sought to deprive the clause of operational meaning by balking at any agreed definition of "heavy." The American proposal was that no missile with a volume larger than the SS-11 could be put into the silos heretofore containing "light" missiles. The Soviets had consistently rejected this limitation or any variant of it. We suspected that they were working on a "light" missile larger than the SS-11 but smaller than the SS-9. Our delegation therefore came up with another formula, to the effect that the dimensions of a silo could not be changed. This would have been a looser constraint than restrictions on the volume of the missile itself, because it would permit the Soviets to increase the size of their missiles by using the existing silos more efficiently. We also ran into trouble because the Pentagon feared that a prohibition on altering silo dimensions might prevent conversion of our silos to MIRV'd missiles (Minuteman III). (This turned out to be wrong, but by then we had already dug ourselves into a position that as it turned out we did not need.)

For all these reasons our delegation had advanced the proposition that it was "significant" increases in silo dimensions that should be banned. The Soviets had agreed to this, but refused to define "significant"; they flatly rejected the US proposal to define it as meaning no more than a 10 to 15 percent increase. Our delegation proposed making a unilateral statement — which would not, of course, be binding on the Soviets — that *we* understood "significant" to mean 10 to 15 percent, precisely what the Soviets refused to accept. To rest an agreement on a unilateral statement which the Soviets had rejected seemed too risky to us at the White House; and therefore we placed the whole issue on the summit agenda.

The third issue, how to count SLBMs, was more complex still. My April trip had settled that the Soviets would be permitted 950 SLBMs on sixty-two submarines, but it had left open which missiles and submarine types would be included. The Soviets took the position that some thirty missiles on older nuclear H-class submarines as well as some sixty missiles on the even more ancient diesel-powered G-class submarines were not "modern," and hence should not count against the total. In other words, they wanted ninety older missiles essentially outside of the agreement.

It had also been agreed with Brezhnev in April — following Laird's scheme of January — that to expand from their current numbers to reach the permitted total of 950 the Soviets would have to dismantle older ICBMs and SLBMs. But the point where this dismantling would start — in the SALT jargon, the "baseline" — had been left to the negotiators at Helsinki. Predictably, the Soviets wanted the baseline at as high a number as possible, which would have required a minimum of dismantling; we wanted it as low as possible, so as to get rid of all older ICBMs and SLBMs. Calculations were complicated further because our first attempt was to establish the baseline at the number of modern submarines the Soviet would possess when the treaty was signed. The Soviets claimed they had forty-eight; we estimated forty-three. Even had we been able to agree on this number, we would still have been wrestling over how many missiles this amounted to. For the Soviets had two types of modern submarine: The D-class carried twelve missiles each; the Y-class, sixteen. In short, there was confusion aplenty when Brezhnev and Nixon got down to work the afternoon of Tuesday, May 23.

Two meetings took place, the first from 4:00 to 6:00 P.M. in St. Catherine's Hall, the second from 7:20 to 9:50 in the General Secretary's office in the Kremlin. Only I accompanied Nixon to the first session — officially as a note-taker; since I found myself heavily involved in the negotiation I had difficulty performing my official function. Hence, for the second session we brought along Hal Sonnenfeldt as note-taker. Brezhnev at both meetings was accompanied by his close aide Andrei Aleksandrov, who never spoke, and by the interpreter Sukhodrev.

The meetings demonstrated that heads of government should not negotiate complex subjects. Neither Brezhnev nor Nixon had mastered the technical issues; both were lagging hours behind the delegations in Helsinki, who were going merrily ahead on the very same points.

The first meeting took the leaders into the bog of seeking to define "heavy" missiles. To my amazement Brezhnev adopted a view constantly rejected by the Soviet delegation, to the effect that there was no need to change the dimensions of Soviet silos and that the Soviets had no intention of increasing the diameter of their missiles; this implied that they would accept a freeze on silo dimensions as well as on missile volume. In other words, he seemed to lean to our original proposal of months earlier, heretofore adamantly rejected by the Soviet SALT delegation. Moreover, Brezhnev seemed to be favoring a proposal incompatible with the weapons the Soviets were actually building. His disclaimer of Soviet intentions to increase the diameter of Soviet missiles also turned out to be contrary to the facts. To establish the point clearly, I explained to Brezhnev that we wanted an unambiguous limit on silo modification because new launch techniques could improve the capabilities of missiles. This was not simply a theoretical argument; we had good reason to believe that this was precisely what the Soviets were up to. Brezhnev strenuously denied what we knew to be true; he even drew diagrams to prove I was talking nonsense; of course we could not contradict him, lest we reveal the extent or source of our knowledge. In addition, he took umbrage whenever I described the characteristics of Soviet weapons; the Soviet passion for secrecy was such that whenever we revealed *our* knowledge of *their* capabilities the Soviet leaders became visibly flustered and irritated. As a gesture of good faith, however, Brezhnev formally proposed dropping the word "significant" altogether from the article prohibiting increases in silo dimensions; this would have prevented *any* silo increase.

Brezhnev's complete reversal of the Soviet position in accepting a freeze on missile dimensions seemed to create a problem for us, since according to recent Pentagon calculations — later shown to be erroneous — a freeze on silo size would prevent our installing the MIRV'd Minuteman III in existing Minuteman silos. So we turned Brezhnev's astonishing proposal aside, producing the surrealistic result that the leaders seemed to have switched roles: Brezhnev was veering toward the American position of some months before while Nixon appeared to be adopting the view of the Soviet SALT delegation in Helsinki. Four days later the Joint Chiefs decided that we could have lived with it, after all. By then the Soviets had withdrawn Brezhnev's suggestion, as they were bound to, no matter how Nixon responded, in view of its incompatibility with projected Soviet programs.

The discussion of SLBMs was less at variance with the positions at Helsinki; neither was it distinguished by precision. On this issue Brezhnev coincided with his delegation: Forty-eight Soviet submarines should be the baseline for starting to trade in older submarines and ICBMs for newer submarine-launched missiles. Nixon asked me to handle this part of the discussion. I suggested that we might accept forty-eight submarines as a baseline if it included the nine older H-class submarines. This proposal irritated Brezhnev not a little, since even by Soviet calculations it would have reduced the Soviet baseline figure to thirty-nine modern submarines; and it would have forced the Soviets either to scrap the H-class altogether or to forgo one new modern submarine (with twelve to sixteen missiles each) for each H-class submarine (with three missiles each) retained. He therefore shifted the discussion to the number of US submarines permitted under the agreement. We insisted on an upper limit of forty-four, allowing us a number of missiles equal to the Soviet baseline. (To reach that number we would have to trade in forty-eight of our older Titan ICBMs, which the Pentagon had been wanting to scrap for years and I had kept in service for trading purposes.) But since we in fact had only forty-one missile-carrying submarines and our Joint Chiefs of Staff had rejected building new ones until the Trident series was ready, Nixon could tell Brezhnev painlessly that we would not exercise the option to add three additional submarines during the five-year term of the agreement.

The mind now boggling at all the numbers on the table, both sides agreed to a recess of an hour. I used the time to telegraph Gerard Smith an account of the surprising turn of events.

We reassembled at 7:20 P.M. in Brezhnev's Kremlin office, which was located in a baroque-facaded building in a far corner of the Kremlin down the street from the Grand Kremlin Palace. One entered through a fairly narrow carpeted hallway and went up some steps to a rickety elevator. The third floor was used by the Politburo; the second floor housed the Council of Ministers. Brezhnev's office was at least thirty yards long, and contained a table large enough for the Politburo members and their alternates, usually a total of twenty-one. At the end of that table and perpendicular to it was Brezhnev's enormous desk, one side of which was taken up with a telephone console containing so many buttons that it created the impression that only a trained organist would be able to manipulate it.

The two principals plunged right back into the thick of things. Brezhnev opened the meeting by accepting our proposed distance of 1,500 kilometers between ABM sites. Unfortunately, unknown to either leader, the American delegation in Helsinki had already settled for the Soviet

proposal of 1,300 kilometers that morning. Brezhnev had offered us a
better deal than our negotiators had already accepted. It made no difference; we were finally stuck with the version negotiated at Helsinki;
the difference was marginal anyway.

After this misfire the leaders charged once again into the tricky area
of defining "heavy" missiles. During the recess I had warned Nixon
that because of the MIRV problem he should not stray from the position
of our delegation until we heard from Smith; but he should try to get the
Soviets to agree to our definition of "significant." Therefore Nixon told
Brezhnev that we insisted on a provision that there be no "significant"
increase in silo dimensions (which the Soviets had already accepted) and
defined "significant" as 15 percent (which the Soviets had rebuffed).
Brezhnev, having offered a total freeze on silo size in the earlier meeting, seemed a little baffled that we would not go along with what had
been our position months earlier and would take care of our fear of an
upgrading of Soviet missiles. At that point I thought there was no harm
in resurrecting an old American idea, thus far flatly rejected by the Soviets, that agreed limitations apply not only to silo dimensions but also
to the volume of missiles. This would have put a much sharper constraint on the Soviets' missile development, since they would not have
been able to improve their use of the existing silo space. Brezhnev
seemed to go along with that as well. It was the last time we encountered him in a SALT negotiation without advisers.

I still cannot understand what Brezhnev thought he was doing. Was
he offering us genuine concessions? Did he know enough of our Minuteman conversion program to expect us to turn his suggestions down?
Or did he simply become confused by the technical details and fail to
grasp the distinction between silo dimension and missile volume?

When the two leaders turned to SLBMs they simply repeated the
arguments of the earlier session. It was left that Gromyko and I would
meet the next morning to see whether we could formulate joint instructions to the delegations. But before this meeting actually took place
there came the tense and slightly bizarre encounter between Nixon and
the Soviet leadership at Brezhnev's dacha.

Confrontation at the Dacha

THIS dramatic confrontation began when the General Secretary of the
Central Committee of the Soviet Communist Party kidnapped the
President of the United States. Brezhnev had invited Nixon to dinner on
May 24 to take up "outstanding issues"; he had indicated that only the
top Soviet leadership would be present. The exclusion of Gromyko was
a signal to confine attendance on our side to members of the NSC staff.
We were told first that Brezhnev meant to discuss the Middle East, but

during the afternoon Dobrynin told me that the most likely subject on his leader's mind was Vietnam; at that point the issue had not come up except for the incantation about how "difficult" it had been for the Soviet leaders to receive Nixon. I therefore designated Winston Lord, my aide for all the most sensitive negotiations, and John Negroponte, now the Vietnam expert on my staff, to accompany me to the dacha. The plan had been to leave about an hour after the daily signing ceremony (this time on cooperation in space), proceeding in a motorcade even then being assembled by the Secret Service.

Brezhnev crossed everybody up. As he and Nixon were leaving the signing ceremony he suddenly suggested that they go together to the dacha immediately. Nixon accepted — there was little else he could do, since Brezhnev was physically propelling him into his car — and off the two leaders sped in Brezhnev's big ZIL limousine. Presidential Assistants learn rather quickly to stay close to their chiefs, especially on foreign trips. I jumped into a Soviet follow-up car, shouting to an aide that Lord and Negroponte should make their way to the dacha on their own.

It was an absurd order. No American knew where the dacha was. No Soviet official would tell them. No American car was immediately available. Lord and Negroponte turned frantically to a series of Soviet bureaucrats for assistance. They stoically pretended ignorance — either not understanding English or refusing to take the responsibility to order a car to go to the heavily guarded dacha. Nearly desperate, for no Presidential aide willingly misses a high-level meeting — and they had all my briefing papers — Lord and Negroponte finally managed (with Bill Hyland's help) to reach General Antonov, head of the section of the KGB responsible for foreign leaders' security. He authorized their departure for the dacha and provided a car — but this was not arranged until Brezhnev and Nixon (and I) had already reached the dacha. For in the meantime the small motorcade containing Nixon and Brezhnev in one car and me in another had sped out of Moscow. It was followed by Nixon's own car, full of Secret Service agents beside themselves that the President of the United States had been abducted in front of their very eyes by the Soviet Union's Number One Communist.

Next to riding in foreign airplanes, the Secret Service abhor foreign drivers and cars. They had good reason in this case. It turned out to be a harrowing trip. The main avenues in Moscow have at least six lanes, of which the inside lane is reserved for the highest level of VIPs. Any car on the inside lane has automatic precedence at each intersection. If the Soviet public were less disciplined or less aware of regulations, no member of the Politburo would survive for long, for their chauffeurs cruise through Moscow at seventy miles an hour and pay not the slightest attention to traffic lights, relying on the fact that each intersection will be cleared at their approach. Furthermore, the cars in the motorcade closely tailgate each other at racing-car speeds. The accompanying security cars swing back and forth in a scissorslike motion. If the front car were to stop suddenly, carnage would be inevitable. It is an invigorating experience. After a while fatalism sets in. The only place where I never completely conquered a queasy feeling was at the entrance to the Kremlin, where one hurtles first across a wide boulevard through heavy traffic coming from both directions, and, having survived that crossing, speeds through the fifteenth-century Borovitsky Gate, which is barely wide enough for one-way traffic. If anyone were to miss a signal, the odds in favor of survival at the speed at which Soviet VIP cars travel are negligible.

The dacha was about a forty-minute drive, even at immodest speed, from the Kremlin. It was set on a little rise in a heavily wooded area along the Moscow River. There was no other house in sight. It was heavily guarded by uniformed KGB personnel. The dacha was built in classic Soviet style not too different from the guest houses in Lenin Hills. It was two stories high, comfortable without either appearing lavish or rising to elegance. The ground floor had on one side a little office and a comfortably appointed living room overlooking a lawn leading to a boat landing on the Moscow River. On the other side of the hall was a movie projection room. Next to it there was a small conference room furnished very sparsely with an oval table and a grandfather clock by the wall. The conference room, like the sitting room, overlooked the river.

The evening was to be marked by sudden, unpredictable changes. Having successfully "kidnapped" the President once, Brezhnev, in high good spirits on our arrival at the dacha, then whisked him down to the boat landing for a hydrofoil ride. I followed in another hydrofoil with Aleksandrov.* Far behind, wallowing uncomfortably in our wake, was a conventional vessel loaded with the same Secret Service agents who had now seen their charge abducted a second time by the wily Soviet leaders, this time by water.

The hydrofoil clearly sought to break the speed record of the official limousines, and, for all I know, succeeded. Yet, despite the commotion and the obvious frenzy of those whose procedures were being so totally violated, the excursion gave me a feeling of extraordinary serenity. On both sides of the river there were birch groves that punctuated a softly undulating landscape extending in green waves to the far horizon. The view was consoling rather than spectacular. It was a glimpse of that ocean of land which is Russia. Across this expanse have streamed invading hordes from both East and West over the centuries; in the end, each was overcome by the enduring patience of a people stubbornly

---

*Brezhnev gave Nixon one of these hydrofoils as a gift, in return for the Cadillac that we gave him for his auto collection.

clinging to its native soil and preserving its own identity amidst all violence and cruelty — even that inflicted by its own leaders.

When we returned to the dacha about an hour later, Kosygin and Podgorny had arrived, as had the considerably put-upon Lord and Negroponte. But before our meeting could start I had first to settle a dispute between the KGB and the Secret Service. Determined not to let their charge be carted off on yet another wild ride, and doubtless smarting with indignation at their Soviet counterparts, the Secret Service had driven the President's car right up the portico of the dacha, blocking its entrance and constituting a potential danger to all in case of fire. The KGB, needless to say, were now as irate as the Secret Service had been half an hour earlier. In a negotiation as fraught diplomatically as any in my career, I finally persuaded the Secret Service to move the President's car from Brezhnev's front door in return for a promise that Nixon would use no foreign-made limousine or heathen driver on his return to Moscow. In fairness to the Secret Service one must stress that they have one of the most anguishing jobs in the world. Only a group with rare dedication to duty can take on responsibility for protecting the President — an assignment in which they cannot afford a single mistake. They must follow their own procedures; they cannot allow exceptions. My humorous anecdotes about them in this book should not conceal my admiration and indeed affection for the agents I knew and who also protected me. They are a first-rate, talented, and professional corps.

At last the Soviet leaders and Nixon moved into the conference room to face each other across the oval table. The discussion started harmlessly enough with Brezhnev reviewing the status of various negotiations. He suggested that Gromyko and I pick up the SALT discussions to distill some common instructions for the delegations in Helsinki. Nixon fell in with the spirit of the exchange and listed some issues on which progress seemed possible, such as the establishment of a US–Soviet economic commission. Finally, when Brezhnev mentioned in passing that the Middle East and Vietnam might be worth discussion at some point, and it seemed as if the shadowboxing might go on all night, Nixon decided to put Vietnam squarely on the table. If he had not, the Soviet leaders surely would have; they were loaded for bear.

Nixon began by arguing that the "collateral issue" of Vietnam should not interrupt the basic progress in our relations which was being achieved. (The side that seeks a free hand always claims that linkage does not apply to it.) He then gave a concise and firm summary of our position. He was aware that the Soviet Union had an ideological affinity with Hanoi. But we did not choose this moment for the "flare-up" in Vietnam. Hanoi, aided by Soviet equipment, had. Once the offensive took place, "we had to react as we did." We could not reconsider our policy unless Hanoi indicated new flexibility in its negotiating stance. Moscow, he needled, should use the influence it acquired through sup-

plying military equipment to make Hanoi think again. As for us, we
were determined to bring the war to a conclusion, preferably by negotiation, if necessary by military means.

Now that the subject was Vietnam, the easy camaraderie vanished;
the atmosphere clouded suddenly from one second to the other. Each of
the three Soviet leaders in turn unleashed a diatribe against Nixon, who,
except for two one-sentence interruptions, endured it in dignified silence. Not only was the substance tough but the tone was crudely hectoring. Brezhnev led off. He complained not only about our "cruel"
bombing but about the whole history of our involvement in Vietnam,
which seemed to him designed to embarrass the Soviet Union. He recalled that North Vietnam had first been bombed in 1965 while Kosygin was visiting Hanoi. He denied that military actions were needed to
end the war. Hanoi was eager to negotiate; all we had to do was to get
rid of Thieu and accept Hanoi's "reasonable" political program. There
were several not too subtle allusions that barely stopped short of comparing American policy with Hitler's. In effect confirming the validity
of our strategy, Brezhnev explained the Soviet reasoning for going
ahead with the summit:

> It was certainly difficult for us to agree to hold this meeting under present
> circumstances. And yet we did agree to hold it. I want to explain why. We felt
> that preliminary work prior to the meeting warranted the hope that two powers
> with such economic might and such a high level of civilization and all the other
> necessary prerequisites could come together to promote better relations between
> our two nations.

In a non sequitur that revealed again the Soviets' raw nerve about
China, Brezhnev assailed the Chinese for an immoral foreign policy and
cited the Shanghai Communiqué as supporting evidence; in his view the
fact that each party had stated its own position without defining a
common stand made the whole document unprincipled.

Before we could penetrate the logic of this curious attack on a document we had signed, it was Kosygin's turn. Where Brezhnev had been
emotional, he was analytical; where Brezhnev had pounded the table,
Kosygin was glacially correct, though, as I said, in substance the most
aggressive of the troika. He recalled his conversations with Lyndon Johnson, who had first predicted victory and failed. He implied the same fate
for Nixon. He complained bitterly about damage to Soviet ships and
loss of Soviet lives in Haiphong harbor. He hinted that Hanoi might reconsider its previous refusal to permit forces of other countries to fight
on its side — prompting Nixon to retort that we were not frightened by
that threat. Kosygin turned this into a dig at China by pointing out that
Peking had been prepared to send in troops in 1965 but had been rebuffed by the North Vietnamese. Kosygin suggested that we get rid of
Thieu; the Moscow summit was a logical place to come together on

such a proposal; he was reasonably sure it would be accepted by Hanoi. (So were we. We did not think we required Soviet help to surrender.)

Podgorny concluded the presentations. The third leader in a row now demonstrated the Soviet insecurity about China. There is something about their huge, complex neighbor that unsettles Soviet reasoning. He was in Hanoi, he said, when he learned of my secret trip to China the previous summer. He was able to reassure the North Vietnamese by telling them that Nixon was planning to visit Moscow too — as if a double sellout and isolation was better for Hanoi than one! He then seconded his colleagues' remarks: The war in Vietnam was "unlawful," and "sheer aggression." Podgorny's epithets were the equal of his colleagues', though his delivery was blander and his tone actually milder. While Podgorny was talking, Brezhnev was marching up and down behind his back, muttering to himself. It was not fully clear whether he was trying to lend emphasis to Podgorny's remarks or was getting bored.

Suddenly the thought struck me that for all the bombast and rudeness, we were participants in a charade. While the tone was bellicose and the manner extremely rough, none of the Soviet statements had any operational content. The leaders stayed well clear of threats. Their so-called proposals were the simple slogans of the Paris plenary sessions, which they knew we had repeatedly rejected and which we had no reason to accept now that the military situation was almost daily altering in our favor. The Soviet leaders were not pressing us except with words. They were speaking for the record, and when they had said enough to have a transcript to send to Hanoi, they would stop.

And so it was. Nixon, who behaved with remarkable dignity throughout, replied calmly but firmly, saying that he trusted the war would be settled soon. He noted coldly that the USSR had been "instrumental" in April in getting the secret talks resumed; we were then "somewhat disappointed" when the North Vietnamese were "more intransigent than ever before." He referred pointedly to Brezhnev's cease-fire offer, which we had accepted but Hanoi had rejected out of hand. He proposed that we take up Vietnam again later in the week. We would continue to negotiate with the North Vietnamese, but it was pointless if they were not willing to make peace. We were not expecting the Soviets to solve the problem, but, he said, "maybe you can help us." Kosygin commented sharply that a new proposal was needed, and the President replied equally sharply that the discussion had already gone on too long.

At this point Brezhnev obviously decided that the record was complete. He allowed that we had had a "most serious discussion on a problem of world importance," as if it were an abstract debate among professors. He said he drew the conclusion from Nixon's remarks that the United States was prepared to look for a reasonable solution — a proposition hard to argue with. Kosygin chimed in that not a single ship carrying military equipment was on the way to Vietnam; ''only flour and foodstuffs, no armament whatever.'' This might suggest that Moscow was bringing pressure on Hanoi, or it might mean nothing since all of North Vietnam's harbors were in any event closed by mines.

The fact was that except for their bullying tone in this session the Soviet leaders treated Vietnam as a subsidiary issue during the summit. The top leaders reverted to Vietnam only once more when Brezhnev asked Nixon whether we could modify our proposal of January 25 by having Thieu resign *two* months before a new election rather than one as we had proposed. Nixon hinted that he might be willing to suggest this if Hanoi would accept our other terms.

As for the evening at the dacha, by the time the Soviet leaders had spoken their Vietnam piece for three hours, it was 11:00 P.M. The mood thereupon shifted as suddenly to congeniality as it had to animosity a few hours earlier. We were escorted upstairs to a dining room that appeared to occupy virtually the entire second floor. Despite the late hour a full four-course meal was served, preceded by the usual groaning assortment of hors d'oeuvres.

Brezhnev was now uncharacteristically reserved, perhaps fatigued, although he entered the play jovially on several occasions. Immediately upon the start of the dinner, Kosygin began to offer toasts, trying to get his guests to put away as much Soviet cognac as possible. During the course of the meal he drank at least two glasses of cognac for each American guest. He jokingly disparaged the drinking capacities of the two youngest members of the American side when he noticed that Lord and Negroponte were not emptying their glasses entirely at each toast. Everyone gratefully steered clear of serious talk. There were wisecracks and anecdotes throughout, although the joviality was at times somewhat forced. It was as if there was tacit mutual agreement to restore the good personal relations that had obtained before the Vietnam discussion and that were now to last through the remainder of the summit. The Russians spoke romantically and proudly of Lake Baikal — its huge size, its beauty, and above all its cleanliness. Brezhnev complained that Nixon had inaccurately described it as polluted when seeking to demonstrate the global nature of the environmental problem in a speech. The Great Lakes were very dirty, Brezhnev said, but not Lake Baikal. Nixon's remarks, he said, had probably been drafted by Dr. Kissinger — I was to blame and should be exiled. Nixon suggested Siberia. Brezhnev offered Lake Baikal so that I could learn its wonders firsthand. Sending people to Siberia was a subject of raucous merriment, at least on the Soviet side of the table.

Seriousness surfaced, however, when Brezhnev advanced the proposition that, despite the late hour, Gromyko and another senior Soviet official were waiting for me in Moscow to resume SALT negotiations. I was not eager, after the motorcade, the hydrofoil ride, the brutal Vietnam discussion, and the heavy meal, to meet a fresh Soviet team headed by the indefatigable Gromyko. Though it was already past midnight Nixon, feeling no pain, made me available. This meant that I now faced the prospect of serious talks beginning at about 1:00 A.M. Kosygin said that if I failed, Lake Baikal would be too good for my exile. I suggested that he was goading me to see whether an intoxicated diplomat could keep his numbers straight. I made up my mind that I would stall the evening session unless the Soviets unexpectedly accepted our terms.

We had gone from good humor to bellicosity back to joviality in five hours. The Soviet leaders boisterously escorted us downstairs. To the nearly audible relief of the Secret Service we sped off in an *American* motorcade with Soviet motorcycle escort. I rode with the President back to the Kremlin. He could look forward to bed, I to a fresh Soviet negotiating team.

The SALT Negotiations Conclude

B REZHNEV and Nixon had concluded their SALT discussion on May 23 by suggesting that Gromyko and I would meet to continue the work the next morning; in the event Gromyko did not show up. And no wonder. For clearly the Soviet negotiators would have to regroup after the various concessions offered by their mercurial General Secretary. Gerard Smith thought that we must have misunderstood Brezhnev. His Soviet colleagues may well have been afraid that we had understood him only too well. While the Soviets caucused, negotiations on SALT remained in abeyance for nearly thirty hours. That is when I was thrown into the fray, after the dacha session, during the early morning of May 25.

The interval gave us an opportunity to solicit Smith's advice. This was time-consuming because communications with Helsinki were astonishingly cumbersome. The White House communications center, as on all Presidential trips, moved with the President; it was now located in the Kremlin. The State Department communications center was with Rogers in the Rossiya Hotel. Delay in keeping everyone informed was inherent in the physical arrangements; getting the same documents into the hands of all principals was almost impossible. The normal reporting cables from Helsinki went through State Department channels to Washington, with a copy to the Embassy in Moscow. They were then routed to the Rossiya Hotel, where the State Secretariat combined them with numerous other "interesting" cables and sent them to the NSC office at the Kremlin. There they were put in reading files, which the NSC staff examined between meetings and other work. If the material was judged sufficiently important, summaries were prepared for the President.

For more sensitive messages Smith could use the backchannel to me through the White House Situation Room in Washington. This added hours of delay, because the Situation Room had to retransmit Smith's message with special security restrictions to the White House communications room in the Kremlin. There was an open telephone line to Helsinki, which did not allow any serious discussion. There was a secure telephone located at the Embassy, several miles away.

In retrospect it would have been better to have brought both delegations to Moscow and let them continue their work there in synchronization with the summit. Given Nixon's feelings about who should get credit, I doubt that he would have agreed if I had proposed it. We shall never know because I did not put forward the idea, not uninfluenced by vanity and the desire to control the final negotiation. It was understandably maddening for the delegation to be excluded from the culmination of their patient and skillful efforts over so many years. And we paid the price that negotiators, excluded from a process they consider their prerogative, are likely to take a harder position after the fact than when they conduct the talks themselves. (Until we reached Moscow the delegation had almost invariably taken a "softer" position than the White House, which is normal for overseas negotiators.)

This showed up in Smith's reaction to the problems of silo size and SLBMs. Smith thought it would be a great idea to marry Brezhnev's idea of including missile volume to our arithmetic of how to define a "significant" change in silo size:

> If at Moscow [he wired me] you can get agreement that there will be no significant increase (a) in the size of ICBM silo launcher, or (b) in the volume of ICBMs beyond that of the largest light ICBM currently deployed by either side, and you get the word "significant" further defined to be no more than ten to fifteen percent, that would be great improvement.

Smith was less clear about SLBMs. He insisted on compulsory replacement of older missiles from the start of the agreement. He offered no precise method for calculating the baseline; I suspected that he was keeping open his options. If we could not get an adequate submarine deal, argued Smith, we should confine the offensive freeze to ICBMs. The last sentence of his cable showed the frustrations of being far from the scene of decision and the perennial — if misguided — conviction that Presidential Assistants prevail by keeping from the President the views of key subordinates: "I trust you will put these considerations to the President." All these considerations were indeed placed before the President as soon as they arrived, as was every other backchannel message from Smith.

I reviewed all this with Nixon on the ride back to the Kremlin from the dacha. I did not think the issue of silo dimensions was ready for a Presidential decision. We would first have to see if and how the Soviets would slide off Brezhnev's suggestions; if they slid off them, we should try to nail down an agreed definition of "significant" as meaning 10 to 15 percent; a unilateral statement, as the delegation had suggested, would in my view be unenforceable. Only if the Soviets proved adamant in maintaining the Helsinki position would the President have to involve himself.

It was different with the SLBMs. There was no dispute that it was in our interest to bring about the dismantling of the largest number of older Soviet missiles. But it was also important to keep in mind the realities of our negotiating position. If we excluded SLBMs, as Smith proposed, we would wind up with a theoretical Soviet capability to produce at least 200 more modern SLBMs than were permitted under the agreement (on the basis of the eight submarines under construction each year, which had been the Soviet program for the past five years). In addition, they would keep all of the 209 older ICBMs and ninety old SLBMs. Striking a tough pose was easy enough. The practical question was how we could possibly be better off with no SLBM freeze and up to 500 additional Soviet missiles when, no matter what the outcome in Moscow, our Joint Chiefs of Staff were opposed to any new American submarine building program during the five-year lifetime of the proposed agreement.

In order to avoid the impossible numbers game of agreeing on how many submarines the Soviets actually had, the highly esoteric debates about what constituted a submarine actually "under construction," and the dispute over how many were in the D-class and Y-class, my staff and I had worked out a different approach. We established priorities among the Soviet missiles we wanted to have dismantled, and then subtracted these from the permitted total of 950. We would then express the "baseline" in numbers of missiles rather than of submarines. Of the most urgent priority were the seventy older SS-7 ICBMs located in "hardened" silos. These had very large throwweight and, in their silos, a considerable invulnerability; if they were not dismantled, they might eventually be modernized and add considerably to Soviet capabilities. Next in priority were the roughly 135 SS-7 and SS-8 ICBMs on "soft" launch pads. Their vulnerability made them dangerous as first-strike weapons and their throwweight gave them considerable potential for destruction. The third priority were the missiles in H-class submarines, numbering about thirty. Their range (900 miles) was relatively short, but the submarine was nuclear and therefore capable of sustained operations. The lowest priority for destruction were the sixty missiles on old G-class submarines. Their range was short (300 to 700 miles); the G-class was diesel-powered and noisy and had limited endurance. It was improbable that a country possessing 1,500 ICBMs and nearly 1,000 modern SLBMs would cart sixty short-range missiles across the Atlantic on easily detected submarines that had to surface before they could fire.

In fact, no G-class submarine had operated off our shores since 1966.

The proposal I put before Nixon on the trip back to the Kremlin was to establish the baseline at 740 "modern" SLBMs, beyond which the Soviets would have to start trading in old missiles. This would force the Soviets to destroy all of their older ICBMs if they wanted to reach the agreed SLBM total of 950. We would then insist that the baseline of 740 include all of the thirty missiles on the H-class submarines, giving the Soviets the choice of trading them in later or counting them against the 950 ceiling. We would do the best we could with the G-class, but I warned Nixon that we might have to come back to him for further decisions. Nixon said he would think about this approach and let me know before I left for the meeting with Gromyko, scheduled to take place at the Foreign Ministry.

When I returned to the NSC office in the Kremlin, I found that our domestic base was in danger of collapsing. On May 24 Bernard Gwertzman of the *New York Times* had been the recipient of a major leak that enabled him to give the basic numbers under discussion at Helsinki and in Moscow. Suddenly all hell broke loose. Senators Goldwater and Jackson reacted with expressions of grave concern. A conservative revolt loomed. The canard that we had "conceded" numerical superiority to the Soviets made its first appearance. The Joint Chiefs, Haig reported, were getting restless; they were close to abandoning the position which they had endorsed before our departure, and which included most of their urgent recommendations.

The argument about "conceding" numerical inequality was due either to a misunderstanding or to demagoguery. Inequality stemmed in the first instance from our predecessors' decision to respond to the Soviet buildup not by increasing the number of launchers but by augmenting our warheads through MIRVs. The Johnson Administration had had a strategic doctrine of "assured destruction." Abandoning counterforce, it calculated our program on the basis of our ability to inflict industrial and civilian damage. So long as Soviet accuracies were poor and they had no MIRVs — so that our ICBMs were virtually invulnerable — our strategic capacity was not impaired by the size of the Soviet force; hence, during the Soviet buildup of the Sixties we did not add to our missiles. Even the MIRVs were developed not as an answer to the Soviets' missile program but as a riposte to their ABM. We had then made a deliberate decision to concentrate on a new submarine program, the Trident, rather than produce more of our existing submarines. Since it takes from six to nine years to develop new weapons, the Nixon Administration was in a serious bind in the early Seventies, made worse when the Congress each year opposed new strategic programs and cut the defense budget even below the minimum levels proposed by the Administration. The freeze in offensive weapons had been first urged by Deputy Defense Secretary Packard in the summer of 1970 *to keep the existing numerical gap against us from growing.* It had been requested again by Secretary Laird in his memorandum of January 18, 1972, as being essential to give us the opportunity to redress the strategic balance. It had been known to be under negotiation since May 1971 without any sort of protest. If we aborted the negotiations now, the numerical gap would widen. The agreement at hand would make the Soviets *reduce* their numbers. No program we were developing would be affected by the five-year freeze. We had no choice except to proceed.

These were the considerations I put to Nixon, whom I found stretched out on a massage table after our return from the dacha around one in the morning. He was having his back treated by Dr. Kenneth Riland, who, for his magic in treating sore backs and relieving symptoms of tension, was one of the more valuable members of the Presidential entourage. My explanations required considerable circumlocution because Nixon refused to use the babbler, and we could be sure that the Soviets were listening in. I doubt that my evasions fooled many. In any event it could do no damage for the Soviet leaders to realize that our domestic opposition set limits to our flexibility. (Would that such a limitation had been equally apparent to our opponents in Hanoi!)

Lying naked on the rubbing table, Nixon made one of the more courageous decisions of his Presidency. In danger of losing the support of the right, which he considered his essential base, faced by a SALT negotiator recommending that he drop submarine limits from the negotiation, and with the Joint Chiefs of Staff wobbling, Nixon had the strength of purpose — after the grueling Vietnam session at the dacha — to order me to proceed along the lines I had outlined. For all he knew, nobody would support the approach of freezing both ICBMs and SLBMs. Nevertheless, he told me to ignore Pentagon objections if they went beyond previously agreed positions, and to stand firm against Smith. He would not be swayed by politics at home; and he would not be pushed by the Soviets beyond what I had suggested. Nixon took a heroic position from a decidedly unheroic posture.

Before leaving for the Foreign Ministry, I sent a sharp cable to Haig telling him of the President's decision. His job was to rally support, not simply to transmit concerns. He should, in the process, ask the Joint Chiefs and Deputy Defense Secretary Rush about Smith's proposal to drop SLBMs from the agreement.

Thus prepared, I at last faced Gromyko at 1:15 A.M. in the Stalinist-style wedding-cake skyscraper that houses the Soviet Foreign Ministry in seedy opulence. Gromyko was accompanied by a personality new to all Americans present. He was introduced as Deputy Premier L. V. Smirnov. Though Brezhnev had mentioned his name during dinner I did not know exactly who he was. It required an exchange of notes with my colleagues Sonnenfeldt and Hyland to determine that he held the position of chairman of the Soviet Military-Industrial Commission, a Party-state organization in charge of all defense industries. Smirnov turned out to be bullet-headed, heavyset, and brilliant; he made it clear that only superior orders could have landed him now in a position that so severely taxed his limited resources of self-control. Given Soviet security consciousness, it is doubtful that he had met many foreigners. Surely he had never negotiated with potential adversaries. My style of easy banter at first drove him up the wall; it was clearly inconsistent with his image of the solemnity of the occasion. When I started describing the characteristics of Soviet weapons, Smirnov's irritation turned to frenzy. It was not completely clear whether he was appalled that a capitalist should know so many details of the Soviet weapons program, or that his own colleagues — including probably Gromyko — were learning from me what the Soviet system had successfully kept from them. Whatever the reason, Smirnov became so angry that Gromyko had to take him out of the room and calm him down. When the meeting reassembled — by which point it was 2:30 — I picked up where I had left off, producing another outburst as well as the need for yet another recess. Yet after the cultural shock had worn off, Smirnov and I got along famously. He turned out to be one of the ablest and most intelligent Soviet leaders with whom I dealt. Once he had grasped that pomposity is not a prerequisite for diplomacy, he exhibited a wicked sense of humor.

In that late-night session, however, we faced the problem that Smirnov knew everything about weapons and little about diplomacy, while of Gromyko — not yet a Politburo member — exactly the opposite was true. His skill was diplomacy; his briefing on weapons system had obviously been rudimentary. He could put forward the official Soviet position but not negotiate it; this was a task left to Smirnov and me. Gromyko found himself in the unusual position of making soothing noises whenever matters between me and Smirnov threatened to get out of control.

To begin with, Gromyko was in a frame of mind dour even by his standards. For on him fell the painful duty of withdrawing almost everything put forward by Brezhnev during his meeting with Nixon the previous day. He handled it masterfully by passing around papers that summed up the alleged state of play on various issues — all of them at variance with Brezhnev's position. He avoided any comparison with what Brezhnev had said; he left the discovery of any discrepancies to me. One paper stated that the distance between ABM sites would be 1,300 kilometers. Another paper spoke of banning "significant" changes in silo dimensions but made no reference to missile volume nor defined the term "significant." On SLBMs Gromyko gave me the standard Soviet position establishing forty-eight modern submarines as the Soviet baseline. I saw the differences immediately and put Gromyko through his paces over them; this was less in the hope that he might go back on them — which was not possible, given the realities of the Soviet weapons program — than in the hope of placing him on the defensive and to allow me to waste enough time to avoid a serious negotiation in my general state of fatigue. I needled the Soviets about the change in their position, asking clarifying questions and professing astonishment and outrage that a statement by the General Secretary was not conclusive. All this took up the better part of the meeting and established the principle that the Soviets owed us something.

Gromyko's formulations were a return to orthodoxy. As I have pointed out already, the difference of 200 kilometers on the distance between ABM sites was not important; eventually I would yield on that, but not without establishing some claim to reciprocity. With respect to silo dimensions I was determined to transform our delegation's nonbinding unilateral statement into a binding mutual definition. But my major concern was to get the Soviets to dismantle the largest possible number of launchers as part of the SLBM freeze.

To achieve this I had two assets. The discrepancy between what Brezhnev had said and what Gromyko now put forward was the first. Second, Brezhnev had indicated at the dacha that he was eager to sign the SALT agreement on Friday evening (by then only thirty-six hours away) and all Soviet officials would take this as a firm directive. It was not Nixon but Brezhnev who was under pressure with respect to SALT. Apart from the self-imposed deadline, he had permitted the summit to proceed despite the bombing and mining of North Vietnam. He had purged Shelest from the Politburo. He, much more than Nixon, who had achieved his triumph simply by arriving in Moscow, needed a success. As in Peking, I therefore slowed down the process of negotiations to test whose nerves would prove to be stronger. (I was armed, in any event, by Nixon's comment to me — provided he really meant it — that he was prepared to leave Moscow without a SALT agreement.)

Around three in the morning when there was no time left for real negotiation I introduced an outline of our position with a baseline of 740 SLBM launchers. Before Smirnov could explode a third time, I let the Soviets win one by confirming our delegation's acceptance of 1,300 kilometers as the distance between ABM sites. Gromyko mercifully put an end to the meeting by dryly suggesting that it was getting to be either too early or too late. We left it that we would meet again in six hours' time to resolve the remaining differences.

I returned to the Kremlin around 4:00 A.M. In late spring at that northern latitude, the first rays of sunlight were falling on its golden domes, ochre walls, and red brick battlements. Below me in the stillness lay Moscow, merging into the Great Russian plain with no natural obstacle to interrupt one's gaze. In the silence of that early morning I walked through the vast, empty squares of the Kremlin, seized by one of those rare moments of hope that makes the endless struggle with the contingent endurable for statesmen. Though we were not yet agreed, the tone of the meeting made it likely that we would be able to negotiate a treaty within the guidelines approved by Nixon. There was a chance that we were participating in an event that would give mankind a breathing space, and with luck start a process that could lead to a more tranquil future.

But before we could afford sentimentality, some tough negotiating lay ahead. Gromyko did not appear at 10:00 A.M. Instead, Dobrynin informed us that the Soviet leadership was reviewing the SALT position once again. Brezhnev did not show up for the plenary session that afternoon in the elegant St. Catherine's Hall which dealt with economics, not Nixon's best or favorite subject. Kosygin chaired the Soviet side, and was analytical and precise, which was more than could be said of the Americans, who stuck to familiar generalities. Brezhnev was clearly working on the Soviet SALT position.

My staff and I were frantically analyzing various combinations of figures; the permutations seemed endless, but we had to ensure that the Soviets dismantled the maximum number of missiles. The numbers game of submarine baselines — how many could be traded in, and when they would reach different levels by various combinations of twelve-tube and sixteen-tube boats — forced us into numerous computations on long yellow pads, drawn up between sessions and then quickly scratched up and consumed during meetings. We never could figure out how the Soviets could reach a level of 950 SLBMs on sixty-two submarines.* They did it by the simple device of assuming that most of their submarines had sixteen tubes, even though they had several with twelve tubes.

The SALT discussions resumed at 5:20 P.M. in St. Catherine's Hall — with, as usual, only a half hour's warning. We were prepared and so, it transpired, were the Soviets. The Soviet side was represented by Smirnov, Gromyko, Dobrynin, and Georgi Korniyenko (Chief of the USA Division of the Foreign Ministry). The American group was composed of me, Sonnenfeldt, Hyland, and Rodman. Both delegations were scheduled to go to the ballet performance in Nixon's honor. On the Soviet side neither Gromyko nor Dobrynin could escape this ceremonial duty; we had thus an hour for negotiation. The discussion was brisk; there was no time for either banter or formalistic positions. After a day of agonizing exchanges with Washington and Helsinki it had been concluded that a prohibition on any changes in silo dimension was compatible with our Minuteman III program, after all. But, as I have said, it was too late. Gromyko offered us as a "concession" the position of our

---

*For example, some of these calculations yielded mystifying results: 34 Y-class submarines × 16 missiles = 544; plus 28 D-class submarines × 12 missiles = 336, for a total of 880; plus 30 missiles on the H-class, equaled 910.

delegation in Helsinki, forbidding only "significant" changes; the Soviets were prepared also to note a unilateral American interpretation of
the term "significant." I insisted that "significant" had to be mutually
accepted as not exceeding 15 percent. Gromyko and Smirnov said they
would think it over.

We then turned to the unsolved issue of the baseline from which to
calculate the dismantling of old missiles. Smirnov accepted my proposal
of the previous night, to express it in terms of missile launchers rather
than submarines. But he simply converted the forty-eight submarines the
Soviets claimed they had into launchers by multiplying them by sixteen
(representing launch tubes). Thus the Soviets claimed 768 missiles for
the baseline and excluded missiles on older submarines. This was
clearly nonsense, since we knew they had a number of D-class submarines with only twelve missiles each. After one quick exchange — during which I said, "I understand the arithmetic. The arithmetic is not
hard, the politics is hard" — Smirnov accepted 740 as a baseline.

That left only the question of which SLBMs were included in it. My
suggestion that missiles on both H- and G-class submarines be counted
brought an explosion from Smirnov, who insisted that the idea of counting sixty missiles with a 300- to 700-mile range on diesel-powered submarines that had to surface before firing must be a joke. I tried to ease
the atmosphere by suggesting that maybe the Soviets should put their
monster SS-9 on the G-class submarine, thus solving two problems for
us at once. Smirnov understood the joke (that this would sink the submarines), but Gromyko thought I had come up with a new idea. "Please
be specific," he said. Smirnov and I got things back on track so we
could resume our own sparring. Finally, as the clock chimed six-thirty,
Smirnov asked me what exactly I meant by H-class submarines since it
was an American, not a Soviet term. I told him that we gave this designation to the older nuclear-powered submarines carrying three missiles
each. Smirnov innocently stated that he had always meant those to be
counted in the baseline — a point that had hitherto eluded both me and
our negotiators in Helsinki. Thus were the H-class submarines included
in the total. The Soviets would now have to dismantle a total of 240
older missiles to reach the agreed level of 950 modern SLBMs, including dismantling *all* of the older heavy-throwweight ICBMs. (Or else
they could keep the thirty H-class missiles, in which case they would
have only 920 modern SLBMs; this is in fact what they did.)

Two issues now stood between us and a completed agreement: how to
deal with the missiles on the G-class submarines, and with silo modernization. We agreed to reconvene after the ballet.

The Bolshoi ballet performed *Swan Lake* in its usual acrobatic,
slightly florid style. Between acts supper was served to the Presidential
party in a VIP room. Kosygin and Podgorny did the honors; Brezhnev,

as Party Secretary, kept out of ceremonial events. He was also probably reviewing the SALT negotiations with Smirnov. Just before the third act began, while the lights were already dimming, the wife of an Italian journalist in the audience shouted an anti-Vietnam slogan at Nixon. It was an unheard-of event for Moscow. Podgorny immediately had the lights turned on again, and he and Nixon rose in the official box to the applause of the audience. It was a gallant gesture.

After the performance I explained to Nixon that we were within sight of an agreement if we could reconcile the issue of the sixty old missiles on G-class boats. My colleagues and I had come up with a possible solution that we wanted to submit in the evening session. It was a compromise. We would not insist on counting the sixty old missiles on G-class submarines in the totals, *unless* they were modernized; but existing missiles on G-class boats could not be "traded in" for missiles on new submarines. This served two purposes: To stay below the ceiling of 950, the Soviets would have to dismantle ICBMs and missiles on nuclear-powered submarines; and they could not put modern missiles on diesel boats except by counting them — unlikely as this was, considering the relative ease with which such boats are detected and the short time they can stay on station. Nixon approved.

The two negotiating teams met again at 11:30 P.M. in St. Catherine's Hall. We began with the SLBM baseline. I summed up my understanding that the Soviets accepted the figure of 740 missiles as the baseline and would include the thirty missiles on the H-class submarines. When the Soviet side confirmed this, I raised again the issue of missiles on G-class submarines. Smirnov claimed that the Soviets had accepted our basic proposal and that we were stalling an agreement by constantly raising frivolous new issues. I had read the Soviets a cable from Haig stating that the Defense Department and the Chiefs insisted that the 950 Soviet SLBMs had to include missiles on G-, H-, and Y-class submarines.* Washington also rejected the concept of a freeze confined to ICBMs, as Smith had proposed. It would prefer no agreement to one that let SLBMs run free. Smirnov, who was getting into the spirit of things, rejoined that he had some hair-raising cables of his own and would bring them to the next meeting (it was probably true). Gromyko insisted that the Soviets had reached the limit of their concessions; no further compromise was possible.

I put forward our compromise anyway. The Soviets were without instructions, so the discussion veered back to the silo dimension problem. The Soviets held fast to the tentative agreement worked out in Helsinki, the prohibition against a "significant" increase of silo dimensions. The

---

*The Chiefs' position actually would have enabled the Soviets to trade in sixty short-range G-class missiles and keep seventy heavy-throwweight ICBMs in silos. It was less favorable to us than the compromise the President approved.

US could make its own unilateral statement on the meaning of "significant," which would not, of course, bind the Soviets. I insisted that the Soviets should stop quoting the delegation against the President when it served their purpose; he had the right to overrule his subordinates. We would agree to the ban on "significant" increases in silo dimensions only if there were an agreed and binding definition of what it meant. Gromyko suggested that there would have to be a high-level meeting for the Soviets to consider our position on silo dimensions and G-class submarines. I pointed out that this would prevent the signing the next evening (Friday), which Brezhnev seemed to have in mind. Gromyko agreed. Saturday, it turned out, would be unsuitable since the President was going to Leningrad. We tentatively agreed to slip the signing to Sunday evening, May 28, provided, of course, all the issues were settled before then. It was 12:32 A.M. when the meeting broke up.

I reported to Nixon that we were at an impasse that only the Soviets could break. We could make no further concessions. There could be no signing ceremony on Friday night; it would take place, if at all, on Sunday. Nixon was disappointed but raised no objections. He mumbled that the signing ceremony of SALT might overshadow his television address to the Soviet people, which had also been arranged for Sunday night. He was restless but determined to stay the course.

It is important to keep this sequence in mind because critics later argued that a self-imposed deadline made for hasty negotiation. The fact was that we set no deadlines; we used Brezhnev's own deadline to bring pressure on the Soviets; we even suggested delaying the signing by forty-eight hours. When the meeting broke up on Thursday night, the outcome of the negotiation depended on a Soviet decision; I had left no doubt that we had reached the limit of our concessions. These were identical for all practical purposes with the position of the Helsinki delegation or (as in the case of silo dimensions) an improvement.* None of the issues that gave rise to controversy later over Soviet compliance — unfairly in all cases except one — was negotiated at Moscow.

We had reached the point where all the American summit team could do was to await the outcome of the Soviet high-level meeting on Friday. I was fairly confident that the Soviets would accept our "final" proposal. They could not permit a negotiation that had lasted nearly three years to go down the drain over the issues of silo dimension (on which

---

* The delegation in Helsinki was working on a different SLBM formula that would have reached much the same practical result by redefining the term "under construction." The delegation also tried to achieve an agreed definition of a "heavy ICBM" — since the Interim Agreement prohibited the conversion of "light" ICBM launchers into launchers for "heavy ICBMs." When the Soviets did not agree, our delegation was authorized to issue a unilateral statement declaring our preferred definition and our expectation that the Soviet side would "give due account to this consideration." We overestimated the restraining effect of such a unilateral statement. (See my Congressional briefing of June 15, 1972.)

their own vacillation demonstrated that it was a close call), and the replacement of missiles on G-class diesel submarines (which any analysis indicated it made no sense to modernize anyway).

I therefore sent a cable to Haig requesting that he obtain a formal JCS position on the compromise. It stated our reasoning in firm language. After summing up our proposal I stated:

President is unwilling to see some 60 300-mile SLBMs stand in the way of an agreement that will clearly impose ceilings on Soviets in regard to ICBMs and SLBMs which they could readily exceed in five-year period without freeze — not to mention the retirement of 240 launchers this agreement would bring about.

It should also be understood that base figure now formulated gets Soviets down to 710 on Y-class boats. Thus the Soviets will have to retire some 240 launchers including all of H-class subs to reach permitted total.

The reply of the Joint Chiefs was a classic of Pentagon politics. It agreed to our proposal (which in turn was only a slight modification of what the Chiefs had approved *before* our departure). But they attached a price tag. The President would have to pledge "action necessary to ensure acceleration of our ongoing offensive programs as well as improvements to existing systems." This we were determined to do anyhow. It was one reason why we had promoted the freeze in the first place. But the argument of the Chiefs was not without its logical flaws: Their insistence on an acceleration of our strategic programs was grounded not on a Soviet buildup extending over a decade, but on sixty antiquated Soviet missiles of minimal range on diesel submarines. Had the Soviets known about this reasoning they might well have thrown in the sixty G-class missiles in return for a promise not to accelerate our strategic programs. (We would have resisted this, but it would have had much Congressional support in America.)

We settled down to wait for the outcome of the Soviets' deliberations, with our domestic base apparently secure except for rumblings from Helsinki, where Smith seemed convinced that we were holding out on him. (In fact, we communicated what we knew immediately. It was the Soviets who took their time making decisions.) This led to a testy exchange. Smith, having first accepted my G-class formula, changed his mind and called it a "free ride" for the Soviets to maintain these boats. This was a position I was convinced, perhaps unfairly, he would never have taken but for the frustration of being so far from the conclusion of what he had every reason to consider his own negotiation. We were, however, at a stage where the salving of bruised feelings would have to wait, and I sent a sharp reply:

Can you explain how 60 missiles of 300–700 mile range, barred from modernization in diesel submarines that have to surface to fire, representing less than three percent of the total Soviet force, could represent a free ride? What are we giving up that we were going to do? The Soviets in turn get a ceiling on their SLBMs, a ban on modernization of the G class and lose 240 launchers. If the Soviets refuse to accept the compromise I want someone to explain how our security is enhanced when we then confront the Gs, the Hs, 240 more launchers, and a larger number of SLBMs.

The Soviet decision came with stunning suddenness. Around 10:00 A.M. Dobrynin came to my room in the Kremlin to tell me that the Politburo had been in session since 8:00; there was no telling how long it would last. At 11:00 A.M. we were informed that Gromyko and Smirnov wanted to meet me urgently in St. Catherine's Hall. We assembled at 11:15. Without further ado Gromyko *accepted* not only our position on the G-class and silo dimension problem; he also agreed to our formulation of it. The Soviets would go along with a common definition of "significant."

Gromyko then stunned us even more by insisting on a signing ceremony that very evening as originally scheduled. I have to this day not understood the reason for this Soviet haste. It may have been due to the characteristic of Soviet negotiators that no matter how much they may have haggled, once an agreement is in sight they seem panicked that the results of their labors might be hazarded by some last-minute accident or trick of the inscrutable capitalists. Perhaps I had been too persuasive in presenting our domestic pressures and they feared that some unforeseen objection would sweep away all the painful adjustments. Perhaps they had analyzed our phone calls to Washington. It was tough enough for them to make most of the concessions; it would be humiliating to have them fail at the last minute. Probably the Soviets simply wanted to humor Brezhnev, who earlier in the week had staked his prestige on a Friday ceremony.

Whatever the Soviet reasons, we had little basis for refusing. After all, they were accepting *our* proposals in *our* formulation. The only valid objection was that the final drafting of two clauses (all the rest having been completed) would be rushed (one of them, however, being our delegation's proposal) and that damaged egos would be all over the landscape from Helsinki to Moscow. At 11:30 I asked for a recess to obtain the President's approval. At 11:47 I returned to inform Gromyko that we would proceed. He and I reviewed the texts carefully. We agreed to send joint instructions to Helsinki; both sides' instructions would be identical so that no time would be wasted in clarification. Sonnenfeldt and Korniyenko set about drafting them for Gromyko's and my approval. The summit was now guaranteed to be historic: Never before had identical instructions been sent to Soviet and American negotiators.

Then there came that feeling of serenity which accompanies the conclusion of all great exertions in foreign policy. "I think this is a very important milestone in the relations between our two countries," I said. "And I am very proud to have had the opportunity to work with you gentlemen on it."

Gromyko, not given to hyperbole, replied in Russian: "We are satisfied with the manner in which business was conducted on your part, and we tried to reciprocate. They were really difficult and delicate matters we were working on; specialist delegations have spent almost three years, as of this August, on it. It is really a good end, a real milestone." And then he joked in English: "We are significantly satisfied, even more than fifteen percent."

So ended the negotiation on SALT I.

But it was not yet the end of our labors. As in China, we paid the price for our administrative practices, being called upon again to placate the group that had been excluded from the consummation of its own negotiation. We were no more successful in Moscow than in Hangchow. Part of the tension was caused by technical malfunctions. When Gromyko and I agreed around noon to send joint instructions, I had Sonnenfeldt call Smith on an open line to inform him that instructions were on the way. Since only two issues were involved, and perhaps five to ten sentences, we thought the delegations could conclude their work and return afterward to Moscow on the American plane in time for a signing ceremony at 8:30. We did not realize that our delegation's plane had piston engines and therefore would take two and a half hours to reach Moscow. Nor did we calculate the delay in transmission due to routing the instructions through the White House Situation Room — where, to make matters worse, through a mix-up they were given no special priority. As a result, while the Soviet instructions reached Helsinki within forty minutes, ours had not yet arrived after two hours. Smith, now thoroughly aroused, rightly refused to work from the Soviet text, though assured by Sonnenfeldt that the instructions were joint. Nevertheless, after repeated phone conversations which threw security to the winds (there was no harm in it since the Soviets and we had agreed) and the final unsnarling of communications, the two delegations set to work and completed a joint document on the American delegation's plane to Moscow. It was a Herculean effort crowning years of dedicated labor.

In the meantime, we had pushed back the signing ceremony to 11:00 P.M. to enable our delegation to participate and Smith to join me in a press briefing scheduled for 10:00 P.M. Nixon's dinner for Brezhnev and other Soviet leaders, long planned for that evening, was moved up an hour to fill the interval.

Unhappily, when Smith and his colleagues arrived at the airport, another indignity frayed their already taut nerves even further. We had sent Embassy cars to pick them up. But for some reason these had been denied entry to the tarmac. Whether this was a deliberate Soviet ploy or a bullheaded application of local rules by a minor functionary — I suspect the latter — it meant that no American greeted Smith after making what he had every reason to consider a major contribution to a proud achievement. (Of course, all the senior Americans in Moscow were at Nixon's dinner for Brezhnev, which only exacerbated matters.) Rather than look for the American cars, Smith asked his Soviet colleague Semenov to help out. Smith wanted to go to our Embassy to join me in the briefing, but the Soviet driver insisted on taking him to the Kremlin. Moreover, Smith's notes for his briefing remarks were with another colleague who had departed in another car for the Embassy. Nothing was happening at the Kremlin, since most of the American party had left for Spaso House, the residence of our Ambassador, where the dinner was ending and the briefing was to take place. There I delayed the start of the briefing to wait for Smith, wondering what had happened to him; Smith not only was to join me in the briefing but (I thought) had the official texts for the signing ceremony.

At the Kremlin, Peter Rodman of my staff obtained a Soviet motorpool car and took Smith to the Embassy. Finally, Smith showed up, enraged to the point of incoherence — and not without reason. I have not been able to this day to convince him that what happened was not deliberate but a succession of compounding errors. The summit party was nearly as discomfited by his delay as he. He was the victim of honest bungling, though it must be admitted that the administrative practices of the Nixon Administration tended to inflict this sort of indignity on decent and able men, usually by accident, occasionally by design. There is no question but that Smith deserved better.

Having stated that Smith had a case, I must also recount that he wore his unhappiness on his sleeve. Wounded pride and rage were so ill-concealed that he nearly turned the briefing into a shambles. The briefing took place in the cafeteria of the Embassy, next to Spaso House. I began, but Smith in a stage whisper grumbled that he did not know exactly what the treaty contained. This was not likely to inspire confidence in the press; so I interrupted my presentation to take Smith into an anteroom to try to calm him down. That barely accomplished, I resumed, explaining the general principles of the agreement. Smith then followed with a brief analysis of its provisions that made up in detailed precision what it lacked in passionate advocacy. There was time for only one or two questions before everybody had to leave for the signing ceremony. Max Frankel of the *New York Times,* one of the ablest journalists I know, stressed that he felt bound to tell us the treaty would turn into a public relations fiasco unless the press could ask more questions and clear up ambiguities on which opponents were sure to focus.

The signing ceremony went off smoothly enough, with the Soviet participants winning yet again the daily race into the hall. Smith returned to his hotel; I went to my quarters in the Kremlin; the staff scattered to celebrate. I saw no sense in further briefings, which would produce only additional evidence of tensions within our official party.

Well after midnight, Ziegler called to the effect that Frankel had been right. The SALT story had the makings of a disaster. The terms of the agreement were too technical, the tensions in the American delegation too obvious. Murrey Marder phoned a few minutes later with the same impressions. Journalists pretend that they are not involved in their stories. This is nonsense. Their test of professional excellence is objectivity regardless of involvement. And the best journalists passionately believed in SALT; they wanted to have been present when a beginning was made on turning around the nuclear arms race. They would report the truth as they saw it, but on this occasion they would give us every opportunity to explain that truth.

Haldeman had received the same reports from Ziegler and through him Nixon was informed. Haldeman was near panic that the treaty would not be properly received. Nixon feared a revolt by his constituency on the right, and saw in Smith's conduct an example of the Georgetown and Eastern Establishment conspiracy against him — which was highly unfair. Smith *had* been ill-used (and later defended the agreement with vigor and skill). Nixon and Haldeman therefore insisted that I alone give another briefing to place the treaty in a better context.

This was the origin of the bizarre press conference that began at 1:00 A.M., the morning of Saturday, May 27, my forty-ninth birthday. I stood on the bandstand of the Starry Sky nightclub of the Intourist Hotel, which was the headquarters of the traveling press. The nightclub has been described as looking "like the Roseland Ballroom, vintage 1935. Kissinger stood on the dance floor, the Frank Sinatra of diplomacy, occasionally clutching his only prop, a standing microphone." [2] For an hour I described, as well as I could in my exhaustion after the three all-night sessions, the provisions of the ABM treaty and the offensive freeze, answered questions and sought to explain the significance of a package of complex documents that were either a turning point or another impulse to the superpower arms race, either an augury of a more peaceful international order or a pause before a new set of crises.

The terms of the agreement were compatible with either evolution. They froze the deployment of ABM, in which we had a technological edge though Congress would not have let us exploit it. We suffered here the same disability as in Vietnam. We had enough support to put through our basic program but its opponents were sufficiently powerful to emasculate it. Hence our bargaining position was weaker than it might have been. We did well to freeze Soviet deployments of offensive weapons, in which they had an advantage that was likely to continue to grow in the absence of a freeze. The Soviets gave up 240 older weapons of large throwweight and had to count any modernization of G-class submarines. Since we had no programs that could be deployed during the period of the offensive freeze, it basically did not affect us at all. We traded the defensive for the offensive limitations.

We needed the agreement if we wanted to catch up in offensive weapons. But we also needed SALT if we were ever to explore the possibilities of peaceful coexistence. We would have to be vigilant to maintain the strategic balance. But SALT also gave us the opportunity to determine whether détente was a tactic or a new turn in Soviet policy. We were determined to avoid ever again being in a situation where only the Soviets had strategic programs under way.* But equally we were prepared to seek rules of mutual restraint. We rejected the argument that the nuclear age had made the balance of power irrelevant. But neither did we accept the proposition that it was possible to stake the nation's security entirely on a policy of nuclear confrontation.

These views forced us into a fine balancing act. The result was that we were vulnerable to accusations by liberals of doing too little for arms control and too much for defense, and by conservatives for being too conciliatory in our negotiations. What we sought was a policy to preserve both our strength and our options for a new international order. We were prepared to walk a narrow path, demonstrably dedicated to peace but making clear that our desire for it could not be used as blackmail; aware that we could not afford the miscalculations that in every generation of this century had produced global conflicts but still always ready to confront Soviet expansion and assaults on the balance of power. To preserve peace and to defend justice, to be resolute without bellicosity, to be vigilant without being provocative, would henceforth be the test of our foreign policy. Or so I tried to suggest to the fatigued correspondents during that long night in the weird setting of a Moscow ballroom.

In the event, SALT was well received by many of Nixon's old nemeses — with the *Washington Post* and the *New York Times* leading the applause. It was also attacked by some of his traditional supporters for its alleged "inequality." A military equation that had seemed acceptable when there was no agreement, even though the numbers had become more ominous with every passing year, was suddenly castigated when it stopped the Soviet buildup and restrained no American programs. Few critics addressed a question I raised at the Moscow briefing: The issue was not "what situation [the agreement] perpetuates, but what situation it prevents. The question is where we would be without the freeze." The Soviets were giving up an additional offensive capability; we were not.

---

* After we returned to Washington, I had a conversation with Mel Laird on June 2: "The way to use this freeze is for us to catch up," I told him. "If we don't do this we don't deserve to be in office." Laird fully agreed.

There was another criticism less easily dealt with. Some thoughtful observers feared that our public might be lulled by a false euphoria and fail to support the effort needed for defense. At the outset, this did not turn out to be so. In the year immediately after SALT we started a number of new strategic programs to catch up: the B-1 bomber, the MX missile, the cruise missile, and the Trident submarine-missile system. Indeed, one Senator expostulated to me that we couldn't afford another SALT agreement financially if it led to such an expansion of our strategic budget as this one. Later on, the tragedy of Watergate, through the weakness of the Executive Branch in its battles with Congress, caused our foreign policy to lose much momentum.

But the concern should not be lightly dismissed. Can a democracy combine both resolution and hope, both strength and conciliation? I cannot accept the counsel of despair that we are doomed to extremes of either euphoria or intransigence. I shall say more about this question in assessing the overall impact of the summit. I also owe it here to Gerry Smith to stress that after the understandable flare-up in Moscow, he fought for the ratification of the SALT agreements with tenacity and skill.

Gromyko and the Middle East

AFTER SALT was settled, any remaining tension disappeared from the summit. No serious effort was made afterward to resolve any outstanding international problem. Significantly, the only discussion on the Middle East between Nixon and the Soviet troika took place during the afternoon that preceded the signing of the SALT treaty, guaranteeing that the Soviets would not rock the boat and that we would stick to our strategy of keeping the Middle East on ice until the Soviets were willing to talk compromise. Nixon therefore considered this discussion primarily a holding action. He suggested that Gromyko and Kissinger talk again in the fall, and that in the meantime we try to agree on some general principles to guide further negotiations. (Nixon gave even the unflappable Sukhodrev a problem of translation when he suggested that all this would be preparatory to the "nutcutting stage," which Sukhodrev interpreted literally as the cutting of fruit from a tree, to the obvious mystification of Nixon's interlocutors.) The principals also passed the communiqué treatment of the subject back to Gromyko and me.

Gromyko and I turned to the task quite literally as the last item of our discussions on Sunday afternoon (we were scheduled to leave the next day). The Soviets were in a difficult position — more difficult, in fact, than we realized. Egypt was becoming restive at Moscow's failure to deliver progress toward a settlement. But the Kremlin's pedantic negotiating style and rigid adherence to extreme positions prevented it from formulating proposals that we could have any incentive to support. The Soviets never were able to resolve the dilemma that we had spent three years in trying to sharpen. So long as they endorsed the radical Arab program we could have no reason for joint action with them. Without us the program could be achieved only by a war that the Soviet clients would lose. Thus the Kremlin's rigid Middle East policy turned into a demonstration to the Arab world of its inability to affect events and to a progressive loss of its influence.

So far as we were concerned, our objectives were served if the status quo was maintained until either the Soviets modified their stand or moderate Arab states turned to us for a solution based on progress through attainable stages. Once it was clear that Moscow would not modify its stand, I sought the blandest possible Middle East formulation in the communiqué. And the deadline inherent in a summit ran in our favor; in communiqué haggling the side that is prepared to stand pat is in the stronger position. Its opposite number can achieve its aims only by threatening to wreck the whole exercise — an option that was practically excluded by the agreements on SALT and the "Basic Principles of US–Soviet Relations." The upshot was a meaningless paragraph that endorsed Security Council Resolution 242 and put the two sides on record as favoring peace in the Middle East. Calling as it did for "peaceful settlement" and "military relaxation" in the area, it was practically an implicit acceptance of the status quo and was bound to be taken ill not only in Cairo but elsewhere in the Arab world. (The text of the Middle East portion of the communiqué is in the notes.) [3] We will have to await the memoirs of the Soviet leaders for an explanation of why they chose the route of an agreed text rather than the "our side– your side" formulation of the Shanghai Communiqué. A split text would have given the Soviets greater latitude in expressing their views and placed the onus for thwarting them more clearly on us. Probably the Soviet bureaucracy considered the traditional form sacrosanct, and the Soviet leaders' hatred of the Chinese may have prevented their following a model associated with Nixon's Peking trip.

Almost as inexplicably, Gromyko spent four hours with me that last Sunday trying to agree on "general principles" for a Middle Eastern settlement. Why he should have thought that we would be prepared to couple a bland communiqué with a set of specific principles is not clear. At any rate, the same strategy that governed our approach to the communiqué was bound to determine our attitude toward principles. I conducted what was in effect a delaying tactic. Gromyko was experienced enough to know what I was doing; he put on no real pressure; the Soviets clearly wanted no crisis over the Middle East. The upshot was a tentative agreement on a number of "principles" that in fact did not go beyond the existing United Nations resolutions or were so vague as to leave wide scope for negotiation in implementation. (Their text is in the notes.)[4] Their practical consequence was to confirm the deadlock. Dobrynin and I were supposed to refine them after we were both back in the United States. The Soviets, probably having tried them on their Arab clients and been rebuffed, never pressed them. Neither did we. They came up again at the 1973 summit, with the same lack of result.

The most serious obstacle to my delaying tactics came from my own staff. In order to waste as much time as possible in my meeting with Gromyko, I made Gromyko repeat some of his formulations over and over again so that I could "understand them better." Peter Rodman, who was keeping the record for our side, obviously considered this an aspersion on his reliability, and kept interrupting me to hand me the precise text of Gromyko's proposal, which he had written down verbatim the first time it had been put forward. My repeated elbows in his side would not deter Peter each time we came to a new "principle" on Gromyko's list. I raised so much cain with him afterward over his excess of zeal that never again would either he or Winston Lord hand over a document to me in front of another delegation during a negotiation — even when I asked for it. They never could be sure, they argued, whether I really wanted the document or an excuse for procrastination. In China a month later, I turned to Lord for a document; he had it but pretended otherwise rather than risk another blunder. I went without the document. Peter and Winston begged me in vain to work out some system of hand signals, code words, or even flash cards so they could know whether I really wanted what I was asking for. In later years, an occasional request by me to Lord or Rodman for a document would send them both into paroxysms of laughter, which must have left the head of state or foreign minister I was negotiating with dumbfounded at the apparent total breakdown of discipline on my supposedly browbeaten staff.

As it turned out, the summit proved the last straw for Sadat. On July 18, six weeks later, he culminated months of growing disenchantment with Moscow by expelling the Soviet military advisers and technicians — one of the seminal events in recent Middle Eastern history. I shall discuss this further in Chapter XXX.

Vietnam, as far as we were concerned, was in the same category as the Middle East. We thought events were running favorably. A successful summit was bound to increase Hanoi's sense of isolation. Basically, we wanted no more from the Soviets than acquiescence in our unilateral course and we were well on the way to achieving this. The Soviets, in turn, sought some kind of joint statement in the communiqué, partly to mollify their outraged ally, partly because Brezhnev at the dacha had declared that formulating opposing views as in the Shanghai Communiqué was "unprincipled." Gromyko and I both knew that the only common language possible would likely hurt both sides; but in fact we spent two sessions, Saturday afternoon and Sunday morning, in its vain pursuit. Since this record was clearly not designated for Hanoi, there was none of the hortatory bombast of the dacha meeting; Gromyko, as was his style, engaged in no grandiose speeches; he wasted no time in recriminations. He, of course, would have liked to be able to send some new "concession" to Hanoi as having been extracted from us at the summit. But it was impossible for us to accommodate him. Hanoi would never settle unless convinced that we would yield no further. It had to be deprived of all expectation that its procrastination improved our offers.

I therefore sharply rejected Gromyko's repeated probes urging a coalition government. I pointed out the curious fact that Hanoi was seeking to keep us *in* Vietnam so that we could overthrow Thieu on its behalf. This would never happen. There were only two routes to a settlement — the military terms of our May 31, 1971, proposal (essentially cease-fire, US withdrawals, and return of prisoners) as refurbished on May 8, 1972, or the overall military and political program of the President's January 25 speech. If either approach failed, we would pursue the war's end by military means. Gromyko did not debate these points.

When we met again the next morning, I handed over a bland three-sentence paragraph for an agreed statement on Vietnam. (In the working draft of the whole communiqué, a space had been left blank for it. I suggested that perhaps we should leave it that way; it would certainly be a new approach. Gromyko looked pained.) Predictably, Gromyko rejected our draft. There was no choice except to return to the "unprincipled" format of the Shanghai Communiqué. Each side stated its own position; Soviet support for Hanoi was mildly expressed; there was no common view. Hanoi, in short, was on its own.

So Gromyko and I proceeded through the whole communiqué while Nixon visited Leningrad. My missing the excursion to Leningrad led to a standing joke between Gromyko and me. The Soviets promised to make up for it by taking me to Leningrad on my next trip to the Soviet Union. On each of my many succeeding visits to the USSR, Leningrad was on my original schedule. But each time, we were obliged to cancel the excursion because of the pressure of work in Moscow. I finally told Gromyko that I doubted Leningrad really existed; it was basically a come-on to make me cooperative. Gromyko, rebutting this, asked me, "But where did our Revolution take place?" "In St. Petersburg," I could not resist replying.

The communiqué contained a favorable reference to a European Security Conference similar to that in declarations Moscow had signed with our European allies; it committed us to no date. Our strategy was to tie the European Security Conference to talks on troop reductions and both of them to an end of the Vietnam war. Our approach to expanded economic relations was similar; it would be a carrot for restrained Soviet political behavior. No attempt was made to negotiate specific commercial arrangements; a US–Soviet economic commission was set up to facilitate expanded trade in a general way. A visit by Commerce Secretary Peter Peterson to Moscow was scheduled for July to begin discussions on the related issues of settlement of Soviet Lend-Lease debts and Most Favored Nation status for the Soviet Union. The drafting of the communiqué proceeded smoothly and for once without internal strains in the American delegation.

I had learned enough from the China trip to invite State Department participation. Assistant Secretary of State for European Affairs Martin Hillenbrand was assigned the task, which he discharged with unruffled skill. In the waning hours of the summit, Gromyko surfaced without explanation the "Basic Principles of US–Soviet Relations" agreed to in April. Hillenbrand, a professional too, knew these principles could not possibly have emerged in their existing form from Soviet draftsmen; but he was too wise to make an issue of it. And so we navigated a summit for once without a White House–State confrontation.

Statements of principles tend to get short shrift in our pragmatic society; clearly, they are not self-enforcing. The principles signed in Moscow affirmed the importance of avoiding confrontation; the need for mutual restraint; the rejection of attempts to exploit tensions in other areas to gain unilateral advantages; the renunciation of claims to special privileges by either country in any region (which we interpreted as a denial of the Brezhnev Doctrine); the willingness, on this basis, to coexist peacefully and to strive for a more constructive long-term relationship.

Of course, these principles were not a legal contract. They were intended to establish a standard of conduct by which to judge whether real progress was being made and in the name of which we could resist their violation. For four years we had affirmed our conviction that statesmen had no higher duty than to reduce the dangers of nuclear war; compared to its perils, the gains to be achieved by constant encroachment were bound to be marginal. But in our minds efforts to reduce the danger of nuclear war by the control of arms had to be linked to an end of the constant Soviet pressure against the global balance of power. We were dedicated to peaceful coexistence; we were equally determined to defend the balance of power and the values of freedom. If we fulfilled *our* responsibility to block Soviet encroachments, coexistence could be reliable and the principles of détente could be seen to have marked the path to a more hopeful future.

Only three events stood between us and the end of the summit: a private meeting between Nixon and Brezhnev (which I attended); a brief plenary session of the two delegations; and a gala reception in the vast St. George's Hall of the Kremlin.

Nixon and I walked from the Tsars' Apartments to the General Secretary's office a few hundred yards away through a light rain. We were leaving in the same ambiguous weather as when we arrived. All day long the sun and the clouds were contesting for preeminence. We were in high spirits. We had succeeded in maintaining the summit despite our strong stand in Vietnam. We had achieved all our objectives in Moscow. To be sure, the future was murky; Soviet intentions were in delicate suspense and we still had to end the Vietnam war. But we were on the verge of mastering our domestic crisis. And we were laying foundations of international order. More of our future appeared to be subject to our control than in quite some time.

The last private conversation between Brezhnev and Nixon was relaxed; it was a summing up. Brezhnev asked if we would consider it helpful if a Soviet leader — specifically Podgorny — visited Hanoi. Gromyko had told me the day before that Brezhnev was likely to raise the subject (giving Nixon and me a chance to discuss it first). We thought it unlikely that Moscow would make the travels of one of its senior leaders depend on our preference. Hence there was no sense in objecting; Brezhnev wanted to get some points for checking the inevitable with us. Podgorny was no doubt being sent to placate Hanoi's outrage. On the other hand, such a visit could do little damage. If Moscow were indeed prepared to restrain Hanoi, it would accelerate its isolation. Nixon said that he would welcome Podgorny's journey. Brezhnev, never able to forgo the temptation to pick up some loose change, proposed a bombing halt over all of North Vietnam during the Podgorny visit. Nixon, who had anticipated the request, agreed only not to bomb Hanoi and Haiphong — provided Podgorny did not stay for three months. Brezhnev then asked whether Thieu could be induced to resign two months rather than one month before the election; Podgorny could present this as a result of the summit. Nixon indicated that if all our other terms were accepted he would be prepared to recommend this modification of his January 25 speech. No doubt Brezhnev communicated it to Hanoi. We never heard of it again. For later in the summer Hanoi decided to go another route.

Brezhnev and Nixon came back to the idea of an understanding on the nonuse of nuclear weapons. Nixon skillfully put it back into the special Channel; the subject as outlined was bound to raise havoc within NATO and in our relations with China. Brezhnev volunteered a reaffirmation of the "understanding" on Cuba in general and with regard to submarines in particular. He threw in an assurance of the peaceful intentions of North Korea for good measure. (We thus had obtained assurances regarding Korea in both Peking and Moscow within the space of three months.) Brezhnev then delicately introduced what may well have been the Kremlin's deepest interest in détente. He hinted that both countries might usefully keep an eye on the nuclear aspirations of Peking. Nixon gave him no encouragement. Both leaders finally agreed to restrain propaganda aimed at the other country to the greatest extent possible.

One should not place too much emphasis on the personal relations of leaders, especially in a relaxed atmosphere after a series of events that had strengthened the domestic position of both of them. Obviously, the Soviet Union had also achieved some of its purposes; only rank amateurs believe that a negotiation among major powers can lead to a series of unilateral victories. Even if achievable, such an outcome is rarely desirable; no country will indefinitely keep to any agreement that serves none of its interests. A wise statesman will seek a balance of purposes; some "victories" are not worth achieving, for they mortgage the future. It clearly served Soviet purposes to give its people hope for better relations with the West. The Kremlin no doubt hoped that détente would sap the will to resistance of the democracies. But some hard-liners in the Kremlin had opposed it (for example, Shelest), fearing the risks to the Soviet Union. Brezhnev in my view had several motives. He wanted peace; he would pay some price for it, though he was not abandoning hope for advancing the prospects of a global Communist victory. And like many national leaders he probably sought to avoid a final choice for as long as possible. But this is no more than saying that the future seemed open. Nixon and Brezhnev, in short, were each betting on their ability to shape events in accordance with the purposes and values of their respective societies. No outcome was foreordained.

These prospects gave a strange and exuberant impetus to the final reception. The white and gleaming St. George's Hall of the Kremlin, lit by great chandeliers, swarmed with Soviet VIPs (Anastas Mikoyan was there, and Dmitri Shostakovich), middle- and high-level Soviet bureaucrats, leading foreign journalists, the diplomatic corps. Brezhnev and Nixon entered together and marched through the throng to the end of the room that was cordoned off for the top leadership. The anthems of the two nations were played. The tensions of the past months dissolved in that stirring moment, and many of us in that room were seized by the hope that perhaps we had indeed participated in the birth of a better era. Despite all reservations, it was possible in Moscow that evening to discern at least the distant outlines of a world in which mankind would transcend its doomed march through crises and risks into a realm of restraint and cooperation.

What Did the Summit Accomplish?

NIXON's return from Moscow on June 1 was dramatic. After landing at Andrews Air Force Base, he helicoptered to Capitol Hill. He was greeted by the Congressional leadership and taken immediately to report to a joint session of the Congress. He spoke with a blend of hope (occasionally flirting with exultation) and caution. He asserted that the "foundation has been laid for a new relationship between the two most powerful nations in the world." But he also emphasized that "concrete results, not atmospherics, would be our criterion for meetings at the highest level." He listed the various bilateral agreements, including the SALT accords, which represented "the first step toward a new era of mutually agreed restraint and arms limitations between the two principal nuclear powers." But he also stressed the vital importance of a strong national defense, pointing out that the SALT accords limited no US offensive programs. The "Basic Principles of Relations" were described as a "road map," marking the path that both sides should take if peace was to be lasting. But he reminded his listeners that "maintaining the strength, integrity, and steadfastness of our free world alliances is the foundation on which all of our other initiatives for peace and security in the world must rest. As we seek better relations with those who have been our adversaries, we will not let down our friends and allies around the world."

It was a fair summary of our achievements, our challenges, and our opportunities. Still, it seemed to be inherent in Nixon's life — it was his tragedy — that he was unable to close any chapter or find acceptance with any new departure. Every step he took was immediately subsumed again in the controversies and distrust he had accumulated over a lifetime. He soon found himself in the paradoxical position of a former Cold Warrior accused of being too committed to easing relations with the Soviet Union. What was the reality?

The context as well as the content of the summit made it a major success for American policy. The fact that we had faced down Hanoi and yet completed major negotiations with Moscow (three months after the spectacular in Peking) evoked the prospect of a more hopeful future and thus put Vietnam into perspective. The summits helped us complete the isolation of Hanoi by giving Moscow and Peking a stake in their ties with us. What was even more novel, we were freed for the better part of the year from the domestic turmoil on which thus far Hanoi had always been able to count. This, together with the military defeat of the North Vietnamese offensive, led to a breakthrough in the peace negotiations within months. The summit was equally significant for the evolution of the Middle East. As I will show, it marked a turning point at which moderate Arab leaders began to move toward Washington; it was a step in the process that eighteen months later saw former enemies start on the tortuous journey toward peace under an American aegis.

But the fundamental achievement was to sketch the outline on which coexistence between the democracies and the Soviet system must be based. SALT embodied our conviction that a wildly spiraling nuclear arms race was in no country's interest and enhanced no one's security;

the "Basic Principles" gave at least verbal expression to the necessity of responsible political conduct. The two elements reinforced each other; they symbolized our conviction that a relaxation of tensions could not be based exclusively on arms control; the ultimate test would be restrained international behavior. And here the bilateral agreements signed each day in Moscow — on environment, space, technical cooperation, incidents at sea, the establishment of an economic commission — could over time establish vested interests in peace. It was sure to be a long road and yet it reflected the imperative of peace of the nuclear age.

We were involved in a delicate balancing act: to be committed to peace without letting the quest for it become a form of moral disarmament, surrendering all other values; to be prepared to defend freedom while making clear that unconstrained rivalry could risk everything, including freedom, in a nuclear holocaust. Only a leader firm in his authority, secure in his public support, could walk this tightrope — one prone neither to the sentimentality of identifying coexistence with good personal relations, nor to reckless posturing for its own sake. Whether this would have had the requisite public support in an Administration led by Richard Nixon we will never know. I believe his unsentimental grasp of international affairs was a valuable asset. In any event Watergate prevented the full fruition of the prospects then before us, not only in nurturing US–Soviet relations but more generally in developing a new structure of international relations.

For as far ahead as we can see, America's task will be to re-create and maintain the two pillars of our policy toward the Soviet Union that we began to build in Moscow: a willingness to confront Soviet expansionism and a simultaneous readiness to mark out a cooperative future. A more peaceful world is prevented if we lean too far in either direction. When conciliation becomes an end in itself, a ruthless Soviet policy can turn it, as it occasionally has, into an instrument of blackmail and a cover for unilateral gains. When the more hopeful US–Soviet dialogue is closed off by our action, a price is paid in domestic support and allied cohesion. A successful policy needs both elements: incentives for Soviet restraint (such as economic links), and penalties for adventurism (such as firm US counteraction, including military assistance to friends resisting Soviet or Cuban or radical pressures).

To maintain the dual track of firmness and conciliation required a disciplined Executive Branch and a Congress and public with confidence in their government; a sophisticated understanding of the national interest and a grasp of how events and problems in one sphere are related to those in another. It was a task complex beyond any previous experience. I, too, was ambivalent, profoundly distrustful of Soviet motives, determined to prevent Soviet expansion, scornful of those critics who abjectly accepted Soviet advances or relied on history to undo them. To some extent my interest in détente was tactical, as a device to maximize Soviet dilemmas and reduce Soviet influence as in the Middle East; in part it was domestic, to outmanuever the "peace" pressures so we could rally our public if a showdown proved unavoidable. And yet there was a residue reflecting the unprecedented challenge of our period; a conviction that the moral imperative of leadership in our time was to keep open the prospect, however slim, of a fundamental change, of doing our utmost so that Armageddon did not descend on us through neglect or lack of foresight.

Unfortunately, the erosion of Nixon's domestic base prevented us from fully implementing our vision or our strategy. Relations with the Soviet Union grew increasingly controversial under an attack by both liberals and conservatives. Liberals who for three years had assaulted Nixon for bellicosity and intransigence now found it convenient to criticize, if not détente itself, then its "overselling" in America. Significantly, the criticism was little heard in 1972 and early 1973, in the heyday of US–Soviet détente. It appeared first in the second half of 1973, as the Soviets cracked down on dissidents, Andrei Sakharov made his appeal of August 1973 endorsing the Jackson amendment, the October 1973 Middle East war broke out (which some decided was instigated by the Soviets) — and as Watergate erupted and weakened the Presidency. No evidence was ever adduced to show what this "overselling" consisted of. Indeed, even a casual reading of the stream of speeches, press statements, and interviews during this period will show a pattern of Administration caution, constantly pointing out the limits, the ambiguities, the competition inherent in the relationship, the requirement of vigilance, as well as the very real progress that had been made.

It was a symptom of our domestic divisions that this criticism could have been raised at all about an Administration that had faced down the Soviets over Cienfuegos, had resisted proxy wars by India and Syria, had established the principles of linkage, had begun Presidential visits to Eastern Europe, had fought for a strong defense, and had shouldered the commitments of its predecessors in Indochina in order to maintain American global credibility against aggression — all in the face of some of the most bitter domestic assaults in a century.

To be sure, Nixon's penchant for hyperbole was unlikely to be restrained in an election year. He started out expressing the "hope" for a generation of peace. Soon he came to claim it as an "accomplishment." And in the closing days of the 1972 election campaign he even escalated the goal to be a "century of peace." His public relations people were indefatigable in propounding these propositions — over my frequently expressed, but rather ineffective, dissent. But campaign oratory aside, Nixon's formal statements never failed to stress the competitiveness between the Soviet and American systems and the profound ideological gulf intensifying the rivalry. A good example is the President's Foreign Policy Report of May 3, 1973. It stressed the need for a balance of power and also for international restraint. It reemphasized our Alliance ties. It warned that détente did not mean the end of danger. It affirmed that America was prepared to share its responsibilities, but not to abdicate them.

Moscow, SALT, and détente, however, did give rise to a deeper and more legitimate concern, not one so frivolous and cynical as that expressed by Nixon's traditional opponents on the left who suddenly converted to anti-Communism when Nixon embraced détente. Many conservatives who had previously backed Nixon began to worry not about the policy of the Administration but about the psychological consequences of the process. America was yearning for relief from years of bitterness and turmoil. Spectacular events such as Nixon's visits to Peking and Moscow, while embodying real achievements and sober calculation, also served as dramatic emotional contrasts for the American people after a decade of upheaval and guilt. There was bound to be exuberance, relief, exultation after the fatigue and backbiting that were wearing us down. The conservatives feared that the American people, in its historical alternation between optimism and gloom about Soviet purposes, was swinging too far toward a euphoria that over time would sap its will. They foresaw an erosion of all distinctions, a decay of convictions, when American and Soviet (or for that matter Chinese Communist) leaders were displayed in easy camaraderie on American television screens. They wondered how we would maintain our vigilance — whatever the saving clauses in Presidential statements — when we proclaimed a new era. They doubted whether America could sustain both the willingness to confront and the readiness to cooperate at the same time.

They had a point; they had the historical record on their side. No period of coexistence with the Soviet system has proved permanent. Each has been used by the Kremlin as a springboard for a new advance. And yet in our period this was a counsel of despair. The quest for peaceful coexistence clearly had its perils; it did not follow that a crusading policy of confrontation would prove more successful. The former might sap our vigilance; the latter would risk our national cohesion and our alliances as our government would be denounced with increasing vehemence as the cause of international tensions. We would not accept that the American people could maintain their vigilance only by a strident militance that conceded to our adversaries a monopoly on the global yearning for peace, and that would gradually maneuver the United States government into isolation. Americans would have to learn to live with the geopolitical challenge of maintaining the global balance of power; it was our duty to block Soviet expansionism; these sober convictions animated our policy. But precisely because the conflict was also ideological and political, we thought that we would weaken ourselves by not looking beyond the military balance. Amid the national hysteria on Vietnam, it would almost certainly have been self-defeating. As détente came under attack, the US Congress did not prove any more willing to confront Soviet adventurism in Angola in 1975 — and many hawks joined the majority blocking the American effort there. We were determined to resist Soviet aggressiveness, but we thought the chances better if our policy also gave expression to hope. It remains to be seen whether, given our historical experience and the bitterness of our recent past, it is possible to walk this narrow path; whether we are doomed to oscillate erratically between excessive conciliation and excessive bellicosity. It continues as the fundamental task of any administration.

In briefing a bipartisan group of Congressional leaders about SALT on June 15, 1972, I defined our challenge:

> The deepest question we ask is not whether we can trust the Soviets, but whether we can trust ourselves. Some have expressed concern about the agreements not because they object to their terms, but because they are afraid of the euphoria that these agreements might produce. But surely we cannot be asked to maintain avoidable tension just to carry out programs which our national survival should dictate in any event. We must not develop a national psychology by which we can act only on the basis of what we are against and not on what we are for.
>
> Our challenges then are: Can we chart a new course with hope but without illusion, with large purposes but without sentimentality? Can we be both generous and strong? It is not often that a country has the opportunity to answer such questions meaningfully.

The Moscow summit gave us an opportunity to begin an answer. Destiny willed that we could not complete it, but that we consumed ourselves in controversy. Perhaps it is impossible to give a conclusive answer in any brief period. For US–Soviet relations are now a permanent challenge for the American people, whose response will decide our security but also the prospects for a better world.

XXIX

Summit Aftermath

A Visit to the Shah of Iran

THE ravages of time, emotion, and upheaval have cast into a starkly different context the pleasant journey I made with Nixon after we concluded the Moscow summit. From Kiev, we flew to Tehran on May 30, to be greeted by one of America's closest allies, the Shah of Iran.

At the airport stood a slight, erect figure, Mohammed Reza Pahlavi, Shahanshah Aryamehr, imperial by title, imperious by bearing. America has little to be proud of in our reaction to his overthrow many years later. History is written by the victors; and the Shah is not much in vogue today. Yet it hardly enhances our reputation for steadfastness to hear the chorus today against a leader whom eight Presidents of both parties proclaimed — rightly — a friend of our country and a pillar of stability in a turbulent and vital region.

The institution of shah or emperor was not a personal invention of the Pahlavis; its roots are deep in Iran's past. Located centrally amid all the world's great cultures — reaching from the Indian subcontinent with its conglomerate of color, passion, and endurance to the monochromatic exaltation of Arabia; bordered by Soviet Central Asia in the North; and separated from Africa only by a narrow span of ocean — Iran has inevitably been at the vortex of world history. Conquerors have issued from this stern land of forbidding mountains and parched deserts, of fertile seashores and stark colors; foreign conquerors have added it to their dominion. Indians, Mongols, Afghans, Arabs, Cossacks, Greeks, Europeans, have washed across the edifices of its glorious past, sometimes to stay, occasionally to pass onward. All receded in time, leaving a residue that merged into a population which never lost its Persian identity; the grandeur of Persian aspirations and culture imposed its own consciousness, transcending the national origin, race, or purpose of the invaders. The result was not a national state in the European sense but a potpourri of Persians, Kurds, Baluchis, Afghans, Jews, Turkomans, Arabs, and many others.

For twenty-five hundred years Iran has been governed as an empire even as the dynasties changed; the state needed a unifying principle beyond that of the many nationalities composing it. In one of the ironies of history, the most individualistic peoples and centrifugal societies sometimes create the most absolute forms of rule, as if only the most exalted authority could justify subordination. In Iran, whatever the dynasty, the authority of governance ultimately resided in the remoteness of the emperor: It was his historical strength, as well as his weakness. Without doubt the Shah was an authoritarian ruler. This was in keeping with the traditions, perhaps even the necessities, of his society. It was for a time the source of his strength just as it became later a cause of his downfall.

As time went on and I got to know the Shah better, I realized that he was not by nature a domineering personality. Indeed, he was rather shy and withdrawn. I could never escape the impression that he was a gentle, even sentimental man who had schooled himself in the maxim that the ruler must be aloof and hard, but had never succeeded in making it come naturally. His majestic side was like a role rehearsed over the years. In this he was a prisoner, I suspect, of the needs of his state, just as he was ultimately the victim of his own successes.

The Shah was — despite the travesties of retroactive myth — a dedicated reformer. He was "progressive" in the sense that he sought to industrialize his society; one of the prime causes of his disaster, in fact, was that he modernized too rapidly and that he did not adapt his political institutions sufficiently to the economic and social changes he had brought about. He carried out a vast land reform. He fostered literacy far beyond what was even attempted in neighboring countries. Hundreds of thousands of students were sent on government scholarships to foreign countries where many of them joined radical movements. Women's rights were broadened. The Iranian Gross National Product grew by 10 percent a year from 1967 to 1972, after which the pell-mell advance was replaced by a more sustainable 6 percent. To be sure, there were also darker sides: high-level corruption which blighted the noble aspirations and methods of repression unworthy of the enlightened goals.

Basically, the Shah was applying axioms of all the more "advanced" literature of the West. Even his neglect of political institutions had roots in Western thinking about the relationship between economic development and political stability. Much of the American theory about economic development reflected the experience of the Marshall Plan. Political stability was supposed to follow from economic advance; it was assumed by many Western economists, and believed by the Shah, that the government which raised the standard of living would thereby gain public approbation. In other words, economic progress was itself a contribution to political stability. This theory proved to be disastrously wrong and misguided.

In Europe and Japan, where political institutions and a functioning bureaucracy had developed over the centuries, the threat to stability was indeed the gap between reality and expectation; there, economic progress enhanced the acceptability of the government that brought it about. But in underdeveloped countries economic growth tends to have the opposite effect; it compounds political unrest. Established institutions are undermined, and if it happens before new ones are put in their place upheaval is inevitable. The mass migration from the countryside into the cities separates the workers from traditional patterns of life before new relationships can take their place. Precisely when economic development gains its greatest momentum, the existing political and social structures grow most fragile and the accepted values of tradition are most threatened. Fortunate is the country that can manage a transition to new political forms without turmoil. Wise is the ruler who understands that economic development, far from strengthening his position, carries with it the imperative of building new political institutions to accommodate the growing complexity of his society.

It cannot be said that either the Shah or his friends possessed this wisdom; but, it must be remarked, neither did his enemies. The most implacable opposition came not from those who wanted greater political participation in government but from traditional quarters who were being forced to yield to the thrust of modernism — the landowners, the mullahs deprived of privileges, the votaries of the old order. Or else it came from radicals who found hereditary authoritarianism irksome primarily because they wished to replace it with a more efficient structure of power based on ideology. Ground up between these forces were the genuine believers in democracy and tolerance — a small group of Western-educated intellectuals whose destiny it was to be persecuted by whatever regime governed Iran. So the Shah found himself progressively undermined by his successes, for the further he advanced the more enemies he created. And he was not farsighted enough to create new political institutions or to enlist new loyalties to sustain political stability.

Nor can it be said that the Shah's arms purchases diverted resources from economic development, the conventional criticism of arms sales to developing countries. The Shah did both. Iran's economic growth was not slowed nor was its political cohesion affected by its defense spending. Cut off from military supplies — an impossibility anyway, in light of the ready availability of British and French arms — Iran might have grown more vulnerable to outside pressures without gaining in domestic stability. Perhaps it is history's tragic lesson that only two kinds of structure seem able to survive the stresses of modernization: either totalitarian governments imposing their will and national discipline, or else democratic governments where pluralism and a constitutional tradition were already in place *before* industrialization began. Regrettably, the recent period finds few new examples of democratic evolution in the developing world. For developing countries, one of the attractions of Marxism (or, now, reversion to theocracy) is that it provides a rationale for the exercise of power and a rigid structure of discipline and authority amidst the disintegration of traditional forms.

Whatever the failings of the Shah, wrestling perhaps with forces beyond any man's control, he was for us that rarest of leaders, an unconditional ally, and one whose understanding of the world situation enhanced our own. Over the years I had many conversations with him. In his grasp of the international trends and currents he was among the most impressive leaders that I met. He had a sure grasp of the importance of both the global and the regional balance of power. He understood that the dangers to Iranian independence had historically come from the north rather than from across the sea. With a border of 1,500 miles with the Soviet Union, and confronted by increasingly radical governments in both Iraq and Afghanistan, he knew that he had to find some equipoise to the growing pressure on all his frontiers except that with Pakistan. He could have sought to deflect pressures by becoming the Soviet Union's spokesman in the area through a policy technically nonaligned but operationally anti-West. He could have sought to preserve his independence by maneuvering between the blocs — much as India did — always careful, however, not to antagonize the superpower to the north. He could have leaned toward us but taken our protection for granted, and striven, as had other leaders, to pick up whatever loose change could be found by manipulating the rivalry of the superpowers for short-term ends. Instead, the Shah of Iran chose friendship with the United States. He had been restored to the throne in 1953 by American influence when a leftist government had come close to toppling him. He never forgot that; it may have been the root of his extraordinary trust in American purposes and American goodwill, and of his psychological disintegration when he sensed that friendship evaporating. On some levels excessively, even morbidly, suspicious of possible attempts to diminish his authority, he nevertheless retained an almost naive faith in the United States. By the same token he was unprepared for an America vacillating in his hour of tragedy.

The Shah sought to shape his country's destiny and make Iran a major partner in the West. He believed in assuming the burden of his own defense, at least to the point where he balanced the strength of his radical neighbors, like Iraq, and where he would force Moscow, if it ever sought to subdue Iran, to launch a direct invasion of a magnitude that the United States could not ignore. And he tried to earn our support not only by taking seriously the defense of his country — which was, after all, of crucial strategic importance — but also by displaying his friendship to us at times when he might well have stood aside.

Under the Shah's leadership, the land bridge between Asia and Europe, so often the hinge of world history, was pro-American and pro-West beyond any challenge. Alone among the countries of the region — Israel aside — Iran made friendship with the United States the starting point of its foreign policy. That it was based on a cold-eyed assessment that a threat to Iran would most likely come from the Soviet Union, in combination with radical Arab states, is only another way of saying that the Shah's view of the realities of world politics paralleled our own. Iran's influence was always on our side; its resources reinforced ours even in some distant enterprises — in aiding South Vietnam at the time of the 1973 Paris Agreement, helping Western Europe in its economic crisis in the 1970s, supporting moderates in Africa against Soviet-Cuban encroachment, supporting President Sadat in the later Middle East diplomacy. In the 1973 Middle East war, for example, Iran was the *only* country bordering the Soviet Union not to permit the Soviets use of its air space — in contrast to several NATO allies. The Shah absorbed the energies of radical Arab neighbors to prevent them from threatening the moderate regimes in Saudi Arabia, Jordan, and the Persian Gulf. He refueled our fleets without question. He never used his control of oil to bring political pressure; he never joined any oil embargo against the West or Israel.* Iran under the Shah, in short, was one of America's best, most important, and most loyal friends in the world. The least we owe him is not retrospectively to vilify the actions that eight American Presidents — including the present incumbent — gratefully welcomed.

Thus, on our arrival in Tehran in May 1972, all of us felt almost a physical sense of relief. However friendly the reception had been in Moscow and however successful the US–Soviet summit, there hung over our Soviet visit that miasma of totalitarianism which invariably depresses the visitor, that heavy uniformity which warns the human spirit of the future that awaits it if free peoples lose faith in their liberties and cease defending their values and institutions. In Tehran, the warm goodwill was tangible.

The visit, though humanly engaging, was not without its awkward moments. Nixon was indeed like the Shah in his withdrawn shyness.

---

* He sought, of course, the best possible price for his oil, and was partly responsible for the severe OPEC price rise of 1973. But several things must be said: When he realized the damage done to the West by this action, he helped keep the price stable for the next five years. In fact, the real price of oil *declined* by 15 percent from 1973 to 1978. His motive for the original price rise was not political but economic; unlike some other countries, he wanted the maximum revenues for the development of his country. And he never sought to manipulate the oil price by restricting his production; he always kept his oil production at maximum capacity, thus permitting the law of supply and demand to operate in favor of stable prices.

The Shah tendered the President a lavish white-tie dinner. At its conclusion Nixon had to improvise a toast because the glare of the television lights blinded him and vanity prevented him from wearing glasses when he was being televised. The toast went along well enough but Nixon did not quite know how to conclude it. Three times he came to what could have served as an excellent stopping point, but decided to go around the track again. On the fourth attempt he thought he had hit upon a felicitous conclusion: He quoted an observation of President Eisenhower that, whatever their differences, one thing all successful political leaders seemed to have in common was "the ability to marry above themselves." He then proposed a toast to the Shah and "to his lovely Empress, who has been by his side . . ." The King of Kings looked off into the distance with melancholy.

But even though Nixon was exhausted by his exertions in the Soviet Union and there was little time in Tehran for a deeper dialogue, the conversations between the Shah and Nixon were those of close allies. The disaster for the West that has accompanied the Shah's downfall has led to a feverish quest to find some way to blame Richard Nixon for events that occurred seven years later. Nixon's 1972 visit has retroactively been made a scapegoat; it was blamed for inducing overconfidence in an Emperor who had already been in power for thirty years, supported by several American administrations of both parties.*

It is not obvious, of course, that self-assurance in an ally is a bad thing. Nor was this how the problem appeared in 1972. The real issue in 1972 was that the required balance within an area essential for the security, and even more the prosperity, of all industrial democracies appeared in grave jeopardy. More than 15,000 Soviet troops were still in Egypt, with which we had as yet no diplomatic relations and which was tied to the Soviet Union by a Friendship Treaty signed a year earlier. Just seven weeks before, on April 9, the Soviet Union had concluded a similar Friendship Treaty with Iraq, followed by massive deliveries of the most advanced modern weapons. Syria had long since been a major recipient of Soviet arms — and had invaded moderate Jordan twenty months earlier. Britain at the end of 1971 had just completed the historic withdrawal of its forces and military protection from the Persian Gulf at the precise moment when radical Iraq was being put into a position by Soviet arms to assert traditional hegemonic aims. Our friends — Saudi Arabia, Jordan, the Emirates — were being encircled.

It was imperative for our interests and those of the Western world that the regional balance of power be maintained so that moderate forces

---

*The accusations are made with a certain defensiveness, which suggests to me that the crucial question remains: Was it wrong to support one of our most valuable allies in 1972, or was it wrong to fail to support him effectively in 1978 and 1979? [1]

would not be engulfed nor Europe's and Japan's (and as it later turned out, our) economic lifeline fall into hostile hands. We could either provide the balancing force ourselves or enable a regional power to do so. There was no possibility of assigning any American military forces to the Indian Ocean in the midst of the Vietnam war and its attendant trauma. Congress would have tolerated no such commitment; the public would not have supported it. Fortunately, Iran was willing to play this role. The vacuum left by British withdrawal, now menaced by Soviet intrusion and radical momentum, would be filled by a local power friendly to us. Iraq would be discouraged from adventures against the Emirates in the lower Gulf, and against Jordan and Saudi Arabia. A strong Iran could help damp India's temptations to conclude its conquest of Pakistan. And all of this was achievable without any American resources, since the Shah was willing to pay for the equipment out of his oil revenues. To have failed to match the influx of Soviet arms into neighboring countries would have accelerated the demoralization of moderate forces in the Middle East and speeded up the radicalization of the area, including Iran's. I daresay that it might have prevented or made far more difficult Sadat's later turn toward the West.

The specific decision facing Nixon was the Shah's wish for F-14 or F-15 aircraft and associated equipment. There had been opposition: some Defense Department reluctance to part with advanced technology and State Department fears that the sale might be provocative. The Shah's alternative was to purchase the slightly less advanced French Mirage plane. Nixon overrode the objections and added a proviso that in the future Iranian requests should not be second-guessed. To call this an ''open-ended'' commitment is hyperbole, considering the readiness and skill with which our bureaucracy is capable of emasculating directives it is reluctant to implement — a quality repeatedly demonstrated in the Nixon Administration (as during the India-Pakistan crisis) and soon compounded by the erosion of Nixon's authority as a result of Watergate. Later decisions were shaped less by Nixon's directive than by the judgment of our government as they came up. During the Ford Administration, for example, Secretary of Defense James Schlesinger had a senior official assigned to the Shah for liaison and for vetting arms requests. His conclusion obviously was not affected by a directive from Nixon by then over two years old. He reached the same judgment for much the same reason as Nixon had in 1972. Subsequently, arms continued to be sold in substantial quantities because of the judgment of all senior officials — and of our successors — that they were needed for the balance of power and that Iran was a vital ally carrying burdens which otherwise we would have had to assume. Nothing has occurred to change this judgment in the interval.

Nixon agreed also to encourage the Shah in supporting the autonomy of the Kurds in Iraq. The Kurdish affair and its tragic outcome in the 1973–1975 period are, of course, outside the scope of this volume. The excited polemics published on this subject have neglected to mention that they were written without any evidence of White House decisions and reasoning. I shall explain these in a second volume.* In 1972, in any case, this was all in the future. The benefit of Nixon's Kurdish decision was apparent in just over a year: Only one Iraqi division was available to participate in the October 1973 Middle East war.

The visit to Tehran thus marked an important step in maintaining the balance of power in the Middle East. Our friendship with Iran served us well in the crises soon to descend on us. The geopolitical importance of that country must impel any administration into seeking good relations with whatever group governs Iran. But this imperative need not be pursued by ignoring those who were our friends in their travail. It cannot be in our country's interest to indulge in petty and retrospective denigration of associates of a generation or to show insensitivity to their human needs in their hour of travail. We were willing enough to have the Shah cooperate with us as friend and ally for thirty-seven years; we impress no one by condemning him now. We cannot always assure the future of our friends; we have a better chance of assuring our future if we remember who our friends are.

Return through Warsaw

THE Communist world would not let go of Nixon so easily. On the way home from Iran he stopped in Poland, the largest and most populous of the Soviet-dominated states of Eastern Europe. What drew Nixon there was a combination of nostalgia, domestic politics, and foreign policy. Nixon was nostalgic about Poland because in 1959 it had given him a tumultuous welcome when he visited as Vice President; he never forgot the rare occasions in his life when he had evoked spontaneous enthusiasm. If anything like it could be repeated in a Presidential election year, it would surely not be overlooked by millions of Polish-American voters. And finally, it was our policy to encourage sentiments of national independence in Eastern Europe. That goal had taken us to

---

* Suffice it here to mention, first, that the decision to discourage the Kurds from launching a diversionary offensive during the October 1973 war was based on the unanimous view of our intelligence officials and the Shah that the Kurds would be *defeated* in such an offensive; this judgment was concurred in by the Israeli government. The Shah's decision in 1975 to settle the Kurdish problem with Iraq was based on the judgment, almost certainly correct, that the Kurds were about to be overwhelmed; they could not have been saved without the intervention of two Iranian divisions and $300 million in assistance from us. The Shah was not willing to commit the former; this was his sovereign decision to make. To imagine that Congress would have appropriated the latter sum in the month that Vietnam was collapsing would be fatuous. If we had sought this escalation of our covert intelligence operation, many of those later mourning the Kurds' tragic fate would have probably led the charge against it.

Bucharest in 1969 and to Belgrade in 1970. It brought us to Warsaw in 1972.

There is no country in Europe in which the aspiration to national independence is so inseparable from its history. Poland's past has been as glorious as it has been tragic, as inspiring as its suffering has been immense. Rarely have a people combined such exalted dedication to liberty with such a fierce refusal to subordinate themselves to foreign authority, with such a quixotic willingness continually to hazard their freedom in pursuit of a romantic vision of freedom. Located in the same plain without natural boundaries as Russia but without the buffer afforded by Russia's vast spaces, Poland has been drawn into the maelstrom of all contending forces in Europe and exposed to periodic pressures from both East and West. Its very borders testify to the fluctuations of historical fortune; Poland has been moved around on the map almost like a chair in a room; it has been shifted westward or eastward with the historical tides. As recently as 1945 Poland was in effect moved westward by 150 miles; Russia took Poland's eastern provinces and Poland was compensated by the gift of Germany's eastern provinces. This extraordinary rearrangement, mortgaging Poland's future in both directions, was done by a decision of the victorious powers in which Poles did not participate.

For nearly 150 years, from the late eighteenth century until the end of World War I, the state of Poland, once one of the most important in Europe, disappeared from the map of Europe altogether; Poland was partitioned by Prussia, Austria, and Russia. But in one of the most extraordinary feats of national faith, Poland remained engraved in the hearts of its people even as they were divided among neighboring states. Indeed, in keeping with the nation's wildly romantic and individualistic character, Poland's contribution to the liberty of Europe increased during the years of its national oppression. In the eighteenth and nineteenth centuries Polish patriots were seized with the heroic and moving notion that they could restore freedom to their people only by enhancing freedom everywhere. There was no war for national independence — including America's — that was not ennobled by the participation of Polish volunteers who, in risking their lives for the principle of independence of faraway countries, believed they were vindicating the right to freedom of their own.

Faith in the nation was buttressed in that heroic country by faith in God. Poland was the Eastern outpost of the Catholic Church, whose priests became at the same time the representatives of the spirit of a nation whose oppressors in the main professed a different religion. The Church in Poland was a rallying point for national sentiment as nowhere else. No country had suffered more in the Second World War than Poland, whose political and intellectual vitality seemed to inspire such

terror in its neighbors that its leaders were being systematically liquidated now by the Germans, now by the Soviets. The Nazis ordered the
murder of millions of what they considered Poland's elite. Stalin had
executed several hundred of the Polish officer corps in the Katyn Forest
during the time of the Molotov-Ribbentrop Pact. The Red Army had
stood idly by across the Vistula River while the Germans suppressed the
Warsaw revolt of 1944, calculating that Polish patriots were bound to be
an obstacle to Soviet postwar plans. And so Poland emerged from
World War II with unfamiliar boundaries both in the east and the west,
with an alien regime imposed upon it, and with Soviet troops stationed
seemingly permanently in the country. And yet even its Communist
rulers, put into power by foreign arms, could sustain themselves only by
enlarging the margin of national decision to the maximum extent.
Grudgingly, the Communist superstructure was forced into an accommodation with the Catholic Church, which exacted a large measure of
spiritual autonomy, in return performing its historic role of symbolizing
that some virtues are beyond the reach of political decisions. Uprisings
in 1956 and 1970 warned that the Polish spirit could be quelled only by
a massive display of military power from which the Soviet Union re-
coiled on both occasions.

The fierce devotion to Polish identity was reflected in the rebuilding
of the beautiful old city of Warsaw. So powerful was the national tradition that even the Communist rulers inheriting the heap of rubble that
had once been Warsaw (90 percent destroyed) began their task of reconstruction by rebuilding the city of Poland's past: Sixteenth-century Warsaw rose lovingly re-created from ancient plans before the Communists
dared to impose their own gingerbread Stalinist Gothic on their subjects.

Poland needed from us no lectures on the importance of freedom. All
it required was the psychological assurance that its aspirations were understood by old friends. And therefore our presence in Warsaw was
more important than the substance of the conversations.

We arrived at the airport to a horrendous foul-up. As part of the arrival ceremony, a gaudy Polish army marching band had begun its drill
at the far end of the airport tarmac and was heading toward the reviewing stand in an intricate spit-and-polish maneuver. The ceremony must
have been rehearsed many times, but apparently not with an airplane
present. As the band approached us it became sickeningly clear that it
was heading straight for the engine pods under the wings of *Air Force
One;* indeed, had the pilot started the engines, the entire band would
have been blown away or incinerated. But the band proved equal to the
occasion. Without breaking stride or interrupting the music, it executed
a sharp ninety-degree turn, marched under the wings parallel to the
fuselage, its ranks parting around the engine pods, its melody and personnel unimpaired. To prove that routine is hard to break, the band did

not change the procedure upon our departure; it followed the same precise route, marching into the airplane and under the engines.

Our advance men could not permit such ingenuity to go unmatched. The problem was the perennial one: how to bring about a photo opportunity involving "spontaneous" crowds. It was complicated in Poland because our hosts insisted that we use their cars, thus depriving our advance team of control over the creation of traffic jams, which had worked so well in Rome and Belgrade in 1970. But the advance men were up to the challenge. On the way to his residence from the airport, Nixon stopped to lay a wreath at the Tomb of the Unknown Soldier. Fortunately for our public relations men's composure, in Warsaw this is located in the center of town so that a good-sized crowd had assembled. As Nixon completed the wreath-laying, the President's American limousine suddenly came into view with its regular Secret Service driver. Nixon entered it before our hosts could recover from their surprise. The driver moved the car slowly off the street and onto the sidewalk, that is to say, right into the crowd. Even the most hostile photographer found it impossible to avoid a picture of Nixon's car inundated by Polish crowds. I had been given another lesson in the creation of photo opportunities.

The conversations with Polish leaders could not compete with so much ingenuity. I was much impressed with Edward Gierek, the General Secretary of the Polish Communist Party, who had come to power after the 1970 riots. He was a dedicated Communist and a patriotic Pole. He left the impression that an ideology which destroyed the national character of his people would be meaningless to him and that in the end he would resist if it came to that. He knew that Poland would commit suicide if it challenged its powerful neighbor to the East. And no Pole could totally overcome the distrust of Germany after the suffering of the Second World War. Gierek would maneuver between these two national nightmares, seeking the greatest autonomy in the process, without giving up the Communist principles to which he had devoted his life.

And there was no doubt about his happiness with the outcome of the Moscow summit. Soviet leaders were surely ambivalent about détente, undecided whether to use it as an offensive tactic to tranquilize the West or to make a serious turn toward mutual restraint. Gierek had no such ambivalence. He wanted a code of international conduct in which the strong were restrained from imposing their will on the weak. Poland's autonomy could thrive best under conditions of relaxation of tension. Confrontation involved regimentation; peace was not only an abstract preference but a condition of national survival. And so the stop in Warsaw reminded us of some fundamentals that ultimately make statesmanship worthwhile.

The Soviet Grain Deal

IT must be conceded that in one respect the Soviet Union played a cool hand and outwitted us at the summit. This involved its purchase of American grain a few weeks later.

Every President since Kennedy had considered that it would be a major political success to demonstrate the superiority of our system by selling the Soviet Union the grain it could not grow for itself. For a while our labor unions had prevented such sales by refusing to load Soviet ships and by requiring shipment in American bottoms, which were far too expensive for the Soviets. But those issues were resolved soon after the summit. Nothing now stood in the way except Soviet willingness to buy. Fundamentally, the Soviet purchase of grain in our markets was seen as a domestic matter, an element of our agricultural policy; the NSC staff was kept informed only in general terms. Furthermore, nobody familiar with Secretary of Agriculture Earl Butz's protective attitude toward the agricultural community would believe for one moment that he would accept foreign policy directives gracefully. Butz was the equal of Mel Laird in bureaucratic maneuvering and even more deadly because he represented a single-minded constituency.

When Butz visited Moscow in April 1972, he was told that the Soviet Union might consider a three-year agreement to purchase grain, provided adequate credits were available. By June, Butz had come up with a formula for subsidized credit. During the summit Nixon had commented several times to Brezhnev and Kosygin about the beneficial impact of grain sales on our public opinion, but the Soviet leaders had feigned little interest. Kosygin told Rogers that as a special favor the Soviets might buy $150 million. I advised Nixon that this sum was too insignificant to merit inclusion in the summit communiqué.

After we returned home Soviet interest suddenly picked up. We know now, but did not then, that in 1972 the Soviets were confronting a catastrophic crop failure; their need for American grain was critical. No report accurately pointing to the scale of the Soviet failure reached the White House then or until long after the unprecedentedly massive purchases of that crop year had been completed. We might have suspected that something was wrong; the Soviets abandoned their usual haggling tactics and moved the negotiations forward on the grain issue after the summit on an expert level without polemics or publicity. In retrospect we should have guessed perhaps that Moscow wanted to avoid both political scrutiny and the risks of driving up prices in the grain market if the scale of their crop failure became known. By the last week of June a Deputy Minister from the Soviet Agriculture Ministry had slipped quietly into Washington. Peterson and Butz quickly worked out with him a three-year arrangement involving $750 million in credits. The extent of our ignorance is shown by a conversation I had then with Peterson, who was pleasantly surprised that the Soviets seemed to be considering a purchase of "up to $500 million" worth of grain during the first year.

The Soviets, however, were quick to take advantage of the competitiveness of our grain companies. They gave us a lesson in the handicaps a market economy has in negotiating with a state trading enterprise. Each of our grain companies, trying to steal a march on its competitors, sold the largest amount possible and kept its sale utterly secret, even from the US government. Not for several weeks did we realize that the Soviets had, by a series of separate transactions, bought up nearly one billion dollars' worth of grain in one year — nearly our entire stored surplus. And we had subsidized the deals at a time when the Soviet Union quite literally had no other choice than to buy our grain at market prices or face mass starvation.

It was painful to realize that we had been outmaneuvered, even more difficult to admit that the methods which gained that edge were those of a sharp trader skillfully using our free market system. We had no one to blame but ourselves. Our intelligence about Soviet needs was appalling. Our knowledge of what was happening in our markets was skimpy. The US government was simply not organized at that time to supervise or even monitor private grain sales as a foreign policy matter. The Soviets beat us at our own game.

At first the sale was hailed as a political masterstroke. It led to the usual maneuvering as to who should get credit. I held a briefing in San Clemente for the White House to get some credit for Nixon, but was neatly scooped by Earl Butz at Agriculture, fulfilling the tradition of the Nixon Cabinet of letting the President share only in the bad news. Soon, however, no one wanted any credit; the grain sale rapidly became a political scandal: Nixon was accused of selling at bargain rates to our adversaries and driving up the price for American consumers.* The charge was largely unfair. Nixon favored a grain sale and was not oblivious to its political advantages in a Presidential election year. But he had nothing to do with the terms or the size of the sale. Indeed, the Soviets got away with it because no senior official — except possibly Butz — understood what they were doing. At best, it can be said that we learned from the experience. From then on, all such transactions were treated as foreign policy matters and subjected to interagency monitoring. By 1975, in President Ford's Administration, a five-year agreement was signed with

---

* Part of the scandal was that the government paid a subsidy to American farmers to make up the difference between the domestic price and the world price. When both prices skyrocketed (because of worldwide crop shortages and the increase in demand due to devaluation of the dollar, as well as Soviet purchases), these "hardship" payments continued to be made long after they were warranted. This, of course, was outside the purview of the foreign policy agencies. But it justifiably fueled public resentment against the grain sale.

the Soviet Union regulating its purchases and guarding against any new disruption of our market. But by then, of course, the political, economic, and psychological damage of the earlier deal was done.

We made rapid, and on the whole satisfactory, progress with the Soviet Union on a number of other economic issues. In July, Secretary of Commerce Peter Peterson visited Moscow to review a number of them: the settlement of Lend-Lease debts, the extension of Most Favored Nation status, the possibility of credits, and the establishment of commercial facilities in each other's capitals. These negotiations went so well that Peterson and his staff drafted a basic agreement, leaving open only the final figures on the Lend-Lease debt.

I settled these with Brezhnev during a visit to Moscow from September 10 to 13, the purpose of which was a general review of all aspects of US–Soviet relations. Familiar now with Soviet tactics, we started at a figure on Lend-Lease repayments considerably higher than what we expected to get and spent several evenings consenting to reduce it by increments of $10 million, to a final $722 million — or $25 million more than our formal fallback position; Brezhnev quit before we did. (It was not a famous victory, amounting to less than $1 million a year over the duration of the agreements.) As in the Azores with Pompidou, my ignorance of the subject matter turned into a negotiating asset because it made it impossible for me to be flexible. Nothing so encourages firmness as lack of an alternative. James Lynn, Under Secretary of Commerce, who had joined our delegation, provided the impetus with endlessly ingenious formulas.

In the light of this progress, Nixon and I were dumbfounded when, in August, the Soviets suddenly placed an exit tax on Jewish emigration. Starting in 1969, we had begun to make overtures to Moscow to ease Jewish emigration, emphasizing that such a policy would improve the atmosphere of US–Soviet relations. We did so privately, believing that public confrontation would defeat our ends. We had no great hopes of success. Somewhat to our surprise, Jewish emigration increased from 400 a year in 1968 to 35,000 in 1973, parallel with the improvement in US–Soviet relations. As the total figures increased I turned also to hardship cases — individuals denied visas or arrested or harassed for various offenses that the West would consider political. I privately handed Dobrynin from time to time long lists of Soviet Jewish "refuseniks," or prisoners of conscience, given to me by American Jewish groups coordinating the public effort. I gave these to him "unofficially"; I never asked for a formal reply. In the last year for which I have figures (which was 1973), some 550 out of 800 hardship cases were then quietly released by these methods. The Panovs, for example, were released somewhat later when I made a special appeal to Dobrynin.

The 1972 exit tax was inexplicable in this context; it threatened to reverse a hopeful trend, and for no self-evident purpose. I have never heard a satisfactory explanation. The most plausible is that panicked by the expulsion of their advisers from Egypt, the Soviets decided to take no further chances with their relations with the Arabs. Dobrynin claimed that the decision was made not in the Politburo but by the relevant ministry on its own. It seems unlikely but is not totally impossible; foreign governments, particularly totalitarian ones, always appear more homogeneous than one's own but may not be.

Whatever the motive, the exit tax provoked outrage that focused on the Administration's decision to open up East-West trade. On October 4, Senator Henry M. Jackson and seventy-one cosponsors introduced an amendment making the granting of MFN status dependent on increased emigration. Three-quarters of both houses endorsed it.

But old habits die hard. On October 21, three days after the trade package with the USSR — the Lend-Lease settlement and the MFN clause — was signed, the *Washington Post* was still grousing about our tendency to use trade as a lever on Vietnam. The *Post* maintained its opposition to linkage: "Regardless, the trade agreement can stand by itself. We salute Mr. Nixon and Mr. Brezhnev for acting to their countries' mutual benefit." The *Wall Street Journal* wrote in an October 20 editorial that "the principle of expanded trade between the two countries and of expanded trade and contact between the United States and other Communist nations is nonetheless a worthy principle."

Almost imperceptibly, however, attitudes were beginning to change. Now that Nixon had embraced East-West trade, some of its former acolytes developed second thoughts, apparently on the theory that if Nixon went along with an idea it needed reexamination. For four years the *New York Times* had castigated the Administration for making trade with the Soviets depend on changes in their international conduct. As late as September 13, 1972, the *Times* thought that expanded trade "is sufficiently beneficial to both sides that it ought to be considered . . . on its own merits, independent of particular secondary disputes in other areas." Less than a month later, however, it was edging up to the proposition that we should seek to link trade with changes in the Soviet *domestic* structure — a far more ambitious form of linkage. On October 6 its editorialist was still dubious about the prospects of using economic pressure for domestic change, but warned the "realists in the Kremlin" to take heed of American public opinion. But by November 25 the *Times* had virtually reversed its position: "it will be a serious mistake if American business, the Nixon Administration or, for that matter, Soviet officials, become so eager to expand Soviet-American trade as to forget the continuing sensitivity of the American people — and of Congress — to Soviet political behavior both inside and outside the U.S.S.R.'s borders." The *Washington Post*, which had once denounced trade discrimination against Communist countries as a "costly anachronism" and "cold-war thinking," now praised the Jackson amendment and was soon to urge that MFN status be detached from the trade bill until the Soviets permitted Jewish emigration.[2]

In 1972 these were still distant squalls on an otherwise serene horizon. On the whole, US–Soviet relations were at their best in many years. The Berlin settlement, the SALT agreement, Soviet restraint in the Mideast and in Vietnam, and the wide range of cooperative technical agreements and ongoing negotiations augured well. Yet the Nixon Administration's carefully calculated approach to East-West trade was to run into increasingly strident opposition from the right over the next few years, just as it had been attacked by the left in the previous period. And most ironically the right's traditional anti-Communism found an ally in the left's antipathy to Nixon and growing concern with human rights.

European Attitudes

THERE was yet another constituency to be heard from after the Moscow summit: our European allies. For over three years, at every meeting with every European leader, they had pressed us toward negotiation with the Soviets. They had been lukewarm about linkage, far ahead of us in East-West trade, eager for the European Security Conference, increasingly impatient to start negotiations with respect to mutual and balanced force reductions. Tactfully — but also publicly — they had let it be known that they thought we were too slow in improving our relations with Moscow and that we were running needless risks of war.

Suddenly, now that we had followed their advice, the Europeans revealed their schizophrenia. We heard that some Europeans complained about the "Basic Principles of US–Soviet Relations" because of the use of the phrase "peaceful coexistence" — an astonishing criticism considering that the similar declaration signed by France and in the German treaties went far beyond our formulations. There was disquiet that some of our principles of restraint preempted the European Security Conference — that is, that we had agreed to what our allies wanted to give away in their own name.

These criticisms did not come from heads of government, all of whom wrote warmly congratulatory letters (which may or may not have accorded with their private views). But there was an influential stratum of middle-level officials and publicists who gave vent to a lingering uneasiness, which reflected in part Europe's inability to articulate its own objectives. At a time when the United States was focusing on devising new relationships with Moscow and Peking, the Europeans were unable to reach a consensus on how to organize a new Community. In such circumstances it was understandable, if uncharitable, that they should find a convenient ground for unity in complaining of our alleged collusion with the Soviet Union. Apprehensions about our new cooperation in several technical fields with the Soviets combined with fears about our general propensity to reduce overseas commitments, a tendency more evident than ever in an election year in which the challenger was George McGovern.

On August 21 I wrote Nixon that the situation was remediable:

The media and European publics are unaware of your continuous confidential exchanges with Heath, Brandt, and Pompidou. In their replies to your post-Summit messages, they all have shown confidence in your European policies and in the benefits for their countries from a more cooperative relationship between us and the Soviets. This we cannot advertise, of course. But our problem is less with these leaders than with the lower officials and political observers in Europe. . . .

The requirement to convince these people that we are not going to withdraw from Europe is a continuing one. . . . We will have to pay unusually close attention to the views of our major allies and develop positions for these negotiations which they feel will not damage their security.

Equally important, we will need to explain our decisions. At some point you may want to consider another round of personal discussions to accomplish this.

The root dilemma was that whatever course we chose, whether confrontation or conciliation, would run up against the reality that Atlantic relations had reached a plateau. The postwar generation's goals of security and prosperity had substantially been met. Remaining was a residue of tactical problems imposed by events; there was lacking an agreed strategy for either confrontation or conciliation, for either long-term security or the attainment of other long-range purposes. These would now have to grow out of a dialogue with allies much better able to insist on their own perceptions than ever before.

In the summer of 1972 we could do no more than maintain the dialogue on the tactical level. I had extensive meetings with Helmut Schmidt (then German Finance Minister), Sir Burke Trend, the British Cabinet Secretary, and Michel Debré and Maurice Schumann, French Defense and Foreign Minister respectively. We achieved understanding for our current policies, but all allied visitors to Washington agreed that the Atlantic relationship needed a fresh impetus. And Nixon as well as I believed deeply that whatever we achieved in negotiations with adversaries, our priority was to devote ourselves to strengthening the cohesion and advancing the common purposes of the free peoples. It was another reason to get Vietnam finally behind us. A new generation had come to take security for granted and saw economic progress as inevitable. It was time to match our 1972 summits with Communist leaders with demonstrative reaffirmation of our Alliance commitments and a redefinition of Alliance purposes. Only thus would we be able to judge individual negotiations with the East and reestablish confidence in each other's ultimate goals. It would provide a sense of direction and pride for the community of free peoples. Such was the origin of the Year of Europe that we undertook in 1973.

XXX

Sadat Expels the Soviets

T HE Moscow summit had one further important consequence: Anwar Sadat's expulsion of the Soviet Union from Egypt in July 1972.

Even before the summit, Nixon, like me, was aware of Sadat's mounting disillusionment with the Soviet Union. For all Egypt's dependence on Soviet military support, the USSR had failed to bring about any progress toward a settlement or Israeli withdrawal from Arab territory. Sadat himself had been in Moscow in February and April. Between those two visits, Cairo had opened a secret channel to us. This was one of the factors in our determination to ensure that the Moscow summit communiqué remained insipid on the Middle East, to see what other results our strategy might produce. We were not to know until later how well our strategy had worked. To trace this momentous change in the Middle East, it is necessary to go back almost two years.

The Death of Nasser

T HE end of 1970 was in a way a turning point in the Middle East, though we did not know it then. The Jordan crisis and even the tensions along the Suez Canal were stages in the evolution of Arab perception that the key to a Middle East settlement lay in Washington, not in Moscow. But perhaps the most decisive event was the death of Gamal Abdel Nasser and the accession to power of Anwar Sadat.

Anwar el-Sadat was then little known to us. He was one of the original band of army officers who overthrew King Farouk in 1952; but through the years he was not considered a major figure by our experts. At first, it was not even clear that he would be made the President of Egypt in his own right. Anyone succeeding after the death of so towering a personality as Nasser would have a hard time filling his shoes; in addition, in the case of Sadat the outside world misjudged him because of his informal oratorical style and his village origin, as well as his relatively minor role in Egyptian politics under Nasser. Nasser died on September 28, 1970, when I was with the President on his Mediterranean trip. A day later, a journalist asked me about Sadat. I said I thought he was an interim figure who would not last more than a few weeks. That was among my wildest misjudgments! Over the course of 1971 Sadat would gradually outmaneuver his opponents, accomplishing in May a stunning purge of a formidable group of pro-Soviet rivals who had been plotting to eliminate him. Gradually he established his domestic position and his international freedom of action. Few outsiders even then (certainly not I) understood with what courage, vision, and determination he would later move his country and his region toward a revolution in international affairs, and thus emerge as one of the great leaders of our period. (Another less noticed though significant result of the autumn of crises was the accession of Hafez Asad to power in Syria in November 1970. Less visionary than Sadat, he nevertheless gave Syria unprecedented stability and, against the background of the turbulent history of his people, emerged as a leader of courage and relative moderation.)

Policies well established in our government tend to appear (and sometimes to be) impervious to change. Typically enough, the change of leaders in Egypt seemed to bring no alteration in the State Department's desire to push the diplomatic initiative it had earlier devised. The Department's efforts had stalemated in 1969; they had been revived in June 1970 with the US proposal of a standstill cease-fire along the Suez Canal, only to be immediately submerged again by Nasser's violations of the standstill agreement and the Jordan crisis. At the end of 1970, the initiative was picked up again as if nothing had happened in the interval. That positions had probably hardened and that no new element had been added were not regarded as reasons to forgo the eager diplomacy.

By the end of December 1970, the State Department — buttressed by a reassuring letter of December 3 to Mrs. Meir, urged on Nixon by Rogers — finally managed to persuade the Israelis to return to the Jarring negotiations, from which they had bowed out in September because of Egypt's violations of the standstill cease-fire. But even before Israeli agreement had been secured, Joe Sisco was already sending instructions — without White House clearance — that urged Jarring to renew his mediating mission along the lines of our proposals of 1969 on final borders and peace terms (the Rogers Plan). Sisco had no reason to believe that the parties were about to compromise their heretofore irreconcilable positions, but, as he told me in early January, not much would be lost if Jarring at least made a try. A diplomat should not be faulted for leaving room for the miraculous.

Pacified by a new $90 million American arms package approved by Nixon in October, the Israelis seized the initiative in early 1971 by inviting Jarring to begin his mission with a journey to Israel. Immediately, Jarring faced the problem that had stalemated negotiations the year before: Israel insisted on "peace"; Egypt on withdrawal. The

Israelis handed the Swedish mediator on January 8 a paper listing the "essentials of peace" — including the ending of belligerency, terrorism, economic blockade, and boycott, and establishment of "good neighborly relations and cooperation." In return, Israel sought "secure, recognized, and agreed boundaries" with suitable security provisions — in other words, Israel proposed to acquire Egyptian territory as part of the peace process. Nothing, in short, had changed in the standard Israeli position.

Jarring passed the Israeli document to the Egyptians on January 13. Cairo responded a few days later with a document reiterating the standard Egyptian position, which called for a full Israeli withdrawal to the 1967 boundaries and for Israel to repudiate the policy of "territorial expansion." In a desperate maneuver to reconcile the incompatible by procedural gimmick, Jarring "softened" the Egyptian paper before passing it to the Israelis for their comment; he omitted some of Cairo's more offensive preambular language, which had dismissed the Israeli paper as adding "no new element" to previous Israeli positions. Jarring was attempting to calm suspicions; his tactics achieved the opposite result. As part of the propaganda war that Egypt and Israel were waging against each other, each side eventually leaked its position to the press. It could not have helped the Israelis' confidence when they saw in the press a different version of the Egyptian paper from what they had officially received from Jarring.

As I had predicted, the result of the first round of Jarring talks was a deadlock. Joe Sisco told me on January 21 that he had not expected much more; the purpose of the effort, he now said, was to encourage the Egyptians to renew the cease-fire when it expired at the beginning of February. It did achieve this purpose, but within two weeks Jarring, with State Department encouragement, was putting forward substantive ideas of his own in an effort to break the deadlock.

The scenario we were witnessing was an exact replay of 1969 — activity for its own sake amid self-generated deadlines that could be met only by papering over irreconcilable differences that, in turn, made a blowup all the more inevitable. Drawing on the papers traded in January, Jarring presented a new proposal to both parties on February 8, asking Israel to withdraw to the 1967 border with Egypt (subject to practical security arrangements) and Egypt to sign a peace agreement with Israel. The Israelis were furious; they saw Jarring's paper (with good reason) as based on the Rogers Plan of 1969, which they had rejected then; they also challenged Jarring's mandate to put forward ideas of his own rather than serve as a courier and confine himself to asking questions. To Israel, the Jarring paper was not only objectionable in substance; the mere fact of its presentation obviated, in Israeli minds, any need for Sadat to respond to the Israeli position that had focused on the "peace" provisions.

All this diplomacy was conducted without any real coordination with the White House. For example, Jarring presented his own paper to the two parties on the very day of a Senior Review Group meeting that I had convened presumably to discuss future strategy. Also, a series of important communications in January between Secretary Rogers and Egyptian Foreign Minister Mahmoud Riad were not shown to the White House until after the fact — a procedure my able staff expert Hal Saunders did his best to monitor. These communications included Rogers's assurance to Riad that the United States would make "an all-out effort" to secure a settlement in 1971 — for which there was no White House support at all — on the basis of the Rogers Plan. If the Israelis were inflamed by the substance of Jarring's presentations, the Egyptians would soon grow disillusioned when the proposals we had encouraged Jarring to offer received little US support. Both sides were now angry at us, as the deadlock of 1969 repeated itself. In late February, Jarring's explorations foundered on the Israeli refusal to accept the principle of return to the 1967 borders and the Egyptian insistence on such a principle. Jarring had made some progress, however; Egypt had agreed to a peace agreement, rather than a mere declaration of non-belligerency, if Israel returned to the 1967 borders. But since that was adamantly refused, the Jarring mission was in effect over.

There was some sentiment in the US government for imposing the Rogers Plan on the Israelis. But the President had no stomach for it in the middle of the Laotian crisis. And it made no strategic sense. As long as Egypt was in effect a Soviet military base, we could have no incentive to turn on an ally on behalf of a Soviet client. This is why I was always opposed to comprehensive solutions that would be rejected by both parties and that could only serve Soviet ends by either demonstrating our impotence or being turned into a showcase of what could be exacted by Moscow's pressure. My aim was to produce a stalemate until Moscow urged compromise or until, even better, some moderate Arab regime decided that the route to progress was through Washington.

In fact, had we been more finely attuned to the subtleties of Mideast diplomacy we might have discerned the first hints of fundamental changes in the Egyptian position. In a speech to the Egyptian Parliament on February 4, in which he accepted an extension of the cease-fire, Sadat had surfaced the idea of an interim agreement: a partial Israeli withdrawal from the Suez Canal, permitting the reopening of the Canal, as the "first stage of a timetable which will be prepared later to implement the other provisions of the Security Council resolution [242]." And as noted, Egypt's February 15 reply to Jarring included, for the first time, the willingness to sign a peace agreement with Israel. (Of course, it was conditioned on Israeli withdrawal to the 1967 borders, which Israel would not accept.)

Sadat considered these steps of February 1971 as the beginning of his long, arduous, and extraordinary journey toward peace.[1] His proposal to discuss an interim agreement along the Suez Canal became the focus of diplomacy in 1971 — and a version of the concept eventually was reflected in the January 1974 disengagement agreement that began the peace process after the 1973 war. His willingness to sign a peace agreement with Israel was to become a dramatic reality eight years later. Our perception of the significance of Sadat's moves then was unfortunately still beclouded by the presence of over 15,000 Soviet troops in Egypt and his signing of a Friendship Treaty with Moscow.

The Idea of an Interim Settlement

THE concept of an interim withdrawal from the Canal had been born in the fertile mind of Israeli Defense Minister Moshe Dayan during the late summer of 1970. In Dayan's formulation it required a mutual withdrawal or thinning-out of military forces on *both* sides of the Canal. Dayan's concept was not then an official proposal of the Israeli government, however, and when Dayan visited Washington in December 1970 he was obliged to disavow it except as a "theoretical alternative" to the standard Israeli position, which was that Israel would not grant Egypt the boon of a reopened Suez Canal until a final peace agreement. In fact, Mrs. Meir had asked me what I thought of Dayan's idea when I met with her at the Shoreham Hotel on October 25, 1970, during her visit to Washington in conjunction with the UN's twenty-fifth anniversary. I told her that I had not studied it in detail but it seemed a good idea. The proposal was revived at the beginning of 1971 when an Egyptian general on January 11 approached the head of our mission in Cairo and, speaking in Sadat's name, expressed interest in Dayan's proposal. Next, Sadat repeated it publicly in his February 4 speech.

The reason why an interim accord never materialized in 1971 was the same that thwarted the comprehensive approach: The two sides had radically different purposes in pursuing it. Egypt wanted an interim agreement as the first step toward a total withdrawal; Dayan put it forward as a means to forestall that prospect. To Dayan, a partial disengagement had the attraction of both short-circuiting the Jarring diplomacy and reducing the negotiation to a limited scheme that could be more easily managed by Israel's domestic policies. Above all, it would postpone discussion of the final borders. If implemented, an interim accord would stabilize the Suez front and reduce the possibility of hostilities; Egypt would be less likely to launch a war if it stood to lose the economic benefit of the reopened Canal. This reasoning persuaded Mrs. Meir to accept Sadat's suggestion of a pullback along the Canal in a speech on February 9.

To Sadat, however, disengagement included a much more extensive

Israeli withdrawal than the limited pullback Dayan envisioned. Dayan proposed a withdrawal or thinning out of forces on *each* side; Sadat suggested in *Newsweek* of February 22 that the Israelis should pull back to "a line behind El Arish" (more than halfway across the Sinai) and allow a UN force to take over Sharm el-Sheikh. Sadat also insisted that Egyptian military forces had to cross the Canal, where Dayan saw it as a *mutual* withdrawal *from* the Canal. Most important, Sadat made the agreement conditional on an agreed timetable for total withdrawal along the lines of the Rogers Plan. This the Israelis totally rejected.

Disengagement had no chance of success as long as it had to be negotiated together with an overall settlement. And if there was no chance of success, I saw no reason for us to involve ourselves. Our ace in the hole was that if we played our cards right, we could produce tangible progress in diplomacy while the Soviets could promise only help in war. But for this strategy to work we had to be effectual; we could not waste our prestige on futile maneuvers. To succeed, an interim agreement therefore had to be separated from the comprehensive settlement; if they were linked, we would merely dissipate our influence by chasing a mirage that had all the difficulties of the comprehensive schemes it purported to replace and that we were no more able to produce than Moscow.

Nevertheless, in the absence of any other alternative, the State Department energetically picked up the interim agreement as soon as Jarring's mission collapsed at the end of February. State in the first week of March began privately discussing the merits of a possible interim step with the Israelis, broaching specific ideas with Rabin as early as March 6. The speed with which State moved — only eight days after Israel, on February 26, had rejected the Jarring proposal and with barely time for an assessment on next steps — could hardly alleviate Israel's congenital apprehension that it would again be rushed headlong into a diplomacy which would link an interim with a final settlement along lines it opposed. In the absence of agreed objectives it proved impossible to bridge the gulf between the two sides' conceptions by procedural legerdemain. At various times each side was led to believe that we sympathized with its version of the interim concept; disillusionment, frustration, and stalemate were the inevitable result.

My idea was to use an interim agreement to break the impasse. Once achieved, such a step would ease the way to further advances. But I also parted company with those in Israel who regarded an interim disengagement as a way to avoid any further withdrawals. On the contrary, the chief utility of a disengagement along the Canal in my view was to launch a process of negotiation that might ultimately lead to peace with some or all of the Arab states. (This was, of course, the concept of "step-by-step" progress, which unlocked the peace process in 1974.)

Nixon had given me a mandate to explore what was feasible but not to negotiate it. In pursuit of this, I broached the idea of a separate interim agreement with Dobrynin on March 22, 1971, to see whether the Soviets were prepared to abandon the linkage to a detailed comprehensive plan. I pursued the concept with Abba Eban in mid-March and with Egypt's representative in Washington, Ashraf Ghorbal, on March 25. My approach was to use an initial step to get the process of withdrawal and mutual acceptance under way even without a commitment to ultimate goals. Since Dobrynin was unwilling to discuss my approach, negotiations returned to regular channels and there, not unexpectedly, it turned out that the parties were not yet ready to agree on *even* a limited accord.

The Israelis in mid-April produced a paper with the details of their approach: an Israeli pullback of unspecified (but short) distance from the Canal; *no* Egyptian troops to cross the Canal; some thinning out of Egyptian troops on the Egyptian side of the Canal; a cease-fire of indefinite duration; and *no* linkage whatever to further withdrawals. Rabin, in fact, showed me the proposed Israeli position paper before surfacing it at the State Department. I persuaded him to convince his government to modify some elements that would have made the negotiation a total nonstarter. As it was, the final Israeli version was certain to be unacceptable to Egypt.

Rogers was nevertheless determined to accelerate what he believed to be a hopeful venture. On April 19 he secured the President's authorization to visit several Middle East countries to find common ground between Egypt and Israel on an interim settlement. I expressed my doubts to Nixon in a memorandum of April 22:

> It would be especially worrisome were his presence to accelerate the diplomatic process and further to intensify the current stalemate between Israel, the Arabs, the US and USSR. For this reason, I believe it is important that you caution the Secretary not to depart from the current state of play without keeping us fully apprised and receiving your specific approval for any departure from the status quo.

But I could do no more than warn. Since he was unwilling to confront his Secretary on this issue, Nixon had no way to enforce the above strictures even if he agreed with my analysis, which was far from a foregone conclusion.

Rogers visited the Middle East at the beginning of May 1971. His discussions in Israel and Egypt made the fundamental differences explicit. Sadat wanted Egyptian troops to be able to take up positions on *both* sides of the Canal; Israel violently disagreed (except for Dayan, who thought, wisely, that some Egyptian police presence might be permissible). Sadat insisted on an Israeli commitment in principle to the 1967 borders linked to the Canal accord. Israel would make no such commitment (although Dayan told Sisco that he was one of the few in the government who did see the interim step as part of a continuing peace process). Rogers's trip had no result except to get Dayan in some trouble at home when the differences between his government's position and his own became publicly known. In an astute analysis, Hal Saunders wrote me on May 19 that he feared Sadat might have been counting on Rogers to deliver a Canal agreement; Sadat, who had just carried out the massive purge of pro-Soviet elements in his government, probably needed diplomatic progress "to make his policy work and survive politically. . . . The door is open for a major letdown if there is no movement now." When Rogers sent Nixon a report on his trip, I attached my own analysis in the same vein:

> The sobering thought in all of this is that, while Sadat moved [to purge his opponents] mainly to secure his own position, the US has become unintentionally but closely involved. By coincidence of timing, the Secretary's visit and the expectation of a Canal settlement will be linked in many minds with Sadat's big move. If he cannot demonstrate success for his policy of seeking negotiation, the US — regardless of the merits of the case — may bear much of the onus.

The Phantom Memorandum

A T this point, the quest for an interim agreement turned into a detective story. It was becoming increasingly difficult to find out who was proposing what to whom. The White House could no longer tell whether the parties were putting forward their own views or else interpretations of ours to force us into supporting publicly what we had told them privately. In the process, some of our diplomats carried out an extraordinary maneuver of which the White House was completely ignorant. In a follow-up to the Rogers trip, our diplomatic representative in Cairo helped the Egyptians draft their own counterproposal on an interim settlement. The incident not only revealed the State Department's bias toward an interim accord that was a stage toward an agreed (and unattainable) comprehensive settlement; more worrisome, the American inability to implement the proposal (after the Egyptians had put it forward with what they felt was our blessing) magnified Cairo's disillusionment with American diplomacy; they thought us either incompetent or deceitful.

Only three weeks afterward did the White House have any inkling of what had taken place in Cairo. Evidently what happened was that Donald Bergus, head of the US Interests Section in Cairo,* met with Egyptian Foreign Ministry officials on May 23 to discuss an Egyptian

---

* This was not an embassy since we officially had no diplomatic relations.

position paper. When the Egyptians sought Bergus's advice, he apparently wrote out detailed ideas and left his notes with the Egyptians. Bergus's draft, when it became known, bore a striking resemblance to the formal Egyptian proposal that was ultimately submitted to us by Sadat on June 4. It was an extraordinary procedure, which I remain convinced no professional diplomat of Bergus's experience would have undertaken without authorization from higher-ups. It was also bound to fail and leave us out on a limb. When word of the Bergus memorandum later leaked to the press, the State Department disavowed it, saying that it did not represent an official US position.[2] The Egyptians were now doubly angry, stung by the disavowal and bitter that we could not deliver on what they had assumed represented our own idea. The Israelis were enraged that we were encouraging Egypt to put forward terms which they had told us they would never accept. I was annoyed — to put it mildly — that none of these moves had been disclosed to the President of the United States.

Then came another bombshell, of even greater importance. On May 27, 1971, Sadat signed a Friendship Treaty with the Soviet Union. In his autobiography, Sadat treats this agreement as a kind of sop to Soviet sensibilities after he had purged and jailed all the top pro-Soviet elements in Egyptian politics.[3] I now believe this to have been the principal motive — though none of us understood Sadat at the time. But surely it reflected also a new Soviet boldness and Sadat's frustration with erratic American diplomacy. It was bound to alarm the Israelis and make an interim settlement even harder to achieve. Not surprisingly, State had a more sanguine assessment. Rogers reported to Nixon that the Friendship Treaty "strengthens [Sadat's] hand vis-à-vis his own military by its emphasis on long-range military support. It could help maintain [his] flexibility on a Suez Canal settlement." (State and the CIA made exactly the same analysis of the Soviet Union's Friendship Treaty with India, signed less than three months later.) I wrote the President on May 31 that I disagreed with Rogers's assessment:

The Egyptian Army is dependent on Soviet support. In turn, Sadat is at the moment dependent on his military for his base of power, having purged the party and the bureaucracy. Rather than strengthening Sadat's flexibility with respect to negotiating the Canal settlement, the treaty could give the Soviet Union a veto over the future negotiations. Thus, whatever the outcome of the negotiations — and after all, the Soviets are the chief beneficiaries of a Suez settlement — recent events may have enhanced Soviet long-term influence. Certainly the Soviets are committed to engage themselves as never before in case of resumption of hostilities.

I cannot tell whose interpretation Nixon accepted. My only clue is that in the margin of my memorandum he expressed his worry that "we must not allow this to be a pretext for escalation of arms to Israel. We should assist only in response to incontrovertible evidence of Soviet military aid which we evaluate as significantly changing the balance of power.'' Nixon said more or less the same thing in a news conference on June 1. We were in danger of confrontation with Egypt, Israel, and the Soviet Union simultaneously.

Not knowing Sadat, I had to conclude that he was still playing Nasser's game. Furthermore, Sadat's impatience was becoming evident in repeated declarations that 1971 had to be the "year of decision" in the Middle East. Our strategy had to be to frustrate any Egyptian policy based on military threats and collusion with the Soviet Union. Therefore Sadat's Friendship Treaty with the Soviets, whatever its motives, did not galvanize us to help him as he might have hoped. On the contrary, it reinforced my determination to slow down the process even further to demonstrate that Soviet threats and treaties could not be decisive.

Nevertheless, the State Department remained eager to press ahead. On the day I left for Asia (and China), July 1, Sisco sounded out Ambassador Rabin about a visit to Israel to discuss an interim settlement. (It was hardly a coincidence that this new State Department initiative came when I was leaving for a twelve-day absence abroad!) While in Asia, I managed, as I have described, to persuade the President to hold any major Mideast decisions in abeyance until I returned; he used the pretext of calling an NSC meeting on the subject for July 16, which any new initiatives would have to await. The July 16 NSC meeting, when it convened, was characterized by Presidential complaints about the pro-Israel lobby; Laird's objections to further aircraft supply to Israel; and Rogers's eagerness for Sisco to visit Israel. At the end of the meeting, Nixon authorized the Sisco trip to explore whether there was any flexibility in the Israeli position. There was not. His trip produced so little that Sisco did not even bother to stop in Cairo on the way home.

At this point, after my trip to China and the collapse of the State Department's pursuit of an interim settlement, I became operationally active in Middle East diplomacy for the first time.

Becoming Involved

W HAT finally got me involved in the execution of Middle East diplomacy was that Nixon did not believe he could risk recurrent crises in the Middle East in an election year. He therefore asked me to step in, if only to keep things quiet. My first move was to explore whether the Soviets were in fact willing to moderate their proposals; if not, I intended to draw them into protracted and inconclusive negotiations until either they or some Arab country changed their position. The Soviets were still complaining about unilateral American diplomacy in the Middle East, which reflected not so much Moscow's resentment at being left out as its eagerness to dramatize our failure to bring any progress. I therefore temporized in my talks with Dobrynin in the first half of 1971. But after the July 15 China announcement we held out the prospect of superpower cooperation in the Middle East in a soothing letter that Nixon sent to Brezhnev on August 5. Nixon had made a similar suggestion in a news conference the night before. Dobrynin asked me on August 5 what we had in mind. Having no concrete ideas in mind (nor yet a mandate to offer any), I said it simply reflected our general readiness for broadly based negotiations. Brezhnev replied to Nixon on September 7, reaffirming Soviet interest in a Middle East settlement. Brezhnev expressed dismay that we had broken off earlier direct dealings with Moscow on the subject.

These Soviet overtures came against the backdrop of a step-up of Soviet military activity in Egypt. For example, in September Israel shot down a Soviet attack bomber — an SU-7 jet — over the Canal; an Egyptian surface-to-air missile destroyed an Israeli reconnaissance plane. Egypt had moved some of its SAM sites even farther forward; this could not have been done without Soviet concurrence and cooperation. At the same time, the State Department was hinting that we would delay further aircraft shipments to Israel unless Israel showed greater flexibility. Mrs. Meir wrote Nixon on September 17, reiterating Israel's concept of an interim settlement, but also expressing "grave concern" over the stoppage of delivery of Phantom jets to Israel at a time of an increasing Soviet military presence in Egypt.

If a negotiation on an interim accord was to break, rather than harden, this impasse, perhaps a new tack was required. I wrote Nixon on September 23:

> The problem with the interim settlement is that too much has been attempted. The initial idea was simply a mutual thinning out on both sides. From that it mushroomed to Sadat insisting on moving his forces to the key Sinai passes. To achieve that, the US would have to press Israel almost as hard as to get an overall settlement.
>
> The main hope now, it would seem to me, would be to reduce Egyptian expectations to a point where changes that might realistically be expected in Israel's position could produce an understanding. Because official positions are tied to greater expectations, it may be that the only way of achieving this — if it were possible at all — would be through less official exchanges to see what might be possible.

My mention of "less official exchanges" was prompted by, among other things, a Soviet overture to me. Dobrynin forewarned me on September 20 that Gromyko, when he met with the President on September 29, would propose putting the Mideast issue into the special Channel. I warned Dobrynin, in turn, that at best this would be a slow process, requiring some exploration to see if it was worthwhile. The Middle East was much more complex than even Berlin (which we had just concluded successfully in the Channel); the factors were much less in our control and the indiscretion of the parties involved was of epic proportion.

The prospect of another backchannel negotiation would also require contact with Egypt. I had had a talk on September 16 with a former student of mine, Ali Hamdi el-Gammal, director of the prestigious Cairo newspaper *Al Ahram,* who tried to set up a confidential meeting between me and his chief editor, Mohamed Heikal, a confidant of Sadat. Gammal invited me to Cairo; he discussed as an alternative taking up the offer of a private business executive to host a meeting at his home between me and Heikal.* Then, in early October, Yitzhak Rabin, too, urged me to get involved personally in the interim accord negotiations; he told me confidentially that Israel might be more flexible in its terms if I were involved and it had Presidential assurances that the demands would not be open-ended. I told both Gammal and Rabin that if I decided to engage myself, their respective governments would have to face up to the hard decisions required. Egypt would have to give up its precondition of a commitment to total withdrawal; Israel would have to be prepared to put forward a reasonable package. The only point in staking Presidential prestige was to make progress.

By this time, the President himself was pushing the idea of my more active involvement — if only for the damage-limiting purpose of keeping things quiet until after the 1972 election. When Foreign Minister Gromyko met with Nixon on September 29, 1971, we went through the usual ritual by which a larger meeting including State Department participants was cut short so that Nixon and Gromyko could then talk privately in his hideaway in the Executive Office Building. Nixon accepted Gromyko's suggestion that Dobrynin and I undertake a serious exploration of Middle East issues — though not without linking it again to Soviet help on Vietnam.

I subsequently visited the Soviet Embassy on the evening of September 30 for a two-hour private meeting with Gromyko. I repeated to him the difficulties of settling the Middle East in the Channel, in contrast to Berlin. On Berlin, the parties affected all wanted an agreement; this was less than clear in the Middle East. I pointed out that I did not want to get involved on behalf of the President unless there was a good chance of achieving an agreement; this was why I proposed exploratory talks first. The real issue was not the detail of whether the Israelis withdrew forty kilometers or twenty kilometers from the Canal, but the

---

* Heikal later turned down the invitation and the meeting never took place. Not until the spring of 1972 did Cairo find a reliable channel.

fact that an Israeli withdrawal would be of tremendous symbolic significance. Egypt had to decide whether it wanted substance or theory; there was no possibility of agreeing now on the shape of the final settlement. The more theology we included in the interim settlement, the less likely it would be achieved. Indeed, if I wanted to waste time, I would urge that the interim accord be specific about the final settlement because it would never be agreed to by the parties. If the President and I were to get involved, it would have to be on the basis that progress was possible; this meant to me that there should be some vagueness as to the final destination.

Gromyko rejected this approach. He insisted that an interim agreement be linked specifically and in detail to a final settlement. He argued that there could be no first stage until a final settlement had been worked out and a precise timetable had been established. The final settlement in the Soviet view should occur no later than a year after the interim agreement, though the length of the interval was negotiable. (Gromyko did not explain what value an interim agreement had in these circumstances.) He maintained that a final settlement had to involve total Israeli withdrawal from the occupied territories of all Arab states. In other words, the Soviet Union was still backing the maximum Arab position, oblivious to the fact that in such circumstances Israel had no motive for an interim agreement and we had no incentive to proceed jointly with Moscow. There was no sign of the Soviet Union's willingness to press its clients toward flexibility. However, Gromyko had put forward to Nixon in the hideaway office a proposal that on the surface was a tantalizing modification of the standard Soviet position. In the event of a comprehensive settlement, Gromyko said, the Soviets would be prepared to withdraw their forces from the Middle East, join in an arms embargo in the area, and participate in guarantees of a settlement. But as usual there was less to these proposals than met the eye. We were still being asked to force Israel to accept borders it considered incompatible with its security. The promised withdrawal of Soviet forces would come at the *end* of the entire process; in other words, we would have to execute our entire contribution to this arrangement before the Soviets had to do anything. And even then the Soviets made their withdrawal from Egypt conditional on the withdrawal of American advisers from Iran. All this at a time when Sadat was threatening to settle the issue by war in 1971 or 1972. (This was one of the reasons why we had reacted so strongly to the Indian assault on Pakistan; we wanted to make sure that the Soviet Union understood that a Soviet-sponsored attack in the Middle East would result in an even sharper response.)

But Gromyko had at least added enough new ingredients to fuel "exploratory" discussions between Dobrynin and me. This in turn would give the Soviets an incentive to keep the Middle East calm over the next year — a strategy that would only magnify Egyptian restlessness with Soviet policy.

With the annual gathering in New York of foreign leaders for the General Assembly, State sprang into action again to try to bridge the gap between Egypt and Israel. Rogers, in a UN speech in early October, unveiled American ideas on an interim Suez Canal agreement. This was coupled with the proposal of "proximity talks," a procedure by which an American diplomat would shuttle between the two delegations housed in nearby hotel rooms in New York. Needless to say, neither Egypt nor Israel expected any good to come out of this since the two sides' positions remained irreconcilable; neither side was likely to be maneuvered into a concession by a hyperactive negotiation. The Israelis especially were concerned that they would again be pressed into a futile diplomatic effort without adequate American assurances on arms supply or final destination; their fears were not eased when Sadat visited Moscow in October and returned with a communiqué that pledged new Soviet efforts to "strengthen" Egypt's military might. (Even Rogers was moved to "deplore" that pledge publicly.)

By the end of 1971, the divisions within our government, the State Department's single-minded pursuit of unattainable goals — and the Soviet Union's lack of imagination — had produced the stalemate for which I had striven by design.

Then, in December 1971, Nixon took a step that began to establish my operational control of Middle East diplomacy. Mrs. Meir visited Nixon on December 2 and the two leaders reached a crucial understanding on both strategy and tactics: The quest for a comprehensive settlement would be abandoned for the time being. (Even the State Department had concluded that the road had come to a dead end.) Instead, the effort would be continued to reach an interim agreement with Egypt. Sisco would conduct the "proximity talks" between Egypt and Israel in frontchannels. But the real negotiations would be carried out between Israeli Ambassador Rabin and me, and also between Dobrynin and me. If progress were made in these backchannels, we could feed the results into the "proximity" forum. In other words, we had finally established in the Middle East the same dual-track approach that characterized our other negotiations. Only the Egyptians were as yet missing; I had every confidence that sooner or later they would join.

Backchannel Explorations

EVEN with the new negotiating channels, I saw no need for haste. First, in early 1972, Sisco and Rabin had to settle the annual question of military aid for Israel in order to avoid the periodic brawls that had resulted from trying, futilely, to keep Israel on a short leash. We had always wound up granting Israel's requests, but only after political disputes at home that did not advance negotiations, yet made the Administration appear impotent. After this was finally settled, Israel, in early February, agreed to State's "proximity talks" — only to have the idea rejected by Egypt. In the meantime, I sought to explore what the Soviets really had in mind. Were the overtures for an interim agreement a device to change the existing diplomatic pattern or to demonstrate our alleged pro-Israeli bias to their clients? Above all, I calculated that the longer the process went on, the more likely Sadat would seek to deal with us directly. The Soviets as intermediaries were definitely our second choice.

The answer was soon forthcoming. I began my discussions with Dobrynin in the middle of January 1972 and quickly confirmed that Gromyko's flexibility had been more apparent than real. The Soviets were still as muscle-bound as they had been all through Nixon's Administration. Inflexibly advocating the maximum Arab program, unwilling to run any risks, they retreated to standard positions even when discussing an interim agreement along the Suez Canal. Dobrynin, like Gromyko, was willing enough to explore a disengagement, provided it was integrally linked to an overall settlement. I summed up Moscow's dilemma again in a memorandum to the President:

> Their client cannot win a war with the Israelis. Therefore a continuation of the present simmering crisis can only lead to one of two situations: either a conviction on the part of the Arabs that their alliance with the Soviet Union is inadequate to produce a settlement, or a war by the Egyptians which would face the Soviets with a decision on military support and a risk out of all proportion to anything that could be achieved.

I suggested a strategy to break the logjam. The most significant element — which later reappeared in some early proposals of the Carter Administration — was an attempt to bridge the gulf between Israel's insistence on border changes and the Arab demand for the 1967 frontiers. The notion was to separate the issue of security from that of sovereignty: Egypt would regain sovereignty over the entire Sinai, but Israel would be permitted to maintain certain defense posts in a defined belt on Egyptian soil. I pursued this in the private channel with the Israelis. Rabin and Dayan accepted the approach and by early in 1972 certain principles had been established: Israel said it would agree to withdraw to the western side of the Sinai passes in return for an agreed cease-fire to last until early 1974; Egypt could cross the Suez Canal with police but no military forces; the linkage to a final settlement would be kept vague; Israel would not interfere with the reopening of the Suez Canal. (Many of these provisions found their way into the first disengagement agreement finally negotiated in January 1974.)

The Soviet Union, meanwhile, was still stuck. Dobrynin indicated in February 1972 that Moscow might be willing to discuss the concept of separating security from sovereignty, but, like Gromyko four months earlier, Moscow retreated as soon as it understood that we might be ready to explore the subject seriously. I now think that it had no understanding of any kind with Cairo that gave it flexibility. Dobrynin never came back to the subject.

During March, Dobrynin was pressing me to formulate a more comprehensive peace program of our own; it would be easier for Moscow, he said, to react to our proposals than to deviate from the Arab position on its own initiative. This was undoubtedly true. At the same time, we already knew what the Arab reaction would be to any proposals endorsed by Israel; they had rejected them often enough publicly. If we put forward a position different from Israel's in a so-called private channel through Moscow, Moscow would use it to demonstrate what could be achieved with its assistance and we would be caught once again in crossfire between the two parties. But if we put forward through Moscow a proposal identical with Israel's, Moscow would use it to show the futility of dealing with us.

My strategy had not changed. Until some Arab state showed a willingness to separate from the Soviets, or the Soviets were prepared to dissociate from the maximum Arab program, we had no reason to modify our policy. The Soviets never managed to square this circle. In the meantime, they increased our disquiet by signing, on April 9, 1972, the Friendship Treaty with Iraq, which was soon followed by a substantial flow of modern military equipment. While negotiating on the basis of maximum terms, the Soviets were also creating the conditions for maximum military pressure.

After the start of Hanoi's Easter offensive on March 30, I interrupted the private Middle East talks with Dobrynin as a sign of displeasure with the Soviet arms shipments that had made the North Vietnamese offensive possible. Exchanges on the Mideast were not resumed until my visit to Moscow, April 20–24, to prepare for the summit. On that occasion Gromyko presented a document for a comprehensive settlement that implied the most rigid interpretation of the concessions he had made during the previous fall. He argued that a separate Egyptian-Israeli negotiation was admissible but only if accompanied by a settlement of the "global" issues. And again, whatever the Soviets promised would not be carried out until every provision of an overall agreement — which Israel would never sign without the most massive American pressure — had been implemented. Gromyko continued to drain the previously offered withdrawal of Soviet military personnel of much of its significance. First, it would not be carried out until a comprehensive settlement had been achieved (in other words, after a process that in our estimate was certain to be so prolonged as to make the agreement nearly meaningless); even then, Soviet troops would stay in Arab countries in proportion to American personnel in Iran. Depending on how that was calculated, there might be no withdrawals at all.

Gromyko then helpfully offered a way around our domestic obstacles. He suggested that we might negotiate an agreement on disengagement along the Suez Canal publicly as long as he and I simultaneously reached a *secret* understanding on the terms of a comprehensive settlement, which would be surfaced and implemented immediately after our 1972 Presidential election. Even with legendary self-confidence and devotion to secrecy, I did not believe that this could possibly work. The suggestion was refused.

The bane of Soviet diplomacy is its persistent quest for maximum advantage. Sometimes the constant pressure erodes resistance; but often it backfires by removing any incentive for a serious dialogue. In the midst of a Vietnam offensive fueled by Soviet arms, buffeted by already massive divisions at home, and facing an election, no President could be tempted by a proposition that imposed on us all the burdens of forcing a settlement on an ally in return for no discernible benefit. And it was based on a wrong estimate of our strategy and our possibilities. The Soviet leaders acted as if their presence in the Arab world were permanent, to be manipulated at will by the Kremlin. Earlier, on March 17, I had pointed out to Dobrynin that their position was not as brilliant as he was wont to picture it; the Kremlin's current policy guaranteed its clients only stalemate, or, in fact, defeat in a war. Dobrynin had replied that Moscow also had the option to increase its military presence in Egypt dramatically. I was skeptical: first, because I was convinced that Moscow would stop well short of committing its own forces in what could easily escalate into a direct confrontation with the United States; second, and principally, because I began to sense that our strategy was beginning to work, at least with respect to Egypt.

Egypt Opens a Secret Channel to the United States

S ADAT had visited Moscow in February 1972. Things were not going smoothly between Egypt and the Soviet Union. On April 8, I felt confident enough to advise Nixon that the Soviet-Egyptian relationship was clearly more reserved than in Nasser's time. We understood that Sadat had asked for advanced weapons and Soviet diplomatic and military support on a scale reminiscent of what was extended to India during its conflict with Pakistan, including help to enable Egypt to build its own arms; he had been given assurances of weapons but no blank check of diplomatic or military support. Egypt was pressuring Moscow, but Moscow had clearly calculated — as we had hoped — that since we had gone to the brink over Pakistan, a challenge to the survival of Israel would create uncontrollable risks. And the Kremlin did not stand to gain from building up in Egypt an arms industry that would drastically reduce Cairo's dependence on Soviet supplies. I told Nixon my impression was that the Soviets were holding Sadat at arm's length, fearful of the risks of all-out support, and awaiting my talks with Dobrynin. As usual, they wanted everything: Egyptian subservience, minimum risk, and the complete Arab program. But diplomacy rarely works that way: Those who grab for everything, who forget that politics is the art of the possible, in the end may lose all.

A more tangible reason for my confidence was that in the first week of April 1972 Egypt had opened a secret channel to the White House.

On April 5, a high Egyptian officer told an American official in Cairo that Egypt was dissatisfied with existing diplomatic channels to the United States. In his government's view it was essential we communicate at the Presidential level, bypassing both foreign ministries. The Egyptians suggested that either Helms or I visit Cairo; alternatively, Hafiz Ismail, my opposite number as national security adviser to President Sadat, might come to Washington. I cannot say that I was shocked or offended by the proposition that both sides bypass the foreign ministers. Indeed, I considered it the precondition of success. When the report of the new Egyptian approach reached me on April 8, I immediately wrote on it a note to Al Haig, my deputy: "Al: How about Ismail to Washington?"

Yet, preoccupied with the Vietnam offensive and then my forthcoming trip to Moscow, we did not respond immediately. We wanted to see what Moscow would have to offer in the Channel. We also heard that Sadat would visit Moscow again at the end of April and we did not propose to give the Egyptian party a response which might leak to the Soviets. Above all, a measured pace fitted in with our strategy of creating in Egypt the maximum restlessness with the status quo. So it was not until April 29, while Sadat was in Moscow, that we finally sent a reply to await him on his return. We said that we were indeed interested in a secret high-level meeting; a representative of President Sadat would be welcome in the United States for that purpose. But no meeting could take place until after the Moscow summit. We calculated that the prospect of a meeting after the summit would serve as a greater incentive for restraint than an earlier talk which in the nature of first contacts was bound to be inconclusive. Two weeks later the Egyptians replied that our proposal was being studied, and that we would receive a formal reply in June after the summit. This fitted in nicely with our strategy.

In the meantime, there were mounting indications that tensions between Egypt and the Soviet Union were growing. Sadat's April visit to Moscow apparently heightened his worry that the Soviet Union might settle for the status quo in the Middle East. Even an airlift of advanced Soviet equipment in April and May did not reduce his underlying uneasiness. On May 22 I sent Nixon my assessment that the relationship between Sadat and the Soviets was now one of a worried client to his patron rather than that of equal partners with confidence in each other.

Later on, I came to know Sadat as one of the few truly outstanding leaders I have met. He possessed that combination of insight and courage which marks a great statesman. He had the boldness to go to a war no one thought he could sustain; the moderation to move to peace immediately afterward; and the wisdom to reverse attitudes hardened by decades. But in 1972 none of this was apparent. Sadat had made many threats that he had not carried out. In the Jarring negotiations he had been more flexible than his predecessor, but he had apparently not yet renounced Nasser's delusion that he could insist on unfulfillable demands because of the backing of Soviet arms. We had no regular dialogue with him. None of our emissaries had ever managed to penetrate the charming manner to discover what Sadat really thought. Until the secret channel opened in April 1972, most of our serious dealings had been through Moscow. My reaction to this overture, therefore, was largely tactical: to continue to bring home to Sadat the futility of his course while opening a dialogue by which we hoped to change it.

This was also the background to our Moscow summit discussions on the Middle East. Because of Vietnam and SALT preoccupations, these came only at the end of the summit, when, as we saw in Chapter XXVIII, in a long-night session, Gromyko and I worked out some "general working principles" for an overall settlement; their vagueness was bound to raise additional questions in Sadat's mind.[4] The principles were weaker than Resolution 242; they stated that border rectifications were possible (omitting the modifier "minor," which had become sacramental in official documents); the formulations were ambiguous about the extent of intended Israeli withdrawals. I have never understood why Gromyko accepted them, unless it was exhaustion — after all, he attended even more meetings than I did in Moscow and worked even longer hours. In all events, the principles quickly found their way into the overcrowded limbo of aborted Middle East schemes — as I had intended.

Gromyko and I also agreed on the text of a final communiqué that did no more than urge a peaceful settlement and endorse the Jarring mission; it offered no concrete guidelines for it or any other negotiations. This bland communiqué was to have historic consequences. It was a "violent shock" to Egypt, Sadat records in his memoirs.[5] It proved to be a decisive blow to his relations with the Soviet Union.

All this time, the Egyptians were being treated to the unnerving experience of our three-tiered diplomacy. They were exchanging messages with us through the secret channel; they were receiving the Soviet version of our summit conversations and my talks with Dobrynin;* and they were exposed to the regular State Department overtures to win Egypt's agreement to enter the proximity talks. It must have been a bewildering set of procedures — though it left Cairo in a better position to know what messages were being passed than either the White House or State. For key State cables were not only not shown to the White House for clearance; so far as I can tell now, records of State talks with key Arabs were not even sent to the White House after the event. We therefore often learned what had been transmitted in State channels only after it had been played back in a reporting telegram from some Arab capital briefed by Cairo. Thus, for example, we did not learn of a secret overture to Cairo for proximity talks until well after the fact, nor did we know of a conversation between Sisco and Prince Sultan of Saudi Arabia in June — in which Sisco sought to engage Sultan's help in persuading Egypt to agree to such talks — until it was mentioned in a report from Riyadh on July 18. Equally, State did not know of our secret channel to Cairo. (I doubt that many textbooks on political science will commend these procedures.)

Strangely enough, except for the nervous strain on the participants, our procedures did no damage. Egypt had, after all, initiated the secret White House contact because it had lost confidence in normal diplomatic procedures. And in June, Cairo turned down the State proposal for proximity talks — without, however, significantly reducing State's legendary dedication to the unattainable.

Sadat was now playing for higher stakes. On July 13, we received an ambiguous message through the secret channel. It reiterated the willingness to send a senior representative to Washington, provided we had something new to propose. In the absence of any different initiative Cairo saw no point in a meeting. The corollary was, of course, that we could produce a high-level Egyptian representative by the simple device of indicating that we were willing to explore new approaches.

Before we could fully assess the implications of this Delphic missive came the July 18, 1972, bombshell of Sadat's announcement that he had terminated the mission of the more than 15,000 Soviet military advisers and experts in Egypt. They were to be withdrawn within a week; military installations and equipment set up in Egypt since 1967 were to become Egyptian property.

The decision came as a complete surprise to Washington. (That day I was on my way to Paris for a secret meeting with the North Vietnamese.) To be sure, my strategy had sought to induce Cairo to lessen its re-

---

*The Soviets did not brief Sadat on the summit conversations until five weeks afterward, which compounded his disillusionment with Soviet policy.[6]

liance on the Soviet Union. I had expected that at some point down the
road, Sadat would be prepared to offer to trade Soviet withdrawal for
progress with us. But, still handicapped by my underestimation of the
Egyptian President, I never guessed that he would settle the issue with
one grand gesture, and unilaterally. My first reaction on hearing the
news was that he had acted impetuously and forfeited an important
negotiating asset, for no return. Two days later I prepared a longer and
more reflective analysis:

It has been apparent in the last two months that the Egyptians have resigned
themselves to the fact that there will be little diplomatic movement on the
Arab-Israeli problem this year because of the US elections. . . . Despite this
apparently rational calculation, Sadat has faced the dilemma of how to avoid
allowing inaction to produce a permanent freeze of the situation. . . . Frustration over the lack of movement on the Arab-Israeli issue has been high in
Cairo.

The US–USSR Summit confirmed the sense that nothing was going to happen this year and brought to a head criticism of the Soviet role that had been
going on in Cairo even before the summit. Heikal, the influential editor of *Al
Ahram* who favored talks with the US last summer on an interim settlement,
began a series of public debates about the Soviet-Egyptian relationship in
April. . . .

By then I had come to the conclusion that Sadat's decision might not be
nearly so precipitate as I had thought at first. I noted that Sadat explicitly rejected any restrictions on the use of arms supplied by the Soviets.
I speculated that this statement "may well refer to the possible fact that
the presence of Soviet advisers with Egyptian units could serve as a
Soviet brake on Egyptian offensive movements." My overall assessment summed up four possible motives on the part of Sadat, one of
which was to improve his military options for the following year (that is
to say, 1973):

(a) the necessity to respond politically to internal frustrations; (b) the necessity
to keep, and show himself keeping, the Middle East from becoming completely
frozen in this year of indecision; (c) the desirability of seeking greater Soviet
support for offensive action next year; (d) the opportunity in taking these steps
to offer an enticement to the US by showing that he could cut back on the Soviet relationship.

Sadat made two more speeches on July 24 and 27. Though he alleged
that he had been lied to in 1971 by the United States, he reserved his
heaviest fire for the Soviet Union. Sadat pointed out that he had warned
Moscow before the US–Soviet summit that Cairo could not accept a
continuing state of "no war–no peace"; the summit demonstrated that
Soviet support for Egypt fell far short of American support for Israel.

Sadat's second speech was an indirect appeal to the Soviets to learn from the shock and to enable Cairo to develop an adequate military option for use in the future. Egypt, proclaimed Sadat, did not want Soviet soldiers fighting its battles. Egypt had no interest in causing a confrontation between the superpowers. But Moscow had to understand that for Egypt, the Middle East problem was its top priority, wherever it might rank on the Soviet agenda:

> Our friend must know and appreciate this. To him, the problem might be number four or five. . . . Hence, the pause with the friend so that he will really appreciate the battle. Perhaps when Soviet/Egyptian cooperation runs in this field the way it does in the technological field, everything will be wonderful.

Much has been written and said about the failure of the Soviet Union to live up to the principles of restraint to which it pledged itself at the Moscow summit. Most of the criticism is valid. But the record would be neither complete nor fair without pointing out that the Soviet Union paid heavily in Egypt and throughout the Middle East for its essentially putting the Mideast on ice at the summit. Certainly it did not exercise this restraint out of altruism. Doubtless Israel's strength was the principal deterrent. The Kremlin also assessed that a war risked a direct confrontation with the United States. And the Soviet leaders, needing American grain and our support for ratification of the German treaties, could not afford generating a crisis in so sensitive an area. But it is precisely in this way that a strategy of détente, posing both risks and incentives to encourage Soviet restraint, is supposed to work. In 1972, a year when the United States was heavily engaged in Vietnam, the Soviet Union held back from endorsing its clients' positions in the Middle East and this decision cost Moscow dearly. Our demonstrations of firmness on India-Pakistan and on Vietnam (not to mention the conflicts in the autumn of 1970) must have convinced the Kremlin that one more crisis would overload the circuit. Coupled with this firmness, our conciliatory posture in Moscow and the prospect of further moves on trade helped produce Soviet restraint.

Whatever the reasons for the Soviets' embarrassment, we were intent on making use of the opportunity. My first need was to calm down Dobrynin. On July 20, I told him truthfully, if a bit coyly, that we did not know what was going on in Egypt; we had had no advance warning. We were prepared to continue our exploration of the "principles" discussed in Moscow; Dobrynin must have recognized this as essentially a placebo. That afternoon he brought me a letter to Nixon from Brezhnev. With amazing chutzpah, Brezhnev's letter argued that the Soviet departure from Egypt was in part an implementation of the troop withdrawal proposal presented by Gromyko to Nixon in September 1971; a down payment, as it were, on the offer to withdraw Soviet forces! Thus, it was argued, the United States was now under an obligation to fulfill its part of the bargain, namely to influence Israel toward a settlement "whose centerpiece should be the liberation of all Arab territories occupied by it in 1967." I saw no point in debating this mind-boggling demand; I repeated my offer to explore the Moscow principles. It was the best way to gain time to find out what Cairo was thinking.

We did not have long to wait. The same day I received a report that the chief of Egyptian Intelligence had the day before approached us in the secret channel. He stressed that we should take seriously Cairo's invitation to come up with new ideas as a prelude to a secret high-level meeting. The Egyptians, we were told, were especially interested in an interim agreement along the Suez Canal.

I still did not want to get involved in offering "new" ideas that might only disappoint Sadat and abort the contact at the beginning. I preferred a general exploration to enable us to determine what was feasible before committing ourselves to a course of action. On July 29, therefore, I returned a reply to Cairo reaffirming our willingness to conduct confidential talks, which I described as "potentially extremely important":

With respect to the Egyptian statement that these talks can proceed only on the basis of new U.S. proposals, the U.S. view is as follows: In all the previous successful negotiations conducted at the White House level, the parties have first sought and achieved in preliminary discussion an understanding on the principles and general direction of an agreement before engaging in concrete negotiation. New proposals that led only to a new stalemate would serve neither side's purpose. Therefore, the U.S. side proposes that initial contacts concentrate on a detailed discussion of what is realistically achievable. This is the essence of the matter, and the only justification for the direct involvement of the President. If detailed agreement can be reached on this, then detailed proposals can be devised.

Nothing significant was heard from Sadat during August. Two new prospective intermediaries made their appearance: an Egyptian who claimed to be a friend of Sadat, and a European businessman asserting high-level Egyptian contacts. While in the early phases of approaching another government I was generally prepared to explore many different avenues, I never undermined the integrity of a valid channel once it was established. The two self-appointed intermediaries were therefore gently turned aside. That Egypt had not yet settled its course became apparent on August 22 when we were told in the secret channel that Sadat was still considering his response, but it would come soon; then we were told that a few more days would be needed. On September 4 we were advised that Sadat accepted the talks in principle but would ask for some "clarifications" in a few days.

Finally, on September 7, we received a long and extremely subtle message from Cairo. It informed us that the expulsion of Soviet advisers was a purely national decision, not taken "to please or displease anyone"; in other words, Egypt asked for no special consideration because of it. The message complained of the disproportionate influence that Israel appeared to have on American policy; it recited Egypt's disappointment with the diplomatic exchanges of the previous years, and Egypt's willingness to reopen the Suez Canal. None of this, it was said, was put forward as a precondition for talks.

It was all, as I would come to realize, vintage Sadat. His negotiating tactic was never to haggle over detail but to create an atmosphere that made disagreement psychologically difficult. He (like Chou En-lai) laid stress on a philosophical understanding, recognizing that the implementation of agreements between sovereign states cannot be enforced; it requires a willingness on both sides. Agreement on concepts is sometimes more important than on details. I cannot say that I fully understood Sadat's insight then. Great men are so rare that they take some getting used to.

The next day I replied, accepting the principle of a secret meeting with Hafiz Ismail and promising a fuller reply on my return from another visit to Moscow. My lengthier reply of September 18 once again avoided the specific issues raised by Egypt, because I wanted to reserve these for a face-to-face meeting. I put forward some housekeeping details, such as a possible venue for secret talks, and concluded with a general statement of our intent:

> The US wishes to reassure the Government of Egypt of its firm determination to seek the termination of the cycle of violence in the Middle East and to stress that it places the greatest importance on the forthcoming discussions between representatives of the two governments to achieve this purpose.

By then, the messages were taking on a more than procedural content. For example, Egypt used the private channel to voice its unhappiness about the tone of our public condemnation of the terrorist attack on Israeli athletes at the Olympic Games; it expressed fear that Israeli retaliation against Lebanon might cause some other Arab countries to invite Soviet military help — an interesting indication that Sadat was in fact opposed to Soviet military action in the Middle East. On September 30, we received another Egyptian message complaining that our call for realism was too reminiscent of Israel's position. All Egypt wanted, we were told, was some assurance that we would meet with "open hearts." I knew too little about Egyptian psychology then to respond with comparable humanity; somewhat less poetically, I stated that we were prepared to enter the talks "with an open mind to determine what useful role [we] can play in promoting a just settlement."

These secret talks are designed to develop a course of action that can lead to the implementation of Security Council Resolution 242. The big issue is to define practical measures to accomplish this. It serves nobody's interest to make empty promises. This is the meaning of the term realistic.

The two sides, meeting in a spirit of goodwill, should explore all possibilities with a view to beginning a continued exchange of serious and open views.

While these exchanges were taking place, Soviet Foreign Minister Gromyko paid his annual visit to the United Nations General Assembly. In meetings with both the President and me he repeated the standard Soviet line as if absolutely nothing had changed. He was loath to abandon sacramental positions, even though he had no idea how to implement them. He deprecated an interim settlement, claiming that Egypt would reject it. (We knew better.) And he ritualistically pressed for an overall arrangement in which Israel would get only a declaration of non-belligerency in return for the 1967 frontiers. I was too immersed in Vietnam and Nixon in the campaign to do any serious negotiating. Nixon told Gromyko simply that he would give personal attention to the Middle East after Vietnam was settled. I went back to my proposal of taking Moscow's ''general working principles'' — which Gromyko was trying to bury — and applying them to each of Israel's neighbors (Egypt, Jordan, Syria). I knew that the procedure would certainly not work quickly; it would give us further time to explore the Egyptian channel. The US–Soviet dialogue on the Middle East remained in abeyance, which was where we wanted it.

All that remained was to set a date for my secret talk with Sadat's representative. Sadat showed great understanding when I was too heavily engaged in the chaotic final phase of the Vietnam negotiation to accept the Egyptians' proposed dates of October 16 or 23. My meeting with Hafiz Ismail, Sadat's national security adviser, did not take place until February 1973. The seminal opportunity to bring about a reversal of alliances in the Arab world would have to wait until we had finally put the war in Vietnam behind us.

XXXI

From Stalemate to Breakthrough

Hanoi's Discomfiture

B Y the time we returned home from Moscow, Hanoi's offensive had run out of steam. Several factors had contributed. The North Vietnamese did not follow up the capture of Quang Tri with an assault on the old imperial capital of Hué, whose fall might have been decisive. As in 1968, Hanoi opted for psychological rather than military impact by launching a countrywide offensive, which, as then, led to its military defeat. Three fronts proved too difficult to synchronize and even more complicated to supply; hence Saigon was able to switch its small strategic reserve to meet each threat as it developed. The dispersal of effort also meant that the North Vietnamese needed nearly three weeks to bring up reinforcements for the attack on Hué. By then part of the South's strategic reserve had moved in. Saigon's airborne division fought both at An Loc and near Hué. The marines were used in both the Central Highlands and in Military Region 1. And the South Vietnamese divisions fought better than in any previous battle. Our massive reinforcement of B-52s, raising the total to over 200 by the end of May, exposed the attacking forces to a formidable concentration of firepower, making mass attacks increasingly difficult. Hanoi's problems multiplied further because its commanders were not experienced in handling large units. Attacks by tanks, artillery, and armor frequently bogged down as the various elements lost contact with one another. So by the middle of June, with our bombing and mining making themselves felt, the North Vietnamese army was stalled.

On June 9, in an appraisal for the President of what the blockade begun on May 8 had achieved, I said the prospects for South Vietnam looked "substantially brighter." The blockade had forced all supplies to come by rail, and the railroad lines were being cut by our air attacks. More than 1,000 railroad cars were backed up on the Chinese side of the border. As a result, supplies had to be transferred to trucks, which required time-consuming loading and unloading and encountered extreme difficulties during the rainy season. Enemy communications spoke of ammunition shortages; our pilots reported a noticeable reduction in surface-to-air missile firings, indicating that Hanoi might be rationing its stocks. Radio Hanoi lamented "a number of difficulties" in providing labor for agriculture, industry, and transport. Corruption and black marketeering were provoking angry North Vietnamese exhortations to their people.

Moreover, my memorandum continued, Hanoi could see Moscow's and Peking's reactions to our May 8 measures only as exasperatingly circumspect and limited. Soviet refusal to cancel the summit deeply disturbed and angered the North Vietnamese. On the eve of our trip, Hanoi had publicly warned (unnamed) fellow Communists not to "set national interests against the interests of world revolution" (that is, against Hanoi's interests). Several days later, on May 21 — while we were on the way to Moscow — a Soviet spokesman had made clear that Moscow knew who was meant; he warned bluntly that Hanoi was adopting an "extremely arbitrary interpretation" of the Soviet Union's "duty" to North Vietnam and pointed out that the rest of the Communist world, even including China, favored "peaceful coexistence." Since the Moscow summit, Hanoi had constantly if indirectly attacked the summit and the agreements reached there.

Our twin summits had undoubtedly engendered a sense of isolation in the North. We were seeing their effects on the morale of the North Vietnamese leadership, population, and armed forces. And they had greatly strengthened Nixon's domestic position, thus removing Hanoi's key weapon of leverage on us. In June we received the first inconclusive hints that Hanoi might be engaged in cease-fire planning. During the summer the evidence became clearer. By the middle of September, as I shall show, it was unmistakable.

Morale in South Vietnam had reached its nadir after the fall of Quang Tri. Wild rumors that the United States had agreed to turn over the northern part of the country to Hanoi — almost certainly disseminated by Communist cadres — had been ended by Nixon's decision to mine North Vietnamese harbors. With a revived hope and purpose, Thieu rallied his population. We were, in my view, in a strong position to resume secret talks.

Many consider negotiations as a sign of weakness. I always looked at them as a weapon for seizing the moral and psychological high ground. Some treat willingness to talk when there is no pressure as an unnecessary concession; to me it is a device to improve one's strategic position, because one's interlocutor is aware that one faces no necessity to make concessions. It was, however, not for theoretical but practical reasons that Nixon approved an approach to Hanoi on June 12. We proposed a private meeting with Le Duc Tho for June 28, when I had a weekend free between a trip to China and a sojourn in San Clemente.

Our message invited a repetition of the games of the previous spring by suggesting that the secret talk should *precede* a plenary session. If Hanoi followed its script of demanding a plenary before a private meeting, we were ready to accept July 13 for a plenary and July 18 for the private talk. Nixon preferred this timing because of the Democratic Convention's opening on July 10. We would be able to announce that a meeting was about to take place, whereas my own preference of June 29 hazarded announcing a failure of the talks just before the Democrats met.

While we were waiting for Hanoi's reply, two events underscored North Vietnam's isolation.

On June 8 I had asked Dobrynin what had happened to Podgorny's mission to Hanoi, of which we had been told in Moscow. He said the Soviets were still waiting for an official invitation — an explanation that, given my knowledge of the Kremlin's prickly and obstreperous clients, was clearly plausible. Finally, on June 11, while I was paying a brief visit to Japan, Dobrynin told Haig that Podgorny would leave for Hanoi on June 13 and requested that we stop the bombing of North Vietnam while he was there. We replied, as Nixon had indicated to Brezhnev, that during Podgorny's stay we would not bomb within ten miles of Hanoi and within five miles of Haiphong; no other restrictions would be observed. On June 22 Brezhnev reported to Nixon that Hanoi's leadership had listened with "an attentive attitude" to Podgorny's exposition of the American negotiating position; they were prepared to resume negotiations on a businesslike basis; they did not insist on discussing only North Vietnamese proposals. If accurate, this was a tone we had never heard from North Vietnam. Previously, Hanoi had dismissed any deviation from its various "points" as not "reasonable and logical." Brezhnev's letter concluded with the suggestion that the United States should propose a date for the resumption of negotiations.

This was puzzling since we had made precisely such a proposal to Hanoi on June 12. Was Hanoi keeping Moscow in the dark? Or was Brezhnev urging us to reply promptly to a message from Hanoi that reached us on June 20? That reply had turned out to be much milder than usual. Contrary to the assumptions of our critics, bombing and mining had greatly improved Hanoi's manners. After perfunctorily cataloguing grievances — the bombing and mining and the suspension of plenary sessions — it got to the heart of the problem in near-biblical language: "The DRV side, clothed by its goodwill, agrees to private meetings." Its goodwill did not, however, extend to abandoning its insistence on a prior plenary session. Hanoi's message claimed that Le Duc Tho and Xuan Thuy, being "engaged in work previously scheduled in Hanoi," could not attend a plenary before July 13. This was another interesting sign; Hanoi was not in the habit of giving such explanations. July 15 was proposed for the private meeting; thus Hanoi neatly solved Nixon's political problem for him by proposing a date *after* the Democratic Convention.

Hanoi's isolation was dramatized also by the fact that this message reached me in Peking, where from June 19 to 23 I briefed the Chinese leaders on the Moscow summit, generally to maintain momentum in our new relationship and to discomfit Hanoi. My visit brought no new developments on Vietnam. As always, Chou En-lai showed more interest in a cease-fire than in a political settlement. He understood well enough that a cease-fire was the easier to arrange, and he was eager to remove the irritant of Vietnam from US–Chinese relations. Unlike Moscow, Peking had no interest in a demonstration that the United States was prepared to dump its friends; in its long-range perspective of seeking a counterweight to the Soviet Union, Peking in fact had a stake in our reputation for reliability. And there was always an undercurrent of Chinese uneasiness about Hanoi's hegemonic aspirations in Indochina. Chou asked pointed questions about Nixon's May 8 proposal (which was in effect a cease-fire offer), repeated the standard line of China's historical debt to Hanoi, avoided any implication of any Chinese national interest in the war, and implied that most of China's supplies to Vietnam were foodstuffs. This paralleled what Kosygin had told us about Soviet deliveries four weeks earlier. Given China's more rudimentary armaments industry, Chou was the more likely to be telling the truth. Hanoi was not in a brilliant position when its two patrons were in effect telling its adversary that they were no longer supplying military equipment.

On the day of my return (June 23) we replied to the North Vietnamese. We accepted July 13 for the resumption of plenary sessions and suggested July 19 for the private meeting, largely because it fitted in better with Nixon's travel schedule. We dismissed Hanoi's complaints curtly: "In order to help create the proper atmosphere for these discussions the US will not respond to the allegations in the DRV note of June 20." On June 26 Dobrynin came to the White House in his compulsive quest to find out what I had been doing in Peking. In the process he inquired about Vietnam. Our four-day postponement of the private meeting would, he said, arouse profound suspicions in Hanoi. (This implied a new urgency in our adversary, who earlier in the year had procrastinated for four months before setting a date.) Dobrynin gave me his guess that Hanoi might be waiting until American electoral prospects were clearer before making a final decision on whether to conclude the war.

It was a prescient remark. Hanoi was indeed watching our election campaign, though I was not then sure whether it would hold out on negotiation until after the election in November or opt to negotiate

seriously just before. It would not decide, I told Nixon in a memorandum on June 26, "until it believes it has a clearer picture of whether or
not you will be re-elected." I sent him a summary of a June 10 article in
the Hanoi party newspaper that spoke favorably of McGovern but refrained from flatly predicting his victory. North Vietnam's anger at its
own allies was thinly concealed in the denunciation of Nixon for having
remained a hawk even when he "borrowed dove's wings for distant
trips."

The "hawk" was meanwhile faced with another troop withdrawal
decision. Our numbers were now so low that when the deadline came up
at the end of June there was no room for any dramatic reductions. But
Nixon decided to announce the withdrawal of 10,000 troops over two
months — and told Ziegler to add that no more draftees would be sent
unless they volunteered. The draft, which had been at the heart of so
much campus unrest, no longer threatened students with Vietnam service; when schools reopened in the fall the student protest was over.
Nixon enjoyed announcing the resumption of plenaries at a press conference on June 29, one day after the troop withdrawal news, a week and a
half before the Democratic Convention. Predictably, the *New York
Times* complained that this coincided with the political calendar. I
pointed out to a journalist that Hanoi had picked the date. Hence only
two conclusions were possible: Either Hanoi wanted to promote the
reelection of Nixon, an unlikely prospect; or else Hanoi wanted to
preserve the option of a settlement *before* the election. And that was exactly the case.

Testing the Stalemate

THE resumption of negotiations was of considerable symbolic importance: It showed that Hanoi no longer took for granted either a military victory or Nixon's electoral defeat. If Hanoi had been confident of
winning, it would have timed the negotiations to coincide with some
spectacular new offensive. If it had believed that it could bring about the
political demise of Nixon, it would have stonewalled and published ambiguous peace proposals to stir up our domestic opposition and paint the
Administration as an obstacle to peace — as it had done before the
Easter offensive. That Hanoi insisted on resuming plenaries, even
though they would coincide with the Democratic Convention, was a
demonstration of Hanoi's growing doubt that total victory was possible.

I had reckoned all along that Hanoi's offensive would culminate in a
serious negotiation, whatever happened. If Hanoi were to prevail on the
battlefield, Nixon would be forced to settle on Hanoi's terms; if the offensive were halted and the probable Democratic candidate, Senator
George McGovern, looked as if he was winning the election, Hanoi

would wait; it would gamble on the extremely favorable terms he was offering. (McGovern's terms were much better for Hanoi than what it was asking for in our private talks.) If the offensive were blunted and Nixon looked like the probable winner, Hanoi would make a major effort to settle with us. My private prediction also was that if Nixon were more than ten points ahead in the public opinion polls by September 15, Hanoi would substantially change its negotiating strategy and seek an immediate settlement. But to maintain that option Hanoi would have two tasks: It would have to reconnoiter our intentions to find out our objectives; and it would have to try to narrow the differences in the interval so that a final agreement could be put together quickly, if it so chose, in the few weeks remaining until the election.

I did not agree with those of my staff who thought Hanoi would choose protracted warfare after the offensive. Having committed its regular forces, it would find it technically difficult to revert to guerrilla warfare. And such a course would face psychological obstacles as well. It would be an admission that after ten years of bloody warfare which had drained its country, North Vietnam was back to where it had started. Hanoi might adopt such a strategy if everything else failed; it would not choose it if other options were available.

But if Hanoi's position was militarily precarious, ours was difficult psychologically and politically. The President had gained some maneuvering room with his bold decision to bomb and mine, but if it did not bring results fairly quickly, it would be increasingly attacked as a "failure." The demands for "political" alternatives would mount. And given the way our domestic debate had evolved, this would mean in practice acceptance of Hanoi's demand for a coalition government and a fixed deadline for our withdrawals, conditional only on the release of prisoners of war. (And McGovern was prepared not to insist even on the latter as a formal condition, expressing merely the "expectation" that our withdrawal would lead to their release.) May, June, and July saw the height of the favorable public reaction to the combination of the successful summit and the bombing and mining. Nevertheless, in that same period there were nineteen votes in the House and Senate on various end-the-war amendments. Not all of them were equally objectionable. Some contained elements of our position; none embraced it completely. All were variations on offering withdrawal for the return of our prisoners. The difference between supporters and opponents had narrowed to one issue, whether we should insist on a cease-fire or settle simply for the return of our prisoners in conjunction with our withdrawal.

There were three schools of thought in the Senate on that issue. A growing minority (about thirty Senators) favored setting an unconditional deadline for American withdrawal in the "expectation" that this would lead Hanoi to free our prisoners. About forty Senators favored making withdrawal contingent only on release of our prisoners. A dwindling minority favored making our withdrawal depend also on a cease-fire. By the end of 1971 a majority on behalf of the withdrawal-for-prisoners option had developed; it grew through 1972. Requiring a cease-fire before withdrawal had become a conservative proposal; amendments including it in a settlement were consistently defeated in both houses. Thus, the dominant "peace" position in the Senate now was for us to get out of Vietnam even while the war among the Vietnamese continued. We would end ten years of war in return for our prisoners, while leaving our allies to their fate.

We managed to block the various demands for unconditional withdrawal, but by ever-smaller margins. On July 24 a Cooper-Brooke amendment insisting on a withdrawal in return only for the release of prisoners passed in the Senate by five votes; the same day an attempt by Senator James Allen of Alabama to make our withdrawal contingent on a supervised cease-fire as well was *defeated* by five votes. Sooner or later, one of the amendments to cut off funds would pass. At a minimum Hanoi had every reason to believe that it had a guaranteed safety valve: If it offered us our prisoners, the Congress would probably stop the war. Whatever the parliamentary arithmetic, all of the recurring resolutions, differing as they did from our negotiating position, obviously weakened us for the bargaining that was now inevitable. And we could not go along with the Senate view. We were committed to tying withdrawal to a cease-fire. It remained our view that it would be inhumane, ignoble, and destructive of larger interests elsewhere to withdraw while fighting continued against those who had relied on us. Abandoning our allies to be overrun would mock our sacrifice and discredit our nation's foreign policy.

We were therefore determined to seek a fair compromise. The military situation was improving, but nothing like total victory seemed in sight. By June, even though Saigon had assumed the offensive, the pace of South Vietnamese military operations offered no prospect of either a drastic or a rapid improvement. Not until the middle of September was Quang Tri retaken; the road to An Loc was never completely reopened, although a fresh division was moved up from the Delta to the area around Saigon. While it had performed well in Military Region 4, the 21st Division conducted itself as any other South Vietnamese formation did when shifted out of the area of its recruitment: It turned sluggish and unenterprising. We were approaching a military stalemate. From the vantage point of Hanoi, so recently sure of total victory, this would be a major setback. But we would be running grave risks if we interpreted it as an augury of total victory.

Still, we entered the negotiations in the best position ever. If my analysis were correct, the public opinion polls during September would tip the balance. No concessions on our part in July, therefore, were very likely to affect Hanoi's calculations. And, in fact, our margin for concession was severely circumscribed. If we were true to our principles, we could not, except cosmetically, go beyond our military proposals of May 8, 1972 (or May 31, 1971), and our political proposals of January 25, 1972. So I prepared for the negotiations in an optimistic and relaxed frame of mind; the fundamental decisions would have to be made by Hanoi, not by us. Until Hanoi had analyzed the likely electoral outcome, our best strategy would be to stay cool, offer nothing significantly new, and thus hope to intensify the pressures on Hanoi. The critical moment would come only after Hanoi had made its final judgment of Nixon's electoral prospects.

Later on, the myth developed that Nixon for domestic political reasons was eager to end the war before the election. Nothing could be further from the truth. As I have repeatedly shown, Nixon was exceedingly suspicious of negotiations in general (unless he had a nearly ironclad guarantee of success) and especially with the North Vietnamese. He doubted that anything would ever come of them; as his election prospects improved, he saw no domestic reason to pursue them. In July he still saw some benefit in keeping his Democratic opposition off balance by periodically announcing my private meetings with Le Duc Tho. But after the debacle of McGovern's Vice Presidential nominee, Senator Thomas Eagleton, Nixon lost interest even in that. As the weeks went by he became convinced that he had narrowed McGovern's support to a far-out liberal fringe that would oppose him regardless of what he did on Vietnam. On the other hand, settling even on the terms we had earlier put forward publicly might well put at risk his support among conservative groups whom he considered his base. Nixon saw no possibility of progress until *after* the election and probably did not even desire it. Even then, he preferred another escalation before sitting down to negotiate.

I thought that if things broke right, our election would serve as an unchangeable deadline for Hanoi, the equivalent of an ultimatum. Its fear of what the "hawk" might do with a new mandate for four years might lead it to prefer a settlement before our election. Hanoi might have to abandon its habit of trying to wear us down by propagandistic proposals and mobilizing media and the Congress, and seek a real negotiation. And none too soon, perhaps. For I thought — contrary to both Hanoi's probable analysis and our own conventional wisdom — that we would actually be *worse* off after the election. All the polls I had seen suggested that the composition of the new Congress would be substantially the same as of the old or even slightly less favorable — a prospect reinforced by Nixon's decision to separate his campaign as much as possible from the Congressional race in order to obtain the largest Presidential electoral margin in history. Thus in reality the pressures for ending the war by legislation were certain to resume after November. And the opposition would have a convenient target when we submitted a supplementary budget in January to pay for the costs of reinforcements during the offensive. Laird estimated that we might have to request four to six billion dollars. Nixon already had before him a proposal by Laird to withdraw our augmentation forces after January 1, 1973, to keep the supplementary costs from growing unmanageable. Specifically, Laird proposed withdrawing ninety-eight B-52s and three squadrons of F-4s as of January. Once Hanoi understood that our forces were declining, it could revert to waiting us out. And once the composition of the Congress became clear, Hanoi would resume its psychological warfare.

In any event, I was persuaded that it was not wholly our choice whether to negotiate or not. If Hanoi perceived us as stonewalling, it could "go public." If it accepted the framework of our proposals and disclosed it (which in effect it finally did in October), this would put us in an impossible position domestically, no matter how big Nixon's lead in the polls. We would then be repeating the classic syndrome of the Vietnam war, of appearing to be pushed step by step toward concessions, a process that undermined authority whatever the outcome. The war had to be ended, in my view, by a demonstration that our government was in control of events, and this required maintaining the diplomatic initiative. For all these reasons, I proceeded to the negotiations, with Nixon's acquiescence, if not his enthusiasm.

In June the North Vietnamese were crowing that the return to the plenaries represented a great victory over the United States. And they went back to their old tactics of bringing pressure by inviting to Hanoi those whom they considered leading Americans, in this case labor leaders and journalists. I warned Dobrynin on June 30 that if Hanoi repeated the performance of the previous year — stonewalling in public while talking seriously in private — we would break off the talks. Dobrynin clucked sympathetically (at least I assumed his clucking was sympathetic; in any case there was a good chance the message would be transmitted to Hanoi).

Our basic strategy in the private meetings starting July 19 would be to make no new proposals until Hanoi's intentions became clearer. I would try to drain Hanoi's political proposals gradually of operational content, for example, countering their coalition government with our anodyne proposal for a joint electoral commission. If Hanoi played along, we might gradually emerge with the dual-track approach we had offered originally: settling the military issues, and leaving the political issues essentially to future negotiations among the parties. Such a settlement would preserve our allies and give them an opportunity to determine their future — which is in effect what we had always sought.

Early in July we sent Haig to Saigon to assess the war and to consult with Thieu about the positions we proposed to take. Haig saw Thieu on July 3, but he encountered a different leader from the one we had dealt with thus far. Thieu's army had now been tested in battle; he thought that Hanoi would no longer be able to defeat him, certainly so long as our airpower was available to back him. He calculated — nearly correctly — that he could make our election work for him by playing on Nixon's often repeated reluctance to repeat Johnson's pressure tactics of 1968. Moreover, Thieu understood Hanoi far better than we did. Through all the years of the Nixon Administration, the real reason he had never challenged any of our negotiating proposals was that he calculated that all of them would be rejected by Hanoi. He considered them the price he had to pay for continued American support. But in 1972 he smelled compromise even before most Americans did. Like me, he seemed convinced that a serious negotiation was imminent. But our problem and the one he faced were entirely different. A compromise would be the beginning, not the end, of massive problems in South Vietnam. We would withdraw; South Vietnam would remain. Hanoi would never give up its implacable quest for victory; sooner or later South Vietnam would have to fight alone. Going on to total victory seemed more sensible to Thieu and probably no more costly than the compromises now achievable. Unfortunately, that was not our choice. Even if Hanoi did not suddenly accept our proposals, the new Congress would force us to settle on worse terms — withdrawal for prisoners — than those we would seek to negotiate. It was understandable that Thieu would continue to demand victory, which would have required several years of further American as well as South Vietnamese exertion. But we had no margin at home for such a course. We would be lucky if we could obtain the terms Nixon had put forward on May 8 before the Congress voted us out of the war.

All of this emerged only indistinctly during Haig's visit, like the first rumbles of a distant storm. On July 3, reading from talking points prepared by me and Win Lord, Haig briefed Thieu on the Vietnam discussions of the Moscow summit and my June trip to Peking. He described our new proposal — a cease-fire, the return of POWs, a four-month withdrawal, and Thieu's resignation two months before a new presidential election. The sole difference from previous proposals was the earlier timing provided for Thieu's resignation, as Nixon had half-promised Brezhnev. Haig explained our strategy: "The U.S. had been attempting to combine the firm measures taken on the military front with a demonstration of reasonableness on the negotiating front." He raised to Thieu the possibility preoccupying me, that Hanoi might be considering a softer stance in the near future "on the assumption that President Nixon would win in November and would possibly be easier to deal with before rather than following his reelection."

Thieu's response showed that he was not quite on our wavelength. He did not make this explicit because, according to him, Hanoi's leaders did not feel the pressure to negotiate that Haig was predicting. They would not settle, he argued, unless they obtained a coalition government. A permanent cease-fire would guarantee their defeat because they would never be able to start the war up again — a point Thieu forgot when Hanoi accepted precisely such a cease-fire three months later. Thieu seemed concerned that our bureaucrats might press for a temporary cease-fire during the election period; this, he argued, must be rejected. He opposed an unsupervised cease-fire of any kind; we did not catch the implication — entirely new — that Thieu considered any in-place cease-fire unsupervisable. He was subtly rejecting what we had been offering with his concurrence since October 7, 1970, and what the President had reaffirmed as late as May 8. (Of course, the Senate would soon go on record for a total American withdrawal in return for prisoners without any cease-fire whatsoever.) Thieu had no problem over offering to resign two months before a new election in South Vietnam; he was willing to step down even four months before, if that helped the negotiation. He seemed at one with his brethren in Hanoi in the conviction that whoever controlled the election machinery would win in the end.

Haig promised to convey these thoughts to Washington. In closing, he reassured Thieu once again that "under no circumstances would the United States turn to a solution at the negotiating table which belittled the successes achieved on the battleground, or which offered Hanoi advantages that it could not gain through military action." Thieu extended his warmest regards to Nixon and me, possibly not realizing that Haig's final "reassurance" foreshadowed the in-place cease-fire which Thieu had just rejected, for its corollary was that *we* could seek no advantages beyond the military situation on the ground. Haig had just participated in raising the curtain on one of the most searing dramas in the quest for ending the war in Vietnam.

As I left for Paris on July 19 the differences among the principal actors on our side lay in nuances, in hints whose full import we did not yet grasp. At least in July, Nixon accepted the negotiations largely for their utility in confusing his domestic opponents. Thieu believed that the refusal of a coalition government offered a safe haven from the risks of negotiation and the uncertainty of defending South Vietnam without us. And I did not think any break in the deadlock — which I expected — would occur until the second half of September. Thus we could all rally behind a negotiating strategy that essentially held to established positions and sought to garner whatever concessions Hanoi might offer in seeking to narrow the gap before making its final decision.

I met Le Duc Tho on July 19 in the dingy residence at 11 rue Darthé, which had been the site of all but the first of our previous fourteen meetings. The small dining room overlooking the garden had again been set up with a square conference table covered with green baize. Some at home fancied the North Vietnamese as peace-loving, essentially gentle creatures offended by any demonstration of American power and eager above all to reciprocate gestures of American goodwill. Our experience was otherwise. We knew that the North Vietnamese had wantonly invaded all neighboring countries; that their form of warfare depended in part on terror. Displays of American strength never failed to be taken seriously by them even as they resisted them. Acts of goodwill that did not reflect the existing balance of forces were treated as signs of moral weakness, even as they scorned them. They had been insolent on May 2, when they thought they were winning. They were benign and friendly now, even though in the interval their harbors had been mined and all restrictions on our bombing had been removed.

I began with an analysis of why our previous talks had failed. Hanoi's refusal to distinguish between what could be settled by negotiation and what had to be left to history guaranteed a war to the end. I proceeded at a very deliberate pace and spoke in largely philosophical terms to remove any thought that we felt under the pressure of an approaching election. I stressed (though I did not in fact believe it) that our situation would improve after the election; I warned that any attempt to manipulate the negotiations to influence our elections would lead to an immediate rupture. I closed my opening remarks with a statement of general principles. We were willing to coexist with Hanoi after the war. We had no desire to retain permanent bases in Southeast Asia. We would not impose our preferences on a freely elected government in Saigon. I withheld any concrete proposals.

Le Duc Tho conducted most of the conversation for the North Vietnamese, an indication that they were serious. This was a different "Ducky" — one I had seen only once before, in the previous July, when he had tried to get us to jettison Thieu during the South Vietnamese election. Now he was all conciliation in substance and in style. He laughed at my banter; he subtly flattered my academic credentials. We were spared the epic poem of Vietnam's heroic struggle for independence. Instead, Le Duc Tho insisted that Hanoi was eager to settle the war during Nixon's first term. He asked repeatedly if we would respect whatever agreements were reached, signed or unsigned. He would make a "great effort" to have this meeting become a turning point, he said, provided *both* sides reexamined their positions — an unprecedented disclaimer of infallibility. Hanoi, he averred, would keep in mind our responsibilities in other parts of the world even though these were of no direct concern to the Vietnamese themselves — another startling departure. He dwelt only briefly and perfunctorily on the bombing and mining; amazingly, he did not even ask us to stop them, resorting instead to the refrain of 1968 that ending these activities would create a "propitious" atmosphere for negotiations. I had been half-persuaded by that proposition in 1968; after four years of experience I now knew the opposite was true.

After sparring for a while, I put forward our May 8 proposal — omitting, however, the part about extending the time limit for Thieu's resignation. Ducky turned it down, though much less polemically than in the past. He reiterated Hanoi's standard proposal of a three-part provisional coalition Government of National Concord but modified it in one respect: He implied that once Thieu resigned, the rest of the government could stay and even receive American help, pending a final negotiation with the Communists. Our meeting had lasted for six and a half hours — the longest ever. We agreed to meet again on August 1.

As I left, I told Le Duc Tho that my movements were too well observed now to have the meetings remain secret. There would be too many journalistic inquiries to which we would have to reply either evasively or untruthfully. So I suggested that we announce each meeting after it had been held but give no details. When Nixon had revealed the secret talks in January, Hanoi had declared with bravado that it had only reluctantly and at our urging agreed to keep them confidential. Now, when put to the test, Le Duc Tho grumbled. Obviously, he was loath to give up the advantage of probing our position secretly while depriving our people of hope by stalemating the visible diplomacy. I gave him no choice now. The fact of the talks would be made public. For the remainder of the negotiations we blunted one of the psychological weapons in Hanoi's arsenal by announcing each meeting. In fact, no serious attempt was made by the media to cover the negotiations or to follow either my movements or Le Duc Tho's. It was symptomatic of widespread cynicism about peace prospects. Two announced secret meetings in eleven days, coupled with a trip to Saigon, did little to shake the widespread conviction that it was all an electoral maneuver. No one explained why Hanoi would cooperate in playing such a game.

I summed up the results of the first meeting in a memorandum to the President:

> While they have said nothing which precludes their returning strictly to their old positions, they were about as positive in this first session as we could expect if they do want to settle, especially since we must have thrown them off-stride by withholding the total package discussed in the USSR.
>
> If they do move, it could be in the direction of a ceasefire coupled with political principles along the lines of our January 25 proposal, but this would not surface before several more meetings at the earliest. The other possibility is their using the talks to elaborate a position which makes Thieu alone the obstacle to a comprehensive settlement. . . .

Upon my return I briefed both Dobrynin and Huang Hua about what had happened. And in the interval between the meetings came another of the periodic media assaults, this time to the effect that we were deliberately bombing North Vietnamese dikes and imperiling millions of lives. It was one of the perennials of the antiwar debate, ready-made for a "credibility gap" and for the implication that no immoral act was beyond the Nixon Administration. If we denied it, Hanoi would produce a bomb crater or two on some embankment; if we "admitted" that a stray bomb aimed at a missile site might have hit a dike by accident, we evoked headlines such as this from the *New York Times* of July 16: "How to Bomb a Dike But Not Target It." Nixon in news conferences on June 29 and July 27 and Laird on July 6 firmly denied that our policy was to attack dikes. The assurance should, of course, have been inherently plausible, or the dikes would long since have been destroyed. Nixon also asked on July 27 why there was so much concern about hypothetical attacks on dikes when so little had been said about the 860,000 South Vietnamese made homeless by the most recent North Vietnamese offensive. After a few weeks the dike story went away, not to reappear for the rest of the war.

In the interval, too, we had another exchange with Thieu. It was an indicator of things to come — though once again we took for a tactical misunderstanding what turned out to be a fundamental disagreement. We had told Thieu routinely that we would present during the next plenary session what we had withheld on July 19: Thieu's proposed resignation two months rather than one month before a new election. We also proposed to insist that the cease-fire go into effect on the signature of an agreement in principle, contrary to Hanoi's constant insistence that a cease-fire be deferred until agreement on political issues had been reached. We wanted to avoid a trap in which an agreement in principle would turn into a swap of prisoners for our withdrawal, leaving Hanoi free to pursue the war against South Vietnam.

Though Thieu had agreed to the resignation proposal in his conversation with Haig on July 3 (suggesting that he could even agree to resign sooner) and though the second provision for immediate cease-fire seemed to us entirely to his benefit, he now objected to both. He said that we could indicate the two-month resignation interval informally but not in writing. He tied the cease-fire to a withdrawal of all North Vietnamese forces within three months. The first objection would easily be handled by offering a neutral formulation and a specific private assurance. The withdrawal point was new. With his agreement, a cease-fire in place had been proposed publicly on October 7, 1970. With his concurrence also, we had formally abandoned the demand for mutual withdrawal in our secret proposal of May 31, 1971, and Nixon had urged a cease-fire without withdrawal on January 25 and May 8, 1972.

Thieu's new proposal was unfulfillable. Hanoi would not yield at the conference table what it had not been forced to give up on the battlefield. After having based our whole public position on an unconditional cease-fire, we would never be able to sustain a continuation of the war on this issue; a majority of our Senate was opposed even to making unilateral withdrawal conditional on a cease-fire. On May 31, 1971, we had put forward a proposal prohibiting further infiltration into South Vietnam after a cease-fire. This would have the practical consequence of causing the North Vietnamese forces in the South to atrophy owing to normal attrition. Even this position had next to no public support in the United States, but we were determined to stick to it. Further than that it would be senseless to go; it would just elicit a Congressional resolution forcing us to abandon all conditions. But we did not pursue the disagreement with Thieu since it seemed irrelevant to the deadlocked negotiations.

My August 1 meeting in Paris with Le Duc Tho turned out to be the longest yet; it lasted eight hours. I described it in a memorandum to the President as "the most interesting session we have ever had." Le Duc Tho was not yet so eager for a settlement as to give up his tactic of opening with an assault on our good faith, concentrating his fire this time on our announcements of the private meetings. Then, after an hour-long wrangle, Ducky yielded to the inevitable. He knew very well that there was no way of keeping the fact of the meetings secret if we were determined to publicize them — unless, of course, he was prepared to threaten to break off the conversations.

And this, it transpired, he was not at all willing to do. For on August 1 Le Duc Tho continued the retreat that he had begun on July 19. I presented our new "plan," but Le Duc Tho realized that it consisted mainly of cosmetic modifications. For once his charge that I was offering "nothing new" was accurate. After we had consumed nearly three hours, first in haggling and then in going over familiar ground, Le Duc Tho asked for a recess. It lasted an hour and a quarter, the longest interruption yet. The break brought to light an interesting change in atmosphere observed first by Peter Rodman, who, as note-taker, was most in need of sustenance. At previous meetings, the North Vietnamese had laid out modest snacks, which consisted of Vietnamese spring rolls (*cha gio*) and soft drinks. At the meeting of August 1, fruit, cookies, and a greater variety of light edibles were served, which led Rodman to record for posterity that "the snacks were more lavish and the *cha gio* somewhat thicker than the previous meeting" — an indication both of Rodman's legendary appetite and of the tea-leaf reading to which we had been reduced by four years of frustrating negotiations. (On August 14, wine and rice cakes would appear.)

After the recess, Ducky read me a little lecture on the mining and bombing. When I showed impatience he finally came to the point. He had a whole new set of North Vietnamese proposals.

For two and a half years Hanoi had been tormenting us with the unconditional-withdrawal deadline. We were asked to commit ourselves to a withdrawal schedule that would then have to be kept regardless of what else happened in the negotiations. There would be a cease-fire with our forces while the fighting would go on in South Vietnam. We had countered by agreeing on a schedule for withdrawal contingent on other terms, in effect, a general cease-fire throughout Indochina. One-sided, indeed insolent, as was Hanoi's proposal, it had been gaining momentum within the United States. Several Senate resolutions embodied it; it was McGovern's campaign position. Now Le Duc Tho withdrew it. He was willing to settle for less than he was being offered by the opposition candidate — a pretty clear indication of how Hanoi was reading the forthcoming election. Le Duc Tho agreed that whatever schedule we agreed upon would not start running until *after* all issues were settled; the unconditional deadline, which had rent our domestic debate, was dead.

Le Duc Tho began also to modify his political demands. He still insisted on a coalition government, but he put forward two concessions. Hanoi up to now had demanded a *provisional* coalition government in which the Communists appointed a third of the members and had a veto over the other two-thirds. That disarmed government was supposed then to negotiate with the fully armed Communist shadow government for a definitive solution. Le Duc Tho now proposed making the tripartite coalition government in effect the *definitive* government; it would not have to engage in additional negotiations with the Communists. Reflecting Hanoi's sense of urgency, Le Duc Tho gave up, in addition, the veto over the composition of the non-Communist segments of his proposed structure. In the three-part coalition the Communists and Saigon would each appoint their third, and also one-half of the allegedly "neutral" third. In other words, the tripartite coalition had become a fifty-fifty split — with Saigon thus having a veto — rather than a grab for total power. We were opposed to any form of coalition government, but we were certain that we had not seen the last of Hanoi's flexibility.

Once Le Duc Tho started making concessions, he proved as inventive as he had been obnoxious while stonewalling. He next submitted a procedural proposal for speeding up the negotiation, so complete that it required an advanced degree in metaphysics to understand the bewildering series of forums he was now putting before us. Saigon and the South Vietnamese Communists would negotiate on political issues; the three Vietnamese parties would discuss subjects affecting all of Vietnam; all four parties (including the United States) would treat the questions relating to the cease-fire. To us, the significant feature of this procedural cornucopia was that in each of the forums the *existing* South Vietnamese government, *including* Thieu, could participate as an equal. Hanoi was obviously in full retreat from its ancient position that Thieu would have to resign *before* anything else happened.

I thought Le Duc Tho's proposals sufficiently serious to send the whole voluminous text to Bunker and Thieu for their consideration. In a memorandum to the President — on which Nixon wrote skeptical marginal comments about the tedium of the exercise — I pointed out that Hanoi's new formulations could be a first step toward separating the military and political issues, the approach that I had recommended in my 1968 *Foreign Affairs* article, and that Harriman and Vance had urged on us in the transition period. Le Duc Tho had heretofore adamantly rejected this course. But if it were now the case that North Vietnam was beginning to move, our strategy had to be to continue to reject any coalition government proposal. In time this could end up as some face-saving formulation in which the military issues such as cease-fire, prisoner exchange, and withdrawals would be settled conclusively, while the political issues would be left to prolonged, and possibly inconclusive, negotiations among the various Vietnamese parties.

We were, of course, entering dangerous waters. As long as Hanoi asked us to overthrow an allied government, we were on moral high ground in rejecting it. But with Hanoi now moving toward the gray area of accepting a genuine political contest, the dividing lines would begin to blur. Symbolism and substance would merge. And the former might be more dangerous to our vulnerable allies in Saigon, who would have to remain to fight for their freedom after we had withdrawn, than to us ten thousand miles away. As the private talks — still unnoticed by the media — grew progressively more serious, what emerged more and more as the key issue was something intangible: the psychological resilience of Saigon.

For the time being, we were not compelled to decide. Hanoi had not yet moved far enough to test our consistent position that the only obstacle to a settlement was our refusal to overthrow an allied government. Nixon saw no point in making more concessions because he would just as soon have put the whole negotiating process on ice until after the election. I agreed we should sit tight, because I wanted to conserve for the final push the marginal adjustments in our position we were still capable of making. Hanoi would not make the final decision, in my analysis, until well into September, when Nixon's prospects would be clearer. This assessment, interestingly enough, was shared by Dobrynin, who seemed well informed on our negotiations. All we should do, I thought, was make minor responses to North Vietnamese initiatives and from time to time submit our own written formulations, which should be just forthcoming enough to deny Hanoi any pretext to go public and trigger another bitter domestic controversy in America. Nixon agreed.

To keep the pressure on Hanoi for further dilution of its political position and to coordinate policy with our ally, Nixon agreed that I should visit Saigon immediately following the next meeting in Paris, scheduled for August 14. This had the additional advantage of supporting our strategy of procrastination; it gave me a pretext to delay a reply to Hanoi's August 1 proposals for at least another two weeks. If my assessment of the pressures posed by our election deadline was correct, Hanoi would find itself forced to disclose its hand rapidly. For the first time in the war it was our opponents, not ourselves, who were under the compulsion of time.

As it turned out Le Duc Tho, too, was going to travel; he told us that he had been called back to Hanoi. This confirmed that fundamental decisions were in the offing. As a result, the meeting on August 14 turned into a holding action on both sides. I gave the North Vietnamese a number of documents that made up in legalistic complexity for what they lacked in substance: a statement of general principles drawn from the two preceding meetings; a ten-point negotiating document answering the ten points they had put forward on August 1; and a procedural paper accepting the principle of the different forums they had suggested on August 1 but changing the topics assigned to particular groups. The military issues were straightforward; we had been close to settling them during the previous year. We changed the formulation but not the substance. We put forward no political proposals *at all;* my pending visit to Saigon was the excuse. We agreed to meet again on September 15 on my way back from a long-planned trip to Moscow.

After three meetings, then, there had been significant movement, entirely by Hanoi; it was moving in the right direction but not at a pace that would keep it from reversing course later. Hanoi had given up the demand for Thieu's immediate removal. It had agreed to negotiating forums in which the Saigon government would participate, thus in a sense recognizing its legitimacy. It had abandoned the absurd demand for an unconditional deadline for the withdrawal of American forces. The proposed coalition government, heretofore a transparent front for a Communist takeover, had been reduced to a fifty-fifty split of power.

Moreover, Hanoi seemed to me to have lost some of its previously sure grasp. Le Duc Tho moved almost too urgently; various proposals succeeded each other so rapidly as practically to tempt me to wait to see what else he might have in reserve. And the procedural plan almost invited delay because it created a plethora of forums, each of which could bog down on technicalities and yet, according to Hanoi, *all* of which had to finish before a cease-fire could go into effect. This procedure was more appropriate for the side prepared on the whole to wait rather than for the one in a hurry to settle — which was, suddenly, the North Vietnamese.

But Hanoi had left itself plenty of loopholes. The concept of a coalition government, even on the terms suggested by Hanoi, remained unacceptable. It gave the side that controlled perhaps 10 percent of the population 50 percent of the power. And a fifty-fifty split between groups that had been killing each other for two decades was bound to be a sham. It was certain to turn into a starting point for a new contest, and we would have psychologically weakened our allies for that contest through withdrawing and giving their opponents a share of power disproportionate to their real public support. The procedural forums were as compatible with Thieu's being asked to negotiate his own demise as with accepting his legitimacy. Hanoi had not yet made a decisive choice; it still had a lot of running room.

I reported to the President after my August 14 meeting:

The North Vietnamese will be watching the polls in our country and the developments in South Vietnam and deciding whether to compromise before November. They have an agonizing choice. They can make a deal with an Administration that will give them a fair chance to jockey for power in the South, but refuses to guarantee their victory. Or they can hold out, knowing that this course almost certainly means they will face the same Administration with a fresh four-year mandate that reflects the American people's refusal to cap ten years of sacrifice with ignominy. . . . During this process we have gotten closer to a negotiated settlement than ever before; our negotiating record is becoming impeccable; and we still have a chance to make an honorable peace.

And Nixon's real attitude was reflected in the notes he wrote to Al Haig on the margin of my report:

Which means we have no progress in 15 meetings!*

Al — It is obvious that no progress was made and that none can be expected. Henry must be discouraged — as I have always been on this front until after the election. We have reached the stage where the mere *fact* of private talks helps us very little — if at all. We can soon expect the opposition to begin to make that point.

Disillusionment about K's talks *could* be harmful politically — particularly in view of the fact that the Saigon trip, regardless of how we downplay it, may raise expectations.

What we need most now is a P.R. game plan to either stop talks or if we continue them to give some hope of progress.

Clearly, Nixon would not have been pained if I had recommended halting all negotiations until after the election. I did not do that because my analysis was different.

A Visit to Saigon

In this mood of expectancy I arrived in Saigon on August 17, after having spent a day in Switzerland to celebrate my parents' fiftieth

---

* Actually, it had been my sixteenth secret meeting with the North Vietnamese.

wedding anniversary with them and my children. It was a peaceful respite from the fanatics from Hanoi and the desperate men in Saigon, each groping for a maneuver that would open the road to victory. We were caught seeking compromise from parties united only in their conviction that there was no middle ground, pressed by a public tired of its exertions, harassed by domestic opponents committed to end our involvement on nearly any terms.

Saigon was teeming with rumors that I had come to impose peace. The city wore its incongruous, characteristic air of hysterical lassitude, noisy with motorbikes and military vehicles, flaunting its desire for the good life so ostentatiously as to raise the question whether it could ever mobilize the dedication to prevail against enemies whose only profession, perhaps even avocation, was war. Ambassador Ellsworth Bunker greeted me at Tan Son Nhut airport, unflappable as always. He was convinced that Thieu felt stronger than ever but also that his newfound strength would make him more recalcitrant. Thieu thought that South Vietnam had the upper hand militarily; concessions to which he had agreed in less promising times appeared senseless to him now. He seemed, according to Bunker, genuinely afraid of peace. All his life, he too had known only war; his entire career had been based on American support. A world in which the South Vietnamese would have to stand entirely on their own was full of terrors that his pride would not let him admit.

My meetings with Thieu did not at first seem to support Bunker's forebodings. We met in the modernistic Presidential Palace, flung into the center of Saigon at the juncture of two broad boulevards as if to defy the legacies of both French colonialism and a Vietnamese past (which was, in truth, tenuous at best in this section of the country, taken only a little more than a century before from Cambodia). He was accompanied by Nguyen Phu Duc, who was more or less my equivalent on his staff, and Hoang Duc Nha, his nephew, press assistant, and confidant. Duc, a splendid product of the French educational system, moved from abstract definition to irrelevant conclusion with maddening, hairsplitting ingenuity. America had to take some responsibility for the egregious Nha. He was in his early thirties; he had been educated in the United States and in the process had seen too many movies of sharp young men succeeding by their wits; he came on like the early Alan Ladd in a gangster role. He was dressed in the fanciest Hollywood style, spoke American English fluently, and had retained from his Vietnamese background only an infinite capacity for intrigue. He reinforced Thieu's inherent suspiciousness. Both Bunker and I were convinced that he did much mischief in exacerbating every misunderstanding.

Thieu greeted us with his unvarying dignity and courtesy. His sparkling eyes gave no clue to his inner thoughts, which could not have been free of contempt for a superpower eager to settle for compromise when total victory seemed to him attainable. I assured him that the United States would not crown its long Vietnam effort with dishonor; that we would never join those Americans who regarded Thieu as the obstacle to peace. I hoped to leave Saigon with an agreed assessment and position. The North Vietnamese might have missed the opportunity for a cease-fire before the election, I thought. Too much remained to be negotiated; Hanoi's proposed procedure would make for delay. But whatever Hanoi's intentions, it was essential for Washington and Saigon to adopt a conciliatory posture if public support were to be maintained. And "if we can get a reasonable settlement we will, of course, accept it as you would."

To achieve these objectives I submitted for Thieu's consideration the proposal I planned to make to Le Duc Tho on September 15. We would not change our military proposals except to reduce our withdrawal deadline from four to three months. This did not make much difference, since over four months of actual withdrawals would have elapsed since we had offered the four-month deadline on May 8. On the political side we would reject a coalition government but spell out the composition of the joint electoral commission we had been offering for three years, since May 14, 1969.

Every American plan since that time had proposed an electoral commission on which the Communists would be represented, together with all other political forces; in other words, some sort of tripartite formula. My present idea was to finish off the scheme of coalition government by renaming the electoral commission a Committee of National Reconciliation, without changing its function. And I proposed to spell out its composition as tripartite in theory (the Communist formulation, only implicit in our previous proposals). However, each side would appoint half of the third segment — that is, the fifty-fifty split offered by Le Duc Tho. The renamed electoral commission would make decisions on the principle of unanimity. Thus Saigon had a double veto: in the composition of the Committee and in its operation. It never occurred to me that Thieu might object to a formula which represented only the thinnest pretense of a joint body and reduced the electoral commission to impotence. To underline further that the Committee had no function beyond supervising the election, another provision in our new plan permitted the Communists to participate in the government emerging from the election but only in proportion to the votes they polled. We estimated that this might give the Communists two out of twenty seats. As I explained to Thieu: "In our country political opponents are taken into the cabinet not to be given influence but to be deprived of it." That particular argument Thieu understood.

I was rather proud of this scheme. I thought it put to rest once and for all the idea of a coalition government, yet gave us a defensible position at home if Hanoi turned down our proposal. Thieu, it eventually transpired, did not share my high opinion of my drafting abilities.

A new and important dimension of Thieu now emerged. He had never before faced an American offer that he thought had any chance of being accepted by Hanoi. He had gone along with us before to establish a claim on continued support. But with serious negotiation approaching, his views and ours began increasingly to diverge. Schemes that only made our previous proposals more palatable he now treated as major deviations; what we considered tactical maneuvers he escalated into confrontations. He was looking for a retroactive justification to undo the negotiating record of the past three years.

We did not grasp what was happening right away. We still thought we were operating in tandem with Thieu and therefore blamed his reserve on drafting difficulties and shortsighted advisers. We were prepared to be patient in finding a solution. And Thieu confused us further by applying to us the elusive tactics Vietnamese reserve for foreigners: He never actually made an issue of anything; he simply sought to grind us down by keeping his agreement ever tantalizingly close but always out of reach. I should have recognized the methods from Le Duc Tho. Thieu raised no immediate objections to my presentation. Following a pattern with which we were to become only too familiar, he heard us out with seeming sympathy, asked penetrating questions, suggested modifications, discussed details of implementation. He said he agreed with me that the prospects for negotiations were not very bright; this had a relaxing effect on him. Thieu doubted that Hanoi would offer a cease-fire. A cease-fire worked too one-sidedly in our favor, he said. It would be a "gift" to President Nixon and it would be a psychological setback to the morale of the Communists, since they would be laying down their arms without any political achievement (arguments he would bitterly reject five weeks later). I agreed that Hanoi would probably not give up its political demands, but I reminded him that we were in fact committed to what we had proposed publicly: "If they come back — I don't want to mislead you — and say that there should be a cease-fire, we must accept it."

Thieu handed me an eight-page memorandum criticizing Le Duc Tho's August 1 proposal. It had been crafted in meticulous, nitpicking detail by Duc. After skimming it, I said with irony that I was left with the unavoidable impression that Saigon was not accepting every detail of Hanoi's proposal, but then neither would we. At the end of the conversation I noted again — for the third time — that if Hanoi accepted our May 8 proposal we would have no choice but to go along.

The next day, August 18, again at the Presidential Palace, Thieu handed me a new memorandum, this one of four pages, containing some twenty proposed changes in our plan. About fifteen of these were easily assimilated; others presented greater difficulty. Thieu wanted to alter the phrase "standstill cease-fire" to "general cease-fire" for reasons never made clear unless it was that the South Vietnamese forces had no intention of standing still after a cease-fire. Thieu objected to the tripartite Committee of National Reconciliation even in our fifty-fifty version. It would enshrine the Communists' tripartite principle, he said; it was bound to raise doubts among the population of South Vietnam. I responded by explaining our strategy once again. We wanted to gain time. We wanted to protect ourselves against Hanoi's going public with its proposals. We were merely spelling out what we had offered for over two years. We had always stated publicly that all elements including Communists would be represented on the electoral commission. We were in effect burying the coalition government. For these purposes we wanted to keep some formulations ambiguous; we could not afford to have the talks break down over theological points. On the other hand, I pointed out, for yet a fourth time, that if Hanoi proposed an unconditional cease-fire we would have to accept. Thieu reiterated (again, with later irony) his belief that the North Vietnamese were afraid of a cease-fire because "once they accept a cease-fire they can never start again and we will prolong the political talks forever." Thieu seemed above all afraid that we might make political concessions; the cease-fire timing concerned him less. This turned out to be a misapprehension; Thieu opposed whatever aspect appeared close to a solution. In any event, we finally decided not to alter the existing language on the cease-fire.

But there was a deeper reason for Thieu's ambivalance. He had no difficulty pointing out ambiguities in negotiating documents designed to bridge the gap between mortal enemies. But none of these drafting changes went to the heart of the problem, which for Thieu was domestic and ultimately involved the survival of the non-Communist political structure in South Vietnam: "My duty to the people, the army, political groups and the National Assembly is first of all not to shock them." He had to convince his people that an agreement was not a defeat nor a threat to South Vietnam's internal stability. For this he would always need time. "Even if we accept your proposal we have to study how to explain it." In this Thieu was quite right, and we were to end up pressing him too quickly for his own domestic stability. But it was also to be true that Thieu's own infuriating negotiating style deprived us of any real insight into his thinking.

Only gradually did it dawn on us that we faced not a drafting difficulty but a fundamental philosophical division. The root fact was that Thieu and his government were simply not ready for a negotiated peace. They had a few vague ideas that amounted to an unconditional surrender by Hanoi. They were not satisfied with survival; they wanted a guarantee that they would prevail. They preferred to continue the military contest rather than face a political struggle. As Bunker said on August 31 when he, the President, and I met in Honolulu to review the bidding: "They fear that they are not yet well enough organized to compete politically with such a tough disciplined organization."

But we had our own imperatives. We had struggled and suffered for four years over a war from which we were trying to disengage. We had accepted nearly unbearable fissures in our society to maintain our honor and credibility. We had sustained our effort only by convincing our public that the one issue on which we would not compromise was to impose a Communist government on an ally. But if Hanoi were to accept our offer of a cease-fire, we would not be able to respond with an open-ended commitment to continue the war in pursuit of unconditional victory. If Nixon decided otherwise, the Congress would make our nightmare real and vote us out of the war without any significant conditions, undermining the authority of the American Presidency in every corner of the globe.

Neither Thieu — nor I, for that matter — could come up with a convincing military strategy to change the basic balance of forces in Indochina should negotiations break down. I played with the idea of a two-day South Vietnamese landing operation along the North Vietnamese coast to draw North Vietnamese regular units away from South Vietnam. Thieu was mildly interested, but we both recognized that this was a gimmick, not a strategy. Nor did Thieu's crystal ball show a clear-cut alternative. He expressed the view that by December 1973 — fifteen months away — "if we don't sign anything . . . they will have less supplies, less manpower and less regular units in December 1973 than they had in December 1971 or March of 1972." In other words, after another long stretch of fighting presumably backed by unimpaired American airpower, we could look forward to a balance of forces similar to that which had produced only stalemates in the past. We did not think that either our public or the Congress would hold still for this prospect. And I knew that budgetary stringency would soon force us to reduce our augmentation forces.

The dialogue between Saigon and Washington thus developed like a Greek tragedy in which each side in pursuit of its own necessities produces what it most dreads. For in essence both sides were right. Thieu was a patriot and a highly intelligent man. He had seen his country through a searing war with ability and dedication. He did not deserve the opprobrium American opponents of the war heaped on him as an outlet for their frustration and as an alibi for the surrender they wanted to force on their government. But the imperatives on him were almost diametrically the opposite of ours.

He was, in his view and ours, the legitimate head of the government of South Vietnam. For him to accept the potential legitimacy of those seeking to subvert it was to undermine the psychological basis of his rule. Yet their acceptance in some form was inherent in even the most attenuated compromise proposal. Thieu's domestic imperatives imposed intransigence. We could sustain our support for him only by a show of conciliation. Our goal was honor; we could (as the phrase went) run a risk for peace. But Thieu's problem was survival; he and his people would be left indefinitely after we departed; he had no margin for error.

Nor were Thieu's premonitions unfounded. In the process of meeting the demands of our insatiable opponents in the media and the Congress, we had already reduced our terms to a level far below that which had been thought necessary to maintain the security of South Korea under much more favorable circumstances and over twenty years after the end of the Korean War. Whereas 50,000 American combat troops were still stationed in Korea, we proposed to withdraw *all* our troops from Vietnam, which had much longer and much less easily defended frontiers and an even more implacable enemy. All Thieu would get while the military balance was basically in his favor was a cease-fire with an enemy who had observed no agreement since 1954. In exchange the United States would totally withdraw, not likely to return. Thieu would have most liked unabated United States support until his enemy disintegrated.

Our constant search for some compromise formula illuminated the cultural gap between us and the Vietnamese because the very concept of compromise was alien to both Vietnamese parties.

We had no way of understanding the primeval hatred that animated the two sides. They had fought each other for a generation. They had assassinated each other's officials, tortured each other's prisoners. The chasm of distrust and mutually inflicted suffering was unbridgeable by goodwill or the sort of compromise formulas toward which Americans incline. Each Vietnamese party saw in a settlement the starting point of a new struggle sometime in the not too distant future. Every deliberately vague formula I put forward was tested by each side to determine to what extent it represented an opportunity to inflict a humiliation on the despised opponent. And both sides were marvelously subtle and ingenious in changing phraseology to score such victories, particularly in the Vietnamese language with its finely shaded meanings quite beyond our grasp.

Luckily, none of this was apparent to me at the end of August or else I might not have had the courage to launch myself into what followed; even Thieu may have grasped it only dimly. In fact, he and I had engaged in a minuet, stately in its careful avoidance of the real issues, courtly in its pretense of continued partnership, inherently inconclusive in confining itself to traditional, now irrelevant, patterns. Thieu certainly complicated matters by never making his objections explicit. Instead, like Le Duc Tho in Paris, he fought with characteristic Vietnamese opaqueness and with a cultural arrogance compounded by a French Cartesianism that defined any deviation from abstract, unilaterally proclaimed principles as irreconcilable error.

I left Saigon with a false sense of having reached a meeting of the minds. Thieu and I had decided that we would settle the few remaining disagreements over our draft proposal by exchanging messages through Bunker. There was plenty of time — nearly four weeks until my next meeting on September 15.

Instead, Thieu enveloped himself in silence; we heard absolutely nothing from the Palace. And Nha began to play his little games with the media. After what we had endured in our domestic debate on behalf of Saigon, we were perhaps overly sensitive to the attacks on our motives that found their way increasingly into the Saigon newspapers from the office of the egregious Nha. Certainly their treatment of Ellsworth Bunker, who, then in his seventies, had sustained Saigon for five years, verged on the despicable. Bunker's requests for appointments with Thieu went unanswered or were granted after so much delay that their subject matter had become moot. For example, we had invited Bunker to come on August 31 to Honolulu where Nixon was meeting with the new Japanese Prime Minister, Kakuei Tanaka. The purpose was to review my negotiations with Le Duc Tho. Bunker was to consult with the South Vietnamese so we would have the benefit of their thinking. I was hoping to use the occasion to complete the draft proposal to be submitted on September 15. But despite repeated efforts, Bunker failed to obtain an appointment with Thieu in time. Nor would Saigon reply to our comments on the memorandum handed to me by Thieu, which we had wired from the plane on August 19.

Once again we accepted most of Duc's quibbles, including some that in our judgment were more favorable to Hanoi than our original draft. (We did not, for example, accept a change proposed by Saigon that would have singled out American POW pilots for early release; we did not think it proper to make distinctions among branches of our services.) But that was not the heart of the matter. No sooner had we solved one issue than the indefatigable Duc and Nha would come up with another nitpick. The major bone of contention was Saigon's objection to our proposed composition of the Committee of National Reconciliation. The difference depended on the hairsplitting issue of whether its three segments should be specifically named, as we suggested, or referred to only in a general manner, as Saigon wished. (Graduate students who are interested may read the formulations in the notes at the back.)[1]

At our meeting in Hawaii, Bunker stressed to Nixon and me that he thought we were on the right course. I told Bunker that we counted on him to tell us if we went too far; he was our conscience. "We have not sacrificed all these years in order to sell out now," I told him. "If you think this is unreasonable, we'll change it. And we'll pay whatever price we have to." Bunker reaffirmed his view that out policy was sound; it was indeed the only one possible. As a result of our conversations with Bunker, a Presidential letter to Thieu was drafted and Nixon signed it. It reassured Thieu that "we will not do now what we have refused to do in the preceding three and a half years," that is, abandon South Vietnam. The proposals in question, Nixon argued, would safeguard Saigon's interests if accepted by the enemy and if rejected would strengthen support in the United States for our joint course.

Bunker returned to Saigon on September 5. Armed with the Presidential letter, he was at last received by Thieu on September 6, only to be told that the response to our memoranda would be given the next day. We were now only a week away from my meeting with Le Duc Tho and only two days from my leaving for Moscow. I wired Bunker, pointing out that our "new" proposal was in effect the January 25 proposal with the composition of the electoral commission — in which we had always stated the Communists would be represented — spelled out in somewhat more detail.

On September 7, Thieu applied his now familiar tactics to Bunker. He asked Bunker perceptive questions about our draft and what we would do if it were rejected. He listened as Bunker carefully pointed out the revisions we had made in our proposal in response to Saigon's suggestions. He left Bunker with the impression that he would go along, which prompted me to congratulate Bunker on the "encouraging" results. Then on September 9 Duc and Nha gave Bunker a new draft that reopened additional issues. On September 10 — already en route to Moscow — I accepted most of them, asking for some discretionary flexibility only on the composition of the Committee of National Reconciliation. On September 13, after a month of back-and-forthing and forty-eight hours before my meeting with Le Duc Tho, Thieu again rejected our proposal for, the composition of the Committee. Thieu turned it down not because the Committee bothered him, but because he was not ready for a cease-fire.

Insolence is the armor of the weak; it is a device to induce courage in the face of one's own panic. But that is clearer to me now than it was then. In September 1972 a second Vietnamese party — our own ally — had managed to generate in me that impotent rage by which the Vietnamese have always tormented physically stronger opponents. After a month of exchanges Thieu had dug in on a point so peripheral to the final result that we would never be able to justify to our people breaking up a negotiation over it. If we simply stonewalled on September 15 and Hanoi went public, we would start from a much worse position. If we accepted Thieu's conduct, all coordinated diplomacy would vanish; we would have reached the condition that our domestic critics had accused us of permitting: Thieu would have an absolute veto over our policy.

Our strategy at this juncture was simply what I had advocated in my 1968 *Foreign Affairs* article and in innumerable memoranda and negotiations since: to separate the military and political issues; to settle the military issues (cease-fire, prisoners, withdrawal) first, and to leave the political issues for negotiation between the Vietnamese — giving our allies in Saigon, whom we had strengthened for many years, the opportunity to flourish by their own efforts.

I had explained my strategy at great length to Thieu on August 17 and 18. I had also outlined it in a memorandum to Nixon on August 25:

(1) We want to conclude a negotiated settlement, or at least a breakthrough in principle, on honorable terms. In these efforts, we draw the line at imposing a communist government or making its emergence inevitable.

(2) If a reasonable solution is not possible, we want to make the best possible record for public opinion. In this case, we have to ensure that the negotiations break up over the other side's exorbitant political demands so as to isolate those in our country who would have us accept ignominious terms.

Hanoi and Saigon both rejected my strategy precisely because it involved compromise and because both Vietnamese parties still yearned for a decisive victory. Dobrynin told me on August 22 that Le Duc Tho objected for reasons surprisingly similar to those of Thieu. Le Duc Tho, according to Dobrynin, was convinced that all my formulations had one overriding purpose: to end the military phase of the war while defining the political outcome in general principles whose implementation Hanoi would then have to negotiate with the South Vietnamese, "a process which might take forever." The upshot would be that the South Vietnamese political structure would survive. Hanoi found this impossible to swallow. Thieu had the same objection to the possibilities of physical survival of the Communists. Neither party felt secure enough to risk any letup in the demand for total victory. *Both* seemed to fear the political struggle that would follow a cease-fire. Both strove mightily to push me off the narrow line I was trying to walk in giving Hanoi a face-saving political formula to arrange what amounted to a settlement of the military issues only and the preservation of the political structure of our allies.

Le Duc Tho tried to get me to go beyond form into a substance that would in fact undermine Saigon. Thieu sought to block my concessions on form to avoid having to face the cease-fire, which was his real concern and which would spell the withdrawal of American forces and an end to our bombing. So at the end of the war we managed to "unite" the two Vietnamese parties after all — in their common alarm at American objectives and eventually their common dislike and distrust of the principal American negotiator.

If my analysis was correct, we had to make some cosmetic concession again at the September 15 meeting lest Hanoi conclude that we were stalling and go public with seemingly conciliatory positions that would unravel our domestic support.

We now had three strategic choices: first, to attempt to settle before our election; second, to bring matters to a head by drastic escalation immediately after the election; third, to continue the conflict at its current pace in the hope that somewhere along the line Hanoi would crack and offer even better terms. I favored the first course; Nixon the second. He sought essentially the same terms as I, but he preferred to achieve them by a dramatic show of force immediately after winning a new popular mandate. The third option was more apparent than real. Obstacles to our continuing on the current course were growing, both within and outside the government. In August, Mel Laird, seeking to ease the strain on his defense budget, had sent a memorandum to the President recommending an immediate 20 percent cut in our augmentation forces (those sent since the enemy offensive began), a 40 percent reduction in the rate of aircraft sorties, and a cut in the ammunition supplies. When Nixon refused, Laird put forward the proposal for an even deeper cut effective January 1 (described earlier). Such pressures would be bound to accelerate as the budgetary process went forward.

Moreover, we were again locked into the withdrawal syndrome. On August 29 Nixon announced another withdrawal of 12,000 men, which reduced our forces in Vietnam to 27,000 (well below what we still had in South Korea). The President and I wanted to leave open the public possibility that this might be a permanent residual force which Hanoi could get us to remove only by making concessions. But the Pentagon immediately leaked that it did not consider this the end of the withdrawals. In six months' time we would undoubtedly face budgetary pressures, led by Laird, and Congressional and media demands to complete a total unilateral withdrawal, depriving ourselves of another negotiating asset.

As soon as Congress returned in January we would be inevitably confronted by a new flood of resolutions setting a terminal date for our involvement, at best on terms less favorable than those we might be able to achieve in Paris. In short, I thought Hanoi was miscalculating when it judged that Nixon would be much stronger after the election. If we did not strike while the iron was hot *before* November 7, Hanoi would soon see the fragility of our position. We would then confront again the maddening mixture of procrastination, ambiguous concession, and occasional military "high points" with which Hanoi had sought to grind us down.

I could favor Nixon's option of escalating dramatically *after* the election only as a last resort in case of a total negotiating deadlock; it was preferable to the interminable agony of another long stretch of open-ended conflict. But it could not be our preferred strategy. It would mean that Nixon would begin his second term amid domestic uproar; the wounds that the Vietnam war caused in our society would become even more difficult to heal. Congressional pressures would be accelerated; and we would be pushed up against the January 3 deadline of Congress's return. And for all this we would not achieve terms significantly better than what at last was beginning to appear possible. We could not at this late stage raise the ante in Paris beyond what we had been proposing for two years and most explicitly on January 25 and May 8 — all of which went beyond the Congressional consensus.

Thus if Hanoi decided to settle before the election, we had, in my view, an opportunity that might be unlikely to return. After November 7, whichever course we chose — endurance or escalation — would have to be pursued without a deadline on Hanoi; *we* would be pushed against the grindstone of Congressional pressures. We might not even be able to count on Soviet and Chinese acquiescence indefinitely, or we might be asked to pay some price for it in our relations with them. I thought it wiser to exploit a unique conjunction of circumstances that put us in the strongest domestic, military, and international positions in many years. It was time to seek to extract the maximum concessions from Hanoi.

These were the reasons that induced me to recommend to Nixon that on September 15 we submit a proposal that was only a minor elaboration of the electoral commission, which had been the staple of our position since May 1969. It included the provision on the composition of the Committee of National Reconciliation that Thieu had not accepted. I cabled Nixon, requesting his approval:

> If the other side accepts our proposal, which we believe quite unlikely, then the fact that GVN was not totally on board to the last detail will be obscured by myriad other complexities in what will essentially be a new ballgame. In such an eventuality, it is inconceivable that GVN would find it in its interest to surface what few differences we may have had. . . .

> If on the other hand [the] other side rejects our offer, as we think far more likely, GVN will have absolutely every incentive to go along with us. We cannot imagine that they would want to publicly intimate the existence of any past divergences with us once our reasonable offer is out in the open, Hanoi has declined it, and we are in an excellent position to counter any public efforts by the other side by pointing to negotiating initiative of our own.

Nixon was far from enthusiastic. He was bolstered by a Lou Harris public opinion poll published on September 11, which disclosed that a substantial majority of American voters (55 percent to 32 percent) supported the continued heavy bombings of North Vietnam, and a 64-to-22 majority supported the mining of North Vietnamese harbors. A 47-to-35 plurality was opposed to a coalition government in South Vietnam (the widest plurality ever on that question). By 51 percent to 26 percent, a majority of the public did not agree with McGovern's charge that "Henry Kissinger's travels to Paris and Saigon were no more than a publicity stunt that falsely raised hopes for peace." And by 51 percent to 33 percent, more voters agreed with President Nixon's approach to bringing home American forces from Vietnam than with McGovern's approach. (Twelve days earlier, on August 30, the Gallup Poll had showed the following election preferences: Nixon, 64 percent; McGovern, 30 percent; undecided, 6 percent.)

In these circumstances Nixon saw no political advantage in adopting my recommendations. But as was his custom where national security was concerned, he accepted the foreign policy rationale though not without reminding me that it was really against his political interests. Haig cabled to me in Moscow:

> He [the President] stated that the NSC does not seem to understand that the American people are no longer interested in a solution based on compromise, favor continued bombing and want to see the United States prevail after all these years. I pointed out that this very attitude was fragile and had been accomplished simply because we had been able to carefully blend a series of strong and forthcoming measures in a way that reestablished Presidential credibility. . . . The President finally agreed but insisted that in conveying his approval to you that I emphasize to you his wish that the record you establish tomorrow in your discussions be a tough one which in a public sense would appeal to the Hawk and not to the Dove. I again told the President that the record thus far of these meetings was unassailable and that I was confident that it would remain that way following tomorrow's meeting.

With the advantage of hindsight I believe we could have risked proceeding with Saigon's formulation and without the modification I proposed. Hanoi would almost surely not have broken off the talks fearing the clear prospect of Nixon's reelection. I now think also that this course would have been tactically wise; it would perhaps have reduced Thieu's mistrust, though given our different perspectives nothing could have prevented the final blowup. In the negotiation, it made no difference. For our proposal was never even discussed. On September 15 Le Duc Tho made our proposal irrelevant by presenting the third new North Vietnamese proposal in the four meetings since July.

Interlude: Meetings of September 15 and 27

O N the way back from Moscow I stopped at Chequers on the evening of September 14 to brief Prime Minister Heath about my conversations with the Soviet leaders. We had announced that I would also go to Paris to brief Pompidou. But habits of secrecy are hard to break. In order to gain the six hours needed for meeting Le Duc Tho I flew to Paris by a small plane from a British military airport early in the morning of September 15. To mask my movements, Do Not Disturb signs were left on the doors of our suites at Claridge's Hotel, and the Presidential plane remained at Heathrow until it flew off to Paris later in the day. It was a pointless — even juvenile — game not worth playing, since we would announce the meeting with Le Duc Tho later in the day in any event. From then until the end of the negotiations we made no special efforts to mask my movements, and indeed toward the end began to announce them in advance.

As was the case so often in the history of Vietnam negotiations, the meeting itself mocked all the carefully laid plans. Le Duc Tho continued in the mild, almost pleasant tone that he had displayed since the July 19 meeting. There was again none of the bravado of the first three years, of how American and world opinion would force us to settle. Almost plaintively, he repeatedly inquired whether we were willing to settle rapidly. I was vaguely reassuring, intentionally magnifying his uneasiness. Finally, I brought forward our overall plan, including the paragraph to which Thieu objected. Le Duc Tho dismissed it as nothing basically new, which was close to the mark. But instead of sticking to his previous position, he tabled a new ten-point proposal. Its major feature was to deprive the Government of National Concord (as outlined by him at only our last session) of some of its power. Whereas on August 14 Hanoi had agreed that the Saigon government could continue until the Government of National Concord was formed, Tho now proposed that the two existing administrations continue even *after* a settlement. The Government of National Concord would be confined to supervising compliance with the provisions of the agreement and the conduct of foreign policy; it was again "provisional," to last until a final settlement for which, however, there was no clear-cut procedure. Committees of National Concord would be set up in each province; they would govern all contested areas. Saigon would be in charge of domestic policy in all areas controlled by it. But Tho added — not prepared to give up a debating point even when he was in a hurry — that since most areas were contested, the Committees of National Concord would take over most of the country. Le Duc Tho also put forward a number of cosmetic concessions such as extending the deadline for our withdrawal from his original thirty days to forty-five days (as against the three months in our proposal).

As Le Duc Tho must have expected, I rejected his political proposal outright. We would accept no coalition government in any guise, I told him. Contrary to his previous practice, he responded with only the mildest ritual complaints about our "sincerity," and even seemed to redouble his efforts. Was I prepared to aim for an agreement in principle by a certain timetable? he suddenly wanted to know. After such an agreement the various forums proposed in his August 1 draft would begin to negotiate its implementation. I saw no harm in agreeing to a target date so long as we were making no additional concessions. We settled on October 15. The various forums would still leave plenty of room to refine aspects of the basic agreement.

To gain more time and thereby bring more pressure on Le Duc Tho, I proposed that we devote the next meeting to nailing down language on the already agreed points. These were mostly on the military questions. Tho was the model of conciliation. He agreed, though pointing out that progress on the political question would facilitate the solution of the military issues; it was no longer a precondition. He next proposed a *two-day* meeting, preferably *within a week's time*. I accepted this unprecedented request, but pushed the date back to September 26. The more we squeezed Le Duc Tho against what was more clearly than ever his self-imposed deadline (our Presidential election), the more forthcoming he was likely to be. In a summary memorandum prepared for Nixon immediately after the meeting I wrote:

It is not entirely clear what they have to gain by being so eager to pursue the dialogue. Their dilemma is that further talks strengthen our domestic position and negotiating record without in any way restricting our military flexibility, while if they break them off, they have no hope of settling before November, which I sense from our meeting is their strong preference.

My surmise is that they are deeply concerned about your re-election and its implications for them but, with their collective leadership, they may be having deep difficulties coming to grips with the very political concessions they will have to make to move the talks off dead center. They continue to pose unacceptable demands, perhaps because they lack imagination, perhaps because they wish to defer the necessary concessions to the last possible moment.

We were, in fact, in the strongest bargaining position of the war. September 15 was the day that South Vietnamese forces recaptured Quang Tri, the one provincial capital taken by Hanoi in its offensive. It was the week of polls showing growing American public support for Nixon's handling of the war and the widest Nixon lead over McGovern ever. And it was the time (we learned a few weeks later) that COSVN Directive 06 informed Communist cadres that an effort would be made to "force" Nixon to settle the war before election day — which was Hanoi's way of preparing its people for an agreement essentially on our terms.

The September 15 meeting turned out to be the last regular session held at 11 rue Darthé in Choisy-le-Roi. Although I had masked my movements, Le Duc Tho was not so successful — or careful. His presence in Paris was known; a few days earlier he had even hinted to journalists about a meeting with me, which, however, gave us no difficulty. (While I was in Moscow, Tho had replied to a newsman's query about meeting me: "You will have an answer in a few days' time.") An enterprising CBS-TV film crew followed Le Duc Tho from his residence to the meeting place and ended up with film of my entering and leaving the hitherto secret house. It was left to the North Vietnamese to find a new venue for subsequent meetings.

I left the September 15 meeting satisfied that we had again turned down a coalition government and convinced that Hanoi was well on the way to separating the military and political issues as we wanted. Hanoi, having come this far, would sooner or later table its rock-bottom position. This same prospect filled Thieu with renewed dismay. Bunker was again unable to obtain an appointment with Thieu to report on my meeting with Tho. But Bunker gave me his own assessment that our "patience and persistence seems to be paying off." He added: "I think we have been understanding and very forbearing in deferring to his [Thieu's] views and I believe that we should now be firm in making clear that we also have imperatives."

Instead of getting to see Thieu, Bunker on September 16 was handed a letter from Thieu to Nixon ostensibly in reply to Nixon's letter of August 31. It was artfully written (probably by the American-educated Nha), expressing agreement with all the President's general points. Characteristically, it voiced no appreciation for our having held the line on the key issues of coalition government, supervised cease-fire, and no further infiltration; rather, it warned that no further concessions should be made:

> . . . the Communists should not be encouraged to apply a more ingenious and less expensive method to take over countries through so-called negotiated and political peace solutions. . . . Therefore to continue to make concessions to the Communists in a very illogical way serves only to encourage them in being more stubborn in their position and their pursuit of aggression.

Not acknowledging that *all* our previous proposals had had his concurrence, Thieu said that the terms we had already offered were "indeed too forthcoming, very reasonable and logical, and on which we have gone too far." (Calling our previous proposals "reasonable and logical" was a chilling echo of North Vietnamese phraseology.) Thieu's strictures were as unnecessary as they were wounding, for we had no intention of offering anything new at the next meeting.

Thieu finally deigned on September 17 to receive Bunker's briefing on my meeting with Le Duc Tho. Thieu saw two possibilities: The North Vietnamese might be preparing to reach an agreement in principle prior to our elections, or else they were uncertain about our strategy.

Still half-believing that Thieu's hostility must reflect a misunderstanding, I sent Bunker an even more detailed report of the September 15 session and added a report on my discussions of Vietnam in Moscow, which were in fact superficial since I saw little that Moscow could contribute to the intense exchanges taking place in Paris. But the prospect of success seemed only to heighten Thieu's intransigence. On September 20 in a speech in Hué, he pointedly declared: "No one has a right to negotiate for or accept any solution" except the people of South Vietnam. On September 23 I made one more effort to heal the breach, wiring Bunker:

It is also important that Thieu understand that in the sensitive period facing us, his discernible attitude on the negotiations could have a major influence on Hanoi's strategy. If Thieu is genuinely worried that we might settle prematurely, he must understand that the appearance of differences between Washington and Saigon could have the practical consequence of influencing Hanoi toward a rapid settlement in the secret talks so as to exploit what they might perceive as a split between the U.S. and GVN and the resulting political disarray in Saigon. This would disrupt the carefully measured pace we are attempting to maintain. Our strategy at this point is to force further movement in Hanoi's position and maintain the appearance of constructive activity in Paris while continuing to apply maximum military pressure. Therefore it is essential that Thieu stay close to us so that we demonstrate solidarity to Hanoi.

For the meeting of September 26–27 the North Vietnamese, somewhat sheepish about their responsibility for blowing the cover of the Rue Darthé meeting place, had found a new site. To get there we had to follow a route seemingly designed to remind one of the past, present, and future of our host country, France. We drove southwest out of Paris through the Bois de Boulogne, past the racetrack of Longchamp; then we skirted the monument marking the route of General Leclerc's liberation of Paris in 1944, traversed the intersection at Le Petit Clamart where de Gaulle escaped an assassination attempt in 1962, and passed the nuclear research center at Saclay. In the small quiet country town of Gif-sur-Yvette, at number 108 avenue de Général Leclerc, behind a high green wooden fence, was a one-story white stucco house with a large garden. This was our new meeting site. We had graduated to more pleasant and elegant surroundings.

The North Vietnamese would not say how they found the house, only that it was lent to them by "friends." It turned out that the "friends" were the French Communist Party. It had been the home and studio of the cubist painter Fernand Léger, who had been a Party member or fellow traveler and had bequeathed his house to his grateful Party when he died in 1955. Thus incongruously amid striking reproductions (and perhaps some originals) of Léger's abstract paintings and tapestries, we began a crucial round of increasingly concrete negotiations to end the war. Our new location was to remain peacefully undiscovered for two more months until, after my "peace is at hand" press conference of October 26, the world's journalists laid on massive and unshakable pursuit when we returned to Gif-sur-Yvette in late November.

Le Duc Tho and Xuan Thuy displayed the same sense of urgency for an early end to the war that they had on September 15. They spent the first two hours laying out a work program (a "shed*yule,*" according to Nguyen Dinh Phuong, the North Vietnamese interpreter) * designed to complete a settlement *within the month*. This "shedyule" soon took the place of the epic poem of Hanoi's struggle for liberation as the opening ritual of our talks. Tho would put forward his recommendations for accelerated negotiation like an opening prayer. I would respond. We would haggle, since I considered this as good a subject as any other on which to waste time so as to push Hanoi against its own deadline. At last I would agree to the "shedyule." Tho would then write it down personally in a little notebook whose pages were lined with blue squares, thereby conferring additional solemnity on it. The next time we met the process would be repeated. The "shedyule," however, would be slipped by the interval of time that had since elapsed. Once in exasperation Tho called out: "I am writing it down but I want you to know that I don't believe it."

When we finally turned to substance, Le Duc Tho came back to the idea of a visit by me to Hanoi to overcome final differences. This was included in the "shedyule" hypothetically if we completed the negotiations. After a businesslike point-by-point review of the differences and similarities between the two sides' positions, Le Duc Tho submitted yet another new comprehensive proposal, their fourth in five meetings. (In the past they had stuck to their plans for at least six months.) He did this even after I had said that I would withhold any new ideas to reflect on his comments overnight. (It was just as well; all I had were minor drafting changes.)

Le Duc Tho's new plan — which he called his "final" offer — stripped away further layers from the Communist demand for a tripartite coalition government and moved again toward our proposal, which reduced this essentially to a mixed electoral commission. He still called for a "Provisional Government of National Concord" without Thieu, but once again he had reduced its functions; the Government of National Concord was to be *advisory* to the existing governments with a vague responsibility to mediate between the two sides, and with neither en-

---

* Far be it from me to make fun of anyone's accent — he was an excellent interpreter. But the schedule that Le Duc Tho insisted on became a crucial point in the breakdown of the negotiation in October. The word "schedule" — pronounced in the British way but with the stress oddly on the last syllable — was repeated so many times by Le Duc Tho that it remains indelibly in my memory in Mr. Phuong's pronunciation.

forcement powers nor the right to conduct foreign policy. It, like our proposed Committee of National Reconciliation, would "operate in accordance with the principle of unanimity" — that is, any member had a veto, guaranteeing its impotence even for its limited functions. It remained unacceptable, but "from Hanoi's perspective it represents major movement," I later reported to the President. It was "not inconsistent," I observed, "with their eventually turning their coalition government into an irrelevant committee in order to give a face-saving cover to a standstill cease-fire and de facto territorial control by both sides."

An even more stunning concession was Le Duc Tho's suggestion that after a settlement Hanoi's troops would withdraw from both Laos and Cambodia and that our prisoners in Laos would be released. (He said there were no American prisoners in Cambodia.) It was a remarkable breakthrough. We had insisted on an Indochina-wide cease-fire; we had pressed for the release of all our prisoners held in Indochina; we had demanded North Vietnamese withdrawal from the other countries of Indochina. None of these requirements, except the return of prisoners, had much domestic support in America; yet all were on the way to being realized. Even the quality of the snacks served to us escalated dramatically. On the second day, September 27, they served us caviar, shrimp flour chips, white wine and sherry, in addition to fruit and spring rolls.

Since our strategy seemed to be working, I confined myself to handing over short drafts on such questions as international guarantees, the technicalities of international supervision of a cease-fire, and the exchange of prisoners. As Le Duc Tho pressed harder and harder for rapid progress, he expressed irritation that I was only inching forward and concentrating on peripheral issues — which was true.

I told Le Duc Tho that many of his new proposals were steps forward. However, the continuing requirement that Thieu would have to leave office after the signature of a final agreement was ridiculous. I emphasized again that we would never overthrow our allies, directly or by some subterfuge. Le Duc Tho stressed the "finality" of their offer. I reiterated that the American people would never stand for our ending a war which had cost so much by imposing a Communist government. The final outcome would have to be left to the free decision of the people — a concept that Tho had great difficulty in grasping. He seemed bothered by the winner-take-all aspect of Saigon's presidential elections; he wondered whether the proposed election could not be for a Constituent Assembly instead of for the President. Finally, Le Duc Tho asked whether our proposed Committee of National Reconciliation could be given any function beyond supervising elections. He was prepared for a *three*-day session next time. He proposed October 7 — ten days away. He said that the meeting would be "decisive." To step up the pressure slightly I accepted for October 8.

All this made it increasingly obvious that we were approaching a crucial point. We had in principle settled all military issues: cease-fire, infiltration, withdrawals, release of prisoners, international supervision, Laos. We lacked agreement on Cambodia. Le Duc Tho was still pushing political formulas designed to undermine Saigon. But his eagerness for a three-day meeting in early October left no doubt that we had not yet heard the last word. That might prove unacceptable and when we came to drafting what had been agreed in principle the whole process might evaporate. But we had come a long way. The next meeting would bring either a breakthrough or a commitment to another military test.

I had no doubt what Thieu preferred. Defiant leaks from Saigon were multiplying. Appreciation for services rendered is not a Vietnamese trait; Thieu took our dogged rearguard action on behalf of his country for granted; or else he wanted to shift the onus for any concessions onto our shoulders. But as we approached this climactic moment, another consultation with Thieu was clearly necessary.

Nixon was campaigning on the West Coast. Within hours of my return from Paris on September 27 I reached Haldeman in Los Angeles and proposed that we send Al Haig to Saigon to review with Thieu the various contingencies that might arise in my next meeting with Le Duc Tho. Nixon agreed.

I recommended that we put a number of options before Thieu as political proposals for the next meeting. We might agree to elections for a Constituent Assembly instead of presidential elections; withdrawing the proposal for a presidential election would remove any need for Thieu's resignation. We might ask the proposed Committee of National Reconciliation to review the Constitution one year after a peace agreement for consistency with its terms. This seemed to me the safest course since Saigon would have an absolute veto in this body.

As it turned out, all ingenuity was wasted. Haig could have saved himself the trip. A great admirer of Thieu, Haig this time found himself exposed to the standard Thieu treatment, which in turn was very similar to Le Duc Tho's tactics in Paris when Hanoi thought it was in a strong position. When the two men met first on October 2, for two hours and forty minutes in the Presidential Palace, Thieu was calm and conciliatory, asking thoughtful questions designed to elicit as much information as possible. Haig followed talking points drafted by me and my staff that laid out our strategy of exploiting Hanoi's impatience to elicit further concessions. Conversely, a continuing stalemate that could be attacked at home as resulting from our failure to seize opportunities for peace would in the long run threaten our capacity to aid South Vietnam. Haig explained why we had proceeded as we did on September 15. Our willingness to put forward something marginally new had been important to keep the process going; Hanoi had in fact made a "dramatically revised proposal." We needed something marginally new for the next negotiating session, for the same purpose. Haig outlined the options Nixon had approved.

Haig assumed from Thieu's reaction that Thieu was reassured. (Thieu seemed to be expecting that we would ask again for his commitment to resign before a new election.) Haig reported that Thieu's frame of mind was ''as constructive as we could have hoped for and he will be inclined to be more cooperative than otherwise would have been the case.''

He was soon to learn otherwise. His scheduled appointment with Thieu for October 3 was abruptly canceled. In the meantime Nixon had met with Gromyko at Camp David on October 2. Under the impact of Haig's optimistic report, Nixon had told Gromyko that we would make our final offer at the meeting of October 8. If it were rejected, there would be no further negotiation during the election period. Afterward, we would turn to ''other methods.''

On October 4, Thieu dropped the other shoe. He confronted Haig with his entire National Security Council and bitterly attacked almost every aspect of the American proposal, including those he had long since accepted. He would discuss none of the variants we had put before him. Thieu was in tears at some moments. (I was to be subjected to the identical procedure less than three weeks later.) Haig reported:

> We have just completed 3 hour, 50 minute session with President Thieu and his National Security Council, including Vice President Huong, Prime Minister Khiem, Foreign Minister Lam, Foreign Policy Assistant Duc, and Special Assistant Nha. It was very apparent to Bunker and myself as we approached the Palace that a confrontation was in the offing. Traffic had apparently been stopped for some time and as we entered the Palace there was clear evidence of an atmosphere of crisis. When Bunker and I were called to the President's office, we were instead ushered straight to the conference room where the National Security Council was in waiting. Thieu introduced the meeting in Vietnamese with Nha standing at a chalk board and serving as translator. . . . It was evident from the outset that we were being confronted by solid, unified GVN opposition to US counter-proposals.

Nixon's reaction was far from the sympathy for Thieu that he recalls in his memoirs.[2] On the morning of October 4, Nixon told me that Haig had made a mistake returning home as had always been planned; he should have stayed to work over Thieu. Bunker had better have another ''cold turkey'' talk with Thieu; Thieu had to be made to understand that Nixon refused to be placed in so untenable a position. Nixon authorized me to proceed with the October 8 meeting, consoling himself that Hanoi would probably turn down our proposals anyway. As during the Cienfuegos crisis, he wanted to stall until after the election. ''And we're just going to have to break it off with him [Thieu] after the election, I can see that. You know, if he's going to be this unreasonable, I mean the tail can't wag the dog here.'' I warned Nixon that there was a fifty-fifty chance that Hanoi would finally accept our September 15 proposal (in turn a combination of our proposals going back sixteen months). I thought this was the best chance we would get: ''We can't improve that by another year of bombing.'' Nixon said he agreed. I repeated my view of the strategy: We had ''the clock running on the North Vietnamese.'' I wondered aloud whether Thieu did not really *want* to be pressured by us so that we would bear the onus.

The upshot was a decision that I would stick with our September 15 position and not present any of the variations rejected by Thieu; there was no sense in straining our relations with Thieu even further. Hanoi would be asked to be more specific about military issues before we could offer any new political program. If Hanoi accepted our September 15 proposal, I would ask for a recess to go to Saigon. Nixon told me that then I should ''cram it down his [Thieu's] throat.''

Nixon was clearly hoping that this eventuality — which we had been resisting for nearly four years — would not happen before the election. I was not so sure. For on September 30 we had received a note from Hanoi that showed yet again that Hanoi was eager to settle rapidly and might offer additional new concessions:

The DRVN side [Hanoi] considers that the next meeting which should last three days is of vital importance and that it is time to take a clear decision concerning the orientation of the negotiations: Either, both sides will arrive at an agreement on the essentials of the questions which have been raised, thus permitting the realization of the schedule of the negotiations already understood between the two parties, that is to say to end the war and sign the global accord towards the end of October 1972 or even earlier which would be better.

Or, both sides will not be able to agree, the negotiations will remain at an impasse and the war will be prolonged, in which case the American side must accept the entire responsibility. . . .

For its part, the DRVN side will study in detail the 27 September 1972, 10 point proposition by the American side and will attend the next meeting in a constructive spirit and a serious attitude, in a last effort at arriving at an agreement of the essentials with the American side.

In the meantime, our task was to prepare the context of the October 8 meeting as well as possible. We had to prevent Thieu from making our dispute public, which could undermine both our negotiating position with Hanoi and our domestic position with Nixon's constituency on the right. But we also had to put him on notice that the evolving negotiations might force us to return to some of the political proposals that Haig had discussed with him. On October 5 I drafted a message to Thieu, in Nixon's name, promising consultation before any final decision. The next day I cabled Bunker that Thieu should study the political proposals — for a presidential election, election for the Constituent Assembly, or even review of the Constitution by the electoral commission — left by Haig "so that he cannot complain that he has not had sufficient time to consider the various aspects of these proposals should it be necessary to do so."

In preparation for the October 8 meeting I brought in the State Department. Under Secretary Alex Johnson and Deputy Assistant Secretary for East Asia William Sullivan produced working papers on international supervisory machinery and cease-fire implementation that were enormously useful. And then at last on the morning of Saturday, October 7, I set off for Paris and what turned out to be the climax of four years of negotiations with Hanoi to end the war.

The Breakthrough: The October 8 Meeting

THIS time my entire party stayed at Ambassador Watson's residence, the newly renovated mansion on the fashionable Rue du Faubourg St. Honoré. It was expected to be a three- or four-day session. Al Haig accompanied me because he had a recent, firsthand sense of what the traffic might bear in Saigon and because he would be able to help me to sell any possible agreement to Nixon. Richard T. Kennedy of my staff was left to run my NSC office.

Sunday, October 8, was a crisp, clear autumn day in Paris. With Haig in tow, I arrived at the still-secret white stucco house at Gif-sur-Yvette at 10:30 A.M. The meeting opened with bantering good humor. I apologized to Le Duc Tho and Xuan Thuy for having made them miss church on Sunday — or alternatively a big horse race that was taking place at Longchamp. The North Vietnamese were willing enough to enter into the spirit of the occasion:

KISSINGER: In France they run the opposite way around the track than in America. And I am told there's one race track in Paris, in Auteuil, where when they get around the other side they're behind the trees so you can't see them, and I'm told that that's where the jockeys decide who will win.

LE DUC THO: But we, are we making now a race to peace or to war?

KISSINGER: To peace, and we're behind the trees!

LE DUC THO: But shall we overcome those trees or we shall be hindered by these trees?

KISSINGER: No, we will settle.

LE DUC THO: But if you get out of these trees we will too.

KISSINGER: We'll both come out from behind the trees and we will settle.

LE DUC THO: And then both the horses will have the same road.

KISSINGER: But as we get across the finish line you will be saying, "You have not been sufficiently concrete."

After these opening pleasantries I noticed two big green folders in front of Le Duc Tho and asked him whether he wanted to read them to me. Xuan Thuy invited me to speak first — obviously they wanted to see whether I had brought an offer better than what they were prepared to concede. I replied that we found some positive elements in Le Duc Tho's latest political proposal, such as the principle of unanimity, but it still had major drawbacks:

You would remove the incumbent President upon signature of an agreement; you would abolish the present constitutional structure; you would create new quasi-governmental organs from Saigon right down to the village level.

. . . The cumulative impact of these various elements is clear. Even if any particular one would not necessarily prove decisive, the combination of them all occurring simultaneously has to give us concern.

I concluded sarcastically that I knew that the resultant undermining of Saigon was not intentional; my comments were offered purely in a spirit of cooperation.

I then turned to the military issues, which, I stressed, had taken on "a particular urgency." There were many unresolved problems in Hanoi's latest proposal, particularly in the modalities of a cease-fire, the withdrawal of North Vietnamese forces from Laos and Cambodia, an end of infiltration through Laos and Cambodia into South Vietnam, and the release of US prisoners in Laos and Cambodia. There had been hints but no concrete proposals. We would insist on cease-fires throughout Indochina, although we were open-minded as to the specific arrangements. Even if the cease-fires in Laos and Cambodia had to be arranged separately, they should go into effect simultaneously. I handed over a series of short explanatory papers on all the technical topics — substantially what the State Department had drafted.

I also handed over a "new" peace proposal, which offered in reality only a slight cosmetic change by spelling out somewhat more specifically the functions of the Committee of National Reconciliation; it was to supervise elections and anything else the Committee might agree on, which was not likely to be much because of Saigon's veto. The nature of the elections it was to supervise was not formally specified. If this was our "last offer," as Nixon had told Gromyko, then it could only have signaled to Le Duc Tho that we were standing fast on our position of maintaining the existing structure in Saigon and were making no further significant political concessions.

Apparently Le Duc Tho drew the same conclusion. Instead of exploding as he would have at any point during the previous three years, he said: "I propose now a break and afterward I shall express my views." The meeting broke up at 12:38 P.M. A generous array of luncheon snacks was available while the North Vietnamese disappeared upstairs. At 1:00 P.M. Le Duc Tho reentered the room and chatted with me near the snack table. "When the war ends, some day I will show you the Ho

Chi Minh Trail," he joked. He left again for a few moments to rejoin his colleagues. Then he returned to say that since I had given them "so many papers," the North Vietnamese preferred to have a longer break. He suggested that the meeting resume at 4:00 P.M. I agreed.

My staff and I strolled a bit in the clear autumn air in the garden, whispering softly (in case the bushes were bugged). Then, to pass the time, I thought of taking a drive. Someone (perhaps it was Colonel Guay) suggested Rambouillet, the forest and château about fourteen miles away. I agreed, and the seven members of the team piled into two cars driven by Guay and his associate and headed westward down Route Nationale 306. We never reached Rambouillet. After ten minutes' drive, restless and wanting to confer more privately with Haig, I asked Colonel Guay to stop the car at a place where Haig and I could walk. Guay pulled over at a spot where the trees lining the road suddenly opened up to reveal a small lake, which also seemed to be a picnic area. Picnickers were spreading out their food on checkered tablecloths; couples were lying under the trees. The sky had the mellow blue of the early French autumn. And none of these Parisians paid the slightest attention to this odd group of self-absorbed Americans who were walking along the narrow footpaths lined by tall grass. Haig and I walked briskly part of the way around the lake, reviewing the bidding, then turned and headed back. Other members of our delegation were equally preoccupied, tense over what was to come in two hours' time.

For us the contrast between the matter-of-fact peacefulness of that scene and our own anxiety was almost beyond bearing. At 4:00 P.M. we would know whether the agony endured by so many for nearly a decade would have purchased an honorable end to the war in Vietnam.

The meeting resumed on schedule. Le Duc Tho did not beat around the bush. He turned immediately to his green folders. "I think we cannot negotiate in the way we are doing now," he said, if we were going to keep the schedule that had been agreed upon and rapidly settle the war. All the procedures and multiforum scenarios that he had originally introduced into the negotiation (and I had reluctantly gone along with) Tho now decided were inadequate. They were "very complicated" and would take "a long time for these discussions, many weeks." Therefore: "In order to show our good will and to ensure a rapid end to the war, rapid restoration of peace in Vietnam, as all of us wish for, today we put forward a new proposal regarding the content as well as the way to conduct negotiations, a very realistic and very simple proposal."

Le Duc Tho suggested that the United States and North Vietnam sign an agreement settling the military questions between them — withdrawal, prisoners, cease-fire. On the political problems of South Vietnam, "we shall only agree on the main principles. After the signing of this agreement a cease-fire will immediately take place." The political problem — "that is the most thorny, the most difficult problem" — would not be allowed to prolong our negotiations ("prolonge" as Mr. Phuong, the interpreter, put it). Le Duc Tho now no longer demanded the formation of a coalition Government of National Concord before the cease-fire. Indeed, he dispensed with the entire concept of a coalition government. It was now only an "Administration of National Concord," to be set up within three months by the two South Vietnamese parties and charged with implementing the signed agreements, achieving national concord (whatever that meant), and "organizing" unspecified general and local elections. The two "administrations" in South Vietnam — the Saigon government and the Communist PRG — would continue in existence, with their armies.

This "Administration of National Concord" might never even be set up at all, since it required the approval of the two South Vietnamese parties; its functions were yet to be negotiated by the two mortal enemies, and afterward it would operate on the principle of unanimity.* This pale shadow of their former demands for a coalition government was not much to show for a decade of heroic exertion and horrendous suffering by the North Vietnamese. I was sure I could further reduce the importance of this "Administration" in the negotiations yet to come. After four years of implacable insistence that we dismantle the political structure of our ally and replace it with a coalition government, Hanoi had now essentially given up its political demands.

And there were other provisions that also helped meet our concerns. For three years Hanoi had insisted that an end of American military aid to South Vietnam was an absolute precondition of settlement. Le Duc Tho now scrapped this proposal. "Replacement of armament" (that is, military aid) was permitted; in other words, we could continue to supply South Vietnam. While Hanoi said nothing about withdrawing its troops (indeed, not even admitting that they were there), it accepted our proposal of May 31, 1971, that infiltration into South Vietnam cease; if observed, this would guarantee the erosion of its strength in the South. There would be international control and supervision — although Le Duc Tho considered this "not a pressing question" and proposed to discuss it *after* the cease-fire. There were, inevitably, still some gaps. Le Duc Tho was as yet silent about North Vietnamese troops in Laos and Cambodia (although he had conceded their withdrawal previously); he would not commit Hanoi to cease-fires there because this was contrary to the principle of noninterference in these countries. "But so is the presence of your troops," I cracked. But if Le Duc Tho was sincere in his profession that he would now work as resolutely for peace as he had

---

* This element of unanimity was, in fact, not in Le Duc Tho's October 8 written plan, but he mentioned it in his oral presentation and I was sure he would accept it since it had been in his proposal of September 27. He did.

previously fought the war, these issues could be settled in the next few days. He knew there would be no agreement otherwise. At the end of his presentation Le Duc Tho handed me the text of a draft agreement.

Time and again Le Duc Tho insisted that his plan represented an acceptance of our own proposals:

And this is what you yourself have proposed, the same proposal. . . . So our proposal has shown our good will, our real desire to rapidly end the war. And it is the same proposal made by President Nixon himself — ceasefire, release of prisoners, and troop withdrawal. . . . As to the internal political and military questions of South Vietnam we agree on principles and the South Vietnamese parties will discuss. . . . We do this with a view to reducing the thorny questions. So our aim is to do what you proposed previously: ceasefire and cessation of hostilities, troop withdrawal, release of prisoners. . . . And it is your proposal, and we met it with great good will, in order to end the war. . . . Because this new proposal is exactly what President Nixon has himself proposed: ceasefire, end of the war, release of the prisoners, and troop withdrawal. . . . and we propose a number of principles on political problems. You have also proposed this. And we shall leave to the South Vietnamese parties the settlement of these questions. . . .

And so it was. Hanoi had finally separated the military and political questions, which I had urged nearly four years earlier as the best way to settle. It had accepted Nixon's May 8 proposal and conceded that the South Vietnamese government need not be overthrown as the price of a cease-fire. Having ignored our offer of a presidential election, Hanoi even removed the necessity of Thieu's temporary withdrawal before it. The demand for a coalition government was dropped; the political structure of South Vietnam was left to the Vietnamese to settle.

For nearly four years we had longed for this day, yet when it arrived it was less dramatic than we had ever imagined. Peace came in the guise of the droning voice of an elderly revolutionary wrapping the end of a decade of bloodshed into legalistic ambiguity.

At once I and most of my colleagues understood the significance of what we had heard. In the immediate recess I asked for, Lord and I shook hands and said to each other: "We have done it." Haig, who had served in Vietnam, declared with emotion that we had saved the honor of the military men who had served, died, and suffered there. Le Duc Tho's paper still had many unacceptable elements, to be sure. And others of my colleagues, especially John Negroponte, focused on these in the half-hour break after our interlocutor finished his presentation. But I knew that its essence was a cease-fire, withdrawal of US forces, release of prisoners, plus no further infiltration — the basic program we had offered and insisted was essential since May 1971.

I have often been asked for my most thrilling moment in public service. I have participated in many spectacular events; I have lived with power; I have seen pomp and ceremony. But the moment that moved me most deeply has to be that cool autumn Sunday afternoon while the shadows were falling over the serene French landscape and that large quiet room, hung with abstract paintings, was illuminated only at the green baize table across which the two delegations were facing each other. At last, we thought, there would be an end to the bloodletting in Indochina. We stood on the threshold of what we had so long sought, a peace compatible with our honor and our international responsibilities. And we would be able to begin healing the wounds that the war had inflicted on our own society.

But negotiators must not betray emotion; it becomes a weapon in the hands of the other side. When we resumed, all I could say for tactical reasons at that moment of nearly exultant hope was: "I of course have not had an opportunity to study your paper. From your presentation I believe that you have opened an important new chapter in our negotiations and one that could bring us to a rapid conclusion." I warned Le Duc Tho that whatever was negotiated would have to be approved first by President Nixon, then by Saigon. Only then could we speak of a visit by me to Hanoi as he urged. The earliest date for that could be October 20. I asked to spend the evening and the next morning studying the paper and to meet again at 2:00 P.M. on Monday, October 9. Le Duc Tho assented. I had dinner with a friend. I returned to the Embassy residence and gave directions to Winston Lord and John Negroponte to redraft Le Duc Tho's document, weakening the political provisions even further, strengthening our right to assist South Vietnam, tightening the provisions against infiltration with language drawn from earlier American proposals, and insisting on North Vietnamese withdrawal from Laos and Cambodia.

Afterward I walked alone through the streets of Paris, along the left bank of the Seine to Notre-Dame. I crossed the river near Sainte-Chapelle, turned past the Louvre, and walked across the Place de la Concorde to return to the Ambassador's residence. There is no city in which the past and the present are in such harmonious balance as in Paris. Some cities are older, but less relevant to current reality; others are more overwhelmingly modern, but fail to inspire a sense of continuity. In Paris history lives easily in the contemporary world; it inspires but it does not overwhelm. The Left Bank recalls the human scale of Paris's origin; Notre-Dame breathes of a faith that made a peasant society raise edifices to its vision of God and its sense of the eternal; and the Paris of the nineteenth century shows how nature can be made to serve art (even though the purpose of the broad avenues was more utilitarian — to provide a clear field of fire against rebellious subjects and to complicate the Parisians' temptation to build barricades). All these views of Paris passed by as I paced its streets, lost in reflection. We stood within sight of an exhilarating goal; a great deal would depend on what I did and recommended and pursued over the next few days.

I had three choices. I could reject Le Duc Tho's plan in principle as inadequate; I could accept it in principle and negotiate its improvement; I could stall, perhaps by returning to Washington for consultations.

I decided to proceed. Over the years, we had defined our terms precisely: We would not overthrow an allied government directly or indirectly; we wanted the fighting to end throughout Indochina; we would insist on the return of our prisoners and an accounting for those missing in action. We wanted North Vietnam to remove its forces from neighboring countries. We demanded an end to infiltration into South Vietnam. Le Duc Tho's draft agreement met all of these terms; it in effect accepted what we had put forward on May 31, 1971, and on May 8, 1972. Indeed, the political provisions of the new proposal were much better for us than what Nixon had offered on January 25, 1972. The general elections provided for in Tho's plan were so vague as to be unachievable in practice (as compared with our proposal of presidential elections within six months and Thieu's withdrawal two months before). The "Administration of National Concord" had less power than even the joint electoral commission which we had been urging for over three years, because there was no agreed election to supervise. And I was certain that in a rapid negotiation we could water down the political provisions even further.

As for the military terms, the offer of the cease-fire in place in Vietnam was unqualified. Le Duc Tho had hinted that it could be extended to Laos and Cambodia. The draft be handed over included a provision requiring the withdrawal of all foreign forces from Laos and Cambodia; I would have to try to pin down the timing and make certain that Le Duc Tho considered North Vietnamese forces "foreign." And Hanoi was prepared to return our prisoners as our remaining forces left. There was, admittedly, no provision for the withdrawal of North Vietnamese troops from the South. But we ourselves had abandoned this demand — with Thieu's concurrence — in our cease-fire proposal of October 7, 1970; in our secret seven-point plan of May 31, 1971; and in Nixon's public offers of January 25, 1972, and May 8, 1972. It is worth remembering that nobody — hawk or dove or Thieu, for that matter — objected when the earlier proposals without this provision were put forward. In principle a demand for North Vietnamese withdrawal was certainly equitable. But in practice it had proven unobtainable through ten years of war and three administrations. It was an objective we could reach only by the total defeat of Hanoi, through all-out war, which in turn our public and the Congress would not support. Thus, while we continued to press for it in the coming days, we could not make it a condition for a final settlement. We had long passed that threshold. The best we could do was to insist on the provision of our May 31, 1971, plan that prohibited the infiltration of additional men and material into South Vietnam and which Le Duc Tho now accepted. If observed, this commitment would lead to the attrition of North Vietnamese forces; if violated, we would be no better off with an equally unobserved provision calling for withdrawal.

I also reflected on what would happen if we rejected the proposal and Hanoi then published it — a near certainty. (And indeed Hanoi did go public in late October.) One could imagine the public outcry if we rejected Hanoi's acceptance of our own proposals. It would almost certainly have forced us back to the bargaining table and this time we would have been negotiating under the clamor of Congressional and media accusations of cynicism and bad faith in welshing on our own proposals. In my judgment, our best chance was to proceed, continuing to push Hanoi against its self-imposed deadline of our election, and using its now palpable desire for speed to extract even further improvements.

I was aware, of course, that Nixon on the whole preferred to string out the talks until after our election and then go for broke with both Hanoi and Saigon. But this option was not, in fact, available. Procrastination would force Hanoi into the public arena where our case would be weak. We had no possible basis for refusing or even delaying. The offer was much more favorable than anything imagined by our Congress, media, and public to be achievable, and better than what we had asked for. If Hanoi did publish its proposal, it would become the starting point of negotiations *without* the improvements I was practically certain I could achieve in three or four days of intensive secret negotiations under the pressure of a deadline.

Equally important, the option of escalation — implied in going for broke after the election — was dramatic but not realistic. Our military possibilities would not then be different from now; they might be poorer. We were already doing everything to North Vietnam we were capable of doing except massive B-52 bombing in the northern third of the country. But to begin B-52 attacks there after Hanoi had published its acceptance of our terms would be impossible to justify. And shortly after our election Hanoi would rediscover not only our domestic fragility but also the budgetary pressures that would force us to reduce our forces unilaterally, in line with Laird's fiscal planning. We would then have to settle disagreements with Hanoi by testing each other's endurance through a series of additional deadlocks — a process that would further divide our country and make ending the war as searing as its conduct.

That to me seemed the most crucial point, as I walked the streets of Paris that fateful night. We had a moral duty to our allies in Saigon not to bargain with the fate of those millions who had put their trust in our word. But we had no duty to them to guarantee them a total victory that they were unable to define, whose achievement required an open-ended commitment extending over many years more, and that we had publicly forsworn for the past three years. We had sent millions of Americans and billions of dollars of equipment to South Vietnam and bled our society for ten years. We had bought time while strengthening South Vietnam's capacity to defend itself. But, finally, we had a moral obligation as well to our own people: not to prolong their division beyond the point demanded by honor and our international responsibility; to end the war in a manner that would heal rather than divide. For this, speed was essential before the opportunity was submerged in the morass of our domestic suspicions. If we could bring off a settlement no one had thought possible, achieving the essential terms that we had put forward for years, there was at last a chance for reconciliation in our country. Doves could rejoice in the end of the war. Hawks could take pride in the preservation of America's dignity. If we acted decisively, we might end the war in a manner that gave some meaning to the sacrifices that had been made: as an exercise of our own will rather than through the exhaustion of endless discord. And in this manner I would have repaid a small part of the debt I owed to the country that had sheltered my family and me from persecution, hatred, and tyranny.

For all these reasons I chose the second course — to accept Le Duc Tho's plan in principle and immediately proceed to negotiate to improve it further. I knew that when the chips were down Nixon would back me. He would not forgo a settlement for electoral considerations. He would understand that he risked more by waiting than proceeding. Haldeman would no doubt argue for delay in order not to stir up the conservatives. But apart from the fact that we did not really have this choice, Nixon had never listened to such arguments previously on an issue as crucial as Vietnam and he would not now. Al Haig agreed when I discussed my conclusions with him upon my return to the Embassy residence. Like me, he was moved by the occasion, and by the thought that our military establishment could at last be disengaged with honor from a wretched and ambiguous conflict. Assuming one could negotiate the improvements we still needed, which I was confident of achieving, he did not believe better terms were available short of another year or more of intensive bombing and anguishing turmoil at home.

Well past midnight I sent a cryptic message to Haldeman: ''Tell the President that there has been some definite progress at today's first session and that he can harbor some confidence the outcome will be positive.'' While giving no details, it offered Nixon every opportunity to call a halt or to request additional information if delay was what he wanted. As I had expected, there was no response. Simultaneously, a short message was sent to Ellsworth Bunker to forewarn President Thieu that "the other side may surface a ceasefire proposal during these meetings" and therefore it was "essential that Thieu instruct his commanders to move promptly and seize the maximum amount of critical territory." Bunker, as was becoming customary, was unable to pass on this message because Thieu was unavailable. Thieu had gone waterskiing on October 8, stepped on a nail, been given a tetanus inoculation, and was in bed with a high fever — or so Nha claimed. Bunker noted, however, that Thieu had told him on October 6 that his corps commanders were already under orders to seize territory.

I delayed the session with Le Duc Tho until 4:00 P.M. because we needed the time to prepare a counterdraft designed to use his obsession with a "shedyule" to elicit the maximum concessions. When the meeting of October 9 began, I handed Xuan Thuy a regimental necktie as a reward for having worked on Sunday. He said he would wear it when the agreement was completed. (He did.) I opened the meeting by stressing that Le Duc Tho had given us "a very important document, which I believe will bring us to an agreement." I handed over our new proposal and went over its provisions point by point. We accepted some provisions, reformulated others, dropped some, and added new ones to our own, tightening the provisions on infiltration, replacement of material, and Laos and Cambodia. Le Duc Tho reserved his position until he could study the document, but vocally protested his eagerness to settle with the same intensity that had previously marked his procrastinations:

So the circumstances are propitious. And now we, both you and us, should make an effort to reach an agreement expeditiously, rapidly and with good results. Therefore if each of us have some issue to raise for settlement we should do that with an open heart, frankly and to come to a quick settlement. What we can record in the agreement we shall do that. What we can't record in the agreement, we shall make an understanding with each other.

After two hours we adjourned. This time the North Vietnamese needed the morning to study our draft. The next meeting was set for 4:00 P.M. the following day.

As we were breaking up Tho handed me a lengthy document that he proposed should be signed by the United States and Hanoi; it set down guidelines for the political negotiations of the two South Vietnamese parties. This was, of course, totally contrary to our strategy of separating the political and military issues; it could not possibly be negotiated within the "shedyule" on which Tho set so much store. He must have known this, but perhaps his Viet Cong colleagues in South Vietnam insisted and he did it for the record. I took note of the document, indicated that I would study it, and never returned to it. Neither did Tho.

I sent another terse cable to Haldeman:

At this juncture I believe we have chance to obtain significant progress by maintaining firm position and anticipate progress at tomorrow's session. The essential aspect of issue is to be sure now that no public statements are made which would suggest either anxiety or concern for the current rounds of talks. It is even more important to be silent as to substance. We are at a crucial point. We will have firm prognostication at the end of tomorrow's session.

Again there was no reply, nor a request for further information.

There were two principal reasons for our sparse reporting. There was no Vietnam expert left in the White House who could have analyzed the various provisions for the President. The members of the NSC staff who would normally do this were all with me. The President distrusted the State Department too much to consult it; its Vietnam experts, in any event, were not informed about the state of play. More important, those whom the President saw most frequently in these closing weeks of the campaign were public relations "experts" and political operatives who would be sorely tempted to exploit the negotiations for short-term ends. Both Haig and I knew that Nixon might show a particularly interesting cable to whoever happened into his office. If that person were Charles Colson — with whom he was spending an increasing amount of time — there was no telling what would happen.* I was especially concerned because George McGovern was slated to announce his Vietnam program within twenty-four hours, on the evening of October 10. He was certain to offer Hanoi far more than it was demanding. I did not think it desirable to put before Nixon's political advisers the temptation to risk four years of negotiations for a fleeting headline to make McGovern look ridiculous. In any event, I was sure that in a fast-moving tactical situation I was operating well within Presidential guidelines (particularly those in our conversation of October 4). The October 8 draft was much more favorable to us than what Haig had taken to Thieu, with Nixon's approval, less than a week before. And there were no decisions needed from Nixon at this point.

To avoid misunderstandings in Hanoi, I told Le Duc Tho that all our negotiations were *ad referendum* until they were approved by the President. And to prevent uneasiness in Washington I sent the President a personal cable:

The negotiations during this round have been so complex and sensitive that we have been unable to report their content in detail due to the danger of compromise. We know exactly what we are doing, and just as we have not let you down in the past, we will not do so now. Pending our return and my direct report to you it is imperative that nothing be said in reply to McGovern or in any other context bearing on the current talks.

---

* In December, Nixon did show some of my cables to Colson, which did no damage at the time, though Colson, totally misunderstanding them, later gave them prominence in his own book.[3]

I added a postscript for Haldeman's eyes only: "Please hold everything steady. I recognize the uncertainties there but excessive nervousness can only jeopardize the outcome here."

Few Presidents would have acquiesced in such a procedure. But maddening as Nixon's conduct could be in calm times, it verged on the heroic when really critical issues were at stake. He must have been tense; he could not avoid being uneasy. But at this crucial moment he was prepared to entrust to an adviser far away the outcome of a conflict that had divided the nation he was trying to lead and that might threaten his own Presidency. It took unusual fortitude not to try to affect a negotiation that might decide the election and that would certainly determine whether or not his second term would be tranquil or ridden by crisis. Such was Nixon's self-control that he refrained even from indulging natural human curiosity by a phone call.

The two delegations convened again on Tuesday, October 10, at 4:00 P.M. at Gif-sur-Yvette. Overnight I had had a message delivered to Le Duc Tho enumerating our requirements about security and Laos and Cambodia. This was designed to press him to be as forthcoming as possible in these areas when he presented his counterdraft. Tho grumbled that they "complicated" matters and that I was bringing "pressures" — as if such a procedure were foreign to the tender hearts of the men from Hanoi. But we then got down to cases and in a six-hour session started the tedious process of comparing the two drafts, reconciling them, temporarily putting aside insoluble issues, and starting the negotiation of separate written understandings on topics, such as Laos, that did not fit into a Vietnam peace agreement.

The next day, October 11, we continued, launching ourselves (though we did not realize it) into a marathon session that lasted sixteen hours, from 9:50 A.M. until after 2:00 the following morning. The transcript of that session covers 122 single-spaced pages. The hope and dedication that animated every member of our delegation was shown by my secretary, Irene Derus, who took the stenographic notes throughout the meeting. She declined offers to relieve her, partly because the meeting seemed constantly on the verge of concluding when some other issue would crop up, but more truly because she wanted to participate in the historic event of ending the Vietnam war.

No useful purpose would be served by recounting the ebb and flow of these detailed negotiations. The setting did not lack its surrealistic quality. Surrounded by abstract paintings, we would go through the two drafts point by point. When a disagreement arose, the two delegations would caucus to see whether they could suggest an alternative formulation. This would then have to be typed and translated. While waiting, Tho and I would often chat. I blamed all deadlocks on Xuan Thuy, whom I proposed to banish from the room. Tho threatened to take my chair at

Harvard away from me if I were not more reasonable (his threat turned out to be more meaningful than mine). The heavy-handed joking could not obscure either the tension or the exhilaration, the consciousness of our responsibility, and the hope that we would at last reach the elusive goal which we had pursued with hope and anguish for all these years.

We quickly agreed on a cease-fire, an American withdrawal in two months, and a simultaneous release of prisoners. Our principal objective was to drain the political provisions of whatever vestiges of coalition government remained and to phrase the remnant political obligations of both sides in such a way that failure to fulfill them would give Hanoi no pretext for resuming hostilities. We therefore changed Hanoi's provision that the two South Vietnamese parties had to agree on a political settlement within three months to a weaker formulation — they would "do their utmost" to reach such a settlement — transforming an objective obligation into a subjective promise to make an effort. We added the principle of unanimity. The "Administration of National Concord," formerly a coalition government, was diluted and turned into a nebulous body closer to our electoral commission, called (melding the titles of the two sides' proposals) a "National Council of National Reconciliation and Concord." (The political paragraph in Le Duc Tho's draft of October 8 and the end result as of October 11 are given in the notes.)[4] I later characterized the political provisions at a meeting in Saigon with Thieu and his advisers on October 19:

So let me sum up the political provisions which we consider a major collapse of the Communist position. . . . The demand for the institution of a Provisional Government of National Concord has been dropped. The demand for the amalgamation of ARVN and communist forces has been dropped. The existing government can continue with unlimited amounts of economic aid and American replacement military aid of a very large force. And the only requirement is that it negotiate with the other side to set up a Council. If the Council ever comes into being, it has no jurisdiction that I can determine, except over elections to which you must agree, for institutions which you are to decide, within a framework which depends on your negotiating it. In other words, we have preserved the cardinal position that we leave the future of South Vietnam to the South Vietnamese people and that the government we have recognized is the government of the Republic of South Vietnam and its President.

The reverse side of this was, of course, that Hanoi bargained all the more insistently about the military issues. So it was only after great effort that we were able to achieve Le Duc Tho's agreement that all infiltration of personnel into South Vietnam would cease and that equipment could be replaced on a one-for-one basis under international supervision. (Tho had asked for "equality," meaning that the Communists would have the right to introduce weapons in the South equal to what we were giving to Saigon. Since Saigon's army was much larger, we insisted on our formulation, which meant that existing equipment could be replaced but not augmented. And we prevailed — perhaps because Hanoi had no intention of abiding by the provision.)

At every meeting and with various formulations we kept demanding a North Vietnamese commitment to withdraw their troops from the South. We never obtained it. Le Duc Tho resisted as a matter of principle because he did not regard South Vietnam as a foreign country, and because such a clause would have represented a total surrender. We finally settled for the ban on infiltration and a formulation that after the cease-fire the two South Vietnamese parties would discuss "steps to reduce the military numbers on both sides and to demobilize the troops being withdrawn." I had no illusions. Whenever either we or Hanoi were looking for an elegant way to bury an issue, we left its resolution to the two South Vietnamese parties, who we knew might never agree on anything. We acquiesced because we had been offering a cease-fire in place for two years and because Hanoi was accepting our own compromise formula prohibiting any further infiltration of personnel. This would gradually eliminate North Vietnamese forces in the South through attrition, assuming that the provisions were observed by Hanoi or enforced by us. (That caveat applied to the entire agreement; if doubts as to compliance were to be allowed to block a satisfactory agreement, then the war could never come to a negotiated end; it would have to be fought to the finish.)

Much time was spent on Laos and Cambodia. There were three issues that were not to be settled for several weeks: in what legal form to express whatever obligations were undertaken; the status of foreign forces, including North Vietnamese; and how to establish a cease-fire there. The first issue arose because Tho claimed that internal Laotian and Cambodian matters could not be dealt with in a Vietnamese peace treaty. We settled that by reflecting our understanding in separate written documents. Le Duc Tho accepted that the withdrawal of foreign forces from Cambodia and Laos *should* be part of the Vietnam agreement; after much debate he accepted that all foreign troops would be withdrawn from Laos and Cambodia *and* that Vietnamese troops would be considered foreign for that purpose. We did less well on the cease-fires in Laos and Cambodia. I insisted that these be established by a fixed date that would precede our complete withdrawal. Le Duc Tho agreed to promise a cease-fire in Laos within thirty days after signing the agreement; he insisted that Hanoi's influence on the Cambodian Communists was not decisive. We were skeptical. As subsequent events have made clear, it turned out to be one occasion when Tho was telling the truth.

The major bone of contention was the alleged 30,000 civilian prisoners in South Vietnamese prisons, about 10,000 of them Viet Cong cadres, the rest criminals. Le Duc Tho's October 8 draft required that they be released together with all prisoners of war. I saw no possibility of Saigon's releasing the core of the Viet Cong guerrillas. I proposed that this issue be left to the two South Vietnamese parties, who would "do their utmost" to settle it. Le Duc Tho objected, as well he might, since it in effect left all South Vietnamese Communist prisoners in Saigon's jails. It was obviously a sensitive point for his Viet Cong allies. Yet it was totally unacceptable for us to allow the release of American POWs to be made conditional on our ability to persuade Thieu to release Viet Cong prisoners. A week later the North Vietnamese dropped their demand — an example of a major concession we extracted by making a rapid conclusion of the agreement depend on it.

Finally, Le Duc Tho and I agreed to put into the agreement a general statement reflecting what had first been offered by President Johnson in 1965 and repeated by Nixon explicitly on January 25 and May 8, 1972: that after the war America would contribute to the economic reconstruction of Indochina, "to heal the wounds of war" as the document phrased it somewhat more poetically. I made clear that we would do this as in our own interest, for humane reasons, and to increase the prospects for improved bilateral relations between our countries (and in turn to give Hanoi a greater incentive to honor the agreement). But we rejected then, and continually thereafter, any principle of guilt or reparation; I also made clear that the Congress would have to approve.

There were endless technical discussions about other issues, including international control machinery and the participants at an international peace conference. But at last, at 2:00 A.M. on October 12 — after having negotiated nonstop for sixteen hours, and twenty-two out of the last thirty — Le Duc Tho and I were prepared to call it a day. We had settled all principal Vietnam issues except the formulation on the right of the United States to replace military equipment for South Vietnamese forces and the question of civilians detained by Saigon. We also still needed to formulate a more precise commitment to a cease-fire in Laos and Cambodia. But we had come so far that a conclusion was now inevitable. We were doomed to success, even if it took time. I joked — presciently — that it might achieve no more than to unite all the Vietnamese parties in their opposition to me.

There came over us at last the relief of the end of strenuous exertions accompanied by excruciating tension. For over three years Le Duc Tho and I had tested each other's endurance, tried to break down each other's defenses, sought to deprive each other of options. Diplomacy among adversaries can be a deadly business, all the more for being clothed in conciliatory forms. Both sides had risked not only foreign policy goals but domestic cohesion; both had been forced to put aside the vast objectives with which they had entered the struggle; both were gambling on the future. We were not so naive as to believe that Hanoi's dour leaders had abandoned the aspirations of a lifetime. But having fought for the freedom and independence of those who had relied on us and joined their efforts to ours, we could now hope that similar joint exertions would preserve the peace.

At that early morning hour, overcome by the prospect that had been so elusive for so long, we were in a mood approaching euphoria. And so Le Duc Tho and I both made little speeches in total contrast to the occasionally bitter clashes that had characterized our encounters for three years. Le Duc Tho spoke in the idiom with which we had become all too familiar over these years:

We have made great effort, and you too, you have made great effort. And the efforts are the biggest during the last few days. And sometime during the course of the negotiations, our discussions were hot; on many occasions the impression left was that the negotiations might break. But our efforts have been great, and it can be said that our negotiations have brought about basic agreements on many questions, although the agreement has not been completed in that there are still two or three questions left. But through our effort, no doubt we will reach our objective of peace.

If peace is restored, I can say that there is a new page turned in the history of the relationship of our peoples, a new page turned from the relationship of hostility to a relationship of friendship; not only for the immediate period but for the long term. And the day of signing of the settlement and the day of the end of the war will be a day of festivity for our two peoples. You and us can undertake to firmly keep the agreement we have made here. When we achieve the agreement, then we will undertake to honor what we have signed. So that is what I would like to express before I leave for Hanoi in two or three days.

And I replied, without seeking to match the Homeric quality of Le Duc Tho's last sentences:

Mr. Special Adviser, I greatly appreciate your comments. I have personally negotiated on the problem of Vietnam now since 1967 and with the Special Adviser since 1969. We have had very difficult periods, but we have surmounted them, because we have both realized, as our people have realized, that peace is the most important objective to be achieved. As I told you yesterday, our two countries have on several occasions made an armistice with each other but this time we must make a permanent peace.

But as we move from hostility to friendship, we should remember that there has been a great deal of suffering on both sides and that we owe it to those who have suffered that we not characterize the war in any particular way and that neither of us proclaim victory or defeat.

The real victory for both, of course, will now be the durable relations we can establish with each other. So when my colleagues and I come to Hanoi, we will come to pay our respects to the heroic people of North Vietnam and to begin a new era in our relationships.

This was the mood we carried back to Washington. Lord and David Engel (our able interpreter) stayed behind to make certain the North Vietnamese and we were working from the same texts and to clear up some technical points. After our just-completed marathon, having averaged about three hours sleep a night for four days, they were to spend ten straight hours the following afternoon and evening on painstaking, nit-picking technical and linguistic issues. The rest of us on the return journey were suspended between euphoria and exhaustion.

I had heard nothing from Nixon during the entire period, though my cables left little doubt that I thought the end might be in sight. At the conclusion of the session of October 10 I had sent another cryptic message indicating that a breakthrough was imminent: "Please pass following message to Haldeman for the President: We have decided to stay one more day in expectation that we may score a major breakthrough. Either way we will return tomorrow afternoon. In my judgment we are sufficiently close to a breakthrough to run the risk of another day here." Immediately after returning from the sixteen-hour negotiating session I sent another message to Haldeman unremarkable for its illuminating detail: "Have just completed extremely long session here. It is essential that I have ample time with President tomorrow for thorough review of situation since careful game plan is now required." Haldeman replied that the President was on a campaign trip and that therefore I should not arrive before 5:00 P.M., after which Nixon wished to have dinner with Haig and me.

We had not been much more explicit with Saigon, except to stress with increasing urgency the probability of a cease-fire. Somewhat disingenuously, I wanted to leave Thieu with the impression that Hanoi had insisted on more of its political demands than was in fact the case, to obtain more credit for the collapse of Hanoi's position when I showed Thieu the final agreement, and to enhance his incentive for accepting it. Thieu could not be in any doubt about the imminence of a cease-fire even if he did not yet know the emasculated political terms that would accompany it.

On October 11 I cabled Bunker:

At risk of sounding repetitive he [Thieu] must make absolutely maximum effort to seize as much territory as possible. This is especially true of key populated areas in III Corps surrounding Saigon [MR 3].

At this juncture I see no chance of cease-fire in time frame shorter than two weeks. Thus while there is no reason for panic there is also little time for procrastination on part of ARVN commanders.

I followed it up next day with a lengthier cable summing up where we stood and concluding:

> My judgment at this juncture would be that they appear ready to accept a cease-fire in place in the near future. This, of course, is corroborated by field intelligence and it is for this reason that you cannot overemphasize upon Thieu:
>
> (1) the need to regain as much territory as possible and
>
> (2) the need for greater flexibility on the political side.
>
> We, of course, intend to hold firm in the political area but for tactical reasons we may have to discuss some obligations in this area.

The second point was substantially devious; it was to deflect Thieu's attention to the political provisions where I knew we were getting most of what we asked for. To magnify Thieu's concern over the political provisions I sent Bunker the "guidelines" paper submitted by Le Duc Tho on October 9 and long since buried. It was not a very elevated method; nor did it work, though for quite a different reason.

I had decided not yet to send the complete text of our agreement to Thieu partly because of security; because of our growing distrust of his entourage; because we thought (correctly) that further improvements were possible; and above all because I supposed he would be pleased by the outcome and therefore there was no need to engage him in detail before we were clear on our own game plan. Haig and I believed, indeed, that Thieu would be so delighted at our success in laying the ghost of a coalition government that his acceptance of a standstill cease-fire — which he had, after all, endorsed for two years — would be a formality. The biggest obstacles in our view would be the outrageous Nha and the pedantic Duc, who would nitpick the agreement to death and would not understand that it represented the finest compromise available. John Negroponte was considerably more worried about Thieu's reaction. He proved to be more prescient than the rest of us.

On October 10, George McGovern had put forward his own peace program for Vietnam. It asked much less of Hanoi than Hanoi had already conceded to us. But even the vast majority of moderate American critics had given up any hope of achieving the terms of our various peace offers, much less the better terms of the draft. We were bringing home a document that would vindicate the prayers of those who had endured the course in support of their government, and thus halt the erosion of confidence that had marked the past decade. And yet our opponents could join in supporting it because it achieved at last the goal of peace for which they had striven with dedication. So we hoped that not the least significant result of the last few days would be to salvage a spirit of unity and conciliation from our national ordeal. We could heal our own wounds of war.

The national reaction when this progress became known later in October, and when the agreement was signed in January 1973, was indeed one of relief, and of the first stirrings toward national reconciliation. There were sour notes, however, though they could not drown out the satisfaction that the country could feel in completing our withdrawal from Vietnam. Some claimed that we settled in 1972 for terms available in 1969. Not even the slightest acquaintance with the record sustains that argument. Never before October 8, 1972, had Hanoi agreed to abandon its unacceptable demand for a coalition government. (It had edged away from an insistence on overthrowing the South Vietnamese government only a few weeks before that.) The existence of a South Vietnamese army, continued American military and economic aid to Saigon, withdrawal from Laos and Cambodia, a cease-fire in Laos, and several other major concessions emerged only in the negotiations starting on October 8.

Nor is it correct that all we sought was a "decent interval" before a final collapse of Saigon. All of us who negotiated the agreement of October 12 were convinced that we had vindicated the anguish of a decade not by a "decent interval" but by a decent settlement. We thought with reason that Saigon, generously armed and supported by the United States, would be able to deal with moderate violations of the agreements; that the United States would stand by to enforce the agreement and punish major violations; that Hanoi might be tempted also by economic aid into choosing reconstruction of the North if conquest of the South was kept out of reach; that we could use our relations with Moscow and Peking, in addition, to encourage Hanoi's restraint; and that with our aid the South Vietnamese government would grow in security and prosperity over the time bought by the agreement, and compete effectively in a political struggle in which without question it had the loyalty of most of the population. Perhaps the Vietnamese parties could even work out a peaceful modus vivendi.

We could not know that soon Watergate would nullify most of these assumptions. In blissful ignorance of the future we landed in Washington, near joyous that we had brought home both peace and dignity.

XXXII

The Troubled Road to Peace

ON our return to Washington on October 12 Haig and I went immediately to Nixon's refuge in the Executive Office Building.
It was a two-room suite. The outer office contained a round table and some chairs; its walls were covered with originals of cartoons having Nixon as their subject. There was no desk or receptionist. I never saw the anteroom used for any purpose. One was not invited to the hideaway except by direct Presidential command, transmitted either by Nixon or by Haldeman; there was no need therefore of a waiting room. Nixon's office was a rather long rectangular room with a fireplace at the far end. Its windows opened on a porch overlooking West Executive Avenue, a narrow enclosed street separating the White House from the Executive Office Building. Almost invariably the blinds were drawn. Nixon liked his working offices to convey the atmosphere of a cocoon. There was a very large desk in front of the window and in the corner next to it an easy chair with a settee in front. To its right, as one stood facing it, were a smallish round table and a number of wooden chairs with armrests.

Nixon generally sat in the easy chair with his legs propped up, even when working. His aides sat in the wooden chairs. They could grow uncomfortable if the meeting was prolonged, as it frequently was when the President was in a ruminating mood.

But that was not the case on October 12. Affecting nonchalance, Nixon asked Haig and me to report. Somewhat exultantly, I told him that it looked as if we had achieved all three of our major goals for 1972 — the first two being the visit to Peking and the Moscow summit. I then went through the provisions of the Vietnam agreement in great detail, explaining the differences with our own January and May proposals, almost all in our favor. Nixon's principal concern was Thieu's reaction. I was — naively — optimistic, for we had done better than what we had jointly proposed over the years. Nixon remembers Haig as worried;[1] I have no such recollection. It made no difference, for Haig strongly endorsed the agreement.

Nixon ordered steak and wine to celebrate the event. I outlined the tentative "shedyule" I had agreed to with Le Duc Tho. I would return to Paris on October 17 for a meeting with Xuan Thuy to try to make progress on the two remaining issues of civilian detainees in South Vietnam and replacement of military equipment for the South Vietnamese armed forces. We would also need to work out the understandings on cease-fires in Laos and Cambodia. I would then fly from Paris to Saigon, where I would stay from October 18 through the twenty-second. On the evening of October 22 I would go to Hanoi, returning to Washington on October 24. The agreement would be announced on October 26 and signed on October 31. It was a tight schedule and, as it turned out, a wildly optimistic one. It was one that Hanoi was pressing upon us. At no point did I seek to speed up the process. Our basic purpose was not, of course, to please Hanoi but to use its impatience and a short deadline to force it into rapid agreement on disputed issues. From that point of view my tactic worked.

The President agreed, and we began immediately to squeeze Hanoi. Winston Lord, who was still in Paris collating the Vietnamese and American texts, was instructed to tell Xuan Thuy that Nixon consented to the basic draft provided Hanoi agreed to four changes "without which the US side cannot accept the document." These changes included more precise formulations on such questions as the ban on infiltration, military aid to South Vietnam, and the weakened powers of the National Council. We had had these texts ready in Paris before I left; and they could have been submitted there. They were sent from Washington to add a sense of urgency, to give them Presidential authority, and to make the "shedyule" work for us.

A word is in order here about the messages that passed between Washington and Hanoi during this period. *All* of them were drafted by my staff and me. Some were sent as unsigned notes; when we wanted to lend emphasis they were dispatched in the name of the President. As in all other negotiations I conducted on his behalf, Nixon was given a copy of everything sent in his name; he certainly had an opportunity to countermand any message. He never did so. Once he had given general guidelines, he had no desire to involve himself in the process of negotiating. Nor would the text of documents interest him. He would sometimes comment on my oral account of a document, but the fine points and the specifics of language and nuance held no interest for him. At this stage in the Vietnam negotiations he did not intervene; the stories leaked at the time that his sharp legal eye spotted loopholes were pure fiction. He endorsed the draft agreement without any change. He understood that the viability of the agreement depended on the vigor with which it was enforced and not on the clever exegesis of legal formulas.

What continued to concern him was the possibility of a blowup with Saigon. This he was determined to avoid at almost all costs. If Thieu balked, I was to back off and conclude the agreement after the election. The instruction was more easily issued than implemented, for Hanoi could still force us to take a stand by publishing the texts. Nor did I think matters would reach that point. As yet I enjoyed the illusion that Thieu would happily go along with an agreement better in almost all essentials than the terms we had been offering with his concurrence for two years.

Nixon was quite positive that an agreement was unnecessary for the election; its benefit would be too marginal to warrant any risks. Haldeman, whom I saw directly after Nixon, went further. He thought that an agreement was a potential liability; he was certain that McGovern's support had been reduced to fanatics that would not vote for Nixon even if he arranged the Second Coming. On the other hand, an agreement might disquiet conservative supporters and thus shrink Nixon's margin of victory. The Vietnam negotiations, in short, were not used to affect the election; the election was used to accelerate the negotiations. It performed the role normally carried out by an ultimatum — except that it raised no issue of prestige and, being fixed by the Constitution, was not subject to alteration.

With Haig, I briefed Rogers over breakfast on October 13. He was enthusiastic; he considered the agreement a complete vindication of the US position. Given our strained professional relations, this was high praise indeed — and magnanimous. With a cease-fire in sight, I realized that we were reaching the limit of my small staff's resources. Many technical protocols would have to be prepared that required specialized competence. I asked Rogers for help, something I was not in the habit of doing but should have been. Rogers agreed and assigned Deputy Assistant Secretary William Sullivan to me for that purpose. A former Ambassador to Laos, then head of the Department's Vietnam Working Group, Sullivan had carried out many thankless assignments with skill, daring, and an unusual willingness to assume responsibility. He performed on my staff with panache. He accompanied me on my October around-the-world trip as my deputy. He briefed the Laotian and Thai leaders on our negotiations. And he headed the technical discussions with the Vietnamese in the last phase. Sullivan's contribution to the final round of negotiations was indispensable.

My schedule for October 13 shows the intensity of our preparations. I spent from 10:45 to 11:05 A.M. with Sullivan and Negroponte; 11:05 to 11:09 with Sullivan alone; 12:40 to 1:05 P.M. with Sullivan and Negroponte; 2:40 to 3:30 with Sullivan and Negroponte; 3:35 to 4:09 with the President; 5:36 to 6:24 with Sullivan, Lord (just returned from Paris), and Negroponte; and 8:20 to 8:55 with Lord and Negroponte.

That day a cable arrived from Ellsworth Bunker with a warning that, whatever the agreement, we might be sailing into stormy seas in Saigon.

As had become customary Thieu was unavailable to be briefed; his stalling was now part of every exchange — last time it had been a tetanus shot, now it was an upset stomach. Nha helpfully supplied another reason: Thieu was surprised that the American Embassy was open on Friday the thirteenth. Bunker replied dryly that he had cleared the problem with his astrologer. He warned me, however, that Thieu was settling into a siege mentality reminiscent of 1968. He would almost surely try to stare us down, whatever we brought him. He seemed convinced that if the war continued he would be "in position to make a better settlement a year or two years from now," but he gave us no idea in what respect it would be better or how we could sustain a war with no goal the American public could understand after Hanoi had accepted our own proposals on October 8.

I told Bunker to give Thieu a summary of where we were heading:

Prior to my arrival in Saigon, now tentatively scheduled for Wednesday night, I will be seeing Minister Xuan Thuy and anticipate that the other side will propose a political formula which will require far less of Thieu than the alternate arrangements outlined to him by Haig during his recent visit. This would be combined with a cease-fire in place to go into effect as early as two weeks from the time that an overall agreement in principle is arrived at. In view of this likelihood, it is essential that Thieu understand now that we could have settled the conflict long ago under terms which would have removed him from power. Therefore, he cannot approach his upcoming meeting with me in the context of a confrontation but rather with a positive attitude in which we can confirm arrangements which will consolidate and solidify his future control. I am confident that such political arrangements are in the offing from Hanoi and Thieu must be put off his current confrontation course with us and at the same time be prepared, in return for Hanoi's political concessions, to show a reasonable flexibility on the modalities of a cease-fire in place.

Bunker conveyed this outline of the proposed settlement to Thieu on October 14. We never received a response.

On both October 14 and 15 I stressed to Dobrynin the importance we attached to the outstanding issues. I asked for a Soviet assurance of restraint in arms supply after a settlement. Dobrynin, who had received the text of the draft agreement from Hanoi, evaded the point. A Nixon letter to Brezhnev asking for a similar assurance was also evaded. Even more worrisome was the fact that Hanoi had obviously played games with the translation of the agreed draft. The Vietnamese version of the draft agreement, according to Dobrynin, called the proposed National Council of National Reconciliation and Concord a "political structure." Le Duc Tho and I had spent hours in Paris agreeing to denote it in English as an "administrative structure" to emphasize its nongovernmental character; the Vietnamese translation was unsettled.* I impressed on Dobrynin that Hanoi's version was totally unacceptable.

We also sent a note asking for weapons restraint to Peking; there was no reply. But then the Chinese contribution to Hanoi's arsenal was too marginal to affect the outcome in the South.

On October 16 I breakfasted with Haig, who would hold the fort while I was gone, and Under Secretary of State Alex Johnson. I then saw the President for forty-five minutes. At 11:00 A.M. I left for Andrews Air Force Base on the mission on which all our hopes had been concentrating for four years: the end of the war in Indochina. On the plane a handwritten note from Nixon was waiting for me. It read:

> Dear Henry, As you leave for Paris I thought it would be useful for you to have some guidance that we were talking about on paper. First, do what is right without regard to the election. Secondly, we cannot let a chance to end the war honorably slip away. As far as the elections are concerned, a settlement that did not come unstuck would help among young voters, but we do not need it to win. A settlement that became unstuck would hurt, but would not be fatal. At all costs we must avoid the fact or the impression that we have imposed or agreed to a coalition government. In sum, getting back to my original instruction, do what is right to secure an honorable peace, but do not let the timing be affected by the election.

Interlude in Paris

MY meeting with Xuan Thuy on October 17 lacked the drama of the previous week's sessions with Le Duc Tho. Xuan Thuy had no authority to make major changes. We improved the political provisions further by making explicit that the National Council of National Reconciliation and Concord could supervise the elections; it had no authority to order them. Any new election that might be held would first have to be agreed unanimously by the South Vietnamese parties — the all-purpose formula for burying an issue. The National Council — the last vestige of the coalition government — not only gave a veto to Saigon; it was deprived of anything to do. Hanoi's political program was dead.

With respect to replacement of military equipment, Xuan Thuy insisted on the principle of equality, and we on the principle of a one-for-one replacement for worn-out equipment. Xuan Thuy finally accepted our formulation, but made it contingent on the release of civilian

---

*In the October agreement, Le Duc Tho and I settled on a phrase committing the parties "to set up an administrative structure called the National Council of National Reconciliation and Concord. . . ." Hanoi sought to translate "administrative structure" in Vietnamese by a phrase implying a governmental authority. In the technical meeting in Paris on October 12, Lord and Engel had explicitly rejected this Vietnamese translation and insisted on a weaker phrase with no governmental connotations. The matter was left for later resolution. Hanoi would almost certainly have conceded the point soon afterward had not its publication of the agreement on October 26 turned all unresolved issues, however minor, into issues of prestige.

detainees in South Vietnam. I rejected the proposition; Saigon would never accept it; this was a political matter to be settled between the Vietnamese parties. Moreover, we found Hanoi's assurances regarding a cease-fire in Laos and Cambodia unsatisfactory. I told Xuan Thuy that I could not go to Hanoi unless we had settled the text of the agreement as well as the associated understandings. And his leaders should be clear that we could not proceed except with the approval of Saigon. It might thus be necessary for me to return from Saigon to Paris for another round of negotiations. Alternatively, it might be desirable to meet with Le Duc Tho again, say in Vientiane, after completing my Saigon stop. Xuan Thuy grumbled, but clearly had no authority to give a definitive reply.

Meanwhile in Washington, Nixon was polling his senior advisers. On October 16, he consulted with Secretary Laird and General Abrams. Both, Haig informed me, strongly endorsed the agreement. Abrams stressed that we would not be significantly better off militarily if we fought another year at the present scale (and it was, of course, highly improbable that we could maintain the present scale). On October 18 Rogers and Alex Johnson told Nixon that they considered the draft agreement a "total surrender" by Hanoi, especially on the political points. Haig reported that Nixon was enthusiastic. The President suggested that I treat the forthcoming meetings with Thieu as a "poker game" in which I should hold back the "trump card" until the last trick. Thus I should not show the political portion of the agreement to Thieu immediately. I should imply that Hanoi was asking for more than it actually was. Then, when I tabled the actual text as our "rock-bottom position," Thieu would have a maximum incentive to go along. I did not follow this advice. I had concluded that simply too many people had seen the text of the agreement for us to play games. Playing it straight, it turned out, did not do much good either.

On the way to Saigon I sent a message to Hanoi in my name reiterating what I had said to Xuan Thuy: that a visit to Hanoi could take place "only in the context of an agreement." I included our proposed texts for the disputed points. For emphasis I sent another message to Hanoi later that day, October 18 — this time in the President's name — repeating the impossibility of visiting Hanoi while any points were outstanding and proposing a meeting between Le Duc Tho and me, preferably in Vientiane, if necessary in Paris. Hanoi's cherished "shedyule" would thereby slip by another three or four days.

I had already agreed with Le Duc Tho that we would decrease the bombing of the North during the final phase of the negotiations. Upon my departure for Paris we had reduced the level of bombing north of the twentieth parallel; with the text of the agreement completed, the note said, we would stop bombing the North altogether twenty-four hours before my arrival in Hanoi. At the same time, Washington was making final preparations to beef up Saigon's inventories, to have as high a base as possible for one-for-one replacement. The massive airlift of military equipment into South Vietnam for once had a code name that made sense: it was called "Enhance Plus."

The mood on the long ride to Saigon was optimistic. All of us except John Negroponte thought that Thieu would be overjoyed by the agreement. Again, we reviewed the terms. The cease-fire in place would give Saigon 90 percent of the population; infiltration into South Vietnam was barred; the ghost of the coalition government had been laid to rest; there was international supervision; Viet Cong cadres would probably remain in South Vietnam's jails; US military assistance to Saigon could continue. To be sure, we had not obtained Hanoi's agreement to withdraw its forces from the South. But if the no-infiltration clause was observed, attrition would ease that threat. All this assumed that the agreement would be carried out and above all that the Vietnamese parties were making rational calculations of their prospects. But they had suffered too much for that, and inflicted too much pain on each other. Maddened by hatred and suspicion, incapable of imagining peace, the two Vietnamese parties finally found common ground only in their obsession with humiliating each other and in their effort to draw us into the vortex of their passions. Each seemed willing to destroy itself so long as it could take its hated opponent with it into oblivion.

Consultation with Thieu

ELLSWORTH BUNKER always had a soothing effect in a crisis. When one saw at the foot of the ramp that tall, erect, thin figure, immaculately dressed as if no suit of his would dare rumple even in the tropical heat of Saigon, one knew there was no risk of failure from either excess of impetuosity or lack of dedication. Ellsworth was one of our great diplomats. He came to government service relatively late in life after a distinguished business career; he had no need to prove anything to himself or to others. His ambition was to make a contribution to the foreign policy of his country, whose well-being he identified with the security and hope of all free peoples. His values were reflected not in self-serving rhetoric but in the matter-of-fact performance of a high standard of duty. He was a quintessential American in the optimism that made him appear youthful even then, in his late seventies. For five years he had been in Saigon, serving two Presidents of different parties and earning their unqualified trust and admiration. Through the worst of our domestic travails he never flinched. He supported his government on television and in print when others with far greater responsibility for our involvement were running for cover. He had shared in all of my secret diplomacy involving Vietnam; he had received full summaries of every private meeting and detailed briefings when he visited Washington. For all my years of service, he had stood by the government to which he was accredited, defending it within official councils and in public against the charge that it was the principal obstacle to peace. Nobody deserved less the shoddy treatment to which Thieu was subjecting him — the endless waiting, the postponed appointments, the evasive if not downright deceptive answers he was given. Throughout all this Ellsworth Bunker uttered rarely a word of complaint. He performed his chores with gentleness, discipline, and selfless skill. He had nursed matters to this point; like all of us he yearned for peace with honor. No one who knew him could doubt that he would interpret the requirements of honor strictly.

Bunker, his deputy Charles Whitehouse, General Abrams, and I met soon after our arrival in the small library of the Ambassador's modest residence, selected not for its elegance but for its location on a dead-end street, which eased the security dangers. It was my first opportunity to show Bunker and his associates the current draft of the agreement. Bunker's reaction was that it exceeded what he had thought attainable; less would still have been practically and morally justifiable. His opinion was shared by General Abrams; Abe reiterated what he had told Nixon, that there was no gain to be had in fighting another year on the present scale — adding that if we reduced our effort by withdrawing the augmentation forces, conditions might well deteriorate. He reported the disquieting news that the North Vietnamese had launched a "high point" of offensive activities, especially around Saigon, obviously trying (as I was urging Saigon to try) to seize as much territory as possible before a cease-fire. Abrams thought this offensive would be troublesome, but also that it could be defeated without significant loss of territory.

Charles Whitehouse was the only one present to raise a word of caution. He shared his colleagues' judgment of the agreement, but he doubted that Thieu would accept it before our election. For Saigon to cut the umbilical cord with the United States would be a wrenching psychological blow. Thieu would need many weeks to prepare himself and his people for it. No matter what the terms, Thieu would prevaricate and delay as long as possible. Whitehouse turned out to be right on the mark.

I also consulted Phil Habib, our Ambassador to Korea, whom I had asked to join me in Saigon. Habib's opinion meant a great deal to me. Born in Brooklyn of Lebanese origin, educated at the University of Idaho, he was the antithesis of the public stereotype of the elegant, excessively genteel Foreign Service Officer. He was rough, blunt, direct, as far from the "striped-pants" image as it is possible to be. He had served in Vietnam or dealt with Vietnam problems for nearly ten years. He had been deputy ambassador to a succession of ambassadors at the

Paris peace talks and the one element of continuity on the delegation. He had selected most of the dedicated young Foreign Service Officers who had served in the provinces of South Vietnam. A man of total integrity, he had ridden the roller coaster from hopeful idealism to bleak despair. He wanted us to leave the graveyard of so many hopes, but with dignity. He owed it to his Service and his colleagues to end the war in a manner compatible with our international obligations. He had always urged flexibility but also realism; serious negotiations but no surrender, disguised or otherwise. He would have to sell the agreement to South Korea, an ally that had sent 50,000 troops to Vietnam and whose security also depended on confidence in our reliability. He was exultant about the draft agreement; it exceeded his highest hopes. It would be considered a victory by our Korean allies. With that, every American senior official familiar with the negotiations and with Vietnamese affairs had endorsed our effort.

Had Thieu been able to bring himself to say, even privately, what Whitehouse had outlined, much of the turmoil of the next few weeks would have been avoided. Had we understood immediately that Thieu objected not to specific terms but to the *fact* of an agreement, we would certainly have maneuvered differently. However unreasonable Thieu's position, I was clear in my mind that Nixon did not want a blowup before the election. But Thieu never engaged in a conceptual discussion. Instead, he fought in the Vietnamese manner: indirectly, elliptically, by methods designed to exhaust rather than to clarify, constantly needling but never addressing the real issue — methods by which through the centuries the Vietnamese have sought to break the spirit of foreigners before tackling them physically in one of their heroic charges. One cannot say that it has not worked; unfortunately, it inspires little confidence; it is especially tough on allies. But then no Vietnamese, North or South, would believe that confidence or trust or friendship is decisive. They have survived foreigners for centuries not by trusting but by manipulating them.

The meeting on October 19 was in this mode. On arrival at the Presidential Palace I was kept waiting for fifteen minutes in full view of the press. Then Thieu's aide Hoang Duc Nha appeared to usher me and Bunker into the presidential presence. Thieu extended no greetings. Impassively, he accepted a letter by Nixon, which stated, *inter alia:*

Dr. Kissinger will explain to you in the fullest detail the provisions of the proposed agreement which he carries with him and I will therefore not provide further elaboration in this message. I do, however, want you to know that I believe we have no reasonable alternative but to accept this agreement. It represents major movement by the other side, and it is my firm conviction that its implementation will leave you and your people with the ability to defend yourselves and decide the political destiny of South Vietnam. . . .

Finally, I must say that, just as we have taken risks in war, I believe we must take risks for peace. Our intention is to abide faithfully by the terms of the agreements and understandings reached with Hanoi, and I know this will be the attitude of your government as well. We expect reciprocity and have made this unmistakably clear both to them and their major allies. I can assure you that we will view any breach of faith on their part with the utmost gravity; and it would have the most serious consequences.

To the typed text drafted by my staff and me, Nixon had added the following handwritten note:

Dr. Kissinger, General Haig and I have discussed this proposal at great length. I am personally convinced it is the best we will be able to get and that it meets my *absolute* condition — that the GVN must survive as a free country. Dr. Kissinger's comments have my total backing.

If ever, this was the time for Thieu to state his real concerns and to have a heart-to-heart talk with the emissary of a President who had, after all, staked his political future and his country's credibility on supporting South Vietnam. Instead, Thieu read the letter without comment. He invited me into the next room where, just as during Haig's trip three weeks earlier, his National Security Council was assembled, augmented by the South Vietnamese ambassadors to Washington and the Paris peace talks. Our side, in addition to me, included Bunker, Whitehouse, Abrams, Sullivan, Lord, and interpreter David Engel. The mood was set immediately when Thieu, without a word of introduction, opened the session by announcing that Nha would serve as interpreter. Considering that every Vietnamese present at least understood English, this indicated that Thieu was not going to make things easy for us. Nha proceeded to mock his role by condensing all my remarks to about half their length. This caused me to point out that either Vietnamese was a more concise language than English or else Nha was abbreviating (in which case it would have been interesting to know what he was leaving out). "I am a master of contraction," said Nha humbly.

I began by outlining our strategy. Our Vietnam effort, I argued, had been held together by a very few people against massive domestic pressures seeking to liquidate our involvement in exchange for only the return of American prisoners. Those pressures would become uncontainable if we were perceived to abandon a reasonable negotiating position, especially when it was one we ourselves had put forward. I recognized that in this respect there was a difference between Thieu's imperatives and ours. He had to demonstrate to his people that he was firm; we had to demonstrate that we were flexible. I stressed that our concern was not the two weeks before our elections but the months that would follow. The additional costs of the military augmentation after the offensive — amounting already to $4.1 billion — would have to be submitted to the

Congress in January. It would provide a convenient occasion for cutting off support. For over two years we had made a clearly defined set of proposals with Saigon's concurrence; these had been accepted by Hanoi. Even our supporters in the Congress would never understand if we now dragged our feet. That was the real deadline against which we were working. Forgetting Nixon's "trump card" suggestion, I spent an hour reviewing the entire draft, showing how in the cease-fire section it met every proposal we had put forward, and in its political provisions was far better than the terms we had offered publicly or privately. I concluded with what I considered the central issue:

> We have fought together for eight years and longer. You have sacrificed a great deal and so have we. And now if we could make peace together we can vindicate all the suffering and build together the sort of structure in Vietnam for which we have all suffered so much. It is in this spirit that the President has asked me to speak to you, and I come to you as a friend to deal with a joint problem so we can continue our friendship and continue our cooperation.

Thieu proved as resistant to the eloquence of foreigners as had Le Duc Tho for the three previous years in Paris — or maybe I simply overestimated my persuasiveness. He adopted the tactic I should have recognized from his previous encounters with Haig and me. He raised a number of intelligent questions, none of them going to the heart of the agreement. Thieu wanted to know to what extent I thought the terms compatible with our May 8 proposal; the modalities of signing the agreement; when the international supervisory machinery would go into operation; what schedule I recommended — all of which suggested that if the answers were satisfactory, he would go along. Suddenly he asked whether the agreement was needed for Nixon's reelection. I responded by reading the handwritten note from Nixon that was given to me on the plane as I left Washington.

We agreed to resume the discussion with his full NSC the next morning. Another meeting was scheduled for the afternoon with Thieu, Abrams, General Cao Van Vien (Chairman of the South Vietnamese Joint General Staff), and me to discuss the additional military supplies foreseen by Enhance Plus. My colleagues, Bunker, and I were at this point very optimistic. Thieu's questions and his eagerness to discuss Enhance Plus suggested that he was moving toward a settlement. I sent off a report to Nixon outlining prospects more cautiously than all of us really felt. Any halfway experienced emissary will promise less than he hopes to deliver; it will mitigate the disappointment in case of unexpected failure; it will — let us be frank — heighten his achievement if he succeeds. The report read:

> It is too early to tell Thieu's reaction; we have learned from past trips that he doesn't show his hand until the second meeting. My instinct is that we face the

difficult task we all predicted; it remains to be seen whether we can pull it off.
. . . In sum I made emphatically clear that we considered this an excellent
agreement that would redeem years of sacrifice and fully protect both the GVN
and Thieu. It was a much better settlement than anyone could have expected
and resulted from our firm military and diplomatic support.

At the meeting on the afternoon of October 19, Abrams described to
Thieu the matériel we would leave for the South Vietnamese forces and
the additions we would provide through the Enhance Plus program
before the cease-fire. This included over 150 additional planes, to be delivered in a fourteen-day period. Once again Thieu asked perceptive
questions; to our unsubtle minds it sounded as if he were inching toward
agreement. For example, he raised no direct objection to my proposed
stop in Hanoi; if he accepted the agreement, he said, he would not consider such a journey inappropriate.

Before the next meeting the other Vietnam was heard from. Hanoi's
messages to me now had to travel to Saigon — only 800 miles away —
over a distance of 20,000 miles. Hanoi delivered them in Paris to Colonel Guay. He sent them to Haig in Washington through White House
backchannels. Haig retransmitted them — again in White House backchannels — to Saigon. When we contacted Hanoi, the procedure was
reversed. Our messages went from Saigon to Washington to Paris and
then on to Hanoi.

The message that came late on October 19 nonetheless represented
a reply within twenty-four hours. It made clear that Hanoi did not want
another meeting either in Vientiane or in Paris. Rather, it suggested
that we stick to the original schedule. To enable us to do so it *conceded*
the two remaining points on civilian prisoners and replacement; Hanoi accepted not only the substance of our position but also the text we had sent
from the plane. The practical result was that a cease-fire would free all
prisoners *except* Viet Cong cadres in South Vietnamese jails. And the
replacement provision, coupled with the massive augmentation of South
Vietnamese forces even then under way, permitted what amounted to
unlimited American military assistance to Saigon.

When Haig cabled the North Vietnamese reply to me, he added accurately: ''I recognize this message adds immeasurably to your burdens
at today's meeting.'' It was the height of irony that Hanoi's total acceptance of our demands was thought to add to my burdens. But indeed it
did. Coupled with Hanoi's stepped-up land-grabbing operations, which
Haig also pointed out, it left us with a massive problem. Hanoi's military offensive would make it much harder to persuade Thieu to come
along; Hanoi's message would make it nearly impossible for us to sustain our position domestically if he did not. Saigon held the key; its attitude would determine whether the war would end quickly.

Saigon was in no hurry. But when one is on a tightrope, the most dangerous course is to stop. Once launched on the journey I had no choice except to go forward. We had used the "shedyule" to exact concessions; in the process we had given up scope for procrastination. Until our election, delay, if judiciously used, could improve our bargaining position. Afterward, procrastination would work increasingly in Hanoi's favor. As it became apparent that our military and political position would not improve after November 7, Hanoi would reverse the process and discover that it had every incentive to push us up against our own deadline of a returning Congress and our need for a four- to six-billion-dollar supplementary appropriation. So our alternatives were now narrow indeed. Hanoi always had the option of going public. And in my view — which I have not changed with hindsight — we would not be able to achieve anything like the concessions that were falling to us almost daily now if negotiations were conducted semipublicly under the pressure of a domestic uproar. We would be forced to accept the agreement, whatever Thieu's views. Our real choice was not between delay and agreement. It was between making an agreement exacted by the pressures of Hanoi, Congress, and public opinion, and ending the war as an act of policy, demonstrating that we had mastered events and given some purpose to our sacrifices.

I therefore returned a cable to Hanoi "on behalf of the President" through the White House Situation Room. It declared the text of the agreement "complete" but also pointed to unsettled issues remaining in three areas that had been left to "understandings": American prisoners in Laos and Cambodia; an end to the war in Laos; and the future of Cambodia. Our proposed text for each of these topics was sent to Paris for transmission to Hanoi. On Laos, we asked for an understanding that a cease-fire would follow there within thirty days of that in Vietnam. With respect to Cambodia, where Hanoi insisted — as it turned out, truthfully — that its influence was not conclusive, we asked for confirmation in writing of statements by Le Duc Tho that offensive operations would be stopped, North Vietnamese troops withdrawn, and infiltration ended. While we were at it, we proposed a new "shedyule," which delayed my arrival in Hanoi by forty-eight hours.

Saigon was not eager to have me meet any timetable. What was success for us — the withdrawal of American forces — was a nightmare for our allies; even with a cease-fire they simply could not imagine how they would be better off without us. The meeting scheduled with Thieu and his National Security Council for October 20 slipped from 9:00 A.M. to 2:00 P.M. The session lasted three and a half hours. The composition of the Vietnamese side was the same as the day before. Our delegation was also identical except for Bill Sullivan, whom I had sent to Bangkok and Vientiane to brief the Thai and Laotian leaders about the draft agreement.

Thieu opened the meeting, once again without a word of grace to the American delegation, by expressing profound skepticism about Hanoi's motives and the danger of what he called "ambushes." Nha then went through a list of extremely intelligent questions that centered on the North Vietnamese forces in the South, on clarification of the arms replacement provision, on the composition and functions of the National Council of National Reconciliation and Concord, and on the American attitude if the agreement were violated. I replied in detail, repeating the arguments of the previous day that the ban on infiltration should cause the attrition of the North Vietnamese forces; that the replacement provision would mean in effect unlimited American military aid because of Saigon's large inventories, augmented by Enhance Plus; that the functions of the National Council were to be negotiated by Saigon, which would also have a veto over its composition and operation.

As to the American response to violations, I reiterated Nixon's assurance that in the event of massive North Vietnamese violations the United States would act to enforce the agreement. The argument was later advanced that it was not within the President's power to give such assurances without explicit authorization by the Congress. This idea not only did not occur to us; it would have struck us as inconceivable that the United States should fight for years and lose 45,000 men in an honorable cause, and then stand by while the peace treaty, the achievement of their sacrifice, was flagrantly violated. Diplomacy could not survive such casuistry. Negotiations would become exercises in cynicism; no agreement would ever be maintained. In Vietnam this meant the agreement would have been a blatant subterfuge for surrender. We could have done that earlier and with much less pain. Honor, decency, credibility, and international law all combined to make it seem beyond controversy that we should promise to observe the treaty and see it enforced. What else could be the meaning of a solemn compact ending a war, ratified by an international conference? The point was made privately to Thieu and his associates. It was also made publicly by Nixon, Elliot Richardson (when he was Secretary of Defense), me, and other officials.[2] It seemed to us the least controversial of the issues raised by the agreement. We thought we would be in a better moral and political position to assist Saigon to maintain its freedom in the name of a peace program in which the American people could take pride than in the context of open-ended warfare tearing our country apart. Whether the judgment would have been vindicated in normal times will remain forever unknown. Soon after the agreement was signed, Watergate undermined Nixon's authority, and the dam holding back Congressional antiwar resolutions burst. This unleashed once again the divisive passions we had sought to still by making peace. It gave those who were interested above all in vindicating the argument of a decade of protest one more opportunity — and this time a successful one — to make their case on the ruins of South Vietnam's independence.

First Rumblings

No member of the American team in the Presidential Palace in Saigon that October dreamed of any such sequel. We sincerely believed we were preserving both America's principles and South Vietnam's freedom. We were frustrated not by doubts about opinion at home but by Thieu's seeming inability to grasp his opportunity. Even General Abrams, normally so taciturn, intervened on October 20 to urge that Thieu accept the draft agreement:

I am confident that the structure here as it stands today is capable of securing this country and this government. I echo the sentiments of Dr. Kissinger that no agreement will secure this country — only vigilance and determination will secure it.

When President Nixon on Monday afternoon of this week called me to his office with Secretary Laird and asked me what I thought about this . . . I told him that I thought it was time to take the next step. It was a difficult step to make the first withdrawal and each subsequent one, but as confidence and capabilities and skill developed, it became practicable. So more and more as time has gone on the defense of South Vietnam has been by the South Vietnamese themselves. I have always had great respect and admiration for the South Vietnamese people and military, but I have always believed from the beginning that the day had to come for you and for your own pride and your people when the security and the political strength was all yours, with eventually our air power standing in the wings and our equipment and supplies coming into your ports.

At this point Thieu let it slip that the real anxiety was not the agreement but a lack of just that self-confidence Abrams had defined as so essential. Abrams had urged Thieu not to overestimate Hanoi because the North Vietnamese had made grave errors; they had misjudged the situation repeatedly. Had they moved the two divisions that besieged Khe Sanh in 1968 to Hué, we would never have been able to relieve the city. Similarly, Hanoi "stupidly" dispersed its forces during the 1972 offensive: "They are making an offer because they have lost and they know it. This is the first time they have gotten smart about the war." Unfortunately, Thieu drew the opposite conclusion from Abrams's presentation and turned Abrams's argument against him: "This fact, General Abrams, about how they could have dispatched two divisions from Khe Sanh toward Hué, the fact they didn't means that this is due to the talent of our generals, and the fact that the Communists have lost is due to the talent of our generals." This apparent avowal of self-confidence masked a deeper doubt; Thieu refused to accept Abrams's claim of Communist ineptitude. Listing North Vietnamese failures did not reassure him if success derived from the more contingent factor of South Vietnamese skill (or luck).

That was the heart of the problem which no systems analysis or proclamations about Vietnamization could erase. The South Vietnamese, after eight years of American participation, simply did not feel ready to confront Hanoi without our direct involvement. Their nightmare was not this or that clause but the fear of being left alone. For Saigon's leaders a cease-fire meant the departure of our remaining forces; they could not believe that Hanoi would abandon its implacable quest for the domination of Indochina. In a very real sense they were being left to their own future; deep down, they were panicky at the thought and too proud to admit it. And they were not wrong. We have considered the presence of American forces in Korea essential for the military and psychological balance on that peninsula.

It was not Thieu's fault that we had simply come to the end of our road — largely as the result of our domestic divisions. But even if he understood our position intellectually, he could not, as a Vietnamese patriot, bring himself to accept it publicly. The terms we had obtained were the best possible; they were indeed better than what we had asked for; theoretically they gave South Vietnam the means to survive. But they did not of themselves provide the sinews of confidence and cohesion in Saigon essential to maintain the equilibrium which had in fact been achieved on the battlefield.

This being so, much of the discussion in Saigon's Presidential Palace turned out to be beside the point. The South Vietnamese raised a number of drafting proposals that once more led the American side — ever unequal to the complexities of Vietnamese psychology — to believe that Saigon was feeling its way toward an agreement. That impression was reinforced when Thieu at the end of the meeting stated that he would be busy next morning consulting leaders of the National Assembly and other key political figures to prepare them for what might be ahead. We scheduled the next meeting, then, for 2:00 P.M., October 21; in the meantime, there would be technical discussions between a group of experts headed by Foreign Minister Tran Van Lam and the American team to develop a common position on drafting changes to be proposed to Hanoi. Having told Hanoi that the text of the agreement was "complete" — though not the associated understandings (or protocols) — we knew that this would be a formidable task.

At the end of the three-and-a-half-hour discussion with Thieu, I reported to Washington:

> It was clear from the sober, somewhat sad, mood of the session that they are having great psychological difficulty with cutting the American umbilical cord. They probably realize that the deal is a good one by American standards, but

their focus is on remaining North Vietnamese forces and the likelihood of violations of the agreement. While they showed pride in the talents of their generals, they continued to exhibit awe of Communist cunning and a lack of self-confidence. They undoubtedly feel they need more time, but one senses they will always feel that way. They know what they have to do and it is very painful. They are probably even right. If we could last two more years they would have it made.

. . . . I have the sense that they are slowly coming along and are working themselves into the mental frame of accepting the plan, but their self-respect requires a sense of participation.

As on my secret visit to Moscow in April, I now found myself locked into a communications cycle with Washington that made an effective exchange of views extremely difficult and, as events speeded up, produced escalating misunderstanding, all compounded by the pressures of deadlines, the large stakes involved, and the emotion connected with the homestretch of the war. Saigon was thirteen hours ahead of Washington. My evening reports of meetings would thus arrive in Washington during the middle of the morning. For security we had a complicated system of double-coding at each end that required two sets of communicators. Because of Saigon's curfew our messengers had to arrange for a special escort each time we sent or received a message. All this caused additional delay, so that Washington lagged far behind our deliberations. By the time Haig could discuss our messages with the President, draft a reply for Nixon's consideration, and send it off, the Washington working day was usually over. I would get Washington's reaction during the morning of the next day, generally while I was already involved in another meeting. Thus each end was continually commenting or reporting out of cycle, on events or recommendations already overtaken.

It was hardly surprising that I began to develop the classic neurotic syndrome that comes sooner or later to all those diplomats who work in the field. There were times when Washington seemed to me more interested in positioning itself over what had already happened than in sharing responsibility for our critical decisions. For instance, after my relatively hopeful report of October 19, Nixon helpfully cabled me to tell Thieu that:

I have personally studied in great depth the draft agreement which has been worked out with Hanoi, and I am convinced that it is in the best interest of the government and the people of South Vietnam that this proposal be accepted. Also advise President Thieu in the strongest terms that for the four years I have been in office and, indeed, for the period before that when I was out of office, no American public figure has stood up more staunchly for the proposition that there can be no Communist government imposed on the people of South Vietnam. Furthermore, no U.S. public figure has been a stronger supporter of President Thieu himself. You should assure the President that he can unreservedly rely on the continuation of that support in the days ahead.

But the next day Nixon, as part of his consultation with senior advisers, met with General William Westmoreland, on the verge of retiring as Army Chief of Staff, who suddenly surfaced objections to the very concept of a cease-fire in place. This was amazing, since a standstill cease-fire had been part of our position since October 1970 and had been endorsed then by the Joint Chiefs of Staff, of whom Westmoreland was one. Without telling me of that conversation, Nixon now sent me yet another cable, for the fifth time in four days telling me not to pay any attention to the forthcoming election and to emphasize solidarity with Thieu:

As you continue discussions with Thieu, I wish to re-emphasize again that nothing that is done should be influenced by the U.S. election deadline. I have concluded that a settlement which takes place before the election which is, at best, a washout has a high risk of severely damaging the U.S. domestic scene, if the settlement were to open us up to the charge that we made a poorer settlement now than what we might have achieved had we waited until after the election. The essential requirement is that Thieu's acceptance must be wholehearted so that the charge cannot be made that we have forced him into a settlement which was not in the interest of preventing a Communist takeover of a substantial part of the territory of South Vietnam.

As I outlined yesterday, we must have Thieu as a willing partner in making any agreement. It cannot be a shotgun marriage. I am aware of the risk that Hanoi might go public but am confident that we can handle this eventuality much easier than we could handle a preelection blow-up with Thieu or an agreement which would be criticized as a pretext for U.S. withdrawal.

The first time I had heard this injunction I was moved; now I began to be nagged by the unworthy notion that I was being set up as the fall guy in case anything went wrong. Of all of Nixon's Assistants I was the least involved in the election campaign. I had been out of the country almost constantly since early September. I never participated in meetings dealing with political strategy. On the principle that foreign policy was bipartisan I had refused to attend any fund-raising functions. I had turned aside repeated requests by John Ehrlichman, who alleged that he was transmitting orders from Nixon, to declassify embarrassing documents involving previous administrations to help in the campaign. (This was before the Freedom of Information Act made such matters routine.) On one such missive in August 1972 I had written by hand: "I am opposed — it is cheap politics." Nixon had never pursued the subject with me, but he could be under no misapprehension about my view. My strategy — explained in innumerable memoranda — had been to take advantage of Hanoi's expressed desire to settle before our election, using it as an inflexible deadline with which to extract concessions. Never either orally or in writing had I argued the reverse, that concluding the agreement would help our electoral prospects. Nixon ironically was implying the same charge against me that others were to make against Nixon — that I was rushing it for the election. To him, in fact, the electoral considerations counseled delay. Exhausted by two weeks of working fifteen to eighteen hours a day, testy from jet lag, and touchy from being assailed by two monomaniacal groups of Vietnamese, I returned a sarcastic reply to Haig:

I am grateful for the helpful comments that I have been receiving. It must be kept in mind that any settlement will at best be precarious and usher in a messy period. Nor in the best of circumstances can the South Vietnamese be expected to be enthusiastic since they are losing our military presence and then have to adjust to a situation they have not faced since 1962.

If I am being told to stop this process, then this should be made unambiguous. On the other hand, it is everyone's judgment here — including Bunker, Abrams, Habib and Sullivan — that this is the best deal we are ever going to get. We have to weigh the electoral considerations against the fact that I cannot imagine the prisoner issue being settled in less than a matter of weeks under normal conditions.

In any event I am prepared to stall this operation if I receive a clear signal to do so.

No such signal was forthcoming; nor in fairness could one have been issued. For events in Saigon began to accelerate beyond the capacity of our communications system to handle.

Showdown with Thieu

O N October 21, as I have indicated, we still supposed that we were inching to an understanding with Saigon, if with pain and little grace on the part of Thieu. In the morning I met with the South Vietnamese team of experts headed by Foreign Minister Lam to go over their suggested changes in the draft.

There were twenty-three. Some were of major significance. Saigon wanted to delete the phrase describing the National Council of National Reconciliation and Concord as an "administrative structure" in order to avoid haggling about translation. It urged that the reference to the Demilitarized Zone be strengthened to emphasize its character as a dividing line and to make assaults across it illegal. It insisted that there be no reference in the text to the Provisional Revolutionary Government (Hanoi's political arm in the South). Other changes were seemingly minor, though the notoriously unsubtle Western mind might well not grasp the wounding nature of clearly ambiguous and apparently insignificant phrases. My associates and I had no illusions about the difficulties of obtaining that many changes in a text we had already declared "completed." But we promised Saigon we would try, in good faith. We spent the morning seeking to discover the rationale behind the proposed changes so that we could determine some priority when we took up Saigon's proposals in Hanoi. The atmosphere was professional, marked by a serious attempt to assess the attainable and calculate the practical.

I had lunch with Bunker. We both were quite optimistic as we repaired to his office shortly before 2:00 P.M. to await the summons to the Presidential Palace to meet again the South Vietnamese National Security Council. No call came at the appointed hour. About an hour later Nha called Bunker to say that we should stand by; the meeting had been moved to 5:00 P.M. We would be notified when Thieu was ready. There was no apology for the delay nor an explanation. Nha simply delivered his message and hung up; he must have seen Humphrey Bogart do this in some movie. At 4:30 P.M. — or two and a half hours after our scheduled meeting — Thieu's motorcade passed the Embassy with sirens at full blast. By 5:30 P.M. we had not yet had a word from the Palace, giving rise to an historic occasion: a show of temper by Bunker. He tried to reach Thieu by telephone and was told the President was in a Cabinet meeting. When he asked to speak to Nha, he was told that the press secretary had left the building also and was unreachable. An hour later, or nearly five hours after the scheduled meeting time, Thieu called Bunker to tell him that he would see us right after the Cabinet meeting, which was still taking place. After another three-quarters of an hour Nha telephoned to say that Thieu would see Bunker and me at 8:00 A.M. the next morning. When Bunker remonstrated that the time difference would now mean a delay of at least twenty-four hours in Washington decision time, Nha simply hung up.

We returned to Bunker's residence. Seated in his small library, we tried to understand what was happening. Clearly, the South Vietnamese needed time to deliberate over major decisions. But their insolent manner implied an imminent confrontation. And over what? Thieu had not yet stated a position; he had confined himself to asking questions. The experts' meeting in the morning seemed to have gone well. We had promised to raise all of Saigon's points in Hanoi; we could not, of course, guarantee the outcome. Neither Thieu nor any of his associates had as yet invoked any issue of principle, though the provisions regarding North Vietnamese troops obviously bothered them. Whatever their concerns, no ally had a right to treat an emissary of the President of the United States this way. And the injustice of the conduct toward Bunker was monumental. We felt that impotent rage so cunningly seeded in foreigners by the Vietnamese. Thieu must have sensed that our strategy could not proceed without him; the more his indispensability was brought home to us — however outrageous the conduct — the more he could humiliate Hanoi, the more he could appeal to Vietnamese nationalism, and the better would be his bargaining position.

This was not just paranoia on my part; the emotional frenzy in the Presidential Palace quickly revealed itself. Around 9:00 P.M. — or seven hours after our original appointment — Thieu phoned Bunker. Nearly hysterical, he complained bitterly that Haig's mission three weeks earlier had been to organize a coup against him; members of my team were now continuing the effort. He demanded that we desist. Bunker and I had been among Thieu's principal supporters for years, resisting demands from Hanoi and from antiwar critics that we do away with the Saigon government. Haig had fought in Vietnam; he was a staunch admirer of Thieu's. It was a bitter pill to be accused of trying to overthrow a leader for whose survival we had undergone no little travail. Bunker came as close to indignation as his gentle nature permitted in rebutting Thieu's charges. But we had no time for outrage; nor did we have any option except to endure — as Thieu had correctly calculated. We were locked into a schedule that was to take me to Hanoi in seventy-two hours while our Vietnamese ally was disintegrating emotionally. The phone calls from the Palace could leave no doubt that the mood was turning hostile and, in the absence of specific objections, we did not even know how to resolve matters or what there was to resolve. We began to hope that Hanoi might make the issue academic by refusing the texts on Laos and Cambodia that we had communicated on October 20, but I immediately doubted it. I reported to Washington:

A familiar pattern is beginning to emerge. This puts us into an enormously precarious position. If Hanoi caves again on our latest message and I then refuse to make the trip, they will clearly know what the difficulty is. They would then have every incentive to go public and demand that we sign a settlement to which we have already agreed.

My prediction proved correct. On the evening of October 21, Hanoi once again *accepted* all our demands. The North Vietnamese agreed to all our formulations with respect to Laos and Cambodia. They informed us that there were no American prisoners in Cambodia, but that the prisoners in Laos would be released together with all Americans held in North and South Vietnam. They agreed, too, to the new "shedyule" I had transmitted on October 20. Our strategy was working everywhere with dazzling success — except with our own allies in Saigon. The fact was, as Haig pointed out in a cable, that "we are now at the hard point, and your meeting with Thieu this morning becomes crucial."

Fortunately (given the circumstances), Hanoi made one mistake that provided a real justification for procrastination. The distinguished journalist Arnaud de Borchgrave suddenly had been granted a visa to visit Hanoi. What made the event even more remarkable was that he had not asked for it. Once there, he was granted an interview by Prime Minister Pham Van Dong, which he had not requested. The interview was to be published on October 23, while I was still in Saigon, when Hanoi knew I would be in the process of obtaining South Vietnamese concurrence.* Perhaps Hanoi had arranged the story when it was still operating on the earlier "shedyule" that would have seen me already in Hanoi on the date of publication. The interview in either case was an insulting act of bad faith, and because of the delay, a nearly fatal one. For Pham Van Dong in his interview put forth a tendentious North Vietnamese interpretation of the draft agreement at variance not only with our interpretation but with the text of what had been negotiated. Thieu was described as "overtaken by events"; a "three-sided coalition of transition" would be set up; all detainees on both sides (including civilians) would be released; America had to pay reparations. De Borchgrave reported that Hanoi was already informing foreign diplomats of the completed agreement and was preparing festivities that looked to him like "victory celebrations." The Pham Van Dong interview was bound to provoke the South Vietnamese and compound their gravest suspicions. It also put us on notice that Tho's recent flexibility had been imposed by necessity, not a change of heart. But the interview exhibited weakness as well as duplicity. Pham Van Dong admitted that Thieu would stay after a settlement. Underneath the tendentious phraseology he had made it clear that the agreement was essentially a standstill cease-fire, heretofore contemptuously rejected by Hanoi. The "two armies and two administrations" would remain in existence in the South.

At about the same time a telegram arrived from Nixon instructing me for what we all agreed would be the decisive meeting with Thieu on the morning of October 22. I was to push Thieu to the limit without causing a blowup. I was to do the same with Hanoi. The best solution would be to defer the final agreement until after election day and to keep the two Vietnamese parties quiet until then. The instructions were not illuminating as to how I was to accomplish all this. (They reminded me of the man who during World War II said that the way to solve the submarine problem was to heat the ocean and boil them to the surface. When asked how to do this he replied: "I have given you the idea, the technical implementation is up to you.") But if Nixon's instructions provided no clear-cut course of action, they left no doubt that electoral considerations were driving Nixon more and more to *defer* a settlement, not, as his critics later would have it, to accelerate it.

More helpful was a letter from Nixon to Thieu, drafted by the Presi-

---

* We received an advance text on October 21; de Borchgrave traded his unexpurgated version for Ambassador Godley's permitting him to use Embassy communications in Vientiane to transmit his story to New York, no other quick and reliable cable facilities being available.

dent himself. In it Nixon repeated that he considered the agreement as it stood fully acceptable. And he added a grave warning that must have been extremely painful after all we had done to support Thieu:

Were you to find the agreement to be unacceptable at this point and the other side were to reveal the extraordinary limits to which it has gone in meeting demands put upon them, it is my judgment that your decision would have the most serious effects upon my ability to continue to provide support for you and for the Government of South Vietnam.

Nothing in Vietnam works as expected. The meeting with Thieu at 8:00 A.M. the next morning — Sunday, October 22 — did not, after the ominous preliminaries, produce a confrontation. Indeed, it almost seemed as if Thieu had staged the melodrama of the previous day to establish a posture of independence that would make it possible for him to go along with us at the last moment. Thieu and Nha were on the Vietnamese side, and Bunker was with me. Thieu restated his by now familiar objections to the agreement. He focused on the continued presence of North Vietnamese troops and on the composition of the National Council — which had no functions, in which he was to have a veto, and which, as it turned out, never came into being. I answered Thieu's concerns point by point and gave him Nixon's letter. Thieu responded with some dignity that for us the problem was how to end our participation in the war; for him it was a matter of life and death for his country. He had to consider not only the terms of the agreement but the perception of it by the people of South Vietnam. He was therefore consulting with the leaders of the National Assembly. He also wanted to hear a full report from his advisers on our reaction to the changes they proposed. He would meet Bunker and me again at 5:00 P.M. to give us his final reply.

Bunker and I left the meeting encouraged. "I think we finally made a breakthrough," I optimistically cabled Washington. I asked Bunker to send a fuller report to Washington, since I was leaving for the airport to visit Phnom Penh. Bunker cabled that "we both left with the impression that we had finally made a breakthrough. . . . we both left the meeting more encouraged that Thieu will be trying to find a way through his problems." While Bunker was at it, he also pointed out that Hanoi's attempt to seize as much territory as possible before the cease-fire was a complete failure. There was a large gap, he reported, between the enemy's capabilities and his intentions. "Our conclusion is that despite Communist instructions and efforts by the enemy to carry out these instructions, he has been unable to do so effectively and has suffered casualties in the effort."

To keep the other Vietnamese party quiet I sent a disingenuous message to Hanoi that its reply had been received while I was in Phnom Penh. The answer would have to wait for my return late in the day.

Now that the war was coming to a close, the arrangements for Cambodia were the most complex, and by far the least airtight, of all the settlements.

Laos and Cambodia were being dealt with in two sets of documents. Hanoi took the position that in the draft Vietnam agreement it could obligate itself only with respect to its own actions. Thus it could commit itself to withdraw its own troops from Laos and Cambodia. As for cease-fires between the belligerent parties, or securing pledges of releasing American prisoners, Le Duc Tho could only promise Hanoi's best efforts to persuade its allies. And it would promise these best efforts in written private understandings with us, not in the text of the Vietnam agreement. Thus, under Article 20 of the Vietnam agreement, Hanoi pledged to withdraw its forces from Cambodia and Laos and to refrain from using the territory of Cambodia and Laos for military operations against any of the signatories of the agreement, that is to say, South Vietnam.

The private understandings proved more complex. Hanoi was confident of its influence with its ally in Laos, the Pathet Lao. Le Duc Tho therefore promised to bring about a cease-fire in Laos within thirty days of the Vietnam cease-fire and to sign an understanding to that effect. With respect to Cambodia, Le Duc Tho claimed to have less influence over the Khmer Rouge. He gave only general oral assurances that once the war stopped in Laos and Vietnam, "there is no reason for the war to continue in Cambodia." After repeated efforts to secure a more explicit commitment to a cease-fire in Cambodia, I could achieve no more than Hanoi's written acknowledgment of what Le Duc Tho had told me orally. I decided to urge Lon Nol to offer a cease-fire unilaterally as soon as the Paris Agreement was signed (which he did), and I warned Le Duc Tho that if the Khmer Rouge responded with a new offensive, this would be "contrary . . . to the assumptions on which this Agreement is based."[3] I was willing to gamble that Lon Nol's forces with our modest support could contain the indigenous Cambodian Communists if North Vietnamese troops were withdrawn and North Vietnamese infiltration ended. Indeed, we had little choice. There would have been no support whatever at home for refusing an agreement in Vietnam that returned our prisoners and led to the withdrawal of the North Vietnamese from the countries of Indochina simply because the cease-fire in Cambodia was less than airtight.

I had sent Bill Sullivan to Bangkok and Vientiane, because he knew the leaders of Thailand and Laos, having worked with them when he served as Ambassador to Laos. He had returned with their enthusiastic endorsement. According to Sullivan Souvanna Phouma had exclaimed: "They are totally defeated." The reaction of the Thai leaders was similar. But because of our limited aid and the ambiguous settlement provision for Cambodia, I thought I owed it to Lon Nol to brief him personally.

It was a shaming encounter. Though Lon Nol had genuine cause for uneasiness, there was none of the nitpicking of Saigon, or the insolence. The Cambodians, who had received such a microscopic fraction of the annual aid given to Saigon, continued to place their trust in us. Lon Nol endorsed what we were doing even though he understood that his was the one country in Indochina not given a specific date for a cease-fire — though the North Vietnamese were firmly obligated to withdraw. Lon Nol even promised to put out a statement of strong support for the agreement when it was announced.

The trip to Phnom Penh was therefore painful in a way exactly the opposite of my Saigon sessions. Of all the leaders who had counted on us, none had been so shortchanged as Lon Nol. Of all the victims of North Vietnam's quest for hegemony in Indochina, none had resisted with more of a national spirit and had been left so much to their own devices as the people of Cambodia. In a very real sense Cambodia bore the heaviest burden of the irreconcilability of our domestic debate. After our troops had withdrawn from the sanctuaries, those who had denounced the 1970 incursion did their utmost to forestall any effective assistance to the beleaguered country, as if to punish the free Cambodians for not living up to the role of victim to which they had been consigned. The argument that we must not get bogged down in Cambodia had caused the Congress in 1971 and 1972 to limit all aid to Cambodia to the paltry sum of around $300 million (about 3 percent of our expenditures in Vietnam), to place a ceiling on the number of military attachés to be posted in our Phnom Penh Embassy, and to prohibit the sending of military advisers. Indeed, even our military attachés were prevented by our laws from visiting Cambodian troops. The argument about our getting bogged down in Cambodia was specious or based on a false parallel with Vietnam. The North Vietnamese forces in the South were overextended as it was; Hanoi was in no position to reinforce them; any improvement of Cambodian capabilities was bound to press them hard. And the Khmer Rouge were insignificant at first. All that our self-denial accomplished was to leave poor Cambodia to its own meager resources against its implacable enemy in Hanoi, and to give time to the murderous indigenous Khmer Rouge to build up their forces for their final conquest. It need not have happened. We shunned the opportunity to arm those who were eager to resist and who in doing so could have bogged down the North Vietnamese — not us — in a war of attrition. Whatever one's view about the wisdom of our original incursion, it is not easy to follow the logic of those who based their outrage on Cambodia's independence and then, once North Vietnam and the Khmer Rouge determined on conquest, made impossible an effective resistance to preserve that independence.

In the event, Lon Nol magnanimously endorsed the agreement, declared a unilateral cease-fire, and called for negotiations. His genocidal enemies ignored the appeal; and the American Congress within a year legislated a prohibition against using our air power to assist him. The Cambodian people deserved better.

It was characteristic of Vietnam that a simple failure never seemed to satisfy the vengeful gods arranging its destiny; they had to break one's heart as well. I returned to Saigon excited at the prospect of success. With Lon Nol in accord I thought we were on the homestretch. Bunker and I saw Thieu and Nha at 5:00 P.M. as scheduled, for nearly two hours. At the end of the talk I telegraphed Haig with the disastrous news: "Thieu has just rejected the entire plan or any modification of it and refuses to discuss any further negotiations on the basis of it."

It had been a bizarre encounter. Thieu, who spoke English fluently, refused to use it. While talking he frequently burst into tears — of rage rather than sorrow, Bunker and I thought. Nha translated and at the appropriate passages he too wept.

The meeting began with my briefing Thieu on our successful consultations in Phnom Penh, Bangkok, and Vientiane. Thieu dismissed this with the comment that he was not surprised; those countries had not been "sacrificed." He said that the United States had obviously "connived" with the Soviets and China to sell out South Vietnam. He would not be a party to it. For the first time he revealed that his sense of betrayal went back at least a year, to our proposal asking him to agree to resign one month before a new presidential election. Though he had accepted it without protest, and reiterated it not three months earlier, it obviously had rankled deeply:

Ever since the U.S. asked me to resign and bargained with me on the time of my resignation, had I not been a soldier I would have resigned. Because I see that those whom I regard as friends have failed me. However great the personal humiliation for me I shall continue to fight. My greatest satisfaction will be when I can sign a peace agreement. I have not told anyone that the Americans asked me to resign, since they would share my humiliation, but have made it appear voluntary on my part.

I replied calmly:

I admire the courage, dedication and heroism which have characterized your speech. However, as an American, I can only deeply resent your suggestion that we have connived with the Soviets and the Chinese. How can you conceive this possible when the President on May 8 risked his whole political future to come to your assistance? When we talked with the Soviets and Chinese, it was to pressure them to exert pressure on Hanoi. We genuinely believed that the proposed agreement preserved South Vietnam's freedom — our principles have been the same as yours and we have defended them. You have only one problem. President Nixon has many. Your conviction that we have undermined you will be understood by no American, least of all by President Nixon.

As to specifics: we have not recognized the right of North Vietnam to be in the South. We have used the language of the Geneva Accords, since we thought this the best way to work out a practical solution. Had we wanted to sell you out, there have been many easier ways by which we could have accomplished this.

I pointed out that we now had a practical problem: "We have fought for four years, have mortgaged our whole foreign policy to the defense of one country. What you have said has been a very bitter thing to hear." Obviously the negotiations could not continue without his agreement. I would return to Washington. It was in the interest of both our countries to avoid a confrontation if we were not to mock all we had sacrificed. I suggested that I pay a farewell call before my departure. We set the time for eight the next morning, Monday, October 23.

If October 8, when Hanoi had finally yielded on all its political demands, was the most moving moment of my government service, this was perhaps the saddest — at least to that point. Whatever happened now, Thieu's reaction guaranteed that the war would not end soon, or in a way that would heal the divisions of our country. My fervent hope had been that we could bring peace in a way that those who had sacrificed would find justified their suffering and that those who had opposed the war could accept as a culmination of their efforts. As a united people, we could then turn our energies to the positive tasks awaiting us in a newly hopeful international order. Thieu's conduct made it likely that the negotiation of the peace would haunt our future as the conduct of the war had mortgaged our past. If we failed to keep the "shedyule" of a settlement by October 31, Hanoi would certainly attack us publicly for having reneged on a peace agreement. If Hanoi published the peace terms, which it undoubtedly would, our critics — who had been asking us to settle for *less* — would accept no excuses for our failure to sign, all the more so as Hanoi had accepted our own proposals. Hanoi could accurately point to the repeated concessions it had made, beginning on October 8 and continuing up to October 21. Anybody who knew anything about Vietnam knew that we would be able to achieve a better agreement only by an extended conflict which the Congress had made clear it would never support. If we did not settle on close to the terms now available to us, we would be forced out of the war by a Congress legislating a simple trade of prisoners for our withdrawal. Having given up its political formula, Hanoi would surely jump at the opportunity; it was much better for it than the existing scheme. The war would end messily after all, in a way much less promising for Saigon and infinitely more divisive for our country.

And yet I had no margin for regrets. Outrageous as Thieu's conduct had been, our struggle had been over a principle: that America did not betray its friends. I agreed with Nixon that turning on Thieu would be incompatible with our sacrifice. My duty was to manage affairs, and not let them slide into chaos. Thieu bore a heavy responsibility for luring us deeper and deeper into the bog over four days. Had he revealed his real attitude the day I arrived, we would surely have sent different messages to Hanoi. Still, we could not disintegrate, out of personal irritation, everything for which millions of Americans had endured and suffered for ten years. Nor could we risk allowing Thieu's hysteria to turn into such despair that he would make our split public, tempting Hanoi into a new cycle of intransigence. But neither could we let him believe that he had stared us down and that we would be deflected from our larger objectives. We had to leave no doubt in his mind that any delay now was tactical, to give him a chance to paper over our differences and to exact marginal improvements but not a strategic reversal of our determination to settle the war.

A similarly fine line had to be walked with Hanoi. We had to convince the North Vietnamese Politburo that we were determined to conclude the agreement on substantially existing terms. But we also had to make Hanoi understand it would not be able to use our differences with Saigon to jockey us at the last moment into doing what we had refused for four years: overthrowing the political structure in South Vietnam.

These were the considerations at the heart of the exchanges between me and Lord in Saigon and the President and Haig in Washington as we communicated continually through the night over a distance of ten thousand miles. Dramatic events often take place in incongruous settings. Our headquarters was my small bedroom in Bunker's residence. We had no rapid means of communication with Washington. The secure phone did not work; the open phone was not secure. The double-coding system slowed communications to a point where Washington was generally responding to a message that had already been overtaken by another one. It was the middle of the night in Saigon. Lord would take down my instructions sitting on my bed while I was pacing up and down; he would then go to the next room and draft a message by hand. In the courtyard a driver and communicator were standing by to take Lord's handwritten telegram to the Embassy communications center — after having made sure they would not be challenged because of the curfew. Between messages Lord and I would ponder our dilemma and our choices. Our most important consideration was to get back to Washington before Hanoi blew up. Tempers were further frayed because telegraphic exchanges permit only one set of considerations to be put forward at a time. The give-and-take of conversation not being possible, tentative thoughts become enshrined as formal proposals and treated accordingly. On several occasions both ends of the line changed their minds, but by the time this fact could be communicated, the White House and I were responding to already superseded messages.

Immediately after my disastrous meeting with Thieu on Sunday, around 8:00 P.M. Saigon time, I cabled Haig that we now had two options. I could proceed to Hanoi as originally scheduled, present Saigon's changes, and go back and forth (the term "shuttle diplomacy" did not yet exist) until I had gained the concurrence of both sides. The second option was for me to return immediately to Washington; Haig meanwhile would tell Dobrynin that we had encountered major obstacles in Saigon which we were duty bound to present to the other side in another meeting with Le Duc Tho. We wanted Soviet assistance to keep Hanoi on a restrained course. I advised: "Obviously I favor the second course, but have offered the first [trip to Hanoi] only for intellectual completeness."

The more I thought about it, the less appealing a trip to Hanoi became. I would be trapped there in almost certainly inconclusive meetings; communications with Washington would be difficult; it was hard to foretell to what harassments we would be exposed. At best I would be in transit if things blew up. It was important for me to return to Washington as quickly as possible. The irony — it transpired — was that while Nixon in Washington began to worry that I might proceed to Hanoi, I began to grow anxious in Saigon that *against* my recommendation he might accept the first of the two options and order me to go there. Before I had received a reply to my first message, therefore, I sent off another cable: "I have thought the situation over and there is no viable route except the Soviet Union option which must be taken immediately in order to get ahead of the following message which has to be delivered in Paris at 11 p.m., today, Sunday, Paris time" (about 7:00 A.M. Monday, Saigon time, or some ten hours away).

The message — in the President's name — to be delivered in Paris was for Hanoi, and was designed to stall for enough time to enable me to get back to Washington before Hanoi blew up. It read:

The President notes with appreciation the message from the Prime Minister of the Democratic Republic of Vietnam which satisfied all his points with respect to Laos and Cambodia as well as U.S. prisoners.

As the DRV side knows, the U.S. side has made strenuous efforts in Saigon, Vientiane, Phnom Penh and Bangkok to secure an agreement. As the DRV side also knows, the U.S. side has always taken the position that it could not proceed unilaterally. Unfortunately the difficulties in Saigon have proved somewhat more complex than originally anticipated. Some of them concern matters which the U.S. side is honor-bound to put before the DRV side.

The President wishes the Prime Minister to know that under these circumstances he has asked Dr. Kissinger to return to Washington immediately to consult on what further steps to take.

The President must point out that the breach of confidence committed by the DRV side with respect to the Arnaud de Borchgrave interview bears considerable responsibility for the state of affairs in Saigon.

The President requests that the DRV side take no public action until he can submit a longer message with his considerations which will be transmitted within the next 24 hours.

The U.S. side reaffirms its commitment to the substance and basic principles of the draft agreement.

At that point, when as far as we were concerned we had already selected the course of returning to Washington and indeed had already informed Hanoi of that fact, the White House answered my *first* message. Nixon vehemently rejected the option of going to Hanoi that even then had been put forward only "for intellectual completeness" and with a specific recommendation against it.[4] A flood of cables from Haig in Nixon's name emphasized to me the unwisdom of proceeding to Hanoi. Tempers rose dangerously on both sides of the Pacific Ocean. I cabled back:

In the period now before us I think it is absolutely imperative that we not show any nervousness. Everyone should exude optimism and give the impression that we may be very close to an agreement. If we are hard-pressed by questions we should simply say that technical details always arise in the last stage of negotiations. And if we are really pressed to the wall we should concentrate on the question of North Vietnamese forces in the South. At all cost we must avoid letting Thieu become the object of public scorn, not for his sake but for our own. If Thieu emerges as the villain, even if we finally overcome his objections, everything that we have done for the past eight years will be thrown into question.

I believe that over a period of weeks we can still bring this to a reasonable conclusion. I have asked Bunker to get to work on Thieu. All intelligence indicates that he is making active preparations for a cease-fire. It is therefore likely that he will yield; especially if we remain firm after the election. On the other hand, if he does not yield there is still a good chance that Hanoi and we could sign an agreement which we would recommend to the other parties that they accept. This would give Thieu an opportunity to claim that he was raped but in the end he would yield. We should do a purely bilateral deal only as a last resort.

By the time confusion over my (now canceled) trip to Hanoi had been settled, another controversy arose, this time over my proposal that we stop all bombing of North Vietnam. We had indicated to the North Vietnamese that we would do so twenty-four hours before my arrival in

Hanoi. I did not think that we could fail to carry out this promise and continue full-scale bombing after Hanoi had accepted all our proposals. (Bombing north of the twentieth parallel was to have been stopped when I arrived in Saigon.) On the other hand, I should have known that a bombing halt before the election would touch one of Nixon's rawest nerves. Despite his generally high regard for President Johnson, he had convinced himself that the 1968 bombing halt had been an electoral ploy designed to deprive him at the last second of a certain victory. He never ceased describing it to his associates as an unreciprocated sellout. It was too much to expect Nixon to repeat what looked like the same ploy. He rejected my proposal, though he agreed it was unthinkable to continue bombing north of the twentieth parallel when it was Saigon that had blocked the agreement and when we were the party not fulfilling the schedule.

With respect to my trip to Hanoi and the attitude toward Thieu, Washington and I agreed and yet argued heatedly. On the bombing halt, over which there was a genuine disagreement, the discussion, paradoxically, proceeded calmly and resulted in a sensible solution. Nixon was right. I had overreacted. Bombing of North Vietnam below the twentieth parallel, interdicting supplies relevant to the continuing war in the South, continued.

After no more than three hours' sleep I paid my farewell call on Thieu, accompanied by Bunker, at 8:00 A.M., Monday, October 23. It was a melancholy encounter. I tried to remove the bitterness. Thieu, for all his faults, was a patriot who had fought courageously for his country's independence. And I thought it important not to push him over the brink into rash acts and public confrontation. I informed Thieu that I had requested another meeting with Le Duc Tho to present Saigon's proposals. I hoped that Thieu would not engage in open debate with us in the meantime. There would be no public criticism of Thieu from our side. In order not to raise false hopes I emphasized that we considered the draft agreement a good one and that we would proceed within its framework. We would try to obtain as many of the proposed changes as possible, but we would not abandon the basic draft. I concluded by stressing my respect for the redoubtable South Vietnamese President as a patriot and as a soldier. Still, I had to tell him "in anguish" that if the war went on at the present scale for another six months, the Congress would cut off our funds:

What is important is that all the sacrifices that have been made should not have been made in vain. If we continue our confrontation you will win victories, but we will both lose in the end. It is a fact that in the United States all the press, the media and intellectuals have a vested interest in our defeat. If I have seemed impatient in the last days it is because I saw opportunity slipping away. . . . I am not trying to convince you, but I want you to understand what we have attempted to do. Had it not been for the importance we place on our relationship, we would not have to make new plans — that is why I leave with such a sense of tragedy. We will do our best and Bunker will be in touch with you.

Thieu, much calmer now, reviewed his objections to the agreement once more. They had been softened slightly. He now concentrated on strengthening the provisions regarding the Demilitarized Zone (important because they affected infiltration and reinforcements) and the composition of the impotent National Council of National Reconciliation and Concord (essentially frivolous). He agreed that the question of North Vietnamese troops in the South could be settled on a de facto basis by unannounced North Vietnamese withdrawals. (While we did not have Hanoi's agreement to this, there would be in fact a withering away of North Vietnamese forces if the proposed agreement were observed and infiltration ceased.) Thieu, with dignity, even agreed with my analysis of the American domestic situation. But for South Vietnam it was a matter of survival, he said. He would never take a public position critical of the United States:

I promised [yesterday] to avoid any confrontation and said that I would not publicly acknowledge any disagreement between President Nixon and myself. . . .

I still consider President Nixon a friend and a comrade in arms. Whether or not I am President I will strive to create conditions so that the United States can help Vietnam. If I am an obstacle to American aid or to peace, I will not stay on as President. I had no intention of criticizing President Nixon. I only wish to point out that compared to the situation which would prevail in Cambodia and Laos I find the proposal disadvantageous to South Vietnam, but there is no reason for hatred and enmity among friends and I propose that we forget what has been said.

After making it clear to Saigon that we would proceed with the agreement, we had to convince Hanoi of the same thing without tempting it to exploit the rifts between Saigon and Washington. Just before leaving Saigon I sent a message in the President's name to Colonel Guay in Paris for transmission to Hanoi's representatives. The time selected was 3:00 P.M. Paris time, which was 10:00 P.M. in Saigon, or when I was well on the way back to Washington. Allowing time for transmission, I might with luck reach Washington before Hanoi could respond. The message read in its key passages:

The President of the United States wishes to inform the Prime Minister of the Democratic Republic of Vietnam of the following urgent matters.
The United States has proceeded in good faith to implement the general prin-

ciples and substance discussed with the DRV in Paris. The DRV must certainly have been informed of the strenuous efforts made by Dr. Kissinger and his associates in Laos, Cambodia, Thailand and above all in Saigon.

At the same time the DRV side is aware of the fact that the constant U.S. position has been that it will not impose a unilateral solution on its allies and that it will move ahead only on the basis of consultation. . . .

The President reiterates his firm belief that an agreement is obtainable in the very near future. It is essential that the DRV and US sides mutually explore existing difficulties in the same spirit of good will which has characterized discussions thus far.

To this end the President proposes that special advisor Le Duc Tho and Dr. Kissinger meet again at the earliest opportunity in Paris, to reconcile the remaining issues. Dr. Kissinger will come to Paris on any date set by the DRV. In the present circumstances it is impossible for Dr. Kissinger to go to Hanoi until these additional discussions have been completed.

In order to demonstrate its good faith, the U.S. side will maintain the current restrictions on the bombing until the negotiations are concluded.

The U.S. side must warn that any attempt to exploit the present, temporary difficulties publicly can only lead to prolongation of the negotiations.

It is inevitable that in the war that has lasted so long and has generated such deep passions there should be some temporary obstacles on the way to a final resolution.

The U.S. remains determined to pursue every avenue for peace and urges the leadership of the Democratic Republic of Vietnam to join with it in the same spirit of good will and cooperative effort which has brought the negotiations so close to a solution. If this same attitude is maintained, the current problems will surely be surmounted and there should be an early settlement on the basis of agreements that have already been achieved.

The Journey Home

IT had been a dramatic and exhausting week. We had started on the morning of October 16 with the vision of returning with a peace compatible with our values and an end to our national anguish. We had not achieved it. We had, it is true, made some progress. Hanoi's original draft of October 8, which was in itself such a breakthrough, was greatly improved in the intervening two weeks, and we could take pride in a draft peace treaty exceeding the terms we ourselves had put forward for two years. And though our return journey was clouded by disappointment, it was also marked by determination. Having come this close, both sides had too big an investment in the process to turn back now. In the days following, we would strive to put the pieces back together. We owed it to all the hopes that had been invested in our efforts not to lose heart now.

I have often thought about this stormy period, wondering whether more compassionate treatment of Thieu might have led to a different result. Ideally, perhaps, we should have given him more time to prepare for what was coming. But speed also greatly improved the terms, and, personal respect for him aside, I do not believe that a more deliberate schedule and earlier consultation would have altered his conduct. That was the stuff of tragedy, not a trifling error in human calculation. At that point both sides, on courses they had to take, were doomed to collision. The logic of Thieu's position required a posture of defiant intransigence to prove that Washington and Hanoi could not decide his fate — just as Hanoi's procedure with us, forcing the pace, was partly designed to demonstrate that he was our puppet. Whatever we did, Thieu would have maneuvered to gain time and found a way to confront us, as indeed he had confronted Haig and me on previous visits.

Our disappointment arose from a misapprehension: We failed early enough to grasp that Thieu's real objection was not to the terms but the fact of *any* compromise. Conflict between us and Thieu was built into the termination of the war on any terms less than Hanoi's total surrender. By definition sovereignty cannot be divided. Any outcome that left Thieu in less than total control of his entire territory was therefore for him a setback. He might not be able to change the balance of power on the ground, but this was a far cry from accepting it as a legal obligation. He had gone along with various compromise offers suggesting the contrary, not out of conviction, but as the price for continued American support. We had sustained our backing for Saigon in America by a series of proposals — all of which he had accepted — designed to prove our willingness to walk the extra mile. But the cumulative impact of these proposals — cease-fire in place, new elections, American withdrawal — all amounted to giving Saigon a legal status different from Hanoi's. This is what rankled deeply. And from his point of view Thieu was right. He fought by Vietnamese methods. Tenacity, defiance, and indirection were his weapons. It was not his fault that in 1961 we had launched ourselves on an enterprise by a strategy that our people were to find they could not sustain; in 1963 he had been one of the officers whom we had encouraged to overthrow Ngo Dinh Diem. Probably he had overestimated our subtlety and our power; he had assumed we understood his reservations. We in turn exaggerated his literalness; we had taken for granted that he meant what he told us. By the end of 1972, however, these contradictions were beyond immediate solution. A different procedure might have simply multiplied his possibilities of procrastination. It would not have avoided the impasse. Indeed, it might well have brought it about earlier and made it the more inextricable. Thieu sought total victory; we, an honorable compromise. By October 1972 these two positions could not be reconciled.

On the trip home I knew that there would be strong temptations in Washington to jettison the draft peace treaty and to go for broke after the election. I was determined to preserve the draft against all the passions that would soon descend on us — against the pressure of Hanoi to sign the existing text; against the demand of Saigon to abandon the agreement; and against proclivities in Washington to reverse course, the result of which would be to lose control over events. I had had an inkling of those inclinations in a cable from Haig on October 21 when the first hints of Thieu's later stubbornness appeared. Haig suggested that in case of a blowup we should denounce the National Council of National Reconciliation and Concord as a coalition government and challenge the agreement as an effort by Hanoi to improve its security while giving nothing but fuzzy reassurances. I considered this course inconceivable. We had been offering less favorable terms for years. Nixon had approved a worse draft on October 12. Hanoi had just accepted our language on all major sections. On October 22 I replied that we should not "poormouth an agreement that we will not be able to improve significantly and which we should use instead as a tremendous success." I sent another sharp cable to Haig on October 23:

As for your characterization of the content of the agreement I would like to recall your view that it was a good agreement when we concluded it. It has since been greatly improved with respect to Cambodia, Laos, the International Conference, American prisoners, South Vietnamese prisoners and the replacement provision. As for asking Thieu to give up sovereignty over his territory just what has a cease-fire always added up to? We proposed this way back in October 1970 and again in January 1972 and May 1972. What else were these plans going to lead to except precisely the situation we now have? . . .

Many wars have been lost by untoward timidity. But enormous tragedies have also been produced by the inability of military people to recognize when the time for a settlement had arrived.

In my view that time had come. I cabled Washington from the plane that if Hanoi went public I should give a press conference, acknowledge the agreement, indicate that it represented major progress, but insist that some details remained to be worked out free of any artificial deadline. I would put Hanoi on notice that the basic agreement was not being dropped, but that some changes were necessary; I would put Saigon on notice that we would give it more time and seek some changes, but that the basic structure was not subject to modification.

This strategy, which the President accepted, was to propel me after my arrival home into my first appearance at a televised press conference: the dramatic event summed up in the phrase, "peace is at hand."

XXXIII

"Peace Is at Hand"

Hanoi Goes Public

I T was uncanny returning to Washington from Saigon on October 23.
My colleagues and I were obsessed with the detail of the stalled draft
peace treaty; it was the last thing Nixon wanted to hear about. He
was in the final throes of his reelection campaign, the last campaign of a
compulsive twenty-five-year career. His ambition was to win with the
largest majority in American history. He thought this certain so long as
nothing unprovided for was allowed to happen in the last two months of
the campaign. Therefore, he wanted no fresh electoral issue out of Vietnam. He wanted that problem to go away for two weeks so that he could
deal with it right after the election. His instructions to me were to try to
keep things quiet. This, I was certain, neither our enemies nor allies in
Vietnam would allow.

Electoral considerations aside, Nixon was of course eager to end the
war in Vietnam. But with his eye for essentials he understood that a
preelection peace, if Thieu rebelled, might seem opportunistic and turn
sour. The hawks would then lose heart in upholding the settlement, and
the doves would have a pretext for not supporting it. The trouble was
that while Nixon's analysis was correct, it was Hanoi — not we or
Thieu — that controlled the timing of a confrontation.

I did my best, if with increasingly frayed nerves. By October 23 my
colleagues and I had been in motion for over two weeks — Paris,
Washington, Paris again, Saigon, Phnom Penh, and back to Washington, rarely getting more than four hours of sleep and riding an emotional
roller coaster from hope to frustration, from elation to despair. Nor
could we let up now. The danger was that the draft agreement, so
laboriously put together, could be wrecked by the two monomaniacal
Vietnamese parties; the United States could be pulled off course by
electoral obsession and party passion in Washington. We could not
know how long Moscow and Peking would stay quiet if we returned to
the treadmill of an inconclusive war in which their ally was being
bombed and blockaded after having accepted the terms we ourselves had
put forward.

I sought to hold things together. I had told Hanoi on October 23 that I was returning to Washington but stood ready to meet Le Duc Tho to complete the negotiations. On October 24 I urged Bunker in Saigon to stay in close touch with Thieu and Foreign Minister Lam. He should leave no doubt that we intended to push to a conclusion. We could tolerate a certain amount of "domestic posturing" by Thieu, but he had to remember that his basic support was our confidence in him: ". . . No matter what the concessions he gets in what is now essentially a very workable formula [they] will in no way be a substitute for the ultimate collapse of American support. . . ." The same day, Moscow sent a somewhat plaintive note suggesting that if I went to Hanoi we would still be able to "complete the whole matter." That was clearly impossible while Saigon was in its present frame of mind; but at least it indicated that the North Vietnamese continued eager to proceed. I told Dobrynin that we were prepared to complete the agreement, an offer that would stand even after the election. I also briefed China's Huang Hua in New York, reminding him of the final negotiation of the Shanghai Communiqué during the night session in Hangchow. Chou had permitted us to reopen the communiqué then and thereby guaranteed its widespread acceptance in the United States. If China used its influence with Hanoi to resume negotiations with the same wisdom, the result would be satisfactory. On October 25 Peking weighed in with a message — obviously drafted before it could have received Huang Hua's report of my conversation — urging us to seize this "extremely opportune time to end the Vietnam war." The Chinese explicitly blamed Saigon for the difficulties, affirmed their confidence in our good faith — an extraordinary gesture — but asked rhetorically: ". . . how can the world be forbidden to have its doubts?"

Meanwhile, Hanoi had rejected my message of October 23, accusing us of being not "really serious." It added ominously:

> If the U.S. side continues to use one pretext after another to prolong the negotiations, delay the signing of the agreement, the war in Vietnam will certainly continue, and the U.S. side must bear full responsibility for all the consequences brought about by the United States.
>
> If the U.S. side is really serious and has good will, it must strictly carry out its commitments regarding the agreement and the time schedule agreed upon by the two parties. This statement of the DRVN side is a very serious one. The U.S. side should pay full attention to the views of the DRVN side expounded in this message.

Though firm, the message fell short of the fire-breathing arrogance of previous communications from Hanoi. It stayed well clear of threatening to abrogate the agreement. Hanoi had requested a reply during the day of October 24 Hanoi time — impossible, since by the time we received their message it was already October 25 in North Vietnam. We nevertheless returned an immediate and very calm reply on October 25. The constant repetition of unfounded charges, we said, could only make things worse. We proposed another meeting during the week of October 30; I would attend "with instructions to bring about a final settlement." As soon as agreement was reached, even without Saigon, we would stop the bombing of North Vietnam:

The course adopted during the private meetings in October represents settled U.S. policy. The U.S. is determined to end the war in the nearest future, and it will work with the greatest energy to remove the obstacles that have arisen in any event before the end of November.

A copy of the note was sent to the Chinese via courier the same day. I kept Dobrynin informed. In any case, our message affected no decisions in Hanoi. For during the night of October 25, before the message could have reached there, Hanoi went public.

I was awakened around 5:30 A.M. on Thursday, October 26, to learn that Radio Hanoi had been broadcasting its version of events for hours, first in Vietnamese, then in French, finally in English. Radio Hanoi revealed the negotiating record of the preceding month: On October 8 in a secret meeting, North Vietnam had taken "a new, extremely important initiative" by offering a new draft peace agreement. The broadcast accurately summarized the key points of the draft agreement. "The DRV side proposed that the Democratic Republic of Vietnam and the United States sign this agreement by mid-October 1972" — acknowledging that Hanoi, not we, had pushed for signing before our election. It quoted me as admitting that the new proposal "was indeed an important and very fundamental document." It described the US messages of October 20 and October 22 in which the President had called the text of the agreement "complete," and expressed satisfaction with Hanoi's concessions. It next recited the "shedyule" and the continual slippage to which Hanoi had agreed at American behest. But the United States had failed, on various "pretexts," to keep the schedule. Therefore Hanoi "strongly denounces the Nixon Administration's lack of good will and seriousness," and demanded that the agreement be signed by October 31. It ended with a rather defensive exhortation to its "fighters throughout the country" to persevere in the face of "all hardships and sacrifices."

As it was, Hanoi barely beat the *New York Times* to the story. That same morning, October 26, the paper had cease-fire stories from three places — Paris, Saigon, and Washington — and a five-column headline: "U.S. Is Said to Agree with Hanoi on Framework of a Cease-fire; Expects Saigon to Accept Soon." The most blatant leak came from Paris, where Flora Lewis had picked up from "a high-ranking French

source'' that Le Duc Tho and I had reached ''a wide measure of understanding on a cease-fire and a subsequent political settlement.'' (These
French sources almost certainly had been informed by the North Vietnamese, as de Borchgrave had foreshadowed.) Stories had been leaking
out of Saigon for a week as Thieu denounced Hanoi's proposals as unacceptable. He declared in a speech on October 24 that ''a cease-fire
may come in the near future,'' though this sentence was buried in a long
string of pointed denunciations of any plan that did not include North
Vietnamese withdrawal from South Vietnam or did include a three-sided
coalition government. From Washington, Max Frankel had a story citing ''American officials'' as believing there would be a cease-fire ''in
the next few weeks, perhaps even before election day, Nov. 7, barring a
supreme act of folly in Saigon or Hanoi.'' I had lunched with Frankel
on October 25, giving him only this general picture without going into
details, to reassure Hanoi and keep the pressure on Saigon.

My press conference of October 26 came to be denounced as a Nixon
electoral ploy to raise hopes for peace during the last stages of the
Presidential campaign. The impossible ''shedyule'' that triggered the
whole affair was Hanoi's, not ours. As late as mid-September I could see
no way to conclude the negotiations rapidly. It was Hanoi's October 8
proposal in Paris, abandoning its demand for a coalition government,
that had unlocked the negotiations. It was Hanoi that had insisted on a
signing by October 31 as a condition for a settlement; I had gone along
with it in order to exploit Hanoi's eagerness. Now it was Hanoi, not the
United States, that announced the peace agreement. Nixon at this point
clearly would have preferred keeping the agreement secret until *after* the
election and before undertaking the final round of negotiations. Only
when accused by Hanoi, two weeks before a Presidential election, of
having reneged on a peace settlement did the Administration respond.

Once Hanoi had gone public we had no choice except to state our
case. The purpose of my press conference was to rescue from Vietnamese hatreds a fragile agreement that would end a decade of agony.
Nixon and I agreed that I had to reply to Radio Hanoi's broadcast. I had
two objectives. One was to reassure Hanoi that we would stand by the
basic agreement, while leaving open the possibility of raising Saigon's
suggested changes. The second was to convey to Saigon that we were
determined to proceed on our course. This was not easy without causing
the South Vietnamese to appear as the sole obstacle to peace, thus
triggering renewed assaults by our critics that would disintegrate the political structure of an ally. Nixon and I did not discuss the domestic political implications. Nixon's one instruction in this respect asked me to
stress that the terms we had already agreed with Hanoi were better than
what McGovern was willing to settle for (which of course was true). In
any event, the opportunity to make this point never arose.

So it happened that I appeared for the first time on national television at the very end of Nixon's first term. Until December 1971, except for the announcement of my second China trip, all my press briefings had been on a background basis, which meant that I was identified as either a White House or Administration spokesman, but never by name. After the *Washington Post* had broken the background rules during the India-Pakistan crisis, most of my press conferences were on the record. The White House public relations people, however, were convinced that my accent might disturb Middle America; they therefore permitted pictures but no sound at my on-the-record press conferences. On October 26 they finally took a chance on my pronunciation.

Since my return from Saigon I had, in fact, feared that Hanoi would go public once it was clear that the October 31 signing as agreed in the "shedyule" would not be kept. Therefore I was prepared. My staff had suggested answers to the most likely press questions, with a compilation of the many times I had forewarned Le Duc Tho that Saigon had to be consulted, and also with a summary of intelligence reports of Communist designs to grab the maximum amount of land just before the cease-fire. I went over this material with Nixon in advance of my press conference. I would reaffirm the basic agreement; insist on some changes within its framework; assure Hanoi of our goodwill and warn it against pressure; defend Saigon's right to ask for changes and caution it against fundamental revision; and commit us to a rapid conclusion of the agreement. I did not go over my precise language, which was extemporaneous, but we discussed my general themes. With his one extra request to get in a dig at McGovern (which I in fact avoided), Nixon approved the approach.

And this is the line I followed. In my opening remarks I uttered the phrase ("peace is at hand") that was to haunt me from then on:

We have now heard from both Vietnams and it is obvious that a war that has been raging for ten years is drawing to a conclusion, and that this is a traumatic experience for all of the participants. . . .

We believe that peace is at hand. We believe that an agreement is within sight, based on the May 8th proposal of the President and some adaptation of our January 25th proposal which is just to all parties. It is inevitable that in a war of such complexity . . . there should be occasional difficulties in reaching a final solution, but we believe that by far the longest part of the road has been traversed and what stands in the way of an agreement now are issues that are relatively less important than those that have already been settled.

I defended the right of the people of South Vietnam, "who have suffered so much, . . . who will be remaining in that country after we have departed," to participate in the making of their peace. The concerns of their government deserved great respect. We would insist on changes, but they were soluble in a brief period of time. As for the American people, we were conscious of the anguish the war had caused:

We have been very conscious of the division and the anguish that the war has caused in this country. One reason why the President has been so concerned with ending the war by negotiation, and ending it in a manner that is consistent with our principles, is because of the hope that the act of making peace could restore the unity that had sometimes been lost at certain periods during the war, and so that the agreement could be an act of healing rather than a source of new division. This remains our policy.

And I ended with a warning to both Hanoi and Saigon:

We will not be stampeded into an agreement until its provisions are right. We will not be deflected from an agreement when its provisions are right. And with this attitude, and with some cooperation from the other side, we believe that we can restore both peace and unity to America very soon.

October 26 was a day of high emotion and complicated maneuver. My overwhelming anxiety was to hold the agreement together. If the war went on, the divisions in our country would deepen for no fundamental purpose. But we were not sure that either Vietnamese party would return to the conference table. There is no doubt that in this press briefing I gave hostages to fortune. The drama of the phrase "peace is at hand" would provide a handy symbol of governmental duplicity in the continued bitter atmosphere of the Vietnam debate, as would my repeating publicly what I had already told the parties privately, that I would seek to conclude the agreement in one more session. In fairness to Nixon, he was not aware that I would use the words "peace is at hand." It was a pithy message — too optimistic, as it turned out — to the parties of our determination to persevere; a signal to Hanoi that we were not reneging and to Saigon that we would not be derailed.

And despite all the opprobrium heaped on it later, the statement was essentially true — though clearly if I had to do it over I would choose a less dramatic phrase. Negotiations resumed on November 20 (Hanoi delayed nearly four weeks before allowing resumption). The breakthrough that settled all issues of principle occurred on January 9, 1973; the agreement was initialed on January 23. Semanticists may argue whether a six-week negotiation stretches the meaning of "at hand." The fact is that a bitter war that had lasted ten years and cost untold lives was settled within weeks of that statement.

The major problem was to get Hanoi back to the negotiating table. Just before my press conference I had cabled Bunker to make sure Thieu would not blast the entire agreement; Thieu had to keep his comments compatible with mine. I informed Dobrynin of my intentions. He seemed to think — without instructions — that after a cooling-off period negotiations might resume. We now launched into several days of frantic exchanges, complicated by Nixon's frequent absence on campaign trips. I solved this by sending some messages on my own and checking the broad content of letters in his name by telephone. We could then proceed, and he would sign the text on his return after it had already been communicated electronically.

A rather mystifying note later on October 26 from the North Vietnamese sought to explain why they had gone public. It seemed to refuse another meeting with me, though without the usual combative rhetoric. It proposed that the "best" (but not, note, the "only") procedure was to sign the text of the agreement as it stood. But it concluded with two paragraphs that strongly suggested that Hanoi might after all be prepared to continued negotiations:

> While giving information about the private meetings between the Democratic Republic of Vietnam and the United States, the government of the Democratic Republic of Vietnam still affirms that the best way to rapidly end the war, restore peace in Vietnam is to negotiate seriously. . . .

> The DRVN side will continue the negotiations with its consistent good will and serious attitude, with a view to bringing an early end to the war, restoring peace in Vietnam, in accordance with the aspirations of the Vietnamese people, the American people and the world people. This will create favourable conditions for establishing a new relationship based on equality and mutual interest between the Democratic Republic of Vietnam and the United States.

But the next day, October 27, the North Vietnamese spokesman in Paris, Nguyen Thanh Le, seemed to pull back. He told newsmen that Le Duc Tho and Xuan Thuy would receive me again only if the United States was prepared to sign the October agreement: "If the date of signature is the 31st, then if on the 30th Kissinger wants to meet Le Duc Tho or Xuan Thuy to drink champagne while awaiting the signature, I think the response would be positive." Instead of "peace is at hand," Le offered "peace is at the end of a pen." We responded instead to Hanoi's note of the previous day, reiterating our proposal for a final negotiation and promising a full bombing halt forty-eight hours after a settlement. I sent a copy to the Chinese.

Next, a Soviet note arrived, mildly accusing the United States of deviating from the agreed schedule and implying that the differences with Thieu might be manufactured (Moscow, of course, had no experience of serious disagreements with governments where the Red Army was stationed). We drafted a reply in Nixon's name (he was campaigning in Kentucky) reiterating our basic proposal and asking Moscow's help in resuming negotiations. My staff and I demonstrated that we had learned more felicitous phrasing in the twenty-four hours since my press conference: Nixon's letter told Brezhnev that the goal of peace was certainly "within reach."

Now Thieu was heard from. On October 28 a lengthy and querulous memorandum by Nha pointed out alleged discrepancies between Hanoi's broadcast and my press conference on the one hand, and on the other, what Saigon had been told. The memorandum claimed "surprise" at the various schedules disclosed by Hanoi. (In fact, Thieu knew very well of my intention to fly from Saigon to Hanoi, a plan canceled when he rejected the agreement.) While Nha was at it, he repeated Saigon's objections to the phrase "administrative structure," which he claimed proved that the National Council of National Reconciliation and Concord was a "disguised coalition government." We learned that Thieu had sent emissaries to our other Asian allies to set out his objections to the agreement. This produced another Nixon letter to Thieu, in the drafting of which the President took a personal hand. Nixon gallantly pointed out that my press conference of October 26 reflected his own views. He emphasized that he would not change course after the election:

Just as our unity has been the essential aspect of the success we have enjoyed thus far in the conduct of hostilities, it will also be the best guarantee of future success in a situation where the struggle continues within a more political framework. If the evident drift towards disagreement between the two of us continues, however, the essential base for U.S. support for you and your Government will be destroyed. In this respect the comments of your Foreign Minister that the U.S. is negotiating a surrender are as damaging as they are unfair and improper.

You can be assured that my decisions as to the final character of a peace settlement are in no way influenced by the election in the United States, and you should harbor no illusions that my policy with respect to the desirability of achieving an early peace will change after the election.

That same day I made sure that Bill Sullivan at State would continue to work on the preparation of the technical protocols to implement the basic agreements. I also had Haig send a directive to the Pentagon to prepare shipment of crucial military items if Operation Enhance Plus (the building up of Saigon's inventories) were resumed. (I had slowed down these shipments to Saigon after Thieu rejected the agreement.)

On October 30 it was Hanoi's turn again: Our proposal was being studied very carefully and would receive a reply later, we were told. I considered this on the whole a hopeful sign: Hanoi clearly did not want to agree to a new negotiation before its own publicly proposed deadline of October 31 had passed. It would lose face if it did; it would probably devote October 31 to a big propaganda attack on us. I told Haldeman, who was traveling with the President, that there were three possibilities: Hanoi would cancel the agreement and break off all talks; it would stand on the agreement but refuse any renegotiation; or it would resume talks. I considered the last most likely, given a suitable interval after the proposed signing date.

Next day — October 31 — Peking weighed in again, though with the usual nuance of difference from its North Vietnamese allies. Whereas Hanoi had put the blame squarely on the United States, the Chinese again reserved their angriest rhetoric for Saigon, demanding that we "put a firm stop" to Saigon's behavior. More challenging was a reference apparently linking our Vietnam conduct and our relations with China. If we prolonged the war and protracted the negotiations, the note read, "then how are people to view the U.S. statements about its preparedness to make efforts for the relaxation of tension in the Far East?"

When one is committed, a demonstration of implacability is the only safe course. Hesitation simply invites further pressure. There was no policy — beyond peace in Vietnam — to which I was more committed than better relations with Peking. But we could not permit this to be used against us. We therefore sent a firm note (as always with the Chinese, on unsigned paper with no letterhead or watermark):

The Chinese side, considering all the conversations it has had with the U.S. side about respecting basic principles, must surely understand that the U.S. cannot treat an ally as a puppet. This would accord neither with reality nor principle. The constant assumption and public reiteration by the DRV that the U.S. has complete mastery over its friends has been one of the root causes of present difficulties. The U.S. side would like to remind the Chinese side of the many conversations between Dr. Kissinger and the Prime Minister in which Dr. Kissinger expressed understanding and respect for the Chinese meticulous treatment of Prince Sihanouk, a friendly leader who was a guest on Chinese soil. The U.S. side points out that its problems with its friends are no easier and its principles no different.

While we struggled to hold the agreement together, our public debate on Vietnam heated up once again. We seemed fated to end the war as divisively as it had been conducted. The disclosures of October 26, after a moment of stunned surprise, produced jubilation nationally; the vast majority of our public felt enormous relief. At the same time the bitterness of a decade was not to be stilled even by the end of hostilities. To claim peace with honor seemed an insult to many of our critics. Two main lines of attack developed: that the whole thing was a fraud to help Nixon win the election, which all polls showed was nonsense; that the same terms had been attainable four years earlier, which was totally untrue. Some antiwar critics with breathtaking hypocrisy parroted Thieu's criticism of the inadequacy of the accords, especially regarding the disposition of North Vietnamese troops. They had pressed us for a unilateral deadline for total withdrawal. They had long since given up on cease-fire; on North Vietnamese withdrawal from Laos and Cambodia; on a ban on infiltration into South Vietnam; on continued aid to Saigon. They had castigated these terms as examples of bellicosity and worse. Now that much more had been achieved they could not bring themselves to admit that possibly their government had not been so immoral and stupid as their folklore had it; perhaps it had had a rational strategy after all.

George McGovern took the first line. On October 29 he alleged on "Meet the Press" that he was "puzzled as to why the settlement comes in the closing hours of this campaign. . . . It is really not clear to me what fundamental change has taken place in the last few days which enables Mr. Nixon to announce, now, that we have a settlement just before we go to the polls." McGovern ignored that Hanoi had made the announcement. He was sterner with Thieu than he was with Hanoi; he would reserve the right to renegotiate any agreement that committed the United States to aid Thieu after the war ended.* By November 5 McGovern's suspicion had hardened in his mind into certainty. He told an airport crowd in Moline, Illinois:

> When Dr. Kissinger came out and said that peace was "at hand," he was misleading the people of this country. He knew what he said was false. He and Mr. Nixon know that it was a deliberate deception designed to fool the American people for the sake of Republican votes.
>
> Peace is not at hand, it is not even in sight. . . .[2]

The *Washington Post* in its first reaction on October 27 implied that similar terms might have been available in 1969 in the light of Hanoi's "post-Tet military prostration." A week later, on November 3, the *Post* argued that in any case the terms of the agreement did not justify four years of war after 1969. Clearly, the editorialist did not intend to draw the conclusion that we should fight on for better terms; nor did he mention that the terms were substantially what we had put forward for two years — to the editorialist's displeasure because we were asking for too much. Other papers, such as the *St. Louis Post-Dispatch* on October 27, combined the theme that the same terms were available earlier — for which there was not the slightest evidence — with the argument that whatever credit there was should go to McGovern for having kept the peace issue alive.

---

* The draft agreement indeed, as Nixon argued, included terms in many respects far better for the United States than McGovern's stated position: McGovern insisted on a unilateral end of US military action; the agreement included a mutual cease-fire for all sides. McGovern insisted on US withdrawal from Thailand and offshore; the agreement included no such limits on US forces outside of Indochina. McGovern expressed only the "expectation" of a release of POWs and accounting for the missing in action if we withdrew; the agreement required both within sixty days. McGovern insisted on the disavowal of Thieu; the agreement left the South Vietnamese government intact. McGovern insisted on an end of US military and economic aid to the South Vietnamese; the agreement allowed it to continue. McGovern would not insist on Hanoi's withdrawal from Laos and Cambodia; the agreement pledged it. McGovern did not mention international supervision of a cease-fire; the agreement included it.[1]

By the first week of November the phrase "peace is at hand" was being used to ask why it should take so long to arrange a cease-fire; the fact that Hanoi was refusing to talk was not known, but should have been apparent from Hanoi's public statements. On November 6 the *New York Times* gave editorial expression to its impatience and implied that the promised peace might be a cover for new escalation. By November 9 Murrey Marder in the *Washington Post* had discovered unnamed Administration officials willing to pretend to supposed knowledge that Nixon had never intended to consummate the agreement before the election; it would have been too "messy"; Nixon had therefore decided to risk Hanoi's rebuke despite firm promises and had refused to sign on October 31. On November 10 the *Post* wrote an editorial castigating the Nixon Administration for misleading the American people.

The national mood was far less cynical; there was no widespread hope that the war would soon end. My own attitude was one of determination to overcome the remaining obstacles; Nixon was seized by the unease that always beset him in the last stages of any effort, especially of electoral campaigns, as if it were the premonition of some unspecifiable disaster. One could see the beginnings of the withdrawal that marked his reaction to his overwhelming electoral victory. On November 4, three days before the voting, I accompanied him to San Clemente, stopping off in Albuquerque for the last stage of his campaign. That day we at last received Hanoi's acceptance of our offer to resume negotiations — on November 14 or "another date which may be proposed by the U.S. side." Hanoi gratuitously reaffirmed that it would abide by the text of the agreement — in other words, that it would seek no changes of its own. No North Vietnamese message could be complete without a reference to its legendary "consistent good will and seriousness," to the export of which the peoples of Indochina had been unremittingly exposed for over a decade and would be again in subsequent years.

Because we had been kept waiting for over a week, and to avoid further exchanges before the election, we replied on November 7 proposing November 15. We wanted to give ourselves a slight cushion to enable Haig to go to Saigon to concert our approach with Thieu's. We also warned Hanoi that we expected it to desist from "tendentious public comment or selective releases from earlier documents of the negotiations which can only complicate the task of arriving at a final agreement." On November 8, Hanoi replied, suggesting a postponement to November 20 because Le Duc Tho was "ill." (There can be little doubt that it must have been a rough time for him. All the Communist forces that had geared up for land-grabbing operations in the pre–cease-fire period were now being decimated.) Because it would take Le Duc Tho a week to reach Paris, Hanoi asked for a reply "as quickly as possible."

We accepted the proposed date on November 9. Negotiations were once again in train.

Election Interlude

THE strangest period in Nixon's Presidency followed his overwhelming victory on November 7, 1972. He had achieved a series of spectacular successes in 1971 and 1972: the Berlin agreement, the Peking summit, the Moscow summit and the SALT agreement, the imminent end of the war in Vietnam. The outcome of the election promised to be the biggest landside in our history. And yet as his hour of triumph approached, Nixon withdrew ever more, even from some of his close advisers. His resentments, usually so well controlled, came increasingly to the surface. It was as if victory was not an occasion for reconciliation but an opportunity to settle the scores of a lifetime.

Nixon's mood came to expression the morning after the election, on November 8. The White House staff had been awake much of the previous night celebrating his victory, though even then the festivities I attended seemed to me to lack the boisterous spontaneity that usually marked such events. The President was too withdrawn and shadowy a figure for most of his followers; few of the celebrants had actually met him. His achievements were associated more with solitary discipline and remote courage than with personal inspiration; they followed him more out of admiration for stern competence than personal affection. And yet there was great pride in an Administration that had steered the country through crisis into a period of hopeful tranquillity, perhaps even of national unity.

The good feeling was shattered within twelve hours. The White House staff had been asked to assemble at 11:00 A.M. in the Roosevelt Room. At the dot Nixon strode in through the door closest to the Oval Office. He seemed not at all elated. Rather, he was grim and remote as if the more fateful period of his life still lay ahead. Nothing in his demeanor betrayed that he was meeting associates from perilous and trying times; he acted as if they were from a past now irrevocably finished. Without sitting down, he thankèd the assembled group in a perfunctory manner. After about five minutes he turned the meeting over to Haldeman and left.

Haldeman wasted no time getting to the point. Every member of the White House staff was to submit his resignation immediately; we were to fill out a form listing the documents in our possession. The President would announce his personnel decisions for the new term within a month. The audience was stunned. It was the morning after a triumph and they were being, in effect, fired. Victory seemed to have released a pent-up hostility so overwhelming that it would not wait even a week to surface; it engulfed colleagues and associates as well as opponents. As we left the meeting, Bill Safire, who had been planning to leave at this time anyway, said to me: "You know, if McGovern had won they could have stayed another two months; they would not have been fired until January 20." The same appalling performance was repeated with the Cabinet an hour later.

What propelled Nixon into a course so degrading to his closest associates has never been satisfactorily explained. I had known, of course, that he had always felt cheated because the narrowness of his 1968 victory and the pressures of Vietnam had prevented him from accomplishing a thorough housecleaning of the bureaucracy, which he had attacked and mistrusted as packed with holdover Democrats. He certainly did not receive the wholehearted support extended by the permanent civil service to more charismatic leaders. Still, it does not explain the frenzied, almost maniacal sense of urgency about this political butchery. Had Nixon waited a few weeks it is certain that all Assistants and Cabinet members would of their own accord have followed custom and submitted their resignations. Nixon could then have proceeded at his leisure, retaining or removing as suited his plans. But to ask for resignations en masse within hours of being elected, to distribute forms obviously mimeographed during a campaign in which many of the victims had been working themselves to a frazzle, was wounding and humiliating. It made removal from office appear to be not the result of Presidential reflection about the future but a grudge from the past. Nixon's later troubles had other immediate causes, of course; yet he surely deprived himself of much sympathy then by conveying in his hour of triumph an impression of such total vindictiveness and insensitivity to those who were basically well-disposed to him. (I was not directly affected, having been told by Haldeman right after the Roosevelt Room meeting that my letter of resignation would be a mere formality.)

Whether wiser counsel could have kept Nixon from this course, or whether he was adamantly determined to consummate at last the vendettas of a lifetime must await the memoirs of those who were consulted at the time. They must also explain why Nixon began the housecleaning not with his old adversaries — the regular bureaucracy — but with his own associates and staff.

The afternoon of November 8 I flew with Nixon, Haldeman, and Ehrlichman to Key Biscayne. Again, I was struck that triumph seemed to bring no surcease to this tortured man. He fretted that his popular margin had been a shade less than Johnson's over Goldwater. Above all, he occupied himself with planning the removal or reshuffling of most of his Cabinet, with the exception of George Shultz, who had recently replaced Connally at the Treasury. Rogers was slated to go in the summer, tentatively to be replaced by Kenneth Rush. I was struck by how restless Nixon was, now that he had achieved the overwhelming electoral approval which had been the ambition of a lifetime. It was almost as if it had been sought for its own sake; as if, standing on the pinnacle, Nixon no longer had any purpose left to his life.

As soon as we arrived in Key Biscayne, Nixon withdrew into his compound. From there he went to Camp David with Haldeman and Ehrlichman to plan his new Administration. I saw him only twice in the next nine days, including a session on November 17, when I met with him briefly at Camp David before leaving for Paris. He was difficult to reach. We spoke occasionally on the telephone. To others he was totally inaccessible. The leader who had just won 61 percent of the popular vote cut himself off from his own people. At a moment when, by reaching out, he might have engraved himself in America's heart, as he already had left his mark on its mind, he withdrew into a seclusion even deeper and more impenetrable than in his years of struggle. Isolation had become almost a spiritual necessity to this withdrawn, lonely, and tormented man who insisted so on his loneliness and created so much of his own torment. It was hard to avoid the impression that Nixon, who thrived on crisis, also craved disasters.

Ever since the secret trip to China, my own relationship with him had grown complicated. Until then I had been an essentially anonymous White House Assistant. There was some resentment of the independence of my staff, some suspicion that the principal criterion of their selection had not been rigid conformity. But this was counterbalanced by realization that their skills enabled foreign policy to be conducted from the White House. The interdepartmental machinery gave Nixon control of decision-making while shielding him from the need to issue direct orders. And my backgrounders had conveyed the picture of a President in charge of events that flattered Nixon's conception of himself and corresponded essentially to reality. He might be restless over my friendship with what he called the Georgetown crowd; his associates were unhappy, and not without reason, that some journalists were giving me perhaps excessive credit for the more appealing aspects of our foreign policy while blaming Nixon for the unpopular moves. But this was treated as the necessary price for indispensable services.

After the secret trip to China I became much more visible, and this hit the White House on its rawest nerve: public relations. Of course, every President carefully nurtures his own image; the obsessive pursuit of it, after all, brought him to where he is. No Chief Executive would take kindly to an appointee who is cast by the media as the source of all constructive actions. In Nixon's case this was compounded by his conviction that he faced a lifelong conspiracy of the old Establishment determined to destroy him and that all media attention was ultimately due to public relations, in which, inexplicably, his staff was sadly deficient.

Hence, he grew increasingly convinced that I was needlessly trafficking with his enemies in the "Georgetown set" and at the same time was using my public relations skills to furbish my image and not his. He had a point, though matters were much less in my control than he believed. In any event, the problem was insoluble for the moment. Since Nixon did not have confidence in the State Department as an institution, he felt compelled to entrust the conduct of negotiations to me. But starting with the India-Pakistan crisis in 1971, the White House public relations machinery avoided few opportunities to cut me down to size. And Nixon himself grew testy. His cables to me sometimes seemed written more for a record of dissociation than for conveying instructions, even while (or perhaps because) he was giving me ever-growing authority.

During the last phase of the Vietnam negotiations, Nixon and I never differed on the substance of our negotiating position. Stories leaked by the public relations side of the White House that Nixon's legal training had enabled him to spot flaws in the drafting are supported by no documents or other evidence. (Nixon may or may not have known of individual leaks; but the stories would never have surfaced without confidence that they would receive Presidential favor.) Our only difference, if any, was his desire to avoid a showdown before election day and my conviction that, however desirable, Hanoi would not permit us to avoid it. Privately, his views about the South Vietnamese President were no more charitable than mine; he was determined to prevail but not until after election day. The publicity I received caused him to look for ways of showing that he was in charge, even while usually endorsing the strategy I devised. One had to deduce these latent tensions from vague clues; they were never made explicit in our personal contacts, which were unfailingly courteous and in which no disagreement surfaced. (Of course, I had seen enough of Nixon with others to realize that this was no proof of Presidential favor.) But I was beginning to sense an emerging competitiveness that was certain sooner or later to destroy my effectiveness as a Presidential Assistant and that was accelerated by the emotions of the concluding phase of the Vietnam war.

These tendencies were given impetus by an interview I granted to the Italian journalist Oriana Fallaci, which was without doubt the single most disastrous conversation I ever had with any member of the press. I saw her briefly on November 2 and 4 in my office, constantly interrupted by the frenzies of stitching the negotiations together again. I did so largely out of vanity. She had interviewed leading personalities all over the world. Fame was sufficiently novel for me to be flattered by the company I would be keeping in her journalistic pantheon. I had not bothered to read her writings; her evisceration of other victims was thus unknown to me. Her article appeared in an Italian magazine later in November.

I paid the price for my naiveté. Without doubt the quotes ascribed to me, statements of marginal taste gathered together in what she presented as a conversation, were the most self-serving utterances of my entire public career. It should be noted that I said some very complimentary things about Nixon. According to the published text I praised him for his courage in selecting a chief adviser whom he did not know and in sending him to Peking; I lauded Nixon's expertise in foreign affairs, and his strength: "What I've done has been possible because he made it possible for me." But even that was rather too much for Nixon, and what drove him up the wall was a quotation Fallaci put in my mouth: "Americans like the cowboy . . . who rides all alone into the town, the village, with his horse and nothing else. . . . This amazing, romantic character suits me precisely because to be alone has always been part of my style or, if you like, my technique." I do not believe that I said this in that context or that it was about myself. I am convinced that I may have been the subject of some skillful editing; and Ms. Fallaci has consistently refused to make the tapes available to other journalists. And yet she was on to something. While Nixon was concerned by the rumblings of the right and his congenital premonitions of disaster, I was carried away by the relief and joy that spread across the country among the vast majority eager to believe that an early and honorable end of the war was indeed imminent. Whatever the niggling in the editorial pages, the "peace is at hand" press conference had had an electric effect. Coming on top of a year of successful negotiations on a wide array of subjects with different countries, it was for me a moment of unusual pride not leavened by humility. Fallaci caught that mood even if she took liberties with my pronouncements (which I cannot prove). She wrote history in the Roman style; she sought psychological, not factual, truth.[3]

The implied claim that mine was the central role was bound to be an affront to any President. It was especially hurtful to Nixon, who was convinced, and not without reason, that his opponents gave me a disproportionate amount of credit in order to diminish him. There were no immediate consequences. The interview appeared in America just as I was leaving for my November 20 meeting with Le Duc Tho; thus Nixon could give me no direct sign of his displeasure. He would not see me on November 18, the day before I took off, even though he was in the White House; we only spoke briefly on the telephone. The astute political commentator of the *New Republic,* John Osborne, picked up the warning signals, however, from his acute textual exegesis.[4] And as Nixon and I headed into the turbulent waters of a new negotiation, a steady course was not aided by the latent disaffection between the helmsman and his principal navigator.

Haig Visits Saigon Again

WITH negotiations about to resume, our overriding problem was in Saigon. We had committed ourselves to Hanoi, Moscow, and Peking, as well as to the American public, to settle the agreement in one more session. Of course, Thieu felt no such compulsion. The longer he could keep our forces in the war, the further he put off the nightmare of being left alone. Moreover, as noted, the collapse of the "shedyule" had led the Communists to expose their cadres prematurely in land-grabbing operations before October 31; their forces were being cut down and Thieu wanted the process to continue. The insolence of his pronouncements was unabated. Despite Nixon's letters, in a public speech on November 1 he called the draft agreement a "surrender" document. And yet our information was that he was preparing for a cease-fire and privately speaking about the agreement to his associates in much more generous terms.

On November 10 Xuan Thuy gave an interview that for a change was helpful: He confirmed that the National Council of National Reconciliation and Concord was not a coalition government in disguise. The National Council "will not yet be a government," he told Agence France Presse; the two existing governments would continue to exist until new elections. Thieu was not visibly appeased. In an effort to enlist his support, we sent Haig to Saigon carrying a letter from Nixon, dated November 8, that committed us to continue on our course. The letter expressed disappointment with Thieu's public statements; it affirmed that we considered the draft agreement sound. We promised to improve on some provisions. For example, we would ensure that the Vietnamese translation of the phrase "administrative structure" was changed to remove any implication that the National Council was a governmental body. We would also make explicit what was now implied, that equal numbers of the Council would be appointed from each side. We would attempt to strengthen the provisions to respect the Demilitarized Zone in order to emphasize the distinctive character of South Vietnam. There was a provision that Vietnamese forces would be demobilized; we would seek to turn this into a formula for withdrawal of at least some North Vietnamese troops. "We will use our maximum efforts," wrote Nixon, "to effect these changes in the agreement. I wish to leave you under no illusion, however, that we can or will go beyond these changes in seeking to improve an agreement that we already consider to be excellent." Nixon urged Thieu to "take the political and psychological initiative by hailing the settlement and carrying out its provisions in a positive fashion." He asked for an unambiguous answer.

But lack of ambiguity was precluded by Vietnamese culture and Thieu's personality. Thieu followed the procedure that had by now become stereotyped. He met with Haig on November 10, listened thoughtfully to his explanation of the President's letter, asked intelligent questions, and promised to think about it overnight. Then on November 11 he confronted Haig and Ambassador Bunker with his entire National Security Council and flatly turned down our suggestion to establish priorities among the textual changes he sought. He insisted on *all* of them; he demanded the withdrawal of North Vietnamese forces, which, as I have repeatedly mentioned, had not been part of any of our joint proposals since 1970. He toughened even this unattainable demand by spelling out how the withdrawal should take place and what weapons had to be taken along. He gave Haig a letter to Nixon restating these demands, as well as requiring changes in the proposed composition of the international supervisory machinery.

Between the two meetings I had sent Haig a cable: "You should point out composition of our new Senate to Thieu. No matter what happens, there will be fund cutoff if we do not move in this direction." Haig made the point, but Thieu was either playing chicken or was on a deliberate collision course.

Haig stopped in Phnom Penh to visit the orphan of our Indochina effort, Lon Nol. He who had every reason to feel abandoned once again supported our strategy. He agreed to announce a unilateral cease-fire as soon as the agreement went into effect. (This would at least seize the diplomatic initiative, since the Khmer Rouge had rejected a cease-fire.)

On November 14 Nixon answered Thieu's letter (using, as always, a draft prepared by my staff and me). It explained how we proposed to deal in the peace document with the problem of North Vietnamese forces in the South. We would do our best to obtain changes, but it would be "unrealistic" to expect to obtain what Thieu wanted. Nixon continued:

> But far more important than what we say in the agreement on this issue is what we do in the event the enemy renews its aggression. You have my absolute assurance that if Hanoi fails to abide by the terms of this agreement it is my intention to take swift and severe retaliatory action.

This was another of the letters later released by South Vietnamese officials in April 1975 in a desperate attempt to obtain American aid to prevent the fall of South Vietnam. They had a right to consider that they had relied on these assurances when they signed the agreement. Unfortunately, release of the letters in the spring of 1975 only played into the hands of those who found in them another excuse for abandoning South Vietnam, not a reason for saving it. In 1972 we had every intention of carrying out these assurances. We believed that an honorable agreement earned at the cost of 45,000 American lives was not signed in order to be flouted by the North Vietnamese. We did not intend to sign a surrender. We considered that we had a right to enforce a solemn agreement signed by Hanoi and confirmed at an international conference by twelve nations in March 1973. Nixon said so when meeting with Thieu on April 3, 1973. Secretary of Defense Richardson said so to the press and testified to that effect before the Congress. I emphasized it at various press conferences.[5] Six months later the Congress, under the impact of Watergate, passed a law prohibiting us from exercising what international law recognizes (and what the United States formally confirmed in conjunction with the Israeli-Egyptian peace treaty): the right to enforce a peace agreement. That destroyed the balance of risks on which observers of the agreement rested and mocked the sacrifices which had been made.

To avoid any misunderstanding and to show our good faith, I sent Bunker on November 17 another summary of the changes we would seek that took into account Thieu's comments to Haig. As was becoming habitual, Bunker could not get an appointment to present them for twenty-four hours. Finally, on November 18, the day before I was to leave for Paris, Thieu had the obnoxious Nha submit another memorandum. It showed that three strong Presidential letters and the visit of two Presidential emissaries had made no impression whatever. Instead of establishing priorities among its demands, Saigon now proposed sixty-nine modifications, leaving almost no paragraph of the draft document untouched. Thieu offered to send a representative to Washington to explain the proposed changes to Nixon — a slap at me and another blatant stalling tactic because there was no way an emissary could arrive before I had to leave. We returned an icy Presidential letter warning again that these changes could not possibly all be achieved, and refusing to receive an emissary until the next round of negotiations with Hanoi had been completed. Nearly four weeks of exchanges had failed to narrow the gap between Washington and Saigon. Thieu knew that he would have to yield but would do so only at the last moment. He would force us to put maximum pressure on Hanoi, in the meantime exploiting our reluctance to have a public rupture.

There was another meeting to prepare for my encounter with Le Duc Tho. On November 13 I had dinner with Chinese Deputy Foreign Minister Ch'iao Kuan-hua at the Century Club in New York. He was heading the Chinese delegation to the UN General Assembly. I brought him up to date on our intentions in Paris. If Le Duc Tho stopped in Peking on the way to Paris, I hoped that the Chinese leaders would use their influence in the direction of moderation. Ch'iao gave no such promise. But neither did he support Hanoi's point of view. He urged us to make concessions because great powers could afford a generous attitude: "One should not lose the whole world just to gain South Vietnam." On the other hand, no one should be humiliated. Ch'iao's line was an even softer version of what we had come to recognize as the standard Chinese position: sympathy for Hanoi, but no expenditure of Chinese capital on its ally's behalf. (Except for slightly cruder tactics, this was exactly Moscow's attitude.)

What elicited Ch'iao's particular interest was Cambodia. In appealing again for a cease-fire in Cambodia, I emphasized that American and Chinese interests in Cambodia were congruent because we both wanted a neutral, independent Cambodia free of the domination of any one country. He did not dispute this. Instead, he asked whether I would be prepared to meet Sihanouk on my next visit to China (then scheduled for January 1973). I evaded the specific question but replied in general terms that we were not opposed to Sihanouk provided he was able to establish an independent country:

> I can tell you now on a confidential basis it would be possible to arrive at an understanding with the Prime Minister that does justice to the concerns of Prince Sihanouk. If the war continues in Cambodia, then we have to maintain our present position. But what we want in Cambodia, to be very blunt, is . . . to preserve it from becoming an appendage of Hanoi. Whoever can best preserve it as an independent neutral country, is consistent with our policy, and we believe consistent with yours.

The next day, when I reported the conversation to Nixon, I repeated my view that after there was a cease-fire in Cambodia, Sihanouk would become a factor again and "could come back at the right moment."

The failure of the Vietnam agreement to include a cease-fire in Cambodia was clearly one of its tragedies. But there should be no doubt where the fault lies. I constantly pressed Le Duc Tho for a cease-fire in Cambodia; he pleaded his lack of influence with the Khmer Rouge. And the attitude of the Khmer Rouge was summed up best by none other than Sihanouk himself: "In 1973 the [North] Vietnamese tried to make them negotiate with Lon Nol but it was too dangerous for them. They would then have had to share power and they wanted it all alone. They got it in 1975."[6] I would have been interested in a meeting with Sihanouk to arrange a cease-fire, but negotiations with him could not succeed so long as he was titular head of the Communist forces insisting on total victory. My next trip to Peking, which eventually took place in February 1973, was the earliest occasion for such a meeting. (As it turned out, Sihanouk was not there at that time.) As an indication of our attitude and the Chinese perception of it, Chou En-lai asked us to look after Sihanouk's security in view of rumored plots against the Prince on his foreign travels. We readily agreed. (We also arranged later for the safe departure of Sihanouk's mother from Phnom Penh for Peking.)

A genuine solution involving Sihanouk's return required a balance of forces and the prospect of a cease-fire — as it had in Vietnam and Laos.

There was no way Sihanouk could resume his pre-1970 balancing role unless there were two parties left to balance. Paradoxically, Sihanouk needed some non-Communist forces to survive in Phnom Penh. With total victory in sight the murderous Khmer Rouge would have no need for him. Starting in the spring of 1973, we sought to bring about Sihanouk's return based on a cease-fire. We were willing; the Khmer Rouge refused. The record shows (as I shall make clear in a second volume) that we were prepared, indeed eager, for Sihanouk's return under such conditions and that a negotiation was beginning. What ended the 1973 negotiation was a Congressionally mandated halt to our bombing in the middle of the year; at that point, certain of victory, the Khmer Rouge lost all interest in negotiations — and Sihanouk's role as balancer was doomed.

The Meetings with Le Duc Tho Resume

M Y meeting with Le Duc Tho on the morning of Monday, November 20, was the first since the sixteen-hour marathon of October 12 and its emotional conclusion. The interval had not been kind to either of us. To a group of men so morbidly suspicious as his colleagues in the Hanoi Politburo, Le Duc Tho must have appeared guilty of the unforgivable sin of having been tricked by a wily capitalist. Relying on our acceptance of the draft peace treaty, the North Vietnamese had started land-grabbing operations. So had the South. The North had suffered fearful punishment and perhaps irreplaceable losses when it surfaced its cadres. We had used Hanoi's own October 31 deadline to extract concessions that, had Hanoi followed its usual negotiating style, would not have been made for many months, if ever, and we had done this only to confront the North Vietnamese at the end of the process with yet another series of demands of unspecified magnitude. I believed Dobrynin when he told me that the North Vietnamese were angry.

On the other hand, our situation was not exactly brilliant either. As I had foreseen, when the outline of the agreement became known, what was left of Congressional support for continuing the war evaporated. I had always believed that this was inherent in Hanoi's October 8 proposal. Once it was apparent that it *improved* the terms we had put forward on January 25 and May 8, 1972, we would lose all public and Congressional support if we did not sign. One of the Congressional resolutions cutting off funds provided Hanoi released our prisoners would surely have passed, as nearly had happened earlier in 1972.

My "peace is at hand" press conference had prevented our being stampeded. But the decision publicly to acknowledge the near agreement rather than disavow it put us under pressure once negotiations resumed. Nixon believed that our options had been substantially reduced by my press conference; I was of the view that Le Duc Tho's October 8 proposal was the turning point, and that once it was made our only choice was between dominating events by going through with our own program or being pushed inexorably toward a Congressional cutoff of funds. Probably there was an element of truth in both Nixon's perception and mine; the fact that we both believed we were running out of options — if for different reasons — weighed heavily on us.

The fears of Congressional attitudes were not based on intuition but evidence. On November 27 Laird told me that it was impossible to "keep that thing going right now." He based his judgment on meetings with Senators and House members during the preceding weekend. Laird repeated this conclusion in a meeting which Nixon convened with the Joint Chiefs of Staff on November 30. It was not contested by any of the Chiefs; it was confirmed by Nixon, who estimated that the aid cutoff would take place within two weeks of the return of Congress. John Lehman, responsible for Congressional liaison on my staff, estimated that the new Senate elected in November represented a net loss of three votes to us, which would grow in significance because of the declining influence of Southern chairmen of key committees. For whatever reason, we were facing the nightmare I had dreaded since the summer: of negotiating against the deadline of the return of Congress with no additional leverage on Hanoi to hold the process together.

In this (for us) unpromising context Le Duc Tho greeted me on November 20 at the door of the residence at Gif-sur-Yvette. Since our meeting had been announced on November 17, the press was fully alerted. They had staked out both the US Embassy residence and the North Vietnamese compound. I managed to shake off the pursuit with the aid of a death-defying French motorcycle escort. (Why I was willing to hazard our safety in the high-speed maneuvers this required I cannot now recall; probably the ritual of the secret meetings had become a habit even though they were now being announced in advance.) It was all in vain. Le Duc Tho had made no effort to avoid pursuit, so when I arrived I found journalists and photographers of many nationalities camped across the street. They were to remain for the entire six hours of the meeting and to return for all subsequent meetings — five more days in November, thirteen days in December, and four days in early January. Léger's house stood alone; it was surrounded by a large garden bounded by a high wall. The journalists set up a scaffolding across the road from the house so the photographers could peer down over the wall into the garden and — hopefully but in vain — into the house itself. Through the cold, rain, and snow of the Parisian winter, bearing witness to the intensity of hope around the world in our struggle to end a bitter war, they kept a lonely vigil, never given any concrete information, never able to see much more than my arrivals and departures, or occasionally Le Duc Tho or me walking in the garden during a break. There were no briefings, and few pictures of Le Duc Tho and me together because we were usually greeted at the door by a lower ranking member of the delegation and the two teams arrived and departed separately.

To ease the atmosphere I had brought some gifts for Le Duc Tho and Xuan Thuy. Le Duc Tho received some picture books of Harvard, to prepare him if he ever took up my suggestion to teach a seminar in Marxism-Leninism there, and a pen and pencil set to sign the agreement. To Xuan Thuy I gave a picture book of America and a Steuben glass horse's head in honor of his reputed love of horseracing. The gesture failed to take the sting out of the encounter. Le Duc Tho led off with a long recitation of Hanoi's goodwill and US duplicity in failing to keep the "shedyule." Reading from a prepared statement, he warned us against attempts to coerce North Vietnam; he complained that while North Vietnam had been deceived many times by the French and Japanese and Americans, never had it been deceived as it had this time. (This was said almost with admiration!)

I replied truthfully that Hanoi's previous four years of stonewalling had not prepared us for the suddenness of Hanoi's willingness to settle in October. I read to Le Duc Tho my many previous caveats that the agreement required the concurrence of both Washington and Saigon. I cited the difficulties caused by the de Borchgrave interview (speaking, as I said, "as somebody who has recently been the victim of an interview myself"). It was time to look to the future and to conclude the agreement.

It was a stirring speech whose impact was immediately vitiated by my putting forward all the sixty-nine changes requested by Saigon. This proved to be a major tactical mistake. The list was so preposterous, it went so far beyond what we had indicated both publicly and privately, that it must have strengthened Hanoi's already strong temptation to dig in its heels and push us against our Congressional deadlines. I put them forward in order to avoid the charge that we were less than meticulous in guarding Saigon's concerns — and to ease the task of obtaining Thieu's approval. As often happens when one acts for the record, we achieved neither objective. Since there was no possibility whatever of obtaining this many changes — as we had warned Thieu — every one we abandoned he could use to demonstrate our lack of vigilance and as another pretext for recalcitrance. And once we started the process of retreat we tempted Hanoi to delay in order to see what other concessions might be forthcoming.

Le Duc Tho's first reaction was predictable. He stated that if these changes were presented as an ultimatum the war would go on another four years. He then asked for an overnight recess to study our proposals. One day of negotiation had elapsed without any progress whatever and with the clock now running against us.

When we met again in the afternoon of November 21, Le Duc Tho emphasized the obvious: The changes I was demanding were not just "technical" but substantive, not few but many. He rejected the overwhelming majority; he accepted a few technical ones. More worrying, he began demanding changes of his own. He withdrew the vitally important concession that American prisoners would be released without linkage to Saigon's release of Viet Cong civilian prisoners. Press reports had appeared, based on leaks from the Pentagon, that civilian technicians might be assisting the South Vietnamese after our military left; Le Duc Tho therefore now added a demand that all American civilian technicians be withdrawn along with our military forces. He insisted on the North Vietnamese translation of "administrative structure." All this was old-fashioned hard bargaining; it was also the stuff of which deadlocks are made. Obviously, this was not the Le Duc Tho of the late summer, relentlessly driving toward a settlement. Mercifully, his conduct was also not yet the insolent political warfare of the previous three years. At a minimum Le Duc Tho kept his options open. He could settle quickly, but he could also hang us up indefinitely.

The latter prospect gave no pain to the three South Vietnamese diplomats whom Thieu had assigned to keep an eye on me: Saigon's ambassadors to Washington, London, and the Paris talks were all in Paris. I briefed them every evening at my residence. Their instructions were simple. They were authorized to accept Hanoi's surrender on all the sixty-nine changes proposed by the inventive Nha. They had no authority to consider less or to discuss any compromise or to entertain any alternative language. Hanoi was keeping open the option of insisting on the October text, knowing that whatever its merit Thieu would not be able to survive the humiliation of obtaining no changes whatever. Saigon insisted on all of its counterproposals, many of which were designed for no other purpose than to humiliate the hated enemy from the North. We were caught in the vortex of the decades-long passions of the Vietnamese civil war and we faced an imminent flare-up of our own conflicts at home.

At the three-and-a-half-hour session of November 22, therefore, I returned to essentials, in the process separating myself from Saigon's position — and running the risk of reinvoking the dilemma we faced in October. In the guise of going through the agreement paragraph by paragraph, I dropped many of Saigon's less important nitpicks and reduced our demands to those Nixon had declared essential in his letter to Thieu of November 8, which I had fleshed out in my memorandum to Saigon of November 14. These were clearing up the translation of the phrase "administrative structure" to describe the National Council; strengthening the provisions on respect for the DMZ; finding some solution to the problem of North Vietnamese forces in the South; in addition we wanted a cease-fire in Laos closer to the time of the cease-fire in Vietnam (it now stood at thirty days later), to have the international control machinery in place at the time the cease-fire went into effect, and to clarify further provisions for introducing weapons into South Vietnam.

Le Duc Tho played cat and mouse. In response to my requests he agreed to a looser clause on replacement of weapons. It had read that weapons "worn out or damaged" could be replaced. He now permitted us to add the phrases "destroyed" and "used up," as in the 1954 Geneva Agreement. The practical consequence was in Le Duc Tho's words: "It means that you will have a free hand to introduce armaments." But the flexibility was more apparent than real, for Le Duc Tho maintained his demands that Viet Cong prisoners be released at the same time as American POWs and that American civilian technicians be withdrawn along with US forces. At this rate we would be in Paris all winter.

Meanwhile, Washington was heard from. Relations between Nixon and me now were wary and strained. I knew of his conviction that my October 26 press conference had weakened our bargaining position. This was true — though I believed that it had saved the negotiations and rallied the public. At any event it was now irrelevant; we had to deal with the situation as it was. Ensconced at Camp David, surrounded only by public relations experts, Nixon was still deep in the bog of the resentments that had produced the darkest and perhaps most malevolent frame of mind of his Presidency. Nixon now dispatched a tough-sounding instruction explicitly marked "not a directive — for possible use with the North Vietnamese." It read:

The President is very disappointed at the tone as well as the substance of the last meeting with Le Duc Tho. Under the circumstances, unless the other side shows the same willingness to be reasonable that we are showing, I am directing you to discontinue the talks and we shall then have to resume military activity until the other side is ready to negotiate. They must be disabused of the idea they seem to have that we have no other choice but to settle on their terms. You should inform them directly without equivocation that we do have another choice and if they were surprised that the President would take the strong action he did prior to the Moscow summit and prior to the election, they will find now, with the election behind us, he will take whatever action he considers necessary to protect the United States' interest.

Another message from Haldeman recommended that I should present a sterner appearance in the television pictures with Le Duc Tho. In other words, smiles in Paris were frowned on in Camp David. I knew from experience that tough rhetoric was not an invariable clue to Presidential intention; and threats seemed premature after only forty-eight hours of negotiation. So I took advantage of the specific statement that the message was not a directive and sought to keep the negotiation going.

On November 23 in another six-hour session, I concentrated on strengthening the provisions regarding the DMZ in order to create a legal barrier to infiltration from the North. Le Duc Tho offered a semi-concession on the DMZ in return for altering other parts of the agreement, especially the political sections, prisoners, and American civilian technicians. Le Duc Tho suggested that we settle for a de facto withdrawal of some of their forces from the northernmost part of South Vietnam in return for the release of political prisoners. He refused to tell us how many would withdraw, rejected my proposal of 100,000, and would not put the promise in writing. I thought this package a significant degradation of the October document, because the regression on the prisoners provision was balanced only by a nebulous assurance — in the form of an "understanding" — of the removal of an unspecified number of North Vietnamese troops a short distance across the DMZ.*

It was Thanksgiving Day. Thoughtfully, the North Vietnamese served a lavish lunch of roast beef and chicken in honor of the occasion. Afterward I cabled Nixon that while we had achieved some marginal improvements, the North Vietnamese had pulled back somewhat, leaving the overall agreement slightly *worse* than the one negotiated in October. I gave the President two options: break off the talks and resume bombing north of the twentieth parallel (in effect, the course he had asked me to put to Le Duc Tho twenty-four hours before); or else settle for the improvements in the draft agreement already achieved on the DMZ and weapons provisions, plus a few changes in the political sections as a face-saver for Saigon; the rest of the agreement would remain as it stood in October. I had, of course, no way of knowing whether Hanoi would accept this; I was certain Saigon would refuse. It was symptomatic of the wary relationship growing up between Nixon and me that I offered no recommendation between the two options.† Rather pettily, I added that events so far had confirmed my original analysis: "It appears that our earlier judgments were correct that now the November 7 deadline has passed so has the incentive for Hanoi to proceed in the same panicky fashion which motivated them in October."

But Nixon was no slouch at one-upmanship. He cabled back that "because of expectations that have been built up in this country" (translation: my "peace is at hand" press conference), the break-off of the talks, which he had put forward twenty-four hours earlier, was no longer

---

*In retrospect I believe that this proposal perhaps deserved a fuller examination than it received. I still do not consider it a fair trade for South Vietnam's freeing of thousands of Viet Cong cadres, a far more irrevocable act.

†Nixon claims that I recommended the first option.[7] The evidence does not sustain this; in fact, I hinted at a preference for the second.

possible. He chose the second option, asking me to play the hand as hard as I could:

In my view the October 8 agreement was one which certainly would have been in our interest. You should try to improve it to take account of Saigon's conditions as much as possible. But most important we must recognize the fundamental reality that we have no choice but to reach agreement along the lines of the October 8 principles.

Rather than pressure Hanoi, Nixon preferred now to put the heat on Saigon:

You should inform the Saigon representatives that all military and economic aid will be cut off by the Congress if an agreement is not reached. Inform them also that, under these circumstances, I will be unable to get the Congressional support that is needed.

The next morning, Nixon had second thoughts; I do not know what changed his mind. He sent another cable suggesting that I interrupt the talks after all, on the pretext of giving the negotiators an opportunity to consult their principals. In that case he would authorize a massive air strike against North Vietnam during the recess. This was not my preference. I favored resumption of bombing north of the twentieth parallel only if the talks broke down altogether, and we had not yet reached that point. In any case, Nixon was now prepared to brave the domestic storm if we stuck to a firm line:

Our aim will continue to be to end the war with honor. And if because of the pursuit of our strategy and the accident of the timing of the election we are now in a public relations corner, we must take our lumps and see it through.

In giving this direction, we all must realize that there is no way whatever that we can mobilize public opinion behind us as in the case of November 3 [1969], Cambodia [1970] and May 8 [1972]. But at least with the election behind us, we owe it to the sacrifice that has been made to date by so many to do what is right even though the cost in our public support will be massive.

The net result of all these instructions was to leave the decision up to me. All this time the Saigon contingent of ambassadors had taken an adamant stand, not budging from their demand for the sixty-nine changes. On November 23 we learned that Thieu's aide, Nguyen Phu Duc, was coming to Paris to reinforce the team. If Saigon were to show any flexibility, we would have to await his arrival. I also judged that it would be a mistake for the American and North Vietnamese delegations to keep meeting on the established pattern, formally working our way through the agreement. In the absence of new instructions for Le Duc Tho or "give" from Saigon, we would merely confirm the deadlock. And we would not hear from Saigon for another twenty-four hours.

I therefore proposed to Le Duc Tho that he and I, each accompanied by just one adviser, meet at our old place at Rue Darthé in Choisy-le-Roi. He agreed. Haig and I met him and Xuan Thuy for one and a half hours on November 24 for a philosophical discussion. I read to my interlocutors the starchier of Nixon's telegrams, especially those emphasizing his willingness to run military risks. I stressed that we would in no circumstances accept provisions weaker than those already published — thus rejecting Le Duc Tho's request for changes in Hanoi's favor. Le Duc Tho maintained his position. After this meeting I cabled Nixon that I leaned toward a week's postponement. It would show Hanoi that we were not excessively anxious. It would give us another week to work on Saigon unless Duc brought a fundamental change. As it stood, whatever was negotiable in Paris could not be sold in Saigon. I would wait for my meeting with Nguyen Phu Duc before making a final decision.

Duc brought nothing. Nixon's cable describing Congressional attitudes impressed Duc but obviously could not change his instructions. I decided to ask for a week's recess the next day. In these circumstances a meeting of the two delegations again seemed unwise. Le Duc Tho and Xuan Thuy thus met Haig and me for two hours on the morning of November 25 at Rue Darthé. Le Duc Tho granted a recess grudgingly; I did not have the impression that he was prepared for additional serious talks. We agreed to announce December 4 for a resumption.

This first round of talks thus ended with twelve improvements — some marginal — in the text, balanced against three or four demands by Hanoi for major changes in its favor. We were not clear about Hanoi's ultimate intentions. Le Duc Tho's tactics might be tough negotiating or they could reflect a growing confidence that the psychological tide was running in Hanoi's favor. The North Vietnamese might calculate that we would try to force Saigon to go back to the October text if they held on long enough, shattering the morale of Thieu's government. Or else the Congress would force us out of the war. Nixon meanwhile had changed his mind again. He now thought I should keep the talks going. He had sent me a "suggestion" to that effect late on November 24 after the recess had already been agreed. It was uncharacteristic of Nixon and showed how isolated he was at Camp David. No political leader I have met understood the dynamics of negotiations better than Nixon. He knew that the process of talking rarely produces solutions by itself; only a balance of incentives and penalties can produce progress. We needed to have Hanoi give up its demands for release of Viet Cong political prisoners and for the withdrawal of American civilian technicians. We had to hear from Saigon what modifications of its sixty-nine points it could live with. All the evidence was that neither Vietnamese party was prepared to budge at this moment. We needed the respite if only to avoid having us dug into an intractable stalemate, and to see what pressures could be brought to bear.

I had begun to be seized with a premonition of disaster independent of the issues involved. An experienced negotiator develops a sixth sense for when the other side is ready to settle. The signals are usually matters of nuance: Some issues are not pressed to the absolute limit; some claims are marginally modified; the doors to compromise are always kept tangentially ajar. None of these indicators appeared in the November round of talks; indeed, all the signs were contrary: Hanoi's concessions were marginal and inconclusive; they kept the goal of a settlement always tantalizingly out of reach. One telltale sign was Tho's persistent reluctance to let experts from both sides discuss the protocols — documents that were to spell out in detail the arrangements for implementing general clauses in the main agreements, such as the timing and supervision of the cease-fire, and the composition and authority of the international control machinery. I repeatedly asked for North Vietnamese drafts or ideas on these protocols and said that our experts headed by Ambassador Sullivan were ready to negotiate on them. Tho evaded each of our requests with the lame excuse that the North Vietnamese drafts were not ready. This was amazing in light of Hanoi's insistence three weeks earlier that we sign the basic agreement by October 31. (It also shows how absurd the "shedyule" was in the absence of the implementing documents.) If my instincts were right, worse was yet to come; Hanoi would be embarked on a course of procrastination and we had little leverage to jolt them out of it. In this uneasy mood, I flew home.

Predictably, Washington proved inhospitable to incipient failure. It is a city that thrives on tales of prominence and decline. The raw material of its social life and day-to-day conversation is the rise and fall of the powerful. I had been protected for nearly four years — except for a brief storm during the India-Pakistan crisis — by the unambiguous support of the President. I had been associated with a whole series of successful negotiations. The media had treated me perhaps excessively gently — partly as a contrast to Nixon. I was now to suffer the corresponding penalty. I had made my share of enemies among those in the bureaucracy who thought me unduly dominant and among members of the White House staff jealous of my access to Nixon or wary of the publicity I was receiving. And not even my severest critics have accused me of excesses of humility, the lack of which is bound to invite challenges when vulnerability appears. In Washington, Nixon was clearly getting restive. The prospect of imminent disaster always activates the network of gossip, leak, and innuendo that murmurously determines one's fate through the attitude of the spectators, much as in a Roman circus. One is condemned to the contest like a gladiator and it ends only with one's public career.

Failure in Washington requires a sacrificial offering. I was the logical candidate. The media reminded their audiences of my "peace is at hand" statement, though they treated me, I must say, compassionately at this stage. The same could not be said of some White House aides who began to take precautions to dissociate the President from a possible collapse of the negotiations. Stories began to appear — in columns as different as those of John Osborne, Evans and Novak, and Jack Anderson — that I had exceeded my instructions in the October round, that Nixon's legal-eagle eye had spotted drafting flaws in the original agreement, that Nixon was siding with Thieu against me. Much of it was self-serving nonsense. I had had no instructions to exceed in October; Nixon had not raised a single objection to any provision of the agreement. His private view of Thieu was if anything less charitable than mine, though he was worried about offending the Republican right wing. But in Washington the fact of such leaks is often more interesting than their truth; they indicate, if not Presidential displeasure, at least that some aides consider it safe to attack a close associate of the President. And foreign governments will draw their own conclusions from an appearance of division in high councils. In that respect White House politics is not so different from life at royal courts.

As always in those matters, personal and policy considerations were closely linked. It is natural for a President to want to put some daylight between himself and possible disaster; in my case there was the complicating factor of pent-up — and not unjustified — resentment over what Nixon and his closest associates considered the disproportionate credit for foreign policy successes given to me. As for me, injured pride merged with a real concern that we could see the looming crisis through only if we stayed united and kept our nerve. I tried to make this point to Haldeman and Ziegler; I also pointed out that an attempt to dissociate the President too much from my efforts would backfire; the odds were, after all, quite high that we would succeed eventually and the President would then not wish to appear too far removed from the negotiation. As in the previous year over India-Pakistan, Haldeman and Ziegler were noncommittal.

All this was good clean bureaucratic fun, but it had a massively pernicious impact in the negotiations. It encouraged Thieu in his intransigence and in his seeking to exploit the presumed split between Nixon and me. And it was bound to tempt Hanoi to stonewall in the talks. It would be a disaster for us if Hanoi returned to its time-honored strategy of wearing us down, hoping to lull us into imposing terms on Saigon that would at least achieve Hanoi's long-standing aim of undermining the morale and survival of our ally. This we were determined to avoid. And in fact on substance Nixon and I remained close; as always in crisis Nixon was calm and analytical. But there was no doubt we were caught in a vise. Thieu, on one side, was determined to give us no leeway; Hanoi, on the other side, all the more saw the divisions looming between Saigon and Washington — as well as within our own government — as an opportunity to delay to see what benefits might be waiting down the road. We decided to bring matters to a head, first with Saigon.

On November 26 I asked Bunker to tell Thieu yet again that our minimum conditions remained unchanged. To reinforce our position we now accepted Thieu's earlier suggestion that he should send an emissary and requested the immediate dispatch of Nguyen Phu Duc to Washington from Paris so that Nixon could go over our final position with him. (The point was to disabuse Thieu of any hope that he could play on a Nixon-Kissinger split.) Bunker endorsed the approach; he shared our conviction that Thieu would do nothing to ease our task, would assume no responsibility for the negotiation, and yet would accept the result.

Duc arrived on November 29 to meet a determined Nixon. The President, in fact, thought my proposed talking points were somewhat "too soft." He wanted to show me how to achieve a clear-cut result. Having no experience with the Vietnamese negotiating style, he did not appreciate that it avoids showdown, that its pliant obtuseness often makes it impossible to determine the precise nature of the issue or what exactly has been agreed. Duc carried an extremely long, eloquent letter from Thieu to Nixon. It recounted all the concessions extracted from Saigon over the years with the promise — broken, it alleged — that no other sacrifice would be demanded. Thieu had a point, of course; the tragedy was that what Thieu considered intolerable pressure by us had been regarded by our critics as crass intransigence. We had to navigate in this gulf; to adopt Thieu's view at this late hour would have guaranteed the collapse of all remaining support at home. For the rest, Thieu's letter was oblivious to the intervening negotiations or our domestic dilemma. It restated all his arguments of October, as if repetition could force us on a course not trodden at least since October 1970. Thieu suggested an appeal to world opinion if his "just" demands were not met. This was a forlorn hope; world opinion had been oblivious to Hanoi's transgressions while its troops were trampling the sovereignty of every neighbor; Hanoi had made stick its claim to be the victim of American "oppression" when it had started every war in Indochina since 1954. World opinion was pressuring us, not Hanoi, and was bound to accelerate its pressures.

Nixon succinctly explained to Duc the impossibility of such a course. We could not now abandon peace proposals we had jointly put forward for nearly three years. It was absurd to describe as a coalition government an organization operating by unanimity, selected jointly, and with few specified functions. Our strategy in any case was set. Nixon would proceed on it whatever Saigon's attitude; the latter would determine not the outcome of the negotiation but our ability to provide help afterward and to enforce the agreement. It was strong stuff but not strong enough to elicit a clear-cut reaction. Duc denied any desire for a confrontation. On the contrary, his aim was close cooperation. On the other hand, he had no authority to go beyond the settled views of his President. Nixon grandly suggested that Duc and I sit down to work out a practical solution; his decision had been made. In other words, we were right back where we had started. Duc had no authority to settle and Thieu would never yield to me.

The result was foreordained. I met Duc twice in my office, and in between our two sessions was another brief meeting with Nixon. Nixon stressed to Duc yet again that his ability to enforce the agreement was more important than any changes in the clauses, though he was prepared to seek some further improvements. He told Duc he was confident we could detect infiltration; he told him of contingency plans he had discussed that very morning with the Joint Chiefs. Without an agreement, Nixon said, there was no chance for continuing US aid. He offered to meet with Thieu to reaffirm our support after the agreement was concluded. The optimum course was to "pull together, get the best possible agreement, and then go forward together with U.S. economic and military aid and, above all, strong assurances that the agreement will be enforced." Nixon informed Duc, finally, that if the agreement failed, Congress would probably cut off funds by mid-January. All this fell on the stolid Duc without any noticeable effect. When it was all over, Nixon remarked resignedly to me that Thieu was playing "chicken" and that we had probably no choice except to turn on him.

On the morning of November 30, as he told Duc, Nixon had met with Laird and the Joint Chiefs of Staff. Laird estimated that the Congress would surely vote to cut off funds.

We had sent a message to Hanoi on November 27 saying that we would make a maximum effort on December 4 and to show our goodwill, we were reducing air operations over North Vietnam. The President, on my recommendation, ordered a cut of 25 percent in our sorties. It was probably a mistake; I can remember no instance where the North Vietnamese reciprocated gestures of unilateral restraint. More likely, they saw such moves as impelled by weakness. Hanoi's response of November 30 in any case pocketed the gesture while dismissing it: North Vietnam deemed it necessary to point out "that so far ferocious U.S. air attacks against the Democratic Republic of Vietnam, especially with B-52 planes, in fact have not been reduced." For the rest Hanoi blamed the impasse entirely on American and South Vietnamese actions. We returned a tart reply on the same day:

As the U.S. has consistently pointed out, the one-sided presentation by the DRV of the reasons for the current difficulties cannot contribute to the rapid settlement of the war. . . . Clearly the two sides will be at a point where choices will have to be made between an early peace or a prolongation of the conflict with unforeseeable consequences. The U.S. will make its maximum effort but this cannot succeed without similar effort by the DRV.

Amid looming Congressional disenchantment, caught between two implacable Vietnamese sides who specialized in tormenting each other, stung by leaks at home that my position as negotiator was not all that secure, I was not in a brilliant position from which to resume the negotiation on December 4.

The December Talks: Breakdown of the Negotiation

THERE seemed not much point in beginning the round on December 4 by repeating our sterile exchanges, especially before two delegations now swollen by technical experts on both sides. I therefore proposed by cable that Le Duc Tho and I should begin with another "open-hearted" private discussion. Hanoi accepted, and suggested the original meeting place at 11 rue Darthé. What took place between Le Duc Tho and Xuan Thuy on one side and Haig and me on the other deserves many appellations, but "open-hearted" is not likely to be one of them. Contrary to his usual insistence that I speak first, Le Duc Tho launched into an opening statement harking back to the fiery rhetoric of our early encounters. He accused us of seeking to strengthen what he called the "puppet administration" of Saigon. He criticized the refusal to release Viet Cong political prisoners — which he had accepted in October. He repeated the epic tale of North Vietnamese imperviousness to military pressure. My reply tried to put before Le Duc Tho our sincere commitment to peace — an enterprise that had always proved futile in the past and was to do so again:

The Special Adviser has resorted to his usual tactics, accusing us of supposed bad faith and evil motives. There is a time for suspicion but there is also a time for understanding. What is the reality as we look at it? I have publicly acknowledged [on October 26] something you have never done: that you made an important proposal in October. If the Special Adviser reflects for a few minutes he will recognize that it was a great temptation then, and we received much advice that we should just break the negotiations and accuse you of bad faith. We resisted this advice and put ourselves in a publicly disadvantageous position in order to maintain the momentum toward peace and, quite frankly, to put the other Vietnamese parties under an obligation to move more rapidly. . . . You made an important proposal on October 8. What would you have done if I had said that I would have to go to Saigon to discuss it and we could not meet for two or three more weeks? We have managed to spend three years with each other. You know that it would have been easy to waste many more months. It was a great temptation. We deliberately agreed to an accelerated schedule, knowing very well what risks were involved. Risks for our country, since you would have the opportunity to do what you are now doing, and personal risks for all involved. So you must understand that when you accuse us of bad faith, that is extremely offensive to us. . . . Considering what we have already achieved it would be an historical tragedy, an historical absurdity if we could not conclude an agreement. If we analyze the agreement in terms of who has to do what, the specific obligations, we have settled nearly everything already. So there is really not much more to negotiate about. Either we will settle this week or we will never settle.

So that's how it looks to us. I know it looks different to you. I am sure we can spend the whole week discussing history, good will and serious intent. But what we need now is wisdom to see whether we can settle in the short term because we understand the long term already. We will make a maximum effort. You may not consider this enough. I actually think we could settle very quickly. We have two plans, one for war and one for peace. There is no sense giving you our plan for war. We have talked about this often enough. Let me tell you about our plan for peace.

The plan was to settle the remaining issues within two days, that is by the evening of December 5. The morning after Le Duc Tho and I concluded an agreement, Vice President Agnew, accompanied by General Haig, would leave for Saigon to brief Thieu. Within forty-eight hours we would stop all bombing of North Vietnam. We would sign the agreement no later than December 22. And I presented a stripped-down version of the minimum changes for which we would settle.

But as on every previous occasion Le Duc Tho proved unmoved by eloquence; he was a specialist in the balance of power; he could not be swayed by words when he saw the balance tilting toward him. In turn, he indulged in one of his maddening verbal games. He called on me to make a "great effort"; he promised that he would make an "effort." When he had said it often enough, I asked whether he was not entitled to an adjective for himself. No, replied that stalwart from Hanoi's Politburo, because recently he had made "great efforts" and I had only reciprocated with "efforts." Lest I miss the point, he repeated: "We have already made great efforts and exhausted the possibilities. There remains only little effort [for us] to make."

So on the afternoon of December 4, our two delegations met again — this time in a new location picked by the North Vietnamese, in Sainte Gemme, about an hour's drive west of Paris. My speech of the morning had clearly left no impression. Le Duc Tho did not even make little efforts; he made none at all. He seized the floor for a violent denunciation of our tactics. He then rejected all our proposals from the morning's private session. While he was at it, he also withdrew nine of the twelve changes he had *accepted* during the previous sessions in November. At the same time he maintained all *his* demands for changes in the October agreement. As I reported to the President:

He rejected every change we asked for, asked for a change on civilian prisoners, demanded the withdrawal of American civilians from South Vietnam thus making the maintenance of the Vietnam air force impossible, and withdrew some concessions from last week. In short, we would wind up with an agreement significantly worse than what we started with. I told him flatly that his approach did not provide the basis for a settlement. In the ensuing dialogue Tho stuck firmly by his intransigent position. The only alternative he offered to his presentation this afternoon was to go back to the October agreement literally with no changes by either side.

I did not believe that Le Duc Tho would have dared to put forward such propositions unless he was willing to risk a break-off in the talks. Back at the Embassy residence my associates and I spent hours poring over the records of the meetings, seeking to distill some ray of hope from some arcane formulation. We could not find any. We had taken over the entire residence, since Ambassador Watson had resigned and his successor (John Irwin) had not yet taken up his post. Staff members were frantically rewriting documents; secretaries were collating materials. The dining room stayed open the better part of each night serving outstanding meals that were consumed in deepening gloom.

That first night I concluded that the only hope of averting a collapse would be messages to Moscow and Peking informing Hanoi's Communist backers of the prospects before them. I asked Dick Kennedy, manning my office in Washington, to tell Dobrynin that we were approaching a situation comparable to last May, requiring the same kind of reaction. To give Moscow time to make its influence felt, I asked Le Duc Tho on December 5 for a twenty-four-hour postponement of the meeting scheduled for that afternoon "because of the grave situation resulting from the December 4 meeting."

My report to Nixon made clear that I did not see how we could accept returning to the October text (not to speak of one even worse, as Hanoi proposed). Though I considered the agreement a good one then, intervening events would turn acceptance of it into a debacle. If we could not bring about a single change requested by Saigon (or worse still, accepted a less favorable agreement), it would be tantamount to wrecking the South Vietnamese government. Worst of all, "it would deprive us of any ability to police the agreement, because if the Communists know we are willing to swallow this backdown, they will also know that we will not have the capacity to react to violations."

Thus our only real choice was to pursue a course that involved a high risk of a break-off. Two realistic possibilities existed: First, we could drop all additional requests and sign the agreement with the twelve changes to which the North Vietnamese had agreed in November. Second, we could persevere in seeking some of the additional changes requested by Thieu, reducing them down to two: dropping the phrase "administrative structure," and including some clause that denied Hanoi the legal right to intervene in the internal affairs of South Vietnam. "If, as seems totally unlikely, the other side buys this package, we would have gained a significant change in both the political and military areas. Thus this extra round would have been justified and we would be in a stronger position versus Saigon, although our problems there would still be massive." I favored the second course. However, I warned the President, Hanoi would almost certainly reject either approach:

The central issue is that Hanoi has apparently decided to mount a frontal challenge to us such as we faced last May. If so, they are gambling on our unwillingness to do what is necessary; they are playing for a clearcut victory through our split with Saigon or our domestic collapse rather than run the risk of a negotiated settlement. This is the basic question; the rest is tactics. If they were willing to settle now, I could come up with acceptable formulas and would not need to bother you. Assuming they are going the other route, we are faced with the same kind of hard decisions as last spring.

I considered a breakup probable and I recognized my own responsibility in having forced the pace since October: "If this happens, I will talk to you upon my return about my own responsibility and role. The immediate task now, of course, is to save our national honor and position ourselves as best we can with our people and the world so as to pursue a principled policy in Southeast Asia." I added another page saying that if the President accepted my recommendation he should explain the decision in a television address to the American people. Haig, Lord, and I discussed this addendum in a strategy session in my bedroom overlooking the residence's elegant garden. Haig especially thought it essential that the President be faced with the implications of a deadlock not only in terms of military escalation but also as a means to discourage some of the starchier recommendations of amateurs, now Nixon's sole regular contacts in the strange mood that had settled over him since the election.

Breaking such news to the American public was not their idea of what to do with his overwhelming electoral victory. But there was no disagreement between us as to substance. Nixon therefore rejected it even though he agreed with my analysis. He cabled back on December 5 approving my negotiating tactics. He had no trouble with my view that in case of a breakup we would have to step up military pressure. Indeed, he was eager to order an attack by B-52s on the Hanoi-Haiphong complex even before my talks resumed on December 6. He asked my judgment on whether he should order Admiral Moorer to increase the readiness of our forces and also whether I wanted to buy more time by returning to Washington for consultation. My idea of the television appearance, however, found no favor at all: "I think, however, that the option of raising this to the Presidential level forces the Russians and the Chinese to react, would get at best a mixed reaction here in the U.S., and might make Saigon more difficult to deal with than they presently are."

Each of us, Nixon and his advisers on one side and I on the other, were imprisoned in a world of his own, which touched that of the other only peripherally. I was sensitive to the negotiating situation; he understood what the traffic would bear domestically. I thought I knew the balance of incentives affecting the diplomacy. Nixon was less on top of the tactical situation, but he had a fine sense of public strategy — or thought he did. He was convinced that a television speech would be futile. If he was right, I saw no way of sustaining an effective negotiating strategy; for only the fear of resumed military operations would keep Hanoi on course. We would surely be whipsawed. In any event, I opposed reactions taken out of pique that would unsettle the public mood without offering prospects of success.

I replied to Nixon that I thought it premature to increase the readiness of our forces, that there should be no bombing while the talks were going on, and that a return to Washington after only one day of negotiation would heighten a sense of crisis that would play into Hanoi's hands. Suicidally, I repeated my recommendation that if the talks broke off or recessed, he would have to go on television to explain it. In the best Nixon style, Haldeman was deputized to overrule me. A highly unusual message from the White House Chief of Staff made explicit what Nixon only hinted at. If the talks stalemated, Haldeman suggested, they should be recessed rather than broken off. In that case I was to give a low-key briefing. He offered no clue as to how to give a "low-key" briefing on the collapse of Vietnam peace efforts.

Nixon may have been right in his judgment that there was no public opinion left to rally; if so, and if Hanoi shared the judgment, the negotiations were doomed and prolonging the talks was useless. On December 6 I replied to Haldeman:

Thank you for your message of December 5. We had better face the facts of life. If there is no agreement in the next 48 hours, we may be able to pretend that the talks are in recess long enough to permit me to give a briefing after my return. But soon after, there will be no way to keep either of the Vietnamese parties from making the stalemate evident. Furthermore if we resume all-out bombing this will be even more true. Thus in the event of a stalemate we have only two choices: to yield or to rally American support for one more effort which I do not believe the North Vietnamese can withstand. If we are to attempt to rally the American people only the President can adequately do that eventually. But if it is your judgment that I should go on first, I will of course be glad to attempt it. We can then discuss the President's possible involvement later.

Before my next meeting with Le Duc Tho, Moscow replied to our message. The Kremlin counseled patience, expressed confidence in Hanoi's desire for peace, and assured us — forty-eight hours after Le Duc Tho — that the North Vietnamese were still ready to sign an agreement within the October framework. Dobrynin added privately that Moscow was in touch with Hanoi and that he recommended I keep the talks going to give the Kremlin more time to make its influence felt.

My meeting with Le Duc Tho on December 6 brought no change. Both sides reviewed their positions. There was some tinkering with individual clauses, but we were simply treading water. The best proof of Hanoi's reluctance to settle was Le Duc Tho's continuing refusal to permit a meeting of the experts to negotiate the detailed protocols even on provisions not in dispute. Le Duc Tho said they were "studying our documents" and theirs were not ready. Hence, no matter what he and I decided, it could not be implemented until the experts had concluded a task the North Vietnamese refused to begin. We agreed to make a final effort the next day, December 7; each side should present its minimum position. It was a vainglorious maneuver, almost bound to fail, for it tempted each side to await the concessions of the other. I told the President what I planned to give as our rock-bottom position, and I warned of what we would face even if there were a last-minute breakthrough:

As I have consistently told you since mid-September, this is a very high-risk operation. The eventual outcome of any settlement will essentially turn on the confidence and political performance of the two sides. Having seen the total hatred and pathological distrust between the Vietnamese parties, and knowing as well that Hanoi has no intention of giving up its strategic objectives, we must face the reality that this agreement may lack the foundation of minimum trust that may be needed. Thus it could well break down. It will certainly require from us a posture of constant readiness and willingness to intervene to keep Hanoi and its South Vietnamese allies from nibbling at the edges. . . .

Haig simultaneously alerted the Vice President to be ready to leave for Saigon if there should be a breakthrough the next day.

Nixon's reply directed me to open the next meeting with a series of questions much in the style of a prosecuting attorney, to try to pin Hanoi to a series of intransigent positions to strengthen the record in case the talks should recess or break up. I was then to invite Hanoi to make its final offer.[8] Nixon's approach had merit, though I thought he vastly overrated my ability to pin down Le Duc Tho to unambiguous answers. I had a different view of the tactics, which I communicated to Nixon. My stiff tone could be said to reflect a certain lack of spontaneous warmth in the relationship between President and adviser:

Thank you for your message of December 6. Your instructions are understood and will be followed. However, I believe the tactical sequence in carrying them out should be different. At this afternoon's session I will first push for Hanoi's acceptance of our minimum position which you approved (Option 1). If Le Duc Tho rejects this position I will ask the series of questions you have listed in the first paragraph of your message to me including the one about withdrawal. I will then ask for a recess to enable me to return to Washington and consult with you, following which we will be in touch with them next week on when to resume. I believe it would be a serious mistake to launch today's session with the questions since this process would be likely to result in an outright rejection and place us in a stalemated position at the outset of the session.

I could picture Nixon, cut off from the most knowledgeable senior advisers, all of whom (including Haig) were with me. He would ruminate, writing out the issues on his yellow pad, all the while showered with the advice of his public relations geniuses. Richard Kennedy, who was holding the fort for me, though not an expert on Vietnam, was meticulous and precise. I had asked Haig on December 7 to send him a summary of the situation so he could exert a steadying influence. The PR temptation to evade admitting that there was a deadlock, I was convinced, would make it much harder later to manage the now nearly inevitable recess of the talks. Paradoxically, Hanoi was likely to make its final concessions only if it was convinced that we were willing to risk failure and take the consequences. No one had more to lose from such an eventuality than the author of "peace is at hand." But there was no way of hiding a deadlock indefinitely, no chance of overcoming it if we were not willing to brave its implications. Haig's message to Kennedy, in his best Army prose, read in part:

Henry recognizes that you have been in a difficult position this week and therefore felt you should have the benefit of his personal views on the situation as it now stands. I would emphasize that his experience with the President during crisis periods confirms the fact that most of the President's counsel in the absence of Dr. Kissinger would come from elements within the White House whose orientation and background would cause them to focus primarily on public relations considerations which, while perfectly understandable, can leave a serious substantive gap during vital deliberations. . . . You, of course, must be the sole source of substantive counsel. Henry hopes that you will not make any other kind of assessments or join in any comments [on] Congressional attitudes or public opinion which are available to the President from people whose tasks are precisely that. Your counsel must therefore always be in terms of national security substance. In this context it is now evident that we will need some time to position the public opinion at home in the event the talks break down. But there is no need to allow these considerations to affect our strategy vis-à-vis Hanoi. Hanoi has known for some time what the issues are and what minimum needs of ours they must meet. The question is simply: can they bring themselves to do so? Tactical ploys from our side indicating that we are inclined to avoid facing up to the fact of their intransigence can only make matters worse and their resolve to hang tough even firmer. . . .

Hanoi knows exactly what they have to do. If they meet our minimum demands the management of the agreement itself is going to take the most determined and decisive Presidential leadership to enforce an agreement which we are now convinced both sides will enter into with a minimum of good will. If, on the other hand, the talks break down because Hanoi could not even accept our minimum demands, there is little doubt that we can succeed only as a result of the most courageous and determined national leadership which is not dominated by PR considerations but rather the same realistic assessments of the national interest which have brought us to this point. . . .

The four-hour meeting on December 7 suggested that the basic problem was precisely Hanoi's continued procrastination. Hanoi's apparent calculation was that the lapse of time could only improve its position; that we were hopelessly cornered. Though this was not apparent right away and we continued to cling to the hope that a "concession" heralded a breakthrough, the fact was that December 7 marked the beginning of the real deadlock. Le Duc Tho changed his style somewhat. He abandoned the obvious stonewalling of the previous sessions. He started giving some ground — but always made sure to keep the conclusion of the text just out of reach. He adamantly refused to allow the experts to discuss the protocols; this gave him another means to prevent a conclusion and also added a surrealistic abstractness to the main negotiations. And a bullying tone crept into his presentations, indicating that he thought Hanoi was gaining the upper hand psychologically.

Le Duc Tho's "concessions" were of a peculiar kind. On the first day he had reneged on nine of the twelve changes he had agreed to in November; he now gave back six; he also dropped the crucial demand for the release of civilian prisoners in South Vietnam (which Hanoi had conceded in late October and reneged on in November). On the other hand, he raised ominous concerns on the DMZ provision. In November he had accepted an important change strengthening the obligation to respect the Demilitarized Zone as the demarcation line between North and South Vietnam. Le Duc Tho now wanted a sentence to the effect that North and South Vietnam would discuss the legal status of the DMZ. This had the effect, as I repeated to Nixon, of "placing into question the whole status of the DMZ," not to mention the ban on infiltration. The number of unsettled issues in the agreement was somewhat smaller than the day before, but we had not yet recovered all the November concessions that Le Duc Tho had retracted four days earlier. I was correct in cabling Nixon that we might well achieve one or two of our minimum additions in another session, but it was also true that this was precisely where Le Duc Tho wanted us: tantalizingly close enough to an agreement to keep us going and prevent us from using military force, but far enough away to maintain the pressure that might yet at the last moment achieve Hanoi's objectives of disintegrating the political structure in Saigon. I was more and more concerned about the whole context of the agreement. As I reported to Nixon:

It is now obvious as the result of our additional exploration of Hanoi's intentions that they have not in any way abandoned their objectives or ambitions with respect to South Vietnam. What they have done is decide to modify their strategy by moving from conventional and main force warfare to a political and insurgency strategy within the framework of the draft agreement.

Thus, we can anticipate no lasting peace in the wake of a consummated agreement, but merely a shift in Hanoi's modus operandi. We will probably have little chance of maintaining the agreement without evident hair-trigger U.S. readiness, which may in fact be challenged at any time, to enforce its provisions. Thus we are now down to my original question: is it better to continue to fight on by scuttling the agreement now; or be forced to react later, vindicated by the violation of a solemnly entered agreement?

I recommended the latter course, but Le Duc Tho was rapidly draining the prospect of peace of its exhilaration.

As I had expected, Nixon accepted the recommendation; his reply indicated that he would prefer almost any agreement to a recess. I should seek "some" (unspecified) improvement over the October draft. The message followed a meeting at Camp David of the President, Deputy Secretary of Defense Kenneth Rush, and Admiral Moorer to review contingency plans for a step-up of military operations. Rush and Moorer agreed wholeheartedly that the October agreement was sound and that the Congress would cut off funds, certainly after June 30, if it were not implemented. Nixon, after having told me for months that his main concern was the right-wing constituency, was now coming around to the view that the continuation of the war had no public support. Of course, I was aware from the cabled innuendos that this erosion of public support was being blamed on my "peace is at hand" press conference. Needless to say, I considered this an excuse; I thought the loss of support inherent in Hanoi's October 8 acceptance of our program — and exacerbated by Saigon's intransigence. We were both right and it made no difference. For neither on October 8 nor on October 26 did we have a choice. Whatever the ultimate penalties, the course we took was daring but avoided worse dangers.

Fundamentally, Nixon's and my attempts to shift responsibility back and forth were as meaningless as they were unworthy. If the negotiations succeeded, there would be the same scramble for credit as there was now to avoid blame. If they failed, I was the logical victim — and justifiably so whatever the merits of my analysis. I had pushed the course that had produced the existing situation; Presidential associates have an obligation to protect their chief. I had incurred a special responsibility in this regard by my solitary procedures.

Reflections such as these were, of course, of little help in Paris. My dilemma was that I was caught between Saigon's obstreperousness, the subtle insolence of Hanoi, and a soggy set of perceptions in Washington, which, by trying to keep negotiations going at nearly all cost, was depriving us of the leverage to bring matters to a head.

The four-and-a-half-hour session of December 8 saw Tho's continuing refusal to discuss the protocols, coupled with grudging but not quite conclusive concessions. Tho and I agreed finally to drop the whole phrase "administrative structure," translation of which had caused so much anguish.* He also confirmed his willingness to go back to the original text on civilian prisoners. These were major steps forward. But Le Duc Tho left himself sufficient running room. He remained adamant on defining the DMZ in a manner that threw its status into question and therefore indirectly provided a legal justification for permanent intervention by Hanoi in the South. And he reiterated his demand for a total withdrawal of American civilian technicians working with the South Vietnamese armed forces, which would have the practical effect of paralyzing all the sophisticated equipment of Saigon's military establishment. Still, we were now down essentially to two issues: the DMZ and American civilian personnel. Compared with what had already been settled, these could be dealt with in one session provided the desire was there. On this assumption I asked Haig to return to Washington. If we settled on December 9, I wanted him ready to leave for Saigon the next morning with the Vice President to obtain Thieu's concurrence.

But Le Duc Tho proved as wily in achieving delays as he had been

---

* In the October agreement, the parties agreed "to set up an administrative structure called the National Council of National Reconciliation and Concord. . . ." Dropping the phrase entirely, the parties now simply agreed "to set up a National Council. . . ."

ferocious in producing deadlocks or, briefly, flexible in moving toward a settlement in October. A three-and-a-half-hour meeting on December 9 seemed to produce further progress. But each apparent success confirmed the sinking feeling that our interlocutor was leading us through an endless maze, for no matter what was settled, Le Duc Tho managed to keep alive at least one more issue at each session.

On this occasion Le Duc Tho "gave" us what we already had in October, the right to have American civilians service sophisticated South Vietnamese military equipment. But he hung firm on the DMZ because he knew that permitting military movement through it vitiated the ban on infiltration, which was so important a part of the agreement. He now made a claim novel in our experience with Communist negotiators. He said that the Politburo in Hanoi had overruled him when in November he had agreed to the clause that the DMZ must be respected. He was still awaiting new instructions, he said; he could go no further. It was unprecedented for a member of any Communist Politburo to claim that he had exceeded instructions. Given our knowledge of North Vietnamese procedures, it was also highly improbable. (At least I think so now; then, for reasons I find hard to understand, I tended to believe him.)

I offered a compromise. The language about respecting the DMZ should stay as agreed two weeks before. But I would be prepared to add a sentence to another paragraph which provided that, pending reunification, North and South Vietnam should promptly start negotiations to establish normal relations in various fields. The sentence was: "Among the questions to be discussed will be the authorization of *civil* movement across the Provisional Military Demarcation Line." This had the advantage of implying that all movement across the DMZ was barred, pending agreement between the parties, and that military transit would be prohibited permanently. Le Duc Tho, afraid that he might have difficulty finding an argument for rejecting this compromise, resorted to yet another novel gimmick. He suddenly complained of a headache, high blood pressure, general debility; he seemed to be an elderly man in distress. So convincing was the performance that I offered to adjourn the meeting. Never one to give up an edge, Tho suggested that he would need the entire next day to recover, thereby neatly stalling talks for another forty-eight hours and, of course, aborting the Vice President's trip to Saigon. He generously agreed, however, to have the experts meet — not yet, to be sure, to begin work on the protocols (he had not yet even given us Hanoi's drafts) but to conform the language of the existing texts of the agreement. As soon as I agreed to this procedure — and, indeed, I had little choice when faced with an obvious invalid — Ducky, his purpose accomplished, magically recovered and we spent another hour in insolent banter.

With only *one* issue now remaining I had every hope of finishing

when we next met on Monday, December 11. But I still underestimated
Le Duc Tho. The experts' meeting of the day before had gone reasonably well, though it took seven hours to conform texts that had already
been agreed half a dozen times. There was a cloud on the horizon when
the North Vietnamese sought to change the provision in the agreement
which stated that the parties "shall strictly respect" the 1954 and 1962
accords on Cambodia and Laos. The North Vietnamese proposed to
drop the "shall," thus turning the sentence not into an obligation but
into a statement of fact — an extremely unsettling proposition when one
reflected on the over 100,000 North Vietnamese troops even then running amok in these two countries.

Overnight, from December 9 to 10, I had sent a brief note to Le Duc
Tho in the President's name telling him that Nixon was still considering
my compromise language on the DMZ and had not yet approved it. The
President would far prefer to stick with the original text. I thought that
in this manner what I had proposed could appear as a genuine concession in Hanoi.* Le Duc Tho would not fall for transparent ploys, however. On December 10 he returned a brief note indicating that *his* superiors in Hanoi considered that *their* position — putting the very status of
the DMZ into question — was "a most correct and reasonable proposal."

The happiest group in Paris was the Saigon ambassadorial delegation
assigned to keep an eye on me. Their only duty was to listen to my
briefings each evening; their instructions were to hold fast to each of
Saigon's sixty-nine changes and to listen to no compromise — clearly
to test whatever Le Duc Tho had left of my emotional equilibrium.
There were no compromises to discuss. The increasing depression of the
American delegation caused scarcely concealed elation among the South
Vietnamese.

On December 10 I received also Haig's account of a series of bewildering moves by Nixon, which illuminated the difficulty of guiding
complex negotiations from a distance. First he called Dobrynin to tell
him that he had rejected my compromise language on the DMZ and
asked Moscow to help us bring Hanoi back to the formulation agreed to
in November (respect for the DMZ with no provision for even civilian
movement across it). He then developed second thoughts about Agnew's going to Saigon, fearing that once there he might side with Thieu
against his own Administration; he now wanted to send Connally. Haig
argued him out of that because no private emissary could possibly carry
the clout of the holder of a constitutional office (Connally no longer
being Treasury Secretary), and because Agnew's known proclivities to

---

*I was to be caught on my own cunning: Nixon cites this instruction as his own although he
never saw it until afterward.[9]

the right would give added weight to his support of the agreement. Finally, Haig sent me the President's instructions for the conduct of the talks:

Assuming you are able to slip Monday's meeting to late Monday afternoon, you should then hold tough on the DMZ issue, confirming that the President remains adamant. If Moscow's assistance is evident, we may then find Hanoi caving. If not, the President believes, and I know you do as well, that we must not break off the talks on Monday. In that event you should return for a new session hopefully as early as possible on Tuesday morning, thus giving me [Haig] maximum time to leave Tuesday night with the Vice President. This will enable us to manage the Vice President's personal schedule, the low-keyed announcement and coordination with Bunker and Thieu. Also on Tuesday you should again enter the talks in a tough posture by which time Moscow's ultimate leverage should be evident if, in fact, they exercise it at all. If Le Duc Tho is still intransigent, you should then try our compromise as the final US concession. If even this fails, the President, as we predicted, would even be willing to cave completely with the hopes that we can still bring Thieu around.

In other words, Nixon had disavowed to Dobrynin my compromise proposal as being too soft. At the same time he instructed me to put it forward and to accept Hanoi's formulation as a last resort. He wanted to prevail by bluffing Dobrynin but was ultimately prepared to cave in. A bluff in which the gap between the formal position and what one will accept is so wide cannot work.

In any event, Le Duc Tho was one step ahead of us when we met on December 11. He wanted no agreement, at least on this round. The possibility that we might cave in had obviously occurred to him as well; he therefore moved decisively to escape the embarrassing situation wherein there was only one issue left on which we might yield. He moved quickly to remove this danger. First, he rejected signing procedures that we had assumed settled. (This was a complex arrangement by which Saigon could sign without recognizing the Communist Provisional Revolutionary Government.) Next, forty-eight hours after conceding the issue of American civilian technicians assisting South Vietnamese armed forces, he insisted that this applied only to the public text of the agreement to avoid embarrassing us. He now asked for a written private understanding that our technicians would be withdrawn. He also, regretfully, was not yet ready to discuss any of the protocols. And his instructions on the DMZ would not arrive until next day. Le Duc Tho, in short, made it clear that he would not settle that day, nor (given the outstanding issues) was a settlement likely on the morrow. This behavior was in itself irritating. It was doubly insulting to delay a conclusion when the North Vietnamese had known that for the last forty-eight hours the Vice President had been poised to leave Washington to impose the negotiated agreement on a recalcitrant ally. I reported to the President through Haig:

It is not impossible that we could conclude the agreement tomorrow, but nothing in their behavior suggests any urgency and much in their manner suggests cock-sure insolence. . . .

It is obvious that an agreement was easily achievable on any day since last Thursday. Hanoi may well have concluded that we have been outmaneuvered and dare not continue the war because of domestic and international expectations. They may believe that Saigon and we have hopelessly split and that the imminence of Christmas makes it impossible for us to renew bombing the North. If this is the case we will face a decision of major magnitude. I believe a total collapse by us now would make an agreement unenforceable. The President must also understand that an agreement at this point and under conditions that led to the collapse of South Vietnam would have grave consequences for his historic position later.

All these December meetings now alternated between the Communist meeting place in Gif-sur-Yvette (the Léger house) and the elegant townhouse of an American businessman in Neuilly. Every day we sped to the appropriate site in a hair-raising motorcade with an heroic French police escort. Wooden stands had been thrown up at both places from which the assembled journalists could observe the negotiators pacing during breaks. Ironically, the grimmer the situation inside, the more cordial now was the demeanor of the North Vietnamese welcoming us and bidding us farewell outside the house; no doubt they wanted to give enough of an impression that progress was being made to forestall any thoughts of military escalation on our part. Mindful of my instructions to give no indication of an imminent break, I occasionally chatted in a friendly way with Le Duc Tho within sight of photographers — earning me another reproof from Haldeman.

A cable I received from Haig after the December 11 meeting further elucidated Washington's frame of mind. The President wanted me to stay as long as there was any hope of a settlement; to return for consultations if I judged the deadlock to be unbreakable; to recess but not to adjourn the talks; and to brief the press if he decided to resume bombing. Haig at my request told Dobrynin about the status of our negotiations and let him know that the promised Soviet intercession was clearly ineffective. Dobrynin made ambiguously helpful noises. I kept briefing the Chinese Ambassador to Paris, Huang Chen. He did not even pretend that Peking was doing anything, though he could not have been friendlier. Before my next meeting with Le Duc Tho I learned of a very tough speech by Thieu to his National Assembly that rejected once again the existing framework of negotiations.

As I think about the events of that period, I admire the courage of that dauntless leader who, assaulted by hundreds of thousands of enemy troops and pressed by his only ally, nevertheless persevered in his complicated game of maneuvering between contending necessities. Relentlessly, he sought to demonstrate to his own people simultaneously that he was a genuine Vietnamese nationalist and not a puppet of the United States; that he was capable of providing the leadership even in peace to resist the Communist invaders (under whose rule the vast majority of the population did not then and do not now wish to live); and that he was not an obstacle to peace. He navigated these shoals with skill and determination, on the whole to the benefit of his people. At the time, our needs differed. And so on us the impact of his ruthless egocentricity was to mock our sacrifices, to undo his own position in America, and to impose on us mounting financial and human costs.

Nixon armed me for the meeting of December 12 with a message to read to Le Duc Tho that contradicted his instruction of the previous day to cave in as a last resort and that showed that whatever his maneuvers, once he had analyzed the problem Nixon would do what was right. Written in expectation of a recess, it instructed me to tell Le Duc Tho that in no circumstances would we make the wrong kind of settlement and that until there was an end to North Vietnamese intransigence there would be no further American concessions.

On December 12 the experts, headed by Sullivan on our side and Vice Foreign Minister Nguyen Co Thach on the other, met again in the morning. The North Vietnamese still refused either to discuss our draft protocols or to give us versions of their own. Le Duc Tho had meanwhile received instructions on the DMZ. He had a proposal that omitted the phrase "civilian" from my formula for permitted movement across the DMZ. In other words, Hanoi wanted to leave open the right of military transit through a Demilitarized Zone — one of the neater tricks of diplomacy, and one that raised even further doubts about the ban on infiltration. To ease our pain, Tho finally produced protocols for the cease-fire and international control machinery. He now preempted our plans by informing me that he had decided to leave Paris for Hanoi on Thursday, December 14, taking four or five days to get there. He would not be able to settle unless he could personally convert the recalcitrants in the Politburo who were constantly giving him a hard time, especially on the DMZ. He offered to return if necessary, but thought we could settle the remaining issues by an exchange of messages — a patent absurdity given the many technical details still requiring attention. The idea of a pacific Tho constrained by his bellicose peers from making concessions was mind-boggling; but it served Tho's purpose of stalling without (he hoped) giving us an excuse to retaliate. Le Duc Tho agreed to meet once again the next day in a now forlorn hope for a breakthrough, and to review the conclusions of the experts who would be at last reviewing the protocols.

I reported to Washington at the end of December 12:

All of this sounds mildly encouraging; but I have come to the following conclusion. Hanoi has decided to play for time, either because of the public split between us and Saigon; or because they have a pipeline into the South Vietnamese and know about our exchanges; or because their leadership is divided and they are still making up their minds on whether to conclude the agreement. Their consistent pattern is to give us just enough each day to keep us going but nothing decisive which could conclude an agreement. On the other hand, they wish to insure that we have no solid pretext for taking tough actions. They keep matters low-key to prevent a resumption of bombing. They could have settled in three hours any time these past few days if they wanted to, but they have deliberately avoided this. . . .

They have reduced the issues to a point where a settlement can be reached with one exchange of telegrams. I do not think they will send this telegram, however, in the absence of strong pressures.

Overnight we studied the North Vietnamese drafts of the protocols. They were "outrageous," as I reported to Nixon. The one spelling out the size, composition, and functions of the International Commission of Control and Supervision (ICCS) left the supervisory machinery subject to so many multiple vetos that it was inconceivable how it could possibly inspect anything. The ICCS, which would have two members proposed by the Communists (Hungary and Poland) and two by our side (Canada and Indonesia), would require unanimity to make any investigation or to file any report; no member would have the right to file a minority report. Moreover, the ICCS would have no transport of its own but would have to ask the party being inspected for its approval as well as for any jeeps or telephones or other equipment. Le Duc Tho joked cynically that in Communist areas they might have to travel by buffalo cart. In case a loophole had been left unintentionally, the number of ICCS inspectors would be limited to 250, including support personnel, to inspect infiltration across seven hundred miles of jungle and an even longer shoreline. Hanoi's draft foresaw that the Two-Party Joint Military Commission (consisting of the Viet Cong and Saigon), which we had conceived as having primarily liaison function, would be as strong as the international inspection machinery was weak. This body was to have subgroups down to the district level, thus intruding a Communist presence into every area of South Vietnam in the guise of liaison machinery. I explained our objection sarcastically to Le Duc Tho on the next day:

We feel that your draft exaggerates the traditional Vietnamese hospitality to a point where these [ICCS] teams will find it almost impossible to observe anything, finding themselves surrounded as they are by their Vietnamese hosts at every moment. [Laughter.] As we analyze it, there are about four times as many liaison officers as there are Commission members, and Westerners not used to your standards of hospitality may confuse it with being taken prisoner. [Laughter.] So I believe that some greater possibility for initiative should be given to these members. Secondly, as we understand your draft — and I am afraid we understand it — it provides for all communications and support of the Commission to be furnished by the party in whose area the Commission operates. Now the Special Adviser has already pointed out that they may have to move by buffalo cart. But our basic concern is the purposes of the Commission, and its incentive to find violations may be higher than that of the party committing the violation. And you have set it up not only that the party has to agree to the investigation to begin with but that it has to supply all the communications and transportation.

The cease-fire provisions were equally absurd. They provided for the grounding of every South Vietnamese airplane and the immobilization of every military vessel even in South Vietnamese waters. In the pretense of defining the cease-fire, Hanoi proposed to deprive the South Vietnamese of any capacity for self-defense. No wonder my staff expert on Vietnam, John Negroponte, called Hanoi's negotiating tactics in the December round "clumsy, blatant, and essentially contemptuous of the United States" as well as "tawdry, petty, and at times transparently childish."

All these qualities were apparent in my last meeting with Le Duc Tho on December 13. This was the day that finally exploded the negotiation. It was the first meeting with Le Duc Tho attended by the head of our delegation to the peace talks, Ambassador William Porter. It made him yearn for the calmer if equally sterile atmosphere of the plenary sessions. That morning the language experts had met again to ensure that both sides were working from the same texts of what had been agreed. Whereas earlier experts' meetings had been more or less businesslike, in this meeting the North Vietnamese threw in seventeen brand-new gratuitous phrases that in effect reintroduced earlier North Vietnamese demands which had been dropped by Le Duc Tho in his talks with me. My whole session with him on December 13 was wasted in the exercise of renegotiating all the substantive issues.

One of the linguistic tricks he had been playing all along can serve as an example. In October Le Duc Tho had proposed that the National Council of National Reconciliation and Concord should "direct" certain specified activities. I had rejected this as implying a governmental authority for the Council incompatible with the premise of the agreement. Le Duc Tho then tried "oversee" or "supervise," all of which happened to have the same Vietnamese translation. These too I refused. Finally, we agreed on the weaker word "promote." When we checked the Vietnamese text of the protocols, we found that Hanoi had kept the offending Vietnamese word throughout.

More serious was that the North Vietnamese in the translators' meeting reopened the dispute over the use of the future tense in the clause "the parties shall respect the 1954 and 1962 Geneva Agreements" on Laos and Cambodia; they again dropped the "shall." This was not only reneging on what Le Duc Tho had conceded the day before; it was also decidedly unnerving because Le Duc Tho again rested his objection on the ground that North Vietnam was *already* respecting these agreements and therefore the future tense was misleading. In this insolent interpretation, the agreement to respect the neutrality of Laos and Cambodia turned into a confirmation of Hanoi's right to maintain forces in Laos and Cambodia.

I had come to Paris on December 4 with instructions from Nixon to settle. Le Duc Tho had kept me there ten days, our longest negotiating session ever, and each day we seemed farther away from an agreement. At the end of Saturday, December 9, Le Duc Tho and I agreed there was only one issue left (the DMZ). At the end of Monday, December 11, there were two new issues (civilian technicians and signing procedures). At the end of Tuesday, December 12, there were many more (the three from Saturday and Monday, some others in the text, and several new ones in the protocols). Each day several issues that we thought had been settled in the agreement emerged again in loaded North Vietnamese drafts of either the understandings or the protocols. Le Duc Tho would then yield on most of these in a long day of negotiation, but made sure that enough were left over, or new ones reopened, to prevent a conclusion. The issues left over usually varied from day to day. There was no intractable substantive issue separating the two sides, but rather an apparent North Vietnamese determination *not to allow the agreement to be completed*. This was the insoluble problem over which we began the Christmas bombing five days later.

I concluded the December 13 meeting with a warning to Le Duc Tho of the growing impatience in Washington:

We came here twice, each time determined to settle it very quickly, each time prepared to give you a schedule which we would then have kept absolutely. We kept the Vice President standing by for ten days, in order to start the schedule which we had given you. And we believe that in the last week there has been just enough progress each day to prevent a breakup but never enough to bring about a settlement. I admire the Special Adviser's skill in keeping the negotiations going.

We agreed to tell the press that we would stay in contact about when to meet again. Experts from both sides would continue to meet on the protocols.

It was, to put it mildly, a somber trip back to Washington. No VIP aircraft being available, we had to use an airborne command post. It was an uncomfortable and noisy plane, with no windows, crammed with communications equipment — none of which, it turned out, could be made to communicate with the White House. Encapsuled in that gloomy cocoon, cut off from the world practically and symbolically, we could reflect on the ups and downs of the past two months. No goal in my public life had drawn such an emotional commitment from me. We had been negotiating for ten days on matters that with any goodwill could have been settled in two. Hanoi had quite simply decided that the split between Washington and Saigon, the evident divisions within our government, and the imminent return of a Congress even more hostile to the Administration than its predecessor provided too good an opportunity to pass up. Hanoi, recently so eager for a settlement, had returned to its traditional tactic of psychological warfare. Whether in making war or peace, Vietnam seemed destined to break American hearts.

But self-pity, whatever the cause, could not be more than a transient indulgence. Somehow we had to master events, not simply deplore them. I still thought that the war could be brought to an end quickly, but it would now require another time of trial that would deepen the domestic wounds. The peace process would not, as I had hoped, be a time of healing. We had been frustrated essentially because our eagerness to settle enabled each of the Vietnamese sides to blackmail us while depriving us of effective sanctions against them. Our first obligation was to reestablish a better balance of risks; to bring home to them both that we meant to determine our own destiny. I summed up our options in my final cable from Paris:

Where then does this leave us? I explained our basic dilemma yesterday. Hanoi is almost disdainful of us because we have no effective leverage left, while Saigon in its short-sighted devices to sabotage the agreement knocks out from under us our few remaining props. . . . We will soon have no means of leverage at all while pressures will build up domestically if we fail to reach an agreement or get our prisoners back. We will neither get an agreement nor be able to preserve Saigon.

We now have two essential strategic choices. The first one is to turn hard on Hanoi and increase pressure enormously through bombing and other means. This would include measures like reseeding the mines, massive two-day strikes against the power plants over this weekend, and a couple of B-52 efforts. This would make clear that they paid something for these past ten days. Concurrently . . . pressures on Saigon would be essential so that Thieu does not think he has faced us down, and we can demonstrate that we will not put up with our ally's intransigence any more than we will do so with our enemy.

The second course is to maintain present appearances by scheduling another meeting with Le Duc Tho in early January. This would test the extremely unlikely hypothesis that Tho might get new instructions. If we were once again stonewalled, we would then turn hard on Hanoi. We would give up the current effort, blaming both Vietnamese parties but placing the major onus on Hanoi. We would offer a bilateral deal of withdrawal and an end of bombing for prisoners. Under this course as well we would have to move on Saigon, to bring Thieu aboard in the event of an agreement in January or in the likely event of failure, to lay the basis for going the bilateral route [with Hanoi].

The Christmas Bombing

WHAT has been called the Christmas bombing has been portrayed too often as a massive orgy of destruction, senseless in its purpose, malign in its conception. This is a myth in several respects. My description of the December negotiations can leave little doubt that Hanoi had in effect made a strategic decision to prolong the war, abort all negotiations, and at the last moment seek unconditional victory once again. Nixon and I returned with the utmost reluctance to the consideration of military actions.

For me December 1972 was a melancholy period. Whatever happened now, it was likely that the end of the war would in divisiveness parallel the conduct of it. If we took no decisive step, the two Vietnamese parties would drift farther apart; the brief near-agreement of October would have unraveled; we would not again be able to get such terms except through military exertion of a scale and duration which the Congress and public would never sustain or which, if they did, would tear our country apart. We could, in my view, overcome the dilemma only by an immediate showdown simultaneously with both Hanoi and Saigon.

During the December round of negotiations I had tried to impress on Nixon that a breakup (or a recess) would mean that we would have to step up military pressures on Hanoi if we did not want either an endless war or an unenforceable peace likely to wreck Saigon. I had wanted Nixon to explain the impasse to the public and to escalate military operations. Preoccupied with the negotiations, I had no time to think through what kind of military measures I would recommend when the time came. Haig had requested planning papers from the NSC staff that concentrated mostly on lifting our self-imposed bombing restrictions of the previous October; in other words, to confine B-52s to south of the twentieth parallel and to attack the populated areas with fighter bombers. I made no specific recommendation from Paris.

Nixon's attitude was more complex. Basically, he now wanted the war over on almost any terms. Though I frequently received bellicose-sounding instructions intended to be read to the North Vietnamese, operational recommendations were much softer. I was told to keep on negotiating, which, given the situation, could only confirm the deadlock; to go beyond even our fallback positions and on the DMZ to accept the Communist formulation. I am positive that had Hanoi in December given us one or two minimal, essentially window-dressing, propositions on the DMZ or civilian technicians, Nixon would have accepted them with alacrity — far more so than I. He was not anxious to resume bombing. He had a horror of appearing on television to announce that he was beginning his new mandate by once again expanding the war.

But Hanoi had become greedy. Encouraged by the evident discord between Washington and Saigon, probably perceiving accurately what the new Congress would do in January, the North Vietnamese thought that they could take everything, make us cave in, and demoralize Saigon. The North Vietnamese committed a cardinal error in dealing with Nixon: They cornered him. Nixon was never more dangerous than when he seemed to have run out of options. He was determined not to have his second term tormented like the first by our national trauma — especially when a settlement had seemed so near.

There was another person not quite of the inner circle but getting ever closer to it who played a significant role in the decision: my deputy Al Haig, who was soon to be promoted to Vice Chief of Staff of the Army. He had originally supported the negotiations, but had become more skeptical as Thieu balked and Hanoi stalled. The December round had convinced him that only massive military pressure could overcome Hanoi's disdainful obstruction. He favored large-scale B-52 raids in the North and made these views clear to me at Andrews Air Force Base on Wednesday evening, December 13, on my return from Paris.

Nixon, Haig, and I met on the morning of December 14 to consider our course. We were agreed that if we did nothing we would wind up paralyzed, in effect prisoners of whatever maneuver Hanoi might choose to inflict on us. There was no reason to expect Hanoi to change its tactics if talks did resume in January. Pressures on us to settle for the October draft would mount. After all that had happened, to do so would represent a massive defeat; it would be psychologically devastating in Saigon; having collapsed so completely, we would certainly lose our ability to enforce the agreement. That, of course, was precisely the reason for Hanoi's contemptuous behavior. Saigon, for its part, would see no point in flexibility; with Congress undoubtedly pressing cutoffs of funds it would run no additional risks by sticking to its course. We knew that there was no support for military action elsewhere in the Administration, and that it would provoke a violent uproar in the Congress and the media. And given the President's reluctance to explain his case personally to the public, this was bound to erode whatever popular support was left. While I was on the way back from Paris, Laird had sent a memorandum to Nixon opposing a military response; he claimed to be

supported in this judgment by Rush and Moorer. Haig, checking with
Moorer, found that the Chairman considered his views "misunderstood."

All of us in the December 14 Oval Office meeting agreed that *some*
military response was necessary. But we were not at first in accord
about what kind, and it is difficult to reconstruct now because there
seem to be no written records. Nixon remembers that I urged intensified
bombing south of the twentieth parallel and in southern Laos[10] but no
bombing at all in the populated areas. I have no such recollection; my
memory is that I favored resuming bombing on the scale of that before
the October self-imposed restrictions, over all of North Vietnam but
using fighter-bombers over the populated areas. Haig, on the other
hand, favored B-52 attacks, especially north of the twentieth parallel, on
the ground that only a massive shock could bring Hanoi back to the conference table. Nixon accepted Haig's view. I went along with it — at
first with slight reluctance, later with conviction. For Nixon and Haig
were, I still believe, essentially right. We had only two choices: taking a
massive, shocking step to impose our will on events and end the war
quickly, or letting matters drift into another round of inconclusive negotiations, prolonged warfare, bitter national divisions, and mounting casualties. There were no other options.

Nixon chose the road of forcing a conclusion — resuming heavy
bombing and using B-52s on a sustained basis for the first time over the
northern part of North Vietnam. The choice of B-52s was partly for
shock effect but also because our other aircraft had no all-weather capability. I have mentioned before that about half our planned missions
over North Vietnam in the summer were aborted because of weather.
Moorer estimated that weather difficulties would be even worse in December. (As it turned out, during the two-week period that B-52s were
used over North Vietnam, there were only twelve hours when fighter-
bombers could have operated.) Nixon reasoned, correctly, that he would
pay a serious domestic price for lifting the self-imposed bombing restrictions; but it would become unmanageable only if he failed. He
preferred a massive brief effort to a prolonged inconclusive one.

Later there were stories of a rift between Nixon and me over the use
of B-52s. They were false. The fact is that I agreed with, indeed recommended, stepping up military pressure in the wake of Hanoi's conduct at
the Paris talks. I saw the force of Nixon's and Haig's arguments in the
use of B-52s and concurred. Once Nixon had made the decision, I
implemented it with pain and regret over the receding prospects of
peace, but without hesitation, as the best of difficult alternatives.

If I admired Nixon's decision, I was less enthusiastic about his refusal
to explain it to the public. He had ordered reseeding of the mines for
December 17 and resumption of bombing for December 18. These

events were bound to produce a tremendous furor. But Nixon was determined to take himself out of the line of fire. I was asked to give a low-key briefing of the reasons for the recessing of the Paris talks; how to be low-key about such a dramatic event was no more apparent to me in Washington than it had been in Paris. I had no objection to this assignment; indeed, I volunteered for it. But if there was a major uproar, only the President would be able to quiet it and give the public a sense of where we were headed. It was proper that I should be the butt of attack, as I had been and would be again the focal point of success. I had decided to resign and assume responsibility for the failure if the negotiations collapsed irretrievably.

But the overriding, immediate need would be to calm public fears and rescue national self-confidence out of the bedlam certain to follow Nixon's decision. Nixon explains that he was concerned not to jeopardize the negotiations; silence enabled him to avoid giving our actions the character of an ultimatum and thus permitted Hanoi to return to the conference table without loss of face.[11] This was part of his concern; but I also think there were other, more complex, reasons. Nixon was still seized by the withdrawn and sullen hostility that had dominated his mood since his electoral triumph. He resented having to face once again the emotional travail of an expanded war at the very start of his new Administration. He was much less certain of success than I; he told me his doubts repeatedly. And deep down he was ready to give up by going back to the October draft. He did not want to be identified with a negotiating program that might conflict with this. The B-52 bombing was in this sense *his* last roll of the dice, as the March offensive had been Hanoi's — helpful if it worked; a demonstration to the right wing if it failed that he had done all he could. The paradox of Nixon's relationship with me during that period was that he favored the tougher military measures but the softer negotiating stance, while my position was somewhat the opposite. I favored a stronger negotiating position and, at first, more flexible military tactics (though, I must repeat, once I thought about it I concurred in the B-52 decision).

The necessity of military measures was being powerfully reinforced in our mind every day by the conduct of the North Vietnamese at the experts' meetings continuing in Paris. Sullivan had stayed behind to negotiate on the protocol concerning the release of POWs, one of the most important documents for us. The North Vietnamese stalled all day on December 14; they finally submitted a Vietnamese-language text too late in the day to permit any negotiation. Their draft followed the pattern of the previous sessions of putting back into the protocols objectionable clauses Le Duc Tho had agreed to delete from the basic agreement. Thus the release of South Vietnamese civilian detainees appeared once again as a specific obligation, after having been dropped by Le Duc Tho on at least three previous occasions, the last time five days earlier. Sullivan reported sarcastically: "We expect to receive an English language text of this horror when we meet at Gif tomorrow and will transmit it immediately through this channel. At Gif, we will make a great effort" (Tho's code phrase).

Sullivan then returned to Washington, and Ambassador William Porter, head of our Paris peace delegation, was left to negotiate with Xuan Thuy on both protocols and understandings. They met on December 16; Xuan Thuy carried Le Duc Tho's arrogance to new heights. Instead of stalling on substance he refused to discuss it with respect to any subject, on the Catch-22 pretext that he could not discuss any of the outstanding problems until he had dealt with all of them. (And of course he could not deal with *all* of them except by addressing the parts.) Porter's report described the atmosphere:

We met with DRV at Neuilly from 1530 to 1815. Xuan Thuy stonewalled from beginning to end.

Despite fact we had agreed yesterday on agenda which consisted of a) understanding on Laos and Cambodia, and b) ICCS protocol, Xuan Thuy took position he was unprepared to discuss either.

We handed over our revised understanding on Laos and Cambodia and asked for their comments on it as well as on mutual understanding on cessation of hostilities in Cambodia which we had previously handed over. Xuan Thuy acknowledged receipt of both, but said he would have no comment until all understandings had been discussed.

Xuan Thuy then launched into lengthy exegesis on DRV conception of control and supervision features of our agreement, which made it clear that Two-Party commission was to be multitudinous and ubiquitous, while ICCS was to be minuscule and cloistered. . . .

When meeting closed, Xuan Thuy rather lamely said DRV wished proceed as rapidly as possible. This comment only served to emphasize fact that today's session was a total DRV stall, building a record of Kleberized intransigence [a reference to the four years of futile plenary sessions taking place in the International Conference Center on Avenue Kléber].

This was the context in which I stepped into the White House press room on December 16 to explain the stalemated negotiations. I had been given detailed guidance by Nixon, who had sent me two personal memoranda on December 15 and December 16; the first took up five, the second two, single-spaced pages. Their essence was that I should not try to defend my October 26 "peace is at hand" briefing; there were various subtle digs blaming that briefing for our difficulties. Nixon's advice was to stress the President's consistency, unflappability, firmness, patience, and farsightedness in carrying us through this difficult period. Later on, it was noted that I had mentioned the President fourteen times in my December press conference, whereas I had mentioned him only three times on October 26.¹² Knowing that a count would be kept by one of Haldeman's minions, I had little choice in view of Nixon's instructions.

The aim of my briefing as I conceived it was to place the blame where it belonged — on Hanoi — and again to leave no doubt in Saigon of our determination to conclude the agreement. I explained the reasons for the breakdown in some detail, stressing that Hanoi had raised one frivolous issue after another. "We will not be blackmailed into an agreement," I said. "We will not be stampeded into an agreement, and, if I may say so, we will not be charmed into an agreement until its conditions are right." Again I had two principal audiences — Hanoi and Saigon — but I also knew the hopes of the American people were riding on the outcome of the present impasse:

So, we are in a position where peace can be near,* but peace requires a decision. This is why we wanted to restate once more what our basic attitude is.

With respect to Saigon, we have sympathy and compassion for the anguish of their people and for the concerns of their government. But if we can get an agreement that the President considers just, we will proceed with it.

With respect to Hanoi, our basic objective was stated in the press conference of October 26th. We want an end to the war that is something more than an armistice. We want to move from hostility to normalization and from normalization to cooperation. But we will not make a settlement which is a disguised form of continued warfare and which brings about, by indirection, what we have always said we would not tolerate.

We have always stated that a fair solution cannot possibly give either side everything that it wants. We are not continuing a war in order to give total victory to our allies. We want to give them a reasonable opportunity to participate in a political structure, but we also will not make a settlement which is a disguised form of victory for the other side. . . .

Nothing that I have done since I have been in this position has made me feel more the trustee of so many hopes as the negotiations in which I have recently participated. It was painful at times to think of the hopes of millions and, indeed, of the hopes of many of you ladies and gentlemen who were standing outside these various meeting places expecting momentous events to be occurring, while inside one frivolous issue after another was surfaced in the last three days.

So, what we are saying to Hanoi is, we are prepared to continue in the spirit of the negotiations that were started in October. We are prepared to maintain an agreement that provides for the unconditional release of all American and allied prisoners, that imposes no political solution on either side, that brings about an

---

* I was getting better at careful formulations.

internationally supervised cease-fire and the withdrawal of all American forces within sixty days. It is a settlement that is just to both sides and that requires only a decision to maintain provisions that had already been accepted and an end to procedures that can only mock the hopes of humanity.

On that basis, we can have a peace that justifies the hopes of mankind and the sense of justice of all participants.

The first reaction by the media was measured and balanced though not overly generous. Few neglected to contrast it to my earlier "peace is at hand" statement. They now had another word to play with; I had said that I was speaking to avoid a "charade." The *Baltimore Sun* of December 18 titled an editorial: "End of the Vietnam 'Charade' ''; the *Washington Post* ("The Great Peace Charade," December 19) concluded that at a minimum the Administration had been "taken for a long hard ride by the North Vietnamese." The *New York Times* of the same date was more explicit, heading its editorial "Deception or Naivete?" and on the whole leaning to the former interpretation of the Administration's motivation.

What none of these learned commentators contributed was any sense of what the United States should do in its present impasse, or, for that matter, how we should have responded to the North Vietnamese offer of October 8. There was a marked ambivalence. On December 14, when matters seemed to be progressing, if painfully, the *New York Times* under the heading "Who's Winning What?" criticized the White House for its unwillingness to admit that the proposed agreement would "perilously weaken Saigon's position." (The terms were, of course, far more favorable than the coalition government and unilateral withdrawal that the *New York Times* had been urging for years.) Once the deadlock became apparent, all the critics were back at their old stand: The only legitimate war aim left for the United States was to get its prisoners back. Few challenged the proposition or asked what might be left of the confidence in us of others who depended on us if we simply abandoned an ally to retrieve our prisoners. And if we were prepared to insist on some minimum conditions beyond slinking out with our prisoners while leaving the peoples of Indochina to the tender mercies of the invading North Vietnamese, what else could we do except to pursue the strategy Nixon had ordered? We were right back to the perennial debate: Whatever the claims made previously, were there any minimum terms that defined our honor?

Such questions as these were rapidly submerged in mounting rage over the bombing that resumed on December 18 and lasted for twelve days, immortalized as the "Christmas bombing." The *Christian Science Monitor* of December 20 expressed the common view that bombs not having worked before, they could not possibly lead to results now (a dubious premise and one that in any event Hanoi did not hold). The *St. Louis Post-Dispatch* of December 19 urged us to drop the ''contemptible'' President Thieu of South Vietnam and urged Congress to legislate us out of the war.

The moral indignation rose with each day. The proposition that the United States government was deliberately slaughtering civilians in a purposeless campaign of terror went unchallenged. Some headlines of editorials tell the story: ''New Madness in Vietnam'' (the *St. Louis Post-Dispatch*, December 19); ''The Rain of Death Continues'' (the *Boston Globe*, December 20); ''This Will End the War?'' (the *Chicago Daily News*, December 22); ''Terror from the Skies'' (the *New York Times*, December 22); ''Shame on Earth'' (Tom Wicker, the *New York Times*, December 26); ''Terror Bombing in The Name of Peace'' (the *Washington Post*, December 28); ''The Untold Horror'' (the *New York Post*, December 28); ''Beyond All Reason'' (the *Los Angeles Times*, December 28). These are a small sample. I received incredibly bitter letters from erstwhile friends, from angry citizens. (None of them wrote me in January when the agreement was reached.) Charges of immorality and deception were thrown around with abandon; ''barbaric'' was another favorite adjective. It seemed to be taken for granted that North Vietnam was blameless and that we were embarked on a course of exterminating civilians.

Congressional criticism, though more muted, was also mounting. Senator Muskie called the bombing ''disastrous'' and said he would ''demand an explanation.'' Senator Javits threatened a cutoff of funds, warning that White House freedom of action was measured in weeks; Senator Saxbe suggested that Nixon appeared to have ''taken leave of his senses.'' Senate Majority Leader Mansfield called it ''a Stone Age tactic'' and promised to introduce legislation for a terminal date of the war. Representative Lester Wolff echoed the sentiment. ''Monstrous outrage,'' said Representative Don Riegle. Senator Kennedy said, ''This should outrage the conscience of all Americans.'' Jerry Gordon, coordinator of the National Peace Action Coalition, told a press conference: ''The American people have been lied to once again. Instead of peace being at hand, there is intensified war. Instead of the slaughter in Vietnam ending, it has escalated.''[13] There was no doubt anymore that Congress would move rapidly toward a cutoff in aid.

Foreign criticism based on the same assumptions was equally vocal. The Swedish government compared us with the Nazis (having, of course, been neutral during the Second World War). The Danish, Finnish, Dutch, and Belgian governments also castigated the alleged bombing of cities. The French Foreign Minister made allusively critical comments. Not one NATO ally supported us or even hinted at understanding of our point of view — especially painful from countries who were insisting in their own defenses on a strategy involving massive attacks on civilian targets. Interestingly, Peking and Moscow, while critical, were much more balanced, probably because they knew better what we were up against in Hanoi. In Peking a Foreign Ministry statement and a commentary from the New China News Agency castigated the "new barbarous crime" because the bombings had occurred just when "the talks were about to enter their final stage" — a far cry from the allegations rampant in the West that the negotiation was a fraud. Moscow, too, in its formalistic denunciations, emphasized the need to conclude the agreement. If our tea-leaf reading was correct, Moscow and Peking were telling Hanoi that it would not be able to use our bombing to extract another open-ended commitment for continued warfare. Hanoi was being told by its patrons, subtly but unmistakably, to settle. And the countries that had contributed troops to our effort, such as Thailand and South Korea, applauded; those in the direct line of Communist advance, like Indonesia and Malaysia, expressed no opposition to our action publicly, while supporting it privately. Saigon, of course, was delighted; its official spokesman could not restrain himself from an unsubtle dig to the effect that the whole sequence of events had left me in an "embarrassed position."

"Indiscriminate carpet bombing of heavily populated areas" was the principal accusation. Once the phrase caught on among commentators, it took on a life of its own. The facts were otherwise. A scholar who has examined the evidence writes:

These charges are disproven by evidence available then and by later reports from the scene. The North Vietnamese themselves at the time claimed between 1,300 and 1,600 fatalities, and even though both Hanoi and Haiphong were partially evacuated, such a number of victims — regrettable as any civilian casualties always are — is surely not indicative of terror-bombing. Attacks explicitly aimed at the morale of the population took place against Germany and Japan during World War II and killed tens of thousands. According to an East German estimate, 35,000 died in the triple raid on Dresden in February 1945; the official casualty toll of the bombing of Tokyo with incendiaries on 9–10 March 1945, stands at 83,793 dead and 40,918 wounded. The Hanoi death toll, wrote the London *Economist*, "is smaller than the number of civilians killed by the North Vietnamese in their artillery bombardment of An Loc in April or the toll of refugees ambushed when trying to escape from Quang Tri at the beginning of May. This is what makes the denunciation of Mr. Nixon as another Hitler sound so unreal." Part of the death toll was undoubtedly caused by the North Vietnamese themselves, for they launched about 1,000 SAMs, many of which impacted in the cities of Hanoi and Haiphong and took their toll on their own people. . . .

Malcolm W. Browne of the *New York Times* was greatly surprised by the condition in which he found Hanoi and wrote that "the damage caused by American bombing was grossly overstated by North Vietnamese propaganda. . . ." "Hanoi has certainly been damaged," noted Peter Ward of the *Baltimore Sun* on 25 March 1973 after a visit, "but evidence on the ground disproves charges of indiscriminate bombing. Several bomb loads obviously went astray into civilian residential areas, but damage there is minor, compared to the total destruction of selected targets."[14]

Whatever the military facts, in Washington I was in the eye of a hurricane whose elemental force derived not only from the hatreds of the two Vietnams and the hysteria of domestic critics but also from the painful rift between Nixon and me. Even before the Christmas bombing, the White House had taken pains to distance itself from me. I use the words "White House" because I doubt that Nixon ever gave the order explicitly. At the same time he was bound to become restless with an Assistant who was beginning to compete with him for public attention. In early December, *Time* magazine, with the best will in the world, added to earlier irritations by selecting Nixon and me as joint "Men of the Year." I learned of the plan just before going off for the December round of negotiations. I knew immediately how this would go down with my chief, whose limited capacity for forgiveness surely did not include being upstaged (and being giving equal billing as Man of the Year with his Assistant was tantamount to that). After consulting with Ron Ziegler, who shared my perception of the probable reaction, I appealed all the way up the *Time* hierarchy to the editor-in-chief, Hedley Donovan, with the probably unprecedented request to take me off the cover. Donovan put an end to it by replying that if my importuning did not stop I would be made Man of the Year in my own right.

Nixon's brooding disquietude with my newfound celebrity inevitably transmitted itself to his staff, only too eager to build him up and relishing the bonus of cutting me down to size after years of riding so high.[15] And a Presidential Assistant soon learns that his only strength is the President's confidence; without it, his position will rapidly erode. Articles appeared as I was leaving for the December round of negotiations and throughout my stay in Paris that I was being downgraded and losing influence. Laurence Stern had a story to that effect in the *Washington Post* on December 4. He quoted a former White House aide as saying: "If something comes unstuck in Paris, the onus for this particular settlement, as things stand, lies fully on Henry. There is quite a bit of water between Kissinger and the President on the agreement." (To maintain this distance was no doubt a major factor in Nixon's reluctance to explain the negotiating stalemate on national television.) The *Detroit Free Press* had a similar article, carried in all Newhouse papers, on December 7. Stewart Alsop had a story to that effect in *Newsweek* of

December 18. Victor Zorza and Bernard Gwertzman, two experienced Kremlinologists, ruminated on my imminent purge on December 20. In Washington such speculation tends to be self-fulfilling. A common theme of all these stories was that I had exceeded my instructions in the negotiations in October and gone beyond the limits of prudence in the "peace is at hand" conference. Nixon had reined me in; he had made me toughen our stand.

All this nonsense was great so long as the public relations geniuses leaking it had reason to believe that the negotiation would succeed and they would therefore be able to claim afterward that any improvement was due to the President's intercession. But when the negotiation disintegrated, they were hoisted by their own petard. Inevitably, Nixon was being blamed for intransigence; I was identified with the more conciliatory line. (This was in fact untrue. Insofar as Nixon addressed negotiating terms at all, which was only during the December round, he consistently urged greater concessions than I thought prudent, especially on the DMZ. In general, we had no real tactical disagreements between October and December.) And when the bombing started, many journalists applied the very categories so assiduously fed out by White House PR people in the preceding weeks: Nixon was identified with the "hard," I with the "softer" position.

I did not indicate to any journalist that I had opposed the decision to use B-52s. But I also did little to dampen the speculation, partly in reaction to the harassment of the previous weeks, partly out of a not very heroic desire to deflect the assault from my person. Some of the journalists may have mistaken my genuine depression about the seeming collapse of the peace efforts for a moral disagreement. Though I had much provocation and though I acted mainly by omission and partly through emotional exhaustion, it is one of the episodes of my public life in which I take no great pride.

Nixon was justifiably infuriated by the assertion by columnists that I had opposed the bombing. Though our relationship remained professional in the inevitable daily contacts between security adviser and President, there were many telltale signs of Presidential disfavor. I read years later that Nixon had asked Colson to obtain for him daily records of my telephone calls; they were given to the President, I cannot judge for how long.[16] Nor can I be certain whether they included the content of my conversations or simply a listing of my callers. But I sensed enough to conclude that my period in office should draw to a close. As I have mentioned, if the negotiations collapsed I would resign immediately, assuming full responsibility. If they suceeded, I would see the settlement through until it was firmly established and then resign toward the end of 1973. I have no doubt that except for Watergate I would have carried out this plan; throughout the early months of 1973 I moved in that direction.

However, in the middle of a crisis my obligation was to try to hold things together. This meant getting us back to the conference table.

Negotiations Resume

THE prediction that the bombing was destroying all prospects for negotiation was as common and as false as the accusation that it was a massacre of civilians. Exactly the opposite happened. On the morning of December 18, coincident with the resumption of bombing, we sent a message to Hanoi via our Paris channel accusing North Vietnam of "deliberately and frivolously delaying the talks." We proposed both a solution to the negotiating impasse and a date for resuming talks. We suggested returning to the text as it stood at the end of the first round of negotiations on November 23 (before Le Duc Tho withdrew his concessions), and retaining from the December round only the deletion of the phrase "administrative structure" and the proposed signing procedures. I would be prepared to meet Le Duc Tho anytime after December 26.

The first North Vietnamese reaction to the resumed bombing surfaced on December 20 at the technical meetings in Paris where Heyward Isham (sitting in for Porter, who had influenza) was still trying futilely to make progress on the protocols with Hanoi's Vice Foreign Minister Nguyen Co Thach. Thach read a protest that by Hanoi's standards was extremely mild. He "firmly" rejected the allegation of frivolity and adjourned the technical meeting to December 23, a minimum gesture under the circumstances.

On December 22 we took Thach's protest as a pretext for another message to Hanoi. We did not back off; we added the charge of misrepresentation to that of frivolity. Matters had reached a watershed, and we therefore proposed another meeting — this time under a deadline:

> The choice is whether to slide into a continuation of the conflict or to make a serious final effort to reach a settlement at a time when agreement is so near. The U.S. side, preferring the latter course, proposes a meeting between Special Adviser Le Duc Tho and Dr. Kissinger January 3, 1973. Dr. Kissinger could set aside three days for the purpose of concluding the settlement.

If Hanoi agreed to a meeting on these terms, we said that bombing north of the twentieth parallel would stop as of midnight December 31 for the duration of the negotiations.

Thach showed up as promised at the December 23 meeting of the experts; he read another protest and called for another adjournment, this time not setting a new date but inviting us to propose one — a minimal "escalation" of protest, dramatically revealing Hanoi's reluctance to be charged with breaking off the talks.

On December 26 — the day of one of the biggest B-52 raids — we heard directly from Hanoi. It rejected the "ultimatum language" of our previous message — while accepting our terms. It went on for a few pages, summarizing its version of events since October in — for Hanoi — a nonpolemic manner. It then agreed that talks between experts could resume as soon as the bombing stopped. It pleaded that Le Duc Tho could not attend a meeting before January 8 — because of his health. Hanoi affirmed "its constantly serious negotiating attitude" and its willingness "to settle the remaining questions with the U.S. side." We had not heard such a polite tone from the North Vietnamese since the middle of October.

I informed Nixon, who was in Key Biscayne. He wanted to make sure we would stay one jump ahead of the returning Congress. He therefore pressed for an announcement of resumed meetings at the same time as the ending of the bombing. I suggested that we tie down the understandings firmly. I suggested that we, first, demand that the experts resume meetings on January 2; second, reaffirm our proposal put forward on December 18; and third, insist on limiting my meeting with Le Duc Tho to three or four days. In the meantime we would continue bombing. Nixon reluctantly agreed. Musing about possible outcomes he grew quite enthusiastic about his TV appearance should the negotiations succeed; if Hanoi stonewalled again, I was to do the honors in a briefing. I assured him that given Hanoi's soft reaction it would not come to that.

How eager Hanoi was for a bombing halt was shown the next day, when we received another message expressing readiness to resume technical talks as soon as bombing stopped and reaffirming Le Duc Tho's willingness to meet me on January 8.

We replied on December 27, stating the conditions I had outlined to Nixon: Technical meetings would have to resume on January 2; Le Duc Tho and I would meet on January 8; a time limit would be set on the talks. We warned against introducing into the protocols "matters adequately covered by the basic agreement." The resumed negotiations would be announced coincident with the end of the bombing. In order to give Hanoi the maximum incentive to reply speedily (and to meet Nixon's cherished aim of announcing the resumption of negotiations before the return of Congress on January 3), we offered to stop bombing within thirty-six hours of receiving the final confirmation of these procedures. And we ended our message with another warning:

The U.S. side wishes to reaffirm its readiness to reach a rapid settlement. But this requires an end by the DRV of the methods which prevented the conclusion of a settlement in December. If both sides now return to the attitude of good will shown in October, the remaining problems can be rapidly solved. This will be the spirit with which the U.S. side will approach this final effort to conclude the October negotiations.

Hanoi's reply took less than twenty-four hours — an amazing feat considering the time needed for transmission to and from Paris and the time differences. On December 28 it confirmed our proposals as well as its "constantly serious negotiating attitude."

Next day we told Hanoi we were stopping the bombing as of 7:00 P.M. Washington time. We concluded sternly again:

> The U.S. side wants to again affirm that it will make one final major effort to see whether a settlement within the October framework can be worked out. The U.S. side wants to point out that Dr. Kissinger will not be able to spend more than four days in Paris on this occasion. A repetition of the procedures followed in December could lead to a collapse of the talks.
>
> The U.S. side enters these renewed negotiations with goodwill but urges the DRV side to study carefully the U.S. message of December 18, 1972. The decision must be made now whether it is possible to move from a period of hostility to one of normalization. This remains the U.S. goal which will be pursued with great seriousness.
>
> In the interim it is essential that both sides show the maximum restraint in their public pronouncements.

The announcement was made on December 30. I was positive we had won our gamble and that the next round of negotiations would succeed. We could now move into the final phase of ending the war.

There remained our recalcitrant ally in Saigon. We did not want Thieu to believe that the attacks on the North heralded a new period of open-ended warfare; nor did we want him to be misled by the critical outcry against us. On December 17 Nixon, whose disenchantment with Thieu equaled mine, had asked me to prepare a draft letter for General Haig to deliver on another mission to Saigon: "I don't want him to take any heart from the fact that we are hitting Hanoi. . . ."

I submitted a very firm draft to Nixon. Contrary to his habit of signing my drafts without change, Nixon toughened it nearly to the point of brutality. The letter was his "final" considered judgment; it was his "irrevocable" decision to proceed; he did not want Thieu "under any circumstances" to gain the mistaken impression that the military actions against Hanoi signaled a "willingness or intent to continue U.S. military involvement if Hanoi meets the requirements for a settlement which I have set." Nixon drafted the final sentence in his own hand:

> I have asked General Haig to obtain your answer to this absolutely final offer on my part for us to work together in seeking a settlement along the lines I have approved or to go our separate ways. Let me emphasize in conclusion that General Haig is not coming to Saigon for the purpose of negotiating with you. The time has come for us to present a united front in negotiating with our enemies, and you must decide now whether you desire to continue our alliance or

whether you want me to seek a settlement with the enemy which serves U.S. interests alone.

Even this draft was not strong enough for Nixon; he asked me to have it typed up double-spaced, so he could sharpen it even further.

Haig flew to Saigon and met with Thieu on December 19. Haig had sent a message to the Palace beforehand insisting on a private meeting with Thieu and refusing to meet with his entire National Security Council. Whatever one's views of Thieu's attitude one had to admire his constancy. Nha attended Thieu; Bunker accompanied Haig. Thieu orchestrated a replay of the previous dramas. He listened to Haig; he commented perceptively. He said (correctly) that Haig's mission came down to a negotiation for continued American support. He predicted that after all American forces were withdrawn, Hanoi would resume its guerrilla warfare, keeping its provocation below the level that would justify American retaliation (which also proved to be totally correct). He characterized Nixon's letter as an ultimatum, and promised a reply for the next day.

In the meantime Haig visited Lon Nol for our usual shaming encounter. Lon Nol expressed confidence as long as the North Vietnamese kept to the agreement and withdrew their forces from his country. He reaffirmed his willingness to offer a unilateral cease-fire. It was designed to put the onus for continuing the war on the Khmer Rouge. It was nevertheless a most courageous decision by a man who, with all his faults, represented well the aspirations of his people for peace.

The next day, December 20, Haig cabled me: "I am delighted to join the same club that you were initiated into in October." He had had a tentative appointment with Thieu for 11:00 A.M. It was canceled and Haig was asked to stand by. At 3:30 he was finally received and handed a letter that looked to us like a rejection of Nixon's proposal. Thieu withdrew his objections to the political provisions, but he could not accept the continued presence of North Vietnamese forces in the South. Haig and I both recommended to Nixon that we proceed with the negotiations with Hanoi anyway. If Thieu still refused to come along, we would make a bilateral agreement with North Vietnam to withdraw in return for our prisoners. I believe now that Thieu's message was more subtle than we gave him credit for. At no point in his letter did he say he would refuse to sign an agreement. He rejected what he considered — correctly — a derogation of his sovereignty; he was willing to yield to *force majeure,* but not become part of it. From his point of view he was right; and he was in effect giving us — though we did not understand it — the go-ahead for the final act.

No foreign policy event of the Nixon Presidency evoked such outrage as the Christmas bombing. On no issue was he more unjustly treated. It was not a barbarous act of revenge. It did not cause exorbitant casualties by Hanoi's own figures; certainly it cost much less than the continuation of the war, which was the alternative. It is hard to avoid the impression that a decade of frustration with Vietnam, a generation of hostility to Nixon, and — let me be frank — frustration over his electoral triumph coalesced to produce a unanimity of editorial outrage that suppressed all judgment in an emotional orgy. Any other course would almost certainly have witnessed an endless repetition of the tactics of December. Faced with the prospect of an open-ended war and continued bitter divisions, considering that the weather made the usual bombing ineffective, Nixon chose the only weapon he had available. His decision speeded the end of the war; even in retrospect I can think of no other measure that would have.

The January Round

THE renewed negotiations started inauspiciously. On January 2, 1973, the House Democratic caucus voted 154 to 75 to cut off all funds for Indochina military operations contingent only upon the safe withdrawal of American forces and the release of our prisoners. There was no provision for a cease-fire for any of the countries of Indochina, including Vietnam, nor for the DMZ nor for an end to infiltration. The Congress was threatening to abandon *all* our allies in Indochina. On January 4 the Senate Democratic caucus passed a similar resolution by 36 to 12. It was a measure of the extremity in which Hanoi found itself that it felt it could not wait for the almost certain aid cutoff and proceeded with the negotiations.

The technical talks on the protocols reconvened on January 2, led by Bill Sullivan on the American side and Vice Foreign Minister Nguyen Co Thach for Hanoi. The mood at the outset was "deeply somber," Sullivan reported, but eventually the two teams got down to business. On my instructions Sullivan made clear at the outset that the stalling tactics of December were no longer acceptable, and this led to a generally businesslike session. After an opening statement condemning the bombing, the North Vietnamese delegation did not refer to it again. Sullivan reported: "DRV delegation did not repeat not comport itself like a victorious outfit which had just 'defeated the U.S. Strategic Air Force.' It was generally hang dog, although Thach thawed a bit as afternoon wore on."

Over the next few days Thach and Sullivan settled four contentious issues, leaving four others to me and Le Duc Tho. All of this was mildly encouraging. Obviously Hanoi would not show its full hand until Le Duc Tho was on the scene.

On January 4 Nixon met with Rogers, Moorer, Laird, and me. Most of the time was spent on a briefing by Laird and Moorer on the recent bombing, using pictures that showed the success of "smart bombs" against military targets. The rest concerned public relations, with each participant riding his own hobbyhorse: Nixon stressed the hypocrisy and double standard of the media, especially the TV networks; Laird wanted to talk about bombing results; Rogers was looking for material for Congressional briefings; I pleaded that everyone should avoid statements of eagerness that might undermine a negotiation about which I was now quite optimistic.

On January 5 there was another exchange of letters between Nixon and Thieu. Our letter (staff-drafted) reiterated the conditions for which we would settle and concluded:

I can only repeat what I have so often said: The best guarantee for the survival of South Vietnam is the unity of our two countries which would be gravely jeopardized if you persist in your present course. The actions of our Congress since its return have clearly borne out the many warnings we have made.

Should you decide, as I trust you will, to go with us, you have my assurance of continued assistance in the post-settlement period and that we will respond with full force should the settlement be violated by North Vietnam. So once more I conclude with an appeal to you to close ranks with us.

Thieu replied evasively, on January 7, urging Nixon to instruct me to put forward his concerns and stopping far short of endorsing our program. On the other hand he did not say he would refuse to sign.

On January 6 Nixon and I met at Camp David to review final strategy. He urged me to settle on whatever terms were available. Belying his image-makers, he even said he would settle for the October terms. I demurred, pointing out that whatever their merit — and I thought them adequate — they would now inevitably lead to Saigon's collapse. The South Vietnamese had to have something to show for their confrontations with Hanoi and us. At any rate, I was sure it would not come to that. On that day Le Duc Tho arrived in Paris, issuing a bloodcurdling statement whose apparent intransigence actually enhanced our optimism. Tho announced grandly that he had come to Paris to make a "final" effort for a "rapid" settlement. Since this was the precise condition under which we had agreed to resume negotiations, he was simply putting as an ultimatum what we had insisted on as a precondition. He also adamantly rejected any "unreasonable" changes in the October draft, leaving open a door as wide as a barn for "reasonable" changes.

And so on January 8 Le Duc Tho and I met again at Gif-sur-Yvette for what we both had promised would be our last round of negotiations. The ubiquitous journalists were perched on their improvised bleachers and there was the same confusion between appearance and reality. In

December, when he was stalling, Le Duc Tho had been ostentatiously cordial with me outside while being obnoxious at the conference table. Now, to play to our media's outrage at the bombing, he avoided any joint public handshakes with me at all. In fact, no Vietnamese appeared to greet me at the door. It was simply opened from the inside by an unseen factotum. All this evoked many self-satisfied media stories of a chilly atmosphere after our bombing. In fact, relations on the inside, out of sight of the press, were rather warm. All the North Vietnamese were lined up to greet us. Le Duc Tho was brisk and businesslike on the first day, escalating the cordiality when we began to race toward agreement.

The first day's meeting, lasting four and a half hours, was inconclusive. Tho condemned our bombing along standard lines and in a perfunctory manner; the tone was much milder than his airport statement. After my brief rebuttal we got into a procedural wrangle about which issues remained to be settled. We finally agreed that they were the DMZ and the method of signing, which was complicated by the need to avoid putting Saigon into the position of having to recognize the South Vietnamese Communists. Both sides having restated their proposals, we adjourned. Though obviously not yet prepared to reveal how far he was willing to go, Le Duc Tho took pains to foreshadow flexibility. As the meeting broke up he stressed that he would take our requirements into account when speaking the next day — something we had never heard before. (During the lunch break he had taken me aside to stress again that he was having difficulty with his colleagues in the Politburo who thought him too flexible. If this were true, it was beyond my imagination what his hard-line colleagues might be like.) I reported cautiously to the President:

It is impossible to draw any meaningful conclusion from this meeting. Realistically it would be impossible for them to cave on the issues on the first day at the conference table after intensive B-52 bombing. Thus they could be following the essential procedure of the technical talks at which they didn't give much ground the first day. On the other hand, it is equally possible that they are stonewalling us again as they did in December. Under this hypothesis the progress this past week on technical talks would only be their way of removing the propaganda vulnerability of their position concerning international control machinery. We meet again tomorrow at 10 a.m. and should have clearer indications of their intentions at that session.

The breakthrough came at the next session on January 9. As in December, the meetings now alternated between a Vietnamese and an American location. Colonel Guay had discovered the residence of an American businessman located on a golf course in Saint-Nom-la-Bretèche, not too far from Versailles. There, in verdant surroundings where we could stroll in relative tranquillity during breaks, it quickly became apparent that Tho had come to settle. He proposed that Thach and Sullivan be assigned to work full-time on the protocols and not participate in our main talks. I agreed. He then said:

In order to prove our seriousness and good will to find a rapid solution, we should adequately take into account each other's attitude. Naturally, there should be mutual concession and there should be reciprocity. If one keeps one's own stand then no settlement is possible. Do you agree with me on these lines?

I did indeed; though in fact my goodwill was scarcely tested, for Le Duc Tho in effect accepted our proposal of December 18. He agreed to the draft as it stood on November 23 at the end of the first session after the election, including all the twelve changes he had made during that session. He agreed to my compromise formulation on the Demilitarized Zone, which he had adamantly rejected in December. It was Nixon's sixtieth birthday. I reported to Washington:

We celebrated the President's birthday today by making a major breakthrough in the negotiations. In sum, we settled all the outstanding questions in the text of the agreement, made major progress on the method of signing the agreement, and made a constructive beginning on the associated understandings. . . .

The Vietnamese have broken our heart several times before, and we just cannot assume success until everything is pinned down, but the mood and the businesslike approach was as close to October as we have seen since October.

Despite the tensions with Nixon of recent weeks I owed him a heartfelt recognition:

What brought us to this point is the President's firmness and the North Vietnamese belief that he will not be affected by either Congressional or public pressures. Le Duc Tho has repeatedly made these points to me. So it is essential that we keep our fierce posture during the coming days. The slightest hint of eagerness could prove suicidal.

Nixon flashed back: "I greatly appreciated your birthday greetings and your report. . . . If the other side stays on this track and doesn't go downhill tomorrow, what you have done today is the best birthday present I have had in sixty years."

Great events rarely have a dramatic conclusion. More frequently, they dissolve into a host of technical details. So it was in Paris in January. After the DMZ issue was settled there remained primarily the theological issue of how to sign the documents so that Saigon did not have to acknowledge the Communist-front Provisional Revolutionary Government. After several days of haggling we devised a formula according to which the PRG was not mentioned in the document; the agreement to end the war in Vietnam has the distinction of being the only document with which I am familiar in diplomatic history that does not mention all of the main parties. Nor was it signed on the same page by the parties making peace. The South Vietnamese Communists signed together with Hanoi on one page, Saigon and the United States on another. The negotiations had begun in 1968 with a haggle over the shape of the table; they ended in 1973 with a haggle, in effect, over the same problem.

Once the deadlock was broken, the tension all but vanished. Barring a sudden change in signals from Hanoi, a settlement was now inevitable; and Le Duc Tho held course. He now agreed that Hanoi would bring about a cease-fire in Laos within fifteen days of the Vietnam cease-fire. Only poor Cambodia had to be satisfied with verbal assurances. Le Duc Tho repeated Hanoi's difficulty with the Khmer Rouge:

> I told you on many occasions that we want peace, we want peace in Vietnam and in Laos, and after peace is restored in Vietnam and in Laos we also want peace to be restored in Cambodia. Therefore I told you that when peace is restored in Vietnam then the objective conditions, partly, and our subjective desire on our part, will contribute to the peace in Cambodia. But practically speaking, when discussing with our allies in Cambodia it is not as easy as when we discuss with our allies in Laos. But I am firmly convinced that the restoration of peace in Vietnam and in Laos will create favorable conditions for the restoration of peace in Cambodia, some objective conditions for that. But as far as we are concerned when we have a peace in Vietnam and when our allies in Laos have peace in their country, it is illogical that we still want war in another place.

Hanoi may have had its troubles with the Khmer Rouge, but there would be no possible Congressional or public support for holding up a cease-fire over its ambiguity on Cambodia. I had pressed as hard as I could, for months, for a cease-fire in Cambodia, to no avail. It was a pity. Of all the countries in Indochina the Cambodians behaved most nobly and suffered for their patriotism in the most cruel fashion — not least at the hand of those in our country who professed to be outraged at our alleged violation of their neutrality and who then moved heaven and earth to prevent adequate support for them when North Vietnamese divisions and the Khmer Rouge were despoiling that innocent country long after our troops had left.

As we approached a conclusion there was no longer in our group that elation which accompanied the breakthrough in October. The December negotiations had brought home to us the abiding mutual hatred of the two Vietnams. We knew that a bitter struggle with Thieu still lay ahead. We had learned how thin was the veneer of affability of Hanoi's leadership, whose single-minded quest for hegemony, we were certain, would continue after a settlement. But while we knew that preserving the agreement would involve a struggle, we also had confidence of being able to do so. We were now beyond illusion, but not beyond a sense of grateful relief at the peril we had so nearly overcome and of hope that after all a time of healing might be ahead of us at home.

I and my colleagues — Bill Sullivan, Winston Lord, John Negroponte, David Engel, and Peter Rodman, joined toward the end by George Aldrich, Deputy Legal Adviser at the State Department — worked fifteen hours a day in negotiating sessions, reviewing drafts, briefing the South Vietnamese, exchanging cables with Washington. (We were comforted not a little by Dr. Kenneth Riland, whom the ever-thoughtful Nelson Rockefeller had sent along to minister to backs tight with tension.) It was agreed that Haig would leave for Saigon within twenty-four hours after we completed all texts in Paris. Within forty-eight hours all bombing of the North would stop. About January 18 it would be announced that I would return to Paris around January 23 to complete the agreement. The White House, liberated from the nightmare of failure, turned with a will to the public relations scenario. The President was looking to a role for himself prior to the January 23 initialing. Frantic cables went back and forth; Inauguration festivities complicated the problem of finding a time for an announcement both pregnant with meaning and sufficiently low-key not to tempt the North Vietnamese into another fit of stonewalling. Saigon perversely solved the problem by withholding its concurrence until January 20; Nixon judged wisely that he should not risk the prestige of the Presidency until all parties were irrevocably signed up.

At last on Saturday, January 13, at our meeting place in Saint-Nom-la-Bretèche, the draft agreement was once again complete, together with all understandings and protocols. The two delegations had never had any social contact except for brief bantering during breaks. In the first meetings little food was served. Afterward each delegation served meals at its place but in separate dining facilities. On January 13, 1973, we ate for the first time as a group. I had a meal brought in; Vietnamese and Americans sat alternately around the table. Tho and I made toasts to a lasting peace and friendship between our peoples.

In the negotiations since November 20 a number of changes had been achieved. The provision for our continued military support for Saigon had been expanded to permit in effect unrestricted military assistance. The phrase "administrative structure" to describe the National Council of National Reconciliation and Concord had been dropped, underlining its essential impotence. The functions of the Council had been further reduced, by taking away from it any role in "the maintenance of the cease-fire and the preservation of peace" that had been in the earlier draft. The Demilitarized Zone was explicitly reaffirmed in the precise terms of the provisions that established it in the Geneva Accords. A provision had been added that the parties undertook to refrain from using Cambodia and Laos "to encroach on the sovereignty and security of one another and of other countries." This provision, aimed at the establishment of sanctuaries, was intended to reinforce the earlier one requiring the withdrawal of foreign forces. The international control machinery, now expanded to 1,160 people, was ready to begin operating on the day the agreement was signed. A number of invidious references to the United States had been eliminated; a few additional technical improvements were made. All the protocols and understandings essential to implementing the agreement effectively were completed.

Was it worth it? Were the changes significant enough to justify the anguish and bitterness of those last months of the war? Probably not for us; almost surely for Saigon, about whose survival the war had, after all, been fought. Obviously, we thought the agreement of October adequate or we would not have proceeded with it. But the viability of any agreement depends on the willing cooperation of the parties. Once Thieu balked, we were doomed to what actually followed. We could not in all conscience end a war on behalf of the independence of South Vietnam by imposing an unacceptable peace on our ally. Had we attempted to do so in the last two weeks before the election, we would have been justly accused of playing politics with the destiny of millions. And the attempt would have failed. As it was, it required nearly three months, about twenty changes in the text of the agreement, and the threat of an American aid cutoff to obtain Thieu's acquiescence.

Peace involving American withdrawal was a traumatic event for the South Vietnamese. It could not be sprung on a people who for over a decade had suffered from Communist terrorism and the ravages of war. Thieu had to prepare it carefully and in such a way as to stamp himself as a Vietnamese nationalist. Thieu had to inure his people to our physical absence and he had to steel them to their psychological independence by a show of defiance. That his methods were obnoxiously Vietnamese, that in the process he nearly wrecked our own internal cohesion, does not alter the reality that he fought valiantly, that he was right by his lights and the realities of what he knew of Hanoi's purposes. None of this excuses his egregious, almost maniacal, tactics and his total insensitivity to our necessities.

I have wrestled with the question in my own mind whether if I had dealt with Thieu in a more forthcoming way in October, the problems would have been avoided. Perhaps if I had brought him into the process earlier, he would have had one less grievance against me. But had I brought the original proposal of October 8 to Thieu, his reaction would have been no different and since it was not yet improved he would have resisted even more fiercely. Saigon's guerrilla warfare against the agreement would have started immediately; the improvements we ruthlessly extorted in return for accepting a "shedyule" would have evaporated.

Hanoi would have published its text earlier. We would have been under enormous pressure to accept and our bargaining position would have eroded. Hanoi's December performance would have come sooner, and we would have had no base from which to negotiate. Paradoxically, therefore, a more deliberate pace would almost surely have produced a much worse agreement, not changed Saigon's attitude, increased our domestic division, and magnified the risk of collapse. Nailing down the agreement in October may have been indispensable to holding the pieces together later through what was bound to be a chaotic denouement of a bitter war.

As for the anguish in December, the responsibility is Hanoi's. The sixty-nine changes sought by Saigon, galling as they may have been, had almost all been disposed of by then. We were on the verge of completion — until Hanoi, for reasons I am still not sure I fully understand, made an evident strategic decision to halt the negotiation. The "improvement" at stake at that point was thus not some particular disputed clause but the difference between a settlement and no settlement at all. *That,* to my mind, was worth the agony of December.

Thieu Relents

I RETURNED to the United States on January 13, stopping in Washington only to pick up Haig for the trip to Key Biscayne. The White House public relations exercise to cut me down to size was still perceptible. A large press contingent was waiting, but my plane was ordered by the control tower to a distant corner of Homestead Air Force Base, out of range of even telescopic lenses.

The weird part of my relationship with Nixon during this period, as I have said, was that despite its latent tensions — which I could deduce from the attitude of his associates and which found their way into most of their memoirs — we dealt with each other in a most cordial manner. That strange man who could be so ruthless, fierce, and devious in defending his turf was capable of considerable gentleness in his personal dealings. I reported to Nixon around midnight; we met for over two hours until 2:30 A.M. (it was 8:30 A.M. by my inner clock), reviewing the negotiation and the long ordeal that had brought us to this point. Though I was unhappy with some of Nixon's actions toward me, though I objected to some of his tactics, I felt that night an odd tenderness toward him. He had seen our country through perilous times. He had reached his decisions by arcane processes. But he had honored me by his trust, and at the end of the day he had sought to sustain our country's strength and dignity as he saw it, and he revolutionized international diplomacy. Much intelligence and much knowledge lay behind his accomplishments. He was entitled in an hour of triumph to the limelight that had so pitilessly beaten down on him through all his adversities. And in this mellow mood we reviewed where we stood and how to proceed toward the peace that was now so near. We spoke to each other in nearly affectionate terms, like veterans of bitter battles at a last reunion, even though we both sensed somehow that too much had happened between us to make the rest of the journey together.

Haig would leave the next evening (January 14) for Saigon with an ultimatum that we would sign the document, if necessary without Thieu. On January 15 the White House would announce the end of bombing; on January 18 it would be announced that I would return to Paris on January 23 to "complete the agreement." Nixon would address the nation that evening. The formal signature by foreign ministers would take place in Paris on January 27. As a sop to Rogers I had agreed not to attend the final culmination of these efforts. What we had struggled prayed, hoped, and perhaps even hated for — the end of our involvement in Indochina, and peace — was about to be celebrated.

But we still did not have the agreement of that doughty little man in Saigon, President Thieu. Nixon was determined to prevail. "Brutality is nothing," he said to me. "You have never seen it if this son-of-a-bitch doesn't go along, believe me." Haig delivered a scorching letter from Nixon to Thieu on January 16. It summed up all the advantages of the agreement and listed the improvements which had been achieved in the November and December negotiations. Its crucial paragraph read:

I have therefore irrevocably decided to proceed to initial the Agreement on January 23, 1973 and to sign it on January 27, 1973 in Paris. I will do so, if necessary, alone. In that case I shall have to explain publicly that your Government obstructs peace. The result will be an inevitable and immediate termination of U.S. economic and military assistance which cannot be forestalled by a change of personnel in your government. I hope, however, that after all our two countries have shared and suffered together in conflict, we will stay together to preserve peace and reap its benefits.

Haig, as instructed, demanded an answer by the evening of January 17.

But Thieu would not yield yet. He complained that the draft still lacked "balance." He now admitted that his forces would be able to handle the North Vietnamese remaining in the South; but their continued presence was a psychological challenge that he was duty-bound to resist. Haig thought, as we had so often before, that at the end of the day Thieu would agree to join us.

Thieu once again surprised us. On January 17 he handed Haig a letter to Nixon asking for one more effort to bring about some changes, this time in the protocols. But it was futile, as Thieu must have known. The texts were now frozen; no further negotiation could take place. Nixon replied the same day. The letter summed up once again all the arguments and threats of the previous message. It demanded a reply by the morning of January 20 — Inauguration Day — when Haig would return to Saigon after having briefed the other countries of the area. Failure to answer by that time would be treated as a refusal. "The responsibility for the consequences rests with the Government of Vietnam."

On January 18, at our suggestion, Senators John Stennis and Barry Goldwater, both staunch supporters of Saigon, warned publicly that if Saigon blocked the agreement it would imperil its relations with the United States. We heard from Thieu right on the deadline Nixon had set him, January 20. He was sending Foreign Minister Lam to Paris, he said, to take personal charge of the final round of negotiations, almost certainly a face-saving formula indicating that he would sign. He still demanded a few textual changes, a gesture that again he must have known was only for the record. Nixon riposted that he would need Thieu's agreement by noon the next day or else he would brief legislative leaders that Thieu had refused to go along, with the all the attendant consequences. (These letters, like almost all communications except the one on December 17, were written by me and my associates and approved by Nixon.) On January 21 Thieu relented with dignity, requesting only some unilateral statements by the United States that we recognized Saigon as the legal government of South Vietnam and that Hanoi had no right to maintain troops there. This was consistent with our interpretation of the agreement; the treaty gave no sanction to foreign troops and referred in several places to the "sovereignty of South Vietnam." We gave these assurances.

I believed then, and I believe now, that the agreement could have worked. It reflected a true equilibrium of forces on the ground. If the equilibrium were maintained, the agreement could have been maintained. We believed that Saigon was strong enough to deal with guerrilla war and low-level violations. The implicit threat of our retaliation would be likely to deter massive violations. We hoped that with the program of assistance for all of Indochina, including North Vietnam, promised by two Presidents of both parties, we might possibly even turn Hanoi's attention (and manpower) to tasks of construction if the new realities took hold for a sufficient period of time. Hanoi was indeed instructing its cadres in the South to prepare for a long period of *political* competition. We would use our new relationships with Moscow and Peking to foster restraint.

We had no illusions about Hanoi's long-term goals. Nor did we go through the agony of four years of war and searing negotiations simply to achieve a "decent interval" for our withdrawal. We were determined to do our utmost to enable Saigon to grow in security and prosperity so that it could prevail in any political struggle. We sought not an interval before collapse, but lasting peace with honor. But for the collapse of executive authority as a result of Watergate, I believe we would have succeeded.

XXXIV

Peace at Last

RICHARD NIXON's second Inaugural took place on a day much like his first, cold and clear and blustery. I sat on the platform behind the Cabinet with my eighty-six-year-old father. I was no longer surprised at being there, but I was somewhat stunned by the emotional events of the past months. The war would now soon be over and hope was pervasive. Senators and Congressmen came over to chat and to congratulate; my father, whose life's efforts had been destroyed when Nazism took over his native land, was beaming. He could not really believe what had happened; in a strange way all the anguish of his life seemed vindicated.

There was a blare of trumpets and Nixon appeared to the tune of "Hail to the Chief." He too seemed as if he could not really believe it had all happened; a term in office had not abated his sense of wonder at being there. And he seemed, if not really happy, indeed quite detached.

Triumph seemed to fill Nixon with a premonition of ephemerality. He was, as he never tired of repeating, at his best under pressure. Indeed, it was sometimes difficult to avoid the impression that he needed crises as a motivating force — and that success became not a goal but an obsession so that once achieved he would not know what to do with it. The festivities surrounding the Inauguration were large but not buoyant. Participants acted as if they had earned their presence rather than as if they shared in a new common purpose. Through it all Richard Nixon moved as if he were himself a spectator, not the principal. He had brought off spectacular successes. He had achieved the international goals he had set for the first term. He had before him a blank canvas, one of the rare times in history that a President could devote himself substantially to new and creative tasks of diplomacy. The legacies of the past were being overcome, the international environment was fluid, as happens at most once in a generation — waiting to be shaped. And yet there was about him this day a quality of remoteness, as if he could never quite bring himself to leave the inhospitable and hostile world that he inhabited, that he may have hated but at least had come to terms with. Perhaps it was simple shyness or fatalism; perhaps it was the consciousness of a looming catastrophe.

Two days later, January 22, I left for Paris for the final meeting with Le Duc Tho. It was to take place for the first time on neutral and ceremonial ground in a small conference room at Avenue Kléber, the scene of 174 futile plenary sessions since 1968. Even now it would be used for only a symbolic event. Sullivan and Thach had spent several days checking all the texts. In a final paranoiac gesture the North Vietnamese insisted that on completion each text be bound by string and the string sealed — I suppose to prevent us from deviously slipping in new pages overnight.

When I arrived in Paris, I learned that Lyndon Johnson had died that day. He was himself a casualty of the Vietnam war, which he had inherited and then expanded in striving to fulfill his conception of our nation's duty and of his obligation to his fallen predecessor. There was nothing he had wanted less than to be a war President, and this no doubt contributed to his inconclusive conduct of the struggle. In retirement he had behaved with dignity not untinged by melancholy, burdened with the terrible truth that the only pursuit he really cared about, that of public service, was now closed to him — like a surgeon who at the height of his prowess is barred forever from entering a hospital. Haldeman had phoned him on January 15 to tell him that the bombing would stop. (I had briefed him on Nixon's behalf many times in the past, but, now reduced to a "lower profile," I had been requested by Haldeman not to do so.) But I had sent him a copy of the peace agreement, with a warm note. It was symbolic that this hulking, imperious, vulnerable, expansive, aspiring man, so full of life, should die with the war that had broken his heart.

The meeting started at 9:35 A.M., Tuesday, January 23. Le Duc Tho managed even on this solemn occasion to make himself obnoxious by insisting on ironclad assurances of American economic aid to North Vietnam. I told him that this could not be discussed further until after the agreement was signed; it also depended on Congressional approval and on observance of the agreement. Finally, at a quarter to one, we initialed the various texts and improvised brief closing statements. Le Duc Tho said:

Mr. Adviser, we have been negotiating for almost five years now. I can say this is now the beginning of a new atmosphere between us. It is also the first stone [sic] which marks our new relationship between our two countries, although the official signing ceremony will take place in a few days time. The restoration of peace is the aspiration of the Vietnamese people, the American people and also the people of the world.

So today we have accomplished our work. I talked to your Government through you and you talked to my Government through me. We, both of us, should not forget this historical day. Because it is a long distance and difficult way before we come to this, but now we have overcome all these difficulties. It is a subject for satisfaction between us, for you and for me. And the Agreement will be officially signed in a few days. I solemnly respect [*sic*] here to you that we will strictly implement the Agreement. I think that both of us should do the same, if lasting peace is to be maintained in Vietnam and in Southeast Asia.

And I replied:

Mr. Special Adviser, our two peoples have suffered a great deal. There have been many painful moments and much destruction. You and I have had the great honor of putting an end to this. It is something we can never forget.

But our work will not be complete unless we bring a lasting peace to the people of Indochina, and an atmosphere of reconciliation between the people of North Vietnam and the people of the United States. I would like also solemnly to promise you that we will strictly implement the Agreement. Beyond that, we shall dedicate ourselves to the improvement of the relationship between our two countries. I think you and I have a special relationship and a special obligation in this respect. So our work today completes our negotiations. And I hope that we will be able to look back to this day as the point which marked the beginning of friendship between the people of North Vietnam and the United States.

After this Le Duc Tho and I stepped out on the street in a cold misty rain, and shook hands for the benefit of photographers. I lunched with Foreign Minister Lam of South Vietnam. He behaved with dignity and courage, giving no hint of the bitter dispute of recent months.

America's Vietnam war was over.

Postlude

ON January 23, Washington was, as always before great events, consumed in technicalities. I arrived back in my office around 6:35 P.M. the same day, a few hours before Nixon was to announce the agreement and the cease-fire. For once I was not asked to brief the press until the next day. It was felt, correctly, that the President's speech would require no elaboration. The President briefed the Congressional leaders in the Cabinet Room, doing most of the explaining himself.

I sat alone in my office, waiting for Nixon's speech to the nation. It was the culmination of all we had endured and endeavored for four years. Over two million Americans had given parts of their lives to that distant land. Over forty-five thousand had laid down their lives for it; several hundred thousand had been wounded. They and their families could now take some pride that it had not all been in vain. Those who had opposed the effort in Indochina would, we could hope, close ranks now that their goal of peace had finally been achieved. And the peoples of South Vietnam, Laos, and Cambodia would perhaps attain at long last a future of tranquillity, security, and progress, a future worthy of their sacrifices.

We stood, I fervently hoped, at the threshold of a period of national reconciliation that would be given impetus by the unique opportunity for creativity I saw ahead. Perhaps America had found the way to merge the idealism of the early Sixties with the sterner pragmatism of the recent past. China was now an important friend; we had built a new basis for stable relations with the Soviet Union through a Berlin agreement, the first strategic arms limitation treaty, and an agreed code of international conduct. The diplomatic revolution that had been brought about opened up an extraordinary opportunity for American diplomacy. This, in addition to the dispelling of our Vietnam trauma, was a reason for enormous hope. We had eased relations with adversaries; it was now time to turn to reinvigorating relations with friends, and to resolving unsolved problems. We had decided to make 1973 the Year of Europe, to reaffirm our Alliance ties with the Atlantic Community — and also Japan. We would show that these ties were stronger and deeper than the tentative new relations with Communist countries. On the basis of Alliance cohesion and vitality we would test the real opportunities for détente. We were at a moment of extraordinary opportunity in the Middle East; I was set to meet with President Sadat's national security adviser, Hafiz Ismail, in February — my first step as a Middle East negotiator. Nixon entered his second term with an overwhelming public mandate, a strong executive at the height of his prestige.

Only rarely in history do statesmen find an environment in which all factors are so malleable; before us, I thought, was the chance to shape events, to build a new world, harnessing the energy and dreams of the American people, and mankind's hopes. Almost certainly I would not be able to take part in the whole enterprise over four years; after the peace was well established I would leave — perhaps toward the end of the year. I was grateful for the opportunity I had enjoyed to help prepare the ground.

Nixon spoke at 10:00 P.M. briefly and with conciliation. He paid tribute to Lyndon Johnson, who had yearned for that day, and he asked Americans to consecrate themselves to "make the peace we have achieved a peace that would last."

I called Nixon immediately afterward, as I had done after every major speech, to congratulate him. He seemed incapable of resting on any achievement. He was already worrying about the Congressional briefings that would start next day.

Mrs. Nixon took the phone to congratulate me. It took stout hearts to see it through, she said. What a gallant lady she had been. With pain and stoicism, she had suffered the calumny and hatred that seemed to follow her husband. Unlike the President, she was not capable of the fantasy life in which romantic imaginings embellished the often self-inflicted daily disappointments. She was totally without illusions and totally insistent on facing her trials in solitude. Her dignity never wavered. And if she seemed remote, who could know what fires had had to be banked in her stern existence. She made no claims on anyone; her fortitude had been awesome and not a little inspiring because one sensed that it had been wrested from an essential gentleness.

A few minutes later Nelson Rockefeller called. He had introduced me to public life and sustained me throughout. In a strange way he was both inarticulate and a bit shy, and yet enveloping in his warmth. One had to know him well to understand the tactile manner in which he communicated — the meanings of the little winks, nudges, and mumbles by which he conveyed that he cared, and conferred comfort and inward security. And he was quintessentially American in his unquenchable optimism. He could never imagine that a wrong could not be righted or that effort could not conquer obstacles in the way of honorable goals. He was always encouraging, supportive. He had been there matter-of-factly, unasked, through every crisis of those years. And in this spirit he spoke to me with pride of what his country had accomplished. He saw in America's strength a blessing conferring a duty — to defend the free, to give hope to the disadvantaged, and to walk truly in the paths of justice and mercy.

Around midnight, when I was at home, Nixon called from the Lincoln Sitting Room, where he was brooding alone. He was wondering whether the press would appreciate what had been done; probably not. But that was not what he really had on his mind. He knew that every success brings a terrific letdown, he said. I should not let it get to me. I should not be discouraged. There were many battles yet to fight; I should not weaken. In fact, I was neither discouraged nor did I feel let down. Listening to him, I could picture the scene: Nixon would be sitting solitary and withdrawn, deep in his brown stuffed chair with his legs on a settee in front of him, a small reading light breaking the darkness, and a wood fire throwing shadows on the wall of the room. The loudspeakers would be playing romantic classical music, probably Tchaikovsky. He was talking to me, but he was really addressing himself.

What extraordinary vehicles destiny selects to accomplish its design. This man, so lonely in his hour of triumph, so ungenerous in some of his motivations, had navigated our nation through one of the most anguishing periods in its history. Not by nature courageous, he had steeled himself to conspicuous acts of rare courage. Not normally outgoing, he had forced himself to rally his people to its challenge. He had striven for a revolution in American foreign policy so that it would overcome the disastrous oscillations between overcommitment and isolation. Despised by the Establishment, ambiguous in his human perceptions, he had yet held fast to a sense of national honor and responsibility, determined to prove that the strongest free country had no right to abdicate. What would have happened had the Establishment about which he was so ambivalent shown him some love? Would he have withdrawn deeper into the wilderness of his resentments, or would an act of grace have liberated him? By now it no longer mattered. Enveloped in an intractable solitude, at the end of a period of bitter division, he nevertheless saw before him a vista of promise to which few statesmen have been blessed to aspire. He could envisage a new international order that would reduce lingering enmities, strengthen friendships, and give new hope to emerging nations. It was a worthy goal for America and mankind. He was alone in his moment of triumph on a pinnacle, that was soon to turn into a precipice. And yet with all his insecurities and flaws he had brought us by a tremendous act of will to an extraordinary moment when dreams and possibilities conjoined.

These things passed through my mind that evening after at long last I had placed my initials on the Paris Agreement on Ending the War and Restoring Peace in Vietnam. And I was at peace with myself, neither elated nor sad.

Chapter Notes

II
PERIOD OF INNOCENCE: THE TRANSITION

1. Michel Crozier, *The Bureaucratic Phenomenon* (Chicago: University of Chicago Press, 1964), pp. 44–55, 187–198.
2. Melvin R. Laird, intro., *The Conservative Papers* (Garden City, N.Y.: Anchor Books, Doubleday & Co., 1964).
3. See, e.g., Roger Morris, *Uncertain Greatness* (New York: Harper and Row, 1977), chapter II, "*Coup d'Etat* at the Hotel Pierre."
4. The relevant passage in Nixon's first Inaugural address reads:

    After a period of confrontation, we are entering an era of negotiation.

    Let all nations know that during this Administration our lines of communication will be open.

    We seek an open world — open to ideas, open to the exchange of goods and people — a world in which no people, great or small, will live in angry isolation.

    We cannot expect to make everyone our friend, but we can try to make no one our enemy.

    Those who would be our adversaries, we invite to a peaceful competition — not in conquering territory or extending dominion, but in enriching the life of man.

    As we explore the reaches of space, let us go to the new worlds together — not as new worlds to be conquered, but as a new adventure to be shared.

    With those who are willing to join, let us cooperate to reduce the burden of arms, to strengthen the structure of peace, to lift up the poor and the hungry.

    But to all those who would be tempted by weakness, let us leave no doubt that we will be as strong as we need to be for as long as we need to be.

III
THE CONVICTIONS OF AN APPRENTICE STATESMAN

1. I have discussed the concept of "containment" in *Nuclear Weapons and Foreign Policy* (New York: Harper and Bros., 1957), chapter 2. An excellent analysis may be found in Coral Bell, *Negotiation from Strength* (New York: Alfred A. Knopf, Inc., 1963).
2. US Congress, Senate, Committee on Armed Services and Committee on Foreign Relations, *Hearings on the Military Situation in the Far East,* 82d Cong., 1st sess., 1951, p. 2083.
3. Speech at Llandudno, Wales, Oct. 9, 1948, quoted in *New York Times,* Oct. 10, 1948.
4. "Central Issues of American Foreign Policy," in Kermit Gordon, ed., *Agenda for the Nation* (Washington: The Brookings Institution, 1968), p. 614.

IV
EUROPEAN JOURNEY

1. "Central Issues of American Foreign Policy," in Kermit Gordon, ed., *Agenda for the Nation* (Washington: The Brookings Institution, 1968), p. 595.
2. *The Troubled Partnership: A Re-appraisal of the Atlantic Alliance* (New York: McGraw-Hill, 1965), p. 40.
3. See Walt W. Rostow, "Limits and Responsibilities of American Power," speech at Texas A

& M University, Dec. 4, 1968 (in *Department of State Bulletin*, vol. LX, no. 1541, Jan. 6, 1969).

4. See Francis M. Bator, "The Politics of Alliance: The United States and Western Europe," in Gordon, ed., *Agenda for the Nation*, p. 339.

5. Alastair Buchan, *Europe's Futures, Europe's Choices* (New York: Columbia University Press, 1969), p. vii.

6. See André Malraux, *Felled Oaks: Conversation with de Gaulle* (New York: Holt, Rinehart and Winston, 1971), p. 30.

7. "Central Issues of American Foreign Policy," in Gordon, ed., *Agenda for the Nation*, p. 599.

8. Address by President de Gaulle on May 31, 1960, in *Major Addresses, Statements and Press Conferences of General Charles de Gaulle, May 19, 1958–January 31, 1964* (New York: French Embassy, Press and Information Division, 1964), p. 75.

9. Ibid., p. 78.

10. Press conference of May 15, 1962, *Major Addresses*, p. 176.

11. Press conference of Sept. 5, 1960, *Major Addresses*, pp. 92–93.

V
OPENING MOVES WITH MOSCOW

1. V. I. Lenin, *Selected Works* (New York: International Publishers, 1943), vol. 9, pp. 242 and 267, quoted by Nathan Leites, *A Study of Bolshevism* (Glencoe, Ill.: The Free Press, 1953), p. 347.

2. Nikita Khrushchev, Report to the Twentieth Party Congress of the CPSU, February 1956, *Current Digest of the Soviet Press*, vol. 8 (March 7, 1956), pp. 11–12.

3. Nikolai Podgorny, in *Pravda*, November 20, 1973.

4. Lenin, *Selected Works*, vol. 10, p. 119, quoted by Leites, p. 495.

5. Michael T. Florinsky, *World Revolution and the USSR* (New York: The Macmillan Co., 1933), p. 216.

6. *New York Times*, May 23, 1943.

7. Sumner Welles, *The Time for Decision* (Cleveland and New York: The World Publishing Co., 1944), p. 406.

8. Averell Harriman, *Peace with Russia* (New York, 1959), p. 168.

9. "Why We Treat Different Communist Countries Differently," address by Secretary Rusk, Washington, D.C., Feb. 25, 1964 (in *Department of State Bulletin*, vol. L, no. 1290, March 16, 1964, p. 393).

10. Robert E. Sherwood, *Roosevelt and Hopkins: An Intimate History* (New York: Harper and Bros., 1948), p. 870.

11. See Max Frankel, "Where Do We Go From Victory?" *The Reporter*, Nov. 22, 1962, p. 24.

12. Macmillan's closing statement at Geneva Foreign Ministers' Conference, Nov. 16, 1955, quoted in *Documents on International Affairs 1955* (Oxford: Royal Institute of International Affairs, 1958), pp. 73–77.

13. "Central Issues of American Foreign Policy," in Kermit Gordon, ed., *Agenda for the Nation* (Washington: The Brookings Institution, 1968), p. 609.

14. *The Necessity for Choice* (New York: Harper and Bros., 1961), pp. 195–196.

15. Zbigniew Brzezinski, "Peace and Power," *Encounter*, vol. XXXI, no. 5 (November 1968), p. 13.

16. Marshall D. Shulman, "The Future of the Soviet-American Competition," in *Soviet-American Relations and World Order: The Two and the Many*, Adelphi Paper No. 66 (London: Institute for Strategic Studies, March 1970), p. 10.

17. Clifford speech quoted by Senator Albert Gore in US Congress, Senate, Committee on Foreign Relations, *Strategic and Foreign Policy Implications of ABM Systems, Hearings before the Subcommittee on International Organization and Disarmament Affairs*, 91st Cong., 1st sess., March 21, 1969, p. 165.

18. See, e.g., Stephen S. Rosenfeld, "Nixon's Trip Plans May Affect Talks," *Washington Post*, July 6, 1969; James Reston, "President Nixon's Avoidable Blunders," *New York Times*, June 29, 1969; and editorial in *New York Times*, June 30, 1969.

VI
FIRST STEPS TOWARD CHINA

1. *U.S. News & World Report,* Sept. 16, 1968, p. 48.
2. *The Necessity for Choice* (New York: Harper and Bros., 1961), p. 202. In my book on Europe, published in 1965, I saw some merit in President de Gaulle's conception of China as a necessary counterweight to the Soviet Union, though I tended also to regard China as an objective problem for the United States' "global responsibilities." *The Troubled Partnership* (New York: McGraw-Hill, 1965), pp. 59–60.
3. Most of what we know of what took place on the Ussuri River is based on the published accounts of both sides. These accounts are analyzed in Thomas W. Robinson, *The Sino-Soviet Border Dispute: Background, Development, and the March 1969 Clashes,* The Rand Corp., August 1970 (RM–6171–PR). See also Neville Maxwell, "The Chinese Account of the 1969 Fighting at Chenpao," *The China Quarterly,* no. 56 (October–December 1973), p. 730.
4. Maxwell, "The Chinese Account," p. 731.
5. See the *Washington Star* of Aug. 28 and 29, 1969. The *Star* felt free to break the "background" rule because it had not been invited to the luncheon.

VII
DEFENSE POLICY AND STRATEGY

1. Kuznetsov quoted in Charles E. Bohlen, *Witness to History 1929–1969* (New York: W. W. Norton and Co., 1973), pp. 495–496.
2. Albert Wohlstetter, "Is There a Strategic Arms Race?" *Foreign Policy,* no. 15 (Summer 1974), pp. 3–20; "Rivals But No 'Race,' " *Foreign Policy,* no. 16 (Fall 1974), pp. 48–81.
3. This was the title of a book by Senator J. William Fulbright: *The Pentagon Propaganda Machine* (New York: Random House, 1970, and Vintage Books, 1971).
4. Erwin Knoll and Judith Nies McFadden, eds., *American Militarism 1970* (New York: The Viking Press, 1969), p. 11. See also John W. Finney, "45 in Congress Seek Rein on Military," *New York Times,* June 3, 1969.
5. Neil Sheehan, "Congress Group Hopes to Use ABM Fight to Curb Other Arms," *New York Times,* July 10, 1969.
6. See *Congressional Quarterly,* May 30, 1969, p. 847. See also the editorial in the March 8, 1969, *Saturday Review* ("The Anti-Ballistic Missile Decision: President Nixon's Vietnam?"), reprinted in the *New York Times,* March 11, 1969, p. 19.
7. Carl Kaysen, "Military Strategy, Military Forces, and Arms Control," in Kermit Gordon, ed., *Agenda for the Nation* (Washington: The Brookings Institution, 1968), pp. 549–584 (quote is at 549–550); Charles L. Schultze, "Budget Alternatives after Vietnam," ibid., pp. 13–48.
8. Graham Allison, Ernest May, and Adam Yarmolinsky, "Limits to Intervention," *Foreign Affairs,* vol. 48, no. 2 (January 1970), p. 246.
9. *New York Times,* April 21, 1969.
10. *New York Times,* May 18, 1969.
11. *New York Times* editorials, Feb. 7 and Feb. 9, 1969.
12. Abram Chayes and Jerome B. Wiesner, eds., *ABM: An Evaluation of the Decision to Deploy an Antiballistic Missile System,* with an introduction by Senator Edward M. Kennedy (New York: Harper and Row, 1969).
13. Statement by Senator Edward M. Kennedy to the Committee on National Priorities, Democratic Policy Council, Feb. 24, 1970. See also *New York Times,* Feb. 25, 1970.
14. Nixon's remarks, while originally made on a background basis, were later released for publication in the 1969 volume of *Public Papers of the Presidents of the United States: Richard Nixon: 1969* (Washington: US Government Printing Office, 1971), pp. 544–556.

VIII
THE AGONY OF VIETNAM

1. That all the key decisions even in the early 1960s were public knowledge is demonstrated convincingly by Henry Fairlie, "We Knew What We Were Doing When We Went Into Vietnam," *Washington Monthly* (May 1973).
2. "The Viet Nam Negotiations," *Foreign Affairs,* vol. 47, no. 2 (January 1969), pp. 211–234.
3. Addicts of secret documents may read this NSC staff summary of the agencies' responses to NSSM 1 in the *Washington Post* of April 25, 1972.

4. See Chapter XII, note 11.

5. Under the Hague Convention of 1907, a neutral country has the obligation not to allow its territory to be used by a belligerent. If the neutral country is unwilling or unable to prevent this, the other belligerent has the right to take appropriate counteraction. See the address by State Department Legal Adviser John Stevenson to the Bar Association of the City of New York on May 28, 1970, explaining our legal position with respect to operations in Cambodia by US and South Vietnamese forces from April 30 to June 30, 1970 (in *Department of State Bulletin*, vol. LXII, June 22, 1970, pp. 765–770).

6. The full House Judiciary Committee voted 26–12 *not* to put forward this proposed article of impeachment. The colorful phrases quoted, and others, may be found in US Congress, House, *Report of the Committee on the Judiciary on the Impeachment of Richard M. Nixon, President of the United States*, 93d Cong., 2d sess., Aug. 20, 1974: p. 298 (Rep. Waldie, "massive bombing of neutral Cambodia"); p. 308 (Rep. Drinan, "Presidential conduct more shocking . . . ," etc.); see also pp. 307, 312 (Rep. Drinan, "a massive bombing," "massive bombing in a neutral country"); and p. 328 (Rep. Holtzman joined by nine others, "the systematic bombing of a neutral country").

7. Robert F. Kennedy, *To Seek a Newer World* (Bantam Books, April 1968), especially pp. 207–218. Kennedy wrote: "Withdrawal is now impossible" (p. 186) and "A negotiated settlement must be less than a victory for either side. . . . For either side to yield its minimum conditions would be in fact to surrender" (pp. 196–197).

8. See John W. Finney, "Rockefeller Coup Gave Platform a Dovish Tone," *New York Times*, Aug. 6, 1968.

9. Clark M. Clifford, "A Viet Nam Reappraisal," *Foreign Affairs*, vol. 47, no. 4 (July 1969).

10. The text of Nixon's July 15 letter to Ho Chi Minh and of Ho's reply was released by the White House at the time of Nixon's Nov. 3, 1969, speech on Vietnam.

11. MEMORANDUM FOR THE PRESIDENT September 10, 1969
FROM: Henry A. Kissinger
SUBJECT: Our Present Course in Vietnam

I have become deeply concerned about our present course on Vietnam. This memorandum is to inform you of the reasons for my concern. It does not discuss alternative courses of action, but is provided for your background consideration. You know my recommendations.

While time acts against both us and our enemy, it runs more quickly against our strategy than against theirs. This pessimistic view is based on my view of Hanoi's strategy and the probable success of the various elements of our own.

I. *U.S. Strategy*

In effect, we are attempting to solve the problem of Vietnam on three highly interrelated fronts; (1) within the U.S., (2) in Vietnam, and (3) through diplomacy. To achieve our basic goals through diplomacy, we must be reasonably successful on *both* of the other two fronts.

a. *U.S.*

The pressure of public opinion on you to resolve the war quickly will increase — and I believe increase greatly — during the coming months. While polls may show that large numbers of Americans now are satisfied with the Administration's handling of the war, the elements of an evaporation of this support are clearly present. The plans for student demonstrations in October are well known, and while many Americans will oppose the students' activities, they will also be reminded of their own opposition to the continuation of the war. As mentioned below, I do not believe that "Vietnamization" can significantly reduce the pressures for an end to the war, and may, in fact, increase them after a certain point. Particularly significant is the clear opposition of many "moderate" leaders of opinion, particularly in the press and in the East (e.g., *Life* Magazine). The result of the recrudescence of intense public concern must be to polarize public opinion. You will then be somewhat in the same position as was President Johnson, although the substance of your position will be different. You will be caught between the Hawks and the Doves.

The effect of these public pressures on the U.S. Government will be to accentuate the internal divisiveness that has already become apparent to the public and Hanoi. Statements by government officials which attempt to assuage the Hawks or Doves will serve to confuse Hanoi but also to confirm it in its course of waiting us out.

b. *Vietnam*

Three elements on the Vietnam front must be considered — (1) our efforts to "win the war" through military operations and pacification, (2) "Vietnamization," and (3) the political position of the GVN.

(1) I do not believe that with our current plans we can win the war within two years, although our success or failure in hurting the enemy remains very important.

(2) "Vietnamization" must be considered both with regard to its prospects for allowing us to turn the war over to the Vietnamese, and with regard to its effect on Hanoi and U.S. public opinion. I am not optimistic about the ability of the South Vietnamese armed forces to assume a larger part of the burden than current MACV plans allow. These plans, however, call for a thirty-month period in which to turn the burden of the war over to the GVN. I do not believe we have this much time.

In addition, "Vietnamization" will run into increasingly serious problems as we proceed down its path.

— Withdrawal of U.S. troops will become like salted peanuts to the American public: the more U.S. troops come home, the more will be demanded. This could eventually result, in effect, in demands for unilateral withdrawal — perhaps within a year.

— The more troops are withdrawn, the more Hanoi will be encouraged — they are the last people we will be able to fool about the ability of the South Vietnamese to take over from us. They have the option of attacking GVN forces to embarrass us throughout the process or of waiting until we have largely withdrawn before doing so (probably after a period of higher infiltration).

— Each U.S. soldier that is withdrawn will be relatively more important to the effort in the south, as he will represent a higher percentage of U.S. forces than did his predecessor. (We need not, of course, continue to withdraw combat troops but can emphasize support troops in the next increments withdrawn. Sooner or later, however, we must be getting at the guts of our operations there).

— It will become harder and harder to maintain the morale of those who remain, not to speak of their mothers.

— "Vietnamization" may not lead to reduction in U.S. casualties until its final stages, as our casualty rate may be unrelated to the total number of American troops in South Vietnam. To kill about 150 U.S. soldiers a week, the enemy needs to attack only a small portion of our forces.

— "Vietnamization" depends on broadening the GVN, and Thieu's new government is not significantly broader than the old (see below). The best way to broaden the GVN would be to create the impression that the Saigon government is winning or at least permanent. The more uncertainty there is about the outcome of the war, the less the prospect for "Vietnamization."

(3) We face a dilemma with the GVN: The present GVN cannot go much farther towards a political settlement without seriously endangering its own existence; but at the same time, it has not gone far enough to make such a settlement likely.

Thieu's failure to "broaden" his government is disturbing, but not because he failed to include a greater variety of Saigon's Tea House politicians. It is disturbing because these politicians clearly do not believe that Thieu and his government represent much hope for future power, and because the new government does not offer much of a bridge to neutralist figures who could play a role in a future settlement. This is not to mention his general failure to build up political strength in non-Catholic villages. In addition, as U.S. troops are withdrawn, Thieu becomes more dependent on the political support of the South Vietnamese military.

c. *Diplomatic Front*

There is not therefore enough of a prospect of progress in Vietnam to persuade Hanoi to make real concessions in Paris. Their intransigence is also based on their estimate of growing U.S. domestic opposition to our Vietnam policies. It looks as though they are prepared to try to wait us out.

II. *Hanoi's Strategy*

There is no doubt that the enemy has been hurt by allied military actions in the South, and is not capable of maintaining the initiative on a sustained basis there. Statistics on enemy-initiated activities, as well as some of Giap's recent statements, indicate a conscious decision by Hanoi to settle down to a strategy of "protracted warfare." This apparently consists of small unit actions with "high point" flurries of activity, and emphasis on inflicting U.S. casualties (particularly through rocket and mortar attacks). This pattern of actions seems clearly to indicate a low-cost strategy aimed at producing a psychological, rather than military, defeat for the U.S.

This view of their strategy is supported by our estimates of enemy infiltration. They *could* infiltrate more men, according to intelligence estimates, despite growing domestic difficulties. The only logical reason for their not having done so is that more men were not needed in the pipeline — at least for a few months — to support a lower-cost strategy of protracted warfare. It seems most unlikely that they are attempting to "signal" to us a desire for a *de facto* mutual withdrawal, although this cannot be discounted. There is no diplomatic sign of this — except in Xuan Thuy's linkage of points two and three of the PRG program — and I do not believe they trust us enough to "withdraw" a larger percentage of their men than we have of ours, as they would be doing.

Hanoi's adoption of a strategy designed to wait us out fits both with its doctrine of how to fight a revolutionary war and with its expectations about increasingly significant problems for the U.S.

III. *Conclusion*

In brief, I do not believe we can make enough evident progress in Vietnam to hold the line within the U.S. (and the U.S. Government), and Hanoi has adopted a strategy which it should be able to maintain for some time — barring some break like Sino-Soviet hostilities. Hence my growing concern.

12. My memorandum for the President of Sept. 11, 1969, argued, *inter alia:*

Given the history of over-optimistic reports on Vietnam the past few years, it would be practically impossible to convince the American people that the other side is hurting and therefore with patience, *time could be on our side.* First of all we are not sure about our relative position — we have misread indicators many times before. Secondly, even if we conclude that the allied military position is sound, we don't know how to translate this into political terms — and the political prospects in South Vietnam are much shakier. Thirdly, the Administration faces an extremely skeptical and cynical American audience — the President is rightly reluctant to appear optimistic and assume his own credibility gap. Finally, to a large and vocal portion of the dissenters in this country, the strength of the allied position is irrelevant — they want an end to the war at any price.

13. *The New York Times Magazine,* Sept. 21, 1969.

14. For example, on March 1, 1969, the *Times* cited the easing of the Communist offensive as an occasion to pursue negotiation. The Communists' conciliatory response to Nixon's May 14 speech was cited on May 18 as a reason for the US to commence withdrawal. On June 10, an editorial cited the closeness of the NLF Ten Points and the Nixon program as a reason for the US to discuss a coalition government. Editorials of July 28, Aug. 25, and Aug. 31 pointed to the lull in the fighting as an argument for American de-escalation and a cease-fire proposal.

15. An editorial of March 9, 1969, argued that the enemy's spring offensive only proved that a US military victory was impossible and the peace talks had to be pursued. On July 28, Hanoi's stalling in the Paris talks was a reason to accelerate US withdrawals. The enemy's August 11–12 wave of attacks prompted the *Times* on August 16 to urge US de-escalation and a cease-fire proposal.

16. See editorials of Dec. 26, 1968, and Jan. 19, 1969 (mutual withdrawal); Jan. 30 and March 21 (US to initiate mutual withdrawals); May 18 (unilateral US withdrawals); and May 31 (timetable for US withdrawal).

17. Jan. 30, 1969 ("initiate"); March 21 ("begin"); May 31 (50–100,000 as "substantial"); June 10 ("step toward disengagement"); Sept. 17 ("timid," not "significant"); Sept. 27 (not "adequate"); Oct. 2 ("token").

18. See editorials of May 14, 1969 (coalition electoral commission); June 10 (interim coalition).

19. April 3, 1969 (cutback of search-and-destroy missions); Aug. 5, Oct. 15, 1969 (call for cease-fire).

20. Jan. 19, 1969 (mutual troop withdrawal); Jan. 30 (US troop withdrawal); April 3 (reduction of search-and-destroy missions; US troop withdrawal); May 14, May 15, June 10 (coalition elec-

toral commission); May 18 (US troop withdrawal); Aug. 5, Aug. 16, Aug. 30 (cutback of offensive operations; standstill cease-fire); Sept. 7 (cease-fire for Ho's funeral).

21. E.g., July 28, 1969 (US troop withdrawal).

22. Jan. 19, Jan. 30, 1969 (troop withdrawal, after bombing halt); April 3, 1969 (reduction of search-and-destroy missions, after B-52 cutback); May 15 (coalition electoral commission, after May 14 speech); May 18 (unilateral troop withdrawal, after May 14 speech); June 10 (interim coalition, after June withdrawal announcement); Aug. 5, Aug. 16, Aug. 30 (cease-fire, defensive ground tactics, after June withdrawal announcement); Oct. 2 (after September withdrawal announcement).

23. E.g., May 5, 1969 (continued pursuit of military victory); May 17 (failure to slow down offensive operations; delay in withdrawing troops); Aug. 16 (failure to propose cease-fire or de-escalation); Aug. 25 (delay in withdrawing troops); Aug. 31 (continued military pressure; ignoring lull; delay in withdrawing troops); Oct. 2 (aggressive ground tactics; tokenism of withdrawals, ignoring Ho funeral truce).

24. E.g., May 5, 1969 (jailing of opponents; procrastination with land reform); May 17 (jailing of opponents); Aug. 25 (choice of new Premier); Sept. 12 (balking at Ho funeral truce).

25. E.g., March 1, 1969 (total bombing halt); May 15, May 17, 1969 (May 14 speech); Aug. 16, Oct. 2, 1969 (troop withdrawal, etc.).

26. E.g., March 1, 1969 (easing of Communist attacks); May 9, 1969 (Front's Ten Points); May 18, 1969 (initial response to May 14 speech); July 28, Aug. 25, Aug. 31, 1969 (lulls); Aug. 16, 1969 ("virtual cessation" of infiltration).

27. March 9, May 5, 1969 (step-up in allied attacks); Aug. 25, Aug. 31, 1969 (lull in fighting).

28. E.g., April 3, 1969 (cutback of search-and-destroy missions); May 5, May 17 (defensive posture, US withdrawal); May 18 (US withdrawal); June 10 (interim coalition); Sept. 5 (Ho Chi Minh funeral truce).

29. *New York Times,* May 15, 1969; *Washington Post,* June 23, 1969.

30. *New York Times,* May 15, May 30, 1969.

IX
Early Tests in Asia

1. Information in this paragraph is from the unclassified testimony of General Earle Wheeler to a subcommittee of the House Armed Services Committee, April 25, 1969.

2. This portion of the Nixon-Sato communiqué reads as follows:

    The Prime Minister described in detail the particular sentiment of the Japanese people against nuclear weapons and the policy of the Japanese Government reflecting such sentiment. The President expressed his deep understanding and assured the Prime Minister that, *without prejudice to the position of the United States Government with respect to the prior consultation system under the Treaty of Mutual Cooperation and Security,* the reversion of Okinawa would be carried out in a manner consistent with the policy of the Japanese Government as described by the Prime Minister. [Emphasis added.]

3. See, e.g., I. M. Destler, et al., *Managing an Alliance: The Politics of US-Japanese Relations* (Washington: The Brookings Institution, 1976), p. 156, a book that I found otherwise a useful summary of the public events.

4. See, e.g., Roger Morris, *Uncertain Greatness* (New York: Harper and Row, 1977), pp. 104–105.

X
Words and Shadows

1. Fatah policy statement of Oct. 19, 1968, reported in the *New York Times,* Oct. 20, 1968.

2. See the report of Andrei Zhdanov to the conference of Communist Parties establishing the Cominform, September 1947, reprinted in US Congress, House, Committee on Foreign Affairs, *The Strategy and Tactics of World Communism, Report to Subcommittee, No. 5 on National and International Movements,* House Document No. 619, Supplement I, 80th Cong., 2d session, 1948, p. 211. Zhdanov essentially treated the Middle East as in transition from the British to the American sphere of influence.

3. See Arnaud de Borchgrave's interview with Nasser in *Newsweek* of Feb. 10, 1969, and his interview with Eshkol in *Newsweek* of Feb. 17, 1969.

XI
The Uneasy Alliance

1. See, e.g., a column by C. L. Sulzberger in the *New York Times*, Dec. 7, 1969.
2. See, e.g., *Congressional Record* (daily ed.), May 18, 1971, p. S7217, quoted in John Newhouse et al., *US Troops in Europe: Issues, Costs, and Choices* (Washington: The Brookings Institution, 1971), p. 5.
3. See US Congress, Senate, Committee on Foreign Relations, *United States Security Agreements and Commitments Abroad: United States Forces in Europe, Hearings before the Subcommittee on United States Security Agreements and Commitments Abroad*, 91st Cong., 2d sess., Pt. 10, testimony of June 24, 1970, p. 2243.
4. Willy Brandt, *People and Politics: The Years 1960–1975* (Boston: Little, Brown & Co., 1978), p. 248.
5. Ibid., p. 289.

XII
The War Widens

1. Walters's richly detailed account is in Vernon A. Walters, *Silent Missions* (Garden City, N.Y.: Doubleday & Co., 1978), chapters 24 and 28.
2. Ibid., pp. 580–582.
3. On earlier Vietnamese dominance of Laos and Cambodia, see Bernard Fall, *The Two Vietnams*, rev. ed. (London: Pall Mall Press, 1965), pp. 12–19, 33.
4. Ibid., p. 386.
5. See, e.g., *New York Times*, Feb. 25, 1970.
6. Sihanouk interview in *New York Times*, March 12, 1970.
7. See his memoirs, *My War with the CIA: The Memoirs of Prince Norodom Sihanouk as Related to Wilfred Burchett* (New York: Random House, Pantheon Books, 1973), p. 24. See also pp. 21–22, 24–26, 42–43, 50, 54, 201–202.
8. William Shawcross, *Sideshow: Kissinger, Nixon and the Destruction of Cambodia* (New York: Simon and Schuster, 1979), p. 165.
9. Following is the text of the entire message:
   MEMORANDUM FOR Henry Kissinger
   FROM THE PRESIDENT
   I think we need a bold move in Cambodia, assuming that I feel the way today (it is five AM, April 22) at our meeting as I feel this morning to show that we stand with Lon Nol. I do not believe he is going to survive. There is, however, some chance that he might and in any event we must do something symbolic to help him survive. We have really dropped the ball on this one due to the fact that we were taken in with the line that by helping him we would destroy his "neutrality" and give the North Vietnamese an excuse to come in. Over and over again we fail to learn that the Communists never need an excuse to come in. They didn't need one in Hungary in 1956 when the same argument was made by the career State people and when Dulles bought it because he was tired and it was during the campaign. They didn't need one in Czechoslovakia when the same argument was made by the State people, and they didn't need one in Laos where we lost a precious day by failing to make the strike that might have blunted the whole offensive before it got started, and in Cambodia where we have taken a completely hands-off attitude by protesting to the Senate that we have only a "delegation of seven State Department jerks" in the Embassy and would not provide any aid of any kind because we were fearful that if we did so it would give them a "provocation" to come in. They are romping in there and the only government in Cambodia in the last 25 years that had the guts to take a pro-Western and pro-American stand is ready to fall. I am thinking of someone like Bob Murphy who would be sent there on a trip to report back to me and who would go in and reassure Lon Nol. This, of course, would be parallel to your activities which will be undertaken immediately after the NSC meeting, in the event that I decide to go on this course, with some of the lily-livered Ambassadors from our so-called friends in the world. We are going to find out who our friends are now, because if we decide to stand up here some of the rest of them had better come along fast.
   I will talk to you about this after the NSC meeting.
10. John Mitchell took notes of the meeting and wrote a concise two-page memorandum:

MEMORANDUM OF MEETING   April 28, 1970
PRESENT: The President, Secretary of State, Secretary of Defense, Attorney General
SUBJECT: Cambodia/South Vietnam

The subject meeting was held in the Oval Office of The President on Tuesday, April 28, 1970, commencing at 10:20 a.m. and lasting for approximately twenty minutes.

The President stated that the purpose of the meeting was to advise those present of the decisions he had reached with respect to the developing situation in South Vietnam and Cambodia. The President further stated that he had had the subject under constant consideration for the past ten days and had taken into consideration all of the information provided by the Director of Central Intelligence, the Joint Chiefs of Staff and Admiral McCain and his staff at the briefing in Hawaii. The President further stated that, in arriving at his decision, he had taken into consideration the positions taken by the Secretary of State and Secretary of Defense in opposition to the use of U.S. Forces in Cambodia and the fact that Dr. Kissinger was leaning against the recommendation of such use.

The President further stated that the previous day he had made certain inquiries of Ambassador Bunker and General Abrams. The President read his communication to Ambassador Bunker and the Ambassador's reply received late Monday evening.

The President further stated that, based upon his review of the general Cambodian situation, he had decided not to change the current U.S. position with respect to military assistance to Cambodia or his authorization for the ARVN operation in the Parrot's Beak. The President further stated that he had decided to confirm the authorization for a combined U.S./GVN operation against COSVN headquarters in Fish Hook in order to protect U.S. Forces in South Vietnam. The President expressed the opinion that the COSVN operation was necessary in order to sustain the continuation of the Vietnamization Program and would possibly help in, but not detract from, U.S. efforts to negotiate peace.

The President further stated that he had taken into consideration, in arriving at his decisions, the probable adverse reaction in some Congressional circles and some segments of the public. The President further stated that, in order to establish the record of the events leading to his decisions and the advice he had received concerning the subject matter thereof, the previous evening he had dictated a tape which included the contrary recommendations of the Secretary of State and the Secretary of Defense.

At the close of the President's statements he left the Oval Office to attend another meeting in the Cabinet Room. There was no discussion of the subject matter of the meeting by others in attendance during the presence of the President.

[Signed:] J. N. Mitchell

11. See Elizabeth Becker, "Cambodia: A Look at Border War with Vietnam," *Washington Post,* Dec. 27, 1978; Henry Kamm, "Pol Pot Confirmed Assertion by Nixon," *New York Times,* March 18, 1979, p. 7.

12. *New York Times,* May 18, 1970.

13. See e.g., Stanley Karnow, "Cambodia: Nixon's the One," *Washington Post,* Jan. 12, 1979.

14. See e.g., William Shawcross, "Cambodia: The Blame," *The Sunday Times* (London), Dec. 12, 1976; "Who 'Lost' Cambodia?" *New York Times,* Feb. 6, 1979; *Sideshow,* passim.

15. E.g., Shawcross, *Sideshow,* pp. 372–373, 389. Shawcross, who thus excused the Khmer Rouge atrocities, was amazingly upbraided in turn by another writer who alleged that there was insufficient evidence the atrocities ever took place. Richard Dudman, *The New York Times Book Review,* April 22, 1979. Some of our critics seem to be ready to give Pol Pot the benefit of the doubt before their own government.

16. See also Sihanouk's interview in the *Far Eastern Economic Review,* May 11, 1979, p. 14, in which he described Pol Pot as a "butcher" responsible for the deaths of two million Cambodians.

17. An excellent analysis of the Khmer Rouge's methodical application of ideological doctrine is by Francois Ponchaud, *Cambodia: Year Zero* (New York: Holt, Rinehart and Winston, 1977). The quotation from Khieu Samphan's dissertation is on p. 87.

18. *Congressional Record* (daily ed.), Dec. 16, 1970, pp. S20283, 20289 ff.

XIII
THE SOVIET RIDDLE

1. Charles L. Schultze with Edward K. Hamilton and Allen Schick, *Setting National Priorities: The 1971 Budget* (Washington: The Brookings Institution, 1970), chapter 2.

2. Quoted in the *New York Times,* Feb. 24, 1970.
3. See, e.g., an article in *Commentary* in March 1970 that denounced Nixon for his ABM program, MIRV testing, and laxity in pursuing limitations in SALT: Maurice J. Goldbloom, "Nixon So Far," *Commentary* (March 1970), pp. 30–31.
4. My staff summed up for me Dave Packard's recommendations that it was urgent that we negotiate limits on offensive systems as soon as possible:

> Secretary Packard has sent you a memo on SALT objectives and tactics. In it he argues that the Delegation should be given new instructions "with which we can attempt to achieve an agreement at Vienna by mid-October or, at the latest, November." He says an early, though limited, agreement is important because the coming "squeeze on the national budget" which is "likely" to result in "large reductions in defense programs, including strategic forces," has a "significant effect on the timing of our SALT tactics." This, he says, is because cuts dictated by the budget will be more acceptable in the U.S. and a "sign of good intentions" to the USSR if there has been progress at SALT but would "decrease our bargaining leverage" if there had not.
>
> (It would be interesting to know what cuts in strategic programs DOD plans which would "decrease our bargaining leverage" this fall.)

XV
THE AUTUMN OF CRISES: JORDAN

1. See Henry Brandon, *The Retreat of American Power* (Garden City, N.Y.: Doubleday & Co., 1973), p. 134.

XVI
THE AUTUMN OF CRISES: CIENFUEGOS

1. *RN: The Memoirs of Richard Nixon* (New York: Grosset & Dunlap, 1978), pp. 220–221.
2. Reported, for example, in the *Baltimore Sun,* Sept. 3, 1970.
3. *New York Times,* Jan. 6, 1971.

XVII
THE AUTUMN OF CRISES: CHILE

1. See Paul E. Sigmund, *The Overthrow of Allende and the Politics of Chile, 1964–1976* (Pittsburgh: University of Pittsburgh Press, 1977), p. 89. The text of the Popular Unity program may be found in J. Ann Zammit, ed., *The Chilean Road to Socialism* (Austin: University of Texas Press, 1973), pp. 255–284.
2. See Régis Debray, *The Chilean Revolution: Conversations with Allende* (New York: Random House, Pantheon Books, 1971), p. 159.
3. Ibid., p. 119.
4. Ibid., p. 120.
5. Ibid., p. 118.
6. Ibid., p. 117.
7. Ibid., p. 118.
8. Ibid., pp. 122–123.
9. Ibid., p. 82.
10. Under President Ford's intelligence reorganization of 1976 it was renamed the Operations Advisory Group; under President Carter the same functions are carried out by a similar committee called the NSC Special Coordination Committee, under Executive Order 12036, Jan. 24, 1978.
11. US Congress, Senate, Select Committee to Study Governmental Operations with Respect to Intelligence Activities, *Alleged Assassination Plots Involving Foreign Leaders; An Interim Report,* 94th Cong., 1st sess., November 1975, p. 229.
12. Debray, *The Chilean Revolution,* pp. 123–125.
13. Interview with Mexico City newspaper *Excelsior,* published on Nov. 4, 1970.
14. See *New York Times,* Nov. 9, 1970.
15. Chile received during the Allende period a total of $947.9 million in new credits extended by Communist and Western sources, which included $620 million from Soviet and other Communist-bloc countries. These figures do not include ongoing disbursements under previous commitments. For example, the Inter-American Development Bank (IDB) disbursed $46.2 million to Chile in the Allende period, with the yearly average during that period in fact larger than the disbursements by the IDB to Chile during any single year from 1964 to 1970. See US

Congress, House, Committee on Foreign Affairs, *United States and Chile During the Allende Years, 1970–1973, Hearings before the Subcommittee on Inter-American Affairs of the House Committee on Foreign Affairs*, 1975, pp. 324, 447; US Congress, Senate, Select Committee to Study Governmental Operations with Respect to Intelligence Activities, *Covert Action in Chile, 1963–1973*, Staff Report, 94th Cong., 1st sess., 1975, p. 32; Report by the Inter-American Committee on the Alliance for Progress, Jan. 28, 1974, on Chile's internal situation and external financing needs (Organization of American States Series H/XIV, CIAP/650), pp. V14–V15.

XVIII
An Invitation to Peking

1. Roger Morris, *Uncertain Greatness* (New York: Harper and Row, 1977), p. 97.
2. See *New York Times*, June 18, 1970.
3. Edgar Snow, "China Will Talk from a Position of Strength," *Life*, July 30, 1971, p. 24.
4. *Time*, Oct. 5, 1970.
5. *RN: The Memoirs of Richard Nixon* (New York: Grosset & Dunlap, 1978), p. 546.
6. Nixon records that we learned of Mao's statement "within a few days after he made it." *RN*, p. 547. After looking over my records, I believe that neither Nixon nor I knew of the comments by Mao until they were published by *Life* on April 30, 1971, after the Ping-Pong episode. The earliest reference in my records to the fact of a Snow interview is in a low-level State Department report of April 1, 1971, to the effect that in an interview with Snow Mao had shown some flexibility regarding Taiwan. Snow wrote again on the same subject in *Life*, July 30, 1971. Nixon must have meant that he was aware of the Snow interview before my secret trip, which is correct.
7. This account is from a UPI story by Arnold Dibble published July 16, 1971.
8. Armin Meyer, our Ambassador in Tokyo, gives this account and justly praises Cunningham for his role. Armin H. Meyer, *Assignment Tokyo: An Ambassador's Journal* (Indianapolis: Bobbs-Merrill, 1974), pp. 130–131.
9. Snow, "China Will Talk from a Position of Strength," p. 24.
10. *RN*, p. 552.

XIX
The Journey to Peking

1. *New York Times*, July 26, 1971, p. 6.
2. Brandon tells the story with grace and humor in Henry Brandon, *The Retreat of American Power* (Garden City, N.Y.: Doubleday & Co., 1973), chapter 11.
3. Armin H. Meyer, *Assignment Tokyo* (Indianapolis: Bobbs-Merrill, 1974), pp. 133–137.
4. *New York Times*, Oct. 31, 1971.

XX
Breakthrough on Two Fronts

1. E.g., *RN: The Memoirs of Richard Nixon* (New York: Grosset & Dunlap, 1978), p. 523. See also Marquis Childs, *Washington Post*, June 1, 1971.
2. "U.S. Split on Defense Costs, Muskie Told Soviet Premier," *Washington Star*, Jan. 26, 1971.
3. "Senate Panel to Be Informed on Progress in Arms Talks," *Washington Star*, Feb. 2, 1971.
4. "U.S. Negotiator Testifies on Limiting ABMs," *Washington Post*, Feb. 4, 1971; "Foster Asks Total Ban on A-Tests," *Washington Post*, Feb. 28, 1971.
5. United Press International, May 4, 1971.
6. "Senate Reopens Debate Over ABM," *New York Times*, April 20, 1971.
7. "Harvard–M.I.T. Arms Experts Pleased by Nixon's Move on Talks," *New York Times*, May 27, 1971.

XXI
The Tilt: The India-Pakistan Crisis of 1971

1. SEATO's membership included the United States, Britain, France, Australia, New Zealand, Pakistan, the Philippines, Thailand (and South Vietnam as a protocol state). CENTO grouped the countries of the so-called Northern Tier, Turkey, Iran, and Pakistan, with Britain; the United States was a member in all but name.
2. *Washington Star*, May 19, 1971.

3. The State Department acknowledged on June 22 that its original announcement of the embargo on April 15 did not mention the fact that earlier transactions would not necessarily be affected by it. See the *New York Times,* June 23, 1971.

4. Dobrynin also gave the gestation period as a year. Jha told Rogers it was two years, and Foreign Minister Singh gave t'.is figure publicly. After Nixon's July 15 China announcement, Singh had told the Indian Parliament cryptically that India had been considering countermeasures to a possible Sino-American rapprochement "for some time" (see Chapter XIX).

5. Sydney H. Schanberg, "India Sets Range for Retaliations in East Pakistan," *New York Times,* Nov. 29, 1971.

6. The Article read: "The Government of Pakistan is determined to resist aggression. In case of aggression against Pakistan, the Government of the United States of America, in accordance with the Constitution of the United States of America, will take such appropriate action, including the use of armed forces, as may be mutually agreed upon and as is envisaged in the Joint Resolution to Promote Peace and Stability in the Middle East, in order to assist the Government of Pakistan at its request."

7. Assurances were given by the Kennedy and Johnson administrations, including a letter from President John F. Kennedy to Pakistani President Mohammed Ayub Khan on Jan. 26, 1962; an aide-mémoire presented by the US Ambassador on Nov. 5, 1962; a public statement by the State Department on Nov. 17, 1962; and an oral promise by President Lyndon Johnson to Ayub Khan on Dec. 15, 1965.

8. See the Anderson column in the *Washington Post,* Dec. 21, 1971, and the minutes of the Dec. 8 WSAG meeting published in the *New York Times,* Jan. 15, 1972.

9. The *Washington Post* of Dec. 8, 1971, reported on my background briefing with a column headlined, "White House Softens Pro-Pakistan Stance." Senator Barry Goldwater was so carried away by my briefing that he inserted it *in toto* into the *Congressional Record* without informing us. *Congressional Record* (daily ed.), Dec. 9, 1971, p. S21012.

10. Milton Viorst, "War Odious, but Not Always Evil," *Washington Star,* Dec. 11, 1971.

11. See the *New York Times,* Jan. 6, 1972; *Washington Post,* Jan. 6, 1972.

XXII
CRISIS IN THE ALLIANCE

1. Raymond Aron, *The Imperial Republic: The United States and the World 1945–1973* (Cambridge, Mass.: Winthrop Publishers, 1974), pp. 293–295.

XXIII
VIETNAM 1970–71: FORCING HANOI'S HAND

1. *Washington Post* editorials, Aug. 28 and Sept. 1, 1970.

2. See the *New York Times,* June 16, 1969; *The New York Times Magazine,* Sept. 21, 1969.

3. See, e.g., *New York Times* editorials, Aug. 5, Aug. 21, Aug. 24, Oct. 15, 1969.

4. They included Henry Jackson, who drafted the letter, Hugh Scott, Mike Mansfield, Barry Goldwater, Jacob Javits, Warren Magnuson, Bob Doyle, Alan Bible, Thomas J. McIntyre, Winston Prouty, Birch Bayh, Charles Percy, Milton Young, and Ted Stevens.

5. "Peace Plan Gets Wide Praise from Hill Leaders and Media," *Washington Post,* Oct. 9, 1970.

6. "Peace Initiative Backed By The Press," *Philadelphia Inquirer,* Oct. 11, 1970.

7. Proposed, for example by Morton Halperin and Leslie Gelb in the *Washington Post,* Oct. 11, 1970, and by Halperin again in the *New York Times,* Nov. 7, 1970.

8. Benjamin F. Schemmer, *The Raid* (New York: Harper and Row, 1976), pp. 243–244.

9. A handy schedule of a dozen separate planned antiwar rallies and campaigns was published in the *Washington Daily News:* see Judy Luce, "Demonstration Timetable Here," March 31, 1971, p. 3.

10. Address to the Nation, April 7, 1971; see also news conferences of Feb. 17 and March 4, 1971.

11. The May 31 proposal as I read it to Xuan Thuy was as follows:

> First, we are prepared to set a terminal date for the withdrawal of all our forces from South Vietnam. We would, as I have indicated earlier, arrange for roughly the same timetable for the withdrawal of other Allied forces.
>
> Second, the Vietnamese and the other peoples of Indochina should discuss among themselves the manner in which all other outside forces would withdraw from the countries of Indochina.

Third, there should be a ceasefire in place throughout Indochina, to become effective at the time when U.S. withdrawals based on the final agreed timetable begin.

Fourth, as part of the ceasefire, there should be no further infiltration of outside forces into the countries of Indochina.

Fifth, there should be international supervision of the ceasefire and its provisions.

Sixth, both sides should renew their pledge to respect the 1954 and 1962 Geneva Accords, to respect the neutrality, territorial integrity, and independence of Laos and Cambodia. This could be formalized at an international conference.

Seventh, I want to reiterate our proposal for the immediate release of all prisoners of war and innocent civilians held by both sides throughout Indochina. We believe this issue should be settled immediately on a humanitarian basis. If this is not done, the men must be released as an integral part of the settlement we are proposing in our final offer. We would expect:

— Your side would present a complete list of all prisoners held throughout Indochina on the day an agreement is reached.

— The release of the prisoners would begin on the same day as our withdrawals under the agreed timetable.

— The release of prisoners would be completed at least two months before the completion of our final withdrawals.

We are prepared to talk concretely and to make rapid progress. We have framed this offer to respond to your proposals. We expect that you will deal with our final proposals in a constructive spirit.

12. Walters handed over the text of our new eight points:

1. The United States agrees to the total withdrawal from South Vietnam of all U.S. forces and other foreign forces allied with the government of South Vietnam. This withdrawal will be carried out in the following manner:

— All American and allied forces, except for a small number of personnel needed for technical advice, logistics, and observance of the ceasefire mentioned in point 6, will be withdrawn by July 1, 1972, provided that this statement of principles is signed by December 1, 1971. The terminal date for these withdrawals will in no event be later than seven months after this statement of principles is signed.

— The remaining personnel, in turn, will be progressively withdrawn beginning one month before the Presidential election mentioned in point 3 and simultaneously with the resignations of the incumbent President and Vice President of South Vietnam also provided for in point 3. These withdrawals will be completed by the date of the Presidential election.

2. The release of all military men and innocent civilians captured throughout Indochina will be carried out in parallel with the troop withdrawals mentioned in point 1. Both sides will present a complete list of military men and innocent civilians held throughout Indochina on the day this statement of principles is signed. The release will begin on the same day as the troop withdrawals and will be completed by July 1, 1972, provided this statement is signed by December 1, 1971. The completion of this release will in no event be later than seven months after this statement is signed.

3. The following principles will govern the political future of South Vietnam:

The political future of South Vietnam will be left for the South Vietnamese people to decide for themselves, free from outside interference.

There will be a free and democratic Presidential election in South Vietnam within six months of the signature of the final agreement based on the principles in this statement. This election will be organized and run by an independent body representing all political forces in South Vietnam which will assume its responsibilities on the date of the final agreement. This body will, among other responsibilities, determine the qualification of candidates. All political forces in South Vietnam can participate in the election and present candidates. There will be international supervision of this election.

One month before the Presidential election takes place, the incumbent President and Vice President of South Vietnam will resign. A caretaker Administration, headed by the Chairman of the Senate, will assume administrative responsibilities except for those pertaining to the election, which will remain with the independent election body.

The United States, for its part, declares that it:

— will support no candidate and will remain completely neutral in the South Vietnamese election.

— will abide by the outcome of this election and any other political processes shaped by the South Vietnamese people themselves.

— is prepared to define its military and economic assistance relationship with any government that exists in South Vietnam.

Both sides agree that:

— South Vietnam, together with the other countries of Indochina, should adopt a foreign policy of neutrality.

— Reunification of Vietnam should be decided on the basis of discussions and agreements between North and South Vietnam without constraint and annexation from either party, and without foreign interference.

4. Both sides will respect the 1954 Geneva Agreements on Indochina and those of 1962 on Laos. There will be no foreign intervention in the Indochinese countries and the Indochinese peoples will be left to settle by themselves their own affairs.

5. The problems existing among the Indochinese countries will be settled by the Indochinese parties on the basis of mutual respect for independence, sovereignty, territorial integrity and non-interference in each other's affairs. Among the problems that will be settled is the implementation of the principle that all armed forces of the countries of Indochina must remain within their national frontiers.

6. There will be a general ceasefire throughout Indochina, to begin when the final agreement is signed. As part of the ceasefire, there will be no further infiltration of outside forces into any of the countries of Indochina.

7. There will be international supervision of the military aspects of this agreement including the ceasefire and its provisions, the release of prisoners of war and innocent civilians and the withdrawal of outside forces from Indochina.

8. There will be an international guarantee for the fundamental national rights of the Indochinese peoples, the neutrality of all the countries in Indochina, and lasting peace in this region.

Both sides express their willingness to participate in an international conference for this and other appropriate purposes.

13. McGovern quoted in *Washington Post*, Jan. 4, 1972.
14. Muskie and Humphrey quoted in *Newsweek*, Feb. 7, 1972.

XXIV
NIXON'S TRIP TO CHINA

1. *RN: The Memoirs of Richard Nixon* (New York: Grosset & Dunlap, 1978), pp. 560–564.
2. Ross Terrill, *Flowers on an Iron Tree: Five Cities of China* (Boston: Little, Brown & Co., 1975), p. 171.
3. The complete text of the Shanghai Communiqué is as follows:

JOINT COMMUNIQUE

February 28, 1972
Shanghai, People's Republic
of China

President Richard Nixon of the United States of America visited the People's Republic of China at the invitation of Premier Chou En-lai of the People's Republic of China from February 21 to February 28, 1972. Accompanying the President were Mrs. Nixon, U.S. Secretary of State William Rogers, Assistant to the President Dr. Henry Kissinger, and other American officials.

President Nixon met with Chairman Mao Tse-tung of the Communist Party of China on February 21. The two leaders had a serious and frank exchange of views on Sino–U.S. relations and world affairs.

During the visit, extensive, earnest and frank discussions were held between President Nixon and Premier Chou En-lai on the normalization of relations between the United States of America and the People's Republic of China, as well as on other matters of interest to both sides. In addition, Secretary of State William Rogers and Foreign Minister Chi P'eng-fei held talks in the same spirit.

President Nixon and his party visited Peking and viewed cultural, industrial and agricultural sites, and they also toured Hangchow and Shanghai where, continuing discussions with Chinese leaders, they viewed similar places of interest.

The leaders of the People's Republic of China and the United States of America found it beneficial to have this opportunity, after so many years without contact, to present candidly to one another their views on a variety of issues. They reviewed the international situation in which important changes and great upheavals are taking place and expounded their respective positions and attitudes.

The U.S. side stated: Peace in Asia and peace in the world requires efforts both to reduce immediate tensions and to eliminate the basic causes of conflict. The United States will work for a just and secure peace: just, because it fulfills the aspirations of peoples and nations for freedom and progress; secure, because it removes the danger of foreign aggression. The United States supports individual freedom and social progress for all the peoples of the world, free of outside pressure or intervention. The United States believes that the effort to reduce tensions is served by improving communication between countries that have different ideologies so as to lessen the risks of confrontation through accident, miscalculation or misunderstanding. Countries should treat each other with mutual respect and be willing to compete peacefully, letting performance be the ultimate judge. No country should claim infallibility and each country should be prepared to re-examine its own attitudes for the common good. The United States stressed that the peoples of Indochina should be allowed to determine their destiny without outside intervention; its constant primary objective has been a negotiated solution; the eight-point proposal put forward by the Republic of Vietnam and the United States on January 27, 1972 represents a basis for the attainment of that objective; in the absence of a negotiated settlement the United States envisages the ultimate withdrawal of all U.S. forces from the region consistent with the aim of self-determination for each country of Indochina. The United States will maintain its close ties with and support for the Republic of Korea; the United States will support efforts of the Republic of Korea to seek a relaxation of tension and increased communication in the Korean peninsula. The United States places the highest value on its friendly relations with Japan; it will continue to develop the existing close bonds. Consistent with the United Nations Security Council Resolution of December 21, 1971, the United States favors the continuation of the ceasefire between India and Pakistan and the withdrawal of all military forces to within their own territories and to their own sides of the ceasefire line in Jammu and Kashmir; the United States supports the right of the peoples of South Asia to shape their own future in peace, free of military threat, and without having the area become the subject of great power rivalry.

The Chinese side stated: Wherever there is oppression, there is resistance. Countries want independence, nations want liberation and the people want revolution — this has become the irresistible trend of history. All nations, big or small, should be equal; big nations should not bully the small and strong nations should not bully the weak. China will never be a superpower and it opposes hegemony and power politics of any kind. The Chinese side stated that it firmly supports the struggles of all the oppressed people and nations for freedom and liberation and that the people of all countries have the right to choose their social systems according to their own wishes and the right to safeguard the independence, sovereignty and territorial integrity of their own countries and oppose foreign aggression, interference, control and subversion. All foreign troops should be withdrawn to their own countries.

The Chinese side expressed its firm support to the peoples of Vietnam, Laos and Cambodia in their efforts for the attainment of their goal and its firm support to the seven-point proposal of the Provisional Revolutionary Government of the Republic of South Vietnam and the elaboration of February this year on the two key problems in the proposal, and to the Joint Declaration of the Summit Conference of the Indochinese Peoples. It firmly supports the eight-point program for the peaceful unification of Korea put forward by the Government of the Democratic People's Republic of Korea on April 12, 1971, and the stand for the abolition of the "U.N. Commission for the Unification and Rehabilitation of Korea." It firmly opposes the revival and outward expansion of Japanese militarism and firmly supports the Japanese people's desire to build an independent, democratic, peaceful and neutral Japan. It firmly maintains that India and Pakistan should, in accordance with the United Nations resolutions on the India-Pakistan question, immediately withdraw all their forces to their respective territories and to their own sides of the ceasefire line in

Jammu and Kashmir and firmly supports the Pakistan Government and people in their struggle to preserve their independence and sovereignty and the people of Jammu and Kashmir in their struggle for the right of self-determination.

There are essential differences between China and the United States in their social systems and foreign policies. However, the two sides agreed that countries, regardless of their social systems, should conduct their relations on the principles of respect for the sovereignty and territorial integrity of all states, non-aggression against other states, non-interference in the internal affairs of other states, equality and mutual benefit, and peaceful coexistence. International disputes should be settled on this basis, without resorting to the use or threat of force. The United States and the People's Republic of China are prepared to apply these principles to their mutual relations.

With these principles of international relations in mind the two sides stated that:

— progress toward the normalization of relations between China and the United States is in the interests of all countries;

— both wish to reduce the danger of international military conflict;

— neither should seek hegemony in the Asia-Pacific region and each is opposed to efforts by any other country or group of countries to establish such hegemony; and

— neither is prepared to negotiate on behalf of any third party or to enter into agreements or understandings with the other directed at other states.

Both sides are of the view that it would be against the interests of the peoples of the world for any major country to collude with another against other countries, or for major countries to divide up the world into spheres of interest.

The two sides reviewed the long-standing serious disputes between China and the United States. The Chinese side reaffirmed its position: The Taiwan question is the crucial question obstructing the normalization of relations between China and the United States; the Government of the People's Republic of China is the sole legal government of China; Taiwan is a province of China which has long been returned to the motherland; the liberation of Taiwan is China's internal affair in which no other country has the right to interfere; and all U.S. forces and military installations must be withdrawn from Taiwan. The Chinese Government firmly opposes any activities which aim at the creation of "one China, one Taiwan," "one China, two governments," "two Chinas," and "independent Taiwan" or advocate that "the status of Taiwan remains to be determined."

The U.S. side declared: The United States acknowledges that all Chinese on either side of the Taiwan Strait maintain there is but one China and that Taiwan is a part of China. The United States Government does not challenge that position. It reaffirms its interest in a peaceful settlement of the Taiwan question by the Chinese themselves. With this prospect in mind, it affirms the ultimate objective of the withdrawal of all U.S. forces and military installations from Taiwan. In the meantime, it will progressively reduce its forces and military installations on Taiwan as the tension in the area diminishes.

The two sides agreed that it is desirable to broaden the understanding between the two peoples. To this end, they discussed specific areas in such fields as science, technology, culture, sports and journalism, in which people-to-people contacts and exchanges would be mutually beneficial. Each side undertakes to facilitate the further development of such contacts and exchanges.

Both sides view bilateral trade as another area from which mutual benefit can be derived, and agreed that economic relations based on equality and mutual benefit are in the interest of the people of the two countries. They agree to facilitate the progressive development of trade between their two countries.

The two sides agreed that they will stay in contact through various channels, including the sending of a senior U.S. representative to Peking from time to time for concrete consultations to further the normalization of relations between the two countries and continue to exchange views on issues of common interest.

The two sides expressed the hope that the gains achieved during this visit would open up new prospects for the relations between the two countries. They believe that the normalization of relations between the two countries is not only in the interest of the Chinese and American peoples but also contributes to the relaxation of tension in Asia and the world.

President Nixon, Mrs. Nixon and the American party expressed their appreciation for the gracious hospitality shown them by the Government and people of the People's Republic of China.

XXV
HANOI THROWS THE DICE

1. Safire's account, from the speech-writing perspective, is in *Before the Fall* (Garden City, N.Y.: Doubleday & Co., 1975), pp. 417–420.
2. See, e.g., *RN: The Memoirs of Richard Nixon* (New York: Grosset & Dunlap, 1978), p. 591.
3. *RN*, pp. 590–591.

XXVI
THE SECRET TRIP TO MOSCOW

1. See Elmo R. Zumwalt, Jr., *On Watch: A Memoir* (New York: Quadrangle Books/The New York Times Book Co., 1976), pp. 152–163.
2. *New York Times*, Feb. 9, 1972. The *Los Angeles Times* on Feb. 4 even returned to the concept of an ABM-only agreement.
3. See, e.g., Tad Szulc, in "How Kissinger Did It: Behind the Vietnam Cease-Fire Agreement," *Foreign Policy*, no. 15 (Summer 1974), and in *The Illusion of Peace* (New York: The Viking Press, 1978), pp. 544–545. Szulc claims this was the first explicit US proposal of a cease-fire in place that dropped the demand for mutual withdrawal. In fact, a cease-fire in place had been proposed in the President's speech of Oct. 7, 1970. Any expectation of negotiating a mutual withdrawal was dropped in the secret proposal of May 31, 1971 — and indeed implicitly in our acceleration of unilateral withdrawals. A cease-fire in place was offered again in our secret proposal of Oct. 11, 1971, and publicly in the President's January 25, 1972, speech. All that was left of mutual withdrawal in our 1971–72 proposals was the provision that "the problems existing among the Indochinese countries will be settled by the Indochinese parties on the basis of mutual respect for independence, sovereignty, territorial integrity and non-interference in each other's affairs. Among the problems that will be settled is the implementation of the principle that all armed forces of the countries of Indochina must remain within their national frontiers."
4. See *RN*, p. 592.

XXVII
THE SHOWDOWN

1. *New York Times*, Jan. 5, 1973.
2. Excerpts from Nixon's April 30 memorandum to me are printed in *RN: The Memoirs of Richard Nixon* (New York: Grosset & Dunlap, 1978), pp. 593–594.
3. See *RN*, p. 594.
4. I was not present at the May 8 leadership meeting. An account of it is in William Safire, *Before the Fall* (Garden City: Doubleday & Co., 1975), pp. 422–427.
5. The Senators are quoted in *Congressional Quarterly*, May 13, 1972.
6. *New York Times* editorial, May 9, 1972.
7. *New York Times, Washington Post, Christian Science Monitor,* and *Boston Globe* editorials of May 10, 1972.
8. Marvin Kalb and Bernard Kalb, *Kissinger* (Boston: Little, Brown & Co., 1974), p. 310.
9. This memorandum is quoted in *RN*, pp. 606–607.

XXVIII
THE MOSCOW SUMMIT

1. See, e.g., *Washington Post*, May 18, 1972.
2. Marvin Kalb and Bernard Kalb, *Kissinger* (Boston: Little, Brown & Co., 1974), p. 328.
3. The text of the Middle East section of the 1972 US–Soviet communiqué was as follows:

   The two Sides set out their positions on this question. They reaffirm their support for a peaceful settlement in the Middle East in accordance with Security Council Resolution 242.
   Noting the significance of constructive cooperation of the parties concerned with the Special Representative of the UN Secretary General, Ambassador Jarring, the US and the USSR confirm their desire to contribute to his mission's success and also declare their readiness to play their part in bringing about a peaceful settlement in the Middle East. In the view of the US and the USSR, the achievement of such a settlement would open prospects for the normalization of the Middle East situation and would permit, in particular, consideration of further steps to bring about a military relaxation in that area.

4. The "general working principles" worked out with Gromyko as a result of the May 1972 summit discussions read as follows:

   1. The final agreement should be comprehénsive, covering all parties and issues. This does not preclude that the implementation occurs in stages or that some issues and disputes are resolved on a priority basis.

   2. The agreement should contain provisions for the withdrawal of Israeli forces from Arab territories occupied in 1967.

   3. Any border rectifications, which may take place, should result from voluntary agreement among the parties concerned.

   4. Mutual arrangements for security could include demilitarized zones, the temporary stationing of UN personnel at Sharm el-Sheikh, and the most effective international guarantees with the appropriate participation of the Soviet Union and the United States.

   5. The agreements should lead to an end of a state of belligerency and the establishment of peace.

   6. Freedom of navigation through the Straits of Tiran and the Suez Canal should be assured. This is fully consistent with Egyptian sovereignty over the Canal.

   7. Recognition of the independence and sovereignty of all states in the Middle East, including Israel, is one of the basic principles on which the settlement must be based.

Unilateral Points:

   The US position is that completion of the agreements should at some stage involve negotiations among the signatories.

   The Soviet position is that the problem of the Palestinian refugees should be solved on a just basis and in accordance with the appropriate UN decisions.

XXIX
SUMMIT AFTERMATH

1. The conventional revisionist view is well exemplified by the series of articles by George W. Ball in the *Washington Star*, March 14–16, 1979; and Ball's letter to the editor of *The Economist*, Feb. 17, 1979.
2. Compare the *Washington Post* editorials of June 7 and July 27, 1971, with its editorials of Oct. 7, 1972, and Feb. 21, 1973.

XXX
SADAT EXPELS THE SOVIETS

1. See Anwar el-Sadat, *In Search of Identity* (New York: Harper and Row, 1978), pp. 219, 221–222. Sadat made the same point in his address to the Israeli Knesset on Nov. 20, 1977.
2. See Marilyn Berger, "Envoy 'Paper' Compromises U.S. in Mideast," *Washington Post*, June 29, 1971.
3. Sadat, *In Search of Identity*, p. 225.
4. See Chapter XXVIII, note 4.
5. Sadat, *In Search of Identity*, p. 229.
6. Ibid.

XXXI
FROM STALEMATE TO BREAKTHROUGH

1. The US draft of the relevant article was as follows:
   The Composition of the Committee will be as follows:
   — Representatives of the Republic of Vietnam to be designated by the Government of the Republic of Vietnam;
   — Representatives of the NLF to be designated by the NLF;
   — Representatives of various political and religious tendencies in South Vietnam associated neither with the Government of the Republic of Vietnam nor the NLF but designated by mutual agreement between the Government of the Republic of Vietnam and the NLF.
   President Thieu and his staff gave us a proposed redraft, as follows:
   The Committee will be composed of representatives of all the political, religious forces and tendencies in SVN [South Vietnam]. The NLF is considered as one of the above. The representatives will be designated by mutual agreement.

We preferred to be specific because it gave Hanoi the tripartite form while draining it of substance. Our scheme transformed the coalition government into an electoral commission with a fifty-fifty split and a Saigon veto. In our judgment Saigon's formulation was less favorable to its own cause because it would have given the NLF a veto over even the Saigon representatives on the Committee.

2. See *RN: The Memoirs of Richard Nixon* (New York: Grosset & Dunlap, 1978), p. 690.
3. See Charles W. Colson, *Born Again* (Old Tappan, N.J.: Chosen Books, Inc., 1976), p. 76.
4. The result can best be judged by comparing Hanoi's original draft with the version that emerged on October 11. Le Duc Tho's draft of October 8 read:

Immediately after the cease-fire, the two South Vietnamese parties shall hold consultations in a spirit of national concord, equality, mutual respect, and mutual non-elimination to set up the three-segment administration of national concord and to settle all other internal matters of South Viet Nam in keeping with the South Viet Nam people's aspirations for peace, independence, democracy, and neutrality. The two South Vietnamese parties shall as soon as possible sign an agreement on the internal matters of South Viet Nam, and not later than three months after the enforcement of cease-fire.

The version on October 11 read:

Immediately after the cease-fire, the two South Vietnamese parties shall hold consultations in a spirit of national reconciliation and concord, mutual respect, and mutual non-elimination to set up an administrative structure called the National Council of National Reconciliation and Concord of three equal segments. The Council shall operate on the principle of unanimity. After the National Council of National Reconciliation and Concord has assumed its functions, the two South Vietnamese parties will consult about the formation of councils at lower levels. The two South Vietnamese parties shall sign an agreement on the internal matters of South Vietnam as soon as possible and do their utmost to accomplish this within three months after the cease-fire comes into effect, in keeping with the South Vietnamese people's aspirations for peace, independence and democracy.

This was weakened further in later negotiations by dropping the phrase "administrative structure," the Vietnamese translation of which was controversial. See Chapter XXXIII.

XXXII
THE TROUBLED ROAD TO PEACE

1. *RN: The Memoirs of Richard Nixon* (New York: Grosset & Dunlap, 1978), p. 693.
2. See, e.g., Nixon's news conference of March 15, 1973; his address of March 29, 1973; the joint statememt of Presidents Nixon and Thieu, April 3, 1973; Secretary of Defense Richardson on "Meet the Press," April 1, 1973; Richardson testimony to the Senate Armed Services Committee, April 2, 1973; Richardson remarks to newsmen prior to appearing before the House Appropriations Committee, April 3, 1973; my interview with Marvin Kalb, CBS-TV, February 1, 1973; remarks of Ambassador William Sullivan on "Meet the Press," Jan. 28, 1973; and other sources collected in US Congress, Senate, Committee on Appropriations, *Emergency Military Assistance and Economic and Humanitarian Aid to South Vietnam, 1975, Hearings before the Committee on Appropriations*, 94th Cong., 1st sess., 1975, pp. 19–24.
3. The relevant assurances I had recited back to Hanoi in a message on October 20 read:

With respect to Cambodia, the U.S. side operates on the basis of the following statements made by Special Advisor Le Duc Tho at private meetings with Dr. Kissinger on September 26 and 27 and October 8 and 11, 1972:

— "The questions of the war in Vietnam and Cambodia are closely linked: when the war is settled in Vietnam, there is no reason for the war to continue in Cambodia" (September 27);

— "Once the Vietnam problem is settled, the question of Cambodia certainly will be settled; and the end of the Vietnamese war will create a very great impact that will end the war in Cambodia perhaps immediately" (October 8);

— "It is an understanding between us that the DRV will abide by the principle that all foreign forces, including its own, must put an end to their military activities in Cambodia and be withdrawn from Cambodia and not be reintroduced" (September 26);

— "The DRV will follow the same principles in Cambodia that it will follow in South Vietnam and Laos, that is, it will refrain from introducing troops, armament, and war material into Cambodia" (October 11); and

— "As Article 18 [later 23] states, the obligations of this agreement come into force on the day of its signing" (October 11).

The United States reiterates its view as expounded by Dr. Kissinger on October 11, 1972, that if, pending a settlement in Cambodia, offensive activities are taken there which would jeopardize the existing situation, such operations would be contrary to the spirit of Article 15(b) [later 20(b)] and to the assumptions on which this Agreement is based.

Hanoi confirmed these statements in a written message on October 21 and added a written assurance that it would ''actively contribute to restoring peace in Cambodia.''

4. What complicated matters even further is that Nixon seemed to be reacting also to messages sent the day before dealing with an entirely different problem. He seemed to believe that I was determined to go to Hanoi, which the record does not sustain. And he quotes in his memoirs as a proof (*RN*, p. 699) a cable from October 21 dealing with quite a different situation.

On the morning of October 21, when the South Vietnamese team had submitted its twenty-three proposed changes in the agreement, we were faced with the question of where and how to raise them with the North Vietnamese. In order to keep Hanoi from going public, I suggested that I might maintain the ''shedyule,'' go to Hanoi, put forward the requested changes, and try thus to use my visit as a means to delay a conclusion of the agreement until after the election. That message arrived in Washington during the night and was thus not acted on for about twelve hours. (The quote from my cable in *RN*, p. 699, is from a still earlier cable I sent when I was under the impression that Saigon would accept the document provided it could get some changes.) By that time Thieu had canceled the meeting scheduled for later that day and subjected Bunker to the indignities already described. Under these circumstances I *withdrew* my original recommendation. Before having any response to my first message I cabled Haig: ''I will do my utmost to prevent a blowup here. In any event I do not see what Thieu has to gain from it. I will find some pretext for cancelling the trip to Hanoi.'' For some reason that second cable was neither acknowledged nor did it receive a reply. But the first one suggesting the trip to Hanoi be maintained was the subject of passionate exchanges all the more infuriating because they had meanwhile become irrelevant.

XXXIII
''Peace Is at Hand''

1. McGovern's position was spelled out in his speech of Oct. 10, 1972; see also his appearance on the ''Today'' show, April 4, 1972, and his remarks in New Hampshire reported by UPI on Feb. 9, 1972 (re Laos and Cambodia).

2. *New York Times*, Nov. 6, 1972. McGovern's remarks on ''Meet the Press'' are reported in the *Washington Post*, Oct. 30, 1972.

3. Oriana Fallaci, *Interview with History* (Boston: Houghton Mifflin Co., 1977), chapter 1.

4. See John Osborne in *The New Republic*, Dec. 16, 1972, reprinted in Osborne, *The Fourth Year of the Nixon Watch* (New York: Liveright, 1973), pp. 200–201.

5. See Chapter XXXII, note 2.

6. Quoted in William Shawcross, ''Sihanouk's Case,'' *The New York Review of Books*, Feb, 22, 1979.

7. *RN: The Memoirs of Richard Nixon* (New York: Grosset & Dunlap, 1978), p. 721.

8. The full text of the President's message to me of Dec. 6 is in *RN*, pp. 729–730.

9. *RN*, p. 731.

10. *RN*, p. 733.

11. *RN*, p. 736.

12. E.g., Marvin Kalb and Bernard Kalb, *Kissinger* (Boston: Little, Brown & Co., 1974), p. 413.

13. *Christian Science Monitor*, Dec. 21, 1972; *Washington Post*, Dec. 21, 1972.

14. Guenter Lewy, *America in Vietnam* (New York: Oxford University Press, 1978), pp. 413–414 (footnotes omitted).

15. A good account of the mood of the White House staff can be found in William Safire, *Before the Fall* (Garden City, N.Y.: Doubleday & Co., 1975), pp. 666–670.

16. Charles W. Colson, *Born Again* (Old Tappan, N.J.: Chosen Books, Inc., 1976), pp. 79–80.

Index